CIVIL PROCEDURE

ASPEN CASEBOOK SERIES

CIVIL PROCEDURE CASES AND PROBLEMS

Fifth Edition

Allan Ides
Christopher N. May Professor of Law
Loyola Law School

Christopher N. May
Professor Emeritus
Loyola Law School

Simona Grossi
Professor of Law & Theodore A. Bruinsma Fellow
Loyola Law School

 Wolters Kluwer

Printed in the United States of America.

1 2 3 4 5 6 7 8 9 0

ISBN 978-1-4548-6331-1

Library of Congress Cataloging-in-Publication Data

Names: Ides, Allan, 1949- author. | May, Christopher N., author. | Grossi, Simona, author.
Title: Civil procedure : cases and problems / Allan Ides, Loyola Law School, Christopher N. May Professor of Law, Christopher N. May, Loyola Law School, Professor Emeritus, Simona Grossi, Loyola Law School, Professor of Law & Theodore A. Bruinsma Fellow.
Description: Fifth edition. | New York : Wolters Kluwer, [2016] | Series: Aspen casebook series
Identifiers: LCCN 2016004895 | ISBN 9781454863311
Subjects: LCSH: Civil procedure—United States—Cases. | LCGFT: Casebooks.
Classification: LCC KF8839 .I34 2016 | DDC 347.73/5—dc23
LC record available at http://lccn.loc.gov/2016004895

About Wolters Kluwer Legal & Regulatory Solutions U.S.

Wolters Kluwer Legal & Regulatory Solutions U.S. delivers expert content and solutions in the areas of law, corporate compliance, health compliance, reimbursement, and legal education. Its practical solutions help customers successfully navigate the demands of a changing environment to drive their daily activities, enhance decision quality and inspire confident outcomes.

Serving customers worldwide, its legal and regulatory solutions portfolio includes products under the Aspen Publishers, CCH Incorporated, Kluwer Law International, ftwilliam.com and MediRegs names. They are regarded as exceptional and trusted resources for general legal and practice-specific knowledge, compliance and risk management, dynamic workflow solutions, and expert commentary.

For Matthew, Joel, and Kate

For a dear friend and former colleague
Dean Fred Lower,
who forty years ago gave me the chance
to begin teaching Civil Procedure

For Aaron

SUMMARY OF CONTENTS

Contents   *xi*

Preface   *xxxi*

Acknowledgments   *xxxiii*

Introduction   1

I.   **Pleadings and Related Motions**   13

II.   **Personal Jurisdiction**   115

III.   **Service of Process and Notice**   245

IV.   **Subject Matter Jurisdiction**   303

V.   **Venue, Transfer, and *Forum Non Conveniens***   407

VI.   **The *Erie* Doctrine and Related Problems**   465

VII.   **Discovery**   553

VIII.   **Joinder of Claims and Parties**   633

IX.   **Class Actions**   749

X.   **Adjudication Without Trial**   885

XI.   **Trial**   965

XII.   **Appellate Review**   1045

XIII.   **The Binding Effect of a Final Judgment**   1131

Table of Cases   1233

Table of Authorities   1253

Index   1261

CONTENTS

Preface   *xxxi*

Acknowledgments   *xxxiii*

Introduction   1

A. The State and Federal Judicial Systems   1
   1. State Judicial Systems   2
   2. The Federal Judicial System   3
B. State and Federal Court Caseloads   6
   1. State Court Caseloads   6
   2. Federal Court Caseloads   9

Chapter I. Pleadings and Related Motions   13

A. Code Pleading   14
            Epstein v. M. Blumenthal & Co.   17
            Notes and Questions   19
            Problem 1-1   20
            Doe v. City of Los Angeles   21
            Notes and Questions   28
            Problem 1-2   29
B. Notice Pleading and the Federal Rules of Civil Procedure   30
   1. The Complaint   32
      a. Rule 8   32
      b. Foundational Cases and Developments   32
            Conley v. Gibson   32
            Notes and Questions   34
            Problems 1-3–1-5   36
            A Note on Exceptions to Rule 8   36
            Leatherman v. Tarrant County Narcotics
                Intelligence and Coordination Unit   38
            Notes and Questions   40
            Problems 1-6–1-7   41
      c. Recent Developments   42
            Bell Atlantic Corp. v. Twombly   42
            Notes and Questions   53
            Problem 1-8   55
            Ashcroft v. Iqbal   55
            Notes and Questions   66
            A Note on Plausibility, Inferences, and
                Pleading Sufficiency   67

	d.	*Twombly* and *Iqbal* Applied	70
		Swanson v. Citibank, N.A.	70
		Notes and Questions	76
		McCleary-Evans v. Maryland Department of Transportation	77
		Notes and Questions	83
		Littlejohn v. City of New York	84
		Notes and Questions	95
		Problem 1-9	95
	2.	The Answer	96
		King Vision Pay Per View, Ltd. v. J.C. Dimitri's Restaurant, Inc.	98
		Notes and Questions	100
		Problems 1-10–1-11	100
	3.	Rule 12(b) Motions to Dismiss	101
		Johnson v. City of Shelby	103
		Notes and Questions	104
		Kirksey v. R.J. Reynolds Tobacco Co.	104
		Notes and Questions	107
		Problems 1-12–1-13	108
C.	Pleading Review Problem		109
		Problem 1-14	109

Chapter II.   Personal Jurisdiction — 115

A.	*Pennoyer v. Neff* and the Rule of Territoriality		116
		Pennoyer v. Neff	116
		Notes and Questions	124
		Problems 2-1–2-3	126
B.	Traditional Bases of Personal Jurisdiction		127
	1.	Personal Jurisdiction	127
		a. Domicile	127
		b. Voluntary Appearance	128
		c. Consent to Service on an Agent	129
		d. Transient or Tag Jurisdiction	129
	2.	*In Rem* and *Quasi in Rem* Jurisdiction	130
		Harris v. Balk	131
		Notes and Questions	134
		Problem 2-4	135
	3.	The Advent of Fictions	135
C.	The Modern Law of Jurisdiction		137
	1.	*International Shoe* — Jurisdiction Beyond Fictions and Tradition	138
		International Shoe Co. v. Washington	138
		Notes and Questions	143

2. Establishing a Statutory Basis for Jurisdiction beyond
   the Traditional Forms   145
3. Due Process: The Nonresident Defendant's Connections
   with the Forum State   148
   a. Contracts   149
        McGee v. International Life Insurance Co.   149
        Notes and Questions   150
        Hanson v. Denckla   151
        Notes and Questions   156
        Burger King Corp. v. Rudzewicz   157
        Notes and Questions   166
        Problems 2-5–2-7   167
   b. Torts   168
        Calder v. Jones   168
        Notes and Questions   171
        Problems 2-8–2-10   173
        Walden v. Fiore   174
        Notes and Questions   180
        A Note on the "Stream of Commerce"
          Theory   181
        J. McIntyre Machinery, Ltd. v. Nicastro   182
        Notes and Questions   197
        A Note on the Stream-of-Commerce
          Theory Today   199
        Problems 2-11–2-12   200
        A Note on Personal Jurisdiction and the
          Internet   201
        Problems 2-13–2-14   203
4. Due Process: The Relatedness Requirement   204
        Nowak v. Tak How Investments, Ltd.
          [Part I]   204
        Notes and Questions   210
        Problem 2-15   212
5. Due Process: The Reasonableness Requirement   212
        Asahi Metal Industry Co., Ltd. v.
          Superior Court of California   213
        Notes and Questions   216
        Nowak v. Tak How Investments, Ltd.
          [Part II]   216
        Notes and Questions   218
        Problems 2-16–2-17   219
6. Due Process: General Jurisdiction   220
        Daimler A.G. v. Bauman   220
        Notes and Questions   230

	Problems 2-18–2-19	230
D.	Minimum Contacts and the Traditional Bases of Jurisdiction	231
	Problem 2-20	233
E.	Exercising Jurisdiction Under Federal Long-Arm Provisions	234
	1. Federal Long-Arm Provisions	235
	2. Minimum Contacts at the National Level	235
	Problem 2-21	236
F.	Challenging Lack of Personal Jurisdiction over the Defendant	237
	1. The Burden of Proof	237
	2. Direct Attack	237
	3. Collateral Attack	239
	Problems 2-22–2-23	240
G.	Personal Jurisdiction Review Problems	241
	Problems 2-24–2-25	241

Chapter III.   Service of Process and Notice   245

A.	The Mechanics of Service: Rule 4	246
	1. Request for Waiver of Service	246
	Problem 3-1	247
	2. Formal Service of Summons and Complaint	247
	a. Individuals	248
	Problem 3-2	248
	b. Corporations, Partnerships, and Associations	249
	American Institute of Certified Public Accountants v. Affinity Card, Inc.	249
	Notes and Questions	253
	c. Defendants Served in a Foreign Country	254
	d. Substantial Compliance	254
	Problem 3-3	255
	3. Time Limit for Effecting Service: Rule 4(m)	256
B.	The Due Process Right to Notice	257
	Mullane v. Central Hanover Bank & Trust Co.	257
	Notes and Questions	263
	Problems 3-4–3-5	265
	Jones v. Flowers	266
	Notes and Questions	274
	Problems 3-6–3-7	276
	A Note on Challenging Service of Process	277
	You've Got Mail	278
C.	Pre-filing Waiver and Consent	280
	Underwood Farmers Elevator v. Leidholm	281
	Notes and Questions	283

D.   Policy-Based Immunities and Exemptions   284
     1.   Participation in Legal Proceedings in the Forum State   285
     2.   Trickery or Fraud   285
              Problems 3-8–3-9   286
E.   Notice and Hearing When Property Is Attached   287
              Connecticut v. Doehr   288
              Notes and Questions   295
              Problems 3-10–3-12   298
F.   Service of Process and Notice Review Problems   300
              Problem 3-13–3-15   300

     Chapter IV.   Subject Matter Jurisdiction   303

A.   Subject Matter Jurisdiction in Federal Courts   304
     1.   The Constitutional and Statutory Dimensions
          of Subject Matter Jurisdiction in Federal Courts   304
     2.   Federal Question Jurisdiction   306
          a.   Article III "Arising Under" Jurisdiction   306
                   Problem 4-1   308
          b.   Statutory "Arising Under" Jurisdiction: The
               Federal Question Jurisdiction of U.S.
               District Courts   308
                   The Foundations of Statutory
                      Arising-Under Jurisdiction   309
                   Shoshone Mining Co. v. Rutter   310
                   Notes and Questions   312
                   *American Well Works Co. v. Layne
                      & Bowler Co.*   312
                   Notes and Questions   314
                   Smith v. Kansas City Title and Trust Co.   314
                   Notes and Questions   317
                   Gully v. First National Bank   317
                   Notes and Questions   321
                   Problems 4-2–4-4   321
                   A Note on Declaratory Judgments and
                      Statutory Arising-Under Jurisdiction   322
                   Problems 4-5–4-6   323
                   A Note on Concurrent and Exclusive
                      Federal Question Jurisdiction   324
                   The Modern Approach to Statutory
                      Arising-Under Jurisdiction   325
                   Gunn v. Minton   326
                   Notes and Questions   332
                   Problem 4-7   333

3. Diversity Jurisdiction   333
    a. Introduction   333
    b. Diversity of State Citizenship   335
            Rodríguez v. Señor Frog's de La Isla, Inc.   335
            Notes and Questions   339
            Problem 4-8   340
            A Note on 28 U.S.C. § 1359 and
                "Collusive" Transfers or Assignments
                to Create Diversity Jurisdiction   341
            A Note on the Citizenship of Artificial
                Entities   342
            Problem 4-9   343
            A Note on Statutes Allowing for
                Minimal Diversity   344
    c. Cases Involving Aliens   345
            Eze v. Yellow Cab Co. of Alexandria,
                Virginia, Inc.   345
            Notes and Questions   346
            Grupo Dataflux v. Atlas Global Group,
                L.P.   347
            Notes and Questions   352
            Problems 4-10–4-11   355
            A Note on U.S. Citizens with Dual
                Nationality   356
            A Note on U.S. Corporations with Their
                Principal Place of Business Abroad   357
            Problems 4-12–4-13   357
    d. Amount in Controversy   358
            Coventry Sewage Associates v. Dworkin
                Realty Co.   359
            Notes and Questions   365
            A Note on Aggregation of Claims   366
            Problems 4-14–4-15   368
            A Note on Computing the Amount in
                Controversy in Suits for Declaratory
                or Injunctive Relief   368
            Problem 4-16   370
4. Supplemental Jurisdiction   370
    a. Overview and Introduction   370
    b. Pendent and Ancillary Jurisdiction   371
            United Mine Workers of America v. Gibbs   371
            Notes and Questions   375
            Owen Equipment and Erection Co.
                v. Kroger   377
            Notes and Questions   382

A Note on *Kroger* and Potential Evasions
of the Complete Diversity Principle   384
A Note on Pendent-Party Jurisdiction   386
c.   Supplemental Jurisdiction: § 1367   387
Problems 4-17–4-19   389
5.   Removal Jurisdiction   390
a.   Section 1441(a): Removability in General   390
b.   Section 1441(b): Limits on the Removal of
Diversity Cases   391
Problems 4-20–4-21   391
c.   Section 1441(c): Removal of Federal Questions
Joined with Nonremovable Claims   392
d.   Section 1446: Procedure for Removal of
Civil Actions   393
e.   Section 1447: Procedure after Removal Generally   394
Ettlin v. Harris   394
Notes and Questions   398
Problems 4-22–4-23   399
B.   Challenging a Court's Subject Matter Jurisdiction   400
1.   Direct Attack   400
2.   Collateral Attack   401
Problems 4-24–4-25   403
C.   Subject Matter Jurisdiction Review Problems   404
Problems 4-26–4-27   404

**Chapter V.   Venue, Transfer, and *Forum
Non Conveniens***   407

A.   Venue in Federal Courts   408
1.   The General Venue Statute: 28 U.S.C. § 1391   408
Subsection (b)(1)—Residence of
Defendants   409
Subsection (b)(2)—Substantial Part
of Events   409
First of Michigan Corp. v. Bramlet   409
Notes and Questions   413
Problems 5-1–5-3   415
Subsection (b)(3)—Fallback Provision   416
Problems 5-4–5-5   416
Subsections (c)(2) and (d)—Residence
of Corporate and Noncorporate
Entities   417
Problems 5-6–5-7   419
Notes and Questions   420
Problem 5-8   421

2. Transfer of Venue in Federal Court   421
      Skyhawke Technologies, LLC v. DECA
        International Corp.   *421*
      Notes and Questions   428
      Graham v. Dyncorp International, Inc.   430
      Notes and Questions   435
      A Note on Transfer When Originating
        Court Lacks Personal Jurisdiction   436
      Problems 5-9–5-10   436
      A Note on Multidistrict Litigation   437
      A Note on Forum-Selection Clauses   438
      Atlantic Marine Construction Co., Inc.
        v. United States District Court   *439*
      Notes and Questions   448
      Problems 5-11–5-12   448
B. *Forum Non Conveniens*   450
      Piper Aircraft Co. v. Reyno   *451*
      Notes and Questions   459
      A Note on an Available Alternate Forum   460
      A Note on *Forum Non Conveniens* in
        State Courts   460
      Problems 5-13–5-15   461
C. Venue, Transfer, and *Forum Non Conveniens*
    Review Problems   463
      Problems 5-16–5-17   464

Chapter VI.   The *Erie* Doctrine and Related Problems   465

A. The Law to Be Applied in Federal and State Courts   465
B. The *Erie* Doctrine: The Law to Be Applied in Diversity
    and Supplemental Jurisdiction Cases   467
    1. A Brief History of the Pre-*Erie* Landscape   467
    2. The Demise of "Federal General Common Law"   470
          Erie Railroad Co. v. Tompkins   470
          Notes and Questions   474
          Problems 6-1–6-2   477
C. A Survey of the Three-Track Approach to the *Erie* Doctrine   478
    1. Is There a Conflict?   479
    2. Is the Federal Law Valid?   482
          Track One: The Validity of Federal
            Procedural Statutes   482
          Track Two: The Validity of Formal
            Federal Procedural Rules   483
          Track Three: The Validity of
            Judge-Made Procedural Law   486

D. Three Tracks of Analysis: Procedural Statutes, Formal
Rules, and Judge-Made Laws 490
   1. Track One: Federal Statutes and the Supremacy Clause 490
      a. The Standard Model 490
         Stewart Organization, Inc. v. Ricoh Corp. 490
         Notes and Questions 495
         Problems 6-3–6-4 496
      b. A Variation on Track One: The Continuing
        Validity of "Specialized" Federal Common Law 497
         Problem 6-5 502
   2. Track Two: The Federal Rules of Civil Procedure 502
         Sibbach v. Wilson & Co., Inc. 503
         Notes and Questions 505
         Problem 6-6 507
         A Note on the Omnipresence of *Erie* 508
         Hanna v. Plumer [Part I] 509
         Notes and Questions 513
         Problems 6-7–6-8 515
         Shady Grove Orthopedic Associates,
           P.A. v. Allstate Insurance Co. 516
         Notes and Questions 527
         Problems 6-9–6-11 527
   3. Track Three: Federal Procedural Common Law 529
         Guaranty Trust Co. v. York 529
          Notes and Questions 531
         Problem 6-12 532
         A Note on *Byrd* and Refining the
          Erie/York Formula 533
         Problem 6-13 533
         Hanna v. Plumer [Part II] 534
         Notes and Questions 536
         Problems 6-14–6-15 537
         Gasperini v. Center for Humanities, Inc. 538
         Notes and Questions 546
         A Note on Federal Law in State Courts 547
         Problems 6-16–6-17 549
E. *Erie* Review Problems 550
         Problems 6-18–6-20 550

Chapter VII.   Discovery 553

A. Pragmatic Preliminary—Devising a Discovery Plan 555
B. The Scope of Formal Discovery 557
   1. Discovery Relevance 557
         Problems 7-1–7-2 558

		2.	Privilege		559
			Jaffee v. Redmond		560
			Notes and Questions		566
			Problem 7-3		568
			Upjohn Company v. United States [Parts I and II]		568
			Notes and Questions		573
			Problem 7-4		574
		3.	The Work-Product Doctrine		574
			Hickman v. Taylor		574
			Notes and Questions		581
			Upjohn Company v. United States [Part III]		582
			Problems 7-5–7-6		584
			A Note on Information Obtained from Experts		585
	C.	The Formal Discovery Process in Federal Court			586
		1.	Mandatory Conference and Mandatory Disclosures		587
			a.	The Discovery Conference	587
			b.	Mandatory Disclosure	588
				Advance Financial Corp. v. Utsey	589
		2.	Methods to Discover Additional Materials		591
			a.	Depositions	591
			b.	Interrogatories	593
			c.	Requests for Production and Inspection	594
				Problem 7-7	596
				Notes and Questions	597
			d.	E-Discovery	597
				Wood v. Capital One Services, LLC	599
				Notes and Questions	607
			e.	Physical and Mental Examinations	608
				Schlagenhauf v. Holder	609
				Notes and Questions	615
				Problems 7-8–7-9	616
			f.	Requests for Admissions	616
			g.	Discovery Related to Experts	617
				Problem 7-10	619
			h.	Duty to Supplement or Correct	619
			i.	Protective Orders, Motions to Compel, and Sanctions	620
				Seattle Times Co. v. Rhinehart	621
				Notes and Questions	627
				A Note on Federal Discovery to Assist Foreign and International Tribunals	627

D.   Discovery Review Problem   628
        Problem 7-11   628

Chapter VIII.   Joinder of Claims and Parties   **633**

A.   Precursors to Modern Joinder: Joinder at Common
     Law, Equity, and Under the Codes   633
     1.   Joinder at Common Law   633
     2.   Joinder in Equity   634
     3.   Joinder Under the Codes   635
B.   Joinder of Claims by Plaintiffs and Defendants Under
     the Federal Rules   637
     1.   Claims and Counterclaims   637
               Problems 8-1–8-2   637
               Law Offices of Jerris Leonard, P.C. v.
                  Mideast Systems, Ltd.   638
               Notes and Questions   641
               Burlington Northern Railroad Co.
                  v. Strong   643
               Notes and Questions   645
               A Note on Supplemental Jurisdiction
                  and Counterclaims   646
               Hart v. Clayton-Parker and Associates, Inc.   647
               Notes and Questions   649
               Problem 8-3   650
               A Note on Parallel Federal Proceedings   651
     2.   Crossclaims   651
               Rainbow Management Group, Ltd. v.
                  Atlantis Submarines Hawaii, L.P.   651
               Notes and Questions   654
               Harrison v. M.S. Carriers, Inc.   656
               Notes and Questions   658
               Problem 8-4   659
C.   Permissive Joinder of Parties by Plaintiffs   659
               Exxon Mobil Corp. v. Allapattah
                  Services, Inc.   660
               Notes and Questions   669
               Problems 8-5–8-8   672
               A Note on the Real-Party-in-Interest
                  Requirement   673
D.   Joinder of Parties by Defendants   674
     1.   Joinder of Third Parties Under Rule 13(h)   675
               Schoot v. United States   675
               Notes and Questions   677

Hartford Steam Boiler Inspection and
    Insurance Co. v. Quantum Chemical
    Corp.   677
Notes and Questions   682
Problems 8-9–8-10   682
2.   Joinder of Third Parties Under Rule 14   683
Wallkill 5 Associates II v. Tectonic
    Engineering, P.C.   683
Notes and Questions   686
Problem 8-11   687
Guaranteed Systems, Inc. v. American
    National Can Co.   687
Notes and Questions   690
Problem 8-12   690
E.   Intervention by Absentees   691
Great Atlantic & Pacific Tea Co. v.
    Town of East Hampton   691
Notes and Questions   696
Problems 8-13–8-14   699
Mattel, Inc. v. Bryant   701
Notes and Questions   703
Problem 8-15   703
F.   Interpleader   704
Indianapolis Colts v. Mayor and City
    Council of Baltimore   707
Notes and Questions   710
Problems 8-16–8-17   712
Geler v. National Westminster Bank USA   712
Notes and Questions   716
Problems 8-18–8-19   718
G.   Compulsory Joinder   719
1.   Rule 19(a)(1)   722
Temple v. Synthes Corp., Ltd.   722
A Note on the "Complete Relief"
    Clause of Rule 19(a)(1)(A)   723
Problem 8-20   724
Maldonado-Viñas v. National Western
    Life Ins. Co.   725
Notes and Questions   730
A Note on the Feasibility of Joinder   730
2.   Rule 19(b)   731
Provident Tradesmens Bank & Trust Co. v.
    Patterson   731
Notes and Questions   740

	Problems 8-21–8-23	744
H.	Joinder of Claims and Parties Review Problem	745
	Problem 8-24	745

Chapter IX.   Class Actions   **749**

A.	Constitutional Limitations on the Use of Class Actions	750
	1. Adequate Representation	750
	Hansberry v. Lee	750
	Notes and Questions	754
	2. Notice and Right to Appear or Opt Out	755
	Phillips Petroleum Co. v. Shutts	755
	Notes and Questions	761
	Problem 9-1	763
B.	Federal Subject Matter Jurisdiction	763
	1. Ordinary Class Actions	763
	Problem 9-2	765
	2. "CAFA" Class Actions and Mass Actions	765
	a. The Federal Court's Original Jurisdiction	765
	b. Cases Removed from State Courts	766
	c. Exceptions to the Federal Court's Jurisdiction	768
	d. Nonreliance on CAFA	769
	e. Mass Actions	770
	f. The Impact of CAFA	771
	Problems 9-3–9-4	772
C.	Requirements for Bringing a Federal Class Action Under Rule 23	773
	1. Satisfying the Prerequisites of Rule 23(a)	775
	Chandler v. Southwest Jeep-Eagle, Inc.	775
	Notes and Questions	780
	A Note on Class Certification	782
	A Note on Class Actions and the Statute of Limitations	782
	Problem 9-5	783
	Robidoux v. Celani	784
	Notes and Questions	788
	A Note on Subclasses	790
	Problems 9-6–9-7	791
	Wal-Mart Stores, Inc. v. Dukes [Part I]	792
	Notes and Questions	803
	2. Satisfying Rule 23(b)(1), (2), or (3)	805
	a. Rule 23(b)(1)(A) and (B)	805
	Boggs v. Divested Atomic Corp.	806
	Notes and Questions	811
	In re Telectronics Pacing Systems, Inc.	813

		Notes and Questions	820
		Problems 9-8–9-9	822
		A Note on Settlement Classes	823
	b.	Rule 23(b)(2)	824
		Wal-Mart Stores, Inc. v. Dukes [Part II]	825
		Notes and Questions	829
		A Note on the Preclusive Effect of Class Action Judgments	832
		Problems 9-10–9-12	833
	c.	Rule 23(b)(3)	834
		i. Predominance	834
		ii. Superiority	835
		iii. Four Non-exhaustive Factors	837
		iv. Notice to Class Members	838
		Hanlon v. Chrysler Corporation [Part I]	840
		Notes and Questions	847
		Problem 9-13	850
		A Note on Enjoining Competing Actions	850
		Problems 9-14–9-16	852
D.	Settlement or Dismissal of Class Actions		853
		Hanlon v. Chrysler Corp. [Part II]	855
		Notes and Questions	860
		Problem 9-17	864
E.	Class Arbitration Waivers		865
		AT&T Mobility LLC v. Concepcion	867
		Notes and Questions	878
F.	Class Action Review Problem		880
		Problem 9-18	880

Chapter X.   Adjudication Without Trial   885

A.	Summary Judgment		886
	1.	Introduction	886
	2.	The Basic Requirements for Summary Judgment	887
		a. Federal Rule of Civil Procedure 56	887
		b. Foundational Cases	888
		Anderson v. Liberty Lobby, Inc.	889
		Notes and Questions	897
		Problem 10-1	900
		Celotex Corporation v. Catrett	901
		Notes and Questions	908
		Matsushita Electric Industrial Co., Ltd. v. Zenith Radio Corp.	909

	Notes and Questions	921
	Problems 10-2–10-3	922
3.	Summary Judgment for the Plaintiff	923
	Problem 10-4	924
	Johnson v. Tuff N Rumble Management, Inc.	926
	Notes and Questions	934
	Problem 10-5	935
4.	Summary Judgment *Sua Sponte*	936
	Goldstein v. Fidelity and Guaranty Insurance Underwriters, Inc.	937
	Notes and Questions	941
	Problems 10-6–10-8	942
B.	Default Judgments	944
	Rogers v. Hartford Life and Accident Insurance Co.	945
	Notes and Questions	950
	Problem 10-9	952
C.	Dismissal of Actions	952
1.	Voluntary Dismissal	953
	Problem 10-10	956
2.	Dismissal for Failure to Prosecute	956
	Problems 10-11–10-12	958
3.	Dismissal as a Judicial Sanction	960
	Problem 10-13	961
D.	Adjudication Without Trial Review Problem	961
	Problem 10-14	961
Chapter XI.	**Trial**	**965**
A.	The Pretrial Conference	966
B.	The Right to a Trial by Jury	969
	Beacon Theatres, Inc. v. Westover	971
	Notes and Questions	975
	Problems 11-1–11-2	976
	Chauffeurs, Teamsters & Helpers Local No. 391 v. Terry	976
	Notes and Questions	984
	Problem 11-3	985
	Markman v. Westview Instruments, Inc.	986
	Notes and Questions	992
	Problem 11-4	992
	A Note on the Composition of Juries	993
	A Note on the Ongoing Debate over the Jury System	995

C. Jury Instructions and Verdicts   996
        Mitchell v. Gonzales   998
        Notes and Questions   1004
        Problem 11-5   1004
        A Note on Verdicts   1005
        Problem 11-6   1007
D. Motions for Judgment as a Matter of Law   1007
        Honaker v. Smith   1010
        Notes and Questions   1021
        Problem 11-7   1022
        Weisgram v. Marley Co.   1023
        Notes and Questions   1027
E. Motions for a New Trial   1028
        Tesser v. Board of Education   1029
        Notes and Questions   1039
F. Trial Review Problem   1041
        Problem 11-8   1041

Chapter XII.   Appellate Review   **1045**

A. Overview and Basic Terminology   1045
B. The Timing of an Appeal   1046
    1. Final Decisions and the Collateral-Order Doctrine 1046
            *Cohen v. Beneficial Industrial
                Loan Corp.*   1047
            Notes and Questions   1048
            Mohawk Industries, Inc. v. Carpenter   1050
            Notes and Questions   1056
            Problem 12-1   1058
            Quackenbush v. Allstate Insurance Co.   1058
            Notes and Questions   1060
            Problems 12-2–12-4   1061
            A Note on Appealability Under
                State Law   1062
    2. Statutory Exceptions to the Final Decision Rule 1063
        a. Interlocutory Appeals Under § 1292(a)(1)   1063
                Carson v. American Brands, Inc.   1064
                Notes and Questions   1067
                Problem 12-5   1068
        b. Interlocutory Appeals Under § 1292(b)   1068
                *Ahrenholz v. Board of Trustees of the
                    University of Illinois*   1070
                Notes and Questions   1072
                Problem 12-6   1073
        c. Review Under the All Writs Act   1073
                Will v. United States   1074

*Silver Sage Partners, Ltd. v. United
States District Court* 1079
Notes and Questions 1081
Problem 12-7 1082
d. Certification Under Rule 54(b) 1083
*Olympia Hotels Corp. v. Johnson Wax
Development Corp.* 1084
Notes and Questions 1086
C. Standards of Review on Appeal 1086
Questions Involving District-Court
Discretion 1087
Questions of Fact 1088
Questions of Law 1089
Mixed Questions of Law and Fact 1089
Pullman-Standard v. Swint 1090
Notes and Questions 1097
*Cooper Industries, Inc. v. Leatherman
Tool Group, Inc.* 1098
Notes and Questions 1105
Problems 12-8–12-9 1107
D. Review in the U.S. Supreme Court 1107
1. Section 1253 1108
2. Section 1254 1109
3. Section 1257 1111
Redrup v. New York 1111
Notes and Questions 1113
a. The Final-Judgment Rule 1114
Cox Broadcasting Corp. v. Cohn 1114
Notes and Questions 1119
Flynt v. Ohio 1120
Notes and Questions 1122
Problems 12-10–12-13 1123
b. Federal Question Raised and Decided 1124
Cardinale v. Louisiana 1124
A Note on the Adequate and
Independent State Ground Doctrine 1126
c. The Highest State Court in Which a Decision
Could Be Had 1126
E. Appeals Review Problem 1127
Problem 12-14 1127

Chapter XIII. The Binding Effect of a Final Judgment 1131

A. Claim Preclusion or Res Judicata 1132
1. The Same Claim 1133
*Porn v. National Grange Mutual
Insurance Co.* 1137

			Notes and Questions	1143
			Los Angeles Branch NAACP v. Los Angeles	
			Unified School District	*1144*
			Notes and Questions	1149
			A Note on Continuing Conduct	1149
			Problems 13-1–13-2	1151
			A Note on Intersystem Preclusion	1152
			State-to-State	1152
			State-to-Federal	1153
			Federal-to-State	1153
			Problem 13-3	1155
	2.	Final, Valid, and on the Merits		1155
		a. Finality		1155
			Federated Department Stores, Inc. v.	
			Moitie	*1156*
			Notes and Questions	1160
			Problems 13-4–13-5	1161
		b. Validity		1162
		c. On the Merits		1163
			Problems 13-6–13-7	1164
	3.	Same Parties and Persons Who Should Be Treated as Such		1165
			Taylor v. Sturgell	*1165*
			Notes and Questions	1174
			Problems 13-8–13-11	1177
B.	Issue Preclusion or Collateral Estoppel			1179
	1.	Same Issue		1180
			Commissioner of Internal Revenue v.	
			Sunnen	*1182*
			Notes and Questions	1186
			Some Further Thoughts on the Dimensions of an Issue	1188
			Lumpkin v. Jordan	*1189*
			Notes and Questions	1194
			A Note on Foreseeability—The *Evergreens* Problem	1195
			Problems 13-12–13-14	1195
	2.	Actually Litigated		1197
			Problem 13-15	1198
	3.	Decided and Necessary		1198
			Cunningham v. Outten	*1200*
			Notes and Questions	1202
			Problems 13-16–13-17	1203

	A Note on Potential Exceptions Based on the Nature of the Prior Proceedings	1203
	A Note on Alternative Determinations	1205
	Aldrich v. State of New York	1205
	Notes and Questions	1207
4.	Same Parties: The Principles of Mutuality and Nonmutuality	1208
	Bernhard v. Bank of America National Trust & Savings Association	1208
	Notes and Questions	1211
	Problem 13-18	1212
	Parklane Hosiery Co., Inc. v. Shore	1212
	Notes and Questions	1217
	Smith v. Bayer Corporation	1219
	Notes and Questions	1227
	A Note on Nonmutuality and Intersystem Preclusion	1228
C.	Claim and Issue Preclusion Review Problems	1230
	Problems 13-19–13-20	1230

Table of Cases	1233
Table of Authorities	1253
Index	1261

Preface

Most first-year law students find Civil Procedure to be one of their most challenging courses. While other first-year courses such as Contracts, Torts, Property, and Criminal Law present their own difficulties, they at least address roughly familiar turf—the making of enforceable agreements, the vindication of personal injuries, the ownership of property, and the commission and punishment of crimes—areas to which many of you have been exposed on television or at the movies, if not in real life. Civil Procedure, on the other hand, introduces us to a new language of process, and in a sense a new way of thinking, premised on rules and principles that occur and recur daily, but within the much less visible realms of civil litigation and formal dispute resolution. Because it has no "real world" counterpart, Civil Procedure is in some ways like a foreign language, possessing a linguistic culture of its own. As a student, your first challenge is thus to learn the basics of this new language—one in which you will soon find yourself to be surprisingly fluent.

While the doctrines of Civil Procedure may at times seem highly technical or more than moderately perplexing in their application, don't despair! The fog of one's initial encounter with procedure is natural, yet it is neither permanent nor impenetrable. To succeed at Civil Procedure, you need patience, discipline, and a willingness to appreciate the inherent play of some of the underlying doctrines. In our over 70 years of combined teaching experience, we have found that students who accept this challenge often, and to their surprise, find Civil Procedure to be one of their most enjoyable and rewarding courses. What at first glance might appear to be a subject that is dry and far removed from human experience may, with patience and effort on your part, turn out to be rich in its intellectual and practical possibilities. You might think of Civil Procedure as a series of puzzles, each with its own special rules and nuances. Like an intricate game, as you master one level, you will move on to a new and more challenging stage. If you learn to take one step at a time, you will proceed nicely to the finish.

We have, frankly, loved (and continue to love) teaching Civil Procedure. There is a deep pleasure in watching students learn to navigate an initially mysterious but almost always fascinating labyrinth. This casebook reflects our rich and satisfying experience. It embodies the thousands of hours we've spent in the classroom and in our offices—working with students, learning what works and what doesn't, trying new approaches. One thing of which we're certain is this: The only way to learn Civil Procedure is through an active process of applying the doctrines to the solution of real Problems. It is for this reason that this book contains well over 200 Problems interspersed throughout the text. We urge students who use the book to do the Problems as they appear in their assignments. Given the amount of material that must be covered, it is unlikely your professor will be able to cover all of the Problems in class. Yet this is a boon for you, for by doing the Problems your-self you will reap tremendous benefits. Make a habit of doing all of the Problems, either by yourself or with a small group of your fellow students. Then take the time to review the actual cases on which many of the Problems are based, the citations to which appear at the end of the Problem. If the court took a different approach than you did, ask yourself why. In short, make a habit of first learning the language of Civil Procedure by doing the reading and listening to your professor. Then practice using that language by applying it to the Problems as they appear in the book. This process of reading, thinking, doing—and sometimes redoing—is the one sure way to master Civil Procedure.

Good luck to you on this new adventure. We hope that these materials will serve as a useful learning tool, and that they will provide you with the knowledge and the confidence necessary to use the civil litigation system as a means of fur-thering justice.

Allan Ides
Christopher N. May
Simona Grossi

February 2016

Acknowledgments

First, we would like to thank David Burcham, the former dean of Loyola Law School and current President of Loyola Marymount University, whose friendship, leadership, and support have made the successful completion of this project a reality. We also express our gratitude to Professors Georgene Vairo and Lawrence Solum, both of whom read and provided helpful comments on draft chapters of this casebook, and to the Hon. Wm. Matthew Byrne, Jr., for his invaluable insights into the pretrial litigation process. Professor Michael Wolfson deserves special thanks for his contributions to the materials on discovery. Thanks also go to our research assistants, Gabriel Avina, Kasha Harshaw, Kate Ides, Amy Lerner, Susy Li, Ian Mackinnon, Meegan Moloney, Dara Tang, and Monica Vu for their many helpful contributions in preparing the First Edition of this book; to Mary Adams, Robert Briseno, Caitlin Comstock, Jamie Crute, Melissa Daghighian, Nina Kim, Jessica Levinson, Megan Moore, Tony Sain, and Jasmine Shoukry for their assistance in preparing the Second Edition; to Brittany Grunau, Megan Loebl, Ryan Rappeport, Anne Rawlinson, and Alejandro Ruiz for for their assistance in preparing the Third Edition; to Asaf Agazanof, Erin Murphy, Kelly Laffey, Bora Panduku, Danielle Perry, Paul Rezvani, Ivan Vuckovic, Maxwell Wright, and Rowena Zirbel for their assistance in preparing the Fourth Edition, with a special thanks to Elena DeCoste Grieco for her detailed copyediting on the Fourth Edition; and to Patrick Albasha, Dylan Bensinger, and Hope Satterthwaite for their assistance in preparing the Fifth Edition. Thanks, too, to our secretaries, Ruth Busch and Liz Luk, for all their help. We are also grateful to Pam Buckles and all the members of Faculty Support for their willingness to pitch in whenever asked.

We also want to thank the American Law Institute for granting us permission to reprint the Restatement (Second) of Judgments, §13 Comment b, §20, §24, §27, §35, §36, and §37, © 1982.

Finally, we would thank the thousands of wonderful students who over many years have given us inspiration and a better understanding of the learning process, and without whom we would never have undertaken such a project.

CIVIL PROCEDURE

INTRODUCTION

In this course we will study the court procedures that apply to civil lawsuits—suits in which a plaintiff seeks monetary or other relief against a defendant who has breached a contract, committed a tort, or in some other way violated the plaintiff's rights. While our principal focus will be on the procedures that govern civil actions in federal court, we will also look at some of the contrasting approaches followed by state courts. Each state is free to establish its own procedural rules, so long as these do not violate the federal Constitution. Yet many states have gradually modified their procedural rules so that they now closely resemble those of the federal courts. As a result, an understanding of the procedures that govern civil actions in the federal courts will often afford an excellent insight into state civil proceedings as well.

A.   The State and Federal Judicial Systems

In each of the 50, two sets of courts operate side by side, yet quite independently of each other. The states operate the first set while the federal government maintains the second. Although their structures vary, these systems invariably include at least one set of trial courts and one or two levels of appellate tribunals. Most state and federal courts hear both civil and criminal actions. In the criminal setting, prosecutors have no choice but to institute suit in a court operated by the government whose criminal laws are being enforced. A state prosecutor must therefore file a criminal action in one of the state's courts, while a U.S. Attorney can bring a federal criminal prosecution only in federal court. The picture is quite different—and considerably more interesting—with respect to civil suits. In the civil context, a plaintiff often has the choice of bringing her suit in either a state or a federal court. This would occur when the state and federal courts have "concurrent" jurisdiction over the type of suit being filed. As we will see, this is not an uncommon situation. In addition, she may be able to file her suit in any number of different states so long as the defendant is subject to the judicial authority of those states, and there may be multiple such states. Moreover, the plaintiff's choice of forum can be critical. While the state and federal judicial systems are similar in many respects, there are also important differences between them. The same is true among the different state courts whose applicable substantive and procedural law may differ in ways that can sometimes significantly affect a case's outcome.

1.   State Judicial Systems

Each state has its own system of trial and appellate courts. Most states have multiple levels of trial courts, each designed to hear certain types of suits. In these states, a court's "subject matter jurisdiction"—*i.e.*, the types of cases it is allowed to hear—often depends on the amount at stake and sometimes on the nature of the suit. In Florida, for example, the county courts hear actions involving up to $15,000, while the circuit courts have jurisdiction over suits that exceed this amount. In those states with only one level of trial courts, the trial court may hear all civil cases regardless of the amount in dispute. Such "unified" court systems are found in Illinois, whose circuit court is the state's only trial court, and in California, where the superior court hears all types of civil suits. Regardless of how many levels of trial courts a state maintains, the number of courts at each level is usually considerable. These tribunals are dispersed throughout the state so as to make litigation as convenient as possible.

If we shift our focus from the trial court to the appellate court level, we find similar variations among the states. About a dozen states have only one appellate court, usually called the supreme court. This is the case in Delaware, Nevada, and Vermont. However, most states maintain two levels of appellate courts, typically consisting of a supreme court and a set of intermediate courts of appeal. California, Florida, and Illinois are among the states falling into this latter category. Some states have several distinct intermediate appellate courts, each designed to hear certain types of cases. Alabama and Tennessee, in addition to a supreme court, each have two types of intermediate appellate tribunals, one for civil cases and the other for criminal cases. Finally, states such as Oklahoma and Texas have only one level of intermediate appellate court, but two courts of last resort—one for criminal cases (the Court of Criminal Appeals) and the other for civil cases (the Supreme Court). *See* Court Statistics Project, State Court Structure Charts (National Center for State Courts 2013) (*available at* http:www.courtstatistics.org/other-pages/state_court_structure_charts.aspx).

State judicial systems differ not only in terms of their structure but also with respect to the procedures that govern the handling of civil cases in their courts. The U.S. Constitution, particularly the Fourteenth Amendment Due Process Clause, places some limitations on the procedures state courts may employ in handling civil cases. Beyond this, each state is largely free to develop its own procedural rules for civil litigation. Not surprisingly, countless variations exist among state procedures, some trivial but others critical. They include such things as the paper size for pleadings, the need to number the lines on each page, the persons who may be included in a lawsuit, the ability to assert jurisdiction over those located outside the state, the amount of time a defendant has to respond to a complaint, the available discovery devices for gathering information, the procedures for summary adjudication, the right to a jury trial, the amount of time to appeal an adverse judgment, the preclusive effect of a judgment, and the need to employ alternatives like mediation or arbitration before proceeding with a lawsuit.

In bringing a lawsuit, plaintiffs often have the option of filing in several different states, due to the fact that courts in each of those states could acquire jurisdiction over the defendants. In these situations, the choice may be a critical one because of differences in the procedures that the court will follow and in the substantive law that the court will use to resolve the dispute. While it may be no surprise that the applicable procedures might vary depending on which court a case proceeds in, it may be less obvious that the substantive law used to resolve the dispute may also hinge on where the case proceeds. The reason for this is that when a suit has connections with more than one state, a court will apply its "choice of law" rules to decide which state's body of substantive law should be used. Since the states use different choice-of-law rules, the applicable substantive law—and thus the outcome of the case—may turn on where the suit proceeds. The subject of choice of law is not part of the basic Civil Procedure course. Yet it is important to realize that these issues, along with differences in the governing procedures, often play an important role in a lawyer's decision as to where to file suit. On the differences in state court systems, see generally COURT STATISTICS PROJECT, EXAMINING THE WORK OF STATE COURTS: AN OVERVIEW OF 2012 STATE TRIAL COURT CASELOADS (NATIONAL CENTER FOR STATE COURTS 2014) (hereinafter STATE TRIAL COURT CASELOADS, 2012).

2.   The Federal Judicial System

The ratification of the U.S. Constitution in 1788 brought into being the U.S. government, one of whose branches is the federal judiciary. Article III of the Constitution itself created the U.S. Supreme Court. However, the Framers left it for Congress to decide whether there should be any federal "inferior Courts," or whether all cases should instead commence in state court with the possibility of ultimate review by the Supreme Court on appeal. The first Congress was quick to resolve this issue. Through the Judiciary Act of 1789, it created a system of lower federal trial and appellate courts. These courts have continued to the present day, though their structure and jurisdiction have changed considerably over the years.

Article III strictly limits the kinds of cases the Supreme Court and any lower federal courts may hear. When Congress creates inferior federal courts, it must decide which of the Article III cases those courts can hear. Without such congressional authorization, cases falling within Article III cannot be brought in the lower federal courts but must instead be filed in state court. Congress may, if it wishes, then allow the Supreme Court to review those state court decisions that fall within Article III's scope. In this section, we consider the structure of the federal judicial system as it exists today and the types of cases the federal courts are authorized to hear. Later, we will take a brief look at the nature and extent of the federal courts' current caseload.

One can visualize the federal judicial system as a pyramid that consists of three levels of tribunals—the district courts, the courts of appeals, and the Supreme Court. The district courts are trial courts that have original jurisdiction over those

Article III cases Congress has authorized them to hear. The circuit courts of appeals are intermediate appellate tribunals that may review decisions of the federal district courts. The Supreme Court, which sits at the top of the federal judicial pyramid, may review decisions of the federal courts of appeals and state court decisions that involve questions of federal law or otherwise fall within Article III. Because Article III provides that the judges and justices on these courts shall hold their offices "during good Behaviour," they may be removed only by impeachment. In addition to these three courts, Congress has from time to time created specialized federal tribunals, including the court of federal claims, the court of international trade, customs and patent courts, military courts, territorial courts, tax courts, and bankruptcy courts. These tribunals, many of which still exist today, are beyond the scope of this course. Our focus will be on the district courts, the courts of appeals, and the Supreme Court.

At the federal district court level, Congress has divided the 50 states and the District of Columbia into roughly 90 districts; each state has at least one federal district court. No district embraces more than a single state, but in the more populous states each district includes only part of the state. Approximately half of the states consist of only one federal district (*e.g.*, the District of Colorado), whereas California, New York, and Texas are each divided into four federal districts (*e.g.*, the Northern, Eastern, Central, and Southern Districts of California). Congress determines the number of federal judgeships for each district based on the district's size and caseload. Idaho and North Dakota, for example, each encompass one federal district (*i.e.*, the District of Idaho and the District of North Dakota), and each has only two federal district judges. At the other end of the spectrum, the district courts for the Central District of California (Los Angeles) and the Southern District of New York (Manhattan) each have more than 25 federal judges. *See* 28 U.S.C. §§ 81-131. The total number of authorized federal district court judgeships is 677, though only about 600 of these positions are currently filled. In addition, nearly 350 senior district judges still handle cases. *See* Administrative Office of the U.S. Courts, Judicial Facts and Figures 2013, at tbl. 1.1; ADMIN. OFFICE OF THE U.S. COURTS, JUDICIAL BUSINESS OF THE U.S. COURTS 2014, at tbl. 3 (2014) (hereinafter JUDICIAL BUSINESS OF THE U.S. COURTS 2014). These figures contrast sharply with the 13 federal district court judgeships created by the Judiciary Act of 1789. *Compare* 28 U.S.C. § 133 *with* Judiciary Act of 1789, 1 Stat. 73, at §§ 2-3.

Turning to the intermediate appellate level, Congress has created 12 federal circuit courts of appeals. Eleven of these are numbered circuits (*i.e.*, First Circuit, Second Circuit, etc.), each embracing anywhere from three to nine states, and a circuit for the District of Columbia. Each circuit court hears appeals from the federal district courts in its designated geographic area. The number of judgeships for each circuit varies depending on its appellate caseload. For example, the First Circuit, which embraces four New England states and Puerto Rico, has only six circuit judges, while the Ninth Circuit—which includes seven western states plus Alaska, Guam, and Hawaii—has 29 circuit judges. *See* 28 U.S.C. §§ 41, 44. In addition to the 12 circuit courts of appeals, Congress created the Court of Appeals for the Federal Circuit, which reviews lower federal court decisions from around the country in certain types of cases such as those involving patents, claims against the United States, and international trade. *See* 28 U.S.C. § 1295.

At the top of the federal judicial pyramid sits the Supreme Court. While the Constitution created this tribunal, the Framers left it for Congress to decide how many Justices would sit on the Court. Over the years, the number has increased from its original six to its current level of nine. In terms of what cases the Supreme Court can hear, the Constitution itself defined the Supreme Court's "original" jurisdiction, *i.e.*, the small handful of Article III cases that may be commenced there rather than having to be appealed from a lower state or federal court. While the Constitution provided that the Supreme Court might take all of the other Article III cases in its appellate capacity, the Framers gave Congress the power to decide which of these cases the Court could actually hear. Congress has never allowed the Supreme Court to review on appeal all of the cases allowed under Article III.

The federal courts are courts of limited subject matter jurisdiction. Unlike their state counterparts, they cannot hear suits of all types but are limited to those that Article III, § 2 defines as falling within the federal judicial power. In the Framers' eyes, it was only in these limited categories of cases that there was a need to provide an alternative to or a check on the state courts. Not surprisingly, cases within Article III's federal judicial power include those involving the laws of the United States (embracing criminal and civil matters), those affecting foreign ambassadors and ministers, those between different states, and those between a state and citizens of another state. In each of these instances, there are obvious reasons as to why a litigant might not trust a state court to resolve the matter as fairly or as wisely as a federal tribunal might. From the standpoint of ordinary private litigants, the most important types of civil cases federal courts may hear are those "arising under" the Constitution, laws, or treaties of the United States ("federal question" cases), those between citizens of different states ("diversity" cases), and those between citizens and aliens ("alienage" cases).

The purpose of federal question jurisdiction is to provide a forum that will ensure the full, fair, and uniform enforcement of federally created rights regardless of where filed. Diversity and alienage jurisdiction afford litigants who are citizens of another state or country the option of proceeding in a forum that may be less influenced by local bias than a state court might be. Because state judges are usually chosen by popular election, they may be less immune to local pressure and prejudice than federal judges who hold their positions for life. The federal courts' jurisdiction in most federal question cases and in all diversity and alienage cases is concurrent with that of the state courts, rather than exclusive. This means that if the litigants wish to proceed with these cases in state rather than federal court, they are free to do so.

Federal question cases may be filed in a district court regardless of the amount that is in dispute. For diversity cases, however, the amount in controversy must exceed a congressionally established jurisdictional minimum. When this was raised in 1997 from $50,000 to $75,000, it had the initial effect of reducing the number of diversity cases filed in federal court. Yet the decline was only temporary.

By 2010, diversity filings had climbed to the point where they were nearly double their 1997 level. *See* Administrative Office of the U.S. Courts, Federal Judicial Caseload Statistics, 1997 and 2010, at tbl. C-2.

B.   State and Federal Court Caseloads

We have seen that a plaintiff can sometimes institute a particular lawsuit in either state or federal court. In addition, the plaintiff may often be able to do so in any of several different states. When deciding where to bring a suit, one of the factors a plaintiff's counsel may consider is the extent of a court's caseload and how long it is likely to take for the case to come to trial. In this section, we will take a brief look at the state and federal court caseloads. As we will see, while the variations are considerable, a court's caseload does not always determine the length of time it will take for a case to reach trial. In addition to their potential impact on a party's choice of forum, caseload figures may give us a deeper appreciation of the challenge that judges face, and a better sense of why lawsuits don't always move as swiftly as the parties might desire. These figures also help to explain the growing efforts in recent years to find ways of resolving civil disputes through means other than formal litigation.

1.   State Court Caseloads

Most state trial courts, at least those of the highest level, hear both civil and criminal cases. The proportion that each occupies in the overall caseload varies from state to state. During 2012, civil cases constituted 40 percent of the cases filed in all state courts combined, excluding traffic cases. State court civil filings leveled off in the 1990s after having increased steadily for many years. However, since the 2008 recession, civil filings have declined steadily, in part due to courthouse closures and reduced hours of business. *See* State Trial Court Caseloads, 2012, at 3-8.

The number of new civil filings (excluding domestic relations cases) varies dramatically from state to state. In 2012, more than 1 million new civil cases were filed in the state courts of California, New York, and Texas, as compared with fewer than 35,000 new filings in Alaska, North Dakota, and Vermont. While these differences are partly attributable to differences in states' populations, this is not the sole explanatory factor, for the number of new civil filings per 100,000 residents varies sharply from state to state—suggesting that some states are simply more litigious than others. For example, during 2012, there were over 9,000 new civil filings per 100,000 residents in Maryland, New Jersey, Virginia, and the District of Columbia, while in ten states—Alabama, Alaska, Arkansas, California, Hawaii, Maine, Minnesota, New Hampshire, Pennsylvania, and Vermont—the figure was less than half of that. *See* Court Statistics Project, 2012 Trial Courts—Civil

CASELOADS (Statewide Civil Caseloads and Rates), at 10 (NATIONAL CENTER FOR STATE COURTS 2014) (hereinafter STATE TRIAL COURTS—CIVIL CASELOADS, 2012).

The impact of new filings on the litigation process depends on both the number of cases filed and the number of judges available to hear them. A critical figure is therefore the number of new filings per judge. Since the principal state trial courts hear both civil and criminal cases, assessing a judge's workload necessitates taking both types of cases into account. During 2010, new civil and criminal filings (exclusive of traffic cases) ranged from fewer than 600 new filings per judge in Alaska, Idaho, Massachusetts, Mississippi, and West Virginia, to over 5,000 cases per judge in South Carolina. The median new filings per judge for all state courts that year was just under 1,800. *See* COURT STATISTICS PROJECT, AN ANALYSIS OF 2010 STATE COURT CASELOADS, at 5 (NATIONAL CENTER FOR STATE COURTS, rev. DEC. 2012).

While these figures may seem staggering, it is important to realize that a majority of the civil cases filed are dismissed, settled, or otherwise disposed of before they ever reach trial, thus consuming much less judicial time and attention than fully litigated actions. In California, for example, state trial courts processed over 900,000 civil suits during the 2012-2013 fiscal year, including more than 175,000 that were handled by the state's small claims court (which can hear claims by individuals of up to $7,500 and claims by other entities of up to $5,000). More than three-quarters of the California civil suits ended prior to trial. With respect to those that did go to trial, there is no right to a jury in small claims court. But of the civil cases that went to trial in the superior court where that right is fully protected, only 2 percent involved juries. The rest were tried to a judge, a far more expeditious procedure. The significant number of cases disposed of prior to trial, coupled with the low percentage of jury trials, helps explain the fact that in 2012-2013, over 80 percent of the California superior court's general civil cases were disposed of in less than a year, while more than 90 percent had been pending fewer than 18 months. Nor is California unique. In 2013, fewer than 5 percent of the civil cases disposed of by the New York Supreme Court—the state's principal trial court—went all the way through trial. And during 2002, for 21 reporting states (that did not include New York), 92 percent of the civil cases that terminated were disposed of prior to trial (with less than 1 percent involving jury trials). *See* JUDICIAL COUNCIL OF CALIFORNIA, 2014 COURT STATISTICS REPORT: STATEWIDE CASELOAD TRENDS 2003-2004 THROUGH 2012-2013, at 72-74 (2014) (hereinafter 2014 CALIFORNIA COURT STATISTICS REPORT); NEW YORK STATE UNIFIED COURT SYSTEM, ANNUAL REPORT 2013, at 23 (2014); COURT STATISTICS PROJECT, EXAMINING THE WORK OF STATE COURTS, 2003, at 22 (NATIONAL CENTER FOR STATE COURTS 2004) (hereinafter EXAMINING THE WORK OF STATE COURTS, 2003).

At the state appellate level, 39 states have intermediate appellate courts as well as a state high court; indeed, a few of these states—*e.g.*, Oklahoma and Texas— have two courts of last resort, one for civil cases and the other for criminal cases. In states with several levels of appellate tribunals, review at the first level is often mandatory if a timely appeal is filed, while further review by the state high court is usually discretionary. The remaining 11 states and the District of Columbia have a state high court but no intermediate appellate tribunals. In three of these states—Delaware, Nevada, and Wyoming—the high court has no discretion to reject a timely appeal, thus guaranteeing the right to appellate review. *See* COURT STATISTICS PROJECT, STATE COURT STRUCTURE CHARTS (NATIONAL CENTER FOR STATE COURTS 2013).

State appellate court caseloads vary dramatically. At the state high court level, the number of cases received each year is affected by several factors, including the state's population, how many lawsuits were instituted in the lower courts, and whether the state has any intermediate appellate courts. Many of the cases a high court receives are resolved summarily, *e.g.*, by simply denying a petition for discretionary review. In 2012-2013, while the California Supreme Court disposed of over 8,000 cases, it issued written opinions in only 94 (or 1.1 percent) of them. Similarly, the Illinois Supreme Court in 2012 processed almost 2,800 appeals, while issuing written opinions in only 81 (or 2.9 percent) of them. By contrast, in 2012 the Rhode Island Supreme Court—a much less busy tribunal even though it is the state's only appellate court—disposed of fewer than 400 appeals, while issuing written opinions in nearly 150 (or 39 percent) of them. There is no question but that in heavy-caseload states like California and Illinois, "[t]he Supreme Court's exercise of discretion to grant or deny petitions for review constitutes a significant part of its workload." *See* COURT STATISTICS PROJECT, 2012 APPELLATE CASELOAD TABLES (*Grand Total Appellate Court Caseloads*) (NATIONAL CENTER FOR STATE COURTS 2015) (hereinafter STATE APPELLATE CASELOADS 2012).

At the intermediate appellate level, caseloads again depend on the volume of litigation in the state trial courts and on the extent to which the appellate tribunal has discretion to deny review. During 2012, the number of cases over which jurisdiction was exercised by those intermediate appellate courts authorized to hear both civil and criminal cases ranged from highs of over 300 cases per judge in Florida to a low of about 50 cases per judge in Mississippi—both states in which the intermediate appellate courts have little if any discretion to deny review. *See* STATE APPELLATE CASELOADS 2012 (Opinions Reported by State Appellate Courts).

A significant percentage of state appellate decisions take the form of written but "unpublished" opinions that do not appear in any of the official court reports. During 2000, state high courts published about 40 percent of their opinions, with the figures varying sharply from state to state. In California, Illinois, Massachusetts, Ohio, Texas, and Washington, 100 percent of the state high court opinions were published. At the other end of the spectrum, the publication rates in Nevada and New Jersey that year were below 7 percent, while for the Arizona Supreme Court, the rate was less than 3 percent. *See* B. OSTROM, N. KAUDER & N. LAFOUNTAIN, COURT STATISTICS PROJECT, EXAMINING THE WORK OF STATE COURTS, 2001: A NATIONAL PERSPECTIVE 84-86 (NATIONAL CENTER FOR STATE COURTS 2002). The U.S. Supreme Court, by contrast, publishes all of the roughly 75 to 90 opinions it issues each year.

At the intermediate state appellate court level, the national publication rate tends to be a little higher than at the state high court level, averaging around 52 percent. However, in states whose high court publishes virtually all of its opinions, the publication rate at the intermediate appellate level may be much lower. Thus, in California during 2012-2013, the state supreme court published all 94 of its opinions, but the state's intermediate appellate courts published only 9 percent of their decisions. *See* Court Statistics Project, Examining the Work of State Courts, 1999-2000: A National Perspective 88 (National Center for State Courts 2001); 2014 California Court Statistics Report, at 13, 27.

There was a time when "unpublished" appellate opinions were not generally accessible to the public. This is no longer true, for while these decisions do not appear in the official court reporters, they are now often retrievable from computer databases such as LEXIS and Westlaw. This raises the issue of whether such officially unpublished decisions may be cited by counsel as authority in other cases. The answer varies depending on the court. Court rules in some states provide that such opinions have absolutely no precedential value and may not be cited in any other case, unless they are relevant for claim or issue preclusion purposes. *See, e.g.,* Cal. R. Ct. 8.1115(b) (eff. Jan. 1, 2007) (unpublished opinions may be cited only if "the opinion is relevant under the doctrines of law of the case, res judicata, or collateral estoppel" or when "the opinion is relevant to a criminal or disciplinary action because it states reasons for a decision affecting the same defendant or respondent in another such action").

However, because unpublished opinions that cannot be cited in other lawsuits raise fundamental questions of fairness, some states have begun to relax their restrictions on using such opinions for persuasive purposes. Kentucky, which previously banned the citation of unpublished decisions, now permits them to be cited "if there is no published opinion that would adequately address the issue before the court." Ky. R. Civ. P. 76.28(4)(c) (eff. Jan. 1, 2003). *See also* Alaska R. App. P. 214(d)(1) (eff. Apr. 15, 2008) (while citation of unpublished decisions "is not encouraged," they may be cited if "there is no published opinion that would serve as well"); Ariz. Sup. Ct. R. 111(c) (eff. Jan. 1, 2015) (unpublished opinions may be cited "if no opinion adequately addresses the issue before the court" and the opinion has not been ordered "depublished"); Tenn. Sup. Ct. R. 4(G)(1) (unpublished court of appeals opinions may be cited as persuasive authority unless designated "Not for Citation" by state supreme court); Ohio S. Ct. R. Rep. Ops. 3.4 (all court of appeals opinions, whether published or unpublished, "may be cited as legal authority and weighted as deemed appropriate by the courts"). Texas has gone much further. It no longer permits its appellate courts to issue "unpublished" opinions in civil cases, and treats all opinions rendered in civil cases as having precedential value. *See* Tex. R. App. P. 47.2(c) (eff. Jan. 1, 2003) and 47.7(b) (eff. Sept. 30, 2008).

2.   Federal Court Caseloads

When we turn from the state to the federal courts, we find that the number of civil filings in federal district courts pales in comparison with that of many state trial courts. During 2013-2014, there were roughly 295,000 new civil suits filed in the federal district courts—fewer than the number of new civil filings in many state courts during the previous year, even including relatively small states like Colorado, Kentucky, and Washington. The federal figure was dwarfed by that of the state courts of California, New York, and Texas, each of which had over one million new civil filings in 2012. And, when we look at all of the state trial courts combined, their total new civil filings in 2012 were about 18 million—more than 60 times the federal figure. *See* ADMINISTRATIVE OFFICE OF THE U.S. COURTS, FEDERAL JUDICIAL CASELOAD STATISTICS, 2014, at tbl. C-2 (hereinafter FEDERAL JUDICIAL CASELOAD STATISTICS, 2014); STATE TRIAL COURT CASELOADS, 2012, at 4.

Not only is the federal judiciary's total civil caseload smaller than that of many state courts, but federal judges' individual dockets—including both civil and criminal cases—tend to be far more manageable than that of their state counter-parts. We saw earlier that state trial court judges averaged nearly 1,800 new civil and criminal filings apiece during 2010. For federal judges, the figure was less than a third of that. And while the numbers vary considerably between federal districts, the disparities tend to be less extreme than at the state level. At the high end of the federal spectrum, the District of Arizona and the Southern District of West Virginia each had over 1,100 new filings per judge in 2013-2014—a figure that is still far lower than that of a typical state court judge. At the opposite end of the federal spectrum, there were nine federal districts where new filings that year averaged fewer than 300 cases per judge, with the Districts of Alaska and the District of Columbia each having fewer than 180 new cases per judge. *See* FEDERAL JUDICIAL CASELOAD STATISTICS, 2014, at tbl. X-1A.

These reduced disparities within the federal system reflect the fact that Congress has been sensitive in this area, from time to time creating new federal judgeships for those districts whose caseloads become unusually high. Thus, in 1999-2000, the Southern District of California had 871 new filings per judge, as compared with that year's national average of 488. In 2002, Congress responded by increasing the number of judgeships for that district from eight to 13. As a result, though total new filings in that district were higher in 2003-2004 than they were four years earlier, the number of new filings per judge averaged only 632, well below the 871 figure for 1999-2000. *See* Pub. L. No. 107-273, 116 Stat. 1786-1787 (Nov. 2, 2002); ADMINISTRATIVE OFFICE OF THE U.S. COURTS, JUDICIAL BUSINESS OF THE U.S. COURTS 2000 and 2004, at tbls. X-1A.

As in state court, the overwhelming majority of federal civil cases are resolved without ever going to trial. Thus, in 2013-2014, only about 1 percent of the cases that terminated involved a trial; of these, nearly 70 percent were jury trials. Since so few federal cases reached the trial stage, the median disposition time for civil cases that terminated that year was less than nine months. For cases that did go to trial, the typical time from the filing of the complaint to the completion of trial was only about two years, though the times varied sharply among federal districts—ranging from lows of 12 to 14 months in the Northern District of Florida and the Eastern District of Virginia, to over four and a half years in the Eastern

District of Tennessee. JUDICIAL BUSINESS OF THE U.S. COURTS 2014, at tbls. C-4 & C-5. The trials themselves tend to be brief. In 2013-2014, more than half of all federal civil trials took but a day, while over 75 percent were completed within three days. *See* JUDICIAL BUSINESS OF THE U.S. COURTS 2014, at tbl. T-2.

The length of time it takes for a civil case to be resolved through trial is not necessarily a function of the court's caseload. Thus, in 2013-2014, the Southern District of Ohio and the Northern District of New York each averaged about 450 new filings per judge, yet the median time to trial in the two courts differed by over a year—*i.e.*, 20 months in the Southern District of Ohio as compared to 35 months in the Northern District of New York. *See* JUDICIAL BUSINESS OF THE U.S. COURTS 2014, at tbls. C-5 & X-1A. The anticipated time to trial may influence a plaintiff's initial choice of forum, both between state and federal court, and among federal courts. It may also affect a defendant's decision whether or not to seek removal of a case from state to federal court. Even more fundamentally, it may influence the parties' willingness to forgo the judicial system entirely and to instead resolve their dispute through less formal means such as arbitration or mediation.

At the federal appellate level, the number of cases filed in the U.S. Circuit Courts of Appeals has declined slightly over the past five years. There has also been a steady drop in the percentage of court of appeals opinions that are published. In 2000-2001, the publication rate was 20 percent but by 2012-2013 it had fallen to 13.5 percent. Publication rates vary dramatically between federal circuits. During 2013-2014, the District of Columbia Circuit and the Eighth Circuit each published about half of their opinions, while the publication rate in the Fourth Circuit was below 7 percent. *See* JUDICIAL BUSINESS OF THE U.S. COURTS 2001, 2014, at tbl. B-12.

With respect to unpublished appellate court opinions, while it is agreed that they are not to be treated as *binding* precedent in other cases, the circuits differ in terms of what if any *persuasive* value they should have. Until recently, the circuits also varied in terms of when unpublished opinions could be cited, but the adoption of Federal Rule of Appellate Procedure 32.1 in 2006 eliminated those disparities. Rule 32.1 now provides that a federal court of appeals "may not prohibit or restrict the citation of federal judicial opinions, orders, judgments, or other written dispositions," whether they have been "designated as 'unpublished,' 'not for publication,' 'non-precedential,' or the like," if they were "issued on or after January 1, 2007." Yet it still remains for each circuit to decide how much weight it will accord such "unpublished" opinions, with some circuits giving them no precedential effect while others give them some persuasive value. *See* George C. Pratt, *Citing Judicial Dispositions*, in 20A MOORE'S FEDERAL PRACTICE §§ 332.1.01 *et seq.* (3d ed. 2015).

I

PLEADINGS AND RELATED MOTIONS

The basic unit of litigation in federal courts is the claim. It generates the litigation, controls the scope of discovery, provides the focal point for summary judgment, and determines the relevance of evidence to be presented at trial, should there be one. It is the heartbeat of the case. But it is much more than that. A claim presents a demand for justice under the law and, as such, the judicial recognition and enforcement of claims of right are essential components of the rule of law. As famously stated in *Marbury v. Madison*, 5 U.S. (1 Cranch) 137, 163 (1803):

> The very essence of civil liberty certainly consists in the right of every individual to claim the protection of the laws, whenever he receives an injury. One of the first duties of government is to afford that protection. . . .
>
> The government of the United States has been emphatically termed a government of laws, and not of men. It will certainly cease to deserve this high appellation, if the laws furnish no remedy for the violation of a vested legal right.

While there is no constitutional or statutory definition of what constitutes a claim, the Federal Rules of Civil Procedure, which were adopted in 1938 and which apply to all civil actions filed in federal court, are built around a precise understanding of that term. In this regard, Rule 8(a)(2) provides, "A pleading that states a claim for relief must contain . . . a short and plain statement of the claim showing that the pleader is entitled to relief. . . ." FED. R. CIV. P. 8(a)(2). We will study this rule in detail, but our focus now is on the word "claim." The use of that word reflected a conscious effort by the drafters of the federal rules to avoid an ongoing dispute over what constituted a "cause of action" and to use a word that signified a pragmatic understanding of the basic litigation unit as being comprised of "a group of operative facts giving rise to one or more rights of action." CHARLES E. CLARK, HANDBOOK OF THE LAW OF CODE PLEADING 477 (2d ed. 1947) (hereinafter "CLARK, HANDBOOK").*

---

* As to the controversy over the meaning of "cause of action," some argued that it referred to the distinct legal theory on which the case was premised, *e.g.*, a negligence or breach of contract theory; some thought that it referred to the invasion of a specified primary right, *e.g.*, causes of action for personal injuries as distinct from causes of action for property injuries; and others suggested that the cause of action embraced no more than a statement of the facts that had generated the legal action and that was suggestive of the pleader's legal theories justifying judicial relief. *See generally* Charles E. Clark, *The Code Cause of Action*, 33 YALE L.J. 817 (1924).

Think of "operative facts" as constituting a coherent story in which the narrator describes an event or a series of related events in which she claims to have suffered one or more injuries to her person and/or her property at the hands of the defendant. Our narrator's "rights of action" constitute the legal theories that may entitle her to some form of judicial redress. Her claim is a composite of the operative facts and the multiple rights of action arising out of those facts.

Hence, a claim is not merely a specified right of action, though the word is sometimes used colloquially in that fashion. Rather, a claim is the confluence of the facts and the rights of action arising out of them, which is to say that a claim in federal court is a collection of related facts giving rise to one or more rights of action. Together, the narrative facts and the rights arising out of them constitute the "cause" of the "action." So conceived, the term "claim" conveys the idea behind the phrase "cause of action," without generating the confusion that had previously accompanied the latter term. And indeed, the operative-facts definition is consistent with the idea of natural lawyering and judging that animated the drafters of the Federal Rules of Civil Procedure, under which pragmatic considerations of convenience, efficiency, and fairness would play a central role in the procedural system. *See* FED. R. CIV. P. 1 (endorsing the "just, speedy, and inexpensive determination of every action and proceeding").

The operative-facts definition of a claim plays an essential role in a wide range of procedural doctrines, many of which we will examine in this course. In this chapter, we examine the claim from the perspective of the pleadings. Pleadings are written documents through which a party to a civil action either asserts a claim or defense, or denies the legitimacy of an opposing party's claim or defense. In essence, the pleadings in a civil action are the documents through which the parties present their case to the court and define the basic scope of the controversy between them. Our primary focus will be on pleadings in federal court. We begin, however, with an examination of an alternate pleading model that existed prior to the adoption of the federal rules and that is still followed in some state judicial systems.

A.   Code Pleading

American colonial courts and their successor state and federal courts were modeled on the British judicial system. That system, which was more a product of history than of logic, adhered to a complicated procedural formula that divided judicial power between common law courts and courts of equity. Common law courts exercised jurisdiction over 11 precisely defined "forms of action," covering much of what we now know as tort, contract, and property law, and provided complainants basic remedies such as money damages and the return of improperly withheld property. Courts of equity exercised jurisdiction over any action that fell outside the 11 forms of action or that sought a remedy not available under those forms, such as an injunction or an accounting. While the system of pleading in equity was somewhat flexible, the system of pleading at common law was ritualistic, formal, and highly technical. The goal of common law pleading was to reduce every case to a single issue of law or fact; hence, common law pleading was sometimes referred to as issue pleading. It accomplished this goal through a lengthy and serpentine pleading process. *See generally* CHARLES A. KEIGWIN, CASES IN COMMON LAW PLEADING (2d ed. 1934); JOSEPH H. KOFFLER & ALISON REPPY, COMMON LAW PLEADING (1969); JOHN JAY MCKELVEY, PRINCIPLES OF COMMON LAW PLEADING (2d ed. 1917); BENJAMIN J. SHIPMAN, HANDBOOK OF COMMON-LAW PLEADING (3d ed. 1923).

The perceived defects in the common law pleading system led to calls for its abandonment. New York was the first state to do so. The revised New York Constitution adopted in 1846 began this process by merging the courts of law and equity into one court of general jurisdiction. A commission was then formed to abolish the common law system of pleading. The commission's work was adopted in 1848 and became known as the Field Code, after David Dudley Field, one of its principal authors. The Field Code was adopted or emulated by a majority of the states within 25 years. Even those states that retained some vestige of common law pleading altered their rules of pleading to conform to certain features of the code model.

The new codes had several important features and innovations. First, like New York, most code jurisdictions merged their courts of law and equity and created one court of general jurisdiction that could take cognizance of all forms of relief. Next, the codes abolished the common law "forms of action," replacing them with a single form typically described as a "civil action." The civil action was designed to accommodate common law, statutory, and equitable rights of action, *i.e.*, most lawsuits of a civil nature. In essence, under a code, one form fit all causes of action. Third, the codes liberalized rules regarding joinder of causes of action and parties, making it possible for litigants to receive a more complete resolution of their dispute in a single proceeding. In this respect, the codes borrowed heavily from equity practice. Finally, the codes simplified and shortened the pleading process by limiting the types of pleadings that could be filed to complaints, answers, demurrers, and replies, as well as by replacing "issue pleading" with "fact pleading."

Under the codes, the plaintiff initiated the lawsuit by filing a complaint (or in some jurisdictions a "petition"). The Field Code, which operated as a model for other states, provided that the complaint was to contain:

> (1) The title of the cause, specifying the name of the court in which the action is brought, the name of the county in which the plaintiff desires the trial to be had, and the names of the parties to the action, plaintiff and defendant.
>
> (2) A statement of the facts constituting the cause of action, in ordinary and concise language, without repetition, and in such a manner as to enable a person of common understanding to know what is intended.
>
> (3) A demand of the relief, to which the plaintiff supposes himself entitled. If the recovery of money be demanded, the amount thereof shall be stated.

N.Y. COMMISSIONERS ON PRACTICE & PLEADINGS, FIRST REPORT § 120 (1848). With respect to (2), a statement of facts in a complaint is built on "allegations."

An allegation is an assertion of a fact or facts that the pleader believes to be true. As such, an allegation is not proof of the fact or facts asserted.

Once properly served with a summons and a copy of the complaint, the defendant had two pleading options. She could file an answer in which she admitted or denied each "material" allegation in the complaint, and through which she alleged any "new matter" constituting a defense or counterclaim. *See id.* §§ 128-130. Alternatively, the defendant could file a "demurrer" through which she could challenge the legal sufficiency of the action, including that "the complaint does not state facts sufficient to constitute a cause of action." *Id.* § 122. The demurrer assumed that the facts were as the plaintiff stated them, but if the demurrer were overruled, the defendant could then challenge the facts by filing an answer and proceeding with the litigation process.

Once the answer was filed, the plaintiff could file a "reply" to any new matter asserted in the answer. In some code jurisdictions, however, a reply was unnecessary; new matter was assumed to have been denied. The reply (or an absence of one) ended the pleadings in most code jurisdictions. The matters contested would then be prepared for trial.

Although the code-pleading model had an elegant simplicity, the goal of pleading facts became somewhat more complicated than the authors of the codes had anticipated. The parties were expected to plead only the so-called ultimate facts, and not the evidentiary facts or conclusions of law. There were, however, no clear distinctions between these ill-defined categories. The result was that fact pleading began to take on some of the complexities of common law pleading, with numerous cases being won or lost on a court's belated perception of what did or did not constitute an ultimate fact. Thus an allegation that one was "entitled" to specific property might be treated as an impermissible conclusion of law, while an allegation that one was the owner of property and entitled to possession might be treated as a permissible ultimate fact. As one leading critic of fact pleading observed:

> The ultimate facts are supposed to be somewhere between the law and the evidence. But facts do not easily disentangle themselves from conclusions or from details. The pleader is attempting to restate or reconstruct past happenings; and, like individuals generally, he may be garrulous or he may be taciturn, he may be talkative or he may be reticent.

CLARK, HANDBOOK, *supra*, at 231. Clark's point was that the pleader should be given wide latitude to state her case, the only limiting principle being that the pleading provide notice of the underlying claim to the opposing side. *Id.* at 233.

In addition, while the phrase "cause of action" may initially have been conceived as something akin to the "operative-facts" definition of a claim, *see* Charles E. Clark, *The Code Cause of Action*, 33 YALE L.J. 817, 820-822 (1924), it evolved into a more technical meaning that equated it with a primary right (*e.g.*, personal injury, property injury, contractual rights, etc.) and with specified legal theories that would entitle the pleader to redress for a violation of the right at issue. As such, one set of facts could give rise to several theories of legal obligation, each of which had to be identified separately and fully justified by factual allegations that conformed to the essential elements of the asserted obligation. More generally, some jurisdictions began to treat fact pleading as an end in itself and not simply as the initiating stage of the litigation process. The consequence was that fact pleading in some states evolved into a highly technical and sometimes arcane art that all too often elevated the formalities of pleading above the merits of the underlying controversy and the efficient delivery of justice.

Epstein v. M. Blumenthal & Co.

158 A. 234 (Conn. 1932)

MALTBIE, C.J.

In this action M. Blumenthal & Co., Incorporated, and Maurice Rundbaken were made defendants. The complaint alleged in substance that on January 17, 1930, the plaintiff was walking on the sidewalk on Main street in the city of Hartford, and about 2 o'clock in the afternoon was passing the store of the defendant Blumenthal Company; that, when she was three or four feet from the building, a servant, agent, or employee of these defendants "suddenly and without warning of any kind, came out of the entrance carrying a ladder which he held in a horizontal position, holding the same with his hands, and which ladder extended in front of him about three feet. As the agent, servant or employee of the defendants, came out of this entrance with the ladder in this position onto the public highway, which at that time was considerably crowded, the plaintiff was passing this particular place, and he smashed into her with said ladder with great force and speed and struck her at about the knees with the end of said ladder, knocking her to the ground with great force and violence, causing her severe, painful and permanent injury and doing some damage to her clothing." The specifications of negligence read as follows: "The defendants were negligent in that their agent, servant or employee failed to act as a reasonable and prudent man having in mind the circumstances of his entrance into said public thoroughfare in the center of the shopping district at a period of the day when he knew, or should have known, that pedestrians were continually passing and re-passing said entrance; in that he carried with him a ladder which extended out into said street and which was below the eyes of any persons upon whom he would suddenly or sharply come upon; in that he entered said highway without looking to ascertain whether or not the circumstances or conditions warranted his entrance into said highway at that particular time with the object that he had in his hands and the manner in which he was carrying the same; in that he failed to give a warning or notice of any kind of his intention to enter said thoroughfare; and in that he carried with him an article which he should have known would do injury to any person upon which he might suddenly come under the circumstances of his unexpected entrance into said highway and the position in which he was carrying said article."

Upon the trial, the plaintiff offered evidence and claimed to have proved that the defendant Blumenthal Company operated a store on Main street in Hartford in its busiest section; that on the day of the accident the defendant Rundbaken had sent some men to place a large sign on the front of the store; that just prior to the accident they were using a ladder in hanging it; that one of them, as the plaintiff was passing upon the sidewalk, descended the ladder, and, when he reached the sidewalk, lowered it, and, holding it parallel with the sidewalk, walked toward the entrance of the store; that he changed his course in order to enter, and in so doing swung the ladder around so that it struck the plaintiff. The trial court charged the jury upon the issues of negligence, contributory negligence, and damages presented by the plaintiff's claims of proof, but it also called their attention to the allegations of the complaint, and instructed them that, before they could bring in a verdict for the plaintiff, they must find that she had been injured in the way mentioned in the complaint, and that the defendants or either of them were negligent in the way mentioned. The jury returned a verdict which the court refused to accept, and then adjourned the case until the next morning. It then stated that it was in accord with the verdict as regarded the defendant Blumenthal Company, but asked further consideration as regarded the defendant Rundbaken, and then gave them further instructions. In these it emphasized that the negligence proved must be the negligence alleged in the complaint; it told them it was their duty to examine its allegations; and it stated that it was proof of the allegations of negligence alleged, not of some negligence not alleged, which must support a verdict for the plaintiff. Thereafter the jury brought in a verdict for both defendants.

The purport of these instructions was that the jury could not bring in a verdict for the plaintiff, unless she had proved the particular cause of action she had alleged. Obviously the verdict was the result of this charge, and, if the trial court committed error in it, the judgment cannot stand. On the other hand, if it was correct, any errors it may have committed in the charge given before the jury first retired are not of any consequence. Reduced to its essence, the question is, Could proof of an injury suffered in the way the plaintiff's evidence indicated sustain a verdict upon the allegations of the complaint? The complaint not merely recited that a servant of the defendants, holding the ladder, suddenly and without warning came out of the entrance of the building as the plaintiff was passing and as he was doing this struck her with it, but the particular acts of negligence specified are expressly predicated upon his conduct in coming out upon the sidewalk. There is no suggestion in them of negligence upon his part in swinging the ladder around while upon the sidewalk nor of his management of it in proceeding toward the entrance of the store after he had descended from it. We have departed very far from the strictness of the old common-law doctrine of variance, and now discourage claims based upon it, regarding them only where there is a disagreement between the allegations and the proof in some matter essential to the charge or claim. *Maguire v. Kiesel*, 86 Conn. 453, 457. "However, it remains true that the plaintiff's allegations are the measure of his right of recovery. This is necessary in order to maintain regularity in procedure, and it makes for just decisions that the plaintiff should not be allowed to recover for a cause which he has not fairly alleged in his pleadings." *Mazziotti v. Di Martino*, 103 Conn. 491, 496. In this instance the plaintiff in her complaint has made the conduct of the defendant's servant in coming out upon the sidewalk the very basis and essence of her claim. Under these circumstances, a recovery based upon his negligence in swinging the ladder around after he descended from it and when he was proceeding toward the entrance of the store would be to go beyond the scope of the variations which we can overlook and permit a recovery upon a cause of action not alleged. After becoming satisfied that there was a fatal variance between the allegations and the proof, the trial court might well have suggested or even directed an amendment to the complaint. But it did not do this, and "it is our duty under the circumstances to accept the issue as framed by the pleadings, and review the court's determination of it." *Andrews v. Peck*, 83 Conn. 666, 668. The trial court committed no error in its instructions to the jury on returning them to reconsider their verdict as the case stood before it.

There is no error.

In this opinion the other Judges concurred.

NOTES AND QUESTIONS

1. *The fatal variance.*   What, precisely, was the "fatal variance" between the plaintiff's allegations and her proof at trial? Why do you think the plaintiff's lawyer presented proof at trial that differed from the complaint's allegations? Do you think that the defendants were surprised or prejudiced by this variance? The court recognized that some variances between allegations and proof would be permitted but concluded that this particular variance crossed the line of tolerability. As a consequence, the variance was deemed *material* and hence fatal. Why? Did you find the court's reasoning persuasive?

2. *The modern code approach to variances.*   In most jurisdictions today, the potential harshness of the rule against material variances has been substantially ameliorated by a number of developments. First, a variance will generally not be treated as material "unless it has actually misled the adverse party to his prejudice in maintaining his action or defense upon the merits." CAL. CIV. PROC. CODE § 469. How would the variance in *Epstein* have fared under this standard? Next, even material variances can be cured by an amendment to the pleadings, including an amendment to conform to proof, so long as this can be accomplished "upon such terms as may be just." *Id.* Under this standard the court might allow the opposing party additional time to prepare a response to the nonconforming evidence. That party might also be awarded the additional costs associated with the new preparation. Finally, a material variance can be "cured" by a party's failure to object to the nonconforming evidence at trial. In essence, the theory of the trial operates as an amendment of the pleadings.

This overall liberality toward variances is not, however, completely elastic. For example, in *Brautigan v. Brooks*, 38 Cal. Rptr. 784 (Ct. App. 1964), the defendant initially pleaded contributory negligence as a defense but then withdrew the plea before trial. After the evidence was in, some of which arguably supported that defense, the defendant moved to amend the pleadings to conform to proof. The trial court granted the motion. In reversing, the appellate court explained that the plaintiff, who had produced no evidence on this issue, had been placed in an untenable position. He could have either presented no response to the belated defense and run the risk inherent in such silence, or he could have reopened the case limited to the question of contributory negligence and thereby placed undue emphasis on that defense. The appellate court refused to place the plaintiff in this dilemma. Notice, however, that the appellate court did not base its ruling on the technicalities of pleading but on fairness and substantial justice between the parties. Was the remedy of amending her pleadings to conform to proof one that was available to the plaintiff in *Epstein*? Had she sought to make such an amendment, should she have been allowed to do so?

3. *Ultimate facts, evidentiary facts, and conclusions of law.*   A pleader must plead ultimate facts, as opposed to evidentiary facts or conclusions of law. Stated at a general level, the ultimate facts are those factual propositions on which liability will be directly established. Evidentiary facts are the raw data through which the ultimate facts will be proven. Conclusions of law are mere recitations of the legal standards applicable to the cause of action asserted. A California practice manual provides the following example: "A complaint in a personal injury case alleges that: (1) defendant drove his car immediately after having consumed a fifth of vodka; (2) defendant drove while under the influence of alcohol; and (3) defendant drove in violation of California drunk driving law." 1 ROBERT I. WEIL & IRA A. BROWN, JR., CALIFORNIA PRACTICE GUIDE: CIVIL PROCEDURE BEFORE TRIAL 6-33 (2010). Allegation (1) is an evidentiary fact; allegation (3) is a conclusion of law; and allegation (2) is an ultimate fact. *Id.* While it may be difficult to draw a bright line between these categories, you must try to develop a sense of the distinction since conclusions of law will not count in determining whether the facts are sufficient to state a cause of action, and evidentiary facts are not necessary and may even narrow the scope of what a party is permitted to prove at trial. How would your characterize Epstein's allegations? Was the excessive detail a factor in the court's conclusion that the variance was fatal?

PROBLEM

1-1. Read Federal Rule of Civil Procedure 15(b) in your supplement. It has been said that Rule 15(b) was designed "to avoid the tyranny of formalism." *In re Santa Fe Downs, Inc.*, 611 F.2d 815, 817 (10th Cir. 1980). Using the facts of *Epstein*, would a federal court following Rule 15(b) have granted a motion to conform the pleadings to the evidence? Would it have done so even after the judgment had been entered? *See* 6A CHARLES ALAN WRIGHT, ARTHUR R. MILLER & MARY KAY KANE, FEDERAL PRACTICE AND PROCEDURE § 1491 (3d ed. 2010 & Supp. 2015).

Modern jurisdictions that adhere to the fact-pleading model have eliminated much of the formalism that infected fact pleading in the early part of the twentieth century. For example, California Code of Civil Procedure § 452 provides: "In the construction of a pleading, for the purpose of determining its effect, its allegations must be liberally construed, with a view to substantial justice between the parties." CAL. CIV. PROC. CODE § 452. However, a complaint still must allege facts sufficient to state a cause of action. As phrased in § 425.10(a)(1) of the California Code of Civil Procedure, a complaint shall contain "a statement of the *facts* constituting the cause of action, in ordinary and concise language." *Id.* § 425.10(a)(1) (emphasis added); *see Committee on Children's Television, Inc. v. General Foods Corp.,* 673 P.2d 660, 669 (Cal. 1983); 4 B.E. WITKIN, CALIFORNIA PROCEDURE §§ 378-397 (5th ed. 2008).

The following case presents an example of a state supreme court—the California Supreme Court—assessing the sufficiency of a complaint under contemporary fact-pleading standards. In order to appreciate the court's application of those standards, two preliminary points must be considered. First, the court makes reference to allegations made on "information and belief." An allegation made on information and belief is one about which the pleader lacks personal knowledge, as when the pleader reasonably relies on information supplied by a third party, or when the pleader lacks the means of obtaining that knowledge, typically because the relevant information is in the adverse party's possession. Allegations premised on information and belief are permitted, but the party must premise them on something more than mere conjecture or the boilerplate recitation of the claim's substantive elements. *See 4* WITKIN, supra, §§ 398-399.

Second, as noted previously, fact pleading requires the pleader to allege the "ultimate facts" as opposed to evidentiary facts or conclusions of law.

Doe v. City of Los Angeles

169 P.3d 559 (Cal. 2007)

MORENO, J.

Code of Civil Procedure § 340.1, which extends the statute of limitations within which a victim of childhood sexual abuse may sue a person or entity who did not perpetrate the abuse but was a legal cause of it, requires that such actions be brought before the victim's 26th birthday, unless the defendant "knew or had reason to know, or was otherwise on notice, of any unlawful sexual conduct by an employee, volunteer, representative, or agent, and failed to take reasonable steps, and to implement reasonable safeguards, to avoid acts of unlawful sexual conduct in the future by that person. . . ." (Code Civ. Proc., § 340.1, subd. (b)(2).)

Plaintiffs, John Doe and John Doe 2, now in their 40's, sued the City of Los Angeles ["City"] and the Boy Scouts of America ["BSA"] alleging they had been sexually abused by David Kalish, a police officer, while they were participants in the Los Angeles Police Department ["LAPD"] Explorer Scout Program in the 1970s. The superior court dismissed their actions on the ground that the statute of limitations had lapsed because plaintiffs failed to adequately plead that defendants "knew or had reason to know, or [were] otherwise on notice, of any unlawful sexual conduct" by Kalish. The Court of Appeal affirmed.

We granted review to examine whether the pleadings in these cases are sufficient to invoke the extended statute of limitations set forth in subdivision (b)(2). . . .

I.   FACTS

A.   *Doe 1's Complaint*

Doe 1's operative pleading . . . alleges that Kalish sexually abused him "between approximately 1974 through 1979" when he was under 18 years old and a participant in the "Law Enforcement Explorer Scout program" at LAPD's Devonshire division. Kalish, who was a supervisor of that program and allegedly used his position as supervisor to molest Doe 1, is not a party to this appeal. The complaint further alleges causes of action against the City [and] BSA . . . for negligent vetting, supervision, training and retention of Kalish, negligent supervision and management of the Explorer Scout program, negligent failure to warn and negligent failure to supervise and protect Doe 1.

Doe 1 alleges that he first met Kalish while Doe 1 was a participant in the Deputy Auxiliary Police (DAP) program at LAPD's Devonshire division. The DAP program was sponsored by the police department and provided social and athletic activities to at-risk children between the ages of 12 and 14. According to Doe 1, it was common knowledge among LAPD officers that Kalish sought out and befriended boys in the DAP program who "bec[a]me his eventual victims." Kalish encouraged some of these boys to join the Explorer Scout program after they completed the DAP program "so that he could have further access to them in subsequent years." Doe 1 joined the Devonshire Explorer Scout program in 1975, when he was 14 years old, and remained a participant until sometime in 1979, when he was 17. . . .

Doe 1 alleges that Kalish was a pedophile and a friend of Vince Pirelli, a known pornographer who specialized in pornographic movies featuring boys. According to Doe 1, Pirelli was present at Kalish's house at the same time as some of the Explorer Scouts, and Kalish pressured Doe 1 to participate in Pirelli's pornographic movies. Another of Kalish's victims was also pressured into making pornographic movies for Pirelli. On information and belief, Doe 1 alleges that Kalish filmed sexual encounters at his home with victims other than Doe 1 and had a preference for "young slight blond boys," a description that fit at least two of his victims from the Explorer Scout program.

Doe 1 alleges on information and belief that it was "commonly known" that Kalish invited Explorer Scouts into his home outside of sanctioned program events and activities. Kalish would pick up plaintiff and other Explorer Scouts, at least one of whom Kalish also sexually abused, and drive them to his house. There, he allowed Explorer Scouts to drink and watch pornography. On one occasion, a boy who had been drinking at Kalish's house became drunk and was involved in a traffic incident that resulted in a police report.

Kalish also drank with some of his victims in the parking lot of Devonshire station after his victims had completed their evening shift at the Communications Division. On one occasion, Kalish became intoxicated and asked another victim, who was an unlicensed 15 year old, to drive him home. Kalish took the same boy to the police academy to watch Kalish complete his monthly firearm qualification, and then bought his victim gifts at the police academy gift shop. At other times, he took the boy to the police academy to play racquetball or jog, after which they showered together, and then Kalish would take the boy home at 3:00 or 4:00 A.M. Kalish showed favoritism to this boy and others, including Doe 1, by buying them LAPD jackets and shirts, some of which were unavailable to the public, and openly giving them these gifts at Devonshire station. He also showed favoritism by providing "additional ride-alongs, ride-alongs in the downtown patrol division, and commendations."

Doe 1 alleges that other police officers from Devonshire station participated in unauthorized activities and trips with Kalish and Explorer Scouts. Additionally, it was "commonly known" that Kalish traveled to Thailand which is "a known heaven for pedophiles." Doe 1 alleges on information and belief that, on one of these trips, other LAPD officers observed Kalish with a young Thai boy.

Doe 1 alleges that on one occasion Kalish molested him at a sanctioned Explorer Scout activity and on another occasion as Kalish was driving Doe 1 home from a sanctioned activity. A third incident occurred at Doe 1's home. Doe 1 was afraid of what would happen to his Explorer Scout career and his hope to become a police officer if he resisted Kalish. Additionally, Kalish had threatened at least one other victim to keep him silent and constantly asked whether that victim had confided in anyone.

On information and belief, Doe 1 alleges that nationwide there have been at least 31 reported incidents of the sexual abuse of Explorer Scouts by police officers participating in the Explorer Scout program. With respect to the Devonshire program, Doe 1 alleges that, prior to the incidents involving Kalish, there were "other instances of misconduct . . . between Advisors and Scouts involving drinking and sexual fraternization" that should have put those in charge of the program on notice of the need to make changes to protect the scouts against sexual exploitation. He alleges further that "other LAPD officers viewed the Explorer/Scout program as a 'time bomb' because of lax supervision and inadequate oversight, the nature of the program, and other known incidents of improper fraternization between officers and scouts."

Based on Kalish's improper conduct with scouts including unauthorized fraternization, favoritism and engaging in prohibited one-on-one contact with targeted scouts, "[d]efendants and each of them knew or should have known that Kalish presented a risk of sexual exploitation to boys in the Devonshire Explorer/Scout program. . . . Defendants and each of them further knew or should have known that Kalish had a friendship and/or business interests with known pornographer

Vince Pirelli, and that Kalish traveled on more than one occasion to Thailand, both of which should have prompted immediate inquiry as the nature of those friendships and trips posed a risk to the young boys in the Explorer/Scouts."

B.   Doe 2's Complaint

Doe 2's operative pleading is his first amended complaint. It contains the same causes of action alleged in Doe 1's fourth amended complaint against the same defendants, and its allegations closely track those made in Doe 1's complaint. Like Doe 1, Doe 2 alleges that he was molested by Kalish between 1974 and 1979 while he was a participant in the Explorer Scout program. The complaint also identifies Doe 2 as the other victim referred to in Doe 1's complaint whom Kalish allegedly had driven him home because Kalish was too intoxicated to drive and whom Kalish took to the police academy to watch Kalish complete his monthly firearm qualifications and to play racquetball and jog.

Doe 2's complaint contains additional allegations regarding defendants' knowledge. Doe alleges that "BSA knew and the LAPD should have known, prior to the incidents complained of here, that pedophiles were active in its organization and the programs it sponsored." Additionally, Doe 2 alleges on information and belief that "since the early part of the last century—the BSA has maintained 'Confidential Files' on questionable scout leaders, including those suspected of child molestation." The complaint further alleges that since 1971, "more than half of all leaders placed in the Confidential Files have been put there for child abuse," and these statistics "represent only a small number of the suspected pedophiles in the BSA organization." Doe 2 alleges that prior to his molestation by Kalish, "numerous adults in BSA programs, were investigated, arrested and/or tried for child sexual abuse." He alleges further that statistics maintained by BSA since 1980 show "more than one incident of sexual abuse per week for the past two decades involving scouts and scout leaders, that is, more than 1000 reported incidents since 1980." He alleges that BSA knew or had reason to know of comparable numbers of sexual abuse occurring before 1980.

Doe 2 alleges that LAPD and BSA knew or should have known that, prior to Kalish's molestation of Doe 2, "sexual exploitation and sexual abuse of Explorer Scouts had occurred in its Hollywood and Devonshire programs." Specifically, Doe 2 alleges that "in the late 1960's and early 1970's . . . Defendant LAPD knew and Defendant BSA should have known of the following: a) that a police officer was having sex with an Explorer Scout in the Hollywood Division's Explorer Scout Program[;] b) that another two police officers were having sex with a different Explorer Scout in the Hollywood Division's Explorer Scout Program; and c) that another police officer had sex with an Explorer Scout in the Devonshire Division's Explorer Scout Program while on a sanctioned scout camping trip and got her pregnant."

Accordingly, Doe 2 alleges on information and belief that defendants "knew or should have known, prior to the incidents complained of here, that numerous incidents of sexual abuse and sexual exploitation occurred in BSA-sponsored programs and in the LAPD Explorer Scout program; that pedophiles were active in the BSA organization and the programs it sponsored; that the subject Explorer Scout program is a program of such nature so as to create an especial risk of sexual exploitation and sexual abuse to the minor scouts participating in them; that pedophiles seduce their victims in ways similar to that of adults; and that training, education, warnings and supervision would prevent or at least minimize the likelihood of sexual exploitation and abuse."

C.   The Demurrers

Both the City and BSA demurred to the plaintiffs' operative complaints. As relevant here, BSA argued that the complaints were barred by the statute of limitations, which ordinarily precludes an action against a nonperpetrator defendant after the plaintiff's 26th birthday. BSA acknowledged that § 340.1, subdivisions (b) and (c) revived such actions against a nonperpetrator defendant for a one-year period, but argued that plaintiffs had failed to comply with the statute's knowledge or notice requirements because they had not pled "that Boy Scouts of America knew or had reason to know in advance of unlawful sexual conduct by Kalish and that he was an employee, volunteer, representative, or agent." The City also cited plaintiffs' failure to sufficiently allege knowledge or notice as a ground for its demurrers.

The trial court agreed with the defendants and sustained the demurrers without leave to amend. . . .

The Court of Appeal affirmed the dismissal of plaintiffs' action. We granted review.

II.   ANALYSIS . . .

A.   The Purpose and Scope of Subdivision (b)(2) . . .

Thus, construing [subdivision (b)(2)] as a whole, the knowledge or notice requirement refers to knowledge or notice of *past* unlawful sexual conduct by the individual currently accused of other unlawful sexual conduct. [T]his construction of the statute is supported by the legislative history. In an analysis of the policy reasons supporting Senate Bill No. 1779, it was noted: "According to the proponents, many of the victims that would be covered under this bill were abused for years during their childhood, enduring hundreds of assaults from employees or agents that the employer knew or had reason to know had committed *past* unlawful sexual conduct but failed to take reasonable steps to prevent *future* occurrences." (Assem. Com. on Judiciary, Rep. on Sen. Bill No. 1779, as amended June 6, 2002, p. 9.)

Fairly construed, then, subdivision (b)(2) requires the victim to establish that the nonperpetrator defendant had actual knowledge, constructive knowledge (as measured by the reason to know standard), or was otherwise on notice that the perpetrator had engaged in past unlawful sexual conduct with a minor and, possessed of this knowledge or notice, failed to take reasonable preventative steps or implement reasonable safeguards to avoid acts of future unlawful sexual conduct by the perpetrator.

B.   Are Plaintiffs' Pleadings Sufficient to Satisfy the Knowledge or Notice Requirements of Subdivision (b)(2)?

Preliminarily, the parties disagree as to the level of specificity required of plaintiffs' knowledge and notice pleadings. Characterizing subdivision (b)(2) as a "defense" to the statute of limitations, the Court of Appeal held that plaintiffs must allege specific facts, although it did not explain what this entailed. Defendants adopt this position. Plaintiffs, by contrast, contend that the doctrine of "less particularity" applies to the knowledge and notice pleadings. This doctrine provides that "[l]ess particularity [in pleading] is required when it appears that defendant has superior knowledge of the facts, so long as the pleading gives notice of the issues sufficient to enable preparation of a defense." (*Okun v. Superior Court* (1981) 29 Cal. 3d 442, 458, 175 Cal. Rptr. 157, 629 P.2d 1369.) Thus, plaintiffs contend that "pleading ultimate facts is sufficient since the particularized knowledge lies with the defendant and the defendant does not need more information for evaluation of the action brought against it."

We disagree with any implication in the Court of Appeal's analysis that plaintiffs seeking the shelter of subdivision (b)(2) are required to plead evidentiary, as opposed to ultimate facts, and may not include allegations based on information and belief. Contrary to the Court of Appeal's characterization, the subdivision is not a defense to a statute of limitations but, as we have observed, an expansion of the limitations period, the purpose of which is to expand access to the courts by victims of childhood sexual abuse. It would be inconsistent with this purpose, or with the mandate to broadly construe these provisions, to apply more stringent rules of pleading than those that ordinarily apply. Thus, the complaint ordinarily is sufficient if it alleges ultimate rather than evidentiary facts. Moreover, "[p]laintiff may allege on information and belief any matters that are not within his personal knowledge, if he has information leading him to believe that the allegations are true." (*Pridonoff v. Balokovich* (1951) 36 Cal. 2d 788, 792, 228 P.2d 6.)

Furthermore, we agree with plaintiffs that the doctrine of less particularity may be especially appropriate in this setting. The legislative history of Senate Bill No. 1779 demonstrates the Legislature was particularly sensitive to cases of childhood sexual abuse in which the nonperpetrator defendant concealed from victims of that abuse its knowledge of the perpetrator's past acts of unlawful sexual conduct. "[C]laims of some victims were delayed because the employer withheld information from victims or lied to victims so the employers' negligence and wrongful conduct would not be discovered. This is a key distinction and policy justification for holding these wrongdoing employers liable past the victim's 26th birthday. In these cases, the evidence is not lost because the perpetrator of the abuse could not be found or his memories faded. Instead, the evidence is in the possession of the wrongdoing employer or third party, who knew or had reason to know of complaints of sexual misconduct against the employee or agent but failed to take reasonable steps to avoid future unlawful acts by that employee or agent." (Assem. Com. on Judiciary, Rep. on Sen. Bill No. 1779, as amended June 6, 2002, p. 9.)

This recognition by the Legislature that one reason a plaintiff may remain ignorant of the nonperpetrator defendant's wrongdoing is because that defendant has withheld or concealed evidence of its wrongdoing argues strongly in favor of broader, rather than more restrictive, standards of pleading where subdivision (b)(2) is alleged to apply. In the appropriate case, a plaintiff should be able to rely on the doctrine of less particularity where he or she can plausibly allege that the nonperpetrator defendant withheld or concealed evidence of its knowledge or notice of the perpetrator's past unlawful sexual conduct with minors.[5]

Nothing in the foregoing discussion, however, assists these plaintiffs because no degree of broad construction of their pleadings can supply what is missing from them—allegations that defendants knew, had reason to know, or were otherwise on notice of past incidents of unlawful sexual conduct by Kalish with minors that triggered the duty on defendant's part to take preventive measure to avoid acts of unlawful sexual conduct by Kalish in the future.

Plaintiffs' repetitive and rambling allegations regarding the knowledge or notice requirement can be distilled into five categories. First, there are numerous allegations to the effect that defendants inadequately supervised the Explorer Scout program at Devonshire station during the time period that plaintiffs participated in the program and, as a result, it was staffed by unqualified officers who engaged in improper activity with the participants. Second, there are general allegations that the BSA was aware of past incidents involving sexual molestation of scouts by scout leaders along with more specific allegations that, prior to Kalish's molestation of plaintiffs, defendants were aware of incidents of sexual misconduct by other officers involved in the Explorer Scout programs at the Hollywood and Devonshire stations. Third, there are general allegations that BSA was aware that sexual predators were active in its programs. In this connection, plaintiffs allege that there were significant reported incidents of sexual misconduct by scout leaders after 1980 from which they infer that a comparable number of such incidents was known to the BSA before 1980. Fourth, there are allegations that other police officers were aware of Kalish's pedophilic tendencies—these are the "commonly known" allegations—because of his open interest in young boys, the favoritism he showed to certain of the scouts, including the plaintiffs, his inappropriate fraternization with some scouts, including plaintiffs, both on the job and at his home, his alleged association with a known pornographer, and his trips to Thailand, where

---

5. On the other hand, the pleading must conform to "the general rule that a complaint must contain only allegations of ultimate facts as opposed to allegations of . . . legal conclusions. . . ." (*Burke v. Superior Court* (1969) 71 Cal. 2d 276, 279, fn. 4, 78 Cal. Rptr. 481, 455 P.2d 409.) Thus a pleading that did no more than assert boilerplate allegations that defendants knew or were on notice of the perpetrator's past unlawful sexual conduct would not be sufficient nor would allegations of information and belief that merely asserted the facts so alleged without alleging such information that "lead[s] [the plaintiff] to believe that the allegations are true." (*Pridonoff v. Balokovich, supra,* 36 Cal. 2d at p. 792, 228 P.2d 6.)

he was observed in the company of a young boy, among other allegations. Fifth, there are the allegations pertaining to Kalish's molestation of plaintiffs while he was on duty.

Plaintiffs argue that these allegations satisfy the knowledge or notice requirement of subdivision (b)(2) because that subdivision requires nothing more than constructive knowledge or notice by the nonperpetrator defendant of a single incident of sexual misconduct "no matter how minor," by "*any* of [the nonperpetrator defendant's] employees, volunteers, representatives or agents" to "subject [the defendant] to the provisions of subdivision (b)(2)." This argument, however, wrenches out of context particular words in the provision—"*any* unlawful sexual conduct by *an* employee, volunteer, representative, or agent"—in a manner incompatible with the principles of statutory construction to which we have previously referred and also with the legislative intent behind the subdivision as expressed in the plain language of the statute and the legislative history. Plaintiffs' argument impliedly concedes what is plain on the face of their complaints: that their complaints fail to allege that defendants had knowledge of Kalish's past unlawful sexual conduct with minors, which is the prerequisite for imposing upon these defendants liability for his subsequent sexual abuse of plaintiffs. That defendants had knowledge or notice of misconduct by Kalish that created a risk of sexual exploitation is not enough under the express terms of the statute. In the absence of sufficient allegations of knowledge or notice on the part of these defendants, their demurrers were correctly sustained and the actions against them properly dismissed.

III.   DISPOSITION

We affirm the judgment of the Court of Appeal.

NOTES AND QUESTIONS

1. Demurrer.   The City and the BSA filed "demurrers" to the plaintiffs' complaints. A demurrer is a type of motion used to attack the legal sufficiency of a pleading. There are several grounds on which a demurrer can be based, including, among others, lack of subject matter jurisdiction, lack of capacity to sue, and misjoinder of parties. *See, e.g.,* CAL. CIV. PROC. CODE § 430.10(a)-(i) (listing grounds for a demurrer). The demurrers in Doe asserted that the complaints filed by Doe 1 and Doe 2 failed to "state facts sufficient to constitute a cause of action." *Id.* § 430.10(e). If a court sustains a failure-to-state-facts-sufficient demurrer (also known as a "general demurrer"), the court will usually give the plaintiff at least one opportunity to file an amended complaint that attempts to cure the pleading deficiency.

2. Identifying the focal point of the pleading deficiency.   At issue in *Doe v. City of Los Angeles* was whether the plaintiffs' complaint against the City and the BSA contained sufficient allegations to extend the statute of limitations pursuant to

§ 340.1(b)(2) of the California Code of Civil Procedure on claims of nonperpetrator liability. To be clear, the question was not whether the plaintiffs' allegations were sufficient to state a claim for negligent supervision or the like, but whether those allegations were sufficient to extend the statute of limitations on such a claim. Hence, the critical allegations in the complaint were only those allegations relevant to the legal standard established by § 340.1(b)(2). What was that standard and why did the court conclude that the plaintiffs' allegations failed to satisfy it? More specifically, why did the court deem the allegations referenced in the penultimate paragraph of Part II inadequate?

3. *Doctrine of less particularity.*   The court mentions the doctrine of less particularity. What are the requirements of that doctrine? And how does it alter the pleading standard in a code system like California's? Was the court's conclusion that the plaintiffs' allegations failed to satisfy the standard under § 340.1(b)(1) consistent with the court's earlier observation that the "doctrine of less particularity may be especially appropriate in this setting"? Or did the flaw in the plaintiffs' pleadings have nothing to do with the degree of particularity?

4. *Information and belief.*   The court voices its disagreement with "any implication in the Court of Appeal's analysis that plaintiffs seeking the shelter of subdivision (b)(2) are required to plead evidentiary, as opposed to ultimate facts, and may not include allegations based on information and belief." What was the basis for this disagreement? What does it mean to plead on "information and belief"? How would you distinguish allegations based on information and belief from allegations of ultimate facts or allegations of evidentiary facts? Would it have been sufficient for the plaintiffs to have alleged, based on information and belief, that both the City and the BSA knew Kalish had engaged in sexual misconduct in the past? Is there any hint in the court's opinion as to how it would have ruled had the plaintiffs done so?

5. *Pleading standard and the applicable rules.*   The court acknowledged that "[t]his recognition by the Legislature that one reason a plaintiff may remain ignorant of the nonperpetrator defendant's wrongdoing is because that defendant has withheld or concealed evidence of its wrongdoing argues strongly in favor of broader, rather than more restrictive, standards of pleading where subdivision (b)(2) is alleged to apply." Treating the statute of limitations as a substantive rule for the purpose of pleading analysis, can you see how the applicable substantive standard might affect the pleading standard, by relaxing it (as in this case), or by making it more demanding? Can you think of reasons why this might occur? Why, notwithstanding this relaxed standard, did the court find the plaintiffs' complaints deficient? Did the complaints lack evidentiary support? Should a complaint have to have evidentiary support to pass the applicable pleading test?

PROBLEM

1-2. The plaintiffs' daughter was brutally murdered by a prison parolee who had just been released from a New York state prison. The plaintiffs sued the state in a New York state court. Their complaint described their daughter's murder and then made the following allegations:

> That their daughter's death was a result of the negligent acts and omissions to act of the State of New York, its parole board, parole division, agents, servants, and employees; that after the parolee's release the state, its agents, servants, and employees neglected and omitted to restrain, control, survey, treat, and keep in custody said parolee whom it was required by law to restrain, control, survey, treat, and keep under custodial control and surveillance; that the state, its agents, servants, and employees had actual or constructive notice of the parolee's rapist and homicidal tendencies, as well as knowledge of his propensities, his record of molestation, sexual perversion, deviation, and sexual crime, as well as his homicidal tendencies; that as a result of such failure and neglect to act it did thereby cause, permit, and allow the murder of their daughter.

Assuming that the state may be sued for negligence under such circumstances, do the allegations meet the standards of fact pleading? In answering this question, use the opinion in *Doe* as your guide. *See Taylor v. State*, 320 N.Y.S.2d 343 (N.Y. App. Div. 1971).

B.   Notice Pleading and the Federal Rules of Civil Procedure

Over time, the perceived deficiencies in fact pleading led to yet another movement for reform. One of the leading proponents of that effort was Charles E. Clark, Dean of the Yale Law School and later a federal judge on the Second Circuit Court of Appeals. *See generally* CLARK, HANDBOOK, *supra*, at 54-71, 225-245 (outlining the various criticisms and describing the "modern" move toward pleading reform). Clark argued that "[t]he aim of pleadings should be . . . to give reasonable notice of the pleader's case to the opponent and to the court." *Id.* at 57. To ask more was to risk elevating the technicalities of pleading over the delivery of justice. Furthermore, Clark and other critics of code pleading believed that the genuine need to develop the legal and factual issues underlying a legal controversy—the goals of issue and fact pleading—could be accommodated by post-pleading devices, including discovery, pretrial conferences, and summary judgment. The aim of Clark's reform efforts, therefore, was to treat pleadings largely as documents that initiate a lawsuit and not as the primary devices through which to resolve the underlying dispute.

The movement for further pleading reform in the United States bore fruit in 1938 with the adoption of the Federal Rules of Civil Procedure. Prior to 1938, procedure in federal court had been divided between matters at law and matters in equity. In the former context, each federal court followed the procedural law of the state in which it sat, creating a wide divergence in federal practice throughout the nation. In equity proceedings, on the other hand, all federal courts followed a uniform set of federal rules. The first accomplishment of the new Federal Rules of Civil Procedure was to eliminate this perplexing dichotomy by providing a single body of rules to govern all civil proceedings in federal courts. Beyond this major change in federal practice, the federal rules built on and refined their code-pleading predecessors. Thus the new federal rules merged law and equity, provided for a single form of action — "the civil action" — and limited permissible pleadings to complaints, answers, and the like. (Read FED. R. CIV. P. 1, 2, and 7 in your supplement.)

The federal rules differed from the state codes in two substantial respects. First, the federal rules were adopted pursuant to a congressional delegation to the Supreme Court to "prescribe general rules of practice and procedure . . . for cases in the United States district courts. . . ." Rules Enabling Act of 1934, 28 U.S.C. § 2072(a). Pursuant to that delegation, the Court appointed an Advisory Committee of lawyers and academics to assist it in formulating the new rules. (Not coincidentally, Charles Clark was the reporter for the first Advisory Committee.) The rules recommended by the committee were eventually approved by the Court and became operative on September 16, 1938. The power to revise the rules remains with the Supreme Court, and the Court continues to use an Advisory Committee to consider amendments to the rules. This process of court-centered rulemaking (with some congressional oversight) permits flexibility and a relatively streamlined method for revising and adjusting the rules. Changes in the state codes, on the other hand, depend on the more cumbersome process of legislation. The federal method of court-centered rulemaking, therefore, was itself a major innovation.

Second, and directly pertinent to the present topic, the federal rules rejected fact pleading. In its place they provided a simplified form of pleading that has become known as "notice pleading." To this end, Rule 8(a) provides: "A pleading that states a claim for relief must contain: (1) a short and plain statement of the grounds for the court's jurisdiction . . . ; (2) a short and plain statement of the claim showing that the pleader is entitled to relief; and (3) a demand for the relief sought. . . ." FED. R. CIV. P. 8(a).

A majority of states have now adopted notice (or simplified) pleading as their general pleading standard for most civil actions. In addition, many of the remaining code states use "notice" as at least a partial measure of the sufficiency of pleadings, thereby somewhat softening the edges of fact pleading. New York, the birthplace of fact pleading, has adopted a hybrid approach that combines the notice standard with the principles of code pleading: "Statements in a pleading shall be sufficiently particular to give the court and parties notice of the transactions, occurrences, or series of transactions or occurrences, intended to be proved and the material elements of each cause of action or defense." N.Y. CIV. PRAC. L. & R. § 3013 (McKinney 1991); *see also Committee on Children's Television, Inc. v. General Foods Corp.*, 673 P.2d 660 (1983) (emphasizing the role of notice in pleading in a code jurisdiction).

There is a small wrinkle here. Federal notice pleading standards are currently in somewhat of a developmental mode, with recent decisions by the U.S. Supreme Court imposing what appear to be stricter standards that emphasize the importance of pleading facts. This development may eventually erase the distinction between notice pleading and contemporary versions of fact pleading (such as the New York version noted in the previous paragraph).

1.   The Complaint

a.   Rule 8

In federal court, "[a] civil action is commenced by filing a complaint with the court." FED. R. CIV. P. 3. Under Rule 8(a), the complaint must contain "a short and plain statement" of the court's jurisdiction and of the plaintiff's claim, as well as a demand for relief. (Jurisdiction in this context refers only to subject matter jurisdiction, a topic we will address in Chapter IV, *infra*.) Rule 8(d)(1) also provides that "[e]ach allegation must be simple, concise, and direct. No technical form is required." Moreover, "[p]leadings must be construed so as to do justice." *Id.* at 8(e). In this sense, the federal rules, on their face, reflect a flexible attitude toward pleading that was not evident under most codes at the time the federal rules were adopted. And it is this attitude of liberality toward the pleadings that truly differentiates classic notice pleading from traditional fact or code pleading. Modern codes are in accord. *See, e.g.,* N.Y. CIV. PRAC. L. & R. § 3026 (McKinney 1991) ("Pleadings shall be liberally construed. Defects shall be ignored if a substantial right of a party is not prejudiced.").

The pleading rules described in Rule 8(a) also apply to other claim-initiating pleadings such as counterclaims (a claim filed by defendant against plaintiff), cross-claims (a claim filed by a defendant against a co-defendant), and third-party complaints (a claim for indemnity filed by defendant against a third party).

b.   Foundational Cases and Developments

Conley v. Gibson

355 U.S. 41 (1957)

MR. JUSTICE BLACK delivered the opinion of the Court.

Once again Negro employees are here under the Railway Labor Act asking that their collective bargaining agent be compelled to represent them fairly. In a series of cases beginning with *Steele v. Louisville & Nashville R. Co.*, 323 U.S. 192, this Court has emphatically and repeatedly ruled that an exclusive bargaining agent under the Railway Labor Act is obligated to represent all employees in the bargaining unit fairly and without discrimination because of race and has held that the courts have power to protect employees against such invidious discrimination.

This class suit was brought in a Federal District Court in Texas by certain Negro members of the Brotherhood of Railway and Steamship Clerks, petitioners here, on behalf of themselves and other Negro employees similarly situated against the Brotherhood, its Local Union No. 28 and certain officers of both. In summary, the complaint made the following allegations relevant to our decision: Petitioners were employees of the Texas and New Orleans Railroad at its Houston Freight House. Local 28 of the Brotherhood was the designated bargaining agent under the Railway Labor Act for the bargaining unit to which petitioners belonged. A contract existed between the Union and the Railroad which gave the employees in the bargaining unit certain protection from discharge and loss of seniority. In May 1954, the Railroad purported to abolish 45 jobs held by petitioners or other Negroes all of whom were either discharged or demoted. In truth the 45 jobs were not abolished at all but instead filled by whites as the Negroes were ousted, except for a few instances where Negroes were rehired to fill their old jobs but with loss of seniority. Despite repeated pleas by petitioners, the Union, acting according to plan, did nothing to protect them against these discriminatory discharges and refused to give them protection comparable to that given white employees. The complaint then went on to allege that the Union had failed in general to represent Negro employees equally and in good faith. It charged that such discrimination constituted a violation of petitioners' right under the Railway Labor Act to fair representation from their bargaining agent. And it concluded by asking for relief in the nature of declaratory judgment, injunction and damages.

The respondents appeared and moved to dismiss the complaint on several grounds: (1) the National Railroad Adjustment Board had exclusive jurisdiction over the controversy; (2) the Texas and New Orleans Railroad, which had not been joined, was an indispensable party defendant; and (3) the complaint failed to state a claim upon which relief could be given. The District Court granted the motion to dismiss holding that Congress had given the Adjustment Board exclusive jurisdiction over the controversy. The Court of Appeals for the Fifth Circuit, apparently relying on the same ground, affirmed. Since the case raised an important question concerning the protection of employee rights under the Railway Labor Act we granted certiorari.

[On the question of jurisdiction, the Supreme Court reversed the lower courts. It also concluded that the Texas and New Orleans Railroad was not an indispensable party.]

Turning to respondents' final ground, we hold that under the general principles laid down in *Steele* [and the cases following it] the complaint adequately set forth a claim upon which relief could be granted. In appraising the sufficiency of the complaint we follow, of course, the accepted rule that a complaint should not be dismissed for failure to state a claim unless it appears beyond doubt that the plaintiff can prove no set of facts in support of his claim which would entitle him to relief. Here, the complaint alleged, in part, that petitioners were discharged wrongfully by the Railroad and that the Union, acting according to plan, refused to protect their jobs as it did those of white employees or to help them with their grievances all because they were Negroes. If these allegations are proven there has been a manifest breach of the Union's statutory duty to represent fairly and without hostile discrimination all of the employees in the bargaining unit. This Court squarely held in *Steele* and subsequent cases that discrimination in representation because of race is prohibited by the Railway Labor Act. The bargaining representative's duty not to draw "irrelevant and invidious" distinctions among those it represents does not come to an abrupt end, as the respondents seem to contend, with the making of an agreement between union and employer. Collective bargaining is a continuing process. Among other things, it involves day-to-day adjustments in the contract and other working rules, resolution of new problems not covered by existing agreements, and the protection of employee rights already secured by contract. The bargaining representative can no more unfairly discriminate in carrying out these functions than it can in negotiating a collective agreement. A contract may be fair and impartial on its face yet administered in such a way, with the active or tacit consent of the union, as to be flagrantly discriminatory against some members of the bargaining unit. . . .

The respondents . . . argue that the complaint failed to set forth specific facts to support its general allegations of discrimination and that its dismissal is therefore proper. The decisive answer to this is that the Federal Rules of Civil Procedure do not require a claimant to set out in detail the facts upon which he bases his claim. To the contrary, all the Rules require is "a short and plain statement of the claim" that will give the defendant fair notice of what the plaintiff's claim is and the grounds upon which it rests. . . . Such simplified "notice pleading" is made possible by the liberal opportunity for discovery and the other pretrial procedures established by the Rules to disclose more precisely the basis of both claim and defense and to define more narrowly the disputed facts and issues. Following the simple guide of Rule [8(e)] that ["pleadings must be construed so as to do justice]," we have no doubt that petitioners' complaint adequately set forth a claim and gave the respondents fair notice of its basis. The Federal Rules reject the approach that pleading is a game of skill in which one misstep by counsel may be decisive to the outcome and accept the principle that the purpose of pleading is to facilitate a proper decision on the merits.

The judgment is reversed and the cause is remanded to the District Court for further proceedings not inconsistent with this opinion.

It is so ordered.

NOTES AND QUESTIONS

1. The sufficiency of the complaint.   The final two substantive paragraphs of the Court's opinion focus on the sufficiency of the complaint. The first of these paragraphs addresses the legal sufficiency of the claim. It asks whether the plaintiffs had asserted a recognized right to relief under the Railway Labor Act. Given this focus on legal sufficiency, what do you think the Court meant when it said, "In appraising the sufficiency of the complaint we follow, of course, the accepted rule that a complaint should not be dismissed for failure to state a claim unless it appears beyond doubt that the plaintiff can prove no set of facts in support of his claim which would entitle him to relief"? If legal sufficiency was the subject of the first paragraph, what is the subject of the second paragraph? In other words, what different issue is being addressed in the second of these two paragraphs? Does the second paragraph have something to do with the generality at which the allegations in the complaint were stated? What principle of pleading emerges from this paragraph?

2. The essential allegations.   The plaintiffs' Railway Labor Act claim required that they show purposeful racial discrimination by their union representatives. In their brief to the Supreme Court, the plaintiffs described their complaint as alleging "a planned course of conduct designed to discriminate against [them] and those similarly situated, solely because of their race or color." Petitioner's Brief, *Conley v. Gibson*, 1957 WL 87661, at *5. This is apparently what the Court was referring to when it said that the union was alleged to have taken action "according to plan." Is this according-to-plan allegation sufficient for purposes of pleading a Railway Labor Act claim under Rule 8(a)(2)? Why or why not?

3. A call for stricter standards.   Shortly before the decision in *Conley*, the Rules Advisory Committee addressed efforts to require stricter pleading standards than those embodied in Rule 8(a)(2). This effort was in part generated by *Dioguardi v. Durning*, 139 F.2d 774 (2d Cir. 1944), a decision authored by Charles E. Clark who had by then been appointed as a judge on the Second Circuit Court of Appeals. The district court in *Dioguardi* had dismissed plaintiff's complaint for "fail[ure] to state facts sufficient to state a cause of action." In an opinion reversing that ruling, Judge Clark described and applied federal pleading standards quite generously:

> It would seem . . . that [plaintiff] has stated enough to withstand a mere formal motion, directed only to the face of the complaint, and that here is another instance of judicial haste which in the long run makes waste. Under the new rules of civil procedure, there is no pleading requirement of stating "facts sufficient to constitute a cause of action," but only that there be "a short and plain statement of the claim showing that the pleader is entitled to relief," Federal Rules of Civil Procedure, Rule 8(a); and the motion for dismissal under Rule 12(b) is for failure to state "a claim upon which relief can be granted."

Id. at 775. It was enough for Judge Clark that the allegations of plaintiff's "home drawn" pleading, "however inartistically they may be stated," had arguably "disclosed" the rights of action on which he asserted a claim for relief. *Id.* at 774, 775. In other words, as was the case in *Conley*, the focus in *Dioguardi* was not on the technical sufficiency of the pleading, but on whether the pleading provided the opposing party fair notice of the right or rights being asserted by the plaintiff.

In response to the call for stricter standards, the Advisory Committee reaffirmed its commitment to simplified pleading with the following observation:

> The criticisms appear to be based on the view that the rule does not require the averment of any information as to what has actually happened. That Rule 8(a) envisages the statement of circumstances, occurrences, and events in support of the claim presented is clearly indicated not only by the forms appended to the rules showing what should be considered as sufficient compliance with the rule, but also by other intermeshing rules. . . . Rule 12(e), providing for a motion for a more definite statement, also shows that the complaint must disclose information with sufficient definiteness. The intent and effect of the rules is to permit the claim to be stated in general terms; the rules are designed to discourage battles over mere form of statement and to sweep away the needless controversies which the codes permitted that served either to delay trial on the merits or to prevent a party from

having a trial because of mistakes in statement. The decision in *Dioguardi* . . . to which proponents of any amendment to Rule 8(a) have especially referred, was not based on any holding that a pleader is not required to supply information disclosing a ground for relief. The complaint in that case stated a plethora of facts and the court so construed them as to sustain the validity of the pleading.

Advisory Committee Report of October, 1955 on Rule 8(a)(2), reprinted in 5 CHARLES ALAN WRIGHT & ARTHUR R. MILLER, FEDERAL PRACTICE AND PROCEDURE § 1201, p. 86 n.11 (3d ed. 2004).

PROBLEMS

1-3. Using the facts of *Epstein* (page 17, *supra*), draft a short and plain statement of the plaintiff's claim showing that she is entitled to relief.

1-4. Do the allegations described in Problem 1-2, page 29, *supra*, satisfy the pleading standards of Rule 8(a)(2)?

1-5. The following allegations were contained in a complaint, filed by a prisoner against a clerk at the prison, alleging that the defendant had interfered with the plaintiff's right of access to the courts:

> Plaintiff was about to board a bus to travel to a judicial hearing when defendant, a clerk at the prison, informed plaintiff that a box of documents the plaintiff was carrying could not be taken on the bus. A brief argument between the defendant and the plaintiff ensued. The warden intervened and promised the plaintiff that the box would be shipped separately. After the plaintiff boarded the bus, the clerk deliberately shipped the box to the wrong location. The box and its contents were lost.

Assuming that the plaintiff's complaint would state a claim for which relief could be granted only if the clerk had acted deliberately (*i.e.*, no claim would be stated if the clerk acted only negligently), are the above allegations sufficient under Rule 8(a)(2)? Isn't the allegation that the clerk acted deliberately merely a conclusion? *See Nance v. Vieregge*, 147 F.3d 589 (7th Cir.), *cert. denied*, 525 U.S. 973 (1998).

A NOTE ON EXCEPTIONS TO RULE 8

Although Federal Rule 8(a) establishes a generally applicable standard of simplified pleading for all civil actions filed in federal court, the federal rules create an exception for allegations of fraud or mistake: "In alleging fraud or mistake, a party must state with particularity the circumstances constituting fraud or mistake." FED. R. CIV. P. 9(b). The purpose of Rule 9(b) is "to protect a defending party's reputation from harm, to minimize strike suits, and to provide detailed notice of a fraud claim to a defending party." Jeffrey A. Parness, *Pleading Special Matters*, in 2 MOORE'S FEDERAL PRACTICE § 9.03[1][a] (3d ed. 2015). The rule also discourages meritless fraud accusations that can do serious damage to the goodwill of a business person. *See generally id.* § 9.03; 5A CHARLES ALAN WRIGHT

& ARTHUR R. MILLER, FEDERAL PRACTICE AND PROECURE §§ 1296 *et seq.* (3d ed. 2004 & Supp. 2015). For an example of a case applying Rule 9(b), *see Varney v. R.J. Reynolds Tobacco Co.*, 118 F. Supp. 2d 63 (D. Mass. 2000). *Cf.* N.Y. CIV. PRAC. L. & R. § 3016 (McKinney Supp. 2005) (imposing particularity requirements in a wider array of cases including libel or slander, fraud or mistake, separation or divorce, sale of goods or services, and certain personal injury actions).

Congress has also created statutory exceptions to Rule 8(a). Most notably, in the Private Securities Litigation Reform Act (PSLRA), passed in 1995, Congress imposed fact-pleading requirements in civil actions seeking to enforce the Securities Exchange Act of 1934 (SEA). The SEA prohibits the use of any manipulative or deceptive device in the sale of a security. Under the PSLRA, a complaint in such a case must "specify each statement alleged to have been misleading, the reason or reasons why the statement is misleading, and, if an allegation regarding the statement or omission is made on information and belief, the complaint shall state with particularity all the facts on which that belief is formed." 15 U.S.C. § 78u-4(b)(1). Moreover, the complaint must "state with particularity facts giving rise to a strong inference that the defendant acted with the required state of mind." *Id.* § 78u-4(b)(2)(A). The primary purpose of this statutory pleading requirement is to prevent the filing of "frivolous, lawyer-driven litigation." *Tellabs, Inc. v. Makor Issues & Rights, Ltd.*, 551 U.S. 308, 322 (2007). The *Tellabs* Court imposed three "prescriptions" on the application of the PSLRA pleading standard:

> First, faced with a Rule 12(b)(6) motion to dismiss . . . courts must . . . accept all factual allegations in the complaint as true. Second, courts must consider the complaint in its entirety, as well as other sources courts ordinarily examine when ruling on Rule 12(b)(6) motions to dismiss. . . . Third, in determining whether the pleaded facts give rise to a "strong" inference of scienter, the court must take into account plausible opposing inferences.

Id. at 322-323; *see* 2 MOORE'S FEDERAL PRACTICE, *supra*, §§ 9.03[6][a][ii], 9.10[1]. For a recent application of the PSLRA pleading standard, see *Matrixx Initiatives, Inc. v. Siracusano*, 563 U.S. 27 (2011). Similarly strict pleading requirements are required by the federal "Y2K Act" of 1999, 15 U.S.C. §§ 6601, 6607.

In addition to the Rule 9(b) and statutory heightened pleading standards, commencing in the 1970s and picking up steam thereafter, lower federal courts began creating common law exceptions to Rule 8(a) by imposing heightened pleading requirements in certain other types of actions. Thus, in actions deemed "disfavored," such as those sounding in libel, slander, or defamation, some courts required plaintiffs to make certain allegations with more specificity or particularity than otherwise required by Rule 8(a)(2). Similarly, some courts imposed heightened pleading requirements in civil rights actions brought under 42 U.S.C. § 1983, a post–Civil War statute that creates a private right of action for any person who claims to have been deprived of a federal constitutional or statutory right by those acting "under color of state law." And still other courts required more particularized pleadings in cases deemed complex. *See generally* Richard L. Marcus, *The Revival of Fact Pleading Under the Federal Rules of Civil Procedure*,

86 COLUM. L. REV. 433, 450 (1986). The next case presents the Supreme Court's response to one such judicially created heightened pleading standard.

Leatherman v. Tarrant County Narcotics Intelligence and Coordination Unit
507 U.S. 163 (1993)

CHIEF JUSTICE REHNQUIST delivered the opinion of the Court.

We granted certiorari to decide whether a federal court may apply a "heightened pleading standard"—more stringent than the usual pleading requirements of Rule 8(a) of the Federal Rules of Civil Procedure—in civil rights cases alleging municipal liability under 42 U.S.C. § 1983. We hold it may not.

We review here a decision granting a motion to dismiss, and therefore must accept as true all the factual allegations in the complaint. This action arose out of two separate incidents involving the execution of search warrants by local law enforcement officers. Each involved the forcible entry into a home based on the detection of odors associated with the manufacture of narcotics. One homeowner claimed that he was assaulted by the officers after they had entered; another claimed that the police had entered her home in her absence and killed her two dogs. Plaintiffs sued several local officials in their official capacity and the county and two municipal corporations that employed the police officers involved in the incidents, asserting that the police conduct had violated the Fourth Amendment to the United States Constitution. The stated basis for municipal liability under *Monell v. New York City Dept. of Social Services*, 436 U.S. 658 (1978), was the failure of these bodies to adequately train the police officers involved. [With respect to this latter claim, the complaint alleged that the defendants "failed to formulate and implement an adequate policy to train [their] officers on the Constitutional limitations restricting the manner in which search warrants may be executed." No further details of this failure to train were described in the complaint.]

The United States District Court for the Northern District of Texas ordered the complaints dismissed because they failed to meet the "heightened pleading standard" required by the decisional law of the Court of Appeals for the Fifth Circuit. The Fifth Circuit, in turn, affirmed the judgment of dismissal, and we granted certiorari to resolve a conflict among the Courts of Appeals concerning the applicability of a heightened pleading standard to § 1983 actions alleging municipal liability. We now reverse.

Respondents seek to defend the Fifth Circuit's application of a more rigorous pleading standard on two grounds. First, respondents claim that municipalities' freedom from *respondeat superior* liability, see *Monell, supra,* necessarily includes immunity from suit. In this sense, respondents assert, municipalities are no different from state or local officials sued in their individual capacity. Respondents reason that a more relaxed pleading requirement would subject municipalities to expensive and time-consuming discovery in every § 1983 case, eviscerating their immunity from suit and disrupting municipal functions.

This argument wrongly equates freedom from liability with immunity from suit. To be sure, we reaffirmed in *Monell* that "a municipality cannot be held liable under § 1983 on a *respondeat superior* theory." 436 U.S., at 691. But, contrary to respondents' assertions, this protection against liability does not encompass immunity from suit. Indeed, this argument is flatly contradicted by *Monell* and our later decisions involving municipal liability under § 1983. In *Monell*, we overruled *Monroe v. Pape*, 365 U.S. 167 (1961), insofar as it held that local governments were wholly immune from suit under § 1983, though we did reserve decision on whether municipalities are entitled to some form of limited immunity. Yet, when we took that issue up again in *Owen v. City of Independence*, 445 U.S. 622, 650 (1980), we rejected a claim that municipalities should be afforded qualified immunity, much like that afforded individual officials, based on the good faith of their agents. These decisions make it quite clear that, unlike various government officials, municipalities do not enjoy immunity from suit—either absolute or qualified—under § 1983. In short, a municipality can be sued under § 1983, but it cannot be held liable unless a municipal policy or custom caused the constitutional injury. We thus have no occasion to consider whether our qualified immunity jurisprudence would require a heightened pleading in cases involving individual government officials.

Second, respondents contend that the Fifth Circuit's heightened pleading standard is not really that at all. See Brief for Respondents Tarrant County Narcotics Intelligence and Coordination Unit et al. 9-10 ("[T]he Fifth Circuit's so-called 'heightened' pleading requirement is a misnomer"). According to respondents, the degree of factual specificity required of a complaint by the Federal Rules of Civil Procedure varies according to the complexity of the underlying substantive law. To establish municipal liability under § 1983, respondents argue, a plaintiff must do more than plead a single instance of misconduct. This requirement, respondents insist, is consistent with a plaintiff's Rule 11 obligation to make a reasonable prefiling inquiry into the facts.

But examination of the Fifth Circuit's decision in this case makes it quite evident that the "heightened pleading standard" is just what it purports to be: a more demanding rule for pleading a complaint under § 1983 than for pleading other kinds of claims for relief. This rule was adopted by the Fifth Circuit in *Elliott v. Perez*, 751 F.2d 1472 (1985), and described in this language:

> "In cases against governmental officials involving the likely defense of immunity we require of trial judges that they demand that the plaintiff's complaints state with factual detail and particularity the basis for the claim which necessarily includes why the defendant-official cannot successfully maintain the defense of immunity." *Id.*, at 1473.

In later cases, the Fifth Circuit extended this rule to complaints against municipal corporations asserting liability under § 1983. See, *e.g.*, *Palmer v. San Antonio*, 810 F.2d 514 (1987).

We think that it is impossible to square the "heightened pleading standard" applied by the Fifth Circuit in this case with the liberal system of "notice pleading" set up by the Federal Rules. Rule 8(a)(2) requires that a complaint include only "a short and plain statement of the claim showing that the pleader is entitled to relief." In *Conley v. Gibson*, 355 U.S. 41 (1957), we said in effect that the Rule meant what it said:

> "[T]he Federal Rules of Civil Procedure do not require a claimant to set out in detail the facts upon which he bases his claim. To the contrary, all the Rules require is 'a short and plain statement of the claim' that will give the defendant fair notice of what the plaintiff's claim is and the grounds upon which it rests." *Id.*, at 47 (footnote omitted).

Rule 9(b) does impose a particularity requirement in two specific instances. It provides that "[i]n all averments of fraud or mistake, the circumstances constituting fraud or mistake shall be stated with particularity." Thus, the Federal Rules do address in Rule 9(b) the question of the need for greater particularity in pleading certain actions, but do not include among the enumerated actions any reference to complaints alleging municipal liability under § 1983. *Expressio unius est exclusio alterius.*

The phenomenon of litigation against municipal corporations based on claimed constitutional violations by their employees dates from our decision in *Monell, supra*, where we for the first time construed § 1983 to allow such municipal liability. Perhaps if Rules 8 and 9 were rewritten today, claims against municipalities under § 1983 might be subjected to the added specificity requirement of Rule 9(b). But that is a result which must be obtained by the process of amending the Federal Rules, and not by judicial interpretation. In the absence of such an amendment, federal courts and litigants must rely on summary judgment and control of discovery to weed out unmeritorious claims sooner rather than later.

The judgment of the Court of Appeals is reversed, and the case is remanded for further proceedings consistent with this opinion.

It is so ordered.

NOTES AND QUESTIONS

1. The presumption of truth.   The *Leatherman* Court began its analysis by observing that, "We review here a decision granting a motion to dismiss, and therefore must accept as true all the factual allegations in the complaint." What did the Court mean by that? Why do you think the Court adopted this presumption? Is it consistent with the idea of notice pleading?

2. Notice pleading and heightened pleading standards.   What was it about the Fifth Circuit standard that led the *Leatherman* Court to conclude that that standard was "heightened"? How did the respondents defend that heightened standard? On what basis did the *Leatherman* Court conclude that this heightened standard was inappropriate? What role did Rule 9(b) play in that conclusion? Does the *Leatherman* Court's analysis leave any room for judicially created heightened pleading standards? By refusing to apply a heightened pleading standard, did the Court invite discovery abuse?

3. *Variable pleading standards.*   Did the Court agree with the argument that "the degree of factual specificity required of a complaint by the Federal Rules of Civil Procedure varies according to the complexity of the underlying substantive law"? Why or why not?

4. *The principle of* Leatherman *reaffirmed.*   In *Swierkiewicz v. Sorema N.A.*, 534 U.S. 506 (2002), a unanimous Supreme Court refused to impose a heightened pleading requirement in employment discrimination cases filed under Title VII of the Civil Rights Act. It was sufficient that plaintiff alleged that he was terminated from his employment on account of his national origin and that he described some of the facts surrounding his termination, all of which were consistent with his claim. The Court explained that under Rule 8(a)(2), the plaintiff "must simply 'give the defendant fair notice of what the plaintiff's claim is and the grounds upon which it rests.'" *Conley v. Gibson*, 355 U.S. 41, 47 (1957)." 534 U.S. at 512. In response to the argument that "allowing lawsuits based on conclusory allegations of discrimination to go forward will burden the courts and encourage disgruntled employees to bring unsubstantiated suits," the Court replied, "Whatever the practical merits of this argument, the Federal Rules do not contain a heightened pleading standard for employment discrimination suits. A requirement of greater specificity for particular claims is a result that 'must be obtained by the process of amending the Federal Rules, and not by judicial interpretation.'" *Id.* at 514-515 (quoting *Leatherman*).

PROBLEMS

1-6. Bennett, an African-American woman, filed an employment discrimination claim against members of a public school board who had refused to hire her. She claimed a violation of the Fourteenth Amendment Equal Protection Clause, which prohibits public institutions from intentionally discriminating on the basis of race. In her complaint, she included a single factual allegation: "I was turned down for a job because of my race." The defendant school board members filed a motion to dismiss under Rule 12(b)(6). What should the district court do? *See Bennett v. Schmidt*, 153 F.3d 516 (7th Cir. 1998).

1-7. Wynder filed a civil rights complaint in a New York federal district court. His complaint alleged race discrimination and attendant violations of his rights under a cavalcade of federal constitutional and statutory provisions, including the First, Fourth, Fifth, Sixth, Eighth, and Fourteenth Amendments to the U.S. Constitution. The plaintiff's claims all stemmed from a variety of alleged adverse employment actions occurring between 1992 and 1998. His complaint, totaling 14 pages with 64 paragraphs, described a wide array of acts and decisions by the defendants that, he believed, collectively constituted a "common conspiratorial scheme" to harass and drive him out of the state police force, all on account of his race. The district court dismissed Wynder's complaint for failure "to articulate in a logical way what his theory of the case is and what his statutory claim is." The court ordered Wynder to provide a "very detailed complaint against each person, separately numbered, stating what your claim is against that person and what evidence you have as of this date as against that person, and what legal theory you're going [to assert] against that person." The court added: "You've sued five people. Each one is to be dealt with separately. Each of them, you're going to have to allege whatever evidence you have in detail as to that person, and your legal theories, and your cite of authority, statutory and case law." When Wynder's amended complaint failed to comply with these requirements, the district court dismissed the case without leave to amend. In so ruling, did the judge act within the discretion given him under Rule 8? *See Wynder v. McMahon*, 360 F.3d 73 (2d Cir. 2004).

c.   *Recent Developments*

Bell Atlantic Corp. v. Twombly
550 U.S. 544 (2007)

[The breakup of the American Telephone & Telegraph Company in 1984 led to the creation of a system of regional telecommunications service providers, the so-called Baby Bells, each with monopolistic power over local telecommunications within a specified geographic region. In 1996, Congress sought to introduce competition into these regional markets by requiring, among other things, that each of the four remaining Baby Bells share its respective regional network and infrastructure with start-up competitors ("CLECs"). The Baby Bells resisted these efforts and one of the responses to that resistance was the consumer class action filed in *Bell Atlantic Corporation v. Twombly*. The *Bell Atlantic* complaint, which consisted of 96 numbered paragraphs, alleged that the named defendants, each a regional telecommunications service provider, *i.e.*, a Baby Bell, entered into a conspiracy designed to thwart the de-monopolization of their respective regional markets. The conspiracy was said to violate § 1 of the Sherman Act. That section provides: "Every contract, combination in the form of trust or otherwise, or conspiracy, in restraint of trade or commerce among the several States, or with foreign nations, is declared to be illegal." Concerted action, *i.e.*, an agreement, is the key to the statutory proscription. It is not, in other words, sufficient to show that a defendant or defendants restrained trade or engaged in anticompetitive practices. They must have agreed among themselves to do so.

[The pleading controversy in *Bell Atlantic* centered directly on the adequacy of plaintiffs' allegations of concerted action among the defendants. The relevant allegations were stated in paragraphs 37 through 51 of the complaint. Those paragraphs detailed two patterns of anticompetitive "parallel conduct," *i.e.*, similar conduct engaged in by each of the defendants. The first pattern involved similar actions undertaken by each defendant to prevent competitors from entering its respective market or service area ("territory-protection pattern"); the second pattern involved the failure of any defendant to attempt to compete within the market or service area of another defendant ("non-competition pattern"). Paragraph 51 then offered the following conclusion:

> In the absence of any meaningful competition between the [defendants] in one another's markets [the non-competition pattern], and in light of the parallel course of conduct that each engaged in to prevent competition from [potential market entrants] within their respective local telephone and/or high speed internet services markets [the territory-protection pattern] and other facts and market circumstances alleged above, Plaintiffs allege upon information and belief that Defendants have entered into a contract, combination or conspiracy to prevent competitive entry in their respective local telephone and/or high speed internet services markets and have agreed not to compete with one another and otherwise allocated customers and markets to one another.

[The district court dismissed the complaint, concluding that parallel business conduct allegations, taken alone, do not state a claim under § 1 of the Sherman Act; plaintiffs must allege additional facts tending to exclude independent self-interested conduct as an explanation for the parallel actions. Reversing, the Second Circuit held that plaintiffs' parallel conduct allegations were sufficient to withstand a motion to dismiss because the Baby Bells failed to show that there is no set of facts that would permit plaintiffs to demonstrate that the particular parallelism asserted was the product of collusion rather than coincidence.]

JUSTICE SOUTER delivered the opinion of the Court.

Liability under § 1 of the Sherman Act, 15 U.S.C. § 1, requires a "contract, combination . . . , or conspiracy, in restraint of trade or commerce." The question in this putative class action is whether a § 1 complaint can survive a motion to dismiss when it alleges that major telecommunications providers engaged in certain parallel conduct unfavorable to competition, absent some factual context suggesting agreement, as distinct from identical, independent action. We hold that such a complaint should be dismissed. . . .

II

A

Because § 1 of the Sherman Act "does not prohibit [all] unreasonable restraints of trade . . . but only restraints effected by a contract, combination, or conspiracy," *Copperweld Corp. v. Independence Tube Corp.*, 467 U.S. 752, 775 (1984), "[t]he crucial question" is whether the challenged anticompetitive conduct "stem[s] from independent decision or from an agreement, tacit or express," [*Theatre Enterprises, Inc. v. Paramount Film Distributing Corp.*, 346 U.S. 537, 540 (1954)]. While a showing of parallel "business behavior is admissible circumstantial evidence from which the fact finder may infer agreement," it falls short of "conclusively establish[ing] agreement or . . . itself constitut[ing] a Sherman Act offense." *Id.*, at 540-541. Even "conscious parallelism," a common reaction of "firms in a concentrated market [that] recogniz[e] their shared economic interests and their interdependence with respect to price and output decisions" is "not in itself unlawful." *Brooke Group Ltd. v. Brown & Williamson Tobacco Corp.*, 509 U.S. 209, 227 (1993).

The inadequacy of showing parallel conduct or interdependence, without more, mirrors the ambiguity of the behavior: consistent with conspiracy, but just as much in line with a wide swath of rational and competitive business strategy unilaterally prompted by common perceptions of the market. Accordingly, we have previously hedged against false inferences from identical behavior at a number of points in the trial sequence. An antitrust conspiracy plaintiff with evidence showing nothing beyond parallel conduct is not entitled to a directed verdict, see *Theatre Enterprises, supra*; proof of a § 1 conspiracy must include evidence tending to exclude the possibility of independent action; and at the summary judgment stage a § 1 plaintiff's offer of conspiracy evidence must tend to rule out the possibility that the defendants were acting independently.

B

This case presents the antecedent question of what a plaintiff must plead in order to state a claim under § 1 of the Sherman Act. Federal Rule of Civil Procedure 8(a)(2) requires only "a short and plain statement of the claim showing that the pleader is entitled to relief," in order to "give the defendant fair notice of what the . . . claim is and the grounds upon which it rests," *Conley v. Gibson*, 355 U.S. 41, 47 (1957). While a complaint attacked by a Rule 12(b)(6) motion to dismiss does not need detailed factual allegations, a plaintiff's obligation to provide the "grounds" of his "entitle[ment] to relief" requires more than labels and conclusions, and a formulaic recitation of the elements of a cause of action will not do. Factual allegations must be enough to raise a right to relief above the speculative level on the assumption that all the allegations in the complaint are true (even if doubtful in fact).[1]

In applying these general standards to a § 1 claim, we hold that stating such a claim requires a complaint with enough factual matter (taken as true) to suggest that an agreement was made. Asking for plausible grounds to infer an agreement does not impose a probability requirement at the pleading stage; it simply calls for

---

1. The dissent greatly oversimplifies matters by suggesting that the Federal Rules somehow dispensed with the pleading of facts altogether. See *post* (opinion of Stevens, J.) (pleading standard of Federal Rules "does not require, or even invite, the pleading of facts"). While, for most types of cases, the Federal Rules eliminated the cumbersome requirement that a claimant "set out *in detail* the facts upon which he bases his claim," *Conley v. Gibson*, 355 U.S. 41, 47 (1957) (emphasis added), Rule 8(a)(2) still requires a "showing," rather than a blanket assertion, of entitlement to relief. Without some factual allegation in the complaint, it is hard to see how a claimant could satisfy the requirement of providing not only "fair notice" of the nature of the claim, but also "grounds" on which the claim rests. See 5 Wright & Miller § 1202, at 94, 95 (Rule 8(a) "contemplate[s] the statement of circumstances, occurrences, and events in support of the claim presented" and does not authorize a pleader's "bare averment that he wants relief and is entitled to it").

enough fact to raise a reasonable expectation that discovery will reveal evidence of illegal agreement. And, of course, a well-pleaded complaint may proceed even if it strikes a savvy judge that actual proof of those facts is improbable, and "that a recovery is very remote and unlikely." *Ibid.* In identifying facts that are suggestive enough to render a § 1 conspiracy plausible, we have the benefit of the prior rulings and considered views of leading commentators, already quoted, that lawful parallel conduct fails to bespeak unlawful agreement. It makes sense to say, therefore, that an allegation of parallel conduct and a bare assertion of conspiracy will not suffice. Without more, parallel conduct does not suggest conspiracy, and a conclusory allegation of agreement at some unidentified point does not supply facts adequate to show illegality. Hence, when allegations of parallel conduct are set out in order to make a § 1 claim, they must be placed in a context that raises a suggestion of a preceding agreement, not merely parallel conduct that could just as well be independent action.

The need at the pleading stage for allegations plausibly suggesting (not merely consistent with) agreement reflects the threshold requirement of Rule 8(a)(2) that the "plain statement" possess enough heft to "sho[w] that the pleader is entitled to relief." A statement of parallel conduct, even conduct consciously undertaken, needs some setting suggesting the agreement necessary to make out a § 1 claim; without that further circumstance pointing toward a meeting of the minds, an account of a defendant's commercial efforts stays in neutral territory. An allegation of parallel conduct is thus much like a naked assertion of conspiracy in a § 1 complaint: it gets the complaint close to stating a claim, but without some further factual enhancement it stops short of the line between possibility and plausibility of "entitle[ment] to relief." Cf. *DM Research, Inc. v. College of Am. Pathologists,* 170 F.3d 53, 56 (C.A.1 1999) ("[T]erms like 'conspiracy,' or even 'agreement,' are borderline: they might well be sufficient in conjunction with a more specific allegation—for example, identifying a written agreement or even a basis for inferring a tacit agreement, . . . but a court is not required to accept such terms as a sufficient basis for a complaint").

We alluded to the practical significance of the Rule 8 entitlement requirement in *Dura Pharmaceuticals, Inc. v. Broudo,* 544 U.S. 336 (2005), when we explained that something beyond the mere possibility of loss causation must be alleged, lest a plaintiff with "'a largely groundless claim'" be allowed to "'take up the time of a number of other people, with the right to do so representing an *in terrorem* increment of the settlement value.'" *Id.,* at 347. So, when the allegations in a complaint, however true, could not raise a claim of entitlement to relief, "'this basic deficiency should . . . be exposed at the point of minimum expenditure of time and money by the parties and the court.'" 5 WRIGHT & MILLER, *supra,* § 1216, at 233-234.

Thus, it is one thing to be cautious before dismissing an antitrust complaint in advance of discovery, cf. *Poller v. Columbia Broadcasting System, Inc.,* 368 U.S. 464 (1962), but quite another to forget that proceeding to antitrust discovery can be expensive. . . .

It is no answer to say that a claim just shy of a plausible entitlement to relief can, if groundless, be weeded out early in the discovery process through "careful case management," given the common lament that the success of judicial supervision in checking discovery abuse has been on the modest side. And it is self-evident that the problem of discovery abuse cannot be solved by "careful scrutiny of evidence at the summary judgment stage," much less "lucid instructions to juries"; the threat of discovery expense will push cost-conscious defendants to settle even anemic cases before reaching those proceedings. Probably, then, it is only by taking care to require allegations that reach the level suggesting conspiracy that we can hope to avoid the potentially enormous expense of discovery in cases with no "'reasonably founded hope that the [discovery] process will reveal relevant evidence'" to support a § 1 claim.

Plaintiffs do not, of course, dispute the requirement of plausibility and the need for something more than merely parallel behavior explained in *Theatre Enterprises* . . . , and their main argument against the plausibility standard at the pleading stage is its ostensible conflict with an early statement of ours construing Rule 8. Justice Black's opinion for the Court in *Conley v. Gibson* spoke not only of the need for fair notice of the grounds for entitlement to relief but of "the accepted rule that a complaint should not be dismissed for failure to state a claim unless it appears beyond doubt that the plaintiff can prove no set of facts in support of his claim which would entitle him to relief." 355 U.S., at 45-46. This "no set of facts" language can be read in isolation as saying that any statement revealing the theory of the claim will suffice unless its factual impossibility may be shown from the face of the pleadings; and the Court of Appeals appears to have read *Conley* in some such way when formulating its understanding of the proper pleading standard, see 425 F.3d, at 106, 114 (invoking *Conley*'s "no set of facts" language in describing the standard for dismissal).

On such a focused and literal reading of *Conley*'s "no set of facts," a wholly conclusory statement of claim would survive a motion to dismiss whenever the pleadings left open the possibility that a plaintiff might later establish some "set of [undisclosed] facts" to support recovery. . . . It seems fair to say that this approach to pleading would dispense with any showing of a "'reasonably founded hope'" that a plaintiff would be able to make a case, see *Dura*, 544 U.S., at 347; Mr. Micawber's optimism would be enough.

Seeing this, a good many judges and commentators have balked at taking the literal terms of the *Conley* passage as a pleading standard. [Citations omitted.]

We could go on, but there is no need to pile up further citations to show that *Conley*'s "no set of facts" language has been questioned, criticized, and explained away long enough. To be fair to the *Conley* Court, the passage should be understood in light of the opinion's preceding summary of the complaint's concrete allegations, which the Court quite reasonably understood as amply stating a claim for relief. But the passage so often quoted fails to mention this understanding on the part of the Court, and after puzzling the profession for 50 years, this famous observation has earned its retirement. The phrase is best forgotten as an incomplete, negative gloss on an accepted pleading standard: once a claim has been stated adequately, it may be supported by showing any set of facts consistent with the allegations in the complaint. *Conley*, then, described the breadth of opportunity to prove what an adequate complaint claims, not the minimum standard of adequate pleading to govern a complaint's survival. . . .

III

When we look for plausibility in this complaint, we agree with the District Court that plaintiffs' claim of conspiracy in restraint of trade comes up short. To begin with, the complaint leaves no doubt that plaintiffs rest their § 1 claim on descriptions of parallel conduct and not on any independent allegation of actual agreement among the ILECs [the Baby Bells]. Although in form a few stray statements speak directly of agreement, on fair reading these are merely legal conclusions resting on the prior allegations. Thus, the complaint first takes account of the alleged "absence of any meaningful competition between [Baby Bells] in one another's markets," "the parallel course of conduct that each [Baby Bell] engaged in to prevent competition from CLECs," "and the other facts and market circumstances alleged [earlier]"; "in light of" these, the complaint concludes "that [the Baby Bells] have entered into a contract, combination or conspiracy to prevent competitive entry into their . . . markets and have agreed not to compete with one another." Complaint ¶ 51, App. 27. The nub of the complaint, then, is the [Baby Bells'] parallel behavior, consisting of steps to keep the CLECs out and manifest disinterest in becoming CLECs themselves, and its sufficiency turns on the suggestions raised by this conduct when viewed in light of common economic experience.

We think that nothing contained in the complaint invests either the action or inaction alleged with a plausible suggestion of conspiracy. As to the [Baby Bells'] supposed agreement to disobey the 1996 Act and thwart the CLECs' attempts to compete, we agree with the District Court that nothing in the complaint intimates that the resistance to the upstarts was anything more than the natural, unilateral reaction of each ILEC intent on keeping its regional dominance. The 1996 Act did more than just subject the [Baby Bells] to competition; it obliged them to subsidize their competitors with their own equipment at wholesale rates. The economic incentive to resist was powerful, but resisting competition is routine market conduct, and even if the [Baby Bells] flouted the 1996 Act in all the ways the plaintiffs allege, there is no reason to infer that the companies had agreed among themselves to do what was only natural anyway; so natural, in fact, that if alleging parallel decisions to resist competition were enough to imply an antitrust conspiracy, pleading a § 1 violation against almost any group of competing businesses would be a sure thing.

The complaint makes its closest pass at a predicate for conspiracy with the claim that collusion was necessary because success by even one CLEC in [a Baby Bell's] territory "would have revealed the degree to which competitive entry by CLECs would have been successful in the other territories." *Id.*, ¶ 50, App. 26-27.

But, its logic aside, this general premise still fails to answer the point that there was just no need for joint encouragement to resist the 1996 Act; as the District Court said, "each [Baby Bell] has reason to want to avoid dealing with CLECs" and "each [Baby Bell] would attempt to keep CLECs out, regardless of the actions of the other ILECs." 313 F. Supp. 2d, at 184.

Plaintiffs' second conspiracy theory rests on the competitive reticence among the [Baby Bells] themselves in the wake of the 1996 Act, which was supposedly passed in the "'hop[e] that the large incumbent local monopoly companies . . . might attack their neighbors' service areas, as they are the best situated to do so.'" Complaint ¶ 38, App. 20. Contrary to hope, the [Baby Bells] declined "'to enter each other's service territories in any significant way,'" Complaint ¶ 38, App. 20, and the local telephone and high speed Internet market remains highly compartmentalized geographically, with minimal competition. Based on this state of affairs, and perceiving the [Baby Bells] to be blessed with "especially attractive business opportunities" in surrounding markets dominated by other [Baby Bells], the plaintiffs assert that the [Baby Bells'] parallel conduct was "strongly suggestive of conspiracy." Id., ¶ 40, App. 21.

But it was not suggestive of conspiracy, not if history teaches anything. In a traditionally unregulated industry with low barriers to entry, sparse competition among large firms dominating separate geographical segments of the market could very well signify illegal agreement, but here we have an obvious alternative explanation. In the decade preceding the 1996 Act and well before that, monopoly was the norm in telecommunications, not the exception. The [Baby Bells] were born in that world, doubtless liked the world the way it was, and surely knew the adage about him who lives by the sword. Hence, a natural explanation for the noncompetition alleged is that the former Government-sanctioned monopolists were sitting tight, expecting their neighbors to do the same thing.

In fact, the complaint itself gives reasons to believe that the [Baby Bells] would see their best interests in keeping to their old turf. Although the complaint says generally that the [Baby Bells] passed up "especially attractive business opportunit[ies]" by declining to compete as CLECs against other [Baby Bells], Complaint ¶ 40, App. 21, it does not allege that competition as CLECs was potentially any more lucrative than other opportunities being pursued by the [Baby Bells] during the same period, and the complaint is replete with indications that any CLEC faced nearly insurmountable barriers to profitability owing to the [Baby Bells'] flagrant resistance to the network sharing requirements of the 1996 Act, id., ¶ 47; App. 23-26. Not only that, but even without a monopolistic tradition and the peculiar difficulty of mandating shared networks, "[f]irms do not expand without limit and none of them enters every market that an outside observer might regard as profitable, or even a small portion of such markets." The upshot is that Congress may have expected some ILECs to become CLECs in the legacy territories of other [Baby Bells], but the disappointment does not make conspiracy plausible. We agree with the District Court's assessment that antitrust conspiracy was not suggested by the facts adduced under either theory of the complaint, which thus fails to state a valid § 1 claim.[14]

Plaintiffs say that our analysis runs counter to *Swierkiewicz v. Sorema N. A.*, 534 U.S. 506, 508 (2002), which held that "a complaint in an employment discrimination lawsuit [need] not contain specific facts establishing a prima facie case of discrimination under the framework set forth in *Douglas Corp. v. Green*, 411 U.S. 792 (1973)." They argue that just as the prima facie case is a "flexible evidentiary standard" that "should not be transposed into a rigid pleading standard for discrimination cases," *Swierkiewicz, supra*, at 512, "transpos[ing] 'plus factor' summary judgment analysis woodenly into a rigid Rule 12(b)(6) pleading standard . . . would be unwise," Brief for Respondents 39. As the District Court correctly understood, however, "*Swierkiewicz* did not change the law of pleading, but simply re-emphasized . . . that the Second Circuit's use of a heightened pleading standard for Title VII cases was contrary to the Federal Rules' structure of liberal pleading requirements." 313 F. Supp. 2d, at 181 (citation and footnote omitted). Even though Swierkiewicz's pleadings "detailed the events leading to his termination, provided relevant dates, and included the ages and nationalities of at least some of the relevant persons involved with his termination," the Court of Appeals dismissed his complaint for failing to allege certain additional facts that Swierkiewicz would need at the trial stage to support his claim in the absence of direct evidence of discrimination. *Swierkiewicz*, 534 U.S., at 514. We reversed on the ground that the Court of Appeals had impermissibly applied what amounted to a heightened pleading requirement by insisting that Swierkiewicz allege "specific facts" beyond those necessary to state his claim and the grounds showing entitlement to relief. *Id.*, at 508.

Here, in contrast, we do not require heightened fact pleading of specifics, but only enough facts to state a claim to relief that is plausible on its face. Because the plaintiffs here have not nudged their claims across the line from conceivable to plausible, their complaint must be dismissed.

* * *

The judgment of the Court of Appeals for the Second Circuit is reversed, and the cause is remanded for further proceedings consistent with this opinion.

It is so ordered.

Justice Stevens, with whom Justice Ginsburg joins except as to Part IV, dissenting. . . .

---

14. In reaching this conclusion, we do not apply any "heightened" pleading standard, nor do we seek to broaden the scope of Federal Rule of Civil Procedure 9, which can only be accomplished "'by the process of amending the Federal Rules, and not by judicial interpretation.'" *Swierkiewicz v. Sorema N. A.*, 534 U.S. 506, 515 (2002) (quoting *Leatherman v. Tarrant County Narcotics Intelligence and Coordination Unit*, 507 U.S. 163, 168 (1993)). On certain subjects understood to raise a high risk of abusive litigation, a plaintiff must state factual allegations with greater particularity than Rule 8 requires. Fed. Rules Civ. Proc. 9(b)-(c). Here, our concern is not that the allegations in the complaint were insufficiently "particular[ized]"; rather, the complaint warranted dismissal because it failed *in toto* to render plaintiffs' entitlement to relief plausible.

I

Rule 8(a)(2) of the Federal Rules requires that a complaint contain "a short and plain statement of the claim showing that the pleader is entitled to relief." The rule did not come about by happenstance and its language is not inadvertent. . . .

Under the relaxed pleading standards of the Federal Rules, the idea was not to keep litigants out of court but rather to keep them in. The merits of a claim would be sorted out during a flexible pretrial process and, as appropriate, through the crucible of trial. Charles E. Clark, the "principal draftsman" of the Federal Rules, put it thus:

> "Experience has shown . . . that we cannot expect the proof of the case to be made through the pleadings, and that such proof is really not their function. We can expect a general statement distinguishing the case from all others, so that the manner and form of trial and remedy expected are clear, and so that a permanent judgment will result." The New Federal Rules of Civil Procedure: The Last Phase—Underlying Philosophy Embodied in Some of the Basic Provisions of the New Procedure, 23 A.B.A.J. 976, 977 (1937) (hereinafter Clark, New Federal Rules). . . .

II

It is in the context of this history that *Conley v. Gibson*, 355 U.S. 41 (1957), must be understood. The *Conley* plaintiffs were black railroad workers who alleged that their union local had refused to protect them against discriminatory discharges, in violation of the National Railway Labor Act. The union sought to dismiss the complaint on the ground that its general allegations of discriminatory treatment by the defendants lacked sufficient specificity. Writing for a unanimous Court, Justice Black rejected the union's claim as foreclosed by the language of Rule 8. *Id.*, at 47-48. In the course of doing so, he articulated the formulation the Court rejects today: "In appraising the sufficiency of the complaint we follow, of course, the accepted rule that a complaint should not be dismissed for failure to state a claim unless it appears beyond doubt that the plaintiff can prove no set of facts in support of his claim which would entitle him to relief." *Id.*, at 45-46.

Consistent with the design of the Federal Rules, *Conley*'s "no set of facts" formulation permits outright dismissal only when proceeding to discovery or beyond would be futile. Once it is clear that a plaintiff has stated a claim that, if true, would entitle him to relief, matters of proof are appropriately relegated to other stages of the trial process. Today, however, in its explanation of a decision to dismiss a complaint that it regards as a fishing expedition, the Court scraps *Conley*'s "no set of facts" language. Concluding that the phrase has been "questioned, criticized, and explained away long enough," the Court dismisses it as careless composition.

If *Conley*'s "no set of facts" language is to be interred, let it not be without a eulogy. That exact language, which the majority says has "puzzl[ed] the profession for 50 years," has been cited as authority in a dozen opinions of this Court and four separate writings. In not one of those 16 opinions was the language "questioned," "criticized," or "explained away." Indeed, today's opinion is the first by any Member of this Court to express *any* doubt as to the adequacy of the

Conley formulation. Taking their cues from the federal courts, 26 States and the District of Columbia utilize as their standard for dismissal of a complaint the very language the majority repudiates: whether it appears "beyond doubt" that "no set of facts" in support of the claim would entitle the plaintiff to relief.

Petitioners have not requested that the *Conley* formulation be retired, nor have any of the six *amici* who filed briefs in support of petitioners. I would not rewrite the Nation's civil procedure textbooks and call into doubt the pleading rules of most of its States without far more informed deliberation as to the costs of doing so. Congress has established a process—a rulemaking process—for revisions of that order. See 28 U.S.C. §§ 2072-2074 (2000 ed. and Supp. IV).

Today's majority calls *Conley*'s "'no set of facts'" language "an incomplete, negative gloss on an accepted pleading standard: once a claim has been stated adequately, it may be supported by showing any set of facts consistent with the allegations in the complaint." *Ante*, at 1969. This is not and cannot be what the *Conley* Court meant. First, as I have explained, and as the *Conley* Court well knew, the pleading standard the Federal Rules meant to codify does not require, or even invite, the pleading of facts. The "pleading standard" label the majority gives to what it reads into the *Conley* opinion—a statement of the permissible factual support for an adequately pleaded complaint—would not, therefore, have impressed the *Conley* Court itself. Rather, that Court would have understood the majority's remodeling of its language to express an *evidentiary* standard, which the *Conley* Court had neither need nor want to explicate. Second, it is pellucidly clear that the *Conley* Court was interested in what a complaint *must* contain, not what it *may* contain. In fact, the Court said without qualification that it was "appraising the *sufficiency* of the complaint." 355 U.S., at 45 (emphasis added). It was, to paraphrase today's majority, describing "the minimum standard of adequate pleading to govern a complaint's survival." . . .

We again spoke with one voice against efforts to expand pleading requirements beyond their appointed limits in *Leatherman v. Tarrant County Narcotics Intelligence and Coordination Unit*, 507 U.S. 163 (1993). Writing for the unanimous Court, Chief Justice Rehnquist rebuffed the Fifth Circuit's effort to craft a standard for pleading municipal liability that accounted for "the enormous expense involved today in litigation," *Leatherman v. Tarrant Cty. Narcotics Intelligence and Coordination Unit*, 954 F.2d 1054, 1057 (1992) (internal quotation marks omitted), by requiring a plaintiff to "state with factual detail and particularity the basis for the claim which necessarily includes why the defendant-official cannot successfully maintain the defense of immunity." *Leatherman*, 507 U.S., at 167 (internal quotation marks omitted). We found this language inconsistent with Rules 8(a)(2) and 9(b) and emphasized that motions to dismiss were not the place to combat discovery abuse: "In the absence of [an amendment to Rule 9(b)], federal courts and litigants must rely on summary judgment and control of discovery to weed out unmeritorious claims sooner rather than later." *Id.*, at 168-169.

Most recently, in *Swierkiewicz*, 534 U.S. 506, we were faced with a case more similar to the present one than the majority will allow. In discrimination cases, our precedents require a plaintiff at the summary judgment stage to produce either direct evidence of discrimination or, if the claim is based primarily on circumstantial evidence, to meet the shifting evidentiary burdens imposed under the framework articulated in *McDonnell Douglas Corp. v. Green*, 411 U.S. 792 (1973). Swierkiewicz alleged that he had been terminated on account of national origin in violation of Title VII of the Civil Rights Act of 1964. The Second Circuit dismissed the suit on the pleadings because he had not pleaded a prima facie case of discrimination under the *McDonnell Douglas* standard.

We reversed in another unanimous opinion, holding that "under a notice pleading system, it is not appropriate to require a plaintiff to plead facts establishing a prima facie case because the *McDonnell Douglas* framework does not apply in every employment discrimination case." *Swierkiewicz*, 534 U.S., at 511. We also observed that Rule 8(a)(2) does not contemplate a court's passing on the merits of a litigant's claim at the pleading stage. Rather, the "simplified notice pleading standard" of the Federal Rules "relies on liberal discovery rules and summary judgment motions to define disputed facts and issues and to dispose of unmeritorious claims." *Id.*, at 512.

As in the discrimination context, we have developed an evidentiary framework for evaluating claims under § 1 of the Sherman Act when those claims rest on entirely circumstantial evidence of conspiracy. See *Matsushita Elec. Industrial Co. v. Zenith Radio Corp.*, 475 U.S. 574 (1986). Under *Matsushita*, a plaintiff's allegations of an illegal conspiracy may not, at the summary judgment stage, rest solely on the inferences that may be drawn from the parallel conduct of the defendants. In order to survive a Rule 56 motion, a § 1 plaintiff "must present evidence 'that tends to exclude the possibility' that the alleged conspirators acted independently.' " *Id.*, at 588 (quoting *Monsanto Co. v. Spray-Rite Service Corp.*, 465 U.S. 752, 764 (1984)). That is, the plaintiff "must show that the inference of conspiracy is reasonable in light of the competing inferences of independent action or collusive action." 475 U.S., at 588.

Everything today's majority says would therefore make perfect sense if it were ruling on a Rule 56 motion for summary judgment and the evidence included nothing more than the Court has described. But it should go without saying in the wake of *Swierkiewicz* that a heightened production burden at the summary judgment stage does not translate into a heightened pleading burden at the complaint stage. The majority rejects the complaint in this case because—in light of the fact that the parallel conduct alleged is consistent with ordinary market behavior—the claimed conspiracy is "conceivable" but not "plausible." I have my doubts about the majority's assessment of the plausibility of this alleged conspiracy. See Part III, *infra*. But even if the majority's speculation is correct, its "plausibility" standard is irreconcilable with Rule 8 and with our governing precedents. As we made clear in *Swierkiewicz* and *Leatherman*, fear of the burdens of litigation does not justify factual conclusions supported only by lawyers' arguments rather than sworn denials or admissible evidence.

This case is a poor vehicle for the Court's new pleading rule, for we have observed that "in antitrust cases, where 'the proof is largely in the hands of the alleged conspirators,' . . . dismissals prior to giving the plaintiff ample opportunity for discovery should be granted very sparingly." *Hospital Building Co. v. Trustees of Rex Hospital*, 425 U.S. 738, 746 (1976). Moreover, the fact that the Sherman Act authorizes the recovery of treble damages and attorney's fees for successful plaintiffs indicates that Congress intended to encourage, rather than discourage, private enforcement of the law. It is therefore more, not less, important in antitrust cases to resist the urge to engage in armchair economics at the pleading stage.

The same year we decided *Conley*, Judge Clark wrote, presciently,

> "I fear that every age must learn its lesson that special pleading cannot be made to do the service of trial and that live issues between active litigants are not to be disposed of or evaded on the paper pleadings, i.e., the formalistic claims of the parties. Experience has found no quick and easy short cut for trials in cases generally *and antitrust cases in particular.*" Special Pleading in the "Big Case"? in Procedure — The Handmaid of Justice 147, 148 (C. Wright & H. Reasoner eds. 1965) (hereinafter Clark, Special Pleading in the Big Case) (emphasis added).

<h2 style="text-align:center">III . . .</h2>

To be clear, if I had been the trial judge in this case, I would not have permitted the plaintiffs to engage in massive discovery based solely on the allegations in this complaint. On the other hand, I surely would not have dismissed the complaint without requiring the defendants to answer the charge that they "have agreed not to compete with one another and otherwise allocated customers and markets to one another." Even a sworn denial of that charge would not justify a summary dismissal without giving plaintiffs the opportunity to take depositions from . . . at least one responsible executive representing each of the . . . defendants. . . .

I fear that the unfortunate result of the majority's new pleading rule will be to invite lawyers' debates over economic theory to conclusively resolve antitrust suits in the absence of any evidence. It is no surprise that the antitrust defense bar — among whom "lament" as to inadequate judicial supervision of discovery is most "common," — should lobby for this state of affairs. But "we must recall that their primary responsibility is to win cases for their clients, not to improve law administration for the public." Clark, Special Pleading in the Big Case 152. As we did in our prior decisions, we should have instructed them that their remedy was to seek to amend the Federal Rules — not our interpretation of them. . . .

Accordingly, I respectfully dissent.

NOTES AND QUESTIONS

1. *The claim in* Twombly.   Using the operative-facts definition of a claim, how would you describe the plaintiffs' claim in *Twombly*? In answering this question, think about the narrative of the complaint. What story were the plaintiffs telling? Did the operative facts give rise to a potential right of action? If so, what substantive law governed that right of action? What were the essential elements of the asserted right? Did the facts pleaded by the plaintiffs support each of those elements? Does your answer depend on the generality at which a fact may be alleged?

2. *Conclusory allegations.* In its discussion of pleading standards, the Court makes several references to the pleading relevance of "legal conclusions" and "conclusory allegation[s]." It states, for example, that "a conclusory allegation of agreement at some unidentified point does not supply facts adequate to show illegality." What is a conclusory allegation and why does the Court discount its use in judging the sufficiency of a complaint? Isn't an allegation that the defendants conspired a factual allegation? If so, what makes it conclusory? Was the allegation in *Conley v. Gibson* that the union had acted in a racially discriminatory "planned course of conduct" conclusory? Consider the same question with respect to the "failure to train" allegation in *Leatherman v. Tarrant County.* See also Note 4, following *Leatherman, supra,* page 41.

3. *The presumption of truth.* Did the *Twombly* Court adhere to the principle endorsed in *Leatherman v. Tarrant County* that, in considering a Rule 12(b)(6) motion to dismiss, a court must accept as true all allegations of fact in a plaintiff's complaint? Given the decision in *Twombly,* how should a judge read the pleadings on a motion to dismiss? What does the Court mean when it says that "a well-pleaded complaint may proceed even if it strikes a savvy judge that actual proof of those facts is improbable, and 'that a recovery is very remote and unlikely'"?

4. *Sufficiency of the claim.* In Part III of its opinion, the Court employs a "plausibility" standard in assessing the sufficiency of the complaint. Why did the Court conclude that the complaint did not meet this standard? In applying that standard, the Court also focused its attention on allegations that the defendants had engaged in "parallel conduct." Is such conduct an essential element of the Sherman Act claim? If not, what was the relevance of parallel conduct with respect to the *Twombly* complaint? Did the Court introduce a "plus factor" into its assessment of pleading sufficiency? Or was the plus factor requirement a product of the law of the Sherman Act? Was the Court requiring proof of a plus factor? If not, what was lacking with respect to that factor?

5. *A heightened pleading standard?* Did the *Twombly* Court impose a heightened pleading standard or turn the federal pleading system into a fact-pleading system? The Court says it did not do so: "Here, in contrast, we do not require heightened fact pleading of specifics, but only enough facts to state a claim to relief that is plausible on its face. Because the plaintiffs here have not nudged their claims across the line from conceivable to plausible, their complaint must be dismissed." Do you agree? Can you distinguish this case from *Conley v. Gibson* and *Leatherman v. Tarrant County*? Is the pleading standard endorsed in *Twombly* more or less strict than the pleading standard endorsed by the California Supreme Court in *Doe v. City of Los Angeles*?

6. *A hasty retreat or a subtle distinction?* Two weeks after deciding *Twombly,* the Supreme Court issued a per curiam opinion that seemed to be in tension with *Twombly.* At issue in *Erickson v. Pardus,* 551 U.S. 89 (2007), was the sufficiency of a complaint filed by a prisoner who charged that he was being subjected to cruel and unusual punishment. His complaint alleged that a prison doctor had removed him from a hepatitis C treatment plan under circumstances "endangering [his] life." The District Court dismissed the complaint for failure to allege that

the doctor's actions had caused him "substantial" and "independent" harm, *i.e.*, harm beyond that which was being caused by the hepatitis C itself. The Court of Appeals affirmed, concluding that the prisoner's allegations of harm were "conclusory." The Supreme Court reversed, explaining:

> It was error for the Court of Appeals to conclude that the allegations in question, concerning harm caused petitioner by the termination of his medication, were too conclusory to establish for pleading purposes that petitioner had suffered "a cognizable independent harm" as a result of his removal from the hepatitis C treatment program.
>
> Federal Rule of Civil Procedure 8(a)(2) requires only a "short and plain statement of the claim showing that the pleader is entitled to relief." Specific facts are not necessary; the statement need only "give the defendant fair notice of what the . . . claim is and the grounds upon which it rests."

Id. at 93. The prisoner, therefore, was not required to allege specific facts pertaining to the substantiality or the independence of the harm. Is *Erickson* distinguishable from *Twombly*? Are the cases distinguishable based on the nature and complexity of the respective claims in each case? If so, does this mean that there is a variable pleading standard that is dependent on the complexity of the underlying claim? If the latter is true, does this suggest that in cases where a higher pleading standard is to be imposed, plaintiffs should be given the opportunity to engage in at least some discovery before the court rules on a Rule 12(b)(6) motion to dismiss? For a critique and evaluation of *Bell Atlantic v. Twombly* and *Erickson v. Pardus*, see Allan Ides, Bell Atlantic *and the Principle of Substantive Sufficiency Under Federal Rule of Civil Procedure 8(a)(2): Toward a Structured Approach to Federal Pleading Practice*, 243 F.R.D. 604 (2007).

PROBLEM

1-8. Reconsider the facts in Problems 1-6 and 1-7. Would those problems be resolved differently under *Bell Atlantic v. Twombly* and *Erickson v. Pardus*?

Ashcroft v. Iqbal

556 U.S. 662 (2009)

JUSTICE KENNEDY delivered the opinion of the Court.

Respondent Javaid Iqbal is a citizen of Pakistan and a Muslim. In the wake of the September 11, 2001, terrorist attacks he was arrested in the United States on criminal charges and detained by federal officials. Respondent claims he was deprived of various constitutional protections while in federal custody. To redress the alleged deprivations, respondent filed a complaint against numerous federal officials, including John Ashcroft, the former Attorney General of the United States, and Robert Mueller, the Director of the Federal Bureau of Investigation (FBI). Ashcroft and Mueller are the petitioners in the case now before us. As to these two petitioners, the complaint alleges that they adopted an unconstitutional policy that subjected respondent to harsh conditions of confinement on account of his race, religion, or national origin.

In the District Court petitioners raised the defense of qualified immunity and moved to dismiss the suit, contending the complaint was not sufficient to state a claim against them. The District Court denied the motion to dismiss, concluding the complaint was sufficient to state a claim despite petitioners' official status at the times in question. Petitioners brought an interlocutory appeal in the Court of Appeals for the Second Circuit. The court, without discussion, assumed it had jurisdiction over the order denying the motion to dismiss; and it affirmed the District Court's decision.

Respondent's account of his prison ordeal could, if proved, demonstrate unconstitutional misconduct by some governmental actors. But the allegations and pleadings with respect to these actors are not before us here. This case instead turns on a narrower question: Did respondent, as the plaintiff in the District Court, plead factual matter that, if taken as true, states a claim that petitioners deprived him of his clearly established constitutional rights? We hold respondent's pleadings are insufficient.

I

Following the 2001 attacks, the FBI and other entities within the Department of Justice began an investigation of vast reach to identify the assailants and prevent them from attacking anew. The FBI dedicated more than 4,000 special agents and 3,000 support personnel to the endeavor. By September 18 "the FBI had received more than 96,000 tips or potential leads from the public." Dept. of Justice, Office of Inspector General, The September 11 Detainees: A Review of the Treatment of Aliens Held on Immigration Charges in Connection with the Investigation of the September 11 Attacks 1, 11-12 (Apr. 2003) (hereinafter OIG Report).

In the ensuing months the FBI questioned more than 1,000 people with suspected links to the attacks in particular or to terrorism in general. Of those individuals, some 762 were held on immigration charges; and a 184-member subset of that group was deemed to be "of 'high interest'" to the investigation. The high-interest detainees were held under restrictive conditions designed to prevent them from communicating with the general prison population or the outside world.

Respondent was one of the detainees. According to his complaint, in November 2001 agents of the FBI and Immigration and Naturalization Service arrested him on charges of fraud in relation to identification documents and conspiracy to defraud the United States. Pending trial for those crimes, respondent was housed at the Metropolitan Detention Center (MDC) in Brooklyn, New York. Respondent was designated a person "of high interest" to the September 11 investigation and in January 2002 was placed in a section of the MDC known as the Administrative Maximum Special Housing Unit (ADMAX SHU). As the facility's name indicates, the ADMAX SHU incorporates the maximum security conditions allowable under Federal Bureau of Prison regulations. ADMAX SHU detainees were kept in lockdown 23 hours a day, spending the remaining hour outside their cells in handcuffs and leg irons accompanied by a four-officer escort.

Respondent pleaded guilty to the criminal charges, served a term of imprisonment, and was removed to his native Pakistan. He then filed a *Bivens* action in the United States District Court for the Eastern District of New York against 34 current and former federal officials and 19 "John Doe" federal corrections officers. See *Bivens v. Six Unknown Fed. Narcotics Agents*, 403 U.S. 388 (1971). The defendants range from the correctional officers who had day-to-day contact with respondent during the term of his confinement, to the wardens of the MDC facility, all the way to petitioners—officials who were at the highest level of the federal law enforcement hierarchy.

The 21-cause-of-action complaint does not challenge respondent's arrest or his confinement in the MDC's general prison population. Rather, it concentrates on his treatment while confined to the ADMAX SHU. The complaint sets forth various claims against defendants who are not before us. For instance, the complaint alleges that respondent's jailors "kicked him in the stomach, punched him in the face, and dragged him across" his cell without justification; subjected him to serial strip and body-cavity searches when he posed no safety risk to himself or others; and refused to let him and other Muslims pray because there would be "[n]o prayers for terrorists."

The allegations against petitioners are the only ones relevant here. The complaint contends that petitioners designated respondent a person of high interest on account of his race, religion, or national origin, in contravention of the First and Fifth Amendments to the Constitution. The complaint alleges that "the [FBI], under the direction of Defendant Mueller, arrested and detained thousands of Arab Muslim men . . . as part of its investigation of the events of September 11." It further alleges that "[t]he policy of holding post-September-11th detainees in highly restrictive conditions of confinement until they were 'cleared' by the FBI was approved by Defendants Ashcroft and Mueller in discussions in the weeks after September 11, 2001." Lastly, the complaint posits that petitioners "each knew of, condoned, and willfully and maliciously agreed to subject" respondent to harsh conditions of confinement "as a matter of policy, solely on account of [his] religion, race, and/or national origin and for no legitimate penological interest." The pleading names Ashcroft as the "principal architect" of the policy, and identifies Mueller as "instrumental in [its] adoption, promulgation, and implementation."

Petitioners moved to dismiss the complaint for failure to state sufficient allegations to show their own involvement in clearly established unconstitutional conduct. The District Court denied their motion. . . . Invoking the collateral-order doctrine petitioners filed an interlocutory appeal in the United States Court of Appeals for the Second Circuit. While that appeal was pending, this Court decided *Bell Atlantic Corp. v. Twombly*, 550 U.S. 544 (2007), which discussed the standard for evaluating whether a complaint is sufficient to survive a motion to dismiss.

The Court of Appeals considered *Twombly*'s applicability to this case. Acknowledging that *Twombly* retired the *Conley* no-set-of-facts test relied upon by the District Court, the Court of Appeals' opinion discussed at length how to apply this Court's "standard for assessing the adequacy of pleadings." It concluded that *Twombly* called for a "flexible 'plausibility standard,' which obliges a pleader to amplify a claim with some factual allegations in those contexts where such amplification is needed to render the claim *plausible.*" The court found that petitioners' appeal did not present one of "those contexts" requiring amplification. As a consequence, it held respondent's pleading adequate to allege petitioners' personal involvement in discriminatory decisions which, if true, violated clearly established constitutional law. . . .

. . . We granted certiorari and now reverse. . . .

III

In *Twombly*, the Court found it necessary first to discuss the antitrust principles implicated by the complaint. Here too we begin by taking note of the elements a plaintiff must plead to state a claim of unconstitutional discrimination against officials entitled to assert the defense of qualified immunity. . . .

The factors necessary to establish a *Bivens* violation [*i.e.*, an implied cause of action for violation of an individual's constitutional rights by an agent of the federal government] will vary with the constitutional provision at issue. Where the claim is invidious discrimination in contravention of the First and Fifth Amendments, our decisions make clear that the plaintiff must plead and prove that the defendant acted with discriminatory purpose. Under extant precedent purposeful discrimination requires more than "intent as volition or intent as awareness of consequences." *Personnel Administrator of Mass. v. Feeney*, 442 U.S. 256, 279 (1979). It instead involves a decisionmaker's undertaking a course of action "'because of,' not merely 'in spite of,' [the action's] adverse effects upon an identifiable group." It follows that, to state a claim based on a violation of a clearly established right, respondent must plead sufficient factual matter to show that petitioners adopted and implemented the detention policies at issue not for a neutral, investigative reason but for the purpose of discriminating on account of race, religion, or national origin.

. . . [E]ach Government official, his or her title notwithstanding, is only liable for his or her own misconduct. In the context of determining whether there is a violation of clearly established right to overcome qualified immunity, purpose rather than knowledge is required to impose *Bivens* liability on the subordinate for unconstitutional discrimination; the same holds true for an official charged with violations arising from his or her superintendent responsibilities.

IV

A

We turn to respondent's complaint. Under Federal Rule of Civil Procedure 8(a)(2), a pleading must contain a "short and plain statement of the claim showing that the pleader is entitled to relief." As the Court held in *Twombly*, the pleading standard Rule 8 announces does not require "detailed factual allegations," but it demands more than an unadorned, the-defendant-unlawfully-harmed-me accusation. A pleading that offers "labels and conclusions" or "a formulaic recitation of the elements of a cause of action will not do." Nor does a complaint suffice if it tenders "naked assertion[s]" devoid of "further factual enhancement."

To survive a motion to dismiss, a complaint must contain sufficient factual matter, accepted as true, to "state a claim to relief that is plausible on its face." A claim has facial plausibility when the plaintiff pleads factual content that allows the court to draw the reasonable inference that the defendant is liable for the misconduct alleged. The plausibility standard is not akin to a "probability requirement," but it asks for more than a sheer possibility that a defendant has acted unlawfully. *Ibid.* Where a complaint pleads facts that are "merely consistent with" a defendant's liability, it "stops short of the line between possibility and plausibility of 'entitlement to relief.'" Two working principles underlie our decision in *Twombly*. First, the tenet that a court must accept as true all of the allegations contained in a complaint is inapplicable to legal conclusions. Threadbare recitals of the elements of a cause of action, supported by mere conclusory statements, do not suffice. (Although for the purposes of a motion to dismiss we must take all of the factual allegations in the complaint as true, we "are not bound to accept as true a legal conclusion couched as a factual allegation.") Rule 8 marks a notable and generous departure from the hyper-technical, code-pleading regime of a prior era, but it does not unlock the doors of discovery for a plaintiff armed with nothing more than conclusions. Second, only a complaint that states a plausible claim for relief survives a motion to dismiss. Determining whether a complaint states a plausible claim for relief will, as the Court of Appeals observed, be a context-specific task that requires the reviewing court to draw on its judicial experience and common sense. But where the well-pleaded facts do not permit the court to infer more than the mere possibility of misconduct, the complaint has alleged—but it has not "show[n]"—"that the pleader is entitled to relief." Fed. Rule Civ. Proc. 8(a)(2).

In keeping with these principles a court considering a motion to dismiss can choose to begin by identifying pleadings that, because they are no more than conclusions, are not entitled to the assumption of truth. While legal conclusions can provide the framework of a complaint, they must be supported by factual allegations. When there are well-pleaded factual allegations, a court should assume their veracity and then determine whether they plausibly give rise to an entitlement to relief.

Our decision in *Twombly* illustrates the two-pronged approach. There, we considered the sufficiency of a complaint alleging that incumbent telecommunications providers had entered an agreement not to compete and to forestall competitive entry, in violation of the Sherman Act, 15 U.S.C. § 1. Recognizing that § 1 enjoins only anticompetitive conduct "effected by a contract, combination, or conspiracy," the plaintiffs in *Twombly* flatly pleaded that the defendants "ha[d] entered into a contract, combination or conspiracy to prevent competitive entry . . . and ha[d] agreed not to compete with one another." The complaint also alleged that the defendants' "parallel course of conduct . . . to prevent competition" and inflate prices was indicative of the unlawful agreement alleged.

The Court held the plaintiffs' complaint deficient under Rule 8. In doing so it first noted that the plaintiffs' assertion of an unlawful agreement was a "'legal conclusion'" and, as such, was not entitled to the assumption of truth. Had the Court simply credited the allegation of a conspiracy, the plaintiffs would have stated a claim for relief and been entitled to proceed perforce. The Court next addressed the "nub" of the plaintiffs' complaint—the well-pleaded, nonconclusory factual allegation of parallel behavior—to determine whether it gave rise to a "plausible suggestion of conspiracy." Acknowledging that parallel conduct was consistent with an unlawful agreement, the Court nevertheless concluded that it did not plausibly suggest an illicit accord because it was not only compatible with, but indeed was more likely explained by, lawful, unchoreographed free-market behavior. Because the well-pleaded fact of parallel conduct, accepted as true, did not plausibly suggest an unlawful agreement, the Court held the plaintiffs' complaint must be dismissed.

B

Under *Twombly*'s construction of Rule 8, we conclude that respondent's complaint has not "nudged [his] claims" of invidious discrimination "across the line from conceivable to plausible."

We begin our analysis by identifying the allegations in the complaint that are not entitled to the assumption of truth. Respondent pleads that petitioners "knew of, condoned, and willfully and maliciously agreed to subject [him]" to harsh conditions of confinement "as a matter of policy, solely on account of [his] religion, race, and/or national origin and for no legitimate penological interest." The complaint alleges that Ashcroft was the "principal architect" of this invidious policy, and that Mueller was "instrumental" in adopting and executing it. These bare assertions, much like the pleading of conspiracy in *Twombly*, amount to nothing more than a "formulaic recitation of the elements" of a constitutional discrimination claim, namely, that petitioners adopted a policy "'because of,' not merely 'in spite of,' its adverse effects upon an identifiable group." As such, the allegations are conclusory and not entitled to be assumed true. To be clear, we do not reject these bald allegations on the ground that they are unrealistic or nonsensical. We do not so characterize them any more than the Court in *Twombly* rejected the plaintiffs' express allegation of a "'contract, combination or conspiracy to prevent competitive entry,'" because it thought that claim too chimerical to be maintained. It is the conclusory nature of respondent's allegations, rather than their extravagantly fanciful nature, that disentitles them to the presumption of truth.

We next consider the factual allegations in respondent's complaint to determine if they plausibly suggest an entitlement to relief. The complaint alleges that "the [FBI], under the direction of Defendant Mueller, arrested and detained thousands of Arab Muslim men . . . as part of its investigation of the events of September 11." It further claims that "[t]he policy of holding post-September-11th detainees in highly restrictive conditions of confinement until they were 'cleared' by the FBI was approved by Defendants Ashcroft and Mueller in discussions in the weeks after September 11, 2001." Taken as true, these allegations are consistent with petitioners' purposefully designating detainees "of high interest" because of their race, religion, or national origin. But given more likely explanations, they do not plausibly establish this purpose.

The September 11 attacks were perpetrated by 19 Arab Muslim hijackers who counted themselves members in good standing of al Qaeda, an Islamic fundamentalist group. Al Qaeda was headed by another Arab Muslim—Osama bin Laden—and composed in large part of his Arab Muslim disciples. It should come as no surprise that a legitimate policy directing law enforcement to arrest and detain individuals because of their suspected link to the attacks would produce a disparate, incidental impact on Arab Muslims, even though the purpose of the policy was to target neither Arabs nor Muslims. On the facts respondent alleges the arrests Mueller oversaw were likely lawful and justified by his nondiscriminatory intent to detain aliens who were illegally present in the United States and who had potential connections to those who committed terrorist acts. As between that "obvious alternative explanation" for the arrests, and the purposeful, invidious discrimination respondent asks us to infer, discrimination is not a plausible conclusion.

But even if the complaint's well-pleaded facts give rise to a plausible inference that respondent's arrest was the result of unconstitutional discrimination, that inference alone would not entitle respondent to relief. It is important to recall that respondent's complaint challenges neither the constitutionality of his arrest nor his initial detention in the MDC. Respondent's constitutional claims against petitioners rest solely on their ostensible "policy of holding post-September-11th detainees" in the ADMAX SHU once they were categorized as "of high interest." To prevail on that theory, the complaint must contain facts plausibly showing that petitioners purposefully adopted a policy of classifying post-September-11 detainees as "of high interest" because of their race, religion, or national origin.

This the complaint fails to do. Though respondent alleges that various other defendants, who are not before us, may have labeled him a person of "of high interest" for impermissible reasons, his only factual allegation against petitioners accuses them of adopting a policy approving "restrictive conditions of confinement" for post-September-11 detainees until they were "'cleared' by the FBI." Accepting the truth of that allegation, the complaint does not show, or even intimate, that petitioners purposefully housed detainees in the ADMAX SHU due to their race, religion, or national origin. All it plausibly suggests is that the Nation's top law enforcement officers, in the aftermath of a devastating terrorist attack, sought to keep suspected terrorists in the most secure conditions available until the suspects could be cleared of terrorist activity. Respondent does not argue, nor can he, that such a motive would violate petitioners' constitutional obligations. He would need to allege more by way of factual content to "nudg[e]" his claim of purposeful discrimination "across the line from conceivable to plausible." *Twombly*, 550 U.S. at 570.

To be sure, respondent can attempt to draw certain contrasts between the plead-ings the Court considered in *Twombly* and the pleadings at issue here. In *Twombly*, the complaint alleged general wrongdoing that extended over a period of years, whereas here the complaint alleges discrete wrongs—for instance, beatings—by lower level Government actors. The allegations here, if true, and if condoned by petitioners, could be the basis for some inference of wrongful intent on petition-ers' part. Despite these distinctions, respondent's pleadings do not suffice to state a claim. Unlike in *Twombly*, where the doctrine of *respondeat superior* could bind the corporate defendant, here, as we have noted, petitioners cannot be held liable unless they themselves acted on account of a constitutionally protected character-istic. Yet respondent's complaint does not contain any factual allegation sufficient to plausibly suggest petitioners' discriminatory state of mind. His pleadings thus do not meet the standard necessary to comply with Rule 8.

It is important to note, however, that we express no opinion concerning the sufficiency of respondent's complaint against the defendants who are not before us. Respondent's account of his prison ordeal alleges serious official misconduct that we need not address here. Our decision is limited to the determination that respondent's complaint does not entitle him to relief from petitioners.

C

Respondent offers three arguments that bear on our disposition of his case, but none is persuasive.

1

Respondent first says that our decision in *Twombly* should be limited to plead-ings made in the context of an antitrust dispute. This argument is not supported by *Twombly* and is incompatible with the Federal Rules of Civil Procedure. Though *Twombly* determined the sufficiency of a complaint sounding in antitrust, the decision was based on our interpretation and application of Rule 8. That Rule in turn governs the pleading standard "in all civil actions and proceedings in the United States district courts." Fed. Rule Civ. Proc. 1. Our decision in *Twombly* expounded the pleading standard for "all civil actions," and it applies to antitrust and discrimination suits alike.

2

Respondent next implies that our construction of Rule 8 should be tempered where, as here, the Court of Appeals has "instructed the district court to cabin dis-covery in such a way as to preserve" petitioners' defense of qualified immunity "as much as possible in anticipation of a summary judgment motion." We have held, however, that the question presented by a motion to dismiss a complaint for insuf-ficient pleadings does not turn on the controls placed upon the discovery process. *Twombly*, *supra*, ("It is no answer to say that a claim just shy of a plausible enti-tlement to relief can, if groundless, be weeded out early in the discovery process through careful case management given the common lament that the success of judicial supervision in checking discovery abuse has been on the modest side").

Our rejection of the careful-case-management approach is especially important in suits where Government-official defendants are entitled to assert the defense of qualified immunity. . . .

. . . Because respondent's complaint is deficient under Rule 8, he is not entitled to discovery, cabined or otherwise.

3

Respondent finally maintains that the Federal Rules expressly allow him to allege petitioners' discriminatory intent "generally," which he equates with a conclusory allegation. Iqbal Brief 32 (citing Fed. Rule Civ. Proc. 9). It follows, respondent says, that his complaint is sufficiently well pleaded because it claims that petitioners discriminated against him "on account of [his] religion, race, and/or national origin and for no legitimate penological interest." Were we required to accept this allegation as true, respondent's complaint would survive petitioners' motion to dismiss. But the Federal Rules do not require courts to credit a complaint's conclusory statements without reference to its factual context.

It is true that Rule 9(b) requires particularity when pleading "fraud or mistake," while allowing "[m]alice, intent, knowledge, and other conditions of a person's mind [to] be alleged generally." But "generally" is a relative term. In the context of Rule 9, it is to be compared to the particularity requirement applicable to fraud or mistake. Rule 9 merely excuses a party from pleading discriminatory intent under an elevated pleading standard. It does not give him license to evade the less rigid—though still operative—strictures of Rule 8. And Rule 8 does not empower respondent to plead the bare elements of his cause of action, affix the label "general allegation," and expect his complaint to survive a motion to dismiss.

V

We hold that respondent's complaint fails to plead sufficient facts to state a claim for purposeful and unlawful discrimination against petitioners. The Court of Appeals should decide in the first instance whether to remand to the District Court so that respondent can seek leave to amend his deficient complaint.

The judgment of the Court of Appeals is reversed, and the case is remanded for further proceedings consistent with this opinion.

It is so ordered.

JUSTICE SOUTER, with whom JUSTICE STEVENS, JUSTICE GINSBURG, and JUSTICE BREYER join, dissenting.

. . . The majority . . . misapplies the pleading standard under *Bell Atlantic* . . . to conclude that the complaint fails to state a claim. I respectfully dissent. . . .

II

[T]he complaint satisfies Rule 8(a)(2). Ashcroft and Mueller admit they are liable for their subordinates' conduct if they "had actual knowledge of the assertedly discriminatory nature of the classification of suspects as being 'of high interest' and they were deliberately indifferent to that discrimination." Iqbal alleges that after the September 11 attacks the Federal Bureau of Investigation (FBI) "arrested and detained thousands of Arab Muslim men," that many of these men were designated by high-ranking FBI officials as being " 'of high interest,' " and that in many cases, including Iqbal's, this designation was made "because of the race, religion, and national origin of the detainees, and not because of any evidence of the detainees' involvement in supporting terrorist activity." The complaint further alleges that Ashcroft was the "principal architect of the policies and practices challenged," and that Mueller "was instrumental in the adoption, promulgation, and implementation of the policies and practices challenged." According to the complaint, Ashcroft and Mueller "knew of, condoned, and willfully and maliciously agreed to subject [Iqbal] to these conditions of confinement as a matter of policy, solely on account of [his] religion, race, and/or national origin and for no legitimate penological interest." The complaint thus alleges, at a bare minimum, that Ashcroft and Mueller knew of and condoned the discriminatory policy their subordinates carried out. Actually, the complaint goes further in alleging that Ashcroft and Muller affirmatively acted to create the discriminatory detention policy. If these factual allegations are true, Ashcroft and Mueller were, at the very least, aware of the discriminatory policy being implemented and deliberately indifferent to it.

Ashcroft and Mueller argue that these allegations fail to satisfy the "plausibility standard" of *Twombly*. They contend that Iqbal's claims are implausible because such high-ranking officials "tend not to be personally involved in the specific actions of lower-level officers down the bureaucratic chain of command." But this response bespeaks a fundamental misunderstanding of the enquiry that *Twombly* demands. *Twombly* does not require a court at the motion-to-dismiss stage to consider whether the factual allegations are probably true. We made it clear, on the contrary, that a court must take the allegations as true, no matter how skeptical the court may be. The sole exception to this rule lies with allegations that are sufficiently fantastic to defy reality as we know it: claims about little green men, or the plaintiff's recent trip to Pluto, or experiences in time travel. That is not what we have here.

Under *Twombly*, the relevant question is whether, assuming the factual allegations are true, the plaintiff has stated a ground for relief that is plausible. That is, in *Twombly*'s words, a plaintiff must "allege facts" that, taken as true, are "suggestive of illegal conduct." In *Twombly*, we were faced with allegations of a conspiracy to violate § 1 of the Sherman Act through parallel conduct. The difficulty was that the conduct alleged was "consistent with conspiracy, but just as much in line with a wide swath of rational and competitive business strategy unilaterally prompted by common perceptions of the market." We held that in that sort of circumstance, "[a]n allegation of parallel conduct is . . . much like a naked assertion of conspiracy in a § 1 complaint: it gets the complaint close to stating a claim, but without some further factual enhancement it stops short of the line between possibility and plausibility of 'entitlement to relief.' " Here, by contrast, the allegations in the complaint are neither confined to naked legal conclusions nor consistent with legal conduct. The complaint alleges that FBI officials discriminated against Iqbal solely on account of his race, religion, and national origin, and it alleges the knowledge and deliberate indifference that, by Ashcroft and Mueller's own admission, are sufficient to make them liable for the illegal action. Iqbal's complaint therefore contains "enough facts to state a claim to relief that is plausible on its face."

I do not understand the majority to disagree with this understanding of "plausibility" under *Twombly*. Rather, the majority discards the allegations discussed above with regard to Ashcroft and Mueller as conclusory, and is left considering only two statements in the complaint: that "the [FBI], under the direction of Defendant Mueller, arrested and detained thousands of Arab Muslim men . . . as part of its investigation of the events of September 11," and that "[t]he policy of holding post-September-11th detainees in highly restrictive conditions of confinement until they were 'cleared' by the FBI was approved by Defendants Ashcroft and Mueller in discussions in the weeks after September 11, 2001." I think the majority is right in saying that these allegations suggest only that Ashcroft and Mueller "sought to keep suspected terrorists in the most secure conditions available until the suspects could be cleared of terrorist activity," and that this produced "a disparate, incidental impact on Arab Muslims." And I agree that the two allegations selected by the majority, standing alone, do not state a plausible entitlement to relief for unconstitutional discrimination.

But these allegations do not stand alone as the only significant, nonconclusory statements in the complaint, for the complaint contains many allegations linking Ashcroft and Mueller to the discriminatory practices of their subordinates. See Complaint ¶ 10 (Ashcroft was the "principal architect" of the discriminatory policy); *id.*, ¶ 11 (Mueller was "instrumental" in adopting and executing the discriminatory policy); *id.*, ¶ 96 (Ashcroft and Mueller "knew of, condoned, and willfully and maliciously agreed to subject" Iqbal to harsh conditions "as a matter of policy, solely on account of [his] religion, race, and/or national origin and for no legitimate penological interest").

The majority says that these are "bare assertions" that, "much like the pleading of conspiracy in *Twombly*, amount to nothing more than a 'formulaic recitation of the elements' of a constitutional discrimination claim" and therefore are "not entitled to be assumed true." The fallacy of the majority's position, however, lies in looking at the relevant assertions in isolation. The complaint contains specific allegations that, in the aftermath of the September 11 attacks, the Chief of the FBI's International Terrorism Operations Section and the Assistant Special Agent in Charge for the FBI's New York Field Office implemented a policy that discriminated against Arab Muslim men, including Iqbal, solely on account of their race, religion, or national origin. Viewed in light of these subsidiary allegations, the allegations singled out by the majority as "conclusory" are no such thing. Iqbal's claim is not that Ashcroft and Mueller "knew of, condoned, and willfully and maliciously agreed to subject" him to a discriminatory practice that is left undefined; his allegation is that "they knew of, condoned, and willfully and maliciously agreed to subject" him to a particular, discrete, discriminatory policy detailed in the complaint. Iqbal does not say merely that Ashcroft was the architect of some amorphous discrimination, or that Mueller was instrumental in an ill-defined constitutional violation; he alleges that they helped to create the discriminatory policy he has described. Taking the complaint as a whole, it gives Ashcroft and Mueller "'fair notice of what the . . . claim is and the grounds upon which it rests.'" . . .

I respectfully dissent.

JUSTICE BREYER, dissenting.

I agree with Justice Souter and join his dissent. I write separately to point out that, like the Court, I believe it important to prevent unwarranted litigation from interfering with "the proper execution of the work of the Government." But I cannot find in that need adequate justification for the Court's interpretation of *Bell Atlantic Corp. v. Twombly*, and Federal Rule of Civil Procedure 8. The law, after all, provides trial courts with other legal weapons designed to prevent unwarranted interference. As the Second Circuit explained, where a Government defendant asserts a qualified immunity defense, a trial court, responsible for managing a case and "mindful of the need to vindicate the purpose of the qualified immunity defense," can structure discovery in ways that diminish the risk of imposing unwarranted burdens upon public officials. A district court, for example, can begin discovery with lower level government defendants before determining whether a case can be made to allow discovery related to higher level government officials. Neither the briefs nor the Court's opinion provides convincing grounds for finding these alternative case-management tools inadequate, either in general or in the case before us. For this reason, as well as for the independently sufficient reasons set forth in Justice Souter's opinion, I would affirm the Second Circuit.

NOTES AND QUESTIONS

1. The presumption of truth.   What role do "judicial experience and common sense" play in the *Iqbal* Court's approach to the presumption of truth? Is this consistent with the approach adopted in either *Leatherman* or *Twombly*? As to the latter, how does *Twombly*'s "savvy judge" differ from *Iqbal*'s experienced judge? Is the one more or less deferential than the other? If the alleged facts are presumed to be true, shouldn't all inferences from those facts be drawn in the pleader's favor? Cf. *Anderson v. Liberty Lobby*, 477 U.S. 242, 245 (1986) (inferences from the facts are to be drawn in favor of the non-moving party in summary judgment motions and in motions for judgment made during or after trial).

2. A three-step test.   The Court adopts a three-step approach to assessing the sufficiency of the complaint, the first step of which is inferred from the two identified by the Court. What are those three steps? Does this approach introduce a type of analysis that differs from the one endorsed by the Court in *Twombly*? Is it similar to the approach used by the California Supreme Court in *Doe v. City of Los Angeles*? Where would you place this approach on a spectrum between the most pragmatic and the most formal? Did the allegations of intent in *Iqbal* differ in any significant way from the allegations of intent in *Conley*?

3. *Rule 9(b).*   What was the relevance of Iqbal's Rule 9(b) argument? On what basis did the Court reject this argument? Do you agree with the Court's reasoning? How would you describe the difference between a general allegation of intent and a conclusory allegation of intent? Might we say that the Rule 9(b) standard for state-of-mind allegations invites conclusory allegations?

4. *Justice Souter's dissenting opinion.*   How does Justice Souter's reading of Iqbal's complaint differ from that of the majority? How should conclusory allegations be read, according to Justice Souter? How does he distinguish *Iqbal* from *Twombly?* Is that distinction convincing?

5. *Justice Breyer's dissenting opinion.*   On what basis does Justice Breyer disagree with the majority? What are the "other legal weapons" he would have used to prevent unwarranted interference with "the proper execution of the work of the Government"? Would his approach be more consistent with the original spirit of Rule 8(a)(2) than the majority's approach?

In *Turkmen v. Hasty,* 789 F.3d 218 (2d Cir. 2015), the Second Circuit revisited the *"Iqbal"* story in a putative class action suit brought against John Ashcroft and Robert Mueller, among others, by Arab and Muslim males who had also been detained in the post-9/11 sweeps in New York. The *Turkmen* plaintiffs' complaint, the initial version of which was filed in 2002, asserted a variety of due process and equal protection claims against the defendants. The claims asserted were virtually identical to those asserted by the plaintiff in *Iqbal.* The primary distinction between *Iqbal* and *Turkmen* was that the *Turkmen* complaint included allegations that relied on two reports issued by the Office of the Inspector General of the United States Department of Justice ("OIG reports") and on information gathered by the plaintiffs during discovery.

As a consequence, the allegations in the *Turkmen* complaint—a fourth amended complaint—provided a more detailed account of the role played by Ashcroft and Mueller in creating and enforcing the challenged policies and practices. Those evidentiary details led a divided panel of the Second Circuit to conclude that the plaintiffs had plausibly pleaded both due process and equal protections claims against Ashcroft, Mueller, and others. More specifically, the panel concluded that there were sufficient allegations in the complaint to support an inference that Ashcroft and Mueller had created and enforced a detention policy that was intentionally based on the race, religion, and/or ethnicity of the persons detained. Thus the pleadings stated a plausible claim upon which relief could be granted, warranting denial of defendants' Rule 12(b)(6) motion to dismiss.

A NOTE ON PLAUSIBILITY, INFERENCES, AND PLEADING SUFFICIENCY

As we will see in the next three principal cases, lower courts have struggled with the Supreme Court's new "plausibility" standard. This is no surprise. Neither

Twombly nor *Iqbal* is a model of clarity. Nor, as Justice Souter's dissent in *Iqbal* makes clear, are they entirely consistent with one another. But, like them or not, they do inform the law in this area and, as lawyers, we must find a workable method through which to navigate that law. This is not to deny the flaws in these opinions; rather, it is to find a way to co-exist with those flaws until such time as they can be remedied. In addition, the effort might reveal precisely where the confusion lies and where we, as lawyers, must be most attentive in drafting or responding to a pleading.

The Court's resolution of the pleading issue in *Twombly* provides our starting point. The precise question there was whether the plaintiffs had adequately pleaded the existence of an agreement to restrain competition, an essential element of their Sherman Act claim. The plaintiffs asked the Court to infer the existence of such an agreement from their allegations showing that the defendants had engaged in parallel, non-competitive conduct. But the substantive law of the Sherman Act did not permit such an inference to be drawn. Under the Sherman Act, a plaintiff cannot establish the existence of an unlawful agreement solely based on parallel conduct. Rather, parallel conduct will support the inference of an unlawful agreement only if the plaintiff pleads additional facts rebutting the presumption that parallel conduct is driven by market considerations ("plus factor" allegations). The *Twombly* complaint did not include any allegations directly supportive of this necessary plus factor; nor did it contain any factual allegations from which an inference of a plus factor could be drawn. In short, the plaintiffs' complaint contained no factual allegation that either directly or by inference supported their theory of the case. The complaint was therefore deficient. The *Twombly* Court made clear that it was not imposing a probability standard; nor was it requiring proof sufficient to sustain a claim, though at times it seemed to stray into that realm. Instead, the flaw in the *Twombly* plaintiffs' complaint was simply that it failed to allege factual matter reasonably suggestive of the existence of an agreement to restrain competition.

In *Iqbal*, the question was whether the plaintiff had adequately alleged that the defendants intentionally discriminated against him on the basis of his religion, race, and national origin. The *Iqbal* Court described the framework through which a court is to assess that question. Under this framework, a court must identify the elements of the plaintiff's claim under the applicable substantive law. Next, it must accept as true all factual allegations in the complaint. Conclusory allegations, however, are not entitled to the presumption of truth, since they are "formulaic" and merely recite the elements of the claim. Finally, the court must determine whether the non-conclusory factual allegations are suggestive of a plausible claim for relief. As to this final step, the *Iqbal* Court instructed:

> To survive a motion to dismiss, a complaint must contain sufficient factual matter, accepted as true, to "state a claim to relief that is plausible on its face." A claim has facial plausibility when the plaintiff pleads factual content that allows the court to draw the reasonable inference that the defendant is liable for the misconduct alleged. The plausibility standard is not akin to a "probability requirement," but it asks for more than a sheer possibility that a defendant has acted unlawfully.

556 U.S. at 678. The Court concluded that Iqbal's complaint failed to meet this "plausibility" standard since the complaint contained no non-conclusory allegations from which to infer invidious intent.

Thus, following *Twombly* and *Iqbal*, the question is not one of probability or proof, but whether the factual matter asserted by the plaintiff states a "plausible" claim for relief. We might say that "plausibility" lies somewhere between the possible and the probable, and that its satisfaction requires a careful consideration of the facts alleged and the reasonable inferences that can be drawn from those facts.

To this point, and stated at this general level, the *Twombly/Iqbal* method is straightforward: Identify the cause of action and its essential elements; set aside the conclusory allegations as not entitled to the presumption of truth; and then assess whether the non-conclusory allegations directly or by inference provide support for each operative element of the identified cause. So much is clear, but now we have arrived at the point where carefully honed lawyering skills will be most essential. How do we determine whether an inference is reasonably suggestive of an element of the cause of action thus rendering the claim plausible?

In the discipline of logic, an inference can be established in three ways: deductively, inductively, or abductively. A *deductive* inference is a product of the classic syllogism and flows ineluctably from its major and minor premises (*e.g.*, all humans are mortal; Socrates is a human; Socrates is mortal). If the premises are true, then the logical deduction provides absolute proof of its conclusion. An *inductive* inference is one for which the premise—a set of facts thought to be true—makes it probable that a particular conclusion is also true (*e.g.*, most adult humans are taller than two feet; Bob is an adult human; Bob is most likely taller than two feet). Finally, an *abductive* inference seeks to establish the best or most likely explanation for an observed set of facts; the inference is the precondition for the thing observed (*e.g.*, the ground is wet; it must have rained).

A legally sustainable inference may employ any or all of the above techniques, but its legitimacy is measured at one step removed in the sense that it does not require absolute proof, definitive probability, or the best choice. Rather, a legitimate inference at law is one that a reasonable fact-finder *could* rationally draw from the facts (or evidence). 1 CLIFFORD S. FISHMAN & ANNE T. MCKENNA, JONES ON EVIDENCE § 4:1 (7th ed. 2014) ("An inference is a factual conclusion that can rationally be drawn from other facts. If fact A rationally supports the conclusion that fact B is also true, then B may be *inferred* from A.").

This appears to be the approach adopted by the Court in *Twombly*, where the Court observed that "the complaint should survive a Rule 12(b)(6) motion 'even if it strikes a savvy judge that actual proof of those facts is improbable, and 'that a recovery is very remote and unlikely.'" Thus, an inference drawn from the facts alleged in a pleading—which facts must be assumed to be true—does not need to be deductively proven, inductively probable, or even abductively optimal. Rather, to survive a Rule 12(b)(6) motion, an inference need only be reasonable, and reasonableness permits a range of alternative inferences, that is, inferences on which reasonable minds may differ. Discovery and trial will then reveal which of these competing and factually supported inferences is, in fact, true (or should be accepted as true). In *Twombly*, given the law of the Sherman Act, there were no facts from which a reasonable fact-finder could infer an agreement in restraint of competition. Therefore, there were no competing inferences with the presumed inference that the defendants' actions were motivated by their shared perceptions of the marketplace. In short, there was nothing from which a court could deduce, induce, or abduce the necessary plus factor. This was also true in *Doe v. City of Los Angeles* with respect to the knowledge of the defendants.

The Court in *Iqbal* seems to have endorsed an approach to inferences that is less deferential to the pleader than what we have described. Thus it found that an inference of discriminatory intent for the post-9/11 dragnet arrest of Arabs and Muslims was "implausible" since there were "more likely explanations" for the defendant's conduct. Specifically, the Court found that the "obvious alternative explanation" for the arrest and detention of Arabs and Muslims was the "nondiscriminatory intent to detain aliens who were illegally present in the United States and who had potential connections to those who committed terrorist acts." At a more general level, the Court invited trial court judges "to draw on [their] judicial experience and common sense" in assessing inferences from the allegations in a complaint, a somewhat more active assessment of the complaint than contemplated by *Twombly*'s "savvy," but deferential judge. In this way, the *Iqbal* Court seemed to allow judges to engage in a type of abductive reasoning under which the "most likely" premise for an event could trump a reasonable inference to the contrary. Presumably, this more rigorous examination of inferences would apply to inductive reasoning as well.

Lower federal courts have adopted conflicting interpretations of the plausibility standard. Our hunch is that much of this confusion is a product of the contrasting approaches to inferences adopted by the respective majority opinions in *Twombly* and *Iqbal*. See what you think when you read the next three principal cases, each of which attempts to apply the new plausibility standard.

d. Twombly *and* Iqbal *Applied*

Swanson v. Citibank, N.A.

614 F.3d 400 (7th Cir. 2010)

Wood, Circuit Judge

Gloria Swanson sued Citibank, Andre Lanier, and Lanier's employer, PCI Appraisal Services, because she believed that all three had discriminated against her on the basis of her race (African-American) when Citibank turned down her application for a home-equity loan. . . .

Swanson based her complaint on the following set of events, which we accept as true for purposes of this appeal. In February 2009 Citibank announced a plan to make loans using funds that it had received from the federal government's Troubled Assets Relief Program. Encouraged by this prospect, Swanson went to a Citibank branch to apply for a home-equity loan. A representative named Skertich told Swanson that she could not apply alone, because she owned her home jointly with her husband; he had to be present as well. Swanson was skeptical, suspecting that Skertich's demand was a ploy to discourage loan applications from African-Americans. She therefore asked to speak to a manager. When the manager joined the group, Swanson disclosed to both Skertich and the manager that Washington Mutual Bank previously had denied her a home-equity loan. The manager warned Swanson that, although she did not want to discourage Swanson from applying for the loan, Citibank's loan criteria were more stringent than those of other banks.

Still interested, Swanson took a loan application home and returned the next day with the necessary information. She was again assisted by Skertich, who entered the information that Swanson had furnished into the computer. When he reached a question regarding race, Skertich told Swanson that she was not required to respond. At some point during this exchange, Skertich pointed to a photograph on his desk and commented that his wife and son were part African-American.

A few days later Citibank conditionally approved Swanson for a home-equity loan of $50,000. It hired Andre Lanier, who worked for PCI Appraisal Services, to visit Swanson's home for an onsite appraisal. Although Swanson had estimated in her loan application that her house was worth $270,000, Lanier appraised it at only $170,000. The difference was critical: Citibank turned down the loan and explained that its conditional approval had been based on the higher valuation. Two months later Swanson paid for and obtained an appraisal from Midwest Valuations, which thought her home was worth $240,000.

Swanson saw coordinated action in this chain of events, and so she filed a complaint (later amended) charging that Citibank, Lanier, and PCI disfavor providing home-equity loans to African-Americans, and so they deliberately lowered the appraised value of her home far below its actual market value, so that they would have an excuse to deny her the loan. She charges that in so doing, they violated the Fair Housing Act, and the Equal Credit Opportunity Act. The district court granted the defendants' motions to dismiss both theories. . . . Initially, the court liberally construed Swanson's complaint to include a common-law fraud claim and declined to dismiss that aspect of the case. Later, however, the defendants moved to dismiss the fraud claim as well, and the district court granted the motion on the grounds that the statements on which Swanson relied were too indefinite and her reliance was unreasonable. This appeal followed.

Before turning to the particulars of Swanson's case, a brief review of the standards that apply to dismissals for failure to state a claim is in order. It is by now well established that a plaintiff must do better than putting a few words on paper that, in the hands of an imaginative reader, *might* suggest that something has happened to her that *might* be redressed by the law. Cf. *Conley v. Gibson*, 355 U.S. 41, 45-46 (1957), disapproved by *Bell Atlantic Corp. v. Twombly*, 550 U.S. 544, 563 (2007) ("after puzzling the profession for 50 years, this famous observation [the 'no set of facts' language] has earned its retirement"). The question with which courts are still struggling is how much higher the Supreme Court meant to set the bar, when it decided not only *Twombly*, but also *Erickson v. Pardus*, 551 U.S. 89 (2007) and *Ashcroft v. Iqbal*, 556 U.S. 662 (2009). This is not an easy question to answer, as the thoughtful dissent from this opinion demonstrates. On the one hand, the Supreme Court has adopted a "plausibility" standard, but on the other hand, it has insisted that it is not requiring fact pleading, nor is it adopting a single pleading standard to replace Rule 8, Rule 9, and specialized regimes like the one in the Private Securities Litigation Reform Act ("PSLRA").

Critically, in none of the three recent decisions . . . did the Court cast any doubt on the validity of Rule 8 of the Federal Rules of Civil Procedure. To the contrary: at all times it has said that it is interpreting Rule 8, not tossing it out the window. It is therefore useful to begin with a look at the language of the rule:

> (a) Claim for Relief. A pleading that states a claim for relief must contain:

> * * *

> (2) a short and plain statement of the claim showing that the pleader is entitled to relief. . . .

FED. R. CIV. P. 8(a)(2). As one respected treatise put it in 2004,

> all that is necessary is that the claim for relief be stated with brevity, conciseness, and clarity. . . . [T]his portion of Rule 8 indicates that a basic objective of the rules is to avoid civil cases turning on technicalities and to require that the pleading discharge the function of giving the opposing party fair notice of the nature and basis or grounds of the pleader's claim and a general indication of the type of litigation that is involved. . . .

5 CHARLES A. WRIGHT & ARTHUR R. MILLER, FEDERAL PRACTICE AND PROCEDURE § 1215 at 165-173 (3d ed. 2004).

Nothing in the recent trio of cases has undermined these broad principles. As *Erickson* underscored, "[s]pecific facts are not necessary." The Court was not engaged in a *sub rosa* campaign to reinstate the old fact-pleading system called for by the Field Code or even more modern codes. We know that because it said so in *Erickson*: "the statement need only give the defendant fair notice of what the . . . claim is and the grounds upon which it rests." Instead, the Court has called for more careful attention to be given to several key questions: what, exactly, does it take to give the opposing party "fair notice"; how much detail realistically can be given, and should be given, about the nature and basis or grounds of the claim; and in what way is the pleader expected to signal the type of litigation that is being put before the court?

This is the light in which the Court's references in *Twombly*, repeated in *Iqbal*, to the pleader's responsibility to "state a claim to relief that is plausible on its face" must be understood. "Plausibility" in this context does not imply that the district court should decide whose version to believe, or which version is more likely than not. Indeed, the Court expressly distanced itself from the latter approach in *Iqbal*, "the plausibility standard is not akin to a probability requirement." As we understand it, the Court is saying instead that the plaintiff must give enough details about the subject-matter of the case to present a story that holds together. In other words, the court will ask itself *could* these things have happened, not *did* they happen. For cases governed only by Rule 8, it is not necessary to stack up inferences side by side and allow the case to go forward only if the plaintiff's inferences seem more compelling than the opposing inferences.

The Supreme Court's explicit decision to reaffirm the validity of *Swierkiewicz v. Sorema, N.A.*, 534 U.S. 506 (2002), which was cited with approval in *Twombly*, indicates that in many straightforward cases, it will not be any more difficult today for a plaintiff to meet that burden than it was before the Court's recent decisions. A plaintiff who believes that she has been passed over for a promotion because of her sex will be able to plead that she was employed by Company X, that a promotion was offered, that she applied and was qualified for it, and that the job went to someone else. That is an entirely plausible scenario, whether or not it describes what "really" went on in this plaintiff's case. A more complex case involving financial derivatives, or tax fraud that the parties tried hard to conceal, or antitrust violations, will require more detail, both to give the opposing party notice of what the case is all about and to show how, in the plaintiff's mind at least, the dots should be connected. Finally, as the Supreme Court warned in *Iqbal* and as we acknowledged later in *Brooks v. Ross*, 578 F.3d 574 (7th Cir. 2009), "abstract recitations of the elements of a cause of action or conclusory legal statements," do nothing to distinguish the particular case that is before the court from every other hypothetically possible case in that field of law. Such statements therefore do not add to the notice that Rule 8 demands. . . .

Returning to Swanson's case, we must analyze her allegations defendant-by-defendant. We begin with Citibank. On appeal, Swanson challenges only the dismissal of her Fair Housing Act and fraud claims. The Fair Housing Act prohibits businesses engaged in residential real estate transactions, including "[t]he making . . . of loans or providing other financial assistance . . . secured by residential real estate," from discriminating against any person on account of race. Swanson's complaint identifies the type of discrimination that she thinks occurs (racial), by whom (Citibank, through Skertich, the manager, and the outside appraisers it used), and when (in connection with her effort in early 2009 to obtain a home-equity loan). This is all that she needed to put in the complaint.

The fact that Swanson included other, largely extraneous facts in her complaint does not undermine the soundness of her pleading. She points to Citibank's announced plan to use federal money to make more loans, its refusal to follow through in her case, and Skertich's comment that he has a mixed-race family. She has not pleaded herself out of court by mentioning these facts; whether they are particularly helpful for proving her case or not is another matter that can safely be put off for another day. It was therefore error for the district court to dismiss Swanson's Fair Housing Act claim against Citibank.

Her fraud claim against Citibank stands on a different footing. Rule 9(b) of the Federal Rules of Civil Procedure provides that "[i]n alleging fraud or mistake, a party must state with particularity the circumstances constituting fraud or mistake. Malice, intent, knowledge, and other conditions of a person's mind may be alleged generally." Of special relevance here, a plaintiff must plead actual damages arising from her reliance on a fraudulent statement. Without a contract, only out-of-pocket losses allegedly arising from the fraud are recoverable. Swanson asserts that Citibank falsely announced plans to make federal funds available in the form of loans to all customers, when it actually intended to exclude African-American customers from those who would be eligible for the loans. Swanson relied, she says, on that false information when she applied for her home-equity loan. But she never alleged that she lost anything from the process of applying for the loan. We do not know, for example, whether there was a loan application fee, or if Citibank or she covered the cost of the appraisal. This is the kind of particular information that Rule 9 requires, and its absence means that the district court was entitled to dismiss the claim.

We now turn to Swanson's claims against Lanier and PCI. Here again, she pursues only her Fair Housing Act and fraud claims. . . . The Fair Housing Act makes it "unlawful for any person or other entity whose business includes engaging in residential real estate-related transactions to discriminate against any person in making available such a transaction, or in the terms or conditions of such a transaction, because of race. . . ." The statute goes on to define the term "residential real estate-related transaction" to include "the selling, brokering, or appraising of residential real property." There is an appraisal exemption also . . . but it provides only that nothing in the statute prohibits appraisers from taking into consideration factors other than race or the other protected characteristics.

Swanson accuses the appraisal defendants of skewing their assessment of her home because of her race. It is unclear whether she believes that they did so as part of a conspiracy with Citibank, or if she thinks that they deliberately undervalued her property on their own initiative. Once again, we find that she has pleaded enough to survive a motion under Rule 12(b)(6). The appraisal defendants knew her race, and she accuses them of discriminating against her in the specific business transaction that they had with her. When it comes to proving her case, she will need to come up with more evidence than the mere fact that PCI (through Lanier) placed a far lower value on her house than Midwest Valuations did. All we hold now is that she is entitled to take the next step in this litigation.

This does not, however, save her common-law fraud claim against Lanier and PCI. She has not adequately alleged that she relied on their appraisal, nor has she pointed to any out-of-pocket losses that she suffered because of it.

We therefore Reverse the judgment of the district court insofar as it dismissed Swanson's Fair Housing Act claims against all three defendants, and we Affirm insofar as it dismissed the common-law fraud claims against all three. Each side will bear its own costs on appeal.

POSNER, Circuit Judge, dissenting in part.

I join the majority opinion except with respect to reversing the dismissal of the plaintiff's claim of housing discrimination. I have difficulty squaring that reversal with *Ashcroft v. Iqbal*. . . .

There is language in my colleagues' opinion to suggest that discrimination cases are outside the scope of *Iqbal*, itself a discrimination case. The opinion says that "a plaintiff who believes that she has been passed over for a promotion because of her sex will be able to plead that she was employed by Company X, that a promotion was offered, that she applied and was qualified for it, and that the job went to someone else." Though this is not a promotion case, the opinion goes on to say that "Swanson's complaint identifies the type of discrimination that she thinks occurs (racial), by whom (Citibank, through Skertich, the manager, and the outside appraisers it used), and when (in connection with her effort in early 2009 to obtain a home equity loan). This is all that she needed to put in the complaint." In contrast, "a more complex case involving financial derivatives, or tax fraud that the parties tried hard to conceal, or antitrust violations, will require more detail, both to give the opposing party notice of what the case is all about and to show how, in the plaintiff's mind at least, the dots should be connected." The "more complex" case to which this passage is referring is *Twombly*, an antitrust case. But *Iqbal*, which charged the defendants with having subjected Pakistani Muslims to harsh conditions of confinement because of their religion and national origin, was a discrimination case, as is the present case, and was not especially complex.

Suppose this *were* a promotion case, and several people were vying for a promotion, all were qualified, several were men and one was a woman, and one of the men received the promotion. No complexity; yet the district court would "draw on its judicial experience and common sense," [quoting *Ascroft v. Iqbal*], to conclude that discrimination would not be a plausible explanation of the hiring decision, without additional allegations.

This case is even stronger for dismissal because it lacks the competitive situation—man and woman, or white and black, vying for the same job and the man, or the white, getting it. . . .

There is no allegation that the plaintiff in this case was competing with a white person for a loan. It was the low appraisal of her home that killed her chances for the $50,000 loan that she was seeking. The appraiser thought her home worth only $170,000, and she already owed $146,000 on it (a first mortgage of $121,000 and a home-equity loan of $25,000). A further loan of $50,000 would thus have been undersecured. We must assume that the appraisal was a mistake, and the house worth considerably more, as she alleges. But errors in appraising a house are common because "real estate appraisal is not an exact science,"—common enough to have created a market for "Real Estate Appraisers Errors & Omissions" insurance policies. The Supreme Court would consider error the plausible inference in this case, rather than discrimination, for it said in *Iqbal* that "as between that 'obvious alternative explanation' for the [injury of which the plaintiff is complaining] and the purposeful, invidious discrimination [the plaintiff] asks us to infer, discrimination is not a plausible conclusion." . . .

The plaintiff has an implausible case of discrimination, but she will now be permitted to serve discovery demands that will compel elaborate document review by Citibank and require its executives to sit for many hours of depositions. (Not that the plaintiff is capable of conducting such proceedings as a pro se, but on remand she may—indeed she would be well advised to—ask the judge to help her find a lawyer.) The threat of such an imposition will induce Citibank to consider settlement even if the suit has no merit at all. That is the pattern that the Supreme Court's recent decisions are aimed at disrupting.

We should affirm the dismissal of the suit in its entirety.

NOTES AND QUESTIONS

1. *Separating the rights of action for purposes of analysis.*   The court in *Swanson* clustered the defendants into two groups. It then performed a distinct analysis of each of the two rights of action asserted by Swanson against both of those groups. One of the most common mistakes law students make is to aggregate a plaintiff's rights of action against the defendant(s) for purposes of pleading analysis. In general, the claims against each defendant and the rights of action arising out of those claims should be analyzed separately. In *Swanson*, however, it made sense to treat each of the two groups of defendants collectively since the rights asserted against the members of each group would rise or fall for identical reasons. Usually, however, you should assume that the claims against each defendant should be assessed independently of one another and that the same should be done for each right of action arising out of those claims.

2. *The savvy judge and the experienced judge.*   How do you think Justice Souter, the author of the majority opinion in *Twombly* and the principal dissent in *Iqbal*, would have resolved this case? And how do you think Justice Kennedy, the author of the majority opinion in *Iqbal*, would have ruled?

3. *The* Iqbal *standard interpreted.*   The *Swanson* court offered the following interpretation of *Iqbal*: "As we understand it, the Court is saying . . . that the plaintiff must give enough details about the subject-matter of the case to present a story that holds together. In other words, the court will ask itself *could* these things have happened, not *did* they happen. For cases governed only by Rule 8, it is not necessary to stack up inferences side by side and allow the case to go forward only if the plaintiff's inferences seem more compelling than the opposing inferences." Is this reading consistent with the *Iqbal* analysis and outcome? Did the *Swanson* majority apply a deferential reasonableness standard to the range of inferences that could be drawn from the plaintiff's complaint—the savvy, but deferential judge? Did the *Swanson* dissent look for the most likely explanation of events alleged in the complaint—the experienced judge applying common sense?

4. *Distinguishing simple cases from more complex ones.*   The *Swanson* court distinguished the case of a plaintiff "who believes that she has been passed over for a promotion because of her sex" from the "more complex case" involving financial derivatives, tax fraud, or antitrust violations. Does the court also suggest that different pleading standards should apply to the cases depending on their different level of complexity? Or is the court suggesting something else? Is the court's approach consistent with *Leatherman v. Tarrant County*? Is it warranted by the decisions in *Twombly, Erickson,* and *Iqbal*?

5. Plaintiff's fraud claims. Why did the court apply Rule 9(b) to the plaintiff's fraud claims? Are the details required by the court part of the circumstances constituting the fraud? A leading treatise provides this guidance:

> [T]he reference to "circumstances" in the rule is to matters such as the time, place, and contents of the false representations or omissions, as well as the identity of the person making the misrepresentation or failing to make a complete disclosure and what that defendant obtained thereby.

5A WRIGHT & MILLER, *supra*, § 1297, at 74.

McCleary-Evans v. Maryland Department of Transportation

780 F.3d 582 (4th Cir. 2015), *petition for cert.* (S. Ct., No. 15-573, filed Nov. 3, 2015)

NIEMEYER, Circuit Judge:

Dawnn McCleary-Evans commenced this action against the Maryland Department of Transportation's State Highway Administration, alleging that the Highway Administration failed or refused to hire her for two positions for which she applied because of her race (African American) and her sex (female), in violation of Title VII of the Civil Rights Act of 1964. In her complaint, she alleged that she was highly qualified for the positions, but that the decisionmakers were biased and had "predetermined" that they would select white candidates to fill the positions.

The district court granted the Highway Administration's motion to dismiss under Federal Rule of Civil Procedure 12(b)(6), concluding that the complaint failed to allege facts that plausibly support a claim of discrimination. Because we agree that McCleary-Evans failed to include adequate factual allegations to support a claim that the Highway Administration discriminated against her *because* she was African American or female, we accordingly affirm.

I

McCleary-Evans worked for over 20 years as a project manager on environmental regulatory compliance projects while employed at the Maryland Department of Natural Resources and the Maryland Transit Administration. In late 2009 and early 2010, she applied for two open positions in the Highway Administration's Environmental Compliance Division, interviewing first for a position as an assistant division chief and later for a position as an environmental compliance program manager. Despite her prior work experience and education, which she alleged made her "more than qualified" for the two positions, she was not selected for either position. Instead, as the complaint asserted, "The positions in question were filled by non-Black candidates."

McCleary-Evans' claim that the Highway Administration did not hire her "because of the combination of her race and gender" relies essentially on two paragraphs of her complaint. In one, she alleged that her applications were "subject to a review panel significantly influenced and controlled by . . . Gregory Keenan, a White male in the Office of Environmental Design ('OED') who worked under the supervision of OED Director, Sonal Sangahvi, a non-Black woman," and that "[d]uring the course of her interview, and based upon the history of hires within OED, . . . both Keenan and Sangahvi predetermined to select for both positions a White male or female candidate." In the other paragraph, she similarly alleged that, "although African American candidates had been among the selection pool," "Keenan and Sangahvi, for reasons of race and gender, overlooked the African American candidates to select White male, preferably, and White female candidates." In short, she claimed in conclusory fashion that the decisionmakers were biased when making the decision. And the complaint did not include any allegations regarding the qualifications or suitability of the persons hired to fill the two positions.

In dismissing her claim, the district court concluded that McCleary-Evans had failed to "allege facts that plausibly support a claim of discrimination." The court reasoned that because this was a case with "no direct evidence of discrimination," McCleary-Evans needed to allege facts sufficient to "state a prima facie case of discrimination for failure to hire by showing: (1) that she is a member of the protected class; (2) that the employer had an open position for which she applied or sought to apply; (3) that she was qualified for the position; and (4) that she was rejected under circumstances giving rise to an inference of unlawful discrimination." It noted that, while McCleary-Evans had sufficiently alleged the first three prongs of the prima facie case, she had not "stated facts sufficient to meet the pleading requirements as to the fourth prong." Her complaint, the court said, "offer[ed] nothing to support her conclusory assertions [of discrimination] beyond an unsubstantiated mention of 'a history of hires' within the division and statements identifying her race, the races of the two members of the hiring review panel, and the races of the two applicants hired for the positions." The court concluded that, "[b]ecause discrimination cannot be presumed simply because one candidate is selected over another candidate, McCleary-Evans ha[d] not pled adequate facts to give rise to a reasonable inference of discrimination."

From the district court's order dismissing her complaint, McCleary-Evans filed this appeal.

II

McCleary-Evans contends that the district court imposed on her a pleading standard "more rigorous" than *Swierkiewicz v. Sorema, N.A.*, 534 U.S. 506 (2002), allows, by analyzing her claim under the standard set forth in *McDonnell Douglas Corp. v. Green*, 411 U.S. 792 (1973), for proving a prima facie case of discrimination. She maintains that the "District Court's decision fails to demonstrate the deficiency of the Complaint as *a pleading*, but rather offers authority that only works as a challenge to demonstrate deficiency as evidentiary proof." (Emphasis added).

In *Swierkiewicz*, the Supreme Court held that "an employment discrimination plaintiff need not plead a prima facie case of discrimination . . . to survive [a] motion to dismiss" because "[t]he prima facie case . . . is an evidentiary standard, not a pleading requirement" that may require demonstrating more elements than are otherwise required to state a claim for relief. The Court stated that requiring a plaintiff to plead a prima facie case would amount to a "heightened pleading standard" that would conflict with Federal Rule of Civil Procedure 8(a)(2). As the Court explained:

> [I]t is not appropriate to require a plaintiff to plead facts establishing a prima facie case because the *McDonnell Douglas* framework does not apply in every employment discrimination case. For instance, if a plaintiff is able to produce direct evidence of discrimination, he may prevail without proving all the elements of a prima facie case.

Accordingly, the Court concluded that "the ordinary rules for assessing the sufficiency of a complaint apply," referring to Federal Rule of Civil Procedure 8(a)(2).

In light of *Swierkiewicz*, McCleary-Evans appropriately argues that the district court erred in its analysis by requiring her to plead facts establishing a prima facie case of discrimination to survive a motion to dismiss. But the district court's erroneous analysis in this case will not save the complaint if, under the "ordinary rules for assessing the sufficiency of a complaint," it fails to state a plausible claim for relief under Title VII.

Federal Rule of Civil Procedure 8(a)(2) "requires only a short and plain statement of the claim showing that the pleader is entitled to relief, in order to give the defendant fair notice of what the . . . claim is and the grounds upon which it rests." *Twombly*, 550 U.S. at 555. But this rule for pleading "requires more than labels and conclusions, and a formulaic recitation of the elements of a cause of action will not do." Instead, a complaint must contain "[f]actual allegations [sufficient] to raise a right to relief above the speculative level." Id. The Supreme Court has accordingly held that Rule 8(a)(2) requires that "a complaint . . . contain sufficient factual matter, accepted as true, to 'state a claim to relief that is *plausible* on its face' " in the sense that the complaint's factual allegations must allow a "court to draw the reasonable inference that the defendant is liable for the misconduct alleged." *Iqbal*, 556 U.S. at 678.

In her complaint, McCleary-Evans purported to state a claim under Title VII, which means that she was required to allege facts to satisfy the elements of a cause of action created by that statute—i.e., in this case, that the Highway Administration "fail[ed] or refus[ed] to hire" her "*because of* [her] race . . . [or] sex." While she did allege that the Highway Administration failed to hire her, she did not allege facts sufficient to claim that the reason it failed to hire her was because of her race or sex. To be sure, she repeatedly alleged that the Highway Administration did not select her because of the relevant decisionmakers' bias against African American women. But those "naked" allegations—a "formulaic recitation" of the necessary elements—"are no more than conclusions" and therefore do not suffice. *Iqbal*, 556 U.S. at 678-79. For example, she alleged that "[d]uring the course of her interview, and based upon the history of hires within [the Office of Environmental Design], . . . both Keenan and Sangahvi predetermined to select for both positions a White male or female candidate." But she alleged no factual basis for what happened "during the course of her interview" to support the alleged conclusion. The allegation that the Highway Administration did not hire her because its decision makers were biased is simply too conclusory. Only speculation can fill the gaps in her complaint—speculation as to why two "non-Black candidates" were selected to fill the positions instead of her. While the allegation that non-Black decisionmakers hired non-Black applicants instead of the plaintiff is *consistent* with discrimination, it does not alone support a *reasonable inference* that the decisionmakers were motivated by bias. McCleary-Evans can only speculate that the persons hired were not better qualified, or did not perform better during their interviews, or were not better suited based on experience and personality for the positions. In short, McCleary-Evans' complaint "stop[ped] short of the line between possibility and plausibility of entitlement to relief." *Id.*

In his dissent, Judge Wynn asserts that our holding "ignores the factual underpinnings" of *Swierkiewicz*, which approved an employment discrimination complaint that, he claims, contained allegations less detailed than those made by McCleary-Evans in this case. A closer look at *Swierkiewicz*, however, reveals that it does not support this position. Swierkiewicz claimed that he had been subject to discrimination based on his age and national origin, alleging that he had been employed by a reinsurance company that was "principally owned and controlled by a French parent corporation" for about six years as the chief underwriting officer when the company's CEO demoted him and "transferred the bulk of his underwriting responsibilities" to an employee who, like the CEO, was a French national and who was also significantly younger than Swierkiewicz. He alleged further that, about a year later, the CEO "stated that he wanted to 'energize' the underwriting department" and appointed the younger French national to serve as the company's new chief underwriting officer. Finally, Swierkiewicz alleged specifically that the new chief underwriting officer was "less experienced and less qualified" for the position because he "had only one year of underwriting experience at the time he was promoted," whereas Swierkiewicz "had 26 years of experience in the insurance industry." *Id.* As this last detail is precisely the kind of allegation that is missing from McCleary-Evans' complaint, the fact that the Supreme Court found Swierkiewicz's allegations sufficient to state a claim ultimately says little about the sufficiency of McCleary-Evans' complaint.

Moreover, in finding the complaint sufficient, the Supreme Court in *Swierkiewicz* applied a different pleading standard than that which it now requires under *Iqbal* and *Twombly*. To be sure, those cases did not overrule *Swierkiewicz*'s holding that a plaintiff need not plead the *evidentiary* standard for proving a Title VII claim—indeed, *Twombly* expressly reaffirmed *Swierkiewicz*'s holding that the "'use of a heightened pleading standard for Title VII cases was contrary to the Federal Rules' structure of liberal pleading requirements.'" But *Twombly* and *Iqbal* did alter the criteria for assessing the sufficiency of a complaint in at least two respects. First, the *Twombly* Court explicitly overruled the earlier standard articulated in *Conley v. Gibson*, 355 U.S. 41 (1957)—and repeated in *Swierkiewicz*—that "'a complaint should not be dismissed for failure to state a claim unless it appears beyond doubt that the plaintiff can prove no set of facts in support of his claim which would entitle him to relief.'" Moreover, *Iqbal* and *Twombly* articulated a new requirement that a complaint must allege a *plausible* claim for relief, thus rejecting a standard that would allow a complaint to "survive a motion to dismiss whenever the pleadings left open the *possibility* that a plaintiff might later establish some 'set of [undisclosed] facts' to support recovery." *Twombly*, 550 U.S. at 56.

In short, in addition to the fact that the *Swierkiewicz* complaint contained more relevant factual allegations for stating a Title VII claim than does McCleary-Evans' complaint, the *Swierkiewicz* Court also applied a pleading standard more relaxed than the plausible-claim standard required by *Iqbal* and *Twombly*. At bottom, therefore, the Supreme Court has, with *Iqbal* and *Twombly*, rejected the sufficiency of complaints that merely allege the possibility of entitlement to relief, requiring plausibility for obtaining such relief and thus rejecting a complaint in which the plaintiff relies on speculation. See *Twombly*, 550 U.S. at 555 ("Factual allegations must be enough to raise a right to relief *above* the speculative level" (emphasis added)).

Thus, contrary to Judge Wynn's assertions about the applicability of *Swierkiewicz*, it is clear that that decision does not control the outcome here because: (1) the complaint in *Swierkiewicz* alleged that the plaintiff was *more qualified* than the younger French person appointed to replace him—an allegation that McCleary-Evans has not made; and (2) *Swierkiewicz* in any event applied a more lenient pleading standard than the plausible-claim standard now required by *Twombly* and *Iqbal*.

Applying the *Twombly/Iqbal* standard here reveals that McCleary-Evans' complaint suffers from the same deficiencies that defeated the complaint in *Iqbal*. In *Iqbal*, the plaintiff, a Muslim citizen of Pakistan who was detained after 9/11, alleged in a conclusory fashion that he was treated harshly pursuant to a policy adopted by the Attorney General and the Director of the FBI solely on account of his race, religion, or national origin. The Supreme Court found the complaint insufficient because it had "not 'nudged [his] claims' of invidious discrimination 'across the line from conceivable to plausible,'" explaining that his factual allegations did not "plausibly suggest" that the Attorney General and the FBI Director had acted with a "discriminatory state of mind."

Similarly, McCleary-Evans' complaint leaves open to speculation the cause for the defendant's decision to select someone other than her, and the cause that she asks us to infer (*i.e.*, invidious discrimination) is not plausible in light of the "'obvious alternative explanation'" that the decisionmakers simply judged those hired to be more qualified and better suited for the positions. Indeed, the consequence of allowing McCleary-Evans' claim to proceed on her complaint as stated would be that any qualified member of a protected class who alleges nothing more than that she was denied a position or promotion in favor of someone outside her protected class would be able to survive a Rule 12(b)(6) motion. Such a result cannot be squared with the Supreme Court's command that a complaint must allege "more than a sheer possibility that a defendant has acted unlawfully." [*Iqbal*, 556 U.S. at 678.]

In sum, while the district court improperly applied the *McDonnell Douglas* evidentiary standard in analyzing the sufficiency of McCleary-Evans' complaint, contrary to *Swierkiewicz*, the court nonetheless reached the correct conclusion under *Twombly* and *Iqbal* because the complaint failed to state a plausible claim for relief, as required by Federal Rule of Civil Procedure 8(a)(2). Accordingly, we affirm.

Affirmed.

WYNN, Circuit Judge, dissenting in part.

I do not agree with that part of the majority's opinion that affirms the dismissal of Dawnn McCleary-Evans's claim that she was discriminated against because of her race. . . .

In evaluating the allegations in McCleary-Evans's complaint . . . we are not limited to the sparse guidance to be gleaned from *Twombly* and *Iqbal*. In 2002 the Supreme Court decided *Swierkiewicz*, a case involving the sufficiency of a wrongful termination claim under Title VII. 534 U.S. 506. In a *unanimous* opinion authored by Justice Thomas, the Court held that "a complaint in an employment discrimination lawsuit [need] not contain specific facts establishing a prima facie case of discrimination. . . ." *Id*. at 508. To the contrary, the plaintiff "easily satisfie[d]" Rule 8(a)(2) when he "detailed the events leading to his termination, provided relevant dates, and included the ages and nationalities of at least some of the relevant persons involved with his termination." Id. at 514. The Court held that such allegations "give respondent fair notice of what petitioner's claims are and the grounds upon which they rest." *Id.* Five years later, the Court told us that *Swierkiewicz* remains good law, specifically referencing the factual allegations that the *Swierkiewicz* Court deemed sufficient to state "grounds showing entitlement to relief." *Twombly*, 550 U.S. at 569-570. . . .

The apparent tension between the Court's decisions in *Iqbal* and *Swierkiewicz* is well-documented. Despite this tension, however, "we have no authority to overrule a Supreme Court decision no matter . . . how out of touch with the Supreme Court's current thinking the decision seems." This is particularly true where, as here, the Supreme Court has said loud and clear that its prior decision has not been overruled. . . .

Turning to McCleary-Evans's complaint, it is clear that her allegations go beyond what *Swierkiewicz* . . . found sufficient to satisfy Rule 8(a)(2). McCleary-Evans contends that she applied for two positions with the Maryland Department of Transportation's State Highway Administration. She lays out in immense detail her qualifications for these positions. She identifies the Highway Administration employees responsible for denying her applications, and states that both were non-African American. She alleges that she and other African Americans who applied for positions with the Highway Administration were denied employment in favor of non-African American applicants. Finally, she alleges that based on her interview experience and what she apparently perceived as a discriminatory history of hires within the Highway Administration, her race played a role in the decision to hire non-African-American candidates over her. In this particular context, drawing on "judicial experience and common sense," *Iqbal*, 556 U.S. at 679, McCleary-Evans's claim of race discrimination is eminently plausible. . . .

Finally, I must take issue with the majority's suggestion that by "retiring" the *Conley v. Gibson* "no set of facts" standard in *Twombly*, the Supreme Court all but retired *Swierkiewicz*. Under the majority's view, what remains of *Swierkiewicz* after *Twombly* is the bare holding that courts should not use the magic words of *McDonnell Douglas* to assess the sufficiency of Title VII claims at the 12(b)(6) stage. Thus, the majority would render *Swierkiewicz* a hollow shell and mute its primary thrust—namely, that discriminatory intent need not be pled with specific facts. But the Supreme Court in *Swierkiewicz* specifically forbade using judicial interpretation to limit the scope of its holding. Indeed, in *Swierkiewicz*, in response to the argument that the Court's holding would "burden the courts" by "allowing lawsuits based on conclusory allegations of discrimination to go forward," *Swierkiewicz*, 534 U.S. at 514, Justice Thomas, writing for a unanimous Court, stated that "[a] requirement of greater specificity for particular claims is a result that 'must be obtained by the process of amending the Federal Rules, and not by judicial interpretation.' " *Id.* (quoting *Leatherman v. Tarrant County Narcotics Intelligence and Coordination Unit*, 507 U.S. 163, 168-169 (1993)). As far as I am aware, no amendment to the Federal Rules has taken effect since the Court's ruling in *Swierkiewicz* that would require the level of specificity that the majority by its own "judicial interpretation" demands from McCleary-Evans.

Because McCleary-Evans's complaint states a plausible claim of discrimination on the basis of race, I respectfully dissent.

NOTES AND QUESTIONS

1. *An uncertain pleading standard.*   As the decisions in *Swanson* and *McCleary-Evans* demonstrate, the scope of the new plausibility standard is far from clear. Three of the six judges who participated in those cases appeared to have adopted a deferential reasonable-inference standard—the majority in *Swanson* and the dissent in *McCleary-Evans*. Their approach most closely reflects Justice Souter's opinions in *Twombly* and *Iqbal*. The three other judges—the majority in *McCleary-Evans* and the dissent in *Swanson*—seem more like Justice Kennedy's opinion in *Iqbal* by either drawing inferences favorable to the defendant or perceived as being more likely from the perspective of the reviewing judge. Is there a *Twombly/Iqbal* standard? As a lawyer tasked with drafting a complaint, what lesson would you draw from these cases?

2. *The* McDonnell Douglas *burden-shifting standard.*   In *McDonnell Douglas v. Green*, 411 U.S. 792 (1973), the Supreme Court created a framework establishing "the order and allocation of proof in a private, non-class action challenging employment discrimination." *Id.* at 800. The purpose of the framework, as

originally conceived, was to provide a "sensible, orderly way to evaluate the evidence" of intentional discrimination in disparate-treatment cases. *Furnco Constr. Corp. v. Waters*, 438 U.S. 567, 577 (1978). The *McDonnell Douglas* Court described its framework as follows:

> [A plaintiff] in a Title VII trial must carry the initial burden under the statute of establishing a prima facie case of racial discrimination. This may be done by showing (i) that he belongs to a racial minority; (ii) that he applied and was qualified for a job for which the employer was seeking applicants; (iii) that, despite his qualifications, he was rejected; and (iv) that, after his rejection, the position remained open and the employer continued to seek applicants from persons of complainant's qualifications.

411 U.S. at 802. Once the plaintiff makes the above showing, a presumption of intent is established and the burden "shift[s] to the employer to articulate some legitimate, nondiscriminatory reason for the employee's rejection." *Id.* If the employer meets its burden of rebuttal, the plaintiff will be given an opportunity to show that the employer's asserted reason was, in fact, a pretext for discrimination.

The *McCleary-Evans* court held, consistently with *Swierkiewicz*, that a plaintiff in a Title VII case is not required to allege a "prima facie" case under the *McDonnell Douglas* standard. But does *McDonnell Douglas* impose a heightened pleading requirement or does it simply offer a method through which to establish an inference of intent? Even though it is not necessary to establish a prima facie case at the pleading stage, would it be sufficient to do so for purposes of alleging intent? Should it be relevant that the Court has held that the *McDonnell Douglas* framework cannot, in and of itself, establish the requisite intent to discriminate? *See St. Mary's Honor Center v. Hicks*, 509 U.S. 502, 510-511 (1993).

Littlejohn v. City of New York

795 F.3d 297 (2d Cir. 2015)

DRONEY, Circuit Judge.

Plaintiff Dawn F. Littlejohn appeals from a judgment of the United States District Court for the Southern District of New York (Sweet, J.) entered on February 28, 2014. Littlejohn alleged that, while employed by the New York City Administration for Children's Services ("ACS"), she was subjected to a hostile work environment and disparate treatment based on her race, and retaliated against because of complaints about such discrimination, in violation of Title VII of the Civil Rights Act of 1964 ("Title VII") and 42 U.S.C. §§ 1981 and 1983. . . . Defendants, the City of New York ("the City") and three individuals who supervised Littlejohn at ACS, moved to dismiss Littlejohn's amended complaint pursuant to Rule 12(b)(6) of the Federal Rules of Civil Procedure. The district court granted Defendants' motion to dismiss in its entirety, and Littlejohn appealed.

For the reasons set forth below, we VACATE the district court's judgment granting Defendants' motion to dismiss with respect to (1) Littlejohn's disparate treatment and retaliation claims against the City under Title VII, (2) Littlejohn's disparate treatment claim against Defendant Amy Baker under §§ 1981 and 1983, and (3) Littlejohn's retaliation claim against Baker under § 1981; AFFIRM the dismissal of the other claims; and REMAND for proceedings consistent with this opinion.

BACKGROUND

I.   Factual Background

Littlejohn is an African-American woman with a master's degree in Industrial/Organizational Psychology from Columbia University. She began working at ACS on April 27, 2009, as the Director of its Equal Employment Opportunity ("EEO") Office. As Director, Littlejohn conducted investigations of claims of discrimination, trained staff, monitored hiring, counseled agency employees, organized diversity activities, and advised staff on EEO policy, duties which she alleges she performed satisfactorily.

From April to December 2009, Littlejohn's supervisor was ACS Deputy Commissioner Anne Williams-Isom, an African-American woman. Before Williams-Isom left ACS in December 2009, she gave Littlejohn an above-average performance review for her work over the previous eight months. Littlejohn does not allege that any discrimination or harassment occurred during the period in which she reported to Williams-Isom.

After Williams-Isom left ACS in late December 2009, Littlejohn began reporting to Defendant Amy Baker, a white woman and the Chief of Staff to ACS Commissioner and Defendant John B. Mattingly, a white man. Littlejohn's relationship with Baker quickly deteriorated. According to Littlejohn's complaint, Baker asked another employee "for negative information about [Littlejohn]"; "physically distanc[ed] herself from [Littlejohn] at meetings"; "increased [Littlejohn's] reporting schedule from an as-needed basis . . . to twice-weekly"; "wrongful[ly] and unnecessar[il]y reprimand[ed]" Littlejohn; "required [Littlejohn] to re-create reasonable accommodation and EEO logs even though these logs were already in place"; became "noticeably impatient, shook her head, blew air out of her mouth when [Littlejohn] talked in the presence of other managers"; "held her head in disbelief, got red in the face, used harsh tones, removed [Littlejohn's] name from the regularly scheduled management meeting lists"; "refused to meet with [Littlejohn] face-to-face, diminished [Littlejohn's] duties and responsibilities as EEO Director"; "changed meetings that were supposed to be scheduled as in person bi-monthly meetings to twice a week over the phone discussions with [Littlejohn]"; and "replaced [Littlejohn] at management meetings with [her] white male subordinate." Compl. ¶¶ 34, 53, 71, 74-75. Littlejohn also alleges that Baker sarcastically told her "you feel like you are being left out," and that Littlejohn did not "understand the culture" at ACS. *Id.* ¶¶ 36, 49.

Shortly after Littlejohn began reporting to Baker, the City announced in January 2010 that ACS would merge with the City's Department of Juvenile Justice ("DJJ"). As a result of the merger, numerous employees from DJJ would be laid off, demoted, reassigned, or terminated. Littlejohn asked Baker to be included in the process of deciding which DJJ employees would be transferred or terminated "to ensure that procedures were in accordance with established . . . guidelines and policies," but Baker and other white managers allegedly "impeded, stymied, and suffocated" Littlejohn's effort to become involved in those decision-making meetings. *Id.* ¶¶ 44-45. Only after an Assistant Commissioner for the Department of Citywide Administrative Services demanded that Littlejohn be included in the meetings was she allowed to attend.

According to Littlejohn, Baker and Mattingly showed preferential treatment to white DJJ employees during the ACS/DJJ merger, while at the same time terminating, demoting, or unfavorably reassigning African-American and Latino/a DJJ employees. Littlejohn alleges that she complained to Baker and Mattingly about the "selection process and failure to abide by proper anti-discrimination policies and procedures." *Id.* ¶ 64. Specifically, Littlejohn believed that Defendants were improperly and purposefully failing to conduct an "adverse impact review and analysis," which was mandated by the City's Department for Citywide Administrative Services layoff manual. *Id.* ¶ 61. Around the same time, Littlejohn also complained to Baker about the lack of African-American women in management positions, lower management levels for African-American employees compared to white employees, and pay disparities between African-American men and their white counterparts. Littlejohn's complaints, however, were "to no avail." *Id.* ¶ 64.

In March 14, 2011, Littlejohn was involuntarily transferred from the EEO Office to the Office of Personnel Services ("OPS") and was allegedly demoted to the civil service non-managerial title of Administrative Staff Analyst, incurring a pay cut of $2,000. Littlejohn was replaced as Director of the EEO Office by Fredda Monn, a white female, who allegedly had no prior EEO experience, received more pay than Littlejohn did as EEO Director, and was provided with a "deputy EEO officer" to help with her work. *Id.* ¶ 78. Littlejohn claimed that the transfer and demotion were in retaliation for her complaints to Baker and Mattingly about "racial discrimination and violations of law" during the ACS/DJJ merger, and for her complaints about "her lack of involvement from an EEO perspective in the decision-making process of DJJ and ACS Job actions." *Id.* ¶¶ 52, 68. . . .

II. Procedural History

Littlejohn commenced this lawsuit *pro se* on February 15, 2013, and filed an amended complaint on September 23, 2013, after she retained counsel. The amended complaint alleged causes of action for hostile work environment and disparate treatment based on Littlejohn's race, and retaliation because of complaints about such discrimination, in violation of Title VII and 42 U.S.C. §§ 1981 and 1983. . . . The Defendants are the City of New York, Mattingly, [and] Baker. . . .

On December 6, 2013, Defendants moved to dismiss all of Littlejohn's claims pursuant to Federal Rule of Civil Procedure 12(b)(6). The district court granted Defendants' motion in its entirety on February 28, 2014, concluding that Littlejohn failed to exhaust her administrative remedies as to her sexual harassment claim and failed to adequately plead her hostile work environment, disparate treatment, and retaliation claims. As to her §§ 1981 and 1983 claims, the district court held in the alternative that Littlejohn failed to allege personal responsibility with respect to individual [Defendant Mattingly], and did not state a claim against the City pursuant to *Monell v. Department of Social Services*, 436 U.S. 658 (1978).

DISCUSSION

I.   Standard of Review

   This Court reviews *de novo* a district court's grant of a motion to dismiss under Rule 12(b)(6). On a motion to dismiss, all factual allegations in the complaint are accepted as true and all inferences are drawn in the plaintiff's favor.

   Determining the propriety of the dismissal of an employment discrimination complaint under Rule 12(b)(6) requires assessment of the interplay among several Supreme Court precedents. *McDonnell Douglas Corp. v. Green*, 411 U.S. 792 (1973), and three subsequent Supreme Court rulings clarifying it, established the nature of a prima facie case of discrimination under Title VII. *Swierkiewicz v. Sorema N.A.*, 534 U.S. 506 (2002), specifically addressed the requirements for *pleading* such a case. And *Ashcroft v. Iqbal*, 556 U.S. 662 (2009), later asserted general pleading requirements (not specifically addressed to discrimination cases), in arguable tension with the holding of *Swierkiewicz*. We discuss each of these.

   McDonnell Douglas . . . established that the requirements of a prima facie case for a plaintiff alleging employment discrimination change as the case progresses. Ultimately, the plaintiff will be required to prove that the employer-defendant acted with discriminatory motivation. However, in the first phase of the case, the prima facie requirements are relaxed. Reasoning that fairness required that the plaintiff be protected from early-stage dismissal for lack of evidence demonstrating the employer's discriminatory motivation before the employer set forth its reasons for the adverse action it took against the plaintiff, the Supreme Court ruled that, in the initial phase of the case, the plaintiff can establish a prima facie case without evidence sufficient to show discriminatory motivation. If the plaintiff can show (1) that she is a member of a protected class; (2) that she was qualified for employment in the position; (3) that she suffered an adverse employment action; and, in addition, has (4) some minimal evidence suggesting an inference that the employer acted with discriminatory motivation, such a showing will raise a temporary "presumption" of discriminatory motivation, shifting the burden of production to the employer and requiring the employer to come forward with its justification for the adverse employment action against the plaintiff. However, once the employer presents evidence of its justification for the adverse action, joining issue on plaintiff's claim of discriminatory motivation, the presumption "drops out of the picture" and the *McDonnell Douglas* framework "is no longer relevant." At this point, in the second phase of the case, the plaintiff must demonstrate that the proffered reason was not the true reason (or in any event not the sole reason) for the employment decision, which merges with the plaintiff's ultimate burden of showing that the defendant intentionally discriminated against her.

For the initial phase, in which the plaintiff benefited from the presumption, the Supreme Court's precedents left unclear how much evidence a plaintiff needed to shift the burden of production to the employer. It suggested in *McDonnell Douglas* that it would be sufficient for a disappointed job seeker who was a member of a protected class to show that she was qualified for the position, that the position remained open, and that the employer continued to seek applicants for the position, without need for any further evidence of discriminatory intent. In [*Texas Department of Community Affairs v. Burdine*, 450 U.S. 248 (1980)], the Court held that it was sufficient for the disappointed applicant to show that the job went to one who was not a member of her protected class. The Court characterized this initial burden as "not onerous," and as "minimal."

The next pertinent Supreme Court precedent is *Swierkiewicz*. In *Swierkiewicz*, the plaintiff was a Hungarian national, 53 years of age, who had been dismissed by his employer, a French company. He brought suit alleging national origin discrimination under Title VII, and age discrimination. His complaint included little in the way of factual allegations supporting an inference of national origin discrimination, other than his Hungarian nationality in a French company, and very little to support his claim of age discrimination. The district court granted the defendant's motion to dismiss the complaint for failure to make out a prima facie case, apparently assuming that the requirements of the prima facie case applied to pleading as well as proof, and that the plaintiff's allegations were insufficient to meet even the reduced prima facie standards at the initial phase of the case. Referring to a memorandum that was incorporated into the complaint and upon which the plaintiff relied, the district court explained that "[t]here is nothing in the memorandum from which age or national origin discrimination can be inferred." Addressing the allegations of both age and national origin discrimination, the court characterized them as "conclusory" and "insufficient as a matter of law to raise an inference of discrimination." Our Court affirmed.

The Supreme Court reversed. The Supreme Court clarified that the standard espoused by the *McDonnell Douglas* line of cases for prima facie sufficiency was "an evidentiary standard, not a pleading requirement." The Court characterized our ruling as unwarrantedly imposing a "heightened pleading standard in employment discrimination cases [that] conflicts with Federal Rule of Civil Procedure 8(a)(2)." The Court explained that "under a notice pleading system, it is not appropriate to require a plaintiff to plead facts establishing a prima facie case." The complaint needed only to "'give the defendant fair notice of what the plaintiff's claim is and the grounds upon which it rests.'" The Court thus concluded that the plaintiff's allegation "that he had been terminated on account of his national origin in violation of Title VII and on account of his age in violation of the ADEA" gave the employer "fair notice of what [the plaintiff's] claims are and the grounds upon which they rest." Reading *Swierkiewicz* on its face, it appears to have meant that a Title VII plaintiff is not required to plead facts supporting even a minimal inference of discriminatory intent.

The final Supreme Court precedent that bears on the standard for determining the sufficiency of a Title VII complaint is *Ashcroft v. Iqbal*, 566 U.S. 622 (2009). The plaintiff in *Iqbal* alleged that governmental defendants, including the Attorney General of the United States, had unconstitutionally discriminated against him by reason of his Pakistani nationality and Muslim religion, resulting in his detention under harsh conditions. The Court found the complaint insufficient to state a claim that the defendants had acted with a "discriminatory state of mind." The Supreme Court had recently determined in *Bell Atlantic Corp. v. Twombly*, 550 U.S. 544 (2007), that a complaint alleging an unlawful agreement in restraint of trade must include "enough factual matter (taken as true) to suggest [plausibly] that an agreement was made," or otherwise include "enough facts to state a claim to relief that is plausible on its face." The issue in *Iqbal* was whether the earlier ruling in *Twombly* applied only in the antitrust context or more broadly. The Court decided that the *Twombly* ruling did not apply solely in the antitrust context. It ruled that, "[t]o survive a motion to dismiss, a complaint must contain sufficient factual matter, accepted as true, to state a claim to relief that is plausible on its face."

The question then arises whether *Iqbal*'s requirement applies to Title VII complaints falling under the *McDonnell Douglas* framework. At least two arguments can be advanced that the *Iqbal* requirement does not apply to such cases. The first is that the requirement to allege facts would appear contradictory to the Supreme Court's ruling a few years earlier in *Swierkiewicz*. The second is that the *Iqbal* ruling of otherwise general applicability might not apply to a particular area for which the Supreme Court in the *McDonnell Douglas* quartet had devised a set of special rules that deviate from the customary prima facie rules.

The best argument that the *Iqbal* requirement does apply to Title VII complaints is that the *Iqbal* ruling is broad, and the Court gave no suggestion that it should not apply to cases falling under *McDonnell Douglas*. As for whether the applicability of *Iqbal* to Title VII pleadings would be contradictory to *Swierkiewicz*, this depends on how one interprets *Swierkiewicz*. Reading that case on its face, it appears to hold that under the notice pleading regime of the Federal Rules, a Title VII discrimination complaint need not assert facts supporting an inference of discriminatory intent, but may simply use the word discrimination, thereby adequately communicating to the defendant the nature of the claim. On the other hand, in *Twombly*, the Supreme Court cast doubt on whether *Swierkiewicz* should be interpreted as meaning that a Title VII complaint did not need to allege facts giving minimal support to an inference of discrimination. The plaintiff in *Twombly* argued against a requirement to plead facts, asserting that such a requirement would be contrary to the *Swierkiewicz* holding. The Court rejected the plaintiff's argument. The Court characterized *Swierkiewicz* as meaning nothing more than that the plaintiff's pleadings contained sufficient factual allegations to satisfy the "liberal pleading requirements" of the Federal Rules and that our Circuit had improperly invoked a "heightened pleading standard for Title VII cases" by requiring the plaintiff "to allege certain additional facts that [he] would need at the trial stage."

As for the argument that the Supreme Court was unlikely to have intended in *Iqbal* to add new wrinkles to the special field of Title VII suits, which the Supreme Court had so extensively covered in the *McDonnell Douglas* quartet of cases, arguably there is no incompatibility, or even tension, between the burden-shifting framework of *McDonnell Douglas* and a requirement that the complaint include reference to sufficient facts to make its claim plausible—at least so long as the requirement to plead facts is assessed in light of the presumption that arises in the plaintiff's favor under *McDonnell Douglas* in the first stage of the litigation.

It is uncertain how the Supreme Court will apply *Iqbal*'s requirement of facts sufficient to support plausibility to Title VII complaints falling under the *McDonnell Douglas* framework. We conclude that *Iqbal*'s requirement applies to Title VII complaints of employment discrimination, but does not affect the benefit to plaintiffs pronounced in the *McDonnell Douglas* quartet. To the same extent that the *McDonnell Douglas* temporary presumption reduces the facts a plaintiff would need to *show* to defeat a motion for summary judgment prior to the defendant's furnishing of a non-discriminatory motivation, that presumption also reduces the facts needed to be *pleaded* under *Iqbal*.

The *Iqbal* requirement is for facts supporting "plausibility." The Supreme Court explained that "[t]he plausibility standard is not akin to a 'probability requirement,' but it asks for more than a sheer possibility that a defendant has acted unlawfully." The question we face is what, in the Title VII context, must be plausibly supported by factual allegations when the plaintiff does not have direct evidence of discriminatory intent at the outset. Answering this question requires attention to the shifting content of the prima facie requirements in a Title VII employment discrimination suit. Recapitulating what we have spelled out above, while the plaintiff ultimately will need evidence sufficient to prove discriminatory motivation on the part of the employer-defendant, at the initial stage of the litigation—prior to the employer's coming forward with the claimed reason for its action—the plaintiff does not need substantial evidence of discriminatory intent. If she makes a showing (1) that she is a member of a protected class, (2) that she was qualified for the position she sought, (3) that she suffered an adverse employment action, and (4) can sustain a *minimal* burden of showing facts suggesting an inference of discriminatory motivation, then she has satisfied the prima facie requirements and a presumption of discriminatory intent arises in her favor, at which point the burden of production shifts to the employer, requiring that the employer furnish evidence of reasons for the adverse action. At this stage, a plaintiff seeking to defeat a defendant's motion for summary judgment would not need evidence sufficient to sustain her ultimate burden of showing discriminatory motivation, but could get by with the benefit of the presumption if she has shown evidence of the factors entitling her to the presumption.

The discrimination complaint, by definition, occurs in the first stage of the litigation. Therefore, the complaint also benefits from the temporary presumption and must be viewed in light of the plaintiff's minimal burden to show discriminatory intent. The plaintiff cannot reasonably be required to allege more facts in the complaint than the plaintiff would need to defeat a motion for summary judgment made prior to the defendant's furnishing of a non-discriminatory justification.

In other words, absent direct evidence of discrimination, what must be plausibly supported by facts alleged in the complaint is that the plaintiff is a member of a protected class, was qualified, suffered an adverse employment action, and has at least minimal support for the proposition that the employer was motivated by discriminatory intent. The facts alleged must give plausible support to the reduced requirements that arise under *McDonnell Douglas* in the initial phase of a Title VII litigation. The facts required by *Iqbal* to be alleged in the complaint need not give plausible support to the ultimate question of whether the adverse employment action was attributable to discrimination. They need only give plausible support to a minimal inference of discriminatory motivation.

We now turn to the assessment of the sufficiency of Littlejohn's several claims.

II.   Disparate Treatment Claim

Littlejohn alleges disparate treatment based on race as a result of her demotion from EEO Director to a lower-paying, non-managerial analyst position in March 2011. Littlejohn's disparate treatment claim under Title VII, § 1981 and § 1983 is subject to the burden-shifting evidentiary framework set forth in *McDonnell Douglas*. As set forth above, because this appeal involves review of a motion to dismiss, we focus only on whether the allegations in the complaint give plausible support to the reduced prima facie requirements that arise under *McDonnell Douglas* in the initial phase of a litigation.

A.   Littlejohn's Disparate Treatment Allegations

The parties do not dispute that Littlejohn's allegations would be sufficient to establish the first three prongs of a prima facie case of discrimination in the initial phase, as the complaint alleges that she belongs to a protected class (black), was qualified for the EEO Director position at issue, and suffered an adverse employment action through her demotion. Rather, the parties dispute whether the allegations give plausible support to the conclusion that the demotion occurred under circumstances giving rise to an inference of discrimination.

An inference of discrimination can arise from circumstances including, but not limited to, "the employer's criticism of the plaintiff's performance in ethnically degrading terms; or its invidious comments about others in the employee's protected group; or the more favorable treatment of employees not in the protected group; or the sequence of events leading to the plaintiff's discharge." As pleaded, none of Defendants' actions directly indicates racial bias. . . .

However, an inference of discrimination also arises when an employer replaces a terminated or demoted employee with an individual outside the employee's protected class. As we have explained, "the evidence necessary to satisfy th[e] initial burden" of establishing that an adverse employment action occurred under circumstances giving rise to an inference of discrimination is "minimal." The fact that a plaintiff was replaced by someone outside the protected class will ordinarily suffice for the required inference of discrimination at the initial prima facie stage of the Title VII analysis, including at the pleading stage.

Littlejohn alleges that she was replaced by a white ACS employee, Fredda Monn, after she was demoted from EEO Director. Littlejohn also alleges that Monn was less qualified for the position. According to Littlejohn's complaint, Monn had "no prior EEO experience," as she "was previously the Director of the Accountability/Review Unit that had nothing to do with EEO matters" but rather "involved the comprehensive review of child welfare case practices." Compl. ¶ 78. Littlejohn's factual allegations are more than sufficient to make plausible her claim that her demotion occurred under circumstances giving rise to an inference of discrimination. Accordingly, we hold that Littlejohn's complaint alleges sufficient facts to satisfy the requirements of *Iqbal*. The district court therefore erred in dismissing this claim. . . .

B.   Liability of the Individual and City Defendants

We must now determine, based on these allegations, which Defendants must face Littlejohn's disparate treatment claim under Title VII and §§ 1981 and 1983. . . .

In sum, Littlejohn's disparate treatment claim with respect to her demotion survives against the City under Title VII, and against Defendant Baker under §§ 1981 and 1983. Littlejohn's disparate treatment claim against [Defendant Mattingly] was properly dismissed by the district court [because Mattingly was not alleged to have been responsible for that disparate treatment.]

III.   Retaliation Claim

Littlejohn also claims she was retaliated against because of her complaints about racial discrimination in the reorganization process following the merger of ACS and DJJ. Retaliation claims under Title VII and § 1981 are both analyzed pursuant to Title VII principles and the *McDonnell Douglas* burden-shifting evidentiary framework. Section 704(a) of Title VII includes an anti-retaliation provision that makes it unlawful "for an employer to discriminate against any . . . employee . . . because [that individual] opposed any practice" made unlawful by Title VII or "made a charge, testified, assisted, or participated in" a Title VII investigation or proceeding. To establish a presumption of retaliation at the initial stage of a Title VII litigation, a plaintiff must present evidence that shows "(1) participation in a protected activity; (2) that the defendant knew of the protected activity; (3) an adverse employment action; and (4) a causal connection between the protected activity and the adverse employment action." As with our analysis of the disparate treatment claim, the allegations in the complaint need only give plausible support to the reduced prima facie requirements that arise under *McDonnell Douglas* in the initial phase of a Title VII litigation.

The parties do not dispute that Littlejohn's allegations, taken as true, would suffice to establish the second and third prongs of a prima facie case of retaliation. Defendants certainly knew of Littlejohn's complaints of discrimination in the ACS/DJJ merger process, and Littlejohn's demotion constitutes an adverse employment action. The parties dispute, however, whether Littlejohn's actions constitute protected activities, and whether Littlejohn has plausibly alleged a causal connection between the protected activities and the adverse employment action.

A. Protected Activities Under § 704(a)

We first examine whether Littlejohn participated in a "protected activity" under the retaliation provisions of Title VII. . . .

Here, Littlejohn alleges that she, "in her capacity as Director of EEO[,] repeatedly objected and complained to defendants Mattingly and Baker about defendants' selection process and failure to abide by proper anti-discrimination policies and procedures." Compl. ¶ 64. Littlejohn also alleges that she "objected to defendants Mattingly and Bakers' discriminatory policies during scheduled meetings with them" over the course of more than a year. *Id.* ¶ 65. Littlejohn argues on appeal that she stepped outside her role as EEO Director when she advocated for minority DJJ employees, but regardless of whether she made these complaints in her capacity as EEO Director, "§ 704(a)'s opposition clause protects" such "complaints to management" and "protest[s] against discrimination." Littlejohn was not simply conveying others' complaints of discrimination to Mattingly and Baker or alerting them to Title VII's mandates; she was complaining about what she believed was unlawful discrimination in the personnel decision-making process during the ACS/DJJ merger. Her complaints of discrimination were protected activities under § 704(a)'s opposition clause.

B. Causal Connection Between the Protected Activity and the Adverse Employment Action

We next consider whether Littlejohn pleaded a causal connection between the protected activities and her demotion. . . .

A causal connection in retaliation claims can be shown either "(1) indirectly, by showing that the protected activity was followed closely by discriminatory treatment, or through other circumstantial evidence such as disparate treatment of fellow employees who engaged in similar conduct; or (2) directly, through evidence of retaliatory animus directed against the plaintiff by the defendant." As discussed above, none of Defendants' actions directly indicates racial bias, nor do those actions directly establish retaliatory animus based on Littlejohn's complaints of discrimination during the ACS/DJJ merger.

However, Littlejohn sufficiently pleaded facts that would indirectly establish causation. According to Littlejohn's complaint, her demotion closely followed her protests of discrimination. Although the district court concluded that Littlejohn's complaints of discrimination began over a year before her March 2011 demotion, Littlejohn alleges that she "objected and complained" to Defendants through March 14, 2011—the day of her demotion—and described in her complaint specific instances in which she objected to discrimination during the year preceding her demotion. Compl. ¶¶ 48-51, 65. At the motion to dismiss stage, we accept these allegations as true and draw all inferences in Littlejohn's favor. We have "not drawn a bright line to define the outer limits beyond which a temporal relationship is too attenuated to establish a causal relationship between the exercise of a federal constitutional right and an allegedly retaliatory action." But Littlejohn's allegations that the demotion occurred within days after her complaints of discrimination are sufficient to plausibly support an indirect inference of causation.

Because Littlejohn's complaint alleges that her "protected activity was followed closely by discriminatory treatment," and because Littlejohn alleges facts that would be sufficient to establish the other elements of a prima facie case of retaliation, her allegations were more than sufficient to withstand the instant motion to dismiss. The district court erred in dismissing this claim. Littlejohn's retaliation claim therefore survives against the City under Title VII and survives against Defendant Baker under § 1981. As with her disparate treatment claim, Littlejohn's retaliation claim against [Defendant Mattingly] was properly dismissed because [he was] not involved in her demotion.

IV. Hostile Work Environment Claim . . .

To establish a hostile work environment under Title VII, § 1981, or § 1983, a plaintiff must show that "the workplace is permeated with discriminatory intimidation, ridicule, and insult that is sufficiently severe or pervasive to alter the conditions of the victim's employment and create an abusive working environment." "This standard has both objective and subjective components: the conduct complained of must be severe or pervasive enough that a reasonable person would find it hostile or abusive, and the victim must subjectively perceive the work environment to be abusive." "The incidents complained of must be more than episodic; they must be sufficiently continuous and concerted in order to be deemed pervasive." In determining whether a plaintiff suffered a hostile work environment, we must consider the totality of the circumstances, including "the frequency of the discriminatory conduct; its severity; whether it is physically threatening or humiliating, or a mere offensive utterance; and whether it unreasonably interferes with an employee's work performance."

Littlejohn's hostile work environment claim is predicated on the following allegations: Baker made negative statements about Littlejohn to Mattingly; Baker was impatient and used harsh tones with Littlejohn; Baker distanced herself from Littlejohn when she was nearby; Baker declined to meet with Littlejohn; Baker required Littlejohn to recreate reasonable accommodation logs; Baker replaced Littlejohn at meetings; Baker wrongfully reprimanded Littlejohn; and Baker increased Littlejohn's reporting schedule. Baker also sarcastically told Littlejohn "you feel like you are being left out," and that Littlejohn did not "understand the culture" at ACS. Compl. ¶¶ 49, 77.

These allegations could not support a finding of hostile work environment that is so severe or pervasive as to have altered the conditions of Littlejohn's employment. The claim was therefore properly dismissed. . . .

CONCLUSION

For the foregoing reasons, we VACATE the district court's judgment granting Defendants' motion to dismiss with respect to (1) Littlejohn's disparate treatment and retaliation claims against the City under Title VII, (2) Littlejohn's disparate treatment claim against Defendant Baker under §§ 1981 and 1983, and (3) Littlejohn's retaliation claim against Baker under § 1981; AFFIRM the dismissal of the other claims; and REMAND for proceedings consistent with this opinion.

NOTES AND QUESTIONS

1. *Solving the* Swierkiewicz *puzzle.*   The court in *Littlejohn*, like the court in *McCleary-Evans*, attempts to reconcile the Supreme Court's decisions in *Iqbal* and *Swierkiewicz* in the particular context of Title VII claims. Both courts agree that *Iqbal* is fully applicable in such cases, but they resolve the tension between *Iqbal* and *Swierkiewicz* somewhat differently. The *McCleary-Evans* court ruled that the plaintiff was not required to plead facts sufficient to establish a prima facie case of discrimination—the *McDonnell Douglas* standard—but was required to adhere to *Iqbal* and plead facts from which an inference of intentional discrimination could be drawn. The *Littlejohn* court, on the other hand, held that the plaintiff was not required to plead facts from which an inference of intent could be drawn, but could satisfy Rule 8(a)(2) by pleading facts sufficient to support a prima facie case under *McDonnell Douglas*. What is the logic of applying the *McDonnell Douglas* standard, which was designed for use at summary judgment, at the pleading stage?

2. *Revisiting* McCleary-Evans.   How would the *Littlejohn* court have decided the *McCleary-Evans* case? How would the *McCleary-Evans* court have decided the *Littlejohn* case? Which approach do you find more persuasive? Which is more consistent with *Twombly* and *Iqbal*?

PROBLEM

1-9. P sued her former employer, UPMC, for violations of the federal Rehabilitations Act (RA). In her complaint she alleged (1) that she was injured at work and placed on leave for a short-term disability; (2) that her doctor certified that she was available to engage in sedentary work; (3) that UPMC provided her with a light-duty clerical position; (4) that there was an opening for a telephone operator at UPMC, for which she applied; (5) that UPMC never contacted her about that position or any other open positions; (6) that UPMC eliminated the clerical position at which she was employed and then terminated P's employment solely for reason of her disability; and (7) that UPMC receives federal funding. The RA provides: "No otherwise qualified individual with a disability in the United States . . . shall, solely by reason of her or his disability, be excluded from participation in, be denied the benefits of, or be subjected to discrimination under any program or activity receiving Federal financial assistance. . . ." Employers subject to the RA are required to make "reasonable accommodation" for a disabled employee's limitations, including the transfer of a disabled employee to a vacant position as an accommodation of his or her disability. Consistent with the standards applied in *Iqbal*, are P's allegations sufficient to state a claim under the RA? *See Fowler v. UPMC Shadyside*, 578 F.3d 203 (3d Cir. 2009). *But see Guirguis v. Movers Specialty Servs., Inc.*, 346 Fed. App'x 774, 776 n.6 (3d Cir. 2009).

2. The Answer

Once the defendant has been served with a summons and a copy of the complaint, her response is normally due within 21 days. *See* FED. R. CIV. P. 12(a)(1)(A)(i).* She may file either an answer or one or more of a number of pretrial motions permitted under Rule 12. If she fails to do either, she risks default and the entry of a default judgment. See Chapter X, part B, *infra*.

Our present focus is on the answer; we will consider Rule 12 motions in the next section and in subsequent chapters. The general rules and principles of pleading set forth in Rule 8, as well as the particularity exceptions in Rule 9, apply fully to the assertion of an affirmative defense. Some courts have also applied the "plausibility" standards of *Iqbal*, *supra*, to the pleading of affirmative defenses; whether this will become standard practice remains to be seen. *See* Jeffrey A. Parness, *General Rules of Pleading*, in 2 MOORE'S FEDERAL PRACTICE § 8.08[1] (3d ed. 2015) (noting the potential unfairness of imposing a plausibility requirement on a defendant who is required to respond to the complaint within 21 days).

In her answer, the defendant must "admit or deny" each allegation in the complaint. FED. R. CIV. P. 8(b)(1)(B). In so doing, she must "fairly respond to the substance of the allegation." FED. R. CIV. P. 8(b)(2). Typically, this is done by admitting or denying each specific allegation. FED. R. CIV. P. 8(b)(3). A "general" denial, *i.e.*, a denial to the entire complaint, may be entered only if the defendant wishes to controvert every allegation in the complaint, including those relating to subject matter jurisdiction. *Id.* If the pleader wishes to deny only part of an allegation, she must specify the admitted part and deny the rest. FED. R. CIV. P. 8(b)(4). A denial may also be based on the pleader's lack of "knowledge or information sufficient to form a belief about the truth of an allegation. . . ." FED. R. CIV. P. 8(b)(5). The denial of an allegation is sometimes referred to as a "negative defense." It challenges the plaintiff's ability to prove one or more of the necessary elements of his claim, *i.e.*, it attempts to negate that element or allegation. Most importantly,

---

*Note that Rule 12(a)(1) applies to all responsive pleadings. The phrase "responsive pleading" includes an answer to a complaint, an answer to a counterclaim, an answer to a cross-claim, and an answer to a third-party claim. FED. R. CIV. P. 7(a). We will cover these other types of claims in Chapter VIII, *infra*.

a failure to deny an allegation and an ineffective denial are both treated as admissions. FED. R. CIV. P. 8(b)(6). Note that some denials, *e.g.*, those challenging the plaintiff's capacity or the performance of a condition precedent, must be made with specificity. FED. R. CIV. P. 9(a)(2), (c).

Suppose the defendant has been properly served with a complaint that alleges as follows:

1. On November 2, 2011, at approximately 2 P.M., the defendant, driving a car westbound on York Avenue, ran a red light at the corner of Figueroa Street and York Avenue.
2. At that same time, plaintiff was driving her truck southbound on Figueroa Street and crossing the intersection at York Avenue with a green light.
3. Defendant's car collided with plaintiff's truck in the middle of the intersection, causing damage to the truck and inflicting injuries on plaintiff.

If the defendant chooses to answer the complaint (as opposed to filing a motion to dismiss under Rule 12(b)), the appropriate admissions and denials might look like this:

1. Defendant admits that he was driving westbound on York Avenue at the given time and date but denies that he ran a right light as he entered the intersection.
2. Defendant admits that at the given time and date, plaintiff was driving her truck southbound on Figueroa Street, but denies that plaintiff entered the intersection with a green light.
3. Defendant admits that his car and plaintiff's truck collided with each other at the intersection of Figueroa Street and York Avenue; admits that plaintiff's truck suffered damage as the result of the collision, but based on a lack of knowledge and belief, denies that plaintiff suffered personal injuries as a result of the collision and otherwise denies all other allegations in Paragraph 3 of plaintiff's complaint not herein admitted.

The answer must also contain any "affirmative defenses" the defendant may have against the plaintiff. FED. R. CIV. P. 8(c). An affirmative defense does not deny (*i.e.*, negate) any of the allegations supporting the plaintiff's right of action; rather, it alleges new facts that will, if proven, defeat that action. In this sense, an affirmative defense is the modern equivalent of the common law's "confession and avoidance," the difference being that a plaintiff under modern practice need not "confess" to plaintiff's allegations but may instead assert both negative and affirmative defenses in a single pleading. *See* FED. R. CIV. P. 8(d)(2)-(3) (rules permit the assertion of alternative and inconsistent claims and defenses).

Rule 8(c) lists a number of common affirmative defenses, such as failure of consideration and contributory negligence, etc. But the list is illustrative only. Any defense that is affirmative in the sense that it is not premised on a denial of plaintiff's allegations but on additional facts giving rise to the defense must be pleaded in the answer. The failure to do so operates as a waiver of the defense, although a court may permit an amendment of the answer to cure the defect if the plaintiff will suffer no prejudice. FED. R. CIV. P. 15; *cf. Sanderson-Cruz v. United States*, 88 F. Supp. 2d 388, 392-393 (E.D. Pa. 2000) (allowing defense to be raised for first time in defendant's motion for summary judgment when plaintiff suffers no prejudice). Some federal circuits also allow affirmative defenses to be raised by way of a motion to dismiss under Rule 12 (*see infra*).

It is sometimes difficult to distinguish between a negative defense and an affirmative defense. The best approach is to assess the extent to which the defense is analogous to one of the listed affirmative defenses, *i.e.*, does it operate as an avoidance by not controverting the plaintiff's proof and, as is typically the case with affirmative defenses, would the defendant bear the burden of proof on the defense at trial. *See, e.g., Brunswick Leasing Corp. v. Wisconsin Cent., Ltd.*, 136 F.3d 521, 530 (7th Cir. 1998). In close cases, fairness is the guide. If a plaintiff is taken by surprise or somehow prejudiced by the defendant's failure to plead what is arguably an affirmative defense, the unpleaded defense will not be allowed. As one court put it, "A defendant should not be permitted to 'lie behind a log' and ambush a plaintiff with an unexpected defense." *Ingraham v. United States*, 808 F.2d 1075, 1079 (5th Cir. 1987). When in doubt, err on the side of treating an ambiguous defense as an affirmative defense. Plead it.

Returning to the hypothetical answer above, the defendant might assert the following affirmative defenses:

Affirmative Defenses

1. *Statute of Limitations.* Plaintiff's complaint was filed after the expiration of the applicable statute of limitations.
2. *Contributory Negligence.* Plaintiff was inebriated at the time of the collision and as a result of that inebriation drove through the intersection of Figueroa Street and York Avenue against a red light.

Finally, the answer must also contain any related counterclaims the defendant wishes to assert against the plaintiff. FED. R. CIV. P. 13(a). We will examine counterclaims in Chapter VIII, *infra*, but a counterclaim in our hypothetical case might be premised on plaintiff's alleged negligence in causing the collision and any resulting harm to the defendant.

The plaintiff is not required to file a reply to an answer unless ordered by the court to do so. FED. R. CIV. P. 7(a)(7). If no reply is filed, affirmative allegations in the answer are deemed denied. FED. R. CIV. P. 8(b)(6). A response is required, however, if the defendant files a counterclaim. Under such circumstances the plaintiff may file either an answer to the counterclaim or a proper motion under Rule 12.

King Vision Pay Per View, Ltd. v. J.C. Dimitri's Restaurant, Inc.
180 F.R.D. 332 (N.D. Ill. 1998)

SHADUR, Senior District Judge.

J.C. Dimitri's Restaurant, Inc. ("Dimitri's") and James Chelios ("Chelios") have filed what purports to be a Response to Complaint that addresses the Complaint filed against them by King Vision Pay Per View, Ltd. This sua sponte opinion is triggered by the Response's pervasive and impermissible flouting of the crystal-clear directive of Fed. R. Civ. P. ("Rule") 8(b) as to how *any* responsive pleading to a federal complaint must be drafted.

This is it. For too many years and in too many hundreds of cases this Court has been reading, and has been compelled to order the correction of, allegedly responsive pleadings that are written by lawyers who are either unaware of or who choose to depart from Rule 8(b)'s plain roadmap. It identifies only three alternatives as available for use in an answer to the allegations of a complaint: to admit those allegations, to deny them or to state a disclaimer (if it can be made in the objective and subjective good faith demanded by Rule 11) in the express terms of the second sentence of Rule 8(b), which then entitles the pleader to the benefit of a deemed denial.

Here Dimitri's' and Chelios' counsel has engaged in a particularly vexatious violation of that most fundamental aspect of federal pleading. It is hard to imagine, but fully 30 of the Response's 35 paragraphs (its express statements in Response §§ 6-12, 17, 25-26 and 33-34, plus the incorporation by reference of such earlier paragraphs in Response §§ 19 and 28) contain this nonresponse, in direct violation of Rule 8(b)'s express teaching: "Neither admit nor deny the allegations of said Paragraph—, but demand strict proof thereof." *Gilbert* [*v. Johnston*, 127 F.R.D. 145, 146 (N.D. Ill. 1989),] and a host of this Court's unpublished opinions since then speak not only of the unacceptability of any such Rule 8(b) violation but also to the equally unacceptable "demand" for "strict proof," a concept that to this Court's knowledge is unknown to the federal practice or to any other system of modern pleading.

This Court's efforts at lawyer education through the issuance of repeated brief opinions or oral rulings, or through faculty participation in seminars and symposia on federal pleading and practice,[4] have proved unavailing. It is time for this Court to follow the Rules itself, in this instance Rule 8(d): "Averments in a pleading to which a responsive pleading is required, other than those as to the amount of damage, are admitted when not denied in the responsive pleading."*. . .

Accordingly all of the allegations of Complaint §§ 6-12, 17, 25-26 and 33-34 are held to have been admitted by Dimitri's and Chelios, and this action will proceed on that basis. And although the same phenomenon referred to in n.4 probably makes it quite unlikely that the lawyers who are most prone to commit the same offense will be lawyers who are regular (or even sporadic) readers of F. Supp. or F.R.D., this opinion is being sent to West Publishing Company for publication.

---

4. Unfortunately those seminars and symposia usually turn out to involve preaching to the converted. Lawyers who really need such continuing legal education rarely attend (they must be too busy making mistakes).

* [The current version is found in Rule 8(b)(6), which provides: "An allegation—other than one relating to the amount of damages—is admitted if a responsive pleading is required and the allegation is not denied." FED. R. CIV. P. 8(b)(6).—EDS.]

Future Rule 8(b) violators are hereby placed on constructive notice that their similarly defective pleadings will encounter like treatment.

NOTES AND QUESTIONS

1. *The roadmap of Rule 8.* Judge Shadur aptly criticized the defendants' attorney for failure to comply with "Rule 8(b)'s plain roadmap." But by construing the defendants' flawed answer in such a technical fashion didn't the judge, too, fail to comply with Rule 8(d)(1)'s equally "plain roadmap," which provides that "[n]o technical form is required"? To the same apparent effect is Rule 8(e), which states that "[p]leadings must be construed so as to do justice." Or was Judge Shadur constrained by the fact that Rule 8(b)(1)(B) requires that each averment be admitted or denied and that the defendant did neither? Even if Judge Shadur were correct, shouldn't he have allowed the defendant to amend its answer pursuant to Rule 15(a)(2)? Maybe that's what happened. *See Peyton v. Otis Elevator Co.*, 1998 WL 574378 (N.D. Ill. Aug. 31, 1998), in which Judge Shadur, citing his decision in *King Vision*, granted leave to amend under roughly identical circumstances but instructed defendant's counsel not to charge the client for the cost of drafting and filing the amended answer. *See also Frank v. Wilbur-Ellis Co. Salaried Emps. LTD Plan*, 2008 WL 4370095 (E.D. Cal. Sept. 24, 2008) (defendant's response that a document relied on by plaintiff in his complaint "speaks for itself" is not a proper denial under Rule 8(b), for "[t]his Court has been attempting to listen to such written materials for years (in the forlorn hope that one will indeed give voice) — but until some such writing does break its silence, this Court will continue to require pleaders to employ one of the three alternatives that are permitted by Rule 8(b) . . .").

PROBLEMS

1-10. An employees' benefit fund brought an action against a coal company seeking to hold the company liable for delinquent beneficiary premiums under the federal Coal Industry Retiree Health Benefit Act of 1992. The coal company filed an answer denying its liability under the act. One year later, after the close of discovery, the plaintiff filed a motion for summary judgment. In response to that motion, the defendant asserted for the first time that imposition of liability under the act would violate the Takings Clause of the Fifth Amendment of the U.S. Constitution, which states, "nor shall private property be taken for public use, without just compensation." Is this belated assertion an affirmative defense? Does it operate as an avoidance? Who would bear the burden of establishing a violation of the Takings Clause? If it is an affirmative defense, should the court allow the defendant to amend its answer to include the defense? To what extent might "surprise" be a factor in that determination? *See Holland v. Cardiff Coal Co.*, 991 F. Supp. 508, 515 (S.D. W. Va. 1997).

1-11. P sustained a workplace injury while employed at GM's metal-stamping plant and was unable to work for a year. He sued GM asserting a workplace intentional tort, and GM properly removed the case to federal court. In the meantime P returned to work and shortly thereafter GM announced a voluntary buyout opportunity. P accepted GM's buyout offer and signed two documents, one of which was a release that provided, among other things, for the release of all claims, demands, or causes of action, known or unknown, related to his employment. GM's answer to P's complaint (which was due after the date the release was signed) neither asserted an affirmative defense based on the release, nor referenced the release in any manner. Defense counsel discovered the release in producing the plaintiff's personnel file during discovery. It then alerted the plaintiff's counsel that GM would assert the release as a bar to the intentional tort claim. GM did not move to amend its answer, however, until after filing a motion for summary judgment at the close of discovery. P has challenged GM's motion to amend, arguing that GM waived the release defense by failing to include it in its answer. Is the release defense an affirmative defense? Assuming a positive answer to that question, how should the district court rule on GM's motion to amend? *See Seals v. General Motors Corp.*, 546 F.3d 766 (6th Cir. 2008).

3.   Rule 12(b) Motions to Dismiss

Rule 12(b) permits a defendant to raise certain specified defenses by motion, prior to filing an answer. (Read Rule 12 in your supplement.) The filing of such a motion tolls the time for filing the answer until 14 days after the defendant receives notice of the court's denial of the motion. FED. R. CIV. P. 12(a)(4)(A). Thus, under Rule 12(b), the defendant may assert any of the following defenses by motion:

(1) Lack of subject matter jurisdiction;
(2) Lack of personal jurisdiction;
(3) Improper venue;
(4) Insufficient process;
(5) Insufficient service of process;
(6) Failure to state a claim upon which relief can be granted; and
(7) Failure to join a party under Rule 19.

The legal standards pertinent to six of these seven motions are covered extensively in other chapters: subject matter jurisdiction (Chapter IV); personal jurisdiction (Chapter II); improper venue (Chapter V); insufficiency of process and insufficiency of service of process (Chapter III); and Rule 19 joinder of parties (Chapter VIII). We will not dwell on them here. For present purposes, that leaves us with motions made under Rule 12(b)(6) for failure to state a claim upon which relief can be granted.

We have already seen Rule 12(b)(6) in operation in the context of challenges to the adequacy of a plaintiff's complaint. In fact, a second look at the Court's decision in *Iqbal, supra,* should be helpful. In that case, the Court began by describing the elements of the right of action asserted by the plaintiff—intentional discrimination based on race, religion, and/or national origin. Next, the Court identified the conclusory allegations in the complaint and pronounced that those allegations were not entitled to the presumption of truth. Finally, the Court asked whether the remaining non-conclusory allegations were sufficient to state a plausible claim for relief. That question was answered by comparing the elements of the right of action with the non-conclusory factual allegations. The middle step of this inquiry presents a pleadings problem, *i.e.,* the determination of whether an allegation is factual or conclusory—factual sufficiency. The first and the third steps address the legal sufficiency of the claim, namely, whether the complaint alleges facts sufficient to show that the pleader is entitled to relief. In *Iqbal,* the answer was "No" since the non-conclusory allegations were insufficient to support an inference of intentional discrimination. As suggested previously, this approach to legal sufficiency looks very much like a general demurrer under a code-pleading regime, where the complaint is dismissed if it fails to allege facts sufficient to constitute a cause of action.

It is quite unlikely that Rule 12(b)(6) was intended to operate as a type of general demurrer, for the federal rules intentionally excluded demurrers from the range of allowable pleadings. *See Dioguardi v. Durning,* 139 F.2d 774, 775 (2d Cir. 1944) ("Under the new rules of civil procedure, there is no pleading requirement of stating 'facts sufficient to constitute a cause of action.'"). As originally conceived, Rule 12(b)(6) would permit only a limited type of challenge to the legal sufficiency of a complaint. Thus, if a complaint, on its face, revealed an absence of any right to relief, the otherwise disfavored motion would stand. The drafters of the federal rules assumed that challenges to the legal sufficiency of the claim would be raised through "talking" motions, *i.e.,* motions accompanied by affidavits or other forms of proof. The 1948 amendments converted such motions into motions for summary judgments. FED. R. CIV. PROC. 12(d). Indeed, at the time the original rules were drafted, summary judgment was expected to be the primary vehicle for framing and challenging both the factual and legal sufficiency of a claim. The inclusion of Rule 12(b)(6) was seen as something of an inconsequential pacifier for those practitioners accustomed to the array of code-pleading motions. Charles E. Clark, *Pleading Under the Federal Rules,* 12 WYO. L.J. 177, 193-194 (1958). But the evolution of Rule 12(b)(6), as reflected in *Twombly* and *Iqbal,* is to the contrary. It is now a powerful motion that can be used to challenge both the factual and legal sufficiency of a pleading.

A Rule 12(b)(6) motion can also be used to dispose of an asserted right that is subject to a dispositive affirmative defense, such as the statute of limitations. If, for example, the defendant asserts the bar of the statute of limitations in a Rule 12(b)(6) motion and the complaint reveals that as a matter of law the plaintiff's claim was filed (or served) beyond the applicable statutory period, the claim, or those parts of it subject to the statute of limitations, will be dismissed. More generally, if the plaintiff's complaint itself reveals the deficiency of the plaintiff's claim, the proper response is a Rule 12(b)(6) motion to dismiss.

For a general overview of Rule 12(b)(6), see Milton I. Shadur & Mary P. Squiers, *Defenses and Objections: When and How Presented; Motion for Judgment on the Pleadings; Consolidating Motions; Waiving Defenses; Pretrial Hearing, in* 2 Moore's Federal Practice § 12.34 (3d ed. 2015); 5B Charles Alan Wright & Arthur R. Miller, Federal Practice and Procedure §§ 1355-1357 (3d ed. 2004 & Supp. 2015).

Johnson v. City of Shelby

135 S. Ct. 346 (2014)

Per Curiam.

Plaintiffs below, petitioners here, worked as police officers for the city of Shelby, Mississippi. They allege that they were fired by the city's board of aldermen, not for deficient performance, but because they brought to light criminal activities of one of the aldermen. Charging violations of their Fourteenth Amendment due process rights, they sought compensatory relief from the city. Summary judgment was entered against them in the District Court, and affirmed on appeal, for failure to invoke 42 U.S.C. § 1983 in their complaint.

We summarily reverse. Federal pleading rules call for "a short and plain statement of the claim showing that the pleader is entitled to relief," Fed. Rule Civ. Proc. 8(a)(2); they do not countenance dismissal of a complaint for imperfect statement of the legal theory supporting the claim asserted. In particular, no heightened pleading rule requires plaintiffs seeking damages for violations of constitutional rights to invoke § 1983 expressly in order to state a claim. See *Leatherman v. Tarrant County Narcotics Intelligence and Coordination Unit*, 507 U.S. 163, 164 (1983) (a federal court may not apply a standard "more stringent than the usual pleading requirements of Rule 8(a)" in "civil rights cases alleging municipal liability"); *Swierkiewicz v. Sorema N.A.*, 534 U.S. 506, 512 (2002) (imposing a "heightened pleading standard in employment discrimination cases conflicts with Federal Rule of Civil Procedure 8(a)(2)").

The Fifth Circuit defended its requirement that complaints expressly invoke § 1983 as "not a mere pleading formality." 743 F.3d 59, 62 (2013). The requirement serves a notice function, the Fifth Circuit said, because "[c]ertain consequences flow from claims under § 1983, such as the unavailability of *respondeat superior* liability, which bears on the qualified immunity analysis." *Ibid.* This statement displays some confusion in the Fifth Circuit's perception of petitioners' suit. No "qualified immunity analysis" is implicated here, as petitioners asserted a constitutional claim against the city only, not against any municipal officer.

Our decisions in *Bell Atlantic Corp. v. Twombly*, 550 U.S. 544 (2007), and *Ashcroft v. Iqbal*, 556 U.S. 662 (2009), are not in point, for they concern the *factual* allegations a complaint must contain to survive a motion to dismiss. A plaintiff, they instruct, must plead facts sufficient to show that her claim has substantive plausibility. Petitioners' complaint was not deficient in that regard. Petitioners stated simply, concisely, and directly events that, they alleged, entitled them to damages from the city. Having informed the city of the factual basis for their complaint, they were required to do no more to stave off threshold dismissal for want of an adequate statement of their claim. See Fed. Rules Civ. Proc. 8(a)(2) and (3), (d)(1), (e). For clarification and to ward off further insistence on a punctiliously stated "theory of the pleadings," petitioners, on remand, should be accorded an opportunity to add to their complaint a citation to § 1983. See 5 Wright & Miller, *supra*, § 1219, at 277-278 ("The federal rules effectively abolish the restrictive theory of the pleadings doctrine, making it clear that it is unnecessary to set out a legal theory for the plaintiff's claim for relief."; Fed. Rules Civ. Proc. 15(a)(2) ("The court should freely give leave [to amend a pleading] when justice so requires.").

* * *

For the reasons stated, the petition for certiorari is granted, the judgment of the United States Court of Appeals for the Fifth Circuit is reversed, and the case is remanded for further proceedings consistent with this opinion.

It is so ordered.

NOTES AND QUESTIONS

1. *Stating the legal theory supporting the claim asserted.*   Does it make sense that a plaintiff can state a claim upon which relief can be granted without identifying the legal theory arising out of that claim? Did *Iqbal* require the plaintiff to identify the legal basis for his claim? Can you reconcile *City of Shelby* with *Iqbal*?

Kirksey v. R.J. Reynolds Tobacco Co.

168 F.3d 1039 (7th Cir. 1999)

POSNER, Chief Judge.

The plaintiff appeals from the dismissal, on the defendants' motion under Fed. R. Civ. P. 12(b)(6), of a personal-injury suit that she brought against two cigarette manufacturers as the executor of the estate of her husband, who, she alleges, smoked cigarettes manufactured by the defendants. The complaint, captioned "complaint for damages for wrongful death and emotional distress," charges that the defendants accelerated Mr. Kirksey's death from lung cancer by falsely advertising that their cigarettes were not addictive and by adding addicting agents to their cigarettes without informing him either that they were doing this or that cigarettes (with or without such agents) are addictive. Had it not been for these acts or omissions, the complaint alleges, Kirksey would have smoked less and lived longer.

The motion to dismiss claimed that the facts alleged in the complaint do not add up to a tort under Illinois law, which supplies the substantive law governing this diversity case. The motion characterized the plaintiff's claim as one of products liability or false advertising and argued that it was either preempted by federal law or barred by the cases interpreting Illinois' tort law. The plaintiff responded to the motion by arguing that her claim

> is not susceptible to those labels or the analysis of the prior cases in light of the allegations that Defendant[s] deliberately tampered with the cigarettes which made them more dangerous than Plaintiff's decedent knew or could have known. Plaintiff further submits that her claim is a species of intentional tort which cannot be easily cabined in the traditional civil wrong categories.

The plaintiff says that she was not "required at this stage of the litigation to specifically characterize or identify the legal basis of the claims in the complaint. . . . Rather, what Plaintiff is required to do at the initial pleading stage, and what Plaintiff has done, is to assert a colorable claim that has some factual support." The plaintiff renews these arguments in this court, the district judge having held that because the plaintiff had "fail[ed] to make any legal argument in support of any claim, her claims are waived." The plaintiff's essential contention is that in requiring her to specify the legal theory underlying her complaint, the judge violated Fed. R. Civ. P. 8(a)(2), which requires only that the complaint contain "a short and plain statement of the [plaintiff's] claim showing that the [plaintiff] is entitled to relief" — not a long-winded statement of legal theories replete with citations to cases or statutes. To require more, the plaintiff argues, would be inconsistent with the "notice pleading" philosophy of the civil rules.

Her characterization of Rule 8(a)(2) is correct. All that's required to state a claim in a complaint filed in a federal court is a short statement, in plain (that is, ordinary, nonlegalistic) English, of the legal claim. . . . The courts keep reminding plaintiffs that they don't have to file long complaints, don't have to plead facts, don't have to plead legal theories. And the plaintiff in this case heeded the advice: her complaint is admirably succinct.

Where the plaintiff has gone astray is in supposing that a complaint which complies with Rule 8(a)(2) is immune from a motion to dismiss. This confuses form with substance. Rule 8(a)(2) specifies the conditions of the formal adequacy of a pleading. It does not specify the conditions of its substantive adequacy, that is, its legal merit. Suppose the complaint had alleged that the defendants had violated Illinois or federal law by failing to obtain a license to manufacture cigarettes. The complaint would comply with Rule 8(a)(2), but, assuming no such license is required, it would be highly vulnerable to dismissal under Rule 12(b)(6). If the defendants filed a motion to dismiss in which they pointed out that there was no such licensing requirement, it would not be responsive of the plaintiff to say that she was not "required at this stage of the litigation to specifically characterize or identify the legal basis of the claims in the complaint." The defendants would have given reasons for dismissing the complaint despite its formal beauties, and she would have to give reasons against. Our system of justice is adversarial, and our judges are busy people. If they are given plausible reasons for dismissing a complaint, they are not going to do the plaintiff's research and try to discover whether there might be something to say against the defendants' reasoning. An unresponsive response is no response. In effect the plaintiff was defaulted for refusing to respond to the motion to dismiss. And rightly so.

At argument the plaintiff's lawyer suggested that such a position is inconsistent with a proper regard for judicial creativity. It is true that a claim should not be dismissed out of hand just because it is so novel that it cannot be fitted into an existing legal category; to deny this would be to argue for returning to the days of the forms of action, when every new claim had to be shoehorned into an existing writ because the issuance of new writs had been brought to a halt in order to curb the power of the writ issuer, the Lord Chancellor. 2 Frederick Pollock & Frederic William Maitland, *The History of English Law Before the Time of Edward I* 563-64 (2d ed. 1968); J.H. Baker, *An Introduction to English Legal History* 51 (2d ed. 1979). But a claim that does not fit into an existing legal category requires more argument by the plaintiff to stave off dismissal, not less, if the defendant moves to dismiss on the ground that the plaintiff's claim has no basis in law. The plaintiff has to show that while her claim has no basis in *existing* law, or at least the law's current pigeonholes, it lies in the natural line of the law's development and should now be recognized as a part of the law. It is absurd to suppose that it is a *sufficient* answer to a motion to dismiss — the end rather than the beginning of analysis — that although the plaintiff cannot identify an existing legal category for his claim, the categories of the law are not closed.

We imagine that the plaintiff's lawyer knows all this, that his problem is that he really cannot think of a viable legal basis for his client's claim, that he hopes that the current legal ferment in the world of tobacco litigation will brew him up a theory at some future date if only he can stave off immediate dismissal under Rule 12(b)(6).

The natural characterization of the claim is as one for the consequences of fraudulent advertising. Suppose that smoking cigarettes were so addictive that if a person smoked a single cigarette, he would be hooked for life; nothing could break him of the habit. And suppose that, knowing this, and knowing that no one would smoke his first cigarette who knew how addictive cigarette smoking is, cigarette manufacturers advertised cigarettes as being nonaddictive, or, knowing that people like Mr. Kirksey didn't realize that cigarettes were addictive, kept mum and by doing so enticed them to take the fatal first step. Suppose further that the addictive properties of cigarettes were not natural to tobacco or to the process of manufacturing cigarettes, but were added by the manufacturers surreptitiously during the process. In combination with the false advertising and the misleading silence, this would be a fraudulent device for getting people to buy more cigarettes. More precisely, it would be a component of the overall fraud, since unless the addictive properties of the product were denied or concealed, no one would buy cigarettes.

So characterized, the plaintiff's claim falls into a familiar tort category, that of fraud or deceit, but it is a category that in the cigarette area has, though to an uncertain degree, been preempted by the federal cigarette labeling and advertising law. See Cigarette Labeling and Advertising Act, § 5(b), 15 U.S.C. § 1334(b);

Cipollone v. Liggett Group, 505 U.S. 504, 527-29 (1992) (plurality opinion).* The plaintiff tries to skirt this pit by intimating that a new tort should be recognized for making food or related products addictive. But this doesn't make any sense without deception, and so we return to the possibly preempted fraud theory. Suppose that some people are doughnut addicts because they cannot resist food rich in sugar, even though it is bad for them, or at least for their physical health. Since sugar, and even doughnuts, are legal substances, the manufacturer could not be accused of wrongdoing if he advertised his doughnuts, even though by doing so he might be causing harm to some people's health. It might be different if he had jiggered the doughnut recipe to make it even more addictive than normal and failed to disclose this fact, though we cannot find any case adopting such a liability theory. But, good or bad, this too would be a fraud theory, and if the product were cigarettes rather than doughnuts the theory might well be preempted by federal law.

Some states, though not Illinois (not yet anyway), *Barry Gilberg, Ltd. v. Craftex Corp.,* 665 F. Supp. 585, 596-97 (N.D. Ill. 1987), recognize an animal called a "prima facie tort," a catchall for harmful intentional misconduct that eludes the familiar categories. But if one thing is certain, it is that if a particular state-law tort is preempted by federal law, it cannot be resuscitated by being given a new name.

We are straying from the main point, which is not that the plaintiff has failed to identify a legal basis for her claim, and not even that she has failed to try to do so in this court; it is that by failing to respond responsively to the motion to dismiss—by standing on her complaint as if, provided only that it complied with the formal requirements of Rule 8(a)(2), it was the last piece of paper she would have to file in the district court—she forfeited her right to continue litigating her claim.

Affirmed.

NOTES AND QUESTIONS

1. *The distinction between formal sufficiency and substantive sufficiency.*   Judge Posner held that the plaintiff's complaint, although spare, met the formal requirements of Rule 8(a)(2). Why? Nevertheless, he also held that dismissal of the complaint under Rule 12(b)(6) was proper. How can a complaint satisfy Rule 8(a)(2) and yet run afoul of Rule 12(b)(6)? If an answer to this question does not spring forth, re-read paragraph four of the court's opinion. Is Judge Posner's approach similar to the three-step approach applied by the Court in *Iqbal*? (The answer is yes, but you should be able to explain why that is so.)

2. *Plaintiff's burden to provide a legal theory for her claim—round two.*   Did Judge Posner hold that the plaintiff had the burden of identifying a legal theory for

---

*[Section 5(b) of the Cigarette Labeling and Advertising Act provides: "No requirement or prohibition based on smoking and health shall be imposed under State law with respect to the advertising or promotion of any cigarettes the packages of which are labeled in conformity with the provisions of this chapter." 15 U.S.C. § 1334(b).—EDs.]

her claim? If so, isn't that inconsistent with the decision in *City of Shelby*? Or can *Kirksey* and *City of Shelby* be reconciled on the notion that the burden of identifying a legal theory shifts to the plaintiff once the defendant plausibly demonstrates that no legal theory is available to provide relief under the facts asserted? In *City of Shelby*, the plaintiffs met that burden since their factual assertions aligned perfectly with a § 1983 claim. In *Kirksey*, the plaintiff simply failed to identify any recognized legal theory or potential development in the law that would support her case.

3. *The problem of novel legal theories.*   It has been observed that courts should be reluctant to grant a Rule 12(b)(6) motion to dismiss in a case involving a novel legal theory: "It is perhaps ironic that the more extreme or even far-fetched is the asserted theory of liability, the more important it is that the conceptual legal theories be explored and assayed in the light of actual facts, not a pleader's supposition." *Shull v. Pilot Life Ins. Co.*, 313 F.2d 445, 447 (5th Cir. 1963). Did Judge Posner's opinion for the court in *Kirksey* transgress this principle by too readily assuming that any potential claim by the plaintiff might be preempted by federal law? Should the plaintiff perhaps have argued more strongly against the use of a preemption defense?

PROBLEMS

1-12. Case had a contractual relationship with State Farm under which he worked as an independent contractor selling State Farm insurance policies. When Case refused to refrain from seeking or holding public office, State Farm terminated his contract. Case sued State Farm for breach of contract. He alleged the above facts and attached the written contract to his complaint as an exhibit that was incorporated by reference into his allegations. The contract provided that State Farm could terminate the contract at will, *i.e.*, without any reason. State Farm has moved to dismiss Case's complaint under Rule 12(b)(6). What should the district court do? *See Case v. State Farm Mut. Auto Ins. Co.*, 294 F.2d 676 (5th Cir. 1961).

1-13. Dorothy, an elderly widow, lived alone in a single-family home in Kankakee, Illinois. In 1999, Larry approached her and recommended that she allow him to make repairs to her home. Dorothy told him she still owed money on the house and advised him of the terms of her mortgage. Larry offered to help her obtain a new home loan at a better rate than she was then paying. The loan that Larry was pushing would pay him $17,000 for the home repairs, and would consolidate some of Dorothy's other outstanding debt. On September 23, 1999, Larry came to Dorothy's home with Frank, an agent of Mortgage Express. Dorothy did not receive a good faith estimate in connection with the Mortgage Express loan and did not receive a copy of the closing documents. She nevertheless signed the loan documents that Larry and Frank presented to her under pressure, without being allowed to read them and without understanding their terms. Under their terms, Dorothy had borrowed $87,000, of which $33,000 went to settlement charges and $17,000 was paid to Larry. Dorothy's monthly loan payments were $780.64, though her monthly income was only $1,100. She later sued Mortgage Express, asserting various state law claims, and won a judgment of $136,500.

However, she was unable to collect on that judgment because Mortgage Express had gone out of business and her loan sold to National Bank. In 2007, National Bank instituted foreclosure proceedings against her. She responded to the foreclosure action by suing National Bank in federal court, claiming that its foreclosure efforts were unconscionable as a matter of Illinois law. Her unconscionability claim focused on the circumstances surrounding the formation of the contract, and the allegations in her complaint alleged all of the above-referenced facts. Illinois law recognizes unconscionable-in-the-formation claims, but such claims must be brought within five years of the formation of the contract. National Bank has filed a Rule 12(b)(6) motion to dismiss. What should the district court do? *See Estate of Davis v. Wells Fargo Bank*, 633 F.3d 529 (7th Cir. 2011).

C.   Pleading Review Problem

1-14. The following complaint was filed in United States District Court in Oregon:

COMPLAINT

Marc Michaels, Beth Abrams, and Tanya Bond,

Plaintiffs

v.

United States Secret Service, Tom Pine, and Bob Raven,

Defendants

INTRODUCTION

1. The Plaintiffs, all citizens of the United States and residents of Oregon, were in Jacksonville, Oregon, on October 14, 2004, assembled on the public sidewalks in front of and across the street from an inn where President George W. Bush was dining. At the time, Plaintiffs were participating in a lawful and peaceful demonstration to protest the President's policies. The Defendants, members of the United States Secret Service, directed state and local police officers to force Plaintiffs, and others assembled with them, to vacate the sidewalks in front of the inn in violation of the Plaintiffs' First Amendment rights to freedom of speech.

PARTIES

Plaintiffs

2. At all times material hereto, Plaintiff Marc Michaels (hereafter "Plaintiff Michaels") was a resident of Jacksonville, Oregon, participating in the demonstration.

3. At all times material hereto, Plaintiff Beth Abrams (hereafter "Plaintiff Abrams") was a resident of Jacksonville, Oregon, and was a co-organizer of and participant in the demonstration.

4. At all times material hereto, Plaintiff Tanya Bond (hereafter "Plaintiff Bond") was a resident of Jacksonville, Oregon, and was a co-organizer of and participant in the demonstration.

Defendants

5. Defendant United States Secret Service (hereafter "Defendant Secret Service") is and at all times material hereto was the federal agency responsible for providing security for the President of the United States.

6. Defendants Tom Pine (hereafter "Defendant Pine") and Bob Raven (hereafter "Defendant Raven") were Secret Service agents at the scene of the demonstration, acting within the scope of their employment and under color of law, assigned to provide security for the President, and directing, requesting and communicating with state and local law enforcement agencies in their operations related to the demonstration.

FACTS

The Forcible Breakup of the Anti-Bush Demonstration

7. On October 14, 2004, President George W. Bush made a campaign appearance in Central Point, Oregon. President Bush was scheduled to spend the evening at the Jacksonville Inn Honeymoon Cottage located on Main Street, west of Third Street, and south of California Street, approximately two blocks from the Jacksonville Inn, in Jacksonville, Oregon.

8. Plaintiffs Abrams and Bond organized a demonstration to take place in Jacksonville on the afternoon and evening of October 14, 2004. The demonstrators planned to gather during the afternoon in Griffin Park, located on South Fifth Street in Jacksonville, about two blocks from the Jacksonville Inn, and then, beginning at about 5:30 P.M., to march from Griffin Park to the sidewalks in front of and across from the Jacksonville Inn. Abrams and Bond received permission from local police authorities with respect to the route of the march and the location of the demonstration.

9. Beginning about 5:00 P.M. on October 14, 2004, Plaintiffs Michaels, Abrams, and Bond, together with about 200 to 300 other anti-Bush demonstrators, including elderly people, families, children, and babes in arms, assembled in Griffin Park.

10. At about 6:00 P.M., the anti-Bush demonstrators left Griffin Park and proceeded to California Street between Third and Fourth Streets, the location of the Jacksonville Inn.

11. At that time, the anti-Bush demonstrators did not know that the President would decide to come to the Jacksonville Inn on California Street for dinner.

12. Immediately adjacent to the anti-Bush demonstrators was a similarly sized group of pro-Bush demonstrators, also chanting and exhibiting signs. The pro-Bush demonstrators began at the western curbs of Third Street and extended west

along California toward Second Street. The two groups were separated only by the 37-foot width of Third Street. Interactions between the anti-Bush demonstrators and the pro-Bush demonstrators were courteous and even jovial.

13. At about 7:00 P.M., the pro-Bush and anti-Bush demonstrators learned that the President was coming to dine at the Jacksonville Inn on the north side of California Street between Third and Fourth Streets.

14. After learning of the President's dinner plans, the participants in both the pro-Bush and anti-Bush demonstrations clustered more on the north side of California Street than on the south side. Both sets of demonstrators had equal access to the President during his arrival at the Jacksonville Inn and would have had equal access during his departure had the anti-Bush demonstrators not been moved two blocks east as alleged below. See Diagram A below.

15. Shortly after 7:00 P.M., just prior to the President's arrival at the patio dining area at the rear of the Jacksonville Inn, at the request of the Defendants Pine and Raven, a group of state and local police officers dressed in riot gear cleared the Third Street alley all the way to the patio dining area directly behind the Jacksonville Inn. Police also blocked Third Street, including both sidewalks, north of California Street. Riot-geared police officers cleared the California Street alley running along the east side of the Inn and were stationed at the entrance of the California Street alley to prevent any unauthorized persons from entering the alley. No demonstrators attempted to enter the California Street alley at any time after the police cleared the alley. At the intersection of Third and California Streets, the police officers began barring members of both groups of demonstrators from crossing the streets, and confining each to the respective sidewalk on which they were standing.

16. The anti-Bush demonstrators along California Street did not have any access to the President or any line of sight to the dining patio at the rear of the Jacksonville Inn. As shown on Diagram A, the anti-Bush demonstrators were blocked by the buildings along California Street and by the riot-geared police officers stationed at the entrance of the California Street alley.

17. President Bush and his party arrived at the back of the Jacksonville Inn at approximately 7:15 P.M. The patio dining area was enclosed by a 6-foot high wooden fence, blocking a view of those in the patio dining area from the sight of all those outside that area.

18. Also present inside the Inn and the patio dining area were dozens of guests and diners. Defendants did not screen these persons or order or force them to leave the patio. Also present, just upstairs from the patio dining area, was a group of approximately thirty persons participating in a medical conference. Some members of the medical group, who came downstairs to get a glance at the President, found an unguarded door leading into the patio dining area, opened that door and stood looking at the President from a distance of about 15 feet.

19. Fifteen minutes later at about 7:30 P.M., after class members' anti-Bush chants and slogans could be heard on the patio where the President was dining, Defendants Pine and Raven requested or directed state and local police officers to clear California Street of all persons between Third and Fourth Streets—that is, anti-Bush demonstrators—and to move them to the east side of Fourth Street and subsequently to the east side of Fifth Street.

20. Defendants Pine and Raven told state and local police officials that the reason for the request or direction was that they did not want anyone within handgun or explosive range of the President.

21. Had that been the true reason for the request or direction, Defendants Pine and Raven would have requested or directed that all persons dining, staying at, or visiting the Inn who had not been screened by the Secret Service be removed from the Inn. Likewise, had that been the true reason for the request or direction, Pine and Raven would have requested or directed that the pro-Bush demonstrators at the corner of Third and California be moved further to the west so that they, too, would not be in range of the President as he travelled from the Inn to the Honeymoon Cottage where he was staying.

22. Instead, Defendants Pine and Raven left the pro-Bush demonstrators on the northwest and southwest corners of Third and California Streets to cheer for President Bush as he traveled to the Honeymoon Cottage, while causing the anti-Bush demonstrators to be moved two blocks east, well out of the President's view.

23. During the entire time these actions were being taken against the anti-Bush demonstrators, the Defendants took no action to move the pro-Bush demonstrators or to move the unscreened diners, hotel guests, and other visitors, including the assembled medical group, who were inside the Inn.

The Secret Service Pattern and Practice

24. This action by the Secret Service Defendants did not comport with normal, lawful Secret Service security measures during Presidential public appearances or visits to hotels, restaurants, or other publicly accessible buildings, absent threats, reports or other special circumstances suggesting the need for unusual security measures. Specifically: (a) There had been no reports, threats, or other information suggesting a potential attempt to harm the President, or any other special circumstances suggesting the need for unusual security measures. (b) It is not the general practice of the Secret Service, in the absence of special circumstances to establish a security zone extending an entire city or town block around hotels, restaurants, or other buildings the President may be visiting in the United States. (c) On information and belief, the criterion of keeping people out of handgun range of the President was made up for this particular occasion, having no precedent in any prior security zones or Presidential appearances, in the absence of special circumstances. (d) On information and belief, the criterion of keeping people out of explosive range of the President was made up for this particular occasion, having no precedent in any prior security zones or Presidential appearances, in the absence of special circumstances.

25. This policy of isolating anti-Bush demonstrators was set out in some detail in the official "Presidential Advance Manual," dated October 2002, instructing the White House Advance Team on how to keep protesters out of the President's vicinity and sight. Viewpoint discrimination by the Secret Service in connection with President Bush was the official policy of the White House. To this end, the Advance Manual provides, "There are several ways the advance person can prepare a site to minimize demonstration. First, as always, work with the Secret Service and have them ask the local police department to designate a protest area

where demonstrators can be placed, preferably not in view of the event site or motorcade route." The Advance Manual also includes discussions about how to deal with protesters, how to disrupt protests, and how to insure that protesters are kept out of sight or hearing of the President and the media.

26. According to published reports, the Secret Service has engaged in these kinds of actions against anti-government expressive activity on numerous other occasions. [In this paragraph, the complaint describes 12 incidents taking place between 2001 and 2004 where the Secret Service appears to have subjected anti-Bush demonstrators to viewpoint discrimination.]

CLAIMED VIOLATION OF THE FIRST AMENDMENT

27. Defendants Pine and Wood ordered the anti-Bush demonstrators removed from the vicinity of the Jackson Inn because of the message the anti-Bush demonstrators were expressing. In so acting, Defendant Pine and Wood, acting in their official capacities and under color of federal law, violated Plaintiffs' right to Freedom of Speech as protected by the First Amendment to the United States Constitution.

DIAGRAM A

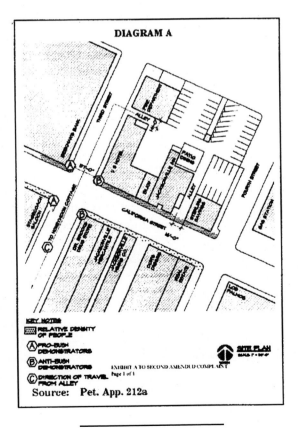

Source: Pet. App. 212a

MOTION TO DISMISS

Defendants Pine and Raven have filed a Rule 12(b)(6) motion to dismiss the complaint filed against them. For purposes of this motion, assume that to prevail on their First Amendment claim, Plaintiffs must ultimately prove that Defendants Pine and Raven intentionally discriminated against them because of the anti-Bush message they were expressing.

Assess the potential arguments that each side will make in support of or in opposition to Defendants' motion. How do you think the district court will (or should) rule? *See Moss v. United States Secret Service*, 711 F.3d 941 (9th Cir. 2013), *rev'd*, 134 S. Ct. 2056 (2014) (on non-pleading grounds).

II

PERSONAL JURISDICTION

The phrase "personal jurisdiction" denotes the power of a court to enter a binding, final judgment against a defendant (or any other party brought into a lawsuit). At its heart, the law of personal jurisdiction is simple and elegant. It is premised on two fundamental concepts: *connecting factors* and *reasonable expectations*. The essential question is whether the defendant has established meaningful connections with the forum state sufficient to put her on notice of a potential lawsuit against her there.

The doctrines governing personal jurisdiction have evolved since the late eighteenth century when the American colonies separated from England and became independent states. At first, jurisdiction depended upon a court's being able to exercise physical power over the defendant or his property within the territorial limits of the "forum state," *i.e.*, the state in which the court sits. This rule of territoriality was based on the public international law principle that a nation's sovereignty stops at its borders. Just as English courts could not exercise power in France, a state like New York could not exercise judicial power over persons or property located in Massachusetts. One notable exception to the rule of territoriality allowed a state to assert jurisdiction over its own citizens or residents by serving them wherever they might be found, whether or not they were within the state at the time of service.

The rule of territoriality became increasingly unworkable as developments in transportation and technology enhanced individual mobility and made the states more and more economically interdependent. A nonresident who committed a wrong in a particular state could avoid being sued there simply by departing the state and leaving no property behind. An injured plaintiff would then be forced to bring suit in a state where the defendant or defendant's property could be found. That state, however, might be so inconvenient in terms of distance or access to evidence and witnesses that the plaintiff would effectively be deprived of a remedy.

Aware of these difficulties, by the mid-twentieth century courts began to move away from strict adherence to the rule of territoriality. Though the presence of the defendant or her property within a state was still *sufficient* for the exercise of jurisdiction, such physical presence was no longer *necessary* when the state had a sufficient connection to the defendant and the lawsuit. Today, courts routinely exercise jurisdiction over defendants who are served with process outside the forum state. This "extraterritorial" jurisdiction is valid so long as the defendant has established contacts with the forum state sufficient to create a reasonable expectation of being sued there. The doctrines governing jurisdiction have thus evolved from an exclusive focus on territoriality to a more flexible concern with fairness centered on the nature and extent of a party's connections with the forum state.

A.   *Pennoyer v. Neff* and the Rule of Territoriality

Pennoyer v. Neff
95 U.S. 714 (1877)

ERROR to the Circuit Court of the United States for the District of Oregon.

[Marcus Neff filed this action against Sylvester Pennoyer in the U.S. Circuit Court in 1874 to recover possession of a 320-acre tract of land in Multnomah County, Oregon, alleged to be worth $15,000. Neff claimed title to the land based on a patent issued to him by the United States on March 19, 1866. Pennoyer claimed title based on a sheriff's sale of the property in execution of a judgment entered against Neff by an Oregon state court on February 19, 1866. The state court suit had been filed in November 1865 by John H. Mitchell, an Oregon attorney who sought to recover fees for services rendered to Neff a few years earlier. Mitchell lived in Oregon and Neff lived in California. Mitchell obtained a court order allowing him to notify Neff of the suit by publishing the summons in the *Pacific Christian Advocate*, a weekly Oregon newspaper, without mailing the summons to Neff's residence. The court granted this order based on Mitchell's affidavit stating that Neff "resides somewhere in the state of California, at what place affiant knows not, and he cannot be found in this state." In the same affidavit, Mitchell asserted that "the defendant has property in this county and state." The newspaper's editor later submitted an affidavit stating that the summons had been published for six consecutive weeks. After Neff failed to respond to the suit, the court, on February 19, 1866, entered a default judgment against him for $294.98. To execute this judgment, the sheriff seized Neff's land on July 9, 1866. On August 7, 1866, the land was sold at a sheriff's sale to Mitchell, for the sum of $341.60. A few days later Mitchell assigned his interest in the land to Pennoyer. The sheriff issued Pennoyer a deed to the land in January 1867. In the U.S. circuit court, Neff argued that Pennoyer had not acquired title to the land because the judgment in *Mitchell v. Neff* on which Pennoyer's title rested was invalid. Neff claimed that the judgment was invalid because (1) the Oregon court had no jurisdiction over him or his property; (2) Mitchell's affidavit supporting the order for publication was defective because he did not use due diligence to ascertain Neff's place of residence; and (3) the editor's affidavit was defective because Oregon law required proof of publication by the printer rather than by the editor. In March 1875, the circuit court issued a decision in Neff's favor. While it rejected his jurisdictional argument, the court ruled that because both affidavits were defective, Neff was entitled to possession of the land. Pennoyer sought review in the U.S. Supreme Court by petition for writ of error.]

Mr. Justice Field delivered the opinion of the court.

This is an action to recover the possession of a tract of land, of the alleged value of $15,000, situated in the State of Oregon. The plaintiff asserts title to the premises by a patent of the United States issued to him in 1866, under the act of Congress of Sept. 27, 1850, usually known as the Donation Law of Oregon. The defendant claims to have acquired the premises under a sheriff's deed, made upon a sale of the property on execution issued upon a judgment recovered against the plaintiff in one of the circuit courts of the State. The case turns upon the validity of this judgment.

It appears from the record that the judgment was rendered in February, 1866, in favor of J. H. Mitchell, for less than $300, including costs, in an action brought by him upon a demand for services as an attorney; that, at the time the action was commenced and the judgment rendered, the defendant therein, the plaintiff here, was a non-resident of the State; that he was not personally served with process, and did not appear therein; and that the judgment was entered upon his default in not answering the complaint, upon a constructive service of summons by publication.

The Code of Oregon provides for such service when an action is brought against a non-resident and absent defendant, who has property within the State. It also provides, where the action is for the recovery of money or damages, for the attachment of the property of the non-resident. And it also declares that no natural person is subject to the jurisdiction of a court of the State, unless he appear in the court, or be found within the State, or be a resident thereof, or have property therein; and, in the last case, only to the extent of such property at the time the jurisdiction attached." Construing this latter provision to mean, that, in an action for money or damages where a defendant does not appear in the court, and is not found within the State, and is not a resident thereof, but has property therein, the jurisdiction of the court extends only over such property, the declaration expresses a principle of general, if not universal, law. The authority of every tribunal is necessarily restricted by the territorial limits of the State in which it is established. Any attempt to exercise authority beyond those limits would be deemed in every other forum, as has been said by this court, an illegitimate assumption of power, and be resisted as mere abuse. In the case against the plaintiff, the property here in controversy sold under the judgment rendered was not attached, nor in any way brought under the jurisdiction of the court. Its first connection with the case was caused by a levy of the execution. It was not, therefore, disposed of pursuant to any adjudication, but only in enforcement of a personal judgment, having no relation to the property, rendered against a non-resident without service of process upon him in the action, or his appearance therein. The court below did not consider that an attachment of the property was essential to its jurisdiction or to the validity of the sale, but held that the judgment was invalid from defects in the affidavit upon which the order of publication was obtained, and in the affidavit by which the publication was proved.

There is some difference of opinion among the members of this court as to the rulings upon these alleged defects. The majority are of opinion that inasmuch as the statute requires, for an order of publication, that certain facts shall appear by affidavit *to the satisfaction of the court or judge*, defects in such affidavit can only be taken advantage of on appeal, or by some other direct proceeding, and cannot be urged to impeach the judgment collaterally. The majority of the court are also of opinion that the provision of the statute requiring proof of the publication in a newspaper to be made by the "affidavit of the printer, or his foreman, or his principal clerk," is satisfied when the affidavit is made by the editor of the paper. The term "printer," in their judgment, is there used not to indicate the person who sets up the type,—he does not usually have a foreman or clerks,—it is rather used as synonymous with publisher. . . .

   If, therefore, we were confined to the rulings of the court below upon the defects in the affidavits mentioned, we should be unable to uphold its decision. But it was also contended in that court, and is insisted upon here, that the judgment in the State court against the plaintiff was void for want of personal service of process on him, or of his appearance in the action in which it was rendered and that the premises in controversy could not be subjected to the payment of the demand of a resident creditor except by a proceeding *in rem*; that is, by a direct proceeding against the property for that purpose. If these positions are sound, the ruling of the Circuit Court as to the invalidity of that judgment must be sustained, notwithstanding our dissent from the reasons upon which it was made. And that they are sound would seem to follow from two well-established principles of public law respecting the jurisdiction of an independent State over persons and property. The several States of the Union are not, it is true, in every respect independent, many of the rights and powers which originally belonged to them being now vested in the government created by the Constitution. But, except as restrained and limited by that instrument, they possess and exercise the authority of independent States, and the principles of public law to which we have referred are applicable to them. One of these principles is, that every State possesses exclusive jurisdiction and sovereignty over persons and property within its territory. As a consequence, every State has the power to determine for itself the civil *status* and capacities of its inhabitants; to prescribe the subjects upon which they may contract, the forms and solemnities with which their contracts shall be executed, the rights and obligations arising from them, and the mode in which their validity shall be determined and their obligations enforced; and also to regulate the manner and conditions upon which property situated within such territory, both personal and real, may be acquired, enjoyed, and transferred. The other principle of public law referred to follows from the one mentioned; that is, that no State can exercise direct jurisdiction and authority over persons or property without its territory. The several States are of equal dignity and authority, and the independence of one implies the exclusion of power from all others. And so it is laid down by jurists, as an elementary principle, that the laws of one State have no operation outside of its territory, except so far as is allowed by comity; and that no tribunal established by it can extend its process beyond that territory so as to subject either persons or property to its decisions. . . .

But as contracts made in one State may be enforceable only in another State, and property may be held by non-residents, the exercise of the jurisdiction which every State is admitted to possess over persons and property within its own territory will often affect persons and property without it. To any influence exerted in this way by a State affecting persons resident or property situated elsewhere, no objection can be justly taken; whilst any direct exertion of authority upon them, in an attempt to give ex-territorial operation to its laws, or to enforce an ex-territorial jurisdiction by its tribunals, would be deemed an encroachment upon the independence of the State in which the persons are domiciled or the property is situated, and be resisted as usurpation.

Thus the State, through its tribunals, may compel persons domiciled within its limits to execute, in pursuance of their contracts respecting property elsewhere situated, instruments in such form and with such solemnities as to transfer the title, so far as such formalities can be complied with; and the exercise of this jurisdiction in no manner interferes with the supreme control over the property by the State within which it is situated.

So the State, through its tribunals, may subject property situated within its limits owned by non-residents to the payment of the demand of its own citizens against them; and the exercise of this jurisdiction in no respect infringes upon the sovereignty of the State where the owners are domiciled. Every State owes protection to its own citizens; and, when non-residents deal with them, it is a legitimate and just exercise of authority to hold and appropriate any property owned by such non-residents to satisfy the claims of its citizens. It is in virtue of the State's jurisdiction over the property of the non-resident situated within its limits that its tribunals can inquire into that non-resident's obligations to its own citizens, and the inquiry can then be carried only to the extent necessary to control the disposition of the property. If the non-resident have no property in the State, there is nothing upon which the tribunals can adjudicate. . . .

. . . If, without personal service, judgments *in personam*, obtained *ex parte* against non-residents and absent parties, upon mere publication of process, which, in the great majority of cases, would never be seen by the parties interested, could be upheld and enforced, they would be the constant instruments of fraud and oppression. Judgments for all sorts of claims upon contracts and for torts, real or pretended, would be thus obtained, under which property would be seized, when the evidence of the transactions upon which they were founded, if they ever had any existence, had perished.

Substituted service by publication, or in any other authorized form, may be sufficient to inform parties of the object of proceedings taken where property is once brought under the control of the court by seizure or some equivalent act. The law assumes that property is always in the possession of its owner, in person or by agent; and it proceeds upon the theory that its seizure will inform him, not only that it is taken into the custody of the court, but that he must look to any proceedings authorized by law upon such seizure for its condemnation and sale. Such service may also be sufficient in cases where the object of the action is to reach

Subject to personal jurisdiction in the State of domicile.

and dispose of property in the State, or of some interest therein, by enforcing a contract or a lien respecting the same, or to partition it among different owners, or, when the public is a party, to condemn and appropriate it for a public purpose. In other words, such service may answer in all actions which are substantially proceedings *in rem*. But where the entire object of the action is to determine the personal rights and obligations of the defendants, that is, where the suit is merely *in personam*, constructive service in this form upon a non-resident is ineffectual for any purpose. Process from the tribunals of one State cannot run into another State, and summon parties there domiciled to leave its territory and respond to proceedings against them. Publication of process or notice within the State where the tribunal sits cannot create any greater obligation upon the non-resident to appear. Process sent to him out of the State, and process published within it, are equally unavailing in proceedings to establish his personal liability.

The want of authority of the tribunals of a State to adjudicate upon the obligations of non-residents, where they have no property within its limits, is not denied by the court below: but the position is assumed, that, where they have property within the State, it is immaterial whether the property is in the first instance brought under the control of the court by attachment or some other equivalent act, and afterwards applied by its judgment to the satisfaction of demands against its owner; or such demands be first established in a personal action, and the property of the non-resident be afterwards seized and sold on execution. But the answer to this position has already been given in the statement, that the jurisdiction of the court to inquire into and determine his obligations at all is only incidental to its jurisdiction over the property. Its jurisdiction in that respect cannot be made to depend upon facts to be ascertained after it has tried the cause and rendered the judgment. If the judgment be previously void, it will not become valid by the subsequent discovery of property of the defendant, or by his subsequent acquisition of it. The judgment, if void when rendered, will always remain void: it cannot occupy the doubtful position of being valid if property be found, and void if there be none. Even if the position assumed were confined to cases where the non-resident defendant possessed property in the State at the commencement of the action, it would still make the validity of the proceedings and judgment depend upon the question whether, before the levy of the execution, the defendant had or had not disposed of the property. If before the levy the property should be sold, then, according to this position, the judgment would not be binding. This doctrine would introduce a new element of uncertainty in judicial proceedings. The contrary is the law: the validity of every judgment depends upon the jurisdiction of the court before it is rendered, not upon what may occur subsequently. . . .

The force and effect of judgments rendered against non-residents without personal service of process upon them, or their voluntary appearance, have been the subject of frequent consideration in the courts of the United States and of the several States, as attempts have been made to enforce such judgments in States other than those in which they were rendered, under the provision of the Constitution requiring that "full faith and credit shall be given in each State to the public acts, records, and judicial proceedings of every other State" [Art. IV, § 1]; and the act of Congress providing for the mode of authenticating such acts, records, and proceedings, and declaring that, when thus authenticated, "they shall have such faith and credit given to them in every court within the United States as they have by law or usage in the courts of the State from which they are or shall or taken." In the earlier cases, it was supposed that the act gave to all judgments the same effect in other States which they had by law in the State where rendered. But this view was afterwards qualified so as to make the act applicable only when the court rendering the judgment had jurisdiction of the parties and of the subject-matter, and not to preclude an inquiry into the jurisdiction of the court in which the judgment was rendered, or the right of the State itself to exercise authority over the person or the subject-matter. . . . [T]he doctrine of this court is, that the act "was not designed to displace that principle of natural justice which requires a person to have notice of a suit before he can be conclusively bound by its result, nor those rules of public law which protect persons and property within one State from the exercise of jurisdiction over them by another." *The Lafayette Insurance Co. v. French*, 59 U.S. (18 How.) 404 (1855).

. . . In all the cases brought in the State and Federal courts, where attempts have been made under the act of Congress to give effect in one State to personal judgments rendered in another State against non-residents, without service upon them, or upon substituted service by publication, or in some other form, it has been held, without an exception, so far as we are aware, that such judgments were without any binding force, except as to property, or interests in property, within the State, to reach and affect which was the object of the action in which the judgment was rendered, and which property was brought under control of the court in connection with the process against the person. The proceeding in such cases, though in the form of a personal action, has been uniformly treated, where service was not obtained, and the party did not voluntarily appear, as effectual and binding merely as a proceeding *in rem*, and as having no operation beyond the disposition of the property, or some interest therein. And the reason assigned for this conclusion has been that which we have already stated, that the tribunals of one State have no jurisdiction over persons beyond its limits, and can inquire only into their obligations to its citizens when exercising its conceded jurisdiction over their property within its limits. . . .

. . . In several of the cases, the decision has been accompanied with the observation that a personal judgment thus recovered has no binding force without the State in which it is rendered, implying that in such State it may be valid and binding. But if the court has no jurisdiction over the person of the defendant by reason of his nonresidence, and, consequently, no authority to pass upon his personal rights and obligations; if the whole proceeding, without service upon him or his appearance, is *coram non judice* and void; if to hold a defendant bound by such a judgment is contrary to the first principles of justice,—it is difficult to see how the judgment can legitimately have any force within the State. The language used can be justified only on the ground that there was no mode of directly reviewing such judgment or impeaching its validity within the State where rendered; and that, therefore, it could be called in question only when its enforcement was elsewhere attempted. In later cases, this language is repeated with less frequency than formerly, it beginning to be considered, as it always ought to have been, that a judgment which can be treated in any State of this Union as contrary to the first principles of justice, and as an absolute nullity, because rendered without any jurisdiction of the tribunal over the party, is not entitled to any respect in the State where rendered.

Be that as it may, the courts of the United States are not required to give effect to judgments of this character when any right is claimed under them. Whilst they are not foreign tribunals in their relations to the State courts, they are tribunals of a different sovereignty, exercising a distinct and independent jurisdiction, and are bound to give to the judgments of the State courts only the same faith and credit which the courts of another State are bound to give to them.

Since the adoption of the Fourteenth Amendment to the Federal Constitution [in 1868], the validity of such judgments may be directly questioned, and their enforcement in the State resisted, on the ground that proceedings in a court of justice to determine the personal rights and obligations of parties over whom that court has no jurisdiction do not constitute due process of law. Whatever difficulty may be experienced in giving to those terms a definition which will embrace every permissible exertion of power affecting private rights, and exclude such as is forbidden, there can be no doubt of their meaning when applied to judicial proceedings. They then mean a course of legal proceedings according to those rules and principles which have been established in our systems of jurisprudence for the protection and enforcement of private rights. To give such proceedings any validity, there must be a tribunal competent by its constitution—that is, by the law of its creation—to pass upon the subject-matter of the suit; and, if that involves merely a determination of the personal liability of the defendant, he must be brought within its jurisdiction by service of process within the State, or his voluntary appearance.

Except in cases affecting the personal *status* of the plaintiff, and cases in which that mode of service may be considered to have been assented to in advance, as hereinafter mentioned, the substituted service of process by publication, allowed by the law of Oregon and by similar laws in other States, where actions are brought against non-residents, is effectual only where, in connection with process against the person for commencing the action, property in the State is brought under the control of the court, and subjected to its disposition by process adapted to that purpose, or where the judgment is sought as a means of reaching such property or affecting some interest therein; in other words, where the action is in the nature of a proceeding *in rem*. . . .

It is true that, in a strict sense, a proceeding *in rem* is one taken directly against property, and has for its object the disposition of the property, without reference to the title of individual claimants; but, in a larger and more general sense, the terms are applied to actions between parties, where the direct object is to reach and dispose of property owned by them, or of some interest therein. Such are cases commenced by attachment against the property of debtors, or instituted to partition real estate, foreclose a mortgage, or enforce a lien. So far as they affect property in the State, they are substantially proceedings *in rem* in the broader sense which we have mentioned. . . .

It follows from the views expressed that the personal judgment recovered in the State court of Oregon against the plaintiff herein, then a non-resident of the State, was without any validity, and did not authorize a sale of the property in controversy.

To prevent any misapplication of the views expressed in this opinion, it is proper to observe that we do not mean to assert, by any thing we have said, that a State may not authorize proceedings to determine the *status* of one of its citizens towards a non-resident, which would be binding within the State, though made without service of process or personal notice to the non-resident. The jurisdiction which every State possesses to determine the civil *status* and capacities of all its inhabitants involves authority to prescribe the conditions on which proceedings affecting them may be commenced and carried on within its territory. The State, for example, has absolute right to prescribe the conditions upon which the marriage relation between its own citizens shall be created, and the causes for which it may be dissolved. One of the parties guilty of acts for which, by the law of the State, a dissolution may be granted, may have removed to a State where no dissolution is permitted. The complaining party would, therefore, fail if a divorce were sought in the State of the defendant; and if application could not be made to the tribunals of the complainant's domicile in such case, and proceedings be there instituted without personal service of process or personal notice to the offending party, the injured citizen would be without redress.

Neither do we mean to assert that a State may not require a non-resident entering into a partnership or association within its limits, or making contracts enforceable there, to appoint an agent or representative in the State to receive service of process and notice in legal proceedings instituted with respect to such partnership, association, or contracts, or to designate a place where such service may be made and notice given, and provide, upon their failure, to make such appointment or to designate such place that service may be made upon a public officer designated for that purpose, or in some other prescribed way, and that judgments rendered upon such service may not be binding upon the non-residents both within and without the State. . . . Nor do we doubt that a State, on creating corporations or other institutions for pecuniary or charitable purposes, may provide a mode in which their conduct may be investigated, their obligations enforced, or their charters revoked, which shall require other than personal service upon their officers or members. . . .

In the present case, there is no feature of this kind, and, consequently, no consideration of what would be the effect of such legislation in enforcing the contract of a non-resident can arise. The question here respects only the validity of a money judgment rendered in one State, in an action upon a simple contract against the resident of another, without service of process upon him, or his appearance therein.

Judgment affirmed.

[The dissenting opinion of Mr. Justice Hunt is omitted.]

NOTES AND QUESTIONS

1. *Statutory bases for jurisdiction.*   Courts may take jurisdiction over defendants only as permitted by a statute or court rule. The Oregon Code, for example, permitted the state's courts to take jurisdiction if the defendant (i) appeared in court, (ii) was found (and served) within the state, (iii) was a resident of the state (regardless of where defendant was served), or (iv) had property in the state. On which of these grounds did the Oregon court rely in *Mitchell v. Neff*? Did Neff fit within any of the first three statutory bases for jurisdiction? As to the fourth part of the statute, what property did Neff own in Oregon in November 1865, when the suit was commenced? What property did he own there in February 1866, when a default judgment was entered against him? Under the fourth part of the statute, when did the Oregon court obtain jurisdiction over Neff?

2. In personam *versus* in rem *jurisdiction.*   If an Oregon court proceeded under any of the first three statutory bases, it acquired "*in personam*" jurisdiction over a defendant. *In personam* jurisdiction allows a court to enter a judgment ordering the defendant to pay the plaintiff a specified sum of money. Such a judgment may be enforced against any property the defendant owned or later came to own. Under the Full Faith and Credit Clause (U.S. Const. art. IV, § 1), a plaintiff may take an in personam judgment to other states and have it enforced against a defendant's property there. An *in personam* judgment is in effect an "open box" that the plaintiff may use to attach property belonging to the defendant until the full amount of the judgment has been collected.

By contrast, if an Oregon court obtained jurisdiction under the fourth part of the statute, it acquired jurisdiction "only to the extent of such property at the time the jurisdiction attached." Jurisdiction of this type is known as "*in rem.*" Unlike an *in personam* judgment, an *in rem* judgment does not order the defendant to pay the plaintiff any money. Instead, it simply awards the plaintiff the property (or a portion of the property) that was attached as the basis for jurisdiction. In contrast to an *in personam* judgment, an in rem judgment is in effect a "sealed box" that cannot be used to reach any other property belonging to the defendant.

3. *Blurring the lines.*   As *Mitchell v. Neff* reveals, Oregon allowed a plaintiff to proceed under the statute by merely alleging that the "defendant has property in this . . . state," but without forcing the plaintiff to identify that property or attach it until after a judgment had been entered. Doesn't such an approach blur the distinction between *in rem* and *in personam* jurisdiction? The judgment in *Mitchell v. Neff* was *in personam* in form, for rather than awarding the plaintiff a specified piece of property, it ordered Neff to pay Mitchell the sum of $294.98. The Oregon courts treated this judgment as an "open box" that could be enforced against any of the defendant's property, including property that Neff did not even own at the time the judgment was entered.

Oregon was not the only state that blurred the distinction between *in rem* and *in personam* jurisdiction. In *Kilborn v. Woodworth*, 5 Johns. 37 (N.Y. 1809), a Massachusetts court took jurisdiction over a New Yorker by attaching a bedstead that allegedly belonged to the defendant. After the Massachusetts court entered a default judgment for the sum of $118.40, the plaintiff sought to enforce that judgment against the defendant's property in New York. The New York court treated the judgment as *in rem* rather than *in personam* and thus held that it could not reach any property other than the bedstead that was attached in Massachusetts.

4. *Refusal to honor the Oregon judgment.*   Even if Oregon exceeded the territorial limits of her sovereignty in issuing the judgment against Neff, why wasn't the circuit court required to honor the judgment? What allowed the federal courts to second-guess the Oregon judgment's validity? The Act of Congress implementing Article IV, § 1's Full Faith and Credit Clause, 28 U.S.C. § 1738, required "every court within the United States" — including the federal courts — to give the Oregon judgment the same faith and credit it would have in the courts of Oregon. Since the Oregon courts treated the judgment as being valid and enforceable against Neff's property, why wasn't the circuit court likewise bound to do so? How did the Supreme Court construe the full faith and credit statute to justify its refusal to honor the judgment in *Mitchell*?

5. *The effect of the Fourteenth Amendment.*   In *Pennoyer*, the Supreme Court declared that a state court judgment issued without proper jurisdiction over the defendant violates the Due Process Clause of the Fourteenth Amendment. However, the Fourteenth Amendment was ratified in 1868, two years after the judgment in *Mitchell*. It did not have the retroactive effect of invalidating judgments entered prior to its adoption. As a result, the Fourteenth Amendment could not serve as the basis for finding the judgment in *Mitchell* to be invalid; instead, the Court had to rely on the rule of territoriality derived from "principles of public law." Though its discussion of the Fourteenth Amendment was dictum, did the Court in *Pennoyer* interpret the Due Process Clause as incorporating the rule of territoriality? If *Mitchell* had been filed after the Fourteenth Amendment was adopted, could Oregon's courts still have deemed the judgment to be valid, or would the state's duty to honor the U.S. Constitution now require that even her own courts treat the judgment as being invalid for lack of jurisdiction?

6. *Notice.*   To what extent was the problem in *Mitchell* the method of notice used to inform Neff of the suit? Would the result have been any different if a process server had personally delivered the summons and complaint to Neff in California, or was adequacy of notice only part of the problem? Would notice by publication in the *Pacific Christian Advocate* have sufficed if the Oregon court had acquired valid in rem jurisdiction over Neff? If so, why would notice by publication be proper in one case but not in the other?

7. *Collateral versus direct attack.*   Neff's suit against Pennoyer involved a "collateral attack" on the prior Oregon judgment. The attack was "collateral" rather than "direct" because it occurred in a separate lawsuit. A "direct attack" is one that occurs as part of—or in a continuation of—the original suit. The most common form of direct attack is an appeal to a higher court, asking that it review a ruling or the judgment of a lower court. Strict time limits apply to most forms of direct attack. Appeals, for example, must usually be filed within 20 to 60 days of entry of the lower court judgment. By contrast, there is often no time limit on bringing a collateral attack. Neff filed suit to recover possession of his land in 1874, eight

years after the judgment was entered in *Mitchell v. Neff*. Because of the potential for upsetting judgments on which people may have relied in good faith, collateral attacks are permitted only on very limited grounds. In *Pennoyer*, the Supreme Court thus held that any alleged defects in Mitchell's affidavit supporting the order for publication had to be raised "on appeal, or by some other direct proceeding, and cannot be urged to impeach the judgment collaterally." Was the same true of Neff's assertion that the Oregon court lacked jurisdiction over him?

8. *Epilogue.*   After Neff recovered possession in 1875, he sued Pennoyer for damage done to the land during Pennoyer's eight years of occupancy. *Neff v. Pennoyer*, 17 F. Cas. 1291 (C.C.D. Or. 1875) (No. 10,085). Pennoyer, who was an 1854 graduate of Harvard Law School, later served as governor of Oregon (1887-1895) and mayor of Portland (1896-1898). Though Neff disappeared from view, his attorney, John H. Mitchell, attained notoriety. In 1905, while serving his fourth term in the U.S. Senate, an Oregon federal court convicted Mitchell of land fraud. He was fined and sentenced to prison but died in 1905 before the U.S. Supreme Court could review his case. *See United States v. Mitchell*, 141 F. 666 (1905), *appeal dismissed*, 199 U.S. 616 (1905); Theodore T. Geer, Fifty Years in Oregon 471 (1916); 1 Harvey W. Scott, History of the Oregon Country 96, 104, 346-348 (1924); 3 Robert Scott & John Raimo, Biographical Directory of the Governors of the United States, 1789-1978, at 1267-1268 (1988). For more information on *Pennoyer*'s cast of characters, see Wendy C. Perdue, *Sin, Scandal, and Substantive Due Process: Personal Jurisdiction and Pennoyer Reconsidered*, 62 Wash. L. Rev. 479 (1987).

PROBLEMS

2-1. Would the Oregon court have acquired jurisdiction over Neff if he had seen a copy of the *Pacific Christian Advocate* and returned to Oregon to contest the suit? If so, what kind of jurisdiction would this have given the court?

2-2. Would the result have been different if Mitchell had sued Neff in April 1866, rather than in November 1865? If Mitchell had thus waited, what steps would the Oregon court have needed to take to obtain valid jurisdiction over Neff?

2-3. Smith sued Farley in a Minnesota state court seeking $5,000 for breach of contract. Smith is a citizen of Minnesota. Farley is a citizen of Wisconsin. At the commencement of the suit, the sheriff attached a $1,000 pig belonging to Farley that was on exhibit at the Minnesota State Fair. Farley, who did not attend the fair, was personally served with the summons and complaint at his farm in Wisconsin. Farley chose to ignore the Minnesota proceedings. The Minnesota court, after finding that Smith's claim was meritorious, entered a default judgment against Farley for $5,000 and awarded the pig to Smith. Analyze the following problems under the principles established in *Pennoyer*.

A. While Smith was on his way home from the fair, the pig somehow managed to escape from the back of his wagon. Two months later Smith learned that the pig had found its way back to Farley's farm in Wisconsin. Smith sued Farley in a Wisconsin state court, seeking return of the pig. Farley claimed that the pig still belonged to him. How should the Wisconsin court rule on the question of who is entitled to the pig?

B. In an effort to collect the remaining $4,000 owed to him by Farley, Smith brought an action in Illinois to enforce the Minnesota judgment by attaching a bank account that Farley maintains with an Illinois bank. Farley asked the court to dismiss the action on the ground that the Minnesota judgment is not entitled to full faith and credit. How should the Illinois court rule on Farley's motion to dismiss?

C. Even if the Minnesota judgment is not entitled to full faith and credit, is there any basis on which Smith can still attach Farley's bank account in Illinois?

B.   Traditional Bases of Personal Jurisdiction

The traditional bases of jurisdiction are typically (and correctly) treated as a product of the sovereignty principle described in *Pennoyer v. Neff*. Thus, consistent with *Pennoyer*, a state may exercise jurisdiction over persons or property found within its borders, but may not, in the usual case, assert judicial authority over persons or property found or located elsewhere. As you will see below, the traditional bases of jurisdiction revolve around these twin propositions of territoriality. But they can also be seen as reflecting a slightly different principle, namely, that jurisdiction should be premised on a defendant's meaningful connections with the forum state, *i.e.*, on those connections that lead to a reasonable expectation of suit there. As you read the materials on the traditional bases of jurisdiction, consider the extent to which this is the case. In doing so, you may sense that one or more of the traditional forms might not be consistent with these principles (at least under some circumstances). Which one(s)? *See* Simona Grossi, *Personal Jurisdiction: A Doctrinal Labyrinth with No Exit*, 47 AKRON L. REV. 617, 621-622 (2014).

1.   Personal Jurisdiction

a.   Domicile

As the Court in *Pennoyer* recognized, a court may exercise jurisdiction over a domiciliary of the forum state even when that person is not found or served within the territory of the forum. An individual's domicile is the state where he or she has taken up residence with the intent to remain permanently or indefinitely. People may have more than one residence, but we each have only one domicile. Moreover, we do not shed our current domicile until we acquire a new one. Thus, even if a person leaves her state of domicile vowing never to return, she retains that domicile until she settles permanently somewhere else.

In *Milliken v. Meyer*, 311 U.S. 457 (1940), for example, Colorado had to give full faith and credit to a Wyoming judgment entered against Meyer, a Wyoming domiciliary who had been living in Colorado for seven years. Despite his lengthy stay in Colorado, Meyer failed to show that he had resided there with the intent necessary to change his domicile. Wyoming therefore properly acquired personal jurisdiction over him on the basis of domicile, through service of process in Colorado. According to the Supreme Court:

> Meyer's domicile in Wyoming was a sufficient basis for that extraterritorial service. As in [the] case of the authority of the United States over its absent citizens, the authority of a state over one of its citizens is not terminated by the mere fact of his absence from the state. . . . The responsibilities of that citizenship arise out of the relationship to the state which domicile creates. . . . The attendant duties, like the rights and privileges incident to domicile, are not dependent on continuous presence in the state. One such incident of domicile is amenability to suit within the state even during sojourns without the state. . . .

Id. at 463-464.

The principle that a state may exercise personal jurisdiction over its absent domiciliaries stems from the sovereign's inherent authority over its citizens or subjects. In *Blackmer v. United States*, 284 U.S. 421 (1932), the Supreme Court invoked this principle to uphold the federal government's exercise of personal jurisdiction over a U.S. citizen living in Paris, France. As the Court explained,

> [T]he United States possesses the power inherent in sovereignty to require the return to this country of a citizen, resident elsewhere, whenever the public interest requires it, and to penalize him in case of refusal. What in England was the prerogative of the sovereign in this respect, pertains under our constitutional system to the national authority which may be exercised by the Congress by virtue of the legislative power to prescribe the duties of the citizens of the United States. It is also beyond controversy that one of the duties which the citizen owes to his government is to support the administration of justice by attending its courts and giving his testimony whenever he is properly summoned.

Id. at 437-438. The Court was careful to distinguish cases like *Pennoyer* in which the absentee is not one of the state's own citizens and where, therefore, "obligations inherent in allegiance are not involved." *Id.* at 438 n.5.

Most states today authorize their courts to exercise personal jurisdiction over persons who are domiciled in the state, regardless of where service of process occurs. *See, e.g.*, N.C. GEN. STAT. § 1-75.4(1)(b); WIS. STAT. ANN. § 801.05(1)(b).

b.   *Voluntary Appearance*

If a defendant voluntarily appears in court without making a timely objection to the court's jurisdiction, the defendant will be deemed to have assented to the court's jurisdiction. For example, if the defendant files an answer to the complaint without challenging the court's jurisdiction, any potential objection to jurisdiction is waived. This traditional basis for the exercise of jurisdiction is consistent with the rule of territoriality since the defendant, either personally or by attorney, has appeared in court within the forum state.

A second form of voluntary appearance is contractual. For example, a contract may include a "forum selection clause" by which the parties agree that any lawsuits between them that arise from the contract may or must be brought in a particular sovereignty's courts. *See, e.g., Interfund Corp. v. O'Byrne,* 462 N.W.2d 86 (Minn. Ct. App. 1990) (holding that Minnesota court had jurisdiction over Washington defendant based on contract provision specifying Minnesota as a proper forum for suits arising under the contract). Through such agreements, the parties in effect agree to appear voluntarily in the designated forum's courts, waiving any objection they might otherwise have had to that court's jurisdiction.

The principle of voluntary appearance is followed in all states. In addition, courts routinely enforce forum selection clauses under principles of contract law and in the absence of policy considerations to the contrary. See Chapter V, *infra,* at page 439.

c.   Consent to Service on an Agent

In *Pennoyer,* the Court noted that a court could acquire personal jurisdiction over a nonresident defendant by service on an in-state agent or representative appointed by that defendant for the purpose of receiving service of process in legal proceedings. By appointing an agent for the receipt of service of process, a defendant consents in advance to being sued in the state's courts. Such consent is typically limited to lawsuits that relate to a defendant's business dealings or activities in the forum state. Since the appointed agent is located in the forum state, service on that agent satisfies *Pennoyer's* rule of territoriality.

For example, in *Kane v. New Jersey,* 242 U.S. 160 (1916), the Supreme Court upheld a New Jersey nonresident-motorist statute that provided that before nonresident drivers could use the state's highways, they had to execute a formal appointment naming the Secretary of State as their agent to receive service of process "in any action or legal proceeding caused by the operation of his registered motor vehicle within this state. . . ." *Id.* at 161. And in *National Equipment Rental, Ltd. v. Szukhent,* 375 U.S. 311 (1964), the Court held that a New York court could assert personal jurisdiction over two Michigan farmers who had signed an equipment lease in Michigan designating "Florence Weinberg, 47-21 Forty-first Street, Long Island City, N.Y., as agent for the purpose of accepting service of any process within the State of New York." *Id.* at 313.

d.   Transient or Tag Jurisdiction

Under the "transient rule" of personal jurisdiction, defendants can be tagged with process no matter how fleeting their presence in the state, even as to lawsuits that bear no relationship to the state. In *Peabody v. Hamilton*, 106 Mass. 217 (1870), for example, a British plaintiff sued a New York defendant in Massachusetts on a claim having no apparent connection to Massachusetts. The defendant was served while aboard a British mail steamer that had docked briefly in Boston Harbor, en route from Nova Scotia to New York. The Massachusetts Supreme Court rejected the defendant's contention that he "was a mere bird of passage from Nova Scotia to New York," *id.* at 218, and therefore not subject to the state's jurisdiction. Instead, said the court, "When the party is in the state, however transiently, and the summons is actually served upon him there, the jurisdiction of the court is complete, as to the person of the defendant." *Id.* at 220.

Today, virtually all states authorize the assertion of personal jurisdiction over a defendant who is served while present in the state. *See, e.g.*, N.C. Gen. Stat. §§ 1-75.4(1)(a); Wis. Stat. Ann. § 801.05(1)(a).

2.   *In Rem* and *Quasi in Rem* Jurisdiction

In rem jurisdiction may be based on the attachment of either tangible or intangible property belonging to the defendant. Tangible property embraces things like real estate, jewelry, vehicles, and farm animals. Intangible property includes items such as shares of corporate stock, bonds, bank accounts, unpaid wages, and other debts or obligations owed to the defendant by someone in the forum state.

There are two types of *in rem* jurisdiction—"true *in rem*" (or "*in rem*") and "*quasi in rem*." A true *in rem* action is one that establishes rights or interests in property as "against all the world." It binds everyone, wherever they reside, whether or not they are parties to the suit, even if their identity or interest in the property is unknown to the court. We will see later that due process may require individualized notice in true *in rem* proceedings to those whose interest in the property is known or readily ascertainable. However, the hallmark of a true *in rem* judgment is that it also binds those who never received notice and were never made parties to the suit. Only a few types of suits qualify as true *in rem*. These include actions to register or quiet title, to condemn or confiscate property, libels in admiralty, probate actions, and bankruptcy proceedings. In these limited situations, the need for finality and certainty has justified use of true *in rem* proceedings even though they may offer less protection to interested claimants than do *quasi in rem* and *in personam* actions. In *Tilt v. Kelsey*, 207 U.S. 43, 56 (1907), the Supreme Court explained the necessity for true in rem jurisdiction, in the context of distributing decedents' estates:

> [S]omewhere the power must exist to decide finally as against the world all questions which arise in the settlement of the succession. Mistakes may occur and sometimes do occur, but it is better that they should be endured than that, in a vain search for infallibility, questions shall remain open indefinitely. . . . "The world must move on, and those who claim an interest in persons and things must be charged with knowledge of their status and condition, and of the vicissitudes to which they are subject. This is the foundation of all judicial proceedings *in rem*." It is therefore

within the power of the sovereign to give to its courts the authority . . . to determine finally as against the world all questions which arise therein.

However, most suits based on the attachment of property are *quasi in rem*. Unlike true *in rem* proceedings, *quasi in rem* actions only affect the interests of particular persons in the attached property—namely, those who have been made parties to the suit. In *Freeman v. Alderson*, 119 U.S. 185 (1886), Justice Field thus observed that there is

> a large class of cases which are not strictly actions *in rem*, but are frequently spoken of as actions *quasi in rem*, because, though brought against persons, they only seek to subject certain property of those persons to the discharge of the claims asserted. . . . But they differ, among other things, from actions which are strictly *in rem*, in that the interest of the defendant is alone sought to be affected, that citation to him is required, and that judgment therein is only conclusive between the parties.

Id. at 187-188. Examples of *quasi in rem* actions include suits to foreclose on a mortgage or lien, suits to repossess goods, and suits for money damages instituted by attaching a defendant's house, farm, car, bank account, or other real or personal property. While courts often use the term *"in rem"* broadly to embrace both true *in rem* and *quasi in rem* actions, you should be aware of the difference between the two.

An *in rem* judgment, whether true *in rem* or *quasi in rem*, can only determine interests in the specific property that was attached as the basis for jurisdiction. In this sense an *in rem* judgment is a "closed box," for unlike an in personam judgment, it cannot be used to collect or reach any other property. Thus, if a plaintiff obtains a *quasi in rem* judgment against a defendant and the property attached was worth less than the amount of the plaintiff's claim, in order to collect the balance of her claim, the plaintiff will have to bring a new lawsuit. In that suit, the plaintiff will have to reprove her case and cannot rely on her victory in the *quasi in rem* suit. On the other hand, since a *quasi in rem* judgment has claim preclusive effect only as to the property attached as the basis for jurisdiction, if the plaintiff had lost the first *quasi in rem* suit, she could still sue again on the same claim— either *in personam* or *quasi in rem*—as long as she does not seek to attach the same property that was involved in the first suit.

Harris v. Balk

198 U.S. 215 (1905)

The plaintiff in error brings the case here in order to review the judgment of the Supreme Court of North Carolina, affirming a judgment of a lower court against him for $180, with interest, as stated therein. . . .

The facts are as follows: The plaintiff in error, Harris, was a resident of North Carolina at the time of the commencement of this action in 1896, and prior to that time was indebted to the defendant in error, Balk, also a resident of North Carolina, in the sum of $180, for money borrowed from Balk by Harris during the year 1896. . . . During the year above mentioned one Jacob Epstein, a resident of Baltimore, in the State of Maryland, asserted that Balk was indebted to him in the sum of over $300. In August, 1896, Harris visited Baltimore for the purpose of purchasing merchandise, and while he was in that city temporarily on August 6, 1896, Epstein [sued Balk and] caused to be issued out of a proper court in Baltimore a foreign or non-resident writ of attachment against Balk, attaching the debt due Balk from Harris, which writ the sheriff at Baltimore laid in the hands of Harris, with a summons to appear in the court at a day named. With that attachment, a writ of summons and a short declaration against Balk . . . were also delivered to the sheriff and by him set up at the court house door, as required by the law of Maryland. Before the return day of the attachment writ Harris left Baltimore and returned to his home in North Carolina. He did not contest the garnishee process, which was issued to garnish the debt which Harris owed Balk. After his return Harris made an affidavit on August 11, 1896, that he owed Balk $180, and stated that the amount had been attached by Epstein of Baltimore, and by his counsel in the Maryland proceeding Harris consented therein to an order of condemnation against him as such garnishee for $180, the amount of his debt to Balk. Judgment was thereafter entered against the garnishee [Harris], and in favor of the plaintiff, Epstein, for $180. After the entry of the garnishee judgment, . . . Harris paid the amount of the judgment. . . . On August 11, 1896, Balk commenced an action against Harris before a justice of the peace in North Carolina, to recover the $180 which he averred Harris owed him. The plaintiff in error, by way of answer to the suit, pleaded in bar the recovery of the Maryland judgment and his payment thereof, and contended that it was conclusive against the defendant in error in this action, because that judgment was a valid judgment in Maryland, and was therefore entitled to full faith and credit in the courts of North Carolina. This contention was not allowed by the trial court, and judgment was accordingly entered against Harris for the amount of his indebtedness to Balk, and that judgment was affirmed by the Supreme Court of North Carolina. The ground of such judgment was that the Maryland court obtained no jurisdiction to attach or garnish the debt due from Harris to Balk, because Harris was but temporarily in the State, and the *situs* of the debt was in North Carolina. . . .

MR. JUSTICE PECKHAM, after making the foregoing statement, delivered the opinion of the court.

The state court of North Carolina has refused to give any effect in this action to the Maryland judgment. . . . If the Maryland court had jurisdiction to award it, the judgment is valid and entitled to the same full faith and credit in North Carolina that it has in Maryland as a valid domestic judgment.

The defendant in error contends that the Maryland court obtained no jurisdiction to award the judgment of condemnation, because the garnishee, although at the time in the State of Maryland, and personally served with process therein, was a non-resident of that State, only casually or temporarily within its boundaries; that the *situs* of the debt due from Harris, the garnishee, to the defendant in error herein was in North Carolina, and did not accompany Harris to Maryland; that, consequently, Harris, though within the State of Maryland, had not possession of any property of Balk, and the Maryland state court therefore obtained no jurisdiction over any property of Balk in the attachment proceedings, and the consent of Harris to the entry of the judgment was immaterial. The plaintiff in error, on the contrary, insists that, though the garnishee were but temporarily in Maryland, . . . the judgment, condemning the debt from Harris to Balk, was a valid judgment, provided Balk could himself have sued Harris for the debt in Maryland. This, it is asserted, he could have done, and the judgment was therefore entitled to full faith and credit in the courts of North Carolina. . . .

. . . We do not see how the question of jurisdiction *vel non* can properly be made to depend upon the so-called original *situs* of the debt, or upon the character of the stay of the garnishee, whether temporary or permanent, in the State where the attachment is issued. Power over the person of the garnishee confers jurisdiction on the courts of the State where the writ issues. If, while temporarily there, his creditor might sue him there and recover the debt, then he is liable to process of garnishment, no matter where the *situs* of the debt was originally. We do not see the materiality of the expression "*situs* of the debt," when used in connection with attachment proceedings. If by *situs* is meant the place of the creation of the debt, that fact is immaterial. If it be meant that the obligation to pay the debt can only be enforced at the *situs* thus fixed, we think it plainly untrue. The obligation of the debtor to pay his debt clings to and accompanies him wherever he goes. He is as much bound to pay his debt in a foreign State when therein sued upon his obligation by his creditor, as he was in the State where the debt was contracted. . . . It would be no defense to such suit for the debtor to plead that he was only in the foreign State casually or temporarily. . . . It is nothing but the obligation to pay which is garnished or attached. This obligation can be enforced by the courts of the foreign State after personal service of process therein, just as well as by the courts of the domicil of the debtor. If the debtor leave the foreign State without appearing, a judgment by default may be entered, upon which execution may issue, or the judgment may be sued upon in any other State where the debtor might be found. . . .

There can be no doubt that Balk, as a citizen of the State of North Carolina, had the right to sue Harris in Maryland to recover the debt which Harris owed him. Being a citizen of North Carolina, he was entitled to all the privileges and immunities of citizens of the several States, one of which is the right to institute actions in the courts of another State. . . .

It thus appears that Balk could have sued Harris in Maryland to recover his debt, notwithstanding the temporary character of Harris' stay there. . . .

It seems to us, therefore, that the judgment against Harris in Maryland, condemning the $180 which he owed to Balk, was a valid judgment, because the court had jurisdiction over the garnishee by personal service of process within the State of Maryland.

It ought to be and it is the object of courts to prevent the payment of any debt twice over. Thus, if Harris, owing a debt to Balk, paid it under a valid judgment against him, to Epstein, he certainly ought not to be compelled to pay it a second time, but should have the right to plead his payment under the Maryland judgment. . . .

The judgment of the Supreme Court of North Carolina must be reversed and the cause remanded for further proceedings not inconsistent with the opinion of this court.

Reversed.

Mr. Justice Harlan and Mr. Justice Day dissented.

NOTES AND QUESTIONS

1. Jurisdiction over Balk.   In the Maryland action, Epstein was the plaintiff and Balk was the defendant. What type of jurisdiction did the Maryland court acquire over Balk? On what theory did the Supreme Court conclude that Balk had intangible property in Maryland that was subject to attachment there? Was the case any different than if Balk had a $180 bank account with a Baltimore bank? Could Maryland likewise have obtained jurisdiction over Balk if his prized pig named "Harris," worth $180, had wandered into Maryland and was seized there? Quite apart from the presence and attachment of Balk's property in Maryland, did he have meaningful connections with the State of Maryland such that he could have anticipated being sued there under the circumstances presented? Is your answer to that question dependent on Harris being "tagged" while in the forum state?

2. Jurisdiction over Harris.   Harris was a so-called garnishee, *i.e.*, someone like a caretaker, an employer, or a bank who holds tangible or intangible property belonging to the defendant. Through the process of garnishment, such property is brought under the court's control and awarded to the plaintiff if she wins the suit. Did the Maryland court obtain jurisdiction over Harris? Was a judgment entered against him? If Harris had not paid Epstein the $180 that he owed to Balk, what steps could Epstein have taken against Harris?

3. Notice to Balk.   Even if a court has a valid basis for obtaining jurisdiction over a defendant, the Due Process Clause also requires that the defendant be given adequate notice and an opportunity to defend the action. Balk was not notified of the Maryland suit until shortly after the default judgment was entered against him. In an omitted portion of its opinion, the Court suggested that the lack of prior notice to Balk might have been fatal were it not for a Maryland statute that gave him a year and a day to appear in the Maryland court and challenge the judgment by showing that Epstein's claim against him was without merit. We will explore the question of notice in Chapter III, *infra.*

4. Epstein's next moves.   In the Maryland suit, Epstein recovered only $180 of the $344 Balk owed him. How might he recover the remaining $164? What if before ruling in Epstein's favor, the Maryland court had included a finding that Balk owed Epstein $344; could Epstein take this Maryland judgment to North Carolina and use it as the basis for attaching Balk's property there? If so, would this be giving the Maryland judgment more than quasi in rem effect?

Suppose instead that to recover the remaining $164 on his claim, Epstein filed an *in personam* action against Balk in North Carolina. Balk appears and denies that he owed Epstein anything. If the court rules for Balk, finding that Epstein's claim is without merit, may it order Epstein to refund the $180 he collected from Balk in the Maryland suit? While the Maryland court had only *quasi in rem* jurisdiction over Balk, did this give it the authority to dispose of the $180 debt? If so, can a North Carolina court undo that judgment by ordering Epstein to return that property? What kind of an attack would this represent on the Maryland judgment? Is a *quasi in rem* judgment thus entitled to full faith and credit as to the specific property that was attached and disposed of in the action?

PROBLEM

2-4. While vacationing in Italy last summer, Alex, who lives in Missouri, was involved in an automobile accident with Paulo, an Italian citizen who lives in Rome. In the accident, Alex suffered $250,000 in personal injuries. Upon returning to Missouri, Alex hired an investigator to determine whether Paulo, who exports wine to the United States, has any assets in this country. The investigator found that Paulo has bank accounts in California, Illinois, Oregon, and Massachusetts, with balances ranging between $25,000 and $50,000. The investigator also learned that Vintage Spirits, Inc., a New York company, buys $100,000 of wine from Paulo each year. Under the principles of *Pennoyer* and *Balk*, what actions might Alex take to collect from Paulo? What can Paulo do to prevent Alex from suing him repeatedly on the same personal injury claim?

3.   The Advent of Fictions

The traditional forms of jurisdiction, each in some way premised on sovereignty and territoriality, were both mechanical and limited. They also became increasingly outmoded as modern technology, including emerging forms of transportation, made interstate commerce more and more pervasive. As a consequence, courts began to devise ways to circumvent the strictures of the traditional forms. This process of circumvention began by the creation of various fictions that would allow the exercise of jurisdiction in a manner that ostensibly complied with the traditional forms but which, in fact, altered those forms.

One such fiction was "*implied consent.*" The Court's decision in *Hess v. Pawloski*, 274 U.S. 352 (1927), provides an apt example. There, a Massachusetts nonresident-motorist statute provided that "operation by a non-resident of a motor vehicle" on a public highway in the state was "equivalent to" appointing the state's registrar of motor vehicles as the driver's agent to receive service of process "in any action or proceeding against him, growing out of any accident or collision in which said non-resident may be involved while" driving in the state. *Id.* at 354. Massachusetts invoked the statute to take personal jurisdiction over a Pennsylvania

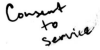

citizen who was involved in an auto accident while driving in the state. The Court upheld the statute even though Massachusetts did not require nonresident motorists to expressly appoint an agent to receive process there.

> Motor vehicles are dangerous machines. . . . The State's power to regulate the use of its highways extends to their use by non-residents as well as by residents. And, in advance of the operation of a motor vehicle on its highway by a non-resident, the State may require him to appoint one of its officials as his agent on whom process may be served in proceedings growing out of such use . . . . The difference between the formal and implied appointment is not substantial so far as concerns the application of the due process clause of the Fourteenth Amendment.

Id. at 356-357. In this way, the fiction of implied consent was used to align the exercise of personal jurisdiction over the nonresident defendant with the traditional forms of jurisdiction, specifically, consent to service on an in-state agent.

The fiction-based approach was also used to justify the exercise of jurisdiction over out-of-state corporations. A corporation is an artificial entity that is created by the law of some state or country. While a corporation may have officers, employees, agents, or property in various locations, the corporation itself exists only on paper and is not literally present anywhere. It was relatively simple for a state to assert jurisdiction over a "domestic" corporation, *i.e.*, one created under its own laws. As the Court noted in *Pennoyer*, "[A] State, on creating corporations, . . . may provide a mode in which their conduct may be investigated, their obligations enforced, or their charters revoked, which shall require other than personal service upon their officers or members." *Pennoyer*, 95 U.S. at 735. States have routinely required domestic corporations to designate a person or entity in the state as their agent to receive service of process and to file that designation with the Secretary of State. *See, e.g.,* CAL. CORP. CODE § 1502(b). Consent to service on a corporate agent within the state operated in the same manner as a natural person's express consent to service on an agent. Even without such consent, states could justify taking jurisdiction over a domestic corporation on the theory that its legal domicile was in the state of its creation. As the Court said in *Bank of Augusta v. Earle*, 38 U.S. (13 Pet.) 519 (1839), "[A] corporation can have no legal existence out of the boundaries of the sovereignty by which it is created. . . . It must dwell in the place of its creation, and cannot migrate to another sovereignty." *Id.* at 588.

It was more difficult to justify taking jurisdiction over "foreign" corporations, *i.e.*, those created under the laws of some other state or country. While some foreign corporations may have expressly consented to service on an agent in the forum (*see, e.g.,* CAL. CORP. CODE § 2105(a)(5)), the Commerce Clause, U.S. Const. art. I., § 8, cl. 3, prohibited states from extracting such consent as a condition for engaging in interstate commerce there. *International Textbook Co. v. Pigg*, 217 U.S. 91 (1910). In the absence of express consent, unless a foreign corporation voluntarily appeared in court, the only other traditional basis for jurisdiction literally applicable to it was *in rem* or *quasi in rem* jurisdiction based on attachment of the corporation's property in the forum state. Such "foreign attachment" was unavailable if the out-of-state corporation had no property in the forum state and was of only limited use if plaintiff's claim exceeded the value of any corporate property located there.

To rectify these shortcomings, courts began indulging in the fiction that a foreign corporation had "consented" to jurisdiction or was "present" in a state if its activities there were deemed sufficient to warrant exercising personal jurisdiction. Yet since the corporation did not actually consent to service and was not really present there, these approaches involved stretching the traditional bases of jurisdiction to cover situations not literally falling within their terms.

In employing the fictions of "consent" or "presence," courts asked whether the foreign corporation was "doing business" in the state. "Doing business" was a term of art that depended on the nature and extent of activity conducted by the corporation's agents and employees in the state. If a corporation was found to be "doing business" in a state, it was subject to personal jurisdiction there. *See, e.g., Philadelphia & Reading Ry. v. McKibbin*, 243 U.S. 264, 265 (1917). Courts often used quantitative or mechanical formulas to decide whether a foreign corporation was "doing business" in the state. Thus, while the mere solicitation of business did not suffice, *Green v. Chicago, Burlington & Quincy Ry.*, 205 U.S. 530 (1907), solicitation *plus* some other activity was enough to find "doing business." *Reynolds v. Missouri, K. & T. Ry.*, 113 N.E. 413 (Mass. 1916). Under another formula, "doing business" could be established by showing that a foreign corporation had engaged in a "continuous course of business" in the state. *International Harvester Co. v. Kentucky*, 234 U.S. 579, 585-586 (1914). *See* Note, *Developments in the Law—State Court Jurisdiction*, 73 HARV. L. REV. 911, 919-923 (1960).

These approaches obviously permitted courts to take jurisdiction over out-of-state corporations even though none of the traditional bases for jurisdiction was satisfied. To preserve the appearance that they were adhering to *Pennoyer* and its rule of territoriality, courts often stated their conclusions in terms of "consent" or "presence." Yet the truth was that courts were exercising jurisdiction over foreign corporations based simply on an analysis of the corporations' activities in the forum state. In 1930, Judge Learned Hand urged courts to confront this reality and employ a "practical test." In his view, the "controlling consideration" in deciding whether a state could take jurisdiction over a foreign corporation should be "whether the extent and continuity of what it has done in the state in question makes it reasonable to bring it before one of its courts." *Hutchinson v. Chase & Gilbert, Inc.*, 45 F.2d 139, 141 (2d Cir. 1930). Fifteen years later in *International Shoe Co. v. Washington*, 326 U.S. 310 (1945), the Supreme Court effectively adopted Hand's position and in so doing obliterated the need to employ fictions as a justification for the exercise of personal jurisdiction.

C.   The Modern Law of Jurisdiction

The modern law of jurisdiction, which employs a less formal and more pragmatic approach to jurisdiction, is traceable to the foundational opinion in

International Shoe Co. v. Washington, our next principal case. But the modern approach does not wholly supplant the traditional forms of jurisdiction. Rather, it provides a means of establishing jurisdiction *in addition* to those forms (with the exception of attaching property found within the state, which will no longer automatically suffice as a basis for obtaining jurisdiction). *See* part D, *infra.* Thus it remains sufficient for purposes of jurisdiction that a person is a domiciliary or citizen of the forum state; voluntarily appears or agrees to appear before a court of the forum state; expressly consents to service on an agent in the forum state; or is found and served while voluntarily present in the forum state. Yet the modern approach and the traditional approaches share two things in common: first, concerns pertaining to sovereignty and the legitimate scope of state power; and second, the express or implicit requirement of meaningful connections with the forum state—*i.e.,* connections that create a reasonable expectation of suit in the forum state.

1. *International Shoe*—Jurisdiction Beyond Fictions and Tradition

International Shoe Co. v. Washington
326 U.S. 310 (1945)

Appeal from the Supreme Court of the State of Washington.

MR. CHIEF JUSTICE STONE delivered the opinion of the Court.

The questions for decision are (1) whether, within the limitations of the due process clause of the Fourteenth Amendment, appellant, a Delaware corporation, has by its activities in the State of Washington rendered itself amenable to proceedings in the courts of that state to recover unpaid contributions to the state unemployment compensation fund exacted by state statutes, and (2) whether the state can exact those contributions consistently with the due process clause of the Fourteenth Amendment.

The statutes in question set up a comprehensive scheme of unemployment compensation, the costs of which are defrayed by contributions required to be made by employers to a state unemployment compensation fund. The contributions are a specified percentage of the wages payable annually by each employer for his employees' services in the state. The assessment and collection of the contributions and the fund are administered by appellees. [A Washington statute] authorizes appellee Commissioner to issue an order and notice of assessment of delinquent contributions upon prescribed personal service of the notice upon the employer if found within the state, or, if not so found, by mailing the notice to the employer by registered mail at his last known address. . . .

In this case notice of assessment for the years in question was personally served upon a sales solicitor employed by appellant in the State of Washington, and a copy of the notice was mailed by registered mail to appellant at its address in St. Louis, Missouri. Appellant appeared specially before the office of unemployment and moved to set aside the order and notice of assessment on the ground that the service upon appellant's salesman was not proper service upon appellant; that appellant was not a corporation of the State of Washington and was not doing business within the state; that it had no agent within the state upon whom service could be made; and that appellant is not an employer and does not furnish employment within the meaning of the statute.

The motion was heard on evidence and a stipulation of facts by the appeal tribunal which denied the motion and ruled that appellee Commissioner was entitled to recover the unpaid contributions. That action was affirmed by the Commissioner; both the Superior Court and the Supreme Court affirmed. . . . The cause comes here on appeal, . . . appellant assigning as error that the challenged statutes as applied infringe the due process clause of the Fourteenth Amendment . . . .

The facts . . . are not in dispute. Appellant is a Delaware corporation, having its principal place of business in St. Louis, Missouri, and is engaged in the manufacture and sale of shoes and other footwear. It maintains places of business in several states, other than Washington, at which its manufacturing is carried on and from which its merchandise is distributed interstate through several sales units or branches located outside the State of Washington.

Appellant has no office in Washington and makes no contracts either for sale or purchase of merchandise there. It maintains no stock of merchandise in that state and makes there no deliveries of goods in intrastate commerce. During the years from 1937 to 1940, now in question, appellant employed eleven to thirteen salesmen under direct supervision and control of sales managers located in St. Louis. These salesmen resided in Washington; their principal activities were confined to that state; and they were compensated by commissions based upon the amount of their sales. The commissions for each year totaled more than $31,000. Appellant supplies its salesmen with a line of samples, each consisting of one shoe of a pair, which they display to prospective purchasers. On occasion they rent permanent sample rooms, for exhibiting samples, in business buildings, or rent rooms in hotels or business buildings temporarily for that purpose. The cost of such rentals is reimbursed by appellant.

The authority of the salesmen is limited to exhibiting their samples and soliciting orders from prospective buyers, at prices and on terms fixed by appellant. The salesmen transmit the orders to appellant's office in St. Louis for acceptance or rejection, and when accepted the merchandise for filling the orders is shipped f.o.b. from points outside Washington to the purchasers within the state. All the merchandise shipped into Washington is invoiced at the place of shipment from which collections are made. No salesman has authority to enter into contracts or to make collections.

The Supreme Court of Washington was of opinion that the regular and systematic solicitation of orders in the state by appellant's salesmen, resulting in a continuous flow of appellant's product into the state, was sufficient to constitute doing business in the state so as to make appellant amenable to suit in its courts. But it was also of opinion that there were sufficient additional activities shown to bring the case within the rule frequently stated, that solicitation within a state by the agents of a foreign corporation plus some additional activities there are sufficient to render the corporation amenable to suit brought in the courts of the state to enforce an obligation arising out of its activities there. *International Harvester Co. v. Kentucky.* . . . The court found such additional activities in the salesmen's display of samples sometimes in permanent display rooms, and the salesmen's residence within the state, continued over a period of years, all resulting in a substantial volume of merchandise regularly shipped by appellant to purchasers within the state . . . .

Appellant . . . insists that its activities within the state were not sufficient to manifest its "presence" there and that in its absence the state courts were without jurisdiction, that consequently it was a denial of due process for the state to subject appellant to suit. It refers to those cases in which it was said that the mere solicitation of orders for the purchase of goods within a state, to be accepted without the state and filled by shipment of the purchased goods interstate, does not render the corporation seller amenable to suit within the state. *See Green v. Chicago, Burlington & Quincy R. Co.* And appellant further argues that since it was not present within the state, it is a denial of due process to subject it to taxation or other money exaction. It thus denies the power of the state to lay the tax or to subject appellant to a suit for its collection.

Historically the jurisdiction of courts to render judgment *in personam* is grounded on their de facto power over the defendant's person. Hence his presence within the territorial jurisdiction of a court was prerequisite to its rendition of a judgment personally binding him. *Pennoyer v. Neff.* But now that the *capias ad respondendum* has given way to personal service of summons or other form of notice, due process requires only that in order to subject a defendant to a judgment *in personam,* if he be not present within the territory of the forum, he have certain minimum contacts with it such that the maintenance of the suit does not offend "traditional notions of fair play and substantial justice." *Milliken v. Meyer,* 311 U.S. 457, 463 (1940).

Since the corporate personality is a fiction, although a fiction intended to be acted upon as though it were a fact, it is clear that unlike an individual its "presence" without, as well as within, the state of its origin can be manifested only by activities carried on in its behalf by those who are authorized to act for it. To say that the corporation is so far "present" there as to satisfy due process requirements, for purposes of taxation or the maintenance of suits against it in the courts of the state, is to beg the question to be decided. For the terms "present" or "presence" are used merely to symbolize those activities of the corporation's agent within the state which courts will deem to be sufficient to satisfy the demands of due process. L. Hand, J., in *Hutchinson v. Chase & Gilbert.* Those demands may be met by such contacts of the corporation with the state of the forum as make it reasonable, in the context of our federal system of government, to require the corporation to defend the particular suit which is brought there. An "estimate of the inconveniences" which would result to the corporation from a trial away from its "home" or principal place of business is relevant in this connection.

"Presence" in the state in this sense has never been doubted when the activities of the corporation there have not only been continuous and systematic, but also give rise to the liabilities sued on, even though no consent to be sued or authorization to an agent to accept service of process has been given. Conversely it has been generally recognized that the casual presence of the corporate agent or even his conduct of single or isolated items of activities in a state in the corporation's behalf are not enough to subject it to suit on causes of action unconnected with the activities there. To require the corporation in such circumstances to defend the suit away from its home or other jurisdiction where it carries on more substantial activities has been thought to lay too great and unreasonable a burden on the corporation to comport with due process.

While it has been held, in cases on which appellant relies, that continuous activity of some sorts within a state is not enough to support the demand that the corporation be amenable to suits unrelated to that activity, . . . there have been instances in which the continuous corporate operations within a state were thought so substantial and of such a nature as to justify suit against it on causes of action arising from dealings entirely distinct from those activities.

Finally, although the commission of some single or occasional acts of the corporate agent in a state sufficient to impose an obligation or liability on the corporation has not been thought to confer upon the state authority to enforce it, other such acts, because of their nature and quality and the circumstances of their commission, may be deemed sufficient to render the corporation liable to suit. Cf. *Kane v. New Jersey, Hess v. Pawloski.* True, some of the decisions holding the corporation amenable to suit have been supported by resort to the legal fiction that it has given its consent to service and suit, consent being implied from its presence in the state through the acts of its authorized agents. But more realistically it may be said that those authorized acts were of such a nature as to justify the fiction.

It is evident that the criteria by which we mark the boundary line between those activities which justify the subjection of a corporation to suit, and those which do not, cannot be simply mechanical or quantitative. The test is not merely, as has sometimes been suggested, whether the activity, which the corporation has seen fit to procure through its agents in another state, is a little more or a little less. Whether due process is satisfied must depend rather upon the quality and nature of the activity in relation to the fair and orderly administration of the laws which it was the purpose of the due process clause to insure. That clause does not contemplate that a state may make binding a judgment *in personam* against an individual or corporate defendant with which the state has no contacts, ties, or relations.

But to the extent that a corporation exercises the privilege of conducting activities within a state, it enjoys the benefits and protection of the laws of that state. The exercise of that privilege may give rise to obligations; and, so far as those obligations arise out of or are connected with the activities within the state, a procedure which requires the corporation to respond to a suit brought to enforce them can, in most instances, hardly be said to be undue.

Applying these standards, the activities carried on in behalf of appellant in the State of Washington were neither irregular nor casual. They were systematic and continuous throughout the years in question. They resulted in a large volume of interstate business, in the course of which appellant received the benefits and protection of the laws of the state, including the right to resort to the courts for the enforcement of its rights. The obligation which is here sued upon arose out of those very activities. It is evident that these operations establish sufficient contacts or ties with the state of the forum to make it reasonable and just, according to our traditional conception of fair play and substantial justice, to permit the state to enforce the obligations which appellant has incurred there. Hence we cannot say that the maintenance of the present suit in the State of Washington involves an unreasonable or undue procedure.

We are likewise unable to conclude that the service of the process within the state upon an agent whose activities establish appellant's "presence" there was not sufficient notice of the suit, or that the suit was so unrelated to those activities as to make the agent an inappropriate vehicle for communicating the notice. It is enough that appellant has established such contacts with the state that the particular form of substituted service adopted there gives reasonable assurance that the notice will be actual. Nor can we say that the mailing of the notice of suit to appellant by registered mail at its home office was not reasonably calculated to apprise appellant of the suit. . . .

Appellant having rendered itself amenable to suit upon obligations arising out of the activities of its salesmen in Washington, the state may maintain the present suit *in personam* to collect the tax laid upon the exercise of the privilege of employing appellant's salesmen within the state. For Washington has made one of those activities, which taken together establish appellant's "presence" there for purposes of suit, the taxable event by which the state brings appellant within the reach of its taxing power. The state thus has constitutional power to lay the tax and to subject appellant to a suit to recover it. The activities which establish its "presence" subject it alike to taxation by the state and to suit to recover the tax.

Affirmed.

MR. JUSTICE JACKSON took no part in the consideration or decision of this case.

MR. JUSTICE BLACK delivered the following opinion.

Congress, pursuant to its constitutional power to regulate commerce, has expressly provided that a State shall not be prohibited from levying the kind of unemployment compensation tax here challenged. We have twice decided that this Congressional consent is an adequate answer to a claim that imposition of the tax violates the Commerce Clause. . . .

The criteria adopted [by the majority] insofar as they can be identified read as follows: Due process does permit State courts to "enforce the obligations which appellant has incurred" if it be found "reasonable and just according to our traditional conception of fair play and substantial justice." And this in turn means that we will "permit" the State to act if upon "an 'estimate of the inconveniences'" which would result to the corporation from a trial away from its 'home' or principal place of business," we conclude that it is "reasonable" to subject it to suit in a State where it is doing business. . . .

I believe that the Federal Constitution leaves to each State, without any "ifs" or "buts," a power to tax and to open the doors of its courts for its citizens to sue corporations whose agents do business in those States. Believing that the Constitution gave the States that power, I think it a judicial deprivation to condition its exercise upon this Court's notion of "fair play," however appealing that term may be. Nor can I stretch the meaning of due process so far as to authorize this Court to deprive a State of the right to afford judicial protection to its citizens on the ground that it would be more "convenient" for the corporation to be sued somewhere else.

There is a strong emotional appeal in the words "fair play," "justice," and "reasonableness." But they were not chosen by those who wrote the original Constitution or the Fourteenth Amendment as a measuring rod for this Court to use in invalidating State or Federal laws passed by elected legislative representatives. No one, not even those who most feared a democratic government, ever formally proposed that courts should be given power to invalidate legislation under any such elastic standards. Express prohibitions against certain types of legislation are found in the Constitution, and under the long-settled practice, courts invalidate laws found to conflict with them. This requires interpretation, and interpretation, it is true, may result in extension of the Constitution's purpose. But that is no reason for reading the due process clause so as to restrict a State's power to tax and sue those whose activities affect persons and businesses within the State, provided proper service can be had. . . . For application of this natural law concept, whether under the terms "reasonableness," "justice," or "fair play," makes judges the supreme arbiters of the country's laws and practices. This result, I believe, alters the form of government our Constitution provides. I cannot agree. . . .

NOTES AND QUESTIONS

1. *The Washington long-arm statute.* International Shoe was served with process under a Washington law that allowed jurisdiction over foreign corporations "doing business" in the state. *International Shoe Co. v. State*, 154 P.2d 801, 803 (Wash. 1945). This was a "long-arm statute," for it authorized Washington courts to reach beyond the state's borders to take personal jurisdiction over nonresident defendants who were not actually present in Washington and who had neither consented to service on an agent there nor voluntarily appeared in the action. As we will see, satisfaction of a long-arm or other jurisdictional statute is a prerequisite to the exercise of personal jurisdiction.

2. *Minimum contacts and reasonableness.* The Washington court found that International Shoe was "doing business" in Washington based on its "regular and systematic solicitation of orders" in the state and because its activities met the "solicitation-plus" rule. According to the Supreme Court what was wrong with these approaches? Under the old "consent," "presence," and "doing business" tests, a court's ability to take jurisdiction over a foreign corporation turned on an analysis of the activities conducted in the state by the corporation's employees

and agents. Under the new minimum-contacts approach, isn't it still necessary to analyze the corporation's forum activities to see whether those activities "make it reasonable" for the state to assert jurisdiction? If so, was the Court's concern that the previous approaches had focused too much on the *quantity* of the defendant's contacts with the forum without also looking at the *quality and nature* of those contacts? Why did Justice Black object to the Court's new approach?

3. *Meaningful connections and reasonable expectations.* What claim did the State of Washington assert against International Shoe? What was the factual premise for that claim and to what extent was the claim based on activities that took place within the state? Was International Shoe responsible for those in-state activities? How would you characterize International Shoe's connections with the forum? Were they intentional or fortuitous? Were they systematic or sporadic? Were they related or unrelated to the claim? Taking all your answers into account, were International Shoe's connections with the forum state "meaningful" in the sense that they created in the company a reasonable expectation that it might be sued in Washington on the asserted claim? Was the exercise of jurisdiction over the International Shoe Company fair?

4. *Activities in the state.* Sections 35 and 36 of Restatement (Second) of Judgments (1971) address the scope of jurisdiction over a nonresident defendant who engages in activities in the forum state. Section 35 thus provides that:

> (1) A state has power to exercise judicial jurisdiction over an individual who does business in the state with respect to causes of action arising from the business done in the state.
>
> (2) A state has power to exercise judicial jurisdiction over an individual who has done business in the state, but has ceased to do business there at the time when the action is brought, with respect to causes of action arising from the business done in the state.
>
> (3) A state has power to exercise judicial jurisdiction over an individual who does business in the state with respect to causes of action that do not arise from the business done in the state if this business is so continuous and substantial as to make it reasonable for the state to exercise such jurisdiction.

Id. § 35. Section 36 provides that:

> (1) A state has power to exercise judicial jurisdiction over an individual who has done, or has caused to be done, an act in the state with respect to any cause of action in tort arising from the act.
>
> (2) A state has power to exercise judicial jurisdiction over an individual who has done, or has caused to be done, an act in the state with respect to any cause of action not in tort arising from the act unless the nature of the act and of the individual's relationship to the state and to other states make the exercise of such jurisdiction unreasonable.

Id. at 36. Do these sections fully capture the minimum contacts test with respect to activities undertaken by a nonresident defendant in the forum state?

5. *Implied presence and implied consent.* While the Court says several times that International Shoe had established its "presence" in Washington, the Court

placed the word in quotation marks to emphasize its fictional nature as applied to corporations. The Court noted that jurisdiction over a foreign corporation had in the past been "supported by resort to the legal fiction that it has given its consent to service and suit. . . ." Do these fictional bases for acquiring jurisdiction over out-of-state defendants have continuing validity after the decision in *International Shoe*? For example, after *International Shoe*, how would a court assess the Massachusetts nonresident motorist statute involved in *Hess v. Pawloski*, page 21, *supra*? Would the outcome of the case be the same?

6. *Specific versus general jurisdiction.* The Court noted that while the minimum-contacts analysis "cannot be simply mechanical or quantitative," the extent of a defendant's contacts with the forum is relevant for it may affect the range of lawsuits that can be brought against a defendant there. If a defendant's contacts with a state are "casual," "single, or isolated," this may permit jurisdiction only in suits relating to those activities. Cases in which the claim arises out of or relates to the defendant's forum activities involve the exercise of "specific jurisdiction."

On the other hand, if a defendant's forum activities are "continuous and systematic," these contacts may be "so substantial and of such a nature as to justify suits . . . on causes of action arising from dealings entirely distinct from those activities." Cases in which the claim is totally unrelated to the defendant's forum contacts involve the exercise of "general jurisdiction." The vast majority of cases in which personal jurisdiction is asserted under a long-arm statute involve specific rather than general jurisdiction. Which type was involved in *International Shoe*?

7. *Adequacy of notice.* How was International Shoe notified of the suit filed against it? Note that the company had not appointed an agent in Washington for the receipt of service of process. If such an agent had existed, would it have been necessary to apply a minimum contacts analysis? If none of the company's Washington employees were authorized to receive service of process, how could service on one of them provide adequate notice of suit? Is there a difference between using such service as the basis for acquiring jurisdiction and employing it as a means of giving notice when another basis for jurisdiction exists? Was it necessary for the state to serve one of the company's employees in Washington?

2. Establishing a Statutory Basis for Jurisdiction beyond the Traditional Forms

As noted above, there is a preliminary step that must be considered in deciding whether a court may exercise extra-territorial jurisdiction over a nonresident defendant, namely, whether there is a statute or formal rule that authorizes the exercise of jurisdiction over the nonresident defendant. Unless the defendant falls within the scope of the applicable statute, jurisdiction is improper and that remains true even when the exercise of jurisdiction would otherwise satisfy due process. In *International Shoe*, for example, the defendant was served with process at its Missouri headquarters under a Washington law that allowed the exercise of jurisdiction over foreign corporations "doing business" in the state. *International*

Shoe Co. v. State, 154 P.2d 801, 803 (Wash. 1945). See also Note 1 following *Pennoyer v. Neff*, at page 124, *supra*. Of course, once the statutory basis for jurisdiction is established, a court must then determine whether the exercise of statutory jurisdiction comports with due process, as the Court did in *International Shoe*. In other words, the exercise of jurisdiction over a nonresident defendant requires both the satisfaction of a jurisdictional statute or formal rule and the satisfaction of due process.

Statutes that permit a court of a state to exercise jurisdiction over a nonresident defendant beyond the traditional forms are known as "long-arm" statutes.* The "arm" of the state is "long" in the sense that it can authoritatively reach beyond the territorial limits of the state. There are two types of long-arm statutes: *"tailored"* (or "specific-act") statutes, which carefully delineate the circumstances under which extraterritorial jurisdiction may be exercised; and "due-process" statutes, which authorize a court of the state to assert long-arm jurisdiction to the maximum extent permitted by the Constitution.

For example, New York has adopted a typical tailored long-arm statute that identifies the specific activities and circumstances under which a nonresident defendant may be subject to jurisdiction in the state:

§ 302. Personal jurisdiction by acts of non-domiciliaries.

(a) Acts which are the basis of jurisdiction. As to a cause of action arising from any of the acts enumerated in this section, a court may exercise personal jurisdiction over any non-domiciliary, or his executor or administrator, who in person or through an agent:

1. transacts any business within the state or contracts anywhere to supply goods or services in the state; or

2. commits a tortious act within the state, except as to a cause of action for defamation of character arising from the act; or

3. commits a tortious act without the state causing injury to person or property within the state, except as to a cause of action for defamation of character arising from the act, if he

(i) regularly does or solicits business, or engages in any other persistent course of conduct, or derives substantial revenue from goods used or consumed or services rendered, in the state, or

(ii) expects or should reasonably expect the act to have consequences in the state and derives substantial revenue from interstate or international commerce; or

4. owns, uses or possesses any real property situated within the state.

N.Y. Civ. Prac. L. § 302(a).

---

* The authority to exercise the traditional forms of jurisdiction is typically governed by state laws pertaining to service of process (*e.g.*, authorizing out-of-state service on a citizen of the state, in-state service on a non-domiciliary found within the state, or service on an in-state agent expressly appointed by the defendant). State laws also define the consequences of a failure to make a timely objection to jurisdiction or of a pre-litigation waiver of the right to make any such objection.

In states that have adopted a tailored long-arm statute, the jurisdictional analysis proceeds in two steps. It begins with the statute and, if the statute is satisfied, proceeds to the minimum contacts test. A court may sometimes skip the statutory analysis if it is clear that, under the facts presented, due process would not be satisfied even if the case were found to fall within the scope of the statute.

By way of contrast, California has adopted a due-process-style long-arm statute: "A court of this state may exercise jurisdiction on any basis not inconsistent with the Constitution of this state or of the United States." CAL. CIV. PROC. CODE § 410.10. Under a California approach, the statutory question and the due process question merge into a single inquiry: Would the exercise of jurisdiction over the nonresident defendant satisfy the minimum contacts test?

Other states have adopted variations on the above models. The Maine legislature took a curious approach, adopting a tailored long-arm statute, ME. REV. STAT. ANN. tit. 14, § 704-A(2), but directing that "to insure maximum protection to citizens of this State, [the statute] shall be applied so as to assert jurisdiction over nonresident defendants to the fullest extent permitted by the due process clause of the United States Constitution, 14th amendment." *Id.* § 704-A(1). Maine's courts have read the statute to mean that "the exercise of personal jurisdiction is permissible as long as it is consistent with the Due Process Clause of the federal constitution, and therefore when applying the statute a court need only consider whether due process requirements have been satisfied." *Suttie v. Sloan Sales, Inc.*, 711 A.2d 1285, 1286 (Me. 1998). Other states have likewise included in their tailored long-arm statutes a provision allowing jurisdiction to be exercised on any other basis permitted by the Constitution. *See, e.g.*, ILL. ANN. STAT. ch. 735, § 5/2-209(c); LA. REV. STAT. ANN. § 13:3201(B); 42 PA. CONS. STAT. ANN. § 5322(a)-(b).

Courts in many other states have simply construed their tailored long-arm statutes as going to the limits of the Due Process Clause. In these states, the courts' ability to assert jurisdiction over out-of-state defendants is thus far broader than would appear from a reading of the jurisdictional statutes. States whose courts have unilaterally transformed their tailored long-arm statutes into due-process-type statutes include Alaska (*Polar Supply Co., Inc. v. Steelmaster Indus., Inc.*, 127 P.3d 52, 54-55 (Alaska 2005)); Minnesota (*Lorix v. Crompton Corp.*, 680 N.W.2d 574, 577 (Minn. Ct. App. 2004)); Missouri (*State ex rel. Newport v. Wiesman*, 627 S.W.2d 874, 876 (Mo. 1982)); New Mexico (*Tercero v. Catholic Diocese of Norwich*, 48 P.3d 50, 54 (N.M. 2002)); Oklahoma (*Gilbert v. Security Fin. Corp. of Okla., Inc.*, 152 P.3d 165, 173 (Okla. 2006)); Texas (*Hall v. Helicopteros Nacionales de Colombia, S.A.*, 638 S.W.2d 870, 872 (Tex. 1982)); Virginia (*Peninsula Cruise, Inc. v. New River Yacht Sales, Inc.*, 512 S.E.2d 560, 562 (Va. 1999)); and Washington (*Shute v. Carnival Cruise Lines*, 783 P.2d 78, 79-80 (Wash. 1989)). *And see Mackey v. Compass Mktg., Inc.*, 892 A.2d 479, 492-493 & n.6 (Md. 2006) (a state's tailored long-arm statute will be read as going to the limits of due process unless barred by canons of statutory construction).

The exercise of personal jurisdiction by federal courts is similarly constrained. In the vast majority of suits brought in federal court, the federal court will "borrow" the jurisdictional statute of the state in which it sits. This approach is a product of Federal Rule of Civil Procedure 4, which states that federal courts may exercise personal jurisdiction over a defendant "who is subject to the jurisdiction of a court of general jurisdiction in the state where the district court is located. . . ." FED R. CIV. P. 4(k)(1)(A). Thus, if a state court could obtain personal jurisdiction over an out-of-state defendant under the state's long-arm statute and consistently with the Fourteenth Amendment, the federal court may do so as well. Conversely, if the state court could not obtain personal jurisdiction because its long-arm statute is tailored or because the defendant lacks minimum contacts with the state, the federal court normally cannot do so either.

Later in this chapter we will see that federal courts may sometimes exercise jurisdiction under a federal long-arm statute or federal rule rather than having to borrow the statutes of the state in which they sit. For now, however, the important thing to remember is that in most suits filed in federal court, the federal court is in no better position than a state court when it comes to acquiring jurisdiction over the defendant.

3. Due Process: The Nonresident Defendant's Connections with the Forum State

Once it appears that an applicable long-arm statute authorizes the assertion of jurisdiction over a defendant, the next question is whether the defendant has minimum contacts with the state in which the court sits. There is only one minimum contacts test, but it applies across a wide array of circumstances. It uniformly requires that we examine the nonresident defendant's connections with the forum, both in terms of quantity and quality; that we consider the relationship between those connections and the claim at issue in the suit; that we determine whether, given the circumstances, the nonresident defendant could have expected to be sued in the forum on that claim; and whether there are any other factors counseling against the exercise of jurisdiction. Thus, the minimum contacts test provides a uniform method through which to measure the legitimacy of the exercise of personal jurisdiction when a nonresident defendant is engaged in activities in the state, either personally or through an agent (as in *International Shoe*); when a nonresident defendant has entered a contractual relationship with a forum resident; when a nonresident defendant may have caused an injury in the state through activities taking place elsewhere; when a nonresident defendant may have shipped, directly or indirectly, a dangerous product into the state; etc. In fact, the minimum contacts test applies to any and every type of claim that may be asserted against a nonresident defendant. In this section, we examine the first aspect of the minimum contacts test: the nonresident defendant's connections to the forum state.

a.   Contracts

McGee v. International Life Insurance Co.
355 U.S. 220 (1957)

Opinion of the Court by Mr. Justice Black, announced by Mr. Justice Douglas.

Petitioner, Lulu B. McGee, recovered a judgment in a California state court against respondent, International Life Insurance Company, on a contract of insurance. Respondent was not served with process in California but by registered mail at its principal place of business in Texas. The California court based its jurisdiction on a state statute which subjects foreign corporations to suit in California on insurance contracts with residents of that State even though such corporations cannot be served with process within its borders.

Unable to collect the judgment in California petitioner went to Texas where she filed suit on the judgment in a Texas court. But the Texas courts refused to enforce her judgment holding it was void under the Fourteenth Amendment because service of process outside California could not give the courts of that State jurisdiction over respondent. Since the case raised important questions, not only to California but to other States which have similar laws, we granted certiorari. It is not controverted that if the California court properly exercised jurisdiction over respondent the Texas courts erred in refusing to give its judgment full faith and credit.

The material facts are relatively simple. In 1944, Lowell Franklin, a resident of California, purchased a life insurance policy from the Empire Mutual Insurance Company, an Arizona corporation. In 1948 the respondent agreed with Empire Mutual to assume its insurance obligations. Respondent then mailed a reinsurance certificate to Franklin in California offering to insure him in accordance with the terms of the policy he held with Empire Mutual. He accepted this offer and from that time until his death in 1950 paid premiums by mail from his California home to respondent's Texas office. Petitioner Franklin's mother was the beneficiary under the policy. She sent proofs of his death to the respondent but it refused to pay claiming that he had committed suicide. It appears that neither Empire Mutual nor respondent has ever had any office or agent in California. And so far as the record before us shows, respondent has never solicited or done any insurance business in California apart from the policy involved here.

Since *Pennoyer v. Neff*, this Court has held that the Due Process Clause of the Fourteenth Amendment places some limit on the power of state courts to enter binding judgments against persons not served with process within their boundaries. But just where this line of limitation falls has been the subject of prolific controversy, particularly with respect to foreign corporations. In a continuing process of evolution this Court accepted and then abandoned "consent," "doing business," and "presence" as the standard for measuring the extent of state judicial power over such corporations. More recently in *International Shoe Co. v. State of Washington*, the Court decided that "due process requires only that in order to subject a defendant to a judgment *in personam*, if he be not present within the territory of the forum, he have certain minimum contacts with it such that the maintenance of the suit does not offend 'traditional notions of fair play and substantial justice.' "

Looking back over this long history of litigation a trend is clearly discernible toward expanding the permissible scope of state jurisdiction over foreign corporations and other nonresidents. In part this is attributable to the fundamental transformation of our national economy over the years. Today many commercial transactions touch two or more States and may involve parties separated by the full continent. With this increasing nationalization of commerce has come a great increase in the amount of business conducted by mail across state lines. At the same time modern transportation and communication have made it much less burdensome for a party sued to defend himself in a State where he engages in economic activity.

Turning to this case we think it apparent that the Due Process Clause did not preclude the California court from entering a judgment binding on respondent. It is sufficient for purposes of due process that the suit was based on a contract which had substantial connection with that State. The contract was delivered in California, the premiums were mailed from there and the insured was a resident of that State when he died. It cannot be denied that California has a manifest interest in providing effective means of redress for its residents when their insurers refuse to pay claims. These residents would be at a severe disadvantage if they were forced to follow the insurance company to a distant State in order to hold it legally accountable. When claims were small or moderate individual claimants frequently could not afford the cost of bringing an action in a foreign forum—thus in effect making the company judgment proof. Often the crucial witnesses—as here on the company's defense of suicide—will be found in the insured's locality. Of course there may be inconvenience to the insurer if it is held amenable to suit in California where it had this contract but certainly nothing which amounts to a denial of due process. There is no contention that respondent did not have adequate notice of the suit or sufficient time to prepare its defenses and appear . . . .

The judgment is reversed and the cause is remanded to the Court of Civil Appeals of the State of Texas, First Supreme Judicial District, for further proceedings not inconsistent with this opinion.

It is so ordered.

The CHIEF JUSTICE took no part in the consideration or decision of this case.

NOTES AND QUESTIONS

1. *Enforcing a judgment.* McGee first sued the defendant in a California court, which entered a judgment in her favor. What does that mean? To what did the judgment entitle her? Why, as a practical matter, do you think she went to Texas to enforce that judgment? Are the courts of one state required to honor the judgments of the courts of another state? Always? On what basis did the Texas

court refuse to honor the judgment of the California court? How should we determine whether the Texas court was correct in so refusing?

2. *Applying the standards of* International Shoe. In what way(s) do *International Shoe* and *McGee* differ from one another? In what way(s) are they similar? Does it matter that *International Shoe* involved the collection of employment taxes, while *McGee* involved a contract of insurance? Do you think that the *McGee* Court properly applied the *International Shoe* standards? Why or why not?

3. *Meaningful connections and reasonable expectations.* What claim did McGee assert in the California proceeding? What was the factual premise for that claim? To what extent is that claim premised on events that took place in California? Did International Life engage in any activity in or directed toward the State of California? Was that activity systematic or sporadic? Was it related or unrelated to the claim? Taking all of your answers into account, were International Life's connections with the forum state "meaningful" in the sense that they put International Life on notice of the possibility of being sued there on the claim asserted by McGee?

Hanson v. Denckla

357 U.S. 235 (1958)

Mr. Chief Justice Warren delivered the opinion of the Court.

This controversy concerns the right to $400,000, part of the corpus of a trust established in Delaware by a settlor who later became domiciled in Florida. One group of claimants . . . urge that this property passed under the residuary clause of the settlor's will, which was admitted to probate in Florida. The Florida courts have sustained this position. Other claimants . . . contend that the property passed pursuant to the settlor's exercise of the *inter vivos* power of appointment created in the deed of trust. The Delaware courts adopted this position and refused to accord full faith and credit to the Florida determination because the Florida court had not acquired jurisdiction over an indispensable party, the Delaware trustee. . . . [Both cases are now before the Court for review.]

The trust whose validity is contested here was created in 1935. Dora Browning Donner, then a domiciliary of Pennsylvania, executed a trust instrument in Delaware naming the Wilmington Trust Co., of Wilmington, Delaware, as trustee. The corpus was composed of securities. Mrs. Donner reserved the income for life, and stated that the remainder should be paid to such persons or upon such trusts as she should [later] appoint. . . . Thereafter she left Pennsylvania, and in 1944 became domiciled in Florida, where she remained until her death in 1952. Mrs. Donner's will was executed Dec. 3, 1949. On that same day she executed the *inter vivos* power of appointment whose terms are at issue here. After making modest appointments in favor of a hospital and certain family retainers, . . . she appointed the sum of $200,000 to each of two trusts previously established . . . with the Delaware Trust Co. [for the benefit of the children of her daughter Elizabeth

Donner Hanson]. The balance of the trust corpus, over $1,000,000 at the date of her death, was appointed to her executrix. That amount passed under the residuary clause of her will [in equal shares to her other two daughters, Katherine Denckla and Dorothy Stewart] and is not at issue here. . . .

Mrs. Donner died Nov. 20, 1952. Her will . . . was admitted to probate in Florida . . . .

. . . Residuary legatees Denckla and Stewart, already the recipients of over $500,000 each [under the will], urge that the power of appointment over the $400,000 appointed to sister Elizabeth's children was not "effectively exercised" and that the property should accordingly pass to them [under the residuary clause]. Fourteen months after Mrs. Donner's death these parties petitioned a Florida chancery court for a declaratory judgment "concerning what property passes under the residuary clause" of the will. . . . [Some of the] defendants were nonresidents and could not be personally served. These included the Wilmington Trust Co. ("trustee") [and] the Delaware Trust Co. (to whom the $400,000 had been paid shortly after Mrs. Donner's death). . . .

The appearing defendants (Elizabeth Donner Hanson and her children) moved to dismiss the suit because the exercise of jurisdiction over indispensable parties, the Delaware trustees, would offend . . . the Fourteenth Amendment. The Chancellor ruled that he lacked jurisdiction over these nonresident defendants. . . . The cause was dismissed as to them. As far as parties before the court were concerned, however, he ruled that the power of appointment was . . . void under the applicable Florida law. In a decree dated Jan. 14, 1955, he ruled that the $400,000 passed under the residuary clause of the will [to Denckla and Stewart].

After the Florida litigation began, but before entry of the decree, the executrix instituted a declaratory judgment action in Delaware to determine who was entitled to participate in the trust assets held in that State. [T]he parties were substantially the same as in the Florida litigation. . . . When the Florida decree was entered [Denckla and Stewart] unsuccessfully urged it as *res judicata* of the Delaware dispute. In a decree dated Jan. 13, 1956, the Delaware Chancellor ruled that the trust and power of appointment were valid under the applicable Delaware law, and that the trust corpus had properly been paid to the Delaware Trust Co. and the other appointees.

. . . [The Florida Supreme Court held that under Florida law] the trust was invalid because the settlor had reserved too much power over the trustee and trust corpus, and the power of appointment was not independently effective to pass the property because it . . . was not accompanied by the requisite formalities. The Chancellor's conclusion that there was no jurisdiction over the trust companies . . . was reversed. . . .

The issues for our decision are, *first*, whether Florida erred in holding that it had jurisdiction over the nonresident defendants, and *second*, whether Delaware erred in refusing full faith and credit to the Florida decree. We need not determine whether Florida was bound to give full faith and credit to the decree of the Delaware Chancellor since the question was not seasonably presented to the Florida court. . . .

. . . Florida adheres to the general rule that a trustee is an indispensable party to litigation involving the validity of the trust. In the absence of such a party a Florida court may not proceed to adjudicate the controversy. . . . [S]tate law required the acquisition of jurisdiction over the [Wilmington Trust Co.][8] before the court was empowered to proceed with the action. . . .

. . . [Appellees] urge that the circumstances of this case amount to sufficient affiliation with the State of Florida to empower its courts to exercise personal jurisdiction over this nonresident defendant. Principal reliance is placed upon *McGee v. International Life Ins. Co.* In *McGee* the Court noted the trend of expanding personal jurisdiction over nonresidents. As technological progress has increased the flow of commerce between States, the need for jurisdiction over nonresidents has undergone a similar increase. At the same time, progress in communications and transportation has made the defense of a suit in a foreign tribunal less burdensome. In response to these changes, the requirements for personal jurisdiction over nonresidents have evolved from the rigid rule of *Pennoyer v. Neff* to the flexible standard of *International Shoe*. But it is a mistake to assume that this trend heralds the eventual demise of all restrictions on the personal jurisdiction of state courts. Those restrictions are more than a guarantee of immunity from inconvenient or distant litigation. They are a consequence of territorial limitations on the power of the respective States. However minimal the burden of defending in a foreign tribunal, a defendant may not be called upon to do so unless he has had the "minimal contacts" with that State that are a prerequisite to its exercise of power over him.

We fail to find such contacts in the circumstances of this case. The defendant trust company has no office in Florida, and transacts no business there. None of the trust assets has ever been held or administered in Florida, and the record discloses no solicitation of business in that State either in person or by mail.

The cause of action in this case is not one that arises out of an act done or transaction consummated in the forum State. In that respect, it differs from *McGee v. International Life Ins. Co.* . . . In *McGee*, the nonresident defendant solicited a reinsurance agreement with a resident of California. The offer was accepted in that State, and the insurance premiums were mailed from there until the insured's death. Noting the interest California has in providing effective redress for its residents when nonresident insurers refuse to pay claims on insurance they have solicited in that State, the Court upheld jurisdiction because the suit "was based on a contract which had substantial connection with that State." In contrast, this action involves the validity of an agreement that was entered without any connection with the forum State. The agreement was executed in Delaware by a trust company incorporated in that State and a settlor domiciled in Pennsylvania. The first relationship Florida had to the agreement was years later when the settlor became domiciled there, and the trustee remitted the trust income to her in that State. From Florida Mrs. Donner carried on several bits of trust administration

---

8. . . . It is unnecessary to determine whether the Delaware Trust Co., to which the $400,000 . . . was paid after Mrs. Donner's death, is also an indispensable party to this proceeding.

that may be compared to the mailing of premiums in *McGee*. But the record discloses no instance in which the *trustee* performed any acts in Florida that bear the same relationship to the agreement as the solicitation in *McGee*. Consequently, this suit cannot be said to be one to enforce an obligation that arose from a privilege the defendant exercised in Florida. This case is also different from *McGee* in that there the State had enacted special legislation . . . to exercise what *McGee* called its "manifest interest" in providing effective redress for citizens who had been injured by nonresidents engaged in an activity that the State treats as exceptional and subjects to special regulation.

The execution in Florida of the powers of appointment . . . does not give Florida a substantial connection with the contract on which this suit is based. It is the validity of the trust agreement, not the appointment, that is at issue here. . . . The unilateral activity of those who claim some relationship with a nonresident defendant cannot satisfy the requirement of contact with the forum State. The application of that rule will vary with the quality and nature of the defendant's activity, but it is essential in each case that there be some act by which the defendant purposefully avails itself of the privilege of conducting activities within the forum State, thus invoking the benefits and protections of its laws. *International Shoe Co. v. Washington*. The settlor's execution in Florida of her power of appointment cannot remedy the absence of such an act in this case.

. . . [Florida] does not acquire that jurisdiction by being the "center of gravity" of the controversy, or the most convenient location for litigation. The issue is personal jurisdiction, not choice of law. It is resolved in this case by considering the acts of the trustee. As we have indicated, they are insufficient to sustain the jurisdiction.

. . . [T]he Florida Supreme Court has repeatedly held that a trustee is an indispensable party without whom a Florida court has no power to adjudicate controversies affecting the validity of a trust. For that reason the Florida judgment must be reversed not only as to the nonresident trustees but also as to appellants, over whom the Florida court admittedly had jurisdiction.

. . . The same reasons that compel reversal of the Florida judgment require affirmance of the Delaware one. Delaware is under no obligation to give full faith and credit to a Florida judgment invalid in Florida because offensive to the Due Process Clause of the Fourteenth Amendment. . . . Since Delaware was entitled to conclude that Florida law made the trust company an indispensable party, it was under no obligation to give the Florida judgment any faith and credit—even against parties over whom Florida's jurisdiction was unquestioned. . . .

The judgment of the Delaware Supreme Court is affirmed, and the judgment of the Florida Supreme Court is reversed and the cause is remanded for proceedings not inconsistent with this opinion.

It is so ordered.

Mr. Justice Black, whom Mr. Justice Burton and Mr. Justice Brennan join, dissenting.

I believe the courts of Florida had power to adjudicate the effectiveness of the appointment made in Florida by Mrs. Donner with respect to all those who were notified of the proceedings and given an opportunity to be heard without violating the Due Process Clause of the Fourteenth Amendment. If this is correct, it follows that the Delaware courts erred in refusing to give the prior Florida judgment full faith and credit. . . .

The same day the 1949 appointment was made Mrs. Donner executed a will, which after her death was duly probated in a Florida court. The will contained a residuary clause providing for the distribution of all of her property not previously bequeathed, including "any and all property, rights and interest over which I may have power of appointment which prior to my death has not been effectively exercised by me. . . ." Thus if the 1949 appointment was ineffective the property involved came back into Mrs. Donner's estate to be distributed under the residuary clause of her will. As might be anticipated the present litigation arose when legatees brought an action in the Florida courts seeking a determination whether the appointment was valid. . . .

In light of the foregoing circumstances it seems quite clear to me that there is nothing in the Due Process Clause which denies Florida the right to determine whether Mrs. Donner's appointment was valid as against its statute of wills. This disposition, which was designed to take effect after her death, had very close and substantial connections with that State. Not only was the appointment made in Florida by a domiciliary of Florida, but the primary beneficiaries also lived in that State. In my view it could hardly be denied that Florida had sufficient interest so that a court with jurisdiction might properly apply Florida law, if it chose, to determine whether the appointment was effectual. True, the question whether the law of a State can be applied to a transaction is different from the question whether the courts of that State have jurisdiction to enter a judgment, but the two are often closely related and to a substantial degree depend upon similar considerations. It seems to me that where a transaction has as much relationship to a State as Mrs. Donner's appointment had to Florida its courts ought to have power to adjudicate controversies arising out of that transaction, unless litigation there would impose such a heavy and disproportionate burden on a nonresident defendant that it would offend what this Court has referred to as "traditional notions of fair play and substantial justice." So far as the nonresident defendants here are concerned I can see nothing which approaches that degree of unfairness. Florida, the home of the principal contenders for Mrs. Donner's largess, was a reasonably convenient forum for all. Certainly there is nothing fundamentally unfair in subjecting the corporate trustee to the jurisdiction of the Florida courts. It chose to maintain business relations with Mrs. Donner in that State for eight years, regularly communicating with her with respect to the business of the trust including the very appointment in question.

Florida's interest in the validity of Mrs. Donner's appointment is made more emphatic by the fact that her will is being administered in that State. It has traditionally been the rule that the State where a person is domiciled at the time of his death is the proper place to determine the validity of his will, to construe its provisions and to marshal and distribute his personal property. Here Florida was seriously concerned with winding up Mrs. Donner's estate and with finally determining what property was to be distributed under her will. . . .

The Court's decision that Florida did not have jurisdiction over the trustee . . . stems from principles stated the better part of a century ago in *Pennoyer v. Neff*. . . . But as the years have passed the constantly increasing ease and rapidity of communication and the tremendous growth of interstate business activity have led to a steady and inevitable relaxation of the strict limits on state jurisdiction announced in that case. In the course of this evolution the old jurisdictional landmarks have been left far behind so that in many instances States may now properly exercise jurisdiction over nonresidents not amenable to service within their borders. Yet further relaxation seems certain. Of course we have not reached the point where state boundaries are without significance, and I do not mean to suggest such a view here. There is no need to do so. For we are dealing with litigation arising from a transaction that had an abundance of close and substantial connections with the State of Florida. . . .

[The dissenting opinion of MR. JUSTICE DOUGLAS is omitted.]

NOTES AND QUESTIONS

1. "Unilateral activity" and "purposeful availment." Consider this passage from the majority opinion:

> The unilateral activity of those who claim some relationship with a nonresident defendant cannot satisfy the requirement of contact with the forum State. The application of that rule will vary with the quality and nature of the defendant's activity, but it is essential in each case that there be some act by which the defendant purposefully avails itself of the privilege of conducting activities within the forum State, thus invoking the benefits and protections of its laws.

Page 154, *supra*. What does the Court mean by "unilateral activity"? Can you identify the activity in *Hanson* that the Court deemed unilateral? Were the forum-related connections in *International Shoe* and *McGee* unilateral? To what extent may "unilateral activity" play a part in the jurisdictional analysis?

The second sentence of the above quotation uses the phrase "purposefully avails." What does that mean? Must a plaintiff seeking to establish minimum contacts now show that the nonresident defendant has received "benefits and protections" from the laws of the forum state? In *International Shoe*, the Court made the following observation:

> But to the extent that a corporation exercises the privilege of conducting activities within a state, it enjoys the benefits and protection of the laws of that state. The exercise of that privilege may give rise to obligations; and, so far as those obligations arise out of or are connected with the activities within the state, a procedure which requires the corporation to respond to a suit brought to enforce them can, in most instances, hardly be said to be undue.

International Shoe, 326 U.S. at 316, and page 141, *supra*. Does the above text establish "purposeful availment" as a necessary condition of jurisdiction? If not, what is the import of this text? Did the Court in *Hanson* treat "purposeful availment" as a necessary condition of jurisdiction? Or is the *Hanson* Court simply emphasizing that defendant (not the plaintiff) must have a meaningful connection with the forum state? *See* Allan Ides & Simona Grossi, *The Purposeful Availment Trap*, 7 FED. CTS. L. REV. 118 (2013).

2. *Distinguishing* McGee.   On what basis did the *Hanson* Court distinguish *McGee*? Would the *Hanson* Court have found jurisdiction over the trustee if Dora Donner had been a domiciliary of Florida when the trust was first created? Would *McGee* have been decided differently if Franklin had resided in Arizona when International Life reinsured him and he had only later moved to California? In short, are the two cases distinguishable in terms of the foreseeability of being haled into a court of the forum state?

3. *Justice Black.*   What are Justice Black's disagreements with the majority? What alternate approach to jurisdiction does he propose? If the majority's principal concern is assuring fairness to defendants, what is the primary focus of Justice Black's approach? Do you agree with Justice Black that there was no fundamental unfairness to the Delaware trustee in the Florida proceeding? Is there anything in Justice Black's opinion that suggests that the Delaware trustee did purposefully direct his activities toward the State of Florida? As between the majority and the dissent, which opinion more closely aligns with the meaningful connections and reasonable expectations principle?

Burger King Corp. v. Rudzewicz

471 U.S. 462 (1985)

JUSTICE BRENNAN delivered the opinion of the Court.

means "among other things"

The State of Florida's long-arm statute extends jurisdiction to "[a]ny person, whether or not a citizen or resident of this state," who, *inter alia*, "[b]reach[es] a contract in this state by failing to perform acts required by the contract to be performed in this state," so long as the cause of action arises from the alleged contractual breach. The United States District Court for the Southern District of Florida, sitting in diversity, relied on this provision in exercising personal jurisdiction over a Michigan resident who allegedly had breached a franchise agreement with a Florida corporation by failing to make required payments in Florida. . . .

I

A

Burger King Corporation is a Florida corporation whose principal offices are in Miami. . . . Burger King conducts approximately 80% of its business through a franchise operation that the company styles the "Burger King System"—"a comprehensive restaurant format and operating system for the sale of uniform and quality food products." Burger King licenses its franchisees to use its trademarks and service marks for a period of 20 years and leases standardized restaurant facilities to them for the same term. . . . They also receive market research and advertising assistance; ongoing training in restaurant management;[2] and accounting, cost-control, and inventory-control guidance. . . .

In exchange for these benefits, franchisees pay Burger King an initial $40,000 franchise fee and commit themselves to payment of monthly royalties, advertising and sales promotion fees, and rent computed in part from monthly gross sales. . . .

Burger King oversees its franchise system through a two-tiered administrative structure. The governing contracts provide that the franchise relationship is established in Miami and governed by Florida law, and call for payment of all required fees and forwarding of all relevant notices to the Miami headquarters. The Miami headquarters sets policy and works directly with its franchisees in attempting to resolve major problems. Day-to-day monitoring of franchisees, however, is conducted through a network of 10 district offices which in turn report to the Miami headquarters.

The instant litigation grows out of Burger King's termination of one of its franchisees. . . . The appellee John Rudzewicz, a Michigan citizen and resident, is the senior partner in a Detroit accounting firm. In 1978, he was approached by Brian MacShara, the son of a business acquaintance, who suggested that they jointly apply to Burger King for a franchise in the Detroit area. MacShara proposed to serve as the manager of the restaurant if Rudzewicz would put up the investment capital; in exchange, the two would evenly share the profits. . . .

Rudzewicz and MacShara jointly applied for a franchise to Burger King's Birmingham, Michigan, district office in the autumn of 1978. Their application was forwarded to Burger King's Miami headquarters, which entered into a preliminary agreement with them in February 1979. During the ensuing four months it was agreed that Rudzewicz and MacShara would assume operation of an existing facility in Drayton Plains, Michigan. MacShara attended the prescribed management courses in Miami during this period, and the franchisees purchased $165,000 worth of restaurant equipment from Burger King's Davmor Industries division in Miami. Even before the final agreements were signed, however, the parties began to disagree. . . . During these disputes Rudzewicz and MacShara negotiated both with the Birmingham district office and with the Miami headquarters.[7] With some misgivings, Rudzewicz and MacShara finally obtained limited concessions from the Miami headquarters, signed the final agreements, and commenced operations in June 1979. By signing the final agreements, Rudzewicz

---

2. Mandatory training seminars are conducted at Burger King University in Miami and at Whopper College Regional Training Centers around the country.

7. Although Rudzewicz and MacShara dealt with the Birmingham district office on a regular basis, they communicated directly with the Miami headquarters in forming the contracts; moreover, they learned that the district office had "very little" decisionmaking authority and accordingly turned directly to headquarters in seeking to resolve their disputes.

obligated himself personally to payments exceeding $1 million over the 20-year franchise relationship.

. . . Rudzewicz and MacShara soon fell far behind in their monthly payments to Miami. . . . After several Burger King officials in Miami had engaged in prolonged but ultimately unsuccessful negotiations with the franchisees by mail and by telephone,[9] headquarters terminated the franchise and ordered Rudzewicz and MacShara to vacate the premises. They refused and continued to occupy and operate the facility as a Burger King restaurant.

B

Burger King commenced the instant action in the United States District Court for the Southern District of Florida in May 1981. . . . Burger King sought damages, injunctive relief, and costs and attorney's fees. Rudzewicz and MacShara entered special appearances and argued, *inter alia*, that . . . the District Court lacked personal jurisdiction over them. The District Court denied their motions after a hearing, holding that, pursuant to Florida's long-arm statute, "a non-resident Burger King franchisee is subject to the personal jurisdiction of this Court in actions arising out of its franchise agreements." . . .

After a 3-day bench trial, the court again concluded that it had "jurisdiction over the subject matter and the parties to this cause." Finding that Rudzewicz and MacShara had breached their franchise agreements with Burger King and had infringed Burger King's trademarks and service marks, the court entered judgment against them, jointly and severally, for $228,875 in contract damages. . . .

Rudzewicz appealed to the Court of Appeals for the Eleventh Circuit. A divided panel of that Circuit reversed the judgment, concluding that the District Court could not properly exercise personal jurisdiction over Rudzewicz. . . .

Burger King appealed the Eleventh Circuit's judgment to this Court. . . . [W]e grant the petition and now reverse.

II

A

The Due Process Clause protects an individual's liberty interest in not being subject to the binding judgments of a forum with which he has established no meaningful "contacts, ties, or relations." *International Shoe Co. v. Washington*. By requiring that individuals have "fair warning that a particular activity may subject [them] to the jurisdiction of a foreign sovereign," the Due Process Clause "gives a degree of predictability to the legal system that allows potential defendants to

---

9. Miami's policy was to "deal directly" with franchisees when they began to encounter financial difficulties, and to involve district office personnel only when necessary. In the instant case, for example, the Miami office handled all credit problems, ordered cost-cutting measures, negotiated for a partial refinancing of the franchisees' debts, communicated directly with the franchisees in attempting to resolve the dispute, and was responsible for all termination matters.

structure their primary conduct with some minimum assurance as to where that conduct will and will not render them liable to suit."

Where a forum seeks to assert specific jurisdiction over an out-of-state defendant who has not consented to suit there, this "fair warning" requirement is satisfied if the defendant has "purposefully directed" his activities at residents of the forum, and the litigation results from alleged injuries that "arise out of or relate to" those activities.[15] . . .

We have noted several reasons why a forum legitimately may exercise personal jurisdiction over a nonresident who "purposefully directs" his activities toward forum residents. A State generally has a "manifest interest" in providing its residents with a convenient forum for redressing injuries inflicted by out-of-state actors. Moreover, where individuals "purposefully derive benefit" from their interstate activities, it may well be unfair to allow them to escape having to account in other States for consequences that arise proximately from such activities; the Due Process Clause may not readily be wielded as a territorial shield to avoid interstate obligations that have been voluntarily assumed. And because "modern transportation and communications have made it much less burdensome for a party sued to defend himself in a State where he engages in economic activity," it usually will not be unfair to subject him to the burdens of litigating in another forum for disputes relating to such activity. *McGee v. International Life Insurance Co.*

Notwithstanding these considerations, the constitutional touchstone remains whether the defendant purposefully established minimum contacts in the forum State. Although it has been argued that foreseeability of causing *injury* in another State should be sufficient to establish such contacts there when policy considerations so require, the Court has consistently held that this kind of foreseeability is not a "sufficient benchmark" for exercising personal jurisdiction. Instead, "the foreseeability that is critical to due process analysis . . . is that the defendant's conduct and connection with the forum State are such that he should reasonably anticipate being haled into court there." . . .

This "purposeful availment" requirement ensures that a defendant will not be haled into a jurisdiction solely as a result of "random," "fortuitous," or "attenuated" contacts, or of the "unilateral activity of another party or a third person." Jurisdiction is proper, however, where the contacts proximately result from actions by the defendant *himself* that create a "substantial connection" with the forum State.[18] Thus where the defendant "deliberately" has engaged in significant activities within a State, or has created "continuing obligations" between himself and residents of the forum, he manifestly has availed himself of the privilege of conducting business there, and because his activities are shielded by "the benefits and

---

15. "Specific" jurisdiction contrasts with "general" jurisdiction, pursuant to which "a State exercises personal jurisdiction over a defendant in a suit not arising out of or related to the defendant's contacts with the forum."

18. So long as it creates a "substantial connection" with the forum, even a single act can support jurisdiction. *McGee v. International Life Insurance Co.* . . .

protections" of the forum's laws it is presumptively not unreasonable to require him to submit to the burdens of litigation in that forum as well.

Jurisdiction in these circumstances may not be avoided merely because the defendant did not *physically* enter the forum State. Although territorial presence frequently will enhance a potential defendant's affiliation with a State and reinforce the reasonable foreseeability of suit there, it is an inescapable fact of modern commercial life that a substantial amount of business is transacted solely by mail and wire communications across state lines, thus obviating the need for physical presence within a State in which business is conducted. So long as a commercial actor's efforts are "purposefully directed" toward residents of another State, we have consistently rejected the notion that an absence of physical contacts can defeat personal jurisdiction there.

Once it has been decided that a defendant purposefully established minimum contacts within the forum State, these contacts may be considered in light of other factors to determine whether the assertion of personal jurisdiction would comport with "fair play and substantial justice." Thus courts in "appropriate case[s]" may evaluate "the burden on the defendant," "the forum State's interest in adjudicating the dispute," "the plaintiff's interest in obtaining convenient and effective relief," "the interstate judicial system's interest in obtaining the most efficient resolution of controversies," and the "shared interest of the several States in furthering fundamental substantive social policies." These considerations sometimes serve to establish the reasonableness of jurisdiction upon a lesser showing of minimum contacts than would otherwise be required. On the other hand, where a defendant who purposefully has directed his activities at forum residents seeks to defeat jurisdiction, he must present a compelling case that the presence of some other considerations would render jurisdiction unreasonable. Most such considerations usually may be accommodated through means short of finding jurisdiction unconstitutional. For example, the potential clash of the forum's law with the "fundamental substantive social policies" of another State may be accommodated through application of the forum's choice-of-law rules. Similarly, a defendant claiming substantial inconvenience may seek a change of venue.[20] Nevertheless, minimum requirements inherent in the concept of "fair play and substantial justice" may defeat the reasonableness of jurisdiction even if the defendant has purposefully engaged in forum activities. . . .

B

(1)

Applying these principles to the case at hand, we believe there is substantial record evidence supporting the District Court's conclusion that the assertion of personal jurisdiction over Rudzewicz in Florida for the alleged breach of his

20. See, *e.g.*, 28 U.S.C. § 1404(a) . . . .

franchise agreement did not offend due process. At the outset, we note a continued division among lower courts respecting whether and to what extent a contract can constitute a "contact" for purposes of due process analysis. If the question is whether an individual's contract with an out-of-state party *alone* can automatically establish sufficient minimum contacts in the other party's home forum, we believe the answer clearly is that it cannot. The Court long ago rejected the notion that personal jurisdiction might turn on "mechanical" tests, or on "conceptualistic . . . theories of the place of contracting or of performance." Instead, we have emphasized the need for a "highly realistic" approach that recognizes that a "contract" is "ordinarily but an intermediate step serving to tie up prior business negotiations with future consequences which themselves are the real object of the business transaction." It is these factors—prior negotiations and contemplated future consequences, along with the terms of the contract and the parties' actual course of dealing—that must be evaluated in determining whether the defendant purposefully established minimum contacts within the forum.

In this case, no physical ties to Florida can be attributed to Rudzewicz other than MacShara's brief training course in Miami.[22] Rudzewicz did not maintain offices in Florida and, for all that appears from the record, has never even visited there. Yet this franchise dispute grew directly out of "a contract which had a *substantial* connection with that State." Eschewing the option of operating an independent local enterprise, Rudzewicz deliberately "reach[ed] out beyond" Michigan and negotiated with a Florida corporation for the purchase of a long-term franchise and the manifold benefits that would derive from affiliation with a nationwide organization. Upon approval, he entered into a carefully structured 20-year relationship that envisioned continuing and wide-reaching contacts with Burger King in Florida. In light of Rudzewicz's voluntary acceptance of the long-term and exacting regulation of his business from Burger King's Miami headquarters, the "quality and nature" of his relationship to the company in Florida can in no sense be viewed as "random," "fortuitous," or "attenuated." Rudzewicz's refusal to make the contractually required payments in Miami, and his continued use of Burger King's trademarks and confidential business information after his termination, caused foreseeable injuries to the corporation in Florida. For these reasons it was, at the very least, presumptively reasonable for Rudzewicz to be called to account there for such injuries.

---

22. The Eleventh Circuit held that MacShara's presence in Florida was irrelevant to the question of Rudzewicz's minimum contacts with that forum, reasoning that "Rudzewicz and MacShara never formed a partnership" and "signed the agreements in their individual capacities." The two did jointly form a corporation through which they were seeking to conduct the franchise, however. They were required to decide which one of them would travel to Florida . . . and Rudzewicz participated in the decision that MacShara would go there. We have previously noted that when commercial activities are "carried on in behalf of" an out-of-state party those activities may sometimes be ascribed to the party, at least where he is a "primary participan[t]" in the enterprise and has acted purposefully in directing those activities. Because MacShara's matriculation at Burger King University is not pivotal to the disposition of this case, we need not resolve the permissible bounds of such attribution.

[handwritten margin notes at top: "trial appeals US Supreme BurgerKing → Rud → Burger court Can you only appeal once? courts decisions"]

The Court of Appeals concluded, however, that in light of the supervision emanating from Burger King's district office in Birmingham, Rudzewicz reasonably believed that "the Michigan office was for all intents and purposes the embodiment of Burger King" and that he therefore had no "reason to anticipate a Burger King suit outside of Michigan." This reasoning overlooks substantial record evidence indicating that Rudzewicz most certainly knew that he was affiliating himself with an enterprise based primarily in Florida. The contract documents themselves emphasize that Burger King's operations are conducted and supervised from the Miami headquarters, that all relevant notices and payments must be sent there, and that the agreements were made in and enforced from Miami. Moreover, the parties' actual course of dealing repeatedly confirmed that decision-making authority was vested in the Miami headquarters and that the district office served largely as an intermediate link between the headquarters and the franchisees. When problems arose over building design, site-development fees, rent computation, and the defaulted payments, Rudzewicz and MacShara learned that the Michigan office was powerless to resolve their disputes and could only channel their communications to Miami. Throughout these disputes, the Miami headquarters and the Michigan franchisees carried on a continuous course of direct communications by mail and by telephone, and it was the Miami headquarters that made the key negotiating decisions out of which the instant litigation arose.

[handwritten margin note: "evidence that the franchisees knew that business was conducted in the Miami location"]

Moreover, we believe the Court of Appeals gave insufficient weight to provisions in the various franchise documents providing that all disputes would be governed by Florida law. The franchise agreement, for example, stated:

> "This Agreement shall become valid when executed and accepted by BKC at Miami, Florida; it shall be deemed made and entered into in the State of Florida and shall be governed and construed under and in accordance with the laws of the State of Florida. The choice of law designation does not require that all suits concerning this Agreement be filed in Florida."

The Court of Appeals reasoned that choice-of-law provisions are irrelevant to the question of personal jurisdiction, relying on *Hanson v. Denckla* for the proposition that "the center of gravity for choice-of-law purposes does not necessarily confer the sovereign prerogative to assert jurisdiction." This reasoning misperceives the import of the quoted proposition. The Court in *Hanson* and subsequent cases has emphasized that choice-of-law *analysis*—which focuses on all elements of a transaction, and not simply on the defendant's conduct—is distinct from minimum-contacts jurisdictional analysis—which focuses at the threshold solely on the defendant's purposeful connection to the forum. Nothing in our cases, however, suggests that a choice-of-law *provision* should be ignored in considering whether a defendant has "purposefully invoked the benefits and protections of a State's laws" for jurisdictional purposes. Although such a provision standing alone would be insufficient to confer jurisdiction, we believe that, when combined with the 20-year interdependent relationship Rudzewicz established with Burger King's Miami headquarters, it reinforced his deliberate affiliation with the forum State and the reasonable foreseeability of possible litigation there. . . .

(2)

Nor has Rudzewicz pointed to other factors that can be said persuasively to outweigh the considerations discussed above and to establish the *unconstitutionality* of Florida's assertion of jurisdiction. We cannot conclude that Florida had no "legitimate interest in holding [Rudzewicz] answerable on a claim related to" the contacts he had established in that State.[25] Moreover, although Rudzewicz has argued at some length that Michigan's Franchise Investment Law governs many aspects of this franchise relationship, he has not demonstrated how Michigan's acknowledged interest might possibly render jurisdiction in Florida *unconstitutional*.[26] Finally, the Court of Appeals' assertion that the Florida litigation "severely impaired [Rudzewicz's] ability to call Michigan witnesses who might be essential to his defense and counterclaim" is wholly without support in the record. And even to the extent that it is inconvenient for a party who has minimum contacts with a forum to litigate there, such considerations most frequently can be accommodated through a change of venue. Although . . . inconvenience may at some point become so substantial as to achieve *constitutional* magnitude, this is not such a case.

The Court of Appeals also concluded, however, that the parties' dealings involved "a characteristic disparity of bargaining power" and "elements of surprise," and that Rudzewicz "lacked fair notice" of the potential for litigation in Florida because the contractual provisions suggesting to the contrary were merely "boilerplate declarations in a lengthy printed contract." Rudzewicz presented many of these arguments to the District Court, contending that Burger King was guilty of misrepresentation, fraud, and duress; that it gave insufficient notice in its dealings with him; and that the contract was one of adhesion. After a 3-day bench trial, the District Court found that Burger King had made no misrepresentations, that Rudzewicz and MacShara "were and are experienced and sophisticated businessmen," and that "at no time" did they "ac[t] under economic duress or disadvantage imposed by" Burger King. Federal Rule of Civil Procedure 52(a) requires that "[f]indings of fact [must] not be set aside unless clearly erroneous," and neither Rudzewicz nor the Court of Appeals has pointed to record evidence that would support a "definite and firm conviction" that the District Court's findings are mistaken. To the contrary, Rudzewicz was represented by counsel throughout these complex transactions and . . . was himself an experienced accountant. . . .

---

25. Complaining that "when Burger King is the plaintiff, you won't 'have it your way' because it sues all franchisees in Miami," Rudzewicz contends that Florida's interest in providing a convenient forum is negligible given the company's size and ability to conduct litigation anywhere in the country. We disagree. Absent compelling considerations, a defendant who has purposefully derived commercial benefit from his affiliations in a forum may not defeat jurisdiction there simply because of his adversary's greater net wealth.

26. Rudzewicz has failed to show how the District Court's exercise of jurisdiction in this case might have been at all inconsistent with Michigan's interests. . . . In any event, minimum-contacts analysis presupposes that two or more States may be interested in the outcome of a dispute, and the process of resolving potentially conflicting "fundamental substantive social policies" can usually be accommodated through choice-of-law rules rather than through outright preclusion of jurisdiction in one forum.

III

Notwithstanding these considerations, the Court of Appeals apparently believed that it was necessary to reject jurisdiction in this case as a prophylactic measure, reasoning that an affirmance of the District Court's judgment would result in the exercise of jurisdiction over "out-of-state consumers to collect payments due on modest personal purchases" and would "sow the seeds of default judgments against franchisees owing smaller debts." We share the Court of Appeals' broader concerns and therefore reject any talismanic jurisdictional formulas; "the facts of each case must [always] be weighed" in determining whether personal jurisdiction would comport with "fair play and substantial justice." The "quality and nature" of an interstate transaction may sometimes be so "random," "fortuitous," or "attenuated" that it cannot fairly be said that the potential defendant "should reasonably anticipate being haled into court" in another jurisdiction. We also have emphasized that jurisdiction may not be grounded on a contract whose terms have been obtained through "fraud, undue influence, or overweening bargaining power" and whose application would render litigation "so gravely difficult and inconvenient that [a party] will for all practical purposes be deprived of his day in court." Just as the Due Process Clause allows flexibility in ensuring that commercial actors are not effectively "judgment proof" for the consequences of obligations they voluntarily assume in other States, so too does it prevent rules that would unfairly enable them to obtain default judgments against unwitting customers.

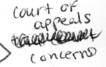

For the reasons set forth above, however, these dangers are not present in the instant case. Because Rudzewicz established a substantial and continuing relationship with Burger King's Miami headquarters, received fair notice from the contract documents and the course of dealing that he might be subject to suit in Florida, and has failed to demonstrate how jurisdiction in that forum would otherwise be fundamentally unfair, we conclude that the District Court's exercise of jurisdiction pursuant to [Florida's long-arm statute] did not offend due process. The judgment of the Court of Appeals is accordingly reversed, and the case is remanded for further proceedings consistent with this opinion.

It is so ordered.

JUSTICE POWELL took no part in the consideration or decision of this case.

JUSTICE STEVENS, with whom JUSTICE WHITE joins, dissenting.

In my opinion there is a significant element of unfairness in requiring a franchisee to defend a case of this kind in the forum chosen by the franchisor. . . . [A]ppellee did business only in Michigan, his business, property, and payroll taxes were payable in that State, and he sold all of his products there.

Throughout the business relationship, appellee's principal contacts with appellant were with its Michigan office. Notwithstanding its disclaimer, the Court seems ultimately to rely on nothing more than standard boilerplate language contained in various documents to establish that appellee " 'purposefully availed himself of the benefits and protections of Florida's laws.' " Such superficial analysis creates a potential for unfairness not only in negotiations between franchisors and their franchisees but, more significantly, in the resolution of the disputes that inevitably arise from time to time in such relationships. . . .

NOTES AND QUESTIONS

1. *What about* McGee?   Given the 1957 decision in *McGee*, why wasn't it clear that a state could assert personal jurisdiction over an "out-of-stater" who entered into and breached a contract with a forum resident? How was *Burger King* arguably distinguishable from *McGee*? What weight should be given to such factors as whether the defendant was a buyer rather than a seller, whether the defendant is financially weaker than the plaintiff, and whether the defendant dealt with the plaintiff's agents in the defendant's home state?

2. *Purposeful connections.*   The *Burger King* Court used the words "purposeful" and "purposefully" numerous times throughout its opinion, *e.g.*, "purposefully directed his activities at residents of the forum"; "purposefully derive benefit from their interstate activities"; "purposefully established minimum contacts in the forum State"; "purposefully engaged in forum activities"; "purposeful connection to the forum"; "purposefully invoked the benefits and protections of a State's laws"; "purposefully derived commercial benefit"; and, of course, "purposeful availment." It summed up its views of "purposefulness" by observing that:

> Jurisdiction is proper . . . where the contacts proximately result from actions by the defendant *himself* that create a "substantial connection" with the forum State. Thus where the defendant "deliberately" has engaged in significant activities within a State, or has created "continuing obligations" between himself and residents of the forum, he manifestly has availed himself of the privilege of conducting business there, and because his activities are shielded by "the benefits and protections" of the forum's laws it is presumptively not unreasonable to require him to submit to the burdens of litigation in that forum as well.

Pages 160-161, *supra*. Using *Burger King* as your guide, is "purposeful availment" an independent requirement of the minimum contacts test or is it a descriptive label that applies when the nonresident defendant has deliberately affiliated herself with the forum? In other words, is the key concept "availment" (and the implicit benefits and protections), or is it the nonresident defendant's creation of a meaningful, intentional connection with the forum state? Regardless of your answers, you should be aware that many courts will treat purposeful availment as a critical element of the minimum contacts test.

3. *Meaningful connections and reasonable expectations.*   What was Burger King's claim against Rudzewicz? What was the factual premise for that claim and to what extent was the claim based on activities that took place (or failed to take place) within the forum state? Was Rudzewicz responsible for those connections? How would you characterize his connections with Florida? Were they intentional or fortuitous? Were they systematic or sporadic? Were they related or unrelated to the claim? Taking all of your answers into account, were Rudzewicz's connections

with Florida "meaningful" in the sense that they created in him a reasonable expectation that he might be sued there on a claim arising out of them?

4. Boilerplate contract language.   Is Justice Stevens correct that the Court's finding of "purposeful availment" rested "on nothing more than standard boilerplate language" designating Florida as the place where the contract was made and payments were due, and as the state whose laws would govern the agreement? Did the Court suggest that other factors besides the contract language were also critical to its finding that Rudzewicz had purposefully directed his conduct toward the forum? If so, what were they?

5. A presumption of jurisdiction.   The Court in Part II-A indicates that in the case of specific jurisdiction, once a plaintiff establishes that defendant satisfies the contacts and relatedness standards, the exercise of jurisdiction is presumptively reasonable. To overcome this presumption, a defendant must "present a compelling case" that the exercise of jurisdiction would be "unreasonable." How would a defendant rebut that presumption? Why was Rudzewicz not successful in doing so?

PROBLEMS

2-5. Vetro, Inc., is a Pennsylvania corporation engaged in the manufacture and sale of various fiberglass reinforcement products. In early 1992, Vetro found itself with a marketable supply of chopped fiberglass strands ("CFS") and offered to supply Glass, Inc., a California corporation engaged in the manufacture of fiberglass roofing products, with its basic needs for CFS. Representatives of Vetro and Glass met shortly thereafter in California where the essential terms of an agreement were negotiated. While no Glass representatives traveled to Pennsylvania, representatives of the company did place several telephone calls to Vetro's offices in Valley Forge, Pennsylvania, as part of the negotiation process. The final agreement was prepared by Vetro in Pennsylvania and sent to Glass in California, where it was signed by Glass. The agreement provided a two-year term during which Vetro would supply all of Glass's CFS needs. The agreement would automatically renew for an additional one-year term commencing April 1, 1994, unless canceled at least 60 days before then. Under the agreement, Vetro agreed to ship CFS directly from its plant in Wichita Falls, Texas, to Glass's manufacturing facility in Bakersfield, California. Vetro's invoicing for the product sold under the agreement was handled by Vetro's Southern California office, and all payments for the CFS were sent to Vetro's office in Los Angeles, California. Glass's primary contact at Vetro was Jerry Leland, a sales representative working at Vetro's Santa Ana, California office. In 1993, Vetro decided to withdraw from the CFS supply business and sought to terminate its contract with Glass. Vetro claims that it canceled the agreement by telephone on December 2, 1993, more than 60 days prior to the April 1, 1994 deadline. According to Glass, however, it was only on March 23, 1994 that Vetro telephoned Glass and announced its intent to cancel the agreement. Vetro ceased delivery of CFS, and Glass withheld payment on outstanding invoices. Vetro then sued Glass in a Pennsylvania court, seeking to recover $303,595.35 in withheld payments. Glass has filed a timely motion to dismiss for lack of personal jurisdiction. How should the court rule on the motion? *See Vetrotex Certainteed Corp. v. Consolidated Fiber Glass Products Co.*, 75 F.3d 147 (1996).

2-6. HL is a California corporation with its principal place of business in California. It operates the Casino Royale on the internet. The website, which is advertised over the internet as the World's Largest Internet Casino, can be accessed from anywhere in the world. The server is in California. Once they access the site, players enter into a contract to play poker, blackjack, roulette, and other games, using their credit cards to buy game tokens that are redeemable for cash. Tom is a Texas domiciliary. While in Texas, he accessed the Casino Royale and contracted to play games on the website. By the end of the day he had won $193,728. When HL refused to pay Tom his winnings, he sued HL in a Texas court. HL moved to dismiss for lack of personal jurisdiction, arguing that it did not direct any of its internet advertising specifically toward Texas residents. How should the court rule on the motion? *See Thompson v. Handa-Lopez, Inc.*, 998 F. Supp. 738 (W.D. Tex. 1998).

2-7. After criminal charges were filed against him in Florida, Seymour, who lives in California, went to Florida and interviewed several law firms there. Before returning to California, he hired the Florida law firm of Paul, Joe & Michael ("PJ&M") to represent him and gave them a $50,000 retainer. Thereafter, PJ&M communicated with Seymour primarily by telephone and mail, but on three occasions a PJ&M lawyer met with him in California. Seymour was convicted in the Florida suit, but an appellate court later reversed his conviction due to incompetence of counsel. Seymour then sued PJ&M for legal malpractice in a California federal court. PJ&M moved to dismiss the suit on the ground that it lacked purposeful availment with California. How should the court rule on the motion? Would your answer differ if, in order to secure payment for legal expenses, PJ&M had required Seymour to give the law firm a deed of trust on his California residence? *See Sher v. Johnson*, 911 F.2d 1357 (9th Cir. 1990).

b.   Torts

Calder v. Jones
465 U.S. 783 (1984)

Justice Rehnquist delivered the opinion of the Court.

Respondent Shirley Jones brought suit in California Superior Court claiming that she had been libeled in an article written and edited by petitioners in Florida. The article was published in a national magazine with a large circulation in California. Petitioners were served with process by mail in Florida and caused special appearances to be entered on their behalf, moving to quash the service of process for lack of personal jurisdiction. . . .

Respondent lives and works in California. She . . . brought this suit against the National Enquirer, Inc., its local distributing company, and petitioners for libel, invasion of privacy, and intentional infliction of emotional harm. The Enquirer is a Florida corporation with its principal place of business in Florida. It publishes a national weekly newspaper with a total circulation of over 5 million. About 600,000 of those copies, almost twice the level of the next highest State, are sold in California. Respondent's . . . claims were based on an article that appeared in the Enquirer's October 9, 1979 issue. . . .

Petitioner South is a reporter employed by the Enquirer. He is a resident of Florida, though he frequently travels to California on business. South wrote the first draft of the challenged article, and his byline appeared on it. He did most of his research in Florida, relying on phone calls to sources in California for the information contained in the article. Shortly before publication, South called respondent's home and read to her husband a draft of the article so as to elicit his comments upon it. Aside from his frequent trips and phone calls, South has no other relevant contacts with California.

Petitioner Calder is also a Florida resident. He has been to California only twice—once, on a pleasure trip, prior to the publication of the article and once after to testify in an unrelated trial. Calder is president and editor of the Enquirer. He "oversee[s] just about every function of the Enquirer." He reviewed and approved the initial evaluation of the subject of the article and edited it in its final form. He also declined to print a retraction requested by respondent. Calder has no other relevant contacts with California.

In considering petitioners' motion to quash service of process, the Superior Court surmised that the actions of petitioners in Florida, causing injury to respondent in California, would ordinarily be sufficient to support an assertion of jurisdiction over them in California. But the court felt that special solicitude was necessary because of the potential "chilling effect" on reporters and editors which would result from requiring them to appear in remote jurisdictions to answer for the content of articles upon which they worked. The court also noted that respondent's rights could be "fully satisfied" in her suit against the publisher without requiring petitioners to appear as parties. The Superior Court, therefore, granted the motion.

The California Court of Appeal reversed. . . . [T]he court concluded that a valid basis for jurisdiction existed on the theory that petitioners intended to, and did, cause tortious injury to respondent in California. The fact that the actions causing the effects in California were performed outside the State did not prevent the State from asserting jurisdiction over a cause of action arising out of those effects.[6] The court rejected the Superior Court's conclusion that First Amendment considerations must be weighed in the scale against jurisdiction. . . .

_____

6. The Court of Appeal further suggested that petitioner South's investigative activities . . . formed an independent basis for an assertion of jurisdiction over him in this action. In light of our approval of the "effects" test employed by the California court, we find it unnecessary to reach this alternate ground.

. . . In judging minimum contacts, a court properly focuses on "the relationship among the defendant, the forum, and the litigation." *Shaffer v. Heitner*. The plaintiff's lack of "contacts" will not defeat otherwise proper jurisdiction, but they may be so manifold as to permit jurisdiction when it would not exist in their absence. Here, the plaintiff is the focus of the activities of the defendants out of which the suit arises.

The allegedly libelous story concerned the California activities of a California resident. It impugned the professionalism of an entertainer whose television career was centered in California.[9] The article was drawn from California sources, and the brunt of the harm, in terms both of respondent's emotional distress and the injury to her professional reputation, was suffered in California. In sum, California is the focal point both of the story and of the harm suffered. Jurisdiction over petitioners is therefore proper in California based on the "effects" of their Florida conduct in California . . . ; Restatement (Second) of Conflicts of Law § 37 (1971).

Petitioners argue that they are not responsible for the circulation of the article in California. A reporter and an editor, they claim, have no direct economic stake in their employer's sales in a distant State. Nor are ordinary employees able to control their employer's marketing activity. The mere fact that they can "foresee" that the article will be circulated and have an effect in California is not sufficient for an assertion of jurisdiction. They do not "in effect appoint the [article their] agent for service of process." *World-Wide Volkswagen Corp. v. Woodson*. Petitioners liken themselves to a welder employed in Florida who works on a boiler which subsequently explodes in California. Cases which hold that jurisdiction will be proper over the manufacturer should not be applied to the welder who has no control over and derives no direct benefit from his employer's sales in that distant State.

Petitioners' analogy does not wash. Whatever the status of their hypothetical welder, petitioners are not charged with mere untargeted negligence. Rather, their intentional, and allegedly tortious, actions were expressly aimed at California. Petitioner South wrote and petitioner Calder edited an article that they knew would have a potentially devastating impact upon respondent. And they knew that the brunt of that injury would be felt by respondent in the State in which she lives and works and in which the National Enquirer has its largest circulation. Under the circumstances, petitioners must "reasonably anticipate being haled into court there" to answer for the truth of the statements made in their article. An individual injured in California need not go to Florida to seek redress from persons who, though remaining in Florida, knowingly cause the injury in California.

Petitioners are correct that their contacts with California are not to be judged according to their employer's activities there. On the other hand, their status as employees does not somehow insulate them from jurisdiction. Each defendant's contacts with the forum State must be assessed individually. In this case, petitioners are primary participants in an alleged wrongdoing intentionally directed at a California resident, and jurisdiction over them is proper on that basis.

---

9. The article alleged that respondent drank so heavily as to prevent her from fulfilling her professional obligations.

We also reject the suggestion that First Amendment concerns enter into the jurisdictional analysis. The infusion of such considerations would needlessly complicate an already imprecise inquiry. . . . *—> so no 1st amd. right?*

We hold that jurisdiction over petitioners in California is proper because of their intentional conduct in Florida calculated to cause injury to respondent in California. The judgment of the California Court of Appeal is

Affirmed.

NOTES AND QUESTIONS

1. *The Restatement (Second) of Conflict of Laws.*   The *Calder* Court referred to the Restatement (Second) of Conflict of Laws § 37. That section provides:

> A state has power to exercise judicial jurisdiction over an individual who causes effects in the state by an act done elsewhere with respect to any cause of action arising from these effects unless the nature of the effects and of the individual's relationship to the state make the exercise of such jurisdiction unreasonable.

Id. Reduced to its essentials, § 37 endorses the exercise of personal jurisdiction over a nonresident defendant when the claim asserted against that defendant arises out of the foreseeable in-forum effects of defendant's out-of-forum activities and the exercise of jurisdiction is otherwise reasonable. This approach to jurisdiction, sometimes referred to as "the effects test," should not be read as an alternative to the minimum contacts test but as a contextualized version of it, another way to determine if the defendant's connections with the forum are meaningful. Section 37 should also be read in conjunction with §§ 35 and 36 of the Restatement, quoted in Note 4 following *International Shoe v. Washington,* page 144, *supra.*

2. *Purposeful availment and beyond.*   Notice that the *Calder* Court did not use the phrase "purposeful availment" or any variation of it. Did Calder and South purposefully avail themselves of the benefits and protections of the laws of California? If not, on what basis did the Court conclude that their connections with California were sufficient to satisfy due process standards? What role do "aim" and "brunt of the injury" play in that determination? And for that matter, what do those terms mean? Were the defendants' connections with the state meaningful in the sense that those connections created a reasonable expectation of suit in the forum? Calder and South did not deliver the offending article into California, but might we say that they were responsible for its publication there? If they are liable in tort under California law by virtue of the article having been published there, does it make sense to say that they should be subject to jurisdiction in California to answer for that tort?

3. *The scope of the* Calder *effects test.*   Lower courts have given *Calder*'s effects test a narrow sweep. There appears to be a growing consensus that the test will be satisfied only when:

(1) The defendant committed an intentional tort; (2) The plaintiff felt the brunt of the harm in the forum such that the forum can be said to be the focal point of the

EFFECTS

harm suffered by the plaintiff as a result of that tort; (3) The defendant expressly aimed his tortious conduct at the forum such that the forum can be said to be the focal point of the tortious activity.

Marten v. Godwin, 499 F.3d 290, 297 (3d Cir. 2007) (quoting *IMO Indus., Inc. v. Kiekert AG*, 155 F.3d 254, 265-266 (3d Cir. 1998)); *accord Pavlovich v. Superior Court*, 58 P.3d 2, 8-9 (Cal. 2002) (effects test requires express aiming at or intentional targeting of the forum; foreseeability of in-state effect insufficient); *Bancroft & Masters, Inc. v. Augusta National Inc.*, 223 F.3d 1082, 1087 (9th Cir. 2000) (*Calder* "cannot stand for the broad proposition that a foreign act with foreseeable effects in the forum state always gives rise to specific jurisdiction"); *but see Yahoo! Inc. v. La Ligue Contre Le Racisme Et L'Antisemitisme*, 433 F.3d 1199, 1206 (9th Cir.) (en banc), *cert. denied*, 547 U.S. 1163 (2006) (adopting a formula similar to the quoted passage but replacing the "brunt of the harm" standard with a "harm . . . likely to be suffered in the forum state" standard).

The Fifth Circuit has adopted an even narrower reading of the "effects test," requiring that for "specific jurisdiction in a libel action, the 'aim' of the plaintiff under the *Calder* test must be demonstrated by showing that (1) the subject matter of and (2) the sources relied upon for the article were in the forum state." *Fielding v. Hubert Burda Media, Inc.*, 415 F.3d 419, 426 (5th Cir. 2005). Some courts have gone even further, suggesting that the effects test "was specifically designed for use in a defamation case" and that it was never "intended to apply to numerous others torts . . . or breach of contract" claims. *United States v. Swiss American Bank, Ltd.*, 274 F.3d 610, 624 (1st Cir. 2001). Finally, *Janmark, Inc. v. Reidy*, 132 F.3d 1200, 1202 (7th Cir. 1997), the one case that read *Calder* much more broadly ("there can be no serious doubt after [*Calder*] that the state in which the victim of a tort suffers the injury may entertain a suit against the accused tortfeasor"), has been called into question by the very circuit that issued the opinion. *See Advanced Tactical Ordnance Systems, LLC v. Real Action Paintball, Inc.*, 751 F.3d 796, 802 (7th Cir. 2014), and *Tamburo v. Dworkin*, 601 F.3d 693, 704-706 (7th Cir.), *cert. denied*, 562 U.S. 1029 (2010). Is this narrowing sweep consistent with § 37 of the Restatement?

4. Calder *and the contracts cases.* Would the decisions in *Hanson v. Denckla*, *McGee v. International Life Ins. Co.*, and *Burger King v. Rudzewicz* come out differently under the narrow version of the effects test described in the preceding note? Consider whether each of the defendants in those cases acted intentionally, whether they aimed their out-of-state activity at the forum state, and whether they acted with an awareness that the brunt of the injury would be felt there. Is it appropriate to use a "torts" test for a contract claim? It might surprise you to learn that the effects test was originally conceived to encompass the decisions in *Hanson* and *McGee*. *See* Restatement (Second) of Conflict of Laws § 37 (1971), comments a & b.

5. *Jurisdiction over National Enquirer, Inc.*   In *Calder*, the writer and the editor challenged jurisdiction but their employer, the National Enquirer, did not. Note that the Court treated each of the defendants separately and did not attribute

the Enquirer's actions to its employees. Had the Enquirer also challenged jurisdiction, how would the issue have been resolved? Would the Court have needed to invoke the effects test? *See Keeton v. Hustler Magazine, Inc.*, 465 U.S. 770 (1984), Note 6, page 199, *infra* (upholding New Hampshire court's jurisdiction in a libel action brought by a New York plaintiff against an Ohio corporation that had sold its magazines in the forum state).

PROBLEMS

2-8. Suppose that A owns and operates a gravel quarry in Nevada. The quarry is located approximately a hundred yards from the border with California. B owns a small ranch in California just across from A's quarry. As part of quarry operations, A is sometimes required to detonate an explosive device. On one such occasion, the detonation sent rocks flying across the border into California, causing significant damage to B's ranch house. B has sued A in a California court, based on a theory of negligence (breach of the duty of due care). Was A's detonation of the explosive in Nevada a sufficiently meaningful connection with California to permit the California court to exercise jurisdiction over A? Would the exercise of jurisdiction over A be consistent with the standards established in the "contract" cases? Would the exercise of jurisdiction over A be consistent with § 37 of the Restatement? Finally, would the exercise of jurisdiction over A be consistent with the *Calder* effects text, as described in Note 3 above? Which of these approaches makes the most sense to you?

2-9. Skin Care, Inc., is a Texas corporation involved in the research, advertising, marketing, and sale of a skin care product called "Natural Care," which is sold throughout the United States. John Sanders is a California-based physician and scientist who maintains a noncommercial website, SkinTruth.com. The website is dedicated to providing educational material, including information and scientific research relating to skin care. In June 2012, Sanders published blog entries on his website that questioned the science behind Natural Care and criticized Skin Care's marketing organization. In response to these blogs, Doug Bick, a high-level representative of Skin Care, posted the following entry on his Facebook page:

> BOY DOES THIS BLOGGING SCORPION HAVE A LOT TO HIDE! More to come shortly about the Truth and Facts about this Blogging Scorpion, things like: Why he lost his medical license (yes we have the documents directly from the Medical Board of California); Why he personally uses multiple social security numbers; How many times has he been charged with domestic violence. Stay tuned as we reveal the REAL truth behind this Blogging Scorpion.

It was clear from the posting that Bick was referring to Sanders. In addition, Bick was aware that Sanders was a resident of California. Aside from this incident, Bick has no other contacts with the State of California. Sanders sued Bick for defamation in a California court. Bick has filed a motion to dismiss. How should the court rule on the motion? *See Burdick v. Superior Court*, 183 Cal. Rptr. 3d 1 (Ct. App. 2015).

2-10. Craig, a resident of Pennsylvania, where he is a licensed pharmacist, enrolled in a Kansas University ("KU") online internet-based Advanced Pharmacy Degree program that he learned of from KU's website. All of his communications and dealings with KU were by e-mail. During his first year in the program, Craig complained to the program director and to the dean about his grades and about KU's three-year time limit for completing the degree requirements; he also objected that school officials were not sufficiently attentive to his complaints. In response, the program director threatened to dismiss Craig from the program. The following year, Professor James accused Craig of plagiarizing several writing assignments. After the dean and the program director investigated these allegations, Craig was expelled from KU on grounds of academic misconduct. He then filed suit in a Pennsylvania federal court against the dean, the program director, and Professor James, seeking reinstatement and damages. The complaint alleges that the defendants violated Craig's First Amendment rights by falsely accusing him of plagiarism and by expelling him in retaliation for his having criticized the KU program. After the defendants were served in Kansas under Pennsylvania's long-arm statute, they moved to dismiss the action for lack of personal jurisdiction. The defendants have never visited Pennsylvania nor have they sought to promote the program to pharmacists there. Can Craig successfully invoke the effects test to support the Pennsylvania court's taking jurisdiction over the defendants? *See Marten v. Godwin*, 499 F.3d 290 (3d Cir. 2007).

Walden v. Fiore

134 S. Ct. 1115 (2014)

Justice Thomas delivered the opinion of the Court.

This case asks us to decide whether a court in Nevada may exercise personal jurisdiction over a defendant on the basis that he knew his allegedly tortious conduct in Georgia would delay the return of funds to plaintiffs with connections to Nevada. Because the defendant had no other contacts with Nevada, and because a plaintiff's contacts with the forum State cannot be "decisive in determining whether the defendant's due process rights are violated," *Rush v. Savchuk*, 444 U.S. 320, 332 (1980), we hold that the court in Nevada may not exercise personal jurisdiction under these circumstances.

I

Petitioner Anthony Walden serves as a police officer for the city of Covington, Georgia. In August 2006, petitioner was working at the Atlanta Hartsfield-Jackson Airport as a deputized agent of the Drug Enforcement Administration (DEA). As part of a task force, petitioner conducted investigative stops and other law enforcement functions in support of the DEA's airport drug interdiction program.

On August 8, 2006, Transportation Security Administration agents searched respondents Gina Fiore and Keith Gipson and their carry-on bags at the San Juan airport in Puerto Rico. They found almost $97,000 in cash. Fiore explained to DEA agents in San Juan that she and Gipson had been gambling at a casino known as the El San Juan, and that they had residences in both California and Nevada (though they provided only California identification). After respondents were cleared for departure, a law enforcement official at the San Juan airport notified petitioner's task force in Atlanta that respondents had boarded a plane for Atlanta, where they planned to catch a connecting flight to Las Vegas, Nevada.

When respondents arrived in Atlanta, petitioner and another DEA agent approached them at the departure gate for their flight to Las Vegas. In response to petitioner's questioning, Fiore explained that she and Gipson were professional gamblers. Respondents maintained that the cash they were carrying was their gambling "'bank'" and winnings. After using a drug-sniffing dog to perform a sniff test, petitioner seized the cash. Petitioner advised respondents that their funds would be returned if they later proved a legitimate source for the cash. Respondents then boarded their plane.

After respondents departed, petitioner moved the cash to a secure location and the matter was forwarded to DEA headquarters. The next day, petitioner received a phone call from respondents' attorney in Nevada seeking return of the funds. On two occasions over the next month, petitioner also received documentation from the attorney regarding the legitimacy of the funds.

At some point after petitioner seized the cash, he helped draft an affidavit to show probable cause for forfeiture of the funds and forwarded that affidavit to a United States Attorney's Office in Georgia. According to respondents, the affidavit was false and misleading because petitioner misrepresented the encounter at the airport and omitted exculpatory information regarding the lack of drug evidence and the legitimate source of the funds. In the end, no forfeiture complaint was filed, and the DEA returned the funds to respondents in March 2007.

Respondents filed suit against petitioner in the United States District Court for the District of Nevada, seeking money damages under *Bivens v. Six Unknown Fed. Narcotics Agents*, 403 U.S. 388 (1971). Respondents alleged that petitioner violated their Fourth Amendment rights by (1) seizing the cash without probable cause; (2) keeping the money after concluding it did not come from drug-related activity; (3) drafting and forwarding a probable cause affidavit to support a forfeiture action while knowing the affidavit contained false statements; (4) willfully seeking forfeiture while withholding exculpatory information; and (5) withholding that exculpatory information from the United States Attorney's Office.

The District Court granted petitioner's motion to dismiss. Relying on this Court's decision in *Calder v. Jones*, the court determined that petitioner's search of respondents and his seizure of the cash in Georgia did not establish a basis to exercise personal jurisdiction in Nevada. The court concluded that even if petitioner caused harm to respondents in Nevada while knowing they lived in Nevada, that fact alone did not confer jurisdiction. Because the court dismissed the complaint for lack of personal jurisdiction, it did not determine whether venue was proper.

On appeal, a divided panel of the United States Court of Appeals for the Ninth Circuit reversed. The Court of Appeals assumed the District Court had correctly determined that petitioner's search and seizure in Georgia could not support exercise of jurisdiction in Nevada. The court held, however, that the District Court could properly exercise jurisdiction over "the false probable cause affidavit aspect of the case." According to the Court of Appeals, petitioner "expressly aimed" his submission of the allegedly false affidavit at Nevada by submitting the affidavit with knowledge that it would affect persons with a "significant connection" to Nevada. After determining that the delay in returning the funds to respondents caused them "foreseeable harm" in Nevada and that the exercise of personal jurisdiction over petitioner was otherwise reasonable, the court found the District Court's exercise of personal jurisdiction to be proper. The Ninth Circuit denied rehearing en banc, with eight judges, in two separate opinions, dissenting.

We granted certiorari to decide whether due process permits a Nevada court to exercise jurisdiction over petitioner. We hold that it does not and therefore reverse.

II

A

[The Court's discussion of Nevada's long-arm statute, which allows its courts to exercise jurisdiction "on any basis not inconsistent with . . . the Constitution," is omitted.]

B

1 . . .

This case addresses the "minimum contacts" necessary to create specific jurisdiction. The inquiry whether a forum State may assert specific jurisdiction over a nonresident defendant "focuses on 'the relationship among the defendant, the forum, and the litigation.'" *Keeton v. Hustler Magazine, Inc.* For a State to exercise jurisdiction consistent with due process, the defendant's suit-related conduct must create a substantial connection with the forum State. Two related aspects of this necessary relationship are relevant in this case.

First, the relationship must arise out of contacts that the "defendant himself" creates with the forum State. *Burger King Corp. v. Rudzewicz.* Due process limits on the State's adjudicative authority principally protect the liberty of the non-resident defendant—not the convenience of plaintiffs or third parties. We have consistently rejected attempts to satisfy the defendant-focused "minimum contacts" inquiry by demonstrating contacts between the plaintiff (or third parties) and the forum State. We have thus rejected a plaintiff's argument that a Florida court could exercise personal jurisdiction over a trustee in Delaware based solely on the contacts of the trust's settlor, who was domiciled in Florida and had executed powers of appointment there. *Hanson v. Denckla.* We have likewise held that Oklahoma courts could not exercise personal jurisdiction over an automobile distributor that supplies New York, New Jersey, and Connecticut dealers based only on an automobile purchaser's act of driving it on Oklahoma highways. *World-Wide Volkswagen Corp. v. Woodson*. Put simply, however significant the plaintiff's contacts with the forum may be, those contacts cannot be "decisive in determining whether the defendant's due process rights are violated."

Second, our "minimum contacts" analysis looks to the defendant's contacts with the forum State itself, not the defendant's contacts with persons who reside there. Accordingly, we have upheld the assertion of jurisdiction over defendants who have purposefully "reach[ed] out beyond" their State and into another by, for example, entering a contractual relationship that "envisioned continuing and wide-reaching contacts" in the forum State, *Burger King*, or by circulating magazines to "deliberately exploi[t]" a market in the forum State, *Keeton*. And although physical presence in the forum is not a prerequisite to jurisdiction, *Burger King*, *supra*, at 476, physical entry into the State—either by the defendant in person or through an agent, goods, mail, or some other means—is certainly a relevant contact.

But the plaintiff cannot be the only link between the defendant and the forum. Rather, it is the defendant's conduct that must form the necessary connection with the forum State that is the basis for its jurisdiction over him. To be sure, a defendant's contacts with the forum State may be intertwined with his transactions or interactions with the plaintiff or other parties. But a defendant's relationship with a plaintiff or third party, standing alone, is an insufficient basis for jurisdiction. Due process requires that a defendant be haled into court in a forum State based on his own affiliation with the State, not based on the "random, fortuitous, or attenuated" contacts he makes by interacting with other persons affiliated with the State. *Burger King*, 471 U.S., at 475.

2

These same principles apply when intentional torts are involved. In that context, it is likewise insufficient to rely on a defendant's "random, fortuitous, or attenuated contacts" or on the "unilateral activity" of a plaintiff. A forum State's exercise of jurisdiction over an out-of-state intentional tortfeasor must be based on intentional conduct by the defendant that creates the necessary contacts with the forum. *Calder v. Jones* illustrates the application of these principles. In *Calder*, a California actress brought a libel suit in California state court against a reporter and an editor, both of whom worked for the National Enquirer at its headquarters in Florida. The plaintiff's libel claims were based on an article written and edited by the defendants in Florida for publication in the National Enquirer, a national weekly newspaper with a California circulation of roughly 600,000.

We held that California's assertion of jurisdiction over the defendants was consistent with due process. Although we recognized that the defendants' activities "focus[ed]" on the plaintiff, our jurisdictional inquiry "focuse[d] on 'the relationship among the defendant, the forum, and the litigation.'" Specifically, we examined the various contacts the defendants had created with California (and not just with the plaintiff) by writing the allegedly libelous story.

We found those forum contacts to be ample: The defendants relied on phone calls to "California sources" for the information in their article; they wrote the story about the plaintiff's activities in California; they caused reputational injury in California by writing an allegedly libelous article that was widely circulated in the State; and the "brunt" of that injury was suffered by the plaintiff in that State. "In sum, California [wa]s the focal point both of the story and of the harm suffered." Jurisdiction over the defendants was "therefore proper in California based on the 'effects' of their Florida conduct in California."

The crux of *Calder* was that the reputation-based "effects" of the alleged libel connected the defendants to California, not just to the plaintiff. The strength of that connection was largely a function of the nature of the libel tort. However scandalous a newspaper article might be, it can lead to a loss of reputation only if communicated to (and read and understood by) third persons. Accordingly, the reputational injury caused by the defendants' story would not have occurred but for the fact that the defendants wrote an article for publication in California that was read by a large number of California citizens. Indeed, because publication to third persons is a necessary element of libel, the defendants' intentional tort actually occurred in California. In this way, the "effects" caused by the defendants' article—*i.e.*, the injury to the plaintiff's reputation in the estimation of the California public—connected the defendants' conduct to California, not just to a plaintiff who lived there. That connection, combined with the various facts that gave the article a California focus, sufficed to authorize the California court's exercise of jurisdiction.

III

Applying the foregoing principles, we conclude that petitioner lacks the "minimal contacts" with Nevada that are a prerequisite to the exercise of jurisdiction over him. It is undisputed that no part of petitioner's course of conduct occurred in Nevada. Petitioner approached, questioned, and searched respondents, and seized the cash at issue, in the Atlanta airport. It is alleged that petitioner later helped draft a "false probable cause affidavit" in Georgia and forwarded that affidavit to a United States Attorney's Office in Georgia to support a potential action for forfeiture of the seized funds. Petitioner never traveled to, conducted activities within, contacted anyone in, or sent anything or anyone to Nevada. In short, when viewed through the proper lens—whether the defendant's actions connect him to the forum—petitioner formed no jurisdictionally relevant contacts with Nevada.

The Court of Appeals reached a contrary conclusion by shifting the analytical focus from petitioner's contacts with the forum to his contacts with respondents. Rather than assessing petitioner's own contacts with Nevada, the Court of Appeals looked to petitioner's knowledge of respondents' "strong forum connections." In the court's view, that knowledge, combined with its conclusion that respondents suffered foreseeable harm in Nevada, satisfied the "minimum contacts" inquiry.

This approach to the "minimum contacts" analysis impermissibly allows a plaintiff's contacts with the defendant and forum to drive the jurisdictional analysis. Petitioner's actions in Georgia did not create sufficient contacts with Nevada simply because he allegedly directed his conduct at plaintiffs whom he knew had Nevada connections. Such reasoning improperly attributes a plaintiff's forum connections to the defendant and makes those connections "decisive" in the jurisdictional analysis. It also obscures the reality that none of petitioner's challenged conduct had anything to do with Nevada itself.

Relying on *Calder*, respondents emphasize that they suffered the "injury" caused by petitioner's allegedly tortious conduct (*i.e.*, the delayed return of their gambling funds) while they were residing in the forum. This emphasis is likewise misplaced. As previously noted, Calder made clear that mere injury to a forum resident is not a sufficient connection to the forum. Regardless of where a plaintiff lives or works, an injury is jurisdictionally relevant only insofar as it shows that the defendant has formed a contact with the forum State. The proper question is not where the plaintiff experienced a particular injury or effect but whether the defendant's conduct connects him to the forum in a meaningful way.

Respondents' claimed injury does not evince a connection between petitioner and Nevada. Even if we consider the continuation of the seizure in Georgia to be a distinct injury, it is not the sort of effect that is tethered to Nevada in any meaningful way. Respondents (and only respondents) lacked access to their funds in Nevada not because anything independently occurred there, but because Nevada is where respondents chose to be at a time when they desired to use the funds seized by petitioner. Respondents would have experienced this same lack of access in California, Mississippi, or wherever else they might have traveled and found themselves wanting more money than they had. Unlike the broad publication of the forum-focused story in *Calder*, the effects of petitioner's conduct on respondents are not connected to the forum State in a way that makes those effects a proper basis for jurisdiction.[9]

The Court of Appeals pointed to other possible contacts with Nevada, each ultimately unavailing. Respondents' Nevada attorney contacted petitioner in Georgia, but that is precisely the sort of "unilateral activity" of a third party that "cannot satisfy the requirement of contact with the forum State." *Hanson*, 357 U.S., at 253. Respondents allege that some of the cash seized in Georgia "originated" in Nevada, but that attenuated connection was not created by petitioner, and the cash was in Georgia, not Nevada, when petitioner seized it. Finally, the funds were eventually returned to respondents in Nevada, but petitioner had

---

9. Respondents warn that if we decide petitioner lacks minimum contacts in this case, it will bring about unfairness in cases where intentional torts are committed via the Internet or other electronic means (*e.g.*, fraudulent access of financial accounts or "phishing" schemes). As an initial matter, we reiterate that the "minimum contacts" inquiry principally protects the liberty of the nonresident defendant, not the interests of the plaintiff. In any event, this case does not present the very different questions whether and how a defendant's virtual "presence" and conduct translate into "contacts" with a particular State. To the contrary, there is no question where the conduct giving rise to this litigation took place: Petitioner seized physical cash from respondents in the Atlanta airport, and he later drafted and forwarded an affidavit in Georgia. We leave questions about virtual contacts for another day.

nothing to do with that return (indeed, it seems likely that it was respondents' uni-lateral decision to have their funds sent to Nevada).

* * *

Well-established principles of personal jurisdiction are sufficient to decide this case. The proper focus of the "minimum contacts" inquiry in intentional-tort cases is "'the relationship among the defendant, the forum, and the litigation.'" And it is the defendant, not the plaintiff or third parties, who must create contacts with the forum State. In this case, the application of those principles is clear: Petitioner's relevant conduct occurred entirely in Georgia, and the mere fact that his conduct affected plaintiffs with connections to the forum State does not suffice to authorize jurisdiction. We therefore reverse the judgment of the Court of Appeals.

It is so ordered.

NOTES AND QUESTIONS

1. Applying Burger King. Did you notice that the *Walden* Court relied on *Burger King* in describing and applying the standards under which to assess personal jurisdiction? Does this suggest that the minimum contacts test does not vary from one context to another? See Note 2, page 171 (following *Calder v. Jones*). *Burger King* required the plaintiff to show that the nonresident defendant had established purposeful connections with the forum state; that purposefulness was demonstrated in the context of a contractual relationship. Did either *Calder* or *Walden* require anything different, *i.e.*, anything other than a purposeful connection with the forum state? Might we say that in *Burger King* and *Calder* the purposeful connection was found, while in *Walden* it was not? If that is so, the critical distinction is not between contract cases and tort cases, but between those cases in which a purposeful connection is found and those in which it is not.

With the foregoing in mind, let's compare *Burger King* and *Walden*. What did the defendant in *Burger King* do to affiliate himself with the forum state? In other words, on what basis did the *Burger King* Court find the necessary purposeful connection with the forum state? Did the defendant in *Walden* do anything comparable? How, if at all, did he affiliate himself with the forum state? Suppose in *Burger King* that the contract between the defendant and Burger King was negotiated and signed in the defendant's home state, Michigan, and that all business transactions between the plaintiff and the defendant occurred there. Suppose too that the defendant's only connection with Burger King was that he knew that his failure to make the required payments under the contract would have an impact on Burger King at its headquarters in Florida. Would the Court have upheld jurisdiction under those circumstances? Were the facts in *Walden* significantly distinguishable from this hypothetical?

A NOTE ON THE "STREAM OF COMMERCE" THEORY

"Stream of commerce" is a theory (or metaphor) used in product liability cases to describe multi-state or multi-nation "streams" of commercial transactions that begin when a manufacturer delivers its product into the "stream of commerce" in one state—*e.g.*, by delivering the product to a distributor—and ends when the product is purchased at retail in another state. The question is whether such a manufacturer (or other party in the chain of distribution) can be subject to personal jurisdiction on a claim of product liability in the state of retail sale. As we will see, this question cannot be resolved independently from the more fundamental question of whether the defendant has established a meaningful connection with the forum state. *See, e.g.*, *Gray v. American Radiator & Standard Sanitary Corp.*, 176 N.E.2d 761 (Ill. 1961) (an Illinois court could take personal jurisdiction over an Ohio valve manufacturer that sold a valve to a Pennsylvania company that installed the valve in a water heater that was sold to a retailer in Illinois who then sold the heater to a customer who was injured when the heater exploded there).

In *World-Wide Volkswagen Corp. v. Woodson*, 444 U.S. 286 (1980), the Supreme Court appeared to endorse the stream-of-commerce theory. The precise question in *World-Wide* was whether a New York auto retailer and its New York wholesale distributor could be subject to personal jurisdiction in Oklahoma when a car manufactured in Germany and sold at retail in New York was driven by the New York buyer to Oklahoma where it was involved in an automobile accident. Despite the Court's apparent endorsement of the stream-of-commerce theory, the Court held that the theory could not be used to establish jurisdiction in the case before it since the "stream" ended when the product was sold to the retail purchaser in New York. More fundamentally, the Court held that neither the New York auto retailer nor the New York wholesale distributor had established any meaningful connections with the State of Oklahoma, either by virtue of the stream of commerce or otherwise.

The Court again addressed the stream-of-commerce theory in *Asahi Metal Industry Co., Ltd. v. Superior Court of California*, 480 U.S. 102 (1987). That case presented the question of whether a California court could exercise personal jurisdiction over a Japanese tire valve manufacturer that sold one of its valve assemblies to a Taiwanese tire manufacturer. The tire manufacturer incorporated the valve into a finished motorcycle tire tube that it then shipped and sold to a California cycle shop where a customer purchased it. That customer was severely injured (and his wife killed) after his motorcycle collided with a truck. The Court deadlocked on the question of whether placing goods in the stream of commerce was by itself enough to establish a meaningful connection with the state where the product finally reaches a retail buyer, or whether something more was required on the manufacturer's part. Four Justices (Justices Brennan *et al.*) said that placing a product in the stream was by itself enough, so long as defendant was aware that the final product was being marketed in the forum state as part of a "regular and anticipated flow of products from manufacture to distribution to retail sale" (the "pure stream of commerce" theory). Four other Justices (Justices O'Connor *et al.*) insisted that a more "substantial connection" was required, *i.e.*, some additional "action of the defendant purposely directed toward the forum State," such as advertising or soliciting sales in the forum state, establishing channels for providing regular advice to customers in the forum state, or creating or controlling the distribution system that brought its products into the forum state (the "stream of commerce plus" theory). The ninth Justice (Justice Stevens) declined to endorse either approach, but emphasized the importance of taking the volume, value, and hazardous nature of the product into account.

Due to its lack of any clear holding, *Asahi* left state and lower federal courts in disarray concerning the use of the stream-of-commerce theory. In the case that follows, decided more than 20 years after the Justices had deadlocked on the issue in *Asahi*, the Court returned to the stream-of-commerce theory in hopes of clarifying the law. You will notice that once again, however, there is no majority opinion for the Court.

J. McIntyre Machinery, Ltd. v. Nicastro
131 S. Ct. 2780 (2011)

JUSTICE KENNEDY announced the judgment of the Court and delivered an opinion, in which THE CHIEF JUSTICE, JUSTICE SCALIA, and JUSTICE THOMAS join.

Whether a person or entity is subject to the jurisdiction of a state court despite not having been present in the State either at the time of suit or at the time of the alleged injury, and despite not having consented to the exercise of jurisdiction, is a question that arises with great frequency in the routine course of litigation. The rules and standards for determining when a State does or does not have jurisdiction over an absent party have been unclear because of decades-old questions left open in *Asahi Metal Industry Co. v. Superior Court of Cal., Solano Cty.*, 480 U.S. 102 (1987).

Here, the Supreme Court of New Jersey, relying in part on *Asahi*, held that New Jersey's courts can exercise jurisdiction over a foreign manufacturer of a product so long as the manufacturer "knows or reasonably should know that its products are distributed through a nationwide distribution system that might lead to those products being sold in any of the fifty states." Applying that test, the court concluded that a British manufacturer of scrap metal machines was subject to jurisdiction in New Jersey, even though at no time had it advertised in, sent goods to, or in any relevant sense targeted the State.

That decision cannot be sustained . . . . Due process protects the defendant's right not to be coerced except by lawful judicial power. As a general rule, the exercise of judicial power is not lawful unless the defendant "purposefully avails itself of the privilege of conducting activities within the forum State, thus invoking the benefits and protections of its laws." *Hanson v. Denckla* . . . . [T]he general rule is applicable in this products-liability case, and the so-called "stream-of-commerce" doctrine cannot displace it.

I

This case arises from a products-liability suit filed in New Jersey state court. Robert Nicastro seriously injured his hand while using a metal-shearing machine manufactured by J. McIntyre Machinery, Ltd. (J. McIntyre). The accident occurred in New Jersey, but the machine was manufactured in England, where J. McIntyre is incorporated and operates. The question here is whether the New Jersey courts have jurisdiction over J. McIntyre, notwithstanding the fact that the company at no time either marketed goods in the State or shipped them there. Nicastro was a plaintiff in the New Jersey trial court and is the respondent here; J. McIntyre was a defendant and is now the petitioner.

At oral argument in this Court, Nicastro's counsel stressed three primary facts in defense of New Jersey's assertion of jurisdiction over J. McIntyre.

First, an independent company agreed to sell J. McIntyre's machines in the United States. J. McIntyre itself did not sell its machines to buyers in this country beyond the U.S. distributor, and there is no allegation that the distributor was under J. McIntyre's control.

Second, J. McIntyre officials attended annual conventions for the scrap recycling industry to advertise J. McIntyre's machines alongside the distributor. The conventions took place in various States, but never in New Jersey.

Third, no more than four machines (the record suggests only one), including the machine that caused the injuries that are the basis for this suit, ended up in New Jersey.

In addition to these facts emphasized by respondent, the New Jersey Supreme Court noted that J. McIntyre held both United States and European patents on its recycling technology. It also noted that the U.S. distributor "structured [its] advertising and sales efforts in accordance with" J. McIntyre's "direction and guidance whenever possible," and that "at least some of the machines were sold on consignment to" the distributor.

In light of these facts, the New Jersey Supreme Court concluded that New Jersey courts could exercise jurisdiction over petitioner without contravention of the Due Process Clause. Jurisdiction was proper, in that court's view, because the injury occurred in New Jersey; because petitioner knew or reasonably should have known "that its products are distributed through a nationwide distribution system that might lead to those products being sold in any of the fifty states"; and because petitioner failed to "take some reasonable step to prevent the distribution of its products in this State."

Both the New Jersey Supreme Court's holding and its account of what it called "[t]he stream-of-commerce doctrine of jurisdiction" were incorrect, however. This Court's *Asahi* decision may be responsible in part for that court's error regarding the stream of commerce, and this case presents an opportunity to provide greater clarity.

II

The Due Process Clause protects an individual's right to be deprived of life, liberty, or property only by the exercise of lawful power. This is no less true with respect to the power of a sovereign to resolve disputes through judicial process than with respect to the power of a sovereign to prescribe rules of conduct for those within its sphere. As a general rule, neither statute nor judicial decree may bind strangers to the State.

A court may subject a defendant to judgment only when the defendant has sufficient contacts with the sovereign "such that the maintenance of the suit does not offend 'traditional notions of fair play and substantial justice.'" *International Shoe Co. v. Washington.* Freeform notions of fundamental fairness divorced from traditional practice cannot transform a judgment rendered in the absence of authority into law. As a general rule, the sovereign's exercise of power requires some act by which the defendant "purposefully avails itself of the privilege of conducting activities within the forum State, thus invoking the benefits and protections of its laws," though in some cases, as with an intentional tort, the defendant might well fall within the State's authority by reason of his attempt to obstruct its laws. In products-liability cases like this one, it is the defendant's purposeful availment that makes jurisdiction consistent with "traditional notions of fair play and substantial justice."

A person may submit to a State's authority in a number of ways. There is, of course, explicit consent. Presence within a State at the time suit commences through service of process is another example. Citizenship or domicile—or, by analogy, incorporation or principal place of business for corporations—also indicates general submission to a State's powers. Each of these examples reveals circumstances, or a course of conduct, from which it is proper to infer an intention to benefit from and thus an intention to submit to the laws of the forum State. These examples support exercise of the general jurisdiction of the State's courts and allow the State to resolve both matters that originate within the State and those based on activities and events elsewhere. By contrast, those who live or operate primarily outside a State have a due process right not to be subjected to judgment in its courts as a general matter.

There is also a more limited form of submission to a State's authority for disputes that "arise out of or are connected with the activities within the state." *International Shoe Co.* Where a defendant "purposefully avails itself of the privilege of conducting activities within the forum State, thus invoking the benefits and protections of its laws," *Hanson,* it submits to the judicial power of an otherwise foreign sovereign to the extent that power is exercised in connection with the defendant's activities touching on the State. In other words, submission through contact with and activity directed at a sovereign may justify specific jurisdiction "in a suit arising out of or related to the defendant's contacts with the forum."

. . . The stream of commerce, like other metaphors, has its deficiencies as well as its utility. It refers to the movement of goods from manufacturers through distributors to consumers, yet beyond that descriptive purpose its meaning is far from exact. This Court has stated that a defendant's placing goods into the stream of commerce "with the expectation that they will be purchased by consumers within the forum State" may indicate purposeful availment. *World-Wide Volkswagen Corp. v. Woodson,* 444 U.S. 286, 298 (1980) (finding that expectation lacking). But that statement does not amend the general rule of personal jurisdiction. It merely observes that a defendant may in an appropriate case be subject to jurisdiction without entering the forum—itself an unexceptional proposition—as where manufacturers or distributors "seek to serve" a given State's market. The principal inquiry in cases of this sort is whether the defendant's activities manifest an intention to submit to the power of a sovereign. In other words, the defendant must "purposefully avai[l] itself of the privilege of conducting activities within the forum State, thus invoking the benefits and protections of its laws." *Hanson.* Sometimes a defendant does so by sending its goods rather than its agents. The defendant's transmission of goods permits the exercise of jurisdiction only where the defendant can be said to have targeted the forum; as a general rule, it is not enough that the defendant might have predicted that its goods will reach the forum State.

In *Asahi*, an opinion by Justice Brennan for four Justices outlined a different approach. It discarded the central concept of sovereign authority in favor of considerations of fairness and foreseeability. As that concurrence contended, "jurisdiction premised on the placement of a product into the stream of commerce [without more] is consistent with the Due Process Clause," for "[a]s long as a participant in this process is aware that the final product is being marketed in the forum State, the possibility of a lawsuit there cannot come as a surprise." It was the premise of the concurring opinion that the defendant's ability to anticipate suit renders the assertion of jurisdiction fair. In this way, the opinion made foreseeability the touchstone of jurisdiction.

The standard set forth in Justice Brennan's concurrence was rejected in an opinion written by Justice O'Connor; but the relevant part of that opinion, too, commanded the assent of only four Justices, not a majority of the Court. That opinion stated: "The 'substantial connection' between the defendant and the forum State necessary for a finding of minimum contacts must come about by an action of the defendant purposefully directed toward the forum State. The placement of a product into the stream of commerce, without more, is not an act of the defendant purposefully directed toward the forum State."

Since *Asahi* was decided, the courts have sought to reconcile the competing opinions. But Justice Brennan's concurrence, advocating a rule based on general notions of fairness and foreseeability, is inconsistent with the premises of lawful judicial power. This Court's precedents make clear that it is the defendant's actions, not his expectations, that empower a State's courts to subject him to judgment.

The conclusion that jurisdiction is in the first instance a question of authority rather than fairness explains, for example, why the principal opinion in *Burnham* "conducted no independent inquiry into the desirability or fairness" of the rule that service of process within a State suffices to establish jurisdiction over an otherwise foreign defendant. As that opinion explained, "[t]he view developed early that each State had the power to hale before its courts any individual who could be found within its borders." Furthermore, were general fairness considerations the touchstone of jurisdiction, a lack of purposeful availment might be excused where carefully crafted judicial procedures could otherwise protect the defendant's interests, or where the plaintiff would suffer substantial hardship if forced to litigate in a foreign forum. That such considerations have not been deemed controlling is instructive.

Two principles are implicit in the foregoing. First, personal jurisdiction requires a forum-by-forum, or sovereign-by-sovereign, analysis. The question is whether a defendant has followed a course of conduct directed at the society or economy existing within the jurisdiction of a given sovereign, so that the sovereign has the power to subject the defendant to judgment concerning that conduct. Personal jurisdiction, of course, restricts "judicial power not as a matter of sovereignty, but as a matter of individual liberty," for due process protects the individual's right to be subject only to lawful power. But whether a judicial judgment is lawful depends on whether the sovereign has authority to render it.

The second principle is a corollary of the first. Because the United States is a distinct sovereign, a defendant may in principle be subject to the jurisdiction of the courts of the United States but not of any particular State. This is consistent with the premises and unique genius of our Constitution . . . . For jurisdiction, a litigant may have the requisite relationship with the United States Government but not with the government of any individual State. That would be an exceptional case, however. If the defendant is a domestic domiciliary, the courts of its home State are available and can exercise general jurisdiction. And if another State were to assert jurisdiction in an inappropriate case, it would upset the federal balance, which posits that each State has a sovereignty that is not subject to unlawful intrusion by other States . . . .

It must be remembered, however, that although this case and *Asahi* both involve foreign manufacturers, the undesirable consequences of Justice Brennan's approach are no less significant for domestic producers. The owner of a small Florida farm might sell crops to a large nearby distributor, for example, who might then distribute them to grocers across the country. If foreseeability were the controlling criterion, the farmer could be sued in Alaska or any number of other States' courts without ever leaving town. And the issue of foreseeability may itself be contested so that significant expenses are incurred just on the preliminary issue of jurisdiction. Jurisdictional rules should avoid these costs whenever possible.

The conclusion that the authority to subject a defendant to judgment depends on purposeful availment, consistent with Justice O'Connor's opinion in *Asahi*, does not by itself resolve many difficult questions of jurisdiction that will arise in particular cases. The defendant's conduct and the economic realities of the market the defendant seeks to serve will differ across cases, and judicial exposition will, in common-law fashion, clarify the contours of that principle.

III

In this case, petitioner directed marketing and sales efforts at the United States. It may be that, assuming it were otherwise empowered to legislate on the subject, the Congress could authorize the exercise of jurisdiction in appropriate courts. That circumstance is not presented in this case, however, and it is neither necessary nor appropriate to address here any constitutional concerns that might be attendant to that exercise of power . . . . Here the question concerns the authority of a New Jersey state court to exercise jurisdiction, so it is petitioner's purposeful contacts with New Jersey, not with the United States, that alone are relevant.

Respondent has not established that J. McIntyre engaged in conduct purposefully directed at New Jersey. Recall that respondent's claim of jurisdiction centers on three facts: The distributor agreed to sell J. McIntyre's machines in the United States; J. McIntyre officials attended trade shows in several States but not in New Jersey; and up to four machines ended up in New Jersey. The British manufacturer had no office in New Jersey; it neither paid taxes nor owned property there; and it neither advertised in, nor sent any employees to, the State. Indeed, after discovery the trial court found that the "defendant does not have a single contact with New Jersey short of the machine in question ending up in this state." These facts may reveal an intent to serve the U.S. market, but they do not show that J. McIntyre purposefully availed itself of the New Jersey market.

It is notable that the New Jersey Supreme Court appears to agree, for it could "not find that J. McIntyre had a presence or minimum contacts in this State—in any jurisprudential sense—that would justify a New Jersey court to exercise jurisdiction in this case." The court nonetheless held that petitioner could be sued in New Jersey based on a "stream-of-commerce theory of jurisdiction." As discussed, however, the stream-of-commerce metaphor cannot supersede either the mandate of the Due Process Clause or the limits on judicial authority that Clause ensures. The New Jersey Supreme Court also cited "significant policy reasons" to justify its holding, including the State's "strong interest in protecting its citizens from defective products." That interest is doubtless strong, but the Constitution commands restraint before discarding liberty in the name of expediency.

* * *

Due process protects petitioner's right to be subject only to lawful authority. At no time did petitioner engage in any activities in New Jersey that reveal an intent to invoke or benefit from the protection of its laws. New Jersey is without power to adjudge the rights and liabilities of J. McIntyre, and its exercise of jurisdiction would violate due process. The contrary judgment of the New Jersey Supreme Court is

Reversed.

JUSTICE BREYER, with whom JUSTICE ALITO joins, concurring in the judgment.

The Supreme Court of New Jersey adopted a broad understanding of the scope of personal jurisdiction based on its view that "[t]he increasingly fast-paced globalization of the world economy has removed national borders as barriers to trade." I do not doubt that there have been many recent changes in commerce and communication, many of which are not anticipated by our precedents. But this case does not present any of those issues. So I think it unwise to announce a rule of broad applicability without full consideration of the modern-day consequences.

In my view, the outcome of this case is determined by our precedents. Based on the facts found by the New Jersey courts, respondent Robert Nicastro failed to meet his burden to demonstrate that it was constitutionally proper to exercise jurisdiction over petitioner J. McIntyre Machinery, Ltd . . . . On that basis, I agree with the plurality that the contrary judgment of the Supreme Court of New Jersey should be reversed.

I . . .

None of our precedents finds that a single isolated sale, even if accompanied by the kind of sales effort indicated here, is sufficient . . . . The Court has held that a single sale to a customer who takes an accident-causing product to a different State (where the accident takes place) is not a sufficient basis for asserting jurisdiction. See *World-Wide Volkswagen Corp. v. Woodson.* And the Court, in separate opinions, has strongly suggested that a single sale of a product in a State does not constitute an adequate basis for asserting jurisdiction over an out-of-state defendant, even if that defendant places his goods in the stream of commerce, fully aware (and hoping) that such a sale will take place. See *Asahi Metal Industry Co. v. Superior Court of Cal., Solano Cty.* (opinion of O'Connor, J.) (requiring "something more" than simply placing "a product into the stream of commerce," even if defendant is "awar[e]" that the stream "may or will sweep the product into the forum State"); (Brennan, J., concurring in part and concurring in judgment) (jurisdiction should lie where a sale in a State is part of "the regular and anticipated flow" of commerce into the State, but not where that sale is only an "edd[y]," *i.e.*, an isolated occurrence); (Stevens, J., concurring in part and concurring in judgment) (indicating that "the volume, the value, and the hazardous character" of a good may affect the jurisdictional inquiry and emphasizing Asahi's "regular course of dealing").

Here, the relevant facts found by the New Jersey Supreme Court show no "regular . . . flow" or "regular course" of sales in New Jersey; and there is no "something more," such as special state-related design, advertising, advice, marketing, or anything else. Mr. Nicastro, who here bears the burden of proving jurisdiction, has shown no specific effort by the British Manufacturer to sell in New Jersey. He has introduced no list of potential New Jersey customers who might, for example, have regularly attended trade shows. And he has not otherwise shown that the British Manufacturer "purposefully avail[ed] itself of the privilege of conducting activities" within New Jersey, or that it delivered its goods in the stream of commerce "with the expectation that they will be purchased" by New Jersey users.

There may well have been other facts that Mr. Nicastro could have demonstrated in support of jurisdiction. And the dissent considers some of those facts. But the plaintiff bears the burden of establishing jurisdiction, and here I would take the facts precisely as the New Jersey Supreme Court stated them.

Accordingly, on the record present here, resolving this case requires no more than adhering to our precedents.

II

I would not go further. Because the incident at issue in this case does not implicate modern concerns, and because the factual record leaves many open questions, this is an unsuitable vehicle for making broad pronouncements that refashion basic jurisdictional rules.

A

The plurality seems to state strict rules that limit jurisdiction where a defendant does not "inten[d] to submit to the power of a sovereign" and cannot "be said to have targeted the forum." But what do those standards mean when a company targets the world by selling products from its Web site? And does it matter if, instead of shipping the products directly, a company consigns the products through an intermediary (say, Amazon.com) who then receives and fulfills the orders? And what if the company markets its products through popup advertisements that it knows will be viewed in a forum? Those issues have serious commercial consequences but are totally absent in this case.

B

But though I do not agree with the plurality's seemingly strict no-jurisdiction rule, I am not persuaded by the absolute approach adopted by the New Jersey Supreme Court and urged by respondent and his *amici*. Under that view, a producer is subject to jurisdiction for a products-liability action so long as it "knows or reasonably should know that its products are distributed through a nationwide distribution system that *might* lead to those products being sold in any of the fifty states." In the context of this case, I cannot agree.

For one thing, to adopt this view would abandon the heretofore accepted inquiry of whether, focusing upon the relationship between "the defendant, the *forum*, and the litigation," it is fair, in light of the defendant's contacts *with that forum*, to subject the defendant to suit there. *Shaffer v. Heitner* (emphasis added). It would ordinarily rest jurisdiction instead upon no more than the occurrence of a product-based accident in the forum State. But this Court has rejected the notion that a defendant's amenability to suit "travel[s] with the chattel." *World-Wide Volkswagen*.

For another, I cannot reconcile so automatic a rule with the constitutional demand for minimum contacts and "purposefu[l] avail[ment]," each of which rest upon a particular notion of defendant-focused fairness. A rule like the New Jersey Supreme Court's would permit every State to assert jurisdiction in a products-liability suit against any domestic manufacturer who sells its products (made anywhere in the United States) to a national distributor, no matter how large or small the manufacturer, no matter how distant the forum, and no matter how few the number of items that end up in the particular forum at issue. What might appear fair in the case of a large manufacturer which specifically seeks, or expects, an equal-sized distributor to sell its product in a distant State might seem unfair in the case of a small manufacturer (say, an Appalachian potter) who sells his product (cups and saucers) exclusively to a large distributor, who resells a single item (a coffee mug) to a buyer from a distant State (Hawaii). I know too little about the range of these or in-between possibilities to abandon in favor of the more absolute rule what has previously been this Court's less absolute approach.

Further, the fact that the defendant is a foreign, rather than a domestic, manufacturer makes the basic fairness of an absolute rule yet more uncertain . . . .

It may be that a larger firm can readily "alleviate the risk of burdensome litigation by procuring insurance, passing the expected costs on to customers, or, if the risks are too great, severing its connection with the State." But manufacturers come in many shapes and sizes. It may be fundamentally unfair to require a small Egyptian shirt maker, a Brazilian manufacturing cooperative, or a Kenyan coffee farmer, selling its products through international distributors, to respond to products-liability tort suits in virtually every State in the United States, even those in respect to which the foreign firm has no connection at all but the sale of a single (allegedly defective) good. And a rule like the New Jersey Supreme Court suggests would require every product manufacturer, large or small, selling to American distributors to understand not only the tort law of every State, but also the wide variance in the way courts within different States apply that law. See, *e.g.*, Dept. of Justice, Bureau of Justice Statistics Bulletin, Tort Trials and Verdicts in Large Counties, 2001, p. 11 (reporting percentage of plaintiff winners in tort trials among 46 populous counties, ranging from 17.9% (Worcester, Mass.) to 69.1% (Milwaukee, Wis.)).

C

At a minimum, I would not work such a change to the law in the way either the plurality or the New Jersey Supreme Court suggests without a better understanding of the relevant contemporary commercial circumstances . . . .

. . . I would adhere strictly to our precedents and the limited facts found by the New Jersey Supreme Court. And on those grounds, I do not think we can find jurisdiction in this case. Accordingly, though I agree with the plurality as to the outcome of this case, I concur only in the judgment of that opinion and not its reasoning.

JUSTICE GINSBURG, with whom JUSTICE SOTOMAYOR and JUSTICE KAGAN join, dissenting.

A foreign industrialist seeks to develop a market in the United States for machines it manufactures. It hopes to derive substantial revenue from sales it makes to United States purchasers. Where in the United States buyers reside does not matter to this manufacturer. Its goal is simply to sell as much as it can, wherever it can. It excludes no region or State from the market it wishes to reach. But, all things considered, it prefers to avoid products liability litigation in the United States. To that end, it engages a U.S. distributor to ship its machines stateside. Has it succeeded in escaping personal jurisdiction in a State where one of its products is sold and causes injury or even death to a local user?

Under this Court's pathmarking precedent in *International Shoe Co. v. Washington* and subsequent decisions, one would expect the answer to be unequivocally, "No." But instead, six Justices of this Court, in divergent opinions, tell us that the manufacturer has avoided the jurisdiction of our state courts, except perhaps in States where its products are sold in sizeable quantities. Inconceivable as it may have seemed yesterday, the splintered majority today "turn[s] the clock back to the days before modern long-arm statutes when a manufacturer, to avoid being hauled into court where a user is injured, need only Pilate-like wash its hands of a product by having independent distributors market it." Weintraub, A Map Out of the Personal Jurisdiction Labyrinth, 28 U.C. Davis L. Rev. 531, 555 (1995).

I

On October 11, 2001, a three-ton metal shearing machine severed four fingers on Robert Nicastro's right hand. Alleging that the machine was a dangerous product defectively made, Nicastro sought compensation from the machine's manufacturer, J. McIntyre Machinery Ltd. (McIntyre UK). Established in 1872 as a United Kingdom corporation, and headquartered in Nottingham, England, McIntyre UK "designs, develops and manufactures a complete range of equipment for metal recycling." . . .

The machine that injured Nicastro, a "McIntyre Model 640 Shear," sold in the United States for $24,900 in 1995, and features a "massive cutting capacity." According to McIntyre UK's product brochure, the machine is "use[d] throughout the [w]orld." . . . The instruction manual advises "owner[s] and operators of a 640 Shear [to] make themselves aware of [applicable health and safety regulations]," including "the American National Standards Institute Regulations (USA) for the use of Scrap Metal Processing Equipment."

Nicastro operated the 640 Shear in the course of his employment at Curcio Scrap Metal (CSM) in Saddle Brook, New Jersey . . . .

CSM's owner, Frank Curcio, "first heard of [McIntyre UK's] machine while attending an Institute of Scrap Metal Industries [(ISRI)] convention in Las Vegas in 1994 or 1995, where [McIntyre UK] was an exhibitor." . . .

McIntyre UK representatives attended every ISRI convention from 1990 through 2005. These annual expositions were held in diverse venues across the United States . . . . McIntyre UK exhibited its products at ISRI trade shows, the company acknowledged, hoping to reach "anyone interested in the machine from anywhere in the United States."

Although McIntyre UK's U.S. sales figures are not in the record, it appears that for several years in the 1990's, earnings from sales of McIntyre UK products in the United States "ha[d] been good" in comparison to "the rest of the world." . . .

From at least 1995 until 2001, McIntyre UK retained an Ohio-based company, McIntyre Machinery America, Ltd. (McIntyre America), "as its exclusive distributor for the entire United States." Though similarly named, the two companies were separate and independent entities with "no commonality of ownership or management." In invoices and other written communications, McIntyre

America described itself as McIntyre UK's national distributor, "America's Link" to "Quality Metal Processing Equipment" from England.

In a November 23, 1999 letter to McIntyre America, McIntyre UK's president spoke plainly about the manufacturer's objective in authorizing the exclusive distributorship: "All we wish to do is sell our products in the [United] States—and get paid!" Notably, McIntyre America was concerned about U.S. litigation involving McIntyre UK products, in which the distributor had been named as a defendant. McIntyre UK counseled McIntyre America to respond personally to the litigation, but reassured its distributor that "the product was built and designed by McIntyre Machinery in the UK and the buck stops here—if there's something wrong with the machine." Answering jurisdictional interrogatories, McIntyre UK stated that it had been named as a defendant in lawsuits in Illinois, Kentucky, Massachusetts, and West Virginia. And in correspondence with McIntyre America, McIntyre UK noted that the manufacturer had products liability insurance coverage.

. . . To achieve McIntyre UK's objective, *i.e.,* "to sell [its] machines to customers throughout the United States," "the two companies [were acting] closely in concert with each other." McIntyre UK never instructed its distributor to avoid certain States or regions of the country; rather, as just noted, the manufacturer engaged McIntyre America to attract customers "from anywhere in the United States."

In sum, McIntyre UK's regular attendance and exhibitions at ISRI conventions was surely a purposeful step to reach customers for its products "anywhere in the United States." At least as purposeful was McIntyre UK's engagement of McIntyre America as the conduit for sales of McIntyre UK's machines to buyers "throughout the United States." Given McIntyre UK's endeavors to reach and profit from the United States market as a whole, Nicastro's suit, I would hold, has been brought in a forum entirely appropriate for the adjudication of his claim . . . . The machine arrived in Nicastro's New Jersey workplace not randomly or fortuitously, but as a result of the U.S. connections and distribution system that McIntyre UK deliberately arranged. On what sensible view of the allocation of adjudicatory authority could the place of Nicastro's injury within the United States be deemed off limits for his products liability claim against a foreign manufacturer who targeted the United States (including all the States that constitute the Nation) as the territory it sought to develop?

II

A few points . . . bear statement at the outset. First, all agree, McIntyre UK surely is not subject to general (all-purpose) jurisdiction in New Jersey courts, for that foreign-country corporation is hardly "at home" in New Jersey. The question, rather, is one of specific jurisdiction, which turns on an "affiliatio[n] between the forum and the underlying controversy."

Second, no issue of the fair and reasonable allocation of adjudicatory authority among States of the United States is present in this case. New Jersey's exercise of personal jurisdiction over a foreign manufacturer whose dangerous product caused a workplace injury in New Jersey does not tread on the domain, or diminish the sovereignty, of any sister State . . . .

Third, the constitutional limits on a state court's adjudicatory authority derive from considerations of due process, not state sovereignty. As the Court clarified in *Insurance Corp. of Ireland v. Compagnie des Bauxites de Guinee*, 456 U.S. 694 (1982):

> "The restriction on state sovereign power described in *World–Wide Volkswagen Corp* . . . must be seen as ultimately a function of the individual liberty interest preserved by the Due Process Clause. That Clause is the only source of the personal jurisdiction requirement and the Clause itself makes no mention of federalism concerns. Furthermore, if the federalism concept operated as an independent restriction on the sovereign power of the court, it would not be possible to waive the personal jurisdiction requirement: Individual actions cannot change the powers of sovereignty, although the individual can subject himself to powers from which he may otherwise be protected."

But see *ante* (plurality opinion) (asserting that "sovereign authority," not "fairness," is the "central concept" in determining personal jurisdiction).

Finally, in *International Shoe* itself, and decisions thereafter, the Court has made plain that legal fictions, notably "presence" and "implied consent," should be discarded, for they conceal the actual bases on which jurisdiction rests.

Whatever the state of academic debate over the role of consent in modern jurisdictional doctrines, the plurality's notion that consent is the animating concept draws no support from controlling decisions of this Court. Quite the contrary, the Court has explained, a forum can exercise jurisdiction when its contacts with the controversy are sufficient; invocation of a fictitious consent, the Court has repeatedly said, is unnecessary and unhelpful . . . .[5]

III

This case is illustrative of marketing arrangements for sales in the United States common in today's commercial world. A foreign-country manufacturer engages a U.S. company to promote and distribute the manufacturer's products, not in any particular State, but anywhere and everywhere in the United States the distributor can attract purchasers. The product proves defective and injures a user in the State where the user lives or works. Often, as here, the manufacturer will have liability insurance covering personal injuries caused by its products.

When industrial accidents happen, a long-arm statute in the State where the injury occurs generally permits assertion of jurisdiction, upon giving proper notice,

---

5. . . . The plurality's notion that jurisdiction over foreign corporations depends upon the defendant's "submission" seems scarcely different from the long-discredited fiction of implied consent. It bears emphasis that a majority of this Court's members do not share the plurality's view.

over the foreign manufacturer. For example, the State's statute might [like] New York's long-arm statute [be tailored].* Or, the State might simply provide, as New Jersey does, for the exercise of jurisdiction "consistent with due process of law."[8]

The modern approach to jurisdiction over corporations and other legal entities, ushered in by *International Shoe*, gave prime place to reason and fairness. Is it not fair and reasonable, given the mode of trading of which this case is an example, to require the international seller to defend at the place its products cause injury? Do not litigational convenience and choice-of-law considerations point in that direction? On what measure of reason and fairness can it be considered undue to require McIntyre UK to defend in New Jersey as an incident of its efforts to develop a market for its industrial machines anywhere and everywhere in the United States? Is not the burden on McIntyre UK to defend in New Jersey fair, *i.e.*, a reasonable cost of transacting business internationally, in comparison to the burden on Nicastro to go to Nottingham, England to gain recompense for an injury he sustained using McIntyre's product at his workplace in Saddle Brook, New Jersey?

McIntyre UK dealt with the United States as a single market. Like most foreign manufacturers, it was concerned not with the prospect of suit in State X as opposed to State Y, but rather with its subjection to suit anywhere in the United States . . . . If McIntyre UK is answerable in the United States at all, is it not "perfectly appropriate to permit the exercise of that jurisdiction . . . at the place of injury"? See . . . Degnan & Kane, The Exercise of Jurisdiction Over and Enforcement of Judgments Against Alien Defendants, 39 Hastings L.J. 799, 813-815 (1988) (noting that "[i]n the international order," the State that counts is the United States, not its component States, and that the fair place of suit within the United States is essentially a question of venue).

In sum, McIntyre UK, by engaging McIntyre America to promote and sell its machines in the United States, "purposefully availed itself" of the United States market nationwide, not a market in a single State or a discrete collection of States. McIntyre UK thereby availed itself of the market of all States in which its products were sold by its exclusive distributor . . . . How could McIntyre UK not have intended, by its actions targeting a national market, to sell products in the fourth largest destination for imports among all States of the United States and the largest scrap metal market? But see *ante* (plurality opinion) (manufacturer's purposeful

---

* [For the cited portion of New York's tailored long-arm statute, which reaches a defendant whose "tortious act without the state caus[es] injury to person or property within the state," see page 146, *supra*. — EDS.]

8. State long-arm provisions allow the exercise of jurisdiction subject only to a due process limitation in Alabama, Arkansas, California, Colorado, Georgia, Illinois, Indiana, Iowa, Kansas, Kentucky, Louisiana, Maryland, Michigan, Minnesota, Missouri, Nevada, North Dakota, Oregon, Pennsylvania, Puerto Rico, South Carolina, South Dakota, Tennessee, Texas, Utah, Washington, and West Virginia. 4 C. Wright & A. Miller, Federal Practice & Procedure § 1068, pp. 577-578, n.12 (3d ed. 2002).

efforts to sell its products nationwide are "not . . . relevant" to the personal jurisdiction inquiry).

Courts, both state and federal, confronting facts similar to those here, have rightly rejected the conclusion that a manufacturer selling its products across the USA may evade jurisdiction in any and all States, including the State where its defective product is distributed and causes injury. They have held, instead, that it would undermine principles of fundamental fairness to insulate the foreign manufacturer from accountability in court at the place within the United States where the manufacturer's products caused injury.

IV

A

While this Court has not considered in any prior case the now-prevalent pattern presented here—a foreign-country manufacturer enlisting a U.S. distributor to develop a market in the United States for the manufacturer's products—none of the Court's decisions tug against the judgment made by the New Jersey Supreme Court. McIntyre contends otherwise, citing *World-Wide Volkswagen*, and *Asahi Metal Industry Co. v. Superior Court of Cal., Solano County.*

World-Wide Volkswagen concerned a New York car dealership that sold solely in the New York market, and a New York distributor who supplied retailers in three States only: New York, Connecticut, and New Jersey . . . . [T]his Court observed that the defendants had done nothing to serve the market for cars in Oklahoma. Jurisdiction, the Court held, could not be based on the *customer's* unilateral act of driving the vehicle to Oklahoma.

Notably, the foreign manufacturer of the Audi in *World-Wide Volkswagen* did not object to the jurisdiction of the Oklahoma courts and the U.S. importer abandoned its initially stated objection. And most relevant here, the Court's opinion indicates that an objection to jurisdiction by the manufacturer or national distributor would have been unavailing. To reiterate, the Court said in *World-Wide Volkswagen* that, when a manufacturer or distributor aims to sell its product to customers in several States, it is reasonable "to subject it to suit in [any] one of those States if its allegedly defective [product] has there been the source of injury."

Asahi arose out of a motorcycle accident in California. Plaintiff, a California resident injured in the accident, sued the Taiwanese manufacturer of the motorcycle's tire tubes, claiming that defects in its product caused the accident. The tube manufacturer cross-claimed against Asahi, the Japanese maker of the valve assembly, and Asahi contested the California courts' jurisdiction. . . .

The decision was not a close call. The Court had before it a foreign plaintiff, the Taiwanese manufacturer, and a foreign defendant, the Japanese valve-assembly maker, and the indemnification dispute concerned a transaction between those parties that occurred abroad. All agreed on the bottom line: The Japanese valve-assembly manufacturer was not reasonably brought into the California courts to litigate a dispute with another foreign party over a transaction that took place outside the United States.

. . . How the Court would have "estimate[d] . . . the inconveniences" had the injured Californian originally sued Asahi is a debatable question. Would this Court have given the same weight to the burdens on the foreign defendant had those been counterbalanced by the burdens litigating in Japan imposed on the local California plaintiff?

In any event, Asahi, unlike McIntyre UK, did not itself seek out customers in the United States, it engaged no distributor to promote its wares here, it appeared at no tradeshows in the United States, and, of course, it had no Web site advertising its products to the world. Moreover, Asahi was a component-part manufacturer with "little control over the final destination of its products once they were delivered into the stream of commerce." . . . To hold that *Asahi* controls this case would, to put it bluntly, be dead wrong.[15]

B

The Court's judgment also puts United States plaintiffs at a disadvantage in comparison to similarly situated complainants elsewhere in the world. Of particular note, within the European Union, in which the United Kingdom is a participant, the jurisdiction New Jersey would have exercised is not at all exceptional. The European Regulation on Jurisdiction and the Recognition and Enforcement of Judgments provides for the exercise of specific jurisdiction "in matters relating to tort . . . in the courts for the place where the harmful event occurred." The European Court of Justice has interpreted this prescription to authorize jurisdiction either where the harmful act occurred or at the place of injury. See *Handelskwekerij G.J. Bier B.V. v. Mines de Potasse d'Alsace S. A.*, 1976 E.C.R. 1735, 1748-1749.

V

The commentators who gave names to what we now call "general jurisdiction" and "specific jurisdiction" anticipated that when the latter achieves its full growth, considerations of litigational convenience and the respective situations of the parties would determine when it is appropriate to subject a defendant to trial in the plaintiff's community. See [von Mehren & Trautman, Jurisdiction to Adjudicate: A Suggested Analysis, 79 Harv. L. Rev. 1121, 1166-1179 (1966)]. Litigational considerations include "the convenience of witnesses and the ease of ascertaining the governing law." As to the parties, courts would differently appraise two situations: (1) cases involving a substantially local plaintiff, like Nicastro, injured by the

---

15. The plurality notes the low volume of sales in New Jersey. A $24,900 shearing machine, however, is unlikely to sell in bulk worldwide, much less in any given State. By dollar value, the price of a single machine represents a significant sale. Had a manufacturer sold in New Jersey $24,900 worth of flannel shirts, see *Nelson v. Park Industries, Inc.*, 717 F.2d 1120 (C.A.7 1983), cigarette lighters, see *Oswalt v. Scripto, Inc.*, 616 F.2d 191 (C.A.5 1980), or wire-rope splices, see *Hedrick v. Daiko Shoji Co.*, 715 F.2d 1355 (C.A.9 1983), the Court would presumably find the defendant amenable to suit in that State.

activity of a defendant engaged in interstate or international trade; and (2) cases in which the defendant is a natural or legal person whose economic activities and legal involvements are largely home-based, *i.e.*, entities without designs to gain substantial revenue from sales in distant markets.[18] [C]ourts presented with von Mehren and Trautman's first scenario—a local plaintiff injured by the activity of a manufacturer seeking to exploit a multistate or global market—have repeatedly confirmed that jurisdiction is appropriately exercised by courts of the place where the product was sold and caused injury.

* * *

For the reasons stated, I would hold McIntyre UK answerable in New Jersey for the harm Nicastro suffered at his workplace in that State using McIntyre UK's shearing machine. While I dissent from the Court's judgment, I take heart that the plurality opinion does not speak for the Court, for that opinion would take a giant step away from the "notions of fair play and substantial justice" underlying *International Shoe.*

NOTES AND QUESTIONS

1. What about the effects test?   The effects test measures the legitimacy of personal jurisdiction when out-of-state activity causes a tortious effect in the forum state. Courts have limited the scope of that test to intentional torts that are aimed at the forum with the awareness that the brunt of the harm will be suffered there. See Note 2, page 173 (following *Calder v. Jones*). The stream-of-commerce theory involves out-of-state activity (manufacturing in a state other than the forum) that causes a tortious effect in the forum. Might we then ask whether the manufacturing and marketing of the product was aimed at the forum with the awareness that the brunt of any harm caused by the product would be suffered there? What does the stream-of-commerce theory add to this? Let's take this question a step further. We have already considered whether there is any significant difference between the "contracts" version of minimum contacts and the "torts" version of that standard (*i.e.*, the effects test). See Note 1, page 180, *supra* (following *Walden v. Fiore*). If "contract" analysis and "tort" analysis are essentially interchangeable, shouldn't we expect two different versions of "tort" analysis to be equally so? That being the case, isn't the fundamental question in each of these categories whether the nonresident has established a meaningful connection with the forum state? And shouldn't that require a careful and realistic examination of the facts? Of the three opinions issued by the Court in *McIntyre*, which comes the closest to doing that?

18. Assigning weight to the local or international stage on which the parties operate would, to a considerable extent, answer the concerns expressed by JUSTICE BREYER (opinion concurring in judgment).

2. *The role of the claim.*   Nicastro sued J. McIntyre on a theory of product liability. In order to prevail, he would have to prove that a dangerously defective product manufactured by the defendant caused his injury. In what location was that tort completed? Was it in the nation of manufacture or in the state in which the machine was being operated? With the correct answer to these questions in hand, does the suit filed by Nicastro more closely resemble the suit filed in *Calder v. Jones* or the one filed in *Walden v. Fiore?* Should the locus of the tort have any bearing on the reasonableness of the exercise of jurisdiction? If J. McIntyre was responsible for Nicastro's injuries, wouldn't it make sense to say that it was answerable for those injuries in the jurisdiction where the tort was completed?

3. *The plurality's stream-of-commerce theory.*   What do you make of the plurality's focus on sovereignty? Does it harken back to *Pennoyer v. Neff?* The sovereignty principle leads the plurality to insist on purposeful availment. Does it make sense in a tort case to require purposeful availment? Is doing so consistent with the approach adopted in *Calder?* Why, according to the plurality, must a manufacturer that targets the entire U.S. market also target the specific state in which the tort occurs? Is that truly the "genius" of our federal system? Did the plurality do anything other than adopt a version of Justice O'Connor's "plus" theory of stream of commerce? Might it even be a stricter version of that test? For a detailed criticism of the plurality opinion (and of the concurring and dissenting opinions), *see* Allan Ides, *A Critical Appraisal of the Supreme Court's Decision in* J. McIntyre Machinery, Ltd. v. Nicastro, 45 LOY. L. REV. 341 (2012).

4. *The concurrence's stream-of-commerce theory.*   In their concurring opinion, why did Justices Breyer and Alito reject the New Jersey Supreme Court's finding that jurisdiction was proper under the stream-of-commerce approach? Does the concurrence's emphasis on the fact that there was but "a single sale" in the forum suggest that these Justices might be inclined to adopt the Brennan stream-of-commerce test in a case in which a larger volume of a defendant's goods had reached the forum state? Or does the concurrence endorse a stream-of-commerce-plus model? As to the "single sale" rationale, is it correct to say that a single contact with the forum is inadequate to establish personal jurisdiction over the party instigating the contact? Have we considered any cases that hold to the contrary? Do you think that the concurrence adequately addressed the facts of the case?

5. *The dissent's "reason and fairness" approach.*   In the dissent's view, why was this an inappropriate case for employing the Court's traditional approach with its exclusive focus on a defendant's contacts with the forum state? Based on the given facts, do you think the dissent could have constructed an argument in favor of jurisdiction under a more established approach? How would you describe the dissent's approach to minimum contacts? In answering this question consider the factors deemed critical to the dissent in concluding that assertion of jurisdiction over McIntyre UK would be reasonable and fair. If a defendant who has engaged in a national marketing campaign satisfies the dissent's test, is the minimum contacts standard then satisfied with respect to all 50 states? In which states would the dissent's approach have allowed a plaintiff like Nicastro to sue? What was the relevance of the dissent's discussion of the European approach to jurisdiction?

Finally, do you see a similarity between the jurisdictional model endorsed by the dissent and the one endorsed by Justice Black in his *Hanson v. Denckla* dissent?

6. *Defendant's distribution of products in the forum.* The Court's stream-of-commerce cases in no way undermine the states' ability to assert jurisdiction over a defendant whose products reach the forum state through the defendant's own distribution efforts, and where the claim can be said to have arisen from the product's presence there. In *Keeton v. Hustler Magazine, Inc.*, 465 U.S. 770 (1984), the Court held that a New Hampshire federal court could assert jurisdiction over *Hustler* magazine, an Ohio corporation whose principal place of business was in California, in a libel action filed by a resident of New York. Noting that Hustler sold 10,000 to 15,000 magazines a month in New Hampshire, the Court explained that the defendant's

> regular circulation of magazines in the forum State is sufficient to support an assertion of jurisdiction in a libel action based on the contents of the magazine. . . .
>
> The District Court found that "[t]he general course of conduct in circulating magazines throughout the state was purposefully directed at New Hampshire, and inevitably affected persons in the state." Such regular monthly sales of thousands of magazines cannot by any stretch of the imagination be characterized as random, isolated, or fortuitous. It is, therefore, unquestionable that New Hampshire jurisdiction over a complaint based on those contacts would ordinarily satisfy the requirement[s] of the Due Process Clause. . . .

Id. at 773-774.

The Court rejected Hustler's argument that New Hampshire had no legitimate interest in a case filed by a New Yorker who sued there only because the statute of limitations had run in every other state.

> New Hampshire may rightly employ its libel laws to discourage the deception of its citizens. . . .
>
> New Hampshire may also extend its concern to the injury that in-state libel causes within New Hampshire to a nonresident. The tort of libel is generally held to occur wherever the offending material is circulated. . . . The communication of the libel may create a negative reputation among the residents of a jurisdiction where the plaintiff's previous reputation was, however small, at least unblemished.

Id. at 776-777. Would *Keeton* have been decided differently if Hustler had a policy of not distributing its magazines in New Hampshire, and copies reached the state only because people who bought them elsewhere took them to New Hampshire? Would the dissenters in *McIntyre Machinery* have been willing to uphold jurisdiction in *Keeton* even though it involved a plaintiff who was able to forum shop among all 50 states?

A NOTE ON THE STREAM-OF-COMMERCE THEORY TODAY

Justice Kennedy's plurality opinion in *McIntyre* expressed hope that the Court would be able to "provide greater clarity" to "the decades-old questions left open in *Asahi*." Did the Court succeed in that endeavor? Only six Justices addressed the stream-of-commerce theory. The four-Justice plurality adopted what appears to be a potentially heightened version of Justice O'Connor's "stream of commerce plus" theory articulated in *Asahi*. The two concurring Justices were less clear, though as we noted there are hints that they thought Justice Brennan's less-demanding "pure stream of commerce" test might be the appropriate one. The dissent, however, never even mentioned the stream-of-commerce theory since, in its view, the case called for use of a novel reason-and-fairness test. But would the dissent agree that if the "pure stream of commerce" test were satisfied, the exercise of jurisdiction would be reasonable and fair?

McIntyre Machinery has left the state and lower federal courts in the same position they were in after *Asahi*. Following that decision, some courts adopted Justice O'Connor's "stream of commerce plus" theory. *See, e.g., Bridgeport Music Inc. v. Still N the Water Publ'g*, 327 F.3d 472, 479-480 (6th Cir.), *cert. denied*, 540 U.S. 948 (2003); *Lesnick v. Hollingsworth & Vose Co.*, 35 F.3d 939 (4th Cir. 1994), *cert. denied*, 513 U.S. 1151 (1995); *Boit v. Gar-Tec Prods., Inc.*, 967 F.2d 671 (1st Cir. 1992). Others followed Justice Brennan's approach. *See, e.g., Barone v. Rich Bros. Interstate Display Fireworks Co.*, 25 F.3d 610, 613-615 (8th Cir.), *cert. denied*, 513 U.S. 948 (1994); *Ruston Gas Turbines, Inc. v. Donaldson Co.*, 9 F.3d 415 (5th Cir. 1993); *Dehmlow v. Austin Fireworks*, 963 F.2d 941, 946-947 (7th Cir. 1992). A third group declined to make a definitive choice between the two theories, instead deciding each case on its own facts and sometimes testing jurisdiction under both theories. *See, e.g., Pennzoil Prods. Co. v. Colelli & Assocs., Inc.*, 149 F.3d 197 (3d Cir. 1998); *Beverly Hills Fan Co. v. Royal Sovereign Corp.*, 21 F.3d 1558, 1565-1566 (Fed. Cir. 1994); *Tobin v. Astra Pharm. Prods., Inc.*, 993 F.2d 528, 543 (6th Cir.), *cert. denied*, 510 U.S. 914 (1993); *Vermeulen v. Renault, U.S.A., Inc.*, 985 F.2d 1534, 1546-1551 (11th Cir.), *cert. denied*, 508 U.S. 907 (1993); *Etchieson v. Central Purchasing, LLC*, 232 P.3d 301, 306 (Colo. Ct. App. 2010); *A.O. Smith Corp. v. American Alt. Ins. Corp.*, 778 So. 2d 615, 618-619 (La. Ct. App. 2000); *CMMC v. Salinas*, 929 S.W.2d 435 (Tex. 1996).

The variety of approaches that these courts have developed for handling stream-of-commerce cases will likely continue to be employed, until such time as the Supreme Court is finally able to resolve the issue. *See, e.g., Book v. Doublestar Dongfeng Tyre Co., Ltd.*, 860 N.W.2d 576, 585 (Iowa 2015) (post-*McIntyre* courts remain divided on scope of stream-of-commerce test); *AFTG-TG, LLC v. Nuvoton Tech. Corp.*, 689 F.3d 1358, 1362-1363 (Fed. Cir. 2012) (*per curiam*) (Court in *McIntyre* "declined to resolve [the Supreme Court's] long-standing split" on stream-of-commerce theory); *Sproul v. Rob & Charlies, Inc.*, 304 P.3d 18, 25-26 (N.M. Ct. App. 2012) (noting post-*McIntyre* confusion over the scope of stream-of-commerce theory).

PROBLEMS

2-11. Dylan owns and operates an auto repair shop in Iowa. In October 2009, while working on a car, he was seriously injured when a 10-ply Treadstone tire he was inflating exploded. Dylan had purchased the tire, which was manufactured in China by Doublestar, Inc., from an Iowa retailer. Doublestar is a Chinese corporation with its principal place of business in China. It has no employees or offices in the United States and does not advertise in this country. In the year preceding the accident, Doublestar produced nearly 3.2 million tires, of which 180,000 were sold in the United States through Voma, Inc., an American distributor. Voma is a Tennessee corporation with its principal place of business in Memphis. When ordering tires from Doublestar, Voma provided it with detailed shipping requirements. Doublestar then delivered the tires to a port in Wuhan, China, where a shipping company then placed the tires in containers to be loaded onto freighters destined for the United States. Of the 180,000 tires purchased by Voma from Doublestar, 7,000 were the 10-ply Treadstone model involved in Dylan's accident. Of these 7,000 tires, 999 were then sold by Voma to Holt, an Iowa distributor. These included 300 10-ply Treadstone tires sold to Holt in the month immediately preceding the accident. Voma shipped all of these 10-ply tires to Holt from its warehouse in Tennessee. Holt in turn sold and delivered them to various retailers throughout the state. The DOT number stamped on the accident-causing tire indicates that Doublestar manufactured that tire in China in early June 2009. Dylan has sued several defendants, including Doublestar, in an Iowa state court on a theory of product liability. Doublestar has filed a motion to dismiss for lack of personal jurisdiction. How should the trial court rule on its motion? In answering this question, consider alternative ways to determine whether this nonresident defendant has established a meaningful connection with the forum state. See Book v. Doublestar Dongfeng Tyre Co., Ltd., 860 N.W.2d 576 (Iowa 2015).

2-12. Bernie was injured while setting up a fireworks display in Nebraska where fireworks are legal. He brought suit in a Nebraska court against several defendants, including Hosoya, the Japanese maker of the fireworks. Hosoya does not advertise in Nebraska, has never sent employees there, and has made no direct sales to the state. Seventy percent of its fireworks are sold in the United States through nine regional distributors, all of which are located in the United States, but none of which is located in Nebraska. One of the distributors, Rich Brothers, is a South Dakota firm with sales personnel in six states, including Nebraska, where its sales of Hosoya fireworks average $16,000 a year. Hosoya sends catalogs to Rich Brothers and once sent a representative to the company's South Dakota offices. Hosoya had no actual knowledge that its fireworks were being sold in Nebraska. It has moved to dismiss the suit for lack of jurisdiction. How should the court rule on the motion? In answering this question, consider alternative ways to determine whether the nonresident defendant has established a meaningful connection with the forum state. See Barone v. Rich Bros. Interstate Display Fireworks Co., 25 F.3d 610 (8th Cir.), cert. denied, 513 U.S. 948 (1994).

A NOTE ON PERSONAL JURISDICTION AND THE INTERNET

An increasingly large number of personal jurisdiction cases involve the internet, the typical question being the extent to which a particular posting—e.g., a posting on a blog or on Facebook—has established a meaningful connection with the forum state. The new and evolving technology aside, this question does not differ in any significant way from the one we consider when the potential connections with the forum state are more tangible or premised on the old media. In both circumstances we ask whether the nonresident defendant has engaged in activity, either in the forum state or elsewhere, that has created a meaningful connection with the forum state. Given that common inquiry, our common sense should instruct us that a posting on the internet, which is potentially accessible anywhere in the world, does not automatically establish a meaningful connection in every forum in which the posting has been or can be accessed. As one court explained,

> If we were to conclude as a general principle that a person's act of placing information on the Internet subjects that person to personal jurisdiction in each State in which the information is accessed, then the defense of personal jurisdiction, in the sense that a State has geographically limited judicial power, would no longer exist. The person placing information on the Internet would be subject to personal jurisdiction in every State.

ALS Scan, Inc. v. Digital Serv. Consultants, Inc., 293 F.3d 707, 712 (4th Cir. 2002), *cert. denied*, 537 U.S. 1105 (2003). We don't need a new doctrine for the new technology. As we've pointed out, the key question remains the same regardless of technological context. Hence, the same principles and precedents we use in non-internet cases should inform our determination of whether personal jurisdiction is satisfied in internet cases. In fact, Problems 2-6, 2-9, and 2-10, pages 168, 173, and 174, *supra*, each of which involved internet-based connections, may be solved without reference to any novel doctrine.

Of course, one must be sensitive to the reality of the internet in determining whether a web-based contact with the forum is sufficiently meaningful for purposes of establishing personal jurisdiction. To that end, some courts have found it useful to characterize the web page at issue as falling into one of three categories: commercial and interactive websites through which the nonresident defendant engages in business on a regular basis (*e.g.*, amazon.com); interactive websites through which users of the site can exchange information but on which no business transactions occur (*e.g.*, reddit.com); and passive websites that do little more than make information available to those who access them (*e.g.*, photobucket. com). *Zippo Manufacturing Co. v. Zippo Dot Com, Inc.*, 952 F. Supp. 1119, 1124 (W.D. Pa. 1997). Many courts have used this framework as a prelude to their minimum contacts analysis. *See, e.g., Best Van Lines, Inc. v. Walker*, 490 F.3d 239, 251-252 (2d Cir. 2007); *Toys "R" Us, Inc. v. Step Two, S.A.*, 318 F.3d 446, 452-455 (3d Cir. 2003); *Neogen Corp. v. Neo Gen Screening, Inc.*, 282 F.3d 883, 890 (6th Cir. 2002); *ALS Scan, Inc., supra*, 293 F.3d at 713-714; *Soma Med. Int'l v. Standard Chartered Bank*, 196 F.3d 1292, 1296-1297 (10th Cir. 1999); *Mink v. AAAA Dev. LLC*, 190 F.3d 333, 336 (5th Cir. 1999); *Cybersell, Inc. v. Cybersell, Inc.*, 130 F.3d 414, 417-419 (9th Cir. 1997); *Snowney v. Harrah's Entertainment, Inc.*, 112 P.3d

28, 33-36 (Cal.), *cert. denied*, 546 U.S. 1015 (2005). But this framework should not be treated as an alternate method through which to assess jurisdiction, as a few courts have suggested. *See, e.g., Sioux Pharm, Inc. v. Summit Nutritionals Int'l, Inc.*, 859 N.W.2d 182 (Iowa 2015). Rather, the framework merely offers its own perspective through which to apply the minimum contacts test.

PROBLEMS

2-13. Panavision, a California-based company that produces motion picture camera equipment, holds registered trademarks to the names "Panavision" and "Panaflex." In 1995, it sought to register an internet website with the domain name Panavision.com, only to find that a website using the Panavision trademark had already been established by Dennis, who lives in Illinois. Dennis's Panavision website displayed photos of the City of Pana, Illinois. When Panavision's attorney sent Dennis a letter advising him to cease using Panavision's trademark and the domain name Panavision.com, Dennis wrote to Panavision in California, stating that he had the right to use the name and suggesting that the company buy the name from him for $13,000, rather than "fund[ing] your attorney's purchase of a new boat." When Panavision refused, Dennis then registered Panavision's other trademark as the domain name Panaflex.com. Thereafter, Panavision sued Dennis in a California federal district court. Dennis has filed a motion to dismiss under Rule 12(b)(2). How should the court rule on the motion? *See Panavision Int'l, L.P. v. Toeppen*, 141 F.3d 1316 (9th Cir. 1998). For a more recent Ninth Circuit application of *Panavision*, see *Rio Properties, Inc. v. Rio International Interlink*, 284 F.3d 1007 (9th Cir. 2002).

2-14. Pebble Beach is a well-known golf course and resort located in California. Pebble Beach contends that its trade name has acquired secondary meaning in the United States and in the United Kingdom. Caddy, a resident of the United Kingdom, occupies and runs a three-room bed and breakfast, restaurant, and bar located on a cliff overlooking the pebbly beaches of England's south shore in a town called Barton-on-Sea. The name of Caddy's operation is "Pebble Beach," which, given its location, is no surprise. Caddy advertises his services, which do not include a golf course, at his website, www.pebblebeach-uk.com. Caddy's website includes general information about the accommodations he provides, including lodging rates in pounds sterling, a menu, and a wine list. Visitors to the website who have questions about Caddy's services may fill out an online inquiry form. However, the website neither has a reservation system nor allows potential guests to book rooms or pay for services online. Pebble Beach sued Caddy in a U.S. district court sitting in California for intentional infringement and dilution of its "Pebble Beach" trademark. Caddy has filed a motion to dismiss for lack of personal jurisdiction. Assuming there is no applicable federal long-arm provision, how should the federal court rule on Caddy's motion? *See Pebble Beach Co. v. Caddy*, 453 F.3d 1151 (9th Cir. 2006).

4. Due Process: The Relatedness Requirement

To establish specific jurisdiction, it is not sufficient for the plaintiff to establish that the nonresident defendant has engaged in activity in, or directed toward, the forum state. The plaintiff must also show that her claim is related to the defendant's forum contacts. A "meaningful connection" is one that links the claim to defendant's purposeful forum contacts. In each of the cases previously covered in this chapter, where personal jurisdiction was upheld, this relatedness requirement was satisfied. Thus, for example, in *International Shoe Co. v. Washington* (page 138, *supra*), the Washington state court suit to collect taxes arose from the defendant's employment of sales representatives in the state. In *McGee v. International Life Insurance Co.* (page 149, *supra*), the California suit to collect under a life insurance policy involved a policy the defendant had solicited from a California resident. In *Burger King Corp. v. Rudzewicz* (page 157, *supra*), the Florida lawsuit sought to enforce a contract that the Michigan defendant had made with the Florida plaintiff. And in *Calder v. Jones* (page 168, *supra*), the plaintiff's libel action was a product of the defendants' having published the article in California. The following case examines and applies this requirement.

Nowak v. Tak How Investments, Ltd. [Part I]*
94 F.3d 708 (1st Cir. 1996), *cert. denied*, 520 U.S. 1155 (1997)

CUMMINGS, Circuit Judge.

A Massachusetts resident who accompanied her husband on a business trip to Hong Kong drowned in their hotel's swimming pool. Plaintiffs later brought this wrongful death diversity action against the Hong Kong corporation that owns the hotel—a corporation that has no place of business outside of Hong Kong. Defendant moved for dismissal, arguing that a Massachusetts court could not exercise personal jurisdiction consistently with due process and, alternatively, that the case should be dismissed on the grounds of *forum non conveniens*. The district court denied both motions, and we now affirm.

I.

Tak How is a Hong Kong corporation with its only place of business in Hong Kong. Its sole asset is the Holiday Inn Crowne Plaza Harbour View in Hong Kong ("Holiday Inn"), where the accident in this case took place. Tak How has no assets, shareholders, or employees in Massachusetts. Sally Ann Nowak ("Mrs. Nowak") was at all relevant times married to plaintiff Ralph Nowak ("Mr. Nowak") and was the mother of their two children. . . . The Nowaks lived in Marblehead,

---

* [Those parts of the court's opinion dealing with purposeful direction and relatedness appear here. Later, we will look at the court's discussion of reasonableness.—EDS.]

Massachusetts, and Mr. Nowak was employed by Kiddie Products, Inc., which has its place of business in Avon, Massachusetts. Kiddie Products does extensive business in Hong Kong. . . . Mr. Nowak customarily made two business trips to Hong Kong each year, accompanied by his wife on one of those trips.

Kiddie Products employees had made trips to Hong Kong since at least 1982, but the company's relationship with Tak How and the Holiday Inn began only in 1992. John Colantuone, a vice-president, was one such employee who had travelled to Hong Kong since 1982 and had stayed at various other hotels. Colantuone was acquainted with the Holiday Inn through advertisements on Hong Kong radio in 1983 or 1984, but only decided to stay there in 1992 after becoming dissatisfied with the rates at other hotels. On his first visit, Colantuone met with the Holiday Inn's sales manager to negotiate a corporate discount for Kiddie Products employees. Holiday Inn agreed to the discount and wrote a letter confirming the arrangement based on a minimum number of room nights per year. Marie Burke, Colantuone's administrative assistant, made all hotel reservations for the company's employees. Although Kiddie Products regularly compared rates at other hotels, Burke was told to book all reservations at the Holiday Inn until instructed otherwise. Since 1992, Kiddie Products employees have stayed exclusively at the Holiday Inn.

In June 1993, the Holiday Inn telecopied Colantuone a message announcing new corporate rates and other promotional materials. Burke requested additional information, and the hotel promptly responded. In July 1993, after a series of exchanges by telecopier, Burke sent a reservation request to the Holiday Inn for several employees for September and October 1993. One of the reservations was for Mr. and Mrs. Nowak to arrive on September 16. On September 18, while the Nowaks were registered guests at the hotel, Mrs. Nowak drowned in the hotel swimming pool. The specific facts surrounding her death are not relevant here.[*] It is uncontested that in 1992 and 1993, prior to Mrs. Nowak's death, Tak How advertised the Holiday Inn in certain national and international publications, some of which circulated in Massachusetts. In addition, in February 1993, Tak How sent direct mail solicitations to approximately 15,000 of its previous guests, including previous guests residing in Massachusetts.

The Nowaks filed this wrongful death action in Massachusetts state court in June 1994. Tak How then removed the case to federal district court and filed two motions to dismiss — one for lack of personal jurisdiction under Fed. R. Civ. P. 12(b)(2) and the other for *forum non conveniens*. The district court initially denied the motion to dismiss for *forum non conveniens*, and then, after allowing time for jurisdictional discovery, issued a memorandum and order denying the Rule 12(b)(2) motion. . . . [B]elieving that a resulting judgment would not be enforceable in

---

[*] [The district court's opinion notes that at the time Mrs. Nowak was using the pool, neither of the two lifeguards "on duty" was watching the pool. Mrs. Nowak was alive when they later found her at the bottom of the pool, but the lifeguards declined to administer mouth-to-mouth CPR for fear of contracting a disease. Neither of them was equipped with a "mouth-to-mouth" faceguard commonly carried by lifeguards. — Eds.]

Hong Kong, Tak How did not answer the Nowaks' complaint. Accordingly, the district court entered a default judgment against Tak How for $3,128,168.33. Tak How appeals the denial of its Rule 12(b)(2) motion and its motion to dismiss the case for *forum non conveniens*.

II.

We first review the denial of Tak How's motion to dismiss for lack of personal jurisdiction. The district court employed a prima facie standard in making its determination rather than adjudicating the jurisdictional facts. . . . Both the court's decision to use the prima facie standard and its conclusion under that standard are reviewed *de novo*. To begin, we find no error in the district court's choice of the prima facie standard. A full-blown evidentiary hearing was not necessary in this case because the facts were, in all essential respects, undisputed. In such circumstances, the prima facie standard is both appropriate and preferred. . . .

[The court agreed with the district court that the case fit within the Massachusetts long-arm statute's terms.]

Turning to the constitutional restraints, this Court follows a tripartite analysis for determining the existence of specific personal jurisdiction (plaintiffs do not allege general personal jurisdiction):

> First, the claim underlying the litigation must directly arise out of, or relate to, the defendant's forum-state activities. Second, the defendant's forum-state contacts must represent a purposeful availment of the privilege of conducting activities in the forum state, thereby invoking the benefits and protections of that state's laws and making the defendant's involuntary presence before the state's court foreseeable. Third, the exercise of jurisdiction must, in light of the Gestalt factors, be reasonable.

Pritzker v. Yari, 42 F.3d 53, 60-61 (1st Cir. 1994) (quoting *United Elec. Workers v. 163 Pleasant St. Corp.*, 960 F.2d 1080, 1089 (1st Cir. 1992)), *cert denied*, 314 U.S. 1108 (1995).

A.   Relatedness

What this Court calls the "relatedness" test is one aspect of demonstrating minimum contacts pursuant to *International Shoe Co. v. Washington* . . . . Tak How's principal argument on appeal is that relatedness requires a proximate cause relationship between its contacts with Massachusetts and the Nowaks' cause of action.

In arguing for a proximate cause relatedness test, Tak How relies on a series of First Circuit cases beginning with *Marino v. Hyatt Corp.*, 793 F.2d 427 (1st Cir. 1986). In each of these cases, this Court construed the language of a state long-arm statute requiring, as does the Massachusetts statute . . . , that the cause of action "arise" from the forum-state contacts. Construing those statutes, we rejected plaintiffs' arguments that the injury at issue would not have occurred "but for" the forum-state contacts. Instead, we held that the defendant's conduct must be the legal or proximate cause of the injury.

[T]he Supreme Judicial Court of Massachusetts dealt our restrictive interpretation a fatal blow in [*Tatro v. Manor Care, Inc.*, 625 N.E.2d 549 (Mass. 1994)].

The Court decided that the "but for" test is more consistent with the language of the long-arm statute and explicitly rejected our interpretation of the statute. . . . Personal jurisdiction was proper in *Tatro* because the California hotel had solicited business in Massachusetts and had agreed to provide the plaintiff with accommodations; but for those acts, the plaintiff would not have been injured.

Tak How . . . concedes, as it must, that *Tatro* is controlling insofar as it deals with the construction of the Massachusetts long-arm statute, but insists that the relatedness discussion in *Marino* had constitutional significance as well. . . .

As an initial matter, "[w]e know . . . that the [relatedness] requirement focuses on the nexus between the defendant's contacts and the plaintiff's cause of action." The requirement serves two purposes.

> First, relatedness is the divining rod that separates specific jurisdiction cases from general jurisdiction cases. Second, it ensures that the element of causation remains in the forefront of the due process investigation.

Most courts share this emphasis on causation, but differ over the proper causative threshold. Generally, courts have gravitated toward one of two familiar tort concepts—"but for" or "proximate cause."

The Ninth Circuit is the most forceful defender of the "but for" test. In *Shute v. Carnival Cruise Lines*,* the court stated that "but for" serves the basic function of relatedness by "preserv[ing] the essential distinction between general and specific jurisdiction." 897 F.2d 377, 385 (9th Cir. 1990). A more stringent standard, the court asserted, "would represent an unwarranted departure from the core concepts of 'fair play and substantial justice,'" because it would preclude jurisdiction in cases where it would be reasonable. In turn, in those cases where "but for" might lead to an unreasonable result, the court predicted that the third prong— the reasonableness inquiry—would guard against unfairness. . . .

The Sixth Circuit applies a "substantial connection" standard. *See Third Nat'l Bank v. WEDGE Group Inc.*, 882 F.2d 1087, 1091 (6th Cir. 1989), *cert. denied*, 493 U.S. 1058. The court's discussion in *Lanier v. American Board of Endodontics*, 843 F.2d 901, 908-911 (6th Cir. 1988), however, suggests that a "but for" relationship survives the due process inquiry.

Finally, the Seventh Circuit has upheld jurisdiction . . . for claims that "lie in the wake of the commercial activities by which the defendant submitted to the jurisdiction of the Illinois courts." See *Deluxe Ice Cream Co. v. R.C.H. Tool Corp.*, 726 F.2d 1209, 1215-1216 (7th Cir. 1984) (breach of warranty). Whether this indeterminate standard would encompass tortious negligence committed outside the forum is unknown.

---

* [In *Shute*, 897 F.2d 377 (9th Cir. 1990), *rev'd on other grounds*, 499 U.S. 585 (1991), a Washington plaintiff, who was injured aboard a ship in Mexican waters on a cruise from California to Mexico, sued the cruise line, a Panamanian corporation whose principal place of business was in Florida, in a Washington federal court. The Ninth Circuit allowed jurisdiction, reasoning that "but for" the defendant's promotional and advertising activities directed at Washington travel agents, the plaintiff would not have taken the cruise and the accident would not have occurred.—EDS.]

On the other hand, the Second and Eighth Circuits, as well as this one, appear to approve a proximate cause standard. *See Pleasant Street*, 960 F.2d at 1089; *Pearrow v. National Life & Accident Ins. Co.*, 703 F.2d 1067, 1069 (8th Cir. 1983); *Gelfand v. Tanner Motor Tours, Ltd.*, 339 F.2d 317, 321-322 (2d Cir. 1964). The courts in *Pearrow* and *Gelfand* found that, for purposes of the long-arm statute at issue, non-forum negligence claims did not arise from in-forum solicitation or ticket sales. District courts from the Third and Tenth Circuits have reached similar results.

This circuit, whether accurately or not, has been recognized as the main proponent of the proximate cause standard. We think the attraction of proximate cause is two-fold. First, proximate or legal cause clearly distinguishes between foreseeable and unforeseeable risks of harm. Foreseeability is a critical component in the due process inquiry, particularly in evaluating purposeful availment, and we think it also informs the relatedness prong. . . . Adherence to a proximate cause standard is likely to enable defendants better to anticipate which conduct might subject them to a state's jurisdiction than a more tenuous link in the chain of causation. Certainly, jurisdiction that is premised on a contact that is a legal cause of the injury underlying the controversy—*i.e.*, that "form[s] an 'important, or [at least] material, element of proof' in the plaintiff's case"—is presumably reasonable, assuming, of course, purposeful availment.

[W]e think the proximate cause standard better comports with the relatedness inquiry because it so easily correlates to foreseeability, a significant component of the jurisdictional inquiry. A "but for" requirement, on the other hand, has in itself no limiting principle; it literally embraces every event that hindsight can logically identify in the causative chain. True, as the Ninth Circuit has noted, courts can use the reasonableness prong to keep Pandora's jar from opening too wide. But to say that the harm that might be done by one factor can be prevented by another is not, after all, an affirmative justification for the former.

That being said, we are persuaded that strict adherence to a proximate cause standard in all circumstances is unnecessarily restrictive. The concept of proximate cause is critically important in the tort context because it defines the scope of a defendant's liability. In contrast, the [relatedness] prong of the jurisdictional tripartite test is not as rigid: it is, "relatively speaking, . . . a 'flexible, relaxed standard.'" We see no reason why, in the context of a relationship between a contractual or business association and a subsequent tort, the absence of proximate cause per se should always render the exercise of specific jurisdiction unconstitutional.

When a foreign corporation directly targets residents in an ongoing effort to further a business relationship, and achieves its purpose, it may not necessarily be unreasonable to subject that corporation to forum jurisdiction when the efforts lead to a tortious result. The corporation's own conduct increases the likelihood that a specific resident will respond favorably. If the resident is harmed while engaged in activities integral to the relationship the corporation sought to establish, we think the nexus between the contacts and the cause of action is sufficiently strong to survive the due process inquiry at least at the relatedness stage.

This concept represents a small overlay of "but for" on "proximate cause." In a sense it is a narrower and more specific identification of the Seventh Circuit's formulation for jurisdiction-worthiness of claims lying "in the wake" of commercial activities in the forum. . . .

This case is illustrative of our reasoning. Through its ongoing correspondence with Kiddie Products, Tak How knew that Kiddie Products employees would stay at its hotel, and could easily anticipate that they might use the pool, a featured amenity of the hotel. The district court thoroughly described this connection.

> The Hotel's solicitation of Kiddie's business and the extensive back-and-forth resulting in Burke's reserving a set of rooms for Kiddie employees and their spouses set in motion a chain of reasonably foreseeable events resulting in Mrs. Nowak's death. The possibility that the solicitation would prove successful and that one or more of the guests staying at the Hotel as a result would use the pool was in no sense remote or unpredictable; in fact, the Hotel included the pool as an attraction in its promotional materials.

While the nexus between Tak How's solicitation of Kiddie Products' business and Mrs. Nowak's death does not constitute a proximate cause relationship, it does represent a meaningful link between Tak How's contact and the harm suffered. Given these circumstances, we think it would be imprudent to reject jurisdiction at this early stage of the inquiry.

By this approach, we intend to emphasize the importance of proximate causation, but to allow a slight loosening of that standard when circumstances dictate. We think such flexibility is necessary in the jurisdictional inquiry: relatedness cannot merely be reduced to one tort concept for all circumstances. . . .

We recognize it will not always be easy to apply this flexible approach to particular circumstances, but that is a function of the complexity of this area of the law. The jurisdictional inquiry is often a difficult fact specific analysis. . . .

B.   Purposeful Availment

The next issue is whether Tak How's contacts with Massachusetts constitute purposeful availment. . . .

We think that Tak How's unprompted June 1993 correspondence with Kiddie Products, which led directly to the ill-fated Hong Kong trip in September 1993, was at least minimally sufficient to satisfy this requirement. The June 1993 correspondence contained promotional materials from the Holiday Inn designed to further entice Kiddie Products employees to stay at the hotel. Even if it may be said that the materials were sent as part of an on-going relationship between the two companies that was originally instigated by Kiddie Products, the continued correspondence by Tak How to Massachusetts does not amount to the kind of unilateral action that makes the forum-state contacts involuntary. Tak How had an obvious financial interest in continuing business with Kiddie Products, and the June 1993 correspondence is the best example of an unprompted solicitation designed to facilitate that business relationship. In order to be subject to Massachusetts' jurisdiction, a defendant need only have one contact with the forum state, so long as that contact is meaningful. *McGee v. International Life Ins. Co., . . . Burger King. . . .*

. . . That Tak How might have to defend itself in a Massachusetts court is certainly foreseeable based on its direct correspondence with Kiddie Products, but its other contacts with Massachusetts reveal an even more substantial attempt by Tak How to purposefully avail itself of the privilege of conducting business activities in the state: Tak How advertised its hotel in national and international publications that circulated in Massachusetts; it solicited by direct mail some of its previous guests residing in Massachusetts; and Tak How listed its hotel in various hotel guides used at travel agencies in Massachusetts. Exercising jurisdiction is appropriate where the defendant purposefully derives economic benefits from its forum-state activities.

[The court then held that exercising jurisdiction would not be unreasonable; see part C.5 of this chapter, page 212, *infra*. The court also upheld the district court's refusal to dismiss the case on grounds of forum non conveniens.]

NOTES AND QUESTIONS

1. *Relatedness as a spectrum.*   Many courts view relatedness as a flexible concept that varies with the extent of a defendant's meaningful contacts with the forum state. *See, e.g., Chew v. Dietrich*, 143 F.3d 24, 29 (2d Cir.), *cert. denied*, 525 U.S. 948 (1998); *Shute v. Carnival Cruise Lines, Inc.*, 897 F.2d 377, 385 n.7 (9th Cir. 1990). If a defendant has only limited contacts with the forum, the plaintiff's claim must usually "arise from" those contacts. As a defendant's forum contacts increase, the relatedness requirement is often relaxed so that the plaintiff's claim must "relate to" but need not "arise from" those contacts. As the court in *Nowak* noted, courts use several approaches in deciding whether a claim "relates to" a defendant's forum contacts, including the "but for," the "substantial connection," and the "lie in the wake of" tests.

2. *Arising from and proximate cause.*   In its strictest form, the relatedness requirement insists that a plaintiff's claim arise directly out of the defendant's purposeful contacts with the forum state. This strict standard would be satisfied if a defendant's forum contacts constitute a necessary element of the plaintiff's claim for relief. In *Nowak*, this "substantive relevance" approach to arising from was not met since Tak How's Massachusetts solicitation activities were not relevant to, much less an important element of, the plaintiffs' wrongful death claim against the hotel. Would the substantive-relevance test have been met in a suit by Kiddie Products against Tak How, alleging that the company's employees had been charged higher rates than Tak How promised in its earlier correspondence?

  Another strict version of the arising-from test is phrased in terms of "proximate cause." Under this test for relatedness, a defendant's purposeful contacts with the forum must constitute both the "cause in fact" and the "legal cause" of the harm for which the plaintiff seeks to recover. *See Peckham v. Continental Casualty Ins. Co.*, 895 F.2d 830, 836-837 (1st Cir. 1990). The cause-in-fact element is met simply by showing that "but for" the defendant's forum contacts, the plaintiff's claim would not have arisen. This element was met in *Nowak* since were it not for the defendant's solicitation aimed at Massachusetts, the Nowaks would not have stayed at the hotel and Mrs. Nowak would not have drowned.

The legal-cause element is more difficult to satisfy. It requires that the defendant's forum contacts were a substantial factor in bringing about the harm to the plaintiff, as opposed to an insignificant cause in comparison with other factors that produced the harm. The notion of "substantial" is used in a popular sense, embracing what an ordinary, reasonable person would regard as the cause of the harm. While there are myriad but-for causes of any particular harm, only a few of them are likely to be substantial enough to qualify as a legal cause of the harm. In *Nowak*, the hotel's Massachusetts advertising, its failure to properly equip the lifeguards, and the lifeguards' absence from the pool area were all but-for causes of Mrs. Nowak's drowning. Yet only the last two of these would qualify as legal or proximate causes. Thus, as the court noted, "the nexus between Tak How's solicitation of Kiddie Products' business and Mrs. Nowak's death does not constitute a proximate cause relationship. . . ." *Nowak*, 94 F.3d at 716.

From a conceptual perspective, the proximate-cause test, which is borrowed from the law of negligence, seems most appropriate in the tort context, while substantive relevance can be effectively applied across a broad spectrum of claims. Both tests are similarly strict in that they insist on a tight relationship between the contact and the claim.

3. The but-for test. Some courts use the but-for or cause-in-fact test by itself to assess relatedness, without insisting that there also be a legal or proximate-cause relationship. If the proximate-cause test represents one of the strictest approaches to relatedness, the but-for test is one of the loosest. As the *Nowak* court observed, the but-for test itself contains "no limiting principle; it literally embraces every event that hindsight can logically identify in the causative chain." *Id.* at 715. The but-for test would seem to allow a New York plaintiff to sue his New York doctor for medical malpractice in a California court simply because the doctor graduated from a California high school 40 years earlier. The but-for test would be met here since but for the doctor's having completed high school, she could not have attended college, which in turn allowed her to attend medical school and practice medicine.

Because of the seemingly limitless reach of the but-for test, the First Circuit was unwilling to adopt it as such. Instead, the court agreed to permit "a slight loosening" of the "proximate cause" standard on a case-by-case basis, "when circumstances dictate"—a loosening that will embrace some, but by no means all, but-for cases. In agreeing to relax the proximate cause standard in this way, the court repeatedly emphasized the element of "foreseeability." Unlike many but-for causes that produce harms that are "remote and unpredictable," Tak How's Massachusetts-related activities "set in motion a chain of reasonably foreseeable events resulting in Mrs. Nowak's death." This suggests that the First Circuit may employ the but-for relatedness test as a gloss on the "proximate cause" standard only when the injury for which the plaintiff sues is one that the defendant could "easily anticipate" as resulting from its purposeful contacts with the forum state.

The Third Circuit has likewise used the but-for test as a starting point in the relatedness analysis, rather than as a test that can be used on its own, out of concern that "[i]f but-for causation sufficed" by itself, "defendants' jurisdictional obligations would bear no meaningful relationship to the scope of the 'benefits and protection' received from the forum." *O'Connor v. Sandy Lane Hotel Co., Ltd.*, 496 F.3d 312, 322-323 (3d Cir. 2007) (tempering the but-for test with a quid pro quo principle in order to ensure that a party's "jurisdictional exposure" is proportional to and reasonably foreseeable from its contacts with the forum).

4. *The "substantial connection" test.* The "substantial connection" test, referred to in *Nowak*, falls on the spectrum somewhere between the "proximate-cause" and the "but-for" tests. It is used by some federal courts and was adopted by the California Supreme Court in *Cornelison v. Chaney*, 545 P.2d 264 (Cal. 1976). That case involved a Nevada auto accident in which a California plaintiff collided with a truck driven by a Nebraskan. At the time of the accident the defendant was engaged in a delivery business that, in the previous seven years, had brought him to California 20 times a year. Though the California Supreme Court held that these contacts were insufficient to allow general jurisdiction, it upheld specific jurisdiction. The court reasoned that since "[t]he accident arose out of the driving of the truck, the very activity which was the essential basis of defendant's contacts with this state," the plaintiff's claim "has a substantial connection with a business relationship defendant has purposefully established with California." *Id.* at 267. How would *Cornelison* have been decided under the strict "proximate cause" test? Under the relaxed but-for test?

PROBLEM

2-15. Elaine, a citizen of Connecticut, sued Walt Disney World in a Connecticut federal court to recover for injuries suffered when she slipped on a stairway at Disney World in Florida. For several years prior to taking the trip, Elaine had seen advertisements for Disney World in a Connecticut newspaper and on local television. In addition to advertising in Connecticut, Disney World had held two promotional events in Connecticut shortly before the suit was filed. Disney World has moved to dismiss the suit for lack of personal jurisdiction. Is Elaine's claim related to Disney's contacts with Connecticut? In answering this question, use the full range of relatedness tests. *See Mallon v. Walt Disney World Co.*, 42 F. Supp. 2d 143 (D. Conn. 1998).

5.   Due Process: The Reasonableness Requirement

A plaintiff's satisfaction of the contacts and relatedness components of personal jurisdiction analysis gives rise to a strong presumption that the exercise of personal jurisdiction would be reasonable under the circumstances presented. The defendant, however, may rebut that presumption by providing a compelling showing that the exercise of jurisdiction would be so unreasonable and unfair that the exercise of jurisdiction would violate the Due Process Clause of the Fourteenth Amendment. *See, e.g., Gordy v. Daily News, L.P.*, 95 F.3d 829, 835-836 (9th Cir. 1996).

In *World-Wide Volkswagen Corp. v. Woodson*, 444 U.S. 286 (1980), and *Burger King Corp. v. Rudzewicz*, 471 U.S. 462 (1985), the Court identified five factors that may be considered in the reasonableness determination: (1) the burden on the defendant; (2) the forum state's interest in adjudicating the dispute; (3) the plaintiff's interest in obtaining convenient and effective relief; (4) the interstate judicial system's interest in the most efficient resolution of controversies; and (5) the interests of other states in furthering their substantive policies. Although this list is not exhaustive, these factors constitute the essence of the reasonableness inquiry. *Id.* at 476-477; *World-Wide Volkswagen, supra*, 444 U.S. at 292. Many courts refer to these as the "gestalt factors." *Burger King* suggested that it will be unusual for jurisdiction to be defeated on reasonableness grounds since most of the relevant concerns "usually may be accommodated through means short of finding jurisdiction unconstitutional," such as applying the law of another state or country, or changing venue. *Burger King Corp., supra*, 471 U.S. at 477. Yet defendants are sometimes successful in demonstrating unreasonableness.

Asahi Metal Industry Co., Ltd. v. Superior Court of California
480 U.S. 102 (1987)

[This suit arose out of a motorcycle accident in California. Gary Zurcher, the motorcycle driver, filed a products liability action in a California state court against Cheng Shin, the Taiwanese manufacturer of the tire tube, claiming that the tube had been defective. In the same action, Cheng Shin filed an indemnity claim against Asahi, the Japanese manufacturer of the tire valve. Zurcher then settled his claims and was dropped from the suit, leaving only Cheng Shin's claim against Asahi. After the California courts refused to dismiss that claim for lack of jurisdiction, the Supreme Court granted review. As in *J. McIntyre*, the *Asahi* Justices were equally divided on the proper scope of the stream-of-commerce inquiry. JUSTICE O'CONNOR and three members of the Court concluded that Asahi had not met purposeful availment vis-à-vis California since it had done no more than place its goods in the stream of commerce. JUSTICE BRENNAN and three other members of the Court disagreed, finding that purposeful availment was satisfied based on the stream-of-commerce theory. The ninth member of the Court, JUSTICE STEVENS, agreed that there was purposeful availment, but did not endorse or reject any particular version of the stream-of-commerce theory. Though JUSTICE O'CONNOR concluded that purposeful availment was not met, Part II.B of her opinion went on to consider whether taking jurisdiction would have been reasonable had there been purposeful availment. This section of JUSTICE O'CONNOR's opinion was joined by seven other Justices.]

II

B

The strictures of the Due Process Clause forbid a state court to exercise personal jurisdiction over Asahi under circumstances that would offend "'traditional notions of fair play and substantial justice.'" *International Shoe Co. v. Washington.*

We have previously explained that the determination of the reasonableness of the exercise of jurisdiction in each case will depend on an evaluation of several factors. A court must consider the burden on the defendant, the interests of the forum State, and the plaintiff's interest in obtaining relief. It must also weigh in its determination "the interstate judicial system's interest in obtaining the most efficient resolution of controversies; and the shared interest of the several States in furthering fundamental substantive social policies." *World-Wide Volkswagen.*

A consideration of these factors in the present case clearly reveals the unreasonableness of the assertion of jurisdiction over Asahi, even apart from the question of the placement of goods in the stream of commerce.

Certainly the burden on the defendant in this case is severe. Asahi has been commanded by the Supreme Court of California not only to traverse the distance between Asahi's headquarters in Japan and the Superior Court of California . . . , but also to submit its dispute with Cheng Shin to a foreign nation's judicial system. The unique burdens placed upon one who must defend oneself in a foreign legal system should have significant weight in assessing the reasonableness of stretching the long-arm of personal jurisdiction over national borders.

When minimum contacts have been established, often the interests of the plaintiff and the forum in the exercise of jurisdiction will justify even the serious burdens placed on the alien defendant. In the present case, however, the interests of the plaintiff and the forum in California's assertion of jurisdiction over Asahi are slight. All that remains is a claim for indemnification asserted by Cheng Shin, a Taiwanese corporation, against Asahi. The transaction on which the indemnification claim is based took place in Taiwan; Asahi's components were shipped from Japan to Taiwan. Cheng Shin has not demonstrated that it is more convenient for it to litigate its indemnification claim against Asahi in California rather than in Taiwan or Japan.

Because the plaintiff is not a California resident, California's legitimate interests in the dispute have considerably diminished. The Supreme Court of California argued that the State had an interest in "protecting its consumers by ensuring that foreign manufacturers comply with the state's safety standards." The State Supreme Court's definition of California's interest, however, was overly broad. The dispute between Cheng Shin and Asahi is primarily about indemnification rather than safety standards. Moreover, it is not at all clear at this point that California law should govern the question whether a Japanese corporation should indemnify a Taiwanese corporation on the basis of a sale made in Taiwan and a shipment of goods from Japan to Taiwan. The possibility of being haled into a California court as a result of an accident involving Asahi's components undoubtedly creates an additional deterrent to the manufacture of unsafe components; however, similar pressures will be placed on Asahi by the purchasers of its components as long as those who use Asahi components in their final products, and sell those products in California, are subject to the application of California tort law.

World-Wide Volkswagen also admonished courts to take into consideration the interests of the "several States," in addition to the forum State, in the efficient judicial resolution of the dispute and the advancement of substantive policies. In the present case, this advice calls for a court to consider the procedural and substantive policies of other *nations* whose interests are affected by the assertion of jurisdiction by the California court. The procedural and substantive interests of other nations in a state court's assertion of jurisdiction over an alien defendant will differ from case to case. In every case, however, those interests, as well as the Federal interest in its foreign relations policies, will be best served by a careful inquiry into the reasonableness of the assertion of jurisdiction in the particular case, and an unwillingness to find the serious burdens on an alien defendant outweighed by minimal interests on the part of the plaintiff or the forum State. "Great care and reserve should be exercised when extending our notions of personal jurisdiction into the international field."

Considering the international context, the heavy burden on the alien defendant, and the slight interests of the plaintiff and the forum State, the exercise of personal jurisdiction by a California court over Asahi in this instance would be unreasonable and unfair. . . .

JUSTICE BRENNAN, with whom JUSTICE WHITE, JUSTICE MARSHALL, and JUSTICE BLACKMUN join, concurring in part and concurring in the judgment.

I do not agree with the interpretation in Part II-A of the stream-of-commerce theory, nor with the conclusion that Asahi did not "purposely avail itself of the California market." I do agree, however, with the Court's conclusion in Part II-B that the exercise of personal jurisdiction over Asahi in this case would not comport with "fair play and substantial justice." This is one of those rare cases in which "minimum requirements inherent in the concept of 'fair play and substantial justice' . . . defeat the reasonableness of jurisdiction even [though] the defendant has purposefully engaged in forum activities." *Burger King Corp. v. Rudzewicz.* . . .

JUSTICE STEVENS, with whom JUSTICE WHITE and JUSTICE BLACKMUN join, concurring in part and concurring in the judgment.

The judgment of the Supreme Court of California should be reversed for the reasons stated in Part II-B of the Court's opinion. . . . Part II-B establishes, after considering the factors set forth in *World-Wide Volkswagen Corp.*, that California's exercise of jurisdiction over Asahi in this case would be "unreasonable and unfair." This finding alone requires reversal; this case fits within the rule that "minimum requirements inherent in the concept of 'fair play and substantial justice' may defeat the reasonableness of jurisdiction even if the defendant has purposefully engaged in forum activities." Accordingly, I see no reason in this case for the plurality to articulate "purposeful direction" or any other test as the nexus between an act of a defendant and the forum State that is necessary to establish minimum contacts. . . .

NOTES AND QUESTIONS

1. Foreign defendants.   Eight members of the *Asahi* Court suggested that when the defendant who contests jurisdiction is a truly foreign entity or individual, due process requires courts to proceed with additional caution. Yet the Court also made it clear that a defendant's foreign citizenship is not a bar to exercising jurisdiction. The Court stressed that because Cheng Shin was also a foreign entity, neither it nor the forum state had as strong an interest in having the suit proceed in California as might otherwise have been the case. Suppose that in *Asahi*, Gary Zurcher, the California motorcycle driver, had sued both Cheng Shin and Asahi. Would the reasonableness analysis have favored dismissing his case against Asahi? In her dissenting opinion in *McIntyre Machinery*, Justice Ginsburg suggested that how *Asahi* would have been decided had Zurcher originally sued Asahi was "a debatable question." See page 196, *supra*.

2. A variable standard?   As we will see in the next case, some courts treat the defendant's burden in demonstrating unreasonableness as one that varies with the strength of the plaintiff's minimum contacts showing.

Nowak v. Tak How Investments, Ltd. [Part II]
94 F.3d 708 (1st Cir. 1996), *cert. denied*, 520 U.S. 1155 (1997)

[Earlier, at page 204, *supra*, we read the parts of this opinion addressing the contacts and relatedness elements of specific jurisdiction. In the part that follows, the court then concluded that it would not be unreasonable for the Massachusetts federal court to exercise jurisdiction.]

II . . .

C.   The Gestalt Factors

Our conclusion that minimum contacts exist in this case does not end the inquiry. Personal jurisdiction may only be exercised if it comports with traditional notions of "fair play and substantial justice." Out of this requirement, courts have developed a series of factors that bear on the fairness of subjecting a nonresident to a foreign tribunal . . . . The purpose of the gestalt factors is to aid the court in achieving substantial justice, particularly where the minimum-contacts question is very close. In such cases, the gestalt factors may tip the constitutional balance. The Supreme Court's decision in *Asahi Metal Indus. Co. v. Superior Court* is one such example. In *Asahi*, the question of minimum contacts divided the Court, but eight of the Justices agreed that exercising personal jurisdiction would not comport with notions of fair play and substantial justice. This Court has thus adopted a sliding scale approach: "[T]he weaker the plaintiff's showing on the first two prongs (relatedness and purposeful availment), the less a defendant need show in terms of unreasonableness to defeat jurisdiction." The reverse is equally true: a strong showing of reasonableness may serve to fortify a more marginal showing of relatedness and purposefulness.

1. The Burden of Appearance.   It would undoubtedly be burdensome for Tak How to defend itself in Massachusetts: Tak How's only place of business is in Hong Kong. This Court has recognized, however, that it is almost always inconvenient and costly for a party to litigate in a foreign jurisdiction. Thus for this particular gestalt factor to have any significance, the defendant must demonstrate that "exercise of jurisdiction in the present circumstances is onerous in a special, unusual, or other constitutionally significant way." Tak How alleges nothing special or unusual about its situation beyond the ordinary cost and inconvenience of defending an action so far from its place of business. . . . [T]hat is not enough: it simply cannot be the case that every Hong Kong corporation is immune from suit in Massachusetts. We are also persuaded that the burden on Tak How will be minimized by, for example, the availability of transcripts from the Coroner's Court for use in the Massachusetts proceeding.

We have also noted that the burden of appearance is an important gestalt factor primarily because it allows a court to guard against harassing litigation. Were there any indication in the record that the Nowaks brought the present suit to harass Tak How, the burden of appearance in Massachusetts might weigh in Tak How's favor; however, the record does not so indicate.

2. Interest of the Forum.   Although a forum state has a significant interest in obtaining jurisdiction over a defendant who causes tortious injury within its borders, that interest is diminished where the injury occurred outside the forum state. Nonetheless, our task is not to compare the interest of the two sovereigns — the place of the injury and forum state — but to determine whether the forum state *has* an interest. While it is true that the injury in this case occurred in Hong Kong, it is equally true . . . that significant events took place in Massachusetts giving it an interest in this litigation. Tak How solicited business in the state. As the district court noted, Massachusetts has a strong interest in protecting its citizens from out-of-state solicitations for goods or services that prove to be unsafe, and it also has an interest in providing its citizens with a convenient forum in which to assert their claims. Given the forum-state activities that took place prior to Mrs. Nowak's death, we conclude that Massachusetts has a strong interest in exercising jurisdiction even though the injury took place in Hong Kong.

3. The Plaintiffs' Convenience.   This Court must accord deference to the Nowaks' choice of a Massachusetts forum. Regardless, it is obvious that a Massachusetts forum is more convenient for the Nowaks than another forum, particularly a Hong Kong forum. Further, there exists substantial doubt that the Nowaks could adequately resolve the dispute in Hong Kong: Hong Kong's laws regarding contingency fees and posting of security bonds with the court make litigation economically onerous for plaintiffs, and the future of Hong Kong's political system is also uncertain.

4. The Administration of Justice.   This factor focuses on the judicial system's interest in obtaining the most effective resolution of the controversy. Usually this factor is a wash, but in one case we held that preventing piecemeal litigation might favor one jurisdiction over another. Tak How argues that a Massachusetts action would require the application of Hong Kong law, the use of interpreters, and the transportation of key witnesses from Hong Kong that are not subject to compulsory process. On the other hand, the Nowaks point to possible political instability in Hong Kong as the British Colony prepares to revert to Chinese sovereignty. Interpreters and transportation of witnesses would likely also be necessary in Hong Kong. We conclude that the question of efficient administration of justice favors a Massachusetts forum. Given the likelihood that the Nowaks would face great obstacles in Hong Kong due to possible political instability, as well as Hong Kong laws on contingency fees and security bonds, efficiency concerns require a Massachusetts forum.

5. Pertinent Policy Arguments.   The final gestalt factor addresses the interests of the affected governments in substantive social policies. Massachusetts has an interest in protecting its citizens from out-of-state providers of goods and services as well as affording its citizens a convenient forum in which to bring their claims. These interests are best served by the exercise of jurisdiction in Massachusetts. On the other hand, Hong Kong has an interest in protecting visitors to promote and preserve its tourism industry, in protecting its businesses, and in providing all parties with a convenient forum. Only one of Hong Kong's interests—protecting its businesses—might be compromised by a Massachusetts forum, while Massachusetts' primary interest—protecting its citizens—might be compromised by a Hong Kong forum. We thus conclude that the final gestalt factor tips only slightly in the Nowaks' favor.

On balance, we think the gestalt factors weigh strongly in favor of a Massachusetts forum. When considered in combination with the Nowaks' adequate showing on the first two prongs of the constitutional test, we think that, on the specific facts of this case, the exercise of jurisdiction in Massachusetts is reasonable and does not offend the notions of fair play and substantial justice. The district court therefore properly denied Tak How's Rule 12(b)(2) motion to dismiss for lack of personal jurisdiction. . . .

NOTES AND QUESTIONS

1. Plaintiff's alternatives and the statute of limitations.   One of the factors the *Nowak* court considered was that if plaintiffs could not sue in Massachusetts, they might not be able to sue anywhere else. We saw earlier that the element of necessity may also play a role in deciding whether a court can exercise general jurisdiction—*e.g.*, if the court in question is the only one in which all potential defendants may be sued together; or if it is the only U.S. forum available to an American plaintiff; or if there is no other forum in the world in which the plaintiff can afford to litigate. Several of these considerations came into play in *Nowak*.

However, the Supreme Court has made it clear that a plaintiff cannot invoke an argument of necessity based merely on the fact that the chosen forum is now the only one in which the statute of limitations may not yet have run. For in such a case, the plaintiff has presumably created his or her own predicament by neither filing the lawsuit earlier nor filing a protective action. In *Keeton v. Hustler Magazine, Inc.*, 465 U.S. 770, 778-779 (1984), the Court thus wrote: "[T]he fact that the statutes of limitations in every [other] jurisdiction . . . had run on plaintiff's claim in this case" was a factor that simply "does not alter the jurisdictional calculus. . . ."

PROBLEMS

2-16. Lillian was injured while operating a stamping press at her job in New York. The press was built by Navitas, a Japanese company, which sold it to Kurz, a Pennsylvania company, which in turn sold it to Lillian's employer, Forbes, in New York. After Lillian sued Kurz in a New York court, Kurz filed a third-party claim for indemnity against Navitas. Navitas moved to dismiss the claim for lack of jurisdiction. It has had no contracts or direct dealings with New York. Navitas gave Kurz the exclusive right to distribute its products in North America. Pursuant to that agreement, it sent several hundred machines to Kurz in Pennsylvania but had no specific knowledge as to where they would be resold. Assuming that Navitas falls within New York's long-arm statute, can Kurz demonstrate that Navitas had meaningful contacts with New York? If it does so, can Navitas carry its burden of showing that it would be unreasonable to assert jurisdiction under the circumstances presented? *See Kernan v. Kurz-Hastings, Inc.*, 175 F.3d 236 (2d Cir. 1999).

2-17. Amanda, a resident of New Hampshire, filed a medical malpractice action against the Maine Medical Center ("MMC") in the New Hampshire federal court, based on diversity. She seeks damages on behalf of her infant daughter, EC, who was born in a New Hampshire hospital and transferred to MMC's intensive care unit in Portland, Maine, four hours after her birth. EC's physician initiated the transfer. An MMC medical transport team then picked EC up in New Hampshire and drove her the 50 miles back to MMC's facility in Maine. Two weeks after the transfer, an MMC employee placed a hot, wet diaper on EC's heel, causing scarring and requiring EC to receive additional medical services. MMC has filed a Rule 12(b)(2) motion to dismiss.

MMC is a nonprofit Maine corporation with its sole place of business in Portland, Maine. It participates in the Regional Emergency System (RES), a 24-hour communication center that facilitates transfers to MMC from other hospitals and caregivers, including those in New Hampshire. It was pursuant to the RES that EC was transferred to Portland. MMC has no agreement with any New Hampshire physicians under which patients are directed to MMC for medical services. It does not purchase ads in any New Hampshire–based newspapers, telephone directories, or television or radio stations. MMC issues periodic press releases to a range of media outlets, including several in New Hampshire. It also operates an interactive website that provides information about services and staff, and allows users to make online charitable donations, complete patient pre-registration, register for classes, find doctors, and apply for jobs. MMC is registered in New Hampshire as a foreign nonprofit corporation, which allows it to advertise its Poison Control Center (PCC) services. While all PCC services are rendered at MMC's Maine facilities, it has one New Hampshire employee who educates people about PCC services. In the two years before the suit was filed, New Hampshire residents made up 3 percent of MMC's in-patient admissions and accounted for $72 million in income (3.25 percent of its total revenue). Assume that MMC falls within New Hampshire's long-arm statute.

A. Does MMC have meaningful connections with New Hampshire?
B. On what bases might Amanda argue that her lawsuit satisfies the requirements for specific jurisdiction? How likely are any of those arguments to succeed?
C. If Amanda is able to show the existence of meaningful connections, *i.e.*, connections that are significant and related to the plaintiff's claim (specific jurisdiction), can MMC carry its burden of showing that the exercise of jurisdiction here would be unreasonable under the circumstances?

See Cossaboon v. Maine Medical Center, 600 F.3d 25 (1st Cir. 2010).

6. Due Process: General Jurisdiction

In *International Shoe Co. v. Washington*, the Court observed, "[T]here have been instances in which the continuous corporate operations within a state were thought so substantial and of such a nature as to justify suit against it on causes of action arising from dealings entirely distinct from those activities." See page 141, *supra*. This type of jurisdiction is now called "general jurisdiction," sometimes aptly referred to as "all-purpose jurisdiction." It requires that the nonresident defendant's contacts with the forum be so extensive as to treat the defendant as if it were domiciled in the forum, and therefore subject to personal jurisdiction on all claims asserted against it, without any inquiry into either relatedness or reasonableness.

Daimler A.G. v. Bauman

134 S. Ct. 746 (2014)

JUSTICE GINSBURG delivered the opinion of the Court.

This case concerns the authority of a court in the United States to entertain a claim brought by foreign plaintiffs against a foreign defendant based on events occurring entirely outside the United States. The litigation commenced in 2004, when twenty-two Argentinian residents filed a complaint in the United States District Court for the Northern District of California against DaimlerChrysler

[handwritten margin note: Contacts so substantial court acted like D was domiciled ¥ in forum state.]

Aktiengesellschaft (Daimler), a German public stock company, headquartered in Stuttgart, that manufactures Mercedes-Benz vehicles in Germany. The complaint alleged that during Argentina's 1976-1983 "Dirty War," Daimler's Argentinian subsidiary, Mercedes-Benz Argentina (MB Argentina) collaborated with state security forces to kidnap, detain, torture, and kill certain MB Argentina workers, among them, plaintiffs or persons closely related to plaintiffs. Damages for the alleged human-rights violations were sought from Daimler under the laws of the United States, California, and Argentina. Jurisdiction over the lawsuit was predicated on the California contacts of Mercedes-Benz USA, LLC (MBUSA), a subsidiary of Daimler incorporated in Delaware with its principal place of business in New Jersey. MBUSA distributes Daimler-manufactured vehicles to independent dealerships throughout the United States, including California.

The question presented is whether the Due Process Clause of the Fourteenth Amendment precludes the District Court from exercising jurisdiction over Daimler in this case, given the absence of any California connection to the atrocities, perpetrators, or victims described in the complaint. Plaintiffs invoked the court's general or all-purpose jurisdiction. California, they urge, is a place where Daimler may be sued on any and all claims against it, wherever in the world the claims may arise. . . . [U]nder the proffered jurisdictional theory, if a Daimler-manufactured vehicle overturned in Poland, injuring a Polish driver and passenger, the injured parties could maintain a design defect suit in California. Exercises of personal jurisdiction so exorbitant, we hold, are barred by due process constraints on the assertion of adjudicatory authority.

In *Goodyear Dunlop Tires Operations, S.A. v. Brown*, 131 S. Ct. 2846 (2011), we addressed the distinction between general or all-purpose jurisdiction, and specific or conduct-linked jurisdiction. As to the former, we held that a court may assert jurisdiction over a foreign corporation "to hear any and all claims against [it]" only when the corporation's affiliations with the State in which suit is brought are so constant and pervasive "as to render [it] essentially at home in the forum State." Instructed by *Goodyear*, we conclude Daimler is not "at home" in California, and cannot be sued there for injuries plaintiffs attribute to MB Argentina's conduct in Argentina.

I

In 2004, plaintiffs (respondents here) filed suit in the United States District Court for the Northern District of California, alleging that MB Argentina collaborated with Argentinian state security forces to kidnap, detain, torture, and kill plaintiffs and their relatives during the military dictatorship in place there from 1976 through 1983, a period known as Argentina's "Dirty War." Based on those allegations, plaintiffs asserted claims under the Alien Tort Statute, 28 U.S.C. § 1350, and the Torture Victim Protection Act of 1991, as well as claims for wrongful death and intentional infliction of emotional distress under the laws of California and Argentina. The incidents recounted in the complaint center on MB Argentina's plant in Gonzalez Catan, Argentina; no part of MB Argentina's alleged collaboration with Argentinian authorities took place in California or anywhere else in the United States.

Plaintiffs' operative complaint names only one corporate defendant: Daimler, the petitioner here. Plaintiffs seek to hold Daimler vicariously liable for MB Argentina's alleged malfeasance. Daimler is a German Aktiengesellschaft (public stock company) that manufactures Mercedes-Benz vehicles in Germany and has its headquarters in Stuttgart. At times relevant to this case, MB Argentina was a subsidiary wholly owned by Daimler's predecessor in interest.

Daimler moved to dismiss the action for want of personal jurisdiction. Opposing the motion, plaintiffs submitted declarations and exhibits purporting to demonstrate the presence of Daimler itself in California. Alternatively, plaintiffs maintained that jurisdiction over Daimler could be founded on the California contacts of MBUSA, a distinct corporate entity that, according to plaintiffs, should be treated as Daimler's agent for jurisdictional purposes.

MBUSA, an indirect subsidiary of Daimler, is a Delaware limited liability corporation. MBUSA serves as Daimler's exclusive importer and distributor in the United States, purchasing Mercedes-Benz automobiles from Daimler in Germany, then importing those vehicles, and ultimately distributing them to independent dealerships located throughout the Nation. Although MBUSA's principal place of business is in New Jersey, MBUSA has multiple California-based facilities, including a regional office in Costa Mesa, a Vehicle Preparation Center in Carson, and a Classic Center in Irvine. According to the record developed below, MBUSA is the largest supplier of luxury vehicles to the California market. In particular, over 10% of all sales of new vehicles in the United States take place in California, and MBUSA's California sales account for 2.4% of Daimler's worldwide sales.

The relationship between Daimler and MBUSA is delineated in a General Distributor Agreement, which sets forth requirements for MBUSA's distribution of Mercedes-Benz vehicles in the United States. That agreement established MBUSA as an "independent contracto[r]" that "buy[s] and sell[s] [vehicles] . . . as an independent business for [its] own account." The agreement "does not make [MBUSA] . . . a general or special agent, partner, joint venturer or employee of DAIMLERCHRYSLER or any DaimlerChrysler Group Company"; MBUSA "ha[s] no authority to make binding obligations for or act on behalf of DAIMLERCHRYSLER or any DaimlerChrysler Group Company."

After allowing jurisdictional discovery on plaintiffs' agency allegations, the District Court granted Daimler's motion to dismiss. Daimler's own affiliations with California, the court first determined, were insufficient to support the exercise of all-purpose jurisdiction over the corporation. Next, the court declined to attribute MBUSA's California contacts to Daimler on an agency theory, concluding that plaintiffs failed to demonstrate that MBUSA acted as Daimler's agent.

The Ninth Circuit at first affirmed the District Court's judgment. Addressing solely the question of agency, the Court of Appeals held that plaintiffs had not shown the existence of an agency relationship of the kind that might warrant attribution of MBUSA's contacts to Daimler. Judge Reinhardt dissented. In his view, the agency test was satisfied and considerations of "reasonableness" did not bar the exercise of jurisdiction. Granting plaintiffs' petition for rehearing, the panel withdrew its initial opinion and replaced it with one authored by Judge Reinhardt, which elaborated on reasoning he initially expressed in dissent. . . .

We granted certiorari to decide whether, consistent with the Due Process Clause of the Fourteenth Amendment, Daimler is amenable to suit in California courts for claims involving only foreign plaintiffs and conduct occurring entirely abroad.

II

Federal courts ordinarily follow state law in determining the bounds of their jurisdiction over persons. See Fed. Rule Civ. Proc. 4(k)(1)(A) (service of process is effective to establish personal jurisdiction over a defendant "who is subject to the jurisdiction of a court of general jurisdiction in the state where the district court is located"). Under California's long-arm statute, California state courts may exercise personal jurisdiction "on any basis not inconsistent with the Constitution of this state or of the United States." Cal. Civ. Proc. Code Ann. § 410.10 (West 2004). California's long-arm statute allows the exercise of personal jurisdiction to the full extent permissible under the U.S. Constitution. We therefore inquire whether the Ninth Circuit's holding comports with the limits imposed by federal due process.

III

In *Pennoyer v. Neff*, 95 U.S. 714 (1878), decided shortly after the enactment of the Fourteenth Amendment, the Court held that a tribunal's jurisdiction over persons reaches no farther than the geographic bounds of the forum. In time, however, that strict territorial approach yielded to a less rigid understanding, spurred by "changes in the technology of transportation and communication, and the tremendous growth of interstate business activity." *Burnham v. Superior Court of Cal., County of Marin*, 495 U.S. 604, 617 (1990) (opinion of Scalia, J.).

"The canonical opinion in this area remains *International Shoe* in which we held that a State may authorize its courts to exercise personal jurisdiction over an out-of-state defendant if the defendant has 'certain minimum contacts with [the State] such that the maintenance of the suit does not offend "traditional notions of fair play and substantial justice."'" *Goodyear*, 131 S.Ct., at 2853 (quoting *International Shoe*, 326 U.S., at 316). Following *International Shoe*, "the relationship among the defendant, the forum, and the litigation, rather than the mutually exclusive sovereignty of the States on which the rules of *Pennoyer* rest, became the central concern of the inquiry into personal jurisdiction."

International Shoe's conception of "fair play and substantial justice" presaged the development of two categories of personal jurisdiction. The first category is represented by *International Shoe* itself, a case in which the in-state activities of the corporate defendant "ha[d] not only been continuous and systematic, but also g[a]ve rise to the liabilities sued on." *International Shoe* recognized, as well, that "the commission of some single or occasional acts of the corporate agent in a state" may sometimes be enough to subject the corporation to jurisdiction in that State's tribunals with respect to suits relating to that in-state activity. Adjudicatory authority of this order, in which the suit "aris[es] out of or relate[s] to the defendant's contacts with the forum," *Helicopteros Nacionales de Colombia, S.A. v. Hall*, 466 U.S. 408, 414, n.8 (1984), is today called "specific jurisdiction."

International Shoe distinguished between, on the one hand, exercises of specific jurisdiction, as just described, and on the other, situations where a foreign corporation's "continuous corporate operations within a state [are] so substantial and of such a nature as to justify suit against it on causes of action arising from dealings entirely distinct from those activities." As we have since explained, "[a] court may assert general jurisdiction over foreign (sister-state or foreign-country) corporations to hear any and all claims against them when their affiliations with the State are so 'continuous and systematic' as to render them essentially at home in the forum State." *Goodyear*, 131 S. Ct., at 2851.

Since *International Shoe*, "specific jurisdiction has become the centerpiece of modern jurisdiction theory, while general jurisdiction [has played] a reduced role." *Goodyear*, 131 S. Ct., at 2854. *International Shoe*'s momentous departure from *Pennoyer*'s rigidly territorial focus, we have noted, unleashed a rapid expansion of tribunals' ability to hear claims against out-of-state defendants when the episode-in-suit occurred in the forum or the defendant purposefully availed itself of the forum. Our subsequent decisions have continued to bear out the prediction that "specific jurisdiction will come into sharper relief and form a considerably more significant part of the scene."

Our post-*International Shoe* opinions on general jurisdiction, by comparison, are few. "[The Court's] 1952 decision in *Perkins v. Benguet Consol. Mining Co.* remains the textbook case of general jurisdiction appropriately exercised over a foreign corporation that has not consented to suit in the forum." *Goodyear*, 131 S. Ct., at 2856. The defendant in *Perkins*, Benguet, was a company incorporated under the laws of the Philippines, where it operated gold and silver mines. Benguet ceased its mining operations during the Japanese occupation of the Philippines in World War II; its president moved to Ohio, where he kept an office, maintained the company's files, and oversaw the company's activities. *Perkins v. Benguet Consol. Mining Co.*, 342 U.S. 437, 448 (1952). The plaintiff, an Ohio resident, sued Benguet on a claim that neither arose in Ohio nor related to the corporation's activities in that State. We held that the Ohio courts could exercise general jurisdiction over Benguet without offending due process. That was so, we later noted, because "Ohio was the corporation's principal, if temporary, place of business." *Keeton v. Hustler Magazine, Inc.*, 465 U.S. 770, 780, n.11 (1984).

The next case on point, *Helicopteros*, arose from a helicopter crash in Peru. Four U.S. citizens perished in that accident; their survivors and representatives brought suit in Texas state court against the helicopter's owner and operator, a Colombian corporation. That company's contacts with Texas were confined to "sending its chief executive officer to Houston for a contract-negotiation session; accepting into its New York bank account checks drawn on a Houston bank; purchasing helicopters, equipment, and training services from [a Texas-based helicopter company] for substantial sums; and sending personnel to [Texas] for training." Notably, those contacts bore no apparent relationship to the accident that gave rise to the suit. We held that the company's Texas connections did not resemble the "continuous and systematic general business contacts . . . found to exist in *Perkins*." "[M]ere purchases, even if occurring at regular intervals," we clarified, "are not enough to warrant a State's assertion of *in personam* jurisdiction over a nonresident corporation in a cause of action not related to those purchase transactions."

Most recently, in *Goodyear*, we answered the question: "Are foreign subsidiaries of a United States parent corporation amenable to suit in state court on claims unrelated to any activity of the subsidiaries in the forum State?" That case arose from a bus accident outside Paris that killed two boys from North Carolina. The boys' parents brought a wrongful-death suit in North Carolina state court alleging that the bus's tire was defectively manufactured. The complaint named as defendants not only The Goodyear Tire and Rubber Company (Goodyear), an Ohio corporation, but also Goodyear's Turkish, French, and Luxembourgian subsidiaries. Those foreign subsidiaries, which manufactured tires for sale in Europe and Asia, lacked any affiliation with North Carolina. A small percentage of tires manufactured by the foreign subsidiaries were distributed in North Carolina, however, and on that ground, the North Carolina Court of Appeals held the subsidiaries amenable to the general jurisdiction of North Carolina courts.

We reversed, observing that the North Carolina court's analysis "elided the essential difference between case-specific and all-purpose (general) jurisdiction." Although the placement of a product into the stream of commerce "may bolster an affiliation germane to specific jurisdiction," we explained, such contacts "do not warrant a determination that, based on those ties, the forum has general jurisdiction over a defendant." As *International Shoe* itself teaches, a corporation's "continuous activity of some sorts within a state is not enough to support the demand that the corporation be amenable to suits unrelated to that activity." Because Goodyear's foreign subsidiaries were "in no sense at home in North Carolina," we held, those subsidiaries could not be required to submit to the general jurisdiction of that State's courts.

As is evident from *Perkins*, *Helicopteros*, and *Goodyear*, general and specific jurisdiction have followed markedly different trajectories post-*International Shoe*. Specific jurisdiction has been cut loose from *Pennoyer*'s sway, but we have declined to stretch general jurisdiction beyond limits traditionally recognized. As this Court has increasingly trained on the "relationship among the defendant, the forum, and the litigation," *Shaffer*, *i.e.*, specific jurisdiction, general jurisdiction has come to occupy a less dominant place in the contemporary scheme.

IV

With this background, we turn directly to the question whether Daimler's affiliations with California are sufficient to subject it to the general (all-purpose) personal jurisdiction of that State's courts. In the proceedings below, the parties agreed on, or failed to contest, certain points we now take as given. Plaintiffs have never attempted to fit this case into the specific jurisdiction category. Nor did plaintiffs challenge on appeal the District Court's holding that Daimler's own contacts with California were, by themselves, too sporadic to justify the exercise of general jurisdiction. While plaintiffs ultimately persuaded the Ninth Circuit to impute MBUSA's California contacts to Daimler on an agency theory, at no point have they maintained that MBUSA is an alter ego of Daimler.

Daimler, on the other hand, failed to object below to plaintiffs' assertion that the California courts could exercise all-purpose jurisdiction over MBUSA. We will assume then, for purposes of this decision only, that MBUSA qualifies as at home in California.

A

In sustaining the exercise of general jurisdiction over Daimler, the Ninth Circuit relied on an agency theory, determining that MBUSA acted as Daimler's agent for jurisdictional purposes and then attributing MBUSA's California contacts to Daimler. The Ninth Circuit's agency analysis derived from Circuit precedent considering principally whether the subsidiary "performs services that are sufficiently important to the foreign corporation that if it did not have a representative to perform them, the corporation's own officials would undertake to perform substantially similar services."

This Court has not yet addressed whether a foreign corporation may be subjected to a court's general jurisdiction based on the contacts of its in-state subsidiary. Daimler argues, and several Courts of Appeals have held, that a subsidiary's jurisdictional contacts can be imputed to its parent only when the former is so dominated by the latter as to be its alter ego. The Ninth Circuit adopted a less rigorous test based on what it described as an "agency" relationship. Agencies, we note, come in many sizes and shapes: "One may be an agent for some business purposes and not others so that the fact that one may be an agent for one purpose does not make him or her an agent for every purpose." 2A C. J. S., Agency § 43, p. 367 (2013). A subsidiary, for example, might be its parent's agent for claims arising in the place where the subsidiary operates, yet not its agent regarding claims arising elsewhere. The Court of Appeals did not advert to that prospect. But we need not pass judgment on invocation of an agency theory in the context of general jurisdiction, for in no event can the appeals court's analysis be sustained.

The Ninth Circuit's agency finding rested primarily on its observation that MBUSA's services were "important" to Daimler, as gauged by Daimler's hypothetical readiness to perform those services itself if MBUSA did not exist. Formulated this way, the inquiry into importance stacks the deck, for it will always yield a pro-jurisdiction answer: "Anything a corporation does through an independent contractor, subsidiary, or distributor is presumably something that the corporation would do 'by other means' if the independent contractor, subsidiary, or distributor did not exist." The Ninth Circuit's agency theory thus appears to subject foreign corporations to general jurisdiction whenever they have an in-state subsidiary or affiliate, an outcome that would sweep beyond even the "sprawling view of general jurisdiction" we rejected in *Goodyear*.

B

Even if we were to assume that MBUSA is at home in California, and further to assume MBUSA's contacts are imputable to Daimler, there would still be no basis to subject Daimler to general jurisdiction in California, for Daimler's slim contacts with the State hardly render it at home there.

Goodyear made clear that only a limited set of affiliations with a forum will render a defendant amenable to all-purpose jurisdiction there. "For an individual, the paradigm forum for the exercise of general jurisdiction is the individual's domicile; for a corporation, it is an equivalent place, one in which the corporation is fairly regarded as at home." With respect to a corporation, the place of incorporation and principal place of business are "paradig[m] . . . bases for general jurisdiction." Those affiliations have the virtue of being unique—that is, each ordinarily indicates only one place—as well as easily ascertainable. Cf. *Hertz Corp. v. Friend*, 559 U.S. 77, 94 (2010) ("Simple jurisdictional rules . . . promote greater predictability."). These bases afford plaintiffs recourse to at least one clear and certain forum in which a corporate defendant may be sued on any and all claims.

Goodyear did not hold that a corporation may be subject to general jurisdiction *only* in a forum where it is incorporated or has its principal place of business; it simply typed those places paradigm all-purpose forums. Plaintiffs would have us look beyond the exemplar bases *Goodyear* identified, and approve the exercise of general jurisdiction in every State in which a corporation "engages in a substantial, continuous, and systematic course of business." That formulation, we hold, is unacceptably grasping.

As noted, the words "continuous and systematic" were used in *International Shoe* to describe instances in which the exercise of specific jurisdiction would be appropriate. Turning to all-purpose jurisdiction, in contrast, *International Shoe* speaks of "instances in which the continuous corporate operations within a state [are] so substantial and of such a nature as to justify suit . . . *on causes of action arising from dealings entirely distinct from those activities.*" Accordingly, the inquiry under *Goodyear* is not whether a foreign corporation's in-forum contacts can be said to be in some sense "continuous and systematic," it is whether that corporation's "affiliations with the State are so 'continuous and systematic' as to render [it] essentially at home in the forum State." 131 S. Ct., at 2851.[19]

Here, neither Daimler nor MBUSA is incorporated in California, nor does either entity have its principal place of business there. If Daimler's California activities sufficed to allow adjudication of this Argentina-rooted case in California, the same global reach would presumably be available in every other State in which

---

19. We do not foreclose the possibility that in an exceptional case, a corporation's operations in a forum other than its formal place of incorporation or principal place of business may be so substantial and of such a nature as to render the corporation at home in that State. But this case presents no occasion to explore that question, because Daimler's activities in California plainly do not approach that level. It is one thing to hold a corporation answerable for operations in the forum State, quite another to expose it to suit on claims having no connection whatever to the forum State.

MBUSA's sales are sizable. Such exorbitant exercises of all-purpose jurisdiction would scarcely permit out-of-state defendants "to structure their primary conduct with some minimum assurance as to where that conduct will and will not render them liable to suit." *Burger King Corp.*, 471 U.S., at 472.

It was therefore error for the Ninth Circuit to conclude that Daimler, even with MBUSA's contacts attributed to it, was at home in California, and hence subject to suit there on claims by foreign plaintiffs having nothing to do with anything that occurred or had its principal impact in California.[20]

C

Finally, the transnational context of this dispute bears attention. The Court of Appeals emphasized, as supportive of the exercise of general jurisdiction, plaintiffs' assertion of claims under the Alien Tort Statute (ATS) and the Torture Victim Protection Act of 1991 (TVPA). Recent decisions of this Court, however, have rendered plaintiffs' ATS and TVPA claims infirm.

The Ninth Circuit, moreover, paid little heed to the risks to international comity its expansive view of general jurisdiction posed. Other nations do not share the uninhibited approach to personal jurisdiction advanced by the Court of Appeals in this case. In the European Union, for example, a corporation may generally be sued in the nation in which it is "domiciled," a term defined to refer only to the location of the corporation's "statutory seat," "central administration," or "principal place of business." European Parliament and Council Reg. 1215/2012, Arts. 4(1), and 63(1), 2012 O.J. (L. 351) 7, 18. See also *id.*, Art. 7(5), 2012 O.J. 7 (as to "a dispute *arising out of the operations of a branch, agency or other establishment*," a corporation may be sued "in the courts for the place where the branch, agency or other establishment is situated" (emphasis added)). The Solicitor General informs us, in this regard, that "foreign governments' objections to some domestic courts' expansive views of general jurisdiction have in the

---

20. To clarify . . . , the general jurisdiction inquiry does not "focu[s] solely on the magnitude of the defendant's in-state contacts." General jurisdiction instead calls for an appraisal of a corporation's activities in their entirety, nationwide and worldwide. A corporation that operates in many places can scarcely be deemed at home in all of them. Otherwise, "at home" would be synonymous with "doing business" tests framed before specific jurisdiction evolved in the United States. Nothing in *International Shoe* and its progeny suggests that "a particular quantum of local activity" should give a State authority over a "far larger quantum of . . . activity" having no connection to any in-state activity.

Justice Sotomayor would reach the same result, but for a different reason. Rather than concluding that Daimler is not at home in California, Justice Sotomayor would hold that the exercise of general jurisdiction over Daimler would be unreasonable "in the unique circumstances of this case." In other words, she favors a resolution fit for this day and case only. True, a multipronged reasonableness check was articulated in *Asahi*, but not as a free-floating test. Instead, the check was to be essayed when *specific* jurisdiction is at issue. First, a court is to determine whether the connection between the forum and the episode-in-suit could justify the exercise of specific jurisdiction. Then, in a second step, the court is to consider several additional factors to assess the reasonableness of entertaining the case. When a corporation is genuinely at home in the forum State, however, any second-step inquiry would be superfluous. . . .

past impeded negotiations of international agreements on the reciprocal recognition and enforcement of judgments." Considerations of international rapport thus reinforce our determination that subjecting Daimler to the general jurisdiction of courts in California would not accord with the "fair play and substantial justice" due process demands. *International Shoe*, 326 U.S., at 316.

* * *

For the reasons stated, the judgment of the United States Court of Appeals for the Ninth Circuit is
Reversed.

JUSTICE SOTOMAYOR, concurring in the judgment.

I agree with the Court's conclusion that the Due Process Clause prohibits the exercise of personal jurisdiction over Daimler in light of the unique circumstances of this case. I concur only in the judgment, however, because I cannot agree with the path the Court takes to arrive at that result. . . .

. . . The Court can and should decide this case on the . . . ground that, no matter how extensive Daimler's contacts with California, that State's exercise of jurisdiction would be unreasonable given that the case involves foreign plaintiffs suing a foreign defendant based on foreign conduct, and given that a more appropriate forum is available. . . .

Until today, our precedents had established a straightforward test for general jurisdiction: Does the defendant have "continuous corporate operations within a state" that are so substantial and of such a nature as to justify suit against it on causes of action arising from dealings entirely distinct from those activities"? *International Shoe*. In every case . . . we have focused solely on the magnitude of the defendant's in-state contacts, not the relative magnitude of those contacts in comparison to the defendant's contacts with other States. . . .

Had the majority applied our settled approach, it would have had little trouble concluding that Daimler's California contacts rise to the requisite level . . . .

The majority today concludes otherwise. . . . [It] announces the new rule that in order for a foreign defendant to be subject to general jurisdiction, it must not only possess continuous and systematic contacts with a forum State, but those contacts must also surpass some unspecified level when viewed in comparison to the company's "nationwide and worldwide" activities." . . .

[T]o the extent the majority is concerned with the modern-day consequences of *International Shoe*'s conception of personal jurisdiction, there remain other judicial doctrines available to mitigate any resulting unfairness to large corporate defendants. Here, for instance, the reasonableness prong may afford petitioner relief. In other cases, a defendant can assert the doctrine of *forum non conveniens* if a given State is a highly inconvenient place to litigate a dispute. In still other cases, the federal change of venue statute can provide protection. See 28 U.S.C. § 1404(a) . . . .

. . . Because I would reverse the Ninth Circuit's decision on the narrower ground that the exercise of jurisdiction over Daimler would be unreasonable in any event, I respectfully concur in the judgment only.

NOTES AND QUESTIONS

1. *The locus of general jurisdiction.* The *Daimler* Court describes the paradigm example of general jurisdiction over natural persons as domicile. Domicile is, of course, one of the traditional bases under which a court of a state may exercise jurisdiction over a natural person who is a permanent resident of that state. Such jurisdiction is "general" in that it encompasses claims having no relationship to the forum state, other than the fact that the individual is domiciled there (even if not found and served there). The *Daimler* Court then describes the locus of general jurisdiction over a corporation as the rough equivalent of corporate domicile, *i.e.*, the place where the corporation is "at home." The paradigmatic "home" of a corporation, the Court tells us, is the corporation's state of incorporation and/or its principal place of business. The "state of incorporation" is the state under whose law the corporation has been chartered. A corporation's "principal place of business" is typically the state in which its corporate headquarters are located. *See Hertz v. Friend*, 559 U.S. 77 (2010). Does the Court leave open the possibility that a corporation might be "at home" in states other than its states of incorporation or principal place of business? Would general jurisdiction have been satisfied in any of the specific jurisdiction cases we've read?

2. *Emerging trends in specific and general jurisdiction.* The *Daimler* Court describes specific jurisdiction as the centerpiece of modern jurisdiction and general jurisdiction as a more limited and exceptional form of jurisdiction. Clearly, the Court's "at home" metaphor is meant to curtail the circumstances under which general jurisdiction may be exercised. But, given the Court's 2011 decision in *J. McIntyre Machinery, Ltd. v. Nicastro*, page 182, *supra*, isn't the Court restricting both specific and general jurisdiction? Does this make sense? Consider Justice Ginsburg's dissent in *J. McIntyre*, page 190, *supra*, where she calls for a more expansive approach to specific jurisdiction. Is her *J. McIntyre* dissent consistent with her majority opinion in *Daimler*?

3. *Specific jurisdiction compared.* Given the Court's opinion in *Daimler*, how would you describe the differences between specific and general jurisdiction?

PROBLEMS

2-18. In November 2012, Carmouche, a passenger on a cruise operated by Carnival Inc., a Florida corporation, was injured in Belize during a shore excursion operated by Tamborlee. Carmouche sued Tamborlee for negligence in a federal district court in Florida. Tamborlee moved to dismiss Carmouche's complaint for lack of personal jurisdiction. Tamborlee is a corporation registered in Panama that provides shore excursions for tourists in Belize. Tamborlee has never operated a shore excursion in Florida, advertised to potential customers in Florida, or been incorporated or licensed to do business in Florida. Tamborlee's connections with Florida include insurance policies with several Florida companies; a bank account with Citibank that is handled by a department in Miami; membership in the Florida Caribbean Cruise Association, a nonprofit trade organization; and a long-term contract with Carnival to provide shore excursions for Carnival passengers in Belize. That contract includes a forum-selection clause under which Tamborlee consented to jurisdiction in any court in the State of Florida as to any claim between it and Carnival arising out of the contract. Is Tamborlee subject to general jurisdiction in Florida? *See Carmouche v. Tamborlee Mgmt., Inc.*, 789 F.3d 1201 (11th Cir. 2015).

2-19. L.L. Bean ("Bean") is a Maine corporation with its principal place of business in that state. It sells over $1 billion in clothing and outdoor equipment annually to consumers in 50 states and 150 countries. Bean's corporate offices, distribution facilities, and manufacturing facilities are all in Maine. It has stores in Maine, Delaware, New Hampshire, Oregon, and Virginia. Bean ships 200 million catalogs each year and has a toll-free number for placing orders. It also maintains an interactive website that allows customers to view and purchase products online, and to interact "live" with Bean customer service representatives. Gator.com Corp. (Gator), a Delaware corporation with its principal place of business in California, develops and distributes software programs to consumers who buy goods and services on the internet. When a Gator program user visits a retail website, the program may display a pop-up window offering a coupon for a competitor. For example, a Gator user who visits Bean's interactive website is offered a coupon for one of Bean's competitors, Eddie Bauer. After Bean advised Gator that its pop-up window violated Bean's rights under federal and state law, Gator sued Bean in a California federal court, seeking a declaratory judgment that its program does not violate any of Bean's rights under federal or state law. After Bean was served under California's long-arm statute, it moved to dismiss under Rule 12(b)(2), claiming an absence of minimum contacts with California. Bean supported its motion with a declaration stating that it is not authorized to do business in California; has no stores or facilities there; has no agent for service of process there; is not required to pay taxes there; and does not target any national print or broadcast marketing efforts at the state. In opposition to the motion, Gator contended that Bean was subject to general jurisdiction in California. Its supporting papers show that as a result of Bean's catalog mailings, its toll-free number, and its website, 6 percent of its sales are to California residents. In addition, Gator notes that Bean targets Californians with direct e-mail solicitation and maintains relationships with many California vendors from whom it purchases products. Are Bean's contacts with California sufficient to allow the court to assert general jurisdiction? *See Gator.com Corp. v. L.L. Bean, Inc.*, 341 F.3d 1072 (9th Cir. 2003), *vacated as moot*, 398 F.3d 1125 (9th Cir. 2005).

D.   Minimum Contacts and the Traditional Bases of Jurisdiction

The minimum contacts test developed in *International Shoe* and its progeny was designed to determine when a court could exercise personal jurisdiction beyond the traditional bases for doing so. Recall that those traditional bases included physical presence or transient jurisdiction; voluntary appearance; consent to service on an agent in the state; domicile; and, in the context of *in rem* or *quasi in rem* jurisdiction, property found within the state. Yet, since the minimum contacts test was an attempt to articulate the requirements of the Due Process Clause, the question naturally arose as to whether the same due process requirements should apply as well to some or all of the traditional bases for acquiring jurisdiction. The Supreme Court addressed that question in two cases. In *Shaffer v. Heitner*, 433 U.S. 1986 (1977), the Court was asked to consider whether the Due Process Clause imposed additional limitations on the exercise of jurisdiction when the only basis for doing so was that the nonresident defendant's property was found within the state. And in *Burnham v. Superior Court*, 495 U.S. 604 (1990), the Court was asked the same due-process question with respect to the exercise of transient jurisdiction. In *Shaffer*, the Court held that the exercise of *quasi in rem* jurisdiction was subject to the standards of the minimum contacts test. In *Burnham*, it held that no such limitations were imposed on the exercise of transient jurisdiction.

In *Shaffer*, a Delaware trial court had acquired *quasi in rem* jurisdiction over the shares of stock owned by several directors of a Delaware corporation. The shares were deemed to be present in Delaware by virtue of a Delaware law that made Delaware the *situs* of the shares of stock held in a Delaware corporation, regardless of where the certificates of stock were physically located. The shares in question bore no relationship to the claim asserted against the directors. The *Shaffer* Court offered the following explanation for its decision to subject the exercise of *in rem* jurisdiction to the minimum contacts test:

> The case for applying to jurisdiction *in rem* the same test of "fair play and substantial justice" as governs assertions of jurisdiction *in personam* is simple and straightforward. It is premised on recognition that "[t]he phrase, 'judicial jurisdiction over a thing,' is a customary elliptical way of referring to jurisdiction over the interests of persons in a thing." Restatement (Second) of Conflict of Laws § 56, Introductory Note (1971) (hereafter Restatement). This recognition leads to the conclusion that in order to justify an exercise of jurisdiction *in rem*, the basis for jurisdiction must be sufficient to justify exercising "jurisdiction over the interests of persons in a thing." The standard for determining whether an exercise of jurisdiction over the interests of persons is consistent with the Due Process Clause is the minimum-contacts standard elucidated in *International Shoe*.
>
> This argument, of course, does not ignore the fact that the presence of property in a State may bear on the existence of jurisdiction by providing contacts among the forum State, the defendant, and the litigation. For example, when claims to the property itself are the source of the underlying controversy between the plaintiff and the defendant, it would be unusual for the State where the property is located not to have jurisdiction. In such cases, the defendant's claim to property located in the State would normally indicate that he expected to benefit from the State's protection of his interest. The State's strong interests in assuring the marketability of property within its borders and in providing a procedure for peaceful resolution of disputes about the possession of that property would also support jurisdiction, as would the likelihood that important records and witnesses will be found in the

State. The presence of property may also favor jurisdiction in cases such as suits for injury suffered on the land of an absentee owner, where the defendant's ownership of the property is conceded but the cause of action is otherwise related to rights and duties growing out of that ownership.

It appears, therefore, that jurisdiction over many types of *in rem* actions which now are or might be brought *in rem* would not be affected by a holding that any assertion of state-court jurisdiction must satisfy the *International Shoe* standard. For the type of *quasi in rem* action typified by *Harris v. Balk* and the present case, however, accepting the proposed analysis would result in significant change. These are cases where the property which now serves as the basis for state-court jurisdiction is completely unrelated to the plaintiff's cause of action. Thus, although the presence of the defendant's property in a State might suggest the existence of other ties among the defendant, the State, and the litigation, the presence of the property alone would not support the State's jurisdiction. If those other ties did not exist, cases over which the State is now thought to have jurisdiction could not be brought in that forum . . . .

We are left, then, to consider the significance of the long history of jurisdiction based solely on the presence of property in a State. Although the theory that territorial power is both essential to and sufficient for jurisdiction has been undermined, we have never held that the presence of property in a State does not automatically confer jurisdiction over the owner's interest in that property. This history must be considered as supporting the proposition that jurisdiction based solely on the presence of property satisfies the demands of due process, but it is not decisive. "[T]raditional notions of fair play and substantial justice" can be as readily offended by the perpetuation of ancient forms that are no longer justified as by the adoption of new procedures that are inconsistent with the basic values of our constitutional heritage. The fiction that an assertion of jurisdiction over property is anything but an assertion of jurisdiction over the owner of the property supports an ancient form without substantial modern justification. Its continued acceptance would serve only to allow state-court jurisdiction that is fundamentally unfair to the defendant.

433 U.S. at 207-212.

PROBLEM

2-20. Paul owns a canary-yellow Bentley automobile worth $95,000. A year ago, while driving the car near his home in Iowa, he collided with a car driven by Tom who lives in Chicago, Illinois. The Bentley suffered minor damage but Tom's car was destroyed. While Paul was recently out of the country, his sister borrowed the Bentley without his knowledge or permission and drove it to Chicago for a week. When Tom spotted the Bentley in the garage of a Chicago hotel, he sued Paul in an Illinois court, seeking $35,000 for the damage to his own car. The Illinois court asserted jurisdiction over Paul by attaching the Bentley. Paul has moved to release the car and dismiss the case on the ground that the Illinois court does not have jurisdiction over him. How should the court rule on his motion?

In *Burnham v. Superior Court,* "the question presented [was] whether the Due Process Clause of the Fourteenth Amendment denies California courts jurisdiction over a nonresident, who was personally served with process while temporarily in that State, in a suit unrelated to his activities in the State." 495 U.S. at 607 (Scalia, J., opinion for plurality). The Court was unable to assemble a majority opinion, but all nine members of the Court affirmed the authority of a state court to exercise transient jurisdiction without reference to the minimum contacts test. Justice Scalia, writing for a four-person plurality, concluded that the well-established tradition of transient jurisdiction was in itself sufficient to establish the due process pedigree of the practice. "The short of the matter is that jurisdiction based on physical presence alone constitutes due process because it is one of the continuing traditions of our legal system that define the due process standard of 'traditional notions of fair play and substantial justice.'" *Id.* at 619. Justice White, who joined much of the plurality opinion, limited his approval to cases where, as here, the nonresident's "presence in the forum State is intentional." *Id.* at 627 (White, J., concurring). Justice Brennan, also writing for four members of the Court, questioned Justice Scalia's singular focus on tradition and history, but agreed "that the Due Process Clause of the Fourteenth Amendment generally permits a state court to exercise jurisdiction over a defendant if he is served with process while voluntarily present in the forum State." *Id.* at 628-629 (Brennan, J., concurring). Finally, Justice Stevens, writing for himself, explained, "For me, it is sufficient to note that the historical evidence and consensus identified by Justice Scalia, the considerations of fairness identified by Justice Brennan, and the common sense displayed by Justice White, all combine to demonstrate that this is, indeed, a very easy case. Accordingly, I agree that the judgment should be affirmed." *Id.* at 640 (Stevens, J., concurring) (The rule that emerges from this collection of opinions is that the exercise of transient jurisdiction is consistent with due process—traditional notions of fair play and substantial justice—when a nonresident defendant is served with process while voluntarily in the state.)

E.   Exercising Jurisdiction Under Federal Long-Arm Provisions

We noted earlier that federal courts normally borrow the long-arm and other jurisdictional statutes of the state in which they sit. *See* FED. R. CIV. P. 4(k)(1)(A). When they do so, federal courts must assess the constitutionality of jurisdiction by applying the same Fourteenth Amendment Due Process Clause standards that would govern a state court across the street. This dependence on state jurisdictional statutes holds true even in many cases brought to vindicate federal rights. When Congress creates such rights it seldom enacts special provisions for securing jurisdiction over defendants. As a result, plaintiffs seeking to enforce their federal rights must often, though not always, look to state jurisdictional statutes to bring the defendant into federal court.

1. Federal Long-Arm Provisions

However, there are a number of important exceptions that allow federal courts to utilize federal rather than state provisions to obtain jurisdiction over parties. First, Rule 4(k)(1)(C) allows federal courts to exercise personal jurisdiction "when authorized by a federal statute." One of the most important of these federal statutory provisions is the federal interpleader statute, which provides for nationwide service of process. *See* 28 U.S.C. §§ 1335, 2361. Interpleader enables a person who is unsure as to which of several claimants may be entitled to a fund or a piece of property to sue all of the claimants in one action, rather than having to litigate separately with the risk of being found liable to more than one of the claimants. For example, an insurance company faced with rival claims to the proceeds of a life insurance policy might wish to bring an action against all of the competing claimants. Section 1335 may permit a federal court to obtain jurisdiction over all of the claimants, including those who are not amenable to service under the state's long-arm statute. See Chapter VIII, part G ("Interpleader"), *infra.* Other federal statutes that authorize federal courts to effect nationwide or worldwide service include § 27 of the Securities and Exchange Act (15 U.S.C. § 78aa(b)), which has been construed to permit worldwide service of process in suits brought under the securities acts, as well as § 12 of the Clayton Antitrust Act (15 U.S.C. § 22).

Second, Rule 4(k)(2) allows federal courts to obtain personal jurisdiction through worldwide service of process on claims brought to vindicate federal rights, if the plaintiff can show that the defendant is not subject to jurisdiction under the laws of any state and that the exercise of jurisdiction is constitutional. This provision operates like a long-arm statute. It seeks to enhance the ability of plaintiffs suing on federally created rights to do so in the United States instead of having to sue abroad or forsake their claims entirely. As one court explained,

> Before Rule 4(k)(2) was conceived [in 1993], federal courts "borrowed" from state law when a federal statute did not otherwise provide a mechanism for service of process. . . . Accordingly, foreign defendants who lacked single-state contacts sufficient to bring them within the reach of a given state's long-arm statute (whether by reason of the paucity of the contacts or of limitations built into the statute itself), but who had enough contacts with the United States as a whole to make personal jurisdiction over them in a United States court constitutional, could evade responsibility for civil violations of federal laws that did not provide specifically for service of process.
>
> To close this loophole, the drafters designed the new Rule 4(k)(2) to function as a species of federal long-arm statute.

United States v. Swiss Am. Bank, Ltd., 191 F.3d 30, 40 (1st Cir. 1999).

2. Minimum Contacts at the National Level

If a federal court uses a federal long-arm provision, the constitutionality of the exercise of jurisdiction is measured by the Due Process Clause of the Fifth

Amendment. Though the Supreme Court has yet to address this matter, the lower federal courts are in virtual agreement that in federal long-arm cases in which the minimum contacts test applies, the focus under the Fifth Amendment must be on a defendant's national contacts, not just its contacts with the state in which the federal court is located. *See, e.g., Medical Mut. of Ohio v. deSoto,* 245 F.3d 561, 566-568 (6th Cir. 2001); *SEC v. Carrillo,* 115 F.3d 1540, 1542-1544 (11th Cir. 1997) (collecting authorities); 4 CHARLES ALAN WRIGHT & ARTHUR R. MILLER, FEDERAL PRACTICE AND PROCEDURE § 1068.1 (3d ed. 2002 & Supp. 2015).

As in cases involving state long-arm statutes, a defendant may seek to rebut the presumption that arises once the contacts and relatedness requirements of due process have been satisfied. While this is a difficult showing to make, ironically, it may more often succeed at the national level than at the state level. For one thing, if the defendant is an alien, the burdens of litigating under a foreign legal system may reach the level that prevailed in *Asahi.* In addition, given the vast size of the United States, the fact that a defendant has meaningful contacts with one part of the country may not make it fair to have to litigate in another part of the country thousands of miles away. As the drafters of Rule 4(k)(2) noted, a "district court should be especially scrupulous to protect aliens who reside in a foreign country from forum selections so onerous that injustice could result." Advisory Committee Note, 1993 Amendments, 146 F.R.D. 401, 572 (1993). *See, e.g., Aerogroup Int'l, Inc. v. Marlboro Footworks, Ltd.,* 956 F. Supp. 427, 442 (S.D.N.Y. 1996) (refusing to exercise jurisdiction under Rule 4(k)(2) over Canadian defendants who otherwise had minimum contacts with the United States, where "[e]xercising jurisdiction . . . would offend fair play and substantial justice" and where the New Jersey plaintiff could bring suit in Canada).

PROBLEM

2-21. The U.S. Securities and Exchange Commission ("SEC") filed suit in a Florida federal district court against Bosque, a Costa Rican corporation that owns and operates a teak plantation in Costa Rica. The complaint alleged that Bosque fraudulently offered and sold unregistered securities to U.S. residents in order to finance its operations in Costa Rica. Bosque advertised the securities in American Airlines' in-flight magazine, mailed information to investors in California and New York, and maintained a bank account in Florida to process payments from U.S. investors. If you were representing the SEC in this matter, on what possible bases might the court obtain personal jurisdiction over Bosque? Assume Florida has a tailored long-arm statute authorizing personal jurisdiction over nonresidents on claims that "arise from" contacts that the nonresident has with the state. *See SEC v. Carrillo,* 115 F.3d 1540 (11th Cir. 1997).

F. Challenging Lack of Personal Jurisdiction over the Defendant

A defendant can challenge the court's personal jurisdiction either "directly" or "collaterally." In a direct attack, the jurisdictional objection is raised in the same proceeding in which jurisdiction is sought to be exercised. By contrast, in a collateral attack, the jurisdictional challenge is raised in a different or collateral proceeding, often in a different court from the one that heard the suit in question.

1. The Burden of Proof

Whether jurisdiction is challenged directly or collaterally, the general rule is that the plaintiff must ultimately show, by a preponderance of the evidence, that the court has jurisdiction over the defendant.

At the outset of a case, a plaintiff may know very little about the full nature and extent of a defendant's contacts with the forum state. Thus federal district courts "are to assist the plaintiff by allowing jurisdictional discovery unless the plaintiff's claim is 'clearly frivolous.'" *Toys "R" Us, Inc. v. Step Two, S.A.*, 318 F.3d 446, 456 (3d Cir. 2003). Once a plaintiff has been afforded an opportunity for reasonable jurisdictional discovery, the judge must rule on the defendant's motion to dismiss.

2. Direct Attack

A direct attack on the court's authority to exercise personal jurisdiction over the defendant may be made by a pretrial motion to dismiss or by raising the jurisdictional objection in the answer to the complaint. Regardless of which approach is adopted, the objection must be asserted within the time allotted to respond to the complaint. In general, a failure to raise the objection at the defendant's first appearance constitutes a waiver of the objection.

In federal court, the principles governing the timing, manner, and waiver of challenges to personal jurisdiction are set out in Rule 12. Under the federal rules, a party served with a summons and complaint must normally file a responsive pleading within 21 days of service. FED. R. CIV. PROC. 12(a)(1)(A). Within that time frame, a party may object to the court's exercise of personal jurisdiction either in a responsive pleading or in a Rule 12(b)(2) motion to dismiss for "lack of personal jurisdiction." A failure to raise the objection in a timely fashion constitutes a waiver. The objection is also waived if the defendant files a responsive pleader and/or a Rule 12(b) motion, neither of which challenge the court's exercise of personal jurisdiction. *Id.*, 12(g)(2) & 12(h)(1). The objection is not waived, however, "by joining it with one or more other defenses or objections in a responsive pleading or in a motion." *Id.*, 12(b).

In short, a defendant who is sued in federal court must challenge the court's jurisdiction over her through a motion to dismiss under Rule 12(b) or in her answer, *whichever is filed first*, or she waives any objection to the exercise of personal jurisdiction.

If a trial court overrules a timely objection to the exercise of personal jurisdiction, most judicial systems, including the federal system, permit the defendant to seek review of the trial court's ruling—but only after a final decision or judgment has been entered in the case, which could take years. If the defendant wants immediate review of the jurisdictional ruling, she must take a default and allow a judgment to be entered against her. If she does this, however, she waives her right to challenge the judgment on the merits, for the only objection preserved is the jurisdictional one.

Some states provide for interlocutory review of the trial court's personal jurisdiction ruling. Indeed, some insist upon it if a defendant wishes to pursue the objection. In California, for example, a defendant whose motion to quash—the state's equivalent of a Rule 12(b)(2) motion to dismiss—has been denied must immediately petition the appellate court for a writ of mandate. CAL. CIV. PROC. CODE § 418.10(c). Failure to do so waives any objection to jurisdiction (*see, e.g., McCorkle v. City of Los Angeles*, 449 P.2d 453 (Cal. 1969); *State Farm Gen. Ins. Co. v. JT's Frames, Inc.*, 104 Cal. Rptr. 3d 573, 578-584 (Ct. App. 2010)); *i.e.*, unlike federal court, it cannot be raised as part of an appeal from a final judgment.

A defendant who failed to object to jurisdiction in the trial court can still directly attack jurisdiction as long as she did not appear at all in the proceedings and had a default judgment entered against her. However, such a defendant cannot raise the jurisdictional issue by way of *appeal*, for the objection was not presented to the trial court and thus cannot be used as the basis for seeking appellate review. Instead, at least in the federal system, a defaulting defendant can make a motion under Rule 60(b)(4), asking the *trial court* to set aside its judgment on the ground that it is "void." FED. R. CIV. P. 60(b)(4). This is consistent with the principle recognized in *Pennoyer v. Neff*, 95 U.S. 714, 728 (1877), that a judgment rendered by a court that lacks jurisdiction over the defendant is "void."

Though Rule 60(c) literally requires that 60(b) motions seeking relief from judgments be made "within a reasonable time," and usually within a year after judgment was entered, these restrictions do not apply to motions based on the court's lack of jurisdiction over the defendant. Thus even a defendant who had timely notice of the suit but who totally ignored the proceedings may go back into the trial court *at any time* and ask to have the judgment set aside for lack of jurisdiction. If the court concludes that jurisdiction did not exist, whether because the defendant did not fit within an applicable long-arm statute or because minimum contacts were lacking, it must set aside the judgment and dismiss the case. *See, e.g., "R" Best Produce, Inc. v. DiSapio*, 540 F.3d 115, 122-124 (2d Cir. 2008) (holding that Rule 60(b)(4) motion to set aside judgment for lack of jurisdiction filed 18 months after entry of default was proper even though defendant had timely notice of suit); *Sea-Land Serv., Inc. v. Ceramica Europa II, Inc.*, 160 F.3d 849 (1st Cir. 1998) (holding that trial court had to entertain motion under Rule 60(b)(4) to set aside default judgment for lack of jurisdiction despite unreasonable delay by the defendant); 11 CHARLES ALAN WRIGHT, ARTHUR R. MILLER & MARY KAY

KANE, FEDERAL PRACTICE AND PROCEDURE § 2862 (3d ed. 2012 & Supp. 2015). However, in contrast to the rule that the plaintiff normally has the burden of showing a statutory basis for jurisdiction and the existence of minimum contacts, some courts in this setting place the burden on the defendant to prove that jurisdiction was lacking, at least when the defendant had timely notice of the original proceedings. *See, e.g., Bally Export Corp. v. Balicar, Ltd.*, 804 F.2d 398 (7th Cir. 1986) (holding that motion to set aside default judgment for lack of jurisdiction could be made under Rule 60(b)(4) nearly four years after entry of judgment, but defendant failed to carry its burden of proving that jurisdiction did not exist); *"R" Best Produce, Inc., supra*, 540 F.3d at 126 (holding that on remand defendant would have burden of showing that jurisdiction did not exist).

3. Collateral Attack

If a defendant appears in a proceeding and waives an objection to jurisdiction by failing to raise it in a proper manner, the defendant cannot later *collaterally* attack the judgment on jurisdictional grounds. The same is true of a defendant who appears and makes a jurisdictional objection but loses on the issue; while the defendant may pursue her *direct* attack by appealing the trial court's adverse ruling to a higher court, she cannot litigate the jurisdictional issue again in a collateral proceeding. Indeed, in *Baldwin v. Iowa State Traveling Men's Assn.*, 283 U.S. 522 (1931), the Supreme Court explained:

> Public policy dictates that there be an end of litigation; that those who have contested an issue shall be bound by the result of the contest, and that matters once tried shall be considered forever settled as between the parties. We see no reason why this doctrine should not apply in every case where one voluntarily appears, presents his case and is fully heard, and why he should not, in the absence of fraud, be thereafter concluded by the judgment of the tribunal to which he has submitted his cause.

Id. at 525-526.

Thus, in order to collaterally attack a judgment on the ground that the rendering court lacked jurisdiction, a defendant must have totally ignored the proceeding and allowed a default judgment to be entered against her. "A party that simply refuses to appear may contend in a later case that the first tribunal lacked jurisdiction—though jurisdiction is the *only* issue thus preserved, and if the first court had jurisdiction then the judgment must be enforced." *United States v. County of Cook, Ill.*, 167 F.3d 381, 388 (7th Cir.), *cert. denied*, 528 U.S. 1019 (1999). This is obviously a high-stakes strategy, for the only objection that can be asserted in the collateral proceeding is lack of jurisdiction; the defendant waives any other possible defenses to the plaintiff's claim. This strategy makes sense only if a defendant is absolutely certain that the court lacks jurisdiction (a certainty that will be rare given the ambiguous nature of the law of jurisdiction), or if the defendant has no legitimate way to oppose the claim.

If a defendant is successful in collaterally attacking a judgment for lack of personal jurisdiction, this will preclude the plaintiff from seeking to further enforce that judgment in other states. In other words, the finding that jurisdiction did not exist will be given *res judicata* effect in each and every subsequent enforcement proceeding the plaintiff brings. *See Board of Trustees, Sheet Metal Workers' Nat'l Pension Fund v. Elite Erectors, Inc.*, 212 F.3d 1031, 1034-1035 (7th Cir. 2000). If the original judgment was that of a federal court, the defendant need not wait for the plaintiff to bring additional enforcement actions. Instead, the defendant can go back to the original federal court and ask it to set aside the default judgment under Rule 60(b)(4). In this set-aside proceeding, the earlier finding that the court lacked jurisdiction over the defendant must be given *res judicata* effect. The plaintiff cannot relitigate the jurisdiction issue, and thus the federal court has no choice but to set aside its previous default judgment. *See, e.g., Drexler v. Kozloff*, 2000 WL 376608 (10th Cir. Apr. 13, 2000) (unanimous unpublished opinion). A similar avenue may be available if the first judgment was rendered by a state court that follows procedures like those set out in Federal Rule 60(b).

An even simpler solution may be possible if the default judgment and the first enforcement action both happen to involve federal courts. In this setting, most federal circuits will allow a defendant to file, in the *enforcing* court, a Rule 60(b)(4) motion to set aside the *rendering* court's earlier default judgment, if it is found that the rendering court lacked jurisdiction over the defendant. This eliminates any need for the defendant to go back to the original federal court for set-aside relief. As the Fifth Circuit explained in *Harper Macleod Solicitors v. Keaty & Keaty*, 260 F.3d 389 (5th Cir. 2001):

> We join the majority of circuits and hold that [enforcing] courts may use Rule 60(b)(4) to sustain jurisdictional challenges to default judgments issued by another district court . . . . That one district court may exercise such authority over another is a necessary consequence of the established rule that a defendant may challenge a rendering court's personal jurisdiction in a court in which enforcement of a default judgment is attempted. Such authority also reflects the federal system's disdain for default judgments.

Id. at 395; *see also On Track Transp., Inc. v. Lakeside Warehouse & Trucking, Inc.*, 245 F.R.D. 213, 216-220 (E.D. Pa. 2007) (collecting authorities); 11 WRIGHT, MILLER & KANE, *supra*, § 2865.

PROBLEMS

2-22. Phillip sued Arthur for $250,000 in a Colorado federal court, alleging that Arthur stole the registration papers for Phillip's racehorse, Quizzical, thereby preventing Phillip from selling the horse or entering him in races. Phillip lives in Colorado. Arthur is a citizen of Maryland, where he runs a farm at which Phillip sometimes boards Quizzical. Copies of the summons and complaint were served on Arthur at the Maryland farm. Arthur filed an answer denying that he stole Quizzical's papers. The case went to trial and resulted in a judgment in Phillip's favor for $250,000. Phillip has taken the judgment to Maryland to enforce it against Arthur's assets there. Arthur has consulted a Maryland attorney for whom you are clerking. The attorney has asked you to prepare a memo discussing whether there is any way to prevent enforcement of the judgment on the ground that the Colorado court lacked jurisdiction over Arthur.

2-23. Linda and Harold were involved in an automobile accident ten years ago in New Mexico. Harold, who then resided in Indiana, was driving home from a vacation in southern California. Two months after the accident, Linda, who lived in California, sued Harold in a California federal court, seeking $1 million for injuries she suffered in the accident. Harold was personally served with process in Indiana but ignored the suit because his only property consisted of a six-year-old car that was exempt from attachment under Indiana law. The California court then entered a default judgment against Harold for $1 million. A year later, Harold's aunt died and left him $500,000 in cash, a condominium in Florida, and some farmland in Wisconsin. Linda's attorney has now sued Harold in a Florida court to enforce the California judgment against his condominium there. What options does Harold have for protecting the condominium and his other property interests?

G.   Personal Jurisdiction Review Problems

2-24. AM Inc., a Rhode Island corporation, manufactures, sells, and distributes instruments for the science of sleep technology. Although the identity of some of its customers is well known, AM's financial arrangements with its sales people, its marketing strategy, and its pricing and cost structures are all highly confidential, and AM takes efforts to protect its trade secrets and other confidential information. In 2002, AM hired Kevin as a Product Specialist, responsible for the demonstration and training of its Grass Technologies product line. When he was hired, Kevin signed an Employee Agreement that contained a non-competition clause that provided:

> I recognize that the Company sells its products throughout North America and Europe; as such, upon termination of my employment at the Company, for whatever reason, I shall not directly or indirectly enter into or engage in a business that competes with the Company in a territory consisting of North America and Europe for a period of one year thereafter.

The Agreement also contained the following trade secrets clause:

> I hereby agree that any inventions, discoveries or improvements and any technical data, trade secrets (including, but not limited to, customer lists), information or know-how, made, discovered or conceived or acquired by me during the period of my employment, whether patentable, patented or not, are to be and remain the property of the Company; that, without the written authorization of the Company, I will neither use nor disclose to any person other than my superiors in the Company, any information, trade secrets, technical data or know-how relating to the Company's

products, processes, methods, equipment and business practices, which I have acquired during my employment.

In addition, the Employee Agreement contained a choice-of-law and forum-selection clause, which stated that it shall be governed by the laws of the State of Rhode Island and that Kevin consented to personal jurisdiction in Rhode Island for any dispute arising out of the Agreement.

In 2004, AM transferred Kevin to its Florida offices where he became a District Sales Manager. In that capacity, Kevin had access to and used AM's trade secrets, including confidential marketing, pricing, and customer information, as well as AM's research and development efforts.

NK, a California corporation, competes with AM in the sleep technology market. In 2006, NK hired Kevin as its Florida-based sales director. Before doing so, NK became aware of AM's Employment Agreement with Kevin and referred the contract to counsel for review. NK's lawyer advised NK that there was some risk in hiring Kevin; notwithstanding that advice, NK hired Kevin to sell its products in competition with AM, in the sales territory he had covered for AM. You may assume that Kevin, as an employee of NK, used the knowledge he had acquired while employed by AM, including confidential trade secrets, and that NK fully expected him to do so.

AM sued Kevin in a Rhode Island federal court, claiming breach of contract and misappropriation of trade secrets. AM later amended its complaint and added a third claim of unfair competition. In that amended complaint, it also joined NK as a defendant, against whom it alleged claims of tortious interference with contract and misappropriation of trade secrets. Both Kevin and NK have filed motions to dismiss pursuant to Rule 12(b)(2). How should the district court rule on those motions? You may assume that Rhode Island has adopted a due process style long-arm statute. *See Astro-Med, Inc. v. Nihon Kohden America, Inc.*, 591 F.3d 1 (1st Cir. 2009).

2-25. Arnold Brickenblocker ("Arnold") is a citizen and well-known resident of California. He is best known for his roles as a muscle-bound hero of action films and for his distinctively bizarre accent. Arnold is often cast as the lead character in so-called star-driven films (*i.e.*, bad movies with big names). One of Arnold's most popular and readily recognizable film roles is that of the title character in *The Exterminator*. Throughout much of the film, Arnold, as the Exterminator, maintains a stern demeanor and wears black sunglasses. This image of him is highly distinctive, really cool, and immediately recognizable by much of the public.

The Fred Flintstone Motor Company ("Fred") is an automobile dealership incorporated under the laws of Ohio and located in Bedrock, Ohio, a few miles southwest of Akron. There is no evidence in the record that Fred has had any operations or employees in California, has ever advertised in California, or has ever sold a car to anyone in California. Fred maintains an internet website that is available for viewing in California. The website is used solely to post information and advertisements regarding vehicles and services available at the Bedrock dealership.

In early 2002, Fred placed a full-page color advertisement in the *Bedrock Daily*, a local Bedrock-based newspaper. The advertisement ran in the *Bedrock Daily* five times in April 2002. Most of the advertisement consists of small photographs and descriptions of various cars available for purchase or lease from Fred. Just below a large-font promise that Fred "WON'T BE BEAT," the advertisement includes a small, but clearly recognizable, photograph of Arnold as the Exterminator. A "bubble quotation," like those found in comic strips, is drawn next to Arnold's mouth, reading, "Arnold says: 'Exterminate EARLY at Fred's!'" This part of the advertisement refers to a special offer inviting customers to close out their current leases before the expected termination date and to buy or lease a new car from Fred. The advertisement, which was also posted on Fred's website, was never circulated outside of Ohio other than through the website.

Fred regularly purchases Asian-made automobiles that are imported by California entities. However, in purchasing these automobiles, Fred deals directly with representatives of those entities in Illinois and New Jersey and never with the California-based importers themselves. Some of Fred's sales contracts with its automobile suppliers include a choice-of-law provision specifying California law. In addition, Fred regularly retains the services of a California-based direct-mail marketing company.

Fred never sought or received Arnold's permission to use the Exterminator photograph in the advertisement or on the website.

Arnold brought suit against Fred in a federal court sitting in Los Angeles, California, alleging six state law causes of action arising out of Fred's unauthorized use of his image in the advertisement. He claims that Fred caused him financial harm in that the use of Arnold's photograph to endorse Fred's business "diminishes [Arnold's] hard earned reputation as a major motion picture star, and risks the potential for overexposure of his image to the public, thereby potentially diminishing the compensation he would otherwise garner from his career as a major motion picture star."

According to Arnold's complaint, his compensation as the lead actor in star-driven films was based on his ability to draw crowds to the box office, and his ability to do so depended in part on the scarcity of his image. If Arnold's image were to become ubiquitous—in advertisements and on television, for example—the movie-going public would be less likely to spend their money to see his films, and his compensation would diminish accordingly. Therefore, Arnold maintains, it is vital for him to avoid "over-saturation of his image." To this end, he has steadfastly refused to endorse any products in the United States, despite being offered substantial sums to do so.

Fred has filed a motion to dismiss the complaint for lack of personal jurisdiction pursuant to Rule 12(b)(2). Assess the arguments that each side would make with respect to Fred's motion. How should the district court rule? *See Schwarzenegger v. Fred Martin Motor Co.*, 374 F.3d 797 (9th Cir. 2004).

III

SERVICE OF PROCESS AND NOTICE

The Due Process Clause entitles a defendant in a civil action to notice of the action and an opportunity to be heard. This chapter examines the notice part of that equation. Typically, notice of a lawsuit is accomplished through "service of process," *i.e.*, through the formal delivery to the defendant ("service") of the legal documents ("process") that summon him or her to court. Absent waiver, proper service of process is a prerequisite to the exercise of personal jurisdiction. As the Supreme Court observed,

> Before a . . . court may exercise personal jurisdiction over a defendant, the procedural requirement of service of summons must be satisfied. "[S]ervice of summons is the procedure by which a court . . . asserts jurisdiction over the person of the party served."

Omni Capital Int'l, Ltd. v. Rudolf Wolff & Co., Ltd., 484 U.S. 97, 104 (1987) (quoting *Mississippi Publ'g Corp. v. Murphree*, 326 U.S. 438, 444-445 (1946)). Thus a judgment rendered in the absence of adequate service of process is unenforceable, even if a valid basis for personal jurisdiction otherwise exists.

The adequacy of service of process turns on two factors: compliance with a statute (or rule) authorizing the form of service used, and compliance with the standards imposed by the Fifth and Fourteenth Amendment Due Process Clauses. Service-of-process statutes/rules allow a range of customary methods through which to serve a defendant, the most common of which is personal service on the defendant. If the statutory/rule component of proper service is satisfied, the question then becomes whether that statute/rule, either on its face or as applied, comports with the standards of due process. Those standards require notice "reasonably calculated" to apprise the defendant of the pending action.

In the materials that follow, we will examine Federal Rule of Civil Procedure 4, which governs service of process in federal courts. While Rule 4 applies only to federal court proceedings, many of its provisions find counterparts in state service-of-process statutes. In addition, Rule 4 borrows state service-of-process methods as an alternative means of securing proper service. Hence, Rule 4 provides an opportunity to study an array of service methods. We will also examine the standards of due process, which, of course, apply uniformly to both state and federal courts.

A.   The Mechanics of Service: Rule 4

1.   Request for Waiver of Service

Perhaps the most striking thing about Rule 4 is its effort to eliminate issues concerning service of process by inducing the defendant to waive formal service of the summons and complaint. *See* FED. R. CIV. P. 4(d). The "waiver of service" provision allows a plaintiff to send a copy of the complaint to the defendant by first-class mail or other reliable means, accompanied by a "Notice of a Lawsuit and Request to Waive Service of Summons" and a "Waiver of the Service of Summons." (*See* forms appended to FED. R. CIV. P. 4.) The defendant must be given at least 30 days to respond unless she is located outside the United States, in which case the period is 60 days. If the defendant signs and returns the Waiver of Service within the allowed time, no service of a summons occurs. As Rule 4(d)(1) indicates, the waiver procedure may be used only with certain types of defendants.

What incentive does a defendant have to waive service? Rule 4(d)(1) imposes on defendants "a duty to avoid unnecessary expenses of serving the summons." Thus, unless the defendant waives service in a timely manner, "the court must impose on the defendant . . . the expenses later incurred in making service; and . . . the reasonable expenses, including attorney's fees, of any motion required to collect those service expenses." FED. R. CIV. P. 4(d)(2). If a defendant agrees to waive service, she does not have to answer the complaint until 60 days after the request for waiver was sent, *i.e.*, 30 days after the waiver is due. *See* FED. R. CIV. P. 4(d)(3). To be sure, a defendant can gain additional time by refusing to return the waiver, but this is at the cost of having to pay for formal service.

By waiving service, a defendant does not surrender any of her defenses, including lack of jurisdiction over the person herself. *See* FED. R. CIV. P. 4(d)(5). Nor does she waive a statute of limitations defense. If the applicable statute is tolled only by service of the summons and complaint, as opposed to merely filing the complaint, Rule 4(d)(4) states that service is deemed to have occurred on the date the plaintiff files the signed waiver with the court.

There is one situation in which a defendant may have an incentive *not* to waive service. When the statute of limitations is tolled only by service (or by the filing of a waiver), a defendant may be able to run out the clock by refusing to waive service. If, at the end of the 30-day waiver period, the plaintiff has not received a signed waiver, she must attempt formal service. By the time this is effected, however, the statute of limitations may have run. That the defendant received actual notice of the suit through receipt of the request for waiver is not enough to toll the statute. Thus, if a plaintiff files suit near the end of the limitations period and if the applicable statute is tolled only by service on the defendant, it is a mistake to seek a waiver. Instead, as the Federal Rules Advisory Committee warned, "[u]nless there is ample time, the plaintiff should proceed directly to the formal methods for service identified in [Rule 4]." FED. R. CIV. P. 4, Advisory Committee Notes to 1993 Amendments, 146 F.R.D. 401, 565 (1993).

Nor can a plaintiff in this situation argue that her unsuccessful attempt to obtain a waiver happened to satisfy a state service rule (which federal courts may often borrow) that authorizes service by mail. Instead, Rule 4(d) envisions a two-step process: first seeking a waiver, and second effecting formal service if no waiver is obtained. "That the first step under the Rule might otherwise meet the requirements of some other method of service, such as service under [state law], is pure serendipity. Such coincidence cannot by hindsight be converted to a valid service—and a 'gotcha' for the unsuspecting defendant." *Carimi v. Royal Caribbean Cruise Line, Inc.*, 959 F.2d 1344, 1347 (5th Cir. 1992); *see also* 4A Charles A. Wright & Arthur R. Miller, Federal Practice and Procedure § 1092.1 (4th ed. 2015). Otherwise, a defendant who was told that not signing a waiver would later result in formal service might instead have a default judgment entered against her because she did not answer the complaint accompanying the waiver request within the 21 days allowed by Rule 12(a).

PROBLEM

3-1. On August 12, an arbitrator entered an award sustaining certain grievances filed by Local 633 of the United Mine Workers Union on behalf of workers at Eagle Energy, Inc. ("Eagle"). On November 7, Eagle filed a complaint in a West Virginia federal court to vacate the arbitrator's award. Three days later, on November 10, it mailed a copy of the summons and complaint to James Miller, president of Local 633, with a request for waiver of service. Miller received the letter on November 11 but did not sign the waiver. In December, Local 633 moved to dismiss the suit on the ground that it is barred by the statute of limitations. The applicable statute of limitations requires that service be made on the defendant within three months after the arbitration award was entered, *i.e.*, by November 12. Eagle opposed this motion on the grounds that Local 633 received notice of the suit within the limitations period and that the November 10 mailing constituted valid service under West Virginia law. Eagle notes that Rule 4(h)(1), which governs service on unincorporated associations such as labor unions, allows a federal court to borrow the service rules of the state in which it sits. Should the court grant the union's motion to dismiss? Would the result be different if the November 10 mailing had not included a request to waive service? *See Eagle Energy, Inc. v. District 17, United Mine Workers of Am.*, 177 F.R.D. 357 (S.D. W. Va. 1998).

2. Formal Service of Summons and Complaint

Federal Rule 4 specifies the methods for effecting formal service of the summons and complaint for each of six different types of defendants: (1) individuals in the United States (Rule 4(e)); (2) individuals in a foreign country (Rule 4(f)); (3) minors or incompetents (Rule 4(g)); (4) corporations, partnerships, or associations (Rule 4(h)); (5) the United States, its agencies and officers (Rule 4(i)); and (6) foreign states, or American state and local governments (Rule 4(j)). The important thing is to realize that the authorized means of service depends on the character of the particular defendant. Note that the waiver of service provisions of Rule 4(d)(1) may be employed only with respect to defendants described in subdivisions (e), (f), and (h); defendants in the other three categories must be served formally.

a.   Individuals

If the defendant is an individual located within the United States, Rule 4(e)(2) allows the plaintiff to serve the defendant "personally"; to leave the summons and complaint at the defendant's "dwelling or usual place of abode with someone of suitable age and discretion who resides there"; or to deliver copies to an agent who has been "authorized by appointment or by law to receive service" on the defendant's behalf. Not surprisingly, each of these methods has spawned litigation. For example: Does throwing the summons and complaint at a defendant's feet constitute personal delivery? What qualifies as the dwelling house or usual place of abode of a defendant who has more than one residence? Who is a person of suitable age or discretion, and what does it take for that person to reside there? Was an alleged agent properly appointed to receive process for the defendant? These questions become particularly critical if, in the event service was defective, it is too late to re-serve the defendant due to the running of the statute of limitations.

In addition to the above methods of service, Rule 4(e)(1) allows the plaintiff to employ any mode of service authorized by the law of either the state in which the federal court sits or the state in which service is to be effected. If the federal court borrows a state service provision, it must look to state law to see how that provision has been construed.

PROBLEM

3-2. The LSJ Investment Co. (LSJ) filed suit in an Ohio federal court against Fell and Friedman, charging them with engaging in a video-game-store investment swindle in violation of federal law. LSJ sent separate summonses and complaints by certified mail to Fell c/o Diehard Marketing Group, 5137 Clareton Drive, Suite 210, Agoura Hills, California, and to Friedman at 22615 Mobile Street, West Hills, California. The certified mail to Fell was returned marked "Attempted Not Known." The certified mail to Friedman was initially signed for by someone named Carol Ponder but was later returned as "opened in error" and "not at this address." Ms. Ponder operates a message center and mail drop for a number of businesses at the Mobile Street address, which Friedman has often given as his own. LSJ's lawyer then re-sent the summons and complaint to both defendants by regular mail, with a waiver of service form. The post office did not return the mailings, but neither defendant signed the waiver form. Ten months later, after the defendants failed to respond to the suit, LSJ asked the court to enter a default judgment, claiming that both defendants had been properly served.

Ohio law provides for out-of-state service by certified mail and allows service to be evidenced by a return receipt "signed by any person." Ohio law also provides for ordinary mail service when certified mail is returned unclaimed; such ordinary mail service must be sent by a postal clerk and evidenced by a certificate of mailing completed by the clerk. California law allows service by mail when there is a written acknowledgment of receipt; if no acknowledgment is returned, another method of service must be used.

Was valid service made on Fell and on Friedman? *See LSJ Investment Co., Inc. v. O.L.D., Inc.*, 167 F.3d 320 (6th Cir. 1999). Would your answer be different if the regular mailings had been sent by a postal clerk rather than by LSJ's lawyer?

b.   Corporations, Partnerships, and Associations

Rule 4(h) governs service on corporations, partnerships, and unincorporated associations. If the entity is served within the United States, subdivision (h)(1)(A) allows the plaintiff to borrow state law rules of service, as permitted when serving individuals under Rule 4(e)(1). Alternatively, Rule 4(h)(1)(B) allows the plaintiff to deliver a copy of the summons and complaint to "an officer, a managing or general agent, or any other agent authorized by appointment or by law to receive service of process. . . ." While courts are often flexible in deciding whether the person served qualifies as a "managing or general agent," the individual must be sufficiently connected with the company's operations to render it likely that service on that individual will provide notice to the defendant.

American Institute of Certified Public Accountants v. Affinity Card, Inc.

8 F. Supp. 2d 372 (S.D.N.Y. 1998)

SCHEINDLIN, DISTRICT JUDGE

Plaintiff, The American Institute of Certified Public Accountants ("AICPA"), filed a complaint sounding in breach of contract against defendant, Affinity Card, Inc. ("Affinity"), on March 24, 1998. An affidavit of service was filed on April 7, 1998. The defendant did not move or answer in the time permitted, and the plaintiff applied for a default judgment pursuant to Fed. R. Civ. P. 55 and Local Civil Rule 55.1. On May 11, 1998, a default judgment was entered against the defendant. The defendant now moves pursuant to Fed. R. Civ. P. 55(c) and 60(b)(4) to vacate the judgment of default as void for lack of personal jurisdiction due to ineffective service of process. For the reasons stated below, the motion is granted.

I.   Background

This action arises out of a tripartite contract entered into on November 5, 1992, by the plaintiff, defendant, and Marine Midland Bank. The contract established a Visa credit card marketed to AICPA members with Affinity's promotional assistance and issued by Marine Midland. AICPA and Affinity are entitled to a share in the fees collected from the program's participants. The plaintiff alleges that the defendant has improperly withheld information concerning these fees and has failed to make payments as obligated.

The plaintiff attempted service upon the defendant on March 30, 1998. Peter Murphy, a professional process server, handed the summons and complaint to one Patrick McDonald at Affinity's principal place of business in Wellesley, Massachusetts. See Affidavit of Peter Murphy in Support of Motion to Vacate Default Judgment ("Murphy Aff.") at ¶¶ 1-8. The plaintiff subsequently filed an affidavit of service that identified McDonald as Assistant Vice-President of Affinity. McDonald, however, is not employed by Affinity. He is the Assistant Vice-President of Primecard Corporation ("Primecard").

Affinity shares a suite of offices with three other companies, including Primecard. See Affidavit of Greg Miller (President and CEO, Affinity) in Support of Motion to Vacate Default Judgment ("Miller Aff.") at ¶ 15. The four companies share a receptionist's area, but the most significant link joining them is Greg Miller, president, treasurer, and at least a partial owner of all.

According to the plaintiff, Murphy entered the office and was greeted by McDonald at the receptionist's area. He asked McDonald "if Gregory Miller, Affinity Card's president, was there." After being informed that Miller was out, he told McDonald that he had some important legal papers for Affinity Card and Miller, and asked whether there was anyone there who could accept the papers for Affinity Card. McDonald said he could accept the papers and would make sure Miller received them that afternoon. Murphy then showed the summons and complaint to McDonald and asked for his name and title. McDonald said he was Assistant Vice-President, and Murphy assumed that McDonald meant Assistant Vice-President of Affinity. After that exchange, Murphy handed the summons and complaint to McDonald. . . .

The defendant's version of the events is slightly different. The defendant contends that after McDonald identified himself as Assistant Vice-President, Murphy said "that will do," or words to that effect, and handed over a sealed white envelope addressed to Miller. See Affidavit of Patrick McDonald (Assistant Vice-President, Primecard) in Support of Motion to Vacate Default Judgment ("McDonald Aff.") at ¶ 3. According to the defendant, Murphy did ask for Miller, but never asked McDonald if he could accept service for Affinity Card or Miller, never indicated the nature or purpose of the delivery, and never showed the documents to McDonald. McDonald placed the sealed, unopened envelope in Miller's box later that day.

II.   *Discussion*

Defendant now moves for an order vacating the default judgment pursuant to Federal Rules of Civil Procedure 55(c) and 60(b)(4). After the entry of a default judgment, Rule 55(c) grants a litigant the right to petition a court to vacate the judgment upon a showing of good cause and in accordance with Rule 60(b).

Subsection four of Rule 60(b) provides that a court may relieve a party from a final judgment if the judgment is void. *See* Fed. R. Civ. P. 60(b)(4). . . . A motion predicated on subsection four is unique, however, in that relief is not discretionary and a meritorious defense is not necessary as on motions made pursuant to other 60(b) subsections.

Valid service of process is a prerequisite to a district court's assertion of personal jurisdiction over a defendant. *See Omni Capital Int'l v. Rudolf Wolff & Co., Ltd.,* 484 U.S. 97, 103 (1987). A judgment entered against a party not subject to the personal jurisdiction of the court is a nullity. Hence, a judgment obtained by way of defective service is void for lack of personal jurisdiction and must be set aside as a matter of law.

In a federal diversity action, service of process upon a corporation may be made pursuant to Fed. R. Civ. P. [4(h)(1)(B)], or pursuant to the law of either the state in which the district court sits, or in which service is effected. *See* Fed. R. Civ. P. 4(e)(1), [4(h)(1)(A)]. The issue raised here is therefore straightforward: was service of process effective pursuant to Fed. R. Civ. P. 4(h)(1), New York's long arm statute, or the laws of Massachusetts?

Before analyzing the sufficiency of the attempted service, it should be noted that the Second Circuit has expressed on numerous occasions its "preference that litigation disputes be resolved on the merits, not by default." Default judgments have been described as "the most severe sanction which the court may apply, and its use must be tempered by the careful exercise of judicial discretion to assure that its imposition is merited." Although there is no judicial discretion when considering a jurisdictional question such as the sufficiency of process, when confronted with equally reliable but conflicting accounts, courts should resolve any doubts in favor of the party seeking relief under Rule 60(b). Accordingly, where the parties' accounts of the attempted service differ but both are inherently plausible, and there is nothing in the record upon which to judge the veracity of either version, a court should credit the version of the party seeking to vacate the default.

A.   Service of Process Under Federal Rule 4(h)(1)

According to the Federal Rules of Civil Procedure, service of process may be made upon a corporation by delivering copies of the summons and complaint to an officer, a managing or general agent, or to any other agent authorized to receive service of process. *See* Fed. R. Civ. P. [4(h)(1)(B)]. The burden is on the plaintiff to show a basis for an inference that the defendant has authorized a particular person to accept service of process on its behalf.

McDonald does not come within the letter of the statute. He is neither employed by nor expressly authorized to accept service on behalf of the defendant. The plaintiff argues that service was nevertheless effective and cites to several cases that have construed service of process rules liberally. Indeed, Rule 4(h)(1) does not require rigid formalism, and there are many cases where courts have exercised personal jurisdiction over defendants although service of process was delivered to someone other than the persons listed in the rule.

The rule does not require that service be made solely on a restricted class of formally titled officials, but rather permits it to be made upon a representative so integrated with the organization that he will know what to do with the papers. Generally, service is sufficient when made upon an individual who stands in such a position as to render it fair, reasonable and just to imply the authority on his part to receive services . . . .

McDonald had been working at Primecard for just a few months, he had no responsibilities for Affinity, and had never even heard of it. He did not hold himself out as a representative of Affinity or authorized to receive service on its behalf. Nor did he learn that the envelope which he placed in Miller's mailbox contained important legal documents until several weeks later. He was not sufficiently "integrated" with Affinity to allow the inference that he had authority to receive service.

In every case cited by the plaintiff, the person served was employed by the defendant corporation. As stated, McDonald was not employed by Affinity. . . .

Many of the rulings cited by the plaintiff were made on motions to dismiss, not on motions to vacate default judgments. Given the courts' preference for resolution on the merits, the procedural posture is of paramount importance. . . . Of course on a motion to dismiss, all doubts are resolved in favor of the nonmoving party.

The plaintiff places great weight on the fact that Greg Miller, the President of Affinity, actually received the summons and complaint on the very same day that the papers were delivered to McDonald. In *Durant v. Traditional Invs., Ltd.*, 1990 WL 33611 (S.D.N.Y. Mar. 22, 1990), this Court recognized the significance of actual notice. Citing to a procedural treatise, Judge Leisure wrote that "when a defendant receives actual notice of a lawsuit brought against him, technical imperfections with service will rarely invalidate the service." Id. at *3 (*citing* Wright & Miller, Federal Practice & Procedure, § 1063 at 225).

The actual receipt of the summons and complaint is an important factor in determining the effectiveness of service. However, actual notice of the action will not, in itself, cure an otherwise defective service. *See Omni Capital Int'l v. Rudolf Wolff and Co., Ltd.*, 484 U.S. 97, 104 (1987). . . .

B.   Service Under New York's Long Arm Statute

New York provides for specific jurisdiction over a foreign corporation that "transacts any business within the state or contracts anywhere to supply goods or services in the state," but only where the cause of action arises out of the aforesaid transaction. N.Y. C.P.L.R. § 302(a)(1). If these conditions are met, service may be made outside New York in the same manner as service is made within the state. Under New York law, service may be made upon a corporation by delivering the summons to an officer, director, managing or general agent, cashier, or anyone authorized by appointment or law to receive service.

Affinity is amenable to service pursuant to New York's long arm statute, having contracted to provide services in New York. It is well settled under New York law that service is effective where the process server reasonably relies on an employee's representations that she is authorized to receive service of process on behalf of the defendant. As under the federal rules, service of process upon a non-employee who makes no representations as to authorization to receive service is not effective. Thus, plaintiff's service of process was ineffective under New York law.

C. Service Under Massachusetts Law

Massachusetts provides that service upon a corporation may be made by delivering a copy of the summons and complaint "to an officer, to a managing or general agent, or to a person in charge of the business at the principal place of business thereof within the Commonwealth, if any; or by delivering such copies to any other agent authorized by appointment or by law to receive service of process . . . ." This language largely parallels the federal rules, but Massachusetts courts have construed the language narrowly. *See, e.g., Kane & Kane, Inc. v. Norwood Racquetball Dev. Corp.*, 1992 Mass. App. Div. 189 (1992) (process ineffective where employee of defendant corporation upon whom complaint was served was neither clerk nor agent). Given the relatively restrictive interpretation of the Massachusetts courts, service upon a non-employee is ineffective under Massachusetts standards.

More Narrow

III. *Conclusion*

The motion to vacate the default judgment is granted. The plaintiff technically has failed to effect proper service of process. Until proper service is effected, this Court has no jurisdiction over the defendant. However, as the Court may grant relief "upon such terms as are just," Fed. R. Civ. P. 60(b), and in light of the plaintiff's good faith belief that service had been properly effected, this vacatur is conditioned upon defendant's agreement to accept service on its attorney. Such service shall be made within seven (7) days of this Order. . . .

NOTES AND QUESTIONS

1. *Burden of proof.*   If the propriety of service is challenged, the burden of proving its validity normally rests with the party on whose behalf service was made — usually the plaintiff. *See* 4A WRIGHT & MILLER, *supra*, § 1083, at 437-439. If the facts concerning service are in dispute, as they were here, the court must decide which facts to use in determining whether the plaintiff has carried its burden of showing that service was proper. Since the court here did not conduct a hearing at which witnesses testified orally, but instead accepted testimony in the form of written affidavits, was it able to assess credibility and decide who was telling the truth? If not, what facts did the court use to determine whether service was proper?

2. *Procedural posture.*   What did the court mean when it said that the procedural posture of the case was of critical importance? Suppose that instead of allowing a default judgment to be entered against it, Affinity had filed a motion to dismiss the action under Rule 12(b)(5) for insufficiency of service of process. Assuming that the court conducted a hearing on this motion based solely on

affidavits without testimony from live witnesses, what facts would the court have used in deciding whether service was proper? Might the court have then reached a different conclusion concerning the adequacy of service than it reached in the actual case? If so, does this make sense? Do the differing approaches both further the same goal of resolving lawsuits on their merits rather than by default or by dismissal for procedural reasons?

c.   Defendants Served in a Foreign Country

If a defendant is to be served in a foreign country, a federal court must exercise caution so as not to intrude on another nation's sovereignty. At the same time, however, the court must be certain that the manner of service ensures fair notice to interested parties. The drafters of Rule 4 were aware of this tension, noting: "Inasmuch as our Constitution requires that reasonable notice be given, an earnest effort should be made to devise a method of communication that is consistent with due process and minimizes offense to foreign law." FED. R. CIV. P. 4, Advisory Committee Notes to 1993 Amendments, 146 F.R.D. 401, 569 (1993).

Accordingly, Rule 4 authorizes special and highly flexible procedures for serving defendants in foreign countries, whether the defendant is an individual (subdivisions (f)-(g)), or a corporation, partnership, or association (subdivision (h)(2)). If the situation is covered by a federal treaty or agreement, such as the Hague Convention on the Service Abroad of Judicial and Extrajudicial Documents, those procedures must be employed. *See* FED. R. CIV. P. 4(f)(1). *But see Volkswagenwerk Aktiengesellschaft v. Schlunk*, 486 U.S. 694 (1988) (excluding application of the Convention when the forum state service provision permits service on an instate subsidiary of the defendant as an involuntary agent). Nations signing the Hague Convention agree to designate a Central Authority to receive and transmit requests for service coming from other contracting nations, and to then certify that service has been made. If there is no federal treaty or agreement that applies, or if an applicable accord does not provide the exclusive means of service, a district court has a range of other options. It may borrow the law of the country in which service is effected; it may follow procedures suggested by that foreign country; or, if not prohibited by foreign law, it may employ personal service, have the court send mail return receipt requested, or use any other means not contrary to international agreement. *See* FED. R. CIV. P. 4(f)(2) & Advisory Committee Notes to 1993 Amendments, 146 F.R.D. at 566-569; 4B CHARLES ALAN WRIGHT, ARTHUR R. MILLER & ADAM N. STEINMAN, FEDERAL PRACTICE AND PROCEDURE §§ 1133-1136 (4th ed. 2015).

d.   Substantial Compliance

State and federal courts often take a liberal approach to service of process, accepting "substantial compliance" with the service rules rather than demanding strict adherence to all of their technicalities. *See* 4A WRIGHT & MILLER, *supra*, § 1083. "Rule 4 is a flexible rule that should be liberally construed so long as a party receives sufficient notice of the complaint. . . . Nonetheless, without substantial compliance with Rule 4, neither actual notice nor simply naming the defendant in the complaint will provide personal jurisdiction." *Direct Mail Specialists, Inc. v. Eclat Computerized Tech., Inc.*, 840 F.2d 685, 688 (9th Cir. 1988) (internal quotation marks omitted).

The flexibility of a court's approach turns on a variety of factors including the procedural posture of the case; the type of service involved; whether the plaintiff made a reasonable, good faith mistake; whether the defendant was evading service; whether the relevant service provision is inherently ambiguous (*e.g.*, "usual place of abode"; "managing or general agent"); whether the defendant received actual notice; and whether justice would be served by a relaxed construction. In addition, some courts may simply tolerate more elasticity than others. For example, in contrast to the *Affinity Card* case that we read earlier, the court in *Direct Mail Specialists, Inc.*, *supra*, refused to set aside a default judgment, finding that leaving process with a receptionist at the defendant's office substantially complied with Rule 4(h)(1)(B)'s provision for delivery to "a managing or general agent," even though the receptionist was employed by a related company that shared the same office. Yet there are limits on how much flexibility is permitted. As one court put it, a judge "has discretion to distinguish between mere technical errors and a complete disregard for Rule 4." *Weaver v. New York*, 7 F. Supp. 2d 234, 237 (W.D.N.Y. 1998) (dismissing, without prejudice, suit filed by layperson when the mode of service reflected no attempt to comply with Rule 4).

PROBLEM

3-3. Rabbi Weiss, a New York resident, brought a defamation action against Polish Cardinal Glemp based on a sermon Glemp had delivered in Poland in 1989. After unsuccessfully pursuing the claim in Poland and New York, Weiss filed suit in Washington in 1993 during Glemp's three-day visit to that state. A process server and a Polish translator went to the rectory at which Glemp was staying and asked to see the cardinal, explaining that they had important legal papers to give him. They were told by Glemp's secretary that the cardinal was not available and were asked to leave. Two hours later, the process server and the interpreter returned and saw Glemp through a large plate glass window. They shouted to him in Polish that he was being served with official documents. As they did so, Glemp turned and looked at them. They then placed the documents on a concrete windowsill four feet from where Glemp was sitting and left. Four months later, Glemp's lawyers moved to dismiss the action on the ground that service of process was improper. Washington law provides that the summons may be served by "delivering a copy . . . to the defendant personally, or by leaving a copy of the summons at the house of his usual abode with some person of suitable age and discretion then resident therein." Weiss's lawyers contend that there was substantial compliance with the service statute. How should the court rule? *See Weiss v. Glemp*, 903 P.2d 455 (Wash. 1995) (en banc). What if process had instead been handed to Glemp's secretary at the rectory?

3.   Time Limit for Effecting Service: Rule 4(m)

Rule 4(m) authorizes a federal court to dismiss an action "without prejudice" as to any defendant in the United States who is not served "within 90 days after the complaint is filed. . . ." The court must extend the time for service "if the plaintiff shows good cause for the failure. . . ." *Id.* The Advisory Committee Notes explain that Rule 4(m) also "authorizes the court to relieve a plaintiff of the consequences of an application of this subdivision even if there is no good cause shown. . . . Relief may be justified, for example, if the applicable statute of limitations would bar the refiled action, or if the defendant is evading service or conceals a defect in attempted service [until after the 90-day period has expired]." FED. R. CIV. P. 4, Advisory Committee Notes to 1993 Amendments, 146 F.R.D. 401, 573 (1993). The Supreme Court, citing the Advisory Committee Notes, has reiterated that this rule gives federal courts the discretion to extend a plaintiff's time "even if there is no good cause shown." *Henderson v. United States*, 517 U.S. 654, 658 n.5, 662-663 (1996).

Yet "the running of the statute of limitations does not require the district court to extend time for service of process. Rather, absent a finding of good cause, a district court may in its discretion still dismiss the case. . . ." *Petrucelli v. Bohringer & Ratzinger*, 46 F.3d 1298, 1306-1308 (3d Cir. 1995). In such cases, while a court may be required to at least consider the fact that the statute of limitations has run, *Lepone-Dempsey v. Carroll Cnty. Comm'rs*, 476 F.3d 1277 (11th Cir. 2007), there is no guaranty that an extension will be granted. In *Zapata v. City of New York*, 502 F.3d 192 (2d Cir. 2007), *cert. denied*, 552 U.S. 1243 (2008), for example, the court of appeals affirmed a Rule 4(m) dismissal of the plaintiff's federal civil rights claim against the city and one of its prison guards when service was effected four days after the then-operative 120-day limit. Though a refiled action would be time barred, the court upheld the dismissal on the bases that the plaintiff had made no effort to effect service within the prescribed period and that the defendant guard would now be prejudiced by having to defend the suit.

Rule 4(m)'s caveat that a dismissal under the rule is "without prejudice" will not protect a plaintiff from the effects of the statute of limitations. The phrase "without prejudice" means only that a dismissal is not on the merits, so that if the plaintiff refiles the suit, it will not be barred by the doctrine of res judicata or claim preclusion. Thus, "[t]hat a dismissal is 'without prejudice' under Rule 4(m) does not mean the dismissal is 'without consequence,' if the statute of limitations has run." *Conover v. Lein*, 87 F.3d 905, 908-909 (7th Cir. 1996) (upholding dismissal, on statute of limitations grounds, of action that was refiled after a prior dismissal under Rule 4(m), where the first action was filed on the last day of the two-year statute of limitations period).

Thus, despite its seeming generosity in terms of extending time to effect service, Rule 4(m)'s 90-day limit is one that plaintiffs should treat seriously. If a good portion of this period has elapsed without service having been effected, it is a mistake for a plaintiff to seek a waiver of service under Rule 4(d). For if no waiver is received after the end of 30 days, the plaintiff will have to make actual service—by which time the 90-day period may have expired.

B.   The Due Process Right to Notice

To be valid, the method of service must comply with the relevant statutes or rules and satisfy the Due Process Clause of the Fifth or Fourteenth Amendment to the U.S. Constitution. While the Fifth Amendment applies to the federal courts and the Fourteenth Amendment applies to the state courts, their notice requirements are identical.

One of the fundamental requirements of due process is that a person who is made a party to a lawsuit be afforded adequate notice of that suit. Thus a judgment rendered in the absence of adequate notice is void. The Due Process Clause does not prescribe any particular method of notification to be applied in all cases and under all circumstances. To be sure, certain standard methods such as in-hand service of process will satisfy due process in almost all cases. Yet due process does not insist that the means chosen be 100 percent certain to inform a party of the lawsuit, even though actual notice almost always satisfies due process. Instead, the adequacy of notice depends on the particular case's circumstances and the likelihood that the method of service employed will either be effective, or no less effective than any other reasonably available means. In essence, to satisfy due process, the form of notice used must be reasonable in light of the specific practicalities and peculiarities of the case at hand.

Mullane v. Central Hanover Bank & Trust Co.

339 U.S. 306 (1950)

MR. JUSTICE JACKSON delivered the opinion of the Court.

This controversy questions the constitutional sufficiency of notice to beneficiaries on judicial settlement of accounts by the trustee of a common trust fund established under the New York Banking Law. The New York Court of Appeals considered and overruled objections that the statutory notice contravenes requirements of the Fourteenth Amendment and that by allowance of the account beneficiaries were deprived of property without due process of law. . . .

Common trust fund legislation is addressed to a problem appropriate for state action. Mounting overheads have made administration of small trusts undesirable to corporate trustees. In order that donors and testators of moderately sized trusts may not be denied the service of corporate fiduciaries, the District of Columbia and some thirty states other than New York have permitted pooling small trust estates into one fund for investment administration. The income, capital gains, losses and expenses of the collective trust are shared by the constituent trusts in proportion to their contribution. By this plan, diversification of risk and economy of management can be extended to those whose capital standing alone would not obtain such advantage.

Statutory authorization for the establishment of such common trust funds is provided in the New York Banking Law. Under this Act a trust company may . . . establish a common fund and . . . invest therein the assets of an unlimited number of estates, trusts or other funds of which it is trustee. Each participating trust shares ratably in the common fund, but exclusive management and control is in the trust company as trustee, and neither a fiduciary nor any beneficiary of a participating trust is deemed to have ownership in any particular asset or investment of this common fund. . . . Provisions are made for accountings twelve to fifteen months after the establishment of a fund and triennially thereafter. The decree in each such judicial settlement of accounts is made binding and conclusive as to any matter set forth in the account upon everyone having any interest in the common fund or in any participating estate, trust or fund.

In January, 1946, Central Hanover Bank and Trust Company established a common trust fund in accordance with these provisions, and in March, 1947, it petitioned the Surrogate's Court for settlement of its first account as common trustee. During the accounting period a total of 113 trusts . . . participated in the . . . fund, the gross capital of which was nearly three million dollars. The record does not show the number or residence of the beneficiaries, but they were many and it is clear that some of them were not residents of the State of New York.

The only notice given beneficiaries of this specific application was by publication in a local newspaper in strict compliance with the minimum requirements of N.Y. Banking Law: "After filing such petition [for judicial settlement of its account] the petitioner shall cause to be issued by the court in which the petition is filed and shall publish not less than once in each week for four successive weeks in a newspaper to be designated by the court a notice or citation addressed generally without naming them to all parties interested in such common trust fund and in such estates, trusts or funds mentioned in the petition, all of which may be described in the notice or citation only in the manner set forth in said petition and without setting forth the residence of any such decedent or donor of any such estate, trust or fund." Thus the only notice required, and the only one given, was by newspaper publication setting forth merely the name and address of the trust company, the name and the date of establishment of the common trust fund, and a list of all participating estates, trusts or funds.

At the time the first investment in the common fund was made on behalf of each participating estate, however, the trust company . . . had notified by mail each person of full age and sound mind whose name and address were then known to it and who were "entitled to share in the income therefrom . . . [or] . . . who would be entitled to share in the principal if the event upon which such estate, trust or fund will become distributable should have occurred at the time of sending such notice." Included in the notice was a copy of those provisions of the Act relating to the sending of the notice itself and to the judicial settlement of common trust fund accounts.

Upon the filing of the petition for the settlement of accounts, appellant was . . . appointed special guardian and attorney for all persons known or unknown not otherwise appearing who had or might thereafter have any interest in the income of the common trust fund; and appellee Vaughan was appointed to represent those similarly interested in the principal. There were no other appearances on behalf of any one interested in either interest or principal.

Appellant appeared specially, objecting that notice and the statutory provisions for notice to beneficiaries were inadequate to afford due process under the Fourteenth Amendment, and therefore that the court was without jurisdiction to render a final and binding decree. Appellant's objections were entertained and overruled. . . . A final decree accepting the accounts has been . . . affirmed . . . by the Court of Appeals of the State of New York.

The effect of this decree, as held below, is to settle "all questions respecting the management of the common fund." We understand that every right which beneficiaries would otherwise have against the trust company, either as trustee of the common fund or as trustee of any individual trust, for improper management of the common trust fund during the period covered by the accounting is sealed and wholly terminated by the decree.

We are met at the outset with a challenge to the power of the State—the right of its courts to adjudicate at all as against those beneficiaries who reside without the State of New York. It is contended that the proceeding is one *in personam* in that the decree affects neither title to nor possession of any *res*, but adjudges only personal rights of the beneficiaries to surcharge their trustee for negligence or breach of trust. Accordingly, it is said, under the strict doctrine of *Pennoyer v. Neff*, the Surrogate is without jurisdiction as to nonresidents upon whom personal service of process was not made.

Distinctions between actions *in rem* and those *in personam* are ancient and originally expressed in procedural terms what seems really to have been a distinction in the substantive law of property under a system quite unlike our own. . . . American courts have sometimes classed certain actions as *in rem* because personal service of process was not required, and at other times have held personal service of process not required because the action was *in rem*.

Judicial proceedings to settle fiduciary accounts have been sometimes termed *in rem*, or more indefinitely *quasi in rem*, or more vaguely still, "in the nature of a proceeding *in rem*." It is not readily apparent how the courts of New York did or would classify the present proceeding, which has some characteristics and is wanting in some features of proceedings both *in rem* and *in personam*. But in any event we think that the requirements of the Fourteenth Amendment to the Federal Constitution do not depend upon a classification for which the standards are so elusive and confused generally and which, being primarily for state courts to define, may and do vary from state to state. Without disparaging the usefulness of distinctions between actions *in rem* and those *in personam* . . . we do not rest the power of the State to resort to constructive service in this proceeding upon how its courts or this Court may regard this historic antithesis. It is sufficient to observe that, whatever the technical definition of its chosen procedure, the interest of each state in providing means to close trusts that exist by the grace of its laws and are administered under the supervision of its courts is so insistent and rooted in custom as to establish beyond doubt the right of its courts to determine the interests of all claimants, resident or nonresident, provided its procedure accords full opportunity to appear and be heard.

Quite different from the question of a state's power to discharge trustees is that of the opportunity it must give beneficiaries to contest. Many controversies have raged about the cryptic and abstract words of the Due Process Clause but there can be no doubt that at a minimum they require that deprivation of life, liberty or property by adjudication be preceded by notice and opportunity for hearing appropriate to the nature of the case.

In two ways this proceeding does or may deprive beneficiaries of property. It may cut off their rights to have the trustee answer for negligent or illegal impairments of their interests. Also, their interests are presumably subject to diminution in the proceeding by allowance of fees and expenses to one who, in their names but without their knowledge, may conduct a fruitless or uncompensatory contest. Certainly the proceeding is one in which they may be deprived of property rights and hence notice and hearing must measure up to the standards of due process.

Personal service of written notice within the jurisdiction is the classic form of notice always adequate in any type of proceeding. But the vital interest of the State in bringing any issues as to its fiduciaries to a final settlement can be served only if interests or claims of individuals who are outside of the State can somehow be determined. A construction of the Due Process Clause which would place impossible or impractical obstacles in the way could not be justified.

Against this interest of the State we must balance the individual interest sought to be protected by the Fourteenth Amendment. This is defined by our holding that "The fundamental requisite of due process of law is the opportunity to be heard." This right to be heard has little reality or worth unless one is informed that the matter is pending and can choose for himself whether to appear or default, acquiesce or contest.

The Court has not committed itself to any formula achieving a balance between these interests in a particular proceeding or determining when constructive notice may be utilized or what test it must meet. Personal service has not in all circumstances been regarded as indispensable to the process due to residents, and it has more often been held unnecessary as to nonresidents. . . .

An elementary and fundamental requirement of due process in any proceeding which is to be accorded finality is notice reasonably calculated, under all the circumstances, to apprise interested parties of the pendency of the action and afford them an opportunity to present their objections. The notice must be of such nature as reasonably to convey the required information, and it must afford a reasonable time for those interested to make their appearance. But if with due regard for the practicalities and peculiarities of the case these conditions are reasonably met the constitutional requirements are satisfied. . . .

But when notice is a person's due, process which is a mere gesture is not due process. The means employed must be such as one desirous of actually informing the absentee might reasonably adopt to accomplish it. The reasonableness and hence the constitutional validity of any chosen method may be defended on the ground that it is in itself reasonably certain to inform those affected, or, where conditions do not reasonably permit such notice, that the form chosen is not substantially less likely to bring home notice than other of the feasible and customary substitutes.

It would be idle to pretend that publication alone as prescribed here, is a reliable means of acquainting interested parties of the fact that their rights are before the courts. It is not an accident that the greater number of cases reaching this Court on the question of adequacy of notice have been concerned with actions founded on process constructively served through local newspapers. Chance alone brings to the attention of even a local resident an advertisement in small type inserted in the back pages of a newspaper, and if he makes his home outside the area of the newspaper's normal circulation the odds that the information will never reach him are large indeed. The chance of actual notice is further reduced when, as here, the notice required does not even name those whose attention it is supposed to attract, and does not inform acquaintances who might call it to attention. In weighing its sufficiency on the basis of equivalence with actual notice, we are unable to regard this as more than a feint.

Nor is publication here reinforced by steps likely to attract the parties' attention to the proceeding. It is true that publication traditionally has been acceptable as notification supplemental to other action which in itself may reasonably be expected to convey a warning. The ways of an owner with tangible property are such that he usually arranges means to learn of any direct attack upon his possessory or proprietary rights. Hence, libel of a ship, attachment of a chattel or entry upon real estate in the name of law may reasonably be expected to come promptly to the owner's attention. When the state within which the owner has located such property seizes it for some reason, publication or posting affords an additional measure of notification. A state may indulge the assumption that one who has left tangible property in the state either has abandoned it, in which case proceedings against it deprive him of nothing, or that he has left some caretaker under a duty to let him know that it is being jeopardized. . . .

In the case before us there is, of course, no abandonment. On the other hand these beneficiaries do have a resident fiduciary as caretaker of their interest in this property. But it is their caretaker who in the accounting becomes their adversary. Their trustee is released from giving notice of jeopardy, and no one else is expected to do so. Not even the special guardian is required or apparently expected to communicate with his ward and client, and, of course, if such a duty were merely transferred from the trustee to the guardian, economy would not be served and more likely the cost would be increased.

This Court has not hesitated to approve of resort to publication as a customary substitute in another class of cases where it is not reasonably possible or practicable to give more adequate warning. Thus it has been recognized that, in the case of persons missing or unknown, employment of an indirect and even a probably futile means of notification is all that the situation permits and creates no constitutional bar to a final decree foreclosing their rights.

Those beneficiaries represented by appellant whose interests or whereabouts could not with due diligence be ascertained come clearly within this category. As to them the statutory notice is sufficient. However great the odds that publication will never reach the eyes of such unknown parties, it is not in the typical case much more likely to fail than any of the choices open to legislators endeavoring to prescribe the best notice practicable.

Nor do we consider it unreasonable for the State to dispense with more certain notice to those beneficiaries whose interests are either conjectural or future or, although they could be discovered upon investigation, do not in due course of business come to knowledge of the common trustee. Whatever searches might be required in another situation under ordinary standards of diligence, in view of the character of the proceedings and the nature of the interests here involved we think them unnecessary. We recognize the practical difficulties and costs that would be attendant on frequent investigations into the status of great numbers of beneficiaries, many of whose interests in the common fund are so remote as to be ephemeral; and we have no doubt that such impracticable and extended searches are not required in the name of due process. The expense of keeping informed from day to day of substitutions among even current income beneficiaries and presumptive remaindermen, to say nothing of the far greater number of contingent beneficiaries, would impose a severe burden on the plan, and would likely dissipate its advantages. These are practical matters in which we should be reluctant to disturb the judgment of the state authorities.

Accordingly we overrule appellant's constitutional objections to published notice insofar as they are urged on behalf of any beneficiaries whose interests or addresses are unknown to the trustee.

As to known present beneficiaries of known place of residence, however, notice by publication stands on a different footing. Exceptions in the name of necessity do not sweep away the rule that within the limits of practicability notice must be such as is reasonably calculated to reach interested parties. Where the names and post office addresses of those affected by a proceeding are at hand, the reasons disappear for resort to means less likely than the mails to apprise them of its pendency.

The trustee has on its books the names and addresses of the income beneficiaries represented by appellant, and we find no tenable ground for dispensing with a serious effort to inform them personally of the accounting, at least by ordinary mail to the record addresses. Certainly sending them a copy of the statute months and perhaps years in advance does not answer this purpose. The trustee periodically remits their income to them, and we think that they might reasonably expect that with or apart from their remittances word might come to them personally that steps were being taken affecting their interests.

We need not weigh contentions that a requirement of personal service of citation on even the large number of known resident or nonresident beneficiaries would, by reasons of delay if not of expense, seriously interfere with the proper administration of the fund. Of course personal service even without the jurisdiction of the issuing authority serves the end of actual and personal notice, whatever power of compulsion it might lack. However, no such service is required under the circumstances. This type of trust presupposes a large number of small interests. The individual interest does not stand alone but is identical with that of a class. The rights of each in the integrity of the fund and the fidelity of the trustee are shared by many other beneficiaries. Therefore notice reasonably certain to reach most of those interested in objecting is likely to safeguard the interests of all, since any objection sustained would inure to the benefit of all. We think that under such circumstances reasonable risks that notice might not actually reach every beneficiary are justifiable. . . .

The statutory notice to known beneficiaries is inadequate, not because in fact it fails to reach everyone, but because under the circumstances it is not reasonably calculated to reach those who could easily be informed by other means at hand. However it may have been in former times, the mails today are recognized as an efficient and inexpensive means of communication. Moreover, the fact that the trust company has been able to give mailed notice to known beneficiaries at the time the common trust fund was established is persuasive that postal notification at the time of accounting would not seriously burden the plan.

. . . Publication may theoretically be available for all the world to see, but it is too much in our day to suppose that each or any individual beneficiary does or could examine all that is published to see if something may be tucked away in it that affects his property interests. . . .

We hold that the notice of judicial settlement of accounts required by the New York Banking Law is incompatible with the requirements of the Fourteenth Amendment as a basis for adjudication depriving known persons whose whereabouts are also known of substantial property rights. Accordingly the judgment is reversed and the cause remanded for further proceedings not inconsistent with this opinion.

Reversed.

[The dissenting opinion of Mr. Justice Burton is omitted.]

NOTES AND QUESTIONS

1. Jurisdiction. How did the New York court obtain jurisdiction over those trust beneficiaries who lived outside New York? Without jurisdiction, the issue of notice would never have arisen. The settlement proceeding by the trustee against the beneficiaries sought to award the trustee fees and expenses out of the trust funds and cut off all claims the beneficiaries might have against the trustee for mismanagement or fraud during the accounting period. The award of fees and expenses can be thought of as involving an *in rem* proceeding, for it gives the trustee a piece of the trust property located in New York. Is the same true of the portion of the decree exonerating the trustee from any claims against it? If the trustee's mismanagement depleted the trust fund to 25 percent of its true worth, would the value of the claims cut off by the decree be limited to the value of the remaining trust assets? If not, is this aspect of the proceeding merely *in rem*, or is it more like an *in personam* action? Does the type of notice required by due process turn on whether the proceeding is characterized as being *in rem* or *in personam*?

2. *No formula.*   *Mullane* rejects a rigid formula as to the type of notice required by the Due Process Clause and instead requires "notice reasonably calculated, under all the circumstances, to apprise interested parties of the pendency of the action. . . ." *Mullane*, 339 U.S. at 314. The form of notice chosen must either be "reasonably certain to inform those affected, . . . or, where conditions do not reasonably permit such notice," must not be "substantially less likely to bring home notice than other of the feasible and customary substitutes." *Id.* at 315. A court must consider the "practicalities and peculiarities of the case" and balance the defendant's interest in receiving perfect notice through in-hand service of process against the interests of the plaintiff and the state in being able to proceed without encountering "impossible or impractical obstacles . . . ." *Id.* at 314. What would have been the consequence of requiring the trustee to try to identify, locate, and serve all of the beneficiaries? From the beneficiaries' perspective, what would have been gained by requiring such efforts? Why was notice by publication adequate with respect to unknown beneficiaries if it was virtually certain that this mechanism would not afford them actual notice? Would the court still have upheld notice by mere publication to those beneficiaries whose names or addresses were unknown to the trustee if there had been only three participating trusts, and if, instead of hundreds of beneficiaries, there had been only a dozen? Why might this have mattered?

3. *First-class mail.*   In *Mullane*, the Court endorsed the use of "ordinary" mail to notify the "known present beneficiaries of known place of residence." Will service via ordinary or first-class mail always satisfy due process? If the defendant admits having received the summons and complaint by mail, due process is satisfied because the plaintiff used a method of service that resulted in actual notice. *See, e.g., Snider Int'l Corp. v. Town of Forest Heights*, 739 F.3d 140, 145-148 (4th Cir.), *cert. denied*, 134 S. Ct. 2667 (2014) (municipalities' exclusive reliance on ordinary first-class mail to provide notice to those violating traffic laws satisfied due process as a method of service "reasonably calculated to confer actual notice," in a setting where no plaintiffs claimed they had not received a citation that had been mailed to them). But what if mail service results in a default judgment against a defendant who later denies having received notice of the suit? Is ordinary first-class mail so reliable as to warrant the conclusion that the defendant received the summons and complaint? Might the constitutionality of such notice depend

on the nature of the lawsuit and the potential consequences for the defendant if notice is not received? Should it matter whether the plaintiff first attempted notice by more reliable methods? Courts are divided on these questions, though most are reluctant to uphold the use of first-class mail by itself unless other more certain and verifiable means of service have first been attempted and failed. *Compare Miserandino v. Resort Properties, Inc.*, 691 A.2d 208, 218-219 (Md.), *cert. denied*, 522 U.S. 953 (1997) (refusing to give full faith and credit to a default judgment where service had been effected by first-class mail) *with Weigner v. City of New York*, 852 F.2d 646 (2d Cir. 1988), *cert. denied*, 488 U.S. 1005 (1989) (upholding service by regular mail when supplemented with publication and posting).

4. *Tailoring notice to a defendant's needs. Mullane* insisted that "[t]he means employed must be such as one desirous of actually informing the absentee might reasonably adopt to accomplish it." 339 U.S. at 315. Will this sometimes require that notice be tailored to a defendant's special needs when the plaintiff knows that generally acceptable forms of notice are unlikely to be effective in the defendant's case? Does the answer depend on how much of a burden such tailoring of notice would impose on the plaintiff?

In *Covey v. Town of Somers*, 351 U.S. 141 (1956), a city brought foreclosure proceedings against a woman whom it knew was mentally incompetent, lived alone, and had no relatives in the state. The city notified her of the action by direct mail to her home, by posting at the post office, and by publication in two local papers. Five days after the property was deeded to the city under a default judgment, a local court certified the woman to be of unsound mind and committed her to a state hospital for the insane. Citing *Mullane*, the Supreme Court held that the notice used would have been "sufficient in the case of the ordinary taxpayer" but that it did not constitute due process with respect to "a person known to be an incompetent who is without the protection of a guardian. . . ." *Id.* at 146-147. *See also Deutsche Bank National Trust Co. v. Goldfeder*, 86 A.3d 1118 (Del. 2014) (relying on *Covey* to vacate sheriff's sale of Goldfeder's home where bank, nearly four years earlier, had obtained a default judgment in a mortgage foreclosure action after giving constructive notice that complied with state law, on the basis that Goldfeder, who had no legal guardian, "was incompetent at the time and could not defend the action" and that the bank would suffer only "limited prejudice," even though there was no evidence that the bank knew of Goldfeder's condition). Does this suggest that it might be in plaintiff's best interest to ensure that the defendant has received notice of the suit, rather than automatically seeking a default judgment when defendant fails to respond in a timely manner?

PROBLEMS

3-4. After Delores slipped and fell in a parking lot that Clifford owns in South Dakota, she sued Clifford in a South Dakota court for negligent maintenance of the property. Clifford suffers from Alzheimer's disease. Although he has not been legally adjudged incompetent and has no judicially appointed guardian, his wife handles all of his business affairs under a power of attorney. At the time the sheriff attempted to serve Clifford at his South Dakota home, his wife was in Nevada. Gordon, a family friend, was caring for Clifford in her absence. Gordon answered the door and told the sheriff that Clifford was mentally incompetent, that Clifford's wife was away, and that he was staying with Clifford until she returned. The sheriff left the papers with Gordon, who said he would see that Clifford's attorney received them. After the statute of limitations had run, making it too late for Delores to re-serve Clifford, Clifford's attorney moved to dismiss the suit for improper service of process. Assuming service complied with South Dakota law, did it satisfy the Due Process Clause? *See Wagner v. Truesdell,* 574 N.W.2d 627 (S.D. 1998).

3-5. Union Bank sued A.J. in a New York court to recover monies owed under five promissory notes. An identical earlier suit had been dismissed on a technicality without prejudice to its being refiled. In the second suit, a process server went to A.J.'s home in New York and was advised that A.J. was there and that he should wait. After 30 minutes, however, he was told that A.J. was unavailable. Two days later the same process server returned and saw A.J. in his car in the driveway. A.J. saw the process server but kept the windows up and refused to speak with him. A.J. then maneuvered his car around the process server's car, which partly blocked the driveway, and managed to drive away. The process server chased him on foot and succeeded in placing the summons and complaint "on or about the windshield" of A.J.'s car; it is unclear whether the papers were placed under the windshield wiper. A.J. has moved to dismiss the suit for inadequate service of process. Assuming that service complied with New York law, did it satisfy due process? *See Union Nat'l Bank v. Pacamor Bearings, Inc.,* 503 N.Y.S.2d 671 (Sup. Ct. 1986).

Jones v. Flowers
547 U.S. 220 (2006)

CHIEF JUSTICE ROBERTS delivered the opinion of the Court.

Before a State may take property and sell it for unpaid taxes, the Due Process Clause of the Fourteenth Amendment requires the government to provide the owner "notice and opportunity for hearing appropriate to the nature of the case." *Mullane v. Central Hanover Bank & Trust Co.* We granted certiorari to determine whether, when notice of a tax sale is mailed to the owner and returned undelivered, the government must take additional reasonable steps to provide notice before taking the owner's property.

I

In 1967, petitioner Gary Jones purchased a house at 717 North Bryan Street in Little Rock, Arkansas. He lived in the house with his wife until they separated in 1993. Jones then moved into an apartment in Little Rock, and his wife continued to live in the North Bryan Street house. Jones paid his mortgage each month for

30 years, and the mortgage company paid Jones' property taxes. After Jones paid off his mortgage in 1997, the property taxes went unpaid, and the property was certified as delinquent.

In April 2000, respondent Mark Wilcox, the Commissioner of State Lands (Commissioner), attempted to notify Jones of his tax delinquency, and his right to redeem the property, by mailing a certified letter to Jones at the North Bryan Street address. The packet of information stated that unless Jones redeemed the property, it would be subject to public sale two years later on April 17, 2002. Nobody was home to sign for the letter, and nobody appeared at the post office to retrieve the letter within the next 15 days. The post office returned the unopened packet to the Commissioner marked "unclaimed."

Two years later, and just a few weeks before the public sale, the Commissioner published a notice of public sale in the Arkansas Democrat Gazette. No bids were submitted, which permitted the State to negotiate a private sale of the property. Several months later, respondent Linda Flowers submitted a purchase offer. The Commissioner mailed another certified letter to Jones at the North Bryan Street address, attempting to notify him that his house would be sold to Flowers if he did not pay his taxes. Like the first letter, the second was also returned to the Commissioner marked "unclaimed." Flowers purchased the house, which the parties stipulated in the trial court had a fair market value of $80,000, for $21,042.15. Immediately after the 30-day period for postsale redemption passed, Flowers had an unlawful detainer notice delivered to the property. The notice was served on Jones' daughter, who contacted Jones and notified him of the tax sale.

Jones filed a lawsuit in Arkansas state court against the Commissioner and Flowers, alleging that the Commissioner's failure to provide notice of the tax sale and of Jones' right to redeem resulted in the taking of his property without due process . . . . The trial court granted summary judgment in favor of the Commissioner and Flowers. It concluded that the Arkansas tax sale statute, which set forth the notice procedure followed by the Commissioner, complied with constitutional due process requirements.

Jones appealed, and the Arkansas Supreme Court affirmed the trial court's judgment. The court noted our precedent stating that due process does not require actual notice, see *Dusenbery v. United States*, 534 U.S. 161, 170 (2002), and it held that attempting to provide notice by certified mail satisfied due process in the circumstances presented.

We granted certiorari to resolve a conflict among the Circuits and State Supreme Courts concerning whether the Due Process Clause requires the government to take additional reasonable steps to notify a property owner when notice of a tax sale is returned undelivered. We hold that when mailed notice of a tax sale is returned unclaimed, the State must take additional reasonable steps to attempt to provide notice to the property owner before selling his property, if it is practicable to do so. Under the circumstances presented here, additional reasonable steps were available to the State. We therefore reverse the judgment of the Arkansas Supreme Court.

II

A

Due process does not require that a property owner receive actual notice before the government may take his property. *Dusenbery*. Rather, we have stated that due process requires the government to provide "notice reasonably calculated, under all the circumstances, to apprise interested parties of the pendency of the action and afford them an opportunity to present their objections." *Mullane*. The Commissioner argues that once the State provided notice reasonably calculated to apprise Jones of the impending tax sale by mailing him a certified letter, due process was satisfied. The Arkansas statutory scheme is reasonably calculated to provide notice, the Commissioner continues, because it provides for notice by certified mail to an address that the property owner is responsible for keeping up to date. The Commissioner notes this Court's ample precedent condoning notice by mail, see, *e.g., Dusenbery, Tulsa Professional Collection Services, Inc., Mennonite Bd. of Missions, Mullane,* and adds that the Arkansas scheme exceeds constitutional requirements by requiring the Commissioner to use certified mail.

It is true that this Court has deemed notice constitutionally sufficient if it was reasonably calculated to reach the intended recipient when sent. See, *e.g., Dusenbery; Mullane*. In each of these cases, the government attempted to provide notice and heard nothing back indicating that anything had gone awry, and we stated that "[t]he reasonableness and hence the constitutional validity of [the] chosen method may be defended on the ground that it is in itself reasonably certain to inform those affected." But we have never addressed whether due process entails further responsibility when the government becomes aware prior to the taking that its attempt at notice has failed. That is a new wrinkle, and we have explained that the "notice required will vary with circumstances and conditions." *Walker v. City of Hutchinson*. The question presented is whether such knowledge on the government's part is a "circumstance and condition" that varies the "notice required."

The Courts of Appeals and State Supreme Courts have addressed this question on frequent occasions, and most have decided that when the government learns its attempt at notice has failed, due process requires the government to do something more before real property may be sold in a tax sale.[1] Many States already require in their statutes that the government do more than simply mail notice to delinquent owners, either at the outset or as a followup measure if initial mailed notice is ineffective.

In *Mullane*, we stated that "when notice is a person's due . . . [t]he means employed must be such as one desirous of actually informing the absentee might reasonably adopt to accomplish it," and that assessing the adequacy of a particular

---

1. Most Courts of Appeals have also concluded that the Due Process Clause of the Fifth Amendment requires the Federal Government to take further reasonable steps in the property forfeiture context . . . .

form of notice requires balancing the "interest of the State" against "the individual interest sought to be protected by the Fourteenth Amendment." Our leading cases on notice have evaluated the adequacy of notice given to beneficiaries of a common trust fund, *Mullane*, a mortgagee, *Mennonite*, owners of seized cash and automobiles, *Dusenbery*, creditors of an estate, *Tulsa Professional*, and tenants living in public housing, *Greene v. Lindsey*. In this case, we evaluate the adequacy of notice prior to the State extinguishing a property owner's interest in a home.

We do not think that a person who actually desired to inform a real property owner of an impending tax sale of a house he owns would do nothing when a certified letter sent to the owner is returned unclaimed. If the Commissioner prepared a stack of letters to mail to delinquent taxpayers, handed them to the postman, and then watched as the departing postman accidentally dropped the letters down a storm drain, one would certainly expect the Commissioner's office to prepare a new stack of letters and send them again. No one "desirous of actually informing" the owners would simply shrug his shoulders as the letters disappeared and say "I tried." Failure to follow up would be unreasonable, despite the fact that the letters were reasonably calculated to reach their intended recipients when delivered to the postman.

By the same token, when a letter is returned by the post office, the sender will ordinarily attempt to resend it, if it is practicable to do so. This is especially true when, as here, the subject matter of the letter concerns such an important and irreversible prospect as the loss of a house. Although the State may have made a reasonable calculation of how to reach Jones, it had good reason to suspect when the notice was returned that Jones was "no better off than if the notice had never been sent." Deciding to take no further action is not what someone "desirous of actually informing" Jones would do; such a person would take further reasonable steps if any were available.

In prior cases, we have required the government to consider unique information about an intended recipient regardless of whether a statutory scheme is reasonably calculated to provide notice in the ordinary case. In *Robinson v. Hanrahan*, we held that notice of forfeiture proceedings sent to a vehicle owner's home address was inadequate when the State knew that the property owner was in prison. In *Covey v. Town of Somers*, we held that notice of foreclosure by mailing, posting, and publication was inadequate when town officials knew that the property owner was incompetent and without a guardian's protection.

The Commissioner points out that in these cases, the State was aware of such information *before* it calculated how best to provide notice. But it is difficult to explain why due process would have settled for something less if the government had learned after notice was sent, but before the taking occurred, that the property owner was in prison or was incompetent. Under *Robinson* and *Covey*, the government's knowledge that notice pursuant to the normal procedure was ineffective triggered an obligation on the government's part to take additional steps to effect notice. That knowledge was one of the "practicalities and peculiarities of the case" that the Court took into account in determining whether constitutional requirements were met. It should similarly be taken into account in assessing the adequacy of notice in this case. The dissent dismisses the State's knowledge that its notice was ineffective as "learned long after the fact," but the notice letter was promptly returned to the State two to three weeks after it was sent, and the Arkansas statutory regime precludes the State from taking the property for two *years* while the property owner may exercise his right to redeem.

It is certainly true, as the Commissioner and Solicitor General contend, that the failure of notice in a specific case does not establish the inadequacy of the attempted notice; in that sense, the constitutionality of a particular procedure for notice is assessed *ex ante*, rather than *post hoc*. But if a feature of the State's chosen procedure is that it promptly provides additional information to the government about the effectiveness of notice, it does not contravene the *ex ante* principle to consider what the government does with that information in assessing the adequacy of the chosen procedure. After all, the State knew *ex ante* that it would promptly learn whether its effort to effect notice through certified mail had succeeded. It would not be inconsistent with the approach the Court has taken in notice cases to ask, with respect to a procedure under which telephone calls were placed to owners, what the State did when no one answered. Asking what the State does when a notice letter is returned unclaimed is not substantively different.

The Commissioner has three further arguments for why reasonable followup measures were not required in this case. First, notice was sent to an address that Jones provided and had a legal obligation to keep updated. See Ark. Code Ann. § 26-35-705 (1997). Second, "after failing to receive a property tax bill and pay property taxes, a property holder is on inquiry-notice that his property is subject to governmental taking." Third, Jones was obliged to ensure that those in whose hands he left his property would alert him if it was in jeopardy. None of these contentions relieves the State of its constitutional obligation to provide adequate notice.

The Commissioner does not argue that Jones' failure to comply with a statutory obligation to keep his address updated forfeits his right to constitutionally sufficient notice, and we agree . . . . Although Ark. Code Ann. § 26-35-705 provides strong support for the Commissioner's argument that mailing a certified letter to Jones at 717 North Bryan Street was reasonably calculated to reach him, it does not alter the reasonableness of the Commissioner's position that he must do nothing more when the notice is promptly returned "unclaimed."

As for the Commissioner's inquiry notice argument, the common knowledge that property may become subject to government taking when taxes are not paid does not excuse the government from complying with its constitutional obligation of notice before taking private property . . . . Arkansas affords even a delinquent taxpayer the right to settle accounts with the State and redeem his property, so Jones' failure to pay his taxes in a timely manner cannot by itself excuse inadequate notice.

Finally, the Commissioner reminds us of a statement from *Mullane* that the State can assume an owner leaves his property in the hands of one who will inform him if his interest is in jeopardy . . . . An occupant, however, is not charged with acting as the owner's agent in all respects, and it is quite a leap . . . to conclude that it is an obligation of tenancy to follow up with certified mail of unknown content addressed to the owner. In fact, the State makes it impossible for the occupant to learn why the Commissioner is writing the owner, because an occupant cannot call for a certified letter without first obtaining the owner's signature . . . . In any event, there is no record evidence that notices of attempted delivery were left at 717 North Bryan Street.

Jones should have been more diligent with respect to his property, no question. People must pay their taxes, and the government may hold citizens accountable for tax delinquency by taking their property. But before forcing a citizen to satisfy his debt by forfeiting his property, due process requires the government to provide adequate notice of the impending taking.

B

In response to the returned form suggesting that Jones had not received notice that he was about to lose his property, the State did—nothing. For the reasons stated, we conclude the State should have taken additional reasonable steps to notify Jones, if practicable to do so. The question remains whether there were any such available steps. While "[i]t is not our responsibility to prescribe the form of service that the [government] should adopt," if there were no reasonable additional steps the government could have taken upon return of the unclaimed notice letter, it cannot be faulted for doing nothing.

We think there were several reasonable steps the State could have taken. What steps are reasonable in response to new information depends upon what the new information reveals. The return of the certified letter marked "unclaimed" meant either that Jones still lived at 717 North Bryan Street, but was not home when the postman called and did not retrieve the letter at the post office, or that Jones no longer resided at that address. One reasonable step primarily addressed to the former possibility would be for the State to resend the notice by regular mail, so that a signature was not required. The Commissioner says that use of certified mail makes actual notice more likely, because requiring the recipient's signature protects against misdelivery. But that is only true, of course, when someone is home to sign for the letter, or to inform the mail carrier that he has arrived at the wrong address. Otherwise, . . . the use of certified mail might make actual notice less likely in some cases—the letter cannot be left like regular mail to be examined at the end of the day, and it can only be retrieved from the post office for a specified period of time. Following up with regular mail might also increase the chances of actual notice to Jones if—as it turned out—he had moved. Even occupants who ignored certified mail notice slips addressed to the owner (if any had been left) might scrawl the owner's new address on the notice packet and leave it for the postman to retrieve, or notify Jones directly.

Other reasonable followup measures, directed at the possibility that Jones had moved as well as that he had simply not retrieved the certified letter, would have been to post notice on the front door, or to address otherwise undeliverable mail to "occupant." . . . Occupants who might disregard a certified mail slip not addressed to them are less likely to ignore posted notice, and a letter addressed to them (even as "occupant") might be opened and read. In either case, there is a significant chance the occupants will alert the owner, if only because a change in ownership could well affect their own occupancy. In fact, Jones first learned of the State's effort to sell his house when he was alerted by one of the occupants—his daughter—after she was served with an unlawful detainer notice.

Jones believes that the Commissioner should have searched for his new address in the Little Rock phonebook and other government records such as income tax rolls. We do not believe the government was required to go this far . . . . An open-ended search for a new address—especially when the State obligates the taxpayer to keep his address updated with the tax collector—imposes burdens on the State significantly greater than the several relatively easy options outlined above.

The Commissioner complains about the burden of even those additional steps, but his argument is belied by . . . the fact that Arkansas transfers the cost of notice to the taxpayer or the tax sale purchaser. The Commissioner has offered no estimate of how many notice letters are returned, and no facts to support the dissent's assertion that the Commissioner must now physically locate "tens of thousands of properties every year." Citing our decision in *Greene v. Lindsey*, the Solicitor General adds that posted notice could be taken down by children or vandals. But in *Greene*, we noted that outside the specific facts of that case, posting notice on real property is "a singularly appropriate and effective way of ensuring that a person . . . is actually apprised of proceedings against him." Successfully providing notice is often the most efficient way to collect unpaid taxes, but rather than taking relatively easy additional steps to effect notice, the State undertook the burden and expense of purchasing a newspaper advertisement, conducting an auction, and then negotiating a private sale of the property to Flowers.

The Solicitor General argues that requiring further effort when the government learns that notice was not delivered will cause the government to favor modes of providing notice that do not generate additional information—for example, starting (and stopping) with regular mail instead of certified mail. We find this unlikely, as we have no doubt that the government repeatedly finds itself being asked to prove that notice was sent and received. Using certified mail provides the State with documentation of personal delivery and protection against false claims that notice was never received. That added security, however, comes at a price—the State also learns when notice has *not* been received. We conclude that, under the circumstances presented, the State cannot simply ignore that information in proceeding to take and sell the owner's property—any more than it could ignore the information that the owner in *Robinson* was in jail, or that the owner in *Covey* was incompetent.

. . . [T]he Commissioner . . . reminds us that the State did make some attempt to follow up with Jones by publishing notice in the newspaper a few weeks before the public sale. Several decades ago, this Court observed that "[c]hance alone" brings a person's attention to "an advertisement in small type inserted in the back pages of a newspaper," *Mullane,* and that notice by publication is adequate only where "it is not reasonably possible or practicable to give more adequate warning." Following up by publication was not constitutionally adequate under the circumstances presented here because, as we have explained, it was possible and practicable to give Jones more adequate warning of the impending tax sale.

. . . [W]e disclaim any "new rule" that is "contrary to *Dusenbery* and a significant departure from *Mullane*." In *Dusenbery*, the Government was aware that someone at the prison had signed for the prisoner's notice letter, and we determined that this attempt at notice was adequate, despite the fact that the State could have made notice more likely by requiring the prisoner to sign for the letter himself. In this case, of course, the notice letter was returned to the Commissioner, informing him that his attempt at notice had failed.

As for *Mullane*, it directs that "when notice is a person's due . . . [t]he means employed must be such as one desirous of actually informing the absentee might reasonably adopt to accomplish it." Mindful of the dissent's concerns, we conclude, at the end of the day, that someone who actually wanted to alert Jones that he was in danger of losing his house would do more when the attempted notice letter was returned unclaimed, and there was more that reasonably could be done.

. . . In prior cases finding notice inadequate, we have not attempted to redraft the State's notice statute. The State can determine how to proceed in response to our conclusion that notice was inadequate here, and the States have taken a variety of approaches to the present question. It suffices for present purposes that we are confident that additional reasonable steps were available for Arkansas to employ before taking Jones' property.

* * *

There is no reason to suppose that the State will ever be less than fully zealous in its efforts to secure the tax revenue it needs. The same cannot be said for the State's efforts to ensure that its citizens receive proper notice before the State takes action against them. In this case, the State is exerting extraordinary power against a property owner—taking and selling a house he owns. It is not too much to insist that the State do a bit more to attempt to let him know about it when the notice letter addressed to him is returned unclaimed.

The Commissioner's effort to provide notice to Jones of an impending tax sale of his house was insufficient to satisfy due process given the circumstances of this case. The judgment of the Arkansas Supreme Court is reversed, and the case is remanded for proceedings not inconsistent with this opinion.

It is so ordered.

Justice Alito took no part in the consideration or decision of this case.

Justice Thomas, with whom Justice Scalia and Justice Kennedy join, dissenting . . . .

Arkansas' attempts to contact petitioner by certified mail at his "record address," without more, satisfy due process. Because the notices were sent to the address provided by petitioner himself, the State had an especially sound basis for determining that notice would reach him. Moreover, Arkansas exceeded the constitutional minimum by additionally publishing notice in a local newspaper. Due process requires nothing more—and certainly not here, where petitioner had a statutory duty to pay his taxes and to report any change of address to the state taxing authority.

My conclusion that Arkansas' notice methods satisfy due process is reinforced by the well-established presumption that individuals, especially those owning property, act in their own interest . . . . Consistent with this observation, Arkansas was free to "indulge the assumption" that petitioner had either provided the state taxing authority with a correct and up-to-date mailing address—as required by state law—"or that he . . . left some caretaker under a duty to let him know that [his property was] being jeopardized."

The Court does not conclude that certified mail is inherently insufficient as a means of notice, but rather that "the government's knowledge that notice pursuant to the normal procedure was ineffective triggered an obligation on the government's part to take additional steps to effect notice." I disagree.

First, whether a method of notice is reasonably calculated to notify the interested party is determined *ex ante, i.e.,* from the viewpoint of the government agency at the time its notice is sent. This follows from *Mullane,* where this Court rested its analysis on the information the sender had "at hand" when its notice was sent. Relatedly, we have refused to evaluate the reasonableness of a particular method of notice by comparing it to alternative methods that are identified after the fact. See *Dusenbery.* Today the Court appears to abandon both of these practices. Its rejection of Arkansas' selected method of notice—a method this Court has repeatedly concluded is constitutionally sufficient—is based upon information that was unavailable when notice was sent . . . .

Second, implicit in our holding that due process does not require "actual notice" is that when the "government becomes aware . . . that its attempt at notice has failed," it is not required to take additional steps to ensure that notice has been received . . . . Under the majority's logic, each time a doubt is raised with respect to whether notice has reached an interested party, the State will have to consider additional means better calculated to achieve notice. Because this rule turns on speculative, newly acquired information, it has no natural end point, and, in effect, requires the States to achieve something close to actual notice. The majority's new rule is contrary to *Dusenbery* and a significant departure from *Mullane* . . . .

NOTES AND QUESTIONS

1. The need for additional notice.   Does *Jones* stand for the proposition that whenever restricted delivery mail is returned unclaimed, a plaintiff must take additional steps to afford the defendant notice? If not, what was it that rendered the state's method of notice constitutionally infirm in that case? There were two distinct stages in these proceedings at which the commissioner was required to give notice to the property owner: first, at the tax delinquency stage, to warn the owner that unless the delinquent taxes were paid within two years, the property would be sold; and second, if the two years expired without full payment, at the tax sale stage, to apprise the owner that a purchase offer had been received and that the property would be sold unless the taxes were paid immediately. Was the state's notice procedure the same at each of these stages? Did the Court hold that the procedures were unconstitutional at both stages? If not, under *Mullane*'s balancing test, is there a difference in terms of what is at stake to the property owner at each stage? Are you satisfied that this is enough to warrant different levels of constitutional protection? *See Pagonis v. United States*, 575 F.3d 809, 814-815 (8th Cir. 2009) (holding that *Jones*'s notice requirements do not apply at the tax delinquency stage because no deprivation of property occurs at that point).

2. *Acceptable additional notice.* What "additional reasonable steps" were available that would have cured the constitutional defect in Arkansas's existing notice procedure? Does the Court specify which of these additional reasonable steps the state must adopt? After *Jones*, what is the simplest way to provide notice in tax delinquency cases involving real property that would pass constitutional muster? Would you have to effect personal service? Would you feel comfortable relying solely on unrestricted first-class mail? Since *Jones* was decided, state and federal courts have held that in cases in which restricted delivery mail was returned "unclaimed," due process is usually satisfied if notice was also sent—either concurrently or subsequently—by regular mail that was not returned. *See, e.g., Nicholson v. HF05*, 2009 WL 4842472 (Iowa App. Dec. 17, 2009); *Borkon v. City of Phila.*, 2008 WL 4058694 (E.D. Pa. Aug. 29, 2008); *Morris v. LandNpulaski, LLC*, 309 S.W.3d 212, 216-218 (Ark. Ct. App. 2009). Plaintiffs wanting to play it even safer might, at little extra expense, follow the suggestion in *Jones* that separate sets of restricted delivery and first-class mail be addressed to the defendant, one by name and the other as "Occupant"—for a total of four mailings. *See, e.g., Griffin v. Bierman*, 941 A.2d 475 (Md. 2008).

3. *Posting.* In *Jones*, the Court recognized that one acceptable way to supplement notice by restricted-delivery mail would have been "to post notice on the front door" of Jones's house. In *Greene v. Lindsey*, 456 U.S. 444 (1982), the Court held that as an alternative to personal service, posting on the door of a defendant's home or apartment—not the county courthouse—"would, in many or perhaps most instances, constitute not only a constitutionally acceptable means of service, but indeed a singularly appropriate and effective way of ensuring that a person who cannot conveniently be served personally is actually apprised of proceedings against him." *Id.* at 452-453. *Greene* rejected use of posting as the sole form of notice in that particular case, for it involved a public housing project at which notices tacked to apartment doors "were 'not infrequently' removed by children or other tenants before they could have their intended effect." *Id.* at 453. In that setting, said the Court, "posted service *accompanied by* mail service, is constitutionally preferable to posted service alone." *Id.* at 455 n.9. In light of the Court's statement in *Greene*, do you think posting alone would have satisfied due process in *Jones*, or would "a person who actually desired to inform" Jones that his property was about to be sold have had good reason to doubt that mere posting would inform him of this fact?

4. Supplementing service by mail.   The Court in *Jones* held that on the facts of that case, the unsuccessful use of restricted-delivery mail had to be supplemented by some other form of notice. Under the balancing test's evaluation of the private interest at stake, was it significant there that "the State [was] extinguishing a property owner's interest in a home"? 547 U.S. at 229. And on the state's side of the balance, did it matter that under the statutory scheme in question, time was not critical since Arkansas law afforded a two-year redemption period before the property could be sold? Might the result be different in other types of cases? For example, under *Jones*, would the government have to attempt additional notice if restricted delivery mail were returned unclaimed in a case involving (a) the sale of an impounded vehicle when notice was sent to the owner's address as listed by the State Department of Motor Vehicles (*Wilson v. Farris*, 2010 WL 3463442 (M.D. Fla. Aug. 30, 2010)); or (b) the 20-day suspension of a pilot's license when notice was sent to the pilot's home address and someone there refused delivery (*Yi Tu v. National Transp. Safety Bd.*, 470 F.3d 941 (9th Cir. 2006)). In these cases, how would you balance the competing public and private interests in deciding whether restricted-delivery mail alone was sufficient? Would it matter what post-deprivation remedies might be available if the government's action turned out to have been mistaken?

PROBLEMS

3-6. While driving in West Virginia, Diane lost control of her car and hit Hartwell, who was trying to repair his truck at the side of the road. Diane is a resident of Illinois. Her actual whereabouts are unknown. Three months after the accident, Hartwell sued Diane in a West Virginia court for personal injuries suffered in the accident. In accord with the state's nonresident motorist statute, process was served on the Secretary of State who in turn sent it to Diane by certified mail, return receipt requested, to the address she had given at the scene of the accident. After the mail was returned "unclaimed," the Secretary then sent the summons and complaint by certified mail to Gallant, Diane's insurer, as authorized by a West Virginia law that deems a defendant's insurance company to be her agent for service of process in these circumstances. The statute did not require the company to notify the defendant. Gallant received and signed for the papers. After no responsive pleading was filed on behalf of Diane, Hartwell obtained a default judgment against her in the amount of $449,067, plus interest. Ten months later Gallant moved to set aside the default judgment, claiming that the method of service on Diane violated the Due Process Clause. How should the court rule on the motion? *See Hartwell v. Marquez*, 498 S.E.2d 1 (W. Va. 1997).

3-7. In October 2007, Les was handed a letter at the New York public school at which he had worked as a tenured math teacher for 28 years, notifying him that pursuant to a recently issued disciplinary proceeding decision, "you are hereby terminated immediately from your employment position with New York School District." Notices of the proceeding had been mailed to Les in May and in

August, by both certified mail and regular mail, but to an address from which he had moved five years earlier. The district's payroll office had his correct current address, but the human resources office, which handled the disciplinary proceeding, had only the old address, which it had no reason to believe was inaccurate. While the certified-mail notices had been returned "unclaimed," the regular-mail notices did not come back. Les first learned of the proceeding when the final, unappealable termination notice was handed to him at school. Les has filed a 42 U.S.C. § 1983 action against the school district seeking reinstatement and back pay. He alleges that as a tenured teacher, he had a protected property interest in his job, of which he cannot be deprived without due process of law. The district has moved to dismiss on the basis that it respected Les's procedural due process rights by having provided him with notice by both certified and regular mail. It was Les's duty, says the district, to officially update his address with the district's main office, something he did not do until after he was terminated. How should the court rule and why? *See Norgrove v. Board of Educ. of City Sch. Dist. of City of N.Y.*, 881 N.Y.S.2d 802 (Sup. Ct. 2009).

A NOTE ON CHALLENGING SERVICE OF PROCESS

A party that wishes to challenge the sufficiency of service of process, whether on statutory or constitutional grounds, must do so in a timely manner or the defect is waived. The objection may be raised by a motion to dismiss under Rule 12(b)(5) or in the answer, whichever is filed first. *See* FED. R. CIV. P. 12(b). As with an objection to jurisdiction over the defendant, a challenge to the adequacy of service is waived if it is omitted from a pre-answer motion to dismiss or, when no such motion is filed, if it is omitted from the answer. *See* FED. R. CIV. P. 12(g)(1) & (h)(1); Advisory Committee Notes to 1966 Amendment, 39 F.R.D. 69, 78-79 (1966). In short, an objection to the sufficiency of service of process must be included in a party's first response to the proceedings in federal court. *See, e.g., Resolution Trust Corp. v. Starkey*, 41 F.3d 1018, 1021 (5th Cir. 1995) (holding that defendant waived objection to sufficiency of service by omitting the objection from his answer and only later moving to dismiss on this ground). A party may also file a motion to dismiss for "insufficient process." FED. R. CIV. P. 12(b)(4). Such a motion addresses the sufficiency of the content of the summons. As is the case with a challenge to the sufficiency of the method of service, any such challenge is waived if not asserted in the timely fashion described above.

However, a defendant who makes no appearance in the action and has a default judgment entered against her may later challenge the sufficiency of service of process either by filing a motion to vacate the judgment under Rule 60(b)(4) on the basis that it is "void," *see, e.g., American Inst. of Certified Pub. Accountants v. Affinity Card Inc.*, page 249, *supra*), or through a collateral attack on the judgment, *see, e.g., Mennonite Bd. of Missions v. Adams*, 462 U.S. 791 (1983). In either case, there is no time limit on when such relief may be sought. As a result, a judgment based on inadequate service may be attacked years after it was entered, during which time the parties and others may have relied on it to their detriment.

Because of the risks that flow from inadequate service of process, responsible attorneys will err on the side of ensuring that service is properly effected, rather than using less-effective methods that may enhance the chances of obtaining a default judgment, only to have it set aside years after the fact. Does this help explain why the Supreme Court in *Jones v. Flowers, supra,* suggested that it may not be wise to rely solely on first-class mail service simply to avoid the additional burdens associated with using certified or registered mail?

YOU'VE GOT MAIL

In *Rio Properties, Inc. v. Rio International Interlink*, 284 F.3d 1007 (9th Cir. 2002), the Ninth Circuit upheld the use of e-mail as an alternate method for service of process. The underlying controversy involved a trademark infringement suit between a Las Vegas hotel and casino operator ("RIO") and a Costa Rican internet gambling business ("RII"). RIO was unable to serve RII in the United States, there being no domestic agent for service of process, and RIO's efforts to serve RII in Costa Rica proved fruitless as well. RIO's investigator did learn, however, that RII preferred communication through its e-mail address — *email@betrio. com*. RII also had two potential "snail mail" addresses in the United States, neither of which was authorized as an agent to accept service of process. Unable to serve RII by conventional means, RIO filed an emergency motion for alternate service of process pursuant to Rule 4(f)(3) and 4(h)(2). The district court granted RIO's motion and ordered service of process on RII at the two domestic mail addresses, and via RII's e-mail address. The Ninth Circuit upheld all three methods of service, concluding that each was reasonably calculated, under the circumstances, to apprise RII of the action. As to service by e-mail, the Ninth Circuit observed:

> Finally, we turn to the district court's order authorizing service of process on RII by email at *email@betrio.com*. We acknowledge that we tread upon untrodden ground. The parties cite no authority condoning service of process over the Internet or via email, and our own investigation has unearthed no decisions by the United States Courts of Appeals dealing with service of process by email and only one case anywhere in the federal courts. Despite this dearth of authority, however, we do not labor long in reaching our decision. Considering the facts presented by this case, we conclude not only that service of process by email was proper—that is, reasonably calculated to apprise RII of the pendency of the action and afford it an opportunity to respond—but in this case, it was the method of service most likely to reach RII.
>
> To be sure, the Constitution does not require any particular means of service of process, only that the method selected be reasonably calculated to provide notice and an opportunity to respond. In proper circumstances, this broad constitutional principle unshackles the federal courts from anachronistic methods of service and permits them entry into the technological renaissance. . . .
>
> Although communication via email and over the Internet is comparatively new, such communication has been zealously embraced within the business community. RII particularly has embraced the modern e-business model and profited immensely from it. In fact, RII structured its business such that it could be contacted *only* via its email address. RII listed no easily discoverable street address in the United States

or in Costa Rica. Rather, on its website and print media, RII designated its email address as its preferred contact information. . . .

Despite our endorsement of service of process by email in this case, we are cognizant of its limitations. In most instances, there is no way to confirm receipt of an email message. Limited use of electronic signatures could present problems in complying with the verification requirements of Rule 4(a) and Rule 11, and system compatibility problems may lead to controversies over whether an exhibit or attachment was actually received. Imprecise imaging technology may even make appending exhibits and attachments impossible in some circumstances. We note, however, that, except for the provisions recently introduced into Rule 5(b), email service is not available absent a Rule 4(f)(3) court decree. Accordingly, we leave it to the discretion of the district court to balance the limitations of email service against its benefits in any particular case. In our case, the district court performed the balancing test admirably, crafting methods of service reasonably calculated under the circumstances to apprise RII of the pendency of the action.[8]

Id. at 1017-1019.

Has the Ninth Circuit contorted the rules of notice, or did it seek to adapt them to a new and previously uncharted realm that courts will continue to explore? In *Hollow v. Hollow*, 747 N.Y.S.2d 704 (Sup. Ct. 2002), a New York court—citing *Rio Properties*—allowed e-mail service to be made in a divorce action on a husband who had relocated to Saudi Arabia, where he lived and worked in a high-security, company-owned compound at which attempted service even on armed guards was criminally punishable, and where the company refused to accept service or in any way cooperate on his behalf. The court, finding that the "defendant has in essence secreted himself behind a steel door, bolted shut, communicating with the plaintiff and his children exclusively through e-mail," held that "service directed to the defendant's last known e-mail address as well as service by international registered air mail and international mail standard, is sufficient to satisfy . . . due process. . . ." *Id.* at 708. *See also D.Light Design, Inc. v. Boxin Solar Co., Ltd.*, 2015 WL 526835 (N.D. Cal. Feb. 6, 2015) (allowing service by e-mail under Rule 4(f)(3) in suit against two China-based companies where plaintiffs' "diligent efforts" to identify defendants' mailing addresses failed, where defendants used their e-mail addresses as their "preferred contact information," and where plaintiffs employed e-mail tracking to confirm that e-mails to those addresses were sent successfully, the court finding that "service by email is reasonably calculated to provide actual notice to Defendants" and that "[s]uch service may, in fact, be the method most likely to alert the Defendants to this action"); *Craigslist, Inc. v. Meyer*, 2010 WL 2975938 (N.D. Cal. July 26, 2010) (permitting service by e-mail under Rule 4(f)(3) on defendant thought to live in Thailand after more than ten unsuccessful attempts to serve defendant by other means); *Bank Julius Baer & Co. Ltd. v. WikiLeaks*, 2008 WL 413737 (N.D. Cal. Feb. 13, 2008) (permitting service

---

8. Notably, RII does not argue that it did not receive notice of the present lawsuit or that such notice was incomplete, delayed or in any way prejudicial to its ability to respond effectively and in a timely manner.

by e-mail under Rule 4(f)(3) when defendants' physical addresses could not be found and defendants' purported agents refused to accept service); *Philip Morris USA Inc. v. Veles Ltd.*, 2007 WL 725412 (S.D.N.Y. Mar. 12, 2007) (permitting service by e-mail and by fax under Rule 4(f)(3) when defendant conducted business extensively if not exclusively on the internet, and had no discoverable physical address or operable phone numbers).

In *F.T.C. v. Pecon Software Ltd.*, 2013 WL 4016272 (S.D.N.Y. Aug. 7, 2013), the court considered whether, under Rule 4(f)(3), it should authorize service via e-mail and Facebook. The plaintiff sought these alternative methods after its efforts to serve several business entities and individuals located in India, under the Hague Convention on Service, had failed. After finding that "service by means of email and Facebook is not prohibited by international agreement," the district court concluded that it had discretion "to authorize service by such means, provided that due process is also satisfied." *Id.* at *5. The court then allowed service on some of the defendants by e-mail and Facebook, but declined to permit service by Facebook alone since it was not "highly likely" that the latter would reach these defendants. *Id.* at *8. By way of contrast, in a recent matrimonial action, a state court held that the plaintiff could serve a divorce summons on the defendant solely by private message to her spouse's Facebook account, after plaintiff demonstrated she would be unable to effect personal service on the defendant. *Baidoo v. Blood-Dzraku*, 5 N.Y.S.3d 709 (Sup. Ct. 2015).

C.   Pre-filing Waiver and Consent

We have seen that Rule 4(d) allows a plaintiff, after filing suit, to request that the defendant waive service of process. On occasion, defendants waive their right to service and notice of suit long before a lawsuit is brought against them. Such pre-filing waiver of the right to notice may occur when a party has signed an agreement containing a "confession of judgment" clause. A confession-of-judgment clause "is the ancient legal device by which the debtor consents in advance to the holder's obtaining a judgment without notice or hearing, and possibly even with the appearance, on the debtor's behalf, of an attorney designated by the holder." *D.H. Overmyer Co. v. Frick Co. Inc.*, 405 U.S. 174, 176 (1972). When permitted by state law, it

> authorizes an attorney to confess judgment against the person or persons signing it. It is written authority of a debtor and a direction by him for the entry of a judgment against him if the obligation set forth in the note is not paid when due. Such a judgment may be taken by any person or any company holding the note, and it cuts off every defense which the maker of the note may otherwise have. It likewise cuts off all rights of appeal from any judgment taken on it.

Id. at 176 n.2. A critical issue is whether such clauses are constitutionally valid.

Underwood Farmers Elevator v. Leidholm

460 N.W.2d 711 (N.D. 1990)

VANDE WALLE, JUSTICE

Ron Leidholm appealed from an order denying his motion to vacate a judgment against him in favor of Underwood Farmers Elevator. We reverse and remand for further proceedings.

Leidholm contracted with the Elevator to deliver 25,000 bushels of oats at $1.50 per bushel. The contract did not specify a delivery date. In June 1988 Leidholm advised the Elevator that, due to drought conditions, he would be unable to deliver the oats. He requested to "buy out" his contract [by paying the difference between the contract price and] the then current market price of $1.53 per bushel. The Elevator refused. . . . Leidholm was finally allowed to buy out a month later when the price of oats had soared to $2.67 per bushel because of widespread drought conditions. Leidholm asserts that this delay caused him to incur a $29,750 liability, rather than a $750 liability if he had been allowed to buy out at $1.53 per bushel.

At the Elevator's request, Leidholm on December 28, 1988, signed a confession of judgment in favor of the Elevator for $29,750 plus twelve percent interest. Leidholm also signed a statement verifying that he had read the confession of judgment and that the statements therein were true. Leidholm now asserts that he signed the confession of judgment with the manager's assurance that it was just a formality, and that the Elevator would not attempt to collect but would later work out repayment terms, including a reduction of the amount.

Judgment was entered on the confession of judgment on May 23, 1989, and Leidholm was given notice of entry of judgment. When the Elevator sought collection of the judgment, Leidholm moved for vacation of the judgment under Rule 60(b), N.D. R. Civ. P. The district court denied the motion and Leidholm appealed.

The dispositive issue on appeal is whether there has been a sufficient showing that Leidholm voluntarily, knowingly, and intelligently waived his due-process rights to pre-judgment notice and a hearing when he signed the confession of judgment. . . .

Statutes or rules authorizing confession of judgment have historically been viewed with skepticism, and, because they are in derogation of the common law, have been strictly construed.

The United States Supreme Court has addressed due process in the context of a confession of judgment pursuant to a cognovit clause in *D.H. Overmyer Co., Inc., of Ohio v. Frick Company*, 405 U.S. 174 (1972). A cognovit clause is essentially a confession of judgment included in a note whereby the debtor agrees that, upon default, the holder of the note may obtain judgment without notice or a hearing.

The *Overmyer* Court noted that the due-process rights to notice and a hearing prior to a civil judgment may be waived. In determining the adequacy of the waiver, the Court "assumed" that the standard applicable to waiver in a criminal proceeding would apply: The waiver must be voluntary, knowing, and intelligently made. The Court further cautioned that there is no presumed acquiescence in the loss of fundamental rights.

The Court concluded that cognovit clauses are not, *per se*, violative of due process. The Court stressed that such cases should be reviewed on a case-by-case basis, with the factual setting being of paramount importance in determining whether due process is satisfied in each case.

After reviewing the factual circumstances, the Court held that Overmyer had voluntarily, knowingly, and intelligently waived its rights, and stressed that the parties were experienced business entities of equal bargaining power, the cognovit clause was clearly bargained for, and each party had been represented by counsel. The Court also noted that the applicable Ohio law provided a post-judgment hearing through which the debtor could raise defenses and seek vacation of the judgment.

The Elevator asserts that *Overmyer* is inapplicable because it involved a cognovit clause in a note, whereas this case involves a confession of judgment after default. For purposes of due-process analysis, however, we find little significant difference between the cognovit situation and the circumstances present in this case. We believe it is significant that no lawsuit was commenced before the Elevator asked Leidholm to sign the confession of judgment. Leidholm was never served with a summons and complaint, and accordingly did not receive the notice and opportunity to be heard which is part and parcel of those documents. In this respect, Leidholm was in the same position as a party to a cognovit note.

California, construing a statutory provision strikingly similar to our Rule 68(c), has held that *Overmyer* applies to this type of confession of judgment. In *Isbell v. County of Sonoma*, 21 Cal. 3d 61, 577 P.2d 188 (en banc), *cert. denied*, 439 U.S. 996 (1978), the plaintiffs were accused of fraudulently receiving excess welfare benefits. At the urging of the county, they signed confessions of judgment in the amount of the alleged overpayments. Relying upon *Overmyer*, the court concluded that a judgment entered pursuant to such a confession was constitutional only if the debtor validly waived his due-process rights to pre-judgment notice and a hearing.

We conclude that the *Overmyer* due-process analysis applies to Leidholm's confession of judgment.

In analyzing this issue, we note that the Court in *Overmyer* assumed, without deciding, that the criminal standard would apply . . . . Other courts relying upon *Overmyer* have, however, consistently applied the "voluntary, knowing, and intelligent waiver" test to due-process challenges in civil cases. We will apply the same standard in this case and, accordingly, the judgment is valid only if Leidholm voluntarily, knowingly, and intelligently waived his due-process rights to pre-judgment notice and a hearing.

The order denying the motion to vacate judgment was entered without a hearing. . . . We conclude that in order to satisfy the *Overmyer* requirement of a case-by-case, fact-specific review, it is necessary in this instance to remand to the district court for a hearing to determine whether Leidholm voluntarily, knowingly, and intelligently waived his due-process rights to notice and a hearing when he signed the confession of judgment.

The dissent contends that whether Leidholm voluntarily, knowingly, and intelligently waived his due-process rights to pre-judgment notice and a hearing when he signed the confession of judgment was not raised below. Although the motion to vacate the judgment was not phrased in those precise terms, it alleged the following reasons for relief:

"1. Defendant signed a Confession of Judgment at the request of the Plaintiff's manager because he was informed that it was the only way the Plaintiff could keep the debt on its books for any extended period of time.

"2. The manager told Defendant that they would work out the terms of payment at a later date.

"3. The Defendant erroneously believed he owed the debt for which he signed the Confession of Judgment; however, Defendant does not owe the amount set forth in the Judgment as more specifically set out in Defendant's Affidavit and the attached Brief and his belief that he owed $29,750.00 is erroneous."

In the affidavit in support of the motion Leidholm states: "The manager explained that if I signed a confession of judgment the Elevator would hold my debt until a later date when I was able to pay. He further explained that we could work out the terms of repayment at a later date."

The terminology that Leidholm did not "voluntarily, knowingly, and intelligently" waive his due-process rights to pre-judgment notice and hearing when he signed the confession of judgment was not used in the motion. But it is unduly legalistic to conclude that Leidholm was not alleging a lack of knowledge that judgment would be entered against him when he contended he signed because he believed the Elevator would hold the debt until a later date when he was able to pay and that the terms of repayment would be worked out at a later date. Those allegations belie knowledge that judgment would be entered against him without any further negotiations or proceedings. . . . Furthermore, as the Court cautioned in *Overmyer*, there is no presumed acquiescence in the loss of fundamental rights. Under these circumstances we believe the issue, although not artfully raised or briefed below, was raised sufficiently to permit us to consider it on appeal. . . . Our remand is for the purpose of permitting the trial court to consider Leidholm's motion in light of the "voluntarily, knowingly, and intelligently" standard. . . .

[The dissenting opinion of JUSTICE LEVINE is omitted.]

NOTES AND QUESTIONS

1. *Waiver of rights.* What constitutional rights does a person waive by agreeing to a confession-of-judgment or cognovit clause? Is there more at stake than just notice of suit and an opportunity to be heard? Could such a judgment be sought in a court with which defendant lacks minimum contacts? In *First Summit Bank*

v. Samuelson, 580 N.W.2d 132 (N.D. 1998), the confession-of-judgment clause provided: "The undersigned hereby authorizes and empowers any . . . attorney of any court of record within the United States or elsewhere, to appear for the undersigned, and, with or without complaint filed, confess judgment against the undersigned, . . . without any . . . right of appeal." *Id.* at 134 n.1. In terms of its effect, what is the difference between the waiver effected by a confession-of-judgment clause and that involved under Rule 4(d)? Re-read Rule 4(d) and the "Waiver of the Service of Summons" form that follows it in the supplement.

   2. *Full faith and credit.*   While confession-of-judgment or cognovit clauses are illegal in some states and heavily regulated in others, the clauses' broad wording may give the plaintiff a choice of states in which to have a judgment entered. Once a confessed judgment is entered in accord with the laws of the rendering state, it will often be enforced by other states, including those that would not have entered a judgment under the clause. *See, e.g., Dollar Sav. & Trust Co. v. Trocheck*, 725 N.E.2d 710, 713-714 (Ohio Ct. App. 1999) (honoring confessed judgment from Pennsylvania under clause that was invalid under Ohio law); *First Summit Bank, supra,* 580 N.W.2d at 137 ("Although *Leidholm* stands for the proposition that we will enforce our own requirements for confession of judgment before allowing a judgment by a court of this State to be entered, it does not translate into a holding that we will require compliance with our procedures in a foreign state, which has different procedures, before a judgment of that state may be filed and enforced in North Dakota."). However, when a sister state is asked to enforce such a judgment, if its courts conclude that the cognovit clause is invalid under the law of the state in which the judgment was entered, then it may deny full faith and credit to the judgment. *See also Gardiner v. Tallmadge,* 700 S.E.2d 755 (N.C. Ct. App. 2010), *aff'd per curiam,* 721 S.E.2d 928 (N.C. 2011) (refusing to honor Ohio confessed judgment on basis that it would be found invalid under Ohio law, even though Ohio's courts were never asked to rule on that question).

D.   Policy-Based Immunities and Exemptions

   A defendant who is served with process while physically present in the forum state is normally subject to in personam jurisdiction, regardless of whether he or she has minimum contacts with the state. *See Burnham v. Superior Court*, 495 U.S. 604 (1990), pages **232, 234,** *supra* (rejecting use of minimum-contacts test when defendant was served while briefly present in the forum state). Yet for policy reasons a court may decline to exercise jurisdiction over that defendant if he or she entered the state to participate in a legal proceeding there, or if the plaintiff lured the defendant into the state with trickery or fraud. In these situations, a court may grant the defendant immunity from service of process while present in the state.

1.   Participation in Legal Proceedings in the Forum State

As a matter of federal procedural law, a nonresident party, witness, or lawyer, who is present in the forum to participate in a federal judicial proceeding, is immune from service of process in a different case. In *Stewart v. Ramsay*, 242 U.S. 128 (1916), the Supreme Court explained that this immunity "is the privilege of the court, rather than of the defendant. It is founded in the necessities of the judicial administration, which would be often embarrassed, and sometimes interrupted, if the suitor might be vexed with process while attending upon the court for the protection of his rights, or the witness while attending to testify." *Id.* at 130. The immunity extends to pretrial proceedings, such as depositions and settlement conferences, and presumably to any court-related activities that require the individual's presence in the state. 4A WRIGHT & MILLER, *supra*, §§ 1076 & 1077.

Not all states recognize this type of immunity from service of process. *See, e.g.,* *Silverman v. Superior Court*, 249 Cal. Rptr. 724, 727 (Ct. App. 1988) (declaring that the immunity-from-service rule for nonresident parties and nonresident witnesses is "no longer the law in California"). In addition, some courts will deny a nonresident defendant immunity from service if that defendant is otherwise amendable to service under the state's long-arm statute. *See, e.g., Weichert v. Kimber*, 645 N.Y.S.2d 674 (App. Div. 1996).

2.   Trickery or Fraud

Courts usually refuse to exercise jurisdiction over a defendant who was served with process only after being lured into the state through trickery or fraud on the part of the plaintiff or her attorney. As the Mississippi Supreme Court explained:

> It is well established as a general rule that in a civil case a court will not take jurisdiction based on a service of process on a defendant who was brought within the reach of its process wrongfully or fraudulently, or by deceit or any other improper device, provided of course the wrong or deceit is chargeable to plaintiff. This rule is based not on a lack of jurisdiction but on the view that it is improper for a court to exercise a jurisdiction so obtained.

McClellan v. Rowell, 99 So. 2d 653, 656 (Miss. 1958) (refusing to exercise jurisdiction when defendant and her child had been tricked into entering state by plaintiff's false statement that the child's grandmother had suffered a heart attack, was not expected to live, and wanted to see the child before she died); *see also* RESTATEMENT (SECOND) OF CONFLICT OF LAWS § 82, comment f (1971) ("Subject to rare exceptions, a state may exercise judicial jurisdiction over all persons . . . within its territory," but "this jurisdiction is not usually exercised over a defendant who has been induced to enter the state by fraudulent misrepresentations, or through the use of unlawful force. . . . These rules, however, are not jurisdictional.").

There may be times when a plaintiff's having lured the defendant into the forum through trickery or fraud may also destroy jurisdiction. If the basis for obtaining personal jurisdiction is the defendant's physical presence in the state, the Court in *Burnham v. Superior Court*, 495 U.S. 604 (1990), suggested that exercising jurisdiction might violate due process when the defendant's presence in the state was involuntary, unknowing, or unintentional. Depending on the circumstances, a defendant who was tricked into the state by the plaintiff may be able to challenge jurisdiction on that basis, in which case dismissal would be mandatory rather than discretionary. *See, e.g., Stanko v. LeMond*, 1991 WL 152940 (E.D. Pa. Aug. 6, 1991) (holding that when defendant was lured into forum state by trickery and fraud, *Burnham* barred exercise of jurisdiction based on physical presence and that defendant did not have sufficient minimum contracts to allow exercise of long-arm jurisdiction based on prior extraterritorial service). However, if jurisdiction does not depend on the defendant's physical presence in the state, the plaintiff's use of trickery or fraud implicates policy rather than jurisdictional concerns.

Most courts allow a plaintiff to employ trickery or fraud to serve a defendant who is already in the state, even though resort to such tactics to lure a defendant into the state is generally disallowed. Does a defendant who has voluntarily entered the state have a constitutional or statutory right to avoid service? Is the same true of a defendant located outside the state? In permitting fraud or deceit to flush a defendant from hiding, courts have suggested that "there is a duty upon persons within the jurisdiction to submit to the service of process. Although that duty is not legally enforceable, it is, broadly speaking, none the less an obligation which ought not to be evaded by a defendant whom it is attempted to serve." *Gumperz v. Hofmann*, 283 N.Y.S. 823, 825 (App. Div. 1935), *aff'd*, 2 N.E.2d 687 (N.Y. 1936) (approving use of deceit to serve an Argentine physician who was visiting New York by luring him from his New York hotel room). *See also USHA Holdings, LLC v. Franchise India Holdings Ltd.*, 11 F. Supp. 3d 244, 258-261 (E.D.N.Y. 2014) (use of trickery to serve foreign defendants at a particular New York hotel permissible where trickery was not used to lure defendants into the state); *Hammett v. Hammett*, 424 N.Y.S.2d 913 (App. Div. 1980) (approving use of deception to effect service when defendant is in state of own free will).

PROBLEMS

3-8. A New York art gallery sued Daniel Moquay in a New York federal court alleging that he wrongfully interfered with the plaintiff's ability to acquire a certain painting. Moquay, a citizen of France who has a residence in Arizona, was served at Kennedy Airport in New York while changing planes on a trip from Arizona to France. Three months earlier one of the plaintiff's agents telephoned Moquay in Arizona and asked whether he would be in New York again. Moquay said he would be stopping briefly there to change planes. The plaintiff's agent asked Moquay for the arrival date and flight number, falsely stating that he wanted to discuss a settlement with him. Moquay was then served with process as he stepped off the plane in New York. He has moved to dismiss the suit, claiming that the plaintiff used fraud and deceit to obtain jurisdiction over him in New York. How should the court rule? *See American-European Art Assocs., Inc. v. Moquay*, 1995 WL 317321 (S.D.N.Y. May 24, 1995).

3-9. Mary was a passenger in a car driven by her brother, John, when the car was struck by another vehicle in Florida. John's daughter was also a passenger in the car. Mary later sued John in a Connecticut court to recover for personal injuries suffered in the accident. John, a Florida resident, has moved to dismiss Mary's suit on the ground that jurisdiction was obtained over him by trickery and fraud. In support of the motion he asserts that his daughter invited him to visit her home in Connecticut and paid his plane fare for the visit. While at her home he was served with process in Mary's suit and in a separate suit filed against him by his daughter. How should the court rule? *See McIntosh v. McIntosh*, 1996 WL 689948 (Conn. Super. Ct. Nov. 20, 1996), *aff'd per curiam*, 701 A.2d 351 (Conn. App. Ct. 1997).

E.   Notice and Hearing When Property Is Attached

The statutory and constitutional requirements for service of process are designed to afford the defendant an opportunity to contest the merits of the plaintiff's claim before the entry of judgment. Service of process rules thus reflect the "root requirement" of the Due Process Clause "that an individual be given an opportunity for a hearing *before* he is deprived of any significant property interest, except for extraordinary situations where some valid governmental interest is at stake that justifies postponing the hearing until after the event." *Boddie v. Connecticut*, 401 U.S. 371, 378-379 (1971). The "prior hearing" requirement ensures that the right to be heard is "granted at a time when the deprivation can still be prevented," for "no later hearing and no damage award can undo the fact that the arbitrary taking . . . has already occurred." *Fuentes v. Shevin*, 407 U.S. 67, 81-82 (1972).

Yet assuring a defendant the right to contest the plaintiff's claim during a lawsuit's pretrial and trial phases will not always prevent the mistaken deprivation of property. This might occur when a plaintiff seeks to attach a defendant's property at the very outset of the case, before the suit is underway. Pre-judgment attachment may be sought for any of several reasons. First, it may serve as the basis for obtaining *in rem* or *quasi in rem* jurisdiction over the defendant. Second, the plaintiff may be seeking to repossess goods that the defendant was allowed to use while purchasing them under an installment sales contract. Finally, the plaintiff may attach the property as security for a judgment she is seeking but has not yet obtained, in order to prevent the defendant from disposing of the property during the pendency of the suit. The fact that in each of these instances the defendant will eventually have a chance to be heard on the merits of the plaintiff's claim does not eliminate the need for some procedural protection in connection with a prejudgment attachment, for the attachment may in fact be mistaken or improper.

In a series of decisions in the 1970s, the Supreme Court suggested that regardless of the reason for a pre-judgment attachment, states have the option of either providing prior notice and an opportunity for a pre-seizure hearing, or of dispensing with a pre-attachment hearing and instead employing three alternative safeguards. These alternative procedures, recognized in *Mitchell v. W.T. Grant Co.*, 416 U.S. 600 (1974), and in *North Georgia Finishing, Inc. v. Di-Chem, Inc.*, 419 U.S. 601 (1975), consisted of the following: (1) the plaintiff must allege specific facts as to why attachment is warranted; (2) these allegations must be reviewed by a judge rather than by a clerk; and (3) the defendant must be afforded an opportunity for a prompt post-seizure hearing. Yet as the following case, *Connecticut v. Doehr*, 501 U.S. 1 (1991), indicates, the Court has narrowed the circumstances under which summary pre-judgment attachment is permitted. In doing so, the Court articulated a method for deciding when the *Mitchell* approach may be used in place of a pre-deprivation hearing. It appears that the new *Doehr* analysis applies to all pre-judgment seizures, regardless of the reason for the attachment.

Connecticut v. Doehr

501 U.S. 1 (1991)

JUSTICE WHITE delivered an opinion, Parts I, II, and III of which are the opinion of the Court.[*]

This case requires us to determine whether a state statute that authorizes prejudgment attachment of real estate without prior notice or hearing, without a showing of extraordinary circumstances, and without a requirement that the person seeking the attachment post a bond, satisfies the Due Process Clause of the Fourteenth Amendment. We hold that, as applied to this case, it does not.

I

On March 15, 1988, petitioner John F. DiGiovanni submitted an application to the Connecticut Superior Court for an attachment in the amount of $75,000 on respondent Brian K. Doehr's home in Meriden, Connecticut. DiGiovanni took this step in conjunction with a civil action for assault and battery that he was seeking to institute against Doehr in the same court. The suit did not involve Doehr's real estate, nor did DiGiovanni have any pre-existing interest either in Doehr's home or any of his other property.

Connecticut law authorizes prejudgment attachment of real estate without affording prior notice or the opportunity for a prior hearing to the individual whose property is subject to the attachment. The State's prejudgment remedy statute provides, in relevant part:

---

[*] THE CHIEF JUSTICE, JUSTICE BLACKMUN, JUSTICE KENNEDY, and JUSTICE SOUTER join Parts I, II, and III of this opinion, and Justice Scalia joins Parts I and III.

"The court . . . may allow the prejudgment remedy to be issued by an attorney without hearing . . . upon verification by oath of the plaintiff or of some competent affiant, that there is probable cause to sustain the validity of the plaintiff's claims and (1) that the prejudgment remedy requested is for an attachment of real property. . . ."

The statute does not require the plaintiff to post a bond to insure the payment of damages that the defendant may suffer should the attachment prove wrongfully issued or the claim prove unsuccessful.

As required, DiGiovanni submitted an affidavit in support of his application. In five one-sentence paragraphs, DiGiovanni stated that the facts set forth in his previously submitted complaint were true; that "I was willfully, wantonly and maliciously assaulted by the defendant, Brian K. Doehr"; that "[s]aid assault and battery broke my left wrist and further caused an ecchymosis to my right eye, as well as other injuries"; and that "I have further expended sums of money for medical care and treatment." The affidavit concluded with the statement, "In my opinion, the foregoing facts are sufficient to show that there is probable cause that judgment will be rendered for the plaintiff."

On the strength of these submissions the Superior Court Judge, by an order dated March 17, found "probable cause to sustain the validity of the plaintiff's claim" and ordered the attachment on Doehr's home "to the value of $75,000." The sheriff attached the property four days later, on March 21. Only after this did Doehr receive notice of the attachment. He also had yet to be served with the complaint. . . . As the statute further required, the attachment notice informed Doehr that he had the right to a hearing: (1) to claim that no probable cause existed to sustain the claim; (2) to request that the attachment be vacated, modified, or dismissed or that a bond be substituted; or (3) to claim that some portion of the property was exempt from execution.

Rather than pursue these options, Doehr filed suit against DiGiovanni in Federal District Court, claiming that [the statute] was unconstitutional under the Due Process Clause of the Fourteenth Amendment. The District Court upheld the statute and granted summary judgment in favor of DiGiovanni. On appeal, a divided panel of the United States Court of Appeals for the Second Circuit reversed. . . .

II

With this case we return to the question of what process must be afforded by a state statute enabling an individual to enlist the aid of the State to deprive another of his or her property by means of the prejudgment attachment or similar procedure. Our cases reflect the numerous variations this type of remedy can entail. In *Sniadach v. Family Finance Corp. of Bay View*, 395 U.S. 337 (1969), the Court struck down a Wisconsin statute that permitted a creditor to effect prejudgment garnishment of wages without notice and prior hearing to the wage earner. In *Fuentes v. Shevin* (1972), 407 U.S. 67, the Court likewise found a due process violation in state replevin provisions that permitted vendors to have goods seized through an *ex parte* application to a court clerk and the posting of a bond.

Conversely, the Court upheld a Louisiana *ex parte* procedure allowing a lien-holder to have disputed goods sequestered in *Mitchell v. W.T. Grant Co.*, 416 U.S. 600 (1974). *Mitchell*, however, carefully noted that *Fuentes* was decided against "a factual and legal background sufficiently different . . . that it does not require the invalidation of the Louisiana sequestration statute." Those differences included Louisiana's provision of an immediate postdeprivation hearing along with the option of damages; the requirement that a judge rather than a clerk determine that there is a clear showing of entitlement to the writ; the necessity for a detailed affidavit; and an emphasis on the lienholder's interest in preventing waste or alien-ation of the encumbered property. In *North Georgia Finishing, Inc. v. Di-Chem, Inc.*, 419 U.S. 601 (1975), the Court again invalidated an *ex parte* garnishment statute that not only failed to provide for notice and prior hearing but also failed to require a bond, a detailed affidavit setting out the claim, the determination of a neutral magistrate, or a prompt postdeprivation hearing.

These cases "underscore the truism that '[d]ue process, unlike some legal rules, is not a technical conception with a fixed content unrelated to time, place and cir-cumstances.'" *Mathews v. Eldridge*, [424 U.S. 319, 334 (1976)]. In *Mathews*, we drew upon our prejudgment remedy decisions to determine what process is due when the government itself seeks to effect a deprivation on its own initiative. That analysis resulted in the now familiar threefold inquiry requiring consideration of "the private interest that will be affected by the official action"; "the risk of an erro-neous deprivation of such interest through the procedures used, and the probable value, if any, of additional or substitute safeguards"; and lastly "the Government's interest, including the function involved and the fiscal and administrative bur-dens that the additional or substitute procedural requirement would entail."

Here the inquiry is similar, but the focus is different. Prejudgment remedy statutes ordinarily apply to disputes between private parties rather than between an individual and the government. . . . For this type of case, therefore, the relevant inquiry requires, as in *Mathews*, first, consideration of the private interest that will be affected by the prejudgment measure; second, an examination of the risk of erroneous deprivation through the procedures under attack and the probable value of additional or alternative safeguards; and third, in contrast to *Mathews*, principal attention to the interest of the party seeking the prejudgment remedy, with, nonetheless, due regard for any ancillary interest the government may have in providing the procedure or forgoing the added burden of providing greater protections.

We now consider the *Mathews* factors in determining the adequacy of the pro-cedures before us, first with regard to the safeguards of notice and a prior hearing, and then in relation to the protection of a bond.

III

We agree with the Court of Appeals that the property interests that attachment affects are significant. For a property owner like Doehr, attachment ordinarily clouds title; impairs the ability to sell or otherwise alienate the property; taints any credit rating; reduces the chance of obtaining a home equity loan or additional mortgage; and can even place an existing mortgage in technical default where there is an insecurity clause. Nor does Connecticut deny that any of these consequences occurs.

Instead, the State correctly points out that these effects do not amount to a complete, physical, or permanent deprivation of real property; their impact is less than the perhaps temporary total deprivation of household goods or wages. But the Court has never held that only such extreme deprivations trigger due process concern. To the contrary, our cases show that even the temporary or partial impairments to property rights that attachments, liens, and similar encumbrances entail are sufficient to merit due process protection . . . .

We also agree with the Court of Appeals that the risk of erroneous deprivation that the State permits here is substantial. By definition, attachment statutes premise a deprivation of property on one ultimate factual contingency—the award of damages to the plaintiff which the defendant may not be able to satisfy. For attachments before judgment, Connecticut mandates that this determination be made by means of a procedural inquiry that asks whether "there is probable cause to sustain the validity of the plaintiff's claim." . . . What probable cause means in this context, however, remains obscure. The State initially took the position . . . that the statute requires a plaintiff to show the objective likelihood of the suit's success. Doehr, citing ambiguous state cases, reads the provision as requiring no more than that a plaintiff demonstrate a subjective good-faith belief that the suit will succeed. At oral argument, the State shifted its position to argue that the statute requires something akin to the plaintiff stating a claim with sufficient facts to survive a motion to dismiss.

We need not resolve this confusion since the statute presents too great a risk of erroneous deprivation under any of these interpretations. . . . Permitting a court to authorize attachment merely because the plaintiff believes the defendant is liable, or because the plaintiff can make out a facially valid complaint, would permit the deprivation of the defendant's property when the claim would fail to convince a jury, when it rested on factual allegations that were sufficient to state a cause of action but which the defendant would dispute, or in the case of a mere good-faith standard, even when the complaint failed to state a claim upon which relief could be granted. The potential for unwarranted attachment in these situations is self-evident and too great to satisfy the requirements of due process absent any countervailing consideration.

Even if the provision requires the plaintiff to demonstrate, and the judge to find, probable cause to believe that judgment will be rendered in favor of the plaintiff, the risk of error was substantial in this case. . . . [O]nly a skeletal affidavit need be, and was, filed. The State urges that the reviewing judge normally reviews the complaint as well, but concedes that the complaint may also be conclusory. It is self-evident that the judge could make no realistic assessment concerning the likelihood of an action's success based upon these one-sided, self-serving, and conclusory submissions. And . . . in a case like this involving an alleged assault, even a detailed affidavit would give only the plaintiff's version of the confrontation. Unlike determining the existence of a debt or delinquent payments, the issue does not concern "ordinarily uncomplicated matters that lend themselves to documentary proof." *Mitchell*. The likelihood of error that results illustrates that "fairness can rarely be obtained by secret, one-sided determination of facts decisive of rights. . . . [And n]o better instrument has been devised for arriving at truth than to give a person in jeopardy of serious loss notice of the case against him and opportunity to meet it." *Joint Anti-Fascist Refugee Comm. v. McGrath*, 341 U.S. 123, 170-172 (1951) (Frankfurter, J., concurring).

What safeguards the State does afford do not adequately reduce this risk. Connecticut points out that the statute also provides an "expeditiou[s]" postattachment adversary hearing; notice for such a hearing; judicial review of an adverse decision; and a double damages action if the original suit is commenced without probable cause. Similar considerations were present in *Mitchell*, where we upheld Louisiana's sequestration statute despite the lack of predeprivation notice and hearing. But in *Mitchell*, the plaintiff had a vendor's lien to protect, the risk of error was minimal because the likelihood of recovery involved uncomplicated matters that lent themselves to documentary proof, and the plaintiff was required to put up a bond. None of these factors diminishing the need for a predeprivation hearing is present in this case. It is true that a later hearing might negate the presence of probable cause, but this would not cure the temporary deprivation that an earlier hearing might have prevented. . . .

Finally, we conclude that the interests in favor of an *ex parte* attachment, particularly the interests of the plaintiff, are too minimal to supply such a consideration here. The plaintiff had no existing interest in Doehr's real estate when he sought the attachment. His only interest in attaching the property was to ensure the availability of assets to satisfy his judgment if he prevailed on the merits of his action. Yet there was no allegation that Doehr was about to transfer or encumber his real estate or take any other action during the pendency of the action that would render his real estate unavailable to satisfy a judgment. Our cases have recognized such a properly supported claim would be an exigent circumstance permitting postponing any notice or hearing until after the attachment is effected. See *Mitchell*. . . . Absent such allegations, however, the plaintiff's interest in attaching the property does not justify the burdening of Doehr's ownership rights without a hearing to determine the likelihood of recovery.

No interest the government may have affects the analysis. The State's substantive interest in protecting any rights of the plaintiff cannot be any more weighty than those rights themselves. Here the plaintiff's interest is *de minimis*. . . .

Historical and contemporary practices support our analysis. Prejudgment attachment is a remedy unknown at common law. . . . [A]ttachment measures in both England and this country had several limitations that reduced the risk of erroneous deprivation which Connecticut permits. Although attachments ordinarily did not require prior notice or a hearing, they were usually authorized only where the defendant had taken or threatened to take some action that would place the satisfaction of the plaintiff's potential award in jeopardy. . . .

Connecticut's statute appears even more suspect in light of current practice. A survey of state attachment provisions reveals that nearly every State requires either a preattachment hearing, a showing of some exigent circumstance, or both, before permitting an attachment to take place. . . .

We do not mean to imply that any given exigency requirement protects an attachment from constitutional attack. . . . We do believe, however, that the procedures of almost all the States confirm our view that the Connecticut provision before us, by failing to provide a preattachment hearing without at least requiring a showing of some exigent circumstance, clearly falls short of the demands of due process.

IV

A

Although a majority of the Court does not reach the issue, JUSTICES MARSHALL, STEVENS, O'CONNOR, and I deem it appropriate to consider whether due process also requires the plaintiff to post a bond or other security in addition to requiring a hearing or showing of some exigency. . . .

Without a bond, at the time of attachment, the danger that . . . property rights may be wrongfully deprived remains unacceptably high even with such safeguards as a hearing or exigency requirement. The need for a bond is especially apparent where extraordinary circumstances justify an attachment with no more than the plaintiff's *ex parte* assertion of a claim. . . . Until a postattachment hearing . . . a defendant has no protection against damages sustained where no extraordinary circumstance in fact existed or the plaintiff's likelihood of recovery was nil. Such protection is what a bond can supply. . . .

But the need for a bond does not end here. A defendant's property rights remain at undue risk even when there has been an adversarial hearing to determine the plaintiff's likelihood of recovery. At best, a court's initial assessment of each party's case cannot produce more than an educated prediction as to who will win. This is especially true when, as here, the nature of the claim makes any accurate prediction elusive. In consequence, even a full hearing under a proper probable-cause standard would not prevent many defendants from having title to their homes impaired during the pendency of suits that never result in the contingency that ultimately justifies such impairment, namely, an award to the plaintiff. Attachment measures currently on the books reflect this concern. All but a handful of States require a plaintiff's bond despite also affording a hearing either before, or (for the vast majority, only under extraordinary circumstances) soon after, an attachment takes place. . . .

Nor is there any appreciable interest against a bond requirement. [The statute] does not require a plaintiff to show exigent circumstances nor any pre-existing interest in the property facing attachment. A party must show more than the mere existence of a claim before subjecting an opponent to prejudgment proceedings that carry a significant risk of erroneous deprivation.

B

Our foregoing discussion compels the four of us to consider whether a bond excuses the need for a hearing or other safeguards altogether. If a bond is needed to augment the protections afforded by preattachment and postattachment hearings, it arguably follows that a bond renders these safeguards unnecessary. That conclusion is unconvincing, however, for it ignores certain harms that bonds could not undo but that hearings would prevent. . . .

The necessity for at least a prompt postattachment hearing is self-evident because the right to be compensated at the end of the case, if the plaintiff loses, for all provable injuries caused by the attachment is inadequate to redress the harm inflicted, harm that could have been avoided had an early hearing been held. . . .

If a bond cannot serve to dispense with a hearing immediately after attachment, neither is it sufficient basis for not providing a preattachment hearing in the absence of exigent circumstances even if in any event a hearing would be provided a few days later. The reasons are the same: a wrongful attachment can inflict injury that will not fully be redressed by recovery on the bond after a prompt postattachment hearing determines that the attachment was invalid. . . .

V

Because Connecticut's prejudgment remedy provision violates the requirements of due process by authorizing prejudgment attachment without prior notice or a hearing, the judgment of the Court of Appeals is affirmed, and the case is remanded to that court for further proceedings consistent with this opinion.

It is so ordered.

CHIEF JUSTICE REHNQUIST, with whom JUSTICE BLACKMUN joins, concurring in part and concurring in the judgment.

I agree with the Court that the Connecticut attachment statute, "as applied to this case," fails to satisfy the Due Process Clause. . . . I therefore join Parts I, II, and III of its opinion. Unfortunately, the remainder of the opinion does not confine itself to the facts of this case, but enters upon a lengthy disquisition as to what combination of safeguards are required to satisfy due process in hypothetical cases not before the Court. I therefore do not join Part IV.

As the Court's opinion points out, the Connecticut statute allows attachment not merely for a creditor's claim, but for a tort claim of assault and battery; it affords no opportunity for a predeprivation hearing; it contains no requirement that there be "exigent circumstances," such as an effort on the part of the defendant to conceal assets; no bond is required from the plaintiff; and the property attached is one in which the plaintiff has no pre-existing interest. The Court's opinion is, in my view, ultimately correct when it bases its holding of unconstitutionality of the Connecticut statute as applied here on our cases of *Sniadach,*

Fuentes, *Mitchell*, and *Di-Chem*. But I do not believe that the result follows so inexorably as the Court's opinion suggests. All of the cited cases dealt with personality—bank deposits or chattels—and each involved the physical seizure of the property itself, so that the defendant was deprived of its use. . . . In the present case, on the other hand, Connecticut's prejudgment attachment on real property statute, which secures an incipient lien for the plaintiff, does not deprive the defendant of the use or possession of the property. . . .

. . . [Some courts have held] that the mere imposition of a lien on real property, which does not disturb the owner's use or enjoyment of the property, is not a deprivation of property calling for procedural due process safeguards. I agree with the Court, however, that upon analysis the deprivation here is a significant one, even though the owner remains in undisturbed possession. . . .

It is both unwise and unnecessary, I believe, for the plurality to proceed, as it does in Part IV, from its decision of the case before it to discuss abstract and hypothetical situations not before it. . . .

The two elements of due process with which the Court concerns itself in Part IV—the requirements of a bond and of "exigent circumstances"—prove to be upon analysis so vague that the discussion is not only unnecessary, but not particularly useful. Unless one knows what the terms and conditions of a bond are to be, the requirement of a "bond" in the abstract means little. The amount to be secured by the bond and the conditions of the bond are left unaddressed—is there to be liability on the part of a plaintiff if he is ultimately unsuccessful in the underlying lawsuit, or is it instead to be conditioned on some sort of good-faith test? The "exigent circumstances" referred to by the Court are admittedly equally vague; nonresidency appears to be enough in some States, an attempt to conceal assets is required in others, an effort to flee the jurisdiction in still others. We should await concrete cases which present questions involving bonds and exigent circumstances before we attempt to decide when and if the Due Process Clause of the Fourteenth Amendment requires them as prerequisites for a lawful attachment.

[JUSTICE SCALIA's concurring opinion is omitted.]

NOTES AND QUESTIONS

1. *The balancing test.*   *Doehr* adopted the three-prong balancing test from *Mathews v. Eldridge*, 424 U.S. 319 (1976), to decide when courts may use *Mitchell's ex parte* procedure instead of giving defendants an opportunity for a pre-deprivation hearing. The first two *Mathews* factors focus on the defendant. They consider the nature of the property interest of which the defendant is being deprived and the risk that an *ex parte* proceeding could impose that deprivation erroneously. These considerations are balanced against the third factor, which looks to the plaintiff's interests and asks if there are any "exigent circumstances," *Doehr*, 501 U.S. at 21, or "countervailing consideration[s]," *id.* at 14, that justify dispensing with a prior hearing. Under this balancing approach, the more serious

the deprivation to the defendant and/or the greater the risk of error from an *ex parte* proceeding, the stronger the showing the plaintiff must make to warrant dispensing with a pre-deprivation hearing.

How would the analysis in *Doehr* have differed (and which *Mathews* factors would be affected) if (a) the plaintiff had sued to collect the balance due under a written loan agreement?; (b) the plaintiff had attached the bank account defendant uses to run his business?; (c) the defendant had a history of evading his creditors; (d) the plaintiff had sued to repossess goods that defendant was buying under an installment sales contract?

2. *Security for judgment.*   In *Doehr*, the Court noted that the plaintiff attached Doehr's property as security, *i.e.*, "to ensure the availability of assets to satisfy his judgment if he prevailed on the merits of his action." *Doehr*, 501 U.S. at 16. In doing so, however, the plaintiff relied on a Connecticut statute that allowed pre-judgment attachment whenever the property attached is real estate. Other parts of the same statute allowed *ex parte* attachment if the defendant "is about to fraudulently dispose of or has fraudulently disposed of any of his property with intent to hinder, delay or defraud his creditors or . . . has fraudulently hidden or withheld money, property or effects which should be liable to the satisfaction of his debts. . . ." *Doehr*, 501 U.S. at 5 n.1. Had the plaintiff instead proceeded under one of these parts of the statute, would the security-for-judgment rationale have allowed use of the *Mitchell* approach? As Justice Rehnquist observed in *Doehr*, some states allow attachment to secure a judgment whenever the defendant is a nonresident. Should this, without more, constitute an exigent circumstance sufficient to warrant *ex parte* attachment?

3. *In rem attachment.*   In *United States v. James Daniel Good Real Property*, 510 U.S. 43 (1993), the federal government brought an *in rem* action seeking the forfeiture of a house and four acres of land in Hawaii years after its owner had been found guilty of having illegal drugs on the premises. The government seized the property, which at the time was rented out to tenants, without giving its owner prior notice or an opportunity to be heard. Upon seizure, the government allowed the tenants to remain in possession but directed that future rents be paid to the U.S. marshal. The Supreme Court held this *ex parte* procedure to be unconstitutional. Applying the *Mathews/Doehr* balancing test, the Court concluded that because there was a significant risk of erroneous attachment, the *ex parte* attachment was valid only if exigent circumstances were present. None were found to exist. As for the need to obtain in rem jurisdiction, the Court acknowledged that "seizure of the *res* has long been considered a prerequisite to the initiation of *in rem* forfeiture proceedings," but concluded that "[b]ecause real property cannot abscond, the court's jurisdiction can be preserved without prior seizure." *Id.* at 57. Instead, "[i]n the case of real property, the *res* may be brought within the reach of the court simply by posting notice on the property and leaving a copy of the process with the occupant" — "without physical seizure. . . ." *Id.* at 58. The Court also rejected the government's claim that the risk of transfer, concealment, or destruction of the property was an exigent circumstance justifying *ex parte* seizure. "To establish exigent circumstances" that would allow *ex parte* seizure, said the Court, "the

Government must show that less restrictive measures—*i.e.*, a *lis pendens*, restraining order, or bond—would not suffice to protect the Government's interests in preventing the sale, destruction, or continued unlawful use of the real property." *Id.* at 62. The Court distinguished *Calero-Toledo v. Pearson Yacht Leasing Co.*, 416 U.S. 663 (1974), a civil forfeiture action involving the *ex parte* seizure of a drug-running yacht, noting that because the property there was movable, it "might have disappeared had the Government given advance warning of the forfeiture action. . . ." *Id.* at 57; *see also United States v. Any and All Radio Station Equip. Located at 9613 Madison Ave., Cleveland, Ohio*, 218 F.3d 543, 550 (6th Cir. 2000) (declining to apply *James Daniel Good's* prior hearing requirement to *in rem* attachment of "easily moveable personal property").

James Daniel Good thus suggests that when *in rem* or *quasi in rem* actions involve real property, a defendant must be given notice and an opportunity to be heard before the property is seized, unless the plaintiff can show exigent circumstances that warrant an *ex parte* seizure. Does the case also suggest that merely giving the defendant an opportunity for a pre-attachment adversarial hearing might not suffice to satisfy due process? Wouldn't a full trial further reduce the risk of erroneous attachment, compared to a mere adversarial hearing? If procedures short of attachment are available to prevent the transfer, concealment, or destruction of the property, what exigent circumstances justify attaching the property before there has been a full trial on the merits of the plaintiff's claim? Might this suggest that pre-judgment attachment in some *in rem* cases may be unconstitutional?

4. *Attachment to satisfy a judgment.*   *Doehr* involved a plaintiff who attached the defendant's property prior to the entry of judgment. A plaintiff may also seek to attach property to satisfy or execute an *in personam* judgment that the plaintiff has already obtained. Several questions arise in this post-judgment context. First, is the defendant entitled to any additional notice and opportunity to be heard since she presumably already had notice of the suit and a chance to defend it on the merits? The answer to this question is yes. The fact that a defendant was given notice and an opportunity to be heard on the merits of the plaintiff's claim does nothing to prevent a possibly erroneous or mistaken post-judgment attachment of the defendant's property. For example, the defendant may have already satisfied the judgment, the seized property may not belong to the defendant, or the property may be legally exempt from attachment. Courts have thus uniformly held that defendants have a constitutional right to notice and an opportunity to be heard concerning the propriety of the attachment. *See, e.g., Dorwart v. Caraway*, 966 P.2d 1121 (Mont. 1998), *cert. denied*, 526 U.S. 1051 (1999); *Dionne v. Bouley*, 757 F.2d 1344 (1st Cir. 1985); *Finberg v. Sullivan*, 634 F.2d 50 (3d Cir. 1980) (en banc), *motion to vacate judgment denied*, 658 F.2d 93 (3d Cir. 1981).

Second, if there is a right to notice and an opportunity to be heard when property is attached to satisfy a judgment, may a court employ *Mitchell's ex parte* procedures, or must the defendant be given pre-attachment notice and hearing? Applying the *Mathews* balancing test, courts have been virtually unanimous in concluding that in this setting, notice and hearing may be postponed until after a defendant's property has been attached. On the defendant's side of the balance, while attachment may cause a deprivation of a valuable property interest, the risk of erroneous attachment is lower than in the pre-judgment setting since the plaintiff's claim has been adjudicated and reduced to judgment. As for the plaintiff's interests, without an *ex parte* summary attachment, there is a serious risk the defendant will secrete, diminish, or destroy the property rather than allow it to fall into the plaintiff's hands. In short, the due process is therefore satisfied if the defendant is given prompt post-seizure notice of the attachment and an opportunity for a prompt hearing at which the attachment can be challenged.

PROBLEMS

3-10. The Shawmut Bank brought a foreclosure action against Rick in a Rhode Island court to collect the amount he owed on a promissory note. The note was secured by a mortgage on Rick's Rhode Island home. Besides seeking to foreclose on the mortgage, the bank sought a deficiency judgment in case the house sold for less than the amount owed. In connection with filing the suit, the bank obtained an *ex parte* writ attaching the house. In addition, to secure the deficiency judgment, it obtained the *ex parte* attachment of a $1,000 coin collection that Rick had in the house. A state statute provides that an attachment may issue only after a judge has reviewed specific sworn allegations as to why the attachment is sought. The statute gives persons whose property is attached an opportunity to challenge the attachment at a hearing within ten days after the attachment occurs. Rick seeks to have both attachments lifted on the ground that they violate the Due Process Clause. How should the court rule? *See Shawmut Bank of R.I. v. Costello,* 643 A.2d 194 (R.I. 1994).

3-11. A municipal code provision authorizes New York City ("City") to seize the motor vehicles of those accused of driving while intoxicated (DWI) or committing other crimes for which a motor vehicle was an instrumentality. The City retains possession of the vehicle until the criminal proceedings are completed and the City decides either not to bring or loses a civil forfeiture suit. During this period, which can take months or years to complete, the owner—who may not have been the driver at the time, in which case the vehicle is usually not subject to forfeiture—is deprived of all use of a vehicle that may be essential to his or her daily life. And even if the owner were the driver, he or she may end up pleading to a lesser charge that does not trigger forfeiture. Because DWI is a misdemeanor rather than a felony, state law provides no post-arrest determination of probable cause, thus depriving the owner of any opportunity to promptly challenge the continued retention of the vehicle. Instead, the owner must wait for the City to either release the vehicle if it elects not to seek forfeiture, or raise the challenge in the ensuing forfeiture proceeding, which may not occur until long after the vehicle was seized. Seven plaintiffs whose vehicles were seized after they (or the driver of the vehicle) were arrested for DWI have sued the City under 42 U.S.C. § 1983, alleging that its vehicle seizure and retention policy violates their Fourteenth

Amendment rights by failing to provide an opportunity for a prompt post-seizure retention hearing. Under *Mathews v. Eldridge*, is the City's policy constitutional? *See Krimstock v. Kelly*, 306 F.3d 40 (2d Cir. 2002), *cert. denied*, 539 U.S. 969 (2003), *and subsequent appeal*, 464 F.3d 246 (2d Cir. 2006).

3-12. A state statute provides that a plaintiff who brings a lawsuit in which the judgment sought would affect the title to, or the possession, use, or enjoyment of real property in which the plaintiff has a preexisting interest—*e.g.*, an action to foreclose a mortgage, to quiet title, to enjoin violation of a zoning ordinance, or to enforce an easement—may file with the complaint a *lis pendens* with respect to the property. The *lis pendens* (or notice of pendency of a lawsuit) does not restrain the use or transfer of the property. Rather, it merely provides constructive notice to prospective buyers or interest holders that if they acquire the property while the suit is pending, they will take it subject to the outcome of the action. A *lis pendens* is designed to prevent a defendant from effectively nullifying a judgment in the plaintiff's favor by conveying disputed property during the pendency of a suit. While a *lis pendens* does not restrain the owner in any way, it may result in lowering the value of the property should the owner wish to mortgage or sell it while the *lis pendens* is in effect. Under state law, a *lis pendens* may be issued *ex parte*, but the defendant must be given notice within 30 days. The defendant can move to cancel a *lis pendens* on the ground that the plaintiff did not commence (or has not prosecuted) the action "in good faith"; however, a court in ruling on such a motion does not assess the merits of the plaintiff's claim or the plaintiff's likelihood of success. A defendant can move to substitute a bond for the *lis pendens* if the bond is adequate.

Several homeowners have brought a 42 U.S.C. § 1983 action against the state officials who enforce the *lis pendens* statute, alleging that it violates the Fourteenth Amendment Due Process Clause. Plaintiffs each had a *lis pendens* placed on their property by a lender, after falling behind in their mortgage payments. In several instances, the *lis pendens* was filed only after the owner had attempted to transfer the property. Plaintiffs claim that the failure to afford them notice and an opportunity to be heard before a *lis pendens* was imposed injured them in several ways: Some were denied home equity loans needed for repairs, while others had difficulty selling their property or had to do so at a reduced price, before their motions to cancel the *lis pendens* could be heard. Defendants have moved to dismiss under Rule 12(b)(6) on the basis that the *lis pendens* law passes muster under the *Mathews v. Eldridge* balancing test. They argue that the case is sharply distinguishable from *Connecticut v. Doehr*.

    A. To what extent have the plaintiffs' property interests been impaired here? How does the impairment compare with those in cases such as *Sniadach*, *Fuentes*, *Mitchell*, *James Daniel Good*, and *Doehr*? Is the impairment here sufficient to trigger the protections of procedural due process? If yes, how much weight should it be given?

    B. What is the risk of erroneous deprivation, *i.e.*, that a *lis pendens* issued *ex parte* will be imposed improperly? Under state law, when is a party entitled to a *lis pendens*? Is the risk that an *ex parte lis pendens* will be issued erroneously higher or lower than the risk of erroneous attachment in *Doehr*? To what extent would allowing a prior hearing reduce the risk of error, given the standard for obtaining a *lis pendens*?

C. What interests of private parties and of the state are furthered by using an *ex parte* procedure? To what extent would these interests be undermined if a *lis pendens* could issue only after the property owner were given notice and an opportunity to be heard?

On balance, is the state's *lis pendens* procedure constitutional under *Mathews v. Eldridge*? *See Diaz v. Paterson*, 547 F.3d 88 (2d Cir. 2008), *cert. denied*, 557 U.S. 903 (2009).

F.   Service of Process and Notice Review Problems

3-13. Alonzo, a State Y citizen, was injured while riding a roller coaster on a pier located in State X. The accident took place on January 1, 2004, and was subject to State X's one-year statute of limitations, which is tolled only by service of process. The operator and owner of the coaster, Bob, is a citizen of State X. On December 10, 2004, Alonzo filed a diversity action against Bob in a U.S. district court sitting in State X. On that same date, Alonzo's lawyer, using certified mail, mailed Bob a copy of the complaint, a "Notice of Lawsuit and Request to Waive Service of Summons" and a "Waiver of the Service of Summons," all in compliance with Rule 4(d). State X law permits service of process to be effected either by a certified mailing or by personal service. Bob received and read the materials mailed by Alonzo's lawyer on December 12. He did not, however, respond in any fashion. On January 15, 2005, Bob was personally served by a process server at great expense to Alonzo. Bob's attorney immediately filed a motion to dismiss based on the running of the statute of limitations. Alonzo responded, claiming that the certified mailing was effective as a matter of State X law. How should the court rule on Bob's motion to dismiss?

3-14. Phyllis, a resident of State X, was injured when the water heater in her home exploded. She had just recently purchased the water heater at a local appliance store in State X. The water heater was manufactured by American Radiator, Inc. ("American"), a State Y corporation. The pressure valve on the water heater was manufactured in State Z by Titan Valve, Inc. ("Titan"), a State Z corporation. Titan shipped the valve to American in State Y, where it was fabricated onto the water heater. Phyllis sued American in a State X federal court on a theory of products liability. American then brought Titan into the lawsuit pursuant to Rule 14(a), seeking indemnity from Titan and claiming that the defective Titan valve caused the explosion.

Titan was served at its headquarters in State Z by Macduff, a professional process server, who handed a copy of the summons and complaint (American's

Rule 14 complaint) to a receptionist seated in Titan's main lobby. According to Macduff, he told the receptionist, Hecate, that he was handing her legal process to be delivered to Titan's chief executive officer. Also according to Macduff, he asked Hecate if she was authorized to accept process on behalf of the corporation and she replied that she was. According to Hecate, however, Macduff simply walked in, tossed some papers at her, said, "Take these to your leader," and walked out. Hecate denies that she was authorized to accept service of process, having only been recently hired. She did deliver the papers to the chief executive officer, who received them that day. Both Macduff and Hecate have signed affidavits attesting to their respective versions of the event.

Titan, believing that service of process was ineffective, has filed a timely motion to dismiss pursuant to Rule 12(b)(5). How should the court rule on this motion? (Assume that the standards of personal jurisdiction have otherwise been satisfied.)

3-15. Carrie and Miranda own and operate a small casino in Nevada. Miranda has filed a lawsuit against Carrie in a Nevada state court in which she alleges that Carrie embezzled over $500,000 in firm assets. Miranda further alleges that Carrie used the embezzled funds to purchase a new home and that it is possible Carrie will sell that home and abscond with the money. As part of her filing, and pursuant to Nevada law, Miranda requested and received an *ex parte* attachment of Carrie's home. Such attachments must be approved by a court clerk (as it was here), and may be issued only if plaintiff attests under oath that the allegations of her complaint are true and that the assets are "at risk." Carrie was notified of the attachment when she was served with a copy of the summons and complaint. The attachment will not affect her possession or use of the home in any fashion. It does, however, prevent Carrie from transferring title or otherwise encumbering the property pending resolution of the lawsuit. Carrie can have the attachment removed by posting a bond or by demanding a hearing "to be held no later than 45 days after the service of summons." If she elects the latter course, the attachment will be lifted if Carrie shows by a preponderance of the evidence that there is no risk she will sell or encumber the attached asset. Carrie has filed a lawsuit in a U.S. district court challenging the attachment. Assuming the court has jurisdiction, how should it rule on the merits of Carrie's due process claim?

IV

SUBJECT MATTER JURISDICTION

"Jurisdiction to resolve cases on the merits requires both authority over the category of claim in suit (subject-matter jurisdiction) and authority over the parties (personal jurisdiction), so that the court's decision will bind them." *Ruhrgas AG v. Marathon Oil Co.*, 526 U.S. 574, 577 (1999). In Chapter II we looked at the statutory and constitutional principles that govern a court's ability to obtain jurisdiction over the parties to a suit. We now look at the rules that pertain to a court's subject matter jurisdiction.

Subject matter jurisdiction defines and limits judicial authority by prescribing the class of cases a particular court may hear. The boundaries of a court's subject matter jurisdiction are typically found in a constitution, a statute, or some combination of the two. And those boundaries are usually defined by reference to one or more of the following three factors: (1) the type of legal issue that may be presented; (2) a minimum or maximum amount in controversy; and (3) the characteristics of the parties to the case. "Type" refers to the nature of the controversy, *e.g.*, civil claims in general, probate proceedings, marriage dissolution, etc. The "amount in controversy" refers to the monetary value of the dispute between the parties. And "characteristics" pertain to some identifying attribute of one or more of the parties to the suit, *e.g.*, the plaintiff is the U.S. government, the defendant is a minor, etc. Thus a state statute might define and limit the subject matter jurisdiction of a family law court to cases involving marriage dissolution and child custody. Or Congress might grant federal district courts the authority to adjudicate civil cases in which the parties to the dispute are citizens of different states.

Despite the wide variety of possibilities, from the perspective of subject matter jurisdiction, there are only two types of trial courts—courts of general jurisdiction and courts of limited jurisdiction. A court of general jurisdiction is presumed competent to adjudicate all civil disputes except those specifically excluded from its authority. Many states have trial courts of general jurisdiction, such as the Superior Court in California or the Circuit Court in Illinois. Such courts exercise jurisdiction over a wide range of matters from torts to civil rights to business disputes. They may not exercise jurisdiction over cases that fall under federal patent or copyright laws since federal law specifically excludes such cases from the jurisdiction of state courts. Courts of limited jurisdiction, on the other hand, may exercise judicial power only over those subject matters that are specifically vested in them. All federal courts are courts of limited jurisdiction. They may exercise only that subject matter jurisdiction that is permitted by the Constitution and conferred on them by statute. Some state courts are also courts of limited jurisdiction, such as the family law court described in the previous paragraph.

By defining the range of cases over which a court may exercise power, subject matter jurisdiction directs cases to an appropriate forum. It also prohibits courts lacking subject matter jurisdiction from adjudicating cases outside their defined range of competence. As a consequence, the presence or absence of subject matter jurisdiction presents a critical threshold issue that must be resolved expressly or impliedly before a court proceeds to a dispute's merits. A court's lack of subject matter jurisdiction may be raised at any time during the direct proceeding, including while on appeal, and occasionally even through collateral attack made in a separate proceeding.

Subject matter jurisdiction plays a critical role within the federal judicial system. Through a combination of constitutional and statutory provisions, it defines the constitutional limits of federal judicial authority and further confines the exercise of that authority to those specific matters Congress has statutorily conferred on federal courts. There is no presumption of jurisdiction. In every case filed in federal court, the party invoking the court's jurisdiction has the burden of establishing the constitutional and statutory basis for that jurisdiction. If at any time during a proceeding filed in federal court, the court concludes that it lacks subject matter jurisdiction, it will dismiss the case. The consequence of incorrectly filing in federal court therefore can be quite costly to the client in terms of lost time, wasted resources, and perhaps even the loss of a claim.

The allocation of subject matter jurisdiction within each state judicial system is largely a product of that state's laws, with some additional limitations imposed by federal law. State judicial systems vary from the simple to the complex. Typically, a combination of state constitutional and statutory law establishes the overall architecture of the state's judicial system and provides for specific allocations of power within that system. The consequences of improperly invoking a state court's subject matter jurisdiction can be severe, though the remedy in many situations will be to transfer the case to the proper judicial forum within the state. The focus of this chapter, however, will be on federal subject matter jurisdiction.

A. Subject Matter Jurisdiction in Federal Courts

1. The Constitutional and Statutory Dimensions of Subject Matter Jurisdiction in Federal Courts

Article III of the Constitution establishes the federal judicial power and defines the entire range of circumstances under which that power may be exercised. To this end, Article III, § 1 provides: "The judicial Power of the United States, shall be vested in one supreme Court, and in such inferior Courts as the Congress may from time to time ordain and establish." U.S. CONST. art. III, § 1. This language mandates the existence of a Supreme Court and provides Congress with the discretionary power to create and design a system of lower federal courts. Article III, § 2 then lists the nine categories of "cases" and "controversies" that may be heard within the federal judicial system, namely, those

- arising under the Constitution, laws, and treaties of the United States;
- between citizens of different states;
- between a state, or citizens thereof, and foreign states, citizens, or subjects;
- affecting ambassadors, other public ministers, and consuls;
- in admiralty and maritime jurisdiction;
- to which the United States shall be a party;
- between two or more states;
- between a state and citizens of another state; and
- between citizens of the same state claiming lands under grants from different states.

U.S. Const. art. III, § 2.

The above categories define the potential and constitutionally permissible range of federal court subject matter jurisdiction, while congressionally enacted statutes specify the cases or controversies within that range that any particular federal court may in fact hear. Both elements must be satisfied before a federal court may exercise subject matter jurisdiction. In other words, an Article III federal court may only exercise subject matter jurisdiction over those matters that are both listed in Article III and statutorily authorized by Congress. The only exception to this rule pertains to the Supreme Court's original jurisdiction, which is constitutionally self-executing and requires no statutory authorization.

In contrast to personal jurisdiction, which is designed simply to protect individual litigants' interests, "[s]ubject-matter limitations on federal jurisdiction serve institutional interests. They keep the federal courts within the bounds the Constitution and Congress have prescribed." *Ruhrgas AG v. Marathon Oil Co.*, 526 U.S. 574, 583 (1999). Unlike personal jurisdiction, therefore, these constitutional and statutory limitations on federal judicial power cannot be waived. Instead, they "must be policed by the courts on their own initiative" whether or not the parties object. *Id.*

Our examination of federal court subject matter jurisdiction will focus on two particular subject matters, "federal question" cases and "diversity" cases. The first involves cases "arising under" the Constitution, laws, or treaties of the United States. The second deals with suits between citizens of different states, or between citizens of a state and citizens or subjects of a foreign country. Between them, these two categories account for almost 85 percent of the civil actions filed in federal courts, federal question cases being the slightly more numerous of the two groups. *See* Administrative Office of the U.S. Courts, Federal Judicial Caseload Statistics 2014, at tbl. C-2 (hereinafter Federal Judicial Caseload Statistics). Each of these forms of subject matter jurisdiction is authorized by Article III, and each is conferred on the federal court system by statute. Our task is to define the scope of the Article III grants of power and to learn the extent to which Congress has conferred that power on the modern federal judiciary.

2.   Federal Question Jurisdiction

Stated at its most general level, a federal question case is a case in which an issue of federal law is properly presented to a court for judicial resolution. The constitutional authority for vesting this type of jurisdiction in the federal judiciary derives from Article III, § 2's authorization of federal judicial power over cases "arising under" the Constitution, laws, or treaties of the United States. Title 28 U.S.C. § 1331, the so-called general federal question statute, confers federal question jurisdiction on federal district courts, using language virtually identical to that in Article III's arising-under clause. We will see, however, that the meanings attributed to Article III "arising under" and to statutory "arising under" differ from one another. In general, while Article III defines a broad range of federal judicial power, § 1331 has been interpreted to confer only a portion of that range on federal district courts.

a.   Article III "Arising Under" Jurisdiction

As we have already noted, Article III, § 2 of the Constitution extends federal judicial power to all cases "arising under this Constitution, the Laws of the United States, and Treaties made, or which shall be made, under their Authority." U.S. CONST. art. III, § 2. These three categories encompass the entire range of federal law possibilities, including constitutional law, statutory law, treaties, executive agreements, federal common law, federal administrative rules, and certain executive branch orders. For convenience, we will refer to these various possibilities under the collective title of "federal law." Thus Article III extends federal judicial power to all cases arising under federal law. The critical task is to discover what the cryptic phrase "arising under" means within the context of Article III.

The leading case on this subject is *Osborn v. Bank of the United States,* 22 U.S. (9 Wheat.) 738 (1824). In that case, the Bank of the United States, a private corporation chartered by an act of Congress, filed suit in a federal circuit court (one of the earliest federal trial courts) seeking to enjoin a state auditor from collecting an allegedly unconstitutional state tax on the bank. Specifically, the bank claimed that the tax violated the Supremacy Clause by obstructing the implementation of valid federal law. U.S. CONST. art. VI, cl. 2. The preliminary issue before the Court was whether the circuit court could exercise subject matter jurisdiction over the case. In an opinion by Chief Justice John Marshall, the Supreme Court upheld the circuit court's jurisdiction. In doing so, the Chief Justice first noted that the act chartering the bank conferred jurisdiction on federal circuit courts over any case to which the bank was a party.

The statutory element of jurisdiction having been satisfied, Chief Justice Marshall then considered whether the statutory grant came within the range of subject matters authorized by Article III, *i.e.,* whether the case was one arising under federal law. In answering this question in the affirmative, Marshall endorsed a broad reading of the phrase, "arising under." In his words:

> We think, then, that when a question to which the judicial power of the Union is extended by the constitution, forms an ingredient of the original cause, it is in the power of Congress to give the Circuit Courts jurisdiction of that cause, although other questions of fact or law may be involved in it.

Id. at 823. Applying this "ingredient" principle to the case before it, Marshall concluded that every case to which the bank was a party was one arising under federal law, since implicit in any such case was a question of federal law pertaining to the legitimacy and scope of the bank's federal charter. This remained so even when the federal ingredient would play no direct role in the proceeding at hand. *Id.* at 824. In other words, in any case to which the bank was a party there was an implicit federal ingredient that somehow "federalized" the case regardless of whether that ingredient was contested or was a matter of dispute between the parties. In so ruling, Marshall wrote much more broadly than necessary to resolve the case before him, as the bank's claim was itself premised on an assertion that the state tax was unconstitutional, a clear federal issue at the forefront of the litigation. But the scope of Marshall's opinion was not inadvertent, and he made the breadth of the holding clear by noting that even in cases of breach of contract that are not directly built on any question of federal law, the presence of the bank in the suit would transform the case into one arising under federal law within the meaning of Article III.

Put succinctly, under *Osborn*, a case arises under federal law for purposes of Article III whenever the original "cause" (or claim) implicitly includes a *federal ingredient*, even if that ingredient plays no active role in the pending case. The scope of Marshall's interpretation can be narrowed slightly if one takes into account the fact that the legitimacy of the Bank of the United States was a matter of considerable political and constitutional controversy at the time *Osborn* was decided. In fact, the tax imposed by the State of Maryland was itself a challenge to that legitimacy. Hence, the federal nature of the controversy was palpable. But still the language of *Osborn* is broad enough to validate any statute that confers jurisdiction on federal courts premised solely on the existence of a federal ingredient somehow blended into the background of the plaintiff's claim.

Although *Osborn*'s interpretation of Article III may seem overbroad, it makes sense from a constitutional perspective. It enables Congress to ensure that certain federal questions will always have a federal forum, even in those cases in which the federal question may play no direct part in the resolution of the case. Thus, in *Osborn*, the Court honored Congress's intent to create a federal forum that would protect the Bank of the United States, an institution that was designed to promote specific federal policies, from the potential local prejudices of state court judges. Of course, Article III does not itself vest federal district courts with such a broad-based form of jurisdiction. Rather, it merely provides Congress with the tools to do so.

The Supreme Court has never tested the limits of the *Osborn* decision, and some members of the Court have questioned the breadth of Marshall's opinion. *See Verlinden B.V. v. Central Bank of Nigeria*, 461 U.S. 480, 492-493 (1983) (discussing authorities). But one thing is clear. There is universal agreement that the Article III arising-under standard will be satisfied when the federal ingredient is itself the subject of the dispute, which was in fact the case in *Osborn* where a state law was challenged under the Supremacy Clause. *Id*. We might say, consistently with *Osborn*, that Article III arising-under jurisdiction is definitively satisfied when the case is truly about federal law, but also when federal law exists only as a potential issue lodged in the foundational background of the case.

PROBLEM

4-1. Lon was injured when the car in which he was driving overturned while he was making a routine left-hand turn. He filed suit against the vehicle's manufacturer, Fast Autos, in a state court of general jurisdiction, seeking actual damages for personal injuries and punitive damages on the theory that Fast Autos was aware of this dangerous design defect. After a jury trial, Lon was awarded $100,000 in personal injury damages and an additional $50 million in punitive damages. Fast Autos immediately filed a motion to reduce the punitive damages, arguing that the award was excessive and in violation of the Due Process Clause of the Fourteenth Amendment. The trial court rejected this argument, as did the state court of appeals and the state supreme court. Fast Autos now seeks review in the U.S. Supreme Court under a statute that provides, "Final judgments or decrees rendered by the highest court of a State in which a decision could be had, may be reviewed by the Supreme Court by writ of certiorari . . . where any title, right, privilege, or immunity is specially set up or claimed under the [U.S.] Constitution. . . ." 28 U.S.C. § 1257. Assuming the parties are from the same state, would the Supreme Court have jurisdiction over this appeal? Remember you must break down this question into its statutory and constitutional components.

b.   Statutory "Arising Under" Jurisdiction: The Federal Question Jurisdiction of U.S. District Courts

Statutory arising-under jurisdiction defines an important component of the U.S. district courts' original jurisdiction. Indeed, it addresses one of the most important functions of a federal district court, namely, the authority to hear cases involving matters of federal law and to ensure the uniform interpretation and enforcement of federal law throughout the nation. This was, after all, the primary reason the Constitution granted Congress the power to create inferior courts. What is surprising, however, is that Congress did not vest lower federal courts with jurisdiction over general federal question cases until 1875, with a minor and short-lived exception in 1801-1802.* Today, however, federal question cases make up a substantial

---

* The Circuit Court Act of 1801, adopted during the final days of President John Adams' administration, vested federal circuit courts with a broad jurisdiction over cases "arising under the constitution and laws of the United States . . . ." Act of February 13, 1801, § 11, 2 Stat. 89, 92. The newly elected administration of Thomas Jefferson saw the act as an effort by the defeated Federalist Party to create a Federalist stronghold in the judicial branch, which was largely composed of Federalist judges. Congress, at President Jefferson's request, repealed the Circuit Court Act less than a week after Jefferson took office. Act of March 8, 1802, § 1, 2 Stat. 132.

majority of all civil cases filed by private litigants in federal district courts. The range of topics falling within this realm is as extensive as the panoramic landscape of federal law.

There are a number of jurisdictional statutes that vest federal question jurisdiction in the district courts. Some of these statutes address specific areas of federal concern such as civil rights, commerce, postal laws, etc. However, most of these specific grants have been rendered redundant by 28 U.S.C. § 1331, which grants subject matter jurisdiction over federal question cases in general, regardless of the specific category of federal law.

The text of § 1331 provides in full: "The district courts shall have original jurisdiction of all civil actions arising under the Constitution, laws, or treaties of the United States." 28 U.S.C. § 1331. Given the close parallel between this language and Article III's text, one is tempted to conclude that Congress intended to confer on district courts the entire range of Article III arising-under jurisdiction as defined in *Osborn*. The modern Court, however, has been somewhat more circumspect in its interpretations of § 1331. Hence, the phrase "arising under" has two meanings, a potentially broad one, premised on Article III of the Constitution, and a more focused, statutory one, premised on § 1331.

The Foundations of Statutory Arising-Under Jurisdiction

General arising-under jurisdiction was conferred on federal courts in the aftermath of the Civil War, in part to provide a neutral federal tribunal to ensure the fair and equal vindication of federal civil rights. Act of March 3, 1875, 18 Stat. 470. The limited legislative history of the 1875 Act suggests that Congress may have meant to "confer the whole [Article III] power" on lower federal courts. 2 Cong. Rec. 4986 (1874) (remarks of Sen. Carpenter). But even so, it is doubtful that there was a congressional consensus on exactly what that "whole power" entailed. In any event, the Supreme Court's initial decisions construing the 1875 Act reflect an approach to statutory arising-under jurisdiction that is at least somewhat narrower than the Article III vision endorsed in *Osborn*. In other words, through the 1875 Act and its succeeding iterations, Congress appears to have vested less than the whole Article III power in lower federal courts. Thus, in *Little York Gold Washing & Water Co. v. Keyes*, 96 U.S. 199 (1877), the Court observed:

> Before, therefore, a circuit court can be required to retain a cause under this jurisdiction, it must in some form appear upon the record, by a statement of facts, "in legal and logical form," such as is required in good pleading, that the suit is one which "really and substantially involves a dispute or controversy" as to a right which depends upon the construction or effect of the Constitution, or some law or treaty of the United States.

Id. at 203-204; *accord Carson v. Dunham*, 121 U.S. 421, 429 (1887). Under this approach, jurisdiction could not be sustained based on a dormant question of federal law that lurked somewhere in the background of plaintiff's case. Rather, to support jurisdiction, the federal ingredient had to play an active role in the litigation. In addition, the Court's early interpretations of statutory arising-under jurisdiction made it clear that jurisdiction was to be measured solely from the perspective of the plaintiff's claim, unaided by the defendant's answer or any affirmative defenses the defendant might assert. *Tennessee v. Union & Planters' Bank,* 152 U.S. 454 (1894). Consistent with the foregoing, under the "well-pleaded complaint rule," allegations in the complaint that anticipated a federal defense would therefore not count in the jurisdictional calculus. *Louisville & Nashville Railroad Co. v. Mottley,* 211 U.S. 149 (1908). In short, the entire focus of the jurisdictional inquiry in statutory arising-under cases was on the plaintiff's unadorned claim and whether resolution of the plaintiff's prima facie claim itself depended on the construction or effect of federal law.

Shoshone Mining Co. v. Rutter
177 U.S. 505 (1900)

Mr. Justice Brewer delivered the opinion of the Court. . . .

By the Constitution (art. 3, § 2) the judicial power of the United States extends "to all cases, in law and equity, arising under this Constitution, the laws of the United States" and to controversies "between citizens of different states." By article 4, § 3, cl. 2, Congress is given "power to dispose of and make all needful rules and regulations respecting the territory or other property belonging to the United States." Under these clauses Congress might doubtless provide that any controversy of a judicial nature arising in or growing out of the disposal of the public lands should be litigated only in the courts of the United States. The question, therefore, is not one of the power of Congress, but of its intent. It has so constructed the judicial system of the United States that the great bulk of litigation respecting rights of property, although those rights may in their inception go back to some law of the United States, is in fact carried on in the courts of the several states. . . .

When in § 2326, Rev. Stat., Congress authorized that which is familiarly known in the mining regions as an "adverse suit," it simply declared that the adverse claimant should commence proceedings "in a court of competent jurisdiction."* It did not in express language prescribe either a Federal or a state court, and did not provide for exclusive or concurrent jurisdiction. If it had intended that the jurisdiction should be vested only in the Federal courts, it would undoubtedly have said so. If it had intended that any new rule of demarcation between the jurisdiction of the Federal and state courts should apply, it would likewise undoubtedly have said so. Leaving the matter as it did, it unquestionably meant

---

* [Section 2326 provided: "It shall be the *duty* of the adverse claimant, within thirty days after filing his claim, to commence proceedings in a court of competent jurisdiction, to determine the question of the right of possession, and prosecute the same with reasonable diligence to final judgment; and a failure so to do shall be a waiver of his adverse claim."—Eds.]

that the competency of the court should be determined by rules theretofore prescribed in respect to the jurisdiction of the Federal courts. . . .

In the present case, diverse citizenship does not exist. Jurisdiction must therefore depend upon the question whether the suit is one arising under the Constitution or laws of the United States.

[I]t was well settled that a suit to enforce a right which takes its origin in the laws of the United States is not necessarily one arising under the Constitution or laws of the United States, within the meaning of the jurisdiction clauses; for if it did, every action to establish title to real estate (at least in the newer states) would be such a one, as all titles in those states come from the United States or by virtue of its laws. As said by Mr. Chief Justice Waite, in *Little York Gold-Washing & Water Co. v. Keyes*, 96 U.S. 199, 203:

> The suit must, in part at least, arise out of a controversy between the parties in regard to the operation and effect of the Constitution or laws upon the facts involved. . . . Before, therefore, a circuit court can be required to retain a cause under this jurisdiction, it must, in some form, appear upon the record, by a statement of facts, "in legal and logical form," such as is required in good pleading, . . . that the suit is one which "really and substantially involves a dispute or controversy" as to a right which depends upon the construction or effect of the Constitution or some law or treaty of the United States.

The adverse suit, Rev. Stat. § 2326, is "to determine the question of the right of possession." That right may or may not involve the construction or effect of the Constitution or a law or treaty of the United States. By §§ 2319, 2324 and 2332, Revised Statutes, it is expressly provided that this right of possession may be determined by "local customs of rules of miners in the several mining districts, so far as the same are applicable and not inconsistent with the laws of the United States;" or "by the statute of limitations for mining claims of the state or territory where the same may be situated." So that in a given case the right of possession may not involve any question under the Constitution or laws of the United States, but simply a determination of local rules and customs, or state statutes, or even only a mere matter of fact.

The recognition by Congress of local customs and statutory provisions as at times controlling the right of possession does not incorporate them into the body of Federal law. . . .

Inasmuch, therefore, as the "adverse suit" to determine the right of possession may not involve any question as to the construction or effect of the Constitution or laws of the United States, but may present simply a question of fact as to the time of the discovery of mineral, the location of the claim on the ground, or a determination of the meaning and effect of certain local rules and customs prescribed by the miners of the district, or the effect of state statutes, it would seem to follow that it is not one which necessarily arises under the Constitution and laws of the United States. . . .

So, we conclude . . . that although these suits may sometimes so present questions arising under the Constitution or laws of the United States that the Federal courts will have jurisdiction, yet the mere fact that a suit is an adverse suit authorized by the statutes of Congress is not in and of itself sufficient to vest jurisdiction in the Federal courts . . . .

MR. JUSTICE WHITE did not hear the argument and took no part in the decision of this case.

MR. JUSTICE MCKENNA dissents.

NOTES AND QUESTIONS

1. *Identify the plaintiff's claim.*   The plaintiff in *Shoshone* filed an adverse claim to a mining patent, essentially arguing that he held superior title to the subject property. Property claims typically present questions of state law. Did the plaintiff's claim of ownership depend on the construction, effect, or validity of federal law? Can you imagine circumstances where that might have been the case? Would jurisdiction have been established under such circumstances?

2. *The effect of § 2326.*   Did § 2326 create a federal right of action? Did it create any right of action? If not, what did it accomplish? What might its purpose have been? To answer these questions you must carefully read the statute's text, quoted in the footnote on page 310, *supra*.

3. *The statutory arising-under standard.*   How would you characterize the arising-under standard applied by the Court in *Shoshone*? What must a plaintiff demonstrate to satisfy that standard? Would you say that the standard is centered on the claim? Is it consistent with the standard described in the introductory text preceding the case?

American Well Works Co. v. Layne & Bowler Co.
241 U.S. 257 (1916)

MR. JUSTICE HOLMES delivered the opinion of the court:

This is a suit begun in a state court, removed to the United States court, and then, on motion to remand by the plaintiff, dismissed by the latter court, on the ground that the cause of action arose under the patent laws of the United States, that the state court had no jurisdiction, and that therefore the one to which it was removed had none. There is a proper certificate and the case comes here direct from the district court.

Of course the question depends upon the plaintiff's declaration. That may be summed up in a few words. The plaintiff alleges that it owns, manufactures, and sells a certain pump, has or has applied for a patent for it, and that the pump is known as the best in the market. It then alleges that the defendants have falsely and maliciously libeled and slandered the plaintiff's title to the pump by stating that the pump and certain parts thereof are infringements upon the defendant's pump and certain parts thereof, and that without probable cause they have brought suits against some parties who are using the plaintiff's pump, and that they are threatening suits against all who use it. The allegation of the defendants' libel or slander is repeated in slightly varying form, but it all comes to statements to various people that the plaintiff was infringing the defendants' patent, and that the defendant would sue both seller and buyer if the plaintiff's pump was used. Actual damage to the plaintiff in its business is alleged to the extent of $50,000, and punitive damages to the same amount are asked.

It is evident that the claim for damages is based upon conduct; or, more specifically, language, tending to persuade the public to withdraw its custom from the plaintiff, and having that effect to its damage. Such conduct, having such effect, is equally actionable whether it produces the result by persuasion, by threats, or by falsehood, and it is enough to allege and prove the conduct and effect, leaving the defendant to justify if he can. If the conduct complained of is persuasion, it may be justified by the fact that the defendant is a competitor, or by good faith and reasonable grounds. If it is a statement of fact, it may be justified, absolutely or with qualifications, by proof that the statement is true. But all such justifications are defenses, and raise issues that are no part of the plaintiff's case. In the present instance it is part of the plaintiff's case that it had a business to be damaged; whether built up by patents or without them does not matter. It is no part of it to prove anything concerning the defendants' patent, or that the plaintiff did not infringe the same—still less to prove anything concerning any patent of its own. The material statement complained of is that the plaintiff infringes, —which may be true notwithstanding the plaintiff's patent. That is merely a piece of evidence. Furthermore, the damage alleged presumably is rather the consequence of the threat to sue than of the statement that the plaintiff's pump infringed the defendants' rights.

A suit for damages to business caused by a threat to sue under the patent law is not itself a suit under the patent law. And the same is true when the damage is caused by a statement of fact,—that the defendant has a patent which is infringed. What makes the defendants' act a wrong is its manifest tendency to injure the plaintiff's business; and the wrong is the same whatever the means by which it is accomplished. But whether it is a wrong or not depends upon the law of the state where the act is done, not upon the patent law, and therefore the suit arises under the law of the state. A suit arises under the law that creates the cause of action. The fact that the justification may involve the validity and infringement of a patent is no more material to the question under what law the suit is brought than it would be in an action of contract. If the state adopted for civil proceedings the saying of the old criminal law: the greater the truth, the greater the libel, the validity of the patent would not come in question at all. In Massachusetts the truth would not be a defense if the statement was made from disinterested malevolence. The state is master of the whole matter, and if it saw fit to do away with actions of this type altogether, no one, we imagine, would suppose that they still could be maintained under the patent laws of the United States.

Judgment reversed.

MR. JUSTICE MCKENNA dissents, being of opinion that the case involves a direct and substantial controversy under the patent laws.

NOTES AND QUESTIONS

1. Identify the plaintiff's claim.   What was the plaintiff's claim? Did the resolution of that precise claim depend on the construction, effect, or validity of federal patent law? Was it jurisdictionally relevant that the case involved a dispute about a patent? Had the plaintiff asserted a claim of patent infringement, would the arising-under standard have been satisfied?

2. The statutory arising-under standard.   Was the result in *American Well Works* consistent with the decision in *Shoshone*? Were the approaches to subject matter jurisdiction the same? If not, how do they differ? Did the Court in *American Well Works* endorse a new standard for measuring subject matter jurisdiction? If so, what is the standard?

Smith v. Kansas City Title & Trust Co.

255 U.S. 180 (1921)

Mr. Justice Day delivered the opinion of the Court.

A bill was filed in the United States District Court for the Western Division of the Western District of Missouri by a shareholder in the Kansas City Title & Trust Company to enjoin the company, its officers, agents and employees, from investing the funds of the company in farm loan bonds issued by Federal Land Banks or Joint-Stock Land Banks under authority of the Federal Farm Loan Act of July 17, 1916.

The relief was sought on the ground that these acts were beyond the constitutional power of Congress. The bill avers that the board of directors of the company are about to invest its funds in the bonds to the amount of $10,000 in each of the classes described, and will do so unless enjoined by the court in this action . . . .

Section 27 of the act provides that farm loan bonds issued under the provisions of the act by Federal Land Banks or Joint-Stock Land Banks shall be a lawful investment for all fiduciary and trust funds, and may be accepted as security for all public deposits. The bill avers that the defendant Trust Company is authorized to buy, invest in and sell government, state and municipal and other bonds, but it cannot buy, invest in or sell any such bonds, papers, stocks or securities which are not authorized to be issued by a valid law or which are not investment securities, but that nevertheless it is about to invest in farm loan bonds; that the Trust Company has been induced to direct its officers to make the investment by reason of its reliance upon the provisions of the Farm Loan Acts, especially sections 21, 26 and 27, by which the farm loan bonds are declared to be instrumentalities of the government of the United States, and as such, with the income derived therefrom, are declared to be exempt from federal, state, municipal and local taxation, and are further declared to be lawful investments for all fiduciary and trust funds. The bill further avers that the acts by which it is attempted to authorize the bonds are wholly illegal, void and unconstitutional, and of no effect, because unauthorized by the Constitution of the United States.

The bill prays that the acts of Congress authorizing the creation of the banks, especially sections 26 and 27 thereof, shall be adjudged and decreed to be unconstitutional, void and of no effect, and that the issuance of the farm loan bonds, and the taxation exemption feature thereof, shall be adjudged and decreed to be invalid . . . .

No objection is made to the federal jurisdiction, either original or appellate, by the parties to this suit, but that question will be first examined. The company is authorized to invest its funds in legal securities only. The attack upon the proposed investment in the bonds described is because of the alleged unconstitutionality of the acts of Congress undertaking to organize the banks and authorize the issue of the bonds. No other reason is set forth in the bill as a ground of objection to the proposed investment by the board of directors acting in the company's behalf. As diversity of citizenship is lacking, the jurisdiction of the District Court depends upon whether the cause of action set forth arises under the Constitution or laws of the United States.

The general rule is that, where it appears from the bill or statement of the plaintiff that the right to relief depends upon the construction or application of the Constitution or laws of the United States, and that such federal claim is not merely colorable, and rests upon a reasonable foundation, the District Court has jurisdiction under this provision.

At an early date, considering the grant of constitutional power to confer jurisdiction upon the federal courts, Chief Justice Marshall said:

> "A case in law or equity consists of the right of the one party, as well as of the other, and may truly be said to arise under the Constitution or a law of the United States, whenever its correct decision depends upon the construction of either," *Cohens v. Virginia*, 6 Wheat. 264, 379; and again, when "the title or right set up by the party, may be defeated by one construction of the Constitution or law of the United States, and sustained by the opposite construction." *Osborn v. Bank of the United States*, 9 Wheat. 738, 822.

These definitions were quoted and approved in *Patton v. Brady*, 184 U.S. 608, 611, citing *Gold Washing Co. v. Keyes*, 96 U.S. 199, 201; *Tennessee v. Davis*, 100 U.S. 257; *White v. Greenhow*, 114 U.S. 307; *Railroad Co. v. Mississippi*, 102 U.S. 135, 139.

This characterization of a suit arising under the Constitution or laws of the United States has been followed in many decisions of this and other federal courts. . . .

The jurisdiction of this court is to be determined upon the principles laid down in the cases referred to. In the instant case the averments of the bill show that the directors were proceeding to make the investments in view of the act authorizing the bonds about to be purchased, maintaining that the act authorizing them was constitutional and the bonds valid and desirable investments. The objecting shareholder avers in the bill that the securities were issued under an unconstitutional law, and hence of no validity. It is therefore apparent that the controversy concerns the constitutional validity of an act of Congress which is directly drawn in question. The decision depends upon the determination of this issue.

. . . We are therefore of the opinion that the District Court had jurisdiction under the averments of the bill and that a direct appeal to this court upon constitutional grounds is authorized.

We come to examine the questions presented by the attack upon the constitutionality of the legislation in question. . . .

. . . For the reasons stated, we think the contention of the government and the appellees that these banks are constitutionally organized and the securities here involved legally exempted from taxation, must be sustained.

It follows that the decree of the District Court is
Affirmed.

MR. JUSTICE BRANDEIS took no part in the consideration or decision of this case.

MR. JUSTICE HOLMES, dissenting. . . .

It is evident that the cause of action arises not under any law of the United States but wholly under Missouri law. The defendant is a Missouri corporation and the right claimed is that of a stockholder to prevent the directors from doing an act, that is, making an investment, alleged to be contrary to their duty. But the scope of their duty depends upon the charter of their corporation and other laws of Missouri. If those laws had authorized the investment in terms the plaintiff would have had no case, and this seems to me to make manifest what I am unable to deem even debatable, that, as I have said, the cause of action arises wholly under Missouri law. If the Missouri law authorizes or forbids the investment according to the determination of this Court upon a point under the Constitution or Acts of Congress, still that point is material only because the Missouri law saw fit to make it so. The whole foundation of the duty is Missouri law, which at its sole will incorporated the other law as it might incorporate a document. The other law or document depends for its relevance and effect not on its own force but upon the law that took it up, so I repeat once more the cause of action arises wholly from the law of the State.

But it seems to me that a suit cannot be said to arise under any other law than that which creates the cause of action. It may be enough that the law relied upon creates a part of the cause of action although not the whole, as held in *Osborn v. Bank of United States*, 9 Wheat. 738, 819-823, which perhaps is all that is meant by the less guarded expressions in *Cohens v. Virginia*, 6 Wheat. 264, 379. I am content to assume this to be so, although the *Osborn Case* has been criticized and regretted. But the law must create at least a part of the cause of action by its own force, for it is the suit, not a question in the suit, that must arise under the law of the United States. The mere adoption by a State law of a United States law as a criterion or test, when the law of the United States has no force proprio vigore, does not cause a case under the State law to be also a case under the law of the United States, and so it has been decided by this Court again and again. *Miller v. Swann*, 150 U.S. 132, 136, 137; *Louisville & Nashville R. R. Co. v. Western Union Telegraph Co.*, 237 U.S. 300, 303. See, also, *Shoshone Mining Co. v. Rutter*, 177 U.S. 505, 508, 509.

. . . I am confirmed in my view . . . that "a suit arises under the law that creates the cause of action." That was the ratio decidendi of *American Wells Works Co. v. Layne & Bowler Co.*, 241 U.S. 257, 260. I know of no decisions to the contrary and see no reason for overruling it now.

MR. JUSTICE MCREYNOLDS concurs in this dissent. In view of our opinion that this Court has no jurisdiction we express no judgment on the merits.

NOTES AND QUESTIONS

1. Identify the plaintiff's claim.   The plaintiff-shareholder in *Smith* claimed that Kansas City Title & Trust was failing to conform its conduct to the law by purchasing what he considered "unlawful" securities. This was a claim for breach of the fiduciary duty owed by Kansas City Title & Trust to its shareholders. The legal foundations for Smith's claim were in the company's charter and in applicable state law, and yet the Court held that the case was one arising under federal law. Why?

2. The statutory arising-under standard.   Did the *Smith* Court follow a similar jurisdictional analysis to the one endorsed by the Court in *Shoshone*? Assuming the respective approaches to jurisdiction were similar, is there anything that distinguishes the one case from the other? Why did Justice Holmes dissent? Did *American Well Works* establish a "creation test" as the exclusive measure of arising-under jurisdiction? If so, did the *Smith* Court overrule *American Well Works*? Or was Holmes mistaken as to the actual scope of the *American Well Works* decision?

Gully v. First National Bank
299 U.S. 109 (1936)

MR. JUSTICE CARDOZO delivered the opinion of the Court.

Whether a federal court has jurisdiction of this suit as one arising under the Constitution and laws of the United States is the single question here.

Petitioner, plaintiff in the court below, sued the respondent in a state court in Mississippi to recover a money judgment. The following facts appear on the face of the complaint: In June, 1931, the assets of the First National Bank of Meridian, a national banking association, were conveyed to the respondent, the First National Bank in Meridian, under a contract whereby the debts and liabilities of the grantor, insolvent at the time and in the hands of a receiver, were assumed by the grantee, which covenanted to pay them. Among the debts and liabilities so assumed were moneys owing to the petitioner, the state collector of taxes, or now claimed to be owing to him, for state, county, city, and school district taxes. In form the assessment was imposed upon the shares or capital stock of the bank, its surplus and undivided profits, exclusive of the value of the real estate. In law, so the pleader states, all taxes thus assessed were debts owing by the shareholders, which the bank was under a duty to pay as their agent out of moneys belonging to them, then in its possession. The new bank, in violation of its covenant, failed to pay the taxes of the old bank, which it had thus assumed and made its own. Judgment is demanded for the moneys due under the contract.

A petition was filed by the respondent for the removal of the cause to the federal court upon the ground that the suit was one arising "under the Constitution or laws of the United States." The state court made an order accordingly, and the federal District Court denied a motion to remand. Later, after a trial upon the merits, the complaint was dismissed. The Circuit Court of Appeals for the Fifth Circuit affirmed the judgment of dismissal, overruling the objection that the cause was one triable in the courts of Mississippi. The decision was put upon the ground that the power to lay a tax upon the shares of national banks has its origin and measure in the provisions of a federal statute, and that by necessary implication a plaintiff counts upon the statute in suing for the tax. Because of the importance of the ruling, this Court granted certiorari, "limited to the question of the jurisdiction of the District Court."

How and when a case arises "under the Constitution or laws of the United States" has been much considered in the books. Some tests are well established. To bring a case within the statute, a right or immunity created by the Constitution or laws of the United States must be an element, and an essential one, of the plaintiff's cause of action. *Starin v. New York*, 115 U.S. 248, 257; *First National Bank v. Williams*, 252 U.S. 504, 512. The right or immunity must be such that it will be supported if the Constitution or laws of the United States are given one construction or effect, and defeated if they receive another. A genuine and present controversy, not merely a possible or conjectural one, must exist with reference thereto, and the controversy must be disclosed upon the face of the complaint, unaided by the answer or by the petition for removal. (*Tennessee v. Union & Planters' Bank*, 152 U.S. 454; *Louisville & Nashville R. Co. v. Mottley*, 211 U.S. 149). Indeed, the complaint itself will not avail as a basis of jurisdiction in so far as it goes beyond a statement of the plaintiff's cause of action and anticipates or replies to a probable defense.

Looking backward we can see that the early cases were less exacting than the recent ones in respect of some of these conditions. If a federal right was pleaded, the question was not always asked whether it was likely to be disputed. This is seen particularly in suits by or against a corporation deriving its charter from an act of Congress. *Osborn v. Bank of the United States*, 9 Wheat. 738, 817-828. Modern statutes have greatly diminished the importance of those decisions by narrowing their scope. Federal incorporation is now abolished as a ground of federal jurisdiction except where the United States holds more than one-half the stock. Partly under the influence of statutes disclosing a new legislative policy, partly under the influence of more liberal decisions, the probable course of the trial, the real substance of the controversy, has taken on a new significance. "A suit to enforce a right which takes its origin in the laws of the United States is not necessarily, or for that reason alone, one arising under those laws, for a suit does not so arise unless it really and substantially involves a dispute or controversy respecting the validity, construction, or effect of such a law, upon the determination of which the result depends." *Shulthis v. McDougal*, 225 U.S. 561, 569; . . . *Shoshone Mining Co. v. Rutter*, 177 U.S. 505, 507 . . . .

Viewing the case at hand against this background of established principle, we do not find in it the elements of federal jurisdiction.

1. The suit is built upon a contract which in point of obligation has its genesis in the law of Mississippi. A covenant for a valuable consideration to pay another's debts is valid and enforceable without reference to a federal law. For all that the complaint informs us, the failure to make payment was owing to lack of funds or to a belief that a stranger to the contract had no standing as a suitor or to other objections nonfederal in their nature. There is no necessary connection between the enforcement of such a contract according to its terms and the existence of a controversy arising under federal law.

2. The obligation of the contract being a creation of the state, the question remains whether the plaintiff counts upon a federal right in support of his claim that the contract has been broken. The performance owing by the defendant was payment of the valid debts, and taxes are not valid debts unless lawfully imposed. From this defendant argues that a federal controversy exists, the tax being laid upon a national bank or upon the shareholders therein, and for that reason being void unless permitted by the federal law.

Not every question of federal law emerging in a suit is proof that a federal law is the basis of the suit. The tax here in controversy, if valid as a tax at all, was imposed under the authority of a statute of Mississippi. The federal law did not attempt to impose it or to confer upon the tax collector authority to sue for it. True, the tax, though assessed through the action of the state, must be consistent with the federal statute consenting, subject to restrictions, that such assessments may be made. It must also be consistent with the Constitution of the United States. If there were no federal law permitting the taxation of shares in national banks, a suit to recover such a tax would not be one arising under the Constitution of the United States, though the bank would have the aid of the Constitution when it came to its defense. . . . *Louisville & Nashville R. Co. v. Mottley, supra*. That there is a federal law permitting such taxation does not change the basis of the suit, which is still the statute of the state, though the federal law is evidence to prove the statute valid.

The argument for the respondent proceeds on the assumption that, because permission at times is preliminary to action, the two are to be classed as one. But the assumption will not stand. A suit does not arise under a law renouncing a defense, though the result of the renunciation is an extension of the area of legislative power which will cause the suitor to prevail. Let us suppose an amendment of the Constitution by which the states are left at liberty to levy taxes on the income derived from federal securities, or to lay imposts and duties at their pleasure upon imports and exports. If such an amendment were adopted, a suit to recover taxes or duties imposed by the state law would not be one arising under the Constitution of the United States, though in the absence of the amendment the duty or the tax would fail. We recur to the test announced in *Puerto Rico v. Russell & Co.*: "The federal nature of the right to be established is decisive — not the source of the authority to establish it." Here the right to be established is one created by the state. If that is so, it is unimportant that federal consent is the source of state authority. To reach the underlying law we do not travel back so far. By unimpeachable authority, a suit brought upon a state statute does not arise under an act of Congress or the Constitution of the United States because prohibited thereby. *Louisville & Nashville R. Co. v. Mottley, supra.* With no greater reason can it be said to arise thereunder because permitted thereby.

Another line of reasoning will lead us to the same conclusion. The Mississippi law provides, in harmony with the act of Congress, that a tax upon the shares of national banks shall be assessed upon the shareholders, though the bank may be liable to pay it as their agent, charging their account with moneys thus expended. Petitioner will have to prove that the state law has been obeyed before the question will be reached whether anything in its provisions or in administrative conduct under it is inconsistent with the federal rule. If what was done by the taxing officers in levying the tax in suit did not amount in substance under the law of Mississippi to an assessment of the shareholders, but in substance as well as in form was an assessment of the bank alone, the conclusion will be inescapable that there was neither tax nor debt, apart from any barriers that Congress may have built. On the other hand, a finding upon evidence that the Mississippi law has been obeyed may compose the controversy altogether, leaving no room for a contention that the federal law has been infringed. The most one can say is that a question of federal law is lurking in the background, just as farther in the background there lurks a question of constitutional law, the question of state power in our federal form of government. A dispute so doubtful and conjectural, so far removed from plain necessity, is unavailing to extinguish the jurisdiction of the states.

This Court has had occasion to point out how futile is the attempt to define a "cause of action" without reference to the context. To define broadly and in the abstract "a case arising under the Constitution or laws of the United States" has hazards of a kindred order. What is needed is something of that common-sense accommodation of judgment to kaleidoscopic situations which characterizes the law in its treatment of problems of causation. One could carry the search for causes backward, almost without end. Instead, there has been a selective process which picks the substantial causes out of the web and lays the other ones aside. As in problems of causation, so here in the search for the underlying law. If we follow the ascent far enough, countless claims of right can be discovered to have their source or their operative limits in the provisions of a federal statute or in the Constitution itself with its circumambient restrictions upon legislative power. To set bounds to the pursuit, the courts have formulated the distinction between controversies that are basic and those that are collateral, between disputes that are necessary and those that are merely possible. We shall be lost in a maze if we put that compass by.

The judgment should be reversed and the cause remitted to the District Court, with instructions to remand it to the court in Mississippi from which it was removed.

Reversed.

MR. JUSTICE STONE took no part in the consideration or decision of this case.

NOTES AND QUESTIONS

1. The standard to be applied.   Re-read the fourth and fifth paragraphs of the Court's opinion. They purport to describe the standards for statutory arising-under jurisdiction. Would this standard validate the exercise of jurisdiction in *Smith*? Would it have altered the results in *Shoshone* and *American Well Works*?

2. The standard applied.   Notice that Justice Cardozo carefully identified the plaintiff's claim. What was that claim? Was the claim a product of state law or federal law? Did the resolution of the claim depend on the construction, validity, or effect of federal law? The Court seems to agree that there was a potential federal issue lurking in the background of the case. What was that issue and why was it not sufficient to validate the exercise of jurisdiction? Was that finding of insufficiency a rebuke of the decision in *Osborn v. United States*? Or can the two cases be distinguished?

PROBLEMS

4-2. Eric commutes daily through the City of Beverly Glen. Over the past six months, he has been stopped eight times by members of the Beverly Glen Police Department, yet never once has he been cited for a traffic infraction or any other illegal activity. His car, however, was searched on four of these occasions. Eric claims that the city has adopted a policy of racial profiling under which African-American males between the ages of 18 and 30 years of age, a category into which Eric falls, are routinely stopped for "investigatory purposes." Eric has filed suit against the city in federal district court. He claims a violation of his equal protection rights under the Fourteenth Amendment and seeks an injunction against the practice of racial profiling. His claim for relief is premised on 42 U.S.C. § 1983, which provides that certain persons acting under color of state law, including a city or a county, who deprive another person of a constitutional right "shall be liable to the party injured in an action at law, suit in equity, or other proper proceeding for redress." Does Eric's civil rights claim arise under federal law within the meaning of § 1331?

4-3. Duke was injured while traveling on the A-Train, a passenger train owned and operated by Railways, Inc. He released his claim against Railways in consideration for a promise that Railways would provide him free transportation for life. Railways honored this obligation until Congress passed a statute that prohibited railroads from providing free transportation. When Railways refused to honor its agreement with Duke, he sued Railways in a federal district court claiming breach of contract. His complaint correctly predicted that Railways would interpose the federal statute as an affirmative defense. He also asserted that application of the statute to his agreement would violate the Fifth Amendment to the U.S. Constitution as an uncompensated taking of his property. Does Duke's breach of contract claim arise under federal law within the meaning of § 1331? *See Louisville & Nashville Railroad Co. v. Mottley*, 211 U.S. 149 (1908).

4-4. Ormet, Inc. has filed a breach of contract action against Ohio Power (OP) in federal court, alleging that OP failed to transfer to it certain "emission allowances" issued to OP by the federal Environmental Protection Agency (EPA) as part of the Acid Rain Program. The allowances are extremely valuable for they permit their owner to emit air pollutants that would otherwise exceed federally imposed limits. According to Ormet, it agreed to buy electrical power from OP's West Virginia generating plant, in exchange for which Ormet agreed to pay a proportionate share of the plant's operating and maintenance expenses. Ormet's complaint alleged that since it was paying a share of OP's plant expenses, under § 408(i) of the federal Clean Air Act, it was entitled to a proportionate share of the emission allowance that the EPA had issued OP for that plant. Ormet further alleged that the failure to convey these emission allowances was a breach of the underlying contract. Does Ormet's breach of contract action arise under federal law within the meaning of § 1331? *See Ormet Corp. v. Ohio Power Co.*, 98 F.3d 799 (4th Cir. 1996).

A NOTE ON DECLARATORY JUDGMENTS AND STATUTORY ARISING-UNDER JURISDICTION

A declaratory judgment is a statutorily created remedy that allows a court to declare the parties' rights and obligations without imposing any form of coercive relief such as monetary damages or an injunction. The underlying presumption is that the parties will abide by the court's judgment announcing what their respective rights and duties are. Either side of a controversy may file an action for declaratory relief. Thus, suppose A asserts that certain conduct B is about to engage in will breach a contract that exists between them. B denies that the conduct will have this effect. Either A or B may file an action for declaratory relief. Whoever prevails will be awarded a favorable and binding declaration as to the legality of the challenged conduct.

The Declaratory Judgment Act, 28 U.S.C. §§ 2201-2202, vests federal district courts with the power to enter declaratory judgments in cases over which they would otherwise have jurisdiction. The Declaratory Judgment Act does not, however, expand subject matter jurisdiction. *See Skelly Oil Co. v. Phillips Petroleum Co.*, 339 U.S. 667, 673-674 (1950). Whether an action for declaratory relief arises under federal law for purposes of § 1331 depends on whether it would have so arisen if one of the parties had been seeking coercive relief—*i.e.*, monetary damages or an injunction. We must therefore determine which of the parties would have been the plaintiff in a coercive suit for damages or an injunction on the same issues, and then ask whether that suit would have arisen under federal law by virtue of either the creation test or the essential federal ingredient test. *See ABB Inc. v. Cooper Indus., LLC*, 635 F.3d 1345, 1349-1351 (Fed. Cir. 2011).

For example, suppose Jerry claims that the Kramer Company has violated the federal Clean Air Act (CAA) by emitting pollutants into the ambient air surrounding Jerry's community. Assume also that the CAA creates a private right of action permitting persons such as Jerry to seek injunctive relief for violations of the act and that Jerry threatens such a suit. May Kramer file a claim for declaratory relief in federal court? Yes. The potential plaintiff in a coercive suit under the CAA would be Jerry, who could seek an injunction. Jerry's hypothetical well-pleaded complaint would state a claim arising under federal law since the CAA creates Jerry's cause of action.

On the other hand, suppose Jerry relied only on a state environmental statute and that Kramer, in seeking declaratory relief, asked the court to rule that its federally issued license preempts the state law. Under the preemption doctrine, a product of the Supremacy Clause of the Constitution (art. VI, § 2), valid federal law trumps any state law to the contrary. In most cases, preemption operates as an affirmative defense to a state-law claim. Will Kramer's suit for declaratory relief arise under federal law? No. Even though Kramer raises a federal issue in its complaint for declaratory relief—the preemption issue—that issue would arise only as a defense in a coercive suit and therefore cannot serve as a basis for statutory arising-under jurisdiction. This is because, as we have seen in the several cases above, the determination of subject matter jurisdiction focuses on the complaint only (the "well-pleaded complaint" rule). The potential plaintiff in a coercive suit would still be Jerry, but his claim is now state created and no federal issues would be part of his well-pleaded complaint.

PROBLEMS

4-5. Cooper is the registered owner of a federal patent that uses dielectric fluid to insulate electrical transformers. ABB produces a vegetable oil version of dielectric fluid that operates in a similar fashion. When Cooper learned that ABB had contacted Dow Chemical Co. to manufacture ABB's vegetable-oil dielectric fluid, Cooper wrote to Dow noting a potential infringement of the Cooper patent and advising: "We wish to formally put Dow on notice that Cooper will vigorously defend its rights should Dow attempt to make products covered by one or more of Cooper's patents." ABB then filed a declaratory judgment action against Cooper in a federal court, seeking a declaration that its product "does not infringe, and has not infringed directly, indirectly, willfully or otherwise, any valid enforceable claim" of the Cooper dielectric-fluid patent. Cooper filed a Rule 12(b)(1) motion to dismiss, arguing that ABB has not itself asserted a claim arising under federal patent laws. (Note: 28 U.S.C. § 1338(a) vests federal courts with exclusive jurisdiction over cases arising under federal patent laws; you may assume that the phrase "arising under" as used in § 1338(a) operates in the same fashion as that phrase operates in § 1331.) What should the district court do? *See ABB Inc. v. Cooper Indus., LLC,* 635 F.3d 1345 (Fed. Cir. 2011).

4-6. Opera Plaza is a privately owned condominium complex. The Opera Plaza Residential Parcel Homeowners Association ("Association") has authority to create and enforce covenants, conditions, and restrictions pertaining to the common areas of the complex. One such restriction prohibits the placement of satellite dishes in common areas of a condominium complex. The Hoangs, who own an Opera Plaza condominium unit, installed a satellite dish in a common area on the exterior of that unit. In so doing, they contended that the satellite-dish restriction was inconsistent with regulations issued by the Federal Communications Commission (FCC). In essence, they contended that the state laws permitting the restriction were preempted by FCC regulations. The Association, asserting jurisdiction under § 1331, sued the Hoangs in federal court. The Association sought an injunction and damages for breach of contract, as well as a declaration that FCC regulations did not bar the satellite-dish restriction. (You may assume that the FCC regulations do not support a private right of action.) The Hoangs have filed a motion to dismiss under Rule 12(b)(1). How should the court rule? *See Opera Plaza Residential Parcel Homeowners Assn. v. Hoang*, 376 F.3d 831 (9th Cir. 2004).

A NOTE ON CONCURRENT AND EXCLUSIVE FEDERAL QUESTION JURISDICTION

State courts, and particularly state courts of general jurisdiction, are presumptively competent to adjudicate cases arising under federal law. Indeed, until the enactment of § 1331 in 1875, state courts had exclusive jurisdiction over most federal question cases. With passage of the Act of 1875, jurisdiction over such cases became concurrent between state and federal courts. That remains true today. In most federal question cases, the litigants have a choice between a federal and a state forum. Congress may rebut this presumption of concurrent jurisdiction by granting federal courts exclusive jurisdiction over any or all cases arising under federal law. A grant of exclusive jurisdiction divests state courts of authority over all cases falling within the specified exclusive realm. *Tafflin v. Levitt*, 493 U.S. 455, 458-459 (1990). Congress has granted federal courts exclusive jurisdiction over only a few types of federal question cases. *See, e.g.*, 28 U.S.C. § 1333 (admiralty, maritime, and prize cases); § 1334 (bankruptcy); § 1338 (patents and copyrights). As a consequence, state courts are without jurisdiction to preside over such cases. Jurisdiction over the vast majority of federal question cases, however, remains concurrent between state and federal courts.

Where state courts have concurrent jurisdiction over federal claims, they may not refuse to exercise that jurisdiction if the federal claim falls within the general range of matters that the state court is otherwise empowered to hear. Essentially, the Supremacy Clause, article VI, clause 2, imposes on "the Judges in every State" an obligation to adjudicate federal cases that fall within their general range of competence. U.S. CONST. art. VI, cl. 2. A state court of general jurisdiction therefore may not decline to hear a federal civil claim if the only basis for doing so is the federal nature of the claim. *See Howlett v. Rose*, 496 U.S. 356, 380-381 (1990).

The Modern Approach to Statutory Arising-Under Jurisdiction

In *Franchise Tax Board v. Construction Laborers Vacation Trust*, 463 U.S. 1 (1983), the Supreme Court summarized the law of statutory arising-under jurisdiction as it stood in 1983:

> The most familiar definition of the statutory "arising under" limitation is Justice Holmes' statement, "A suit arises under the law that creates the cause of action." *American Well Works Co. v. Layne & Bowler Co.*, 241 U.S. 257, 260 (1916). However, it is well settled that Justice Holmes' test is more useful for describing the vast majority of cases that come within the district courts' original jurisdiction than it is for describing which cases are beyond district court jurisdiction. We have often held that a case "arose under" federal law where the vindication of a right under state law necessarily turned on some construction of federal law, see, *e.g.*, *Smith v. Kansas City Title & Trust Co.*, 255 U.S. 1807 (1921); *Hopkins v. Walker*, 244 U.S. 486 (1917). Leading commentators have suggested that for purposes of § 1331 an action "arises under" federal law "if in order for the plaintiff to secure the relief sought he will be obliged to establish both the correctness and the applicability to his case of a proposition of federal law." P. Bator, P. Mishkin, D. Shapiro & H. Wechsler, Hart & Wechsler's The Federal Courts and the Federal System 889 (2d ed. 1973).
>
> One powerful doctrine has emerged, however—the "well-pleaded complaint" rule—which as a practical matter severely limits the number of cases in which state law "creates the cause of action" that may be initiated in or removed to federal district court, thereby avoiding more-or-less automatically a number of potentially serious federal-state conflicts.
>
> > [W]hether a case is one arising under the Constitution or a law or treaty of the United States, in the sense of the jurisdictional statute, . . . must be determined from what necessarily appears in the plaintiff's statement of his own claim in the bill or declaration, unaided by anything alleged in anticipation of avoidance of defenses which it is thought the defendant may interpose. *Taylor v. Anderson*, 234 U.S. 74, 75-76 (1914).
>
> Thus, a federal court does not have original jurisdiction over a case in which the complaint presents a state-law cause of action, but also asserts that federal law deprives the defendant of a defense he may raise, *Taylor v. Anderson, supra*; *Louisville & Nashville R. Co. v. Mottley*, 211 U.S. 149 (1908), or that a federal defense the defendant may raise is not sufficient to defeat the claim, *Tennessee v. Union & Planters' Bank*, 152 U.S. 454 (1894). "Although such allegations show that very likely, in the course of the litigation, a question under the Constitution would arise, they do not show that the suit, that is, the plaintiff's original cause of action, arises under the Constitution." *Louisville & Nashville R. Co. v. Mottley, supra*, 211 U.S., at 152. . . . "[A] right or immunity created by the Constitution or laws of the United States must be an element, and an essential one, of the plaintiff's cause of action." *Gully v. First National Bank*, 299 U.S. 109, 112 (1936).

483 U.S. at 8-10.

The above description should have a familiar feel. To satisfy statutory arising-under jurisdiction, the plaintiff's claim must depend on the construction, validity, or effect of federal law. This formula is elegant and sufficient to guide the subject matter jurisdiction analysis. However, by dividing the jurisdictional landscape into two distinct fields—cases that fall within the "creation test" and those that involve an essential federal ingredient—the *Franchise Tax Board* Court introduced a mechanical distinction into the formula. The *Franchise Tax Board* Court also added an additional policy wrinkle to arising-under standards. In the Court's words: "We have always interpreted . . . 'the current of jurisdictional legislation since the Act of March 3, 1875,' with an eye to practicality and necessity." 463 U.S. at 20 (quoting *Skelly Oil Co. v. Phillips Petroleum Co.*, 339 U.S. 667, 673 (1950)). On its face, this observation may seem innocuous but, in effect, it creates a potential policy-based trump on the exercise of federal question jurisdiction, which has now been folded into the arising-under doctrine. *See* Simona Grossi, *A Modified Theory of the Law of Federal Courts: The Case of Arising Under Jurisdiction*, 88 WASH. L. REV. 961, 987-990 (2013).

Gunn v. Minton

133 S. Ct. 1059 (2013)

CHIEF JUSTICE ROBERTS delivered the opinion of the Court.

Federal courts have exclusive jurisdiction over cases "arising under any Act of Congress relating to patents." 28 U.S.C. § 1338(a). The question presented is whether a state law claim alleging legal malpractice in the handling of a patent case must be brought in federal court.

I

In the early 1990s, respondent Vernon Minton developed a computer program and telecommunications network designed to facilitate securities trading. In March 1995, he leased the system—known as the Texas Computer Exchange Network, or TEXCEN—to R.M. Stark & Co., a securities brokerage. A little over a year later, he applied for a patent for an interactive securities trading system that was based substantially on TEXCEN. The U.S. Patent and Trademark Office issued the patent in January 2000.

Patent in hand, Minton filed a patent infringement suit in Federal District Court against the National Association of Securities Dealers, Inc. (NASD) and the NASDAQ Stock Market, Inc. He was represented by Jerry Gunn and the other petitioners. NASD and NASDAQ moved for summary judgment on the ground that Minton's patent was invalid under the "on sale" bar, 35 U.S.C. § 102(b). That provision specifies that an inventor is not entitled to a patent if "the invention was . . . on sale in [the United States], more than one year prior to the date of the application," and Minton had leased TEXCEN to Stark more than one year prior to filing his patent application. Rejecting Minton's argument that there were differences between TEXCEN and the patented system that precluded application of the on-sale bar, the District Court granted the summary judgment motion and declared Minton's patent invalid.

Minton then filed a motion for reconsideration in the District Court, arguing for the first time that the lease agreement with Stark was part of ongoing testing of TEXCEN and therefore fell within the "experimental use" exception to the on-sale bar. The District Court denied the motion.

Minton appealed to the U.S. Court of Appeals for the Federal Circuit. That court affirmed, concluding that the District Court had appropriately held Minton's experimental-use argument waived.

Minton, convinced that his attorneys' failure to raise the experimental-use argument earlier had cost him the lawsuit and led to invalidation of his patent, brought this malpractice action in Texas state court. His former lawyers defended on the ground that the lease to Stark was not, in fact, for an experimental use, and that therefore Minton's patent infringement claims would have failed even if the experimental-use argument had been timely raised. The trial court agreed, holding that Minton had put forward "less than a scintilla of proof" that the lease had been for an experimental purpose. It accordingly granted summary judgment to Gunn and the other lawyer defendants.

On appeal, Minton raised a new argument: Because his legal malpractice claim was based on an alleged error in a patent case, it "aris[es] under" federal patent law for purposes of 28 U.S.C. § 1338(a). And because, under § 1338(a), "[n]o State court shall have jurisdiction over any claim for relief arising under any Act of Congress relating to patents," the Texas court—where Minton had originally brought his malpractice claim—lacked subject matter jurisdiction to decide the case. Accordingly, Minton argued, the trial court's order should be vacated and the case dismissed, leaving Minton free to start over in the Federal District Court.

A divided panel of the Court of Appeals of Texas rejected Minton's argument. Applying the test we articulated in *Grable & Sons Metal Products, Inc. v. Darue Engineering & Mfg.*, 545 U.S. 308, 314 (2005), it held that the federal interests implicated by Minton's state law claim were not sufficiently substantial to trigger § 1338 "arising under" jurisdiction. It also held that finding exclusive federal jurisdiction over state legal malpractice actions would, contrary to Grable's commands, disturb the balance of federal and state judicial responsibilities. Proceeding to the merits of Minton's malpractice claim, the Court of Appeals affirmed the trial court's determination that Minton had failed to establish experimental use and that arguments on that ground therefore would not have saved his infringement suit.

The Supreme Court of Texas reversed . . . . The Court concluded that Minton's claim involved a "substantial federal issue" within the meaning of *Grable* [and that his case therefore fell within the exclusive jurisdiction of the federal courts]. . . .

We granted certiorari.

II

"Federal courts are courts of limited jurisdiction," possessing "only that power authorized by Constitution and statute." There is no dispute that the Constitution permits Congress to extend federal court jurisdiction to a case such as this one, *see Osborn v. Bank of United States*, 9 Wheat. 738, 823-824 (1824); the question is whether Congress has done so.

As relevant here, Congress has authorized the federal district courts to exercise original jurisdiction in "all civil actions arising under the Constitution, laws, or treaties of the United States," 28 U.S.C. § 1331, and, more particularly, over "any civil action arising under any Act of Congress relating to patents," § 1338(a). Adhering to the demands of "[l]inguistic consistency," we have interpreted the phrase "arising under" in both sections identically, applying our § 1331 and § 1338(a) precedents interchangeably. For cases falling within the patent-specific arising under jurisdiction of §1338(a), however, Congress has not only provided for federal jurisdiction but also eliminated state jurisdiction, decreeing that "[n]o State court shall have jurisdiction over any claim for relief arising under any Act of Congress relating to patents." § 1338(a) (2006 ed., Supp. V). To determine whether jurisdiction was proper in the Texas courts, therefore, we must determine whether it would have been proper in a federal district court—whether, that is, the case "aris[es] under any Act of Congress relating to patents."

For statutory purposes, a case can "aris[e] under" federal law in two ways. Most directly, a case arises under federal law when federal law creates the cause of action asserted. See *American Well Works Co. v. Layne & Bowler Co.*, 241 U.S. 257, 260 (1916) ("A suit arises under the law that creates the cause of action"). As a rule of inclusion, this "creation" test admits of only extremely rare exceptions, *see, e.g., Shoshone Mining Co. v. Rutter*, 177 U.S. 505 (1900), and accounts for the vast bulk of suits that arise under federal law. Minton's original patent infringement suit against NASD and NASDAQ, for example, arose under federal law in this manner because it was authorized by 35 U.S.C. §§ 271, 281.

But even where a claim finds its origins in state rather than federal law—as Minton's legal malpractice claim indisputably does—we have identified a "special and small category" of cases in which arising under jurisdiction still lies. In outlining the contours of this slim category, we do not paint on a blank canvas. Unfortunately, the canvas looks like one that Jackson Pollock got to first.

In an effort to bring some order to this unruly doctrine several Terms ago, we condensed our prior cases into the following inquiry: Does the "state law claim necessarily raise a stated federal issue, actually disputed and substantial, which a federal forum may entertain without disturbing any congressionally approved balance of federal and state judicial responsibilities"? *Grable*, 545 U.S., at 314. That is, federal jurisdiction over a state law claim will lie if a federal issue is: (1) necessarily raised, (2) actually disputed, (3) substantial, and (4) capable of resolution in federal court without disrupting the federal-state balance approved by Congress. Where all four of these requirements are met, we held, jurisdiction is proper because there is a "serious federal interest in claiming the advantages thought to be inherent in a federal forum," which can be vindicated without disrupting Congress's intended division of labor between state and federal courts.

III

Applying *Grable*'s inquiry here, it is clear that Minton's legal malpractice claim does not arise under federal patent law. Indeed, for the reasons we discuss, we are comfortable concluding that state legal malpractice claims based on underlying patent matters will rarely, if ever, arise under federal patent law for purposes of § 1338(a). Although such cases may necessarily raise disputed questions of patent law, those cases are by their nature unlikely to have the sort of significance for the federal system necessary to establish jurisdiction.

A

To begin, we acknowledge that resolution of a federal patent question is "necessary" to Minton's case. Under Texas law, a plaintiff alleging legal malpractice must establish four elements: (1) that the defendant attorney owed the plaintiff a duty; (2) that the attorney breached that duty; (3) that the breach was the proximate cause of the plaintiff's injury; and (4) that damages occurred. In cases like this one, in which the attorney's alleged error came in failing to make a particular argument, the causation element requires a "case within a case" analysis of whether, had the argument been made, the outcome of the earlier litigation would have been different. To prevail on his legal malpractice claim, therefore, Minton must show that he would have prevailed in his federal patent infringement case if only petitioners had timely made an experimental-use argument on his behalf. That will necessarily require application of patent law to the facts of Minton's case.

B

The federal issue is also "actually disputed" here—indeed, on the merits, it is the central point of dispute. Minton argues that the experimental-use exception properly applied to his lease to Stark, saving his patent from the on-sale bar; petitioners argue that it did not. This is just the sort of "'dispute . . . respecting the . . . effect of [federal] law'" that *Grable* envisioned.

C

Minton's argument founders on *Grable*'s next requirement, however, for the federal issue in this case is not substantial in the relevant sense. In reaching the opposite conclusion, the Supreme Court of Texas focused on the importance of the issue to the plaintiff's case and to the parties before it. As our past cases show, however, it is not enough that the federal issue be significant to the particular parties in the immediate suit; that will always be true when the state claim "necessarily raise[s]" a disputed federal issue, as *Grable* separately requires. The substantiality inquiry under *Grable* looks instead to the importance of the issue to the federal system as a whole.

In *Grable* itself, for example, the Internal Revenue Service had seized property from the plaintiff and sold it to satisfy the plaintiff's federal tax delinquency. Five years later, the plaintiff filed a state law quiet title action against the third party that had purchased the property, alleging that the IRS had failed to comply with certain federally imposed notice requirements, so that the seizure and sale were invalid. In holding that the case arose under federal law, we primarily focused not on the interests of the litigants themselves, but rather on the broader significance of the notice question for the Federal Government. We emphasized the Government's "strong interest" in being able to recover delinquent taxes through seizure and sale of property, which in turn "require[d] clear terms of notice to allow buyers . . . to satisfy themselves that the Service has touched the bases necessary for good title." The Government's "direct interest in the availability of a federal forum to vindicate its own administrative action" made the question "an important issue of federal law that sensibly belong[ed] in a federal court."

A second illustration of the sort of substantiality we require comes from *Smith v. Kansas City Title & Trust Co.*, 255 U.S. 180 (1921), which *Grable* described as "[t]he classic example" of a state claim arising under federal law. In *Smith*, the plaintiff argued that the defendant bank could not purchase certain bonds issued by the Federal Government because the Government had acted unconstitutionally in issuing them. We held that the case arose under federal law, because the "decision depends upon the determination" of "the constitutional validity of an act of Congress which is directly drawn in question." Again, the relevant point was not the importance of the question to the parties alone but rather the importance more generally of a determination that the Government "securities were issued under an unconstitutional law, and hence of no validity."

Here, the federal issue carries no such significance. Because of the backward-looking nature of a legal malpractice claim, the question is posed in a merely hypothetical sense: If Minton's lawyers had raised a timely experimental-use argument, would the result in the patent infringement proceeding have been different? No matter how the state courts resolve that hypothetical "case within a case," it will not change the real-world result of the prior federal patent litigation. Minton's patent will remain invalid.

Nor will allowing state courts to resolve these cases undermine "the development of a uniform body of [patent] law." Congress ensured such uniformity by vesting exclusive jurisdiction over actual patent cases in the federal district courts and exclusive appellate jurisdiction in the Federal Circuit. See 28 U.S.C. §§ 1338(a), 1295(a)(1). In resolving the nonhypothetical patent questions those cases present, the federal courts are of course not bound by state court case-within-a-case patent rulings. In any event, the state court case-within-a-case inquiry asks what would have happened in the prior federal proceeding if a particular argument had been made. In answering that question, state courts can be expected to hew closely to the pertinent federal precedents. It is those precedents, after all, that would have applied had the argument been made.

As for more novel questions of patent law that may arise for the first time in a state court "case within a case," they will at some point be decided by a federal court in the context of an actual patent case, with review in the Federal Circuit. If the question arises frequently, it will soon be resolved within the federal system, laying to rest any contrary state court precedent; if it does not arise frequently, it is unlikely to implicate substantial federal interests. The present case is "poles apart from *Grable*," in which a state court's resolution of the federal question "would be controlling in numerous other cases." *Empire Healthchoice Assurance, Inc.*, 547 U.S., at 700.

Minton also suggests that state courts' answers to hypothetical patent questions can sometimes have real-world effect on other patents through issue preclusion. Minton, for example, has filed what is known as a "continuation patent" application related to his original patent. He argues that, in evaluating this separate application, the patent examiner could be bound by the Texas trial court's interpretation of the scope of Minton's original patent. It is unclear whether this is true. The Patent and Trademark Office's Manual of Patent Examining Procedure provides that res judicata is a proper ground for rejecting a patent "only when the earlier decision was a decision of the Board of Appeals" or certain federal reviewing courts, giving no indication that state court decisions would have preclusive effect. In fact, Minton has not identified any case finding such preclusive effect based on a state court decision. But even assuming that a state court's case-within-a-case adjudication may be preclusive under some circumstances, the result would be limited to the parties and patents that had been before the state court. Such "fact-bound and situation-specific" effects are not sufficient to establish federal arising under jurisdiction.

Nor can we accept the suggestion that the federal courts' greater familiarity with patent law means that legal malpractice cases like this one belong in federal court. It is true that a similar interest was among those we considered in *Grable*. But the possibility that a state court will incorrectly resolve a state claim is not, by itself, enough to trigger the federal courts' exclusive patent jurisdiction, even if the potential error finds its root in a misunderstanding of patent law.

There is no doubt that resolution of a patent issue in the context of a state legal malpractice action can be vitally important to the particular parties in that case. But something more, demonstrating that the question is significant to the federal system as a whole, is needed. That is missing here.

D

It follows from the foregoing that *Grable*'s fourth requirement is also not met. That requirement is concerned with the appropriate "balance of federal and state judicial responsibilities." We have already explained the absence of a substantial federal issue within the meaning of *Grable*. The States, on the other hand, have "a special responsibility for maintaining standards among members of the licensed professions." Their "interest . . . in regulating lawyers is especially great since lawyers are essential to the primary governmental function of administering justice, and have historically been officers of the courts." We have no reason to suppose that Congress—in establishing exclusive federal jurisdiction over patent cases—meant to bar from state courts state legal malpractice claims simply because they require resolution of a hypothetical patent issue.

* * *

As we recognized a century ago, "[t]he Federal courts have exclusive jurisdiction of all cases arising under the patent laws, but not of all questions in which a patent may be the subject-matter of the controversy." In this case, although the state courts must answer a question of patent law to resolve Minton's legal malpractice claim, their answer will have no broader effects. It will not stand as binding precedent for any future patent claim; it will not even affect the validity of Minton's patent. Accordingly, there is no "serious federal interest in claiming the advantages thought to be inherent in a federal forum." Section 1338(a) does not deprive the state courts of subject matter jurisdiction.

The judgment of the Supreme Court of Texas is reversed, and the case is remanded for further proceedings not inconsistent with this opinion.

It is so ordered.

[The concurring opinion of MR. JUSTICE THOMAS is omitted.]

NOTES AND QUESTIONS

1. Identify the plaintiff's claim.   What was Gunn's claim? Will the resolution of that claim depend on the construction, validity, or effect of federal law? Under the standard endorsed by the Court in *Gully v. First Bank of Meridian, supra,* would Gunn's claim have been one arising under federal law for purposes of § 1331? Would it have satisfied the standard endorsed by Justice Holmes in his dissent in *Smith v. Kansas City Title & Trust?* Did the *Gunn* majority endorse the Holmes standard?

2. A four-step approach.   The *Gunn* Court describes a four-step approach to assessing jurisdiction in cases where the plaintiff's claim is not itself created by federal law: "[F]ederal jurisdiction over a state-law claim will lie if a federal issue is: (1) necessarily raised, (2) actually disputed, (3) substantial, and (4) capable of resolution in federal court without disrupting the federal-state balance approved by Congress." Page 328, *supra.* The first step describes what we might call the *Smith/Gully* standard, namely, that resolution of a state-law claim will depend on the construction, validity, or effect of federal law. The second step, "actually disputed," has a surface appeal, but is a bit difficult to understand since jurisdiction must be measured on the face of the complaint, and under the well-pleaded complaint rule we cannot know or anticipate the defendant's response to the claim. Thus this step appears suspect, or enigmatic at best. Third, the federal issue must be "substantial," *i.e.,* important to the federal system as a whole. Here the focus turns away from the plaintiff's interest in a federal forum and centers on the interest of the federal system. Does the *Gunn* Court offer any insight into how a court is to measure this federal interest? Finally, even if the first three requirements are met, the case must be dismissed if the district court determines that the exercise of subject matter jurisdiction will upset the congressionally mandated balance between state and federal jurisdiction. How will a district court make that determination? What facts should it rely on? Would resolution of this question be better suited to the legislative process?

3. *Implications for the creation test?* Is it possible that the Court's emphasis on the substantiality of the federal question raised – the third element in its test – could likewise be used to limit federal jurisdiction in cases that would otherwise satisfy the creation test? Might this be a tempting means of reducing federal court caseloads, particularly where, in the Court's eyes, declining jurisdiction over the particular type of case involved would not upset the proper balance between state and federal jurisdiction? If not all cases that would otherwise meet the essential federal ingredient satisfy the arising under test for federal question jurisdiction, why shouldn't the same be true of some cases that would seem to satisfy the creation test? What role would congressional intent play in answering the questions?

PROBLEM

4-7. Bobby McAdams ("plaintiff") filed a wrongful death action in a federal court, asserting jurisdiction under § 1331, against Medtronic, Inc. ("Medtronic"), for products liability and negligence premised on alleged manufacturing, design, and marketing defects in a pain pump manufactured by Medtronic that the plaintiff believes caused his daughter, Tina McAdams, to die of morphine toxicity three days after her discharge from the hospital following implantation of the pump. With respect to both claims, plaintiff relies on the Medical Device Amendments ("MDA") to the federal Food, Drug and Cosmetics Act (FDCA), which establish specific compliance standards for medical devices such as the pain pump implanted in Ms. McAdams. Neither the MDA nor the FDCA creates a private right of action. The plaintiff argues, however, that the failure to comply with the MDA standards constituted a breach of the duty of due care. Medtronic denies that it failed to comply with the federal standards and has filed a motion to dismiss under Rule 12(b)(1). What should the district court do? *See McAdams v. Medtronic, Inc.*, 2010 WL 3909958 (S.D. Tex. Sept. 29, 2010).

3. Diversity Jurisdiction

a. Introduction

Article III, § 2, of the Constitution extends the federal judicial power to so-called diversity cases, *i.e.*, (1) controversies between citizens of different states, and (2) controversies between a citizen of a state and a citizen or subject of a foreign country (sometimes referred to as "alienage jurisdiction"). The Founders authorized the federal courts to entertain diversity cases out of fear that state courts might favor their own citizens in disputes with citizens from other states or from other countries. The possibility of such discrimination against outsiders posed several dangers. First, as Alexander Hamilton wrote in The Federalist No. 80, it threatened "the peace of the confederacy" as a potential source of "bickering and animosities . . . among the members of the union" and even of war with foreign nations. THE FEDERALIST No. 80 (Alexander Hamilton). Secondly, the feared partiality of state courts jeopardized the new nation's economic growth. During the Pennsylvania ratification debates, James Wilson, a member of the Constitutional Convention, thus warned that the expansion of commerce could be stunted if out-of-state merchants and creditors were entirely at state courts' mercy, without "proper security . . . for the regular discharge of contracts." Wilson asked, "[I]s it not necessary, if we mean to restore either public or private credit, that foreigners, as well as ourselves, have a just and impartial tribunal to which they may resort?" 2 ELLIOT'S DEBATES 489-494.

While diversity jurisdiction may have served an important role in 1789, many question the need for its continued existence today. Diversity cases—consisting mainly of tort, contract, and property disputes founded on state law—now comprise about one-third of the federal civil docket. More than 100,000 diversity cases were filed in federal court in 2014, twice the number of such cases filed in 2001. *See* FEDERAL JUDICIAL CASELOAD STATISTICS (2001) & (2014), *supra*, at tbl. C-2. These cases compete on crowded court calendars with lawsuits that are arguably more deserving of federal judicial attention, including federal criminal cases, civil rights actions, and suits to vindicate other federal statutory rights. In addition, diversity cases raise problems of federalism, for they require federal judges to interpret and apply state law, a task for which state judges are much better equipped. Finally, as we will see, diversity jurisdiction can lead to inefficiency because federal courts must often resolve issues of federal judicial power that would not arise in state court.

Given these drawbacks, modern critics argue that diversity jurisdiction is no longer justified by any realistic danger that state courts will be prejudiced against outsiders. Yet studies continue to show that experienced trial lawyers often regard such bias as a reason to prefer federal court over state court. This is particularly true in most of the South, in the less industrialized parts of the Midwest, and in some Rocky Mountain states. *See, e.g.*, Neal Miller, *An Empirical Study of Forum Choices in Removal Cases Under Diversity and Federal Question Jurisdiction*, 41 AM. U. L. REV. 369, 407-412, 423-430 (1992). Whether these fears of local bias are well founded is another matter, and one that is extremely difficult to document. Nevertheless, it is clear that federal diversity jurisdiction continues to provide many litigants with access to a system of justice that preserves the appearance of fairness.

Title 28 U.S.C. § 1332(a) authorizes federal district courts to take original jurisdiction over four categories of diversity cases, *i.e.*, those between

(1) citizens of different States;
(2) citizens of a State and citizens or subjects of a foreign state, except that the district courts shall not have original jurisdiction under this subsection of an action between citizens of a State and citizens or subjects of a foreign state who are lawfully admitted for permanent residence in the United States and are domiciled in the same State;
(3) citizens of different States and in which citizens or subjects of a foreign state are additional parties; and
(4) a foreign state . . . as plaintiff and citizens of a State or of different States.

Id. The first category embraces interstate diversity cases. The second category involves alienage jurisdiction. The third category entails a mix of the first two in the sense that there is interstate diversity as well as the presence of aliens. The fourth category covers suits by a foreign government or foreign government entity against citizens of one or more states. Our principal focus is on the first three types of diversity cases. It is important to remember that under § 1332, none of these cases may be brought in federal court unless "the matter in controversy exceeds the sum or value of $75,000, exclusive of interest and costs. . . ." *Id.*

b. Diversity of State Citizenship

Section 1332(a)(1)'s grant of jurisdiction over cases "between citizens of different States" would, on its face, appear to allow a federal court to hear a suit brought by a citizen of New York against a citizen of California and a citizen of New York, since the plaintiff and one of the defendants are from different states. However, in *Strawbridge v. Curtiss,* 7 U.S. (3 Cranch) 267 (1806), Chief Justice Marshall construed § 1332's predecessor statute as requiring that there be "complete diversity" between the parties, such that no plaintiff is a citizen of the same state as any defendant. This interpretation of the diversity statute still holds today. Because our example involves only "minimal diversity"—the plaintiff is diverse from one but not all of the defendants—it does not meet the diversity requirement of § 1332. The Supreme Court has made clear that *Strawbridge* was merely an interpretation of the diversity statute and that Article III, § 2's grant of judicial power to cases "between Citizens of different States" does not require the presence of complete diversity. In *State Farm Fire & Casualty Co. v. Tashire,* 386 U.S. 523 (1967), the Court thus explained that "Article III poses no obstacle to the legislative extension of federal jurisdiction, founded on diversity, so long as *any two* adverse parties are not co-citizens." *Id.* at 531 (emphasis added). While Congress could amend § 1332 to require some form of minimal rather than complete diversity, it has not done so. In applying the diversity statute, it is therefore imperative that no plaintiff be a citizen of the same state as any defendant. This brings us to the critical question of how we determine a party's citizenship for diversity purposes.

Rodríguez v. Señor Frog's de La Isla, Inc.

642 F.3d 28 (1st Cir. 2011)

THOMPSON, Circuit Judge.

This is a diversity-based personal-injury case. A jury returned a $450,000 verdict for Paloma Rodríguez against Señor Frog's de la Isla, Inc. ("Señor Frog," for short) in Puerto Rico's federal district court. Señor Frog now appeals, challenging nearly every aspect of the district judge's performance. Unable to find any reversible error in the judge's actions, we affirm.

How It All Began

San Juan, Puerto Rico, early in the pre-dawn morning of December 5, 2004. Cruising in her Mazda 323 on the Muñoz Rivera Expressway, 21-year-old Rodríguez hit a pothole—a collision that cost her two tires and killed the engine. But the worst was yet to come.

Turning her hazards on, Rodríguez somehow got her car to the side of the road, completely out of the way of oncoming traffic. A police officer patrolling that stretch of highway spotted her and pulled over. He left the cruiser's flashing lights on. A tow-truck driver also showed up, parked his truck in front of Rodríguez's car, activated the truck's flashing lights, pointed a spotlight on the work area, and put out cones to caution drivers passing by. As the truck driver lowered the truck's platform, Rodríguez got back into the Mazda either to grab some personal items or to do something to help out with the towing process.

That is when Carlos Estrada closed in, speeding in a Mitsubishi Mirage registered to Señor Frog. His headlights were off. He had a blood-alcohol level nearly double the legal limit in Puerto Rico. And he smashed that Mitsubishi right into the rear of Rodríguez's Mazda. Rodríguez was hurt, and apparently hurt badly. "She was thrown inside the vehicle," the officer later said. Covered in blood, she had no vital signs—"she appeared to be dead." But she survived and sued Señor Frog in district court under diversity jurisdiction, *see* 28 U.S.C. § 1332, alleging negligence and negligent entrustment. She sued other defendants too (including Estrada), but they were later dismissed for reasons that are not important here, so we skip them . . . .

The Diverse-Citizenship Issue

The diversity-jurisdiction statute empowers federal courts to hear and decide suits between citizens of different states, provided the amount in controversy is more than $75,000. *See* 28 U.S.C. § 1332(a). Puerto Rico is a state for diversity-jurisdiction purposes. *See id.* § 1332(e). And Señor Frog is a citizen of Puerto Rico, *see id.* § 1332(c)(1), so Rodríguez's suit is untenable if she was a Puerto Rico citizen when she filed her December 1, 2005 complaint. Señor Frog argues that she *was*, though it did not press this argument until after Rodríguez had rested her case. But after an evidentiary hearing, the judge deemed Rodríguez a citizen of California when she sued, and this conclusion survives clear-error review.

Citizenship for diversity purposes is domicile, and domicile is the place where one is present and intends to stay. As the party invoking diversity jurisdiction, Rodríguez had to prove domicile by a preponderance of the evidence—and she did just that, presenting enough evidence to show that she was a domiciliary (and thus a citizen) of California.

Rodríguez was the only witness at the hearing on the diversity issue—Señor Frog called no one. Rodríguez testified that she had moved from Puerto Rico to California in September 2005, roughly three months before she filed this suit. She was pregnant, and she and her boyfriend Adrian Peralta wanted to start their lives together in the Golden State. Since they had very little money, the couple lived in a San Francisco Bay area home owned by Peralta's grandmother. And by the time she sued Señor Frog, she had fully relocated from Puerto Rico to California: she was physically present in California (with her clothes, books, furniture, household items, *etc.*), had opened up a California bank account (she had no money in any Puerto Rico banks), had gotten a California driver's license and job, and had hired a California lawyer to fight on her behalf. And though she had not registered to vote in California (actually, she was not registered to vote anywhere) and did not attend church there, she had settled on living in the Golden State permanently. *Cf. Bank One, Texas, N.A. v. Montle*, 964 F.2d 48, 50 (1st Cir. 1992) (holding that factors that can help an inquiring court determine a party's intent include where the party exercises civil and political rights, pays taxes, has real and personal property, has a driver's or other license, has bank accounts, has a job or owns a business, attends church, and has club memberships—for simplicity we call these the "*Bank One* factors").

Post-complaint events cast no doubt on the earnestness of Rodríguez's intent either. Rodríguez told the judge that she gave birth to a baby boy in California, turned to a California pediatrician to treat him, and put him in a California daycare for a spell. She also enrolled in three California community college courses and got a cell phone with a California area code (she may have acquired the cell phone pre-complaint, but we cannot tell for certain). True, starting in 2007, Rodríguez spent several semesters at the InterAmerican University in Puerto Rico (she could get her bachelor's degree faster if she studied there, she said), and she was still taking classes there at the time of trial. But she made clear that she returned to California whenever school was not in session (during winter, spring, and summer breaks, for example), and she provided copies of plane tickets to prove that point. She also reaffirmed that she intended to live in California for the rest of her life (she hoped to land a teaching job there once she got her degree).

Having the exclusive ability to assess Rodríguez's demeanor and tone, the district judge was best positioned to separate true from false testimony. The judge found Rodríguez credible, and after carefully canvassing the testimony, she meticulously detailed findings of fact, which she supported with specific references to the evidence. Because we cannot say that these findings were clearly erroneous, her ruling that there was diverse citizenship must stand.

Undaunted, Señor Frog insists that the district judge botched her ruling in several respects. For openers, Señor Frog protests that Rodríguez did not have enough *Bank One* factors on her side, given that she had not registered to vote in California and had no religious affiliation there. Also, Rodríguez produced no documentary evidence—no bank statements, driving records, college transcripts, *etc.*—to support key claims, and, given the best-evidence rule, *see* Fed. R. Evid. 1002, the judge had no business accepting her "self-serving" comments about her intent to stay in California indefinitely. Searching for a "gotcha!" moment, Señor Frog notes too that Rodríguez said at trial that she "lived in Mayaguez," Puerto Rico, "all my life"—testimony it says should have caused the judge to dismiss the case for lack of diversity jurisdiction straightaway, without bothering with an evidentiary hearing.

We cannot buy into these arguments. For one thing, a party need not check off *every Bank One* factor to satisfy her burden, and, in any event, Rodríguez checked off more than enough of them — the California bank account, driver's license, job, and personal-property location sync up nicely with key *Bank One* factors.

For another thing, the district judge did not blindly accept Rodríguez's statement that she intended to make California her home. Rather, the judge sifted the testimony and grounded her ruling in facts that *confirmed* Rodríguez's intent claim. And Señor Frog's best-evidence theory changes nothing. With exceptions not relevant here, the best-evidence rule requires a party trying to prove the "content" of a written document to introduce the document itself. *See* Fed. R. Evid. 1002. Think of a will contest where the will is not in evidence and a witness tries to discuss the document's words from memory — that is the sort of situation that the rule was designed to address. But that is not our case. Rodríguez never tried to give the exact terms of her California bank account, driver's license, or college transcripts. She simply tried to prove, through her own direct testimony, certain facts that she had direct knowledge of — that she had opened a California bank account, acquired a California license, and taken several California community-college courses *pre*-complaint. Consequently, this case falls outside the compass of the best-evidence rule.

Last but not least, Rodríguez's trial testimony in no way short-circuited her diverse-citizenship claim. Consider the context. Thrilled beyond words that his daughter had survived the collision, Rodríguez's father hosted a Christmas Day party at his Mayaguez home in 2004 — roughly three weeks after Estrada had rear-ended Rodríguez and one year before she filed this action. Rodríguez was deeply depressed, he said, and he thought a small soirée with family and friends might lift her spirits. At trial, Rodríguez's counsel asked her whether any party-goers had come from San Juan (we are not sure why this mattered). "No," she replied, "I *lived in Mayaguez all my life*, so most of my friends are from Mayaguez." Señor Frog makes much of this language, suggesting that it proved her California-domicile claim was a lie — so, the argument goes, the judge should have kicked her case to the curb without further ado. We think not. Again, diversity of citizenship is determined as of the time of suit. And, fairly read, Rodríguez's testimony went to her *pre-suit* living situation, which means that her statement could not and did not sabotage diversity jurisdiction.

That ends this phase of the case. Standing by what we said moments ago — that we cannot call the judge's diverse-citizenship conclusion clearly wrong . . . .

[The court's discussion of non-jurisdictional issues raised by Señor Frog have been omitted.]

What This All Means

For the reasons recited above, we *affirm* the judgment below in all respects. Costs to Rodríguez.

So Ordered.

NOTES AND QUESTIONS

1. *State citizenship and domicile.* For diversity purposes, a U.S. citizen is deemed to be a citizen of the state in which he or she is domiciled. A person has only one domicile even if he or she has residences in several different states. A person acquires a domicile by taking up residence in a place with the intent to remain there indefinitely. He or she then retains that domicile until acquiring a new one.

2. *Burden of pleading and proving jurisdiction.* Rule 8(a)(1) of the Federal Rules of Civil Procedure requires that the complaint contain "a short and plain statement of the grounds for the court's jurisdiction. . . ." FED. R. CIV. P. 8(a)(1). While detailed jurisdictional allegations are not required, the allegations of jurisdiction in a diversity case should identify each party's citizenship. The federal rules thus place the burden of *pleading* the existence of subject matter jurisdiction on a plaintiff who files in federal court. If subject matter jurisdiction is challenged, as it was in *Rodríguez*, the plaintiff then bears the additional burden of *proving* the existence of jurisdiction. How did the plaintiff in *Rodríguez* attempt to carry this burden?

When a party seeks to establish jurisdiction by asserting that there has been a change in domicile, he or she encounters an additional hurdle as well:

> There is a presumption of continuing domicile that applies whenever a person relocates. In order to defeat the presumption and establish a new domicile (the "domicile of choice"), the person must demonstrate both (1) residence in a new state, and (2) an intention to remain in that state indefinitely. There is no durational residency requirement in the establishment of domicile; once presence in the new state and intent to remain are met, the new domicile is instantaneously established.

Acridge v. Evangelical Lutheran Good Samaritan Soc'y, 334 F.3d 444, 448 (5th Cir. 2003).

3. *U.S. citizens domiciled abroad.* Since citizenship for diversity purposes is based partly on domicile, a U.S. citizen who is not domiciled in one of the United States—or in the District of Columbia, Puerto Rico, or a U.S. territory, *see* 28 U.S.C. § 1332(e)—is not a "citizen" of any "state" within the meaning of § 1332. Nor does such a person qualify as a "citizen or subject" of a "foreign state" for diversity purposes, since the latter terms encompass only foreign nationals. The result is that a U.S. citizen domiciled abroad cannot sue or be sued in a federal court on the basis of diversity. *See, e.g., Freidrich v. Davis*, 767 F.3d 374 (3d Cir. 2014) (holding that federal court lacked jurisdiction under § 1332 over suit by citizen of Ohio against U.S. citizen who had changed his domicile from Pennsylvania to Germany); *Twentieth Century-Fox Film Corp. v. Taylor*, 239 F. Supp. 913, 914 (S.D.N.Y. 1965) (noting that Elizabeth Taylor, who made her home in England, "is a citizen of the United States, but is not a citizen of any state").

4. *Standard of appellate review.* Once a federal district court has ruled on the absence or presence of diversity, what standard does the court of appeals apply in reviewing that determination? If the district court had found that Rodríguez

was domiciled in Puerto Rico and that diversity therefore did not exist, would the court of appeals likely have reversed? If not, does this mean that a trial court's ruling on diversity jurisdiction is effectively unreviewable, or was the issue here simply so close that a ruling either way would have been upheld?

5. *Domestic relations and probate exception.* Even if the standards of complete diversity are satisfied, a federal district court will not exercise subject matter jurisdiction over domestic relations proceedings (*i.e.*, divorce, alimony, and child custody proceedings) or probate proceedings. *Ankenbrandt v. Richards*, 504 U.S. 689 (1992). Note, however, that not every case that touches on the topic of either domestic relations or the ownership of a decedent's property will necessarily fall within this exception. For example, the Supreme Court found that the probate exception did not apply to a tortious interference claim filed by Anna Nicole Smith against an individual who had contested Ms. Smith's right to receive an inter vivos gift from her late husband. Ms. Smith was not seeking to probate or annul a will; nor was she seeking property that was otherwise in a state probate court's custody. Hers was simply a suit seeking an *in personam* judgment against an alleged tortfeasor. Hence, the probate exception did not apply. *See Marshall v. Marshall*, 547 U.S. 293 (2006).

PROBLEM

4-8. Courtney Lundquist filed an action on March 20, 1987, in a federal district court against William Fawcett, to recover on a series of promissory notes. Lundquist's complaint alleged federal jurisdiction on the basis of diversity of citizenship. On November 5, 1990, Fawcett filed a motion to dismiss for lack of subject matter jurisdiction on the ground that complete diversity of citizenship did not exist. The motion, which included affidavits and other evidentiary documents, alleged that Lundquist, like the defendant, was a citizen of New Hampshire. Lundquist filed an objection to the motion to dismiss, in which he alleged that he was a citizen of Florida. As proof, Lundquist presented affidavits of himself and his wife setting forth primarily the following evidence that he was a citizen not of New Hampshire but of Florida: (1) that he purchased real property in Florida and moved there in 1984, keeping his New Hampshire property as a summer home; (2) that since 1984, he had maintained several Florida bank accounts; (3) that he had a Florida driver's license; (4) that his wife had run a horse farm continuously in Florida since 1984; (5) that he and/or his wife belonged to several social organizations in Florida; (6) that he had summered in New Hampshire, in some years spending as few as two to three weeks there; (7) that all of his personal belongings were in Florida except for certain bank accounts and for sparse furnishings in the Melvin Village, New Hampshire, residence; and (8) that he listed a Florida residence on his federal tax returns for 1987, 1988, and 1989.

Fawcett's evidence that Lundquist was a New Hampshire citizen was as follows: (1) that he owned real property in Melvin Village, New Hampshire, and paid taxes on that property; (2) that he maintained a functioning telephone in Melvin

Village; (3) that he had had a New Hampshire driver's license since 1986; (4) that he was registered to vote in New Hampshire from 1976 until at least 1990, and had actually voted in New Hampshire during that time; and (5) that he or his wife stated his address to be in Melvin Village, New Hampshire, on 1986, 1987, and 1988 annual reports filed with the New Hampshire Secretary of State on behalf of a corporation of which he was sole director, president, and treasurer, and his wife was secretary.

The district court concluded that Lundquist was a citizen of New Hampshire at the time the suit was filed and granted the defendant's motion to dismiss. Lundquist has appealed. How should the court of appeals rule? In answering this question consider the relevant date from which to determine citizenship as well as the standard of review that the appellate court should apply. *See Lundquist v. Precision Valley Aviation, Inc.*, 946 F.2d 8 (1st Cir. 1991).

A NOTE ON 28 U.S.C. § 1359 AND "COLLUSIVE" TRANSFERS OR ASSIGNMENTS TO CREATE DIVERSITY JURISDICTION

If a claim is transferred from one party to another through subrogation or a valid assignment, the assignee may sue to enforce that claim. This may create an incentive for parties to deliberately assign claims in order to create diversity of citizenship, thereby allowing the claim to be filed in federal rather than in state court. In 1948, Congress sought to block such attempts to manufacture diversity by enacting 28 U.S.C. § 1359, which provides: "A district court shall not have jurisdiction of a civil action in which any party, by assignment or otherwise, has been improperly or collusively made or joined to invoke the jurisdiction of such court." Because of § 1359, an assignment that may be valid as a matter of state law will not necessarily suffice to create federal diversity jurisdiction. In *Kramer v. Caribbean Mills, Inc.*, 394 U.S. 823 (1969), for example, the Supreme Court held that federal subject matter jurisdiction did not exist over a breach of contract action brought by a Texas lawyer against a Haitian corporation, even though the suit appeared to satisfy § 1332(a)(2) as one between a citizen of a state and a citizen of a foreign country. The claim had been assigned to the lawyer for $1 by a Panamanian corporation that, under a separate agreement, was entitled to receive 95 percent of any net recovery on the claim. The suit could not otherwise have been brought in federal court since it would have been between two alien corporations. The plaintiff "candidly admit[ted] that the 'assignment was in substantial part motivated by a desire . . . to make diversity jurisdiction available. . . .'" *Kramer*, 394 U.S. at 828. Even though the assignment was valid under Texas law and the lawyer probably qualified as the real party in interest, the Court ruled that "[s]uch 'manufacture of Federal jurisdiction' was the very thing which Congress intended to prevent when it enacted § 1359. . . ." *Id.* at 829. Because the assignor in *Kramer* had retained a substantial (95 percent) interest in the claim, the Court declined to reconsider its earlier decisions that an absolute or complete transfer of a claim does not offend § 1359 "regardless of the transferor's motive." *Id.* at 829 n.9.

In determining whether a transfer or assignment runs afoul of § 1359, federal courts consider a variety of factors, including whether the assignee lacked a prior interest in the claim or litigation; whether the assignment is between closely affiliated business entities; whether the assignment occurred close to the time the suit was commenced; whether there was a lack of meaningful consideration for the assignment; whether the assignment was partial rather than complete; whether the assignor controls the litigation; and whether there is direct evidence of a motive to create diversity jurisdiction. Affirmative answers to these questions increase the likelihood that § 1359 will be triggered. Courts do not insist on proof of subjective motive, however; instead, they will often infer a collusive motive from the objective criteria enumerated above. *See* Richard D. Freer, *Plaintiff and Defendant; Capacity; Public Officers, in* 4 MOORE'S FEDERAL PRACTICE § 17.13[3][b] (3d ed. 2015).

While § 1359 applies only to assignments made to *create* federal diversity jurisdiction, some courts take a similar approach when there has been an assignment or transfer to *defeat* diversity jurisdiction. In such cases, courts—using factors similar to those employed to see if there has been an improper creation of diversity—may treat the assignor or transferor as the real party in interest and therefore the party whose citizenship is determinative for diversity purposes. *See, e.g., Attorneys Trust v. Videotape Computer Prods., Inc.*, 93 F.3d 593 (9th Cir. 1996) (rejecting challenge to subject matter jurisdiction by nondiverse plaintiff against whom judgment had been entered by trial court, on basis that pre-filing assignment to plaintiff was insufficient to make assignee the real party in interest); *Grassi v. Ciba-Geigy, Ltd.*, 894 F.2d 181 (5th Cir.), *reh'g denied*, 899 F.2d 11 (5th Cir. 1990) (upholding defendant's removal of case from state to federal court based on diversity when there had been a collusive assignment of the claim to destroy diversity); *see also HDNet MMA 2008, LLC v. Zuffa, LLC*, 2008 WL 958067, at *45 (N.D. Tex. Apr. 9, 2008) (noting that "[r]ecently . . . federal courts have protected their jurisdiction with increasing vigilance, invoking the authority to examine the underlying nature of transactions that have the effect of manipulating diversity jurisdiction," but also noting that "there is hardly a consistent body of law addressing attempts to *defeat* jurisdiction") (emphasis in original).

A NOTE ON THE CITIZENSHIP OF ARTIFICIAL ENTITIES

Up to this point we have been considering the citizenship of natural persons for purposes of establishing diversity. A similar question arises with respect to artificial persons such as corporations and unincorporated associations. Section 1332(c)(1) addresses that question with respect to corporations. It provides that "a corporation shall be deemed to be a citizen of every State or foreign state by which it has been incorporated and of the State or foreign state where it has its principal place of business. . . ." 28 U.S.C. § 1332(c)(1). That means that a corporation is a citizen of *every* state or foreign state in which it is incorporated (though most corporations are only incorporated in one such place) *and* of the state or foreign state in which the corporation's principal place of business is located. If a corporation is incorporated in the same state or foreign state as its principal place of business, it has only one place of citizenship. If the place(s) of incorporation and the principal place of business are in different states or foreign states, the corporation has dual (or multiple) states of citizenship. In the case of dual (or multiple) corporate citizenship, each of the places of citizenship will count in the determination of diversity. Hence complete diversity would be defeated if a citizen of State A sued a corporation incorporated in State A with its principal place of business in State B. The same result would follow if the states of incorporation and principal place of business were reversed.

The state or foreign state of incorporation is usually easy to identify. It is the state or foreign state under whose laws the corporation was organized and created. Determining the principal place of business has proved a bit trickier. At one time, lower courts followed a variety of tests in making that determination—nerve center, business activities, total activities, and a number of hybrid approaches. Eventually, the Supreme Court intervened and endorsed a single test:

> We conclude that "principal place of business" is best read as referring to the place where a corporation's officers direct, control, and coordinate the corporation's activities. It is the place that Courts of Appeals have called the corporation's "nerve center." And in practice it should normally be the place where the corporation maintains its headquarters—provided that the headquarters is the actual center of direction, control, and coordination, *i.e.*, the "nerve center," and not simply an office where the corporation holds its board meetings (for example, attended by directors and officers who have traveled there for the occasion). . . .
>
> We recognize that there may be no perfect test that satisfies all administrative and purposive criteria. We recognize as well that, under the "nerve center" test we adopt today, there will be hard cases. For example, in this era of telecommuting, some corporations may divide their command and coordinating functions among officers who work at several different locations, perhaps communicating over the Internet. That said, our test nonetheless points courts in a single direction, towards the center of overall direction, control, and coordination.

Hertz Corp. v. Friend, 559 U.S. 77, 92-93, 95-96 (2010). In short, in all but the most unusual case, a corporation's principal place of business is the place in the state or foreign state where the corporate headquarters is located.

Section 1332(c)(1) applies only to corporations. Organizations and associations that are not incorporated—such as membership organizations, voluntary associations, partnerships, and many labor unions—are deemed, for diversity purposes, to be citizens of every state and foreign state of which any member is a citizen. *See, e.g., Carden v. Arkoma Assocs.*, 494 U.S. 185 (1990) (holding that citizenship of a partnership is determined by looking to the citizenship of all of its partners, including both general and limited partners).

PROBLEM

4-9. Central Energy, Inc. ("Central Energy") sued the Wheeling Steel Corporation ("Wheeling Steel") in a federal district court, invoking that court's diversity jurisdiction. Central Energy is a West Virginia corporation, West Virginia being both its state of incorporation and its sole place of business. Wheeling Steel is a Delaware corporation. All of Wheeling Steel's day-to-day operations take place in Wheeling, West Virginia, where the company operates a steel plant. These day-to-day operations include purchasing materials, selling products, managing environmental compliance, and administering human resource matters, including payroll. In addition, Wheeling Steel has an employee credit union established in Wheeling, is a member of the Wheeling Chamber of Commerce, and participates actively in the Wheeling business community. Seven of Wheeling Steel's corporate officers maintain offices in Dearborn, Michigan, including the chief executive officer and the chief financial officer. These corporate officers set corporate policies and direct the company's "strategic decision making" from the Dearborn offices. Day-to-day operations, however, are overseen in Wheeling. Wheeling Steel has filed a motion to dismiss, arguing that its principal place of business is West Virginia, thereby destroying diversity. How should the court rule on the motion? *See Central W. Va. Energy Co., Inc. v. Mountain State Carbon, LLC*, 636 F.3d 101 (4th Cir. 2011).

A NOTE ON STATUTES ALLOWING FOR MINIMAL DIVERSITY

In recent years Congress has authorized the federal courts to hear certain specialized types of cases even if there is only minimal rather than complete diversity. The first of these recent statutes, the Multiparty, Multiforum Trial Jurisdiction Act of 2002, 28 U.S.C. § 1369 applies to certain civil actions that arise from a single accident, such as a plane crash, in which at least 75 people died at a discrete location. The act allows a suit to be filed in or removed to federal court if there is "minimal diversity," *i.e.*, "if any party is a citizen of a State and any adverse party is a citizen of another State, a citizen or subject of a foreign state, or a foreign state. . . ." 28 U.S.C. § 1369(c)(1). However, Congress limited the act to cases that do not lend themselves to litigation in a particular state's court. The act thus applies only if a substantial part of the accident occurred in a state other than the state in which a defendant resides, or if at least two defendants reside in different states, or if substantial parts of the accident occurred in different states. For similar reasons, the act does not apply to suits in which a "substantial majority of all plaintiffs are citizens of a single State of which the primary defendants are also citizens" and if "the claims asserted will be governed primarily by the laws of that State." 28 U.S.C. § 1369(b). For a recent example of a court applying the act, *see Pettitt v. Boeing Co.*, 606 F.3d 340 (7th Cir. 2010) (regarding a plane crash in Cameroon).

An even more recent federal statute allowing for minimal diversity is the Class Action Fairness Act of 2005 ("CAFA"). This act permits some class actions to be filed in or removed to federal court if the matter in controversy exceeds $5 million, and if "any member of [the] class of plaintiffs" is diverse from "any defendant. . . ." 28 U.S.C. § 1332(d)(2)(A). However, CAFA cannot be invoked if the suit is particularly well suited for litigation in state court as, for example, when at least two-thirds of the class members are from the state in which the suit was filed, at least one defendant is a citizen of that state, and most of the injuries occurred there. 28 U.S.C. § 1332(d)(3). Moreover, a federal court may decline jurisdiction over a class action that otherwise meets the act's requirements if more than one-third (but less than two-thirds) of the class members and defendants are citizens of the forum state and if, "looking at the totality of the circumstances," the action is one that is better suited for litigation in state court. 28 U.S.C. § 1332(d)(3). We will look at CAFA more closely in Chapter IX.

c. Cases Involving Aliens

In the previous section we considered diversity jurisdiction in suits between citizens of different states. Section 1332 also gives the federal courts jurisdiction over certain cases involving aliens, *i.e.*, persons who are "citizens or subjects of a foreign state." 28 U.S.C. § 1332(a). Specifically, § 1332(a) provides for original jurisdiction over controversies that meet the amount-in-controversy requirement and that are between "(2) citizens of a State and citizens or subjects of a foreign state . . . ; [or] (3) citizens of different States and in which citizens or subjects of a foreign state are additional parties." *Id.*

The importance of alienage jurisdiction is suggested by the fact that in 2010, there were more than 22 million aliens living in the United States, accounting for 7.3 percent of the nation's population. U.S. Census Bureau, tbl. 1.1, *Population by Sex, Age, Nativity, and U.S. Citizenship Status* (2014). In New York and New Jersey, noncitizens made up over 12 percent of their population that year, while in California, nearly one out of every six residents was an alien. *See U.S. Census Bureau, The Foreign-Born Population in the United States: 2010*, at 1-4 (2012). We will focus on two particular issues concerning alienage jurisdiction. One concerns the extent to which these provisions allow jurisdiction if aliens are present on both sides of a case. The other issue concerns who is deemed to be an alien for diversity purposes. As we will see, the two issues are sometimes closely related. We will also look at an issue that potentially affects both state citizenship diversity and alienage diversity, namely whether a post-filing change in citizenship can retroactively cure a diversity defect that existed at the time of filing.

Eze v. Yellow Cab Co. of Alexandria, Virginia, Inc.
782 F.2d 1064 (D.C. Cir. 1986)

Per Curiam:

Plaintiffs are citizens of Nigeria. They commenced a personal injury action based on an automobile accident alleged to have occurred in the District of Columbia. Their complaint names two defendants: Yellow Cab Company of Alexandria, Va., Inc.; and Godwin Sam Okakpa (correct name: Akakpo), the alleged driver of the

Yellow Cab vehicle in which plaintiffs were passengers at the time of the accident. Plaintiffs invoked federal court jurisdiction on the basis of "alienage."

Defendant Yellow Cab moved to dismiss for lack of jurisdiction over the subject matter, contending that the requisite diversity of citizenship had not been asserted. Yellow Cab emphasized that plaintiffs had not alleged the citizenship of the defendant taxicab driver, but had simply stated that Akakpo "has a residence which is presently unknown to the Plaintiffs."

Plaintiffs failed to answer the motion to dismiss within the 10 days prescribed by D.D.C. Rule 1-9(d). Nor did plaintiffs request a time extension. The district court therefore treated the motion as conceded and dismissed the complaint. In its dismissal order, the court observed that plaintiffs "ha[d] failed to allege the citizenship of the defendant Godwin Sam [Akakpo] such that 28 U.S.C. § 1332 could be applied to afford jurisdiction."

We affirm, as indeed we must in view of the representation at oral argument made by counsel for plaintiff-appellants that Akakpo is an alien, a citizen of Ghana. See also Brief for Appellee Akakpo at 3 n. * (noting that appellee Akakpo had informed his own counsel that "he is a citizen of the State of Ghana").

Federal jurisdiction is authorized where there is a suit between a citizen of a state and citizens or subjects of a foreign state. 28 U.S.C. § 1332(a)(2). Congress has also authorized federal jurisdiction in suits between citizens of different states in which citizens of foreign countries are additional parties. *Id.* at § 1332(a)(3). But under long-held precedent, diversity must be "complete." *Strawbridge v. Curtiss,* 7 U.S. (3 Cranch) 267 (1806). A diversity suit, in line with the *Strawbridge* rule, may not be maintained in federal court by an alien against a citizen of a state and a citizen of some other foreign country.

Plaintiffs here had abundant notice of the jurisdictional defect urged in support of the motion to dismiss. They now acknowledge that their two-defendant lawsuit does not meet the complete diversity requirement. They did not move in the district court to drop the individual defendant as a party. Instead, they did nothing to overcome the impediment to federal court adjudication of their case. Under these circumstances, the district court's order was entirely proper and is accordingly

Affirmed.

NOTES AND QUESTIONS

1. *"Complete diversity" under § 1332(a)(2).*   Wouldn't it have been possible to construe § 1332(a)(2) so as to allow jurisdiction in *Eze,* since the suit was *partially* between citizens of a state (Yellow Cab) and citizens of a foreign state (plaintiffs)? However, a parallel reading of § 1332(a)(1) would allow federal jurisdiction over a suit by an Ohio citizen against citizens of Maine and Ohio, as one that is partially between citizens of different states. *Strawbridge,* by insisting on *complete* diversity, rejected such a reading of § 1332(a)(1). Under similar considerations, courts have read § 1332(a)(2) to require "complete alienage," such that aliens may not appear on both sides of controversy.

2. Section 1332(a)(3). In *Eze*, if the injured plaintiffs had consisted of Nigerian citizens as well as a citizen of Maryland, would the federal court have had jurisdiction under § 1332? Section 1332(a)(2) would not work for there would still be aliens on both sides of the suit, wrecking complete diversity. But what about § 1332(a)(3)? With the addition of a Maryland plaintiff, and assuming Yellow Cab is a citizen of Virginia, the case is now one between "citizens of different States and in which citizens or subjects of a foreign state are additional parties . . ." 28 U.S.C. § 1332(a)(3). Most courts agree that the presence of aliens on both sides of a dispute, though fatal to jurisdiction under § 1332(a)(2), is not fatal under § 1332(a)(3) as long as there is a genuine dispute between the citizens of different states. *See, e.g., Dresser Indus., Inc. v. Underwriters at Lloyd's of London*, 106 F.3d 494, 496-500 (3d Cir. 1997); *Transure, Inc. v. Marsh and McLennan, Inc.*, 766 F.2d 1297, 1298-1299 (9th Cir. 1985). The same is true even if the aliens happen to be citizens of the same country. *See, e.g., Tango Music, LLC v. DeadQuick Music, Inc.*, 348 F.3d 244 (7th Cir. 2003) (upholding jurisdiction under § 1332(a)(3) when U.S. parties were diverse, but citizens of the United Kingdom were present on both sides of case).

3. Curing lack of complete diversity. In a case like *Eze* in which there is partial but not complete diversity, the plaintiff may avoid dismissal of the case by agreeing to drop the nondiverse parties from the suit, as long as they are not indispensable to the action. This may be done even at the appellate court level in order to preserve, as to the parties who are diverse, a judgment rendered by the trial court. *See Newman-Green, Inc. v. Alfonzo-Larrain*, 490 U.S. 826 (1989). In *Eze*, the court of appeals noted that the plaintiffs had made no effort to drop Akakpo, the nondiverse party.

Grupo Dataflux v. Atlas Global Group, L.P.

541 U.S. 567 (2004)

JUSTICE SCALIA delivered the opinion of the Court.

This case presents the question whether a party's post-filing change in citizenship can cure a lack of subject-matter jurisdiction that existed at the time of filing in an action premised upon diversity of citizenship. *See* 28 U.S.C. § 1332.

I

Respondent Atlas Global Group, L.P., is a limited partnership created under Texas law. In November 1997, Atlas filed a state-law suit against petitioner Grupo Dataflux, a Mexican corporation, in the United States District Court for the Southern District of Texas. The complaint contained claims for breach of contract and *in quantum meruit*, seeking over $1.3 million in damages. It alleged that "[f]ederal jurisdiction is proper based upon diversity jurisdiction pursuant to [28 U.S.C. § 1332(a)(2)], as this suit is between a Texas citizen [Atlas] and a citizen or subject of Mexico [Grupo Dataflux]." Pretrial motions and discovery consumed almost three years. In October 2000, the parties consented to a jury trial presided over by a Magistrate Judge. On October 27, after a 6-day trial, the jury returned a verdict in favor of Atlas awarding $750,000 in damages.

On November 18, before entry of the judgment, Dataflux filed a motion to dismiss for lack of subject-matter jurisdiction because the parties were not diverse at the time the complaint was filed. *See* Fed. Rules Civ. Proc. 12(b)(1), (h)(3). The Magistrate Judge granted the motion. The dismissal was based upon the accepted rule that, as a partnership, Atlas is a citizen of each state or foreign country of which any of its partners is a citizen. Because Atlas had two partners who were Mexican citizens at the time of filing, the partnership was a Mexican citizen. (It was also a citizen of Delaware and Texas based on the citizenship of its other partners.) And because the defendant, Dataflux, was a Mexican corporation, aliens were on both sides of the case, and the requisite diversity was therefore absent. *See* *Mossman v. Higginson*, 4 Dall. 12, 14 (1800).

On appeal, Atlas did not dispute the finding of no diversity at the time of filing. It urged the Court of Appeals to disregard this failure and reverse dismissal because the Mexican partners had left the partnership in a transaction consummated the month before trial began. Atlas argued that, since diversity existed when the jury rendered its verdict, dismissal was inappropriate. The Fifth Circuit agreed. It acknowledged the general rule that, for purposes of determining the existence of diversity jurisdiction, the citizenship of the parties is to be determined with reference to the facts as they existed at the time of filing. However, relying on our decision in *Caterpillar Inc. v. Lewis*, 519 U.S. 61 (1996), it held that the conclusiveness of citizenship at the time of filing was subject to exception when the following conditions are satisfied:

> "(1) [A]n action is filed or removed when constitutional and/or statutory jurisdictional requirements are not met, (2) neither the parties nor the judge raise the error until after a jury verdict has been rendered, or a dispositive ruling has been made by the court, and (3) before the verdict is rendered, or ruling is issued, the jurisdictional defect is cured."

The opinion strictly limited the exception as follows: "If at any point prior to the verdict or ruling, the issue is raised, the court must apply the general rule and dismiss regardless of subsequent changes in citizenship."

The jurisdictional error in the present case not having been identified until after the jury returned its verdict; and the post-filing change in the composition of the partnership having (in the Court's view) cured the jurisdictional defect; the Court reversed and remanded with instructions to the District Court to enter judgment in favor of Atlas. We granted certiorari.

II

It has long been the case that "the jurisdiction of the Court depends upon the state of things at the time of the action brought." *Mollan v. Torrance*, 9 Wheat. 537, 539 (1824). This time-of-filing rule is hornbook law (quite literally) taught to first-year law students in any basic course on federal civil procedure. It measures all challenges to subject-matter jurisdiction premised upon diversity of citizenship against the state of facts that existed at the time of filing—whether the challenge be brought shortly after filing, after the trial, or even for the first time on appeal. (Challenges to subject-matter jurisdiction can of course be raised at any time prior to final judgment. *See Capron v. Van Noorden*, 2 Cranch 126 (1804).)

We have adhered to the time-of-filing rule regardless of the costs it imposes. . . .

It is uncontested that application of the time-of-filing rule to this case would require dismissal, but Atlas contends that this Court "should accept the very limited exception created by the Fifth Circuit to the time-of-filing principle." The Fifth Circuit and Atlas rely on our statement in *Caterpillar* that "[o]nce a diversity case has been tried in federal court . . . considerations of finality, efficiency, and economy become overwhelming." This statement unquestionably provided the *ratio decidendi* in *Caterpillar*, but it did not augur a new approach to deciding whether a jurisdictional defect has been cured.

Caterpillar broke no new ground, because the jurisdictional defect it addressed had been cured by the dismissal of the party that had destroyed diversity. That method of curing a jurisdictional defect had long been an exception to the time-of-filing rule. . . . Federal Rule of Civil Procedure 21 provides that "[p]arties may be dropped or added by order of the court . . . at any stage of the action and on such terms as are just." . . . Indeed, the Court held in [*Newman-Green, Inc. v. Alfonzo-Larrain*, 490 U.S. 826, 837 (1989)] that courts of appeals also have the authority to cure a jurisdictional defect by dismissing a dispensable nondiverse party.

Caterpillar involved an unremarkable application of this established exception. Complete diversity had been lacking at the time of removal to federal court, because one of the plaintiffs shared Kentucky citizenship with one of the defendants. Almost three years after the District Court denied a motion to remand, but before trial, the diversity-destroying defendant settled out of the case and was dismissed. The case proceeded to a 6-day jury trial, resulting in judgment for the defendant, Caterpillar, against Lewis. This Court unanimously held that the lack of complete diversity at the time of removal did not require dismissal of the case.

The sum of *Caterpillar's* jurisdictional analysis was an approving acknowledgment of Lewis's admission that there was "complete diversity, and therefore federal subject-matter jurisdiction, at the time of trial and judgment." 519 U.S., at 73. . . .

III

To our knowledge, the Court has never approved a deviation from the rule articulated by Chief Justice Marshall in 1829 that "[w]here there is *no* change of party, a jurisdiction depending on the condition of the party is governed by that condition, as it was at the commencement of the suit." [*Conolly v. Taylor*, 27 U.S. (2 Pet.) 556 (1829)] (emphasis added). Unless the Court is to manufacture a brand-new exception to the time-of-filing rule, dismissal for lack of subject-matter jurisdiction is the only option available in this case. The purported cure arose not from a change in the parties to the action, but from a change in the citizenship of a continuing party. Withdrawal of the Mexican partners from Atlas did not change the fact that Atlas, the single artificial entity created under Texas law, remained a party to the action. True, the composition of the partnership, and consequently its citizenship, changed. But allowing a citizenship change to cure the jurisdictional defect that existed at the time of filing would contravene the principle articulated by Chief Justice Marshall in *Conolly*.[5] We decline to do today what the Court has refused to do for the past 175 years. . . .

IV

The dissenting opinion rests on two principal propositions: (1) the jurisdictional defect in this case was cured by a change in the composition of the partnership; and (2) refusing to recognize an exception to the time-of-filing rule in this case wastes judicial resources, while creating an exception does not. We discuss each in turn.

A

Unlike the dissent, our opinion does not turn on whether the jurisdictional defect here contained at least "minimal diversity." Regardless of how one characterizes the acknowledged jurisdictional defect, it was never cured. The only two ways in which one could conclude that it had been cured would be either (1) to acknowledge that a party's post-filing change of citizenship can cure a time-of-filing jurisdictional defect, or (2) to treat a change in the composition of a partnership like a change in the parties to the action. The Court has never, to our knowledge, done the former; and not even the dissent suggests that it ought to do so in this case. The dissent diverges from our analysis by adopting the latter approach, stating that "this case seems . . . indistinguishable from one in which there is a change in the parties to the action."

This equation of a dropped partner with a dropped party is flatly inconsistent with *Carden* [v. *Arkoma Associates*, 494 U.S. 185 (1990)]. The dissent in *Carden* sought to apply a "real party to the controversy" approach to determine which partners counted for purposes of jurisdictional analysis. The *Carden* majority rejected that approach, reasoning that "[t]he question presented today is not which of various parties before the Court should be considered for purposes of determining whether there is complete diversity of citizenship. . . . There are not . . . multiple respondents before the Court, but only one: the artificial entity called Arkoma Associates, a limited partnership." 494 U.S., at 188, n. 1.

---

5. The dissent acknowledges that "[t]he Court has long applied [Chief Justice] Marshall's time-of-filing rule categorically to post-filing changes that otherwise would *destroy* diversity jurisdiction," but asserts that "[I]n contrast, the Court has not adhered to a similarly steady rule for post-filing changes in the party line-up, alterations that *perfect* previously defective statutory subject-matter jurisdiction." . . . The dissent identifies five cases in which the Court permitted a post-filing change to cure a jurisdictional defect. Every one of them involved a *change of party*. The dissent does not identify a single case in which the Court held that a single party's post-filing change of citizenship cured a previously existing jurisdictional defect.

There was from the beginning of this action a single plaintiff (Atlas), which, under *Carden*, was not diverse from the sole defendant (Dataflux). Thus, this case fails to present "two adverse parties [who] are not co-citizens." *State Farm Fire & Casualty Co. v. Tashire*, 386 U.S. 523, 531 (1967). Contrary to the dissent's characterization, then, this is not a case like *Caterpillar* or *Newman-Green* in which "party line-up changes . . . simply trimmed the litigation down to an ever present core that met the statutory requirement." Rather, this is a case in which a single party changed its citizenship by changing its internal composition. . . .

B

We now turn from consideration of the conceptual difficulties with the dissent's disposition to consideration of its practical consequences. The time-of-filing rule is what it is precisely because the facts determining jurisdiction are subject to change, and because constant litigation in response to that change would be wasteful. The dissent would have it that the time-of-filing rule applies to establish that a court has jurisdiction (and to protect that jurisdiction from later destruction), but does not apply to establish that a court lacks jurisdiction (and to prevent post-filing changes that perfect jurisdiction). But whether destruction or perfection of jurisdiction is at issue, the policy goal of minimizing litigation over jurisdiction is thwarted whenever a new exception to the time-of-filing rule is announced, arousing hopes of further new exceptions in the future. That litigation-fostering effect would be particularly strong for a new exception derived from such an expandable concept as the "efficiency" rationale relied upon by the dissent.

The dissent argues that it is essential to uphold jurisdiction in this and similar cases because dismissal followed by refiling condemns the parties to "an almost certain replay of the case, with, in all likelihood, the same ultimate outcome." But if the parties expect "the same ultimate outcome," they will not waste time and resources slogging through a new trial. They will settle, with the jury's prior verdict supplying a range for the award. Indeed, settlement instead of retrial will probably occur even if the parties do not expect the same ultimate outcome. When the stakes remain the same and the players have been shown each other's cards, they will not likely play the hand all the way through just for the sake of the game. And finally, even if the parties run the case through complete "re-litigation in the very same District Court in which it was first filed in 1997," the "waste" will not be great. Having been through three years of discovery and pretrial motions in the current case, the parties would most likely proceed promptly to trial.

Looked at in its overall effect, and not merely in its application to the sunk costs of the present case, it is the dissent's proposed rule that is wasteful. Absent uncertainty about jurisdiction (which the dissent's readiness to change settled law would preserve for the future), the obvious course, for a litigant whose suit was dismissed as Atlas's was, would have been immediately to file a new action. That is in fact what Atlas did, though it later dismissed the new case without prejudice. Had that second suit been pursued instead of this one, there is little doubt that the dispute would have been resolved on the merits by now. Putting aside the time that has passed between the Fifth Circuit's decision and today, there were two years of wasted time between dismissal of the action and the Fifth Circuit's reversal of that dismissal—time that the parties could have spent litigating the merits (or engaging in serious settlement talks) instead of litigating jurisdiction. . . .

We decline to endorse a new exception to a time-of-filing rule that has a pedigree of almost two centuries. Uncertainty regarding the question of jurisdiction is particularly undesirable, and collateral litigation on the point particularly wasteful. The stability provided by our time-tested rule weighs heavily against the approval of any new deviation. The judgment of the Fifth Circuit is reversed.

It is so ordered.

[The dissenting opinion of JUSTICE GINSBURG, joined by JUSTICES STEVENS, SOUTER, and BREYER, is omitted.]

NOTES AND QUESTIONS

1. *Time of filing.* The critical question in determining the existence of diversity jurisdiction is whether diversity was satisfied at the time suit was filed. If that requirement is met, post-filing changes in party citizenship cannot destroy subject matter jurisdiction. In *Grupo Dataflux*, the Court reaffirmed the parallel rule that if diversity jurisdiction is not satisfied at the time of filing, post-filing changes in a party's citizenship will not cure that defect.

2. *Dropping parties versus dropping partners.* The Court notes that in a case of partial but not complete diversity, a plaintiff may avoid dismissal of the action by agreeing, even at the appellate stage, to drop the nondiverse parties, so long as they are not indispensable to the suit. Why didn't that principle work here when the partnership's composition changed just prior to trial to eliminate the lack of complete diversity? Had the Court allowed this, wouldn't the same principle allow federal courts to hear and decide state-law claims between nondiverse parties, and then cure the lack of jurisdiction retroactively if, prior to entry of a final judgment or while the case was on appeal, one of the parties' citizenship changed so as to cure the lack of diversity? Would such an approach pose Article III problems if, as the Fifth Circuit's rule would have allowed, federal courts could proceed with cases even "when constitutional . . . jurisdictional requirements are not met," as in a suit in which not even minimal diversity existed? By contrast, when an appellate court allows a party who wrecked subject matter jurisdiction to be dropped from the case, is the court acting to *preserve* a judgment between the nondiverse parties, or is it allowing surgery that will *jettison* that part of the case the court lacked statutory authority to hear? Could Congress override *Grupo Dataflux* by authorizing federal courts to make exceptions to § 1332's complete diversity requirement, at least in cases in which minimal diversity existed at the time of filing? As a practical matter, is Congress likely to expand federal diversity jurisdiction in this way?

3. *Section 1332(a)(3).*   Suppose Atlas had initially sued both Dataflux and its U.S. agent, Hector, a citizen of California. Would jurisdiction have then existed under § 1332? Since two of Atlas's partners are Mexican citizens, would the case satisfy § 1332(a)(2)? If not, might it satisfy § 1332(a)(3), as a suit between "citizens of different States . . . in which citizens . . . of a foreign state are additional parties"? As a partnership, Atlas is treated as a citizen of Delaware, Texas, and Mexico—the states of its partners' citizenship. Since Hector, one of the defendants, is a citizen of California, does the case qualify as being one between citizens of different states (Delaware and Texas versus California), with citizens of Mexico (Atlas's Mexican partners and Dataflux, a Mexican corporation) as additional parties? If so, § 1332(a)(3) would seem to be met. However, this approach—which involves fragmenting the partnership and treating its members as distinct parties—is barred by *Carden v. Arkoma Associates*, 494 U.S. 185, 187 n.1 (1990), which held that in determining the citizenship of a partnership, a court may not fragment the entity: "There are *not* . . . multiple respondents before the Court, but only *one*: the artificial entity called Arkoma Associates, a limited partnership." Thus our hypothetical would not qualify as a § 1332(a)(3) suit between citizens of different states with aliens as "additional parties," for that would require treating each partner as a separate party to the suit rather than viewing the partnership entity as a whole.

4. *Risks to the plaintiff.*   What risks does the plaintiff run by filing suit in federal court without first making sure there is a valid basis for subject matter jurisdiction? In *Grupo Dataflux*, the plaintiffs' $750,000 judgment was wiped out, forcing them to start over. Since complete diversity by now existed, they could bring a new suit in federal court for it appears that under applicable state law, the statute of limitations was suspended during the six-and-a-half years the first federal suit was pending. *See Grupo Dataflux*, 541 U.S. at 595 n.11 (Ginsburg, J., dissenting). Yet starting over will not always be possible, as when the statute of limitations has run in the interim and the plaintiff did not file a timely protective action in a court that had subject matter jurisdiction. *See also International Shipping Co., S.A. v. Hydra Offshore, Inc.*, 875 F.2d 388 (2d Cir.), *cert. denied*, 493 U.S. 1003 (1989) (dismissing case for lack of complete diversity and imposing $10,000 Rule 11 sanction on plaintiffs' attorney).

The last half of the twentieth century witnessed a dramatic rise in the degree of political and economic integration among the nations of the world. As countries become more and more heavily dependent on a global market, individuals and companies are increasingly likely to operate across national boundaries, perhaps even conducting the bulk of their activities in a foreign nation. In Chapter II we saw the impact that globalization has had in shaping the law of personal jurisdiction. It has also had an effect on subject matter jurisdiction, challenging our traditional notions of who should be deemed a "citizen" and who an "alien" for purposes of ascertaining diversity.

The issue comes into play with respect to individuals as well as corporations. A person may be a citizen of one country but reside permanently in another country. Some individuals are legal citizens of several countries and thus possess dual or multiple nationalities. Similarly, corporations created under one nation's laws may conduct all or most of their activities elsewhere. Of what country should such persons and entities be deemed citizens for diversity purposes?

In the case of individuals, we saw earlier that a U.S. citizen domiciled abroad is, for diversity purposes, treated as being neither a citizen of any state nor a citizen or subject of a foreign state. What about a citizen or subject of a foreign country who is domiciled in the United States? Until recently, an alien was not deemed to be a state citizen for diversity purposes even if she were domiciled in that state. This meant that a French citizen living permanently in California could file a tort action in federal court against her next-door neighbor, invoking § 1332(a)(2) even though both parties were California domiciliaries. In 1988 Congress amended § 1332(a) to exclude such suits from federal court by providing that "an alien admitted to the United States for permanent residence shall be deemed a citizen of the State in which such alien is domiciled." 28 U.S.C. § 1332(a). The amendment thus narrowed federal diversity jurisdiction, for suits between permanent resident aliens and U.S. citizens domiciled in the same state would no longer satisfy § 1332(a)(2).

The 1988 amendment to § 1332(a) could also have had the opposite effect of expanding diversity jurisdiction. Consider two examples. First, suppose that the Nigerian plaintiffs in *Eze* were domiciled in Maryland and that they had been admitted to the United States as permanent resident aliens (*i.e.*, that the United States had issued them green cards). Assume that Yellow Cab is a Virginia corporation and that Akakpo, a citizen of Ghana, was not admitted to the United States for permanent residence but was instead here on a temporary visa. Would the federal court have had subject matter jurisdiction over this suit under § 1332(a)(3)? Under the 1988 amendment to § 1332(a), the suit is arguably one between citizens of different states (Maryland and Virginia) and in which an alien (Akakpo) is an additional party.

As a second example, suppose that before filing suit, the Ezes had settled their claims with Yellow Cab, leaving only their claims against Akakpo. In light of the 1988 amendment, would their suit against Akakpo fall within § 1332(a)(2), assuming the Ezes are permanent resident aliens domiciled in Maryland? If we read the amendment as having intended to treat such aliens as being citizens or subjects of a foreign state *and* of their U.S. state of domicile, complete diversity would be lacking under § 1332(a)(2) since aliens would appear on both sides of the suit. However, if we read the amendment literally as treating permanent resident aliens *solely* as citizens of their U.S. state of domicile, § 1332(a)(2) would seem to be met since the suit would be one between Maryland citizens and a citizen of Ghana. Do the diversity provisions of Article III, § 2 allow federal courts to hear nonfederal claims between citizens of other countries when no U.S. citizens are parties to the case?

In an effort to avoid this constitutional conundrum and, at the same time, to preserve the limitation on permanent resident aliens invoking diversity jurisdiction against residents of the state in which the alien resides, Congress in 2011 amended § 1332(a) by eliminating the sentence that defined permanent resident aliens as citizens of the state in which they reside and by adding the following language to subsection (a)(2):

> [T]he district courts shall not have original jurisdiction under this subsection of an action between citizens of a State and citizens or subjects of a foreign state who are lawfully admitted for permanent residence in the United States and are domiciled in the same State.

28 U.S.C. § 1332(a)(2). Did Congress succeed in its dual mission?

PROBLEMS

4-10. Consider the following parties:

- Ursula, a citizen of the United States domiciled in California.
- Lary, a citizen of the United States domiciled in Arizona.
- Piotr, a citizen of Poland and a permanent legal resident of New York.
- Indira, a citizen of India and a permanent legal resident of California.
- Anahita, a citizen of Iran.
- Michiko, a citizen of Japan.
- An, a citizen of China.
- Aden, a citizen of Ireland.
- Bayami, a citizen of the Philippines.

In which of the following cases would a federal court be empowered to exercise diversity or alienage jurisdiction? (Assume the amount-in-controversy requirement is satisfied in each case.) To the extent there may be a jurisdictional defect, how, if at all, might that defect be remedied?

A. Ursula versus Anahita.
B. Ursula versus Piotr.
C. Ursula versus Indira.
D. Ursula versus Aden and Bayami. A2 - YES
E. Ursula and An versus Michiko. A2 - NO
F. Ursula and An versus Michiko and Lary. A3 - YES
G. Piotr versus Indira. A2 - NO

4-11. China Nuclear Energy Industry Corp. ("China Nuclear") filed suit in federal court against Arthur Andersen ("Andersen"), a partnership, alleging that Andersen issued a false and misleading report on which China Nuclear relied to its detriment. China Nuclear is a foreign corporation whose principal place of business is overseas. Some of Andersen's partners are permanent resident aliens domiciled in the United States; the other partners are U.S. citizens domiciled in the United States. Andersen has moved to dismiss the suit for lack of subject matter jurisdiction. What arguments would each party make in supporting or opposing this motion? *See China Nuclear Energy Indus. Corp. v. Andersen, LLP*, 11 F. Supp. 2d 1256 (D. Colo. 1998).

A NOTE ON U.S. CITIZENS WITH DUAL NATIONALITY

If a person is both a U.S. citizen and a citizen or subject of another country, should she be treated as a foreign national for diversity purposes, or can her foreign citizenship be ignored? For example, suppose Melissa, a U.S. citizen domiciled in New York, is also a citizen of Greece. Paul, a French citizen, sues her in federal court. Does the case fall within § 1332(a)(2) as a suit between a citizen of France and a citizen of New York, or does Melissa's Greek citizenship wreck diversity because citizens of foreign states appear on both sides of the dispute? To the extent that alienage jurisdiction is designed to protect aliens from possible local prejudice and avoid friction with foreign governments, these concerns carry less weight when the foreign national is also a U.S. citizen. Moreover, treating Melissa as a citizen of both New York and Greece would mean that Paul could sue her only in state court where, as a "true" foreigner, he might well be the victim of prejudice. For these reasons, a growing number of federal courts have ignored the foreign citizenship of a U.S. citizen who has dual nationality. *See, e.g., Swiger v. Allegheny Energy, Inc.*, 540 F.3d 179, 185 (3d Cir. 2008); *Coury v. Prot*, 85 F.3d 244 (5th Cir. 1996); *Acton S.A. v. Marc Rich & Co.*, 951 F.2d 504, 507 (2d Cir. 1991), *cert. denied*, 503 U.S. 1006 (1992); *Falken Indus., Ltd. v. Johnson*, 360 F. Supp. 2d 208, 210 (D. Mass. 2005).

The Supreme Court has suggested that it remains an open question whether, under § 1332(a)(2), a federal court in a two-party case may ignore the foreign citizenship of a U.S. citizen with dual nationality, if the opposing party is a citizen or subject solely of a foreign county. In *Grupo Dataflux v. Atlas Global Group, L.P.*, 541 U.S. 567 (2004), the Court said in a footnote:

> We understand "minimal diversity" to mean the existence of at least *one* party who is diverse in citizenship from one party on the other side of the case, even though the extraconstitutional "complete diversity" required by our cases is lacking. It is possible, though far from clear, that one can have opposing parties in a two-party case who are co-citizens, and yet have minimal Article III jurisdiction because of the multiple citizenship of one of the parties.

Id. at 577 n.6. While the last sentence of the quoted paragraph addresses a diversity of state citizenship case, the same question would be posed by a two-party alienage jurisdiction case in which there are foreign citizens or subjects on both sides of the suit, one of whom is also a U.S. citizen domiciled in the United States. In this alienage situation, the "minimal diversity" required by Article III would be lacking if that provision requires that there be at least two parties who are *entirely* diverse from each other. Such an Article III requirement would pose no problem in a case like *Eze* in which the Nigerian plaintiffs were entirely diverse from defendant Yellow Cab, even though they were not diverse from defendant Akakpo. While Congress could amend § 1332(a)(2) to allow diversity jurisdiction in *Eze*-type cases, it is less clear that Congress—or a federal court—could allow diversity jurisdiction in our hypothetical in which Paul, a French citizen, sues Melissa, who is a citizen of both Greece and the United States and domiciled in New York, for here there is not the requisite minimum of two parties who are entirely diverse from one another.

A NOTE ON U.S. CORPORATIONS WITH THEIR PRINCIPAL PLACE OF BUSINESS ABROAD

If a corporation is created under the laws of one of the 50 states but has its principal place of business in another country, should it, pursuant to § 1332(c)(1), be treated as a dual citizen of both its domestic state of incorporation and the foreign state in which its principal business exists? If so, a "true" foreign national would often be barred from suing these U.S. corporations in federal court since, as in *Eze* and *China Nuclear Energy*, aliens would appear on both sides of the dispute. The foreign plaintiff would have to sue the American corporation in state court where the plaintiff could face real prejudice. A careful reading of § 1332 would seem to compel this result. As we noted earlier, § 1332(c)(1) provides that a corporation is a citizen of "every State" in which it is incorporated and of "the State or foreign state" of its principal place of business. This suggests that the drafters of the recently amended § 1332(c)(1) intended to treat a U.S. corporation whose principal place of business is abroad as being a citizen of that foreign state. Under the earlier version of § 1332(c)(1), some courts had ruled that such corporations were citizens only of their state of incorporation. *See Cabalceta v. Standard Fruit Co.*, 883 F.2d 1553, 1556-1561 (11th Cir. 1989) (holding that Florida corporation whose principal place of business was in Central America was a citizen of Florida only; complete diversity therefore existed in suit filed by Costa Rican plaintiffs for pesticide exposure at banana plantation in Costa Rica). That is no longer the rule.

PROBLEMS

4-12. Fima Candy Co. ("Fima") is an Israeli corporation whose principal place of business is in Nazareth, Israel. Fima brought suit in a North Carolina federal court against Mike's Foods and its president, Michael Gonen, alleging that they failed to pay for chocolates ordered from Fima. Mike's Foods is a North Carolina corporation with its principal place of business in Durham, North Carolina. Michael is a naturalized U.S. citizen who has retained his original Israeli citizenship. He lives with his family in Durham and owns a house in Israel, which he visits twice a year. The defendants have moved to dismiss the case for lack of subject matter jurisdiction. How should the court rule on the motion? *See Nazareth Candy Co., Ltd. v. Sherwood Grp., Inc.*, 683 F. Supp. 539 (M.D.N.C. 1988).

4-13. BDS, a Delaware corporation with its sole place of business in France, produces and sells computers. Pierre, the company's president, is a French citizen who lives in Paris. BDS's computer warehouse in France was covered by two policies of insurance, both negotiated in New York. One was issued by Liberty Insurance, a New York corporation located in New York; the other was issued by Boyds, an English corporation. After the warehouse was destroyed by fire, BDS filed claims with both insurers for $2 million. Liberty and Boyds then sued BDS and Pierre in a New York federal court, seeking declaratory judgment that because the fire was the result of arson committed by Pierre, the policies did not cover the loss. What arguments will each side make in addressing the issue of subject matter jurisdiction?

d.   Amount in Controversy

Though Article III, § 2 authorizes the federal judiciary to entertain diversity cases regardless of the size of the dispute, Congress has always insisted that the amount in controversy exceed a specified minimum. In 1789, the first Congress set this threshold at $500. The current version of § 1332 requires that, in diversity cases, "the matter in controversy exceeds the sum or value of $75,000, exclusive of interest and costs. . . ." As with the existence of diversity, a plaintiff who invokes diversity jurisdiction must allege in the complaint that the amount in controversy exceeds the statutory minimum.

The amount alleged by the plaintiff will be accepted as being the true amount in controversy if it is apparently made in "good faith." *St. Paul Mercury Indem. Co. v. Red Cab Co.*, 303 U.S. 283 (1938). The good faith requirement has both a subjective and an objective component. The first focuses on what the plaintiff actually knew or believed, while the second looks at what a reasonable person would have known. Both components must be satisfied to establish good faith. In other words, the plaintiff must believe that she is entitled to recover at least the jurisdictional minimum and her belief must be objectively reasonable.

A plaintiff's good faith is often measured under a "legal certainty" test. Under that test, if it is legally certain that plaintiff cannot recover the jurisdictional minimum, it usually follows that the amount in controversy has not been alleged in good faith. For example, suppose that Eileen brought a diversity action against Hotel Six, seeking $100,000 for jewelry that was stolen from her room. If the hotel can show that a valid statute or contractual provision limits its liability to $2,500, it would be clear to a legal certainty that the amount in controversy does not meet the threshold for bringing a diversity action in federal court. While Eileen's damages claim for $100,000 might well have met the subjective component of the good faith test—she believed she was entitled to $100,000—it would not satisfy the objective component since a reasonable plaintiff would have been aware of the statutory or contractual limitation on the hotel's liability.

As the next case demonstrates, however, there may be circumstances where it is legally certain that plaintiff cannot recover the jurisdictional minimum, but where she can nonetheless establish her good faith in alleging that the matter in controversy exceeds the sum or value of $75,000.

Coventry Sewage Associates v. Dworkin Realty Co.

71 F.3d 1 (1st Cir. 1995)

STAHL, Circuit Judge.

Appellants, Coventry Sewage Associates ("Coventry") and Woodland Manor Improvement Association ("Woodland") brought a diversity action against appellees, Dworkin Realty Co. ("Dworkin") and The Stop & Shop Supermarket Company ("Stop & Shop"). The United States District Court for the District of Rhode Island found that the amount-in-controversy requirement of 28 U.S.C. § 1332(a) was not met and dismissed the case, pursuant to appellees' motion under Fed. R. Civ. P. 12(b)(1), for lack of subject matter jurisdiction.* For the reasons stated below, and because of the unusual facts of this case, we reverse.

I.   Factual Background and Prior Proceedings

Coventry and Woodland own and operate a private sewer line and sewage pumping station servicing, among others, a supermarket run by Stop & Shop, located on property owned by Dworkin, a wholly-owned subsidiary of Stop & Shop (hereinafter appellees will be referred to collectively as "Stop & Shop").[1] In June 1992, Coventry and Woodland (hereinafter, collectively "Coventry") entered into a "Sewer Connection Agreement" with Stop & Shop, whereby Stop & Shop agreed to pay a service fee for sewer-main usage. The service fee was based, in part, upon the number of cubic feet of water consumed on the property. To determine the amount of water consumed, the parties' contract relied on invoices from the Kent County Water Authority ("KCWA"). The KCWA sent these invoices to Stop & Shop, and Stop & Shop in turn forwarded them to Coventry.

Because of a dispute over the reasonableness of an increase in the service fee—an increase Coventry claimed was permitted by the contract—Stop & Shop refused to pay Coventry's bills which accumulated beginning in early 1994. In October 1994, Coventry filed this action seeking recovery of $74,953.00, the amount it claimed to be due based upon water-usage numbers obtained from the KCWA invoices and what Coventry claimed was the correct new service fee rate. Coventry also sought contractual attorneys' fees. It is undisputed that, at the time Coventry commenced the action, it alleged the amount in controversy in the belief that it exceeded the jurisdictional minimum, and not as a ruse to invoke federal jurisdiction.

---

* [At the time this case was decided, the amount in controversy needed only to exceed the sum of $50,000, exclusive of interest and costs.—EDS.]

1. The existence of diversity of citizenship is undisputed.

Shortly after the complaint was filed, but before Stop & Shop filed its answer, Stop & Shop contacted the KCWA about the invoices underlying Coventry's fee calculations. The KCWA then sent an employee to the property who discovered that there had been a misreading of Stop & Shop's water meters, essentially caused by the adding of an extra zero to the number of cubic meters actually consumed. By letter dated November 18, 1994, the KCWA notified Stop & Shop that it was correcting the billing error by changing the amounts of the invoices.

Based upon the KCWA's corrected invoices, Coventry reduced the sum of its bills to Shop & Stop to only $18,667.88, an amount that included the disputed fee increase. Subsequently, Stop & Shop paid the undisputed portion of the fee, $10,182.48, initially withholding the disputed balance of $8,485.40. Stop & Shop ultimately paid this remaining sum as well, reserving the right to recoup the amount should it prevail in its challenge to the reasonableness of the service fee. Stop & Shop, presumably doubting the existence of diversity jurisdiction, asked Coventry to voluntarily dismiss the federal action; Coventry refused, however, apparently because of its intention to pursue in federal court its claim for contractual attorneys' fees.[2]

Stop & Shop moved to dismiss the action under Fed. R. Civ. P. 12(b)(1) for lack of subject matter jurisdiction. The district court granted the motion, finding that, "to a legal certainty," the amount in controversy did not exceed $50,000 as required by 28 U.S.C. § 1332(a). Notwithstanding the small amount actually in controversy, Coventry appeals the dismissal of the action. At oral argument before this court, counsel for Coventry stated that the reason for the insistence upon federal jurisdiction was that the case would get to an earlier trial in federal court (including the appeal proceedings) than if the case were pursued in state court.

II.   Discussion

We review *de novo* the district court's dismissal for lack of subject matter jurisdiction under Fed. R. Civ. P. 12(b)(1). *Murphy v. United States*, 45 F.3d 520, 522 (1st Cir.), *cert. denied*, 515 U.S. 1144 (1995). Although the facts pertinent to this appeal are undisputed, we are nonetheless "mindful that the party invoking the jurisdiction of a federal court carries the burden of proving its existence." *Taber Partners, I v. Merit Builders, Inc.*, 987 F.2d 57, 60 (1st Cir.), *cert. denied*, 510 U.S. 823 (1993).

Coventry argues that at the time it filed the action, it claimed, in good faith, damages in excess of $50,000; thus, the subsequent reduction of the amount in controversy did not divest the district court of jurisdiction. Coventry contends that

---

2. We note that although attorneys' fees usually will not constitute a portion of the amount in controversy, there is an exception where, as here, the fees are contractual. *Department of Recreation v. World Boxing Ass'n*, 942 F.2d 84, 89 (1st Cir. 1991). In this case, Coventry cannot avail itself of this exception as a basis for federal jurisdiction because, not only are there no specifics in the record as to the amount of such fees, [but] Coventry informed this court at oral argument that its estimation of attorneys' fees was only $10,000.

the KCWA's post-filing discovery of the billing error and changing of the invoice amounts was a "subsequent event" that neither undermined its good faith in filing, nor disturbed the court's jurisdiction once it attached. Shop & Stop [sic] argues that the billing error was a mere "subsequent revelation" that proved, to a legal certainty, that the amount in controversy had always been below the jurisdictional minimum and thus the court properly dismissed the case for lack of subject matter jurisdiction.

This case illustrates the competing policies that operate when a court makes an amount-in-controversy determination. On the one hand, a federal court should rigorously enforce the jurisdictional limits that Congress chooses to set in diversity cases. On the other hand, preliminary jurisdictional determinations should neither unduly delay, nor unfairly deprive a party from, determination of the controversy on the merits. As a policy matter, the "which court" determination ought to be made with relative dispatch so that the parties may proceed to resolution of the dispute's merits.

For the purpose of establishing diversity jurisdiction, the amount in controversy is determined by looking to the circumstances at the time the complaint is filed. Moreover, it has long been the rule that a court decides the amount in controversy from the face of the complaint, "unless it appears or is in some way shown that the amount stated in the complaint is not claimed 'in good faith.'" *Horton v. Liberty Mut. Ins. Co.*, 367 U.S. 348, 353 (1961) (quoting *St. Paul Mercury Indem. Co. v. Red Cab Co.*, 303 U.S. 283, 288 (1938)). When a plaintiff initiates an action in federal court, the plaintiff knows or should know whether the claim surpasses the jurisdictional minimum. *St. Paul*, 303 U.S. at 290.

> [The plaintiff's] good faith in choosing the federal forum is open to challenge not only by resort to the face of the complaint, but by the facts disclosed at trial, and if from either source it is clear that his claim never could have amounted to the sum necessary to give jurisdiction, there is no injustice in dismissing the suit.

Id. . . .

In a portion of *St. Paul* crucial to the instant case, and from which the parties before us parse their favorite phrases, the Court wrote:

> The intent of Congress drastically to restrict federal jurisdiction in controversies between citizens of different states has always been rigorously enforced by the courts. The rule governing dismissal for want of jurisdiction in cases brought in the federal court is that, unless the law gives a different rule, the sum claimed by the plaintiff controls if the claim is apparently made in good faith. It must appear to a legal certainty that the claim is really for less than the jurisdictional amount to justify dismissal. The inability of plaintiff to recover an amount adequate to give the court jurisdiction does not show his bad faith or oust the jurisdiction. Nor does the fact that the complaint discloses the existence of a valid defense to the claim. But if, from the face of the pleadings, it is apparent, to a legal certainty, that the plaintiff cannot recover the amount claimed or if, from the proofs, the court is satisfied to a like certainty that the plaintiff never was entitled to recover that amount, and that his claim was therefore colorable for the purpose of conferring jurisdiction, the

suit will be dismissed. Events occurring subsequent to the institution of suit which reduce the amount recoverable below the statutory limit do not oust jurisdiction.

Id. at 288-89 (footnotes and citations omitted).

The rules gleaned from the foregoing passage may be summarized as follows. First, federal courts must diligently enforce the rules establishing and limiting diversity jurisdiction. Second, unless the law provides otherwise, the plaintiff's damages claim will control the amount in controversy for jurisdictional purposes if it is made "in good faith." If the face of the complaint reveals, to a legal certainty, that the controversy cannot involve the requisite amount, jurisdiction will not attach. Moreover, if later evidence shows, to a legal certainty, that the damages never could have exceeded the jurisdictional minimum such that the claim was essentially feigned (colorable) in order to confer jurisdiction, the action must be dismissed. *See also id.* at 290 (noting that plaintiff's good faith in choosing a federal forum may be challenged by trial facts which establish that the "claim never could have amounted to the sum necessary to give jurisdiction"). Finally, if events subsequent to commencement of the action reduce the amount in controversy below the statutory minimum, the federal court is not divested of jurisdiction.

A careful review of *St. Paul* evinces its primary concern for the plaintiff's "good faith" in alleging the amount in controversy. When discerning a plaintiff's good faith, a court may look to whether it "appear[s] to a legal certainty that the claim is really for less than the jurisdictional amount." *St. Paul*, 303 U.S. at 289. The parties in the instant case spill much ink over the meaning of "good faith": whether it includes an objective as well as subjective component, and if so, whether "objective" good faith includes "objective facts" as opposed to "actual facts," etc. Stop & Shop argues that the "objective facts" were always the same: that it consumed much less water than originally shown on KCWA's invoices, and that although the claimed amount in controversy was over $50,000 at the time of filing, the "actual" amount in controversy is, indisputably, less than the jurisdictional minimum. Coventry counters that not only did it file with subjective good faith, but, because a wholly independent third party's actions were relied upon (indeed, it was Stop & Shop that forwarded KCWA's invoices to Coventry), there is no reason that Coventry "should have known" about the "actual" amount in controversy and thus, it claimed the damages in "objective" good faith as well.

This court has found that "good faith" in the amount-in-controversy context includes an element of "objective" good faith. In *Jimenez Puig v. Avis Rent-A-Car Sys.*, 574 F.2d 37, 40 (1st Cir. 1978), we found that, although the plaintiff had not acted "in deliberate bad faith" in filing his damages claim for mental anguish, "[t]he question, however, is whether to anyone familiar with the applicable law this claim could objectively have been viewed as worth [the jurisdictional minimum]." *Id.* (viewing evidence in light most favorable to plaintiff, and finding that, from the outset, plaintiff had no chance of recovering statutory minimum). We find that here, there is no dispute as to good faith, subjective or objective. It is undisputed that Coventry alleged the amount in controversy believing its accuracy at the time. Furthermore, there is no evidence, and Stop & Shop does not argue otherwise, that Coventry had any reason to believe, at the time of filing, that

KCWA's invoices, upon which the service fee was calculated, were factually incorrect. We find that, objectively viewed, at the time of its filing, Coventry's claim was worth more than the jurisdictional minimum.

This case fits well within the rule that once jurisdiction attaches, it is not ousted by a subsequent change of events. In *Thesleff v. Harvard Trust Co.*, 154 F.2d 732, 732 n.1 (1st Cir. 1946), we noted that although plaintiff filed remittiturs that reduced the amount in controversy below the jurisdictional minimum, the facts at the time the action was commenced conferred jurisdiction which subsequent events could not divest. . . .

In the instant case, Coventry filed the complaint because Stop & Shop refused to pay its bills totaling $74,953.00. The amount in controversy, at the time of filing, exceeded the statutory minimum regardless of the then unknown "actual facts" of Stop & Shop's water consumption. It was not until Coventry filed the action that Stop & Shop inquired about KCWA's invoices and KCWA subsequently changed them to reflect accurately the amount of water usage. Presumably, had the billing error never been detected, the action would have proceeded on Coventry's damages claim of $74,953.00. The fact that an independent third party's error initially inflated the amount in controversy above the jurisdictional minimum does not lead to the inevitable result that the third party's correction, subsequent to the filing of the complaint, affects the propriety of the jurisdiction once it attached.

Stop & Shop insists that, in this case, we should draw a distinction between "subsequent events" and "subsequent revelations." Stop & Shop argues that the subsequent revelation that the actual amount of damages never met the jurisdictional minimum—as opposed to a subsequent event that reduces that amount—divests the court of jurisdiction, regardless of what the parties knew or should have known at the time of filing. At oral argument before this court, counsel for Stop & Shop acknowledged that the logical extension of this argument is that the court would have been without jurisdiction over the case even if KCWA's error had not been discovered until trial.

To support this argument, Stop & Shop cites three cases that are factually distinguishable from the instant one, and that, in any event, are not controlling upon this court. First, in *American Mutual Liab. Ins. Co. v. Campbell Lumber Mfg. Corp.*, 329 F. Supp. 1283, 1284 (N.D. Ga. 1971), the plaintiff filed an action for amounts due on insurance contracts. The plaintiff was forced to estimate its damages claim because certain of defendant's records were not available to it. During post-filing discovery, the plaintiff learned that the actual amount in controversy was below the statutory minimum. The court found that the maximum amount recoverable on the plaintiff's theory never varied, and noted that the correct amount in controversy was ascertainable at the time the action was filed. Thus, in dismissing the action, the court reasoned that the plaintiff's realization that its earlier estimation of damages was erroneous was not an "event," under *St. Paul*, that reduced the amount recoverable. *Id.* at 1286.

Second, in *Jones v. Knox Exploration Corp.*, 2 F.3d 181, 182 (6th Cir. 1993), the plaintiffs revealed in their appellate brief that "it was not discovered until this appeal that the amount in controversy is actually less than $50,000." The court acknowledged that subsequent events that reduce the amount in controversy, such as an amendment to the complaint or an application of a post-discovery legal defense, would not oust federal jurisdiction. The court reasoned that "[a] distinction must be made, however, between subsequent events that change the amount in controversy and subsequent revelations that, in fact, the required amount was or was not in controversy at the commencement of the action." *Id.* at 183. The court found that there was no subsequent event that occurred to reduce the amount; instead, there was only a subsequent revelation that, in fact, the required amount was not in controversy at the time the action was filed. Thus, the court ordered dismissal based on lack of subject matter jurisdiction.

Third, in *Tongkook America, Inc. v. Shipton Sportswear Co.*, 14 F.3d 781, 782-83 (2d Cir. 1994), the parties realized during pre-trial discovery that, one year prior to filing suit, the plaintiff had drawn a certain amount upon a letter of credit that was erroneously [not subtracted from] the damages claim. The court rejected plaintiff's argument that the discovery of the failure to credit the amount withdrawn was an "event subsequent to the institution of the suit." *Id.* at 784-85. The court deemed the plaintiff's previous withdrawal upon the letter of credit an "event which preceded the commencement of the suit [that] objectively altered the amount of [plaintiff's] claim." *Id.* at 786. Thus, the sum certain in controversy was lower than the jurisdictional minimum and the court ordered the case dismissed for lack of subject matter jurisdiction.

In the instant case, Coventry did not base its damages claim on a faulty estimation that required recalculation during discovery, as in *American Mutual*; rather, it alleged the amount in controversy based upon a third-party's information that neither party had any reason to know was erroneous. Unlike the "mere revelation" in *Jones* that there was never the requisite amount in controversy, the reduction in the amount in controversy here occurred only after KCWA's affirmative acts of checking the water meters and changing the invoice amounts. Finally, . . . in *Tongkook*, the parties themselves made the error affecting the amount in controversy approximately one year prior to commencement of the suit. Thus, it appears that the plaintiff in that case should have known that its claim did not exceed the jurisdictional minimum. . . . In the instant case, an independent third party with otherwise no connection to the case made an apparently non-obvious error so that the amount-in-controversy at the time of filing, in fact, exceeded the jurisdictional minimum. Coventry had no reason to know that its claimed amount of damages was in error. Moreover, the reduction of the amount in controversy resulted from acts occurring wholly after the action commenced. We hold that, under these extraordinary circumstances, the district court's jurisdiction was not disturbed by the subsequent reduction of the amount in controversy.

III. *Conclusion*

For the foregoing reasons, we vacate the judgment of the district court, and remand for further proceedings consistent with this opinion. Each party shall bear its own costs.

NOTES AND QUESTIONS

1. *Subsequent events versus subsequent revelations.* A subsequent event is an event that takes place after the filing of the complaint. Such subsequent events might include the abandonment or dismissal of some of the plaintiff's claims, or the defendant's payment of a portion of the plaintiff's demand. A subsequent event altering the amount in controversy never divests the court of jurisdiction. A subsequent revelation, which also occurs after the filing of the complaint, does not alter the amount in controversy but instead reveals what that amount actually was at the time the complaint was filed. Such revelations might consist of newly discovered information showing that the amount in controversy is less than it was originally thought to be. A subsequent revelation of the true amount in controversy will affect the court's jurisdiction only if that revelation establishes the plaintiff's lack of good faith. Do you agree with the *Coventry* court that the parties' discovery of KCWA's error was a "subsequent event"—"reduction of the amount in controversy resulted from acts occurring wholly after the action commenced"—rather than a "subsequent revelation"? Didn't discovery of the mistake reveal that the defendant never owed the plaintiff more than $18,667.88?

2. *Legal certainty and objective good faith.* In order to uphold jurisdiction, was it necessary for the court to treat the discovery of KCWA's error as a subsequent event? Even if it were a subsequent revelation, doesn't the court's opinion suggest that the plaintiff met both the subjective and the objective requirements of the good faith test since its reliance on KCWA's figures was innocent as well as the type of error a reasonable person might have made? Would the result in *Coventry* have been the same if one of the plaintiff's employees, rather than a third party, had been responsible for the mistake that led to inflating the damages claim? In *Tongkook America, Inc. v. Shipton Sportswear*, 14 F.3d 781 (2d Cir. 1994), the court dismissed the suit, based on a legal certainty that the plaintiff could not recover the jurisdictional minimum, when the plaintiff's innocent mistake resulted from a failure to carefully review its own business records. *See also State Farm Mut. Auto. Ins. Co. v. Powell*, 87 F.3d 93 (3d Cir. 1996) (dismissing action by insurer for judgment that it was not liable on two policies totaling $100,000 after plaintiff discovered from its own records that only one policy, worth $50,000, was at issue).

3. *Attorneys' fees.* In calculating the amount in controversy, § 1332(a) states that "interest and costs" shall not be taken into account, even though a successful party may usually recover interest and certain costs of litigation from the defendant. 28 U.S.C. § 1332(a); *see* 28 U.S.C. § 1961 (interest); 28 U.S.C. § 1920 (costs); FED. R. CIV. P. 54(d). Under the so-called American rule, the prevailing party must ordinarily pay its own attorneys' fees without reimbursement from the other side. However, there are situations where either a contract or a statute allows a successful litigant to recover attorneys' fees from her adversary. *See, e.g.,* 42 U.S.C. § 1988(b) (allowing recovery of attorneys' fees in civil rights actions). In these limited situations—because such fees are not generally deemed to be part of "costs"—a reasonable estimate of the plaintiff's attorneys' fees may be included

in computing the amount in controversy. In *Coventry*, since the contract between the parties expressly allowed for the recovery of attorneys' fees, why didn't this enable the plaintiff to meet the amount-in-controversy requirement?

4. Disincentives to overstating the amount in controversy.   Are there any considerations that might keep a plaintiff from inflating the amount in controversy in order to bring a diversity suit in federal court? First, if the court in *Coventry* had dismissed the action, concluding that the amount alleged by the plaintiff was not claimed in good faith, might the plaintiff have then been barred from refiling in state court? *See Tongkook Am., Inc. v. Shipton Sportswear*, 14 F.3d 781, 786 (2d Cir. 1994) (reversing judgment for plaintiff and ordering case dismissed when plaintiff mistakenly inflated the amount in controversy, noting that the statute of limitations might now prevent plaintiff from pursuing the case in state court). Second, in addition to possible statute of limitations problems if the case is dismissed, plaintiffs' attorneys can be sanctioned under Rule 11 for misstating the amount in controversy. *See, e.g., Arends v. Mitchell Sav. Bank*, 1997 WL 754118 (N.D. Ill. Nov. 21, 1997); *Wood v. Brosse U.S.A., Inc.*, 149 F.R.D. 44 (S.D.N.Y. 1993). Third, even if as in *Coventry* a plaintiff can meet the good faith rule and avoid dismissal, might the plaintiff nonetheless elect to refile in state court assuming the statute of limitations has not run? If such a plaintiff stays in federal court and even if it wins a favorable judgment, could the court still refuse to award the plaintiff its costs? Could it also force the plaintiff to reimburse the defendant for the defendant's costs, even though the plaintiff won the case?

5. Standard of review.   The appellate court in *Coventry* applied a *"de novo"* standard of review. In essence, the appellate court made an independent determination as to whether subject matter jurisdiction had been satisfied. The district court's judgment on this issue was essentially irrelevant. However, in *Rodríguez v. Señor Frog's de La Isla, Inc.*, page 355, *supra*, the appellate court applied a "clearly erroneous" standard of review in determining whether a district court had properly resolved a diversity issue. That standard requires an appellate court to defer to the initial judgment made by the district court unless the lower court was clearly wrong in its judgment. Why were different appellate review standards applied in these two cases? What type of error did the trial court make in each case? Does that justify the adoption of two different standards of review?

A NOTE ON AGGREGATION OF CLAIMS

In computing the amount in controversy, a plaintiff may aggregate all of her claims against a single defendant, whether or not the claims are related to one another. As long as the total or aggregate of damages exceeds the jurisdictional minimum, the amount-in-controversy requirement is satisfied. Thus, if Harriet brings a diversity action against Charlie seeking $10,000 for breach of contract, $40,000 for defamation, $20,000 for personal injuries, and $10,000 in punitive damages as authorized by state law, the amount-in-controversy requirement of § 1332 is satisfied since the amounts, when added together, exceed $75,000.

Aggregation is normally allowed only with respect to the claims of one plaintiff against one defendant. If there is more than one plaintiff, each plaintiff usually must independently satisfy the amount-in-controversy requirement. In our prior example, if Harriet's sister Rose had joined as a co-plaintiff in the suit, her claims against Charlie would have to exceed $75,000 on their own; if her claims totaled less than this amount, she could not add her claims to Harriet's to meet the jurisdictional minimum. Similarly, when one plaintiff sues several defendants, the plaintiff must ordinarily satisfy § 1332's amount-in-controversy requirement separately as to each defendant; a plaintiff cannot usually add her claims against one defendant to those against another defendant. [Note: This specific rule will be subject to modification when we examine permissive joinder of parties in Chapter VIII, part D.2.]

The only exception to the rule against aggregation of claims by or against separate parties is if the claims involve a "single title or right" in which the parties have "a common and undivided interest." *Troy Bank v. G.A. Whitehead & Co.*, 222 U.S. 39 (1911). In these relatively rare situations, aggregation is allowed by multiple plaintiffs suing one defendant.

Suppose that in his will, Mario gave each of his four children a one-quarter, undivided interest in his $80,000 vintage video game collection. After Mario's death, the collection was destroyed in a fire caused by his brother Luigi. If Mario's children are of diverse citizenship from Luigi, they may join together in suing Luigi in federal court. Though each child's interest in the collection is worth only $20,000, the claims may be aggregated to meet § 1332's amount-in-controversy requirement because the ownership of the entire collection is common and undivided among the children, and involves a single title or right, namely Mario's will. However, the common-and-undivided-interest requirement would not have been met if, in his will, Mario had divided up his video collection by bequeathing each child specific games worth $20,000. Under these circumstances, each child would now have a separate and distinct claim to the specific games allotted to him or her, even though their claims still derive from a single title or right, the will.

Aggregation is likewise permitted in situations involving joint and several liability. Even if each defendant caused only a portion of the harm to the plaintiff, each may be held liable for the total damage caused by the defendants as a group, and the individual claims may therefore be aggregated. For example, suppose Larry, Moe, and Curly were jointly responsible for removing a stand of timber worth $120,000 from Jack's land. If complete diversity exists, Jack may sue them in federal court and can aggregate his claims against the defendants to satisfy § 1332, even if each defendant removed only $40,000 worth of timber. Jack is enforcing a single title or right to the stand of timber; and, as far as their liability to Jack is concerned, the defendants have a common and undivided interest since each is liable for the total harm caused, not just his own $40,000 share. If Jack later collects the full $120,000 from one defendant, that defendant may seek contribution from the others for their share of the damages, but this does not alter the fact that vis-à-vis Jack, the defendants' interests are common and undivided.

Rather than viewing the above examples as exceptions to the rule against aggregation, one might think of them as cases in which the amount in controversy is simply measured by the value of the entire single title or right in issue, without regard to the share possessed by the individual litigants.

PROBLEMS

4-14. Pat and Oscar were injured when Pat's car in which they were riding was rammed by Ted. Pat and Oscar sued Ted in federal court based on diversity of citizenship. Pat seeks $60,000 for personal injuries and $20,000 for damage to her car. Oscar seeks $50,000 for personal injuries, $10,000 for income lost during his recuperation, and $10,000 in punitive damages, plus interest, costs, and attorneys' fees. In addition, Oscar seeks $5,000 for a laptop computer that Ted had borrowed from him and lost several months prior to the accident. If complete diversity exists, does the court have subject matter jurisdiction over the case?

4-15. Rachel, a citizen of Maine, owns a parcel of land in Colorado. She recently learned that for the past few years the land has been a dumpsite for old tires, motor oil, and garbage. Rachel filed suit in a Colorado federal court against Manny, Moe, and Jack, alleging that they dumped this debris on her land without permission. The complaint alleges that Manny was responsible for the tires, Moe for the oil, and Jack for the garbage. The complaint seeks damages of $92,000, the estimated total cost of cleaning up the land. Of this sum, $7,000 is the cost of removing the tires, $80,000 the cost of cleaning up the oil, and $5,000 the cost of disposing of the garbage. Under state law, anyone who contributes to the physical or chemical pollution of land may be held liable for the full amount of the cleanup costs. Manny, Moe, and Jack are Colorado citizens. Does the court have subject matter jurisdiction over the suit?

A NOTE ON COMPUTING THE AMOUNT IN CONTROVERSY IN SUITS FOR DECLARATORY OR INJUNCTIVE RELIEF

If a plaintiff seeks relief in the form of money damages, it is relatively easy to ascertain the amount in controversy for purposes of § 1332. The task is more difficult if the complaint seeks declaratory and/or injunctive relief, since these remedies do not usually involve a specified amount of money. And, in contrast to a suit for money damages in which the plaintiff's gain is equal to the defendant's loss, the value of declaratory or injunctive relief may differ for the two parties. For example, suppose a shipowner brings a diversity action against a railroad seeking a declaration that the defendant's bridge over a river constitutes a nuisance and an order that the bridge be removed. What is the amount in controversy? In a case involving these facts, the Supreme Court stated that "the want of a sufficient amount of damage having been sustained to give the Federal Courts jurisdiction, will not defeat the remedy, as the removal of the obstruction is the matter in controversy, and the value of the object must govern." *Mississippi & Mo. R.R. Co. v. Ward*, 67 U.S. (2 Black) 485, 492 (1862). The Court did not explain what it meant by "the value of the object." Was it the value to the plaintiff of being able to navigate the river freely? The cost to the defendant of removing the obstruction? Or the value of the bridge itself? As the case suggests, there are a number of ways of measuring the amount in controversy in suits for declaratory or injunctive relief. The courts are sharply divided as to which approach to use.

Three principal approaches are employed today. First, under the "plaintiff-viewpoint rule," the amount in controversy is the value or benefit to the plaintiff of obtaining the relief sought. This rule is consistent with the principle that in suits for monetary relief courts look to the allegations in the plaintiff's complaint to ascertain the amount in controversy. A court adopted this approach in *Ericsson GE Mobile Communications, Inc. v. Motorola Communications & Electronics, Inc.*, 120 F.3d 216 (11th Cir. 1997), in which it dismissed a suit by an unsuccessful bidder to enjoin execution of a municipal contract for a police communications system between a city and the successful bidder. Because there was no assurance that the contract would be awarded to the plaintiff in the rebidding process, § 1332's jurisdictional minimum was not met even though an injunction would set aside a contract worth $11 million to the defendant. *Accord Morrison v. Allstate Indem. Co.*, 228 F.3d 1255, 1268-1271 (11th Cir. 2000).

A second and much more widely used approach is the "either-viewpoint rule," under which "the amount in controversy is the pecuniary result to either party which the judgment would directly produce." *Ronzio v. Denver & Rio Grande W. R.R. Co.*, 116 F.2d 604, 606 (10th Cir. 1940) (finding diversity jurisdiction over suit to quiet title to water rights when value of rights to defendant but not to plaintiffs met the jurisdictional minimum). This approach is consistent with § 1332's goal of permitting significant diversity cases to enter federal court. The "either-viewpoint rule" was used in *City of South Bend, Indiana v. Consolidated Rail Corp.*, 880 F. Supp. 595 (N.D. Ind. 1995), a suit by two cities to enjoin a railroad from violating local ordinances that outlawed the sounding of train whistles at rail crossings. The cities could not show that the benefit to them of securing compliance with the laws exceeded $50,000, but jurisdiction nonetheless existed because the defendant faced potential fines of more than $7 million a day if it ignored the ordinances.

Finally, a few courts consider the value of the suit to the party invoking federal jurisdiction, *i.e.*, the plaintiff in a suit initiated in federal court, and the defendant in a suit removed from state to federal court. Although the removal statute, 28 U.S.C. § 1441(a), permits a defendant to remove a case only if the plaintiff could have filed it originally in federal court, this approach would sometimes allow removal of cases that the plaintiff could not have instituted in federal court. Despite this difficulty, the approach is occasionally used. *Bedell v. H.R.C. Limited*, 522 F. Supp. 732 (E.D. Ky. 1981), involved a suit commenced in state court to enjoin construction of a low-income housing project. After the defendant removed the case to federal court, the court stated that since it was the defendant who was invoking federal jurisdiction, the amount in controversy would be measured solely from the defendant's perspective. The jurisdictional minimum was satisfied because if an injunction were issued, the defendant would lose more than $400,000 that it had already spent on construction.

PROBLEM

4-16. Sandstone, Inc. ("Sandstone") operates a highly popular restaurant near the beach in California. It recently expanded its outdoor eating area, adding a dozen new spotlights to illuminate the area at night. Ten nearby property owners have sued Sandstone in a California state court, alleging that the restaurant failed to comply with a local zoning ordinance. Plaintiffs seek to enjoin the defendant from using the new lights until the expansion project is submitted to and approved by the zoning board. Once such an application is submitted, it will take the board at least 60 days to review the restaurant expansion. Sandstone is a Delaware corporation with restaurants in all 50 states; its corporate offices are in Chicago, Illinois. Plaintiffs are all citizens of California. They claim that use of the new spotlights has reduced their property value in amounts ranging from $10,000 to $50,000 apiece. Without use of the new spotlights, Sandstone estimates it will lose an average of $1,500 per day. Sandstone has removed the case to federal court, based on diversity of citizenship. Does the case meet the requirements of § 1332?

4.   Supplemental Jurisdiction

a.   Overview and Introduction

Under the doctrine of "supplemental jurisdiction," a federal court may sometimes adjudicate rights of action that do not fall within the court's federal question or diversity jurisdiction. For example, suppose Sara and Ben were involved in an automobile accident that caused $500 damage to Sara's car. Even if she and Ben are of diverse citizenship, Sara could not sue Ben in federal court for the damage to her car since her claim would not meet § 1332's amount-in-controversy requirement. However, if Ben sues Sara in federal court seeking $250,000 for injuries he suffered in the accident, Sara could file a counterclaim against him for the $500 damage to her car. While there is no independent basis of jurisdiction over her $500 claim, it falls within the court's supplemental jurisdiction because it is factually related to Ben's claim over which jurisdiction exists pursuant to § 1332. In essence, Ben's and Sara's claims are part of the same case. As long as a federal court has proper subject matter jurisdiction over a "case," it may decide—as part of that case—some questions and even entire claims that could not have entered the federal courts on their own. Without supplemental jurisdiction, federal litigation would be highly inefficient, since claims like Ben's and Sara's would often have to be heard as separate lawsuits, even though they are closely related and involve many of the same witnesses.

Supplemental jurisdiction is governed by 28 U.S.C. § 1367, a statute that was adopted in 1990. This statute codified and replaced the previous judge-made doctrines of "pendent jurisdiction" and "ancillary jurisdiction." In studying supplemental jurisdiction we will start with pendent and ancillary jurisdiction, for without an understanding of these doctrines it is difficult to comprehend the operation of § 1367. We will then look more closely at supplemental jurisdiction, first as it applies in federal question cases and then as it applies in diversity cases. However, because supplemental jurisdiction in diversity cases depends heavily on which joinder rule the would-be supplemental claim was asserted under, a full discussion of § 1367's operation in diversity cases is saved for Chapter VIII, dealing with joinder of claims and parties.

b. Pendent and Ancillary Jurisdiction

The judge-made doctrine of pendent jurisdiction permitted federal courts to take jurisdiction over rights of action asserted by the *original plaintiff* for which there was no independent basis of subject matter jurisdiction. Ancillary jurisdiction, on the other hand, usually involved claims by a person *other than the original plaintiff*, again when no independent basis of jurisdiction existed. Examples of ancillary jurisdiction include claims by the defendant against the plaintiff (counterclaims); claims by a defendant against a co-defendant (cross-claims); claims by someone wishing to intervene in the suit as an additional plaintiff (intervention); and claims by a defendant against a third party who might be liable to the defendant for all or part of the plaintiff's claim (impleader).

United Mine Workers of America v. Gibbs
383 U.S. 715 (1966)

Mr. Justice Brennan delivered the opinion of the Court.

Respondent Paul Gibbs was awarded compensatory and punitive damages in this action against petitioner United Mine Workers of America (UMW) for alleged violations of § 303 of the Labor Management Relations Act, 1947, 61 Stat. 158, as amended and of the common law of Tennessee. The case grew out of the rivalry between the United Mine Workers and the Southern Labor Union over representation of workers in the southern Appalachian coal fields. Tennessee Consolidated Coal Company, not a party here, laid off 100 miners of the UMW's Local 5881 when it closed one of its mines in southern Tennessee during the spring of 1960. Late that summer, Grundy Company, a wholly owned subsidiary of Consolidated, hired respondent as mine superintendent to attempt to open a new mine on Consolidated's property at nearby Gray's Creek through use of members of the Southern Labor Union. As part of the arrangement, Grundy also gave respondent a contract to haul the mine's coal to the nearest railroad loading point.

On August 15 and 16, 1960, armed members of Local 5881 forcibly prevented the opening of the mine, threatening respondent and beating an organizer for the rival union. The members of the local believed Consolidated had promised them the jobs at the new mine; they insisted that if anyone would do the work, they would. . . . There was no further violence at the mine site; a picket line was maintained there for nine months; and no further attempts were made to open the mine during that period.

Respondent lost his job as superintendent, and never entered into performance of his haulage contract. He testified that he soon began to lose other trucking contracts and mine leases he held in nearby areas. Claiming these effects to be the result of a concerted union plan against him, he sought recovery not against Local 5881 or its members, but only against petitioner, the international union. The suit was brought in the United States District Court for the Eastern District of Tennessee, and jurisdiction was premised on allegations of secondary boycotts under § 303. The state law claim, for which jurisdiction was based upon the doctrine of pendent jurisdiction, asserted "an unlawful conspiracy and an unlawful boycott aimed at him and [Grundy] to maliciously, wantonly and willfully interfere with his contract of employment and with his contract of haulage."

The trial judge refused to submit to the jury the claims of pressure intended to cause mining firms other than Grundy to cease doing business with Gibbs; he found those claims unsupported by the evidence. The jury's verdict was that the UMW had violated both § 303 and state law. Gibbs was awarded $60,000 as damages under the employment contract and $14,500 under the haulage contract; he was also awarded $100,000 punitive damages. On motion, the trial court set aside the award of damages with respect to the haulage contract on the ground that damage was unproved. It also held that union pressure on Grundy to discharge respondent as supervisor would constitute only a primary dispute with Grundy, as respondent's employer, and hence was not cognizable as a claim under § 303. Interference with the employment relationship was cognizable as a state claim, however, and a remitted award [totaling $75,000] was sustained on the state law claim. The Court of Appeals for the Sixth Circuit affirmed. We granted certiorari. We reverse. . . .

A threshold question is whether the District Court properly entertained jurisdiction of the claim based on Tennessee law. . . .

The fact that state remedies were not entirely pre-empted [by federal law] does not, however, answer the question whether the state claim was properly adjudicated in the District Court absent diversity jurisdiction. The Court held in *Hurn v. Oursler*, 289 U.S. 238, that state law claims are appropriate for federal court determination if they form a separate but parallel ground for relief also sought in a substantial claim based on federal law. The Court distinguished permissible from non-permissible exercises of federal judicial power over state law claims by contrasting "a case where two distinct grounds in support of a single cause of action are alleged, one only of which presents a federal question, and a case where two separate and distinct causes of action are alleged, one only of which is federal in character. In the former, where the federal question averred is not plainly wanting in substance, the federal court, even though the federal ground be not established, may nevertheless retain and dispose of the case upon the nonfederal ground; in the latter it may not do so upon the nonfederal *cause of action*." The question is into which category the present action fell.

Hurn was decided in 1933, before the unification of law and equity by the Federal Rules of Civil Procedure. At the time, the meaning of "cause of action" was a subject of serious dispute; the phrase might "mean one thing for one purpose and something different for another." *United States v. Memphis Cotton Oil Co.*, 288 U.S. 62, 67-68. The Court in *Hurn* identified what it meant by the term by citation of *Baltimore S.S. Co. v. Phillips*, 274 U.S. 316, a case in which "cause of action" had been used to identify the operative scope of the doctrine of *res judicata*. In that case the Court had noted that "'the whole tendency of our decisions is to require a plaintiff to try his whole cause of action and his whole case at one time,'". . . . Had the Court found a jurisdictional bar to reaching the state claim in *Hurn*, we assume that the doctrine of *res judicata* would not have been applicable in any subsequent state suit. But . . . the Court found that the weighty policies of judicial economy and fairness to parties reflected in *res judicata* doctrine were in themselves strong counsel for the adoption of a rule which would permit federal courts to dispose of the state as well as the federal claims.

With the adoption of the Federal Rules of Civil Procedure and the unified form of action, Fed. Rule Civ. Proc. 2, much of the controversy over "cause of action" abated. The phrase remained as the keystone of the *Hurn* test, however, and . . . has been the source of considerable confusion. Under the Rules, the impulse is toward entertaining the broadest possible scope of action consistent with fairness to the parties; joinder of claims, parties and remedies is strongly encouraged. Yet because the *Hurn* question involves issues of jurisdiction as well as convenience, there has been some tendency to limit its application to cases in which the state and federal claims are, as in *Hurn*, "little more than the equivalent of different epithets to characterize the same group of circumstances."

This limited approach is unnecessarily grudging. Pendent jurisdiction, in the sense of judicial *power*, exists whenever there is a claim "arising under [the] Constitution, the Laws of the United States, and Treaties made, or which shall be made, under their Authority . . . ," U.S. Const., Art. III, § 2, and the relationship between that claim and the state claim permits the conclusion that the entire action before the court comprises but one constitutional "case." The federal claim must have substance sufficient to confer subject matter jurisdiction on the court. The state and federal claims must derive from a common nucleus of operative fact. But if, considered without regard to their federal or state character, a plaintiff's claims are such that he would ordinarily be expected to try them all in one judicial proceeding, then, assuming substantiality of the federal issues, there is power in federal courts to hear the whole.

That power need not be exercised in every case in which it is found to exist. It has consistently been recognized that pendent jurisdiction is a doctrine of discretion, not of plaintiff's right. Its justification lies in considerations of judicial economy, convenience and fairness to litigants; if these are not present a federal court should hesitate to exercise jurisdiction over state claims, even though bound to apply state law to them. Needless decisions of state law should be avoided both as a matter of comity and to promote justice between the parties, by procuring for them a surer-footed reading of applicable law. Certainly, if the federal claims are dismissed before trial, even though not insubstantial in a jurisdictional sense, the state claims should be dismissed as well. Similarly, if it appears that the state issues substantially predominate, whether in terms of proof, of the scope of the issues raised, or of the comprehensiveness of the remedy sought, the state claims may be dismissed without prejudice and left for resolution to state tribunals. There may, on the other hand, be situations in which the state claim is so closely tied to questions of federal policy that the argument for exercise of pendent jurisdiction is particularly strong. In the present case, for example, the allowable scope of the state claim implicates the federal doctrine of pre-emption; while this interrelationship does not create statutory federal question jurisdiction, *Louisville & N.R. Co. v. Mottley*, 211 U.S. 149, its existence is relevant to the exercise of discretion. Finally, there may be reasons independent of jurisdictional considerations, such as the likelihood of jury confusion in treating divergent legal theories of relief, that would justify separating state and federal claims for trial, Fed. Rule Civ. Proc. 42(b). If so, jurisdiction should ordinarily be refused.

The question of power will ordinarily be resolved on the pleadings. But the issue whether pendent jurisdiction has been properly assumed is one which remains open throughout the litigation. Pretrial procedures or even the trial itself may reveal a substantial hegemony of state law claims, or likelihood of jury confusion, which could not have been anticipated at the pleading stage. Although it will of course be appropriate to take account in this circumstance of the already completed course of the litigation, dismissal of the state claim might even then be merited. For example, it may appear that the plaintiff was well aware of the nature of his proofs and the relative importance of his claims; recognition of a federal court's wide latitude to decide ancillary questions of state law does not imply that it must tolerate a litigant's effort to impose upon it what is in effect only a state law case. Once it appears that a state claim constitutes the real body of a case, to which the federal claim is only an appendage, the state claim may fairly be dismissed.

We are not prepared to say that in the present case the District Court exceeded its discretion in proceeding to judgment on the state claim. We may assume for purposes of decision that the District Court was correct in its holding that the claim of pressure on Grundy to terminate the employment contract was outside the purview of § 303. Even so, the § 303 claims based on secondary pressures on Grundy relative to the haulage contract and on other coal operators generally were substantial. . . . [T]he state and federal claims arose from the same nucleus of operative fact and reflected alternative remedies. Indeed, the verdict sheet sent in to the jury authorized only one award of damages, so that recovery could not be given separately on the federal and state claims.

It is true that the § 303 claims ultimately failed and that the only recovery allowed respondent was on the state claim. We cannot confidently say, however, that the federal issues were so remote or played such a minor role at the trial that in effect the state claim only was tried. Although the District Court dismissed as unproved the § 303 claims that petitioner's secondary activities included attempts to induce coal operators other than Grundy to cease doing business with respondent, the court submitted the § 303 claims relating to Grundy to the jury. The jury returned verdicts against petitioner on those § 303 claims, and it was only on petitioner's motion for a directed verdict and a judgment *n.o.v.* that the verdicts on those claims were set aside. The District Judge considered the claim as to the haulage contract proved as to liability, and held it failed only for lack of proof of damages. Although there was some risk of confusing the jury in joining the state and federal claims—especially since, as will be developed, differing standards of proof of UMW involvement applied—the possibility of confusion could be lessened by employing a special verdict form, as the District Court did. Moreover, the question whether the permissible scope of the state claim was limited by the doctrine of pre-emption afforded a special reason for the exercise of pendent jurisdiction; the federal courts are particularly appropriate bodies for the application of pre-emption principles. We thus conclude that although it may be that the District Court might, in its sound discretion, have dismissed the state claim, the circumstances show no error in refusing to do so.

[After holding that pendent jurisdiction existed over the state law claims, the Supreme Court reversed the judgment on the ground that there was insufficient proof of UMW involvement to find the union liable for its members' conduct.]

NOTES AND QUESTIONS

1. *Identifying the claim in Gibbs.*   What were the operative facts of the claim asserted by Gibbs? What rights of action arose out of those facts? Under Federal Rule of Civil Procedure 8(a)(2), would it matter that one of those rights was based on federal law and that others were based on state law? Setting aside jurisdictional issues for the moment, would it make sense to adjudicate the three rights of action asserted by Gibbs in a single proceeding? If the case filed by Gibbs is treated as a direct product of his claim, wouldn't it also make sense to say that the entire case arose under federal law since resolution of Gibbs's claim would depend, in part, on the construction, validity, and/or effect of federal law? Indeed, federal law created one of the rights of action asserted by Gibbs. In other words, the operative-facts definition of a claim may have rendered the doctrine of pendent claim jurisdiction superfluous. At a minimum, does this suggest that there is a close affinity between the operative-facts definition of a claim and the doctrinal definition of pendent jurisdiction? (Note that courts in this particular context tend to use the word "claim" in a non-technical sense as interchangeable with "right of action.")

2. *A single constitutional case.*   Why was it important in *Gibbs* that the federal and state law rights of action (or claims) arose from "a common nucleus of operative fact"? Would the court have had the constitutional power to take pendent

jurisdiction over a state law right of action by Gibbs against the UMW based on an unrelated incident that had occurred two years earlier? Would that right of action present a different claim, *i.e.*, a different set of operative facts? Is there a relationship between the operative-facts definition of a claim and the common-nucleus-of-operative-facts definition of what constitutes a case?

3. *Common nucleus of operative fact.*   Courts differ as to what constitutes a common nucleus of operative fact. Some courts require only a "loose" factual connection while others insist on a much closer nexus. *Compare Baer v. First Options of Chicago Inc.*, 72 F.3d 1294, 1299-1301 (7th Cir. 1995) (applying "loose connection" test in upholding supplemental jurisdiction over claims between plaintiff's attorneys concerning who was entitled to fees in a Title VII case), *with Lyon v. Whisman*, 45 F.3d 758, 761-763 (3d Cir. 1995) (rejecting "loose nexus" test and finding no supplemental jurisdiction between a federal right of action for overtime wages and state right of action for a promised bonus). Is this debate over the relative "looseness" or "tightness" of the connection helpful? Is it consistent with *Gibbs*? Did the *Gibbs* Court offer a method through which to determine if separate claims or rights of action arise out of a common nucleus of operative facts? In answering this question, consider this observation by the *Gibbs* Court: "But if, considered without regard to their federal or state character, a plaintiff's claims are such that he would ordinarily be expected to try them all in one judicial proceeding, then, assuming substantiality of the federal issues, there is power in federal courts to hear the whole."

4. *Power and discretion.*   The exercise of pendent jurisdiction involves two separate questions. First, does the federal court have the constitutional power to hear the state-law claims? Second, if the power exists, should the court in its discretion assert pendent jurisdiction? The first question is sometimes described as comprising three elements: (1) a federal question that is sufficiently substantial to confer jurisdiction; (2) a common nucleus of operative facts; and (3) separate claims that one would expect to be tried in one judicial proceeding. The first element merely restates the substantiality requirement for federal question jurisdiction. The second element we have already described, and the third, although often described as "cumulative" with the second, helps define the range of that second element by suggesting a common-sense approach to the factual relationship between claims that ought to be tried together. *See* 13D Charles Alan Wright, Arthur R. Miller, Edward H. Cooper & Richard D. Freer, Federal Practice and Procedure: Jurisdiction and Related Matters § 3567.1 (3d ed. 2008 & Supp. 2015).

As to the second question, what factors did the *Gibbs* Court suggest a trial court should take into account in exercising its discretion? Suppose that two years after a suit was filed but before trial begins, the plaintiff's federal right of action (*i.e.*, the jurisdiction-conferring aspect of the claim) is dismissed. Must the federal court dismiss the pendent state-law right of action? Would dismissal under such circumstances necessarily represent a sensible use of judicial resources? What additional facts might be relevant to resolving this question?

Owen Equipment and Erection Co. v. Kroger

437 U.S. 365 (1978)

MR. JUSTICE STEWART delivered the opinion of the Court.

In an action in which federal jurisdiction is based on diversity of citizenship, may the plaintiff assert a claim against a third-party defendant when there is no independent basis for federal jurisdiction over that claim? . . .   —issue

I

'No

On January 18, 1972, James Kroger was electrocuted when the boom of a steel crane next to which he was walking came too close to a high-tension electric power line. The respondent [Geraldine Kroger] (his widow, who is the administratrix of his estate) filed a wrongful-death action in the United States District Court for the District of Nebraska against the Omaha Public Power District (OPPD). Her complaint alleged that OPPD's negligent construction, maintenance, and operation of the power line had caused Kroger's death. Federal jurisdiction was based on diversity of citizenship, since the respondent was a citizen of Iowa and OPPD was a Nebraska corporation.

OPPD then filed a third-party complaint pursuant to Fed. Rule Civ. Proc. 14(a)* against the petitioner, Owen Equipment and Erection Co. (Owen), alleging that the crane was owned and operated by Owen, and that Owen's negligence had been the proximate cause of Kroger's death. OPPD later moved for summary judgment on the respondent's complaint against it. While this motion was pending, the respondent was granted leave to file an amended complaint naming Owen as an additional defendant. Thereafter, the District Court granted OPPD's motion for summary judgment in an unreported opinion. The case thus went to trial between the respondent and the petitioner alone.

The respondent's amended complaint alleged that Owen was "a Nebraska corporation with its principal place of business in Nebraska." Owen's answer admitted that it was "a corporation organized and existing under the laws of the State of Nebraska," and denied every other allegation of the complaint. On the third day of trial, however, it was disclosed that the petitioner's principal place of business was in Iowa, not Nebraska,[5] and that the petitioner and the respondent were thus both citizens of Iowa. The petitioner then moved to dismiss the complaint for lack of jurisdiction. The District Court reserved decision on the motion, and the jury thereafter returned a verdict in favor of the respondent. . . . [A]fter the trial, the District Court denied the petitioner's motion to dismiss the complaint.

---

* [Rule 14 impleader allows the defendant to file a third-party complaint against one not already a party to the suit, seeking indemnity in the event the defendant is found liable to the plaintiff.—EDS.]

5. The problem apparently was one of geography. Although the Missouri River generally marks the boundary between Iowa and Nebraska, Carter Lake, Iowa, where the accident occurred and where Owen had its main office, lies west of the river, adjacent to Omaha, Neb. Apparently the river once avulsed at one of its bends, cutting Carter Lake off from the rest of Iowa.

The judgment was affirmed on appeal. The Court of Appeals held that under this Court's decision in *Mine Workers v. Gibbs*, the District Court had jurisdictional power, in its discretion, to adjudicate the respondent's claim against the petitioner because that claim arose from the "core of 'operative facts' giving rise to both [respondent's] claim against OPPD and OPPD's claim against Owen." It further held that the District Court had properly exercised its discretion in proceeding to decide the case even after summary judgment had been granted to OPPD, because the petitioner had concealed its Iowa citizenship from the respondent. . . .

II

It is undisputed that there was no independent basis of federal jurisdiction over the respondent's state-law tort action against the petitioner, since both are citizens of Iowa. And although Fed. Rule Civ. Proc. 14(a) permits a plaintiff to assert a claim against a third-party defendant, it does not purport to say whether or not such a claim requires an independent basis of federal jurisdiction. Indeed, it could not determine that question, since it is axiomatic that the Federal Rules of Civil Procedure do not create or withdraw federal jurisdiction.

In affirming the District Court's judgment, the Court of Appeals relied upon the doctrine of ancillary jurisdiction, whose contours it believed were defined by this Court's holding in *Mine Workers v. Gibbs*. The *Gibbs* case differed from this one in that it involved pendent jurisdiction, which concerns the resolution of a plaintiff's federal- and state-law claims against a single defendant in one action. By contrast, in this case there was no claim based upon substantive federal law, but rather state-law tort claims against two different defendants. Nonetheless, the Court of Appeals was correct in perceiving that *Gibbs* and this case are two species of the same generic problem: Under what circumstances may a federal court hear and decide a state-law claim arising between citizens of the same State? But we believe that the Court of Appeals failed to understand the scope of the doctrine of the *Gibbs* case. . . .

It is apparent that *Gibbs* delineated the constitutional limits of federal judicial power. But even if it be assumed that the District Court in the present case had constitutional power to decide the respondent's lawsuit against the petitioner,[10] it does not follow that the decision of the Court of Appeals was correct. Constitutional power is merely the first hurdle that must be overcome in determining that a federal court has jurisdiction over a particular controversy. For the jurisdiction of the federal courts is limited not only by the provisions of Art. III of the Constitution, but also by Acts of Congress.

---

10. Federal jurisdiction in *Gibbs* was based upon the existence of a question of federal law. The Court of Appeals in the present case believed that the "common nucleus of operative fact" test also determines the outer boundaries of constitutionally permissible federal jurisdiction when that jurisdiction is based upon diversity of citizenship. We may assume without deciding that the Court of Appeals was correct in this regard.

That statutory law as well as the Constitution may limit a federal court's juris-diction over nonfederal claims[11] is well illustrated by two recent decisions of this Court, *Aldinger v. Howard*, 427 U.S. 1 (1976) and *Zahn v. International Paper Co.*, 414 U.S. 291 (1973). In *Aldinger* the Court held that a Federal District Court lacked jurisdiction over a state-law claim against a county, even if that claim was alleged to be pendent to one against county officials under 42 U.S.C. § 1983. In *Zahn* the Court held that in a diversity class action under Fed. Rule Civ. Proc. 23(b)(3), the claim of each member of the plaintiff class must independently sat-isfy the minimum jurisdictional amount set by 28 U.S.C. § 1332(a), and rejected the argument that jurisdiction existed over those claims that involved $10,000 or less as ancillary to those that involved more. In each case, despite the fact that fed-eral and nonfederal claims arose from a "common nucleus of operative fact," the Court held that the statute conferring jurisdiction over the federal claim did not allow the exercise of jurisdiction over the nonfederal claim.

The *Aldinger* and *Zahn* cases thus make clear that a finding that federal and nonfederal claims arise from a "common nucleus of operative fact," the test of *Gibbs*, does not end the inquiry into whether a federal court has power to hear the nonfederal claims along with the federal ones. Beyond this constitutional mini-mum, there must be an examination of the posture in which the nonfederal claim is asserted and of the specific statute that confers jurisdiction over the federal claim, in order to determine whether "Congress in [that statute] has . . . expressly or by implication negated" the exercise of jurisdiction over the particular nonfed-eral claim. *Aldinger v. Howard, supra*, 427 U.S., at 18.

III

The relevant statute in this case, 28 U.S.C. § 1332(a)(1), confers upon federal courts jurisdiction over "civil actions where the matter in controversy exceeds the sum or value of $10,000 . . . and is between . . . citizens of different States." This statute and its predecessors have consistently been held to require complete diver-sity of citizenship. That is, diversity jurisdiction does not exist unless *each* defen-dant is a citizen of a different State from each plaintiff. Over the years Congress has repeatedly re-enacted or amended the statute conferring diversity jurisdiction, leaving intact this rule of complete diversity. Whatever may have been the origi-nal purposes of diversity-of-citizenship jurisdiction, this subsequent history clearly demonstrates a congressional mandate that diversity jurisdiction is not to be avail-able when any plaintiff is a citizen of the same State as any defendant.[16]

---

11. As used in this opinion, the term "nonfederal claim" means one as to which there is no independent basis for federal jurisdiction. Conversely, a "federal claim" means one as to which an independent basis for federal jurisdiction exists.

16. Notably, Congress enacted § 1332 as part of the Judicial Code of 1948, shortly after Rule 14 was amended in 1946. When the Rule was amended, the Advisory Committee noted that "in any case where the plaintiff could not have joined the third party originally because of jurisdictional limitations such as lack of diversity of citizenship, the majority view is that any attempt by the plain-tiff to amend his complaint and assert a claim against the impleaded third party would be unavail-ing." 28 U.S.C. App., p. 7752. The subsequent re-enactment without relevant change of the diversity statute may thus be seen as evidence of congressional approval of that "majority view."

not the only requirement

   Thus it is clear that the respondent could not originally have brought suit in federal court naming Owen and OPPD as codefendants, since citizens of Iowa would have been on both sides of the litigation. Yet the identical lawsuit resulted when she amended her complaint. Complete diversity was destroyed just as surely as if she had sued Owen initially. In either situation, in the plain language of the statute, the "matter in controversy" could not be "between . . . citizens of different States."

   It is a fundamental precept that federal courts are courts of limited jurisdiction. The limits upon federal jurisdiction, whether imposed by the Constitution or by Congress, must be neither disregarded nor evaded. Yet under the reasoning of the Court of Appeals in this case, a plaintiff could defeat the statutory requirement of complete diversity by the simple expedient of suing only those defendants who were of diverse citizenship and waiting for them to implead non-diverse defendants.[17] If a "common nucleus of operative fact" were the only requirement for ancillary jurisdiction in a diversity case, there would be no principled reason why the respondent in this case could not have joined her cause of action against Owen in her original complaint as ancillary to her claim against OPPD. Congress' requirement of complete diversity would thus have been evaded completely.

   It is true, as the Court of Appeals noted, that the exercise of ancillary jurisdiction over nonfederal claims has often been upheld in situations involving impleader, cross-claims or counterclaims.[18] But in determining whether jurisdiction over a nonfederal claim exists, the context in which the nonfederal claim is asserted is crucial. And the claim here arises in a setting quite different from the kinds of nonfederal claims that have been viewed in other cases as falling within the ancillary jurisdiction of the federal courts.

   First, the nonfederal claim in this case was simply not ancillary to the federal one in the same sense that, for example, the impleader by a defendant of a third-party defendant always is. A third-party complaint depends at least in part upon the resolution of the primary lawsuit. Its relation to the original complaint is thus not mere factual similarity but logical dependence. The respondent's claim against the petitioner, however, was entirely separate from her original claim against OPPD, since the petitioner's liability to her depended not at all upon

---

   17. This is not an unlikely hypothesis, since a defendant in a tort suit such as this one would surely try to limit his liability by impleading any joint tortfeasors for indemnity or contribution. Some commentators have suggested that the possible abuse of third-party practice could be dealt with under 28 U.S.C. § 1359 which forbids collusive attempts to create federal jurisdiction. The dissenting opinion today also expresses this view. But there is nothing necessarily collusive about a plaintiff's selectively suing only those tortfeasors of diverse citizenship, or about the named defendants' desire to implead joint tortfeasors. Nonetheless, the requirement of complete diversity would be eviscerated by such a course of events.

   18. The ancillary jurisdiction of the federal courts derives originally from cases such as *Freeman v. Howe*, 24 How. 450, which held that when federal jurisdiction "effectively controls the property or fund under dispute, other claimants thereto should be allowed to intervene in order to protect their interests, without regard to jurisdiction." *Aldinger v. Howard*, 427 U.S., at 11. More recently, it has been said to include cases that involve multiparty practice, such as compulsory counterclaims; impleader; cross-claims; or intervention as of right.

whether or not OPPD was also liable. Far from being an ancillary and dependent claim, it was a new and independent one.

Second, the nonfederal claim here was asserted by the plaintiff, who voluntarily chose to bring suit upon a state-law claim in a federal court. By contrast, ancillary jurisdiction typically involves claims by a defending party haled into court against his will, or by another person whose rights might be irretrievably lost unless he could assert them in an ongoing action in a federal court. A plaintiff cannot complain if ancillary jurisdiction does not encompass all of his possible claims in a case such as this one, since it is he who has chosen the federal rather than the state forum and must thus accept its limitations. "[T]he efficiency plaintiff seeks so avidly is available without question in the state courts."[20]

It is not unreasonable to assume that, in generally requiring complete diversity, Congress did not intend to confine the jurisdiction of federal courts so inflexibly that they are unable to protect legal rights or effectively to resolve an entire, logically entwined lawsuit. Those practical needs are the basis of the doctrine of ancillary jurisdiction. But neither the convenience of litigants nor considerations of judicial economy can suffice to justify extension of the doctrine of ancillary jurisdiction to a plaintiff's cause of action against a citizen of the same State in a diversity case. Congress has established the basic rule that diversity jurisdiction exists under 28 U.S.C. § 1332 only when there is complete diversity of citizenship. . . . To allow the requirement of complete diversity to be circumvented as it was in this case would simply flout the congressional command.

Accordingly, the judgment of the Court of Appeals is reversed. *It is so ordered.*

Mr. Justice White, with whom Mr. Justice Brennan joins, dissenting. . . .

In the present case, the only indication of congressional intent that the Court can find is that contained in the diversity jurisdictional statute, 28 U.S.C. § 1332(a). . . . Because this statute has been interpreted as requiring complete diversity of citizenship between each plaintiff and each defendant, *Strawbridge v. Curtiss*, the Court holds that the District Court did not have ancillary jurisdiction over Mrs. Kroger's claim against Owen. In so holding, the Court unnecessarily expands the scope of the complete-diversity requirement while substantially limiting the doctrine of ancillary jurisdiction.

The complete-diversity requirement, of course, could be viewed as meaning that in a diversity case, a federal district court may adjudicate only those claims that are between parties of different States. Thus, in order for a defendant to implead a third-party defendant, there would have to be diversity of citizenship; the same would also be true for cross-claims between defendants and for a third-party defendant's claim against a plaintiff. Even the majority, however, refuses to read the complete-diversity requirement so broadly; it recognizes with seeming approval the exercise of ancillary jurisdiction over nonfederal claims in situations

---

20. Whether Iowa's statute of limitations would now bar an action by the respondent in an Iowa court is, of course, entirely a matter of state law. . . .

involving impleader, cross-claims, and counterclaims. Given the Court's willingness to recognize ancillary jurisdiction in these contexts, despite the requirements of § 1332(a), I see no justification for the Court's refusal to approve the District Court's exercise of ancillary jurisdiction in the present case.

It is significant that a plaintiff who asserts a claim against a third-party defendant is not seeking to add a new party to the lawsuit. In the present case, for example, Owen had already been brought into the suit by OPPD, and, that having been done, Mrs. Kroger merely sought to assert against Owen a claim arising out of the same transaction that was already before the court. . . .

Because in the instant case Mrs. Kroger merely sought to assert a claim against someone already a party to the suit, considerations of judicial economy, convenience, and fairness to the litigants—the factors relied upon in *Gibbs*—support the recognition of ancillary jurisdiction here. Already before the court was the whole question of the cause of Mr. Kroger's death. Mrs. Kroger initially contended that OPPD was responsible; OPPD in turn contended that Owen's negligence had been the proximate cause of Mr. Kroger's death. In spite of the fact that the question of Owen's negligence was already before the District Court, the majority requires Mrs. Kroger to bring a separate action in state court in order to assert that very claim. Even if the Iowa statute of limitations will still permit such a suit, considerations of judicial economy are certainly not served by requiring such duplicative litigation.[4] . . .

We have previously noted that "[s]ubsequent decisions of this Court indicate that *Strawbridge* is not to be given an expansive reading." *State Farm Fire & Cas. Co. v. Tashire*, 386 U.S. 523, 531 n.6 (1967). In light of this teaching, it seems to me appropriate to view § 1332 as requiring complete diversity only between the plaintiff and those parties he actually brings into the suit. Beyond that, I would hold that in a diversity case the District Court has power, both constitutional and statutory, to entertain all claims among the parties arising from the same nucleus of operative fact as the plaintiff's original, jurisdiction-conferring claim against the defendant. Accordingly, I dissent from the Court's disposition of the present case.

NOTES AND QUESTIONS

1. Jurisdiction over third-party complaint.   OPPD's third-party complaint seeking indemnity against Owen was based on state law. Did complete diversity exist between these two parties? If not, how did subject matter jurisdiction exist over

---

4. It is true that prior to trial OPPD was dismissed as a party to the suit and that, as we indicated in *Gibbs*, the dismissal prior to trial of the federal claim will generally require the dismissal of the nonfederal claim as well. Given the unusual facts of the present case, however—in particular, the fact that the actual location of Owen's principal place of business was not revealed until the third day of trial—fairness to the parties would lead me to conclude that the District Court did not abuse its discretion in retaining jurisdiction over Mrs. Kroger's claim against Owen. . . .

this claim? As footnote 18 observes, ancillary jurisdiction is often used in situations of this type involving the defendant's impleader of a third-party defendant.

2. *Ancillary or pendent jurisdiction?*   The lower courts here treated Kroger's claim against Owen as involving ancillary jurisdiction. Yet, as the Court notes, ancillary jurisdiction "typically" involves claims by defendants or by those intervening in a suit to protect their interests. If, as here, the claim is asserted by the original plaintiff, doesn't it really involve a form of pendent jurisdiction? Does the Court suggest that it will be more sympathetic toward typical ancillary claims than to those asserted by the original plaintiff? How does the Court rationalize this difference in treatment?

3. *The issue of power.*   In *Gibbs* we saw that pendent jurisdiction involved two questions: power and discretion. The question of power turned on whether the federal and state rights of action were part of the same constitutional case, *i.e.*, whether they arose from a common nucleus of operative fact. If they did, a court had discretion to hear the entire claim. In *Kroger*, was there any doubt that Geraldine Kroger's claim against Owen involved the same constitutional case as her claim against OPPD? (Note that Kroger's rights of action against Owen and OPPD are, in fact, separate "claims" since they are asserted against different parties.) If it would have been constitutional for the court to hear her claim against Owen, why did the district court lack jurisdiction over it? Did the Supreme Court rule that the lower courts merely abused their discretion in deciding to exercise jurisdiction over that claim, or was the problem one of power? Has the Court now added a second step to the power analysis, one not discussed in *Gibbs*? How would you describe that step? Did *Kroger* implicitly overrule *Gibbs*? Or does the perceived congressional intent justify different results in the two cases?

4. *Circumventing § 1332.*   The *Kroger* majority repeatedly warned that if it allowed ancillary or pendent jurisdiction over claims by a plaintiff against a nondiverse third-party defendant, plaintiffs like Kroger could easily circumvent the complete diversity requirement of § 1332. Indeed, the Court analyzes the case as though Kroger had originally sued both OPPD and Owen. Had she done so, her suit presumably would have been dismissed (unless the claim against Owen were dropped) since complete diversity would not have existed. But could Kroger have asked the court to take pendent jurisdiction over her nondiversity claim against Owen? The case resembled *Gibbs* in that Kroger asserted two rights of action arising out of the same set of operative facts, one that had an independent basis of jurisdiction and one that did not. Yet there was a critical difference between the two cases, for unlike *Gibbs*, Kroger was not asserting her rights of action against the same party. Instead, the pendent right of action (or claim) in *Kroger* involved a defendant (Owen) who was not a party to the jurisdiction-conferring right of action against OPPD; it would thus have involved using pendent jurisdiction to add a new *party* to the suit, not just an additional right of action against a defendant who was otherwise properly before the court. Courts refer to this as "pendent party" jurisdiction. The *Kroger* Court was obviously reluctant to allow pendent-party jurisdiction when doing so would evade the complete diversity requirement of § 1332.

A NOTE ON *KROGER* AND POTENTIAL EVASIONS OF THE COMPLETE DIVERSITY PRINCIPLE

The complete diversity principle precludes a plaintiff in a diversity case from filing a claim against a nondiverse defendant. A "plaintiff" is a person named as such in the complaint, or so designated by the court on entry into the case, or as a consequence of realignment by the court. Similarly, a "defendant" is a person named as such in the complaint (and properly served), or so designated by the court on entry into the case, or as a consequence of realignment by the court. In other words, the status of being either a plaintiff or a defendant is a technical and literal one that arises from the party's actual status in the case. By way of contrast, a party brought into a case pursuant to Rule 14 is a "third-party defendant," which is a status separate and distinct from the status of either a plaintiff or a defendant (as defined above). Hence, the complete-diversity rule does not technically apply to parties brought in under Rule 14, for such a party is neither a plaintiff nor a defendant. Thus there is no violation of the complete-diversity principle when a party impleads a nondiverse third-party defendant. In *Kroger*, for example, there was no violation of the complete diversity principle when the OPPD impleaded Owen Equipment ("Owen"), even though both parties were from the same state. In short, the complete-diversity rule pertains only to claims filed by literal plaintiffs against literal defendants.

The *Kroger* decision does not alter the complete-diversity principle, but it extends it. Under *Kroger*, and as a direct consequence of the complete-diversity principle, neither pendent nor ancillary jurisdiction (collectively "supplemental jurisdiction") may be used in a manner that circumvents that principle. For example, if a plaintiff were to sue two defendants, only one of whom was diverse from the plaintiff, supplemental jurisdiction could not be invoked to establish jurisdiction over the claim asserted against the nondiverse defendant. To rule otherwise would circumvent the complete-diversity principle, for it would literally allow the plaintiff to do that which the principle forbids, namely, assert a diversity claim against a nondiverse defendant. But the majority opinion in *Kroger* went a step further than this by precluding the exercise of supplemental jurisdiction in situations that do not technically violate the complete-diversity principle but that may operate as an evasion of that principle.

The situation in *Kroger* is instructive. OPPD impleaded Owen pursuant to Rule 14. Kroger then sought to assert an affirmative claim against Owen (as is permitted by Rule 14). The assertion of a Rule 14 claim under such circumstances would not technically violate the complete-diversity principle, even if both parties were from the same state, since it does not involve a claim by a plaintiff against a defendant; rather, it is a claim asserted by the plaintiff against a third-party defendant. Nonetheless, the Court concluded that allowing Kroger to assert her claim against Owen would, at least potentially, operate as an evasion of the complete-diversity principle. The potential evasion would work like this: (1) the plaintiff sues a diverse party, anticipating that the party will implead a third-party defendant who is not diverse from the plaintiff; (2) the defendant does, in fact, implead that third-party defendant; and (3) the plaintiff responds by filing a Rule 14 claim against the third-party defendant. The problem in *Kroger* was not that the plaintiff there engaged in such a tactic, but that the claim against the impleaded, nondiverse party would create a potential for circumventing the jurisdictional requirements of § 1332. Thus *Kroger* stands for the proposition that a federal court may not exercise supplemental jurisdiction under circumstances that violate the complete-diversity principle or that create the potential for evading that principle. *Kroger* does not completely foreclose the exercise of supplemental jurisdiction over a claim filed by a plaintiff against a nondiverse party. Rather, the decision forecloses the filing of such claims only when doing so either violates the complete diversity principle — plaintiff versus nondiverse defendant — or sanctions a joinder device that risks evasion of the complete-diversity principle.

Consider two examples. First, using the basic alignment of the parties in *Kroger*, suppose that before Kroger filed her claim against Owen. Owen, pursuant to Rule 14, filed a claim against her. If Kroger were to respond to that claim with a compulsory counterclaim, could the court exercise supplemental jurisdiction over her counterclaim? It should be clear that Kroger's claim does not violate the complete-diversity principle, for her claim, although asserted against a nondiverse party, is not asserted against a defendant and is filed in response to another claim. Nonetheless, would the exercise of jurisdiction over this responsive claim operate (at least potentially) as an evasion of the complete-diversity principle? The key distinction between this scenario and the actual situation in *Kroger* is the intermediate claim filed by Owen against Kroger. Does that additional step in the process sufficiently ameliorate the potential for evasion? After the decision in *Kroger*, the consensus view among lower courts was that the potential for evasion in such cases was sufficiently ameliorated to allow a federal court to exercise supplemental jurisdiction over the plaintiff's counterclaim. *See Finkle v. Gulf & W. Mfg. Co.*, 744 F.2d 1015 (3d Cir. 1984); 6 CHARLES ALAN WRIGHT, ARTHUR R. MILLER & MARY KAY KANE, FEDERAL PRACTICE AND PROCEDURE § 1444.1 & nn.17-19 (3d ed. 2010 & Supp. 2015). In short, there was no violation of the complete-diversity principle and an insufficient potential that the principle would be evaded.

Second, again using the basic alignment of the parties in *Kroger*, suppose that OPPD, the named defendant, filed a counterclaim against Kroger and that in response Kroger sought to implead Owen on a theory of indemnity — Rule 14(b) specifically allows a plaintiff to file an impleader under such circumstances. Would Kroger's impleader violate the evasion principle and, hence, foreclose the exercise of supplemental jurisdiction over her indemnity claim against Owen? Stated slightly differently, would the counterclaim filed by OPPD against Kroger sufficiently ameliorate the potential for evasion such that the exercise of supplemental jurisdiction would be appropriate? Again, after the decision in *Kroger*, lower federal courts viewed this type of situation as sufficiently distinguishable from the *Kroger* scenario, such that the exercise of supplemental jurisdiction would be appropriate. Indeed, as in the first scenario, Kroger's claim is filed in response to another claim, thus ameliorating the potential for evasion of the § 1332 jurisdictional requirements. *See Brown & Caldwell v. Institute for Energy Funding, Ltd.*, 617 F. Supp. 649 (C.D. Cal. 1985).

A NOTE ON PENDENT-PARTY JURISDICTION

As we have seen, *Kroger* in effect rejected pendent-party jurisdiction over Geraldine Kroger's claim against Owen. Though her claims against OPPD and Owen were part of the same constitutional case, the Court held that congressional limitations on federal jurisdiction, as embodied in § 1332's complete-diversity requirement, prohibited a federal court from exercising jurisdiction over a state-law claim between citizens of the same state.

In two other cases, the Supreme Court again rejected pendent-party jurisdiction on the ground that it would be inconsistent with congressional intent. The first case, *Aldinger v. Howard*, 427 U.S. 1 (1976), was a suit brought in federal court by Monica Aldinger after she was fired from her job with Spokane County for living with her boyfriend. She sued several defendants, including the county and her boss, Merton Howard. Because Aldinger, the county, and Howard were all citizens of Washington, there was no diversity jurisdiction. Her principal claim against Howard was based on the Federal Civil Rights Act, 42 U.S.C. § 1983, over which the district court had jurisdiction pursuant to 28 U.S.C. § 1343. The claims against the county were based entirely on state law. Though they lacked an independent basis of jurisdiction, Aldinger urged that since these claims arose from the same common nucleus of operative fact as her claims against Howard, pendent-party jurisdiction allowed the court to hear them. The Supreme Court rejected the argument. After examining the legislative history of the jurisdiction-conferring statute, § 1343, it concluded that Congress did not wish that statute to be used to bring counties into federal court. Pendent-party jurisdiction in this setting would thus have been contrary to congressional intent. Moreover, since Aldinger could have filed all her claims in state court, the denial of pendent-party jurisdiction here did not result in judicial inefficiency or hardship to litigants.

The *Aldinger* Court pointedly left the door open for pendent-party jurisdiction in other contexts, stating:

> [W]e decide here only the issue of so-called "pendent party" jurisdiction with respect to a claim brought under §§ 1343(3) and 1983. Other statutory grants and other alignments of parties and claims might call for a different result. When the grant of jurisdiction to a federal court is exclusive, for example, as in the prosecution of tort claims against the United States under 28 U.S.C. § 1346, the argument of judicial economy and convenience can be coupled with the additional argument that *only* in a federal court may all of the claims be tried together. . . . [I]t would be as unwise as it would be unnecessary to lay down any sweeping pronouncement upon the existence or exercise of such jurisdiction.

Aldinger, 427 U.S. at 18. In deciding whether or not to exercise pendent-party jurisdiction, lower courts were told to make sure that "Congress in the statutes conferring jurisdiction has not expressly or by implication negated its existence." *Id.*

Finley v. United States, 490 U.S. 545 (1989), presented the Court with the very case that it had contemplated in *Aldinger*. Barbara Finley brought the suit on behalf of her husband and two children who were killed in a plane crash at a

San Diego, California, airport. The defendants were the United States, the City of San Diego, and a utility company that maintained power lines near the airport. The claim against the United States was made under the Federal Tort Claims Act (FTCA) over which the federal court had exclusive jurisdiction pursuant to 28 U.S.C. § 1346(b). The city and the utility were sued under state tort law. Though no diversity of citizenship existed, Finley urged that pendent-party jurisdiction existed over her state tort claims against the two nonfederal defendants. In a five-to-four decision, the Supreme Court rejected the argument, even though it meant that a plaintiff like Barbara Finley would have to split her lawsuit in two, bringing her FTCA claim against the United States in federal court while proceeding against the other defendants in state court.

Unlike *Kroger* and *Aldinger*, there was no evidence in *Finley* that Congress had *rejected* the proposed exercise of pendent-party jurisdiction. Instead, the *Finley* Court proceeded by analyzing the language of § 1346(b) and concluding that Congress had not expressly *authorized* jurisdiction over the pendent parties; the lack of such an authorization was fatal. The Court's earlier cases had assumed the existence of pendent-party jurisdiction in the absence of evidence that Congress had expressly or impliedly negated it. *Finley* proceeded from the opposite assumption, insisting on an express congressional authorization before allowing such jurisdiction. By requiring an express statutory authorization, *Finley* sounded the death knell for pendent-party jurisdiction; for with such a statute there is no need to invoke the doctrine, and without such a statute the doctrine may not be employed.

c.   Supplemental Jurisdiction: § 1367

The *Finley* Court invited Congress to respond if it was unhappy with the Court's rejection of pendent-party jurisdiction in that case: "Whatever we say regarding the scope of jurisdiction conferred by a particular statute can of course be changed by Congress." *Finley*, 490 U.S. at 556. Congress accepted the invitation, but not just as to the "particular statute" involved in *Finley*. Instead, Congress in 1990 enacted 28 U.S.C. § 1367, which provides for "supplemental jurisdiction." This statute codifies and replaces the former common law doctrines of pendent and ancillary jurisdiction, and allows in many instances for the exercise of what was previously referred to as pendent-party jurisdiction. The difference is that with the adoption of § 1367, all of these jurisdictional doctrines are now governed by statute, and all are now referred to as involving "supplemental jurisdiction." The full text of § 1367 appears in your supplement.

Section 1367(a) provides as follows:

> Except as provided in subsections (b) and (c) or as expressly provided otherwise by Federal statute, in any civil action of which the district courts have original jurisdiction, the district courts shall have supplemental jurisdiction over all other claims that are so related to claims in the action within such original jurisdiction that they form part of the same case or controversy under Article III of the United States

Constitution. Such supplemental jurisdiction shall include claims that involve the joinder or intervention of additional parties.

28 U.S.C. § 1367(a). As we noted previously, a complete exploration of § 1367 will be undertaken in Chapter VIII, which addresses joinder of claims and parties. Three important aspects of this statute, however, warrant special mention here. First, § 1367(a) incorporates *Gibbs*'s recognition that a federal court's ability to hear claims over which there is no independent basis of jurisdiction is limited to rights of action that are part of the same constitutional case or controversy as the jurisdiction-conferring claim. Thus, most courts define "same case or controversy" in terms of the common-nucleus-of-operative-fact principle articulated in *Gibbs*. *See, e.g., Rodriguez v. Doral Mortg. Corp.*, 57 F.3d 1168, 1175-1176 (1st Cir. 1998). However, some courts have given § 1367(a) a broader reading that would allow the exercise of supplemental jurisdiction over claims that have only "a loose factual connection" to the jurisdiction-conferring claim and that would not satisfy the *Gibbs* common-nucleus test. *See Channell v. Citicorp Nat'l Servs., Inc.*, 89 F.3d 379, 385-386 (7th Cir. 1996); *see also Jones v. Ford Motor Credit Co.*, 358 F.3d 205, 212-213 (2d Cir. 2004). Second, the last sentence of § 1367(a) expressly allows the addition of new parties, as was often true of ancillary jurisdiction and as would have occurred with pendent-party jurisdiction. Third, though the statute recognizes the importance of congressional intent in deciding whether to allow supplemental jurisdiction, a court may no longer infer or imply an intent to negate. Rather, a court must find that Congress has "*expressly* provided otherwise by *Federal statute*," 28 U.S.C. § 1367(a) (emphasis added). Without such express statutory language to the contrary, supplemental jurisdiction must be allowed when it meets the requirements under § 1367.

Section 1367(b) bars supplemental jurisdiction, in certain circumstances, when a district court's jurisdiction is "founded solely on section 1332," the diversity statute. Section 1367(b) poses no obstacle to the exercise of supplemental jurisdiction in cases entering federal court on other bases such as § 1331, the federal question statute. We will defer discussion of § 1367(b) to Chapter VIII, which deals with joinder of claims and parties, for it is only in certain joinder settings that supplemental jurisdiction is barred in diversity cases. However, at this point, it's worth noting that § 1367(b) attempted to codify the holding in *Kroger* so as to disallow supplemental (formerly pendent-party) jurisdiction in diversity cases over claims by plaintiffs that would destroy or evade complete diversity.

Section 1367(c) sets out four grounds on which a district court may decline to exercise supplemental jurisdiction. As you read this subdivision, ask yourself how these grounds compare in scope to the discretion recognized in *Gibbs* as part of the common law doctrine of pendent jurisdiction. Does § 1367(c) give a court as much latitude as it had before? Should § 1367(c)(4) be read as a catch-all, or was the phrase "exceptional circumstances" meant to exclude consideration of factors such as judicial economy, efficiency, or fairness that played a role under *Gibbs*? There is a sharp split among the federal circuits on these questions. Most courts appear to have adopted the view that § 1367(c) preserves the full range of discretion recognized in *Gibbs*. *See, e.g., Enochs v. Lampasas Cnty.*, 641 F.3d 155, 165

& n.5 (5th Cir. 2011). Some, however, take the position that the statute strictly cabins a court's discretion to decline supplemental jurisdiction. *See, e.g., Rivera v. Rochester Genesee Regional Trans. Auth.*, 743 F.3d 11, 27 (2d Cir. 2012).

Section 1367(d) seeks to ease the hardship formerly faced by parties like Geraldine Kroger whose would-be pendent or ancillary claims were dismissed by a federal court after the applicable statute of limitations might have run. Now, if a federal court refuses to exercise supplemental jurisdiction, the statute of limitations is tolled for the period during which the federal suit was pending and for at least 30 days after the dismissal. This allows a party to refile the dismissed claim—and the rest of its case, if it chooses—in a state court. As long as the statute of limitations had not run at the time the federal suit was commenced, the claims will not be time barred in state court. Section 1367(d), however, will toll the applicable statute of limitations only if the state-law claim in question in fact fell within the court's § 1367(a) supplemental jurisdiction. Otherwise, dismissal of the would-be supplemental claims will not qualify for the § 1367(d) tolling provision. In *Barry Aviation, Inc. v. Land O'Lakes Municipal Airport Commission*, 366 F. Supp. 2d 792 (W.D. Wis. 2005), the court dismissed the plaintiff's federal constitutional and statutory claims and, there being no diversity between the parties, it then declined supplemental jurisdiction over several accompanying state-law claims. Yet the court then noted that § 1367(d)'s

> tolling provision applies only to claims for which the court has supplemental jurisdiction. It does not apply to plaintiff's claims that defendants breached the parties' contract . . . because these claims are not part of the same case or controversy as its federal claims. Although this may mean that plaintiff will be time barred from bringing the contract claims in state court, it is not within this court's discretion to exercise jurisdiction over those claims.

Id. at 812. Thus § 1367(d) will not always save a plaintiff when courts decline to exercise supplemental jurisdiction.

PROBLEMS

4-17. How would *Aldinger v. Howard*, page 389, *supra*, and *Finley v. United States*, pages 386-387, *supra*, be decided under § 1367?

4-18. Lucille, a citizen of Florida, has sued the Everglades Bank and Trust Co. in a Florida federal district court. The bank is a Delaware corporation whose principal place of business is in Miami, Florida. Lucille seeks $5,000 damages under the Federal Truth in Lending Act (FTLA), alleging that the bank failed to make disclosures required by the act when it made her a loan. The FTLA was designed to promote active consumer enforcement of the provisions of the act. Lucille also seeks $50,000 under Florida libel law, claiming that the bank injured her reputation when it told a local newspaper Lucille was a "swindler" because she had not repaid the loan. The bank has filed a counterclaim against Lucille for $85,000, the unpaid portion of the loan. Does the district court have jurisdiction over the case, *i.e.*, over the claims filed by Lucille and by the bank?

4-19. Phillip bought a new car from Baxter Chevrolet ("Baxter") in Chicago, Illinois. When he fell behind in his payments, Phillip began receiving threatening letters from Baxter. These were followed by telephone calls in the middle of the night. Phillip was no longer able to sleep and began to lose weight. One day while he was at a Chicago Cubs baseball game, a Baxter employee broke into Phillip's garage and removed a late-model Chevrolet. As it turned out, the car belonged to Phillip's brother, Reggie, who had asked Phillip to store the car for him while he was on a fishing trip in Minnesota. Phillip and Reggie sued Baxter Chevrolet in an Illinois federal district court. Phillip seeks damages of $10,000 under the federal Fair Debt Collection Practices Act, claiming that Baxter's letters and phone calls violated provisions of that act. Phillip seeks an additional $30,000 under Illinois trespass law. In the same action, Reggie seeks $45,000 under state law for the conversion of his car. Baxter has filed a third-party complaint against Art Fox, a private investigator who informed Baxter that the car in Phillip's garage belonged to Phillip; the third-party complaint, which was filed under Rule 14, seeks indemnity from Fox in the event Baxter is found liable to Reggie. Phillip, Reggie, Baxter, and Fox are all citizens of Illinois. Does the federal court have subject matter jurisdiction?

5.   Removal Jurisdiction

To this point we have been focusing on the original jurisdiction of the federal district courts, *i.e.*, their authority to hear cases that a plaintiff initiates in a federal court under statutes such as §§ 1331, 1332, and 1367. We turn now to the federal courts' removal jurisdiction, *i.e.*, their ability to hear cases that a plaintiff initiates in state court but which the defendant wishes to remove to federal court. Removal allows a defendant to override the plaintiff's original choice of forum. It is an exception to the general rule that the plaintiff may choose from among the available courts where litigation will occur. While Congress has provided for removal jurisdiction since the first federal trial courts were created in 1789, the conditions under which removal may occur have changed with time.

The current general removal statute, 28 U.S.C. § 1441, specifies when a defendant may elect to remove a case from state to federal court. Other statutes address the removability of certain specific types of suits. *See, e.g.*, 28 U.S.C. § 1442 (federal officer sued or prosecuted); § 1442a (member of armed forces sued or prosecuted); § 1443 (civil rights cases); § 1444 (foreclosure actions against the United States); and § 1445 (nonremovable actions). The procedure for removal is set forth in § 1446, while the procedure followed after removal is described by § 1447 and Rule 81(c). Our attention will be devoted to § 1441, the general removal statute, and to the procedures for removal and following removal under §§ 1446 and 1447.

a.   Section 1441(a): Removability in General

Section 1441(a), which applies to both federal question and diversity cases, allows a defendant or the defendants to remove a civil action from state court to federal court if the case is one that could have been filed in federal court origi-nally, *i.e.*, if the federal court would have had original jurisdiction over the entire action if the plaintiff had filed it there. Note that while the plaintiff could have originally filed the case in federal court, the plaintiff has no authority to then remove the case from state court once it has been filed there. In other words, removal is exclusively a privilege of the defendant or defendants.

Under 1441(a), a case may be removed only to the federal district court embracing the place in which the state suit is pending; it cannot be *removed* to any other federal court. For example, if the plaintiff initiates a suit in the California Superior Court in Los Angeles and all of the requirements for removal are satisfied, the defendant may remove the case only to the U.S. District Court for the Central District of California, the district that embraces Los Angeles. In addition, proper removal makes venue automatically proper in the court to which the case has been removed, and, in this respect, §1441(a) operates as a venue provision.

b. *Section 1441(b): Limits on the Removal of Diversity Cases*

Section 1441(b)(2) bars removal in diversity cases if any "properly joined and served" defendant is a citizen of the forum state. This means that even if com-plete diversity is satisfied and the case could have been filed originally in federal court, it may not be removed from state court if any defendant is domiciled in the forum state. The idea behind § 1441(b)(2) is that the presence of a defendant from the forum state reduces the risk of potential bias against out-of-staters that diversity jurisdiction was designed to guard against. In addition, subsection § 1441 (b)(1) provides that "the citizenship of defendants sued under fictitious names shall be disregarded." This provision prevents a plaintiff from rendering a case non-removable by naming Doe defendants. But "[i]f the plaintiff has described the Doe defendants so that their identity is clear, or if the defendants are better equipped than are plaintiffs to ascertain the Doe defendants' citizenship, or if the Doe defendant is an agent of a company, a few federal courts have permitted the actual identity of a non-diverse Doe defendant to destroy diversity jurisdiction upon removal." *See* 14B CHARLES ALAN WRIGHT, ARTHUR R. MILLER, EDWARD H. COOPER & JOAN E. STEINMAN, FEDERAL PRACTICE AND PROCEDURE § 3723 (4th ed. 2009 & Supp. 2015). And the First and Fifth Circuits have held that § 1441(b)(1)'s "direction to disregard the citizenship of defendants sued under fictitious names does not continue to apply to parties substituted for John Doe defendants, and that § 1447(e) requires remand to state court upon the substitu-tion or addition of non-diverse defendants." *Id.*

PROBLEMS

4-20. The case of *United Mine Workers v. Gibbs*, page 371, *supra*, was instituted by Paul Gibbs against the UMW in a Tennessee federal district court. If the suit had instead been filed in a Tennessee state court located in Nashville, Tennessee, could the UMW have removed the case to a Tennessee federal court under § 1441(a)? To which federal court in Tennessee would it have been removable? Would § 1441(b)(2) have barred removal if the defendant UMW had members who reside in Tennessee?

4-21. *Owen Equipment v. Kroger*, page 377, *supra*, was initiated by Geraldine Kroger in a Nebraska federal district court. Assume that she had instead brought the action in the Nebraska state court in Omaha. Could defendant OPPD, prior to its joinder of Owen, have removed the case to federal court under § 1441(a) and (b)? If removable, to which federal court could the suit have been removed?

c.   Section 1441(c): Removal of Federal Questions Joined with Nonremovable Claims

Even if a case cannot be removed under § 1441(a) as one over which the district court would have had original jurisdiction, there is a possibility that it can be removed under § 1441(c). Suppose Mary sues Bill in state court claiming that he failed to pay her the minimum wage required by federal law. In the same suit she seeks damages from Bill for breach of contract based on his failure to reimburse her for job-related travel expenses. If Mary and Bill are citizens of the same state, can Bill remove the case to federal court? Since there is no diversity, the only way the case could come within the federal court's original jurisdiction is based on the federal wage claim. This claim presumably arises under federal law and could enter federal court under § 1331. The breach of contract claim, however, could enter federal court only under supplemental jurisdiction. Yet it is doubtful this claim satisfies § 1367(a) as it does not seem to share a common nucleus of operative fact with the minimum-wage claim. Hence, the case is not one that could have been filed originally in federal court. As such, the case cannot be removed under § 1441(a) as a case over which the district court would have original jurisdiction. However, § 1441(c) may still provide a basis for removing this case to federal court.

Section 1441(c) provides in full:

> (1) If a civil action includes—
>   (A) a claim arising under the Constitution, laws, or treaties of the United States (within the meaning of section 1331 of this title), and
>   (B) a claim not within the original or supplemental jurisdiction of the district court or a claim that has been made nonremovable by statute, the entire action may be removed if the action would be removable without the inclusion of the claim described in subparagraph (B).
> (2) Upon removal of an action described in paragraph (1), the district court shall sever from the action all claims described in paragraph (1)(B) and shall remand the severed claims to the State court from which the action was removed. Only defendants against whom a claim described in paragraph (1)(A) has been asserted are required to join in or consent to the removal under paragraph (1).

28 U.S.C. § 1441(c).

Essentially, removal under § 1441(c) is available for cases in which federal claims have been joined with a claim or claims that render the case nonremovable under § 1441(a). Once a case is removed under § 1441(c), the federal court must sever the nonremovable claim(s) and remand them to the state court. Here the federal court has no discretion. 28 U.S.C. § 1441(c)(2). In other words, the only claims that will remain in the district court are the federal claims. This subsection also makes it clear that only the defendants on the federal claims—the "claim described in paragraph (1)(A)"—must "join in or consent to the notice of removal." *Id.*

d.   Section 1446: Procedure for Removal of Civil Actions

Section 1446 describes the removal procedure. Under § 1446(a), the defendant or defendants must file a notice of removal in the district court or division of the district court in which the action is pending, *i.e.*, in the district court or division that embraces the geographic region in which the state court sits. Pursuant to subsection (b), the notice must generally be filed within 30 days of receipt of the complaint (with variations for later served defendants and with an extension for cases in which removability only becomes apparent subsequent to the initial pleading). In addition, if removal is premised on §1441(a) (as opposed to § 1441(c)), all defendants properly joined and served "must join in or consent to the removal of the action." 28 U.S.C. § 1446(b)(2)(A).

Section 1446(c) addresses special concerns that arise in the context of diversity removals. Subsection (c)(1) limits any time extension for the removal of a diversity case to "1 year after commencement of the action, unless the district court finds that the plaintiff has acted in bad faith in order to prevent a defendant from removing the action." In addition, § 1446(c)(2) provides a method for calculating the amount in controversy:

> [T]he sum demanded in good faith in the initial pleading shall be deemed to be the amount in controversy, except that—
>
> (A) the notice of removal may assert the amount in controversy if the initial pleading seeks—
> (i)   nonmonetary relief; or
> (ii) a money judgment, but the State practice either does not permit demand for a specific sum or permits recovery of damages in excess of the amount demanded; and
> (B) removal of the action is proper on the basis of an amount in controversy asserted under subparagraph (A) if the district court finds, by the preponderance of the evidence, that the amount in controversy exceeds the amount specified in section 1332(a).

28 U.S.C § 1446(c)(2). Notice that under § 1446(c) there are two standards in operation—the familiar "good faith" standard, *see* page 358, *supra*, when the removing party relies on the sum demanded in the plaintiff's complaint, and a stricter "preponderance of the evidence" standard when the removing party makes

an independent assertion of the amount in controversy. Why would (or should) the standard be more demanding in the latter context?

Finally, § 1446(d) requires the removing party or parties to provide prompt written notice of the removal to "all adverse parties" and to "file a copy of the notice with the clerk of [the] State court." This notice "shall effect the removal and the State court shall proceed no further unless and until the case is remanded." *Id.*

e. Section 1447: Procedure after Removal Generally

Sections 1447(a) and (b) authorize the district court to take control over the removed case by asserting its authority over the parties and the records to that proceeding. Subsection (c) addresses the potential "remand" of a case improvidently removed. Under that subsection, a motion to remand the case to state court for any defect in the removal procedure (other than on subject matter jurisdiction grounds) must be made within 30 days of the filing of the notice of removal. As to subject matter jurisdiction, § 1447(c) provides that if at any time after removal but "before final judgment" the court concludes that it in fact "lacks subject matter jurisdiction, the case shall be remanded."

An order remanding a case based on either a defect in the removal procedure or for a lack of subject matter jurisdiction "is not reviewable on appeal or otherwise." 28 U.S.C. § 1447(d); *see generally* 14C Charles Alan Wright, Arthur R. Miller, Edward H. Cooper & Joan E. Steinman, Federal Practice and Procedure § 3740 (4th ed. 2009 & Supp. 2015) (describing the rule and potential exceptions to it). Section 1447(d) does not, however, apply to discretionary remands. For example, in *California Dept. of Water Resources v. Powerex Corp.*, 533 F.3d 1087 (9th Cir. 2008), the Ninth Circuit upheld the exercise of appellate jurisdiction over a discretionary remand order made pursuant to 28 U.S.C. § 1367(c) (supplemental jurisdiction). As the court explained, the remand was not based on a defect in the removal procedure or on the absence of subject matter jurisdiction, but on the district court's exercise of discretion. Hence, the appellate review restriction of § 1447(d) did not apply.

Finally, if after removal, "the plaintiff seeks to join an additional defendant whose joinder would destroy subject matter jurisdiction, the court may deny joinder, or permit joinder and remand the action to the State court." 28 U.S.C. § 1447(e).

Ettlin v. Harris

2013 WL 6178986 (C.D. Cal. Nov. 22, 2013)

The Honorable David O. Carter, District Judge. . . .

I. BACKGROUND

Over the years, pro se plaintiff, Mr. Ettlin, has been waging a quixotic campaign against a judicial compensation policy that he believes to be unconstitutional. This action is the latest chapter; these defendants are the latest windmills.

A. Occupy Los Angeles

During the fall of 2011, as part of the national "Occupy" Movement, activists established and occupied tents in front of Los Angeles City Hall. Mr. Ettlin participated in the events by, among other things, holding a "press conference."

On November 29, 2011, Mr. Ettlin was "visiting" with one of the "occupants." He also "carried a large three-foot by five-foot sign with his free speech message printed thereon." While he was walking with his sign, he observed a large police presence, including Sheriff's Department buses and barricades.

He watched as police dismantled the tents and placed personal belongings into garbage bags. Mr. Ettlin could not hear any of the police instructions and was frightened, so he left. As he was leaving, he encountered a police officer, who told him to move in the direction of a crowd. Mr. Ettlin believed that he would be arrested if he moved in that direction, so he went another way. At around 2 A.M., Mr. Ettlin finally got to his car and drove home.

Based on the events of that night, Mr. Ettlin filed suit in Los Angeles Superior Court [claiming violations of his rights under both federal and state law]. . . .

C.   The Present Lawsuit

On August 22, 2013, Mr. Ettlin filed the present action in state court. Mr. Ettlin served Defendants Attorney General Harris, Judge Levine, County Supervisors, and Chris Ryan Legal. There is no proof that he served Defendants Judge Gee, Judge King, Judge Otero, or Judge Wright, and he did not serve the United States of America, State of California, or the County of Los Angeles. . . .

On September 26, 2013, County Supervisors—four of the fourteen named defendants—removed the action to federal court. County Supervisors did not aver that any other defendants consented, but did aver that Judge Levine's counsel "declined to join but [did] not oppose removal."

As of November 20, 2013, no other defendant has consented to the removal.

II.   MOTION TO REMAND

Mr. Ettlin moves this Court to remand the action to state court because County Supervisors failed to comply with the rule of unanimity.

A court will remand a removed action if the removal was procedurally defective. 28 U.S.C. § 1447(c). "[V]iolation of the unanimity rule" is one such defect.

A century ago, the Supreme Court announced the rule of unanimity, which requires that all defendants in a state court action consent to removal. In 2011, Congress codified the requirement, providing that: "When a civil action is removed solely under section 1441(a), all defendants who have been properly joined and served must join in or consent to the removal of the action." 28 U.S.C. § 1446(b)(2)(A).

A.   Removal Under Section 1441(c)

There is no dispute that only four of the fourteen defendants consented to or joined the removal. Rather, removing defendants, County Supervisors, contend that they were not bound by the rule of unanimity because they removed the state court action under 28 U.S.C. § 1441(c), not "solely under Section 1441(a)." The Court disagrees because the Federal Courts Jurisdiction and Venue Clarification Act (JVCA) foreclosed the possibility of removal under 1441(c) when state law claims would otherwise come within the court's supplemental jurisdiction.

1.   JVCA, Section 1441(c), and Supplemental Jurisdiction

County Supervisors direct the court's attention to cases that construe language that no longer exists. For example, County Supervisors rely heavily on [cases that] analyze the "separate and independent" clause of 1441(c)—a clause that was deleted in 2011.

Prior to 2011, 1441(c) provided that:

> Whenever a *separate and independent* claim or cause of action within the jurisdiction conferred by section 1331 of this title is joined *with one or more otherwise nonremovable claims or causes of action*, the entire case may be removed and the district court may determine all issues therein, or, in its discretion, may remand all matters in which State law predominates.

28 U.S.C. § 1441(c) (1990) (emphasis added). . . .

In 2011, Congress enacted the JVCA, which . . . provides:

> (1) If a civil action includes—
>   (A)   a claim arising under the Constitution, laws, or treaties of the United States (within the meaning of [28 U.S.C. § 1331]), and
>   (B)   *a claim not within the original or supplemental jurisdiction of the district court* . . . , the entire action may be removed if the action would be removable without the inclusion of the claim described in subparagraph (B).

28 U.S.C. § 1441(c) (emphasis added).

A plain reading of the new text makes clear that an action is removable under 1441(c) only if there is at least one claim that is "not within the original or supplemental jurisdiction of the district court."

This reading is supported by the legislative history of the JVCA. . . . Now, when an action includes a claim under § 1331 and a claim not within the original or supplemental jurisdiction of the court, then courts "shall sever [the latter claim] and shall remand the severed claims to the State court from which the action was removed." 28 U.S.C. § 1441(c)(2). The new provision makes the sever-and-remand approach mandatory, not discretionary. More importantly for this action, the legislative history makes clear that 1441(c) is a provision that is concerned only with the case where the district court lacks subject matter jurisdiction over at least one claim. . . .

Finally, this is the only construction of 1441(c) that preserves the rule of unanimity, which the JVCA codified in 2011. If defendants were given the choice to remove under either 1441(a) or 1441(c), the rule of unanimity would be a nullity—all defendants would remove under 1441(c), avoid the rule of unanimity, and 1441(a) would have no purpose.

In sum, removal under 1441(c) is appropriate only if at least one of the claims is not within the district court's original or supplemental jurisdiction. Removal under 1441(a) and 1441(c) are mutually exclusive, not redundant.

2.   Applicability of § 1441(c) to this Action

The question now turns on whether any of Mr. Ettlin's claims are "not within the original or supplemental jurisdiction of [this court]." 28 U.S.C. § 1441(c)(1)(B).

If a district court has original jurisdiction over some claims in a civil action, it also has supplemental jurisdiction over all related claims that are part of the same case or controversy. 28 U.S.C. § 1367(a). "A state law claim is part of the same case or controversy when it shares a 'common nucleus of operative fact' with the federal claims, and the state and federal claims would normally be tried together." *Bahrampour v. Lampert*, 356 F.3d 969, 978 (9th Cir. 2012); *accord United Mine Workers v. Gibbs*, 383 U.S. 715, 725 (1966).

Here, Mr. Ettlin asserts several causes of action that undoubtedly fall within the Court's original jurisdiction: claims under § 1983 and RICO. Those federal claims arise out of two sets of events: the § 1983 claims arise out of an encounter with police during an Occupy LA event in November 2011; and his other federal claims, such as one under RICO, arise out of his attempts to litigate his § 1983 claims. Each of Mr. Ettlin's state law claims arise[s] out of one of those two sets of events; they share a "common nucleus of operative fact" with the federal claims.

County Supervisors specifically identify Mr. Ettlin's claim for "elder abuse" as one that is non-removable. The Court, however, disagrees. Mr. Ettlin's elder abuse claim is premised on police conduct during an Occupy LA event—the same basis for his § 1983 claims. Both claims "arise out of exactly the same facts," and this court, therefore, has jurisdiction over the state law claims pursuant to 28 U.S.C. 1367(a).

Because this Court has jurisdiction over all of Mr. Ettlin's claims, County Supervisors cannot remove the action under 1441(c). Frankly, any other outcome would permit defendants to do an end run around the rule of unanimity.

B.   Removal Under 1441(a)

County Supervisors' opposition rests almost entirely on the assertion that the unanimity rule does not apply to them because they removed the action under 1441(c). The Court disagrees with this assertion. *Supra* Part II-A. But, this does not end the inquiry. Although they do not make the argument, the Court turns to whether County Supervisors complied with the unanimity requirement if they had "removed solely under 1441(a)." *See* 28 U.S.C. § 1446(b)(2)(A).

In a case involving multiple defendants, "[a]ll defendants must join in a removal petition." Although circuits are split as to what form a co-defendant's joinder in removal must take, the Ninth Circuit has adopted the position that "'at least one attorney of record' [must] sign the notice and certify that the remaining defendants consent to removal; it does not insist that each defendant submit written notice of such consent." *Proctor v. Vishay Intertechnology Inc.*, 584 F.3d 1208, 1224-25 (9th Cir. 2009). In general, courts should resolve doubts in favor of remand.

Here, County Supervisors did not aver that any of the ten other defendants consented to removal. They contacted only Defendant Judge Levine, and she "declined to join but [did] not oppose removal[.]" Notice of Removal at 2. So, at first blush, they failed to comply with the Ninth Circuit's rule that "at least one attorney of record . . . certify that the remaining defendants consent to removal."

County Supervisors' excuse seems to be that Mr. Ettlin did not file his proofs of service in a timely manner, and so it was impossible to contact the other defendants. The Court finds this excuse unavailing for four reasons.

First, even if Mr. Ettlin failed to file proofs of service, it was clear that at least two [other] defendants were properly joined and served: Attorney General Harris and Judge Levine. Both Attorney General Harris and Judge Levine filed demurrers in the state court action prior to removal. It appears that County Supervisors did not contact Attorney General Harris, and Judge Levine expressly declined to provide consent.

Second, Attorney General Harris and Judge Levine manifested an intent to have the matter adjudicated in state court. "A state court defendant may lose or waive the right to remove a case to a federal court by taking some substantial offensive or defensive action in the state court action, indicating a willingness to litigate in the state tribunal." . . . Here, Attorney General Harris and Judge Levine both filed demurrers in state court, and neither has consented to the removal. Although the demurrers alone did not constitute waiver, the Court notes that at least two defendants "manifest[ed] [an] intent to have the matter adjudicated [in state court]."

Third, during the month and a half that this action has been in federal court, no other defendants have consented to removal.

Finally, as a practical matter, it is hard for this Court to believe that County Supervisors could not find the contact information for four federal judges and the California Attorney General within the month prescribed for timely removal. It does not appear that County Supervisors made much of an effort to comply with the rule of unanimity.

The Court holds that the non-opposition of one other defendant—and the non-response of nine—cannot qualify as "unanimous."

III.   DISPOSITION

County Supervisors' removal would be appropriate only under 1441(a). However, they did not comply with the rule of unanimity required for 1441(a) removal. Therefore, this court GRANTS Plaintiff Dennis Ettlin's Motion to Remand. . . .

NOTES AND QUESTIONS

1. The scope of § 1441(a).   Did the district court properly conclude that the case was potentially removable under § 1441(a)? Since this case involved state-law claims, did §1441(b) have any bearing on the question of removability? If the case was removable under §1441(a), why did the district court order the case remanded to state court?

2. *The scope of § 1441(c).* Why wasn't this case removable under §1441(c)? And why did that matter? Given the text of § 1441(c) and the district court's ruling in *Ettlin v. Harris*, under what circumstances may a defendant remove a case pursuant to § 1441(c)? Will the effect of such a removal always result in a splitting of the case between the federal and state tribunals?

3. *Appealability.* Could the County Supervisors in *Ettlin v. Harris* appeal or otherwise seek review of the district court's remand order?

PROBLEMS

4-22. Will brought suit in a Michigan state court against his employer, Bread Basket, Inc. ("Bread Basket"), claiming that the company failed to pay him over-time, in violation of the federal Fair Labor Standards Act ("FLSA"), and that it breached an implied contract of employment by firing him. He does not allege that he was fired in retaliation for complaining about overtime pay. Bread Basket is a Michigan corporation with its principal place of business in Michigan. Will is a citizen of Wisconsin. The defendant has removed the action to federal court. Was the case properly removed under § 1441(a) and (b)? Under § 1441(c)? If you decided that the case was properly removed, may the court in its discretion retain the entire case? *See Nesbitt v. Bun Basket, Inc.,* 780 F. Supp. 1151 (W.D. Mich. 1991).

4-23. When Tom's car had a flat tire he called Classic Cars to send a tow truck to repair it. After the tire was fixed, Ryan, the tow truck operator, demanded that Tom pay him $25 cash on the spot. Tom did not have $25 in cash but offered to pay by other means. An altercation ensued and Ryan called the police. Police officer Kenney arrived on the scene and arrested Tom for disorderly conduct. Tom later sued Kenney and Classic Cars in Massachusetts state court seeking $25,000 in damages from each defendant. The parties are all citizens of Massachusetts. Tom's claims against Kenney alleged a violation of his federal constitutional rights, as well as false arrest, false imprisonment, and malicious prosecution in violation of state law. His claim against Classic Cars alleged unfair and deceptive trade practices under state law, based on the company's failure to inform him in advance of the $25 cash fee and its use of a police officer to resolve a contract dispute. The defendants removed the suit to federal court. Was removal proper under § 1441(a) and (b)? Under § 1441(c)? If the case was properly removed, may the court elect to retain jurisdiction over all of the claims? If the court decides to remand any of the state-law claims, what statutes, if any, authorize it to do so? Would any of those remand orders be appealable? *See Rey v. Classic Cars,* 762 F. Supp. 421 (D. Mass. 1991).

B. Challenging a Court's Subject Matter Jurisdiction

1. Direct Attack

A direct attack on a court's subject matter jurisdiction in a pending case may be made at any time prior to the completion of the appellate process in that proceeding. The challenge may be raised by either party—including the party who invoked the court's jurisdiction—or by the court itself acting *sua sponte*. An objection to subject matter jurisdiction cannot be waived. Nor may the parties' consent or the court's acquiescence establish subject matter jurisdiction. In short, a potential challenge to a court's subject matter jurisdiction remains viable throughout the lawsuit's entire life.

In a case originally filed in federal court, a challenge to subject matter jurisdiction may be raised in the district court through a pretrial motion to dismiss under Rule 12(b)(1) or thereafter by either party or the court itself. FED. R. CIV. P. 12(h)(3). The parties or the court may suggest a lack of subject matter jurisdiction at any time, "even initially at the highest appellate instance." *Grupo Dataflux v. Atlas Global Grp., L.P.*, 541 U.S. 567, 576 (2004) (quoting *Kontrick v. Ryan*, 540 U.S. 443, 455 (2004)). In *Louisville & Nashville Railroad Co. v. Mottley*, 211 U.S. 149 (1908), for example, the issue of subject matter jurisdiction was raised for the first time in the Supreme Court by the Court itself. Regardless of the timing of the objection, should subject matter jurisdiction be found to have been wanting at the time the suit was commenced, the remedy is dismissal, no matter how much time and effort has gone into the litigation.

In the context of a case removed from state to federal court, § 1447 provides: "If at any time before final judgment it appears that the district court lacks subject matter jurisdiction, the case shall be remanded. An order remanding the case may require payment of just costs and any actual expenses, including attorney fees, incurred as a result of the removal." 28 U.S.C. § 1447(c).

If the defendant in a federal court action challenges both personal jurisdiction and subject matter jurisdiction, the federal court will normally resolve the issue of subject matter jurisdiction first. If this is found to be lacking, the case will be dismissed (or in the case of removal, remanded to state court), without reaching the issue of personal jurisdiction. This sequencing reduces the federal court's interference with a state court's ability to hear the same case, for a finding that personal jurisdiction did not exist would prevent the parties from relitigating that same issue in state court, forcing a dismissal of the state suit as well. However, the Supreme Court has held that "there is no unyielding jurisdictional hierarchy" for resolving these issues. *Ruhrgas AG v. Marathon Oil Co.*, 526 U.S. 574, 578 (1999). If, in a particular case, the subject matter jurisdiction question is unusually complex while the personal jurisdiction issue is straightforward, considerations of judicial efficiency allow a federal court to reverse the usual preference for resolving subject matter jurisdiction first. In *Ruhrgas*, the Court thus held that the federal judge in a case removed from state court did not abuse his discretion by dismissing the case for lack of personal jurisdiction, without reaching a "difficult and novel question" concerning subject matter jurisdiction. *Id.* at 588.

Turning to the state courts, most states provide that a lack of subject matter jurisdiction may be challenged at any time during the litigation process, including while on appeal. For example, in California a lack of subject matter jurisdiction is not waived if not raised by demurrer or answer to the complaint. CAL. CIV. PROC. CODE § 430.80(a). Yet rather than outright dismissal, a successful attack on a state court's subject matter jurisdiction may often result in nothing more than a transfer to the proper tribunal within the state. *See* CAL. CIV. PROC. CODE § 396 (mandating transfer to a court of competent jurisdiction in lieu of dismissal). Of course, if no such tribunal is available, dismissal is the proper remedy. For example, if a state court is asked to exercise jurisdiction over an exclusive federal matter, the only remedy is to dismiss. Suffice it to say that the more complicated the architecture of the state's judicial system, the more likely one is to encounter challenges to any particular court's subject matter jurisdiction.

Regardless of whether a court is ultimately found to have lacked subject matter jurisdiction, a court generally has jurisdiction to determine its own jurisdiction. Thus the parties must obey orders entered by the court prior to its determination of subject matter jurisdiction, at least when the asserted claim of jurisdiction is not flagrantly beyond the bounds of the court's authority. Moreover, even if a federal court concludes that it lacks subject matter jurisdiction, it may award attorneys' fees to the defendant "as an appropriate deterrent to future frivolous suits." *Tancredi v. Metropolitan Life Ins. Co.*, 378 F.3d 220, 225 (2d Cir. 2004) (internal citations omitted); *see* 11A CHARLES ALAN WRIGHT, ARTHUR R. MILLER & MARY KAY KANE, FEDERAL PRACTICE AND PROCEDURE § 2960 (3d ed. 2013 & Supp. 2015).

2. Collateral Attack

Under the traditional approach, the judgment of a court lacking subject matter jurisdiction was deemed to be void. The original parties or even a stranger to the initial suit could attack that judgment through a separate or "collateral" proceeding. In essence, the jurisdictionally defective judgment was treated as a nullity.

Although one can find some recent applications of the traditional approach, the common approach today is somewhat more circumspect, emphasizing the importance of the finality of judgments over the niceties of jurisdiction. In federal courts the policy against permitting collateral attacks on subject matter jurisdiction is very strong. In *Chicot County Drainage District v. Baxter State Bank*, 308 U.S. 371 (1940), the Court refused to allow a collateral attack on a federal district court's subject matter jurisdiction when the jurisdictional issue could have been raised in the initial proceeding:

> The lower federal courts are all courts of limited jurisdiction, that is, with only the jurisdiction which Congress has prescribed. But none the less they are courts with

authority, when parties are brought before them in accordance with the requirements of due process, to determine whether or not they have jurisdiction to entertain the cause and for this purpose to construe and apply the statute under which they are asked to act. Their determinations of such questions, *while open to direct review, may not be assailed collaterally.*

Id. at 376 (emphasis added). The fact that the parties had not challenged jurisdiction during the direct proceeding did not alter the Court's conclusion. *Id.* at 378. In essence, the prior judgment was treated as having implicitly and finally decided that issue.

Yet in *Kalb v. Feuerstein*, 308 U.S. 433 (1940), a case decided the same day as *Chicot County*, the Court reached a different conclusion. In *Kalb*, a farmer filed a petition in federal bankruptcy court for an extension of time to pay his debts under the federal Frazier-Lemke Act. While the bankruptcy proceeding was pending, Wisconsin's Walworth County Court entered a judgment of foreclosure on the farmer's property. The farmer made no direct attack on the state court's jurisdiction but filed two separate suits collaterally attacking the foreclosure sale. The Supreme Court upheld the collateral attack:

> It is generally true that a judgment by a court of competent jurisdiction bears a presumption of regularity and is not thereafter subject to collateral attack. But Congress, because its power over the subject of bankruptcy is plenary, may by specific bankruptcy legislation create an exception to that principle and render judicial acts taken with respect to the person or property of a debtor whom the bankruptcy law protects nullities and vulnerable collaterally. Although the Walworth County Court had general jurisdiction over foreclosures under the law of Wisconsin, a peremptory prohibition by Congress in the exercise of its supreme power over bankruptcy that no state court have jurisdiction over a petitioning farmer-debtor or his property, would have rendered the confirmation of sale and its enforcement beyond the County Court's power and nullities subject to collateral attack. . . .
>
> We think the language and broad policy of the Frazier-Lemke Act conclusively demonstrate that Congress intended to, and did deprive the Wisconsin County Court of the power and jurisdiction to continue or maintain in any manner the foreclosure proceedings against appellants without the consent after hearing of the bankruptcy court in which the farmer's petition was then pending.

Id. at 438-440. What might account for the different results in *Chicot County* and *Kalb*? Remember that *Chicot County* states the general rule against allowing collateral attacks, while *Kalb* represents an exception to it.

Might the different results also be explained by the fact that *Chicot County* involved an attack on a prior federal court judgment, while in *Kalb* the earlier judgment was that of a state court? The italicized language in the *Chicot County* excerpt quoted above suggests that federal judgments can never be collaterally attacked on subject matter jurisdiction grounds. The Supreme Court unanimously, albeit in dictum, stated recently that while a federal court's subject matter jurisdiction can be challenged directly at any time, "even initially at the highest appellate instance," federal "subject-matter jurisdiction, however, may not be attacked collaterally." *Kontrick v. Ryan*, 540 U.S. 443, 455 & n.9 (2004) (citing

Des Moines Navigation & R. Co. v. Iowa Homestead Co., 123 U.S. 552 (1887), and RESTATEMENT (SECOND) OF JUDGMENTS § 12 (1982)). If *Chicot County* and *Kontrick* mean what they say, the absolute "no collateral attack" rule would appear to be one that applies only to federal court judgments. The more flexible *Kalb* approach would then still allow collateral attacks on state court judgments, such as those rendered in violation of a federal statute that stripped state courts of jurisdiction over certain types of cases, as was true in *Kalb*. However, the matter remains unresolved. Shortly after *Kontrick* was decided, the U.S. Court of Appeals for the Federal Circuit, in a suit brought against the United States, permitted a collateral attack on judgments rendered by a Texas federal district court and by the U.S. Court of Appeals for the Fifth Circuit, on the ground that the federal Tucker Act required such actions to be filed in the Court of Federal Claims in Washington, D.C. *Christopher Village, L.P. v. United States*, 360 F.3d 1319 (Fed. Cir. 2004), *cert. denied*, 543 U.S. 1146 (2005), *reh'g denied*, 544 U.S. 992 (2005).

PROBLEMS

4-24. Durfee brought an action against Duke in a Nebraska state court to quiet title to certain land situated on the Missouri River. The main channel of that river forms the boundary between the states of Nebraska and Missouri. The Nebraska court had jurisdiction over the subject matter of the controversy only if the land in question was in Nebraska. Whether the land was in Nebraska depended entirely on a factual question—whether avulsion or accretion had caused a shift in the river's course. After the parties had fully litigated that issue, the court concluded that the land was in Nebraska. The court also awarded title to Durfee. Shortly thereafter, Duke filed an action against Durfee in a Missouri state court seeking title to that same land. The action was removed to federal district court. Should Duke now be allowed to challenge the validity of the Nebraska judgment by arguing that the land was located in Missouri and that the Nebraska court therefore lacked subject matter jurisdiction? Would it make any difference if the land were in fact on the Missouri side of the river? *See Durfee v. Duke*, 375 U.S. 106 (1963).

4-25. Willy sued Coastal Corporation ("Coastal") in a Texas state court, raising a variety of claims relating to Coastal's decision to terminate his employment as in-house counsel. He alleged that he had been fired due to his refusal to participate in Coastal's violation of various federal and state environmental laws. Coastal, relying on the essential federal ingredient test, removed the case to federal district court. The district court upheld the removal over Willy's objection; however, the court did subsequently grant Coastal's motion to dismiss for failure to state a claim. At the same time, the district court granted Coastal's motion for Rule 11 sanctions, awarding attorneys' fees of approximately $20,000 against Willy and his attorney. The district court found that the filings made by the plaintiff's counsel "create[d] a blur of absolute confusion." These included a 1,200-page, unindexed, unnumbered pile of materials that the district court determined "to be a conscious and wanton affront to the judicial process, this court, and opposing counsel," the filing of which was "irresponsible at a minimum and at worst intentionally harassing." Willy's sanctionable behavior also included careless pleading, such as reliance on a nonexistent Federal Rule of Evidence. None of the sanctionable conduct was related to Willy's effort to convince the district court that it was without subject matter jurisdiction. On appeal, the court of appeals concluded that the district court had lacked subject matter jurisdiction because the complaint raised no claims arising under federal law. Given this lack of subject matter jurisdiction, can the award of Rule 11 sanctions stand? *See Willy v. Coastal Corp.*, 503 U.S. 131 (1992).

C.   Subject Matter Jurisdiction Review Problems

4-26. Paula, who was born and raised in Alaska, graduated from the University of Texas in 1998. By that time, her family had all moved from Alaska, and she had no plans to return. She worked in Texas for one year after graduating. In September 1999, she moved to Nashville, Tennessee, where she accepted a permanent position designing web pages for Webfoot Websites, Inc. ("Webfoot"), a Tennessee corporation with its principal place of business in Nashville. In December, Paula was promoted, given a modest raise, and transferred to a new department. She then made a down payment on a small home in Nashville and looked forward to continuing success at Webfoot. Within a month of her promotion, however, her new supervisor, Milt, began making unwanted sexual advances toward her. Paula kept Milt's behavior to herself because she knew he had been a valued employee in the Nashville office since the company opened its doors in 1992. After several months of Milt's innuendoes and threats, Paula suffered what she described as a "private breakdown." On June 1, 2000, she resigned her position at Webfoot, sold her home, and moved back to Texas where she hoped to enroll in graduate school in the fall. Fortunately, she got her old job back, although her annual salary was $5,000 less than what she had been making at Webfoot.

In July 2000, Paula sued Webfoot and Milt in a federal district court in Nashville, asserting jurisdiction under 28 U.S.C. §§ 1331, 1332, and 1367. She claimed that Webfoot violated the Federal Sexual Harassment Prevention Act ("FSHPA") by not maintaining a work environment free of sexual harassment. FSHPA expressly provides a private remedy against employers who violate the act. Paula made no allegation that Webfoot was aware of Milt's behavior; rather, her claim under FSHPA was based on a theory of strict liability. Her claim against Milt was based solely on the state common law tort of intentional infliction of emotional distress, for which there is a one-year statute of limitations. In her suit, Paula sought actual damages against Webfoot totaling $100,000, based on her lost earnings, the cost of relocating to Texas, and the severe depression from which she currently suffers. She sought an identical amount from Milt.

Eighteen months after Paula filed her suit and on the eve of trial, the U.S. Supreme Court decided the case of *More v. Less*, holding in a five-to-four decision that FSHPA does not impose employer liability without proof that the employer had actual knowledge of the sexual harassment. On learning of the Supreme Court decision, Webfoot immediately filed a motion to dismiss Paula's FSHPA claim under Rule 12(b)(6) ("failure to state a claim"). The motion was granted by the district court. Milt has now filed a motion to dismiss Paula's claim against him under Rule 12(b)(1). What should the district court do?

4-27. In 2005, Lance, an Australian national who currently lives in Portland, Oregon, sold his skateboard manufacturing company to Radical Industries ("Rad") for $5 million. Rad is a Delaware corporation with its corporate headquarters in Los Angeles, California. The company's manufacturing and warehouse facilities are in Portland, Oregon. Managers at the Portland office oversee day-to-day operations, including purchases, sales, employment decisions and company payroll. The Los Angeles office does retain complete authority over company policy and strategic planning. However, the management philosophy practiced from that office tends to allow the Portland managers a wide range of operational discretion. Lance's company had a reputation for producing skateboards of the highest quality. Its trade name, "Lance-A-Lot," was known and respected by skateboarders from the Venice bike path to the Great Wall of China. Use of that trade name was likely to produce annual sales of at least $500,000 per year. Given the easy marketability of the "Lance-A-Lot" name, Lance feared that Rad might try to profit from the "Lance-A-Lot" reputation while producing boards of inferior quality. To guard against this, the contract of sale provided that all skateboards sold by Rad under the "Lance-A-Lot" name must meet the standards of the Federal Skateboard Safety Act ("FSSA"). If Rad violated this provision of the contract, its rights to the "Lance-A-Lot" name would automatically revert to Lance, who would then be free to use or sell the "Lance-A-Lot" name as he saw fit. In general, Lance felt very strongly about both his reputation and compliance with the FSSA standards. The FSSA was enacted in 2003 to stem the tide of serious skateboard injuries that had reached epidemic proportions, and Lance was one of FSSA's most vocal supporters. Section 301 of the FSSA provides a private right of action for any person injured by a violation of FSSA standards.

The August 2010 issue of *Skateboard World* magazine revealed that the "Lance-A-Lot" skateboards being sold by Rad were defective and of inferior quality. In particular, the boards split under light impact and the wheels tended to fall off on sharp turns. A short time later, the Half Pipe Skateboard Company contacted Lance, inquiring whether it might acquire rights to the "Lance-A-Lot" name for the next two years, for which Half Pipe was willing to pay $50,000. Lance expressed great interest in the deal but explained to Half Pipe that he had to first make certain the rights to the "Lance-A-Lot" name had reverted to him.

Lance immediately wrote to Rad, noting that from the *Skateboard World* article, it was apparent that Rad had manufactured and sold "Lance-A-Lot" skateboards that were not in compliance with FSSA standards. Lance advised Rad that under the terms of their contract, all rights to the "Lance-A-Lot" name had now reverted to him. Several days later, Lance received an angry reply from Rad denying the

Skateboard World allegations and declaring that Rad continued to hold exclusive rights to the "Lance-A-Lot" name.

On the advice of counsel, Lance sued Rad in California Superior Court, seeking a declaratory judgment that "Lance-A-Lot" skateboards manufactured by Rad failed to meet FSSA standards, and that all rights to the "Lance-A-Lot" trade name had therefore reverted to him. Rad, after having been served on October 1, 2010, filed a timely notice of removal in the appropriate U.S. district court. As grounds for removal, Rad alleged federal question jurisdiction under § 1331 and diversity jurisdiction under § 1332. Lance has filed a motion to remand. What should the district court do?

Suppose that Rad filed its notice of removal on November 1, 2010. What additional arguments might Lance make regarding remand? If Lance were to succeed on these arguments, could Rad appeal the appropriate district court order?

V

VENUE, TRANSFER, AND *FORUM NON CONVENIENS*

The "venue" of a lawsuit refers to the geographic location of the court in which the lawsuit is filed. *See, e.g.*, 28 U.S.C. § 1390(a) ("geographic specification of the proper court"). The rules of venue, which are largely statutory, determine which location or locations are proper for any particular lawsuit. In state judicial systems, proper venues are usually keyed to political subdivisions such as counties or cities, *i.e.*, to the courts of those counties or cities. In more populous states, venue might be further refined to focus on specific sections of those political subdivisions. Within the federal judicial system, venue is determined by reference to federal judicial districts, at least one of which is located in each state. Larger federal judicial districts are sometimes further divided into divisions.

The factors used to determine proper venue vary from jurisdiction to jurisdiction in their specific details, but not significantly in their general characteristics. Typical factors include where a cause of action arose or where substantial events giving rise to it occurred, where the property that is the subject of the dispute is located, where the defendant resides or is doing business or may be found, where the plaintiff resides or is doing business, and, in the case of suits against the government, where the seat of government is located. In addition, most jurisdictions have a "general" venue statute designed to cover the bulk of all civil litigation, as well as a number of narrower venue provisions designed to apply to specific types of claims.

Although one of the primary purposes of venue is to provide the parties with a convenient forum, the "convenience" of any particular venue is not established through a case-by-case, ad hoc analysis, as in the case of personal jurisdiction. Rather, convenience is codified in a statute. Thus, if a statute provides that venue is proper only where the defendant resides, the legislature has defined that location as presumptively convenient. Only when a party seeks a transfer to another proper venue or a dismissal under the doctrine of *forum non conveniens* will the *relative* convenience of the alternative forum be considered. We will explore both of those possibilities below. In general, however, the propriety of venue is determined by the applicable venue statutes.

A. Venue in Federal Courts

1. The General Venue Statute: 28 U.S.C. § 1391

There are two types of federal venue statutes: a general statute that applies to all diversity cases and to most federal question cases, 28 U.S.C. § 1391, and a vast array of special venue statutes that apply to specific types of lawsuits. *See, e.g.*, 28 U.S.C. § 1394 (suits by banking association against Comptroller of the Currency); § 1395 (suits to recover a pecuniary fine, penalty, or forfeiture); § 1396 (suits to collect internal revenue taxes); § 1397 (interpleader actions); § 1400 (actions arising under patent or copyright laws); 15 U.S.C. §§ 15(a), 22 (suits arising under the Clayton Antitrust Act). Most of these special venue statutes are considered supplemental to the general venue statute. *Pure Oil Co. v. Suarez*, 384 U.S. 202, 204-205 (1966). In other words, they provide venues in addition to those provided by § 1391. *See, e.g., Monument Builders of Greater Kan. City, Inc. v. American Cemetery Assn.* 891 F.2d 1473, 1477 (10th Cir. 1989), *cert. denied*, 495 U.S. 930 (1990) (holding that Clayton Act venue provisions were supplemental to general venue provisions). Some special venue statutes, however, are exclusive in that they preclude reliance on the general venue statute. *See, e.g.*, 28 U.S.C. § 1402 (specified suits in which the United States is a defendant).

The focus of our attention will be on the general venue statute since it is the most widely applicable and since it provides a good model for developing an overall approach to solving venue problems. We begin with the first two subsections of § 1391, the current version of which provides as follows:

> (a) APPLICABILITY OF SECTION. Except as otherwise provided by law—(1) this section shall govern the venue of all civil actions brought in district courts of the United States; and (2) the proper venue for a civil action shall be determined without regard to whether the action is local or transitory in nature.*
>
> (b) VENUE IN GENERAL. A civil action may be brought in—(1) a judicial district in which any defendant resides, if all defendants are residents of the State in which the district is located; (2) a judicial district in which a substantial part of the events or omissions giving rise to the claim occurred, or a substantial part of property that is the subject of the action is situated; or (3) if there is no district in which an action may otherwise be brought as provided in this section, any judicial district in which any defendant is subject to the court's personal jurisdiction with respect to such action.

28 U.S.C. § 1391(a)-(b). Previously, § 1391 drew a distinction between venue provisions applicable in diversity cases and those applicable in federal question cases.

---

* A "local action" is a proceeding that directly affects the ownership or possession of real property, *e.g.*, a mortgage foreclosure proceeding or a quiet title action. At common law, a local action could only be filed in the venue where the property is located. Some states have enlarged the scope of local actions to include actions that are simply related to real property, *e.g.*, trespass actions or those involving damage to real property. If an action is not local, it is deemed "transitory" and need not be tied to any particular location. As § 1391(a)(2) makes clear, the distinction between local and transitory actions is now irrelevant for purposes of establishing venue in federal courts.

The distinction was largely cosmetic since the actual operation of the seemingly distinct venue provisions was virtually identical. The current version of § 1391, quoted above and enacted in 2011, eliminates the distinction and provides a unified framework to identify the proper venue for each action.

Subsection (b)(1) — Residence of Defendants

For purposes of venue, the residence of "a natural person, including an alien lawfully admitted for permanent residence in the United States, [is] the judicial district in which that person is domiciled." 28 U.S.C. § 1391(c)(1). In the case of a solitary defendant, subsection (b)(1) permits venue to be laid in the judicial district where that defendant is domiciled (resides). In the case of multiple defendants, all of whom reside in the same state, venue will be proper in a judicial district in which any one of them resides. Hence, if the plaintiff sues three defendants, all of whom reside in California, but in three different judicial districts — the Central, the Northern and the Southern — the case may be filed in any one of those districts. On the other hand, if the defendants do not reside in the same state, subsection (b)(1) is not available, since subsection (b)(1) only applies if all defendants reside in the same state.

Subsection (b)(2) — Substantial Part of Events

Under subsection (b)(2), venue is proper in a judicial district "in which a substantial part of the events or omissions giving rise to the claim occurred. . . ." 28 U.S.C. § 1391(b)(2). This language replaced the phrase "where the claim arose." That phrase implied that there was only one such district, but provided no guidance for those cases in which facts giving rise to the claim occurred in multiple districts. Some lower courts interpreted that phrase generously to identify the proper venue as being wherever substantial events giving rise to the claim occurred. Other courts were reluctant to accept such a broad interpretation of the statutory text. The newly adopted language eliminates that difficulty by recognizing that events or omissions giving rise to a claim may occur in more than one district.

First of Michigan Corp. v. Bramlet

141 F.3d 260 (6th Cir. 1998)

COLE, Circuit Judge.

Appellants, First of Michigan Corporation ("First of Michigan") and Michael Sobol, appeal the district court's dismissal based on improper venue of their case against Appellees, Carlton and Dolores Bramlet ("the Bramlets").

The sole issue on appeal is whether the district court erred in dismissing the plaintiffs' case based on improper venue. . . .

I.

Between September 1989 and August 1991, the Bramlets invested approximately $62,000 in an Individual Retirement Account ("IRA") with First of Michigan pursuant to the advice of Michael Sobol, an investment broker. The Bramlets' June 1, 1996, IRA statement indicated a loss of $37,556. On June 24, 1996, the Bramlets, residents of Florida, initiated an arbitration action against First of Michigan and Sobol by filing a Uniform Submission Agreement with the National Association of Securities Dealers ("NASD") in Florida. In their arbitration complaint, the Bramlets alleged that First of Michigan and Sobol failed to provide them with periodic statements of their IRA's value, thereby concealing the account's steady loss until it was too late to mitigate the damage. The terms of the arbitration agreement provided that any arbitration hearing between the parties would be conducted in accordance with "the Constitution, By-Laws, Rules, Regulations and/or NASD Code of Arbitration Procedures of the sponsoring organization."

Subsequently, First of Michigan and Sobol filed this action in the district court for the Eastern District of Michigan, seeking to enjoin and dismiss the Bramlets' arbitration claims as ineligible for arbitration, pursuant to NASD Code of Arbitration § 15, which bars arbitration of claims relating to investments more than six years old. First of Michigan and Sobol asserted jurisdiction in the federal district court based on the parties' diversity of citizenship and 28 U.S.C. § 1391(a), which establishes the proper venue for diversity cases.*

The Bramlets responded that the district court in Michigan was an improper venue and moved to dismiss the case against them. . . . The Bramlets reasoned that in 1989, when they began investing with Sobol and First of Michigan, they lived in Texas, and the majority of incidents giving rise to their claim took place in 1990, after they had moved to Florida. First of Michigan and Sobol contended that "a substantial part of the events or omissions giving rise to the claim occurred" in Michigan. Specifically, in 1989, the Bramlets met Sobol in Michigan in order to solicit his advice in converting Carlton Bramlet's 401(k) funds. Further, Sobol originated and received all of his telephone calls with the Bramlets and established the IRAs at issue in Michigan.

On March 13, 1997, the district court dismissed the plaintiffs' case based on improper venue, reasoning that "the most substantial event giving rise to plaintiffs' complaint for declaratory relief was the Bramlets' filing of an arbitration action, which they initiated in Florida." The district court concluded that because the Bramlets did not reside in Michigan, and a "substantial part of the events giving rise to the plaintiffs' complaint" did not occur in Michigan, venue in Michigan was improper. This timely appeal followed.

---

* [As noted in the text, § 1391 no longer distinguishes between diversity and federal question cases. The then § 1391(a) standards referenced by the court are now embodied in § 1391(b).—Eds.]

II.

We have not specifically addressed the standard of review which we apply to a district court's order dismissing a complaint based on improper venue. Whether the district court erred in dismissing for improper venue frequently implicates the related question of whether the district court also erred in failing to transfer the case to a proper venue pursuant to 28 U.S.C. § 1406(a) rather than dismiss. The decision of whether to dismiss or transfer is within the district court's sound discretion, and accordingly, we review such a decision for an abuse of discretion.

However, in this case, the plaintiffs do not claim that the district court erred by dismissing their case rather than transferring it to a proper venue; they instead contend that the district court applied an obsolete standard in determining that venue was improper in the first instance, thereby challenging the district court's interpretation of the venue statute. As the district court's determination of whether a plaintiff has filed his action in the proper venue involves an interpretation of the venue statute, it is a question of law subject to *de novo* review. We therefore review *de novo* the district court's determination that the plaintiffs filed their case in an improper venue.

III.

First of Michigan and Sobol contend that the district court applied an "incorrect, obsolete" standard in granting the motion to dismiss on the basis of improper venue. The plaintiffs refer to the district court's finding that "the most substantial event giving rise to plaintiffs' complaint . . . was the Bramlets' filing of an arbitration action, which they initiated in Florida." First of Michigan and Sobol argue that proper venue is not limited to the district where the most substantial event giving rise to the complaint arose. Rather, the plaintiffs cite 28 U.S.C. § 1391(a)(2) to support their argument that venue is proper wherever "a substantial part" of the events giving rise to the claim occurred.

28 U.S.C. § 1391(a) states in relevant part: A civil action wherein jurisdiction is founded only on diversity of citizenship may, except as otherwise provided by law, be brought only in . . . (2) a judicial district in which a substantial part of the events or omissions giving rise to the claim occurred. . . . The statute was amended in 1990 in order to broaden the venue provisions. The commentary following the 1990 revisions to § 1391(a)(2) states:

> The fact that substantial activities took place in district B does not disqualify district A as proper venue as long as "substantial" activities took place in A, too. Indeed, district A should not be disqualified even if it is shown that the activities in district B were more substantial, or even the most substantial. Any other approach would restore the pinpointing problem that created the difficulties under the now discarded "claim arose" standard. If the selected district's contacts are "substantial," it should make no difference that another's are more so, or the most so.

David D. Siegel, Commentary on the 1988 and 1990 Revisions of Section 1391, Subdivision (a), Clause (2), 28 U.S.C.A. §1391 (1993).

Before 1990, § 1391 limited proper venue to . . . "*the* judicial district in which the claim arose." *Onderik v. Morgan*, 897 F.2d 204, 206 (6th Cir. 1989) (emphasis added). The amended version of § 1391 replaced this standard in favor of proper venue in "a judicial district in which a *substantial part* of the events giving rise to the claim arose." 28 U.S.C. § 1391(a)(2) (emphasis added).

The 1990 amendment to § 1391(a)(2) renders the *Onderik* standard obsolete. *See Setco Enterprises Corp. v. Robbins*, 19 F.3d 1278, 1280-81 (8th Cir. 1994) (stating that under the amended statute, courts "no longer ask which district among the two or more potential forums is the 'best' venue. Rather, [they] ask whether the district the plaintiff chose had a substantial connection to the claim, whether or not other forums had greater contacts"); *Bates v. C & S Adjusters, Inc.*, 980 F.2d 865, 866-68 (2d Cir. 1992) (noting that "the new statute does not, as a general matter, require the District Court to determine the best venue"). We have not previously reviewed the determination of venue under the amended version of § 1391.

In light of the amended language of § 1391(a)(2), we hold that in diversity of citizenship cases the plaintiff may file his complaint in any forum where a substantial part of the events or omissions giving rise to the claim arose; this includes any forum with a substantial connection to the plaintiff's claim. *See* 28 U.S.C. § 1391(a). We thus conclude that the district court misapplied the statute in determining that the plaintiffs filed their action in an improper venue. The district court cited the amended version of § 1391(a)(2). However, in its order dismissing the plaintiffs' claim, the district court referred to "the most substantial event giving rise to" the complaint. This phrase echos the pre-1990 standard for the determination of appropriate venue. The district court reasoned that the only event triggering First of Michigan and Sobol's lawsuit seeking to enjoin the Bramlets' arbitration claim was the filing of the arbitration claim in Florida, and that the plaintiffs' case was not based on First of Michigan and Sobol's handling of the Bramlets' investments. The district court stated that "[d]espite the fact that the Bramlets purchased the disputed investments through a Michigan broker, the case at bar would not exist had the Bramlets not instigated the arbitration in Florida." This analysis indicates that the district court based its determination that venue was improper on a single occurrence which directly gave rise to the plaintiffs' action, rather than considering whether the forum the plaintiffs chose had a substantial connection to their claim.

An application of the amended § 1391(a)(2), which allows plaintiffs to file a diversity case wherever a substantial part of the events giving rise to their claim occurred, would have allowed First of Michigan and Sobol's claim to proceed in the district court for the Eastern District of Michigan. Most of the transactions relating to the Bramlets' investments took place in Michigan or resulted from contact the Bramlets had with Sobol, who at all times conducted business in Michigan. We have held in similar circumstances that venue is proper where the underlying transactions and investments took place and is not limited to the forum where the defendants filed a request for arbitration. Under § 1391(a)(2), we reiterate that the appropriate forum for a case is any forum in which a substantial part of the events or omissions giving rise to the claim occurred. With this standard in mind, we conclude that the district court erred in dismissing the plaintiffs' case based on an outdated interpretation of the venue statute.

IV.

For the foregoing reasons, we REVERSE the judgment of the district court and REMAND for further proceedings consistent with this opinion.

NOTES AND QUESTIONS

1. Standards of review. The court in *Bramlet* stated that a district court's order dismissing a suit for improper venue is normally reviewed under an abuse-of-discretion standard. Why should that be the normal standard of review for venue dismissals? What type of error by a district court would lead to a reversal under that standard? Why did the *Bramlet* court nonetheless review the district court's venue decision under a "de novo" standard? And how does that standard differ from the abuse-of-discretion standard?

2. The requirement of substantiality. By using the word "substantial," § 1391(b)(2) requires something more than an incidental relationship between the district and the cause of action. As one court observed, "Events or omissions that might only have some tangential connection with the dispute in litigation are not enough . . . . The test . . . is not the defendant's 'contacts' with a particular district, but rather the location of those 'events or omissions giving rise to the claim'. . . ." *Cottman Transmission Sys., Inc. v. Martino*, 36 F.3d 291, 294 (3d Cir. 1994). "Substantiality is intended to preserve the element of fairness so that a defendant is not haled into a remote district having no real relationship to the dispute." *Id.* Do you think that this "element of fairness" might prevent venue from being exercised even though the reasonableness element of personal jurisdiction has been satisfied? Reconsider the facts of *Burger King Corp. v. Rudzewicz*, Chapter II, at page 157, *supra*. The defendants in that case operated a Burger King franchise in Michigan. Burger King, which was headquartered in Miami, Florida, sued the defendants for breach of the franchise agreement. The suit was filed in the Southern District of Florida, which embraces the city of Miami. The Supreme Court upheld personal jurisdiction over the defendants on the theory that the defendants' business dealings with Burger King were purposefully directed toward Burger King's headquarters in the State of Florida. Does it necessarily follow that "a substantial part of the events or omissions giving rise to the claim occurred" in the Southern District of Florida? Would it make any difference to your arguments that "a substantial part of the events or omissions giving rise to the claim occurred" in the Michigan district in which the defendants operated their Burger King franchise? For more recent applications of the substantiality test, see *Bockman v. First American Marketing Corp.*, 459 Fed. App'x

157 (3d Cir. 2012); *Astro-Med, Inc. v. Nihon Kohden America, Inc.*, 591 F.3d 1, 11-12 (1st Cir. 2009).

3. *Burden of pleading and burden of proof.* In federal court, the plaintiff does not have the burden of pleading proper venue, although it is a good practice to do so. Moreover, a federal court will not usually raise an objection to venue on its own motion, although under exceptional circumstances it might. Thus the burden is typically on the defendant to challenge the propriety of venue. A defendant may do so by filing a timely motion to dismiss for improper venue under Federal Rule of Civil Procedure 12(b)(3). Any objection to venue is waived if defendant files a responsive pleading or a motion to dismiss that does not include the objection. *See* FED. R. CIV. P. 12(h)(1) (covering waiver or preservation of certain defenses). If a timely objection to venue is raised, most federal courts hold that the plaintiff then has the burden of establishing that venue is proper. *See* 14D CHARLES ALAN WRIGHT, ARTHUR R. MILLER, EDWARD H. COOPER & RICHARD D. FREER, FEDERAL PRACTICE AND PROCEDURE § 3826, at 499-507 & n.24 (4th ed. 2013 & Supp. 2015). *But see* Georgene M. Vairo, *Determination of Proper Venue, in* 17 MOORE'S FEDERAL PRACTICE § 110.01[5][c] (3d ed. 2015) (arguing that a defendant objecting to venue should have the burden of proving that venue is improper).

4. *Multiple parties and multiple claims.* As we will learn in more detail in Chapter VIII, cases often involve multiple plaintiffs, multiple defendants, multiple claims, and multiple rights of action. In federal court, venue must be satisfied for all original parties and claims. This can be accomplished through a combination of venue provisions, such as the "residence" and "substantial part" provisions of § 1391(b). If we adhere to the operative-facts definition of a claim, it would be an unusual case in which all the rights of action arising out of those facts were not each tied to the same district or districts under the substantial-part standard. Of course, if the rights of action arise out of different operative facts, then they arise from different claims and venue for each such claim must be established separately.

5. *Time frame from which venue is measured.* In general, the propriety of venue is assessed at the time the action is commenced. Hence, if venue is proper when a case is filed, venue remains proper regardless of any reconfiguration of the case or any change in residency of the parties. *Exxon Corp. v. F.T.C.*, 588 F.2d 895, 899 (3d Cir. 1978). For example, if venue is premised on the defendant's residency, a post-filing change of that defendant's residence will not render a previously established venue improper. Note, however, that the time-of-commencement rule does not necessarily apply when a plaintiff attempts to cure a defect in venue. Thus, in cases involving multiple defendants when venue is asserted under the residency provision of § 1391 (b)(1), a plaintiff may dismiss a nonresident (venue-destroying) defendant from the case to cure a defect in venue. In this particular context, venue is not assessed as of the time of commencement but in accord with the case's post-dismissal configuration. *See Knowlton v. Allied Van Lines, Inc.*, 900 F.2d 1196, 1200-1201 (8th Cir. 1990); 14D WRIGHT, MILLER, COOPER & FREER, *supra*, § 3807.

PROBLEMS

5-1. Re-read the facts of Problem 2-24, at page 241, *supra*. Would venue be proper in the district court for the District of Rhode Island? Where else might venue be proper? *See Astro-Med, Inc. v. Nihon Kohden America, Inc.*, 591 F.3d 1, 11-12 (1st Cir. 2009).

5-2. Hawes was involved in trademark litigation with L'Oreal in France. At issue in that litigation was whether a website domain name that Hawes had registered with Network Solutions, Inc. ("Network Solutions"), infringed the L'Oreal trademark. As part of that litigation, control over the domain name was deposited into the registry of the French court. While that action was pending, Hawes, who resided in Massachusetts, entered into an oral contract with Mitrano, who resided in New Hampshire. Under this contract, Mitrano agreed to provide legal services for Hawes pertaining to the domain name's ownership and control. The contract was formed and signed in Massachusetts. Initial services on the contract were performed in Massachusetts and in France. Payments for the services rendered were made from Massachusetts. Subsequently, Mitrano moved to Virginia, where he continued to provide legal services under the contract. Specifically, he filed a lawsuit on Hawes's behalf against Network Solutions and L'Oreal in the Eastern District of Virginia ("Eastern District"), in which he challenged the transfer of the domain name into the French court registry. That lawsuit was partially successful. Hawes now refuses to pay Mitrano for services rendered under the contract, particularly those services related to the filing of the suit in the Eastern District. In response, Mitrano has filed a breach of contract diversity action against Hawes in the Eastern District, claiming that Hawes owes him over $400,000 for legal services rendered. Hawes has moved to dismiss, arguing that venue is improper in the Eastern District. Is he correct? *See Mitrano v. Hawes*, 377 F.3d 402 (4th Cir. 2004).

5-3. McDaniel is a hog farmer from Alabama. In 1997, he sold over 700 hogs to Smithfield Foods, Inc. ("Smithfield"), a Delaware corporation with its corporate headquarters in Smithfield, Virginia. McDaniel negotiated the sales of the hogs to Smithfield over the telephone and delivered the hogs to the company's buying station in Georgia. McDaniel now claims that as a result of practices undertaken by Smithfield and other packers, cash markets for hogs have been destroyed, competition among packers has been dramatically reduced or eliminated, illegal price coordination among packers has been effectuated, and prices paid for hogs have been depressed. He has filed suit against Smithfield in the U.S. District Court for the Middle District of Alabama—the location of McDaniel's farm—claiming a violation of the federal Packers and Stockyards Act. The specific actions of which McDaniel complains include Smithfield's (1) acquiring or increasing its interest in several hog growers, (2) purchasing numerous meat packing and processing plants, and (3) having long-term contracts for supplying hogs to its subsidiaries. These actions did not take place in Alabama. McDaniel alleges that the strategy for these activities was coordinated from Smithfield's headquarters in Virginia. Is venue proper in the Middle District of Alabama under § 1391(b)(2)? *See McDaniel v. IBP, Inc.*, 89 F. Supp. 2d 1289, 1293-1297 (M.D. Ala. 2000).

Subsection (b)(3)—Fallback Provision

Section 1391(b)(3) provides that "if there is no district in which an action may otherwise be brought as provided in this section, [venue may be laid in] any judicial district in which any defendant is subject to the court's personal jurisdiction with respect to such action." In one sense, subsection (b)(3) appears to be a very generous venue provision since it requires only that personal jurisdiction be satisfied as to any one defendant. But that apparent generosity is a bit misleading. Subsection (b)(3) is a "fallback" provision. Thus a party may successfully invoke subsection (b)(3) only when there is no federal judicial district in which venue would be proper under either the "residence" or "substantial part" clauses of § 1391(b). *See Daniel v. American Bd. of Emergency Med.*, 428 F.3d 408, 434-435 (2d Cir. 2005). To be clear, to rely on the fallback provision it is insufficient that neither (b)(1) nor (b)(2) would be satisfied in the particular district in which the plaintiff has filed her suit. Rather, there must be no federal district anywhere in the United States in which either of those sections would be satisfied. Basically, the purpose of the fallback provision is to provide a federal forum for cases where the events giving rise to the claim occurred outside the country. In this limited circumstance, personal jurisdiction over one of the defendants serves as a substitute for the usual venue criteria.

PROBLEMS

5-4. During her junior year in college at Nevada State University ("NSU"), Katerina spent her spring semester in Florence, Italy, as part of NSU's semester abroad program. While there she met Jeremy and Gavin, who were also NSU students. The three were inseparable during the semester, often taking road trips together to various parts of Europe. On one such trip, Katerina was seriously injured when Jeremy drove his rented Fiat off the road into an embankment. Katerina believes that the accident was caused in part by Jeremy's excessive speed and in part by Gavin, who had distracted Jeremy by mooning a pedestrian just before the accident. Katerina has filed a lawsuit against Jeremy and Gavin in the U.S. District Court for the District of Nevada. Assume that § 1332's required amount in controversy is met. Although all three students are currently attending NSU, none is a resident of Nevada. Katerina lives with her family in New Mexico, while Jeremy and Gavin are domiciled in Oregon and Arizona, respectively. The suit was filed a week prior to the beginning of the fall semester following the accident. Jeremy and Gavin were both served during the first week of classes. Is venue in the District of Nevada proper?

5-5. Hassan was arrested by U.S. forces in Pakistan in 2002 and subsequently incarcerated at the U.S. detention center in Guantanamo Bay, Cuba, where he spent the next five years. Hassan was not charged with a crime and in 2007 he was released to Pakistan. In 2008, he filed a federal civil rights claim in the U.S. District Court for the Western District of Washington. There were three possible defendants. The first was Robert, the Secretary of Defense during a substantial part of Hassan's incarceration, who was responsible for some of the policies pertaining to Hassan's incarceration. The second was James, a military officer who authorized Hassan's arrest in Pakistan. The third was Daniel, an FBI agent who interrogated Hassan at the Guantanamo Bay detention center. Although Robert currently lives and works in Fairfax County, Virginia (the location of the Pentagon), his permanent residence is in Seattle, Washington, and has been there for the past 20 years. James, now retired, has moved to Virginia, where he lived prior to joining the military; James was, however, stationed at a military base near Spokane, Washington from 1999 through 2008, where he lived with his family. Daniel is also domiciled in Fairfax County, Virginia, where he has lived since 1998. Seattle is in the Western District of Washington; Spokane is in the Eastern District of Washington; Fairfax County is in the Eastern District of Virginia. Assume that Hassan can state a valid claim against each of the three possible defendants; assume (unless the question otherwise indicates) that there are no issues pertaining to personal jurisdiction.

A. Suppose Hassan sued only Robert. Would venue be proper in the Western District of Washington under § 1391(b)(1)?

B. Suppose that Hassan sued Robert and James, and that the suit was filed prior to James's retirement. How might you argue that venue was proper in the Western District of Washington under § 1391(b)(1)? Might subsection (b)(1) allow Hassan to file his suit in any other district in Washington? Suppose that after the filing of the suit, James retired and moved to Virginia. Explain how those events would or would not be relevant to the question of venue in the Western District of Washington?

C. Suppose Hassan sued all three defendants. Would either § 1391(b)(1) or (b)(2) suffice to establish venue in the Western District of Washington?

D. Suppose again that Hassan sued all three defendants. Could Hassan rely on subsection (b)(3) to establish venue in the Western District of Washington? In answering this question, consider how the defendants might respond to Hassan's assertion of (b)(3) venue. If the defendants challenged Hassan's use of (b)(3), which party (or parties) would have the burden of establishing the propriety or impropriety of that usage?

E. Assume that Hassan sued all three defendants in the Western District of Washington, but that the court granted Daniel's motion to dismiss for lack of personal jurisdiction. Given that ruling, from what point in time should the court resolve the question of venue? Would venue now be proper in the Western District of Washington?

See Hamad v. Gates, 2010 WL 4511142 (W.D. Wash. Nov. 2, 2010) (encompassing comparable facts but not necessarily "correct" in all aspects of the decision).

Subsections (c)(2) and (d) — Residence of Corporate and Noncorporate Entities

For purposes of venue, § 1391(c)(2) provides that "an entity with the capacity to sue and be sued . . . under applicable law . . . , whether or not incorporated, shall be deemed to reside, if a defendant, in any judicial district in which such defendant is subject to the court's personal jurisdiction with respect to the civil action in question. . . ." In cases where the entity is a plaintiff, subsection (c)(2) defines residence as "the judicial district in which the entity maintains its principal place of business. . . ." This provision covers corporations and unincorporated associations, including partnerships. It is relatively easy to apply in those states that have only a single judicial district. In such states, a defendant entity is a resident of the state's federal judicial district if the entity's contacts with the state satisfy the due process standards of either specific or general jurisdiction.

The venue landscape is slightly more complicated in multidistrict states. Section 1391(d) provides:

> For purposes of venue under this chapter, in a State which has more than one judicial district and in which a defendant that is a corporation is subject to personal jurisdiction at the time an action is commenced, such corporation shall be deemed to reside in any district in that State within which its contacts would be sufficient to subject it to personal jurisdiction if that district were a separate State. . . .

Here, the personal jurisdiction analysis is redirected toward contacts with a district, treating the district as a hypothetical state. Of course, there may be more than one district that satisfies this test, in which case the corporate defendant is deemed to reside in any such district. The section also addresses the rare case in which the contacts with the state may be so dispersed throughout a multidistrict state that personal jurisdiction would not be satisfied in any single district. In such a case, "the corporation shall be deemed to reside in the district within which it has the most significant contacts." *Id.*

Some lower federal courts have held that the phrase "personal jurisdiction" as used in § 1391(c) requires the court to apply the state's long-arm statute's standards in addition to a due process analysis. *See, e.g., Vesuvius Technologies, LLC v. SilverCentral, Inc.,* 2013 WL 1879107, at *1 (E.D. Wis. May 3, 2013); *Grynberg v. Goldman Sachs Group, Inc.,* 2013 WL 1192585, at *2 (D.N.J. Mar. 22, 2013). In single-district states, this approach has little impact since the state's long-arm statute must usually be satisfied in any event to establish personal jurisdiction over the corporate defendant. In multidistrict states, however, applying the state long-arm standards on a district-by-district basis may operate as a limit on the scope of federal venue provisions if the long-arm statute's standards cannot be satisfied in any specific district. Other lower federal courts apply only the due process standards, reasoning that venue in federal courts presents a question of federal law to which state law is irrelevant. *See, e.g., Graham v. Dyncorp Int'l, Inc.,* 973 F. Supp. 2d 698, 701-702 (S.D. Tex. 2013); *New York Access Billing, LLC v. ATX Communications, Inc.,* 289 F. Supp. 2d 260, 266-267 (N.D.N.Y. 2013). The leading commentators are in accord with this latter approach. *See* 17 MOORE'S FEDERAL PRACTICE, *supra,* § 110.03[4][c]; 14D WRIGHT, MILLER, COOPER & FREER, *supra,* § 3811.1. Until this issue is resolved, however, one must be aware of the conflict.

There is a slight wrinkle. Subsection (d) references only *corporate* defendants. In this sense, it appears to be narrower than subsection (c)(2), which covers both corporations and unincorporated associations, leaving open the question of how one is to measure the residency of an unincorporated association in a multidistrict state. If we adhere to the text of § 1391(d), which narrows a plaintiff's choice only as to corporate defendants, it would seem that an unincorporated association could be deemed a resident of any district in a multidistrict state, regardless of its contacts with the district, so long as the standards of personal jurisdiction over that unincorporated association have been satisfied statewide. In *Graham v. Dyncorp Int'l, Inc., supra*, the district court addressed this anomaly and offered a solution:

> Contrast section 1391(d)'s use of "corporation" with section 1391(c)'s much broader reference to "an entity with the capacity to sue and be sued in its common name under applicable law." 28 U.S.C. § 1391(c)(2). Basic principles of statutory construction—namely the requirement to follow plain language and to give meaning to different language in the same statute—would seem to require applying section 1391(d) only to corporations.
>
> The development of this different language also warrants consideration. Prior to the Federal Courts Jurisdiction and Venue Clarification Act of 2011, both of these provisions were contained in 1391(c), and both used only the term "corporation." *See* 28 U.S.C. § 1391(c) (2010). Courts, however, including the Supreme Court, had long interpreted the term "corporation" in section 1391(c) to include unincorporated associations like partnerships and LLCs. In the Clarification Act, Congress codified this judicial interpretation by including the "whether or not incorporated" language in section 1391(c)'s general residence definition, which applies in single-district states. But Congress also moved the multi-district rule into a separate section 1391(d), which retained the prior use of "corporation." *See* 14D Charles Alan Wright *et al.*, FEDERAL PRACTICE & PROCEDURE § 3812 (describing this history and calling section 1391(d)'s failure to include unincorporated associations an "oversight"). So much for "clarification" of venue law.
>
> Despite this distinction in the current statute, [this court] feels compelled to follow the precedent that reads the "corporation" language to refer to unincorporated entities like LLCs.

973 F. Supp. 2d at 701 n.2. Does that interpretive accommodation make sense?

PROBLEMS

5-6. Reconsider the facts of Problem 5-3, page 415, *supra*. Applying 28 U.S.C. § 1391(c)-(d), construct an argument that venue would have been proper in the Middle District of Alabama. Think of it this way: On what basis would McDaniel argue that a federal court sitting in Alabama would have personal jurisdiction over Smithfield?

5-7. Nissan Motor Co., Ltd. ("Nissan Motor") is a large Japanese auto maker. Its subsidiary, Nissan North America, Inc. ("Nissan North America"), which has its principal place of business in Gardena, California, markets and distributes Nissan vehicles in the United States. Nissan Motor owns, and Nissan North America is the exclusive licensee of, various registered trademarks using the word "Nissan" in connection with automobiles and other vehicles. The first such trademark was registered in 1959. The defendant, Nissan Computer Corporation (NCC), is a North

Carolina corporation with its principal place of business in North Carolina. NCC is in the business of computer sales and services. The company was incorporated in 1991 by Uzi Nissan, its current president. NCC registered the internet domain names "nissan.com" and "nissan.net" in May 1994 and March 1996, respectively. In July 1995, Nissan Motor and Nissan North America sent Uzi Nissan a letter expressing "great concern" about use of the word Nissan in NCC's domain name. Subsequently, NCC altered the content of its "nissan.com" website and displayed a "Nissan Computer" logo that was confusingly similar to Nissan Motor's logo. In addition, the website displayed banner advertisements and web links to various search engines and merchandising companies, including links to automobile merchandisers. Uzi Nissan did offer to sell the disputed domain names to Nissan Motor for several million dollars. However, Nissan Motor declined. Instead, Nissan Motor and Nissan North America filed a suit against NCC in the U.S. District Court for the Central District of California ("Central District") where Gardena is located, charging NCC with trademark infringement. Venue was purportedly established under § 1391(b)(1). Is venue in the Central District proper under that section? Is there any other provision of § 1391 that would permit venue in the Central District? *See Nissan Motor Co., Ltd. v. Nissan Computer Corp.*, 89 F. Supp. 2d 1154, 1161-1162 (C.D. Cal.), *aff'd*, 246 F.3d 675 (9th Cir. 2000).

NOTES AND QUESTIONS

1. The practical utility of subsection (c)(2). What, if anything, is the practical difference between establishing that an entity is subject to personal jurisdiction within a particular district and establishing that the district is one "in which a substantial part of the events or omissions giving rise to the claim occurred"? 28 U.S.C. § 1391(b)(2). Does general jurisdiction or consent to service on an agent factor into your answer?

2. The residence of political subdivisions. Cities, counties, and other state or local government subdivision units are residents of the judicial district in which they are located. In addition, some courts have also used § 1391(c) as a measure of political subdivision residence. *See, e.g.*, *Rodriguez-Torres v. American Airlines Corp.*, 8 F. Supp. 2d 150, 151-152 (D.P.R. 1998).

3. Venue and nonresident alien defendants. Under § 1391(c)(3), "a defendant not resident in the United States may be sued in any judicial district, and the joinder of such a defendant shall be disregarded in determining where the action may be brought with respect to other defendants." This provision apparently covers any individual alien who has not been admitted for permanent residence to the United States. *Cf.* 28 U.S.C. § 1391(c)(1) (residence of alien admitted for permanent residence). It also applies to corporations incorporated in a foreign nation. In addition, given the breadth of the language, it applies to United States citizens who are domiciled abroad, though there are no cases addressing this possibility.

4. Removal and venue. Recall that under appropriate circumstances, 28 U.S.C. § 1441 allows a case originally filed in a state court to be removed from that court to the federal court embracing the place in which the state court sits. *See* Chapter IV, part A.5, page 390, *supra*. Upon proper removal, venue in the federal court is automatically proper. This remains true even if venue would not have been proper in that federal court had the case originally been filed there. *See* 28 U.S.C. § 1390(c) (federal venue statutes do "not determine the district court to which a civil action pending in State court may be removed"). Removal under the Class Action Fairness Act, 28 U.S.C. § 1453, has the same effect with respect to establishing venue in the federal court to which the action was properly removed.

PROBLEM

5-8. Nine expatriate citizens of Guatemala brought suit in the U.S. District Court for the District of Massachusetts ("District of Massachusetts") under the federal Torture Victim Protection Act of 1991 against Hector Gramajo, formerly Guatemala's Minister of Defense. The plaintiffs sought compensatory and punitive damages for devastating injuries they suffered from the conduct of Guatemalan military forces. The plaintiffs alleged that Gramajo was personally responsible for numerous acts of gruesome violence and torture inflicted by military personnel who were under his direct command. All of the activities giving rise to the suit took place in Guatemala. The complaint was served on Gramajo while he was in Massachusetts attending Harvard University's Kennedy School of Government. Is venue proper in the District of Massachusetts? Suppose the plaintiffs named as a co-defendant a U.S. citizen who is a resident of Florida. Assuming personal jurisdiction could be established over that defendant in Massachusetts, on what theory might venue be proper there? *See Xuncax v. Gramajo*, 886 F. Supp. 162, 193 (D. Mass. 1995).

2. Transfer of Venue in Federal Court

Skyhawke Technologies, LLC v. DECA International Corp.

2011 WL 1806511 (S.D. Miss. May 11, 2011)

PARKER, United States Magistrate Judge.

This matter is before the court on the Motion to Change Venue filed by Defendant DECA International Corporation (DECA). Having duly considered the motion, the applicable legal standards, and the other submissions by the parties, the court finds that the motion should be DENIED.

Factual Background

Plaintiff Skyhawke Technologies, LLC (Skyhawke) accuses DECA of infringing on two patents of which Skyhawke is the assignee—Patent No. 6,456,938 (hereinafter the "938 patent"), entitled "Personal DGPS Golf Course Cartographer,

Navigator and Internet Web Site with Map Exchange and Tutor," and Patent No. 7,118,498 (hereinafter the "498 patent"), entitled "Personal Golfing Assistant and Method and System for Graphically Displaying Golf Related information and for Collection, Processing and Distribution of Golf Related Data." Skyhawke is a limited liability company with its principal place of business in Ridgeland, Mississippi. DECA is a California corporation with its principal place of business in La Palma, California. DECA is a wholly owned subsidiary of DECA System Inc., a Korean corporation.

Skyhawke alleges that DECA has made, caused to be made, imported, caused to be imported, used, offered to sell, sold, and caused to be sold products (*i.e.*, the Golfbuddy World Platinum product) in Mississippi, which has infringed, induced infringement, and/or contributed to infringement on the 938 patent and the 498 patent.

In the instant motion, DECA asks the court to transfer this case from the Southern District of Mississippi (hereinafter "Southern District") to the Central District of California (hereinafter "Central District").

Transfer of Venue Standard

For the convenience of parties and witnesses and in the interest of justice, a district court may transfer any civil action to any other district or division where it might have been brought. 28 U.S.C.A. § 1404(a). "[T]he plaintiff's choice of forum is clearly a factor to be considered but in and of itself it is neither conclusive nor determinative." *In re Horseshoe Entm't*, 337 F.3d 429, 434 (5th Cir. 2003).

[W]hen the transferee venue is not clearly more convenient than the venue chosen by the plaintiff, the plaintiff's choice should be respected. When the movant demonstrates that the transferee venue is clearly more convenient, however, it has shown good cause and the district court should therefore grant the transfer. *In re Volkswagen of Am., Inc.*, 545 F.3d 304, 315 (5th Cir. 2008) ("Volkswagen II"). A decision to transfer venue under Section 1404 is committed to the sound discretion of the transferring judge.

The threshold issue is whether the claim could have been filed in the judicial district to which the movant is seeking to transfer the case. *In re Volkswagen AG*, 371 F.3d 201, 203 (5th Cir. 2004) ("Volkswagen I"). Venue is proper in any district in which any defendant resides [if all defendants are residents of the state in which the district is located]. 28 U.S.C.A. § 1391(b)(1). A defendant corporation is deemed to reside in any district in which it is subject to personal jurisdiction at the time the action is commenced. *Id.* at [§ 1391(d)].

In order to determine the convenience to the parties and witnesses the court applies private and public interest factors. The private interest factors include:

(1) the relative ease of access to sources of proof; (2) the availability of compulsory process to secure the attendance of witnesses; (3) the cost of attendance for willing witnesses; and (4) all other practical problems that make trial of a case easy, expeditious and inexpensive.

The public interest factors are as follows:

> (1) the administrative difficulties flowing from court congestion; (2) the local interest in having localized interests decided at home; (3) the familiarity of the forum with the law that will govern the case; and (4) the avoidance of unnecessary problems of conflict of laws of the application of foreign law.

Analysis

The court answers the threshold question of whether suit may have been brought against DECA in the Central District in the affirmative, given that DECA is headquartered in the Central District; thus, transfer of venue to the Central District is permissible under 28 U.S.C. § 1404(a). Accordingly, the court finds it necessary to weigh the applicable private interest and public interest factors to determine whether the Central District is the clearly more convenient venue versus the plaintiff's chosen venue, the Southern District.

Private Interest Factors

(1) Access to sources of proof

DECA avers that this factor weighs in its favor because the documents relating to design, development, testing, and marketing of the product at issue, as well as product models and prototypes, are located in its California headquarters. *In re Genentech, Inc.*, 566 F.3d 1338, 1345 (Fed. Cir. 2009), states: "In patent infringement cases, the bulk of the relevant evidence usually comes from the accused infringer. Consequently, the place where the defendant's documents are kept weighs in favor of transfer to that location." DECA argues that transport of the documents for trial will impose a significant and unnecessary burden. *See id.* at 1346 (holding that district court erred in denying a transfer where the plaintiff's chosen venue would impose a significant and unnecessary burden on the petitioners to transport documents that would not be incurred in the requested venue).

DECA claims that other sources of proof are located at the facility of DECA System in Bundang, Korea. DECA argues that the Central District is 1,850 miles closer to Korea than the Southern District, and thus, the more convenient forum. Conversely, Skyhawke argues that sources of proof found in Korea are located outside of the Central District, thus this does not weigh in favor of transfer.

DECA also highlights the fact that Skyhawke's 938 patent is for a product developed in Wayne City, Illinois, and suggests that all documents relating to this product's development will be found in Illinois—not Mississippi. Skyhawke denies this, and claims all documents related to the 938 patent were transferred to Skyhawke's possession.

Skyhawke further argues that in addition to having its principal place of business in the Southern District and employing ninety-six residents of the Southern District, all documents, records, and other evidence relating to the inventions and prosecution histories of the two Skyhawke patents at issue are located in the Southern District at its Ridgeland facility. Additionally, Skyhawke claims that documents relating to the development of the 498 product, financial records relating to damages incurred, documents relating to the commercial success of the products at issue, and the alleged infringing devices that DECA sold in Mississippi are all located in the Southern District. Accordingly, Skyhawke urges this court to find that this factor does not weigh in DECA's favor where Skyhawke would be equally as inconvenienced should its choice of venue be disturbed.

While the court agrees with the observation in the *Genentech* case that the bulk of the evidence in patent matters is often presented by the alleged infringer—in this case DECA—it is clear that Skyhawke maintains records in the Southern District that will be relevant. Moreover, while DECA has certainly not waived its rights to contest venue by filing an answer and counterclaim, its pleadings suggest that Skyhawke's records will also be relevant. For example, DECA claims, *inter alia*, that the patents at issue are invalid for Skyhawke's failure to satisfy the statutory requirements of 35 U.S.C. §§ 101, et seq. Records and other evidence regarding Skyhawke's compliance, or lack thereof, with the statutory requirements are more likely to be in Skyhawke's possession.

On balance, this factor is either neutral or very slightly favors DECA.

(2) *Compulsory process* ~WITNESSES~   ~100 MILE CIRCLE~

DECA alleges that this court's subpoena powers will not extend to any of the witnesses in this case, given that a number of their identified witnesses reside in or near the Central District. DECA contends the fact that the Central District is "a venue with usable subpoena power . . . weighs in favor of transfer, and not only slightly." *In re Genentech*, 566 F.3d at 1345. Conversely, Skyhawke argues that the Southern District has subpoena power over party witnesses and that the analysis of this factor only applies to non-party witnesses. Skyhawke further asserts that this factor is neutral—and if not, weighs against transfer—because neither the Central District nor the Southern District has compulsory process over any of the identified witnesses from Korea or over Mr. Kent Barnard, the inventor of the 938 patent and a resident of Indiana.

Skyhawke is correct in its assessment that the compulsory process factor involves a factual analysis of non-party witnesses versus party witnesses. It is unclear whether the identified witnesses at the DECA System facility in Korea are non-party witnesses rather than party witnesses. Assuming they are non-party witnesses, neither the Central District nor the Southern District could compel them to appear at trial. The same can be said of the inventor of the 938 patent, an Indiana resident.

Accordingly, this factor is essentially neutral as to both parties. It is worth noting, however, that "if this court cannot compel a witness's attendance at trial, neither party is prevented from using the witness's videotaped deposition at trial." *Symbol Technologies, Inc. v. Metrologic Instruments Inc.*, 450 F. Supp. 2d 676, 679 (E.D. Tex. 2006).

(3) *Cost of attendance for witnesses*

This factor has been referred to as the most important private interest. DECA estimates the distance between the two forums to be 1,850 miles, which makes travel for DECA's witnesses inconvenient. The Fifth Circuit has established the "100-mile rule," which states: "When the distance between an existing venue for trial of a matter and a proposed venue under § 1404(a) is more than 100 miles, the factor of inconvenience to witnesses increases in direct relationship to the additional distance to be traveled." *Volkswagen II*, 545 F.3d at 317.

DECA identified three of its officers as material witnesses on the subjects of design, development, and marketing of the alleged infringing product, all of whom reside in the Central District of California. DECA argues that these witnesses will incur a "dramatic burden in terms of cost, time away from family, and time away from other personal and professional obligations" if required to travel to the Southern District for trial. *Id.* To the extent that former employees of DECA may be necessary witnesses, those former employees are said to currently reside in the Los Angeles and Seattle, Washington areas—much closer to the Central District than the Southern District. The Fifth Circuit has recognized that witnesses who must travel for trial incur not only a monetary burden, "but also the personal costs associated with being away from work, family, and community." *Volkswagen II*, 545 F.3d at 317.

DECA argues that the previously identified witnesses who live in Korea will incur greater costs due to a lack of direct flights from Seoul to Jackson, Mississippi. DECA identifies three officers from its parent-corporation DECA System as material witnesses—Junha Park (Software Development Manager), Gisu Lee (Hardware Development Manager), and Suk Chul Ham (Global Marketing Manager)—who may have knowledge regarding the design, development, and/or marketing of the alleged infringing product. According to DECA, the fact that there are no direct flights from Seoul, Korea to Jackson, Mississippi and no direct flights from Los Angeles, California to Jackson, Mississippi should weigh in its favor since this means increased costs and increased travel time for DECA's witnesses.

Additionally, DECA suggests that should the inventor or anyone else involved in securing the patent be identified as necessary third-party witnesses those witnesses would have no connection to the Southern District. As a result, DECA argues that the Southern District would be no more convenient for those potential witnesses than the Central District.

For all of the aforementioned reasons, DECA argues that this factor overwhelmingly weighs in its favor.

Conversely, Skyhawke has identified as material witnesses three of its officers, who are inventors of the 498 product, and who all reside in the Southern District. Skyhawke contends that their witnesses will be equally inconvenienced by traveling to the Central District should venue be changed. Ultimately, Skyhawke argues that where a transfer in venue would simply shift the inconvenience from one party to another, this factor is neutral and does not support granting DECA's motion.

The Fifth Circuit has recognized that pursuant to the 100-mile rule the additional distance to be traveled for trial in a proposed venue "means additional travel time; additional travel time increases the probability for meal and lodging expenses; and additional travel time with overnight stays increases the time which these fact witnesses must be away from their regular employment." *Volkswagen I*, 371 F.3d at 205. However, where a transfer in venue serves to shift inconvenience from one party to the next, this factor does not weigh in favor of granting the movant's request given that the convenience of all parties and witnesses should be considered. *See id.* at 204. Thus, where DECA has identified three of its officers as essential witnesses and Skyhawke has identified three of its officers as essential witnesses, this factor is neutral given that a transfer of venue would result in transferring the increased costs and inconvenience to Skyhawke.

A typical patent case involves witnesses who come from all over the country or world. With regard to the DECA System witnesses traveling from Korea, the court finds the increased travel time of the witnesses from the DECA System facility in Korea may weigh in DECA's favor, but only slightly, as foreign travel will likely inconvenience these witnesses regardless of whether they are traveling to the Central District or the Southern District. "Thus, regardless of where the trial is held, many witnesses, including third-party witnesses, will likely need to travel a significant distance." *Symbol Technologies*, 450 F. Supp. at 679 (citation omitted).

(4) *Other practical problems*

DECA again argues that all documentary evidence and witnesses in this case are located in either California and Korea and that in granting a transfer to a venue in closer proximity to the relevant witnesses and evidence this court will further the interests of ease, expediency and cost of trial. Conversely, Skyhawke avers that to the extent DECA argues in favor of a transfer because witnesses and evidence from Korea are closer to the Central District, DECA is incorrect as a matter of law. *See In re Genentech*, 566 F.3d at 1344 (finding that district court erred in giving significant weight to the inconvenience of European witnesses where witnesses would be traveling a significant distance no matter where they testified).

The factual considerations asserted by DECA in support of its contention that this factor weighs in its favor are essentially restatements of previously asserted facts, namely that the majority of the documents and witnesses in the instant case may be found in or in closer proximity to the Central District. Given that DECA has not made any novel arguments nor identified any other practical problems for the court's consideration, the court finds this factor is neutral.

Public Interest Factors:

(1) *Local interest*

DECA argues that its company employs over thirty local residents and has become a prominent presence in the local economy of the Central District—generating $10 million in sales in 2010 alone. DECA emphasizes the fact that promotional events for its product are held in conjunction with local golf retail stores and Southern–California–based golf publications and that it has contributed to various local charitable organizations. DECA contends that because the reputation and business activities of its officers and employees are at issue in this case, the Central District has an interest in the outcome.

According to DECA, the only connection between the accused product and the Southern District is the fact that the product is sold here. DECA purports sales in the Southern District to be less than 0.12% of its nationwide sales in 2010. DECA avers that sale of the allegedly infringing product, without more, is insufficient to demonstrate a local interest for the purposes of a transfer of venue analysis. In support of this argument, DECA cites *In re TS Tech USA Corp.*, 551 F.3d 1315, 1321 (Fed. Cir. 2008), a patent infringement case which held that there was no local interest in the original venue merely because the accused product was sold there given that none of the parties had an office in the plaintiff's chosen venue, no witnesses resided there, and no evidence was located there.

Skyhawke argues that its chosen venue is the venue wherein its sole facility was founded in 1998, and as such Skyhawke's presence in the Southern District is not "recent, ephemeral, [or] an artifact of litigation." *In Re Zimmer Holdings, Inc.*, 609 F.3d 1378, 1381 (Fed. Cir. 2010). Skyhawke submits that ninety-six residents of the Southern District, as well as all of its officers and directors, work at its Ridgeland facility. Moreover, Skyhawke emphasizes that DECA intended for its infringing product to be sold and used in Mississippi, as evidenced by the digital maps of approximately one-hundred-fifty Mississippi golf courses contained on its product. For all of the aforementioned reasons, Skyhawke argues that there is a strong local interest in prosecuting this matter in the Southern District.

The Federal Circuit in *TS Tech* found no local interest in the plaintiff's chosen venue because the only connection to that venue was that the infringing product was sold there. In so finding, the court noted that there were no witnesses, no principal places of business of any party, and no evidence located in the original venue. Conversely, in the instant case, Skyhawke has a facility in Ridgeland, Mississippi, witnesses reside here, and Skyhawke's physical evidence is located at its facility. Moreover, as pointed to by Skyhawke, DECA has presumably directed its product at Mississippi consumers given that the product contains digital maps of Mississippi golf courses. Accordingly, while DECA makes a valid argument that the Central District has a local interest in this matter, the court finds the Southern District likewise has a local interest that is equal to that of the Central District in that Skyhawke's sole facility, witnesses and documents are located in the Southern District and given that the alleged infringing product is being sold here. Thus, the court finds this factor to be neutral.

(2) Administrative difficulties

DECA argues that disposition and trial timelines are slightly shorter in the Central District as opposed to the Southern District. DECA cites Administrative Office of the United States Courts data, which lists the Central District median disposition time as 5.6 months and median time to trial as 18.5 months. The Southern District's median disposition time is listed as 8.1 months with a median time to trial of 23.9 months. Thus, the Southern District's median time to trial is 5.4 months behind that of the Central District. Skyhawke argues that this slightly shorter time frame should be accorded minimal weight, if any. Moreover, Skyhawke notes that the Federal Circuit has referred to this as the "most speculative" factor in the analysis. *See In re Genentech,* 566 F.3d at 1347. "To the extent that court congestion is relevant, the speed with which a case can come to trial and be resolved may be a factor." *Id.* (citation omitted). The Federal Circuit in *In re Genentech* further noted:

> Without attempting to predict how this case would be resolved and which court might resolve it more quickly . . . when . . . several relevant factors weigh in favor of transfer and others are neutral, then the speed of the transferee district court should not alone outweigh all of those other factors.

While recognizing that this factor is clearly the most speculative, the court finds that a difference of approximately five months in average time of disposition is significant enough to slightly weigh in favor of DECA. However, given that the other factors are essentially neutral, the court, in keeping with the reasoning of *Genentech,* affords this factor little weight.

(3)   *Forum's familiarity with the governing law and (4) Conflict of law problems*

Both parties agree that the two remaining factors in the transfer of venue analysis are neutral as to both parties.

Conclusion

This case could have been brought in either of the two jurisdictions at issue. This is not a case such as *TS Tech* where the plaintiff had no real connection with the chosen forum, or such as *Genentech* where a substantial number of material witnesses resided in the transferee venue and no witnesses resided in the original forum. Here, SkyHawke has a substantial presence in this District, a number of witnesses are located in this District and some key records are located in this District.

While not determinative, a plaintiff's choice of venue is afforded deference. DECA has the burden of showing that its preferred venue is clearly more convenient. It failed to meet the burden as most of the factors in the analysis are neutral. Only one or two slightly favor a transfer. A change of venue would simply transfer any inconvenience DECA might suffer to SkyHawke. The plaintiff's choice of forum should be upheld.

IT IS, THEREFORE, ORDERED, that Defendant DECA's Motion to Transfer Venue is DENIED.

NOTES AND QUESTIONS

1. Transfers between federal courts.   If venue is proper in the federal court in which a case has been filed, both the plaintiff and the defendant retain the option of requesting that the case be transferred to another federal court "where it might have been brought," *i.e.*, where both venue and personal jurisdiction would have been satisfied at the time of filing the original suit. 28 U.S.C. § 1404(a). Was this a case where defendant was entitled to invoke § 1404(a)? That statute provides: "For the convenience of parties and witnesses, in the interest of justice, a district court may transfer any civil action to any other district or division where it might have been brought or to any district or division to which all parties have consented." Did the Central District of California meet that test? Whether to grant a motion to transfer under § 1404(a) is within the originating court's discretion. In exercising that discretion courts consider a number of private interest factors, including a strong preference for the plaintiff's choice of forum, ease of access to sources of proof, the availability of compulsory process for unwilling witnesses, the cost of obtaining attendance of willing witnesses, and practical problems that make trial of a case easy, expeditious, and inexpensive. The court also considers various public interest factors, including the relative congestion of court dockets, choice-of-law considerations, and the relationship of the community in which the respective courts and jurors are located to the occurrences that gave rise to the litigation. *See In re Genentech, Inc.*, 566 F.3d 1338 (Fed. Cir. 2009), *In re Volkswagen of America, Inc.*, 545 F.3d 304 (5th Cir. 2008), *cert. denied*, 555 U.S. 1172 (2009). Did the magistrate judge abuse his discretion in denying the motion to transfer in *Skyhawke Technologies*?

For cases in which venue is improper in the originating court, 28 U.S.C. § 1406(a) provides: "The district court of a district in which is filed a case laying venue in the wrong division or district shall dismiss, or if it be in the interest of justice, transfer such case to any district or division in which it could have been brought." The choice of whether to dismiss or transfer under § 1406(a) is also within the originating court's discretion. Why wasn't *Skyhawke* a § 1406(a) case? In determining whether to dismiss or transfer under § 1406(a), the court will not examine the private and public interest factors applicable to a potential transfer under § 1404(a). The question presented in a § 1406(a) motion to transfer is not which of two potential forums provides the optimal venue; rather, the question is whether dismissal or transfer will best serve the interests of justice. Thus, if the impropriety of venue in the original court is clear, the court will be more likely to dismiss despite potential adverse consequences to the plaintiff.

2. Consensual transfers. In *Hoffman v. Blaski*, 363 U.S. 335 (1960), the Supreme Court held that a case could not be transferred under § 1404(a) to a district in a state that lacked personal jurisdiction over the defendants at the commencement of the lawsuit, even if the defendants were now willing to waive any objection to jurisdiction there. Such a district was literally not one where the suit "might have been brought." A 2011 amendment to § 1404(a) modified this rule to now allow such a transfer if "all parties have consented." The new language encompasses transfers to district courts that would have initially lacked personal jurisdiction, proper venue, or both. By contrast, a transfer under § 1406(a) can still only be made to a district or division where the case "could have been brought."

Graham v. Dyncorp International, Inc.

973 F. Supp. 2d 698 (S.D. Tex. 2013)

GREGG COSTA, District Judge.

This case arises from an accident at Camp Davis, an American military base in Afghanistan. Plaintiff Angela Graham, a resident of Oklahoma, filed suit against DynCorp International, Inc. (DynCorp Inc.) and DynCorp International, LLC (DynCorp LLC). Both DynCorp entities move to dismiss for improper venue on the ground that they lack continuous and systematic general business contacts in this forum. Alternatively, they seek a convenience transfer to the Eastern District of Virginia. Having reviewed the parties' pleadings and briefing, the facts, and the law, this Court determines that venue is improper in this District. In deciding how to respond to that deficiency, the Court dismisses DynCorp, Inc. but exercises its option of transferring the case against DynCorp, LLC, and concludes that the Northern District of Texas, Fort Worth Division, is the most convenient forum in which venue lies against that defendant.

I.   BACKGROUND

On April 10, 2011, while stationed at Camp Davis, Graham sustained injuries when a vehicle driven by a DynCorp employee hit the portable laundry container where Graham was located. Graham claims that the collision resulted in serious injuries to her back, neck, and jaw. The accident worksheet lists the cause as inattentive driving and indicates that the accident was drug or alcohol related.

Although the injury occurred in Afghanistan and Graham is a resident of Oklahoma, Graham brought this action for negligence in federal court in the Southern District of Texas. The original complaint named only DynCorp, Inc. as a defendant. That entity filed a motion to dismiss for lack of venue, or in the alternative, to transfer venue to the Eastern District of Virginia. Graham then filed an amended complaint adding DynCorp, LLC as a defendant. The LLC then filed a motion to dismiss mirroring the arguments made in the first motion to dismiss.

II.   LEGAL STANDARD

A party may move to dismiss an action based on improper venue pursuant to Rule 12(b)(3). Once a defendant challenges venue, the plaintiff has the burden of demonstrating that the chosen venue is proper. "On a Rule 12(b)(3) motion to dismiss for improper venue, the court must accept as true all allegations in the complaint and resolve all conflicts in favor of the plaintiff." If venue is lacking, section 1406 instructs district courts to "dismiss, or if it be in the interest of justice, transfer such case to any district or division in which it could have been brought." 28 U.S.C. § 1406 (a). The decision to dismiss or transfer lies within the court's discretion.

III. DISCUSSION

A. The Venue Standard

Graham contends that venue is proper in the Southern District of Texas because the DynCorp entities [reside] in this district. *See* 28 U.S.C. § 1391(b)(1). Venue is proper in a district "in which any defendant resides, if all defendants are residents of the State in which the district is located." 28 U.S.C. § 1391(b). The statute then defines residence for various types of parties, including business entities: "[A]n entity with the capacity to sue and be sued in its common name under applicable law, whether or not incorporated, shall be deemed to reside, if a defendant, in any judicial district in which such defendant is subject to the court's personal jurisdiction with respect to the civil action in question." *Id.* § 1391(c)(2). The venue analysis thus largely collapses into a personal jurisdiction analysis.

There is a twist, however, in states like Texas with multiple federal judicial districts. In this situation, a "corporation shall be deemed to reside in any district in that State within which its contacts would be sufficient to subject it to personal jurisdiction if that district were a separate State."[2] *Id.* § 1391(d). The Court will thus conduct a personal jurisdiction "contacts" analysis, but with the Southern District of Texas, rather than the State of Texas, being the relevant jurisdiction.

Note the emphasis on a "contacts" analysis. Some courts applying section 1391(d)'s multi-district residence rule undertake a full personal jurisdiction inquiry, with the first step of considering the forum state's long arm statute and then proceeding to the Due Process Clause's "minimum contacts" analysis. This Court will follow the better-reasoned approach that recognizes the venue statute only refers to the "*contacts* [that] would be sufficient to subject it to personal jurisdiction if that district were a separate State." 28 U.S.C. 1391(d) (emphasis added).

With respect to that "minimum contacts" analysis, "the canonical opinion . . . remains [*International Shoe*], in which [the Supreme Court] held that a State may authorize its courts to exercise personal jurisdiction over an out-of-state defendant if the defendant has 'certain minimum contacts with [the State] such that the maintenance of the suit does not offend traditional notions of fair play and substantial justice.'" *Goodyear Dunlop Tires Operations, S.A. v. Brown*, 131 S. Ct. 2846, 2853 (2011). "There are two types of 'minimum contacts': those that give rise to specific personal jurisdiction and those that give rise to general personal jurisdiction." In this case, Graham rightly does not contend that specific jurisdiction exists, given that the injury occurred in Afghanistan, so the sole issue is general jurisdiction.

General personal jurisdiction is "all-purpose" and grants a court the power "to hear any and all claims against" a party regardless of where the events at issue took

---

2. [Here the court explains that the omission of unincorporated associations from the text of § 1391(d) was an oversight and, consistently with the perceived congressional intent, concludes that § 1391(d) should be interpreted as also being applicable to unincorporated associations. The text of this footnote is quoted at page 419, *supra*. — EDS.]

place. As highlighted by recent Supreme Court decisions, general jurisdiction requires a substantially higher degree of contacts than specific jurisdiction.

A court has general jurisdiction over a nonresident defendant "when their affiliations with the State are so 'continuous and systematic' as to render them essentially at home in the forum State." "The 'continuous and systematic contacts test is a difficult one to meet, requiring extensive contacts between a defendant and a forum.'" Under this test, the defendant's "contacts must be reviewed in toto, and not in isolation from one another." Continuous or repeated contacts will not be sufficient unless they are "so substantial and of such a nature as to justify suit against it on causes of action arising from dealings entirely distinct from those activities." "Random, fortuitous, or attenuated contacts are not sufficient to establish jurisdiction."

B.   General Jurisdiction Analysis

The venue statute's requirement of conducting a "contacts" analysis for the judicial district rather than the forum state turns out to doom Graham's attempt to subject Defendants to this Court's jurisdiction. While the Court concludes that DynCorp, LLC has sufficient contacts to be subject to general jurisdiction in Texas because of its substantial presence in Fort Worth, *see infra* Section III.C, its contacts limited to the Southern District do not meet the high level required for general jurisdiction.

1.   *DynCorp, Inc.*

With respect to DynCorp, Inc., the Court sees few, if any, contacts with this District or with Texas. The government contracts in Texas that Graham attributes to the Defendants are contracts entered into by DynCorp, LLC. Based on the record before the Court and a review of public filings, DynCorp, Inc. appears to be nothing more than a shell holding company. . . . The Court can therefore easily conclude that DynCorp, Inc. does not have contacts with this forum that would subject it to venue. Moreover, because DynCorp, Inc.'s apparent inactivity complicates the venue transfer analysis discussed below, the more efficient resolution is to dismiss it from this case for lack of venue pursuant to Rule 12(b)(3).

2.   *DynCorp, LLC*

The contacts Graham identifies as a basis for venue involve DynCorp, LLC. That entity has performed a great deal of work for NASA in this District. . . . However, [DynCorp] argues in response that it merely uses NASA facilities at no cost and with no maintenance responsibilities, and the income it derives here is but a small fraction of its total revenue.

The few Supreme Court cases addressing general jurisdiction demonstrate that the above contacts do not rise to the level of the "continuous and systematic" ones required to confer general jurisdiction. *See Helicopteros Nacionales de Colom., S.A. v. Hall*, 466 U.S. 408 (1984). . . . [J]ust as the defendant's contacts in *Helicopteros* were limited to its interactions with a single Texas helicopter company, DynCorp, LLC's identified contacts in the Southern District are limited to contracts with a single entity—NASA—that though large in absolute dollar terms constitute a small fraction of its operations.

Perkins v. Benguet Consolidated Mining Co., 342 U.S. 437 (1952), the only case in which the Supreme Court has found general jurisdiction, also demonstrates that DynCorp, LLC is not "at home" in the Southern District of Texas. In *Perkins*, after relocating from the Philippines because of World War II, the defendant conducted all of its business in Ohio. . . .

DynCorp, LCC was hardly conducting all of its business in the Southern District of Texas. The $47 million in revenue from services provided at Ellington Field accounted for only 1.2% of its 2012 Revenue. . . . The case law requires more consistent and extensive contacts to support the exercise of general jurisdiction. . . .

Accordingly, Graham has failed to demonstrate that venue is proper over DynCorp, LLC in this district.

C.   Dismissal or Transfer of Claims Against DynCorp LLC

Given the finding that venue is improper in this District over DynCorp, LLC, the Court has discretion to dismiss or transfer the case in the interest of justice to any district where it could have been brought. *See* 28 U.S.C. § 1406(a). In general, the interest of justice "requires transferring such cases to the appropriate judicial district rather than dismissing them." This Court finds that transferring the case would be in the interest of justice because "[t]ransfer would facilitate a more expeditious resolution of the merits of the controversy in a concededly proper forum and would avoid the costs and delay that would result from dismissal and refiling." Transfer also avoids any potential statute of limitations problems that might arise if Graham were required to refile this case involving an event in 2011.

The Court finds that are at least two districts where venue would be proper and the case could have been brought: the Eastern District of Virginia and the Northern District of Texas. DynCorp, LLC concedes venue is proper in the Eastern District of Virginia, and sought a convenience transfer to that venue in the event the Court had found venue proper in this district.

But venue is also proper in the Northern District of Texas under section 1391(b)(1) because, although DynCorp, LCC's contacts in this district do not meet the continuous and systematic contacts required for general jurisdiction, it is "at home" in that other part of this State. DynCorp, LLC's contacts in the Northern District of Texas are equal to or greater than the contacts found sufficient by the Court in *Perkins*. It maintains a large office in Fort Worth and has an agent for service of process in the Northern District. In addition, public filings with the SEC reveal extensive contacts with Fort Worth. The company leases 218,925 square feet of office space, described as executive offices for the company's finance and administration departments, in Fort Worth. Notably, this is more than twice the 105,814 square feet of office space that the company leases for its official headquarters in Falls Church, Virginia. Moreover, within the Northern District of Texas, DynCorp, LLC also leases 96,000 square feet of space, described as warehouse logistics headquarters, in Coppell, and has contracted to provide aircraft maintenance services at Sheppard Air Force Base in Wichita Falls. A review of SEC filings also indicates that the company has used external auditors in Fort Worth to review its filings.

With venue lying in both the Northern District of Texas and the Eastern District of Virginia, the question becomes which is more convenient for the parties and witnesses. The Court is not aware of any cases providing guidance on selecting between two competent forums for transfer under section 1406(a), but finds that it would be appropriate to apply the factors used in assessing a convenience transfer under section 1404. In that context, the Fifth Circuit has articulated the following factors:

> The private interest factors are: (1) the relative ease of access to sources of proof; (2) the availability of compulsory process to secure the attendance of witnesses; (3) the cost of attendance for willing witnesses; and (4) all other practical problems that make trial of a case easy, expeditious and inexpensive. The public interest factors are: (1) the administrative difficulties flowing from court congestion; (2) the local interest in having localized interests decided at home; (3) the familiarity of the forum with the law that will govern the case; and (4) the avoidance of unnecessary problems of conflict of laws or in the application of foreign law.

In re Volkswagen of Am., Inc., 545 F.3d 304, 315 (5th Cir. 2008) (en banc).

The *Volkswagen* factors lead the Court to conclude that transfer to the Northern District is appropriate. Most of the factors are neutral between the two districts, either because the accident occurred in Afghanistan or because neither of the parties have provided evidence showing one forum to be more convenient than the other. DynCorp, LLC, for example, has not identified which of its employees or contractors are likely witnesses at trial. Moreover, both districts have a similar local interest in the case given DynCorp, LLC's extensive presence in each.

The Court ultimately finds most persuasive the fact that the one person who is certain to be a witness and present throughout a trial—Plaintiff Graham—is a resident of Oklahoma. A transfer to the Northern District of Texas would make prosecuting this case substantially more convenient for Graham than if the Court transferred the case to Virginia, halfway across the country from where she lives. And transferring to another district within the state in which Graham chose to sue is appropriate given that, to the extent possible, the Court should defer to her choice of forum.

After weighing the factors, the Court concludes that the Northern District of Texas is a more convenient forum than the Eastern District of Virginia. The Court will therefore exercise its discretion under 28 U.S.C. § 1406(a) to transfer the claims against DynCorp, LLC to the Northern District of Texas, Fort Worth Division.

IV.   CONCLUSION

For the reasons discussed above, DynCorp, Inc.'s motion to dismiss is GRANTED. A separate order of dismissal will issue.

DynCorp, LLC's motion to dismiss is GRANTED IN PART and DENIED IN PART and the case against it is TRANSFERRED to the Northern District of Texas, Fort Worth Division. A separate order of transfer will issue.

NOTES AND QUESTIONS

1. *The intersection between personal jurisdiction, venue, and transfer analysis.* In what ways are personal jurisdiction analysis and venue analysis similar and distinct? How is transfer analysis distinct from both? Was DynCorp, LLC subject to personal jurisdiction in Texas? If so, why was venue improper in the Southern District? Why would it have been proper in the Northern District? Did a substantial part of the events giving rise to the claim occur there? Since venue was improper in the Southern District, under what authority did the court transfer the case against DynCorp, LLC to the Northern District? Why didn't the court dismiss the case against DynCorp, LLC for improper venue as it did with respect to DynCorp, Inc.? Finally, if venue was improper in the Southern District, why did the court engage in a § 1404(a) convenience analysis? Is that appropriate in a § 1406(a) transfer?

2. *The law to be applied in transferred cases.*   As we will learn in Chapter VI, in resolving cases filed within their diversity jurisdiction, federal courts must apply state substantive law. More specifically, a federal court sitting in diversity must apply the same substantive law that would be applied by a state court of the forum state. Thus a State X federal court sitting in diversity will apply the same substantive law a State X state court would have applied had the case been filed there. What happens if a case is initially filed in a federal court sitting in State X but is then transferred to a federal court in State Y? If the transfer is made under § 1404(a), then the federal court sitting in State Y will apply the same substantive law a state court sitting in State X would have applied. *Van Dusen v. Barrack*, 376 U.S. 612 (1964). In other words, the substantive law of the transferor court follows the case. This remains true regardless of whether the plaintiff or the defendant initiates the transfer. *Ferens v. John Deere Co.*, 494 U.S. 516 (1990). On the other hand, if the transfer is under § 1406(a), the federal court sitting in State Y will follow the same substantive law that a state court sitting in State Y would apply to the case. Thus, under a § 1406(a) transfer, the substantive law of the transferor court does not follow the case. *See* 15 CHARLES ALAN WRIGHT, ARTHUR R. MILLER, EDWARD H. COOPER & RICHARD D. FREER, FEDERAL PRACTICE AND PROCEDURE § 3846 (4th ed. 2013 & Supp. 2015). Can you see a reason for this distinction?

The *Van Dusen* rule does not apply in federal question cases. In part this is based on the fiction that federal law is uniform throughout the nation, so a transfer from one federal forum to another should make no difference. However, there are in fact numerous conflicts among the circuits over the meaning and applicability of federal law. Nonetheless, regardless of whether a transfer is accomplished under § 1404(a) or under § 1406(a), the federal law of the circuit in which the transferee or receiving court sits will be applied. There are some exceptions to this rule, as when federal law itself permits a lack of uniformity. For a discussion of these exceptions, see Georgene M. Vairo, *Change of Venue, in* 17 MOORE'S FEDERAL PRACTICE § 111.02[2] (3d ed. 2015).

A NOTE ON TRANSFER WHEN ORIGINATING COURT LACKS PERSONAL JURISDICTION

If a court lacks personal jurisdiction over a defendant, the standard remedy is to dismiss the case as to that party. In federal court, however, there is another possibility. In *Goldlawr, Inc. v. Heiman*, 369 U.S. 463 (1962), the Supreme Court held that a federal district court that lacked personal jurisdiction over the defendant could transfer the case to another federal court in which venue would be proper and service of process could be effected. Although *Goldlawr* has been criticized for ignoring the due process rights of the "non-jurisdictional" defendant, courts continue to follow the basic principle of the case.

If venue is proper in the original court, but personal jurisdiction is lacking, the motion to transfer should be made pursuant to § 1404(a). If the motion is granted, the *Van Dusen* rule will not apply, *i.e.*, the substantive law will not travel with the transfer due to the lack of personal jurisdiction in the original court. If both venue and personal jurisdiction are lacking in the original court, the motion should be made pursuant to § 1406(a), as was done in *Goldlawr*. As with all § 1406 transfers, the substantive law does not travel with the transfer.

A few courts have held that once a district court grants a motion to dismiss for lack of personal jurisdiction, it can no longer order a transfer. *See, e.g., HollyAnne Corp. v. TFT, Inc.*, 199 F.3d 1304, 1306-1307 (Fed. Cir. 1999). In other words, the transfer must be ordered as an alternative to dismissal, not as an afterthought.

PROBLEMS

5-9. Hall, a resident of Kings County, New York, part of the Eastern District of New York, was allegedly kidnapped by Young, a retired police officer and resident of South Orange, New Jersey. On Sunday, May 24, 1998, Young abducted Hall while the latter was leaving the Hampden Inn in Elmsford, New York, in the Southern District of New York. Young, who falsely identified himself as a police officer and member of a New Jersey fugitive squad, produced documents purporting to be an outstanding warrant for Hall's arrest from Union City, New Jersey, and a criminal history report from the South Orange Police Department. Young and an accomplice handcuffed Hall, threw him into the back seat of their car, injuring his shoulder, and transported him to a warehouse in Newark, New Jersey, where he was bound and blindfolded with duct tape. At the warehouse, Young and his accomplice dragged Hall to a forklift and tied him to a roll bar with electrical cord. Hall was left in the New Jersey warehouse for three hours, until the Newark police freed him. A member of the South Orange Police Department, one Collum, also a resident of South Orange, had supplied Young with access to certain law enforcement resources that were used in the kidnapping. Hall has filed suit in the Southern District of New York against Young, Collum, and the South Orange Police Department for false imprisonment—a state tort—and for violation of his federal constitutional rights. As to the South Orange Police Department, Hall alleges that its failure to train and properly supervise its officers contributed to the kidnapping. The defendants have moved to dismiss the case on grounds of improper venue, or in the alternative to transfer it to the District of New Jersey pursuant to either § 1404(a) or § 1406(a). What should the district court do? *See Hall v. South Orange*, 89 F. Supp. 2d 488 (S.D.N.Y. 2000). If the court transfers the case to New Jersey, what substantive law should the New Jersey court apply? Note that New York is in the Second Circuit, while New Jersey is in the Third Circuit.

5-10. Lindley, a citizen of Florida, purchased a boat equipped with an engine manufactured by Caterpillar, Inc. ("Caterpillar"). Caterpillar is incorporated under the laws of Delaware with its principal place of business in Peoria, Illinois. Lindley used the boat in his commercial diving and fishing business located in Jacksonville Beach, Florida. After the engine broke down twice, Caterpillar replaced it with a new engine. That engine, in turn, broke down four times and was replaced again. The third engine broke down twice; on the second occasion, Caterpillar refused to rebuild the engine unless Lindley paid for it. All of the repair and replacement activity was performed by a Caterpillar-approved repair shop located in Jacksonville Beach. Asserting damages in excess of $500,000, Lindley filed suit against Caterpillar in the Western District of Pennsylvania, the residence of Lindley's lawyer, alleging products liability, negligence, breach of warranties, breach of contract, fraud, misrepresentation, violation of the Florida Deceptive and Unfair Trade Practices Act, and violation of the Illinois Consumer Fraud and Deceptive Business Practices Act. Caterpillar, which does business in all 50 states, has moved to have the case transferred to the U.S. District Court for the Middle District of Florida, which encompasses Jacksonville Beach. How should the district court rule? *See Lindley v. Caterpillar, Inc.*, 93 F. Supp. 2d 615 (E.D. Pa. 2000). If transfer is to occur, should it be under § 1404(a), § 1406(a), or § 1631?

A NOTE ON MULTIDISTRICT LITIGATION

Multidistrict litigation is a procedural device established by 28 U.S.C. § 1407 through which the federal judicial system may coordinate or consolidate pretrial proceedings in factually related lawsuits that have been filed in different federal judicial districts. For example, the harm caused by the inhalation of asbestos led to the filing of over 26,000 cases in 87 federal districts. *See In re Asbestos Prods. Liab. Litig.*, 771 F. Supp. 415, 417-424 (J.P.M.L. 1991). Section 1407 permitted consolidation of pretrial matters in those cases given the substantial factual overlap among them and the overall complexity of the issues presented. To require every federal court in which such a case was filed to oversee a separate pretrial process, including discovery, would be duplicative and wasteful of both private and public resources. Section 1407 provides a means through which the federal judiciary may coordinate or consolidate pretrial proceedings in the interests of justice and efficiency. There is no comparable device for cases filed in a multiplicity of state courts, unless those cases can be and are removed to federal court.

The determination of whether to order a § 1407 transfer is made by the Judicial Panel on Multidistrict Litigation (JPML), which comprises seven federal judges appointed by the Chief Justice of the United States. Section 1407(a) permits the JPML to order a transfer "[w]hen civil actions involving one or more common questions of fact are pending in different districts," if doing so "will be for the convenience of parties and witnesses and will promote the just and efficient conduct of such actions." 28 U.S.C. § 1407(a). Whether these factors are satisfied is within the JPML's broad discretion. In general, the panel has focused on the final factor—the just and efficient conduct of such actions—emphasizing that the purpose of § 1407 is to streamline the pretrial process when truly complex cases have been filed in more than one district and when the transfer can promote judicial efficiency. Thus, although all types of civil suits may be subject to a § 1407 transfer, the typical cases in which transfer occurs involve such matters as mass torts, airline disasters, complex antitrust or securities cases, and the like.

In deciding whether to issue a § 1407 order to transfer, the JPML can act on its own initiative or at the behest of a party in a pending case. 28 U.S.C. § 1407(c). If the JPML determines that a § 1407 transfer is appropriate, it assigns the affected cases to a single federal district court for pretrial proceedings. The transferee court is vested with complete authority to determine all pretrial matters under the Federal Rules of Civil Procedure, including discovery and dispositive pretrial motions such as motions to dismiss or motions for summary judgment. After the pretrial proceedings are complete, the cases are remanded for trial to the federal district courts from which they were transferred. The transferee court's rulings are then binding on the originating court. *See generally* Georgene M. Vairo, *Multidistrict Litigation, in* 17 MOORE'S FEDERAL PRACTICE, at ch. 112 (3d ed. 2015); 15 WRIGHT, MILLER, COOPER & FREER, *supra,* §§ 3861-3868.

A NOTE ON FORUM-SELECTION CLAUSES

A "forum selection clause" is a provision in a contract under which the parties to the contract designate an appropriate forum in which any lawsuits specified in the contract may or must be filed. If the forum-selection clause merely provides that the suit *may* be filed in the identified forum, the clause is "permissive" in the sense that it allows either party to file a suit in the chosen forum. A permissive clause does not, however, preclude filing the suit in other proper venues. In this sense, a permissive forum-selection clause merely creates a possible additional venue beyond those provided by statute. On the other hand, if the forum-selection clause requires that any specified lawsuit be filed in a particular forum (as in "must be" filed), the clause is deemed "exclusive" in the sense that it designates the only forum in which the suit can be brought. Conceptually, this seems to suggest that the exclusive forum renders all other venues "wrong." But as we'll see that is not quite right.

The way in which a forum-selection clause identifies the selected forum may also be significant. Such a clause might identify the selected forum by reference to a particular geographic region—*e.g.*, any state or federal court in the State of Montana. Such a clause gives the filing party two forum options, one state and the other federal. Alternatively, the clause might identify a specific court within the identified region—*e.g.*, the High Court of London or the Superior Court of the County of Los Angeles. In each of these contexts, there is one option only, neither of which is federal.

In order to determine whether a forum-selection clause controls in any particular case, two preliminary questions must be examined. First, does the lawsuit fall within the terms of the clause at issue? If not, quite obviously, the forum-selection clause is irrelevant. Second, if the suit does come within the clause's terms, is the clause enforceable? In general, there is a strong presumption of enforceability. Thus, in federal court a forum-selection clause will be deemed enforceable unless the objecting party can "clearly show that enforcement would be unreasonable and unjust, or that the clause was invalid for such reasons as fraud or overreaching . . . [or that] enforcement would contravene a strong public policy of the forum in which suit is brought . . . [or that] the chosen forum is seriously inconvenient for the trial of the action." *M/S Bremen v. Zapata Off-Shore Co.*, 407 U.S. 1, 15 (1972); *see, e.g., Evolution Online Sys., Inc. v. Koninklijke PTT Nederland N.V.*, 145 F.3d 505, 510-511 & n.10 (2d Cir. 1998). *See generally* 17 MOORE'S FEDERAL PRACTICE, *supra*, § 111.04[3][b]. Under this standard, the vast majority of such clauses are enforced.*

Atlantic Marine Construction Co., Inc. v. United States District Court
134 S. Ct. 568 (2013)

JUSTICE ALITO delivered the opinion of the Court.

The question in this case concerns the procedure that is available for a defendant in a civil case who seeks to enforce a forum-selection clause. We reject

---

* In federal question cases, federal law, *i.e.*, the *Bremen* standard, governs the enforceability of forum-selection clauses. *See* 17 MOORE'S FEDERAL PRACTICE, *supra*, § 111.04[4][a] (noting that although *Bremen* was an admiralty case, "lower courts have routinely imported its standards to a wide variety of non-admiralty cases"). In the context of diversity, though, there is a circuit split. *See M.B. Restaurants, Inc. v. CKE Restaurants, Inc.*, 183 F.3d 750, 752 n.4 (8th Cir. 1999) (collecting authorities); *compare General Engineering Corp. v. Martin Marietta Alumina, Inc.*, 783 F.2d 352, 356-358 (3d Cir. 1986) (holding that state law governs), *with Lighthouse MGA, LLC v. First Premium Ins. Group, Inc.*, 448 Fed. App'x 512, 514 & n.6 (5th Cir. 2011) (holding that federal law governs). Yet the practical consequences of this split have been relatively trivial given that state law on this point tends to mirror the federal standard. *See Servewell Plumbing, LLC v. Federal Ins. Co.*, 439 F.3d 786, 789 (8th Cir. 2006); *Lambert v. Kysar*, 983 F.2d 1110, 1116-1122 (1st Cir. 1993).

petitioner's argument that such a clause may be enforced by a motion to dismiss under 28 U.S.C. § 1406(a) or Rule 12(b)(3) of the Federal Rules of Civil Procedure. Instead, a forum-selection clause may be enforced by a motion to transfer under § 1404(a), which provides that "[f]or the convenience of parties and witnesses, in the interest of justice, a district court may transfer any civil action to any other district or division where it might have been brought or to any district or division to which all parties have consented." When a defendant files such a motion, we conclude, a district court should transfer the case unless extraordinary circumstances unrelated to the convenience of the parties clearly disfavor a transfer. In the present case, both the District Court and the Court of Appeals misunderstood the standards to be applied in adjudicating a § 1404(a) motion in a case involving a forum-selection clause, and we therefore reverse the decision below.

I

Petitioner Atlantic Marine Construction Co., a Virginia corporation with its principal place of business in Virginia, entered into a contract with the United States Army Corps of Engineers to construct a child-development center at Fort Hood in the Western District of Texas. Atlantic Marine then entered into a subcontract with respondent J-Crew Management, Inc., a Texas corporation, for work on the project. This subcontract included a forum-selection clause, which stated that all disputes between the parties " 'shall be litigated in the Circuit Court for the City of Norfolk, Virginia, or the United States District Court for the Eastern District of Virginia, Norfolk Division.' " *In re Atlantic Marine Constr. Co.*, 701 F.3d 736, 737-738 (C.A.5 2012).

When a dispute about payment under the subcontract arose, however, J-Crew sued Atlantic Marine in the Western District of Texas, invoking that court's diversity jurisdiction. Atlantic Marine moved to dismiss the suit, arguing that the forum-selection clause rendered venue in the Western District of Texas "wrong" under § 1406(a) and "improper" under Federal Rule of Civil Procedure 12(b)(3). In the alternative, Atlantic Marine moved to transfer the case to the Eastern District of Virginia under § 1404(a). J-Crew opposed these motions.

The District Court denied both motions. It first concluded that § 1404(a) is the exclusive mechanism for enforcing a forum-selection clause that points to another federal forum. The District Court then held that Atlantic Marine bore the burden of establishing that a transfer would be appropriate under § 1404(a) and that the court would "consider a nonexhaustive and nonexclusive list of public and private interest factors," of which the "forum-selection clause [was] only one such factor." Giving particular weight to its findings that "compulsory process will not be available for the majority of J-Crew's witnesses" and that there would be "significant expense for those willing witnesses," the District Court held that Atlantic Marine had failed to carry its burden of showing that transfer "would be in the interest of justice or increase the convenience to the parties and their witnesses."

Atlantic Marine petitioned the Court of Appeals for a *writ of mandamus* directing the District Court to dismiss the case under § 1406(a) or to transfer the case to the Eastern District of Virginia under § 1404(a). The Court of Appeals denied Atlantic Marine's petition because Atlantic Marine had not established a "'clear and indisputable'" right to relief. Relying on *Stewart Organization, Inc. v. Ricoh Corp.*, 487 U.S. 22 (1988), the Court of Appeals agreed with the District Court that § 1404(a) is the exclusive mechanism for enforcing a forum-selection clause that points to another federal forum when venue is otherwise proper in the district where the case was brought. The court stated, however, that if a forum-selection clause points to a nonfederal forum, dismissal under Rule 12(b)(3) would be the correct mechanism to enforce the clause because § 1404(a) by its terms does not permit transfer to any tribunal other than another federal court. The Court of Appeals then concluded that the District Court had not clearly abused its discretion in refusing to transfer the case after conducting the balance-of-interests analysis required by § 1404(a). That was so even though there was no dispute that the forum-selection clause was valid. We granted certiorari.

II

Atlantic Marine contends that a party may enforce a forum-selection clause by seeking dismissal of the suit under § 1406(a) and Rule 12(b)(3). We disagree. Section 1406(a) and Rule 12(b)(3) allow dismissal only when venue is "wrong" or "improper." Whether venue is "wrong" or "improper" depends exclusively on whether the court in which the case was brought satisfies the requirements of federal venue laws, and those provisions say nothing about a forum-selection clause.

A

Section 1406(a) provides that "[t]he district court of a district in which is filed a case laying venue in the wrong division or district shall dismiss, or if it be in the interest of justice, transfer such case to any district or division in which it could have been brought." Rule 12(b)(3) states that a party may move to dismiss a case for "improper venue." These provisions therefore authorize dismissal only when venue is "wrong" or "improper" in the forum in which it was brought.

This question—whether venue is "wrong" or "improper"—is generally governed by 28 U.S.C. § 1391. That provision states that "[e]xcept as otherwise provided by *law* . . . this section *shall* govern the venue of *all civil actions* brought in district courts of the United States." § 1391(a)(1) (emphasis added). It further provides that

> "[a] civil action may be brought in—(1) a judicial district in which any defendant resides, if all defendants are residents of the State in which the district is located; (2) a judicial district in which a substantial part of the events or omissions giving rise to the claim occurred, or a substantial part of property that is the subject of the action is situated; or (3) if there is no district in which an action may otherwise be brought as provided in this section, any judicial district in which any defendant is subject to the court's personal jurisdiction with respect to such action."

§ 1391(b). When venue is challenged, the court must determine whether the case falls within one of the three categories set out in § 1391(b). If it does, venue is proper; if it does not, venue is improper, and the case must be dismissed or transferred under § 1406(a). Whether the parties entered into a contract containing a forum-selection clause has no bearing on whether a case falls into one of the categories of cases listed in § 1391(b). As a result, a case filed in a district that falls within § 1391 may not be dismissed under § 1406(a) or Rule 12(b)(3).

Petitioner's contrary view improperly conflates the special statutory term "venue" and the word "forum." It is certainly true that, in some contexts, the word "venue" is used synonymously with the term "forum," but § 1391 makes clear that venue in "all civil actions" must be determined in accordance with the criteria outlined in that section. That language cannot reasonably be read to allow judicial consideration of other, extrastatutory limitations on the forum in which a case may be brought.

The structure of the federal venue provisions confirms that they alone define whether venue exists in a given forum. In particular, the venue statutes reflect Congress' intent that venue should always lie in *some* federal court whenever federal courts have personal jurisdiction over the defendant. The first two paragraphs of § 1391(b) define the preferred judicial districts for venue in a typical case, but the third paragraph provides a fallback option: If no other venue is proper, then venue will lie in "*any judicial district* in which any defendant is subject to the court's personal jurisdiction" (emphasis added). The statute thereby ensures that so long as a federal court has personal jurisdiction over the defendant, venue will always lie somewhere. As we have previously noted, "Congress does not in general intend to create venue gaps, which take away with one hand what Congress has given by way of jurisdictional grant with the other." *Smith v. United States*, 507 U.S. 197, 203 (1993) (internal quotation marks omitted). Yet petitioner's approach would mean that in some number of cases—those in which the forum-selection clause points to a state or foreign court—venue would not lie in any federal district. That would not comport with the statute's design, which contemplates that venue will always exist in some federal court.

The conclusion that venue is proper so long as the requirements of § 1391(b) are met, irrespective of any forum-selection clause, also follows from our prior decisions construing the federal venue statutes. In *Van Dusen v. Barrack*, 376 U.S. 612 (1964), we considered the meaning of § 1404(a), which authorizes a district court to "transfer any civil action to any other district or division where it might have been brought." The question in *Van Dusen* was whether § 1404(a) allows transfer to a district in which venue is proper under § 1391 but in which the case could not have been pursued in light of substantive state-law limitations on the suit. In holding that transfer is permissible in that context, we construed the phrase "where it might have been brought" to refer to "the federal laws delimiting the districts in which such an action 'may be brought,'" noting that "the phrase 'may be brought' recurs at least 10 times" in §§ 1391-1406. We perceived "no valid reason for reading the words 'where it might have been brought' to narrow the range of permissible federal forums beyond those permitted by federal venue statutes."

As we noted in *Van Dusen*, § 1406(a) "shares the same statutory context" as § 1404(a) and "contain[s] a similar phrase." It instructs a court to transfer a case from the "wrong" district to a district "in which it could have been brought." The most reasonable interpretation of that provision is that a district cannot be "wrong" if it is one in which the case could have been brought under § 1391. Under the construction of the venue laws we adopted in *Van Dusen*, a "wrong" district is therefore a district other than "those districts in which Congress has provided *by its venue statutes* that the action 'may be brought.'" If the federal venue statutes establish that suit may be brought in a particular district, a contractual bar cannot render venue in that district "wrong."

Our holding also finds support in *Stewart*. As here, the parties in *Stewart* had included a forum-selection clause in the relevant contract, but the plaintiff filed suit in a different federal district. The defendant had initially moved to transfer the case or, in the alternative, to dismiss for improper venue under § 1406(a), but by the time the case reached this Court, the defendant had abandoned its § 1406(a) argument and sought only transfer under § 1404(a). We rejected the plaintiff's argument that state law governs a motion to transfer venue pursuant to a forum-selection clause, concluding instead that "federal law, specifically 28 U.S.C. § 1404(a), governs the District Court's decision whether to give effect to the parties' forum-selection clause." We went on to explain that a "motion to transfer under § 1404(a) . . . calls on the district court to weigh in the balance a number of case-specific factors" and that the "presence of a forum-selection clause . . . will be a significant factor that figures centrally in the district court's calculus."

The question whether venue in the original court was "wrong" under § 1406(a) was not before the Court, but we wrote in a footnote that "[t]he parties do not dispute that the District Court properly denied the motion to dismiss the case for improper venue under 28 U.S.C. § 1406(a) because respondent apparently does business in the Northern District of Alabama. See 28 U.S.C. § 1391(c) (venue proper in judicial district in which corporation is doing business)." In other words, because § 1391 made venue proper, venue could not be "wrong" for purposes of § 1406(a). Though *dictum*, the Court's observation supports the holding we reach today. A contrary view would all but drain *Stewart* of any significance. If a forum-selection clause rendered venue in all other federal courts "wrong," a defendant could always obtain automatic dismissal or transfer under § 1406(a) and would not have any reason to resort to § 1404(a). *Stewart*'s holding would be limited to the presumably rare case in which the defendant inexplicably fails to file a motion under § 1406(a) or Rule 12(b)(3).

B

Although a forum-selection clause does not render venue in a court "wrong" or "improper" within the meaning of § 1406(a) or Rule 12(b)(3), the clause may be enforced through a motion to transfer under § 1404(a). That provision states that "[f]or the convenience of parties and witnesses, in the interest of justice, a district court may transfer any civil action to any other district or division where it might have been brought or to any district or division to which all parties have consented." Unlike § 1406(a), § 1404(a) does not condition transfer on the initial forum's being "wrong." And it permits transfer to any district where venue is also proper (*i.e.*, "where [the case] might have been brought") or to any other district to which the parties have agreed by contract or stipulation.

Section 1404(a) therefore provides a mechanism for enforcement of forum-selection clauses that point to a particular federal district. And for the reasons we address in Part III, *infra*, a proper application of § 1404(a) requires that a forum-selection clause be "given controlling weight in all but the most exceptional cases."

Atlantic Marine argues that § 1404(a) is not a suitable mechanism to enforce forum-selection clauses because that provision cannot provide for transfer when a forum-selection clause specifies a state or foreign tribunal, and we agree with Atlantic Marine that the Court of Appeals failed to provide a sound answer to this problem. The Court of Appeals opined that a forum-selection clause pointing to a nonfederal forum should be enforced through Rule 12(b)(3), which permits a party to move for dismissal of a case based on "improper venue." As Atlantic Marine persuasively argues, however, that conclusion cannot be reconciled with our construction of the term "improper venue" in § 1406 to refer only to a forum that does not satisfy federal venue laws. If venue is proper under federal venue rules, it does not matter for the purpose of Rule 12(b)(3) whether the forum-selection clause points to a federal or a nonfederal forum.

Instead, the appropriate way to enforce a forum-selection clause pointing to a state or foreign forum is through the doctrine of *forum non conveniens*. Section 1404(a) is merely a codification of the doctrine of *forum non conveniens* for the subset of cases in which the transferee forum is within the federal court system; in such cases, Congress has replaced the traditional remedy of outright dismissal with transfer. For the remaining set of cases calling for a nonfederal forum, § 1404(a) has no application, but the residual doctrine of *forum non conveniens* "has continuing application in federal courts." And because both § 1404(a) and the *forum non conveniens* doctrine from which it derives entail the same balancing-of-interests standard, courts should evaluate a forum-selection clause pointing to a nonfederal forum in the same way that they evaluate a forum-selection clause pointing to a federal forum.

C

An *amicus* before the Court argues that a defendant in a breach-of-contract action should be able to obtain dismissal under Rule 12(b)(6) if the plaintiff files suit in a district other than the one specified in a valid forum-selection clause. Petitioner, however, did not file a motion under Rule 12(b)(6), and the parties did not brief the Rule's application to this case at any stage of this litigation. We therefore will not consider it. Even if a defendant could use Rule 12(b)(6) to enforce a forum-selection clause, that would not change our conclusions that § 1406(a) and Rule 12(b)(3) are not proper mechanisms to enforce a forum-selection clause and that § 1404(a) and the *forum non conveniens* doctrine provide appropriate enforcement mechanisms.

III

Although the Court of Appeals correctly identified § 1404(a) as the appropriate provision to enforce the forum-selection clause in this case, the Court of Appeals erred in failing to make the adjustments required in a § 1404(a) analysis when the transfer motion is premised on a forum-selection clause. When the parties have agreed to a valid forum-selection clause, a district court should ordinarily transfer the case to the forum specified in that clause.[5] Only under extraordinary circumstances unrelated to the convenience of the parties should a § 1404(a) motion be denied. And no such exceptional factors appear to be present in this case.

A

In the typical case not involving a forum-selection clause, a district court considering a § 1404(a) motion (or a *forum non conveniens* motion) must evaluate both the convenience of the parties and various public-interest considerations. Ordinarily, the district court would weigh the relevant factors and decide whether, on balance, a transfer would serve "the convenience of parties and witnesses" and otherwise promote "the interest of justice." § 1404(a).

The calculus changes, however, when the parties' contract contains a valid forum-selection clause, which "represents the parties' agreement as to the most proper forum." The "enforcement of valid forum-selection clauses, bargained for by the parties, protects their legitimate expectations and furthers vital interests of the justice system." For that reason, and because the overarching consideration under § 1404(a) is whether a transfer would promote "the interest of justice," "a valid forum-selection clause [should be] given controlling weight in all but the most exceptional cases." The presence of a valid forum-selection clause requires district courts to adjust their usual § 1404(a) analysis in three ways.

First, the plaintiff's choice of forum merits no weight. Rather, as the party defying the forum-selection clause, the plaintiff bears the burden of establishing that transfer to the forum for which the parties bargained is unwarranted. Because plaintiffs are ordinarily allowed to select whatever forum they consider most advantageous (consistent with jurisdictional and venue limitations), we have termed their selection the "plaintiff's venue privilege." But when a plaintiff agrees by contract to bring suit only in a specified forum—presumably in exchange for other binding promises by the defendant—the plaintiff has effectively exercised its "venue privilege" before a dispute arises. Only that initial choice deserves deference, and the plaintiff must bear the burden of showing why the court should not transfer the case to the forum to which the parties agreed.

---

5. Our analysis presupposes a contractually valid forum-selection clause.

Second, a court evaluating a defendant's § 1404(a) motion to transfer based on a forum-selection clause should not consider arguments about the parties' private interests. When parties agree to a forum-selection clause, they waive the right to challenge the preselected forum as inconvenient or less convenient for themselves or their witnesses, or for their pursuit of the litigation. A court accordingly must deem the private-interest factors to weigh entirely in favor of the preselected forum. As we have explained in a different but "'instructive'" context, "[w]hatever 'inconvenience' [the parties] would suffer by being forced to litigate in the contractual forum as [they] agreed to do was clearly foreseeable at the time of contracting." *The Bremen v. Zapata Off-Shore Co.*, 407 U.S. 1, 17-18 (1972).

As a consequence, a district court may consider arguments about public-interest factors only. Because those factors will rarely defeat a transfer motion, the practical result is that forum-selection clauses should control except in unusual cases. Although it is "conceivable in a particular case" that the district court "would refuse to transfer a case notwithstanding the counterweight of a forum-selection clause," such cases will not be common.

Third, when a party bound by a forum-selection clause flouts its contractual obligation and files suit in a different forum, a § 1404(a) transfer of venue will not carry with it the original venue's choice-of-law rules—a factor that in some circumstances may affect public-interest considerations. A federal court sitting in diversity ordinarily must follow the choice-of-law rules of the State in which it sits. See *Klaxon Co. v. Stentor Elec. Mfg. Co.*, 313 U.S. 487, 494-496 (1941). However, we previously identified an exception to that principle for § 1404(a) transfers, requiring that the state law applicable in the original court also apply in the transferee court. We deemed that exception necessary to prevent "defendants, properly subjected to suit in the transferor State," from "invok[ing] § 1404(a) to gain the benefits of the laws of another jurisdiction . . . ."

The policies motivating our exception to the *Klaxon* rule for § 1404(a) transfers, however, do not support an extension to cases where a defendant's motion is premised on enforcement of a valid forum-selection clause. To the contrary, those considerations lead us to reject the rule that the law of the court in which the plaintiff inappropriately filed suit should follow the case to the forum contractually selected by the parties. In *Van Dusen*, we were concerned that, through a § 1404(a) transfer, a defendant could "defeat the state-law advantages that might accrue from the exercise of [the plaintiff's] venue privilege." But as discussed above, a plaintiff who files suit in violation of a forum-selection clause enjoys no such "privilege" with respect to its choice of forum, and therefore it is entitled to no concomitant "state-law advantages." Not only would it be inequitable to allow the plaintiff to fasten its choice of substantive law to the venue transfer, but it would also encourage gamesmanship. Because "§ 1404(a) should not create or multiply opportunities for forum shopping," we will not apply the *Van Dusen* rule when a transfer stems from enforcement of a forum-selection clause: The court in the contractually selected venue should not apply the law of the transferor venue to which the parties waived their right.

When parties have contracted in advance to litigate disputes in a particular forum, courts should not unnecessarily disrupt the parties' settled expectations. A forum-selection clause, after all, may have figured centrally in the parties' negotiations and may have affected how they set monetary and other contractual terms; it may, in fact, have been a critical factor in their agreement to do business together in the first place. In all but the most unusual cases, therefore, "the interest of justice" is served by holding parties to their bargain.

B

The District Court's application of § 1404(a) in this case did not comport with these principles. The District Court improperly placed the burden on Atlantic Marine to prove that transfer to the parties' contractually preselected forum was appropriate. As the party acting in violation of the forum-selection clause, J-Crew must bear the burden of showing that public-interest factors overwhelmingly disfavor a transfer.

The District Court also erred in giving weight to arguments about the parties' private interests, given that all private interests, as expressed in the forum-selection clause, weigh in favor of the transfer. The District Court stated that the private-interest factors "militat[e] against a transfer to Virginia" because "compulsory process will not be available for the majority of J-Crew's witnesses" and there will be "significant expense for those willing witnesses." But when J-Crew entered into a contract to litigate all disputes in Virginia, it knew that a distant forum might hinder its ability to call certain witnesses and might impose other burdens on its litigation efforts. It nevertheless promised to resolve its disputes in Virginia, and the District Court should not have given any weight to J-Crew's current claims of inconvenience.

The District Court also held that the public-interest factors weighed in favor of keeping the case in Texas because Texas contract law is more familiar to federal judges in Texas than to their federal colleagues in Virginia. That ruling, however, rested in part on the District Court's belief that the federal court sitting in Virginia would have been required to apply Texas' choice-of-law rules, which in this case pointed to Texas contract law. But for the reasons we have explained, the transferee court would apply Virginia choice-of-law rules. It is true that even these Virginia rules may point to the contract law of Texas, as the State in which the contract was formed. But at minimum, the fact that the Virginia court will not be required to apply Texas choice-of-law rules reduces whatever weight the District Court might have given to the public-interest factor that looks to the familiarity of the transferee court with the applicable law. And, in any event, federal judges routinely apply the law of a State other than the State in which they sit. We are not aware of any exceptionally arcane features of Texas contract law that are likely to defy comprehension by a federal judge sitting in Virginia.

* * *

We reverse the judgment of the Court of Appeals for the Fifth Circuit. Although no public-interest factors that might support the denial of Atlantic Marine's motion to transfer are apparent on the record before us, we remand the case for the courts below to decide that question.

It is so ordered.

NOTES AND QUESTIONS

1. *The proper mechanism.*   Did the Court hold that § 1404(a) is the exclusive vehicle through which to seek a transfer from a district court where venue is proper to a district court designated in a forum-selection clause? Why? If the parties have contractually agreed to file their dispute in a particular forum, doesn't it follow that all other forums are rendered "wrong" or "improper"? Does the application of § 1404(a) in this context differ from its application in *Skyhawke Technologies, LLC v. DECA International Corp.*, page 421, *supra*? Does the choice-of-law consequence of a § 1404(a) forum-selection-clause transfer differ from what occurs under a standard § 1404(a) transfer? Given these differences in application and consequence, doesn't a § 1404(a) forum-selection-clause transfer operate more like a § 1406(a) motion and transfer?

2. *Remand.*   Did the Supreme Court hold that the forum-selection clause had to be enforced here, with the result that the case must be transferred to the Eastern District of Virginia, Norfolk Division? On remand, what discretion if any does the Texas district court have in terms of retaining jurisdiction over the case? When the district court first ruled on Atlantic Marine's motion to transfer under § 1404(a), it ruled that the only public interest factor favoring transfer was the fact that the Eastern District of Virginia was a slightly more efficient forum because, on average, it disposed of civil cases 2.3 months more quickly, a difference that the Texas court described as being "negligible." 2012 WL 8499879, at *7 (W.D. Tex. Aug. 6, 2012). All of the other public interest factors, it said, "weigh in favor of denying transfer"—including the fact that § 1404(a) transfers effect "but a change of courtrooms"; as a result, a Virginia federal court would have to apply the same law a Texas court would have applied, possibly that of Texas with which the Texas court would be much more familiar. *Id.* at *8. Was the district court correct, or on remand might this public interest factor weigh in favor of transfer?

PROBLEMS

5-11. Eulala Shute, a resident of the State of Washington, purchased passage for a seven-day cruise on a Carnival Cruise Line ("Carnival") ship, the *Tropicale*, through a local travel agent. Carnival advertised its cruises in the state and provided travel agents in the state with brochures and seminars promoting Carnival's cruises. Shute paid the fare to the agent who forwarded the payment to Carnival's headquarters in Miami, Florida. Carnival then prepared the tickets and sent them to Shute in the state of Washington. The face of each ticket, at its left-hand lower corner, contained this admonition: "SUBJECT TO CONDITIONS OF CONTRACT ON LAST PAGES. IMPORTANT!" Those pages contained the following clause:

> It is agreed by and between the passenger and the Carrier that all disputes and matters whatsoever arising under, in connection with or incident to this Contract shall be litigated, if at all, in and before a Court located in the State of Florida, U.S.A., to the exclusion of the Courts of any other state or country.

Shute boarded the *Tropicale* in Los Angeles, California. The ship sailed to Puerto Vallarta, Mexico, and then returned to Los Angeles. While the ship was in international waters off the Mexican coast, Shute was injured when she slipped on a deck mat during a guided tour of the ship's galley. She filed suit against Carnival in the U.S. District Court for the Western District of Washington, claiming that her injuries had been caused by the negligence of Carnival and its employees.

Carnival moved to dismiss or transfer the suit to the federal district court for the Southern District of Florida pursuant to 28 U.S.C. § 1406(a) and Rule 12(b)(3), or in the alternative to transfer the case there pursuant to 28 U.S.C. § 1404(a), contending that the forum-selection clause on the ticket required Shute to bring her suit in a court in Florida.

A. Was venue proper in the Western District of Washington? (Note that there is also an interesting personal jurisdiction issue presented.)

B. Was the forum-selection clause permissive or exclusive? Did the clause include a federal option? If so, in which court or courts could that option be exercised?

C. Did the forum-selection clause apply to Ms. Shute's lawsuit?

D. What arguments regarding enforceability might the parties make? To what extent would it matter that Ms. Shute's injuries could make it difficult or impossible for her to travel to Florida? Who bears the burden of persuasion on this issue?

E. If the forum-selection clause applies and is enforceable, what should the district court do?

F. If the district court transfers the case to the Southern District of Florida, what substantive law should that court apply in resolving the dispute?

See Carnival Cruise Lines, Inc. v. Shute, 499 U.S. 585 (1991).

5-12. Terra International, Inc. ("Terra") manufactures and distributes a variety of agricultural products including nitrogen-based fertilizers. Terra is a Delaware corporation with its principal place of business in Sioux City, Iowa. In the late 1970s, Mississippi Chemical Corporation ("MCC"), a Mississippi corporation with its principal place of business in Yazoo City, Mississippi, developed an ammonium neutralization process that reduces the emissions of ammonium nitrate into the environment and increases the efficiency of the ammonium-nitrate manufacturing process. MCC and Terra entered into a license agreement under which Terra agreed to pay MCC $40,000 to use MCC's neutralizer technology at Terra's manufacturing facility in Iowa. One section of the license agreement contained a forum-selection clause: "Any dispute or disputes arising between the parties hereunder, insofar as the same cannot be settled by friendly agreement, will be determined in the District Court of the United States for the Southern District of Mississippi." On December 13, 1994, 14 years after Terra and MCC entered into the license agreement, an explosion occurred at Terra's factory. The explosion killed four people, injured 18 others, and leveled the facility's ammonium nitrate plant. Terra filed a diversity action against MCC in the U.S. District Court for the Northern District of Iowa, the district in which the explosion occurred. In its complaint, Terra limited its cause of action to two tort claims. The first claim alleged that MCC negligently designed its neutralizer technology and failed to train and properly warn Terra employees regarding the technology. The second claim asserted that MCC's neutralizer technology was unreasonably dangerous and defective and that MCC should therefore be held strictly liable for the damages the explosion caused. Terra did not assert any parallel claims for breach of contract. MCC filed a motion to transfer the case to Mississippi pursuant to 28 U.S.C. § 1404(a).

    A. Does the forum-selection clause apply to this lawsuit?

    B. Is there any argument here that the forum-selection clause is invalid? Would your answer to this question change if an Iowa statute provided: "A forum selection clause is invalid and unenforceable to the extent that it would deprive a court located in Iowa of the ability to hear a lawsuit brought by individuals seeking to recover for personal injuries suffered in this state"?

    C. Assuming the clause is valid, on what bases might plaintiffs argue that it should be found unenforceable? Is it at all relevant to this analysis that some of the plaintiffs were so badly injured that they cannot travel to Mississippi? Would a state statute barring the enforcement of such clauses factor into the analysis?

    D. Would it be an abuse of discretion for the court to grant the motion to transfer?

    E. Would your answer to any of the above questions differ if the clause had specified that any lawsuit between the parties "must be filed in the Circuit Court of Yazoo County, Mississippi"?

See Terra Int'l, Inc. v. Mississippi Chem. Corp., 119 F.3d 688 (8th Cir.), *cert. denied*, 522 U.S. 1029 (1997).

B.   *Forum Non Conveniens*

   Forum non conveniens is a common law doctrine that permits a court to decline the exercise of jurisdiction if the suit may be filed in another more convenient forum. It can be used by federal courts when the more convenient forum is in a foreign country. And it may be employed in state court if the more convenient forum is in a sister state or abroad. For example, in Problem 3-9, at page 287, *supra*, while the Connecticut court denied defendant John's motion to dismiss the suit brought against him by his sister, Mary, since it was not Mary who lured him into the state by trickery or fraud, the court granted his motion to dismiss based on *forum non conveniens*, since the lawsuit arose out of a multi-vehicle automobile accident that took place in Florida. *See McIntosh v. McIntosh*, 1996 WL 689948, at *2-*3 (Conn. Super. Ct., Nov. 20, 1996), *aff'd per curiam*, 701 A.2d 351 (Conn. App. Ct. 1997).

A party seeking a *forum non conveniens* dismissal must usually meet a heavy burden of persuasion to overcome the strong presumption in favor of the plaintiff's choice of forum. This is the same burden that a defendant must carry in a § 1404(a) transfer case that does not involve a forum-selection clause. *Cf. Atlantic Marine Construction Co., Inc., supra*, 134 S. Ct. at 581 n.6. To meet this burden, the moving party must usually show (1) that there is an available alternate forum; and (2) that the balance of private and public concerns implicated by the choice of forum weighs heavily in favor of dismissal.

Piper Aircraft Co. v. Reyno
454 U.S. 235 (1981)

JUSTICE MARSHALL delivered the opinion of the Court.

These cases arise out of an air crash that took place in Scotland. Respondent, acting as representative of the estates of several Scottish citizens killed in the accident, brought wrongful-death actions against petitioners that were ultimately transferred to the United States District Court for the Middle District of Pennsylvania. Petitioners moved to dismiss on the ground of *forum non conveniens*. After noting that an alternative forum existed in Scotland, the District Court granted their motions. The United States Court of Appeals for the Third Circuit reversed. The Court of Appeals based its decision, at least in part, on the ground that dismissal is automatically barred where the law of the alternative forum is less favorable to the plaintiff than the law of the forum chosen by the plaintiff. Because we conclude that the possibility of an unfavorable change in law should not, by itself, bar dismissal, and because we conclude that the District Court did not otherwise abuse its discretion, we reverse.

I

A

In July 1976, a small commercial aircraft crashed in the Scottish highlands during the course of a charter flight from Blackpool to Perth. The pilot and five passengers were killed instantly. The decedents were all Scottish subjects and residents, as are their heirs and next of kin. There were no eyewitnesses to the accident. At the time of the crash the plane was subject to Scottish air traffic control.

The aircraft, a twin-engine Piper Aztec, was manufactured in Pennsylvania by petitioner Piper Aircraft Co. (Piper). The propellers were manufactured in Ohio by petitioner Hartzell Propeller, Inc. (Hartzell). At the time of the crash the aircraft was registered in Great Britain and was owned and maintained by Air Navigation and Trading Co., Ltd. (Air Navigation). It was operated by McDonald Aviation, Ltd. (McDonald), a Scottish air taxi service. Both Air Navigation and McDonald were organized in the United Kingdom. The wreckage of the plane is now in a hangar in Farnsborough, England.

The British Department of Trade investigated the accident shortly after it occurred. A preliminary report found that the plane crashed after developing a spin, and suggested that mechanical failure in the plane or the propeller was responsible. At Hartzell's request, this report was reviewed by a three-member Review Board, which held a 9-day adversary hearing attended by all interested parties. The Review Board found no evidence of defective equipment and indicated that pilot error may have contributed to the accident. The pilot, who had obtained his commercial pilot's license only three months earlier, was flying over high ground at an altitude considerably lower than the minimum height required by his company's operations manual.

In July 1977, a California probate court appointed respondent Gaynell Reyno administratrix of the estates of the five passengers. Reyno is not related to and does not know any of the decedents or their survivors; she was a legal secretary to the attorney who filed this lawsuit. Several days after her appointment, Reyno commenced separate wrongful-death actions against Piper and Hartzell in the Superior Court of California, claiming negligence and strict liability. Air Navigation, McDonald, and the estate of the pilot are not parties to this litigation. The survivors of the five passengers whose estates are represented by Reyno filed a separate action in the United Kingdom against Air Navigation, McDonald, and the pilot's estate. Reyno candidly admits that the action against Piper and Hartzell was filed in the United States because its laws regarding liability, capacity to sue, and damages are more favorable to her position than are those of Scotland. Scottish law does not recognize strict liability in tort. Moreover, it permits wrongful-death actions only when brought by a decedent's relatives. The relatives may sue only for "loss of support and society."

On petitioners' motion, the suit was removed to the United States District Court for the Central District of California. Piper then moved for transfer to the United States District Court for the Middle District of Pennsylvania, pursuant to 28 U.S.C. § 1404(a). Hartzell moved to dismiss for lack of personal jurisdiction, or in the alternative, to transfer.[5] In December 1977, the District Court quashed service on Hartzell and transferred the case to the Middle District of Pennsylvania. Respondent then properly served process on Hartzell.

---

5. The District Court concluded that it could not assert personal jurisdiction over Hartzell consistent with due process. However, it decided not to dismiss Hartzell because the corporation would be amenable to process in Pennsylvania.

B

In May 1978, after the suit had been transferred, both Hartzell and Piper moved to dismiss the action on the ground of *forum non conveniens*. The District Court granted these motions in October 1979. It relied on the balancing test set forth by this Court in *Gulf Oil Corp. v. Gilbert*, 330 U.S. 501 (1947), and its companion case, *Koster v. Lumbermens Mut. Cas. Co.*, 330 U.S. 518 (1947). In those decisions, the Court stated that a plaintiff's choice of forum should rarely be disturbed. However, when an alternative forum has jurisdiction to hear the case, and when trial in the chosen forum would "establish . . . oppressiveness and vexation to a defendant . . . out of all proportion to plaintiff's convenience," or when the "chosen forum [is] inappropriate because of considerations affecting the court's own administrative and legal problems," the court may, in the exercise of its sound discretion, dismiss the case. To guide trial court discretion, the Court provided a list of "private interest factors" affecting the convenience of the litigants, and a list of "public interest factors" affecting the convenience of the forum.[6]

After describing our decisions in *Gilbert* and *Koster*, the District Court analyzed the facts of these cases. It began by observing that an alternative forum existed in Scotland; Piper and Hartzell had agreed to submit to the jurisdiction of the Scottish courts and to waive any statute of limitations defense that might be available. It then stated that plaintiff's choice of forum was entitled to little weight. The court recognized that a plaintiff's choice ordinarily deserves substantial deference. It noted, however, that Reyno "is a representative of foreign citizens and residents seeking a forum in the United States because of the more liberal rules concerning products liability law," and that "the courts have been less solicitous when the plaintiff is not an American citizen or resident, and particularly when the foreign citizens seek to benefit from the more liberal tort rules provided for the protection of citizens and residents of the United States."

The District Court next examined several factors relating to the private interests of the litigants, and determined that these factors strongly pointed towards Scotland as the appropriate forum. Although evidence concerning the design, manufacture, and testing of the plane and propeller is located in the United States, the connections with Scotland are otherwise "overwhelming." The real parties in interest are citizens of Scotland, as were all the decedents. Witnesses who could testify regarding the maintenance of the aircraft, the training of the pilot, and the

---

6. The factors pertaining to the private interests of the litigants included the "relative ease of access to sources of proof; availability of compulsory process for attendance of unwilling, and the cost of obtaining attendance of willing, witnesses; possibility of view of premises, if view would be appropriate to the action; and all other practical problems that make trial of a case easy, expeditious and inexpensive." *Gilbert*, 330 U.S., at 508. The public factors bearing on the question included the administrative difficulties flowing from court congestion; the "local interest in having localized controversies decided at home"; the interest in having the trial of a diversity case in a forum that is at home with the law that must govern the action; the avoidance of unnecessary problems in conflict of laws, or in the application of foreign law; and the unfairness of burdening citizens in an unrelated forum with jury duty. *Id.*, at 509.

investigation of the accident—all essential to the defense—are in Great Britain. Moreover, all witnesses to damages are located in Scotland. Trial would be aided by familiarity with Scottish topography, and by easy access to the wreckage.

The District Court reasoned that because crucial witnesses and evidence were beyond the reach of compulsory process, and because the defendants would not be able to implead potential Scottish third-party defendants, it would be "unfair to make Piper and Hartzell proceed to trial in this forum." The survivors had brought separate actions in Scotland against the pilot, McDonald, and Air Navigation. "[I]t would be fairer to all parties and less costly if the entire case was presented to one jury with available testimony from all relevant witnesses." Although the court recognized that if trial were held in the United States, Piper and Hartzell could file indemnity or contribution actions against the Scottish defendants, it believed that there was a significant risk of inconsistent verdicts.[7]

The District Court concluded that the relevant public interests also pointed strongly towards dismissal. The court determined that Pennsylvania law would apply to Piper and Scottish law to Hartzell if the case were tried in the Middle District of Pennsylvania.[8] As a result, "trial in this forum would be hopelessly complex and confusing for a jury." In addition, the court noted that it was unfamiliar with Scottish law and thus would have to rely upon experts from that country. The court also found that the trial would be enormously costly and time-consuming; that it would be unfair to burden citizens with jury duty when the Middle District of Pennsylvania has little connection with the controversy; and that Scotland has a substantial interest in the outcome of the litigation.

In opposing the motions to dismiss, respondent contended that dismissal would be unfair because Scottish law was less favorable. The District Court explicitly rejected this claim. It reasoned that the possibility that dismissal might lead to an unfavorable change in the law did not deserve significant weight; any deficiency in the foreign law was a "matter to be dealt with in the foreign forum."

---

7. The District Court explained that inconsistent verdicts might result if petitioners were held liable on the basis of strict liability here, and then required to prove negligence in an indemnity action in Scotland. Moreover, even if the same standard of liability applied, there was a danger that different juries would find different facts and produce inconsistent results.

8. Under *Klaxon v. Stentor Electric Mfg. Co.*, 313 U.S. 487 (1941), a court ordinarily must apply the choice-of-law rules of the State in which it sits. However, where a case is transferred pursuant to 28 U.S.C. § 1404(a), it must apply the choice-of-law rules of the State from which the case was transferred. *Van Dusen v. Barrack*, 376 U.S. 612 (1946). Relying on these two cases, the District Court concluded that California choice-of-law rules would apply to Piper, and Pennsylvania choice-of-law rules would apply to Hartzell. It further concluded that California applied a "governmental interests" analysis in resolving choice-of-law problems, and that Pennsylvania employed a "significant contacts" analysis. The court used the "governmental interests" analysis to determine that Pennsylvania liability rules would apply to Piper, and the "significant contacts" analysis to determine that Scottish liability rules would apply to Hartzell.

C

On appeal, the United States Court of Appeals for the Third Circuit reversed and remanded for trial. The decision to reverse appears to be based on two alternative grounds. First, the Court held that the District Court abused its discretion in conducting the *Gilbert* analysis. Second, the Court held that dismissal is never appropriate where the law of the alternative forum is less favorable to the plaintiff. . . .

II

The Court of Appeals erred in holding that plaintiffs may defeat a motion to dismiss on the ground of *forum non conveniens* merely by showing that the substantive law that would be applied in the alternative forum is less favorable to the plaintiffs than that of the present forum. The possibility of a change in substantive law should ordinarily not be given conclusive or even substantial weight in the *forum non conveniens* inquiry. . . .

The Court of Appeals' approach is not only inconsistent with the purpose of the *forum non conveniens* doctrine, but also poses substantial practical problems. If the possibility of a change in law were given substantial weight, deciding motions to dismiss on the ground of *forum non conveniens* would become quite difficult. Choice-of-law analysis would become extremely important, and the courts would frequently be required to interpret the law of foreign jurisdictions. First, the trial court would have to determine what law would apply if the case were tried in the chosen forum, and what law would apply if the case were tried in the alternative forum. It would then have to compare the rights, remedies, and procedures available under the law that would be applied in each forum. Dismissal would be appropriate only if the court concluded that the law applied by the alternative forum is as favorable to the plaintiff as that of the chosen forum. The doctrine of *forum non conveniens*, however, is designed in part to help courts avoid conducting complex exercises in comparative law. As we stated in *Gilbert*, the public interest factors point towards dismissal where the court would be required to "untangle problems in conflict of laws, and in law foreign to itself."

Upholding the decision of the Court of Appeals would result in other practical problems. At least where the foreign plaintiff named an American manufacturer as defendant, a court could not dismiss the case on grounds of *forum non conveniens* where dismissal might lead to an unfavorable change in law. The American courts, which are already extremely attractive to foreign plaintiffs, would become even more attractive. The flow of litigation into the United States would increase and further congest already crowded courts. . . .

We do not hold that the possibility of an unfavorable change in law should *never* be a relevant consideration in a *forum non conveniens* inquiry. Of course, if the remedy provided by the alternative forum is so clearly inadequate or unsatisfactory that it is no remedy at all, the unfavorable change in law may be given substantial weight; the district court may conclude that dismissal would not be in the interests of justice.[22] In these cases, however, the remedies that would be provided by the Scottish courts do not fall within this category. Although the relatives of the decedents may not be able to rely on a strict liability theory, and although their potential damages award may be smaller, there is no danger that they will be deprived of any remedy or treated unfairly.

III

The Court of Appeals also erred in rejecting the District Court's *Gilbert* analysis. The Court of Appeals stated that more weight should have been given to the plaintiff's choice of forum, and criticized the District Court's analysis of the private and public interests. However, the District Court's decision regarding the deference due plaintiff's choice of forum was appropriate. Furthermore, we do not believe that the District Court abused its discretion in weighing the private and public interests.

A

The District Court acknowledged that there is ordinarily a strong presumption in favor of the plaintiff's choice of forum, which may be overcome only when the private and public interest factors clearly point towards trial in the alternative forum. It held, however, that the presumption applies with less force when the plaintiff or real parties in interest are foreign.

The District Court's distinction between resident or citizen plaintiffs and foreign plaintiffs is fully justified. In *Koster*, the Court indicated that a plaintiff's choice of forum is entitled to greater deference when the plaintiff has chosen the home forum. When the home forum has been chosen, it is reasonable to assume that this choice is convenient. When the plaintiff is foreign, however, this assumption is much less reasonable. Because the central purpose of any *forum non conveniens* inquiry is to ensure that the trial is convenient, a foreign plaintiff's choice deserves less deference.

B

The *forum non conveniens* determination is committed to the sound discretion of the trial court. It may be reversed only when there has been a clear abuse of discretion; where the court has considered all relevant public and private interest

---

22. At the outset of any *forum non conveniens* inquiry, the court must determine whether there exists an alternative forum. Ordinarily, this requirement will be satisfied when the defendant is "amenable to process" in the other jurisdiction. *Gilbert*, 330 U.S., at 506-507. In rare circumstances, however, where the remedy offered by the other forum is clearly unsatisfactory, the other forum may not be an adequate alternative, and the initial requirement may not be satisfied. Thus, for example, dismissal would not be appropriate where the alternative forum does not permit litigation of the subject matter of the dispute. Cf. *Phoenix Canada Oil Co. Ltd. v. Texaco, Inc.*, 78 F.R.D. 445 (Del. 1978) (court refuses to dismiss, where alternative forum is Ecuador, it is unclear whether Ecuadorean tribunal will hear the case, and there is no generally codified Ecuadorean legal remedy for the unjust enrichment and tort claims asserted).

factors, and where its balancing of these factors is reasonable, its decision deserves substantial deference. Here, the Court of Appeals expressly acknowledged that the standard of review was one of abuse of discretion. In examining the District Court's analysis of the public and private interests, however, the Court of Appeals seems to have lost sight of this rule, and substituted its own judgment for that of the District Court.

(1)

In analyzing the private interest factors, the District Court stated that the connections with Scotland are "overwhelming." This characterization may be somewhat exaggerated. Particularly with respect to the question of relative ease of access to sources of proof, the private interests point in both directions. As respondent emphasizes, records concerning the design, manufacture, and testing of the propeller and plane are located in the United States. She would have greater access to sources of proof relevant to her strict liability and negligence theories if trial were held here. However, the District Court did not act unreasonably in concluding that fewer evidentiary problems would be posed if the trial were held in Scotland. A large proportion of the relevant evidence is located in Great Britain.

The Court of Appeals found that the problems of proof could not be given any weight because Piper and Hartzell failed to describe with specificity the evidence they would not be able to obtain if trial were held in the United States. It suggested that defendants seeking *forum non conveniens* dismissal must submit affidavits identifying the witnesses they would call and the testimony these witnesses would provide if the trial were held in the alternative forum. Such detail is not necessary. Piper and Hartzell have moved for dismissal precisely because many crucial witnesses are located beyond the reach of compulsory process, and thus are difficult to identify or interview. Requiring extensive investigation would defeat the purpose of their motion. Of course, defendants must provide enough information to enable the District Court to balance the parties' interests. Our examination of the record convinces us that sufficient information was provided here. Both Piper and Hartzell submitted affidavits describing the evidentiary problems they would face if the trial were held in the United States.

The District Court correctly concluded that the problems posed by the inability to implead potential third-party defendants clearly supported holding the trial in Scotland. Joinder of the pilot's estate, Air Navigation, and McDonald is crucial to the presentation of petitioners' defense. If Piper and Hartzell can show that the accident was caused not by a design defect, but rather by the negligence of the pilot, the plane's owners, or the charter company, they will be relieved of all liability. It is true, of course, that if Hartzell and Piper were found liable after a trial in the United States, they could institute an action for indemnity or contribution against these parties in Scotland. It would be far more convenient, however, to resolve all claims in one trial. The Court of Appeals rejected this argument. Forcing petitioners to rely on actions for indemnity or contributions would be "burdensome" but not "unfair." Finding that trial in the plaintiff's chosen forum would be burdensome, however, is sufficient to support dismissal on grounds of *forum non conveniens*.

(2)

The District Court's review of the factors relating to the public interest was also reasonable. On the basis of its choice-of-law analysis, it concluded that if the case were tried in the Middle District of Pennsylvania, Pennsylvania law would apply to Piper and Scottish law to Hartzell. It stated that a trial involving two sets of laws would be confusing to the jury. It also noted its own lack of familiarity with Scottish law. Consideration of these problems was clearly appropriate under *Gilbert*; in that case we explicitly held that the need to apply foreign law pointed towards dismissal.[29] The Court of Appeals found that the District Court's choice-of-law analysis was incorrect, and that American law would apply to both Hartzell and Piper. Thus, lack of familiarity with foreign law would not be a problem. Even if the Court of Appeals' conclusion is correct, however, all other public interest factors favored trial in Scotland.

Scotland has a very strong interest in this litigation. The accident occurred in its airspace. All of the decedents were Scottish. Apart from Piper and Hartzell, all potential plaintiffs and defendants are either Scottish or English. As we stated in *Gilbert*, there is "a local interest in having localized controversies decided at home." Respondent argues that American citizens have an interest in ensuring that American manufacturers are deterred from producing defective products, and that additional deterrence might be obtained if Piper and Hartzell were tried in the United States, where they could be sued on the basis of both negligence and strict liability. However, the incremental deterrence that would be gained if this trial were held in an American court is likely to be insignificant. The American interest in this accident is simply not sufficient to justify the enormous commitment of judicial time and resources that would inevitably be required if the case were to be tried here.

IV

The Court of Appeals erred in holding that the possibility of an unfavorable change in law bars dismissal on the ground of *forum non conveniens*. It also erred in rejecting the District Court's *Gilbert* analysis. The District Court properly decided that the presumption in favor of the respondent's forum choice applied with less than maximum force because the real parties in interest are foreign. It did not act unreasonably in deciding that the private interests pointed towards trial in Scotland. Nor did it act unreasonably in deciding that the public interests favored trial in Scotland. Thus, the judgment of the Court of Appeals is
   Reversed.

[JUSTICES POWELL and O'CONNOR took no part in the decision; JUSTICE WHITE concurred in part and dissented in part; JUSTICES STEVENS and BRENNAN dissented.]

---

29. Many *forum non conveniens* decisions have held that the need to apply foreign law favors dismissal. Of course, this factor alone is not sufficient to warrant dismissal when a balancing of all relevant factors shows that the plaintiff's chosen forum is appropriate.

NOTES AND QUESTIONS

1. *Prelude to dismissal.* *Piper* was originally filed in a Los Angeles Superior Court and then removed to the U.S. District Court for the Central District of California. On what basis was the case removed? On what basis, if any, was venue proper in the Central District of California? Both Piper and Hartzell moved to transfer the case to the Middle District of Pennsylvania. Was that a district in which the case could have been brought? Why was Piper's motion to transfer based on § 1404(a) while Hartzell's was based on § 1406(a)? Finally, why did the district court in the Middle District conclude that Pennsylvania law would apply to the claims against Piper while Scottish law would apply to the claims against Hartzell?

2. *Plaintiff's choice of forum.* The *Piper* Court noted that the plaintiff's choice of forum is usually given substantial weight in the balancing of interests under a *forum non conveniens* analysis. A nonresident foreign plaintiff's choice of a U.S. forum is, however, entitled to less deference. Why? Doesn't the United States have an interest in providing a judicial forum for foreigners injured by Americans doing business abroad? *See In re Union Carbide Corp. Gas Plant Disaster at Bhopal, India*, 634 F. Supp. 842, 867 (S.D.N.Y. 1986), *aff'd as modified*, 809 F.2d 195 (2d Cir.) (rejecting as imperialistic the notion that the United States ought to provide a forum to redress injuries caused by an American company doing business in India), *cert. denied*, 484 U.S. 871 (1987).

3. *Abuse of discretion.* The *Piper* Court held that it was not an abuse of discretion for the district court to dismiss the suit. Would it have been an abuse of discretion for the district court to have instead retained the suit?

4. *Venue or jurisdiction?* *Forum non conveniens* is often described as a venue doctrine. *See American Dredging Co. v. Miller*, 510 U.S. 443, 453 (1993). Yet, might it not be more properly characterized as jurisdictional? Consider the extent to which *forum non conveniens* analysis resembles the reasonableness aspect of personal jurisdiction. *See* Simona Grossi, Forum Non Conveniens *as a Jurisdictional Doctrine*, 75 U. PITT. L. REV. 1, 32-33 (2013). If a court were to find that the exercise of personal jurisdiction over the defendant would be reasonable, might it nonetheless conclude that the case should be dismissed on *forum non conveniens* grounds? On what bases might a court so rule? Court congestion? Inconvenience to the court? Would a dismissal on such grounds be consistent with a court's obligation to exercise the jurisdiction conferred on it by law? Or might these *forum non conveniens* concerns in fact qualify as the kind of "other considerations" that *Burger King Corp. v. Rudzewicz*, 471 U.S. 462, 477 & n.20 (1985), suggested might establish a "compelling case that . . . would render jurisdiction unreasonable"?

5. *The timing of the determination.* In *Sinochem International Co. Ltd. v. Malaysia International Shipping Corp.*, 549 U.S. 422 (2007), the Supreme Court held that a district court may decide the question of *forum non conveniens* before determining any questions of subject matter or personal jurisdiction. In essence, the Court held that the questions pertaining to jurisdiction are only vital if the

lower court decides to proceed to the controversy's merits". The Court explained its ruling as follows:

> A *forum non conveniens* dismissal "den[ies] audience to a case on the merits"; it is a determination that the merits should be adjudicated elsewhere . . . . A district court therefore may dispose of an action by a *forum non conveniens* dismissal, bypassing questions of subject-matter and personal jurisdiction, when considerations of convenience, fairness, and judicial economy so warrant.

Id. at 432. In essence, the Court held that the questions pertaining to jurisdiction are only vital if the lower court decides to proceed to the controversy's merits. *See also Ruhrgas AG v. Marathon Oil Co.*, 526 U.S. 574 (1999) (sequencing of decisions regarding subject matter and personal jurisdiction within the discretion of the district court).

A NOTE ON AN AVAILABLE ALTERNATE FORUM

The *Piper* Court emphasized that in federal courts the availability of an alternate forum is a prerequisite to any application of the doctrine of *forum non conveniens*. At a minimum, this means that there must be an alternate forum that would have jurisdiction over both the parties and the controversy. Beyond these jurisdictional requirements, however, the Court gave little guidance as to what constitutes an adequate alternate forum. In footnote 22 of its opinion, page 456, *supra*, the Court did observe: "In rare circumstances . . . where the remedy offered by the other forum is clearly unsatisfactory, the other forum may not be an adequate alternative, and the initial requirement may not be satisfied." *Piper*, 454 U.S. at 254 n.22. However, this is a very difficult standard to satisfy. Most courts have found that an alternate forum is adequate so long as it provides *some* remedy for the plaintiff. Stated differently, unless the foreign forum provides no remedy at all, it is unlikely that a federal court will find the alternative forum to be unavailable. *See El-Fadl v. Central Bank of Jordan*, 75 F.3d 668, 677-678 (D.C. Cir. 1996) (holding that alternative forum is unavailable when defendant is immunized from suit there); 17 MOORE'S FEDERAL PRACTICE, *supra*, § 111.74[2].

A NOTE ON *FORUM NON CONVENIENS* IN STATE COURTS

In state courts, the doctrine of *forum non conveniens* is a matter of state law. While most states follow the same general principles that the Supreme Court applied in *Piper*, there are differences. For example, some states are much more hospitable to foreign plaintiffs suing domestic corporations than was the Court in *Piper*. In *Bochetto v. Piper Aircraft Co.*, 94 A.3d 1044 (Pa. Super. Ct. 2014), *appeal denied*, 112 A.3d 648 (Pa. 2015), a case involving the crash of an American-built plane in Portugal, the court reversed the *forum non conveniens* dismissal of a suit brought by foreign plaintiffs in Pennsylvania state court, explaining that in this "international setting" federal precedent was not "persuasive authority" and that in contrast to *Piper*, under Pennsylvania's forum non conveniens law, "[w]hile foreign plaintiffs enjoy 'less deference' with regard to their choice of forum, their choice is still entitled to solicitude." 94 A.3d at 1050-1051, 1056.

At the opposite extreme, some states are even less hospitable to plaintiffs than was Supreme Court in *Piper*. In New York the availability of an alternate forum is not an absolute requirement for invoking the doctrine, but is instead simply an "important factor" to be weighed in the balancing of private and public interests. In *Islamic Republic of Iran v. Pahlavi*, 467 N.E.2d 245 (N.Y. 1984), *cert. denied*, 469 U.S. 1108 (1985), New York's high court thus held that it was not an abuse of discretion to dismiss a multibillion dollar lawsuit brought against the former Shah of Iran by the Islamic Republic of Iran, even though there was apparently no other tribunal available to hear the case. The court reasoned that given the complex and burdensome nature of the case and the lack of any real connection with New York, the suit was properly dismissed. However, *Pahlavi* appears not to have been followed by any other states and even in New York, it "has been limited to its own facts by lower New York courts." *Vicknair v. Phelps Dodge Industries, Inc.*, 767 N.W.2d 171, 176-180 (N.D. 2009). *See also Binder v. Shepard's Inc.*, 133 P.3d 276, 278-280 (Okla. 2006) (rejecting *Pahlavi* and holding that "the existence of a viable alternate forum is a prerequisite to the application of the doctrine of *forum non conveniens*").

PROBLEMS

5-13. In October 1993, Robert Guidi, Coby Hoffman, and Merrill Kramer were in Egypt on business. While eating dinner in the restaurant of a hotel managed by IHC, a Delaware corporation with its principal place of business in New York City, all three men were shot by an Egyptian gunman named Farahat who had entered the hotel without arousing the suspicion of hotel security. In addition to the three Americans, Farahat shot a Syrian lawyer, a French lawyer, and an Italian judge. Of his six victims, four died, including Robert Guidi and Coby Hoffman. Immediately after the shooting, Farahat surrendered to hotel security and the Egyptian police. His claimed motivation for the shootings was religious scruples directed against foreigners. In the criminal prosecution that followed, Farahat was adjudged insane and committed to a government hospital in January 1994. He escaped from the hospital in September 1997 and the same day, with the help of at least one other person, killed ten more people in an attack on a tour bus.

Karen Guidi, Eve Hoffman, Merrill Kramer, and Lois Kramer filed a diversity suit against IHC in the Southern District of New York seeking damages for wrongful death and personal injuries. IHC moved for dismissal on the ground of forum non conveniens, arguing that information critical to its defense regarding hotel security could be obtained only in Egypt, that the cost of defending itself in New York would be prohibitive, that it would be unable to implead the Egyptian government, and that an Egyptian court would be better able to apply Egyptian tort law. In addition, the families of the Italian judge and the French lawyer whom

Farahat had killed in the same incident had already commenced wrongful death actions in the Egyptian courts. The plaintiffs opposed IHC's motion on several fronts, including that American plaintiffs should not be compelled to sue an American defendant in a foreign country and that the plaintiffs were emotionally unable to travel to Egypt for a trial, in part because of continuing terrorist activity in Egypt directed against foreigners—50 tourists had been killed at Luxor, Egypt, in November 1997. The district court granted the motion and dismissed. Was it an abuse of discretion to do so? More specifically, is this case distinguishable from *Piper*? Finally, how would a California state court rule on this issue? *See Guidi v. Inter-Continental Hotels Corp.*, 224 F.3d 142 (2d Cir. 2000). *Compare Iragorri v. International Elevator, Inc.*, 203 F.3d 8 (1st Cir. 2000) (affirming *forum non conveniens* dismissal of Maine federal court suit by U.S. citizen against U.S. corporation, arising from elevator accident in Colombia, although alternative Colombian forum was subject to U.S. travel advisory), *with Iragorri v. United Technologies Corp.*, 274 F.3d 65 (2d Cir. 2001) (en banc) (ordering Connecticut federal court to reconsider its *forum non conveniens* dismissal of same plaintiff's suit against two other U.S. defendants arising from same Colombian accident).

5-14. Urvashi, a six-year-old Indian national, was seriously injured while traveling on the high seas as a passenger aboard the Apj Karan, an Indian registered cargo ship. At the time, she was accompanying her father who was a crew member. After the accident, Urvashi was flown to New York where she underwent numerous operations to repair her injuries. During her convalescence she and her family were granted temporary medical visas to remain in the United States. She is now attending elementary school in the United States and is waiting to undergo one further operation. Through her parents, she has filed an admiralty lawsuit in federal district court against the vessel and its owners, Surrendra, Ltd. ("Surrendra"), an Indian shipping company. Urvashi claims that her injuries were due to the negligence of certain crew members on the Apj Karan. Assume that subject matter jurisdiction and venue are both satisfied, and that Indian common law, which is founded on British common law, must be applied to resolve this controversy. Surrendra has moved to dismiss the case under the doctrine of *forum non conveniens*. In response, the plaintiff submitted affidavits from two experts on Indian law, both of whom concluded that the Indian judicial system is in a state of "collapse" and that it would likely take 25 years to resolve the case within that system. Specifically, they asserted that the court in which this case would be filed has only two judges and a backlog of over 150,000 cases. The defendant responded with an expert of its own who agreed that while there were significant delays in the Indian judicial system, there were ways in which a case could be expedited. The defendants' expert opined that "given the tender age of the child, the Calcutta High Court (which would be the court in which the action would have to be filed, given the amount of compensation claimed) would undoubtedly grant an 'expedited hearing' request." Surrendra also offered the affidavit of the company's General Manager, who promised that if the district court dismissed the case, Surrendra would cooperate in seeking expedited treatment of any suit brought in India. How should the district court rule on the motion? In answering this question, be sure to apply each step of the *forum non conveniens* analysis. *See Bhatnagar v. Surrendra Overseas Ltd.*, 52 F.3d 1220 (3d Cir. 1995), *aff'g* 820 F. Supp. 958 (E.D. Pa. 1993).

5-15. Thirteen minor league baseball players ("the players") from the Dominican Republic brought a sexual harassment suit against the San Francisco Giants and Luis Rosa, the Giants' former Latin American scout. The suit was filed in the U.S. District Court for the Northern District of California. The players had each signed a seven-year minor league contract with the Giants. Although the contracts initially assigned the players to the San Pedro Giants in the Dominican Republic, playing for the San Francisco Giants or some other U.S. team was each player's common goal. All 13 players claimed that Rosa expressly conditioned their continued employment and/or reassignment to U.S. teams on their submitting to his sexual advances, and that he appropriated part of their earnings or signing bonuses for his own use. They also alleged that the Giants' management knew or had reason to know of the scout's misconduct. Based on these same allegations, a combined criminal and civil suit against the Giants and Rosa was instituted in the Dominican Republic. The defendants have moved to dismiss the federal district court proceeding under the doctrine of *forum non conveniens.* Rosa is currently in California with no immediate plans to return to the Dominican Republic. What should the district court do? *See Monegro v. Rosa*, 211 F.3d 509 (9th Cir. 2000), *cert. denied*, 531 U.S. 1112 (2001).

C. Venue, Transfer, and *Forum Non Conveniens* Review Problems

5-16. In 1988, Leonardo Martino, a Michigan resident, entered into a franchise agreement with A-1 Transmissions, Inc. ("A-1"), also a Michigan corporation, under which Martino would operate an A-1 franchise in the State of Michigan. Three years later, A-1 assigned its franchises to Cottman Transmission Systems, Inc. ("Cottman"), a Pennsylvania corporation with its principal place of business in the Eastern District of Pennsylvania. In conformance with that assignment, Martino executed a franchise agreement with Cottman on August 26, 1991, which included a forum-selection clause providing that "any legal proceedings arising out of this Agreement shall be filed in a state or federal court located in the State of Pennsylvania." Cottman also retained authority to enforce the original A-1 agreement. Under this arrangement, transactions between the parties included payments made by Martino to Cottman in Pennsylvania, the ordering of parts and supplies by Martino from Cottman's Pennsylvania offices, and the imposition of long-term and exacting regulation of Martino's business by Cottman.

Because the Cottman agreement signed by Martino and others failed to comply with a provision of a Michigan statute, in April 1992 Cottman offered its franchisees the opportunity to rescind their contracts. Martino accepted that offer.

Thereafter, in December 1992, Cottman filed suit against Martino in the U.S. District Court for the Eastern District of Pennsylvania, asserting two causes of action: (1) unauthorized use of Cottman's trademarks after spring 1992—a federal claim; and (2) breach of the A-1 franchise agreement's covenant not to compete—a state-law claim.

A. Was the forum-selection clause that was included in the Cottman franchise agreement permissive or exclusive?
B. Did it contain a federal option?
C. Was that clause applicable to the suit filed by Cottman?
D. Assuming the clause was applicable, would it likely be deemed enforceable?
E. Assuming the forum-selection clause does not apply (or was not enforceable), what motions might Martino file and how might the district court rule on those motions?

See Cottman Transmission Systems, Inc. v. Martino, 36 F.3d 291 (3d Cir. 1994).

5-17. Erica was seriously injured by a land mine explosion in Kabul, Afghanistan. At the time, she was working as a surveyor for Rebuild, Inc. ("Rebuild"), a Delaware corporation with an office in Delaware, and its main office and principal place of business in Los Angeles, California. Rebuild is engaged in reconstructing highways in and around Kabul. Erica claims that her injury was due to the negligence of her supervisors who failed to warn her that the area in which she was working was infested with land mines. Erica, who is a British citizen, has come to California on a temporary visa for extensive plastic surgery. The procedures are expected to take up to four years. She has sued Rebuild in the U.S. District Court for the Central District of California, asserting claims for negligence. Rebuild has filed a motion to dismiss under Rule 12(b)(3), alternative motions to transfer to Delaware pursuant to § 1404(a) or § 1406(a), and a motion to dismiss under the doctrine of *forum non conveniens*. As to the motions to transfer, Rebuild argues that the Delaware forum will be significantly more convenient since most of its operational employees, some of whom might be called as witnesses, work out of that office. As to the *forum non conveniens* motion, Rebuild asserts that the proper forum is in Kabul where the accident took place, where several witnesses reside, and where much of the evidence can be found. As part of this latter motion, Rebuild has agreed to submit to the jurisdiction of the Kabul judicial system and has waived any statute of limitations defense. Erica's opposition to the motion cites her physical condition as making travel difficult, the dangers in Afghanistan, the instability of the judicial system there, and the fact that most of the witnesses were American citizens employed by Rebuild. What should the district court do?

VI

THE *ERIE* DOCTRINE AND RELATED PROBLEMS

In this chapter, we study the *"Erie* doctrine." *Erie* at bottom is simple and elegant. It establishes the common-sense principle that a federal court sitting in diversity should apply state substantive law to the resolution of the state claims presented to it. Although this principle is easy to state (and seemingly obvious), students sometimes find it difficult to grasp. The goal of this chapter is to demystify *Erie*. We will proceed step by step, beginning with a brief overview of the contexts in which *Erie* might apply and then study the *Erie* decision and the related problem of federal common law. With this background as our foundation, we will examine a three-track analytical structure that should leave you with a solid and confident understanding of the *Erie* doctrine.

A. The Law to Be Applied in Federal and State Courts

Suppose a party files a gender discrimination claim in a U.S. district court under 42 U.S.C. § 1983. In a case like this, the federal law created by § 1983 and cases construing it will provide the substantive standards used to resolve the controversy. Similarly, federal procedural law will dictate the procedures followed in achieving that resolution. Neither of these propositions is startling. One would expect a federal claim filed in a federal court to be decided by reference to federal law. So, too, when a state court adjudicates a purely state law claim such as a tort action between private parties, that state court will generally look to state law, both substantive and procedural, to resolve the dispute. These simple scenarios do not, however, describe the full range of possibilities. Federal courts must sometimes adjudicate state law issues and state courts must sometimes adjudicate federal law issues.

Imagine, for example, a diversity case in which the underlying claim is for breach of contract. What law—federal or state—will the federal court apply to resolve that claim? The basic answer is simple. A federal court sitting in diversity will generally apply federal procedural law and state substantive law. In essence, the federal court operates as an alternative forum for the adjudication of the state-created right. Since the character of the federal forum is in large part defined by the procedures it applies, those procedures remain relatively constant regardless of the underlying claim's nature. On the other hand, this alternative forum is not the machine through which to create or redesign state law. As a consequence, a breach of contract claim premised on state law remains a state law claim even when filed in federal court. The federal court, therefore, will apply state-created contract law to resolve the dispute. In this way, the essential character of the state-created right does not depend on whether that right is adjudicated in a state or a federal court. In other words, federal courts sitting in diversity do not make state law, but instead merely apply that law through the lens of federal procedure.

The opposite situation occurs when a federal claim is filed in state court. Just as a federal court may sometimes operate as an alternative forum for the adjudication of a state-created claim, a state court may operate as an alternative forum for federally created claims. For example, state courts have concurrent jurisdiction with federal courts over § 1983 claims. This grant of jurisdiction does not, however, alter the substantive law applicable to such claims. In exercising jurisdiction over a § 1983 claim, a state court must therefore apply the same principles of substantive law as would be applied had the case been filed in federal court. On the other hand, the state-filed claim usually will be processed within the state system by reference to state procedural law.

The foregoing description of federal and state court practices brings us closer to the reality of actual practice, but we are still not quite there. We have assumed to this point that the realms of substantive law and procedural law occupy wholly distinct, clearly demarcated spheres. While this assumption holds true in most cases, it is not universally accurate. As a general matter, substantive rules define the standards of conduct applicable to everyday life, while procedural rules specify the manner or means through which claims arising under the substantive law may be adjudicated. Thus the law of negligence provides "substantive" standards against which to measure our everyday duties to one another, while the law of personal jurisdiction creates a "procedural" framework within which to determine whether a specific person is amenable to suit in a particular forum for breach of those duties. Sometimes, however, the distinction between substance and procedure is far from clear, making the choice of which law to apply more problematic than our bright-line models may suggest.

Consider the following situation: A federal court exercising its diversity or supplemental jurisdiction is asked to adjudicate a state-created tort claim. The claim is filed beyond the state's statute of limitations but within the time limits ostensibly allowed by federal law. Should the federal court follow the more generous federal rule and proceed to the merits, or must it apply state law and dismiss the suit?

Under the initial approach described above, the label applied to these laws would be crucial. If we were to label statutes of limitations as procedural, the federal court would follow federal law and allow the case to proceed. The reason? Federal courts sitting in diversity apply federal procedural law. On the other hand, if statutes of limitations were deemed substantive, the federal court sitting in diversity would follow state law and dismiss the lawsuit. A fair argument can be made for both labels. Statutes of limitations are procedural in that they provide a reasonable time frame within which a substantive claim can be filed. Yet they are also substantive to the extent that they afford individuals peace of mind after a designated period of time by barring otherwise legitimate substantive claims from being vindicated. Clearly, the labels "substantive" and "procedural" provide little normative guidance in this area of ambiguity; rather, they represent at best conclusions. We thus need a method for determining how to arrive at the proper conclusion, *i.e.*, a method through which to determine which law should be followed regardless of formal labels.

The bulk of this chapter focuses on how federal courts sitting in diversity or exercising supplemental jurisdiction resolve potential conflicts between state substantive law and federal procedural law. The foundation for this examination rests, as we have seen, on the proposition that federal courts adjudicating state law claims must generally apply state substantive law and federal procedural law. We will consider various applications of that rule and also examine potential exceptions to it, as well as problems that may arise when the lines between substance and procedure are blurred, *i.e.*, when an ostensibly procedural rule appears to operate substantively.

The chapter begins with a foundational case, *Erie Railroad Co. v. Tompkins*, 304 U.S. 64 (1938). There the Supreme Court established what was at the time a remarkable proposition: Federal courts exercising diversity jurisdiction are not free to devise principles of substantive common law (such as tort or contract law) but are instead required to apply state law, including state common law, to the resolution of such quintessentially state claims. We will then look at problems that arise in diversity and supplemental jurisdiction cases when federal procedural law appears to conflict with state law and will examine the extent to which the principles of *Erie* are implicated by such conflicts. Here we will discover that the *Erie* analysis is premised on three separate tracks or approaches, each dependent on the type of federal procedural law at issue—statutes, formal rules, or judge-made doctrines. In this context, we will see some overlap as well as some bright-line distinctions between and among the tracks. We will also explore the relatively limited sphere of legitimate federal common law that survived *Erie*. This should help define the actual scope of the *Erie* decision, which in essence leaves the creation of state law to the states and federal law to the organs of the national government. For useful discussions of the *Erie* doctrine, see Allan Ides, *The Supreme Court and the Law to Be Applied in Diversity Cases: A Critical Guide to the Development and Application of the* Erie *Doctrine and Related Problems*, 163 F.R.D. 19 (1995); Stephan B. Burbank, *The Rules Enabling Act of 1934*, 130 U. Pa. L. Rev. 1015 (1982); and John Hart Ely, *The Irrepressible Myth of* Erie, 87 Harv. L. Rev. 693 (1974).

B.   The *Erie* Doctrine: The Law to Be Applied in Diversity and Supplemental Jurisdiction Cases

1.   A Brief History of the Pre-*Erie* Landscape

Prior to 1938, the year of the Court's decision in *Erie*, federal courts followed a very different choice-of-law model than the one described in the preceding overview. Procedure in federal court depended on whether the court was sitting in law or in equity. Roughly speaking, cases at law were those in which a party sought monetary relief, while cases in equity included those in which a party sought some type of nonmonetary relief such as an injunction or an equitable accounting. In cases at law, the federal Conformity Act of 1872, 17 Stat. 197, required that federal courts follow the procedures mandated by the respective state in which they sat. In equity proceedings, however, federal courts followed a uniform body of federal rules promulgated pursuant to the federal Process Act of 1792, 1 Stat. 275.

The choice of which substantive law to apply in a federal court was even more complicated. With respect to federal question or arising-under cases, federal law provided the relevant legal standards for most such cases, but in diversity suits the law to be applied combined elements of state law and federal judge-made law. More particularly, while federal courts sitting in diversity were generally required to apply state constitutional, statutory, and local customary law, they were not required to follow state judge-made or common law. This meant that a federal judge sitting in Georgia adjudicating a tort claim that arose in Georgia would not necessarily apply Georgia common law to the claim. Instead, the federal judge would be free to look to general principles of the common law that were thought to transcend state lines. As a consequence, the accident of diversity jurisdiction often provided federal court litigants a different body of governing law than would be applied by a state court of the forum state. Not surprisingly, this potential disparity led to abuse, unfairness, and forum shopping between the federal and state courts.

These complications can be traced to *Swift v. Tyson*, 41 U.S. (16 Pet.) 1 (1842). The precise issue presented in *Swift* was whether an individual who had purchased a bill of exchange (a type of promissory note) for value and in good faith could be barred from recovering on the bill due to the original holder's fraud. Under New York common law, the person obligated on the bill could raise the fraud defense even against a bona fide purchaser, while under general principles of common law, at least as perceived by the Supreme Court, he could not. The Court held that the federal trial court was free to ignore the common law of New York and instead apply its own view of general common law.

In arriving at this conclusion, the *Swift* Court construed and applied § 34 of the Judiciary Act of 1789. That section (now referred to as the Rules of Decision Act (RDA) and codified at 28 U.S.C. § 1652) provided: "[T]he laws of the several states, except where the Constitution, treaties, or statutes of the United States otherwise require or provide, shall be regarded as rules of decision in trials at common law, in the Courts of the United States, in cases where they apply." Judiciary Act of 1789, ch. 20, 1 Stat. 73, § 34 (codified as amended at 28 U.S.C. § 1652). Given this language, why was a federal court allowed to ignore state common law decisions? Simple: According to the *Swift* Court, the word "laws" as used in the RDA did not embrace state common law decisions:

> In the ordinary use of language, it will hardly be contended, that the decisions of courts constitute laws. They are, at most, only evidence of what the laws are, and are not, of themselves, laws. They are often reexamined, reversed, and qualified by the

courts themselves, whenever they are found to be either defective, or ill-founded, or otherwise incorrect. The laws of a state are more usually understood to mean the rules and enactments promulgated by the legislative authority thereof, or long-established local customs having the force of laws. In all the various cases, which have hitherto come before us for decision, this court have uniformly supposed, that the true interpretation of the 34th section limited its application to state laws, strictly local, that is to say, to the positive statutes of the state, and the construction thereof adopted by the local tribunals, and to rights and titles to things having a permanent locality, such as the rights and titles to real estate, and other matters immovable and intra-territorial in their nature and character. It never has been supposed by us, that the section did apply, or was designed to apply, to questions of a more general nature, not at all dependent upon local statues or local usages of a fixed and permanent operation, as, for example, to the construction of ordinary contracts or other written instruments, and especially to questions of general commercial law, where the state tribunals are called upon to perform the like functions as ourselves, that is, to ascertain, upon general reasoning and legal analogies, what is the true exposition of the contract or instrument, or what is the just rule furnished by the principles of commercial law to govern the case. And we have not now the slightest difficulty in holding, that this section, upon its true intendment and construction, is strictly limited to local statutes and local usages of the character before stated, and does not extend to contracts and other instruments of a commercial nature, the true interpretation and effect whereof are to be sought, not in the decisions of the local tribunals, but in the general principles and doctrines of commercial jurisprudence.

Swift, 41 U.S. at 18-19. In short, while the RDA required a federal court to follow state statutes and certain fixed local customs, there was no such requirement with respect to state common law.

Justice Story, the author of the *Swift* opinion, had hoped that this new regime of federal general common law would promote uniformity throughout the nation, and particularly so in the area of commercial law. Federal courts would, in essence, help create a coherent body of modern law that would be uniform throughout the United States, thus promoting commerce and the development of an integrated nation-state.

Yet Story's vision of uniformity was not to be realized. The regime of *Swift*, which lasted just short of a hundred years, produced a body of law, sometimes referred to as federal general common law, which was anything but uniform or coherent. Nice and elusive distinctions were drawn between local matters, *i.e.*, those in which a federal court sitting in diversity would follow state decisional law, and general common law matters, *i.e.*, those in which the federal court could ignore state court decisions. For example, torts were deemed matters of general law, while most issues concerning real property were considered local. In addition, federal courts sometimes refused to honor state court interpretations of state constitutions and statutes, to the extent that those interpretations did not comport with what was perceived as the general common law. And to make matters even more confusing, federal courts created a body of general common law that was not even uniform within the federal sphere. Thus a tort recognized by one federal court would not necessarily be accepted by another. In short, despite its grand pretensions, the legacy of *Swift* was a chaotic system under which federal and state courts in the same state often applied different substantive principles to identical controversies involving what we now recognize as quintessential matters of state law. By the end of the nineteenth century, demands for *Swift*'s demise had become widespread.

2.   The Demise of "Federal General Common Law"

Erie Railroad Co. v. Tompkins
304 U.S. 64 (1938)

MR. JUSTICE BRANDEIS delivered the opinion of the Court.

The question for decision is whether the oft-challenged doctrine of *Swift v. Tyson*, [41 U.S. (16 Pet.) 1 (1842),] shall now be disapproved.

Tompkins, a citizen of Pennsylvania, was injured on a dark night by a passing freight train of the Erie Railroad Company while walking along its right of way at Hughestown in that state. He claimed that the accident occurred through negligence in the operation, or maintenance, of the train; that he was rightfully on the premises as licensee because on a commonly used beaten footpath which ran for a short distance alongside the tracks; and that he was struck by something which looked like a door projecting from one of the moving cars. To enforce that claim he brought an action in the federal court for Southern New York, which had jurisdiction because the company is a corporation of that state. It denied liability; and the case was tried by a jury.

The Erie insisted that its duty to Tompkins was no greater than that owed to a trespasser. It contended, among other things, that its duty to Tompkins, and hence its liability, should be determined in accordance with the Pennsylvania law; that under the law of Pennsylvania, as declared by its highest court, persons who use pathways along the railroad right of way—that is, a longitudinal pathway as distinguished from a crossing—are to be deemed trespassers; and that the railroad is not liable for injuries to undiscovered trespassers resulting from its negligence, unless it be wanton or willful. Tompkins denied that any such rule had been established by the decisions of the Pennsylvania courts; and contended that, since there was no statute of the state on the subject, the railroad's duty and liability is to be determined in federal courts as a matter of general law.

The trial judge refused to rule that the applicable law precluded recovery. The jury brought in a verdict of $30,000; and the judgment entered thereon was affirmed by the Circuit Court of Appeals, which held, 90 F.2d 603, 604 [2d Cir. 1937], that it was unnecessary to consider whether the law of Pennsylvania was as contended, because the question was one not of local, but of general, law, and that "upon questions of general law the federal courts are free, in absence of a local statute, to exercise their independent judgment as to what the law is; and it is well settled that the question of the responsibility of a railroad for injuries caused by its servants is one of general law. . . . Where the public has made open and notorious use of a railroad right of way for a long period of time and without objection, the company owes to persons on such permissive pathway a duty of care in the operation of its trains. . . . It is likewise generally recognized law that a jury may find that negligence exists toward a pedestrian using a permissive path on the railroad right of way if he is hit by some object projecting from the side of the train."

The Erie had contended that application of the Pennsylvania rule was required, among other things, by § 34 of the Federal Judiciary Act of September 24, 1789, which provides: "The laws of the several States, except where the Constitution, treaties, or statutes of the United States otherwise require or provide, shall be regarded as rules of decision in trials at common law, in the courts of the United States, in cases where they apply."

Because of the importance of the question whether the federal court was free to disregard the alleged rule of the Pennsylvania common law, we granted certiorari.

First. Swift v. Tyson held that federal courts exercising jurisdiction on the ground of diversity of citizenship need not, in matters of general jurisprudence, apply the unwritten law of the state as declared by its highest court; that they are free to exercise an independent judgment as to what the common law of the state is — or should be; . . .

. . . The federal courts assumed, in the broad field of "general law," the power to declare rules of decision which Congress was confessedly without power to enact as statutes. Doubt was repeatedly expressed as to the correctness of the construction given § 34, and as to the soundness of the rule which it introduced. But it was the more recent research of a competent scholar, who examined the original document, which established that the construction given to it by the Court was erroneous; and that the purpose of the section was merely to make certain that, in all matters except those in which some federal law is controlling, the federal courts exercising jurisdiction in diversity of citizenship cases would apply as their rules of decision the law of the state, unwritten as well as written.[5]

Criticism of the doctrine became widespread after the decision of *Black & White Taxicab Co. v. Brown & Yellow Taxicab Co.*, 276 U.S. 518 [(1928)]. There, Brown and Yellow, a Kentucky corporation owned by Kentuckians, and the Louisville and Nashville Railroad, also a Kentucky corporation, wished that the former should have the exclusive privilege of soliciting passenger and baggage transportation at the Bowling Green, Kentucky, railroad station; and that the Black and White, a competing Kentucky corporation, should be prevented from interfering with that privilege. Knowing that such a contract would be void under the common law of Kentucky, it was arranged that the Brown and Yellow reincorporate under the law of Tennessee, and that the contract with the railroad should be executed there. The suit was then brought by the Tennessee corporation in the federal court for western Kentucky to enjoin competition by the Black and White; an injunction issued by the District Court was sustained by the Court of Appeals;

5. Charles Warren, New Light on the History of the Federal Judiciary Act of 1789 (1923) 37 Harv. L. Rev. 49, 51-52, 81-88, 108.

and this Court, citing many decisions in which the doctrine of *Swift v. Tyson* had been applied, affirmed the decree.

Second. Experience in applying the doctrine of *Swift v. Tyson*, had revealed its defects, political and social; and the benefits expected to flow from the rule did not accrue. Persistence of state courts in their own opinions on questions of common law prevented uniformity; and the impossibility of discovering a satisfactory line of demarcation between the province of general law and that of local law developed a new well of uncertainties.

On the other hand, the mischievous results of the doctrine had become apparent. Diversity of citizenship jurisdiction was conferred in order to prevent apprehended discrimination in state courts against those not citizens of the state. *Swift v. Tyson* introduced grave discrimination by non-citizens against citizens. It made rights enjoyed under the unwritten "general law" vary according to whether enforcement was sought in the state or in the federal court; and the privilege of selecting the court in which the right should be determined was conferred upon the non-citizen. Thus, the doctrine rendered impossible equal protection of the law. In attempting to promote uniformity of law throughout the United States, the doctrine had prevented uniformity in the administration of the law of the State.

The discrimination resulting became in practice far-reaching. This resulted in part from the broad province accorded to the so-called "general law" as to which federal courts exercised an independent judgment. In addition to questions of purely commercial law, "general law" was held to include the obligations under contracts entered into and to be performed within the State, the extent to which a carrier operating within a State may stipulate for exemption from liability for his own negligence or that of his employee; the liability for torts committed within the State upon persons resident or property located there, even where the question of liability depended upon the scope of a property right conferred by the State; and the right to exemplary or punitive damages. Furthermore, state decisions construing local deeds, mineral conveyances, and even devises of real estate, were disregarded.

In part the discrimination resulted from the wide range of persons held entitled to avail themselves of the federal rule by resort to the diversity of citizenship jurisdiction. Through this jurisdiction individual citizens willing to remove from their own state and become citizens of another might avail themselves of the federal rule. And, without even change of residence, a corporate citizen of the State could avail itself of the federal rule by reincorporating under the laws of another State, as was done in the *Taxicab* case.

The injustice and confusion incident to the doctrine of *Swift v. Tyson* have been repeatedly urged as reasons for abolishing or limiting diversity of citizenship jurisdiction. Other legislative relief has been proposed. If only a question of statutory construction were involved, we should not be prepared to abandon a doctrine so widely applied throughout nearly a century. But the unconstitutionality of the course pursued has now been made clear and compels us to do so.

Third. Except in matters governed by the Federal Constitution or by Acts of Congress, the law to be applied in any case is the law of the State. And whether the law of the State shall be declared by its Legislature in a statute or by its highest court in a decision is not a matter of federal concern. There is no federal general common law. Congress has no power to declare substantive rules of common law applicable in a State whether they be local in their nature or "general," be they commercial law or a part of the law of torts. And no clause in the Constitution purports to confer such a power upon the federal courts. As stated by Mr. Justice Field when protesting in *Baltimore & Ohio R. Co. v. Baugh*, 149 U.S. 368, 401 [(1893)], against ignoring the Ohio common law of fellow-servant liability: "I am aware that what has been termed the general law of the country—which is often little less than what the judge advancing the doctrine thinks at the time should be the general law on a particular subject—has been often advanced in judicial opinions of this court to control a conflicting law of a State. I admit that learned judges have fallen into the habit of repeating this doctrine as a convenient mode of brushing aside the law of a State in conflict with their views. And I confess that, moved and governed by the authority of the great names of those judges, I have, myself, in many instances, unhesitatingly and confidently, but I think now erroneously, repeated the same doctrine. But, notwithstanding the great names which may be cited in favor of the doctrine, and notwithstanding the frequency with which the doctrine has been reiterated, there stands, as a perpetual protest against its repetition, the Constitution of the United States, which recognizes and preserves the autonomy and independence of the States—independence in their legislative and independence in their judicial departments. Supervision over either the legislative or the judicial action of the States is in no case permissible except as to matters by the Constitution specifically authorized or delegated to the United States. Any interference with either, except as thus permitted, is an invasion of the authority of the State, and, to that extent, a denial of its independence."

The fallacy underlying the rule declared in *Swift v. Tyson* is made clear by Mr. Justice Holmes. The doctrine rests upon the assumption that there is "a transcendental body of law outside of any particular State but obligatory within it unless and until changed by statute," that federal courts have the power to use their judgment as to what the rules of common law are; and that in the federal courts "the parties are entitled to an independent judgment on matters of general law":

> "But law in the sense in which courts speak of it today does not exist without some definite authority behind it. The common law so far as it is enforced in a State, whether called common law or not, is not the common law generally but the law of that State existing by the authority of that State without regard to what it may have been in England or anywhere else.

* * *

> "The authority and only authority is the State, and if that be so, the voice adopted by the State as its own [whether it be of its Legislature or of its Supreme Court] should utter the last word."

Thus the doctrine of *Swift v. Tyson* is, as Mr. Justice Holmes said, "an unconstitutional assumption of powers by the Courts of the United States which no lapse of time or respectable array of opinion should make us hesitate to correct." In disapproving that doctrine we do not hold unconstitutional § 34 of the Federal Judiciary Act of 1789 or any other Act of Congress. We merely declare that in applying the doctrine this Court and the lower courts have invaded rights which in our opinion are reserved by the Constitution to the several States.

Fourth. The defendant contended that by the common law of Pennsylvania as declared by its highest court in *Falchetti v. Pennsylvania R. Co.*, 307 Pa. 203; 160 A. 859, the only duty owed to the plaintiff was to refrain from willful or wanton injury. The plaintiff denied that such is the Pennsylvania law. In support of their respective contentions the parties discussed and cited many decisions of the Supreme Court of the State. The Circuit Court of Appeals ruled that the question of liability is one of general law; and on that ground declined to decide the issue of state law. As we hold this was error, the judgment is reversed and the case remanded to it for further proceedings in conformity with our opinion.

Reversed.

Mr. Justice Cardozo took no part in the consideration or decision of this case.

Mr. Justice Butler (dissenting) [joined by Mr. Justice McReynolds] . . . .

Mr. Justice Reed (concurring in part).

I concur in the conclusion reached in this case, in the disapproval of the doctrine of *Swift v. Tyson*, and in the reasoning of the majority opinion, except in so far as it relies upon the unconstitutionality of the "course pursued" by the federal courts.

The "doctrine of *Swift v. Tyson*," as I understand it, is that the words "the laws," as used in § 34, line one, of the Federal Judiciary Act of September 24, 1789, do not include in their meaning "the decisions of the local tribunals." Mr. Justice Story, in deciding that point, said, "Undoubtedly, the decisions of the local tribunals upon such subjects are entitled to, and will receive, the most deliberate attention and respect of this court; but they cannot furnish positive rules, or conclusive authority, by which our own judgments are to be bound up and governed."

To decide the case now before us and to "disapprove" the doctrine of *Swift v. Tyson* requires only that we say that the words "the laws" include in their meaning the decisions of the local tribunals. As the majority opinion shows, by its reference to Mr. Warren's researches and the first quotation from Mr. Justice Holmes, that this Court is now of the view that "laws" includes "decisions," it is unnecessary to go further and declare that the "course pursued" was "unconstitutional," instead of merely erroneous . . . .

NOTES AND QUESTIONS

1. Interpreting Erie. The precise holding in *Erie* is quite simple: Federal courts sitting in diversity must follow the substantive legal standards imposed by state law, including the state's common law. This makes sense. Claims brought in diversity are by definition state-created and the accident of diversity jurisdiction does not alter the fundamental state law character of the underlying rights and obligations. This holding is now so interwoven with modern federal practice that in most diversity cases *Erie* merits at best a passing reference.

Despite the relative simplicity of the *Erie* holding, the underlying rationales for the decision may be somewhat elusive. Clearly, there was something more at stake than the reversal of an erroneous statutory construction. At its core, *Erie* rejects the notion that the common law represents a transcendent body of principles that can be discovered through pure reason. Rather, the common law, like all law, is seen as nothing more than the product of legitimate sovereign power. In other words, law is made, not discovered. And the common law is judge-made law. From this perspective, the "unconstitutional course" pursued under the regime of *Swift* becomes more apparent. Under the reserved powers doctrine, a doctrine you will examine in more detail in your course on Constitutional Law, the federal government is deemed to be one of limited powers, which means it may exercise only those powers expressly granted to it. All other government powers are reserved to the people or to the states. Since there is no expressly granted federal power to create basic tort law, that power is reserved to the people or to the states. In other words, the federal government lacks the sovereign authority to make such law.

The *Swift* doctrine had invited federal courts to violate this principle of federalism by allowing them to create what was in essence state law. Moreover, even when the general common law created by the federal courts under *Swift* happened to parallel the federal government's lawmaking power (*e.g.*, liability standards for interstate railroads), that lawmaking power was given by the Constitution to Congress, not to the courts. Therefore, for the courts to exercise such lawmaking authority would violate the principle of separation of powers.

2. *Which state's law applies?*   The Court in *Erie* held that a federal court sitting in diversity must apply the substantive law of the state. But the law of which state? The complaint in *Erie* was filed in a federal court in New York. The accident, however, had taken place in Pennsylvania. Did New York or Pennsylvania law apply? Such choice-of-law dilemmas occur whenever all or part of the activity that gives rise to a claim has taken place in a state other than the one in which the suit is filed. To resolve such conflicts, state courts refer to their own so-called choice-of-law principles. On the facts of *Erie*, a New York state court might well conclude that under New York choice-of-law principles, Pennsylvania tort law should apply since the accident occurred in Pennsylvania. The *Erie* Court assumed (largely because the parties had done so as well) that on remand the New York federal district court would apply the law of Pennsylvania. But had the parties disagreed on the applicability of Pennsylvania law, what principles would the federal district court have relied on to resolve that dispute?

In *Klaxon Co. v. Stentor Electric Manufacturing Co.*, 313 U.S. 487 (1941), the Supreme Court answered that question. At issue in *Klaxon* was a contract dispute between a New York company and a Delaware company. Suit was filed in the federal district court for the District of Delaware. The parties disagreed over whether New York or Delaware law applied to the underlying contractual dispute. *Klaxon* held that a federal district court must apply the choice-of-law principles followed by the courts of the forum state. Thus the federal district court sitting in

Delaware was required to apply the same choice-of-law principles that a Delaware state court would apply. That did not mean that Delaware substantive law necessarily applied to the underlying controversy. Rather, it meant that the federal district court would apply the same substantive law as would a Delaware state court. Therefore, if a Delaware court would apply New York law to the contractual dispute, a federal district court sitting in Delaware must do the same.

After *Klaxon*, we can restate the *Erie* rule as follows: A federal district court exercising jurisdiction over a state-law claim must apply the same substantive law as would be applied by the courts of the state in which the federal district court sits. A federal district court sitting in State X thus does not necessarily apply State X substantive law. Rather, it applies the substantive law that a State X court would use. *See generally* 19 Charles Alan Wright, Arthur R. Miller & Edward H. Cooper, Federal Practice and Procedure § 4506 (2d ed. 1996 & Supp. 2015).

3. *Determining the content of state law.*   Once a federal court determines which state's law to apply in a diversity case, the court must then ascertain the content of that law. In many cases this task is relatively easy. The court merely refers to the appropriate sources of state law — state constitutions, statutes, administrative rules, and judicial decisions — and attempts to predict how the state's highest court would currently rule on the point presented. If the federal court discovers a dispositive answer, say a recent decision by the state's highest court, the federal court will simply apply that law to the controversy. The problem becomes more complicated when there is no dispositive state law. This most often occurs when the state's highest court has yet to decide the question presented. It may also occur when although the question has been decided, time and later developments in the law have since eroded that earlier decision's precedential value. Remember, the goal is to predict what the state's highest court would do if it were confronted with the issue today.

To alleviate the difficulty of accurate prediction under such circumstances, many states provide a method through which a federal court may certify an open question of state law to the state's highest court. *See* Uniform Certification of Questions of Law Act § 3 (1995) ("The [Supreme Court] of this State may answer a question of law certified to it by a court of the United States . . . if the answer may be determinative of an issue in pending litigation in the certifying court and there is no controlling appellate decision, constitutional provision, or statute of this State."). While federal courts take different approaches as to when certification is appropriate, some judges have suggested that as a matter of federalism, certification should occur "whenever there is a question of state law that is even possibly in doubt . . . ." Guido Calabresi, *Federal and State Courts: Restoring a Workable Balance*, 78 N.Y.U. L. Rev. 1293, 1301 (2003). When a federal court does certify a question, it will sometimes express its own tentative view on the issue, thereby relieving the state high court of the need to address the matter if it agrees with the provisional federal resolution. *See Briggs Ave. LLC v. Insurance Corp. of Hanover*, 516 F.3d 42 (2d Cir. 2008). If the state high court accepts certification, once it has answered the certified question, the federal court then proceeds to resolve the controversy in accord with that answer. See, e.g., Briggs Ave. LLC v. Insurance Corp. of Hanover, 550 F.3d 246 (2d Cir. 2008) (per curiam opinion affirming district judgment after state high court accepted certification and answered the certified question as the district court had).

In states in which certification is not available or when it is not appropriate under the circumstances, the federal court remains under a duty to resolve the case. In essence, it must use the best available information to predict the current content of state law. This requires a careful reading of all relevant sources of state law, including patterns in high court opinions, dicta from those opinions, information in concurring and dissenting opinions, and even the opinions of lower state courts or of the courts in sister states. While none of these sources is binding in a technical sense, they all may provide useful guidance in determining the scope of a state's law. Keep in mind that the goal is not to construct the "best" law for the state, but to predict how the state's highest court would now rule. Given that the federal prediction of state law is not revisable by state appellate courts in the particular case, the federal court must take special care to neither expand nor contract the scope of state law. Instead, it must remain true to *Erie* and attempt to decide the case in accord with state law as filtered through the predicted vantage point of the state's highest court. *See generally* 19 WRIGHT, MILLER & COOPER, *supra*, § 4507.

PROBLEMS

6-1. Alice designs interactive web pages for small businesses. Her company, Alice's Cyberspace Restaurant, is located outside Providence, Rhode Island. Alice entered a contract with Cowpatty Burgers, a fast-food chain doing business in southwest Virginia. The contract was negotiated over the internet and signed by the parties in their respective states. Under the agreement, Alice was to receive a set fee for designing a web page promoting "the world" of Cowpatty Burgers. After completing the project according to contractual specifications, Alice e-mailed a bill for services rendered to Cowpatty Burgers. The client, however, refused to pay, claiming that it no longer needed a website, the market for cowpatties having dried up. Alice has filed a breach of contract suit against Cowpatty Burgers in a federal district court in Roanoke, Virginia. Assume that the requisites of diversity jurisdiction and venue have been satisfied. How is the federal district court to determine which body of substantive law to apply to this dispute? Would your answer be different if the suit had been filed in a federal court sitting in Rhode Island? Does it matter that Virginia choice-of-law principles and Rhode Island choice-of-law principles might lead to the application of different bodies of substantive law?

6-2. Two semi-trucks collided on an interstate highway in Illinois. The driver of one truck left his vehicle in the lane of traffic. The driver of the other truck pulled onto the shoulder. Minutes later a pickup truck driven by K collided with the truck parked in the lane of traffic, killing K. K's wife filed a diversity suit in an Illinois federal district court against the drivers of both trucks, arguing that their negligence in colliding with one another was a proximate cause of her husband's death. The Illinois Supreme Court has never decided whether a driver's negligence in causing one accident can be treated as the proximate cause of a subsequent accident. Nor are there any Illinois statutes on point. Three intermediate Illinois appellate courts have, however, addressed this issue. The first such decision was in 1966 and the most recent one was in 1988. In all three decisions the respective courts found that proximate cause could be established under such circumstances. In this case, the defendant drivers have moved to dismiss the wife's wrongful death suit for failure to state a claim. What should the federal district court do? *See Knoblauch v. DEF Express Corp.*, 86 F.3d 684 (7th Cir. 1996).

C.   A Survey of the Three-Track Approach to the *Erie* Doctrine

The primary question explored in this section involves how one resolves conflicts between federal procedural law and state substantive law. We have already established that federal courts sitting in diversity generally apply state substantive law and federal procedural law. But what happens when federal procedural law conflicts with state substantive law? Which trumps the other? *Erie* did not directly address these questions since no such conflict existed there, the Court having found that the purported federal standard was invalid as a matter of the reserved powers doctrine. Yet such conflicts do arise, and their resolution depends in part on whether the conflicting federal procedure derives from a federal statute, from a federal rule, or from federal judge-made law. There are, in essence, three tracks of analysis, one for resolving each type of conflict.

The three-track model is founded on the Supremacy Clause of the U.S. Constitution, which provides:

> This Constitution, and the Laws of the United States which shall be made in Pursuance thereof; and all Treaties made, or which shall be made, under the Authority of the United States, shall be the supreme Law of the Land; and the Judges in every State shall be bound thereby, any Thing in the Constitution or Laws of any State to the Contrary notwithstanding.

U.S. CONST. art. VI, cl. 2. This language translates into a fundamental principle of our constitutional system of government: State law must conform to the dictates of the U.S. Constitution, and must yield to *constitutionally* valid federal law whenever a conflict between state and federal law arises. This is true for all varieties of federal law, both substantive and procedural. The principle applies in federal question cases, diversity cases, and cases filed in state courts. Regardless of the context, valid federal law is the supreme law of the land and trumps any state law to the contrary. *Erie* did not hold otherwise. According to *Erie*, the flaw in the regime of *Swift v. Tyson* was that the federal general common law was constitutionally invalid, *i.e.*, not in pursuance of the Constitution. This constitutionally invalid "federal general common law" could not trump contrary state law. The Rules of Decision Act, 28 U.S.C § 1652 (the modern, codified version of § 34 of the Judiciary Act of 1789), as reinterpreted by the *Erie* Court, was to the same effect, for it requires federal courts to apply state law as the "rule of decision" in the absence of any valid conflicting federal law.

This section presents an overview of the three-track model, as informed by the Supremacy Clause, and should provide you with a basic understanding of how that model operates within the federal judicial system. In the next section, we will examine each of the tracks in detail.

As noted, the separate tracks are a product of the type of procedural law at issue. Track One pertains to federal statutes; Track Two pertains to formal federal rules; and Track Three pertains to judge-made doctrines. In this sense, the tracks are technically distinct and, as a consequence, each track has its own unique characteristics. Yet the commonalities among the tracks may be more significant than the differences. Those commonalities are a consequence of the fact that each of the tracks, in its own way, attempts to answer the same two questions: First, is there truly a conflict between the federal procedural law at issue and some provision of state law? And, second, assuming there is such a conflict, is the federal law valid? It is with respect to this latter question that the tracks diverge slightly from one another. Most importantly, however, if the two fundamental questions (conflict and validity) are answered affirmatively, regardless of which track, the result is the same: The federal law must be applied as a matter of federal supremacy. Let's begin with the first question.

1.   Is There a Conflict?

Regardless of the type of federal procedural law at issue, we must initially determine whether any perceived conflict between that law and state law is a real conflict, for if there is in fact no such conflict, the choice-of-law problem disappears and the federal court simply applies the federal law in question. As noted above, this "real conflict" determination is made in an identical fashion regardless of whether we are dealing with a federal statute, a formal federal rule, or federal judge-made law. In other words, in this respect, the three tracks do not diverge from one another.

The real-conflict inquiry consists of three steps: (1) identify the potential conflict, (2) identify the issue to be resolved, and (3) determine whether the federal standard is sufficiently broad to control resolution of that issue. Consider three examples:

Example 1: State X law provides that citizens of State X have an absolute right to a state court forum in State X for adjudicating claims that arise under State X law (the "State X forum law"). P, a citizen of State X, sues D, a citizen of State Y, in a State X court on a breach of contract claim arising under State X law. The amount in controversy exceeds $100,000. D files a timely and procedurally proper petition for removal to federal court under 28 U.S.C. §§ 1441(a), 1446. After the case is removed, P files a motion to remand, arguing that the State X forum law controls and that the case must be returned to state court. There is clearly a potential conflict between federal and state law since federal law appears to permit removal while State X law guarantees P a state court forum. Is that conflict real? To answer that question we must identify the issue presented to the district court and ask whether § 1441(a) is sufficiently broad to control resolution of that issue. The issue presented is whether D was entitled to remove the case to federal court. Section 1441(a) provides that a defendant may remove a case to federal court if the district court would have "original jurisdiction" over that case. Courts have interpreted this provision to mean that a defendant may remove a case to federal court if that case could have been filed in federal court as an original matter. Given that interpretation, it would seem that § 1441(a) is sufficiently broad to control the issue presented—*i.e.*, whether D was entitled to remove the case to federal court. In short, the potential conflict is a real conflict.

Example 2: The service of process standards of State X provide that in all lawsuits brought against an estate, the executor of the estate must be served by "delivering a copy of the summons and complaint to the executor personally," within one year of the incident that gave rise to the lawsuit. Federal Rule of Civil Procedure 4(e)(2)(B) allows service on an individual by "leaving a copy of [the summons and complaint] at the individual's dwelling or usual place of abode with someone of suitable age and discretion who resides there." P, a citizen of State Y, filed a diversity suit in a federal court sitting in State X against the estate of a driver who was involved in an automobile accident with P. The accident took place in State X, and both the decedent and the executor of the estate reside in State X. P effected service on the executor within one year of the accident in accord with Rule 4(e)(2)(B) by leaving a copy of the summons and complaint with the executor's spouse at the executor's home. After being so served and 13 months after the accident, the executor filed a motion to quash service of process, arguing that under State X law she was entitled to personal service within one year of the accident, which she had not received. There is a potential conflict between the federal and state laws since Rule 4(e)(2)(B) appears to permit a form of substituted service while state law does not. Is that conflict real? To answer that question we must identify the issue presented to the district court and ask whether Rule 4(e)(2)(B) is sufficiently broad to control its resolution. The issue presented to the district court is whether service on the executor's spouse was proper. Rule 4(e)(2)(B) specifically allows for this method of service. The rule is, therefore, sufficiently broad to resolve the issue presented. Given that the state rule is to the contrary, the potential conflict is a real conflict.

Example 3: P was injured in State X while employed by Subcontractor on a project undertaken by Subcontractor on behalf of D. P sued D for negligence, claiming that D was responsible for P's injuries. D countered by arguing that P should be treated as D's "statutory employee" within the meaning of the State X workers' compensation law, thereby precluding P from receiving any compensation from D other than that provided by the workers' compensation law. P's suit was filed in a federal court in State X under that court's diversity jurisdiction. In federal court, even though the Seventh Amendment does not guaranty a right to jury trial in such cases, by virtue of tradition and practice, the decision as to whether P was a statutory employee would be allocated to the jury as a mixed question of law and fact. In a State X court, however, a judge would decide that issue. Given these differing allocations of decision-making authority, there is at least a potential conflict between the federal and state standards. Is the conflict real? To answer that question we must identify the issue presented to the district court and ask whether the federal judge-made (tradition and practice) allocation is sufficiently broad to control resolution of that issue. The issue presented is whether a jury or a judge should decide a particular mixed question of law and fact. The federal principle clearly allocates that authority to the jury. The federal principle is, therefore, sufficiently broad to control that issue. The conflict is real.

Notice that the approach in each of these examples is identical (obsessively so!) even though the first example involves a federal statute (28 U.S.C. § 1441(b)), the second involves a formal federal rule (Rule 4(e)(2)(B)), and the third involves federal judge-made law (the traditional allocation of decision-making authority between judge and jury). In each situation, we

- identified a potential conflict between federal procedural law and state law;
- identified the issue to be resolved; and
- determined whether the federal standard was sufficiently broad to control resolution of that issue, making the conflict with state law real.

If, in going through these steps, we find that the federal law is sufficiently broad to control resolution of the identified issue, we must then determine (in the next phase of the analysis) whether the federal law is valid. On the other hand, if we conclude that the federal law is not sufficiently broad to control, the inquiry is at an end since there is no relevant federal law to apply. In that event—*i.e.*, in the absence of a real conflict—state law controls.

In each of the above examples, we concluded that the federal law was sufficiently broad to control. Do not, however, assume that this will always be the case. In many instances, the potentially applicable federal principle will not speak to the issue presented. In fact, a court might interpret an ambiguous federal standard narrowly to avoid a conflict with state law. Consider the following example:

> P filed a tort claim against D in a federal court sitting in State X, properly invoking that court's diversity jurisdiction. While P filed her complaint within the applicable State X statute of limitations, she did not serve D until after that limitations period had run. Under State X law, a statute of limitations is not tolled until the defendant has been properly served. Relying on this provision of state law, D filed a motion to dismiss, arguing that P's claim was time barred. In objecting to D's motion, P relies on Rule 3 of the Federal Rules of Civil Procedure, which provides, "A civil action is commenced by filing a complaint with the court." She argues that under Rule 3, commencement of the suit (*i.e.*, filing a complaint with the court) tolls any applicable statute of limitations. There is a potential conflict between Rule 3, as so interpreted, and the State X rule that requires service for purposes of tolling. The issue presented is whether the statute of limitations was tolled when P filed her complaint. The question, therefore, is whether Rule 3 is sufficiently broad to control resolution of that issue. The text of the rule is at least ambiguous in this regard, for it makes no mention of either "tolling" or "statutes of limitations." The word "commences" could embrace the concept of tolling, but that interpretation is

far from necessary. In a similar case, the Supreme Court held that Rule 3 was not sufficiently broad to control the question of whether the statute of limitations had been tolled, perhaps, in part, to avoid the potential conflict with state law. *Walker v. Armco Steel Corp.*, 446 U.S. 740 (1980). In short, the potential conflict was not a real conflict.

In sum, in every case in which you perceive a potential conflict between a federal procedural law (whether a statute, a formal rule, or judge-made law), you must carefully examine that perception, using the above three-step formula, to determine whether the conflict is in fact real. If there is a real conflict, you will then test the validity of the federal law, under standards described below. If there is no conflict, you may apply the state law (as was done in the *Walker* case cited in the last example above).

2.   Is the Federal Law Valid?

At this step of the inquiry, we assume that the perceived conflict between federal and state law is real. That being the case, we must determine whether the federal law is valid. If it is, then under principles of federal supremacy, the federal law must be applied; if it is not valid, then it may not be applied, in which case we would again turn to state law as the rule of decision.

At this stage of our analysis, the tracks diverge, for the measure of validity as to each type of federal procedural law differs. We will see, however, that despite the technical differences, the seemingly distinct measures of validity also share much in common.

Track One: The Validity of Federal Procedural Statutes

Articles I and III of the Constitution vest Congress with the power to create courts inferior to the Supreme Court and to regulate the procedures followed in those courts. We have seen numerous examples of such procedural statutes, such as those pertaining to subject matter jurisdiction (28 U.S.C. §§ 1331, 1332, 1367, 1441) and venue (*id.* §§ 1391, 1404(a), 1406(a)).

In general, every measure enacted by Congress must fall within the defined scope of an enumerated power vested in Congress by the Constitution. With respect to the power to create federal procedural law, the scope of congressional authority is quite broad. Any exercise of that authority will be upheld if the enacted provision is "rationally classifiable" as procedural. That does not mean that the measure must be clearly procedural, but only that a member of Congress could rationally have concluded that it was. Keep in mind that a statute can be rationally classifiable as being both procedural and substantive and still fall within the defined scope of the congressional power to create federal procedural law. In essence, the potential characterization of the law as "substantive" is irrelevant so long as the law is also rationally classifiable as procedural. Thus we never ask whether the measure is substantive, or whether it might more properly be considered substantive, or even whether application of the federal statute will affect a substantive right. Instead, the sole focus of the inquiry is on the potential rationality of the procedural characterization. Not surprisingly, no ostensibly procedural federal statute has ever failed this very low threshold test.

Although the odds are slim that you will ever come across a federal statute that purports to be procedural but that is not rationally classifiable as such, you must, whenever the issue arises, explain why the particular statute under consideration satisfies the rationally-classifiable test. (In other words, don't skip this part of the analysis.) To perform this task, simply ask yourself how the statute operates within the federal procedural system. What does it do? For example, 28 U.S.C. § 1404(a) permits the transfer of a case from one proper venue to another proper venue if the district court concludes that the case may be more conveniently or efficiently litigated in the second venue. Section 1404(a) thus operates within the procedural system as a method through which to assess and promote the relative convenience or efficiency of alternate venues. As such, § 1404(a) is rationally classifiable as procedural, for it operates only within the federal litigation system and at least arguably (rationally) promotes fairness and efficiency within that system.

Given that virtually all real-world federal procedural statutes will easily satisfy the rationally classifiable test, it is all the more important that you carefully consider the initial real-conflict inquiry, for in Track One that is most likely where the battle over which law to apply, federal or state, will be won or lost.

For an instructive case on Track One, see *Stewart Organization, Inc. v. Ricoh Corp.*, 487 U.S. 22 (1988), at page 490, *infra*; *see also* Problems 6-3 and 6-4, at pages 496-497, *infra*.

Track Two: The Validity of Formal Federal Procedural Rules

The 1934 Rules Enabling Act (REA), 20 U.S.C. § 2072, delegated to the Supreme Court a broad authority to prescribe rules of "practice and procedure" for cases in inferior federal courts—district courts and courts of appeals. The REA further provides, however, that "[s]uch rules shall not abridge, enlarge or modify any substantive right." The Supreme Court promulgated both the Federal Rules of Civil Procedure (FRCP) and the Federal Rules of Appellate Procedure (FRAP) under the authority vested in it by the REA.

The validity of a rule promulgated pursuant to the REA requires a two-step inquiry that is designed to ensure that the rule at issue is consistent with the REA's delegation of rulemaking authority to the Court. Consistent with that delegation, any such rule must (step one) be a rule of practice or procedure (*see* § 2072(a)) that (step two) does not abridge, enlarge, or modify any substantive right (*see* § 2072(b)).

The step-one inquiry is virtually identical to the rationally-classifiable-as-procedural test used to measure the validity of federal procedural statutes. This makes sense given that the power delegated to the Supreme Court by Congress is the congressional power to create procedural law for inferior federal courts. Hence step one of the REA analysis replicates the Track One validity test, and just as no statute has ever fallen victim to that low-threshold test, no formal federal rule has ever failed to satisfy step one of the Track Two test. But as was true in Track One, a careful lawyer, judge, or student will still address this question by explaining how the rule at issue operates within the federal procedural system.

Step two of the REA analysis requires a slight change of perspective. Here we ask whether a rule that we've already concluded to be rationally classifiable as procedural might nonetheless abridge, enlarge, or modify a substantive right. As we know from the preceding discussion of Track One, federal procedural statutes are not subject to such an inquiry. Congress, however, apparently wanted to impose a limitation on its delegation of rulemaking authority, one that would help ensure that the rules promulgated by the Supreme Court pursuant to its delegated authority did not inadvertently cross the line between procedure and substance. In short, a congressional statute may cross that line; a rule promulgated by the Supreme Court may not.

We begin step two of the REA analysis by asking whether there is a substantive right that might be abridged, enlarged, or modified by the federal rule at issue. Typically, this will be the substantive right underlying the plaintiff's claim—*e.g.*, the right to enforce contractual obligations or the right to enforce the standards of negligence. We then ask whether the federal rule has altered that right in some significant fashion. More specifically, has the rule changed any of the elements of that claim? Or has it altered the remedies, including any applicable time limitations, available for that claim's enforcement? Keep in mind, we are not asking whether the rule has simply affected the claim in some way but whether the rule has significantly altered the nature or enforceability of that claim. It will be a rare federal rule that crosses this line, in part because the federal rules carry a strong presumption of validity. Indeed, the Supreme Court has never found a federal rule to have violated this principle—remember, it's the Supreme Court that promulgates these rules!—and lower court cases finding such a violation have been few and far between.

Let's consider an example. Recall Example 2 above, in which state law required personal service on an executor, while Federal Rule 4(e)(2)(B) permitted service at the executor's usual place of abode. We concluded that the federal rule was sufficiently broad to control resolution of the issue presented—the propriety of service—and that there was a real conflict between the state and federal rules. We must now ask whether Rule 4(e)(2)(B) is valid. To make this determination we apply the two-step approach mandated by the REA: Is the rule rationally classifiable as procedural (§ 2072(a))? If so, does the rule nonetheless abridge, enlarge, or modify a substantive right (§ 2072(b))? For the rule to be valid, the first question must be answered affirmatively (easy) and the second question must be answered negatively (relatively easy).

As to the first question, Rule 4(e)(2)(B) operates within the federal procedural system as a method through which to notify a defendant of a pending lawsuit against her and, as such, is rationally classifiable as procedural, for notice provides the defendant an opportunity to be heard. As to the second question, we must first identify the substantive right at issue; in this example, it would be the right to redress of personal injuries sustained in an automobile accident. Rule 4(e)(2)(B) does not change any elements of that right, does not alter the time frame within which a suit seeking redress for violation of that right may be brought, and does not alter the remedies available for redress of that right. It does have an effect on the parties' underlying rights and obligations, however, for if the executor ignores the summons, a default may be entered against the estate. But such an effect will not transgress the abridge-enlarge-modify proscription. And while we could say that the federal rule alters the executor's right to in-hand service, that is a procedural right—*i.e.*, a right that arises only in the context of litigation—and the REA does not preclude the alteration of state-created procedural rights. Rather, the abridge-enlarge-modify proscription applies only to significant alterations of substantive rights. In short, Rule 4(e)(2)(B) is valid, for it is rationally capable of being classified as procedural and it does not abridge, enlarge, or modify any substantive right.

Suppose, however, that Rule 4(e)(2)(B) permitted service on the executor after the lapse of the one-year limitation imposed by state law, so long as the case itself was filed within the applicable limitations period. (In the example, State X law required service on the executor within one year of the incident giving rise to the claim.) Would the federal rule, as so construed, remain valid under the terms of the REA? The rule would likely pass the low hurdle of the rationally classifiable test, since one could rationally conclude that an extended period of time for service of process post-filing would advance the orderly administration of justice by allowing the plaintiff sufficient time to effect proper service. Yet, even if this were so, the rule might nonetheless enlarge and modify a substantive right—*i.e.*, the right to recover from the estate. While the rule would not alter any elements of the underlying tort claim, it could significantly alter the time frame within which that claim may be asserted, for it could indefinitely extend that time frame beyond the one-year service limit imposed by state law. In essence, the federal rule would permit a claim to be vindicated through federal litigation even though the right to do so would have expired as a matter of state law prior to service of process. *See* Problem 6-10, at page 528, *infra*.

There is an important open question in Track Two. In 2010, a four-Justice plurality of the Supreme Court concluded that the abridge-enlarge-modify limitation imposed by the REA applied only to facial challenges to the federal rules and did not, therefore, permit any as-applied challenges to those rules based on a particular case's facts. *Shady Grove Orthopedic Assocs. v. Allstate Ins. Co.*, 559 U.S. 393 (2010); *see* page 516, *infra*. The basic idea behind the plurality's position was that the federal rules should be uniformly valid (or invalid) throughout the United States and not dependent on the nuances of state law or on the particular circumstances of the pending case. Given the careful process through which the federal rules are adopted, which includes extensive input from lawyers, judges, academics, and the public at large—both before the rules are promulgated and then before the promulgated rules can take effect—it is quite unlikely that a federal rule will ever, on its face, abridge, enlarge, or modify a substantive right. Hence, this approach would render the abridge-enlarge-modify limitation largely, if not completely, superfluous. Indeed, it eliminates any practical distinction between Track One and Track Two. One Justice, however, expressed strong disagreement with the plurality's approach, arguing that the REA's text clearly permits as-applied challenges to the federal rules. He noted, however, that a successful as-applied challenge to a federal rule would still be rare given the overall presumption of validity that attaches to the federal rules. Four other Justices did not address this issue. Hence we are left with an open question: May the validity of a federal rule be challenged on an as-applied basis? To be on the safe side of this equation, and until further instruction from the Supreme Court, one should proceed as if both facial and as-applied challenges are allowed, but be aware that the latter may not be permitted.

For an instructive case on Track Two, *see Hanna v. Plumer (Part I)*, 380 U.S. 460 (1965), at page 509, *infra*; *see also* Problem 6-7, at page 515, *infra*, and Problems 6-9 and 6-10, at pages 527-528, *infra*.

Track Three: The Validity of Judge-Made Procedural Law

Federal judges have an inherent authority to create and enforce principles of federal procedural law that address matters not controlled by the Constitution, statutes, or formal rules. Given the limited nature of this authority, the range within which such judge-made law operates tends to be circumscribed. There are, however, some significant aspects of federal procedure that remain dependent on doctrines of judge-made law. The doctrine of *forum non conveniens*, which we examined in Chapter V, part B, at page 450, *supra*, is one such example; the related doctrines of claim and issue preclusion, which are the topics of Chapter XIII, are another.

As was the case in Track Two, validity under Track Three requires applying a two-step inquiry. As to the first step, since the inherent judicial authority to make law in this context is an authority to make federal *procedural* law, it follows that the law created must, at the very least, be arguably procedural, for if it is not, the judge-made law does not fall within the vested power's scope. Yet, somewhat surprisingly, in addressing potential conflicts between federal judge-made procedural law and state law, courts rarely consider this preliminary point. In fact, there is no clearly established doctrinal test for assessing whether a principle of judge-made law can be properly characterized as procedural. Still, given the procedure-only limitation on the lawmaking authority at issue here, it would seem prudent to subject judge-made procedural law to the test we use to measure the validity of federal procedural statutes and formal rules. Thus we must ask whether the applicable principle of judge-made law is rationally classifiable as procedural.

Using the doctrine of *forum non conveniens* as an example, we might say that the doctrine is rationally classifiable as procedural for the same reasons that support the procedural rationality of 28 U.S.C. § 1404(a) — namely, that the doctrine of *forum non conveniens* provides a method through which a judge can determine whether a pending case would be more fairly, conveniently, and efficiently litigated in a different forum. In short, although this preliminary question is often overlooked, a careful lawyer (or student) will want to determine whether the judge-made law at issue can be properly characterized as procedural, for if it cannot be so characterized, it does not represent a valid exercise of the inherent judicial authority to create federal procedural law. (And even if it might fall within the scope of some other federal power, those are powers that the Constitution has assigned to the legislative or executive branch, not to the judiciary.)

Step two of our Track Three analysis assumes that the judge-made law is rationally classifiable as procedural and then asks whether, despite that characterization, the law nevertheless functions substantively in the sense that its application significantly alters the underlying substantive rights at issue in the case. You are right to think (if you do) that this sounds something like the abridge-enlarge-modify test used in Track Two (without the facial versus as-applied debate). Basically, both tests seek to measure the validity of an arguably procedural law (formal rule or judge-made law, respectively) by determining whether that law crosses, in some significant way, the line between procedure and substance. The method for doing so under Track Three is, however, somewhat different from that employed in Track Two.

The validity test that has emerged under Track Three is itself judge-made and has evolved through fits and starts over the past several decades. The current version, which appears firmly established, is sometimes referred to as the "refined outcome determinative test," or as pertaining to outcome determination "at the forum shopping stage." Essentially, this test asks us to view the case from a pre-filing point in time when the plaintiff is contemplating a choice between federal and state court. The question we then ask, having adopted the forum-shopping perspective, is whether a plaintiff confronted with this choice would choose the federal forum in order to gain a distinct, substantive advantage that would not be available in state court. Three examples should help clarify the nature of this inquiry.

First, let's return to our service of process example in which federal law permitted substituted service at the party's usual place of abode, while state law required personal service. Assume that the federal standard is not found in a formal rule but is a product of judge-made procedure. The refined outcome-determinative test requires that we ask, from the perspective of the plaintiff at the forum-shopping stage, whether the choice between these methods of service would lead a plaintiff to choose the federal forum in order to gain a substantive advantage that would be unavailable in the state forum. The answer here is clearly no. While a plaintiff may conclude that substituted service would be more convenient and perhaps less costly, nothing in that cost-benefit analysis pertains to the substance of the plaintiff's claim. No elements of the claim are changed, no remedies are altered, and there is no alteration of the time frame within which the suit may be brought. As such, the choice between the federal and state forums would not be deemed outcome determinative at the forum-shopping stage. Might the answer be different if the statute of limitations were about to run and the plaintiff knew that the defendant was out of the country on vacation?

Second, suppose that the plaintiff, a trust beneficiary, files a diversity case in a State X federal court seeking an equitable accounting of the trust's assets. In seeking that accounting, the plaintiff asserts that as a matter of State X law, the trustee breached its fiduciary duty to the trust beneficiaries. Suppose, too, that the suit was filed after the applicable State X statute of limitations had run. Should the federal court honor the State X statute of limitations, or may the federal court give the plaintiff the benefit of the federal judge-made doctrine of laches that would allow the case to proceed as a matter of equity? (You may want to consider whether there is a real conflict and, if so, whether the federal doctrine is rationally classifiable as procedural. We'll assume an affirmative answer to each of these inquiries.) Examining this conflict from the plaintiff's perspective at the forum-shopping stage, the plaintiff would clearly choose the federal forum over the state forum since the former is open to adjudicate the plaintiff's claim while the latter is not. Should this choice be deemed outcome determinative at the forum-shopping stage? Yes. There are two ways of explaining this conclusion. First, the federal judge-made doctrine of laches as applied in this case would operate (or function) to create a right under state law that was not otherwise enforceable as a matter of state law. This rationale invokes a classic application of the *Erie* principle that federal courts have no constitutional warrant to create or alter state law. Second, by in effect extending the State X statute of limitations, the federal judge-made doctrine of laches would significantly alter, *i.e.*, here extend, the enforceability of a state-created right. Regardless of which rationale we rely on, it should be clear that choice of the federal forum would give the plaintiff a significant substantive advantage that would not be available in state court.

Finally, suppose that federal judges are allowed, under a principle of judge-made law, to reduce the amount of a potentially excessive jury verdict, but only if the amount of the damages awarded can be said to "shock the conscience." This standard is highly deferential toward the jury's judgment, the consequence being that federal judges rarely alter jury-based damage awards. In State X courts, however, a judge must reduce the size of a jury-based damage award if the amount awarded "deviates materially" from damages awarded in similar cases. This state standard is far less deferential toward the jury and leads to larger and more frequent reductions of jury-based damage awards. In a diversity case filed in a federal court sitting in State X and to which State X substantive law applies, should the federal court, when faced with a motion to reduce the size of the jury verdict, apply the federal shocks-the-conscience standard or the State X deviates-materially standard? (Again, we will assume a real conflict and that the federal law principle is rationally classifiable as procedural.) Viewed from the forum-shopping stage, might the plaintiff choose the federal forum over the state forum in order to gain a potential substantive advantage? Arguably, yes. While this is not as clear a case of outcome determination at the forum-shopping stage as was the previous example in which the federal court door was "open" while the state court door was "shut," it is a much stronger case for finding outcome determination than was presented by the choice between different methods of service in the first example. Indeed, this third example falls somewhere between the first two.

The conclusions in these Track Three examples are reflective of controlling decisions by the Supreme Court. *Hanna v. Plumer (Part II)*, 380 U.S. 460 (1965) (service of process example), at page 534, *infra*; *Guaranty Trust Co. v. York*, 326 U.S. 99 (1945) (doctrine of laches example), at page 529, *infra*; and *Gasperini v. Center for Humanities, Inc.*, 518 U.S. 415 (1996) (reduction of jury verdict example), at page 538, *infra*. These examples thus provide a spectrum of possibilities that define the rough contours of the refined outcome-determinative test. The first example describes a situation in which the test is clearly not satisfied; hence the federal judge-made law is valid and must be applied. The second example describes a situation in which the test is clearly satisfied; hence the federal judge-made law may not be validly applied. The third example describes a situation that falls in between these two extremes; in the actual case, the Court in essence concluded that the state deviates-materially standard must be applied. You should use this spectrum of possibilities as a template against which to measure the application of the refined outcome-determinative test to other facts. *See also* Problem 6-14, at page 537, *infra*.

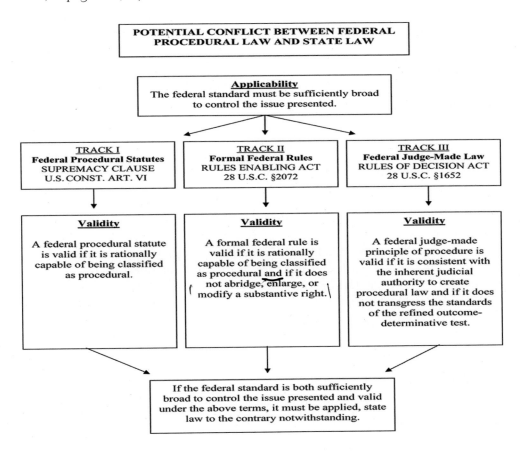

POTENTIAL CONFLICT BETWEEN FEDERAL PROCEDURAL LAW AND STATE LAW

Applicability
The federal standard must be sufficiently broad to control the issue presented.

TRACK I	**TRACK II**	**TRACK III**
Federal Procedural Statutes SUPREMACY CLAUSE U.S. CONST. ART. VI	**Formal Federal Rules** RULES ENABLING ACT 28 U.S.C. §2072	**Federal Judge-Made Law** RULES OF DECISION ACT 28 U.S.C. §1652

Validity

A federal procedural statute is valid if it is rationally capable of being classified as procedural.

Validity

A formal federal rule is valid if it is rationally capable of being classified as procedural and if it does not abridge, enlarge, or modify a substantive right.

Validity

A federal judge-made principle of procedure is valid if it is consistent with the inherent judicial authority to create procedural law and if it does not transgress the standards of the refined outcome-determinative test.

If the federal standard is both sufficiently broad to control the issue presented and valid under the above terms, it must be applied, state law to the contrary notwithstanding.

Note: "Validity" in each track presumes that the federal standard is otherwise constitutional in the sense that it does not transgress limitations on federal power such as those found in the Bill of Rights.

D.   Three Tracks of Analysis: Procedural Statutes, Formal Rules, and Judge-Made Laws

1.   Track One: Federal Statutes and the Supremacy Clause

a.   *The Standard Model*

Stewart Organization, Inc. v. Ricoh Corp.
487 U.S. 22 (1988)

JUSTICE MARSHALL delivered the opinion of the Court.

This case presents the issue whether a federal court sitting in diversity should apply state or federal law in adjudicating a motion to transfer a case to a venue provided in a contractual forum-selection clause.

I

The dispute underlying this case grew out of a dealership agreement that obligated petitioner company, an Alabama corporation, to market copier products of respondent, a nationwide manufacturer [incorporated in New York] with its principal place of business in New Jersey. The agreement contained a forum-selection clause providing that any dispute arising out of the contract could be brought only in a court located in Manhattan. [The agreement also included a choice-of-law clause designating New York law as controlling disputes arising under the agreement.] Business relations between the parties soured under circumstances that are not relevant here. In September 1984, petitioner brought a complaint in the United States District Court for the Northern District of Alabama. The core of the complaint was an allegation that respondent had breached the dealership agreement, but petitioner also included claims for breach of warranty, fraud, and antitrust violations.

Relying on the contractual forum-selection clause, respondent moved the District Court either to transfer the case to the Southern District of New York under 28 U.S.C. § 1404(a) or to dismiss the case for improper venue under 28 U.S.C. § 1406. The District Court denied the motion. It reasoned that the transfer motion was controlled by Alabama law and that Alabama looks unfavorably upon contractual forum-selection clauses. The court certified its ruling for interlocutory appeal, and the Court of Appeals for the Eleventh Circuit accepted jurisdiction.

On appeal, a divided panel of the Eleventh Circuit reversed the District Court. The panel concluded that questions of venue in diversity actions are governed by federal law, and that the parties' forum-selection clause was enforceable as a matter of federal law. The panel therefore reversed the order of the District Court and remanded with instructions to transfer the case to a Manhattan court. After petitioner successfully moved for rehearing en banc, the full Court of Appeals proceeded to adopt the result, and much of the reasoning, of the panel opinion. . . . We now affirm under somewhat different reasoning.

II

. . . Our cases indicate that when the federal law sought to be applied is a congressional statute, the first and chief question for the district court's determination is whether the statute is "sufficiently broad to control the issue before the Court." *Walker v. Armco Steel Corp.*, 446 U.S. 740, 749-750 (1980); *Burlington Northern R. Co. v. Woods*, 480 U.S. 1, 4 (1987). This question involves a straightforward exercise in statutory interpretation to determine if the statute covers the point in dispute.[4]

If the district court determines that a federal statute covers the point in dispute, it proceeds to inquire whether the statute represents a valid exercise of Congress' authority under the Constitution. If Congress intended to reach the issue before the District Court, and if it enacted its intention into law in a manner that abides with the Constitution, that is the end of the matter; "[f]ederal courts are bound to apply rules enacted by Congress with respect to matters . . . over which it has legislative power." *Prima Paint Corp. v. Flood & Conklin Mfg. Co.*, 388 U.S. 395, 406 (1967). Thus, a district court sitting in diversity must apply a federal statute that controls the issue before the court and that represents a valid exercise of Congress' constitutional powers.

III

Applying the above analysis to this case persuades us that federal law, specifically 28 U.S.C. § 1404(a), governs the parties' venue dispute.

A

At the outset we underscore a methodological difference in our approach to the question from that taken by the Court of Appeals. The en banc court determined that federal law controlled the issue based on a survey of different statutes and judicial decisions that together revealed a significant federal interest in questions of venue in general, and in choice-of-forum clauses in particular. The Court of Appeals then proceeded to apply the standards announced in our opinion in *The Bremen v. Zapata Off-Shore Co.*, 407 U.S. 1 (1972), to determine that the forum-selection clause in this case was enforceable. But the immediate issue before the District Court was whether to grant respondent's motion to transfer the action under § 1404(a), and . . . the immediate issue before the Court of Appeals

---

4. Our cases at times have referred to the question at this stage of the analysis as an inquiry into whether there is a "direct collision" between state and federal law. Logic indicates, however, and a careful reading of the relevant passages confirms, that this language is not meant to mandate that federal law and state law be perfectly coextensive and equally applicable to the issue at hand; rather, the "direct collision" language, at least where the applicability of a federal statute is at issue, expresses the requirement that the federal statute be sufficiently broad to cover the point in dispute. It would make no sense for the supremacy of federal law to wane precisely because there is no state law directly on point.

was whether the District Court's denial of the § 1404(a) motion constituted an abuse of discretion. Although we agree with the Court of Appeals that the *Bremen* case may prove "instructive" in resolving the parties' dispute, we disagree with the court's articulation of the relevant inquiry as "whether the forum selection clause in this case is unenforceable under the standards set forth in *The Bremen*." Rather, the first question for consideration should have been whether § 1404(a) itself controls respondent's request to give effect to the parties' contractual choice of venue and transfer this case to a Manhattan court. For the reasons that follow, we hold that it does.

B

Section 1404(a) provides: "For the convenience of parties and witnesses, in the interest of justice, a district court may transfer any civil action to any other district or division where it might have been brought." Under the analysis outlined above, we first consider whether this provision is sufficiently broad to control the issue before the court. That issue is whether to transfer the case to a court in Manhattan in accordance with the forum-selection clause. We believe that the statute, fairly construed, does cover the point in dispute.

Section 1404(a) is intended to place discretion in the district court to adjudicate motions for transfer according to an "individualized, case-by-case consideration of convenience and fairness." *Van Dusen v. Barrack*, 376 U.S. 612, 622 (1964). A motion to transfer under § 1404(a) thus calls on the district court to weigh in the balance a number of case-specific factors. The presence of a forum-selection clause such as the parties entered into in this case will be a significant factor that figures centrally in the district court's calculus. In its resolution of the § 1404(a) motion in this case, for example, the District Court will be called on to address such issues as the convenience of a Manhattan forum given the parties' expressed preference for that venue, and the fairness of transfer in light of the forum-selection clause and the parties' relative bargaining power. The flexible and individualized analysis Congress prescribed in § 1404(a) thus encompasses consideration of the parties' private expression of their venue preferences.

Section 1404(a) may not be the only potential source of guidance for the District Court to consult in weighing the parties' private designation of a suitable forum. The premise of the dispute between the parties is that Alabama law may refuse to enforce forum-selection clauses providing for out-of-state venues as a matter of state public policy. If that is so, the District Court will have either to integrate the factor of the forum-selection clause into its weighing of considerations as prescribed by Congress, or else to apply, as it did in this case, Alabama's categorical policy disfavoring forum-selection clauses. Our cases make clear that, as between these two choices in a single "field of operation," *Burlington Northern R. Co. v. Woods*, 480 U.S., at 7, the instructions of Congress are supreme. Cf. *ibid.* (where federal law's "discretionary mode of operation" conflicts with the nondiscretionary provision of Alabama law, federal law applies in diversity).

It is true that § 1404(a) and Alabama's putative policy regarding forum-selection clauses are not perfectly coextensive. Section 1404(a) directs a district court to take account of factors other than those that bear solely on the parties' private ordering of their affairs. The district court also must weigh in the balance the convenience of the witnesses and those public-interest factors of systemic integrity and fairness that, in addition to private concerns, come under the heading of "the interest of justice." It is conceivable in a particular case, for example, that because of these factors a district court acting under § 1404(a) would refuse to transfer a case notwithstanding the counterweight of a forum-selection clause, whereas the coordinate state rule might dictate the opposite result.[10] But this potential conflict in fact frames an additional argument for the supremacy of federal law. Congress has directed that multiple considerations govern transfer within the federal court system, and a state policy focusing on a single concern or a subset of the factors identified in § 1404(a) would defeat that command. Its application would impoverish the flexible and multifaceted analysis that Congress intended to govern motions to transfer within the federal system. The forum-selection clause, which represents the parties' agreement as to the most proper forum, should receive neither dispositive consideration (as respondent might have it) nor no consideration (as Alabama law might have it), but rather the consideration for which Congress provided in § 1404(a). Cf. *Norwood v. Kirkpatrick*, 349 U.S. 29, 32 (1955) (§ 1404(a) accords broad discretion to district court, and plaintiff's choice of forum is only one relevant factor for its consideration). This is thus not a case in which state and federal rules "can exist side by side . . . each controlling its own intended sphere of coverage without conflict." *Walker v. Armco Steel Corp.*, 446 U.S., at 752.

Because § 1404(a) controls the issue before the District Court, it must be applied if it represents a valid exercise of Congress' authority under the Constitution. The constitutional authority of Congress to enact § 1404(a) is not subject to serious question. As the Court made plain in *Hanna*, "the constitutional provision for a federal court system . . . carries with it congressional power to make rules governing the practice and pleading in those courts, which in turn includes a power to regulate matters which, though falling within the uncertain area between substance and procedure, are rationally capable of classification as either." 380 U.S., at 472. Section 1404(a) is doubtless capable of classification as a procedural rule, and indeed, we have so classified it in holding that a transfer pursuant to § 1404(a) does not carry with it a change in the applicable law. *See Van Dusen v. Barrack*, 376 U.S., at 636-637 ("[B]oth the history and purposes of § 1404(a) indicate that it should be regarded as a federal judicial housekeeping measure"). It therefore falls comfortably within Congress' powers under Article III as augmented by the Necessary and Proper Clause.

---

10. The dissent does not dispute this point, but rather argues that if the forum-selection clause would be *unenforceable* under state law, then the clause cannot be accorded any weight by a federal court. Not the least of the problems with the dissent's analysis is that it makes the applicability of a federal statute depend on the content of state law. See n.4, *supra*. If a State cannot pre-empt a district court's consideration of a forum-selection clause by holding that the clause is automatically enforceable, it makes no sense for it to be able to do so by holding the clause automatically void.

We hold that federal law, specifically 28 U.S.C. § 1404(a), governs the District Court's decision whether to give effect to the parties' forum-selection clause and transfer this case to a court in Manhattan.[11] We therefore affirm the Eleventh Circuit order reversing the District Court's application of Alabama law. The case is remanded so that the District Court may determine in the first instance the appropriate effect under federal law of the parties' forum-selection clause on respondent's § 1404(a) motion.

It is so ordered.

[The concurring opinion of JUSTICE KENNEDY, joined by JUSTICE O'CONNOR, is omitted.]

JUSTICE SCALIA, dissenting. . . .

When a litigant asserts that state law conflicts with a federal procedural statute or formal Rule of Procedure, a court's first task is to determine whether the disputed point in question in fact falls within the scope of the federal statute or Rule. In this case, the Court must determine whether the scope of § 1404(a) is sufficiently broad to cause a direct collision with state law or implicitly to control the issue before the Court, *i.e.*, validity between the parties of the forum-selection clause, thereby leaving no room for the operation of state law. I conclude that it is not.

Although the language of § 1404(a) provides no clear answer, in my view it does provide direction. The provision vests the district courts with authority to transfer a civil action to another district "[f]or the convenience of parties and witnesses, in the interest of justice." This language looks to the present and the future. As the specific reference to convenience of parties and witnesses suggests, it requires consideration of what is likely to be just in the future, when the case is tried, in light of things as they now stand. Accordingly, the courts in applying § 1404(a) have examined a variety of factors, each of which pertains to facts that currently exist or will exist: *e.g.*, the forum actually chosen by the plaintiff, the current convenience of the parties and witnesses, the current location of pertinent books and records, similar litigation pending elsewhere, current docket conditions, and familiarity of the potential courts with governing state law. In holding that the validity between the parties of a forum-selection clause falls within the scope of § 1404(a), the Court inevitably imports, in my view without adequate textual foundation, a new *retrospective* element into the court's deliberations, requiring examination of what the facts were concerning, among other things, the bargaining power of the parties and the presence or absence of overreaching at the time the contract was made.

The Court largely attempts to avoid acknowledging the novel scope it gives to § 1404(a) by casting the issue as how much *weight* a district court should give a forum-selection clause as against other factors when it makes its determination

---

11. Because a validly enacted Act of Congress controls the issue in dispute, we have no occasion to evaluate the impact of application of federal judge-made law on the "twin aims" that animate the *Erie* doctrine.

under § 1404(a). I agree that if the weight-among-factors issue were before us, it would be governed by § 1404(a). That is because, while the parties may decide who between them should bear any inconvenience, only a court can decide how much weight should be given under § 1404(a) to the factor of the parties' convenience as against other relevant factors such as the convenience of witnesses. But the Court's description of the issue begs the question: what law governs whether the forum-selection clause is a *valid* or *invalid* allocation of any inconvenience between the parties. If it is invalid, *i.e.*, should be voided, between the parties, it cannot be entitled to any weight in the § 1404(a) determination. Since under Alabama law the forum-selection clause should be voided, see *Redwing Carriers, Inc. v. Foster*, 382 So. 2d 554, 556 (Ala. 1980), in this case the question of what weight should be given the forum-selection clause can be reached only if as a preliminary matter federal law controls the issue of the validity of the clause between the parties.

Second, § 1404(a) was enacted against the background that issues of contract, including a contract's validity, are nearly always governed by state law. It is simply contrary to the practice of our system that such an issue should be wrenched from state control in absence of a clear conflict with federal law or explicit statutory provision. . . . Section 1404(a) is simply a venue provision that nowhere mentions contracts or agreements, much less that the validity of certain contracts or agreements will be matters of federal law. It is difficult to believe that state contract law was meant to be preempted by this provision that we have said "should be regarded as a federal judicial housekeeping measure," *Van Dusen v. Barrack*, 376 U.S. 612, 636-637 (1964), that we have said did not change "the relevant factors" which federal courts used to consider under the doctrine of *forum non conveniens*, and that we have held can be applied retroactively because it is procedural. It seems to me the generality of its language— "[f]or the convenience of parties and witnesses, in the interest of justice" —is plainly insufficient to work the great change in law asserted here.

. . . [I]n deciding whether a federal procedural statute or Rule of Procedure encompasses a particular issue, a broad reading that would create significant disuniformity between state and federal courts should be avoided if the text permits. As I have shown, the interpretation given § 1404(a) by the Court today is neither the plain nor the more natural meaning; at best, § 1404(a) is ambiguous. I would therefore construe it to avoid the significant encouragement to forum shopping that will inevitably be provided by the interpretation the Court adopts today. . . .

NOTES AND QUESTIONS

1. The Track One test.   Notice the simplicity of the analytical structure in the *Ricoh* opinion. In terms of approach, a two-part test emerges from the Court's opinion. The Court first asked whether the federal statute, § 1404(a), was "sufficiently broad to control the issue before the Court." *Ricoh*, 487 U.S. at 26. The method here was one of basic statutory construction, *i.e.*, a combination of what the text appears to say and any evidence of what Congress may have intended the text to accomplish. There is certainly room for disagreement over the Court's interpretation of § 1404(a)'s scope, but the essential question of whether the statute was "sufficiently broad to control" is unremarkable. Stated otherwise, the Court was simply asking, "Does the statute apply to the issue presented?" or "Is the statute pertinent to resolution of that issue?" Implicit in this inquiry is the subsidiary question of whether the federal statute and the state law actually conflict. Once the Court determined that the statute did apply and that there was a conflict, the only remaining question was whether the statute was constitutional, *i.e.*, did Congress have the constitutional authority to pass such a law? If so, under the Supremacy Clause, the federal statute would trump state law to the contrary. What was the power exercised by Congress to pass § 1404(a)? What test did the Court use to measure whether § 1404(a) was a proper exercise of that power?

2. *Track One and* Erie.   What is the difference between the problem presented in *Ricoh* and that presented in *Erie*? Why wasn't *Erie* pertinent to the decision in *Ricoh*? Think in terms of the specific language of the RDA, 28 U.S.C. § 1652, and of the Supremacy Clause. *See also Ricoh*, 487 U.S. at 32 n.11, *supra*, at page 494.

3. *Erie's subtle influence.*   Despite the relative simplicity and elegance of the *Ricoh* Track One analysis, the Court has on occasion deviated from the standards of that track. Most such deviations appear in cases decided prior to 1965 and can be considered part of an abandoned jurisprudence in which *Erie* was applied well beyond its reserved-powers foundation. Yet even today the Court occasionally refers to the *Erie* doctrine when considering the scope or applicability of a federal procedural statute that potentially conflicts with state law. Most often, such allusions to *Erie* operate only as a reminder of the importance of adhering to state substantive law in diversity cases. In this sense, *Erie* functions as an interpretive principle that may invite a narrow reading of the federal statute in order to avoid a conflict with state law or policy. *See, e.g., Ferens v. John Deere Co.*, 494 U.S. 516 (1990) (suggesting the relevance of *Erie* to statutory analysis). In this regard, notice that Justice Scalia's opinion in *Ricoh* interprets § 1404(a) narrowly in order to avoid a conflict with what he perceives as state substantive law. The point here is that although *Erie* is technically irrelevant to a Track One analysis—again, consider the language of § 1652—the underlying philosophy of *Erie*, which reflects a principle of federalism, may nonetheless operate as a factor in determining the scope of the federal statute under review.

PROBLEMS

6-3. Lester, who lived in State X, met Lisa at a beach party during spring break in State Y. Lisa had no interest in pursuing any type of a relationship with Lester, but Lester pestered her for two days and insisted that she give him her phone number. She finally relented and wrote a fake number on the back of a matchbook. When Lester called the number, the voice at the other end of the line bellowed, "Woof! Woof! You've reached the Spay and Neuter Clinic." Lester was enraged.

He filed a diversity suit against Lisa in a State Y federal district court, claiming negligent infliction of emotional distress. The parties agreed that the law of State Y applied to the case. Lisa filed a motion to dismiss for failure to state a claim since a recent decision by State Y's highest court specifically held that State Y did not recognize claims for negligent infliction of emotional distress. The district court granted Lisa's motion. Lester appealed, arguing that the district court should have ignored the State Y decision and "forged new law." The court of appeals affirmed the dismissal and is considering whether to assess double costs against Lester for filing a frivolous appeal. Apropos of this possibility, 28 U.S.C. § 1912 provides: "Where a judgment is affirmed by the Supreme Court or a court of appeals, the court in its discretion may adjudge to the prevailing party just damages for his delay, and single or double costs." The purpose of § 1912 is to discourage frivolous appeals. Lester has objected that had the case been filed in state court, the award of double costs would not have been permitted under any circumstances. May the federal court of appeals impose double costs on Lester?

6-4. Nathan filed a diversity suit against the Boeing Company in a U.S. district court in Seattle, claiming that he had been unlawfully fired by Boeing in violation of the laws of the state of Washington. During voir dire of the prospective jury panel, Nathan learned that two of the panel's potential members worked for Boeing. Under Washington law these employees would have been automatically stricken from the panel for "cause," rather than forcing Nathan to use his limited number of peremptory challenges to remove. Nathan argued that the district court was required to adhere to this state-law principle. The trial judge rejected that argument and permitted the Boeing employees to remain on the panel, subject only to peremptory challenges. In so ruling, the judge relied on 28 U.S.C. § 1870, which states in part: "All challenges for cause or favor, whether to the array or panel or to individual jurors, shall be determined by the court." In the judge's view, this statute vested her with discretion to determine whether "cause" for removal had been established under the particular facts presented. On appeal, Nathan argues that the district court had no discretion on this issue and was required to remove the employees from the jury panel in accord with the principles of the law of the State of Washington. How should the appellate court rule? *See Nathan v. Boeing Co.*, 116 F.3d 422 (9th Cir. 1997).

b.   *A Variation on Track One: The Continuing Validity of "Specialized" Federal Common Law*

The Court in *Erie* announced, "There is no federal general common law." *Erie*, 304 U.S. at 78. By "general common law," the Court referred to those legally binding principles of judge-made law that arise in contexts normally reserved to the states. Typically, this would include such matters as basic contract, tort, and property law. Since the Constitution does not grant the federal government a general power to make such law, the *Erie* Court reasoned quite sensibly that federal courts have no business doing so either.

Yet, by sounding the death knell for federal *general* common law, the *Erie* Court did not announce or even suggest the demise of what may be called "specialized" federal common law or more simply, federal common law. In fact, on the day *Erie* was decided, the Supreme Court applied principles of federal common law to resolve a dispute between two states over an interstate stream—an area of law in which the federal interest is especially strong given the potential for interstate distrust implicit in such controversies. *Hinderlider v. La Plata River & Cherry Creek Ditch Co.*, 304 U.S. 92 (1938).

The distinction between federal general common law and federal common law lies in the nature of the law being created. Just as state courts may create principles of law pertaining to matters reserved to the states, federal courts possess a limited power to develop a common law pertaining to matters over which the Constitution vests authority in the federal government. This common law power is generally subject to revision by Congress, but in the absence of such revision, federal common law is, like all other species of federal law, the "supreme Law of the Land" and is fully binding in cases to which it applies. U.S. Const., art. VI, cl. 2 ("the Supremacy Clause"). As such, federal common law trumps state laws to the contrary. Nor does the RDA, 28 U.S.C. § 1652 (the statute interpreted in *Erie*), require to the contrary. Federal common law is drawn by inference from the Constitution, treaties, and laws of the United States—which it seeks to interpret—and therefore operates as the rule of decision in cases in which it applies. Thus federal common law triggers what is, in essence, a Track One analysis.

The potential range of federal common law is theoretically as broad as the subject areas over which the Constitution vests power in the national government. In practice, however, the actual reach of federal common law is substantially more circumscribed. In part, this stems from a deeply imbedded recognition in the constitutional separation of powers that Congress, and not the federal judiciary, is the primary engine for the making of national policy. *Milwaukee v. Illinois and Michigan*, 451 U.S. 304, 312-313 (1981) ("The enactment of a federal rule in an area of national concern, and the decision whether to displace state law in doing so, is generally made not by the federal judiciary, purposefully insulated from democratic pressures, but by the people through their elected representatives in Congress."). As a consequence, federal common law tends to appear in certain domains in which its propriety is constitutionally driven or when Congress has expressly or implicitly delegated the power to create it to the courts.

One of the easiest ways to comprehend the realm of federal common law is to examine those legal domains in which the phenomenon most often recurs. Our goal here is not to provide an exhaustive taxonomy of federal common law or to provide a precise methodology for assessing every potential exercise of this power. Rather, the purpose is to give a rough idea of specialized federal common law and to contrast it with the *Erie* doctrine's dissolution of federal general common law. Among other things, this contrast should help us to more fully appreciate *Erie* as a doctrine designed to respect the states' reserved powers. A brief survey of the following seven (somewhat overlapping) categories of federal common law should serve these purposes:

- constitutional common law;
- statutory federal common law;
- common law to protect uniquely federal interests;
- foreign relations and customary international law;
- common law of interstate relations;
- admiralty and maritime law; and
- federal procedural common law.

Constitutional common law.   This first category largely comprises Supreme Court interpretations of the U.S. Constitution, augmented somewhat by both state court and lower federal court interpretations of that same text. The topics cover the entire range of federal constitutional issues that may come before federal and state courts for resolution. For all practical purposes constitutional law is what the Court says it is. *See* Allan Ides, *Judicial Supremacy and the Law of the Constitution*, 47 U.C.L.A. L. Rev. 491 (1999). The Court's constitutional interpretations are binding on both federal and state courts. Until revised by the Court or altered by constitutional amendment, they trump all federal and state laws to the contrary. Moreover, constitutional common law is the one area of federal common law in which Congress has no authority to revise the substance of the law, other than through the process of proposing constitutional amendments. The judicially created minimum contacts test of personal jurisdiction and the Court's interpretation of Article III "arising under" are both examples of constitutional common law.

Statutory federal common law.   The second category of federal common law involves the judicial interpretation of federal statutes. Of course, if a judicial "interpretation" of a statute merely tracks the language of the statute, one would be hard pressed to describe the resulting legal principle as judge-made or as federal common law. But to the extent that a judicial interpretation embellishes a statute's text by adding or altering rights or obligations, or by filling a gap in the statutory scheme, the resulting "law" can be fairly described as judge-made and therefore as federal common law. In any event, no matter how one labels such interpretations, *i.e.*, as mere extensions of a statute or as statutory federal common law, these judicial glosses are laws to the same extent as the statutes that they interpret, and they are fully binding in the cases to which they apply. Statutory federal common law, therefore, trumps state law to the contrary. Federal courts do, however, often shape or construe statutory federal common law in a manner that is designed to avoid any such conflicts. *See, e.g.*, Justice Scalia's dissenting opinion in *Ricoh, supra*. Finally, unlike the situation with constitutional common law, Congress is free to revise statutory federal common law through the normal legislative process.

Statutory federal common law comes in two general varieties: interstitial and global. *Interstitial* federal common law is created when a federal court fills a small gap in an otherwise comprehensive legislative scheme. For example, we have already considered the phenomenon of implied rights of action. An implied right of action fills an interstitial gap in a legislative scheme by judicially creating a private enforcement mechanism when Congress has been silent. Similarly, Congress sometimes fails to include a statute of limitations along with an expressly created private right of action. Federal courts can fill this interstitial gap either by borrowing an analogous state statute of limitations or by adopting a federal statute of limitations found in a similar or related federal statutory scheme. Thus, since 42 U.S.C. § 1983 contains no statute of limitations, a federal court enforcing a § 1983 claim will typically—as a matter of federal common law—borrow the state's statute of limitations for personal injury claims to fill this interstitial gap.

However, federal courts are sometimes called upon to create statutory federal common law that does more than fill an interstitial gap. The judicial construction of the 1890 Sherman Antitrust Act, 15 U.S.C. §§ 1-8, provides an example of what we might call *global* statutory federal common law. The act prohibits restraints of trade, monopolies, and the like. The act's terse language does not, however, reveal the circumstances under which these fairly general standards will be enforced. Instead, for more than a century it has been left to the federal judiciary to develop a federal common law of antitrust. This judicial creativity is premised on the presumed intent of Congress to vest federal courts with the authority to do so. *See National Soc'y of Prof'l Eng'rs v. United States*, 435 U.S. 679, 688 (1978) ("Congress . . . did not intend the text of the Sherman Act to delineate the full meaning of the statute or its application in concrete situations. The legislative history makes it perfectly clear that it expected the courts to give shape to the statute's broad mandate by drawing on common-law tradition."). Similarly, the 1947 Labor Management Relations Act, 29 U.S.C. §§ 141-187, which grants federal courts subject matter jurisdiction over suits for violations of collective bargaining agreements, has long been interpreted as authorizing "federal courts to fashion a body of federal law for the enforcement of these collective bargaining agreements. . . ." *Textile Workers Union of Am. v. Lincoln Mills of Ala.*, 353 U.S. 448, 450-451 (1957). Both the federal common law of antitrust and the federal common law of labor/management relations are, like the statutes from which they derive, the supreme law of the land, contrary state law notwithstanding, although they are subject to revision by Congress.

Uniquely federal interests.   A federal court may also create federal common law to protect "uniquely federal interests." One can see this category as another way of approaching statutory federal common law since typically in such cases the unique federal interests stem from a federal statute. At the heart of this category is a potential conflict between state law and some federal policy or interest that the application of state law would undermine. Such uniquely federal interests might involve the rights and obligations of the United States, including its property interests, or they might involve the federal government's ability to exercise some discretionary power vested in it by the Constitution or by federal legislation. This category is often triggered when the liability of the United States itself is at stake. *Compare Clearfield Trust Co. v. United States*, 318 U.S. 363 (1943) (holding that federal common law determines the liability of the United States on a check issued by it), *with Bank of Am. Nat'l Trust & Sav. Assn. v. Parnell*, 352 U.S. 29 (1956) (declining to apply federal common law to a dispute between private parties over their liability on U.S. bearer bonds). But the presence of the United States in the suit is not necessarily required. As with other nonconstitutional federal common law, Congress is free to revise federal common law developed to protect uniquely federal interests.

Foreign relations and customary international law.   The law of foreign relations can be seen as a special instance of the preceding category. Simply put, lawsuits implicating U.S. foreign policy may call for the creation of federal common law to prevent state- or foreign-law interference with those interests. *See Banco Nacional de Cuba v. Sabbatino*, 376 U.S. 398 (1964). Similarly, the Court has recognized the legitimacy of customary international law in the development of a federal common law of human rights. *See Sosa v. Alvarez-Machain*, 542 U.S. 692 (2004).

Common law of interstate relations.   The law of interstate relations, typically addressing border disputes between states or interstate controversies over water rights, is largely a product of Supreme Court decisions. Under Article III, the Supreme Court may exercise original jurisdiction over such cases, and in the absence of congressional legislation, resolution of these controversies depends on the application of federal common law. In essence, the national interest in uniformity allows this federal common law to trump the interests or policies of individual states, but not the overarching authority of Congress. *See Milwaukee v. Illinois and Michigan*, 451 U.S. 304 (1981) (holding that federal statutory law displaces preexisting federal common law).

Admiralty and maritime law.   The power of federal courts to create federal common law in the context of admiralty and maritime suits is well established and derives largely from Article III's grant of admiralty and maritime jurisdiction to the federal courts. *See, e.g., Norfolk Shipbuilding & Drydock Corp. v. Garris*, 531 U.S. 1 (2001) (recognizing maritime wrongful death cause of action for negligent breach of a maritime duty of care). This power is, however, also subject to the paramount power of Congress. *See Southern Pac. Co. v. Jensen*, 244 U.S. 205 (1917). Like other valid federal common law, the common law of admiralty supersedes state law to the contrary, although the test for measuring actual conflicts with state law remains somewhat amorphous. *See American Dredging Co. v. Miller*, 510 U.S. 443 (1994).

Procedural common law.   Finally, the authority to create a nonconstitutional federal common law of procedure derives from the implied power of Article III judges to create a law of procedure for application in federal courts. Such procedural common law includes the doctrine of forum non conveniens, *see* Chapter V, *supra*, and the doctrines of claim and issue preclusion, *see* Chapter XIII, *infra*. Most procedural law used by federal courts today, however, is either statutory or, like the Federal Rules of Civil Procedure, judicially created pursuant to a delegation from Congress. As with most species of federal common law, Congress again holds the ultimate power over nonconstitutional federal procedure. Moreover, as we will see, the federal common law of procedure is the one area of legitimate federal common law that may at times have to yield to conflicting state law under the *Erie* doctrine. *See* part D.3, page 529, *infra*.

PROBLEM

6-5. A Lear Jet crashed shortly after takeoff from Georgia's DeKalb County Airport. The cause of the crash was the ingestion of birds into the aircraft's jet engines. The birds were swarming above a county-owned dump located adjacent to the airport and beneath the plane's takeoff path. Representatives of deceased passengers sued DeKalb County, the operator of the airport, in a U.S. district court based on diversity of citizenship. Assume the requisites of diversity were satisfied. The plaintiffs sought damages for negligence, nuisance, and breach of contract. As to the latter claim, the plaintiffs claimed standing as third-party beneficiaries to contracts between the County and the Federal Aviation Administration (FAA). (A third-party beneficiary to a contract is a person who is not a party to the contract but for whose especial benefit the contract was made.) The FAA contracts required the county to take action to restrict land use in the airport's vicinity to uses compatible with airport use. Under state law, the plaintiffs could sue as third-party beneficiaries to the FAA contract. However, given the interest of the United States in air safety, and given that the United States is a party to the contracts in question, should the district court apply federal common law to the plaintiffs' breach of contract claim? Assume that federal common law would not recognize a third party's right to enforce provisions of the FAA contract. *See Miree v. DeKalb Cnty.*, 433 U.S. 25 (1977).

2. Track Two: The Federal Rules of Civil Procedure

We mentioned earlier that prior to 1938, federal courts followed a complex matrix of procedural rules, some of which were borrowed from the respective state in which the federal court sat and others of which were uniform throughout the nation. The choice of which body of rules to apply depended on whether the federal court was sitting in law or in equity. In 1938, the same year *Erie* was decided, the Federal Rules of Civil Procedure (FRCP) went into effect. These rules merged law and equity and provided a uniform set of federal procedural rules to be applied in all civil cases filed in U.S. district courts. The Supreme Court promulgated the rules pursuant to a delegation from Congress under the Rules Enabling Act (REA), 28 U.S.C. § 2072. That statute as currently written provides in pertinent part:

> (a) The Supreme Court shall have the power to prescribe general rules of practice and procedure and rules of evidence for cases in the United States district courts (including proceedings before magistrates thereof) and courts of appeals.
> (b) Such rules shall not abridge, enlarge or modify any substantive right. . . .

28 U.S.C. § 2072. The constitutional source of power for the REA was the same source examined by the Court in *Stewart Organization v. Ricoh Corp.*, *supra*, namely, Congress's power under Article I's Necessary and Proper Clause to create and prescribe rules of procedure for Article III federal courts. Presumably,

the delegation of that authority to the Supreme Court was within constitutional bounds; at least that delegation has never been the subject of serious doubt.

This leads us to the Track Two analysis. How should a federal district court resolve a potential conflict between a formal federal rule—*i.e.*, a rule promulgated pursuant to the REA—and state law?

Sibbach v. Wilson & Co., Inc.
312 U.S. 1 (1941)

[Hertha Sibbach was injured in an automobile accident in Indiana that she claimed was caused by one of defendant Wilson & Co.'s employees. Sibbach sued the employer in an Illinois federal court, seeking damages for personal injuries. The defendant denied liability and moved for an order requiring that plaintiff submit to a physical examination pursuant to FRCP 35(a). That rule, as then worded, provided: "In an action in which the mental or physical condition of a party is in controversy, the court in which the action is pending may order him to submit to a physical or mental examination by a physician." The district court ordered the examination pursuant to Rule 35, but the plaintiff refused to comply, arguing that the federal rule was invalid since it contravened Illinois law. Under Illinois law, state court judges lacked the power to order physical examinations. The state-law rule operated as a rule of evidence precluding the introduction of judicially ordered examinations into evidence. After a hearing, the district court found the plaintiff in contempt and, pursuant to Rule 37, ordered her committed to the Cook County jail until such time as she complied with the court's order. Sibbach appealed. The court of appeals upheld Rule 35's validity and affirmed the judgment. The Supreme Court granted cert.]

MR. JUSTICE ROBERTS delivered the opinion of the Court.

This case calls for decision as to the validity of Rules 35 and 37 of the Rules of Civil Procedure for District Courts of the United States. . . .

The contention of the petitioner, in [the] final analysis, is that Rules 35 and 37 are not within the mandate of Congress to this court. . . .

Congress has undoubted power to regulate the practice and procedure of federal courts, and may exercise that power by delegating to this or other federal courts authority to make rules not inconsistent with the statutes or Constitution of the United States; but it has never essayed to declare the substantive state law, or to abolish or nullify a right recognized by the substantive law of the state where the cause of action arose, save where a right or duty is imposed in a field committed to Congress by the Constitution. On the contrary it has enacted that the state law shall be the rule of decision in the federal courts.

Hence we conclude that the [Rules Enabling Act] was purposely restricted in its operation to matters of pleading and court practice and procedure. Its two provisos or caveats emphasize this restriction. The first is that the court shall not "abridge, enlarge, nor modify substantive rights," in the guise of regulating procedure. The second is that if the rules are to prescribe a single form of action for cases at law and suits in equity, the constitutional right to jury trial inherent in the former must be preserved. There are other limitations upon the authority to prescribe rules which might have been, but were not mentioned in the Act; for instance, the inability of a court, by rule, to extend or restrict the jurisdiction conferred by a statute.

Whatever may be said as to the effect of the Conformity Act while it remained in force, the rules, if they are within the authority granted by Congress, repeal that statute, and the District Court was not bound to follow the Illinois practice respecting an order for physical examination. On the other hand if the right to be exempt from such an order is one of substantive law, the Rules of Decision Act required the District Court, though sitting in Illinois, to apply the law of Indiana, the state where the cause of action arose, and to order the examination. To avoid this dilemma the petitioner admits, and, we think, correctly, that Rules 35 and 37 are rules of procedure. She insists, nevertheless, that by the prohibition against abridging substantive rights, Congress has banned the rules here challenged. In order to reach this result she translates "substantive" into "important" or "substantial" rights. And she urges that if a rule affects such a right, albeit the rule is one of procedure merely, its prescription is not within the statutory grant of power embodied in the [REA]. She contends that our decisions and recognized principles require us so to hold. . . .

We are thrown back, then, to the arguments drawn from the language of the [REA]. Is the phrase "substantive rights" confined to rights conferred by law to be protected and enforced in accordance with the adjective law of judicial procedure? It certainly embraces such rights. One of them is the right not to be injured in one's person by another's negligence, to redress infraction of which the present action was brought. The petitioner says the phrase connotes more; that by its use Congress intended that in regulating procedure this court should not deal with important and substantial rights theretofore recognized. Recognized where and by whom? The state courts are divided as to the power in the absence of statute to order a physical examination. In a number such an order is authorized by statute or rule. The rules in question accord with the procedure now in force in Canada and England.

The asserted right, moreover, is no more important than many others enjoyed by litigants in District Courts sitting in the several states, before the Federal Rules of Civil Procedure altered and abolished old rights or privileges and created new ones in connection with the conduct of litigation. The suggestion that the rule offends the important right to freedom from invasion of the person ignores the fact that, as we hold, no invasion of freedom from personal restraint attaches to refusal so to comply with its provisions. If we were to adopt the suggested criterion of the importance of the alleged right we should invite endless litigation and confusion worse confounded. The test must be whether a rule really regulates procedure,—the judicial process for enforcing rights and duties recognized by substantive law and for justly administering remedy and redress for disregard or infraction of them. That the rules in question are such is admitted.

Finally, it is urged that Rules 35 and 37 work a major change of policy and that this was not intended by Congress. Apart from the fact already stated, that the policy of the states in this respect has not been uniform, it is to be noted that the authorization of a comprehensive system of court rules was a departure in policy, and that the new policy envisaged in the enabling act of 1934 was that the whole field of court procedure be regulated in the interest of speedy, fair and exact determination of the truth. The challenged rules comport with this policy. Moreover, in accordance with the Act, the rules were submitted to the Congress so that that body might examine them and veto their going into effect if contrary to the policy of the legislature. . . .

The District Court treated the refusal to comply with its order as a contempt and committed the petitioner therefor. Neither in the Circuit Court of Appeals nor here was this action assigned as error. We think, however, that in the light of the provisions of Rule 37 it was plain error of such a fundamental nature that we should notice it. Section (b)(2)(iv) of Rule 37 exempts from punishment as for contempt the refusal to obey an order that a party submit to a physical or mental examination. The District Court was in error in going counter to this express exemption. The remedies available under the rule in such a case are those enumerated in Section (b)(2)(i)(ii) and (iii). For this error we reverse the judgment and remand the cause to the District Court for further proceedings in conformity to this opinion.

Reversed.

MR. JUSTICE FRANKFURTER, dissenting [joined by JUSTICES BLACK, DOUGLAS, and MURPHY]:

. . .

So far as national law is concerned, a drastic change in public policy in a matter deeply touching the sensibilities of people or even their prejudices as to privacy, ought not to be inferred from a general authorization to formulate rules for the more uniform and effective dispatch of business on the civil side of the federal courts. I deem a requirement as to the invasion of the person to stand on a very different footing from questions pertaining to the discovery of documents, pre-trial procedure and other devices for the expeditious, economic and fair conduct of litigation. That disobedience of an order under Rule 35 cannot be visited with punishment as for contempt does not mitigate its intrusion into an historic immunity of the privacy of the person. Of course the Rule is compulsive in that the doors of the federal courts otherwise open may be shut to litigants who do not submit to such a physical examination. . . .

NOTES AND QUESTIONS

1. The text of the REA and the elements of the Track Two test. The first sentence of the REA, § 2072 (a), provides: "The Supreme Court shall have the power to prescribe general rules of practice and procedure and rules of evidence for cases in the

United States district courts (including proceedings before magistrates thereof) and courts of appeals." Pursuant to this delegation, the Court is empowered to promulgate rules of "practice and procedure" for lower federal courts—the Federal Rules of Civil Procedure and the Federal Rules of Appellate Procedure being obvious examples of this delegated authority in action. Of course, any rule promulgated pursuant to this delegation must, in order to be deemed valid, fall within the scope of the delegated authority. Hence a formal federal rule will be found valid only if it can be properly characterized as being a rule of "practice" or "procedure." Not surprisingly, the method for making that determination is, in practical effect, identical to the method used for determining whether a federal statute falls within the scope of the congressional power to regulate federal procedure. Thus, to be valid, a federal rule must be rationally capable of being classified as procedural. The inquiry may, as in *Sibbach*, be phrased as whether the rule "really regulates procedure," but regardless of phrasing the inquiry is essentially the same. Moreover, given the strong presumption of validity that attaches to the federal rules, and given that every one of those rules purports to regulate some aspect of procedure, it would be extraordinary to find one that could not be described as either rationally capable of being classified as procedural or as really regulating procedure.

The second sentence of the REA, § 2072(b), imposes an additional limitation on the scope of the REA's delegation to the Court: "Such rules shall not abridge, enlarge or modify any substantive right." Thus, a rule that satisfies the first sentence of the REA, *i.e.*, a rule that is appropriately characterized as procedural, might still exceed the delegation from Congress if the rule abridges, enlarges, or modifies a *substantive right*. This limitation distinguishes Track Two from Track One, where the only measure of validity pertains to whether the statute at issue can be rationally characterized as procedural. Essentially, Congress delegated less than the whole of its authority to regulate procedure in the federal courts. The result is that validity under Track Two requires a two-step inquiry, the first focused on the procedural nature of the rule and the second focused on the possible substantive operation of that rule.

2. Sibbach *and Track Two.*   In *Sibbach*, the plaintiff conceded that Rule 35 was procedural, and the Court agreed with that concession. Can you explain, in your own words, why Rule 35 is rationally capable of being classified as procedural? In attempting to answer this question, ask yourself how Rule 35 operates within the system of federal procedure. What does it do to advance the litigation process?

Instead of arguing that Rule 35 could not be characterized as procedural, which would have been futile, Sibbach argued that application of the rule transgressed the substantive-rights limitation imposed by the REA. Specifically, she argued that Rule 35, as applied in her case, "abridged" her right to be free from a judicially ordered physical examination—a right she characterized as important or substantial—and she further argued that the Court should equate "substantive" with "important" and "substantial." Justice Frankfurter's dissent appears to agree with the plaintiff on this point. Did the Court fail to appreciate the significance of plaintiff's argument? More importantly, in rejecting that argument, did the Court render § 2072(b)'s abridge-enlarge-modify limitation meaningless?

The answers to these questions are elusive. On the one hand, it can certainly be argued that plaintiff's substantive right to privacy was abridged by the district court's order. She was ordered to relinquish her right to refuse a physical examination, under threat of imprisonment. If this is the proper characterization of the operation of Rule 35(a) in *Sibbach*, it may well be that the Court's "really regulates procedure" formula overlooked the limitations imposed by the second sentence of the REA. In essence, the Court allowed a procedural rule to abridge a substantive right, in direct contravention of the language of the statute.

On the other hand, the Court's opinion can be read as fully comporting with the substantive limitations of the REA. First, the Court rejected the district court's remedy—incarceration—as being too severe and one that might well have abridged a substantive right. Next, in the Court's view, the right claimed by the plaintiff was not substantive. Instead, that "right" arose solely "in connection with the conduct of litigation" and was therefore more properly characterized as a procedural right. Importantly, the judge-made Illinois law on which plaintiff relied was generally described by the Illinois courts as a limitation on the power of state court judges to issue such an order, rather than as being reflective of an affirmative individual right. Moreover, the plaintiff in *Sibbach* was precluded from arguing that the right claimed was truly substantive, since the applicable substantive law—Indiana law—would have permitted the examination. Therefore, the right at issue seems to have been a right derived solely from practice, not from the substantive law. Given that characterization of the case, the application of Rule 35 cannot be said to violate the second sentence of the REA. At most, it abridged a procedural right.

Let us conclude at this point that we are faced with an open question: Did the *Sibbach* Court adhere to or alter the two-step model seemingly mandated by the REA? We will revisit this question when we read *Shady Grove Orthopedic Associates, P.A. v. Allstate Insurance Co.*, 559 U.S. 393 (2010), at page 516, *infra*, the Court's most recent foray into this territory.

PROBLEM

6-6. Harry has filed a diversity suit in a State X federal court claiming that the Quality Cafe served him a contaminated ham, thereby causing him to suffer serious medical harm. Quality denies the claim, but further asserts that if it is liable to Harry, then Prepared Foods, from whom Quality purchased the ham, is required by law to indemnify Quality for any such liability. To this end, and relying on Rule 14, Quality seeks to bring Prepared Foods into the case as a third-party defendant. Rule 14(a)(1) specifically allows a defendant to bring in an absent party "who is or may be liable to [the defendant] for all or part of the claim against it." And, indeed, under State X substantive law, Prepared Foods would be required to indemnify Quality if the latter were found liable to Harry. However, State X law also provides that no claim for indemnification may be filed by a defendant until such time as the defendant's primary liability to the plaintiff has first been established in a final judgment. A State X court would thus not allow Quality to bring Prepared Foods into the lawsuit at this time, since no judgment has yet been entered against Quality. Accordingly, Prepared Foods has asked the U.S. District Court to dismiss Quality's Rule 14(a)(1) claim against it. What should the court do? In answering this question, you must determine whether the federal rule applies, whether it and the state law are in conflict, whether the federal rule can be characterized as a regulation of procedure and, finally, whether application of the federal rule abridges, enlarges, or modifies a substantive right. *See Jeub v. B/G Foods, Inc.*, 2 F.R.D. 238 (D. Minn. 1942).

A NOTE ON THE OMNIPRESENCE OF *ERIE*

The REA's two-step approach to resolving conflicts between the federal rules and state law did not gain immediate and universal acceptance. Many justices and judges interpreted *Erie* as something more than an application of the reserved powers doctrine. For them, *Erie* represented a powerful and omnipresent principle of federalism that could insinuate itself into a wide variety of contexts. By the end of the 1940s, these views dominated the Court, and the simple model established by the REA all but disappeared. *Erie* became instrumental in the resolution of a wide array of conflicts between state and federal law, including those involving both the federal rules and federal procedural statutes. The most notable examples of this tendency came in a trilogy of cases decided on the same day in 1949.

The first, *Ragan v. Merchants Transfer & Warehouse Co.*, 337 U.S. 530 (1949), arose out of a highway accident that occurred in Kansas. The plaintiff, invoking diversity jurisdiction, filed a complaint in the U.S. District Court for the District of Kansas. The complaint was filed within the state's two-year statute of limitations, but service of process was not effected until after the statute of limitations had run. Under Kansas law, the statute of limitations was tolled only by service of process. Under Federal Rule of Civil Procedure 3, however, a civil action was deemed "commenced" merely "by filing a complaint with the court." The question, there-fore, was which tolling standard the district court should follow. Applying *Erie* in a somewhat mechanical fashion, the Court held that since state law created the cause of action, "the measure" of that cause of action must be found in state law as well. Rule 3's definition of commencement, therefore, had to give way to the state tolling provision. The Court made no effort to examine Rule 3 under *Sibbach* and the express standards of the REA.

The second case, *Woods v. Interstate Realty Co.*, 337 U.S. 535 (1949), took *Ragan* a step further and applied *Erie* as a limitation on a federal statute. *Woods* was a diversity suit in which a Tennessee corporation sued a resident of Mississippi in the U.S. District Court for Mississippi, seeking a broker's commission on real estate sold by the corporation on behalf of the resident. The defendant moved for summary judgment, claiming that the contract was void due to the plaintiff corporation's failure to register to do business within the state. The district court agreed and dismissed the lawsuit. The court of appeals reversed, concluding that state law did not render the contract void, but merely denied a noncomplying corporation the privilege of filing suit in state court. The Supreme Court reversed. In the Court's view, regardless of how one interpreted the state law, under *Erie*, since Mississippi denied the corporation a remedy in the courts of the state, access to federal court must be denied as well. In other words, state law operated as a limitation on the federal diversity statute. Contrast this application of *Erie* with the Court's treatment of that doctrine in *Stewart Organization v. Ricoh Corp.*, particularly footnote 4 of that opinion at page 491, *supra*.

Finally, *Cohen v. Beneficial Industrial Loan Corp.*, 337 U.S. 541 (1949), involved a stockholder's derivative action filed against a Delaware corporation in a New Jersey federal court under that court's diversity jurisdiction. The suit alleged extensive corporate mismanagement and fraud. After the suit was filed, the State of New Jersey enacted a statute granting any domestic or foreign corporation subject to any pending or future derivative suit the right to demand that plaintiff post security for reasonable expenses that might be incurred by the corporation in defending the suit. The statute did not create a liability for those expenses, but provided a method through which any resulting liability could be satisfied. Pursuant to this statute, the corporate defendant in *Cohen* filed a motion to require that plaintiff post a $125,000 security bond. The district court denied the motion and the court of appeals reversed. The Supreme Court upheld the appellate court's decision. In so doing, it concluded that although Rule 23, which at the time regulated the filing of derivative actions in federal courts, did not require the posting of a security bond, the federal court under *Erie* was obligated to follow state law, essentially because of the importance of the state policy at stake. Yet as Justice Rutledge pointed out in dissent, there is a significant difference between requiring that a federal court apply state law to determine whether a cause of action exists, and requiring a federal court to adopt state rules regarding the posting of bonds as security. The former involves substantive law in the most obvious sense, while the latter is merely an incident to litigation over the underlying substantive rights and thus well within the regulatory powers of Congress.

The net effect of this trilogy of decisions was to expand the *Erie* formula well beyond its reserved-powers rationale, treating that decision as a mandate for what might be characterized as a reverse form of supremacy, under which state law and policy could even trump otherwise valid federal rules and statutes. The next principal case, *Hanna v. Plumer*, was a response to the somewhat amorphous and confusing legacy of this trilogy.

Hanna v. Plumer [Part I]
380 U.S. 460 (1965)

MR. CHIEF JUSTICE WARREN delivered the opinion of the Court.

The question to be decided is whether, in a civil action where the jurisdiction of the United States district court is based upon diversity of citizenship between the parties, service of process shall be made in the manner prescribed by state law or that set forth in Rule 4(d)(1) of the Federal Rules of Civil Procedure.

On February 6, 1963, petitioner, a citizen of Ohio, filed her complaint in the District Court for the District of Massachusetts, claiming damages in excess of $10,000 for personal injuries resulting from an automobile accident in South Carolina, allegedly caused by the negligence of one Louise Plumer Osgood, a Massachusetts citizen deceased at the time of the filing of the complaint. Respondent, Mrs. Osgood's executor and also a Massachusetts citizen, was named as defendant. On February 8, service was made by leaving copies of the summons and the complaint with respondent's wife at his residence, concededly in compliance with Rule 4(d)(1), which provides:

> "The summons and complaint shall be served together. The plaintiff shall furnish the person making service with such copies as are necessary. Service shall be made as follows:
>
> "(1) Upon an individual other than an infant or an incompetent person, by delivering a copy of the summons and of the complaint to him personally or by leaving copies thereof at his dwelling house or usual place of abode with some person of suitable age and discretion then residing therein. . . ."*

Respondent filed his answer on February 26, alleging, *inter alia*, that the action could not be maintained because it had been brought "contrary to and in violation of the provisions of Massachusetts General Laws." That section provides:

> "Except as provided in this chapter, an executor or administrator shall not be held to answer to an action by a creditor of the deceased which is not commenced within one year from the time of his giving bond for the performance of his trust, or to such an action which is commenced within said year unless before the expiration thereof the writ in such action has been served by delivery in hand upon such executor or administrator or service thereof accepted by him or a notice stating the name of the estate, the name and address of the creditor, the amount of the claim and the court in which the action has been brought has been filed in the proper registry of probate. . . ."

On October 17, 1963, the District Court granted respondent's motion for summary judgment, citing *Ragan v. Merchants Transfer & Warehouse Co.*, 337 U.S. 530, and *Guaranty Trust Co. of New York v. York*, 326 U.S. 99, in support of its conclusion that the adequacy of the service was to be measured by § 9, with which, the court held, petitioner had not complied. On appeal, petitioner admitted noncompliance with § 9, but argued that Rule 4(d)(1) defines the method by which service of process is to be effected in diversity actions. The Court of Appeals for the First Circuit, finding that "[r]elatively recent amendments [to § 9] evince a clear legislative purpose to require personal notification within the year," concluded that the conflict of state and federal rules was over "substantive rather than a procedural matter," and unanimously affirmed. Because of the threat to the

---

* [The current version of Rule 4(d)(1) is now numbered Rule 4(e)(2). — Eds.]

goal of uniformity of federal procedure posed by the decision below, we granted certiorari.

We conclude that the adoption of Rule 4(d)(1), designed to control service of process in diversity actions, neither exceeded the congressional mandate embodied in the Rules Enabling Act nor transgressed constitutional bounds, and that the Rule is therefore the standard against which the District Court should have measured the adequacy of the service. Accordingly, we reverse the decision of the Court of Appeals.

The Rules Enabling Act, 28 U.S.C. § 2072 (1958 ed.), provides, in pertinent part:

> "The Supreme Court shall have the power to prescribe, by general rules, the forms of process, writs, pleadings, and motions, and the practice and procedure of the district courts of the United States in civil actions.
>
> "Such rules shall not abridge, enlarge or modify any substantive right and shall preserve the right of trial by jury. . . ."

Under the cases construing the scope of the Enabling Act, Rule 4(d)(1) clearly passes muster. Prescribing the manner in which a defendant is to be notified that a suit has been instituted against him, it relates to the "practice and procedure of the district courts."

> "The test must be whether a rule really regulates procedure—the judicial process for enforcing rights and duties recognized by substantive law and for justly administering remedy and redress for disregard or infraction of them." *Sibbach v. Wilson & Co.*, 312 U.S. 1, 14.

In *Mississippi Pub. Corp. v. Murphree*, 326 U.S. 438, this Court upheld Rule 4(f), which permits service of a summons anywhere within the State (and not merely the district) in which a district court sits:

> "We think that Rule 4(f) is in harmony with the Enabling Act. . . . Undoubtedly most alterations of the rules of practice and procedure may and often do affect the rights of litigants. Congress' prohibition of any alteration of substantive rights of litigants was obviously not addressed to such incidental effects as necessarily attend the adoption of the prescribed new rules of procedure upon the rights of litigants who, agreeably to rules of practice and procedure, have been brought before a court authorized to determine their rights. *Sibbach v. Wilson & Co.*, 312 U.S. 1, 11-14. The fact that the application of Rule 4(f) will operate to subject petitioner's rights to adjudication by the district court for northern Mississippi will undoubtedly affect those rights. But it does not operate to abridge, enlarge or modify the rules of decision by which that court will adjudicate its rights." *Id.*, at 445-446.

Thus were there no conflicting state procedure, Rule 4(d)(1) would clearly control. However, respondent, focusing on the contrary Massachusetts rule, calls to the Court's attention another line of cases, a line which—like the Federal Rules—had its birth in 1938. *Erie R. Co. v. Tompkins*, 304 U.S. 64, overruling *Swift v. Tyson*, 16 Pet. 1, held that federal courts sitting in diversity cases, when deciding questions of "substantive" law, are bound by state court decisions as well as state statutes. The broad command of *Erie* was therefore identical to that of the

Enabling Act: federal courts are to apply state substantive law and federal procedural law. . . .**

There is, however, a . . . fundamental flaw in respondent's syllogism: the incorrect assumption that the rule of *Erie R. Co. v. Tompkins* constitutes the appropriate test of the validity and therefore the applicability of a Federal Rule of Civil
Procedure.\The *Erie* rule has never been invoked to void a Federal Rule.|It is
true that there have been cases where this Court has held applicable a state rule
in the face of an argument that the situation was governed by one of the Federal
Rules. But the holding of each such case was not that *Erie* commanded displacement of a Federal Rule by an inconsistent state rule, but rather that the scope of
the Federal Rule was not as broad as the losing party urged, and therefore, there
being no Federal Rule which covered the point in dispute, *Erie* commanded the
enforcement of state law. . . . (Here, of course, the clash is unavoidable; Rule
4(d)(1) says—implicitly, but with unmistakable clarity—that inhand service is not
required in federal courts.) At the same time, in cases adjudicating the validity
of Federal Rules, we have not applied the *York* rule or other refinements of *Erie*,
but have to this day continued to decide questions concerning the scope of the
Enabling Act and the constitutionality of specific Federal Rules in light of the
distinction set forth in *Sibbach*.

Nor has the development of two separate lines of cases been inadvertent. The
line between "substance" and "procedure" shifts as the legal context changes.
"Each implies different variables depending upon the particular problem for
which it is used." *Guaranty Trust Co. of New York v. York, supra*, 326 U.S. at 108.
It is true that both the Enabling Act and the *Erie* rule say, roughly, that federal
courts are to apply state "substantive" law and federal "procedural" law, but from
that it need not follow that the tests are identical. For they were designed to control very different sorts of decisions. When a situation is covered by one of the
Federal Rules, the question facing the court is a far cry from the typical, relatively
unguided *Erie* choice: the court has been instructed to apply the Federal Rule,
and can refuse to do so only if the Advisory Committee, this Court, and Congress
erred in their prima facie judgment that the Rule in question transgresses neither
the terms of the Enabling Act nor constitutional restrictions.

We are reminded by the *Erie* opinion that neither Congress nor the federal
courts can, under the guise of formulating rules of decision for federal courts,
fashion rules which are not supported by a grant of federal authority contained
in Article I or some other section of the Constitution; in such areas state law
must govern because there can be no other law. But the opinion in *Erie*, which
involved no Federal Rule and dealt with a question which was "substantive" in
every traditional sense (whether the railroad owed a duty of care to Tompkins as
a trespasser or a licensee), surely neither said nor implied that measures like Rule
4(d)(1) are unconstitutional. For the constitutional provision for a federal court

---

** [The Court at this point explains why application of Rule 4(d)(1) would not violate the
standards developed under *Erie*, assuming that those were applicable. We will examine that discussion when we revisit *Erie* and *Hanna* in our coverage of Track Three analysis, at pages 534-536,
infra. — EDS.]

system (augmented by the Necessary and Proper Clause) carries with it congressional power to make rules governing the practice and pleading in those courts, which in turn includes a power to regulate matters which, though falling within the uncertain area between substance and procedure, are rationally capable of classification as either. Cf. *M'Culloch v. State of Maryland*, 4 Wheat. 316. Neither *York* nor [any other cases applying the *Erie* doctrine] ever suggested that the rule there laid down for coping with situations where no Federal Rule applies is coextensive with the limitation on Congress to which *Erie* had adverted.(Although this Court has never before been confronted with a case where the applicable Federal Rule is in direct collision with the law of the relevant State, courts of appeals faced with such clashes have rightly discerned the implications of our decisions.)

> "One of the shaping purposes of the Federal Rules is to bring about uniformity in the federal courts by getting away from local rules. This is especially true of matters which relate to the administration of legal proceedings, an area in which federal courts have traditionally exerted strong inherent power, completely aside from the powers Congress expressly conferred in the Rules. The purpose of the *Erie* doctrine, even as extended in *York* and *Ragan*, was never to bottle up federal courts with 'outcome-determinative' and 'integral-relations' stoppers—when there are 'affirmative countervailing [federal] considerations' and when there is a Congressional mandate (the Rules) supported by constitutional authority." *Lumbermen's Mutual Casualty Co. v. Wright*, 322 F.2d 759, 764 (C.A. 5th Cir. 1963).

Erie and its offspring cast no doubt on the long-recognized power of Congress to prescribe housekeeping rules for federal courts even though some of those rules will inevitably differ from comparable state rules. . . . Thus, though a court, in measuring a Federal Rule against the standards contained in the Enabling Act and the Constitution, need not wholly blind itself to the degree to which the Rule makes the character and result of the federal litigation stray from the course it would follow in state courts, it cannot be forgotten that the *Erie* rule, and the guidelines suggested in [*Guaranty Trust v. York*], were created to serve another purpose altogether. To hold that a Federal Rule of Civil Procedure must cease to function whenever it alters the mode of enforcing state-created rights would be to disembowel either the Constitution's grant of power over federal procedure or Congress' attempt to exercise that power in the Enabling Act. Rule 4(d)(1) is valid and controls the instant case.

Reversed.

MR. JUSTICE BLACK concurs in the result.

[JUSTICE HARLAN's concurring opinion follows the presentation of the second half of the *Hanna* Court's majority opinion, at page 535, *infra*.]

NOTES AND QUESTIONS

1. *Reinterpreting the precedents.* The Court in *Hanna* engaged in a bit of revisionist history when it declared:

The *Erie* rule has never been invoked to void a Federal Rule. It is true that there have been cases where this Court has held applicable a state rule in the face of an argument that the situation was governed by one of the Federal Rules. But the holding of each such case was not that *Erie* commanded displacement of a Federal Rule by an inconsistent state rule, but rather that the scope of the Federal Rule was not as broad as the losing party urged, and therefore, there being no Federal Rule which covered the point in dispute, *Erie* commanded the enforcement of state law.

In reality, both *Ragan* and *Cohen* specifically relied on *Erie* to resolve the choice-of-law issue presented. True, neither case held that the respective federal rule was "void," but both decisions refused to apply the federal rule in light of what was treated as conflicting state law. But revisionism is not necessarily a bad thing. *Hanna*'s reinterpretation of *Ragan* and *Cohen* at least offered a plausible alternative rationale for those decisions. Neither of the rules at issue in those cases expressly addressed the point "in conflict." Moreover, the reinterpretation polished the rough edges of the REA case law between *Sibbach* and *Hanna*, creating a powerful statement that underscored the FRCP's independent validity. And, as was true in *Sibbach*, *Erie* was again declared irrelevant as a measure of that validity.

2. The return of the two-step REA analysis.   In rejecting *Erie* as providing the proper measure to assess a formal federal rule, the *Hanna* Court returned to the formula that the REA established. As we have noted, the REA imposes two requirements: (1) the rule must be one of procedure or process—*i.e.*, it must be rationally classifiable as procedural; and (2) the rule may not abridge, enlarge, or modify a substantive right. But did the *Hanna* Court actually endorse this two-step interpretation of the REA? It would certainly seem to have done so, though the Court's discussion of the REA is somewhat cryptic. After revisiting and reinterpreting the *Ragan* decision, the Court quotes both provisions of the REA, and then explains how Rule 4(d)(1) "passes muster" under those dual standards. As to the process provision, the Court observes, "Prescribing the manner in which a defendant is to be notified that a suit has been instituted against him, it relates to the 'practice and procedure of the district courts.'" Then, with respect to the potential abridgement of a substantive right, the Court quotes approvingly from its decision in *Mississippi Publishing Corp. v. Murphree*, 326 U.S. 438 (1946), where the Court rejected an REA-based challenge to Rule 4(f), a provision that allowed service of process outside of a judicial district. The quotation explains that while adherence to Rule 4(f) might affect the processing of the defendant's substantive rights, application of that rule did not "operate to abridge, enlarge or modify the rules of decision by which that court will adjudicate its rights." In other words, adherence to Rule 4(f)'s service of process standard did not alter the elements or remedies of the claim asserted against the defendant. The implicit message of this discussion was that the same could be said of Rule 4(d)(1), namely, that its application would not operate to abridge, enlarge, or modify any substantive rights. Indeed, nothing in the *Hanna* opinion suggests that the defendant made an argument to the contrary.

The *Hanna* Court also observed that the federal rules are themselves subject to constitutional restraint. Of course, this is true of all federal and state laws. With respect to the federal rules, however, the primary constitutional constraints are built into the REA. The REA's "practice and procedure" requirement parallels the constitutional power of Congress to regulate procedure in federal courts, while the substantive-rights limitation operates as a limit on the delegation of that power to the Supreme Court. The first component is a product of the principle that the federal government can only exercise those powers granted to it—here, the power to regulate procedure in the federal courts. The second component is a product of the Non-Delegation Doctrine, which limits the extent to which Congress can delegate legislative authority to another branch of the federal government. Hence, satisfaction of the REA standards can be seen as establishing a strong presumption of constitutionality, even though this is rarely, if ever, discussed as such in judicial opinions applying the REA. This presumption of constitutionality would be overcome, however, if the rule at issue were to transgress a constitutional limitation such as those found in the Bill of Rights. There are no published reports of any such cases.

PROBLEMS

6-7. Olga filed suit against a nursing home, claiming that the home failed to protect her from an attack by another resident. She seeks actual and punitive damages. Assume that the suit was properly filed in a U.S. district court based on diversity jurisdiction and that Florida substantive law applies to her claims. The nursing home has moved to dismiss Olga's claim for punitive damages, based on a Florida statute that has been construed to require pre-clearance by a judge before any claim for punitive damages may be asserted. The statute does not, however, alter the standards under which punitive damages may be awarded. Olga argues that Federal Rule 8(a)(2) provides the controlling standards for claims filed in federal courts. It provides: "A pleading that states a claim for relief must contain . . . a short and plain statement of the claim showing that the pleader is entitled to relief; . . ." In addition, Rule 8(a)(3) states that the pleading shall include "a demand for the relief sought. . . ." What should the district court do? See *Cohen v. Office Depot, Inc.*, 184 F.3d 1292, 1297-1300 (11th Cir. 1999), *vacated on other grounds*, 204 F.3d 1069 (11th Cir.), *cert. denied*, 531 U.S. 957 (2000); *Alexander v. Univ./Gainesville Healthcare Ctr., Inc.*, 17 F. Supp. 2d 1291 (N.D. Fla. 1998).

6-8. Margaret filed a diversity action in a U.S. district court sitting in State X, claiming that she had suffered personal injuries while on the defendant's business premises. Her suit named Kirk, the registered owner of the business, as the sole defendant. Her complaint was filed and served within the applicable statute of limitations; however, unbeknownst to Margaret, Kirk had sold the business to George prior to the date on which Margaret was injured. Once she discovered the true facts, which was after the State X statute of limitations had run, Margaret attempted to amend her complaint by dismissing Kirk as a defendant and naming George in his stead. At that time, Federal Rule 15(c) would allow such an amendment to "relate back" to the time of the original filing, thus avoiding any statute of limitations problem, only if the newly named defendant had notice of the pending suit within the statute of limitations; George did not have any such notice. State X law, on the other hand, would allow relation back despite the lack of notice, essentially tolling the statute of limitations from the date of filing. As between Rule 15(c) and the law of State X, which should the district court follow? *See Marshall v. Mulrenin*, 508 F.2d 39, 44-45 (1st Cir. 1974). Read the current Rule 15(c)(1). Is the current version designed to avoid the issue confronting the court in this problem?

Shady Grove Orthopedic Associates, P.A. v. Allstate Insurance Co.
559 U.S. 393 (2010)

JUSTICE SCALIA announced the judgment of the Court and delivered the opinion of the Court with respect to Parts I and II-A, an opinion with respect to Parts II-B and II-D, in which THE CHIEF JUSTICE, JUSTICE THOMAS, and JUSTICE SOTOMAYOR join, and an opinion with respect to Part II-C, in which THE CHIEF JUSTICE and JUSTICE THOMAS join.

New York law prohibits class actions in suits seeking penalties or statutory minimum damages. We consider whether this precludes a federal district court sitting in diversity from entertaining a class action under Federal Rule of Civil Procedure 23.

I

The petitioner's complaint alleged the following: Shady Grove Orthopedic Associates, P. A., provided medical care to Sonia E. Galvez for injuries she suffered in an automobile accident. As partial payment for that care, Galvez assigned to Shady Grove her rights to insurance benefits under a policy issued in New York by Allstate Insurance Co. Shady Grove tendered a claim for the assigned benefits to Allstate, which under New York law had 30 days to pay the claim or deny it. See N.Y. Ins. Law Ann. § 5106(a) (West 2009). Allstate apparently paid, but not on time, and it refused to pay the statutory interest that accrued on the overdue benefits (at 2 percent per month).

Shady Grove filed this diversity suit in the Eastern District of New York to recover the unpaid statutory interest. Alleging that Allstate routinely refuses to pay interest on overdue benefits, Shady Grove sought relief on behalf of itself and a class of all others to whom Allstate owes interest. The District Court dismissed the suit for lack of jurisdiction. It reasoned that N.Y. Civ. Prac. Law Ann. § 901(b), which precludes a suit to recover a "penalty" from proceeding as a class action, applies in diversity suits in federal court, despite Federal Rule of Civil Procedure 23. Concluding that statutory interest is a "penalty" under New York law, it held that § 901(b) prohibited the proposed class action. And, since Shady Grove conceded that its individual claim (worth roughly $500) fell far short of the amount-in-controversy requirement for individual suits under 28 U.S.C. § 1332(a), the suit did not belong in federal court.[3]

The Second Circuit affirmed. The court did not dispute that a federal rule adopted in compliance with the Rules Enabling Act, 28 U.S.C. § 2072, would control if it conflicted with § 901(b). But there was no conflict because (as we will describe in more detail below) the Second Circuit concluded that Rule 23 and § 901(b) address different issues. . . .

We granted certiorari.

II

The framework for our decision is familiar. We must first determine whether Rule 23 answers the question in dispute. If it does, it governs—New York's law notwithstanding—unless it exceeds statutory authorization or Congress's rulemaking power. . . .

A

The question in dispute is whether Shady Grove's suit may proceed as a class action. Rule 23 provides an answer. It states that "[a] class action may be maintained" if two conditions are met: The suit must satisfy the criteria set forth in subdivision (a) (*i.e.*, numerosity, commonality, typicality, and adequacy of representation), and it also must fit into one of the three categories described in subdivision (b). Fed. Rule Civ. Proc. 23(b). By its terms this creates a categorical rule entitling a plaintiff whose suit meets the specified criteria to pursue his claim as a class action . . . . Thus, Rule 23 provides a one-size-fits-all formula for deciding the class-action question. Because § 901(b) attempts to answer the same question— *i.e.*, it states that Shady Grove's suit "may *not* be maintained as a class action" (emphasis added) because of the relief it seeks—it cannot apply in diversity suits unless Rule 23 is ultra vires.

The Second Circuit believed that § 901(b) and Rule 23 do not conflict because they address different issues. Rule 23, it said, concerns only the criteria for determining whether a given class can and should be certified; section 901(b), on the other hand, addresses an antecedent question: whether the particular type of claim is eligible for class treatment in the first place—a question on which Rule 23 is silent. Allstate embraces this analysis.

We disagree. To begin with, the line between eligibility and certifiability is entirely artificial. Both are preconditions for maintaining a class action . . . . Relabeling Rule 23(a)'s prerequisites "eligibility criteria" would obviate Allstate's objection— a sure sign that its eligibility-certifiability distinction is made-to-order. . . .

. . . Rule 23 permits all class actions that meet its requirements, and a State cannot limit that permission by structuring one part of its statute to track Rule 23

---

3. Shady Grove had asserted jurisdiction under 28 U.S.C. § 1332(d)(2), which relaxes, for class actions seeking at least $5 million, the rule against aggregating separate claims for calculation of the amount in controversy.

and enacting another part that imposes additional requirements. Both of § 901's subsections undeniably answer the same question as Rule 23: whether a class action may proceed for a given suit.

The dissent argues that § 901(b) has nothing to do with whether Shady Grove may maintain its suit as a class action, but affects only the *remedy* it may obtain if it wins. Whereas "Rule 23 governs procedural aspects of class litigation" by "prescrib[ing] the considerations relevant to class certification and postcertification proceedings," § 901(b) addresses only "the size of a monetary award a class plaintiff may pursue." Accordingly, the dissent says, Rule 23 and New York's law may coexist in peace.

We need not decide whether a state law that limits the remedies available in an existing class action would conflict with Rule 23; that is not what § 901(b) does. By its terms, the provision precludes a plaintiff from "maintain[ing]" a class action seeking statutory penalties. Unlike a law that sets a ceiling on damages (or puts other remedies out of reach) in properly filed class actions, § 901(b) says nothing about what remedies a court may award; it prevents the class actions it covers from coming into existence at all . . . .

The dissent all but admits that the literal terms of § 901(b) address the same subject as Rule 23—*i.e.*, whether a class action may be maintained—but insists the provision's *purpose* is to restrict only remedies. Unlike Rule 23, designed to further procedural fairness and efficiency, § 901(b) (we are told) "responds to an entirely different concern": the fear that allowing statutory damages to be awarded on a class-wide basis would "produce overkill." . . .

This evidence of the New York Legislature's purpose [relied on by the dissent] is pretty sparse. But even accepting the dissent's account of the Legislature's objective at face value, it cannot override the statute's clear text. Even if its aim is to restrict the remedy a plaintiff can obtain, § 901(b) achieves that end by limiting a plaintiff's power to maintain a class action . . . .

The dissent's approach of determining whether state and federal rules conflict based on the subjective intentions of the state legislature is an enterprise destined to produce "confusion worse confounded," *Sibbach v. Wilson & Co.*, 312 U.S. 1, 14 (1941). It would mean, to begin with, that one State's statute could survive pre-emption (and accordingly affect the procedures in federal court) while another State's identical law would not, merely because its authors had different aspirations. It would also mean that district courts would have to discern, in every diversity case, the purpose behind any putatively pre-empted state procedural rule, even if its text squarely conflicts with federal law. That task will often prove arduous. Many laws further more than one aim, and the aim of others may be impossible to discern . . . . Predictably, federal judges would be condemned to poring through state legislative history—which may be less easily obtained, less thorough, and less familiar than its federal counterpart.

But while the dissent does indeed artificially narrow the scope of § 901(b) by finding that it pursues only substantive policies, that is not the central difficulty of the dissent's position. The central difficulty is that even artificial narrowing cannot render § 901(b) compatible with Rule 23. *Whatever* the policies they pursue, they flatly contradict each other. Allstate asserts (and the dissent implies that we can (and must) *interpret* Rule 23 in a manner that avoids overstepping its authorizing statute. If the Rule were susceptible of two meanings—one that would violate § 2072(b) and another that would not—we would agree. But it is not. Rule 23 unambiguously authorizes *any* plaintiff, in *any* federal civil proceeding, to maintain a class action if the Rule's prerequisites are met. We cannot contort its text, even to avert a collision with state law that might render it invalid. What the dissent's approach achieves is not the avoiding of a "conflict between Rule 23 and § 901(b)," but rather the invalidation of Rule 23 (pursuant to § 2072(b) of the Rules Enabling Act) to the extent that it conflicts with the substantive policies of § 901. There is no other way to reach the dissent's destination. We must therefore confront head-on whether Rule 23 falls within the statutory authorization.

B

Erie involved the constitutional power of federal courts to supplant state law with judge-made rules. In that context, it made no difference whether the rule was technically one of substance or procedure; the touchstone was whether it "significantly affect[s] the result of a litigation." *Guaranty Trust Co. v. York*, 326 U.S. 99, 109 (1945). That is not the test for either the constitutionality or the statutory validity of a Federal Rule of Procedure. Congress has undoubted power to supplant state law, and undoubted power to prescribe rules for the courts it has created, so long as those rules regulate matters "rationally capable of classification" as procedure. *Hanna* [*v. Plumer*], 380 U.S. at 472. In the Rules Enabling Act, Congress authorized this Court to promulgate rules of procedure subject to its review, 28 U.S.C. § 2072(a), but with the limitation that those rules "shall not abridge, enlarge or modify any substantive right," § 2072(b).

We have long held that this limitation means that the Rule must "really regulat[e] procedure, the judicial process for enforcing rights and duties recognized by substantive law and for justly administering remedy and redress for disregard or infraction of them," *Sibbach* [*v. Wilson & Co.*], 312 U.S. at 14. The test is not whether the rule affects a litigant's substantive rights; most procedural rules do. *Mississippi Publishing Corp. v. Murphree*, 326 U.S. 438, 445 (1946). What matters is what the rule itself regulates: If it governs only "the manner and the means" by which the litigants' rights are "enforced," it is valid; if it alters "the rules of decision by which [the] court will adjudicate [those] rights," it is not. *Id.* at 446.

Applying that test, we have rejected every statutory challenge to a Federal Rule that has come before us. We have found to be in compliance with § 2072(b) rules prescribing methods for serving process, and requiring litigants whose mental or physical condition is in dispute to submit to examinations. Likewise, we have upheld rules authorizing imposition of sanctions upon those who file frivolous appeals, or who sign court papers without a reasonable inquiry into the facts asserted. Each of these rules had some practical effect on the parties' rights, but each undeniably regulated only the process for enforcing those rights; none altered the rights themselves, the available remedies, or the rules of decision by which the court adjudicated either.

Applying that criterion, we think it obvious that rules allowing multiple claims (and claims by or against multiple parties) to be litigated together are also valid. See, *e.g.*, Fed. Rules Civ. Proc. 18 (joinder of claims), 20 (joinder of parties), 42(a) (consolidation of actions). Such rules neither change plaintiffs' separate entitlements to relief nor abridge defendants' rights; they alter only how the claims are processed. For the same reason, Rule 23—at least insofar as it allows willing plaintiffs to join their separate claims against the same defendants in a class action—falls within § 2072(b)'s authorization. A class action, no less than traditional joinder (of which it is a species), merely enables a federal court to adjudicate claims of multiple parties at once, instead of in separate suits. And like traditional joinder, it leaves the parties' legal rights and duties intact and the rules of decision unchanged. . . .

Allstate argues that Rule 23 violates § 2072(b) because the state law it displaces, § 901(b), creates a right that the Federal Rule abridges—namely, a "substantive right . . . not to be subjected to aggregated class-action liability" in a single suit. To begin with, we doubt that that is so. Nothing in the text of § 901(b) (which is to be found in New York's procedural code) confines it to claims under New York law; and of course New York has no power to alter substantive rights and duties created by other sovereigns. As we have said, the *consequence* of excluding certain class actions may be to cap the damages a defendant can face in a single suit, but the law itself alters only procedure. In that respect, § 901(b) is no different from a state law forbidding simple joinder. As a fallback argument, Allstate argues that even if § 901(b) is a procedural provision, it was enacted "for *substantive reasons*." Its end was not to improve "the conduct of the litigation process itself" but to alter "the outcome of that process."

The fundamental difficulty with both these arguments is that the substantive nature of New York's law, or its substantive purpose, *makes no difference*. A Federal Rule of Procedure is not valid in some jurisdictions and invalid in others—or valid in some cases and invalid in others—depending upon whether its effect is to frustrate a state substantive law (or a state procedural law enacted for substantive purposes). That could not be clearer in *Sibbach*:

> ". . . If we were to adopt the suggested criterion of the importance of the alleged right we should invite endless litigation and confusion worse confounded. The test must be whether a rule really regulates procedure. . . ." 312 U.S. at 13-14 (footnotes omitted).

Hanna unmistakably expressed the same understanding that compliance of a Federal Rule with the Enabling Act is to be assessed by consulting the Rule itself, and not its effects in individual applications . . . .

In sum, it is not the substantive or procedural nature or purpose of the affected state law that matters, but the substantive or procedural nature of the Federal Rule. We have held since *Sibbach*, and reaffirmed repeatedly, that the validity of a Federal Rule depends entirely upon whether it regulates procedure. If it does, it is authorized by § 2072 and is valid in all jurisdictions, with respect to all claims, regardless of its incidental effect upon state-created rights.

C

A few words in response to the concurrence. . . .

The concurrence would decide this case on the basis, not that Rule 23 is procedural, but that the state law it displaces is procedural, in the sense that it does not "function as a part of the State's definition of substantive rights and remedies." A state procedural rule is not preempted, according to the concurrence, so long as it is "so bound up with," or "sufficiently intertwined with," a substantive state-law right or remedy "that it defines the scope of that substantive right or remedy."

This analysis squarely conflicts with *Sibbach*, which established the rule we apply. The concurrence contends that *Sibbach* did not rule out its approach, but that is not so. Recognizing the impracticability of a test that turns on the idiosyncrasies of state law, *Sibbach* adopted and applied a rule with a single criterion: whether the Federal Rule "really regulates procedure." 312 U.S. at 14. That the concurrence's approach would have yielded the same result in *Sibbach* proves nothing; what matters is the rule we *did* apply, and that rule leaves no room for special exemptions based on the function or purpose of a particular state rule. We have rejected an attempt to read into *Sibbach* an exception with no basis in the opinion, and we see no reason to find such an implied limitation today.

In reality, the concurrence seeks not to apply *Sibbach*, but to overrule it (or, what is the same, to rewrite it). Its approach, the concurrence insists, gives short shrift to the statutory text forbidding the Federal Rules from "abridg[ing], enlarg[ing], or modify[ing] any substantive right," § 2072(b). There is something to that. It is possible to understand how it can be determined whether a Federal Rule "enlarges" substantive rights without consulting State law: If the Rule creates a substantive right, even one that duplicates some state-created rights, it establishes a new *federal* right. But it is hard to understand how it can be determined whether a Federal Rule "abridges" or "modifies" substantive rights without knowing what state-created rights would obtain if the Federal Rule did not exist. *Sibbach*'s exclusive focus on the challenged Federal Rule—driven by the very real concern that Federal Rules which vary from State to State would be chaos—is hard to square with § 2072(b)'s terms.

Sibbach has been settled law, however, for nearly seven decades. Setting aside any precedent requires a "special justification" beyond a bare belief that it was wrong. And a party seeking to overturn a *statutory* precedent bears an even greater burden, since Congress remains free to correct us, and adhering to our precedent enables it do so. We do Congress no service by presenting it a moving target. In all events, Allstate has not even asked us to overrule *Sibbach*, let alone carried its burden of persuading us to do so. Why we should cast aside our decades-old decision escapes us, especially since (as the concurrence explains) that would not affect the result . . . .

* * *

The judgment of the Court of Appeals is reversed, and the case is remanded for further proceedings.

It is so ordered.

JUSTICE STEVENS, concurring in part and concurring in the judgment.

The New York law at issue, N.Y. Civ. Prac. Law Ann. (CPLR) § 901(b) (West 2006), is a procedural rule that is not part of New York's substantive law. Accordingly, I agree with Justice Scalia that Federal Rule of Civil Procedure 23 must apply in this case and join Parts I and II-A of the Court's opinion. But I also agree with Justice Ginsburg that there are some state procedural rules that federal courts must apply in diversity cases because they function as a part of the State's definition of substantive rights and remedies. . . .

If . . . the federal rule is "sufficiently broad to control the issue before the Court," such that there is a "direct collision," the court must decide whether application of the federal rule "represents a valid exercise" of the "rulemaking authority . . . bestowed on this Court by the Rules Enabling Act." *Burlington Northern R. Co.*, 480 U.S. at 5. That Act requires, *inter alia*, that federal rules "not abridge, enlarge or modify *any* substantive right." 28 U.S.C. § 2072(b) (emphasis added). Unlike Justice Scalia, I believe that an application of a federal rule that effectively abridges, enlarges, or modifies a state-created right or remedy violates this command. Congress may have the constitutional power "to supplant state law" with rules that are "rationally capable of classification as procedure," (internal quotation marks omitted), but we should generally presume that it has not done so. Indeed, the mandate that federal rules "shall not abridge, enlarge or modify any substantive right" evinces the opposite intent, as does Congress' decision to delegate the creation of rules to this Court rather than to a political branch.

Thus, the second step of the inquiry may well bleed back into the first. When a federal rule appears to abridge, enlarge, or modify a substantive right, federal courts must consider whether the rule can reasonably be interpreted to avoid that impermissible result. And when such a "saving" construction is not possible and the rule would violate the Enabling Act, federal courts cannot apply the rule. A federal rule, therefore, cannot govern a particular case in which the rule would displace a state law that is procedural in the ordinary use of the term but is so intertwined with a state right or remedy that it functions to define the scope of the state-created right. . . .

Justice Scalia believes that the sole Enabling Act question is whether the federal rule "really regulates procedure," which means, apparently, whether it regulates "the manner and the means by which the litigants' rights are enforced." I respectfully disagree. This interpretation of the Enabling Act is consonant with the Act's first limitation to "general rules of practice and procedure," § 2072(a). But it ignores the second limitation that such rules also "not abridge, enlarge or modify *any* substantive right," § 2072(b) (emphasis added), and in so doing ignores the balance that Congress struck between uniform rules of federal procedure and respect for a State's construction of its own rights and remedies. It also ignores the separation-of-powers presumption, and federalism presumption, that counsel against judicially created rules displacing state substantive law.

Although the plurality appears to agree with much of my interpretation of § 2072, it nonetheless rejects that approach for two reasons, both of which are mistaken. First, Justice Scalia worries that if federal courts inquire into the effect of federal rules on state law, it will enmesh federal courts in difficult determinations about whether application of a given rule would displace a state determination about substantive rights. I do not see why an Enabling Act inquiry that looks to state law necessarily is more taxing than Justice Scalia's.[10] Although, Justice Scalia may generally prefer easily administrable, bright-line rules, his preference does not give us license to adopt a second-best interpretation of the Rules Enabling Act. Courts cannot ignore text and context in the service of simplicity.

Second, the plurality argues that its interpretation of the Enabling Act is dictated by this Court's decision in *Sibbach*, which applied a Federal Rule about when parties must submit to medical examinations. But the plurality misreads that opinion . . . . To understand *Sibbach*, it is first necessary to understand the issue that was before the Court. The petitioner raised only the facial question whether "Rules 35 and 37 [of the Federal Rules of Civil Procedure] are . . . within the mandate of Congress to this court" and not the specific question of "the obligation of federal courts to apply the substantive law of a state." The Court, therefore, had no occasion to consider whether the particular application of the Federal Rules in question would offend the Enabling Act.

Nor, in *Sibbach*, was any further analysis necessary to the resolution of the case because the matter at issue, requiring medical exams for litigants, did not pertain to "substantive rights" under the Enabling Act. . . . We held that "the phrase 'substantive rights'" embraces only state rights, such as the tort law in that case, that are sought to be enforced in the judicial proceedings. If the Federal Rule had in fact displaced a state rule that was sufficiently intertwined with a state right or remedy, then perhaps the Enabling Act analysis would have been different.[13] Our subsequent cases are not to the contrary. . . .

---

10. It will be rare that a federal rule that is facially valid under 28 U.S.C. § 2072 will displace a State's definition of its own substantive rights. See Wright § 4509, at 272 (observing that "unusual cases occasionally might arise in which . . . because of an unorthodox state rule of law, application of a Civil Rule . . . would intrude upon state substantive rights"). Justice Scalia's interpretation, moreover, is not much more determinative than mine. Although it avoids courts' having to evaluate state law, it tasks them with figuring out whether a federal rule is really "procedural." It is hard to know the answer to that question and especially hard to resolve it without considering the nature and functions of the state law that the federal rule will displace. The plurality's "'test' is no test at all—in a sense, it is little more than the statement that a matter is procedural if, by revelation, it is procedural."

13. Put another way, even if a federal rule in most cases "really regulates procedure," *Sibbach*, 312 U.S. at 14[,] it does not "really regulat[e] procedure" when it displaces those rare state rules that, although "procedural" in the ordinary sense of the term, operate to define the rights and remedies available in a case. This is so because what is procedural in one context may be substantive in another.

As I have explained, in considering whether to certify a class action such as this one, a federal court must inquire whether doing so would abridge, enlarge, or modify New York's rights or remedies, and thereby violate the Enabling Act . . . . Faced with a federal rule that dictates an answer to a traditionally procedural question and that displaces a state rule, one can often argue that the state rule was *really* some part of the State's definition of its rights or remedies.

In my view, however, the bar for finding an Enabling Act problem is a high one. The mere fact that a state law is designed as a procedural rule suggests it reflects a judgment about how state courts ought to operate and not a judgment about the scope of state-created rights and remedies. And for the purposes of operating a federal court system, there are costs involved in attempting to discover the true nature of a state procedural rule and allowing such a rule to operate alongside a federal rule that appears to govern the same question. The mere possibility that a federal rule would alter a state-created right is not sufficient. There must be little doubt.

The text of CPLR § 901(b) expressly and unambiguously applies not only to claims based on New York law but also to claims based on federal law or the law of any other State. And there is no interpretation from New York courts to the contrary. It is therefore hard to see how § 901(b) could be understood as a rule that, though procedural in form, serves the function of defining New York's rights or remedies . . . . It is true, as the dissent points out, that there is a limited amount of legislative history that can be read to suggest that the New York officials who supported § 901(b) wished to create a "limitation" on New York's "statutory damages." But, as Justice Scalia notes, that is not the law that New York adopted.

The legislative history, moreover, does not clearly describe a judgment that § 901(b) would operate as a limitation on New York's statutory damages. . . .

Because Rule 23 governs class certification, the only decision is whether certifying a class in this diversity case would "abridge, enlarge or modify" New York's substantive rights or remedies. Although one can argue that class certification would enlarge New York's "limited" damages remedy, such arguments rest on extensive speculation about what the New York Legislature had in mind when it created § 901(b). But given that there are two plausible competing narratives, it seems obvious to me that we should respect the plain textual reading of § 901(b), a rule in New York's procedural code about when to certify class actions brought under any source of law, and respect Congress' decision that Rule 23 governs class certification in federal courts. In order to displace a federal rule, there must be more than just a possibility that the state rule is different than it appears.

Accordingly, I concur in part and concur in the judgment.

Justice Ginsburg, with whom Justice Kennedy, Justice Breyer, and Justice Alito join, dissenting. . . .

The Court reads Rule 23 relentlessly to override New York's restriction on the availability of statutory damages. Our decisions, however, caution us to ask, before undermining state legislation: Is this conflict really necessary? Had the Court engaged in that inquiry, it would not have read Rule 23 to collide with New York's legitimate interest in keeping certain monetary awards reasonably bounded. I would continue to interpret Federal Rules with awareness of, and sensitivity to, important state regulatory policies. Because today's judgment radically departs from that course, I dissent.

I . . .

In 1975, the Judicial Conference of the State of New York proposed a new class-action statute designed "to set up a flexible, functional scheme" that would provide "an effective, but controlled group remedy." Judicial Conference Report on CPLR, reprinted in 1975 N.Y. Laws pp. 1477, 1493 (McKinney). As originally drafted, the legislation addressed only the procedural aspects of class actions; it specified, for example, five prerequisites for certification, eventually codified at § 901(a), that closely tracked those listed in Rule 23. See CPLR § 901(a) (requiring, for class certification, numerosity, predominance, typicality, adequacy of representation, and superiority).

While the Judicial Conference proposal was in the New York Legislature's hopper, "various groups advocated for the addition of a provision that would prohibit class action plaintiffs from being awarded a statutorily-created penalty . . . except when expressly authorized in the pertinent statute." *Sperry v. Crompton Corp.*, 8 N.Y.3d 204, 211 (2007). These constituents "feared that recoveries beyond actual damages could lead to excessively harsh results." *Ibid.* "They also argued that there was no need to permit class actions . . . [because] statutory penalties . . . provided an aggrieved party with a sufficient economic incentive to pursue a claim." *Ibid.* Such penalties, constituents observed, often far exceed a plaintiff's actual damages. "When lumped together," they argued, "penalties and class actions produce overkill."

Aiming to avoid "annihilating punishment of the defendant," the New York Legislature amended the proposed statute to bar the recovery of statutory damages in class actions. In his signing statement, Governor Hugh Carey stated that the new statute "empowers the court to prevent abuse of the class action device and provides *a controlled remedy*." . . .

Shady Grove contends—and the Court today agrees—that Rule 23 unavoidably preempts New York's prohibition on the recovery of statutory damages in class actions. . . .

The Court, I am convinced, finds conflict where none is necessary. Mindful of the history behind § 901(b)'s enactment, the thrust of our precedent, and the substantive-rights limitation in the Rules Enabling Act, I conclude, as did the Second Circuit and every District Court to have considered the question in any detail, that Rule 23 does not collide with § 901(b). As the Second Circuit well understood, Rule 23 prescribes the considerations relevant to class certification and postcertification proceedings—but it does not command that a particular remedy be available when a party sues in a representative capacity. Section 901(b), in contrast, trains on that latter issue. Sensibly read, Rule 23 governs procedural aspects of class litigation, but allows state law to control the size of a monetary award a class plaintiff may pursue.

The Court single-mindedly focuses on whether a suit "may" or "may not" be maintained as a class action. Putting the question that way, the Court does not home in on the reason *why*. Rule 23 authorizes class treatment for suits satisfying its prerequisites because the class mechanism generally affords a fair and efficient way to aggregate claims for adjudication. Section 901(b) responds to an entirely different concern; it does not allow class members to recover statutory damages because the New York Legislature considered the result of adjudicating such claims en masse to be exorbitant. The fair and efficient *conduct* of class litigation is the legitimate concern of Rule 23; the *remedy* for an infraction of state law, however, is the legitimate concern of the State's lawmakers and not of the federal rulemakers . . . .

II

. . . Shady Grove's effort to characterize § 901(b) as simply "procedural" cannot successfully elide this fundamental norm: When no federal law or rule is dispositive of an issue, and a state statute is outcome affective in the sense our cases on *Erie* (pre and post-*Hanna*) develop, the Rules of Decision Act commands application of the State's law in diversity suits. As this case starkly demonstrates, if federal courts exercising diversity jurisdiction are compelled by Rule 23 to award statutory penalties in class actions while New York courts are bound by § 901(b)'s proscription, "substantial variations between state and federal [money judgments] may be expected." *Gasperini*, 518 U.S. at 430 (quoting *Hanna*, 380 U.S. at 467-468 (internal quotation marks omitted)). The "variation" here is indeed "substantial." Shady Grove seeks class relief that is *ten thousand times* greater than the individual remedy available to it in state court. As the plurality acknowledges, forum shopping will undoubtedly result if a plaintiff need only file in federal instead of state court to seek a massive monetary award explicitly barred by state law. See *Gasperini*, 518 U.S. at 431 ("*Erie* precludes a recovery in federal court significantly larger than the recovery that would have been tolerated in state court."). The "accident of diversity of citizenship," *Klaxon Co. v. Stentor Elec. Mfg. Co.*, 313 U.S. 487, 496 (1941), should not subject a defendant to such augmented liability . . . .

III

The Court's erosion of *Erie*'s federalism grounding impels me to point out the large irony in today's judgment. Shady Grove is able to pursue its claim in federal court only by virtue of the recent enactment of the Class Action Fairness Act of 2005 (CAFA), 28 U.S.C. § 1332(d). In CAFA, Congress opened federal-court doors to state-law-based class actions so long as there is minimal diversity, at least 100 class members, and at least $5,000,000 in controversy. By providing a federal forum, Congress sought to check what it considered to be the overreadiness of some state courts to certify class actions. In other words, Congress envisioned fewer—not more—class actions overall. Congress surely never anticipated that CAFA would make federal courts a mecca for suits of the kind Shady Grove has launched: class actions seeking state-created penalties for claims arising under state law-claims that would be barred from class treatment in the State's own courts . . . .

NOTES AND QUESTIONS

1. *Interpreting a federal rule.*   The key dispute between the majority (Parts I and II.A of Justice Scalia's opinion) and the dissent authored by Justice Ginsburg pertains to whether Rule 23 was sufficiently broad to control the issue presented — *i.e.*, whether Rule 23 controlled the question of class certification in the context of a lawsuit to enforce statutory penalties under New York law. Justice Scalia focuses on the rule's text and concludes that the text vests the plaintiff with a right to proceed as a class action (assuming other requisites of the rule are satisfied). To what extent does Justice Ginsburg rely on the text, or does her interpretation of Rule 23 emanate from something other than the text? If so, what principle animates that interpretation? Can you see how Justice Stevens's approach appears to be a hybrid of the approaches adopted by Justices Scalia and Ginsburg? The important point here is that there is no set formula for determining whether a federal rule is sufficiently broad to control the issue presented. Quite often, a combination of factors play into that decision. That combination includes the text of the rule, any Advisory Committee notes on the rule, relevant policy considerations, and a federalism-premised desire to avoid unnecessary conflicts with state law. In this sense, the three approaches in *Shady Grove* describe the range of possibilities that may influence a judge in concluding whether a particular rule is sufficiently broad to control the issue presented. It is less important that you choose among these approaches, than that you recognize the full range of interpretive possibilities.

2. *The plurality and the concurrence.*   Parts II.B and II.C of Justice Scalia's opinion represent a plurality viewpoint with which Justice Stevens disagrees. What is the precise nature of that disagreement? To what extent are the positions of Justices Scalia and Stevens consistent with *Sibbach* and/or *Hanna*? (In answering this question, you might want to review those decisions and the notes following them.) As a practical matter, when, if ever, might this disagreement be of significance? Although Justice Ginsburg takes no part in the debate between Justices Scalia and Stevens, is there any hint in her opinion as to which side of this debate she might favor?

PROBLEMS

6-9. In a case that had been removed from state to federal court based on diversity of citizenship, the plaintiffs won a jury verdict and were awarded a $305,000 judgment. The defendant appealed and procured a stay of judgment pending appeal. On appeal, after the plaintiffs again prevailed, they asked the court of appeals to assess a 10 percent affirmance penalty pursuant to a forum state statute that imposes such a penalty on all unsuccessful appeals in which a stay of judgment has been granted. The purpose of this statute is to discourage frivolous appeals. The Federal Rules of Appellate Procedure do not themselves impose any mandatory penalties. However, Appellate Rule 38 does provide: "If a court of appeals determines that an appeal is frivolous, it may . . . award just damages and single or double costs to the appellee." FED. R. APP. P. 38. Rule 38 was promulgated pursuant to the REA. Is the court of appeals bound by the forum state's mandatory affirmance penalty, or may the court exercise its discretion under Rule 38? In answering this question, consider how the various opinions in *Shady Grove* might factor into your analysis. *See Burlington N. R. Co. v. Woods*, 480 U.S. 1 (1987).

6-10. Federal Rule of Civil Procedure 8 establishes the general rules of pleading applicable in federal courts. As to the contents of a complaint, Rule 8(a)(2) requires only that the complaint contain "a short and plain statement of the claim showing that the pleader is entitled to relief; . . ." This standard, sometimes referred to as "notice" or "simplified" pleading, requires that the complaint simply provide sufficient factual matter to state a claim on which relief can be granted and to apprise the opposing party of that claim. Robin has filed a medical malpractice case in a State X federal court, properly invoking that court's diversity jurisdiction. Her complaint satisfies the requirements of notice pleading imposed by Rule 8(a)(2). The defendant, however, has filed a motion to dismiss Robin's claim for failure to comply with a State X "affidavit of merit" statute. That statute requires a plaintiff in a medical malpractice case to file, within 60 days of the filing of a complaint, an affidavit of a licensed physician verifying that there exists a reasonable probability that the care, skill, or knowledge exercised or exhibited in the treatment that is the subject of the complaint fell outside acceptable professional standards. Should the district court grant the defendant's motion? *See Chamberlain v. Giampapa, M.D.*, 210 F.3d 154 (3d Cir. 2000). Might it make a difference if the affidavit-of-merit statute required that the affidavit be attached to the complaint? *See Estate of C.A. v. Grier*, 752 F. Supp. 2d 763 (S.D. Tex. 2010); *Baird v. Celis*, 41 F. Supp. 2d 1358 (N.D. Ga. 1999).

6-11. Same facts as in the previous problem, but assume that Robin filed her case in a State T federal court. State T law requires that plaintiffs in medical malpractice suits file an "expert report" as to each defendant physician no later than 180 days after the date on which the action is filed. In terms of content, the mandated expert report is essentially the same as the State X affidavit-of-merit requirement described in the previous problem. The expert report may not be used as evidence at trial. If a plaintiff fails to file a timely and satisfactory expert report, the case must be dismissed with prejudice. Assume that Robin failed to file a timely expert report and that the defendant has moved to dismiss. Robin argues that the State T requirement is in "direct collision" with Rule 26(a)(2)(A), which provides that "a party must disclose to the other parties the identity of any witness it may use at trial" as an expert witness. The rule further provides that a "party must make these disclosures at the times and in the sequence that the court orders." FED. R. CIV. P. 26(a)(2)(C). Is there a real conflict between State T law and Rule 26(a)(2)? In answering this question, consider the likely purpose of Rule

26(a)(2)'s expert-disclosure requirement and the likely purpose of State T's expert-report requirement. *Compare Poindexter v. Bonsukan, M.D.*, 145 F. Supp. 2d 800 (E.D. Tex. 2001) (finding a conflict), *with Cruz v. Chang, M.D.*, 400 F. Supp. 2d 906 (W.D. Tex. 2005) (finding no conflict).

3.   Track Three: Federal Procedural Common Law

Most federal procedural law is embodied either in a statute or in a formal federal rule such as the FRCP. There is, however, a modest body of federal procedural common law. Some of this judge-made law stems from the Constitution, *e.g.*, the due process minimum contacts test of personal jurisdiction. Such constitutional federal procedural law trumps state law to the contrary on a straightforward Supremacy Clause analysis. Similarly, some federal procedural common law stems from statutory interpretation, *e.g.*, the judicially created complete diversity requirement of 28 U.S.C. § 1332. This form of federal procedural common law triggers a Track One analysis, *i.e.*, precisely the same analysis that applies to the underlying federal statute itself. There is, however, a third type of federal procedural common law, the content of which is neither constitutionally driven nor statutorily premised. The authority to create such free-standing procedural common law derives from an Article III court's inherent authority to develop rules of procedure when no constitutional, statutory, or formal federal rule exists. Obvious examples of this category include the doctrine of forum non conveniens, *see* Chapter V, *supra*, and the doctrines of claim and issue preclusion, *see* Chapter XIII, *infra*. When this type of federal judge-made procedural law conflicts with state law, Track Three analysis applies. And within this track, the *Erie* doctrine plays a direct and significant role. A word of advice: One must be patient in attempting to understand Track Three. The test and one's confidence in applying it emerge only after careful study of a series of cases that progressively refine the analysis.

Guaranty Trust Co. v. York

326 U.S. 99 (1945)

Mr. Justice Frankfurter delivered the opinion of the Court. . . .

[York filed a diversity suit against Guaranty Trust Company claiming breach of fiduciary duty (a state-created cause of action) and seeking equitable relief. She claimed that Guaranty was trustee over certain notes she held as a beneficiary of the trust relationship and that Guaranty had breached the trust by negotiating a reduction in the value of the notes. The suit was dismissed on Guaranty's motion for summary judgment, the federal district court having concluded that no trust relationship existed. The court of appeals reversed, holding that the company was a trustee with fiduciary obligations to the holders of the notes. The court of appeals also ruled that on remand the trial court was not bound by the otherwise applicable state statute of limitations, which seemed to bar the suit. Instead, the federal district court was free to rely on the equitable doctrine of laches as developed by federal decisional law. That doctrine gave a federal court broad discretion to determine whether a case had been timely filed. The issue before the Supreme Court was whether the trial court was free to apply the flexible doctrine of laches or was instead required to adhere to the state statute of limitations. The Court first ruled that the *Erie* doctrine was as fully applicable to a proceeding in equity as it was to a proceeding at law.] . . .

And so this case reduces itself to the narrow question whether, when no recovery could be had in a State court because the action is barred by the statute of limitations, a federal court in equity can take cognizance of the suit because there is diversity of citizenship between the parties. Is the outlawry, according to State law, of a claim created by the States a matter of "substantive rights" to be respected by a federal court of equity when that court's jurisdiction is dependent on the fact that there is a State-created right, or is such statute of "a mere remedial character," which a federal court may disregard? . . .

Here we are dealing with a right to recover derived not from the United States but from one of the States. When, because the plaintiff happens to be a non-resident, such a right is enforceable in a federal as well as in a State court, the forms and mode of enforcing the right may at times, naturally enough, vary because the two judicial systems are not identic. But since a federal court adjudicating a State-created right solely because of the diversity of citizenship of the parties is for that purpose, in effect, only another court of the State, it cannot afford recovery if the right to recover is made unavailable by the State nor can it substantially affect the enforcement of the right as given by the State.

And so the question is not whether a statute of limitations is deemed a matter of "procedure" in some sense. The question is whether such a statute concerns merely the manner and the means by which a right to recover, as recognized by the State, is enforced, or whether such statutory limitation is a matter of substance in the aspect that alone is relevant to our problem, namely, does it significantly affect the result of a litigation for a federal court to disregard a law of a State that would be controlling in an action upon the same claim by the same parties in a State court?

It is therefore immaterial whether statutes of limitation are characterized either as "substantive" or "procedural" in State court opinions in any use of those terms unrelated to the specific issue before us. *Erie R. Co. v. Tompkins* was not an endeavor to formulate scientific legal terminology. It expressed a policy that touches vitally the proper distribution of judicial power between State and federal courts. In essence, the intent of that decision was to insure that, in all cases where a federal court is exercising jurisdiction solely because of the diversity of citizenship of the parties, the outcome of the litigation in the federal court should be substantially the same, so far as legal rules determine the outcome of a litigation, as it would be if tried in a State court. The nub of the policy that underlies *Erie R. Co. v. Tompkins* is that for the same transaction the accident of a suit by a non-resident litigant in a federal court instead of in a State court a block away, should not lead to a substantially different result. And so, putting to one side abstractions regarding "substance" and "procedure," we have held that in diversity cases the federal courts must follow the law of the State as to burden of proof, as to conflict of laws, as to contributory negligence. *Erie R. Co. v. Tompkins* has been applied with an eye alert to essentials in avoiding disregard of State law in diversity cases in the federal courts. A policy so important to our federalism must be kept free from entanglements with analytical or terminological niceties.

Plainly enough, a statute that would completely bar recovery in a suit if brought in a State court bears on a State-created right vitally and not merely formally or negligibly. As to consequences that so intimately affect recovery or non-recovery a federal court in a diversity case should follow State law. . . . [I]f a plea of the statute of limitations would bar recovery in a State court, a federal court ought not to afford recovery. . . .

Diversity jurisdiction is founded on assurance to non-resident litigants of courts free from susceptibility to potential local bias. The Framers of the Constitution, according to [Chief Justice] Marshall, entertained "apprehensions" lest distant suitors be subjected to local bias in State courts, or, at least, viewed with "indulgence the possible fears and apprehensions" of such suitors. And so Congress afforded out-of-State litigants another tribunal, not another body of law. The operation of a double system of conflicting laws in the same State is plainly hostile to the reign of law. Certainly, the fortuitous circumstance of residence out of a State of one of the parties to a litigation ought not to give rise to a discrimination against others equally concerned but locally resident. The source of substantive rights enforced by a federal court under diversity jurisdiction, it cannot be said too often, is the law of the States. Whenever that law is authoritatively declared by a State, whether its voice be the legislature or its highest court, such law ought to govern in litigation founded on that law, whether the forum of application is a State or a federal court and whether the remedies be sought at law or may be had in equity. . . .

The judgment is reversed and the case is remanded for proceedings not inconsistent with this opinion.

So ordered.

Mr. Justice Roberts and Mr. Justice Douglas took no part in the consideration or decision of this case.

[The dissenting opinion of Mr. Justice Rutledge, joined by Mr. Justice Murphy, is omitted.]

NOTES AND QUESTIONS

1. *The specific holding in* York.   Under *Erie* and *Klaxon*, a federal court sitting in diversity is required to apply the same substantive law that a court of the forum

state would apply. The decision in *York* can be seen as a straightforward application of this principle. While Justice Frankfurter refused to rest his decision on the mere labels "substance" and "procedure," he did not ignore the significance of either concept. The key for him was not the label, but the law's actual operation. According to Frankfurter, if an ostensibly procedural rule operates in a substantive fashion, it will be treated as substantive law for purposes of the *Erie* doctrine. In essence, Frankfurter invites a realistic appraisal of how a particular law functions within the context of diversity jurisdiction. Why did he conclude that the operation of the doctrine of laches was substantive under the facts of *York?* Think of it this way: Under state law the cause of action was "outlawed," while under federal law it was not (at least theoretically). Thus the doctrine of laches operated in a substantive fashion because it recognized a state-created right that, as a practical matter, no longer existed under state law. It created (or revived) a state-law cause of action—a direct violation of the reserved-powers principle on which *Erie* had been decided.

   2. The expansive interpretation of York.   Justice Frankfurter's opinion goes well beyond the simple holding described in the preceding note—*i.e.,* that federal judge-made law may not revive a moribund state cause of action—to create a somewhat elusive test to measure the legitimacy of federal procedure. Near the end of his opinion, in what may well be dicta, he says that the critical question is whether the rule at issue may "significantly affect the result of a litigation." *Erie,* according to Frankfurter, was premised on the notion that when a federal court exercises diversity jurisdiction, "the outcome of the litigation . . . should be substantially the same, so far as legal rules determine the outcome of a litigation, as it would be if tried in a State court." *Id.* This insistence on a rough uniformity of outcomes emerged in subsequent cases as the "outcome-determinative test" under which—for a time, at least—not only federal judge-made law but also federal statutes and formal federal rules were subjected to the Court's *Erie/York* scrutiny. The *Ragan, Woods,* and *Cohen* cases discussed earlier, involving Federal Rules of Civil Procedure, fell prey to this all-encompassing formula, and it took the Supreme Court many years to pull itself out of that jurisprudential quagmire. Why was *York* an appropriate (or inappropriate) vehicle for the discussion of uniformity of outcomes? In other words, was the problem presented in *York* one of outcomes?

PROBLEM

   6-12. A commercial passenger plane crashed in Scotland killing all of the crew and passengers. One of the passengers was from California. Her estate filed a lawsuit against the airline in a California state court. All of the evidence of the crash, including the remains of the aircraft, is in Scotland, and the parties agree that liability must be established under Scottish law. The plaintiff filed suit in California because juries there tend to grant larger damage awards than in Scotland. Assume that personal jurisdiction is satisfied and that after the case was filed, the defendant properly removed it to federal court on the basis of alienage jurisdiction.

Once removed, the defendant then moved to dismiss under the doctrine of forum non conveniens, arguing that a forum in Scotland was available and substantially better suited to resolve the controversy. Assume that the federal law of *forum non conveniens* would permit the district court to grant the defendant's motion. However, California law as it existed at the time prohibited application of the doctrine of *forum non conveniens* when the plaintiff is a California citizen. Does the decision in *York* require the district court to conform its decision to the standards of California law?

A NOTE ON *BYRD* AND REFINING THE *ERIE/YORK* FORMULA

In the years following *York*, the Court sought to prune the perceived excesses of the *Erie/York* "outcome determinative" formula. One of its first attempts to do so was in *Byrd v. Blue Ridge Rural Electric Cooperative, Inc.*, 356 U.S. 525 (1958), a tort action filed in a South Carolina federal district court. The case turned on whether the plaintiff was a "statutory employee" of the defendant, in which event his sole remedy was that provided by South Carolina's Workers' Compensation Act. The question before the Court was whether, on remand, the "statutory employee" issue should be decided by a jury, as was the usual practice in federal court, or whether the district court should follow South Carolina's common law practice of having that issue decided by the judge. The Court held that for three reasons, the district court was not obligated to follow the state rule. First, the state practice was not clearly substantive, for it was not intended to be "bound up with" or an "integral part of" any "rights and obligations created by state law"; instead, it merely represented "a form and mode of enforcing the [employer's] immunity . . . ." Second, even if the practice were deemed to be substantive under the outcome-determinative test, there were "affirmative countervailing considerations" here that would trump any obligation to follow state law—namely, that an "essential characteristic" of the federal system is "the manner in which, in civil common-law actions, it distributes trial functions between judge and jury and, under the influence—if not the command—of the Seventh Amendment, assigns the disputed questions of fact to the jury." Finally, said the Court, this was not a case where the outcome of the litigation would in fact be "substantially affected by whether the issue of immunity is decided by a judge or a jury," for there was no "certainty that a different result would follow, or even the strong possibility that this would be the case."

This approach adopted by the *Byrd* Court is often described as "*Byrd* balancing." How might it have been applied in *York*?

PROBLEM

6-13. In light of *Byrd*, would your analysis of Problem 6-12 be different in any way? Before answering this question, reconsider the discussion of *forum non conveniens* in *Piper Aircraft Co. v. Reyno* in Chapter V, part B, page 451, *supra*.

Hanna v. Plumer [Part II]

380 U.S. 460 (1965)

[As we saw earlier, the issue in *Hanna v. Plumer*, page 509, *supra*, was whether a federal court sitting in diversity must follow the service requirements of Federal Rule 4(d)(1)—now Rule 4(e)(2)—or the more restrictive service requirements imposed by state law. In the previous excerpt from *Hanna*, the Court held that the REA provided the proper framework for the resolution of such conflicts. But before arriving at that conclusion, the Court assumed the applicability of *Erie/York* and in the process modified the rule to be extracted from those cases. The discussion is plainly dicta, but it is dicta that has been treated by both the Supreme Court and lower federal courts as authoritative.]

Respondent, by placing primary reliance on *York* and *Ragan*, suggests that the *Erie* doctrine acts as a check on the Federal Rules of Civil Procedure, that despite the clear command of Rule 4(d)(1), *Erie* and its progeny demand the application of the Massachusetts rule. Reduced to essentials, the argument is: (1) *Erie*, as refined in *York*, demands that federal courts apply state law whenever application of federal law in its stead will alter the outcome of the case. (2) In this case, a determination that the Massachusetts service requirements obtain will result in immediate victory for respondent. If, on the other hand, it should be held that Rule 4(d)(1) is applicable, the litigation will continue, with possible victory for petitioner. (3) Therefore, *Erie* demands application of the Massachusetts rule. The syllogism possesses an appealing simplicity, but is for several reasons invalid.

In the first place, it is doubtful that, even if there were no Federal Rule making it clear that in-hand service is not required in diversity actions, the *Erie* rule would have obligated the District Court to follow the Massachusetts procedure. "Outcome-determination" analysis was never intended to serve as a talisman. *Byrd v. Blue Ridge Rural Elec. Cooperative*, 356 U.S. 525, 537. Indeed, the message of *York* itself is that choices between state and federal law are to be made not by application of any automatic, "litmus paper" criterion, but rather by reference to the policies underlying the *Erie* rule.

The *Erie* rule is rooted in part in a realization that it would be unfair for the character of result of a litigation materially to differ because the suit had been brought in a federal court.

> "Diversity of citizenship jurisdiction was conferred in order to prevent apprehended discrimination in state courts against those not citizens of the state. *Swift v. Tyson* [16 Pet. 1] introduced grave discrimination by noncitizens against citizens. It made rights enjoyed under the unwritten 'general law' vary according to whether enforcement was sought in the state or in the federal court; and the privilege of selecting the court in which the right should be determined was conferred upon the noncitizen. Thus, the doctrine rendered impossible equal protection of the law." *Erie R. Co. v. Tompkins, supra*, 304 U.S. at 74-75.

The decision was also in part a reaction to the practice of "forum-shopping" which had grown up in response to the rule of *Swift v. Tyson*. That the *York* test was an attempt to effectuate these policies is demonstrated by the fact that the opinion framed the inquiry in terms of "substantial" variations between state and federal litigation. Not only are nonsubstantial, or trivial, variations not likely to raise the sort of equal protection problems which troubled the Court in *Erie*; they are also unlikely to influence the choice of a forum. The "outcome-determination" test therefore cannot be read without reference to the twin aims of the *Erie* rule: discouragement of forum-shopping and avoidance of inequitable administration of the laws.

The difference between the conclusion that the Massachusetts rule is applicable, and the conclusion that it is not, is of course at this point "outcome-determinative" in the sense that if we hold the state rule to apply, respondent prevails, whereas if we hold that Rule 4(d)(1) governs, the litigation will continue. But in this sense *every* procedural variation is "outcome-determinative." For example, having brought suit in a federal court, a plaintiff cannot then insist on the right to file subsequent pleadings in accord with the time limits applicable in state courts, even though enforcement of the federal timetable will, if he continues to insist that he must meet only the state time limit, result in determination of the controversy against him. So it is here. Though choice of the federal or state rule will at this point have a marked effect upon the outcome of the litigation, the difference between the two rules would be of scant, if any, relevance to the choice of a forum. Petitioner, in choosing her forum, was not presented with a situation where application of the state rule would wholly bar recovery; rather, adherence to the state rule would have resulted only in altering the way in which process was served. Moreover, it is difficult to argue that permitting service of defendant's wife to take the place of in-hand service of defendant himself alters the mode of enforcement of state-created rights in a fashion sufficiently "substantial" to raise the sort of equal protection problems to which the *Erie* opinion alluded. . . .

MR. JUSTICE HARLAN, concurring. . . .

. . . I have always regarded [*Erie*] as one of the modern cornerstones of our federalism, expressing policies that profoundly touch the allocation of judicial power between the state and federal systems. *Erie* recognized that there should not be two conflicting systems of law controlling the primary activity of citizens, for such alternative governing authority must necessarily give rise to a debilitating uncertainty in the planning of everyday affairs. And it recognized that the scheme of our Constitution envisions an allocation of law-making functions between state and federal legislative processes which is undercut if the federal judiciary can make substantive law affecting state affairs beyond the bounds of congressional legislative powers in this regard. Thus, in diversity cases *Erie* commands that it be the state law governing primary private activity which prevails.

The shorthand formulations which have appeared in some past decisions are prone to carry untoward results that frequently arise from oversimplification. The Court is quite right in stating that the "outcome-determinative" test of *Guaranty Trust Co. v. York*, if taken literally, proves too much, for any rule, no matter how clearly "procedural," can affect the outcome of litigation if it is not obeyed. In turning from the "outcome" test of *York* back to the unadorned forum-shopping rationale of *Erie*, however, the Court falls prey to like oversimplification, for a simple forum-shopping rule also proves too much; litigants often choose a federal forum merely to obtain what they consider the advantages of the Federal Rules of Civil Procedure or to try their cases before a supposedly more favorable judge. To my mind the proper line of approach in determining whether to apply a state or a federal rule, whether "substantive" or "procedural," is to stay close to basic principles by inquiring if the choice of rule would substantially affect those primary decisions respecting human conduct which our constitutional system leaves to state regulation. If so, *Erie* and the Constitution require that the state rule prevail, even in the face of a conflicting federal rule.

The Court weakens, if indeed it does not submerge, this basic principle by finding, in effect, a grant of substantive legislative power in the constitutional provision for a federal court system (compare *Swift v. Tyson*, 16 Pet. 1), and through it, setting up the Federal Rules as a body of law inviolate.

> "[T]he constitutional provision for a federal court system . . . carries with it congressional power . . . to regulate matters which, though falling within the uncertain area between substance and procedure, *are rationally capable of classification as either*." (Emphasis supplied.)

So long as a reasonable man could characterize any duly adopted federal rule as "procedural," the Court, unless I misapprehend what is said, would have it apply no matter how seriously it frustrated a State's substantive regulation of the primary conduct and affairs of its citizens. Since the members of the Advisory Committee, the Judicial Conference, and this Court who formulated the Federal Rules are presumably reasonable men, it follows that the integrity of the Federal Rules is absolute. Whereas the unadulterated outcome and forum-shopping tests may err too far toward honoring state rules, I submit that the Court's "arguably procedural, *ergo* constitutional" test moves too fast and far in the other direction. . . .

NOTES AND QUESTIONS

1. The refined outcome-determinative test.   As we saw in our first excerpt from *Hanna* on page 509, *supra*, the Court rejected *Erie* as a legitimate basis for measuring the validity of a Federal Rule of Civil Procedure. The Court's discussion of *Erie* in this second excerpt from *Hanna*, therefore, is plainly dictum, but it is a dictum that has been adopted as part of the *Erie* jurisprudence. How does this opinion modify the outcome-determinative test? Specifically, from what point in the litigation process is outcome determination to be measured? Why? Can you see how the *Hanna* Court's application of the outcome-determinative test reflects the reserved-powers principles described and applied in *Erie*?

The *Hanna* version of outcome determination is often referred to as the "refined outcome-determinative test." Consider whether *Gasperini*, the next principal case, properly applies the outcome-determinative test as refined by *Hanna*.

2. The elements of Track Three analysis.   Track Three analysis parallels Tracks One and Two to the extent that we must first determine whether the judge-made rule or doctrine is sufficiently broad to control resolution of the issue presented to the court. As noted previously, see page 486, *supra*, there is also an implicit requirement that the judge-made rule pertain to procedure, *i.e.*, the doctrine must be rationally capable of being characterized as procedural. The only additional wrinkle on this latter point is that the judge-made procedural doctrine must be consistent with any federal statutes or formal federal rules. In other words, the common law of procedure cannot trump federal statutes or formal federal rules. Once we determine that the judge-made rule is applicable and within the federal court's power to fashion rules of procedure, we apply *Hanna's* refined outcome-determinative test. Under that test, if application of the judge-made rule would be outcome determinative at the forum-shopping stage, then state law must be followed unless, under *Byrd* balancing, federal policy trumps the application of state law.

PROBLEMS

6-14. Let's reconsider the facts of *Byrd*, discussed at page 533, *supra*. The case was filed in federal court under diversity jurisdiction and the question was whether the injured plaintiff was a "statutory employee" within the meaning of state law. Recall that under state law, a judge would decide this question, while under federal practice it was one for the jury. How would you apply the refined outcome-determinative test to this scenario? Do you need to apply *Byrd* balancing to resolve the *Erie* problem?

6-15. Chambers, the director of a company that operated a television station in Louisiana, agreed to sell the station's facilities and broadcast license to NASCO. When Chambers changed his mind, NASCO filed a diversity action seeking specific performance. Before and during the litigation, Chambers engaged in a series of frivolous actions designed to frustrate the sale's consummation and the district court's ability to resolve the dispute. The court eventually entered judgment for NASCO and, on NASCO's motion, imposed sanctions against Chambers in the form of attorneys' fees and expenses totaling almost $1 million, representing NASCO's total litigation costs paid to its attorneys. In so ruling, the court explained that Chambers had (1) attempted to deprive the court of jurisdiction by acts of fraud; (2) filed false and frivolous pleadings; and (3) "attempted, by other tactics of delay, oppression, harassment and massive expense to reduce [NASCO] to exhausted compliance." In ordering sanctions, the court relied on its inherent power as an Article III court to sanction misconduct in cases filed before it. Louisiana law, however, bars the shifting of attorneys' fees in the absence of express statutory authorization; no such statutory provision was applicable here. On appeal, assuming the outrageousness of Chambers's behavior was established, should the appellate court affirm or reverse the district court's imposition of sanctions? *See Chambers v. NASCO, Inc.*, 501 U.S. 32 (1991).

Gasperini v. Center for Humanities, Inc.

518 U.S. 415 (1996)

JUSTICE GINSBURG delivered the opinion of the Court.

Under the law of New York, appellate courts are empowered to review the size of jury verdicts and to order new trials when the jury's award "deviates materially from what would be reasonable compensation." N.Y. Civ. Prac. Law and Rules (CPLR) § 5501(c). Under the Seventh Amendment, which governs proceedings in federal court, but not in state court, "the right of trial by jury shall be preserved, and no fact tried by a jury, shall be otherwise re-examined in any Court of the United States, than according to the rules of the common law." The compatibility of these provisions, in an action based on New York law but tried in federal court by reason of the parties' diverse citizenship, is the issue we confront in this case. We hold that New York's law controlling compensation awards for excessiveness or inadequacy can be given effect, without detriment to the Seventh Amendment, if the review standard set out in CPLR § 5501(c) is applied by the federal trial court judge, with appellate control of the trial court's ruling limited to review for "abuse of discretion."

I

Petitioner William Gasperini, a journalist for CBS News and the Christian Science Monitor, began reporting on events in Central America in 1984. He earned his living primarily in radio and print media and only occasionally sold his photographic work. During the course of his seven-year stint in Central America, Gasperini took over 5,000 slide transparencies, depicting active war zones, political leaders, and scenes from daily life. In 1990, Gasperini agreed to supply his original color transparencies to The Center for Humanities, Inc. (Center) for use in an educational videotape, Conflict in Central America. Gasperini selected 300 of his slides for the Center; its videotape included 110 of them. The Center agreed to return the original transparencies, but upon the completion of the project, it could not find them.

Gasperini commenced suit in the United States District Court for the Southern District of New York, invoking the court's diversity jurisdiction pursuant to 28 U.S.C. § 1332. . . . The Center conceded liability for the lost transparencies and the issue of damages was tried before a jury.

At trial, Gasperini's expert witness testified that the "industry standard" within the photographic publishing community valued a lost transparency at $1,500. This industry standard, the expert explained, represented the average license fee a commercial photograph could earn over the full course of the photographer's copyright, *i.e.*, in Gasperini's case, his lifetime plus 50 years. Gasperini estimated that his earnings from photography totaled just over $10,000 for the period from 1984 through 1993. He also testified that he intended to produce a book containing his best photographs from Central America.

After a three-day trial, the jury awarded Gasperini $450,000 in compensatory damages. This sum, the jury foreperson announced, "is [$]1500 each, for 300 slides." Moving for a new trial under Federal Rule of Civil Procedure 59, the Center attacked the verdict on various grounds, including excessiveness. Without comment, the District Court denied the motion.

The Court of Appeals for the Second Circuit vacated the judgment entered on the jury's verdict. Mindful that New York law governed the controversy, the Court of Appeals endeavored to apply CPLR § 5501(c), which instructs that, when a jury returns an itemized verdict, as the jury did in this case, the New York Appellate Division "shall determine that an award is excessive or inadequate if it deviates materially from what would be reasonable compensation." . . . Surveying Appellate Division decisions that reviewed damage awards for lost transparencies, the Second Circuit concluded that testimony on industry standard alone was insufficient to justify a verdict; prime among other factors warranting consideration were the uniqueness of the slides' subject matter and the photographer's earning level.

Guided by Appellate Division rulings, the Second Circuit held that the $450,000 verdict "materially deviates from what is reasonable compensation." Some of Gasperini's transparencies, the Second Circuit recognized, were unique, notably those capturing combat situations in which Gasperini was the only photographer present. But others "depicted either generic scenes or events at which other professional photojournalists were present." No more than 50 slides merited a $1,500 award, the court concluded, after "[g]iving Gasperini every benefit of the doubt." Absent evidence showing significant earnings from photographic endeavors or concrete plans to publish a book, the court further determined, any damage award above $100 each for the remaining slides would be excessive. Remittiturs "presen[t] difficult problems for appellate courts," the Second Circuit acknowledged, for court of appeals judges review the evidence from "a cold paper record." Nevertheless, the Second Circuit set aside the $450,000 verdict and ordered a new trial, unless Gasperini agreed to an award of $100,000. . . .

II

Before 1986, state and federal courts in New York generally invoked the same judge-made formulation in responding to excessiveness attacks on jury verdicts: courts would not disturb an award unless the amount was so exorbitant that it "shocked the conscience of the court." . . .

In both state and federal courts, trial judges made the excessiveness assessment in the first instance, and appellate judges ordinarily deferred to the trial court's judgment.

In 1986, as part of a series of tort reform measures, New York codified a standard for judicial review of the size of jury awards. Placed in CPLR § 5501(c), the prescription reads:

"In reviewing a money judgment . . . in which it is contended that the award is excessive or inadequate and that a new trial should have been granted unless a stipulation is entered to a different award, the appellate division shall determine that an award is excessive or inadequate if it deviates materially from what would be reasonable compensation."

As stated in Legislative Findings and Declarations accompanying New York's adoption of the "deviates materially" formulation, the lawmakers found the "shock the conscience" test an insufficient check on damage awards; the legislature therefore installed a standard "invit[ing] more careful appellate scrutiny." . . .

New York state-court opinions confirm that § 5501(c)'s "deviates materially" standard calls for closer surveillance than "shock the conscience" oversight.

Although phrased as a direction to New York's intermediate appellate courts, § 5501(c)'s "deviates materially" standard, as construed by New York's courts, instructs state trial judges as well. Application of § 5501(c) at the trial level is key to this case.

To determine whether an award "deviates materially from what would be reasonable compensation," New York state courts look to awards approved in similar cases. Under New York's former "shock the conscience" test, courts also referred to analogous cases. The "deviates materially" standard, however, in design and operation, influences outcomes by tightening the range of tolerable awards.

III

In cases like Gasperini's, in which New York law governs the claims for relief, does New York law also supply the test for federal-court review of the size of the verdict? The Center answers yes. The "deviates materially" standard, it argues, is a substantive standard that must be applied by federal appellate courts in diversity cases. The Second Circuit agreed. Gasperini, emphasizing that § 5501(c) trains on the New York Appellate Division, characterizes the provision as procedural, an allocation of decisionmaking authority regarding damages, not a hard cap on the amount recoverable. Correctly comprehended, Gasperini urges, § 5501(c)'s direction to the Appellate Division cannot be given effect by federal appellate courts without violating the Seventh Amendment's Reexamination Clause.

As the parties' arguments suggest, CPLR § 5501(c), appraised under *Erie R. Co. v. Tompkins*, 304 U.S. 648 (1938), and decisions in *Erie*'s path, is both "substantive" and "procedural": "substantive" in that § 5501(c)'s "deviates materially" standard controls how much a plaintiff can be awarded; "procedural" in that § 5501(c) assigns decisionmaking authority to New York's Appellate Division. Parallel application of § 5501(c) at the federal appellate level would be out of sync with the federal system's division of trial and appellate court functions, an allocation weighted by the Seventh Amendment. The dispositive question, therefore, is whether federal courts can give effect to the substantive thrust of § 5501(c) without untoward alteration of the federal scheme for the trial and decision of civil cases.

A

Federal diversity jurisdiction provides an alternative forum for the adjudication of state-created rights, but it does not carry with it generation of rules of substantive law. . . . Under the *Erie* doctrine, federal courts sitting in diversity apply state substantive law and federal procedural law.

Classification of a law as "substantive" or "procedural" for *Erie* purposes is sometimes a challenging endeavor. *Guaranty Trust Co. v. York*, 326 U.S. 99 (1945), an early interpretation of *Erie*, propounded an "outcome-determination" test: "[D]oes it significantly affect the result of a litigation for a federal court to disregard a law of a State that would be controlling in an action upon the same claim by the same parties in a State court?" . . . A later pathmarking case, qualifying *Guaranty Trust*, explained that the "outcome-determination" test must not be applied mechanically to sweep in all manner of variations; instead, its application must be guided by "the twin aims of the *Erie* rule: discouragement of forum-shopping and avoidance of inequitable administration of the laws." *Hanna v. Plumer*, 380 U.S. 460, 468 (1965).

Informed by these decisions, we address the question whether New York's "deviates materially" standard, codified in CPLR § 5501(c), is outcome affective in this sense: Would "application of the [standard] . . . have so important an effect upon the fortunes of one or both of the litigants that failure to [apply] it would [unfairly discriminate against citizens of the forum State, or] be likely to cause a plaintiff to choose the federal court"? *Id.*, at 468, n.9.

We start from a point the parties do not debate. Gasperini acknowledges that a statutory cap on damages would supply substantive law for *Erie* purposes. Although CPLR § 5501(c) is less readily classified, it was designed to provide an analogous control.

New York's Legislature codified in § 5501(c) a new standard, one that requires closer court review than the common-law "shock the conscience" test. More rigorous comparative evaluations attend application of § 5501(c)'s "deviates materially" standard. To foster predictability, the legislature required the reviewing court, when overturning a verdict under § 5501(c), to state its reasons, including the factors it considered relevant. We think it a fair conclusion that CPLR § 5501(c) differs from a statutory cap principally "in that the maximum amount recoverable is not set forth by statute, but rather is determined by case law." In sum, § 5501(c) contains a procedural instruction, but the State's objective is manifestly substantive.

It thus appears that if federal courts ignore the change in the New York standard and persist in applying the "shock the conscience" test to damage awards on claims governed by New York law, "'substantial' variations between state and federal [money judgments]" may be expected. We therefore agree with the Second Circuit that New York's check on excessive damages implicates what we have called *Erie*'s "twin aims." Just as the *Erie* principle precludes a federal court from giving a state-created claim "longer life . . . than [the claim] would have had in the state court," *Ragan*, 337 U.S., at 533-534, so *Erie* precludes a recovery in federal court significantly larger than the recovery that would have been tolerated in state court.

B

CPLR § 5501(c), as earlier noted, is phrased as a direction to the New York Appellate Division. Acting essentially as a surrogate for a New York appellate forum, the Court of Appeals reviewed Gasperini's award to determine if it "deviate[d] materially" from damage awards the Appellate Division permitted in similar circumstances. The Court of Appeals performed this task without benefit of an opinion from the District Court, which had denied "without comment" the Center's Rule 59 motion. Concentrating on the authority § 5501(c) gives to the Appellate Division, Gasperini urges that the provision shifts fact-finding responsibility from the jury and the trial judge to the appellate court. Assigning such responsibility to an appellate court, he maintains, is incompatible with the Seventh Amendment's Reexamination Clause, and therefore, Gasperini concludes, § 5501(c) cannot be given effect in federal court. Although we reach a different conclusion than Gasperini, we agree that the Second Circuit did not attend to "[a]n essential characteristic of [the federal court] system," *Byrd v. Blue Ridge Rural Elec. Cooperative, Inc.*, 356 U.S. 525, 537 (1958), when it used § 5501(c) as "the standard for [federal] appellate review."

That "essential characteristic" was described in *Byrd*, a diversity suit for negligence in which a pivotal issue of fact would have been tried by a judge were the case in state court. The *Byrd* Court held that, despite the state practice, the plaintiff was entitled to a jury trial in federal court. In so ruling, the Court said that the *Guaranty Trust* "outcome-determination" test was an insufficient guide in cases presenting countervailing federal interests. The Court described the countervailing federal interests present in *Byrd* this way:

> "The federal system is an independent system for administering Justice to litigants who properly invoke its jurisdiction. An essential characteristic of that system is the manner in which, in civil common-law actions, it distributes trial functions between judge and jury and, under the influence—if not the command—of the Seventh Amendment, assigns the decisions of disputed questions of fact to the jury."

The Seventh Amendment, which governs proceedings in federal court, but not in state court, bears not only on the allocation of trial functions between judge and jury, the issue in *Byrd*; it also controls the allocation of authority to review verdicts, the issue of concern here. The Amendment reads:

> "In Suits at common law, where the value in controversy shall exceed twenty dollars, the right of trial by jury shall be preserved, and no fact tried by a jury, shall be otherwise re-examined in any Court of the United States, than according to the rules of the common law."

Byrd involved the first Clause of the Amendment, the "trial by jury" Clause. This case involves the second, the "re-examination" Clause. In keeping with the historic understanding, the Reexamination Clause does not inhibit the authority of trial judges to grant new trials "for any of the reasons for which new trials have heretofore been granted in actions at law in the courts of the United States." Fed. Rule Civ. Proc. 59(a). . . . "The trial judge in the federal system," we have reaffirmed, "has . . . discretion to grant a new trial if the verdict appears to [the judge] to be against the weight of the evidence." *Byrd*, 356 U.S., at 540. This discretion includes overturning verdicts for excessiveness and ordering a new trial without qualification, or conditioned on the verdict winner's refusal to agree to a reduction (remittitur).

In contrast, appellate review of a federal trial court's denial of a motion to set aside a jury's verdict as excessive is a relatively late, and less secure, development. Such review was once deemed inconsonant with the Seventh Amendment's Reexamination Clause. We subsequently recognized that, even in cases in which the *Erie* doctrine was not in play—cases arising wholly under federal law—the question was not settled; we twice granted certiorari to decide the unsettled issue, but ultimately resolved the cases on other grounds.

Before today, we have not "expressly [held] that the Seventh Amendment allows appellate review of a district court's denial of a motion to set aside an award as excessive." *Browning-Ferris Industries of Vt., Inc. v. Kelco Disposal, Inc.*, 492 U.S. 257, 279, n.25 (1989). But in successive reminders that the question was worthy of this Court's attention, we noted, without disapproval, that courts of appeals engage in review of district court excessiveness determinations, applying "abuse of discretion" as their standard. . . .

As the Second Circuit explained, appellate review for abuse of discretion is reconcilable with the Seventh Amendment as a control necessary and proper to the fair administration of justice: "We must give the benefit of every doubt to the judgment of the trial judge; but surely there must be an upper limit, and whether that has been surpassed is not a question of fact with respect to which reasonable men may differ, but a question of law." *Dagnello v. Long Island R. Co.*, 289 F.2d 797, 806 (CA2 1961). . . . We now approve this line of decisions. . . .

C

In *Byrd*, the Court faced a one-or-the-other choice: trial by judge as in state court, or trial by jury according to the federal practice. In the case before us, a choice of that order is not required, for the principal state and federal interests can be accommodated. The Second Circuit correctly recognized that when New York substantive law governs a claim for relief, New York law and decisions guide the allowable damages. But that court did not take into account the characteristic of the federal court system that caused us to reaffirm: "The proper role of the trial and appellate courts in the federal system in reviewing the size of jury verdicts is . . . a matter of federal law." *Donovan v. Penn Shipping Co.*, 429 U.S. 648, 649 (1977) (*per curiam*).

New York's dominant interest can be respected, without disrupting the federal system, once it is recognized that the federal district court is capable of performing the checking function, *i.e.*, that court can apply the State's "deviates materially" standard in line with New York case law evolving under CPLR § 5501(c).[22] We

---

22. Justice Scalia finds in Federal Rule of Civil Procedure 59 a "federal standard" for new trial motions in "'direct collision'" with, and "'leaving no room for the operation of,'" a state law like CPLR § 5501(c). The relevant prescription, Rule 59(a), has remained unchanged since the adoption of the Federal Rules by this Court in 1937. Rule 59(a) is as encompassing as it is uncontroversial. It is indeed "Hornbook" law that a most usual ground for a Rule 59 motion is that "the damages are excessive." See C. Wright, Law of Federal Courts 676-677 (5th ed. 1994). Whether damages are excessive for the claim-in-suit must be governed by some law. And there is no candidate for that governance other than the law that gives rise to the claim for relief—here, the law of New York.

recall, in this regard, that the "deviates materially" standard serves as the guide to be applied in trial as well as appellate courts in New York.

Within the federal system, practical reasons combine with Seventh Amendment constraints to lodge in the district court, not the court of appeals, primary responsibility for application of § 5501(c)'s "deviates materially" check. Trial judges have the "unique opportunity to consider the evidence in the living courtroom context," *Taylor v. Washington Terminal Co.*, 409 F.2d 145, 148 (C.A.D.C. 1969), while appellate judges see only the "cold paper record."

District court applications of the "deviates materially" standard would be subject to appellate review under the standard the Circuits now employ when inadequacy or excessiveness is asserted on appeal: abuse of discretion. In light of *Erie*'s doctrine, the federal appeals court must be guided by the damage-control standard state law supplies, but as the Second Circuit itself has said: "If we reverse, it must be because of an abuse of discretion. . . . The very nature of the problem counsels restraint. . . . We must give the benefit of every doubt to the judgment of the trial judge." *Dagnello*, 289 F.2d, at 806.

IV

It does not appear that the District Court checked the jury's verdict against the relevant New York decisions demanding more than "industry standard" testimony to support an award of the size the jury returned in this case. As the Court of Appeals recognized, the uniqueness of the photographs and the plaintiff's earnings as photographer — past and reasonably projected — are factors relevant to appraisal of the award. Accordingly, we vacate the judgment of the Court of Appeals and instruct that court to remand the case to the District Court so that the trial judge, revisiting his ruling on the new trial motion, may test the jury's verdict against CPLR § 5501(c)'s "deviates materially" standard.

It is so ordered.

JUSTICE STEVENS, dissenting.

While I agree with most of the reasoning in the Court's opinion, I disagree with its disposition of the case. I would affirm the judgment of the Court of Appeals. I would also reject the suggestion that the Seventh Amendment limits the power of a federal appellate court sitting in diversity to decide whether a jury's award of damages exceeds a limit established by state law. . . .

JUSTICE SCALIA, with whom THE CHIEF JUSTICE and JUSTICE THOMAS join, dissenting. . . .

[The bulk of Justice Scalia's opinion criticizes the Court's interpretation of the Seventh Amendment. The portion printed below responds to the Court's *Erie* analysis.]

The Court . . . holds today that a state practice that relates to the division of duties between state judges and juries must be followed by federal courts in diversity cases. On this issue, . . . our prior cases are directly to the contrary. . . .

The Court acknowledges that state procedural rules cannot, as a general matter, be permitted to interfere with the allocation of functions in the federal court system. Indeed, it is at least partly for this reason that the Court rejects direct application of § 5501(c) at the appellate level as inconsistent with an " 'essential characteristic' " of the federal court system — by which the Court presumably means abuse-of-discretion review of denials of motions for new trials. But the scope of the Court's concern is oddly circumscribed. The "essential characteristic" of the federal jury, and, more specifically, the role of the federal trial court in reviewing jury judgments, apparently counts for little. The Court approves the "accommodat[ion]" achieved by having district courts review jury verdicts under the "deviates materially" standard, because it regards that as a means of giving effect to the State's purposes "without disrupting the federal system." But changing the standard by which trial judges review jury verdicts *does* disrupt the federal system, and is plainly inconsistent with the "strong federal policy against allowing state rules to disrupt the judge-jury relationship in federal court." *Byrd v. Blue Ridge Rural Elec. Cooperative, Inc.*, 356 U.S. 525, 538 (1958). The Court's opinion does not even acknowledge, let alone address, this dislocation.

. . . It seems to me quite wrong to regard [§ 5501(c)] as a "substantive" rule for *Erie* purposes. The "analog[y]" to "a statutory cap on damages" fails utterly. There is an absolutely fundamental distinction between a *rule of law* such as that, which would ordinarily be imposed upon the jury in the trial court's instructions, and a *rule of review*, which simply determines how closely the jury verdict will be scrutinized for compliance with the instructions. A tighter standard for reviewing jury determinations can no more plausibly be called a "substantive" disposition than can a tighter appellate standard for reviewing trial-court determinations. The one, like the other, provides additional assurance *that the law has been complied with*; but the other, like the one, *leaves the law unchanged*.

The Court commits the classic *Erie* mistake of regarding whatever changes the outcome as substantive. That is not the only factor to be considered. Outcome determination "was never intended to serve as a talisman," *Hanna v. Plumer*, 380 U.S. 460, 466-467 (1965), and does not have the power to convert the most classic elements of the *process* of assuring that the law is observed into the substantive law itself. . . .

In any event, the Court exaggerates the difference that the state standard will make. It concludes that the different outcomes are likely to ensue depending on whether the law being applied is the state "deviates materially" standard of § 5501(c) or the "shocks the conscience" standard. Of course it is not the federal *appellate* standard but the federal *district-court* standard for granting new trials that must be compared with the New York standard to determine whether substantially different results will obtain — and it is far from clear that the district-court standard *ought* to be "shocks the conscience." . . . What seems to me far more likely to produce forum-shopping is the consistent difference between the state and federal *appellate* standards, which the Court leaves untouched. Under the Court's disposition, the Second Circuit reviews only for abuse of discretion, whereas New York's appellate courts engage in a *de novo* review for material deviation, giving the defendant a double shot at getting the damages award set aside. The only result that would produce the conformity the Court erroneously believes *Erie* requires is the one adopted by the Second Circuit and rejected by the Court: *de novo* federal appellate review under the § 5501(c) standard. . . .

The foregoing describes why I think the Court's *Erie* analysis is flawed. But in my view, one does not even reach the *Erie* question in this case. The standard to be applied by a district court in ruling on a motion for a new trial is set forth in Rule 59 of the Federal Rules of Civil Procedure, which provides that "[a] new trial may be granted . . . for any of the reasons for which new trials have heretofore been granted in actions at law *in the courts of the United States*." (Emphasis added.) That is undeniably a federal standard. Federal District Courts in the Second Circuit have interpreted that standard to permit the granting of new trials where "'it is quite clear that the jury has reached a seriously erroneous result'" and letting the verdict stand would result in a "'miscarriage of Justice.'" *Koerner v. Club Mediterranee, S.A.,* [833 F. Supp. 327, 331 (S.D.N.Y. 1993)] (quoting *Bevevino v. Saydjari,* 574 F.2d 676, 684 (CA2 1978)). Assuming (as we have no reason to question) that this is a correct interpretation of what Rule 59 requires, it is undeniable that the Federal Rule is "'sufficiently broad' to cause a 'direct collision' with the state law or, implicitly, to 'control the issue' before the court, thereby leaving no room for the operation of that law." *Burlington Northern R. Co. v. Woods,* 480 U.S. 1, 4-5 (1987). It is simply not possible to give controlling effect both to the federal standard and the state standard in reviewing the jury's award. That being so, the court has no choice but to apply the Federal Rule, which is an exercise of what we have called Congress's "power to regulate matters which, though falling within the uncertain area between substance and procedure, are rationally capable of classification as either," *Hanna,* 380 U.S., at 472. . . .

NOTES AND QUESTIONS

1. Multiple courts review. As amended in 1986, New York's CPLR § 5501(c) allowed both the trial court and the state court of appeals to review a jury's verdict for excessiveness. What standard of review did they each employ? Was the state's choice of standard constrained in any way by the Seventh Amendment? How did the state's standard compare with that usually employed by federal district and appellate courts? Which standard made it easier for an unhappy defendant to have a jury verdict set aside on the grounds of excessiveness?

2. Which track? In *Gasperini,* arguments were made in favor of all three tracks of the *Erie* analysis. Gasperini urged that because use of New York's deviates-materially standard at the federal appellate level would violate the Seventh Amendment's Reexamination Clause, the conflict should be analyzed under

Track One. In the Court's eyes, did the Seventh Amendment in fact go that far, or did it simply allow for federal appellate review but without clearly delineating the appropriate standard of review?

In his dissent, Justice Scalia argued that, properly viewed, this was a Track Two case due to the fact that Federal Rule of Civil Procedure 59 specifies a "federal standard" for granting a new trial, to wit, "for any of the reasons for which new trials have heretofore been granted in actions at law in the courts of the United States." Did the majority agree with Justice Scalia that in a case like this, involving "excessiveness," Rule 59 was in "direct collision" with CPLR § 5501(c), "leaving no room for the operation of that law"? Or, was this a case where excessiveness under Rule 59 would in fact be determined by reference to state law?

The majority rejected the Track One and Track Two analyses for the reasons suggested above, and treated this as therefore being a Track Three case. Under Track Three, which of *Erie*'s "twin aims" were implicated here? Was this a case where failure to follow state law at the federal trial and/or appellate court levels could lead to forum shopping and/or an inequitable administration of the laws? If so, did that mean that New York's deviates-materially standard had to be applied at both the federal district court and appellate court levels? Were there any countervailing federal interests present here that tempered that conclusion, and if so, to what extent?

3. *A backward glance.*   One useful way to fully appreciate the *Gasperini* decision is to begin with the specific holding. What did the Court rule with respect to the standard to be applied by federal district courts in assessing the excessiveness of jury verdicts? Consider the same question regarding the standard to be applied by the federal courts of appeals. Now work backward from those holdings to see how Track Three analysis allowed the Court to reach these conclusions.

A NOTE ON FEDERAL LAW IN STATE COURTS

As we noted at the beginning of this chapter, state courts are sometimes called on to decide federal issues. This may occur if a plaintiff chooses to file a federal claim in state court; recall that jurisdiction over federal claims is presumed to be concurrent between federal and state courts unless Congress expressly provides to the contrary. See "A Note on Concurrent and Exclusive Federal Question Jurisdiction," at page 324, *supra*. Or it might occur if a defendant in a state court proceeding raises a federal defense to the plaintiff's state-law cause of action or files a federal counterclaim. Under any of these circumstances, the state court must apply federal substantive law to resolve the federal claim or defense. However, the state court will generally be allowed to apply state procedural law in processing those federal issues. In other words, state courts adjudicating "federal questions" usually apply federal substantive law and state procedural law. This, of course, mirrors the practice of federal courts adjudicating state-law claims.

We have already noted that under the Supremacy Clause, valid and applicable federal law trumps conflicting state law. This was the basis for our Track

One analysis. The same principles apply when a state court adjudicates a federal claim or defense. Indeed, the language of the Supremacy Clause is directed to the judges of state courts: "This Constitution, and the Laws of the United States which shall be made in Pursuance thereof . . . shall be the supreme Law of the Land; and the Judges in every State shall be bound thereby, any Thing in the Constitution or Laws of any State to the Contrary notwithstanding." U.S. CONST. art. VI, cl. 2. Thus, if confronted with a federal claim—*e.g.*, a Title IX (20 U.S.C. § 1681(a)) gender discrimination claim—a state court must apply the appropriate principles of federal substantive law to resolve that claim. On the other hand, since most federal procedural law, with the notable exception of constitutionally mandated procedures, does not by its very nature apply in state proceedings, state courts normally follow state procedural law to process both federal and state claims and defenses.

Most importantly, also by virtue of the Supremacy Clause, a state court may not decline to adjudicate a federal claim on the ground that federal and not state law creates the claim. So long as the federal claim falls within the range of matters generally within that state court's competence, the court is obligated to adjudicate that claim. *Testa v. Katt*, 330 U.S. 386 (1947). For example, if a state court of general jurisdiction is competent to adjudicate civil rights claims premised on state law, then that court must also entertain civil rights claims premised on federal law. *Howlett v. Rose*, 496 U.S. 356 (1990). Moreover, a state cannot circumvent this principle by divesting its courts of jurisdiction over both the disfavored federal claim and an equivalent state-law claim if the state's action is motivated by hostility to the type of claim involved. *Haywood v. Drown*, 556 U.S. 729 (2009) (invalidating New York law that barred state courts from hearing certain § 1983 damages claims and equivalent state-law claims against state corrections officers).

This brings us to a critical question. If a state court must apply federal substantive law to the resolution of a federal claim or defense, but may apply state procedural law to the processing of that claim or defense, what happens when the federal substantive law and the state procedural law seem to conflict? This presents what is sometimes referred to as a "reverse-*Erie*" problem. The analysis, however, is much simplified. If state procedural law actually conflicts with applicable and valid federal law, the state law must give way. Thus what we truly have is a reverse Track One analysis. Valid and applicable federal law trumps state law to the contrary. This does not mean that state procedural law cannot affect the proceedings or even the outcome of litigation. It means only that state procedural law may not operate in a manner that significantly alters the federal right.

The Court applied the foregoing principle in *Felder v. Casey*, 487 U.S. 131 (1988). There, the plaintiff filed a federal civil rights claim in state court, alleging that several police officers had beaten him severely during an arrest, in violation of his federal constitutional rights. His claim was premised on 42 U.S.C. § 1983. In filing the suit, however, the plaintiff had failed to comply with the state's "notice-of-claim" statute. That statute required that at least 120 days prior to the filing of any lawsuit against a government officer in a state court, the plaintiff must "notify the [officer] of the circumstances giving rise to the claim, the amount of the claim, and his or her intent to hold the named [officer] liable." 487 U.S. at 134. As a consequence of the plaintiff's failure to comply with this provision, the state supreme court ordered the trial court to dismiss the plaintiff's § 1983 claim. The U.S. Supreme Court reversed. It concluded that application of this state "practice" rule undermined the broad remedial purposes of § 1983 by creating an obstacle to vindicating the underlying constitutional rights. As such, the notice-of-claim provision, as applied, ran afoul of the Supremacy Clause. The state trial court was therefore required to adjudicate the plaintiff's federal claim. In short, state procedural law was not permitted to trump federal substantive law.

Consider another example. Suppose State X's rules of civil procedure provide that the failure to plead an affirmative defense in an answer will constitute a waiver of that defense in the absence of good cause shown. As a consequence, if a defendant fails to plead federal preemption in her answer, under State X rules, she will not be permitted to raise that defense at trial unless good cause for the default can be shown. In this way, application of State X rules eliminates the federal defense and may well affect the litigation's outcome. But that does not necessarily mean that the State X rules alter the federal right. Unless the defendant can show that Congress intended to permit this particular preemption defense to be raised at any time during the litigation, the Supremacy Clause will not be offended by application of the State X waiver rule. In other words, unless the right to raise the defense after the pleading stage is considered part of the substantive right conferred by Congress, adherence to state procedure will not run afoul of the Supremacy Clause. In general, so long as the state rules of procedure neither alter the underlying substantive federal right nor create an insurmountable or unreasonable obstacle to the assertion of a federal claim or defense, the state procedure can be followed.

PROBLEMS

6-16. Dice, a railroad fireman, was injured when an engine in which he was riding jumped the track. Claiming that the railroad's negligence caused the accident, he brought an action against the railroad under the Federal Employers' Liability Act (FELA) in a state court of general jurisdiction. The purpose of the FELA was to ensure that injured employees covered by the act are fully compensated for injuries negligently inflicted by their employers. The railroad denied its negligence and claimed that Dice had signed a release as to all damages beyond $1,000. Dice admitted to signing several documents but claimed that he had done so relying on the railroad's deliberately false statement that he was only signing a receipt for wages. The jury found in favor of Dice, awarding him $25,000, implicitly finding that the railroad had procured the release through fraud. The trial court, however, entered a judgment notwithstanding the verdict. The judge concluded that state law governed the release's validity and that under state law the plaintiff, a man of ordinary intelligence, was bound by the signed release in the absence of a showing of fraud. The judge also held that under state law, whether fraud had been shown was a fact question to be decided by the judge and not the jury. He concluded that the evidence here was insufficient to establish fraud. Was the trial court correct in determining that state law governed the release's validity? If federal law controls, how would you design the content of that law? Was the trial court correct in following state procedures regarding the allocation of fact finding between the judge and the jury on the issue of fraud? *See Dice v. Akron, Canton & Youngstown R.R. Co.*, 342 U.S. 359 (1952).

6-17. Carl died while confined in a South Carolina county jail. His widow, Susan, brought an action against the County in a South Carolina federal district court. She asserted a claim under 42 U.S.C. § 1983 for a violation of her husband's constitutional rights, as well as supplemental claims for wrongful death and survival under South Carolina law. All claims were filed within the applicable statutes of limitations. Thereafter, in response to a summary judgment motion filed by the County, the district court dismissed the § 1983 claim. Two weeks later, acting pursuant to 28 U.S.C. § 1367(c)(3), the court then issued an order declining to exercise jurisdiction over the remaining state law claims. Importantly, § 1367(d) tolls the running of any applicable statute of limitations for 30 days after a subsection (c) dismissal, thus granting the plaintiff a 30-day safe harbor within which to refile the dismissed claims in state court. However, South Carolina state law does not recognize any such tolling provision. Rather, upon dismissal of the federal action, the statute of limitations on the state law claims begins to run immediately. Following the federal court dismissal, Susan re-filed her wrongful death and survival claims in state court within the 30-day safe harbor window. However, the state court nonetheless dismissed those claims as time barred because the state's statute of limitations had expired during the two-week interim between the federal dismissal and the filing of her state lawsuit. On appeal, should the state appellate court apply state or federal law in determining whether the statute of limitations was tolled for 30 days after dismissal of the federal suit? In answering this question, use the Track One model, but note that the federal statute here, 28 U.S.C. § 1367(d), purports to apply to proceedings in state court, *i.e.*, it does not directly regulate proceedings in federal court. This observation does not resolve the problem. It only makes the resolution of this "reverse-*Erie*" problem somewhat more difficult to explain. *See Jinks v. Richland Cnty., S.C.*, 538 U.S. 456 (2003).

E.   *Erie* Review Problems

6-18. California's anti-SLAPP statute provides for the pretrial dismissal of certain actions—so-called strategic lawsuits against public participation or SLAPP suits—that may masquerade as ordinary lawsuits but that are intended to deter people from exercising their right to comment on public issues or to punish them for doing so. The statute is designed to protect the rights of petition and free speech and prevent abusive use of the judicial process to impair those rights. A defendant sued in a potential SLAPP suit may, within 60 days of service of the complaint, file a special motion to strike (an "anti-SLAPP motion"). To prevail on this anti-SLAPP motion, the defendant must show that the plaintiff's cause of action is one arising out of protected expressive activity engaged in by the defendant, *i.e.*, that the plaintiff's claim is premised on the defendant's expressive activity. If the defendant makes this showing, the case will be dismissed with prejudice unless plaintiff can show a reasonable probability of success on the merits of the asserted cause of action. May the defendant in a diversity case filed in a California federal court file an anti-SLAPP motion to strike a plaintiff's complaint that is premised on the defendant's expressive activity? In answering this question, consider the potential relationship between the anti-SLAPP motion and Rules 8(a)(2) and 12(b)(6).

Suppose, in addition, that under California law, once a defendant files an anti-SLAPP motion, discovery must be stayed unless the plaintiff can show good cause, namely, a need for information in the hands of the defendant that is necessary to meet plaintiff's burden on the anti-SLAPP motion. Assuming the anti-SLAPP statute applies in federal proceedings, must a federal court adhere to this stay-of-discovery requirement? In answering this question, consider Rules 26(d) & (f) and 56(d). *See Makaeff v. Trump University, LLC*, 715 F.3d 254 (9th Cir.), *reh'g (en banc) denied*, 736 F.3d 1180 (9th Cir. 2013).

6-19. Bob was injured when the car he was driving in State X collided with a truck being driven by Carol. The accident occurred at an intersection with a traffic light. Both drivers claim that the other ran a red light and caused the accident. Bob sued Carol in a State X federal court, properly invoking that court's diversity jurisdiction, and seeking $80,000 for injuries incurred in the accident. The case was tried before a jury, the sole question being who ran the red light. At trial, Bob testified that he entered the intersection when his light turned green. He further testified that his vehicle was struck when Carol's truck "barreled" into the intersection against a red light. Carol testified that she entered the intersection slowly and only after her light had turned green, and that she was surprised when Bob's vehicle sped into the intersection and crashed into her truck. She also called two credible and disinterested eyewitnesses, Ted and Alice, both of whom corroborated Carol's version of the events. The jury entered a verdict for Bob and awarded him $80,000 in damages. Carol sought to overturn the jury verdict by filing a motion for judgment as a matter of law pursuant to Rule 50 of the Federal Rules of Civil Procedure, in which she argued that, given the evidence, no reasonable juror could have ruled in favor of Bob. Bob objected to Carol's motion based on her failure to have filed a motion for judgment prior to submission of the case to the jury, as required (according to Bob) by Rule 50(a)(2). Carol has responded to this argument by pointing out that State X law does not require a party seeking a post-verdict judgment to have filed a motion for judgment prior to submission of the case to the jury. She urges the district court to follow State X law in this regard. What should the district court do? How would the district court's analysis of the problem differ if the standards of Rule 50(a)(2) had been embodied in a statute? What if instead they were merely the product of federal judge-made doctrine?

6-20. The County of Orange, California ("the County"), entered into a contract with Tata America, Inc. ("Tata") in which Tata agreed to develop a computerized property tax management system for the County. Their contract contained a clause providing that the parties "hereby expressly and knowingly waive all rights to trial by jury in any action between them arising out of or in any way connected with this contract." The contract also contained a California choice-of-law clause. In 2013, after Tata allegedly failed to perform under the contract, the County brought a diversity action against Tata in a California federal district court, and filed a demand for jury trial. California law and federal law treat pre-dispute jury trial waivers differently. Under long-standing California contract law, such waivers are invalid unless expressly authorized by statute, *see Grafton Partners, LP v. Superior Court*, 116 P.3d 479 (Cal. 2003), whereas the Seventh Amendment to the U.S. Constitution permits such waivers so long as each party knowingly and voluntarily waived its rights. *See Palmer v. Valdez*, 560 F.3d 965, 968 (9th Cir. 2009), *cert. denied*, 559 U.S. 906 (2010). No California statute authorized the waiver executed here. No federal statute or federal rule of civil procedure addresses such waivers that are knowing and voluntary. Federal Rule of Civil Procedure 38(a) provides: "The right of trial by jury as declared by the Seventh Amendment to the Constitution—or as provided by a federal statute—is preserved to the parties inviolate." While the County concedes that its waiver of the right to jury trial was both knowing and voluntary, it argues that the federal court should apply California law, under which the waiver would be held invalid. Tata has moved to strike the County's demand for a jury trial. How should the court rule on the motion to strike? In answering this question, consider the possible application of each of the three tracks of *Erie*. Does the case arguably fit into more than one of them? *See In re County of Orange*, 784 F.3d 520 (9th Cir. 2015), *pet. for cert. filed* (No. 15-509), 84 USLW 3223 (Oct. 16, 2015).

VII

DISCOVERY

"If you scrutinize a legal rule, you will see that it is a conditional statement referring to facts. Such a rule seems to say, in effect 'If such and such a fact exists, then this or that legal consequence should follow.'" JEROME FRANK, COURTS ON TRIAL: MYTH AND REALITY IN AMERICAN JUSTICE 14 (1949). In other words, the law supplies the principle, but the facts determine whether that principle will apply. Moreover, in the vast majority of cases, the applicable legal principle is not in dispute, or at least not at the center of the dispute. The fight is more often over the facts and how to interpret them in light of what all agree are the potentially applicable principles of law. In most negligence cases, for example, both sides agree on the legal standards; they disagree over the facts and whether those facts impose liability under the given standards.

One of a litigator's fundamental responsibilities, therefore, is to gather the facts and to develop them, creatively but honestly, into a comprehensible narrative that favorably reflects the client's position by supporting the legal theories on which the client relies. The process of doing so usually begins with the client's story, which may be a simple, linear story of the events that have led her to seek legal advice, or a complex stream of consciousness more akin to a James Joyce novel. The client's story, regardless of its narrative quality or complexity, however, is only the first step in the fact-gathering process. That process includes preliminary fact gathering from readily available sources (*e.g.*, public records, libraries, eyewitnesses, etc.), the development of a flexible discovery plan, further fact investigation, and formal discovery. Of course, all of these steps interact with one another during what must be an ongoing and evolving process of fact gathering. This process of fact gathering is called discovery. It includes both informal fact gathering by the attorney or her agents and the formal exchange of factual information between parties to a lawsuit. This latter aspect of discovery, sometimes called "formal discovery," is the primary topic of this chapter.

The purpose of formal discovery is to allow the parties to prepare their case with a shared knowledge of the relevant facts. Mutual discovery promotes fairness by taking much of the surprise out of litigation; by assisting in narrowing the dispute alleged in the pleadings through disclosure of those matters not in controversy; and by encouraging an early resolution of the controversy through pretrial motion (*e.g.*, summary judgment) or settlement. Although parties to a lawsuit are free to voluntarily grant one another open access to all relevant information within their possession, discovery may also proceed along more formal lines, in accordance with the rules of discovery established for the court in which the lawsuit is filed.

At early common law, there was virtually no formal discovery. The pleading process was designed not to provide access to information but to limit the scope of the dispute to a single legal or factual issue. Beyond the pleadings, there were no formal discovery devices. Fact gathering was a private endeavor. A party could seek a "bill of particulars" for a more definite statement, but this device rarely provided more than a clarification of the adversary's legal claim or defense.

The opportunity for discovery at equity was somewhat better. The "interrogative" component of a party's pleading posed questions to her adversary that had to be answered. The answers formed part of the record on which the chancellor decided the case. Importantly, discovery at equity was limited to information relevant to the allegations of the party seeking the information (the "propounding" party). In other words, a party answering an interrogatory was not required to disclose information relevant to his own allegations, but only information relevant to the propounding party's allegations. Eventually, equity also permitted the inspection of documents under limited circumstances, and the pretrial examination of witnesses who might not be available at the time of trial. In addition, a litigant at common law who wanted to "discover" facts from an adversary could seek a "bill of discovery" in equity, but the process was cumbersome for it required the filing of a separate lawsuit. In short, both at law and in equity, formal discovery was either nonexistent or of very limited scope.

State and federal courts initially followed the separate common law and equity models. Beginning in the early nineteenth century, however, individual states began to adopt innovations by importing some of the equity discovery devices, such as interrogatories, into actions at law. The adoption and spread of code pleading energized this process of change. Under the influence of the Field Code, many states opted to permit "depositions" as a primary tool of discovery. In a deposition, a party or a witness is questioned by the attorneys representing the parties to the suit, much as at trial, but in a private setting. The testimony is given under oath and is recorded or transcribed in some fashion. In addition, by the 1930s, a majority of states had expanded the scope of discovery to include all relevant information in the possession of the party to whom discovery was directed, rejecting the equity rule that limited discovery to information relevant to the propounding party's allegations. Practices were not, however, uniform. In some states, depositions had become the sole discovery device, in other states interrogatories remained the exclusive means of discovery and in still others a combination of the two was permitted. Eventually, most states also allowed the inspection of documents, but only with the permission of the court.

By contrast, discovery in the federal courts up through the 1930s remained a very limited tool, largely premised on common law and equity practices, though somewhat modified for modern usage. In 1938, however, with adoption of the Federal Rules of Civil Procedure, all of that changed. Just as the federal rules embraced a modern approach to pleading, the rules also adopted a form of discovery that complemented and built on the new rules of pleading.

In the materials that follow, we will examine discovery as practiced under the Federal Rules of Civil Procedure. *See* FED. R. CIV. P. 26-37. Of all the federal civil rules, those relating to discovery have had the most influence on state practices. Indeed, a majority of the states have used the federal discovery rules as a model for their own rules. Hence, although what we say about federal discovery does not technically apply to actions filed in state courts, the federal rules do provide the general model on which most state-based discovery systems are premised. The details do, however, differ from state to state and we will from time to time note some of those differences.

A.   Pragmatic Preliminary—Devising a Discovery Plan

As noted above, formal discovery is not the first step in the information gathering process. Competent attorneys gather facts from their clients and from other available sources before filing suit and embarking on the sometimes expensive and time-consuming intricacies of formal discovery. Moreover, even in the midst of litigation, one does not simply plunge into discovery with the hope of finding some valuable information. Given various limits on the amount of formal discovery that may be undertaken, a point we will examine below, an attorney must use formal discovery devices as efficiently and effectively as possible. This requires the development of a "discovery plan," *i.e.*, an organized approach to the gathering of factual material that will maximize the efficient accumulation of all relevant information.

Let's adopt the perspective of a lawyer who has just completed an initial interview with a client. The client appears to have a number of potential claims against one or more defendants. What steps would our lawyer take to develop a discovery plan for this client? The approach might look something like this:

- Engage in preliminary investigation.
- Create a broad and generous outline of every plausible claim.
- Convert each claim into its component elements.
- Match the component elements with the known facts.
- Measure the probable worth of available evidence in support of the known facts.
- Identify evidence needed to fill "factual" gaps (*i.e.*, to support an element of a claim for which there is no available evidence).
- Identify potential sources for additional evidence and assess probable cost of finding that evidence.
- Engage in further fact investigation.
- Refine outline of potential claims (adding and deleting as necessary).
- Work through each step again.

As this task list suggests, the creation of a discovery plan involves a dynamic and evolutionary process. The potential claims adjust to the accumulating facts until, in the lawyer's judgment, there is adequate information on which to proceed in good faith to the pleading stage. At this point, the attorney should have a sound factual basis for any claims to be asserted, and a clear (or clearer) idea of what formal discovery will be most beneficial to her client's interests. *See* FED. R. CIV. P. 11(b)(3) (imposing a duty on attorneys to ensure that factual allegations have or will have evidentiary support). In essence, the attorney knows both what she absolutely needs to discover and what she would like to discover. Once she files a complaint, the process of formal discovery may then begin. Note that by filing a complaint in federal court, an attorney "certifies" that "the factual contentions have evidentiary support or, if specifically so identified, will likely have evidentiary support after a reasonable opportunity for further investigation or discovery. . . ." FED. R. CIV. P. 11(b)(3). Of course, this process of refinement and investigation continues, with proper concern for costs and benefits, even after formal discovery has begun. The point is that the process of discovery requires forethought, preparation, creativity, and a continual adjustment to the ever-changing body of available information.

Suppose the following facts. Pookie Jones, your client, tells you she was driving her new BMW and proceeding west through an intersection in the City of Lexington, Virginia. The light was green when she entered the intersection. When she reached the middle of the intersection, however, her car was struck by a vehicle that had entered the intersection from the north. The driver of that vehicle was Hippie Smith. Pookie suffered serious injuries and wants money damages to compensate her for them. How would you proceed to develop a discovery plan for her?

First, after a preliminary investigation, which might include procuring the police report and any witness statements, and perhaps re-interviewing Pookie, you would proceed to list a wide range of plausible claims. For example: Hippie might be liable for negligence or even assault (perhaps the accident was the result of road rage); if Hippie were driving on someone else's behalf, that party (*e.g.*, a pizza delivery company) might be liable as well; the manufacturer of Hippie's vehicle might be liable under a theory of products liability if a defect in the car, say a faulty brake system, caused the accident; the manufacturer of Pookie's vehicle might be similarly liable if a defect in it caused or contributed to Pookie's injuries; so too with the manufacturers or suppliers of the component parts and with the dealers who sold the vehicles; the public entity responsible for the lights at the intersection might be liable for negligence if the lights malfunctioned or if some other road condition caused the accident; the emergency medical personnel and doctors who attended to Pookie might be liable if they were negligent in treating her injuries; another driver may have forced Hippie into the intersection; and so forth. You may have scant if any evidence for some of these potential claims, but given your limited information, they are certainly plausible and worth at least preliminary consideration.

Each claim must now be broken down into its component elements, *i.e.*, into the legal propositions that must be proved if the client is to prevail. For example, the elements of a negligence claim are duty, breach, and causation. Therefore, to prevail against Hippie on a negligence claim, Pookie must prove that Hippie *breached a duty* of due care and that Hippie's breach *caused* her injuries.

Next, convert each legal element of each claim into a fact statement and describe the specific evidence that supports that statement. For example, as to breach of duty, the facts available are that Hippie, while driving on a public highway, ran a red light. Evidence in support of this fact might be Pookie's statement, the police report, eyewitness accounts, and so forth. There may be contrary evidence such as a conflicting eyewitness statement.

Having identified the relevant evidence and its potential role in the anticipated litigation, you must then assess the strength of that evidence. Is it direct or circumstantial? "I saw the red light" as opposed to "My light was green, so his must have been red." Is it credible — is it your client's version, or that of a neutral eyewitness? Is the evidence consistent or internally contradictory? And so forth.

At this point you may push some claims to the front of the line and set others aside. It may be, for example, that there are no facts to support a theory that Hippie was driving on someone else's behalf. Most importantly, you can now see with some clarity which remaining potential claims have evidentiary gaps or weaknesses, *i.e.*, elements unsupported by available facts or supported only by relatively weak evidence. For example, as to the products liability claim against the manufacturer of Hippie's car, you may have no evidence of any defect in that vehicle other than the circumstantial evidence that Hippie claims to have tried to stop. More investigation is required. Perhaps research into public documents might reveal a history of problems with some aspect of this vehicle (*e.g.*, government crash tests). Or the services of an expert might uncover some latent defect. In any event, you need more information before you can make a final judgment about whether to proceed with or discard this claim.

By following this process and repeating each step as many times as necessary, you will eventually decide which claims, if any, merit the filing of a lawsuit. Moreover, if you do file a lawsuit on Pookie's behalf, by having worked your way through this discovery plan you will have prepared yourself for the process of formal discovery. You will know the factual strengths and weaknesses of your case and will have a firm idea of the type of information you would like to obtain from your adversary — the whats, the wheres, and the whos that are most important to your case.

B. The Scope of Formal Discovery

Of course, in assessing what you would like to discover from a potential party opponent, you must be aware of the range of information that you will be permitted to discover, *i.e.*, the so-called scope of formal discovery.

1. Discovery Relevance

The Federal Rules of Civil Procedure, as most recently amended in 2015, define the scope of discoverable material as follows:

> Parties may obtain discovery regarding any nonprivileged matter that is relevant to any party's claim or defense and proportional to the needs of the case, considering the importance of the issues at stake in the action, the amount in controversy, the parties' relative access to relevant information, the parties' resources, the importance of the discovery in resolving the issues, and whether the burden or expense of the proposed discovery outweighs its likely benefit. Information within this scope of discovery need not be admissible in evidence to be discoverable.

FED. R. CIV. P. 26(b)(1). Thus, the information must be *relevant* to the parties' claims or defenses and *proportional* to what is at stake in the case, taking into account the respective burdens that granting or denying discovery would impose on the parties involved. And, as the second sentence of the rule makes clear, the information sought through discovery "need not be admissible in evidence to be discoverable."

PROBLEMS

7-1. Eleven people were traveling in a van on a Utah highway when the tread belt on a Cooper tire separated, causing the driver to lose control of the vehicle. As a result, the van went off the road and rolled over several times before coming to a stop. Nine of the eleven individuals in the van died from the injuries they sustained in the accident. The remaining two passengers suffered severe injuries but survived. The survivors and heirs of the deceased passengers brought suit against Cooper in a federal district court. Their complaint asserted various strict products liability, negligence, and breach of warranty claims against Cooper. The plaintiffs alleged that Cooper knew or should have known that the tires used on the van were prone to tread separation within their normal and intended use. Specifically, the plaintiffs claimed that "prior to the production of the van tire, Cooper realized that its tires suffered from an unacceptably high rate of tread separations, but deliberately failed to make design changes to combat this knowledge or warn consumers about the problems with its tires." They further alleged that information available to Cooper before production of the tire even began "confirmed that Cooper knew about these dangerous and defective conditions." To substantiate these claims, the plaintiffs sought discovery from Cooper with respect to tread separation issues pertaining to all substantially similar Cooper tires. In response, Cooper sought a protective order to limit discovery to matters relating to the specific type of tire involved in the accident. What role should discovery relevance and proportionality play in the district court's determination? How would you advise the court to rule? *See In re Cooper Tire & Rubber Co.*, 568 F.3d 1180 (10th Cir. 2009).

7-2. Gary, a former U.S. Congressman, brought a defamation action in a federal district court against Dominick, a well-known writer, alleging that Dominick had made slanderous statements criminally implicating Gary in the disappearance and death of Chandra, Gary's former intern. The statements were premised on the inference that Gary was having an illicit affair with Chandra and that her disappearance was designed to end the relationship and to cover up the affair. Dominick filed an answer in which he asserted an affirmative defense of "substantial truth." As a part of discovery, Dominick's lawyer took Gary's deposition, during which Gary refused to answer the following questions:

> Did you have a sexual relationship with Chandra? Was your relationship with Chandra what people would consider an affair? Was there any change in your relations with Chandra during the period October 2000 to the time she disappeared in 2001? Was there any physical intimacy of any kind in your relationship? Did Chandra ever spend the night in your apartment? Were you ever concerned that any aspect of your friendship or conduct with Chandra might become public knowledge?

Do these questions seek information that is relevant to a claim or defense in the action? Is the discovery request proportional? *See Condit v. Dunne*, 225 F.R.D. 100 (S.D.N.Y. 2004).

2.   Privilege

A "privilege" is a judicially recognized exemption from the duty to disclose relevant information. Significantly, the text of Rule 26(b)(1) expressly limits the scope of discovery to matters that are "nonprivileged." In other words, if a matter is privileged, it is not discoverable. A matter is deemed privileged for purposes of discovery if it would be privileged at trial. *United States v. Reynolds*, 345 U.S. 1, 6 (1953). For this determination we look to the Federal Rules of Evidence, which set the standards for the admissibility of evidence in federal courts. As to privileges, Rule 501 of these evidence rules provides:

> The common law — as interpreted by the United States courts in the light of reason and experience — governs a claim of privilege unless any of the following provides otherwise:
>
> - the United States Constitution;
> - a federal statute; or
> - a rule prescribed by the Supreme Court.
>
> But in a civil case, state law governs privilege regarding a claim or defense for which state law supplies the rule of decision.

Fed. R. Evid. 501.

Notice that Rule 501 refers to five types of privileges: (1) those created by federal common law; (2) those created by the Constitution; (3) those created by federal statute; (4) those created by a rule promulgated by the Supreme Court; and (5) those created by state law. The bulk of the privileges applicable in federal proceedings are created by federal common law. These include the attorney-client privilege, the priest-penitent privilege, spousal privileges, a state secrets privilege, and others. *See generally* Patrick E. Higginbotham, *Duty to Disclose; General*

Provisions Governing Discovery, in 6 MOORE'S FEDERAL PRACTICE §§ 26.47 *et seq.* (3d ed. 2015). State law privileges apply only when the information sought is relevant solely to a claim or defense arising under state law. This would occur in diversity cases in which the parties raise only state-law claims or in the context of supplemental jurisdiction when federal and state claims are joined in one proceeding. When information is relevant to both a federal claim or defense and a state claim or defense, federal law governs. *See* 6 MOORE'S FEDERAL PRACTICE, *supra,* § 26.47[4]. Constitutional privileges include, for example, an individual's Fifth Amendment right against self-incrimination, or the president's right to maintain the confidentiality of communications with close advisors. Examples of statutory and rule-created privileges include the federal government's duty to maintain the confidentiality of tax returns (26 U.S.C. § 6103) and of census data (13 U.S.C. § 9(a)), and its limited duty to maintain the secrecy of grand jury proceedings (FED. R. CRIM. P. 6).

Jaffee v. Redmond
518 U.S. 1 (1996)

JUSTICE STEVENS delivered the opinion of the Court.

After a traumatic incident in which she shot and killed a man, a police officer received extensive counseling from a licensed clinical social worker. The question we address is whether statements the officer made to her therapist during the counseling sessions are protected from compelled disclosure in a federal civil action brought by the family of the deceased. Stated otherwise, the question is whether it is appropriate for federal courts to recognize a "psychotherapist privilege" under Rule 501 of the Federal Rules of Evidence.

I

Petitioner is the administrator of the estate of Ricky Allen. Respondents are Mary Lu Redmond, a former police officer, and the Village of Hoffman Estates, Illinois, her employer during the time that she served on the police force. Petitioner commenced this action against respondents after Redmond shot and killed Allen while on patrol duty.

On June 27, 1991, Redmond was the first officer to respond to a "fight in progress" call at an apartment complex. As she arrived at the scene, two of Allen's sisters ran toward her squad car, waving their arms and shouting that there had been a stabbing in one of the apartments. Redmond testified at trial that she relayed this information to her dispatcher and requested an ambulance. She then exited her car and walked toward the apartment building. Before Redmond reached the building, several men ran out, one waving a pipe. When the men ignored her order to get on the ground, Redmond drew her service revolver. Two other men then burst out of the building, one, Ricky Allen, chasing the other. According to

Redmond, Allen was brandishing a butcher knife and disregarded her repeated commands to drop the weapon. Redmond shot Allen when she believed he was about to stab the man he was chasing. Allen died at the scene. Redmond testified that before other officers arrived to provide support, "people came pouring out of the buildings," and a threatening confrontation between her and the crowd ensued.

Petitioner filed suit in Federal District Court alleging that Redmond had violated Allen's constitutional rights by using excessive force during the encounter at the apartment complex. The complaint sought damages under 42 U.S.C. § 1983, and the Illinois wrongful-death statute. At trial, petitioner presented testimony from members of Allen's family that conflicted with Redmond's version of the incident in several important respects. They testified, for example, that Redmond drew her gun before exiting her squad car and that Allen was unarmed when he emerged from the apartment building.

During pretrial discovery petitioner learned that after the shooting Redmond had participated in about 50 counseling sessions with Karen Beyer, a clinical social worker licensed by the State of Illinois and employed at that time by the Village of Hoffman Estates. Petitioner sought access to Beyer's notes concerning the sessions for use in cross-examining Redmond. Respondents vigorously resisted the discovery. They asserted that the contents of the conversations between Beyer and Redmond were protected against involuntary disclosure by a psychotherapist-patient privilege. The district judge rejected this argument. Neither Beyer nor Redmond, however, complied with his order to disclose the contents of Beyer's notes. At depositions and on the witness stand both either refused to answer certain questions or professed an inability to recall details of their conversations.

In his instructions at the end of the trial, the judge advised the jury that the refusal to turn over Beyer's notes had no "legal justification" and that the jury could therefore presume that the contents of the notes would have been unfavorable to respondents. The jury awarded petitioner $45,000 on the federal claim and $500,000 on her state-law claim. . . .

[The Court of Appeals for the Seventh Circuit held that the communications between Redmond and Beyer were privileged and, hence, not discoverable. Because the trial court's instructions to the jury were therefore erroneous, the appellate court reversed and remanded for a new trial.]

The United States Courts of Appeals do not uniformly agree that the federal courts should recognize a psychotherapist privilege under Rule 501. Because of the conflict among the Courts of Appeals and the importance of the question, we granted certiorari. We affirm.

II

Rule 501 of the Federal Rules of Evidence authorizes federal courts to define new privileges by interpreting ["[t]he common law] . . . in the light of reason and experience." The authors of the Rule borrowed this phrase from our opinion in *Wolfle v. United States*, 291 U.S. 7, 12 (1934), which in turn referred to the oft-repeated observation that "the common law is not immutable but flexible, and by its own principles adapts itself to varying conditions." *Funk v. United States*, 290 U.S. 371, 383 (1933). The Senate Report accompanying the 1975 adoption of the Rules indicates that Rule 501 "should be understood as reflecting the view that the recognition of a privilege based on a confidential relationship . . . should be determined on a case-by-case basis." S. Rep. No. 93-1277, p. 13 (1974). The Rule thus did not freeze the law governing the privileges of witnesses in federal trials at a particular point in our history, but rather directed federal courts to "continue the evolutionary development of testimonial privileges." *Trammel v. United States*, 445 U.S. 40, 47 (1980).

The common-law principles underlying the recognition of testimonial privileges can be stated simply. "For more than three centuries it has now been recognized as a fundamental maxim that the public . . . has a right to every man's evidence. When we come to examine the various claims of exemption, we start with the primary assumption that there is a general duty to give what testimony one is capable of giving, and that any exemptions which may exist are distinctly exceptional, being so many derogations from a positive general rule." *United States v. Bryan*, 339 U.S. 323, 331 (1950). Exceptions from the general rule disfavoring testimonial privileges may be justified, however, by a "public good transcending the normally predominant principle of utilizing all rational means for ascertaining truth." *Trammel*, 445 U.S., at 50.

Guided by these principles, the question we address today is whether a privilege protecting confidential communications between a psychotherapist and her patient "promotes sufficiently important interests to outweigh the need for probative evidence. . . ." 445 U.S., at 51. Both "reason and experience" persuade us that it does.

III

Like the spousal and attorney-client privileges, the psychotherapist-patient privilege is "rooted in the imperative need for confidence and trust." *Ibid.* Treatment by a physician for physical ailments can often proceed successfully on the basis of a physical examination, objective information supplied by the patient, and the results of diagnostic tests. Effective psychotherapy, by contrast, depends upon an atmosphere of confidence and trust in which the patient is willing to make a frank and complete disclosure of facts, emotions, memories, and fears. Because of the sensitive nature of the problems for which individuals consult psychotherapists, disclosure of confidential communications made during counseling sessions may cause embarrassment or disgrace. For this reason, the mere possibility of disclosure may impede development of the confidential relationship necessary for successful treatment. As the Judicial Conference Advisory Committee observed in 1972 when it recommended that Congress recognize a psychotherapist privilege as part of the Proposed Federal Rules of Evidence, a psychiatrist's ability to help her patients "'is completely dependent upon [the patients'] willingness and ability to talk freely. This makes it difficult if not impossible for [a psychiatrist] to function without being able to assure . . . patients of confidentiality and, indeed, privileged communication. Where there may be exceptions to this general rule . . . , there is wide agreement that confidentiality is a *sine qua non* for successful psychiatric treatment.'" Advisory Committee's Notes to Proposed Rules, 56 F.R.D. 183, 242 (1972) (quoting Group for Advancement of Psychiatry, Report No. 45, Confidentiality and Privileged Communication in the Practice of Psychiatry 92 (June 1960)).

By protecting confidential communications between a psychotherapist and her patient from involuntary disclosure, the proposed privilege thus serves important private interests.

Our cases make clear that an asserted privilege must also "serv[e] public ends." *Upjohn Co. v. United States*, 449 U.S. 383, 389 (1981). Thus, the purpose of the attorney-client privilege is to "encourage full and frank communication between attorneys and their clients and thereby promote broader public interests in the observance of law and administration of justice." *Ibid*. And the spousal privilege, as modified in *Trammel*, is justified because it "furthers the important public interest in marital harmony," 445 U.S., at 53. The psychotherapist privilege serves the public interest by facilitating the provision of appropriate treatment for individuals suffering the effects of a mental or emotional problem. The mental health of our citizenry, no less than its physical health, is a public good of transcendent importance.

In contrast to the significant public and private interests supporting recognition of the privilege, the likely evidentiary benefit that would result from the denial of the privilege is modest. If the privilege were rejected, confidential conversations between psychotherapists and their patients would surely be chilled, particularly when it is obvious that the circumstances that give rise to the need for treatment will probably result in litigation. Without a privilege, much of the desirable evidence to which litigants such as petitioner seek access—for example, admissions against interest by a party—is unlikely to come into being. This unspoken "evidence" will therefore serve no greater truth-seeking function than if it had been spoken and privileged.

That it is appropriate for the federal courts to recognize a psychotherapist privilege under Rule 501 is confirmed by the fact that all 50 States and the District of Columbia have enacted into law some form of psychotherapist privilege. We have previously observed that the policy decisions of the States bear on the question whether federal courts should recognize a new privilege or amend the coverage of an existing one. Because state legislatures are fully aware of the need to protect the integrity of the factfinding functions of their courts, the existence of a consensus among the States indicates that "reason and experience" support recognition of the privilege. In addition, given the importance of the patient's understanding that her communications with her therapist will not be publicly disclosed, any State's promise of confidentiality would have little value if the patient were aware that the privilege would not be honored in a federal court. Denial of the federal privilege therefore would frustrate the purposes of the state legislation that was enacted to foster these confidential communications.

It is of no consequence that recognition of the privilege in the vast majority of States is the product of legislative action rather than judicial decision. Although common-law rulings may once have been the primary source of new developments in federal privilege law, that is no longer the case. In *Funk v. United States*, 290 U.S. 371 (1933), we recognized that it is appropriate to treat a consistent body of policy determinations by state legislatures as reflecting both "reason" and "experience." *Id.*, at 376-381. That rule is properly respectful of the States and at the same time reflects the fact that once a state legislature has enacted a privilege there is no longer an opportunity for common-law creation of the protection. . . .

The uniform judgment of the States is reinforced by the fact that a psychotherapist privilege was among the nine specific privileges recommended by the Advisory Committee in its proposed privilege rules. In *United States v. Gillock*, 445 U.S., at 367-368, our holding that Rule 501 did not include a state legislative privilege relied, in part, on the fact that no such privilege was included in the Advisory Committee's draft. The reasoning in *Gillock* thus supports the opposite conclusion in this case. In rejecting the proposed draft that had specifically identified each privilege rule and substituting the present more open-ended Rule 501, the Senate Judiciary Committee explicitly stated that its action "should not be understood as disapproving any recognition of a psychiatrist-patient . . . privileg[e] contained in the [proposed] rules." S. Rep. No. 93-1277, at 13.

Because we agree with the judgment of the state legislatures and the Advisory Committee that a psychotherapist-patient privilege will serve a "public good transcending the normally predominant principle of utilizing all rational means for ascertaining truth," *Trammel*, 445 U.S., at 50, we hold that confidential communications between a licensed psychotherapist and her patients in the course of diagnosis or treatment are protected from compelled disclosure under Rule 501 of the Federal Rules of Evidence.[14]

IV

All agree that a psychotherapist privilege covers confidential communications made to licensed psychiatrists and psychologists. We have no hesitation in concluding in this case that the federal privilege should also extend to confidential communications made to licensed social workers in the course of psychotherapy. The reasons for recognizing a privilege for treatment by psychiatrists and psychologists apply with equal force to treatment by a clinical social worker such as Karen Beyer. Today, social workers provide a significant amount of mental health treatment. Their clients often include the poor and those of modest means who could not afford the assistance of a psychiatrist or psychologist, but whose counseling sessions serve the same public goals. Perhaps in recognition of these circumstances, the vast majority of States explicitly extend a testimonial privilege

---

14. Like other testimonial privileges, the patient may of course waive the protection.

to licensed social workers. We therefore agree with the Court of Appeals that "[d]rawing a distinction between the counseling provided by costly psychotherapists and the counseling provided by more readily accessible social workers serves no discernible public purpose."

We part company with the Court of Appeals on a separate point. We reject the balancing component of the privilege implemented by that court and a small number of States. Making the promise of confidentiality contingent upon a trial judge's later evaluation of the relative importance of the patient's interest in privacy and the evidentiary need for disclosure would eviscerate the effectiveness of the privilege. As we explained in *Upjohn*, if the purpose of the privilege is to be served, the participants in the confidential conversation "must be able to predict with some degree of certainty whether particular discussions will be protected. An uncertain privilege, or one which purports to be certain but results in widely varying applications by the courts, is little better than no privilege at all." 449 U.S., at 393.

These considerations are all that is necessary for decision of this case. A rule that authorizes the recognition of new privileges on a case-by-case basis makes it appropriate to define the details of new privileges in a like manner. Because this is the first case in which we have recognized a psychotherapist privilege, it is neither necessary nor feasible to delineate its full contours in a way that would "govern all conceivable future questions in this area." *Id.*, at 386.[19]

V

The conversations between Officer Redmond and Karen Beyer and the notes taken during their counseling sessions are protected from compelled disclosure under Rule 501 of the Federal Rules of Evidence. The judgment of the Court of Appeals is affirmed.

It is so ordered.

JUSTICE SCALIA, with whom THE CHIEF JUSTICE joins as to Part III, dissenting.

The Court has discussed at some length the benefit that will be purchased by creation of the evidentiary privilege in this case: the encouragement of psychoanalytic counseling. It has not mentioned the purchase price: occasional injustice. That is the cost of every rule which excludes reliable and probative evidence—or at least every one categorical enough to achieve its announced policy objective. In the case of some of these rules, such as the one excluding confessions that have not been properly "Mirandized," see *Miranda v. Arizona*, 384 U.S. 436 (1966), the victim of the injustice is always the impersonal State or the faceless "public

---

19. Although it would be premature to speculate about most future developments in the federal psychotherapist privilege, we do not doubt that there are situations in which the privilege must give way, for example, if a serious threat of harm to the patient or to others can be averted only by means of a disclosure by the therapist.

at large." For the rule proposed here, the victim is more likely to be some individual who is prevented from proving a valid claim—or (worse still) prevented from establishing a valid defense. The latter is particularly unpalatable for those who love justice, because it causes the courts of law not merely to let stand a wrong, but to become themselves the instruments of wrong. . . .

NOTES AND QUESTIONS

1. Privilege under state law.   The plaintiff in *Jaffee* sued Redmond under both federal and state law. The state-law claim was premised on the Illinois wrongful death statute. Assuming that the information conveyed by Redmond to her therapist was relevant to that claim, why didn't the Court simply look to Illinois law to determine if that law recognized the psychotherapist-patient privilege? Suppose that the only claim filed in *Jaffee* were the wrongful death claim and that Illinois did not extend the psychotherapist-patient privilege to licensed social workers. Would the Court have been bound to adhere to the state's more limited version of the privilege? Finally, what role, if any, did state law play in the creation of this federal privilege?

2. The presumption against privileges.   The dominant principle within our adjudicatory justice system is that the public is entitled to every person's evidence. As the *Jaffee* Court points out, privileges are an exception to that rule. The consequence of this hierarchy of principle and exception is that new privileges are rarely recognized. On what basis did the *Jaffee* Court conclude that the presumption against recognizing a new privilege had been overcome? Did the Court adequately explain why federal courts do not recognize a physician-patient privilege? How is that privilege distinguishable from the psychotherapist-patient privilege?

3. Balancing tests and privileges.   The *Jaffee* Court criticized the Seventh Circuit for including a "balancing component" in the psychotherapist-patient privilege. Why? Was this criticism consistent with the Court's own use of a balancing test in determining whether to recognize the privilege? Consider the following comment regarding balancing and privileges:

> [Where balancing points to recognizing the privilege], the resulting rule is to be a bright line, resisting post hoc decision making. However, the underlying tensions balanced out in creating the privilege cannot be escaped entirely. The tensions will surface in applying the bright line rule, at least in the accretive process of defining the scope of the privilege.

6 MOORE'S FEDERAL PRACTICE, *supra*, § 26.47[3]. Does this mean that while balancing defines the scope of the privilege, a bright-line test determines whether the privilege applies? What is the "bright line" test that emerges from *Jaffee*?

4. Asserting and waiving the privilege.   The burden of claiming a privilege and of establishing that a privilege exists is on the privilege holder. This burden will not be satisfied by a general or blanket assertion of privilege. Rather, under Rule

26(b)(5)(A), the privilege holder must "(i) Expressly [make the claim]; and (ii) Describe the nature of the documents, communications, or tangible things not produced or disclosed—and do so in a manner that, without revealing information itself privileged or protected, will enable other parties to assess the [existence of the privilege]." Of course, the submission must also be sufficient for the court to determine if the privilege does in fact apply. *See North River Ins. Co. v. Stefanou*, 831 F.2d 484, 486-487 (4th Cir. 1987), *cert. denied*, 486 U.S. 1007 (1988).

In addition, as the *Jaffee* Court points out in footnote 14, all privileges are subject to waiver, including implied waiver. An implied waiver might occur when the privilege holder puts the otherwise privileged matter in controversy. For example, if a privilege holder sues his psychotherapist for malpractice, he impliedly waives the psychotherapist-patient privilege as to confidential matters relevant to his claim. Similarly, a privilege will be deemed waived if the privilege holder intentionally discloses privileged matter to a third party other than his attorney.

Waiver may also occur during discovery if the privilege holder or a third party inadvertently discloses privileged information. The problem of inadvertent disclosure is particularly acute in the context of the discovery of electronically stored information, when the privileged information may be embedded but not immediately visible in the material displayed on a computer screen (*see* "E-discovery," at page 597, *infra*). Rule 26(b)(5)(B) provides a method for sequestering such inadvertently disclosed information pending the judicial resolution of any claim of privilege. *See* 8 Charles Alan Wright, Arthur R. Miller & Richard L. Marcus, Federal Practice and Procedure § 2016.7 (3d ed. 2010 & Supp. 2015). Federal Rule of Evidence 502(b) establishes the method for determining whether an inadvertent disclosure operates as a waiver of the attorney-client privilege or of the protections afforded attorney work product. Under that rule, an "inadvertent" disclosure will not operate as a waiver if the "the holder of the privilege or protection took reasonable steps to prevent disclosure; and . . . the holder promptly took reasonable steps to rectify the error . . . ." Fed. R. Evid. 502(b)(1)-(3).

With respect to the potential waiver of other privileges, federal courts have taken three different approaches: (1) inadvertent disclosure automatically operates as a waiver; (2) inadvertent disclosure never operates as a waiver; and (3) whether inadvertent disclosure operates as a waiver depends on a balancing of equities. Factors considered by courts adopting the latter approach include the reasonableness of the efforts to avoid disclosure, any delay in correcting the error, the scope and burden of discovery, the extent of disclosure, time constraints related to the production of information, and fairness. 6 Moore's Federal Practice, *supra*, § 26.47[5]; *see also* 8 Wright, Miller & Marcus, *supra*, § 2016.3. The first two approaches have been criticized for their rigidity and the third for its lack of uniformity.

If a privilege holder intends to use the privileged material at trial, should she be allowed to withhold that material during discovery? *See Engl v. Aetna Life Ins. Co.*, 139 F.2d 469, 473 (2d Cir. 1943) (per Judge Charles E. Clark).

PROBLEM

7-3. Virmani, a physician of Indian descent, lost his medical staff privileges at a hospital after an unfavorable peer review concluded that he had created a "life-threatening emergency" during a surgical procedure. Virmani sued the hospital in federal court claiming that its peer review process discriminated against Indian physicians in violation of federal law. As part of discovery, he sought access to peer review records the hospital had compiled over the past 20 years. The hospital claimed that the records were privileged as "medical peer review materials" and sought a protective order to that effect. All 50 states and the District of Columbia have adopted a medical peer review privilege, which typically arises in the context of malpractice claims. Should the federal district court recognize a peer review privilege in this case? *See Adkins v. Christie*, 488 F.3d 1324 (11th Cir. 2007), *cert. denied*, 552 U.S. 1131 (2008); *Virmani v. Novant Health Inc.*, 259 F.3d 284 (4th Cir. 2001).

Upjohn Company v. United States [Parts I and II]
449 U.S. 383 (1981)

JUSTICE REHNQUIST delivered the opinion of the Court.

We granted certiorari in this case to address important questions concerning the scope of the attorney-client privilege in the corporate context. . . .

I

Petitioner Upjohn Co. manufactures and sells pharmaceuticals here and abroad. In January 1976 independent accountants conducting an audit of one of Upjohn's foreign subsidiaries discovered that the subsidiary made payments to or for the benefit of foreign government officials in order to secure government business. The accountants so informed petitioner, Mr. Gerard Thomas, Upjohn's Vice President, Secretary, and General Counsel. Thomas is a member of the Michigan and New York Bars, and has been Upjohn's General Counsel for 20 years. He consulted with outside counsel and R. T. Parfet, Jr., Upjohn's Chairman of the Board. It was decided that the company would conduct an internal investigation of what were termed "questionable payments." As part of this investigation the attorneys prepared a letter containing a questionnaire which was sent to "All Foreign General and Area Managers" over the Chairman's signature. The letter began by noting recent disclosures that several American companies made "possibly illegal" payments to foreign government officials and emphasized that the management needed full information concerning any such payments made by Upjohn. The letter indicated that the Chairman had asked Thomas, identified as "the company's General Counsel," "to conduct an investigation for the purpose of determining the nature and magnitude of any payments made by the Upjohn

Company or any of its subsidiaries to any employee or official of a foreign government." The questionnaire sought detailed information concerning such payments. Managers were instructed to treat the investigation as "highly confidential" and not to discuss it with anyone other than Upjohn employees who might be helpful in providing the requested information. Responses were to be sent directly to Thomas. Thomas and outside counsel also interviewed the recipients of the questionnaire and some 33 other Upjohn officers or employees as part of the investigation.

On March 26, 1976, the company voluntarily submitted a preliminary report to the Securities and Exchange Commission on Form 8-K disclosing certain questionable payments. A copy of the report was simultaneously submitted to the Internal Revenue Service, which immediately began an investigation to determine the tax consequences of the payments. Special agents conducting the investigation were given lists by Upjohn of all those interviewed and all who had responded to the questionnaire. On November 23, 1976, the Service issued a summons pursuant to 26 U.S.C. § 7602 demanding production of:

> "All files relative to the investigation conducted under the supervision of Gerard Thomas to identify payments to employees of foreign governments and any political contributions made by the Upjohn Company or any of its affiliates since January 1, 1971 and to determine whether any funds of the Upjohn Company had been improperly accounted for on the corporate books during the same period.
>
> "The records should include but not be limited to written questionnaires sent to managers of the Upjohn Company's foreign affiliates, and memorandums or notes of the interviews conducted in the United States and abroad with officers and employees of the Upjohn Company and its subsidiaries."

The company declined to produce the documents specified in the second paragraph on the grounds that they were protected from disclosure by the attorney-client privilege and constituted the work product of attorneys prepared in anticipation of litigation. On August 31, 1977, the United States filed a petition seeking enforcement of the summons under 26 U.S.C. §§ 7402(b) and 7604(a) in the United States District Court for the Western District of Michigan. That court adopted the recommendation of a Magistrate who concluded that the summons should be enforced. Petitioners appealed to the Court of Appeals for the Sixth Circuit which rejected the Magistrate's finding of a waiver of the attorney-client privilege, but agreed that the privilege did not apply "[t]o the extent that the communications were made by officers and agents not responsible for directing Upjohn's actions in response to legal advice . . . for the simple reason that the communications were not the 'client's.'" . . .

II

Federal Rule of Evidence 501 provides that "the privilege of a witness . . . shall be governed by the principles of the common law as they may be interpreted by the courts of the United States in light of reason and experience." The attorney-client privilege is the oldest of the privileges for confidential communications known to the common law. Its purpose is to encourage full and frank communication between attorneys and their clients and thereby promote broader public interests in the observance of law and administration of justice. The privilege recognizes that sound legal advice or advocacy serves public ends and that such advice or advocacy depends upon the lawyer's being fully informed by the client. As we stated last Term in *Trammel v. United States*, 445 U.S. 40, 51 (1980): "The lawyer-client privilege rests on the need for the advocate and counselor to know all that relates to the client's reasons for seeking representation if the professional mission is to be carried out." And in *Fisher v. United States*, 425 U.S. 391, 403 (1976), we recognized the purpose of the privilege to be "to encourage clients to make full disclosure to their attorneys." This rationale for the privilege has long been recognized by the Court, see *Hunt v. Blackburn*, 128 U.S. 464, 470 (1888) (privilege "is founded upon the necessity, in the interest and administration of justice, of the aid of persons having knowledge of the law and skilled in its practice, which assistance can only be safely and readily availed of when free from the consequences or the apprehension of disclosure"). Admittedly complications in the application of the privilege arise when the client is a corporation, which in theory is an artificial creature of the law, and not an individual; but this Court has assumed that the privilege applies when the client is a corporation. *United States v. Louisville & Nashville R. Co.*, 236 U.S. 318, 336 (1915), and the Government does not contest the general proposition.

The Court of Appeals, however, considered the application of the privilege in the corporate context to present a "different problem," since the client was an inanimate entity and "only the senior management, guiding and integrating the several operations, . . . can be said to possess an identity analogous to the corporation as a whole." The first case to articulate the so-called "control group test" adopted by the court below, *Philadelphia v. Westinghouse Electric Corp.*, 210 F. Supp. 483, 485 (ED Pa.), reflected a similar conceptual approach:

> "Keeping in mind that the question is, Is it the corporation which is seeking the lawyer's advice when the asserted privileged communication is made?, the most satisfactory solution, I think, is that if the employee making the communication, of whatever rank he may be, is in a position to control or even to take a substantial part in a decision about any action which the corporation may take upon the advice of the attorney, . . . then, in effect, *he is (or personifies) the corporation* when he makes his disclosure to the lawyer and the privilege would apply." (Emphasis supplied.)

Such a view, we think, overlooks the fact that the privilege exists to protect not only the giving of professional advice to those who can act on it but also the giving of information to the lawyer to enable him to give sound and informed advice. The first step in the resolution of any legal problem is ascertaining the factual background and sifting through the facts with an eye to the legally relevant. See ABA Code of Professional Responsibility, Ethical Consideration 4-1:

> "A lawyer should be fully informed of all the facts of the matter he is handling in order for his client to obtain the full advantage of our legal system. It is for the lawyer in the exercise of his independent professional judgment to separate the relevant and important from the irrelevant and unimportant. The observance of the ethical

obligation of a lawyer to hold inviolate the confidences and secrets of his client not only facilitates the full development of facts essential to proper representation of the client but also encourages laymen to seek early legal assistance."

See also *Hickman v. Taylor*, 329 U.S. 495, 511 (1947).

In the case of the individual client the provider of information and the person who acts on the lawyer's advice are one and the same. In the corporate context, however, it will frequently be employees beyond the control group as defined by the court below—"officers and agents . . . responsible for directing [the company's] actions in response to legal advice"—who will possess the information needed by the corporation's lawyers. Middle-level—and indeed lower-level—employees can, by actions within the scope of their employment, embroil the corporation in serious legal difficulties, and it is only natural that these employees would have the relevant information needed by corporate counsel if he is adequately to advise the client with respect to such actual or potential difficulties. This fact was noted in *Diversified Industries, Inc. v. Meredith*, 572 F.2d 596 (CA8 1978) (en banc):

"In a corporation, it may be necessary to glean information relevant to a legal problem from middle management or non-management personnel as well as from top executives. The attorney dealing with a complex legal problem 'is thus faced with a "Hobson's choice". If he interviews employees not having "the very highest authority," their communications to him will not be privileged. If, on the other hand, he interviews *only* those employees with the "very highest authority", he may find it extremely difficult, if not impossible, to determine what happened.'" *Id.*, at 608-609.

The control group test adopted by the court below thus frustrates the very purpose of the privilege by discouraging the communication of relevant information by employees of the client to attorneys seeking to render legal advice to the client corporation. The attorney's advice will also frequently be more significant to non-control group members than to those who officially sanction the advice, and the control group test makes it more difficult to convey full and frank legal advice to the employees who will put into effect the client corporation's policy.

The narrow scope given the attorney-client privilege by the court below not only makes it difficult for corporate attorneys to formulate sound advice when their client is faced with a specific legal problem but also threatens to limit the valuable efforts of corporate counsel to ensure their client's compliance with the law. In light of the vast and complicated array of regulatory legislation confronting the modern corporation, corporations, unlike most individuals, "constantly go to lawyers to find out how to obey the law," Burnham, The Attorney-Client Privilege in the Corporate Arena, 24 Bus. Law. 901, 913 (1969), particularly since compliance with the law in this area is hardly an instinctive matter, see, *e.g.*, *United States v. United States Gypsum Co.*, 438 U.S. 422, 440-441 (1978) ("the behavior proscribed by the [Sherman] Act is often difficult to distinguish from the gray zone of socially acceptable and economically justifiable business conduct"). The test adopted by the court below is difficult to apply in practice, though no abstractly formulated and unvarying "test" will necessarily enable courts to decide questions such as this with mathematical precision. But if the purpose of the attorney-client privilege is to be served, the attorney and client must be able to predict with some degree of certainty whether particular discussions will be protected. An uncertain privilege, or one which purports to be certain but results in widely varying applications by the courts, is little better than no privilege at all. The very terms of the test adopted by the court below suggest the unpredictability of its application. The test restricts the availability of the privilege to those officers who play a "substantial role" in deciding and directing a corporation's legal response. Disparate decisions in cases applying this test illustrate its unpredictability.

The communications at issue were made by Upjohn employees to counsel for Upjohn acting as such, at the direction of corporate superiors in order to secure legal advice from counsel. As the Magistrate found, "Mr. Thomas consulted with the Chairman of the Board and outside counsel and thereafter conducted a factual investigation to determine the nature and extent of the questionable payments *and to be in a position to give legal advice to the company with respect to the payments.*" (Emphasis supplied.) Information, not available from upper-echelon management, was needed to supply a basis for legal advice concerning compliance with securities and tax laws, foreign laws, currency regulations, duties to shareholders, and potential litigation in each of these areas. The communications concerned matters within the scope of the employees' corporate duties, and the employees themselves were sufficiently aware that they were being questioned in order that the corporation could obtain legal advice. The questionnaire identified Thomas as "the company's General Counsel" and referred in its opening sentence to the possible illegality of payments such as the ones on which information was sought. A statement of policy accompanying the questionnaire clearly indicated the legal implications of the investigation. The policy statement was issued "in order that there be no uncertainty in the future as to the policy with respect to the practices which are the subject of this investigation." It began "Upjohn will comply with all laws and regulations," and stated that commissions or payments "will not be used as a subterfuge for bribes or illegal payments" and that all payments must be "proper and legal." Any future agreements with foreign distributors or agents were to be approved "by a company attorney" and any questions concerning the policy were to be referred "to the company's General Counsel." This statement was issued to Upjohn employees worldwide, so that even those interviewees not receiving a questionnaire were aware of the legal implications of the interviews. Pursuant to explicit instructions from the Chairman of the Board, the communications were considered "highly confidential" when made, and have been kept confidential by the company. Consistent with the underlying purposes of the attorney-client privilege, these communications must be protected against compelled disclosure.

The Court of Appeals declined to extend the attorney-client privilege beyond the limits of the control group test for fear that doing so would entail severe burdens on discovery and create a broad "zone of silence" over corporate affairs. Application of the attorney-client privilege to communications such as those involved here, however, puts the adversary in no worse position than if the communications had never taken place. The privilege only protects disclosure of communications; it does not protect disclosure of the underlying facts by those who communicated with the attorney:

> "[T]he protection of the privilege extends only to *communications* and not to facts. A fact is one thing and a communication concerning that fact is an entirely different thing. The client cannot be compelled to answer the question, 'What did you say or write to the attorney?' but may not refuse to disclose any relevant fact within his knowledge merely because he incorporated a statement of such fact into his communication to his attorney." *Philadelphia v. Westinghouse Electric Corp.*, 205 F. Supp. 830, 831 (ED Pa. 1962).

Here the Government was free to question the employees who communicated with Thomas and outside counsel. Upjohn has provided the IRS with a list of such employees, and the IRS has already interviewed some 25 of them. While it would probably be more convenient for the Government to secure the results of petitioner's internal investigation by simply subpoenaing the questionnaires and notes taken by petitioner's attorneys, such considerations of convenience do not overcome the policies served by the attorney-client privilege. As Justice Jackson noted in his concurring opinion in *Hickman v. Taylor*, 329 U.S., at 516: "Discovery was hardly intended to enable a learned profession to perform its functions . . . on wits borrowed from the adversary."

Needless to say, we decide only the case before us, and do not undertake to draft a set of rules which should govern challenges to investigatory subpoenas. Any such approach would violate the spirit of Federal Rule of Evidence 501. See S. Rep. No. 93-1277, p. 13 (1974) ("the recognition of a privilege based on a confidential relationship . . . should be determined on a case-by-case basis"); *Trammel*, 445 U.S., at 47. While such a "case-by-case" basis may to some slight extent undermine desirable certainty in the boundaries of the attorney-client privilege, it obeys the spirit of the Rules. At the same time we conclude that the narrow "control group test" sanctioned by the Court of Appeals, in this case cannot, consistent with "the principles of the common law as . . . interpreted . . . in the light of reason and experience," Fed. Rule Evid. 501, govern the development of the law in this area. . . .

Accordingly, the judgment of the Court of Appeals is reversed, and the case remanded for further proceedings.

It is so ordered.

[The concurring opinion of CHIEF JUSTICE BURGER is omitted.]

NOTES AND QUESTIONS

1. Defining the attorney-client privilege.   What precisely is the attorney-client privilege and under what circumstances does it apply? Judge Charles E. Wyzanski aptly described its basic contours in an oft-quoted passage:

> The privilege applies only if (1) the asserted holder of the privilege is or sought to become a client; (2) the person to whom the communication was made (a) is a member of the bar of a court, or his subordinate and (b) in connection with

this communication is acting as a lawyer; (3) the communication relates to a fact of which the attorney was informed (a) by his client (b) without the presence of strangers (c) for the purpose of securing primarily either (i) an opinion on law or (ii) legal services or (iii) assistance in some legal proceeding, and not (d) for the purpose of committing a crime or tort; and (4) the privilege has been (a) claimed and (b) not waived by the client.

United States v. United Shoe Mach. Corp., 89 F. Supp. 357, 358-359 (D. Mass. 1950). What, according to the Court in *Upjohn*, is the policy behind this privilege and what is the scope of the protection it affords? Finally, how if at all was the policy behind the doctrine advanced by the decision in *Upjohn*?

2. *Unincorporated associations.* The rule established in *Upjohn* regarding communications between corporate counsel and an employee of the corporation has been applied to similar communications within unincorporated associations. *See In re Bieter Co.*, 16 F.3d 929, 935-940 (8th Cir. 1994) (extending privilege to communications between attorney for a partnership and an independent consultant hired by the partnership).

PROBLEM

7-4. Diana is concerned that she might be sued by Lester, whom she recently discharged as an employee. Lester has complained publicly that Diana terminated his employment in retaliation for his labor organizing activities. Nervous about the potential suit, Diana calls an attorney friend seeking advice. She tells her friend that Lester's termination was at least in part due to his labor-related activities, but she also explains that Lester was habitually late for work and generally unreliable. Diana concedes, however, that Lester's personnel file contains only positive reviews of his work. The attorney friend asks Diana to mail the personnel file to her for safekeeping. When asked what the "charge" will be, the attorney friend replies, "Charge it to friendship." Assuming a lawsuit is subsequently filed by Lester, may he require the "attorney friend" to disclose what Diana told her regarding Lester's termination? Assuming the attorney friend possesses the personnel file (and represents Diana in the lawsuit), would the attorney-client privilege shield the file from discovery? In answering these questions, you might use the framework described by Judge Wyzanski in Note 1, *supra*.

3. The Work-Product Doctrine

Hickman v. Taylor

329 U.S. 495 (1947)

MR. JUSTICE MURPHY delivered the opinion of the Court.

This case presents an important problem under the Federal Rules of Civil Procedure as to the extent to which a party may inquire into oral and written statements of witnesses, or other information, secured by an adverse party's counsel in the course of preparation for possible litigation after a claim has arisen. Examination into a person's files and records, including those resulting from the professional activities of an attorney, must be judged with care. It is not without reason that various safeguards have been established to preclude unwarranted excursions into the privacy of a man's work. At the same time, public policy supports reasonable and necessary inquiries. Properly to balance these competing interests is a delicate and difficult task.

On February 7, 1943, the tug "J. M. Taylor" sank while engaged in helping to tow a car float of the Baltimore & Ohio Railroad across the Delaware River at Philadelphia. The accident was apparently unusual in nature, the cause of it still being unknown. Five of the nine crew members were drowned. Three days later the tug owners and the underwriters employed a law firm, of which respondent Fortenbaugh is a member, to defend them against potential suits by representatives of the deceased crew members and to sue the railroad for damages to the tug.

A public hearing was held on March 4, 1943, before the United States Steamboat Inspectors, at which the four survivors were examined. This testimony was recorded and made available to all interested parties. Shortly thereafter, Fortenbaugh privately interviewed the survivors and took statements from them with an eye toward the anticipated litigation; the survivors signed these statements on March 29. Fortenbaugh also interviewed other persons believed to have some information relating to the accident and in some cases he made memoranda of what they told him. At the time when Fortenbaugh secured the statements of the survivors, representatives of two of the deceased crew members had been in communication with him. Ultimately claims were presented by representatives of all five of the deceased; four of the claims, however, were settled without litigation. The fifth claimant, petitioner herein, brought suit in a federal court under the Jones Act on November 26, 1943, naming as defendants the two tug owners, individually and as partners, and the railroad.

One year later, petitioner filed 39 interrogatories directed to the tug owners. The 38th interrogatory read: "State whether any statements of the members of the crews of the Tugs 'J. M. Taylor' and 'Philadelphia' or of any other vessel were taken in connection with the towing of the car float and the sinking of the Tug 'John M. Taylor'. Attach hereto exact copies of all such statements if in writing, and if oral, set forth in detail the exact provisions of any such oral statements or reports."

Supplemental interrogatories asked whether any oral or written statements, records, reports or other memoranda had been made concerning any matter relative to the towing operation, the sinking of the tug, the salvaging and repair of the tug, and the death of the deceased. If the answer was in the affirmative, the tug owners were then requested to set forth the nature of all such records, reports, statements or other memoranda.

The tug owners, through Fortenbaugh, answered all of the interrogatories except No. 38 and the supplemental ones just described. While admitting that statements of the survivors had been taken, they declined to summarize or set forth the contents. They did so on the ground that such requests called "for privileged matter obtained in preparation for litigation" and constituted "an attempt to obtain indirectly counsel's private files." It was claimed that answering these requests "would involve practically turning over not only the complete files, but also the telephone records and, almost, the thoughts of counsel."

In connection with the hearing on these objections, Fortenbaugh made a written statement and gave an informal oral deposition explaining the circumstances under which he had taken the statements. But he was not expressly asked in the deposition to produce the statements. The District Court for the Eastern District of Pennsylvania, sitting *en banc*, held that the requested matters were not privileged. The court then decreed that the tug owners and Fortenbaugh, as counsel and agent for the tug owners forthwith "Answer Plaintiff's 38th interrogatory and supplemental interrogatories; produce all written statements of witnesses obtained by Mr. Fortenbaugh, as counsel and agent for Defendants; state in substance any fact concerning this case which Defendants learned through oral statements made by witnesses to Mr. Fortenbaugh whether or not included in his private memoranda and produce Mr. Fortenbaugh's memoranda containing statements of fact by witnesses or to submit these memoranda to the Court for determination of those portions which should be revealed to Plaintiff." Upon their refusal, the court adjudged them in contempt and ordered them imprisoned until they complied.

The Third Circuit Court of Appeals, also sitting *en banc*, reversed the judgment of the District Court. It held that the information here sought was part of the "work product of the lawyer" and hence privileged from discovery under the Federal Rules of Civil Procedure. The importance of the problem, which has engendered a great divergence of views among district courts, led us to grant certiorari.

The pre-trial deposition-discovery mechanism established by Rules 26 to 37 is one of the most significant innovations of the Federal Rules of Civil Procedure. Under the prior federal practice, the pre-trial functions of notice-giving issue-formulation and fact-revelation were performed primarily and inadequately by the pleadings. Inquiry into the issues and the facts before trial was narrowly confined and was often cumbersome in method. The new rules, however, restrict the pleadings to the task of general notice-giving and invest the deposition-discovery process with a vital role in the preparation for trial. The various instruments of discovery now serve (1) as a device, along with the pre-trial hearing under Rule 16, to narrow and clarify the basic issues between the parties, and (2) as a device for ascertaining the facts, or information as to the existence or whereabouts of facts, relative to those issues. Thus civil trials in the federal courts no longer need be carried on in the dark. The way is now clear, consistent with recognized privileges, for the parties to obtain the fullest possible knowledge of the issues and facts before trial. . . .

In urging that he has a right to inquire into the materials secured and prepared by Fortenbaugh, petitioner emphasizes that the deposition-discovery portions of the Federal Rules of Civil Procedure are designed to enable the parties to discover the true facts and to compel their disclosure wherever they may be found. It is said that inquiry may be made under these rules, epitomized by Rule 26, as to any relevant matter which is not privileged; and since the discovery provisions are to be applied as broadly and liberally as possible, the privilege limitation must be restricted to its narrowest bounds. On the premise that the attorney-client privilege is the one involved in this case, petitioner argues that it must be strictly confined to confidential communications made by a client to his attorney. And since the materials here in issue were secured by Fortenbaugh from third persons rather than from his clients, the tug owners, the conclusion is reached that these materials are proper subjects for discovery under Rule 26. . . .

We agree, of course, that the deposition-discovery rules are to be accorded a broad and liberal treatment. No longer can the time-honored cry of "fishing expedition" serve to preclude a party from inquiring into the facts underlying his opponent's case. Mutual knowledge of all the relevant facts gathered by both parties is essential to proper litigation. To that end, either party may compel the other to disgorge whatever facts he has in his possession. The deposition-discovery procedure simply advances the stage at which the disclosure can be compelled from the time of trial to the period preceding it, thus reducing the possibility of surprise. But discovery, like all matters of procedure, has ultimate and necessary boundaries. As indicated by [Rules 26(c), 30, and 37(a)], limitations inevitably arise when it can be shown that the examination is being conducted in bad faith or in such a manner as to annoy, embarrass or oppress the person subject to the inquiry. And as Rule 26(b) provides, further limitations come into existence when the inquiry touches upon the irrelevant or encroaches upon the recognized domains of privilege.

We also agree that the memoranda, statements and mental impressions in issue in this case fall outside the scope of the attorney-client privilege and hence are not protected from discovery on that basis. It is unnecessary here to delineate the content and scope of that privilege as recognized in the federal courts. For present purposes, it suffices to note that the protective cloak of this privilege does not extend to information which an attorney secures from a witness while acting for his client in anticipation of litigation. Nor does this privilege concern the memoranda, briefs, communications and other writings prepared by counsel for his own use in prosecuting his client's case; and it is equally unrelated to writings which reflect an attorney's mental impressions, conclusions, opinions or legal theories.

But the impropriety of invoking that privilege does not provide an answer to the problem before us. Petitioner has made more than an ordinary request for relevant, non-privileged facts in the possession of his adversaries or their counsel. He has sought discovery as of right of oral and written statements of witnesses whose identity is well known and whose availability to petitioner appears unimpaired. He has sought production of these matters after making the most searching inquiries of his opponents as to the circumstances surrounding the fatal accident, which inquiries were sworn to have been answered to the best of their information and belief. Interrogatories were directed toward all the events prior to, during and subsequent to the sinking of the tug. Full and honest answers to such broad inquiries would necessarily have included all pertinent information gleaned by Fortenbaugh through his interviews with the witnesses. Petitioner makes no suggestion, and we cannot assume, that the tug owners or Fortenbaugh were incomplete or dishonest in the framing of their answers. In addition, petitioner was free to examine the public testimony of the witnesses taken before the United States Steamboat Inspectors. We are thus dealing with an attempt to secure the production of written statements and mental impressions contained in the files and the mind of the attorney Fortenbaugh without any showing of necessity or any indication or claim that denial of such production would unduly prejudice the preparation of petitioner's case or cause him any hardship or injustice. For aught that appears, the essence of what petitioner seeks either has been revealed to him already through the interrogatories or is readily available to him direct from the witnesses for the asking.

The District Court, after hearing objections to petitioner's request, commanded Fortenbaugh to produce all written statements of witnesses and to state in substance any facts learned through oral statements of witnesses to him. Fortenbaugh was to submit any memoranda he had made of the oral statements so that the court might determine what portions should be revealed to petitioner. All of this was ordered without any showing by petitioner, or any requirement that he make a proper showing, of the necessity for the production of any of this material or any demonstration that denial of production would cause hardship or injustice. The court simply ordered production on the theory that the facts sought were material and were not privileged as constituting attorney-client communications.

In our opinion, neither Rule 26 nor any other rule dealing with discovery contemplates production under such circumstances. That is not because the subject matter is privileged or irrelevant, as those concepts are used in these rules. Here is simply an attempt, without purported necessity or justification, to secure written statements, private memoranda and personal recollections prepared or formed by an adverse party's counsel in the course of his legal duties. As such, it falls outside the arena of discovery and contravenes the public policy underlying the orderly prosecution and defense of legal claims. Not even the most liberal of discovery theories can justify unwarranted inquiries into the files and the mental impressions of an attorney.

Historically, a lawyer is an officer of the court and is bound to work for the advancement of justice while faithfully protecting the rightful interests of his clients. In performing his various duties, however, it is essential that a lawyer work with a certain degree of privacy, free from unnecessary intrusion by opposing parties and their counsel. Proper preparation of a client's case demands that he assemble information, sift what he considers to be the relevant from the irrelevant facts, prepare his legal theories and plan his strategy without undue and needless interference. That is the historical and the necessary way in which lawyers act within the framework of our system of jurisprudence to promote justice and to protect their clients' interests. This work is reflected, of course, in interviews, statements, memoranda, correspondence, briefs, mental impressions, personal beliefs, and countless other tangible and intangible ways—aptly though roughly termed by the Circuit Court of Appeals in this case as the "Work product of the lawyer." Were such materials open to opposing counsel on mere demand, much of what is now put down in writing would remain unwritten. An attorney's thoughts, heretofore inviolate, would not be his own. Inefficiency, unfairness and sharp practices would inevitably develop in the giving of legal advice and in the preparation of cases for trial. The effect on the legal profession would be demoralizing. And the interests of the clients and the cause of justice would be poorly served.

We do not mean to say that all written materials obtained or prepared by an adversary's counsel with an eye toward litigation are necessarily free from discovery in all cases. Where relevant and non-privileged facts remain hidden in an attorney's file and where production of those facts is essential to the preparation of one's case, discovery may properly be had. Such written statements and documents might, under certain circumstances, be admissible in evidence or give clues as to the existence or location of relevant facts. Or they might be useful for purposes of impeachment or corroboration. And production might be justified where the witnesses are no longer available or can be reached only with difficulty. Were production of written statements and documents to be precluded under such circumstances, the liberal ideals of the deposition-discovery portions of the Federal Rules of Civil Procedure would be stripped of much of their meaning. But the general policy against invading the privacy of an attorney's course of preparation is so well recognized and so essential to an orderly working of our system of legal procedure that a burden rests on the one who would invade that privacy to establish adequate reasons to justify production through a subpoena or court order. That burden, we believe, is necessarily implicit in the rules as now constituted.

[Rule 26(c)], as presently written, gives the trial judge the requisite discretion to make a judgment as to whether discovery should be allowed as to written statements secured from witnesses. But in the instant case there was no room for that discretion to operate in favor of the petitioner. No attempt was made to establish any reason why Fortenbaugh should be forced to produce the written statements. There was only a naked, general demand for these materials as of right and a finding by the District Court that no recognizable privilege was involved. That was insufficient to justify discovery under these circumstances and the court should have sustained the refusal of the tug owners and Fortenbaugh to produce.

But as to oral statements made by witnesses to Fortenbaugh, whether presently in the form of his mental impressions or memoranda, we do not believe that any showing of necessity can be made under the circumstances of this case so as to justify production. Under ordinary conditions, forcing an attorney to repeat or write out all that witnesses have told him and to deliver the account to his adversary gives rise to grave dangers of inaccuracy and untrustworthiness. No legitimate purpose is served by such production. The practice forces the attorney to testify as to what he remembers or what he saw fit to write down regarding witnesses' remarks. Such testimony could not qualify as evidence; and to use it for impeachment or corroborative purposes would make the attorney much less an officer of the court and much more an ordinary witness. The standards of the profession would thereby suffer.

Denial of production of this nature does not mean that any material, non-privi-leged facts can be hidden from the petitioner in this case. He need not be unduly hindered in the preparation of his case, in the discovery of facts or in his anticipa-tion of his opponents' position. Searching interrogatories directed to Fortenbaugh and the tug owners, production of written documents and statements upon a proper showing and direct interviews with the witnesses themselves all serve to reveal the facts in Fortenbaugh's possession to the fullest possible extent consistent with public policy. Petitioner's counsel frankly admits that he wants the oral state-ments only to help prepare himself to examine witnesses and to make sure that he has overlooked nothing. That is insufficient under the circumstances to permit him an exception to the policy underlying the privacy of Fortenbaugh's profes-sional activities. If there should be a rare situation justifying production of these matters, petitioner's case is not of that type.

We fully appreciate the wide-spread controversy among the members of the legal profession over the problem raised by this case. It is a problem that rests on what has been one of the most hazy frontiers of the discovery process. But until some rule or statute definitely prescribes otherwise, we are not justified in permit-ting discovery in a situation of this nature as a matter of unqualified right. When Rule 26 and the other discovery rules were adopted, this Court and the members of the bar in general certainly did not believe or contemplate that all the files and mental processes of lawyers were thereby opened to the free scrutiny of their adversaries. And we refuse to interpret the rules at this time so as to reach so harsh and unwarranted a result.

We therefore affirm the judgment of the Circuit Court of Appeals.
Affirmed.

MR. JUSTICE JACKSON, concurring [joined by JUSTICE FRANKFURTER]. . . .

The primary effect of the practice advocated here would be on the legal pro-fession itself. But it too often is overlooked that the lawyer and the law office are indispensable parts of our administration of justice. Law-abiding people can go nowhere else to learn the ever changing and constantly multiplying rules by which they must behave and to obtain redress for their wrongs. The welfare and tone of the legal profession is therefore of prime consequence to society, which would feel the consequences of such a practice as petitioner urges secondarily but certainly. . . .

The real purpose and the probable effect of the practice ordered by the district court would be to put trials on a level even lower than a "battle of wits." I can conceive of no practice more demoralizing to the Bar than to require a lawyer to write out and deliver to his adversary an account of what witnesses have told him . . . . Whenever the testimony of the witness would differ from the "exact" state-ment the lawyer has delivered, the lawyer's statement would be whipped out to impeach the witness . . . .

NOTES AND QUESTIONS

1. *The distinction between the attorney-client privilege and the work-product doctrine.*   The attorney-client privilege protects confidential communications between an attorney and her client, while the work-product doctrine protects the preparation an attorney undertakes on behalf of her client in anticipation of litigation or trial. The purpose of the former is to promote full disclosure of all relevant information between the attorney and client. What, according to the *Hickman* Court, is the purpose of the latter? As made clear in *Hickman*, however, neither doctrine shields against discovery of the underlying material facts.

2. *Written statements signed by a witness and written or mental impressions of oral statements made by a witness.*   Interrogatory 38 in *Hickman* sought production of two separate types of material or information: (1) written statements signed by the witnesses; and (2) Fortenbraugh's notes or impressions of oral statements made by the witnesses. The Court held that the former—commonly referred to as "fact work product," "ordinary work product," or "qualified work product"—were discoverable only upon a showing of good cause but that the latter—commonly referred to as "opinion work product" or "absolute work product"—were rarely if ever discoverable. Why the distinction?

3. *Rule 26(b)(3).*   At the time *Hickman* was decided, the federal rules did not provide specific protection from discovery for an attorney's work product. The decision in *Hickman*, therefore, was essentially based on common law principles of privilege (though technically work product is not considered a privilege). Today, however, the *Hickman* rule is embodied in part in Rule 26(b)(3). That rule provides:

> Ordinarily, a party may not discover documents and tangible things that are prepared in anticipation of litigation or for trial by or for another party or its representative (including the other party's attorney, consultant, surety, indemnitor, insurer, or agent). But, subject to Rule 26(b)(4), those materials may be discovered if: (i) they are otherwise discoverable under Rule 26(b)(1); and (ii) the party shows that it has substantial need for the materials to prepare its case and cannot, without undue hardship, obtain their substantial equivalent by other means.

FED. R. CIV. P. 26(b)(3)(A). If a court permits discovery under this standard, it "must protect against disclosure of the mental impressions, conclusions, opinions, or legal theories of a party's attorney or other representative concerning the litigation." *Id.* 26(b)(3)(B). Does this mean that a party may never discover the opinion work product prepared by another party's attorney? Notice that the rule covers only documents and other tangible things. It does not pertain to intangible things (thoughts, impressions, etc.) except to the extent that those intangibles are embodied in a document or tangible thing. Is this significant? Does this mean that "disembodied" intangibles are never discoverable? Or does *Hickman* resolve this problem? The lower federal courts are not of one mind, and the second part of *Upjohn*—the next principal case below—addresses the discoverability of opinion work product and the underlying conflict over the scope of Rule 26(b)(3). As to the overall scope and application of Rule 26(b)(3), see generally 6 MOORE'S FEDERAL PRACTICE, *supra*, § 26.70; 8 WRIGHT, MILLER & MARCUS, *supra*, §§ 2021-2028.

4. *Judicial duty to limit discovery.* Even if a party's discovery is directed toward material that is discovery-relevant, nonprivileged, and not subject to the work-product doctrine, a court must nonetheless, either on motion or its own initiative, "limit the frequency or extent" of otherwise permissible discovery if:

> (i) the discovery sought is unreasonably cumulative or duplicative, or can be obtained from some other source that is more convenient, less burdensome, or less expensive; (ii) the party seeking discovery has had ample opportunity to obtain the information by discovery in the action; or (iii) the proposed discovery is outside the scope permitted by Rule 26(b)(1).

FED. R. CIV. P. 26(b)(2)(C).

Upjohn Company v. United States [Part III]
449 U.S. 383 (1981)

JUSTICE REHNQUIST delivered the opinion of the Court. . . .

[Parts I and II of the Court's opinion in this case appear at page 568, *supra*.]

III

Our decision that the communications by Upjohn employees to counsel are covered by the attorney-client privilege disposes of the case so far as the responses to the questionnaires and any notes reflecting responses to interview questions are concerned. The summons reaches further, however, and Thomas has testified that his notes and memoranda of interviews go beyond recording responses to his questions. To the extent that the material subject to the summons is not protected by the attorney-client privilege as disclosing communications between an employee and counsel, we must reach the ruling by the Court of Appeals that the work-product doctrine does not apply to summonses issued [by the IRS] under 26 U.S.C. § 7602.

The Government concedes, wisely, that the Court of Appeals erred and that the work-product doctrine does apply to IRS summonses. This doctrine was announced by the Court over 30 years ago in *Hickman v. Taylor*, 329 U.S. 495 (1947). In that case the Court rejected "an attempt, without purported necessity or justification, to secure written statements, private memoranda and personal recollections prepared or formed by an adverse party's counsel in the course of his legal duties." *Id.*, at 510 . . . . The "strong public policy" underlying the work-product doctrine . . . has been substantially incorporated in Federal Rule of Civil Procedure 26(b)(3).

As we stated last Term, the obligation imposed by a tax summons remains "subject to the traditional privileges and limitations." *United States v. Euge*, 444 U.S.

707, 714 (1980). Nothing in the language of the IRS summons provisions or their legislative history suggests an intent on the part of Congress to preclude application of the work-product doctrine. Rule 26(b)(3) codifies the work-product doctrine, and the Federal Rules of Civil Procedure are made applicable to summons enforcement proceedings by [Rule 81(a)(5)]. While conceding the applicability of the work-product doctrine, the Government asserts that it has made a sufficient showing of necessity to overcome its protections. The Magistrate apparently so found. The Government relies on the following language in *Hickman*:

> "We do not mean to say that all written materials obtained or prepared by an adversary's counsel with an eye toward litigation are necessarily free from discovery in all cases. Where relevant and nonprivileged facts remain hidden in an attorney's file and where production of those facts is essential to the preparation of one's case, discovery may properly be had. . . . And production might be justified where the witnesses are no longer available or can be reached only with difficulty." 329 U.S., at 511.

The Government stresses that interviewees are scattered across the globe and that Upjohn has forbidden its employees to answer questions it considers irrelevant. The above-quoted language from *Hickman*, however, did not apply to "oral statements made by witnesses . . . whether presently in the form of [the attorney's] mental impressions or memoranda." *Id.*, at 512. As to such material the Court did "not believe that any showing of necessity can be made under the circumstances of this case so as to justify production. . . . If there should be a rare situation justifying production of these matters petitioner's case is not of that type." *Id.*, at 512-513. Forcing an attorney to disclose notes and memoranda of witnesses' oral statements is particularly disfavored because it tends to reveal the attorney's mental processes, 329 U.S., at 513 ("what he saw fit to write down regarding witnesses' remarks"); *id.*, at 516-517 ("the statement would be his [the attorney's] language, permeated with his inferences") (Jackson, J., concurring).

Rule 26 accords special protection to work product revealing the attorney's mental processes. The Rule permits disclosure of documents and tangible things constituting attorney work product upon a showing of substantial need and inability to obtain the equivalent without undue hardship. This was the standard applied by the Magistrate. Rule 26 goes on, however, to state that "[i]n ordering discovery of such materials when the required showing has been made, the court shall protect against disclosure of the mental impressions, conclusions, opinions or legal theories of an attorney or other representative of a party concerning the litigation." Although this language does not specifically refer to memoranda based on oral statements of witnesses, the *Hickman* court stressed the danger that compelled disclosure of such memoranda would reveal the attorney's mental processes. It is clear that this is the sort of material the draftsmen of the Rule had in mind as deserving special protection. See Notes of Advisory Committee on 1970 Amendment to Rules, 28 U. S. C. App., p. 442 ("The subdivision . . . goes on to protect against disclosure the mental impressions, conclusions, opinions, or legal theories . . . of an attorney or other representative of a party. The *Hickman* opinion drew special attention to the need for protecting an attorney against discovery of memoranda prepared from recollection of oral interviews. The courts have steadfastly safeguarded against disclosure of lawyers' mental impressions and legal theories . . . ").

Based on the foregoing, some courts have concluded that *no* showing of necessity can overcome protection of work product which is based on oral statements from witnesses. Those courts declining to adopt an absolute rule have nonetheless recognized that such material is entitled to special protection.

We do not decide the issue at this time. It is clear that the Magistrate applied the wrong standard when he concluded that the Government had made a sufficient showing of necessity to overcome the protections of the work-product doctrine. The Magistrate applied the "substantial need" and "without undue hardship" standard articulated in the first part of Rule 26(b)(3). The notes and memoranda sought by the Government here, however, are work product based on oral statements. If they reveal communications, they are, in this case, protected by the attorney-client privilege. To the extent they do not reveal communications, they reveal the attorneys' mental processes in evaluating the communications. As Rule 26 and *Hickman* make clear, such work product cannot be disclosed simply on a showing of substantial need and inability to obtain the equivalent without undue hardship.

While we are not prepared at this juncture to say that such material is always protected by the work-product rule, we think a far stronger showing of necessity and unavailability by other means than was made by the Government or applied by the Magistrate in this case would be necessary to compel disclosure. Since the Court of Appeals thought that the work-product protection was never applicable in an enforcement proceeding such as this, and since the Magistrate whose recommendations the District Court adopted applied too lenient a standard of protection, we think the best procedure with respect to this aspect of the case would be to reverse the judgment of the Court of Appeals for the Sixth Circuit and remand the case to it for such further proceedings in connection with the work-product claim as are consistent with this opinion.

Accordingly, the judgment of the Court of Appeals is reversed, and the case remanded for further proceedings.

It is so ordered.

[The concurring opinion of Chief Justice Burger is omitted.]

PROBLEMS

7-5. Smith brought an action to recover for injuries he sustained in an industrial accident when the cab of a crane he was operating became disengaged from its pedestal mounts. The defendant resisted the discovery of three types of evidence: (1) witness statements taken within three days of the accident by a defense investigator; (2) investigative reports by a defense investigator analyzing the accident, including the investigator's on-scene attempt to verify the boom angle of the crane as reported by Smith at the time the accident occurred, as well as the investigator's summaries of his interviews with various witnesses; and (3) any surveillance evidence of Smith undertaken by the defendant after the accident. To what extent, if at all, does the work-product doctrine permit the defendant to refuse to provide these materials? *See Smith v. Diamond Offshore Drilling, Inc.*, 168 F.R.D. 582 (S.D. Tex. 1996).

7-6. Jones is a mortgage broker. In January 2005, a prosecutor with the U.S. Attorney's Office contacted Jones's counsel and indicated that Jones was the subject of a grand jury investigation regarding fraudulent mortgage transactions. Jones and his attorney met with the prosecutor and several federal agents. During this meeting, Jones discussed his role in certain specific mortgage transactions. Jones also indicated that on advice of counsel, he had surreptitiously recorded conversations with a broker named Smith, who was also a subject of the grand jury investigation. These conversations related to one of the mortgage transactions under investigation. The prosecutor requested copies of the recorded conversations, but Jones refused to turn them over. Jones was subsequently served with a subpoena that ordered him to produce, *inter alia*, "[o]riginals of any and all tape recordings of conversations between you and [Smith]." Jones refused to comply, invoking attorney-client privilege and the work-product doctrine. As to the latter, Jones asserted that the recordings are opinion work product and completely immune from discovery. The prosecutor, in a motion to compel, argued that the recordings were unique and that they provided factual matter, otherwise unobtainable, that was highly relevant to her investigation. How should the federal district court rule on the prosecutor's motion? In answering this question, address both the claim of attorney-client privilege and the work-product doctrine. *See In re Grand Jury Subpoena Dated July 6, 2005*, 510 F.3d 180 (2d Cir. 2007), *cert. denied*, 553 U.S. 1094 (2008).

A NOTE ON INFORMATION OBTAINED FROM EXPERTS

Attorneys sometimes use experts to assist them in anticipation of litigation or in preparation for trial, without intending to call the expert as a witness. For example, a lawyer preparing for trial in an antitrust suit against a computer manufacturer might hire experts in computer technology to teach her how various computer operating systems work. If the lawyer plans to use an expert's testimony at trial, the federal rules provide for generous discovery of facts known and opinions held by that expert. FED. R. CIV. P. 26(b)(4)(A). If, however, the expert is "not expected to be called as a witness at trial," discovery is only allowed "on showing exceptional circumstances under which it is impracticable for the party to obtain facts or opinions on the same subject by other means" FED. R. CIV. P. 26(b)(4)(D)(ii). The purpose of this rule is to prevent one party from relying exclusively on the work done by another. The rule also protects against the disclosure of opinion work product since nontestifying experts are often involved in the strategic planning of the litigation for which they were hired.

Given the policies behind the rule, the burden of establishing "exceptional circumstances" is heavy, albeit not insurmountable. In general, courts have recognized two circumstances under which this burden might be satisfied: when the investigation undertaken by the expert cannot be replicated because the object of study is no longer observable; or when the expense of replicating the study is prohibitive. *See, e.g., Braun v. Lorillard, Inc.*, 84 F.3d 230, 236 (7th Cir.), *cert. denied*, 519 U.S. 992 (1996) (permitting discovery of negative test results of presence of asbestos in lung tissue since the tissue examined was destroyed during the testing process); *Castaneda v. Burger King Corp.*, 259 F.R.D. 194, 196-199 (N.D. Cal. 2009) (permitting discovery of surveys prepared by defendant as to the measurements of its restaurants before changes were made to bring them into compliance with the Americans with Disabilities Act where those changes made it impossible for plaintiffs to now obtain the information themselves, where defendant had thwarted plaintiffs' earlier efforts to undertake their own studies, and where the information was not available from any other source); *Bank Brussels Lambert v. Chase Manhattan Bank*, 175 F.R.D. 34, 44-45 (S.D.N.Y. 1997) (permitting discovery of accounting expert's investigation of a financial institution where the institution's records were in a condition that made it impossible to replicate the study). If such discovery is permitted, however, the requesting party must normally "pay the expert a reasonable fee for time spent in responding to discovery . . . and . . . also pay the other party a fair portion of the fees and expenses it reasonably incurred in obtaining the expert's facts and opinions." FED. R. CIV. P. 26(b)(4)(E) (i)-(ii). *See generally* 6 MOORE'S FEDERAL PRACTICE, *supra*, § 26.80; 8A CHARLES ALAN WRIGHT, ARTHUR R. MILLER & RICHARD L. MARCUS, FEDERAL PRACTICE AND PROCEDURE § 2032 (3d ed. 2010 & Supp. 2015). Special provisions address discovery of experts used to perform physical or mental examinations. *See* FED. R. CIV. P. 26(b)(4)(D)(i) & 35(b).

C.   The Formal Discovery Process in Federal Court

Now that we have a sense of the range of information that can be discovered through the use of the formal discovery process, we need to understand the tools through which that discovery can be accomplished. What follows is a summary of the basic tools and techniques used in discovery in civil actions filed in federal court. Some reference to state practice is made as well. Keep in mind, however, that the availability of formal discovery does not end the informal fact-gathering process. Nor does it freeze the pretrial discovery plan. An effective attorney will continue to gather facts, both formally and informally, and to revise and update her discovery plan as new information becomes available.

Read Federal Rules 26 through 37 and 45.

1.   Mandatory Conference and Mandatory Disclosures

a.   *The Discovery Conference*

The formal discovery process usually begins only after a lawsuit has been filed.* In most jurisdictions, a suit having been filed, the parties may commence discovery without leave of court, though the plaintiff may be required to wait a short period of time after the service of the complaint before serving his initial discovery requests. *See, e.g.,* CAL. CIV. PROC. CODE §§ 2025.210 (depositions), 2030.020 (interrogatories), 2033.020 (requests for admission) — each allowing defendants to commence discovery immediately upon being served, while requiring plaintiffs to wait 10 to 20 days after service depending on the type of discovery involved). For most cases filed in federal court, however, discovery may not commence until the parties have first met and conferred to "consider the nature and basis of their claims and defenses and the possibilities for promptly settling or resolving the case; make or arrange for the disclosures required by Rule 26(a)(1); discuss any issues about preserving discoverable information; and develop a proposed discovery plan." FED. R. CIV. P. 26(f)(2); *see also* FED. R. CIV. P. 26(d)(1) (postponing most discovery until parties undertake the Rule 26(f) conference). The parties, through their attorneys, are "jointly responsible" for arranging this conference, which is to be undertaken without the supervision of the court. The purpose of the discovery conference is to encourage a speedy resolution of the controversy and to provide a mechanism through which the parties can mold the discovery process to the particular needs of their case. As to the latter, the subsidiary goal is to obviate the need for judicial intervention in the discovery process.

The discovery plan developed at the Rule 26(f) conference must state the parties' "views and proposals" regarding:

(A)   what changes should be made in the timing, form, or requirement for disclosures under Rule 26(a), including a statement of when initial disclosures were made or will be made;

(B)   the subjects on which discovery may be needed, when discovery should be completed, and whether discovery should be conducted in phases or be limited to or focused on particular issues;

(C)   any issues about disclosure, discovery or preservation of electronically stored information, including the form or forms in which it should be produced;

(D)   any issues about claims of privilege or of protection as trial-preparation materials, including—if the parties agree on a procedure to assert these claims after production—whether to ask the court to include their agreement in an order under Federal Rule of Evidence 502;

---

* Under limited circumstances, a person who expects to be a party to a lawsuit may petition a court for an order to take the deposition of a potential witness who may not be available to testify once the action is commenced. *See* FED. R. CIV. P. 27(a). This might occur, for example, if the potential witness is ill and in danger of dying. The goal of a pretrial deposition is to preserve the testimony.

   (E)   what changes should be made in the limitations on discovery imposed under these rules or by local rule, and what other limitations should be imposed; and

   (F)   any other orders that the court should issue under Rule 26(c) or under Rule 16(b) and (c).

FED. R. CIV. P. 26(f)(3). Notice that the above subsections give the parties the collective right, subject to the court's approval, to alter the rules of discovery and to mold the overall discovery process to their case's needs. *See also* FED. R. CIV. P. 29 (granting parties the right to stipulate to certain alterations of the discovery rules).

    The theory underlying this federal approach, followed also in some state courts (*see, e.g.,* CAL. CIV. PROC. CODE § 2016.030), is that discovery is not a "one size fits all" proposition. Instead, each case is unique and the parties must have a relatively free hand to design a discovery plan that is responsive to their needs. This opportunity to mold discovery provides yet another motivation for the creation of a pre-filing discovery plan. *See supra,* pages 555-557. An attorney who has carefully developed and worked through such a plan will be acutely aware of the factual strengths and weaknesses of her case and will therefore be better prepared to negotiate, in the best interests of her client, the overall design of the Rule 26(f) discovery plan.

    Upon completion of the conference, the parties must submit a "written report outlining the plan" to the court. FED. R. CIV. P. 26(f)(2). Failure of a party or its attorney "to participate in good faith in developing and submitting a proposed discovery plan" may result in the imposition of sanctions. FED. R. CIV. P. 37(f).

b.   Mandatory Disclosure

    One of the most important innovations in the federal rules is found in Rule 26(a)(1)(A), which imposes an initial disclosure requirement on all parties, "without awaiting a discovery request. . . ." The purpose of this requirement is to "accelerate the exchange of basic information about the case and to eliminate the paper work involved in requesting such information. . . ." Advisory Committee Note, 1993 Amendments, 146 F.R.D 401, 628. These initial disclosures must be made to the other parties at, or within 14 days after, the Rule 26(f) conference "unless a different time is set by stipulation or court order" or unless a proper objection is filed. FED. R. CIV. P. 26(a)(1)(C). The disclosures must include identification of all potential witnesses who may be used to support that party's claims or defenses; identification of all documents, electronically stored information, or tangible things in the possession of the disclosing party that may be similarly so used; information regarding the computation of damages; and copies of any applicable insurance agreements. FED. R. CIV. P. 26(a)(1)(A)(i)-(iv). Special rules pertain to the mandatory disclosure of potential expert witness testimony. FED. R. CIV. P. 26(a)(2)(A)-(E).

    This mandatory disclosure requirement was originally adopted in 1993, with a provision allowing federal district courts to opt out by adoption of a local rule. The

2000 amendments to the federal rules eliminated the opt-out provision. Today, mandatory disclosure is required in the vast majority of civil actions filed in federal court. *See* FED. R. CIV. P. 26(a)(1)(B) (listing eight exceptions). *See generally* 6 MOORE'S FEDERAL PRACTICE, *supra*, §§ 26.20-26.28; 8A WRIGHT, MILLER & MARCUS, *supra*, § 2053. For a description of the controversy surrounding the adoption of mandatory disclosure, see Charles W. Sorenson, Jr., *Disclosure Under Federal Rule of Civil Procedure 26(a)—"Much Ado About Nothing?,"* 46 HASTINGS L.J. 679 (1995).

Advance Financial Corp. v. Utsey

2001 WL 102484 (S.D. Ala. Jan. 24, 2001)

ORDER

VOLLMER, Senior J.

After due and proper consideration of all portions of this file deemed relevant to the issues raised, and there having been no objections filed, the Recommendation of the Magistrate Judge . . . is ADOPTED as the opinion of this Court.

It is ORDERED that Plaintiff's Motion for Sanctions be GRANTED, and that judgment by default be entered against the Defendants.

RECOMMENDATION OF MAGISTRATE JUDGE

STEELE, Magistrate J.

[The court ordered the parties to file the "written report" required by Rule 26(f) no later than July 28, 2000.] That deadline was extended until August 18, 2000 to accommodate the schedule of counsel for the Defendants. The deadline passed without the filing of the Rule 26(f) report and, on August 25, 2000, this Court entered a show cause order ordering the parties to file by September 5, 2000, the Rule 26(f) report or show cause by that date why they were unable to do so. On August 30, 2000, a report of the parties' planning meeting was filed by Plaintiff's counsel unsigned by Defendants' counsel. In Plaintiff's Motion for Sanctions, Plaintiff explains that, with regard to the Rule 26(f) report,

> Counsel for the parties met telephonically on August 17, 2000. As a result of the conference, Plaintiff's counsel prepared a draft report of parties' planning meeting, and submitted it to Defendants' counsel for his additions. When no response was forthcoming, Plaintiff's counsel filed the report unilaterally, by the September 5, 2000 deadline without the signature of Defendants' counsel and without the Defendants' narrative statement, when Defendants' counsel failed to submit the Defendants' narrative statement and sign the proposed joint report.

Also, in Plaintiff's Motion for Sanctions, Plaintiff notes that, notwithstanding this Court's Order directing the parties to produce their Fed. R. Civ. P. 26(a)(1) initial disclosures on or before September 29, 2000, Defendants failed to produce their initial disclosures. On October 24, 2000, this Court entered an Order ordering Defendants by November 8, 2000, to show cause why Plaintiff's Motion for

Sanctions should not be granted. In response, on November 9, 2000, Defendants filed a Motion for Extension of Time seeking additional time in which to make the initial disclosures. The motion was granted and Defendants were ordered by November 17, 2000, to produce the Rule 26(a)(1) disclosures. When these disclosures were not forthcoming, Plaintiff filed its Second Motion for Sanctions noting Defendants' failure to produce this information and also noting Defendants' failure to produce documents identified in a deposition notice duces tecum. As a result of Defendants' failure to produce this information, Plaintiff was forced to cancel the depositions. Upon receipt of Plaintiff's Second Motion for Sanctions, this Court entered a show cause order on November 16, 2000 ordering Defendants by November 27, 2000, to show cause why the Second Motion for Sanctions should not be granted. When Defendants failed to respond to this Court's Order, Plaintiff filed Plaintiff's Third Motion for Sanctions on November 28, 2000.

After receiving Plaintiff's Third Motion for Sanctions, and after noting Defendants' failure to respond to this Court's show cause order, this Court set these motions for oral argument on December 15, 2000. Because of recent eye surgery, Defendants' counsel was unable to attend the hearing in person but participated by telephone conference. During the conference, Defendants' counsel was afforded the opportunity to explain why he failed to submit or sign the Report of the Parties' Planning Meeting, why Defendants failed to produce their initial disclosures, why Defendants failed to produce documents requested in the deposition notice duces tecum, and why Defendants failed to respond to this Court's show cause order. Counsel's only offered explanation for these failures was that counsel had experienced some physical problems which resulted in eye surgery during the week preceding the hearing, and that counsel was experiencing communication problems with his clients.

Upon consideration of all matters presented, the Court finds that Defendants have offered no reasonable justification for their failure to submit the Rule 26(f) report, their failure to produce their initial disclosures, their failure to produce documents associated with the scheduled depositions, and their failure to respond to this Court's show cause order. While the Court is sympathetic to Defendants' counsel's physical problems, it is noted that counsel's eye surgery occurred only recently and does not appear to be the cause of Defendants' failure to comply with the orders of this Court. It is noted that the discovery completion date is less than two weeks away. Even assuming that Defendants would respond to an order compelling them to produce documents (which, based on the Defendants' performance to date, is quite uncertain), it is now impossible to complete discovery before the December 29, 2000, discovery completion date. An extension of that date would serve only to reward Defendants' wrongful conduct and punish Plaintiff who, from all appearances, has done everything possible to get the Defendants to comply with the orders of this Court. Therefore, the date will not be extended.

Given the nature of Defendants' actions and failure to act, and given Defendants' failure to proffer any substantial justification for these failures, and after reviewing the sanctions available pursuant to Fed. R. Civ. P. 37(b) and (c), the Court finds that only the sanction of judgment by default is appropriate under these circumstances as no lesser sanction will suffice. Therefore, it is the recommendation of the undersigned that this Court enter a judgment by default against the Defendants. . . .

2. Methods to Discover Additional Materials

Beyond the material provided by mandatory disclosure, a party may seek additional discovery through one or more of the following methods: (a) depositions upon oral examination or written questions; (b) written interrogatories; (c) production of documents or things, or permission to enter land or other property for inspection and other purposes; (d) e-discovery; (e) physical and mental examinations; and (f) requests for admission. We will briefly examine each of these methods. Keep in mind, however, that the Rule 26(f) conference and discovery plan may play a major role in organizing, modifying, and even limiting the manner and extent to which these devices may be used. For a thorough, pragmatic, and generally entertaining discussion of the various discovery devices, see ROGER S. HAYDOCK & DAVID F. HERR, DISCOVERY PRACTICE (4th ed. 2008).

a. Depositions

A *"deposition"* is a procedure through which an attorney may ask questions of an opposing party or a witness ("the deponent"). The questions directed to the deponent must be answered spontaneously and under oath. Although depositions have some disadvantages, including their expense, they are widely considered to be the most effective discovery device for they permit the attorney to probe an opponent's case and to evaluate the opposition players with little interference from opposing counsel. As one commentator has observed, "they without doubt form a key element of civil dispute resolution." Jeffrey W. Stempel, *Depositions upon Oral Examination, in* 7 MOORE'S FEDERAL PRACTICE § 30.02[2], at 15 (3d ed. 2015).

An attorney who wishes to take a deposition must provide written notice to the person who is going to be deposed and to all other parties, describing who is to be deposed and the time and place of the deposition. FED. R. CIV. P. 30(b)(1). The notice may also include a request for the production of documents, electronically stored information, or tangible things that the deponent must then bring to the deposition.* FED. R. CIV. P. 30(b)(2), 34(a)(1)(A). Typically, the deposition will take place in the office of the examining attorney, though she may designate any other convenient location. The deposition must be taken before a

---

* If the deponent is a nonparty and does not consent to attend, her attendance can be compelled by the service of a subpoena. FED. R. CIV. P. 45(a)(1)(B). The subpoena may include a demand that the deponent produce specified documents, electronically stored information, or other tangible things at the deposition. FED. R. CIV. P. 45(a)(1)(C). A subpoena that includes such a demand is called a subpoena duces tecum.

person empowered to administer oaths (the officer), typically a professional court reporter. FED. R. CIV. P. 28(a), 30(b)(5)(A). And the proceedings must be recorded in some fashion (*e.g.*, stenographically or by way of a video or audio recording). FED. R. CIV. P. 30(b)(3). Also typically present at the deposition are the deponent's attorney, if she has one, and the attorneys for the other parties to the action. In the real world of litigation, the arrangements for depositions are usually agreed on by the parties in advance. *See* FED. R. CIV. P. 29(a) ("[T]he parties may stipulate that . . . a deposition may be taken before any person, at any time or place, on any notice, and in the manner specified . . . .").

When the deposition is "upon oral examination," it begins with the administration of an oath to the deponent, after which the attorney who noticed the deposition proceeds to ask questions to which the deponent must respond. The other attorneys present may raise objections to questions, which must be noted in the record, and may cross-examine the deponent. They may not, however, coach the deponent. The standard for relevance is "discovery relevance." Therefore, trial objections such as hearsay and the like have no bearing on a deponent's duty to answer. Indeed, an attorney may instruct her client not to answer "only when necessary to preserve a privilege, to enforce a limitation ordered by the court, or to present a motion" to the court demonstrating the questioner's bad faith. FED. R. CIV. P. 30(c)(2). If a deponent declines to answer a question, the attorney asking the question may seek an order to compel from the appropriate court. FED. R. CIV. P. 37(a). While the deposition may be adjourned until such time as the motion to compel is resolved, the better practice is to complete the deposition before seeking a motion to compel. This promotes efficiency and gives the attorney a better opportunity to determine if the information is truly needed. Significantly, sanctions may be imposed "on a person who impedes, delays, or frustrates the fair examination of the deponent." FED. R. CIV. P. 30(d)(2). In addition, if a deponent refuses to answer a question when directed by a court to do so, she may be held in contempt. FED. R. CIV. P. 37(b)(1). *See generally* 7 MOORE'S FEDERAL PRACTICE, *supra*, §§ 30.01 *et seq.*; 8A WRIGHT, MILLER & MARCUS, *supra*, §§ 2101-2120.

In the absence of a written stipulation by the parties, a party must seek leave of court if a proposed deposition "would result in more than 10 depositions being taken" by her side of the controversy. FED. R. CIV. P. 30(a)(2)(A)(i). Moreover, "[u]nless otherwise stipulated or ordered by the court, a deposition is limited to 1 day of 7 hours." FED. R. CIV. P. 30(d)(1). In the absence of permission from the court, a person can only be deposed one time within the context of a single action. FED. R. CIV. P. 30(a)(2)(A)(ii).

A deposition upon "written questions" is a paper version of an oral deposition in which the questions (direct, cross, redirect, and recross) are prepared in writing in advance of the deposition and then submitted to the designated deposition officer. The questions are read to the deponent by the officer who makes a record of the responses. FED. R. CIV. P. 31. With this format, the deposing attorney loses the opportunity to assess the demeanor of the deponent, as well as the ability to pursue a spontaneous line of questions that may be suggested by an unanticipated response. As a consequence, written depositions are rarely used. They can be useful, however, to depose a relatively insignificant witness, especially one who is out of state and for whom the deposing party has but a few questions. Here, the advantage is that written depositions are much less expensive to conduct or participate in than oral depositions. *See generally* James C. Francis IV, *Depositions upon Written Questions, in* 7 MOORE'S FEDERAL PRACTICE, *supra*, §§ 31.01 *et seq.*; 8A WRIGHT, MILLER & MARCUS, *supra*, §§ 2131-2133.

A party's deposition may be used at trial for any admissible purpose. FED. R. CIV. P. 32(a)(1). The same is true with respect to the deposition of a witness who has since died or who is unavailable to testify. FED. R. CIV. P. 32(a)(4). In addition, depositions may be used at trial to contradict or impeach the testimony of any deponent who appears as a witness. FED. R. CIV. P. 32(a)(2).

b. Interrogatories

An "interrogatory" is a written request for information that may be served on an opposing party and that must be answered by that party in writing and under oath. FED. R. CIV. P. 33(a)-(b). Unlike written depositions, interrogatories may not be used with respect to nonparties. In federal court, a party may serve a maximum of 25 interrogatories on any one party, though the number may be increased by leave of court or by stipulation of the parties. FED. R. CIV. P. 33(a)(1). Many state rules contain similar limitations. *See, e.g.*, CAL. CIV. PROC. CODE § 2030.030 (initial maximum of 35 specially prepared interrogatories with potential bypass provision); MINN. R. CIV. P. 33.01(a) (maximum of 50 interrogatories without permission of the court). Local court rules sometimes impose further limits on the number of interrogatories allowed. In addition, in federal court and in many state courts, a "subpart" of an interrogatory counts as an additional interrogatory. For example, an interrogatory that asked a party to state her height, weight, and age might constitute three interrogatories.

Interrogatories differ from depositions in one very important respect. A question asked at a deposition requires an immediate oral response by the deponent. The answer to an interrogatory, however, may be and usually is drafted by the attorney for the party on whom it was served. As a consequence, a skilled attorney can minimize the amount of useful information provided by an answer to an interrogatory unless the question is drafted with equally skilled precision. On the other hand, one benefit of an interrogatory over a deposition is that the former requires an answer that reflects the knowledge of the party, her agents, and her attorney, while the latter does not. In a deposition, only the actual and present knowledge of the deponent herself can be discovered. In general, however, interrogatories are relatively ineffective devices for probing deeply into the other party's case.

Interrogatories are most useful in discovering specific information, such as the time of day an event occurred, the date on which certain goods were delivered, the speed at which the defendant was driving, and the like. They also can be used to lay the foundation for further discovery by seeking to determine the identity and whereabouts of witnesses, the identity of the custodian of documents, whether a party is insured, and other preliminary matters that will assist an attorney in determining whom to depose, which documents to request, and so forth. In federal court, the need for such preliminary interrogatories is obviated by the initial disclosures required under Rule 26(a)(1). In most states, however, interrogatories provide the primary means, aside from cooperative disclosure, through which such preliminary and foundational information can be discovered.

A party served with interrogatories must serve a written copy of the answers, and any objections stated with specificity, within 30 days after service of the interrogatories. FED. R. CIV. P. 33(b)(2). Grounds for objection include, among others, discovery relevance, privilege, work product, and undue burden or expense. The party submitting the interrogatories may then move for an order to compel answers under Rule 37(a). In addition, a court may impose sanctions for failure to answer properly served interrogatories. FED. R. CIV. P. 37(b) & (d).

See generally Claudia Wilken, *Interrogatories to Parties, in* 7 MOORE'S FEDERAL PRACTICE, *supra,* § 33.01; 8B CHARLES ALAN WRIGHT, ARTHUR R. MILLER & RICHARD L. MARCUS, FEDERAL PRACTICE AND PROCEDURE §§ 2161-2182 (3d ed. 2010 & Supp. 2015).

c.   Requests for Production and Inspection

Many, if not most, civil actions involve documents, electronically stored information, or other tangible things that satisfy the very broad standards of discovery relevance. The range of these materials is as broad as the range of claims and defenses that may be asserted in a civil action, including virtually every imaginable thing that is *not intangible*. Thus, in a case involving a contract, that range might include all drafts and copies of the contract and all correspondence between the parties. In a case involving an automobile accident, the relevant material might include the automobiles themselves or the reported results of crash tests. And in a case involving an accident on private property, discovery requests might include a request to access the property itself. Quite clearly these materials must be discoverable or available for inspection through some device if the parties are to have a complete opportunity to prepare their case for trial.

Of course, in federal court, the parties are subject to the mandatory disclosure of relevant "documents, electronically stored information, and tangible things," even in the absence of any formal discovery requests. FED. R. CIV. P. 26(a)(1)(A)(ii). And more generally, lawyers often cooperate with one another in the exchange of such materials. One purpose of the Rule 26(f) conference is to facilitate such exchanges. Note, however, that the mandatory initial *disclosure* requirement under the federal rules can be satisfied by merely providing a "description by category and location" of such materials, rather than the materials themselves, and then only if the items are ones that the disclosing party "may" use in support of one of her claims or defenses. Mandatory disclosure does not, therefore, assure *automatic access* to the identified materials themselves. Nor does it cover those materials that may support another party's claims or defenses, *i.e.*, so-called inculpatory evidence that might harm the disclosing party. And, as to voluntary cooperative disclosure, there is no guarantee that all relevant materials will be made available. As a consequence, discovery rules in state and federal courts provide parties the right to inspect and copy all nonprivileged and relevant materials in an opposing party's possession, *i.e.*, documents, electronically stored information, and other tangible things that fall within the general scope of discovery relevance. *See* FED. R. CIV. P. 34(a)(1)(A); *see also* CAL. CIV. PROC. CODE § 2031.010.

The device through which to gain access to these materials is a "request for production." Simply put, through a request for production, a party may ask an opposing party to produce or provide access to the designated items. A request can be directed toward the production of "any designated documents or electronically stored information—including writings, drawings, graphs, charts, photographs, sound recordings, images, and other data or data compilations—stored in any medium from which information can be obtained. . . ." FED. R. CIV. P. 34(a)(1)(A). It can also seek an opportunity to inspect, copy, or test any tangible thing, FED. R. CIV. P. 34(a)(1)(B), as well as the right to enter onto land or other property for purposes of inspection, measuring, surveying, testing, photography, and the like. FED. R. CIV. P. 34(a)(2).

A request for production must describe the item or items to be produced, or the property to which access is demanded, with reasonable particularity. The test is one of common sense. "The request should be sufficient to (1) allow a person of ordinary intelligence to say 'I know what they want' and (2) permit a judge to determine whether all the requested items have been produced." HAYDOCK & HERR, *supra*, at § 25.02, p. 25-5. For example, proper requests would include a demand that the defendant produce "all correspondence between the parties pertaining to the August 27, 2000 contract between them," or a request to inspect and test "the chain saw that plaintiff claims was the cause of his injuries," or a request to "enter upon and survey the land over which the easement is claimed." On the other hand, a request to produce all "relevant documents or things in plaintiff's possession" would be inadequate as insufficiently particular. The request for production must also specify a reasonable time, place, and manner for the production, inspection, copying, etc.

Under Rule 34, a request for production may only be directed to a party. If the material is in the possession or custody of a nonparty, the "request" must be accomplished through the issuance of a subpoena directed to the nonparty. FED. R. CIV. P. 34(c), 45(a)(2). A notice of deposition or a subpoena for a deposition may also include a request for the production of documents, electronically stored information, or tangible things which, in the absence of a valid objection, the deponent must then bring to the deposition. FED. R. CIV. P. 30(b)(2), 45(a)(2)(C).

As noted earlier, formal discovery in federal court generally cannot begin until after the parties' Rule 26(f) discovery conference. However, Rule 26(d)(2) makes an exception that allows a request for the production of documents to be "delivered" to or by a party once 21 days have passed since that party was served, with the request then deemed to have been "served" at the first Rule 26(f) conference. Because Rule 34 requests often "involve heavy discovery burdens," it was hoped that this early delivery option, which was added to the rule in 2015, "would facilitate the conference by allowing consideration of actual requests, providing a focus for specific discussion." *See Report of the Advisory Committee on Civil Rules*, http://uscourts.gov/rules-policies/archives/committee-reports/CV05-2013.pdf, at 8-9 (May 8, 2013).

Once a request for production is served (or deemed served under Rule 26(d)(2)), the party to whom it is directed must respond in writing within 30 days, either affirming that the request will be permitted as requested or interposing an objection to the request. FED. R. CIV. P. 34(b)(2). If a party fails to respond to such a request, fails to produce the documents, or interposes an objection to production, the requesting party may move for an order to compel. FED. R. CIV. P. 37(a)(3)(B)(iv). As is true with other discovery devices, sanctions may be imposed for a failure to comply with a court's order directing a party to produce or provide access to the requested materials. FED. R. CIV. P. 37(b)(2). *See, e.g., Washington Met. Area Transit Comm'n v. Reliable Limousine Service, LLC*, 776 F.3d 1 (D.C. Cir. 2015) (affirming entry of default judgment for plaintiff as sanction for defendant's failure to answer interrogatories and respond to requests for the production of documents).

See generally James C. Francis IV, *Production of Documents and Things and Entry upon Land for Inspection and Other Purposes, in* 7 MOORE'S FEDERAL PRACTICE §§ 34.01 *et seq.*; 8B WRIGHT, MILLER & MARCUS, *supra*, §§ 2201-2219.

PROBLEM

7-7. In a products liability suit involving the explosion of a gas tank on a vehicle manufactured by the defendant, the plaintiffs requested that the defendant produce "any report dated between January 1, 1966 and January 13, 1978 that pertains to any alternative fuel system design proposed, suggested, investigated, studied, considered, analyzed, and/or tested for possible incorporation in the 1969 through 1975 X-body series vehicles." In response to this request, the defendant turned over only one such report even though other discovery materials indicated that several fuel system reports had been issued during the relevant time frame. The defendant explained this apparent anomaly by noting that the fuel systems at issue in the other reports were not specifically related to "the 1969 through 1975 X-body series vehicles" but related instead to the entire line of cars manufactured by the defendant. According to the defendant, these other reports and tests related to "overall product improvement" and not to the improvement of a particular product. Should the defendant be subject to sanctions for failure to produce the additional reports? How might the plaintiff have worded the request to ensure that it included all fuel system reports during the relevant time frame? *See Sellon v. Smith*, 112 F.R.D. 9 (D. Del. 1986).

NOTES AND QUESTIONS

1. The destruction of evidence.   What sanctions might a court impose on a party who willfully destroys evidence subject to a discovery request? Clearly, if a party destroys discoverable evidence in violation of a *court order*, the court may impose sanctions on that party. *See* FED. R. CIV. P. 37(b). Should that same rule apply if the destruction, although not in violation of a court order, is designed to avoid compliance with a discovery request? Rule 37(b) does not itself answer this question since its scope is limited to the violation of court orders. A number of federal courts have held, however, that a court retains inherent authority to sanction the destruction of evidence subject to a discovery request, even if that request is not bolstered by a court order. *See, e.g., Webb v. District of Columbia*, 146 F.3d 964, 971 (D.C. Cir. 1998) (citing court's inherent power to preserve the integrity of the judicial process). In addition, some courts have gone further and recognized a duty to preserve evidence that a party reasonably should know *may* be subject to a discovery request in a pending or potential future action, even though no request has yet been made. *See, e.g., Wm. T. Thompson Co. v. General Nutrition Corp., Inc.*, 593 F. Supp. 1443, 1455-1456 (C.D. Cal. 1984), 104 F.R.D. 119 (C.D. Cal. 1985). *See generally* JAMIE S. GORELICK, STEPHEN MARZEN & LAWRENCE SOLUM, DESTRUCTION OF EVIDENCE 65-137 (1989 & Supp. 2014). Finally, as we will see in the next section, Rule 37(e) specifically addresses the failure to preserve, or the deliberate destruction of, electronically stored information.

2. Reasonably accessible form.   When items are produced in response to a request for production, they must be produced in a reasonably accessible form. With respect to documents, Rule 34(b)(2)(E)(i) provides that "[a] party must produce documents as they are kept in the usual course of business or must organize and label them to correspond to the categories in the request. . . ." In other words, a party may not intentionally bury a document in a mass of other unrelated materials. *Rothman v. Emory University*, 123 F.3d 446 (7th Cir. 1997), provides an instructive example. In that case, a former law student sued his law school, claiming that it had violated the Americans with Disabilities Act. In response to a discovery order to produce only documents responsive to the school's discovery requests, the former student produced "three large bankers' boxes of college papers and numerous other unrelated, non-responsive materials." *Id.* at 455. The Seventh Circuit upheld the trial court's imposition of sanctions to cover the costs incurred by the school in sorting through the documents. Shouldn't the student have known better? If the student's production of documents was in response to a request and not a judicial order, could the district court still have imposed sanctions?

d.   E-Discovery

It goes without saying that we are in the midst of a digital information revolution (or explosion). This reality, however one describes it, has had a significant impact on discovery practices. A combination of the sheer volume of electronically stored information ("ESI"),* the wide variety of methods through which that information is stored and retrieved, and the costs associated with those processes present significant challenges to litigants and the judicial system. *See generally* SHIRA A. SCHEINDLIN & DANIEL J. CAPRA, ELECTRONIC DISCOVERY AND DIGITAL EVIDENCE IN A NUTSHELL (2009).

The federal rules were amended in 2006 to make it clear that ESI is subject to discovery under the general standards of discovery established by the federal rules, but with some significant qualifications designed to take into account unique problems associated with e-discovery. Thus, while it is clear that ESI is discoverable under the basic standards of discovery relevance established in Rule 26(b)(1), subsection (b)(2)(B) specifically provides:

> A party need not provide discovery of electronically stored information from sources that the party identifies as not reasonably accessible because of undue burden or cost. On motion to compel discovery or for a protective order, the party from whom discovery is sought must show that the information is not reasonably accessible because of undue burden or cost. If that showing is made, the court may nonetheless order discovery from such sources if the requesting party shows good cause, considering the limitations of Rule 26(b)(2)(C). The court may specify conditions for the discovery.

Note that this section comes into play only when the ESI is "not reasonably accessible." This might occur, for example, when deleted e-mail has been stored on backup recordings that can only be accessed through an expensive process of restoration. On the other hand, it is not likely to occur when an e-mail remains accessible on a hard drive in the possession of the party served with the request to produce.

In addition, all forms of discovery, including e-discovery, are subject to Rule 26(b)(2)(C), which provides,

> On motion or on its own, the court must limit the frequency or extent of discovery otherwise allowed by these rules or by local rule if it determines that: (i) the discovery sought is unreasonably cumulative or duplicative, or can be obtained from some other source that is more convenient, less burdensome, or less expensive; (ii) the party seeking discovery has had ample opportunity to obtain the information by discovery in the action; or (iii) the proposed discovery is outside the scope permitted by Rule 26(b)(1).

With respect to the interplay between, subsections (2)(B) and (2)(C) of Rule 26(b), the Advisory Committee on the Federal Rules offers the following guidance:

> Once it is shown that a source of electronically stored information is not reasonably accessible, the requesting party may still obtain discovery by showing good cause, considering the limitations of Rule 26(b)(2)(C) that balance the costs and potential benefits of discovery. The decision whether to require a responding party to search for and produce information that is not reasonably accessible depends not only on the burdens and costs of doing so, but also on whether those burdens and costs

---

* The amount of that information worldwide, which is growing exponentially, is currently measured in "zettabytes" of information. One zettabyte is the equivalent of one sextillion bytes. To paraphrase the *Hitchhiker's Guide to the Galaxy*, that is a "vastly, hugely, mindboggingly big" number. DOUGLAS ADAMS, THE HITCHHIKER'S GUIDE TO THE GALAXY 75 (2005).

can be justified in the circumstances of the case. Appropriate considerations may include: (1) the specificity of the discovery request; (2) the quantity of information available from other and more easily accessed sources; (3) the failure to produce relevant information that seems likely to have existed but is no longer available on more easily accessed sources; (4) the likelihood of finding relevant, responsive information that cannot be obtained from other, more easily accessed sources; (5) predictions as to the importance and usefulness of the further information; (6) the importance of the issues at stake in the litigation; and (7) the parties' resources.

The responding party has the burden as to one aspect of the inquiry — whether the identified sources are not reasonably accessible in light of the burdens and costs required to search for, retrieve, and produce whatever responsive information may be found. The requesting party has the burden of showing that its need for the discovery outweighs the burdens and costs of locating, retrieving, and producing the information. In some cases, the court will be able to determine whether the identified sources are not reasonably accessible and whether the requesting party has shown good cause for some or all of the discovery, consistent with the limitations of Rule 26(b)(2)(C), through a single proceeding or presentation. The good-cause determination, however, may be complicated because the court and parties may know little about what information the sources identified as not reasonably accessible might contain, whether it is relevant, or how valuable it may be to the litigation. In such cases, the parties may need some focused discovery, which may include sampling of the sources to learn more about what burdens and costs are involved in accessing the information, what the information consists of, and how valuable it is for the litigation in light of information that can be obtained by exhausting other opportunities for discovery.

The good-cause inquiry and consideration of the Rule 26(b)(2)(C) limitations are coupled with the authority to set conditions for discovery. The conditions may take the form of limits on the amount, type, or sources of information required to be accessed and produced. The conditions may also include payment by the requesting party of part or all of the reasonable costs of obtaining information from sources that are not reasonably accessible. A requesting party's willingness to share or bear the access costs may be weighed by the court in determining whether there is good cause. But the producing party's burdens in reviewing the information for relevance and privilege may weigh against permitting the requested discovery.

ADVISORY COMM. NOTES TO THE 2006 AMENDMENTS TO THE FEDERAL RULES OF CIVIL PROCEDURE, 234 F.R.D. 296, 338-339.

Wood v. Capital One Services, LLC

2011 WL 2154279 (N.D.N.Y. Apr. 15, 2011)

DAVID E. PEEBLES, United States Magistrate Judge.

Plaintiff Gareth D. Wood commenced this action against defendants Capital One Services, LLC ("Capital One Services") and NCO Financial Systems, Inc. ("NCO") alleging, *inter alia*, violations of the Federal Debt Collection Practices Act ("FDCPA"), 15 U.S.C. § 1692 *et seq.*, and New York General Business Law

("GBL") § 349. Plaintiff's claims stem from defendants' efforts to collect a consumer debt of a relatively modest amount, although plaintiff has styled the action as a class action being brought on behalf of himself and other similarly situated individuals and has now moved for class certification.

Currently pending before the court are cross-motions related to the issue of pretrial discovery, including electronically stored information ("ESI"). Plaintiff, who has already had the benefit of considerable discovery concerning his claim, seeks extensive discovery some of which involves sweeping searches of ESI using suggested search terms, and requests an order compelling defendants' compliance with his discovery demands. Defendant Capital One Services estimates the expense of responding to plaintiff's demands at as much as $5 million. NCO, while not quantifying the expense of production, also claims that compliance with plaintiff's demands would entail considerable burden. Both defendants therefore oppose plaintiff's application and have lodged mirror motions requesting the issuance of protective orders pursuant to Rule 26(c) of the Federal Rules of Civil Procedure, invoking the rule of proportionality set forth in [Rule 26(b)(1)] . . . .

I. BACKGROUND

On December 31, 2007, plaintiff opened an account with Capital One Bank. Capital One Services, however, has provided all of the necessary support for the servicing of plaintiff's account since its inception, pursuant to an agreement between the two entities and continues to do so even though the account has been charged off. NCO did not at any time service plaintiff's account, although it has supplied debt collection services with regard to the account.

By October of 2009 the plaintiff's account became significantly delinquent with a balance owed of $1731.35. As a result of the delinquency a Pre-Legal Notice, dated October 8, 2009, was generated. The notice was created using a template developed by Capital One Services, and the expense of printing and mailing it were underwritten by Capital One Services. Despite being dated earlier, the Pre-Legal Notice was not delivered to the United States Postal Service until October 12, 2009 and was received by Wood on October 15, 2009.

The Pre-Legal Notice sent to Wood identified the creditor as Capital One Bank, listed Capital One Services as servicing the account, and is signed by that defendant. The letter recited the potential consequences associated with a lawsuit, but stated that "[n]o decision has been made to sue you yet, so you still have options . . . ." The letter advised that those options could be explored or payment arranged by calling a telephone number listed on the notice, or by visiting www. capitalone.com/solutions. Had plaintiff called the telephone number listed on the Pre–Legal Notice he would have first received an automated message welcoming him to Capital One and requesting that he enter his account number. Once the account number was entered his call would have been automatically routed to NCO. After receiving the letter plaintiff did not call the telephone number listed on the letter, although his attorney later did on November 6, 2009, at which time his call was in fact forwarded to NCO.

Plaintiff's account was referred by Capital One Services to NCO for debt collection assistance on October 9, 2009. NCO thereafter sent Wood a letter on October 10, 2009 advising of its involvement and making a series of disclosures pursuant to the FDCPA. The NCO letter was received prior to October 15, 2009, when the Capital One Services Pre-Legal Notice was delivered.

II.   PROCEDURAL HISTORY

Plaintiff commenced this action on December 29, 2009. Plaintiff's complaint named Capital One Services, NCO and Capital One Bank as defendants and asserted claims under the FDCPA and GBL § 349, as well as for common law fraud . . . .

On March 8, 2011, with permission from the court, plaintiff filed a letter motion to compel discovery, and both defendants moved for protective orders shielding them from the requirements of plaintiff's discovery demands. Those motions have now been fully briefed and were argued before the court on March 29, 2011, at which time decision was reserved.

III.   DISCUSSION

A.   Applicable Discovery Standards

. . . Despite the generous breadth of discovery permitted under Rule 26(b)(1), the rules recognize certain specific, potentially overriding considerations that can effectively circumscribe the required production of otherwise pertinent discovery. Of relevance to the pending dispute, [Rule 26(b)(2)(C)(i)] authorizes a court to restrict discovery sought by a party if the information requested "is unreasonably cumulative or duplicative, or [can be obtained] from some other source that is more convenient, less burdensome, or less expensive." . . .

The defendants in this case, while not necessarily conceding the relevance of all of plaintiff's demands, seek refuge in [Rule 26(b)(1)] which, in essence, articulates a rule or principle of proportionality. That section permits a court to limit discovery where "the burden or expense of the proposed discovery outweighs its likely benefit, considering [the amount in controversy, the importance of the issues at stake in the action, and the parties' resources"]. The rule of proportionality serves to protect a party against having to produce voluminous documents of questionable relevance . . . .

The vast majority of plaintiff's requests implicate the search and production of ESI. Generally speaking, "[e]lectronic documents are no less subject to disclosure than paper records." *Rowe Entertainment v. William Morris Agency, Inc.*, 205 F.R.D. 421, 428 (S.D.N.Y. 2002). "This is true not only of electronic documents that are currently in use, but also of documents that may have been deleted and now reside only on backup disks." *Zubulake* [*v. UBS Warburg LLC*, 217 F.R.D. 309, 317 (S.D.N.Y. 2003)]. The rule of proportionality applies with equal force in a case involving requests for the production of ESI.

Ordinarily the presumption is that the party whose ESI is being sought during discovery must bear the expense of complying with the discovery request, just as is the case with regard to any other more traditional discovery. In some cases, however, it is appropriate to shift all or some costs of producing discovery to the requesting party when compliance with demands would impose undue burden or expense on a responding party. The decision of whether to invoke cost-shifting is informed by several relevant factors, including

    (1) [t]he extent to which the request is specifically tailored to discover relevant information;

    (2) [t]he availability of such information from other sources;

    (3) [t]he total cost of production, compared to the amount in controversy;

    (4) [t]he total cost of production, compared to the resources available to each party;

    (5) [t]he relative ability of each party to control costs and its incentive to do so;

    (6) [t]he importance of the issues at stake in the litigation; and

    (7) [t]he relative benefits to the parties of obtaining the information.

Zubulake, 217 F.R.D. at 322. Of these, the first two factors, comprising the marginal utility test, are the most important. *Id.* at 323.

Derived from Judge Scheindlin's opinion in *Zubulake* and the court's earlier decision in *Rowe Entertainment*, the rules drafters have suggested the following considerations for aiding in determining who should bear the expense of e-discovery:

(1) the specificity of the discovery request; (2) the quantity of information available from other and more easily accessed sources; (3) the failure to produce relevant information that seems likely to have existed but is no longer is available on more easily accessed sources; (4) the likelihood of finding relevant responsive information that cannot be obtained from other more easily accessed sources; (5) predictions as to the importance and usefulness of the further information; (6) the importance of the issues at stake in the litigation; and (7) the parties' resources.

Fed. R. Civ. P. 26, Advisory Comm. Notes 2006 Amend.

B.   Underlying Legal Claims and Defenses

As can be seen, the scope of discovery is defined in the first instance by relevance to the claims and defenses in a case. Accordingly, before turning to the specifics of the discovery that has occurred to date and evaluating plaintiff's demands, it is important to lay out as a backdrop the claims and defenses that have been raised in this action.

Plaintiff's complaint asserts causes of action under both the FDCPA and GBL § 349. Generally speaking, the FDCPA prohibits a debt collector from employing any false, deceptive or misleading representation or means when collecting a debt. 15 U.S.C. § 1692e. The Act also specifically prohibits the use of a threat to take action which cannot legally be taken, or is not intended. *Id.* Under the FDCPA the term "debt collector" is defined, in relevant part, to mean

> any person who uses any instrumentality of interstate commerce or the mails in any business that principal purpose of which is the collection of any debts, or who regularly collects or attempts to collect, directly or indirectly, debts owed or due or asserted to be owed to be due another . . . .

15 U.S.C. § 1692a(6). The FDCPA authorizes commencement of a civil suit by an aggrieved debtor and, absent class certification, provides for an award of actual damages plus such additional damages as the court allows up to $1,000, as well as payment of costs, including a reasonable attorney's fee. 15 U.S.C. § 1692k(a).

GBL § 349 provides, in pertinent part, that "[d]eceptive acts or practices in the conduct of any business, trade or commerce or in the furnishing of any service in this state are hereby declared unlawful." N.Y. Gen. Bus. Law § 349. A claim under GBL § 349 is stated when a plaintiff alleges that the defendant engaged in a materially misleading consumer-oriented act resulting in injury to the plaintiff. As relief, a plaintiff establishing a violation of GBL § 349 can recover actual damages and may be entitled to injunctive relief as well as an award of attorney's fees.

In his complaint, Wood asserts that the Pre-Legal Notice he received was deceptive in that it misled him into believing that legal action was imminent when, in fact, there was no present intention on the part of the defendants to initiate suit. Plaintiff also maintains that the letter, though initiated by Capital One Services, was sent on behalf of NCO, and failed to disclose that it was an initial communication from a debt collector, and misled him into believing that it came from Capital One Services and that the telephone number listed was for that defendant, rather than NCO. Plaintiff further asserts that the letter failed to provide the required protective notifications, including of the right to receive information to verify the debt and the right to dispute it.

In [response to] plaintiff's claims, Capital One Services argues that it is not a debt collector within the meaning of the Act and that the letter was not materially misleading. Capital One Services additionally contends that in any event the plaintiff did not suffer any actual injuries as a result of receiving the letter, and any recovery will therefore be limited to the statutory damages provided under the FDCPA. For its part, defendant NCO asserts that it had no involvement in sending the initial letter and therefore cannot be held accountable for any non-compliance with the FDCPA or violation of GBL § 349 related to that communication.

C. *Discovery To Date*

Prior to the filing of the pending motions, the parties engaged in a considerable amount of discovery in the action. To date, plaintiff has served twenty-five interrogatories and forty-three document demands on defendant Capital One Services. In response, defendant Capital One Services has answered plaintiff's interrogatories, twice supplementing those answers, and has produced approximately fifteen hundred pages of documents. In addition, Capital One Services has submitted to two days of a Rule 30(b)(6) deposition, covering not only the merits of the action but also the methods employed to respond to plaintiff's discovery demands.

Defendant NCO has similarly responded to written discovery demands, producing in excess of four hundred pages of e-mails concerning plaintiff's account. The e-mails produced include all non-privileged communications discovered through a search using some, though not all, of plaintiff's proposed search terms of active e-mail boxes of agreed-upon NCO employees. In addition, NCO has produced a Rule 30(b)(6) witness to address that defendant's search for responsive documents.

D.   Specifics Of Plaintiff's Discovery Demands

1.   NCO

[P]laintiff seeks production of all e-mails related to the Pre-Legal Notices and Pre-Legal Program at Capital One Services. Plaintiff makes that request in order to probe an affirmative defense under which NCO asserts that

> [t]he letter at issue is not NCO's letter, but instead Capitol One's letter. As noted above, NCO had no participation in the development or creation of the template from which the letter was generated. NCO has no control over communications from Capital One.

In support of that request, plaintiff notes that a search of archived e-mails was conducted by NCO, utilizing plaintiff's proposed search terms, yielding 12,071 matches, but that the e-mails recovered pursuant to that search have not been produced. Plaintiff also requests similar searches with regard to additional NCO employees . . . .

2.   Capital One Services

Implicated in this motion are plaintiff's requests to defendant Capital One Services . . . . First, plaintiff seeks a search of e-mail accounts of some forty-one employees, utilizing plaintiff's suggested search terms. The second request in issue involves images of hard drives and searches of two specified drives to probe the Pre-Legal Notice and relationship with NCO . . . .

E.   Analysis

In weighing the competing arguments of the parties I have applied the rule of proportionality and considered the factors set out in [Rule 26(b)(1)] as bearing upon whether that rule should be invoked. I have also taken into account the fact that courts are generally more likely to invoke the rule and limit discovery when faced with a request for "voluminous records of questionable relevance."

Two of the factors recited in [Rule 26(b)(1)] weigh in plaintiff's favor. Plainly, Capital One Services and NCO, as large corporations, have resources available to finance the effort that would be required to meet plaintiff's sweeping discovery demands. Similarly, the court recognizes that strong public policy considerations which led to enactment of the FDCPA.

The other relevant factors, however, do not favor the plaintiff. The amount in controversy in this action, absent class certification, is exceedingly modest. Plaintiff essentially has acknowledged that he did not suffer any actual damages as a result of the alleged violations, and thus his recovery in all likelihood will be limited to $1,000 plus costs and attorneys' fees. As will be seen, the relevance of the specific discovery sought is marginal, and the information sought is not likely to play an important role in resolving the material issues in the case.

1. E-mail Searches

The primary thrust of plaintiff's discovery effort with respect to defendant Capital One Services is to obtain e-mail communications relating to the preparation of the Pre-Legal Notice form sent to the plaintiff. Plaintiff's initial search request regarding e-mails sought searches of ten e-mail accounts using the following search terms: "pre-legal," "pre legal," "legal," "legal letter," "legal letters," "pre legal letter," "pre-legal letter," "letterhead," "pre-legal rollout," "cash and legal," "cash letter," "cash letters," "Q2 initiatives," "bkt 6," "B5 accounts," "B6 accounts," "pre-legal notification," "call forwarding" and "routing." Plaintiff has since requested similar searches for six additional Capital One Services employees, identified by Ramon Valdepenas as forming a team "responsible for customer contact strategies" and involved in the creation of the Pre-Legal Notice, as well as the search of the mailboxes of Brad Mason, Niki Howard, Paul Ayres, Esq., John Reece, Esq., and Jeffrey Hansen. According to Capital One Services, the likely volume to be generated by the requested searches, after elimination of duplicates, is as high as 1,753,537 documents, costing in excess of $5,000,000 to process, review, and produce.

Addressing NCO, plaintiff has requested a search of e-mail archive accounts for eleven NCO employees using the following search terms: "pre-legal," "pre legal," "legal letter," "legal letters," "pre legal letter," "pre-legal letter," "pre-legal rollout," "bkt 6," "B5 accounts," "B6 accounts," "pre-legal notification," "call forwarding," and "routing." NCO has refused to carry out the required searches, although it did conduct a modified search using terms deemed relevant, which yielded 12,071 matches estimated to involve 60,000 pages of documents, but has declined to turn those over to plaintiff citing the expense associated with reviewing those e-mails for relevance and privilege.

Neither plaintiff's submissions in support of his motion to compel and in opposition to defendants' protective order motions, nor his oral presentation during the recent hearing shed significant light on the potential relevance of the documents sought. The uncontroverted facts show that the plaintiff received a letter authored and sent by Capital One Services, and the letter speaks for itself. Plaintiff argues that the letter was actually sent on behalf of NCO. Capital One Services has argued that in the end it is likely it will be found exempt from the Act on the grounds that it is not a debt collector, and makes a strong case in arguing that position. Thus, even assuming that the notice came from Capital One Services, plaintiff has cited no case suggesting that an entity that is not a debt collector must still comply with the requirements of the FDCPA. The relevance of the information now sought is therefore not readily apparent; at a minimum, the importance of the discovery sought in resolving the issues in the case is greatly diminished by this fact.

Plaintiff argues that the import of the Pre-Legal Notice was that suit was imminent at the time it was sent, and a least sophisticated consumer would draw that conclusion from reading the letter. While the language of the Pre-Legal Notice sent by Capital One Services does not state that legal action will be commenced if the debt is not paid, and indeed affirmatively states that no decision regarding suit has yet been made, plaintiff is correct that construed from the standpoint of the "least sophisticated consumer" it could potentially regarded as stating an intention to sue. Intent to sue therefore could be potentially relevant, provided Capital One is subject to the FDCPA.

Assuming minimal relevance, however, defendants have clearly identified an inordinate burden associated with responding to the request. Applying the seven factors found in *Zubulake* to inform the decision of whether cost shifting should be applied, I note that plaintiff's request is anything but specifically tailored to discover the necessary information, the sources of the information sought and relevant to plaintiff's claims is available through other means, including by way of deposition, and the cost of production exponentially exceeds the amount in controversy. And, because of the likelihood that Capital One Services is not properly regarded as a debt collector, the importance of the discovery sought and the benefits to plaintiff of obtaining the information all militate against requiring the requested discovery at the expense of Capital One Services.

A similar analysis applies with regard to NCO. While the volume of e-discovery implicated by plaintiff's request to NCO is far less than in the case of Capital One Services, the information sought is no more relevant to issues in the case. There is no evidence currently in the record to suggest that NCO sent the letters in issue or should for some reason be held accountable for their contents. I therefore similarly find that the rule of proportionality should be applied to plaintiff's ESI demands to NCO.

In sum, for the reasons set forth above I will deny plaintiff's request for the ESI searches referenced in his motion, without prejudice to his right to renew the motion to compel in the event he is willing to underwrite the expense associated with any such search.

2.   Hard Drive Searches

In his motion to compel plaintiff requests the production of three files identified on Capital One Services' Knowledge Links Hard Drive . . . . That request is not addressed either in defendant Capital One Services' response to the motion or in its separate motion for a protective order. Accordingly, the request will be granted, and defendant Capital One Services will be required to provide that information . . . .

[The court's discussion of non-ESL discovery-related issues is omitted.]

IV. SUMMARY AND CONCLUSION

Plaintiff has demanded from the defendants large volumes of information, including ESI, some of which defendants acknowledge has at least some small modicum of relevance to the claims and defenses in this case. I am convinced, however, that the marginal relevance associated with plaintiff's requests is far outweighed by the burden of responding, and that the relevant factors to be considered, including the amount at stake, and the importance of the discovery sought to resolution of the issues involved, warrant application of the rule of proportionality to deny the bulk of plaintiff's requests.

Finding that defendants have sustained their burden of demonstrating that the effort and expense associated with searching for and producing the requested information far outweighs any potential relevance, I conclude that absent an agreement by the plaintiff to bear the expense of production, his request should be denied, with one exception and subject to renewal in the event of class certification.

Based upon the foregoing it is hereby

ORDERED as follows:

1) Within thirty days of the date of this order defendant Capital One Services shall produce to plaintiff [the] three files identified on Capital One Services Knowledge Links Hard Drive . . . ;

2) With that exception, plaintiff's motion to compel discovery is DENIED, and defendants' motions for a protective order are GRANTED.

3) These determinations are without prejudice to plaintiff's right to re-apply to the court for all or some of the relief now sought in the event of class certification, and provided plaintiff reasonably believes that class certification renders all or some of the information sought . . . relevant and that the relevance outweighs the burden of production . . . .

NOTES AND QUESTIONS

1. *The discoverability of ESI.* In denying the plaintiff's motion to compel the requested e-mail searches, the *Wood* court relied, in part, on *Zubulake v. UBS Warburg LLC*, 217 F.R.D. 309, 317 (S.D.N.Y. 2003), a very influential district court opinion that predates the 2006 amendments to the federal rules. Can you see how the *Zubulake* seven-factor test is reflected in Rule 26(b)(2)(B) & (C) and in the 2006 Advisory Committee Notes? The defendants in *Wood* did not challenge the plaintiff's motion to compel discovery of information that was available on hard drives. If they had, and assuming discovery relevance, do you think it likely that the court would have ruled in their favor on the same "proportionality" grounds it relied on when it denied the plaintiff's motion to compel production of

employee e-mails? (You should be able to explain why "no" or at least "probably not" is the correct answer.)

2. *The right to discard and the duty to preserve.*   Given the volume of ESI and the problems associated with the storage of ESI, it is not surprising that most large-scale businesses have adopted record-retention protocols that permit the routine purging of ESI. Typically, this would be done according to schedule under which the ESI is transferred from a hard drive to some type of backup recording. After a specified period of time, the backup recording would then be destroyed. Rule 37(e) implicitly recognizes the legitimacy of such routine purging by allowing the imposition of judicial measures only where "electronically stored information that should have been preserved in the anticipation or conduct of litigation is lost because a party failed to take reasonable steps to preserve it, and it cannot be restored or replaced through additional discovery." This rule thus recognizes that once a party "reasonably anticipates litigation," an obligation to preserve evidence arises. *See Pension Comm. of Univ. of Montreal Pension Plan v. Banc of Am. Secs., LLC,* 685 F. Supp. 2d 456, 466 (S.D.N.Y. 2010). At that point, a party "must suspend its routine document retention/destruction policy and put in place a 'litigation hold' to ensure the preservation of relevant documents." *Zubulake v. UBS Warburg LLC,* 220 F.R.D. 212, 218 (S.D.N.Y. 2003). While Rule 37(e) allows a court to take measures to cure any prejudice caused by the destruction, absent a "finding that the party acted with the intent to deprive another party of the information's use in the litigation," FED. R. CIV. P. 37(e)(2), the court may impose corrective measures "no greater than necessary to cure the prejudice . . . ." FED. R. CIV. P. 37(e)(1). *See Report of the Advisory Committee on Civil Rules,* http://uscourts.gov/rules-policies/archives/committee-reports/CV05-2014.pdf, at 263 (May 2, 2014) ("[t]he better rule for the negligent or grossly negligent loss of electronically stored information is to preserve a broad range of measures to cure prejudice caused by its loss, but to limit the most severe measures to instances of intentional loss or destruction"). *See also* SCHEINDLIN & CAPRA, *supra,* at 215-242.

e.   *Physical and Mental Examinations*

If a party's physical or mental condition is placed "in controversy" in a pending case, the parties' attorneys will typically arrange for the administration of an appropriate examination by mutual agreement. Thus, in personal injury lawsuits, the plaintiff will often voluntarily consent to undergo a physical examination by a doctor designated by the defendant. In federal court, the Rule 26(f) conference is the appropriate forum through which to make such arrangements. If, however, no agreement can be reached among the parties, the court in which the case is pending may, on motion and with good cause shown, order the appropriate examination and "must specify the time, place, manner, conditions, and scope of the examination, as well as the person or persons who will perform it." FED. R. CIV. P. 35(a)(2)(B); *see also* CAL. CIV. PROC. CODE § 2032.020.

Schlagenhauf v. Holder

379 U.S. 104 (1964)

MR. JUSTICE GOLDBERG delivered the opinion of the Court.

This case involves the validity and construction of Rule 35(a) of the Federal Rules of Civil Procedure as applied to the examination of a defendant in a negligence action. . . .

An action based on diversity of citizenship was brought in the District Court seeking damages arising from personal injuries suffered by passengers of a bus which collided with the rear of a tractor-trailer. The named defendants were The Greyhound Corporation, owner of the bus; petitioner, Robert L. Schlagenhauf, the bus driver; Contract Carriers, Inc., owner of the tractor; Joseph L. McCorkhill, driver of the tractor; and National Lead Company, owner of the trailer. Answers were filed by each of the defendants denying negligence.

Greyhound then cross-claimed against Contract Carriers and National Lead for damage to Greyhound's bus, alleging that the collision was due solely to their negligence in that the tractor-trailer was driven at an unreasonably low speed, had not remained in its lane, and was not equipped with proper rear lights. Contract Carriers filed an answer to this cross-claim denying its negligence and asserting "[t]hat the negligence of the driver of the . . . bus [petitioner Schlagenhauf] proximately caused and contributed to . . . Greyhound's damages."

Pursuant to a pretrial order, Contract Carriers filed a letter—which the trial court treated as, and we consider to be, part of the answer—alleging that Schlagenhauf was "not mentally or physically capable" of driving a bus at the time of the accident.

Contract Carriers and National Lead then petitioned the District Court for an order directing petitioner Schlagenhauf to submit to both mental and physical examinations by one specialist in each of the following fields:

1. Internal medicine;
2. Ophthalmology;
3. Neurology; and
4. Psychiatry.

For the purpose of offering a choice to the District Court of one specialist in each field, the petition recommended two specialists in internal medicine, ophthalmology, and psychiatry, respectively, and three specialists in neurology—a total of nine physicians. The petition alleged that the mental and physical condition of Schlagenhauf was "in controversy" as it had been raised by Contract Carriers' answer to Greyhound's cross-claim. This was supported by a brief of legal authorities and an affidavit of Contract Carriers' attorney stating that Schlagenhauf had seen red lights 10 to 15 seconds before the accident, that another witness had seen the rear lights of the trailer from a distance of three-quarters to one-half mile, and that Schlagenhauf had been involved in a prior accident.

The certified record indicates that petitioner's attorneys filed in the District Court a brief in opposition to this petition asserting, among other things, that "the physical and mental condition of the defendant Robert L. Schlagenhauf is not 'in controversy' herein in the sense that these words are used in Rule 35 . . . [and] that good cause has not been shown for the multiple examinations prayed for by the cross-defendant. . . ."

While disposition of this petition was pending, National Lead filed its answer to Greyhound's cross-claim and itself "cross-claimed" against Greyhound and Schlagenhauf for damage to its trailer. The answer asserted generally that Schlagenhauf's negligence proximately caused the accident. The cross-claim additionally alleged that Greyhound and Schlagenhauf were negligent

> "[b]y permitting said bus to be operated over and upon said public highway by the said defendant, Robert L. Schlagenhauf, when both the said Greyhound Corporation and said Robert L. Schlagenhauf knew that the eyes and vision of the said Robert L. Schlagenhauf was [sic] impaired and deficient."

The District Court, on the basis of the petition filed by Contract Carriers, and without any hearing, ordered Schlagenhauf to submit to nine examinations—one by each of the recommended specialists—despite the fact that the petition clearly requested a total of only four examinations.[3]

Petitioner applied for a writ of mandamus in the Court of Appeals against the respondent, the District Court Judge, seeking to have set aside the order requiring his mental and physical examinations. The Court of Appeals denied mandamus, one judge dissenting.

We granted certiorari to review undecided questions concerning the validity and construction of Rule 35. . . .

We hold that Rule 35 . . . is free of constitutional difficulty and is within the scope of the Enabling Act. We therefore agree with the Court of Appeals that the District Court had power to apply Rule 35 to a party defendant in an appropriate case.

There remains the issue of the construction of Rule 35. We enter upon determination of this construction with the basic premise "that the deposition-discovery rules are to be accorded a broad and liberal treatment," *Hickman v. Taylor*, [329 U.S. 495, 507 (1947)], to effectuate their purpose that "civil trials in the federal courts no longer need be carried on in the dark." *Id.*, at 501.

Petitioner contends that even if Rule 35 is to be applied to defendants, which we have determined it must, nevertheless it should not be applied to him as he was not a party in relation to Contract Carriers and National Lead—the movants

---

3. After the Court of Appeals denied mandamus, the order was corrected by the District Court to reduce the number of examinations to the four requested. We agree with respondent that the issue of that error has become moot. However, the fact that the District Court ordered nine examinations is not irrelevant, together with all the other circumstances, in the consideration of whether the District Court gave to the petition for mental and physical examinations that discriminating application, which Rule 35 requires.

for the mental and physical examinations—at the time the examinations were sought. The Court of Appeals agreed with petitioner's general legal proposition, holding that the person sought to be examined must be an opposing party *vis-à-vis* the movant (or at least one of them). While it is clear that the person to be examined must be a party to the case, we are of the view that the Court of Appeals gave an unduly restrictive interpretation to that term. Rule 35 only requires that the person to be examined be a party to the "action," not that he be an opposing party *vis-à-vis* the movant. There is no doubt that Schlagenhauf was a "party" to this "action" by virtue of the original complaint. Therefore, Rule 35 permitted examination of him (a party defendant) upon petition of Contract Carriers and National Lead (codefendants), provided, of course, that the other requirements of the Rule were met. Insistence that the movant have filed a pleading against the person to be examined would have the undesirable result of an unnecessary proliferation of cross-claims and counterclaims and would not be in keeping with the aims of a liberal, nontechnical application of the Federal Rules. . . .

Petitioner next contends that his mental or physical condition was not "in controversy" and "good cause" was not shown for the examinations, both as required by the express terms of Rule 35.

The discovery devices sanctioned by Part V of the Federal Rules include the taking of oral and written depositions (Rules 26-32), interrogatories to parties (Rule 33), production of documents (Rule 34), and physical and mental examinations of parties (Rule 35). The scope of discovery in each instance is limited by Rule 26(b)'s provision that "the deponent may be examined regarding any matter, not privileged, which is *relevant to the subject matter involved* in the pending action" (emphasis added), and by the provisions of Rule 30(b) permitting the district court, upon motion, to limit, terminate, or otherwise control the use of discovery devices so as to prevent either their use in bad faith or undue "annoyance, embarrassment, or oppression."

It is notable, however, that in none of the other discovery provisions is there a restriction that the matter be "in controversy," and only in Rule 34 is there Rule 35's requirement that the movant affirmatively demonstrate "good cause."*

This additional requirement of "good cause" was reviewed by Chief Judge Soboloff in *Guilford National Bank of Greensboro v. Southern Ry. Co.*, 297 F.2d 921, 924 (C.A. 4th Cir.), in the following words:

"Subject to . . . [the restrictions of Rules 26(b) and 30(b) and (d)], a party may take depositions and serve interrogatories without prior sanction of the court or even its knowledge of what the party is doing. Only if a deponent refuses to answer in the belief that the question is irrelevant, can the moving party request under Rule 37 a court order requiring an answer."

"Significantly, this freedom of action, afforded a party who resorts to depositions and interrogatories, is not granted to one proceeding under [Rule 35]. Instead, the court must decide as an initial matter, and in every case, whether the motion

---

* [The "good cause" requirement has since been eliminated from Rule 34, but still remains part of Rule 35.—EDS.]

requesting production of documents or the making of a physical or mental examination adequately demonstrates good cause. The specific requirement of good cause would be meaningless if good cause could be sufficiently established by merely showing that the desired materials are relevant, for the relevancy standard has already been imposed by Rule 26(b). Thus, by adding the words '. . . good cause . . . ,' the Rules indicate that there must be greater showing of need under . . . [Rule 35] than under the other discovery rules."

. . . [Thus] the "in controversy" and "good cause" requirements of Rule 35 . . . are not met by mere conclusory allegations of the pleadings—nor by mere relevance to the case—but require an affirmative showing by the movant that each condition as to which the examination is sought is really and genuinely in controversy and that good cause exists for ordering each particular examination. Obviously, what may be good cause for one type of examination may not be so for another. The ability of the movant to obtain the desired information by other means is also relevant.

Rule 35, therefore, requires discriminating application by the trial judge, who must decide, as an initial matter in every case, whether the party requesting a mental or physical examination or examinations has adequately demonstrated the existence of the Rule's requirements of "in controversy" and "good cause," which requirements, as the Court of Appeals in this case itself recognized, are necessarily related. This does not, of course, mean that the movant must prove his case on the merits in order to meet the requirements for a mental or physical examination. Nor does it mean that an evidentiary hearing is required in all cases. This may be necessary in some cases, but in other cases the showing could be made by affidavits or other usual methods short of a hearing. It does mean, though, that the movant must produce sufficient information, by whatever means, so that the district judge can fulfill his function mandated by the Rule.

Of course, there are situations where the pleadings alone are sufficient to meet these requirements. A plaintiff in a negligence action who asserts mental or physical injury places that mental or physical injury clearly in controversy and provides the defendant with good cause for an examination to determine the existence and extent of such asserted injury. This is not only true as to a plaintiff, but applies equally to a defendant who asserts his mental or physical condition as a defense to a claim, such as, for example, where insanity is asserted as a defense to a divorce action.

Here, however, Schlagenhauf did not assert his mental or physical condition either in support of or in defense of a claim. His condition was sought to be placed in issue by other parties. Thus, under the principles discussed above, Rule 35 required that these parties make an affirmative showing that petitioner's mental or physical condition was in controversy and that there was good cause for the examinations requested. This, the record plainly shows, they failed to do.

The only allegations in the pleadings relating to this subject were the general conclusory statement in Contract Carriers' answer to the cross-claim that "Schlagenhauf was not mentally or physically capable of operating" the bus at the time of the accident and the limited allegation in National Lead's cross-claim that, at the time of the accident, "the eyes and vision of . . . Schlagenhauf was [sic] impaired and deficient."

The attorney's affidavit attached to the petition for the examinations provided:

> "That . . . Schlagenhauf, in his deposition . . . admitted that he saw red lights for 10 to 15 seconds prior to a collision with a semi-tractor trailer unit and yet drove his vehicle on without reducing speed and without altering the course thereof.
>
> "The only eye-witness to this accident known to this affiant . . . testified that immediately prior to the impact between the bus and truck that he had also been approaching the truck from the rear and that he had clearly seen the lights of the truck for a distance of three-quarters to one-half mile to the rear thereof.
>
> ". . . Schlagenhauf has admitted in his deposition . . . that he was involved in a [prior] similar type rear end collision. . . ."

This record cannot support even the corrected order which required one examination in each of the four specialties of internal medicine, ophthalmology, neurology, and psychiatry. Nothing in the pleadings or affidavit would afford a basis for a belief that Schlagenhauf was suffering from a mental or neurological illness warranting wide-ranging psychiatric or neurological examinations. Nor is there anything stated justifying the broad internal medicine examination.

The only specific allegation made in support of the four examinations ordered was that the "eyes and vision" of Schlagenhauf were impaired. Considering this in conjunction with the affidavit, we would be hesitant to set aside a visual examination if it had been the only one ordered. However, as the case must be remanded to the District Court because of the other examinations ordered, it would be appropriate for the District Judge to reconsider also this order in light of the guidelines set forth in this opinion.

The Federal Rules of Civil Procedure should be liberally construed, but they should not be expanded by disregarding plainly expressed limitations. The "good cause" and "in controversy" requirements of Rule 35 make it very apparent that sweeping examinations of a party who has not affirmatively put into issue his own mental or physical condition are not to be automatically ordered merely because the person has been involved in an accident—or, as in this case, two accidents—and a general charge of negligence is lodged. Mental and physical examinations are only to be ordered upon a discriminating application by the district judge of the limitations prescribed by the Rule. To hold otherwise would mean that such examinations could be ordered routinely in automobile accident cases. The plain language of Rule 35 precludes such an untoward result.

Accordingly, the judgment of the Court of Appeals is vacated and the case remanded to the District Court to reconsider the examination order in light of the guidelines herein formulated and for further proceedings in conformity with this opinion.

Vacated and remanded.

Mr. Justice Black, with whom Mr. Justice Clark joins, concurring in part and dissenting in part.

I agree with the Court that under Rule 35(a): (1) a plaintiff and a defendant have precisely the same right to obtain a court order for physical or mental examination of the other party or parties to a lawsuit; (2) before obtaining such an order it must be shown that physical or mental health is "in controversy" as to a relevant and material issue in the case; and (3) such an order "may be made only on motion for good cause shown" after "notice to the party to be examined and to all other parties." Unlike the Court, however, I think this record plainly shows that there *was* a controversy as to Schlagenhauf's mental and physical health and that "good cause" was shown for a physical and mental examination of him, unless failure to deny the allegations amounted to an admission that they were true. While the papers filed in connection with this motion were informal, there can be no doubt that other parties in the lawsuit specifically and unequivocally charged that Schlagenhauf was not mentally or physically capable of operating a motor bus at the time of the collision, and that his negligent operation of the bus caused the resulting injuries and damage. The other parties filed an affidavit based on depositions of Schlagenhauf and a witness stating that Schlagenhauf, driving the bus along a four-lane highway in what apparently was good weather, had come upon a tractor-trailer down the road in front of him. The tractor-trailer was displaying red lights visible for at least half a mile, and Schlagenhauf admitted seeing them. Yet after coming in sight of the vehicle Schlagenhauf continued driving the bus in a straight line, without slowing down, for a full 10 or 15 seconds until the bus struck the tractor-trailer. Schlagenhauf admitted also that he had been involved in the very same kind of accident once before. Schlagenhauf has never at any time in the proceedings denied and he does not even now deny the charges that his mental and physical health and his eyes and vision were impaired and deficient. . . .

MR. JUSTICE DOUGLAS, dissenting in part.

While I join the Court in reversing this judgment, I would, on the remand, deny all relief asked under Rule 35.

I do not suppose there is any licensed driver of a car or a truck who does not suffer from some ailment, whether it be ulcers, bad eyesight, abnormal blood pressure, deafness, liver malfunction, bursitis, rheumatism, or what not. If he or she is turned over to the plaintiff's doctors and psychoanalysts to discover the cause of the mishap, the door will be opened for grave miscarriages of justice. When the defendant's doctors examine plaintiff, they are normally interested only in answering a single question: did plaintiff in fact sustain the specific injuries claimed? But plaintiff's doctors will naturally be inclined to go on a fishing expedition in search of *anything* which will tend to prove that the defendant was unfit to perform the acts which resulted in the plaintiff's injury. And a doctor for a fee can easily discover something wrong with any patient—a condition that in prejudiced medical eyes might have caused the accident. Once defendants are turned over to medical or psychiatric clinics for an analysis of their physical well-being and the condition of their psyche, the effective trial will be held there and not before the jury. There are no lawyers in those clinics to stop the doctor from probing this organ or that one, to halt a further inquiry, to object to a line of questioning. And there is no judge to sit as arbiter. The doctor or the psychiatrist has a holiday in the privacy of his office. The defendant is at the doctor's (or psychiatrist's) mercy; and his report may either overawe or confuse the jury and prevent a fair trial. . . .

[The opinion of Mr. Justice Harlan, dissenting on procedural grounds, is omitted.]

NOTES AND QUESTIONS

1. *"In controversy" and "good cause."*   On what grounds did the majority hold that the district court's order violated Rule 35? Was it because Schlagenhauf's physical and mental conditions weren't "in controversy"? Or was it because the defendants had failed to show "good cause" for the requested exams? More specifically, what would the defendants have had to show to demonstrate that Schlagenhauf's physical and mental conditions were in controversy? Did the majority impose a heightened pleading requirement? An evidentiary requirement? Assuming the conditions were in controversy, what more, if anything, would be needed to show good cause for an order requiring the various examinations? The majority seemed to suggest that an examination by the ophthalmologist would be permissible. Why? Finally, the individual plaintiffs suing Greyhound for personal injuries would quite likely be required to submit to physical examinations to assess the extent of their injuries. *See Sibbach v. Wilson & Co., Inc.*, 312 U.S., 1 (1941), page 503, *supra*. If that's true, how does their situation differ from that of Schlagenhauf's?

2. *Abuse-of-discretion standard.*   The decision of whether to order a physical or mental examination is within the district court judge's discretion. A judge's decision to grant or deny a motion under Rule 35(a) will be reversed only if she is found to have abused her discretion. *Herrera v. Lufkin Industries, Inc.*, 474 F.3d 675, 688 (10th Cir. 2007). This is a highly deferential standard that grants a district court broad leeway in applying the principles of the *Schlagenhauf* decision. *Curtis v. Express, Inc.*, 868 F. Supp. 467, 468 (N.D.N.Y. 1994) ("Even if good cause is shown, it is still within the court's discretion to determine whether to order an examination."). Similarly, the district court has broad discretion in determining the scope of any ordered examination and the conditions under which that examination may proceed. In exercising its discretion, the court may take into account the privacy rights of the person to be examined as well as the danger or pain involved in the procedure. *See generally* James C. Francis IV, *Physical and Mental Examinations, in* 7 Moore's Federal Practice, *supra*, § 35.05; 8B Wright, Miller & Marcus, *supra*, §§ 2234.1, 2235.

3. *To whom does Rule 35 apply?*   As the Court stated in *Schlagenhauf*, Rule 35 applies to all persons who are parties to the pending litigation regardless of their adversary status vis-à-vis one another. As currently written, the rule also applies to persons in the "custody" or under the "legal control" of a party. This language

is meant to make it clear that "a parent or guardian suing to recover for injuries to a minor may be ordered to produce the minor for examination." Advisory Committee Note, *1970 Amendments*, 48 F.R.D. 487, 529. A party required to produce another person for a physical or mental examination and who fails to do so may be subject to sanctions unless she has made a good faith effort to produce the absent person. FED. R. CIV. P. 37(b)(2)(B).

PROBLEMS

7-8. Duncan brought an action against the Upjohn Company claiming that the defendant was negligent in the testing and marketing of Halcion, a tranquilizer. Duncan claims that the drug caused him to become psychologically unstable and caused him to undergo a drastic personality change. Further, he alleges that the defendant's negligence caused him permanent medical, psychological, and psychiatric injury. May the district court, pursuant to a motion made under Rule 35, order Duncan to submit to a psychiatric examination? *See Duncan v. Upjohn Co.*, 155 F.R.D. 23 (D. Conn. 1994).

7-9. Robin filed suit against Imperial Stores for wrongful job termination. She claims that she was terminated on account of her race and alleges a violation of Title VII of the 1964 Civil Rights Act, breach of contract, breach of the covenant of good faith and fair dealing, sex discrimination, fraud and deceit, defamation, and a violation of labor law. She requests damages on various grounds, including compensatory damages for losses resulting from "humiliation, mental anguish, and emotional distress." The defendant claims that Robin has put her "mental condition" in controversy within the meaning of Rule 35(a). Do you agree? Can you distinguish this problem from the previous one? *Compare Turner v. Imperial Stores*, 161 F.R.D. 89 (S.D. Cal. 1995), *with Nuskey v. Lambright*, 251 F.R.D 3 (D.D.C. 2008).

f. Requests for Admissions

A "request for admission" is a written device through which one party asks another party to admit or deny the truth of a specific matter relevant to the pending action between them. The effect of an admission is to conclusively establish the matter admitted, which then cannot be contested at trial or be the subject of further discovery. A request may be directed to any matter that falls within the scope of relevant discovery under Rule 26(b)(1) and that relates to "facts, the application of law to fact, or opinions about either," or to "the genuineness of any described documents." FED. R. CIV. P. 36(a)(1)(A)-(B). Thus a defendant being sued for breach of contract for failure to deliver flowers to a wedding might be asked to admit or deny the following: "Neither defendant nor its agents delivered flowers to the Church of Good Feeling on June 23, 2001." Served with such a request, the party must either admit, deny, or explain why it is unable to do either, but the party may choose the latter course only after a "reasonable inquiry" and may not simply rely on a lack of information or knowledge. FED. R. CIV. P. 36(a)(4). If only part of the request is true, the party must specify that which is true and qualify or deny the remainder. *Id.* A failure to respond within the appropriate time frame—usually 30 days—is treated as an admission. FED. R. CIV. P. 36(a)(3). If the matter is admitted, it is deemed "conclusively established" for purposes of the pending action (but only the pending action), unless the court on motion permits withdrawal of the admission. FED. R. CIV. P. 36(b). If the matter is denied and the requesting party thereafter proves its truthfulness, the party who failed to admit may be required to pay the reasonable expenses, including attorneys' fees, incurred in making that proof. FED. R. CIV. P. 37(c)(2).

A request for admission is not technically a discovery device for it does not assist a party in gathering information from another party. Rather, its purpose is to narrow the matters that will be contested at trial.

See generally Claudia Wilken, *Requests for Admissions, in* 7 MOORE'S FEDERAL PRACTICE §§ 36.01 *et seq.*; 8B WRIGHT, MILLER & MARCUS, *supra*, §§ 2251-2265.

g. Discovery Related to Experts

For purposes of discovery, there are five types of experts: (1) experts who have been retained to testify at trial; (2) experts who have been retained in anticipation of litigation or for trial preparation but who are not expected to testify; (3) experts who have been consulted but not retained; (4) experts who are employees of a party and who provide expert advice in the regular course of their employment; and (5) experts who are unaffiliated with any party to the case.

1. Experts retained to testify. Rule 26(a)(2)(A) requires that a party in a federal court proceeding disclose the identity of any retained expert who may testify at trial. The disclosure must be accompanied by a written report prepared and signed by the expert witness.

> The report must contain: (i) a complete statement of all opinions the witness will express and the basis and reasons for them; (ii) the facts or data considered by the witness in forming them; (iii) any exhibits that will be used to summarize or support them; (iv) the witness's qualifications, including a list of all publications authored in the previous 10 years; (v) a list of all other cases in which, during the previous 4 years, the witness testified as an expert at trial or by deposition; and (vi) a statement of the compensation to be paid for the study and testimony in the case.

FED. R. CIV. P. 26(a)(2)(B). These disclosures are required without any party making a request for them. They must be made at the times and in the sequence directed by the court or by stipulation of the parties, or in accord with Rule 26(a)(2)(D). A party may then depose any person who has been identified as an expert who may testify at trial. Rule 26(b)(4)(A). The deposition may not take place, however, until the expert's written report required by Rule 26(a)(2)(B) has been completed. Rule 26(b)(4)(A). The hope is that the report will obviate the need for a deposition.

At the state court level, the discovery rules applicable to trial experts vary from state to state. While the approach adopted in some states closely parallels the federal model, others limit discovery in this context to the use of interrogatories. In California, which roughly parallels the federal model, once the initial trial date is set, any party may demand the mutual and simultaneous exchange of each party's expert list and any preparatory writings or reports made by the experts on those lists. CAL. CIV. PROC. CODE § 2034.210. Any expert on the exchanged list may be deposed by any other party. *Id.* § 2034.410.

2. *Experts retained but not expected to testify.*   This issue was explored above in "A Note on Information Obtained from Experts," at page 585, *supra.* As that note pointed out, the facts known or opinions held by such experts can be discovered through interrogatories or depositions in federal court suits only as provided by Rule 35(b) in the context of physical and mental examinations, or upon "showing exceptional circumstances under which it is impracticable for the party to obtain facts or opinions on the same subject by other means." FED. R. CIV. P. 26(b)(4)(D)(ii). This is a very difficult standard to satisfy, quite similar to the heightened standard for the forced disclosure of work product. Indeed, one can see such experts' contributions as a form of work product. *See* 6 MOORE'S FEDERAL PRACTICE, *supra,* §§ 26.70[5][b]-[c], 26.80[2]; 8A WRIGHT, MILLER & MARCUS, *supra,* § 2032. Most states also severely limit the discoverability of this type of information.

3. *Experts consulted but not retained.*   It often happens that a lawyer will consult several experts before deciding whom to retain. The federal rules do not provide for any discovery concerning those experts who are not retained or their identities. Advisory Committee Note, 1970 Amendments, 48 F.R.D. 487, 504. Moreover, these consultations may well come within the protection of the work-product rule. The states are generally in accord.

4. *Expert employees.*   In both federal and state courts, an expert who is an employee of a party is generally treated as an ordinary fact witness and is not immune from discovery by virtue of her "expert" status. For example, a design engineer employed by an auto manufacturer would be treated as an ordinary witness in a suit against the manufacturer alleging a design defect in a vehicle designed by that engineer. Under limited circumstances, an "employee expert" who has been specially designated to assist in preparation for litigation may be treated as a "retained" expert, and hence relatively immune from discovery. 8 WRIGHT, MILLER & MARCUS, *supra,* § 2033. Yet care would have to be taken to ensure that the party employer was not simply trying to insulate its employee from discovery.

5. *Unaffiliated experts.*   To what extent may a party demand the facts known and opinions held by an expert who is completely unaffiliated with the action? For example, may a party demand information from a scientist who is knowledgeable in the general subject area of the lawsuit, but who has not been retained by any party to the suit? The answer is no. The only way to obtain such information, aside from voluntarily, is by way of subpoena, and Rule 45(d)(3)(B)(ii) provides for the quashing of any subpoena that requires disclosure of "an unretained expert's

opinion or information that does not describe specific occurrences in dispute and results from the expert's study that was not requested by a party."

PROBLEM

7-10. After Jay was injured in an industrial accident involving heavy machinery, he retained Bob as his attorney. In preparing for a lawsuit against the manufacturer of the equipment, Bob retained the services of Reconstruct, Inc. ("Reconstruct"), an accident investigation firm that specializes in reconstructing industrial accidents. Reconstruct prepared a memorandum for Bob in which it described its reconstruction of the accident. Shortly thereafter, Bob filed a civil action on Jay's behalf against the manufacturer in federal court. He also hired Amy to testify as an expert at trial on the specific topic of industrial safety and he so identified her in the disclosures required by Rule 26(a)(2)(A). After hiring Amy, Bob gave her a copy of the Reconstruct memorandum, and she relied on that memorandum in preparing the report required by Rule 26(a)(2)(A). May the defense depose Amy regarding the details of the Reconstruct memorandum over Bob's objection that the memorandum and its contents are protected work product? Would it make any difference if the memorandum revealed some of Bob's impressions about the case? Does Rule 26 (a)(2)(B) or (b)(3) answer these questions? *See Johnson v. Gmeinder*, 191 F.R.D. 638 (D. Kan. 2000).

h.   Duty to Supplement or Correct

As a general matter, a party to a federal action is under a continuing duty, without any demand from another party, to supplement or correct mandatory disclosures and responses to discovery requests if the party learns that the prior disclosure is in some material respect incomplete or incorrect. FED. R. CIV. P. 26(e). This duty only applies if the "corrective information has not otherwise been made known to the other parties during the discovery process or in writing . . . ." FED. R. CIV. P. 26(e)(1)(A). The duty to supplement extends to information gathered from experts who may be called to testify at trial and includes information contained in the expert's report and deposition. The duty also extends to any response to an interrogatory, request for production, or request for admission. It does not extend to nonexperts' deposition testimony. However, if a deponent's testimony at trial varies from her deposition, she may be impeached by that deposition. Depositions aside, the failure to supplement or correct may lead a court to impose evidentiary or monetary sanctions on the offending party, as well as monetary sanctions on counsel. For example, in *Licciardi v. TIG Insurance Group*, 140 F.3d 357 (1st Cir. 1998), the court of appeals held that the testimony of the defendant's medical expert should have been excluded from trial since the testimony contradicted the expert's "uncorrected" earlier report. Given the prejudicial nature of the testimony — it involved a key element of the plaintiff's claim — the case was remanded for a new trial. *See generally* 6 Moore's Federal Practice, *supra*, §§ 26.130-26.132, *et seq.*; 8A Wright, Miller & Marcus, *supra*, §§ 2048-2050.

In many states, there is no continuing duty to supplement or correct responses to discovery. In such jurisdictions, the parties must make periodic requests or demands designed to elicit newly acquired information. *Cf.* Cal. Civ. Proc. Code § 2030.070 (allowing a party to propound supplemental interrogatories to elicit later acquired information).

i. *Protective Orders, Motions to Compel, and Sanctions*

Any litigator will tell you that judges do not like to become involved in discovery disputes. The basic philosophy behind this reluctance, aside from the added strain on a judge's already heavy workload, is that reasonably competent attorneys should be able to manage discovery without the court's aid. The attorneys are in the best position to move the process along in a manner that comports with their clients' needs. The overall structure of the federal discovery rules is designed to accomplish that end. From the discovery conference and mandatory disclosures to the use of post-disclosure discovery tools, attorney initiative is the rule, while judicial intervention is the exception. The ideal approach to discovery, therefore, is for the attorneys on each side to accommodate, within reason, the other side's discovery needs while at the same time respecting their own clients' legitimate interests. Quite often that is precisely the way it works out. Sometimes, however, that noble goal cannot be accomplished and some form of judicial intervention is the only available option.

Courts have three basic tools that can be used to supervise the discovery process. First, a court, on motion, may enter a protective order designed to shield a party or other person subject to discovery from "annoyance, embarrassment, oppression, or undue burden or expense. . . ." Fed. R. Civ. P. 26(c)(i). Second, a court may enter an order compelling a party to provide disclosure or discovery. Fed. R. Civ. P. 37(a)(3). A party seeking an order to compel must certify that she "has in good faith conferred or attempted to confer with the person or party failing to make disclosure or discovery in an effort to obtain it without court action." Fed. R. Civ. P. 37(a)(1). Finally, a court may impose sanctions on a party or an attorney who fails to obey a court order pertaining to disclosure or discovery, who fails to comply with the basic rules of disclosure and discovery, or who fails to participate in the framing of a discovery plan. Fed. R. Civ. P. 37(b)-(f). Sanctions can range from an order to pay the reasonable expenses and fees incurred in contesting the challenged behavior to the outright dismissal of the recalcitrant party's claim or defense. *Id.*; *see Advance Fin. Corp. v. Utsey*, page 589, *supra* (sanction of default judgment). A court may also hold a party, nonparty, or attorney in contempt for failure to comply with a discovery order, except an order to submit to a physical or mental examination. Fed. R. Civ. P. 37(b)(1), 37(b)(2)(A)(vii).

See generally 6 Moore's Federal Practice, *supra*, §§ 26.101-26.108; Wayne D. Brazil, *Failure to Make Disclosures or to Cooperate in Discovery; Sanctions, in*

7 MOORE'S FEDERAL PRACTICE, *supra*, §§ 37.01 *et seq.*; 8A WRIGHT, MILLER & MARCUS, *supra*, §§ 2035-2044.1.

Seattle Times Co. v. Rhinehart

467 U.S. 20 (1984)

JUSTICE POWELL delivered the opinion of the Court.

This case presents the issue whether parties to civil litigation have a First Amendment right to disseminate, in advance of trial, information gained through the pretrial discovery process.

I

Respondent Rhinehart is the spiritual leader of a religious group, the Aquarian Foundation. The Foundation has fewer than 1,000 members, most of whom live in the State of Washington. Aquarian beliefs include life after death and the ability to communicate with the dead through a medium. Rhinehart is the primary Aquarian medium.

In recent years, the Seattle Times and the Walla Walla Union-Bulletin have published stories about Rhinehart and the Foundation. Altogether 11 articles appeared in the newspapers during the years 1973, 1978, and 1979. The five articles that appeared in 1973 focused on Rhinehart and the manner in which he operated the Foundation. They described seances conducted by Rhinehart in which people paid him to put them in touch with deceased relatives and friends. The articles also stated that Rhinehart had sold magical "stones" that had been "expelled" from his body. One article referred to Rhinehart's conviction, later vacated, for sodomy. The four articles that appeared in 1978 concentrated on an "extravaganza" sponsored by Rhinehart at the Walla Walla State Penitentiary. The articles stated that he had treated 1,100 inmates to a 6-hour-long show, during which he gave away between $35,000 and $50,000 in cash and prizes. One article described a "chorus line of girls [who] shed their gowns and bikinis and sang. . . ." The two articles that appeared in 1979 referred to a purported connection between Rhinehart and Lou Ferrigno, star of the popular television program, "The Incredible Hulk."

II

Rhinehart brought this action in the Washington Superior Court on behalf of himself and the Foundation against the Seattle Times, the Walla Walla Union-Bulletin, the authors of the articles, and the spouses of the authors. Five female members of the Foundation who had participated in the presentation at the penitentiary joined the suit as plaintiffs. The complaint alleges that the articles contained statements that were "fictional and untrue," and that the defendants—petitioners here—knew, or should have known, they were false. According to the complaint, the articles "did and were calculated to hold [Rhinehart] up to public scorn, hatred and ridicule, and to impeach his honesty, integrity, virtue, religious philosophy, reputation as a person and in his profession as a spiritual leader." With respect to the Foundation, the complaint also states: "[T]he articles have, or may have had, the effect of discouraging contributions by the membership and public and thereby diminished the financial ability of the Foundation to pursue its corporate purposes." The complaint alleges that the articles misrepresented the role of the Foundation's "choir" and falsely implied that female members of the Foundation had "stripped off all their clothes and wantonly danced naked. . . ." The complaint requests $14,100,000 in damages for the alleged defamation and invasions of privacy.

Petitioners filed an answer, denying many of the allegations of the complaint and asserting affirmative defenses. Petitioners promptly initiated extensive discovery. They deposed Rhinehart, requested production of documents pertaining to the financial affairs of Rhinehart and the Foundation, and served extensive interrogatories on Rhinehart and the other respondents. Respondents turned over a number of financial documents, including several of Rhinehart's income tax returns. Respondents refused, however, to disclose certain financial information, the identity of the Foundation's donors during the preceding 10 years, and a list of its members during that period.

Petitioners filed a motion under the State's Civil Rule 37 requesting an order compelling discovery.[5] In their supporting memorandum, petitioners recognized that the principal issue as to discovery was respondents' "refusa[l] to permit any effective inquiry into their financial affairs, such as the source of their donations, their financial transactions, uses of their wealth and assets, and their financial condition in general." Respondents opposed the motion, arguing in particular that compelled production of the identities of the Foundation's donors and members would violate the First Amendment rights of members and donors to privacy, freedom of religion, and freedom of association. Respondents also moved for a protective order preventing petitioners from disseminating any information gained through discovery. Respondents noted that petitioners had stated their intention to continue publishing articles about respondents and this litigation, and their intent to use information gained through discovery in future articles.

In a lengthy ruling, the trial court initially granted the motion to compel and ordered respondents to identify all donors who made contributions during the five years preceding the date of the complaint, along with the amounts donated. The court also required respondents to divulge enough membership information to substantiate any claims of diminished membership. . . . [T]he court refused to issue a protective order. It stated that the facts alleged by respondents in support of their motion for such an order were too conclusory to warrant a finding of "good cause" as required by Washington Superior Court Civil Rule 26(c) . . . .

Respondents filed a motion for reconsideration in which they renewed their motion for a protective order. They submitted affidavits of several Foundation

---

5. Washington Superior Court Civil Rule 37 [then provided] in relevant part: "A party, upon reasonable notice to other parties and all persons affected thereby, may apply to the court in the county where the deposition was taken, or in the county where the action is pending for an order compelling discovery. . . ."

members to support their request. The affidavits detailed a series of letters and telephone calls defaming the Foundation, its members, and Rhinehart—including several that threatened physical harm to those associated with the Foundation. The affiants also described incidents at the Foundation's headquarters involving attacks, threats, and assaults directed at Foundation members by anonymous individuals and groups. In general, the affidavits averred that public release of the donor lists would adversely affect Foundation membership and income and would subject its members to additional harassment and reprisals.

Persuaded by these affidavits, the trial court issued a protective order covering all information obtained through the discovery process that pertained to "the financial affairs of the various plaintiffs, the names and addresses of Aquarian Foundation members, contributors, or clients, and the names and addresses of those who have been contributors, clients, or donors to any of the various plaintiffs." The order prohibited petitioners from publishing, disseminating, or using the information in any way except where necessary to prepare for and try the case. By its terms, the order did not apply to information gained by means other than the discovery process. In an accompanying opinion, the trial court recognized that the protective order would restrict petitioners' right to publish information obtained by discovery, but the court reasoned that the restriction was necessary to avoid the "chilling effect" that dissemination would have on "a party's willingness to bring his case to court."

Respondents appealed from the trial court's production order, and petitioners appealed from the protective order. The Supreme Court of Washington affirmed both. . . .

III

Most States, including Washington, have adopted discovery provisions modeled on Rules 26 through 37 of the Federal Rules of Civil Procedure. F. James & G. Hazard, Civil Procedure 179 (1977). Rule 26(b)(1) provides that a party "may obtain discovery regarding any matter, not privileged, which is relevant to the subject matter involved in the pending action." It further provides that discovery is not limited to matters that will be admissible at trial so long as the information sought "appears reasonably calculated to lead to the discovery of admissible evidence." Wash. Super. Ct. Civil Rule 26(b)(1).

The Rules do not differentiate between information that is private or intimate and that to which no privacy interests attach. Under the Rules, the only express limitations are that the information sought is not privileged, and is relevant to the subject matter of the pending action. Thus, the Rules often allow extensive intrusion into the affairs of both litigants and third parties. If a litigant fails to comply with a request for discovery, the court may issue an order directing compliance that is enforceable by the court's contempt powers. Wash. Super. Ct. Civil Rule 37(b).[17]

---

17. In addition to its contempt power, Rule 37(b)(2) authorizes a trial court to enforce an order compelling discovery by other means including, for example, regarding designated facts as established for purposes of the action. Cf. Fed. Rule Civ. Proc. 37(b)(2)(A).

Petitioners argue that the First Amendment imposes strict limits on the availability of any judicial order that has the effect of restricting expression. They contend that civil discovery is not different from other sources of information, and that therefore the information is "protected speech" for First Amendment purposes. Petitioners assert the right in this case to disseminate any information gained through discovery. They do recognize that in limited circumstances, not thought to be present here, some information may be restrained. They submit, however:

> "When a protective order seeks to limit expression, it may do so only if the proponent shows a compelling governmental interest. Mere speculation and conjecture are insufficient. Any restraining order, moreover, must be narrowly drawn and precise. Finally, before issuing such an order a court must determine that there are no alternatives which intrude less directly on expression."

We think the rule urged by petitioners would impose an unwarranted restriction on the duty and discretion of a trial court to oversee the discovery process.

IV

It is, of course, clear that information obtained through civil discovery authorized by modern rules of civil procedure would rarely, if ever, fall within the classes of unprotected speech identified by decisions of this Court. In this case, as petitioners argue, there certainly is a public interest in knowing more about respondents. This interest may well include most—and possibly all—of what has been discovered as a result of the court's order under Rule 26(b)(1). It does not necessarily follow, however, that a litigant has an unrestrained right to disseminate information that has been obtained through pretrial discovery. For even though the broad sweep of the First Amendment seems to prohibit all restraints on free expression, this Court has observed that "[f]reedom of speech . . . does not comprehend the right to speak on any subject at any time." *American Communications Assn. v. Douds*, 339 U.S. 382, 394-395 (1950).

The critical question that this case presents is whether a litigant's freedom comprehends the right to disseminate information that he has obtained pursuant to a court order that both granted him access to that information and placed restraints on the way in which the information might be used. In addressing that question it is necessary to consider whether the "practice in question [furthers] an important or substantial governmental interest unrelated to the suppression of expression" and whether "the limitation of First Amendment freedoms [is] no greater than is necessary or essential to the protection of the particular governmental interest involved." *Procunier v. Martinez*, 416 U.S. 396, 413 (1974).

A

At the outset, it is important to recognize the extent of the impairment of First Amendment rights that a protective order, such as the one at issue here, may cause. As in all civil litigation, petitioners gained the information they wish to disseminate only by virtue of the trial court's discovery processes. As the Rules authorizing discovery were adopted by the state legislature, the processes thereunder are a matter of legislative grace. A litigant has no First Amendment right of access to information made available only for purposes of trying his suit. *Zemel v. Rusk*, 381 U.S. 1, 16-17 (1965) ("The right to speak and publish does not carry with it the unrestrained right to gather information"). Thus, continued court control over the discovered information does not raise the same specter of government censorship that such control might suggest in other situations.

Moreover, pretrial depositions and interrogatories are not public components of a civil trial. Such proceedings were not open to the public at common law, and, in general, they are conducted in private as a matter of modern practice. See Marcus, Myth and Reality in Protective Order Litigation, 69 Cornell L. Rev. 1 (1983). Much of the information that surfaces during pretrial discovery may be unrelated, or only tangentially related, to the underlying cause of action. Therefore, restraints placed on discovered, but not yet admitted, information are not a restriction on a traditionally public source of information.

Finally, it is significant to note that an order prohibiting dissemination of discovered information before trial is not the kind of classic prior restraint that requires exacting First Amendment scrutiny. As in this case, such a protective order prevents a party from disseminating only that information obtained through use of the discovery process. Thus, the party may disseminate the identical information covered by the protective order as long as the information is gained through means independent of the court's processes. In sum, judicial limitations on a party's ability to disseminate information discovered in advance of trial implicates the First Amendment rights of the restricted party to a far lesser extent than would restraints on dissemination of information in a different context. Therefore, our consideration of the provision for protective orders contained in the Washington Civil Rules takes into account the unique position that such orders occupy in relation to the First Amendment.

B

Rule 26(c) furthers a substantial governmental interest unrelated to the suppression of expression. The Washington Civil Rules enable parties to litigation to obtain information "relevant to the subject matter involved" that they believe will be helpful in the preparation and trial of the case. Rule 26, however, must be viewed in its entirety. Liberal discovery is provided for the sole purpose of assisting in the preparation and trial, or the settlement, of litigated disputes. Because of the liberality of pretrial discovery permitted by Rule 26(b)(1), it is necessary for the trial court to have the authority to issue protective orders conferred by Rule 26(c). It is clear from experience that pretrial discovery by depositions and interrogatories has a significant potential for abuse. This abuse is not limited to matters of delay and expense; discovery also may seriously implicate privacy interests of litigants and third parties. The Rules do not distinguish between public and private information. Nor do they apply only to parties to the litigation, as relevant information in the hands of third parties may be subject to discovery.

There is an opportunity, therefore, for litigants to obtain—incidentally or purposefully—information that not only is irrelevant but if publicly released could be damaging to reputation and privacy. The government clearly has a substantial interest in preventing this sort of abuse of its processes. As stated by Judge Friendly in *International Products Corp. v. Koons*, 325 F.2d 403, 407-408 (CA2 1963), "[w]hether or not the Rule itself authorizes [a particular protective order] . . . we have no question as to the court's jurisdiction to do this under the inherent 'equitable powers of courts of law over their own process, to prevent abuses, oppression, and injustices.'" The prevention of the abuse that can attend the coerced production of information under a State's discovery rule is sufficient justification for the authorization of protective orders.

C

We also find that the provision for protective orders in the Washington Rules requires, in itself, no heightened First Amendment scrutiny. To be sure, Rule 26(c) confers broad discretion on the trial court to decide when a protective order is appropriate and what degree of protection is required. The Legislature of the State of Washington, following the example of the Congress in its approval of the Federal Rules of Civil Procedure, has determined that such discretion is necessary, and we find no reason to disagree. The trial court is in the best position to weigh fairly the competing needs and interests of parties affected by discovery. The unique character of the discovery process requires that the trial court have substantial latitude to fashion protective orders.

V

The facts in this case illustrate the concerns that justifiably may prompt a court to issue a protective order. As we have noted, the trial court's order allowing discovery was extremely broad. It compelled respondents—among other things—to identify all persons who had made donations over a 5-year period to Rhinehart and the Aquarian Foundation, together with the amounts donated. In effect the order would compel disclosure of membership as well as sources of financial support. The Supreme Court of Washington found that dissemination of this information would "result in annoyance, embarrassment and even oppression." It is sufficient for purposes of our decision that the highest court in the State found no abuse of discretion in the trial court's decision to issue a protective order pursuant to a constitutional state law. We therefore hold that where, as in this case, a protective order is entered on a showing of good cause as required by Rule 26(c), is limited to the context of pretrial civil discovery, and does not restrict the dissemination of the information if gained from other sources, it does not offend the First Amendment.

The judgment accordingly is

Affirmed.

[The concurring opinion of JUSTICE BRENNAN, with whom JUSTICE MARSHALL joined, is omitted.]

NOTES AND QUESTIONS

1. *State rules and federal rules.* It appears that the State of Washington has modeled its discovery rules on the federal rules. As the federal rules are amended, must the State of Washington adopt those amendments? In other words, is the State of Washington now required to alter its standard of discovery relevance from "subject matter" to "claim or defense" as the federal rules have done? Must the State of Washington recognize the privileges that federal law recognizes? Does your answer to the latter question depend on the source of the privilege (constitutional, statutory, or common law)? Although the U.S. Supreme Court upheld the protective order issued by the trial court in *Seattle Times*, it did entertain the possibility that the order might have violated the First Amendment. Does this mean that federal law limits state procedural rules? To what extent and under what circumstances?

2. *Violations of the protective order.* Suppose the Seattle Times violates the trial court's protective order. What remedies will be available to Mr. Rhinehart? What action can the trial court take? (In answering these questions, assume that the State of Washington's Rule 37 is to the same effect as Federal Rule 37.)

A NOTE ON FEDERAL DISCOVERY TO ASSIST FOREIGN AND INTERNATIONAL TRIBUNALS

This chapter has examined the discovery tools available to litigants in ordinary civil actions brought in the U.S. district courts. In addition, federal courts may sometimes allow discovery in connection with legal or quasi-legal proceedings being conducted by a foreign or international tribunal. This is made possible by 28 U.S.C. § 1782(a), a statute that dates from the mid-nineteenth century. In its current form, § 1782(a), which is entitled "Assistance to foreign and international tribunals and to litigants before such tribunals," provides as follows:

> The district court of the district in which a person resides or is found may order him to give his testimony or statement or to produce a document or other thing for use in a proceeding in a foreign or international tribunal, including criminal investigations conducted before formal accusation. The order may be made pursuant to a letter rogatory issued, or request made, by a foreign or international tribunal or upon the application of any interested person and may direct that the testimony or statement be given, or the document or other thing be produced, before a person appointed by the court. . . . To the extent that the order does not prescribe otherwise, the testimony or statement shall be taken, and the document or other thing produced, in accordance with the Federal Rules of Civil Procedure. . . .

28 U.S.C. § 1782(a).

In *Intel Corp. v. Advanced Micro Devices, Inc.*, 542 U.S. 241 (2004), the Supreme Court construed this statute broadly. In that case, Advanced Micro Devices ("AMD") had filed an antitrust complaint against Intel with the directorate-general for Competition of the Commission of the European Communities

("Commission"). The Commission is an administrative body whose decisions are subject to ultimate review by the European Court of Justice. In its complaint, AMD recommended that the directorate-general seek discovery of documents Intel had produced in a private antitrust action filed in the U.S. District Court for the Northern District of Alabama. After the directorate-general declined to do so, AMD filed an action under § 1782(a) in the U.S. District Court for the Northern District of California, where both Intel and AMD are headquartered, seeking the production of these documents. The Supreme Court agreed that AMD should be allowed to invoke § 1782(a) even though the Commission proceedings might not themselves be strictly judicial in nature, noting that AMD had a right both to submit information to the Commission and to seek subsequent judicial review of the Commission's disposition of its complaint. The Supreme Court also held that § 1782(a) permits the discovery of material even if it would not be discoverable were it located in a foreign jurisdiction and even if it might not be discoverable in domestic U.S. litigation analogous to the foreign proceeding.

The *Intel* Court emphasized, however, that federal judges are not required to grant § 1782(a) discovery applications. In deciding whether or not to do so, a court may consider a number of factors. First, if the person from whom discovery is being sought is a participant in the foreign proceeding, as was the case here, there may be less need to invoke § 1782(a) than if they are a nonparticipant who might be outside the foreign tribunal's jurisdictional reach. Second, a federal court may take into account the foreign tribunal's receptivity to the proposed assistance. Third, the Court cautioned that unduly intrusive or burdensome requests could be trimmed or rejected. Finally, the Court suggested that discovery may be less appropriate if application for discovery involves an effort to circumvent foreign proof-gathering restrictions or other policies of a foreign country or of the United States. As to the latter, the Court noted that the Commission's "Leniency Program" allows participants to confess their wrongdoing in return for prosecutorial leniency, a policy that could potentially be undermined by the use of § 1782(a). And, in terms of U.S. policy, it was potentially relevant that the Alabama federal district court had placed the material sought here under a protective order. The Court remanded the case so that the lower federal courts could determine, in light of these considerations, whether and to what extent the discovery sought here should be granted.

On remand the district court applied the above factors and denied the application. In so doing, the court noted that Intel was a participant in the foreign proceeding, that the Commission had filed amicus briefs objecting to the application, that granting the application would circumvent the Commission's discovery rules, and that the request was burdensome. *Advanced Micro Devices v. Intel Corp.*, 2004 WL 2282320 (N.D. Cal. Oct. 4, 2004). No appeal was taken.

D.   Discovery Review Problem

7-11. Fran Kubelik sued her former employer, IBS, Inc., in a federal district court claiming violations of Title VII of the Civil Rights Act of 1964 ("Title VII"), a federal statute that prohibits various forms of discrimination in the workplace. Ms. Kubelik claims that she was fired because of her sex, a protected category under Title VII, and in retaliation for having filed charges against her employer with the Equal Employment Opportunity Commission (EEOC). The EEOC is a federal agency charged with enforcing Title VII. In terms of remedies, Ms. Kubelik seeks back pay and benefits, future pay and benefits (collectively totaling $13 million), punitive damages, and attorneys' fees. At the time she was fired, Ms. Kubelik's annual salary and benefits package exceeded $500,000. By way of contrast, IBS's most recent quarterly profits were over $700 million. In addition, IBS claims that the most Ms. Kubelik could possibly recover in compensatory damages would be $1.2 million.

In the context of an allegedly unlawful termination of employment based on sex, Title VII requires the plaintiff to prove that she was terminated from her employment and that sex was "a" motivating factor—not necessarily "the" motivating factor—in her employer's decision to fire her. In the context of a claim for unlawful retaliation, Title VII requires the plaintiff to show that she engaged in activity protected by Title VII (*e.g.*, filing charges with the EEOC), that an adverse employment action occurred, and that there was a causal connection between the protected activity and the adverse employment action. (These standards present a "streamlined" version of the actual Title VII standards.)

In her complaint, Ms. Kubelik alleged as follows:

1. Defendant IBS is a Delaware corporation engaged in the international sales of securities.
2. Ms. Kubelik was employed by IBS in its New York office from August 23, 1999 until October 23, 2001 when she was fired by her IBS supervisor.
3. Ms. Kubelik was hired by IBS as a senior salesperson in its United States–based Asian Sales Desk ("the Desk"). At that time, the manager of the Desk was C.C. Baxter, who informed Ms. Kubelik, who was already an experienced securities salesperson, that she would be considered to fill his position on the Desk when he returned to his former position at IBS's London office.
4. On January 29, 2001, Mr. Baxter wrote a performance evaluation of Ms. Kubelik's work and indicated that during the year 2000, Ms. Kubelik had either fully met or exceeded all performance objectives. She received the highest possible rating for "teamwork."
5. Ms. Kubelik was awarded a substantial bonus for her work in 2000, the second highest in the history of the Desk.
6. Mr. Baxter relocated to IBS's London office at the end of January 2001.
7. On information and belief, Ms. Kubelik was not considered for Mr. Baxter's replacement. Instead, IBS hired J. Sheldrake to assume Mr. Baxter's responsibilities.
8. During Mr. Sheldrake's tenure as manager, Ms. Kubelik was the only female senior salesperson working the Desk.
9. From the outset, Mr. Sheldrake treated Ms. Kubelik differently than he treated her male counterparts.

10. Among other things, Mr. Sheldrake ridiculed and belittled Ms. Kubelik in front of co-workers, asking her if "anybody liked her"; excluded her from work-related outings with male co-workers and clients; made sexist remarks in her presence, such as stating that he had "yellow fever," meaning he liked Asian women; instructed Ms. Kubelik not to go to the gym during lunch as it would set a bad precedent, yet placed no such restrictions on male co-workers; and isolated Ms. Kubelik from other senior salespersons (all male) by seating her apart from them.

11. On information and belief, Mr. Sheldrake took no similar actions with regard to any male salesperson.

12. Mr. Sheldrake's discriminatory treatment of Ms. Kubelik was part of the "male" culture at IBS.

13. During this same period of time, male-written peer reviews of Ms. Kubelik instructed her to "smile more" and be "softer," reflecting the view that Ms. Kubelik did not comport with the IBS stereotype of women as passive and accommodating toward men.

14. Ms. Kubelik complained about the above unfair treatment to the managing director of International Equity Sales, the managing director of Global Asian Sales, the executive director of Human Resources, and the associate director of Human Resources.

15. On information and belief, the defendant took no action to discipline Mr. Sheldrake, despite the fact that the executive director of Human Resources agreed that Mr. Sheldrake was "a problem."

16. In July 2001, shortly after Ms. Kubelik had complained to the individuals described in paragraph 14, Mr. Sheldrake retaliated against her by criticizing her in that month's performance review and describing her as insubordinate, unsupportive, and abrasive. Although Ms. Kubelik asked Mr. Sheldrake to provide specific examples, he did not do so.

17. On August 16, 2001, Ms. Kubelik filed a charge of discrimination against IBS with the EEOC, describing Mr. Sheldrake's discriminatory treatment of her.

18. On information and belief, Mr. Sheldrake was made aware of the EEOC charges on August 21, 2001.

19. On October 9, 2001, Ms. Kubelik received a letter signed by Mr. Sheldrake stating that her employment with IBS was terminated as of October 23, 2001.

20. IBS, through its agent, J. Sheldrake, terminated Ms. Kubelik's employment because of her sex and in retaliation for her having filed charges with the EEOC.

Ms. Kubelik's attorney has properly served IBS with a request that IBS "produce all electronically stored information concerning any communications by or between five specified UBS employees from August 1999 to December 2001 concerning the plaintiff." The "specified" group includes Mr. Sheldrake, Mr. Sheldrake's supervisor, an IBS human relations officer who had been assigned to handle issues concerning Ms. Kubelik, and two of Ms. Kubelik's coworkers at the Desk. E-mail was an important means of communication at IBS during the relevant time period. Each salesperson on the Desk, received approximately 200 e-mails each day.

A. Does this request to produce satisfy the standards of Rule 26(b)(1) and Rule 34(a)(1)(A)?

B. What should IBS do if some of the e-mails involve discussions between Mr. Sheldrake and an IBS in-house counsel regarding Ms. Kubelik's EEOC charges?

In response to the above request, IBS produced 100 pages of e-mails, all of which were retrieved from readily accessible online sources. IBS did not, however, search its backup system. Under that system, which is required by the Securities and Exchange Commission, "deleted" e-mails are preserved each month to backup tapes. These tapes are kept for three years and then destroyed. Restoration of an undestroyed tape takes approximately five days. A total of 77 backup tapes held by IBS potentially included e-mails that fall within the request to produce. IBS estimates that the cost of doing such a search would be $300,000. Ms. Kubelik has filed a motion to compel IBS to search all 77 backup tapes for purposes of responding to her discovery request.

C. Which sections (or subsections) of the federal rules are relevant to resolving this question? How should the district court rule on this motion?

D. What should IBS do if some of the e-mail exchanges between Mr. Sheldrake and in-house counsel (noted above) were inadvertently included in the 100 pages of e-mails provided to Ms. Kubelik? Which federal rule or rules are pertinent to answering this question?

Suppose that in response to Ms. Kubelik's motion to compel, the district court orders IBS to produce, at its expense, e-mails responsive to the request to produce from any five backup tapes selected by Ms. Kubelik and to prepare an affidavit detailing the results of its search, as well as the time and money spent.

E. Why, in terms of federal discovery principles, would the district court make such an order? (You might want to consult the Advisory Committee Notes quoted at page 598, *supra*.)

IBS has now complied with the district court's order regarding the five backup tapes. The results of that compliance are as follows: The search of the five selected backup tapes reveals 800 pages of e-mails responsive to the request to produce. The total cost of the restoration and search (including attorney and paralegal time) was $20,000. IBS estimates the cost of restoring and searching the remaining 72 tapes to be $275,000; of that figure, $100,000 is attributable to attorney and paralegal time. IBS now requests either that no further restoration be required or that the cost of any further restoration and search be shifted to Ms. Kubelik. In response, Ms.

Kubelik cites 68 e-mails produced in the sample restoration and search as "highly relevant" to her claims. Some of those e-mails reflect facts that refute assertions made by IBS in defense of the EEOC charges, some involve discussions of how to best phrase complaints about Ms. Kubelik, some attest to the positive quality of Ms. Kubelik's performance (including one from Mr. Sheldrake), and others reveal the hostility between Mr. Sheldrake and Ms. Kubelik. In addition, the restoration revealed that Mr. Sheldrake had deleted e-mails from online sources after the EEOC charges had been filed and after IBS attorneys had advised him to save all materials pertaining to Ms. Kubelik. Accordingly, Ms. Kubelik asks the court to order the restoration and search of the remaining 72 backup tapes and that IBS bear the entire cost.

F. How would you advise the court to rule on these matters?

There are seven published opinions from the case on which this problem is (roughly) based. The key (and foundational) e-discovery opinions are *Zubulake v. UBS Warburg, LLC*, 217 F.R.D. 309 (S.D.N.Y. May 13, 2003) and 216 F.R.D. 280 (S.D.N.Y. July 24, 2003). If you're interested in the case overall, the other pretrial opinions, some of which also pertain to discovery and related evidentiary problems, can be found at 382 F. Supp. 2d 536 (S.D.N.Y. Mar. 16, 2005), 231 F.R.D. 159 (S.D.N.Y. Feb. 3, 2005), 229 F.R.D. 422 (S.D.N.Y. July 20, 2004), 220 F.R.D. 212 (S.D.N.Y. Oct. 22, 2003), and 230 F.R.D. 290 (S.D.N.Y. May 13, 2003). The case eventually went to trial and a jury awarded the plaintiff $9.1 million in compensatory damages and $20.1 million in punitive damages. Prior to an appeal, the parties settled for an undisclosed amount.

VIII

JOINDER OF CLAIMS AND PARTIES

In a simple lawsuit, a single plaintiff asserts a single claim or right of action against a single defendant. But lawsuits may be more complex than that, and include multiple parties and multiple claims. The rules on joinder of claims and parties govern these more complicated scenarios. The focus of this chapter is on joinder under the federal rules. In applying those rules, we must also attend to the standards of subject matter jurisdiction, which impose constitutional and statutory limitations on the permissible scope of joinder.

A. Precursors to Modern Joinder: Joinder at Common Law, Equity, and Under the Codes

Early American courts were modeled on the British judicial system. Under that system, courts were divided between courts of law and courts of equity. Each set of courts followed distinct procedures and provided distinct remedies. The common law system of joinder was strict and limited, while joinder under equity was open and flexible. Eventually, American courts adopted a uniform procedural system under which the rules of joinder borrowed heavily from the more liberal system of joinder used by the courts of equity.

1. Joinder at Common Law

The system of joinder used by the English common law courts—*i.e.*, King's Bench, Common Pleas, and the Exchequer—made it difficult for a plaintiff to join together claims that arose from the same underlying incident or to include multiple plaintiffs or multiple defendants as parties in the same action.

Under the common law, a plaintiff could ordinarily join together different claims or causes of action only if they involved the same "form of action." The forms of action were original writs issued by the king's chancellor permitting a plaintiff to bring a lawsuit in the common law courts. Only a limited number of forms were available, each designed for a particular type of suit. The forms covering actions based on contract, for example, included the writs of account, assumpsit, covenant, and debt. Other forms covered tort-type actions, including the writs of replevin, trespass, trespass on the case (or "case"), and trover. "The writs were like doors to the king's courts; there was one for big dogs and a smaller one for little dogs; there were doors for yellow dogs and black dogs, and the door of case for mongrel curs of no particular breed, but just plain dogs." Benjamin J. Shipman, Handbook of Common-Law Pleading 60 n.11 (3d ed. 1923). The plaintiff had to select the form or writ most appropriate for her case. Each form of action was accompanied by its own procedures and its own remedies.

If a plaintiff were suing a single defendant, she could include only those claims that involved the same form of action. Such claims could be joined together even if they arose from entirely unrelated incidents. On the other hand, claims that arose from the same set of facts could not be joined together if they involved different forms of action. In *Cooper v. Bissell*, 16 Johns 146 (N.Y. Sup. Ct. 1819), the court reversed a judgment for a plaintiff who had improperly joined a claim for trespass (alleging that the defendant had entered the plaintiff's land and taken his horse) with a claim for trespass on the case (based on the defendant's having refused to return the horse to the plaintiff).

The common law was equally strict when it came to joinder of parties. Several plaintiffs could join together in suing a defendant only if the rights they sought to enforce were "joint." In such a case, joinder was not merely proper but mandatory. Under the common law, a similar rule barred plaintiffs from including more than one defendant in an action except when the defendants' obligations to the plaintiff were jointly held.

2.   Joinder in Equity

The rules governing joinder of claims and parties in the courts of equity or Chancery were far more liberal than those employed at common law. This reflected a number of fundamental differences between law and equity. First, equity by its nature was flexible, designed to afford justice in situations in which the rigidity of the common law left litigants without adequate remedies. Second, courts of equity were not tied to the forms of action. A plaintiff commenced a suit in equity simply by filing a petition that set forth the facts of her grievance. Unlike the common law, whose procedures and remedies varied depending on which form of action was involved, equity employed the same procedures in all cases, thereby making joinder of different claims far more feasible. Finally, because suits in equity were decided by the chancellor, rather than by a jury as was true of some common law actions, the risk that liberal joinder of claims and parties would lead to confusion was greatly diminished.

Courts of equity sought to resolve an entire controversy in one proceeding. The chancellor had broad discretion to allow joinder of claims and parties when the claims arose from the same transaction or when the claims, though arising from different transactions, all concerned the same subject matter. Equity in fact *required* that plaintiffs join all persons who would be directly affected by a judgment. In addition, it *permitted* plaintiffs to join other parties when the matters could be conveniently tried together. *See* Charles E. Clark, Handbook of the

Law of Code Pleading 353-357, 379, 437 (2d ed. 1947). In explaining equity's liberal approach to joinder, the Supreme Court noted that

> [e]very case must be governed by its own circumstances; and as these are as diversified as the names of the parties, the court must exercise a sound discretion on the subject. Whilst parties should not be subjected to expense and inconvenience, in litigating matters in which they have no interest, multiplicity of suits should be avoided, by uniting in one bill all who have an interest in the principal matter in controversy, though the interests may have arisen under distinct contracts.

Gaines v. Chew, 43 U.S. (2 How.) 619, 642 (1844). For example, equity allowed owners of separate properties to join together as plaintiffs in a suit to enjoin a nuisance that harmed each of them. It also permitted a plaintiff, in seeking to set aside fraudulent conveyances of land he claimed to own, to join as defendants all persons who claimed a portion of the land even if they acquired their interests in the land at different times and under separate conveyances.

3. Joinder Under the Codes

The English rules that governed proceedings at common law and in equity operated in the United States long after the American colonies declared their independence in 1776. Until the mid-nineteenth century, many states maintained separate courts of law and equity. Other states had single courts but administered law and equity separately. Finally in 1846, New York abolished its court of equity and, two years later, enacted the Field Code. The Field Code eliminated the distinction between actions at law and actions in equity. It also abolished the forms of action, by providing that there was "but one form of action, for the enforcement or protection of private rights and the redress of private wrongs, which shall be denominated a civil action." N.Y. Laws 1848, ch. 379, § 69. In merging law and equity, the Field Code sought to ensure that a litigant could obtain all of the relief to which it was entitled in a single lawsuit, instead of having to sue separately at law and in equity, or make a choice between the two systems. By the end of the nineteenth century, more than half the states had followed New York's lead by enacting similar codes of their own. *See* Fleming James, Jr., Civil Procedure 16-17 (1965); Clark, *supra*, at 21-31. One significant feature of the codes was that many of them were influenced by equity's liberal approach to joinder of claims and parties.

The codes divided claims or causes of action into a number of classes. Plaintiffs could assert all claims against a defendant that fell into the same class, regardless of whether the claims were legal or equitable in nature. The typical code provision, modeled after that of New York, contained eight classes. A plaintiff in suing a defendant could "unite in the same complaint several causes of action" when they all involved (1) contracts, express or implied; (2) injuries to the person; (3) injuries to the character; (4) injuries to property; (5) actions to recover real property; (6) actions to recover chattels; (7) claims against a trustee; or (8) actions arising from the same transaction, or transactions connected with the same subject of the action. The codes thus borrowed from the common law by permitting joinder of claims of the same type, *e.g.*, all contract claims, all claims for injury to person, etc. They also borrowed from equity by permitting plaintiffs, under class (8), to join all claims that arose from the same transaction or from distinct transactions that related to the same subject. This last class was added to the New York code in 1852. In each of the code states the number of classes varied. Some combined several classes into one, while only about half of the codes included the equity-based "same transaction" class. CLARK, *supra*, at 441 & n.20.

While the codes sought to liberalize the joinder of *claims*, they were only partly successful in doing so. We noted earlier that a plaintiff at common law could join together all claims for trespass on the case, even if they covered injuries to person, character, and property. Yet under the New York code, for example, these claims fell into separate classes—(2), (3), and (4). A plaintiff would therefore have to sue on them separately unless, under class (8), they were all deemed to arise from the same transaction, or from different transactions connected with the same subject. Moreover, the potentially liberalizing effect of the "same transaction" class was sometimes undermined by courts that interpreted the language of class (8) in a highly restrictive fashion. *See* CLARK, *supra*, at 452-456.

The code provisions governing joinder of *parties* likewise failed to replicate the liberal approach followed by courts of equity. This resulted partly from the fact that, as with joinder of claims by one plaintiff suing one defendant, claims involving multiple plaintiffs or multiple defendants all had to fall within the same code class. In addition, the codes required that each claim had to affect all parties to the action. Finally, under the codes, several plaintiffs could join together only if they each had an interest in the subject of the action *and* in the relief demanded. Essentially, these rules and their restrictive interpretations by the courts allowed joinder of parties only when the parties had joint interests in the subject matter of the suit.

In short, despite the goal of liberalizing joinder of claims and parties, joinder under the codes was often no broader than that permitted at common law and sometimes less so. In many code states, the discretion that courts of equity had enjoyed to effect liberal joinder as a means of settling a controversy in one proceeding all but disappeared. *See* William W. Blume, *The Scope of a Civil Action*, 42 MICH. L. REV. 257, 262-264 (1943); CLARK, *supra*, at 358-368, 380-388; 7 CHARLES ALAN WRIGHT, ARTHUR R. MILLER & MARY KAY KANE, FEDERAL PRACTICE AND PROCEDURE § 1651 (3d ed. 2001 & Supp. 2015).

It was against this backdrop that the federal rules were proposed in 1934 and implemented four years later. Until that time, the Conformity Act of 1872 had required federal courts in actions at law to apply the procedures of the state in which they sat, including the state's rules governing joinder of claims and parties. Learning from the experience of the states, the drafters of the federal rules succeeded in effecting a truly liberal system of joinder that has enabled the federal courts to realize equity's goal of resolving disputes in as efficient a manner as possible.

B. Joinder of Claims by Plaintiffs and Defendants Under the Federal Rules

1. Claims and Counterclaims

The federal rules allow complete and unrestricted joinder of claims between plaintiffs and defendants. Rule 18(a) thus provides that a plaintiff "may join, as independent or alternative claims, as many claims" as she has against a defendant. FED. R. CIV. P. 18(a). The same rule, along with Rule 13(a) and (b), permits a defendant to assert as a "counterclaim" any claim he may have against the plaintiff. Read Rules 18(a) and 13(a) through (c).

As we have noted, even though the rules of *joinder* permit the liberal joinder of claims, a federal court may entertain those claims only if the court has jurisdiction over the claim or claims asserted and the parties joined. Hence any asserted claim must satisfy either an independent basis of jurisdiction, such as federal question or diversity jurisdiction, 28 U.S.C. §§ 1331 & 1332, or must fall within the court's supplemental jurisdiction under § 1367.

In addition, venue must be proper as to each claim asserted by the plaintiff. This usually poses no obstacle to joinder if venue is based on 28 U.S.C. § 1391(b)(1). That section provides that venue is proper in a district in which any defendant resides if all defendants reside in the same state. In these cases, a defendant's residence in the selected district renders venue proper as to all claims asserted against that defendant (or any of the defendants) by the plaintiff. On the other hand, if venue is established under § 1391(b)(2) (a "district in which a substantial part of the events or omissions giving rise to the claim occurred"), venue may be proper for one claim but not for others. In such situations, plaintiff may still ask the court to invoke the discretionary doctrine of "pendent venue" if the claims are otherwise factually related. *See* Georgene Vairo, *Determination of Proper Venue, in* 17 MOORE'S FEDERAL PRACTICE § 110.05 (3d ed. 2015). With respect to a defendant's counterclaims, since the plaintiff chose the federal court in question, the plaintiff is deemed to have waived any objection to venue on those counterclaims. *See* Edward F. Sherman & Mary P. Squiers, *Counterclaim and Cross-Claim, in* 3 MOORE'S FEDERAL PRACTICE § 13.113 (3d ed. 2015); 6 CHARLES ALAN WRIGHT, ARTHUR R. MILLER & MARY KAY KANE, FEDERAL PRACTICE AND PROCEDURE § 1424 (3d ed. 2010 & Supp. 2015).

PROBLEMS

8-1. Paul and Ted were roommates at a college in New York City. During their four years together there, Paul loaned Ted a total of $10,000 that Ted never repaid. In their sophomore year, Ted caused $15,000 damage to Paul's car after borrowing it for a weekend. In their junior year, Ted destroyed Paul's $2,000 computer while testing the law of gravity. By the time the two had graduated and parted company, Ted also owed Paul $50,000 in telephone bills. Paul sued Ted in the federal court for the Southern District of New York, asserting claims to recover for the unpaid loans, the car damage, the destroyed computer, and the telephone bills. Paul is a citizen of California. Ted is a citizen of New Jersey. Under Rule 18, did Paul have a right to join these claims together in his suit against Ted? If joinder was proper, does the federal court have subject matter jurisdiction over the case? Finally, if both joinder and subject matter jurisdiction were proper, is venue satisfied as to each of Paul's claims?

8-2. In Problem 8-1, do the federal rules allow Ted to assert against Paul a claim for $25,000 in injuries suffered in an auto accident when the two were driving in Paul's car in Connecticut the day before graduation? Is Ted required to assert this claim or is his doing so optional? Assuming joinder of Ted's claim is allowed by the federal rules, does the federal court have subject matter jurisdiction and proper venue as to the claim?

Counterclaims are responsive claims in the sense that they are filed in response to a claim previously filed against the counterclaimant in the pending action. For example, and most typically, a defendant might file a counterclaim against a plaintiff as in Problem 8-2. The federal rules distinguish between "compulsory" counterclaims and "permissive" counterclaims. A compulsory counterclaim is one that must be asserted, while a permissive counterclaim is one that may, but need not, be asserted. Rule 13(a)(1) defines a compulsory counterclaim as

> any claim that—at the time of service—the pleader has against an opposing party if the claim: (A) arises out of the transaction or occurrence that is the subject matter of the opposing party's claim; and (B) does not require adding another party over whom the court cannot acquire jurisdiction.

FED. R. CIV. P. 13(a)(1)(A)-(B). Rule 13(a)(2) then provides two exceptions, one for claims that are pending in a previously filed action and one pertaining to *in rem* actions. *See* Note 5, following the next principal case, *infra*. All other counterclaims—*i.e.*, those not compulsory by virtue of Rule 13(a)'s definition and exceptions—are permissive. As to that category, Rule 13(b) provides that "[a] pleading may state as a counterclaim against an opposing party any claim that is not compulsory." FED. R. CIV. P. 13(b). As you will see, the key distinction between compulsory and permissive counterclaims lies in how one interprets and applies the phrase "same transaction or occurrence."

Law Offices of Jerris Leonard, P.C. v. Mideast Systems, Ltd.
111 F.R.D. 359 (D.D.C. 1986)

GASCH, DISTRICT JUDGE . . . .

I.   FACTS

[The Law Offices of Jerris Leonard, P.C. ("Leonard") represented Mideast Systems and China Civil Construction ("MS/CCC") in government contracts litigation with the U.S. Department of the Interior ("Department"), litigation that MS/CCC lost. When MS/CCC failed to pay him his attorneys' fees, Leonard sued MS/CCC in federal court to recover them ("the *Jerris Leonard* matter"). After MS/CCC ignored that proceeding, a default judgment was entered against it in August 1985 for $72,000. Thereafter, in June 1986, MS/CCC sued Leonard for legal malpractice in a New York state court. That malpractice claim alleged that the Department had offered to settle the earlier suit against MS/CCC for $100,000; that on Leonard's advice MS/CCC declined to accept the offer; and that the Department then recovered a much larger judgment against it. After being served in the state court malpractice action, Leonard returned to federal court and sought declaratory relief to the effect that MS/CCC's state court malpractice claim was a compulsory counterclaim in the *Jerris Leonard* matter and that, as a result, the malpractice claim was now barred from being litigated in the New York state court.]

II.   DISCUSSION

Rule 13(a) states in relevant part:

> A pleading shall state as a counterclaim any claim which at the time of serving the pleading the pleader has against any opposing party, if it arises out of the transaction or occurrence that is the subject matter of the opposing party's claim and does not require for its adjudication the presence of third parties of whom the court cannot acquire jurisdiction.*

"The purpose of the rule is 'to prevent multiplicity of actions and to achieve resolution in a single lawsuit of all disputes arising out of common matters.'" The Supreme Court has given the rule's operative terms, "transaction or occurrence," broad meaning: They "may comprehend a series of many occurrences, depending not so much upon the immediateness of their connection as upon their *logical relationship*." *Moore v. New York Cotton Exchange*, 270 U.S. 593, 610 (1926) (emphasis added). Where the factual claims in two actions indicate that evidence offered in both claims is likely to be substantially identical, the claim should be adjudicated in a single forum.

Under this standard, it is hard to imagine a clearer compulsory counterclaim to a complaint for failure to pay legal fees than a legal malpractice claim stemming from the handling of the litigation for which fees are sought. The party raising the malpractice claim is in effect asserting a defense of failure to perform to the lawyer's claim for breach of contract. The testimony and documents necessary to litigate both claims are likely to be substantially the same. Several courts have held that a tort action stemming out of the same transaction as a breach of contract claim is a compulsory counterclaim to the contract action. *Crutcher v. Aetna Life Insurance Co.*, 746 F.2d 1076, 1080 (5th Cir. 1984) (suit for breach of

---

* [Since this case was decided, the language of Rule 13(a) has changed from that quoted in the court's opinion. The change in wording was stylistic only. The current version of the Rule 13(a) appears in the text preceding this case. — EDS.]

fiduciary duty and tortious interference is compulsory counterclaim to action to recover on guaranty); *Cleckner v. Republic Van & Storage Co.*, 556 F.2d 766 (5th Cir. 1977) (negligence claim for damage to goods is compulsory counterclaim to suit by movers for failure to pay); *In re McCoy*, 373 F. Supp. 870, 873 (D. Tex. 1974) (medical malpractice claim is compulsory counterclaim to suit for unpaid doctor's fees); *Black v. Dillon*, 28 Cal. Rptr. 678, 679 (Cal. App. 3rd Dist. 1963) (same). In the case at bar, the legal malpractice claim has a very close logical relationship to the claim for legal fees owed for the same litigation; thus it is a compulsory counterclaim under Rule 13(a).

If a party fails to plead a compulsory counterclaim while litigation is pending, it is forever barred from raising the claim. This is true even if the party defaulted, as did MS/CCC. Defendants who have a valid default judgment entered against them may be barred from raising compulsory counterclaims in subsequent state court litigation.

[MS/CCC] argues that Rule 13(a) is wholly inapplicable to [it] because MS/CCC never served a pleading in the *Jerris Leonard* matter, and the rule speaks of "pleadings." If this is another way of arguing that Rule 13(a) is inapplicable where a party has a default judgment entered against it, [the law is] otherwise . . . . The fact that a party declines to appear does not prevent the default judgment from being set up as res judicata against it, barring subsequent counterclaims. The comments to the rule also make it clear that the rule was designed to prevent just such a scenario as [defense counsel contends] it permits:

> [T]he subdivision . . . insures against the undesirable possibility . . . whereby a party having a claim which would be the subject of a compulsory counterclaim could avoid stating it as such by bringing an independent action in another court after the commencement of the federal action . . . .

Rule 13(a), 1946 Amendment, Note to Subdivision (a).

Rule 13(a) does not bar a party from later raising a compulsory counterclaim that matured after the original pleading. Mr. Abrahams, [MS/CCC's new attorney], appears to argue that MS/CCC's claim for legal malpractice until he, as the entity's new lawyer, discovered facts which would be the basis for such a claim . . . .

Perhaps Mr. Abrahams is attempting to invoke the "discovery rule," which is that a cause of action for legal malpractice does not "until the client knows or should know all material facts essential to show the elements of that cause of action." . . . Examining the complaint filed in [the legal malpractice action in state court], the Court ascertains that all the facts alleged concerning the lawyers' representation of MS/CCC in the district court litigation were known or should have been known to MS/CCC at the time the *Jerris Leonard* suit was filed. . . . When MS/CCC was sued for nonpayment of legal feels in the *Jerris Leonard* matter, it was put on notice that the reasonableness of the fees charged would be an issue. . . .

Furthermore, Mr. Abrahams cites no case, and the Court knows of none, that holds that the discovery rule applies to the date when a plaintiff-client's new attorney discovers the facts underlying a malpractice claim, as opposed to the plaintiff-client itself.

III.   CONCLUSION

In sum, the legal malpractice claim as framed by MS/CCC in the New York complaint [was] a compulsory counterclaim in the *Jerris Leonard* suit. As MS/CCC knew or should have known of the existence of a potential claim at the time its answer was due in this Court, but instead chose to suffer default judgment, the Court finds that MS/CCC is now barred by Rule 13(a) from raising the claim, and it will so declare . . . .

ORDERED that a declaratory judgment be entered in favor of plaintiffs and against defendants holding that the lawsuit initiated by defendant [MS/CCC] against plaintiffs in this action in the Supreme Court of the State of New York on June 12, 1986, should have been brought as a compulsory counterclaim in this action, but now is forever barred under Rule 13(a) of the Federal Rules of Civil Procedure from being raised in this case or in any other legal action because final judgment on this matter was entered against MS/CCC and in favor of plaintiffs by this Court on August 2, 1985 . . . .

NOTES AND QUESTIONS

1. *The "logical relation" test.*   The court in *Jerris Leonard* described the "logical relation" test as setting the framework for determining whether a claim is compulsory within the meaning of Rule 13(a), *i.e.*, using the language of current Rule 13(a)(1)(A), whether that claim "arises out of the transaction or occurrence that is the subject matter of the opposing party's claim." FED. R. CIV. P. 13(a)(1)(A). On what basis did the court determine that the fee claim and the malpractice claim were logically related? Would the litigation of those claims in a single proceeding have promoted efficiency? Was the court's ruling unfair to MS/CCC? In answering this question, keep in mind the vintage of Rule 13(a)—1938—and of the logical-relation test—1926. To what extent is the logical-relation test similar to the operative-facts definition of a claim?

2. *Of defaults and Rule 13(a).*   Rule 13(a)(1)(A) requires that "a pleading state" any transactionally related claim the pleader has against an opposing party. But MS/CCC did not file a pleading. Rather, MS/CCC took a default. Hence MS/CCC argued that the requirements of Rule 13(a) had not been triggered. Why did the court reject this argument? What would be the general consequences if courts were to adopt the view urged by MS/CCC? The approach adopted by the *Jerris Leonard* court with respect to the preclusive effect of defaults reflects the well-established view. *See* 3 MOORE'S FEDERAL PRACTICE, *supra*, § 13.14[3]; 6 WRIGHT, MILLER & KANE, *supra*, § 1417 & n.13.

3. *Consequences of failing to assert a compulsory counterclaim in general.*   Even though the text of Rule 13(a) is silent as to the consequences of failing to plead

a compulsory counterclaim, the Advisory Committee Notes to the original rule state that "[i]f the action proceeds to judgment without the interposition of a counterclaim as required by subdivision (a) . . . the counterclaim is barred." This was the approach adopted by the *Jerris Leonard* court. Why didn't the arguments of MS/CCC warrant the court's granting it relief from the consequences of the compulsory counterclaim rule?

4. *The practical consequences of the declaratory judgment in* Jerris Leonard. The practical effect of the order issued in *Jerris Leonard* was to bar assertion of the malpractice claim in the pending New York lawsuit. While state courts are not bound by the federal rules, they are required to give full faith and credit to a federal court's judgment, just as they must give full faith and credit to the judgments of their sister states' courts. *See* U.S. Const. art. IV, § 1. This means that the state court must give the federal default judgment the same scope and effect as the federal court would give that judgment. In short, the state court must bar the malpractice action. We will examine "intersystem" preclusion further in Chapter XIII, at pages 1152-1155, *infra.*

5. *Exceptions to the compulsory counterclaim rule.* Rule 13(a) identifies a number of situations in which counterclaims are not compulsory and thus need not be asserted even though they arise from the same "transaction or occurrence" as the opposing party's claim:

A. Claims that a defendant (or potential counterclaimant) did not possess at the time she served her responsive pleading and that matured or were acquired only later. Fed. R. Civ. P. 13(a)(1).
B. Claims that require the presence of third parties over whom the court cannot acquire jurisdiction. Fed. R. Civ. P. 13(a)(1)(B).
C. Claims that were the subject of another pending action at the time the federal action was commenced. Fed. R. Civ. P. 13(a)(2)(A).
D. Claims by a defendant over whom the court has obtained only *in rem* or *quasi in rem* jurisdiction, if that defendant has not filed any other counterclaims against the plaintiff. Fed. R. Civ. P. 13(a)(2)(B).

Which one of these exceptions did the defendant in *Jerris Leonard* seek to invoke? Why did the court reject that argument?

6. *Amendment to assert an omitted counterclaim.* The federal rules allow a party some leeway to amend a pleading and to include an omitted counterclaim in that amended pleading. Specifically, a party may amend a pleading "once as a matter of course" so long as the amendment is made within the time constraints specified in Rule 15(a)(1)(A) and (B). Any subsequent attempt to amend a pleading beyond the time constraints imposed by subsection (a)(1) may be made "only with the opposing party's written consent or the court's leave," the latter to be granted "freely . . . when justice so requires." Fed. R. Civ. P. 15(a)(2). If a counterclaim is newly asserted as part of an amended pleading and arises out of the same transaction as the original claim asserted against the counterclaimant, the amendment will "relate back" to the date on which the counterclaimant's initial pleading was filed, thereby avoiding any potential statute of limitations complications that might otherwise result from the omission. Fed. R. Civ. P. 15(c)(1)((B).

In the *Jerris Leonard* case, why couldn't MS/CCC invoke Rule 15 in order to belatedly assert its legal malpractice counterclaim against Jerris Leonard? Had MS/CCC filed a pleading that could have been amended?

Burlington Northern Railroad Co. v. Strong

907 F.2d 707 (7th Cir. 1990)

RIPPLE, Circuit Judge.

John Strong sued his employer, Burlington Northern Railroad Company (Burlington), alleging personal injury tort damages. A jury awarded Mr. Strong $73,000. Thereafter, Burlington moved to set off against the judgment money received by Mr. Strong from a disability insurance program funded by Burlington. The district court denied this motion. Burlington then brought a separate suit to recover the funds. Summary judgment in favor of Burlington for the entire amount of the disability funds was entered on November 30, 1988. Mr. Strong appeals from the district court's judgment in the second suit. For the following reasons, we affirm. . . .

Mr. Strong was a member of the Brotherhood of Maintenance of Way Employees during his employment with Burlington. The union operated under a collective bargaining agreement that applied to all union employees the provisions of the Supplemental Sickness Benefit Agreement of 1973 (1973 Agreement). In turn, the 1973 Agreement provided that the Supplemental Sickness Benefits (SSB) received by employees would not duplicate recovery of lost wages from a disability case.

Mr. Strong was injured in two separate accidents on September 12, 1983 and March 5, 1985 during his employment with Burlington. He brought suit against Burlington to recover for these injuries under the Federal Employers Liability Act (FELA), 45 U.S.C. §§ 51-60. Following a jury trial, Mr. Strong was awarded $73,000 in compensation for the 1983 injury; Burlington was found not liable for the 1985 injury.

After the trial, Burlington moved for a determination that the amount of the judgment ought to be reduced by $11,678.21, the amount paid to Mr. Strong in SSB benefits. The district court held that, "in the absence of a lien or judgment in its favor, [Burlington] is not entitled to withhold the sum of $11,678.21 for any Supplemental Sickness Benefit paid to [Mr. Strong]." . . . However, the district court suggested that Mr. Strong could not succeed in keeping the money if Burlington sued on the contract:

> I note that plaintiff's recalcitrance in refusing to remit the $11,678.21 sum allegedly paid out as Supplemental Sickness Benefit payments may well have adverse consequences for plaintiff himself. . . . [I]t seems clear that defendant can sue on the contract to recover this amount of money from plaintiff, and that if it does so, plaintiff will be subject to additional and probably unnecessary costs for defending a new lawsuit.

Taking its cue from the district court, Burlington sued on the contract to recover the SSB payments. Mr. Strong argued that the railroad's suit was barred by *res judicata* because such a claim should have been brought as a compulsory counterclaim to the previous FELA suit. However, the court decided that the railroad's claim was a permissive, not compulsory, counterclaim: "Burlington Northern's right to recoup the disability benefits does not arise out of the same occurrence (the accidents) that gave rise to Strong's lawsuit; it derives from the provisions of the Supplemental Sickness Benefit Agreement of May 12, 1973." . . . The court further decided that, even if the claim could be said to be related to the same occurrence, an exception for claims that had not matured at the time of filing the answer would apply. . . .

Mr. Strong argues that Burlington's claim for setoff was a compulsory counterclaim that was waived when Burlington failed to raise it during the first trial (Mr. Strong's FELA trial). Rule 13(a) is "in some ways a harsh rule": if a counterclaim is compulsory and the party does not bring it in the original lawsuit, that claim is thereafter barred. . . . But the rule serves a valuable role in the litigation process, especially in conserving judicial resources. As we have noted, Rule 13(a) "is the result of a balancing between competing interests. The convenience of the party with a compulsory counterclaim is sacrificed in the interest of judicial economy." *Martino v. McDonald's Sys., Inc.*, 598 F.2d 1079, 1082 (7th Cir.), *cert. denied*, 444 U.S. 966 (1979). . . .

In order to be a compulsory counterclaim, Rule 13(a) requires that the claim (1) exist at the time of pleading, (2) arise out of the same transaction or occurrence as the opposing party's claim, and (3) not require for adjudication parties over whom the court may not acquire jurisdiction. There is no dispute that the third element—no required third parties—is met in this case. Our disposition therefore must turn on whether the other two requirements are met. We shall discuss them in the same order as the district court: (1) the same transaction and (2) the existence at the time of pleading requirements.

This court has developed a "logical relationship" test to determine whether the "transaction or occurrence" is the same for purposes of Rule 13(a).

> "Courts generally have agreed that the words 'transaction or occurrence' should be interpreted liberally in order to further the general policies of the federal rules and carry out the philosophy of Rule 13(a). . . . As a word of flexible meaning, 'transaction' may comprehend a series of many occurrences, depending not so much upon the immediateness of their connection as upon their logical relationship. . . . [A] counterclaim that has its roots in a separate transaction or occurrence is permissive and is governed by Rule 13(b)."

Gilldorn Sav. Assn. v. Commerce Sav. Assn., 804 F.2d 390, 396 (7th Cir. 1986). Despite this liberal construction, we have stressed that our inquiry cannot be a "'wooden application of the common transaction label.'" [*Id.* at 397.] Rather, we must examine carefully the factual allegations underlying each claim to determine if the logical relationship test is met. . . .

In short, there is no formalistic test to determine whether suits are logically related. A court should consider the totality of the claims, including the nature of the claims, the legal basis for recovery, the law involved, and the respective factual backgrounds.

Even when a counterclaim meets the "same transaction" test, a party need not assert it as a compulsory counterclaim if it has not matured when the party serves his answer. This maturity exception "is derived from the language in the rule limiting its application to claims the pleader has 'at the time of serving the pleading.'" 6 C. Wright, A. Miller & M. Kane, Federal Practice and Procedure § 1411, at 81 (2d ed. 1990). "This exception to the compulsory counterclaim requirement necessarily encompasses a claim that depends upon the outcome of some other lawsuit and thus does not come into existence until the action upon which it is based has terminated." *Id.* at 82.

We believe, in light of the foregoing principles, that the district court correctly concluded that Burlington's claim was not a compulsory counterclaim. We agree with the district court that the claims do not arise out of the same transaction. Burlington's right to recoup does not arise out of the same occurrence that gave rise to Mr. Strong's earlier suit. His suit is grounded in the accidents that resulted in his injury. By contrast, Burlington's suit is grounded in the provisions of the Supplemental Sickness Benefit Agreement of May 12, 1973. The two claims "raise different legal and factual issues governed by different bodies of law." "Judicial economy would not be well served in this case as these two actions are based on separate transactions. . . ." They "lack any shared realm of genuine dispute."

We also agree with the district court that, even if we were to assume, *arguendo*, that these claims involve the same transaction, Burlington's claim need not have been brought as a counterclaim. It did not exist until the conclusion of the first suit when Mr. Strong obtained his judgment. Thus, the so-called "maturity exception" would permit the maintenance of this second suit. Accordingly, the district court properly determined that the railroad's claim is a permissive counterclaim that was not waived by Burlington's failure to plead it in the FELA case. . . .

For the foregoing reasons, we affirm the judgment of the district court.

Affirmed.

NOTES AND QUESTIONS

1. *The "logical relationship" test revisited.* Like the *Jerris Leonard* court, the *Burlington* court relied on the logical-relationship test in applying Rule 13(a). The court in *Jerris Leonard* focused on the factual congruence of the fee and malpractice claims. On what factors did the *Burlington* court focus? What, as a practical matter, do these decisions tell you about the scope and application of the logical-relationship test? Are these decisions reconcilable? Would Burlington's counterclaim have been compulsory if, in his FELA action, Strong had also sought a declaratory judgment that any FELA benefits he recovered should not be reduced by the amount of the SSB benefits he had already received? Would that make the *Burlington* case more like the situation faced by the court in *Jerris Leonard*? In other words, would Strong's additional claim create a more substantial factual congruence with the railroad's potential counterclaim?

A NOTE ON SUPPLEMENTAL JURISDICTION AND COUNTERCLAIMS

As we have noted, every claim asserted in a federal court must satisfy the requirements for subject matter jurisdiction and, of course, this principle applies to counterclaims. Hence a counterclaim must either satisfy an independent basis of jurisdiction—*e.g.*, federal question or diversity—or fall within the scope of supplemental jurisdiction. The focus of this note is on the relationship between counterclaims and supplemental jurisdiction.

In the context of compulsory counterclaims, the inquiry is relatively simple. A counterclaim that satisfies the standards of Rule 13(a)(1)(A) will automatically satisfy the "same-case-or-controversy" (or "common-nucleus-of-fact") standard established in the supplemental jurisdiction statute, 28 U.S.C. § 1367(a). Either the rule and statutory tests are identical or the statutory standard is slightly more generous (*i.e.*, of a broader sweep) than the rule standard and thereby embraces all claims that satisfy the rule. There may be some small jurisdictional wrinkles in a diversity suit when a plaintiff files a counterclaim against a nondiverse third party, but we will attend to those later. Suffice it to say that when a defendant files a counterclaim that arises out of the same transaction or occurrence as the plaintiff's jurisdictionally sufficient claim, the standards of supplemental jurisdiction are satisfied.

The landscape is somewhat more complicated for permissive counterclaims. A counterclaim will be deemed permissive if it does not arise out of the same transaction or occurrence as an opposing party's claim, or if it falls into one of the exceptions listed in Rule 13(a)(1) and (2). If the counterclaim's permissive nature is due to the fact that it does not arise out of the same transaction or occurrence as an opposing party's claim and there is no independent basis of jurisdiction over that counterclaim, the automatic satisfaction of supplemental jurisdiction cannot be presumed. Indeed, up until recently, such permissive counterclaims were automatically deemed jurisdictionally deficient. In essence, Rule 13(a)'s same-transaction test and § 1367(a)'s common-nucleus test were treated as being synonymous, and the failure to satisfy one was deemed a failure to satisfy the other. A majority of courts still follow this view.

However, a growing number of courts, including at least three circuit courts, have adopted a slightly different approach. These courts hold that the § 1367(a) standard is slightly more generous than the same-transaction standard of Rule 13(a)(1)(A). Hence, according to these courts, under a narrow range of circumstances, a counterclaim may not be sufficiently related to an opposing party's claim to satisfy the same transaction test, rendering that counterclaim permissive, but may be sufficiently related to that claim to satisfy the standards of supplemental jurisdiction. *See Global NAPs, Inc. v. Verizon New England Inc.*, 603 F.3d 71 (1st Cir. 2010) *cert. denied*, 562 U.S. 1200 (2011); *Jones v. Ford Motor Credit Co.*, 358 F.3d 205 (2d Cir. 2004); *Channell v. Citicorp Nat'l Servs., Inc.*, 89 F.3d 379 (7th Cir. 1996). Such a counterclaim is, therefore, both permissive and jurisdictionally sufficient. Courts adopting this approach, however, appear to be more willing to decline the exercise of supplemental jurisdiction under the discretionary standards established in § 1367(c). In many cases, therefore, this new twist on permissive counterclaims will make no practical difference.

In sum, a compulsory counterclaim as defined by Rule 13(a)(1)(A) will, by definition, satisfy the jurisdictional standards of § 1367(a). This principle is universally accepted. With respect to permissive counterclaims that are not transactionally related to an opposing party's claim, a majority of courts treat the standards of Rule 13(a)(1)(A) and § 1367(a) as being synonymous and thereby preclude the application of supplemental jurisdiction to those claims. In these courts, a permissive counterclaim may thus be filed only if it rests on an independent basis of jurisdiction. A minority of courts, however, treat the standards of § 1367(a) as slightly more generous than the standards under Rule 13(a)(1)(A). Thus, for these courts, a counterclaim might fail to satisfy the standards of Rule 13(a)(1)(A) but nonetheless satisfy the standards of § 1367(a). *See* 6 WRIGHT, MILLER & KANE, *supra*, § 1422.

Hart v. Clayton-Parker and Associates, Inc.
869 F. Supp. 774 (D. Ariz. 1994)

BROOMFIELD, Chief Judge.

Before the court is plaintiff's motion to dismiss [defendant's] counterclaim. . . .

Plaintiff's complaint states that in 1990, she applied for and received a credit card from J.C. Penney Company. When she was subsequently unable to pay her balance of $1,135.25, J.C. Penney assigned her account to defendant for collection purposes. Plaintiff alleges that defendant engaged in deceptive, unfair and abusive debt-collection practices in violation of the [federal] Fair Debt Collection Practices Act ("FDCPA") and applicable Arizona law prohibiting unreasonable debt collection practices.

Defendant has filed a counterclaim alleging that plaintiff defaulted on her payments owing under her installment credit agreement with J.C. Penney's. Defendant thus seeks $1,135.25 plus interest as well as [their] costs and attorney's fees.

In her motion to dismiss counterclaim, plaintiff argues that the court lacks subject matter jurisdiction over defendant's counterclaim. She maintains that because the counterclaim does not arise under federal law and the parties are not diverse, the court can have jurisdiction over the counterclaim only if it is a compulsory counterclaim under Federal Rule of Civil Procedure 13(a). Plaintiff contends, however, that her cause of action for unlawful debt collection does not arise out of the same transaction or occurrence as defendant's cause of action for the underlying debt because 1) her claim focuses on facts concerning defendant's debt collection practices while the counterclaim focuses on the performance of a contract, 2) the evidence required to support each claim differs, and 3) the claim and counterclaim are not related on a transactional level. Plaintiff finally argues that adjudication of the counterclaim would require the presence of J.C. Penney and that the court cannot acquire jurisdiction over that entity.

Defendant responds that there is a logical relationship between the complaint and counterclaim and that the counterclaim is therefore compulsory. It further contends that the court is competent to adjudicate the counterclaim and that treating the counterclaim as compulsory would avoid a multiplicity of lawsuits. Defendant next avers that Congress has not evinced an intention to insulate FDCPA plaintiffs from the counterclaims of their creditors. Finally, defendant maintains that the court can exercise supplemental jurisdiction over the counterclaim.

The court will first address defendant's argument that the court has supplemental jurisdiction over the counterclaim. The recently-enacted supplemental jurisdiction statute provides, in relevant part:

> Except [as otherwise provided], in any civil action of which the district courts have original jurisdiction, the district courts shall have supplemental jurisdiction over all other claims that are so related to claims in the action within such original jurisdiction that they form part of the same case or controversy under Article III of the United States Constitution.

28 U.S.C. § 1367(a).

Defendant maintains that under section 1367(a), the court may exercise jurisdiction over the counterclaim regardless of whether federal subject matter jurisdictional requirements are independently met. Defendant's argument, however, overlooks the fact that even under section 1367(a), courts must still distinguish between compulsory and permissive counterclaims: federal courts have supplemental jurisdiction over compulsory counterclaims, but permissive counterclaims require their own jurisdictional basis. That is, section 1367(a) itself implicitly recognizes that only a compulsory counterclaim forms a part of the same case or controversy of the claim giving rise to federal jurisdiction. Thus, resolution of the question of the court's jurisdiction over defendant's counterclaim depends on whether the counterclaim is compulsory or permissive.

. . . In determining what constitutes a compulsory counterclaim, the Ninth Circuit applies a "logical relationship" test to determine whether a claim and counterclaim arise out of the same transaction or occurrence. This test analyzes "whether the essential facts of the various claims are so logically connected that considerations of judicial economy and fairness dictate that all the issues be resolved in one lawsuit." *Pochiro v. Prudential Ins. Co. of America*, 827 F.2d 1246, 1249 (9th Cir. 1987) (quotation omitted). Thus, courts should consider whether the facts necessary to prove the claim and counterclaim substantially overlap.

Defendant relies on *Plant v. Blazer Financial Services, Inc. of Georgia*, 598 F.2d 1357 (5th Cir. 1979) for the proposition that its debt collection claim is a compulsory counterclaim to plaintiff's FDCPA claim. In that case, the plaintiff brought an action under the Truth in Lending Act ("TILA"), and the defendant filed a counterclaim to recover the underlying debt. . . .

Every other Court of Appeals to consider the issue has rejected the *Plant* analysis and concluded that TILA claims and underlying loan transactions do not arise out of the same transaction or occurrence and are thus not subject to the compulsory counterclaim provision of Rule 13(a). *See, e.g., . . . Whigham v. Beneficial Finance Co. of Fayetteville*, 599 F.2d 1322 (4th Cir. 1979). . . . [T]he Fourth

Circuit has reasoned that the debt collection claim is not compulsory because (1) the only question in the TILA suit is whether the lender made disclosures required by federal law, while the counterclaim requires the court to determine the parties' contractual rights under state law; (2) the evidence needed to support each claim differs; and (3) the claims are not logically related because the TILA suit does not arise from the obligations created by the contractual relationship. *Whigham*, 599 F.2d at 1324.

More importantly, not only do most courts reject the *Plant* court's analysis of counterclaims in TILA cases, every published decision directly addressing the issue in this case has found that FDCPA lawsuits and lawsuits arising from the underlying contractual debt are not compulsory counterclaims. *Peterson v. United Accounts, Inc.*, 638 F.2d 1134, 1137 (8th Cir. 1981); *Ayres v. National Credit Management Corp.*, 1991 WL 66845, at *4 (E.D. Pa. April 25, 1991); *Gutshall v. Bailey and Assocs.*, 1991 WL 166963, at *2 (N.D. Ill. February 11, 1991); *Leatherwood v. Universal Business Service Company*, 115 F.R.D. 48, 49 (W.D.N.Y. 1987).

The court finds the reasoning in these cases persuasive. As aptly stated by the *Ayres* court:

> Although defendants' right to payment from plaintiff is certainly factually linked to the fairness of defendants' collection practices—there being no attempted collection without an alleged debt—a cause of action on the debt arises out of events different from the cause of action for abuse in collecting. The former centers on evidence regarding the existence of a contract, the failure to perform on a contract, or other circumstances leading to the creation of a valid debt. The latter centers on evidence regarding the improprieties and transgressions, as defined by the FDCPA, in the procedures used to collect the debt, regardless of the debt's validity.

1991 WL 66845, at *1. That is, plaintiff's FDCPA claim relates to the alleged use of abusive debt collection practices, while defendant's counterclaim "encompasses a private duty under state law [requiring] a broad proof of facts establishing the existence and performance of a contract, the validity of the contract's provisions, a breach of the contract by the plaintiff and monetary damages resulting from the breach." *Leatherwood*, 115 F.R.D. at 49. Moreover, plaintiff's FDCPA case turns on the content of defendant's written demand letters, and the validity of the debt itself will not be relevant to plaintiff's case.

The court thus finds that the FDCPA claim and the claim on the underlying debt raise different legal and factual issues governed by different bodies of law. As such, the court concludes that defendant's state-law counterclaim is not logically related to plaintiff's complaint and is therefore not a compulsory counterclaim. Accordingly, the court lacks jurisdiction over defendant's counterclaim and will grant plaintiff's motion to dismiss. . . .

NOTES AND QUESTIONS

1. Jurisdiction over the permissive counterclaim.   In *Hart v. Clayton-Parker*, the district court's decision was based, in part, on the court's adherence to the majority

rule that "federal courts have supplemental jurisdiction over compulsory counterclaims, but permissive counterclaims require their own jurisdictional basis."
Hart, 869 F. Supp. at 776. How might the case have been resolved if the *Hart*
court had applied the "emerging" rule that permits the exercise of supplemental
jurisdiction over some permissive counterclaims? In answering this question, you
might note that toward the end of its opinion, the *Hart* court did at least implicitly recognize that there was some factual connection between the FDCPA and
the debt collection claims—see the block quote from the *Ayres* opinion, at page
649, *supra*. More recently, district courts in the Ninth Circuit have concluded
that while counterclaims seeking to enforce a debt in FDCPA cases are permissive (as in *Hart*), such claims also satisfy the supplemental jurisdiction standards
of § 1367(a). Yet those courts have declined to exercise supplemental jurisdiction
on, among other things, policy considerations related to the chilling effect that
exercising jurisdiction might have on the filing of FDCPA claims. As one court
explained:

> Accepting supplemental jurisdiction . . . will increase both the complexity and
> length of time to resolve Plaintiff's narrow and straightforward FDCPA claim.
> Although the Counterclaim issue is not novel (a debt allegedly owed), the Court,
> sitting in Arizona, will be required to determine choice-of-law questions and, if
> appropriate, apply California law to [Defendant's] state claim. A California court is
> better suited to resolve California state law claims and disputes regarding state law.
> Declining supplemental jurisdiction also reduces the risk of incorrect application
> of California law and furthers the principle of comity. Accepting supplemental
> jurisdiction would also involve this District Court and its limited resources in
> legal questions of no federal significance and may substantially predominate over
> Plaintiff's FDCPA claim. Finally, considering the purpose of the FDCPA is to give
> those harmed by an alleged FDCPA violation a remedy against a debt collector
> regardless of whether the underlying debt is valid, the Court is persuaded to follow
> the majority of the district courts in the Ninth Circuit that strong public policy
> reasons exist for declining to exercise jurisdiction over [Defendant's] Counterclaim.

Randall v. Nelson & Kennard, 2009 WL 2710141, *6 (D. Ariz. Aug. 26, 2009). In
short, under the "emerging" view, courts achieve the same result as in *Hart*, but
via a different route, one that more clearly exposes the policy considerations that
may well have been at the "heart" of the *Hart* decision.

PROBLEM

8-3. In *Hart v. Clayton-Parker*, suppose that Amanda Hart's complaint included
a claim for a declaratory judgment that J.C. Penney's underlying claim was without merit and that she therefore owed the defendant nothing. Would the defendant's counterclaim for $1,135.25 then have been compulsory under Rule 13(a)?
Would the federal court have subject matter jurisdiction over the counterclaim? Is
there an independent basis for jurisdiction over the claim? If not, is it supplemental to any other claim in the suit over which an independent basis of jurisdiction

exists? In the end, which of the claims filed in this suit may the federal court hear? Of course, the answers to these questions depend on whether you apply the majority rule or the emerging rule.

A NOTE ON PARALLEL FEDERAL PROCEEDINGS

The failure to assert a compulsory counterclaim under Federal Rule 13(a) operates as a bar to filing the claim in a second suit only if the first suit has already gone to judgment. A party may therefore attempt to litigate an omitted compulsory counterclaim by filing a second action while the first suit is still pending. Because such parallel actions undermine Rule 13(a)'s goal of promoting judicial efficiency, federal courts have developed techniques for dealing with this situation when both actions are pending in federal courts. Under the so-called first-to-file or first-filed rule, the first court may enjoin the second action, or the second court may stay, dismiss, or transfer the action before it, thus forcing the party to assert the omitted counterclaim in the first suit. *See* 6 WRIGHT, MILLER & KANE, *supra*, § 1418; *Semmes Motors, Inc. v. Ford Motor Company*, 429 F.2d 1197 (2d Cir. 1970).

2.   Crossclaims

We have been considering claims between plaintiffs and defendants. Since the plaintiff is by definition seeking relief against the defendant, the plaintiff and defendant are "opposing" parties within the meaning of Rule 13(a) and (b). We turn now to a consideration of claims asserted by a party against a "co-party" such as those filed by a defendant against a co-defendant. Claims between co-parties are "crossclaims" and are governed by Federal Rule 13(g). Read this rule carefully. As the following case shows, claims between co-defendants do not always constitute crossclaims but may instead sometimes qualify as counterclaims and, thus, be subject to Rule 13(a).

Rainbow Management Group, Ltd. v. Atlantis Submarines Hawaii, L.P.

158 F.R.D. 656 (D. Haw. 1994)

FONG, District Judge. . . .

Introduction

Plaintiff Rainbow Management Group ("RMG") has sued defendants Atlantis Submarines Hawaii, L.P. ("Atlantis") and George A. Haydu ("Haydu") for damages to and loss of use of RMG's vessel Elua, sustained when the Elua collided with Haydu's vessel. Defendant Atlantis has filed the instant motion for summary judgment. Atlantis argues that RMG's claims are barred because they were compulsory counterclaims not pleaded in previous litigation regarding the collision.

Background

Defendant Atlantis operates commercial submarine tours off-shore at Waikiki Beach. At the time of the accident, RMG was under contract with Atlantis to transport passengers back and forth from the shore to the submarine.

On January 27, 1992, RMG's vessel Elua was ferrying passengers from the shore to Atlantis' submarine Atlantis X. The exchange of passengers required the Elua and Atlantis X to come alongside each other to allow their respective crews to secure the two vessels with lines. After the vessels were tied together, a ramp was placed between the two vessels for the passengers to walk on.

That same day, Haydu and four passengers were aboard Haydu's vessel, the Boston Whaler, preparing to scuba dive. The Boston Whaler was moored at an Atlantis reef approximately 200 yards from where Elua and Atlantis X were beginning to transfer passengers.

The Elua collided with the Boston Whaler. The Boston Whaler was destroyed, and several of its passengers suffered personal injuries. The Elua was damaged and repaired.

Plaintiff RMG now seeks recovery against Atlantis for damages to Elua's hull and the resultant loss of use of the vessel. In response, Atlantis asserts that RMG's claim is a compulsory counterclaim that RMG should have asserted in a previous lawsuit by one of the injured Boston Whaler passengers against Atlantis, RMG, and Haydu. See *Berry v. Atlantis Submarines Hawaii, L.P.*, Civil No. 93-00580 SPK ("*Berry*"). The procedural history of *Berry* is set forth below.

Procedural History

George Martin Berry, a passenger on the Boston Whaler on [January] 27, 1992, was injured as a result of the collision. Berry and his wife sued Atlantis and RMG as co-defendants on July 22, 1993. The complaint alleged that both Atlantis and RMG were negligent in the operation of their vessels.

On August 23, 1993 Atlantis filed a cross-claim against RMG and a third-party complaint against Haydu. Its cross-claim against RMG stated two counts, one for breach of contract, and the second for contribution and indemnity.

On September 3, 1993, RMG filed a cross-claim against Atlantis. . . . RMG sought contribution and indemnity, [and] denied any wrongdoing. . . . However, RMG did not assert its claim for damage to or loss of use of the Elua resulting from the January 27, 1992 collision. . . .

In June 1994, RMG filed a second suit (the subject of the instant summary judgment motion). In this suit, RMG sought recovery for damage to the Elua and loss of its use resulting from the collision of [January] 27, 1992. On August 30, 1994, RMG moved [under Rule 42(a)] to consolidate its suit with the still-pending *Berry* case. However, Magistrate Judge Barry Kurren denied the motion, because of delay and prejudice to the opposing parties.

Atlantis and RMG have settled with the parties in the *Berry* case. . . . Thus, the only remaining controversy is between RMG and Atlantis. . . .

Discussion

In support of the instant motion, Atlantis argues that RMG's claims are compulsory counterclaims, barred by Fed. R. Civ. P. 13(a) because RMG failed to assert them in the *Berry* case. Rule 13(a) provides in pertinent part:

> *Compulsory counterclaims.* A pleading shall state as a counterclaim any claim which at the time of serving the pleading the pleader has against any opposing party, if it arises out of the same transaction or occurrence that is the subject matter of the opposing party's claim. . . .

Atlantis argues that, after it filed its initial cross-claim against RMG, RMG became an "opposing party" within the meaning of Rule 13(a), and thereafter was required to plead any claims against Atlantis that arose out of the same transaction or occurrence as the initial cross-claims.

In response, RMG argues that its Elua claim is not a compulsory counterclaim, but is instead a permissive cross-claim pursuant to Fed. R. Civ. P. 13(g). Rule 13(g) provides in pertinent part:

> *Cross-Claim Against a Co-Party.* A pleading may state as a cross-claim any claim by one party against a co-party arising out of the transaction or occurrence that is the subject matter either of the original action or of a counterclaim therein. . . .

RMG argues that Atlantis was a co-party in the *Berry* case, not an opposing party. Thus, RMG could have asserted its Elua claim in the *Berry* case, but it was not required to do so.[3]

This issue appears to be an open question in the Ninth Circuit, and the case law from other circuits is limited and contradictory. See, e.g., *U.S. v. Confederate Acres Sanitary Sewage & Drainage Sys.*, 935 F.2d 796, 799 (6th Cir. 1991) ("cross-claims against co-defendants are permissive"); *Earle M. Jorgenson Co. v. T.I. United States, Ltd.*, 133 F.R.D. 472, 474 (E.D. Penn. 1991) ("[O]nce a cross-claim has been pleaded, the cross-claimant becomes an opposing party, and 'the party against whom the cross-claim is asserted must plead as a counterclaim any right to relief that party has against the cross-claimant that arise from the same transaction or occurrence'" . . .).

Professor James W. Moore addresses this problem in his treatise, and concludes that co-parties become opposing parties within the meaning of Rule 13(a) after one party pleads a cross-claim against the other:

> [A]ssume that A and B sue X on a contract claim; and X pleads a permissive counterclaim for damages caused by the negligence of A and B. A may plead a

---

3. Alternatively, RMG argues that its Elua damage claim does not arise from the same transaction or occurrence as the *Berry* case. This contention is without merit. Both lawsuits resulted from the [January] 27, 1992 collision involving the three vessels, Elua, Boston Whaler, and Atlantis X. Moreover, in its motion for consolidation, RMG itself claimed that "[b]oth lawsuits arise out of the same occurrence, with the underlying facts identical and common fact witnesses."

cross-claim against B to the effect that B is liable to A for all or part of X's claim. A's claim is related to X's counterclaim, but it has certain characteristics of an independent claim, since it in no way affects X. If B, now an *opposing party* to A on the cross-claim also has a claim against A, which arises out of the same transaction or occurrence that is the subject matter of A's cross-claim against him, such a claim is a counterclaim within subdivision (a) and must be pleaded, unless within an exception thereto.

3 James W. Moore and Jo Desha Lucas, *Moore's Federal Practice,* ¶ 13.34, at 13-209-210 (2d. ed. 1985) (emphasis in original, footnotes omitted).

The Supreme Courts of Kansas and Alaska have also adopted this approach. Furthermore, this approach is consistent with the goal of judicial economy and reducing unnecessary litigation, because it encourages parties to plead all claims arising out of a single incident and to resolve such claims in a single lawsuit.

The court finds Professor Moore's approach to this issue to be persuasive, and, accordingly, adopts the following rule: Co-parties become opposing parties within the meaning of Fed. R. Civ. P. 13(a) after one such party pleads an initial cross-claim against the other. The court holds, however, that this rule should be limited to situations in which the initial cross-claim includes a substantive claim (as opposed to merely a claim for contribution and indemnity). The reason for this modification is that an unlimited rule may actually increase the amount or complexity of litigation.

For example, assume in the instant case that Atlantis' initial cross-claim did not include a substantive claim for breach of contract, but merely a claim for contribution and indemnity. In the typical case, RMG would respond with a cross-claim of its own for contribution and indemnity. Such cross-claims would not introduce new issues into the case, and could, in all likelihood, be litigated without substantially increasing the cost or complexity of the litigation.

If the court were to adopt Professor Moore's approach without the limitation discussed above, however, RMG would be forced to file all additional claims against Atlantis arising from the same transaction or occurrence underlying the initial cross-claim. RMG might therefore choose to file claims it might otherwise have chosen *not* to litigate, such as claims for minor damages or other claims for small dollar amounts. The court's modified approach eliminates this problem, because claims against the initial cross-claimant only become compulsory when the initial cross-claim itself includes substantive claims. . . .

In the instant case, Atlantis' initial cross-claim included a claim for contribution and indemnity, as well as an additional substantive claim for breach of contract. RMG was therefore on notice that it would have to defend against claims other than its own original claim. Accordingly, under the rule adopted today, the court GRANTS Atlantis' motion for summary judgment. . . .

NOTES AND QUESTIONS

1. Draw a diagram!   In a complicated case like this that involves multiple claims, multiple parties, and two separate suits, it is impossible to figure out what's going on unless you draw a diagram showing the parties to the litigation, their claims, and the federal rules governing them.

2. *Crossclaims and counterclaims.* What is the difference between a counterclaim and a crossclaim? Some courts have defined a co-party for purposes of Rule 13(g) as being any party who is not an opposing party. *See* 3 MOORE'S FEDERAL PRACTICE, *supra*, § 13.71[1]. Does Rule 13(g)'s "transaction or occurrence" limitation on asserting crossclaims look familiar? Does this mean that crossclaims are always compulsory? May a crossclaim include a claim that has not yet matured, in the sense that it merely seeks indemnification *in the event* that the cross-complainant is found liable to someone else in the suit? Is the same true of counterclaims under Rule 13(a) and (b)?

Was Atlantis's crossclaim against RMG in *Berry* proper under Rule 13(g)? If so, was Atlantis required to assert that claim? In *Berry*, was RMG's claim against Atlantis a crossclaim (as the court at one point describes it) or a counterclaim? Does the answer hinge on whether Atlantis was a "co-party" or an "opposing party" at the time RMG filed its claim? Is it accurate to say that crossclaims themselves are always permissive but that the filing of a crossclaim will sometimes turn additional claims between the same parties into counterclaims—some of which may be compulsory?

3. *When do co-defendants become opposing parties?* According to the district court, if Atlantis had crossclaimed solely for indemnification, would RMG have been barred from later suing Atlantis for damage to the Elua? In formulating its rule as to when defendants become opposing parties, the court was concerned that a broader rule might induce parties like RMG to assert claims in the first suit that they would otherwise never litigate. How realistic is this concern? Isn't it more costly for a party like RMG to bring a damage claim as a separate suit than to include it in ongoing litigation in which similar issues are being litigated? Is a narrow rule as to when defendants become opposing parties likely to encourage a multiplicity of suits involving the same underlying issues? A number of other courts have agreed with *Rainbow Management* that the mere assertion of an indemnity claim is not enough to turn co-defendants into opposing parties. *See, e.g., Paramount Aviation Corp. v. Agusta*, 178 F.3d 132, 146 n.11 (3d Cir.) (dictum), *cert. denied*, 528 U.S. 878 (1999); *City of Colton v. American Promotional Events, Inc.*, 2010 WL 4569038 (C.D. Cal. Nov. 2, 2010); *Hemme v. Bharti*, 183 S.W.3d 593 (Mo. 2006) (so construing Missouri's compulsory counterclaim rule that is based on Rule 13(a)).

4. *Unfairness and complexity.* Is it fair to plaintiffs to let defendants assert crossclaims and counterclaims against one another, since those claims may be of no interest to the plaintiff and may only delay the plaintiff's ability to obtain the relief she seeks? Isn't there also the possibility that the addition of crossclaims and counterclaims between defendants will unduly complicate the case, particularly if it is tried to a jury rather than a judge? Do Rules 13(i), 42(b), and 54(b) give federal judges the ability to address these concerns?

5. *Subject matter jurisdiction.* In *Rainbow Management*, assume that the plaintiffs were citizens of California, that RMG and Atlantis were both citizens of Hawaii, and that the plaintiffs were seeking more than $75,000 from each

defendant. Under these facts, the district court would have had subject matter jurisdiction over the main action on the basis of § 1332(a)(1). While Rule 13 allowed Atlantis and RMG to assert claims against each other, would the court also have had subject matter jurisdiction over those claims? Would either § 1331 or § 1332 have been satisfied? Did the claims between the Atlantis and RMG satisfy § 1367(a) as being part of the "same case or controversy" as the plaintiffs' claims? If so, would § 1367(b) have posed an obstacle due to the lack of diversity between RMG and Atlantis? In answering the latter question, it may help to know that Rule 20 allowed the plaintiffs to join Atlantis and RMG in one lawsuit rather than having to sue them separately.

Harrison v. M.S. Carriers, Inc.
1999 WL 195539 (E.D. La. Apr. 7, 1999)

SEAR, District Judge. . . .

On September 21, 1998, plaintiffs, Mary Gilbert, Cynthia Daniels, and Dave Harrison, Jr., filed suit against defendants as a result of an automobile accident which occurred on September 25, 1997. Plaintiffs allegedly suffered injuries when a car driven by plaintiff Dave Harrison and a M.S. Carriers tractor collided. Plaintiffs seek damages for injuries sustained in connection with the accident.

Plaintiffs originally filed this action in the Civil District Court for the Parish of Orleans ("CDC"). Defendants timely removed this action to this Court on October 28, 1998, based solely on diversity jurisdiction. . . .

On February 4, 1999, plaintiffs then moved to amend their complaint to name their co-plaintiff, Harrison, the driver of the automobile in which they were riding, and his insurer, Guaranty National Insurance Company, as additional defendants. Plaintiffs seek to assert negligence claims against Harrison. Defendants opposed the motion asserting that the proper procedural mechanism by which plaintiffs must assert their claim against co-plaintiff Harrison is a cross-claim.

On February 24, 1999, [Magistrate] Judge Wilkinson denied plaintiffs' motion to amend their complaint. Judge Wilkinson denied the motion, but without prejudice to plaintiffs' assertion of a cross-claim against Harrison and an amended complaint against his insurer. Plaintiffs Gilbert and Daniels now seek review of this order.

Federal Rule of Civil Procedure 72(a) provides that a District Court shall "modify or set aside any portion of the magistrate's order found to be clearly erroneous or contrary to law." A magistrate judge's order is not clearly erroneous or contrary to law unless the reviewing court is left "with the definite and firm conviction that a mistake has been made." The party challenging the magistrate judge's ruling bears the burden of proving that the determination was clearly erroneous or contrary to law.

Judge Wilkinson ruled that a cross-claim is the proper procedure for asserting a claim against co-plaintiff Harrison. Movers, Gilbert and Daniels, contend that a cross-claim is not proper. To support this contention, movers rely on the Third Circuit's ruling in *Danner v. Anskis*, 256 F.2d 123 (3d Cir. 1958).

In *Danner*, the passengers and the driver of one automobile sued the driver of the vehicle with which their vehicle collided. The passenger plaintiffs attempted to file a cross-claim against the driver plaintiff. The Third Circuit held that Federal Rule of Civil Procedure 13(g) does not authorize a plaintiff to state as a cross-claim against a co-plaintiff . . . a claim arising out of a transaction or occurrence which is the subject matter of a common complaint against a defendant. The Court reasoned:

> The purpose of Rule 13(g) is . . . to permit a plaintiff against whom a defendant has filed a counter claim to state as a cross-claim against a co-plaintiff a claim growing out of that transaction or occurrence that is the subject matter of the counter claim or relating to any property that is the subject matter of that counter claim. . . . Unless so limited the rule could have the effect of extending the jurisdiction of the district court to controversies not within the federal judicial power in violation of the Constitution. . . .

The clear language of Rule 13(g) does not support the Third Circuit's holding in *Danner*. "In a statutory construction case, the beginning point must be the language of the statute, and when a statute speaks with clarity to an issue, judicial inquiry into the statute's meaning, in all but the most extraordinary circumstance, is finished." [*First Am. Bank v. Resolution Trust Corp.*, 30 F.3d 644, 647 (5th Cir. 1994).] . . .

The Fifth Circuit has explained that Rule 13(g) "states two prerequisites for a cross-claim: (1) that it be a claim by one party against a co-party and (2) that the claim arise out of the same transaction or occurrence as the original counterclaim." [*McDonald v. Oliver*, 642 F.2d 169, 172 (5th Cir. 1981).]

Additionally the Eastern District of Louisiana has allowed a plaintiff to file a cross-claim in a case nearly identical to this one.[9] Furthermore, *Danner* has been criticized by commentators.

Accordingly, I find that a cross-claim is the proper method of asserting plaintiffs' claim against co-plaintiff Harrison.

Having decided that, it is still necessary that I determine whether Judge Wilkinson properly denied plaintiffs' amendment to the pleadings. In determining whether an amendment to the pleadings should be permitted in a removed case that includes a new non-diverse defendant, Judge Wilkinson relied on the Fifth Circuit's ruling in *Hensgens v. Deere & Co.*, 833 F.2d 1179 (5th Cir. 1987).

In *Hensgens*, the Fifth Circuit held that [in such cases] the district court should scrutinize the amendment more closely than an ordinary amendment. . . .

---

9. See *Butler v. Rigsby*, 1997 WL 655928 (E.D. La., Oct. 20, 1997) (a lawsuit was instituted by a driver and her passengers against the driver of the other vehicle. The plaintiffs who were the passengers sought to file a cross-claim against the plaintiff driver, alleging that she was negligent. District Court Judge Sarah Vance held that "[t]he cross-claims are properly asserted under Rule 13(g) because they are claims 'by one party against a co-party arising out of the transaction or occurrence that is the subject matter . . . of the original action.' Fed. R. Civ. P. 13(g).").

. . . Judge Wilkinson concluded that movant's principal motivation in choosing to add the non-diverse co-plaintiff as a defendant in an amended petition, rather than a cross-claim, was to defeat federal jurisdiction. I agree. Judge Wilkinson's ruling gave the plaintiffs what they sought, a procedure to assert their claims against the co-plaintiff Harrison. There appears no other reason to seek review of the Magistrate Judge's Order than to defeat diversity jurisdiction. . . .

I do not find Judge Wilkinson's ruling to be clearly erroneous or contrary to law.

Accordingly, It Is Ordered that plaintiffs Gilbert and Daniels Motion to Review the Magistrate's Order is Denied.

NOTES AND QUESTIONS

1. Crossclaims between co-plaintiffs.   *Harrison* rejected the reasoning of *Danner v. Anskis*, 256 F.2d 123 (3d Cir. 1958), which held that crossclaims between co-plaintiffs are permitted only by a plaintiff against whom a defendant has filed a counterclaim. Was the *Harrison* court correct in stating that "[t]he clear language of Rule 13(g) does not support the Third Circuit's holding"? Rule 13(g) provides that a crossclaim may be included in a "pleading." If a plaintiff who has not been served with a counterclaim simply files a cross-claim against a co-plaintiff, what "pleading" is then involved? Rule 7(a) lists the various pleadings that are permitted in federal court. The list includes complaints, third-party complaints, and a variety of answers. Crossclaims are not included on the list. *See* 3 Moore's Federal Practice, *supra*, § 13.60. Thus, in the absence of a counterclaim filed against her, the plaintiff has no occasion to file any further pleading that might include a crossclaim. To allow a plaintiff to file a free-standing crossclaim that is not part of any "pleading" might, therefore, be seen as contrary to Rule 13(g)'s plain language. Yet is this technical reading of Rule 13(g) consistent with Rule 1, which states that the federal rules "should be construed, administered, and employed by the court and the parties to secure the just, speedy, and inexpensive determination of every action and proceeding"? Fed. R. Civ. P. 1. Could a plaintiff avoid this textual anomaly by including the cross-claim in the original or an amended complaint?

2. Subject matter jurisdiction.   Since the plaintiffs in *Harrison* were not diverse from one another, how did the court have subject matter jurisdiction over the cross-claim? For purposes of supplemental jurisdiction, while § 1367(a) was clearly satisfied since the cross-claim and the main action involved the same accident, what about § 1367(b)? Since it was Rule 20 that allowed the plaintiffs to join together in one action, does § 1367(b) prohibit the court from exercising supplemental jurisdiction over the crossclaim? Before answering this question read § 1367(b) and carefully consider how one might interpret the phrase "inconsistent with the jurisdictional requirements of section 1332." 28 U.S.C. § 1367(b). In doing so, review *Owen Equipment and Erection Co. v. Kroger*, see page 377, *supra*, and "A Note on *Kroger* and Potential Evasions of the Complete Diversity Principle," at page 384, *supra*.

3. Unrelated crossclaims. Rule 13(g) allows the filing of a crossclaim only if it arises from the "transaction or occurrence" that is the subject matter of the original action or of a counterclaim. Once a party asserts a crossclaim that satisfies this relationship requirement, Rule 18(a) then allows the party to join with that crossclaim any other claims she has against the opposing party, including those that are totally unrelated to the main action or to any counterclaims filed in the suit. Yet while Rule 18(a) allows the assertion of unrelated crossclaims, jurisdiction and venue requirements must still be satisfied for the claim to proceed in federal courts.

PROBLEM

8-4. Diana and Francine were partners in South Productions, Ltd. ("South Productions"), a partnership formed to revive the musical "South Side Story." During its three years of operation, South Productions failed to pay the federal government $200,000 in income and unemployment taxes. The government sued Diana and Francine in federal court to collect these taxes. Diana's answer to the complaint included a crossclaim against Francine, seeking indemnification for any taxes Diana might be found to owe the government. Diana also asserted a crossclaim seeking $250,000 from Francine for loss of investment, legal expenses, mental and emotional anguish, and defamation, all arising from Francine's partnership dealings. Diana and Francine are citizens of New York. As a matter of joinder, did Diana have the right to assert these crossclaims against Francine? Assuming joinder was proper, does the court have subject matter jurisdiction over both crossclaims? *See United States v. West Productions, Ltd.*, 1997 WL 668210 (S.D.N.Y. Oct. 27, 1997).

C.   Permissive Joinder of Parties by Plaintiffs

The circumstances under which a federal lawsuit may be structured to include more than one plaintiff or more than one defendant are set out in Rule 20 ("Permissive Joinder of Parties"). Rule 20(a) provides in pertinent part:

(a) *Persons Who May Join or Be Joined.*
    (1) *Plaintiffs.* Persons may join in one action as plaintiffs if:
        (A) they assert any right to relief jointly, severally, or in the alternative with respect to or arising out of the same transaction, occurrence, or series of transactions or occurrences; and
        (B) any question of law or fact common to all plaintiffs will arise in the action.
    (2) *Defendants.* Persons—as well as a vessel, cargo, or other property subject to admiralty process in rem—may be joined in one action as defendants if:

       (A) any right to relief is asserted against them jointly, severally, or in the alternative with respect to or arising out of the same transaction, occurrence, or series of transactions or occurrences; and

       (B) any question of law or fact common to all defendants will arise in the action.

FED. R. CIV. P. 20(a).

Does the same-transaction-or-occurrence requirement look familiar? It is virtually identical to the wording of Rule 13(a) (compulsory counterclaims) and Rule 13(g) (cross-claims). Not surprisingly, the federal courts employ the same flexible logical-relationship approach to the same-transaction-or-occurrence requirement of Rule 20(a) as they use under Rule 13(a) and (g). Richard D. Freer, *Permissive Joinder of Parties, in* 4 MOORE'S FEDERAL PRACTICE § 20.05[2] (3d ed. 2015). But keep in mind that Rule 20(a) is slightly broader in scope than the same-transaction test used in Rules 13(a) and 13(g), since Rule 20(a) also permits joinder of parties when the separate claims of or against those parties arise out of the same "series" of transactions or occurrences. Yet Rule 20(a) requires a showing that the claims asserted by or against the joined parties share at least one common question of law or of fact. This commonality requirement ensures that claims within a transaction or within a series of transactions are sufficiently linked to make joinder of the relevant parties (and the related claims) a sensible option.

As is the case with joinder of claims, joinder of parties must conform not only to the federal rules but also to jurisdictional and venue requirements.

Exxon Mobil Corp. v. Allapattah Services, Inc.
545 U.S. 546 (2005)

JUSTICE KENNEDY delivered the opinion of the Court.

These consolidated cases present the question whether a federal court in a diversity action may exercise supplemental jurisdiction over additional plaintiffs whose claims do not satisfy the minimum amount-in-controversy requirement, provided the claims are part of the same case or controversy as the claims of plaintiffs who do allege a sufficient amount in controversy. Our decision turns on the correct interpretation of 28 U.S.C. § 1367. The question has divided the Courts of Appeals, and we granted certiorari to resolve the conflict.

We hold that, where the other elements of jurisdiction are present and at least one named plaintiff in the action satisfies the amount-in-controversy requirement, § 1367 does authorize supplemental jurisdiction over the claims of other plaintiffs in the same Article III case or controversy, even if those claims are for less than the jurisdictional amount specified in the statute setting forth the requirements for diversity jurisdiction. . . .

I

In 1991, about 10,000 Exxon dealers filed a class-action suit against the Exxon Corporation in the United States District Court for the Northern District of Florida. The dealers alleged an intentional and systematic scheme by Exxon under which they were overcharged for fuel purchased from Exxon. The plaintiffs invoked the District Court's § 1332(a) diversity jurisdiction. After a unanimous jury verdict in favor of the plaintiffs, the District Court certified the case for interlocutory review, asking whether it had properly exercised § 1367 supplemental jurisdiction over the claims of class members who did not meet the jurisdictional minimum amount in controversy.

The Court of Appeals for the Eleventh Circuit upheld the District Court's extension of supplemental jurisdiction to these class members. *Allapattah Services, Inc. v. Exxon Corp.*, 333 F.3d 1248 (2003). "[W]e find," the court held, "that § 1367 clearly and unambiguously provides district courts with the authority in diversity class actions to exercise supplemental jurisdiction over the claims of class members who do not meet the minimum amount in controversy as long as the district court has original jurisdiction over the claims of at least one of the class representatives." Id., at 1256. This decision accords with the views of the Courts of Appeals for the Fourth, Sixth, and Seventh Circuits. The Courts of Appeals for the Fifth and Ninth Circuits, adopting a similar analysis of the statute, have held that in a diversity class action the unnamed class members need not meet the amount-in-controversy requirement, provided the named class members do. These decisions, however, are unclear on whether all the named plaintiffs must satisfy this requirement.

In the other case now before us the Court of Appeals for the First Circuit took a different position on the meaning of § 1367(a). [*Rosario Ortega v. Star-Kist Foods, Inc.*, 370 F.3d 124 (1st Cir. 2004).] In that case, a 9-year-old girl sued Star-Kist in a diversity action in the United States District Court for the District of Puerto Rico, seeking damages for unusually severe injuries she received when she sliced her finger on a tuna can. Her family joined in the suit, seeking damages for emotional distress and certain medical expenses. The District Court granted summary judgment to Star-Kist, finding that none of the plaintiffs met the minimum amount-in-controversy requirement. The Court of Appeals for the First Circuit, however, ruled that the injured girl, but not her family members, had made allegations of damages in the requisite amount.

The Court of Appeals then addressed whether, in light of the fact that one plaintiff met the requirements for original jurisdiction, supplemental jurisdiction over the remaining plaintiffs' claims was proper under § 1367. The court held that § 1367 authorizes supplemental jurisdiction only when the district court has original jurisdiction over the action, and that in a diversity case original jurisdiction is lacking if one plaintiff fails to satisfy the amount-in-controversy requirement. Although the Court of Appeals claimed to "express no view" on whether the result would be the same in a class action, its analysis is inconsistent with that of the Court of Appeals for the Eleventh Circuit. The Court of Appeals for the First

Circuit's view of § 1367 is, however, shared by the Courts of Appeal for the Third, Eighth, and Tenth Circuits, and the latter two Courts of Appeals have expressly applied this rule to class actions.

II

A

The district courts of the United States, as we have said many times, are "courts of limited jurisdiction. They possess only that power authorized by Constitution and statute," *Kokkonen v. Guardian Life Ins. Co. of America*, 511 U.S. 375, 377 (1994). In order to provide a federal forum for plaintiffs who seek to vindicate federal rights, Congress has conferred on the district courts original jurisdiction in federal-question cases—civil actions that arise under the Constitution, laws, or treaties of the United States. 28 U.S.C. § 1331. In order to provide a neutral forum for what have come to be known as diversity cases, Congress also has granted district courts original jurisdiction in civil actions between citizens of different States, between U.S. citizens and foreign citizens, or by foreign states against U.S. citizens. § 1332. To ensure that diversity jurisdiction does not flood the federal courts with minor disputes, § 1332(a) requires that the matter in controversy in a diversity case exceed a specified amount, currently $75,000.

Although the district courts may not exercise jurisdiction absent a statutory basis, it is well established—in certain classes of cases—that, once a court has original jurisdiction over some claims in the action, it may exercise supplemental jurisdiction over additional claims that are part of the same case or controversy. The leading modern case for this principle is *Mine Workers v. Gibbs*, 383 U.S. 715 (1966). . . .

We have not, however, applied *Gibbs'* expansive interpretive approach to other aspects of the jurisdictional statutes. For instance, we have consistently interpreted § 1332 as requiring complete diversity: In a case with multiple plaintiffs and multiple defendants, the presence in the action of a single plaintiff from the same State as a single defendant deprives the district court of original diversity jurisdiction over the entire action. *Strawbridge v. Curtiss*, 3 Cranch 267 (1806); *Owen Equipment & Erection Co. v. Kroger*, 437 U.S. 365, 375 (1978). The complete diversity requirement is not mandated by the Constitution, *State Farm Fire & Casualty Co. v. Tashire*, 386 U.S. 523, 530-531 (1967), or by the plain text of § 1332(a). The Court, nonetheless, has adhered to the complete diversity rule in light of the purpose of the diversity requirement, which is to provide a federal forum for important disputes where state courts might favor, or be perceived as favoring, home-state litigants. The presence of parties from the same State on both sides of a case dispels this concern, eliminating a principal reason for conferring § 1332 jurisdiction over any of the claims in the action. The specific purpose of the complete diversity rule explains both why we have not adopted *Gibbs'* expansive interpretive approach to this aspect of the jurisdictional statute and why *Gibbs* does not undermine the complete diversity rule. In order for a federal court to invoke supplemental jurisdiction under *Gibbs*, it must first have original jurisdiction over at least one claim in the action. Incomplete diversity destroys original jurisdiction with respect to all claims, so there is nothing to which supplemental jurisdiction can adhere.

In contrast to the diversity requirement, most of the other statutory prerequisites for federal jurisdiction, including the federal-question and amount-in-controversy requirements, can be analyzed claim by claim. True, it does not follow by necessity from this that a district court has authority to exercise supplemental jurisdiction over all claims provided there is original jurisdiction over just one. Before the enactment of § 1367, the Court declined in contexts other than the pendent-claim instance to follow *Gibbs'* expansive approach to interpretation of the jurisdictional statutes. The Court took a more restrictive view of the proper interpretation of these statutes in so-called pendent-party cases involving supplemental jurisdiction over claims involving additional parties-plaintiffs or defendants—where the district courts would lack original jurisdiction over claims by each of the parties standing alone.

Thus, with respect to plaintiff-specific jurisdictional requirements, the Court held in *Clark v. Paul Gray, Inc.*, 306 U.S. 583 (1939), that every plaintiff must separately satisfy the amount-in-controversy requirement. . . . The Court reaffirmed this rule, in the context of a class action brought invoking § 1332(a) diversity jurisdiction, in *Zahn v. International Paper Co.*, 414 U.S. 291 (1973). It follows "inescapably" from *Clark*, the Court held in *Zahn*, that "any plaintiff without the jurisdictional amount must be dismissed from the case, even though others allege jurisdictionally sufficient claims." . . .

In *Finley v. United States*, 490 U.S. 545 (1989), we confronted a similar issue in a different statutory context. The plaintiff in *Finley* brought a Federal Tort Claims Act negligence suit against the Federal Aviation Administration in District Court, which had original jurisdiction under § 1346(b). The plaintiff tried to add related claims against other defendants, invoking the District Court's supplemental jurisdiction over so-called pendent parties. We held that the District Court lacked a sufficient statutory basis for exercising supplemental jurisdiction over these claims. [W]e held in *Finley* that "a grant of jurisdiction over claims involving particular parties does not itself confer jurisdiction over additional claims by or against different parties." While *Finley* did not "limit or impair" *Gibbs'* liberal approach to interpreting the jurisdictional statutes in the context of supplemental jurisdiction over additional claims involving the same parties, *Finley* nevertheless declined to extend that interpretive assumption to claims involving additional parties. *Finley* held that in the context of parties, in contrast to claims, "we will not assume that the full constitutional power has been congressionally authorized, and will not read jurisdictional statutes broadly."

As the jurisdictional statutes existed in 1989, then, here is how matters stood: First, the diversity requirement in § 1332(a) required complete diversity; absent complete diversity, the district court lacked original jurisdiction over all of the claims in the action. Second, if the district court had original jurisdiction over at least one claim, the jurisdictional statutes implicitly authorized supplemental jurisdiction over all other claims between the same parties arising out of the same

Article III case or controversy. Third, even when the district court had original jurisdiction over one or more claims between particular parties, the jurisdictional statutes did not authorize supplemental jurisdiction over additional claims involving other parties.

B

In *Finley* we emphasized that "[w]hatever we say regarding the scope of jurisdiction conferred by a particular statute can of course be changed by Congress." In 1990, Congress accepted the invitation. It passed the Judicial Improvements Act, 104 Stat. 5089, which enacted § 1367, the provision which controls these cases.

Section 1367 provides, in relevant part:

"(a) Except as provided in subsections (b) and (c) or as expressly provided otherwise by Federal statute, in any civil action of which the district courts have original jurisdiction, the district courts shall have supplemental jurisdiction over all other claims that are so related to claims in the action within such original jurisdiction that they form part of the same case or controversy under Article III of the United States Constitution. Such supplemental jurisdiction shall include claims that involve the joinder or intervention of additional parties.

"(b) In any civil action of which the district courts have original jurisdiction founded solely on section 1332 of this title, the district courts shall not have supplemental jurisdiction under subsection (a) over claims by plaintiffs against persons made parties under Rule 14, 19, 20, or 24 of the Federal Rules of Civil Procedure, or over claims by persons proposed to be joined as plaintiffs under Rule 19 of such rules, or seeking to intervene as plaintiffs under Rule 24 of such rules, when exercising supplemental jurisdiction over such claims would be inconsistent with the jurisdictional requirements of section 1332."

All parties to this litigation and all courts to consider the question agree that § 1367 overturned the result in *Finley*. There is no warrant, however, for assuming that § 1367 did no more than to overrule *Finley* and otherwise to codify the existing state of the law of supplemental jurisdiction. We must not give jurisdictional statutes a more expansive interpretation than their text warrants; but it is just as important not to adopt an artificial construction that is narrower than what the text provides. No sound canon of interpretation requires Congress to speak with extraordinary clarity in order to modify the rules of federal jurisdiction within appropriate constitutional bounds. Ordinary principles of statutory construction apply. In order to determine the scope of supplemental jurisdiction authorized by § 1367, then, we must examine the statute's text in light of context, structure, and related statutory provisions.

Section 1367(a) is a broad grant of supplemental jurisdiction over other claims within the same case or controversy, as long as the action is one in which the district courts would have original jurisdiction. The last sentence of § 1367(a) makes it clear that the grant of supplemental jurisdiction extends to claims involving joinder or intervention of additional parties. The single question before us, therefore, is whether a diversity case in which the claims of some plaintiffs satisfy the amount-in-controversy requirement, but the claims of others plaintiffs do not, presents a "civil action of which the district courts have original jurisdiction." If the answer is yes, § 1367(a) confers supplemental jurisdiction over all claims, including those that do not independently satisfy the amount-in-controversy requirement, if the claims are part of the same Article III case or controversy. If the answer is no, § 1367(a) is inapplicable and, in light of our holdings in *Clark* and *Zahn*, the district court has no statutory basis for exercising supplemental jurisdiction over the additional claims.

We now conclude the answer must be yes. When the well-pleaded complaint contains at least one claim that satisfies the amount-in-controversy requirement, and there are no other relevant jurisdictional defects, the district court, beyond all question, has original jurisdiction over that claim. The presence of other claims in the complaint, over which the district court may lack original jurisdiction, is of no moment. If the court has original jurisdiction over a single claim in the complaint, it has original jurisdiction over a "civil action" within the meaning of § 1367(a), even if the civil action over which it has jurisdiction comprises fewer claims than were included in the complaint. Once the court determines it has original jurisdiction over the civil action, it can turn to the question whether it has a constitutional and statutory basis for exercising supplemental jurisdiction over the other claims in the action.

Section 1367(a) commences with the direction that §§ 1367(b) and (c), or other relevant statutes, may provide specific exceptions, but otherwise § 1367(a) is a broad jurisdictional grant, with no distinction drawn between pendent-claim and pendent-party cases. In fact, the last sentence of § 1367(a) makes clear that the provision grants supplemental jurisdiction over claims involving joinder or intervention of additional parties. The terms of § 1367 do not acknowledge any distinction between pendent jurisdiction and the doctrine of so-called ancillary jurisdiction. Though the doctrines of pendent and ancillary jurisdiction developed separately as a historical matter, the Court has recognized that the doctrines are "two species of the same generic problem," *Kroger*, 437 U.S., at 370. Nothing in § 1367 indicates a congressional intent to recognize, preserve, or create some meaningful, substantive distinction between the jurisdictional categories we have historically labeled pendent and ancillary.

If § 1367(a) were the sum total of the relevant statutory language, our holding would rest on that language alone. The statute, of course, instructs us to examine § 1367(b) to determine if any of its exceptions apply, so we proceed to that section. While § 1367(b) qualifies the broad rule of § 1367(a), it does not withdraw supplemental jurisdiction over the claims of the additional parties at issue here. The specific exceptions to § 1367(a) contained in § 1367(b), moreover, provide additional support for our conclusion that § 1367(a) confers supplemental jurisdiction over these claims. Section 1367(b), which applies only to diversity cases, withholds supplemental jurisdiction over the claims of plaintiffs proposed to be joined as indispensable parties under Federal Rule of Civil Procedure 19, or who seek to intervene pursuant to Rule 24. Nothing in the text of § 1367(b), however, withholds supplemental jurisdiction over the claims of plaintiffs permissively joined under Rule 20 (like the additional plaintiffs in *Star-Kist*) or certified as class-action members pursuant to Rule 23 (like the additional plaintiffs in *Exxon*). The natural, indeed the necessary, inference is that § 1367 confers supplemental jurisdiction over claims by Rule 20 and Rule 23 plaintiffs. This inference, at least with respect to Rule 20 plaintiffs, is strengthened by the fact that § 1367(b) explicitly excludes supplemental jurisdiction over claims against defendants joined under Rule 20.

We cannot accept the view, urged by some of the parties, commentators, and Courts of Appeals, that a district court lacks original jurisdiction over a civil action unless the court has original jurisdiction over every claim in the complaint. As we understand this position, it requires assuming either that all claims in the complaint must stand or fall as a single, indivisible "civil action" as a matter of definitional necessity — what we will refer to as the "indivisibility theory" — or else that the inclusion of a claim or party falling outside the district court's original jurisdiction somehow contaminates every other claim in the complaint, depriving the court of original jurisdiction over any of these claims — what we will refer to as the "contamination theory."

The indivisibility theory is easily dismissed, as it is inconsistent with the whole notion of supplemental jurisdiction. If a district court must have original jurisdiction over every claim in the complaint in order to have "original jurisdiction" over a "civil action," then in *Gibbs* there was no civil action of which the district court could assume original jurisdiction under § 1331, and so no basis for exercising supplemental jurisdiction over any of the claims. The indivisibility theory is further belied by our practice — in both federal-question and diversity cases — of allowing federal courts to cure jurisdictional defects by dismissing the offending parties rather than dismissing the entire action. *Clark*, for example, makes clear that claims that are jurisdictionally defective as to amount in controversy do not destroy original jurisdiction over other claims. 306 U.S., at 590 (dismissing parties who failed to meet the amount-in-controversy requirement but retaining jurisdiction over the remaining party). If the presence of jurisdictionally problematic claims in the complaint meant the district court was without original jurisdiction over the single, indivisible civil action before it, then the district court would have to dismiss the whole action rather than particular parties.

We also find it unconvincing to say that the definitional indivisibility theory applies in the context of diversity cases but not in the context of federal-question cases. The broad and general language of the statute does not permit this result. The contention is premised on the notion that the phrase "original jurisdiction of all civil actions" means different things in §§ 1331 and 1332. It is implausible, however, to say that the identical phrase means one thing (original jurisdiction in all actions where at least one claim in the complaint meets the following requirements) in § 1331 and something else (original jurisdiction in all actions where every claim in the complaint meets the following requirements) in § 1332.

The contamination theory, as we have noted, can make some sense in the special context of the complete diversity requirement because the presence of non-diverse parties on both sides of a lawsuit eliminates the justification for providing a federal forum. The theory, however, makes little sense with respect to the amount-in-controversy requirement, which is meant to ensure that a dispute is sufficiently important to warrant federal-court attention. The presence of a single non-diverse party may eliminate the fear of bias with respect to all claims, but the presence of a claim that falls short of the minimum amount in controversy does nothing to reduce the importance of the claims that do meet this requirement.

It is fallacious to suppose, simply from the proposition that § 1332 imposes both the diversity requirement and the amount-in-controversy requirement, that the contamination theory germane to the former is also relevant to the latter. There is no inherent logical connection between the amount-in-controversy requirement and § 1332 diversity jurisdiction. After all, federal-question jurisdiction once had an amount-in-controversy requirement as well. If such a requirement were revived under § 1331, it is clear beyond peradventure that § 1367(a) provides supplemental jurisdiction over federal-question cases where some, but not all, of the federal-law claims involve a sufficient amount in controversy. In other words, § 1367(a) unambiguously overrules the holding and the result in *Clark*. If that is so, however, it would be quite extraordinary to say that § 1367 did not also overrule *Zahn*, a case that was premised in substantial part on the holding in *Clark*. . . .

Finally, it is suggested that our interpretation of § 1367(a) creates an anomaly regarding the exceptions listed in § 1367(b): It is not immediately obvious why Congress would withhold supplemental jurisdiction over plaintiffs joined as parties "needed for just adjudication" under Rule 19 but would allow supplemental jurisdiction over plaintiffs permissively joined under Rule 20. The omission of Rule 20 plaintiffs from the list of exceptions in § 1367(b) may have been an "unintentional drafting gap." If that is the case, it is up to Congress rather than the courts to fix it. The omission may seem odd, but it is not absurd. An alternative explanation for the different treatment of Rule 19 and Rule 20 is that Congress was concerned that extending supplemental jurisdiction to Rule 19 plaintiffs would allow circumvention of the complete diversity rule: A non-diverse plaintiff might be omitted intentionally from the original action, but joined later under Rule 19 as a necessary party. The contamination theory described above, if applicable, means this ruse would fail, but Congress may have wanted to make assurance double sure. More generally, Congress may have concluded that federal jurisdiction is only appropriate if the district court would have original jurisdiction over the claims of all those plaintiffs who are so essential to the action that they could be joined under Rule 19.

To the extent that the omission of Rule 20 plaintiffs from the list of § 1367(b) exceptions is anomalous, moreover, it is no more anomalous than the inclusion of Rule 19 plaintiffs in that list would be if the alternative view of § 1367(a) were to prevail. If the district court lacks original jurisdiction over a civil diversity action where any plaintiff's claims fail to comply with all the requirements of § 1332, there is no need for a special § 1367(b) exception for Rule 19 plaintiffs who do not meet these requirements. Though the omission of Rule 20 plaintiffs from § 1367(b) presents something of a puzzle on our view of the statute, the inclusion of Rule 19 plaintiffs in this section is at least as difficult to explain under the alternative view.

And so we circle back to the original question. When the well-pleaded complaint in district court includes multiple claims, all part of the same case or controversy, and some, but not all, of the claims are within the court's original jurisdiction, does the court have before it "any civil action of which the district courts have original jurisdiction"? It does. Under § 1367, the court has original jurisdiction over the civil action comprising the claims for which there is no jurisdictional defect. No other reading of § 1367 is plausible in light of the text and structure of the jurisdictional statute. Though the special nature and purpose of the diversity requirement mean that a single non-diverse party can contaminate every other claim in the lawsuit, the contamination does not occur with respect to jurisdictional defects that go only to the substantive importance of individual claims.

It follows from this conclusion that the threshold requirement of § 1367(a) is satisfied in cases, like those now before us, where some, but not all, of the plaintiffs in a diversity action allege a sufficient amount in controversy. We hold that § 1367 by its plain text overruled *Clark* and *Zahn* and authorized supplemental jurisdiction over all claims by diverse parties arising out of the same Article III case or controversy, subject only to enumerated exceptions not applicable in the cases now before us.

C

The proponents of the alternative view of § 1367 insist that the statute is at least ambiguous and that we should look to other interpretive tools, including the legislative history of § 1367, which supposedly demonstrate Congress did not intend § 1367 to overrule *Zahn*. We can reject this argument at the very outset simply because § 1367 is not ambiguous. For the reasons elaborated above, interpreting § 1367 to foreclose supplemental jurisdiction over plaintiffs in diversity cases who do not meet the minimum amount in controversy is inconsistent with the text, read in light of other statutory provisions and our established jurisprudence. Even if we were to stipulate, however, that the reading these proponents urge upon us is textually plausible, the legislative history cited to support it would not alter our view as to the best interpretation of § 1367. . . .

As we have repeatedly held, the authoritative statement is the statutory text, not the legislative history or any other extrinsic material. . . . Not all extrinsic materials are reliable sources of insight into legislative understandings, . . . and legislative history in particular is vulnerable to two serious criticisms. First, legislative history is itself often murky, ambiguous, and contradictory. . . . Second, judicial reliance on legislative materials like committee reports, which are not themselves subject to the requirements of Article I, may give unrepresentative committee members—or, worse yet, unelected staffers and lobbyists—both the power and the incentive to attempt strategic manipulations of legislative history to secure results they were unable to achieve through the statutory text. . . . It is clear . . . that in this instance both criticisms are right on the mark. . . .

* * *

The judgment of the Court of Appeals for the Eleventh Circuit is affirmed. The judgment of the Court of Appeals for the First Circuit is reversed, and the case is remanded for proceedings consistent with this opinion.

It is so ordered.

JUSTICE STEVENS, with whom JUSTICE BREYER joins, dissenting. . . .

. . . Not only does the House Report specifically say that § 1367 was not intended to upset *Zahn v. International Paper Co.*, but its entire explanation of the statute demonstrates that Congress had in mind a very specific and relatively modest task—undoing this Court's 5-to-4 decision in *Finley v. United States*. In addition to overturning that unfortunate and much-criticized decision, the statute, according to the Report, codifies and preserves the "the pre-*Finley* understandings of the authorization for and limits on other forms of supplemental jurisdiction," House Report, at 28, with the exception of making "one small change in pre-*Finley* practice," id., at 29, which is not relevant here. . . .

JUSTICE GINSBURG, with whom JUSTICE STEVENS, JUSTICE O'CONNOR, and JUSTICE BREYER join, dissenting. . . .

The Court adopts a plausibly broad reading of § 1367, a measure that is hardly a model of the careful drafter's art. There is another plausible reading, however, one less disruptive of our jurisprudence regarding supplemental jurisdiction. If one reads § 1367(a) to instruct, as the statute's text suggests, that the district court must first have "original jurisdiction" over a "civil action" before supplemental jurisdiction can attach, then *Clark* and *Zahn* are preserved, and supplemental jurisdiction does not open the way for joinder of plaintiffs, or inclusion of class members, who do not independently meet the amount-in-controversy requirement. For the reasons that follow, I conclude that this narrower construction is the better reading of § 1367. . . .

NOTES AND QUESTIONS

1. Rule 20 and § 1367(a).   Suppose two plaintiffs are injured in an explosion at the defendant's plant. They allege that the explosion was a product of the defendant's negligent maintenance of the plant. Both plaintiffs are diverse from the defendant. One plaintiff claims damages in excess of $75,000; the other does not. Would Rule 20 allow these plaintiffs to join together in a suit against this defendant? Assuming that joinder was proper, does it follow that the standards of § 1367(a) will also have been satisfied? More generally, will satisfaction of the Rule 20 standards inevitably satisfy the same-case-or-controversy requirements of § 1367? You should be able to explain, consistently with the *Exxon Mobil* decision, why the answer to the previous two questions is affirmative.

Suppose instead that neither of the plaintiffs in the above hypothetical satisfies the amount-in-controversy requirement, but that by aggregating their separate claims, they together assert more than $75,000 in damages against the defendant. Would Rule 20 still allow them to join together as plaintiffs? Would § 1367(a) confer supplemental jurisdiction over their separate claims? Here, our first answer is yes, but the second is no. Why? In terms of § 1367(a), how does this type of aggregation (neither plaintiff independently satisfies the amount-in-controversy requirement) differ from the type of aggregation at issue in *Exxon Mobil*, over which supplemental jurisdiction may be exercised?

Consider another variation on the original hypothetical. Suppose that each plaintiff meets the amount-in-controversy requirement but only one of them is diverse from the defendant. Would Rule 20 allow their joinder as plaintiffs? Would § 1367(a) confer supplemental jurisdiction? Again we have a yes followed by a no. What aspect of the *Exxon Mobil* opinion mandates a negative answer to the second question? For these purposes, the *Exxon Mobil* Court drew a distinction between the principle of complete diversity and the principle of non-aggregation. What was that distinction? Do you agree with it? Agree or not, it would seem that an absence of complete diversity and situations where neither plaintiff meets the amount-in-controversy requirement will be treated the same for purposes of § 1367(a). In other words, neither will be treated as asserting a case or controversy that falls within a federal district court's original jurisdiction. As a consequence, supplemental jurisdiction is not available under such circumstances.

2. Enter § 1367(b) — diversity cases only.   We've now established that in diversity cases brought by multiple plaintiffs in which some but not all of the plaintiffs satisfy the amount-in-controversy requirement, a federal court may, pursuant to § 1367(a), exercise supplemental jurisdiction over those transactionally related claims that do not meet the amount-in-controversy requirement. There is, however, a caveat. In diversity jurisdiction cases, the exercise of supplemental jurisdiction under § 1367(a) is subject to the restrictions set forth in § 1367(b). That section, which applies only in diversity cases, prohibits the exercise of supplemental jurisdiction

> over claims by plaintiffs against persons made parties under Rule 14, 19, 20, or 24 of the Federal Rules of Civil Procedure, or over claims by persons proposed to be joined as plaintiffs under Rule 19 of such rules, or seeking to intervene as plaintiffs under Rule 24 of such rules, when exercising supplemental jurisdiction over such claims would be inconsistent with the jurisdictional requirements of section 1332.

28 U.S.C. § 1367(b).

Essentially, § 1367(b) prohibits the exercise of supplemental jurisdiction in any of the listed joinder scenarios if, and only if, the joinder violates the jurisdictional requirements of § 1332 (*i.e.*, complete diversity and amount in controversy).

3. Applying § 1367(b) in Exxon Mobil.   Both *Exxon Mobil* and its companion case, *Star-Kist*, were diversity cases. Hence both triggered the application of § 1367(b). Can you explain why § 1367(b) did not preclude the exercise of supplemental jurisdiction in either case? To answer this question you must carefully attend to the text of § 1367(b) and apply that text to the precise circumstances of each case.

4. An anomaly created by the text of § 1367(b).   Suppose that the plaintiffs in *Exxon* and *Star-Kist* had each filed claims against multiple defendants. What rule or rules of joinder would permit them to do this? There are two possibilities. One is Rule 20 (permissive joinder of parties) and the other is Rule 23 (class actions). Let's assume for the moment that the group of defendants was relatively small and that their joinder was accomplished under Rule 20. Assume also that the damages claimed by the plaintiffs were identical as to each defendant, and that some plaintiffs satisfied the amount in controversy while others did not. We know that if the joinder standards of Rule 20 are satisfied, the jurisdictional standards of § 1367(a) will be met as well (*see* Note 1, *supra*). But since this is a diversity case, we must test it against § 1367(b). Here the plaintiffs would be asserting "claims against persons made parties under Rule . . . 20," one of the specific joinder scenarios contemplated by § 1367(b). And the plaintiffs' claims would also be "inconsistent with the jurisdictional requirements under § 1332," as some of those claims would not exceed $75,000. Hence § 1367(b) would not permit the exercise of supplemental jurisdiction over these claims.

Do you see the anomaly? If multiple plaintiffs, only one of whom meets the amount in controversy requirement, join together under Rule 20 to sue a single defendant, supplemental jurisdiction will be allowed over those claims that do not meet § 1332's amount-in-controversy requirement. Why? The claims are part of the same case or controversy under § 1367(a) and, despite the fact that this is a diversity case, nothing in § 1367(b) precludes the exercise of supplemental jurisdiction under such circumstances. That's the precise holding of *Exxon Mobil*. But if those same plaintiffs sue multiple defendants who are joined pursuant to Rule 20, supplemental jurisdiction is not permitted over those claims that do not satisfy the amount-in-controversy requirement. Why? Because, unlike the single-defendant scenario, here one of the specific restrictions found in § 1367(b) applies, *i.e.*, the one relating to claims filed *against* parties joined pursuant to Rule 20.

What if the defendants were so numerous that the plaintiffs could proceed against them as a defendant class under Rule 23? Would supplemental jurisdiction then be permitted? Yes. Nothing in § 1367(b) references claims brought against parties joined pursuant to Rule 23. Hence supplemental jurisdiction is permitted over claims filed against a single defendant or against a group of defendants numerous enough to constitute a class but not against multiple defendants of a smaller number.

Do you think that Congress intended this outcome? Or is this just a textual glitch? If the latter, which appears to have been the case, what should the Court do? Does the *Exxon Mobil* Court provide any clue as to the approach the Court would take to the above-mentioned anomalies?

5. Misjoinder of parties.   Suppose that after a plaintiff has joined multiple plaintiffs or multiple defendants, it appears that joinder was improper under Rule 20(a) because the claims neither arise from the same transaction or occurrence nor share a common question of law or fact. Does the court have any choice but to dismiss the suit? *See* FED. R. CIV. P. 21. If an improperly joined claim has an independent basis of subject matter jurisdiction, may the federal court sever it from the original action and allow it to proceed as a separate lawsuit? What if the severed claim shares a common question of law or fact with the other claims and was misjoined only because it did not arise from the same transaction or occurrence? After severance, could the federal court consolidate the two actions for purposes of conducting a joint hearing or trial on the questions that they do share in common? *See* FED. R. CIV. P. 42(a); 7 WRIGHT, MILLER & KANE, *supra*, § 1653 n.7.

PROBLEMS

8-5. Veruca and Augustus, both citizens of State Hex, were sitting on a lovely park bench sucking on gigantic gobstoppers. In that same park and at the same time, and by the sheerest of coincidences, Violet, a citizen of State Why, was recklessly pumping the pedals of her newly purchased Deluxe Very Stylish Bike as she chewed on a large wad of gum. Unfortunately for all concerned, Violet blew a rather large bubble, which burst in a rather amazing explosion of purple and pink daisies, causing her to crash into the unsuspecting couple, both of whom immediately swallowed their gobstoppers in big, painful gulps. At the time of the accident, Violet was making a delivery of chocolate mice for her employer, Charlie, Inc., a State Why corporation. Veruca sustained $100,000 in personal injuries, while Augustus's damages amounted to a piddling 50,000 bucks. They joined together and sued Violet for negligence in a U.S. district court in which venue was proper.

A. Do the federal rules permit Veruca and Augustus to join together in their suit against Violet?

B. Do either Veruca or Augustus assert a claim over which the district court would have an independent basis of jurisdiction?

C. Is there an independent basis of jurisdiction over Augustus's claim against Violet?

D. Does Augustus's claim against Violet satisfy the standards of § 1367(a)?

E. Might the exercise of jurisdiction over Augustus's claim be inconsistent with the jurisdictional standards of § 1332(a)?

F. May the district court exercise supplemental jurisdiction over Augustus's claim?

G. If Augustus had been from State Why, would your answer to question F be the same? Explain why or why not (no pun intended).

H. Assuming again that Augustus is a citizen of State Hex, would Rule 20 allow Veruca and Augustus to join Violet and Charlie, Inc., as defendants in a single suit, claiming that Charlie, Inc., was liable for the negligence of its employee Violet?

I. May the district court exercise supplemental jurisdiction over the claim against Charlie, Inc.? (In answering this question, you should follow the steps indicated in questions C, D, and E above.)

8-6. Victoria, a Maryland resident, brought suit in a Maryland federal district court to recover $250,000 for injuries suffered while using a water slide in Ocean City, Maryland. She named as defendants Jolly Roger Rides, Inc. ("Jolly Roger"), the company that operates the slide, and Dexter Manufacturing, Inc. ("Dexter"), the slide's manufacturer. Victoria's complaint alleged that her injuries were proximately caused by the defendants' negligence in the design, manufacture, maintenance, and/or operation of the water slide. Jolly Roger is a Maryland corporation. Dexter is a Georgia corporation. Was joinder of the defendants proper under the federal rules? Assuming joinder was proper, does the federal court have subject matter jurisdiction over the case? If the court dismisses the action, should it grant the defendants' motion to impose monetary sanctions on the plaintiff's attorney under Rule 11? *See Ware v. Jolly Roger Rides, Inc.*, 857 F. Supp. 462 (D. Md. 1994).

8-7. Adam rented a truck from U-Drive, Inc. ("U-Drive") to transport from California to New York personal items belonging to Megan, Caitlin, Melissa, Jamie, and himself. While driving through New Jersey, the truck broke down. Adam contacted U-Drive, which towed the vehicle to its facility in Saddle Brook, New Jersey. As the hour was late, U-Drive recommended that Adam spend the night in a local motel, assuring him that the truck and its contents would be safe at its facility. During the night, the truck disappeared. Though it was later found, the contents were never recovered. Adam, Megan, Caitlin, Melissa, and Jamie are now citizens of New York. They have filed a diversity action against U-Drive, a citizen of Oregon, in New Jersey federal court, claiming property loss and emotional distress. Adam seeks damages totaling $90,000; Megan claims damages of $80,000. Caitlin, Melissa, and Jamie seek damages of $35,000, $20,000, and $5,000, respectively. Did the plaintiffs have a right to join together in this action? Assuming they did, does the federal court have subject matter jurisdiction? *See Gandolfo v. U-Haul Int'l, Inc.*, 978 F. Supp. 558 (D.N.J. 1996).

8-8. In Problem 8-7, suppose that in its answer to the complaint, U-Drive included a counterclaim against Adam, alleging that he owed the company the $1,500 rental charge for the trip from California to New York. In his reply to the counterclaim, Adam asserted claims against Megan, Caitlin, Melissa, and Jamie, seeking $300 from each of them as their shares of the $1,500 rental fee. As a matter of joinder, did U-Drive and Adam have a right to assert their claims? If so, does subject matter jurisdiction exist over each of the claims?

A NOTE ON THE REAL-PARTY-IN-INTEREST REQUIREMENT

Federal Rule of Civil Procedure 17(a)(1) provides, "An action must be prosecuted in the name of the real party in interest. . . ." The real party in interest is the person who is vested by law with the right to sue on the asserted claim, either on her own behalf or on behalf of another. For example, an adult injured in an automobile accident is the real party in interest to assert her claim of personal injury arising out of the accident. That same adult might also be the real party in interest to assert a claim of personal injuries to her child who was also injured in that accident. Thus Rule 17(a)(1) provides that executors, administrators, guardians, and other representatives may bring suit in their own name, without having to join the party for whose benefit the action is brought. And as the Advisory Committee Notes explain, "the specific instances enumerated are not exceptions to, but illustrations of, the rule." 39 F.R.D. 69, 84-85 (1966). In other words, in each of the listed instances, the *right to sue* typically belongs to the named representative, even though the suit is ultimately for the benefit of others.

The real-party-in-interest requirement protects the defendant against having to litigate the same claim twice and thus risk multiple vexation or multiple liability. A judgment in a suit filed by someone other than the real party in interest will not preclude a subsequent suit against the defendant by the real party in interest. Thus, if a defendant loses the first suit and pays the plaintiff the amount sought, the defendant could be forced to pay the same amount again in a suit by the real party in interest. Even if the defendant won the first suit, she is still burdened by having to litigate the same claim again. Since the rule is designed for the defendant's benefit, a real-party-in-interest objection is waived unless the defendant raises the defect promptly either by motion or as an affirmative defense in the answer.

Finally, Rule 17 provides that a "court may not dismiss an action for failure to prosecute in the name of the real party in interest until, after an objection, a reasonable time has been allowed for the real party in interest to ratify, join, or be substituted into the action. After ratification, joinder, or substitution, the action proceeds as if it had been originally commenced by the real party in interest." Fed. R. Civ. P. 17(a)(3).

See generally Richard D. Freer, *Plaintiff and Defendant; Capacity; Public Officers, in* 4 Moore's Federal Practice § 17.12[2][a] (3d ed. 2015); 6A Charles Alan Wright, Arthur R. Miller & Mary Kay Kane, Federal Practice and Procedure § 1554 (3d ed. 2010 & Supp. 2015).

D.   Joinder of Parties by Defendants

We have seen that under Rule 13(a), (b), and (g), defendants may assert counterclaims and crossclaims against those who are already parties to a lawsuit. There are two situations in which a defendant can assert a claim against someone who is not already a party to the suit, thus bringing a new or third party into the action. Federal Rule 13(h) sometimes permits a defendant who has filed a counterclaim or a crossclaim against an existing party to join a new party to that claim. And Rule 14(a) allows a defendant to file a third-party complaint against a nonparty who is or may be liable to indemnify the defendant for all or part of the plaintiff's claim against him. If joinder of a third party is permitted under either of these rules, it is also necessary that the court be able to obtain personal jurisdiction over the new party and that subject matter jurisdiction exist over the claim.

1. Joinder of Third Parties Under Rule 13(h)

Schoot v. United States

664 F. Supp. 293 (N.D. Ill. 1987)

ASPEN, District Judge. . . .

On August 8, 1983, Schoot and Vorbau were each assessed a 100% penalty (held jointly and severally liable) of $47,194.53 pursuant to 26 U.S.C. § 6672 for their willful failure to collect, truthfully account for, and pay over withholding and Federal Insurance Contributions Act taxes due and owing from Steelograph Business Interiors, Inc. ("Steelograph") for the second, third, and fourth quarters of 1980, the fourth quarter of 1981 and the first quarter of 1982. Despite the assessments and demands made upon Vorbau by the government, and except for the application of a refund in the amount of $1,807.00, Vorbau has refused or neglected to pay the assessed liability. Despite the assessments and demands made upon Schoot by the government, and except for the application of a refund in the amount of $137.31 and the payment of $50.00, he has refused or neglected to pay the assessed liability.

Steelograph was incorporated in Illinois and had its principal place of business in Illinois. At all relevant times herein, Schoot was an employee of Steelograph and he performed only ministerial duties at the direction of Vorbau. At all relevant times herein, Vorbau was President of Steelograph. Schoot did not have control over the company's payroll or business decisions nor did Schoot decide which creditors Steelograph would pay. Those types of decisions were made by Vorbau, who was solely responsible for payment of the relevant taxes.

Schoot originally filed a claim under 28 U.S.C. §§ 1331, 1346(a)(1) against the United States to recover Internal Revenue taxes and interest allegedly erroneously or improperly assessed or collected from Schoot. The United States counterclaimed against Schoot for the balance due on the penalty. Vorbau was made a party to this action as an additional defendant on the government's counterclaim pursuant to Fed. R. Civ. P. 13(h). . . .

Vorbau seeks dismissal of the United States' counterclaim pursuant to Fed. R. Civ. P. 12(b) for lack of personal jurisdiction, improper venue and improper joinder. We reject this motion for the following reasons.

Vorbau is subject to the personal jurisdiction of this Court by Fed. R. Civ. P. 4(e) and Ill. Rev. Stat. ch. 110 § 2-209 (1985). The Illinois long arm statute provides that if any person, in person or through an agent, does any of the acts enumerated in the statute, they submit to the jurisdiction of the Illinois courts. Section 2-209(a)(1) provides that the transaction of any business within Illinois is such an act. The Government has alleged that Vorbau was president of an Illinois corporation and resided in Illinois at the time the acts, out of which this action arose, took place. The fact that counter-defendant Vorbau has since moved out of state does not insulate him from the long arm jurisdiction of the state of Illinois for acts that took place while he lived and worked in the state. Therefore, it is clear that this Court has personal jurisdiction over Vorbau.

Vorbau contends that improper venue is another ground for dismissal. Venue for Schoot's original complaint against the Government is properly located in this district because pursuant to 28 U.S.C. § 1402 any action against the United States under 28 U.S.C. § 1346 may be prosecuted in the judicial district where the plaintiff resides. Thus, where Schoot resides in the Eastern Division of the Northern District of Illinois, venue is proper in this Court. The issue that Vorbau raises is whether there is proper venue for the Government's counterclaim. However, in the case of compulsory counterclaims, the venue statutes have been construed to apply only to the original claim, and not to the compulsory counterclaims. Therefore, as a third party brought into this action under Fed. R. Civ. P. 13(h), Vorbau cannot object to venue. . . .

Finally, Vorbau contends that the counterclaim against him should be dismissed for improper joinder. First, Vorbau argues that the Government failed to make a proper motion to join Vorbau as an additional counter-defendant under Fed. R. Civ. P. 13(h). A review of the record, however, reveals that the Government in its May 2, 1986 Motion to File Amended Answer and Counterclaim sought leave of this Court "to add Roger C. Vorbau as an additional defendant on the counterclaim." That motion was allowed by this Court by way of a May 2, 1986 minute order.

Vorbau also argues that his joinder is improper under Fed. R. Civ. P. 20 because "the issue of fact to be determined by a fact finder with respect to Vorbau will not be in common with respect to plaintiff Schoot." Rule 20, however, states that joinder is proper "if *any* question of law or fact common to all defendants will arise in the action." ([E]mphasis added). As the Government noted in its brief, there are numerous common questions of law or fact in this action.[3] Therefore, finding that the Government properly joined Vorbau as an additional defendant to the counterclaim under Fed. R. Civ. P. 13(h) and 20, we deny Vorbau's motion to dismiss on that ground.

In sum, we deny counter-defendant Vorbau's motion to dismiss the counterclaim of the United States on all grounds alleged. . . .

---

3. The Government set forth the following as common questions of law or fact in this action:

1. Who was responsible for withholding, accounting for and paying over the withheld taxes?
2. Was the failure to account and pay over those taxes willful?
3. Who had the power to control the decision making process by which Steelograph allocated its funds among creditors?
4. Who prepared or assisted in the preparation of federal tax returns?
5. Who prepared, reviewed or signed financial statements of Steelograph?
6. Who signed checks for Steelograph?
7. Who had authority to hire and fire employees?
8. Who were the officers of Steelograph?
9. What were the responsibilities of those officers?
10. What was the relationship of the officers among themselves in relation to the conduct of the day to day affairs of Steelograph?

NOTES AND QUESTIONS

1. Adopting the defendant's perspective.   In deciding whether Rule 13(h) permitted the government to add Vorbau as an additional party to its counterclaim against Schoot, the court analyzed the situation from the government's perspective, as though the government were instituting an action against Schoot and Vorbau. The question was thus whether in such an action, Rule 20 would have allowed the government to join Schoot and Vorbau as co-defendants. The court found that because the claims arose from the same series of transactions and occurrences and shared some common questions, Rule 20 was satisfied, thereby allowing joinder of the claim against Vorbau under Rule 13(h).

2. Satisfying Rule 19 or 20.   The text of Rule 13(h) provides, "Rules 19 and 20 govern the addition of a person as a party to a counterclaim or crossclaim." FED. R. CIV. P. 13(h). This means that joinder under Rule 13(h) must accord with either Rule 19 *or* 20. *See* 6 WRIGHT, MILLER & KANE, *supra*, § 1434. This explains why in *Schoot*, once the court found that the requirements of Rule 20 were satisfied, it did not have to go on and consider Rule 19.

Hartford Steam Boiler Inspection and Insurance Co. v. Quantum Chemical Corp.

1994 WL 494776 (N.D. Ill. Sept. 8, 1994)

GRADY, District Judge.

Before the court are the memoranda of the parties addressing the question of the court's jurisdiction to hear the claims against the third-party defendants. For the reasons discussed below, we conclude that we do have jurisdiction to hear the claims against the third-party defendants.

Background

This suit arises out of an incident that occurred at the Quantum Chemical Corporation ("Quantum") plant in Morris, Illinois on September 12, 1989, when a heat exchanger failed, causing damage to the heat exchanger and some surrounding property. Defendant Quantum had insurance coverage under a policy issued by plaintiff Hartford Steam Boiler Inspection and Insurance Company ("Hartford"), as well as under policies issued by third-party defendants, Industrial Risk Insurers ("IRI") and DR Insurance Company ("DRI") (collectively, the "Property Insurers"). The central inquiry in this case is which policy covered the heat exchanger failure. The Hartford policy does not cover damages resulting from an explosion, but does cover damages resulting from an "accident" to an "object." Conversely, the Property Insurers policies cover damages resulting from explosions, but do not cover accidents. Following the occurrence, Quantum filed business interruption and property damage claims with both Hartford and

Property Insurers. Hartford maintains that Quantum's losses were caused by an explosion, and therefore denies coverage, while Property Insurers maintain that the losses resulted from a pre-existing crack in the heat exchanger, and accordingly, also deny coverage.

. . . Rather than filing suit against its insurers immediately upon denial of its claims, Quantum encouraged them to arbitrate their disputes regarding coverage. The [P]roperty [I]nsurers agreed to do so, but Hartford, initially, did not. Instead, on October 29, 1991, Hartford instituted this action against Quantum, ("the federal court action"), seeking a declaratory judgment that Quantum's losses were not covered under its policy. This court's jurisdiction over Hartford's claim against Quantum is founded on diversity, pursuant to 28 U.S.C. § 1332.

Rather than answering the complaint and filing any counterclaims in the federal court action, Quantum instead filed another suit against both Hartford and the Property Insurers in Grundy County, Illinois, on April 3, 1992 ("the state court action"). Hartford and the Property Insurers each filed motions to dismiss or stay the state court action because of the concurrently pending suit in this court. On October 2, 1992, the circuit court in Grundy County granted the motions to dismiss. On January 7, 1993, over fourteen months after the filing of the federal court action, and in response to this court's orders of November and December of 1992, Quantum submitted its answer to the complaint in the federal court action, and counterclaimed against Hartford. Quantum also filed a third-party complaint against the Property Insurers . . . .

Discussion . . .

This court's original jurisdiction over the federal court action brought by Hartford against Quantum and the counterclaims brought by Quantum against Hartford lies in diversity pursuant to 28 U.S.C. § 1332. However, because there is not diversity of citizenship between Quantum and the Property Insurers, a question has been raised regarding this court's jurisdiction over Quantum's third-party complaint against the added defendants. . . . Interestingly, it is Quantum, the third-party plaintiff, who argues that this court lacks jurisdiction to hear its claims against the third-party defendants, while Hartford and the Property Insurers all argue that the claims against the Property Insurers can properly be heard in this court under supplemental jurisdiction, pursuant to 28 U.S.C. § 1367.

A.   *The Exercise of Supplemental Jurisdiction under § 1367(a), Unless Prohibited by § 1367(b)*

Quantum filed its counterclaims against Hartford pursuant to Federal Rule of Civil Procedure 13, and added the Property Insurers as third-party defendants to the counterclaims pursuant to Rule 13(h). Rule 13(h) provides that "[p]ersons other than those made parties to the original action may be made parties to a counterclaim . . . in accordance with the provisions of Rules 19 and 20." Rule 19 provides for joinder of persons needed for just adjudication, and Rule 20 provides for permissive joinder of parties as defendants "if there is asserted against them jointly, severally, or in the alternative, any right to relief in respect of or arising out of the same transaction [or] occurrence, . . . and if any question of law or fact common to all defendants will arise in the action."

Hartford and the Property Insurers maintain that this court has jurisdiction over the claims against the third-party defendants, Property Insurers, pursuant to 28 U.S.C. § 1367. That statute provides:

> (a) Except as provided in subsections (b) and (c) or as expressly provided otherwise by Federal statute, in any civil action of which the district courts have original jurisdiction, the district courts shall have supplemental jurisdiction over all other claims that are so related to claims in the action within such original jurisdiction that they form part of the same case or controversy under Article III of the United States Constitution. Such supplemental jurisdiction shall include all claims that involve the joinder or intervention of additional parties.

As discussed above, the court has original jurisdiction based on diversity over both Hartford's claim against Quantum and Quantum's counterclaims against Hartford. Thus, the only question is whether the court has supplemental jurisdiction over Quantum's claims against the third-party defendants. Accordingly, we apply the supplemental jurisdiction analysis only to these claims.

Clearly, the claims against the Property Insurers satisfy the requirement of forming part of the same case or controversy as the claims by Hartford against Quantum and Quantum against Hartford over which we have original jurisdiction. No party raises any significant challenge on this point. Thus, we have supplemental jurisdiction over the claims against the additional parties under § 1367(a), unless either of the exceptions provided in subsection (b) or (c) apply.

Subsection (b) provides:

> In any civil action of which the district courts have original jurisdiction founded solely on section 1332 of this title, the district court shall not have supplemental jurisdiction under subsection (a) over claims by *plaintiffs* against persons made parties under Rule 14, 19, 20, or 24 of the Federal Rules of Civil Procedure, or over claims by persons proposed to be joined as plaintiffs under Rule 19 of such rules, . . . when exercising supplemental jurisdiction over such claims would be inconsistent with the jurisdictional requirements of section 1332 (emphasis added).

By its terms, subsection (b) does not apply to the joinder of the Property Insurers by *defendant* Quantum under Rule 13(h). Rather, subsection (b) applies only to claims by *plaintiffs* against new parties whose addition would destroy diversity. In this way, subsection (b) prevents the original plaintiff from maneuvering a non-federal claim into federal court by initially filing claims against only diverse parties, and then later seeking to add non-diverse parties, whose presence, had plaintiff included them in its original complaint, would have destroyed diversity. As explained in the commentary to § 1367, subsection (b) "carves out only specific instances in which it excludes the supplemental jurisdiction in diversity cases. By no means does it exclude it from diversity cases in general." Rather, subsection (b) "is concerned only with efforts of a plaintiff to smuggle in claims that the plaintiff would not otherwise be able to interpose against certain parties

. . . for want of subject matter jurisdiction. The repetition of the word 'plaintiffs' at several rule-citing junctures in subdivision (b) makes this clear." D. Siegel, 28 U.S.C. § 1367 Practice Commentary, p. 832 (West 1993).

Defendant Quantum makes much of the fact that Hartford did not join the Property Insurers in its original complaint. Quantum suggests that Hartford deliberately did not join the Property Insurers for jurisdictional reasons because their presence in the suit would destroy diversity. It appears to the court, however, that the real reason Hartford did not join the Property Insurers is far more straightforward and simple than Quantum would have us believe: Hartford did not join the Property Insurers because it has no claim against them. In the original suit, Hartford was seeking a declaration of its rights and obligations under its insurance contract with Quantum, a contract to which the Property Insurers are not parties. . . .

. . . Section 1367 does not on its face prohibit a defendant from joining a non-diverse third-party defendant to a compulsory counterclaim, and the courts have allowed such claims. . . .

Support for the exercise of supplemental jurisdiction over additional non-diverse parties to compulsory counterclaims comes also from leading civil procedure authorities. "[W]here a party asserting a . . . counterclaim of the compulsory type seeks to bring in additional parties [as permitted under Fed. R. Civ. P. 13(h)], no diversity of citizenship between the counterclaimant and the added party is required, whether jurisdiction of the main action is founded on diversity or upon a federal matter." 3 J. Moore & R. Freer, *Moore's Federal Practice* ¶ 13.39, p. 13-236 (2d ed. 1993). Similarly, Wright and Miller's *Federal Practice and Procedure* informs us that "[u]ncertainty over the potential restrictions . . . on the ability of the courts to assert ancillary jurisdiction over Rule 13(h) parties joined to a compulsory counterclaim was laid to rest by the enactment of a new statutory form of jurisdiction, supplemental jurisdiction, in 1990. That jurisdiction is available for all related claims that form part of the same case or controversy as the original claims." 6 C. Wright & A. Miller, *Federal Practice and Procedure* § 1436, p. 13 (Supp. 1994). . . . The rationale for allowing supplemental jurisdiction over additional parties to compulsory counterclaims is that, by definition, compulsory counterclaims "involve the same transaction or occurrence as the original action and therefore are closely related to the main claim." Id. at 192 (1971). Permissive counterclaims, by contrast, require independent jurisdictional grounds.

Therefore, if Quantum's counterclaims against Hartford are compulsory, this court will have supplemental jurisdiction over the new parties to the counterclaim, the Property Insurers, regardless of the lack of diversity of citizenship. Rule 13(a) of the Federal Rules of Civil Procedure defines as compulsory any counterclaim

> which at the time of serving the pleading the pleader has against any opposing party, if it arises out of the transaction or occurrence that is the subject matter of the opposing party's claim and does not require for its adjudication the presence of third parties of whom the court cannot acquire jurisdiction.

. . . Quantum makes no argument that its counterclaims against Hartford were not compulsory. Indeed, the fact that Quantum filed counterclaims against Hartford suggests that Quantum considered those claims compulsory; otherwise, presumably, Quantum would not have brought them in this suit. Quantum does not desire to litigate its claims in this court, but filed them here only because it believed them to be compulsory and did not want to waive them altogether.

The mandatory nature of Quantum's counterclaims against Hartford is also made clear by case law interpreting Rule 13(a). . . . A counterclaim is considered as arising out of the same transaction or occurrence as the original claim if it is " 'logically related' to the opposing party's claim." *USM Corp. v. SPS Technologies, Inc.*, 102 F.R.D. 167, 170 (N.D. Ill. 1984) (citations omitted). "[W]here separate trials on each of the respective claims would involve a substantial duplication of effort and time by the parties and the court," a logical relationship exists between the claims. *Id.* "Relevant considerations include whether the claims involve: (1) many of the same factual issues; (2) the same factual and legal issues; or (3) are offshoots of the same basic controversy between the parties." *Id.* Applying this test to the present case, it is clear that a logical relationship exists between Hartford's original declaratory judgment action against Quantum and Quantum's counterclaims against Hartford. Both arise out of the same incident, the failure of the heat exchanger at the Quantum plant, and the same contract, the insurance contract between Hartford and Quantum. There can be no dispute that the counterclaims against Hartford are compulsory. Thus, we have supplemental jurisdiction over the new parties to the counterclaims, the Property Insurers.

Moreover, we note that the existence of supplemental jurisdiction over these new parties to the counterclaims, added pursuant to Rule 13(h), does not depend on whether their joinder was necessary pursuant to Rule 19 or permissive pursuant to Rule 20.[3] Wright and Miller observe that Rule 13(h) does not differentiate between parties added pursuant to Rule 19 and parties added pursuant to Rule 20, and explain that "inasmuch as the claim itself is already within the court's ancillary jurisdiction [now codified in § 1367 as supplemental jurisdiction], the party should be added on the same basis in the interests of maximum judicial efficiency and economy." 6 Wright & Miller, *supra* § 1436, at 192. . . . Thus, it is not necessary for us to determine whether the Property Insurers are "necessary" new parties or merely "permissive" new parties.

B. *Discretionary Denial of Supplemental Jurisdiction Pursuant to § 1367(c)*

[The court rejected Quantum's argument that even if supplemental jurisdiction existed under § 1367(a) and (b), the court should decline to exercise it pursuant to the discretionary exceptions provided in subsection (c).]

Conclusion

For the reasons discussed, we conclude that we have supplemental jurisdiction pursuant to 28 U.S.C. § 1367 over the counterclaims against the third-party defendants, Industrial Risk Insurers and DR Insurance Company. . . .

---

3. There appears to be no debate that the Property Insurers were properly joined under at least one of the two joinder provisions.

NOTES AND QUESTIONS

1. *Satisfying Rule 19 or 20.*   At footnote 3 the court stated that joining the Property Insurers under Rule 13(h) accorded with Rule 19 or 20, or both. Since the parties agreed on this point, the court did not pursue the matter. Can you explain why Rule 20 would have been satisfied here? Though we have not yet studied Rule 19, assume that it would be satisfied if, in the absence of the party to be joined under Rule 13(h) (*i.e.*, here, the Property Insurers), that party's interests could be impaired or an existing party could not obtain complete relief. Would either of these Rule 19 tests have been met here?

2. *Adding parties to permissive counterclaims.*   The court found that because Quantum's counterclaim against Hartford was compulsory, adding Property Insurers to that claim was within the court's supplemental jurisdiction. Would the result have been any different if the counterclaim had been permissive? Doesn't Rule 13(h) also allow a defendant to add additional parties to a permissive counterclaim? And if the court has subject matter jurisdiction over a permissive counterclaim against the plaintiff, won't it ordinarily also have jurisdiction over the claim against a third party added to that claim? Even if the third-party claim lacks an independent basis of jurisdiction, won't it usually satisfy § 1367(a) since it presumably arises from the same transaction or occurrence as the permissive counterclaim against the plaintiff? If so, would § 1367(b) pose any obstacle even in a diversity case?

PROBLEMS

8-9. After Smith's factory was destroyed during a hurricane, he filed a $250,000 claim with his insurance company, Insco, which refused to pay on the ground that the policy did not cover losses caused by natural calamities. When Smith continued to insist that the company pay under the policy, Insco brought a diversity action against him in federal court seeking a declaratory judgment that its policy with Smith did not provide coverage for the loss. Insco is a New York corporation; Smith is a citizen of Iowa. Smith filed a counterclaim against Insco for a declaratory judgment that it is obligated to cover the $250,000 loss. Smith joined Brown as an additional party to the counterclaim. Brown, a citizen of Iowa, is the insurance agent who sold Smith the Insco policy and who advised him that it covered hurricane losses. Smith seeks damages of $250,000 from Brown under theories of detrimental reliance, breach of contract, and negligence. Was joinder of Brown allowed by Rule 13(h)? Assuming it was, does the court have subject matter jurisdiction over the claim against Brown? *See Travelers Ins. Co. v. Intraco, Inc.*, 163 F.R.D. 554 (S.D. Iowa 1995).

8-10. Ted keeps two automobiles at Roy's garage. Roy sued Ted in a Texas federal court seeking $500,000 for personal injuries suffered when Ted hit Roy while returning one of the cars, a BMW, to the garage. Ted filed a counterclaim against Roy for $100,000, asserting that Roy was responsible for failing to contain an earlier fire that destroyed Ted's Rolls Royce at the garage. Ted named Jim as an additional party to the counterclaim, alleging that Jim's negligence started the fire. Roy is a citizen of Texas. Ted and Jim are citizens of Louisiana. Did Ted have a right to assert his claims against Roy and Jim? Assuming that he did, does the court have subject matter jurisdiction over these claims?

2.   Joinder of Third Parties Under Rule 14

Wallkill 5 Associates II v. Tectonic Engineering, P.C.

1997 WL 452252 (D.N.J. July 25, 1997)

WOLIN, District Judge.

This matter is before the Court on the motion of defendant Tectonic Engineering, P.C. ("Tectonic") to dismiss the complaint of plaintiff Wallkill 5 Associates II ("Wallkill") on three grounds: (1) lack of personal jurisdiction pursuant to Federal Rule of Civil Procedure 12(b)(2); (2) improper venue pursuant to Federal Rule of Civil Procedure 12(b)(3) with an alternative request to transfer the action to the Southern District of New York under 28 U.S.C. § 1406(a); and (3) failure to join an indispensable party. Alternatively, if the complaint is not dismissed or transferred, Tectonic requests that the Court grant leave for Tectonic to join Walter Poppe General Contractors, Inc. as a third-party defendant.

. . . For the reasons given below, the Court will deny Tectonic's motion in its entirety. The Court will also deny Tectonic's request to join Poppe as a third-party defendant.

Background

In the early 1990's, S & S Associates ("S & S"), a New Jersey partnership and the predecessor in interest to Wallkill, also a New Jersey partnership, bought property in Wallkill, New York with plans to build and lease a warehouse on the site. S & S hired Tectonic, a New York corporation, and its president Donald Benvie, a New York resident (collectively "Tectonic"), to perform certain geotechnical tests on the property and to issue a formal geotechnical report.

In order to determine the subsurface soil conditions on the property, Tectonic had ten test pits dug and six soil borings done on various parts of the property. . . . The results of these tests were incorporated into the Geotechnical Report (the "Report"), issued on November 29, 1993. In general, Tectonic's Report advised that after some remedial work, the land would be suitable for development.

Wallkill claims that, in reliance on the Report, it exercised its option to purchase the vacant land for $375,000. Wallkill also negotiated with a prospective tenant for a lease of the to-be-constructed warehouse. Wallkill then negotiated a construction contract with Walter Poppe General Contractors, Inc. ("Poppe"), a New Jersey corporation, to have the vacant land developed and a warehouse constructed thereon.

As the general contractor, Poppe hired various subcontractors to perform the contracted work. Poppe performed the initial clearing of the site cutting the trees and burning the brush. . . . Work had been going on for several months when, in October, 1994, Wallkill learned from Poppe that certain areas of the land were unsuitable for building even after implementation of the recommendations in Tectonic's Report, due to the existence of unsuitable organic material, including wood chips, branches and stumps.

Wallkill called Tectonic to evaluate the extent of the problem at the site. Tectonic dug several pits at that time to determine the depth and breadth of the unsuitable material. Tectonic contends that these pits revealed that the unsuitable organic material was not under the property's original soil; rather the pits indicated that the unsuitable material had been placed on top of the original ground. . . .

Wallkill contends that the conclusions in Tectonic's Report were erroneous. Wallkill claims that Tectonic failed to discover or mention unsuitable subsurface soil conditions, despite digging test pits at ten spots on the property. . . .

Wallkill sued Tectonic in this Court alleging: (1) breach of duty of performance (First Count); (2) breach of express and implied warranties (Second Count); (3) breach of contract (Third Count); and (4) breach of professional care (Fourth Count). . . .

Wallkill claims that it would not have exercised its option to purchase the property had it known of the actual condition of the land. Wallkill also claims that it was damaged because of the extra time and money expended to remove the unsuitable organic material: $110,000 to make the land suitable for building; $32,000 to extend the loan agreement on the property; $8,000 per year for a rise in the interest rate on the loan ($120,000 over the fifteen year term of the loan); and loss of rent. . . . Wallkill did not name Poppe . . . as [a] defendant.

Discussion

[The court's discussion and denial of Tectonic's motions to dismiss for lack of personal jurisdiction, to dismiss or transfer for improper venue, and to dismiss on the ground that Poppe was an indispensable party under Rule 19 is omitted.]

As an alternative to joinder under Rule 19, Tectonic requests leave to file a third-party complaint against Poppe pursuant to Federal Rule of Civil Procedure 14(a). Rule 14 provides, in pertinent part:

> [A] defending party, as a third-party plaintiff, may cause a summons and complaint to be served upon a person not a party to the action who is or may be liable to a third-party plaintiff for all or part of the plaintiff's claim against the third-party plaintiff.

Fed. R. Civ. P. 14(a).[6] A third-party plaintiff may not present a claim of the third-party defendant's liability to the plaintiff; rather it must set forth a claim of secondary liability such that, if the third-party plaintiff is found liable, the third-party defendant will be liable to him under a theory of indemnification, contribution, or some other theory of derivative liability recognized by the relevant substantive law. *See Janney Montgomery Scott,* 11 F.3d at 412 (noting that Rule 14 "permits a party defendant who claims a right of indemnity from third persons to protect itself from potentially inconsistent verdicts by impleading the absent party . . .") . . . . Consequently, a theory that another party is the correct defendant is not appropriate for a third-party complaint.

> A defendant sued for negligence, for example, cannot implead a third party whose negligence was totally responsible for plaintiff's injury. When a third party's conduct furnishes a complete defense against the defendant's liability, the defendant may raise that conduct defensively in his answer but may not use it as a foundation for impleader.

[Toberman v. Copas, 800 F. Supp. 1239, 1242 (M.D. Pa. 1992).]

Even if a third-party plaintiff alleges a proper basis to implead an additional party, Rule 14 does not require joinder; "rather the decision to permit joinder rests with the sound discretion of the trial court." *Remington Arms Co. v. Liberty Mut. Ins. Co.,* 748 F. Supp. 1057, 1068 (D. Del. 1990); *see also Somportex Ltd. v. Philadelphia Chewing Gum Corp.,* 453 F.2d 435, 439 n.6 (3d Cir. 1971), *cert. denied,* 405 U.S. 1017 (1972) (declaring that "a court, called upon to exercise its discretion as to impleader, must balance the desire to avoid circuity of actions and to obtain consistent results against any prejudice that the plaintiff might suffer from complications of the case."). In deciding whether to permit impleader, a court must consider (1) prejudice to the original plaintiff; (2) complication of issues at trial; (3) likelihood of trial delay; and (4) timeliness of the motion to implead. *See O'Mara Enter., Inc. v. Mellon Bank,* 101 F.R.D. 668, 670 (W.D. Pa. 1983).

Tectonic fails to show that, if it is found liable to Wallkill, Poppe will be liable to it. Tectonic's theory of recovery is not supported by any allegation that Poppe stands in a joint tortfeasor relationship to Tectonic, or that there is any relationship of contribution or indemnity, which would trigger secondary liability under New Jersey law. Moreover, Tectonic does not allege that Poppe has a contractual

---

6. The Court pauses to note that original plaintiffs cannot use Rule 14 to circumvent the requirements of supplemental jurisdiction. While the district court would have jurisdiction over the third-party plaintiff's claim against a non-diverse party under 28 U.S.C. § 1367(a), § 1367(b) precludes the original plaintiff from using Rule 14 to amend its complaint to include the impleaded party and, thus, litigate the impleaded party's liability to it. *See . . . [Janney Montgomery Scott, Inc. v. Shepard Niles, Inc.,* 11 F.3d 399, 412 n.15 (3d Cir. 1993)] (recognizing that under § 1367(b), district court would not have jurisdiction over claims by a plaintiff against a party impleaded under Rule 14). Thus, if the Court permits Poppe to be joined, adjudicability is limited to the issues raised by joinder. *See Owen Equip., & Erection Co. v. Kroger,* 437 U.S. 365, 376-77 (1978) (holding that in an action based on diversity, any claim asserted by the original plaintiff against the third-party defendant must present an independent jurisdictional basis).

relationship with or owes a duty to Tectonic. Tectonic merely states that because it believes that Poppe either moved the unsuitable organic material to where it was later found or permitted the material to be moved, it has a "good faith basis to believe that Poppe is liable to Tectonic for all of the plaintiff's claim against Tectonic." . . . The Court finds that this is a defense rather than a proper basis for third-party liability under Rule 14. Accordingly, the Court denies Tectonic's motion for permission to join Poppe as a third-party defendant.

Conclusion

For the foregoing reasons, the Court will deny Tectonic's motion to dismiss in its entirety. The Court will also deny Tectonic's request for leave to file a third-party complaint against Poppe. . . .

NOTES AND QUESTIONS

1. *Types of claims allowed by Rule 14.*   Rule 14(a) allows four types of claims: first, under Rule 14(a)(1), an "impleader," or indemnity claim, by the defendant against the third-party defendant; second, under Rule 14(a)(2)(B), counterclaims by the third-party defendant against the third-party plaintiff and crossclaims by the third-party defendant against a co-party third-party defendant; third, under Rule 14(a)(2)(D), claims by the third-party defendant against the original plaintiff; and, fourth, under Rule 14(a)(3), claims by the original plaintiff against the third-party defendant.

2. *Subject matter jurisdiction.*   If Tectonic's claim against the general contractor, Poppe, had satisfied Rule 14(a), would Rule 14(a) have allowed Poppe to assert a claim against Wallkill for monies owed on the project? Would it have permitted Wallkill to assert a claim against Poppe for damages caused to the site? Assuming that these claims could have been asserted under Rule 14(a), would the federal court have had subject matter jurisdiction over each of them? In considering these questions, look at footnote 6, page 685, *supra.*

3. *Mislabeling claims.*   Parties sometimes mistakenly assert claims under Rule 14(a) that should have been brought under Rule 13(h). While both rules allow a defendant to bring in new parties to the action, a Rule 13(h) claim must be part of a counterclaim or crossclaim being asserted against an existing party. A Rule 14 indemnity claim, on the other hand, is asserted solely against the new party to the suit. The other main difference between the two rules is that impleader under Rule 14 is limited to indemnity claims, while claims asserted under Rule 13(h) may seek any form of relief. If a party mistakenly files a claim under Rule 14 that should have been filed under Rule 13(h), courts will usually treat the claim as having been brought under the proper rule without penalizing the party. *See, e.g., FDIC v. Bathgate,* 27 F.3d 850, 873-874 (3d Cir. 1994); *Lasa per L'Industria del Marmo Societa per Azioni v. Alexander,* 414 F.2d 143, 145-147 (6th Cir. 1969). In *Wallkill,* how might Tectonic have asserted a damages claim against Poppe if it

contended that Poppe and Wallkill had injured its business reputation by falsely blaming Tectonic for conditions that developed only after it had tested the site?

4. *Piggybacking under Rule 18(a).*   While Rule 14(a) limits defendants to merely asserting claims for indemnity against a third-party defendant, once such a claim has been asserted, may the defendant join with the indemnity claim any other claims it may have against the third-party defendant? *See* FED. R. CIV. P. 18(a). Will the court necessarily have subject matter jurisdiction over these additional claims?

PROBLEM

8-11. In Problem 8-7, page 673, *supra*, suppose that after Adam and his friends sued U-Drive, Inc. for the loss of their goods, U-Drive, in that same action, filed a claim against Hawkeye Security ("Hawkeye"), alleging that Hawkeye's security guards negligently allowed the truck to be stolen from U-Drive's New Jersey facility. U-Drive seeks indemnification from Hawkeye in the event it is found liable to the plaintiffs. It also seeks $25,000 from Hawkeye for overbilling during the previous two years. After U-Drive brought Hawkeye into the action, the plaintiffs amended their complaint to assert negligence claims against Hawkeye for property loss and emotional distress. Hawkeye is an Oregon corporation with its principal place of business in New York.

   A. Did the federal joinder rules permit U-Drive to assert its claims against Hawkeye? Assuming joinder was proper, does the federal court have subject matter jurisdiction over U-Drive's claims?
   B. As a matter of joinder, did Adam and his friends have a right to assert their claims against Hawkeye? If joinder was proper, does the federal court have subject matter jurisdiction over their claims?

Guaranteed Systems, Inc. v. American National Can Co.

842 F. Supp. 855 (M.D.N.C. 1994)

FRANK W. BULLOCK, JR., Chief Judge.

This civil action is before the court on Third-Party Defendant's motion to dismiss the third-party action for lack of supplemental jurisdiction pursuant to 28 U.S.C. § 1367(b) . . . .

Facts

On March 17, 1993, contractor Guaranteed Systems, Inc., a North Carolina corporation, filed a state court action ("original action") in the Superior Court Division of the General Court of Justice, Rockingham County, North Carolina, against American National Can Company ("National Can"), a Delaware corporation, alleging that National Can had failed to pay Guaranteed Systems for construction work on a National Can facility in Forest Park, Georgia. National Can removed the original action to federal court pursuant to 28 U.S.C. §§ 1441(a) and 1446 because the federal court had original jurisdiction over the original action under 28 U.S.C. § 1332(a). National Can then answered and filed a counterclaim against Guaranteed Systems alleging, *inter alia*, that Guaranteed Systems had been negligent in the performance of its construction work on the National Can facility. On June 30, 1993, Guaranteed Systems, defending against National Can's counterclaim, answered and, pursuant to Rule 14(b) of the Federal Rules of Civil Procedure, filed a third-party action against sub-contractor R.K. Elite-HydroVac Services, Inc. ("HydroVac"), alleging claims for indemnity and contribution for any amount that may be determined to be owed to National Can by Guaranteed Systems as a result of the counterclaim initiated by National Can.

Discussion

Federal courts may exercise original jurisdiction pursuant to 28 U.S.C. § 1331 over cases involving a federal question or pursuant to 28 U.S.C. § 1332 ("the diversity statute") over cases involving citizens of different states, that is, those cases in which the parties are "diverse." They may also exercise supplemental jurisdiction pursuant to 28 U.S.C. § 1367 over all other claims that form part of the same case or controversy as the action within their original jurisdiction, unless that action is within their jurisdiction solely on the basis of the diversity statute. If that action is within their jurisdiction solely on the basis of diversity, federal courts may not exercise supplemental jurisdiction over certain claims, including claims by plaintiffs against persons made parties under Rule 14 of the Federal Rules of Civil Procedure, when so doing would be inconsistent with the jurisdictional requirements of 28 U.S.C. § 1332, for instance, when the plaintiff and the other party are non-diverse.

In the case before the court, it is undisputed that the court's jurisdiction over the original action is founded solely on the diversity statute. It is also undisputed that the third-party action involves a claim that is so related to the original action that it forms "part of the same case or controversy." 28 U.S.C. § 1367(a). The disputed issue is whether the court may exercise supplemental jurisdiction over the third-party state law claim between Plaintiff and Third-Party Defendant, whom Plaintiff, defending the counterclaim, has impleaded for indemnity or contribution in accordance with Rule 14(b) of the Federal Rules of Civil Procedure, when Plaintiff and Third-Party Defendant are non-diverse parties.

The terms of 28 U.S.C. § 1367(b) prohibit the court from exercising jurisdiction over Plaintiff's third-party claim. Guaranteed Systems is clearly a plaintiff in a diversity suit asserting a claim against a non-diverse third-party defendant made a party under Rule 14.

Were it not for the enactment of Section 1367, however, the rationale of the decision in *Owen Equip. & Erection Co. v. Kroger*, 437 U.S. 365 (1978), could allow the court to exercise jurisdiction under these circumstances. *Owen* prohibits the court only from exercising jurisdiction over a state law claim by a plaintiff against a non-diverse third-party defendant impleaded for indemnity purposes by a *defendant*. The principal rationale of both *Owen* and Section 1367(b) is to prevent a plaintiff from "evad[ing] the jurisdictional requirements of 28 U.S.C. § 1332 by the simple expedient of naming initially only those defendants whose joinder satisfies section 1332's requirements and later adding claims not within original federal jurisdiction against other defendants who have intervened or been joined on a supplemental basis." That rationale is inapplicable to the third-party action in this case.

The third-party action in this case corresponds most closely to the typical ancillary impleader claim the Supreme Court used as a benchmark to distinguish the claim the *Owen* plaintiff attempted to assert. In *Owen*, the Supreme Court noted that "in determining whether jurisdiction over a nonfederal claim exists, the context in which the nonfederal claim is asserted is crucial." The Court went on to say that the claim at issue in that case was "simply not ancillary to the federal one in the same sense that, for example, the impleader by a defendant of a third-party defendant *always* is." ([E]mphasis added). An impleader claim has "logical dependence" on the original claim; it is not a "new and independent" claim. Furthermore, Plaintiff here did *not* "voluntarily cho[o]se to bring suit upon a state-law claim in a federal court," as did the plaintiff in *Owen*. Rather, Plaintiff's case was removed to federal court in contravention of Plaintiff's original forum choice.

Essentially, Plaintiff acts as a defendant to National Can's claim when it impleads HydroVac for indemnity. Plaintiff had no logical reason to join HydroVac in the original action because HydroVac's alleged liability to Plaintiff is contingent on Plaintiff's liability to National Can on their counterclaim. Plaintiff cannot be said to have tried to evade the requirements of the diversity statute when it first filed in state court and then impleaded HydroVac only in response to National Can's counterclaim. Plaintiff desires simply and sensibly to avoid the piecemeal and potentially adverse resolution of the liabilities in question.

Before the enactment of Section 1367's supplemental jurisdiction provisions, when cases like the one before the court arose, a court's "decision ultimately [was] based on a weighing of the desire to preserve the integrity of constitutionally based jurisdictional limitations against the desire to dispose of all disputes arising from one set of facts in one action." 6 Charles A. Wright *et al.*, *Federal Practice and Procedure* § 1444 at 319 (2d ed. 1990). If it were not bound by the plain terms of the statute, the court would be swayed by the interests of justice and efficiency to construe Plaintiff's claim as a claim by a *defendant* against a person made party under Rule 14 rather than a claim by a plaintiff, and thus to allow it to proceed under 28 U.S.C. § 1367(b). The court believes, however, that such a construction would reach beyond the limits of Section 1367(b). The jurisdiction of the federal courts is limited not only by Article III of the Constitution, but also by Acts of Congress. The court therefore will grant Third-Party Defendant's motion to dismiss. . . .

NOTES AND QUESTIONS

1. Impleader by plaintiffs.   Even though we tend to think of impleader as a joinder device available to defendants, Rule 14(b) allows plaintiffs against whom a claim has been filed to implead a third party for indemnity on the same basis that a defendant might. Essentially, the plaintiff has been put in the position of a defendant and Rule 14(b) extends to a plaintiff faced with a claim the same opportunity for impleader that it affords a defendant. Of course, as is true with all of the federal joinder rules, joinder under Rule 14(b) must comport with the standards of subject matter jurisdiction.

2. Subject matter jurisdiction.   Judge Bullock concluded that the text of § 1367(b) precluded him from exercising subject matter jurisdiction over Guaranteed Systems' attempt to implead HydroVac. But did it? Judge Bullock premised his ruling on language in the statutory text that precludes plaintiffs in diversity cases from filing claims against persons joined under Rule 14. But that language is only triggered if the exercise of supplemental jurisdiction over the claim "would be inconsistent with the jurisdictional requirements of section 1332." What are those jurisdictional requirements? *See* "A Note on *Kroger* and Potential Evasions of the Complete Diversity Principle," page 384, *supra*. And would the exercise of jurisdiction over the plaintiff's Rule 14(b) impleader have been inconsistent with any of those requirements? Does § 1367(b) change the jurisdictional standards of § 1332? Finally, do you agree with Judge Bullock's resolution of the jurisdictional issue?

3. Successive impleader.   Rule 14(a)(5) allows a third-party defendant who is sued for indemnity to "proceed under this rule against a nonparty who is or may be liable to the third-party defendant for all or part of any claim against it." FED. R. CIV. P. 14(a)(5). The rule thus allows the third-party defendant to implead a fourth-party defendant, and so on. This is true whether the third-party defendant was brought into the case by the defendant under Rule 14(a) or by a plaintiff (against whom a claim was filed) under Rule 14(b).

PROBLEM

8-12. When Viacom sold the Taylor Forge Steel Co. ("Taylor Forge") to Michael, Viacom agreed to conduct an environmental cleanup of the business site. Michael agreed to indemnify Viacom for any cleanup costs in excess of $1.75 million. Viacom, a Delaware corporation with its principal place of business in New York, has sued Michael, a Florida citizen, in a New York federal court for breach of contract, claiming that he failed to reimburse Viacom as agreed. Michael filed a counterclaim, alleging that in obtaining the indemnity agreement Viacom misrepresented the extent of contamination at the Taylor Forge site and that Viacom's delay in cleaning up the site had reduced Taylor Forge's value. Michael also filed a claim against Conolog, a neighboring business, alleging that it had contaminated the site and was liable for the cleanup costs. Conolog, a Delaware corporation with its principal place of business in New Jersey, filed a claim against Taylor Forge for contribution and indemnity. Taylor Forge, a Delaware corporation located in New Jersey, then filed a claim against Viacom essentially identical to Michael's counterclaim against Viacom. Did the federal rules authorize the parties to assert these various claims? If so, does the federal court have subject matter jurisdiction over each of the claims? *See Viacom Int'l, Inc. v. Kearney*, 212 F.3d 721 (2d Cir.), *cert. denied*, 531 U.S. 1051 (2000).

E.   Intervention by Absentees

In certain situations, a stranger to a lawsuit may be allowed to intervene in the action, even over the existing parties' opposition, particularly if the stranger has an interest that may be harmed if the suit were to proceed without her. Intervention was largely unknown to the common law, which operated on the principle that the plaintiff was usually the master of his lawsuit. Under the codes, which borrowed from the European civil law, intervention was allowed in limited settings. *See* FLEMING JAMES, JR., CIVIL PROCEDURE 501-502 (1965). Today, both state and federal courts frequently allow intervention, in accord with the applicable rule or statute.

Rule 24 governs intervention in federal court proceedings. Read this rule carefully. Note that Rule 24(a) provides for intervention of right, while 24(b) deals with permissive intervention. Subdivisions (a)(1) and (b)(1)(A) of Rule 24 allow intervention to the extent provided for by federal statute. Examples of such statutory intervention include 28 U.S.C. § 2403(a) (allowing the United States to intervene in actions involving the constitutionality of a federal law), § 2403(b) (allowing a state to intervene in actions involving the constitutionality of state law), and 42 U.S.C. § 3612(o)(2) (allowing victims of housing discrimination to intervene in suits brought on their behalf by the attorney general under the Fair Housing Act). Nonstatutory intervention under Rule 24 is governed by subdivisions (a)(2) (intervention of right) and (b)(1)(B) (permissive intervention). The material that follows explores intervention under Rule 24.

Great Atlantic & Pacific Tea Co. v. Town of East Hampton

178 F.R.D. 39 (E.D.N.Y. 1998)

WEXLER, District Judge.

In this action challenging the validity of a local zoning law, Group for the South Fork, Inc. (the "Group") requests leave to intervene as defendants either as of right under Fed. R. Civ. P. 24(a)(2), or alternatively, as a matter of discretion under Fed. R. Civ. P. 24(b)(2). For the reasons set forth below, the Group's motion is denied with leave to renew at a later stage of the litigation.

Facts

In 1996, defendant Town of East Hampton adopted and filed with the State of New York a local zoning law, officially known as Local Law No. 17 of 1996 (the "Superstore Law"), amending . . . the East Hampton Town Code to restrict the establishment of very large retail stores within East Hampton outside of the Central Business zone. The Superstore Law provides, *inter alia*, that a building used for a supermarket may not exceed 25,000 square feet in gross floor area and that parking for supermarkets shall be located primarily to the sides or rear of the building. The effect of the Superstore Law was to prevent plaintiff, The Great Atlantic & Pacific Tea Company, Inc. ("A & P"), from proceeding with its proposal to develop a 33,878 square foot supermarket at a site on Montauk Highway formerly occupied by a Stern's department store. The proposed site is in a Neighborhood Business zone.

A & P brings this suit against the Town, seeking a declaratory judgment that the Town's passage of the Superstore Law was beyond its legislative authority, and that the law itself violates the New York and federal constitutions in that it denies A & P due process and equal protection, and interferes with interstate commerce. A & P also asserts that the law violates 42 U.S.C. § 1983 and is an illegal restraint of trade under New York law. The Town has moved to dismiss the complaint for failure to state a claim pursuant to Rule 12(b)(6) of the Federal Rules of Civil Procedure.

Through its president, Robert DeLuca, the Group describes itself as an environmental organization dedicated to preserving the rural character, rural heritage, and natural resources of the South Fork of Long Island, including the East Hampton area. The Group actively supported the Superstore Law, and its members provided extensive testimony during public hearings as well as providing commentary on area planning statements relevant to the law. The Group has also submitted affidavits from some of its members who live near the proposed site of the A & P supermarket, averring that the rural and residential character of the area will be changed to the detriment of their property values.

The Group has filed a proposed answer and proposed memoranda of law in support of its proposed motion to dismiss A & P's complaint. A review of the memoranda of law submitted by the Town and the Group reveals that they raise similar arguments in support of dismissal of plaintiff's complaint. A & P objects to the Group's intervention in this action.

Analysis

I.   Intervention as of Right

To intervene as of right under Rule 24(a)(2), the would-be intervenor must establish the following:

> (1) a timely motion; (2) an interest relating to the property or transaction that is the subject matter of the action; (3) an impairment of that interest without intervention; and (4) the movant's interest is not adequately represented by the other parties to the litigation.

United States v. Pitney Bowes, Inc., 25 F.3d 66, 70 (2d Cir. 1994). Intervention will be denied if any requirement is not met.

A.   Timeliness

The complaint was filed on November 20, 1996, and the Group's motion to intervene was filed on May 9, 1997. A & P does not contest the timeliness of the motion and the Court finds, absent opposition, that the first element of the *Pitney Bowes* test is met.

B.   The Intervenor's Interest in the Transaction that is the Subject of the Action

An intervenor's interest must be "direct, substantial, and legally protectable," rather than "remote or contingent." An organization like the Group has a sufficient interest to support intervention by right where the underlying action concerns legislation previously supported by the organization. This is particularly true where, as here, the personal interests of its members in the continued environmental quality of the area and the continued rural character of East Hampton would be threatened if the Superstore Law is found to be invalid or unconstitutional and A & P proceeds with development of its planned market. The Court finds that the Group has demonstrated a sufficient legal interest in the subject matter of this action to satisfy the second element of the *Pitney Bowes* test.

C.   Effect on Intervenor's Interests

The third element of the intervention by right standard is met where the intervenors demonstrate that, absent intervention, the disposition of the action may, as a practical matter, impede or impair their interests. Here, the interests of the Group and its members would likely be impaired if the Superstore Law is found to be invalid or unconstitutional.

D.   Adequacy of Representation

Although the Group's application to intervene passes the first three steps, it founders on the final element, adequacy of representation. An applicant for intervention as of right must show that it may not be adequately represented by a named party. This showing places only a "minimal burden" on the would-be intervenor. *Trbovich v. United Mine Workers of Am.*, 404 U.S. 528, 538 n.10 (1972). Nonetheless, adequate representation is presumed when the would-be intervenor shares the same ultimate objective as a party to the lawsuit. To overcome the presumption of adequate representation in the face of shared objectives, the would-be intervenor must demonstrate collusion, nonfeasance, adversity of interest, or incompetence on the part of the named party that shares the same interest.

On the facts here, adequate representation is presumed because the Group and the Town share the same ultimate objective in this litigation, namely, a declaration that the Superstore Law was validly enacted and is constitutional. The Group does not suggest that the presumption is overcome because of collusion, nonfeasance, or incompetence by the Town in its defense of the validity of the Superstore Law. Rather, the Group contends that the Town will not adequately represent its interests in defending the Superstore Law because the Group is an environmental organization whose concern is focused on protecting the environment and the rural character of the South Fork of Long Island, whereas the Town must concern itself with other interests such as perceived economic growth and stimulation of tax revenues. Consequently, the Group contends, it will argue the environmental rationale for the Superstore Law more vigorously than would the Town.

Even accepting as true the Group's characterization of these differing concerns, the interests of the Group coincide with the interests of the Town in terms of the single legal issue to be determined by this lawsuit, i.e., the validity and constitutionality of the Superstore Law. To prevail on its theory of inadequate representation, the Group would need to demonstrate that it has a legal interest in maintaining the Superstore Law that not only differs from the Town's interest, but would permit the Group to assert a justification for the law that could not be equally asserted by the Town. This demonstration is lacking. *See Natural Resources Defense Council v. New York State Dep't of Environ. Conservation*, 834 F.2d 60, 62 (2d Cir. 1987) (finding adequate representation where proposed intervenor failed to show that the nature of its interests were related to colorable legal defenses that the state agency would be less able to assert). The fact that the Group and the Town may have different motives behind their joint interest in defending the statute does not lead to the conclusion that the Town will fail to pursue its defense of the Superstore Law with vigor.

To the extent that the Group, by virtue of its environmental expertise, might be more persuasive than the Town in arguing the environmental justification for the Superstore Law, such a notion is speculative (particularly in light of the cooperation between the Group and the Town in passing the Superstore Law) and unsupported by examination of the Group's proposed briefs submitted in support of the Town's motion to dismiss. Both sets of briefs raise the same issues and offer the same arguments. Even assuming that the Group may be better able than the Town to provide environmental expertise and that a need for such expertise will arise during these proceedings, the Group may seek *amicus curiae* status to bring its views before the Court.

The Group further contends that it is inadequately represented because the Town might settle the action on terms that the Group would not approve, or because the Town might not appeal an adverse decision. These arguments are unpersuasive. As the Fifth Circuit has noted with respect to possible future settlement of an action:

The mere possibility that a party may at some future time enter into a settlement cannot alone show inadequate representation. If this were so, the requirement that the would-be intervenor show inadequacy of representation would be effectively written out of the rule, for it is always a possibility that the present parties will settle a lawsuit.

. . . Similarly, the mere fact that a party might fail to appeal does not rise to the level of inadequate representation. "If disagreement with an actual party over trial strategy, including whether to challenge or appeal a court order, were sufficient bases for a proposed intervenor to claim that its interests were not adequately represented, the requirement would be rendered meaningless."

Because the Group has failed to demonstrate that the Town will inadequately represent its interests, the application for intervention as of right pursuant to Rule 24(a)(2) is denied with leave to renew at a later stage of the proceedings in the event the Group can make a factual showing that the Town is not vigorously litigating the case.

II.   Permissive Intervention

The Group also seeks to intervene pursuant to Rule 24(b)(2).* Permissive intervention may be granted "when an applicant's claim or defense and the main action have a question of law or fact in common." Fed. R. Civ. P. 24(b)(2). This threshold test is clearly met because both the Group and the Town seek a declaration that the Superstore Law is valid and constitutional.

Permissive intervention is a matter left to the discretion of the court. The principal consideration for the court in determining whether or not to allow intervention is "whether the intervention will unduly delay or prejudice the adjudication of the rights of the original parties." In exercising its discretion, the court may consider other relevant factors, including the nature and extent of the intervenor's interests; whether the intervenor's interests are adequately represented by the parties; and whether the party seeking intervention will significantly contribute to the full development of the underlying factual issues in the suit and to the just and equitable adjudication of the legal question presented.

It is also clear, however, that intervention should not be used as a means to inject collateral issues into an existing action, particularly where it serves to delay and complicate the litigation. After reviewing the affidavits submitted by the Group in support of its motion to intervene, the Court is troubled by the potential for the injection of collateral issues, in particular, the issue of commercial development at the proposed A & P site even where such development would be within the limits imposed by the Superstore Law.

The affidavit submitted by the Group's president, Robert DeLuca, stresses concerns that go far beyond merely validating the Superstore Law and strongly suggests that any major commercial development which changes the present

---

* [The current version of this rule is designated Rule 24(b)(1)(B). — Eds.]

character of the proposed A & P site would be unacceptable to the Group, even if such development fell within the bounds of the Superstore Law. . . .

The affidavits submitted by other Group members similarly indicate that their concerns are not so much directed to banning superstores in East Hampton areas zoned for Neighborhood Business as they are to banning any major commercial development of the proposed A & P site. . . .

After reviewing the affidavits submitted by the Group, the Court is left with the firm impression that the Group will seek to transform this lawsuit from a test of the validity of the Superstore Law into a contest over the propriety of commercial development in East Hampton in general and at the proposed A & P site in particular. The arguments raised in the Group's affidavits are equally applicable to the proposed A & P supermarket and to the establishment of smaller ventures on the site.

Taking the above considerations into account, the Court finds that the nature and extent of the Group's interest in defending the validity of the Superstore Law is identical to that of the Town and both seek the same ultimate outcome. The Town appears ready, willing and able to vigorously defend the validity of the Superstore Law so that the Group's interests are adequately represented. Moreover, the Group's concerns over commercial development at the proposed site, as opposed merely to its concern to defend the validity of the Superstore Law, injects a collateral issue into this lawsuit that can only serve to delay and complicate the proceedings to the prejudice of plaintiff without assisting in the resolution of the central issue before the Court. . . . Consequently, the Group's motion to intervene pursuant to Rule 24(b)(2) is denied with leave to renew at a later stage of the proceedings in the event the Group can make a factual showing that the Town is not vigorously litigating this action.

Conclusion

For the reasons stated above, the Group's motion to intervene is denied with leave to renew at a later stage of the proceedings in the event the Group can make a factual showing that the Town is not vigorously litigating this action.

So Ordered.

NOTES AND QUESTIONS

1. Procedure for intervention.   Read Rule 24(c). Note that a would-be intervenor must file a motion stating the grounds for intervention, accompanied by the party's proposed pleading. What pleadings and papers did the Group file with its motion to intervene? In what way did this material influence the court's ruling on the motion?

2. Timeliness.   Rule 24(a)(2) imposes four requirements for intervention of right. The first of these is that the motion to intervene must be timely. *See* FED. R. CIV. P. 24(a). While this was not a problem in *Great Atlantic & Pacific*, it was an issue in *Sierra Club v. Espy*, 18 F.3d 1202 (5th Cir. 1994), an action the Sierra Club brought to challenge the U.S. Forest Service's management of national forests in Texas. Eight years after the suit was filed, two trade associations representing purchasers of timber from these forests sought to intervene in the action. The court identified several factors to be considered in resolving the issue of timeliness:

> (1) The length of time during which the would-be intervenor actually knew or reasonably should have known of its interest in the case before it petitioned for leave to intervene; (2) the extent of the prejudice that the existing parties to the litigation may suffer as a result of the would-be intervenor's failure to apply for intervention as soon as it knew or reasonably should have known of its interest in the case; (3) the extent of the prejudice that the would-be intervenor may suffer if intervention is denied; and (4) the existence of unusual circumstances militating either for or against a determination that the application is timely.

Id. at 1205. The court emphasized that

> [t]he analysis is contextual; absolute measures of timeliness should be ignored. The requirement of timeliness is not a tool of retribution to punish the tardy would-be intervenor, but rather a guard against prejudicing the original parties by the failure to apply sooner. Federal courts should allow intervention "where no one would be hurt and greater justice could be attained."

Id. The court rejected "the notion that the date on which the would-be intervenor became aware of the pendency of the action should be used to determine whether it acted promptly," for this would encourage "premature intervention that wastes judicial resources." *Id.* at 1206. Instead, "[a] better gauge of promptness is the speed with which the would-be intervenor acted when it became aware that its interests would no longer be protected by the original parties." *Id.* The court concluded that the motion was timely, for it was filed 15 days after it became clear that the Forest Service would no longer protect the intervenors' interests.

   3. *Intervenor's interest.*   Next, under Rule 24(a)(2) the applicant must have an interest "relating to the property or transaction that is the subject of the action. . . ." How did the intervenors in *Great Atlantic & Pacific* satisfy this element? While courts have provided no clear definition of this requirement, many take an expansive view of it. This is particularly true in cases affecting the public interest when it is important that a diversity of viewpoints be represented. *See Smuck v. Hobson*, 408 F.2d 175 (D.C. Cir. 1969). *See generally* 7C Charles Alan Wright, Arthur R. Miller & Mary Kay Kane, Federal Practice and Procedure § 1908.1 (3d ed. 2007 & Supp. 2015). While the interest prong of Rule 24(a)(2) is by no means met in all cases, a court that is disinclined to allow intervention will often base its denial on the intervenor's failure to satisfy one of the other three requirements for intervention of right. Note, however, that some courts have adopted a somewhat stricter approach to this question, requiring the assertion of an interest that is legally recognized as enforceable. *See Aurora Loan Servs., Inc. v. Craddieth*, 442 F.3d 1018 (7th Cir. 2006); *International Chem. Corp. v. Nautilus Ins. Co.*, 2010 WL 3070101, at *2 (W.D.N.Y. Aug. 3, 2010).

4. Impair or impede.   On what basis did the court find that the intervenors in *Great Atlantic & Pacific* met the third requirement for intervention of right, *i.e.*, that "the action may as a practical matter impair or impede" their ability to protect their interest? FED. R. CIV. P. 24(a)(2). Does the "may as a practical matter" wording of 24(a)(2) suggest that the showing of possible prejudice does not need to be very strong? If a judgment's practical effects are what matter, should the possible *stare decisis* effect of an adverse judgment be enough to satisfy the "impair or impede" requirement? A number of courts have answered this question in the affirmative, at least when the questions of law are very close to those that would arise in a separate action involving the intervenor. *See, e.g., Stone v. First Union Corp.*, 371 F.3d 1305, 1309-1310 (11th Cir. 2004); *United States v. Oregon*, 839 F.2d 635, 638 (9th Cir. 1988); *Oneida Indian Nation of Wis. v. New York*, 732 F.2d 261, 265 (2d Cir. 1984); *Atlantis Dev. Corp. v. United States*, 379 F.2d 818, 828-829 (5th Cir. 1967); *see also* 7C WRIGHT, MILLER & KANE, *supra*, § 1908.2.

5. Adequacy of representation.   The fourth and final requirement for intervention of right asks whether "existing parties adequately represent" the would-be intervenor's interests. FED. R. CIV. P. 24(a)(2). On whom did *Great Atlantic & Pacific* place the burden of persuasion with respect to adequacy of representation? The court cited *Trbovich v. United Mine Workers*, 404 U.S. 528 (1972), in which the Supreme Court said that this requirement "is satisfied *if the applicant shows* that representation of his interest 'may be' inadequate; and the burden of making that showing should be treated as minimal." *Id.* at 538 n.10 (emphasis added). Yet doesn't the wording of Rule 24(a)(2) suggest that those opposing intervention have the burden of showing that the applicant's interest is adequately represented? In contrast to *Great Atlantic & Pacific* and *Trbovich*, some courts place the burden of persuasion on this issue on the party resisting intervention. *See, e.g., United States v. American Tel. & Tel. Co.*, 642 F.2d 1285, 1293 (D.C. Cir. 1980); *United States v. Dep't of Mental Health*, 785 F. Supp. 846, 849 (E.D. Cal. 1992); *CBS Inc. v. Snyder*, 136 F.R.D. 364, 368 (S.D.N.Y. 1991); *see also* 7C WRIGHT, MILLER & KANE, *supra*, § 1909.

In *Great Atlantic & Pacific*, why did the would-be intervenors fail Rule 24(a)(2)'s inadequacy-of-representation requirement? Did the court reach the correct result given the "'may be' inadequate" language of *Trbovich*? If the mere possibility that representation might at some point become inadequate were enough to satisfy the rule, would this requirement have any meaning? The *Great Atlantic & Pacific* court denied the motion to intervene, but "with leave to renew at a later stage of the proceedings." Under what conditions might a renewed motion to intervene succeed? *See, e.g., Americans United for Separation of Church and State v. City of Grand Rapids*, 922 F.2d 303 (6th Cir. 1990) (allowing Chabad House to intervene of right to appeal a district court decision that enjoined the city from displaying a menorah owned by Chabad in a city square during Jewish religious holidays, finding that the city ceased adequately to represent Chabad's interests once it failed to file an appeal).

6. Permissive intervention.   The court in *Great Atlantic & Pacific* also denied the motion to intervene permissively under former Rule 24(b)(2)—current Rule

24(b)(1)(B). What factors did the court look to in exercising its discretion? Rule 24(b)(3) directs a judge to consider "whether the intervention will unduly delay or prejudice the adjudication of the original parties' rights." FED. R. CIV. P. 24(b)(3). Courts consider a number of other factors as well, including whether existing parties adequately represent an applicant's interests (something that *must* be taken into account for intervention of right); whether the applicant's input as a party would significantly help the court in developing the factual or legal issues involved in the case; and whether the applicant raises other issues that might unduly complicate the case. Which of these was dispositive in *Great Atlantic & Pacific*? *See also* 7C WRIGHT, MILLER & KANE, *supra*, §§ 1911, 1913; Edward J. Brunet & Jerry E. Smith, *Intervention, in* 6 MOORE'S FEDERAL PRACTICE §§ 24.10-24.11 (3d ed. 2015).

7. *Conditioning intervention.*   Even when an intervenor meets the four requirements for intervention of right, a court may place "appropriate conditions or restrictions" on the intervenor's participation in the suit, including conditions that promote the "efficient conduct of the proceedings." Advisory Committee's Note to 1966 Amendment, 39 F.R.D. 69, 111; *see* 7C WRIGHT, MILLER & KANE, *supra*, § 1922. For example, if inadequate representation exists with respect to some but not all of the issues that an intervenor wishes to litigate, might a court limit the intervenor's involvement to presenting evidence just on these issues? When intervention is permissive rather than of right, courts are even more likely to limit the extent of an intervenor's participation in the suit.

PROBLEMS

8-13. Several white students who were denied admission to the University of Michigan sued in federal court to enjoin the university's race-conscious admissions policy on the ground that it violates the Equal Protection Clause of the Fourteenth Amendment. Twelve African American and Latino/a individuals who have applied or intend to apply to the university have moved to intervene in the action under Rule 24(a) and (b) to defend the policy. They claim that resolution of the case could impair their access to the university and assert that the university may not adequately represent their interests because it could be reluctant to raise some defenses the intervenors would present. Specifically, the proposed intervenors contend that internal pressures might prevent the university from offering evidence of its past discrimination and of the disparate impact produced by some of its admissions criteria. Should the court grant the motion to intervene under Rule 24(a)(2)? If this is denied, should permissive intervention be allowed under 24(b)(1)(B), and if so, what conditions might the court place on the intervenors' participation in the suit? *See Grutter v. Bollinger*, 188 F.3d 394 (6th Cir. 1999), *rev'd on other grounds, sub nom. Gratz v. Bollinger*, 539 U.S. 244 (2003).

8-14. Aaron, a California citizen, was hurt when his car was hit by a truck owned by Western Trucking, an Oregon corporation. After the accident, Aaron received treatment at Loma Linda Hospital ("Loma Linda") in California, resulting in fees and charges totaling $100,000. Under California law, Loma Linda may assert a statutory lien for the cost of services rendered against any judgment or settlement Aaron obtains from the accident. Aaron filed a diversity action against Western Trucking in a California federal court, seeking $1 million for his injuries. Two years later, Loma Linda learned that the suit was about to settle. It contacted Aaron, who disputed Loma Linda's right to payment. Loma Linda then moved to intervene as a plaintiff in the federal suit to assert its lien against any settlement. Does Loma Linda meet the requirements for intervention under Rule 24(a)(2) or (b)(1)(B)? If so, does it matter whether Loma Linda intervenes as a plaintiff or as a defendant? *See Ghazarian v. Wheeler*, 177 F.R.D. 482 (C.D. Cal. 1997).

———

Prior to the adoption of 28 U.S.C. § 1367, intervention presented perplexing jurisdictional problems in diversity suits if a proposed intervenor under Rule 24(a)(2) was nondiverse from one of the parties against whom that intervenor would be aligned. Could a federal court, consistently with the standards of § 1332, exercise ancillary jurisdiction over such nondiverse intervenors? The answer to that question depended on whether the proposed intervenor's presence in the case was deemed "indispensable." The word "indispensable" was a term of art borrowed from the jurisprudence of Rule 19, a rule pertaining to the "required" joinder of absent parties and to which we will turn shortly. For now, suffice it to say that in the context of a diversity suit, a conclusion of indispensability under Rule 19 is premised on two interrelated findings: (1) complete diversity would have been destroyed had that party been joined as an original party to the suit; and (2) in fairness and justice the case cannot proceed in that party's absence. In essence, the combination of these findings, *i.e.*, the ultimate finding of indispensability, establishes an absence of subject matter jurisdiction by framing the case as if the absent party had been an original party to the proceeding. To put it slightly differently, indispensability asks whether the party was absolutely required to have been joined as an original party and, if so, whether the court would have had jurisdiction over the case had that party been so joined.

In the context of Rule 24(a)(2), lower federal courts borrowed this concept of indispensability for determining whether ancillary jurisdiction could be exercised over the intervention of a nondiverse plaintiff or defendant. If that party was deemed to be indispensable—*i.e.*, one who should have but could not have been joined as an original party (as a consequence of diversity)—ancillary jurisdiction could not be exercised over the intervention. On the other hand, if that party's presence in the suit was not deemed indispensable—*i.e.*, the party need not have been joined at the outset—the court could exercise ancillary jurisdiction over the intervention. Under the latter circumstance, the intervention of a nondiverse and non-indispensable party was not seen as an evasion of the complete diversity principle.

Today courts continue to apply these pre-§ 1367 standards to determine whether they can exercise supplemental jurisdiction over a proposed Rule 24(a)(2) intervention by a nondiverse party.

Mattel, Inc. v. Bryant

446 F.3d 1011 (9th Cir. 2006)

NOONAN, CIRCUIT JUDGE.

Mattel, Inc., a Delaware corporation with headquarters in California, appeals the order of the district court denying Mattel's motion to remand this action to state court in which Mattel had begun this suit against Carter Bryant, a resident of Missouri and a product designer formerly in its employ. Holding that diversity jurisdiction is not defeated by the intervention of MGA Entertainment, Inc., a California corporation not an indispensable party, we conclude that the district court properly retained jurisdiction.*

PROCEEDINGS

On April 27, 2004, Mattel filed a complaint against Bryant in Los Angeles County Superior Court alleging breach of contract and various torts [relating to Byant's creation of the "Bratz" line of dolls]. On May 14, 2004, Bryant removed the case to federal court, but the court held that the monetary requirement for diversity jurisdiction had not been satisfied. After discovery, Bryant again removed the case, and Mattel again moved to remand. On December 7, 2004, MGA Entertainment, Inc. (MGA) intervened as a defendant to protect its rights to Bratz dolls. On March 4, 2005, the district court held that diversity jurisdiction existed. Mattel was a Delaware corporation with headquarters in California, Bryant was a resident of Missouri, and the amount in controversy was over $75,000. The district court held that the intervention of MGA, a California corporation unmentioned in Mattel's complaint, did not destroy the diversity because MGA was not an indispensable party. The district court certified its order for interlocutory review under 28 U.S.C. § 1292(b). On May 12, 2005, a motions panel of this court granted Mattel permission to appeal.

ANALYSIS

An Indispensable Intervenor? Diversity jurisdiction exists in the controversy between Mattel and Bryant unless destroyed by MGA's intervention as a defendant. Intervention destroys diversity if the intervening party is indispensable. *Takeda v. Northwestern Nat'l Life Ins. Co.*, 765 F.2d 815, 819 (9th Cir. 1985). We review a district court's indispensability determination for abuse of discretion. Mattel argues that MGA is indispensable to the case, explaining its failure to name MGA as a defendant by ignorance dispelled only by discovery that rights to Bratz were at stake. There is, therefore, Mattel argues, "a significant risk of prejudice" to

---

* [Background facts: Bryant's drawings were the inspiration for Bratz dolls, a product line developed and marketed by Mattel's competitor, MGA Entertainment. *See* Appellees' Opening Brief, 2005 WL 3227203.—EDS.]

MGA if the ownership of rights to intellectual property, i.e., the Bratz creations, were decided in the absence of MGA. This significant risk of prejudice is sufficient, Mattel concludes, to make MGA indispensable and so defeats diversity. In opposition, MGA in the joint brief it has filed with Bryant denies that its presence is essential to deciding the controversy between Mattel and Bryant; declares that Mattel can obtain complete relief on all the claims it asserts against Bryant without the presence of MGA; notes that Mattel seeks no relief from MGA; and maintains that, in short, MGA is not an indispensable party.

Mattel's solicitude for the rights of MGA appears to be driven by its desire to have the litigation proceed in a California court. The standard for determining whether a party is indispensable is set by the rule which requires the determination to be made "in equity and good conscience." Fed. R. Civ. P. 19(b). MGA disavows its indispensability. When, as in this case, collusion with the plaintiff is manifestly absent, a defendant intervenor's declaration that it is not indispensable satisfies any concern that a decision in its absence would have prejudiced it. MGA does not need Mattel to tell it what its risks were. Undoubtedly, MGA's posture is as much driven by its desire to be in federal court as Mattel's posture is driven by the desire to be in state court. Acknowledging MGA's jurisdictional motive, we accept its disavowal. MGA is not indispensable. The diversity required by 28 U.S.C. § 1332 is satisfied together with the judge-made rule of complete diversity and the judge-made exception for a non-indispensable defendant-intervenor.

The Effect of Section 1367. Mattel relies more heavily on a second objection to diversity jurisdiction, 28 U.S.C. § 1367(b), which reads:

> In any civil action of which the district courts have original jurisdiction founded solely on section 1332 of this title, the district courts shall not have supplemental jurisdiction under subsection (a) over claims by plaintiffs against persons made parties under Rule 14, 19, 20, or 24 of the Federal Rules of Civil Procedure, or over claims by persons proposed to be joined as plaintiffs under Rule 19 of such rules, or seeking to intervene as plaintiffs under Rule 24 of such rules, when exercising supplemental jurisdiction over such claims would be inconsistent with the jurisdictional requirements of section 1332.

MGA has been made a party under Rule 24. In becoming a party, MGA answered Mattel's claims. Therefore, Mattel maintains, § 1367(b)'s prohibition against supplemental jurisdiction over claims made by parties under Rule 24 is violated.

Mattel's argument overlooks the final clause of § 1367(b): the prohibition applies only "when exercising supplemental jurisdiction over such claims would be inconsistent with the jurisdictional requirements of section 1332." This final clause makes the diversity statute, § 1332, decisive. If that statute is not offended, the prohibition of § 1367(b) does not apply. We have already determined that the intervention of MGA does not offend § 1332. Mattel is mistaken in believing that § 1367(b) trumps § 1332. Neither § 1332 nor § 1367 upset the long-established judge-made rule that the presence of a non-diverse and not indispensable defendant intervenor does not destroy complete diversity. The addition of MGA does not destroy diversity jurisdiction.

Conclusion. For the foregoing reasons, the order of the district court is AFFIRMED.

NOTES AND QUESTIONS

1. *Indispensability.*   Since we have yet to examine Rule 19, we cannot fully assess the *Mattel* court's "indispensability" analysis. Nor does the court's opinion provide enough facts to examine the full range of potential prejudice to the parties and to MGA should the case proceed in MGA's absence. But if Mattel were seeking only monetary damages from its former employee, which seems to be the case, it is unlikely that MGA's presence in the suit would be required to fully vindicate either Mattel's or Bryant's claims or defenses. Similarly, as a nonparty, MGA would not be bound by any judgment against Bryant, though such a judgment might place an economic cloud on the company's property interest in the Bratz line of dolls. In short, while it would make sense to have MGA involved in the suit to fully resolve the ownership of the Bratz line of dolls, a court could surely proceed to adjudicate rights and obligations between Mattel and Bryant in MGA's absence. The Ninth Circuit also accepted MGA's representation that it wasn't indispensable, though such a concession seems like a thin thread on which to base a jurisdictional determination, especially since the concession was conveniently consistent with MGA's argument that the court had jurisdiction over the intervention.

2. *Subject matter jurisdiction.* Section 1367(b) provides that in diversity cases, "the district courts shall not have supplemental jurisdiction . . . over claims by persons . . . seeking to intervene as plaintiffs under Rule 24," when doing so would be "inconsistent with the jurisdictional requirements of section 1332." 28 U.S.C. § 1367(b). MGA intervened as a defendant. Wouldn't it have been simpler for the court to say that § 1367(b) places no limits on intervention by a defendant? But would that be fully accurate? After all, when a party intervenes as a defendant, the intervenor-defendant is, almost by definition, subject to a claim asserted by the plaintiff. With that perspective in mind, what other language in § 1367(b) might be relevant to the jurisdictional inquiry? Wouldn't it be safe to say that regardless of whether a nondiverse party in a diversity case seeks to intervene as a plaintiff or as a defendant, we should attend to all of the potential limitations established by § 1367(b)?

PROBLEM

8-15. Aurora filed a mortgage foreclosure suit against Frank in a federal district court, properly invoking that court's diversity jurisdiction. The court entered a judgment in favor of Aurora and scheduled a foreclosure sale. However, three weeks before the sale, Frank secured financing that would allow him to pay off the mortgage and avoid the sale. On the morning of the day of the sale, Frank's lawyer notified the district court that his client had made an alternative arrangement for paying off the loan. But the lawyer mistakenly described the alternative as a "real" sale of the home rather than as a financing arrangement that would allow Frank to keep the home. The judge, thinking that Frank was therefore "going to be out of the house no matter what," refused to stop the foreclosure sale, at which Midwest was the high bidder. Midwest tendered the purchase price to the court official who had conducted the sale, and the official then issued Midwest a certificate of sale, which, while not the equivalent of title, is nonetheless considered a valuable and enforceable property interest under the applicable state law. Before Midwest could take title to the property, the foreclosure sale had to be confirmed by the district court. The district judge convened a hearing on Aurora's motion to confirm the sale to Midwest. During the hearing, at which Midwest was not present, it was revealed that Frank had indeed found a lender who was willing to pay the amount due Aurora on the mortgage. Based on this additional information, the judge denied Aurora's motion to confirm the sale. Eight days later, Midwest filed a motion to intervene as a plaintiff under Rule 24(a)(2), seeking to challenge the district court's refusal to confirm the sale. Both Frank and Midwest are citizens of Illinois. Does Midwest have a right to intervene under Rule 24(a)(2)? If so, would the district court have subject matter jurisdiction over that intervention? To answer this latter question, you must attend to the text of § 1367(b) and to the jurisdictional requirements of § 1332. *See Aurora Loan Servs., Inc. v. Craddieth,* 442 F.3d 1018 (7th Cir. 2006).

F.   Interpleader

Interpleader is a joinder device that comes into play when two or more persons each claim that they are entitled to the same property or "stake." The person holding the property (the "stakeholder"), rather than having to potentially defend separate lawsuits by each of the claimants, may bring an action against all of the claimants, forcing them to "interplead" or litigate amongst themselves to determine which of them is entitled to the stake. Interpleader spares the stakeholder the vexation of multiple lawsuits with respect to the same property and eliminates the risk that in separate suits the stakeholder might be found liable to more than one claimant for the same property.

For example, suppose that upon Wilbur's death, his four children each claimed the entire proceeds of a $100,000 life insurance policy. Each child might conceivably sue the insurance company for the full $100,000, forcing the company to defend four separate suits. Moreover, it is possible that judgments could be rendered against the company in each of these actions, resulting in its having to pay a total of $400,000 on a policy that was worth only $100,000. By bringing an interpleader action, however, the company might sue all four children in one suit to determine which of them is entitled to the policy proceeds.

Interpleader is available even to a stakeholder who has already been sued by one or more of the claimants. Thus, in our example, if one of the children had sued the company in a federal court, the company could interplead defensively by filing a counterclaim for interpleader against the plaintiff under Rule 13(a), joining the other children as additional parties to the counterclaim under Rule 13(h). If one of the children had instead sued the company in state court, it could then file an interpleader action against the four children in federal court. Assuming all of the requirements for interpleader were met, the federal court could then enjoin the children from proceeding with or filing any individual suits against the company, forcing them to litigate their claims to the policy solely in the federal interpleader action.

Originally, interpleader was available only if a stakeholder conceded that it owed the property to someone and simply was unsure of which claimant it should pay. In these cases, the stakeholder deposits the stake with the court and drops out of the suit, leaving the claimants to litigate among themselves. Interpleader was later expanded to cover situations in which a stakeholder believed that it did not in fact owe the property to anyone. Our insurance company, for example, might claim that the policy had lapsed for nonpayment of premiums and that none of the children were therefore entitled to the proceeds. In these latter cases, the court must first decide whether the stakeholder owes the property to anyone. If the answer is in the affirmative, the court dismisses the stakeholder from the suit and then proceeds to determine which of the competing claimants is entitled to the property.

Interpleader comes into play only when a stakeholder is faced with multiple claims involving *a single obligation*. A person who has incurred separate obligations to a number of parties cannot interplead them, for there is no risk that separate suits will result in multiple vexation or multiple liability on a single obligation. Thus, if the driver of an automobile negligently injures five people, the driver has potentially incurred five separate obligations to compensate each of the injured. The driver therefore cannot interplead the five victims even if he might prefer to avoid multiple lawsuits. If the driver is found liable to each of the victims in five separate lawsuits, this would not involve multiple liability on a single obligation, for the driver's total liability is not limited to a specific sum. On the other hand, if the driver carried a $500,000 liability policy, the insurance company could interplead the five victims and force them to litigate *their claims to the policy* in a single suit, for the company has only a single liability as defined by the policy.

Interpleader actions proceed in two stages. In stage one, the court determines whether the stakeholder faces adverse claims to the same stake or property, thereby making interpleader an appropriate remedy. If this requirement is met, the action proceeds to stage two, in which the adverse claimants then litigate against each other to see which of them is entitled to the stake.

There are two distinct avenues for bringing interpleader actions in federal court today—those brought under the interpleader statute, 28 U.S.C. § 1335 (so-called statutory interpleaders), and those brought under Rule 22 (so-called rule interpleaders). The nomenclature is a little misleading, however, since both types of interpleader rely on jurisdictional statutes, and both rely at least in part on the federal rules. The true distinction is between those interpleader cases that satisfy the jurisdictional standards of § 1335 ("statutory interpleader") and those that must satisfy some other jurisdictional statute, most typically § 1332 or § 1367. We will, however, use the accepted nomenclature to distinguish between the two.

Statutory interpleader is governed by its own special provisions concerning subject matter jurisdiction (§ 1335), venue (§ 1397), and personal jurisdiction over the claimants (§ 2361). Rule interpleader, on the other hand, is governed by the normal statutes or rules concerning subject matter jurisdiction (*e.g.*, §§ 1331, 1332, 1367, etc.), venue (*e.g.*, § 1391), and personal jurisdiction (*e.g.*, Rule 4(k)). The following table summarizes the differences between statutory and rule interpleader.

	Statutory Interpleader	**Rule Interpleader**
Subject Matter Jurisdiction	§ 1335: at least two claimants diverse from one another (*i.e.*, "minimal diversity"); stake worth at least $500	Normal rules; *e.g.*, § 1332: stakeholder diverse from all claimants and stake worth over $75,000
Venue	§ 1397: district in which any claimant resides	Normal rules; *e.g.*, § 1391
Personal Jurisdiction	§ 2361: in any district (*i.e.*, nationwide service); *see* Rule 4(k)(1)(C)	Normal rules; *e.g.*, borrow state long-arm statute under Rule 4(k)(1)(A)
Deposit of Stake with Court	§ 1335: must deposit stake or bond with court	Optional
Enjoining Other Proceedings	§ 2361: court may enjoin all other suits against stake	Court may enjoin all other suits against stake

Note that for statutory interpleader under 28 U.S.C. § 1335, diversity is measured "vertically" rather than "horizontally," *i.e.*, there must be diversity between at least two claimants. Thus, if a stakeholder brings an interpleader action against four claimants, § 1335 simply requires that at least two of the claimant-defendants be diverse from one another. This contrasts with the "horizontal" measurement of diversity under § 1332, where the plaintiff must be diverse from all of the defendants. Moreover, under § 1335, diversity need not be complete. In *State Farm Fire & Casualty Co. v. Tashire*, 386 U.S. 523 (1967), a statutory interpleader action in which several of the claimants were citizens of the same state, the Supreme Court ruled that § 1335 requires

> only "minimal diversity," that is, diversity of citizenship between two or more claimants, without regard to the circumstance that other rival claimants may be co-citizens. . . . In *Strawbridge v. Curtiss*[, 3 Cranch (7 U.S.) 267 (1806)], this Court

held that the diversity of citizenship statute required "complete diversity": where co-citizens appeared on both sides of a dispute, jurisdiction was lost. But Chief Justice Marshall there purported to construe only "The words of the act of congress," not the Constitution itself. And in a variety of contexts this Court and the lower courts have concluded that Article III poses no obstacle to the legislative extension of federal jurisdiction, founded on diversity, so long as any two adverse parties are not co-citizens. Accordingly, we conclude that the present case is properly in the federal courts.

386 U.S. at 530-531.

The menus for statutory and rule interpleader are "fixed" and no "substitutions" are allowed. In other words, an interpleader action must satisfy *all* of the requirements under at least one of the two menus. However, before checking to see whether either of these menus is satisfied, one must first make sure that the case involves "adverse claimants" to the same stake, thus making interpleader an appropriate option.

Indianapolis Colts v. Mayor and City Council of Baltimore
741 F.2d 954 (7th Cir. 1984), *cert. denied*, 470 U.S. 1052 (1985)

BAUER, Circuit Judge.

Defendants Mayor and City Council of Baltimore (collectively "Baltimore") appeal from two district court orders entered in this interpleader action Plaintiff Indianapolis Colts filed pursuant to 28 U.S.C. § 1335. The Colts, a football team owning a National Football League franchise, filed the action claiming interpleader jurisdiction on the ground that Baltimore and the Capital Improvement Board of Managers of Marion County, Indiana (CIB), operators of the Indianapolis Hoosier Dome, had conflicting claims against the team. The district court in Indiana granted the Colts' request for an order restraining Baltimore from pursuing its condemnation action against the Colts, which was pending in a federal district court in Maryland. Two weeks later, the district court also enjoined Baltimore from pursuing a Maryland state court action against the NFL in which Baltimore hoped to stop the Colts from moving to Indianapolis. We hold that the district court did not have interpleader jurisdiction to hear this suit, and therefore vacate the orders and remand with instructions to dismiss.

I

Through the 1983 season, the Colts played their home games in Baltimore Memorial Stadium. In February 1984, the Colts and the stadium managers began negotiating a renewal of the Memorial Stadium lease. At the same time, the Colts negotiated with the CIB regarding the possibility of moving the team to the Hoosier Dome.

On March 27, 1984, Colts owner Robert Irsay learned that the Maryland Senate passed a bill granting the City of Baltimore the power to acquire the Colts by eminent domain. Irsay decided to move the team to Indianapolis and promptly executed a lease with the CIB. The Colts fled Baltimore under the cloak of darkness; eight moving vans full of Colts equipment arrived in Indianapolis on March 29.

On March 29, Maryland's governor signed into law the bill authorizing Baltimore to acquire the Colts by condemnation. Baltimore filed a condemnation petition against the Colts on March 30 in Maryland state court. The state court restrained the Colts from transferring any element of the team from Baltimore.

After learning about the condemnation suit by telegram, the Colts took two actions. First, on April 2, the Colts caused removal of the state court condemnation proceeding to federal district court in Maryland. Second, on April 5, the Colts filed this action in the United States District Court for the Southern District of Indiana, claiming that their obligations under the lease with the CIB conflicted with Baltimore's attempts to acquire the team through eminent domain.

II

Our review of this case extends to the question of whether the interpleader was proper. This question is an issue of law entitled to full appellate review.

We hold that the Colts have not successfully satisfied the pleading requirements of 28 U.S.C. § 1335. Despite the Colts' argument that it is unfair for the City of Indianapolis to lose the team by another city's condemnation suit, we find that the CIB and Baltimore do not have conflicting claims over a single stake. Additionally, even assuming the CIB and Baltimore have claims over the same stake, the Colts do not face a reasonable danger of multiple liability or vexatious, conflicting claims from the claimants, and thus interpleader is not justified here.

A

A basic jurisdictional requirement of statutory interpleader is that there be adverse claimants to a particular fund. The CIB and Baltimore are not claimants to the same stake. Baltimore seeks ownership of the Colts franchise, whereas the CIB has no claim to ownership of the franchise. Instead, the CIB has a lease with the Colts that requires the team to play its games in the Hoosier Dome and imposes other obligations to ensure the success of the enterprise.

The Colts argue in part that clause 11 of their lease with the CIB raises an interest in the CIB which conflicts with Baltimore's attempt to obtain the franchise. Clause 11 grants the CIB the first chance to find purchasers for the team if Irsay decides to sell his controlling interest. This right of first refusal is the CIB's contractual guarantee either that Irsay always will control the team or that the CIB will have the right to choose his successor. Yet this provision does not give the CIB a present right to buy the Colts, and thus does not raise a claim against the franchise conflicting with Baltimore's claim.[1]

---

1. Other interests might constitute a claim conflicting with the eminent domain action. For example, if the CIB had signed a contract to purchase the Colts, the CIB might have had rights as equitable owner which would conflict with Baltimore's claim. The right of first refusal and the contractual obligations of the Colts, however, do not raise such a conflict. . . .

. . . Interpleader is warranted only to protect the plaintiff-stakeholder from conflicting liability to the stake.

Interpleader is proper in cases such as a surety confronted by claims of subcontractors and materialmen which exceed the surety's contractual liability, conflicting claims of entitlement to the proceeds of a life insurance policy, or automobile insurers surrendering the maximum sum of their liability to the court for disposition to plaintiffs in an accident case. The issue of whether the interpleaded defendants' claims are adverse does not arise often. The Colts' argument here that the "bottom line" of this case is which city "gets" the Colts clouds the issue of adversity. Only reasonable legal claims can form the adversity to the plaintiff necessary to justify interpleader. The CIB has no reasonable legal claim to ownership of the franchise sought by Baltimore. For the Colts, losing their franchise to Baltimore may lead to breach of the lease claims by the CIB, but this is not a situation for which interpleader was designed.

B

Interpleader is a suit in equity. Because the sole basis for equitable relief to the stakeholder is the danger of exposure to double liability or the vexation of conflicting claims, the stakeholder must have a real and reasonable fear of double liability or vexatious, conflicting claims to justify interpleader. Even assuming that Baltimore and the CIB are fighting over the same stake, the Colts do not have a reasonable fear of double liability or vexatious claims here. The Colts and the CIB foresaw the likelihood of legal obstacles to prevent the Colts from leaving Baltimore, among which was an eminent domain action. The Colts and the CIB thus specifically contracted that the lease obligations will terminate at the Colts' option if the Colts' franchise is acquired by eminent domain. . . . This "escape" clause renders unreasonable the Colts' claim that they will face a second suit over the same stake if Baltimore ultimately succeeds in its eminent domain action. The Colts' characterization of the CIB's claim does not meet a "minimal threshold level of substantiality."

The distinction in this case between the lack of adverse claims and the lack of fear of double liability or vexatious litigation is slight. Other courts, however, have recognized that even if adverse claims exist in theory, still there may be no real fear of multiple lawsuits. In [*Bierman v. Marcus*, 246 F.2d 200 (3d Cir. 1957)], for example, the plaintiffs sought interpleader to resolve claims over a specific sum of money. One claimant asserted a valid claim. The other supposed claimant, however, was a corporation controlled by the plaintiffs. The Third Circuit ruled that the plaintiffs knew that the corporation would make no claim against the money and thus no equitable consideration supported interpleader jurisdiction. . . .

Because the Colts cannot assert a reasonable fear of multiple liability or vexatious, conflicting claims, interpleader jurisdiction was not proper. There is no other basis for federal jurisdiction in the federal district court in Indiana to hear the Colts' action and thus this suit must be dismissed. . . .

COFFEY, Circuit Judge, dissenting.

The issue in this case is whether the Capital Improvement Board ("CIB") and the City Council of Baltimore ("Baltimore") are adverse claimants to a particular stake held by the Indianapolis Colts. . . . I dissent from the majority's strained attempt to simplify this case as merely involving an eminent domain proceeding in Baltimore, Maryland, and a lease agreement in Indianapolis, Indiana. Rather, as characterized by the district court judge, this action involves a struggle over a very unique stake—"the rights and privileges of the [Colts] franchise and the property rights incident to the operation thereof"—with all of the attending social and economic benefits to be derived by two major metropolitan cities competing for the rights and privileges of the Colts' National Football League franchise. . . .

The claim asserted by the CIB is not, as the majority contends, a simple contract interest, rather it involves the rights, benefits, and privileges of a National Football League franchise formerly known as the Baltimore Colts. It is this intangible, but very unique, property right that the CIB seeks to control by enforcing the terms of its Lease. . . . The CIB's interest in enforcing the Lease is not simply to turn a profit for the Hoosier Dome but to enhance the prestige and the economic climate of the City of Indianapolis and the County of Marion, Indiana with a coveted National Football League franchise. . . .

The fact that the City of Indianapolis does not own the Colts and the CIB has only entered into a contract with the present owners of the franchise is of no consequence. . . . The full intent of the CIB as embodied in the Lease is to keep the Colts in Indianapolis and thereby enjoy the rights and privileges of a National Football League franchise. The City of Baltimore also clearly desires these very same rights and privileges and thus, contrary to the majority's simplified analysis, there does exist in this case a common, identifiable stake—the rights and privileges of the Colts' franchise—subject to adverse claims. . . .

The City of Baltimore has fought, and will continue to fight, as is its right, the CIB's interest in the Colts. Thus, the above scenario is certainly sufficient to satisfy the language of 28 U.S.C. § 1335 that two adverse claimants "may claim to be entitled" to the same stake. In light of the liberal construction to be accorded the Federal interpleader statute to protect the stakeholder from the expense and risk of double litigation, I am convinced that the Colts satisfy the jurisdictional requirement of 28 U.S.C. § 1335.

NOTES AND QUESTIONS

1. Adverse claims to the same stake.   How did the majority and the dissent differ in their characterizations of what each defendant was claiming? Why did this matter in deciding whether interpleader was proper? Would interpleader have been appropriate if Indianapolis had threatened to bring eminent domain proceedings against the Colts? Why did the majority conclude that interpleader would have been inappropriate even if the action could be said to involve competing claims to the same stake? Must the stakeholder make a threshold showing that it faces a realistic threat of multiple vexation or multiple liability before a court will allow interpleader?

2. *Statutory versus rule interpleader.*   Why did the Colts invoke only statutory interpleader? Would the suit have met the subject matter jurisdiction, venue, and personal jurisdiction requirements for rule interpleader? The Colts organization was a Delaware corporation; it claimed to have changed its principal place of business from Maryland to Indiana shortly before the Indiana lawsuit was filed.

3. *Unliquidated tort claims.*   Interpleader actions often involve insurance policies that provide a fixed amount of coverage for all claims arising from a particular accident or incident. In most states, an injured party cannot bring a "direct action" against the tortfeasor's insurance company. Instead, the insurer may be sued only if a judgment has first been obtained against the insured. Insurance companies nevertheless frequently seek to bring their own action to interplead all potential claimants to the policy before the claimants have sued the insured or reduced their unliquidated claims to judgment. Does the "may expose" language of Rule 22(a)(1) and the "may claim" language of 28 U.S.C. § 1335 allow this use of interpleader, or must an insurer wait until after judgments have been entered against its insured and claims have been made against the policy? In *State Farm Fire & Casualty Co. v. Tashire, supra,* the Court held that the insurer of one of the drivers in a bus-truck collision could bring a statutory interpleader action against the dozens of injured parties, even though only a few of them had sued the insured and none of their claims had yet been reduced to judgment.

> Were an insurance company required to await reduction of claims to judgment, the first claimant to obtain such a judgment or to negotiate a settlement might appropriate all or a disproportionate slice of the fund before his fellow claimants were able to establish their claims. The difficulties such a race to judgment pose for the insurer, and the unfairness which may result to some claimants, were among the principal evils the interpleader device was intended to remedy.

Tashire, 386 U.S. at 533. Courts have read Rule 22 in a similar fashion. *See* Richard D. Freer, *Interpleader, in* 4 MOORE'S FEDERAL PRACTICE § 22.03[1][e] (3d ed. 2015).

In such a case, how does a court determine whether the claims are adverse to one another? Doesn't this depend on a number of variables including the amount of the policy, the total amount of the claims or anticipated claims, and the likelihood that the claimants will prevail against the insured? In *Tashire,* only four suits had been filed against the insured, but these claims exceeded $1 million, whereas the policy was limited to $20,000. *Cf. CNA Ins. Cos. v. Waters,* 926 F.2d 247 (3d Cir. 1991) (dismissing insurer's attempt to interplead claimants to uninsured motorist policy on ground that claims were not "adverse" when insurer lacked "bona fide fear" that claims would exceed policy limits); *American Family Mut. Ins. Co. v. Roche,* 830 F. Supp. 1241, 1245 n.3 (E.D. Wis. 1993) (expressing doubt that claims were adverse when record failed to show that potential claims would exceed insurance policy limits).

PROBLEMS

8-16. Carl's employer provided group life and accidental death insurance for its employees through Hanford Insurance ("Hanford"), a Delaware corporation whose principal place of business is in Connecticut. Hanford issued Carl a Verification of Coverage certificate stating that the face amount of the Basic Policy was $85,000 and that a Supplemental Policy provided additional coverage of $50,000. Carl, who lived and worked in Texas, initially designated his mother, Ida, an Ohio resident, as the beneficiary under both policies. He later changed the beneficiary under the Basic Policy to Eterna Benefits, a New York partnership, to whom he had sold that policy for $40,000. Carl planned to sell the Supplemental Policy to Eterna as well but was informed by Hanford that the Verification of Coverage certificate was incorrect. According to Hanford, while the Basic Policy had a face value of $85,000, the Supplemental Policy provided no death benefits. After Carl died, Eterna sought payment of $85,000 under the Basic Policy, and Ida sought $50,000 under the Supplemental Policy. May Hanford interplead Eterna and Ida? Would it matter whether Ida, besides claiming benefits under the Supplemental Policy, also asserted that the change of beneficiary under the Basic Policy was invalid? If interpleader is proper, in what federal courts (if any) might Hanford bring the action? In answering this question, be sure to consider each of the requirements for both statutory and rule interpleader. *See Hartford Life & Accident Ins. Co. v. Eterna Benefits LLC*, 1997 WL 726441 (N.D. Tex. Nov. 17, 1997).

8-17. A bus collided with a truck in northern California while en route to Oregon. More than 30 people were hurt. Five of them were from Canada; the rest were from Arizona, California, New York, Oregon, and Texas. The bus company was a California corporation with its principal place of business in Arizona. The bus driver was a citizen of Oregon. The operator of the truck, who was also from Oregon, carried a $20,000 liability policy issued by State Farm, an Illinois corporation with its principal place of business in Illinois. After several suits had been filed against its insured in the California state courts, State Farm filed an interpleader action in an Oregon federal court, naming as defendants the bus company, the bus driver, all of the injured parties, and the operator of the truck. Personal service was effected on each of the U.S. defendants. The five Canadian defendants were served by registered mail, return receipt requested. Can State Farm maintain this action in the Oregon federal court under either statutory or rule interpleader? *See State Farm Fire & Casualty Co. v. Tashire*, 386 U.S. 523 (1967).

Geler v. National Westminster Bank USA

763 F. Supp. 722 (S.D.N.Y. 1991)

ROBERT L. CARTER, District Judge.

This case illustrates how ineptitude and dilatory tactics can complicate a relatively simple matter.

Background

These consolidated actions relate to a 90-day renewable certificate of deposit, in the amount of approximately $500,000, issued by National Westminster Bank (the "Bank"). It is disputed whether the account was held solely by Benjamin Ghitelman or jointly by Benjamin Ghitelman and his wife Susana Ghitelman (a/k/a Shoshana Ghitelman). The account was a so-called *Totten* trust, payable on the death of the depositor or depositors to the named beneficiaries, Ida Geler, Israel Geler and Yacof Geler (the "Gelers").

After Benjamin Ghitelman's death, Susana Ghitelman withdrew the funds deposited in the account. Subsequently, the Gelers attempted to withdraw the money, only to find that Susana Ghitelman had already withdrawn it. Susana Ghitelman returned the money to the Bank upon its demand. She subsequently died. The Gelers then filed against the Bank, the first action herein (the "Geler action"), seeking to recover the disputed funds.

Throughout the discovery period, Marilyn B. Fairberg attended conferences in the Geler action as counsel for Howard Gluckman ("Gluckman" or "Susana Ghitelman's administrator"), who was not a party to the action, and who had not yet received ancillary letters of administration C.T.A. for the Susana Ghitelman estate from the Surrogate's Court of the State of New York, County of New York. Fairberg represented to this court that her client would intervene in the action as soon as he received those letters.

Relying on these representations, Constantine A. Despotakis, then counsel to the Bank, sought to delay the resolution of the Geler action pending the intervention of Susana Ghitelman's administrator. Despite the court's repeated suggestions that the Bank should bring an interpleader claim against the Gelers and the Susana Ghitelman estate, Despotakis, without explanation or excuse, failed to pursue that remedy. . . . Meanwhile, the Geler action proceeded to the point that discovery was completed and a motion for summary judgment by the Gelers was fully submitted.

The Surrogate's Court eventually entered a decree appointing Gluckman as ancillary administrator C.T.A. of Susana Ghitelman's estate. Despite her earlier representations, however, Fairberg did not have Gluckman intervene in the Geler action, but proceeded to file suit against the Bank in the Supreme Court of the State of New York, County of New York (the "state court action"), seeking the proceeds of the certificate of deposit, as well as damages for fraud and breach of fiduciary duty related to the transactions in issue. Fairberg's tactics waste judicial resources and threaten to expose the Bank to multiple liability on a single fund.[3]

Despotakis, on behalf of the Bank, subsequently filed . . . an additional action in this court . . . seeking interpleader of the competing claims of the Gelers and Susana Ghitelman's administrator. At a conference held on April 2, 1991, the court ordered the two actions consolidated.

---

3. Because the Bank is treated as a citizen of New York, the state court action is not removable despite diversity of citizenship. *See* 28 U.S.C. § 1441(b).

The Bank now seeks an injunction staying litigation of the state court action. The Gelers, however, contend that this court lacks power to enjoin proceedings in the state court action. . . .

Discussion

. . . The Anti-Injunction Act, 28 U.S.C. § 2283, generally forbids the federal courts from enjoining state court proceedings. The act admits of only three exceptions: the court may enjoin a pending state court action (1) as expressly authorized by act of Congress, (2) where necessary in aid of its jurisdiction, or (3) where necessary to protect or effectuate its judgments.

The Bank attempts to characterize its claim as one under the federal interpleader statute, 28 U.S.C. § 1335. Title 28 U.S.C. § 2361 expressly authorizes the court to enjoin pending state proceedings in statutory interpleader actions. However, this case cannot proceed as a statutory interpleader action because of a lack of diversity of citizenship among the claimants.

For a stakeholder to maintain a statutory interpleader action, at least two of the claimants must be of diverse citizenship. *State Farm Fire & Cas. Co. v. Tashire*, 386 U.S. 523, 530-31 (1967); *see* 28 U.S.C. § 1335(a)(1). The citizenship of a disinterested stakeholder is irrelevant.

For the purposes of both the interpleader statute and the general diversity jurisdiction statute, Susana Ghitelman's administrator is treated as having the same citizenship as the decedent, an Israeli. *See* 28 U.S.C. § 1332(c)(2). . . . Consequently, the representative of the estate of an alien is treated as an alien for purposes of diversity jurisdiction.

The Gelers are all citizens of Israel. Thus, all of the claimants in this case are aliens or are treated as aliens, and the requisite diversity is lacking.

The Bank is treated as a citizen of New York, the state in which it is located. *See* 28 U.S.C. § 1348. The Bank makes the far-fetched argument that it may be regarded as a claimant because Gluckman, as Susana Ghitelman's administrator, also asserts a claim for fraud and breach of fiduciary duty against it in the state court action. In support of this argument, the Bank cites cases that have held that if the stakeholder has an interest in the fund deposited in court, it is a claimant for purposes of statutory interpleader jurisdiction.

In this case, however, the Bank has disclaimed all interest in the fund deposited in court. Though Susana Ghitelman's administrator claims a potentially larger amount in the state court action, only the amount deposited in court is in issue in the putative statutory interpleader action.[7] Since the Bank has no interest in the money deposited in court, it is in no sense a claimant to it.

Although the court does not have jurisdiction under the interpleader statute, it has jurisdiction if the action is treated as an interpleader under Rule 22, F.R. Civ. P. Since the plaintiff (the Bank) is diverse in citizenship from all the defendants

---

7. As a prerequisite to maintaining a statutory interpleader action, the stakeholder must either post a bond or deposit the amount in controversy into court. 28 U.S.C. § 1335(a)(2).

(Susana Ghitelman's administrator and the Gelers), and the amount in controversy exceeds $50,000, the court has subject-matter jurisdiction under the general diversity-jurisdiction statute. 28 U.S.C. § 1332.

The Gelers object that the Bank's interpleader-related pleadings refer only to the interpleader statute, and argue that the court therefore must not treat them as a rule interpleader. However, pleadings are not to be read narrowly and technically, but are to be construed so as to do "substantial justice." Rule 8(f), F.R. Civ. P. A claim will be dismissed only if its allegations would entitle the claimant to relief on no possible theory, even though the theory of the party asserting the claim was incorrect. Since the Bank alleges all the essential elements of a rule interpleader action, the court will construe its pleadings as stating a claim under Rule 22, F.R. Civ. P.

Although 28 U.S.C. § 2361, which authorizes the court to enjoin pending state proceedings, applies only to statutory interpleader actions, the court has the power to enjoin a pending state proceeding in a rule interpleader action under the "aid of jurisdiction" exception to the Anti-Injunction Act. *Id.* § 2283.

In *General Railway Signal Co. v. Corcoran*, [921 F.2d 700, 702-703 (7th Cir. 1991)], the Court of Appeals for the Seventh Circuit vacated a district court order that had enjoined enforcement of a state court judgment pending the outcome of the federal interpleader action. The court of appeals held that, because there was no diversity between the claimants, the district court had misconstrued the federal action as a statutory interpleader case, and that, therefore, it had erroneously relied on 28 U.S.C. § 2361 to support its entry of an injunction. However, the court of appeals held that the federal action could proceed as a rule interpleader case, and that the district court, on remand, could nonetheless issue the injunction, since "[a] federal court presiding over an interpleader action may stay pending state court proceedings involving the same interpled fund under the 'necessary in aid of its jurisdiction' exception to the Anti-Injunction Act." *Id.* at 707. [T]he court explained:

> Usually interpleader will not be really effective unless all claimants are brought before the same court in one proceeding and restricted to that single forum in the assertion of their claims. To accomplish that end, . . . it is of course essential that the interpleader court enjoin the institution or prosecution of other suits on the same subject matter elsewhere.

Id. at 707.

Commentators agree that where, as here, a federal court can assert conventional *in personam* jurisdiction over the claimants, it has the authority to enjoin a state court proceeding in a rule interpleader case. As Wright, Miller and Kane explain:

> Section 2361 only authorizes injunctions against other judicial proceedings in statutory interpleader actions; it does not apply to rule interpleader. . . . But the mere fact that a nationwide injunction under Section 2361 is not available in a rule interpleader case does not mean that the court does not have discretion in the latter context to issue an order against those claimants that have been subjected to the court's jurisdiction in accordance with the more traditional rules of process

applicable in cases under Rule 22. . . . A preliminary injunction to stay a state court action while the federal court determines the Rule 22 interpleader case might be regarded as "necessary in aid of its jurisdiction" and a permanent injunction at the conclusion of the federal action may be needed "to protect or effectuate its judgments." Accordingly, the proper accommodation between the policy against enjoining state proceedings and the objectives of rule interpleader is to recognize the federal court's power to issue an order whenever a pending state court action represents a threat to the effectiveness of the interpleader suit or the enforceability of its judgment.

7 C. Wright, A. Miller & M. Kane, [FEDERAL PRACTICE AND PROCEDURE] § 1717 at 616-17 (2d ed. 1986). . . .

Allowing litigation to go forward on individual claims while a rule interpleader action is pending in federal court would defeat the entire purpose of the interpleader remedy, which is to avoid the possibility of multiple litigation leading to multiple liability. Concurrent suits on individual claims in state court during the pendency of a federal interpleader action thus uniquely impair the federal court's jurisdiction. Under such circumstances, the "aid of jurisdiction" exception to the Anti-Injunction Act is clearly applicable, and the Anti-Injunction Act poses no barrier to the court's authority to issue an injunction against the state-court action.

Before an injunction in a rule interpleader case can be granted, however, the usual standards for granting a preliminary injunction must be satisfied. That is, the party seeking the injunction must demonstrate (1) irreparable harm if the injunction is not granted, (2) either likelihood of success on the merits or sufficiently serious questions going to the merits to make them fair ground for litigation, and (3) a balance of hardships tipping clearly in favor of the party requesting relief. Moreover, the party against whom the injunction is sought must be afforded notice and a fair opportunity to be heard. Rule 65(a), F.R. Civ. P.

Under the circumstances of this case, comity and respect for the state court system dictate that the Bank should first move in the state court for a stay of the state court action before applying for an injunction in this court. If the state court grants the motion, an injunction from this court will be unnecessary. Thus, the Bank has not made the required showing of irreparable harm.

. . . The motion of the Bank for an injunction staying the state court action is . . . denied, without prejudice to renewal of the motion if the Bank is unable to obtain a stay in state court.

IT IS SO ORDERED.*

NOTES AND QUESTIONS

1. Defensive interpleader.   In *Geler*, did the bank need to file a separate suit to interplead the claimants to the certificate of deposit? Couldn't it have converted

---

* [For the court's subsequent decision on the merits of this interpleader action, *see* 1991 WL 267759 (S.D.N.Y. Dec. 5, 1991), *aff'd*, 970 F.2d 895 (2d Cir. 1992). — EDS.]

the suit brought against it by the Gelers into an interpleader action by counter-claiming against the Gelers under Rule 13(a) and joining Ghitelman's adminis-trator as an additional party to that counterclaim under Rule 13(h)? Federal Rule 22(a)(2) specifically authorizes defensive interpleader "[b]y a defendant" stake-holder whom one of the claimants has sued, "through a crossclaim or counter-claim." While statutory interpleader lacks a similar express provision, courts allow a defendant stakeholder to do so by counterclaim or crossclaim. *See* 4 MOORE'S FEDERAL PRACTICE, *supra*, § 22.02[4]; 7 WRIGHT, MILLER & KANE, *supra*, § 1708.

2. *Enjoining other proceedings.*   Section 2361 allows a federal court to enjoin the claimants from "instituting or prosecuting" any other state or federal suit "affecting the property, instrument or obligation involved in the interpleader action. . . ." 28 U.S.C. § 2361. In *Tashire*, the Court held that § 2361 only allows the interpleader court to enjoin present or future suits that affect the stake. *Tashire* was a statutory interpleader action brought by the insurer of a truck driver involved in a bus-truck accident that injured dozens of people. *See* Problem 8-17, page 712, *supra.* The district court issued an injunction requiring that all claims arising from the accident be litigated in the interpleader action, including claims against the operator of the truck, the bus company, and its driver. The Supreme Court overturned the injunction, ruling that a § 2361 injunction cannot "be employed to accomplish purposes that exceed the needs of orderly contest with respect to the fund" or stake. *Tashire*, 386 U.S. at 534. Statutory interpleader, said the Court, was never intended to function "as a 'bill of peace,' capable of sweeping dozens of lawsuits out of the various state and federal courts in which they were brought and into a single interpleader proceeding." *Id.* at 536. Thus, while the district court could enjoin any other pending or future suits against the insurance policy and require that all such claims be litigated solely in the interpleader action, it could not bar the claimants from litigating other claims arising from the accident in courts of their own choosing.

3. *A federal injunction in* Geler.   Assuming a federal court's injunctive author-ity is the same for statutory and rule interpleader, what injunction could the dis-trict court issue in *Geler* if the state court refuses the bank's request for a stay? Could it enjoin the administrator from further litigating his state court claims to recover the proceeds of the certificate of deposit? Could it enjoin the administra-tor's state court damages claims for fraud and breach of fiduciary duty? Are the latter claims against the stake? Would allowing the fraud and breach of fiduciary duty claims to proceed in state court cause the bank multiple vexation or pose a risk of multiple liability on a single obligation? What if the federal interpleader court awarded the proceeds of the certificate of deposit to the Gelers, while the state court found that the bank had breached its fiduciary duty by not paying those proceeds to Ghitelman? Even if not all of the state-law claims are literally against the stake, are they sufficiently related to the stake that judicial efficiency and the avoidance of inconsistent determinations might still warrant a federal injunction against separate litigation of these state-law claims?

4. *The stakeholder as a claimant.*   As the court in *Geler* noted, if the stake-holder claims an interest in the stake, some courts treat the stakeholder as being a

"claimant" in deciding whether the requirements of statutory interpleader are satisfied. Under this approach, if a stakeholder from New York sues five claimants from California concerning property worth $500 or more, the case will satisfy § 1335 if the stakeholder contends that it does not owe the property to anyone. *See* 7 Wright, Miller & Kane, *supra*, § 1710 & n.25 (citing conflicting authorities). If the value of the stake exceeds $75,000, would subject matter jurisdiction also exist in the preceding hypothetical for purposes of rule interpleader? In *Geler*, the bank sought to invoke statutory interpleader on the basis that it was a "claimant" to the property and that minimal diversity therefore existed among the claimants. Why did the court reject this argument? What are the potential advantages to an interested stakeholder of deeming it a claimant for purposes of statutory interpleader? If the other claimants are all from the same state and the stake is worth $25,000, would the suit otherwise have to be filed in a state court? For venue purposes, would this allow an interested stakeholder to file a statutory interpleader action in the district of its own residence, rather than having to sue where one of the other claimants resides? Does treating an interested stakeholder as a claimant also expand a federal court's ability to obtain personal jurisdiction over the other claimants?

PROBLEMS

8-18. A truck owned by Zephyr, Inc. ("Zephyr") struck a school bus in Louisiana. Moments later two cars following the bus collided with one another. Twenty-five people were hurt, some of them seriously. All of the injured were from Louisiana except for Wells, a passenger in one of the cars, who was from Wisconsin. Zephyr is a Delaware corporation with its principal place of business in Maine. Pan American Insurance ("Pan American"), a Texas corporation with its principal place of business in Dallas, had issued Zephyr a $100,000 policy covering the accident. Elmer, a citizen of Louisiana, sued Pan American and Zephyr in a Louisiana state court seeking $250,000 for injuries suffered as a result of Zephyr's alleged negligence. Louisiana is one of the few states to allow a "direct action" against an insurance company based on the liability of its insured, without the need to first obtain a judgment against the insured. Assume that Louisiana has a tailored long-arm statute that reaches the owners and operators of vehicles involved in accidents in the state. Pan American concedes that if its insured was negligent, the policy covers the accident.

A. May Pan American file a federal interpleader action against all of the injured parties in its home state of Texas?

B. May Pan American file such an action in a Louisiana federal court?

C. Is there any way that Pan American, without filing a new lawsuit of its own, can force the injured parties to interplead in federal court?

D. If a federal court finds that interpleader is proper, may it enjoin the parties from filing or further prosecuting any suits against Pan American or its insured relating to the accident?

See Pan American Fire & Cas. Co. v. Revere, 188 F. Supp. 474 (E.D. La. 1960).

8-19. Bongo Productions ("Bongo"), an Oregon corporation with its principal place of business in New Jersey, arranged a boxing match between Killer Cardigan and Leadfist O'Droole. The winner's purse was $500,000. Five California investors each put up $100,000 of the purse in exchange for a share of the fight revenues. Each fighter agreed to forfeit his share of the purse if he tested positive for drugs within 48 hours of the match. The fight was held on June 3 in New Jersey. In a split decision, Cardigan was declared the winner. A day later, he tested positive for drugs. As a result, Bongo refused to pay him the winner's purse. The investors then insisted that if the purse were not paid to Cardigan, they were each entitled to a refund of their $100,000. They also disputed Bongo's calculation of their share of the fight revenue. Cardigan, who lives in California, sued Bongo in Oregon federal district court, alleging that Bongo falsified his drug test results. Cardigan seeks payment of the $500,000 purse plus $1 million in damages for libel. Meanwhile, the California investors sued Bongo in a California federal court seeking a refund of their investments and a larger share of the fight revenue. May Bongo interplead Cardigan and the five investors in the Oregon action? If so, may the Oregon federal court enjoin the defendants from filing or proceeding with any other lawsuits against Bongo relating to the fight?

G.   Compulsory Joinder

When bringing a lawsuit, the plaintiff must initially decide how the suit is to be structured. For example, suppose Shelley was injured in an auto accident while taking her mother to the doctor's office. In framing her lawsuit against the driver of the other car, Shelley might consider making her mother a co-plaintiff in the action. Depending on the facts, Shelley might also name as additional defendants the garage that serviced her car, the manufacturer whose design of the vehicle may have exacerbated her injuries, and/or the city whose failure to repair the roadway might have contributed to the accident. As a matter of *permissive* joinder, could Shelley have included these other parties in her suit? If these other parties had learned of the action, could they have *intervened* in the suit? Suppose, however, that Shelley did not include any of these additional parties in her suit against the driver of the other car, and that none of them tried to intervene. At the defendant's insistence, or on its own initiative, the court might then order that Shelley amend her complaint to include some or all of these persons, on the basis that they are *required parties* to the suit. Yet such joinder might turn out not to be *feasible*, for the absentee might not be amenable to service or might destroy subject matter jurisdiction. In that event, if the court concludes that it would be unfair to proceed without the absentee, it might dismiss Shelley's lawsuit on the ground that the absentee is an *indispensable party* to the action.

In this section we will look at how courts decide when a plaintiff must expand the scope of her lawsuit to include a person deemed to be a "required party" to the action. (Older cases and prior versions of the federal rules used the phrase "necessary party.") We will also examine avenues available to a court when it is impossible for the plaintiff to join such a party, including the last-resort device of dismissal when the absentee is determined to be an *indispensable party*. While our focus will be on Federal Rule of Civil Procedure 19, many states expressly follow the federal approach in this area. *See, e.g., Lungren v. Community Redevelop. Agency of Palm Springs*, 56 Cal. Rptr. 2d 786, 790 (Ct. App. 1997); *E.I. Dupont de Nemours & Co. v. Shell Oil Co.*, 1983 WL 8942, at *1 (Del. Ch. Dec. 13, 1983); *International Savings and Loan Assn., Ltd. v. Carbonel*, 5 P.3d 454, 461-462 & n.11 (Haw. Ct. App. 2000); *Gibson v. Miami Valley Milk Producers, Inc.*, 299 N.E.2d 631, 639-640 (Ind. Ct. App. 1973); *State v. Lamar Adver. Co. of La., Inc.*, 279 So. 2d 671, 673-677 (La. 1973); *Canal Nat'l Bank v. Old Folks' Home Assn. of Brunswick*, 347 A.2d 428, 441-442 (Me. 1975); *Steers v. Rescue 3, Inc.*, 934 P.2d 532, 534 (Or. Ct. App. 1997); *Landes v. Capital City Bank*, 795 P.2d 1127, 1130 (Utah 1990).

Read Rule 19. You will see that the analysis under the rule consists of three distinct inquiries. The first involves a determination of whether an absent party ought to be joined, *i.e.*, whether that party is *required*. Rule 19(a) defines a required party as person who falls into one of three categories:

- those without whom a court will be unable to accord *complete relief* among the existing parties (Rule 19(a)(1)(A));
- those who claim an interest in the subject of the action and *whose interest might be harmed* in their absence (Rule 19(a)(1)(B)(i)); or
- those who have an interest in the subject of the action and whose absence might harm an existing party by exposing that party to a *substantial risk of incurring double or multiple liability, or otherwise inconsistent obligations* (Rule 19(a)(1)(B)(ii)).

As we will see in the next principal case and the note following it, subsection (a)(1)(A)'s "complete relief" standard refers to complete relief as between the existing parties. This principle would come into play, for example, in a case where the plaintiff seeks an injunction, the success of which requires the cooperation of the absent party. Subsections (a)(1)(B)(i) and (ii) refer respectively to the potential harm that either the absent party or an existing party might suffer if the absent party were not brought into the case. Under subsection (B)(i), the question is one of practical impairment to the absent party, much like the standard for intervention as of right under Rule 24(a)(2). With respect to all three 19(a) categories, the essential question is whether, as a practical matter, the absent party is someone who, in all fairness, ought to be brought in the case. As to the existing parties, the potential risks must be "substantial," which is to say that merely conjectural or hypothetical risks will not suffice. *See, e.g., Bacardi Intern. Ltd. v. V. Suarez & Co., Inc.*, 719 F.3d 1, 13 (1st Cir.), *cert. denied*, 134 S.Ct. 640 (2013) (finding risk of inconsistent obligations "theoretically possible, but . . . not a practical concern.").

If an absent party is deemed "required" under any one of the above criteria under Rule 19(a)(1), the court must order that party joined if it is "feasible" to do so. *Id.* For these purposes, joinder is feasible if the absent party is "subject to service of process" and if joinder will not "deprive the court of subject-matter jurisdiction." *Id.* In addition, venue may become a factor in determining feasibility if a party joined pursuant to Rule 19 raises a timely and proper objection to venue after being brought into the case. Fed. R. Civ. P. 19(a)(3).

If the absent party is deemed required but her joinder is not feasible, under Rule 19(b), the court must "determine whether, in equity and good conscience, the action should proceed among the existing parties or should be dismissed." Rule 19(b) provides a non-exhaustive list of factors that might be considered in making this determination:

> (1) the extent to which a judgment rendered in the person's absence might prejudice that person or the existing parties;
> (2) the extent to which any prejudice could be lessened or avoided by: (A) protective provisions in the judgment; (B) shaping the relief; or (C) other measures;
> (3) whether a judgment rendered in the person's absence would be adequate; and
> (4) whether the plaintiff would have an adequate remedy if the action were dismissed for nonjoinder.

Fed. R. Civ. P. 19(b). Subsection (b)(1) revisits the potential harm to the absent party or to any existing party, but now from the perspective of whether the case can proceed in the absence of the required party. This inquiry is similar to that under Rule 19(a)(1)(B). However, here the court will also consider whether any of the present parties has the same interest as the absent party, such that they can adequately represent that interest.

Subsection (b)(2) requires the court to determine whether there is anything that can be done to avoid the harm identified under subsection (b)(1). For example, a court might consider inviting an absent party who is not subject to service of process to intervene and thus submit to jurisdiction, or it might withhold its judgment until such time as the absent party has had an opportunity to litigate the pertinent issues in another court. The court might also consider whether the objecting party can bring the absent party into the case through other joinder devices such as a counterclaim or a counterclaim in interpleader.

Subsection (b)(3) raises an efficiency concern premised on the "public stake in settling disputes by wholes, whenever possible." *Provident Tradesmens Bank & Trust Co. v. Patterson*, 399 U.S. 102, 111 (1968). Here, the court considers whether resolution of the case in the absence of the required party will fully settle the underlying controversy.

Finally, if application of the above factors suggests dismissal as the appropriate remedy, subsection (b)(4) requires the court to consider the potential harm to the plaintiff if the case is dismissed, essentially calling for a balancing of interests that should inform the ultimate resolution of the joinder dispute.

In sum, an absent party should be brought into a case if in her absence the court cannot accord complete relief among the existing parties or her absence from the suit will cause harm to her or to one of the existing parties. She cannot, however, be forcibly joined if she is not subject to service of process or if her joinder will destroy subject matter jurisdiction. Finally, if she ought to be joined but cannot be, the court must consider whether and under what circumstances it would be fair to proceed without her.

1.   Rule 19(a)(1)

Temple v. Synthes Corp., Ltd.

498 U.S. 5 (1990)

PER CURIAM.

Petitioner Temple, a Mississippi resident, underwent surgery in October 1986 in which a "plate and screw device" was implanted in his lower spine. The device was manufactured by respondent Synthes Corp., Ltd. (U.S.A.) (Synthes), a Pennsylvania corporation. Dr. S. Henry LaRocca performed the surgery at St. Charles General Hospital in New Orleans, Louisiana. Following surgery, the device's screws broke off inside Temple's back.

Temple filed suit against Synthes in the United States District Court for the Eastern District of Louisiana. The suit, which rested on diversity jurisdiction, alleged defective design and manufacture of the device. At the same time, Temple filed a state administrative proceeding against Dr. LaRocca and the hospital for malpractice and negligence. At the conclusion of the administrative proceeding, Temple filed suit against the doctor and the hospital in Louisiana state court.

Synthes did not attempt to bring the doctor and the hospital into the federal action by means of a third-party complaint, as provided in Federal Rule of Civil Procedure 14(a). Instead, Synthes filed a motion to dismiss Temple's federal suit for failure to join necessary parties pursuant to Federal Rule of Civil Procedure 19. Following a hearing, the District Court ordered Temple to join the doctor and the hospital as defendants within 20 days or risk dismissal of the lawsuit. According to the court, the most significant reason for requiring joinder was the interest of judicial economy. The court relied on this Court's decision in *Provident Tradesmens Bank & Trust Co. v. Patterson*, 390 U.S. 102 (1968), wherein we recognized that one focus of Rule 19 is "the interest of the courts and the public in complete, consistent, and efficient settlement of controversies." When Temple failed to join the doctor and the hospital, the court dismissed the suit with prejudice.

Temple appealed, and the United States Court of Appeals for the Fifth Circuit affirmed. The court deemed it "obviously prejudicial to the defendants to have the separate litigations being carried on," because Synthes' defense might be that the plate was not defective but that the doctor and the hospital were negligent, while the doctor and the hospital, on the other hand, might claim that they were not negligent but that the plate was defective. The Court of Appeals found that the claims overlapped and that the District Court therefore had not abused its discretion in ordering joinder under Rule 19. . . .

In his petition for certiorari to this Court, Temple contends that it was error to label joint tortfeasors as indispensable parties under Rule 19(b) and to dismiss the lawsuit with prejudice for failure to join those parties. We agree. Synthes does not deny that it, the doctor, and the hospital are potential joint tortfeasors. It has long been the rule that it is not necessary for all joint tortfeasors to be named as defendants in a single lawsuit. Nothing in the 1966 revision of Rule 19 changed that principle. The Advisory Committee Notes to Rule 19(a) explicitly state that "a tortfeasor with the usual 'joint-and-several' liability is merely a permissive party to an action against another with like liability." There is nothing in Louisiana tort law to the contrary.

The opinion in *Provident Bank*, *supra*, does speak of the public interest in limiting multiple litigation, but that case is not controlling here. There, the estate of a tort victim brought a declaratory judgment action against an insurance company. We assumed that the policyholder was a person "who, under [Rule 19(a)], should be 'joined if feasible'" and went on to discuss the appropriate analysis under Rule 19(b), because the policyholder could not be joined without destroying diversity. After examining the factors set forth in Rule 19(b), we determined that the action could proceed without the policyholder; he therefore was not an indispensable party whose absence required dismissal of the suit.

Here, no inquiry under Rule 19(b) is necessary, because the threshold requirements of Rule 19(a) have not been satisfied. As potential joint tortfeasors with Synthes, Dr. LaRocca and the hospital were merely permissive parties. The Court of Appeals erred by failing to hold that the District Court abused its discretion in ordering them joined as defendants and in dismissing the action when Temple failed to comply with the court's order. For these reasons, we grant the petition for certiorari, reverse the judgment of the Court of Appeals for the Fifth Circuit, and remand for further proceedings consistent with this opinion.

It is so ordered.

A NOTE ON THE "COMPLETE RELIEF" CLAUSE OF RULE 19(a)(1)(A)

In *Temple*, the hospital and LaRocca seemed to satisfy the "complete relief" clause of Rule 19(a)(1)(A), yet the Court held they were not required parties to the suit against Synthes. While the Court relied mainly on the Advisory Committee Note specifically exempting joint tortfeasors from 19(a)(1)(A), courts have generally construed the "complete relief" clause narrowly, seldom finding a party to be required on the basis of this provision alone. If the mere possibility that there could be other lawsuits involving an absentee were enough to trigger Rule 19(a)(1)(A), the traditional principle that a plaintiff may usually structure her lawsuit as she pleases would be eviscerated. Thus, in the view of most courts, "the term complete relief refers only 'to relief as between the persons already parties, and not as between a party and the absent person whose joinder is sought.'" *Arkwright-Boston Mfrs. Mut. Ins. Co. v. City of New York*, 762 F.2d 205, 209 (2d Cir. 1985); *Perrain v. O'Grady*, 958 F.2d 192, 196 (7th Cir. 1992) (same); *see* Richard D. Freer, *Required Joinder of Parties, in* 4 MOORE'S FEDERAL PRACTICE, *supra*, § 19.03[2].

The "complete relief" clause of Rule 19(a)(1)(A) will be met when any relief between the *existing parties* would be hollow or meaningless without the absentee's presence in the suit. This is sometimes true in suits for injunctive relief in which the absentee is vital to effectuating the judgment. For example, in *Kraebel v. New York City Department of Housing Preservation and Development*, 1994 WL 132239 (S.D.N.Y. Apr. 14, 1994), a landlord claimed that the city's delay in processing real estate tax reimbursement claims was unconstitutional. The city argued that the delays were caused by the need to obtain documentation from the DHCR, a state agency, which often took months or even years to provide the information. The court agreed with the city that the Commissioner of the DHCR qualified as a necessary party under Rule 19(a)(1):

> Plaintiff . . . seeks monetary as well as injunctive relief to reduce the unconstitutional delays. Any injunctive relief granted in this case would extend only to [the City] and would have no effect on DHCR's processing of the essential documentation if its Commissioner is not a party. Thus, if DHCR is ultimately found to be partially or wholly responsible for the delays, the injunctive relief would not fully remedy the unconstitutional procedures. Accordingly, because full relief . . . cannot be accorded among the present parties without his joinder, the Commissioner of DHCR is a necessary party within the meaning of Rule 19(a)(1).

Id. at *4. The court found that the Commissioner's joinder was feasible and ordered the plaintiff to join him within 20 days. *Id.*

PROBLEM

8-20. During his lifetime, Bernard and his son Louis owned and operated Prestige Art Inc. ("Prestige") in Chicago. After Bernard's death in 2013, his daughter Klarice took possession of the art work that had been displayed in Bernard's home, including several works that Prestige sold to Aaron in November 2002. Upon making that purchase, Aaron—who was a close friend of Bernard's and Louis's—allowed Bernard to continue displaying the works in Bernard's home, with the understanding they would be turned over to Aaron upon Bernard's death. After Klarice refused to surrender these works to him, Aaron sued Klarice in federal district court, based on diversity. Klarice has moved to dismiss the action under Rule 12(b)(7), claiming that Louis is a required party under Rule 19(a) because Klarice has a number of claims against him that relate to his work at Prestige. Aaron remains good friends with Louis and does not wish to add him as a defendant in the suit. Are Klarice's allegations sufficient to establish that Louis is a required party who must be joined if feasible? *See Young v. Schutz*, 2015 WL 2265465 (N.D. Ill. May 11, 2015).

Maldonado-Viñas v. National Western Life Ins. Co.

303 F.R.D. 177 (D.P.R. 2014)

Besosa, District Judge.

Before the Court is defendant National Western Life Insurance's motion to dismiss pursuant to Federal Rule of Civil Procedure 12(b)(7). For the reasons explained below, the Court DENIES the motion to dismiss.

I.   BACKGROUND

A.   Factual Background as Alleged in the Complaint

On April 30, 2011, Carlos Iglesias-Alvarez ("Carlos Iglesias") submitted $1,467,500 with an annuity application to defendant National Western Life Insurance ("National Western"). Carlos Iglesias named his brother, Francisco Iglesias, as the annuity's beneficiary. This annuity was signed by Marangelis Rivera, who represented herself as National Western's agent but who did not have an agent's license in the Commonwealth of Puerto Rico.

On May 2, 2011, Carlos Iglesias submitted another $1,467,500 with a second annuity application to National Western. This second annuity identified Carlos Iglesias as the annuitant and Francisco Iglesias as the owner and beneficiary. Francisco Iglesias did not sign the second annuity application.

Carlos Iglesias died on November 2, 2011. Damaris Maldonado-Viñas, Juan Carlos Iglesias-Maldonado, and Jose Carlos Iglesias-Maldonado (collectively, "plaintiffs") are Carlos Iglesias's widow and two surviving sons. Plaintiffs first learned of the two annuities through discovery in a Puerto Rico court proceeding.

Francisco Iglesias—Carlos Iglesias's brother who was named as the beneficiary of both annuities and the owner of the second annuity—is a resident of Madrid, Spain, and a citizen of Spain. National Western paid Francisco Iglesias his claim benefits for both annuities on February 23, 2012, and March 13, 2012, sending checks for $1,643,600 and $1,500,000 directly to Francisco Iglesias's address in Spain.

B.   Plaintiffs' Complaint

On March 11, 2014, plaintiffs filed a complaint against National Western seeking $2,935,000, which is the amount Carlos Iglesias paid National Western for the two annuities. Plaintiffs allege: (1) that the first annuity is null and void because it was signed by a person fraudulently claiming to be a licensed agent, in violation of Puerto Rico law; (2) that the second annuity is null and void because it was never perfected insofar as the owner, Francisco Iglesias, never signed the application; and (3) that both annuities are null and void because the payment tendered with the annuity applications came from money of the conjugal partnership between Damaris Maldonado-Viñas and Carlos Iglesias, and Damaris Maldonado-Viñas never consented to the use of the funds for the annuities, as required by Puerto Rico law.

C.   Defendant National Western's Motion to Dismiss

Defendant National Western moved to dismiss the complaint pursuant to Federal Rule of Civil Procedure 12(b)(7) ("Rule 12(b)(7)"). National Western alleges: (1) that pursuant to Federal Rule of Civil Procedure 19(a)(1), Francisco Iglesias is a required party to this action; (2) that joinder of Francisco Iglesias is not feasible because he is a citizen and resident of Spain who does not maintain regular contacts with Puerto Rico, and therefore the Court does not have personal jurisdiction over him; and (3) that pursuant to Federal Rule of Civil Procedure 19(b), the Court should dismiss the action because the action cannot proceed "in equity and good conscience" in Francisco Iglesias's absence. Defendant National Western submitted exhibits to support its motion to dismiss, including the two annuity contracts. Plaintiffs opposed the motion to dismiss, and defendant National Western replied.

II.   DISCUSSION

Federal Rule of Civil Procedure 19 ("Rule 19") outlines a three-step approach to determine whether an action should be dismissed pursuant to Rule 12(b)(7) for failure to join a required party. First, the Court determines whether the absent person is a "required party" to the action. Fed. R. Civ. P. 19(a)(1). If the person is required, then the Court ascertains whether joinder is feasible. *Id.* Finally, if the person is required and joinder is not feasible, then the Court must "determine whether, in equity and good conscience, the action should proceed among the existing parties or should be dismissed." Fed. R. Civ. P. 19(b).

Rule 19 "calls for courts to make pragmatic, practical judgments that are heavily influenced by the facts of each case." *Bacardi Int'l Ltd. v. V. Suarez & Co.*, 719 F.3d 1, 9 (1st Cir. 2013). Courts "should keep in mind the policies that underlie Rule 19, 'including the public interest in preventing multiple and repetitive litigation, the interest of the present parties in obtaining complete and effective relief in a single action, and the interest of absentees in avoiding the possible prejudicial effect of deciding the case without them.'" *Picciotto v. Cont'l Cas. Co.*, 512 F.3d 9, 15-16 (1st Cir. 2008) (citing *Acton Co. v. Bachman Foods, Inc.*, 668 F.2d 76, 78 (1st Cir. 1982)).

A.   Rule 19(a)(1): Required Party

Rule 19(a)(1) sets forth three tests, any one of which, if satisfied, results in deeming an absent person a required party. A person is a required party if:

> (A) in that person's absence, the court cannot accord complete relief among existing parties; or
> (B) that person claims an interest relating to the subject of the action and is so situated that disposing of the action in the person's absence may:
> > (i) as a practical matter impair or impede the person's ability to protect the interest; or
> > (ii) leave an existing party subject to a substantial risk of incurring double, multiple, or otherwise inconsistent obligations because of the interest.

Fed. R. Civ. P. 19(a)(1). The Court proceeds to apply each test to determine whether Francisco Iglesias is a required party to this action.

1.   Rule 19(a)(1)(A): Accord Complete Relief

A person is a required party if, "in that person's absence, the court cannot accord complete relief among existing parties." Fed. R. Civ. P. 19(a)(1)(A). The Court here can accord the relief that plaintiffs seek by voiding both annuities and ordering defendant National Western to return to plaintiffs the sum of the annuity premiums paid by Carlos Iglesias. Granting this relief does not require the presence of Francisco Iglesias, and defendant National Western advances no argument as to why it would. Thus, Francisco Iglesias is not a required party pursuant to Rule 19(a)(1)(A).

2.   *Rule 19(a)(1)(B)(i): Impair Absent Person's Ability to Protect his Interest*

A person is a required party if disposing of the action in the person's absence would "as a practical matter impair or impede" his ability to protect an interest he has in the litigation. Fed. R. Civ. P. 19(a)(1)(B)(i). A court's judgment is not legally enforceable against a nonparty. *Provident Tradesmens Bank & Trust Co. v. Patterson*, 390 U.S. 102, 110 (1968). Accordingly, the parties here do not dispute that if Francisco Iglesias remains a nonparty and the Court issues a judgment voiding the annuities, that judgment will not bind Francisco Iglesias or compel him to return the annuity benefits that he received.

The appropriate inquiry is whether a judgment voiding the annuities would "*as a practical matter* impair or impede" Francisco Iglesias's ability to protect an interest he may claim in this case. *See* Fed. R. Civ. P. 19(a)(1)(B)(i) (emphasis added). To this end, defendant National Western argues that if this Court, in Francisco Iglesias's absence, voids the annuities and orders National Western to return to plaintiffs the premiums paid by Carlos Iglesias, then Francisco Iglesias "will confront a claim to refund [the annuity benefits he collected] in the proper jurisdiction, while possibly facing the disadvantage that a decision by this Court, applying Puerto Rico law in his absence, could be deemed highly persuasive against him." The Court finds National Western's argument unpersuasive in light of plaintiffs' reasoned analysis on this point.

As plaintiffs explain, to prevail in this case, plaintiffs have to establish (1) that only licensed agents can legally sell annuities pursuant to Puerto Rico law, and an unlicensed National Western agent sold Carlos Iglesias the first annuity; (2) that annuity contracts are not perfected until the owner signs them, and National Western failed to get the owner's signature on the second annuity; or (3) that Carlos Iglesias's spouse's consent was necessary to purchase both annuities, and National Western failed to obtain this consent. In other words, based on plaintiffs' specific causes of action, the Court can void one or both annuities only if it finds that National Western illegally or negligently sold the annuities. Francisco Iglesias may actually *benefit* from such a ruling: if National Western brings a claim against Francisco Iglesias to return the benefits he collected, Francisco Iglesias could possibly assert a defense that but for National Western's negligence, the annuities would have remained valid.

This case is easily distinguished from the three cases upon which defendant National Western relies. In *Carbajal v. Dorn*, No. CV-09-283-PHX-DGC, 2009 WL 3756694 (D. Ariz. Nov. 5, 2009), *Belcher ex rel. Belcher v. Prudential Insurance Co. of America*, 158 F. Supp. 2d 777 (S.D. Ohio 2001), and *United States v. Fried*, 183 F. Supp. 371 (E.D.N.Y. 1960), the respective district courts ruled that absent beneficiaries of life insurance policies were required parties in actions that sought to either change the named beneficiary (*Carbajal* and *Belcher*) or order that the cash surrender value of the life insurance policies be paid to the United States to satisfy the insured's arrears of income taxes (*Fried*). None of the defendant insurance companies in these three cases had already paid the absent beneficiaries their benefits. Therefore, even without *res judicata* effect, judgments changing the beneficiary or ordering that the policy funds be paid to someone else would have automatically diminished or extinguished the absent beneficiaries' vested interests in the insurance benefits. Here, because Francisco Iglesias has already received the annuity benefits, a judgment voiding the annuities in his absence would not automatically extinguish his right to the benefits. Thus, National Western's reliance on [these cases] is unpersuasive.

Defendant National Western raises a new argument in its reply to plaintiffs' opposition to the motion to dismiss. It avers that because Francisco Iglesias is the named "owner" of the second annuity, and thus a "direct party to the contract at hand," he must be a required party in this action to void the annuity. The Court is unpersuaded by this argument. Pursuant to Article II, Section 2.1, of the annuity contract, the annuity owner may exercise his or her rights only "while the Annuitant is alive." All of Francisco Iglesias's rights as the "owner," therefore, terminated upon Carlos Iglesias's death. Thus, Francisco Iglesias has no interest in this action to void the second annuity by virtue of his designation as the annuity's "owner."

Francisco Iglesias is not a required party pursuant to Rule 19(a)(1)(B)(i) because disposing of this action in his absence would not, as a practical matter, impair or impede his ability to protect any interest he may claim relating to the subject of this action.

3.   *Rule 19(a)(1)(B)(ii): Risk of Double or Inconsistent Obligations*

A person is a required party if disposing of the action in his absence would "leave an existing party subject to a substantial risk of incurring double, multiple, or otherwise inconsistent obligations." Rule 19(a)(1)(B)(ii). Defendant National Western argues that a decision by the Court ordering National Western to return to plaintiffs the premiums paid by Carlos Iglesias would expose National Western to a risk of incurring inconsistent obligations "should another court deem that [Francisco Iglesias] need not [return the benefits] in open contradiction to a decision here." In raising this argument, however, defendant National Western ignores the distinction between inconsistent obligations and inconsistent adjudications or results that the First Circuit Court of Appeals has explicitly drawn in the Rule 19 context. "'Inconsistent obligations are not . . . the same as inconsistent adjudications or results,' because '[i]inconsistent obligations occur when a party is unable to comply with one court's order without breaching another court's order concerning the same incident.'" *Bacardi Int'l Ltd.*, 719 F.3d at 12 (quoting *Delgado v. Plaza Las Americas, Inc.*, 139 F.3d 1, 3 (1st Cir. 1998)). If the Court orders defendant National Western to return the premiums paid by Carlos Iglesias and another court rules that Francisco Iglesias does not have to return to National Western the benefits he received, National Western could comply with each order without breaching the other. Thus, National Western has failed to explain how it would be subject to a risk of "inconsistent obligations," as the term is narrowly construed by the First Circuit Court of Appeals.

Although defendant National Western never argues that it would be subject to a risk of double obligations, the Court will address this point briefly. If the Court orders National Western to return the premiums paid and another court rules that Francisco Iglesias does not have to return to National Western the benefits he received, then National Western would certainly have paid out double on the annuities. But even this is not the "double obligation" that Rule 19(a)(1)(B)(ii) seeks to avoid. As the First Circuit Court of Appeals explains, "where two suits arising from the same incident involve different causes of action, defendants are not faced with the potential for double liability because separate suits have different consequences and different measures of damages." *Delgado*, 139 F.3d at 3. Any claim that defendant National Western may bring against Francisco Iglesias for a refund would involve a different cause of action and a different theory of recovery than those raised in this case. Therefore, disposing of this case in Francisco Iglesias's absence would not subject National Western to a risk of double obligation.

Thus, Francisco Iglesias is not a required party pursuant to Rule 19(a)(1)(B)(ii) because disposing of this action in his absence would not leave defendant National Western "subject to a substantial risk of incurring double, multiple, or otherwise inconsistent obligations."

B.   Francisco Iglesias Is Not a Required Party

Having not met any of the three tests set forth in Rule 19(a)(1), the Court concludes that Francisco Iglesias is not a required party to this action. This ends the Rule 19 analysis. The Court need not determine whether joinder would be feasible or whether the action should proceed or be dismissed pursuant to Rule 19(b).

III.   CONCLUSION

For the reasons explained above, the Court DENIES defendant National Western's motion to dismiss pursuant to Rule 12(b)(7).

IT IS SO ORDERED.

NOTES AND QUESTIONS

1. *Accord complete relief.*   The district court concluded that the joinder of Francisco Iglesias was not required to accord complete relief within the meaning of Rule 19(a)(1)(A). But wasn't it likely that a judgment against National Western would lead to further litigation between it and Francisco? If so, why did the district court nonetheless conclude that Francisco's joinder was not required?

2. *Impair absent person's ability to protect his interest.*   The district court also concluded that the litigation before it would not, as a practical matter, impair any interest Francisco had in the subject of the action within the meaning of Rule 19(a)(1)(B)(i). Do you agree with that conclusion?

3. *Risk of inconsistent or double obligations.*   The district court drew a distinction between inconsistent obligations and inconsistent adjudications. What is that distinction and how is it relevant for purposes of Rule 19(a)(1)(B)(ii)? *See, e.g., Field v. Volkswagenwerk A.G.*, 626 F.2d 293, 301-302 (3d Cir. 1980) (holding that the "inconsistent obligations" clause of Rule 19(a)(1)(B)(ii) is not triggered by "the possibility of a subsequent adjudication that may result in a judgment that is inconsistent as a matter of logic"). Was the potential inconsistency facing National Western an obligation or an adjudication? Contrast this case with one in which two women claim the exclusive right to use the name "Mrs. Caryl Warner." If the first Mrs. Caryl Warner sues the telephone company to force it to remove the second Mrs. Caryl Warner's name from its directory, the company could face inconsistent obligations if the second Mrs. Caryl Warner were not included in the suit, for in a second action she might obtain an order requiring the company to include her name in the directory. *See Warner v. Pacific Tel. & Tel. Co.*, 263 P.2d 465 (Cal. Ct. App. 1953). Was the inconsistency in *Maldonado-Viñas* of a similar nature?

The district court recognized that it was possible that National Western would pay out "double on the annuities." Yet the court concluded that this possibility did not present a risk that National Western incurred a "double obligation." In the district court's view, what would constitute a risk of double obligation and why wasn't there such a risk in this case?

A NOTE ON THE FEASABILITY OF JOINDER

As we have noted, the joinder of a required party is mandatory if that party "is subject to service of process and [if joinder of that party] will not deprive the court of subject-matter jurisdiction." FED. R. CIV. P. 19(a)(1). The opposite is also true: If the required party is not subject to service of process or if that party's joinder would destroy subject matter jurisdiction, he cannot be joined. Under this circumstance, the court must turn to Rule 19(b) and consider whether and under what circumstances it can proceed in the party's absence.

The phrase "subject to service of process" requires consideration of the usual rules and standards pertaining to service of process and personal jurisdiction, including waiver. There are no additional wrinkles here other than that the court may invite a party with potential objections to personal jurisdiction to intervene and waive those objections. In short, Rule 19 invites a consideration of the law of personal jurisdiction.

The subject matter jurisdiction limitation on Rule 19 joinder appears, as a practical matter, to be limited to diversity and alienage cases. As to federal question cases, it is quite unlikely that the joinder of an additional party would deprive a court of arising-under jurisdiction. At the very least, a claim by or against a "required" party in this context would fall within the court's supplemental jurisdiction, 28 U.S.C. § 1367(a), as part of the same constitutional case. In the context of diversity and alienage jurisdiction, the most likely deprivation of jurisdiction will occur when the required party's joinder would destroy complete diversity. *See* 28 U.S.C. § 1367(b). That defect can sometimes be cured by a careful alignment of that party so as to avoid a violation of the complete diversity rule. This, of course, presumes that the ultimate alignment of that party as a plaintiff or defendant is consistent with her potential role in the case. It is also possible, but less likely, that an amount-in-controversy deficiency will deprive a court of subject matter jurisdiction. *See Exxon Mobil Corp. v. Allapattah Services, Inc.*, page 660, *supra*, and the notes following.

With respect to venue, which is not mentioned in Rule 19(a)(1), there is a potential for a delayed determination of "unfeasibility" if the required party is joined and then files a timely and proper objection to venue. Under that circumstance, the district court must dismiss the party from the case, *see* Rule 19(a)(3), and then consider whether and the extent to which the case can proceed under Rule 19(b). A problem of venue unfeasibility is most likely to occur when the original venue is premised on residency of the defendants, *see* 28 U.S.C. § 1391(b) (1). If venue is premised on substantial events having occurred in the district, *see* § 1391(b)(2), a successful objection to venue by a required party would be remote at best.

2.   Rule 19(b)

Provident Tradesmens Bank & Trust Co. v. Patterson
390 U.S. 102 (1968)

Mr. Justice Harlan delivered the opinion of the Court.

This controversy, involving in its present posture the dismissal of a declaratory judgment action for nonjoinder of an "indispensable" party, began nearly 10 years ago with a traffic accident. An automobile owned by Edward Dutcher, who was not present when the accident occurred, was being driven by Donald Cionci, to whom Dutcher had given the keys. John Lynch and John Harris were passengers. The automobile crossed the median strip of the highway and collided with a truck being driven by Thomas Smith. Cionci, Lynch, and Smith were killed and Harris was severely injured.

Three tort actions were brought. Provident Tradesmens Bank, the administrator of the estate of passenger Lynch and petitioner here, sued the estate of the driver, Cionci, in a diversity action. Smith's administratrix, and Harris in person, each brought a state-court action against the estate of Cionci, Dutcher, the owner, and the estate of Lynch. These Smith and Harris actions, for unknown reasons, have never gone to trial and are still pending. The Lynch action against Cionci's estate was settled for $50,000, which the estate of Cionci, being penniless, has never paid.

Dutcher, the owner of the automobile and a defendant in the as yet untried tort actions, had an automobile liability insurance policy with Lumbermens Mutual Casualty Company, a respondent here. That policy had an upper limit of $100,000 for all claims arising out of a single accident. This fund was potentially subject to two different sorts of claims by the tort plaintiffs. First, Dutcher himself might be held vicariously liable as Cionci's "principal"; the likelihood of such a judgment against Dutcher is a matter of considerable doubt and dispute. Second, the policy by its terms covered the direct liability of any person driving Dutcher's car with Dutcher's "permission."

The insurance company had declined, after notice, to defend in the tort action brought by Lynch's estate against the estate of Cionci, believing that Cionci had not had permission and hence was not covered by the policy. The facts allegedly were that Dutcher had entrusted his car to Cionci, but that Cionci had made a detour from the errand for which Dutcher allowed his car to be taken. The estate of Lynch, armed with its $50,000 liquidated claim against the estate of Cionci, brought the present diversity action for a declaration that Cionci's use of the car had been "with permission" of Dutcher. The only named defendants were the company and the estate of Cionci. The other two tort plaintiffs were joined as plaintiffs. Dutcher, a resident of the State of Pennsylvania as were all the plaintiffs, was not joined either as plaintiff or defendant. The failure to join him was not adverted to at the trial level.

The major question of law contested at trial was a state-law question. The District Court had ruled that, as a matter of the applicable (Pennsylvania) law, the driver of an automobile is presumed to have the permission of the owner. Hence, unless contrary evidence could be introduced, the tort plaintiffs, now declaratory judgment plaintiffs, would be entitled to a directed verdict against the insurance company. The only possible contrary evidence was testimony by Dutcher as to restrictions he had imposed on Cionci's use of the automobile. The two estate plaintiffs claimed, however, that under the Pennsylvania "Dead Man Rule" Dutcher was incompetent to testify on this matter as against them. The District Court upheld this claim. It ruled that under Pennsylvania law Dutcher was incompetent to testify against an estate if he had an "adverse" interest to that of the estate. It found such adversity in Dutcher's potential need to call upon the insurance fund to pay judgments against himself, and his consequent interest in not having part or all of the fund used to pay judgments against Cionci. The

District Court, therefore, directed verdicts in favor of the two estates. Dutcher was, however, allowed to testify as against the live plaintiff, Harris. The jury, nonetheless, found that Cionci had had permission, and hence awarded a verdict to Harris also.

Lumbermens appealed the judgment to the Court of Appeals for the Third Circuit, raising various state-law questions. The Court of Appeals did not reach any of these issues. Instead, after reargument *en banc*, it decided, 5-2, to reverse on two alternative grounds neither of which had been raised in the District Court or by the appellant.

The first of these grounds was that Dutcher was an indispensable party. The court held that the "adverse interests" that had rendered Dutcher incompetent to testify under the Pennsylvania Dead Man Rule also required him to be made a party. The court did not consider whether the fact that a verdict had already been rendered, without objection to the nonjoinder of Dutcher, affected the matter. Nor did it follow the provision of Rule 19 of the Federal Rules of Civil Procedure that findings of "indispensability" must be based on stated pragmatic considerations. It held, to the contrary, that the right of a person who "may be affected" by the judgment to be joined is a "substantive" right, unaffected by the federal rules; that a trial court "may not proceed" in the absence of such a person; and that since Dutcher could not be joined as a defendant without destroying diversity jurisdiction the action had to be dismissed.

Since this ruling presented a serious challenge to the scope of the newly amended Rule 19, we granted certiorari. Concluding that the inflexible approach adopted by the Court of Appeals in this case exemplifies the kind of reasoning that the Rule was designed to avoid, we reverse.

I . . .

We may assume, at the outset, that Dutcher falls within the category of persons who, under [Rule 19(a)(1)], should be "joined if feasible." The action was for an adjudication of the validity of certain claims against a fund. Dutcher, faced with the possibility of judgments against him, had an interest in having the fund preserved to cover that potential liability. Hence there existed, when this case went to trial, at least the possibility that a judgment might impede Dutcher's ability to protect his interest, or lead to later relitigation by him.

The optimum solution, an adjudication of the permission question that would be binding on all interested persons, was not "feasible," however, for Dutcher could not be made a defendant without destroying diversity. Hence the problem was the one to which Rule 19(b) appears to address itself: in the absence of a person who "should be joined if feasible," should the court dismiss the action or proceed without him? Since this problem emerged for the first time in the Court of Appeals, there were also two subsidiary questions. First, what was the effect, if any, of the failure of the defendants to raise the matter in the District Court? Second, what was the importance, if any, of the fact that a judgment, binding on the parties although not binding on Dutcher, had already been reached after extensive litigation? The three questions prove, on examination, to be interwoven.

We conclude, upon consideration of the record and applying the "equity and good conscience" test of Rule 19(b), that the Court of Appeals erred in not allowing the judgment to stand.

Rule 19(b) suggests four "interests" that must be examined in each case to determine whether, in equity and good conscience, the court should proceed without a party whose absence from the litigation is compelled.[2] Each of these interests must, in this case, be viewed entirely from an appellate perspective since the matter of joinder was not considered in the trial court. First, the plaintiff has an interest in having a forum. Before the trial, the strength of this interest obviously depends upon whether a satisfactory alternative forum exists.[3] On appeal, if the plaintiff has won, he has a strong additional interest in preserving his judgment. Second, the defendant may properly wish to avoid multiple litigation, or inconsistent relief, or sole responsibility for a liability he shares with another. After trial, however, if the defendant has failed to assert this interest, it is quite proper to consider it foreclosed.[4]

Third, there is the interest of the outsider whom it would have been desirable to join. Of course, since the outsider is not before the court, he cannot be bound by the judgment rendered. This means, however, only that a judgment is not *res judicata* as to, or legally enforceable against, a nonparty. It obviously does not mean either (a) that a court may never issue a judgment that, in practice, affects a nonparty or (b) that (to the contrary) a court may always proceed without considering the potential effect on nonparties simply because they are not "bound" in the technical sense. Instead, as Rule 19(a) expresses it, the court must consider the extent to which the judgment may "as a practical matter impair or impede his ability to protect" his interest in the subject matter. When a case has reached the appeal stage the matter is more complex. The judgment appealed from may not in fact affect the interest of any outsider even though there existed, before trial, a possibility that a judgment affecting his interest would be rendered. When necessary, however, a court of appeals should, on its own initiative, take steps to protect the absent party, who of course had no opportunity to plead and prove his interest below.

Fourth, there remains the interest of the courts and the public in complete, consistent, and efficient settlement of controversies. We read the Rule's third criterion, whether the judgment issued in the absence of the nonjoined person will

---

2. For convenience, we treat these interests in a different order from that appearing in Rule 19(b). . . .

3. The Advisory Committee . . . in its note on the 1966 Revision of Rule 19 . . . comments as follows on the fourth factor listed in Rule 19(b), the adequacy of plaintiff's remedy if the action is dismissed: "[T]he court should consider whether there is any assurance that the plaintiff, if dismissed, could sue effectively in another forum where better joinder would be possible." . . .

4. The Committee Note comments that "when the moving party is seeking dismissal in order to protect himself against a later suit by the absent person . . . and is not seeking vicariously to protect the absent person against a prejudicial judgment . . . his undue delay in making the motion can properly be counted against him as a reason for denying the motion." . . .

be "adequate," to refer to this public stake in settling disputes by wholes, whenever possible, for clearly the plaintiff, who himself chose both the forum and the parties defendant, will not be heard to complain about the sufficiency of the relief obtainable against them. After trial, considerations of efficiency of course include the fact that the time and expense of a trial have already been spent.

Rule 19(b) also directs a district court to consider the possibility of shaping relief to accommodate these four interests. Commentators had argued that greater attention should be paid to this potential solution to a joinder stymie, and the Rule now makes it explicit that a court should consider modification of a judgment as an alternative to dismissal. Needless to say, a court of appeals may also properly require suitable modification as a condition of affirmance.

Had the Court of Appeals applied Rule 19's criteria to the facts of the present case, it could hardly have reached the conclusion it did. We begin with the plaintiff's viewpoint. It is difficult to decide at this stage whether they would have had an "adequate" remedy had the action been dismissed before trial for nonjoinder: we cannot here determine whether the plaintiffs could have brought the same action, against the same parties plus Dutcher, in a state court. After trial, however, the "adequacy" of this hypothetical alternative, from the plaintiffs' point of view, was obviously greatly diminished. Their interest in preserving a fully litigated judgment should be overborne only by rather greater opposing considerations than would be required at an earlier stage when the plaintiffs' only concern was for a federal rather than a state forum.

Opposing considerations in this case are hard to find. The defendants had no stake, either asserted or real, in the joinder of Dutcher. They showed no interest in joinder until the Court of Appeals took the matter into its own hands. This properly forecloses any interest of theirs, but for purposes of clarity we note that the insurance company, whose liability was limited to $100,000, had or will have full opportunity to litigate each claim on that fund against the claimant involved. Its only concern with the absence of Dutcher was and is to obtain a windfall escape from its defeat at trial.

The interest of the outsider, Dutcher, is more difficult to reckon. The Court of Appeals, concluding that it should not follow Rule 19's command to determine whether, as a practical matter, the judgment impaired the nonparty's ability to protect his rights, simply quoted the District Court's reasoning on the Dead Man issue as proof that Dutcher had a "right" to be joined:

> The subject matter of this suit is the coverage of Lumbermens' policy issued to Dutcher. Depending upon the outcome of this trial, Dutcher may have the policy all to himself or he may have to share its coverage with the Cionci Estate, thereby extending the availability of the proceeds of the policy to satisfy verdicts and judgments in favor of the two Estate plaintiffs. Sharing the coverage of a policy of insurance with finite limits with another, and thereby making that policy available to claimants against that other person is immediately worth less than having the coverage of such policy available to Dutcher alone. By the outcome in the instant case, to the extent that the two Estate plaintiffs will have the proceeds of the policy available to them in their claims against Cionci's estate, Dutcher will lose a measure

of protection. Conversely, to the extent that the proceeds of this policy are not available to the two Estate plaintiffs Dutcher will gain. . . .

There is a logical error in the Court of Appeals' appropriation of this reasoning for its own quite different purposes: Dutcher had an "adverse" interest (sufficient to invoke the Dead Man Rule) because he would have been *benefited* by a ruling *in favor* of the insurance company; the question before the Court of Appeals, however, was whether Dutcher was *harmed* by the judgment *against* the insurance company.

The two questions are not the same. If the three plaintiffs had lost to the insurance company on the permission issue, that loss would have ended the matter favorably to Dutcher. If, as has happened, the three plaintiffs obtain a judgment against the insurance company on the permission issue, Dutcher may still claim that as a nonparty he is not estopped by that judgment from relitigating the issue. At that point it might be argued that Dutcher should be bound by the previous decision because, although technically a nonparty, he had purposely bypassed an adequate opportunity to intervene. We do not now decide whether such an argument would be correct under the circumstances of this case. If, however, Dutcher is properly foreclosed by his failure to intervene in the present litigation, then the joinder issue considered in the Court of Appeals vanishes, for any rights of Dutcher's have been lost by his own inaction.

If Dutcher is not foreclosed by his failure to intervene below, then he is not "bound" by the judgment in favor of the insurance company and, in theory, he has not been harmed. There remains, however, the practical question whether Dutcher is likely to have any need and if so will have any opportunity, to relitigate. The only possible threat to him is that if the fund is used to pay judgments against Cionci the money may in fact have disappeared before Dutcher has an opportunity to assert his interest. Upon examination, we find this supposed threat neither large nor unavoidable.

The state-court actions against Dutcher had lain dormant for years at the pleading stage by the time the Court of Appeals acted. Petitioner asserts here that under the applicable Pennsylvania vicarious liability law there is virtually no chance of recovery against Dutcher. We do not accept this assertion as fact, but the matter could have been explored below. Furthermore, even in the event of tort judgments against Dutcher, it is unlikely that he will be prejudiced by the outcome here. The potential claimants against Dutcher himself are identical with the potential claimants against Cionci's estate. Should the claimants seek to collect from Dutcher personally, he may be able to raise the permission issue defensively, making it irrelevant that the actual monies paid from the fund may have disappeared: Dutcher can assert that Cionci did not have his permission and that therefore the payments made on Cionci's behalf out of Dutcher's insurance policy should properly be credited against Dutcher's own liability. Of course, when Dutcher raises this defense he may lose, either on the merits of the permission issue or on the ground that the issue is foreclosed by Dutcher's failure to intervene in the present case, but Dutcher will not have been prejudiced by the failure of the District Court here to order him joined.

If the Court of Appeals was unconvinced that the threat to Dutcher was trivial, it could nevertheless have avoided all difficulties by proper phrasing of the decree. The District Court, for unspecified reasons, had refused to order immediate payment on the Cionci judgment. Payment could have been withheld pending the suits against Dutcher and relitigation (if that became necessary) by him. In this Court, furthermore, counsel for petitioners represented orally that they, the tort plaintiffs, would accept a limitation of all claims to the amount of the insurance policy. Obviously such a compromise could have been reached below had the Court of Appeals been willing to abandon its rigid approach and seek ways to preserve what was, as to the parties, subject to the appellants' other contentions, a perfectly valid judgment.

The suggestion of potential relitigation of the question of "permission" raises the fourth "interest" at stake in joinder cases—efficiency. It might have been preferable, at the trial level, if there were a forum available in which both the company and Dutcher could have been made defendants, to dismiss the action and force the plaintiffs to go elsewhere. Even this preference would have been highly problematical, however, for the actual threat of relitigation by Dutcher depended on there being judgments against him and on the amount of the fund, which was not revealed to the District Court. By the time the case reached the Court of Appeals, however, the problematical preference on efficiency grounds had entirely disappeared: there was no reason then to throw away a valid judgment just because it did not theoretically settle the whole controversy.

II

Application of Rule 19(b)'s "equity and good conscience" test for determining whether to proceed or dismiss would doubtless have led to a contrary result below. The Court of Appeals' reasons for disregarding the Rule remain to be examined. The majority of the court concluded that the Rule was inapplicable because "substantive" rights are involved, and substantive rights are not affected by the Federal Rules. Although the court did not articulate exactly what the substantive rights are, or what law determines them, we take it to have been making the following argument: (1) there is a category of persons called "indispensable parties"; (2) that category is defined by substantive law and the definition cannot be modified by rule; (3) the right of a person falling within that category to participate in the lawsuit in question is also a substantive matter, and is absolute.

With this we may contrast the position that is reflected in Rule 19. Whether a person is "indispensable," that is, whether a particular lawsuit must be dismissed in the absence of that person, can only be determined in the context of particular litigation. There is a large category, whose limits are not presently in question, of persons who, in the Rule's terminology, should be "joined if feasible," and who, in the older terminology, were called either necessary or indispensable parties. Assuming the existence of a person who should be joined if feasible, the only further question arises when joinder is not possible and the court must decide whether to dismiss or to proceed without him. To use the familiar but confusing terminology, the decision to proceed is a decision that the absent person is merely "necessary" while the decision to dismiss is a decision that he is "indispensable."[15] The decision whether to dismiss (*i.e.*, the decision whether the person missing is "indispensable") must be based on factors varying with the different cases, some such factors being substantive, some procedural, some compelling by themselves, and some subject to balancing against opposing interests. Rule 19 does not prevent the assertion of compelling substantive interests; it merely commands the courts to examine each controversy to make certain that the interests really exist. To say that a court "must" dismiss in the absence of an indispensable party and that it "cannot proceed" without him puts the matter the wrong way around: a court does not know whether a particular person is "indispensable" until it had examined the situation to determine whether it can proceed without him.

The Court of Appeals concluded, although it was the first court to hold, that the 19th century joinder cases in this Court created a federal, common-law, substantive right in a certain class of persons to be joined in the corresponding lawsuits. At the least, that was not the way the matter started. The joinder problem first arose in equity and in the earliest case giving rise to extended discussion the problem was the relatively simple one of the inefficiency of litigation involving only some of the interested persons. A defendant being sued by several cotenants objected that the other cotenants were not made parties. Chief Justice Marshall replied:

> This objection does not affect the jurisdiction, but addresses itself to the policy of the Court. Courts of equity require, that all the parties concerned in interest shall be brought before them, that the matter in controversy may be finally settled. This equitable rule, however, is framed by the Court itself, and is subject to its discretion. . . . [*Elmendorf v. Taylor*, 23 U.S. (10 Wheat.) 152 (1825).]

Following this case there arose three cases, also in equity, that the Court of Appeals here held to have declared a "substantive" right to be joined. It is true that these cases involved what would now be called "substantive" rights. This substantive involvement of the absent person with the controversy before the Court was, however, in each case simply an inescapable fact of the situation presented to the Court for adjudication. The Court in each case left the outsider with no more "rights" than it had already found belonged to him. The question in each case was simply whether, given the substantive involvement of the outsider, it was proper to proceed to adjudicate as between the parties. . . .

The most influential of the cases in which this Court considered the question whether to proceed or dismiss in the absence of an interested but not joinable outsider is *Shields v. Barrow*, [58 U.S. (17 How.) 130 (1854)], referred to in the opinion below. There the Court attempted, perhaps unfortunately, to state general

---

15. The Committee Note puts the matter as follows: "The subdivision [19(b)] uses the word 'indispensable' only in a conclusory sense, that is, a person is 'regarded as indispensable' when he cannot be made a party and, upon consideration of the factors above mentioned, it is determined that in his absence it would be preferable to dismiss the action, rather than to retain it."

definitions of those persons without whom litigation could or could not proceed. In the former category were placed

> "Persons having an interest in the controversy, and who ought to be made parties, in order that the court may act on that rule which requires it to decide on, and finally determine the entire controversy, and do complete justice, by adjusting all the rights involved in it. These persons are commonly termed necessary parties; but if their interests are separable from those of the parties before the court, so that the court can proceed to a decree, and do complete and final justice, without affecting other persons not before the court, the latter are not indispensable parties."

Id. at 139. The persons in the latter category were

> "Persons who not only have an interest in the controversy, but an interest of such a nature that a final decree cannot be made without either affecting that interest, or leaving the controversy in such a condition that its final termination may be wholly inconsistent with equity and good conscience."

Ibid.

These generalizations are still valid today, and they are consistent with the requirements of Rule 19, but they are not a substitute for the analysis required by that Rule. Indeed, the second *Shields* definition states, in rather different fashion, the criteria for decision announced in Rule 19(b). One basis for dismissal is prejudice to the rights of an absent party that "*cannot*" be avoided in issuance of a final decree. Alternatively, if the decree can be so written that it protects the interests of the absent persons, but as so written it leaves the controversy so situated that the outcome may be inconsistent with "equity and good conscience," the suit should be dismissed.

The majority of the Court of Appeals read *Shields v. Barrow* to say that a person whose interests "may be affected" by the decree of the court is an indispensable party, and that all indispensable parties have a "substantive right" to have suits dismissed in their absence. We are unable to read *Shields* as saying either. It dealt only with persons whose interests must, unavoidably, be affected by a decree and it said nothing about substantive rights. Rule 19(b), which the Court of Appeals dismissed as an ineffective attempt to change the substantive rights stated in *Shields*, is, on the contrary, a valid statement of the criteria for determining whether to proceed or dismiss in the forced absence of an interested person. It takes, for aught that now appears, adequate account of the very real, very substantive claims to fairness on the part of outsiders that may arise in some cases. This, however, simply is not such a case. . . .

We think it clear that the judgment below cannot stand. The judgment is vacated and the case is remanded to the Court of Appeals for consideration of those issues raised on appeal that have not been considered, and, should the Court of Appeals affirm the District Court as to those issues, for appropriate disposition preserving the judgment of the District Court and protecting the interests of nonjoined parties.

It is so ordered.

NOTES AND QUESTIONS

1. A required party.   The Court assumed that Dutcher was a required party, *i.e.*, a person who must be joined if feasible. Was he? Which, if any, of Federal Rule 19(a)(1)'s sub-clauses did Dutcher satisfy? As to Rule 19(a)(1)(A) ("complete relief"), in the absence of Dutcher, could the plaintiffs receive all the relief they sought from Lumbermens? Did Dutcher's absence prevent Lumbermens from paying for injuries covered by Dutcher's insurance policy? Is it relevant, for purposes of the complete relief clause, that Dutcher might later sue Lumbermens to enforce the terms of the policy?

Rule 19(a)(1)(B) comes into play only if the absentee claims "an interest relating to the subject of the action." FED. R. CIV. P. 19(a)(1)(B). Presumably, Dutcher had an interest in the proper enforcement of Lumbermens' contractual obligations to him. Carefully consider the scope of that interest. Was it more extensive than the $100,000 maximum payout under the policy? Did it cover any liability Dutcher might incur for damages that exceeded that amount? Might we say that Dutcher had an interest in the enforcement of the policy according to its terms?

Having identified Dutcher's interest in the subject of the action, Rule 19(a)(1)(B)(i) requires that we determine whether proceeding in his absence would "impair or impede" his ability to protect that interest. Our instinctive answer is affirmative. Dutcher's ability to protect or preserve the policy coverage could be impaired by a judgment against Lumbermens since the collective damages of the injured parties might exhaust the policy's coverage limits and subject Dutcher to potential liability for damages in excess of that amount. But is this truly an impairment of Dutcher's interest in the subject of the action, *i.e.*, in the enforcement of Lumbermens' obligations under the contract? True, Dutcher might be held liable for damages in excess of the policy's coverage in the pending state-court proceedings, but his liability in those proceedings would depend on whether Cionci was driving with permission and whether the injured parties could prove damages in excess of $100,000, both of which Dutcher would be free to contest regardless of the outcome of the suit against Lumbermens. Is the fact that Dutcher might be liable for damages that exceed the policy coverage a harm caused by the judgment in the first suit?

We must then consider, under 19(a)(1)(B)(ii), whether there was a risk that Dutcher's absence would cause an existing party—Lumbermens—to incur double, multiple, or inconsistent obligations. If the trial court found (as it did) that Cionci had Dutcher's permission, Lumbermens might have to pay out the entire $100,000 in proceeds to satisfy claims against Cionci's estate. If Dutcher were later found liable in the pending state court suits, he might then seek reimbursement from Lumbermens. If Lumbermens refused to pay him, claiming it had already paid out the full policy proceeds, Dutcher might sue the company. Yet, while Lumbermens would then incur the vexation of a second lawsuit, it seems unlikely that it would incur double or multiple liability. In order to prevail against Lumbermens, Dutcher would have to establish that Cionci was driving with

Dutcher's permission—the opposite of what he actually contended. If Dutcher prevailed on that issue, Lumbermens would have a complete defense to his subsequent claim, for a finding of "with permission" would fully validate the previously made payments to the plaintiffs—payments that exhausted the $100,000 policy limits.

In addition to its concern with double or multiple liability, Rule 19(a)(1)(B)(ii) also asks whether an existing party faces the risk of "inconsistent obligations." FED. R. CIV. P. 19(a)(1)(B)(ii). Did Dutcher's absence pose this danger for Lumbermens? The company's risk of inconsistent obligations stemmed from the possibility that the first suit might find that Cionci had permission, while a second suit might conclude that permission was lacking. Though these judgments would rest on inconsistent *adjudications* or *findings* on the issue of permission, would they impose inconsistent or conflicting *obligations* on Lumbermens? *See* Note 3 following *Maldonado-Viñas v. National Western Life Ins. Co.*, at page 730, *supra*.

We now return to our original question, *i.e.*, was Dutcher a required party within the meaning of Rule 19(a)(1)? The Court assumed that to be the case. What do you think?

2. *Feasibility.*   Why wasn't Dutcher's joinder feasible? Would the trial court have been able to assert personal jurisdiction over him? Would his joinder have been consistent with 28 U.S.C. § 1332(a)(1)? If this suit had arisen after the 1990 enactment of 28 U.S.C. § 1367, would the court have had supplemental jurisdiction if Dutcher were joined as an additional defendant? Could he logically have been aligned as a plaintiff?

3. *Proceed in the absence of the required party.*   In determining whether Dutcher was a party in whose absence the case should be dismissed, the Court rearranged the Rule 19(b) criteria in terms of the four interests involved, *i.e.*, the plaintiff's, the defendant's, the absentee's, and the public's. The Court emphasized that this analysis must be flexible and pragmatic, each interest being "subject to balancing against opposing interests." The Rule 19(b) factors mirror those we considered under Rule 19(a) when deciding whether the absentee should be joined if feasible. Under Rule 19(b), however, the court examines these factors from a different perspective. The question now is not whether the party should be joined in the case, but whether, in equity and good conscience, the court should proceed in his absence. How did Dutcher's absence implicate each or any of these interests?

Let's focus on the text of current Rule 19(b) and consider the extent to which the *Provident* Court's application of Rule 19(b) is consistent with that text. Subsection (b)(1) requires the court to consider "the extent to which a judgment rendered in the person's absence might prejudice that person or the existing parties." In Note 1 we considered whether Dutcher or any of the existing parties would be prejudiced by his absence. Were you able to identify any potential prejudice to Dutcher or Lumbermens? In its application of Rule 19(b), did the Court identify any such prejudice? If there is no such prejudice, what should the court do?

Subsection (b)(2) requires the court to consider "the extent to which any prejudice could be lessened or avoided by: (A) protective provisions in the judgment; (B) shaping the relief; or (C) other measures." Of course, if no prejudice is identified or identifiable, this subsection does not come into play. But assuming there was some potential prejudice to Dutcher, how did the *Provident* Court suggest that prejudice might be avoided or ameliorated? We will examine this subsection further in Note 4 below.

Rule 19(b)(3) asks whether a judgment rendered in the required party's absence—here Dutcher's—would be "adequate." Would it have been adequate from the perspective of the plaintiffs? If they prevailed, would they receive the complete relief they sought? Was there a chance of further litigation between Dutcher and Lumbermens? Given what we know about the complete relief clause of Rule 19(a)(1)(A), would the possibility of future litigation in itself warrant dismissal of the lawsuit in Dutcher's absence?

Finally, Rule 19(b)(4) asks "whether the plaintiff would have an adequate remedy if the action were dismissed for nonjoinder." Notice that this provision changes the focus of Rule 19(b) from any potential harm to the absent party or the objecting defendant to the perspective of the plaintiff. The underlying presumption of this section is that the examination of subsections (b)(1)-(3) revealed a degree of prejudice at least minimally sufficient to warrant consideration of a dismissal. We are now asked to balance the harm to the required party or to the defendant in proceeding in the absence of the required party against the harm to the plaintiff of dismissing the suit. Why did the *Provident* Court think that any alternative remedy for the plaintiff would be inadequate under the circumstances of that case? Did the Court suggest that the balance might be struck differently in a case where the Rule 12(b)(7) motion is made early in the litigation and where the plaintiff could still re-file the case against all interested parties in a convenient state court? (This question assumes that the party filing the motion was able to show a sufficient degree of prejudice to warrant dismissal.)

4. Ameliorating the prejudice.   In the previous note, we briefly considered Rule 19(b)(2), which provides that once a court identifies prejudice to the absent or an existing party, it should consider "the extent to which any prejudice could be lessened or avoided by: (A) protective provisions in the judgment; (B) shaping the relief; or (C) other measures." There are several ways that a court can accomplish this ameliorative goal. The *Provident* Court suggested two possibilities: The trial court could withhold its judgment until Dutcher had an opportunity to litigate the permission issue; or the trial court could enter a judgment that would eliminate any potential prejudice to Dutcher or Lumbermens, *i.e.*, by incorporating the plaintiffs' agreement to a $100,000 cap on total liability. Other possibilities include granting a remedy other than the one sought by the plaintiff. For example, if the remedy of specific performance is sought but would harm an absent party, the court might consider an award of money damages as an alternative. Or a court could limit the scope of its judgment by requiring a prevailing plaintiff to take specific actions to avoid any harm to the absent party. Finally, a court might invite the absent party to intervene or instruct the defendant to use other available joinder devices to bring that absent party into the case. Thus a court might suggest joinder of the absent party to a counterclaim (Rule 13(h)), the impleader of the absent party (Rule 14(a)), or the interpleader of the plaintiffs and the absent party (Rule 22). Of course, these additional joinder devices must also be consistent with the standards of personal and subject matter jurisdiction. *See generally* 7 WRIGHT, MILLER & KANE, *supra*, § 1608.

In *Provident*, if Dutcher's absence had been noted at the trial court level, might the court have solved the problem by inviting (or ordering) Lumbermens to defensively interplead Dutcher and the original plaintiffs, all of whom had potential claims against the insurance policy? Lumbermens might have done this by counterclaiming against the plaintiffs under Rule 13(a) and joining Dutcher as an additional party to the counterclaim under Rule 13(h). Alternatively, could the trial court have solved the feasibility problem by notifying Dutcher of the suit and inviting him to intervene under Rule 24(a)(2)? At the time the case was decided, federal courts often took ancillary jurisdiction over claims involving intervenors. With the 1990 adoption of § 1367, is this still a viable option in diversity cases? *See Mattel, Inc. v. Bryant*, page 701, *supra*.

5. *Waiver.*   Does a defendant waive an objection to the lack of an indispensable party by failing to raise this defect promptly in the trial court? *See* FED. R. CIV. P. 12(h). May the defect be asserted for the first time on appeal? May it be raised by the court *sua sponte* even if none of the parties has done so? Did *Provident Tradesmens Bank* implicitly answer any of these questions?

6. *Procedural posture.*   How was the Rule 19(b) indispensability analysis affected by the fact that Dutcher's absence was not raised until the case had reached the court of appeals? In the balancing process, did this procedural posture increase the plaintiffs' interest in proceeding without Dutcher? Did it lessen or eliminate the concern for any possible prejudice to Lumbermens? How did it affect the public's interest in the efficient use of judicial resources? Would the Rule 19(b) analysis have come out the same way if Lumbermens had promptly objected to Dutcher's absence in the trial court by moving to dismiss under Rule 12(b)(7)? In that event, would there have been another court available to the plaintiffs in which they could have effected more complete joinder? Assuming such a court were available, would the federal trial court have been justified in dismissing the case if there were other ways of bringing Dutcher into the suit?

7. *Collateral attack.*   If a court erroneously decides to proceed without a necessary or an indispensable party, is the judgment later subject to collateral attack? Historically, courts treated the failure to include an indispensable party as depriving the court of all power to proceed with the case, thereby opening the judgment to collateral attack. *See, e.g., Hanson v. Denckla*, 357 U.S. 235, 245 (1958) (Florida judgment subject to collateral attack due to lack of jurisdiction over Delaware trustee, when Florida law deemed the trustee "an indispensable party" in whose "absence . . . a Florida court may not proceed to adjudicate the controversy"). *See* Chapter II, page 151, *supra*. Today, the lack of a necessary or indispensable party still serves as the basis for a direct attack, as in *Provident Tradesmens Bank*. Otherwise, however, the judgment is usually treated as being

valid and binding on those who were made parties to the suit and is not subject to collateral attack. As the Advisory Committee Notes explain, "Even if the court is mistaken in its decision to proceed in the absence of an interested person, it does not by that token deprive itself of the power to adjudicate as between the parties already before it through proper service of process." Advisory Committee Note, 1966 Amendments, 39 F.R.D. 69, 89.

PROBLEMS

8-21. The Keal Company ("Keal") conducted operations in Dublin, Virginia, and Orrville, Ohio. Workers at the Dublin facility were represented by Local 171 of the Teamsters Union, based in Roanoke, Virginia, while those at the Orrville facility were represented by Local 964, based in Cleveland, Ohio. When Keal shut down its Orrville facility, workers there were free to transfer to the Dublin facility to the extent that work was available there. A dispute arose between the two Locals concerning seniority for the transferring workers. Local 171 claimed that the transferring workers should lose their seniority and be placed at the bottom of the Dublin seniority list. Local 964 contended that these workers should retain their seniority and be dovetailed into the Dublin seniority list. To resolve the issue, Local 964 instituted a grievance proceeding against Keal and Local 171 before a Joint Union-Management Seniority Committee ("Committee"). The Committee found in Local 964's favor, ruling that transferring workers should keep their seniority. Local 171 then sued Keal in a Virginia federal court under the federal Labor Management Relations Act. It sought an order vacating the Committee's decision and ordering Keal to place transferring workers at the bottom of the Dublin seniority list. Local 964 was not named in the suit because it could not be served in Virginia. Keal has moved to dismiss the action under Rule 12(b)(7) on the ground that Local 964 is a required party whose joinder is not feasible and without whom the court cannot proceed. How should the court rule on the motion? Is Local 964 a required party based on any of Rule 19(a)'s subdivisions? If so, is joinder feasible? If joinder of Local 964 is not feasible, should the action in equity and good conscience be dismissed, based on a balancing of the relevant 19(b) factors? *See Teamsters Local Union No. 171 v. Keal Driveaway Co.,* 173 F.3d 915 (4th Cir. 1999).

8-22. LTG, a New York partnership, sued Comfed Bank ("Comfed"), a Massachusetts bank, in a Massachusetts federal court, seeking the return of funds that Comfed holds in escrow. Comfed has moved to dismiss under Rule 12(b)(7), claiming that NHC, a New York corporation that is claiming the same funds, is a required party whose joinder is not feasible and without whom the court cannot proceed. How should the court rule? *See Lodge on the Green Assocs. v. Comfed Savings Bank,* 121 F.R.D. 3 (D. Mass. 1988).

8-23. ADG, Inc. ("ADG"), a Virginia corporation with its principal place of business in Missouri, leased five floors of an office building in New York from Fifth Avenue, Inc. ("Fifth Avenue"), a New York corporation. ADG later subleased two of the floors to Towers, a Nevada corporation whose principal place of business was in New York. Fifth Avenue signed an agreement with ADG and Towers consenting to the sublease and promising not to unreasonably withhold or delay its consent to any alterations proposed by Towers. After taking possession, Towers asked that additional electrical power be provided to the floors it had subleased. Fifth Avenue insisted on seeing schematic plans showing the necessary structural changes. However, it denied Towers access to the building's basement, where the electrical equipment was located. Without such access, the necessary plans could not be prepared. Claiming it was unable to use the subleased space as planned, Towers stopped paying rent to ADG and sued Fifth Avenue in a New York state court, seeking an order requiring that Fifth Avenue either consent to the alterations or provide Towers access to the building's basement. Thereafter, ADG sued Towers in a New York federal court for breach of the sublease agreement, based on Towers's failure to pay rent. Towers counterclaimed against ADG, seeking an injunction requiring ADG to provide additional electrical power to the floors it had subleased. Towers has moved to dismiss the federal suit on the ground that Fifth Avenue is a necessary and indispensable party. How should the court rule on the motion? *See Associated Dry Goods Corp. v. Towers Fin. Corp.*, 920 F.2d 1121 (2d Cir. 1990).

H. Joinder of Claims and Parties Review Problem

8-24. In 2002, the City of Memphis, Tennessee ("the City" or "Memphis") decided to construct a new city hall ("the project"). The City awarded the architectural contract on the project to Arch E. Tech ("Archie"), a well-known architect who lives in Ohio. During the four years he worked on the project, Archie relocated his offices to Memphis. The City also hired Southern Builders, Inc. ("SB"), a Tennessee corporation, as the prime contractor on the project. SB, as required by its contract with the City, purchased a $500,000 performance bond from Continental Casualty ("CC"), a Delaware corporation with its principal place of business in Tennessee, under which CC agreed to indemnify SB for any liability incurred by SB as the prime contractor on the project. SB also entered a subcontract with Alexander Marble, Ltd. ("Alexander"), a partnership with partners in Tennessee, Kentucky, and Ohio, under which Alexander agreed to procure and install the marble to be used on the project. Alexander then, with SB's permission, subcontracted with Quarry, Inc. ("Quarry"), a Florida corporation with its principal place of business in Delaware, which agreed to supply the marble for the project.

A number of disputes have arisen out of the project, two of which are significant here. The first is a dispute between Quarry and Alexander regarding the quality of the marble delivered, the timeliness of the deliveries, and the amount of money owed to Quarry under the subcontract. As a result of this dispute, Alexander has withheld payments under the Quarry/Alexander subcontract, including $100,000 that was advanced to Alexander by SB for the purpose of paying Quarry. SB has also refused to advance an additional $50,000 under the Quarry/Alexander sub-contract. A second dispute has arisen between SB and Alexander. This dispute pertains to Alexander's overall performance under the SB/Alexander subcontract, including Alexander's failure to monitor the quality of the marble and to install the marble in a timely fashion. As a result of that dispute, SB has terminated the SB/Alexander subcontract.

Quarry has filed breach of contract claims against Alexander and SB in a U.S. district court in Tennessee ("USDC"). Quarry claims $100,000 in damages from Alexander (the withheld advance) and an additional $50,000 from SB for further payments due under the Quarry/Alexander subcontract. (You may assume that SB is obligated to Quarry under that contract.)

Alexander filed a timely answer denying Quarry's claim. Alexander has also filed the following claims: a breach of contract claim against Quarry, seeking $70,000 in damages based on the allegation that the marble delivered by Quarry was substandard; a breach of contract claim against SB, claiming $500,000 in liquidated damages based on SB's wrongful termination of the SB/Alexander sub-contract; and a tortious interference claim against Archie, seeking $500,000 in damages and alleging that the termination of the SB/Alexander subcontract was due, in part, to false information conveyed by Archie to SB regarding Alexander's work on the project.

SB filed a timely answer denying the claims of both Quarry and Alexander. In response to Alexander's claim against it, SB also filed a $50,000 claim against Alexander for negligence in procuring and installing the marble. Finally, SB filed a third-party claim against CC for indemnification.

A. Under the federal rules, may Quarry join Alexander and SB as defendants in a single proceeding?

B. Assuming for purposes of this question only that Quarry's joinder of Alexander and SB would be allowed under the federal rules, may the court exercise subject matter jurisdiction over those claims?

C. Assuming for purposes of this and all subsequent questions that the federal rules allow Quarry's joinder of Alexander and SB and that the joinder would satisfy federal subject matter jurisdiction standards, would the rules allow Alexander to file its $70,000 claim against Quarry?

D. Would the claim filed by Alexander against Quarry described in the previous question be deemed compulsory or permissive?

E. Would the court have subject matter jurisdiction over the claim filed by Alexander against Quarry despite the fact that the claim does not satisfy the amount-in-controversy requirement and the fact that by filing the claim, Alexander is essentially a "plaintiff" for purposes of supplemental jurisdiction?

F. Would the federal rules allow Alexander to file his claim against SB?

G. Assuming for purposes of this question only that the federal rules would allow the filing of Alexander's claim against SB, would the court have subject matter jurisdiction over that claim?

H. With respect to Alexander's claim against Archie, which of the federal rules, if any, would allow Alexander to bring Archie into this case?

I. Assuming for purposes of this question only that the federal rules would allow Archie's joinder, would the court have subject matter jurisdiction over the claim against Archie?

J. The facts indicate that SB has filed "a $50,000 claim against Alexander for negligence in procuring and installing the marble." What would be the consequences for SB if it had failed to file this claim prior to the date on which a final judgment was entered in the case?

K. Which federal rule, if any, would allow SB to file its claim against CC? If a federal rule does allow this joinder, would the federal court have subject matter jurisdiction over the claim?

L. Assuming for purposes of this question that the joinder of CC was allowed by the federal rules and was consistent with the standards of subject matter jurisdiction, would the federal rules allow Quarry to file a claim against CC asserting a claim for declaratory relief that Quarry was entitled to $50,000 under the SB performance bond?

M. Use the same assumptions as the previous question, and also assume that the federal rules would allow Quarry's claim against CC. Would the court have subject matter jurisdiction over Quarry's claim?

N. For purposes of this question, assume that the federal rules and all applicable standards of subject matter jurisdiction have been satisfied for the following claims: Quarry's claims against Alexander and SB; Alexander's claims against Quarry and SB; and SB's claims against Alexander and CC. The City has filed a timely motion to intervene. Attached to its motion is a complaint naming SB as a defendant and seeking $1 million in damages arising out of SB's "negligent and fraudulent" supervision of the project. Would the federal rules allow the City to intervene under these circumstances?

O. Use the same assumptions as in the previous question, and also assume that CC has filed a motion to dismiss under Rule 12(b)(7), arguing that the absence of the City will subject CC to vexatious and multiple litigation on the performance bond. How should the court respond to this motion?

P. Use the same assumptions as in question N, and also assume that the City has filed a motion to intervene and that the court has concluded that the City was entitled to intervene as of right. Would the court have subject matter jurisdiction over the City's claim?

IX

CLASS ACTIONS

A class action is a type of representative litigation in which one or more parties sue or are sued as representatives of a larger group of similarly situated persons or entities, the so-called class. When a class action is properly filed and certified as such by the court, any resulting judgment will bind all members of the class, except those who may have exercised a right to opt out of the class where such an option is available.

The class action device emerged as a means of promoting the efficient resolution of legal disputes involving large numbers of parties. From a joinder perspective, the numerosity of the interested parties might be so great as to render joinder of each plaintiff or defendant impractical or impossible. Moreover, in the context of a plaintiff's class action, the amount at stake for each of those whom a defendant has wronged may be such that it is not economically feasible for each injured person to sue on her own. In this sense, a class action is often an alternative to no action at all.

Class actions carry certain inherent dangers. For example, in the context of a plaintiffs' class action, a judgment might cut off any separate right of action an absent class member would otherwise have against the defendant. Similarly, in defendant class actions, the judgment may place legal obligations on individual class members who have not literally had their day in court. Thus, unless carefully managed, class actions pose the risk of depriving absent class members of valuable interests under conditions that may violate a member's due process right to notice and the opportunity to be heard. In addition, there may be times when use of a plaintiff class action could impose such heavy financial burdens on a defendant as to raise constitutional and fairness concerns. *See* Linda S. Mullenix, *Ending Class Actions as We Know Them: Rethinking the American Class Action*, 64 Emory L.J. 399 (2014). The law of class actions, therefore, must attend to these risks.

This chapter focuses on Federal Rule of Civil Procedure 23, which governs class actions in the federal courts. While state courts are free to follow rules of their own, most states have adopted class action rules that are at least modeled after Rule 23. Robert H. Klonoff & Edward K. M. Bilich, Class Actions and Other Multi-Party Litigation 439 (2d ed. 2006); Linda S. Mullenix, State Class Actions: Practice and Procedure § 1 (2007). Before looking at Rule 23, however, we will consider a number of the basic constraints that the Constitution imposes on the ability of a court—state or federal—to adjudicate a person's rights through a class action.

A.   Constitutional Limitations on the Use of Class Actions

1.   Adequate Representation

Hansberry v. Lee

311 U.S. 32 (1940)

MR. JUSTICE STONE delivered the opinion of the Court.

The question is whether the Supreme Court of Illinois, by its adjudication that petitioners in this case are bound by a judgment rendered in an earlier litigation to which they were not parties, has deprived them of the due process of law guaranteed by the Fourteenth Amendment.

Respondents brought this suit in the Circuit Court of Cook County, Illinois, to enjoin the breach by petitioners of an agreement restricting the use of land within a described area of the City of Chicago, which was alleged to have been entered into by some five hundred of the land owners. The agreement stipulated that . . . no part of the land should be "sold, leased to or permitted to be occupied by any person of the colored race," and provided that it should not be effective unless signed by the "owners of 95 per centum of the frontage" within the described area. The bill of complaint set up that the owners of 95 per cent of the frontage had signed; that respondents are owners of land within the restricted area who have either signed the agreement or acquired their land from others who did sign and that petitioners Hansberry, who are Negroes, have, with the alleged aid of the other petitioners and with knowledge of the agreement, acquired and are occupying land in the restricted area formerly belonging to an owner who had signed the agreement.

To the defense that the agreement had never become effective because owners of 95 per cent of the frontage had not signed it, respondents pleaded that that issue was *res judicata* by the decree in an earlier suit. *Burke v. Kleiman*, 277 Ill. App. 519 [(1934)]. To this petitioners pleaded, by way of rejoinder, that they were not parties to that suit or bound by its decree, and that denial of their right to litigate, in the present suit, the issue of performance of the condition precedent to the validity of the agreement would be a denial of due process of law guaranteed by the Fourteenth Amendment. It does not appear . . . that any of petitioners is the successor in interest to or in privity with any of the parties in the earlier suit. . . .

The Supreme Court of Illinois, upon an examination of the record in *Burke v. Kleiman, supra*, found that that suit, in the Superior Court of Cook County, was brought by a landowner in the restricted area to enforce the agreement which had been signed by her predecessor in title, in behalf of herself and other property owners in like situation, against four named individuals who had acquired or asserted an interest in a plot of land formerly owned by another signer of the agreement; that upon stipulation of the parties in that suit that the agreement had been signed by owners of 95 per cent of all the frontage, the court had adjudged that the agreement was in force, that it was a covenant running with the land and binding all the land within the described area in the hands of the parties to the agreement and those claiming under them including defendants, and had entered its decree restraining the breach of the agreement by the defendants and those claiming under them, and that the appellate court had affirmed the decree. It found that the stipulation was untrue but held . . . that it was not fraudulent or collusive. . . .

From this the Supreme Court of Illinois concluded in the present case that *Burke v. Kleiman* was a "class" or "representative" suit and that in such a suit "where the remedy is pursued by a plaintiff who has the right to represent the class to which he belongs, other members of the class are bound by the results in the case unless it is reversed or set aside on direct proceedings"; that petitioners in the present suit were members of the class represented by the plaintiffs in the earlier suit and consequently were bound by its decree which had rendered the issue of performance of the condition precedent to the restrictive agreement *res judicata*, so far as petitioners are concerned. . . .

[W]hen the judgment of a state court, ascribing to the judgment of another court the binding force and effect of *res judicata*, is challenged for want of due process it becomes the duty of this Court to examine the course of procedure in both litigations to ascertain whether the litigant whose rights have thus been adjudicated has been afforded such notice and opportunity to be heard as are requisite to the due process which the Constitution prescribes.

It is a principle of general application in Anglo-American jurisprudence that one is not bound by a judgment *in personam* in a litigation in which he is not designated as a party or to which he has not been made a party by service of process. *Pennoyer v. Neff*. . . . A judgment rendered in such circumstances is not entitled to the full faith and credit which the Constitution and statute of the United States prescribe, and judicial action enforcing it against the person or property of the absent party is not that due process which the Fifth and Fourteenth Amendments requires.

To these general rules there is a recognized exception that, to an extent not precisely defined by judicial opinion, the judgment in a "class" or "representative" suit, to which some members of the class are parties, may bind members of the class or those represented who were not made parties to it.

The class suit was an invention of equity to enable it to proceed to a decree in suits where the number of those interested in the subject of the litigation is so great that their joinder as parties in conformity to the usual rules of procedure is impracticable. Courts are not infrequently called upon to proceed with causes in which the number of those interested in the litigation is so great as to make difficult or impossible the joinder of all because some are not within the jurisdiction[,] or because their whereabouts is unknown[,] or where if all were made parties to the suit its continued abatement by the death of some would prevent or unduly delay a decree. In such cases where the interests of those not joined are of the same class as the interests of those who are, and where it is considered that the latter fairly represent the former in the prosecution of the litigation of the issues in which all have a common interest, the court will proceed to a decree.

It is evident that the considerations which may induce a court thus to proceed, despite a technical defect of parties, may differ from those which must be taken into account in determining whether the absent parties are bound by the decree or, if it is adjudged that they are, in ascertaining whether such an adjudication satisfies the requirements of due process and of full faith and credit. Nevertheless there is scope within the framework of the Constitution for holding in appropriate cases that a judgment rendered in a class suit is *res judicata* as to members of the class who are not formal parties to the suit. . . . With a proper regard for divergent local institutions and interests, this Court is justified in saying that there has been a failure of due process only in those cases where it cannot be said that the procedure adopted, fairly insures the protection of the interests of absent parties who are to be bound by it.

It is familiar doctrine of the federal courts that members of a class not present as parties to the litigation may be bound by the judgment where they are in fact adequately represented by parties who are present, or where they actually participate in the conduct of the litigation in which members of the class are present as parties, or where the interest of the members of the class, some of whom are present as parties, is joint, or where for any other reason the relationship between the parties present and those who are absent is such as legally to entitle the former to stand in judgment for the latter.

In all such cases . . . we may assume for present purposes that such procedure affords a protection to the parties who are represented though absent, which would satisfy the requirements of due process and full faith and credit. Nor do we find it necessary for the decision of this case to say that, when the only circumstance defining the class is that the determination of the rights of its members turns upon a single issue of fact or law, a state could not constitutionally adopt a procedure whereby some of the members of the class could stand in judgment for all, provided that the procedure were so devised and applied as to insure that those present are of the same class as those absent and that the litigation is so conducted as to insure the full and fair consideration of the common issue. We decide only that the procedure and the course of litigation sustained here by the plea of *res judicata* do not satisfy these requirements.

The restrictive agreement did not purport to create a joint obligation or liability. If valid and effective its promises were the several obligations of the signers and those claiming under them. The promises ran severally to every other signer. It is plain that in such circumstances all those alleged to be bound by the agreement would not constitute a single class in any litigation brought to enforce it. Those who sought to secure its benefits by enforcing it could not be said to be in the same class with or represent those whose interest was in resisting performance, for the agreement by its terms imposes obligations and confers rights on the owner of each plot of land who signs it. If those who thus seek to secure the benefits of the agreement were rightly regarded by the state Supreme Court as constituting a class, it is evident that those signers or their successors who are interested in challenging the validity of the agreement and resisting its performance are not of the same class in the sense that their interests are identical so that any group who had elected to enforce rights conferred by the agreement could be said to be acting in the interest of any others who were free to deny its obligation.

Because of the dual and potentially conflicting interests of those who are putative parties to the agreement in compelling or resisting its performance, it is impossible to say, solely because they are parties to it, that any two of them are of the same class. Nor without more, and with the due regard for the protection of the rights of absent parties which due process exacts, can some be permitted to stand in judgment for all.

It is one thing to say that some members of a class may represent other members in a litigation where the sole and common interest of the class in the litigation, is either to assert a common right or to challenge an asserted obligation. It is quite another to hold that all those who are free alternatively either to assert rights or to challenge them are of a single class, so that any group merely because it is of the class so constituted, may be deemed adequately to represent any others of the class in litigating their interests in either alternative. Such a selection of representatives for purposes of litigation, whose substantial interests are not necessarily or even probably the same as those whom they are deemed to represent, does not afford that protection to absent parties which due process requires. The doctrine of representation of absent parties in a class suit has not hitherto been thought to go so far. Apart from the opportunities it would afford for the fraudulent and collusive sacrifice of the rights of absent parties, we think that the representation in this case no more satisfies the requirements of due process than a trial by a judicial officer who is in such situation that he may have an interest in the outcome of the litigation in conflict with that of the litigants.

The plaintiffs in the *Burke* case sought to compel performance of the agreement in behalf of themselves and all others similarly situated. They did not designate the defendants in the suit as a class or seek any injunction or other relief against others than the named defendants, and the decree which was entered did not purport to bind others. In seeking to enforce the agreement the plaintiffs in that suit were not representing the petitioners here whose substantial interest is in resisting performance. The defendants in the first suit were not treated by the pleadings or decree as representing others or as foreclosing by their defense the rights of others, and even though nominal defendants, it does not appear that their interest in defeating the contract outweighed their interest in establishing its validity. For a court in this situation to ascribe to either the plaintiffs or defendants the performance of such functions on behalf of petitioners here, is to attribute to them a power that it cannot be said that they had assumed to exercise, and a responsibility which, in view of their dual interests it does not appear that they could rightly discharge.

Reversed.

NOTES AND QUESTIONS

1. Parties, privies, and class members.   If the Hansberrys had purchased their parcel from one of the named parties in *Burke v. Kleiman*, would there have been any question as to their being bound by the prior judgment? As successors in interest to a named party, they would have been in privity and therefore bound by the judgment as though they had been parties to the suit. Since this was not the case, however, the Hansberrys could be bound by the finding in *Burke* that the covenant was enforceable only if that judgment was binding on unnamed class members like their predecessor in interest.

2. Dissenting class members.   According to the Court, why weren't the Hansberrys' interests adequately represented in the prior class action? In virtually all class actions, won't there be some members of the class who oppose bringing the action and who thus side with the class opponent? Courts have recognized that the party opposing the class will often adequately represent the interests of such "dissenting class members." E.g., *Horton v. Goose Creek Indep. Sch. Dist.*, 690 F.2d 470, 486-488 (5th Cir. 1982), *cert. denied*, 463 U.S. 1207 (1983) (holding that in suit by class of children challenging school district's use of dogs to sniff lockers, cars, and students for drugs and alcohol, school district that vigorously defended the suit adequately represented the interests of any dissenting class members who favored the practice). In *Burke v. Kleiman*, why didn't the defendants likewise adequately represent the interests of those like petitioners who opposed enforcement of the racially restrictive covenant? Would the outcome of *Hansberry* have been different if the parties in *Burke* had actually litigated the covenant's validity rather than stipulating that it was binding? Might the result have been different if the defendants had been sued as representatives of a class consisting of all owners who opposed the covenant?

3. Collateral attack for inadequate representation.   It is a "recognized principle that the court conducting [an] action cannot predetermine the *res judicata* effect of the judgment; this can be tested only in a subsequent action." Advisory Committee Note, 1966 Amendments, 39 F.R.D. 69, 106. Whether a class action judgment will bind individual class members thus turns on whether a later court, when asked to give the judgment full faith and credit, determines that the action satisfied the requirements of due process. As in *Hansberry*, class members who believe that the action did not satisfy due process may collaterally attack the judgment in a subsequent proceeding. If the attack succeeds, the party who opposed the class may have to relitigate the matter with individual class members. *See, e.g., Brown v. Ticor Title Ins. Co.*, 982 F.2d 386, 390-391 (9th Cir. 1992), *writ dismissed*, 511 U.S. 117 (1994). Consequently, in a class action, the litigants and the judge have a mutual interest in assuring that the representative parties adequately protect the class; otherwise, their efforts to settle the matter in a single proceeding may prove to have been in vain.

4. Other aspects of fair procedure.   According to *Hansberry*, is adequate representation alone always enough to satisfy the requirements of due process? Besides adequacy, *Hansberry* said it is critical that "the procedure adopted, fairly insures the protection of the interests of absent parties who are to be bound by it. . . ." *Hansberry*, 311 U.S. at 42. Is adequate representation one element of a broader requirement of fair procedure? Might there be other elements as well? For example, are there times when class members are entitled to notice and the opportunity to participate in the suit? Should class members sometimes have a right to opt out of the class so that they can pursue their claims individually? As a separate matter, might there be situations in which the right to adequate representation itself necessitates giving some notice to the class? In this respect, aren't unnamed class members in a position similar to that of the trust beneficiaries in *Mullane v. Central Hanover Bank & Trust Co.*, 339 U.S. 306 (1950)? *See* Chapter III, part B, at page 257, *supra*. There, it was not enough that a court-appointed guardian represented the beneficiaries. The Court held that due process also required sending notice to at least some of them. Is a similar procedure sometimes necessary in a class action so the court can be sure that the class representation is in fact adequate?

2. Notice and Right to Appear or Opt Out

Phillips Petroleum Co. v. Shutts

472 U.S. 797 (1985)

JUSTICE REHNQUIST delivered the opinion of the Court.

Petitioner is a Delaware corporation which has its principal place of business in Oklahoma. During the 1970's it produced or purchased natural gas from leased land located in 11 different States, and sold most of the gas in interstate commerce. Respondents are some 28,000 of the royalty owners possessing rights to the leases from which petitioner produced the gas; they reside in all 50 States, the District of Columbia, and several foreign countries. Respondents brought a class action against petitioner in the Kansas state court, seeking to recover interest on royalty payments which had been delayed by petitioner. They recovered judgment in the trial court, and the Supreme Court of Kansas affirmed the judgment over petitioner's contentions that the Due Process Clause of the Fourteenth Amendment prevented Kansas from adjudicating the claims of all the respondents, and that the Due Process Clause and the Full Faith and Credit Clause of Article IV of the Constitution prohibited the application of Kansas law to all of the transactions between petitioner and respondents. . . . We reject petitioner's jurisdictional claim, but sustain its claim regarding the choice of law. . . .

Respondents Irl Shutts, Robert Anderson, and Betty Anderson filed suit against petitioner in Kansas state court, seeking interest payments on their suspended royalties. . . . Shutts is a resident of Kansas, and the Andersons live in Oklahoma. Shutts and the Andersons own gas leases in Oklahoma and Texas. Over petitioner's objection the Kansas trial court granted respondents' motion to certify the suit as a class action under Kansas law. The class as certified was comprised of 33,000 royalty owners who had royalties suspended by petitioner. The average claim of each royalty owner for interest on the suspended royalties was $100.

After the class was certified respondents provided each class member with notice through first-class mail. The notice described the action and informed each class member that he could appear in person or by counsel; otherwise each member would be represented by Shutts and the Andersons, the named plaintiffs. The notices also stated that class members would be included in the class and bound by the judgment unless they "opted out" of the lawsuit by executing and returning a "request for exclusion" that was included with the notice. The final class as certified contained 28,100 members; 3,400 had "opted out" of the class by returning the request for exclusion, and notice could not be delivered to another 1,500 members, who were also excluded. Less than 1,000 of the class members resided in Kansas. Only a minuscule amount, approximately one quarter of one percent, of the gas leases involved in the lawsuit were on Kansas land.

. . . [T]he case was tried to the court. The court found petitioner liable under Kansas law for interest on the suspended royalties to all class members. . . .

Petitioner raised two principal claims in its appeal to the Supreme Court of Kansas. It first asserted that the Kansas trial court did not possess personal jurisdiction over absent plaintiff class members as required by *International Shoe Co. v. Washington* and similar cases. Related to this first claim was petitioner's contention that the "opt-out" notice to absent class members, which forced them to return the request for exclusion in order to avoid the suit, was insufficient to bind class members who were not residents of Kansas or who did not possess "minimum contacts" with Kansas. Second, petitioner claimed that Kansas courts could not apply Kansas law to every claim in the dispute. . . .

The Supreme Court of Kansas held that the entire cause of action was maintainable under the Kansas class-action statute, and the court rejected both of petitioner's claims. First, it held that the absent class members were plaintiffs, not defendants, and thus the traditional minimum contacts test of *International Shoe* did not apply. The court held that nonresident class-action plaintiffs were only entitled to adequate notice, an opportunity to be heard, an opportunity to opt out of the case, and adequate representation by the named plaintiffs. If these procedural due process minima were met, according to the court, Kansas could assert jurisdiction over the plaintiff class and bind each class member with a judgment on his claim. The court surveyed the course of the litigation and concluded that all of these minima had been met.

The court also rejected petitioner's contention that Kansas law could not be applied to plaintiffs and royalty arrangements having no connection with Kansas
. . . .

I

As a threshold matter we must determine whether petitioner has standing to assert the claim that Kansas did not possess proper jurisdiction over the many plaintiffs in the class who were not Kansas residents and had no connection to Kansas. Respondents claim that a party generally may assert only his own rights, and that petitioner has no standing to assert the rights of its adversary, the plaintiff class, in order to defeat the judgment in favor of the class. . . .

. . . Petitioner seeks to vindicate its own interests. As a class-action defendant petitioner is in a unique predicament. If Kansas does not possess jurisdiction over this plaintiff class, petitioner will be bound to 28,100 judgment holders scattered across the globe, but none of these will be bound by the Kansas decree. Petitioner could be subject to numerous later individual suits by these class members because a judgment issued without proper personal jurisdiction over an absent party is not entitled to full faith and credit elsewhere and thus has no *res judicata* effect as to that party. Whether it wins or loses on the merits, petitioner has a distinct and personal interest in seeing the entire plaintiff class bound by *res judicata* just as petitioner is bound. The only way a class action defendant like petitioner can assure itself of this binding effect of the judgment is to ascertain that the forum court has jurisdiction over every plaintiff whose claim it seeks to adjudicate, sufficient to support a defense of *res judicata* in a later suit for damages by class members.

While it is true that a court adjudicating a dispute may not be able to predetermine the res judicata effect of its own judgment, petitioner has alleged that it would be obviously and immediately injured if this class-action judgment against it became final without binding the plaintiff class. We think that such an injury is sufficient to give petitioner standing on its own right to raise the jurisdiction claim in this Court. . . .

II

Reduced to its essentials, petitioner's argument is that unless out-of-state plaintiffs affirmatively consent, the Kansas courts may not exert jurisdiction over their claims. Petitioner claims that failure to execute and return the "request for exclusion" provided with the class notice cannot constitute consent of the out-of-state plaintiffs; thus Kansas courts may exercise jurisdiction over these plaintiffs only if the plaintiffs possess the sufficient "minimum contacts" with Kansas as that term is used in cases involving personal jurisdiction over out-of-state defendants. Since Kansas had no prelitigation contact with many of the plaintiffs and leases involved, petitioner claims that Kansas has exceeded its jurisdictional reach and thereby violated the due process rights of the absent plaintiffs.

In *International Shoe* we were faced with an out-of-state corporation which sought to avoid the exercise of personal jurisdiction over it as a defendant by a Washington state court. . . . We noted that the Due Process Clause did not permit a State to make a binding judgment against a person with whom the State had no contacts, ties, or relations. If the defendant possessed certain minimum contacts with the State, . . . the State could force the defendant to defend himself in the forum, upon pain of default, and could bind him to a judgment.

The purpose of this test, of course, is to protect a defendant from the travail of defending in a distant forum, unless the defendant's contacts with the forum make it just to force him to defend there. . . .

. . . [P]etitioner claims that the same analysis must apply to absent class-action plaintiffs. In this regard petitioner correctly points out that a chose in action is a constitutionally recognized property interest possessed by each of the plaintiffs. An adverse judgment by Kansas courts in this case may extinguish the chose in action forever through *res judicata*. Such an adverse judgment, petitioner claims, would be every bit as onerous to an absent plaintiff as an adverse judgment on the merits would be to a defendant. Thus, the same due process protections should apply to absent plaintiffs: Kansas should not be able to exert jurisdiction over the plaintiffs' claims unless the plaintiffs have sufficient minimum contacts with Kansas.

We think petitioner's premise is in error. The burdens placed by a State upon an absent class-action plaintiff are not of the same order or magnitude as those it places upon an absent defendant. An out-of-state defendant summoned by a plaintiff is faced with the full powers of the forum State to render judgment *against* it. The defendant must generally hire counsel and travel to the forum to defend itself from the plaintiff's claim, or suffer a default judgment. The defendant may be forced to participate in extended and often costly discovery, and will be forced to respond in damages or to comply with some other form of remedy imposed by the court should it lose the suit. The defendant may also face liability for court costs and attorney's fees. These burdens are substantial, and the minimum contacts requirement of the Due Process Clause prevents the forum State from unfairly imposing them upon the defendant.

A class-action plaintiff, however, is in quite a different posture. The Court noted this difference in *Hansberry v. Lee*, which explained that a "class" or "representative" suit was an exception to the rule that one could not be bound by judgment *in personam* unless one was made fully a party in the traditional sense. . . . The absent parties would be bound by the decree so long as the named parties adequately represented the absent class and the prosecution of the litigation was within the common interest.[1]

Modern plaintiff class actions follow the same goals, permitting litigation of a suit involving common questions when there are too many plaintiffs for proper joinder. Class actions also may permit the plaintiffs to pool claims which would be uneconomical to litigate individually. For example, this lawsuit involves claims averaging about $100 per plaintiff; most of the plaintiffs would have no realistic day in court if a class action were not available.

In sharp contrast to the predicament of a defendant haled into an out-of-state forum, the plaintiffs in this suit were not haled anywhere to defend themselves upon pain of a default judgment. . . .

A plaintiff class in Kansas and numerous other jurisdictions cannot first be certified unless the judge, with the aid of the named plaintiffs and defendant, conducts an inquiry into the common nature of the named plaintiffs' and the absent

---

1. [I]n the present case there is no question that the named plaintiffs adequately represent the class, and that all members of the class have the same interest in enforcing their claims against the defendant.

plaintiffs' claims, the adequacy of representation, the jurisdiction possessed over the class, and any other matters that will bear upon proper representation of the absent plaintiffs' interest. Unlike a defendant in a civil suit, a class-action plaintiff is not required to fend for himself. The court and named plaintiffs protect his interests. Indeed, the class-action defendant itself has a great interest in ensuring that the absent plaintiffs' claims are properly before the forum. In this case, for example, the defendant sought to avoid class certification by alleging that the absent plaintiffs would not be adequately represented and were not amenable to jurisdiction.

The concern of the typical class-action rules for the absent plaintiffs is manifested in other ways. Most jurisdictions, including Kansas, require that a class action, once certified, may not be dismissed or compromised without the approval of the court. In many jurisdictions such as Kansas the court may amend the pleadings to ensure that all sections of the class are represented adequately.

Besides this continuing solicitude for their rights, absent plaintiff class members are not subject to other burdens imposed upon defendants. They need not hire counsel or appear. They are almost never subject to counterclaims or cross-claims, or liability for fees or costs. Absent plaintiff class members are not subject to coercive or punitive remedies. Nor will an adverse judgment typically bind an absent plaintiff for any damages, although a valid adverse judgment may extinguish any of the plaintiff's claims which were litigated.

Unlike a defendant in a normal civil suit, an absent class-action plaintiff is not required to do anything. He may sit back and allow the litigation to run its course, content in knowing that there are safeguards provided for his protection. In most class actions an absent plaintiff is provided at least with an opportunity to "opt out" of the class, and if he takes advantage of that opportunity he is removed from the litigation entirely. This was true of the Kansas proceedings in this case. The Kansas procedure provided for the mailing of a notice to each class member by first-class mail. The notice, as we have previously indicated, described the action and informed the class member that he could appear in person or by counsel, in default of which he would be represented by the named plaintiffs and their attorneys. The notice further stated that class members would be included in the class and bound by the judgment unless they "opted out" by executing and returning a "request for exclusion" that was included in the notice.

Petitioner contends, however, that the "opt out" procedure provided by Kansas is not good enough, and that an "opt in" procedure is required to satisfy the Due Process Clause of the Fourteenth Amendment. Insofar as plaintiffs who have no minimum contacts with the forum State are concerned, an "opt in" provision would require that each class member affirmatively consent to his inclusion within the class.

Because States place fewer burdens upon absent class plaintiffs than they do upon absent defendants in nonclass suits, the Due Process Clause need not and does not afford the former as much protection from state-court jurisdiction as it does the latter. The Fourteenth Amendment does protect "persons," not "defendants," however, so absent plaintiffs as well as absent defendants are entitled to some protection from the jurisdiction of a forum State which seeks to adjudicate their claims. In this case we hold that a forum State may exercise jurisdiction over the claim of an absent class-action plaintiff, even though that plaintiff may not possess the minimum contacts with the forum which would support personal jurisdiction over a defendant. If the forum State wishes to bind an absent plaintiff concerning a claim for money damages or similar relief at law,[3] it must provide minimal procedural due process protection. The plaintiff must receive notice plus an opportunity to be heard and participate in the litigation, whether in person or through counsel. The notice must be the best practicable, "reasonably calculated, under all the circumstances, to apprise interested parties of the pendency of the action and afford them an opportunity to present their objections." *Mullane*. . . . The notice should describe the action and the plaintiffs' rights in it. Additionally, we hold that due process requires at a minimum that an absent plaintiff be provided with an opportunity to remove himself from the class by executing and returning an "opt out" or "request for exclusion" form to the court. Finally, the Due Process Clause of course requires that the named plaintiff at all times adequately represent the interests of the absent class members.

We reject petitioner's contention that the Due Process Clause of the Fourteenth Amendment requires that absent plaintiffs affirmatively "opt in" to the class, rather than be deemed members of the class if they do not "opt out." We think that such a contention is supported by little, if any precedent, and that it ignores the differences between class-action plaintiffs, on the one hand, and defendants in nonclass civil suits on the other. Any plaintiff may consent to jurisdiction. The essential question, then, is how stringent the requirement for a showing of consent will be.

We think that the procedure followed by Kansas, where a fully descriptive notice is sent first-class mail to each class member, with an explanation of the right to "opt out," satisfies due process. Requiring a plaintiff to affirmatively request inclusion would probably impede the prosecution of those class actions involving an aggregation of small individual claims, where a large number of claims are required to make it economical to bring suit. The plaintiff's claim may be so small, or the plaintiff so unfamiliar with the law, that he would not file suit individually, nor would he affirmatively request inclusion in the class if such a request were required by the Constitution.[4] If, on the other hand, the plaintiff's claim is sufficiently large or important that he wishes to litigate it on his own, he will likely

---

3. Our holding today is limited to those class actions which seek to bind known plaintiffs concerning claims wholly or predominately for money judgments. We intimate no view concerning other types of class actions, such as those seeking equitable relief. Nor, of course, does our discussion of personal jurisdiction address class actions where the jurisdiction is asserted against a *defendant* class.

4. In this regard the Reporter for the 1966 amendments to the Federal Rules of Civil Procedure stated: "[R]equiring the individuals affirmatively to request inclusion in the lawsuit would result in freezing out the claims of people—especially small claims held by small people—who for one reason or another, ignorance, timidity, unfamiliarity with business or legal matters, will simply not take the affirmative step." Kaplan, Continuing Work of the Civil Committee: 1966 Amendments of the Federal Rules of Civil Procedure (I), 81 Harv. L. Rev. 356, 397-398 (1967).

have retained an attorney or have thought about filing suit, and should be fully capable of exercising his right to "opt out."

In this case over 3,400 members of the potential class did "opt out," which belies the contention that "opt out" procedures result in guaranteed jurisdiction by inertia. Another 1,500 were excluded because the notice and "opt out" form was undeliverable. We think that such results show that the "opt out" procedure provided by Kansas is by no means *pro forma*, and that the Constitution does not require more to protect what must be the somewhat rare species of class member who is unwilling to execute an "opt out" form, but whose claim is nonetheless so important that he cannot be presumed to consent to being a member of the class by his failure to do so. Petitioner's "opt in" requirement would require the invalidation of scores of state statutes and of the class-action provision of the Federal Rules of Civil Procedure, and for the reasons stated we do not think that the Constitution requires the State to sacrifice the obvious advantages in judicial efficiency resulting from the "opt out" approach for the protection of the *rara avis* portrayed by petitioner.

We therefore hold that the protection afforded the plaintiff class members by the Kansas statute satisfies the Due Process Clause. The interests of the absent plaintiffs are sufficiently protected by the forum State when those plaintiffs are provided with a request for exclusion that can be returned within a reasonable time to the court. Both the Kansas trial court and the Supreme Court of Kansas held that the class received adequate representation, and no party disputes that conclusion here. We conclude that the Kansas court properly asserted personal jurisdiction over the absent plaintiffs and their claims against petitioner.

III

[In this concluding part of its opinion, the Court addressed the question of whether, consistent with the Due Process and the Full Faith and Credit Clauses, Kansas courts could apply "Kansas contract and equity law to every claim in this case, notwithstanding that over 99% of the gas leases and some 97% of the plaintiffs in the case had no apparent connection to the State of Kansas except for this lawsuit." *Shutts*, 472 U.S. 814-815. The Court concluded that "[g]iven Kansas' lack of 'interest' in claims unrelated to that State, and the substantive conflict with jurisdictions such as Texas, . . . application of Kansas law to every claim in this case is sufficiently arbitrary and unfair as to exceed constitutional limits." *Id.* at 822.]

We therefore affirm the judgment of the Supreme Court of Kansas insofar as it upheld the jurisdiction of the Kansas courts over the plaintiff class members in this case, and reverse its judgment insofar as it held that Kansas law was applicable to all of the transactions which it sought to adjudicate. . . .

NOTES AND QUESTIONS

1. *Jurisdiction over class members.* The Court agreed that most members of this nationwide class lacked minimum contacts with Kansas. If it had strictly adhered to the requirements of *International Shoe v. Washington* and its progeny

(*see* Chapter II, *supra*), the Court might have agreed with the defendant that to satisfy due process, class members must affirmatively exercise the "opt in" right in the class action. What would the likely effect of an opt-in rule have been on the viability of nationwide or multi-state class actions?

2. *The basis and scope of* Shutts.   The defendant's objection to the use of a class action in *Shutts* was based on the fact that many plaintiff class members lacked minimum contacts with the forum state of Kansas. Yet in discussing the need to give the individual class members notice and an opportunity to participate or opt out, the Court did not limit this need to members who could show that they were not subject to personal jurisdiction. Instead, the Court seemed to hold that in suits wholly or predominantly for monetary relief, *all members* of a plaintiff class must be given these rights. This suggests that the Court's decision rested on a broader rationale than simply protecting a person's due process right not to be forced to litigate in a forum with which he or she lacks minimum contacts. Nor did the Court link the need for notice to ensuring the adequacy of representation, for this was not at issue in the case. Indeed, adequacy of representation is not dependent on the receipt of notice. What then was the basis of *Shutts*? Was it perhaps that a person with a claim for damages has a right to be heard—a right that normally cannot be impaired by forcing her to litigate her claim as an unnamed class member in a suit that is filed and controlled by others?

In *Ortiz v. Fibreboard Corp.*, 527 U.S. 815 (1999), the Court discussed *Shutts* but did little to clarify its scope. *Ortiz* described *Shutts* as having held that "before an absent class member's right of action was extinguishable due process required that the member 'receive notice plus an opportunity to be heard and participate in the litigation,' and . . . that 'at a minimum . . . an absent plaintiff [must] be provided an opportunity to remove himself from the class.'" *Ortiz*, 527 U.S. at 848. However, the Court quickly qualified this broad reading by adding that "[i]n *Shutts*, as an important caveat to our holding, we made clear that we were only examining the procedural protections attendant on binding *out-of-state* class members whose claims were '*wholly or predominantly for money judgments*.'" *Id.* at 848 n.24 (emphasis added). It thus remains unclear whether the constitutional rights described in *Shutts* apply only to class members who lack minimum contacts with the forum or whether they extend to all class members in cases in which damages are a significant aspect of the relief sought. We will revisit this issue later. *See Wal-Mart Stores, Inc. v. Dukes*, 131 S. Ct. 2541 (2011), at page 792, *infra*.

3. *Denying opt out to avoid prejudice.*   In Chapter VIII, page 741, *supra*, we studied the concept of compulsory joinder. *See* FED. R. CIV. P. 19. We saw that there are times when the risk of prejudice caused by separate lawsuits may require that a person be joined as a required party whether or not he or she wishes to do so. In such cases, any due process right that a person might have to litigate his or her claim separately is trumped by the need to avoid serious harm to others. In the class action setting, might similar concerns warrant denying members of a plaintiff class the right to opt out when doing so would seriously prejudice other class members or the class opponent? In such cases, however, should class members at least be given notice and an opportunity to intervene so that they have the same

ability to protect their interests as someone involuntarily joined under Rule 19? *See* FED. R. CIV. P. 23(d)(1)(B)(iii) (stating that court may require that some or all class members be given notice and opportunity to intervene and present claims or defenses).

4. Failure to receive notice.   *Shutts* also raises the question of whether class members who are entitled to notice and opt-out rights may collaterally attack a judgment adverse to the class by claiming that notice was never received. In *Shutts*, those individuals to whom notice could not be delivered by first-class mail were excluded from the class. Was this constitutionally required? If due process were construed to impose a rigid requirement of actual notice (something it does not compel in other settings), this could seriously undermine the utility of class actions, for it is often impracticable or impossible to identify and/or locate every member of a class. *See* 7AA CHARLES ALAN WRIGHT, ARTHUR R. MILLER & MARY KAY KANE, FEDERAL PRACTICE AND PROCEDURE § 1786 (3d ed. 2005 & Supp. 2015).

PROBLEM

9-1. Clara has filed a gender discrimination suit in a Tennessee federal court against Bell Telephone Company ("Bell") for whom she works in Tennessee. In this suit, she seeks $13,000 in wages lost because Bell reinstated her to a lower-paying job after she returned from maternity leave, in alleged violation of federal law. Bell moved to dismiss the suit on the grounds of *res judicata*, noting that Clara was part of an earlier class action filed in a Louisiana federal court challenging Bell's treatment of its female employees who took maternity leaves. The prior suit resulted in a judgment that entitled class members to payment of wages lost from delays in rehiring when they returned from maternity leave and to the restoration of any seniority lost due to those delays. Clara, who was notified of the class action but given no opt-out right, was awarded $400 in lost wages and eight days' seniority based on Bell's delay in rehiring her. Bell contends that as a matter of *res judicata* the class action judgment bars Clara's current suit. According to Bell, if she wished to assert a claim for $13,000 in wages lost because she was rehired to a lower-paying job, she should have done so by intervening in the Louisiana class action. Can Clara successfully argue that it would violate due process to dismiss her suit based on the prior class action? *See King v. South Central Bell Tel. & Tel. Co.*, 790 F.2d 524 (6th Cir. 1986).

B.   Federal Subject Matter Jurisdiction

1.   Ordinary Class Actions

Like any other suit brought in federal court, class actions must satisfy the requirements for federal subject matter jurisdiction. If a class action seeks to vindicate rights protected by federal law, it can be filed in federal court by invoking Article III, § 2's "arising under" jurisdiction, and 28 U.S.C. § 1331 (the general federal question statute) or one of the other statutes governing federal question cases. *See* Chapter IV, page 306, *supra*. If, in addition to a federal claim, the action asserts claims based on state law, the court may exercise supplemental jurisdiction over the state claims as long as they are part of the same constitutional case, *i.e.*, if they share a common nucleus of operative facts with the federal claims. *See* 28 U.S.C. § 1367(a); Chapter IV, page 370, *supra*. In other words, class actions that include claims arising under federal law are governed by the same subject matter jurisdiction principles that apply in non–class action cases.

Differences exist, however, with respect to class actions that are based on diversity of citizenship. The Supreme Court has long held that in measuring the existence of diversity in class suits, we look solely to the citizenship of the named or representative parties, ignoring the citizenship of unnamed class members. *See Supreme Tribe of Ben-Hur v. Cauble*, 255 U.S. 356, 365 (1921). A plaintiff class action will thus satisfy the complete-diversity requirement of 28 U.S.C. § 1332 as long as the named parties bringing the action on behalf of the class are of diverse citizenship from all of the defendants. The fact that the plaintiff class may include members who are nondiverse from defendants is irrelevant. The same is true if the plaintiff sues a defendant class: So long as the plaintiff and named defendants are diverse, it does not matter that some of the defendant class members are not diverse from the plaintiff.

With respect to the amount-in-controversy requirement, however, the Court in *Snyder v. Harris*, 394 U.S. 332 (1969), held that normally each class member—not just the class representatives—must satisfy § 1332's jurisdictional minimum. Class members may not aggregate their claims, any more than named plaintiffs are allowed to do so, except in the rare case in which they are litigating with respect to a single title or right in which they have a common and undivided interest. *See* "A Note on Aggregation of Claims," page 366, *supra*. Consequently, under *Snyder*, a class action could enter federal court on the basis of diversity only if each member's claim exceeded § 1332's jurisdictional minimum, exclusive of interest and costs. For example, in *Zahn v. International Paper Co.*, 414 U.S. 291, 301 (1973), a class action was brought on behalf of 200 owners and lessees of real property surrounding a lake the defendant had allegedly polluted. While the claims of each of the four named plaintiffs met § 1332's jurisdictional minimum, the Court read § 1332 as requiring that each class member must also meet this requirement. In short, while courts looked solely to the class representatives to measure diversity under § 1332, this was not true with respect to the amount-in-controversy requirement.

The rule in *Zahn* has been modified by 28 U.S.C. § 1367. Clearly, the claims of named plaintiffs and class members in a diversity suit constitute a single constitutional case within the meaning of § 1367(a). Hence, assuming a named plaintiff satisfies the amount-in-controversy requirement, a federal court will have power to hear the claims of class members that do not satisfy that requirement. Indeed, the power of a federal court to exercise supplemental jurisdiction in this context is governed only by § 1367(a), as § 1367(b) makes no reference to Rule 23 or to class actions. Hence, as we saw in *Exxon Mobil Corp. v. Allapattah Services, Inc.*, 545 U.S. 546 (2005), at page 660, *supra*, a federal court sitting in diversity may exercise supplemental jurisdiction over claims by class members that do not satisfy the amount-in-controversy requirement. At least that is true when the class sues only a single defendant. If the class sues multiple defendants, joining them under Rule 20, the limitations of § 1367(b) might well be triggered. See Note 4, following *Exxon*, at page 671, *supra* (discussing the anomalies created by § 1367(b)).

PROBLEM

9-2. Devin and Bryce brought a class action in California state court against Philip Morris, claiming that its deceptive advertising practices violated state law by failing to warn consumers of the addictive nature of tobacco. Plaintiffs allege that as a result of these practices they became addicted to cigarettes, costing each of them from $1,750 to $2,500 per year. The class consists of all Californians who in the past four years would likely have been deceived by the defendant's deceptive practices and who have become addicted to cigarettes due to the addictive nature of nicotine. Plaintiffs seek to recover the cost of buying cigarettes to maintain their smoking addiction. They also seek an injunction barring the defendant from continuing to engage in these practices and request attorneys' fees consisting of 25 percent of the total fund recovered by the class. The defendant removed the suit to federal court on the basis of 28 U.S.C. §§ 1441 and 1332. Plaintiffs have moved to remand the action to state court, claiming that § 1332's jurisdictional minimum has not been met. What will each side argue on the motion to remand? How is the federal court likely to rule on the motion to remand? *See Daniels v. Philip Morris Cos., Inc.*, 18 F. Supp. 2d 1110 (S.D. Cal. 1998).

2.   "CAFA" Class Actions and Mass Actions

a.   The Federal Court's Original Jurisdiction

The Class Action Fairness Act (CAFA) was enacted to make it easier for large-scale class actions to be filed in or removed to federal court based on diversity jurisdiction, even when they would not satisfy § 1332(a)'s jurisdictional requirements. In enacting CAFA, Congress intended to respond to concerns that class actions — particularly those filed in states that had become magnets or "judicial hellholes" for such suits — were being abused in ways that hurt both the class members and the typically out-of-state corporate defendants. Defendants sued in such cases argued that a federal court would be preferable, either because it might be less willing to certify the case as a class action, or because even if it were to do so, a federal tribunal would afford defendant a fairer day in court.

CAFA—which is codified at 28 U.S.C. § 1332(d)—grants federal district courts subject matter jurisdiction over plaintiff class actions involving 100 or more class members if the total value of all claims exceeds $5 million and there is at least minimal diversity between the opposing parties. These requirements are designed to ease the burden of establishing federal jurisdiction. Thus the minimal diversity requirement will be satisfied whenever "any member of a class of plaintiffs is a citizen of a State different from any defendant"; "any member of a class of plaintiffs is a foreign state or a citizen or subject of a foreign state and any defendant is a citizen of a State"; or "any member of a class of plaintiffs is a citizen of a State and any defendant is a foreign state or a citizen or subject of a foreign state." 28 U.S.C. § 1332(d)(2). These minimal diversity alternatives are significantly less difficult to satisfy than the "complete diversity" standard applied under § 1332(a).

With respect to the amount in controversy, CAFA permits the exercise of jurisdiction if "the matter in controversy exceeds the sum or value of $5,000,000, exclusive of interest and costs. . . ." *Id.* For these purposes, CAFA provides that "the claims of the individual class members shall be aggregated," and imposes no requirement that any individual claim exceed a specified minimum. *Id.* § 1332(d)(6). Similarly, in measuring the amount in controversy when the class seeks non-monetary relief, CAFA allows a court to aggregate the value of injunctive relief for the entire class. It has likewise been read by some courts as allowing invocation of the "either viewpoint" rule (*see* Chapter IV, page 369, *supra*), rather than having to view the amount at stake solely through the plaintiffs' eyes. *See, e.g., Keeling v. Esurance Ins. Co.,* 660 F.3d 273 (7th Cir. 2011); *Pagel v. Dairy Farmers of America, Inc.,* 986 F. Supp. 2d 1151, 1158-1161 (C.D. Cal. 2013); *Tomkins v. Basic Research LL,* 2008 WL 1808316 at *4 n.9 (E.D. Cal. Apr. 22, 2008). *But see Ava Acupuncture P.C. v. State Farm Mut. Auto. Ins. Co.,* 592 F. Supp. 2d 522, 527 n.37 (S.D.N.Y. 2008) (expressing doubt that the effect of CAFA was to replace the Second Circuit's "plaintiffs only" perspective with the "either viewpoint" rule).

b.   Cases Removed from State Courts

Responding to the complaints of corporate defendants who were unhappy at having to defend class actions in state courts, CAFA also contains a removal provision, 28 U.S.C. § 1453, that makes the removal of CAFA actions to federal court relatively easy. First, in contrast to § 1446(b)'s one-year time limit for removing ordinary diversity cases from state to federal court, a class action may be removed under CAFA at any time—as long as the defendant acts within 30 days after it becomes clear that the case is or has become removable. For these purposes, a case that was not initially removable becomes removable when the complaint or some later document makes it unambiguously clear that the suit meets CAFA's jurisdictional requirements. *See Thomas v. Bank of Am. Corp.,* 570 F.3d 1280 (11th Cir. 2009). Second, § 1453(b) provides that cases falling within CAFA are removable "without regard to whether any defendant is a citizen of the State in which the action is brought," thus eliminating plaintiff's ability to prevent removal in a diversity case by naming a forum-state defendant. Third, a CAFA action, unlike suits removed under § 1441(a) and (b), may be removed "by any defendant without the consent of all defendants." *Id.* CAFA thus makes it quite easy for a defendant sued in state court to have a class action removed to federal court. Finally, unlike ordinary diversity cases where a plaintiff can prevent removal by seeking less than if a case would otherwise satisfy CAFA's $5 million jurisdictional minimum, a plaintiff's stipulation to limit recovery to less than that amount will not prevent removal, for until a class is certified, a named plaintiff cannot make a stipulation that will bind proposed class members. *Standard Fire Ins. Co. v. Knowles*, 133 S. Ct. 1345 (2013). A plaintiff's post-removal attempts to defeat federal jurisdiction under CAFA are equally likely to fail. *See Louisiana v. American National Property & Casualty Co.*, 746 F.3d 633, 639 (5th Cir. 2014) ("[e]very circuit that has addressed the question has held that" other than in cases of genuine mootness, "post-removal events do not oust CAFA jurisdiction"). Such unavailing efforts include amending a complaint to eliminate class allegations; voluntarily dismissing a removed action and re-filing it in state court; and dismissing claims against diverse defendants. *See* 2 Joseph M. McLaughlin, McLaughlin on Class Actions § 12:1 & nn. 3-4 (2014) (hereinafter McLaughlin on Class Actions).

Plaintiffs' attempts to avoid the application of CAFA may likewise fail if, rather than filing one class action that seeks more than $5 million, they file multiple but related class actions, each seeking no more than $5 million, when "there was no colorable reason for breaking up the lawsuit in this fashion other than to avoid federal jurisdiction." *Freeman v. Blue Ridge Paper Products, Inc.*, 551 F.3d 405, 407 (6th Cir. 2008). In *Freeman*, the plaintiffs filed five separate but virtually identical class suits in state court, each seeking $4.9 million and each covering a different six-month period. The court of appeals held that the suits were removable under CAFA and that they should be treated as a single class action. Otherwise, said the court,

> [i]f such pure structuring permits class plaintiffs to avoid CAFA, then Congress's obvious purpose in passing the statute—to allow defendants to defend large interstate class actions in federal court—can be avoided almost at will. . . . CAFA was clearly designed to prevent plaintiffs from artificially structuring their suits to avoid federal jurisdiction.

Id. As another court explained, a "plaintiff . . . cannot create duplicative class action litigation and arbitrarily 'gerrymander' time frames in order to evade the purview of the CAFA." *Proffitt v. Abbott Labs.*, 2008 WL 4401367, at *3-5 (E.D. Tenn. Sept. 23, 2008) (allowing removal of 11 essentially identical class actions, each covering a one-year period, and each seeking damages of no more than $4,999,000).

While CAFA is designed to make removal easier for defendants, most federal appellate courts have held that the burden of establishing federal jurisdiction, including particularly the $5 million amount-in-controversy requirement, rests "on the party wishing to see the case in federal court." *Lewis v. Verizon Commcns.*,

Inc., 627 F.3d 395, 399 (9th Cir. 2010). But even here, the burden on the defendant is slightly relaxed since "a defendant's notice of removal need include only a plausible allegation that the amount in controversy exceeds the jurisdictional threshold. Evidence establishing the amount is required . . . only when the plaintiff contests, or the court questions, the defendant's allegation." *Dart Cherokee Basin Operating Co., LLC v. Owens*, 135 S. Ct. 547, 554 (2014).

c.   *Exceptions to the Federal Court's Jurisdiction*

Even though CAFA expands the federal courts' subject matter jurisdiction, Congress was sensitive to the fact that state courts have strong and legitimate interests in hearing certain types of class actions, including some that would otherwise fall within the act's scope. To the extent that CAFA sought to prevent plaintiffs' attorneys from shopping for state courts that have no connection to a lawsuit but that simply have a reputation for being extremely favorable to plaintiffs, CAFA's purposes would not be served by displacing state-court jurisdiction as to those class actions that have a genuine link with the state in question. CAFA thus contains a number of exceptions—some discretionary and others mandatory—that allow certain class suits to be heard in state court even though they would otherwise fall within the act's scope. Assuming that a defendant has carried its initial burden of showing that CAFA's requirements for removal to federal court have been met, the burden shifts to the plaintiffs to show that one of CAFA's express jurisdictional exceptions applies. *Westerfeld v. Independent Processing, LLC*, 621 F.3d 819, 822-823 (8th Cir. 2010); *Kaufman v. Allstate N.J. Ins. Co.*, 561 F.3d 144, 153-154 (3d Cir. 2009). Conversely, in a case filed originally in federal court under CAFA, the burden would fall on a defendant wishing to have the suit heard in state court to show that one of CAFA's exceptions allows or requires the federal court to decline jurisdiction. *See, e.g., Hollinger v. Home State Mutual Ins. Co.*, 654 F.3d 564, 571 (5th Cir. 2011).

Under the first of these exceptions—the "local controversy" exception—CAFA allows federal courts, "in the interests of justice and looking at the totality of the circumstances," to decline jurisdiction "over a class action in which greater than one-third but less than two-thirds of the members of all proposed plaintiff classes in the aggregate and the primary defendants are citizens of the State in which the action was originally filed. . . ." 28 U.S.C. § 1332(d)(3). In exercising this discretion courts are instructed to consider a number of factors, including (a) whether there is any national or interstate interest in the claims; (b) whether the claims will be governed by the laws of the state in which the action was originally filed; (c) whether it appears that plaintiffs sought to craft the action to avoid federal jurisdiction; (d) whether the chosen forum has a distinct nexus with the class members, the alleged harm, or the defendants; (e) whether the bulk of those seeking to recover in all of the related proposed plaintiff class actions comprise citizens of the forum state; and (f) whether during the preceding three years other class actions involving the same or similar claims have been filed. *Id.* This last factor addresses the concern that plaintiffs' attorneys might seek to circumvent the act by carving up what could have been a much larger class action into a series of smaller ones that individually do not fall within CAFA's provisions. *See, e.g., Preston v. Tenet Healthsystem Memorial Med. Center, Inc.*, 485 F.3d 804 (5th Cir. 2007) (local controversy exception invoked by Louisiana federal court to remand a class action brought against a New Orleans hospital by and on behalf of patients hospitalized there at the time Hurricane Katrina made landfall).

Second, federal courts are obligated to decline jurisdiction over an action that otherwise meets CAFA's requirements if it qualifies as a "local controversy" because (1) more than two-thirds of the members of the proposed plaintiff class are citizens of the state in which the action was originally filed; (2) at least one principal defendant is a citizen of that state; and (3) the principal injuries resulting from the defendants' conduct were incurred in that state. A "principal defendant" is one whose conduct formed a "significant basis" for the claims asserted and from whom "significant relief" is sought. *Coffey v. Freeport McMoran Copper & Gold*, 581 F.3d 1240, 1243-1246 (10th Cir. 2009). This exception does not apply, however, if during the three years prior to the filing of this class action other similar class actions were brought against any of the defendants. *See* 28 U.S.C. § 1332(d)(4)(A).

Third, under the so-called "home state" exception, federal courts must decline jurisdiction under CAFA if two-thirds or more of the proposed plaintiff class members, as well as each of the primary defendants, are citizens of the state in which the action was originally filed. *See* § 1332(d)(4)(B). Finally, CAFA does not apply to certain types of lawsuits—including, for example, those that arise under various federal securities acts and those that involve the internal affairs of corporations created under the laws of the state in question. *See* 28 U.S.C. § 1332(d)(9).

d.   Nonreliance on CAFA

In light of the fact that CAFA allows, and sometimes requires, a federal judge to decline subject matter jurisdiction over certain cases that otherwise fall within the act's provisions, there may be occasions when a party wishing to have a class action heard in federal court—the defendant in a removed case or the plaintiff in an original action—might seek to bring the suit into federal court without relying on CAFA, thus avoiding the act's jurisdictional limitations. For example, if the named plaintiff is diverse from the defendant and has a claim that exceeds $75,000, federal subject matter jurisdiction exists over that claim pursuant to 28 U.S.C. § 1332(a). Pursuant to § 1367, the court would then have supplemental jurisdiction over the claims of any nondiverse class members and over any of their claims that do not exceed $75,000. *See Exxon Mobil Corp. v. Allapattah Servs., Inc.*, page 660, *supra*. Since such a class suit could have been filed originally in federal court—or removed under § 1441(a)-(b) if the defendant was not from the forum state—the case is one that a federal court might well be able to hear without having to invoke CAFA. If the party invoking federal jurisdiction can make this showing, the federal court's ability to remand the case or decline jurisdiction would be more limited than were the suit brought into federal court under CAFA. For, as with other federal subject matter jurisdiction statutes, a plaintiff whose case does not qualify under one statute (*e.g.*, § 1332, due to a lack of complete diversity), may still enter federal court through another jurisdictional door (*e.g.*, § 1331, due to its arising under federal law). However, a defendant seeking to take this non-CAFA route would then have to comply with the stricter removal requirements of § 1441(a)-(b) and § 1446, including the need for the consent of all defendants and the one-year limitation on removal.

e.   Mass Actions

Even though CAFA is addressed primarily to class actions, its expansion of federal court subject matter jurisdiction is not limited to such cases. The statute also reaches the "mass action," *i.e.*, a civil suit that is not brought as a class action but in which the aggregated monetary claims of 100 or more named plaintiffs exceed $5 million and are "proposed to be tried jointly" because they involve common questions of law or fact. 28 U.S.C. § 1332(d)(11) (providing that a mass action shall be deemed to be a class action for purposes of removal under CAFA). As with CAFA class actions, a mass action may be removed to federal court even if there is only minimal diversity and even if not all defendants wish to remove it. However, in contrast to CAFA's class action provision under which the size of the individual claims is irrelevant, the mass action provision requires that the federal court decline jurisdiction over any individual claims that do not exceed $75,000. *See Lowery v. Alabama Power Co.*, 483 F.3d 1184, 1203-1207 (11th Cir. 2007), *cert. denied*, 553 U.S. 1080 (2008). CAFA's mass action provision is designed to prevent plaintiffs from circumventing the act's class action provision by bringing suits that involve the joinder of 100 or more individual plaintiffs seeking monetary relief through a single trial and "simply choosing not to seek class certification." *Lowery*, 483 F.3d at 1198 n.32. The provision does not apply if the claims were joined at the defendant's request or if the claims are consolidated solely for pretrial purposes. Nor does it apply if, as in the case of a plane crash or other mass disasters, all the claims arise from an event that occurred in the state in which the suit was filed, and the injuries were suffered there or in contiguous states.

Plaintiffs can avoid removal of a mass action to federal court by filing separate, virtually identical suits in state court, each carefully limited to fewer than 100 named plaintiffs. Even if each of these actions is filed in the same state court, removal is barred notwithstanding the fact that minimal diversity exists, and each claim exceeds $75,000. *See Atwell v. Boston Scientific Corp.*, 740 F.3d 1160, 1162-1163 (8th Cir. 2013) (collecting cases). Indeed, plaintiffs can avoid removal even if their separate suits in the same state court have been joined for discovery and other pretrial coordination, as long as they stop short of seeking joinder for trial purposes. *Parson v. Johnson & Johnson*, 749 F.3d 879 (10th Cir. 2014) (affirming the remand of 11 suits involving 650 plaintiffs to Oklahoma state court because defendants failed to show that plaintiffs, in addition to pretrial coordination, had proposed a joint trial of their claims). The federal courts have generally respected plaintiffs' right to shape their lawsuits in this non-class setting, noting that in drafting CAFA, Congress "contemplated that some cases which could have been brought as a mass action would, because of the way in which plaintiffs chose to structure their claim, remain outside of CAFA's grant of jurisdiction." *Anderson v. Bayer Corp.*, 610 F.3d 390, 393 (7th Cir. 2010); *and see* Marc A. Werner, *The Viability and Strategic Significance of Class Action Alternatives Under CAFA's Mass Action Provisions*, 103 GEO. L.J. 465, 486-489 (2015).

f.   The Impact of CAFA

The effect of CAFA and its relaxed federal diversity requirements has been to increase by nearly 75 percent the number of class actions that now enter federal court based on diversity of citizenship. The totals presently exceed 400 cases per year. This increase in the federal courts' diversity class action caseload has been due almost entirely to a rise in the number of cases filed *originally* in federal court, rather than to an increase in the number of class actions that defendants remove from state court. This is a somewhat surprising development, as CAFA was enacted for the primary purpose of enabling defendants to *remove* class actions from state to federal court, particularly from state courts that were viewed as being highly plaintiff friendly. However, once CAFA arrived on the scene, plaintiffs whose class actions fell within the act's parameters have increasingly filed their suits in federal court rather than in a state court from which the defendant might then remove it. Thus, in 2006-2007, the most recent period for which data is available, the total number of diversity class actions filed originally in federal court was almost triple the pre-CAFA level, while the number of diversity class actions removed from state to federal court remained essentially the same. *See* EMERY G. LEE III & THOMAS E. WILLGING, FED. JUDICIAL CTR., THE IMPACT OF THE CLASS ACTION FAIRNESS ACT OF 2005 ON THE FEDERAL COURTS: FOURTH INTERIM REPORT TO THE JUDICIAL CONFERENCE ADVISORY COMMITTEE ON CIVIL RULES 1-2, 6-9 (2008) (hereinafter LEE & WILLGING, FOURTH INTERIM REPORT).

By initiating their class actions in federal court, plaintiffs can avoid the expense and the delay of confronting removal proceedings. And, instead of shopping for a plaintiff-friendly state court from which their suit might simply be removed, class plaintiffs in the post-CAFA world are now more likely to select what they believe will be a favorable or friendly federal court. Among the factors plaintiffs consider in making this selection are the federal district's geographic connection to the litigation, the composition and reputation of its bench, the federal circuit's rules on class certification (some circuits being more class-certification-friendly than others), the substantive law that the court would apply, and the speed with which the action is likely to proceed. Certain federal districts have seen an enormous increase in the number of original diversity class action filings in the wake of CAFA (*e.g.*, E.D. Louisiana—11-fold increase; D. New Jersey and S.D. Florida—7-fold increase; C.D. California—6-fold increase). This is a reverse of the pre-CAFA landscape where it was certain state courts that functioned as class action magnets. *See* Thomas E. Willging & Emery G. Lee III, Fed. Judicial Ctr., The Impact of the Class Action Fairness Act of 2005 on the Federal Courts: Third Interim Report to the Judicial Conference Advisory Committee on Civil Rules 17 (2007); Lee & Willging, Fourth Interim Report, at 23 fig. 5; 2 McLaughlin on Class Actions § 12:6. For an excellent discussion of CAFA, *see* The Class Action Fairness Act: Law and Strategy (Gregory C. Cook ed., 2013); Georgene M. Vairo, Class Action Fairness Act of 2005: A Review and Preliminary Analysis (2005).

PROBLEMS

9-3. *Phillips Petroleum Co. v. Shutts*, 472 U.S. 797 (1985), page 775, *supra*, involved a class action that was brought and litigated in a Kansas state court prior to CAFA's passage. At the time that suit was filed in the early 1980s, could Phillips have removed the action to federal court? If the suit were filed in a Kansas state court today, and if the average claim now amounted to $200 per class member, could Phillips remove the case to federal court? If it were removed, could the federal court decline to exercise jurisdiction, or is this a case over which the exercise of jurisdiction would be mandatory? What, if anything, might the plaintiffs' attorney do today to keep Phillips from litigating this dispute in federal court?

9-4. Janelle rented a truck from a Home Depot store in South Plainfield, New Jersey, where she lives. She signed an agreement stating that she would rent the vehicle for no more than 75 minutes and that it would be returned to the store by 7:38 p.m. that evening. The agreement specified that the rental fee was $19.00 for the first 75 minutes, and $5.00 for each additional 15 minutes; that if the vehicle were returned late, additional charges might apply; and that Home Depot's store hours were 6:00 a.m. to 10 p.m. When Janelle brought the truck back around 7:30 p.m. that evening, store personnel advised her that the rental department had closed and that she would have to return the vehicle the next day. Janelle came back with the truck at 8:00 a.m. the following morning and had to pay a fee totaling $287.14, rather than just $19.00. Janelle then filed a class action in New Jersey state court on behalf of "all New Jersey consumers who rented a vehicle from a Home Depot store with no after-hours rental return facilities and who were unable to return the vehicle after hours, with the result that they were charged 'late' fees for the period during which no vehicles could be returned." Alleging breach of contract, common law fraud, and violation of New Jersey's Consumer Fraud Act (CFA), the complaint sought "damages and compensation to all class members, interest, punitive damages, costs of suit, treble damages, and attorneys' fees as expressly permitted under the CFA." The class was said to comprise "thousands, if not . . . tens or hundreds of thousands, of individuals." Home Depot, a Delaware corporation headquartered in Georgia, promptly removed the case to federal court. Although Janelle filed no motion to remand the suit to state court on the ground that the federal court lacked subject matter jurisdiction, the court raised this issue *sua sponte*. When asked by the federal judge to address the question, Janelle replied that she would "leave it to the defendant to explain its basis for asserting jurisdiction." How should the court rule on the question of subject matter jurisdiction and why? If this case is one that was properly removed under CAFA, does it fall within any of the act's exceptions that might allow or require the case to be remanded to state court? *See Frederico v. Home Depot*, 507 F.3d 188 (3d Cir. 2007).

C. Requirements for Bringing a Federal Class Action Under Rule 23

Rule 23 governs class actions in federal courts—including those cases that are permitted to enter federal court pursuant to CAFA. While subdivisions (a) and (b) set forth the requirements for bringing a federal class action, subdivisions (c) through (h) discuss the procedures the court must follow in managing and conducting a class suit.

No suit may be maintained as a class action unless it satisfies all four prerequisites set forth in Rule 23(a):

- *(a)(1): numerosity*—whether the size of the class is such that joining the individual members as named parties would be impracticable;
- *(a)(2): commonality*—whether there are questions of law or fact that are common to the class and that would thus involve duplication of resources in individual suits;
- *(a)(3): typicality*—whether the claims or defenses of the class representative are typical of those of the class as a whole; and
- *(a)(4): adequacy of representation*—whether the class representative (and their lawyers) will fairly and adequately protect the interests of the class members.

FED. R. CIV. P. 23(a).

In addition to meeting each of the requirements of 23(a), a suit may proceed as a class action in federal court only if it is one of the types of class actions described in Rule 23(b):

- (b)(1): This subdivision covers situations where, without a class action, individual suits could (A) prejudice the party opposing the class by subjecting them to incompatible standards of conduct, or (B) prejudice individual members of the class themselves. An example of (A) would be a class action by prison inmates challenging prison conditions, since separate suits could result in the defendant officials being ordered to implement conflicting reforms. An example of (B) would be a class action by employees challenging the validity of a company pension plan, for a suit by an individual worker might result in invalidating or restructuring the plan to the detriment of other employees.

- *(b)(2):* This subdivision reaches cases where a party has acted or failed to act on grounds generally applicable to a class, so that injunctive or declaratory relief is appropriate respecting the class as a whole based on the illegality of that behavior. A class action by female police officers to enjoin a city from using gender discriminatory promotion practices would fit this category. In (b)(2) cases, because the defendant is typically in a position where it must treat all members of the class similarly, both judicial economy and fairness to the parties support proceeding on a class basis. Otherwise, each class member might have to sue separately to protect her rights, while the opposing party might have to repeatedly litigate the same underlying issue.

- *(b)(3):* In contrast to (b)(1) and (b)(2), where the relief sought must be primarily if not exclusively injunctive or declaratory, this subdivision covers damages actions where the only thing uniting class members is that their claims share some common question of law or fact. A suit qualifies under (b)(3) if the court finds (i) that the common questions predominate over those issues that are unique to each class member, and (ii) that a class action would be superior to other forms of adjudication. For example, in a class action against a drug company by those who consumed one of its products, a court might conclude that the time, effort, and expense saved by litigating the liability question in a single proceeding warrants a (b)(3) class action, despite the presence of individual issues concerning the nature and extent of each member's damages.

See FED. R. CIV. P. 23(b).

The Supreme Court has made it clear that in order to satisfy Rule 23, a plaintiff cannot simply allege that the requirements of the rule have been met.

> Rule 23 does not set forth a mere pleading standard. A party seeking class certification must affirmatively demonstrate his compliance with the Rule — that is, he must be prepared to prove that there are *in fact* sufficiently numerous parties, common questions of law or fact, etc. . . . . [C]ertification is proper only if the trial court is satisfied, after a rigorous analysis, that the prerequisites of Rule 23(a) have been satisfied.

Wal-Mart Stores, Inc. v. Dukes, 131 S. Ct. 2541, 2551 (2011) (internal quotation marks omitted). The same holds true with respect to satisfying Rule 23(b)'s requirements. *See also Halliburton Co. v. Erica P. John Fund, Inc.,* 134 S. Ct. 2398, 2412 (2014) (same).

Besides making sure that Rule 23(a) and (b) have been met, a court must satisfy itself that there is an identifiable class. Though nowhere mentioned in Rule 23, this requirement is implicit in the notion of a class action. Unless there is a class whose membership can be determined with a fair degree of specificity and objectivity, it may be impossible to decide whether that class has met the numerosity, commonality, typicality, and adequacy requirements. Moreover, if the class is only vaguely defined, courts may be unable to ascertain whether or not a particular individual belongs to the class. This in turn could make it difficult to provide notice to class members. And, without a class that is identifiable on the basis of objective criteria, a judgment in the action might not have its proper *res judicata* effect.

If a lawsuit meets all of the requirements of Rule 23 and falls within the federal court's subject matter jurisdiction, it can most likely proceed as a class action in federal court even if the state in which the federal court sits would bar the suit from proceeding on a class basis. In such cases, the federal rule will usually trump the conflicting state law by virtue of the Rules Enabling Act, 28 U.S.C. § 2072. The Court so held in *Shady Grove Orthopedic Associates, P.A. v. Allstate Insurance Co.*, 559 U.S. 393 (2010). In that case, a New York federal court dismissed a class action that satisfied Rule 23, due to the fact that a New York law barred such suits seeking to collect a statutory penalty from proceeding on a class basis. The Supreme Court reversed, holding that Rule 23 controlled because it regulates federal court procedure, and it did not alter any clearly substantive state-created rights, thus satisfying the requirements of 28 U.S.C. § 2072. *See* Chapter VI, page 516, *supra*. As a result of *Shady Grove*, suits that cannot proceed as class actions in state court may proceed as class actions in federal courts if they meet the requirements of Rule 23 and fall within the federal court's subject matter jurisdiction.

In the sections that follow, we will first examine the requirements under Rule 23(a), and then explore the three subdivisions of Rule 23(b). At the same time, we will look at the procedures courts employ in managing class action suits. We will then consider the special problems that arise when a class action lawsuit is settled or dismissed.

1.   Satisfying the Prerequisites of Rule 23(a)

Chandler v. Southwest Jeep-Eagle, Inc.

162 F.R.D. 302 (N.D. Ill. 1995)

CASTILLO, District Judge.

Plaintiff Raymond Chandler ("Chandler") sues defendant Southwest Jeep-Eagle, Inc. ("Southwest") . . . seeking redress for alleged misrepresentations and unfair and deceptive practices in connection with Southwest's standard retail installment contract. . . . Count I alleges that Southwest made certain misrepresentations in its retail installment contracts in violation of the Truth in Lending Act, 15 U.S.C. § 1601 et seq. ("TILA"). Count II alleges that the misrepresentations amounted to deceptive practices under the Illinois Consumer Fraud and Deceptive Business Practices Act . . . ("Consumer Fraud Act"). . . .

Pursuant to Federal Rule of Civil Procedure 23, Chandler moves for class certification with respect to counts I and II. . . .

With respect to count I, the TILA claim, the proposed class includes anyone whose retail installment contract is dated on or after October 12, 1993, one year prior to the date Chandler filed his original complaint. With respect to count II, the Consumer Fraud Act claim, the proposed class includes anyone whose retail installment contract was outstanding on or after October 12, 1991, three years prior to the date Chandler filed his original complaint. The different temporal parameters of the two classes is a product of the different statutes of limitation for TILA and the Consumer Fraud Act. . . .

Background

Southwest operates an automobile dealership. . . . On May 23, 1994, Chandler purchased from Southwest a used Chrysler automobile to be used for personal, family and household purposes. At the time he purchased the car, Chandler signed Southwest's standard motor vehicle retail installment sales contract. . . . Chandler also informed Southwest that he wished to purchase a full warranty from Chrysler that would be transferable to another authorized Chrysler dealership for the purpose of repairs. Southwest informed Chandler that the price for a full warranty was $1,780.40 and provided Chandler with its standard service contract, on which the fee amount was listed under the subheading "Amounts Paid to Others for You," along with taxes, insurance premiums, and license, title, registration and filing fees, none of which were negotiable. Chandler signed the contract and paid the $1,780.40 fee to Southwest.

Chandler alleges, however, that Southwest only transferred a small portion of the $1,780.40 to Chrysler, retaining the balance, and that the fee amount was actually unilaterally determined by Southwest and therefore negotiable. Chandler charges that the method by which the cost was listed on the contract is misleading, unfair and deceptive. He alleges that Southwest intended him and other purchasers to rely on the misleading, unfair and deceptive representation and thus not attempt to negotiate the price of the service contract, allowing Southwest routinely to overcharge customers. He further alleges that had he known that the cost of the service contract was negotiable, neither he nor the average consumer would have paid as much. . . .

Analysis

Class Certification for Counts I and II

The party seeking class certification bears the burden of establishing that certification is proper. *Retired Chicago Police Assn. v. City of Chicago*, 7 F.3d 584, 596 (7th Cir. 1993).

Rule 23 requires a two-step analysis to determine whether class certification is appropriate. First, the action must satisfy all four requirements of Rule 23(a). That is, "the plaintiff must meet the prerequisites of numerosity, commonality, typicality, and adequacy of representation." *Harriston v. Chicago Tribune Co.*, 992 F.2d 697, 703 (7th Cir. 1993) (internal quotation marks omitted). "All of these elements are prerequisites to certification; failure to meet any one of these precludes certification as a class." *Retired Chicago Police*, 7 F.3d at 596. Second, the action must satisfy one of the conditions of Rule 23(b). Chandler seeks certification under Rule 23(b)(3), which requires that questions of law or fact common to class members predominate over questions affecting only individual members, and that a class action be superior to other available methods for the fair and efficient adjudication of the controversy.

Chandler maintains that all of the requirements of Rule 23(a) and (b)(3) are met. Southwest contends that Chandler fails to meet any of Rule 23's requirements. Accordingly, we address each of the requirements for Rule 23(b)(3) certification in turn below.

A.   Numerosity

Rule 23's first express requirement is that the class be "so numerous that joinder of all members is impracticable." FED. R. CIV. P. 23(a)(1). The issue of whether the numerosity requirement is satisfied is extremely fact-specific. Courts have granted class certification to groups smaller than 30, *see Riordan v. Smith Barney*, 113 F.R.D. 60 (N.D. Ill. 1986) (finding 29 class members sufficient in securities fraud case where the class members were geographically diverse), and denied class certification in cases where the proposed class exceeded 100 members. *Marcial v. Coronet Ins. Co.*, 880 F.2d 954 (7th Cir. 1989) (denying certification to proposed class of 400-600 members where class membership could only be determined by an inquiry into the individual circumstances of each member); *In re Cardinal Indus.*, 139 B.R. 703 (Bankr. S.D. Ohio 1991) (holding that 205 class members was not sufficient where joinder is practicable because the majority of class members were controlled by the same corporation); *Liberty Lincoln-Mercury, Inc. v. Ford Marketing Corp.*, 149 F.R.D. 65 (D.N.J. 1993) (finding that 123 class members was not sufficient where the class members were large businesses capable of litigating their claims individually). As a general proposition, although the numerosity analysis does not rest on any magic number, permissive joinder is usually deemed impracticable where the class members number 40 or more. *See* H. Newberg, Class Actions § 305 (1992); *Ikonen v. Hartz Mountain Corp.*, 122 F.R.D. 258, 262 (S.D. Cal. 1988). That standard is met in this case.

Southwest concedes that the proposed class would consist of approximately 50 members for purposes of the TILA claim [count I] and approximately 150 members for purposes of the Consumer Fraud Act claim [count II], but argues that these classes are insufficiently numerous to warrant certification. Southwest cites *Marcial, In re Cardinal Indus.*, and *Liberty Lincoln-Mercury* as support for its argument. However, in each of these cases, class certification was denied for reasons unrelated to numerosity. Moreover, the facts of this case are significantly different than those presented in the cases cited by Southwest. In the instant case, the dispute concerns a standard form document signed by all proposed class members, who are otherwise unrelated and would unlikely be motivated to bring individual actions given the relatively small size of the claim. These factors militate in favor of class certification even where the number of class members is relatively small. *See, e.g., Swanson v. American Consumer Indus.*, 415 F.2d 1326, 1333 n.9 (7th Cir. 1969) (finding 40 class members sufficient for certification where individual class members are widely scattered and the amount at issue too small to warrant undertaking individual actions). In the instant case, the Court finds that the proposed classes are sufficiently numerous to make joinder impracticable. Accordingly, we find the numerosity requirement to be satisfied.

B.   Commonality

Rule 23(a)(2) requires the presence of questions of law or fact common to the class. A "common nucleus of operative fact" is generally enough to satisfy the commonality requirement. *Rosario v. Livaditis*, 963 F.2d 1013, 1018 (7th Cir. 1992) (citing *Franklin v. City of Chicago*, 102 F.R.D. 944, 949-950 (N.D. Ill. 1984)). A common nucleus of operative fact is typically found where, as in the instant case, the defendants have engaged in standardized conduct toward members of the proposed class. *Franklin*, 102 F.R.D. 944, 949 (N.D. Ill. 1984) (citing *Katz v. Carte Blanche Corp.*, 52 F.R.D. 510, 514 (W.D. Pa. 1971)) (finding class certification appropriate where plaintiff challenged city police department's standard method of transporting all arrestees); *Heartland Communications, Inc. v. Sprint Corp.*, 161 F.R.D. 111 (D. Kan. 1995) (granting class certification where the contracts signed by all proposed class members, while not identical, contained virtually the same provision as that challenged by the named class representative). . . .

In the instant case, all proposed class members purchased a standard service contract from Southwest. Thus, their claims all involve the common question of whether the disclosure provisions of Southwest's standard retail installment contract violated TILA and/or the Consumer Fraud Act. Southwest contends that the commonality requirement is not met because each class member must prove reliance and actual damages. It is well-established, however, that the presence of some individualized issues does not overshadow the common nucleus of operative fact presented when the defendant has engaged in standardized conduct toward the class. . . . Accordingly, we find that the commonality requirement is satisfied.

C.   Typicality

Rule 23(a)(3) requires that the representative plaintiff's claims be typical of those of the class. This requirement focuses on whether the named representative's claim has the same essential characteristics of the claims of the class at large. A plaintiff's claim is typical "if it arises from the same event or practice or course of conduct that gives rise to the claims of other class members and his or her claims are based on the same legal theory." *De La Fuente v. Stokely-Van Camp, Inc.*, 713 F.2d 225, 232 (7th Cir. 1983). In this case, the legal theory underlying Chandler's class claims is that the standard retail installment contract provided to him and all other proposed class members violated TILA and/or the Consumer Fraud Act. Plainly, Chandler's TILA and Consumer Fraud Act claims arise out of the same course of conduct giving rise to the claims of the other class members. Southwest maintains, however, that Chandler is an atypical class representative because his own deposition testimony suggests that he did not rely on (or was not misled by) any alleged misrepresentation.

It is clear that Chandler has fairly alleged that he relied upon and was deceived by Southwest's misrepresentation. Furthermore, Southwest reads Chandler's testimony selectively. In his deposition, Chandler clearly states that he believed that the amount charged would be transferred to the service contract provider. Although Southwest may ultimately prove that Chandler did not rely on the alleged misrepresentation, the determination of whether Chandler is a typical class member for purposes of class certification does not depend on the resolution of the merits of the case. The typicality requirement is satisfied.

D. Adequacy of Representation

Rule 23(a)(4)'s adequacy requirement has three elements: (1) the chosen class representative cannot have antagonistic or conflicting claims with other members of the class; (2) the named representative must have a "sufficient interest in the outcome to ensure vigorous advocacy," *Riordan*, 113 F.R.D. 60, 64 (N.D. Ill. 1986); and, (3) counsel for the named plaintiff must be competent, experienced, qualified, and generally able to conduct the proposed litigation vigorously. Southwest challenges Chandler's ability to satisfy the last of these three requirements.[9] Southwest notes that at least one judge has expressed doubt regarding Chandler's counsel's ability to represent a class. Notwithstanding the foregoing, this Court is satisfied that Chandler's attorneys have demonstrated that they possess the necessary qualifications to represent adequately a class of consumers under TILA and the Consumer Fraud Act. Chandler's attorneys have successfully prosecuted numerous consumer class actions—including actions before this Court. In addition, a number of courts have commented favorably on their performance in class actions. Accordingly, we find that Chandler has met his burden of satisfying Rule 23(a)(4)'s adequacy of representation requirement.

E. Predominance of Common Questions of Law or Fact

Class certification pursuant to Rule 23(b)(3) requires a determination that "questions of law or fact common to the members of the class predominate over any questions affecting only individual members, and that a class action is superior to other methods for the fair and efficient adjudication of the controversy." . . . [The court found that both of these requirements were satisfied.]

Having determined that all of the prerequisites of Rule 23(a) are satisfied and that the action also meets the conditions of Rule 23(b)(3), the Court grants plaintiff's motion for class certification for counts I and II. This action may be

---

9. Southwest somewhat half-heartedly asserts that Chandler is not personally motivated to pursue the claims on behalf of the class and that this action is driven by Chandler's counsel. However, Southwest has made no showing that Chandler is not an adequate representative of the class; and, the fact that Chandler's counsel has prosecuted numerous other class actions, standing alone, does not vitiate Chandler's role as a class representative.

maintained as a class action with the class defined, as in plaintiff's motion and memorandum in support of class certification, as follows:

(1) Count I: All individuals who purchased a service contract from the defendant by means of a standard retail installment contract, dated on or after October 12, 1993, in which the TILA disclosures represented that the defendant paid an amount to a third party in exchange for a service contract that was different from the amount actually paid.

(2) Count II: All individuals who purchased a service contract from the defendant by means of a standard retail installment contract, outstanding on or after October 12, 1991, in which the TILA disclosures represented that the defendant paid an amount to a third party in exchange for a service contract that was different from the amount actually paid. . . .

NOTES AND QUESTIONS

1. Numerosity. Rule 23(a)(1)'s focus is not on the size of the class but on whether the class's size makes joinder impracticable. Indeed, numerosity may fail even when the class is numerous, if there is no apparent obstacle to joinder. Thus whether numerosity is met depends on the specific facts of each case. Moreover, even quite small classes may satisfy the numerosity requirement where public policy would be furthered by allowing a class action. *See, e.g., Rannis v. Recchia,* 380 Fed. App'x 646, 650-652 (9th Cir. 2010) (class of 20 satisfied numerosity where proceeding on the basis of individual claims would be "inefficient" (potentially clogging the court's docket) and "costly" (imposing unnecessary financial burdens on class members whose claims were unlikely to exceed $600)). Mere allegations as to numerosity are not enough. Plaintiff "bears the burden of making *some* showing . . . that the class . . . meets the numerosity requirement." *Vega v. T-Mobile USA, Inc.,* 564 F.3d 1256, 1267 (8th Cir. 2009). In *Chandler,* what besides size led the court to find that Rule 23(a)(1) was met?

2. Commonality. Without Rule 23(a)(2)'s insistence that there be questions of law or fact common to the class, there would obviously be no point in litigating the class members' claims together since no judicial efficiency would result. How was the commonality requirement met in *Chandler?* Will the presence of individualized issues peculiar to each class member defeat Rule 23(a)(2)'s commonality requirement? Might the presence of such issues prevent certification of a class under Rule 23(b)(3)? Note that Rule 24(b)(1)(B), allowing permissive intervention if an intervenor's claim or defense shares a common question with the main action, mirrors Rule 23(a)(2). Since all class actions must satisfy Rule 23(a)(2)'s commonality requirement, a court always has the discretion to allow a class member to intervene permissively so as to participate in the suit. *See* FED. R. CIV. P. 23(d)(1)(B)(iii).

3. Typicality. Here the analysis shifts from the characteristics of the class as a whole (numerosity, commonality) to the relationship between the class and the named plaintiffs. To satisfy this requirement, the representative parties' claims or defenses must be typical, *i.e.*, they must arise from the same events or conduct giving rise to the class claims and be reasonably co-extensive with those claims. *See Ault v. Walt Disney World Co.*, 692 F.3d 1212, 1216 (11th Cir. 2012), *cert. denied*, 133 S. Ct. 1806 (2013). Thus, to determine typicality, the court should compare the representative's claims or defenses with those of the absent class members. *See Wolin v. Jaguar Land Rover North America, LLC*, 617 F.3d 1168, 1175 (9th Cir. 2010). Typicality is, in essence, an indirect way of assuring that the class representative is a member of the class. The typicality requirement also helps to ensure that representation of the class will be fair and adequate. Would typicality have been met if Chandler did not allege that he had relied on the defendant's misrepresentations?

4. *Adequacy of representation.*   By requiring that the representative party and class counsel fairly and adequately protect class members' interests, Rule 23(a)(4) helps to ensure the constitutionality of the class action. As we saw in *Hansberry v. Lee*, page 750, *supra*, without adequate representation, a class action judgment will not bind class members. The adequacy requirement focuses on both the class representative and class counsel. As to the former, Rule "23(a)(4) serves to uncover conflicts of interest between named parties and the class they seek to represent." *Amchem Prods., Inc. v. Windsor*, 521 U.S. 591, 625 (1997). The class representatives' interests must not be antagonistic to or conflict with those of class members. For example, "[i]n employment discrimination litigation, conflicts might arise . . . between employees and applicants who were denied employment and who will, if granted relief, compete with employees for fringe benefits or seniority. Under Rule 23, the same plaintiff could not represent these classes." *General Tel. Co. of the Nw. v. E.E.O.C.*, 446 U.S. 318, 331 (1980). Even when there is no conflict of interest with class members, a representative party must not have a relationship with class counsel that could cause it to favor the interests of counsel over those of the class. In *Chandler*, did the defendant suggest this might be a problem? Why did the court reject the contention? What kinds of facts might have strengthened such a contention? On what basis did the court find that class counsel satisfied Rule 23(a)(4)? Once initially approved, if counsel is later found to have provided inadequate representation, this may result in the trial or appellate court decertifying the class or may cause other courts to rule that the judgment is not binding on class members. In assessing the adequacy of class counsel, may a court insist that "the lawyers staffed on the case fairly reflect the class composition in terms of relevant race and gender metrics"? *See Martin v. Blessing*, 134 S. Ct. 402 (2013) (statement of Alito, J.) (suggesting that such a requirement, frequently imposed by one federal district court judge, is unconstitutional).

5. *Class definition.*   In the last paragraph of its opinion, the court carefully defined the classes it was certifying under counts I and II. Why is it necessary to specifically describe those included in the class? Is this critical in (b)(3) actions for deciding who is entitled to individual notice? *See* FED. R. CIV. P. 23(c)(2). Is it also important in later deciding who is bound by the judgment? *See* FED. R. CIV. P. 23(c)(3).

A NOTE ON CLASS CERTIFICATION

If a suit is brought as a class action, Rule 23(c)(1)(A) provides that the district court shall, "at an early practicable time," determine whether the suit may proceed on a class basis. FED. R. CIV. P. 23(c)(1)(A). In *Chandler*, the action was filed on October 12, 1994. The district judge did not issue a certification order until June 8, 1995, approximately eight months later. While this may seem like a long time, a court must develop a record to support its findings as to whether the requirements of Rule 23(a) and (b) have been met, and if so, how the class should be defined. *See Szabo v. Bridgeport Machs., Inc.*, 249 F.3d 672, 675-677 (7th Cir.), *cert. denied*, 534 U.S. 951 (2001). Since Rule 23(f) permits a discretionary interlocutory appeal from an order granting or denying class action certification, the trial court must not move so swiftly that its order is subject to reversal. Several of the cases appearing later in this chapter involved interlocutory appeals. The issue of certification, however, is one that remains subject to modification or withdrawal under Rule 23(c)(1)(C), which allows a court to alter or amend a certification order at any time before final judgment is entered in the case. For these purposes, the court may—before or after certification—solicit input from the class by giving them notice and an "opportunity to signify whether they consider the representation fair and adequate. . . ." FED. R. CIV. P. 23(d)(1)(B)(iii); *see* 7B CHARLES ALAN WRIGHT, ARTHUR R. MILLER & MARY KAY KANE, FEDERAL PRACTICE AND PROCEDURE § 1793 (3d ed. 2005 & Supp. 2015)).

If a federal court rejects class certification on the basis that the case does not satisfy the requirements of Rule 23, what effect will that have on the ability of would-be class members to bring a similar class action of their own in a federal or state court? As long as the plaintiffs in the second action were not named parties to the earlier suit, since that suit did not proceed on a class basis they cannot be bound by the earlier determination that Rule 23 was not satisfied. (As we will see in Chapter XIII, page 1165, *infra*, a judgment can only bind those who were parties to the case or who fall within one of six limited exceptions; though class actions are among those exceptions to this rule, the earlier suit in our scenario was not certified as a class action.) Thus, whether the named plaintiffs in the first would-be class action won or lost their case, others similarly situated can later bring an identical lawsuit of their own and seek to have it certified as a class action. As a result, a defendant who successfully defeats class certification and wins (or loses) on the merits may still face repeated attempts by other similarly situated parties to bring essentially identical suits on an individual or would-be class basis. *Smith v. Bayer Corp.*, 131 S. Ct. 2368 (2011).

A NOTE ON CLASS ACTIONS AND THE STATUTE OF LIMITATIONS

In *Chandler*, the court noted that the proposed class consisted of all persons whose claims were not barred by the applicable one-year and three-year statutes of limitations on the date the suit was filed, October 12, 1994. Suppose that instead of certifying the class on June 8, 1995, as it did, the court had on that date denied certification. Would it then have been too late for those whose claims were now more than one and three years old to file their own actions? The answer is no. If a suit is filed as a class action, this tolls the running of the statute of limitations for all members of the asserted class as defined in the complaint. Without such a rule, the courts would be inundated by protective individual actions and by motions to intervene as named parties filed by putative class members fearful that the class action might not be certified. The statute of limitations will begin to run again if the court denies certification of the class, decertifies a previously certified class, or narrows the class definition to exclude some members. At this point, if those denied class membership wish to pursue their individual claims, they must promptly intervene as named parties in a pending case or file their own actions within the time that remains on the statute of limitations clock. *See American Pipe & Constr. Co. v. Utah*, 414 U.S. 538, 552-556 (1974); *Crown, Cork & Seal Co. v. Parker*, 462 U.S. 345, 353-354 (1983). In *American Pipe*, for example, the proposed class action was filed 11 days before the running of the statute of limitations. When the district court subsequently denied certification, the purported class members had 11 days in which to protect themselves by either intervening in the named plaintiffs' suit or filing separate actions of their own. An order denying, revoking, or modifying class certification may thus have serious and immediate consequences for rejected class members. If these individuals relied on the filing of the class suit in not filing their own claims, a court may order that those denied class status be promptly notified and informed that they may need to act quickly to preserve their rights. It is also possible that a purported class member who then brings an individual action after the statute of limitations has run may, depending on the circumstances of his or her case, be able to invoke the doctrine of equitable tolling to keep the suit from being dismissed. *See* DAVID F. HERR, FED. JUDICIAL CTR., MANUAL FOR COMPLEX LITIGATION § 21.313 (4th ed. 2014) (hereinafter MANUAL FOR COMPLEX LITIGATION); 7B WRIGHT, MILLER & KANE, *supra*, § 1793 & n.47 (Supp. 2014); *see also Bernard v. Gulf Oil Corp.*, 890 F.2d 735, 746 (5th Cir. 1989), *cert. denied*, 497 U.S. 1003 (1990); *Payne v. Travenol Labs., Inc.*, 673 F.2d 798, 813 (5th Cir.), *cert. denied*, 459 U.S. 1038 (1982); *Puffer v. Allstate Ins. Co.*, 614 F. Supp. 2d 905 (N.D. Ill. 2009).

PROBLEM

9-5. Two Hispanic migrant laborers sued the head of the Ohio State Highway Patrol (OSHP) to challenge the constitutionality of OSHP's practice of questioning Hispanic motorists and passengers about their immigration status and seizing their identity papers. The plaintiffs were each questioned about their immigration status during routine traffic stops and had their federal immigration documents confiscated. They seek an injunction against these practices on behalf of a class consisting of "all current and future Hispanic motorists and passengers in Ohio who are involved in traffic stops by the OSHP and are interrogated about their immigration status or suffer the seizure of their lawfully issued immigration documents." Many class members are migrant laborers who live in Ohio only part of the year. Plaintiffs seek an order certifying the case as a class action under Rule 23(a) and (b)(2). Assuming that the suit satisfies (b)(2), does it meet each of the requirements of 23(a)? *See Farm Labor Org. Comm. v. Ohio State Highway Patrol,* 184 F.R.D. 583 (N.D. Ohio 1998).

Robidoux v. Celani
987 F.2d 931 (2d Cir. 1993)

PECKHAM, Senior District Judge

This is an action by three recipients of public assistance in Vermont seeking to represent a class of persons whose applications for public assistance have been delayed unlawfully by the Vermont Department of Social Welfare (Department). Appellants Julie Robidoux, Kathleen Rock and Margaret Bevins appeal from a judgment of the United States District Court for the District of Vermont . . . dismissing their lawsuit brought under 42 U.S.C. § 1983. Appellants challenge the district court's refusal to certify their suit as a class action and the district court's subsequent dismissal of the suit as moot. For the reasons stated below, we vacate the judgment of the district court and remand for further proceedings consistent with this opinion.

I.   Background and Proceedings Below

The Vermont Department of Social Welfare administers several public assistance programs, including the Food Stamp Program, the Aid to Needy Families with Children Program (ANFC) . . . , and the Supplemental Fuel Assistance Program (Fuel Assistance). Federal regulations require state social welfare agencies to determine applicants' eligibility for public assistance programs within certain time periods. . . . [T]he Department must make decisions on both Food Stamp and ANFC applications within 30 days of the date of application. The deadlines do not apply where the Department cannot make a timely decision because of an applicant's delay in completing the application. . . .

The sole source of income for Julie Robidoux, Kathleen Rock, and Margaret Bevins and their families is public assistance, unemployment insurance, or social security benefits. In spring 1991, finding their resources inadequate to support their families, Robidoux, Rock, and Bevins applied for Food Stamp and/or ANFC benefits to supplement their incomes. The Department did not process any of these applications within the 30-day deadlines.

. . . Appellants were . . . referred to Vermont Legal Aid (VLA) in the spring of 1991. Assisted by VLA, Robidoux filed suit in April 1991 alleging delays by the Department in processing applications for ANFC, Food Stamps, and Fuel Assistance and seeking class-based injunctive relief. At the time Robidoux filed suit, she had received her Food Stamps but had not yet received her ANFC benefits. Rock and Bevins later filed motions to intervene in this suit. At the time of their interventions, neither had received her benefits. All three appellants subsequently received benefits retroactive to their applications.

The plaintiff and intervenors moved, pursuant to FED. R. CIV. P. 23(b)(2), to certify as a class "[a]ll current and future Vermont applicants for assistance from the Food Stamp, ANFC, and Fuel Assistance Programs." In support of their motion for class certification, Appellants submitted two documents. One was a letter from the Department's Commissioner to the U.S. Department of Agriculture which indicated that from July to September 1990, 8 percent of the approximately 800 monthly Vermont Food Stamp applications, or about 65 applications per month, had taken more than 30 days to process. The second document was a monitoring record by the U.S. Department of Health and Human Services, which indicated that 71 of 4017, or nearly 2 percent, of quarterly ANFC applications had taken the Department more than 45 days to process during that same period.

The district court denied the motion for class certification. The district court concluded that Appellants had not shown sufficient evidence of numerosity, because

> [p]laintiff has the burden to show that the class is so large that joinder is impossible. Plaintiff has only shown three people who may be affected, and speculatively an undetermined number of future class members.

The court also found that Appellants' situation was not typical of a pattern of delay as to Food Stamp, ANFC, and Fuel Assistance applicants, because there was no showing of any delay or refusal by the Fuel Assistance program. . . .

In support of their motion for reconsideration of the denial of class certification, Appellants submitted a Department report showing overdue applications for May 1990, December 1990, and February 1991. This document indicated that decisions in ANFC were overdue in 22 cases (6% of 365 cases) in May 1990, 74 cases (14% of 528) in December 1990, and 68 cases (13% of 522) in February 1991. Overdue Food Stamp decisions totalled 52 cases (10% of 518) in May 1990, 133 cases (15% of 884) in December 1990, and 113 cases (13% of 867) in February 1991. The study indicated that an increase in applications caused the increase in overdue cases. The district court denied the motion for reconsideration on the same basis as its earlier order.

Appellants then moved for summary judgment, and defendant made a cross-motion for summary judgment. The district court granted summary judgment for defendant, ruling that Appellants' claims were moot. The court found that there was not a reasonable expectation that Appellants would be subjected to the same harm in the future.

II. Discussion

Appellants argue that 1) they have met the requirements for class certification, 2) they have standing, and 3) their claims are not moot. As to the claims with respect to Food Stamps and ANFC, we agree. With respect to alleged delays in processing applications for Fuel Assistance, we conclude that further consideration is warranted.

A.   Class Certification

If the district court has applied the proper legal standards in deciding whether to certify a class, its decision may be overturned only if it has abused its discretion. At the same time, however, abuse of discretion can be found more readily on appeals from the denial of class status than in other areas, for the courts have built a body of case law with respect to class action status. . . .

Rule 23(a) sets forth the requirements for class certification. . . . Appellants challenge the district court's rulings on numerosity and typicality.

1.   Numerosity

Appellants first argue that the district court applied an incorrect legal standard in requiring plaintiffs to show the existence of a class so numerous that "joinder is impossible," while Rule 23(a) requires a finding that the numerosity makes joinder of all class members "impracticable."

Impracticable does not mean impossible. Thus, the district court in the present case, in concluding that numerosity was lacking because plaintiffs had not shown the class to be so large that joinder was "impossible," applied the wrong standard.

Appellants further contend that, under the proper standard, they met the burden of showing numerosity. We agree. Courts have not required evidence of exact class size or identity of class members to satisfy the numerosity requirement. *See, e.g., Barlow v. Marion County Hosp. Dist.*, 88 F.R.D. 619, 625 (M.D. Fla. 1980) (as the bearers of the burden to show joinder is impracticable, "[p]laintiffs must show some evidence of or reasonably estimate the number of class members" but "need not show the exact number"); *see also* 1 Herbert B. Newberg, *Newberg on Class Actions: A Manual for Group Litigation at Federal and State Levels* § 3.05, at 139 (2d ed. 1985).

Appellants presented documentary evidence of delays in 22 to 133 cases per month, depending on the month and whether the assistance sought was Food Stamps or ANFC. Other government benefits cases have held that class representatives who presented similar numbers of potential class members satisfied the numerosity requirement. *See, e.g., Grant v. Sullivan*, 131 F.R.D. 436, 446 (M.D. Pa. 1990) (a court "may certify a class even if it is composed of as few as 14 members"); . . . A leading treatise concludes, based on prevailing precedent, that the difficulty in joining as few as 40 class members should raise a presumption that joinder is impracticable. 1 Newberg, *supra*, § 3.05, at 141-142.

The Department contends on appeal, however, that not all of the delayed cases included in the figures provided to the court can be attributed to Departmental fault. . . . The Department conceded at oral argument that it does not keep records of the reasons for the delays and so cannot provide an exact number of persons delayed by applicant fault. Plaintiffs have presented documentary evidence of delays in a sufficient number of cases to meet the numerosity requirement. . . .

The district court also failed to address other factors relevant to the practicability of joinder. Determination of practicability depends on all the circumstances surrounding a case, not on mere numbers. Relevant considerations include judicial economy arising from the avoidance of a multiplicity of actions, geographic dispersion of class members, financial resources of class members, the ability of claimants to institute individual suits, and requests for prospective injunctive relief which would involve future class members. 1 Newberg, *supra*, § 3.06, at 143; *see Deposit Guar. Nat'l Bank v. Roper*, 445 U.S. 326, 339 (1980) ("Where it is not economically feasible to obtain relief within the traditional framework of a multiplicity of small individual suits for damages, aggrieved persons may be without any effective redress unless they may employ the class-action device."). . . .

Many of these additional factors are present in this case. Consolidating in a class action what could be over 100 individual suits serves judicial economy. Moreover, the potential class members are distributed over the entire area of Vermont. They are also economically disadvantaged, making individual suits difficult to pursue. An injunction requiring the Department to comply with the statutory deadlines would affect all potential class members, and individual suits could lead to potentially inconsistent results.

Thus, the district court abused its discretion in determining that the class was not so numerous that joinder of all members would be impracticable.

2. *Typicality*

Rule 23(a)(3)'s typicality requirement is satisfied when each class member's claim arises from the same course of events and each class member makes similar legal arguments to prove the defendant's liability. When it is alleged that the same unlawful conduct was directed at or affected both the named plaintiff and the class sought to be represented, the typicality requirement is usually met irrespective of minor variations in the fact patterns underlying individual claims. For example, in *Rossini v. Ogilvy & Mather, Inc.*, 798 F.2d 590, 596-598 (2d Cir. 1986), the Second Circuit held that a district court had abused its discretion in decertifying a class in an employment discrimination case. The class representative alleged she was a victim of discriminatory denial of transfers, while she sought to certify a class of women suffering discrimination in advancement generally (*e.g.*, through denial of transfer, fewer training opportunities, or lack of promotion). Evidence indicating that the employer discriminated *in the same general fashion* against the class representatives and against other members of the class was held sufficient to satisfy the typicality requirement. *Id.* at 598. The court relied, among other things, on evidence showing that many of the employment decisions were made by the same, central group of people within the employer's organization. . . .

The district court found that Appellants' claims were not typical of those of the class because there was no showing of delays in processing applications in the Fuel Assistance program. Though this may mean that the class to be certified should not include persons suffering delays with respect only to that program, the typicality requirement plainly was met with respect to persons suffering delays with respect to their applications for benefits under the other two programs. A court is not bound by the class definition proposed in the complaint and should not dismiss the action simply because the complaint seeks to define the class too broadly. Though the court need not take on an onerous burden of identifying issues that may be appropriate for class-action treatment or of constructing sub-classes pursuant to FED. R. CIV. P. [23(c)(4)-(5)] ("class may be divided into sub-classes"; class action may be maintained "with respect to particular issues"), . . . there was no undue burden here. Appellants asserted that there were delays in three well-defined public assistance programs, and it would have required little effort for the court, upon concluding that plaintiffs themselves had no claims with respect to one of the programs, to define the class as comprising persons claiming delays with respect to the other two. We conclude that the district court should have certified a class consisting at least of persons who suffered delays with respect to their applications for Food Stamps and ANFC.

In support of their request to represent persons suffering delays in the Fuel Assistance program, Appellants point out that though none of the named plaintiffs or intervenors had alleged delays in receiving benefits under that program, the Fuel Assistance program is seasonal and was not operating at the time the com-plaint was filed. . . . According to Appellants, the Department, which processes the applications in all three programs, is acting in the same general fashion in all three programs by failing to act on applications within the 30-day deadlines (in the case of ANFC and Food Stamp) or within a time frame mandated by due process (in the case of Fuel Assistance). The evidence shows that this problem stems from the same cause: an increase in the number of applications for public assistance.

We leave the matter of whether the class should include persons who suffered delays with respect to the Fuel Assistance program for further consideration by the district court. If, on remand, plaintiff or any intervenor can assert a claim that he or she is suffering delay in the processing of his or her own application for assistance under that program, the class action should be allowed to proceed with respect to that program. . . .

[The court rejected the Department's contentions that the plaintiffs lacked standing and that their claims had become moot.]

Conclusion

The district court's judgment dismissing the complaint is vacated, and the case is remanded for further proceedings not inconsistent with the foregoing, including (a) certification of a class comprising at least "all current and future Vermont appli-cants for assistance from the Food Stamp, ANFC, and Fuel Assistance Programs," and (b) further consideration of whether the class, or a subclass, may include persons with claims for delays with respect to the Fuel Assistance program. . . .

NOTES AND QUESTIONS

1. Standard of review. Under what standard does a federal appellate court review the trial court's decision granting or denying class certification? Does the standard vary depending on the nature of the trial court's ruling and the basis on which it is challenged?

2. *Numerosity.*   What was wrong with the district court's evaluation of numerosity? The *Robidoux* class included "[a]ll current *and future* Vermont applicants for assistance from the Food Stamp, ANFC, and Fuel Assistance Programs." *Robidoux*, 987 F.2d at 934 (emphasis added). This involves a "fluid class" whose membership is constantly changing. As some members drop out of the class because their applications are no longer pending, new applicants are regularly entering the class. When a suit is brought on behalf of a fluid class seeking injunctive relief against future misconduct, will numerosity be easier to meet because others are steadily flowing into the class? Apart from numerical size, what factors did the court rely on in finding that numerosity was satisfied? If the nature of the claims and/or the resources of the class members make it unlikely they will sue individually, does this support finding that joinder is impracticable?

3. *Curing typicality and adequacy problems.*   What was the problem with the plaintiffs' challenge to delays in processing Fuel Assistance applications? The court suggests several ways of dealing with situations in which the named parties' claims are not typical of those of the class or when they do not adequately represent all class members. One possibility is to amend the complaint and narrow the definition of the class to exclude such members. *See* FED. R. CIV. P. 23(d)(1)(D). Another is to allow a member who is not adequately represented to intervene in the action, *see* FED. R. CIV. P. 23(d)(1)(B)(iii); would such a member satisfy the conditions for intervention of right under Rule 24(a)(2)? *See* FED. R. CIV. P. 24(a)(2).

4. *Fluid classes and mootness.*   One advantage of defining a fluid class is that it may protect against dismissal on grounds of mootness, for even if the class representative's claims become moot, the fluid nature of the class helps to ensure that there will always be class members whose claims remain alive. As long as the class has been certified, a court may allow a member whose claim is still alive to intervene and substitute for a named party whose claim has become moot. In *Robidoux*, this was of no help to the class because the plaintiffs' claims became moot before the class had been certified. However, the court of appeals there invoked the "inherently transitory" doctrine to save the suit from dismissal:

> [T]he fact that the plaintiffs received their unlawfully delayed benefits after the lawsuit was commenced did not mean that the action thereby became moot. Where class claims are inherently transitory, "the termination of a class representative's claim does not moot the claims of the unnamed members of the class." *Gerstein v. Pugh*, 420 U.S. 103, 110 n.11 (1975); *Sosna v. Iowa*, 419 U.S. 393, 401-402 (1975). Even where the class is not certified until after the claims of the individual class representatives have become moot, certification may be deemed to relate back to the filing of the complaint in order to avoid mooting the entire controversy. . . . In the present case, [the class] claims are inherently transitory since the Department will almost always be able to process a delayed application before a plaintiff can obtain relief through litigation.

Robidoux, 987 F.2d at 938-939. *See Genesis Healthcare Corp. v. Symczyk*, 133 S. Ct. 1523, 1530-1531 (2013) (explaining relation-back doctrine as it applies to inherently transitory class action claims).

5. *Class actions by legal services programs.*   The plaintiffs in *Robidoux* were indigents represented by Vermont Legal Aid, Inc. A few years after the case was decided, Congress began prohibiting programs that receive any funding from the national Legal Services Corporation (LSC) from initiating or participating in class action lawsuits. *See* 42 U.S.C. § 2996e(d)(5) (2015); 45 C.F.R. § 1617 (2015). This prohibition, which is still in effect, curtails the ability of lawyers to bring class actions on behalf of low-income clients. Some programs, including Vermont Legal Aid, have continued to offer their clients a full array of legal services by refusing federal LSC funding. Because of the difficulties of raising alternative funds, however, many legal services programs have no choice but to seek LSC funding with the attendant restrictions. Challenges to the constitutionality of the class-action restriction on LSC-fund recipients have been rejected. *See Legal Aid Servs. of Or. v. Legal Servs. Corp.*, 608 F.3d 1084 (9th Cir. 2010); *Brooklyn Legal Servs. Corp. v. Legal Servs. Corp.*, 462 F.3d 219 (2d Cir. 2006), *cert. denied*, 552 U.S. 810 (2007).

A NOTE ON SUBCLASSES

Another possible solution to the typicality problem in *Robidoux* would be to create subclasses pursuant to Rule 23(c)(5), with a specific named party—perhaps an intervenor—charged with representing each particular subgroup's interests. As the Supreme Court has explained, "the adversity among subgroups requires that the members of each subgroup cannot be bound . . . except by . . . those who understand that their role is to represent solely the members of their respective subgroups." *Amchem Prods., Inc. v. Windsor*, 521 U.S. 591, 627 (1997).

In *Amchem Products*, the Supreme Court cited the failure to create subclasses as a basis for denying class action status to a suit brought against asbestos manufacturers on behalf of U.S. residents who had been occupationally exposed to asbestos and who had not already sued the defendants. The Court concluded that the proposed class did not meet Rule 23(a)(4)'s adequacy requirement due to the fact that the class contained persons with conflicting interests, *i.e.*, those with current injuries from asbestos exposure and those who had been exposed but whose injuries had not yet manifested themselves. In certifying the class and approving a settlement of the case, the district court had failed to create subclasses that would ensure the protection of each subgroup. Instead, said the Supreme Court,

> named parties with diverse medical conditions sought to act on behalf of a single giant class rather than on behalf of discrete subclasses. In significant respects, the interests of those within the single class are not aligned. Most saliently, for the currently injured, the critical goal is generous immediate payments. That goal tugs against the interest of exposure-only plaintiffs in ensuring an ample, inflation-protected fund for the future. . . .
>
> The settling parties, in sum, achieved a global compromise with no structural assurance of fair and adequate representation for the diverse groups and individuals affected. Although the named parties alleged a range of complaints, each served

generally as representative for the whole, not for a separate constituency. . . . [There was] no assurance here—either in the terms of the settlement or in the structure of the negotiations—that the named plaintiffs operated under a proper understanding of their representational responsibilities.

Id. at 626-627.

If a court creates subclasses, Rule 23(c)(5) provides that each subclass must independently satisfy the requirements of Rule 23(a) and (b). While the creation of subclasses may be necessary to satisfy typicality and adequacy of representation, might carving up the class result in one or more subclasses that fail to satisfy numerosity because they have so few members that joinder is not impracticable? *See Warren v. Xerox Corp.*, 2004 WL 1562884, at *17-*18 (E.D.N.Y. Jan. 26, 2004) (refusing to create subclasses when it was not clear they would satisfy numerosity); *Chmieleski v. City Prods. Corp.*, 71 F.R.D. 118, 150-151 (W.D. Mo. 1976) (refusing to certify subclass of 22 because joinder was not impracticable).

PROBLEMS

9-6. Eight female students sued Essex College alleging that its varsity athletic and athletic scholarship programs discriminated against women in violation of federal law. Seven of the plaintiffs belonged to the college's "club" lacrosse team while the eighth plaintiff played "club" softball. The college does not sponsor female varsity teams in either of these sports. Such female teams do exist in other sports, but the plaintiffs do not belong to any of them. The plaintiffs seek an injunction requiring that the college create varsity female lacrosse and softball teams and that it provide equal scholarships for male and female varsity athletes. The plaintiffs have moved for certification of a class that includes "all current and future female students who are interested in playing varsity lacrosse or softball at Essex College." How should the court rule on the motion? If subclasses need to be created, how might they be defined? *See Boucher v. Syracuse Univ.*, 164 F.3d 113 (2d Cir. 1999).

9-7. Four plaintiffs sued Falk Auto Sales ("Falk") and JB Collections ("JBC"), alleging that the defendants engaged in a scheme to defraud used car buyers, in violation of federal and state law. According to the complaint, Falk sold cars to customers, financed the purchases, and took security interests in the cars. If a buyer missed a payment, Falk repossessed the vehicle and assigned the buyer's note to JBC. JBC then attempted to collect the balance due from the buyer. Meanwhile, unless the buyer immediately redeemed the car, Falk sought to resell it. If the car was resold, the original buyer was neither informed of the fact nor were the proceeds of the sale credited to the buyer or, if in excess of the amount owed, refunded to him or her. Moreover, buyers were not credited with payments they had made on their notes after repossession. Plaintiffs seek certification of a class consisting of all persons who bought used cars from Falk, financed the purchases with Falk, defaulted on their loans, and failed to redeem their cars after repossession. The proposed class consists of 2,500 people. Defendants object to certification on the ground that the proposed class does not satisfy the commonality, typicality, and adequacy requirements of Rule 23(a). They note that class members' damages will vary with the facts of each case and that defendants' affirmative defenses will differ among members. Moreover, the class is not homogeneous because not all members had their cars sold, not all sales resulted in surplus proceeds, and not all buyers made further payments on their notes. Finally, defendants claim that the named plaintiffs lack characteristics that allow them to represent all members of the class, for none of the named plaintiffs was owed surplus proceeds, and none made further payments on their notes. How should the court rule on the certification motion? *See Chisholm v. TranSouth Fin. Corp.*, 194 F.R.D. 538 (E.D. Va. 2000).

Wal-Mart Stores, Inc. v. Dukes [Part I]*
131 S. Ct. 2541 (2011)

JUSTICE SCALIA delivered the opinion of the Court.

We are presented with one of the most expansive class actions ever. The District Court and the Court of Appeals approved the certification of a class comprising about one and a half million plaintiffs, current and former female employees of petitioner Wal-Mart who allege that the discretion exercised by their local supervisors over pay and promotion matters violates Title VII by discriminating against women. In addition to injunctive and declaratory relief, the plaintiffs seek an award of backpay. We consider whether the certification of the plaintiff class was consistent with Federal Rules of Civil Procedure 23(a) and (b)(2).

I

A

Petitioner Wal-Mart is the Nation's largest private employer. It operates four types of retail stores throughout the country: Discount Stores, Supercenters, Neighborhood Markets, and Sam's Clubs. Those stores are divided into seven nationwide divisions, which in turn comprise 41 regions of 80 to 85 stores apiece. Each store has between 40 and 53 separate departments and 80 to 500 staff positions. In all, Wal-Mart operates approximately 3,400 stores and employs more than one million people.

Pay and promotion decisions at Wal-Mart are generally committed to local managers' broad discretion, which is exercised "in a largely subjective manner." Local store managers may increase the wages of hourly employees (within limits) with only limited corporate oversight. As for salaried employees, such as store

---

* [Those parts of the Court's opinion dealing with Rule 23(a) appear here. Later, we will look at the Court's discussion of Rule 23(b).—EDS.]

managers and their deputies, higher corporate authorities have discretion to set their pay within preestablished ranges.

Promotions work in a similar fashion. Wal-Mart permits store managers to apply their own subjective criteria when selecting candidates as "support managers," which is the first step on the path to management. Admission to Wal-Mart's management training program, however, does require that a candidate meet certain objective criteria, including an above-average performance rating, at least one year's tenure in the applicant's current position, and a willingness to relocate. But except for those requirements, regional and district managers have discretion to use their own judgment when selecting candidates for management training. Promotion to higher office — *e.g.*, assistant manager, co-manager, or store manager — is similarly at the discretion of the employee's superiors after prescribed objective factors are satisfied.

B

The named plaintiffs in this lawsuit, representing the 1.5 million members of the certified class, are three current or former Wal-Mart employees who allege that the company discriminated against them on the basis of their sex by denying them equal pay or promotions, in violation of Title VII of the Civil Rights Act of 1964, 42 U.S.C. § 2000e-1 *et seq.* . . .

[The three named plaintiffs, each a current or former female employee of Wal-Mart stores in Missouri or California, complained of adverse gender discriminatory treatment by Wal-Mart managers.]

These plaintiffs, respondents here, do not allege that Wal-Mart has any express corporate policy against the advancement of women. Rather, they claim that their local managers' discretion over pay and promotions is exercised disproportionately in favor of men, leading to an unlawful disparate impact on female employees. And, respondents say, because Wal-Mart is aware of this effect, its refusal to cabin its managers' authority amounts to disparate treatment. Their complaint seeks injunctive and declaratory relief, punitive damages, and backpay. It does not ask for compensatory damages.

Importantly for our purposes, respondents claim that the discrimination to which they have been subjected is common to *all* Wal-Mart's female employees. The basic theory of their case is that a strong and uniform "corporate culture" permits bias against women to infect, perhaps subconsciously, the discretionary decisionmaking of each one of Wal-Mart's thousands of managers — thereby making every woman at the company the victim of one common discriminatory practice. Respondents therefore wish to litigate the Title VII claims of all female employees at Wal-Mart's stores in a nationwide class action.

C

Class certification is governed by Federal Rule of Civil Procedure 23. Under Rule 23(a), the party seeking certification must demonstrate, first, that:

"(1) the class is so numerous that joinder of all members is impracticable,

"(2) there are questions of law or fact common to the class,

"(3) the claims or defenses of the representative parties are typical of the claims or defenses of the class, and

"(4) the representative parties will fairly and adequately protect the interests of the class."

Second, the proposed class must satisfy at least one of the three requirements listed in Rule 23(b). Respondents rely on Rule 23(b)(2), which applies when "the party opposing the class has acted or refused to act on grounds that apply generally to the class, so that final injunctive relief or corresponding declaratory relief is appropriate respecting the class as a whole."

Invoking these provisions, respondents moved the District Court to certify a plaintiff class consisting of "'[a]ll women employed at any Wal-Mart domestic retail store at any time since December 26, 1998, who have been or may be subjected to Wal-Mart's challenged pay and management track promotions policies and practices.'" As evidence that there were indeed "questions of law or fact common to" all the women of Wal-Mart, as Rule 23(a)(2) requires, respondents relied chiefly on three forms of proof: statistical evidence about pay and promotion disparities between men and women at the company, anecdotal reports of discrimination from about 120 of Wal-Mart's female employees, and the testimony of a sociologist, Dr. William Bielby, who conducted a "social framework analysis" of Wal-Mart's "culture" and personnel practices, and concluded that the company was "vulnerable" to gender discrimination.

Wal-Mart unsuccessfully moved to strike much of this evidence. It also offered its own countervailing statistical and other proof in an effort to defeat Rule 23(a)'s requirements of commonality, typicality, and adequate representation. Wal-Mart further contended that respondents' monetary claims for backpay could not be certified under Rule 23(b)(2), first because that Rule refers only to injunctive and declaratory relief, and second because the backpay claims could not be manageably tried as a class without depriving Wal-Mart of its right to present certain statutory defenses. With one limitation not relevant here, the District Court granted respondents' motion and certified their proposed class.[3]

D

A divided en banc Court of Appeals substantially affirmed the District Court's certification order. The majority concluded that respondents' evidence of commonality was sufficient to "raise the common question whether Wal-Mart's female employees nationwide were subjected to a single set of corporate policies (not merely a number of independent discriminatory acts) that may have worked to unlawfully discriminate against them in violation of Title VII." It also agreed with the District Court that the named plaintiffs' claims were sufficiently typical of the

---

3. . . . [The district court] decided to afford class members notice of the action and the right to opt-out of the class with respect to respondents' punitive-damages claim.

class as a whole to satisfy Rule 23(a)(3), and that they could serve as adequate class representatives, see Rule 23(a)(4). With respect to the Rule 23(b)(2) question, the Ninth Circuit held that respondents' backpay claims could be certified as part of a (b)(2) class because they did not "predominat[e]" over the requests for declaratory and injunctive relief, meaning they were not "superior in strength, influence, or authority" to the nonmonetary claims.[4]

Finally, the Court of Appeals determined that the action could be manageably tried as a class action because the District Court could adopt the approach the Ninth Circuit approved in *Hilao v. Estate of Marcos*, 103 F.3d 767, 782-787 (1996). There compensatory damages for some 9,541 class members were calculated by selecting 137 claims at random, referring those claims to a special master for valuation, and then extrapolating the validity and value of the untested claims from the sample set. The Court of Appeals "s[aw] no reason why a similar procedure to that used in *Hilao* could not be employed in this case." It would allow Wal-Mart "to present individual defenses in the randomly selected 'sample cases,' thus revealing the approximate percentage of class members whose unequal pay or nonpromotion was due to something other than gender discrimination."

We granted certiorari.

II

The class action is "an exception to the usual rule that litigation is conducted by and on behalf of the individual named parties only." In order to justify a departure from that rule, "a class representative must be part of the class and 'possess the same interest and suffer the same injury' as the class members." Rule 23(a) ensures that the named plaintiffs are appropriate representatives of the class whose claims they wish to litigate. The Rule's four requirements—numerosity, commonality, typicality, and adequate representation—"effectively 'limit the class claims to those fairly encompassed by the named plaintiff's claims.'" *General Telephone Co. of Southwest v. Falcon*, 457 U.S. 147, 156 (1982).

A

The crux of this case is commonality—the rule requiring a plaintiff to show that "there are questions of law or fact common to the class." Rule 23(a)(2).[5] That language is easy to misread, since "[a]ny competently crafted class complaint literally

---

4. To enable that result, the Court of Appeals trimmed the (b)(2) class [by remanding] that part of the certification order which included respondents' punitive-damages claim in the (b)(2) class, so that the District Court might consider whether that might cause the monetary relief to predominate.

5. We have previously stated in this context that "[t]he commonality and typicality requirements of Rule 23(a) tend to merge. Both serve as guideposts for determining whether under the particular circumstances maintenance of a class action is economical and whether the named plaintiff's claim and the class claims are so interrelated that the interests of the class members will be fairly and adequately protected in their absence. Those requirements therefore also tend to merge with the adequacy-of-representation requirement, although the latter requirement also raises concerns about the competency of class counsel and conflicts of interest." . . .

raises common 'questions.'" Nagareda, Class Certification in the Age of Aggregate Proof, 84 N.Y.U. L. Rev. 97, 131-132 (2009). For example: Do all of us plaintiffs indeed work for Wal-Mart? Do our managers have discretion over pay? Is that an unlawful employment practice? What remedies should we get? Reciting these questions is not sufficient to obtain class certification. Commonality requires the plaintiff to demonstrate that the class members "have suffered the same injury." This does not mean merely that they have all suffered a violation of the same provision of law. Title VII, for example, can be violated in many ways—by intentional discrimination, or by hiring and promotion criteria that result in disparate impact, and by the use of these practices on the part of many different superiors in a single company. Quite obviously, the mere claim by employees of the same company that they have suffered a Title VII injury, or even a disparate-impact Title VII injury, gives no cause to believe that all their claims can productively be litigated at once. Their claims must depend upon a common contention—for example, the assertion of discriminatory bias on the part of the same supervisor. That common contention, moreover, must be of such a nature that it is capable of classwide resolution—which means that determination of its truth or falsity will resolve an issue that is central to the validity of each one of the claims in one stroke.

> "What matters to class certification . . . is not the raising of common 'questions'—even in droves—but, rather the capacity of a classwide proceeding to generate common *answers* apt to drive the resolution of the litigation. Dissimilarities within the proposed class are what have the potential to impede the generation of common answers." Nagareda, *supra*, at 132.

Rule 23 does not set forth a mere pleading standard. A party seeking class certification must affirmatively demonstrate his compliance with the Rule—that is, he must be prepared to prove that there are *in fact* sufficiently numerous parties, common questions of law or fact, etc. We recognized in *Falcon* that "sometimes it may be necessary for the court to probe behind the pleadings before coming to rest on the certification question," and that certification is proper only if "the trial court is satisfied, after a rigorous analysis, that the prerequisites of Rule 23(a) have been satisfied." Frequently that "rigorous analysis" will entail some overlap with the merits of the plaintiff's underlying claim. That cannot be helped. . . . Nor is there anything unusual about that consequence: The necessity of touching aspects of the merits in order to resolve preliminary matters, *e.g.*, jurisdiction and venue, is a familiar feature of litigation.

In this case, proof of commonality necessarily overlaps with respondents' merits contention that Wal-Mart engages in a *pattern or practice* of discrimination.[7] That

---

7. In a pattern-or-practice case, the plaintiff tries to "establish by a preponderance of the evidence that . . . discrimination was the company's standard operating procedure[,] the regular rather than the unusual practice." If he succeeds, that showing will support a rebuttable inference that all class members were victims of the discriminatory practice, and will justify "an award of prospective relief," such as "an injunctive order against the continuation of the discriminatory practice."

is so because, in resolving an individual's Title VII claim, the crux of the inquiry is "the reason for a particular employment decision." Here respondents wish to sue about literally millions of employment decisions at once. Without some glue holding the alleged *reasons* for all those decisions together, it will be impossible to say that examination of all the class members' claims for relief will produce a common answer to the crucial question *why was I disfavored*.

B

This Court's opinion in *Falcon* describes how the commonality issue must be approached. There an employee who claimed that he was deliberately denied a promotion on account of race obtained certification of a class comprising all employees wrongfully denied promotions and all applicants wrongfully denied jobs. We rejected that composite class for lack of commonality and typicality, explaining:

> "Conceptually, there is a wide gap between (a) an individual's claim that he has been denied a promotion [or higher pay] on discriminatory grounds, and his otherwise unsupported allegation that the company has a policy of discrimination, and (b) the existence of a class of persons who have suffered the same injury as that individual, such that the individual's claim and the class claim will share common questions of law or fact and that the individual's claim will be typical of the class claims."

Falcon suggested two ways in which that conceptual gap might be bridged. First, if the employer "used a biased testing procedure to evaluate both applicants for employment and incumbent employees, a class action on behalf of every applicant or employee who might have been prejudiced by the test clearly would satisfy the commonality and typicality requirements of Rule 23(a)." Second, "[s]ignificant proof that an employer operated under a general policy of discrimination conceivably could justify a class of both applicants and employees if the discrimination manifested itself in hiring and promotion practices in the same general fashion, such as through entirely subjective decisionmaking processes." We think that statement precisely describes respondents' burden in this case. The first manner of bridging the gap obviously has no application here; Wal-Mart has no testing procedure or other companywide evaluation method that can be charged with bias. The whole point of permitting discretionary decisionmaking is to avoid evaluating employees under a common standard.

The second manner of bridging the gap requires "significant proof" that Wal-Mart "operated under a general policy of discrimination." That is entirely absent here. Wal-Mart's announced policy forbids sex discrimination, and as the District Court recognized the company imposes penalties for denials of equal employment opportunity. The only evidence of a "general policy of discrimination" respondents produced was the testimony of Dr. William Bielby, their sociological expert. Relying on "social framework" analysis, Bielby testified that Wal-Mart has a "strong corporate culture," that makes it " 'vulnerable' " to "gender bias." He could not, however, "determine with any specificity how regularly stereotypes play a meaningful role in employment decisions at Wal-Mart. At his deposition . . . Dr.

Bielby conceded that he could not calculate whether 0.5 percent or 95 percent of the employment decisions at Wal-Mart might be determined by stereotyped thinking." . . . If Bielby admittedly has no answer to that question, we can safely disregard what he has to say. It is worlds away from "significant proof" that Wal-Mart "operated under a general policy of discrimination."

C

The only corporate policy that the plaintiffs' evidence convincingly establishes is Wal-Mart's "policy" of *allowing discretion* by local supervisors over employment matters. On its face, of course, that is just the opposite of a uniform employment practice that would provide the commonality needed for a class action; it is a policy *against having* uniform employment practices. It is also a very common and presumptively reasonable way of doing business—one that we have said "should itself raise no inference of discriminatory conduct."

To be sure, we have recognized that, "in appropriate cases," giving discretion to lower-level supervisors can be the basis of Title VII liability under a disparate-impact theory—since "an employer's undisciplined system of subjective decisionmaking [can have] precisely the same effects as a system pervaded by impermissible intentional discrimination." But the recognition that this type of Title VII claim "can" exist does not lead to the conclusion that every employee in a company using a system of discretion has such a claim in common. . . . A party seeking to certify a nationwide class will be unable to show that all the employees' Title VII claims will in fact depend on the answers to common questions.

Respondents have not identified a common mode of exercising discretion that pervades the entire company—aside from their reliance on Dr. Bielby's social frameworks analysis that we have rejected. In a company of Wal-Mart's size and geographical scope, it is quite unbelievable that all managers would exercise their discretion in a common way without some common direction. Respondents attempt to make that showing by means of statistical and anecdotal evidence, but their evidence falls well short. . . .

Even if they are taken at face value, these studies are insufficient to establish that respondents' theory can be proved on a classwide basis. . . . As Judge Ikuta observed in her dissent, "[i]nformation about disparities at the regional and national level does not establish the existence of disparities at individual stores, let alone raise the inference that a company-wide policy of discrimination is implemented by discretionary decisions at the store and district level." A regional pay disparity, for example, may be attributable to only a small set of Wal-Mart stores, and cannot by itself establish the uniform, store-by-store disparity upon which the plaintiffs' theory of commonality depends.

There is another, more fundamental, respect in which respondents' statistical proof fails. Even if it established (as it does not) a pay or promotion pattern that differs from the nationwide figures or the regional figures in *all* of Wal-Mart's 3,400 stores, that would still not demonstrate that commonality of issue exists. Some managers will claim that the availability of women, or qualified women, or interested women, in their stores' area does not mirror the national or regional statistics. And almost all of them will claim to have been applying some sex-neutral, performance-based criteria—whose nature and effects will differ from store to store. . . . Other than the bare existence of delegated discretion, respondents have identified no "specific employment practice"—much less one that ties all their 1.5 million claims together. Merely showing that Wal-Mart's policy of discretion has produced an overall sex-based disparity does not suffice.

Respondents' anecdotal evidence suffers from the same defects, and in addition is too weak to raise any inference that all the individual, discretionary personnel decisions are discriminatory. . . . [R]espondents filed some 120 affidavits reporting experiences of discrimination—about 1 for every 12,500 class members—relating to only some 235 out of Wal-Mart's 3,400 stores. More than half of these reports are concentrated in only six States (Alabama, California, Florida, Missouri, Texas, and Wisconsin); half of all States have only one or two anecdotes; and 14 States have no anecdotes about Wal-Mart's operations at all. Even if every single one of these accounts is true, that would not demonstrate that the entire company "operate[s] under a general policy of discrimination," which is what respondents must show to certify a companywide class.

The dissent misunderstands the nature of the foregoing analysis. It criticizes our focus on the dissimilarities between the putative class members on the ground that we have "blend[ed]" Rule 23(a)(2)'s commonality requirement with Rule 23(b)(3)'s inquiry into whether common questions "predominate" over individual ones. That is not so. We quite agree that for purposes of Rule 23(a)(2) " '[e]ven a single [common] question'" will do. We consider dissimilarities not in order to determine (as Rule 23(b)(3) requires) whether common questions *predominate*, but in order to determine (as Rule 23(a)(2) requires) whether there *is* "[e]ven a single [common] question." And there is not here. Because respondents provide no convincing proof of a companywide discriminatory pay and promotion policy, we have concluded that they have not established the existence of any common question.

In sum, we agree with Chief Judge Kozinski that the members of the class:

> "held a multitude of different jobs, at different levels of Wal-Mart's hierarchy, for variable lengths of time, in 3,400 stores, sprinkled across 50 states, with a kaleidoscope of supervisors (male and female), subject to a variety of regional policies that all differed. . . . Some thrived while others did poorly. They have little in common but their sex and this lawsuit." . . .

* * *

The judgment of the Court of Appeals is

Reversed.

JUSTICE GINSBURG, with whom JUSTICE BREYER, JUSTICE SOTOMAYOR, and JUSTICE KAGAN join, concurring in part and dissenting in part.

The class in this case, I agree with the Court, should not have been certified under Federal Rule of Civil Procedure 23(b)(2). . . .

. . . The Court, however, disqualifies the class at the starting gate, holding that the plaintiffs cannot cross the "commonality" line set by Rule 23(a)(2). In so ruling, the Court imports into the Rule 23(a) determination concerns properly addressed in a Rule 23(b)(3) assessment.

I

A

Rule 23(a)(2) establishes a preliminary requirement for maintaining a class action: "[T]here are questions of law or fact common to the class." The Rule "does not require that all questions of law or fact raised in the litigation be common"; indeed, "[e]ven a single question of law or fact common to the members of the class will satisfy the commonality requirement." See Advisory Committee's 1937 Notes on Fed. Rule Civ. Proc. 23, 28 U.S.C. App., p. 138 (citing with approval cases in which "there was only a question of law or fact common to" the class members).

. . . [A] "question" "common to the class" must be a dispute, either of fact or of law, the resolution of which will advance the determination of the class members' claims.[3]

B

The District Court, recognizing that "one significant issue common to the class may be sufficient to warrant certification," found that the plaintiffs easily met that test. . . .

The District Court certified a class of "[a]ll women employed at any Wal-Mart domestic retail store at any time since December 26, 1998." The named plaintiffs, led by Betty Dukes, propose to litigate, on behalf of the class, allegations that Wal-Mart discriminates on the basis of gender in pay and promotions. . . .

Women fill 70 percent of the hourly jobs in the retailer's stores but make up only "33 percent of management employees." . . . The plaintiffs' "largely uncontested descriptive statistics" also show that women working in the company's stores "are paid less than men in every region" and "that the salary gap widens over time even for men and women hired into the same jobs at the same time."

The District Court identified "systems for . . . promoting in-store employees" that were "sufficiently similar across regions and stores" to conclude that "the manner in which these systems affect the class raises issues that are common to all class members."

Wal-Mart's compensation policies also operate uniformly across stores, the District Court found. The retailer leaves open a $2 band for every position's hourly pay rate. Wal-Mart provides no standards or criteria for setting wages

---

3. The Court suggests Rule 23(a)(2) must mean more than it says. If the word "questions" were taken literally, the majority asserts, plaintiffs could pass the Rule 23(a)(2) bar by "[r]eciting . . . questions" like "Do all of us plaintiffs indeed work for Wal-Mart?" Sensibly read, however, the word "questions" means disputed issues, not any utterance crafted in the grammatical form of a question.

within that band, and thus does nothing to counter unconscious bias on the part of supervisors.

Wal-Mart's supervisors do not make their discretionary decisions in a vacuum. The District Court reviewed means Wal-Mart used to maintain a "carefully constructed . . . corporate culture," such as frequent meetings to reinforce the common way of thinking. . . .

The plaintiffs' evidence . . . suggests that gender bias suffused Wal-Mart's company culture. . . .

Finally, the plaintiffs presented an expert's appraisal to show that the pay and promotions disparities at Wal-Mart "can be explained only by gender discrimination and not by . . . neutral variables." . . . The results, the District Court found, were sufficient to raise an "inference of discrimination."

C

The District Court's identification of a common question, whether Wal-Mart's pay and promotions policies gave rise to unlawful discrimination, was hardly infirm. The practice of delegating to supervisors large discretion to make personnel decisions, uncontrolled by formal standards, has long been known to have the potential to produce disparate effects. Managers, like all humankind, may be prey to biases of which they are unaware. The risk of discrimination is heightened when those managers are predominantly of one sex, and are steeped in a corporate culture that perpetuates gender stereotypes. . . .

We have held that "discretionary employment practices" can give rise to Title VII claims, not only when such practices are motivated by discriminatory intent but also when they produce discriminatory results. . . .

The plaintiffs' allegations state claims of gender discrimination in the form of biased decisionmaking in both pay and promotions. [R]esolving those claims would necessitate examination of particular policies and practices alleged to affect, adversely and globally, women employed at Wal-Mart's stores. Rule 23(a) (2), setting a necessary but not a sufficient criterion for class-action certification, demands nothing further.

II

A

The Court gives no credence to the key dispute common to the class: whether Wal-Mart's discretionary pay and promotion policies are discriminatory. ("Reciting" questions like "Is [giving managers discretion over pay] an unlawful employment practice?" "is not sufficient to obtain class certification."). "What matters," the Court asserts, "is not the raising of common 'questions,'" but whether there are "[d]issimilarities within the proposed class" that "have the potential to impede the generation of common answers."

The Court blends Rule 23(a)(2)'s threshold criterion with the more demanding criteria of Rule 23(b)(3), and thereby elevates the (a)(2) inquiry so that it is no longer "easily satisfied." Rule 23(b)(3) certification requires, in addition to the four 23(a) findings, determinations that "questions of law or fact common to class members predominate over any questions affecting only individual members" and that "a class action is superior to other available methods for . . . adjudicating the controversy."

The Court's emphasis on differences between class members mimics the Rule 23(b)(3) inquiry into whether common questions "predominate" over individual issues. And by asking whether the individual differences "impede" common adjudication, the Court duplicates 23(b)(3)'s question whether "a class action is superior" to other modes of adjudication. Indeed, Professor Nagareda, whose "dissimilarities" inquiry the Court endorses, developed his position in the context of Rule 23(b)(3). "The Rule 23(b)(3) predominance inquiry" is meant to "tes[t] whether proposed classes are sufficiently cohesive to warrant adjudication by representation." If courts must conduct a "dissimilarities" analysis at the Rule 23(a)(2) stage, no mission remains for Rule 23(b)(3).

Because Rule 23(a) is also a prerequisite for Rule 23(b)(1) and Rule 23(b)(2) classes, the Court's "dissimilarities" position is far reaching. Individual differences should not bar a Rule 23(b)(1) or Rule 23(b)(2) class, so long as the Rule 23(a) threshold is met. For example, in *Franks v. Bowman Transp. Co.*, 424 U.S. 747 (1976), a Rule 23(b)(2) class of African-American truckdrivers complained that the defendant had discriminatorily refused to hire black applicants. We recognized that the "qualification[s] and performance" of individual class members might vary. "Generalizations concerning such individually applicable evidence," we cautioned, "cannot serve as a justification for the denial of [injunctive] relief to the entire class."

B

The "dissimilarities" approach leads the Court to train its attention on what distinguishes individual class members, rather than on what unites them. Given the lack of standards for pay and promotions, the majority says, "demonstrating the invalidity of one manager's use of discretion will do nothing to demonstrate the invalidity of another's."

Wal-Mart's delegation of discretion over pay and promotions is a policy uniform throughout all stores. The very nature of discretion is that people will exercise it in various ways. A system of delegated discretion, *Watson* held, is a practice actionable under Title VII when it produces discriminatory outcomes. A finding that Wal-Mart's pay and promotions practices in fact violate the law would be the first step in the usual order of proof for plaintiffs seeking individual remedies for company-wide discrimination. That each individual employee's unique circumstances will ultimately determine whether she is entitled to backpay or damages should not factor into the Rule 23(a)(2) determination.

* * *

The Court errs in importing a "dissimilarities" notion suited to Rule 23(b)(3) into the Rule 23(a) commonality inquiry. I therefore cannot join Part II of the Court's opinion.

NOTES AND QUESTIONS

1. Common question and common answers.   In their motion to certify a nation-wide class, the named plaintiffs asserted that their Title VII claims and those of the 1.5 million women they sought to represent in all 50 states shared the common question of whether Wal-Mart's pay and promotion policies, though facially neutral, were implemented so as to discriminate against women. Why didn't this assertion suffice to satisfy Rule 23(a)(2)'s requirement that there be a question of law or fact common to all members of the class? To answer that question we must approach commonality as the Court did, *i.e.*, by inquiring whether the common question is one that suggests the suitability of the case for classwide resolution. The Court here focused less on the commonality of the question than it did on the answer to that question. Thus, at the class certification stage, it was not enough for the would-be class representatives to assert the mere presence of a common *question*; rather, they were also required to demonstrate that the proposed class members will have a *common answer* to that question — *i.e.*, that they will offer similar evidence and arguments to *prove* a common element of their claims.

Can you see how this distinction between questions and answers pertains to the larger question of whether the common questions are appropriate for classwide resolution? Think of it this way: If each class member would answer the common question differently, seeking to prove discrimination in a myriad of ways, each unique to a particular class member, a particular store, or a particular region, is there any reason to believe that the claims "can productively be litigated at once" through a single class action? Under such circumstances, what is to be gained by combining them all into a single suit, rather than bringing individual claims, or suing on behalf of a more narrowly drawn class that is limited to the particular store, division, or region where a common practice may in fact be demonstrable? Thus Rule 23(a)(2)'s common question requirement will be satisfied only if that question will have a common answer for all members of the proposed class. As the Court notes, making this determination may require a judge, at the class-certification stage, to look at the merits of plaintiffs' claims, *i.e.*, at the evidence that they will offer to prove that their rights were violated; for it is only at this level that the presence or absence of common questions will sometimes be revealed.

Would the *Wal-Mart* Court's "common answers" standard have been satisfied in *Chandler v. Southwest Jeep-Eagle, Inc.*, 162 F.R.D. 302 (N.D. Ill. 1995), at page 775, *supra*?

2. The proposed nationwide class.   What evidence did the *Wal-Mart* plaintiffs present in support of certifying a nationwide class? Did they allege the existence of any written company policy that discriminated against women? Had there been such a policy, might this have satisfied Rule 23(a)(2)? Alternatively, were plaintiffs able to identify any gender-biased, national Wal-Mart testing or evaluation procedure that was used in the compensation and promotion of workers? Would evidence of such a policy have met Rule 23(a)(2)? But didn't the plaintiffs in fact have evidence that supported their allegation that Wal-Mart maintained a gender-biased corporate culture that impeded the hiring and advancement of women?

If so, why didn't this suffice to satisfy Rule 23(a)(2)? Was the Court's problem here that this evidence addressed only 235 (or 7%) of Wal-Mart's 3,400 stores, and that these stores were concentrated in six states—numbers too low and too geographically localized to "identif[y] a common mode of exercising discretion that pervades the entire company" and that would have justified certification of a nationwide class? The Court agreed that had plaintiffs shown that "discrimination was the company's standard operating procedure," and that it was a "regular rather than the unusual practice," then a "rebuttable inference that all class members were victims of the discriminatory practice" would have been warranted. *See* page 796 n.7, *supra*. In the end, was the basic disagreement between the majority and the dissent over how much evidence the plaintiffs needed at the class-certification stage to warrant an inference that Wal-Mart was engaging in gender discrimination on a nationwide rather than a more localized basis? Does the majority leave the door open for nationwide class actions in which plaintiffs can make a stronger showing as to the existence of a common question shared by all members of such a class?

3. *The class representatives' burden.*   As the Court said in *Wal-Mart*, "[a] party seeking class certification must affirmatively demonstrate his compliance with the Rule," with certification warranted "only if the trial court is satisfied, after a rigorous analysis, that the prerequisites of Rule 23(a) have been satisfied." Might it take some time for the named plaintiffs to gather the information necessary to support their motion for class certification? Rule 23(c)(1)(A) sets no fixed time as to when the certification decision must be made, but instead says simply that it be done at "an early practicable time. . . ." FED. R. CIV. P. 23(c)(1)(A). What is practicable will depend on the case's complexity and on the amount of pre-filing investigation the plaintiffs were able to do. In *Wal-Mart*, more than three years elapsed between the filing of the complaint and the trial court hearing on the class-certification question, during which time the plaintiffs engaged in "extensive discovery" on the class question. *Dukes v. Wal-Mart Stores, Inc.*, 222 F.R.D. 137, 142 (N.D. Cal. 2004). *See Pyke v. Cuomo*, 209 F.R.D. 33, 35-37 (N.D.N.Y. 2002) (motion to certify class was timely, though filed ten years after action commenced, where defendants showed no prejudice and court had not yet reached merits of case).

4. *Narrower classes.*   Might the plaintiffs in *Wal-Mart* have been able to satisfy Rule 23(a)(2) if instead of suing on behalf of a nationwide class, they defined the class more narrowly? Following the Supreme Court's decision in that case, plaintiffs did just that, amending their complaint to embrace a much smaller class consisting of the 150,000 women who worked in Wal-Mart's 250 California stores. The district court nonetheless denied certification, for the same reason the Supreme Court had earlier rejected certification of a nationwide class. As the court explained, "[r]ather than identify an employment practice and define a class around it, plaintiffs continue to challenge the discretionary decisions of hundreds of decision makers, while arbitrarily confining their proposed class to corporate regions that include stores in California . . . ." *Dukes v. Wal-Mart Stores, Inc.*, 964 F. Supp. 2d 1115, 1127-1128 (N.D. Cal. 2013). What if plaintiffs had sued just on behalf of women who worked in one of Wal-Mart's stores—one with a particularly

bad record? If the average Wal-Mart store had 400 current and former workers and even the smallest had about 80, might this have satisfied Rule 23(a)(1)'s numerosity requirement? Would Rule 23(a)(2) now be met? Would such a smaller class have been viable given the likely size of any monetary recovery, and even though 42 U.S.C. § 2000(e)-5(k) allows the award of attorneys' fees to successful plaintiffs in Title VII suits?

2.   Satisfying Rule 23(b)(1), (2), or (3)

If a suit meets all four requirements of Rule 23(a), it may proceed as a class action only if it qualifies under one of three types of class actions recognized by Rule 23(b). If the suit is one that proceeds under (b)(3), Rule 23(c)(2) contains special provisions requiring that class members be given notice and a right to opt out of the class. These special (b)(3) procedures reflect a compromise between the competing goals of judicial efficiency and respect for an individual's right to her own day in court. Unlike (b)(1) and (b)(2) actions, in which the relief sought is mainly injunctive or declaratory in nature, (b)(3) actions are predominantly for money damages. Depending on the amount at stake, class members may have the ability and the incentive to litigate such claims with their own lawyers in a forum of their own choosing. Moreover, the fact that the suit did not qualify under (b)(1) means that separate actions will not prejudice the class opponent or other class members. The reasons for proceeding on a class basis may therefore be less compelling in (b)(3) cases than in other class suits. While judicial efficiency might favor having a (b)(3) suit proceed on an all-inclusive basis, fairness to those wishing to proceed separately dictates giving members a chance either to opt out or appear through their own counsel. Although courts in (b)(1) and (b)(2) suits may also afford notice and an opportunity to opt out, this is a matter of judicial discretion rather than a right. For this reason, (b)(1) and (b)(2) suits are sometimes described as being "mandatory" class actions, in contrast to (b)(3) actions in which each member's participation is ultimately voluntary on his or her part.

a.   Rule 23(b)(1)(A) and (B)

An action will qualify under Rule 23(b)(1)(A) or (B) if separate lawsuits by (or against) individual members could prejudice the party opposing the class or harm other class members. Subdivision (1)(A) addresses the risk that individual suits will create incompatible standards of conduct for the party opposing the class. This concern is similar to that which in a non-class setting might make an absentee a necessary party under Rule 19(a)(1)(B)(ii). Subdivision (b)(1)(B) deals with the related risk that separate suits may impair other class members' interests. This provision mirrors Rule 19(a)(1)(B)(i), which recognizes that the risk of harm to absentees may make their joinder necessary. The difference is that in the Rule 19 setting, a court is considering whether to require that absentees be added to the suit, whereas in the Rule 23(b)(1)(B) setting, the "absentees" have been included as unnamed members of a proposed class.

Boggs v. Divested Atomic Corp.
141 F.R.D. 58 (S.D. Ohio 1991)

KINNEARY, District Judge.

I.   Introduction

Teresa Boggs, a resident of Lucasville, Ohio, lives within six miles of the Portsmouth Gaseous Diffusion Plant. The plant, which is located in rural Pike County, Ohio, approximately four miles from the town of Piketon, processes radioactive materials for the United States Department of Energy. It began operating in the early 1950's and has continuously produced enriched uranium since that time.

Ms. Boggs and the other named plaintiffs, residents of either Pike or Scioto Counties who also live within six miles of the plant, claim that they and their properties have been exposed to radioactive materials and non-radioactive hazardous wastes emitted from the Portsmouth plant. They have asked this Court to certify a class of all similarly-situated persons in order that they may present, on a classwide basis, claims for emotional distress, diminution in the value of their real property, medical monitoring for early cancer detection, and injunctive relief against further unlawful emissions of hazardous substances from the plant. . . . For the following reasons, plaintiffs' motion to certify a class consisting of all persons who live, rent, or own property within a six-mile radius of the boundaries of the Portsmouth Gaseous Diffusion Plant will be granted.

II.   Factual Background

The first amended complaint identifies eight individuals as representative of the following class of plaintiffs:

> "All persons, firms, or entities who were residents, property owners or lessees of property within a radius of six miles from the boundary of the Portsmouth Gaseous Plant ('the Portsmouth Plant'), which proximity caused such persons and property to be subject to the harmful effects of airborne particulates and run-off water from defendants' operations at the Portsmouth Plant."

. . . The named defendants are Divested Atomic Corporation, which . . . operated the plant until November 16, 1986, and Martin Marietta Energy Systems, which has operated the plant after that date. . . .

A.   Class Definition

The plaintiffs define the class as all persons living within a six-mile radius of the boundaries of the Portsmouth Plant whose persons or property have been exposed to radioactive or hazardous wastes released from the plant. The defendants claim that this definition of the class is improper because, in their view, it requires the court to decide that each person living within this geographic area, or owning property within it, has suffered some actual injury from exposure to hazardous or radioactive wastes. According to defendants, a trial on the merits would be needed in order to identify persons with actionable injuries. . . .

Plaintiffs argue that defendants misapprehend the definition of the class. They agree that whether certain people have actionable injuries from exposure is a merits issue. However, for purposes of class membership, they assert that it is the *fact of exposure,* in some amount, rather than proof of a compensable injury that is important. The inquiry then becomes [whether] plaintiffs have shown that emissions of potentially harmful materials, without yet deciding what is a harmful quantity of such materials, reasonably may have reached persons and property within a six-mile radius of the plant. In other words, the Court must ask two questions: (1) is there any evidence that the plant has discharged radioactive or hazardous substances beyond its borders? And (2) if so, have those substances traveled up to six miles? The present record suggests the answers to both questions is yes. . . .

B. Class Size

The only other factual issue relates to the size of the class. Factually, this becomes an issue only if exposure to "harmful" levels of radiation is made a part of the class definition. Otherwise, it is apparent that well in excess of a thousand persons, and perhaps between four thousand and five thousand, now live within six miles of the plant. It is reasonable to infer that there has been some sale of property and residential relocation between the early 1950's and today. It cannot seriously be disputed that plaintiffs' class definition fits thousands if not tens of thousands of people. Although plaintiffs' counsel may be required, at some point and for purposes of giving notice, not only to determine the precise size of the class but the names and addresses of all the members, it is sufficient for certification purposes to conclude that the class numbers in the thousands and that there is some geographic dispersion of class members. . . . The Court now turns to a discussion of the legal significance of these facts in the context of the requirements of Rule 23.

III. Discussion . . .

A. Numerosity . . .

Plaintiffs, through the evidence cited above relating to the size of the class and dispersion of radioactive materials originating from the plant, have made a strong *prima facie* showing that there are too many potential plaintiffs to be joined in one lawsuit. The Court has already concluded that defendants' focus on the number of persons who have been harmed by exposure to radioactive emissions is a merits argument, essentially unrelated to the issue of class certification because of the way in which the class has been defined. . . .

. . . [T]he Court finds this class too numerous to make joinder of all its members in a single lawsuit to be practicable. . . .

B.   Commonality

. . . Plaintiffs have identified a substantial number of common questions, both factual and legal, including: (1) how extensive were the emissions from the plant; (2) what caused them; (3) were they foreseeable, (4) what precautions to avoid emissions were taken, or can be taken; (5) what is the economic impact of emissions; and (6) can the defendants be held liable under theories of strict liability, negligence, private nuisance, or willful and wanton misconduct. Defendants have not argued that these questions are not fairly raised by the pleadings, or that they are not common to the class members' claims. The Court has no difficulty in concluding that the commonality requirement has been satisfied.

C.   Typicality

. . . The named plaintiffs have advanced two distinct types of claims arising out of a larger variety of legal theories: (1) that their personal well-being has been affected by exposure to radioactive material, so that they reasonably fear the onset of cancer or other diseases and reasonably require medical monitoring; and (2) that their property interests have been damaged by contamination, affecting their ability to sell their realty for a price unaffected by a purchaser's knowledge of such contamination or apprehension about the safety of living on property near the plant. . . . All of these claims rest on common legal theories of federal statutory violations, strict liability, negligence, private nuisance, and willful or wanton misconduct.

Defendants' arguments stress the many individual differences which exist both among named plaintiffs and between the named plaintiffs as a group and the balance of the class. . . . Finally, they argue that damage claims—which, in their view, are the primary if not only substantial claims in this case—are inherently individualized and therefore atypical. With these differences, defendants claim that the typicality requirement has not and cannot be met. . . .

. . . [T]he Sixth Circuit has stated that "the mere fact that questions peculiar to each individual member of the class remain after the common questions of the defendant's liability have been resolved does not dictate the conclusion that a class action is impermissible." *Sterling v. Velsicol Chemical Co.*, 855 F.2d 1188, 1197 (6th Cir. 1988). That case, like this one, involved a claim by neighbors of a hazardous industrial facility that renegade materials from the facility had contaminated their properties. Although individualized issues existed, the conduct allegedly giving rise to liability was identical for each plaintiff and class member. The Court noted that "where the defendant's liability can be determined on a classwide basis because the cause of the disaster is a single course of conduct which is identical for each of the plaintiffs, a class action may be the best suited vehicle to resolve such a controversy." *Id.*

These statements apply directly to the typicality issue presented in this case. Clearly, people and parcels of real property, like snowflakes, necessarily have different and unique characteristics. The important question is to what extent those differences, when compared to the nature and extent of the shared characteristics of the named plaintiffs' and the class members' claims, will defeat the Court's ability to achieve a considerable efficiency through collective adjudication of those claims. Here, as in *Sterling*, notwithstanding the differences, class treatment is clearly a better way to proceed.

Counsel have taken great pains to minimize individual differences, and heighten typicality, by presenting only certain types of claims. . . . Rather than asking exclusively for money damages, they have also prayed for common forms of relief, including medical monitoring and injunctive relief concerning the plant's continued operation. These claims are common to all members and are typical of each, notwithstanding the fact that each named plaintiff may verbalize his or her subjective fears differently or have a different level of awareness about when emissions occurred, how they manifested themselves, or what elements or compounds were involved. Thus, the typicality requirement has also been satisfied.

D.   Adequacy of Representation

. . . Clearly, counsel in this case are eminently qualified to prepare the case for trial and to try it. Defendants do not dispute that. Thus, the only question presented is whether the named plaintiffs suffer from some infirmity that makes them unsuited to act as class representatives.

Defendants assert that they have "unique" defenses to the claims of each named plaintiff, and that these defenses cut against these plaintiffs' ability adequately to represent the interests of absent class members. . . .

The central problem with defendants' arguments is that none of these defenses are unique to the named plaintiffs. . . . In short, the named plaintiffs have asserted claims both typical of the other class members, and subject to typical defenses. Since there is no suggestion that other factors have caused or may cause conflict between the named plaintiffs and other class members, the named plaintiffs adequately represent the interests of the class as a whole, and the requirements of Rule 23(a)(4) have also been satisfied.

E.   Rule 23(b)

Plaintiffs have argued for class certification under almost all of the separate subtests found in Rule 23(b). Focusing on their claims for injunctive relief, they argue that either a 23(b)(1) or 23(b)(2) class is appropriate because there is a real risk of inconsistent adjudications, and because the defendants have acted in a way common to all class members, so that injunctive relief with respect to the class as a whole is appropriate. They also assert that a 23(b)(3) class could be certified because the common issues identified above do predominate, and a class action is clearly a superior way—indeed, the only possible way—to adjudicate these claims.

Defendants' argument against certification of any class under Rule 23(b) is two-fold. First, . . . defendants insist that plaintiffs truly seek only a monetary award, and that their claims for injunctive relief are either insubstantial or poorly-disguised money damage items. That being the case, certification under Rules 23(b)(1) and 23(b)(2) is unavailable. Turning then to Rule 23(b)(3), defendants reiterate their position that individual issues dominate this case, so that no efficiency would be achieved by consolidating these claims in one judiciary proceeding.

As is evident from the discussion to this point, the Court has rejected defendants' view of the individualized nature of the plaintiffs' claims. Common issues of liability, causation, and remedies not only predominate but overwhelm individualized issues. If these claims were tried separately, the amount of repetition would be manifestly unjustified. To the extent that each claim of each plaintiff depends upon proof concerning the history of operations at the plant, the nature, timing, extent and cause of emissions, the kinds of remedies, if any, appropriate to address potential future emissions, the need for medical monitoring, [and] the generalized impact of the plant's operations on real property values, that proof would be virtually identical in each case. It would be neither efficient nor fair to anyone, including defendants, to force multiple trials to hear the same evidence and decide the same issues. Clearly, a Rule 23(b)(3) class could properly be certified under these circumstances.

A 23(b)(3) class, however, allows class members to opt out of the action if they desire. [I]f there is a real risk of inconsistent adjudications which would subject the defendants to incompatible standards of conduct, the Court should consider certifying a 23(b)(1) class to prevent the possibility of multiple actions being filed. Thus, the Court will also examine this case under Rule 23(b)(1)(A).

Plaintiffs argue that all of their requests for remediation—plant cleanup, for example, medical monitoring or nuisance abatement—can only be handled by a single judicial order. If multiple courts addressed those issues, they could well order defendants to take actions that could not be performed consistently with each other, thus forcing defendants to choose which orders to obey and which to disregard under threat of contempt.

Defendants discount the probability of truly inconsistent adjudications, claiming that any court order would direct them simply to comply with all applicable laws, and that multiple orders to that effect would not be inconsistent. Although Rule 23(b)(1)(A) does embody a policy of protecting a defendant from the dilemma of complying with inconsistent standards of conduct—a protection these defendants seem not to want—it also allows a single court to fashion an appropriate remedy, and to bring a controversy to a final and complete resolution. In addition, this Court . . . perceives the threat of inconsistent adjudication to be real. Any remedy ordered would not be so simplistic as defendants suggest. If plaintiffs can show an entitlement to injunctive relief, it would undoubtedly be in the form of a complex order, addressing many specific features of plant operation. It is unlikely that two different courts would tailor a remedial order in the same fashion, and it is therefore entirely conceivable that different remedial orders would contain incompatible provisions. Therefore, a 23(b)(1)(A) class can also be certified. Since the (b)(1)(A) class is more comprehensive, the Court will certify a class under that subsection.

IV. Conclusion

It is therefore ORDERED that plaintiffs' motion for class certification is GRANTED. A class is hereby CERTIFIED under F.R. Civ. P. 23(b)(1)(A). . . .

NOTES AND QUESTIONS

1. *Class certification and merits.* The defendants objected that the definition of the proposed class was improper because it turned on the merits of the plaintiffs' claims. The court rejected this contention, noting that membership in the class was based on whether individuals had been *exposed to* the defendants' hazardous waste, not on whether they had in fact suffered *a compensable injury*. Courts uniformly hold that class membership may not depend on the merits of an individual's claim. *Eisen v. Carlisle & Jacquelin*, 417 U.S. 156, 177-178 (1974) (holding that courts may not undertake a preliminary consideration of the merits in order to decide whether suit may proceed as a class action). Otherwise, a court would have to either make a determination of the merits at the class-certification stage or defer certification until after a trial on the merits. The first alternative would be time consuming and could be prejudicial to the class opponent, while the latter would allow parties to obtain the benefits of a class action without first satisfying the requirements for it. Moreover, a class definition that turns on the merits of individual members' claims would put the party opposing the class in a "heads you win, tails I lose" position. If the class won the suit, all of its members would benefit. But if the class lost, it would suddenly become devoid of members, for it included only those with meritorious claims. As a result, if the court had previously certified a class, it would have to withdraw that ruling since it would now be clear that the numerosity requirement was not satisfied. The class opponent could then be exposed to fresh suits by all of the unnamed class members.

However, as we saw earlier (at Note 1, page 803, *supra*), in order to ensure that there are questions of law or fact common to the class, as required by Rule 23(a)(2), a court can look at the *merits* of the class members' claims in order to make sure they indeed share both a common question and a common answer. In *Boggs*, the merits of the plaintiffs' claims met this test since they all involved the same legal theories and the same underlying facts. If the merits of the plaintiffs' claims had instead rested on separate and distinct legal theories, or different sets of underlying facts, then it might be less clear that Rule 23(a)(2) was satisfied. But again, this legitimate inquiry into the legal merits or legal basis of the class members' individual claims is very different from requiring that class members at this point prove that their legal claims are in fact meritorious.

2. *Subclasses.* In *Amchem Products, Inc. v. Windsor*, 521 U.S. 591 (1997), see "A Note on Subclasses," page 790, *supra*, the Supreme Court held that subclasses should have been created in a suit filed on behalf of those exposed to

asbestos. In light of *Amchem*, should subclasses have been created in *Boggs*, a suit brought on behalf of those exposed to hazardous waste? Are the two cases distinguishable?

3. *Avoiding (b)(3) certifications.*   Since the court found that the proposed class satisfied both (b)(1)(A) and (b)(3), why did it certify the action solely under (b)(1)(A)? Courts generally hold that if an action qualifies under (b)(1) or (b)(2) as well as (b)(3), then (b)(1) or (b)(2) will control. *See* 7AA WRIGHT, MILLER & KANE, *supra*, § 1772. As one court explained:

> Most suits that qualify as class actions under Rule 23(b)(1) or (b)(2) will also qualify under the more comprehensive Rule 23(b)(3). Unlike members of subdivision (b)(1) or (b)(2) classes, members of Rule 23(b)(3) classes have an automatic right to opt out, that is, to exclude themselves from the binding effect of the judgment. Because of this additional burden on the parties, courts generally prefer to certify a class under Rule 23(b)(1) or (b)(2) if possible.

Specialty Cabinets & Fixtures, Inc. v. American Equitable Life Ins. Co., 140 F.R.D. 474, 477 (S.D. Ga. 1991). However, as we will see, the Supreme Court has since limited the ability of courts to employ Rule 23(b)(1) or (b)(2) in cases like this in which claims for injunctive relief are combined with claims for monetary relief. *See* Notes 2 & 3, at page 829, *infra*.

4. *Notice and opt-out rights.*   While Rule 23(b)(1) suits carry no automatic notice and opt-out rights, Rule 23(d)(1)(B) gives courts discretion to order notice to the class, and Rule 23(d)(1)(E), which authorizes orders concerning other procedural matters, is broad enough to encompass opt-out rights. Would giving class members the right to entirely opt out of a (b)(1)(A) class be consistent with the rule's underlying purposes? Might this expose the class opponent to the very risks the rule was designed to avoid? In cases like *Boggs*, in which the class seeks both injunctive relief and damages, the justification for granting opt-out rights becomes much stronger. *See, e.g., Eubanks v. Billington*, 110 F.3d 87, 94-95 (D.C. Cir. 1997) (stating that "the language of Rule 23 is sufficiently flexible to afford district courts discretion to grant opt-out rights in (b)(1) and (b)(2) class actions" especially "where both injunctive and monetary relief are sought"). In these "hybrid" cases, would granting opt-out rights solely with respect to monetary relief defeat the goals of (b)(1) or (b)(2)? As we will see, the Supreme Court has since made the granting of opt-out rights mandatory in most class actions seeking monetary relief. *See Wal-Mart Stores, Inc. v. Dukes* [Part II], 131 S. Ct. 2541 (2011), at page 825, *infra*.

In contrast to Rule 23(b)(1)(A), which focuses on whether individual suits might expose the class opponent to possibly incompatible forms of relief, Rule 23(b)(1)(B) is concerned with the risk of prejudice to the class if individual members were to bring their own actions. For example, in *Lloyd v. City of Philadelphia*, 121 F.R.D. 246, 251 (E.D. Pa. 1988), a plaintiff class challenged a law mandating that certain categories of city workers belong to a union. The court held that (b)(1)(B) was satisfied because a ruling enjoining the law in a suit by one employee would likely be dispositive of the rights of other workers in the mandatory categories since the city had to treat all of these workers equally. Similarly, in *White v. National Football League*, 822 F. Supp. 1389, 1409 (D. Minn. 1993), *aff'd*, 41 F.3d 402 (8th Cir. 1994), *cert. denied*, 515 U.S. 1137 (1995), an antitrust class action challenging the NFL's employment practices was held to satisfy Rule 23(b)(1)(B) since an injunction restructuring the NFL's practices in an individual suit could prejudice similar challenges by other players. However, most courts hold that the mere risk of an adverse stare decisis effect from individual suits is not enough to trigger Rule 23(b)(1)(B). *See, e.g., Tilley v. TJX Cos., Inc.*, 345 F.3d 34, 40-43 (1st Cir. 2003). For if this were sufficient, virtually every class action would qualify under that provision, something probably not intended by the rule's drafters. *See* Jerold S. Solovy, Ronald L. Marner, Timothy J. Chorvat & David M. Feinberg, *Class Actions*, in 5 Moore's Federal Practice § 23.42[3][b] (3d ed. 2015).

One of the classic uses of Rule 23(b)(1)(B) involves cases in which class members have claims against a limited fund such as an insurance policy or a trust fund, for suits by individual claimants will deplete or exhaust that fund to the detriment of those claimants who might sue later. As the next case explains, however, there are limits to using the "limited fund" rationale to qualify an action under (b)(1)(B).

In re Telectronics Pacing Systems, Inc.

221 F.3d 870 (6th Cir. 2000)

MERRITT, Circuit Judge.

I.   Introduction and Summary

The traditional norm of our legal system is the adversary trial by an individual plaintiff claiming redress for a particular wrong. The question before us is how far the courts should go in allowing class action, mass tort cases to deviate from that tradition. More specifically, this appeal asks us to interpret and apply the recent Supreme Court class action case of *Ortiz v. Fibreboard Corp.*, 527 U.S. 815, 119 S. Ct. 2295 (1999). It holds that a "mandatory" class (a class that generally does not give individual notice to members or allow them to opt out) may not be certified, or a settlement approved, under Federal Rule of Civil Procedure 23(b)(1)(B) based simply on an unconventional "limited fund" created by the defendants through a settlement of their liability. (The traditional "limited fund" is a pool of money coming from an outside source, the amount of which is not subject to manipulation by the parties.) We must apply *Ortiz* to this class action claiming that defective pacemakers were implanted in the hearts of approximately 40,000 individuals. The appeal is from the district court's order certifying, on a "limited fund" rationale, a non-opt-out class and approving a mandatory class-action settlement of $57 million. Members of the class object to the settlement on grounds that it unfairly releases from liability the parent corporations of the manufacturers of the defective pacemakers which hold substantial assets, was not the result of arms-length negotiations among the interested parties and overcompensates the plaintiffs' lawyers as an incentive for them to settle the cases of absent class members. . . . We conclude that the Supreme Court's opinion in *Ortiz* . . . requires that the mandatory Rule 23(b)(1)(B) class certified by the district court here must be decertified and that the settlement approved by the district court must be disapproved.

In *Ortiz* the Supreme Court was again faced with a large class of asbestos claimants suing a manufacturer, which had in turn sued its two insurance carriers for funds to pay the claimants. Negotiations between the lawyers for the class and the manufacturer and the two insurance companies produced a settlement fund of $1.525 billion, contingent on certification under Rule 23(b)(1)(B) as a mandatory class, and approval of the settlement on a limited fund theory. The lower courts certified the claimants as a Rule 23(b)(1)(B) mandatory, non-opt-out class and approved the settlement because they believed that on balance it was in the best interests of the claimants who otherwise stood to lose the fund should the insurance companies win their pending no-coverage cases.

The Supreme Court reversed the Fifth Circuit in *Ortiz* by a 7 to 2 vote. The Court concluded that applicants for certification on a limited fund theory under Rule 23(b)(1)(B) "must show that the fund is limited by more than the agreement of the parties." The Court reached this conclusion because such a mandatory class-action settlement runs head long into long-established principles of due process, the Seventh Amendment right of trial by jury and the "principle of general application in Anglo-American jurisprudence that one is not bound by a judgment *in personam* in a litigation in which he is not a designated party or to which he has not been made a party by service of process."

One of the problems with compromising the rights of absent class members under Rule 23(b)(1)(B) through global mass tort settlements distributed on a mandatory basis arises from the perverse set of incentives it may provide defendants and class action lawyers—"the potential for gigantic fees." The defendants may be able to settle cases by providing, relatively speaking, a small amount of money for seriously injured class members while providing large attorney fees for lawyers for the class as an inducement to settlement. If the courts deviate very far from the traditional or strict limited fund theory by allowing a limited fund to be created purely by settlement, the legal system runs the risk of eliminating adversary trials conducted to redress wrongs individually by actual plaintiffs through a process by which defendants pay off a small group of plaintiffs' class action lawyers who actually represent other parties. . . .

II.   *Facts and Procedural History*

This products liability class-action litigation was brought on behalf of individuals implanted with the Telectronics Accufix Atrial "J" pacemaker lead. The lead is implanted in the atrium of the heart as part of a pacemaker device used to restore normal heartbeat. It was determined in 1994 that some of the lead wires had a tendency to break, coming through the polyurethane coating and potentially causing injury to the heart and blood vessels. TPLC-manufactured leads of this type were implanted in about 40,000 persons world-wide, including about 25,000 persons in the United States.

Defendant TPLC, a Delaware corporation, manufactured and distributed these leads in the United States between 1988 and 1994. Defendant Telectronic Pacing Systems, also a Delaware corporation, is the sole owner of TPLC. . . . Additional named defendants are Pacific Dunlop, Ltd. and Nucleus, Ltd, both Australian companies. . . . Nucleus and Pacific Dunlop were made defendants on the ground that they are alter egos or agents of their subsidiary, TPLC. . . .

Numerous state and federal court actions were filed against defendants. Many of the suits became part of a multi-district litigation proceeding in the Southern District of Ohio. The amended and consolidated master class action complaint asserted claims against TPLC, Nucleus and Pacific Dunlop for negligence, strict liability, failure to warn, breach of implied and express warranty, fraud, medical monitoring, fear of future product failure, intentional and negligent infliction of emotional distress, loss of consortium, misrepresentation and compensatory and punitive damages. A 17-member Plaintiff's Steering Committee was appointed by the district court to coordinate discovery and other pretrial proceedings on behalf of all transferred plaintiffs. . . .

The Australian defendants, Pacific Dunlop and Nucleus, moved to dismiss for lack of personal jurisdiction. In February 1997, the district court denied the motion, finding that the companies maintained sufficient contacts with the United States for the court to exercise personal jurisdiction over them. . . .

Defendants and the Plaintiffs' Steering Committee entered into settlement negotiations. . . . The parties filed a joint motion for certification of a mandatory class and approval of the proposed settlement. On July 22, 1998, the district court preliminarily approved the class action settlement proposed by the parties. TPLC's assets, determined to be about $78 million, were divided into four funds: (1) a Patient Benefit Fund of about $47 million out of which class member[s] would be compensated; (2) an Operating Fund of about $20 million that TPLC will use to pay operating expenses; (3) a Litigation Fund of about $7 million that TPLC would use to pay expenses related to non-lead-related litigation and (4) a Reserve Fund of $4 million to be used by defendants to pay expenses in other, unrelated litigation. Pacific Dunlop agreed to contribute $10 million to the Patient Benefit Fund, raising that fund to $57 million and the parties agreed that any unused funds from the other three funds would be added to the Patient Benefit Fund. The defendants and Plaintiffs' Steering Committee also determined categories of class members, based on the extent of injury to date and whether a lead was still implanted in the class member.

The district court approved the settlement and ultimately certified the class as a mandatory, non-opt-out class under Rule 23(b)(1)(B) as requested by the parties. The district court certified the no-opt out class because it found, based on economic information provided by TPLC, that there was a "limited fund" from which injured plaintiffs could be paid. The district court stated that it did not take into account the assets of Nucleus or Pacific Dunlop in determining the total assets available to the settlement fund because (1) it believed that the court was unlikely to obtain jurisdiction over the Australian companies, (2) the time and cost of litigating against a foreign defendant made litigation infeasible and (3) the jury in [a one-week nonbinding] summary trial had not found the two Australian companies liable. . . .*

As required by Rule 23(e), the district court held a fairness hearing. It reviewed the settlement for fairness, reasonableness and adequacy and found that the settlement as a whole satisfied the standards of Rule 23(e). Fifty-three class members objected to the settlement.

The district court also approved an award of 28%, or about $19 million, of the net Patient Benefit Fund as attorney fees. As part of the settlement agreement, defendants did not object to this fee request. The attorney fee amount was objected to by various unnamed class members.

Five different groups of class members have appealed the approval of the settlement and their appeals have been consolidated. . . .

III.   Discussion

Applying the characteristics of appropriate limited fund actions after *Ortiz*, we are compelled to reject certification of the class under subsection (b)(1)(B) and hold that approval of the settlement was an abuse of discretion. *Ortiz* instructed the lower courts to look to the "traditional" or historical nature of certification under Rule 23(b)(1)(B) and stated that courts should not stray too far from these traditional models in determining if certification is suitable under Rule 23(b)(1)(B). *Ortiz*, 119 S. Ct. at 2311 ("[T]he greater the leniency in departing from the historical limited fund model, the greater the likelihood of abuse. . . ."). As emphasized in *Ortiz*, the limited fund concept in subsection (b)(1)(B) contemplates a fixed fund in the traditional sense: a fixed resource, such as a mineral deposit, or a fixed amount of money, such as a trust.[5] The traditional and most common use of subsection (b)(1)(B) class actions is in "limited fund" cases where claims are aggregated against a *res* or preexisting fund insufficient to satisfy all claims. . . .

. . . Clearly *any* potentially large judgment creates the risk of depletion of a defendant's assets and sets up the possibility that, as a practical matter, adjudication may be "dispositive of the interest of other members not parties to the adjudications" or may "substantially impair or impede their ability to protect their interests." FED. R. CIV. P. 23(b)(1)(B). *Ortiz* confirmed that a literal reading of the Rule is inappropriate and that mandatory class treatment is to be confined to a

---

* [As the district court later noted, while "the summary jury trial is merely advisory, of no binding effect on anyone, . . . it is a settlement device used to assist the Parties in assessing the results of a trial on the merits. From the experience of this Court in other cases, . . . the results have been very instructive in helping the parties negotiate settlements." *In re Telectronics Pacing Sys., Inc.*, 137 F. Supp. 2d 985, 993 n.8 (S.D. Ohio 2001).—EDS.]

5. A limited fund exists when a fixed asset or piece of property exists in which all class members have a preexisting interest. . . . Classic illustrations include claimants to trust assets, a bank account, insurance proceeds, [and] company assets in a liquidation sale. . . .

narrow category of cases. The Supreme Court directed that when looking to limited fund actions, the "object was to stay close to the historical model."

Drawing from the paradigmatic examples identified above, the *Ortiz* Court articulated three "common characteristics" of limited fund class actions that the drafters of Rule 23(b)(1)(B) "must have assumed would be at least a sufficient set of conditions to justify binding absent members of a class." "The first and most distinctive characteristic," the Court explained, "is that the totals of the aggregated liquidated claims and the fund available for satisfying them, set definitely at their maximums, demonstrate the inadequacy of the fund to pay all the claims." The second characteristic of typical limited fund cases is that "the whole of the inadequate fund was to be devoted to the overwhelming claims." "Third, the claimants identified by a common theory of recovery were treated equitably among themselves." The Court reasoned that these characteristics should be treated "as presumptively necessary, and not merely sufficient, to satisfy the limited fund rationale for a mandatory class action."

Significantly, the *Ortiz* Court explicitly refused to decide the ultimate issue of whether, even if these three requirements were met, Rule 23(b)(1)(B) may ever be used to aggregate individual tort claims. Because we find that the settlement in the instant case fails to satisfy all three characteristics of limited fund actions, we need not answer the ultimate question either. We note, however, that the applicability of Rule 23(b)(1)(B) to a fund purporting to liquidate actual and potential tort claims is "subject to question." As the Supreme Court explained, the drafters "would have thought such an application of the Rule surprising." Moreover, as we shall explain in more detail later, there are "serious constitutional concerns that come with any attempt to aggregate individual tort claims on a limited fund rationale."

Release of the Parent Companies

The primary problem with this settlement is that it fails to meet the first "traditional" characteristic set out by the Court in *Ortiz*: "the totals of the aggregated liquidated claims and the fund available for satisfying them, set definitely at their maximums, demonstrate the inadequacy of the fund to pay all the claims." There are no "liquidated" claims here, so the parties must first estimate the total potential liability to TPLC. TPLC maintains that it has inadequate funds to cover even its legal expenses if the claims are brought individually, let alone satisfy any judgments against it. The parties to this appeal apparently agree that TPLC, standing alone, does not have the necessary assets to cover the expected liability. However, establishing the "fund available" for satisfying the claims is the crux of the problem, because TPLC seeks to exclude the assets of its parent corporations from the calculation.

Specifically, the objectors contend that this is not a true "limited fund" case because the Australian defendants—the parent companies of TPLC—are solvent and potentially liable and their assets should not be excluded when determining the amount available to class members as redress for their injuries. . . .

Although we have no factual findings from the district court on the matter, it appears undisputed that the two companies do not have "limited funds" in the traditional sense and would be able to bear the expense of litigation and pay damages if found liable. TPLC informed the district court, however, that it would not settle without the two Australian companies being dismissed. The district court, believing that the settlement was in jeopardy if it did not agree to this part of the settlement, approved it. The district court acknowledged that only TPLC was a limited fund, but held that because TPLC would not settle unless Pacific Dunlop and Nucleus were released, "the loss of settlement can constitute a 'risk' within the meaning of Rule 23(b)(1)(B)" justifying certification under that subsection. Without settlement, the district court worried that some class members might be unable to recover for their injuries because TPLC might run out of funds before all class members could be compensated for their injuries and the parent corporations might not be found liable. . . .

. . . The problem with the district court's approach is that it confuses the ability of plaintiffs to prevail on the merits with the ability to pay a judgment. The issues are separate. If not for the settlement, there would be no limited fund because the class members could pursue their claims against the Australian defendants individually if they chose, as well as against TPLC. . . . We cannot approve a settlement that releases these parent companies from all liability and leaves class members with no recourse against them.

Although not entirely clear, the district court also may have been suggesting that the assets of all three companies—TPLC, Nucleus and Pacific Dunlop—together constituted a limited fund due to the risk that the latter two companies would not be held liable by a jury. In *Ortiz*, the Supreme Court explained the ways in which the insurance assets at issue in that case could have been limited. First, "[t]he insurance assets would obviously be 'limited' in the traditional sense if the total of the demonstrable claims would render the insurers insolvent, or if the policies provided aggregate limits falling short of that total." Because this type of traditional limitation was not present in *Ortiz*, the Court explained that "any limit of the insurance asset here had to be a product of potentially unlimited policy coverage discounted by the risk that Fibreboard would ultimately lose the coverage dispute litigation." The Court did not decide whether "[t]his sense of limit as a value discounted by risk," which it explained to be a step removed from the historical model, would suffice for limited fund treatment. Instead, assuming that such a risk analysis would suffice, the Court concluded that it had not been undertaken in that case. As in *Ortiz*, the district court in the instant case did not undertake an independent risk analysis, but instead accepted the $10 million settlement figure as representing the maximum amount the Australian defendants could be required to pay claimants, which is plainly improper. Moreover, we are doubtful that this "value discounted by risk" theory is sufficient to support a finding that the fund is limited, for there is always risk inherent in litigation.

Threat of Bankruptcy

In addition, the threat of bankruptcy alone, an argument put forth by TPLC as a primary reason to approve the limited fund settlement, cannot be the basis for finding a limited fund. Presumably *all* companies have limited funds at some point—there is always the possibility that a large mass tort action or other litigation will put a company into bankruptcy. Should that eventuality threaten, we have a comprehensive bankruptcy scheme in this country for just such an occurrence. Simply demonstrating that there is a possibility, even a likelihood, that bankruptcy might at some point occur cannot be the basis for finding that there is a "limited fund" in an ongoing corporate concern. . . .

Lack of Arms-length Negotiations

We also cannot approve this settlement because it appears not to be the result of arms-length negotiation among the parties. A significant aspect of this settlement appears to be to limit the liability of the parent companies. The bootstrapping of a Rule 23(b)(3) class into a Rule 23(b)(1)(B) class is impermissible and highlights the problem with defining and certifying class actions by reference to a proposed settlement. *Ortiz* makes clear that subsection (b)(1)(B) was not intended for the lawyers representing the parties essentially to "create" a limited fund by threatening that there would be no settlement unless the deepest pockets are totally released from liability. We therefore agree with the objectors that the Australian parent companies should not be totally released from liability based solely on agreement of the parties and for that reason alone this settlement cannot be approved.

We do not decide whether the other two traditional characteristics of a limited fund case are met here because the first requirement is not met.

Constitutional Considerations

The Supreme Court in *Ortiz* also articulated several constitutional considerations compromised in a non-opt-out class action regarding a mass tort. Both Seventh Amendment jury trial rights and the Fifth Amendment due process principle regarding the right to a "day in court" are implicated in aggregating individual claims sounding in tort. The Supreme Court has repeatedly emphasized the importance of allowing affected persons to opt out of representative suits. *See, e.g., Phillips Petro. Co. v. Shutts*, 472 U.S. 797, 811-812 (1985); *Mullane v. Central Hanover Bank & Trust Co.*, 339 U.S. 306, 314-315 (1950); *Hansberry v. Lee*, 311 U.S. 32, 42-45 (1940).

Class certification, whether mandatory or not, necessarily compromises various rights of absent class members. Rule 23(b)(3), with its notice and opt-out provisions, strikes a balance between the value of aggregating similar claims and the right of an individual to have his or her day in court. Certification under subsection (b)(1)(B), which does not include these protections, must be carefully scrutinized and sparingly utilized. The Supreme Court also stressed that in a proper interpretation of Rule 23, principles of sound judicial management and constitutional considerations of due process and the right to jury trial all lead to the conclusion that in an action for money damages class members are entitled to personal notice and an opportunity to opt out. This entitlement can be overcome only when individual suits would confound the interests of other plaintiffs, such as with a limited fund that must be distributed ratably or an injunction that affects all plaintiffs similarly. . . .

Generally, due process requires that class members bringing particularized tort claims for money damages be provided an opportunity to opt-out of the class. *Shutts*, 472 U.S. at 811-812 & n. 3. From a due process point of view, the opt-out choice is of less concern when there is a definite fund or res from which plaintiffs will receive damages. When there is a true limited fund, the only question is how to divide up the pie. Where defendants have sufficient funds to compensate class members through individual litigation, however, as Pacific Dunlop and Nucleus apparently do, the choice to opt-out becomes much more meaningful and due process demands that class members be afforded that right where possible. If certain plaintiffs wish to opt-out and take their chances at suing a foreign corporation, due process would seem to require that they be allowed to do so absent strong considerations to the contrary not present here. . . .

IV.   *Conclusion*

In light of our disposition, all other issues are pretermitted. Our holding here does not end the matter or foreclose injured plaintiffs from recovery. If TPLC is or becomes insolvent, then, as discussed above, bankruptcy is a partial solution. This would leave open for adjudication the liability of the parent companies, which all parties recognize to be the defendants with the deepest pockets. Our decision here, therefore, should not adversely affect the members of the class who have real injuries to be redressed and compensated.

While there are differences between the settlement in *Ortiz* and the one at issue here, the settlement as approved strays too far from the traditional model and undermines many of the protections built into Rule 23. Moreover, the form of the settlement calls into question its fairness and raises constitutional concerns. While we do not decide if a limited fund class, or any type of class certification, can work in this case, the settlement cannot deprive class members of the protections available under Rule 23 generally and the traditional model of limited fund cases set forth by the Supreme Court in *Ortiz*. For that reason we reverse and remand to the district court.

NOTES AND QUESTIONS

1. Limiting the "limited fund" concept.   What did the *In re Telectronics* court mean when it said, "[t]he bootstrapping of a Rule 23(b)(3) class into a Rule 23(b)(1)(B) class is impermissible"? In the traditional "limited fund" case, when the total of all claims exceeds the size of the fund, there is a risk that those who sue first may exhaust the fund, depriving others of the ability to recover. How was this case different? In *Ortiz v. Fibreboard Corp.*, 527 U.S. 815 (1999), the Court limited the use of the limited-fund concept in mass tort cases — cases that would otherwise qualify only under Rule 23(b)(3) — where class members would have a right to opt out and litigate their claims separately. *Oritz* suggested that expanding the limited-fund concept to embrace mass tort cases was not only contrary to the purposes of Rule 23, but might also deprive class members of their constitutional rights. First, as to Rule 23,

> the Advisory Committee did not contemplate that the mandatory class action codified in subdivision (b)(1)(B) would be used to aggregate unliquidated tort claims on a limited fund rationale. . . . While the Advisory Committee focused much attention on the amenability of Rule 23(b)(3) to such cases, the Committee's debates are silent about resolving tort claims under a mandatory limited fund rationale under Rule 23(b)(1)(B). It is simply implausible that the Advisory Committee, so concerned about the potential difficulties posed by dealing with mass tort cases under Rule 23(b)(3), with its provisions for notice and the right to opt out, . . . would have uncritically assumed that mandatory versions of such class actions, lacking such protections, could be certified under Rule 23(b)(1)(B). We do not . . . decide the ultimate question whether Rule 23(b)(1)(B) may ever be used to aggregate individual tort claims. . . . But we do recognize that the Committee would have thought such an application of the Rule surprising, and take this as a good reason to limit any surprise by presuming that the Rule's historical antecedents identify requirements.

Ortiz, 527 U.S. at 843-845.

Second, said the *Ortiz* Court, "serious constitutional concerns" would arise, under the Seventh Amendment and the Due Process Clause, if the "limited fund" concept were routinely applied in mass tort cases. *Id.* at 845. The Seventh Amendment issue arises only if the class action is brought for the purpose of settling rather than trying the case:

> [T]he certification of a mandatory class followed by settlement of its action for money damages obviously implicates the Seventh Amendment jury trial rights of absent class members. . . . By its nature, . . . a mandatory settlement-only class action with legal issues and future claimants compromises their Seventh Amendment rights without their consent.

Id. at 845-846. Yet even in nonsettlement cases in which a jury trial may occur, use of the limited-fund rationale may violate class members' due process rights:

> [M]andatory class actions aggregating damage claims implicate the due process "principle of general application in Anglo-American jurisprudence that one is not bound by a judgment *in personam* in a litigation in which he is not designated as a party or to which he has not been made a party by service of process," *Hansberry v. Lee*, 311 U.S. 32, 40 (1940), it being "our 'deep-rooted historic tradition that everyone should have his own day in court,'" *Martin v. Wilks*, 490 U.S. 755, 762 (1989). . . .
>
> The inherent tension between representative suits and the day-in-court ideal is only magnified if applied to damages claims gathered in a mandatory class. Unlike

Rule 23(b)(3) class members, objectors to the collectivism of a mandatory subdivision (b)(1)(B) action have no inherent right to abstain. The legal rights of absent class members (which in a class like this one would include claimants who by definition may be unidentifiable when the class is certified) are resolved regardless either of their consent, or, in a class with objectors, their express wish to the contrary.

527 U.S. at 846-847.

2. *The* In re Telectronics *limited fund.* While *Ortiz* stopped short of ruling that the limited-fund rationale may never be used to litigate unliquidated tort claims on a class basis under Rule 23(b)(1)(B), the Court held that the claimed limited fund must at a minimum satisfy the three criteria discussed by the Sixth Circuit in *In re Telectronics.* What was wrong with the limited fund approved by the district court in *In re Telectronics?* Would the result have been the same if the principal defendants were bankrupt and the only other defendants were their insurance companies? Did the court of appeals' opinion leave open any other way the plaintiffs might have established the existence of a limited fund? As we will see, since *Ortiz* was decided the Supreme Court has cast further doubt on the propriety of using the limited-fund rationale to qualify a class action under Rule 23(b)(1), rather than having to use Rule 23(b)(3). *See Wal-Mart Stores, Inc. v. Dukes* [Part II], at page 825, *infra.*

3. *The scope of class members' opt-out rights.*   Earlier we discussed the extent to which due process requires notice and opt-out rights for class members, noting that some courts have read *Ortiz* as mandating opt-out rights whenever substantial damage claims are involved. *See* Note 2, page 762, *supra.* In *In re Telectronics,* how broadly did the Sixth Circuit read *Ortiz?* Under the Sixth Circuit's approach, would opt-out rights have been required in *Boggs v. Divested Atomic Corp.*, page 806, *supra?*

PROBLEMS

9-8. Several plaintiffs sued C&L, a major accounting firm consisting of 1,200 partners and principals, alleging that C&L should have discovered that the financial statements of one of its clients, Far-Out Inc., were fraudulent. During the period of the fraud, C&L instead issued "clean" audit statements on which the plaintiffs relied to their detriment in dealing with Far-Out. The plaintiffs seek damages under federal and state law. Fearing that C&L's insurance funds and partnership assets will be insufficient to satisfy the judgments that may be entered against C&L, plaintiffs seek certification of a defendant class consisting of all C&L partners and principals, with the goal of reaching their personal assets. Under applicable law, each partner and principal of C&L is jointly and severally liable for any judgment against C&L, and for the negligence of any other partner or principal. C&L's professional liability insurance provides limited coverage for suits against partners and principals. Until these policy limits are exhausted, the policy covers both the cost of defending a suit against a partner or principal and any judgment rendered. Assuming that a defendant class consisting of all C&L partners and principals meets the requirements of Rule 23(a), does it satisfy 23(b)? *See In re Phar-Mor, Inc. Securities Litig.*, 875 F. Supp. 277 (W.D. Pa. 1994).

9-9. Forty-eight inmates at Jackson State Prison sued the prison warden, the guards, and the guards' union, alleging that the defendants conspired to cause a riot at the prison and a subsequent lockdown. During these incidents, some of the inmates were injured and many suffered damage to items of personal property. The plaintiffs have moved for certification of a class consisting of the 10,000 inmates who were incarcerated in the prison at the time of the riot. On behalf of the class, plaintiffs seek an injunction barring defendants from authorizing, ratifying, or participating in any future conduct designed to bring about a riot or a lockdown, and from threatening or imposing lockdowns except where legally justified. Plaintiffs also seek damages on behalf of the class to be paid from defendants' personal assets. Most of the defendants have no significant assets and some may have common law immunity from damages liability. On what bases might plaintiffs seek certification of a class? What arguments would the defendants make to oppose certification? *See In re Jackson Lockdown/MCO Cases*, 107 F.R.D. 703 (E.D. Mich. 1985).

A NOTE ON SETTLEMENT CLASSES

In re Telectronics involved a "settlement" or "settlement only" class. Before certification was sought, the Plaintiffs' Steering Committee and defendants had reached a settlement covering 40,000 people. To make this global settlement binding on all members of the proposed class, the parties then filed "a joint motion for certification of a mandatory class and approval of the proposed settlement." In *Amchem Products, Inc. v. Windsor*, 521 U.S. 591, 618-622 (1997), decided several years before *In re Telectronics*, the Supreme Court had recognized the legitimacy of "settlement only" classes, even though they are not mentioned in Rule 23. However, the Court made clear that such classes—and any subclasses (see page 790, *supra*)—may be certified only if they meet the strict requirements of Rule 23(a) and (b). In addition, any settlement must be approved in accordance with 23(e). *Amchem* warned that "proposed settlement classes sometimes warrant more, not less, caution on the question of certification" than ordinary classes. *Id.* at 620 n.16. This is due partly to the fact that in contrast to most class actions, the class "opponent" in the settlement context favors rather than resists certification of the class. As a result, any defects in the proposed class may be more difficult for a court to detect. In addition, there is the danger that class counsel, moved by the prospect of receiving a sizable fee, will agree to a settlement that is less than optimal for the class. This risk is heightened if the settlement is reached before full discovery, for class counsel may not be fully aware of the nature and extent of class members' claims. As one court observed, settlement classes create especially lucrative opportunities for putative class attorneys to generate fees for themselves without any effective monitoring by class members who have not yet been apprised of the pendency of the action. Moreover, because the court does not appoint a class counsel until the case is certified, attorneys jockeying for position might attempt to cut a deal with the defendants by underselling the plaintiffs' claims relative to other attorneys. Unauthorized settlement negotiations occurring before the certification determination thus create the possibility of negotiation from a position of weakness by the attorney who purports to represent the class. Pre-certification negotiations also hamper a court's ability to review the true value of the settlement or the legal services after the fact.

In re General Motors Corp. Pick-Up Truck Fuel Tank Prods. Liab. Litig., 55 F.3d 768, 788 (3d Cir.), *cert. denied*, 516 U.S. 824 (1995).

At one time courts were more lenient in approving a class for settlement purposes, on the theory that the class action was only "provisional," "temporary," or "conditional" in the sense that it depended on what happened with the settlement efforts. Yet the ultimate stakes in such suits are potentially the same as in other class actions — namely a binding disposition of the class members' claims. Rule 23(c) was thus amended in 2003 to delete its reference to "conditional" classes, recognizing that the need for judicial scrutiny is as great — if not greater — in the settlement context as in other class suits. If a settlement class is certified and settlement efforts later collapse, the parties are free to continue the class suit for litigation purposes or they can move to have the class action dismissed without prejudice so that individual suits may be pursued. *See* 5 MOORE'S FEDERAL PRACTICE, *supra*, § 23.161[2][a].

b.   Rule 23(b)(2)

A class action will qualify under Rule 23(b)(2) if the party opposing the class has acted (or refused to act) on grounds generally applicable to the class, thereby making it appropriate for the court to issue injunctive or declaratory relief on behalf of the entire class. *Robidoux v. Celani*, 987 F.2d 931 (2d Cir. 1993), page 784, *supra*, a class suit to compel Vermont officials to process public assistance applications in a timely manner, met the requirements of (b)(2). In that case the class sought only declaratory and injunctive relief. As we have noted, problems may arise if the class in a purported (b)(2) action also seeks damages. Like 23(b)(1) actions, suits brought under (b)(2) are mandatory class actions in which there is no automatic right to opt out. *See* FED. R. CIV. P. 23(c)(2). If the plaintiffs seek damages as well as injunctive or declaratory relief, the question arises as to whether such "hybrid" actions can still qualify under (b)(2) if the damages sought are merely "incidental" to the request for injunctive or declaratory relief. Hybrid (b)(2) actions raise concerns similar to those posed by "limited fund" (b)(1)(B) cases. In both instances, if the suit is allowed to proceed under (b)(1) or (b)(2), it may dispose of monetary claims of class members who have been given no right to opt out and litigate their claims separately.

Wal-Mart Stores, Inc. v. Dukes [Part II]

131 S. Ct. 2541 (2011)

JUSTICE SCALIA delivered the opinion of the Court. . . .

[The facts of this case and the parts that addresses its failure to satisfy Rule 23(a)(2) appear at part C.1, page 792, *supra*. Part III, which follows, addresses Rule 23(b)(2).]

III

We also conclude that respondents' claims for backpay were improperly certified under Federal Rule of Civil Procedure 23(b)(2). Our opinion in *Ticor Title Ins. Co. v. Brown*, 511 U.S. 117, 121 (1994) *(per curiam)* expressed serious doubt about whether claims for monetary relief may be certified under that provision. We now hold that they may not, at least where (as here) the monetary relief is not incidental to the injunctive or declaratory relief.

A

Rule 23(b)(2) allows class treatment when "the party opposing the class has acted or refused to act on grounds that apply generally to the class, so that final injunctive relief or corresponding declaratory relief is appropriate respecting the class as a whole." One possible reading of this provision is that it applies *only* to requests for such injunctive or declaratory relief and does not authorize the class certification of monetary claims at all. We need not reach that broader question in this case, because we think that, at a minimum, claims for *individualized* relief (like the backpay at issue here) do not satisfy the Rule. The key to the (b)(2) class is "the indivisible nature of the injunctive or declaratory remedy warranted — the notion that the conduct is such that it can be enjoined or declared unlawful only as to all of the class members or as to none of them." In other words, Rule 23(b)(2) applies only when a single injunction or declaratory judgment would provide relief to each member of the class. It does not authorize class certification when each individual class member would be entitled to a *different* injunction or declaratory judgment against the defendant. Similarly, it does not authorize class certification when each class member would be entitled to an individualized award of monetary damages.

That interpretation accords with the history of the Rule. Because Rule 23 "stems from equity practice" that predated its codification, *Amchem Products, Inc. v. Windsor*, 521 U.S. 591, 613 (1997), in determining its meaning we have previously looked to the historical models on which the Rule was based. As we observed in *Amchem*, "[c]ivil rights cases against parties charged with unlawful, class-based discrimination are prime examples" of what (b)(2) is meant to capture. In particular, the Rule reflects a series of decisions involving challenges to racial segregation — conduct that was remedied by a single classwide order. In none of the cases cited by the Advisory Committee as examples of (b)(2)'s antecedents did the plaintiffs combine any claim for individualized relief with their classwide injunction. See Advisory Committee's Note, 39 F.R.D. 69, 102 (1966).

Permitting the combination of individualized and classwide relief in a (b)(2) class is also inconsistent with the structure of Rule 23(b). Classes certified under (b)(1) and (b)(2) share the most traditional justifications for class treatment—that individual adjudications would be impossible or unworkable, as in a (b)(1) class, or that the relief sought must perforce affect the entire class at once, as in a (b)(2) class. For that reason these are also mandatory classes: The Rule provides no opportunity for (b)(1) or (b)(2) class members to opt out, and does not even oblige the District Court to afford them notice of the action. Rule 23(b)(3), by contrast, is an "adventuresome innovation" of the 1966 amendments, framed for situations "in which 'class-action treatment is not as clearly called for.'" It allows class certification in a much wider set of circumstances but with greater procedural protections. Its only prerequisites are that "the questions of law or fact common to class members predominate over any questions affecting only individual members, and that a class action is superior to other available methods for fairly and efficiently adjudicating the controversy." Rule 23(b)(3). And unlike (b)(1) and (b)(2) classes, the (b)(3) class is not mandatory; class members are entitled to receive "the best notice that is practicable under the circumstances" and to withdraw from the class at their option. See Rule 23(c)(2)(B).

Given that structure, we think it clear that individualized monetary claims belong in Rule 23(b)(3). The procedural protections attending the (b)(3) class—predominance, superiority, mandatory notice, and the right to opt out—are missing from (b)(2) not because the Rule considers them unnecessary, but because it considers them unnecessary *to a (b)(2) class.* When a class seeks an indivisible injunction benefitting all its members at once, there is no reason to undertake a case-specific inquiry into whether class issues predominate or whether class action is a superior method of adjudicating the dispute. Predominance and superiority are self-evident. But with respect to each class member's individualized claim for money, that is not so—which is precisely why (b)(3) requires the judge to make findings about predominance and superiority before allowing the class. Similarly, (b)(2) does not require that class members be given notice and opt-out rights, presumably because it is thought (rightly or wrongly) that notice has no purpose when the class is mandatory, and that depriving people of their right to sue in this manner complies with the Due Process Clause. In the context of a class action predominantly for money damages we have held that absence of notice and opt-out violates due process. See *Phillips Petroleum Co. v. Shutts.* While we have never held that to be so where the monetary claims do not predominate, the serious possibility that it may be so provides an additional reason not to read Rule 23(b)(2) to include the monetary claims here.

B

Against that conclusion, respondents argue that their claims for backpay were appropriately certified as part of a class under Rule 23(b)(2) because those claims do not "predominate" over their requests for injunctive and declaratory relief. They rely upon the Advisory Committee's statement that Rule 23(b)(2) "does not extend to cases in which the appropriate final relief relates *exclusively or predominantly* to money damages." The negative implication, they argue, is that it *does* extend to cases in which the appropriate final relief relates only partially and nonpredominantly to money damages. Of course it is the Rule itself, not the Advisory Committee's description of it, that governs. And a mere negative inference does not in our view suffice to establish a disposition that has no basis in the Rule's text, and that does obvious violence to the Rule's structural features. The mere "predominance" of a proper (b)(2) injunctive claim does nothing to justify elimination of Rule 23(b)(3)'s procedural protections: It neither establishes the superiority of *class* adjudication over *individual* adjudication nor cures the notice and opt-out problems. We fail to see why the Rule should be read to nullify these protections whenever a plaintiff class, at its option, combines its monetary claims with a request—even a "predominating request"—for an injunction.

Respondents' predominance test, moreover, creates perverse incentives for class representatives to place at risk potentially valid claims for monetary relief. In this case, for example, the named plaintiffs declined to include employees' claims for compensatory damages in their complaint. That strategy of including only back-pay claims made it more likely that monetary relief would not "predominate." But it also created the possibility (if the predominance test were correct) that individual class members' compensatory-damages claims would be *precluded* by litigation they had no power to hold themselves apart from. If it were determined, for example, that a particular class member is not entitled to backpay because her denial of increased pay or a promotion was *not* the product of discrimination, that employee might be collaterally estopped from independently seeking compensatory damages based on that same denial. That possibility underscores the need for plaintiffs with individual monetary claims to decide *for themselves* whether to tie their fates to the class representatives' or go it alone—a choice Rule 23(b)(2) does not ensure that they have. . . .

Finally, respondents argue that their backpay claims are appropriate for a (b)(2) class action because a backpay award is equitable in nature. The latter may be true, but it is irrelevant. The Rule does not speak of "equitable" remedies generally but of injunctions and declaratory judgments. . . .

C

In *Allison v. Citgo Petroleum Corp.*, 151 F.3d 402, 415 (C.A.5 1998), the Fifth Circuit held that a (b)(2) class would permit the certification of monetary relief that is "incidental to requested injunctive or declaratory relief," which it defined as "damages that flow directly from liability to the class *as a whole* on the claims forming the basis of the injunctive or declaratory relief." In that court's view, such "incidental damage should not require additional hearings to resolve the disparate merits of each individual's case; it should neither introduce new substantial legal or factual issues, nor entail complex individualized determinations." We need not decide in this case whether there are any forms of "incidental" monetary relief that are consistent with the interpretation of Rule 23(b)(2) we have announced and that comply with the Due Process Clause. Respondents do not argue that they can satisfy this standard, and in any event they cannot.

Contrary to the Ninth Circuit's view, Wal-Mart is entitled to individualized determinations of each employee's eligibility for backpay. Title VII includes a detailed remedial scheme. If a plaintiff prevails in showing that an employer has discriminated against him in violation of the statute, the court "may enjoin the respondent from engaging in such unlawful employment practice, and order such affirmative action as may be appropriate, [including] reinstatement or hiring of employees, with or without backpay . . . or any other equitable relief as the court deems appropriate." But if the employer can show that it took an adverse employment action against an employee for any reason other than discrimination, the court cannot order the "hiring, reinstatement, or promotion of an individual as an employee, or the payment to him of any backpay."

We have established a procedure for trying pattern-or-practice cases that gives effect to these statutory requirements. When the plaintiff seeks individual relief such as reinstatement or backpay after establishing a pattern or practice of discrimination, "a district court must usually conduct additional proceedings . . . to determine the scope of individual relief." At this phase, the burden of proof will shift to the company, but it will have the right to raise any individual affirmative defenses it may have, and to "demonstrate that the individual applicant was denied an employment opportunity for lawful reasons."

The Court of Appeals believed that it was possible to replace such proceedings with Trial by Formula. A sample set of the class members would be selected, as to whom liability for sex discrimination and the backpay owing as a result would be determined in depositions supervised by a master. The percentage of claims determined to be valid would then be applied to the entire remaining class, and the number of (presumptively) valid claims thus derived would be multiplied by the average backpay award in the sample set to arrive at the entire class recovery—without further individualized proceedings. We disapprove that novel project. Because the Rules Enabling Act forbids interpreting Rule 23 to "abridge, enlarge or modify any substantive right," 28 U.S.C. § 2072(b), a class cannot be certified on the premise that Wal-Mart will not be entitled to litigate its statutory defenses to individual claims. And because the necessity of that litigation will prevent backpay from being "incidental" to the classwide injunction, respondents' class could not be certified even assuming, *arguendo*, that "incidental" monetary relief can be awarded to a 23(b)(2) class. . . .

JUSTICE GINSBURG, with whom JUSTICE BREYER, JUSTICE SOTOMAYOR, and JUSTICE KAGAN join, concurring in part and dissenting in part.

The class in this case, I agree with the Court, should not have been certified under Federal Rule of Civil Procedure 23(b)(2). The plaintiffs, alleging discrimination in violation of Title VII, seek monetary relief that is not merely incidental to any injunctive or declaratory relief that might be available. A putative class of this type may be certifiable under Rule 23(b)(3), if the plaintiffs show that common class questions "predominate" over issues affecting individuals—*e.g.*, qualification for, and the amount of, backpay or compensatory damages—and that a class action is "superior" to other modes of adjudication.

Whether the class the plaintiffs describe meets the specific requirements of Rule 23(b)(3) is not before the Court, and I would reserve that matter for consideration and decision on remand.[1] . . .

NOTES AND QUESTIONS

1. *Due process and individual notice.* In *Phillips Petroleum Co. v. Shutts*, 472 U.S. 797 (1985), page 755, *supra*, it was unclear whether the Due Process Clause requires that class members be given notice and the right to opt out whenever damages are a significant part of the relief sought in a class action. Did the Court finally answer this question in *Wal-Mart*, or did it rest its decision on other grounds?

2. *Rule 23(b)(2) and individualized relief.* The Court unanimously agreed that in a (b)(2) class action, claims for "individualized relief"—as opposed to "classwide relief"—may never be entertained. On what basis does the Court reach this conclusion? What were the claims for individualized relief in this case? May there be less of a need to proceed on a class basis when class members have their own individualized claims for damages? Will this always be true? Does the Court's insistence that if such suits are to proceed on a class basis, they must be certified under (b)(3) rather than (b)(2), allow class members—rather than the class representatives or the court that administers the suit—to individually decide whether they wish to proceed on a class basis? If monetary damages could be sought in a (b)(2) action so long as they do not "predominate" over the claims for declaratory and injunctive relief, what might class representatives and class counsel be tempted to do so as to ensure that the suit will be certified under (b)(2) rather than (b)(3)? While courts sometimes give (b)(2) class members the opportunity to opt out—as did the district court here with respect to the claims for punitive damages—this is neither a matter of right in a (b)(2) action nor is it routinely granted just because money damages are sought.

3. *Rule 23(b)(1) actions.* Even though *Wal-Mart* was a (b)(2) action, does its reasoning and much of its discussion likewise apply to those (b)(1) class actions in which class members seek individualized monetary recovery as well as relief that is common to the class? This was the case in *Boggs v. Divested Atomic Corp.*, 141 F.R.D. 58 (S.D. Ohio 1991), page 806, *supra*, in which the class of residents living near a nuclear power plant sought individual damages for emotional distress

---

1. The plaintiffs requested Rule 23(b)(3) certification as an alternative, should their request for (b)(2) certification fail.

and diminution of property value, in addition to injunctive relief involving plant cleanup, medical monitoring, and nuisance abatement. In light of *Wal-Mart*, was the *Boggs* court's holding that class members could assert their damages claims in their (b)(1)(A) class action proper?

4. *"Incidental" monetary relief.*   Does *Wal-Mart* absolutely rule out the possibility that a class action can be certified under Rule 23(b)(2) when monetary relief is being sought? Might there be times when the monetary relief is sufficiently "incidental to requested injunctive or declaratory relief" that use of a non-opt-out (b)(2) action would be proper? *Wal-Mart*, 131 S. Ct. at 2560. The Court cited *Allison v. Citgo Petroleum Corp.*, 151 F.3d 402 (5th Cir. 1998), which suggested that (b)(2) would be permissible in an "incidental" damages case. The *Allison* court explained that

> incidental damages should be only those to which class members automatically would be entitled once liability to the class (or subclass) as a whole is established. . . . [S]uch damages should at least be capable of computation by means of objective standards and not dependent in any significant way on the intangible, subjective differences of each class member's circumstances. Liability for incidental damages should not require additional hearings to resolve the disparate merits of each individual's case; it should neither introduce new and substantial legal or factual issues, nor entail complex individualized determinations.

Allison, 151 F.3d at 415. *See also In re Monumental Life Ins. Co.*, 365 F.3d 408, 414-420 (5th Cir.), *cert. denied*, 543 U.S. 870 (2004) (approving use of 23(b)(2) under *Allison*'s test where "[t]he prevalence of variables common to the class makes damages computation virtually a mechanical task"); *Arnold v. United Artists Theatre Circuit, Inc.*, 158 F.R.D. 439, 450-453 (N.D. Cal. 1994) (certifying class action under Rule 23(b)(2) when plaintiffs' claims for statutory minimum damages of $250 were deemed merely incidental to their claims for injunctive relief). Assuming that such relief may still be permissible in a (b)(2) action, did the backpay sought by the would-be plaintiff class in *Wal-Mart* qualify as "incidental"? Even if at first blush it did not so qualify, did the named plaintiffs suggest that Wal-Mart's total liability for backpay could be determined in a way that would satisfy *Allison v. Citgo*'s test for "incidental," *i.e.*, by not requiring "additional hearings to resolve the disparate merits of each individual's case"? *Allison*, 151 F.3d at 415. Why did the Court suggest that use of plaintiffs' proposed Trial by Formula solution might violate the Rules Enabling Act, 28 U.S.C. § 2072(b)? *See* Chapter VI, part D. 2, *supra*.

5. *The premise of cohesiveness.*   An unstated premise of (b)(2) actions is that the class is sufficiently cohesive and homogeneous that the members' individual rights will not be sacrificed by requiring them to litigate on a class basis. Lack of cohesiveness may defeat a (b)(2) class action even if, in contrast to *Wal-Mart*, no individual monetary relief is sought. In *Barnes v. American Tobacco Co.*, 161 F.3d 127 (3d Cir. 1998), *cert. denied*, 526 U.S. 1114 (1999), the court cited a lack of cohesiveness in rejecting a (b)(2) class action for medical monitoring brought against tobacco companies by a class of cigarette smokers. The court agreed that

the relief sought—"the establishment of a court-supervised program through which class members would undergo periodic medical examinations in order to promote the early detection of diseases caused by smoking"—was injunctive in nature. 161 F.3d at 132. Yet, noting that in Rule "23(b)(2) class actions . . . the class claims must be cohesive," the court concluded that "addiction, causation, the defenses of comparative and contributory negligence, the need for medical monitoring and the statute of limitations present too many individual issues to permit certification. . . . These disparate issues make class treatment inappropriate." *Id.* at 142-143. We noted earlier that one requirement for a (b)(3) action is that questions common to the class "predominate over" those issues that affect only individual members. By insisting on "cohesiveness," have the courts read a similar requirement into Rule 23(b)(2)?

6. *Courts' options in hybrid cases.* The *Wal-Mart* Court held that in a hybrid class action in which the plaintiffs assert individualized monetary claims along with claims for declaratory or injunctive relief, the monetary claims cannot be heard in a (b)(2) action. Instead, if they are to be heard on a class basis, it must be done under (b)(3). There are several ways a federal court can deal with this situation.

> The first option is certifying the class under Rule 23(b)(3) for all proceedings. Rule 23(b)(3) permits class certification when "questions of law or fact common to the members of the class predominate over any questions affecting only individual members, and that a class action is superior to other available methods for the fair and efficient adjudication of the controversy." In this category of lawsuit, the class members may seek either predominantly legal or equitable remedies, but each member must share common questions of law or fact with the rest of the class, therefore making class-wide adjudication of the common questions efficient compared to repetitive individual litigation of the same questions. In contrast to Rule 23(b)(2), however, certification under Rule 23(b)(3) entails mandatory personal notice and opportunity to opt out for all class members. . . .
>
> The second option is divided certification. The district court could certify a Rule 23(b)(2) class for the portion of the case addressing equitable relief and a Rule 23(b)(3) class for the portion of the case addressing damages. This avoids the due process problems of certifying the entire case under Rule 23(b)(2) by introducing the Rule 23(b)(3) protections of personal notice and opportunity to opt out for the damages claims.

Lemon v. International Union of Operating Eng'rs, Local No. 139, 216 F.3d 577, 581-582 (7th Cir. 2000). The *Lemon* court cited a third option—certifying the entire action under (b)(2) for both monetary and equitable remedies but providing *all* class members with personal notice and an opportunity to opt out. Did the district court in *Wal-Mart* in effect use this option with respect to the class members' punitive damages claims? Does this route give prospective class members the same protections they would have in a (b)(3) certification? Are the criteria for certifying a (b)(3) class more sensitive to class members' interests than those that apply under (b)(1) and (b)(2)? Might this explain why *Wal-Mart* specified that (b)(3) must be used in these cases?

A NOTE ON THE PRECLUSIVE EFFECT OF CLASS ACTION JUDGMENTS

The *Wal-Mart* Court, in Part III.B of its opinion, noted that class representatives often assert only some of the claims class members may have against the opposing party, leaving other claims to be litigated by class members individually. In *Wal-Mart*, the named plaintiffs thus included class members' claims for backpay but omitted their claims for compensatory damages. In other settings, a class may sue for declaratory and injunctive relief while omitting any claims that members may have for monetary relief.

Under normal principles of claim preclusion, a party cannot "split" his claims in this way. Instead, he must assert all of the factually related claims he has against an opposing party in a single suit. *See* Chapter XIII, part A, *infra*. Class actions are an exception to this rule. Courts have recognized that not all claims class members may have against an opposing party are necessarily suitable for litigation on a class basis, even if they all arise from the same underlying transaction or occurrence. Such omitted claims may therefore be sued upon by class members in a later suit, unless perhaps class members were advised by the court that they had to litigate those claims by intervening as named parties in the class action. *See, e.g., Cooper v. Federal Reserve Bank of Richmond*, 467 U.S. 867, 873-874, 880-881 (1984) (class action seeking damages for alleged "pattern and practice" of discrimination did not bar later suits by class members seeking damages for having been discriminated against individually); *see also Hiser v. Franklin*, 94 F.3d 1287, 1291 (9th Cir. 1996), *cert. denied*, 520 U.S. 1103 (1997); *Fortner v. Thomas*, 983 F.2d 1024, 1031 (11th Cir. 1993); *Robinson v. Lattimore*, 946 F.2d 1566 (D.C. Cir. 1991) (per curiam); *Wright v. Collins*, 766 F.2d 841, 847-849 (4th Cir. 1985); *Crowder v. Lash*, 687 F.2d 996, 1007-1009 (7th Cir. 1982); *Johnson v. General Motors Corp.*, 598 F.2d 432, 437 (5th Cir. 1979); 18A Charles Alan Wright, Arthur R. Miller & Edward H. Cooper, Federal Practice and Procedure § 4455 (2d ed. 2002 & Supp. 2015).

However, once a class action goes to judgment, specific issues that were litigated and decided in that suit may have preclusive effect in a subsequent lawsuit between a class member and the party who opposed the class. In other words, even though claim preclusion will not prevent a former class member from bringing a subsequent lawsuit, issue preclusion, or collateral estoppel, may prevent the parties from relitigating an issue that the class action suit resolved. *See* Chapter XIII, part B, *infra*. This may benefit class members or the class opponent, depending on the particular case. As the Court in *Wal-Mart* explained:

> If it were determined . . . that a particular class member is not entitled to backpay because her denial of increased pay or promotion was *not* the product of discrimination, that employee might be collaterally stopped from independently seeking compensatory damages based on that same denial. That possibility underscores the need for plaintiffs with individual monetary claims to decide *for themselves* whether to tie their fates to the class representatives' or go it alone—a choice Rule 23(b)(2) does not ensure that they have.

Wal-Mart, 131 S. Ct. at 2559 (emphasis in original). If, on the other hand, the class won the earlier suit, such use of issue preclusion will benefit rather than harm a former class member. *See, e.g., Stewart v. Cheek & Zeehandelar, LLP,* 252 F.R.D. 387, 396 (S.D. Ohio 2008) (allowing plaintiffs who were members of a prior successful class action seeking declaratory and injunctive relief to individually sue the same defendant for damages and use the prior favorable judgment to collaterally estop the defendant from relitigating an issue on which the defendant lost in the class suit).

PROBLEMS

9-10. Jeffrey sued GC Services ("GC"), a debt collection agency, in federal court alleging that GC violated the Fair Debt Collection Practices Act (FDCPA) by using a form collection letter that created the false impression that GC was affiliated with the government. The FDCPA, which permits class actions, allows a named plaintiff to recover statutory damages of up to $1,000 for herself and statutory damages for the class. The latter are capped at either $500,000, or 1 percent of the defendant's net worth, whichever is less. Jeffrey has moved for certification of a class under Rule 23(b)(2), consisting of 4 million people from whom GC attempted to collect debts during the one-year period before the suit was filed. He seeks a declaratory judgment that GC's form letter violates the FDCPA, an injunction barring further use of the letter, and statutory damages for himself and the class. The FDCPA also authorizes the recovery of actual damages, but none are sought in this case. May the court certify this suit under Rule 23(a) and (b) (2)? *Compare Gammon v. GC Servs. L.P.,* 162 F.R.D. 313 (N.D. Ill. 1995), *with Talbott v. GC Servs. L.P.,* 191 F.R.D. 99 (W.D. Va. 2000).

9-11. Andrew and Eric sued Time-Warner in federal court alleging that the company violated its cable television subscribers' rights by selling personally identifiable information to third parties without giving subscribers clear notice of its disclosure practices, in violation of the federal Cable Communications Policy Act of 1984 (CCPA). The plaintiffs seek to enjoin the defendant from further CCPA violations. In addition, they seek statutory damages under the CCPA of $1,000 per class member, as well as actual and punitive damages. The plaintiffs have asked the court to certify a (b)(2) class consisting of as many as 12 million cable subscribers in 23 states whose privacy rights were allegedly violated by the disclosures. Time-Warner objects to allowing the case to proceed as a class action, particularly with respect to the statutory damages claims, as this would threaten the company with bankruptcy. Does the suit meet the requirements of Rule 23(a)? If so, does it satisfy (b)(2) on the basis that the class is cohesive and that the damages claims, though substantial, are merely "incidental"? Is this a case in which the damages claims are such that class members must be given a right to litigate them individually? If so, how might a court go about certifying a class or classes under Rule 23(b)? In doing so, might the court treat the claims for statutory damages and actual damages differently? *See Parker v. Time Warner Entm't Co., L.P.,* 331 F.3d 13 (2d Cir. 2003).

9-12. Reconsider Problem 9-1, page 763, *supra*. There, Clara sued her employer for $13,000 in lost wages based on her having been rehired to a lower-paying job after returning from maternity leave. In an earlier (b)(2) class action on behalf of female employees who had taken maternity leaves, a federal judgment was entered enjoining the company from delaying its rehiring of women who return from maternity leaves, and requiring it to restore seniority rights and pay any wages lost through such delays. As a result of the class action, Clara, who was notified of that suit, received $400 in back wages and eight days' seniority based on the delay in rehiring her. The class did not seek compensation in the form of income lost by those like Clara who were rehired to lower-paying positions. Does *res judicata* bar Clara's current suit for $13,000 in lost wages? *See King v. South Cent. Bell Tel. & Tel. Co.*, 790 F.2d 524 (6th Cir. 1986).

c.   Rule 23(b)(3)

We turn now to the last of Rule 23(b)'s subdivisions. In order to satisfy Rule 23(a)(2), the class members' claims must share common questions of law or fact. In order to satisfy (b)(3), the court must find that the common questions *predominate* over questions peculiar to each individual's claim and that a class action is *superior* to other ways of handling the matter.

i.   Predominance

The predominance inquiry under Rule 23(b)(3) seeks to ensure that a class action will achieve "economies of time, effort, and expense . . . ." Advisory Committee Note, 1966 Amendments, 39 F.R.D. 69, 102. To satisfy the predominance requirement, there must be "a showing that *questions* common to the class predominate, not that those questions will be answered, on the merits, in favor of the class." *Amgen Inc. v. Connecticut Retirement Plans and Trust Funds*, 133 S. Ct. 1184, 1191 (2013) (emphasis in original). To insist otherwise "would put the cart before the horse" and demand that "[t]o gain certification under Rule 23(b) (3)," plaintiffs "must first establish that they will win the fray . . . . [T]he office of a Rule 23(b)(3) ruling is not to adjudicate the case; rather, it is to select the method best suited to adjudication of the controversy fairly and efficiently." *Id.* (internal quotation marks omitted).

However, if despite the presence of common questions, there are also individual questions that will affect each claimant differently, "an action conducted nominally as a class action [might] degenerate in practice into multiple lawsuits separately tried." 39 F.R.D. at 103. Thus, in *Amchem Products, Inc. v. Windsor*, 521 U.S. 591 (1997), the Court ruled that a nationwide settlement class action brought against asbestos manufacturers, on behalf of those who had been occupationally exposed to asbestos, did not meet the predominance requirement of

Rule 23(b)(3). While the harmfulness of asbestos exposure was clearly a question common to the class,

> [c]lass members were exposed to different asbestos-containing products, for different amounts of time, in different ways, and over different periods. Some class members suffer no physical injury or have only asymptomatic pleural changes, while others suffer from lung cancer, disabling asbestosis, or from mesothelioma. . . . Each has a different history of cigarette smoking, a factor that complicates the causation inquiry.

Id. at 624.

> Given the greater number of questions peculiar to the several categories of class members, and to individuals within each category, and the significance of those uncommon questions, any overarching dispute about the health consequences of asbestos exposure cannot satisfy the Rule 23(b)(3) predominance standard.

Id. at 623-624. The result might have been different had the claims arisen from a single event such as an airplane crash, since "mass tort cases arising from a common cause or disaster may, depending upon the circumstances, satisfy the predominance requirement." *Id.* at 625. Yet even then, while common questions would exist as to the issue of liability, it is possible that "[q]uestions of individual damage calculations will inevitably overwhelm questions common to the class" so as to defeat satisfaction of 23(b)(3). *Comcast Corp. v. Behrend*, 133 S. Ct. 1426, 1433 (2013). In *Comcast*, the Court thus held that Rule 23(b)(3)'s predominance requirement was not met in an antitrust class action where the plaintiffs could not show that damages were capable of measurement on a classwide basis.

ii.   Superiority

If predominance is satisfied, the court must also find that a (b)(3) class action is superior to other approaches that may have "greater practical advantage." Advisory Committee Note, 1966 Amendments. One alternative is for claimants to sue individually or intervene as named parties, thereby allowing them to be represented by their own counsel. Another potential option is for the parties to use a "test case" or "model action," in which one claim is litigated against the class opponent. If the defendant loses that suit, other plaintiffs whose claims turn on the same issue can invoke collateral estoppel or issue preclusion, eliminating the need to relitigate those questions in individual suits. Other possibilities include using Rule 42(a) to consolidate separate actions pending before the same court, or transferring and consolidating for pretrial purposes separate actions pending before different federal courts, pursuant to 28 U.S.C. § 1407. These alternatives presume that members of the would-be class have the incentive and the ability to bring separate actions. If individual claims are small, there may be no satisfactory substitute for a class action. *See* 5 MOORE'S FEDERAL PRACTICE, *supra*, § 23.46; 7AA WRIGHT, MILLER & KANE, *supra*, § 1779; *see also Henry v. Cash Today, Inc.*, 199 F.R.D. 566, 573 (S.D. Tex. 2000) (certifying (b)(3) class action under Truth in Lending Act, despite act's provision for paying up to $1,000 in statutory damages plus attorneys' fees, because this provision was insufficient to motivate the filing of individual actions).

Even in settings where most class members are unlikely to sue individually, courts may be hesitant to conclude that a (b)(3) action meets the superiority test if it would lead to unjust results for the class opponent. In *Parker v. Time Warner Entm't Co., L.P.*, 331 F.3d 13 (2d Cir. 2003) (*see* Problem 9-11, page 833), *supra*, the plaintiffs sued several cable companies under the federal Cable Communications Policy Act (CCPA) for not having fully disclosed their practice of selling subscriber information to third parties. The CCPA authorizes any individual aggrieved by a violation of the act to sue for injunctive and monetary relief—including statutory, actual, and punitive damages—plus costs and attorneys' fees. 47 U.S.C. § 551(f). The plaintiffs sought certification of a nationwide class consisting of as many as 12 million people. They sought to recover millions of dollars in profits that the defendants had earned from selling the information, plus statutory damages of $1,000 per class member or a potential total of $12 billion. The district court certified a (b)(2) class for the plaintiffs' declaratory and injunctive relief claims but refused to certify a (b)(3) class for the damages claims. It concluded that "a class action is not the superior manner of proceeding where the liability a defendant stands to incur is grossly disproportionate to any actual harm sustained by an aggrieved individual," raising constitutional due process concerns. *Parker v. Time Warner Entm't Co., L.P.*, 198 F.R.D. 374, 383 (E.D.N.Y. 2001), *vacated*, 331 F.3d 13 (2d Cir. 2003). To allow a (b)(3) action under such circumstances, said the court, would be a "misuse of the procedural mechanism provided by a class action suit," and would "turn what is fundamentally a consumer protection scheme for cable subscribers into a vehicle for the financial demise of a cable service provider that failed to comply with technical aspects of that scheme." 198 F.R.D. at 384. However, the Second Circuit reversed and remanded the case for further consideration. It agreed that in a (b)(3) suit of this type, "the potential for a devastatingly large damages award, out of all reasonable proportion to the actual harm suffered by members of the plaintiff class, may raise due process issues." *Parker*, 331 F.3d at 22 (citing *State Farm Mut. Auto Ins. Co. v. Campbell*, 538 U.S. 408 (2003)). Yet if use of a class action would have this effect, the solution is "not to prevent certification, but to nullify that effect and reduce the aggregate damage award." 331 F.3d at 22. This solution would seem to be preferable to denying (b)(3) certification entirely, for under that approach, given the slim likelihood of individual suits being filed, "the wrongdoer escapes liability to all except the named plaintiffs." *Id.* at 29 (Jon O. Newman, Circuit Judge, concurring).

Following the Second Circuit's remand of *Parker v. Time Warner* to the district court, the parties reached a settlement and again asked the court to certify a class under Rule 23(b)(3). However, instead of seeking damages of $1,000 per class member, plaintiffs now agreed to accept what amounted to $6.76 per class member. Even adding the plaintiffs' attorneys' fees of $3.3 million, the total value of the settlement came to $10.7 million, less than 1 percent of the $12 billion that was at stake when the plaintiffs had first sought to certify the class under Rule 23(b)(3). This time, 11 years after the suit was filed, the district court approved the certification as well as the settlement. In doing so, the judge expressed some frustration:

> This order brings to a close a case that has raised compelling questions of law arising at the intersection of consumer protection statutes that provide for minimum statutory damages and the class action mechanism. Each of these tools is intended to encourage the prosecution of cases that would otherwise be too costly for an individual plaintiff to pursue. The combination of the two threatens defendants with the multiplication of statutory damages, possibly beyond the contemplation of Congress and the limits of due process. . . .
>
> The settlement, while fair, adequate and reasonable—in that it makes a minimal sum available to the purported victims of a minimal harm—is nonetheless unsatisfying because so much time and labor was expended to achieve so little.

Parker v. Time Warner Entm't Co., L.P., 631 F. Supp. 2d 242, 246-247 (E.D.N.Y. 2009).

iii.   Four Non-exhaustive Factors

Rule 23(b)(3) lists four non-exhaustive factors that a court should consider in conducting the predominance and superiority inquiries. The first of these is the class members' interest in proceeding with separate actions. Fed. R. Civ. P. 23(b)(3)(A). If the claims are for sizable amounts, individuals may be willing and able to sue separately. On the other hand, when individual claims are relatively small in relation to the anticipated litigation costs, a class action may be the only viable means of vindicating the rights involved.

The second factor is the extent and nature of any pending litigation involving the class members. Fed. R. Civ. P. 23(b)(3)(B). If other individual or class suits are already pending and would proceed despite the proposed class action, approving an additional class action might not further judicial economy. Similarly, if a large number of class members exercise their right to opt out and bring their own suits, this may cause the court to reconsider an initial finding that the class action is superior to other approaches.

Third, the court must consider the desirability of concentrating the litigation in the selected forum. Fed. R. Civ. P. 23(b)(3)(C). Given the location of evidence and witnesses, it may be that another court or courts would be more appropriate. But if the selected court is a convenient one, a class action proceeding in that court may be much more efficient than a large number of individual suits.

The fourth factor, and probably the most important one, concerns "manageability," *i.e.*, the difficulties that would be encountered in managing the suit as a class action. Fed. R. Civ. P. 23(b)(3)(D). Since individual notice is required in (b)(3) actions, there may be serious obstacles to identifying and/or contacting class members. Problems may also arise in calculating damages. If this would require a large number of separate trials, a court may conclude that a class action is not manageable. Sometimes damages can be proven on an aggregate or lump-sum basis, either by consulting the defendant's records or by using a mathematical or statistical formula. Yet manageability problems may even arise in attempting to allocate these damages among class members. A formal trial to determine the extent of each member's injury can be avoided if the parties agree to a less formal administrative procedure in which class members submit written claims to determine their individual recovery. But, in cases in which each member of a large class is entitled to only a small amount, the costs of distribution may themselves consume the fund. Or, only a few members of the class may come forward to claim their share of the recovery, leaving much of the fund undistributed.

Courts occasionally solve the latter problem by allowing a *cy pres* ("as near as possible") or "fluid" recovery by which any unclaimed damages are distributed through a market mechanism (*e.g.*, by reducing prices to future buyers of the good or service in question), or given to a government body, trust, or private charitable organization that will indirectly benefit class members. *See, e.g., In re Lupron Marketing and Sales Practices Litig.*, 677 F.3d 21, 31-39 (1st Cir.), *cert. denied*, 133 S. Ct. 338 (2012); *In re Infant Formula Multidistrict Litig.*, 2005 WL 2211312 (N.D. Fla. Sept. 8, 2005); *Jones v. National Distillers*, 56 F. Supp. 2d 355 (S.D.N.Y. 1999); *but see Dennis v. Kellogg Co.*, 697 F.3d 858 (9th Cir. 2012) (rejecting class action settlement where *cy pres* distribution was to charities having no relation to the class or the underlying claims). When allowed by the courts, the *cy pres* device serves to strip a defendant of ill-gotten gains and deter future wrongdoing while seeking to ensure that the class suit does not merely or unduly benefit the lawyers who brought the case. *See* 7AA Wright, Miller & Kane, *supra*, §§ 1780, 1784; 5 Moore's Federal Practice, *supra*, § 23.46[2][e]; Rhonda Wasserman, *Cy Pres in Class Action Settlements*, 88 S. Cal. L. Rev. 97 (2014). *See also Marek v. Lane*, 134 S. Ct. 8 (2013) ("*Cy pres* remedies are a growing feature of class action settlements" which raise "fundamental concerns" of fairness; "[i]n a suitable case, this Court may need to clarify the limits on [their] use . . . .") (statement of C.J. Roberts respecting the denial of certiorari).

iv.   *Notice to Class Members*

In class actions brought under Rule 23(b)(1) or (2), the court has broad discretion concerning what notice, if any, will be given to class members. A court may decide that notice to the class, before or after the initial certification, may help it to evaluate the adequacy of representation, the appropriateness of subclasses, or the need to redefine the class. *See* Fed. R. Civ. P. 23(d)(1)(B). In addition, the court may provide notice in such cases if class members are going to be given an opportunity to opt out. *See* Note 4, page 812, *supra*.

However, in actions brought under Rule 23(b)(3), where each class member has an absolute right to opt out, Rule 23(c)(2)(B) requires that the court "direct to class members the best notice that is practicable under the circumstances, including individual notice to all members who can be identified through reasonable effort." Fed. R. Civ. P. 23(c)(2)(B). The notice must clearly and concisely state in plain, easily understood language: (i) the nature of the action; (ii) the definition of the class certified; (iii) the class claims, issues, or defenses; (iv) that a class member may enter an appearance through an attorney if the member so desires; (v) that the court will exclude from the class any member who requests exclusion; (vi) the time and manner for requesting exclusion; and (vii) the binding effect of a class judgment on members under Rule 23(c)(3).

Id. This notice is usually sent shortly after the court has determined that the class satisfies Rule 23(a) and (b)(3). However, as we saw earlier, while that determination need not be made immediately, it must be made "at an early practicable time. . . ." Fed. R. Civ. P. 23(c)(1)(A). This flexibility reflects the fact that it may take time to determine whether the suit should proceed as a class action and, if so, how the class should be defined. Moreover, it is possible that the case can be settled, in which event the (b)(3) and proposed settlement notices might be combined into one.

Since a (b)(3) notice must be sent individually to every class member whose identity and whereabouts can reasonably be determined, a key question is who must bear the costs of identifying and notifying class members. The Supreme Court has held that these expenses must be borne by the class representative. In *Oppenheimer Fund, Inc. v. Sanders*, 437 U.S. 340 (1978), the Court ruled that the class opponent cannot be forced to absorb the expense of identifying class members, even if it could do so from its own records at relatively little cost. And, in *Eisen v. Carlisle & Jacquelin*, 417 U.S. 156 (1974), the Court held that the cost of sending individual notices to (b)(3) class members must likewise normally be borne by the class representative, even if the consequence is that the class suit must be abandoned. This is what happened in *Eisen*, in which Morton Eisen sued several brokerage houses on behalf of a nationwide class of 3,750,000 people who had purchased and sold "odd lots" on the New York Stock Exchange. The suit was dismissed because Eisen, who stood to recover only $70 in damages, could not afford the $225,000 expense of sending individual notices to the 2,250,000 class members whose names and addresses were ascertainable.

In retrospect, what might Eisen and his attorneys have done to reduce notice costs? Could they have sued on behalf of a smaller class, consisting perhaps of those who lived in a specific geographic area or those who had engaged in transactions during a designated period of time? *See, e.g., Mace v. Van Ru Credit Corp.,* 109 F.3d 338 (7th Cir. 1997) (permitting plaintiffs to bring class action on behalf of residents of a single state rather than on behalf of a nationwide class when the latter would have posed manageability problems that would defeat certification under Rule 23(b)(3)). If the cost of sending notice to a smaller class were affordable, that suit could serve as a model or test case for subsequent actions on behalf of other classes. Alternatively, could Eisen's lawyers themselves have paid the cost of providing notice? *Compare Margolis v. Caterpillar, Inc.,* 815 F. Supp. 1150, 1154 (C.D. Ill. 1991) (allowing lawyers for plaintiff classes to pay and later absorb notice costs if a (b)(3) class action is unsuccessful is in accordance with ABA Model Rule of Professional Conduct 1.8(e)), *with Weber v. Goodman,* 9 F. Supp. 2d 163, 171-174 (E.D.N.Y. 1998) (allowing lawyers in (b)(3) class actions to advance costs is permissible under the New York code of professional responsibility, so long as named plaintiffs agree to pay their pro rata share of costs and expenses if the suit is unsuccessful,).

Hanlon v. Chrysler Corporation [Part I]
150 F.3d 1011 (9th Cir. 1998)

THOMAS, Circuit Judge:

We are presented in this appeal with procedural and substantive objections to the settlement of a nationwide class action against Chrysler Corporation. After examining the settlement in accordance with the guidelines established in *Amchem Products, Inc. v. Windsor*, 521 U.S. 591 (1997), we affirm the district court.

I

In September 1993, the National Highway Traffic Safety Administration ("NHTSA") Office of Defect Investigation learned of a rear liftgate latch problem in 1992 Chrysler minivans. NHTSA opened a preliminary investigation, which was expanded to an "engineering analysis" of all 1984-1994 Chrysler minivans. . . . Despite NHTSA's investigation, Chrysler publicly denied any problem with its rear liftgate latches. . . .

. . . The investigation was finally closed on October 25, 1995. At that time, NHTSA was satisfied that the voluntary ["service action"] taken by Chrysler had been as effective as a formal recall. . . .

Prior to the agreement between NHTSA and Chrysler, plaintiffs' lawyers in several states filed class actions in various state courts seeking latch replacement, as well as damages under various state-law warranties and theories of recovery. The plaintiffs' counsel in the state actions met with engineering experts, conducted and defended depositions, and were proceeding through the normal course of document-intensive discovery. Class counsel in the two California cases and the Texas case moved for class certification; however, the hearings were continued at Chrysler's request.

[While the NHTSA investigation was still pending], Chrysler and counsel from the various state actions began serious settlement discussions. . . . As a result of the settlement discussions, all of the state class actions were consolidated in one large national class action (the *Hanlon* class) in federal court in the Northern District of California under Judge Legge on June 16, 1995. In their complaint the *Hanlon* plaintiffs asserted various claims against Chrysler with regard to an alleged defect in the rear liftgate latches of the minivans. Three days after filing the case, the parties submitted a settlement agreement to the court for approval. The district court held a preliminary hearing on the settlement agreement on August 18, [1995], and issued an Order granting preliminary approval of the settlement and certifying the nationwide class of Minivan owners for settlement purposes only. All personal injury and death cases are excluded from this settlement.

The Order also provided at Paragraph 19:

> Pending final determination of whether the settlement embodied in the Settlement Agreement is to be approved, no member of the Settlement Class, either directly, representatively, derivatively, or in any other capacity, shall commence or prosecute any action or proceeding in any court or tribunal asserting any of the claims [covered by] the Settlement Agreement.

Pursuant to the August 18 Order, the Court-approved notice of the proposed settlement was mailed directly to over 3.3 million Minivan owners. The order granting preliminary approval of the settlement set an objection and opt-out date of October 20, 1995, and all activity on the state actions ceased.

A few weeks after the *Hanlon* action was filed, Robert Kempton, a resident of Georgia and Chrysler minivan owner, filed a similar class action in a Georgia state court. Kempton sought to represent himself and all Georgia residents and entities who purchased or leased a Chrysler minivan in the relevant product years. In direct contravention of the federal district court's August 18 order, Kempton filed a motion to certify the Georgia class on October 17, 1995. Kempton specifically stated that his goal was either to opt out all Georgia residents from the *Hanlon* action or object on their behalf. The *Hanlon* plaintiffs and Chrysler filed a motion to enjoin Kempton from proceeding, and the California district court issued such an order on October 19, 1995.

Kempton expressly ignored the injunction and proceeded with the Georgia class certification, arguing that he had opted out of the *Hanlon* class and therefore was not subject to that court's jurisdiction or bound by its orders. The Georgia state judge entered an order conditionally granting Kempton's motion and certifying the class.

Following notification of the proposed settlement, the district court in California conducted two fairness hearings on the adequacy of the settlement in November 1995. The court made several findings at the second hearing on November 30, 1995, indicating its approval of the settlement. Prior to entering the order, the court gave objectors an opportunity to present arguments on the pending settlement. The objections centered around one primary issue: the adequacy and fairness of the settlement in light of Chrysler's prior agreement with NHTSA to replace all of the defective latches. At the conclusion of the hearing, the court entered a final order of settlement and award of attorneys fees.

In early 1996, Chrysler acknowledged that approximately one million class members never received the notice of settlement and opportunity to opt-out of the settlement class because it had inadvertently failed to include them in the initial mailing. As a result, Chrysler moved to set aside the final order of settlement and reopen the proceedings to allow additional notice to these class members. The court agreed and granted Chrysler's Rule 60(b) Motion to Partially Reopen the Judgment on February 23, 1996.

A third and final fairness hearing was held on April 29, 1996. At the close of that hearing, the court issued a new order that was substantially similar to the November 30 order. The objectors timely appealed to this court.

II

In recent years, the difficulties attendant to consummating settlement of mass tort and consumer lawsuits have caused litigants to instigate lawsuits for the limited purpose of obtaining court approval of a certified class settlement. Although there is nothing inherently wrong with this practice, we must pay "undiluted, even heightened, attention" to class certification requirements in a settlement context. *Amchem Products, Inc. v. Windsor*, 521 U.S. 591, 620 (1997) ("*Amchem*").

A

Our threshold task is to ascertain whether the proposed settlement class satisfies the requirements of Rule 23(a) of the Federal Rules of Civil Procedure applicable to all class actions, namely: (1) numerosity, (2) commonality, (3) typicality, and (4) adequacy of representation. The prerequisite of numerosity is discharged if "the class is so large that joinder of all members is impracticable." None of the objectors contest certification for failure to meet this condition, and as a nationwide class with millions of class members residing in fifty states, this requirement is clearly satisfied.

A class has sufficient commonality "if there are questions of fact and law which are common to the class." The commonality preconditions of Rule 23(a)(2) are less rigorous than the companion requirements of Rule 23(b)(3). . . . The existence of shared legal issues with divergent factual predicates is sufficient, as is a common core of salient facts coupled with disparate legal remedies within the class. Although members of the proposed class in this instance may possess different avenues of redress, their claims stem from the same source: the allegedly defective designed rear liftgate latch installed in minivans manufactured by Chrysler between 1984 and 1995. Thus, the proposed class shares sufficient factual commonality to satisfy the minimal requirements of Rule 23(a)(2).

The typicality prerequisite of Rule 23(a) is fulfilled if "the claims or defenses of the representative parties are typical of the claims or defenses of the class." Under the rule's permissive standards, representative claims are "typical" if they are reasonably co-extensive with those of absent class members; they need not be substantially identical. In this instance, the broad composition of the representative parties vitiates any challenge founded on atypicality. The representative parties comprise persons from every state, representing all models of Chrysler minivans and include minivan owners whose latches remain operable. The narrow focus of the proposed class was to obtain a defect-free rear liftgate latch in Chrysler minivans owned by class members, or receive adequate non-personal injury compensatory damages. Given these limited objectives and the broad composition of the representative parties, the representative claims were sufficiently typical to pass muster under Rule 23(a)(3).

The final hurdle interposed by Rule 23(a) is that "the representative parties will fairly and adequately protect the interests of the class." To satisfy constitutional due process concerns, absent class members must be afforded adequate representation before entry of a judgment which binds them. . . .

Examination of potential conflicts of interest has long been an important prerequisite to class certification. That inquiry is especially critical when the . . . class settlement is tendered along with a motion for class certification. *Amchem* instructs us to give heightened scrutiny to cases in which class members may have claims of different strength.

Amchem was a settlement class action which attempted to settle all pending and future asbestos litigation. The asbestos manufacturers wished to resolve all claims, including those not yet filed or even in existence at the time of the settlement. The class was never divided into sub-classes and additional counsel was never appointed to represent the interests of plaintiffs with as yet undeveloped or undiagnosed injuries. . . .

. . . The [*Amchem*] Court also held that all of the Rule 23 standards for class actions must be met without regard to the presence or terms of a pending settlement agreement.

At the heart of *Amchem* was concern over settlement allocation decisions; asbestos manufacturers had a designated amount of money that was not fairly distributed between present and future claimants. The *Amchem* settlement eliminated all present and future claims against asbestos manufacturers, with class counsel attempting to represent both groups of plaintiffs. The Supreme Court found this dual representation to be particularly troubling, given that present plaintiffs had a clear interest in a settlement that maximized current funds, while future plaintiffs had a strong interest in preserving funds for their future needs and protecting the total fund against inflation.

Unlike the class in *Amchem*, this class of minivan owners does not present an allocation dilemma. Potential plaintiffs are not divided into conflicting discrete categories, such as those with present health problems and those who may develop symptoms in the future. Rather, each potential plaintiff has the same problem: an allegedly defective rear latchgate which requires repair or commensurate compensation. The differences in severity of personal injury present in *Amchem* are avoided here by excluding personal injury and wrongful death claims. Similarly, there is no structural conflict of interest based on variations in state law, for the named representatives include individuals from each state, and the differences in state remedies are not sufficiently substantial so as to warrant the creation of subclasses. Representatives of other potential subclasses are included among the named representatives, including owners of every minivan model. . . .

. . . [T]he proposed settlement does not propose different terms for different class members; on the contrary, treatment of each class member is identical. Given these careful precautions and safeguards, no improper conflict of interest existed which would deny absent class members adequate representation.

Our second adequacy inquiry is directed to the vigor with which the named representatives and their counsel will pursue the common claims. Although there are no fixed standards by which "vigor" can be assayed, considerations include competency of counsel and, in the context of a settlement-only class, an assessment of the rationale for not pursuing further litigation.

The objectors do not seriously challenge the competence of class counsel, and the record dispels any cause for concern. Affidavits submitted to the district court show experience prosecuting dozens of high profile class action cases and products liability litigation. If these attorneys are not equal to the task of prosecuting this case, it is not clear to us who would be. . . .

The *Amchem* Court also noted the problem of counsel "not prepared to try a case." Such counsel is, almost by definition, inadequate because an inability or unwillingness to try a case means the class loses all of the benefits of adversarial litigation. "Class counsel confined to settlement negotiations could not use the threat of litigation to press for a better offer. . . ." *Amchem*, 521 U.S. at 621. District courts must be skeptical of some settlement agreements put before them because they are presented with a "bargain proffered for . . . approval without benefit of an adversarial investigation." *Id.*

These concerns warrant special attention when the record suggests that settlement is driven by fees; that is, when counsel receive a disproportionate distribution of the settlement, or when the class receives no monetary distribution but class counsel are amply rewarded.

These circumstances are not present in this case. . . . We find counsel's prosecution of the case sufficiently vigorous to satisfy any Rule 23(a)(4) concerns.

In sum, the named representatives have fulfilled the threshold requirements of Fed. R. Civ. P. 23(a). . . . The named plaintiffs have also satisfied the heightened scrutiny we must give to Rule 23(a) requirements when considering certification of a settlement-only class.

B

In addition to meeting the conditions imposed by Rule 23(a), the parties seeking class certification must also show that the action is maintainable under Fed. R. Civ. P. 23(b)(1), (2) or (3). In the instant case, the parties propose certification pursuant to Rule 23(b)(3), which is appropriate "whenever the actual interests of the parties can be served best by settling their differences in a single action." 7A Charles Alan Wright, Arthur R. Miller & Mary Kay Kane, *Federal Practice & Procedure* § 1777 (2d ed. 1986). To qualify for certification under this subsection, a class must satisfy two conditions in addition to the Rule 23(a) prerequisites: common questions must "predominate over any questions affecting only individual members," and class resolution must be "superior to other available methods for the fair and efficient adjudication of the controversy."

"The Rule 23(b)(3) predominance inquiry tests whether proposed classes are sufficiently cohesive to warrant adjudication by representation." *Amchem*, 521 U.S. at 623. This analysis presumes that the existence of common issues of fact or law have been established pursuant to Rule 23(a)(2); thus, the presence of commonality alone is not sufficient to fulfill Rule 23(b)(3). In contrast to Rule

23(a)(2), Rule 23(b)(3) focuses on the relationship between the common and individual issues. . . .

A common nucleus of facts and potential legal remedies dominates this litigation. Variations in state law do not necessarily preclude a 23(b)(3) action, but class counsel should be prepared to demonstrate the commonality of substantive law applicable to all class members. In this case, although some class members may possess slightly differing remedies based on state statute or common law, the actions asserted by the class representatives are not sufficiently anomalous to deny class certification. On the contrary, to the extent distinct remedies exist, they are local variants of a generally homogenous collection of causes which include products liability, breaches of express and implied warranties, and "lemon laws." Individual claims based on personal injury or wrongful death were excluded from the class. Thus, the idiosyncratic differences between state consumer protection laws are not sufficiently substantive to predominate over the shared claims. Indeed, at the November 30, 1995, fairness hearing, the objectors acknowledged that independent of any variations in state law, there were still sufficient common issues to warrant a class action, particularly questions of Chrysler's prior knowledge of the latch deficiency, the design defect, and a damages remedy.

Rule 23(b)(3) also requires that class resolution must be "superior to other available methods for the fair and efficient adjudication of the controversy." The superiority inquiry under Rule 23(b)(3) requires determination of whether the objectives of the particular class action procedure will be achieved in the particular case. This determination necessarily involves a comparative evaluation of alternative mechanisms of dispute resolution. In this instance, the alternative methods of resolution are individual claims for a small amount of consequential damages or latch replacement. Further, the statute of limitations has run for owners of older vehicles under many state laws, and state lemon laws almost universally require that the vehicle be defective beyond repair—a condition which is impossible for many owners to demonstrate. Thus, many claims could not be successfully asserted individually. Even if efficacious, these claims would not only unnecessarily burden the judiciary, but would prove uneconomic for potential plaintiffs. In most cases, litigation costs would dwarf potential recovery. In this sense, the proposed class action is paradigmatic. A fair examination of alternatives can only result in the apodictic conclusion that a class action is the clearly preferred procedure in this case.

Assessment of the non-exclusive factors listed in Rule 23(b)(3) which potentially apply to both the predominance and superiority inquiries yields the same result. From either a judicial or litigant viewpoint, there is no advantage in individual members controlling the prosecution of separate actions. There would be less litigation or settlement leverage, significantly reduced resources and no greater prospect for recovery. With a few exceptions, the pre-existing lawsuits were cooperatively managed and can be effectively merged into the instant action. No particular forum stands out as a logical venue for concentration of claims. Thus, consideration of the factors enumerated in Rule 23(b)(3) does not alter the conclusion.

Thus, given the limited focus of the action, the shared factual predicate and the reasonably inconsequential differences in state law remedies, the proposed class was sufficiently cohesive to survive Rule 23(b)(3) scrutiny. A comparative examination of alternatives underscores the wisdom of a class action in this instance. Consideration of the specific, non-exclusive factors identified in Rule 23(b)(3) produces the same result. Thus, the requisite predominance and superiority tests are satisfied, and the conditions of Rule 23(b)(3) have been met. . . .

III

After the federal consolidated class action was filed, but before the settlement agreement was presented to the district court for preliminary approval, Robert Kempton filed a state class action in Georgia. Kempton's theory of recovery was very similar to that of the federal action, but he claimed relief under Georgia state law. He sought to represent himself and all other Georgia consumers who owned or leased a minivan from the relevant model years, and asserted the right to opt-out all Georgia customers from the federal class action.

The district court expressly held that Kempton's actions in proceeding with his state class action, in direct contravention of the district court's injunction against such a proceeding, operated to exclude him from the nationwide class, but his opt-out had no effect on the remaining Georgia class members. Kempton argues on appeal that the district court erred, that his actions were taken on behalf of all Georgia class members, and that the state court's certification of the Georgia action operates to opt-out all Georgia class members from the plaintiff class.

The district court was entirely correct. All class members in a Rule 23(b)(3) action are entitled to due process, including notice. *Phillips Petroleum v. Shutts*, 472 U.S. 797, 810-813 (1985). The procedural due process rights of these members include an opportunity to be excluded from the action. The right to participate, or to opt-out, is an individual one and should not be made by the class representative or the class counsel. There is no class action rule, statute, or case that allows a putative class plaintiff or counsel to exercise class rights en masse, either by making a class-wide objection or by attempting to effect a group-wide exclusion from an existing class. Indeed, to do so would infringe on the due process rights of the individual class members, who have the right to intelligently and individually choose whether to continue in a suit as class members. *Eisen v. Carlisle & Jacquelin*, 417 U.S. 156, 173-77 (1974). Additionally, to allow representatives in variously asserted class actions to opt a class out without the permission of individual class members "would lead to chaos in the management of class actions." *Berry Petroleum Co. v. Adams & Peck*, 518 F.2d 402, 412 (2d Cir. 1975). In this case, all members of the purported Georgia class were notified of this class action and the proposed settlement, and all but twenty-eight elected to remain in the class. By contrast, there is no evidence in the record that any Georgia class member received notice of the Kempton suit and made an intelligent election to join or decline to participate in it. . . .

In addition, the temporary approval of the nationwide settlement stayed the state class actions. The federal court had the power to issue an injunction against continued state proceedings under the All Writs Act, 28 U.S.C. § 1651 ("[t]he All Writs Act . . . empowers the federal courts to enjoin state proceedings that interfere, derogate, or conflict with federal judgments, orders, or settlements." *Keith v. Volpe*, 118 F.3d 1386, 1390 (9th Cir. 1997)) and the Anti-Injunction Act, 28 U.S.C. § 2283 (a federal court may intervene and enjoin state court proceedings in three narrow circumstances, one of which includes when it is necessary to protect the court's jurisdiction). Although comity requires federal courts to exercise extreme caution in interfering with state litigation, federal courts have the power to do so when their jurisdiction is threatened.

Further, Fed. R. Civ. P. Rule 23(d) vests a district court with the authority and discretion to protect the interests and rights of class members and to ensure its control over the integrity of the settlement approval process. . . .

Because a class representative in a state class action, acting at the same time as a federal class action, lacks the power to opt-out an entire class without the permission of individual class members, the district court properly ruled that Kempton's actions served as an individual opt-out for Kempton alone.

[In Parts IV and V of its opinion, the court evaluated and approved the terms of the settlement agreement, including the award of attorneys' fees. These parts of the opinion appear in the next section of this chapter, part D, *infra*.]

VI

The certification of the settlement class, the approval of the class settlement and the fee award were well within the guidelines provided by *Amchem* and Fed. R. Civ. P. 23. Accordingly, we affirm the judgment of the district court.

NOTES AND QUESTIONS

1. *A settlement class.*   Like *In re Telectronics*, page 813, *supra*, *Hanlon* involved a settlement class action. The plaintiffs did not seek to litigate any claims against Chrysler but instead wished to settle the claims of a nationwide class of minivan owners. Three days after the complaint was filed on behalf of the class, the parties submitted a settlement for the court's approval. Two months later, after reviewing the agreement, the court simultaneously notified class members that a class had been certified and that the settlement had been preliminarily approved. How did the fact that this was a settlement class affect the court of appeals' review of the case?

2. *Notice to class members.*   Since *Hanlon* was a (b)(3) action, notice had to be given to every class member whose name and address were reasonably ascertainable. Notice was accordingly sent to 4.3 million people by ordinary first-class mail, the method of notice customarily employed in class action lawsuits. At the then current rate of 32 cents per ounce, postage alone exceeded $1 million. Although the class representative must usually pay the cost of sending notice to the class, do you think that was true here? Suppose that Chrysler's records did not include all current minivan owners and that there was no practicable way to locate them.

Though Rule 23(c)(2)(B) does not require individual notice to such class members, does due process require some effort to notify them? If so, what form of notice might the court direct to class members whose identity or whereabouts was unknown?

3. *Opting out and the statute of limitations.*   Why did the court reject Kempton's efforts to exclude all class members living in Georgia? What's wrong with allowing opt-out rights to be exercised en masse by those wishing to sue on behalf of a subset of the class? When plaintiff class members properly exercise their opt-out rights, does this guarantee that they will be able to bring their own suits against the defendant? We saw earlier that the filing of a class action tolls the statute of limitations for members of the purported class if class certification is later denied. *See* page 782, *supra*. Some courts have also held that filing a class action tolls the statute of limitations for class members who elect to opt out after the class has been certified. *See, e.g., Realmonte v. Reeves,* 169 F.3d 1280, 1283-1284 (10th Cir. 1999) (adopting and noting similar tolling rule in the Third, Eighth, and Ninth Circuits); *and see In re Urethane Antitrust Litig.,* 663 F. Supp. 2d 1067, 1079-1083 (D. Kan. 2009) (state rather than federal tolling rule applies re state law claims). However, this tolling rule only protects members as to whom the statute of limitations had not run at the time the class suit was filed. In *Hanlon,* for example, the limitations period had already expired for the owners of older vehicles, making any prospect of individual actions by them illusory.

4. *Appearing through counsel.*   Rule 23(c)(2)(B)(iv) and (v) give members of a (b)(3) class the rights to opt out, or "enter an appearance through an attorney." Does this mean that class members who opt out may automatically intervene and participate as named parties without having to satisfy Rule 24? While allowing automatic intervention might make the action unwieldy, Rule 23(d)(1)(C) authorizes a court to impose such conditions on intervenors as "may be required for the proper and efficient conduct of the action." Advisory Committee Note, 1966 Amendments, 39 F.R.D. 69, 107. Courts are divided as to whether the Rule 23(c)(2)(B)(iv) right to enter an appearance through an attorney is synonymous with intervention. Most courts hold that this provision merely allows (b)(3) class members to receive copies of all papers filed in the suit so that they can monitor the adequacy of representation and decide whether to seek intervention under Rule 24. *See* 7B WRIGHT, MILLER & KANE, *supra,* § 1799; 5 MOORE'S FEDERAL PRACTICE, *supra,* §§ 23.104[2][a][iii], 23.143.

5. *Omitting claims for personal injury and death.*   Why did the plaintiffs in *Hanlon* omit all claims for personal injury and death resulting from defective latches and instead seek only repair, replacement, and/or compensatory damages for the latch itself? If they had sought damages for personal injury and wrongful death on behalf of a class, would the requirements of Rule 23(a) still have been met? Might it have been necessary to create subclasses? If so, would each subclass have met Rule 23(a)(1)'s numerosity requirement? Would subclasses suing for personal injury or wrongful death have satisfied the predominance and superiority tests of Rule 23(b)(3)? Would such a case have been distinguishable from *Amchem,* discussed by the court in *Hanlon*? Assuming such a class action had

initially satisfied Rule 23(a) and (b)(3), if class members with personal injury or wrongful death claims opted out in large enough numbers, might the court reconsider its certification order in light of new problems with numerosity and superiority? As to those class members who chose not to opt out, since the class did not assert any claims for personal injury or wrongful death, will class members who later sue separately on these claims be met with the defense of *res judicata* because they split their claims for relief? *See* "A Note On the Preclusive Effect of Class Action Judgments," page 832, *supra*; Chapter XIII, part A ("Claim Preclusion or Res Judicata"), page 1132, *infra*.

6. *Why not (b)(1) or (b)(2)?* Could the parties in *Hanlon* have avoided giving class members any opt-out rights and thus made the settlement universal by seeking certification under (b)(1) or (b)(2), rather than under (b)(3)? If the parties had agreed to limit Chrysler's total liability for latch repair, replacement, and compensation to a fixed dollar amount, would this have qualified the suit as a limited-fund case under (b)(1)(B)? Could they also have argued that the suit satisfied (b)(2) since the class sought primarily injunctive relief requiring that Chrysler repair or replace the defective latches? Alternatively, could (b)(2) have been invoked if the settlement agreement included monetary damages at a fixed amount based solely on the year and model of the Chrysler minivan? This case was decided before the Supreme Court handed down its decision in *Wal-Mart*, 131 S. Ct. 2541 (2011), page 825 , *supra*. After *Wal-Mart*, what is the likelihood that (b)(2) could be used in a case like this?

7. *A defendant's preference for (b)(3)?* Plaintiffs' class counsel often prefer having a class certified under (b)(1) or (b)(2) rather than (b)(3), since the former carry no automatic opt-out rights nor do they impose a duty to give individual notice to all class members. One might assume that defendants would likewise favor (b)(1) or (b)(2), for in a (b)(3) plaintiff class action, the defendant faces the prospect of individual suits by those who may choose to exclude themselves from the class. Yet, as in *Hanlon*, defendants will often prefer a (b)(3) certification. *See, e.g., Lemon*, page 831, *supra* (overturning district court's certification of a Title VII suit as a (b)(2) class action because the request for money damages was not incidental). The Seventh Circuit addressed this issue in *Jefferson v. Ingersoll International Inc.*, 195 F.3d 894 (7th Cir. 1999):

> Although class members who want control of their own litigation are vitally concerned about the choice, so too are defendants—for the final resolution of a suit that proceeds to judgment (or settlement) under Rule 23(b)(2) may be collaterally attacked by class members who contend that they should have been notified and allowed to proceed independently. Defendants who want the outcome of a damages action (no matter which side wins) to be *conclusive* favor Rule 23(b)(3), because it alone insulates the disposition from collateral attack by dissatisfied class members.

Id. at 896-897. Thus, had the *Hanlon* class been certified under Rule 23(b)(2), would the settlement judgment necessarily have had the *res judicata* effect of preventing members of that class from later bringing their own individual or class actions to litigate the same claims that were settled earlier? May this help explain why the plaintiffs as well as the defendant in *Hanlon* favored having the class certified under (b)(3)?

PROBLEM

9-13. We saw earlier that in *Wal-Mart Stores, Inc. v. Dukes*, 131 S. Ct. 2541 (2011), the Court held that a class could not be certified under Rule 23(b)(2) because the monetary relief sought by class members was not "incidental" to the injunctive or declaratory relief. Yet as Justice Ginsburg noted, "[t]he plaintiffs requested Rule 23(b)(3) certification as an alternative, should their request for (b)(2) certification fail." *See* page 829 n.1, *supra*. Suppose that the plaintiffs were able to amend their complaint to narrow the proposed class in a way that satisfied Rule 23(a)(2)—e.g., by defining the class as including only current and former Wal-Mart employees in one or more of the six states in which there was strong evidence of gender discrimination by company officials, or as including only those working for certain area supervisors who clearly engaged in discriminatory practices. As in their original suit, the plaintiffs seek declaratory and injunctive relief, backpay, and punitive damages.

  A. Would the suit satisfy the other three requirements of Rule 23(a)?
  B. Would it satisfy Rule 23(b)(3)'s predominance and superiority requirements?
  C. How would Rule 23(b)(3)'s four non-exhaustive criteria figure in the analysis?
  D. Might it be necessary to create subclasses? If so, how would you define them, and would they then individually meet the requirements of Rule 23(a) and (b)(3)?
  E. If (b)(3) is satisfied, should the entire case be certified under (b)(3), or might other Rule 23(b) subdivisions be utilized as well?
  F. Are there parts of this case that may not be suitable for class treatment, such that they should be litigated on an individual basis?

A NOTE ON ENJOINING COMPETING ACTIONS

The *Hanlon* district court enjoined class members from filing or proceeding with other related actions against Chrysler. Despite the impression given by the Ninth Circuit's opinion, it is very unusual for a federal class action court to enjoin a pending state court suit, for the Anti-Injunction Act, 28 U.S.C. § 2283, generally bars this. *See Sandpiper Vill. Condo. Assn. v. Louisiana-Pacific Corp.*, 428 F.3d 831, 842-853 (9th Cir. 2005), *cert. denied*, 548 U.S. 905 (2006) (noting that such injunctions are rarely proper). However, if the federal class action court has approved or is about to approve a class settlement, as was the case in *Hanlon*, some courts hold that this falls within § 2283's exception allowing a federal court to issue an injunction "necessary in aid of its jurisdiction." 28 U.S.C. § 2283.

This exception allows stays "to prevent a state court from so interfering with a federal court's consideration or disposition of a case as to seriously impair the federal court's flexibility and authority to decide the case." *Atlantic Coast Line R.R. v. Brotherhood of Locomotive Eng'rs*, 398 U.S. 281, 295 (1970); *see, e.g., In re Diet Drugs*, 282 F.3d 220 (3d Cir. 2002); *see also Negrete v. Allianz Life Ins. Co. of N. Am.*, 523 F.3d 1091, 1098-1103 (9th Cir. 2008); *Retirement Sys. of Ala. v. J.P. Morgan Chase & Co.*, 386 F.3d 419, 425-428 (2d Cir. 2004); MANUAL FOR COMPLEX LITIGATION, *supra*, §§ 20.32, 21.15; 7B WRIGHT, MILLER & KANE, *supra*, § 1798.1. The Anti-Injunction Act does not bar federal court injunctions against the filing of future—as opposed to pending—state court suits.

Even when the Anti-Injunction Act does not stand in the way, lack of personal jurisdiction may prevent a court from enjoining other related actions by class members. This is especially true in suits like *Hanlon* that are brought on behalf of a nationwide class, for many members may lack minimum contacts with the forum state. In *Hanlon*, the California federal court enjoined Robert Kempton, a Georgia resident, from proceeding with a suit he had filed in a Georgia state court. Yet it does not appear that Kempton had minimum contacts with California nor did he consent to jurisdiction by participating or appearing in the California suit. How then did the California federal court acquire jurisdiction over him so as to allow issuance of the injunction? Had Kempton not opted out of the federal suit after being notified of his right to do so, this would have constituted consent to jurisdiction, *see Phillips Petroleum Co. v. Shutts*, 472 U.S. 797 (1985), at page 755, *supra*, but he did opt out. It is therefore doubtful that the court's order in *Hanlon*, barring class members from filing or proceeding with related actions against Chrysler, was valid as to those members who lacked minimum contacts with the state and who did not consent to jurisdiction by appearing or failing to opt out. *See In re Prudential Ins. Co. Am. Sales Practices Litig.*, 148 F.3d 283, 306 (3d Cir. 1998); *Carlough v. Amchem Prods., Inc.*, 10 F.3d 189, 198-201 (3d Cir. 1993); 7A CHARLES ALAN WRIGHT, ARTHUR R. MILLER & MARY KAY KANE, FEDERAL PRACTICE AND PROCEDURE § 1757 (3d ed. 2005 & Supp. 2015).

Due to the federal courts' limited ability to enjoin pending state court suits, there are occasions when federal and state court class actions involving essentially the same claims are proceeding simultaneously on parallel tracks. In this race-to-judgment setting, whichever of the competing suits first reaches final judgment will have *res judicata* or claim preclusion effect on other pending suits between the parties on the same claims. Does this explain the injunction in *Hanlon*? Did the temporary ban against filing or proceeding with other actions protect the federal court's jurisdiction by assuring that no state suit could reach final judgment before the federal class settlement was approved and reduced to judgment? Thereafter, the injunction could be lifted and those electing to opt out could then pursue their individual or class remedies without jeopardizing the federal settlement.

If competing or overlapping class actions are pending in different federal courts, the court with the more recently filed suit may either stay the case before it or transfer it to the federal district in which the earlier filed class action is pending.

See Tomkins v. Basic Research LL, 2008 WL 1808316, at *5-*6 (E.D. Cal. Apr. 22, 2008). Yet these steps under the so-called first-to-file rule are discretionary, and the second court may decline to stay or transfer if it believes that the case before it is the superior vehicle for resolving the dispute. In this situation, whichever federal suit first reaches final judgment will control the other through *res judicata. See Blair v. Equifax Check Servs., Inc.*, 181 F.3d 832, 838-839 (7th Cir. 1999) (discussing court's options when overlapping class actions are pending in different federal courts).

PROBLEMS

9-14. When we were examining Rule 23(a), we read *Chandler v. Southwest Jeep-Eagle, Inc.*, 162 F.R.D. 302 (N.D. Ill. 1995), a case that qualified as a class action under Rule 23(b)(3). *See* page 775, *supra.* In editing the case, we omitted that portion of the court's opinion finding that the action qualified under Rule 23(b)(3). On what basis might the court have reached that conclusion?

9-15. In *In re Telectronics, see* page 813, *supra,* after the court of appeals held that the suit did not meet the requirements for a limited-fund Rule 23(b)(1)(B) class action, the case was remanded to the district court. There the parties jointly moved for certification of a settlement class under Rule 23(b)(3). How should the court rule on the certification question? Does the suit satisfy the superiority and predominance requirements in light of the four non-exhaustive factors? *See In re Telectronics Pacing Systems Inc.*, 137 F. Supp. 2d 985 (S.D. Ohio 2001).

9-16. Samuel filed a class action against Simon & Shuster, Inc. ("Simon & Shuster") and the North Shore Collection Agency, alleging that they violated the federal Fair Debt Collection Practices Act (FDCPA) and New York law by allegedly sending 420,000 misleading collection letters regarding overdue bills for book purchases. Simon & Shuster sent the letters on North Shore stationery even though North Shore was not involved in collecting debts for the company. The FDCPA allows statutory damages of up to $1,000 in an individual suit, and the lesser of $500,000 or 1 percent of the defendants' net worth in a class suit, plus reasonable attorneys' fees. Samuel seeks declaratory and injunctive relief, maximum statutory damages to be distributed on a fluid-recovery basis if appropriate, and attorneys' fees. He seeks certification of a nationwide class under Rule 23(b)(3). The defendants oppose certification, contending that even if the requirements of Rule 23(a) are met, a class action is not superior to individual actions. They note that the maximum statutory damages recoverable in this class suit are $500,000, less than $2 per class member, whereas individual suits—none of which has yet been filed—would allow each person to recover $1,000 in statutory damages. The defendants argue that the only people who will benefit from a class action are Samuel's lawyers, while the defendants will be subject to heavy administrative costs, and class members will recover only miniscule amounts. Should the court certify the class under Rule 23(b)(3)? *Compare Weber v. Goodman*, 9 F. Supp. 2d 163 (E.D.N.Y. 1998), *as modified*, 1998 WL 1807355 (E.D.N.Y. June 1, 1998), *with Shroder v. Suburban Coastal Corp.*, 729 F.2d 1371 (11th Cir. 1984).

D.   Settlement or Dismissal of Class Actions

Rule 23(e) provides that any settlement, voluntary dismissal, or compromise of the claims, issues, or defenses of a certified class must be approved by the court. Approval is required both when settlement follows class certification and when, as in *Hanlon v. Chrysler Corp.*, 150 F.3d 1011, page 840, *supra*, the rulings on certification and settlement are being made at the same time. The approval process is a rigorous one. While a federal court must accept or reject the settlement in its entirety, the court may advise the parties that judicial approval is contingent on their making certain specified changes. *See* 5 MOORE'S FEDERAL PRACTICE, *supra*, § 23.168.

The importance of judicial approval in the class action settlement context cannot be overstated, for counsel on both sides may be tempted to short-change the class. Nor will the named plaintiffs necessarily represent the best interests of the class if, as is often the case, their individual recovery is more generous than that of unnamed class members. As Judge Richard Posner explained in *Eubank v. Pella Corp.*, 753 F.3d 718 (7th Cir. 2014):

> A high percentage of lawsuits is settled—but a study of certified class actions in federal court in a two-year period (2005 to 2007) found that *all* 30 such actions had been settled. Emery G. Lee III et al., "Impact of the Class Action Fairness Act on the Federal Courts" 2, 11 (Federal Judicial Center 2008). The reasons that class actions invariably are settled are twofold. Aggregating a great many claims (sometimes tens or even hundreds of thousands—occasionally millions) often creates a potential liability so great that the defendant is unwilling to bear the risk, even if it is only a small probability, of an adverse judgment. At the same time, class counsel, ungoverned as a practical matter by either the named plaintiffs or the other members of the class, have an opportunity to maximize their attorneys' fees—which (besides other expenses) are all they can get from the class action—at the expense of the class. The defendant cares only about the size of the settlement, not how it is divided between attorneys' fees and compensation for the class. From the selfish standpoint of class counsel and the defendant, therefore, the optimal settlement is one modest in overall amount but heavily tilted toward attorneys' fees. As we said in *Creative Montessori Learning Centers v. Ashford Gear LLC*, 662 F.3d 913, 918 (7th Cir. 2011), "we and other courts have often remarked [on] the incentive of class counsel, in complicity with the defendant's counsel, to sell out the class by agreeing with the defendant to recommend that the judge approve a settlement involving a meager recovery for the class but generous compensation for the lawyers—the deal that promotes the self-interest of both class counsel and the defendant and is therefore optimal from the standpoint of their private interests."

Id. at 720.

Under Rule 23's approval process, it is imperative that the court obtain input from those class members who did not participate in negotiating the proposed settlement. To this end, Rule 23(e)(1) requires a court to "direct notice in a reasonable manner to all class members who would be bound" by the settlement. In contrast to Rule 23(c)(2)(B), which mandates "individual notice" to all reasonably ascertainable members of a (b)(3) class, regardless of cost, courts have much broader discretion in deciding what constitutes a "reasonable manner" of notice with respect to proposed settlements. The standard is one that takes into account what is practicable under the circumstances. While courts often insist that notice be sent by first-class mail to all known class members, with some form of published notice for the benefit of unknown members, circumstances may allow for less-sweeping individual notice. Since what is at stake is usually not a member's right to opt out but rather a determination of whether a proposed settlement or dismissal is fair and reasonable, it may be enough that the notice reaches a fair cross-section of the class or of each subclass. But this will not always be true. In a settlement class action brought under Rule 23(b)(3), if a single notice is used to advise members of both their opt-out right and the terms of the proposed settlement, the rigorous notice standards of Rule 23(c)(2)(B) then apply. In addition to notifying class members as to the terms of the proposed settlement, Rule 23(e)(3) requires that the parties "file a statement identifying any agreement made in connection with the proposal." This ensures that the court is aware of any additional concessions, stipulations, or waivers the parties may have made concerning the proposed settlement.

Once the parties have complied with these notice and disclosure provisions, the court must conduct a settlement hearing under Rule 23(e)(2), at which class members may appear and object to the proposal. A court may then approve the settlement, dismissal, or compromise only if it finds it to be "fair, reasonable, and adequate." FED. R. CIV. P. 23(e)(2). And, in a (b)(3) class action, Rule 23(e)(4) gives a judge the discretion to withhold approval of the settlement "unless it affords a new opportunity to request exclusion to individual class members who had an earlier opportunity to request exclusion but did not do so." If the court invokes this last option, additional notice must be given to the class members. Together, these provisions seek to ensure that a judge can serve as a fiduciary to protect unnamed class members against a possibly collusive or unjust resolution of the class action. As noted, one potential risk is that the representative parties may try to use the added leverage afforded by a class suit to extract benefits for themselves, while sacrificing the class's interests. Another concern is that class representatives may have grown faint-hearted and decided to abandon the suit on whatever terms the class opponent was willing to offer. It is also possible that conflicts between class counsel and the class, or between differing segments of the class, may lead to a settlement that unfairly favors some individuals or groups at the expense of others. While many of these dangers are also present when a would-be class action is settled or dismissed without ever being certified, since disposition of such a case will not bind anyone except the named parties, the strict notice and approval requirements of Rule 23(e) are not triggered.

We have been looking at the class action settlement restrictions imposed by Rule 23. An additional set of limitations was adopted as part of the Class Action Fairness Act of 2005 (CAFA), 28 U.S.C. §§ 1711-1715. CAFA's settlement provisions apply to all class actions filed in or removed to federal court—not just those that enter under CAFA's special subject matter jurisdiction provisions. The CAFA provisions essentially do four things. First, and most importantly, they limit the amount that may be awarded in attorneys' fees in cases in which a class action settlement involves an award of coupons to class members. Congress adopted this provision after finding that "[c]lass members often receive little or no benefit from class actions, and are sometimes harmed, such as where . . . counsel are awarded large fees, while leaving class members with coupons or other awards of little or no value. . . ." Pub. L. No. 109-2, § 2(a)(3), 119 Stat. 4 (2005). To ensure that such settlements are fair, and that they do not result in the award of unseemly high fees, CAFA requires court approval of attorneys' fees that are paid in any coupon-settlement case. 28 U.S.C. § 1712(e). It also provides that any portion of a fee that is attributable to an award of coupons "shall be based on the value to class members of the coupons that are redeemed," 28 U.S.C. § 1712(a), not on the face value of the coupons issued. Any balance of the fee "shall be based upon the amount of time class counsel reasonably expended working on the action." 28 U.S.C. § 1712(b)(1).

Second, CAFA bars a federal court from approving any settlement in which a class member is obligated to make payment to class counsel, unless the court finds "that nonmonetary benefits to the class member substantially outweigh the monetary loss." 28 U.S.C. § 1713. In addition, CAFA prohibits a federal court from approving a settlement in which class members living in closer geographic proximity to the court receive a larger award than those living farther away, absent some special reason—such as exposure to air or noise pollution—that accounts for the difference in treatment. 28 U.S.C. § 1714. Finally, CAFA requires that before any class action settlement may be approved by a federal court, the defendants must provide information about the case and notice of the proposed settlement to the U.S. Attorney General's Office (or other federal officials), as well as to the state attorney general (or other officials) in every state in which any class member resides. 28 U.S.C. § 1715. This last provision is designed to give federal and state officials an opportunity, if they wish, to request additional information and to inform the court of any problems they may see with the proposed settlement. Class action defendants have a strong incentive to comply with these notification duties, for if they do not, any class member may elect not to be bound by the settlement agreement and may bring a new action of their own—against the same defendants on the same claim—as long as the statute of limitations has not yet run. 28 U.S.C. § 1715(e)(1).

Hanlon v. Chrysler Corp. [Part II]
150 F.3d 1011 (9th Cir. 1998)

THOMAS, Circuit Judge:

[Earlier, we read those parts of the court's opinion holding that this nationwide settlement class action involving a defective Chrysler minivan latch satisfied Rule

23(a) and (b)(3). *See* page 840, *supra*. In the portions of the opinion that appear below, the court went on to review the district court's approval of the settlement and its award of attorneys' fees. You will recall that notice of the suit and proposed settlement was mailed to 4.3 million class members and that the district court held three fairness hearings before it approved the settlement.]

IV

Having concluded independent of settlement considerations that the proposed class passes certification muster, our analysis must turn to the proposed settlement itself. In that determination, we are guided by Rule 23(e). . . .

A

Adequate notice is critical to court approval of a class settlement under Rule 23(e). In this case, the notice provided to the absent class members provided each member with the opportunity to opt-out and individually pursue any state law remedies that might provide a better opportunity for recovery. The objectors contended at oral argument that even if the notice provided to the class met the requirements of Rule 23(c)—which it clearly did—the absent class members still did not understand what they were giving up. There is no evidence of such wide-scale confusion or ignorance in the record.

On the contrary, the text of the notice plainly stated:

> If the proposed settlement is approved, it will be binding and will release Chrysler from any and all claims, including any claims for consumer damages or equitable relief, arising out of or related to the Minivan rear liftgate latches, that were or could have been asserted by Settlement Class members in the Hanlon lawsuit. In addition, if the proposed settlement is approved, it will release any and all claims, arising out of or related to the Minivan rear liftgate latches, that were or could have been asserted for Settlement Class members in certain class action lawsuits pending in various state courts around the United States. The proposed settlement does not, however, release, dismiss, or affect any claims for personal injury or wrongful death as an alleged result of the rear-door latch on the Minivans.

The notice resulted in approximately 971 members of the class exercising their opt-out right. This number reveals two things: (1) at least some portion of the class understood the notice and chose not to participate in the settlement for whatever reason; and (2) the vast majority of the class—over 99.9%—agreed to be bound. . . .

The individual notice sent to each minivan owner, coupled with the pre-trial publicity, NHTSA actions, and nationwide dealer participation was sufficient to bring the urgency of the action to each class member's attention. There is no evidence that the settlement proposed and accepted by the district court did anything to advance the rights of one group of claimants over another and plaintiffs who were at risk of losing what they deemed valuable claims had an opportunity to protect their interests.

B

Fed. R. Civ. P. 23(e) requires the district court to determine whether a proposed settlement is fundamentally fair, adequate, and reasonable. Our review of the district court's decision to approve a class action settlement is extremely limited. It is the settlement taken as a whole, rather than the individual component parts, that must be examined for overall fairness. *Officers for Justice v. Civil Serv. Comm'n of San Francisco*, 688 F.2d 615, 628 (9th Cir. 1982). Neither the district court nor this court have the ability to "delete, modify or substitute certain provisions." *Id.* at 630. The settlement must stand or fall in its entirety. *Id.*

Assessing a settlement proposal requires the district court to balance a number of factors: [1] the strength of the plaintiffs' case; [2] the risk, expense, complexity, and likely duration of further litigation; [3] the risk of maintaining class action status throughout the trial; [4] the amount offered in settlement; [5] the extent of discovery completed and the stage of the proceedings; [6] the experience and views of counsel; [7] the presence of a governmental participant; and [8] the reaction of the class members to the proposed settlement. To survive appellate review, the district court must show it has explored comprehensively all factors. *See Protective Comm. for Indep. Stockholders of TMT Trailer Ferry, Inc. v. Anderson*, 390 U.S. 414, 434 (1968).

Several circuits have held that settlement approval that takes place prior to formal class certification requires a higher standard of fairness. The dangers of collusion between class counsel and the defendant, as well as the need for additional protections when the settlement is not negotiated by a court-designated class representative, weigh in favor of a more probing inquiry than may normally be required under Rule 23(e). . . . *See also Manual for Complex Litigation* § 30.45 (3rd ed. 1995) ("Approval under Rule 23(e) of settlements involving settlement classes . . . requires closer judicial scrutiny than approval of settlements where class certification has been litigated."). [*See id.*, 4th ed. 2014, at § 21.612.] No circuit has held to the contrary. Because settlement class actions present unique due process concerns for absent class members, we agree with our sister circuits and adopt this standard as our own.

We have repeatedly stated that the decision to approve or reject a settlement is committed to the sound discretion of the trial judge because he is "exposed to the litigants, and their strategies, positions and proof." *Officers for Justice*, 688 F.2d at 626. The district court held a hearing in August 1995 in which it granted preliminary approval of the settlement agreement and approved a class-wide notice. Two fairness hearings followed in November 1995, and a third was held in April 1996. The transcripts of the hearings reveal an exhaustive presentation by the objectors raising virtually all of the issues noted in the briefs and in oral argument before this court.

In approving the settlement under Rule 23(e), the district court noted that the class was not giving up any right to challenge the adequacy of the replacement latch and was relieved from any duty to prove that the original latch was defective. The monitoring by class counsel and the additional outreach provided by

Chrysler also worked in favor of the class in terms of extended notification and the fulfillment of all terms. The district court also retains jurisdiction over the implementation of the settlement. Class counsel may return to court if Chrysler is not using its "best efforts" to obtain the latch replacement goals or if the outreach and notification funds are allocated or spent in an inappropriate manner. The court also recognized that the alternatives to settlement were not promising; the parties could return to the bargaining table but that was no guarantee that the class would receive a better deal. Allowing the state court actions to proceed put the entire class at risk of "balkanized decisions" and high expenses—the only benefit being that "a few people would get a little more money."

The judge's decision to approve the settlement was correct on the merits, and reflected the proper deference to the private consensual decision of the parties. As we noted in *Officers for Justice*, "the court's intrusion upon what is otherwise a private consensual agreement negotiated between the parties to a lawsuit must be limited to the extent necessary to reach a reasoned judgment that the agreement is not the product of fraud or overreaching by, or collusion between, the negotiating parties, and that the settlement, taken as a whole, is fair, reasonable and adequate to all concerned." *Id.* at 625. The fairness hearings support such a finding.

There is no evidence to suggest that the settlement was negotiated in haste or in the absence of information illuminating the value of plaintiffs' claims. In fact, settlement negotiations began several months prior to the filing of the consolidated federal action and included numerous meetings. No evidence of collusion was presented to the district court or otherwise evident in the record.

The settlement presented to the district court obligates Chrysler to make the minivans safe. This fact alone sets this case apart from *GM Pick-Up Litig.* and *In re Ford Motor Co. Bronco II Prod. Liab. Litig.*, 981 F. Supp. 969 (E.D. La. 1997))—cases in which a settlement agreement was rejected in large measure because it did nothing to remedy the safety problem with the vehicles. Again and again, the objectors reiterated that their primary concern was the safety of the vehicles and the prevention of injury. Of course it is possible, as many of the objectors' affidavits imply, that the settlement could have been better. But this possibility does not mean the settlement presented was not fair, reasonable or adequate. Settlement is the offspring of compromise; the question we address is not whether the final product could be prettier, smarter or snazzier, but whether it is fair, adequate and free from collusion. In this regard, the fact that the overwhelming majority of the class willingly approved the offer and stayed in the class presents at least some objective positive commentary as to its fairness. There was no disparate treatment between class members; all stood to benefit equally, a fact which lessens the likelihood that the named plaintiffs and their attorneys colluded with Chrysler to increase their own recovery at the expense of the unnamed plaintiffs who class counsel had a duty to represent. No objector stepped forward and suggested that his or her personal claim was being sacrificed for the greater good—and if any thought that was the case, they had the right to opt-out of the class.

The district court's final determination to approve the settlement should be reversed "only upon a strong showing that the district court's decision was a clear abuse of discretion." *In re Pacific Enterprises Sec. Litig.*, 47 F.3d 373, 377 (9th Cir. 1995) (internal quotation omitted). There was no such showing here. . . .

V

We review a district court's award of attorneys fees for an abuse of discretion. *In re Washington Public Power Supply System Sec. Litig.*, 19 F.3d 1291, 1296 (9th Cir. 1994).

At Chrysler's insistence, class counsel and Chrysler did not negotiate or discuss attorneys fees until after the final settlement agreement was presented to the court. The parties then met with retired California Superior Court Judge Coleman Fannin in a fee mediation session. They eventually agreed to a fee of $5 million coupled with $200,000 in costs; Judge Fannin's affidavit indicated that he initially recommended this amount. The mediator's role did not include evaluating the benefits of the settlement so Judge Fannin had no way to ascertain whether $5 million was an appropriate percentage recovery. His affidavit was submitted only to certify that the figure was the result of legitimate arms-length negotiations.

Contrary to the objectors' contention, we do not believe the weight the district court gave to the mediation proceeding was an abrogation of its duty to determine independently whether the fee award was proper. Rather, the court relied on the mediator as independent confirmation that the fee was not the result of collusion or a sacrifice of the interests of the class, an inquiry the court was required to make. More importantly, Judge Legge appears to have reviewed the award using a lodestar methodology by requiring class counsel to submit detailed evidence of their work on behalf of the class. The choice of method for determining attorney fees is also reviewed for an abuse of discretion.

This court has affirmed the use of two separate methods for determining attorneys fees, depending on the case. In "common-fund" cases where the settlement or award creates a large fund for distribution to the class, the district court has discretion to use either a percentage or lodestar method. The percentage method means that the court simply awards the attorneys a percentage of the fund sufficient to provide class counsel with a reasonable fee. This circuit has established 25% of the common fund as a benchmark award for attorney fees. *Six (6) Mexican Workers v. Arizona Citrus Growers*, 904 F.2d 1301, 1311 (9th Cir. 1990).

Although no class member is entitled to a cash recovery—making valuation of the settlement agreement more difficult—Chrysler and class counsel valued the settlement at $115 million. This is the amount Chrysler charged against its earnings in order to account for its voluntary service action and the production and installation of the replacement latches. The fee award of $5.2 million represents roughly 4.5% of this "common fund", significantly less than the 25% commonly used under *Six Mexican Workers*. We note, however, that the court rejected the idea of a straight percentage recovery because of its uncertainty as to the valuation of the settlement.

In employment, civil rights and other injunctive relief class actions, courts often use a lodestar calculation because there is no way to gauge the net value of the settlement or any percentage thereof. The lodestar calculation begins with the multiplication of the number of hours reasonably expended by a reasonable hourly rate. *Blum v. Stenson*, 465 U.S. 886, 897 (1984). The hours expended and the rate should be supported by adequate documentation and other evidence; thus, attorneys working on cases where a lodestar may be employed should keep records and time sheets documenting their work and time spent. The resulting figure may be adjusted upward or downward to account for several factors including the quality of the representation, the benefit obtained for the class, the complexity and novelty of the issues presented, and the risk of nonpayment.

Class counsel presented affidavits to the district court justifying their fees on the basis of their work on the individual state class actions. The fee award also includes all future services that class counsel must provide through the life of the latch replacement program. They must remain available to enforce the contractual elements of the settlement agreement and represent any class members who encounter difficulties. The factual record provides a sufficient evidentiary basis for the district court's approval of the fee request. The lodestar calculation received further support from the mediator's recommendation, although we note that such a recommendation is never the starting point for calculation of a fee award. We find no abuse of discretion.

VI

The certification of the settlement class, the approval of the class settlement and the fee award were well within the guidelines provided by *Amchem* and Fed. R. Civ. P. 23. Accordingly, we affirm the judgment of the district court.

NOTES AND QUESTIONS

1. Approving the settlement.   Did the settlement procedure followed by the district court comply with the provisions of Rule 23(e)? In its opinion, the Ninth Circuit lists eight factors that a district court must consider in reviewing the fairness, adequacy, and reasonableness of a proposed class action settlement. Which of the factors supported the district court's approval of the settlement? Did any of the factors weigh against approval? In addition to the factors listed in *Hanlon*, courts also consider (1) the reasonableness of the settlement fund in light of the best possible recovery; (2) the defendants' ability to withstand a larger judgment; (3) the existence and probable outcomes of claims by other classes and subclasses; (4) whether class members had a right to opt out; (5) the reasonableness of attorneys' fees; and (6) the possible existence of fraud or collusion behind the settlement. *See* 5 MOORE'S FEDERAL PRACTICE, *supra*, § 23.164.

2. Challenging a settlement on appeal.   When the Ninth Circuit reviewed the settlement in this case, did it evaluate each of the factors that it listed as being relevant? Is there a difference between the way trial courts and appellate courts address this issue? Once a federal trial court approves a class action settlement, must an unnamed class member who unsuccessfully objected to that settlement and who now wishes to appeal the district court's approval ruling, formally intervene as a party in the suit in order to file an appeal? Even though only named parties may normally appeal an adverse judgment, the Supreme Court in *Devlin v. Scardelletti*, 536 U.S. 1 (2002), held that this rule does not apply in the class action setting. Instead, said the Court, once a class has been certified, "nonnamed class members . . . who have objected in a timely manner to approval of the settlement at the fairness hearing have the power to bring an appeal without first intervening." *Id.* at 14. *See also Smith v. Bayer Corp.*, 131 S. Ct. 2368, 2379 (2011) (same).

3. *The timing of notice.*   Did the district court send class members a separate notice of the proposed settlement under Rule 23(e), or was this notice combined with the Rule 23(c)(2)(B) notice required in (b)(3) actions? Does this procedure offer any advantages to class members? As one court noted,

> the use of the settlement class [in (b)(3) actions] in some sense enhances plaintiffs' right to opt out. Since the plaintiff is offered the opportunity to opt out of the class simultaneously with the opportunity to accept or reject the settlement offer, which is supposed to be accompanied by all information on settlement, the plaintiff knows exactly what result he or she sacrifices when opting out.

In re Gen. Motors Corp. Pick-Up Truck Fuel Tank Prods. Liab. Litig., 55 F.3d 768, 792 (3d Cir.), *cert. denied*, 516 U.S. 824 (1995). By contrast, in ordinary (b)(3) class actions, the class has been certified and the opt-out period has typically expired before a settlement is reached. If class members don't like its terms, their principal recourse is to object to the settlement and hope that the court will reject it. However, as noted earlier, Rule 23(e)(4) gives a federal court the option in a (b)(3) action to "refuse to approve a settlement unless it affords a new opportunity to request exclusion to individual class members who had an earlier opportunity to request exclusion but did not do so." FED. R. CIV. P. 23(e)(4).

4. *Significance of opt-outs.* Only 971 class members opted out after seeing the proposed settlement. That number represented about one-fiftieth of 1 percent of the 4.3 million class members who received notice. Does the fact that the opt-outs were so few suggest that the settlement was a fair one since, at least in theory, any of the other class members could have opted out as well? Or might it reflect another reality? As one court explained in a case involving a class of those who had purchased defective windows:

> [O]pting out of a class action is very rare. Virtually no one who receives notice that he is a member of a class in a class action suit opts out. He doesn't know what he could do as an opt-out. He's unlikely to hire a lawyer to litigate over a window. . . . A study of other product-liability class actions found that the average opt-out percentage was less than one tenth of one percent. Theodore Eisenberg & Geoffrey Miller, *The Role of Opt-Outs and Objectors in Class Action Litigation: Theoretical and Empirical Issues*, 57 VAND. L. REV. 1529, 1549 (2004) . . . . [A] low opt-out rate is no evidence that a class action settlement was "fair" to the members of the class.

Eubank v. Pella Corp., 753 F.3d 718, 728 (7th Cir. 2014) (and noting that the opt-out rate in that case was "only one twentieth of one percent of the recipients of the notice of approved settlement").

5. *Preferential treatment of class representatives.*   The court in *Hanlon* noted that the settlement involved no disparate treatment of class members and that all were treated in the same manner. Courts are understandably alert to settlements that treat the named parties more favorably than other class members. However, courts often approve "incentive awards" for class representatives. "Such awards are discretionary, and are intended to compensate class representatives for work done on behalf of the class, to make up for financial or reputational risk undertaken in bringing the action, and sometimes to recognize their willingness to act as a private attorney general. Awards are generally sought after a settlement or verdict has been achieved." *Rodriguez v. West Pub. Co.*, 563 F.3d 948, 958-959 (9th Cir. 2008). *See, e.g., Cook v. Niedert*, 142 F.3d 1004, 1016 (7th Cir. 1998) (approving $25,000 incentive award for named plaintiffs in ERISA class action); MANUAL FOR COMPLEX LITIGATION, *supra*, §§ 21.61, 21.62 & n.971 (noting that differentials among awards are not necessarily improper but call for judicial scrutiny); 5 MOORE'S FEDERAL PRACTICE, *supra*, § 23.164[6]. The situation is very different if the named plaintiffs and class counsel enter into an "incentive agreement" at the outset of the case, where the size of a named plaintiff's award turns on the dollar amount of the settlement or verdict. In this latter case, the amount of the award may have nothing to do with the factors courts typically consider in making an award. Moreover, it could create a conflict of interest among the named plaintiffs, class counsel, and the class itself in terms of what type of relief is best in the case. *See Rodriquez v. West Pub. Co., supra* (disapproving *ex ante* incentive agreement where each named plaintiff's award would range from $10,000 to $75,000, depending on the dollar amount of the settlement or verdict).

6. *Attorneys' fees.*   Class action judgments may involve an award of attorneys' fees if such an award was authorized by statute or by a prior agreement between the parties. In the settlement context, the parties' agreement often contains a provision concerning the payment of fees and costs to class counsel. In either case, if the class was certified—whether early on or at the time of the settlement—Rule 23(h) requires that class counsel seek judicial approval of the award, which will be granted only if the award is reasonable. If the award is part of a proposed settlement, the court must accept or reject it as part of the overall agreement. In *Hanlon*, was the agreement as to counsel's fees part of or separate from the class settlement itself? Are there ethical problems for class counsel in negotiating a fee along with a class settlement? Does class counsel face a conflict of interest in terms of how the settlement allocates relief as between the class and its attorneys? How did the parties in *Hanlon* attempt to deal with these problems? These conflicts can be eliminated if the parties let the court award attorneys' fees, to be paid either out of the fund created by the settlement or on top of the class's relief. In the latter case, the parties may agree to a cap on the maximum fee to be awarded.

Whether the court is itself awarding the fees, or simply reviewing fees agreed to by the parties, it will typically employ either the "lodestar" or the "percentage" method. In federal courts, there is a trend in favor of using the latter approach in common-fund cases. *See In re Sumotomo Copper Litig.*, 74 F. Supp. 2d 393, 396-398 (S.D.N.Y. 1999) (noting trend in federal circuits). The argument in favor of the percentage method is that it is simpler to apply and less subject to manipulation by counsel. And, since it rewards counsel based on the amount recovered for the class, it "directly aligns the interests of the class and its counsel and provides a powerful incentive for the efficient prosecution and early resolution of litigation, which clearly benefits both litigants and the judicial system." *In re Am. Bank Note Holographics, Inc. Sec. Litig.*, 127 F. Supp. 2d 418, 431-432 (S.D.N.Y. 2001). The Ninth Circuit's benchmark figure of 25 percent for common-fund cases is typical of that used in other circuits. *See* MANUAL FOR COMPLEX LITIGATION, *supra*, §§ 14.121, 21.7; 5 MOORE'S FEDERAL PRACTICE, *supra*, § 23.124[5][b]. Are there cases that may not lend themselves to the percentage method? Why did the *Hanlon* court use the lodestar approach?

Regardless of the method used, the fees awarded class counsel "may not exceed what is 'reasonable' under the circumstances," and while a district court's determination as to "[w]hat constitutes a reasonable fee . . . will not be overturned absent an abuse of discretion," *Goldberger v. Integrated Res., Inc.*, 209 F.3d 43, 47 (2d Cir. 2000), appellate review is far from perfunctory. *See McDaniel v. County of Schenectady*, 595 F.3d 411, 416 (2d Cir. 2010). Indeed, even when courts using the percentage method award fees far below the 25 percent benchmark, the award may still be set aside on excessiveness grounds. *See, e.g., In re Cendant Corp. PRIDES Litig.*, 243 F.3d 722 (3d Cir.), *cert. denied*, 534 U.S. 889 (2001) (vacating as excessive $19.3 million attorneys' fee award in class action settlement judgment when award, though only 5.7 percent of total class recovery, amounted to compensation of $3,300 per hour — seven times the attorneys' maximum hourly rate — in a fairly noncomplex case).

To avoid these problems, courts employing the percentage-of-recovery method may still "use the lodestar method to cross-check the reasonableness of a percentage-of-recovery fee award. The cross-check is performed by dividing the proposed fee award by the lodestar calculation, resulting in a lodestar multiplier. When the multiplier is too great, the court should reconsider its calculation under the percentage-of-recovery method, with an eye toward reducing the award." *In re AT&T Corp.*, 455 F.3d 160, 164 (3d Cir. 2006) (internal citations omitted). *And see Americana Art China Co., Inc. v. Foxfire Printing and Packaging, Inc.*, 743 F.3d 243 (7th Cir. 2014) (affirming district court's use of lodestar method when percentage method would have resulted in a much larger and possibly inequitable fee).

7. *Coupon settlements under CAFA. Hanlon* was decided in 1998, seven years before CAFA took effect. Had CAFA been in effect at the time, would *Hanlon* have qualified as a "coupon settlement" case so as to be subject to 28 U.S.C. § 1712? Surprisingly, CAFA never defines the term "coupon settlement." While some courts view coupon settlements as limited to those that offer a discount on future purchases, others have found the term satisfied by the free distribution of a new product even without the need for an additional purchase. *See* James M.

Finberg & Laura M. Reich, *CAFA Settlement Provisions, in* THE CLASS ACTION FAIRNESS ACT: LAW AND STRATEGY 309-313 (Gregory C. Cook ed., 2013). Under the latter definition, the settlement in *Hanlon* would likely qualify, for minivan owners were in effect given a coupon entitling them to a new latch without their having to make any additional purchase from Chrysler. If so, would the attorneys' fee award in *Hanlon* have complied with the terms of § 1712?

Under § 1712(a), if attorneys' fees are based on a calculation as to the value of the coupons, a court must look at the value of the coupons *actually redeemed, i.e.,* at the number of Chrysler owners who in fact took advantage of the replacement service, rather than at the face value of the 4.3 million replacement offers issued. Since the fee award in *Hanlon* was made before any replacements had occurred, § 1712(a) would not have been satisfied. To comply with that provision, attorneys' fees could not have been awarded until *after* the period for obtaining replacements had expired. The named plaintiffs and class counsel would then have had a strong incentive—one contrary to the interests of class members—to set a short time period for replacements, after which the offer would expire. Fearing that the court might not approve such a scheme, might the plaintiffs have abandoned the coupon settlement route entirely? One of CAFA's purposes was in fact to discourage the use of coupon settlements and it appears to have had that effect. *See* Finberg & Reich, *supra,* at 308-309, 313.

Even if we treat *Hanlon* as a coupon settlement case, could plaintiffs' attorneys have avoided the strictures of § 1712(a) by calculating their fees not on the basis of the value of the latch replacement offer but rather on "the amount of time class counsel reasonably expended working on the action"? *See* 28 U.S.C. § 1712(b)(1). Did the *Hanlon* court affirm the award of attorneys' fees by looking solely at the value of the latch replacement coupons, or was the award independently justifiable under the lodestar method? Is this alternative approach authorized by § 1712(b)? *See also In re HP Inkjet Printer Litig.,* 2014 WL 4949584 (N.D. Cal. Sept. 30, 2014) (after court of appeals reversed attorneys' fee award made under § 1712(a) because district court did not consider the value of the coupons "actually redeemed," plaintiffs then sought and were awarded attorneys' fees under § 1712(b) by ignoring the coupons entirely and instead looking exclusively at the value of counsel's services using the lodestar method).

We have treated *Hanlon* as a coupon settlement case. Yet the settlement there also "obligate[d] Chrysler to make the minivans safe." To the extent this involves equitable relief, would the case now fall within § 1712(c)? If so, would this change the way attorneys' fees are calculated in the case? In retrospect, was the *Hanlon* court sensitive to the same concerns that later prompted Congress to enact CAFA's class action settlement provisions?

PROBLEM

9-17. Crawford and Blair filed separate federal class actions against Equifax on behalf of debtors who had received collection letters that violated the Fair Debt

Collection Practices Act. Each suit sought to enjoin further use of the letter and to recover statutory damages, which are capped at the lesser of $500,000 or 1 percent of the debt collector's net worth. *Crawford*, which was filed first, was brought on behalf of a nationwide class that includes the *Blair* class, which is limited to debtors living in Illinois. *Crawford* was certified under Rule 23(b)(2); *Blair* was certified under Rule 23(b)(3). The *Blair* court declined to stay the proceedings before it. As a result, the actions proceeded simultaneously before different judges. Due to the difference in class sizes, the maximum possible recovery in *Crawford* was $2.34 per class member, as compared to $250 per class member in *Blair*. While *Blair* was pending, the *Crawford* court tentatively approved a settlement providing that (1) Equifax will cease sending the disputed letter; (2) Crawford will personally receive $500 in damages and a $1,500 incentive award for serving as the class representative; (3) Equifax will donate $5,500 to a law school legal clinic for use in protecting consumers; (4) Equifax will pay attorneys' fees of $78,000 to Crawford's lawyer; (5) class members remain free to file their own suits, but no other suit may proceed as a class action. The settlement contains no finding or concession of liability on Equifax's part. Blair intervened in *Crawford* and objected to the court's certification of the class under Rule 23(b)(2) and to the terms of the settlement. After holding a Rule 23(e) hearing, the *Crawford* court gave final approval to the settlement and refused to alter the basis for certification. Blair has appealed.

A. Should the court of appeals affirm the district court's certification of the *Crawford* class under Rule 23(b)(2)?
B. Should the court of appeals affirm the district court's approval of the *Crawford* settlement?
C. If the court affirms both the certification order and the settlement in *Crawford*, what effect will this have on the pending *Blair* action?

See Crawford v. Equifax Payment Servs., Inc., 201 F.3d 877 (7th Cir. 2000).

E.   Class Arbitration Waivers

We have thus far been looking at the use of class actions to litigate cases in court. There are times, however, when parties may have agreed that any disputes that arise between them shall be resolved through arbitration rather than by resort to litigation. Although arbitration arose as a means for resolving individual disputes, in recent years there has been increasing use of so-called class arbitration, *i.e.*, an arbitration proceeding brought on behalf of a group of similarly situated individuals, each seeking relief for a similar wrong. The use of class arbitration received a green light from the Supreme Court's decision in *Green Tree Financial Corp. v. Bazzle*, 539 U.S. 444 (2003), which held that the Federal Arbitration Act (FAA), 9 U.S.C. §§ 1 *et seq.*, does not preclude arbitration proceedings from being conducted on a classwide rather than an individual basis. Instead, said the Court, the validity of such clauses is to be determined under the *general* principles of state contract law and is not otherwise preempted by the FAA. Where an arbitrator, applying general contract law principles, concludes that an agreement between the parties authorizes class arbitration, that decision is effectively unreviewable by the courts. "The arbitrator's construction holds, however good, bad, or ugly .... [T]he question for a judge is not whether the arbitrator construed the parties' contract correctly, but whether he construed it at all." *Oxford Health Plans LLC v. Sutter*, 133 S. Ct. 2064, 2071 (2013).

The Court in *Bazzle* did not address the separate issue of whether in the absence of an express or fairly implied authorization of the parties, judicially ordered class arbitration was consistent with the FAA. In *Stolt-Nielsen S.A. v. AnimalFeeds International Corp.*, 559 U.S. 662 (2010), the Court answered this question, holding that "a party may not be compelled under the FAA to submit to class arbitration unless there is a contractual basis for concluding that the party *agreed* to do so." *Id.* at 684 (emphasis in original). As the Court explained, "An implicit agreement to authorize class-action arbitration . . . is not a term that the arbitrator may infer solely from the fact of the parties' agreement to arbitrate. This is so because class-action arbitration changes the nature of arbitration to such a degree that it cannot be presumed the parties consented to it by simply agreeing to submit their disputes to an arbitrator." *Id.* at 685. The Court left open the possibility that class arbitration might sometimes be proper even in the absence of an express authorization: "We have no occasion to decide what contractual basis may support a finding that the parties agreed to authorize class-action arbitration. Here, as noted, the parties stipulated that there was 'no agreement' on the issue of class-action arbitration." *Id.* at 687 n.10.

In response to *Bazzle*, and in an effort to eliminate any doubt as to whether class arbitration had been authorized, some companies whose consumer or employment agreements contained compulsory arbitration clauses began including an express class-action waiver provision so as to make clear that arbitration could proceed only on an individual basis. A bank credit card agreement might thus provide that any disputes arising in connection with the card must be resolved by individual arbitration and that the use of class actions in proceedings brought by customers against the bank is prohibited.

The potential value of being able to conduct some arbitrations on a classwide basis stems from the fact that, as with ordinary civil litigation, the amounts at stake for those adversely affected by a company's wrongdoing may be so small as to make it economically infeasible to pursue such arbitration claims on an individual basis. Thus, if a contractual compulsory arbitration clause is coupled with a class-action prohibition, the result may be that a company can in effect avoid all liability for conduct that inflicted relatively small harms on thousands of individuals. Knowing this, a company might be much less deterred from engaging in illegal conduct than it would be were there a likelihood of its being held accountable through class-based arbitration.

The question that remained was whether an agreement that prohibits compulsory arbitration from proceeding on a classwide basis might, consistent with the FAA, be held to be legally unenforceable under general principles of state contract law such as duress or unconscionability. The *Stolt-Nielsen* Court had no need to answer this question, for the parties were "sophisticated business entities" to whom these state law defenses did not apply and the class-arbitration prohibition there was upheld.

AT&T Mobility LLC v. Concepcion
563 U.S. 333 (2011)

JUSTICE SCALIA delivered the opinion of the Court.

Section 2 of the Federal Arbitration Act (FAA) makes agreements to arbitrate "valid, irrevocable, and enforceable, save upon such grounds as exist at law or in equity for the revocation of any contract." 9 U.S.C. § 2. We consider whether the FAA prohibits States from conditioning the enforceability of certain arbitration agreements on the availability of classwide arbitration procedures.

I

In February 2002, Vincent and Liza Concepcion entered into an agreement for the sale and servicing of cellular telephones with AT&T Mobility LCC (AT&T). The contract provided for arbitration of all disputes between the parties, but required that claims be brought in the parties' "individual capacity, and not as a plaintiff or class member in any purported class or representative proceeding."[2] The agreement authorized AT&T to make unilateral amendments, which it did to the arbitration provision on several occasions. . . .

The revised agreement provides that customers may initiate dispute proceedings by completing a one-page Notice of Dispute form available on AT&T's Web site. AT&T may then offer to settle the claim; if it does not, or if the dispute is not resolved within 30 days, the customer may invoke arbitration by filing a separate Demand for Arbitration, also available on AT&T's Web site. In the event the parties proceed to arbitration, the agreement specifies that AT&T must pay all costs for nonfrivolous claims; that arbitration must take place in the county in which the customer is billed; that, for claims of $10,000 or less, the customer may choose whether the arbitration proceeds in person, by telephone, or based only on submissions; that either party may bring a claim in small claims court in lieu of arbitration; and that the arbitrator may award any form of individual relief, including injunctions and presumably punitive damages. The agreement, moreover, denies AT&T any ability to seek reimbursement of its attorney's fees, and, in the event that a customer receives an arbitration award greater than AT&T's last written settlement offer, requires AT&T to pay a $7,500 minimum recovery and twice the amount of the claimant's attorney's fees.

---

2. That provision further states that "the arbitrator may not consolidate more than one person's claims, and may not otherwise preside over any form of a representative or class proceeding."

The Concepcions purchased AT&T service, which was advertised as including the provision of free phones; they were not charged for the phones, but they were charged $30.22 in sales tax based on the phones' retail value. In March 2006, the Concepcions filed a complaint against AT&T in the United States District Court for the Southern District of California. The complaint was later consolidated with a putative class action alleging, among other things, that AT&T had engaged in false advertising and fraud by charging sales tax on phones it advertised as free.

In March 2008, AT&T moved to compel arbitration under the terms of its contract with the Concepcions. The Concepcions opposed the motion, contending that the arbitration agreement was unconscionable and unlawfully exculpatory under California law because it disallowed classwide procedures. The District Court denied AT&T's motion. It described AT&T's arbitration agreement favorably, noting, for example, that the informal dispute-resolution process was "quick, easy to use" and likely to "promp[t] full or . . . even excess payment to the customer *without* the need to arbitrate or litigate"; that the $7,500 premium functioned as "a substantial inducement for the consumer to pursue the claim in arbitration" if a dispute was not resolved informally; and that consumers who were members of a class would likely be worse off. Nevertheless, relying on the California Supreme Court's decision in *Discover Bank v. Superior Court*, 36 Cal. 4th 148, 30 Cal. Rptr. 3d 76, 113 P.3d 1100 (2005), the court found that the arbitration provision was unconscionable because AT&T had not shown that bilateral arbitration adequately substituted for the deterrent effects of class actions.

The Ninth Circuit affirmed, also finding the provision unconscionable under California law as announced in *Discover Bank. Laster v. AT&T Mobility LLC*, 584 F.3d 849, 855 (2009). It also held that the *Discover Bank* rule was not preempted by the FAA because that rule was simply "a refinement of the unconscionability analysis applicable to contracts generally in California." In response to AT&T's argument that the Concepcions' interpretation of California law discriminated against arbitration, the Ninth Circuit rejected the contention that " 'class proceedings will reduce the efficiency and expeditiousness of arbitration'" and noted that " '*Discover Bank* placed arbitration agreements with class action waivers on the *exact same footing* as contracts that bar class action litigation outside the context of arbitration.'"

We granted certiorari.

II

The FAA was enacted in 1925 in response to widespread judicial hostility to arbitration agreements. Section 2, the "primary substantive provision of the Act," *Moses H. Cone Memorial Hospital v. Mercury Constr. Corp.*, 460 U.S. 1, 24 (1983), provides, in relevant part, as follows:

> "A written provision in any maritime transaction or a contract evidencing a transaction involving commerce to settle by arbitration a controversy thereafter arising out of such contract or transaction . . . shall be valid, irrevocable, and enforceable, save upon such grounds as exist at law or in equity for the revocation of any contract." 9 U.S.C. § 2.

We have described this provision as reflecting both a "liberal federal policy favoring arbitration," and the "fundamental principle that arbitration is a matter of contract. . . ." In line with these principles, courts must place arbitration agreements on an equal footing with other contracts, and enforce them according to their terms.

The final phrase of § 2, however, permits arbitration agreements to be declared unenforceable "upon such grounds as exist at law or in equity for the revocation of any contract." This saving clause permits agreements to arbitrate to be invalidated by "generally applicable contract defenses, such as fraud, duress, or unconscionability," but not by defenses that apply only to arbitration or that derive their meaning from the fact that an agreement to arbitrate is at issue. The question in this case is whether § 2 preempts California's rule classifying most collective-arbitration waivers in consumer contracts as unconscionable. We refer to this rule as the *Discover Bank* rule.

Under California law, courts may refuse to enforce any contract found "to have been unconscionable at the time it was made," or may "limit the application of any unconscionable clause." Cal. Civ. Code Ann. § 1670.5(a) (West 1985). A finding of unconscionability requires "a 'procedural' and a 'substantive' element, the former focusing on 'oppression' or 'surprise' due to unequal bargaining power, the latter on 'overly harsh' or 'one-sided' results." *Armendariz v. Foundation Health Psychcare Servs., Inc.*, 24 Cal. 4th 83, 114, 99 Cal. Rptr. 2d 745, 6 P.3d 669, 690 (2000).

In *Discover Bank*, the California Supreme Court applied this framework to class-action waivers in arbitration agreements and held as follows:

> "[W]hen the waiver is found in a consumer contract of adhesion in a setting in which disputes between the contracting parties predictably involve small amounts of damages, and when it is alleged that the party with the superior bargaining power has carried out a scheme to deliberately cheat large numbers of consumers out of individually small sums of money, then . . . the waiver becomes in practice the exemption of the party 'from responsibility for [its] own fraud, or willful injury to the person or property of another.' Under these circumstances, such waivers are unconscionable under California law and should not be enforced." (quoting Cal. Civ. Code Ann. § 1668).

California courts have frequently applied this rule to find arbitration agreements unconscionable.

III

A

The Concepcions argue that the *Discover Bank* rule, given its origins in California's unconscionability doctrine and California's policy against exculpation, is a ground that "exist[s] at law or in equity for the revocation of any contract" under FAA § 2. Moreover, they argue that even if we construe the *Discover Bank* rule as a prohibition on collective-action waivers rather than simply an application of unconscionability, the rule would still be applicable to all dispute-resolution contracts, since California prohibits waivers of class litigation as well.

When state law prohibits outright the arbitration of a particular type of claim, the analysis is straightforward: The conflicting rule is displaced by the FAA. *Preston v. Ferrer*, 552 U.S. 346, 353 (2008). But the inquiry becomes more complex when a doctrine normally thought to be generally applicable, such as duress or, as relevant here, unconscionability, is alleged to have been applied in a fashion that disfavors arbitration. In *Perry v. Thomas*, 482 U.S. 483 (1987), for example, we noted that the FAA's preemptive effect might extend even to grounds traditionally thought to exist " 'at law or in equity for the revocation of any contract.' " We said that a court may not "rely on the uniqueness of an agreement to arbitrate as a basis for a state-law holding that enforcement would be unconscionable, for this would enable the court to effect what . . . the state legislature cannot."

An obvious illustration of this point would be a case finding unconscionable or unenforceable as against public policy consumer arbitration agreements that fail to provide for judicially monitored discovery. The rationalizations for such a holding are neither difficult to imagine nor different in kind from those articulated in *Discover Bank*. A court might reason that no consumer would knowingly waive his right to full discovery, as this would enable companies to hide their wrongdoing. Or the court might simply say that such agreements are exculpatory—restricting discovery would be of greater benefit to the company than the consumer, since the former is more likely to be sued than to sue. And, the reasoning would continue, because such a rule applies the general principle of unconscionability or public-policy disapproval of exculpatory agreements, it is applicable to "any" contract and thus preserved by § 2 of the FAA. In practice, of course, the rule would have a disproportionate impact on arbitration agreements; but it would presumably apply to contracts purporting to restrict discovery in litigation as well.

Other examples are easy to imagine. The same argument might apply to a rule classifying as unconscionable arbitration agreements that fail to abide by the Federal Rules of Evidence, or that disallow an ultimate disposition by a jury (perhaps termed "a panel of twelve lay arbitrators" to help avoid preemption). Such examples are not fanciful, since the judicial hostility towards arbitration that prompted the FAA had manifested itself in "a great variety" of "devices and formulas" declaring arbitration against public policy. And although these statistics are not definitive, it is worth noting that California's courts have been more likely to hold contracts to arbitrate unconscionable than other contracts. . . .

The Concepcions suggest that all this is just a parade of horribles, and no genuine worry. "Rules aimed at destroying arbitration" or "demanding procedures incompatible with arbitration," they concede, "would be preempted by the FAA because they cannot sensibly be reconciled with Section 2." The "grounds" available under § 2's saving clause, they admit, "should not be construed to include a State's mere preference for procedures that are incompatible with arbitration and 'would wholly eviscerate arbitration agreements.' "

We largely agree. Although § 2's saving clause preserves generally applicable contract defenses, nothing in it suggests an intent to preserve state-law rules that stand as an obstacle to the accomplishment of the FAA's objectives. As we have said, a federal statute's saving clause " 'cannot in reason be construed as [allowing] a common law right, the continued existence of which would be absolutely inconsistent with the provisions of the act. In other words, the act cannot be held to destroy itself.'" *American Telephone & Telegraph Co. v. Central Office Telephone, Inc.,* 524 U.S. 214, 227-228 (1998).

We differ with the Concepcions only in the application of this analysis to the matter before us. We do not agree that rules requiring judicially monitored discovery or adherence to the Federal Rules of Evidence are "a far cry from this case." The overarching purpose of the FAA . . . is to ensure the enforcement of arbitration agreements according to their terms so as to facilitate streamlined proceedings. Requiring the availability of classwide arbitration interferes with fundamental attributes of arbitration and thus creates a scheme inconsistent with the FAA.

B

The "principal purpose" of the FAA is to "ensur[e] that private arbitration agreements are enforced according to their terms." This purpose is readily apparent from the FAA's text. Section 2 makes arbitration agreements "valid, irrevocable, and enforceable" as written (subject, of course, to the saving clause); § 3 requires courts to stay litigation of arbitral claims pending arbitration of those claims "in accordance with the terms of the agreement"; and § 4 requires courts to compel arbitration "in accordance with the terms of the agreement" upon the motion of either party to the agreement (assuming that the "making of the arbitration agreement or the failure . . . to perform the same" is not at issue). In light of these provisions, we have held that parties may agree to limit the issues subject to arbitration, to arbitrate according to specific rules, and to limit *with whom* a party will arbitrate its disputes.

The point of affording parties discretion in designing arbitration processes is to allow for efficient, streamlined procedures tailored to the type of dispute. It can be specified, for example, that the decisionmaker be a specialist in the relevant field, or that proceedings be kept confidential to protect trade secrets. And the informality of arbitral proceedings is itself desirable, reducing the cost and increasing the speed of dispute resolution. . . .

Contrary to the dissent's view, our cases place it beyond dispute that the FAA was designed to promote arbitration. They have repeatedly described the Act as "embod[ying] [a] national policy favoring arbitration," and "a liberal federal policy favoring arbitration agreements, notwithstanding any state substantive or procedural policies to the contrary." Thus, in *Preston v. Ferrer,* holding preempted a state-law rule requiring exhaustion of administrative remedies before arbitration, we said: "A prime objective of an agreement to arbitrate is to achieve 'streamlined proceedings and expeditious results,'" which objective would be "frustrated" by requiring a dispute to be heard by an agency first. That rule, we said, would "at the least, hinder speedy resolution of the controversy."

California's *Discover Bank* rule similarly interferes with arbitration. Although the rule does not *require* classwide arbitration, it allows any party to a consumer contract to demand it *ex post*. The rule is limited to adhesion contracts, but the times in which consumer contracts were anything other than adhesive are long past.[6] The rule also requires that damages be predictably small, and that the consumer allege a scheme to cheat consumers. The former requirement, however, is toothless and malleable (the Ninth Circuit has held that damages of $4,000 are sufficiently small, and the latter has no limiting effect, as all that is required is an allegation. Consumers remain free to bring and resolve their disputes on a bilateral basis under *Discover Bank*, and some may well do so; but there is little incentive for lawyers to arbitrate on behalf of individuals when they may do so for a class and reap far higher fees in the process. And faced with inevitable class arbitration, companies would have less incentive to continue resolving potentially duplicative claims on an individual basis.

Although we have had little occasion to examine classwide arbitration, our decision in [*Stolt-Nielsen S.A. v. AnimalFeeds International Corp.*, 130 S. Ct. 1758, 1763 (2010)], is instructive. In that case we held that an arbitration panel exceeded its power under § 10(a)(4) of the FAA by imposing class procedures based on policy judgments rather than the arbitration agreement itself or some background principle of contract law that would affect its interpretation. We then held that the agreement at issue, which was silent on the question of class procedures, could not be interpreted to allow them because the "changes brought about by the shift from bilateral arbitration to class-action arbitration" are "fundamental." This is obvious as a structural matter: Classwide arbitration includes absent parties, necessitating additional and different procedures and involving higher stakes. Confidentiality becomes more difficult. And while it is theoretically possible to select an arbitrator with some expertise relevant to the class-certification question, arbitrators are not generally knowledgeable in the often-dominant procedural aspects of certification, such as the protection of absent parties. The conclusion follows that class arbitration, to the extent it is manufactured by *Discover Bank* rather than consensual, is inconsistent with the FAA.

First, the switch from bilateral to class arbitration sacrifices the principal advantage of arbitration—its informality—and makes the process slower, more costly, and more likely to generate procedural morass than final judgment. "In bilateral arbitration, parties forgo the procedural rigor and appellate review of the courts in order to realize the benefits of private dispute resolution: lower costs, greater efficiency and speed, and the ability to choose expert adjudicators to resolve specialized disputes." But before an arbitrator may decide the merits of a claim in classwide procedures, he must first decide, for example, whether the class itself

---

6. Of course States remain free to take steps addressing the concerns that attend contracts of adhesion—for example, requiring class-action-waiver provisions in adhesive arbitration agreements to be highlighted. Such steps cannot, however, conflict with the FAA or frustrate its purpose to ensure that private arbitration agreements are enforced according to their terms.

may be certified, whether the named parties are sufficiently representative and typical, and how discovery for the class should be conducted. A cursory comparison of bilateral and class arbitration illustrates the difference. According to the American Arbitration Association (AAA), the average consumer arbitration between January and August 2007 resulted in a disposition on the merits in six months, four months if the arbitration was conducted by documents only. As of September 2009, the AAA had opened 283 class arbitrations. Of those, 121 remained active, and 162 had been settled, withdrawn, or dismissed. Not a single one, however, had resulted in a final award on the merits. For those cases that were no longer active, the median time from filing to settlement, withdrawal, or dismissal—not judgment on the merits—was 583 days, and the mean was 630 days.

Second, class arbitration *requires* procedural formality. The AAA's rules governing class arbitrations mimic the Federal Rules of Civil Procedure for class litigation. . . . And while parties can alter those procedures by contract, an alternative is not obvious. If procedures are too informal, absent class members would not be bound by the arbitration. For a class-action money judgment to bind absentees in litigation, class representatives must at all times adequately represent absent class members, and absent members must be afforded notice, an opportunity to be heard, and a right to opt out of the class. *Phillips Petroleum Co. v. Shutts*, 472 U.S. 797, 811-812 (1985). At least this amount of process would presumably be required for absent parties to be bound by the results of arbitration.

We find it unlikely that in passing the FAA Congress meant to leave the disposition of these procedural requirements to an arbitrator. Indeed, class arbitration was not even envisioned by Congress when it passed the FAA in 1925; as the California Supreme Court admitted in *Discover Bank*, class arbitration is a "relatively recent development." And it is at the very least odd to think that an arbitrator would be entrusted with ensuring that third parties' due process rights are satisfied.

Third, class arbitration greatly increases risks to defendants. Informal procedures do of course have a cost: The absence of multilayered review makes it more likely that errors will go uncorrected. Defendants are willing to accept the costs of these errors in arbitration, since their impact is limited to the size of individual disputes, and presumably outweighed by savings from avoiding the courts. But when damages allegedly owed to tens of thousands of potential claimants are aggregated and decided at once, the risk of an error will often become unacceptable. Faced with even a small chance of a devastating loss, defendants will be pressured into settling questionable claims. Other courts have noted the risk of "in terrorem" settlements that class actions entail, and class arbitration would be no different.

Arbitration is poorly suited to the higher stakes of class litigation. In litigation, a defendant may appeal a certification decision on an interlocutory basis and, if unsuccessful, may appeal from a final judgment as well. Questions of law are reviewed *de novo* and questions of fact for clear error. In contrast, 9 U.S.C. § 10 allows a court to vacate an arbitral award *only* where the award "was procured by corruption, fraud, or undue means"; "there was evident partiality or corruption

in the arbitrators"; "the arbitrators were guilty of misconduct in refusing to post-
pone the hearing . . . or in refusing to hear evidence pertinent and material to the
controversy[,] or of any other misbehavior by which the rights of any party have
been prejudiced"; or if the "arbitrators exceeded their powers, or so imperfectly
executed them that a mutual, final, and definite award . . . was not made." The
AAA rules do authorize judicial review of certification decisions, but this review
is unlikely to have much effect given these limitations; review under § 10 focuses
on misconduct rather than mistake. . . . We find it hard to believe that defendants
would bet the company with no effective means of review, and even harder to
believe that Congress would have intended to allow state courts to force such a
decision.[8] . . .

The dissent claims that class proceedings are necessary to prosecute small-dollar claims that might otherwise slip through the legal system. But States cannot
require a procedure that is inconsistent with the FAA, even if it is desirable for
unrelated reasons. Moreover, the claim here was most unlikely to go unresolved.
As noted earlier, the arbitration agreement provides that AT&T will pay claimants
a minimum of $7,500 and twice their attorney's fees if they obtain an arbitration
award greater than AT&T's last settlement offer. The District Court found this
scheme sufficient to provide incentive for the individual prosecution of meritorious claims that are not immediately settled, and the Ninth Circuit admitted that
aggrieved customers who filed claims would be "essentially guarantee[d]" to be
made whole. Indeed, the District Court concluded that the Concepcions were
better off under their arbitration agreement with AT&T than they would have
been as participants in a class action, which "could take months, if not years, and
which may merely yield an opportunity to submit a claim for recovery of a small
percentage of a few dollars."

* * *

Because it "stands as an obstacle to the accomplishment and execution of the
full purposes and objectives of Congress," *Hines v. Davidowitz*, 312 U.S. 52, 67
(1941), California's *Discover Bank* rule is preempted by the FAA. The judgment
of the Ninth Circuit is reversed, and the case is remanded for further proceedings
consistent with this opinion.

It is so ordered.

---

8. The dissent cites three large arbitration awards (none of which stems from classwide arbitration) as evidence that parties are willing to submit large claims before an arbitrator. Those examples
might be in point if it could be established that the size of the arbitral dispute was predictable when
the arbitration agreement was entered. Otherwise, all the cases prove is that arbitrators can give huge
awards—which we have never doubted. The point is that in class-action arbitration huge awards
(with limited judicial review) will be entirely predictable, thus rendering arbitration unattractive. It
is not reasonably deniable that requiring consumer disputes to be arbitrated on a classwide basis will
have a substantial deterrent effect on incentives to arbitrate.

[JUSTICE THOMAS'S concurring opinion is omitted.]

JUSTICE BREYER, with whom JUSTICE GINSBURG, JUSTICE SOTOMAYOR, and JUSTICE KAGAN join, dissenting.

The Federal Arbitration Act says that an arbitration agreement "shall be valid, irrevocable, and enforceable, *save upon such grounds as exist at law or in equity for the revocation of any contract.*" 9 U.S.C. § 2 (emphasis added). California law sets forth certain circumstances in which "class action waivers" in *any* contract are unenforceable. In my view, this rule of state law is consistent with the federal Act's language and primary objective. It does not "stan[d] as an obstacle" to the Act's "accomplishment and execution." And the Court is wrong to hold that the federal Act pre-empts the rule of state law.

I

The California law in question consists of an authoritative state-court interpretation of two provisions of the California Civil Code. The first provision makes unlawful all contracts "which have for their object, directly or indirectly, to exempt anyone from responsibility for his own . . . violation of law." The second provision authorizes courts to "limit the application of any unconscionable clause" in a contract so "as to avoid any unconscionable result."

The specific rule of state law in question consists of the California Supreme Court's application of these principles to hold that "some" (but not "all") "class action waivers" in consumer contracts are exculpatory and unconscionable under California "law." In particular, in *Discover Bank* the California Supreme Court stated that, when a class-action waiver

> "is found in a consumer contract of adhesion in a setting in which disputes between the contracting parties predictably involve small amounts of damages, and when it is alleged that the party with the superior bargaining power has carried out a scheme to deliberately cheat large numbers of consumers out of individually small sums of money, then . . . the waiver becomes in practice the exemption of the party 'from responsibility for [its] own fraud, or willful injury to the person or property of another.'"

In such a circumstance, the "waivers are unconscionable under California law and should not be enforced."

The *Discover Bank* rule does not create a "blanket policy in California against class action waivers in the consumer context." Instead, it represents the "application of a more general [unconscionability] principle." Courts applying California law have enforced class-action waivers where they satisfy general unconscionability standards. And even when they fail, the parties remain free to devise other dispute mechanisms, including informal mechanisms, that, in context, will not prove unconscionable.

II

A

The *Discover Bank* rule is consistent with the federal Act's language. It "applies equally to class action litigation waivers in contracts without arbitration agreements as it does to class arbitration waivers in contracts with such agreements." Linguistically speaking, it falls directly within the scope of the Act's exception permitting courts to refuse to enforce arbitration agreements on grounds that exist "for the revocation of *any* contract." 9 U.S.C. § 2 (emphasis added). The majority agrees.

B

The *Discover Bank* rule is also consistent with the basic "purpose behind" the Act. We have described that purpose as one of "ensur[ing] judicial enforcement" of arbitration agreements. As is well known, prior to the federal Act, many courts expressed hostility to arbitration, for example by refusing to order specific performance of agreements to arbitrate. The Act sought to eliminate that hostility by placing agreements to arbitrate " *'upon the same footing as other contracts.'* "

Congress was fully aware that arbitration could provide procedural and cost advantages. The House Report emphasized the "appropriate[ness]" of making arbitration agreements enforceable "at this time when there is so much agitation against the costliness and delays of litigation." And this Court has acknowledged that parties may enter into arbitration agreements in order to expedite the resolution of disputes.

But we have also cautioned against thinking that Congress' primary objective was to guarantee these particular procedural advantages. Rather, that primary objective was to secure the "enforcement" of agreements to arbitrate.

Thus, insofar as we seek to implement Congress' intent, we should think more than twice before invalidating a state law that does just what § 2 requires, namely, puts agreements to arbitrate and agreements to litigate "upon the same footing."

III

The majority's contrary view (that *Discover Bank* stands as an "obstacle" to the accomplishment of the federal law's objective), rests primarily upon its claims that the *Discover Bank* rule increases the complexity of arbitration procedures, thereby discouraging parties from entering into arbitration agreements, and to that extent discriminating in practice against arbitration. These claims are not well founded.

For one thing, a state rule of law that would sometimes set aside as unconscionable a contract term that forbids class arbitration is not (as the majority claims) like a rule that would require "ultimate disposition by a jury" or "judicially monitored discovery" or use of "the Federal Rules of Evidence." Unlike the majority's examples, class arbitration is consistent with the use of arbitration. It is a form of arbitration that is well known in California and followed elsewhere. Indeed, the AAA has told us that it has found class arbitration to be "a fair, balanced, and efficient means of resolving class disputes." And unlike the majority's examples, the *Discover Bank* rule imposes equivalent limitations on litigation; hence it cannot fairly be characterized as a targeted attack on arbitration.

Where does the majority get its contrary idea—that individual, rather than class, arbitration is a "fundamental attribut[e]" of arbitration? The majority does not explain. And it is unlikely to be able to trace its present view to the history of the arbitration statute itself. . . .

. . . [I]f neither the history nor present practice suggests that class arbitration is fundamentally incompatible with arbitration itself, then on what basis can the majority hold California's law pre-empted?

For another thing, the majority's argument that the *Discover Bank* rule will discourage arbitration rests critically upon the wrong comparison. The majority compares the complexity of class arbitration with that of bilateral arbitration. And it finds the former more complex. But, if incentives are at issue, the *relevant* comparison is not "arbitration with arbitration" but a comparison between class arbitration and judicial class actions. After all, in respect to the relevant set of contracts, the *Discover Bank* rule similarly and equally sets aside clauses that forbid class procedures—whether arbitration procedures or ordinary judicial procedures are at issue.

Why would a typical defendant (say, a business) prefer a judicial class action to class arbitration? AAA statistics "suggest that class arbitration proceedings take more time than the average commercial arbitration, but may take *less time* than the average class action in court." Data from California courts confirm that class arbitrations can take considerably less time than in-court proceedings in which class certification is sought. And a single class proceeding is surely more efficient than thousands of separate proceedings for identical claims. Thus, if speedy resolution of disputes were all that mattered, then the *Discover Bank* rule would reinforce, not obstruct, that objective of the Act.

The majority's related claim that the *Discover Bank* rule will discourage the use of arbitration because "[a]rbitration is poorly suited to . . . higher stakes" lacks empirical support. Indeed, the majority provides no convincing reason to believe that parties are unwilling to submit high-stake disputes to arbitration. . . .

Because California applies the same legal principles to address the unconscionability of class arbitration waivers as it does to address the unconscionability of any other contractual provision, the merits of class proceedings should not factor into our decision. If California had applied its law of duress to void an arbitration agreement, would it matter if the procedures in the coerced agreement were efficient?

Regardless, the majority highlights the disadvantages of class arbitrations, as it sees them. But class proceedings have countervailing advantages. In general agreements that forbid the consolidation of claims can lead small-dollar claimants to abandon their claims rather than to litigate. I suspect that it is true even here, for as the Court of Appeals recognized, AT&T can avoid the $7,500 payout (the payout that supposedly makes the Concepcions' arbitration worthwhile) simply by paying the claim's face value, such that "the maximum gain to a customer for the hassle of arbitrating a $30.22 dispute is still just $30.22."

What rational lawyer would have signed on to represent the Concepcions in litigation for the possibility of fees stemming from a $30.22 claim? See, *e.g., Carnegie v. Household Int'l, Inc.*, 376 F.3d 656, 661 (C.A.7 2004) ("The *realistic* alternative to a class action is not 17 million individual suits, but zero individual suits, as only a lunatic or a fanatic sues for $30"). . . . *Discover Bank* sets forth circumstances in which the California courts believe that the terms of consumer contracts can be manipulated to insulate an agreement's author from liability for its own frauds by "deliberately cheat[ing] large numbers of consumers out of individually small sums of money." Why is this kind of decision—weighing the pros and cons of all class proceedings alike—not California's to make?

Finally, the majority can find no meaningful support for its views in this Court's precedent. The federal Act has been in force for nearly a century. We have decided dozens of cases about its requirements. We have reached results that authorize complex arbitration procedures. *E.g.,* . . . (antitrust claims arising in international transaction are arbitrable). We have upheld nondiscriminatory state laws that slow down arbitration proceedings. *E.g.,* . . . (California law staying arbitration proceedings until completion of related litigation is not pre-empted). But we have not, to my knowledge, applied the Act to strike down a state statute that treats arbitrations on par with judicial and administrative proceedings. . . .

These cases do not concern the merits and demerits of class actions; they concern equal treatment of arbitration contracts and other contracts. Since it is the latter question that is at issue here, I am not surprised that the majority can find no meaningful precedent supporting its decision.

IV

By using the words "save upon such grounds as exist at law or in equity for the revocation of any contract," Congress retained for the States an important role incident to agreements to arbitrate. 9 U.S.C. § 2. Through those words Congress reiterated a basic federal idea that has long informed the nature of this Nation's laws. . . . But federalism is as much a question of deeds as words. It often takes the form of a concrete decision by this Court that respects the legitimacy of a State's action in an individual case. Here, recognition of that federalist ideal, embodied in specific language in this particular statute, should lead us to uphold California's law, not to strike it down. We do not honor federalist principles in their breach.

With respect, I dissent.

NOTES AND QUESTIONS

1. A generally applicable contract defense?   Was the California doctrine of unconscionability on which the lower courts here relied to invalidate the contract's class-arbitration-waiver provision one that California courts employ only in the arbitration setting, or is it a "generally applicable contract defense" that could also be used to invalidate a contractual ban on class-action lawsuits? Is the fact that invocation of the doctrine here resulted in invalidating the arbitration agreement enough to strip it of its "generally applicable" status? Was there any evidence that the unconscionability doctrine on which the lower courts here relied was being deliberately or selectively invoked to discriminate against arbitration agreements? If not, why didn't this case fall within the FAA's § 2 savings clause?

2. *Narrowing the savings clause.*   Does *Concepcion* significantly narrow the scope of the FAA's savings clause by holding that even if a state law doctrine such as unconscionability seems to fall within § 2's exception as a ground that "exist[s] at law or in equity for the revocation of any contract," that doctrine still cannot be invoked if it would "stand as an obstacle to the accomplishment of the FAA's objectives"? Isn't the same likely to be true of other nondiscriminatory state law provisions that, if applied in the arbitration setting, could lead to invalidation of a compulsory arbitration clause?

3. *Inconsistent with the FAA's objectives?*   On what basis did the Court conclude that class arbitration is inconsistent with the FAA's objectives? Does Justice Breyer in his dissent agree with that conclusion? The FAA was enacted in 1925 to encourage arbitration and protect it from what was then viewed as widespread judicial hostility. Does the *Concepcion* decision further the FAA's purpose if, as the dissent suggests, the alternative to class arbitration is in many instances—particularly when individual claims are small—no arbitration at all? While AT&T customers remain free to proceed against the company either through individual arbitration or in small claims court, given the small size of the typical claim (the Concepcions sought only $30.22) and the often complex nature of the issues, only a miniscule number of dissatisfied customers may ever pursue these options. *See* Brief of Civil Procedure and Complex Litigation Professors as Amici Curiae in Support of Respondents at *20-21, *Concepcion*, 563 U.S. 333 (No. 09-893) (Oct. 5, 2010) (during a 14-month period, in the last 12 of which the challenged AT&T procedure was in effect (including its $7,500-minimum-recovery and double-attorneys'-fee provisions), only 10 of AT&T's more than 70 million U.S. customers filed arbitration claims).

4. *An "effective vindication" of federal statutory rights exception?*   The *Concepcion* Court rejected, as being "inconsistent with the FAA," any concern that without a class remedy, plaintiffs' "small-dollar claims . . . might otherwise slip through the legal system." *Concepcion* was a diversity case involving state-created rights. However, when plaintiffs assert federal law claims, they may be able to invoke a judge-made exception to the FAA that "allow[s] courts to invalidate agreements that prevent the 'effective vindication' of a federal statutory right." *American Express Co. v. Italian Colors Restaurant*, 133 S. Ct. 2304, 2310 (2013). This exception has been read narrowly to reach only those agreements that involve "a prospective waiver of a party's *right to pursue* statutory remedies." *Id.* It would thus apply to "an arbitration agreement forbidding the assertion of certain [federal] statutory rights," and perhaps to "filing and administrative fees attached to an arbitration that are so high as to make access to the forum impracticable." *Id.* at 2310-2311. But, said the Court, "the fact that it is not worth the expense involved in *proving* a statutory right does not constitute the elimination of the *right to pursue* the remedy," for even without a class remedy, plaintiffs still retain

the right to proceed on an individual basis. *Id.* at 2311. The *American Express* Court thus upheld a class-arbitration-waiver clause even though plaintiffs established that as a practical matter "they would incur prohibitive costs if compelled to arbitrate under the class action waiver." *Id.* at 2308 (noting that individual arbitration would cost between several hundred thousand and one million dollars in a case where plaintiff's maximum recovery was $38,549). For the same reason, the "effective vindication" exception would not have saved the *Concepcion* plaintiffs had they been suing under federal law, for they still possessed the legal right to pursue that statutory remedy.

5. *Legislative solutions.*   Because *Concepcion* was a decision that simply interpreted the FAA, could Congress amend that statute to provide that "state statutory or common law allowing arbitration to proceed on a classwide basis is not preempted by this act"? Would the right to class arbitration then be guaranteed in all states, or only in those like California where class-action waivers are often deemed unconscionable? *See* Brief for Respondents at 18-24, App. 1a-3a, *Concepcion*, 563 U.S. 333 (No. 09-893) (Sept. 29, 2010) (noting that courts in 20 states have at times held contract provisions barring employees and consumers from pursuing class relief to be unenforceable).

In states where class-arbitration waivers are enforceable, might a compulsory arbitration provision that allows arbitration only on an individual basis leave many with no remedy at all, if their claims are relatively small? In recent years, bills introduced in Congress to amend the FAA have not sought to simply outlaw class-arbitration-waiver provisions, but to instead render unenforceable any pre-dispute arbitration agreement that requires the arbitration of antitrust, civil rights, consumer, or employment disputes. *See, e.g.,* S. 878, 113th Cong., 1st Sess. (2013), § 402(a); H.R. 1844, 113th Cong., 1st Sess. (2013), § 402(a). Under the proposed legislation, while parties could agree to arbitrate such disputes *after* they have arisen, they could not be forced to do so based on a prior agreement.

F.   Class Action Review Problem

9-18. Mary, a citizen of California, filed a class action in the California Superior Court in Sacramento against Basic Research LLC and Dynakor Pharmacal LLC ("Dynakor"), neither of which is a California citizen. In her complaint, Mary seeks to recover on behalf of herself and other "similarly situated" individuals the costs associated with the purchase and use of an allegedly ineffective dietary supplement, Louzit, which defendants advertised as a "foolproof" alternative to weight loss with "guaranteed success" and "without any grueling diet or exercise regimens!" Defendants sell Louzit directly to consumers for $39.99 per bottle. The product is also available online and from a variety of retail stores, including Walgreens and Wal-Mart. The defendants have a collective products liability insurance policy that limits the insurer's combined total liability for claims arising from or related to the use of Louzit to $5 million. Mary's complaint alleges that after purchasing Louzit by mail from Dynakor, she used it for two weeks as directed on the package labeling but did not experience any weight loss. Shortly after she stopped taking it, she became ill and required medical care.

Mary's complaint was filed on December 6, 2007. It asserts claims under three California consumer protection statutes: the Unfair Competition Law; the False Advertising Law; and the Consumers Legal Remedies Act. The complaint states that the suit is being brought on behalf of the "thousands of persons" who purchased or used Louzit in California and that "each individual class member's total claim is for less than $75,000." Plaintiffs seek injunctive relief in the form of a recall or buy-back of Louzit currently on store shelves; corrective advertising to warn those who purchased Louzit that the product is ineffective and perhaps harmful; restitution for any amounts paid or expended on the product; compensatory damages for any injuries sustained by a purchaser as a result of using Louzit; plus punitive damages and attorney's fees as authorized by the California statutes under which the suit is brought. Mary and the proposed class are represented by four experienced attorneys who have previously been involved in major and highly successful plaintiff class actions.

On February 1, 2008, the defendants removed the action to the U.S. District Court for the Eastern District of California in Sacramento. Their removal petition stated that as of January 31, 2008, total California sales of Louzit had thus far exceeded $2 million.

If, in answering the following questions, there are additional facts that you need to know, indicate what those facts are and why they are important.

A. *Removal*

1. Was defendants' notice of removal timely?
2. Was the action removable under 28 U.S.C. § 1441(a)-(b), on the basis that the case is one over which the federal court had original jurisdiction pursuant to § 1332(a)?
3. Would the action have been removable under 28 U.S.C. § 1441(a)-(b) if, in her complaint, Mary had also asserted a claim under the Racketeer Influenced and Corrupt Organizations Act (RICO), 18 U.S.C. §§ 1961-1968?
4. Was this action removable under 28 U.S.C. § 1441(a)-(b) on the basis that it was a case over which the federal court had original jurisdiction pursuant to § 1332(d)?
5. Would your answer to questions 2, 3, or 4 be different if the removal petition had been filed only by defendant Basic Research LLC?
6. Assuming the case was properly removed under § 1332(d), on what bases if any might the plaintiff ask that the suit be remanded to state court?

B. *Dismissal*

7. Mary ordered her package of Louzit directly from Dynakor, using the company's website, which contained the following statement:

By submitting this purchase order, you hereby agree that you will resolve any disputes you may have with Basic Research, Dynakor, or any other entity that manufactures, distributes, or sells Louzit, through binding arbitration, without resort to a court of law. You further agree that any such disputes that may arise between yourself and any of these entities will be resolved on an individual basis, without use of any class action or class-based remedy.

Assume that Mary's suit was successfully removed and that the court declined to remand the case to state court. The defendants have moved to dismiss the suit on the ground that Mary agreed to resolve any disputes through binding arbitration. How should the court rule on this motion, and why?

C. Class Action

Assume that in question 7, the federal court denied the defendants' motion to dismiss Mary's case after finding that the arbitration procedures set forth in the company's policy did not meet minimum requirements of fairness, including that there be a neutral arbitrator, an opportunity for at least minimal discovery, and a written final decision. *See Gilmer v. Interstate/Johnson Lane Corp.*, 500 U.S. 20 (1991). Mary has now moved to certify her suit as a class action in federal court.

8. Does her lawsuit meet each of the provisions of Rule 23(a)? Does it need to satisfy all of them? Is it possible that some aspects of her suit satisfy Rule 23(a), while others do not?

9. Does Mary's lawsuit meet the requirements of Rule 23(b)? Does it need to meet all of them? Assuming the suit satisfies Rule 23(b), might the court invoke more than one subpart of that rule rather than certifying it—to the extent that certification is proper—entirely under just one of them? Is this a case that could call for the creation of subclasses? If so, would the requirements of Rule 23(a) have to be met with respect to each subclass and, if that's so, is it possible the suit could not proceed as a class action as to some of them?

10. Suppose the court is prepared to certify this as a class action under Rule 23. Would notice have to be given to all class members? Would any notice have to include a right to opt out before a class is certified, or is this a case that might not require an opt-out right?

D. Settlement

Suppose that after the class was certified, the parties reached a settlement under which the defendants will issue coupons worth a total of $5 million to class members, allowing them to acquire any of the 50 different products that the defendants sell online and in retail stores around the country. The settlement also requires the defendants to publish a notice in five California and five national publications that includes the following statement:

"CAUTION! Not everyone who uses Louzit finds that it helps them to lose weight, and some users have experienced complications that required medical assistance."

11. In connection with the proposed settlement, must any additional effort be made to contact class members? If so, must they now be afforded a right to opt out if they were previously given that right in the precertification class notice and chose not to exercise it?

12. The settlement agreement contains a clause awarding attorneys' fees to class counsel equal to 5 percent of the $5 million coupon settlement (*i.e.*, $250,000). Is this fee proper?

See Tompkins v. Basic Research LL, 2008 WL 1808316 (E.D. Cal. Apr. 22, 2008) (involving a case with similar but not identical facts and not addressing all of the issues raised here).

X

ADJUDICATION WITHOUT TRIAL

Not all cases go to trial. In recent years, fewer than 10 percent of the civil cases filed in 21 selected states reached the trial stage, while in federal district courts, only about 1 percent of all civil cases did so. *See* Introduction, part B.1, page 6, *supra*, and part B.2, page 9, *supra*. The reasons for this are varied. Some cases settle amicably, often as a result of mediation or nonbinding arbitration. Others are dismissed at an early stage of the litigation on procedural grounds, such as lack of jurisdiction over the defendant, lack of subject matter jurisdiction, improper venue, forum *non conveniens*, absence of an indispensable party, or failure to state a claim upon which relief can be granted. *See* FED. R. CIV. P. 12(b).

Yet even if a plaintiff's case neither settles nor is procedurally dismissed, a trial may still be unnecessary if there is no genuine dispute as to the material facts. The primary means for determining whether such a dispute exists is through a motion for summary judgment. The summary judgment procedure provides the court with a preview of the evidence each side would offer if the case were to go to trial. While the pleadings may have suggested that the parties disagreed as to the facts, that disagreement may not be a genuine one if one party lacks evidence from which a reasonable judge or jury could rule in her favor. In such a case, there is obviously no point in going to trial. Instead, by applying the relevant legal principles to the undisputed facts, the court may enter summary judgment for the moving party if it concludes that the movant is entitled to win the case as a matter of law. *See* FED. R. CIV. P. 56.

Even without a motion for summary judgment it is sometimes clear that there is no need for a trial. For example, if a defendant fails to respond to the complaint within the time allowed, the plaintiff's allegations—other than perhaps those concerning damages—will be accepted as true. Assuming those allegations are legally sufficient to allow the plaintiff to recover, the court may enter a default judgment against the defendant without conducting a trial on the merits. Nor is a trial necessary if a plaintiff voluntarily seeks to dismiss her case, or if the court orders a case dismissed due to the plaintiff's failure to prosecute the action or comply with a court rule or order.

In the present chapter we will consider a number of settings in which lawsuits may be disposed of without trial. Our initial focus will be on summary judgment. We will then consider the circumstances under which judgments may be entered by default. Finally, we will briefly explore voluntary and involuntary dismissals.

A.   Summary Judgment

1.   Introduction

A motion for summary judgment tests the *evidentiary* sufficiency of a claim or defense. Hence the motion is usually filed after the parties have had an ample opportunity for discovery. Summary judgment is to be contrasted with Rule 12(b)(6), which tests the *legal* sufficiency of the pleadings. In a Rule 12(b)(6) motion, the non-conclusory factual allegations in a pleading are presumed to be true. With a summary judgment motion, however, there is no such presumption of truth, and the inquiry extends beyond the pleadings to the evidence gathered and exchanged by the parties. A party whose claim or defense is subject to a summary judgment motion must show that the evidence is such that a reasonable fact-finder could rule in her favor should the case go to trial. *See* Jeffrey W. Stempel & Steven S. Gensler, *Summary Judgment, in* 11 Moore's Federal Practice § 56 App. 100[1]-[2] (3d ed. 2015); 10A Charles Alan Wright, Arthur R. Miller & Mary Kay Kane, Federal Practice and Procedure § 2711 (3d ed. 1998 & Supp. 2015). If she fails to make this showing, summary judgment will be granted against her.

Thus the "mission of the summary judgment procedure is to pierce the pleadings and to assess the proof in order to see whether there is a genuine need for trial." Advisory Committee Note, 1963 Amendments, 31 F.R.D. 587, 648. The motion may be made by either party or by the court *sua sponte*. It allows a judge to look behind what may have been reasonably based allegations to determine whether the parties have admissible evidence that would establish their claims or defenses at trial. *See* Fed. R. Civ. P. 56(c)(1)-(2). If after reviewing the affidavits, depositions, interrogatories, admissions, or other material submitted in connection with the motion, the court concludes that a reasonable jury could find in favor of either party, summary judgment will be denied, and the case will proceed to trial. But if the court concludes that no reasonable jury could find in favor of the non-moving party, it will enter summary judgment against that party. To permit such a case to go to trial would be costly and pointless, for it would likely result in the court entering a judgment as a matter of law—either before the case was sent to the jury or after the jury returned a verdict that the court felt compelled to override. *See* Fed. R. Civ. P. 50.

The entry of summary judgment hinges on whether the parties can carry their respective "burdens of production" on the motion. The party moving for summary judgment has the initial burden of identifying evidence that, if not contradicted, would compel a reasonable fact-finder to rule in that party's favor. If a movant carries this initial burden, the burden of production shifts to the non-moving party to identify evidence that would allow a reasonable fact-finder to find in its favor. If the non-moving party meets this burden, summary judgment will be denied, for this preview of the evidence has revealed that there is indeed a genuine issue of material fact that must be resolved at trial. However, if the non-moving party cannot identify any such evidence, the court will enter summary judgment for the moving party if, based on these undisputed facts, "the movant is entitled to judgment as a matter of law." FED. R. CIV. P. 56(a).

The scope of a party's burden of production on summary judgment turns, in part, on whether that party would have the "burden of persuasion" at trial. As to claims set forth in the complaint, the burden of persuasion at trial normally rests on the plaintiff. As to counterclaims and most defenses, however, the burden of persuasion usually rests with the defendant. A party seeking summary judgment on a claim or defense for which that party has the burden of persuasion at trial must show that she has sufficient proof of each element of her claim or defense such that a reasonable fact-finder could rule in her favor. On the other hand, when a party seeks summary judgment on a claim or defense for which the opposing party has the burden of persuasion at trial, he need only establish that the non-moving party cannot meet its burden of persuasion on one element of that claim or defense. Can you see the reason behind this distinction?

2. The Basic Requirements for Summary Judgment

a. *Federal Rule of Civil Procedure 56*

Federal Rule of Civil Procedure 56 provides federal courts with the authority to enter summary judgments and describes the general standards and circumstances under which a court may do so.

Rule 56(a) authorizes either party to move for summary judgment or partial summary judgment. It requires the moving party to identify the claim or defense, or part thereof, on which summary judgment is sought. The section further provides that the "court shall grant summary judgment if the movant shows that there is no genuine dispute as to any material fact and the movant is entitled to judgment as a matter of law." FED. R. CIV. P. 56(a). A genuine dispute is one on which reasonable minds can differ. A material fact is one that is relevant to a claim or defense. Finally the rule requires that the court "state on the record the reasons for granting or denying the motion." *Id.*

The only time limit imposed by Rule 56 is found in subsection (b), which provides that "a party may file a motion for summary judgment at any time until 30 days after the close of all discovery." FED. R. CIV. P. 56(b). Other time constraints on summary judgment practice may be imposed by local rule or court order. *See* FED. R. CIV. P. 16(c)(2)(E) (pre-trial scheduling order for the filing of summary judgment motion). Typically summary judgments are scheduled to be filed after the close of discovery.

Rule 56(c) outlines the procedures to be followed on a motion for summary judgment. Subsections (c)(1)(A) and (c)(1)(B) describe how the parties must show the presence or absence of a disputed, material fact. To that end the parties may cite to a variety of factual materials in the record, such as depositions, documents, electronically stored information, affidavits or declarations, stipulations, admissions, interrogatory answers, and the like. FED. R. CIV. P. 56(c)(1)(A). Or the parties may show that the evidentiary materials cited by an opponent "do not establish the absence or presence of a genuine dispute, or that an adverse party cannot produce admissible evidence to support the fact." FED. R. CIV. P. 56(c)(1)(B). The method used will ultimately depend on the party's relative burden of production on summary judgment and on that party's burden of persuasion at trial. *See* part A.1, *supra*. Subsection (c)(2) allows a party to object to the material relied on by an opposing party on grounds that it is not reducible to admissible evidence; subsection (c)(3) allows a court to consider materials in the record not cited by the parties, but does not require it to do so; and subsection (c)(4) requires that any affidavit or declaration used to support or oppose a motion for summary judgment be based on personal knowledge, describe facts that would be reducible to admissible evidence, and show that the affiant or declarant is competent to testify to the matters described. FED. R. CIV. P. 56(c)(2)-(4).

Rule 56(d) is designed to address those situations where a motion for summary judgment has been filed before the opposing party had a sufficient opportunity to gather the facts necessary to contest the motion. It vests the court with discretion to "(1) defer considering the motion or deny it; (2) allow time to obtain affidavits or declarations or to take discovery; or (3) issue any other appropriate order." FED. R. CIV. P. 56(d). Similarly, Rule 56(e) vests a court with a range of options when a party has failed to meet its burden of production as to an assertion of fact. The court may give that party an opportunity to meet its burden of production as to that fact, treat the fact as undisputed, grant summary judgment if doing so is otherwise consistent with the standards for granting summary judgment, or "issue any other appropriate order." FED. R. CIV. P. 56(e).

Rule 56(f) allows a court, "[a]fter giving notice and a reasonable time to respond," to "(1) grant summary judgment for a nonmovant; (2) grant the motion on grounds not raised by a party; or (3) consider summary judgment on its own after identifying for the parties material facts that may not be genuinely in dispute." This is sometimes referred to as summary judgment *sua sponte*. Rule 56 also permits a court to grant summary judgment on less than all the relief sought. Thus "it may enter an order stating any material fact . . . that is not genuinely in dispute and treating the fact as established in the case." FED. R. CIV. P. 56(g).

Finally, Rule 56(h) authorizes the imposition of sanctions for the submission of an affidavit or declaration "in bad faith or solely for delay. . . ." FED. R. CIV. P. 56(h).

b.   Foundational Cases

At one time, federal courts treated summary judgment motions as disfavored. While the approach varied somewhat among the circuits, many federal courts took the position that if the party opposing summary judgment created even the "slightest doubt" as to whether there was a colorable issue of fact, the motion would be denied and the case would proceed to trial. CHARLES ALAN WRIGHT

& MARY KAY KANE, THE LAW OF FEDERAL COURTS § 99, at 708 (7th ed. 2011). This hesitant attitude changed radically with the Supreme Court's 1986 decisions in *Matsushita Electric Industrial Co., Ltd. v. Zenith Radio Corp.*, 475 U.S. 574 (1986), *Anderson v. Liberty Lobby, Inc.*, 477 U.S. 242 (1986), and *Celotex Corp. v. Catrett*, 477 U.S. 317 (1986). These three decisions, each of which we will consider below, elevated the pretrial summary judgment motion from a rarely used device to an effective and now often invoked means of disposing of a case prior to trial. As you read these cases, you will see that the current text of Rule 56, as outlined above, is designed to embody many of the summary judgment principles reflected in the trilogy.

Anderson v. Liberty Lobby, Inc.

477 U.S. 242 (1986)

JUSTICE WHITE delivered the opinion of the Court.

In *New York Times Co. v. Sullivan*, 376 U.S. 254, 279-280 (1964), we held that, in a libel suit brought by a public official, the First Amendment requires the plaintiff to show that in publishing the defamatory statement the defendant acted with actual malice — "with knowledge that it was false or with reckless disregard of whether it was false or not." We held further that such actual malice must be shown with "convincing clarity." Id., at 285-286. These *New York Times* requirements we have since extended to libel suits brought by public figures as well. See, *e.g.*, *Curtis Publishing Co. v. Butts*, 388 U.S. 130 (1967).

This case presents the question whether the clear-and-convincing-evidence requirement must be considered by a court ruling on a motion for summary judgment under Rule 56 of the Federal Rules of Civil Procedure in a case to which *New York Times* applies. The United States Court of Appeals for the District of Columbia Circuit held that that requirement need not be considered at the summary judgment stage. We granted certiorari because that holding was in conflict with decisions of several other Courts of Appeals, which had held that the *New York Times* requirement of clear and convincing evidence must be considered on a motion for summary judgment. We now reverse.

I

Respondent Liberty Lobby, Inc., is a not-for-profit corporation and self-described "citizens' lobby." Respondent Willis Carto is its founder and treasurer. In October 1981, The Investigator magazine published [three] articles. . . . These articles portrayed respondents as neo-Nazi, anti-Semitic, racist, and Fascist.

Respondents filed this diversity libel action in the United States District Court for the District of Columbia, alleging that some 28 statements and 2 illustrations in the 3 articles were false and derogatory. Named as defendants in the action were petitioner Jack Anderson, the publisher of The Investigator, petitioner Bill

Adkins, president and chief executive officer of the Investigator Publishing Co., and petitioner Investigator Publishing Co. itself.

Following discovery, petitioners moved for summary judgment pursuant to Rule 56. In their motion, petitioners asserted that because respondents are public figures they were required to prove their case under the standards set forth in *New York Times*. Petitioners also asserted that summary judgment was proper because actual malice was absent as a matter of law. In support of this latter assertion, petitioners submitted the affidavit of Charles Bermant, an employee of petitioners and the author of the two longer articles. In this affidavit, Bermant stated that he had spent a substantial amount of time researching and writing the articles and that his facts were obtained from a wide variety of sources. He also stated that he had at all times believed and still believed that the facts contained in the articles were truthful and accurate. Attached to this affidavit was an appendix in which Bermant detailed the sources for each of the statements alleged by respondents to be libelous.

Respondents opposed the motion for summary judgment, asserting that there were numerous inaccuracies in the articles and claiming that an issue of actual malice was presented by virtue of the fact that in preparing the articles Bermant had relied on several sources that respondents asserted were patently unreliable. Generally, respondents charged that petitioners had failed adequately to verify their information before publishing. Respondents also presented evidence that William McGaw, an editor of The Investigator, had told petitioner Adkins before publication that the articles were "terrible" and "ridiculous."

In ruling on the motion for summary judgment, the District Court first held that respondents were limited-purpose public figures and that *New York Times* therefore applied. The District Court then held that Bermant's thorough investigation and research and his reliance on numerous sources precluded a finding of actual malice. Thus, the District Court granted the motion and entered judgment in favor of petitioners.

On appeal, the Court of Appeals affirmed as to 21 and reversed as to 9 of the allegedly defamatory statements. Although it noted that respondents did not challenge the District Court's ruling that they were limited-purpose public figures and that they were thus required to prove their case under *New York Times*, the Court of Appeals nevertheless held that for the purposes of summary judgment the requirement that actual malice be proved by clear and convincing evidence, rather than by a preponderance of the evidence, was irrelevant: To defeat summary judgment respondents did not have to show that a jury could find actual malice with "convincing clarity." The court based this conclusion on a perception that to impose the greater evidentiary burden at summary judgment "would change the threshold summary judgment inquiry from a search for a minimum of facts supporting the plaintiff's case to an evaluation of the weight of those facts and (it would seem) of the weight of at least the defendant's uncontroverted facts as well." The court then held, with respect to nine of the statements, that summary judgment had been improperly granted because "a jury could reasonably conclude that the . . . allegations were defamatory, false, and made with actual malice."

II

A

Our inquiry is whether the Court of Appeals erred in holding that the heightened evidentiary requirements that apply to proof of actual malice in this *New York Times* case need not be considered for the purposes of a motion for summary judgment. Rule 56(c) of the Federal Rules of Civil Procedure provides that summary judgment "shall be rendered forthwith if the pleadings, depositions, answers to interrogatories, and admissions on file, together with the affidavits, if any, show that there is no genuine issue as to any material fact and that the moving party is entitled to a judgment as a matter of law." [*See current* FED. R. CIV. P. 56(a), (c)(1).] By its very terms, this standard provides that the mere existence of *some* alleged factual dispute between the parties will not defeat an otherwise properly supported motion for summary judgment; the requirement is that there be no *genuine* issue of *material* fact.

As to materiality, the substantive law will identify which facts are material. Only disputes over facts that might affect the outcome of the suit under the governing law will properly preclude the entry of summary judgment. Factual disputes that are irrelevant or unnecessary will not be counted. . . .

More important for present purposes, summary judgment will not lie if the dispute about a material fact is "genuine," that is, if the evidence is such that a reasonable jury could return a verdict for the nonmoving party. In *First National Bank of Arizona v. Cities Service Co.*, 391 U.S. 253 (1968), we affirmed a grant of summary judgment for an antitrust defendant where the issue was whether there was a genuine factual dispute as to the existence of a conspiracy. We noted Rule 56(e)'s provision that a party opposing a properly supported motion for summary judgment "may not rest upon the mere allegations or denials of his pleading, but . . . must set forth specific facts showing that there is a genuine issue for trial." [*See current* FED. R. CIV. P. 56(c)(1).] . . . We went on to hold that, in the face of the defendant's properly supported motion for summary judgment, the plaintiff could not rest on his allegations of a conspiracy to get to a jury without "any significant probative evidence tending to support the complaint." . . .

Our prior decisions may not have uniformly recited the same language in describing genuine factual issues under Rule 56, but it is clear enough from our recent cases that at the summary judgment stage the judge's function is not himself to weigh the evidence and determine the truth of the matter but to determine whether there is a genuine issue for trial. . . . [T]here is no issue for trial unless there is sufficient evidence favoring the nonmoving party for a jury to return a verdict for that party. If the evidence is merely colorable, *Dombrowski v. Eastland*, 387 U.S. 82, 87 (1967), or is not significantly probative, *Cities Service, supra*, at 290, summary judgment may be granted.

That this is the proper focus of the inquiry is strongly suggested by the Rule itself. Rule 56(e) [*see current* FED. R. CIV. P. 56(c)(1)] provides that, when a properly supported motion for summary judgment is made,[4] the adverse party "must set forth specific facts showing that there is a genuine issue for trial."[5] And, as we noted above, Rule 56(c) [*see current* FED. R. CIV. P. 56(a)] provides that the trial judge shall then grant summary judgment if there is no genuine issue as to any material fact and if the moving party is entitled to judgment as a matter of law. There is no requirement that the trial judge make findings of fact. The inquiry performed is the threshold inquiry of determining whether there is the need for a trial—whether, in other words, there are any genuine factual issues that properly can be resolved only by a finder of fact because they may reasonably be resolved in favor of either party.

Petitioners suggest, and we agree, that this standard mirrors the standard for a directed verdict under Federal Rule of Civil Procedure 50(a), which is that the trial judge must direct a verdict if, under the governing law, there can be but one reasonable conclusion as to the verdict. If reasonable minds could differ as to the import of the evidence, however, a verdict should not be directed. As the Court long ago said in *Improvement Co. v. Munson*, 14 Wall. 442, 448 (1872), and has several times repeated:

> "Nor are judges any longer required to submit a question to a jury merely because some evidence has been introduced by the party having the burden of proof, unless the evidence be of such a character that it would warrant the jury in finding a verdict in favor of that party. Formerly it was held that if there was what is called a *scintilla* of evidence in support of a case the judge was bound to leave it to the jury, but recent decisions of high authority have established a more reasonable rule, that in every case, before the evidence is left to the jury, there is a preliminary question for the judge, not whether there is literally no evidence, but whether there is any upon which a jury could properly proceed to find a verdict for the party producing it, upon whom the *onus* of proof is imposed." (Footnotes omitted.)

The Court has said that summary judgment should be granted where the evidence is such that it "would require a directed verdict for the moving party." *Sartor v. Arkansas Gas Corp.*, 321 U.S. 620, 624 (1944). And we have noted that the "genuine issue" summary judgment standard is "very close" to the "reasonable jury" directed verdict standard: "The primary difference between the two motions is procedural; summary judgment motions are usually made before trial and decided on documentary evidence, while directed verdict motions are

---

4. Our analysis here does not address the question of the initial burden of production of evidence placed by Rule 56 on the party moving for summary judgment. See *Celotex Corp. v. Catrett*, 477 U.S. 317 (1986). Respondents have not raised this issue here, and for the purposes of our discussion we assume that the moving party has met initially the requisite evidentiary burden.

5. This requirement in turn is qualified by Rule 56(f)'s [*see current* FED. R. CIV. P. 56(d)] provision that summary judgment be refused where the nonmoving party has not had the opportunity to discover information that is essential to his opposition. In our analysis here, we assume that both parties have had ample opportunity for discovery.

made at trial and decided on the evidence that has been admitted." *Bill Johnson's Restaurants, Inc. v. NLRB*, 461 U.S. 731, 745, n.11 (1983). In essence, though, the inquiry under each is the same: whether the evidence presents a sufficient disagreement to require submission to a jury or whether it is so one-sided that one party must prevail as a matter of law.

B

Progressing to the specific issue in this case, we are convinced that the inquiry involved in a ruling on a motion for summary judgment or for a directed verdict necessarily implicates the substantive evidentiary standard of proof that would apply at the trial on the merits. If the defendant in a run-of-the-mill civil case moves for summary judgment or for a directed verdict based on the lack of proof of a material fact, the judge must ask himself not whether he thinks the evidence unmistakably favors one side or the other but whether a fair-minded jury could return a verdict for the plaintiff on the evidence presented. The mere existence of a scintilla of evidence in support of the plaintiff's position will be insufficient; there must be evidence on which the jury could reasonably find for the plaintiff. The judge's inquiry, therefore, unavoidably asks whether reasonable jurors could find by a preponderance of the evidence that the plaintiff is entitled to a verdict— "whether there is [evidence] upon which a jury can properly proceed to find a verdict for the party producing it, upon whom the *onus* of proof is imposed." *Munson, supra,* 14 Wall., at 448.

In terms of the nature of the inquiry, this is no different from the consideration of a motion for acquittal in a criminal case, where the beyond-a-reasonable-doubt standard applies and where the trial judge asks whether a reasonable jury could find guilt beyond a reasonable doubt. Similarly, where the First Amendment mandates a "clear and convincing" standard, the trial judge in disposing of a directed verdict motion should consider whether a reasonable factfinder could conclude, for example, that the plaintiff had shown actual malice with convincing clarity. . . .

Just as the "convincing clarity" requirement is relevant in ruling on a motion for directed verdict, it is relevant in ruling on a motion for summary judgment. When determining if a genuine factual issue as to actual malice exists in a libel suit brought by a public figure, a trial judge must bear in mind the actual quantum and quality of proof necessary to support liability under *New York Times*. For example, there is no genuine issue if the evidence presented in the opposing affidavits is of insufficient caliber or quantity to allow a rational finder of fact to find actual malice by clear and convincing evidence.

Thus, in ruling on a motion for summary judgment, the judge must view the evidence presented through the prism of the substantive evidentiary burden. This conclusion is mandated by the nature of this determination. The question here is whether a jury could reasonably find *either* that the plaintiff proved his case by the quality and quantity of evidence required by the governing law *or* that he did not. Whether a jury could reasonably find for either party, however, cannot be defined except by the criteria governing what evidence would enable the jury to find for either the plaintiff or the defendant: It makes no sense to say that a jury could reasonably find for either party without some benchmark as to what standards govern its deliberations and within what boundaries its ultimate decision must fall, and these standards and boundaries are in fact provided by the applicable evidentiary standards.

Our holding that the clear-and-convincing standard of proof should be taken into account in ruling on summary judgment motions does not denigrate the role of the jury. It by no means authorizes trial on affidavits. Credibility determinations, the weighing of the evidence, and the drawing of legitimate inferences from the facts are jury functions, not those of a judge, whether he is ruling on a motion for summary judgment or for a directed verdict. The evidence of the non-movant is to be believed, and all justifiable inferences are to be drawn in his favor. Neither do we suggest that the trial courts should act other than with caution in granting summary judgment or that the trial court may not deny summary judgment in a case where there is reason to believe that the better course would be to proceed to a full trial. *Kennedy v. Silas Mason Co.*, 334 U.S. 249 (1948).

In sum, we conclude that the determination of whether a given factual dispute requires submission to a jury must be guided by the substantive evidentiary standards that apply to the case. This is true at both the directed verdict and summary judgment stages. Consequently, where the *New York Times* "clear and convincing" evidence requirement applies, the trial judge's summary judgment inquiry as to whether a genuine issue exists will be whether the evidence presented is such that a jury applying that evidentiary standard could reasonably find for either the plaintiff or the defendant. Thus, where the factual dispute concerns actual malice, clearly a material issue in a *New York Times* case, the appropriate summary judgment question will be whether the evidence in the record could support a reasonable jury finding either that the plaintiff has shown actual malice by clear and convincing evidence or that the plaintiff has not.

III

Respondents argue, however, that whatever may be true of the applicability of the "clear and convincing" standard at the summary judgment or directed verdict stage, the defendant should seldom if ever be granted summary judgment where his state of mind is at issue and the jury might disbelieve him or his witnesses as to this issue. They rely on *Poller v. Columbia Broadcasting System, Inc.*, 368 U.S. 464 (1962), for this proposition. We do not understand *Poller*, however, to hold that a plaintiff may defeat a defendant's properly supported motion for summary judgment in a conspiracy or libel case, for example, without offering any concrete evidence from which a reasonable juror could return a verdict in his favor and by merely asserting that the jury might, and legally could, disbelieve the defendant's denial of a conspiracy or of legal malice. The movant has the burden of showing that there is no genuine issue of fact, but the plaintiff is not thereby relieved of his own burden of producing in turn evidence that would support a jury verdict. Rule 56(e) [*see current* FED. R. CIV. P. 56(c)] itself provides that a party opposing a properly supported motion for summary judgment may not rest upon mere allegation or denials of his pleading, but must set forth specific facts showing that there is a genuine issue for trial. Based on that Rule, *Cities Service*, 391 U.S., at 290, held that the plaintiff could not defeat the properly supported summary judgment motion of a defendant charged with a conspiracy without offering "any significant probative evidence tending to support the complaint." As we have recently said, "discredited testimony is not [normally] considered a sufficient basis for drawing a contrary conclusion." *Bose Corp. v. Consumers Union of United States, Inc.*, 466 U.S. 485, 512 (1984). Instead, the plaintiff must present affirmative evidence in order to defeat a properly supported motion for summary judgment. This is true even where the evidence is likely to be within the possession of the defendant, as long as the plaintiff has had a full opportunity to conduct discovery. We repeat, however, that the plaintiff, to survive the defendant's motion, need only present evidence from which a jury might return a verdict in his favor. If he does so, there is a genuine issue of fact that requires a trial.

IV

In sum, a court ruling on a motion for summary judgment must be guided by the *New York Times* "clear and convincing" evidentiary standard in determining whether a genuine issue of actual malice exists—that is, whether the evidence presented is such that a reasonable jury might find that actual malice had been shown with convincing clarity. Because the Court of Appeals did not apply the correct standard in reviewing the District Court's grant of summary judgment, we vacate its decision and remand the case for further proceedings consistent with this opinion.

It is so ordered.

Justice Brennan, dissenting.

The Court today holds that "whether a given factual dispute requires submission to a jury must be guided by the substantive evidentiary standards that apply to the case." In my view, the Court's analysis is deeply flawed, and rests on a shaky foundation of unconnected and unsupported observations, assertions, and conclusions. . . . Accordingly, I respectfully dissent.

To support its holding that in ruling on a motion for summary judgment a trial court must consider substantive evidentiary burdens, the Court appropriately begins with the language of Rule 56(c) [*see current* FED. R. CIV. P. 56(a)], which states that summary judgment shall be granted if it appears that there is "no genuine issue as to any material fact and that the moving party is entitled to a judgment as a matter of law." The Court then purports to restate this Rule, and asserts that "summary judgment will not lie if the dispute about a material fact is 'genuine,' that is, if the evidence is such that a reasonable jury could return a verdict for the nonmoving party." No direct authority is cited for the proposition that in order to determine whether a dispute is "genuine" for Rule 56 purposes a judge must ask if a "reasonable" jury could find for the non-moving party. . . . The Court maintains that this summary judgment inquiry "mirrors" that which applies in the context of a motion for directed verdict under Federal Rule of Civil Procedure 50(a): "whether the evidence presents a sufficient disagreement to require submission to a jury or whether it is so one-sided that one party must prevail as a matter of law." . . .

As far as I can discern, this conclusion . . . has been reached without the benefit of any support in the case law. Although . . . the Court cites *Adickes* and *Cities Service*, those cases simply do not stand for the proposition that in ruling on a summary judgment motion, the trial court is to inquire into the "one-sidedness" of the evidence presented by the parties. . . .

. . . In neither case is there any intimation that a trial court should inquire whether plaintiff's evidence is "significantly probative," as opposed to "merely colorable," or, again, "one-sided." Nor is there in either case any suggestion that once a nonmoving plaintiff has made out a prima facie case based on evidence satisfying Rule 56(e) [*see current* FED. R. CIV. P. 56(c)(1)] that there is any showing that a defendant can make to prevail on a motion for summary judgment. Yet this is what the Court appears to hold, relying, in part, on these two cases. . . .

. . . [T]he Court purports to restate the summary judgment test, but with each repetition, the original understanding is increasingly distorted. . . .

The Court's opinion is replete with boilerplate language to the effect that trial courts are not to weigh evidence when deciding summary judgment motions. . . .

But the Court's opinion is also full of language which could surely be understood as an invitation—if not an instruction—to trial courts to assess and weigh evidence much as a juror would. . . .

I simply cannot square the direction that the judge "is not himself to weigh the evidence" with the direction that the judge also bear in mind the "quantum" of proof required and consider whether the evidence is of sufficient "caliber or quantity" to meet that "quantum." I would have thought that a determination of the "caliber and quantity," *i.e.*, the importance and value, of the evidence in light of the "quantum," *i.e.*, amount "required," could *only* be performed by weighing the evidence.

If in fact, this is what the Court would, under today's decision, require of district courts, then I am fearful that this new rule—for this surely would be a brand new procedure—will transform what is meant to provide an expedited "summary" procedure into a full-blown paper trial on the merits. It is hard for me to imagine that a responsible counsel, aware that the judge will be assessing the "quantum" of the evidence he is presenting, will risk either moving for or responding to a summary judgment motion without coming forth with *all* of the evidence he can muster in support of his client's case. Moreover, if the judge on motion for summary judgment really is to weigh the evidence, then in my view grave concerns are raised concerning the constitutional right of civil litigants to a jury trial. . . .

In my view, if a plaintiff presents evidence which either directly or by permissible inference (and these inferences are a product of the substantive law of the underlying claim) supports all of the elements he needs to prove in order to prevail on his legal claim, the plaintiff has made out a prima facie case and a defendant's motion for summary judgment must fail regardless of the burden of proof that the plaintiff must meet. In other words, whether evidence is "clear and convincing," or proves a point by a mere preponderance, is for the factfinder to determine. As I read the case law, this is how it has been, and because of my concern that today's decision may erode the constitutionally enshrined role of the jury, and also undermine the usefulness of summary judgment procedure, this is how I believe it should remain.

[The dissenting opinion of JUSTICE REHNQUIST, with whom CHIEF JUSTICE BURGER joined, is omitted.]

NOTES AND QUESTIONS

1. Burdens of production and persuasion.   The burden of production on summary judgment pertains to a party's obligation on summary judgment to show either the absence or presence of a genuine issue of material fact. The burden of production is initially on the moving party but shifts to the opposing party if the moving party meets its burden of production. A moving party meets its burden of production if it demonstrates the presumptive absence of a genuine issue of material fact. If the moving party meets that burden, the opposing party will meet its burden of production only if it rebuts that presumption, *i.e.*, only if it shows that there is a genuine issue of material fact. These showings must be made consistently with the standards of Rule 56(c).

The burden of persuasion at trial identifies the party who must prove the contested factual issue. Typically, a plaintiff has the burden of persuasion on matters relevant to her claim, while the defendant has the burden of persuasion on matters relevant to any affirmative defense or counterclaim.

If the party moving for summary judgment is the party with the burden of persuasion at trial (*e.g.*, the plaintiff on her claim or the defendant on his affirmative defense or counterclaim), that party must produce evidence sufficient to create a presumption that there is no genuine issue of material fact as to any element of its claim or defense. If the moving party meets this burden of production, the burden of production shifts to the opposing party to rebut that presumption by showing that there is a genuine issue of material facts as to at least one element of the moving party's claim or defense.

If the moving party does not bear the burden of persuasion at trial (*e.g.*, a defendant challenging a claim asserted against him by the plaintiff or the plaintiff challenging an affirmative defense or counterclaim raised by the defendant), she may meet her burden of production in one of two ways: (1) offer evidence negating an element of the opposing party's claim or defense (*e.g.*, as to a breach of contract claim, a letter indicating that the plaintiff accepted the defendant's performance under the contract as satisfactory); or (2) show that the opposing party has insufficient evidence to prove one element of her claim or defense (*e.g.*, as to a breach of contract claim, defendant might show that the plaintiff's has no evidence that the parties entered into a contract). (We will examine this second method of meeting the burden of production in the next principal case.) If the moving party meets its burden of production, the burden shifts to the opposing party to show that it has sufficient evidence to create a genuine issue of material fact on the challenged issue. The opposing party may meet this burden of production by (a) rehabilitating the evidence attacked in the moving party's papers with satisfactory opposing evidence; or (b) producing evidence that challenges the moving party's showing that the opposing party lacks sufficient evidence to prove its claim or defense.

2. *The summary judgment procedure in Liberty Lobby.*   What was the claim in Liberty Lobby and who, at trial, would have the burden of persuasion on that claim? How did the defendants in *Liberty Lobby* purport to meet their burden of production for summary judgment? Which element or elements of the plaintiffs' claim did they challenge? Did they meet their burden of production and, if so, how did they do that? Assuming the burden of production shifted to the plaintiffs, what evidence did the plaintiffs offer to satisfy their burden of production and what would they have to demonstrate to meet that burden? On what basis did the court of appeals conclude that summary judgment should not have been granted with respect to nine allegedly defamatory statements? Why did it affirm the entry of summary judgment as to the others?

3. *A variable standard based on the burden of proof.*   In *Liberty Lobby*, the Court held that in ruling on a motion for summary judgment, a judge "must be guided by the substantive evidentiary standards that apply to the case," and must ask whether a jury, applying those standards, "could reasonably find for either the plaintiff or the defendant." *Liberty Lobby, supra,* 477 U.S. at 255. The relative burdens of production will thus vary from case to case in two respects. First, it will depend on the type of case involved, mirroring the evidentiary standard—*i.e.,* the "burden of proof"—that would be employed at trial. In *Liberty Lobby*, what evidentiary standard would the plaintiffs have to satisfy at trial in order to prove actual malice in their public-figure libel action? Would a mere preponderance of the evidence suffice, or would they have to meet a stricter clear-and-convincing-evidence standard? Did this same elevated standard then apply in deciding whether the plaintiffs' evidence of actual malice was sufficient to survive the defendants' motion for summary judgment? Second, even among suits employing the same evidentiary standard of proof, the amount of evidence the nonmovant needs to identify to survive a motion for summary judgment will depend on the strength of the movant's initial showing. In a case like *Liberty Lobby*, the more persuasive the defendants' evidence concerning the amount of care taken in preparing the articles in question, the greater the showing the plaintiff would have to make in order to survive a summary judgment ruling in the defendants' favor. It was in both these senses that the *Liberty Lobby* Court phrased the test as being whether there is a "*genuine* issue of *material* fact." *Id.* at 991.

4. *The remand in* Liberty Lobby.   In Part IV of its opinion, the *Liberty Lobby* Court chose to remand the case rather than deciding for itself whether the evidence identified by the plaintiffs would allow a reasonable jury to find that actual malice had been shown with convincing clarity. On remand, the district court

ruled that, as to seven of the nine allegations at issue, there was insufficient support in the record to allow a reasonable jury to make such a finding; thus, the district court granted the defendants' motion for summary judgment as to those allegations. However, the court denied the defendants' motion as to the other two allegations, concluding that as to them, a reasonable jury could find actual malice by clear and convincing evidence. *Liberty Lobby, Inc. v. Anderson*, 1991 WL 186998 (D.D.C. May 1, 1991).

5. *Judicial exceptions.* Near the end of Part II.B of its opinion, the Court in *Liberty Lobby* noted that even if summary judgment is otherwise warranted, a judge may "deny summary judgment in a case where there is reason to believe that the better course would be to proceed to a full trial." 477 U.S. at 255. What circumstances might justify such a denial? In *Kennedy v. Silas Mason Co.*, 334 U.S. 249 (1948), cited in *Liberty Lobby*, the Court held that while the technical requirements for summary judgment had been met, the motion should have been denied because the novel legal issues posed would benefit from the richer factual record that could be developed at trial. *See also Tovar v. U.S. Postal Service*, 3 F.3d 1271 (9th Cir. 1993) (reversing grant of summary judgment when factual record was insufficient to decide an important question of law); 10A WRIGHT, MILLER & KANE, *supra*, § 2728; 10B CHARLES ALAN WRIGHT, ARTHUR R. MILLER & MARY KAY KANE, FEDERAL PRACTICE AND PROCEDURE §§ 2732-2732.3 (3d ed. 1998 & Supp. 2015). Yet the effect of the Supreme Court's 1986 trilogy of cases, while not entirely eliminating a judge's authority to deny an otherwise properly supported summary judgment motion, has been to reduce the federal courts' willingness to make such exceptions. This presumption against judicial exceptions is reflected in the 2010 amendments to Rule 56(a), which replaced the word "may" with "shall" in describing when summary judgment is to be granted ("The Court *shall* grant summary judgment if. . . ."). *See* Advisory Committee Notes, 2010 Amendments, Rule 56, 266 F.R.D. 502, 541-542, 579-580.

6. *Current state practice.* Since 1986, many states have adopted *Liberty Lobby*'s strengthened approach to summary judgment. *See, e.g., Aguilar v. Atlantic Richfield Co.*, 24 P.3d 493, 509 (Cal. 2001) (noting that as a result of several statutory amendments, "summary judgment law in this state now conforms, largely but not completely, to its federal counterpart as clarified and liberalized in *Celotex, Anderson*, and *Matsushita*"); *Cerberus Int'l, Ltd. v. Apollo Mgmt., L.P.*, 794 A.2d 1141, 1147-1149 (Del. 2002) (adopting *Liberty Lobby*'s "common sense approach" and noting it "appears to be the majority rule"). Yet not all states have elected to follow the federal approach. *See, e.g., Romero v. Philip Morris Inc.*, 242 P.3d 280, 287-288 (N.M. Ct. App. 2010) ("Federal courts . . . following the '*Celotex* trilogy,' have become more inclined to grant summary judgment. . . . We continue to refuse to loosen the reins of summary judgment [and] do not wish to grant trial courts greater authority to grant summary judgment than has been traditionally available in New Mexico."); *Huckabee v. Time Warner Entm't Co. L.P.*, 19 S.W.3d 413, 420-423 & n.2 (Tex. 2000) ("[I]f a fact issue exists at the summary judgment stage, the evaluation about whether a reasonable jury could find the plaintiff's evidence to be clear and convincing is best made after the facts are fully

developed at trial. That most other jurisdictions have accepted *Anderson* should not compel us to adopt a standard that is contrary to our traditional jurisprudence and difficult to apply in practice.").

PROBLEM

10-1. Susan filed a personal injury action in federal court against Celebrity Cruises ("Celebrity") for injuries suffered while aboard the *Zenith*, a Celebrity ship, for a one-week cruise. Her injuries occurred when a beverage container carved from a coconut and weighing nearly four pounds fell from Deck 12 onto Deck 11 below, striking Susan on the head. Under the applicable law, Celebrity may be found liable if it negligently created a situation in which it was foreseeable that an injury of this type could occur, whether or not the defendant actually knew of the dangerous condition. Celebrity filed an answer denying the complaint's principal allegations and later moved for summary judgment. The motion was supported by an affidavit stating that because there had been no prior coconut-related accidents either on the *Zenith* or on any of Celebrity's other ships, the accident was unforeseeable and that Celebrity's conduct was therefore consistent with a standard of reasonable care. In response to the motion, Susan did not dispute that this may have been the first such Celebrity accident. However, she has filed a declaration from the director of the International Bartenders School stating that specialty drinks of this type should be consumed only by seated customers and that to serve beverages in such containers to standing customers on an upper deck was "an accident waiting to happen." Susan also filed her own declaration stating that there were no tables or other places on Deck 12 on which a drink could be rested and that the only feasible spot, widely used by passengers, was a narrow six-inch railing that overlooks Deck 11. Susan contends that because these facts, if proved, are sufficient to establish negligence, Celebrity's motion should be denied.

A. Did Celebrity carry its initial burden of production in moving for summary judgment? As to which material fact or facts does it argue there is no genuine issue? As to each of these facts, is Celebrity's evidence such that, unless successfully rebutted, no reasonable jury could find in the plaintiff's favor?

B. Assuming Celebrity carried its initial burden, has Susan met her burden of production in opposing the motion by showing that there is a genuine dispute as to each of the relevant material facts? How should the court rule on the motion and why?

C. Would your answer to part B be the same if in its motion for summary judgment Celebrity noted that under the applicable law, it can be found liable only if it had actual or constructive notice of the condition that had created the danger, and that it had this notice for a sufficient amount of time to invite corrective measures? In this latter scenario, what if anything could Susan do if, at the time Celebrity filed its motion, she had no knowledge concerning the *Zenith*'s prior history and safety record?

Compare McDonough v. Celebrity Cruises, Inc., 64 F. Supp. 2d 259 (S.D.N.Y. 1999), *with Galentine v. Holland America Line-Westours, Inc.*, 333 F. Supp. 2d 991 (W.D. Wash. 2004).

Celotex Corporation v. Catrett

477 U.S. 317 (1986)

JUSTICE REHNQUIST delivered the opinion of the Court.

The United States District Court for the District of Columbia granted the motion of petitioner Celotex Corporation for summary judgment against respondent Catrett because the latter was unable to produce evidence in support of her allegation in her wrongful-death complaint that the decedent had been exposed to petitioner's asbestos products. A divided panel of the Court of Appeals for the District of Columbia Circuit reversed, however, holding that petitioner's failure to support its motion with evidence tending to *negate* such exposure precluded the entry of summary judgment in its favor. . . . We granted certiorari . . . and now reverse the decision of the District of Columbia Circuit.

Respondent commenced this lawsuit in September 1980, alleging that the death in 1979 of her husband, Louis H. Catrett, resulted from his exposure to products containing asbestos manufactured or distributed by 15 named corporations. Respondent's complaint sounded in negligence, breach of warranty, and strict liability. . . . Petitioner's motion, which was first filed in September 1981, argued that summary judgment was proper because respondent had "failed to produce evidence that any [Celotex] product . . . was the proximate cause of the injuries alleged within the jurisdictional limits of [the District] Court." In particular, petitioner noted that respondent had failed to identify, in answering interrogatories specifically requesting such information, any witnesses who could testify about the decedent's exposure to petitioner's asbestos products. In response to petitioner's summary judgment motion, respondent then produced three documents which she claimed "demonstrate that there is a genuine material factual dispute" as to whether the decedent had ever been exposed to petitioner's asbestos products. The three documents . . . all tend[ed] to establish that the decedent had been exposed to petitioner's asbestos products in Chicago during 1970-1971. Petitioner, in turn, argued that the three documents were inadmissible hearsay and thus could not be considered in opposition to the summary judgment motion.

In July 1982, almost two years after the commencement of the lawsuit, the District Court granted [Celotex's summary judgment motion]. The court explained that it was [doing so] because "there [was] no showing that the plaintiff was exposed to the defendant Celotex's product in the District of Columbia or elsewhere within the statutory period." Respondent appealed . . . and a divided panel of the District of Columbia Circuit reversed. The majority of the Court of Appeals held that petitioner's summary judgment motion was rendered "fatally defective" by the fact that petitioner "made no effort to adduce *any* evidence, in the form of affidavits or otherwise, to support its motion." According to the majority, Rule 56(e)* of the Federal Rules of Civil Procedure, and this Court's decision in *Adickes v. S.H. Kress & Co.*, 398 U.S. 144, 159 (1970), establish that "the party opposing the motion for summary judgment bears the burden of responding *only after* the moving party has met its burden of coming forward with proof of the absence of any genuine issues of material fact." The majority therefore declined to consider petitioner's argument that none of the evidence produced by respondent in opposition to the motion for summary judgment would have been admissible at trial. . . .

We think that the position taken by the majority of the Court of Appeals is inconsistent with the standard for summary judgment set forth in Rule 56(c) of the Federal Rules of Civil Procedure. [*See current* FED. R. CIV. P. 56(a).] Under Rule 56(c), summary judgment is proper "if the pleadings, depositions, answers to interrogatories, and admissions on file, together with the affidavits, if any, show that there is no genuine issue as to any material fact and that the moving party is entitled to a judgment as a matter of law." In our view, the plain language of Rule 56(c) mandates the entry of summary judgment, after adequate time for discovery and upon motion, against a party who fails to make a showing sufficient to establish the existence of an element essential to that party's case, and on which that party will bear the burden of proof at trial. In such a situation, there can be "no genuine issue as to any material fact," since a complete failure of proof concerning an essential element of the nonmoving party's case necessarily renders all other facts immaterial. The moving party is "entitled to a judgment as a matter of law" because the nonmoving party has failed to make a sufficient showing on an essential element of her case with respect to which she has the burden of proof. "[T]h[e] standard [for granting summary judgment] mirrors the standard for a directed verdict under Federal Rule of Civil Procedure 50(a). . . ." *Anderson v. Liberty Lobby, Inc.*, 477 U.S. 242, 250 (1986).

Of course, a party seeking summary judgment always bears the initial responsibility of informing the district court of the basis for its motion, and identifying those portions of "the pleadings, depositions, answers to interrogatories, and admissions on file, together with the affidavits, if any," which it believes demonstrate the absence of a genuine issue of material fact. But unlike the Court of Appeals, we

---

* [There is no direct counterpart to Rule 56(e) in the current version of the Federal Rules. At the time this case was decided, Rule 56(e) provided in pertinent part: "When a motion for summary judgment is made and supported as provided in this rule, an adverse party may not rest upon the mere allegations or denials of the adverse party's pleading, but . . . must set forth specific facts showing that there is a genuine issue for trial." Yet the current Rule makes clear that a nonmovant's burden is triggered only after the movant has properly supported its motion, for it permits a party to oppose the motion by "showing that the materials cited do not establish the absence . . . of a genuine dispute." Rule 56(c)(1)(b).—EDS.]

find no express or implied requirement in Rule 56 that the moving party support its motion with affidavits or other similar materials *negating* the opponent's claim. On the contrary, Rule 56(c), which refers to "the affidavits, *if any*"* (emphasis added), suggests the absence of such a requirement. And if there were any doubt about the meaning of Rule 56(c) in this regard, such doubt is clearly removed by Rules 56(a) and (b),** which provide that claimants and defendants, respectively, may move for summary judgment *"with or without supporting affidavits"* (emphasis added). The import of these subsections is that, regardless of whether the moving party accompanies its summary judgment motion with affidavits, the motion may, and should, be granted so long as whatever is before the district court demonstrates that the standard for the entry of summary judgment, as set forth in Rule 56(c), is satisfied. One of the principal purposes of the summary judgment rule is to isolate and dispose of factually unsupported claims or defenses, and we think it should be interpreted in a way that allows it to accomplish this purpose.

Respondent argues, however, that Rule 56(e)† by its terms, places on the non-moving party the burden of coming forward with rebuttal affidavits, or other specified kinds of materials, only in response to a motion for summary judgment "made and supported as provided in this rule." According to respondent's argument, since petitioner did not "support" its motion with affidavits, summary judgment was improper in this case. But as we have already explained, a motion for summary judgment may be made pursuant to Rule 56 "with or without supporting affidavits." In cases like the instant one, where the nonmoving party will bear the burden of proof at trial on a dispositive issue, a summary judgment motion may properly be made in reliance solely on the "pleadings, depositions, answers to interrogatories, and admissions on file." Such a motion, whether or not accompanied by affidavits, will be "made and supported as provided in this rule," and Rule 56(e) [*see current* FED. R. CIV. P. 56(c)(1), (4)] therefore requires the nonmoving party to go beyond the pleadings and by her own affidavits, or by the "depositions, answers to interrogatories, and admissions on file," designate "specific facts showing that there is a genuine issue for trial."

We do not mean that the nonmoving party must produce evidence in a form that would be admissible at trial in order to avoid summary judgment. Obviously, Rule 56 does not require the nonmoving party to depose her own witnesses. Rule 56(e) [*see current* FED. R. CIV. P. 56(c)(1)] permits a proper summary judgment motion to be opposed by any of the kinds of evidentiary materials listed in Rule 56(c) [*see current* FED. R. CIV. P. 56(c)(1), (4)], except the mere pleadings

---

* [While the "if any" language no longer appears in the Rule, Rule 56(c)(1) makes clear that parties have broad discretion in terms of what materials they may cite or rely on in supporting or opposing a motion for summary judgment. — EDS.]

** [Though the "with or without" language no longer appears in the Rule, Rule 56(c)(1)(A) makes clear that "affidavits" are but one of several ways a party may support or oppose a motion for summary judgment. — EDS.]

† [For the text of former Rule 56(e), see footnote *, page 902, *supra*. — EDS.]

themselves, and it is from this list that one would normally expect the nonmoving party to make the showing to which we have referred.

The Court of Appeals in this case felt itself constrained, however, by language in our decision in *Adickes v. S.H. Kress & Co.*, 398 U.S. 144 (1970). There we held that summary judgment had been improperly entered in favor of the defendant restaurant in an action brought under 42 U.S.C. § 1983. In the course of its opinion, the *Adickes* Court said that "both the commentary on and the background of the 1963 amendment conclusively show that it was not intended to modify the burden of the moving party . . . to show initially the absence of a genuine issue concerning any material fact." . . . But we do not think the *Adickes* language quoted above should be construed to mean that the burden is on the party moving for summary judgment to produce evidence showing the absence of a genuine issue of material fact, even with respect to an issue on which the nonmoving party bears the burden of proof. Instead, as we have explained, the burden on the moving party may be discharged by "showing"—that is, pointing out to the district court—that there is an absence of evidence to support the nonmoving party's case. . . .

Our conclusion is bolstered by the fact that district courts are widely acknowledged to possess the power to enter summary judgments *sua sponte*, so long as the losing party was on notice that she had to come forward with all of her evidence. It would surely defy common sense to hold that the District Court could have entered summary judgment *sua sponte* in favor of petitioner in the instant case, but that petitioner's filing of a motion requesting such a disposition precluded the District Court from ordering it.

Respondent commenced this action in September 1980, and petitioner's motion was filed in September 1981. The parties had conducted discovery, and no serious claim can be made that respondent was in any sense "railroaded" by a premature motion for summary judgment. Any potential problem with such premature motions can be adequately dealt with under Rule 56(f) [*see current* FED. R. CIV. P. 56(d)], which allows a summary judgment motion to be denied, or the hearing on the motion to be continued, if the nonmoving party has not had an opportunity to make full discovery.

In this Court, respondent's brief and oral argument have been devoted as much to the proposition that an adequate showing of exposure to petitioner's asbestos products was made as to the proposition that no such showing should have been required. But the Court of Appeals declined to address either the adequacy of the showing made by respondent in opposition to petitioner's motion for summary judgment, or the question whether such a showing, if reduced to admissible evidence, would be sufficient to carry respondent's burden of proof at trial. We think the Court of Appeals with its superior knowledge of local law is better suited than we are to make these determinations in the first instance.

The Federal Rules of Civil Procedure have for almost 50 years authorized motions for summary judgment upon proper showings of the lack of a genuine, triable issue of material fact. Summary judgment procedure is properly regarded not as a disfavored procedural shortcut, but rather as an integral part of the Federal Rules as a whole, which are designed "to secure the just, speedy and inexpensive determination of every action." Fed. Rule Civ. Proc. 1. Before the shift to "notice pleading" accomplished by the Federal Rules, motions to dismiss a complaint or to strike a defense were the principal tools by which factually insufficient claims or defenses could be isolated and prevented from going to trial with the attendant unwarranted consumption of public and private resources. But with the advent of "notice pleading," the motion to dismiss seldom fulfills this function any more, and its place has been taken by the motion for summary judgment. Rule 56 must be construed with due regard not only for the rights of persons asserting claims and defenses that are adequately based in fact to have those claims and defenses tried to a jury, but also for the rights of persons opposing such claims and defenses to demonstrate in the manner provided by the Rule, prior to trial, that the claims and defenses have no factual basis.

The judgment of the Court of Appeals is accordingly reversed, and the case is remanded for further proceedings consistent with this opinion.

It is so ordered.

JUSTICE WHITE, concurring.

I agree that the Court of Appeals was wrong in holding that the moving defendant must always support his motion with evidence or affidavits showing the absence of a genuine dispute about a material fact. I also agree that the movant may rely on depositions, answers to interrogatories, and the like, to demonstrate that the plaintiff has no evidence to prove his case and hence that there can be no factual dispute. But the movant must discharge the burden the Rules place upon him: It is not enough to move for summary judgment without supporting the motion in any way or with a conclusory assertion that the plaintiff has no evidence to prove his case. . . .

JUSTICE BRENNAN, with whom THE CHIEF JUSTICE and JUSTICE BLACKMUN join, dissenting.

This case requires the Court to determine whether Celotex satisfied its initial burden of production in moving for summary judgment on the ground that the plaintiff lacked evidence to establish an essential element of her case at trial. I do not disagree with the Court's legal analysis. The Court clearly rejects the ruling of the Court of Appeals that the defendant must provide affirmative evidence disproving the plaintiff's case. . . . However, because I believe that Celotex did not meet its burden of production under Federal Rule of Civil Procedure 56, I respectfully dissent from the Court's judgment.

I . . .

The burden of production imposed by Rule 56 requires the moving party to make a prima facie showing that it is entitled to summary judgment. The manner in which this showing can be made depends upon which party will bear the burden of persuasion on the challenged claim at trial. If the *moving* party will bear the burden of persuasion at trial, that party must support its motion with credible evidence—using any of the materials specified in Rule 56(c)—that would entitle it to a directed verdict if not controverted at trial. Such an affirmative showing shifts the burden of production to the party opposing the motion and requires that party either to produce evidentiary materials that demonstrate the existence of a "genuine issue" for trial or to submit an affidavit requesting additional time for discovery. Fed. Rules Civ. Proc. 56(e), (f) [*see current* FED. R. CIV. P. 56(d), (e)].

If the burden of persuasion at trial would be on the *non-moving* party, the party moving for summary judgment may satisfy Rule 56's burden of production in either of two ways. First, the moving party may submit affirmative evidence that negates an essential element of the nonmoving party's claim. Second, the moving party may demonstrate to the court that the nonmoving party's evidence is insufficient to establish an essential element of the nonmoving party's claim. If the nonmoving party cannot muster sufficient evidence to make out its claim, a trial would be useless and the moving party is entitled to summary judgment as a matter of law.

Where the moving party adopts this second option and seeks summary judgment on the ground that the nonmoving party—who will bear the burden of persuasion at trial—has no evidence, the mechanics of discharging Rule 56's burden of production are somewhat trickier. Plainly, a conclusory assertion that that the nonmoving party has no evidence is insufficient. Such a "burden" of production is no burden at all and would simply permit summary judgment procedure to be converted into a tool for harassment. Rather, as the Court confirms, a party who moves for summary judgment on the ground that the nonmoving party has no evidence must affirmatively show the absence of evidence. This may require the moving party to depose the nonmoving party's witnesses or to establish the inadequacy of documentary evidence. If there is literally no evidence in the record, the moving party may demonstrate this by reviewing for the court the admissions, interrogatories, and other exchanges between the parties that are in the record. Either way, however, the moving party must affirmatively demonstrate that there is no evidence in the record to support a judgment for the nonmoving party.

If the moving party has not fully discharged this initial burden of production, its motion for summary judgment must be denied . . . . Accordingly, the nonmoving party may defeat a motion for summary judgment that asserts that the nonmoving party has no evidence by calling the court's attention to supporting evidence already in the record that was overlooked or ignored by the moving party. In that event, the moving party must respond by making an attempt to demonstrate the inadequacy of this evidence, for it is only by attacking all the record evidence allegedly supporting the nonmoving party that a party seeking summary judgment satisfies Rule 56's burden of production.[3] Thus, if the record disclosed that the

---

3. Once the moving party has attacked whatever record evidence—if any—the nonmoving party purports to rely upon, the burden of production shifts to the nonmoving party, who must either (1) rehabilitate the evidence attacked in the moving party's papers, (2) produce additional evidence showing the existence of a genuine issue for trial as provided in Rule 56(e), or (3) submit an affidavit explaining why further discovery is necessary as provided in Rule 56(f). . . .

moving party had overlooked a witness who would provide relevant testimony for the nonmoving party at trial, the court could not find that the moving party had discharged its initial burden of production unless the moving party sought to demonstrate the inadequacy of this witness' testimony. Absent such a demonstration, summary judgment would have to be denied on the ground that the moving party had failed to meet its burden of production under Rule 56. . . .

II

I do not read the Court's opinion to say anything inconsistent with or different than the preceding discussion. My disagreement with the Court concerns the application of these principles to the facts of this case.

Defendant Celotex sought summary judgment on the ground that plaintiff had "failed to produce" any evidence that her decedent had ever been exposed to Celotex asbestos. Celotex supported this motion with a two-page "Statement of Material Facts as to Which There Is No Genuine Issue" and a three-page "Memorandum of Points and Authorities" which asserted that the plaintiff had failed to identify any evidence in responding to two sets of interrogatories propounded by Celotex and that therefore the record was "totally devoid" of evidence to support plaintiff's claim.

Approximately three months earlier, Celotex had filed an essentially identical motion. Plaintiff responded to this earlier motion by producing three pieces of evidence which she claimed "[a]t the very least . . . demonstrate that there is a genuine factual dispute for trial": (1) a letter from an insurance representative of another defendant describing asbestos products to which plaintiff's decedent had been exposed; (2) a letter from T.R. Hoff, a former supervisor of decedent, describing asbestos products to which decedent had been exposed; and (3) a copy of decedent's deposition from earlier workmen's compensation proceedings. Plaintiff also apparently indicated at that time that she intended to call Mr. Hoff as a witness at trial.

Celotex subsequently withdrew its first motion for summary judgment. However, as a result of this motion, when Celotex filed its second summary judgment motion, the record *did* contain evidence—including at least one witness—supporting plaintiff's claim. Indeed, counsel for Celotex admitted to this Court at oral argument that Celotex was aware of this evidence and of plaintiff's intention to call Mr. Hoff as a witness at trial when the second summary judgment motion was filed. Moreover, plaintiff's response to Celotex' second motion pointed to this evidence—noting that it had already been provided to counsel for Celotex in connection with the first motion—and argued that Celotex had failed to "meet its burden of proving that there is no genuine factual dispute for trial."

On these facts, there is simply no question that Celotex failed to discharge its initial burden of production. Having chosen to base its motion on the argument that there was no evidence in the record to support plaintiff's claim, Celotex was not free to ignore supporting evidence that the record clearly contained. Rather, Celotex was required, as an initial matter, to attack the adequacy of this evidence. Celotex' failure to fulfill this simple requirement constituted a failure to discharge its initial burden of production under Rule 56, and thereby rendered summary judgment improper. . . .

[The dissenting opinion of JUSTICE STEVENS is omitted.]

NOTES AND QUESTIONS

1. Celotex's initial burden of production.   The summary judgment motion filed by the defendant in *Celotex* challenged the plaintiff's ability to prove an essential element of her claim, namely, that her husband had been exposed to asbestos manufactured by Celotex during the relevant time frame. This was an issue on which the plaintiff would have had the "burden of persuasion" at trial. How did Celotex purport to meet its burden of production on summary judgment? On what basis did the court of appeals conclude that Celotex failed to meet that burden? Why did the Supreme Court disagree? Under the approach endorsed by the *Celotex* Court, in what two ways could a moving party like Celotex meet its burden of production? Would these same methods of satisfying the burden of production be available to a party who has the burden of persuasion at trial? Why or why not? Does Justice Brennan disagree with Court's overall approach to summary judgment? If not, why does he dissent?

After *Celotex*, is it sufficient for a moving party without the burden of persuasion at trial to simply allege that the non-moving party lacks evidence necessary to prove an essential element of a claim or defense? To what extent does Justice White express concerns on this point? Before seeking summary judgment, Celotex submitted two sets of interrogatories inquiring as to what evidence the plaintiff had to support her claim that the decedent had been exposed to defendant's product. Would the result have been the same if Celotex had not first submitted these interrogatories to the plaintiff? Does the Court's ruling that a defendant may move for summary judgment by simply noting the inadequacy of the plaintiff's evidence, without offering any evidence that negates the plaintiff's claim, follow logically from *Liberty Lobby*'s having equated the standards for summary judgment and directed verdict? In thinking about this, suppose that at trial the plaintiff offered no evidence showing that the decedent had been exposed to the defendant's product. Could the defendant then have successfully moved for a directed verdict based on the plaintiff's lack of evidence? Should the result be the same if the defendant seeks dismissal of the case earlier, through a pretrial motion for summary judgment?

2. On remand.   On remand in *Celotex*, the court of appeals rejected the district court's earlier refusal to consider some of the plaintiff's evidence simply because it was not presented in admissible form. *Catrett v. Johns-Manville Sales Corp.*, 826 F.2d 33 (D.C. Cir. 1987), *cert. denied*, 484 U.S. 1066 (1988). For one thing, the appellate court said that because the defendant in supporting its summary judgment motion did not object to the admissibility of some of the evidence identified by the plaintiff, it waived any objection to that evidence at least for summary judgment purposes. Secondly, the court of appeals noted that even had a timely evidentiary objection been made, it would not have been fatal, for the Supreme Court had expressly stated that evidence not in an admissible form may be considered as long as it can be "reduced to admissible evidence" at trial. *Catrett*, 826 F.2d at 34. In reversing the district court's grant of summary judgment, the court of appeals thus held that even if one critical piece of the plaintiff's evidence—the Hoff letter—was inadmissible hearsay, it could still be considered at the summary judgment stage because the plaintiff had shown that "the substance of the letter is reducible to admissible evidence in the form of trial testimony." *Id.* at 38. Rule 56 has since been amended to recognize this reducible-to-admissible-evidence principle. *See* FED. R. CIV. P. 56(c)(2).

Matsushita Electric Industrial Co., Ltd. v. Zenith Radio Corp.

475 U.S. 574 (1986)

JUSTICE POWELL delivered the opinion of the Court.

This case requires that we again consider the standard district courts must apply when deciding whether to grant summary judgment in an antitrust conspiracy case.

I . . .

A

Petitioners, defendants below, are 21 corporations that manufacture or sell "consumer electronic products" (CEPs)—for the most part, television sets. Petitioners include both Japanese manufacturers of CEPs and American firms, controlled by Japanese parents, that sell the Japanese-manufactured products. Respondents, plaintiffs below, are Zenith Radio Corporation (Zenith) and National Union Electric Corporation (NUE). Zenith is an American firm that manufactures and sells television sets. NUE is the corporate successor to Emerson Radio Company, an American firm that manufactured and sold television sets until 1970, when it withdrew from the market after sustaining substantial losses. Zenith and NUE began this lawsuit in 1974, claiming that petitioners had illegally conspired to drive American firms from the American CEP market. According to respondents, the gist of this conspiracy was a "'scheme to raise, fix and maintain artificially *high* prices for television receivers sold by [petitioners] in Japan and, at the same time, to fix and maintain *low* prices for television receivers exported to and sold in the United States.'" These "low prices" were allegedly at levels that produced substantial losses for petitioners. The conspiracy allegedly began as early as 1953, and according to respondents was in full operation by sometime in the late 1960's. Respondents claimed that various portions of this scheme violated §§ 1 and 2 of the Sherman Act, § 2(a) of the Robinson-Patman Act, § 73 of the Wilson Tariff Act, and the Antidumping Act of 1916.

After several years of detailed discovery, petitioners filed motions for summary judgment on all claims against them. The District Court directed the parties to file, with preclusive effect, "Final Pretrial Statements" listing all the documentary evidence that would be offered if the case proceeded to trial. Respondents filed such a statement, and petitioners responded with a series of motions challenging the admissibility of respondents' evidence. In three detailed opinions, the District Court found the bulk of the evidence on which Zenith and NUE relied inadmissible.

The District Court then turned to petitioners' motions for summary judgment. In an opinion spanning 217 pages, the court found that the admissible evidence did not raise a genuine issue of material fact as to the existence of the alleged conspiracy. At bottom, the court found, respondents' claims rested on the inferences that could be drawn from petitioners' parallel conduct in the Japanese and American markets, and from the effects of that conduct on petitioners' American competitors. After reviewing the evidence both by category and *in toto*, the court found that any inference of conspiracy was unreasonable, because (i) some portions of the evidence suggested that petitioners conspired in ways that did not injure respondents, and (ii) the evidence that bore directly on the alleged price-cutting conspiracy did not rebut the more plausible inference that petitioners were cutting prices to compete in the American market and not to monopolize it. Summary judgment therefore was granted on respondents' claims under § 1 of the Sherman Act and the Wilson Tariff Act. Because the Sherman Act § 2 claims, which alleged that petitioners had combined to monopolize the American CEP market, were functionally indistinguishable from the § 1 claims, the court dismissed them also. Finally, the court found that the Robinson-Patman Act claims depended on the same supposed conspiracy as the Sherman Act claims. Since the court had found no genuine issue of fact as to the conspiracy, it entered judgment in petitioners' favor on those claims as well.

B

The Court of Appeals for the Third Circuit reversed. The court began by examining the District Court's evidentiary rulings, and determined that much of the evidence excluded by the District Court was in fact admissible. These evidentiary rulings are not before us.

On the merits, and based on the newly enlarged record, the court found that the District Court's summary judgment decision was improper. The court acknowledged that "there are legal limitations upon the inferences which may be drawn from circumstantial evidence," but it found that "the legal problem . . . is different" when "there is direct evidence of concert of action." Here, the court concluded, "there is both direct evidence of certain kinds of concert of action and circumstantial evidence having some tendency to suggest that other kinds of concert of action may have occurred." Thus, the court reasoned, cases concerning the limitations on inferring conspiracy from ambiguous evidence were not dispositive. Turning to the evidence, the court determined that a factfinder reasonably could draw the following conclusions:

1. The Japanese market for CEPs was characterized by oligopolistic behavior, with a small number of producers meeting regularly and exchanging

information on price and other matters. This created the opportunity for a stable combination to raise both prices and profits in Japan. American firms could not attack such a combination because the Japanese Government imposed significant barriers to entry.

2. Petitioners had relatively higher fixed costs than their American counterparts, and therefore needed to operate at something approaching full capacity in order to make a profit.

3. Petitioners' plant capacity exceeded the needs of the Japanese market.

4. By formal agreements arranged in cooperation with Japan's Ministry of International Trade and Industry (MITI), petitioners fixed minimum prices for CEPs exported to the American market. The parties refer to these prices as the "check prices," and to the agreements that require them as the "check price agreements."

5. Petitioners agreed to distribute their products in the United States according to a "five company rule": each Japanese producer was permitted to sell only to five American distributors.

6. Petitioners undercut their own check prices by a variety of rebate schemes. Petitioners sought to conceal these rebate schemes both from the United States Customs Service and from MITI, the former to avoid various customs regulations as well as action under the antidumping laws, and the latter to cover up petitioners' violations of the check-price agreements.

Based on inferences from the foregoing conclusions, the Court of Appeals concluded that a reasonable factfinder could find a conspiracy to depress prices in the American market in order to drive out American competitors, which conspiracy was funded by excess profits obtained in the Japanese market. The court apparently did not consider whether it was as plausible to conclude that petitioners' price-cutting behavior was independent and not conspiratorial . . . .

We granted certiorari to determine . . . whether the Court of Appeals applied the proper standards in evaluating the District Court's decision to grant petitioners' motion for summary judgment . . . .

II

We begin by emphasizing what respondents' claim is *not*. Respondents cannot recover antitrust damages based solely on an alleged cartelization of the Japanese market, because American antitrust laws do not regulate the competitive conditions of other nations' economies. Nor can respondents recover damages for any conspiracy by petitioners to charge higher than competitive prices in the American market. Such conduct would indeed violate the Sherman Act, but it could not injure respondents: as petitioners' competitors, respondents stand to gain from any conspiracy to raise the market price in CEPs. Finally, for the same reason, respondents cannot recover for a conspiracy to impose nonprice restraints that have the effect of either raising market price or limiting output. Such restrictions, though harmful to competition, actually *benefit* competitors by making supracompetitive pricing more attractive. Thus, neither petitioners' alleged supracompetitive pricing in Japan, nor the five-company rule that limited distribution in this country, nor the check prices insofar as they established minimum prices in this country, can by themselves give respondents a cognizable claim against petitioners for antitrust damages. The Court of Appeals therefore erred to the extent that it found evidence of these alleged conspiracies to be "direct evidence" of a conspiracy that injured respondents.

Respondents nevertheless argue that these supposed conspiracies, if not themselves grounds for recovery of antitrust damages, are circumstantial evidence of another conspiracy that *is* cognizable: a conspiracy to monopolize the American market by means of pricing below the market level. The thrust of respondents' argument is that petitioners used their monopoly profits from the Japanese market to fund a concerted campaign to price predatorily and thereby drive respondents and other American manufacturers of CEPs out of business. Once successful, according to respondents, petitioners would cartelize the American CEP market, restricting output and raising prices above the level that fair competition would produce. The resulting monopoly profits, respondents contend, would more than compensate petitioners for the losses they incurred through years of pricing below market level.

The Court of Appeals found that respondents' allegation of a horizontal conspiracy to engage in predatory pricing, if proved, would be a *per se* violation of § 1 of the Sherman Act. Petitioners did not appeal from that conclusion. The issue in this case thus becomes whether respondents adduced sufficient evidence in support of their theory to survive summary judgment. We therefore examine the principles that govern the summary judgment determination.

III

To survive petitioners' motion for summary judgment, respondents must establish that there is a genuine issue of material fact as to whether petitioners entered into an illegal conspiracy that caused respondents to suffer a cognizable injury. This showing has two components. First, respondents must show more than a conspiracy in violation of the antitrust laws; they must show an injury to them resulting from the illegal conduct. Respondents charge petitioners with a whole host of conspiracies in restraint of trade. Except for the alleged conspiracy to monopolize the American market through predatory pricing, these alleged conspiracies could not have caused respondents to suffer an "antitrust injury," because they actually tended to benefit respondents. Therefore, unless, in context, evidence of these "other" conspiracies raises a genuine issue concerning the existence of a predatory pricing conspiracy, that evidence cannot defeat petitioners' summary judgment motion.

Second, the issue of fact must be "genuine." Fed. Rules Civ. Proc. 56(c), (e).* When the moving party has carried its burden under Rule 56(c), its opponent must

---

* [The genuineness standard and its role in the parties' respective burdens of production are now addressed in Fed. R. Civ. P. 56(a) & (c). — EDS.]

do more than simply show that there is some metaphysical doubt as to the material facts. In the language of the Rule, the nonmoving party must come forward with "specific facts showing that there is a *genuine issue for trial*." Fed. Rule Civ. Proc. 56(e) (emphasis added). Where the record taken as a whole could not lead a rational trier of fact to find for the non-moving party, there is no "genuine issue for trial."

It follows from these settled principles that if the factual context renders respondents' claim implausible—if the claim is one that simply makes no economic sense—respondents must come forward with more persuasive evidence to support their claim than would otherwise be necessary. [*First National Bank of Arizona v. Cities Service Co.*, 391 U.S. 253 (1968)] is instructive. The issue in that case was whether proof of the defendant's refusal to deal with the plaintiff supported an inference that the defendant willingly had joined an illegal boycott. Economic factors strongly suggested that the defendant had no motive to join the alleged conspiracy. The Court acknowledged that, in isolation, the defendant's refusal to deal might well have sufficed to create a triable issue. But the refusal to deal had to be evaluated in its factual context. Since the defendant lacked any rational motive to join the alleged boycott, and since its refusal to deal was consistent with the defendant's independent interest, the refusal to deal could not by itself support a finding of antitrust liability.

Respondents correctly note that "[o]n summary judgment the inferences to be drawn from the underlying facts . . . must be viewed in the light most favorable to the party opposing the motion." But antitrust law limits the range of permissible inferences from ambiguous evidence in a § 1 case. Thus, in *Monsanto Co. v. Spray-Rite Service Corp.*, 465 U.S. 752 (1984), we held that conduct as consistent with permissible competition as with illegal conspiracy does not, standing alone, support an inference of antitrust conspiracy. To survive a motion for summary judgment or for a directed verdict, a plaintiff seeking damages for a violation of § 1 must present evidence "that tends to exclude the possibility" that the alleged conspirators acted independently. Respondents in this case, in other words, must show that the inference of conspiracy is reasonable in light of the competing inferences of independent action or collusive action that could not have harmed respondents.

Petitioners argue that these principles apply fully to this case. According to petitioners, the alleged conspiracy is one that is economically irrational and practically infeasible. Consequently, petitioners contend, they had no motive to engage in the alleged predatory pricing conspiracy; indeed, they had a strong motive *not* to conspire in the manner respondents allege. Petitioners argue that, in light of the absence of any apparent motive and the ambiguous nature of the evidence of conspiracy, no trier of fact reasonably could find that the conspiracy with which petitioners are charged actually existed. This argument requires us to consider the nature of the alleged conspiracy and the practical obstacles to its implementation.

IV

A

A predatory pricing conspiracy is by nature speculative. Any agreement to price below the competitive level requires the conspirators to forgo profits that free competition would offer them. The forgone profits may be considered an investment in the future. For the investment to be rational, the conspirators must have a reasonable expectation of recovering, in the form of later monopoly profits, more than the losses suffered. As then-Professor Bork, discussing predatory pricing by a single firm, explained:

> "Any realistic theory of predation recognizes that the predator as well as his victims will incur losses during the fighting, but such a theory supposes it may be a rational calculation for the predator to view the losses as an investment in future monopoly profits (where rivals are to be killed) or in future undisturbed profits (where rivals are to be disciplined). The future flow of profits, appropriately discounted, must then exceed the present size of the losses." R. Bork, The Antitrust Paradox 145 (1978).

As this explanation shows, the success of such schemes is inherently uncertain: the short-run loss is definite, but the long-run gain depends on successfully neutralizing the competition. Moreover, it is not enough simply to achieve monopoly power, as monopoly pricing may breed quick entry by new competitors eager to share in the excess profits. The success of any predatory scheme depends on *maintaining* monopoly power for long enough both to recoup the predator's losses and to harvest some additional gain. Absent some assurance that the hoped-for monopoly will materialize, *and* that it can be sustained for a significant period of time, "[t]he predator must make a substantial investment with no assurance that it will pay off." For this reason, there is a consensus among commentators that predatory pricing schemes are rarely tried, and even more rarely successful [citing various authorities].

These observations apply even to predatory pricing by a *single firm* seeking monopoly power. In this case, respondents allege that a large number of firms have conspired over a period of many years to charge below-market prices in order to stifle competition. Such a conspiracy is incalculably more difficult to execute than an analogous plan undertaken by a single predator. The conspirators must allocate the losses to be sustained during the conspiracy's operation, and must also allocate any gains to be realized from its success. Precisely because success is speculative and depends on a willingness to endure losses for an indefinite period, each conspirator has a strong incentive to cheat, letting its partners suffer the losses necessary to destroy the competition while sharing in any gains if the conspiracy succeeds. The necessary allocation is therefore difficult to accomplish. Yet if conspirators cheat to any substantial extent, the conspiracy must fail, because its success depends on depressing the market price for *all* buyers of CEPs. If there are too few goods at the artificially low price to satisfy demand, the would-be victims of the conspiracy can continue to sell at the "real" market price, and the conspirators suffer losses to little purpose.

Finally, if predatory pricing conspiracies are generally unlikely to occur, they are especially so where, as here, the prospects of attaining monopoly power seem slight. In order to recoup their losses, petitioners must obtain enough market power to set higher than competitive prices, and then must sustain those prices long enough to earn in excess profits what they earlier gave up in below-cost prices. Two decades after their conspiracy is alleged to have commenced, petitioners appear to be far from achieving this goal: the two largest shares of the retail market in television sets are held by RCA and respondent Zenith, not by any of petitioners. Moreover, those shares, which together approximate 40% of sales, did not decline appreciably during the 1970's. Petitioners' collective share rose rapidly during this period, from one-fifth or less of the relevant markets to close to 50%. Neither the District Court nor the Court of Appeals found, however, that petitioners' share presently allows them to charge monopoly prices; to the contrary, respondents contend that the conspiracy is ongoing—that petitioners are still artificially *depressing* the market price in order to drive Zenith out of the market. The data in the record strongly suggest that that goal is yet far distant.

The alleged conspiracy's failure to achieve its ends in the two decades of its asserted operation is strong evidence that the conspiracy does not in fact exist. Since the losses in such a conspiracy accrue before the gains, they must be "repaid" with interest. And because the alleged losses have accrued over the course of two decades, the conspirators could well require a correspondingly long time to recoup. Maintaining supracompetitive prices in turn depends on the continued cooperation of the conspirators, on the inability of other would-be competitors to enter the market, and (not incidentally) on the conspirators' ability to escape antitrust liability for their *minimum* price-fixing cartel. Each of these factors weighs more heavily as the time needed to recoup losses grows. If the losses have been substantial—as would likely be necessary in order to drive out the competition—petitioners would most likely have to sustain their cartel for years simply to break even.

Nor does the possibility that petitioners have obtained supracompetitive profits in the Japanese market change this calculation. Whether or not petitioners have the *means* to sustain substantial losses in this country over a long period of time, they have no *motive* to sustain such losses absent some strong likelihood that the alleged conspiracy in this country will eventually pay off. The courts below found no evidence of any such success, and—as indicated above—the facts actually are to the contrary: RCA and Zenith, not any of the petitioners, continue to hold the largest share of the American retail market in color television sets. More important, there is nothing to suggest any relationship between petitioners' profits in Japan and the amount petitioners could expect to gain from a conspiracy to monopolize the American market. In the absence of any such evidence, the possible existence of supracompetitive profits in Japan simply cannot overcome the economic obstacles to the ultimate success of this alleged predatory conspiracy.

B

In *Monsanto*, we emphasized that courts should not permit factfinders to infer conspiracies when such inferences are implausible, because the effect of such practices is often to deter procompetitive conduct. Respondents, petitioners' competitors, seek to hold petitioners liable for damages caused by the alleged conspiracy to cut prices. Moreover, they seek to establish this conspiracy indirectly, through evidence of other combinations (such as the check-price agreements and the five company rule) whose natural tendency is to raise prices, and through evidence of rebates and other price-cutting activities that respondents argue tend to prove a combination to suppress prices. But cutting prices in order to increase business often is the very essence of competition. Thus, mistaken inferences in cases such as this one are especially costly, because they chill the very conduct the antitrust laws are designed to protect. "[W]e must be concerned lest a rule or precedent that authorizes a search for a particular type of undesirable pricing behavior end up by discouraging legitimate price competition."

In most cases, this concern must be balanced against the desire that illegal conspiracies be identified and punished. That balance is, however, unusually one-sided in cases such as this one. As we earlier explained, predatory pricing schemes require conspirators to suffer losses in order eventually to realize their illegal gains; moreover, the gains depend on a host of uncertainties, making such schemes more likely to fail than to succeed. These economic realities tend to make predatory pricing conspiracies self-deterring: unlike most other conduct that violates the antitrust laws, failed predatory pricing schemes are costly to the conspirators. Finally, unlike predatory pricing by a single firm, *successful* predatory pricing conspiracies involving a large number of firms can be identified and punished once they succeed, since some form of minimum price-fixing agreement would be necessary in order to reap the benefits of predation. Thus, there is little reason to be concerned that by granting summary judgment in cases where the evidence of conspiracy is speculative or ambiguous, courts will encourage such conspiracies.

V

As our discussion in Part IV-A shows, petitioners had no motive to enter into the alleged conspiracy. To the contrary, as presumably rational businesses, petitioners had every incentive *not* to engage in the conduct with which they are charged, for its likely effect would be to generate losses for petitioners with no corresponding gains. The Court of Appeals did not take account of the absence of a plausible motive to enter into the alleged predatory pricing conspiracy. It focused instead on whether there was "direct evidence of concert of action." The Court of Appeals erred in two respects: (i) the "direct evidence" on which the court relied had little, if any, relevance to the alleged predatory pricing conspiracy; and (ii) the court failed to consider the absence of a plausible motive to engage in predatory pricing.

The "direct evidence" on which the court relied was evidence of *other* combinations, not of a predatory pricing conspiracy. Evidence that petitioners conspired to raise prices in Japan provides little, if any, support for respondents' claims: a conspiracy to increase profits in one market does not tend to show a conspiracy to sustain losses in another. Evidence that petitioners agreed to fix *minimum* prices (through the check-price agreements) for the American market actually works in petitioners' favor, because it suggests that petitioners were seeking to place a floor under prices rather than to lower them. The same is true of evidence that petitioners agreed to limit the number of distributors of their products in the American market—the so-called five company rule. That practice may have facilitated a horizontal territorial allocation, but its natural effect would be to raise market prices rather than reduce them. Evidence that tends to support any of these collateral conspiracies thus says little, if anything, about the existence of a conspiracy to charge below-market prices in the American market over a period of two decades.

That being the case, the absence of any plausible motive to engage in the conduct charged is highly relevant to whether a "genuine issue for trial" exists within the meaning of Rule 56(e). Lack of motive bears on the range of permissible conclusions that might be drawn from ambiguous evidence: if petitioners had no rational economic motive to conspire, and if their conduct is consistent with other, equally plausible explanations, the conduct does not give rise to an inference of conspiracy. Here, the conduct in question consists largely of (i) pricing at levels that succeeded in taking business away from respondents, and (ii) arrangements that may have limited petitioners' ability to compete with each other (and thus kept prices from going even lower). This conduct suggests either that petitioners behaved competitively, or that petitioners conspired to *raise* prices. Neither possibility is consistent with an agreement among 21 companies to price below-market levels. Moreover, the predatory pricing scheme that this conduct is said to prove is one that makes no practical sense: it calls for petitioners to destroy companies larger and better established than themselves, a goal that remains far distant more than two decades after the conspiracy's birth. Even had they succeeded in obtaining their monopoly, there is nothing in the record to suggest that they could recover the losses they would need to sustain along the way. In sum, in light of the absence of any rational motive to conspire, neither petitioners' pricing practices, nor their conduct in the Japanese market, nor their agreements respecting prices and distribution in the American market, suffice to create a "genuine issue for trial." Fed. Rule Civ. Proc. 56(e).

On remand, the Court of Appeals is free to consider whether there is other evidence that is sufficiently unambiguous to permit a trier of fact to find that petitioners conspired to price predatorily for two decades despite the absence of any apparent motive to do so. The evidence must "ten[d] to exclude the possibility" that petitioners underpriced respondents to compete for business rather than to implement an economically senseless conspiracy. In the absence of such evidence, there is no "genuine issue for trial" under Rule 56(e), and petitioners are entitled to have summary judgment reinstated.

VI . . .

The decision of the Court of Appeals is reversed, and the case is remanded for further proceedings consistent with this opinion.

It is so ordered.

JUSTICE WHITE, with whom JUSTICE BRENNAN, JUSTICE BLACKMUN, and JUSTICE STEVENS join, dissenting

It is indeed remarkable that the Court, in the face of the long and careful opinion of the Court of Appeals, reaches the result it does. The Court of Appeals faithfully followed the relevant precedents, and it kept firmly in mind the principle
that proof of a conspiracy should not be fragmented. After surveying the massive
record, including very significant evidence that the District Court erroneously had
excluded, the Court of Appeals concluded that the evidence taken as a whole creates a genuine issue of fact whether petitioners engaged in a conspiracy in violation
of §§ 1 and 2 of the Sherman Act and § 2(a) of the Robinson-Patman Act. In my
view, the Court of Appeals' opinion more than adequately supports this judgment.

The Court's opinion today, far from identifying reversible error, only muddies the
waters. In the first place, the Court makes confusing and inconsistent statements
about the appropriate standard for granting summary judgment. Second, the Court
makes a number of assumptions that invade the factfinder's province. Third, the
Court faults the Third Circuit for nonexistent errors and remands the case although
it is plain that respondents' evidence raises genuine issues of material fact.

I

The Court's initial discussion of summary judgment standards appears consistent with settled doctrine. I agree that "[w]here the record taken as a whole could
not lead a rational trier of fact to find for the nonmoving party, there is no 'genuine
issue for trial.'" I also agree that "'[o]n summary judgment the inferences to be
drawn from the underlying facts . . . must be viewed in the light most favorable to
the party opposing the motion.'" But other language in the Court's opinion suggests a departure from traditional summary judgment doctrine. Thus, the Court
gives the following critique of the Third Circuit's opinion:

> "[T]he Court of Appeals concluded that a reasonable factfinder could find a
> conspiracy to depress prices in the American market in order to drive out American
> competitors, which conspiracy was funded by excess profits obtained in the Japanese
> market. The court apparently did not consider whether it was as plausible to conclude
> that petitioners' price-cutting behavior was independent and not conspiratorial."

In a similar vein, the Court summarizes *Monsanto Co. v. Spray-Rite Service
Corp., supra,* as holding that "courts should not permit factfinders to infer conspiracies when such inferences are implausible . . . ." Such language suggests
that a judge hearing a defendant's motion for summary judgment in an antitrust
case should go beyond the traditional summary judgment inquiry and decide for
himself whether the weight of the evidence favors the plaintiff. *Cities Service* and
Monsanto do not stand for any such proposition. Each of those cases simply held
that a particular piece of evidence standing alone was insufficiently probative to
justify sending a case to the jury. These holdings in no way undermine the doctrine that all evidence must be construed in the light most favorable to the party
opposing summary judgment.

If the Court intends to give every judge hearing a motion for summary judgment
in an antitrust case the job of determining if the evidence makes the inference of
conspiracy more probable than not, it is overturning settled law. If the Court does

not intend such a pronouncement, it should refrain from using unnecessarily broad and confusing language.

II

In defining what respondents must show in order to recover, the Court makes assumptions that invade the factfinder's province. The Court states with very little discussion that respondents can recover under § 1 of the Sherman Act only if they prove that "petitioners conspired to drive respondents out of the relevant markets by (i) pricing below the level necessary to sell their products, or (ii) pricing below some appropriate measure of cost." This statement is premised on the assumption that "[a]n agreement without these features would either leave respondents in the same position as would market forces or would actually benefit respondents by raising market prices." In making this assumption, the Court ignores the contrary conclusions of respondents' expert DePodwin, whose report in very relevant part was erroneously excluded by the District Court.

The DePodwin Report, on which the Court of Appeals relied along with other material, indicates that respondents were harmed in two ways that are independent of whether petitioners priced their products below "the level necessary to sell their products or . . . some appropriate measure of cost." First, the Report explains that the price-raising scheme in Japan resulted in lower consumption of petitioners' goods in that country and the exporting of more of petitioners' goods to this country than would have occurred had prices in Japan been at the competitive level. Increasing exports to this country resulted in depressed prices here, which harmed respondents. Second, the DePodwin Report indicates that petitioners exchanged confidential proprietary information and entered into agreements such as the five company rule with the goal of avoiding intragroup competition in the United States market. The Report explains that petitioners' restrictions on intragroup competition caused respondents to lose business that they would not have lost had petitioners competed with one another.

The DePodwin Report alone creates a genuine factual issue regarding the harm to respondents caused by Japanese cartelization and by agreements restricting competition among petitioners in this country. No doubt the Court prefers its own economic theorizing to Dr. DePodwin's, but that is not a reason to deny the factfinder an opportunity to consider Dr. DePodwin's views on how petitioners' alleged collusion harmed respondents.

The Court, in discussing the unlikelihood of a predatory conspiracy, also consistently assumes that petitioners valued profit-maximization over growth. In light of the evidence that petitioners sold their goods in this country at substantial losses over a long period of time, I believe that this is an assumption that should be argued to the factfinder, not decided by the Court.

III

In reversing the Third Circuit's judgment, the Court identifies two alleged errors: "(i) [T]he 'direct evidence' on which the [Court of Appeals] relied had little, if any, relevance to the alleged predatory pricing conspiracy; and (ii) the court failed to consider the absence of a plausible motive to engage in predatory pricing." The Court's position is without substance.

A

The first claim of error is that the Third Circuit treated evidence regarding price fixing in Japan and the so-called five company rule and check prices as "'direct evidence' of a conspiracy that injured respondents." The passage from the Third Circuit's opinion in which the Court locates this alleged error makes what I consider to be a quite simple and correct observation, namely, that this case is distinguishable from traditional "conscious parallelism" cases, in that there is direct evidence of concert of action among petitioners. The Third Circuit did not, as the Court implies, jump unthinkingly from this observation to the conclusion that evidence regarding the five company rule could support a finding of antitrust injury to respondents. The Third Circuit twice specifically noted that horizontal agreements allocating customers, though illegal, do not ordinarily injure competitors of the agreeing parties. However, after reviewing evidence of cartel activity in Japan, collusive establishment of dumping prices in this country, and long-term, below-cost sales, the Third Circuit held that a factfinder could reasonably conclude that the five company rule was not a simple price-raising device:

> "[A] factfinder might reasonably infer that the allocation of customers in the United States, combined with price-fixing in Japan, was intended to permit concentration of the effects of dumping upon American competitors while eliminating competition among the Japanese manufacturers in either market."

I see nothing erroneous in this reasoning.

B

The Court's second charge of error is that the Third Circuit was not sufficiently skeptical of respondents' allegation that petitioners engaged in predatory pricing conspiracy. But the Third Circuit is not required to engage in academic discussions about predation; it is required to decide whether respondents' evidence creates a genuine issue of material fact. The Third Circuit did its job, and remanding the case so that it can do the same job again is simply pointless.

The Third Circuit indicated that it considers respondents' evidence sufficient to create a genuine factual issue regarding long-term, below-cost sales by petitioners. The Court tries to whittle away at this conclusion by suggesting that the "expert opinion evidence of below-cost pricing has little probative value in comparison with the economic factors . . . that suggest that such conduct is irrational." But the question is not whether the Court finds respondents' experts persuasive, or prefers the District Court's analysis; it is whether, viewing the evidence in the light most favorable to respondents, a jury or other factfinder could reasonably conclude that petitioners engaged in long-term, below-cost sales. I agree with the Third Circuit that the answer to this question is "yes."

It is misleading for the Court to state that the Court of Appeals "did not disturb the District Court's analysis of the factors that substantially undermine the probative value of [evidence in the DePodwin Report respecting below-cost sales]." The Third Circuit held that the exclusion of the portion of the DePodwin Report regarding below-cost pricing was erroneous because "the trial court ignored DePodwin's uncontradicted affidavit that all data relied on in his report were of the type on which experts in his field would reasonably rely." In short, the Third Circuit found DePodwin's affidavit sufficient to create a genuine factual issue regarding the correctness of his conclusion that petitioners sold below cost over a long period of time. Having made this determination, the court saw no need—nor do I—to address the District Court's analysis point by point. The District Court's criticisms of DePodwin's methods are arguments that a factfinder should consider.

IV

Because I believe that the Third Circuit was correct in holding that respondents have demonstrated the existence of genuine issues of material fact, I would affirm the judgment below and remand this case for trial.

NOTES AND QUESTIONS

1. *The role of the claim in summary judgment analysis.*   What are the operative facts of the plaintiffs' claim? What point is the *Matsushita* Court is making in the first paragraph of Part II of the opinion? Is it attempting to trim the relevant operative facts of the claim? Only one right of action is before the Court. What is it and what are its elements? What facts might be relevant to that right of action? Under what evidentiary standard must that right of action be proven? Can you describe the defendants' burden of production on summary judgment? Did they meet that burden? If so, how? Did the plaintiffs meet their burden of production? Why or why not?

2. *Summary judgment standards.*   The Court describes the summary judgment standards in Part III of its opinion. Is that description consistent with the text of Rule 56? What is the initial burden on the moving party? How must the opposing party respond? What is a "genuine issue of material fact"? Which party must establish that such a fact exists? In whose favor should inferences be drawn? Did the Court adhere to these standards when it applied them in Parts IV and V of its opinion? The dissent asserts that the majority "makes confusing and inconsistent statements about the appropriate standard for granting summary judgment." Is that an accurate criticism of the majority opinion? What other error does the dissent identify in its critique of the majority opinion?

3. *The plus factors.*   In Part III of its opinion, the Court states, "It follows from these settled principles that if the factual context renders respondents' claim implausible—if the claim is one that simply makes no economic sense—respondents must come forward with more persuasive evidence to support their claim than would otherwise be necessary." It further noted that

[t]o survive a motion for summary judgment or for a directed verdict, a plaintiff seeking damages for a violation of § 1 must present evidence "that tends to exclude the possibility" that the alleged conspirators acted independently. Respondents in this case, in other words, must show that the inference of conspiracy is reasonable in light of the competing inferences of independent action or collusive action that could not have harmed respondents.

Does this remind you of the plausibility formula adopted by the Court in *Bell Atlantic Corp. v. Twombly*, 550 U.S. 544 (2007)? Was it appropriate for the *Twombly* Court to import this summary judgment "plus" factor into the pleading analysis? What factors might counsel against applying this aggressive summary judgment standard at the pleading stage?

4. *Inferences on a motion for summary judgment.* How does a judge normally read the underlying facts in a motion for summary judgment? Did that general rule of interpretation apply in *Matsushita*? Why not? Did antitrust law play any peculiar role in this respect? Is there anything about an antitrust case that makes it atypical, and perhaps not the most suitable for elaborating a pleading formula applicable to a broader, wide range of cases?

PROBLEMS

10-2. In Problem 10-1, page 900, *supra*, could Celebrity Cruises have based its motion for summary judgment on its assertion that Susan has no evidence to explain how the coconut came to fall on her, and that it could have resulted from the intentional act of another passenger rather than from any negligence on Celebrity's part? If so, could Celebrity simply assert in its motion that Susan lacks such evidence of causation, or would something more be required on its part? If Susan in fact lacked any such evidence, is there anything she could do at this point to try to redress the situation? Would it matter if more than a year had now transpired since the lawsuit was filed?

10-3. Jeff, a passenger in a car driven by Ken, was injured during a rainstorm when their vehicle spun into the oncoming lane and collided with a car driven by Jan. Jeff sued Ken and Jan in Indiana state court, claiming that each driver was negligent. With respect to Jan, Jeff alleged that she had breached her duty to maintain a proper lookout so as to be able to take precautionary measures to avoid a collision. After filing an answer denying that she had breached any duty of care owed to Jeff, Jan moved for summary judgment. Her motion asserted that Jeff had no evidence demonstrating her negligence and that his claim must therefore fail. In an accompanying affidavit, Jan said she had first seen Jeff's vehicle when it was only two or three car lengths away and that the crash occurred four seconds later. She did not identify any evidence showing that she had been driving at a proper speed, that she had braked in a timely manner, that she had attempted to turn away, that she had honked her horn or blinked her lights, or that otherwise affirmatively showed a lack of negligence on her part. In response to Jan's motion, Jeff did not identify any evidence showing that Jan could have avoided the accident or that she was otherwise negligent. Instead, he argued that the issue of whether Jan acted reasonably under the circumstances was one that a jury should resolve.

A. If Indiana's law of summary judgment mirrors that of the federal courts as set out in *Celotex*, how should the court rule on Jan's motion? Did she carry her initial burden of showing there was no genuine issue as to the material fact of her negligence and that she was therefore entitled to judgment in her favor as a matter of law? Was she required to come forward with answers to interrogatories, affidavits, or other materials that affirmatively showed an absence of negligence on her part? Even if she was not, might the court still be justified in denying her motion?

B. How, if at all, would your answer to part A differ if Indiana's law of summary judgment required a moving party without the burden of persuasion at trial to "negate" an element of the non-moving party's claim?

C. Assume that Indiana's law of summary judgment is the same as that of the federal courts and that Jan has carried her initial burden in moving for summary judgment. Could Jeff successfully defeat the entry of summary judgment by filing the affidavit of Bob, a neighbor, who has stated that a week after the accident occurred, his friend Moe, who had witnessed the accident, told him that Jan at the time appeared to be speeding and that she was using a cellphone. Will Bob's affidavit suffice to defeat Jan's motion for summary judgment, even though his statement would be inadmissible hearsay at trial since he recites statements made to him by a third party rather than his own observations of the accident?

See Cole v. Gohmann, 727 N.E.2d 1111 (Ind. Ct. App. 2000).

3.   Summary Judgment for the Plaintiff

All of the summary judgment cases we have considered so far involved motions made by defendants. Summary judgment motions are sometimes made by plaintiffs, though much less frequently than by defendants. While plaintiffs who have been served with counterclaims often move for summary judgment on those claims, in this setting they occupy the same position as defendants. What is less common is for a plaintiff to move for summary judgment on her own claim. The reason for this disparity is the greater difficulty of prevailing on such a motion than on one made by a defendant. As we have seen, a defendant can obtain summary judgment simply by showing that the plaintiff lacks sufficient evidence to prove *an* essential element of her claim. That the plaintiff may be able to prove all of the other elements is irrelevant, and the defendant need not even address them. By contrast, when a plaintiff moves for summary judgment on her own claim, or more particularly on a right of action to which that claim gives rise, she must show with respect to *every* element of that right that no genuine issue exists. If a genuine issue exists as to even one of them, the plaintiff's motion will be denied and the case will proceed to trial. This is not to say, however, that plaintiffs never move for summary judgment or that such motions always fail. *See, e.g., United States v. $52,000.00, More or Less, in U.S. Currency*, 508 F. Supp. 2d 1036, 1045 (S.D. Ala. 2007) (holding that in a drug money forfeiture action brought by the government, in which the government moved for summary judgment and met its initial burden of showing by a preponderance of the evidence—*i.e.*, that it was more likely than not—that the property in question was subject to forfeiture, the opposing party's mere denials in the form of "bald assertions, absent supporting evidence, affidavits, or citation to the record before this Court or legal authority, do not give rise to a genuine issue of material fact to preclude the entry of summary judgment in favor of the Government").

In terms of timing, Rule 56(b) places no limits on how early a motion for summary judgment may be filed. Thus, just as a defendant may file a motion for summary judgment along with her answer, a plaintiff may file such a motion simultaneously with her complaint. However, Rule 56(d) allows a court to defer considering or deny such a motion if the opposing party can show that it needs more time to prepare its opposition, including "time . . . to take discovery . . . ."

Sometimes a plaintiff moves only for a *partial summary judgment, e.g.,* on the issue of the defendant's liability, if a genuine issue remains as to the amount of damages. As amended in 2010, Rule 56(a) expressly allows a federal court to grant "partial summary judgment," *i.e.*, judgment on just "part of [a] claim or defense. . . ." Fed. R. Civ. P. 56(a). Prior to that amendment, courts treated a motion for partial summary judgment as simply narrowing the range of facts that remain in dispute and that would be resolved at trial, without any actual judgment being entered at the time. *See* 11 Moore's Federal Practice, *supra*, § 56.122; § 56App.08[1], at 56App. 16; 10B Wright, Miller & Kane, *supra*, § 2737.

PROBLEM

10-4. Lodge Hall Music Inc. ("LHM") owns the copyrights to various musical compositions. It filed suit in federal court against Waco, Inc. ("Waco"), a club that serves alcoholic beverages and plays recorded music for its patrons, and against Waco's owners, Chuck and Jane Carter. The complaint alleges that Waco violated federal copyright law by playing four songs whose copyrights the plaintiff owns. LHM seeks $6,000 in statutory damages ($1,500 for each of the four violations), plus costs and attorneys' fees. Under federal law, a business like Waco can play music without violating a copyright if that business purchases a license from the American Society of Composers, Authors, and Publishers (ASCAP). This allows the purchaser to play music owned by ASCAP members without having to obtain separate licenses from the owner of each song that it plays. Waco declined to buy such a license from ASCAP. On October 19, two ASCAP investigators visited the Waco club. In affidavits filed in support of LHM's summary judgment motion, the investigators stated that they were at the club from 8:30 P.M. until 1:35 A.M. that night and that the four songs owned by the plaintiff were played between 10:00 and 11:00 P.M. In opposing LHM's motion, Waco relied on its verified answer to the complaint, which was signed by the Carters. While the answer did not dispute LHM's ownership of the copyrights, it did deny that the plaintiff's songs were played that night and stated that the club had stopped playing music at midnight and closed a short time later. The Carters also relied on their depositions, in which they stated that while they did not personally know which songs were played on October 19, the club's disc jockey had told them that the plaintiff's four songs were not among them. The defendants assert that the plaintiff's affidavits are perjured and unreliable and that summary judgment must therefore be denied.

A. In moving for summary judgment, did plaintiff LHM carry its initial burden of production by showing that there was no genuine dispute as to any material fact? What materials may LHM rely on in seeking to make this showing?

B. In opposing LHM's motion for summary judgment, did the defendants meet their burden of production, *i.e.*, did they show that there was a genuine issue as to any of the material facts and, if so, which ones? What materials can the defendants legitimately rely upon in seeking to make this showing?

C. If summary judgment were appropriate here on the question of liability, could a court enter only a partial summary judgment, or might summary judgment also be appropriate on the question of damages?

See Lodge Hall Music, Inc. v. Waco Wrangler Club, Inc., 831 F.2d 77 (5th Cir. 1987).

Many instances in which a plaintiff seeks summary judgment involve "cross-motions for summary judgment" where the defendant is seeking summary judgment as well. In some of these cases, the parties may agree on all of the critical underlying facts but disagree as to their legal consequences. Such cross-motions often occur, for example, in suits challenging the constitutionality of government action where there is no dispute as to the material facts and the only issue is the validity of the challenged law or conduct. In these cases, as long as no further factual development is needed to clarify the issue, the court may grant summary judgment for whichever party is entitled to win on the constitutional issue. *See, e.g., Bartnicki v. Vopper,* 532 U.S. 514 (2001) (affirming grant of defendant's cross-motion for summary judgment when media defendant's broadcast of plaintiff's stolen tapes was protected by the First Amendment); *Crosby v. National Foreign Trade Council,* 530 U.S. 363 (2000) (affirming grant of plaintiff's cross-motion for summary judgment in suit challenging constitutionality of Massachusetts law that barred state agencies from dealing with companies that did business with Burma). Cross-motions for summary judgment may also occur, however, with respect to entirely different issues, such that a court might end up granting neither motion—with the result that the case may proceed to trial. Thus, suppose that in a breach of contract action, the defendant moves for summary judgment based on the statute of limitations, while the plaintiff files a cross-motion for summary judgment as to the merits of her claim. The court could end up deciding both that the statute of limitations has not run and that material issues of fact remain with respect to the contract claim, in which case both motions will be denied.

Johnson v. Tuff N Rumble Management, Inc.

2000 WL 622612 (E.D. La. May 15, 2000), *appeal dismissed*, 253 F.3d 701 (5th Cir. 2001), *cert. denied*, 535 U.S. 929 (2002)

VANCE, District Judge.

Before the Court are the motions of plaintiffs, Joseph Johnson and Wardell Quezergue, for summary judgment and Rule 11 sanctions against defendant, Joe Jones d/b/a Melder Publishing Co. For the following reasons, plaintiffs' motions are Granted.

I.   Background

This copyright infringement case involves the rights to a song entitled *It Ain't My Fault*. Plaintiffs, Joseph Johnson and Wardell Quezergue, claim that they are the sole composers and copyright owners of the song. Quezergue registered a copyright to *It Ain't My Fault* with the United States Copyright Office on June 22, 1964. On the copyright application, Quezergue listed himself and Johnson as the authors and copyright owners of the song. Plaintiffs attest that they never assigned any of their interest in the copyright of the song to Jones, Melder Publishing, or any other entity, firm or corporation owned by Jones. Jones, appearing herein *pro se*, claims a 50% ownership of the song by transfer from Johnson.

The dispute between plaintiffs and Jones arises out of a Power of Attorney signed by Johnson on April 14, 1992, in which Johnson granted Jones power of attorney in all matters connected with the use of *It Ain't My Fault*. On December 29, 1992, Jones, as Johnson's "authorized agent," filed a copyright registration to *It Ain't My Fault* in the name of Smokey Johnson Publishing Co. & Melder Publishing Co. The registration completed by Jones and the certificate issued by the U.S. Register of Copyrights list Johnson and Quezergue as the authors of the song and indicate that Smokey Johnson Publishing & Melder Publishing had obtained ownership of the copyright "by written agreement." On December 30, 1992, Jones filed two copyright renewals relative to the 1964 and the 1992 registrations. Both renewal documents identify Johnson and Quezergue as authors and Joseph Johnson c/o Melder Publishing and Wardell Quezergue c/o Melder Publishing as copyright owners of *It Ain't My Fault*. . . . Plaintiffs now move for summary judgment on the grounds that no genuine issue of fact exists as to whether Jones owns a copyright interest in *It Ain't My Fault*. Specifically, plaintiffs argue that Jones has failed to produce a valid written assignment as required to establish his ownership under federal copyright law. Plaintiffs also move for sanctions against Jones, arguing that his memoranda submitted in opposition to the summary judgment motion violate Rule 11 of the Federal Rules of Civil Procedure. Jones opposes both motions.

II. Discussion

A. Summary Judgment

1. Legal Standard

Summary judgment is appropriate when there are no genuine issues as to any material facts, and the moving party is entitled to judgment as a matter of law. A court must be satisfied that no reasonable trier of fact could find for the nonmoving party or, in other words, "that the evidence favoring the nonmoving party is insufficient to enable a reasonable jury to return a verdict in her favor." *Lavespere v. Niagara Mach. & Tool Works, Inc.*, 910 F.2d 167, 178 (5th Cir. 1990), *abrogated on other grounds by Little v. Liquid Air Corp.*, 37 F.3d 1069 (5th Cir. 1994). The moving party bears the burden of establishing that there are no genuine issues of material fact.

If the dispositive issue is one for which the nonmoving party will bear the burden of proof at trial, the moving party may satisfy its burden by merely pointing out that the evidence in the record contains insufficient proof concerning an essential element of the nonmoving party's claim. The burden then shifts to the nonmoving party, who must, by submitting or referring to evidence, set out specific facts showing that a genuine issue exists. The nonmovant may not rest upon allegations and denials.

2. Assignment of Copyright

To prevail on a copyright infringement claim, plaintiffs must prove that they own a valid copyright, and that defendants impermissibly copied or otherwise infringed upon that copyright. All of the copyright registration and renewal certificates in the record, including those filed by Jones, state that Johnson and Quezergue authored *It Ain't My Fault*. Accordingly, the Court finds that ownership of the copyright vested initially with plaintiffs as the song's authors.

Jones asserts that he obtained a copyright interest in *It Ain't My Fault* by virtue of a transfer of ownership from Johnson. The Copyright Act permits a copyright owner to transfer his ownership in whole or in part. *See* 17 U.S.C. § 201(d). However, "[a] transfer of copyright ownership, other than by operation of law, is not valid unless an instrument of conveyance, or a note or memorandum of the transfer, is *in writing* and signed by the owner of the rights conveyed or such owner's duly authorized agent." Id. § 204(a) (emphasis added). The writing requirement "ensures that the creator of a work will not give away his copyright inadvertently." *Effects Assocs., Inc. v. Cohen*, 908 F.2d 555, 556-57 (9th Cir. 1990).

Plaintiffs argue that no genuine issue of fact exists as to whether Jones owns a copyright interest in *It Ain't My Fault* because Jones has failed to produce a valid written assignment transferring the copyright from plaintiffs to Jones. Johnson and Quezergue attached affidavits to their summary judgment motion stating that they are the sole composers and copyright owners of *It Ain't My Fault*. Further, they aver that they never assigned any of their copyright interest in the song to Jones, Melder Publishing Co., or any other entity owned by Jones.

A.   PLAINTIFFS' REQUEST FOR ADMISSIONS DEEMED ADMITTED UNDER RULE 36

Plaintiffs assert that Jones' failure to respond to Requests for Admissions regarding the existence of an alleged written assignment warrants summary judgment in their favor pursuant to Federal Rule of Civil Procedure 36. On December 21, 1999, plaintiffs mailed to Jones a Request for Production of Documents, Interrogatories and Admissions, by both certified and first class mail. The Request for Admissions notified Jones to respond within thirty days pursuant to Rule 36. Among other requests, plaintiffs asked Jones to admit or deny that he does not have a signed assignment of copyright from Quezergue, Johnson or Smokey Johnson Publishing relating to *It Ain't My Fault*. Plaintiffs also asked Jones to produce any and all assignments of copyright in the song. A review of the record indicates that Jones has not yet responded to these requests. Plaintiffs allege that the certified mail was returned marked "refused."

Rule 36(a) gives a party served with requests for admissions thirty days in which to respond. If the party to whom the request is directed does not answer or object to the admissions within that time period, the matter is deemed admitted. Rule 36(b) adds that "[a] matter admitted under this rule is conclusively established unless the court, on motion, permits [the admission to be withdrawn or amended]." The conclusive effect of Rule 36(b) "applies equally to those admissions made affirmatively and those established by default, even if the matters admitted relate to material facts that defeat a party's claim." *American Auto. Assn. v. AAA Legal Clinic of Jefferson*, 930 F.2d 1117, 1120 (5th Cir. 1991) (citations omitted).

Here, Jones has still not responded to plaintiffs' Requests for Admissions, more than four months after plaintiffs mailed them to him. Further, Jones has not moved this Court to withdraw the admissions pursuant to Rule 36(b). Jones avers that he did not receive or refuse any mail from plaintiffs, and that he first received the Request for Admissions as an attachment to plaintiffs' summary judgment motion. Jones also asserts that he was in the hospital when the mail was allegedly refused. These arguments do not prevent the admission of the matters requested under Rule 36. When the record demonstrates that the request for admissions was mailed to the party's last known street address in accordance with Federal Rule of Civil Procedure 5(b), the failure to receive a request will not prevent summary judgment based thereon. . . . The Court therefore deems admitted all of the matters raised in plaintiffs' Request for Admissions dated December 29, 1999.

It is well established that admissions, including matters deemed admitted as a result of a party's failure to respond to a request for admission, may form the basis for granting summary judgment. Because the admissions establish that Jones does not have a signed assignment of copyright in *It Ain't My Fault* from Quezergue, Johnson or Smokey Johnson Publishing, no genuine issue of fact exists as to whether Jones owns a copyright interest in the song.

B. No Valid Written Assignment

Even without considering the Rule 36 admissions, the Court finds that summary judgment is appropriate here because Jones has failed to produce any credible summary judgment evidence to rebut plaintiffs' sworn testimony that they did not assign a copyright interest in *It Ain't My Fault* to Jones or any entity under his control. Jones claims to have obtained rights to the published version of the song by virtue of a written assignment from Johnson. In his initial opposition to plaintiffs' summary judgment motion, Jones suggests that because he registered and renewed a copyright in the published version of the song as Johnson's duly authorized agent, a genuine issue exists as to his ownership interest.

Copyright ownership and registration are separate and distinct issues. *See Arthur Rutenberg Homes, Inc. v. Drew Homes, Inc.*, 29 F.3d 1529, 1531 (11th Cir. 1994) (*citing* 17 U.S.C. § 408(a)). "Copyright inheres in authorship and exists whether or not it is ever registered." Id. Jones suggests that his registration and renewal of the copyright in *It Ain't My Fault* on December 29 and 30, 1992 establish that he owns an interest in the song's copyright. It is true that a certificate of registration from the U.S. Register of Copyrights constitutes *prima facie* evidence of the validity of a copyright. However, the statutory presumption of copyright validity codified at Section 410(c) of the Copyright Act applies only to certificates of registration made before or within five years after first publication of the work. As to works published more than five years before registration, the automatic presumption does not apply, and the Court has discretion to determine what weight to give the copyright registrations. Here, the certificate of registration issued to Smokey Johnson & Melder Publishing by the U.S. Register of Copyrights on December 30, 1992 indicates that the work was first published on August 1, 1964, approximately twenty-eight years earlier. Accordingly, the statutory presumption does not apply. In light of plaintiffs' evidence of the invalidity of the registration certificate held by Jones, the Court finds the certificates insufficient to sustain Jones' burden on summary judgment.

As noted above, Jones can have an ownership interest in *It Ain't My Fault* only if plaintiffs or their duly authorized agent assigned that interest to him by written agreement. A written agreement assigning interests in a copyright must clearly establish that the parties intended to transfer a copyright interest. Jones suggests that because Johnson granted him power of attorney and authorized him to act as his agent, an issue of fact exists as to whether Johnson assigned an interest in the song to him. The Court has reviewed the Power of Attorney signed by Johnson on April 20, 1992. Nothing in the Power of Attorney or in the undated "Authorization" signed by Johnson indicates that Johnson intended to assign his interest in *It Ain't My Fault* to Jones. . . .

In his supplemental opposition to plaintiffs' summary judgment motion, Jones produced for the first time an alleged written agreement between Johnson and Smokey Johnson & Melder Publishing. This "Song Writer(s) Contract," dated August 1, 1964, states that Johnson assigned to Smokey Johnson & Melder Publishing all copyrights in *It Ain't My Fault*. Plaintiffs assert that the contract is a forgery. In support, they point to numerous characteristics of the document which challenge its authenticity as a document executed in 1964. First, the document was printed on a computer laser printer and in the same type face as Jones' pleadings. Second, the document exhibits word processing features that did not exist in 1964, including justified text and a word processing file name located in the footer of the first page. Finally, both of Johnson's signatures on the document are identical. After reviewing the Songwriter(s) Contract, the Court agrees with plaintiffs that the contract is an obvious forgery. As plaintiffs observe, laser printers and personal computers did not exist in 1964. No reasonable jury could find that the proffered document is valid.

Because plaintiffs have properly supported their summary judgment motion, the burden shifts to Jones to establish the authenticity of the purported copyright assignment. Jones has presented no evidence establishing the authenticity of the Songwriter(s) Contract and has proffered no other credible evidence that Johnson assigned his copyright interests in *It Ain't My Fault* to him. Accordingly, the Court grants plaintiffs' motion for summary judgment and concludes as a matter of law that Jones does not own a copyright interest in any version, published or unpublished, of *It Ain't My Fault*. . . .

B.   Rule 11 Sanctions

Plaintiffs also move the Court to sanction Jones on the grounds that he filed motions in opposition to summary judgment on February 28, 2000 and March 3, 2000 in violation of Federal Rule of Civil Procedure 11. Plaintiffs assert that Jones filed the opposition motions without conducting a reasonable inquiry into the facts; that the motions are not warranted by existing law; and that Jones interposed the motions for an improper purpose, namely, harassment, delay and increase in the costs of litigation. Plaintiffs also contend that the Songwriter(s) Contract attached as Exhibit 3 to Jones' supplemental opposition motion is a blatant forgery. Jones conclusorily rejects these allegations and asserts that the Court should instead impose Rule 11 sanctions on plaintiffs and their counsel.

Although Jones appears in this case *pro se*, Rule 11 applies equally to attorneys and to unrepresented parties. *See* Fed. R. Civ. P. 11(b) ("By presenting to the court a pleading . . . , an attorney *or unrepresented party* [certifies] . . .") (emphasis added). *See also Hicks v. Bexar County, Texas*, 973 F. Supp. 653, 687 (W.D. Tex. 1997), *aff'd*, 137 F.3d 1352 (5th Cir. 1998) ("The Fifth Circuit has made it clear that Rule 11 applies fully and completely to actions filed by *pro se* litigants.") (collecting cases). The rule requires that a party initiate a motion for sanctions separately from other motions or requests and describe the specific conduct alleged to violate subdivision (b). *See* [Fed. R. Civ. P. 11(c)(2)]. The motion ["must not be filed or be presented to the court if the challenged . . . claim . . . is withdrawn or appropriately corrected within 21 days after service. . . .]" Id. Here, plaintiffs sent Jones a letter dated March 10, 2000, warning him that they intended to seek sanctions unless he withdrew the offending motions and attaching a copy of their Rule 11 motion. When Jones did not withdraw his claims within 21 days, plaintiffs filed a separate Rule 11 motion with this Court. Plaintiffs clearly complied with the provisions of [Rule 11(c)(2)]. By contrast, Jones has not complied with the procedural requirements of Rule 11. Jones did not file a separate motion for Rule 11 sanctions against plaintiffs but instead included the request in his opposition to plaintiffs' motion. The only Rule 11 motion properly before this Court, therefore, is that filed by plaintiffs.

The purpose of Rule 11 is "to deter baseless filings in district court and thus . . . streamline the administration and procedure of the federal courts." *Cooter & Gell v. Hartmarx Corp.*, 496 U.S. 384, 393 (1990). The rule applies to every pleading, written motion, or other paper submitted to the Court. When an unrepresented party submits a pleading to the court, he certifies to the best of his knowledge, information, and belief that: (1) the pleading is not interposed for any improper purpose, such as to harass or to cause unnecessary delay or increase in the costs of litigation; (2) the pleading is warranted by existing law or a good faith argument for modification of existing law; and (3) the litigant has conducted a reasonable inquiry into the factual allegations and denials which support the pleading. The Court applies an objective, not subjective, standard of reasonableness to determine whether a party has violated these duties. The conduct of the attorney or unrepresented party is assessed at the time he submitted the pleading or motion.

Jones has clearly violated Rule 11. First, Jones' allegations that a genuine issue of fact exists as to his ownership of a copyright interest in *It Ain't My Fault* were not warranted by existing law or the extension, modification, or reversal of existing law. In determining whether counsel has made a reasonable *legal* inquiry, the Court considers the following factors: (1) the time available to the attorney; (2) the plausibility of the legal view contained in the document; (3) the *pro se* status of the litigant; and (4) the complexity of the legal and factual issues raised. The Court granted Jones a seven-day extension of time to file his original opposition to plaintiffs' summary judgment motion and then permitted Jones leave to supplement his opposition. Jones thus had sufficient time to make a reasonable inquiry into the applicable law. Further, the legal issue here is not particularly complex and was set forth simply in plaintiffs' motion for summary judgment: Jones can have a copyright interest in *It Ain't My Fault* only if plaintiffs transferred that interest to him by virtue of a written assignment. Jones nevertheless cited no legal authority in support of his copyright ownership allegations. Instead, he suggested that the Power of Attorney granted to him by Johnson and/or the certificates of copyright registration that he received from the U.S. Register of Copyrights raise an issue of fact as to his ownership. This argument is wholly without legal support, as discussed above. Moreover, although the Court considers the special circumstances of Jones' *pro se* status, those circumstances do not weigh in his favor here. A review of the Court's records reveals that Jones has been a party to at least two other copyright infringement actions in this district. . . . Jones' prior experience clearly demonstrates that he is aware of the legal elements required to properly obtain ownership of a copyright, in particular, the necessity of a valid written assignment. All of these factors indicate that Jones submitted the opposition motions at issue without adequate legal support as required by Rule 11.

Jones also violated Rule 11 by failing to conduct a reasonable inquiry into the facts underlying his motions and by interposing those motions for the purposes of delay, harassment, and increasing the costs of litigation. The evidence reveals that the Songwriter(s) Contract that Jones attached as Exhibit 3 to his supplemental opposition is a forgery of a 1964 document. Presenting a forged document to the Court is certainly not reasonable and warrants the imposition of sanctions under Rule 11. Further, Jones asserts that the affidavit properly filed by Johnson in support of plaintiffs' summary judgment motion is the product of fraud and perjury. Jones offers absolutely no factual support for this allegation and a review of the record reveals none.

The following excerpt from Jones' opposition memorandum demonstrates the inadequate factual inquiry and improper purpose underlying the pleading:

> ". . . Johnson's affidavit as you can see is fraud, perjury and corruption by the attorney that prepared this fraudulent and corrupted document for Joseph Johnson to sign. . . ."
>
> "Your Honor, you may want to ask Joseph Johnson if he has a mental problem. . . . This is a vicious act of stealing all his rights and interest at high noon."

The inclusion of scandalous or indecent matter is itself a strong indication that an improper purpose underlies a motion. *See* Fed. R. Civ. P. 11 Adv. Comm. Notes. The Fifth Circuit has held that "[a]busive language towards opposing counsel has no place in documents filed with our courts; the filing of a document containing such language is one form of harassment prohibited by Rule 11." *Coats v. Pierre*, 890 F.2d 728, 734 (5th Cir. 1989). Not only does Jones make disparaging remarks about plaintiffs and their counsel, but he also attacks the integrity of this Court:

> Attorney Gregory P. Eveline should be sanctioned along with Wardell Quezerque for fabricating lies and misleading the Honorable Sara Vance and Magistrate Judge Africk. . . . From my experience this business is usual for these attorneys I have dealt with in New Orleans; they are trickery misusing and abusing citizens, and not being respectful to the code of ethics, and in many cases their behavior is tolerated by a percentage of the judges in our judicial system, including the local parish and federal judges in the state of Louisiana.

Given the compelling evidence of fraud, the unsubstantiated factual allegations, and the abusive language used by Jones, the Court finds that Jones did not conduct a reasonable factual inquiry in this case and that he filed his motions for an improper purpose.

For the foregoing reasons, the Court concludes that Rule 11 sanctions are appropriate here. Plaintiffs assert that the Court should sanction Jones by ordering him to pay attorneys' fees in the amount of $1,250; assessing punitive sanctions against him in the amount of $10,000 per counsel; striking Jones' motions; declaring the Songwriter(s) Contract a forgery; requiring Jones to immediately retain counsel; and barring Jones from filing further documents in this case without an attorney or leave of court.

Once a court finds that counsel or an unrepresented party has violated Rule 11, the Court has discretion to impose an appropriate sanction. Although the district court has broad discretion in fashioning an appropriate sanction, the sanction imposed should be the "least severe sanction" adequate to deter future violations of Rule 11. [*See* FED. R. CIV. P. 11(c)(4).] The purpose of Rule 11 sanctions is to deter rather than to compensate. Sanctions may be monetary or nonmonetary and may include striking the offending paper. The rule expressly provides that a court may also award the movant some or all of the reasonable attorney's fees and other expenses incurred as a direct result of the Rule 11 violation.

. . . [T]he Court finds that a monetary sanction in the amount of plaintiffs' reasonable attorneys' fees and costs is necessary to deter future misconduct by Jones. In so concluding, the Court notes that the Fifth Circuit has imposed sanctions against Jones for filing frivolous pleadings in a prior copyright infringement action. . . . In addition to engaging in similar conduct in other litigation, Jones' actions do not represent an isolated event in this case. On May 27, 1999, Jones filed a motion to dismiss plaintiffs' claims for lack of personal jurisdiction, improper venue, [and] insufficient service of process. Jones attached a one and one-half page memorandum to the motion, which referenced absolutely no law or facts to support his allegations. Nevertheless, the filing of this wholly unsubstantiated motion required a response by plaintiffs as well as an investigation by this Court, which resulted in a six-page opinion denying Jones' motion. The Court has already discussed the implications of Jones' *pro se* status and finds that, after weighing all of the factors outlined above, it does not militate against imposing monetary sanctions here.

. . . The plaintiffs aver that they have expended $1,250 in attorneys' fees, representing 10 hours of work at $125 per hour. The Court finds this amount reasonable under the circumstances. Plaintiffs are also entitled to costs, which they have not yet verified. The Court further notes that, in addition to filing a Rule 11 motion, plaintiffs filed a memorandum in reply to Jones' opposition motions on March 9, 2000. Because the filing of plaintiffs' reply was directly caused by Jones' Rule 11 violation, and plaintiffs have not included the fees incurred in filing this reply, the Court will allow plaintiffs to submit a statement of fees and costs relating thereto. . . .

After considering Jones' fraudulent abuse of the judicial process both in this case and in other cases in this district, the Court recognizes that a monetary sanction alone is unlikely to deter him from filing future frivolous pleadings. Accordingly, the Court also enjoins defendant from filing any paper related to this case with this Court or its personnel until he pays the sanctions associated with plaintiffs' Rule 11 and reply motions in full. . . . The Court further orders that defendant is precluded from asserting any new argument or defense based on a claimed ownership interest in the copyright at issue.

The Court finds no authority for ordering punitive damages under Rule 11 and denies plaintiffs' request for such sanctions. . . . Because the plain language of Rule 11 indicates that reasonable attorney fees should be limited to those fees directly caused by the offending violation, the Court will not impose punitive sanctions here.

Finally, the Court denies plaintiffs' requests that the Court require Jones to immediately retain counsel and prohibit him from filing future pleadings absent this Court's approval.

III.   Conclusion

For the foregoing reasons, the Court grants plaintiffs' motion for summary judgment. The Court also grants plaintiffs' motion for Rule 11 sanctions and sanctions Jones as indicated above. The Clerk of Court is instructed to return, unfiled, any pleadings tendered by Joe Jones in this case until he has satisfied all outstanding awards of sanctions.

NOTES AND QUESTIONS

1. No genuine issue.   Could the court have based its granting of summary judgment for the plaintiffs solely on the defendant's failure to answer their request for admissions? Would such a summary judgment ruling always be appropriate when the non-moving party has failed to respond? What evidence did the defendant ultimately identify in support of his contention that he had a partial ownership interest in the copyright? Why didn't any of this suffice to create a genuine issue of material fact so as to allow the case to go to trial? In holding that the defendant's evidence was insufficient, did the court assess its weight and credibility in relation to the plaintiffs' competing evidence? Under the pre-1986 federal approach to summary judgment, would the result here likely have been the same?

2. Dismissal of appeal.   As the case caption in *Johnson* notes, the defendant appealed the district court's order granting summary judgment. The Fifth Circuit dismissed the appeal on April 11, 2001, without addressing the merits of the trial court's ruling. Why didn't the appellate court entertain the appeal? Did the trial court's order result in the entry of a judgment in the plaintiffs' favor, or did it involve only a partial summary judgment? What issues if any remained to be resolved at trial? If a summary judgment ruling does not dispose of the entire case, it is deemed to involve an "interlocutory" rather than a "final judgment." As such, there is usually no right to immediately appeal the ruling. *See* Chapter XII, part B, page 1045, *infra*. If the defendant in *Johnson* wanted appellate review of the district court's summary judgment ruling, he would thus have had to wait until there was a final judgment disposing of the entire case.

Immediate interlocutory appeal of summary judgment rulings is allowed in limited circumstances, none of which applied here. Such appeals are permitted, for example, when a summary judgment ruling completely disposes of the claims between some but not all of the parties, and the trial court certifies that there is no reason to delay entry of a final judgment between the affected parties. *See* FED. R. CIV. P. 54(b); *see also* Chapter XII, part B.2.d, page 1083, *infra*.

Interlocutory appeals are also allowed under the "collateral order doctrine," when a summary judgment ruling disposes of an important issue unconnected with the merits of the case and when delaying the right to appeal would render appellate review inadequate. *See, e.g., Mitchell v. Forsyth*, 472 U.S. 511, 524-530 (1985) (allowing under collateral order doctrine immediate appeal of order denying defendant's summary judgment motion that was based on assertion that he was absolutely immune from suit). *See* Chapter XII, part B.1, page 1046, *infra*; *see also* 11 Moore's Federal Practice, *supra*, § 56.130[4][a]; 10A Wright, Miller & Kane, *supra*, § 2715; 15A Charles Alan Wright, Arthur R. Miller & Edward H. Cooper, Federal Practice & Procedure § 3914.10 (2d ed. 1992 & Supp. 2015).

3. *Sanctions.*   Read Rule 11 in the supplement. Sanctions may be imposed under Rule 11 on a party who unsuccessfully moves for summary judgment or on one who unsuccessfully opposes such a motion, if the motion or opposition is unjustified. *See, e.g., Clark v. United Parcel Serv., Inc.*, 460 F.3d 1004 (8th Cir. 2006), *cert. denied*, 549 U.S. 1340 (2007) (affirming $21,000 in Rule 11 sanctions imposed on plaintiffs' attorney for frivolous opposition to defendants' motion for summary judgment); *Melrose v. Shearson/Am. Express, Inc.*, 120 F.R.D. 668 (N.D. Ill. 1988), *rev'd*, 898 F.2d 1209 (7th Cir. 1990), *aff'd on reh'g*, 1990 WL 78047 (N.D. Ill. June 1, 1990) (imposing Rule 11 sanctions of $37,212 on defendant's counsel for filing frivolous summary judgment motion). Why did the court impose sanctions on defendant Jones? Were they imposed under what is now Rule 11(c)(2) or under Rule 11(c)(3)? Does Rule 11 mean that whenever a party loses on a summary judgment motion it risks sanctions? If not, what besides the fact that Jones lost on these motions warranted sanctions here? If you had been brought in to represent Jones, what might you have done to avoid his incurring sanctions under Rule 11? The plaintiffs in *Johnson* sought sanctions against Jones solely under Rule 11. Yet Rule 56(h) also permits sanctions, consisting of reasonable expenses and attorneys' fees, to be imposed on a party who files summary judgment affidavits "in bad faith or solely for delay. . . ." Fed. R. Civ. P. 56(h). Would Rule 56(h) have justified the imposition of sanctions on defendant Jones? If so, would it have reached all of the conduct that was sanctioned by the court under Rule 11? Why didn't the *Johnson* court consider Jones's own request for the imposition of sanctions?

PROBLEM

10-5. Carl, an attorney, filed a patent infringement action in federal court on behalf of Pamela, alleging that defendant Imageware, Inc. ("Imageware") had infringed on Pamela's patent. Shortly after the suit was filed, Imageware's attorney telephoned Carl and advised him that Pamela no longer owned the patent, that she had transferred it to someone else, and that the law gave only the patent's owner standing to sue for infringement. When Carl refused to discuss the matter, Imageware's attorney wrote him, asking that he dismiss the complaint with prejudice due to Pamela's lack of standing. The letter concluded, "Please allow this letter to serve as formal notice pursuant to Federal Rule of Civil Procedure 11(c) that, unless the Complaint is dismissed with prejudice forthwith, my client reserves the right to seek appropriate sanctions, including all fees and costs incurred in defending this matter." After Carl ignored the letter, Imageware advised him it would seek Rule 11 sanctions. Imageware then filed a motion for summary judgment supported by affidavits and documents showing that Pamela no longer owned the patent and that she therefore lacked standing to assert that claim in a federal court. Instead of opposing the motion, Carl amended his complaint to add four state-law claims over which he asked the court to take supplemental jurisdiction.

A. How should the court rule on Imageware's motion for summary judgment? Did Imageware carry its initial burden of production with respect to the federal claim? If it did, what was Carl required to do? Was amending his complaint to assert four presumably viable state-law claims a sufficient response to the defendant's motion?

B. If the court were to grant the defendant's motion as to the patent infringement claim, would that dispose of the four state-law claims? Did the defendant move for summary judgment as to them? Might the federal court, once it dismissed the federal claim, then decline to exercise supplemental jurisdiction over the state-law claims (assuming there was no diversity of citizenship between the parties)?

C. Assume that the federal court granted summary judgment for Imageware on the patent claim and that it dismissed the state-law claims, declining to exercise supplemental jurisdiction over them. Imageware then sent Carl a letter stating that it would seek sanctions. A month later it filed a motion for sanctions under Rule 11, which it served on Carl the same day. After conducting a hearing, the district court granted the motion. It found that Carl had violated Rule 11(b)(2) because his client's suit for patent infringement was not warranted by existing law or by a nonfrivolous argument for the extension, modification, or reversal of existing law. The court imposed sanctions requiring Carl to pay Imageware the $25,000 in attorneys' fees and expenses it had incurred as a result of his filing the suit. No sanctions were imposed on Pamela. Carl has appealed, claiming that the district court's imposition of sanctions did not comply with the requirements of Rule 11(c). How should the court rule and why?

See Barber v. Miller, 146 F.3d 707 (9th Cir. 1998).

4. Summary Judgment *Sua Sponte*

As the Supreme Court noted in *Celotex Corp. v. Catrett,* 477 U.S. 317 (1986), page 901, *supra,* federal courts "possess the power to enter summary judgments *sua sponte*"—*i.e.*, on their own initiative—"so long as the losing party was on notice that she had to come forward with all of her evidence." *Id.* at 326. Without such authority, the incompetence of counsel might force a court to proceed to trial in a case that should have been disposed of summarily. This *sua sponte* option is now expressly recognized by Rule 56(f), which was added to the Federal Rules in 2010, and which permits the exercise of such authority after a court has given the parties "notice and a reasonable time to respond. . . ." FED. R. CIV. P. 56(f). The authority may be invoked when one party moves for summary judgment but the court concludes that summary judgment should be entered against, rather than in favor of, the movant. *See* FED. R. CIV. P. 56(f)(1); *see, e.g., Bell v. Marseilles Elementary School*, 160 F. Supp. 2d 883 (N.D. Ill. 2001) (entering summary judgment *sua sponte* for plaintiff after defendant moved for summary judgment). It may also be exercised to grant summary judgment for the moving party but on grounds the movant did not invoke. *See* FED. R. CIV. P. 56(f)(2). And finally, the court may invoke this authority even if none of the parties has moved for summary judgment. *See* FED. R. CIV. P. 56(f)(3); *see, e.g., Lillo ex rel. Estate of Lilo v. Bruhn*, 413 Fed. App'x 161 (11th Cir.), *cert. denied*, 132 S. Ct. 244 (2011) (affirming entry of summary judgment *sua sponte* for defendant police officers, based on officers' qualified immunity, after plaintiff was given opportunity to engage in discovery and brief the issue); *Kellar v. Wills*, 186 Fed. App'x 714 (8th Cir. 2006) (affirming entry of partial summary judgment for defendant *sua sponte* when plaintiff had notice and opportunity to defend the viability of her claims); *Hubbard v. Parker*, 994 F.2d 529 (8th Cir. 1993) (affirming entry of summary judgment *sua sponte* when district court first advised parties of its intentions by telephone and invited their response).

Goldstein v. Fidelity and Guaranty Insurance Underwriters, Inc.

86 F.3d 749 (7th Cir. 1996)

TERENCE T. EVANS, Circuit Judge.

Two fires—one in October of 1992 and the other in April of 1993—combined to destroy a complex of four interconnected buildings at 1775-1825 West Diversey Street in Chicago. The Diversey Street property was one of several commercial properties in Chicago owned by Michael Goldstein and his company, Gold Realty Group. This litigation concerns a claim by Goldstein against his insurance company, whose name we'll shorten by calling it Fidelity, growing out of the fire. Goldstein moved for summary judgment in the district court, but the tables were turned on him when the judge, *sua sponte*, granted summary judgment for Fidelity. Goldstein appeals.

Before addressing the district court's disposition of the substantive issues, we must determine whether it was cricket for the court to enter summary judgment on its own motion. As everyone knows, summary judgment is only appropriate when there are no genuine issues of material fact and the moving party is entitled to judgment as a matter of law. FED. R. CIV. P. 56. And a district court may enter summary judgment in favor of a party even if no motion for relief of that sort has been filed. This course of action, however, raises concerns in addition to the usual ones present in a motion for summary judgment. The party against whom summary judgment is entered must have notice that the court is considering dropping the ax on him before it actually falls. In other words, the entry of summary judgment is inappropriate when it takes a party by surprise.

In our case, of course, Goldstein filed a motion for summary judgment. Both parties, Goldstein in particular, were on notice that summary judgment was being considered. In the motion for summary judgment he chose to present to the district court, Goldstein claimed that no genuine issues of material fact existed in the case. As a general rule, however, a motion for summary judgment is not a waiver of the right to trial if the motion is denied. This means that if the district court disagreed with Goldstein as to the existence of a genuine issue of material fact, Goldstein would not be precluded from arguing the facts at trial. It does not mean that if the district court agreed with his characterization of the facts, Goldstein can wiggle out of his concession and compel a reversal of a judgment against him based on questions of law. Here, Judge Kocoras in the district court thought Goldstein was right about the facts but wrong on his assertion that he was entitled to judgment as a matter of law. Goldstein now claims that the resolution of the legal issues against him was inappropriate because he was not allowed to contest the facts, and that he would have had "greater incentive" to seek out disputed facts had he known summary judgment was being considered in a mode other than in his favor. At oral argument, we asked Goldstein's counsel if this wasn't a bit of lawyerly game-playing. He said it was not. We disagree.

We do not want to encourage district courts to consider summary judgment *sua sponte* because the procedure warrants "special caution," and it's often inappropriate. It is also largely unnecessary, as a district court can always invite a nonmoving party to file a motion for summary judgment in its favor. But while we do not express resounding approval of *sua sponte* summary judgment, it is not always wrong for a district court to resolve certain cases in this fashion. It's just a bit risky. In this case, however, we conclude that Goldstein was afforded the necessary safeguards, and that the potential hazards of the procedure were avoided. No genuine issue of material fact existed, and disposition of the case hinged on the judge's interpretation of the insurance policy. We reject the claim that Judge Kocoras, in this case, was wrong to act *sua sponte*.

Having determined that the entry of summary judgment on the court's own motion was not erroneous in and of itself, we turn to the disposition of Goldstein's substantive claims. We review the district court's grant of summary judgment *de novo*. Here are the facts.

The Diversey Street buildings were one of ten Goldstein properties insured under a Fidelity policy covering a one-year period starting on September 1, 1992. Prior to September 1, 1992, Goldstein's ten properties were insured under two Fidelity policies through the Associated Agency. . . . During the summer of 1992, Goldstein shifted his account from the Associated Agency to the Mesirow Agency, which handled the 1992 renewal of coverage. Mesirow submitted one renewal request to Fidelity, covering all ten Goldstein properties. During the renewal process, Mesirow asked Fidelity (on August 27, 1992) to charge a lower premium rather than a higher "non-sprinklered" rate for the Diversey property because the sprinkler system in the buildings was being restored. Fidelity agreed. The premium thus set, on all ten properties, was $55,497 for the one-year policy. Goldstein apparently paid this sum to Mesirow sometime before October 5, 1992, but it was not sent to Fidelity by Mesirow until November 10, 1992. . . .

Although coverage kicked in on September 1, 1992, the policy itself was not actually issued to Goldstein until October 29, 1992. Between September 1 and October 29, Goldstein's properties were covered under the terms of a binder issued by Mesirow. Also between those dates, on October 5, a fire broke out at the West Diversey property, destroying two buildings and damaging one other.

The binder issued by Mesirow contained a waiver of Fidelity's standard policy provision regarding sprinklers called, in insurance lingo, a "protective safeguards endorsement." If not waived, the endorsement would have required Goldstein to maintain, as a condition of coverage, an automatic sprinkler system to protect the property against fires. . . . The actual policy, when issued at the end of October, did contain the endorsement, which said, "As a condition of this insurance, you are required to maintain the protective devices or services listed in the Schedule." The protective safeguard listed in the schedule was an automatic sprinkler system. . . .

After the October 5 fire, Goldstein and Fidelity started to circle each other as they began shadow-boxing over the claim. Fidelity suspected arson—at least at first. Also, Fidelity was unaware that the binder contained the protective safeguard endorsement waiver. . . .

Goldstein received a copy of a December 16, 1992, letter from . . . Fidelity . . . warning that a future fire might not be covered if the sprinklers were not working. The letter said:

> This letter is to advise you that the sprinkler fire protective system in the six story building is required to be operative and in service under the insurance policy. . . . The intention of this letter is to advise you that should another loss occur IT may not be covered under the referred to policy of insurance.

Beginning in mid-November of 1992, Goldstein requested an advance from Fidelity on the claim. Fidelity advanced $20,000 on November 23, 1992. . . .

On March 12, 1993, Fidelity issued a second advance check . . . for $100,000. . . . This payment was made just after Fidelity finally discovered that the Mesirow Agency had included the waiver of the protective safeguards endorsement in the binder. . . . The arson defense was also scuttled (for lack of evidence), and the fire was then treated by Fidelity as a covered loss. . . .

. . . Added together, a total of $713,314 was paid by Fidelity for the loss stemming from the October 5 fire. The depreciation "holdback" of $391,175 for the October 5 fire was not paid as it was subject to a provision of the policy which required that the property actually be repaired or replaced as a precondition to payment.

On April 25, 1993, the second fire ignited, destroying the remaining structures on the Diversey Street property. It is undisputed, as to this fire, that the sprinkler system was not in operation and that the policy, with the protective safeguard endorsement, replaced the Mesirow binder as of October 29, 1992.

On July 2, 1993, Goldstein submitted a proof of loss for the second fire [claiming more than $8 million]. Fidelity denied the claim based on the by now well-known protective safeguards endorsement as well as other potential defenses not relevant here. Goldstein then demanded the $391,175 holdback for the October 5 fire in a letter of April 20, 1994. A few days later the property (which now was vacant land) was sold for $1,065,000. This suit followed a month later when Goldstein filed a four-count complaint against Fidelity in Illinois state court. . . .

Fidelity removed the case to federal court, invoking the court's diversity jurisdiction. After a year's worth of discovery, Goldstein filed a motion for summary judgment. It was at that time that the district court, as we noted, entered summary judgment, *sua sponte*, in favor of Fidelity on all counts.

Count I of Goldstein's complaint argued that Fidelity was estopped from enforcing the protective safeguards endorsement of the insurance policy, and therefore had a duty to pay Goldstein on his claim for the second fire. Goldstein offered two arguments in support of his estoppel claim. First, he argued he was misled when Fidelity charged him the lower "sprinklered" rate. Because Fidelity didn't charge him the highest rate, he claims, he didn't have to comply with the endorsement. In order for Goldstein to prevail on this claim, he would have to show that Fidelity's failure to charge the higher rate was materially misleading, and that he relied on the misrepresentation to his detriment. Given the undisputed facts, it is not possible for Goldstein to make such a showing. It is absolutely beyond dispute that Goldstein was expressly informed, long before the second fire, that the property would not be covered if it did not comply with the protective safeguards clause in his insurance contract. . . .

Goldstein's second argument in support of his estoppel claim is that he was prevented from complying with the endorsement by Fidelity's failure to advance more money to him on his claim following the first fire. Because Fidelity didn't advance enough money, he argues, it may not enforce the terms of the endorsement. This argument omits a crucial fact: it was Goldstein's responsibility, not Fidelity's, to ensure that [he] was financially solvent. Goldstein's failure to secure the premises and install a sprinkler system after the first fire (or before it for that matter) was not a consequence of any action or inaction on the part of Fidelity. Also, Fidelity was under no obligation to advance funds on Goldstein's claim. Despite this, it is noted that Fidelity did in fact advance Goldstein $120,000 on the claim—not an insignificant sum. . . .

Finally, Fidelity complied with the "loss payment" provision of the policy by paying the October 5 fire loss claim within 30 days after the parties reached agreement. . . . Until that time, legitimate and reasonable disputes existed as to matters like the cause of the fire, the applicability of the endorsement waiver, and the value of the compensable loss.

Count II of the complaint was a breach of contract claim. Goldstein alleged that Fidelity breached the terms of the insurance contract by denying his claim for losses resulting from the second fire. The terms of the contract clearly state that the property will not be covered if the sprinkler system is not in working order. In fact, it is hard to imagine that Fidelity could have expressed itself more clearly than it did in the endorsement. The parties agree that the sprinkler system was not in working order at the time of the second fire. If Fidelity was not estopped from enforcing the protective safeguards endorsement, as we agree with the district court that it was not, the second fire was simply not covered.

A second breach of contract claim was raised in Count III of the complaint. This time, Goldstein argued that Fidelity breached the terms of the insurance policy by not paying the depreciation holdback on fire number one. The insurance policy provides that Fidelity will not pay the depreciation holdback "[u]ntil the lost or damaged property is actually repaired or replaced; and . . . [u]nless the repairs are made as soon as reasonably possible after the loss or damage." Again, the facts are undisputed. Goldstein never replaced or restored the property. The terms of the policy are clear and the district court was correct to grant summary judgment in favor of Fidelity on this issue.

The final count of the complaint sought costs and attorney's fees under . . . the Illinois Insurance Code, claiming that Fidelity vexatiously and unreasonably delayed paying the damage claim from the first fire. . . . The question of whether Fidelity acted vexatiously and unreasonably was within the sound discretion of the district court, and will only be disturbed upon a finding that that discretion was abused.

In determining as a matter of law that Fidelity did not act vexatiously or unreasonably in paying Goldstein's claim when it did, the district court had before it a number of undisputed facts. . . . [T]he policy required Fidelity to remit payment on a claim within 30 days of reaching an agreement as to the amount of loss. It is undisputed that Fidelity paid within the contractual time period. On these undisputed facts, the district court's finding that Fidelity acted neither unreasonably nor vexatiously was correct.

The decision of the district court is affirmed.

NOTES AND QUESTIONS

1. *The plaintiff's motion backfires.*   Had this case gone to trial, the plaintiff's burden of persuasion would have been a mere preponderance of the evidence. As to some of those counts, was there admissible evidence arguably supporting the plaintiff's claim? In rejecting the plaintiff's claims, did the court consider the weight and credibility of the defendant's opposing evidence? In retrospect, was it perhaps a mistake for the plaintiff to have moved for summary judgment? Had he not filed that motion, would summary judgment necessarily have been entered for the defendant anyway? If the case had gone to trial, would it automatically have resulted in a directed verdict or a judgment n.o.v. for the defendant?

PROBLEMS

10-6. Neil sued Cary, a former employee, in Louisiana federal court to recover $192,840 for a loan, credit card charges, and business advances given to Cary during his period of employment. Neil moved for summary judgment. In support of the motion he presented an Acknowledgment of Debt signed by Cary agreeing that he owed Neil $192,840. Cary has opposed the motion on several grounds, supported by his own affidavit. First, he claims that the loan was repaid by Neil's withholding of employment bonuses over several years. Second, Cary disputes the amount sought for business advances. Finally, he claims that the signature on the Acknowledgment of Debt is not his own. Under applicable state law, if the Acknowledgment of Debt is genuine as Neil claims, the other defenses are moot. The Acknowledgment was executed in the presence of a notary public and was signed by Cary, by the notary public, and by two attendant witnesses. Under state law, an Acknowledgment of Debt executed in this manner constitutes full proof of the agreement that it contains, and no external evidence may be used to alter its contents. While the authenticity of such a document can be challenged, the party seeking to do so must offer "convincing proof" of fraud or forgery; a mere preponderance of the evidence will not suffice. Cary claims that the date on the Acknowledgment of Debt had been altered and that on the date that had originally appeared there, he was out of the country. How should the court rule on Neil's motion for summary judgment and why? *See Namas Noor Sdn Bhd v. Williams*, 112 F. Supp. 2d 580 (M.D. La. 2000).

10-7. Robert represented Gary in a suit against General Motors ("GM"), Gary's former employer. The suit alleged that GM had violated the federal civil rights act, 42 U.S.C. § 1981, by subjecting Gary to racial harassment on the job. After the federal district court returned a verdict for Gary in the amount of $555,000, GM appealed. While the case was pending in the court of appeals, the U.S. Supreme Court ruled in another case that § 1981 does not prohibit racial harassment occurring after the formation of an employment contract unless it impairs a worker's ability to enforce contractual rights. Based on this decision, which GM now invoked, the court of appeals reversed the trial court's judgment for Gary. In doing so it noted that in the district court GM had never questioned the applicability of § 1981, even though it was clear that the Supreme Court was reconsidering the statute's scope. However, the court of appeals concluded that because Gary's attorney had not objected to GM's right to raise this argument for the first time on appeal, he had waived his right to prevent GM from doing so. Gary then filed a legal malpractice action against Robert for $555,000, plus interest, alleging that he was negligent in not objecting to GM's right to raise the § 1981 issue for the first time on appeal. In response, Robert moved for summary judgment dismissing the case, while Gary filed a cross-motion for partial summary judgment on the issue of causation. In support of his motion, Robert filed an affidavit stating that he had made a conscious decision not to argue that GM had waived its right to challenge the applicability of § 1981, even though he did not conduct any specific research on the issue. He also cited several cases suggesting that a waiver argument would in any event have failed. In response, Gary cited more recent cases showing that the waiver argument would likely have succeeded, and argued that modest research would have revealed these cases to Robert. How should the court rule on the parties' summary judgment motions? If the court rules in Gary's favor, should its ruling be a partial summary judgment limited to the issue of causation, or should it also extend to the issue of damages? *See McKnight v. Gingras*, 966 F. Supp. 801 (E.D. Wis. 1997).

10-8. While being held in the maximum-security wing of the county jail, Darin was denied the right to engage in worship with other prisoners by yelling through the corner edge of his cell door. He then filed suit in federal court against Rourk, the jail's warden, alleging that her refusal to permit him to engage in group worship violated his rights under (1) the Religious Land Use and Institutionalized Persons Act (RLUIPA), 42 U.S.C. §§ 2000cc *et seq.*; (2) the Free Exercise Clause of the First Amendment; and (3) the state's Penal Code § 4027, which guarantees prison inmates a reasonable opportunity to exercise their religion. Rourk has moved for summary judgment on the RLUIPA claim. In her accompanying memorandum of points and authorities and supporting affidavit, Rourk contends that the jail's ban on group worship does not impose a "substantial burden on religious exercise" within the meaning of RLUIPA because it does not force inmates to act contrary to their religious beliefs and leaves them with alternative means of practicing their religion. She also argues that even if it does impose a "substantial burden," it does not violate the act because it is the "least restrictive means" of preserving prison security. In his response, Darin argues that under a proper interpretation of RLUIPA, the jail's policy substantially burdened his exercise of religion within the meaning of the act, and that the jail's practice of allowing groups of inmates to visit the prison library demonstrates that there were less burdensome means of maintaining prison security than imposing a total ban on group worship.

A. Could the court enter summary judgment for Rourk on the RLUIPA claim if it finds that the prohibition on group worship does not constitute a "substantial burden" on the exercise of religion within the act's meaning?

B. Could the court enter summary judgment for Rourk on the RLUIPA claim if it finds that while the prohibition on group worship constitutes a "substantial burden" within the meaning of the act, it was very likely — though not entirely clear from the record before it — that prison security would be compromised by allowing group worship?

C. Could the court grant summary judgment for Rourk on Darin's First Amendment claim if her motion asserted that she was entitled to summary judgment on Darin's "constitutional claims," but her accompanying memorandum and affidavit, like Darin's written response, was devoted exclusively to the RLUIPA claim?

D. Could the court, acting *sua sponte*, grant summary judgment for Rourk on Darin's Penal Code § 4027 claim even though she did not move for summary judgment as to it?

See Greene v. Solano County Jail, 513 F.3d 982 (9th Cir. 2008).

B.   Default Judgments

If a defendant who was properly served with the summons and complaint fails to respond within the time permitted by the applicable rules, the plaintiff may have a judgment entered by default. Unless set aside, default judgments have the same force and effect as those entered after a full trial. The only difference is that in the default setting, no judge or jury has ever evaluated the merits of the plaintiff's factual allegations concerning the defendant's liability. Instead, those allegations are accepted as true and, assuming they are legally sufficient to entitle the plaintiff to recover, judgment will be entered in the plaintiff's favor. However, the defendant's default conclusively resolves only the issue of liability. If he wishes, a defendant who has defaulted may still contest the plaintiff's allegations concerning the extent of damages. If the defendant does so, the court will conduct a hearing to determine what the amount of the judgment will be.

Rule 55 on default judgments distinguishes between the clerk's entry of a *default*, FED. R. CIV. P. 55(a), and the clerk or the judge's later entry of a *default judgment*, FED. R. CIV. P. 55(b). If a defendant fails to respond to the complaint within the time allowed—usually 21 days as prescribed by Rule 12(a)—Rule 55(a) allows the plaintiff to file a request for the entry of default with the court clerk. This step cuts off the defendant's right to file an answer or otherwise respond to the complaint, unless the court first sets aside the entry of default under the discretion given to it by Rule 55(c).

Once there has been an entry of default under Rule 55(a), a default judgment may then be entered in accord with Rule 55(b). Note that Rule 55(b)(1) sometimes allows the court clerk to enter a default judgment without any participation by a judge. This is limited to cases in which the damages sought are for a sum certain *and* in which the defendant has made no appearance. Unless both of these conditions are met, a default judgment may only be entered by a judge, in accord with Rule 55(b)(2). Unlike Rule 55(b)(1), the entry of a default judgment under (b)(2) is discretionary rather than mandatory. In other words, even if all of the technical requirements for a default judgment have been met, a court under (b)(2) may decline to enter judgment and instead allow the case to proceed.

A defendant can resist the plaintiff's efforts to obtain a default judgment in several ways. First, if the defendant learns of the clerk's entry of default under Rule 55(a) before a default judgment has been entered, the defendant can move to have the default set aside under Rule 55(c), "for good cause. . . ." Since courts prefer to have cases decided on their merits rather than on the basis of a technical default, the "good cause" standard is applied rather liberally, though this is not to say that set-aside motions are always granted. Second, without seeking to set aside the entry of default, a defendant may urge the court not to enter a default judgment if none has yet been entered. To enhance this opportunity, Rule 55(b)(2) requires that if a defendant previously appeared in the case, she must be given written notice at least seven days before a hearing is held on the plaintiff's default judgment motion. This affords the defendant an opportunity to request that the court exercise its discretion by declining to enter a default judgment.

If a default judgment has already been entered, Rule 55(c) provides that the defendant may seek to have it set aside in accord with Rule 60(b). The latter rule allows a court to grant relief from a final judgment under certain circumstances, sometimes only within a year after judgment was entered. *See* FED. R. CIV. P. 60(c)(1). Thus Rule 60(b)(1), to which the one-year limitation applies, allows a judgment to be set aside based on "mistake, inadvertence, surprise, or excusable neglect; . . ." FED. R. CIV. P. 60(b)(1). The Supreme Court has said that "excusable neglect" may "encompass situations in which the failure to comply with the filing deadline is attributable to negligence." *Pioneer Inv. Servs. Co. v. Brunswick Assocs. Ltd. Partnership*, 507 U.S. 380, 394 (1993). And Rule 60(b)(6), which contains no time limit, allows a final judgment to be set aside for "any other reason that justifies relief."

In deciding whether to set aside a default or a default judgment, courts consider several factors including (1) whether and to what extent the default was willful or intentional, rather than a result of negligence or even gross negligence; (2) whether the defendant has a meritorious defense; and (3) whether a set aside would cause prejudice or harm to the plaintiff. *S.E.C. v. McNulty*, 137 F.3d 732, 738 (2d Cir.), *cert. denied*, 525 U.S. 931 (1998). With respect to the second factor, the defendant need not conclusively establish or prove the defense, but must present evidence of facts that, if proven at trial, would constitute a complete defense. *Id.* at 740. As to the third factor, courts have held that "for the setting aside of a default judgment to be considered prejudicial, it must result in more than delay. Rather, the delay must result in tangible harm such as loss of evidence, increased difficulties of discovery, or greater opportunity for fraud or collusion." *Thompson v. American Home Assurance Co.*, 95 F.3d 429, 433-434 (6th Cir. 1996); *see also Microsoft Corp. v. Marturano*, 2008 WL 2622832, at *4 (E.D. Cal. July 1, 2008); *Torres v. Estate of Hill*, 2007 WL 1975440, at *4 (S.D. Cal. Apr. 18, 2007). While the grounds for setting aside defaults and default judgments are similar, it is more difficult to set aside a default judgment than it is to just set aside the clerk's entry of default. This difference is partly explained by the fact that a defendant who seeks merely to set aside the entry of default has acted more promptly than one seeking to set aside a default judgment. In addition, once a default judgment is involved, the plaintiff and third parties may have relied on that judgment so that setting it aside could cause them serious prejudice or harm.

On setting aside defaults and default judgments, see generally Robert M. Bloom, *Default; Default Judgment, in* 10 MOORE'S FEDERAL PRACTICE, *supra*, §§ 55.80-55.84; 10A WRIGHT, MILLER & KANE, *supra*, §§ 2681-2700.

Rogers v. Hartford Life and Accident Insurance Co.

167 F.3d 933 (5th Cir. 1999)

EMILIO M. GARZA, Circuit Judge:

Appellants, Hartford Life and Accident Insurance Company ("Hartford") and Entergy Corporation Companies Benefits Plus Long Term Disability Plan (the

"Plan"), appeal the district court's denial of their motions to set aside the default judgment entered against them. . . . We affirm.

I

Rogers, a former employee of Entergy Corporation, sought long-term disability benefits from the Plan. Hartford insured the long-term disability portion of the Plan. Hartford denied Rogers long-term disability benefits. Rogers then filed a complaint under the Employee Retirement Income Security Act of 1974, 29 U.S.C. § 1001, *et seq.* ("ERISA"), against the Plan and Hartford [in a Mississippi federal district court].

Rogers undertook to serve the Plan with process by sending a copy of the summons and complaint by certified mail, return receipt requested, to the Plan's administrator in New Orleans, Louisiana. With respect to Hartford, Rogers requested that Hartford's agent for process in Mississippi, Elizabeth Coleman, execute a waiver of service of process [pursuant to Rule 4(d)]. She complied with this request, and the waiver of service of process was filed with the district court.

Neither Hartford nor the Plan timely answered Rogers' complaint. On Rogers' request, the district court clerk filed an entry of default. Following a hearing, the district court then entered a default judgment [for $144,305] against both Hartford and the Plan, awarding Rogers expenses for disability benefits, medical benefits, prejudgment interest, and attorney's fees. Over a month later, Hartford and the Plan became aware of the default judgment, and promptly moved for relief. Hartford and the Plan motioned the district court to set aside the default judgment in its entirety, or, in the alternative, to set aside that portion of the judgment relating to medical benefits. The district court denied their motions to set aside the default judgment in its entirety. It decided, however, that Rogers could not recover expenses [of $49,000] for medical treatment, and ordered the default judgment adjusted accordingly. Hartford and the Plan timely appealed. . . .

II

We have adopted a policy in favor of resolving cases on their merits and against the use of default judgments. This policy, however, is "counterbalanced by considerations of social goals, justice and expediency, a weighing process [that] lies largely within the domain of the trial judge's discretion." Accordingly, we review the district court's decision not to set aside the default judgment for abuse of discretion.

A

Hartford argues that the district court should have set aside the default judgment because the court entered the judgment without notice to Hartford. Rule 55(b)(2) provides: ["If the party against whom a default judgment is sought *has appeared personally or by a representative,* that party or its representative must be served with written notice of the application at least 7 days before the hearing"] (emphasis added). Whether the district court should have given Hartford notice of the default judgment depends on whether Hartford "appeared. . . . "

We have taken an expansive view as to what constitutes an appearance under Rule 55(b)(2). We have not construed the phrase ["has appeared"] to require the filing of responsive papers or actual in-court efforts by the defendant. Rather, to qualify as an appearance and trigger Rule 55(b)(2)'s notice requirements, the defendant's actions merely must give the plaintiff a clear indication that the defendant intends to pursue a defense and must "be responsive to the plaintiff's formal Court action." *Baez v. S.S. Kresge Co.*, 518 F.2d 349, 350 (5th Cir. 1975).

According to Hartford, it made an appearance for purposes of Rule 55(b)(2). First, Hartford argues that the waiver of process executed by Coleman qualifies as a response to Rogers' formal court action. Second, Hartford contends that Rogers knew that it intended to contest the suit, because Hartford denied Rogers' claim for disability benefits, and because Rogers included "a completely frivolous count" within his complaint. Thus, according to Hartford, its waiver of process coupled with Rogers' knowledge that it intended to defend the suit entitled it to three days notice of Rogers' application for default judgment. . . .

We note that mere acceptance of formal service of process cannot constitute an appearance for purposes of Rule 55(b)(2). If we construed the phrase that broadly, then every defendant would become entitled to notice, because the act that makes a defendant susceptible to default—acceptance of service—would also constitute an appearance. Under such a reading, a defendant could never default without also appearing in the action. The language of Rule 55, however, evidences an intent to impose a notice requirement in only limited circumstances. We will not interpret the phrase "[has appeared]" so broadly as to eviscerate the appearance requirement of Rule 55(b)(2).

This case, admittedly, presents a different question than whether accepting formal service of process constitutes an appearance. Hartford did not accept service of process, but waived it. . . . A waiver of service of process operates as a substitute for formal service of process. . . . Like formal service of process, a waiver of service of process marks the point in a lawsuit after which the defendant must answer or risk default. Waiver of service of process does not in any way indicate that a defendant intends to defend. Thus, like accepting formal service of process, executing a waiver of service of process does not constitute an appearance for purposes of Rule 55(b)(2).

By executing a waiver of service of process, Hartford did not "appear . . ." for purposes of Rule 55(b)(2). Indeed, none of Hartford's actions rise to the level of an appearance. In this case . . . all of the communications between Hartford and Rogers occurred "[p]rior to the filing of the suit." After Rogers filed his complaint, Hartford did nothing to respond to Rogers' suit, or to demonstrate its intent to defend. Accordingly, we hold that Hartford did not make an appearance such as to bring it within the purview of Rule 55(b)(2).

B

Hartford next argues that the district court abused its discretion in refusing to set aside the default judgment because Hartford's failure to respond to Rogers' complaint constituted excusable neglect. Although Coleman executed a waiver of service of process, and then forwarded it and the complaint by Airborne Express to Hartford's address of record, Hartford never received the delivery. Thus, its failure to respond to Rogers' complaint, Hartford argues, "resulted only from one cause: the unfortunate failure of a reputable overnight package service to deliver the complaint to it and the consequent lack of any documents which would have triggered responsive action by Hartford." In other words, Hartford explains, its failure to reply to Rogers' complaint did not result from either willful or culpable conduct. Hartford contends further that it has a meritorious defense to Rogers' complaint, that proceeding to trial on the merits would not prejudice Rogers, and that other equitable factors support setting aside the default judgment.

Federal Rule of Civil Procedure 60(b)(1) permits relief from a default judgment for "mistake, inadvertence, surprise, or excusable neglect" on a motion made within one year of the judgment. Courts construe Rule 60(b)(1) liberally to ensure that they resolve doubtful cases on the merits. We have directed district courts to consider three factors in determining whether sufficient grounds exist for setting aside a default judgment under Rule 60(b)(1): "(1) the extent of prejudice to the plaintiff; (2) the merits of the defendant's asserted defense; and (3) the culpability of [the] defendant's conduct." *Hibernia Nat'l Bank v. Administracion Central Sociedad Anonima*, 776 F.2d 1277, 1280 (5th Cir. 1985). These factors are not "talismanic." See *CJC Holdings, Inc. v. Wright & Lato, Inc.*, 979 F.2d 60, 64 (5th Cir. 1992). A district court may consider other factors, and the decision of whether to grant relief under Rule 60(b)(1) falls within its sound discretion. . . .

In this case, Coleman executed a waiver of service of process, accepted the complaint, and notified Susan Page, the Senior Claims Examiner in Hartford's claims office in Atlanta, Georgia, that she had received the suit papers. Coleman also informed Page that she intended to send the papers to her immediately. Hartford never received the suit papers, but Hartford also never attempted to obtain another copy of the complaint. Thus, although Airborne Express never delivered the complaint to Hartford, Hartford's neglect—that is, its failure to establish "minimum internal procedural safeguards"—was at least a partial cause of its failure to respond. Once Hartford's registered agent received the complaint and notified Page, Hartford had a responsibility to ensure that "process . . . in fact reached its destination and that action [was] being taken." Hartford, however, did nothing.

On these facts, the district court decided that Hartford's conduct did not constitute excusable neglect, and refused to set aside the default judgment. . . . The district court did not abuse its discretion.

III

A

The Plan argues that we should set aside the default judgment against it because Rogers failed to effect proper service of process, and therefore, the district court lacked personal jurisdiction. As the Plan correctly notes, service of process must occur in accordance with Federal Rule of Civil Procedure 4. Rule 4(e)(1) provides for service ["by . . . following state law for serving a summons in an action brought in courts of general jurisdiction in the state where the district court is located]." Rogers effected service on the Plan by certified mail to the Louisiana office of the Plan's administrator, Entergy Services, Inc., pursuant to Rule 4(c)(5) of the Mississippi Rules of Civil Procedure. Rule 4(c)(5) provides that a plaintiff may use certified mail to serve a "person outside th[e] state." The comments to this rule explain that the "certified mail procedure is not available to serve a person within the state." The Plan argues that because it maintains a registered agent for service of process in Mississippi, it was "within the state" for service or process purposes. Thus, the Plan reasons that, because it was "within the state," the method of service described in Rule 4(c)(5) was not available to Rogers, and Rogers failed to effect proper service of process.[3]

When a district court lacks jurisdiction over a defendant because of improper service of process, the default judgment is void and must be set aside under Federal Rule of Civil Procedure 60(b)(4). No Mississippi court has determined whether Rule 4(c)(5) remains an alternative method of service available to plaintiffs, after a defendant appoints an agent for service of process within the state. We, therefore, must make an "*Erie* guess" as to how the Mississippi Supreme Court would decide this issue. In making an "*Erie* guess" we may consult a variety of sources, including "dicta in [state] court decisions, the general rule on the issue, and the rules in other states that [the state] might look to, as well as treatises and law journals." *State Farm Fire & Cas. Co. v. Fullerton*, 188 F.3d 374, 378 (5th Cir. 1997). . . .

[The court then examined the language of the Mississippi rule and a number of other sources, including a California Court of Appeals decision construing a similar California provision.]

This [California] case, along with a plain reading of Rule 4(c)(5), strongly suggests that if the Mississippi Supreme Court faced the issue, it would decide that Rule 4(c)(5) remains an alternative method of service available to plaintiffs, even though a defendant has appointed an agent for service of process in the state. . . . Thus, we hold that Rule 4(c)(5) remained "among the statutory alternatives open" to Rogers.

In this case, Rogers effected service on the Plan's administrator in Louisiana. The Plan's administrator was located "outside" the state of Mississippi. Rogers, therefore, complied with the service of process requirements of Rule 4(c)(5). . . .

In short, Rogers effected service of process in accordance with Mississippi's Rules of Civil Procedure. The district court, therefore, properly exercised jurisdiction over the Plan. Accordingly, we will not set aside the default judgment under Rule 60(b)(4).

3. We note that Mississippi is the only jurisdiction involved in this case that permits service in the manner conducted by Rogers, and that Rule 4(c)(5) is the only provision of the Mississippi Rules that permits service by certified mail.

B

The Plan also contends that we should set aside the default judgment because Rogers brought this action in a venue not proper under ERISA. As the district court stated, this contention is "patently without merit." The Supreme Court has made clear that if a party defaults by failing to appear or file a timely responsive pleading, the party waives defects in venue. *See, e.g., Hoffman v. Blaski*, 363 U.S. 335, 343 (1960) ("A defendant, properly served with process by a court having subject matter jurisdiction, waives venue by failing seasonably to assert it, or even simply by making default."). . . .

C

Finally, the Plan argues, like Hartford, that its failure to respond timely to Rogers' complaint is attributable to excusable neglect. *See* Fed. R. Civ. P. 60(b)(1). According to the Plan, "a finding of a willful failure to timely respond is necessary to deny a Rule 60(b)(1) motion." It argues that while its conduct was "culpable," it did not "willfully" fail to respond timely to Rogers' complaint. The Plan states that it had adopted "procedures designed to ensure that legal process [was] brought to the attention of the correct person," but that it did not respond timely because the complaint and summons were mistaken for an "internal claim file [ ]." . . . According to the Plan, although it is not "free of fault in failing to discover the complaint," its conduct does not rise to the level of culpability or willfulness that "should prevent a court from setting aside the default judgment." . . .

We note first that the Plan misconstrues the law with respect to Rule 60(b)(1): we do not require the district court to find a "willful" failure to respond in order to deny a Rule 60(b)(1) motion. Contrary to the Plan's position on appeal, the district court properly focused on whether the Plan acted culpably and not on whether it acted willfully. Second, as the district court held and as the facts show, the Plan failed to respond to Rogers' complaint because it carelessly mistook the summons and complaint for an internal appellate file. The Plan simply overlooked the relevant papers. For these reasons, we hold that the district court did not abuse its discretion in refusing to grant relief under Rule 60(b). . . .

For the foregoing reasons, we AFFIRM the district court.

NOTES AND QUESTIONS

1. Right to seven-day notice. Why wasn't the entry of a default judgment against Hartford reversible error due to the plaintiff's failure to give Hartford seven days' notice before that judgment was entered? Since federal courts are quite liberal in deciding whether a defendant "has appeared" in the action for purposes of Rule 55(b)(2), why didn't Hartford's agreeing to waive formal service and its having previously advised the plaintiff that it would contest a lawsuit qualify as an appearance for these purposes? Is the critical question whether the defendant has manifested its intent to *defend the lawsuit*? If so, should it necessarily be fatal that the defendant's only expression of its opposition to the plaintiff's claim occurred before rather than after process was served? Since in most cases the defendant has indicated its opposition to the plaintiff's claim prior to filing, is it critical that even a liberal interpretation of Rule 55(b)(2)'s "has appeared" provision be limited to cases in which a defendant has manifested such an intent *after* the suit was filed?

2. *Refusal to set aside.* Each defendant in *Rogers* offered its own explanation as to why it failed to respond to the complaint in a timely manner. Hartford's reasons are discussed in Part II of the opinion, the Plan's in Part III. In offering these explanations did the defendants have to fit them within one of the subdivisions of Rule 60(b)? Which subdivisions did each defendant rely on? The granting of Rule 60(b) relief is guided by the three factors cited in Part II.B of the court's opinion. *See also S.E.C v. McNulty, supra,* page 945 (listing similar criteria). Which of these did the court focus on in refusing to set aside the default judgment? Are these factors exclusive, or might other considerations have been at work as well? Might setting aside default judgments under these circumstances encourage defendants to rely on sloppy business practices as a basis for obtaining such relief?

3. *You be the judge.* Had you been the district court judge in *Rogers,* how would you have ruled on the defendants' motions to set aside the default judgment? If you had gotten past the "culpability" or "excusable neglect" factor, might any of the other considerations cited by the court as governing set-aside motions have made it difficult to justify setting aside the judgment? Would you have been at all influenced by the fact that the defendants learned of the default judgment only 38 days after it was entered and then promptly sought to have it set aside? Would it have mattered that, as the district court found in the actual case, the plaintiff would not have suffered any cognizable prejudice if the judgment were set aside? *See Rogers v. ITT Hartford Life & Accident Co.,* 178 F.R.D. 476, 480 n.1, 482 n.6 (S.D. Miss. 1997). If you were inclined to grant the set-aside motions, which part or parts of Rule 60(b) would you have relied upon? Had you granted the motions, what is the likelihood that your ruling would have been reversed on appeal?

4. *The "Erie guess."* Why did the court in Part III.A need to ascertain Mississippi's service of process rule in this case? Was this a case in which the Rules of Decision Act, 28 U.S.C. § 1652, as construed in *Erie Railroad Co. v. Tompkins,* 304 U.S. 64 (1938), page 470, *supra,* required the federal court to apply Mississippi's service rule if it were deemed to be a "rule of decision"? Was this a case in which a Federal Rule of Civil Procedure conflicted with state law, and in which applying that rule might violate 28 U.S.C. § 2072(b) by abridging, modifying, or enlarging a substantive state right? Or was this a case in which the federal and state provisions were entirely compatible—thus presenting no *Erie* problem at all—since a federal rule, Rule 4(e)(1), expressly incorporates state law and the only question was how the state provision in question should be construed?

PROBLEM

10-9. John died unexpectedly, leaving a $50,000 life insurance policy issued by Acme Insurance ("Acme"). The proceeds were claimed by his mother, Ann, and by his wife, Ruth. According to Ruth, while Ann was the original beneficiary, John later instructed Acme to make his wife the sole beneficiary. Acme, which had no record of such a change in beneficiary, filed an interpleader action (*see* Chapter VIII, part F, at page 704, *supra*) against Ann and Ruth in a California federal court, asking it to decide which of the two was entitled to the $50,000. Ann and Ruth were both properly served. While Ann answered the complaint, Ruth never did so. In a telephone conversation with Ann's attorney shortly after the suit was filed, Ruth said she was distraught at her husband's death, had not retained counsel, and did not know what she would do about the suit. Ann's attorney advised Ruth to contact the local bar association to find a lawyer. Instead, during her time to respond to the complaint, Ruth sold her California home and moved to Florida with her two-year-old son. Two days after Ruth's answer was due, Ann moved for entry of default, which the clerk entered the next day. Ann then moved for entry of a default judgment, serving Ruth at her new address in Florida. When no response was received within the 21-day period set by local rules, the court entered a default judgment against Ruth. A week later, an attorney whom Ruth had found in Florida wrote the court seeking permission to represent Ruth in the suit, not realizing at the time that a default judgment had just been entered against her. A month later, Ruth filed a motion to set aside the default judgment under Rule 60(b), accompanied by declarations from her and her attorney reciting the circumstances that led to her default. Which subdivisions of Rule 60(b) might Ruth invoke? In terms of the three principal factors courts consider in ruling on such motions, how should the court rule and why? *See TCI Group Life Ins. Plan v. Knoebber*, 244 F.3d 691 (9th Cir. 2001).

C.   Dismissal of Actions

Lawsuits are often dismissed before they reach trial. As we have already seen, the principal means by which a defendant may accomplish this in federal court is by a motion to dismiss under Rule 12(b)—*e.g.*, for lack of subject matter or personal jurisdiction, for improper venue or insufficiency of service of process, for failure to state a claim on which relief can be granted, or due to the absence of a requisite party—or by a motion for summary judgment under Rule 56. In this section, we will briefly note three other situations in which suits may be dismissed. One involves the plaintiff's voluntary dismissal. The other two involve involuntary dismissals ordered by the court either because of the plaintiff's failure to prosecute the action or as a sanction for the plaintiff's misconduct.

1. Voluntary Dismissal

After a suit has been filed, a plaintiff may for any number of reasons decide that it should be dismissed, with or without prejudice to its being filed again. The most common reason for such voluntary dismissals is that the parties have reached a settlement, one of whose conditions is that the plaintiff drop the suit and dismiss the complaint, usually with prejudice to its being filed again. A plaintiff may also elect to voluntarily dismiss a suit if discovery reveals that, at least at the present time, she lacks sufficient evidence to prove her claim, or if she learns that she is not legally entitled to recover under the factual circumstances presented. Indeed, a federal plaintiff may feel pressed to voluntarily dismiss a case that is lacking in merit, out of fear that the defendant might otherwise successfully move for the imposition of sanctions under Rule 11. The Rule 11(c)(2) requirement that a party be given notice of a motion for sanctions at least 21 days before it is filed with the court is

> intended to provide a type of "safe harbor" against motions under Rule 11 in that a party will not be subject to sanctions on the basis of another party's motion unless, after receiving the motion, it refuses to withdraw that position or to acknowledge candidly that it does not currently have evidence to support a specified allegation. . . . [T]he timely withdrawal of a contention will protect a party against a motion for sanctions.

Advisory Committee Note, 1993 Amendments, 146 F.R.D. 401, 591. While voluntary dismissal made within the safe-harbor period will protect a plaintiff against a defendant's motion for sanctions, Rule 11(c)(3) still allows the court to impose sanctions *sua sponte*. However, the Rules Advisory Committee suggested that compliance with the safe-harbor provision would render *sua sponte* sanctions appropriate "only in situations that are akin to a contempt of court. . . ." 146 F.R.D. at 591-592. While many federal courts have endorsed this "akin-to-contempt" or "bad faith" approach, *see, e.g., Kaplan v. DaimlerChrysler, A.G.*, 331 F.3d 1251, 1255-1256 (11th Cir. 2003), others have held that "culpable carelessness" may by itself be enough to warrant judicially initiated sanctions. *See, e.g., Citibank Global Markets, Inc. v. Rodriguez Santana*, 573 F.3d 17, 32 (1st Cir. 2009); *see also Barber v. Miller*, 146 F.3d 707 (9th Cir. 1998); Jerold S. Solovy & Laura A. Kaster, *Signing Pleadings, Motions, and Other Papers; Representations to the Court; Sanctions, in* 2 MOORE'S FEDERAL PRACTICE, *supra*, §§ 11.22[1][b], 11.22[2][a].

Voluntary dismissals in federal court are governed by Rule 41(a). If a suit involves more than one defendant, a plaintiff may dismiss the action against either some or all of the defendants. Under Rule 41(a)(1), a plaintiff may be able to voluntarily dismiss her suit without court approval. This subdivision applies if the plaintiff files a notice of dismissal before the defendant has served the plaintiff with either an answer to the complaint or with the defendant's own motion for summary judgment. FED. R. CIV. P. 41(a)(1)(A)(i). Yet even when a defendant has served one of these items, Rule 41(a)(1) may still be invoked if all parties who have appeared in the action sign a stipulation of dismissal that is filed with the court. FED. R. CIV. P. 41(a)(1)(A)(ii). All other voluntary dismissals require court approval under Rule 41(a)(2), which allows a dismissal to be made subject to "terms that the court considers proper." FED. R. CIV. P. 41(a)(2). Under this provision, a court may refuse to allow a dismissal if the defendant can show that it will suffer serious legal prejudice as a result. However, it is not enough that the defendant may be inconvenienced by having to litigate in another forum or that the plaintiff is seeking to gain some tactical advantage through dismissal. *Smith v. Lenches*, 263 F.3d 972, 975-976 (9th Cir. 2001).

Rule 41(a)(2) is quite liberal. A plaintiff may thus seek dismissal without prejudice in order to avoid an adverse ruling on the defendant's pending motion for summary judgment, to refile his or her case in a court in which the law is more favorable to him or her, or to gain time to gather more evidence once it appears that his or her case may be weak. In *Cutler v. La Crepe Restaurant/Chefs International, Inc.*, 2004 WL 451855 (S.D. Fla. Feb. 18, 2004), for example, the court allowed the plaintiffs to dismiss their personal injury action without prejudice under Rule 41(a)(2) after the defendant had removed the case from state to federal court based on diversity. The court granted the motion even though it appeared that the plaintiffs' ultimate aim was to defeat federal jurisdiction, a goal they could achieve by refiling their suit in state court, this time naming an additional defendant who would wreck complete diversity and thereby defeat removal under 28 U.S.C. § 1441(a) and (b).

In a case in which the defendant can show that serious harm would result from a voluntary dismissal, a court can usually prevent such harm by insisting that any dismissal be with, rather than without, prejudice. Moreover, even if dismissal is to be without prejudice so that the plaintiff may sue again, courts will often condition the dismissal on the plaintiff's agreeing to reimburse the defendant for some or all of the costs and attorneys' fees incurred in litigating the first case. *See, e.g., LeBlang Motors, Ltd. v. Subaru of Am., Inc.*, 148 F.3d 680, 685-687 (7th Cir. 1998) (affirming dismissal without prejudice sought nine days before trial, conditioned on plaintiff's paying defendant costs and reasonable attorneys' fees, later set at $89,032); *Belle-Midwest, Inc. v. Missouri Prop. & Cas. Ins. Guarantee Ass'n*, 56 F.3d 977 (8th Cir. 1995) (affirming dismissal without prejudice conditioned on plaintiff's agreeing to pay $12,027 in costs and attorneys' fees before suit may be refiled). However, if a voluntary dismissal is to be with prejudice, only in "exceptional circumstances" will a court require the plaintiff to pay attorneys' fees since the defendant will never have to defend the same claim again. *See Vanguard Envtl., Inc. v. Kerin*, 528 F.3d 756 (10th Cir. 2008) (suggesting that an "exceptional circumstance" that might warrant requiring the payment of attorneys' fees is when plaintiff has engaged in a practice of bringing actions and then dismissing them with prejudice only after inflicting substantial litigation costs on defendants and the judicial system).

Depending on the conditions imposed, a plaintiff may decide to proceed with a case rather than having it dismissed, for courts have read the terms-and-conditions clause of Rule 41(a)(2) as "grant[ing] plaintiff the option of withdrawing his motion if the district court's conditions are too onerous, and proceeding instead to trial on the merits." *Marlow v. Winston & Strawn*, 19 F.3d 300, 304 (7th Cir. 1994) (citing authorities). For example, in *Westlands Water District v. United States*, 100 F.3d 94, 97 (9th Cir. 1996), the court of appeals ruled that the district judge should have granted the plaintiffs' motion to dismiss without prejudice, but perhaps on the condition that they pay the defendants' costs and attorneys' fees. When the district court, on remand, then conditioned dismissal on the plaintiffs' paying more than $100,000 in attorneys' fees and costs, the plaintiffs elected to proceed with the case on the merits rather than dismiss it. *Westlands Water District v. United States*, 153 F. Supp. 2d 1133, 1140-1141 (E.D. Cal. 2001), *aff'd*, 337 F.3d 1092 (9th Cir. 2003). Courts have also suggested that a plaintiff's right to withdraw a motion to dismiss and instead proceed with a case cannot be conditioned on the plaintiff's having to pay the attorneys' fees the defendant may have incurred in resisting that motion and its withdrawal. *See Marlow v. Winston & Strawn*, 1994 WL 262077 (N.D. Ill. June 10, 1994) (vacating its prior order that plaintiffs' withdrawal of motion to dismiss was conditioned on their paying defendants' attorneys' fees and costs).

There are some limitations on a plaintiff's ability to voluntarily dismiss under Rule 41(a). First, Rule 41(a)(1)(B) specifies that a dismissal under that subdivision will operate with prejudice if an earlier suit based on or including the same claim was previously dismissed by any state or federal court. This prevents a plaintiff from unilaterally invoking voluntary dismissal to harass a defendant against whom the same claim was previously dismissed. However, the two-dismissal rule does not apply if the first dismissal was by court order under Rule 41(a)(2). *See Cunningham v. Whitener*, 182 Fed. App'x 966 (11th Cir. 2006). Second, Rule 41(a)(2) bars a voluntary dismissal by the plaintiff if the effect would be to deprive the court of subject matter jurisdiction over a counterclaim that the defendant filed before being served with the plaintiff's motion to dismiss. This limitation prevents a plaintiff from using voluntary dismissal to defeat a defendant's right to invoke the court's supplemental jurisdiction over related counterclaims. Third, Rule 41(d) gives a second court the discretion to bar relitigation of a suit that the plaintiff earlier voluntarily dismissed in state or federal court, unless and until the plaintiff reimburses the defendant for the "costs" of the first suit. Thus, even if at the time a suit was voluntarily dismissed the plaintiff believed she would be absolutely free to refile the action, her ability to do so in federal court may be subject to monetary conditions first imposed at the time of re-filing—at least in cases where the plaintiff is financially able to do so. In addition, some courts have held that the "costs" referred to in Rule 41(d) also include reasonable attorneys' fees incurred in the first suit, again if the plaintiff is financially able to pay them. *Compare Adams v. New York State Educ. Dep't*, 630 F. Supp. 2d 333, 344-350 (S.D.N.Y. 2009) (staying second action until plaintiffs pay the $11,202.90 in attorneys' fees and costs that defendants incurred in first action), *with Rogers v. Wal-Mart Stores, Inc.*, 230 F.3d 868, 873-875 (6th Cir. 2000), *cert. denied*, 532 U.S. 953 (2001) (holding that the term "costs" in Rule 41(d) does not include attorneys' fees even though "the majority of courts" have held otherwise).

On voluntary dismissals, see generally Charles L. Brieant & Martin H. Redish, *Dismissal of Actions*, *in* 8 MOORE'S FEDERAL PRACTICE, *supra*, §§ 41.10-41.34,

41.70; 9 Charles Alan Wright & Arthur R. Miller, Federal Practice and Procedure §§ 2361-2368 (3d ed. 2008 & Supp. 2015).

PROBLEM

10-10. On the third day of trial, the Duffys voluntarily dismissed their personal injury action against Ford Motor Company under Rule 41(a)(2), after the federal district court barred them from introducing the testimony of an expert witness not listed in the final pretrial order. When the court granted the Duffys' motion to voluntarily dismiss, it advised them that they would be responsible for some of Ford's "costs" if they ever refiled the suit. After the case was dismissed, the court clarified its dismissal order to provide that if the Duffys sued again, they would also have to pay Ford's nonoverlapping attorneys' fees from the first suit, in an amount to be determined later should a second suit be filed. This dismissal was not appealable since it was without prejudice to the Duffys' filing a second action. When the Duffys then hired new lawyers and sued Ford again in federal court, the court ordered them within 30 days to pay Ford $126,431 in attorneys' fees and costs from the first suit, or suffer dismissal of the action. The court at this time also ordered that all rulings from the prior suit would be the "law of the case" in the refiled action, except that the Duffys could name one additional expert witness. The Duffys unsuccessfully objected to both conditions. When they then failed to pay the attorneys' fees and costs, the court dismissed the case. Though the dismissal was without prejudice, the statute of limitations will now bar them from suing again. The Duffys have appealed, claiming that the attorneys' fees and law-of-the-case conditions both exceeded the court's authority under Rule 41. Ford defends the court's action as authorized by Rule 41(a)(2) and (d). What will each party argue? If you were on the court of appeals, how would you rule in this case and why? *See Duffy v. Ford Motor Co.*, 218 F.3d 623 (6th Cir. 2000).

2. Dismissal for Failure to Prosecute

We have been looking at the plaintiffs' ability to voluntarily dismiss a suit under Rule 41(a). We now turn to Rule 41(b), which allows a defendant to file a motion seeking involuntary dismissal of a suit "[i]f the plaintiff fails to prosecute or to comply with these rules or a court order. . . ." Fed. R. Civ. P. 41(b). Our concern here is with dismissals for failure to prosecute. Later we will look at dismissals that are ordered as a sanction. Read Rule 41(b) and (c). Note that "[u]nless the dismissal order states otherwise," most dismissals under Rule 41(b) operate "as an adjudication on the merits," thus barring the plaintiff from filing the same cause of action again. Fed. R. Civ. P. 41(b). However, this presumption does not apply to those procedurally based dismissals specified in the rule.

While Rule 41(b) seems to allow dismissal for failure to prosecute only if a motion to that effect has been filed, courts have read the rule as allowing judges to order such dismissals *sua sponte*, without any formal motion. In such cases, however, courts usually require that the plaintiff have first been given prior warning that their inaction could lead to dismissal. *Rogers v. City of Warren*, 302 Fed. App'x 371, 375-376 (6th Cir. 2008); *Williams v. Combined Ins. Co. of Am.*, 84 Fed. App'x 660 (7th Cir. 2003); *see Link v. Wabash R.R. Co.*, 370 U.S. 626, 630-633 (1962) (upholding *sua sponte* Rule 41(b) dismissal for failure to prosecute, six years after filing, when plaintiff had received no notice or opportunity to be heard concerning dismissal but could be presumed to have known the consequences of his inaction); *Fischer v. Cingular Wireless, LLC*, 446 F.3d 663, 665-666 (7th Cir. 2006) (stating that "although district courts are encouraged to warn litigants before dismissing a case for failure to prosecute, whether they in fact do so is clearly within their discretion"; otherwise "we would in effect be granting each litigant one opportunity to disregard the court's schedule without fear of penalty regardless of the harm done to other litigants"). Rule 41(c) gives courts similar authority to dismiss counterclaims, cross-claims, and third-party complaints when a defendant has failed to prosecute them.

Whether a case should be dismissed for want of prosecution turns on a number of competing policies: "[O]n the one hand, the court's need to manage its docket, the public interest in expeditious resolution of litigation, and the risk of prejudice to defendants from delay; on the other hand, the policy favoring disposition of cases on their merits." *Citizens Utilities Co. v. AT&T*, 595 F.2d 1171, 1174 (9th Cir.), *cert. denied*, 444 U.S. 931 (1979). In deciding whether dismissal is an appropriate remedy for a party's failure to prosecute in a particular case, courts consider a number of factors including (1) whether the failure was due to the party's willfulness, bad faith, or fault; (2) the extent to which the failure prejudiced the opposing party; (3) the length of time in which the plaintiff took no action in the case; (4) whether adequate warning was given that such a failure could lead to dismissal; (5) whether dismissal is necessary to deter future misconduct; and (6) whether less drastic sanctions are appropriate. *See Gardner v. United States*, 211 F.3d 1305, 1309-1310 (D.C. Cir. 2000), *cert. denied*, 531 U.S. 1114 (2001); *Stough v. Mayville Cmty. Schools*, 138 F.3d 612, 615 (6th Cir. 1998). In applying the first and second factors, some courts employ a sliding-scale approach under which the greater the prejudice suffered by the defendant, the better the plaintiff's excuse for the delay must be. *Walker v. City of Lompoc*, 42 F.3d 1404, at *4 (9th Cir. 1994). With respect to the length of time in which the plaintiff has taken no action, local rules in many federal districts specify a period of plaintiff inaction—ranging from three months to one year—after which the case may be dismissed for failure to prosecute. *See, e.g.*, D. DEL. L.R. 41.1 (three months); N.D.N.Y. L.R. 41.2 (four months); N.D. GA. L.R. 41.3(A)(3) (six months); D. KY. C.R. 41.1 (one year); *see also* 8 MOORE'S FEDERAL PRACTICE, *supra*, § 41.51[1] n.2.

Federal courts view dismissal for failure to prosecute as a step that should be taken only in cases of serious abuse. This is particularly true if the dismissal is to be with prejudice to suing again. As the Sixth Circuit has said, "[D]ismissal of a claim for failure to prosecute is a harsh sanction which the court should order only in extreme situations showing a clear record of contumacious conduct by the plaintiff. 'Contumacious' is defined as 'perverse in resisting authority' and 'stubbornly disobedient.'" *Schaefer v. City of Defiance Police Dep't*, 529 F.3d 731, 736 (6th Cir. 2008) (internal citations omitted). Instead, said the court, "[W]e have increasingly emphasized directly sanctioning the delinquent lawyer rather than an innocent client." *Coleman v. American Red Cross*, 23 F.3d 1091, 1095 (6th Cir. 1994) (citation omitted). In *Mulbah v. Detroit Board of Education*, 261 F.3d 586 (6th Cir. 2001), the court thus reversed the dismissal of a civil rights suit for failure to prosecute because lesser sanctions were available to protect the integrity of the pretrial process. Yet such dismissals do occur. In taking such action, courts have rejected the argument that "punishment for the sins of the lawyer should not be visited upon the client. . . ." *Knoll v. American Tel. & Tel. Co.*, 176 F.3d 359, 363 (6th Cir. 1999). Instead, as the Supreme Court said in *Link v. Wabash Railroad Co., supra*:

> There is certainly no merit to the contention that dismissal of petitioner's claim because of his counsel's unexcused conduct imposes an unjust penalty on the client. Petitioner voluntarily chose this attorney as his representative in the action, and he cannot now avoid the consequences of the acts or omissions of this freely selected agent.

370 U.S. at 633-634. In such cases, "if an attorney's conduct falls substantially below what is reasonable under the circumstances, the client's remedy is against the attorney in a suit for legal malpractice," rather than pursuing her suit against the defendant. *Id.* at 633 n.10.

On dismissal for failure to prosecute, see generally 8 MOORE'S FEDERAL PRACTICE, *supra*, § 41.51; 9 WRIGHT & MILLER, *supra*, §§ 2370-2370.1.

PROBLEMS

10-11. In April 2004, David sued American Auto Services ("AAS"), his former employer, in Missouri state court, alleging that AAS in terminating him was guilty of age discrimination in violation of federal and state law. The state court promptly issued a summons but service was not effected on AAS until January 2008, nearly four years after the action was filed. Upon being served, AAS promptly removed the suit to federal court and filed an answer to the complaint. The federal court then issued conference and scheduling orders with which David fully complied. Several months later, AAS filed a Rule 41(b) motion to dismiss the action with prejudice for failure to prosecute. In support of its motion, AAS alleged that during the 44-month delay in effecting service, some of its witnesses, including David's co-workers and managers, had left its employment; that not all records may have been preserved in the regular course of business; and that memories of relevant facts had likely faded. In response, David offered no excuse for his delay in serving AAS but noted that state law imposed no strict deadline for effecting service; that under applicable state law, the filing of the complaint and issuance of the summons were sufficient to toll the applicable statute of limitations; and that he did not violate any state or federal court orders. Assume that the Missouri rule with respect to dismissing a suit due to a plaintiff's failure to prosecute is essentially the same as Federal Rule 41(b).

A. In ruling on AAS's motion, should the federal court consider the amount of time the suit was pending in state court, or should the federal clock start to run for these purposes only once the action was removed? Does your answer depend on the purposes of Rule 41(b)? To the extent that it is a federal housekeeping measure related to the efficient administration of federal judicial business, might the latter approach make sense? To the extent the rule is also designed to protect defendants against any prejudice that may be caused by delay, does ignoring the time the suit was pending in state court make sense?

B. In terms of the specific factors considered in ruling on Rule 41(b) motions, how should the court rule, and why?

C. How might your answer to part B be different if:

1. AAS can show that some of the critical records from the period, and some of the former employees who worked with David at the time, are in fact unavailable?

2. AAS knew of David's age discrimination grievance within two months of his termination due to the fact that before filing suit, David filed charges against AAS with the Equal Employment Opportunity Commission (EEOC)? When the EEOC then denied his claim in January 2004, it advised AAS and David that he had 90 days in which to file a lawsuit—a time period with which he complied.

See Boyle v. American Auto Service, Inc., 571 F.3d 734 (8th Cir. 2009).

10-12. John sued his former employer, AT&T, in federal court alleging that it fired him due to his age, in violation of the Age Discrimination in Employment Act. When the court set October 28, 1996, as the deadline to complete discovery, and February 19, 1997, as the trial date, John's lawyers told the court they had several other cases that might be going to trial then. The court advised them to wait to see how the other cases progressed. It ordered that any motion for a continuance due to an actual conflict be filed within 15 days of counsel's learning of the conflict, and not less than 30 days before trial. In May 1996, John submitted discovery requests to AT&T, some of which were promptly objected to. He did not move to compel discovery until early October 1996, at which time he also asked for an extension of time to complete discovery. The court denied both motions. On January 16, 1997, John's lawyers sent the court a letter stating that they had another trial set for the week of February 18 and asked for "guidance" because their two-lawyer firm could not try both cases at the same time. When the court failed to respond, John on January 24 moved for a continuance of the trial. The court responded a day before the trial was set to start, advising John that his trial would begin several days after the conclusion of the conflicting trial. When that trial ended on February 20, the court then ordered that John's trial would begin on February 25. John's lawyers objected and sought a continuance, which was denied. They then moved to withdraw as counsel, stating that they could not ethically proceed with trial as scheduled due to lack of adequate preparation. The court denied the motion. John's lawyers appeared at trial but did not sit at the counsel table. They were warned that unless they immediately began to present John's case, his suit would be dismissed for lack of prosecution. When nothing happened, the court dismissed the case under Rule 41(b), without prejudice. John has appealed, claiming that dismissal was an abuse of discretion since the statute of limitations will now bar refiling the suit. What will each side argue on appeal? How should the court rule, and why? *See Knoll v. American Tel. & Tel. Co.*, 176 F.3d 359 (6th Cir. 1999).

3. Dismissal as a Judicial Sanction

Besides allowing dismissal of a lawsuit due to a failure to prosecute, Rule 41(b) authorizes dismissal as a sanction for failure to comply with the federal rules or with a court order. Several other federal rules also allow dismissal as a sanction. *See, e.g.,* Fed. R. Civ. P. 4(m) (allowing dismissal without prejudice if plaintiff without good cause fails to serve defendant within 90 days of filing complaint); Fed. R. Civ. P. 16(f)(1) (allowing dismissal as a sanction if a party or party's attorney fails to comply with a scheduling or pretrial order, or fails to participate fully and in good faith in a scheduling or pretrial conference); Fed. R. Civ. P. 37(b)(2) and (d) (allowing dismissal as a sanction for a party's failure to comply with a discovery order, attend its own deposition, respond to interrogatories, or respond to a request for inspection). While dismissal is the "most severe in the spectrum of sanctions," the Supreme Court has stressed that it "must be available to the district court in appropriate cases, not merely to penalize those whose conduct may be deemed to warrant such a sanction, but to deter those who might be tempted to such conduct in the absence of such a deterrent." *National Hockey League v. Metropolitan Hockey Club, Inc.*, 427 U.S. 639, 643 (1976) (affirming dismissal with prejudice when plaintiffs failed to timely answer interrogatories as ordered by district court).

As with dismissal for failure to prosecute, courts consider a number of factors in deciding whether dismissal is an appropriate sanction for a plaintiff's misconduct. These factors, none of which is dispositive, include (1) whether the plaintiff acted intentionally rather than accidentally or involuntarily; (2) whether the plaintiff engaged in a pattern of misconduct rather than just one or two incidents thereof; (3) whether the plaintiff was warned by the court that he was "skating on the thin ice of dismissal"; and (4) whether a less severe sanction would remedy the effect of the plaintiff's transgressions on the defendant and the court. *See, e.g., Hunt v. City of Minneapolis*, 203 F.3d 524, 527-529 (8th Cir. 2000) (citing these factors in affirming dismissal with prejudice of civil rights action when plaintiff "engaged in a persistent pattern of intentional delay by willfully disregarding court orders and violating the Federal Rules"); *Siems v. City of Minneapolis*, 531 F. Supp. 2d

1069 (D. Minn. 2008), *aff'd*, 560 F.3d 824 (8th Cir. 2009) (dismissing suit with prejudice and reporting plaintiff's attorney to the state bar after attorney failed to comply with court order that pretrial documents be filed by a specific date despite repeated warnings from the court). If there has been no intentional or willful conduct on the part of the plaintiff or her attorney, an appellate court may bar resort to dismissal or insist that it be without prejudice so that the plaintiff can perhaps refile the suit. *See Smith v. Gold Dust Casino*, 526 F.3d 402 (8th Cir. 2008) (reversing dismissal with prejudice as inappropriate sanction for failure to comply with discovery deadlines when there was no willful disobedience and no flagrant disregard of any court orders); *Mann v. Lewis*, 108 F.3d 145 (8th Cir. 1997) (affirming dismissal as sanction but ruling that it should have been without prejudice, perhaps coupled with an order personally assessing plaintiff's attorney for defendant's costs). If a case is dismissed under Rule 4(m) due to the plaintiff's failure to serve the defendant within 90 days of filing the complaint, the rule specifies that the dismissal be without prejudice.

On dismissal as a judicial sanction, see generally 8 MOORE'S FEDERAL PRACTICE, *supra*, § 41.52.

PROBLEM

10-13. Bruce, an attorney, sued the Internal Revenue Service (IRS) pro se, alleging that it had violated federal law by attaching his bank account for a claimed tax deficiency without first giving him notice of the deficiency and an opportunity to challenge the assessment in Tax Court. The IRS moved to dismiss his suit for lack of subject matter jurisdiction. A hearing on the motion was set for January 27. On January 21, Bruce moved to continue the hearing because he had the flu and because he had suffered third-degree burns to his hands when his home caught fire on January 18. The district court denied his motion. Bruce failed to appear at the January 27 hearing but telephoned the court that evening and said he had slept through it due to his illness. On January 28, Bruce renewed his motion to continue the hearing and attached a doctor's note explaining his condition and his need for bed rest. The next day, the court denied his request to reschedule the hearing and dismissed the complaint *sua sponte* under Rule 41(b) due to Bruce's failure to attend the January 27 hearing. Bruce has appealed the district court's order dismissing his case. The standard of review is abuse of discretion. How should the court rule and why? *See Gardner v. United States*, 211 F.3d 1305 (D.C. Cir. 2000), *cert. denied*, 531 U.S. 1114 (2001).

D.   Adjudication Without Trial Review Problem

10-14. Ronald Banks is a prisoner confined in the Long Term Segregation Unit ("LTSU") of a Pennsylvania state prison. The LTSU is designed for the "most incorrigible, recalcitrant inmates" and is the most restrictive of the prison's three units for difficult prisoners. The LTSU is itself divided into two levels, Level 2 of which is the most severe. Those assigned to Level 2, which holds up to 40 inmates, must remain at least 90 days and may be housed there indefinitely. While inmates in all three restrictive units have seriously limited privileges, Level 2 inmates are unique in that they (unlike all other prisoners in the state) have no access to newspapers, magazines, or personal photographs.

With the assistance of an attorney, Banks filed a class action in federal court against the Secretary of Pennsylvania's Department of Corrections. The complaint seeks declaratory and injunctive relief on behalf of Banks and all other similarly situated Pennsylvania state prisoners who are or will be confined in LTSU's Level 2. It alleges that the denial of access to newspapers, magazines, and photographs violates the plaintiffs' First Amendment free speech rights because it is not "reasonably related to legitimate penological interests" as required by *Turner v. Safley*, 482 U.S. 78, 89 (1987). Under *Turner*, an inmate challenging a prison regulation on constitutional grounds has the burden of demonstrating that the regulation is unreasonable. The Secretary answered the complaint. After the court certified that the suit could proceed as a class action, the Secretary then moved for summary judgment.

A. Must the Secretary's summary judgment motion be supported by affidavits or other material, or may it simply assert that Banks lacks evidence to show that the challenged Level 2 policy is unreasonable? If this case were governed by California rather than federal summary judgment law, would your answer be any different?

B. If the Secretary's motion relied solely on Banks's lack of evidence in support of his claim, how might Banks avoid having summary judgment entered for defendant? Suppose he submitted a recent *Prison Journal* article whose well-regarded author concluded: "The view of most of the prison wardens and experts I interviewed was that providing prison inmates with access to books and literature imposes but a small burden on prisons, and that affording inmates increased contact with the world generally favors their rehabilitation." Would this suffice to defeat the entry of summary judgment? Is it fatal that Banks has not filed an affidavit from the article's author?

C. Suppose that instead of taking the absence-of-evidence approach, the Secretary supported his summary judgment motion with an affidavit from the prison's superintendent which states that the challenged Level 2 policy was adopted after careful study and that its principal objective is to motivate better behavior on the part of a small group of the most difficult prisoners by giving them an incentive to move out of Level 2. If Banks now responds with the *Prison Journal* article described earlier, is the court's ruling on defendant's motion likely to be the same as it was in part B?

D. If you were representing the Secretary in this case, which of the two approaches would you take in moving for summary judgment? Does each have certain advantages and disadvantages?

E. Suppose the Secretary supported his motion for summary judgment with the affidavit described in part C. Banks believes the justifications offered in the superintendent's affidavit do not satisfy *Turner*. He therefore files a cross-motion for summary judgment, which asserts that "under *Turner*, the policy challenged here is unreasonable as a matter of law." In his accompanying brief in support of the motion, Banks states that only 25 percent of those assigned to Level 2 ever leave the program. He also cites several federal court decisions that note the rehabilitative effect of affording inmates contact with the outside world. Does Banks's motion meet the requirements of Rule 56, whether one treats it as a motion for summary judgment on the plaintiff's behalf, or as an opposition to the defendant's motion for summary judgment?

F. Same assumptions as in part E, but Banks now wants to oppose the motion in a stronger way. What kinds of evidence might he seek to obtain to prevent the entry of summary judgment against him? How might his attorney go about securing such evidence? If you were Banks's counsel and were going to take the prison superintendent's deposition, what kinds of facts might you try to elicit from him, given the justifications the defendant has offered for its policy here?

G. Suppose the Secretary moved for summary judgment five days after filing his answer to the complaint and scheduled a hearing on the motion for 30 days later. Did the Secretary have the right to file his motion so quickly? (If he did, the court's local rules allow a hearing to be scheduled any time after 21 days.) If Banks's lawyer is not sure she can gather sufficient evidence to defeat the Secretary's motion in that period of time, what, if anything, might she do?

H. Assume that Banks was afforded ample time to gather evidence to defeat the entry of summary judgment. However, his attorney, given the limited resources available to her, was unable to find any evidence showing that the prison's treatment of Level 2 inmates violates the *Turner* standards. Once this became clear, the Secretary supplemented his motion for summary judgment with a motion for the imposition of Rule 11 sanctions, asserting that the complaint was filed without an adequate pre-filing inquiry and investigation on the plaintiff's attorney's part. What might the plaintiff's attorney do at this point? How might your answer be affected by the fact that because this has been certified as a class action, a loss on the merits may have both claim and issue preclusion effect, preventing any present or future inmate from again challenging the constitutionality of this Level 2 policy?

See Beard v. Banks, 548 U.S. 521 (2006).

XI

TRIAL

Once the pretrial process is complete, *i.e.*, once all the motions have been filed and resolved and discovery has come to an end, and assuming the litigation has not been dismissed, settled, or otherwise resolved or abandoned, the case, or what remains of it, will be set for trial. While the popular media gives one the sense that most cases go to trial (and often within a matter of days after filing!), in fact, the opposite is true. In federal court, for example, during 2013-2014, only about 1 percent of the decided cases went all the way to trial, with almost 70 percent of those trials being before a jury. ADMIN. OFFICE OF THE U.S. COURTS, JUDICIAL BUSINESS OF THE U.S. COURTS 2014, at tbls. C-4 & C-5. Although the percentage of trial dispositions in state courts is somewhat larger, the overall pattern is the same. The vast majority of civil cases filed in state courts never reach trial; and in contrast to the federal courts, relatively few of those that do are tried to a jury. *See* COURT STATISTICS PROJECT, EXAMINING THE WORK OF STATE COURTS, 2003, at 22 (NATIONAL CENTER FOR STATE COURTS 2004); JUDICIAL COUNCIL OF CALIFORNIA, 2014 COURT STATISTICS REPORT: STATEWIDE CASELOAD TRENDS 2003-2004 THROUGH 2012-2013, at 72-74 (2014); NEW YORK STATE UNIFIED COURT SYSTEM, ANNUAL REPORT 2013, at 23 (2014). Yet trials do take place, and this chapter addresses some of the critical procedural issues that may arise during that process, particularly those pertaining to jury trials.

In both jury trials and bench trials (*i.e.*, cases tried solely to a judge), the judge presides over the trial process, which, of course, includes rulings on questions of law and on the admissibility of evidence. In a bench trial, the judge also decides the facts, while in a jury trial the jury assumes that function. In essence, the role of the jury is to evaluate the admitted evidence and, after having been properly instructed on the law by the judge, to decide the facts in accord with the law and the evidence. Although it is somewhat of an oversimplification, it remains generally true that in a jury trial, the judge decides the law, while the jury decides the facts. This demarcation between law-finder and fact-finder is a direct product of common law practice. *At* common law, the pleadings reduced the controversy to a single issue, either one of law or one of fact. The court decided an issue of law, while the jury decided an issue of fact; so too under our current jury trial system, except that we no longer insist that the parties narrow their dispute to a single issue. *See* Chapter I, part A, at p. 14, *supra*.

While many consider the right to a jury trial to be a foundational principle of our system of civil justice, the right is not an absolute one. The right exists only in certain types of cases, and even then it can be waived by a failure to make a timely demand for a jury trial. *See, e.g.*, FED. R. CIV. P. 38(d) ("A party waives a jury trial unless its demand is properly served and filed."). And once asserted, the right can be circumvented through summary judgment or a directed verdict, and even a favorable jury verdict can be nullified if the judge concludes that the evidence does not support that verdict.

In the material that follows, we will examine the right to a trial by jury in civil cases and the scope of that right, as well as pre-verdict and post-verdict remedies that may be used to avoid or overturn an unfavorable jury verdict. But before examining those issues, we will briefly consider one last pretrial device: the pretrial conference.

A. The Pretrial Conference

One hallmark of common law pleading was the manner in which the pleadings reduced a case to a single issue for decision. In essence, the process of pleading worked as a judicially supervised management device, leading to a relatively specific resolution of the controversy. At least this was the theory. Modern pleading, however, does not perform this winnowing function. Indeed, the opposite is more often the case. Liberal rules of pleading, discovery, and joinder expand the possibilities for complex, multi-issue litigation. Quite often, rather than streamlining a case, the pretrial proceedings can add layers of complexity. Such bloated cases have the potential to bog down in the morass of pretrial proceedings, especially when the lawyers do not give these cases the full attention they deserve. And the eventual trial of such a case runs the risk of overwhelming the trier of fact with a muddled confusion of information and argument. Thus, while modern procedures offer flexibility and a potential for justice that was not available under the rigid single-issue system of common law pleading, the cost of that flexibility may sometimes undermine the actual delivery of justice.

The liberality of modern procedure thus requires some method through which to avoid or ameliorate these potential problems. We have already seen how summary judgment may play a role in the early termination of litigation. *See* Chapter X, part A, *supra*. Another solution, perhaps less drastic from a litigant's perspective, is to vest judges with managerial responsibility over the cases assigned to them. The idea is not to give judges the authority to force the parties toward any particular resolution but to empower a judge to direct the parties to work efficiently and effectively toward resolving the controversy between them, whether that resolution be through settlement, mediation, or a trial on a specified group of issues. This is a delicate balance that requires a careful exercise of judgment, one that accommodates the autonomy of the parties while helping to promote an efficient use of the judicial system.

Consistent with the foregoing, one of the key tools of modern judicial management is the pretrial conference. Although such conferences have their roots in nineteenth-century English practices, the genesis for the modern pretrial conference is often traced to a judicial experiment undertaken by the state courts of Wayne County, Michigan, in 1929. *See* Edson R. Sunderland, *The Theory and Practice of Pre-Trial Procedure*, 36 MICH. L. REV. 215 (1937). At that time, the judicial system in Wayne County, which included the city of Detroit, was experiencing significant case backlogs. The court decided to implement a pretrial hearing procedure through which cases could be streamlined for trial, perhaps even eliminating the necessity for trial. Among other things, the pretrial hearing would resolve evidentiary disputes and establish the actual scope of the controversy between the parties. The success of the program led to its adoption in a number of jurisdictions and, in the federal courts, to the adoption of Rule 16 in 1938. While initially the focus of the Rule 16 conference was on streamlining what would occur at the trial, the rule as now written grants federal judges a broad mandate to supervise the entire pretrial phase of a civil suit. *See* 6A CHARLES ALAN WRIGHT, ARTHUR R. MILLER & MARY KAY KANE, FEDERAL PRACTICE AND PROCEDURE § 1521 (3d ed. 2010 & Supp. 2015). In general, the pretrial conference should be seen as a process rather than as a distinct event. It takes place over the entire course of the pretrial proceedings—a period that is likely to last for at least a year, and in many cases much longer.

There is no universal pretrial conference model, yet the basic contours of the pretrial conference process usually require or permit some version of the following elements:

- a *scheduling conference* that occurs shortly after the litigation's commencement;
- the issuance of a *scheduling order* pertaining to such matters as discovery, joinder of new parties or claims, motions, and the like;
- interim *status conferences* to assess the progress of pretrial preparation and to consider possible alternatives to trial, such as settlement or mediation; and,
- a *final pretrial conference* within a few weeks or even days of the trial, the purpose of which is to determine what the parties will (and will not) present at trial and to further consider potential settlement.

In what follows, we will focus on the federal model for pretrial conferences as provided in Rule 16. State models are generally similar, but do vary in detail from jurisdiction to jurisdiction. *See, e.g.*, ILL. SUP. CT. R. 218; MICH. CT. R. 2.401. But even with respect to the federal model, actual practice under the rule varies from one federal district to another, and even within each district. In general, Rule 16 grants federal district court judges a latitude of discretion in implementing the policies and practices embodied in the rule. This brief review of the rule should provide you with a basic understanding of the role of pretrial conferences in managing the pretrial process. You should read Federal Rule 16 in its entirety.

Rule 16(a) vests the district court with the discretion to

> order the attorneys and any unrepresented parties to appear for one or more pretrial conferences for such purposes as:
>
> (1) expediting disposition of the action;
> (2) establishing early and continuing control so that the case will not be protracted because of lack of management;
> (3) discouraging wasteful pretrial activities;
> (4) improving the quality of the trial through more thorough preparation; and
> (5) facilitating settlement.

FED. R. CIV. P. 16(a). If a district court calls a conference pursuant to Rule 16, attendance by the attorneys and by any unrepresented party is mandatory, as is their good faith participation in that conference and their compliance with any judicial orders emanating from it. *See* FED. R. CIV. P. 16(f) (allowing imposition of sanctions for noncompliance).

Notice that Rule 16(a) gives the court discretion to call more than one pretrial conference. As a consequence, many federal judges calendar an early scheduling conference pertaining to such matters as discovery, anticipated motions, or the like. Other judges may simply wish to send the attorneys a message stating that they have an active interest in the steady progress of the case. Subsection 16(c)(2) lists the range of matters that may be considered at a pretrial conference, including the formulation and simplification of the issues; the possibility of obtaining admissions of fact; the avoidance of unnecessary and cumulative evidence; the timing of summary adjudication; the control and scheduling of discovery; the possibility of settlement and various alternatives to trial; and, more generally, "facilitating in other ways the just, speedy, and inexpensive disposition of the action." FED. R. CIV. P. 16(c)(2)(A)-(P).

Aside from any conferences the district court may call, Rule 16(b)(1) requires the judge to issue a "scheduling order" in all cases not exempted by local rule.* The order may be entered after the court has received the Rule 26(f) discovery plan or after the court has consulted with the attorneys and any unrepresented parties, but, "unless the judge finds good cause for delay," it must be entered "within the earlier of 90 days after any defendant has been served with the complaint or 60 days after any defendant has appeared." FED. R. CIV. P. 16(b)(2). The scheduling order "must limit the time to join other parties, amend the pleadings, complete discovery, and file motions." FED. R. CIV. P. 16(b)(3)(A). It may also include certain other matters appropriate to the circumstances of the case. FED. R. CIV. P. 16(b)(3)(B) (listing permissive contents of order). This scheduling order can only

---

* The exemptions usually cover cases that are deemed sufficiently simple to obviate the need for such detailed supervision, such as cases to review the denial of Social Security benefits and suits brought by the United States to collect on federally insured student loans. *See, e.g.,* C.D. CAL. L.R. 16-12 (listing exemptions including specified Social Security cases).

be modified "for good cause and with the judge's consent." FED. R. CIV. P. 16(b) (4). For these purposes, "[m]ere stipulations by the parties do not constitute good cause." *Hernandez v. Mario's Auto Sales, Inc.*, 617 F. Supp. 2d 488, 492-493 (S.D. Tex. 2009). *And see Rybski v. Home Depot USA, Inc.*, 2012 WL 5416586 (D. Ariz. Oct. 19, 2012) (same).

Once the schedule is set, intermediate status conferences may be called from time to time to review whatever progress the attorneys have made, to ensure that the case development is proceeding in an expeditious fashion, or to simply to remind the attorneys of available alternatives to trial, including settlement and mediation. During the interim between the entry of the scheduling order and the eve of trial, some judges maintain a relatively active oversight role through, for example, regular conference calls with the attorneys, while other judges may be more passive. The degree of judicial involvement is a product of individual philosophy and style. These interim conferences can assist the parties in evaluating the strengths and weaknesses of their respective positions.

Lastly, a final pretrial conference will be scheduled "as close to the start of trial as is reasonable," for the purpose of preparing and fine tuning the case for trial and making one last effort at settlement. FED. R. CIV. P. 16(e). In advance of this final conference, the court may require the parties to file memoranda summarizing their claims, counterclaims, and affirmative defenses, the major elements of each, and their key supporting evidence. They may also be required to file detailed stipulations of fact, memoranda of law on disputed legal questions, and memoranda identifying anticipated evidentiary issues with their position on each. At the final conference, which must be attended by at least one trial attorney for each party and by any unrepresented party, the court may entertain motions in limine to resolve any evidentiary issues the parties anticipate arising at trial. *See, e.g.,* C.D. CAL. L.R. 16-3–16-6, 16-10 (local rules providing detailed pretrial filing requirements). Orders that emanate from this final conference then bind the parties at trial, and may be altered only to "prevent manifest injustice," FED. R. CIV. P. 16(e), although a court can carefully craft its final orders in a manner that leaves it with some flexibility.

Overall, the goal of the pretrial conference is to promote the fair and efficient use of the judicial system, as well as to prepare the case for trial or other resolution in a manner that best promotes the interests of justice.

B. The Right to a Trial by Jury

The Seventh Amendment to the U.S. Constitution provides: "In Suits at common law, where the value in controversy shall exceed twenty dollars, the right of trial by jury shall be preserved. . . ." U.S. CONST. amend. VII; *see also* FED. R. CIV. P. 38(a) ("The right of trial by jury as declared by the Seventh Amendment to the Constitution—or as provided by a federal statute—is preserved to the parties inviolate."). This right is limited to proceedings filed in (or removed to) federal court, for the Seventh Amendment guarantee has not been extended to the states through the Fourteenth Amendment.* Thus, from the perspective of the federal Constitution, the individual states are not obligated to provide jury trials in civil lawsuits. Yet most state constitutions do preserve or protect the right to a jury trial, though not necessarily in a fashion identical to that afforded by the Seventh Amendment. *See, e.g.,* Fla. Const. art. I, § 22 ("The right of trial by jury shall be secure to all and remain inviolate."); Haw. Const. art. I, § 13 ("In suits at common law where the value in controversy shall exceed five thousand dollars, the right of trial by jury shall be preserved."); N.D. Const. art. I, § 13 ("The right of trial by jury shall be secured to all, and remain inviolate."); N.Y. Const. art. I, § 2 ("Trial by jury in all cases in which it has heretofore been guaranteed by constitutional provision shall remain inviolate forever. . . ."); Okla. Const. art. II, § 19 ("The right of trial by jury shall be and remain inviolate, except in civil cases wherein the amount in controversy does not exceed One Thousand Five Hundred Dollars. . . . Provided, however, that the Legislature may provide for jury trial in cases involving lesser amounts."); Tex. Const. art. I, § 15 ("The right of trial by jury shall remain inviolate.").** Our attention here, however, will focus on the Seventh Amendment. By comparison, for an examination of the right to a jury trial under state law, see Jack H. Friedenthal, Mary Kay Kane & Arthur R. Miller, Civil Procedure § 11.7 (4th ed. 2005) (discussing right to jury trial under New York law).

The Seventh Amendment itself does not *create* a right to a jury trial; rather, it *preserves* that right as it existed at common law, which has been interpreted to mean that the scope of the Seventh Amendment is geared to practices extant in the common law courts of England in 1791, the year in which the amendment was ratified. At that time, a jury trial was available only in suits falling within the recognized forms of action at common law and not in equitable proceedings. Thus the Seventh Amendment right to a jury trial clearly attaches to claims seeking money damages for breach of contract or for personal injury. On the other hand, the right just as clearly does not attach to proceedings seeking an injunction, specific performance, or reformation of a contract, for the simple reason that the latter remedies were equitable in nature and not available at common law.

In most cases, the question of whether a litigant is entitled to a jury trial is easily resolved by the standard distinctions between law and equity. However, given the 200-plus years of jurisprudential evolution since the Seventh Amendment's adoption—including the merger of law and equity and the creation of novel rights of action that may borrow from both law and equity—the seemingly distinct line

---

* However, the right to a jury trial in criminal proceedings, protected by the Sixth Amendment to the U.S. Constitution, is fully applicable to the states by virtue of the Fourteenth Amendment. *Duncan v. Louisiana*, 391 U.S. 145 (1968); *see also* U.S. Const. art. III, § 2, cl. 3.

** The Seventh Amendment's $20 minimum has never been adjusted to reflect changes in the value of the dollar since 1791. Using the Consumer Price Index, the original $20 minimum is equivalent to about $500 today. To that extent, our present right to a jury trial in federal court is much broader than what the Framers had in mind, while the right as enshrined in some state constitutions is considerably narrower.

may blur. The three principal cases that follow attempt to navigate that complexity by developing an approach through which to determine, in what may be called nonobvious cases, under what circumstances and to what extent the right to a jury trial attaches. The first case, *Beacon Theatres, Inc. v. Westover*, 359 U.S. 500 (1959), addresses the Seventh Amendment problem that arises when legal and equitable issues are intermingled in a single suit. Next, *Chauffeurs, Teamsters & Helpers, Local No. 391 v. Terry*, 494 U.S. 558 (1990), examines the problem of how one determines whether the right to a jury trial attaches to a claim or remedy that was created post-1791. And finally, *Markman v. Westview Instruments, Inc.*, 517 U.S. 370 (1996), introduces a functional component into the determination of whether to provide a jury trial on a particular issue when there is no clear answer under the guidelines developed in *Terry*. *See generally* 9 CHARLES ALAN WRIGHT & ARTHUR R. MILLER, FEDERAL PRACTICE AND PROCEDURE §§ 2301 *et seq.* (3d ed. 2008 & Supp. 2015); Prentice H. Marshall & Thomas D. Rowe, Jr., *Right to a Jury Trial; Demand, in* 8 MOORE'S FEDERAL PRACTICE §§ 38.01 *et seq.* (3d ed. 2015).

Beacon Theatres, Inc. v. Westover

359 U.S. 500 (1959)

MR. JUSTICE BLACK delivered the opinion of the Court.

Petitioner, Beacon Theatres, Inc., sought by mandamus to require a district judge in the Southern District of California to vacate certain orders alleged to deprive it of a jury trial of issues arising in a suit brought against it by Fox West Coast Theatres, Inc. The Court of Appeals for the Ninth Circuit refused the writ, holding that the trial judge had acted within his proper discretion in denying petitioner's request for a jury. We granted certiorari . . . .

Fox had asked for declaratory relief against Beacon alleging a controversy arising under the Sherman Antitrust Act, 15 U.S.C. §§ 1, 2, and under the Clayton Act, 15 U.S.C. § 15, which authorizes suits for treble damages against Sherman Act violators. According to the complaint Fox operates a movie theatre in San Bernardino, California, and has long been exhibiting films under contracts with movie distributors. These contracts grant it the exclusive right to show "first run" pictures in the "San Bernardino competitive area" and provide for "clearance"—a period of time during which no other theatre can exhibit the same pictures. After building a drive-in theatre about 11 miles from San Bernardino, Beacon notified Fox that it considered contracts barring simultaneous exhibitions of first-run films in the two theatres to be overt acts in violation of the antitrust laws. Fox's complaint alleged that this notification, together with threats of treble damage suits against Fox and its distributors, gave rise to "duress and coercion" which deprived Fox of a valuable property right, the right to negotiate for exclusive first-run contracts. Unless Beacon was restrained, the complaint continued, irreparable harm would result. Accordingly, while its pleading was styled a "Complaint for Declaratory Relief," Fox prayed both for a declaration that a grant of clearance between the Fox and Beacon theatres is reasonable and not in violation of the antitrust laws, and for an injunction, pending final resolution of the litigation, to prevent Beacon from instituting any action under the antitrust laws against Fox and its distributors arising out of the controversy alleged in the complaint. Beacon filed an answer, a counterclaim against Fox, and a cross-claim against an exhibitor who had intervened. These denied the threats and asserted that there was no substantial competition between the two theatres, that the clearances granted were therefore unreasonable, and that a conspiracy existed between Fox and its distributors to manipulate contracts and clearances so as to restrain trade and monopolize first-run pictures in violation of the antitrust laws. Treble damages were asked.

Beacon demanded a jury trial of the factual issues in the case as provided by Federal Rule of Civil Procedure 38(b). The District Court, however, viewed the issues raised by the "Complaint for Declaratory Relief," including the question of competition between the two theatres, as essentially equitable. Acting under the purported authority of Rules 42(b) and 57, it directed that these issues be tried to the court before jury determination of the validity of the charges of antitrust violations made in the counterclaim and cross-claim. A common issue of the "Complaint for Declaratory Relief," the counterclaim, and the cross-claim was the reasonableness of the clearances granted to Fox, which depended, in part, on the existence of competition between the two theatres. Thus the effect of the action of the District Court could be, as the Court of Appeals believed, "to limit the petitioner's opportunity fully to try to a jury every issue which has a bearing upon its treble damage suit," for determination of the issue of clearances by the judge might "operate either by way of res judicata or collateral estoppel so as to conclude both parties with respect thereto at the subsequent trial of the treble damage claim."

The District Court's finding that the Complaint for Declaratory Relief presented basically equitable issues draws no support from the Declaratory Judgment Act. That statute, while allowing prospective defendants to sue to establish their nonliability, specifically preserves the right to jury trial for both parties. It follows that if Beacon would have been entitled to a jury trial in a treble damage suit against Fox it cannot be deprived of that right merely because Fox took advantage of the availability of declaratory relief to sue Beacon first. Since the right to trial by jury applies to treble damage suits under the antitrust laws, and is, in fact, an essential part of the congressional plan for making competition rather than monopoly the rule of trade, the Sherman and Clayton Act issues on which Fox sought a declaration were essentially jury questions.

Nevertheless the Court of Appeals refused to upset the order of the district judge. It held that the question of whether a right to jury trial existed was to be judged by Fox's complaint read as a whole. In addition to seeking a declaratory judgment, the court said, Fox's complaint can be read as making out a valid plea for injunctive relief, thus stating a claim traditionally cognizable in equity. A party who is entitled to maintain a suit in equity for an injunction, said the court, may have all the issues in his suit determined by the judge without a jury regardless of whether legal rights are involved. The court then rejected the argument that equitable relief, traditionally available only when legal remedies are inadequate, was rendered unnecessary in this case by the filing of the counterclaim and cross-claim which presented all the issues necessary to a determination of the right to injunctive relief. . . .

Beacon takes issue with the holding of the Court of Appeals that the complaint stated a claim upon which equitable relief could be granted. . . . Assuming that the pleadings can be construed to support such a request and assuming additionally that the complaint can be read as alleging the kind of harassment by a multiplicity of lawsuits which would *traditionally* have justified equity to take jurisdiction and settle the case in one suit, we are nevertheless of the opinion that, under the Declaratory Judgment Act and the Federal Rules of Civil Procedure, neither claim can justify denying Beacon a trial by jury of all the issues in the antitrust controversy.

The basis of injunctive relief in the federal courts has always been irreparable harm and inadequacy of legal remedies. At least as much is required to justify a trial court in using its discretion under the Federal Rules to allow claims of equitable origins to be tried ahead of legal ones, since this has the same effect as an equitable injunction of the legal claims. And it is immaterial, in judging if that discretion is properly employed, that before the Federal Rules and the Declaratory Judgment Act were passed, courts of equity, exercising a jurisdiction separate from courts of law, were, in some cases, allowed to enjoin subsequent legal actions between the same parties involving the same controversy. This was because the subsequent legal action, though providing an opportunity to try the case to a jury, might not protect the right of the equity plaintiff to a fair and orderly adjudication of the controversy. Under such circumstances the legal remedy could quite naturally be deemed inadequate. Inadequacy of remedy and irreparable harm are practical terms, however. As such their existence today must be determined, not by precedents decided under discarded procedures, but in the light of the remedies now made available by the Declaratory Judgment Act and the Federal Rules.

Viewed in this manner, the use of discretion by the trial court under Rule 42(b) to deprive Beacon of a full jury trial on its counterclaim and cross-claim, as well as on Fox's plea for declaratory relief, cannot be justified. Under the Federal Rules the same court may try both legal and equitable causes in the same action. Fed. Rules Civ. Proc., 1, 2, 18. Thus any defenses, equitable or legal, Fox may have to charges of antitrust violations can be raised either in its suit for declaratory relief or in answer to Beacon's counterclaim. On proper showing, harassment by threats of other suits, or other suits actually brought, involving the issues being tried in this case, could be temporarily enjoined pending the outcome of this litigation. Whatever permanent injunctive relief Fox might be entitled to on the basis of the decision in this case could, of course, be given by the court after the jury renders its verdict. In this way the issues between these parties could be settled in one suit giving Beacon a full jury trial of every antitrust issue. By contrast, the holding of the court below while granting Fox no additional protection unless the avoidance of jury trial be considered as such, would compel Beacon to split his antitrust case, trying part to a judge and part to a jury. Such a result, which involves the postponement and subordination of Fox's own legal claim for declaratory relief as well as of the counterclaim which Beacon was compelled by the Federal Rules to bring, is not permissible.

Our decision is consistent with the plan of the Federal Rules and the Declaratory Judgment Act to effect substantial procedural reform while retaining a distinction between jury and nonjury issues and leaving substantive rights unchanged. Since in the federal courts equity has always acted only when legal remedies were inadequate, the expansion of adequate legal remedies provided by the Declaratory Judgment Act and the Federal Rules necessarily affects the scope of equity. Thus, the justification for equity's deciding legal issues once it obtains jurisdiction, and refusing to dismiss a case, merely because subsequently a legal remedy becomes available, must be re-evaluated in the light of the liberal joinder provisions of the Federal Rules which allow legal and equitable causes to be brought and resolved in one civil action. Similarly the need for, and therefore, the availability of such equitable remedies as Bills of Peace, *Quia Timet* and Injunction must be reconsidered in view of the existence of the Declaratory Judgment Act as well as the liberal joinder provision of the Rules. This is not only in accord with the spirit of the Rules and the Act but is required by the provision in [Rule 38(a)] that "[t]he right to trial by jury as declared by the Seventh Amendment to the Constitution or as given by a statute of the United States shall be preserved . . . inviolate."

If there should be cases where the availability of declaratory judgment or joinder in one suit of legal and equitable causes would not in all respects protect the plaintiff seeking equitable relief from irreparable harm while affording a jury trial in the legal cause, the trial court will necessarily have to use its discretion in deciding whether the legal or equitable cause should be tried first. Since the right to jury trial is a constitutional one, however, while no similar requirement protects trials by the court, that discretion is very narrowly limited and must, wherever possible, be exercised to preserve jury trial. As this Court said in *Scott v. Neely*, 140 U.S. 106, 109-110 [1891]: "In the Federal courts this [jury] right cannot be dispensed with, except by the assent of the parties entitled to it; nor can it be impaired by any blending with a claim, properly cognizable at law, of a demand for equitable relief in aid of the legal action, or during its pendency." This long-standing principle of equity dictates that only under the most imperative circumstances, circumstances which in view of the flexible procedures of the Federal Rules we cannot now anticipate, can the right to a jury trial of legal issues be lost through prior determination of equitable claims. As we have shown, this is far from being such a case. . . .

The judgment of the Court of Appeals is
Reversed.

[The dissenting opinion of JUSTICE STEWART, joined by JUSTICES HARLAN and WHITTAKER, is omitted. JUSTICE FRANKFURTER did not participate in the decision.]

NOTES AND QUESTIONS

1. *Reaffirming the principle.* In *Dairy Queen, Inc. v. Wood*, 369 U.S. 469 (1962), the Court reiterated and reaffirmed the *Beacon Theatres* holding. In that case, the plaintiff, Dairy Queen, Inc., sued a licensee for trademark infringement and breach of contract, seeking both an injunction against future uses of the Dairy Queen trademark and an accounting for money due under the contract. The trial court denied the defendant's demand for a jury trial since, in that court's view, either all of the issues presented were purely equitable, or any potential legal issues were "incidental" to the equitable claims. However, the Supreme Court concluded that the "accounting" was in fact a claim for damages and therefore properly characterized as a legal remedy. As a consequence, regardless of whether one labeled that remedy as incidental to the equitable claims, the defendant was entitled to a jury trial on the factual issues pertaining to that remedy. The *Dairy Queen* Court explained that its ruling in *Beacon Theatres*

> not only emphasizes the responsibility of the Federal Courts of Appeals to grant mandamus where necessary to protect the constitutional right to trial by jury but also limits the issues open for determination here by defining the protection to which that right is entitled in cases involving both legal and equitable claims. The holding in *Beacon Theatres* was that where both legal and equitable issues are presented in a single case, "only under the most imperative circumstances, circumstances which in view of the flexible procedures of the Federal Rules we cannot now anticipate, can the right to a jury trial of legal issues be lost through prior determination of equitable claims." That holding, of course, applies whether the trial judge chooses to characterize the legal issues presented as "incidental" to equitable issues or not. Consequently, in a case such as this where there cannot even be a contention of such "imperative circumstances," *Beacon Theatres* requires that any legal issues for which a trial by jury is timely and properly demanded be submitted to a jury. There being no question of the timeliness or correctness of the demand involved here, the sole question which we must decide is whether the action now pending before the District Court contains legal issues.

Dairy Queen, Inc., 369 U.S. at 472-473.

2. *Imperative circumstances.*   Both *Beacon Theatres* and *Dairy Queen* recognized that under "the most imperative circumstances," the right to a jury trial on a legal claim might give way to a need for a prior determination of an equitable claim. Technically, the Supreme Court has never found such an imperative circumstance. However, in *Katchen v. Landy*, 382 U.S. 323 (1966), the Supreme Court did uphold the power of an Article I bankruptcy court—a tribunal that does not normally use a jury as fact-finder—to resolve a claim by a creditor against the bankrupt's estate, even though the creditor would have been entitled to a jury trial had that claim been filed before an Article III court. *Id.* at 338-339. Was the summary bankruptcy plan an "imperative circumstance" that trumped the creditor's right to a jury trial? Or had the creditor simply waived its right to a jury trial by filing a claim in the bankruptcy proceeding? In *Granfinanciera, S.A. v. Nordberg*, 492 U.S. 33 (1989), the Court appeared to adopt *Katchen*'s "waiver"

interpretation, refusing to extend that case to a circumstance in which the creditor, rather than having itself filed a claim in the bankruptcy proceeding, was instead subject to a claim filed against it by the bankruptcy trustee. *Id.* at 58-59 & nn.13-14. Under these circumstances, the Court held that the creditor had retained its right to a jury trial in the bankruptcy court proceeding.

Lower federal courts appear to be equally chary in finding imperative circumstances. The one case in which a circuit court found an "imperative circumstance," *Leach v. Pan American World Airways*, 842 F.2d 285 (11th Cir. 1988) (holding that imperative circumstance was embodied in federal labor policy), was disapproved by the Supreme Court in *Chauffeurs, Teamsters & Helpers, Local No. 391 v. Terry*, 494 U.S. 558, 563 & n.2 (1990). Hence, to date, authoritative cases satisfying this criterion represent what is essentially a null set.

PROBLEMS

11-1. Alpha and Beta entered into a contract under which Beta was required to deliver a certain amount of produce to Alpha on the first of each month for the next 60 months. The contract also specified the amount Alpha was to pay for the produce. Beta made the deliveries for the first five months, but having concluded that the arrangement was not profitable, Beta made no delivery for the sixth month. Alpha immediately filed a diversity suit against Beta in a federal district court. Alpha seeks specific performance of the contract and monetary damages for losses incurred during the sixth month, when Beta refused to make a delivery. Beta denies the contract's validity and seeks a jury trial on that issue. Is Beta entitled to a jury trial?

11-2. P and D enter into a contract under which D agrees not to compete with P in a specific geographic market. P later sues D claiming a breach of that contract, seeking both damages and injunctive relief. Under *Beacon Theatres* and *Dairy Queen*, is D entitled to a jury trial on the breach-of-contract claim? Does it matter whether the primary relief is for damages or for an injunction? Might there be any "imperative circumstances" under which D would not be entitled to a jury trial? Assuming D is entitled to a jury trial based on the damages remedy, if the jury enters a verdict for D, finding no breach of contract, may the court then enter an injunction if it independently determines that the contract had been breached? *See Ag Servs. of Am., Inc. v. Nielsen*, 231 F.3d 726 (10th Cir. 2000), *cert. denied*, 532 U.S. 1021 (2001).

Chauffeurs, Teamsters & Helpers Local No. 391 v. Terry
494 U.S. 558 (1990)

JUSTICE MARSHALL delivered the opinion of the Court, except as to Part III-A.

This case presents the question whether an employee who seeks relief in the form of backpay for a union's alleged breach of its duty of fair representation has a right to trial by jury. We hold that the Seventh Amendment entitles such a plaintiff to a jury trial.

I

McLean Trucking Company and the Chauffeurs, Teamsters, and Helpers Local No. 391 (Union) were parties to a collective-bargaining agreement that governed the terms and conditions of employment at McLean's terminals. The 27 respondents were employed by McLean as truckdrivers in bargaining units covered by the agreement, and all were members of the Union. In 1982 McLean implemented a change in operations that resulted in the elimination of some of its terminals and the reorganization of others. As part of that change, McLean transferred respondents to the terminal located in Winston-Salem and agreed to give them special seniority rights in relation to "inactive" employees in Winston-Salem who had been laid off temporarily.

After working in Winston-Salem for approximately six weeks, respondents were alternately laid off and recalled several times. Respondents filed a grievance with the Union, contesting the order of the layoffs and recalls. Respondents also challenged McLean's policy of stripping any driver who was laid off of his special seniority rights. Respondents claimed that McLean breached the collective-bargaining agreement by giving inactive drivers preference over respondents. After these proceedings, the grievance committee ordered McLean to recall any respondent who was then laid off and to lay off any inactive driver who had been recalled; in addition, the committee ordered McLean to recognize respondents' special seniority rights until the inactive employees were properly recalled. . . .

McLean continued to engage in periodic layoffs and recalls of the workers at the Winston-Salem terminal. Respondents filed [another] grievance with the Union, but the Union declined to refer the charges to a grievance committee on the ground that the relevant issues had been determined in the prior proceedings.

In July 1983, respondents filed an action in District Court, alleging that McLean had breached the collective-bargaining agreement in violation of § 301 of the Labor Management Relations Act, 1947, 29 U.S.C. § 185, and that the Union had violated its duty of fair representation. Respondents requested a permanent injunction requiring the defendants to cease their illegal acts and to reinstate them to their proper seniority status; in addition, they sought, *inter alia*, compensatory damages for lost wages and health benefits. In 1986 McLean filed for bankruptcy; subsequently, the action against it was voluntarily dismissed, along with all claims for injunctive relief.

Respondents had requested a jury trial in their pleadings. The Union moved to strike the jury demand on the ground that no right to a jury trial exists in a duty of fair representation suit. The District Court denied the motion to strike. After an interlocutory appeal, the Fourth Circuit affirmed the trial court, holding that the Seventh Amendment entitled respondents to a jury trial of their claim for monetary relief. We granted the petition for certiorari to resolve a Circuit conflict on this issue, and now affirm the judgment of the Fourth Circuit.

II

The duty of fair representation is inferred from unions' exclusive authority under the National Labor Relations Act (NLRA), 29 U.S.C. § 159(a), to represent all employees in a bargaining unit. The duty requires a union "to serve the interests of all members without hostility or discrimination toward any, to exercise its discretion with complete good faith and honesty, and to avoid arbitrary conduct." A union must discharge its duty both in bargaining with the employer and in its enforcement of the resulting collective-bargaining agreement. Thus, the Union here was required to pursue respondents' grievances in a manner consistent with the principles of fair representation.

Because most collective-bargaining agreements accord finality to grievance or arbitration procedures established by the collective-bargaining agreement, an employee normally cannot bring a § 301 action against an employer unless he can show that the union breached its duty of fair representation in its handling of his grievance. *DelCostello v. Teamsters*, 462 U.S. 151, 163-164 (1983). Whether the employee sues both the labor union and the employer or only one of those entities, he must prove the same two facts to recover money damages: that the employer's action violated the terms of the collective-bargaining agreement and that the union breached its duty of fair representation.

III

We turn now to the constitutional issue presented in this case—whether respondents are entitled to a jury trial.[3] The Seventh Amendment provides that "[i]n Suits at common law, where the value in controversy shall exceed twenty dollars, the right of trial by jury shall be preserved." The right to a jury trial includes more than the common-law forms of action recognized in 1791; the phrase "Suits at common law" refers to "suits in which *legal* rights [are] to be ascertained and determined, in contradistinction to those where equitable rights alone [are] recognized, and equitable remedies [are] administered." *Parsons v. Bedford*, 3 Pet. 433, 447 (1830); see also *ibid.* ("[T]he amendment then may well be construed to embrace all suits which are not of equity and admiralty jurisdiction, whatever may be the peculiar form which they may assume to settle legal rights"). The right extends to causes of action created by Congress. *Tull v. United States*, 481 U.S. 412, 417 (1987). Since the merger of the systems of law and equity, see Fed. Rule Civ. Proc. 2, this Court has carefully preserved the right to trial by jury where legal rights are at stake. . . .

To determine whether a particular action will resolve legal rights, we examine both the nature of the issues involved and the remedy sought. "First, we compare the statutory action to 18th-century actions brought in the courts of England prior

---

3. Because the NLRA does not expressly create the duty of fair representation, resort to the statute to determine whether Congress provided for a jury trial in an action for breach of that duty is unavailing. . . .

to the merger of the courts of law and equity. Second, we examine the remedy sought and determine whether it is legal or equitable in nature." *Tull, supra,* 481 U.S., at 417-418. The second inquiry is the more important in our analysis.[4]

A

An action for breach of a union's duty of fair representation was unknown in 18th-century England; in fact, collective bargaining was unlawful. We must therefore look for an analogous cause of action that existed in the 18th century to determine whether the nature of this duty of fair representation suit is legal or equitable.

The Union contends that this duty of fair representation action resembles a suit brought to vacate an arbitration award because respondents seek to set aside the result of the grievance process. In the 18th century, an action to set aside an arbitration award was considered equitable. 2 J. Story, Commentaries on Equity Jurisprudence § 1452, pp. 789-790 (13th ed. 1886) (equity courts had jurisdiction over claims that an award should be set aside on the ground of "mistake of the arbitrators"). . . .

The arbitration analogy is inapposite, however, to the Seventh Amendment question posed in this case. No grievance committee has considered respondents' claim that the Union violated its duty of fair representation; the grievance process was concerned only with the employer's alleged breach of the collective-bargaining agreement. Thus, respondents' claim against the Union cannot be characterized as an action to vacate an arbitration award because "[t]he arbitration proceeding did not, and indeed, could not, resolve the employee's claim against the union. . . . Because no arbitrator has decided the primary issue presented by this claim, no arbitration award need be undone, even if the employee ultimately prevails." *DelCostello,* 462 U.S., at 167 (STEVENS, J., concurring in part and dissenting in part).

The Union next argues that respondents' duty of fair representation action is comparable to an action by a trust beneficiary against a trustee for breach of fiduciary duty. Such actions were within the exclusive jurisdiction of courts of equity. 2 Story, *supra,* § 960, p. 266; Restatement (Second) of Trusts § 199(c) (1959). This analogy is far more persuasive than the arbitration analogy. Just as a trustee must act in the best interests of the beneficiaries, a union, as the exclusive representative of the workers, must exercise its power to act on behalf of the employees in good faith. Moreover, just as a beneficiary does not directly control the actions of a trustee, an individual employee lacks direct control over a union's actions taken on his behalf.

---

4. Justice Stevens' analysis emphasizes a third consideration, namely whether "the issues [presented by the claim] are typical grist for the jury's judgment." This Court, however, has never relied on this consideration "as an independent basis for extending the right to a jury trial under the Seventh Amendment." *Tull v. United States,* 481.U.S. 412, 418, n. 4 (1987). . . .

The trust analogy extends to a union's handling of grievances. In most cases, a trustee has the exclusive authority to sue third parties who injure the beneficiaries' interest in the trust, including any legal claim the trustee holds in trust for the beneficiaries. The trustee then has the sole responsibility for determining whether to settle, arbitrate, or otherwise dispose of the claim. Similarly, the union typically has broad discretion in its decision whether and how to pursue an employee's grievance against an employer. Just as a trust beneficiary can sue to enforce a contract entered into on his behalf by the trustee only if the trustee "improperly refuses or neglects to bring an action against the third person," Restatement (Second) of Trusts, *supra*, § 282(2), so an employee can sue his employer for a breach of the collective-bargaining agreement only if he shows that the union breached its duty of fair representation in its handling of the grievance.

Respondents contend that their duty of fair representation suit is less like a trust action than an attorney malpractice action, which was historically an action at law. . . . [W]e find that, in the context of the Seventh Amendment inquiry, the attorney malpractice analogy does not capture the relationship between the union and the represented employees as fully as the trust analogy does. . . .

Nevertheless, the trust analogy does not persuade us to characterize respondents' claim as wholly equitable. The Union's argument mischaracterizes the nature of our comparison of the action before us to 18th-century forms of action. As we observed in *Ross v. Bernhard*, 396 U.S. 531 (1970), "The Seventh Amendment question depends on the nature of the *issue* to be tried rather than the character of the overall action." *Id.*, at 538 (emphasis added) (finding a right to jury trial in a shareholder's derivative suit, a type of suit traditionally brought in courts of equity, because plaintiffs' case presented legal issues of breach of contract and negligence). As discussed above, to recover from the Union here, respondents must prove both that McLean violated § 301 by breaching the collective-bargaining agreement and that the Union breached its duty of fair representation. When viewed in isolation, the duty of fair representation issue is analogous to a claim against a trustee for breach of fiduciary duty. The § 301 issue, however, is comparable to a breach of contract claim—a legal issue.

Respondents' action against the Union thus encompasses both equitable and legal issues. The first part of our Seventh Amendment inquiry, then, leaves us in equipoise as to whether respondents are entitled to a jury trial.

B

Our determination under the first part of the Seventh Amendment analysis is only preliminary. In this case, the only remedy sought is a request for compensatory damages representing backpay and benefits. Generally, an action for money damages was "the traditional form of relief offered in the courts of law." *Curtis v. Loether*, 415 U.S. 189, 196 (1974). This Court has not, however, held that "any award of monetary relief must *necessarily* be 'legal' relief." *Ibid.* (emphasis added). Nonetheless, because we conclude that the remedy respondents seek has none of the attributes that must be present before we will find an exception to the general rule and characterize damages as equitable, we find that the remedy sought by respondents is legal.

First, we have characterized damages as equitable where they are restitutionary, such as in "action[s] for disgorgement of improper profits," *Tull*, 481 U.S., at 424. The backpay sought by respondents is not money wrongfully held by the Union, but wages and benefits they would have received from McLean had the Union processed the employees' grievances properly. Such relief is not restitutionary.

Second, a monetary award "incidental to or intertwined with injunctive relief" may be equitable. *Tull, supra*, 481 U.S., at 424. See, *e.g.*, *Mitchell v. Robert DeMario Jewelry, Inc.*, 361 U.S. 288, 291-292 (1960) (District Court had power, incident to its injunctive powers, to award backpay under the Fair Labor Standards Act; also backpay in that case was restitutionary). Because respondents seek only money damages, this characteristic is clearly absent from the case.[8]

The Union argues that the backpay relief sought here must nonetheless be considered equitable because this Court has labeled backpay awarded under Title VII, of the Civil Rights Act of 1964, 42 U.S.C. § 2000e *et seq.*, as equitable. It contends that the Title VII analogy is compelling in the context of the duty of fair representation because the Title VII backpay provision was based on the NLRA provision governing backpay awards for unfair labor practices. We are not convinced.

. . . Congress specifically characterized backpay under Title VII as a form of "equitable relief." 42 U.S.C. § 2000e-5(g). Congress made no similar pronouncement regarding the duty of fair representation. Furthermore, the Court has noted that backpay sought from an employer under Title VII would generally be restitutionary in nature, in contrast to the damages sought here from the Union. Thus, the remedy sought in this duty of fair representation case is clearly different from backpay sought for violations of Title VII. . . .

We hold, then, that the remedy of backpay sought in this duty of fair representation action is legal in nature. Considering both parts of the Seventh Amendment inquiry, we find that respondents are entitled to a jury trial on all issues presented in their suit.

IV

On balance, our analysis of the nature of respondents' duty of fair representation action and the remedy they seek convinces us that this action is a legal one. Although the search for an adequate 18th-century analog revealed that the claim includes both legal and equitable issues, the money damages respondents seek are the type of relief traditionally awarded by courts of law. Thus, the Seventh Amendment entitles respondents to a jury trial, and we therefore affirm the judgment of the Court of Appeals.

---

8. Both the Union and the dissent argue that the backpay award sought here is equitable because it is closely analogous to damages awarded to beneficiaries for a trustee's breach of trust. Such damages were available only in courts of equity because those courts had exclusive jurisdiction over actions involving a trustee's breach of his fiduciary duties.

The Union's argument, however, conflates the two parts of our Seventh Amendment inquiry. Under the dissent's approach, if the action at issue were analogous to an 18th-century action within the exclusive jurisdiction of the courts of equity, we would necessarily conclude that the remedy sought was also equitable because it would have been unavailable in a court of law. This view would, in effect, make the first part of our inquiry dispositive. We have clearly held, however, that the second part of the inquiry—the nature of the relief—is more important to the Seventh Amendment determination. The second part of the analysis, therefore, should not replicate the "abstruse historical" inquiry of the first part, *Ross v. Bernhard*, 396 U.S. 531, 538, n.10 (1970), but requires consideration of the general types of relief provided by courts of law and equity.

It is so ordered.

JUSTICE BRENNAN, concurring in part and concurring in the judgment.

I agree with the Court that respondents seek a remedy that is legal in nature and that the Seventh Amendment entitles respondents to a jury trial on their duty of fair representation claims. . . . I do not join [Part III-A] of the opinion which reprises the particular historical analysis this Court has employed to determine whether a claim is a "Sui[t] at common law" under the Seventh Amendment, because I believe the historical test can and should be simplified.

The current test, first expounded in *Curtis v. Loether*, requires a court to compare the right at issue to 18th-century English forms of action to determine whether the historically analogous right was vindicated in an action at law or in equity, and to examine whether the remedy sought is legal or equitable in nature. However, this Court, in expounding the test, has repeatedly discounted the significance of the analogous form of action for deciding where the Seventh Amendment applies. I think it is time we dispense with it altogether.[1] I would decide Seventh Amendment questions on the basis of the relief sought. If the relief is legal in nature, *i.e.*, if it is the kind of relief that historically was available from courts of law, I would hold that the parties have a constitutional right to a trial by jury—unless Congress has permissibly delegated the particular dispute to a non-Article III decisionmaker and jury trials would frustrate Congress' purposes in enacting a particular statutory scheme.

I believe that our insistence that the jury trial right hinges in part on a comparison of the substantive right at issue to forms of action used in English courts 200 years ago needlessly convolutes our Seventh Amendment jurisprudence. For the past decade and a half, this Court has explained that the two parts of the historical test are not equal in weight, that the nature of the remedy is more important than the nature of the right. Since the existence of a right to jury trial therefore turns

---

1. I therefore also do not join Part III-A of JUSTICE MARSHALL's opinion because it considers which 18th-century actions are comparable to the modern-day statutory claim brought here.

on the nature of the remedy, absent congressional delegation to a specialized decisionmaker, there remains little purpose to our rattling through dusty attics of ancient writs. The time has come to borrow William of Occam's razor and sever this portion of our analysis. . . .

JUSTICE STEVENS, concurring in part and concurring in the judgment.

Because I believe the Court has made this case unnecessarily difficult by exaggerating the importance of finding a precise common-law analogue to the duty of fair representation, I do not join Part III-A of its opinion. Ironically, by stressing the importance of identifying an exact analogue, the Court has diminished the utility of looking for any analogue. . . .

JUSTICE KENNEDY, with whom JUSTICE O'CONNOR and JUSTICE SCALIA join, dissenting.

This case asks whether the Seventh Amendment guarantees the respondent union members a jury trial in a duty of fair representation action against their labor union. The Court is quite correct, in my view, in its formulation of the initial premises that must govern the case. Under *Curtis v. Loether*, 415 U.S. 189, 194 (1974), the right to a jury trial in a statutory action depends on the presence of "legal rights and remedies." To determine whether rights and remedies in a duty of fair representation action are legal in character, we must compare the action to the 18th-century cases permitted in the law courts of England, and we must examine the nature of the relief sought. I agree also with those Members of the Court who find that the duty of fair representation action resembles an equitable trust action more than a suit for malpractice.

I disagree with the analytic innovation of the Court that identification of the trust action as a model for modern duty of fair representation actions is insufficient to decide the case. The Seventh Amendment requires us to determine whether the duty of fair representation action "is more similar to cases that were tried in courts of law than to suits tried in courts of equity." *Tull v. United States*, 481 U.S. 412, 417 (1987). Having made this decision in favor of an equitable action, our inquiry should end. Because the Court disagrees with this proposition, I dissent. . . .

The Court must adhere to the historical test in determining the right to a jury because the language of the Constitution requires it. The Seventh Amendment "preserves" the right to jury trial in civil cases. We cannot preserve a right existing in 1791 unless we look to history to identify it. Our precedents are in full agreement with this reasoning and insist on adherence to the historical test. No alternatives short of rewriting the Constitution exist. If we abandon the plain language of the Constitution to expand the jury right, we may expect Courts with opposing views to curtail it in the future.

It is true that a historical inquiry into the distinction between law and equity may require us to enter into a domain becoming less familiar with time. Two centuries have passed since the Seventh Amendment's ratification, and the incompleteness of our historical records makes it difficult to know the nature of certain actions in 1791. The historical test, nonetheless, has received more criticism than it deserves. Although our application of the analysis in some cases may seem biased in favor of jury trials, the test has not become a nullity. We do not require juries in all statutory actions. The historical test, in fact, resolves most cases without difficulty.

I would hesitate to abandon or curtail the historical test out of concern for the competence of the Court to understand legal history. We do look to history for the answers to constitutional questions. Although opinions will differ on what this history shows, the approach has no less validity in the Seventh Amendment context than elsewhere.

If Congress has not provided for a jury trial, we are confined to the Seventh Amendment to determine whether one is required. Our own views respecting the wisdom of using a jury should be put aside. Like JUSTICE BRENNAN, I admire the jury process. Other judges have taken the opposite view. See, *e.g.*, J. Frank, Law and the Modern Mind 170-185 (1931). But the judgment of our own times is not always preferable to the lessons of history. Our whole constitutional experience teaches that history must inform the judicial inquiry. Our obligation to the Constitution and its Bill of Rights, no less than the compact we have with the generation that wrote them for us, do not permit us to disregard provisions that some may think to be mere matters of historical form. . . .

NOTES AND QUESTIONS

1. Avoiding the constitutional question.   When, as in *Terry*, a court hears a claim for relief created by federal statute, it may be possible to avoid the Seventh Amendment question by concluding that the statute in question itself provides for the right to a jury trial, or that its legislative history indicates Congress so intended—in which case there is no need to ask whether such a right is constitutionally guaranteed. Was this route available in *Terry*? What if a federal statute expressly provides that there shall be no right to a jury trial for claims brought under its provisions; would a court then likewise be able to avoid the constitutional question?

2. The two-part test.   The *Terry* Court applied a two-part test in deciding whether the Seventh Amendment required a jury trial on the plaintiffs' fair-representation claim. Under the first part of the test, sometimes referred to as the "historical test," a court must determine whether the claimed right has a common law analogue, thus triggering the Seventh Amendment's protections. If so, the Seventh Amendment presumptively applies. The second part of the test requires a court to examine the nature of the remedy being sought and to then determine whether that remedy more closely resembles a legal remedy, such as damages, or an equitable remedy, such as an injunction. If the former, the jury trial right attaches; if the latter, it does not. According to the majority in *Terry*, the second part of the test, *i.e.*, the inquiry into the remedy, is the more important of the two. Why? Is either part of the test susceptible to a bright-line determination?

3. *The historical test.* The so-called historical test—the first prong of the analysis—is purportedly based on the precise language of the Seventh Amendment, which "preserves" the right to a jury trial. Apparently, this particular word choice signifies a constitutional mandate to freeze the scope of the jury trial right to an historically captured meaning. In other words, under this historical approach, the Framers' intent, as reflected in the amendment's language, was to protect the right to a jury trial only insofar as that right was recognized at common law in 1791, neither more nor less. But couldn't we say this of all of the rights found in the text of the Bill of Rights? For example, the First Amendment prohibits Congress from "abridging the freedom of speech." Does this mean that "freedom of speech" is limited to the Framers' perception of that concept? Some would answer this in the affirmative. Others would favor an approach that recognizes constitutional law's evolving nature. Does the absence of the word "preserve" in the other Bill of Rights provisions suggest that they may properly be construed in a more flexible way? You will explore these themes more closely in your Constitutional Law course. *See* CHRISTOPHER N. MAY, ALLAN IDES & SIMONA GROSSI, CONSTITUTIONAL LAW: NATIONAL POWER AND FEDERALISM § 1.6 (7th ed. 2016). In general, why did the dissent argue that the historical test should be the exclusive measure of the Seventh Amendment's scope, and why did Justice Brennan disagree with that approach? Can you see how this debate has broader ramifications for the entire body of constitutional law?

4. *Damages as an equitable remedy.* The plaintiff in *Terry* sought damages for backpay. Damages are most often thought of as a legal remedy. Yet, in applying the remedy half of its Seventh Amendment test, the *Terry* Court did not automatically treat this claim for damages as being legal in nature. Why not? Should a claim for damages always be treated as legal, or only presumptively so? If the latter, under what circumstances will the presumption be rebutted?

5. *State courts and the common law right to a jury trial. Even though they are not bound by the Seventh Amendment,* many states tie their right to a jury trial to the historically perceived scope of that right at common law. For some states, however, the relevant common law is that which existed at the time the state constitution was adopted, rather than 1791. Thus, in California, the scope of the jury trial right is tied to the common law as it existed in 1850. *C & K Engineering Contractors v. Amber Steel Co.*, 587 P.2d 1136, 1139 (Cal. 1978).

PROBLEM

11-3. Several shareholders of Endrun, Inc. ("Endrun"), have filed a shareholders derivative action against Endrun and its board of directors ("the Board"). They claim that the Board breached its fiduciary duty by failing to pursue breach-of-contract and gross-negligence claims against the company's accounting firm. The complaint seeks money damages on the corporation's behalf. Shareholders derivative suits, *i.e.*, suits in which corporate shareholders assert claims on their corporation's behalf, are equitable in origin. This device was unknown at common law. Are the shareholders of Endrun nonetheless entitled to a jury trial on any part of their claim? *See Ross v. Bernhard*, 396 U.S. 531 (1970).

Markman v. Westview Instruments, Inc.
517 U.S. 370 (1996)

JUSTICE SOUTER delivered the opinion for a unanimous Court.

The question here is whether the interpretation of a so-called patent claim, the portion of the patent document that defines the scope of the patentee's rights, is a matter of law reserved entirely for the court, or subject to a Seventh Amendment guarantee that a jury will determine the meaning of any disputed term of art about which expert testimony is offered. We hold that the construction of a patent, including terms of art within its claim, is exclusively within the province of the court.

I . . .

Petitioner in this infringement suit, Markman, owns United States Reissue Patent No. 33,054 for his "Inventory Control and Reporting System for Drycleaning Stores." The patent describes a system that can monitor and report the status, location, and movement of clothing in a dry-cleaning establishment. The Markman system consists of a keyboard and data processor to generate written records for each transaction, including a bar code readable by optical detectors operated by employees, who log the progress of clothing through the dry-cleaning process. Respondent Westview's product also includes a keyboard and processor, and it lists charges for the dry-cleaning services on bar-coded tickets that can be read by portable optical detectors.

Markman brought an infringement suit against Westview and Althon Enterprises, an operator of dry-cleaning establishments using Westview's products (collectively, Westview). Westview responded that Markman's patent is not infringed by its system because the latter functions merely to record an inventory of receivables by tracking invoices and transaction totals, rather than to record and track an inventory of articles of clothing. Part of the dispute hinged upon the meaning of the word "inventory," a term found in Markman's independent claim 1, which states that Markman's product can "maintain an inventory total" and "detect and localize spurious additions to inventory." The case was tried before a jury, which heard, among others, a witness produced by Markman who testified about the meaning of the claim language.

After the jury compared the patent to Westview's device, it found an infringement of Markman's independent claim 1. . . . The District Court nevertheless granted Westview's deferred motion for judgment as a matter of law, one of its reasons being that the term "inventory" in Markman's patent encompasses "both cash inventory and the actual physical inventory of articles of clothing." Under the trial court's construction of the patent, the production, sale, or use of a tracking system for dry cleaners would not infringe Markman's patent unless the product was capable of tracking articles of clothing throughout the cleaning process and generating reports about their status and location. Since Westview's system cannot do these things, the District Court directed a verdict* on the ground that Westview's device does not have the "means to maintain an inventory total" and thus cannot " 'detect and localize spurious additions to inventory as well as spurious deletions therefrom,'" as required by claim 1.

Markman appealed, arguing it was error for the District Court to substitute its construction of the disputed claim term 'inventory' for the construction the jury had presumably given it. The United States Court of Appeals for the Federal Circuit affirmed, holding the interpretation of claim terms to be the exclusive province of the court and the Seventh Amendment to be consistent with that conclusion. Markman sought our review on each point, and we granted certiorari. We now affirm.

II

The Seventh Amendment provides that "[i]n Suits at common law, where the value in controversy shall exceed twenty dollars, the right of trial by jury shall be preserved. . . ." Since Justice Story's day, *United States v. Wonson*, 28 F. Cas. 745, 750 (No. 16,750) (CC Mass. 1812), we have understood that "[t]he right of trial by jury thus preserved is the right which existed under the English common law when the Amendment was adopted." *Baltimore & Carolina Line, Inc. v. Redman*, 295 U.S. 654, 657 (1935). In keeping with our longstanding adherence to this "historical test," we ask, first, whether we are dealing with a cause of action that either was tried at law at the time of the founding or is at least analogous to one that was, see, e.g., *Tull v. United States*, 481 U.S. 412, 417 (1987). If the action in question belongs in the law category, we then ask whether the particular trial decision must fall to the jury in order to preserve the substance of the common-law right as it existed in 1791.

A

As to the first issue, going to the character of the cause of action, "[t]he form of our analysis is familiar. 'First we compare the statutory action to 18th-century actions brought in the courts of England prior to the merger of the courts of law

---

* [A federal court may enter a directed verdict (today, a judgment as a matter of law) under Rule 50, "if under the governing law, there can be but one reasonable conclusion as to the verdict. If reasonable minds could differ as to the import of the evidence, however, a verdict should not be directed." *Anderson v. Liberty Lobby, Inc.*, 477 U.S. 242, 250-251 (1986). — EDS.]

and equity.'" *Granfinanciera, S.A. v. Nordberg*, 492 U.S. 33, 42 (1989). Equally familiar is the descent of today's patent infringement action from the infringement actions tried at law in the 18th century, and there is no dispute that infringement cases today must be tried to a jury, as their predecessors were more than two centuries ago.

B

This conclusion raises the second question, whether a particular issue occurring within a jury trial (here the construction of a patent claim) is itself necessarily a jury issue, the guarantee being essential to preserve the right to a jury's resolution of the ultimate dispute. In some instances the answer to this second question may be easy because of clear historical evidence that the very subsidiary question was so regarded under the English practice of leaving the issue for a jury. But when, as here, the old practice provides no clear answer, we are forced to make a judgment about the scope of the Seventh Amendment guarantee without the benefit of any foolproof test.

The Court has repeatedly said that the answer to the second question "must depend on whether the jury must shoulder this responsibility *as necessary to preserve the 'substance of the common-law right of trial by jury.'*" *Tull v. United States, supra*, at 426 (emphasis added). "Only those incidents which are regarded as fundamental, as inherent in and of the essence of the system of trial by jury, are placed beyond the reach of the legislature." *Id.*

The "substance of the common-law right" is, however, a pretty blunt instrument for drawing distinctions. We have tried to sharpen it, to be sure, by reference to the distinction between substance and procedure. We have also spoken of the line as one between issues of fact and law.

But the sounder course, when available, is to classify a mongrel practice (like construing a term of art following receipt of evidence) by using the historical method, much as we do in characterizing the suits and actions within which they arise. Where there is no exact antecedent, the best hope lies in comparing the modern practice to earlier ones whose allocation to court or jury we do know, seeking the best analogy we can draw between an old and the new.

C

"Prior to 1790 nothing in the nature of a claim had appeared either in British patent practice or in that of the American states," Lutz, Evolution of the Claims of U.S. Patents, 20 J. Pat. Off. Soc. 134 (1938), and we have accordingly found no direct antecedent of modern claim construction in the historical sources. Claim practice did not achieve statutory recognition until the passage of the Act of July 4, 1836, and inclusion of a claim did not become a statutory requirement until 1870, Act of July 8, 1870; see 1 A. Deller, Patent Claims § 4, p. 9 (2d ed. 1971). Although, as one historian has observed, as early as 1850 "judges were . . . beginning to express more frequently the idea that in seeking to ascertain the invention 'claimed' in a patent the inquiry should be limited to interpreting the summary, or 'claim,'" Lutz, *supra*, at 145, "[t]he idea that the claim is just as important if not more important than the description and drawings did not develop until the Act of 1870 or thereabouts." Deller, *supra*, § 4, at 9.

At the time relevant for Seventh Amendment analogies, in contrast, it was the specification, itself a relatively new development, that represented the key to the patent. Thus, patent litigation in that early period was typified by so-called novelty actions, testing whether "any essential part of [the patent had been] disclosed to the public before," *Huddart v. Grimshaw*, Dav. Pat. Cas. 265, 298 (K.B. 1803), and "enablement" cases, in which juries were asked to determine whether the specification described the invention well enough to allow members of the appropriate trade to reproduce it, see, *e.g.*, *Arkwright v. Nightingale*, Dav. Pat. Cas. 37, 60 (C.P. 1785).

The closest 18th-century analogue of modern claim construction seems, then, to have been the construction of specifications, and as to that function the mere smattering of patent cases that we have from this period shows no established jury practice sufficient to support an argument by analogy that today's construction of a claim should be a guaranteed jury issue. . . .

D

Losing, then, on the contention that juries generally had interpretive responsibilities during the 18th century, Markman seeks a different anchor for analogy in the more modest contention that even if judges were charged with construing most terms in the patent, the art of defining terms of art employed in a specification fell within the province of the jury. Again, however, Markman has no authority from the period in question, but relies instead on the later case of *Neilson v. Harford*, Webs. Pat. Cas. 328 (Exch. 1841). There, an exchange between the judge and the lawyers indicated that although the construction of a patent was ordinarily for the court, *id.*, at 349 (Alderson, B.), judges should "leav[e] the question of words of art to the jury," *id.*, at 350 (Alderson, B.). Without, however, in any way disparaging the weight to which Baron Alderson's view is entitled, the most we can say is that an English report more than 70 years after the time that concerns us indicates an exception to what probably had been occurring earlier. In place of Markman's inference that this exceptional practice existed in 1791 there is at best only a possibility that it did, and for anything more than a possibility we have found no scholarly authority.

III

Since evidence of common-law practice at the time of the framing does not entail application of the Seventh Amendment's jury guarantee to the construction of the claim document, we must look elsewhere to characterize this determination of meaning in order to allocate it as between court or jury. We accordingly consult existing precedent and consider both the relative interpretive skills of judges and juries and the statutory policies that ought to be furthered by the allocation.

A

The two elements of a simple patent case, construing the patent and determining whether infringement occurred, were characterized by the former patent practitioner, Justice Curtis. "The first is a question of law, to be determined by the court, construing the letters-patent, and the description of the invention and specification of claim annexed to them. The second is a question of fact, to be submitted to a jury." *Winans v. Denmead*, [15 How. 330, 338 (1854)].

In arguing for a different allocation of responsibility for the first question, Markman relies primarily on two cases, *Bischoff v. Wethered*, 9 Wall. 812 (1870), and *Tucker v. Spalding*, 13 Wall. 453 (1872). These are said to show that evidence of the meaning of patent terms was offered to 19th-century juries, and thus to imply that the meaning of a documentary term was a jury issue whenever it was subject to evidentiary proof. That is not what Markman's cases show, however. . . .

[After discussing the two cases, the Court concluded that] neither *Bischoff* nor *Tucker* indicates that juries resolved the meaning of terms of art in construing a patent, and neither case undercuts Justice Curtis's authority.

B

Where history and precedent provide no clear answers, functional considerations also play their part in the choice between judge and jury to define terms of art. We said in *Miller v. Fenton*, 474 U.S. 104, 114 (1985), that when an issue "falls somewhere between a pristine legal standard and a simple historical fact, the fact/law distinction at times has turned on a determination that, as a matter of the sound administration of justice, one judicial actor is better positioned than another to decide the issue in question." So it turns out here, for judges, not juries, are the better suited to find the acquired meaning of patent terms.

The construction of written instruments is one of those things that judges often do and are likely to do better than jurors unburdened by training in exegesis. Patent construction in particular "is a special occupation, requiring, like all others, special training and practice. The judge, from his training and discipline, is more likely to give a proper interpretation to such instruments than a jury; and he is, therefore, more likely to be right, in performing such a duty, than a jury can be expected to be." *Parker v. Hulme*, [18 F. Cas. 1138, 1140 (No. 10, 740) (CC E.D. Pa. 1849)]. Such was the understanding nearly a century and a half ago, and there is no reason to weigh the respective strengths of judge and jury differently in relation to the modern claim; quite the contrary, for "the claims of patents have become highly technical in many respects as the result of special doctrines relating to the proper form and scope of claims that have been developed by the courts and the Patent Office." Woodward, Definiteness and Particularity in Patent Claims, 46 Mich. L. Rev. 755, 765 (1948).

Markman would trump these considerations with his argument that a jury should decide a question of meaning peculiar to a trade or profession simply because the question is a subject of testimony requiring credibility determinations, which are the jury's forte. It is, of course, true that credibility judgments have to be made about the experts who testify in patent cases, and in theory there could be a case in which a simple credibility judgment would suffice to choose between experts whose testimony was equally consistent with a patent's internal logic. But our own experience with document construction leaves us doubtful that trial courts will run into many cases like that. In the main, we expect, any credibility determinations will be subsumed within the necessarily sophisticated analysis of the whole document, required by the standard construction rule that a term can be defined only in a way that comports with the instrument as a whole. Thus, in these cases a jury's capabilities to evaluate demeanor, to sense the "main-springs of human conduct," or to reflect community standards, are much less significant than a trained ability to evaluate the testimony in relation to the overall structure of the patent. The decisionmaker vested with the task of construing the patent is in the better position to ascertain whether an expert's proposed definition fully comports with the specification and claims and so will preserve the patent's internal coherence. We accordingly think there is sufficient reason to treat construction of terms of art like many other responsibilities that we cede to a judge in the normal course of trial, notwithstanding its evidentiary underpinnings.

C

Finally, we see the importance of uniformity in the treatment of a given patent as an independent reason to allocate all issues of construction to the court. As we noted in *General Elec. Co. v. Wabash Appliance Corp.*, 304 U.S. 364, 369 (1938), "[t]he limits of a patent must be known for the protection of the patentee, the encouragement of the inventive genius of others and the assurance that the subject of the patent will be dedicated ultimately to the public." Otherwise, a "zone of uncertainty which enterprise and experimentation may enter only at the risk of infringement claims would discourage invention only a little less than unequivocal foreclosure of the field," *United Carbon Co. v. Binney & Smith Co.*, 317 U.S. 228, 236 (1942), and "[t]he public [would] be deprived of rights supposed to belong to it, without being clearly told what it is that limits these rights." *Merrill v. Yeomans*, 94 U.S. 568, 573 (1877). It was just for the sake of such desirable uniformity that Congress created the Court of Appeals for the Federal Circuit as an exclusive appellate court for patent cases, H.R. Rep. No. 97-312, pp. 20-23 (1981), observing that increased uniformity would "strengthen the United States patent system in such a way as to foster technological growth and industrial innovation." *Id.*, at 20.

Uniformity would, however, be ill served by submitting issues of document construction to juries. Making them jury issues would not, to be sure, necessarily leave evidentiary questions of meaning wide open in every new court in which a patent might be litigated, for principles of issue preclusion would ordinarily foster uniformity. But whereas issue preclusion could not be asserted against new and independent infringement defendants even within a given jurisdiction, treating interpretive issues as purely legal will promote (though it will not guarantee) intra-jurisdictional certainty through the application of *stare decisis* on those questions not yet subject to interjurisdictional uniformity under the authority of the single appeals court.

* * *

Accordingly, we hold that the interpretation of the word "inventory" in this case is an issue for the judge, not the jury, and affirm the decision of the Court of Appeals for the Federal Circuit.

It is so ordered.

NOTES AND QUESTIONS

1. *A functional approach.*   Did the *Markman* Court abandon the approach adopted and applied by the Court in *Terry*? Or is the approach followed in *Markman* an alternative to *Terry*? If so, when does that alternative apply, and what is the content or method of that alternative?

2. *Uniformity.*   How did the desire for uniformity of treatment shape the Court's decision in this case? If the owner of a patent brings an infringement action and wins, can the owner then use that decision to bind another defendant in a subsequent suit with respect to the first court's finding as to the scope of the patentee's rights? Has the defendant in the second action yet had her day in court? Would allowing the patent owner to invoke so-called issue preclusion or collateral estoppel against the defendant in the second suit violate the latter's right to due process of law? *See* Chapter XIII, at part B.4, *infra*. The Court in Part III.C of its opinion thus notes that "issue preclusion could not be asserted against new and independent infringement defendants. . . ." That being so, how does this support the Court's conclusion that such issues are better resolved by a judge than by a jury, even though the judges in the two cases are unlikely to be the same?

PROBLEM

11-4. DMD, a property developer, sued the City of Monterey under 42 U.S.C. § 1983 after the city rejected five of DMD's applications to develop a parcel of land within the city. With each application, the city imposed increasingly more rigorous requirements on the developer. DMD claimed that the city's action amounted to a "regulatory taking" of property in violation of the Fifth Amendment's Takings Clause and sought just compensation for the taking. Section 1983, on which DMD relied, was enacted after the Civil War to create a cause of action to redress the violation of constitutional rights by persons, including municipalities, acting under color of state law. Should the judge or the jury decide the question of whether the city's action amounted to a regulatory taking? Is it relevant that § 1983 suits are generally deemed "constitutional" torts? Is it also relevant that a landowner has no right to a jury trial in direct condemnation proceedings since there was no such right at common law? *See City of Monterey v. Del Monte Dunes at Monterey, Ltd.*, 526 U.S. 687 (1999).

A NOTE ON THE COMPOSITION OF JURIES

At common law, the standard jury comprised 12 male landowners from the county in which the trial was to take place. Neither women, nor men without property, were permitted to serve on juries. In the earliest cases, the jurors were expected to be familiar with the parties and even with the incident giving rise to the suit. The jurors were, in essence, witnesses. *See* ELLEN E. SWARD, THE DECLINE OF THE CIVIL JURY 76-78 (2001) (hereinafter "SWARD, DECLINE"). Today, however, the ideal juror is drawn from a broad cross section of the adult population and is expected to be an unbiased observer of the trial, having neither any connection with the parties nor any specialized knowledge of the underlying controversy. *See, e.g.*, 28 U.S.C. § 1861 (2006) (requiring jurors to be "selected at random from a fair cross section of the community"); CAL. CIV. PROC. CODE § 197(a) (requiring jurors to be "selected at random, from a source or sources inclusive of a representative cross section of the population of the area served by the court"). Of course, a complete absence of knowledge is sometimes impossible in cases that have received substantial pretrial publicity. Nonetheless, all jurors are expected to approach a case free from any preconceived notions about the appropriate outcome and free from any special information about the parties or the controversy.

In general, in both state and federal courts, all U.S. citizens over the age of 18 are presumed eligible to serve on a jury. Exceptions might include persons with a mental or physical incapacity; persons without the ability to read, write, speak, or understand English; persons convicted of a felony; persons holding certain federal, state, and local public offices, including those pertaining to police and fire safety; and active members of the U.S. armed forces. *See, e.g.*, 28 U.S.C. §§ 1863(b)(6), 1865(b). The jurors for a particular case are then drawn from a pool of the eligible adults living within the relevant community. Thus a federal district court sitting in Los Angeles, California, *i.e.*, within the Central District of California, draws its jurors from the Western Division of that district, which comprises the counties of Los Angeles, Ventura, Santa Barbara, and San Luis Obispo, a relatively large, diverse, and populous region. *See* Central District of California, General Order No. 13-13 (10/25/13). On the other hand, a state superior court located in downtown Los Angeles, a few blocks from the federal courthouse, draws its jurors from a much smaller geographic region, namely, a 20-mile radius of the courthouse. Can you see how the potential difference in jury demographics might play a role in the choice between a federal and a state forum?

The process of selecting jurors begins with the compilation of a master list (sometimes referred to as a "master jury wheel") comprising all adults eligible for jury service within the relevant geographic community. In practice, each judicial district or division keeps its own master list. Such lists are typically based on public records such as voter registration, department of motor vehicle records, tax rolls, and the like. The range of sources on which states draw varies considerably. *Compare* CAL. CIV. PROC. CODE § 197(b) (relying exclusively on department of motor vehicle lists of licensed drivers and identification card holders), *with* 42 PA.

Cons. Stat. Ann. §§ 4521-4521.1 (relying on driver's license lists, voter registration lists, telephone directories, city directories, state taxpayer lists, school census lists, and lists of welfare and food stamp recipients). Next, from time to time individuals randomly selected from the master list are notified of their obligation to report for jury duty at a specified court on a specified day. On the given dates, the summoned jurors wait to be called to various courtrooms for their potential assignments to cases about to go to trial.

At this point, the process of selection shifts to the specific case for which the jurors are to be impaneled. Prospective jurors may be asked in advance to complete a detailed questionnaire. The judge informs the potential jurors as to the nature of the proceeding and introduces the parties and their attorneys. Each prospective juror is then asked a series of questions designed to elicit whether there is any reason not to allow that individual to sit as a juror in the pending case. This process is called "voir dire," *i.e.*, to see what they say. In some jurisdictions, the lawyers perform the voir dire in the presence of the court, while in others the judge asks the questions, some of which the lawyers may have submitted. *Compare* Fed. R. Civ. P. 47(a) (permitting voir dire by court or parties at the option of the court), *with* Cal. Civ. Proc. Code § 222.5 (allowing both court and counsel to question prospective jurors).

If the answers elicited from a prospective juror indicate a basis for disqualification (*e.g.*, prejudice against one of the parties, special knowledge of the case, etc.), either side may challenge that juror *for cause*. It is, however, within the court's discretion to determine whether good cause has been shown. In addition, each side is also granted a specific number of *peremptory* challenges, *i.e.*, challenges that may be exercised without any need for justification or court approval. That number varies from jurisdiction to jurisdiction. *See, e.g.*, 28 U.S.C. § 1870 (allowing three peremptories); Cal. Civ. Proc. Code § 231(c) (allowing six peremptories). Despite their open-ended nature, peremptory challenges may never be made on the basis of race or gender. Although proof of such bias may be difficult to establish, *see, e.g., Edmonson v. Leesville Concrete Co.*, 500 U.S. 614 (1991) (regarding race-based peremptory challenge); *J.E.B. v. Alabama*, 511 U.S. 127 (1994) (regarding gender-based peremptory challenge), the Supreme Court has made it clear that the requisite showing is not an impossibility. *See Snyder v. Louisiana*, 552 U.S. 472 (2008) (finding racial discrimination by prosecution in selecting jury in a first-degree murder case). *And see SmithKline Beecham Corp. v. Abbott Labs.*, 740 F.3d 471, 474 (9th Cir. 2013) ("We . . . hold that equal protection prohibits peremptory strikes based on sexual orientation and remand for a new trial."); Cal. Civ. Proc. Code § 231.5 (peremptory challenges cannot be based on "an assumption that the prospective juror is biased merely because of his or her race, color, religion, sex, national origin, sexual orientation, or similar grounds").

The selection process continues until a sufficient number of jurors have been selected. While the standard 12-person jury remains the norm in many jurisdictions, *see, e.g.*, Cal. Civ. Proc. Code § 220 (stating that a jury shall "consist of 12 or any number less than 12, upon which the parties may agree"), the Supreme Court has permitted federal courts, without the parties' consent, to use juries as small as six persons—*see Colgrove v. Battin*, 413 U.S. 149 (1973) (upholding district court local rule providing for six-person jury); *see also* FED. R. CIV. P. 48(a)—and even smaller if the parties agree. FED. R. CIV. P. 48(b). Some state constitutions permit a similar judicially imposed diminution in jury size. *See, e.g.*, FLA. CONST. art. I, § 22 (minimum six-person jury); N.D. CONST. art. I, § 13 (same); OKLA. CONST. art. II, § 19 (six-person jury for cases in which $10,000 or less is in controversy, and allowing parties to agree to a lesser number).

Since the federal Constitution does not protect the right to a jury trial in state court, it does not require that jury verdicts in state court proceedings be unanimous. As a consequence, some states allow less-than-unanimous jury verdicts without the parties' consent. *See, e.g.*, HAW. CONST. art. I, § 13 (legislature may provide for as low as a three-fourths majority); N.Y. CONST. art. I, § 2 (legislature may provide for as low as a five-sixths majority); OKLA. CONST. art. II, § 19 (requiring only three-fourths majority). In federal court, however, the requirement of juror unanimity remains the exclusive standard unless the parties otherwise stipulate. FED. R. CIV. P. 48(b).

A NOTE ON THE ONGOING DEBATE OVER THE JURY SYSTEM

Our reliance on the jury system is not without controversy. Perhaps the most famous of its critics was the late Judge Jerome Frank who described the jury system as "the quintessence of governmental arbitrariness." JEROME FRANK, COURTS ON TRIAL: MYTH AND REALITY IN AMERICAN JUSTICE 132 (1949) (hereinafter "FRANK, COURTS ON TRIAL"). Frank saw jurors as poorly trained fact-finders and as potentially lawless representatives of the government, essentially empowered to impose their will in an unaccountable fashion. *Id.* at 126-140. He recognized the argument that jurors could soften the otherwise hard edges of the law by ignoring legal principles they thought unjust or unreasonable but observed that "as a rational defense of the jury system, it is surely curious. It asserts that, desirably, each jury is a twelve-man ephemeral legislature, not elected by the voters, but empowered to destroy what the elected legislators have enacted or authorized." *Id.* at 129-130.

On the other hand, others argue with empirical support that jurors are at least as competent as judges at making fact determinations and that juries perform an important social function by importing community values into the sometimes rigid civil justice system. SWARD, DECLINE, *supra*, AT 23-65. These defenders of the jury system also note that jury duty is one of the few places in which the average citizen actually participates in the government process. The literature on this ongoing debate is voluminous. For a small sampling, aside from the above, see REPORT FROM AN AMERICAN BAR ASSOCIATION/BROOKINGS SYMPOSIUM, CHARTING A FUTURE FOR THE CIVIL JURY SYSTEM (1992); VALERIE P. HANS & NEIL VIDMAR, JUDGING THE JURY (1986); HARRY KALVEN, JR. & HANS ZEISEL, THE AMERICAN JURY (1966); Warren E. Burger, *Thinking the Unthinkable*, 31 LOY. L. REV. 205 (1985); Kevin M. Clermont & Theodore Eisenberg, *Trial by Jury or Judge: Transcending Empiricism*, 77 CORNELL L. REV. 1124 (1992); Peter Huber,

Junk Science and the Jury, 1990 U. CHI. LEGAL FORUM 273; *Development in the Law: The Civil Jury*, 110 HARV. L. REV. 1408 (1997).

While some judges and legal scholars may continue to question the jury system's value and/or reliability, many lawyers remain firmly convinced that it serves a valuable function. In 2014, more than two-thirds of the civil cases that went to trial in the federal courts were tried to a jury—a figure that was fairly constant during the prior decade and a half. *See* ADMIN. OFFICE OF THE U.S. COURTS, JUDICIAL BUSINESS OF THE UNITED STATES COURTS, 2000-2014, tbl. C-4. Yet these figures are a bit misleading, for the number of civil cases that went to trial in the federal courts fell by more than 40 percent during this period (from 5,030 civil trials in 2000 to fewer than 3,000 in 2014). *Id.* This dramatic decline in part reflects a steadily increasing use of binding arbitration clauses in employment and consumer contracts. Thus, while the Seventh Amendment protects the right to a jury trial, it—like the right to a trial itself—can be waived. As a result, the number of jury trials in federal civil cases has been declining and is likely to continue to decline.

C.   Jury Instructions and Verdicts

After the parties have completed their presentation of the evidence, and usually after closing arguments, the court instructs or "charges" the jury as to the law to apply in deciding the case. These instructions are meant to guide the jury to the issues that it must decide and to provide it with the legal standards for resolving those issues. For example, the charge in a simple negligence case brought by Doris Daghighian against Carol Crute might include the following instructions:

> A party must persuade you, by the evidence presented in court, that what he or she is required to prove is more likely to be true than not true. This is referred to as "the burden of proof."
>
> After weighing all of the evidence, if you cannot decide that something is more likely to be true than not true, you must conclude that the party did not prove it. You should consider all the evidence, no matter which party produced the evidence.
>
> In criminal trials, the prosecution must prove the defendant's guilt beyond a reasonable doubt. But in civil trials, such as this one, the party who is required to prove something need prove only that it is more likely to be true than not true.
>
> Negligence is the failure to use reasonable care to prevent harm to oneself or to others.
>
> A person is negligent if he or she does something that a reasonably careful person would not do in the same situation.
>
> Ms. Daghighian claims that she was harmed by Ms. Crute's negligence. To establish this claim, Ms. Daghighian must prove all of the following:
>
> 1.   That Ms. Crute was negligent;
> 2.   That Ms. Daghighian was harmed; and
> 3.   That Ms. Crute's negligence was a substantial factor in causing Ms. Daghighian's harm.

A person can be negligent by acting or by failing to act. A person is negligent if he or she does something that a reasonably careful person would not do in the same situation or fails to do something that a reasonably careful person would do in the same situation.

You must decide how a reasonably careful person would have acted in Ms. Crute's situation.

JUDICIAL COUNCIL OF CAL., CIVIL JURY INSTRUCTIONS, Nos. 200, 400, 401 (2015). Of course, the actual instructions would likely be more detailed and much longer, defining causation, addressing affirmative defenses, and instructing on any other legal issues the jury must resolve or consider.

While it is the judge's duty to instruct the jury, typically the parties first submit proposed instructions to the court, which the court may or may not use. The instructions may be specially drafted by the parties or, as is more often the case, premised on *pattern jury instructions* provided in form books or recommended by the court in which the suit is pending. For example, the instructions quoted above were taken from forms developed by the Los Angeles County Superior Court and are widely used throughout the State of California. Prior to closing arguments, the judge informs counsel of the instructions she intends to give, and counsel prepare their respective closing statements with those instructions in mind.

In giving the instructions, judges in many jurisdictions, including federal courts, may comment on the evidence. *But see* MISS. CODE ANN. § 11-7-155 ("The judge in any civil cause shall not sum up or comment on the testimony, or charge the jury as to the weight of evidence."); WASH. CONST. art. 4, § 16 ("Judges shall not charge juries with respect to matters of fact, nor comment thereon, but shall declare the law."). In so commenting when permitted to do so, however, the judge may not become an advocate for either side but must limit her commentary to a description of the evidence presented and should inform the jury that it is free to disagree with her description of the evidence.

Any objections to the judge's instructions or commentary must be made before the jury retires to deliberate. A failure to do so amounts to a waiver of that objection except in the most egregious circumstances. In most jurisdictions, the trial court is given broad discretion to determine the content of its instructions, but an error of law contained in an instruction can lead to the reversal of a verdict if the error is deemed prejudicial. Read Rule 51 ("Instructions to the Jury; Objections; Preserving a Claim of Error"). *See generally* Thomas D. Rowe, Jr., *Instructions to the Jury; Objections; Preserving a Claim of Error, in* 9 MOORE'S FEDERAL PRACTICE §§ 51.01 *et seq.* (3d ed. 2015).

A question of some importance is whether jurors actually understand the instructions given to them. A number of studies have suggested a negative answer. *See, e.g.,* ROBERT G. NIELAND, PATTERN JURY INSTRUCTIONS: A CRITICAL LOOK AT A MODERN MOVEMENT TO IMPROVE THE JURY SYSTEM (1979); Robert P. Charrow & Veda R. Charrow, *Making Legal Language Understandable: A Psycholinguistic Study of Jury Instructions,* 79 COLUM. L. REV. 1306 (1979); William W. Schwarzer, *Communicating with Juries: Problems and Remedies,* 69 CAL. L. REV. 731 (1981). One of the primary problems with jury instructions is that they tend to be premised on language excised from legislation or judicial decisions rather than being written in terms readily comprehensible to someone untrained in the law. There is, as a consequence, a move today to translate jury instructions into language that a typical lay juror is more likely to understand. *See* PETER M. TIERSMA, COMMUNICATING WITH JURIES: HOW TO DRAFT MORE UNDERSTANDABLE JURY INSTRUCTIONS (2006).

Mitchell v. Gonzales

819 P.2d 872 (Cal. 1991)

LUCAS, C.J.—In this case we decide whether BAJI [Book of Approved Jury Instructions] No. 3.75, the so-called proximate cause instruction, which contains a "but for" test of cause in fact, should continue to be given in this state, or whether it should be disapproved in favor of BAJI No. 3.76, the so-called legal cause instruction, which employs the "substantial factor" test of cause in fact.[2]

Plaintiffs James and Joyce Mitchell, the parents of 12-year-old Damechie Mitchell, who drowned in Lake Gregory on July 4, 1985, sued defendants Jose L. Gonzales, Matilde Gonzales, and Mrs. Gonzales's son Luis (hereafter defendants) for damages, claiming defendants' negligence caused Damechie's death. By special verdict, the jury found that defendants were negligent, i.e., they had breached a duty, but that the negligence was not a proximate cause of the death.

BAJI No. 3.76, requested by plaintiffs and refused by the trial court, provides: "A legal cause of [injury] . . . is a cause which is a substantial factor in bringing about the [injury]. . . ."

The Court of Appeal concluded that, under the facts, the trial court erred when it denied plaintiffs' request to instruct the jury pursuant to BAJI No. 3.76 and instead instructed under BAJI No. 3.75. After reviewing both instructions, the Court of Appeal concluded that BAJI No. 3.75 is potentially misleading and should not have been given, and that the trial court committed prejudicial error when it refused to give BAJI No. 3.76.

. . . We conclude that the Court of Appeal was correct and that BAJI No. 3.75 should be disapproved.

I. Facts

[Damechie Mitchell was 12 years old and relatively small. He weighed approximately 90 pounds and could not swim. His friend Luis Gonzales was two years older and outweighed Damechie by 100 pounds. The Gonzales family invited Damechie to accompany them to Lake Gregory in the San Bernardino Mountains for the Fourth of July. Damechie's mother testified that she informed

---

2. BAJI No. 3.75, requested by defendants and given by the trial court, provides: "A proximate cause of [injury] . . . is a cause which, in natural and continuous sequence, produces the [injury] . . . and without which the [injury] . . . would not have occurred." Because of the "without which" language, courts often refer to this instruction as the "but for" instruction of causation.

Mrs. Gonzales that Damechie could not swim, and agreed to allow Damechie to go on the trip only on condition that he be restricted to the edge of the lake. Mrs. Gonzales denied that Mrs. Mitchell told her that Damechie could not swim. At the lake, Damechie, Luis, and a third companion, Yoshi, rented a paddleboard and after lunch the trio paddled across the lake and into deep water. Neither Mr. nor Mrs. Gonzales was aware of this excursion. When the boys began their return trip, Luis stayed in the water pushing the paddleboard while Damechie and Yoshi rode on the board. As they crossed the lake Damechie told Luis he could not swim and Luis promised to help him if he fell off the board. Eventually, Luis tired of pushing and tried to get on the paddleboard. Either as a result of this maneuver or as a result of horseplay related to his effort to climb aboard, the paddleboard tipped over and Damechie fell into the water. Luis testified that Damechie was very scared while the board was rocking and that Damechie asked Luis not to rock the board because he did not want to fall off. Additionally, Luis admitted that at the time, he was being very rowdy and that when he tipped the board, he and Damechie fell off. Damechie struggled to grab on to Luis, but Luis, fearing that he would be pulled under, pushed Damechie away. Damechie's body was not recovered for several days.]

The jury, by special verdict, concluded that defendants were negligent but that the negligence was not a cause of the death. The jury therefore did not reach a special verdict on comparative negligence. . . .

II.   *Discussion*

As explained below, we conclude the Court of Appeal correctly determined that the trial court prejudicially erred when it refused BAJI No. 3.76 and instead gave BAJI No. 3.75. . . .

A.   **Alleged Instructional Error**

As Dean Prosser observed over 40 years ago, "Proximate cause remains a tangle and a jungle, a palace of mirrors and a maze. . . ." Cases "indicate that 'proximate cause' covers a multitude of sins, that it is a complex term of highly uncertain meaning under which other rules, doctrines and reasons lie buried. . . ." (Prosser, *Proximate Cause in California* (1950) 38 Cal. L. Rev. 369, 375.)

One of the concepts included in the term proximate cause is cause in fact, also referred to as actual cause. Indeed, for purposes of BAJI No. 3.75, "so far as a jury is concerned 'proximate cause' *only* relates to causation in fact." (Com. to BAJI No. 3.75, italics added.) "There are two widely recognized tests for establishing cause in fact. The 'but for' or 'sine qua non' rule, unfortunately labeled 'proximate cause' in BAJI No. 3.75, asks whether the injury would not have occurred but for the defendant's conduct. The other test, labeled 'legal cause' in BAJI No. 3.76, asks whether the defendant's conduct was a substantial factor in bringing about the injury." (*Maupin v. Widling* (1987) 192 Cal. App. 3d 568, 574.) . . .

BAJI Nos. 3.75 and 3.76 are *alternative* instructions that should not jointly be given in a single lawsuit. . . . This case presents the issue of whether BAJI 3.75 should be given in *any* negligence action.

Criticism of the term "proximate cause" has been extensive. Justice Traynor once observed, "In all probability the general expectation is the reasonable one that in time courts will dispel the mists that have settled on the doctrine of proximate cause in the field of negligence." (*Mosley v. Arden Farms Co.* (1945) 26 Cal. 2d 213, 222 (conc. opn. of Traynor, J.).) Similarly, while serving on the Court of Appeal, Justice Tobriner commented, "The concept of proximate causation has given courts and commentators consummate difficulty and has in truth defied precise definition." (*State Comp. Ins. Fund v. Ind. Acc. Com.* (1959) 176 Cal. App. 2d 10, 20.)

Nor did Prosser and Keeton hide their dislike for the term: "The word 'proximate' is a legacy of Lord Chancellor Bacon, who in his time committed other sins. The word means nothing more than near or immediate; and when it was first taken up by the courts it had connotations of proximity in time and space which have long since disappeared. It is an unfortunate word, which places an entirely wrong emphasis upon the factor of physical or mechanical closeness." (Prosser & Keeton on Torts, *supra,* § 42, at p. 273, fn. omitted.)

It is reasonably likely that when jurors hear the term "proximate cause" they may misunderstand its meaning or improperly limit their discussion of what constitutes a cause in fact. Prosser and Keeton's concern that the word "proximate" improperly imputes a spatial or temporal connotation is well founded. Webster's Third New International Dictionary (1981) page 1828, defines proximate as "very near," "next," "immediately preceding or following." Yet, "[p]roximity in point of time or space is no part of the definition [of proximate cause] . . . except as it may afford evidence for or against proximity of causation." (*Osborn v. City of Whittier* (1951) 103 Cal. App. 2d 609, 616.)

Given the foregoing criticism, it is not surprising that a jury instruction incorporating the term "proximate cause" would come under attack from courts, litigants, and commentators. In considering a predecessor to BAJI No. 3.75 that included language almost identical to the current instruction, Prosser observed, "There are probably few judges who would undertake to say just what this means, and fewer still who would expect it to mean anything whatever to a jury. The first sentence was lifted by a California opinion long since from *Shearman and Redfield on Negligence,* a text written for lawyers and not expected to be comprehensible to laymen, and none too good a text at that." (Prosser, *Proximate Cause in California, supra,* 38 Cal. L. Rev. 369, 424, fn. omitted.)

The misunderstanding engendered by the term "proximate cause" has been documented. In a scholarly study of 14 jury instructions, BAJI No. 3.75 produced proportionally the most misunderstanding among laypersons. (Charrow, *Making Legal Language Understandable: A Psycholinguistic Study of Jury Instructions* (1979) 79 Colum. L. Rev. 1306, 1353 (hereafter *Psycholinguistic Study*).) The study noted two significant problems with BAJI No. 3.75. First, because the phrase "natural and continuous sequence" precedes "the verb it is intended to modify, the construction leaves the listener with the impression that the cause itself is in a natural and continuous sequence. Inasmuch as a single 'cause' cannot be in a continuous sequence, the listener is befuddled." (*Psycholinguistic Study, supra,*

79 Colum. L. Rev. at p. 1323.) Second, in one experiment, "the term 'proxi-mate cause' was misunderstood by 23% of the subjects. . . . They interpreted it as 'approximate cause,' 'estimated cause,' or some fabrication." (Id., at p. 1353.)

Our Courts of Appeal have recognized the serious problems with the language of BAJI No. 3.75. In *Fraijo v. Hartland Hospital* [(1979)], 99 Cal. App. 3d 331, the court criticized the instruction because it appeared to place an undue empha-sis on "nearness." Nonetheless, "despite the criticism of the 'but for' language in BAJI No. 3.75, the most recent edition of California Jury Instructions (Civil) . . . allow[s] the trial judge to exercise a discretion in selecting his preference between . . . the 'proximate cause' instruction found in BAJI No. 3.75, or the 'legal cause' instruction found in BAJI No. 3.76." (*Id.*, at p. 346.) . . .

We believe the foregoing authorities properly criticize BAJI No. 3.75 for being conceptually and grammatically deficient. The deficiencies may mislead jurors, causing them, if they can glean the instruction's meaning despite the grammat-ical flaws, to focus improperly on the cause that is spatially or temporally closest to the harm.

In contrast, the "substantial factor" test, incorporated in BAJI No. 3.76 and developed by the Restatement Second of Torts, section 431 (com. to BAJI No. 3.76) has been comparatively free of criticism and has even received praise. "As an instruction submitting the question of causation in fact to the jury in intelligi-ble form, it appears impossible to improve on the Restatement's 'substantial factor [test.]'" (Prosser, *Proximate Cause in California, supra*, 38 Cal. L. Rev. 369, 421.) It is "sufficiently intelligible to any layman to furnish an adequate guide to the jury, and it is neither possible nor desirable to reduce it to lower terms." (*Id.*, at p. 379.) . . .

We recognize that BAJI No. 3.76 is not perfectly phrased. The term "legal cause" may be confusing. As part of the psycholinguistic study referred to above, the experimenters rewrote BAJI No. 3.75 to include the term "legal cause." The study found that "25% of the subjects who heard 'legal cause' misinterpreted it as the opposite of an 'illegal cause.' We would therefore recommend that the term 'legal cause' not be used in jury instructions; instead, the simple term 'cause' should be used, with the explanation that the law defines 'cause' in its own par-ticular way."[9] (*Psycholinguistic Study, supra*, 79 Colum. L. Rev. at p. 1353.) . . .

The continued use of BAJI No. 3.75 as an instruction on cause in fact is unwise. The foregoing amply demonstrates that BAJI No. 3.75 is grammatically confusing and conceptually misleading. Continued use of this instruction will likely cause needless appellate litigation regarding the propriety of the instructions in particular

---

9. Although we need not decide whether BAJI No. 3.76 should be rewritten to eliminate the term "legal cause," we do suggest that the Committee on Standard Jury Instructions consider whether the instruction could be improved by adopting the suggestion of the *Psycholinguistic Study* or by otherwise modifying the instruction.

[California later amended BAJI No. 3.76 to eliminate the term "legal cause." Number 3.76 now provides: "The law defines a cause in its own particular way. A cause of [injury] . . . is something that is a substantial factor in bringing about an [injury]. . . ." JUDICIAL COUNCIL OF CAL., CIVIL JURY INSTRUCTIONS (2015).—EDS.]

cases. Use of BAJI No. 3.76 will avoid much of the confusion inherent in BAJI No. 3.75. It is intelligible and easily applied. We therefore conclude that BAJI No. 3.75, the so-called proximate cause instruction, should be disapproved and that the court erred when it refused to give BAJI No. 3.76 and instead gave BAJI No. 3.75.

B.   Prejudicial Effect of Erroneous Instruction

Having determined it was error to refuse to give BAJI No. 3.76 and instead give BAJI No. 3.75, we must decide whether the error was so prejudicial as to require reversal.

Under article VI, section 13 of the California Constitution, if there is error in instructing the jury, the judgment shall be reversed only when the reviewing court, "after an examination of the entire cause, including the evidence," concludes that the error "has resulted in a miscarriage of justice." Under the Constitution, we must determine whether it is reasonably probable that a result more favorable to the appealing party would have been reached in the absence of error. Although there is no precise formula for determining the prejudicial effect of instructional error, we are guided by the five factors enumerated in *LeMons v. Regents of University of California* (1978) 21 Cal. 3d 869, 876.

The first factor we consider is the degree of conflict in the evidence on the critical issue, here cause in fact. The evidence shows that Damechie drowned, not only because he could not swim, but also because he was placed in a position in which his inability to swim resulted in death. The jury's verdict, amply supported by the evidence, indicates that Mr. and Mrs. Gonzales and their son Luis were at least partially responsible for Damechie's predicament. Mr. and Mrs. Gonzales failed to supervise him adequately. Luis, after assuring Damechie he would be careful and knowing that Damechie could not swim, climbed onto the paddleboard, rocked it, causing it to flip over, and failed to call for help despite the presence of adults who might have been able to save Damechie. The conflict in the evidence is not great. If properly instructed, it is reasonably probable that the jury would have found defendants' behavior to have been a substantial factor, and thus a cause in fact, in Damechie's death.

Second, we consider whether the jury asked for a rereading of the erroneous instruction or of related evidence. The jury did not make such a request, but we note that [the] jury received a copy of the instructions, making such a request unnecessary.

Third, we analyze the closeness of the jury's verdict. The jury found on a vote of nine to three that Jose Gonzales and Luis were negligent (i.e., they breached a duty of care to Damechie). Likewise, the jury concluded on a vote of 11 to 1 that Matilde Gonzales was negligent. Yet the jury unanimously concluded that neither the actions of Luis nor Jose Gonzales caused Damechie's death and, on a vote of 10 to 2, the jury found that the actions of Matilde Gonzales were not a cause of the death.

The verdict as to causation was not particularly close. It seems that the jury did follow BAJI No. 3.75 but was misled by the instruction's flaws: Having found the defendants negligent, it is illogical and inconsistent on this record to conclude that they were not a cause in fact of Damechie's death. Accordingly, we conclude it is reasonably probable that the jury was confused by BAJI No. 3.75 and over-emphasized the "but for" nature of the instruction, improperly focusing on the factor operative at the closest temporal proximity to the time of death, Damechie's inability to swim.

Fourth, we consider whether defense counsel's closing argument contributed to the instruction's misleading effect. The closing argument was replete with references to Damechie's inability to swim, his own knowledge that he could not swim, and his decision nevertheless to venture out on the lake. Counsel also argued that Damechie's parents knew he could not swim, yet they permitted him to go with the Gonzaleses without determining whether the Gonzaleses intended to take the children swimming, and argued that but for these facts, Damechie would not have drowned.

The argument thus highlighted the condition temporally closest to the death, Damechie's inability to swim, and factors related to it. As discussed above, BAJI No. 3.75 improperly emphasizes temporal and spatial proximity. The argument thus contributed to the instruction's misleading effect. It is reasonably probable that if the jury had received the substantial factor instruction, counsel's argument would not have misled the jury.

Finally we consider the effect of other instructions in remedying the error. BAJI No. 3.77 was requested by both parties and given by the court.[11] This instruction did not remedy the confusion caused by instructing the jury under BAJI No. 3.75. By frequently repeating the term "proximate cause" and by emphasizing that a cause must be operating at the moment of injury, the instruction buttressed rather [than] counteracted the restrictions on time and place inherent in the word "proximate." Thus, giving BAJI No. 3.77 did not cure the deficiencies of BAJI No. 3.75.

Based on the foregoing analysis, we conclude that it is reasonably probable a result more favorable to the plaintiffs would have resulted if BAJI No. 3.75 had not been given.

Conclusion

We conclude that BAJI No. 3.75 should be disapproved, that the trial court erred when it gave the instruction, and that such error was prejudicial. Accordingly, the decision of the Court of Appeal reversing the judgment in favor of defendants is affirmed.

---

11. BAJI No. 3.77 provides: "There may be more than one [proximate] [legal] cause of an injury. When negligent conduct of two or more persons contributes concurrently as [proximate] [legal] causes of an injury, the conduct of each of said persons is a [proximate] [legal] cause of the injury regardless of the extent to which each contributes to the injury. A cause is concurrent if it was operative at the moment of injury and acted with another cause to produce the injury. [It is no defense that the negligent conduct of a person not joined as a party was also a [proximate] [legal] cause of the injury.]" As read, the instruction included the term "proximate" and the last sentence.

Mosk, J., Panelli, J., Arabian, J., Baxter, J., and George, J., concurred. [The dissent by Kennard, J., is omitted.]

NOTES AND QUESTIONS

1. Translating the law into lay terms. *Mitchell* provides an example of the difficulty a court confronts in attempting to convey complicated legal concepts to a lay jury, a point first-year law students should surely appreciate. How would you explain the principle of proximate cause to someone with no experience in the law? *See* W. Page Keeton, Dan B. Dobbs, Robert E. Keeton & David G. Owen, Prosser and Keeton on Torts 263-280 (5th ed. 1984). As a general matter, should the law be so complicated that a person of average intelligence cannot understand its subtle intricacies?

2. Instructing on proximate cause. William L. Prosser, the well-known torts professor, described proximate cause as a boundary to liability premised on "some social idea of justice or policy." *Id.* at 264. In other words, the line drawn between a factual cause that is proximate and one that is not has nothing to do with proximity in time or place but with a policy judgment that liability should or should not be imposed under the circumstances presented. In your estimation, would it be appropriate to instruct a jury that whether a factual cause is sufficiently proximate presents a question of justice and policy that the jury must decide? Or is that even a question that a jury should consider?

PROBLEM

11-5. Jason suffered from classic hemophilia. As part of his treatment, he was required to take infusions of blood concentrate. One of the prescription products he used was manufactured by Armour and went under the trade name "Factorate." Prior to 1984, the label on Factorate did not include any warnings regarding the potential transmission of the HIV virus. Jason, who used the product in 1983, became infected with HIV in the fall of 1983 and eventually died of complications from AIDS. His parents filed a lawsuit against Armour claiming that the Factorate Jason used had been contaminated with the HIV virus and that Armour had failed to provide adequate warnings. The warning that Armour finally adopted in 1984, and which the Federal Drug Administration approved, provided:

> The possibility exists that Acquired Immune Deficiency Syndrome (AIDS), an immunologic disorder with extremely severe consequences, may be transmitted by blood, blood products and blood derivatives, including clotting factors. However, the causative agent has neither been isolated nor identified. This information should be considered in determining patient care and treatment.

By law, Armour was required to provide such a warning once it had "reasonable evidence" of a potential risk of transmission of HIV from their product. It applied for this new warning in the fall of 1983. Importantly, such warnings are meant to be transmitted to the doctor, not the patient. Jason's parents claimed that Armour was negligent in not seeking approval of the warning at an earlier time because it had known of the product's risk before it sought FDA approval of the new warning. They additionally claimed that Armour had been negligent in failing to send an individual letter to physicians warning of the risk.

As a defense, Armour presented evidence that Jason's prescribing physician had known of the possibility that AIDS might be transmitted by concentrate when he had first treated Jason with Factorate. Given this knowledge, Armour asserted that under the "learned intermediary rule," any failure on its part to have warned Jason's doctor of that possibility at an earlier time had not been the proximate cause of Jason's infection. If proven, the learned-intermediary defense is an absolute defense in the context of harmful prescription pharmaceuticals such as Factorate.

The trial court charged the jury, consistent with Armour's requested learned-intermediary instruction, that to be entitled to the defense, Armour had to prove that Jason's doctor had known at the time of treatment of the "possibility" that blood products might transmit AIDS. The court, however, also instructed the jury that Armour had to prove that Jason's doctor had known of "reasonable evidence of an association of a serious hazard, that is, AIDS, with Factorate concentrate." The reasonable-evidence standard is the standard that compels a drug company to place an appropriate warning on its labels.

The jury entered a verdict for the plaintiffs in the amount of $2 million. On appeal, Armour claims that the reasonable-evidence aspect of the instruction constituted prejudicial error by creating too high a burden on Armour. It forced Armour to prove that Jason's doctor had had a level of knowledge greater than would have been disclosed by even a timely Armour warning, for that warning would have communicated only that the "possibility exists" that blood products could transmit AIDS. Armour argues that such a warning would not have communicated the additional knowledge that there was reasonable evidence of an association of AIDS with Factorate concentrate and that by including this additional language in the jury charge, the court imposed a higher and erroneous layer of proof on its affirmative defense.

Do you think the jury instruction constituted prejudicial error? *See Christopher v. Cutter Labs.*, 53 F.3d 1184 (11th Cir. 1995).

A NOTE ON VERDICTS

After being properly instructed by the court, the jury retires to deliberate and to arrive at a verdict, including, when appropriate, the amount of any compensatory or punitive damages. The most common type of verdict is a *general verdict*. When asked to render a general verdict, the jury is in essence being asked to decide the facts and then apply the law to those facts. In other words, the jury decides the case. The verdict is "general" in the sense that it does not include any specific findings or explanations. Rather, it simply announces which party is entitled to judgment and the amount of damages, if any. Why or how the jury arrived at its decision remains undisclosed.

Critics of the jury system often cite the general verdict as fraught with potential for abuse. FRANK, COURTS ON TRIAL, *supra*, AT 108-145. For one thing, there is no way to determine the basis for the jury verdict. Did the jury actually decide the facts, or did it decide the case based on a whim? In arriving at its conclusion, did the jury follow the law or ignore it? Was the case so complicated that the jury just gave up and made its best guess as to the fair or correct result?

One remedy for these perceived shortcomings in the general verdict is the use of *special verdicts*. With a special verdict the jury is asked merely to decide specific factual contentions. *See, e.g.*, FED. R. CIV. P. 49(a); CAL. CIV. PROC. CODE § 624; TEX. R. CIV. PROC. 290. The jury having found the facts, the judge rather than the jury then applies the law to those facts. *See generally* 7 BERNARD E. WITKIN, CALIFORNIA PROCEDURE: TRIAL §§ 342-346 (5th ed. 2008); 9B CHARLES ALAN WRIGHT & ARTHUR R. MILLER, FEDERAL PRACTICE AND PROCEDURE §§ 2501 *et seq.* (3d ed. 2008 & Supp. 2015); Robert Dudnik, *Special Verdicts: Rule 49 of the Federal Rules of Civil Procedure*, 74 YALE L.J. 483 (1965); Prentice H. Marshall & Thomas D. Rowe, Jr., *Special Verdict; General Verdict and Questions, in* 9 MOORE'S FEDERAL PRACTICE, *supra*, §§ 49.01 *et seq.*; Edmund M. Morgan, *A Brief History of Special Verdicts and Special Interrogatories*, 32 YALE L.J. 575 (1923). On the positive side of the ledger, special verdicts limit the extent to which a jury can ignore or circumvent its duties. On the negative side, a special verdict divests the jury of its ability to bring the common sense of the community into the decision-making process and, some would say, to do substantial justice. *See* Amendments to the Rules of Civil Procedure, 31 F.R.D. 587, 618-619 (1962) (Black, J., and Douglas, J., dissenting) (stating that Rule 49, in allowing for special verdicts, "is but another means utilized by courts to weaken the constitutional power of juries"). In most jurisdictions, including federal courts, a judge has broad discretion in deciding whether to use a special or general verdict. 9 MOORE'S FEDERAL PRACTICE, *supra*, § 49.11[2]; 9B WRIGHT & MILLER, *supra*, § 2505. Special verdicts are most commonly used in complex cases.

In some jurisdictions, a judge may also ask a jury to return a *general verdict with interrogatories*. FED. R. CIV. P. 49(b). *See generally* 9 MOORE'S FEDERAL PRACTICE, *supra*, § 49.20; 9B WRIGHT & MILLER, *supra*, § 2511; 7 WITKIN, *supra*, §§ 347-349. Here the jury is asked to answer specific factual questions as well as to apply the law to the facts. This technique insures that the jury does actually consider and decide the material facts but at the same time preserves the jury's authority to decide the overall case. *See Bills v. Aseltine*, 52 F.3d 596, 605 (6th Cir.), *cert. denied*, 516 U.S. 865 (1995) (using general verdict with interrogatories to ensure close attention to certain factual matters). If the specific factual findings are internally consistent but one or more of them is inconsistent with the general verdict, the court may require the jury to resume deliberations, order a new trial, or enter judgment in accord with the specific findings (*i.e.*, ignore the general verdict). *See* 7 WITKIN, *supra*, § 364; 9B WRIGHT & MILLER, *supra*, § 2513. If the answers to the interrogatories are inconsistent with one another and if one or more of them is also inconsistent with the general verdict, the court may either require the jury to deliberate further or order a new trial. 9 MOORE'S FEDERAL PRACTICE, *supra*, § 49.11[6]. The court may not, however, enter a judgment for either party.

PROBLEM

11-6. The State X Constitution provides a right to a jury trial in all civil actions in which the amount in controversy exceeds $10,000. In addition, the same constitutional provision prohibits the use of special verdicts in jury trials, the right to a general verdict being considered an essential part of the jury trial guarantee. Arnold, a resident of State X, was injured when his Fjord Extravaganza overturned while exiting the freeway. He sued Fjord, Inc. ("Fjord"), in a federal district court in State X, claiming that the vehicle's design was dangerously defective. Assume that the jurisdictional standards of § 1332 were satisfied. At the close of trial, which was to a properly constituted jury, Fjord, relying on Rule 49(a), requests that the court require the jury to return a special verdict on the question of liability. Given the State X constitutional provision on jury trials, may the district court grant Fjord's request? (You might want to refer to the materials in Chapter VI, *supra*, particularly part D.2.) *See Davis v. Ford Motor Co.*, 128 F.3d 631 (8th Cir. 1997). *See generally* 9B WRIGHT & MILLER, *supra*, § 2502 (state law not controlling).

D. Motions for Judgment as a Matter of Law

Even if the right to a jury trial attaches to a particular case and is properly invoked, it does not follow that a jury must decide the case. The jury, as we have seen, is a fact-finder, and that function only comes into play if there are facts to be found, *i.e.*, only when at least some of the material facts are in genuine dispute. An absence of such a dispute might occur, for example, if the parties agree on the material facts or if the party with the burden of proof on a particular claim or defense has insufficient evidence to support her material allegations. In either case, there is nothing for a jury to do, for there are no facts to be found. In such cases, the court may enter a judgment as a matter of law on that claim or defense. In other words, the case will be taken away from the jury, in whole or in part, and decided by the court. In this sense, the right to a jury trial can be viewed as conditioned on the existence of something for the fact-finder to do, that something being the resolution of a genuine factual controversy.

We have already seen this phenomenon in the context of summary judgments. In the absence of a genuine issue of material fact, a court must grant a summary judgment motion if, on the undisputed facts, the movant is entitled to judgment as a matter of law. *Anderson v. Liberty Lobby, Inc.*, 477 U.S. 242 (1986). This remains so regardless of any previous demand for a jury trial. This same "jury-divesting" principle applies after a case has gone to trial and sometimes even after a jury verdict has been rendered. Thus, if the party with the burden of proof at trial fails to satisfy that burden, the court may, on motion, enter a judgment for the opposing party under the same "no reasonable juror" standard applied in the context of summary judgments.

By way of illustration, suppose in a breach-of-contract suit for the sale of land, the plaintiff produces no evidence of a signed writing as required by the applicable statute of frauds. At the close of the plaintiff's case, and on motion by the defendant, the court may enter judgment for the defendant, just as a summary judgment would have been entered if prior to trial it was clear that the plaintiff had lacked the necessary evidence. Under both circumstances, there is nothing for the jury to decide. Moreover, if the court allows the case to go to the jury, and if despite the absence of the critical evidence the jury nonetheless renders a verdict for the plaintiff, the court may enter a judgment for the defendant based on the evidence's inadequacy. In most jurisdictions this can be done only if the defendant renews a previously made "motion for judgment." As an alternative to entering a judgment at either stage of the proceedings, the court might instead order a new trial.

The names given to these motions for judgment vary somewhat from jurisdiction to jurisdiction. Typically, if the motion is made at the close of the plaintiff's case and before the defendant has presented any evidence, it is referred to as a motion for a *nonsuit*, the basic idea being that the plaintiff has introduced insufficient evidence to support her claim. If the motion is made at the close of all of the evidence, it is typically referred to as a motion for a *directed verdict*. Here the idea is that the evidence taken as a whole, including any evidence of affirmative defenses, supports only one outcome. Finally, if the motion is made after a verdict has been rendered, it is often referred to as a motion for *judgment notwithstanding the verdict* (or judgment n.o.v., or simply JNOV). In most jurisdictions, a party may not file a motion for a JNOV unless she has previously moved for a nonsuit or directed verdict on the same grounds. In this sense, a motion for a JNOV renews the previously made motion. In federal court, all three motions are simply referred to as *motions for judgment as a matter of law*, obviating the necessity of navigating the variable nomenclature. See Rule 50, which should be read in its entirety. A motion for a judgment as a matter of law may be made at any time prior to submission to the jury, but only after a "party has been fully heard on an issue. . . ." FED. R. CIV. P. 50(a). If the motion is denied, the movant may then renew the motion after the return of a jury verdict, or may in the alternative move for a new trial. FED. R. CIV. P. 50(b). A motion for judgment may be made on entire claims or defenses, or just as to discrete issues.

Regardless of nomenclature, the same standards apply to all such motions. A party is entitled to a judgment as a matter of law if, on the evidence finally submitted, no reasonable juror could find against that party. This is, of course, the identical standard applied to summary judgments, the only difference being the motion's timing. Thus, in our statute-of-frauds hypothetical, no reasonable juror could find for the plaintiff since there was no evidence of a written contract. Even if the plaintiff had submitted some evidence on this issue, the same result would follow if the evidence submitted were such that no reasonable juror could find by a preponderance of evidence in the plaintiff's favor. In other words, it is not sufficient to merely submit some evidence or a "scintilla" of evidence. Rather, the evidence must be sufficient to meet the applicable standard of proof. *Cf. Anderson v. Liberty Lobby, Inc.*, 477 U.S. 242 (1986), page 889, *supra* (applying this principle in a summary judgment case with the clear-and-convincing standard of proof). But, a judge may neither weigh the evidence in ruling on a motion for judgment, nor assess the witnesses' credibility. Rather, the judge must view the evidence in the light most favorable to the nonmoving party. As the Supreme Court has observed, "[I]n entertaining a motion for judgment as a matter of law, the court should review all of the evidence in the record. In doing so, however, the court must draw all reasonable inferences in favor of the nonmoving party, and it may not make credibility determinations or weigh the evidence." *Reeves v. Sanderson Plumbing Prods., Inc.*, 530 U.S. 133, 150 (2000).

Of course, in a bench trial a party may also move for a judgment as a matter of law, but since the trier of fact is the judge, the standard for granting the motion is not the reasonable-juror standard. Rather, as the trier of fact, the judge is free to weigh the evidence and assess credibility herself. In other words, the judge performs the jury's fact-finding function. FED. R. CIV. P. 52(c).

One final point must be considered: Are motions for judgment as a matter of law constitutional in the context of jury trials? After all, the Seventh Amendment preserves the right to jury trial "[i]n Suits at common law," and provides that "no fact tried by a jury shall be otherwise re-examined in any Court of the United States, than according to the rules of the common law." U.S. CONST. amend. VII. This constitutional problem can be subdivided further into those motions for judgment that operate pre-verdict (*i.e.*, nonsuits and directed verdicts) and those that operate post-verdict (*i.e.*, JNOVs). As to the former, the Supreme Court has held that common law analogues to the pre-verdict motion, extant in 1791, sustain the constitutionality of modern practice even though the earlier devices may have had different "procedural incidents." *Galloway v. United States*, 319 U.S. 372, 390 (1943) (citing demurrers to the evidence and motions for new trials as early counterparts to the directed verdict). In essence, judges at common law had the authority to take a case away from the jury based on the inadequacy of the evidence. The modern exercise of a similar authority, therefore, does not offend the Seventh Amendment. *Id.* at 388-396. The Court has also upheld the federal courts' (including the courts of appeals') constitutional authority to enter post-verdict motions for judgment, though the basis for this conclusion is less clear since this practice was not recognized at common law. Apparently, the notion is that the post-verdict judgment as a matter of law is merely a delayed exercise of the power to grant a nonsuit or directed verdict. *Montgomery Ward & Co. v. Duncan*, 311 U.S. 243, 250-251 (1940); *Baltimore & Carolina Line v. Redman*, 295 U.S. 654, 657-661 (1935). Hence the necessity for an initial motion made before the case was submitted to the jury. *See* FED. R. CIV. P. 50(b); *Exxon Shipping Co. v. Baker*, 554 U.S. 471, 485 n.5 (2008) ("A motion under Rule 50(b) is not allowed unless the movant sought relief on similar grounds under Rule 50(a) before the case was submitted to the jury."). In any event, it is clear that both pre-verdict and post-verdict motions for judgment as a matter of law are deemed constitutional under the "no reasonable juror standard," *i.e.*, so long as the court does not reweigh the evidence or simply second-guess the jury's judgment.

For a discussion of practice under Rule 50, see Martin H. Redish, *Judgment as a Matter of Law in a Jury Trial; Related Motion for a New Trial; Conditional Ruling,* in 9 MOORE's FEDERAL PRACTICE, *supra*, §§ 50.01 *et seq.*

Honaker v. Smith

256 F.3d 477 (7th Cir. 2001)

RIPPLE, Circuit Judge.

Fred Honaker filed a complaint against Gary Smith, the Mayor and Fire Chief of the Village of Lovington, Illinois ("the Village"), regarding the events surrounding a fire that consumed Mr. Honaker's house in Lovington. . . .

I.   Background

A.   Facts

Mr. Honaker owned a house in Lovington that was not his primary residence, but where he would occasionally stay overnight. The utilities were kept on in the house, though the gas and electricity were not activated. Mr. Honaker had begun extensive remodeling on the house including the removal of an interior wall. Because of this ongoing construction, the house was in very poor condition.

Mr. Honaker earned a living by rebuilding pallets[1] on the property where this house was located. As a consequence of that business, wood and other debris were often strewn around the property. Despite the fact that building pallets often creates a great deal of noise, Mr. Honaker kept unusual hours in his work and would occasionally toil into the early morning. Residents often complained about the state of the property to Lovington's City Council, and Mr. Honaker received citations from local police officers due to the property's poor condition. One resident in particular, Mr. Honaker's neighbor Ed Crafton, had a long-running feud with Mr. Honaker. Crafton made a number of formal and informal complaints regarding the noise emanating from Mr. Honaker's property and the physical state of that property to members of the Village government. Members of the City Council often discussed these complaints and expressed their displeasure with the property's condition. As mayor, Mr. Smith was a member of the City Council.

---

1. Pallets are portable wooden platforms used for storing or moving cargo or freight. Mr. Honaker either bought lumber to build his pallets or, more commonly, hauled away previously made pallets from local businesses and rebuilt them . . . .

Mr. Honaker had an acrimonious history with the Village. He had filed a civil rights suit against it in 1995, which was settled the next year. Village personnel also often made derogatory comments to him about the state of his property. Moreover, Mr. Honaker testified that, at some point near Thanksgiving in 1996, he had a rancorous encounter with Mr. Smith outside of a local bar. Mr. Honaker claimed that, on that occasion, Mr. Smith approached him and "told [him] to get [his] stuff and get out of town . . . [or Mr. Smith] would burn [him] out." Mr. Honaker asserted that he told his lawyer about this threat immediately, but did not report it to any law enforcement agency. Mr. Smith denies that the conversation ever took place.

On the night of March 1, 1997, Mr. Honaker's house caught fire. The Village's volunteer Fire Department responded to the call regarding the fire, which came in at 1:51 A.M., within minutes. In total, four fire trucks and twenty volunteer firefighters from the Fire Department arrived at the scene. Additionally, one fire truck and several firefighters were called in from the neighboring Sullivan, Illinois, Fire Department to help extinguish the blaze. As the Village's Fire Chief, Mr. Smith arrived at the scene soon after the call and led the fighting of the fire. He immediately determined that the house's structure was already badly damaged and noticed that a number of floor joists and beams supporting the second floor were cracked and bowed. As a result, Mr. Smith decided that the firefighters should not enter the house to battle the fire because the house's structure was too unstable to risk such entry.[2] After three hours the fire was extinguished; however, it rekindled twice during that day, requiring the firefighters to return each time to quench the flames.

Don Tankersly, an investigator from the Illinois State Fire Marshall's Office, arrived at the scene of the fire at 3:30 A.M. He saw the firefighters actively engaged in attempting to put out the fire, and he believed that they were making every effort to extinguish the blaze. He also noticed that ceiling joists from the first floor of the house appeared to be cracking and that the second floor of the house looked to be sagging downward. Tankersly later completed his investigation of the fire and determined that it was set intentionally, but found no evidence to demonstrate that Mr. Smith or anyone else was specifically responsible for its origin.

Mr. Honaker arrived at his property on the morning of the fire and was visibly upset and distraught; at one point he even began to cry. He was also extremely angry and began yelling and screaming. However, Mr. Honaker did not seek medical treatment at any point for emotional distress that he may have suffered due to the fire.

The Honaker fire was not the first time that dilapidated buildings owned by a Lovington resident had burned down under suspicious circumstances. A few months before the fire to Mr. Honaker's house, buildings in poor condition that belonged to Lovington resident Tom Brewer also had caught fire. As in Mr.

---

2. After the fire . . . Mr. Honaker made repeated efforts to rebuild the house, all of which failed . . . . As a result, Mr. Honaker eventually sold the property and left Lovington.

Honaker's case, the poor condition of Brewer's property had been discussed in the City Council before the fire, and the Village had asked Brewer to tear down those buildings. Before Brewer took any action, the buildings burned down, and the cause of that fire never was determined.

After the Honaker fire, a great deal of speculation in the Village focused on its possible cause. Mr. Honaker initially suspected that either Crafton or Mr. Smith was involved in setting the blaze. Additionally, rumors soon spread that Doug Thomas, a member of the Village government and of its Fire Department, may have had a role in starting the conflagration, allegations that Thomas denied. Jokes regarding the fact that Mr. Honaker's house had burned down, not long after many members of the community had expressed displeasure about the state of his property, were also prevalent around the Village and were made by some residents at City Council meetings. Mr. Smith denied taking part in those jokes; he also consistently maintained that he had nothing to do with starting the fire and that he made every effort as fire chief to put the fire out as quickly as possible.

B.   District Court Proceedings

On December 16, 1998, Mr. Honaker filed a First Amended Complaint ("the complaint") in this matter, which alleged four causes of action against Mr. Smith. Count I[, which included two claims,] maintained that Mr. Smith, in his official capacity as Mayor of Lovington and Fire Chief of the Lovington Fire Department, was liable under Section 1983* for setting the fire at Mr. Honaker's house and for intentionally failing to properly extinguish the fire. Count IV alleged that Mr. Smith was liable under Illinois law for the intentional infliction of emotional distress.[3] A jury trial began on February 14, 2000. At the close of all of the evidence, Mr. Smith filed a motion for judgment as a matter of law on all of the claims in the complaint. With regard to Count I's Section 1983 claims, the court took the motion under advisement, but allowed the action to be submitted to the jury. However, the court granted the motion as to Count IV's emotional distress claim [over which the court had exercised supplemental jurisdiction]. It did so because it found that Mr. Honaker presented "no evidence of emotional distress . . . other than the mere claim that [he] was upset" and "no evidence of any medical treatment . . . [or] any follow-up whatsoever with counseling in any way."

After its deliberations, the jury returned a verdict on Count I in favor of Mr. Honaker in the amount of $45,000. Mr. Smith then filed a renewed motion

---

* [Section 1983 provides a cause of action against any state or local governmental official who, while acting under color of state law, violates a person's federal constitutional rights. 42 U.S.C. § 1983 (2006).—Eds.]

3. Counts II and III of the complaint maintained that Mr. Smith conspired with Doug Thomas and other unnamed individuals to set fire to Mr. Honaker's house and to fail to extinguish properly that fire, in violation of 42 U.S.C. §§ 1983 and 1985, respectively. The district court granted Mr. Smith's motion for judgment as a matter of law at the close of all of the evidence on these claims, based upon its finding that the evidence presented was insufficient to demonstrate a conspiracy. Mr. [Honaker] does not challenge these rulings on appeal.

for judgment as a matter of law, and on May 4, 2000, the district court granted that motion and entered judgment as a matter of law notwithstanding the verdict on Count I. The court determined that, as to the claim that Mr. Smith was involved in setting fire to Mr. Honaker's house, there was no evidence to support that assertion because Mr. Honaker had put forward only unsupported speculation and conjecture on that point. It also ruled that, even assuming the evidence was sufficient to support a finding that Mr. Smith had set the fire, there was no evidence that he did so "under color of state law," a requirement of all Section 1983 claims. The court explained that in no way could Mr. Smith's action in setting such a fire relate to the performance of his official duties as mayor because any such action "would have involved sneaking around in the late night or early morning hours with some kind of incendiary material." Next, the court determined that no evidence supported Mr. Honaker's claim that Mr. Smith failed to extinguish properly the fire in his capacity as Lovington Fire Chief. This was because "[e]very witness who testified on this subject at trial . . . stated that the firefighters did everything they could to put out the fire." Additionally, the court noted that Mr. Honaker presented no evidence to support his assertions that alternative methods should have been used to fight the fire or that the Fire Department should have taken far less time than the three hours it needed to initially extinguish the blaze. As a result, the district court determined that no rational jury could have found in favor of Mr. Honaker on Count I and granted Mr. Smith's motion for judgment as a matter of law on that cause of action.

II. Discussion

Mr. Honaker now appeals the district court's rulings with regard to Count I and Count IV. He alleges that, as to Count I, the district court erred in granting judgment as a matter of law notwithstanding the jury's verdict. He claims that there was sufficient evidence for the jury to have found that Mr. Smith caused Mr. Honaker's house to be set on fire and that he did so under color of state law. He also maintains that he put forward adequate evidence for a jury to find that Mr. Smith failed to use his best efforts to put out the fire in his capacity as Lovington Fire Chief. Additionally, Mr. Honaker asserts that the district court erred in granting judgment as a matter of law on Count IV's intentional infliction of emotional distress claim because sufficient evidence existed to prove the elements of that tort under Illinois law. We shall address each of these arguments in turn.

A. Mr. Honaker's Section 1983 Claims

With respect to Mr. Honaker's claims in Count I, the district court, pursuant to Federal Rule of Civil Procedure 50 ("Rule 50"), granted Mr. Smith's motion for judgment as a matter of law after the jury had returned a verdict for Mr. Honaker. Pursuant to Rule 50, a district court may grant judgment as a matter of law when ["a reasonable jury would not have a legally sufficient evidentiary basis to find for the party on that issue"]. FED. R. CIV. P. 50(a)(1). We review a district court's grant of judgment as a matter of law de novo. After a jury has rendered its verdict, we must engage in this review not to determine whether the jury believed the right people, but only whether it was presented with a legally sufficient amount of evidence from which it could reasonably derive its verdict. In that regard, we must judge whether the evidence in support of the verdict is substantial; the party opposing the motion must have put forward more than a "mere scintilla" of evidence to support that jury verdict. In reviewing the totality of the evidence in the record, we draw all inferences in the light most favorable to the party against whom the motion is directed. If, after reviewing all of the evidence in the case, the nonmoving party did not introduce enough evidence to support his claim, then judgment as a matter of law is appropriate.

1.   Setting the Fire

Mr. Honaker first contends that there was sufficient evidence for a jury to conclude that Mr. Smith played a role in setting fire to his house. As we have noted, Mr. Honaker's claim in this regard was filed under Section 1983. As a result, he must demonstrate not only that Mr. Smith was in fact involved in setting the fire, but also that Mr. Smith did so "under color of state law" and deprived Mr. Honaker of a federally guaranteed right. We have emphasized that "[n]ot every action by a state official or employee is to be deemed as occurring 'under color' of state law." Action is taken under color of state law when it involves a misuse of power, "possessed by virtue of state law and made possible only because the wrongdoer is clothed with the authority of state law." *Walker v. Taylorville Corr. Ctr.*, 129 F.3d 410, 413 (7th Cir. 1997). As a result, acts by a state officer are not made under color of state law unless they are related in some way to the performance of the duties of the state office. . . .

We agree with the district court's conclusion that, on this record, any action taken by Mr. Smith to cause Mr. Honaker's house to burn to the ground was not effectuated under color of state law. Mr. Honaker does not explain how such an act was related to any official duty or activity of Mr. Smith as Mayor of Lovington or as its Fire Chief. Moreover, Mr. Honaker makes no substantive contention that Mr. Smith used the cloak of his authority as mayor or fire chief or any indicia of his office to set such a fire. In one of his briefs, Mr. Honaker appears to suggest that Mr. Smith may have paid Thomas to set the fire. This allegation is not well-formed and, more importantly, Mr. Honaker again does not explain how such an act would be related in any way to the performance of Mr. Smith's duties as a state officer. Under these circumstances, we agree with the district court that there was no basis upon which a reasonable jury could conclude that Mr. Smith violated Section 1983 by causing Mr. Honaker's house to be set afire.

2.   Extinguishing the Fire

Mr. Honaker also asserts that the district court erred when it ruled that no reasonable jury could have found that Mr. Smith, in his role as fire chief, failed to extinguish properly the fire at Mr. Honaker's house. After extensively reviewing the evidence in the record, we must agree with the district court's conclusion. The record does not contain a legally sufficient amount of evidence from which a jury reasonably could have inferred that Mr. Smith and the firefighters on the scene used anything less than their best efforts to extinguish the fire.

As an initial matter, the evidence overwhelmingly demonstrated that, after receiving the call informing them of the fire on March 1, 1997, the Lovington Fire Department arrived at Mr. Honaker's house within minutes . . . . Moreover, despite the fact that the fire occurred in the early morning hours, the Fire Department responded with four fire trucks and twenty volunteer firefighters. Pursuant to a "mutual aid" agreement with the neighboring Sullivan Fire Department, which employs paid personnel, the Lovington firefighters also called for assistance from Sullivan . . . . As a result of this call for assistance, Sullivan dispatched, in addition to several firefighters, an aerial fire truck which enables firefighters to direct ladders and water to the upper floors of homes . . . .

Additionally, all of the testimony at trial suggested that, upon arriving at Mr. Honaker's house, the firefighters consistently and vigorously fought the fire to the best of their ability. Particularly on point was the testimony of Tankersly, the investigator from the Illinois State Fire Marshall's Office, who was called to the scene to determine the cause of the fire. Tankersly, who had 15 years of experience and who had investigated over 1,000 fires in his career, testified that when he arrived at 3:30 A.M., "[f]irefighters were actively engaged in putting out hot spot fires within the structure." He also said that the firefighters had made every effort to put out the fire and that they could not have done anything more than what they did. He also corroborated Mr. Smith's view that structural problems had rendered the house unsafe for entry by firefighters. A number of the firefighters themselves corroborated that the fire had been fought vigorously . . . .

Mr. Honaker points to three facts to support his assertion that Mr. Smith and the firefighters did not use their best efforts in combating the fire. First, he notes that it initially took the firefighters three hours to conquer the flames, a length of time that he suggests was far too great. Next, he submits that the fact that the firefighters did not enter his house to combat the fire suggests that they did not perform their duties properly. Lastly, he cites a piece of trial testimony in which Mr. Smith made the assertion that he did not let the firefighters enter the house because "that house wasn't worth getting hurt for." Mr. Honaker claims that this statement demonstrates that Mr. Smith's animus towards him was the reason why the firefighters did not enter the structure.

As to the amount of time that it took to combat the fire, we have already noted that substantial testimony supported the conclusion that the firefighters made every effort to control the blaze and that Tankersly, an experienced fire investigator, testified that there was nothing more that could have been done. On the other hand, as the district court noted, Mr. Honaker presented "*no* evidence that three hours was too long a time to put out this type of fire." Mr. Smith had explained that the fire raged for that period of time because the firefighters had difficulty in identifying the proper heat source on which to train their hoses and because the great amount of debris in and around the house made it difficult to quickly develop an entryway through which the water could attack the fire. Mr. Honaker did nothing to contest this explanation or to suggest that the firefighters lingered unnecessarily at the fire scene. A jury would have no evidentiary basis from which to infer reasonably that the Fire Department took an unreasonable amount of time to extinguish the fire.

Additionally, as to the claim that the firefighters should have entered the house, Mr. Smith explained that he did not allow them to do so due to the precarious nature of the house's structure. Every witness who testified on the subject confirmed that, during and after the fire, the floor joists supporting the second floor of the house were cracked and that the second floor itself was sagging — presenting the serious threat that, if the firefighters had entered the burning building, the house might have collapsed around them . . . . Additionally, overwhelming evidence established that the dwelling was in great disrepair because Mr. Honaker had been in the process of "gutting the inside of the house." Since he had purchased the house, Mr. Honaker had removed a non-load-bearing wall, had torn the kitchen ceiling out and even had experienced part of the chimney falling down on top of him. Lastly, witnesses with experience in investigating and fighting fires testified that, under the circumstances, it was not improper for the firefighters to combat the flames from outside the building. Tankersly explained that during his investigation, he saw that the collapse of the second floor "shows major cracks beginning to show in the floor joists" and that these cracks "made the structure pretty much unsafe to even be in." Mr. Smith explained that the classes in which he and the other firefighters were trained taught that a fire should be fought "from the outside in" and that if the structure is in danger of collapse, they should not enter the building.

In contrast, no witness, with or without firefighting experience, testified that the Lovington Fire Department should have entered the house under such circumstances. Mr. Honaker argues that, because the frame of the house continued to stand after the fire and because the firefighters later entered the building to hose down fire that had rekindled, the house was not in such precarious condition that the Fire Department could not have entered it when they first arrived. We do not believe that these facts, without more, are sufficient for a reasonable jury to conclude that the firefighters should have entered a burning building that, by all accounts, appeared to be in serious jeopardy of collapsing.

Ultimately, Lovington's volunteer Fire Department responded to a substantial fire in the early morning hours with four trucks, twenty firefighters and significant assistance from a neighboring fire department. Moreover, not only was substantial evidence presented that the firefighters actively fought the flames with their best efforts, but Mr. Honaker offered no testimony from any witness to demonstrate that the firefighters should have or could have done anything differently. As a result, we must agree with the district court's ruling that there was insufficient evidence for a jury to find that Mr. Smith, in his capacity as Lovington's Fire Chief, failed to fight the fire with his best efforts. Therefore, the district court properly granted judgment as a matter of law on Count I.

B.   Intentional Infliction of Emotional Distress

Mr. Honaker's final contention is that the district court erred when it entered judgment as a matter of law at the close of all of the evidence on Count IV, which alleged an Illinois state law claim of intentional infliction of emotional distress. In ruling, the court explained:

> [T]here is no evidence of emotional distress that has been presented in this case other than the mere claim that Mr. Honaker was upset. There is no evidence of any medical treatment, any, any follow-up whatsoever with counseling in any way. So, as to the argument relative to emotional distress, the Court finds no evidence presented and on that issue will be entering judgment in favor of the defendant.

Later, the court reiterated that, although Mr. Honaker produced "some evidence" that he was upset and distraught on the day of the fire, it did not believe that "mere emotional distress [on] the day . . . of the fire with nothing more is sufficient [to sustain a cause of action on this claim]." Additionally, in its Order after the jury's verdict, the court explained that although Mr. Honaker "testified that he was very upset about the fire . . . he did not seek any treatment for emotional distress." For these reasons, the court ruled that "the evidence was insufficient to show that Plaintiff suffered severe emotional distress," and it did not allow the claim to be heard by the jury. Mr. Honaker asserts that the district court's conclusion in this regard was in error.

We review de novo the district court's decision to grant judgment as a matter of law at the close of all the evidence. The district court may grant judgment as a matter of law in such a circumstance when ["a party has been fully heard on an issue . . . and the court finds that a reasonable jury would not have a legally sufficient evidentiary basis to find for the party on that issue . . . "]. FED. R. CIV. P. 50(a)(1). The district court may not resolve any conflicts in the testimony nor weigh the evidence, except to the extent of determining whether substantial evidence could support a jury verdict—a mere scintilla of evidence will not suffice. We shall reverse the district court's judgment "only if enough evidence exists that might sustain a verdict for the nonmoving party."

The tort of intentional infliction of emotional distress has been recognized in Illinois since 1961. . . . More recently, . . . the Illinois Supreme Court set forth three requirements necessary to demonstrate the intentional infliction of emotional distress: (1) the conduct involved must be truly extreme and outrageous; (2) the actor must either intend that his conduct inflict severe emotional distress, or know that there is at least a high probability that his conduct will cause severe emotional distress and (3) the conduct must in fact cause severe emotional distress. . . .

1.   Extreme and Outrageous Conduct

. . . Mr. Honaker claims that Mr. Smith's actions in allegedly setting fire to his house and failing to properly extinguish that blaze suffice to demonstrate extreme and outrageous conduct under Illinois law. As we have previously explained in this opinion, there is insufficient evidence to suggest that Mr. Smith or the

Lovington Fire Department were deficient in any way in putting out the fire at Mr. Honaker's house. However, Mr. Honaker's claim that Mr. Smith played a role in setting the fire deserves further analysis. As an initial matter, setting fire to a person's house because one believes the house's physical appearance is unsightly is similar in character to acts that have been deemed extreme and outrageous under Illinois law . . . . We believe that, like the circumstances in these cases, intentionally causing a person's house to be set on fire in an effort to force him to leave town also would be deemed to "go beyond all possible bounds of decency . . . and be regarded as intolerable in a civilized community." . . .

Mr. Honaker also must have demonstrated a sufficient evidentiary basis for a jury to find that Mr. Smith did in fact engage in such conduct. No physical evidence was found to link Mr. Smith to the fire's origin and no witnesses testified that they knew Mr. Smith to be connected in any way with the blaze. Both Tankersly and an investigator from the Illinois State Police, Rodney Miller, examined the fire's origin and found no evidence linking Mr. Smith to the start of the conflagration. However, Mr. Honaker claims that a few months prior to the fire, Mr. Smith approached him and "told me to get my stuff and get out of town. He'd burn me out."[13]

Moreover, the fire was set under suspicious circumstances. Indeed, the fire inspector concluded that the conflagration was set intentionally. Mr. Honaker clearly had a longstanding history of acrimonious relations with the Village and with Mr. Smith personally. Mr. Honaker had engaged in contentious litigation with the Village in the past and also had been issued citations by local authorities a number of times due to the poor condition of his property. He testified that, at least once a week, Village personnel would walk by his property and make derogatory comments about its physical appearance. A number of Village residents also complained frequently about the property at City Council meetings, meetings at which Mr. Smith and the other members of the City Council discussed what they could do to address those complaints. Jokes were made by some residents and City Council members at these meetings, while Mr. Smith was in attendance, to the effect that, if a fire were to occur at Mr. Honaker's house, it would not be a bad thing for the Village. At one meeting prior to the fire, when Crafton raised a number of complaints about the property's condition, Mr. Smith told Crafton that he would look at the property and do whatever he could to resolve the problem under the law. Lastly, a number of witnesses testified that, due to the problems with the Honaker property, general feelings of animosity existed between Mr. Smith and Mr. Honaker.

In addition, Mr. Honaker's house was not the first troublesome property for the Village that had burned down. Prior to Mr. Honaker's fire, Lovington resident Tom Brewer saw buildings that he had owned catch fire under what even Mr. Smith agreed were suspicious circumstances. Just a few weeks prior to that fire,

---

13. Again, Mr. Smith has emphatically denied that this conversation ever took place, that he ever threatened Mr. Honaker or that he had anything to do with the start of the fire.

the Village had requested that Brewer tear those buildings down, as there had been complaints about their condition at City Council meetings. The parallels between the fire at the Brewer property and that at Mr. Honaker's house are difficult to ignore.

Ultimately, no direct evidence was presented linking Mr. Smith to the fire at Mr. Honaker's house . . . . However, there is also little question that the house burned under questionable circumstances and that many members of the City Council, including Mr. Smith, were upset about the condition of the property and had complained about it for quite a while. Many witnesses testified that there was also longstanding animosity between Mr. Honaker and Mr. Smith. We believe that these facts, viewed in the light most favorable to Mr. Honaker, provide a legally sufficient amount of evidence to suggest that Mr. Smith might have been responsible for setting the fire, such that he could be said to have engaged in "extreme and outrageous" conduct under Illinois law.

2.   Intent to Cause or the High Probability of Distress

The tort's second element inquires as to whether the actor either intended that his conduct inflict severe emotional distress or knew that there was at least a high probability that his conduct would cause such distress. Courts have generally found this element to be satisfied either when a defendant's actions, by their very nature, were likely to cause severe distress or when the defendant knew that a plaintiff was particularly susceptible to such distress and that, because of this susceptibility, the defendant's actions were likely to cause it to occur. In this case, a jury might well conclude that the burning of Mr. Honaker's house would bring with it the high probability of causing severe emotional distress to Mr. Honaker. Having the mayor of one's town suggest that you leave or be burned out, followed by a fire that all but completely destroys your house, is likely to cause significant emotional trauma.

3.   Severity of the Distress

The third element of the tort focuses on the severity of the emotional distress; it was regarding this element that the district court specifically found that Mr. Honaker had not put forward sufficient facts to sustain his claim.

Illinois courts have explained that:

> The emotional distress must be *severe*. Although fright, horror, grief, shame, humiliation, worry, etc. may fall within the ambit of the term "emotional distress," these mental conditions alone are not actionable. "The law intervenes only where the distress inflicted is so severe that no reasonable man could be expected to endure it. The intensity and the duration of the distress are factors to be considered in determining its severity."

Welsh v. Commonwealth Edison Co., 306 Ill. App. 3d 148, 713 N.E.2d 679, 684 (1999) (emphasis in original) . . . . Yet neither physical injury nor the need for medical treatment is a necessary prerequisite to establishing severe emotional distress. In some instances, when no physical manifestation of the emotional distress existed and where no medical treatment was sought, Illinois courts have still found that a plaintiff could establish severe emotional distress. *See, e.g., Amato v. Greenquist,* 287 Ill. App. 3d 921, 679 N.E.2d 446, 455 (1997) (plaintiff satisfactorily alleged that minister's actions caused him distress, when minister abused counseling relationship with plaintiff's wife by engaging in affair with her, causing "depression, despair, insomnia, anxiety, nervousness and emotional trauma" in plaintiff); . . .

Additionally, some Illinois cases have noted the principle, stated in the Second Restatement of Torts, that "[s]evere distress must be proved; but in many cases the extreme and outrageous character of the defendant's conduct is in itself important evidence that the distress has existed." These cases have acknowledged that, even when significant evidence was not presented as to the severity of distress, the very nature of the conduct involved may be evidence of its impact on the victim. In *Bristow v. Drake Street Inc.,* 41 F.3d 345 (7th Cir. 1994), we extensively discussed when emotional distress is sufficiently severe under Illinois law. In the course of that discussion, we also took note that Illinois courts, following the Restatement, have "tend[ed] to merge the issue of the outrageousness of the defendant's conduct with the issue of the severity of the plaintiff's emotional distress, in effect requiring more evidence of outrageousness the weaker the evidence of distress."

In this case, Mr. Honaker testified that when he saw his house burning on the morning of the fire, he was upset and "got mad and started yelling at everybody." Additionally, he points to the testimony of two witnesses to confirm the severity of the emotional distress he suffered. His ex-wife, Virginia Honaker, explained that on the day of the fire, Mr. Honaker was "pissed" and that he was "cussing, raising all kinds of [C]ain, hollering at the neighbors, everybody else, screaming to the top of his lungs because his house was burned." However, she also qualified some of her answers regarding the seriousness of Mr. Honaker's mental state. For example, Virginia Honaker explained that at one point, Mr. Honaker was "bawling," though when asked if that was unusual for him, she replied "Depends." When asked if it took Mr. Honaker a while to get over his house being burned down, she answered "[a]ccording to him, yes." Additionally, James Webb, a neighbor of Mr. Honaker's, testified that on the day of the fire, Mr. Honaker was "visibly upset" and "very distraught, nervous." Webb also observed that he had only seen Mr. Honaker in that emotional state once before, upon his divorce from Virginia Honaker . . . .

The district court took the view that the evidence was, as a matter of law, insufficient to permit a jury to determine that the emotional distress was sufficiently severe to be actionable. In reaching this determination, the court placed great, and perhaps controlling, weight on the fact that this testimony focused on the manifestations of Mr. Honaker's distress on the day of the fire. Although duration is certainly a factor to be weighed in determining the severity of the plaintiff's distress, it is not the only factor that ought to be considered. Here, the district court apparently gave no consideration as to whether the severity of the alleged conduct—being told by the mayor to get out of town or be burned out followed by the burning of the house—permitted the reasonable inference that Mr. Honaker's distress was not only severe but of significant duration. We believe that the magnitude of that conduct, in conjunction with the evidence of emotional distress that Mr. Honaker did put forward, could allow a jury to find that he suffered severe emotional distress in this case.

Accordingly, although we express no view on the ultimate outcome of the case, we cannot sustain the dismissal of this count alleging a cause of action for the intentional infliction of emotional distress under the law of Illinois.

Conclusion

The district court properly determined that insufficient evidence existed for a jury to find that, under color of state law, Mr. Smith played a role in setting fire to Mr. Honaker's house. The court was also correct in its determination that Mr. Honaker did not put forward enough evidence to demonstrate that Mr. Smith, in his role as Lovington's Fire Chief, used less than his best efforts to extinguish that fire. Accordingly, we affirm the district court's grant of judgment as a matter of law in favor of Mr. Smith on the Section 1983 claims.

With respect to the state law-based claim for the intentional infliction of emotional distress, we reverse the judgment of the district court and remand for further proceedings consistent with this opinion.

AFFIRMED in part, REVERSED and REMANDED in part.

NOTES AND QUESTIONS

1. The § 1983 claims.   In Count I of his complaint, Mr. Honaker asserted two § 1983 claims. Under the first claim, he asserted that Mr. Smith, the mayor and fire chief of the Village, set fire to his house, thus depriving him of property without due process of law. Why did the court of appeals affirm the district court's grant of Smith's motion for judgment as a matter of law as to that claim? In other words, what error was reflected in the jury's verdict? In so ruling, did the courts violate Honaker's right to a jury trial? What would Honaker need to have done at trial to avoid this ruling?

In the second § 1983 claim, Honaker asserted that Smith, in performing his duties as fire chief, intentionally failed to properly extinguish the fire. Again, the court of appeals affirmed the district court's entry of judgment for Smith despite the jury verdict. Was the error in the second § 1983 claim the same as the error in the first? If not, what was the flaw in the second claim?

Notice that with respect to both § 1983 claims, the district court granted what was in effect a JNOV. Does Rule 50 allow this? If the court of appeals had reversed on either of these claims, what would the result have been on remand? Would Rule 50 have allowed the district court to grant Smith's post-verdict motion for judgment if Smith had not made a pre-verdict motion for judgment on the same claims?

2. The infliction-of-emotional-distress claim.   What was Honaker's burden in overcoming Smith's motion for judgment as to this Count IV claim? Do you agree that he met that burden on each of the necessary elements of the emotional-distress claim? In other words, do you think that a reasonable juror could have found in Honaker's favor based on the applicable evidentiary standard, *i.e.*, preponderance of the evidence?

The district court granted Smith's motion on the emotional-distress claim before submitting the case to the jury; hence, the motion operated as a motion for a directed verdict. Will this claim now have to be retried? As we have noted, the standard for a pre-verdict motion for judgment is identical to the standard for a post-verdict motion for judgment. But can you see why a district court might be more reluctant to grant the former than the latter, despite the standards being identical? It is often observed that the better practice is for the court to deny the pre-verdict motion and permit the movant to renew that motion later if the jury renders an unfavorable verdict. 9B WRIGHT & MILLER, *supra*, § 2533. The reason is simple: The reversal of a directed verdict requires a new trial, while the reversal of a JNOV merely requires that the verdict be reinstated. Moreover, if the trial court awaits the verdict, it retains the option of granting a new trial instead of entering a judgment against the jury's verdict. Thus, as the Supreme Court has noted,

> while a district court is permitted to enter judgment as a matter of law when it concludes that the evidence is legally insufficient, it is not required to do so. To the contrary, the district courts are, if anything, encouraged to submit the case to the jury, rather than granting such motions.

Unitherm FoodSystems, Inc. v. Swift-Eckrich, Inc., 546 U.S. 394, 405 (2006).

PROBLEM

11-7. Let's return to our hypothetical lawsuit involving a breach of contract for the sale of land. *See* page 1008, *supra.* We have already noted that if by the close of trial the plaintiff fails to produce any evidence of a writing signed by the defendant, the court could properly grant the defendant's motion for judgment as a matter of law. Suppose, however, that the plaintiff testified at trial that she had engaged in such transactions in the past and that it was always her practice to require a written contract, and that although she can't remember any such signed writing for this particular transaction, she's certain there must have been one. At the close of all the evidence, the defendant makes a motion for a judgment as a matter of law. Would the plaintiff's testimony described above be sufficient to overcome that motion? Would your answer be the same if the defendant had testified that he never had signed any such writing but had seemed evasive and disingenuous while on the witness stand? Or suppose that the plaintiff testified that in fact there was a writing signed by the defendant but that it was accidentally destroyed in a fire. Would that evidence be sufficient to overcome the defendant's motion? And, as to the latter question, would it matter that on cross-examination, it became clear that the plaintiff could produce no evidence of the fire other than her own testimony?

Weisgram v. Marley Co.

528 U.S. 440 (2000)

JUSTICE GINSBURG delivered the opinion of the Court.

This case concerns the respective authority of federal trial and appellate courts to decide whether, as a matter of law, judgment should be entered in favor of a verdict loser. The pattern we confront is this. Plaintiff in a product liability action gains a jury verdict. Defendant urges, unsuccessfully before the federal district court but successfully on appeal, that expert testimony plaintiff introduced was unreliable, and therefore inadmissible, under the analysis required by *Daubert v. Merrell Dow Pharmaceuticals, Inc.*, 509 U.S. 579 (1993). Shorn of the erroneously admitted expert testimony, the record evidence is insufficient to justify a plaintiff's verdict. May the court of appeals then instruct the entry of judgment as a matter of law for defendant, or must that tribunal remand the case, leaving to the district court's discretion the choice between final judgment for defendant or a new trial of plaintiff's case?

Our decision is guided by Federal Rule of Civil Procedure 50,* which governs the entry of judgment as a matter of law, and by the Court's pathmarking opinion in *Neely v. Martin K. Eby Constr. Co.*, 386 U.S. 317 (1967). As *Neely* teaches, courts of appeals should "be constantly alert" to "the trial judge's first-hand knowledge of witnesses, testimony, and issues"; in other words, appellate courts should give due consideration to the first-instance decisionmaker's " 'feel' for the overall case." But the court of appeals has authority to render the final decision. If, in the particular case, the appellate tribunal determines that the district court is better positioned to decide whether a new trial, rather than judgment for defendant, should be ordered, the court of appeals should return the case to the trial court for such an assessment. But if, as in the instant case, the court of appeals concludes that further proceedings are unwarranted because the loser on appeal has had a full and fair opportunity to present the case, including arguments for a new trial, the appellate court may appropriately instruct the district court to enter judgment against the jury-verdict winner. Appellate authority to make this determination is no less when the evidence is rendered insufficient by the removal of erroneously admitted testimony than it is when the evidence, without any deletion, is insufficient.

I

Firefighters arrived at the home of Bonnie Weisgram on December 30, 1993, to discover flames around the front entrance. Upon entering the home, they found

---

* [The quotes from Rule 50 in this opinion have been changed to reflect the current version of the Rule, as amended effective Dec. 1, 2007. The 2007 changes from the prior version of the Rule were intended to be stylistic only. — EDS.]

Weisgram in an upstairs bathroom, dead of carbon monoxide poisoning. Her son, petitioner Chad Weisgram, individually and on behalf of Bonnie Weisgram's heirs, brought a diversity action in the United States District Court for the District of North Dakota seeking wrongful death damages. He alleged that a defect in an electric baseboard heater, manufactured by defendant (now respondent) Marley Company and located inside the door to Bonnie Weisgram's home, caused both the fire and his mother's death.

At trial, Weisgram introduced the testimony of three witnesses, proffered as experts, in an endeavor to prove the alleged defect in the heater and its causal connection to the fire. The District Court overruled defendant Marley's objections, lodged both before and during the trial, that this testimony was unreliable and therefore inadmissible under Federal Rule of Evidence 702 as elucidated by *Daubert*. At the close of Weisgram's evidence, and again at the close of all the evidence, Marley unsuccessfully moved under Federal Rule of Civil Procedure 50(a) for judgment as a matter of law on the ground that plaintiffs had failed to meet their burden of proof on the issues of defect and causation. The jury returned a verdict for Weisgram. Marley again requested judgment as a matter of law, and additionally requested, in the alternative, a new trial, pursuant to Rules 50 and 59; among arguments in support of its post-trial motions, Marley reasserted that the expert testimony essential to prove Weisgram's case was unreliable and therefore inadmissible. The District Court denied the motions and entered judgment for Weisgram. Marley appealed.

The Court of Appeals for the Eighth Circuit held that Marley's motion for judgment as a matter of law should have been granted. Writing for the panel majority, Chief Judge Bowman first examined the testimony of Weisgram's expert witnesses, the sole evidence supporting plaintiffs' product defect charge. Concluding that the testimony was speculative and not shown to be scientifically sound, the majority held the expert evidence incompetent to prove Weisgram's case. The court then considered the remaining evidence in the light most favorable to Weisgram, found it insufficient to support the jury verdict, and directed judgment as a matter of law for Marley. In a footnote, the majority "reject[ed] any contention that [it was] required to remand for a new trial." It recognized its discretion to do so under [Rule 50(e)], but stated: "[W]e can discern no reason to give the plaintiffs a second chance to make out a case of strict liability. . . . This is not a close case. The plaintiffs had a fair opportunity to prove their claim and they failed to do so." The dissenting judge disagreed on both points, concluding that the expert evidence was properly admitted and that the appropriate remedy for improper admission of expert testimony is the award of a new trial, not judgment as a matter of law.

Courts of Appeals have divided on the question whether Federal Rule of Civil Procedure 50 permits an appellate court to direct the entry of judgment as a matter of law when it determines that evidence was erroneously admitted at trial and that the remaining, properly admitted evidence is insufficient to constitute a submissible case. We granted certiorari to resolve the conflict, and we now affirm the Eighth Circuit's judgment.

II

Federal Rule of Civil Procedure 50 . . . governs motions for judgment as a matter of law in jury trials. It allows the trial court to remove cases or issues from the jury's consideration "when the facts are sufficiently clear that the law requires a particular result." 9A C. Wright & A. Miller, Federal Practice and Procedure § 2521. Subdivision [(e)] controls when, as here, the verdict loser appeals from the trial court's denial of a motion for judgment as a matter of law:

> "[T]he party who prevailed on that motion may, as appellee, assert grounds entitling the party to a new trial in the event the appellate court concludes that the trial court erred in denying the motion for judgment. If the appellate court reverses the judgment, nothing in this rule precludes it from determining that the appellee is entitled to a new trial, or from directing the trial court to determine whether a new trial shall be granted."

Under this Rule, Weisgram urges, when a court of appeals determines that a jury verdict cannot be sustained due to an error in the admission of evidence, the appellate court may not order the entry of judgment for the verdict loser, but must instead remand the case to the trial court for a new trial determination. Nothing in Rule 50 expressly addresses this question.

In a series of pre-1967 decisions, this Court refrained from deciding the question, while emphasizing the importance of giving the party deprived of a verdict the opportunity to invoke the discretion of the trial judge to grant a new trial. Then, in *Neely*, the Court reviewed its prior jurisprudence and ruled definitively that if a motion for judgment as a matter of law is erroneously denied by the district court, the appellate court does have the power to order the entry of judgment for the moving party.

Neely first addressed the compatibility of appellate direction of judgment as a matter of law (then styled "judgment *n.o.v.*") with the Seventh Amendment's jury trial guarantee. It was settled, the Court pointed out, that a trial court, pursuant to Rule 50(b), could enter judgment for the verdict loser without offense to the Seventh Amendment. "As far as the Seventh Amendment's right to jury trial is concerned," the Court reasoned, "there is no greater restriction on the province of the jury when an appellate court enters judgment *n.o.v.* than when a trial court does"; accordingly, the Court concluded, "there is no constitutional bar to an appellate court granting judgment *n.o.v.*" The Court next turned to "the statutory grant of appellate jurisdiction to the courts of appeals [in 28 U.S.C. § 2106]," which it found "certainly broad enough to include the power to direct entry of judgment *n.o.v.* on appeal." The remainder of the *Neely* opinion effectively complements Rules 50(c) and [50(e)], providing guidance on the appropriate exercise of the appellate court's discretion when it reverses the trial court's denial of a defendant's Rule 50(b) motion for judgment as a matter of law.

Neely represents no volte-face in the Court's understanding of the respective competences of trial and appellate forums. Immediately after declaring that appellate courts have the power to order the entry of judgment for a verdict loser, the Court cautioned:

"Part of the Court's concern has been to protect the rights of the party whose jury verdict has been set aside on appeal and who may have valid grounds for a new trial, some or all of which should be passed upon by the district court, rather than the court of appeals, because of the trial judge's first-hand knowledge of witnesses, testimony, and issues—because of his 'feel' for the overall case. These are very valid concerns to which the court of appeals should be constantly alert."

Nevertheless, the Court in *Neely* continued, due consideration of the rights of the verdict winner and the closeness of the trial court to the case "do[es] not justify an ironclad rule that the court of appeals should never order dismissal or judgment for the defendant when the plaintiff's verdict has been set aside on appeal." "Such a rule," the Court concluded, "would not serve the purpose of Rule 50 to speed litigation and to avoid unnecessary retrials." *Neely* ultimately clarified that if a court of appeals determines that the district court erroneously denied a motion for judgment as a matter of law, the appellate court may (1) order a new trial at the verdict winner's request or on its own motion, (2) remand the case for the trial court to decide whether a new trial or entry of judgment for the defendant is warranted, or (3) direct the entry of judgment as a matter of law for the defendant.

III

The parties before us—and Court of Appeals opinions—diverge regarding *Neely's* scope. Weisgram, in line with some appellate decisions, posits a distinction between cases in which judgment as a matter of law is requested based on plaintiff's failure to produce enough evidence to warrant a jury verdict, as in *Neely*, and cases in which the proof introduced becomes insufficient because the court of appeals determines that certain evidence should not have been admitted, as in the instant case. Insufficiency caused by deletion of evidence, Weisgram contends, requires an "automatic remand" to the district court for consideration whether a new trial is warranted.

Weisgram relies on cases holding that, in fairness to a verdict winner who may have relied on erroneously admitted evidence, courts confronting questions of judgment as a matter of law should rule on the record as it went to the jury, without excising evidence inadmissible under Federal Rule of Evidence 702. These decisions are of questionable consistency with Rule 50(a)(1), which states that in ruling on a motion for judgment as a matter of law, the court is to inquire whether there is any "legally sufficient evidentiary basis to find for [the opponent of the motion]." Inadmissible evidence contributes nothing to a "legally sufficient evidentiary basis."

As *Neely* recognized, appellate rulings on post-trial pleas for judgment as a matter of law call for the exercise of "informed discretion," and fairness to the parties is surely key to the exercise of that discretion. But fairness concerns should loom as large when the verdict winner, in the appellate court's judgment, failed to present sufficient evidence as when the appellate court declares inadmissible record evidence essential to the verdict winner's case. In both situations, the party whose verdict is set aside on appeal will have had notice, before the close of evidence, of the alleged evidentiary deficiency. On appeal, both will have the opportunity to argue in support of the jury's verdict or, alternatively, for a new trial. And if judgment is instructed for the verdict loser, both will have a further chance to urge a new trial in a rehearing petition.

Since *Daubert*, moreover, parties relying on expert evidence have had notice of the exacting standards of reliability such evidence must meet. It is implausible to suggest, post-*Daubert*, that parties will initially present less than their best expert evidence in the expectation of a second chance should their first try fail. We therefore find unconvincing Weisgram's fears that allowing courts of appeals to direct the entry of judgment for defendants will punish plaintiffs who could have shored up their cases by other means had they known their expert testimony would be found inadmissible. In this case, for example, although Weisgram was on notice every step of the way that Marley was challenging his experts, he made no attempt to add or substitute other evidence.

After holding Weisgram's expert testimony inadmissible, the Court of Appeals evaluated the evidence presented at trial, viewing it in the light most favorable to Weisgram, and found the properly admitted evidence insufficient to support the verdict. Weisgram offered no specific grounds for a new trial to the Eighth Circuit. Even in the petition for rehearing, Weisgram argued only that the appellate court had misapplied state law, did not have the authority to direct judgment, and had failed to give adequate deference to the trial court's evidentiary rulings. The Eighth Circuit concluded that this was "not a close case." In these circumstances, the Eighth Circuit did not abuse its discretion by directing entry of judgment for Marley, instead of returning the case to the District Court for further proceedings.

* * *

Neely recognized that there are myriad situations in which the determination whether a new trial is in order is best made by the trial judge. *Neely* held, however, that there are also cases in which a court of appeals may appropriately instruct the district court to enter judgment as a matter of law against the jury-verdict winner. We adhere to *Neely*'s holding and rationale, and today hold that the authority of courts of appeals to direct the entry of judgment as a matter of law extends to cases in which, on excision of testimony erroneously admitted, there remains insufficient evidence to support the jury's verdict.

For the reasons stated, the judgment of the Court of Appeals for the Eighth Circuit is

Affirmed.

NOTES AND QUESTIONS

1. What standard must the court of appeals apply?   Under what standard did the court of appeals in *Weisgram* order entry of judgment for the defendant? Under what standard did the Supreme Court evaluate that decision? Clearly, the *Weisgram* Court rejected an ironclad rule that would have precluded the court of appeals from entering judgment as a matter of law. But did the Supreme Court provide any guidance as to when an appellate court may require the trial court to enter judgment as a matter of law? In this regard, the Supreme Court stated that the court of appeals did not "abuse its discretion" by ordering the entry of a judgment. Would the appellate court have abused its discretion if it had remanded and ordered a new trial? If the answer to that question is a negative, doesn't it follow that the district court should have been allowed to exercise its discretion in deciding whether to enter judgment as a matter of law or order a new trial? Does Rule 50(e) provide any guidance to the appellate court?

2.   *The appellate court's options.* In *Weisgram*, the defendant challenged the sufficiency of the plaintiff's evidence in the district court by first filing a Rule 50(a) motion for judgment as a matter of law before the case went to the jury and then renewing that motion under Rule 50(b) after the jury had returned a verdict in the plaintiff's favor. In ruling on the defendant's post-verdict motion, the district judge was in a position to assess the sufficiency of all the evidence, including the credibility of critical witnesses. The court of appeals stepped in only after the district court had performed these pre- and post-verdict functions.

Suppose a defendant files a Rule 50(a) motion before the case goes to the jury but then fails either to renew that motion under Rule 50(b) after the jury has returned a verdict for the plaintiff or to file an alternative motion for a new trial under Rules 50(b) and 59. May the defendant nonetheless ask the court of appeals to review the sufficiency of the evidence and remand the case for a new trial if the court concludes that the evidence was insufficient? Would this be consistent with the Supreme Court's admonition in *Neely v. Martin K. Eby Constr. Co.*, 386 U.S. 317, 325 (1967), quoted in *Weisgram* at page 1023, *supra*, that "courts of appeals should 'be constantly alert' to the 'trial judge's first-hand knowledge of witnesses, testimony, and issues'; in other words appellate courts should give due consideration to the first-instance decisionmaker's 'feel' for the overall case"? While a district court's ruling does not bind a court of appeals, as *Weisgram* itself makes clear, the appellate tribunal at least has the benefit of the trial judge's input and insight. Based on these concerns, the Supreme Court in *Unitherm Food Systems, Inc.*, *supra*, thus held that "a party is not entitled to pursue a new trial on appeal unless that party makes an appropriate postverdict motion in the district court." 546 U.S. at 404.

E.   Motions for a New Trial

Both state and federal courts permit a party to challenge an adverse judgment by moving for a new trial. The motion may be filed in lieu of or as an alternative to a post-verdict motion for judgment as a matter of law. A *motion for a new trial* differs from the latter in two important ways. First, the specific remedy sought is a new trial, not a judgment in favor of the moving party; and second, the standards for granting a new trial are significantly more flexible than the "no reasonable juror" standard applicable to judgments as a matter of law.

Typically, a party must make a motion for a new trial within a specified number of days of the entry of judgment. The time limits are strictly enforced, depriving a court of the authority to grant a new trial if a motion is not timely filed. In federal courts, for example, Rule 59(b) provides that "[a] motion for a new trial must be filed no later than 28 days after the entry of judgment." FED. R. CIV. P. 59(b). A federal court will not entertain a motion for a new trial filed after the specified period—no matter how unique or compelling the circumstances may be. *Bowles v. Russell*, 551 U.S. 205 (2007). Most state courts have adopted a similar position. *See, e.g., Daitch v. Benson*, 2014 WL 1022110 (Tex. Ct. App. 2014); *Tri-County Elevator Co. v. Superior Court*, 185 Cal. Rtpr. 208, 212 (Ct. App. 1982).

Some state statutes specify the grounds for which a new trial may be granted, while other states, as well as the federal rules, adopt a more general approach, allowing new trials on all grounds previously recognized at common law. Thus Rule 59(a)(1) provides that a motion for a new trial may be granted "(A) after a jury trial, for any reason for which a new trial has heretofore been granted in an action at law in federal court; or (B) after a nonjury trial, for any reason for which a rehearing has heretofore been granted in a suit in equity in federal court." FED. R. CIV. P. 59(a)(1); *cf.* CAL. CIV. PROC. CODE § 657 (specifying seven specific grounds).

Regardless of the approach taken, a motion for a new trial will only be granted to redress prejudicial errors, *i.e.*, errors that affect the fundamental fairness of the trial process and that may therefore have infected the judgment. The range of potential reversible errors is broad. Typical grounds include:

- errors in the jury-selection process;
- erroneous evidentiary rulings;
- erroneous jury instructions;
- verdict as being against the weight of the evidence;
- excessiveness or inadequacy of the verdict;
- misconduct by the judge, jury, attorneys, parties, or witnesses; or
- newly discovered evidence.

In all of the above categories, the trial court is given broad discretion to determine whether the purported error has so infected the trial process as to render the judgment suspect or the process fundamentally unfair. *See generally* Martin H. Redish, *New Trial; Altering or Amending a Judgment, in* 12 MOORE'S FEDERAL PRACTICE §§ 59.01 *et seq.* (3d ed. 2015).

The principal case below provides an example of how a court might approach a motion for a new trial. Notice that the opinion is fact intensive. Why would that be?

Tesser v. Board of Education

190 F. Supp. 2d 430 (E.D.N.Y. 2002), *aff'd*, 370 F.3d 314 (2d Cir. 2004)

GARAUFIS, District Judge.

Now before this court is Plaintiff's post-trial motion for judgment as a matter of law pursuant to Fed. R. Civ. P. 50, or alternatively, a new trial pursuant to Fed. R. Civ. P. 59. For the reasons discussed below, Plaintiff's motion is denied.

I.   Background

Plaintiff Gilda Tesser brought this civil rights action against her former employers ("defendants") by complaint filed November 17, 1997. The complaint included various claims, including religious discrimination under Title VII of the Civil Rights Act of 1964, 42 U.S.C. §§ 2000e *et seq.* ("Title VII") and the New York City Human Rights Law, Administrative Code §§ 8-101 *et seq.*, and retaliation in her terms of employment for having complained about the perceived discrimination. After years of pre-trial discovery and motion practice, the case went to trial before a jury on July 9, 2001. The trial lasted over two weeks, ending on July 25, 2001, when the jury entered a verdict for defendants on all counts.[1] The instant motion for a judgment notwithstanding the verdict pursuant to Fed. R. Civ. P. 50, or in the alternative, a new trial pursuant to Rule 59 followed. . . .

At the time of the allegedly discriminatory actions, Plaintiff was an Assistant Principal in Charge of P.S. 177 in Community School District 21. Defendant Superintendent Weber appointed Plaintiff to this position. At the time, he believed Plaintiff would eventually be promoted to principal when the position became available and intended to support her candidacy for this position.

In 1991, Plaintiff applied for the position of principal at P.S. 177. "In effect at that time was an internal Chancellor's C-30 Regulation requiring community school boards to follow a three-step process in selecting supervisory personnel. Level I involved the establishment of a screening committee consisting of six to ten parents, two teachers, the superintendent, and community school board members. The committee determined the selection criteria and interviewed at least ten candidates. Only the parents and teachers were allowed to vote for at least five of those candidates, who were then recommended to the community superintendent. Level II required the superintendent to evaluate the recommended candidates and recommend two to the community school board. Level III required the community school board either to select one for appointment or to request that the superintendent or committee consider other candidates from the original Level I pool."

Plaintiff testified that prior to, and during her candidacy, she learned that the parents of P.S. 177 were opposed to her appointment because she was Jewish. Plaintiff informed Weber of the anti-Semitic animus she believed was being expressed by the parents. Plaintiff and Weber had several conversations regarding Plaintiff's concerns. Weber testified that over the course of these conversations he began to believe Plaintiff was acting irrationally, that she would be unable to work

---

1. The jury verdict found 1) that plaintiff did not prove that the [defendants] had discriminated against plaintiff on the basis of her religion; 2) that plaintiff did not prove that the defendants retaliated against plaintiff because of her complaints of religious discrimination or because she hired an attorney; and 3) that plaintiff did not prove that information contained in the letter dated November 29, 1994 was false or misleading. Plaintiff moved pursuant to Rules 50 and 59 only with respect to the verdicts on discrimination and retaliation. Therefore, the verdict regarding false or misleading information is not challenged or considered in this memorandum and order.

effectively with the school community, and that her perception of anti-Semitism was unfounded. In explaining why he thought Plaintiff was "unraveling" or acting "irrationally," he testified that Ms. Tesser yelled at him, that he thought she was accusing the parents of anti-Semitism rather than admitting that they simply did not like her, and that she stated she was "going to get" the parents on the selection committee.

Despite the alleged religious discrimination directed at Plaintiff, the parents did not eliminate Plaintiff from consideration and she successfully moved on to the second level of consideration. Moreover, Plaintiff's own witness, a member of the Level I selection committee, testified that no parent indicated a desire to prevent Ms. Tesser's selection because she was Jewish. Plaintiff's witness did testify, however, that the parents thought Ms. Tesser was being given preferential treatment by Weber because she was Jewish. This witness further testified that the parents indicated their preference for another candidate, Mr. Ianniello. The witness thought it was unfair that the parents were attempting to hamper Ms. Tesser's progress to Level II because they did not like Ms. Tesser personally and because they preferred Mr. Ianniello for his popularity rather than for his qualifications.

After passing Level I, Plaintiff hired an attorney because of her concern about religious discrimination affecting the progress of her candidacy. On January 16, 1992, Plaintiff tape recorded a conversation she had with Weber and Plotnick [the president of the Community School Board] in which her decision to hire an attorney was discussed. Weber made it known to Tesser that he did not agree with her decision to hire an attorney. He was later admonished for these statements in a letter from the Chancellor. On June 24, 1992, Weber submitted his two choices for principal of P.S. 177 to the school board. Plaintiff was not one of the two finalists. Therefore, after the completion of Level II, Plaintiff was no longer under consideration for the position of principal. Weber testified that although he did not think it was necessary for Plaintiff to hire an attorney, this was not the basis for his decision not to recommend her to Level III. He further testified that he knew that one finalist, Kathleen Lavin, was not Jewish; however he believed the other finalist, Arlynn Brody, was Jewish. In sum, Weber testified that his decision not to recommend Plaintiff was not based on her religion or in retaliation for hiring an attorney, but was the result of his concern that she could not handle the responsibilities of a principal at P.S. 177.

By letter dated June 30, 1992, Weber informed Plaintiff that instead of remaining at P.S. 177 she had been reassigned to P.S. 128, another school within District 21 in which she had worked prior to coming to P.S. 177. Her assignment was to begin in August 1992. On July 7, 1992, she filed a complaint with the Board of Education of the City of New York ("BOE") alleging discrimination based on her religion in the C-30 selection process. Thus, at the time Plaintiff was beginning her work at P.S. 128, an investigation was ongoing with respect to her complaint and the selection of Lavin as principal at P.S. 177. The Office of Equal Opportunity concluded that the decision not to select Plaintiff was not the result of religious discrimination, and the selection of Lavin was finalized.

During the 1992 school year at P.S. 128, various employment-related actions were taken with respect to Plaintiff, which she alleged were discriminatory. These included a change in office space, change in duties, and a refusal by Principal Miller to allow her to see and revise the faculty notes for the upcoming school year. Plaintiff also testified that within her first few weeks back at P.S. 128, Miller told her that she would not be allowed to remain there and threatened to have her thrown out of the building if she did not leave. Plaintiff claimed to have suffered tremendous emotional stress as a result of this incident, and she was admitted to psychiatric care for treatment. She filed a "line of duty" injury claim, alleging that Mr. Miller's treatment had directly led to her need for therapy and inability to work for some 25 days.

Plaintiff subsequently filed a claim of religious discrimination and retaliation with the New York Human Rights Commission in June 1993, requested a temporary transfer to another district in August of 1993, and applied for, and was granted whistle-blower status on September 21, 1993 by the Special Commissioner of Investigation ("SCOI"). Because the BOE had not granted Plaintiff her requested transfer outside of District 21, on her own initiative she obtained employment in the Plainview Old Bethpage Central School District ("Plainview"). BOE granted her a one-year leave to take this position. She also was granted a leave of absence for child-care immediately following her one-year leave to work in Plainview. When it was discovered that she had been working elsewhere while on child-care leave, in violation of the leave policy, she was ordered to return to work in District 21 or risk being reported as an unauthorized absentee. When Plaintiff did not return to District 21 for work, she was deemed resigned, a less severe status than unauthorized absentee because it allowed her the option of withdrawing her resignation.

At trial, the above facts, as well as those going to damages, were developed in greater detail through the submission of numerous documents, letters, tape recordings, expert opinion, witness testimony, and records from the administrative investigations and proceedings. Included among the testifying witnesses were Plaintiff, Defendant Weber, and Defendant Miller. As in many discrimination cases, ultimately the case turned in significant degree on the respective credibility of Plaintiff and defendants and their explanations for the various events and employment actions. In this case, the jury did not believe that Plaintiff's version was more probable than not, and it returned a verdict in favor of the defendants. The jury unanimously found that Plaintiff did not prove that the BOE, Community School District 21, Donald Weber, or Michael Miller "discriminated against her based on her religion," and it found that Plaintiff had not proven that the BOE, Community School District 21, Donald Weber, or Michael Miller "retaliated against her because of her complaining of religious discrimination or because she hired an attorney."

II.   Discussion

A.   Rule 50 Motion for Judgment as a Matter of Law

In this Circuit, a party seeking to vacate a jury verdict and enter judgment as a matter of law carries a "heavy burden." Judgment as a matter of law is only appropriate when "(1) there is such a complete absence of evidence supporting the verdict that the jury's findings could only have been the result of sheer surmise and conjecture, or (2) there is such an overwhelming amount of evidence in favor of the movant that reasonable and fair minded persons could not arrive at a verdict against it." When considering a Rule 50 motion and deciding whether there was a sufficient evidentiary basis to support the verdict, the court cannot assess the weight of conflicting evidence or substitute its judgment for that of the jury. Rather, it must make all credibility determinations and draw all inferences in favor of the nonmovant.

First, Plaintiff argues for judgment as a matter of law on the basis that there is overwhelming circumstantial evidence to support her claim of religious discrimination by her employers and defendants have failed to supply evidence sufficient to support their asserted legitimate business reason for not promoting Plaintiff. In making this argument, Plaintiff implies that by having established her *prima facie* case, she presented the jury with a presumption of discrimination that shifted the burden of disproving such discrimination to defendants. To the extent Plaintiff relies on this presumption, it mischaracterizes the proper legal burden Plaintiff maintained at trial, and is insufficient for granting judgment as a matter of law.

The Second Circuit has made clear that in employment discrimination cases, as in other civil cases, the ultimate burden of persuasion *always* remains with the plaintiff. *See Fisher v. Vassar College*, 114 F.3d 1332, 1336-1337 (2d Cir. 1997). The presumption created by the [*McDonnell Douglas Corp. v. Green*, 411 U.S. 792 (1973)] burden shifting analysis, so critical in surviving summary judgment or dismissal at the close of plaintiff's case, is not enough to guarantee a plaintiff will win her case, "even if the elements of the prima facie case go unchallenged." *Fisher, supra* at 1336. "[E]vidence sufficient to satisfy the scaled-down requirements of the prima facie case under *McDonnell Douglas* does not necessarily tell much about whether discrimination played a role in the employment decision. The fact that a plaintiff is judged to have satisfied these minimal requirements is no indication that, at the end of the case, plaintiff will have enough evidence of discrimination to support a verdict in his favor." *Id.* at 1337 . . . .

In the instant case, the facts presented by Plaintiff were sufficient to establish a *prima facie* case at the summary judgment stage and to proceed to trial. Those same facts, however, are not necessarily sufficient, as a matter of law, to require a verdict in her favor. Thus, in considering Plaintiff's motion for judgment notwithstanding the verdict, this court does not reapply the *McDonnell Douglas* analysis to Plaintiff's claims. Rather, this court considers the sole determinative issue, whether or not a reasonable jury could have concluded that Plaintiff failed to prove by a preponderance of the evidence that defendants' employment-related actions were motivated by illegal discrimination or retaliation.

In arguing that Plaintiff has proven as a matter of law the defendants' discriminatory motive, Plaintiff essentially reargues the facts presented at trial. Based on these facts she asserts that "the evidence supports but one conclusion: Weber capitulated to the discriminatory will of the parents and declined to pass Ms. Tesser's name on to Level III." She argues that Weber's proffered reasons for not passing on Ms. Tesser's name are incredible, and therefore the only rational conclusion is that he is trying to hide his discriminatory motives. In particular, Plaintiff points to the fact that Weber continued to employ and approve of Ms. Tesser's work during the same period of time he claims that she began acting irrationally and incapable of taking on the position of principal.

As a matter of law, Plaintiff's suggestion that a clear showing of pretext establishes discrimination in this case is wrong. While proof of pretext combined with circumstantial evidence may be sufficient to prove discriminatory intent, it does not require such a finding. In other words, the jury might have disbelieved Weber's proffered reason for his decision, yet still not believed that Plaintiff had proven illegal discrimination was a motivating factor.

As a factual matter, defendants presented sufficient evidence upon which a jury could believe their proffered reasons were true, or at least have concluded that discrimination was not a motivating factor. In explaining his reasoning in not recommending Plaintiff, Weber testified that while he thought Ms. Tesser was still capably performing her current duties, he did not believe that she was demonstrating the skills, especially in relating to the parents and community, necessary for a principal. Based on this assessment, he decided not to pass her name on to Level III. The evidence presented at trial is not wholly inconsistent with this explanation.

On a motion for judgment as a matter of law, I cannot disregard Weber's explanation by passing on his credibility or weighing conflicting evidence. While evidence introduced by Plaintiff could have led a reasonable jury to disbelieve Weber, the evidence was not so "overwhelming[ly] . . . in favor of the movant that reasonable and fair minded persons could not arrive at a verdict against [her]." Further, given the significant conflicting evidence, I do not find that the jury's verdict was based on "sheer surmise and conjecture." Accordingly, I find that a reasonable jury could conclude, as did the jury in this case, that Plaintiff failed to prove by a preponderance of the evidence that defendants acted with a discriminatory motive.

Plaintiff also argues that she has proven retaliation by defendants as a matter of law. With respect to Defendant Miller, Plaintiff argues that this court should find his testimony that he did not have knowledge of her participation in a protected activity as "incredible as a matter of law" and that this court should "infer" that Miller had knowledge because the SCOI determined that Miller had retaliated against Plaintiff.

With respect to Defendant BOE, Plaintiff argues that because the SCOI determined that Miller retaliated against Plaintiff, this finding is "conclusive" and when the BOE accepted this determination it "admitted" retaliation by Miller, for which it is liable. Similarly, she argues that the BOE already "admitted" Weber's retaliatory conduct when it found that Weber acted improperly in calling the Plainview school in violation of BOE's order that Weber not call any of Plaintiff's "prospective employers."

State administrative findings, such as the SCOI investigation, or the finding of probable cause by the New York Human Rights Commission are not preclusive on federal Title VII claims. Therefore, the jury was not bound to find, as Plaintiff would have it, that the SCOI findings or their adoption by the BOE establish retaliatory conduct as a matter of law under the meaning of Title VII. Moreover, the jury was properly instructed on the various elements required for a finding of retaliation, and how those differed as between individual and corporate defendants. The jury was instructed that "[t]o find a defendant liable for retaliation, you must find, by a preponderance of the evidence, that the defendant, motivated by the plaintiff's reasonable and good-faith opposition to discrimination based on her religion, subjected her to an adverse employment action." I further instructed the jurors that they could find retaliation by the BOE, Community School District 21 and Weber "even if Miller denies direct knowledge of the plaintiff's claims of religious discrimination" and the jury received instructions on the meaning of constructive discharge as a form of adverse employment action.

While the SCOI finding was not binding on the jury, it was persuasive evidence in favor of Plaintiff. This court, however, must view the evidence in the light most favorable to defendants and draw all reasonable inferences in their favor. Considering the SCOI was only one piece of evidence among many, I find that a reasonable jury could conclude that the actions taken by the defendants were not retaliatory.

First, Miller testified that when Plaintiff returned to P.S. 128 he did not know of her complaints to the Chancellor and the BOE. I will not second-guess the jury's weighing of his testimony. Second, the defendants presented evidence upon which a reasonable jury could conclude that the various employment-related actions were not "adverse," regardless of defendants' knowledge of Plaintiff's complaints. For instance, although Plaintiff's office at P.S. 128 upon her return there in 1992 was not the same one she had during her prior tenure, Miller testified that the change had occurred after she left in 1990, when a new assistant principal, Mr. Sealey, took over. Based on this evidence, the jury could reasonably conclude that the change in office space, which occurred two years prior, was not an adverse employment action directed at Plaintiff's complaints of religious discrimination. Similarly, the jury could reasonably conclude that the fact that Plaintiff was responsible for more bus and lunchroom duties was not retaliatory since these were the same bus and lunchroom duties that Mr. Sealey had performed as assistant principal prior to Plaintiff's return to this position. Finally, accepting as true Defendant Miller's account of the incident in which he told Plaintiff to leave the building, he was ordering her to go to the district office for a counseling session because of her recent comments about getting back at the superintendent, the school board and the parents. A reasonable jury could find Miller's action appropriate in the given context and conclude that he did not retaliate for any complaints of discrimination by Plaintiff.

While the examples discussed above do not account for every point of fact which Plaintiff raises to support her motion for judgment as a matter of law on the retaliation claim, they amply demonstrate the sufficient conflicting evidence as to the motivations of the defendants. Thus, I find that a reasonable jury could conclude that Plaintiff failed to prove by a preponderance of the evidence that the defendants retaliated against Plaintiff because of her complaints of discrimination.

B.   Plaintiff's Rule 59 Motion for a New Trial

1.   Legal Standard

A motion for a new trial, pursuant to Fed. R. Civ. P. 59, may be granted when the district court is "convinced that the jury has reached a seriously erroneous result or that the verdict is a miscarriage of justice." *Smith v. Lightning Bolt Prods., Inc.*, 861 F.2d 363, 370 (2d Cir. 1988). Unlike the standard for granting judgment as a matter of law, the standard for a new trial permits the trial judge to "weigh the evidence himself, and [he] need not view it in the light most favorable to the verdict winner." *DLC Mgmt. Corp. v. Town of Hyde Park*, 163 F.3d 124, 134 (2d Cir. 1998). Despite this more lenient standard, the Second Circuit has cautioned that a trial court "should rarely disturb a jury's evaluation of a witness's credibility." *Id.* Therefore, "[w]here the resolution of the issues depend[s] on assessment of the credibility of the witnesses, it is proper for the court to refrain from setting aside the verdict and granting a new trial." *Metromedia Co. Fugazy*, 983 F.2d 350, 363 (2d Cir. 1992).

2.   Analysis

First, Plaintiff argues that the complete lack of credibility of defendants Miller and Weber taken together with the substantial evidence in her favor warrant a new trial. In addition, she identifies four other grounds for granting a new trial: the inadequacy of jury deliberations, the limitations on Plaintiff's ability to present her rebuttal case, the admission of irrelevant and prejudicial evidence, and improper statements made by defendants' counsel during summation. Even under the more lenient standard for granting a new trial, this court finds that none of the stated grounds are sufficient, individually or cumulatively, for granting a new trial in this case.

(a)   SUFFICIENCY OF THE EVIDENCE

As already discussed with respect to the Rule 50 motion, there is a significant amount of evidence that if believed as true supports the jury's verdict for defendants. I do not find that defendants Miller and Weber were so lacking in credibility as witnesses that the jury could not have properly believed all, or part, of their testimony. Therefore, I decline to set aside a jury verdict on the basis of witness credibility when the resolution of determinative issues in this case largely depended on the jurors' assessment of those very witnesses' testimony.

(b)   ADEQUACY OF JURY DELIBERATIONS

Second, Plaintiff's claim that the jury deliberations were inadequate is without merit. In *Wilburn v. Eastman Kodak Co.*, 180 F.3d 475 (2d Cir. 1999), the Second Circuit held that the trial judge did not err in denying plaintiff's motion for a new trial where the jury had deliberated for only twenty minutes. The court held, "[a] jury is not required to deliberate for any set length of time. Brief deliberation, by itself, does not show that the jury failed to give full, conscientious or impartial consideration to the evidence." In the instant case, the jury was given comprehensive instructions on the law and then deliberated for approximately two hours. While there was a great deal of documentary evidence to consider, the issues to be resolved in this case were not more complex than the average Title VII employment discrimination case. Moreover, there is no reason to conclude that in considering this case the jury "contemptuously or flippantly disregarded its duty." Accordingly, I find no basis for overturning the jury verdict based on the length of its deliberations.

(c) TRIAL ERRORS

Plaintiff's third through fifth asserted grounds for a new trial all allege some type of evidentiary or trial error. This court considers these grounds for a new trial in the context of the harmless error standard of the Federal Rules of Civil Procedure, which states:

> Unless justice requires otherwise, no error in admitting or excluding evidence— or any other error by the court or a party—is ground for granting a new trial, for setting aside a verdict, or for vacating, modifying, or otherwise disturbing a judgment or order. At every stage of the proceeding, the court must disregard all errors and defects that do not affect any party's substantial rights.

Fed. R. Civ. P. 61*; *see also Perry v. Ethan Allen, Inc.*, 115 F.3d 143, 150 (2d Cir. 1997) (holding that the court "will not conclude that a substantial right was affected unless it is likely that in some material respect the factfinder's judgment was 'swayed by the error'").

Plaintiff's third ground for a new trial is that she suffered substantial prejudice when she took the stand before defendants Weber and Miller, limiting her ability to rebut their testimony. Weber and Miller were called to the stand as Plaintiff's witnesses, but were not called to the stand by Defense. Plaintiff intended to take the stand as part of her case in chief, but only after first placing Weber and Miller on the stand for direct. Despite this court's order, Weber and Miller were not available on the first day of trial, thus Plaintiff took the stand first. Plaintiff argues that this so severely limited her ability to rebut statements made by Weber and Miller that it amounts to grounds for a new trial.

A trial court has discretion to "exercise reasonable control over the mode and order of interrogating witnesses and presenting evidence so as to (1) make the interrogation and presentation effective for the ascertainment of the truth, [and] (2) avoid needless consumption of time. . . ." Fed. R. Evid. 611. Therefore, it was within this court's discretion to move forward once the jury had been selected, rather than delaying the start of trial by a day or more so that Plaintiff would not have to take the stand before Weber and Miller. Moreover, Plaintiff was free to request an opportunity to retake the stand after Weber and Miller testified but before the close of her case-in-chief. She made no such request at trial. Accordingly, I find that the order of presenting evidence and witnesses was

---

* [The quoted text is from the current version of Rule 61, as amended effective Dec. 1, 2007. The 2007 changes from the prior version of the Rule were intended to be stylistic only.—EDS.]

managed in accordance with Rule 611 and that Plaintiff had adequate opportunity at the time of trial to remedy any potential prejudice that she believed would result from the order of witnesses.

Plaintiff's fourth ground for a new trial is based on the admission of two exhibits, her unredacted tax returns and a letter written by the interim Superintendent of the Plainview school, which explained why Plainview was denying Plaintiff tenure. Plaintiff argues that both of these pieces of evidence were irrelevant and unduly prejudicial and that their admission warrants a new trial.

As to the unredacted tax returns, Plaintiff principally argues that the "Jury's access to the entire tax returns only served to tap any latent prejudices the jurors might direct to Ms. Tesser based upon her wealth." I previously considered the issue of relevance and prejudice before deciding to admit the tax returns in dispute. The decision as to whether or not to admit these documents was reserved until after Plaintiff elicited testimony from her expert, Mr. McAteer, on the tax implications of a damages award to Plaintiff. Mr. McAteer testified that he had reviewed Plaintiff's W-2 forms, among other documents, in preparing his report and he testified as to how a lump sum award to Plaintiff would increase her tax bracket and cause her to pay more in taxes than if she had received that sum as pay over several years. Based on this testimony, it was decided to admit the tax forms with the following limiting instructions to the jury: "The amounts earned by plaintiff's spouse and the family's other income and assets as reflected on the joint tax returns may be considered by you only to the extent that you believe they bear on the testimony of Mr. McAteer to the degree that he referred to the tax consequences in calculating damages. These amounts have no other bearing on this case, and I instruct you not to consider them otherwise." In light of this limiting instruction, and the rule that "juries are presumed to follow their instructions," I conclude that any potential prejudice was sufficiently cured and the admission of the tax returns did not create substantial prejudice.

With respect to the admission of . . . the letter by the interim Superintendent of Plainview, Plaintiff withdrew her objections to admission of this exhibit. . . .

Finally, Plaintiff argues that defense counsel made statements in summation which "led the jury over the line from permissible inference to impermissible speculation." Specifically, Plaintiff argues that defendants caused her substantial prejudice by suggesting, without any factual support, that Plaintiff was withholding, or had destroyed, various pieces of evidence or witness testimony that would either fail to support her claim or, alternatively, exonerate Defendants. For instance, Plaintiff objects to statements made in reference to the tape recorded phone conversations, such as "What did she cutout [sic]? She cut something out. She is hiding something from you, snippants[,] she is one to give you little snippants, not the full picture, if you saw the full picture you would realize there was not merit to her claim at all."

In a civil case such as this, speculation by defense counsel, while not proper, does not threaten to impermissibly shift the burden of proof as it would in a criminal case in which the prosecution makes unfounded speculative arguments about a defendant's guilt. Here, defendants were free to argue that Plaintiff had not met her burden and to question the sufficiency of her evidence. While, there was no specific evidentiary basis for suggesting that Plaintiff had "cutout" or withheld other tape-recordings, taken in context the defense was arguing that the recordings presented by Plaintiff did not accurately represent the conversations between her and defendants. Similarly taking in context each of the statements to which Plaintiff points, I do not believe that they were so prejudicial as to have improperly swayed the jury. Moreover, I gave the jury very specific instructions to preclude any impermissible speculation . . . .

I find that any potential prejudice resulting from statements by defense counsel which may have verged on speculation was adequately cured by the instructions to the jury, and in any case, in light of all the other evidence, such statements could not be considered so substantially prejudicial as to "in some material respect" have "swayed" the factfinder's judgment.

Having considered all the evidence presented at trial, and for all the reasons discussed above, I do not believe that the jury reached a "seriously erroneous result" in deciding that Plaintiff had not carried her burden of proof and I do not find that the verdict is a "miscarriage of justice." Accordingly, Plaintiff's motion for a new trial is denied.

III.   Conclusion

For all the reasons discussed above it is hereby ORDERED that Plaintiff's motion for judgment as a matter of law or, in the alternative, for a new trial is DENIED in its entirety. So ORDERED.

NOTES AND QUESTIONS

1. The distinction between a Rule 50 motion and a Rule 59 motion.   As is commonly done, the plaintiff filed a motion for judgment and, in the alternative, a motion for a new trial. In terms of the standards a court must apply in determining whether to grant either motion, what is the difference between the two? What is the justification for that distinction? In what manner or to what degree does the right to a trial by jury affect the court's willingness to grant either motion?

2. Ruling on both motions.   The district court denied the plaintiff's motion for judgment and thus had to go on to consider her alternative motion for a new trial. Suppose that the court had instead granted the plaintiff's motion for judgment, after the jury returned a verdict for the defendants. Since doing so would have given the plaintiff everything that she wanted, would there be any need for the court to rule as well on her alternative motion for a new trial? If the district court did not rule on that motion, and the court of appeals then reversed the district court's entry of judgment for the plaintiff, would that dispose of the case, or would the case have to be remanded to the district court for a ruling on the motion for a new trial? Might the district court judge now have to rule on the question years after the trial had concluded, at a time when the proceedings and the evidence were no longer fresh in the trial judge's mind? Does Rule 50 address this concern? What does it require a district judge to do under these circumstances?

3. *Remittitur.*   If an award of damages is deemed excessive, a court may order a new trial or, in the alternative, may condition its refusal to grant a new trial on the verdict winner's acceptance of a reduction in the verdict. This is known as *remittitur.* The federal standard for determining excessiveness is usually expressed in terms of "shocking the judicial conscience," though some states allow more judicial leeway. *See Gasperini v. Center for Humanities, Inc.*, 518 U.S. 415 (1996) (holding that federal court sitting in diversity must apply state's "materially deviates" standard in measuring excessiveness of verdict); Chapter VI, page 538, *supra.* In federal court, Rule 59 provides the appropriate vehicle for challenging the excessiveness of a verdict. In determining whether a verdict is excessive, the court weighs the evidence and makes an independent determination of excessiveness, much like the process for determining whether the verdict goes against the clear weight of the evidence. *See generally* 12 MOORE'S FEDERAL PRACTICE, *supra,* § 59.13[2][g][iii]. With respect to compensatory damages, a federal district court's determination of excessiveness is then subject to an abuse-of-discretion standard of review on appeal. *Gasperini*, 518 U.S. at 438. However, if a jury has also awarded punitive damages, a federal appellate court will exercise de novo review in determining whether they may be so disproportionate to the gravity of defendant's offense as to violate the Due Process Clause. *See Cooper Industries, Inc. v. Leatherman Tool Group, Inc.*, 532 U.S. 424 (2001), page 1098, *infra.*

4. *Additur.*   Some state courts also allow *additur.* For example, a plaintiff might file a motion for a new trial, arguing that the size of the jury verdict was insufficient. If the court agrees, it may either grant the motion or condition its denial on the defendant's acceptance of a larger verdict. The California Supreme Court has thus upheld the use of additur and ruled that it does not violate the right to a jury trial under the state constitution. *Jehl v. Southern Pac. Co.*, 427 P.2d 988 (Cal. 1967). For other states that allow additur, see, *e.g.*, ARIZ. RULE OF CIV. PROC. 59(i)(1); CONN. GEN. STAT. § 52-216a; WASH. REV. CODE § 4.76.030; *Carney v. Preston*, 683 A.2d 47 (Del. Super. Ct. 1996); *Parrish v. City of Orlando*, 53 So. 3d 1199 (Fla. Dist. Ct. App. 2011); *Watson v. Payne*, 2011 WL 1233499 (Tenn. Ct. App. Apr. 1, 2011). By contrast, the U.S. Supreme Court has held that use of this device is generally not permitted in federal court because it would violate the Seventh Amendment. *Dimick v. Schiedt*, 293 U.S. 474, 486-487 (1935). The *Dimick* Court reasoned that since additur, unlike remittitur, was unavailable at common law, it could not be used to alter a jury's verdict consistent with the Seventh Amendment. Although *Dimick* has been much criticized, it remains good law. *See Earl v. Bouchard Transp. Co., Inc.*, 917 F.2d 1320, 1331 (2d Cir. 1990) (noting "the asymmetric treatment by federal courts of the doctrines of remittitur and additur, despite vigorous criticism of the rule"). However, additur is allowed in federal court if there was an error in verdict calculation that involves a mistake of law. For example, if the size of the verdict was the result of an erroneous jury instruction, a federal judge may condition the denial of a motion for a new

trial on the defendant's acceptance of a verdict that would have been consistent with a proper instruction.

F.   Trial Review Problem

11-8. John and Edgar, who are African American, were employed at a poultry plant owned and operated by Bison Foods ("Bison"). They sought promotions to fill two shift-manager positions at that plant, but the plant manager, Thomas, instead selected two white males from another of the company's plants. John and Edgar then filed suit against Bison in Alabama federal district court.

    A. John and Edgar sued Bison under Title VII of the Civil Rights Act of 1964, claiming that Bison's refusal to promote them involved discrimination on account of race. The relief they seek is promotion to the managerial positions in question, as well as backpay for the difference between their prior compensation and that paid by the higher level positions. The plaintiffs made a timely demand for jury trial. Bison has objected that the plaintiffs have no right to a jury trial in this case. How should the court rule? (You may want to look again at *Terry*, at page 976, *supra*.)

    B. Suppose that in addition to reinstatement and backpay under Title VII, the plaintiffs seek unlimited compensatory and punitive damages under 42 U.S.C. § 1981, a civil rights statute dating from 1870. To recover punitive damages under § 1981, an employer must be shown to have engaged in intentional racial discrimination either knowing that it was violating the plaintiff's federal rights or acting with malice or reckless indifference toward those rights. The plaintiffs made a timely request for a jury trial on their § 1981 claims. Should such a right be available on these damages claims, whether or not it is available on their Title VII claims for promotion and backpay?

    C. Since the relief sought under the Title VII and § 1981 claims is totally different, and since the evidence needed to prove the claims is only partially overlapping, would it be permissible for the district judge to bifurcate the trial, first trying the Title VII claims and then the § 1981 claims? Does your answer to this question hinge in any way on your answers to parts A and B?

    D. Assume that John and Edgar asserted claims under Title VII and § 1981 and that the entire case was tried before a jury. At trial, the plaintiffs introduced evidence that Thomas

- gave shifting reasons for not hiring them;
- used qualifications not required by company policy that had the effect of excluding the plaintiffs;
- only checked references for black candidates;
- did not review the plaintiffs' performance reviews or personnel files;
- lied about a college-degree requirement for the positions;

- offered one of the shift-manager positions to a white employee before interviewing Edgar, despite having said the position would be held open until the plaintiffs' interviews had been completed;
  - made his decision not to promote the plaintiffs in an atmosphere in which black employees were treated differently; and
  - showed a cool demeanor toward the plaintiffs and made statements referring to them as "boys."

At trial, Bison offered the testimony of Thomas, who stated that there were several reasons for not promoting the plaintiffs, none having to do with race, including the fact that while both were experienced, they lacked college degrees and were currently working at the plant for which the hiring was being made, a plant with serious performance problems that needed someone from the outside. Thomas also testified that his use of the term "boy" merely referred to the plaintiffs' gender and that it had no racial overtones because he did not modify it with a racial classification such as "black boy."

1. At the conclusion of the trial, before the case was submitted to the jury, Bison filed a Rule 50(a) motion for a judgment as a matter of law on both the Title VII and the § 1981 claims, arguing that the plaintiffs had not presented evidence from which a reasonable jury could find that the decision not to promote them was racially motivated, much less that it was made with either the intent to violate, or with malice and reckless indifference toward, the plaintiffs' federal rights. What will Bison argue in favor of its motion? What will the plaintiffs argue in response? Does Edgar arguably have a stronger case than John? How should the court rule on Bison's motion and why?

2. Assume that the court denied Bison's motion. The case went to the jury, which returned a verdict awarding each plaintiff $250,000 in compensatory damages and $1.5 million in punitive damages. Bison then renewed its motion for judgment as a matter of law under Rule 50(b). Since the evidence on which this motion is based is identical to that which the court previously reviewed when it denied Bison's Rule 50(a) motion, does not the "law of the case" preclude the court from now reconsidering the question? Is there any reason why a court that previously denied a Rule 50(a) motion might then grant a Rule 50(b) motion that is based on the identical evidentiary record? If you were the judge, how would you rule on Bison's Rule 50(b) motion and why?

3. Suppose you are representing Bison. Is there anything else you might file in the district court besides a Rule 50(b) motion? How would your arguments in this additional filing differ, if at all, from your contentions under Rule 50(b)? To the extent that one of your new objections is to the award of punitive damages, if the court agrees with you that these were improper, does the judge have any alternative besides totally rejecting the jury's verdict?

   4. If the court grants your Rule 50(b) motion, with the result that
      judgment is now entered for the defendant, is there any need for the
      court to consider the alternative arguments that you made in question
      3, including a possible objection to the punitive damages, since that
      verdict has been completely nullified?

See Ash v. Tyson Foods, Inc., 129 Fed. App'x 529 (11th Cir. 2005), *vacated and remanded per curiam*, 546 U.S. 454 (2006), *aff'd in part and rev'd in part*, 190 Fed. App'x 924 (11th Cir. 2006), *cert. denied*, 549 U.S. 1181 (2007), *decision on remand*, 2008 WL 4921515 (N.D. Ala. Sept. 30, 2008), *rev'd*, 392 Fed. App'x 817 (11th Cir. 2010), *reh'g granted and district court decision aff'd*, 664 F.3d 883 (11th Cir. 2011). *And see Hithon v. Tyson Foods, Inc.*, 566 Fed. App'x 827 (11th Cir.), *cert. denied*, 135 S. Ct. 729 (2014) (awarding plaintiffs attorneys' fees and costs under 42 U.S.C. § 1988).

XII

APPELLATE REVIEW

A. Overview and Basic Terminology

In most cases, once a trial court enters a final judgment or issues an appealable order, a party adversely affected by the trial court's action may seek review in a higher court. Most jurisdictions provide for one appeal as of right, usually to an intermediate appellate court, and for a subsequent opportunity to seek discretionary review in the highest court of the jurisdiction. In examining the appellate process, we will use the federal judicial system as our model since, by and large, it conforms to this generally accepted format.

The basic appellate process itself is quite straightforward. What follows is a simplified description of that process within the federal system: Once an appealable order is entered, the adversely affected party files a timely notice of appeal with the district court. *See* FEDERAL RULE OF APPELLATE PROCEDURE 4(a) (FED. R. APP. P.). That party—"the appellant"—then sees to the preparation and transmission of the "record on appeal," which typically consists of the filings, relevant portions of the transcript, and any docket entries. *See* FED. R. APP. P. 10 & 11. The nonappealing party—"the appellee"—may also participate in the preparation of the record. Next, after certain technicalities are satisfied, the clerk of the court of appeals "dockets" the appeal and on receipt of the record, "files" the record in the court of appeals. *See* FED. R. APP. P. 12. Once the record is filed, the appellant and appellee file briefs in compliance with specific rules of form, substance, and timing. *See* FED. R. APP. P. 28 & 31. After the parties have filed their briefs, the clerk schedules oral argument before a three-person panel of the court of appeals. *See* FED. R. APP. P. 34. Following oral argument, in which the parties engage in a dialogue with the court, the court of appeals issues an opinion on which the clerk enters a judgment. *See* FED. R. APP. P. 36. Once the clerk enters judgment, the losing party may seek a discretionary rehearing before the panel or before the entire court ("en banc"). *See* FED. R. APP. P. 35 & 40. The court of appeals may impose sanctions for the filing of a frivolous appeal. *See* FED. R. APP. P. 38. And finally, a party dissatisfied with the court of appeals' decision may petition the U.S. Supreme Court for review under 28 U.S.C. § 1254, though the Court grants review in only a small percentage of the cases in which review is sought. Of course, individual appeals may be more complicated, *e.g.*, both parties may appeal or, in a complex case, there may be several appellants. And there are numerous details that must be attended to that are not evident in the above outline. But this description should give you a general idea of the basic structure of the appellate process.

The matters subject to review on appeal are generally limited to issues that were raised and either expressly or implicitly "passed upon below." *Singleton v. Wulff*, 428 U.S. 106, 120-121 (1976). The purpose of this rule is to promote judicial efficiency by ensuring that the trial court has an opportunity to correct any errors prior to the entry of its decision and to provide a full record of the issue for appellate consideration. The courts of appeals do have discretion to make exceptions to this rule. *See, e.g., Harden v. Roadway Package Sys., Inc.*, 249 F.3d 1137, 1141 (9th Cir. 2001) (recognizing exception for miscarriage of justice). But in the vast majority of cases, an issue not raised or passed on below will be deemed waived. In addition, harmless error, *i.e.*, errors that have no discernible effect on the case's outcome, will not be reviewed, though whether a particular issue is harmless may itself provide an issue for appeal.

In this chapter, we will address three important and sometimes challenging issues pertaining to the appellate process. First, we will examine the question of when an appeal or some alternate mechanism for review can be filed, *i.e.*, the timing of the appeal. The problem is somewhat more complicated than simply waiting for the entry of a final judgment by the trial court, for there are a number of important exceptions to the final-decision rule. Next, we will look at how closely an appellate court examines the district court's decision, *i.e.*, the standard of review. We'll find that sometimes the lower court's decision is treated with deference, while under other circumstances the court of appeals gives the lower court's decision no weight whatsoever. The key will be distinguishing when one or the other standard applies. Finally, we will briefly consider the Supreme Court's jurisdiction to review decisions by lower federal courts and by the courts of the states.

B. The Timing of an Appeal

1. Final Decisions and the Collateral-Order Doctrine

The primary vehicle through which to invoke a federal court of appeals' jurisdiction is 28 U.S.C. § 1291. That section vests the courts of appeals with jurisdiction over "all final decisions of the district courts of the United States. . . ." 28 U.S.C. § 1291. Speaking very generally, a "final decision" is a judicial order that both conclusively resolves some important aspect of a case and, under most circumstances, results in the litigation's termination. Thus, when a district court enters a final judgment, *i.e.*, a formal order that terminates the litigation and awards judgment to one of the parties, *see* FED. R. CIV. P. 58, a party adversely affected by that judgment may file an appeal.

By way of contrast, § 1291 does not grant appellate jurisdiction over "interlocutory orders," *i.e.*, intermediate rulings that may later merge into a final judgment.

A classic interlocutory order would be a ruling on the admissibility of evidence. Interlocutory orders may be reviewed, if at all, only when merged into a subsequent final decision or by virtue of some other statutory provision. *See, e.g.*, 28 U.S.C. § 1292 (allowing for appealability of certain interlocutory orders), discussed at pages 1063 and 1068, *infra*.

In most cases, the distinction between appealable final decisions and nonappealable interlocutory orders is obvious and the parties proceed accordingly. For example, orders dismissing a case for lack of subject matter jurisdiction (Rule 12(b)(1)), lack of jurisdiction over the defendant (Rule 12(b)(2)), or failure to state a claim on which relief can be granted (Rule 12(b)(6)) are clearly final decisions for the simple reason that they terminate the litigation. In the normal course of events, the district court having made such an order will then enter a final judgment dismissing the case. Just as clearly, orders denying motions to dismiss for lack of subject matter jurisdiction, lack of jurisdiction over the defendant, or failure to state a claim are not final decisions since they do not terminate the litigation. The entry of a final judgment must await further proceedings. There are, however, exceptional circumstances under which the final-decision rule may be satisfied by an order that does not technically end the litigation. For such circumstances, a more flexible, pragmatic definition of "final decision" might be in order.

Cohen v. Beneficial Industrial Loan Corp.
337 U.S. 541 (1949)

MR. JUSTICE JACKSON delivered the opinion of the Court. . . .

[Cohen's decedent filed a stockholder's derivative action against Beneficial Industrial Loan Corporation ("Beneficial") in a federal district court sitting in New Jersey. While the suit was pending, New Jersey passed a law that required plaintiffs in derivative actions to post a bond as security for the defendant's potential expenses should the defendant prevail on the merits. The district court refused to require Cohen to post the bond. Beneficial took an immediate appeal. The court of appeals exercised jurisdiction over the appeal and reversed. Cohen then sought review in the Supreme Court, which granted certiorari.]

At the threshold we are met with the question whether the District Court's order refusing to apply the statute was an appealable one. [Section] 1291 provides, as did its predecessors, for appeal only "from all final decisions of the district courts," except when direct appeal to this Court is provided. . . . It is obvious that, if Congress had allowed appeals only from those final judgments which terminate an action, this order would not be appealable.

The effect of the statute is to disallow appeal from any decision which is tentative, informal or incomplete. Appeal gives the upper court a power of review, not one of intervention. So long as the matter remains open, unfinished or inconclusive, there may be no intrusion by appeal. But the District Court's action upon this application was concluded and closed and its decision final in that sense before the appeal was taken.

Nor does the statute permit appeals, even from fully consummated decisions, where they are but steps towards final judgment in which they will merge. The purpose is to combine in one review all stages of the proceeding that effectively may be reviewed and corrected if and when final judgment results. But this order of the District Court did not make any step toward final disposition of the merits of the case and will not be merged in final judgment. When that time comes, it will be too late effectively to review the present order and the rights conferred by the statute, if it is applicable, will have been lost, probably irreparably. We conclude that the matters embraced in the decision appealed from are not of such an interlocutory nature as to affect, or to be affected by, decision of the merits of this case.

This decision appears to fall in that small class which finally determine claims of right separable from, and collateral to, rights asserted in the action, too important to be denied review and too independent of the cause itself to require that appellate consideration be deferred until the whole case is adjudicated. The Court has long given this provision of the statute this practical rather than a technical construction.

We hold this order appealable because it is a final disposition of a claimed right which is not an ingredient of the cause of action and does not require consideration with it. But we do not mean that every order fixing security is subject to appeal. Here it is the right to security that presents a serious and unsettled question. If the right were admitted or clear and the order involved only an exercise of discretion as to the amount of security, a matter the statute makes subject to reconsideration from time to time, appealability would present a different question. . . .

[On the merits, the Court held that the district court was required to apply the forum state's security-for-expenses requirement. JUSTICES DOUGLAS, FRANKFURTER, AND RUTLEDGE dissented on this point.]

NOTES AND QUESTIONS

1. *A definition of finality.* In *Catlin v. United States*, 324 U.S. 229 (1945), the Supreme Court, in a frequently quoted passage, defined a "final decision" as "one which ends the litigation on the merits and leaves nothing for the court to do but execute the judgment." *Id.* at 233. Quite clearly, the order at issue in *Cohen* did not satisfy that standard. What then is the definition of finality adopted and applied in *Cohen*? Is it enough that the decision on which the appeal is based is "concluded and closed," as the *Cohen* Court described the district court's refusal to impose the bond requirement? If not, what more is required? The *Cohen* test, which is often referred to as the "collateral order doctrine," has been described as consisting of three parts. Can you identify those three parts from the Court's opinion and explain how each was satisfied there? After *Cohen*, what is the remaining

significance of the *Catlin* definition of a final decision? (Hint: The answer is not "none.")

2. *Exception or interpretation?* Is the collateral-order doctrine an exception to the final-decision rule or an interpretation of that rule? If it is the former, what authority does the Supreme Court have to create subject matter jurisdiction under circumstances not provided by a statutory authorization? If it is the latter, is the interpretation a legitimate one? In answering this question, to what extent is it relevant that § 1291 refers to final *decisions* and not to final *judgments*?

3. *The efficiency rationale.* The most often cited justification for the final-decision rule, and particularly the *Catlin* version of that rule, is that it promotes efficiency by avoiding piecemeal appeals and the trial process's inevitable delay and disruption. The rule also avoids the premature and unnecessary appellate consideration of orders that may become moot during the course of the lower court proceedings or which may be revised by the district court as those proceedings unfold. The collateral-order doctrine, on the other hand, does permit appeals from judgments that are not technically final. Yet can you see how the doctrine might nonetheless promote efficiency?

4. *Final decisions and the timeliness of an appeal.* We have been examining the final decision rule for purposes of determining when, under § 1291, a party may appeal an order of the district court. But the final-decision rule is more than a permission slip to appeal. A district court order that terminates the litigation also commences the running of a 30-day time frame within which an appeal of that order must be lodged. FED. R. APP. P. 4(a)(1)(A) ("the notice of appeal . . . must be filed . . . within 30 days after entry of the judgment or order appealed from"). In *Ray Haluch Gravel Co. v. Central Pension Fund*, 134 S. Ct. 773 (2014), the Court addressed this timeliness aspect of the final-decision rule. *Haluch* involved a claim filed by a pension fund ("Fund") against an employer for failure to pay employee benefit contributions due under federal law. On June 17, 2011, the district court issued an order ruling that the Fund was "entitled to certain unpaid contributions, though less than had been requested." The district court delayed ruling on the Fund's motion for attorneys' fees and costs, which it finally did on July 25, 2011. On August 15, 2011, the Fund appealed both rulings. In the court of appeals, the employer argued that the Fund's appeal from the June 17 decision was untimely for failure to comply with Rule 4(a)(1)(A). The court of appeals disagreed, holding that in the context of a delayed ruling on contractual attorneys' fees, a prior decision on the merits was not a final decision within the meaning of § 1291. The Supreme Court granted certiorari and reversed, holding that for purposes of § 1291 and Fed. R. App. P. 4(a)(1)(A), an order that terminates the litigation but leaves open the question of attorneys' fees, whether statutory or contractual, is nonetheless a final decision for purposes of appeal. As a consequence, the Fund's failure to file a notice of appeal within 30 days of the district court's June 17 "final decision" terminated the Fund's right to appeal that decision. 134 S. Ct. at 780-783.

5. *Extension of time to appeal.* Federal Rule of Appellate Procedure 4(a)(5) gives a district court limited authority to extend the time for filing a notice of

appeal. What would the Fund have to have done to take advantage of that provision, had it realized there might be a problem? What was the last date on which it could file a motion for such an extension? With a timely motion and a showing of "excusable neglect or good cause," Rule 4(a)(5)(A)(ii), might the Fund have been able to file its notice of appeal as late as August 15, 2011?

Mohawk Industries, Inc. v. Carpenter
558 U.S. 100 (2009)

JUSTICE SOTOMAYOR delivered the opinion of the Court.

Section 1291 of the Judicial Code confers on federal courts of appeals jurisdiction to review "final decisions of the district courts." 28 U.S.C. § 1291. Although "final decisions" typically are ones that trigger the entry of judgment, they also include a small set of prejudgment orders that are "collateral to" the merits of an action and "too important" to be denied immediate review. *Cohen v. Beneficial Industrial Loan Corp.*, 337 U.S. 541, 546 (1949). In this case, petitioner Mohawk Industries, Inc., attempted to bring a collateral order appeal after the District Court ordered it to disclose certain confidential materials on the ground that Mohawk had waived the attorney-client privilege. The Court of Appeals dismissed the appeal for want of jurisdiction.

The question before us is whether disclosure orders adverse to the attorney-client privilege qualify for immediate appeal under the collateral order doctrine. Agreeing with the Court of Appeals, we hold that they do not. Postjudgment appeals, together with other review mechanisms, suffice to protect the rights of litigants and preserve the vitality of the attorney-client privilege.

I

In 2007, respondent Norman Carpenter, a former shift supervisor at a Mohawk manufacturing facility, filed suit in the United States District Court for the Northern District of Georgia, alleging that Mohawk had terminated him in violation of 42 U.S.C. § 1985(2) [conspiracy to interfere with civil rights] and various Georgia laws. According to Carpenter's complaint, his termination came after he informed a member of Mohawk's human resources department in an e-mail that the company was employing undocumented immigrants. At the time, unbeknownst to Carpenter, Mohawk stood accused in a pending class-action lawsuit [the *Williams* case] of conspiring to drive down the wages of its legal employees by knowingly hiring undocumented workers in violation of federal and state racketeering laws. Company officials directed Carpenter to meet with the company's retained counsel in the *Williams* case, and counsel allegedly pressured Carpenter to recant his statements. When he refused, Carpenter alleges, Mohawk fired him under false pretenses.

After learning of Carpenter's complaint, the plaintiffs in the *Williams* case sought an evidentiary hearing to explore Carpenter's allegations. In its response to their motion, Mohawk described Carpenter's accusations as "pure fantasy" and recounted the "true facts" of Carpenter's dismissal. According to Mohawk, Carpenter himself had "engaged in blatant and illegal misconduct" by attempting to have Mohawk hire an undocumented worker. The company "commenced an immediate investigation," during which retained counsel interviewed Carpenter. Because Carpenter's "efforts to cause Mohawk to circumvent federal immigration law" "blatantly violated Mohawk policy," the company terminated him.

As these events were unfolding in the *Williams* case, discovery was underway in Carpenter's case. Carpenter filed a motion to compel Mohawk to produce information concerning his meeting with retained counsel and the company's termination decision. Mohawk maintained that the requested information was protected by the attorney-client privilege.

The District Court agreed that the privilege applied to the requested information, but it granted Carpenter's motion to compel disclosure after concluding that Mohawk had implicitly waived the privilege through its representations in the *Williams* case. The court declined to certify its order for interlocutory appeal under 28 U.S.C. § 1292(b). But, recognizing "the seriousness of its [waiver] finding," it stayed its ruling to allow Mohawk to explore other potential "avenues to appeal . . . , such as a petition for mandamus or appealing this Order under the collateral order doctrine."

Mohawk filed a notice of appeal and a petition for a writ of mandamus to the Eleventh Circuit. The Court of Appeals dismissed the appeal for lack of jurisdiction under 28 U.S.C. § 1291, holding that the District Court's ruling did not qualify as an immediately appealable collateral order within the meaning of *Cohen*. "Under *Cohen*," the Court of Appeals explained, "an order is appealable if it (1) conclusively determines the disputed question; (2) resolves an important issue completely separate from the merits of the action; and (3) is effectively unreviewable on appeal from a final judgment." According to the court, the District Court's waiver ruling satisfied the first two of these requirements but not the third, because "a discovery order that implicates the attorney-client privilege" can be adequately reviewed "on appeal from a final judgment." The Court of Appeals also rejected Mohawk's mandamus petition, finding no "clear usurpation of power or abuse of discretion" by the District Court. We granted certiorari to resolve a conflict among the Circuits concerning the availability of collateral appeals in the attorney-client privilege context.

II

A

By statute, Courts of Appeals "have jurisdiction of appeals from all final decisions of the district courts of the United States, . . . except where a direct review may be had in the Supreme Court." 28 U.S.C. § 1291. A "final decisio[n]" is typically one "by which a district court disassociates itself from a case." *Swint v. Chambers County Comm'n*, 514 U.S. 35, 42 (1995). This Court, however, "has long given" § 1291 a "practical rather than a technical construction." As we held in *Cohen*, the statute encompasses not only judgments that "terminate an action," but also a "small class" of collateral rulings that, although they do not end the litigation, are appropriately deemed "final." "That small category includes only decisions that are conclusive, that resolve important questions separate from the merits, and that are effectively unreviewable on appeal from the final judgment in the underlying action."

In applying *Cohen*'s collateral order doctrine, we have stressed that it must "never be allowed to swallow the general rule that a party is entitled to a single appeal, to be deferred until final judgment has been entered." *Digital Equipment Corp. v. Desktop Direct, Inc.*, 511 U.S. 863, 868 (1994); see also *Will v. Hallock*, 546 U.S. 345, 350 (2006) ("emphasizing [the doctrine's] modest scope"). Our admonition reflects a healthy respect for the virtues of the final-judgment rule. Permitting piecemeal, prejudgment appeals, we have recognized, undermines "efficient judicial administration" and encroaches upon the prerogatives of district court judges, who play a "special role" in managing ongoing litigation. *Firestone Tire & Rubber Co. v. Risjord*, 449 U.S. 368, 374 (1981); see also *Richardson-Merrell Inc. v. Koller*, 472 U.S. 424, 436 (1985) ("[T]he district judge can better exercise [his or her] responsibility [to police the prejudgment tactics of litigants] if the appellate courts do not repeatedly intervene to second-guess prejudgment rulings").

The justification for immediate appeal must therefore be sufficiently strong to overcome the usual benefits of deferring appeal until litigation concludes. This requirement finds expression in two of the three traditional *Cohen* conditions. The second condition insists upon "*important* questions separate from the merits." More significantly, "the third *Cohen* question, whether a right is 'adequately vindicable' or 'effectively reviewable,' simply cannot be answered without a judgment about the value of the interests that would be lost through rigorous application of a final judgment requirement." That a ruling "may burden litigants in ways that are only imperfectly reparable by appellate reversal of a final district court judgment . . . has never sufficed." Instead, the decisive consideration is whether delaying review until the entry of final judgment "would imperil a substantial public interest" or "some particular value of a high order."

In making this determination, we do not engage in an "individualized jurisdictional inquiry." *Coopers & Lybrand v. Livesay*, 437 U.S. 463, 473 (1978). Rather, our focus is on "the entire category to which a claim belongs." As long as the class of claims, taken as a whole, can be adequately vindicated by other means, "the chance that the litigation at hand might be speeded, or a 'particular injustic[e]' averted," does not provide a basis for jurisdiction under § 1291.

B

In the present case, the Court of Appeals concluded that the District Court's privilege-waiver order satisfied the first two conditions of the collateral order doctrine—conclusiveness and separateness—but not the third—effective unreviewability. Because we agree with the Court of Appeals that collateral order appeals are not necessary to ensure effective review of orders adverse to the attorney-client privilege, we do not decide whether the other *Cohen* requirements are met.*

Mohawk does not dispute that "we have generally denied review of pretrial discovery orders." Mohawk contends, however, that rulings implicating the attorney-client privilege differ in kind from run-of-the-mill discovery orders because of the important institutional interests at stake. According to Mohawk, the right to maintain attorney-client confidences—the *sine qua non* of a meaningful attorney-client relationship—is "irreparably destroyed absent immediate appeal" of adverse privilege rulings.

We readily acknowledge the importance of the attorney-client privilege, which "is one of the oldest recognized privileges for confidential communications." By assuring confidentiality, the privilege encourages clients to make "full and frank" disclosures to their attorneys, who are then better able to provide candid advice and effective representation. This, in turn, serves "broader public interests in the observance of law and administration of justice."

The crucial question, however, is not whether an interest is important in the abstract; it is whether deferring review until final judgment so imperils the interest as to justify the cost of allowing immediate appeal of the entire class of relevant orders. We routinely require litigants to wait until after final judgment to vindicate valuable rights, including rights central to our adversarial system. See, *e.g.*, *Richardson-Merrell*, 472 U.S., at 426 (holding an order disqualifying counsel in a civil case did not qualify for immediate appeal under the collateral order doctrine); *Flanagan v. United States*, 465 U.S. 259, 260 (1984) (reaching the same result in a criminal case, notwithstanding the Sixth Amendment rights at stake). In *Digital Equipment*, we rejected an assertion that collateral order review was necessary to promote "the public policy favoring voluntary resolution of disputes." "It defies common sense," we explained, "to maintain that parties' readiness to settle will be significantly dampened (or the corresponding public interest impaired) by a rule that a district court's decision to let allegedly barred litigation go forward may be challenged as a matter of right only on appeal from a judgment for the plaintiff's favor."

We reach a similar conclusion here. In our estimation, postjudgment appeals generally suffice to protect the rights of litigants and assure the vitality of the attorney-client privilege. Appellate courts can remedy the improper disclosure of privileged material in the same way they remedy a host of other erroneous evidentiary rulings: by vacating an adverse judgment and remanding for a new trial in which the protected material and its fruits are excluded from evidence.

Dismissing such relief as inadequate, Mohawk emphasizes that the attorney-client privilege does not merely "prohibi[t] use of protected information at trial";

---

* [Because the *Cohen* requirements go to an appellate court's subject matter jurisdiction, were it necessary here, the Court would have been obliged to assess whether each condition was met, without regard to whether the parties believed each to be satisfied. Since the Court found that the third condition was not met, there was no need for it to address the first two conditions. *See Digital Equip., supra*, 511 U.S. at 869 n.3. — Eds.]

it provides a "right not to disclose the privileged information in the first place." Mohawk is undoubtedly correct that an order to disclose privileged information intrudes on the confidentiality of attorney-client communications. But deferring review until final judgment does not meaningfully reduce the *ex ante* incentives for full and frank consultations between clients and counsel.

One reason for the lack of a discernible chill is that, in deciding how freely to speak, clients and counsel are unlikely to focus on the remote prospect of an erroneous disclosure order, let alone on the timing of a possible appeal. Whether or not immediate collateral order appeals are available, clients and counsel must account for the possibility that they will later be required by law to disclose their communications for a variety of reasons—for example, because they misjudged the scope of the privilege, because they waived the privilege, or because their communications fell within the privilege's crime-fraud exception. Most district court rulings on these matters involve the routine application of settled legal principles. They are unlikely to be reversed on appeal, particularly when they rest on factual determinations for which appellate deference is the norm. The breadth of the privilege and the narrowness of its exceptions will thus tend to exert a much greater influence on the conduct of clients and counsel than the small risk that the law will be misapplied.

Moreover, were attorneys and clients to reflect upon their appellate options, they would find that litigants confronted with a particularly injurious or novel privilege ruling have several potential avenues of review apart from collateral order appeal. First, a party may ask the district court to certify, and the court of appeals to accept, an interlocutory appeal pursuant to 28 U.S.C. § 1292(b). The preconditions for § 1292(b) review—"a controlling question of law," the prompt resolution of which "may materially advance the ultimate termination of the litigation"—are most likely to be satisfied when a privilege ruling involves a new legal question or is of special consequence, and district courts should not hesitate to certify an interlocutory appeal in such cases. Second, in extraordinary circumstances—*i.e.*, when a disclosure order "amount[s] to a judicial usurpation of power or a clear abuse of discretion," or otherwise works a manifest injustice—a party may petition the court of appeals for a writ of mandamus. *Cheney v. United States Dist. Court for D.C.*, 542 U.S. 367, 390 (2004).[3] While these discretionary review mechanisms do not provide relief in every case, they serve as useful "safety valve[s]" for promptly correcting serious errors.

Another long-recognized option is for a party to defy a disclosure order and incur court-imposed sanctions. District courts have a range of sanctions from which to choose, including "directing that the matters embraced in the order or other designated facts be taken as established for purposes of the action," "prohibiting the disobedient party from supporting or opposing designated claims or defenses," or "striking pleadings in whole or in part." FED. R. CIV. P. 37(b)(2)

---

3. Mohawk itself petitioned the Eleventh Circuit for a writ of mandamus. It has not asked us to review the Court of Appeals' denial of that relief.

(i)-(iii). Such sanctions allow a party to obtain postjudgment review without having to reveal its privileged information. Alternatively, when the circumstances warrant it, a district court may hold a noncomplying party in contempt. The party can then appeal directly from that ruling, at least when the contempt citation can be characterized as a criminal punishment.

These established mechanisms for appellate review not only provide assurances to clients and counsel about the security of their confidential communications; they also go a long way toward addressing Mohawk's concern that, absent collateral order appeals of adverse attorney-client privilege rulings, some litigants may experience severe hardship. Mohawk is no doubt right that an order to disclose privileged material may, in some situations, have implications beyond the case at hand. But the same can be said about many categories of pretrial discovery orders, for which collateral order appeals are unavailable. As with these other orders, rulings adverse to the privilege vary in their significance; some may be momentous, but others are more mundane. Section 1292(b) appeals, mandamus, and appeals from contempt citations facilitate immediate review of some of the more consequential attorney-client privilege rulings. Moreover, protective orders are available to limit the spillover effects of disclosing sensitive information. That a fraction of orders adverse to the attorney-client privilege may nevertheless harm individual litigants in ways that are "only imperfectly reparable" does not justify making all such orders immediately appealable as of right under § 1291.

In short, the limited benefits of applying "the blunt, categorical instrument of § 1291 collateral order appeal" to privilege-related disclosure orders simply cannot justify the likely institutional costs. Permitting parties to undertake successive, piecemeal appeals of all adverse attorney-client rulings would unduly delay the resolution of district court litigation and needlessly burden the Courts of Appeals. See . . . *Cunningham v. Hamilton County*, 527 U.S. 198, 209 (1999) (expressing concern that allowing immediate appeal as of right from orders fining attorneys for discovery violations would result in "the very sorts of piecemeal appeals and concomitant delays that the final judgment rule was designed to prevent"). Attempting to downplay such concerns, Mohawk asserts that the three Circuits in which the collateral order doctrine currently applies to adverse privilege rulings have seen only a trickle of appeals. But this may be due to the fact that the practice in all three Circuits is relatively new and not yet widely known. Were this Court to approve collateral order appeals in the attorney-client privilege context, many more litigants would likely choose that route. They would also likely seek to extend such a ruling to disclosure orders implicating many other categories of sensitive information, raising an array of line-drawing difficulties.[4]

---

4. Participating as *amicus curiae* in support of respondent Carpenter, the United States contends that collateral order appeals should be available for rulings involving certain governmental privileges "in light of their structural constitutional grounding under the separation of powers, relatively rare invocation, and unique importance to governmental functions." We express no view on that issue.

C

In concluding that sufficiently effective review of adverse attorney-client privilege rulings can be had without resort to the *Cohen* doctrine, we reiterate that the class of collaterally appealable orders must remain "narrow and selective in its membership." This admonition has acquired special force in recent years with the enactment of legislation designating rulemaking, "not expansion by court decision," as the preferred means for determining whether and when prejudgment orders should be immediately appealable. Specifically, Congress in 1990 amended the Rules Enabling Act, 28 U.S.C. §§ 2071 *et seq.*, to authorize this Court to adopt rules "defin[ing] when a ruling of a district court is final for the purposes of appeal under section 1291." § 2072(c). Shortly thereafter, and along similar lines, Congress empowered this Court to "prescribe rules, in accordance with [§ 2072], to provide for an appeal of an interlocutory decision to the courts of appeals that is not otherwise provided for under [§ 1292]." § 1292(e). These provisions, we have recognized, "warran[t] the Judiciary's full respect."

Indeed, the rulemaking process has important virtues. It draws on the collective experience of bench and bar, see 28 U.S.C. § 2073, and it facilitates the adoption of measured, practical solutions. We expect that the combination of standard postjudgment appeals, § 1292(b) appeals, mandamus, and contempt appeals will continue to provide adequate protection to litigants ordered to disclose materials purportedly subject to the attorney-client privilege. Any further avenue for immediate appeal of such rulings should be furnished, if at all, through rulemaking, with the opportunity for full airing it provides.

* * *

In sum, we conclude that the collateral order doctrine does not extend to disclosure orders adverse to the attorney-client privilege. Effective appellate review can be had by other means. Accordingly, we affirm the judgment of the Court of Appeals for the Eleventh Circuit.

It is so ordered.

[The concurring opinion of Mr. Justice Thomas is omitted.]

NOTES AND QUESTIONS

1. The Cohen *factors.*   The *Mohawk Industries* Court, citing *Cohen*, described the collateral-order doctrine as involving a " 'small class' of collateral rulings that, although they do not end the litigation, are appropriately deemed 'final.'" *Mohawk Indus.*, 558 U.S. at 106. That small category includes only decisions (1) "that are conclusive," (2) "that resolve important questions separate from the merits," and (3) "that are effectively unreviewable on appeal from the final judgment in the underlying action." *Id.* (quoting *Swint v. Chambers Cnty. Comm'n*, 514 U.S. 35, 42 (1995)). In holding that the district court's privilege-waiver order was not a final decision under the collateral-order doctrine, the *Mohawk Industries*

Court focused on the third element of this test, namely, whether the question was "effectively unreviewable" on appeal. How might you argue that the district court order did (or did not) satisfy the other two *Cohen* factors (conclusive, and important question completely separate from the merits)? In answering this question, use the facts of *Cohen* as a template since presumably the order at issue there was both conclusive and involved an important question completely separate from the merits. Consider also *Coopers & Lybrand v. Livesay*, 437 U.S. 463 (1978), cited in *Mohawk Industries,* in which the Court held that an order refusing to certify a class action was neither conclusive, since the trial court could revisit the issue, nor completely separate from the merits, since class certification is always related to the underlying merits; and *Cunningham v. Hamilton County*, 527 U.S. 198 (1999), in which the Court ruled that an order imposing sanctions for discovery abuse under what is now Rule 37(a)(5) was not immediately appealable since discovery sanctions, which are inevitably tied to the underlying claims and defenses, can never be completely separate from the controversy's merits.

2. *Effectively unreviewable.*   Why did the Court conclude that Mohawk Industries' claimed "right to maintain attorney-client confidences" failed the effectively unreviewable standard? Was it certain that alternative mechanisms would in fact protect the petitioner's interests? If not, might the collateral-order doctrine have been invoked had the petitioner made a stronger showing as to the inefficacy of the alternative mechanisms in its particular case, or does the Court focus instead on the category of such claims as a whole?

3. *Importance of the interest in question.*   The Court in *Mohawk Industries* placed some emphasis on the "importance" of the interest in question (part of the second *Cohen* factor), even though the decision was seemingly based just on the test's third factor. The Court thus noted that invocation of the collateral-order doctrine may hinge on "a judgment about the value of the interests that would be lost through rigorous application of a final judgment requirement," *i.e.*, on "whether delaying review until the entry of final judgment 'would imperil a substantial public interest' or 'some particular value of a high order.'" *Mohawk Indus.*, 558 U.S. at 107 (internal citations omitted). Did the Court accept the importance of the interest the petitioner invoked? Was that interest inherently unimportant, or was it simply less important than the value of avoiding piecemeal review? Was the weight ascribed to that interest further lessened by the Court's belief that in many cases, there may be other ways of protecting the interest besides review of a final judgment?

In two earlier cases, the Supreme Court found the collateral-order doctrine satisfied: *Nixon v. Fitzgerald*, 457 U.S. 731, 741-743 (1982) (allowing appeal from order denying petitioner absolute immunity from suit for civil damages arising from actions taken while petitioner was president of the United States); *Mitchell v. Forsyth*, 472 U.S. 511, 524-530 (1985) (allowing appeal from decisions denying government officials qualified immunity from damages suits, where an "essential attribute" of this freedom was an "entitlement not to stand trial or face the other burdens of litigation"). In light of the importance of the interests in question, can *Mohawk Industries* be reconciled with those cases? Thus, as the Court noted in *Will v. Hallock*, 546 U.S. 345, 351-352 (2006), application of the collateral-order doctrine will often in the end turn on "a judgment about the value of the interests that would be lost through rigorous application of a final judgment requirement."

PROBLEM

12-1. Based on a settlement agreement between the parties, the federal district court dismissed a trademark infringement action that Desktop Direct ("Desktop") had filed against Digital Equipment ("Digital"). Several months later, the district court granted Desktop's motion to vacate the dismissal and rescind the agreement, on the ground that Digital had misrepresented material facts during settlement negotiations. After Digital appealed the district court's order vacating the dismissal pursuant to 28 U.S.C. § 1291, Desktop moved to dismiss the appeal for lack of jurisdiction on the basis that the order was not immediately appealable. In opposition to the motion to dismiss, Digital argues that the essence of its settlement agreement is the "right not to stand trial," a right that would be destroyed forever if it cannot be enforced under the collateral-order doctrine. In Digital's words, "[a] fully litigated case can no more be untried than the law's proverbial bell can be unrung." How should the court rule on Desktop's motion to dismiss the appeal? *See Digital Equip. Corp. v. Desktop Direct, Inc.*, 511 U.S. 863 (1994).

Quackenbush v. Allstate Insurance Co.

517 U.S. 706 (1996)

JUSTICE O'CONNOR delivered the opinion of the Court.

In this case, we consider whether an abstention-based remand order is appealable as a final order under 28 U.S.C. § 1291, and whether the abstention doctrine first recognized in *Burford v. Sun Oil Co.*, 319 U.S. 315 (1943), can be applied in a common-law suit for damages. . . .

[The California Insurance Commissioner ("Commissioner"), Charles Quackenbush, as the trustee for an insolvent insurance company, brought an action in state court against a reinsurer to recover reinsurance proceeds due the insolvent company under common law tort and contract theories. Allstate, the defendant reinsurer, removed the case to federal court on grounds of diversity. The Commissioner filed a motion to remand, arguing that under *Burford v. Sun Oil Co.*, 319 U.S. 315 (1943), the district court should abstain from interfering with what was in essence part of a state regulatory scheme pertaining to insurance companies' insolvency. The district court agreed and remanded the case to state court. The defendant then filed an immediate appeal under § 1291. The court of appeals exercised jurisdiction over the appeal, held that the *Burford* abstention was inapplicable in a suit for damages, and vacated the district court's remand order. The Supreme Court granted Quackenbush's petition for certiorari.]

We first consider whether the Court of Appeals had jurisdiction to hear Allstate's appeal under 28 U.S.C. § 1291, which confers jurisdiction over appeals from "final decisions" of the district courts, and 28 U.S.C. § 1447(d), which provides that "[a]n order remanding a case to the State court from which it was removed is not reviewable on appeal or otherwise."

We agree with the Ninth Circuit and the parties that § 1447(d) interposes no bar to appellate review of the remand order at issue in this case. As we held in *Thermtron Products, Inc. v. Hermansdorfer*, [423 U.S. 336, 345-346 (1976)], and reiterated this Term in *Things Remembered, Inc. v. Petrarca*, 516 U.S. 124, 127 (1995), "§ 1447(d) must be read *in pari materia* with § 1447(c), so that only remands based on grounds specified in § 1447(c) are immune from review under § 1447(d)." This gloss renders § 1447(d) inapplicable here: The District Court's abstention-based remand order does not fall into either category of remand order described in § 1447(c), as it is not based on lack of subject matter jurisdiction or defects in removal procedure.

Finding no affirmative bar to appellate review of the District Court's remand order, we must determine whether that review may be obtained by appeal under § 1291. The general rule is that "a party is entitled to a single appeal, to be deferred until final judgment has been entered, in which claims of district court error at any stage of the litigation may be ventilated." *Digital Equipment Corp. v. Desktop Direct, Inc.*, 511 U.S. 863, 868 (1994) (citations omitted). Accordingly, we have held that a decision is ordinarily considered final and appealable under § 1291 only if it "ends the litigation on the merits and leaves nothing for the court to do but execute the judgment." *Catlin v. United States*, 324 U.S. 229, 233 (1945). We have also recognized, however, a narrow class of collateral orders which do not meet this definition of finality but which are nevertheless immediately appealable under § 1291 because they "conclusively determine a disputed question" that is "completely separate from the merits of the action," "effectively unreviewable on appeal from a final judgment," and "too important to be denied review."

The application of these principles to the appealability of the remand order before us is controlled by our decision in *Moses H. Cone Memorial Hospital v. Mercury Constr. Corp.*, [460 U.S. 1 (1983)]. The District Court in that case entered an order under *Colorado River Water Conservation Dist. v. United States*, 424 U.S. 800 (1976), staying a federal diversity suit pending the completion of a declaratory judgment action that had been filed in state court. The Court of Appeals held that this stay order was appealable under § 1291, and we affirmed that determination on two independent grounds.

We first concluded that the abstention-based stay order was appealable as a "final decision" under § 1291 because it put the litigants "effectively out of court," and because its effect was "precisely to surrender jurisdiction of a federal suit to a state court," 460 U.S., at 11, n.11. These standards do not reflect our oft-repeated definition of finality (citing *Catlin, supra*, at 233); but in *Moses H. Cone* we found their application to be compelled by precedent.

. . . [W]e also held that the stay order at issue in *Moses H. Cone* was appealable under the collateral order doctrine. We determined that a stay order based on the

Colorado River doctrine "presents an important issue separate from the merits" because it "amounts to a refusal to adjudicate" the case in federal court; that such orders could not be reviewed on appeal from a final judgment in the federal action because the district court would be bound, as a matter of res judicata, to honor the state court's judgment; and that unlike other stay orders, which might readily be reconsidered by the district court, abstention-based stay orders of this ilk are "conclusive" because they are the practical equivalent of an order dismissing the case.

The District Court's order remanding on grounds of *Burford* abstention is in all relevant respects indistinguishable from the stay order we found to be appealable in *Moses H. Cone*. No less than an order staying a federal court action pending adjudication of the dispute in state court, it puts the litigants in this case "effectively out of court," and its effect is "precisely to surrender jurisdiction of a federal suit to a state court." Indeed, the remand order is clearly more "final" than a stay order in this sense. When a district court remands a case to a state court, the district court disassociates itself from the case entirely, retaining nothing of the matter on the federal court's docket.

The District Court's order is also indistinguishable from the stay order we considered in *Moses H. Cone* in that it conclusively determines an issue that is separate from the merits, namely, the question whether the federal court should decline to exercise its jurisdiction in the interest of comity and federalism. In addition, the rights asserted on appeal from the District Court's abstention decision are, in our view, sufficiently important to warrant an immediate appeal. And, like the stay order we found appealable in *Moses H. Cone*, the District Court's remand order in this case will not be subsumed in any other appealable order entered by the District Court. . . .

Admittedly, remand orders like the one entered in this case do not meet the traditional definition of finality—they do not "en[d] the litigation on the merits and leav[e] nothing for the court to do but execute the judgment," *Catlin*, 324 U.S., at 233. But because the District Court's remand order is functionally indistinguishable from the stay order we found appealable in *Moses H. Cone*, we conclude that it is appealable, and turn to the merits of the Ninth Circuit's decision respecting *Burford* abstention.

[On the merits, the Court affirmed the Ninth Circuit. Concurring opinions by JUSTICES SCALIA and KENNEDY are omitted.]

NOTES AND QUESTIONS

1. A third approach to finality?   In *Quackenbush*, the district court's remand order did not technically terminate the litigation since it would continue in state court. Nonetheless, the Supreme Court found that the remand order was a final decision within the meaning of § 1291. The Court gave two reasons, one of which was based on a familiar but somewhat cryptic application of the collateral-order doctrine. The other reason, however, seemed to expand the definition of finality beyond final judgments and collateral orders. According to the Court, the district court's order was deemed final because it placed the litigants "effectively out of court" and "surrender[ed] jurisdiction of a federal suit to a state court." *Quackenbush*, 517 U.S. at 714 (quoting *Moses H. Cone Mem'l Hosp. v. Mercury Constr. Corp.*, 460 U.S. 1, 11 n.11 (1983)). Given the "surrender" aspect of the rationale, the *Quackenbush* approach may be of limited utility, since aside from abstention orders, remands of removed cases, and dismissals for lack of original subject matter jurisdiction (*e.g.*, lack of complete diversity), there may be no other contexts in which a federal court order surrenders jurisdiction to a state court. Thus *Quackenbush*'s second rationale would not likely apply to a discovery order that effectively put a plaintiff out of court by making the proof of her case impossible, since the order itself would not operate as a surrender of jurisdiction.

2. *Remand orders in removed cases.*   Why didn't 28 U.S.C. § 1447(d) bar the filing of an immediate appeal in *Quackenbush*? More generally, § 1447(d) aside, would an order remanding a removed case for want of subject matter jurisdiction be a final decision under the rule announced in *Quackenbush*? In answering this question, consider *Thermtron Products, Inc. v. Hermansdorfer*, 423 U.S. 336 (1976), in which the district court remanded a properly removed case based on the court's crowded docket. The Supreme Court held that § 1447(d) did not bar immediate review of the remand order since that section only limits remands based on the criteria of § 1447(c), none of which pertain to a district court's workload. Was the remand order by the district court in *Thermtron* a final decision?

3. *The three faces of finality.*   There would seem to be at least three methods through which a district court order might satisfy the final decision rule: (1) the order terminates the litigation in the sense of a final judgment; (2) the order falls within the collateral-order doctrine; or (3) the order surrenders jurisdiction to a state court. The first method is considered the general rule, while the second and third methods are treated as narrow alternatives to that rule. (They are sometimes also described as exceptions.) The presence of these two alternatives does suggest, however, that the concept of finality is one of pragmatism and not of rigid adherence to doctrine, but a pragmatism that is heavily informed by the strong policy against piecemeal appeals.

PROBLEMS

12-2. Jones brought a civil rights action under 42 U.S.C. § 1983 against five police officers, claiming that they used excessive force when they arrested him and later beat him at the police station. As government officials, the officers were entitled to assert a qualified immunity defense. Three of the officers moved for summary judgment arguing that whatever evidence Jones might have about the other two officers, he could point to no evidence that these three had beaten him or had been present during the beatings. Holding that there was sufficient circumstantial evidence supporting Jones's theory of the case, the district court denied the motion. The three officers sought an immediate appeal under § 1291. They argued that evidence in the pretrial record was not sufficient to show a "genuine" issue of material fact on the question of their complicity in the complained of acts. *See* FED. R. CIV. P. 56(c). Does the court of appeals have jurisdiction to hear this appeal? *See Johnson v. Jones*, 515 U.S. 304 (1995).

12-3. The defendant in a products liability suit moved to disqualify J.R. as plaintiff's counsel on the ground that there was a conflict of interest between J.R. and the defendant's insurer since the insurer was also an occasional client of J.R.'s law firm. The defendant argued that this conflict would give J.R. an incentive to structure the plaintiff's claims for relief so as to enable the insurer to avoid any liability, thus increasing the defendant's own potential liability. The district court denied the motion after requiring J.R. to obtain consent from both the plaintiff and the insurer. The defendant immediately appealed under § 1291. Was the district court's order a final decision? If the decision isn't final, will the defendant have any recourse once a judgment is entered? *See Firestone Tire & Rubber Co. v. Risjord*, 449 U.S. 368 (1981). If the motion to disqualify had been granted, would that order have been immediately appealable? In answering this question, consider the practical consequences of allowing (or not allowing) such an appeal to proceed. *See Richardson-Merrell, Inc. v. Koller*, 472 U.S. 424 (1985).

12-4. In the wake of police raids on a nightclub, the club's owners sued a county for alleged civil rights violations under 42 U.S.C. § 1983, claiming that the raids were pursuant to county policy. Unlike individuals, cities and counties are not entitled to qualified immunity for alleged civil rights violations. On the other hand, under § 1983, a city or county can only be held liable for its own policies and not simply for its employees' misdeeds. Thus in this case the county's liability was dependent, in part, on whether the sheriff who authorized the raids was "the county's final policymaker for law enforcement." If the sheriff was not the "final policymaker," the county was not itself liable for his conduct. The county filed a motion for summary judgment on that precise issue, arguing that there was no genuine issue of fact as to the sheriff's policymaking status. The district court denied the motion but stated that it would make a dispositive ruling on the county's potential liability before jury deliberations. Was the denial of summary judgment immediately appealable under § 1291? *See Swint v. Chambers Cnty. Comm'n*, 514 U.S. 35 (1995).

A NOTE ON APPEALABILITY UNDER STATE LAW

Most state judicial systems follow a model of appealability that is similar in operation to the federal model. In California, for example, a party may appeal from "a judgment." CAL. CIV. PROC. CODE § 904.1(a)(1). This has been interpreted as imposing what is in essence a final-decision rule that includes a modified version of the collateral-order doctrine. *See* 9 BERNARD E. WITKIN, CALIFORNIA PROCEDURE, APPEAL, §§ 57-61 (5th ed. 2008). A few states, however, have adopted a much more flexible approach to appealability. Thus in *Goldston v. American Motors Corp.*, 392 S.E.2d 735 (N.C. 1990), an attorney disqualification case, the

North Carolina Supreme Court expressly declined to follow the Supreme Court's ruling in *Richardson-Merrell, Inc.* (see Problem 12-3, *supra*), noting that "our statutes setting forth the appeals process do not include the same jurisdictional 'finality' requirement as does the federal statute." *Id.* at 737. And in New York, a wide array of judgments and interlocutory orders are immediately appealable. N.Y. Civ. Prac. L. & R. § 5701(a)(1)-(2). As one commentator has observed, § 5701(a) "is the source of the broad spectrum of dispositions that may be forthwith appealed . . . even though they affect only some incident of the case and do not put an end to it. Here, in fact, is the major contrast between New York and federal appellate practice." David D. Siegel, *Supplementary Practice Commentaries*, 7B McKinney's Consol. Laws of N.Y. Ann. 518 (West 1995). The one notable exception is evidentiary rulings. What are the potential costs and benefits of a more liberal approach to immediate appealability?

2.   Statutory Exceptions to the Final Decision Rule

a.   Interlocutory Appeals Under § 1292(a)(1)

Congress has created a number of exceptions to the final decision rule, perhaps the most important of which is found in 28 U.S.C. § 1292(a)(1). That section grants the courts of appeals appellate jurisdiction over "*[i]nterlocutory orders* of the district courts of the United States . . . granting, continuing, modifying, refusing or dissolving injunctions, or refusing to dissolve or modify injunctions. . . ." 28 U.S.C. § 1292(a)(1) (emphasis added). For purposes of § 1292(a)(1), an injunction is a judicial order designed to provide some or all of the relief sought in the underlying litigation and that requires a party, under compulsion of contempt, to do or to refrain from doing some specified act. *See also* § 1292(a)(2)-(3), (c)(2) (providing for other interlocutory appeals).

Section 1292(a)(1) applies to both permanent and preliminary injunctions. A permanent injunction is usually entered as part of a final judgment and hence may be appealable under the final-decision rule; in such cases, § 1292(a)(1) is superfluous. In some instances, however, a permanent injunction may be issued before entry of a final judgment, and for these cases § 1292(a)(1) provides a proper vehicle for appeal. In addition, an order that modifies or dissolves a permanent injunction (or refuses to do either) is also immediately appealable under § 1292(a)(1). The most frequent use of § 1292(a)(1), however, is in the context of preliminary injunctions. A preliminary injunction is usually issued after only a brief hearing, the question of its "permanence" being reserved pending a more complete consideration of the merits. To procure a preliminary injunction, however, a party must show a substantial likelihood of success on the merits, that the balance of equities, including the public interest, favors the issuance of the injunction, and that refusal to grant the preliminary relief would lead to irreparable injury. By its terms, § 1292(a)(1) allows an immediate appeal of an order either granting or refusing to grant a preliminary injunction. The purpose is to prevent the harm that might otherwise ensue if the parties were required to await a final judgment. *See generally* George C. Pratt, *Interlocutory Orders, in* 19 MOORE'S FEDERAL PRACTICE §§ 203.10 *et seq.* (3d ed. 2015); 16 CHARLES ALAN WRIGHT, ARTHUR R. MILLER & EDWARD H. COOPER, FEDERAL PRACTICE AND PROCEDURE §§ 3920-3924.2 (3d ed. 2012 & Supp. 2015).

Carson v. American Brands, Inc.
450 U.S. 79 (1981)

JUSTICE BRENNAN delivered the opinion of the Court.

The question presented in this Title VII class action is whether an interlocutory order of the District Court denying a joint motion of the parties to enter a consent decree containing injunctive relief is an appealable order.

I

Petitioners, representing a class of present and former black seasonal employees and applicants for employment at the Richmond Leaf Department of the American Tobacco Co., brought this suit in the United States District Court for the Eastern District of Virginia under 42 U.S.C. § 1981 and Title VII of the Civil Rights Act of 1964. Alleging that respondents had discriminated against them in hiring, promotion, transfer, and training opportunities, petitioners sought a declaratory judgment, preliminary and permanent injunctive relief, and money damages.

After extensive discovery had been conducted and the plaintiff class had been certified, the parties negotiated a settlement and jointly moved the District Court to approve and enter their proposed consent decree. The decree would have required respondents to give hiring and seniority preferences to black employees and to fill one-third of all supervisory positions in the Richmond Leaf Department with qualified blacks. While agreeing to the terms of the decree, respondents "expressly den[ied] any violation of . . . any . . . equal employment law, regulation, or order."

The District Court denied the motion to enter the proposed decree. Concluding that preferential treatment on the basis of race violated Title VII and the Constitution absent a showing of past or present discrimination, and that the facts submitted in support of the decree demonstrated no "vestiges of racial discrimination," the court held that the proposed decree illegally granted racial preferences to the petitioner class. It further declared that even if present or past discrimination had been shown, the decree would be illegal in that it would extend relief to *all* present and future black employees of the Richmond Leaf Department, not just to *actual* victims of the alleged discrimination.

The United States Court of Appeals for the Fourth Circuit, sitting en banc, dismissed petitioners' appeal for want of jurisdiction. It held that the District

Court's refusal to enter the consent decree was neither a "collateral order" under 28 U.S.C. § 1291, nor an interlocutory order "refusing" an "injunctio[n]" under 28 U.S.C. § 1292(a)(1). Three judges dissented, concluding that the order refusing to approve the consent decree was appealable under 28 U.S.C. § 1292(a)(1).

Noting a conflict in the Circuits, we granted certiorari. We hold that the order is appealable under 28 U.S.C. § 1292(a)(1), and accordingly reverse the Court of Appeals.

II

The first Judiciary Act of 1789, established the general principle that only *final* decisions of the federal district courts would be reviewable on appeal. 28 U.S.C. § 1291. Because rigid application of this principle was found to create undue hardship in some cases, however, Congress created certain exceptions to it. One of these exceptions, 28 U.S.C. § 1292(a)(1), permits appeal as of right from "[i]nterlocutory orders of the district courts . . . granting, continuing, modifying, *refusing* or dissolving *injunctions*. . . . "

Although the District Court's order declining to enter the proposed consent decree did not in terms "refus[e]" an "injunctio[n]," it nonetheless had the practical effect of doing so. This is because the proposed decree would have permanently enjoined respondents from discriminating against black employees at the Richmond Leaf Department, and would have directed changes in seniority and benefit systems, established hiring goals for qualified blacks in certain supervisory positions, and granted job-bidding preferences for seasonal employees. Indeed, prospective relief was at the very core of the disapproved settlement.

For an interlocutory order to be immediately appealable under § 1292(a)(1), however, a litigant must show more than that the order has the practical effect of refusing an injunction. Because § 1292(a)(1) was intended to carve out only a limited exception to the final-judgment rule, we have construed the statute narrowly to ensure that appeal as of right under § 1292(a)(1) will be available only in circumstances where an appeal will further the statutory purpose of "permit[ting] litigants to effectually challenge interlocutory orders of serious, perhaps irreparable, consequence." Unless a litigant can show that an interlocutory order of the district court might have a "serious, perhaps irreparable, consequence," and that the order can be "effectually challenged" only by immediate appeal, the general congressional policy against piecemeal review will preclude interlocutory appeal.

In *Switzerland Cheese Assn., Inc. v. E. Horne's Market, Inc.*, 385 U.S. 23 (1966), for example, petitioners contended that the District Court's denial of their motion for summary judgment was appealable under § 1292(a)(1) simply because its practical effect was to deny them the permanent injunction sought in their summary-judgment motion. Although the District Court order seemed to fit within the statutory language of § 1292(a)(1), petitioners' contention was rejected because they did not show that the order might cause them irreparable consequences if not immediately reviewed. The motion for summary judgment sought permanent and not preliminary injunctive relief and petitioners did not argue that a denial of summary judgment would cause them irreparable harm *pendente lite*. Since permanent injunctive relief might have been obtained after trial, the interlocutory order lacked the "serious, perhaps irreparable, consequence" that is a prerequisite to appealability under § 1292(a)(1).

Similarly, in *Gardner v. Westinghouse Broadcasting Co.*, 437 U.S. 478 (1978), petitioner in a Title VII sex discrimination suit sought a permanent injunction against her prospective employer on behalf of herself and her putative class. After the District Court denied petitioner's motion for class certification, petitioner filed an appeal under § 1292(a)(1). She contended that since her complaint had requested injunctive relief, the court's order denying class certification had the effect of limiting the breadth of the available relief, and therefore of "refus[ing] a substantial portion of the injunctive relief requested in the complaint."

As in *Switzerland Cheese*, petitioner in *Gardner* had not filed a motion for a preliminary injunction and had not alleged that a denial of her motion would cause irreparable harm. The District Court order thus had "no direct or irreparable impact on the merits of the controversy." Because the denial of class certification was conditional, and because it could be effectively reviewed on appeal from final judgment, petitioner could still obtain the full permanent injunctive relief she requested and a delayed review of the District Court order would therefore cause no serious or irreparable harm. As *Gardner* stated:

> "The order denying class certification in this case did not have any such 'irreparable' effect. It could be reviewed both prior to and after final judgment; it did not affect the merits of petitioner's own claim; and it did not pass on the legal sufficiency of any claims for injunctive relief." 437 U.S., at 480-481 (footnotes omitted).

III

In the instant case, unless the District Court order denying the motion to enter the consent decree is immediately appealable, petitioners will lose their opportunity to "effectually challenge" an interlocutory order that denies them injunctive relief and that plainly has a "serious, perhaps irreparable, consequence." First, petitioners might lose their opportunity to settle their case on the negotiated terms. As *United States v. Armour & Co.*, 402 U.S. 673, 681 (1971), stated:

> "Consent decrees are entered into by parties to a case after careful negotiation has produced agreement on their precise terms. The parties waive their right to litigate the issues involved in the case and thus save themselves the time, expense, and inevitable risk of litigation. Naturally, the agreement reached normally embodies a compromise; in exchange for the saving of cost and elimination of risk, the parties each give up something they might have won had they proceeded with the litigation."

Settlement agreements may thus be predicated on an express or implied condition that the parties would, by their agreement, be able to avoid the costs and uncertainties of litigation. In this case, that condition of settlement has been radically affected by the District Court. By refusing to enter the proposed consent decree, the District Court effectively ordered the parties to proceed to trial and to have their respective rights and liabilities established within limits laid down by that court. Because a party to a pending settlement might be legally justified in withdrawing its consent to the agreement once trial is held and final judgment entered, the District Court's order might thus have the "serious, perhaps irreparable, consequence" of denying the parties their right to compromise their dispute on mutually agreeable terms.

There is a second "serious, perhaps irreparable, consequence" of the District Court order that justifies our conclusion that the order is immediately appealable under § 1292(a)(1). In seeking entry of the proposed consent decree, petitioners sought an immediate restructuring of respondents' transfer and promotional policies. They asserted in their complaint that they would suffer irreparable injury unless they obtained that injunctive relief at the earliest opportunity. Because petitioners cannot obtain that relief until the proposed consent decree is entered, any further delay in reviewing the propriety of the District Court's refusal to enter the decree might cause them serious or irreparable harm.

In sum, in refusing to approve the parties' negotiated consent decree, the District Court denied petitioners the opportunity to compromise their claim and to obtain the injunctive benefits of the settlement agreement they negotiated. These constitute "serious, perhaps irreparable, consequences" that petitioners can "effectually challenge" only by an immediate appeal. It follows that the order is an order "refusing" an "injunctio[n]" and is therefore appealable under § 1292(a)(1).

Reversed.

NOTES AND QUESTIONS

1. Refusing an "injunction."   Notice that the district court in *Carson* did not expressly refuse to enter an injunction. It refused to honor a settlement. Yet the Supreme Court nonetheless found that the lower court's order constituted a refusal to issue an injunction. On what basis? *See generally* 19 MOORE'S FEDERAL PRACTICE, *supra*, § 203.10[3][b]. Does the Court's determination comport with the definition of an injunction given in the introduction to this section, *i.e.*, that "[a]n injunction is a judicial order designed to provide some or all of the relief sought in the underlying litigation and that requires a party, under compulsion of contempt, to do or to refrain from doing some specified act"?

2. Serious, perhaps irreparable, consequence.   The *Carson* Court did not rest its finding of appealability solely on the fact that the district court order was, in practical effect, an order refusing an injunction. In addition, the Court required the appellant to demonstrate that an immediate appeal was necessary to avoid a "serious, perhaps irreparable consequence." What is the purpose of this additional requirement? How was that requirement satisfied in *Carson*? A majority of circuit courts considering the issue have held that this requirement does not apply when a district court expressly grants or denies an injunction. *See, e.g., Morgenstern v. Wilson*, 29 F.3d 1291, 1294-1295 (8th Cir. 1994), *cert. denied*, 513 U.S. 1150 (1995). Under such circumstances, the right to appeal is automatic. Does this distinction between express injunctions and implied injunctions make sense? Might it be based, in part, on the requirement that a party must show irreparable harm as a prerequisite to obtaining an express preliminary injunction?

3. *Noninjunctive court orders.*   Court orders that pertain only to the judicial management of an action are not treated as injunctions for purposes of § 1292(a)(1) even if they order a party to take or refrain from taking some particular action. Thus orders pertaining to discovery, transfer of venue, the conduct of trial, and remands are not as a matter of course appealable under § 1292(a)(1). *See* 19 MOORE'S FEDERAL PRACTICE, *supra*, at § 203.10[6]. Temporary restraining orders also are not generally treated as injunctions for purposes of interlocutory appeal. *See id.* § 203.10[5].

PROBLEM

12-5. As a form of protest, Huminski decorated his van with two large posters critical of a local judge. He then parked the van in the courthouse parking lot. Court employees asked Huminski to either take the van out of the lot or remove the signs from it. He declined, and after being served with "trespass warning notices," he filed a federal civil rights action against various officers of the city, the county, and the state. Huminski sought money damages and a permanent injunction that would prevent the defendants from interfering with his claimed First Amendment right to engage in a peaceful protest on the premises of a courthouse parking lot. He did not seek a preliminary injunction. The district court dismissed his claims against the city and county defendants under Rule 12(b)(6) (failure to state a claim). A final judgment was not entered since Huminski's claims against the state and several state employees remained pending. Huminski has filed a notice of appeal under § 1292(a)(1). Should (or may) the court of appeals exercise jurisdiction over that appeal? Does *Carson* apply under these circumstances? Would it make any difference if Huminski had sought a preliminary injunction on these claims? *See Huminski v. Rutland City Police Dep't*, 221 F.3d 357 (2d Cir. 2000).

b.   *Interlocutory Appeals Under § 1292(b)*

Section 1292(b) provides an additional but limited means for the review of interlocutory orders that are not otherwise appealable. Under this section, an appeal may be taken from an interlocutory order if a district judge certifies in writing that the "order involves a controlling question of law as to which there is substantial ground for difference of opinion and that an immediate appeal from the order may materially advance the ultimate termination of the litigation," *and* if the court of appeals, "in its discretion," grants permission to appeal. 28 U.S.C. § 1292(b). Some appellate courts, relying on the statute's legislative history, have limited application of § 1292(b) to big or exceptional cases in which an immediate appeal may avoid protracted and expensive litigation. *See, e.g., Koehler v. Bank of Bermuda, Ltd.*, 101 F.3d 863, 865-866 (2d Cir. 1996); *Milbert v. Bison Labs., Inc.*, 260 F.2d 431 (3d Cir. 1958). Yet the language of the statute doesn't require such a narrow interpretation; indeed, § 1292(b) seems to have been designed to ameliorate some of the harsh and inefficient consequences of the final decision rule.

In a frequently quoted passage, Judge John R. Brown of the Fifth Circuit described the policy behind § 1292(b), noting:

> [I]t was a judge-sought, judge-made, judge-sponsored enactment. Federal Judges from their prior professional practice, and more so from experience gained in the adjudication of today's complex litigation, were acutely aware of two principal things. First, certainty and dispatch in the completion of judicial business makes piecemeal appeal as permitted in some states undesirable. But second, there are occasions which defy precise delineation or description in which as a practical matter orderly administration is frustrated by the necessity of a waste of precious judicial time while the case grinds through to a final judgment as the sole medium through which to test the correctness of some isolated identifiable point of fact, of law, of substance or procedure, upon which in a realistic way the whole case or defense will turn. The amendment was to give to the appellate machinery . . . a considerable flexibility operating under the immediate, sole and broad control of Judges so that within reasonable limits disadvantages of piecemeal and final judgment appeals might both be avoided. It is that general approach rather than the use of handy modifiers — which may turn out to be Shibboleths — that should guide us in its application and in determining whether the procedure specified has been substantially satisfied.

Hadjipateras v. Pacificia, S.A., 290 F.2d 697, 702-703 (5th Cir. 1961).

Appeals under § 1292(b) can, in theory, address a wide array of orders that do not satisfy either § 1291 or § 1292(a)(1), including orders relating to discovery, transfer of venue, admissibility of evidence, and joinder of parties and claims; denials of motions to dismiss for lack of personal jurisdiction, subject matter jurisdiction, or venue; and denials of motions to dismiss for failure to state a claim or for summary judgment. Of course, any such order must satisfy the standards of § 1292(b) quoted above, including certification by both the district court and the court of appeals. The trick lies in convincing two courts, both with an almost unlimited discretion to deny certification, to permit such an appeal. While that task is not insurmountable, successful invocations of § 1292(b) have proven rare. In addition to the statistics cited in the case that follows, in *Koehler v. Bank of Bermuda, supra*, 101 F.3d at 866, the court noted that during the previous two years, the Second Circuit had granted only eight of the 32 petitions it had received under § 1292(b). For an interesting survey of successful and unsuccessful invocations of § 1292(b), see Michael E. Solimine, *Revitalizing Interlocutory Appeals in the Federal Courts*, 58 Geo. Wash. L. Rev. 1165 (1990). *See generally* 19 Moore's Federal Practice, *supra*, §§ 203.30-203.34; 16 Wright, Miller & Cooper, *supra*, §§ 3929-3931.

Ahrenholz v. Board of Trustees of the University of Illinois

219 F.3d 674 (7th Cir. 2000)

POSNER, Chief Judge.

Since the beginning of 1999, this court has received 31 petitions for interlocutory appeal under 28 U.S.C. § 1292(b) and has granted only six of them. The majority have been denied or dismissed for jurisdictional reasons but seven have been denied even though the district judge had certified that the order sought to be appealed "involves a controlling question of law as to which there is substantial ground for difference of opinion and that an immediate appeal from the order may materially advance the ultimate termination of the litigation," which is the statutory standard. Although the standard is the same for the district court and for us, some disagreement in its application is to be expected. In several cases, however, including this one, we have been unsure whether the district court was using the correct standard. Because on the one hand merely the filing of a section 1292(b) petition tends to delay the litigation in the district court even though the filing does not cause the litigation to be stayed, and on the other hand the denial of the petition may cause the litigation to be unnecessarily protracted, we think it may be useful to remind the district judges of this circuit of the importance of the careful application of the statutory test.

There are four statutory criteria for the grant of a section 1292(b) petition to guide the district court: there must be a question of *law*, it must be *controlling*, it must be *contestable*, and its resolution must promise to *speed up* the litigation. There is also a nonstatutory requirement: the petition must be filed in the district court within a *reasonable time* after the order sought to be appealed. *Richardson Electronics, Ltd. v. Panache Broadcasting of Pennsylvania, Inc.*, 202 F.3d 957, 958 (7th Cir. 2000). (The statute requires the petition to be filed in *this* court within 10 days of the district court's 1292(b) order, but there is no statutory deadline for the filing of the petition in the district court.) Unless *all* these criteria are satisfied, the district court may not and should not certify its order to us for an immediate appeal under section 1292(b). To do so in such circumstances is merely to waste our time and delay the litigation in the district court, since the proceeding in that court normally grinds to a halt as soon as the judge certifies an order in the case for an immediate appeal.

The criteria, unfortunately, are not as crystalline as they might be, as shown by this case, a suit against university officials by a former employee of a public university, contending that the defendants effected his termination in retaliation for his exercise of his First Amendment right of free speech. The district judge denied summary judgment on the ground that the plaintiff had established a prima facie case of retaliation. He then certified this denial for an immediate appeal under section 1292(b). He recited the statutory standard but did not explain how its criteria were satisfied, except the last—that if the defendants were entitled to summary judgment, granting summary judgment now would bring the suit to an immediate end. The criteria are conjunctive, not disjunctive. "The federal scheme does not provide for an immediate appeal solely on the ground that such an appeal may advance the proceedings in the district court." *Harriscom Svenska AB v. Harris Corp.*, 947 F.2d 627, 631 (2d Cir. 1991). The defendants' petition to us for permission to take an immediate appeal does not deign to discuss the statutory criteria; it merely reargues the case for summary judgment.

Formally, an appeal from the grant or denial of summary judgment presents a question of law (namely whether the opponent of the motion has raised a genuine issue of material fact), which if dispositive is controlling; and often there is room for a difference of opinion. So it might seem that the statutory criteria for an immediate appeal would be satisfied in every case in which summary judgment was denied on a nonobvious ground. But that cannot be right. Section 1292(b) was not intended to make denials of summary judgment routinely appealable, which is the implication of the district court's certification and of the defendants' petition in this court. A denial of summary judgment is a paradigmatic example of an interlocutory order that normally is not appealable.

We think "question of law" as used in section 1292(b) has reference to a question of the meaning of a statutory or constitutional provision, regulation, or common law doctrine rather than to whether the party opposing summary judgment had raised a genuine issue of material fact. We also think, here recurring to our recent order denying permission to take a section 1292(b) appeal in *Downey v. State Farm Fire & Casualty Co.*, No. 00-8009 (7th Cir. May 18, 2000), that the question of the meaning of a contract, though technically a question of law when there is no other evidence but the written contract itself, is not what the framers of section 1292(b) had in mind either. We think they used "question of law" in much the same way a lay person might, as referring to a "pure" question of law rather than merely to an issue that might be free from a factual contest. The idea was that if a case turned on a pure question of law, something the court of appeals could decide quickly and cleanly without having to study the record, the court should be enabled to do so without having to wait till the end of the case. (Similar considerations have shaped the scope of interlocutory appeal from orders denying immunity defenses. See *Johnson v. Jones*, 515 U.S. 304, 317 (1995)). But to decide whether summary judgment was properly granted requires hunting through the record compiled in the summary judgment proceeding to see whether there may be a genuine issue of material fact lurking there; and to decide a question of contract interpretation may require immersion in what may be a long, detailed, and obscure contract, as in *Downey*, which involved a contract of flood insurance.

It is equally important, however, to emphasize the duty of the district court and of our court as well to allow an immediate appeal to be taken when the statutory criteria are met, as in our recent case of *United Airlines, Inc. v. Mesa Airlines, Inc.*, 219 F.3d 605 (7th Cir. 2000), where we took a section 1292(b) appeal to decide whether federal law preempts state business-tort law in suits between air carriers over routes and rates of service. That was an abstract issue of law, timely sought to be appealed under section 1292(b), resolution of which could (because it was indeed a *controlling* issue) head off protracted, costly litigation. And because it was an abstract issue of law, it was suitable for determination by an appellate court without a trial record.

To summarize, district judges should use section 1292(b) when it should be used, avoid it when it should be avoided, and remember that "question of law" means an abstract legal issue rather than an issue of whether summary judgment should be granted. The present case, like *Downey*, is unsuitable for appeal under section 1292(b) because it does not present an abstract legal issue, and the petition for permission to take such an appeal is therefore

DENIED.

NOTES AND QUESTIONS

1. *Pure questions of law.*   Why did the Seventh Circuit draw a distinction between pure questions of law, which could be the subject of a § 1292(b) appeal, and mixed questions of law, which could not be? Under what circumstances, if any, might a denial of a summary judgment amount to a pure question of law? Should a pure question of fact be appealable under § 1292(b)?

2. *Certification of class actions.*   In 1992, Congress enacted legislation empowering the Supreme Court to prescribe rules, consistent with the Rules Enabling Act, that "provide for an appeal of an interlocutory decision to the courts of appeals that is not otherwise provided for under subsection (a), (b), (c), or (d)" of § 1292. 28 U.S.C. § 1292(e). In 1998, the Court exercised this expanded rulemaking authority and promulgated Rule 23(f) which, in its current form, provides, "A court of appeals may permit an appeal from an order granting or denying class-action certification. . . ." FED. R. CIV. P. 23(f). How does this rule differ in operation from § 1292(b)? Is it more or less likely to generate appeals?

In *Tilley v. TJX Cos., Inc.*, 345 F.3d 34 (1st Cir. 2003), the First Circuit described the criteria it would follow in determining whether to allow an interlocutory appeal under Rule 23(f) in a case involving a defendant class:

> To recapitulate, interlocutory appeals of class certification orders in cases involving defendant classes are warranted when one of three circumstances exists: (i) denial of certification effectively disposes of the litigation because the plaintiff's claim would only be worth pursuing as against a full class of defendants; or (ii) an interlocutory appeal would clarify an important and unsettled legal issue that would likely escape effective end-of-case review; or (iii) an interlocutory appeal is a desirable vehicle either for addressing special circumstances or for avoiding manifest injustice. We remind those who seek interlocutory review pursuant to the first criterion limned above that such petitioners also must demonstrate that the district court's ruling on class certification is problematic.

Id. at 38-39. For a general discussion of Rule 23 and its potential scope, see Michael E. Solimine & Christine Oliver Hines, *Deciding to Decide: Class Action*

Certification and Interlocutory Review by the United States Courts of Appeals Under Rule 23(f), 41 Wm. & Mary L. Rev. 1531 (2000); *see also* Chapter IX at page 782.

PROBLEM

12-6. During contentious collective-bargaining negotiations between a union representing teachers at a Pennsylvania high school and the local school board, an unidentified person intercepted and recorded a cell phone conversation between the chief union negotiator and the union president. Shortly thereafter, a local radio commentator played a tape of the intercepted conversation on his public affairs talk show in connection with news reports about the settlement of the labor dispute. The commentator had received the tape from an anonymous source. In response, the union negotiator and the union president filed a damages suit in a U.S. district court against the commentator under federal wiretapping laws that make it unlawful to publish the contents of an illegally intercepted phone conversation. The defendant filed a motion for summary judgment, arguing that application of the federal wiretap statute under the given circumstances would violate his right to freedom of expression as protected by the First Amendment. The district court rejected this argument, but granted the defendant's motion for an interlocutory appeal, pursuant to 28 U.S.C. § 1292(b). It certified as a controlling question of law: "Whether the imposition of liability on the defendant under the wiretapping statute solely for broadcasting the newsworthy tape on a radio news/public affairs program, when the tape was illegally intercepted and recorded by unknown persons who were not agents of [the] defendant, violates the First Amendment?" Should (or may) the court of appeals accept jurisdiction over this appeal? *See Bartnicki v. Vopper*, 532 U.S. 514 (2001).

c. Review Under the All Writs Act

We have been considering appellate review of federal district court rulings under §§ 1291 and 1292. In addition, the All Writs Act provides that the "Supreme Court and all courts established by Act of Congress may issue all writs necessary or appropriate in aid of their respective jurisdictions and agreeable to the usages and principles of law." 28 U.S.C. § 1651(a). Among the writs available under this act are writs of mandamus and prohibition. A *writ of mandamus* commands an officer of the government, including a judge of an inferior court, to undertake some specified action, usually a nondiscretionary duty. A *writ of prohibition*, on the other hand, orders an official or judge to refrain or desist from taking a specified action. In the present context, both writs may be used by a court of appeals to review certain orders issued by a district court. They are sometimes used interchangeably. The circumstances under which either writ is available, however, are quite limited, and neither writ may be used as a substitute for an appeal.

Will v. United States

389 U.S. 90 (1967)

MR. CHIEF JUSTICE WARREN delivered the opinion of the Court.

The question in this case is the propriety of a writ of mandamus issued by the Court of Appeals for the Seventh Circuit to compel the petitioner, a United States District Judge, to vacate a portion of a pretrial order in a criminal case.

Simmie Horwitz, the defendant in a criminal tax evasion case pending before petitioner in the Northern District of Illinois, filed a motion for a bill of particulars, which contained thirty requests for information. The Government resisted a number of the requests. . . . Ultimately the dispute centered solely on defendant's request number 25. This request sought certain information concerning any oral statements of the defendant relied upon by the Government to support the charge in the indictment. It asked the names and addresses of the persons to whom such statements were made, the times and places at which they were made, whether the witnesses to the statements were government agents and whether any transcripts or memoranda of the statements had been prepared by the witnesses and given to the Government. After considerable discussion with counsel for both sides, petitioner ordered the Government to furnish the information. The United States Attorney declined to comply with the order on the grounds that request number 25 constituted a demand for a list of prosecution witnesses and that petitioner had no power under Rule 7(f) of the Federal Rules of Criminal Procedure to require the Government to produce such a list.

Petitioner indicated his intention to dismiss the indictments against Horwitz because of the Government's refusal to comply with his order for a bill of particulars. Before the order of dismissal was entered, however the Government sought and obtained *ex parte* from the Seventh Circuit a stay of all proceedings in the case. The Court of Appeals also granted the Government leave to file a petition for a writ of mandamus and issued a rule to show cause why such a writ should not issue to compel petitioner to strike request number 25 from his bill of particulars order. This case was submitted on the briefs, and the Court of Appeals at first denied the writ. The Government petitioned for reconsideration, however, and the Court of Appeals, without taking new briefs or hearing oral argument, reversed itself and without opinion issued a writ of mandamus directing petitioner "to vacate his order directing the Government to answer question 25 in defendant's motion for bill of particulars." We granted certiorari, because of the wide implications of the decision below for the orderly administration of criminal justice in the federal courts. We vacate the writ and remand the case to the Court of Appeals for further proceedings.

Both parties have devoted substantial argument in this Court to the propriety of petitioner's order. In our view of the case, however, it is unnecessary to reach this question. The peremptory writ of mandamus has traditionally been used in the federal courts only "to confine an inferior court to a lawful exercise of its prescribed jurisdiction or to compel it to exercise its authority when it is its duty to do so." *Roche v. Evaporated Milk Assn.*, 319 U.S. 21, 26 (1943). While the courts have never confined themselves to an arbitrary and technical definition of "jurisdiction," it is clear that only exceptional circumstances amounting to a judicial "usurpation of power" will justify the invocation of this extraordinary remedy. *De Beers Consol. Mines, Ltd. v. United States*, 325 U.S. 212, 217 (1945). Thus the writ has been invoked where unwarranted judicial action threatened "to embarrass the executive arm of the government in conducting foreign relations," *Ex parte Republic of Peru*, 318 U.S. 578, 588 (1943), where it was the only means of forestalling intrusion by the federal judiciary on a delicate area of federal-state relations, where it was necessary to confine a lower court to the terms of an appellate tribunal's mandate, and where a district judge displayed a persistent disregard of the Rules of Civil Procedure promulgated by this Court. And the party seeking mandamus has "the burden of showing that its right to issuance of the writ is 'clear and indisputable.'" *Bankers Life & Cas. Co. v. Holland*, 346 U.S. 379, 384 (1953).

We also approach this case with an awareness of additional considerations which flow from the fact that the underlying proceeding is a criminal prosecution. All our jurisprudence is strongly colored by the notion that appellate review should be postponed, except in certain narrowly defined circumstances, until after final judgment has been rendered by the trial court. This general policy against piecemeal appeals takes on added weight in criminal cases, where the defendant is entitled to a speedy resolution of the charges against him. Moreover, "in the federal jurisprudence, at least, appeals by the Government in criminal cases are something unusual, exceptional, not favored," *Carroll v. United States*, 354 U.S. 394, 400 (1957), at least in part because they always threaten to offend the policies behind the double-jeopardy prohibition. Government appeal in the federal courts has thus been limited by Congress to narrow categories of orders terminating the prosecution, and the Criminal Appeals Act is strictly construed against the Government's right of appeal. Mandamus, of course, may never be employed as a substitute for appeal in derogation of these clear policies. Nor is the case against permitting the writ to be used as a substitute for interlocutory appeal "made less compelling . . . by the fact that the Government has no later right to appeal." *DiBella v. United States*, 369 U.S. 121, 130 (1962). This is not to say that mandamus may never be used to review procedural orders in criminal cases. It has been invoked successfully where the action of the trial court totally deprived the Government of its right to initiate a prosecution. But this Court has never approved the use of the writ to review an interlocutory procedural order in a criminal case which did not have the effect of a dismissal. We need not decide under what circumstances, if any, such a use of mandamus would be appropriate. It is enough to note that we approach the decision in this case with an awareness of the constitutional precepts that a man is entitled to a speedy trial and that he may not be placed twice in jeopardy for the same offense.

In light of these considerations and criteria, neither the record before us nor the cryptic order of the Court of Appeals justifies the invocation of the extraordinary writ in this case.

We do not understand the Government to argue that petitioner was in any sense without "jurisdiction" to order it to file a bill of particulars.[6] Suffice it to note that Rule 7(f) of the Federal Rules of Criminal Procedure specifically empowers the trial court to "direct the filing of a bill of particulars," and that federal trial courts have always had very broad discretion in ruling upon requests for such bills. Furthermore, it is not uncommon for the Government to be required to disclose the names of some potential witnesses in a bill of particulars, where this information is necessary or useful in the defendant's preparation for trial.

The Government seeks instead to justify the employment of the writ in this instance on the ground that petitioner's conduct displays a "pattern of manifest noncompliance with the rules governing federal criminal trials." It argues that the federal rules place settled limitations upon pretrial discovery in criminal cases, and that a trial court may not, in the absence of compelling justification, order the Government to produce a list of its witnesses in advance of trial. It argues further that in only one category of cases, *i.e.*, prosecutions for treason and other capital offenses, is the Government required to turn over to the defense such a list of its witnesses. A general policy of requiring such disclosure without a particularized showing of need would, it is contended, offend the informant's privilege. Petitioner, according to the Government, adopted "a uniform rule in his courtroom requiring the government in a criminal case to furnish the defense, on motion for a bill of particulars, a list of potential witnesses." The Government concludes that since petitioner obviously had no power to adopt such a rule, mandamus will lie under this Court's decision in *La Buy v. Howes Leather Co.*, 352 U.S. 249 (1957), to correct this studied disregard of the limitations placed upon the district courts by the federal rules.[10]

The action of the Court of Appeals cannot, on the record before us, bear the weight of this justification. There is absolutely no foundation in this record for the Government's assertions concerning petitioner's practice. The legal proposition that mandamus will lie in appropriate cases to correct willful disobedience

---

6. Nor do we understand the Government to argue that a judge has no "power" to enter an erroneous order. Acceptance of this semantic fallacy would undermine the settled limitations upon the power of an appellate court to review interlocutory orders. . . . Courts faced with petitions for the peremptory writs must be careful lest they suffer themselves to be misled by labels such as "abuse of discretion" and "want of power" into interlocutory review of nonappealable orders on the mere ground that they may be erroneous. "Certainly Congress knew that some interlocutory orders might be erroneous when it chose to make them nonreviewable." *De Beers Consol. Mines, Ltd. v. United States*, 325 U.S. 212, 223, 225 (1945) (dissenting opinion of MR. JUSTICE DOUGLAS).

10. We note in passing that *La Buy* and the other decisions of this Court approving the use of mandamus as a means of policing compliance with the procedural rules were civil cases. See *Schlagenhauf v. Holder*, 379 U.S. 104 (1964). We have pointed out that the fact this case involves a criminal prosecution has contextual relevance. In view of our reading of the record, however, we need not venture an abstract pronouncement on the question whether this fact imposes a more stringent standard for the invocation of mandamus by the Government where the allegation is that a district judge has deviated from the federal rules.

of the rules laid down by this Court is not controverted. But the position of the Government rests on two central factual premises: (1) that petitioner in effect ordered it to produce a list of witnesses in advance of trial; and (2) that petitioner took this action pursuant to a deliberately adopted policy in disregard of the rules of criminal procedure. Neither of these premises finds support in the record.

Petitioner repeatedly and, we think, correctly emphasized that request number 25 did not call for a list of government witnesses. He carefully noted that it was utterly immaterial under the terms of request number 25 whether the Government planned to call any of the individuals whose names were sought to the witness stand during the trial. . . . Indeed, petitioner excused the Government from answering request number 29(a), which was so broad as to constitute in effect a demand for a list of prosecution witnesses. Finally, it should be noted that in the opinion accompanying the original order, petitioner averred his willingness to narrow the order of disclosure upon a showing by the Government "that such disclosure will involve physical risk to the individuals or prejudice the government in its ability to produce its evidence." He repeated this offer numerous times in the subsequent hearings on the Government's objections to the bill, but the United States Attorney never suggested that such a showing could be made in this case.

The record is equally devoid of support for the notion that petitioner had adopted a deliberate policy in open defiance of the federal rules in matters of pretrial criminal discovery. The extended colloquy between petitioner and government counsel reveals at most that petitioner took a generally liberal view of the discovery rights of criminal defendants. But petitioner was careful never to divorce his ruling from his view of the legitimate needs of the defendant in the case before him, and there is no indication that he considered the case to be governed by a uniform and inflexible rule of disclosure. Thus the most that can be claimed on this record is that petitioner may have erred in ruling on matters within his jurisdiction. But "[t]he extraordinary writs do not reach to such cases; they may not be used to thwart the congressional policy against piecemeal appeals." *Parr v. United States*, 351 U.S. 513, 520-521 (1956). Mandamus, it must be remembered, does not "run the gauntlet of reversible errors." *Bankers Life & Cas. Co. v. Holland*, 346 U.S. 379, 382 (1953). Its office is not to "control the decision of the trial court," but rather merely to confine the lower court to the sphere of its discretionary power. *Id.*, at 383. Thus the record before us simply fails to demonstrate the necessity for the drastic remedy employed by the Court of Appeals.

Even more important in our view, however, than these deficiencies in the record is the failure of the Court of Appeals to attempt to supply any reasoned justification of its action. Had the Government in fact shown that petitioner adopted a policy in deliberate disregard of the criminal discovery rules and that this policy had proved seriously disruptive of the efficient administration of criminal justice in the Northern District of Illinois, it would have raised serious questions under this Court's decision in *La Buy v. Howes Leather Co.*, 352 U.S. 249 (1957).[14] In *La Buy*, however, we specifically relied upon evidence in the record which showed a pattern of improper references of cases to special masters by the District Judge. There is no evidence in this record concerning petitioner's practice in other cases, aside from his own remark that the Government was generally dissatisfied with it, and his statements do not reveal any intent to evade or disregard the rules. We do not know what he ordered the Government to reveal under what circumstances in other cases. This state of the record renders the silence of the Court of Appeals all the more critical. We recognized in *La Buy* that the familiarity of a court of appeals with the practice of the individual district courts within its circuit was relevant to an assessment of the need for mandamus as a corrective measure. But without an opinion from the Court of Appeals we do not know what role, if any, this factor played in the decision below. In fact, we are in the dark with respect to the position of the Court of Appeals on all the issues crucial to an informed exercise of our power of review. . . .

Due regard, not merely for the reviewing functions of this Court, but for the "drastic and extraordinary" nature of the mandamus remedy, *Ex parte Fahey*, 352 U.S. 258, 259 (1947), and for the extremely awkward position in which it places the District Judge, demands that a court issuing the writ give a reasoned exposition of the basis for its action.

Mandamus is not a punitive remedy. The entire thrust of the Government's justification for mandamus in this case, moreover, is that the writ serves a vital corrective and didactic function. While these aims lay at the core of this Court's decisions in *La Buy* and *Schlagenhauf v. Holder*, we fail to see how they can be served here without findings of fact by the issuing court and some statement of the court's legal reasoning. A mandamus from the blue without rationale is tantamount to an abdication of the very expository and supervisory functions of an appellate court upon which the Government rests its attempt to justify the action below.

The preemptory common-law writs are among the most potent weapons in the judicial arsenal. "As extraordinary remedies, they are reserved for really extraordinary causes." *Ex parte Fahey*, 352 U.S. at 260. There is nothing in the record here to demonstrate that this case falls into that category, and thus the judgment below cannot stand. What might be the proper decision upon a more complete record, supplemented by the findings and conclusions of the Court of Appeals, we cannot and do not say. Hence the writ is vacated and the cause is remanded to the Court of Appeals for the Seventh Circuit for further proceedings not inconsistent with this opinion. *It is so ordered.*

---

14. The Government also places reliance on *Schlagenhauf v. Holder*, 379 U.S. 104 (1964), arguing that it "reaffirmed" *La Buy*. Insofar as it did so, the case does not help the Government here, since we have no quarrel with *La Buy*, which is simply inapposite where there is no showing of a persistent disregard of the federal rules. And it cannot be contended that *Schlagenhauf* on its facts supports an invocation of mandamus in this case. The Court there did note that the various questions concerning the construction of Rule 35 were new and substantial, but it rested the existence of mandamus jurisdiction squarely on the fact that there was real doubt whether the District Court had any power at all to order a defendant to submit to a physical examination.

Writ vacated and cause remanded.

MR. JUSTICE MARSHALL took no part in the consideration or decision of this case.

MR. JUSTICE BLACK, concurring.

I concur in the Court's judgment to vacate and agree substantially with its opinion, but would like to add a few words, which I do not understand to be in conflict with what the Court says, concerning the writ of mandamus. I agree that mandamus is an extraordinary remedy which should not be issued except in extraordinary circumstances. And I also realize that sometimes the granting of mandamus may bring about the review of a case as would an appeal. Yet this does not deprive a court of its power to issue the writ. Where there are extraordinary circumstances, mandamus may be used to review an interlocutory order which is by no means "final" and thus appealable under federal statutes. Finality, then, while relevant to the right of appeal, is not determinative of the question when to issue mandamus. Rather than hinging on this abstruse and infinitely uncertain term, the issuance of the writ of mandamus is proper where a court finds exceptional circumstances to support such an order. In the present case it is conceivable that there are valid reasons why the Government should not be forced to turn over the requested names and that compliance with the order would inflict irreparable damage on its conduct of the case. The trouble here, as I see it, is that neither of the courts below gave proper consideration to the possible existence of exceptional facts which might justify the Government's refusal to disclose the names. Having no doubt as to the appropriateness of mandamus, if the circumstances exist to justify it, I would vacate the judgment below and remand the case to the Court of Appeals for further deliberation on whether there are special circumstances calling for the issuance of mandamus.

Silver Sage Partners, Ltd. v. United States District Court

1998 WL 246526 (9th Cir. May 15, 1998)

BEFORE WIGGINS and KLEINFELD, Circuit Judges, and SMITH, District Judge.

Memorandum

Silver Sage Partners, Ltd. ("Silver Sage") petitions this court for a writ of mandamus following a district court order awarding the City of Desert Hot Springs and other defendants (collectively, the "City") a new trial on the issue of damages. We have jurisdiction under 28 U.S.C. § 1651(a), and we deny the petition.

The All Writs Act, 28 U.S.C. § 1651(a), provides that "[t]he Supreme Court and all courts established by Act of Congress may issue all writs necessary or appropriate in aid of their respective jurisdictions and agreeable to the usages and principles of law." A writ of mandamus is an extraordinary remedy. The writ " 'has traditionally been used in the federal courts only to confine an inferior court to a lawful exercise of its prescribed jurisdiction or to compel it to exercise its authority when it is its duty to do so.'" *Credit Suisse v. U.S. District Court*, 130 F.3d 1342, 1345 (9th Cir. 1997). The petitioner must satisfy the "burden of showing that [its] right to issuance of the writ is 'clear and indisputable.'" *Bankers Life & Cas. Co. v. Holland*, 346 U.S. 379, 384 (1953).

We look to five specific guidelines when determining whether a writ should issue:

(1) The party seeking the writ has no other adequate means, such as a direct appeal, to attain the relief he or she desires.

(2) The petitioner will be damaged or prejudiced in a way not correctable on appeal. (This guideline is closely related to the first.)

(3) The district court's order is clearly erroneous as a matter of law.

(4) The district court's order is an oft-repeated error, or manifests a persistent disregard of the federal rules.

(5) The district court's order raises new and important problems, or issues of law of first impression.

Bauman v. United States District Court, 557 F.2d 650, 654-55 (9th Cir. 1977) (citations omitted). None of the guidelines is determinative and all five need not be satisfied for a writ to issue. Indeed, the guidelines will rarely all point in the same direction or all be relevant or applicable.

We conclude that Silver Sage is unable to meet its high burden. The basis of Silver Sage's petition is the district court's award of a new trial. It is well-established that "[a] trial court's ordering of a new trial rarely, if ever, will justify the issuance of a writ of mandamus." *Allied Chem. Corp. v. Daiflon, Inc.*, 449 U.S. 33, 36 (1980) (per curiam). An application of the *Bauman* guidelines confirms that this petition does not present an exception to this general rule.

First, the district court order granting new trial and remittitur and all determinations relating thereto are fully reviewable on appeal from a final judgment. "Consequently, it cannot be said that [Silver Sage] 'has no other adequate means to seek the relief [it] desires.'" [*Id.*] . . .

Second, Silver Sage has failed to show that the district court's order is clearly erroneous as a matter of law. Silver Sage isolates one ambiguous paragraph in the order and uses it to attribute nefarious intentions to the district court. The new trial order, however, was based on such issues as causality, insufficiency of the evidence, and failure to mitigate. Silver Sage has not shown that those findings were clearly erroneous.

Third, the court's order is not an oft-repeated error and does not manifest persistent disregard for the federal rules. The record does not support Silver Sage's allegation that the district court refused to hear it on the merits of the new trial order. Finally, the order does not raise new and important problems or issues of law of first impression.

In sum, Silver Sage has not carried its burden of showing that its right to issuance of the writ is " 'clear and indisputable.'" Any error by the district court in its new trial order is correctable on appeal. We encourage the district court and the parties to strive for promptness in all subsequent proceedings.

Denied.

NOTES AND QUESTIONS

1. *The later appeal from a final judgment.*   By granting the defendant's motion for a new trial on the issue of damages, the district court in *Silver Sage* set aside the 1994 jury verdict that awarded the plaintiff $3,040,439. When the plaintiff's effort to obtain interlocutory review failed, the case was then remanded to the district court, where a new jury awarded the plaintiff nominal damages of $1. The plaintiff again appealed, this time from a final judgment. Despite its previously expressed doubts, the Ninth Circuit now ruled in the plaintiff's favor, ordering that the original verdict handed down seven years earlier be reinstated since it was not against the clear weight of the evidence. *Silver Sage Partners, Ltd. v. City of Desert Hot Springs*, 251 F.3d 814 (9th Cir. 2001). Thus, as the court of appeals promised, the final-judgment rule did not prevent Silver Sage from eventually obtaining review of the district court's new trial order. For the plaintiff's success in collecting on this judgment, *see Silver Sage Partners, Ltd. v. City of Desert Hot Springs*, 339 F.3d 782 (9th Cir. 2003), *cert. denied*, 540 U.S. 1110 (2004); Clay Lambert, *Municipal Bankruptcy Offers Protection, But at a Price*, Half Moon Bay Rev., http://www.hmbreview.com/news/article_da6ab1cf-cfe2-5afa-8153-d2eab91c9170.html.

2. *The exceptional nature of the writ.*   The Supreme Court in *Will* and the Ninth Circuit's memorandum opinion in *Silver Sage* make it abundantly clear that review of a district court's orders by writ is exceptional and not to be used as a ready substitute for an appeal, even if any available appeal must await a final decision. The exceptional nature of proceeding under § 1651(a) should not, however, be taken to suggest that a writ of mandamus or prohibition will never issue against a district court. For example, in *Mallard v. United States District Court*, 490 U.S. 296 (1989), the Supreme Court upheld the use of a writ of mandamus to review a district court's order that an attorney represent an indigent defendant in a civil rights suit pursuant to a statute giving federal courts the power "to request" that attorneys undertake such representation. The attorney, claiming a lack of litigation experience, asked to be relieved of the duty. The district court refused, and the attorney sought review of that order under § 1651(a). The court of appeals denied the writ. The Supreme Court held that review of the district court's order by writ was appropriate and, on the merits, ruled that the statute did not permit the district court to order an attorney to represent an indigent. Can you distinguish *Mallard* from *Will*? Would *Mallard* satisfy the five factors relied on by the Ninth Circuit in *Silver Sage*?

A party may also proceed by writ when a court of appeals remands a case to the district court, and the district court refuses to comply with the mandate issued by the appellate court. *See, e.g., Pit River Tribe v. U.S. Forest Serv.*, 615 F.3d 1069 (9th Cir. 2010); *Vizcaino v. U.S. Dist. Court*, 173 F.3d 713 (9th Cir.), *amended*,

184 F.3d 1070 (9th Cir. 1999), *cert. denied*, 528 U.S. 1105 (2000); *Lights of Am., Inc. v. U.S. Dist. Court*, 130 F.3d 1369 (9th Cir. 1997).

3. *State practices compared.*   In some state courts, the use of writs as an adjunct to the appellate process is more commonplace, particularly in the context of challenges to a court's assertion of personal jurisdiction. In California, for example, if a state trial court denies a motion to quash service of summons, the defendant must immediately file for a writ of mandamus to challenge the ruling. CAL. CIV. PROC. CODE § 418.10(c). If the defendant instead files a pleading and defends on the merits, planning to appeal after the entry of a final judgment, the jurisdictional issue will be deemed waived.

Within the federal system, however, a denial of a motion to dismiss for want of personal jurisdiction must generally await review until a final decision has been entered. For example, in *Burger King Corp. v. Rudzewicz*, 471 U.S. 462 (1985), page 157, *supra*, which was filed in a federal district court, appellate review of the jurisdictional issue was delayed until after entry of final judgment. A federal district court's lack of personal jurisdiction may be attacked by way of writ, however, if the assertion of jurisdiction amounts to clear error or, as sometimes phrased, to a usurpation of judicial power. Yet as is true in other circumstances, the party seeking the writ has the burden of establishing that entitlement to the writ is "clear and indisputable." These same exceptional standards apply when a party seeks a writ challenging an order upholding subject matter jurisdiction or venue, or ordering a case transferred to another district. In other words, the writ is available for such challenges, but only upon a showing of clear error. *See generally* 16 WRIGHT, MILLER & COOPER, *supra*, § 3933.1.

PROBLEM

12-7. Big Mart sued Aaron in a federal district court, claiming that Aaron had defrauded the company in at least 14 transactions in eight different states. Several months after Big Mart filed its complaint, Aaron was criminally indicted in another federal district court for one of the transactions at issue in the Big Mart complaint. Aaron then moved for a protective order in the Big Mart civil suit, seeking a stay of discovery until the close of the criminal proceedings, on the basis that discovery might undermine his Fifth Amendment privilege against self-incrimination. Big Mart objected to the stay on various grounds, including a concern that evidence might be destroyed in the interim. Although discovery in the civil suit would not technically violate Aaron's Fifth Amendment privilege, the district court, acting pursuant to Rule 26(c) ("Protective Orders"), and in the exercise of its discretion, granted the stay in the interests of justice. Big Mart has now filed an appeal and, in the alternative, seeks a writ of mandamus to compel the district court to rescind its order. Does the court of appeals have jurisdiction over the appeal? Assuming it does not, is this an appropriate case for the issuance of a writ of mandamus? *See Kmart Corp. v. Aronds*, 123 F.3d 297 (5th Cir. 1997).

d.   Certification Under Rule 54(b)

Modern litigation often involves multiple claims and multiple parties. *See* Chapter VIII, *supra* ("Joinder of Claims and Parties"). In such cases, it sometimes occurs that a district court will make a final determination on one or more of the claims, or on all of the claims involving one of several parties, without fully resolving the underlying action. For example, in an action involving multiple claims, a district court might enter a summary judgment on one claim, but leave other claims to be resolved at trial. As we've seen, such interlocutory rulings are generally not appealable until a final decision has been entered on the entire case. Under some circumstances, however, judicial efficiency and fairness to the parties may be better promoted by permitting an interlocutory appeal. Title 28 U.S.C. § 1292(a)-(b), discussed *supra*, operates as a statutory recognition of this principle.

Rule 54(b) offers another variation on this same theme. It provides a means through which a district court "dealing with multiple claims or multiple parties [may] direct the entry of final judgment as to fewer than all of the claims or parties," *Curtiss-Wright Corp. v. General Elec. Co.*, 446 U.S. 1, 3 (1980), in essence certifying those matters for immediate appeal. Thus, Rule 54(b) provides:

> When an action presents more than one claim for relief—whether as a claim, counterclaim, cross-claim, or third-party claim—or when multiple parties are involved, the court may direct entry of a final judgment as to one or more, but fewer than all, claims or parties only if the court expressly determines that there is no just reason for delay.

Fed R. Civ. P. 54(b). Importantly, Rule 54(b) does not alter the rules of finality other than to provide special relief in cases involving multiple claims or parties. The order certified under Rule 54(b), therefore, must be one that would have been treated as a final decision if there had been no other claims or parties involved in the suit. *Sears, Roebuck & Co. v. Mackey*, 351 U.S. 427 (1956). The easiest way to test for this is to imagine a hypothetical suit in which the only claim is the one to which the district court's order is directed. If the order satisfies the final-decision rule in a hypothetical "single claim" case, then the district court has discretion to certify the order for immediate appeal under Rule 54(b). *See, e.g., State Street Bank & Trust Co. v. Brockrim, Inc.*, 87 F.3d 1487, 1490 (1st Cir. 1996) (testing finality by "hypothetical independent case"). Thus an order that only partially disposes of a claim, for example by determining liability but not awarding the requested relief, cannot serve as the basis for a Rule 54(b) certification. *See Liberty Mut. Ins. Co. v. Wetzel*, 424 U.S. 737 (1976). Such an order would not constitute a final decision in a case in which only one claim was presented; it cannot, therefore, be treated as final in a case involving multiple claims.

The certification process requires a district court to do two things. First, after entering an order, it must make an express determination that there is no just reason for delaying an appeal of that order. The purpose of this finding, which is within the district court's discretion, is to ensure that the resolved matters are separable from what remains to be decided, such that an appellate court will not have to decide the same issues more than once. *Curtiss-Wright Corp. v. General Elec. Co., supra,* 446 U.S. at 8; *see, e.g., Ebrahimi v. City of Huntsville Bd. of Educ.,* 114 F.3d 162, 165-167 (11th Cir. 1997) (simply repeating language of rule or framing certification in merely conclusory terms is inadequate unless basis for certification is obvious from the record). Second, the court must direct the entry of a final judgment on the order in accord with Rule 58. Both requirements are jurisdictional prerequisites for an appeal under Rule 54(a); an appeal premised on a certification that fails to satisfy these requirements will be dismissed. The absence or failure of a certification under the rule does not, however, preclude resort to other avenues of appeal such as the collateral-order doctrine, or § 1292(a) or (b). *See generally* Fern M. Smith, *Judgment; Costs, in* 10 MOORE'S FEDERAL PRACTICE §§ 54.01 *et seq.* (3d ed. 2015); 10 CHARLES ALAN WRIGHT, ARTHUR R. MILLER & MARY KAY KANE, FEDERAL PRACTICE AND PROCEDURE §§ 2653-2661 (4th ed. 2014).

Olympia Hotels Corp. v. Johnson Wax Development Corp.
908 F.2d 1363 (7th Cir. 1990)

POSNER, Circuit Judge.

Before us are cross-appeals in a suit arising out of a contract dispute. The appeals are rich with issues, and to discuss them intelligibly we shall have to simplify matters brutally.

In 1988, Olympia Hotels Corporation filed suit against Racine Hotel Partners Limited Partnership charging breach of contract and, by a subsequent amendment to the complaint, conspiracy as well, all in violation of Wisconsin law. . . . Racine filed compulsory counterclaims that charged Olympia not only with breach of contract and with fraud in the inducement of the contract—both claims under Wisconsin law—but also with violations of the federal RICO statute. . . .

The principal counterclaims, [including the RICO claims], were not filed until March 23, 1989; and with trial scheduled for May 15, the judge decided to sever the counterclaims (except for Racine's claim for breach of contract) from the plaintiff's claims and try them later . . . . They remain pending in the district court, and there is no trial date. The trial on the plaintiff's claims began as scheduled and lasted two weeks. The voir dire of the jury was conducted by a federal magistrate over Racine's objection. At the close of all the evidence the judge directed a verdict for Olympia on Racine's counterclaim for breach of contract and for Racine on Olympia's claim of civil conspiracy. The jury then returned a verdict for Olympia on its breach of contract claim, awarding $1.2 million in damages. The judge entered judgment for that amount under Rule 54(b) of the Federal Rules of Civil Procedure, and Racine has appealed, with Olympia cross-appealing from the dismissal of its claim of civil conspiracy.

The facts bearing on the legal issues are simple enough. Racine, established to create a first-class hotel in the city of that name, hired Olympia, a hotel-management firm, to build and operate the hotel. The contract had a term of twenty-five years and provided that Olympia would have complete control of the hotel (Racine's principals had no experience in the hotel business) and would use its best efforts to make the hotel a success. The hotel was built and went into operation, but it was not a success and after several years of operation Racine gave Olympia written notice of default. Racine complained that Olympia had not used its best efforts to make a success of the hotel and that it had reimbursed itself out of the hotel's revenues for expenses not actually incurred in the hotel's operation. This suit followed shortly.

The first issue is our appellate jurisdiction. Rule 54(b) authorizes the district court to make immediately appealable a judgment that disposes, with finality, of one or more claims, even though other claims remain pending in the district court so that the suit as a whole has not been finally disposed of by that court. It has seemed to us implicit in the rule that the retained and the appealed claims must be factually distinct, for otherwise the court of appeals may be forced to analyze the same facts in successive appeals, a form of piecemeal appealing not authorized by the rule.

This is a borderline case. The claims for breach of contract and for civil conspiracy that were tried and that the parties are trying to bring before us in their appeals concern the parties' conduct after the contract was signed and the hotel built and in operation, while the counterclaims that await trial in the district court concern promises that Olympia is alleged to have made when the contract was first being negotiated. Yet the claims and counterclaims are of course closely related; if they were not, the counterclaims would not be compulsory; and we shall see that Racine's principal ground of appeal is that the district judge should have let it prove fraud as a defense to Olympia's claim for breach of contract. The fact that one claim appears in the complaint and another in a counterclaim, moreover, does not make them different claims for purposes of Rule 54(b). *Curtiss-Wright Corp. v. General Electric Co.*, 446 U.S. 1, 9 (1980).

This is not, however, a case in which a party "merely gave different legal characterizations to the same facts." It is a case in which although the claims arise from a single dispute or factual setting, there are many factual differences between them . . . . Indeed, it appears that virtually the only facts that overlap are those that are not in dispute. . . .

In the present case, even though the two sets of claims arise out of the same transaction (the contract for the management of Racine's hotel), the pertinent facts—the facts bearing on liability, damages, etc.—are different, so that, in the event that the counterclaims eventually are tried and the judgment appealed to us, we shall not have to reacquaint ourselves with the same facts that we had to learn in order to decide the present appeal. The fact that two claims are one for purposes of res judicata may be relevant in appraising the possibility of a Rule 54(b) judgment . . . . But the res judicata status of the two claims is not conclusive under Rule 54(b), and is probably a diversion from the main issue.

So too we think that some of our previous cases place too much weight on the existence and extent of factual overlap between the two claims. What is true is that if the overlap is complete the claims are the same, the only possible difference being the legal theory in which they have been wrapped. If the same set of facts is alleged as a breach of contract and as a breach of a statutory duty, or as a violation of federal and of state securities laws, or as a fraud and as mutual mistake, then as a practical matter there is only one claim, and a Rule 54(b) judgment cannot be entered. If however there is some but not complete factual overlap between nominally separate claims, this circumstance should invite an exercise of discretion by the district court rather than a determination by us that the retained and appealed claims are or are not separate. "It was therefore proper *for the District Judge* here to consider such factors as . . . whether the nature of the claims already determined was such that no appellate court would have to decide the same issues more than once even if there were subsequent appeals." *Curtiss-Wright Co. v. General Electric Co., supra,* 446 U.S. at 8 (emphasis added).

In sum, it is not a decisive consideration, in determining whether claims are one or more than one for purposes of Rule 54(b), either that they are one claim for purposes of res judicata, or that there is considerable but not complete factual overlap between them. If the claims are legally distinct and involve at least some separate facts, the district court has the *power* to enter a Rule 54(b) judgment, and it becomes a matter of the district judge's *discretion*, reviewable for but only for abuse thereof, whether to exercise the power and enter such a judgment. The conditions that define the district court's power are satisfied here, and there was no abuse of discretion. Not only is "one appropriate use of Rule 54(b) . . . the entry of judgment on the principal claims of the suit while reserving disposition of counterclaims that may require a longer time to resolve," but we shall see that there are compelling pragmatic reasons (the very stuff of discretionary judgments) for deciding this appeal on the merits rather than dismissing it.

[On the merits, the court held that the defendant was entitled to a new trial on the breach-of-contract claim.]

NOTES AND QUESTIONS

1. Factually distinct claims. The defendant in *Olympia Hotels* filed counterclaims based on breach of contract, fraud, and RICO. Only the breach-of-contract claim was tried. Why was it necessary for the Seventh Circuit to determine whether the untried claims were factually distinct from the breach-of-contract claim? On what basis did the court determine that the tried and untried claims were distinct from one another? How does the approach adopted by the court advance the policy of efficiency?

C.   Standards of Review on Appeal

We have been considering the circumstances under which a trial court's ruling or decree may be appealed. We turn now to the question of what standard of review the appellate court should apply to those cases in which a proper appeal has been lodged. A "standard of review" is a conceptual device that dictates the degree of deference a court of appeals must give to a trial court decision. Under the generally accepted view, there are several available standards. Which one to apply depends on the nature of the issue presented vis-à-vis the respective responsibilities of the district court and the court of appeals. In general, if primary responsibility over the issue is lodged in the district court, the standard of review is highly deferential (as was the case in *Olympia Hotels*), whereas if that responsibility is lodged in the court of appeals, no deference is required. The key, therefore, is to discern where the primary decisional responsibility rests.

Unfortunately, the usual approach to determining which standard to apply is more often undertaken mechanically, dividing potential issues on appeal into four seemingly distinct categories:

- questions involving district-court discretion;
- questions of fact;
- questions of law; and
- mixed questions of law and fact.

In theory, each category calls for a specific standard of review, geared to the relative responsibilities of the district and appellate courts with respect to the type of question involved. In other words, the category should determine the standard. As we will see, however, these categories are not nearly as distinct as their descriptions may suggest, and they often operate as mere labels for the conclusion that a particular standard ought to apply. Thus a court might call something a question of fact, not because it is inherently a question of fact but because the standard of review attached to questions of fact appears to be the most appropriate standard given the allocation of decisional responsibilities over that particular type of issue.

We begin with a brief description of each category and its attendant standard. The great majority of issues on appeal can be pigeonholed into one of these categories, making the choice of which standard to apply relatively simple. This basic structure should also create a foundation from which to explore some of the more subtle policy judgments involved in determining which standard to apply in the less obvious and more difficult cases. The next step, therefore, is to determine the extent to which policy considerations may play a significant role in the choice of which standard to apply, with the supposedly bright-line distinctions between discretion, fact, and law serving merely as convenient labels for a more carefully formulated judgment.

Questions Involving District-Court Discretion

The district court is responsible for managing the litigation before it. This often requires an exercise of judgment premised on the pending case's precise contours. For example, whether to grant a motion to transfer venue under 28 U.S.C. § 1404(a) requires the exercise of case-specific managerial judgment.

Similarly, many of the federal rules require the district court to exercise this same type of managerial judgment on a wide range of issues. *See, e.g.,* FED. R. CIV. P. 11 (imposition of sanctions); FED. R. CIV. P. 19 (joinder of persons needed for a just adjudication); FED. R. CIV. P. 26 (management of discovery); FED. R. CIV. P. 42 (consolidation of actions and separate trials); FED. R. CIV. P. 60 (relief from judgment or order). In such circumstances, the district court's decisions are examined under a deferential "abuse of discretion" standard. While there is no specific formula for identifying an abuse of discretion, the basic principle is that the district court will not be reversed under this standard unless it has made either an error of law or a clear error of judgment. *See Cooter & Gell v. Hartmarx Corp.,* 496 U.S. 384, 400 (1990) (holding that abuse-of-discretion standard encompasses a broad range of permissible conclusions). One court has described the standard as follows:

> Abuse of discretion can occur in three principal ways: when a relevant factor that should have been given significant weight is not considered; when an irrelevant or improper factor is considered and given significant weight; and when all proper factors, and no improper ones, are considered, but the court, in weighing those factors, commits clear error of judgment.

Richards v. Aramark Servs., Inc., 108 F.3d 925, 927 (8th Cir. 1997).

Questions of Fact

A question of fact involves a dispute over the objective reality of the event or events in controversy. Questions of fact are examined under two slightly different standards of review. The first pertains to factual findings by juries while the second pertains to factual findings by the district court judge.

If a jury decides a question of fact, the "substantial evidence" or "no reasonable jury" rule applies. Under this highly deferential standard, the scope of appellate review is exceedingly narrow. The jury is considered the quintessential fact finder, and its factual determinations must be upheld unless no rational juror could have so determined. *Cf. Crockett v. Long Island R.R.,* 65 F.3d 274, 278 (2d Cir. 1995) (finding that jury's logically irreconcilable findings were not rational). In applying this standard, the appellate court may not reweigh the evidence. Rather, the court must assess the evidence, and all potential inferences drawn from it, in a light most favorable to the jury's finding. The consequence of this rule is that pure findings of fact by a jury, *i.e.,* factual findings that are unaffected by an erroneously applied legal standard, are rarely if ever overturned on appeal.

The standard of review applicable to questions of fact decided by a judge is embodied in Rule 52(a)(6): "Findings of fact, whether based on oral or other evidence, must not be set aside unless clearly erroneous, and the reviewing court must give due regard to the trial court's opportunity to judge the witnesses' credibility." FED. R. CIV. P. 52(a)(6). This "clearly erroneous" standard is also highly deferential, but at least in theory it is subtly less so than the substantial-evidence rule. The appellate court need not conclude that no reasonable person could have made the factual finding at issue. Rather, a finding is deemed clearly erroneous if the appellate court "is left with the definite and firm conviction that a mistake has been committed." *United States v. U.S. Gypsum Co.*, 333 U.S. 364, 395 (1948). Conversely,

> [i]f the district court's account of the evidence is plausible in light of the record viewed in its entirety, the court of appeals may not reverse it even though convinced that had it been sitting as the trier of fact, it would have weighed the evidence differently. Where there are two permissible views of the evidence, the factfinder's choice between them cannot be clearly erroneous.

Anderson v. City of Bessemer City, 470 U.S. 564, 573-574 (1985). Given the presumed superior expertise of district courts in making factual determinations, the clearly-erroneous standard most often leads to the affirmance of those determinations. That is particularly so when the fact finding is based on a credibility determination by the district judge who, unlike her appellate counterparts, is in a position to observe and assess the witnesses' demeanor. As when reviewing the jury's finding of facts, the appellate court may not reweigh the evidence and must assess the evidence, and all potential inferences drawn from it, in a light most favorable to the judge's finding.

Questions of Law

A question of law is one that pertains to the legal standards under which cases are decided. Questions of law are reviewed under a "de novo standard," which affords "no form of appellate deference" whatsoever to the district court's legal conclusions. *Salve Regina Coll. v. Russell*, 499 U.S. 225, 238 (1991). In essence, the appellate court applies its independent judgment in determining the meaning and content of the law. Of course, district court judges are as fully trained in the law as appellate court judges, and in most cases the district court's interpretations will not differ significantly from those of the appellate court. When the interpretations do differ, however, the district court interpretation is not entitled to any deference, perhaps reflecting the principle that three heads are usually better than one.

Mixed Questions of Law and Fact

A mixed question of law and fact is one "in which the historical facts are admitted or established, the rule of law is undisputed, and the issue is whether the facts satisfy the statutory standard, or to put it another way, whether the rule of law as applied to the established facts is or is not violated." *Pullman-Standard v. Swint*, 456 U.S. 273, 289 n.19 (1982). In short, mixed questions of law and fact involve the application of the accepted law to the established facts. There is no single standard of review for mixed questions of law and fact. Some courts apply the de novo standard, on the theory that the application of the law presents a question of law. Other courts have adopted a sliding-scale approach that focuses on whether the question presented is predominantly one of law or of fact. Still others prefer the clearly-erroneous standard, on the theory that questions of application are essentially fact-bound. *See generally* George C. Pratt, *Standards of Review, in* 19 MOORE'S FEDERAL PRACTICE § 206.04[3] (3d ed. 2015). This range of options is further complicated by the categorical treatment of certain mixed questions of law and fact as being questions of law (*e.g.,* actual malice in a defamation suit) and the treatment of others as being questions of fact (*e.g.,* negligence). We will explore these complications further in the notes following the next case.

Pullman-Standard v. Swint

456 U.S. 273 (1982)

JUSTICE WHITE delivered the opinion of the Court.

Respondents were black employees at the Bessemer, Ala., plant of petitioner Pullman-Standard (the Company), a manufacturer of railway freight cars and parts. They brought suit against the Company and the union petitioners—the United Steelworkers of America, AFL-CIO-CLC, and its Local 1466 (collectively USW)—alleging violations of Title VII of the Civil Rights Act of 1964. As they come here, these cases involve only the validity, under Title VII, of a seniority system maintained by the Company and USW. The District Court found "that the differences in terms, conditions or privileges of employment resulting [from the seniority system] are 'not the result of an intention to discriminate' because of race or color," and held, therefore, that the system satisfied the requirements of § 703(h) of the Act. The Court of Appeals for the Fifth Circuit reversed. . . .

We granted the petitions for certiorari filed by USW and by the Company, limited to the first question presented in each petition: whether a court of appeals is bound by the "clearly erroneous" rule of Federal Rule of Civil Procedure 52(a) in reviewing a district court's findings of fact, arrived at after a lengthy trial, as to the motivation of the parties who negotiated a seniority system; and whether the court below applied wrong legal criteria in determining the bona fides of the seniority system. . . .

I

[The Court reaffirmed that in the context of seniority systems, Title VII requires proof of "discriminatory intent." Moreover, said the Court, a showing of disparate impact on the subject minority group is not in itself sufficient to establish discriminatory intent.] Thus, any challenge to a seniority system under Title VII will require a trial on the issue of discriminatory intent: Was the system adopted because of its racially discriminatory impact?

This is precisely what happened in these cases. . . . [T]he District Court held a . . . trial on the limited question of whether the seniority system was "instituted or maintained contrary to Section 703(h) of the new Civil Rights Act of 1964." That court concluded, as we noted above and will discuss below, that the system was adopted and maintained for purposes wholly independent of any discriminatory intent. The Court of Appeals for the Fifth Circuit reversed.

II

Petitioners submit that the Court of Appeals failed to comply with the command of Rule 52(a) that the findings of fact of a district court may not be set aside unless clearly erroneous. We first describe the findings of the District Court and the Court of Appeals.

Certain facts are common ground for both the District Court and the Court of Appeals. The Company's Bessemer plant was unionized in the early 1940's. Both before and after unionization, the plant was divided into a number of different operational departments. USW sought to represent all production and maintenance employees at the plant and was elected in 1941 as the bargaining representative of a bargaining unit consisting of most of these employees. At that same time, IAM [the International Association of Machinists and Aerospace Workers] became the bargaining representative of a unit consisting of five departments. Between 1941 and 1944, IAM ceded certain workers in its bargaining unit to USW. As a result of this transfer, the IAM bargaining unit became all white.

Throughout the period of representation by USW, the plant was approximately half black. Prior to 1965, the Company openly pursued a racially discriminatory policy of job assignments. Most departments contained more than one job category and as a result most departments were racially mixed. There were no lines of progression or promotion within departments.

The seniority system at issue here was adopted in 1954. Under that agreement, seniority was measured by length of continuous service in a particular department. Seniority was originally exercised only for purposes of layoffs and hirings within particular departments. In 1956, seniority was formally recognized for promotional purposes as well. Again, however, seniority, with limited exceptions, was only exercised within departments; employees transferring to new departments forfeited their seniority. This seniority system remained virtually unchanged until after this suit was brought in 1971.

The District Court approached the question of discriminatory intent in the manner suggested by the Fifth Circuit in *James v. Stockham Valves & Fittings Co.*, 559 F.2d 310 (1977). There, the Court of Appeals stated that "the totality of the circumstances in the development and maintenance of the system is relevant to examining that issue." There were, in its view, however, four particular factors that a court should focus on.

First, a court must determine whether the system "operates to discourage all employees equally from transferring between seniority units." The District Court held that the system here "was facially neutral and . . . was applied equally to all races and ethnic groups." Although there were charges of racial discrimination in its application, the court held that these were "not substantiated by the evidence."

It concluded that the system "applied equally and uniformly to all employees, black and white, and that, given the approximately equal number of employees of the two groups, it was quantitatively neutral as well."

Second, a court must examine the rationality of the departmental structure, upon which the seniority system relies, in light of the general industry practice. The District Court found that linking seniority to "departmental age" was "the modal form of agreements generally, as well as with manufacturers of railroad equipment in particular." Furthermore, it found the basic arrangement of departments at the plant to be rationally related to the nature of the work and to be "consistent with practices which were . . . generally followed at other unionized plants throughout the country." While questions could be raised about the necessity of certain departmental divisions, it found that all of the challenged lines of division grew out of historical circumstances at the plant that were unrelated to racial discrimination. Although unionization did produce an all-white IAM bargaining unit, it found that USW "cannot be charged with racial bias in its response to the IAM situation. [USW] sought to represent all workers, black and white, in the plant." Nor could the Company be charged with any racial discrimination that may have existed in IAM:

> "The company properly took a 'hands-off' approach towards the establishment of the election units. . . . It bargained with those unions which were afforded representational status by the NLRB and did so without any discriminatory animus."

Third, a court had to consider "whether the seniority system had its genesis in racial discrimination," by which it meant the relationship between the system and other racially discriminatory practices. Although finding ample discrimination by the Company in its employment practices and some discriminatory practices by the union, the District Court concluded that the seniority system was in no way related to the discriminatory practices:

> "The seniority system . . . had its genesis . . . at a period when racial segregation was certainly being practiced; but this system was not itself the product of this bias. The system rather came about as a result of colorblind objectives of a union which — unlike most structures and institutions of the era — was not an arm of a segregated society. Nor did it foster the discrimination . . . which was being practiced by custom in the plant."

Finally, a court must consider "whether the system was negotiated and has been maintained free from any illegal purpose." Stating that it had "carefully considered the detailed record of negotiation sessions and contracts which span a period of some thirty-five years," the court found that the system was untainted by any discriminatory purpose. Thus, although the District Court focused on particular factors in carrying out the analysis required by § 703(h), it also looked to the entire record and to the "totality of the system under attack."

The Court of Appeals addressed each of the four factors of the *James* test and reached the opposite conclusion. First, it held that the District Court erred in putting aside qualitative differences between the departments in which blacks were concentrated and those dominated by whites, in considering whether the system applied "equally" to whites and blacks. This is a purported correction of a legal standard under which the evidence is to be evaluated.

Second, it rejected the District Court's conclusion that the structure of departments was rational, in line with industry practice, and did not reflect any discriminatory intent. Its discussion is brief but focuses on the role of IAM and certain characteristics unique to the Bessemer plant. The court concluded:

> "The record evidence, generally, indicates arbitrary creation of the departments by the company since unionization and an attendant adverse affect [*sic*] on black workers. The individual differences between the departmental structure at Pullman-Standard and that of other plants, and as compared with industry practice, are indicative of attempts to maintain one-race departments."

In reaching this conclusion, the Court of Appeals did not purport to be correcting a legal error, nor did it refer to or expressly apply the clearly-erroneous standard.

Third, in considering the "genesis" of the system, the Court of Appeals held that the District Court erred in holding that the motives of IAM were not relevant. This was the correction of a legal error on the part of the District Court in excluding relevant evidence. The court did not stop there, however. It went on to hold that IAM was acting out of discriminatory intent—an issue specifically not reached by the District Court—and that "considerations of race permeated the negotiation and the adoption of the seniority system in 1941 and subsequent negotiations thereafter."

Fourth, despite this conclusion under the third *James* factor the Court of Appeals then recited, but did not expressly set aside or find clearly erroneous, the District Court's findings with respect to the negotiation and maintenance of the seniority system.

The court then announced that "[h]aving carefully reviewed the evidence offered to show whether the departmental seniority system in the present case is 'bona fide' within the meaning of § 703(h) of Title VII, we reject the district court's finding." Elaborating on its disagreement, the Court of Appeals stated:

> "An analysis of the totality of the facts and circumstances surrounding the creation and continuance of the departmental system at Pullman-Standard leaves us with the definite and firm conviction that a mistake has been made. There is no doubt, based upon the record in this case, about the existence of a discriminatory purpose. The obvious principal aim of the I.A.M. in 1941 was to exclude black workers from its bargaining unit. That goal was ultimately reached when maneuvers by the I.A.M. and U.S.W. resulted in an all-white I.A.M. unit. The U.S.W., in the interest of increased membership, acquiesced in the discrimination while succeeding in significantly segregating the departments within its own unit.
>
> "The district court might have reached a different conclusion had it given the I.A.M.'s role in the creation and establishment of the seniority system its due consideration."

Having rejected the District Court's finding, the court made its own findings as to whether the USW seniority system was protected by § 703(h):

"We consider significant in our decision the manner by which the two seniority units were set up, the creation of the various all-white and all-black departments within the U.S.W. unit at the time of certification and in the years thereafter, conditions of racial discrimination which affected the negotiation and renegotiation of the system, and the extent to which the system and the attendant no-transfer rule locked blacks into the least remunerative positions within the company. Because we find that the differences in the terms, conditions and standards of employment for black workers and white workers at Pullman-Standard resulted from an intent to discriminate because of race, we hold that the system is not legally valid under section 703(h) of Title VII, 42 U.S.C. § 2000e-2(h)."

In connection with its assertion that it was convinced that a mistake had been made, the Court of Appeals, in a footnote, referred to the clearly-erroneous standard of Rule 52(a). It pointed out, however, that if findings "are made under an erroneous view of controlling legal principles, the clearly-erroneous rule does not apply, and the findings may not stand." Finally, quoting from *East v. Romine, Inc.*, 518 F.2d 332, 339 (CA5 1975), the Court of Appeals repeated the following view of its appellate function in Title VII cases where purposeful discrimination is at issue:

"'Although discrimination *vel non* is essentially a question of fact it is, at the same time, the ultimate issue for resolution in this case, being expressly proscribed by 42 U.S.C.A. § 2000e-2(a). As such, a finding of discrimination or non-discrimination is a finding of ultimate fact. In reviewing the district court's findings, therefore, we will proceed to make an independent determination of appellant's allegations of discrimination, though bound by findings of subsidiary fact which are themselves not clearly erroneous.'"

III

Pointing to the above statement of the Court of Appeals and to similar statements in other Title VII cases coming from that court, petitioners submit that the Court of Appeals made an independent determination of discriminatory purpose, the "ultimate fact" in this case, and that this was error under Rule 52(a). We agree with petitioners that if the Court of Appeals followed what seems to be the accepted rule in that Circuit, its judgment must be reversed.

Rule 52(a) broadly requires that findings of fact not be set aside unless clearly erroneous. It does not make exceptions or purport to exclude certain categories of factual findings from the obligation of a court of appeals to accept a district court's findings unless clearly erroneous. It does not divide facts into categories; in particular, it does not divide findings of fact into those that deal with "ultimate" and those that deal with "subsidiary" facts.

The Rule does not apply to conclusions of law. The Court of Appeals, therefore, was quite right in saying that if a district court's findings rest on an erroneous view of the law, they may be set aside on that basis. But here the District Court was not faulted for misunderstanding or applying an erroneous definition of intentional discrimination. It was reversed for arriving at what the Court of Appeals thought was an erroneous finding as to whether the differential impact of the seniority system reflected an intent to discriminate on account of race. That question, as we see it, is a pure question of fact, subject to Rule 52(a)'s clearly-erroneous standard. It is not a question of law and not a mixed question of law and fact.

The Court has previously noted the vexing nature of the distinction between questions of fact and questions of law. Rule 52(a) does not furnish particular guidance with respect to distinguishing law from fact. Nor do we yet know of any other rule or principle that will unerringly distinguish a factual finding from a legal conclusion. For the reasons that follow, however, we have little doubt about the factual nature of § 703(h)'s requirement that a seniority system be free of an intent to discriminate.

Treating issues of intent as factual matters for the trier of fact is commonplace. In *Dayton Board of Education v. Brinkman*, 443 U.S. 526, 534 (1979), the principal question was whether the defendants had intentionally maintained a racially segregated school system at a specified time in the past. We recognized that issue as essentially factual, subject to the clearly-erroneous rule. In *Commissioner v. Duberstein*, 363 U.S. 278 (1960), the Court held that the principal criterion for identifying a gift under the applicable provision of the Internal Revenue Code was the intent or motive of the donor—"one that inquires what the basic reason for his conduct was in fact." Resolution of that issue determined the ultimate issue of whether a gift had been made. Both issues were held to be questions of fact subject to the clearly-erroneous rule. In *United States v. Yellow Cab Co.*, 338 U.S. 338, 341 (1949), an antitrust case, the Court referred to "[f]indings as to the design, motive and intent with which men act" as peculiarly factual issues for the trier of fact and therefore subject to appellate review under Rule 52. . . .

This is not to say that discriminatory impact is not part of the evidence to be considered by the trial court in reaching a finding on whether there was such a discriminatory intent as a factual matter. We do assert, however, that under § 703(h) discriminatory intent is a finding of fact to be made by the trial court; it is not a question of law and not a mixed question of law and fact of the kind that in some cases may allow an appellate court to review the facts to see if they satisfy some legal concept of discriminatory intent.[19] Discriminatory intent here means actual motive; it is not a legal presumption to be drawn from a factual showing of something less than actual motive. Thus, a court of appeals may only reverse a district court's finding on discriminatory intent if it concludes that the finding is clearly erroneous under Rule 52(a). Insofar as the Fifth Circuit assumed otherwise, it erred.

---

19. We need not, therefore, address the much-mooted issue of the applicability of the Rule 52(a) standard to mixed questions of law and fact—*i.e.*, questions in which the historical facts are admitted or established, the rule of law is undisputed, and the issue is whether the facts satisfy the statutory standard, or to put it another way, whether the rule of law as applied to the established facts is or is not violated. There is substantial authority in the Circuits on both sides of this question. There is also support in decisions of this Court for the proposition that conclusions on mixed questions of law and fact are independently reviewable by an appellate court.

IV

Respondents do not directly defend the Fifth Circuit rule that a trial court's finding on discriminatory intent is not subject to the clearly-erroneous standard of Rule 52(a). Rather, among other things, they submit that the Court of Appeals recognized and, where appropriate, properly applied Rule 52(a) in setting aside the findings of the District Court. This position has force, but for two reasons it is not persuasive.

First, although the Court of Appeals acknowledged and correctly stated the controlling standard of Rule 52(a), the acknowledgment came late in the court's opinion. The court had not expressly referred to or applied Rule 52(a) in the course of disagreeing with the District Court's resolution of the factual issues deemed relevant under *James v. Stockham Valves & Fittings Co.*, 559 F.2d 310 (1977). Furthermore, the paragraph in which the court finally concludes that the USW seniority system is unprotected by § 703(h) strongly suggests that the outcome was the product of the court's independent consideration of the totality of the circumstances it found in the record.

Second and more fundamentally, when the court stated that it was convinced that a mistake had been made, it then identified not only the mistake but also the source of that mistake. The mistake of the District Court was that on the record there could be no doubt about the existence of a discriminatory purpose. The source of the mistake was the District Court's failure to recognize the relevance of the racial purposes of IAM. Had the District Court "given the I.A.M.'s role in the creation and establishment of the seniority system its due consideration," it "might have reached a different conclusion."

When an appellate court discerns that a district court has failed to make a finding because of an erroneous view of the law, the usual rule is that there should be a remand for further proceedings to permit the trial court to make the missing findings:

> "[F]actfinding is the basic responsibility of district courts, rather than appellate courts, and . . . the Court of Appeals should not have resolved in the first instance this factual dispute which had not been considered by the District Court." *DeMarco v. United States*, 415 U.S. 449, 450 (1974).

Likewise, where findings are infirm because of an erroneous view of the law, a remand is the proper course unless the record permits only one resolution of the factual issue. All of this is elementary. Yet the Court of Appeals, after holding that the District Court had failed to consider relevant evidence and indicating that the District Court might have come to a different conclusion had it considered that evidence, failed to remand for further proceedings as to the intent of IAM and the significance, if any, of such a finding with respect to the intent of USW itself. Instead, the Court of Appeals made its own determination as to the motives of IAM, found that USW had acquiesced in the IAM conduct, and apparently concluded that the foregoing was sufficient to remove the system from the protection of § 703(h).

Proceeding in this manner seems to us incredible unless the Court of Appeals construed its own well-established Circuit rule with respect to its authority to arrive at independent findings on ultimate facts free of the strictures of Rule 52(a) also to permit it to examine the record and make its own independent findings with respect to those issues on which the district court's findings are set aside for an error of law. As we have previously said, however, the premise for this conclusion is infirm: whether an ultimate fact or not, discriminatory intent under § 703(h) is a factual matter subject to the clearly-erroneous standard of Rule 52(a). It follows that when a district court's finding on such an ultimate fact is set aside for an error of law, the court of appeals is not relieved of the usual requirement of remanding for further proceedings to the tribunal charged with the task of factfinding in the first instance.

Accordingly, the judgment of the Court of Appeals is reversed, and the cases are remanded to that court for further proceedings consistent with this opinion.

So ordered.

[JUSTICE STEVENS's concurring opinion is omitted.]

JUSTICE MARSHALL, with whom JUSTICE BLACKMUN joins . . . , dissenting. . . .

As the majority acknowledges, where findings of fact " 'are made under an erroneous view of controlling legal principles, the clearly erroneous rule does not apply, and the findings may not stand.' " Having found that the District Court's findings as to the first and third *James* factors were made under an erroneous view of controlling legal principles, the Court of Appeals was *compelled* to set aside those findings free of the requirements of the clearly-erroneous rule. But once these two findings were set aside, the District Court's conclusion that the departmental system was bona fide within the meaning of § 703(h) also had to be rejected, since that conclusion was based at least in part on its erroneous determinations concerning the first and the third *James* factors.

At the very least, therefore, the Court of Appeals was entitled to remand this action to the District Court for the purpose of reexamining the bona fides of the seniority system under proper legal standards. However, as we have often noted, in some cases a remand is inappropriate where the facts on the record are susceptible to only one reasonable interpretation. In such cases, "[e]ffective judicial administration" requires that the court of appeals draw the inescapable factual conclusion itself, rather than remand the case to the district court for further needless proceedings. Such action is particularly appropriate where the court of appeals is in as good a position to evaluate the record evidence as the district court. . . .

NOTES AND QUESTIONS

1. Misapplication of the law. The court of appeals in *Pullman-Standard* concluded that the district court committed two errors of law: (1) failing to consider the qualitative differences between the departments; and (2) treating IAM's motives as irrelevant. Given that these errors involved questions of law, what standard of review should the court of appeals have applied? Second, given that the court of appeals did find errors of law, and that the Supreme Court did not disagree with that judgment, why did the Supreme Court hold that the court of appeals committed error in reversing the district court's finding of discriminatory intent? In reversing the court of appeals on this point, what standard of review did the Supreme Court apply? Stated somewhat differently, did the court of appeals make an error of law when it failed to treat the issue of discriminatory intent as a question of fact?

2. *The fact of discriminatory intent.*   Given that discriminatory intent was an element of the Title VII cause of action alleged by the plaintiffs in *Pullman-Standard, i.e.,* it was part of the law of Title VII, why did the Court conclude that resolution of that element involved a question of fact? Is discriminatory intent a "fact" in the sense that it involves a component of objective reality? In other words, is the requirement that the plaintiff prove discriminatory intent designed to establish whether as a matter of historical fact the defendants intended to discriminate on the basis of race? Notice that the search for intent was informed by certain factors set forth in *James v. Stockham Valves & Fittings Co.,* 559 F.2d 310 (5th Cir. 1977), *cert. denied,* 434 U.S. 1034 (1978). Yet reliance on those legal standards did not transform the basic question of discriminatory intent from one of fact into one of law. Why not? Furthermore, since the district court's finding on discriminatory intent was based on application of the law (the *James* factors) to the facts, wasn't the question presented to the court of appeals at least a mixed question of fact and law? If the answer to that question is at least "arguably yes," why did the Court nonetheless treat discriminatory intent as a fact question?

3. *Abuse of discretion.*   Why wasn't abuse of discretion the appropriate standard to apply in *Pullman-Standard*? (You can't answer this by saying that "intent" presents a question of fact; that's just a conclusion.) Did the decision on intent involve the type of managerial judgment that might be involved in deciding a motion for transfer of venue? Suppose, for the moment, that the abuse-of-discretion standard had been applied. Would that have altered the outcome in *Pullman-Standard*? (Before answering this, re-read the definition of abuse of discretion in the materials preceding *Pullman-Standard*.) Are you starting to think that there might be less to these "different" standards than meets the eye?

Cooper Industries, Inc. v. Leatherman Tool Group, Inc.
532 U.S. 424 (2001)

Justice Stevens delivered the opinion of the Court.

A jury found petitioner guilty of unfair competition and awarded respondent $50,000 in compensatory damages and $4.5 million in punitive damages. The District Court held that the punitive damages award did not violate the Federal Constitution. The Court of Appeals concluded that "the district court did not abuse its discretion in declining to reduce the amount of punitive damages." The issue in this case is whether the Court of Appeals applied the wrong standard of review in considering the constitutionality of the punitive damages award.

I

The parties are competing tool manufacturers. In the 1980's, Leatherman Tool Group, Inc. (Leatherman or respondent), introduced its Pocket Survival Tool (PST). The Court of Appeals described the PST as an

> "ingenious multi-function pocket tool which improves on the classic 'Swiss army knife' in a number of respects. Not the least of the improvements was the inclusion of pliers, which, when unfolded, are nearly equivalent to regular full-sized pliers. . . . Leatherman apparently created largely and undisputedly now dominates the market for multifunction pocket tools which generally resemble the PST."

In 1995, Cooper Industries, Inc. (Cooper or petitioner), decided to design and market a competing multifunction tool. Cooper planned to copy the basic features of the PST, add a few features of its own, and sell the new tool under the name "ToolZall." Cooper hoped to capture about 5% of the multifunction tool market. The first ToolZall was designed to be virtually identical to the PST, but the design was ultimately modified in response to this litigation. The controversy to be resolved in this case involves Cooper's improper advertising of its original ToolZall design.

Cooper introduced the original ToolZall in August 1996 at the National Hardware Show in Chicago. At that show, it used photographs in its posters, packaging, and advertising materials that purported to be of a ToolZall but were actually of a modified PST. When those materials were prepared, the first of the ToolZalls had not yet been manufactured. A Cooper employee created a ToolZall "mock-up" by grinding the Leatherman trademark from handles and pliers of a PST and substituting the unique fastenings that were to be used on the ToolZall. At least one of the photographs was retouched to remove a curved indentation where the Leatherman trademark had been. The photographs were used, not only at the trade show, which normally draws an audience of over 70,000 people, but also in the marketing materials and catalogs used by Cooper's sales force throughout the United States. Cooper also distributed a touched-up line drawing of a PST to its international sales representatives.

Shortly after the trade show, Leatherman filed this action asserting claims of trade-dress infringement, unfair competition, and false advertising under § 43(a) of the Trademark Act of 1946 (Lanham Act), and a common-law claim of unfair competition for advertising and selling an "imitation" of the PST. In December 1996, the District Court entered a preliminary injunction prohibiting Cooper from marketing the ToolZall and from using pictures of the modified PST in its advertising. Cooper withdrew the original ToolZall from the market and developed a new model with plastic coated handles that differed from the PST. In November 1996, it had anticipatorily sent a notice to its sales personnel ordering a recall of all promotional materials containing pictures of the PST, but it did not attempt to retrieve the materials it had sent to its customers until the following April. As a result, the offending promotional materials continued to appear in catalogs and advertisements well into 1997.

After a trial conducted in October 1997, the jury returned a verdict that answered several special interrogatories. . . . With respect to the advertising claims, it found Cooper guilty of passing off, false advertising, and unfair competition and assessed aggregate damages of $50,000 on those claims. It then answered "Yes" to the following interrogatory:

> "Has Leatherman shown by clear and convincing evidence that by engaging in false advertising or passing off, Cooper acted with malice, or showed a reckless and outrageous indifference to a highly unreasonable risk of harm and has acted with a conscious indifference to Leatherman's rights?"

Because it answered this question in the affirmative, the jury was instructed to determine the "amount of punitive damages [that] should be awarded to Leatherman." The jury awarded $4.5 million.

After the jury returned its verdict, the District Court considered, and rejected, arguments that the punitive damages were "grossly excessive" under our decision in *BMW of North America, Inc. v. Gore*, 517 U.S. 559 (1996). . . .

. . . [T]he Court of Appeals affirmed the punitive damages award. . . .

. . . We now conclude that the constitutional issue merits *de novo* review. Because the Court of Appeals applied an "abuse of discretion" standard, we remand the case for determination of [whether the award violated the Gore criteria] under the proper standard.

II

Although compensatory damages and punitive damages are typically awarded at the same time by the same decisionmaker, they serve distinct purposes. The former are intended to redress the concrete loss that the plaintiff has suffered by reason of the defendant's wrongful conduct. The latter, which have been described as "quasi-criminal," operate as "private fines" intended to punish the defendant and to deter future wrongdoing. A jury's assessment of the extent of a plaintiff's injury is essentially a factual determination, whereas its imposition of punitive damages is an expression of its moral condemnation.

Legislatures have extremely broad discretion in defining criminal offenses, and in setting the range of permissible punishments for each offense. Judicial decisions that operate *within* these legislatively-enacted guidelines are typically reviewed for abuse of discretion.

As in the criminal sentencing context, legislatures enjoy broad discretion in authorizing and limiting permissible punitive damages awards. A good many States have enacted statutes that place limits on the permissible size of punitive damages awards. When juries make particular awards within those limits, the role of the trial judge is "to determine whether the jury's verdict is within the confines set by state law, and to determine, by reference to federal standards developed under Rule 59, whether a new trial or remittitur should be ordered." If no consti-tutional issue is raised, the role of the appellate court, at least in the federal system, is merely to review the trial court's "determination under an abuse-of-discretion standard."

Despite the broad discretion that States possess with respect to the imposi-tion of criminal penalties and punitive damages, the Due Process Clause of the Fourteenth Amendment to the Federal Constitution imposes substantive limits on that discretion. That Clause makes the Eighth Amendment's prohibition against excessive fines and cruel and unusual punishments applicable to the States. The Due Process Clause of its own force also prohibits the States from imposing "grossly excessive" punishments on tortfeasors.

The Court has enforced those limits in cases involving deprivations of life, deprivations of liberty, and deprivations of property.

In these cases, the constitutional violations were predicated on judicial deter-minations that the punishments were "grossly disproportional to the gravity of . . . defendant[s'] offense[s]." We have recognized that the relevant constitutional line is "inherently imprecise," rather than one "marked by a simple mathematical formula." But in deciding whether that line has been crossed, we have focused on the same general criteria: the degree of the defendant's reprehensibility or culpa-bility; the relationship between the penalty and the harm to the victim caused by the defendant's actions; and the sanctions imposed in other cases for comparable misconduct. Moreover, and of greatest relevance for the issue we address today, in each of these cases we have engaged in an independent examination of the relevant criteria.

In [*United States v. Bajakajian*, 524 U.S. 321 (1998)], we expressly noted that the courts of appeals must review the proportionality determination *"de novo"* and specifically rejected the suggestion of the respondent, who had prevailed in the District Court, that the trial judge's determination of excessiveness should be reviewed only for an abuse of discretion. "The factual findings made by the district courts in conducting the excessiveness inquiry, of course, must be accepted unless clearly erroneous. . . . But the question whether a fine is constitutionally excessive calls for the application of a constitutional standard to the facts of a particular case, and in this context *de novo* review of that question is appropriate."

Likewise, in [*Ornelas v. United States*, 517 U.S. 690 (1996)], we held that trial judges' determinations of reasonable suspicion and probable cause should be reviewed *de novo* on appeal. The reasons we gave in support of that holding are equally applicable in this case. First, as we observed in *Ornelas*, the precise meaning of concepts like "reasonable suspicion" and "probable cause" cannot be articulated with precision; they are "fluid concepts that take their substantive con-tent from the particular contexts in which the standards are being assessed." That is, of course, also a characteristic of the concept of "gross excessiveness." Second, "the legal rules for probable cause and reasonable suspicion acquire content only through application. Independent review is therefore necessary if appellate courts are to maintain control of, and to clarify, the legal principles." Again, this is also true of the general criteria set forth in *Gore*; they will acquire more meaningful content through case-by-case application at the appellate level. "Finally, *de novo* review tends to unify precedent" and " 'stabilize the law.' " JUSTICE BREYER made a similar point in his concurring opinion in *Gore*:

> "Requiring the application of law, rather than a decisionmaker's caprice, does more than simply provide citizens notice of what actions may subject them to punishment; it also helps to assure the uniform treatment of similarly situated persons that is the essence of law itself."

Our decisions in analogous cases, together with the reasoning that produced those decisions, thus convince us that courts of appeals should apply a *de novo* standard of review when passing on district courts' determinations of the constitutionality of punitive damages awards.

III

"Unlike the measure of actual damages suffered, which presents a question of historical or predictive fact, the level of punitive damages is not really a 'fact' 'tried' by the jury." Because the jury's award of punitive damages does not constitute a finding of "fact," appellate review of the District Court's determination that an award is consistent with due process does not implicate the Seventh Amendment concerns raised by respondent and its *amicus*. . . .

It might be argued that the deterrent function of punitive damages suggests that the amount of such damages awarded is indeed a "fact" found by the jury and that, as a result, the Seventh Amendment is implicated in appellate review of that award. Some scholars, for example, assert that punitive damages should be used to compensate for the underdeterrence of unlawful behavior that will result from a defendant's evasion of liability.

However attractive such an approach to punitive damages might be as an abstract policy matter, it is clear that juries do not normally engage in such a finely tuned exercise of deterrence calibration when awarding punitive damages. After all, deterrence is not the only purpose served by punitive damages. And there is no dispute that, in this case, deterrence was but one of four concerns the jury was instructed to consider when setting the amount of punitive damages.[12] Moreover, it is not at all obvious that even the *deterrent* function of punitive damages can be served *only* by economically "optimal deterrence." "[C]itizens and legislators may rightly insist that they are willing to tolerate some loss in economic efficiency in

---

12. The jury was instructed to consider the following factors: (1) "The character of the defendant's conduct that is the subject of Leatherman's unfair competition claims"; (2) "The defendant's motive"; (3) "The sum of money that would be required to discourage the defendant and others from engaging in such conduct in the future"; and (4) "The defendant's income and assets." Although the jury's application of these instructions may have depended on specific findings of fact, nothing in our decision today suggests that the Seventh Amendment would permit a court, in reviewing a punitive damages award, to disregard such jury findings.

order to deter what they consider morally offensive conduct, albeit cost-beneficial morally offensive conduct; efficiency is just one consideration among many."[13]

Differences in the institutional competence of trial judges and appellate judges are consistent with our conclusion. In *Gore*, we instructed courts evaluating a punitive damages award's consistency with due process to consider three criteria: (1) the degree or reprehensibility of the defendant's misconduct, (2) the disparity between the harm (or potential harm) suffered by the plaintiff and the punitive damages award, and (3) the difference between the punitive damages awarded by the jury and the civil penalties authorized or imposed in comparable cases. Only with respect to the first *Gore* inquiry do the district courts have a somewhat superior vantage over courts of appeals, and even then the advantage exists primarily with respect to issues turning on witness credibility and demeanor. Trial courts and appellate courts seem equally capable of analyzing the second factor. And the third *Gore* criterion, which calls for a broad legal comparison, seems more suited to the expertise of appellate courts. Considerations of institutional competence therefore fail to tip the balance in favor of deferential appellate review.

IV

It is possible that the standard of review applied by the Court of Appeals will affect the result of the *Gore* analysis in only a relatively small number of cases. Nonetheless, it does seem likely that in this case a thorough, independent review of the District Court's rejection of petitioner's due process objections to the punitive damages award might well have led the Court of Appeals to reach a different result. Indeed, our own consideration of each of the three *Gore* factors reveals a series of questionable conclusions by the District Court that may not survive *de novo* review.

When the jury assessed the reprehensibility of Cooper's misconduct, it was guided by instructions that characterized the deliberate copying of the PST as wrongful. The jury's selection of a penalty to deter wrongful conduct may, therefore, have been influenced by an intent to deter Cooper from engaging in such copying in the future. Similarly, the District Court's belief that Cooper acted unlawfully in deliberately copying the PST design might have influenced its consideration of the first *Gore* factor. But, as the Court of Appeals correctly held, such copying of the functional features of an unpatented product is lawful. The Court of Appeals recognized that the District Court's award of attorney's fees could not be supported if based on the premise that the copying was unlawful, but it did not

---

13. We express no opinion on the question whether [*Gasperini v. Center for Humanities, Inc.*, 518 U.S. 415 (1996)] would govern—and *de novo* review would be inappropriate—if a State were to adopt a scheme that tied the award of punitive damages more tightly to the jury's finding of compensatory damages. This might be the case, for example, if the State's scheme constrained a jury to award only the exact amount of punitive damages it determined were necessary to obtain economically optimal deterrence or if it defined punitive damages as a multiple of compensatory damages (*e.g.*, treble damages).

consider whether that improper predicate might also have undermined the basis for the jury's large punitive damages award.

In evaluating the second *Gore* factor, the ratio between the size of the award of punitive damages and the harm caused by Cooper's tortious conduct, the District Court might have been influenced by respondent's submission that it was not the actual injury—which the jury assessed at $50,000—that was relevant, but rather "the potential harm Leatherman would have suffered had Cooper succeeded in its wrongful conduct." Respondent calculated that "potential harm" by referring to the fact that Cooper had anticipated "gross profits of approximately $3 million during the first five years of sales." Even if that estimate were correct, however, it would be unrealistic to assume that all of Cooper's sales of the ToolZall would have been attributable to its misconduct in using a photograph of a modified PST in its initial advertising materials. As the Court of Appeals pointed out, the picture of the PST did not misrepresent the features of the original ToolZall and could not have deceived potential customers in any significant way. Its use was wrongful because it enabled Cooper to expedite the promotion of its tool, but that wrongdoing surely could not be treated as the principal cause of Cooper's entire sales volume for a 5-year period.

With respect to the third *Gore* factor, respondent argues that Cooper would have been subject to a comparable sanction under Oregon's Unlawful Trade Practices Act. In a suit brought by a State under that Act, a civil penalty of up to $25,000 per violation may be assessed. In respondent's view, *each* of the thousands of pieces of promotional material containing a picture of the PST that Cooper distributed warranted the maximum fine. Petitioner, on the other hand, argues that its preparation of a single "mock-up" for use in a single distribution would have been viewed as a single violation under the state statute. The Court of Appeals expressed no opinion on this dispute. It did, however, observe that the unfairness in Cooper's use of the picture apparently had nothing to do with misleading customers but was related to its inability to obtain a "mock-up" quickly and cheaply. This observation is more consistent with the single-violation theory than with the notion that the statutory violation would have been sanctioned with a multimillion dollar fine.

We have made these comments on issues raised by application of the three *Gore* guidelines to the facts of this case, not to prejudge the answer to the constitutional question, but rather to illustrate why we are persuaded that the Court of Appeals' answer to that question may depend upon the standard of review. The *de novo* standard should govern its decision. Because the Court of Appeals applied a less demanding standard in this case, we vacate the judgment and remand the case for further proceedings consistent with this opinion.

It is so ordered.

[The concurring opinions of Justices Thomas and Scalia are omitted.]

Justice Ginsburg, dissenting.

In *Gasperini v. Center for Humanities, Inc.*, 518 U.S. 415 (1996), we held that appellate review of a federal trial court's refusal to set aside a jury verdict as excessive is reconcilable with the Seventh Amendment if "appellate control [is] limited to review for 'abuse of discretion.'" *Gasperini* was a diversity action in which the defendant had challenged a compensatory damages award as excessive under New York law. The reasoning of that case applies as well to an action challenging a punitive damages award as excessive under the Constitution. I would hold, therefore, that the proper standard of appellate oversight is not *de novo* review, as the Court today concludes, but review for abuse of discretion. . . .

Although *Gasperini* involved compensatory damages, I see no reason why its logic should be abandoned when punitive damages are alleged to be excessive. At common law, as our longstanding decisions reiterate, the task of determining the amount of punitive damages "has [always been] left to the discretion of the jury." The commitment of this function to the jury, we have explained, reflects the historical understanding that "the degree of punishment to be thus inflicted must depend on the peculiar circumstances of each case." The relevant factors include "the conduct and motives of the defendant" and whether, "in committing the wrong complained of, he acted recklessly, or wilfully and maliciously, with a design to oppress and injure the plaintiff." 1 J. Sutherland, Law of Damages 720 (1882). Such inquiry, the Court acknowledges, "is a fact-sensitive undertaking." . . .

. . . I readily acknowledge . . . that the practical difference between the Court's approach and my own is not large. An abuse-of-discretion standard, as I see it, hews more closely to "the strictures of the Seventh Amendment." The Court's *de novo* standard is more complex. It requires lower courts to distinguish between ordinary common-law excessiveness and constitutional excessiveness, and to separate out factfindings that qualify for "clearly erroneous" review. See also *ante*, n.13 (suggesting abuse-of-discretion review might be in order "if a State were to adopt a scheme that tied the award of punitive damages more tightly to the jury's finding of compensatory damages"). The Court's approach will be challenging to administer. Complex as it is, I suspect that approach and mine will yield different outcomes in few cases. . . .

NOTES AND QUESTIONS

1. *A functional approach to standards.*   In *Pullman-Standard*, the issue of discriminatory intent was treated as a question of fact. In *Cooper Industries*, the issue of the excessiveness of a punitive-damage award was treated as a question of law. From the perspective of the *Cooper Industries* Court, what was the distinction between these two issues? Is that distinction based on the inherent nature of the issue, *i.e.*, whether it presents a categorical question of fact or law, or is it based on the allocation of decisional authority between district courts and courts of appeals? If the latter, what is the premise behind that allocation? In *Mucha v.*

King, 792 F.2d 602 (7th Cir. 1986), Judge Posner, writing for the Seventh Circuit, observed that

> the main reason for appellate deference to the findings of fact made by the trial court is not the appellate court's lack of access to the materials for decision but that its main responsibility is to maintain the uniformity and coherence of the law, a responsibility not engaged if the only question is the legal significance of a particular and nonrecurring set of historical events.

Id. at 605-606. Conversely, it would seem to follow that the district court's primary responsibility is to attend to those case-specific aspects of a proceeding that do not implicate the appellate responsibility over uniformity and coherence: managerial decisions, historical fact determinations, and applications of the law that are essentially case-specific. How would you apply Judge Posner's principle to *Pullman-Standard* and *Cooper Industries*?

2. *How many standards?*   Under the traditional view, there are at least four standards of review: abuse of discretion, substantial evidence, clearly erroneous, and de novo—plus whatever standard might apply to mixed questions of law and fact. Yet the substantial-evidence and clearly-erroneous standards are virtually identical in terms of their deference to the initial decision maker; and it should be clear that the abuse-of-discretion standard is just a composite of the clearly-erroneous and de novo standards. It would appear then that there are really only two standards, one that is deferential and one that is not. But let's take this one step further. Are there really even two standards? When a court of appeals reverses a district court's decision under either standard, isn't that reversal always premised on the lower court's failure to comply with the law? If, for example, a finding of fact by the district court is deemed clearly erroneous, hasn't the district court made a legal error? In essence, the district court found a fact to exist when the evidentiary standards, *i.e.*, the applicable law, will not support that finding. Or in the context of a jury finding that a court of appeals reverses under the substantial-evidence standard, isn't the appellate court saying that by deciding the facts inconsistently with the evidence the jury has acted irrationally and violated a principle of law? If this is true, there is only one "standard" of review on appeal: A court of appeals may reverse a decision by the district court (or jury) only when that initial decision maker has made a mistake of law. Under this approach, the sole "standard" to be applied on review is the legal standard that the initial decision maker was required to follow in the court below. That standard and that standard alone pinpoints the question of law presented and defines the potential reversibility of the initial decision.

This one-standard approach may seem like a radical proposition given the orthodox adherence to multiple standards of review on appeal, but think about it as you work through the next set of problems. See if the multiple-standards approach adds anything of value to the determination of whether an error was committed by the initial decision maker.

3. *The decision on remand.*   On remand in *Cooper Industries, Inc.*, the court of appeals, applying the *Gore* criteria, ruled that the jury's $4.5 million punitive damages award violated the Due Process Clause and held that "the maximum

award of punitive damages consistent with due process on the facts of this case is $500,000." *Leatherman Tool Group, Inc. v. Cooper Indus., Inc.*, 285 F.3d 1146, 1151-1152 (9th Cir. 2002).

PROBLEMS

12-8. In 1932, Baumgartner became a naturalized citizen of the United States. In so doing, he took an oath swearing allegiance to the United States and disavowing allegiance to the "German Reich." Ten years later, the U.S. government brought suit to set aside Baumgartner's naturalization decree on the ground that he lied when he took his oath of allegiance because he had in fact not disavowed allegiance to Germany. The standard for revocation of citizenship is evidence of fraud that is "clear, unequivocal, and convincing." Based on the evidence submitted, including diary entries and public statements made by Baumgartner, the district court found that he had committed fraud in taking the oath of allegiance. As a consequence, his naturalization was set aside. Baumgartner has appealed, claiming that the evidence of fraud was not clear, unequivocal, and convincing. Under what standard of review should the court of appeals examine the district court's finding of fraud? In answering this question, first attempt to determine whether the issue falls into one of the set categories (discretion, fact, law, or mixed question of law and fact), then consider whether the issue presented is case-specific (calling for deference) or more generally applicable (calling for uniformity and no deference). In other words, use both the categorical and functional approaches to determining the proper standard of review. Finally, ask whether reversal of the district court could be based on anything other than a mistake of law? *See Baumgartner v. United States*, 322 U.S. 665 (1944).

12-9. Defense counsel filed a Rule 11 motion for sanctions against plaintiff's counsel premised on the latter's alleged failure to engage in an adequate pre-filing inquiry prior to the filing of the complaint. After a hearing on the motion, the district court found that the pre-filing inquiries by plaintiff's counsel were grossly inadequate. The court further concluded that counsel's actions violated Rule 11(b) and awarded monetary sanctions to cover the costs incurred by the defendant in responding to the complaint. Counsel for the plaintiff has appealed the award of sanctions and argues that the court of appeals should apply a clearly-erroneous standard of review to the historical findings of fact, a de novo standard to the question of whether those facts establish a violation of Rule 11, and an abuse-of-discretion standard to the amount of the sanction imposed. Do you agree? *See Cooter & Gell v. Hartmarx Corp.*, 496 U.S. 384 (1990).

D. Review in the U.S. Supreme Court

Article III, § 2, cl. 1 of the U.S. Constitution defines the potential range of cases and controversies over which the federal courts may exercise jurisdiction. It vests the Supreme Court with original jurisdiction over certain of those enumerated cases ("Cases affecting Ambassadors, other public Ministers and Consuls, and those in which a State shall be a Party"), and then provides, "In all the other Cases before mentioned, the supreme Court shall have appellate Jurisdiction, both as to Law and Fact, with such Exceptions, and under such Regulations as the Congress shall make." U.S. CONST. art. III, § 2, cl. 2. The result of this allocation between original and appellate jurisdiction is that the Constitution permits the Supreme Court to exercise a wide range of appellate jurisdiction over the cases and controversies listed in Article III, § 2, including the all-important category of cases "arising under this Constitution, the Laws of the United States, and Treaties. . . ." U.S. CONST. art. III, § 2. The actual scope of the Court's appellate jurisdiction is not, however, coextensive with this constitutional grant. Rather, the Court's appellate jurisdiction is constrained by statutes adopted by Congress pursuant to the Exceptions Clause. In fact, as a practical matter, the Court may exercise its appellate jurisdiction only pursuant to an affirmative grant of authority from Congress. Such grants are constitutional so long as they do not extend the Court's jurisdiction beyond the range permitted by Article III, § 2.

In the vast majority of cases, the Supreme Court's authority to review a case is completely discretionary. In other words, in most cases a party seeking Supreme Court review does not have an appeal as of right. The primary method for seeking this discretionary review is through a petition for a writ of certiorari. In modern usage, certiorari is a writ through which an appellate court orders a lower court to transmit the entire record of a case for appellate review. A petition for a writ of certiorari, however, must identify the specific questions the petitioner would like the Court to review. SUP. CT. R. 14. The Supreme Court now receives 9,000 to 10,000 petitions for certiorari in a typical year. Only about 1 percent of these petitions are granted in any given year, the consequence of which is that the Court decides between 75 and 90 cases each term. *See* JUDICIAL BUSINESS OF THE UNITED STATES COURTS, 2014 ANNUAL REPORT, at tbl. A-1. The Court presides over one term each year, which begins on the first Monday in October and ends in late June or early July of the next calendar year.

The two key statutes pertaining to the Supreme Court's appellate jurisdiction are 28 U.S.C. § 1254 (review of cases in the federal courts of appeals) and § 1257 (review of cases originating in state judicial systems). We will examine the basic rules and principles applicable to each of these avenues of review. First, though, we will briefly mention 28 U.S.C. § 1253, which provides for an appeal as of right to the Supreme Court from three-judge district courts.

1.   Section 1253

Section 1253 provides the primary exception to the general rule of discretionary review by the Supreme Court. The exception, however, is quite limited. Under § 1253, a party has an appeal as of right "from an order granting or denying . . . an interlocutory or permanent injunction in any civil action, suit or proceeding required by any Act of Congress to be heard and determined by a district court of three judges." 28 U.S.C. § 1253. While at one time the array of proceedings requiring the convening of a three-judge district court was quite expansive—and included any case seeking to enjoin the enforcement of a state or federal law on grounds of unconstitutionality (*see* 28 U.S.C. §§ 2281, 2282 (repealed in 1976))—the range today includes only a few exceptional actions, the most notable of which is a case "challenging the constitutionality of the apportionment of congressional districts or the apportionment of any statewide legislative body." 28 U.S.C. § 2284(a). *See generally* Drew S. Days, III, *Authorization for Three-Judge Courts and Direct Appeals to the Supreme Court, in* 22 MOORE'S FEDERAL PRACTICE §§ 404.01 *et seq.* (3d ed. 2015). Thus § 1253's utility is now relatively limited.

2. Section 1254

Section 1254 provides that the Supreme Court may exercise jurisdiction over "cases in the [federal] courts of appeals . . . (1) By writ of *certiorari* granted upon the petition of any party to any civil or criminal case, before or after rendition of judgment or decree," or "(2) By *certification* at any time by a court of appeals of any question of law in any civil or criminal case as to which instructions are desired. . . ." 28 U.S.C. § 1254 (emphasis added). A petition for a writ of certiorari is the usual method for invoking § 1254. The alternative method, certification by the federal court of appeals, is rarely used, for its successful invocation requires an exercise of independent and discretionary judgment by the court of appeals and then acquiescence in that judgment by the Supreme Court. The last case in which the Supreme Court accepted jurisdiction over a certified question was *Iran National Airlines Corp. v. Marschalk Co., Inc.*, 453 U.S. 919 (1981), a case involving the critically important question of the president's power to enter into international settlement agreements. In *United States v. Seale*, 558 U.S. 985 (2009), the Court dismissed a question certified to it by the Fifth Circuit, but Justices Stevens and Scalia filed a statement disagreeing with the dismissal. They noted that "[t]he certification process has all but disappeared in recent decades" and that "it is a newsworthy event these days when a lower court even tries for certification." *Id*. These Justices believed the "certification process serves a valuable, if limited, function," and urged that "[w]e ought to avail ourselves of it in an appropriate case." *Id*. As to certification, see generally STEPHEN M. SHAPIRO, KENNETH S. GELLER, TIMOTHY S. BISHOP, EDWARD A. HARTNETT & DAN HIMMELFARB, SUPREME COURT PRACTICE §§ 9.1 *et seq.* (10th ed. 2014). *See also* SUP. CT. R. 19.

Although certiorari is the usual method for invoking § 1254, that is not to suggest that petitions for certiorari are usually granted. As noted above, the chances of convincing the Court to grant certiorari to a case are quite slim. In deciding whether there are "compelling reasons" to do so, the Court considers whether the questions presented are sufficiently important to warrant review; whether the decision below conflicts with Supreme Court precedent; whether it conflicts with decisions of other federal courts of appeals or state courts of last resort; and whether it "has so far departed from the accepted and usual course of judicial proceedings . . . as to call for an exercise of this Court's supervisory power . . . ." SUP. CT. R. 10. None of these factors constrains the Court's discretion to grant or deny certiorari; rather, they are merely illustrative of what the Court generally deems "certworthy."

Once a petition for certiorari is properly filed with the Court, the opposing party ("the respondent") may file a brief in opposition, and the petitioner may file a reply to that brief. SUP. CT. R. 14-15. The decision on whether to grant the petition is governed by the Court's unwritten "rule of four," which provides that a petition will be granted if at least four of the Court's nine Justices agree to do so. The Justices do not have to state any reason for granting the petition; nor do they have to agree with one another as to why certiorari ought to be granted. They simply must agree to grant. If the rule of four is satisfied, the grant of certiorari may be limited to specific questions designated by the Court, including questions not presented in the petition for certiorari, or the Court may elect to review the entire case. Typically, however, certiorari is limited to some or all of the questions presented in the petition. If the petition is denied (the overwhelmingly usual disposition), that denial is not in any manner to be construed as a decision on the merits or a reflection of the Court's judgment on the merits, though occasionally there are suggestions to the contrary. *See, e.g., United States v. Kras*, 409 U.S. 434, 442-443 (1973) (suggesting that a denial was not without some significance as to the Court's attitude); *cf. Evans v. Stephens*, 544 U.S. 942 (2005) (Stevens, J.) (emphasizing "the fact that a denial of certiorari is not a ruling on the merits of any issue raised by the petition"); *Maryland v. Baltimore Radio Show*, 338 U.S. 912, 917-919 (1950) (Frankfurter, J.) (commenting that a denial of certiorari "carries with it no implication whatever regarding the Court's views on the merits").

Notice that under § 1254 a party may petition for a writ of certiorari before the court of appeals' entry of judgment. This gives the Supreme Court the authority, in extraordinary cases, to take a case out of the court of appeals before a decision has been rendered. *See, e.g., New York Times Co. v. United States* [*The Pentagon Papers Case*], 403 U.S. 713 (1971). The usual course, however, is for the Court (and the parties) to await the court of appeals' entry of judgment.

Other than specifying that a case must be "in" the court of appeals to file a petition for certiorari, § 1254 contains no independent subject matter jurisdiction requirement. The Supreme Court's jurisdiction under § 1254 is thus "derivative" in the sense that it depends on the lower federal courts' jurisdiction. If, for example, the district court exercised jurisdiction over a federal question case in violation of the well-pleaded complaint rule, the Supreme Court would have no authority to hear the case, other than to exercise jurisdiction to determine its jurisdiction, in which event the only appropriate remedy would be a dismissal. *See Louisville & Nashville R.R. Co. v. Mottley*, 211 U.S. 149 (1908). Similarly, if the court of appeals lacks jurisdiction over an appeal, *e.g.*, because of the absence of a "final decision," the Supreme Court under § 1291 is without power to exercise jurisdiction over the case beyond resolving the jurisdictional issue. In other words, the Court may do no more than order the court of appeals to dismiss the case.

3. Section 1257

Section 1257 grants the Supreme Court discretionary jurisdiction by writ of certiorari over "[f]inal judgments" in cases originating within a state judicial system in which a federal question has been raised and decided by the "highest court of a State in which a decision could be had. . . ." 28 U.S.C. § 1257. The same standards and procedures for invoking the Court's certiorari jurisdiction described above with respect to cases arising under § 1254 apply to the consideration of petitions for certiorari filed pursuant to § 1257. *See* Sup. Ct. R. 10 ("Considerations Governing Review on Certiorari"). There are, however, three elements of § 1257 jurisdiction that have no counterpart in § 1254: (1) a final-judgment requirement; (2) a requirement that the federal question have been raised and decided below; and (3) a requirement that the highest state court in which a decision could be had rendered the decision. Before looking at these independent jurisdictional requirements, we will consider a policy question that pertains to certiorari under both §§ 1254 and 1257.

Redrup v. New York

386 U.S. 767 (1967)

Per Curiam.

These three cases arise from a recurring conflict—the conflict between asserted state power to suppress the distribution of books and magazines through criminal or civil proceedings, and the guarantees of the First and Fourteenth Amendments of the United States Constitution.

I.

In No. 3, *Redrup v. New York*, the petitioner was a clerk at a New York City newsstand. A plainclothes patrolman approached the newsstand, saw two paperback books on a rack—Lust Pool, and Shame Agent—and asked for them by name. The petitioner handed him the books and collected the price of $1.65. As a result of this transaction, the petitioner was charged in the New York City Criminal Court with violating a state criminal law. He was convicted, and the conviction was affirmed on appeal.

In No. 16, *Austin v. Kentucky*, the petitioner owned and operated a retail bookstore and newsstand in Paducah, Kentucky. A woman resident of Paducah purchased two magazines from a salesgirl in the petitioner's store, after asking for them by name—High Heels, and Spree. As a result of this transaction the petitioner stands convicted in the Kentucky courts for violating a criminal law of that State.

In No. 50, *Gent v. Arkansas*, the prosecuting attorney of the Eleventh Judicial District of Arkansas brought a civil proceeding under a state statute to have certain issues of various magazines declared obscene, to enjoin their distribution and to obtain a judgment ordering their surrender and destruction. The magazines proceeded against were: Gent, Swank, Bachelor, Modern Man, Cavalcade, Gentleman, Ace, and Sir. The County Chancery Court entered the requested judgment after a trial with an advisory jury, and the Supreme Court of Arkansas affirmed, with minor modifications.

In none of the cases was there a claim that the statute in question reflected a specific and limited state concern for juveniles. In none was there any suggestion of an assault upon individual privacy by publication in a manner so obtrusive as to make it impossible for an unwilling individual to avoid exposure to it. And in none was there evidence of the sort of "pandering" which the Court found significant in *Ginzburg v. United States*, 383 U.S. 463.

II.

The Court originally limited review in these cases to certain particularized questions, upon the hypothesis that the material involved in each case was of a character described as "obscene in the constitutional sense" in *Memoirs v. Massachusetts*, 383 U.S. 413, 418. But we have concluded that the hypothesis upon which the Court originally proceeded was invalid, and accordingly that the cases can and should be decided upon a common and controlling fundamental constitutional basis, without prejudice to the questions upon which review was originally granted. We have concluded, in short, that the distribution of the publications in each of these cases is protected by the First and Fourteenth Amendments from governmental suppression, whether criminal or civil, *in personam* or *in rem*.

Two members of the Court have consistently adhered to the view that a State is utterly without power to suppress, control or punish the distribution of any writings or pictures upon the ground of their "obscenity." A third has held to the opinion that a State's power in this area is narrowly limited to a distinct and clearly identifiable class of material. Others have subscribed to a not dissimilar standard, holding that a State may not constitutionally inhibit the distribution of literary material as obscene unless "(a) the dominant theme of the material taken as a whole appeals to a prurient interest in sex; (b) the material is patently offensive because it affronts contemporary community standards relating to the description or representation of sexual matters; and (c) the material is utterly without redeeming social value," emphasizing that the "three elements must coalesce," and that no such material can "be proscribed unless it is found to be *utterly* without redeeming social value." Another Justice has not viewed the "social value" element as an independent factor in the judgment of obscenity.

Whichever of these constitutional views is brought to bear upon the cases before us, it is clear that the judgments cannot stand. Accordingly, the judgment in each case is reversed. *It is so ordered.*

Judgments reversed.

Mr. Justice Harlan, whom Mr. Justice Clark joins, dissenting.

Two of these cases, *Redrup v. New York* and *Austin v. Kentucky*, were taken to consider the standards governing the application of the scienter requirement announced in *Smith v. California*, 361 U.S. 147, for obscenity prosecutions. There it was held that a defendant criminally charged with purveying obscene material must be shown to have had some kind of knowledge of the character of such material; the quality of that knowledge, however, was not defined. The third case, *Gent v. Arkansas*, was taken to consider the validity of a comprehensive Arkansas anti-obscenity statute, in light of the doctrines of "vagueness" and "prior restraint." The writs of certiorari in *Redrup* and *Austin*, and the notation of probable jurisdiction in *Gent*, were respectively limited to these issues, thus laying aside, for the purposes of these cases, the permissibility of the state determinations as to the obscenity of the challenged publications. Accordingly the obscenity *vel non* of these publications was not discussed in the briefs or oral arguments of any of the parties.

The three cases were argued together at the beginning of this Term. Today, the Court rules that the materials could not constitutionally be adjudged obscene by the States, thus rendering adjudication of the other issues unnecessary. In short, the Court disposes of the cases on the issue that was deliberately excluded from review, and refuses to pass on the questions that brought the cases here.

In my opinion these dispositions do not reflect well on the processes of the Court, and I think the issues for which the cases were taken should be decided. Failing that, I prefer to cast my vote to dismiss the writs in *Redrup* and *Austin* as improvidently granted and, in the circumstances, to dismiss the appeal in *Gent* for lack of a substantial federal question. I deem it more appropriate to defer an expression of my own views on the questions brought here until an occasion when the Court is prepared to come to grips with such issues.

NOTES AND QUESTIONS

1. Discretion.   Does the disposition in *Redrup* suggest that the Supreme Court has plenary authority to determine what to decide and when to decide it? Are there any limits on that discretion? Isn't Justice Harlan correct when he argues that the Court should not decide substantive issues that were neither briefed nor argued before the Court? What is the practical distinction between the Court's disposition and Justice Harlan's suggestion that the writs should have been dismissed as improvidently granted?

2. Lack of a substantial federal question.   Justice Harlan suggested that the appeal in *Gent* should have been dismissed for "lack of a substantial federal question." The distinction between *Gent* and the other two cases decided in *Redrup* is that *Gent* involved an "appeal" from a state court decision. At the time *Redrup* was decided, § 1257(2) allowed an appeal as of right from state court decisions holding a state statute "valid" in the face of a federal constitutional challenge. Although jurisdiction in such cases was "obligatory," the Court frequently circumvented that obligation by dismissing such appeals for lack of a substantial federal question. *Id.* Unlike a denial of certiorari, however, a dismissal of an obligatory appeal was a decision on the merits. For a brief review of the difficulties surrounding § 1257(2), see SHAPIRO, GELLER, BISHOP, HARTNETT & HIMMELFARB, *supra*, § 3.1. Under the current version of § 1257, the method of obligatory review is no longer available.

a.   The Final-Judgment Rule

Cox Broadcasting Corp. v. Cohn
420 U.S. 469 (1975)

MR. JUSTICE WHITE delivered the opinion of the Court.

The issue before us in this case is whether, consistently with the First and Fourteenth Amendments, a State may extend a cause of action for damages for invasion of privacy caused by the publication of the name of a deceased rape victim which was publicly revealed in connection with the prosecution of the crime.

I

In August 1971, appellee's 17-year-old daughter was the victim of a rape and did not survive the incident. Six youths were soon indicted for murder and rape. Although there was substantial press coverage of the crime and of subsequent developments, the identity of the victim was not disclosed pending trial, perhaps because of Ga. Code Ann. § 26-9901 (1972), which makes it a misdemeanor to publish or broadcast the name or identity of a rape victim. In April 1972, some eight months later, the six defendants appeared in court. Five pleaded guilty to rape or attempted rape, the charge of murder having been dropped. The guilty pleas were accepted by the court, and the trial of the defendant pleading not guilty was set for a later date.

In the course of the proceedings that day, appellant Wasell, a reporter covering the incident for his employer, learned the name of the victim from an examination of the indictments which were made available for his inspection in the courtroom. That the name of the victim appears in the indictments and that the indictments were public records available for inspection are not disputed. Later that day, Wassell broadcast over the facilities of station WSB-TV, a television station owned by appellant Cox Broadcasting Corp., a news report concerning the court proceedings. The report named the victim of the crime and was repeated the following day.

In May 1972, appellee brought an action for money damages against appellants, relying on § 26-9901 and claiming that his right to privacy had been invaded by the television broadcasts giving the name of his deceased daughter. Appellants admitted the broadcasts but claimed that they were privileged under both state law and the First and Fourteenth Amendments. The trial court, rejecting appellants' constitutional claims and holding that the Georgia statute gave a civil remedy to those injured by its violation, granted summary judgment to appellee as to liability, with the determination of damages to await trial by jury.

On appeal, the Georgia Supreme Court, in its initial opinion, held that the trial court had erred in construing § 26-9901 to extend a civil cause of action for invasion of privacy and thus found it unnecessary to consider the constitutionality of the statute. The court went on to rule, however, that the complaint stated a cause of action "for the invasion of the appellee's right of privacy, or for the tort of public disclosure"—a "common law tort exist[ing] in this jurisdiction without the help of the statute that the trial judge in this case relied on." Although the privacy invaded was not that of the deceased victim, the father was held to have stated a claim for invasion of his own privacy by reason of the publication of his daughter's name. The court explained, however, that liability did not follow as a matter of law and that summary judgment was improper; whether the public disclosure of the name actually invaded appellee's "zone of privacy," and if so, to what extent, were issues to be determined by the trier of fact. . . . The Georgia Supreme Court did agree with the trial court . . . that the First and Fourteenth Amendments did not, as a matter of law, require judgment for appellants. The court concurred with the statement . . . that "the rights guaranteed by the First Amendment do not require total abrogation of the right to privacy. The goals sought by each may be achieved with a minimum of intrusion upon the other."

Upon motion for rehearing the Georgia court countered the argument that the victim's name was a matter of public interest and could be published with impunity by relying on § 26-9901 as an authoritative declaration of state policy that the name of a rape victim was not a matter of public concern. This time the court felt compelled to determine the constitutionality of the statute and sustained it as a "legitimate limitation on the right of freedom of expression contained in the First Amendment." . . .

We postponed decision as to our jurisdiction over this appeal to the hearing on the merits. We conclude that the Court has jurisdiction, and reverse the judgment of the Georgia Supreme Court.

II . . .

Since 1789, Congress has granted this Court appellate jurisdiction with respect to state litigation only after the highest state court in which judgment could be had has rendered a "[f]inal judgment or decree." Title 28 U.S.C. § 1257 retains this limitation on our power to review cases coming from state courts. The Court has noted that "[c]onsiderations of English usage as well as those of judicial policy" would justify an interpretation of the final-judgment rule to preclude review "where anything further remains to be determined by a State court, no matter how dissociated from the only federal issue that has finally been adjudicated by the highest court of the State." *Radio Station WOW, Inc. v. Johnson*, 326 U.S.

120, 124 (1945). But the Court there observed that the rule had not been administered in such a mechanical fashion and that there were circumstances in which there has been "a departure from this requirement of finality for federal appellate jurisdiction."

These circumstances were said to be "very few," but as the cases have unfolded, the Court has recurringly encountered situations in which the highest court of a State has finally determined the federal issue present in a particular case, but in which there are further proceedings in the lower state courts to come. There are now at least four categories of such cases in which the Court has treated the decision on the federal issue as a final judgment for the purposes of 28 U.S.C. § 1257 and has taken jurisdiction without awaiting the completion of the additional proceedings anticipated in the lower state courts. In most, if not all, of the cases in these categories, these additional proceedings would not require the decision of other federal questions that might also require review by the Court at a later date, and immediate rather than delayed review would be the best way to avoid "the mischief of economic waste and of delayed justice," as well as precipitate interference with state litigation. In the cases in the first two categories considered below, the federal issue would not be mooted or otherwise affected by the proceedings yet to be had because those proceedings have little substance, their outcome is certain, or they are wholly unrelated to the federal question. In the other two categories, however, the federal issue would be mooted if the petitioner or appellant seeking to bring the action here prevailed on the merits in the later state-court proceedings, but there is nevertheless sufficient justification for immediate review of the federal question finally determined in the state courts.

In the first category are those cases in which there are further proceedings—even entire trials—yet to occur in the state courts but where for one reason or another the federal issue is conclusive or the outcome of further proceedings preordained. In these circumstances, because the case is for all practical purposes concluded, the judgment of the state court on the federal issue is deemed final. In *Mills v. Alabama*, 384 U.S. 214 (1966), for example, a demurrer to a criminal complaint was sustained on federal constitutional grounds by a state trial court. The State Supreme Court reversed, remanding for jury trial. This Court took jurisdiction on the reasoning that the appellant had no defense other than his federal claim and could not prevail at trial on the facts or any nonfederal ground. To dismiss the appeal "would not only be an inexcusable delay of the benefits Congress intended to grant by providing for appeal to this Court, but it would also result in a completely unnecessary waste of time and energy in judicial systems already troubled by delays due to congested dockets."

Second, there are cases such as *Radio Station WOW, supra*, . . . in which the federal issue, finally decided by the highest court in the State, will survive and require decision regardless of the outcome of future state-court proceedings. In *Radio Station WOW*, the Nebraska Supreme Court directed the transfer of the properties of a federally licensed radio station and ordered an accounting, rejecting the claim that the transfer order would interfere with the federal license. The federal issue was held reviewable here despite the pending accounting on the "presupposition . . . that the federal questions that could come here have been adjudicated by the State court, and that the accounting which remains to be taken could not remotely give rise to a federal question . . . that may later come here. . . ." The judgment rejecting the federal claim and directing the transfer was deemed "dissociated from a provision for an accounting even though that is decreed in the same order." Nothing that could happen in the course of the accounting, short of settlement of the case, would foreclose or make unnecessary decision on the federal question. Older cases in the Court had reached the same result on similar facts. . . .

In the third category are those situations where the federal claim has been finally decided, with further proceedings on the merits in the state courts to come, but in which later review of the federal issue cannot be had, whatever the ultimate outcome of the case. Thus, in these cases, if the party seeking interim review ultimately prevails on the merits, the federal issue will be mooted; if he were to lose on the merits, however, the governing state law would not permit him again to present his federal claims for review. The Court has taken jurisdiction in these circumstances prior to completion of the case in the state courts. *California v. Stewart*, 384 U.S. 436 (1966), epitomizes this category. There the state court reversed a conviction on federal constitutional grounds and remanded for a new trial. Although the State might have prevailed at trial, we granted its petition for certiorari and affirmed, explaining that the state judgment was "final" since an acquittal of the defendant at trial would preclude, under state law, an appeal by the State. . . .

Lastly, there are those situations where the federal issue has been finally decided in the state courts with further proceedings pending in which the party seeking review here might prevail on the merits on nonfederal grounds, thus rendering unnecessary review of the federal issue by this Court, and where reversal of the state court on the federal issue would be preclusive of any further litigation on the relevant cause of action rather than merely controlling the nature and character of, or determining the admissibility of evidence in, the state proceedings still to come. In these circumstances, if a refusal immediately to review the state court decision might seriously erode federal policy, the Court has entertained and decided the federal issue, which itself has been finally determined by the state courts for purposes of the state litigation.

In *Construction Laborers v. Curry*, 371 U.S. 542 (1963), the state courts temporarily enjoined labor union picketing over claims that the National Labor Relations Board had exclusive jurisdiction of the controversy. The Court took jurisdiction for two independent reasons. First, the power of the state court to proceed in the face of the preemption claim was deemed an issue separable from the merits and ripe for review in this Court, particularly "when postponing review would seriously erode the national labor policy requiring the subject matter of respondents' cause to be heard by the . . . Board, not by the state courts." Second, the Court was convinced that in any event the union had no defense to the entry of a permanent injunction other than the preemption claim that had already been ruled on in the state courts. Hence the case was for all practical purposes concluded in the state tribunals.

In *Mercantile National Bank v. Langdeau*, 371 U.S. 555 (1963), two national banks were sued, along with others, in the courts of Travis County, Tex. The claim asserted was conspiracy to defraud an insurance company. The banks as a preliminary matter asserted that a special federal venue statute immunized them from suit in Travis County and that they could properly be sued only in another county. Although trial was still to be had and the banks might well prevail on the merits, the Court, relying on *Curry*, entertained the issue as a "separate and independent matter, anterior to the merits and not enmeshed in the factual and legal issues comprising the plaintiff's cause of action." Moreover, it would serve the policy of the federal statute "to determine now in which state court appellants may be tried rather than to subject them . . . to long and complex litigation which may all be for naught if consideration of the preliminary question of venue is postponed until the conclusion of the proceedings."

Miami Herald Publishing Co. v. Tornillo, 418 U.S. 241 (1974), is the latest case in this category. There a candidate for public office sued a newspaper for refusing, allegedly contrary to a state statute, to carry his reply to the paper's editorial critical of his qualifications. The trial court held the act unconstitutional, denying both injunctive relief and damages. The State Supreme Court reversed, sustaining the statute against the challenge based upon the First and Fourteenth Amendments and remanding the case for a trial and appropriate relief, including damages. The newspaper brought the case here. We sustained our jurisdiction . . . observing:

> "Whichever way we were to decide on the merits, it would be intolerable to leave unanswered, under these circumstances, an important question of freedom of the press under the First Amendment; an uneasy and unsettled constitutional posture of [the state statute] could only further harm the operation of a free press."

In light of the prior cases, we conclude that we have jurisdiction to review the judgment of the Georgia Supreme Court rejecting the challenge under the First and Fourteenth Amendments to the state law authorizing damage suits against the press for publishing the name of a rape victim whose identity is revealed in the course of a public prosecution. The Georgia Supreme Court's judgment is plainly final on the federal issue and is not subject to further review in the state courts. Appellants will be liable for damages if the elements of the state cause of action are proved. They may prevail at trial on nonfederal grounds, it is true, but if the Georgia court erroneously upheld the statute, there should be no trial at all. Moreover, even if appellants prevailed at trial and made unnecessary further consideration of the constitutional question, there would remain in effect the unreviewed decision of the State Supreme Court that a civil action for publishing the name of a rape victim disclosed in a public judicial proceeding may go forward despite the First and Fourteenth Amendments. Delaying final decision of the First Amendment claim until after trial will "leave unanswered . . . an important question of freedom of the press under the First Amendment," "an uneasy and unsettled constitutional posture [that] could only further harm the operation of a free press." On the other hand, if we now hold that the First and Fourteenth Amendments bar civil liability for broadcasting the victim's name, this litigation ends. Given these factors—that the litigation could be terminated by our decision on the merits and that a failure to decide the question now will leave the press in Georgia operating in the shadow of the civil and criminal sanctions of a rule of law and a statute the constitutionality of which is in serious doubt—we find that reaching the merits is consistent with the pragmatic approach that we have followed in the past in determining finality.

[On the merits, the Court reversed the Georgia Supreme Court on First Amendment grounds holding that: "Once true information is disclosed in public court documents open to public inspection, the press cannot be sanctioned for publishing it. In this instance as in others reliance must rest upon the judgment of those who decide what to publish or broadcast."]

Reversed.

MR. CHIEF JUSTICE BURGER concurs in the judgment.

[The concurring opinions of JUSTICES POWELL and DOUGLAS, both addressing the merits, are omitted.]

MR. JUSTICE REHNQUIST, dissenting.

Because I am of the opinion that the decision which is the subject of this appeal is not a "final" judgment or decree, as that term is used in 28 U.S.C. § 1257, I would dismiss this appeal for want of jurisdiction. . . .

NOTES AND QUESTIONS

1. Final judgments and final decisions.   Do you see the similarities between the final-judgment rule, as explained and applied in *Cox Broadcasting,* and the final-decision rule, as explained and applied in the materials examining appealability under § 1291? Do the same practical considerations that animate the collateral-order doctrine have any bearing on the scope of the final judgment rule? Notice that the final-decision rule involves the exercise of jurisdiction within the federal judicial system, while the final-judgment rule pertains to Supreme Court review of state court decisions. Should "federalism" concerns in the latter setting temper the scope of finality for purposes of § 1257?

2. Principled applications of the fourth category.   Is there a principled way to apply the fourth category described in *Cox Broadcasting?* Doesn't its application require the Court to inquire into the merits before determining the scope of jurisdiction? Doesn't this increase the likelihood that jurisdiction will turn more on the Justices' assessment of the merits than on independent considerations of practical finality?

Flynt v. Ohio

451 U.S. 619 (1981)

PER CURIAM.

On July 14, 1976, criminal complaints were issued against petitioners charging them with disseminating obscenity in violation of Ohio Rev. Code Ann § 2907.32 (1975). The Municipal Court granted petitioners' motions to dismiss the complaints on the ground that petitioners had been subjected to selective and discriminatory prosecution in violation of the Equal Protection Clause of the Fourteenth Amendment. The Court of Appeals of Ohio reversed, finding the evidence insufficient to support petitioners' allegations of selective and discriminatory prosecution. The case was remanded for trial. The Ohio Supreme Court affirmed. We granted certiorari. Because the decision of the Ohio Supreme Court was not a final judgment within the meaning of 28 U.S.C. § 1257, we dismiss the writ for want of jurisdiction.

Consistent with the relevant jurisdictional statute, 28 U.S.C. § 1257, the Court's jurisdiction to review a state-court decision is generally limited to a final judgment rendered by the highest court of the State in which decision may be had. *Cox Broadcasting Corp. v. Cohn*, 420 U.S. 469, 476-477 (1975). In general, the final-judgment rule has been interpreted "to preclude reviewability . . . where anything further remains to be determined by a State court, no matter how dissociated from the only federal issue that has finally been adjudicated by the highest court of the State." *Radio Station WOW, Inc. v. Johnson*, 326 U.S. 120 (1945). Applied in the context of a criminal prosecution, finality is normally defined by the imposition of the sentence. Here there has been no finding of guilt and no sentence imposed.

The Court has, however, in certain circumstances, treated state-court judgments as final for jurisdictional purposes although there were further proceedings to take place in the state court. Cases of this kind were divided into four categories in *Cox Broadcasting Corp. v. Cohn, supra*, and each category was described. We do not think that the decision of the Ohio Supreme Court is a final judgment within any of the four exceptions identified in *Cox*.

In the first place, we observed in *Cox* that in most, if not all, of the cases falling within the four exceptions, not only was there a final judgment on the federal issue for purposes of state-court proceedings, but also there were no other federal issues to be resolved. There was thus no probability of piecemeal review with respect to federal issues. Here, it appears that other federal issues will be involved in the trial court, such as whether or not the publication at issue is obscene.

Second, it is not even arguable that the judgment involved here falls within any of the first three categories identified in the *Cox* opinion, and the argument that it is within the fourth category, although not frivolous, is unsound. The cases falling within the fourth exception were described as those situations:

"[w]here the federal issue has been finally decided in the state courts with further proceedings pending in which the party seeking review here might prevail on the merits on nonfederal grounds, thus rendering unnecessary review of the federal issue by this Court, and where reversal of the state court on the federal issue would be preclusive of any further litigation on the relevant cause of action rather than merely controlling the nature and character of, or determining the admissibility of evidence in, the state proceedings still to come. In these circumstances, if a refusal immediately to review the state-court decision might seriously erode federal policy, the Court has entertained and decided the federal issue, which itself has been finally determined by the state courts for purposes of the state litigation."

Here, it is apparent that if we reversed the judgment of the Ohio Supreme Court on the federal defense of selective enforcement, there would be no further proceedings in the state courts in this case. But the question remains whether delaying review until petitioners are convicted, if they are, would seriously erode federal policy within the meaning of our prior cases. We are quite sure that this would not be the case and that we do not have a final judgment before us.

The cases which the *Cox* opinion listed as falling in the fourth category involved identifiable federal statutory or constitutional policies which would have been undermined by the continuation of the litigation in the state courts. Here there is no identifiable federal policy that will suffer if the state criminal proceeding goes forward. The question presented for review is whether on this record the decision to prosecute petitioners was selective or discriminatory in violation of the Equal Protection Clause. The resolution of this question can await final judgment without any adverse effect upon important federal interests. A contrary conclusion would permit the fourth exception to swallow the rule. Any federal issue finally decided on an interlocutory appeal in the state courts would qualify for immediate review. That this case involves an obscenity prosecution does not alter the conclusion. Obscene material, properly defined, is beyond the protection of the First Amendment. As this case comes to us, we are confronted only with a state effort to prosecute an unprotected activity, the dissemination of obscenity. The obscenity issue has not yet been decided in the state courts, and no federal policy bars a trial on that question. There is no reason to treat this selective prosecution claim differently than we would treat any other claim of selective prosecution.

Accordingly, the writ is dismissed for want of jurisdiction.

So ordered.

JUSTICE STEWART, with whom JUSTICE BRENNAN and JUSTICE MARSHALL join, dissenting.

I believe that a criminal trial of the petitioners under this Ohio obscenity law will violate the Constitution of the United States. It is clear to me, therefore, that "identifiable . . . constitutional polic[y]" will be "undermined by the continuation of the litigation in the state courts."

Accordingly, I think that under the very criteria discussed in the opinion of the Court, the judgment before us is "final for jurisdictional purposes." Believing that the Ohio trial court acted correctly in dismissing the complaints, and that the state appellate courts were in error in overturning that dismissal, I would reverse the judgment.

JUSTICE STEVENS, dissenting.

The decision of a federal question by the highest court of the State is final within the meaning of 28 U.S.C. § 1257 "if a refusal immediately to review the state-court decision might seriously erode federal policy." In the Court's view, this ground does not support reviewability in this case because the Court can discern "no identifiable federal policy that will suffer if the state criminal proceeding goes forward." In my opinion, the interest in protecting magazine publishers from being prosecuted criminally because state officials or their constituents are offended by the content of an admittedly nonobscene political cartoon is not merely "an identifiable federal policy"; it is the kind of interest that motivated the adoption of the First Amendment to the United States Constitution.

Petitioners publish Hustler, a national magazine. The trial court dismissed the criminal complaint against them after hearing evidence tending to establish that Ohio's decision to bring this prosecution was motivated by hostility to a political cartoon that is constitutionally indistinguishable from the rather trite depiction held to be protected by the First Amendment in *Papish v. University of Missouri Curators*, 410 U.S. 667. The Ohio Court of Appeals reversed, and that court's decision was affirmed by the Supreme Court of Ohio over the dissent of Justice Brown.

Because the Court has decided today to dismiss the writ of certiorari for want of jurisdiction, I will not comment on the merits beyond indicating that they concern the standards that a court must apply in determining whether an exercise of prosecutorial discretion has been based on an impermissible criterion such as race, religion, or the exercise of First Amendment rights. Because I place a high value on the federal interest in preventing such prosecutions and because the reinstatement of this criminal complaint may seriously erode that federal interest, I respectfully dissent.

NOTES AND QUESTIONS

1. *The first three categories.*   Was the *Flynt* Court correct when it concluded that the Ohio Supreme Court's decision did not satisfy any of the first three categories described in *Cox Broadcasting*? Explain why (or why not) as to each category.

2. *The fourth category.*   Compare the facts and circumstances of *Flynt* with those in *Cox Broadcasting* and in the other examples of the fourth category described in *Cox*. Is *Flynt* truly distinguishable from those cases? Or does the decision in *Flynt* merely reflect the unbounded nature of the fourth category? Think of it this way: If on remand Larry Flynt were found innocent, would the Ohio Supreme Court's decision rejecting his selective-prosecution argument undermine federal policy or constitutional principles? Can you explain how *Flynt* differs from *Cox Broadcasting* in this regard?

PROBLEMS

12-10. While officers were investigating marijuana sales and making arrests at a Florida home, Thomas drove up and parked in the driveway. An officer met him there and asked his name and whether he had a driver's license. After a check of Thomas's license revealed an outstanding warrant, the officer arrested him and took him inside the home. The officer then went back outside and searched Thomas's car, finding several bags containing methamphetamine. Thomas was charged with illegal possession of a controlled substance. The trial court granted his motion to suppress the evidence of narcotics as being the fruit of an unreasonable search in violation of the Fourth Amendment. An intermediate appellate court reversed, ruling that the search was lawful under the Fourth Amendment standards applicable to car searches. The Florida Supreme Court reversed, finding that the car search precedents did not apply. But instead of affirming the trial court's ruling that the search was unreasonable, the Florida Supreme Court remanded for a determination as to whether the search may have been constitutionally permissible on the basis that it was a "search incident to an arrest." Under Florida law, the state can appeal any adverse ruling by the trial court on the "search incident" issue. The State of Florida sought certiorari review in the U.S. Supreme Court, challenging the Florida Supreme Court's ruling on the scope of the Fourth Amendment with respect to car searches. May the U.S. Supreme Court exercise jurisdiction over the state's petition? *See Florida v. Thomas*, 532 U.S. 774 (2001).

12-11. Guillen, whose wife was killed in an automobile accident in Pierce County, Washington, filed a complaint against the county in a Washington state court seeking access to accident reports and other materials and data held by the county relating to the traffic intersection at which his wife was killed. His suit was filed under the state's Public Disclosure Act (PDA), which mandates the disclosure of such materials. The county resisted disclosure, arguing that a provision of federal law limited the PDA's scope and created a privilege of nondisclosure under the circumstances presented. The state trial court rejected the county's argument and ordered the county to turn over the requested materials. It also ruled that Guillen was entitled to attorneys' fees under the PDA. The Washington Supreme Court affirmed, holding that the federal statute on which the county relied was unconstitutional as being in excess of the authority granted to Congress under the Commerce Clause. The case was remanded for an assessment of attorneys' fees. The county has filed a petition for a writ of certiorari in the U.S. Supreme Court, in which it challenges the state supreme court's interpretation and application of the Commerce Clause. May the U.S. Supreme Court exercise jurisdiction over that petition? *See Pierce Cnty. v. Guillen*, 537 U.S. 129 (2003).

12-12. Brady and Boblit were charged with murder in the first degree. Their trials were separate, Brady being tried first. At his trial Brady took the stand and admitted his participation in the crime but claimed that Boblit did the actual killing. Brady was found guilty and sentenced to death. Prior to the trial, Brady's counsel had requested that the prosecution allow him to examine Boblit's extrajudicial statements. Several of those statements were shown to him, but the prosecution withheld one in which Boblit admitted the actual homicide, and it did not come to Brady's notice until after he had been tried, convicted, and sentenced. Thereafter, Brady moved the trial court for a new trial based on the evidence that the prosecution had suppressed. The motion was denied and Brady appealed both his conviction and the denial of his motion for a new trial. The state supreme court affirmed the conviction but held that the withholding of the evidence by the prosecution denied Brady due process of law and remanded the case for a retrial solely on the question of punishment. Brady seeks certiorari claiming that he is also entitled to a new trial on the question of guilt. Is the state supreme court's decision a final judgment within the meaning of § 1257? Does it fall within any of the *Cox Broadcasting* categories? *See Brady v. Maryland*, 373 U.S. 83 (1963).

12-13. Musso was convicted of perjury in state court. At trial, the government introduced incriminatory statements Musso had made to an undercover police officer after the charges against him had been filed. The evidence was introduced over Musso's objection that the statements had been elicited in violation of his Sixth and Fourteenth Amendment right to counsel. On appeal, the state supreme court reversed the conviction, agreeing with Musso on his Sixth Amendment claim. The case was then remanded for a new trial. In response, the prosecution seeks review of the Sixth Amendment issue in the U.S. Supreme Court. Is the state supreme court decision a final judgment within the meaning of § 1257? Does it fall within any of the *Cox Broadcasting* categories?

b.   Federal Question Raised and Decided

The Supreme Court may exercise jurisdiction over cases originating in state courts only when the federal matters that are "drawn in question" or "specially set up" have been expressly or implicitly decided. 28 U.S.C. § 1257(a). This rule is sometimes described as requiring that the federal question be "substantial," but in the context of discretionary review one can assume that if the Court grants the petition for certiorari, the question or questions over which review was granted are deemed substantial. If after granting certiorari, however, the Court concludes that the federal question was insubstantial, not properly raised below, not decided below, or is otherwise foreclosed from review, it will dismiss the writ as improvidently granted.

Cardinale v. Louisiana
394 U.S. 437 (1969)

MR. JUSTICE WHITE delivered the opinion of the Court.

Petitioner brutally murdered a woman near New Orleans, and then fled the State. He had been seen with his victim, and a warrant was issued for his arrest. In the course of his flight petitioner came to Tucson, Arizona, where he decided to surrender. He flagged down a police car and, after an interruption by the police to warn him that he need not speak, that his speech might be used against him, and that he had a right to contact an attorney, was taken to the station house where he poured out a confession. His confession was introduced in its entirety in the subsequent trial for murder in which petitioner was convicted and sentenced to death. Petitioner does not now contend that his confession was involuntary or that his admission of guilt to the Tucson police was inadmissible in evidence. He objects solely to the admission of those parts of his confession which he argues were both irrelevant and prejudicial in his trial for murder. A Louisiana statute requires that confessions must be admitted in their entirety, La. Rev. Stat. § 15:450, and petitioner contends that this is unconstitutional.

Although certiorari was granted to consider this question, the fact emerged in oral argument that the sole federal question argued here had never been raised, preserved, or passed upon in the state courts below. It was very early established that the Court will not decide federal constitutional issues raised here for the first time on review of state court decisions. In *Crowell v. Randell*, 10 Pet. 368 (1836), Justice Story reviewed the earlier cases commencing with *Owings v. Norwood's Lessee*, 5 Cranch 344 (1809), and came to the conclusion that the Judiciary Act of 1789, c. 20, § 25, 1 Stat. 85, vested this Court with no jurisdiction unless a federal question was raised and decided in the state court below. "If both of these do not appear on the record, the appellate jurisdiction fails." 10 Pet. 368, 391. The Court has consistently refused to decide federal constitutional issues raised here for the first time on review of state court decisions both before the *Crowell* opinion, and since.

In addition to the question of jurisdiction arising under the statute controlling our power to review final judgments of state courts, 28 U.S.C. § 1257, there are sound reasons for this. Questions not raised below are those on which the record is very likely to be inadequate, since it certainly was not compiled with those questions in mind. And in a federal system it is important that state courts be given the first opportunity to consider the applicability of state statutes in light of constitutional challenge, since the statutes may be construed in a way which saves their constitutionality. Or the issue may be blocked by an adequate state ground. Even though States are not free to avoid constitutional issues on inadequate state grounds, they should be given the first opportunity to consider them.

In view of the petitioner's admitted failure to raise the issue he presents here in any way below, the failure of the state court to pass on this issue, the desirability of giving the State the first opportunity to apply its statute on an adequate record, and the fact that a federal habeas remedy may remain if no state procedure for raising the issue is available to petitioner, the writ is dismissed for want of jurisdiction.

It is so ordered.

Mr. Justice Black, Mr. Justice Douglas, and Mr. Justice Fortas concur in the dismissal of the writ, believing it to have been improvidently granted.

A NOTE ON THE ADEQUATE AND INDEPENDENT STATE GROUND DOCTRINE

If a state court decision is based on alternative grounds—one premised on state law and one premised on federal law—the Supreme Court may not review the federal question if the state law basis for the decision is "adequate and independent." *See Michigan v. Long*, 463 U.S. 1032 (1983). This is what the *Cardinale* Court meant when it observed that a federal issue "may be blocked by an adequate state ground." *Cardinale, supra*, 394 U.S. at 439. A state ground is *adequate* if it fully disposes of the case without itself violating any principle of federal law. A state ground is *independent* if it is based solely on an interpretation of state law that is not in any manner intertwined with principles of federal law. Both requirements must be satisfied in order to preclude Supreme Court review.

For example, suppose a teacher is fired from her job after a newspaper published a letter she wrote that was critical of the local school board. She files a lawsuit in state court against the school district, claiming a violation of her state and federal rights of free speech. The state high court holds that the firing violated both the state and federal constitutions and enters judgment for the teacher. In construing the state constitutional provision, the state high court relied on a mixture of state and federal precedent, treating both as binding authority. If the school board now seeks review of the federal claim in the Supreme Court, the state ground of decision will be deemed "adequate" in the sense that it fully resolves the controversy by overturning the board's action, and does not violate any provision of federal law. States are free to grant their citizens more freedom of speech under state law than may be provided by federal law. The state ground is not, however, "independent" since the state court relied on federal precedent in interpreting the state constitutional provision's scope. To the extent that the state court was mistaken as to what federal precedent establishes, that error may have influenced its reading of the state constitution as well. Had the state court instead relied only on state precedent, or made it clear that any federal precedent cited was merely persuasive and not controlling, the state ground would then have been independent. As it stands, however, the state ground is not both adequate *and* independent; therefore, the U.S. Supreme Court may review the federal issue if it wishes to grant certiorari in the case.

In the foregoing hypothetical, would the state ground have been adequate and independent if the state high court had ruled in favor of the school board on both state and federal claims? Assume that in this situation, the state high court relied only on state precedent in construing the state constitution's free speech provision.

c.   *The Highest State Court in Which a Decision Could Be Had*

Title 28 U.S.C. § 1257 also requires that the decision being reviewed must be one made by the "highest court of a State in which a decision could be had." 28

U.S.C. § 1257. This does not mean that a state court of last resort had to have rendered the decision. Rather, it means simply that the party seeking Supreme Court review has exhausted all appeals of right within the state judicial system and has also properly petitioned for any available discretionary review in the state's higher courts. *See generally* SHAPIRO, GELLER, BISHOP, HARTNETT & HIMMELFARB, *supra*, §§ 3.11-3.14. Thus, if a state does not provide any right of appeal and discretionary review is denied, the trial court may be treated as the highest court of the state in which a decision could be had. Most often, however, the "highest court" will be at least an intermediate appellate court if not the state's court of last resort.

E.   Appeals Review Problem

12-14. Bessemer City appointed a committee of four men and one woman to hire a new recreation director. Eight people applied for the position, including Phyllis Anderson, the only female applicant. Anderson was a 39-year-old schoolteacher with college degrees in social studies and education. She had experience as a recreation director and was knowledgeable in the areas of athletics, arts, and crafts. The committee, however, gave the position to Don Kincaid, a 24-year-old male applicant who had recently graduated from college with a degree in physical education, avowedly because of his superior experience in athletics. The four men on the committee voted for Kinkaid, while the sole female member voted for Anderson.

Anderson filed suit against the city in federal district court, claiming gender discrimination under Title VII of the 1964 Civil Rights Act. She sought monetary relief and a preliminary injunction. As to the latter, the court held a brief hearing and denied the preliminary relief. The parties then engaged in discovery, at the close of which the city moved for summary judgment. The motion was denied, the court concluding that there was a genuine issue of material fact with respect to whether the male members of the committee engaged in intentional sex discrimination. The case then went to trial, at the end of which the court found that the written job description, although ambiguous, included substantial responsibilities beyond athletics, and that Anderson was the most qualified candidate to perform the full range of required duties. The court also made several findings regarding potential bias by the male members of the committee, including a finding that during her interview, Anderson was asked whether her husband, Jim, would approve of her working late, while no comparable questions were asked of male applicants. This latter finding was controversial, for there was some evidence that Kincaid had been asked such a question by the female member of the committee, as suggested by the following cross-examination of that committee member:

> "Q: Did the committee members ask that same kind of question regarding
>   night work of the other applicants?
> "A: Not that I recall.

"*Q:* Do you deny that the other applicants, aside from the plaintiff, were asked about the prospect of working at night in that position?

"*A:* Not to my knowledge.

"*Q:* Are you saying they were not asked that?

"*A:* They were not asked, not in the context that they were asked of Phyllis. I don't know whether they were worried because Jim wasn't going to get his supper or what. You know, that goes both ways.

"*Q:* Did you tell Phyllis Anderson that Donnie Kincaid was not asked about night work?

"*A:* He wasn't asked about night work.

"*Q:* That answers one question. Now, let's answer the other one. Did you tell Phyllis Anderson that, that Donnie Kincaid was not asked about night work?

"*A:* Yes, after the interviews—I think the next day or sometime, and I know—may I answer something?

"*Q:* If it's a question that has been asked; otherwise, no. It's up to the judge to say.

"*A:* You asked if there was any question asked about—I think Donnie was just married, and I think I made the comment to him personally—and your new bride won't mind.

"*Q:* So, you asked him yourself about his own wife's reaction?

"*A:* No, no.

"*Q:* That is what you just said.

"Mr. Gibson: Objection, Your Honor.

"The Court: Sustained. You don't have to rephrase the answer."

The district court concluded that the question about Kincaid's spouse was meant to be facetious, given the female committee member's objections to similar questions posed to Anderson. Based on these findings, the district court ruled that the committee had intentionally discriminated against Anderson on the basis of sex. The court then entered an order requiring the city to hire her and set a hearing to determine the amount of damages to which she was entitled.

A. Was the district court order denying the preliminary injunction immediately appealable? If so, under what statute?

B. Was the district court order denying the city's motion for summary judgment immediately appealable? In the alternative, could the city seek review of that order under the All Writs Act, 28 U.S.C. § 1651(a)?

C. Could the district court have certified its disposition of the summary judgment motion for immediate appeal under either § 1292(b) or Rule 54(b)?

D. Was the district court order requiring the city to hire Anderson immediately appealable? If not, when will the order be appealable and under what statute?

E. Once an appeal is properly lodged, under what standard of review should the trial court's decision be reviewed? In answering this question, use both a categorical approach and a functional approach. Does the same standard apply to all the findings? May the court of appeals reverse if it concludes that a more plausible interpretation of the written job description was that the central function of the director was to oversee athletics? Could the court of appeals reasonably conclude from the testimony that the question asked of Kincaid was not facetious? If it so found, could it reverse that finding?

F. For purposes of this question only, assume that the case had been filed in state court and that on interlocutory appeal, a state intermediate appellate court affirmed the trial court's ruling in favor of Anderson and then remanded for a hearing on the amount of damages. Could the U.S. Supreme Court review that decision on certiorari? Assuming the Court could grant certiorari, do you think it would?

See Anderson v. City of Bessemer City, 470 U.S. 564 (1985).

XIII

THE BINDING EFFECT OF A FINAL JUDGMENT

Once a court renders a final judgment in a civil action, the judgment binds the parties to the underlying action unless the judgment is reversed on appeal or otherwise vacated. This means, in general, that the claims and issues resolved and decided within the judgment may not be the subject of further litigation between these parties. Their legal dispute is effectively over. The policy behind this principle of finality is twofold. First, it provides the parties assurance that, at least as between them, the claims and issues involved in their dispute have been finally resolved. Second, it conserves finite judicial resources for those disputes that have yet to be adjudicated. While there are exceptions to this rule, the general principle of finality is critical to the integrity of the litigation process. Indeed, some form of this principle is part of virtually every legal system. *See* Robert von Moschzisker, *Res Judicata*, 38 YALE L.J. 299 (1929).

In our legal system, the principle of finality is embodied in the concept of res judicata, which roughly translated means the thing or matter has been decided. In general, res judicata prevents parties from relitigating matters that have been expressly or implicitly decided between them. Res judicata actually encompasses two related but technically distinct doctrines. The first, sometimes also referred to as "res judicata," but now more commonly called "claim preclusion," defines the circumstances under which a claim or cause of action resolved in one case may operate to preclude further litigation on that claim in a subsequent case. The second doctrine, sometimes referred to as "collateral estoppel," but now usually called "issue preclusion," defines the extent to which discrete issues decided in a prior suit may be binding in subsequent litigation involving different claims.

The following example illustrates the distinction between these two doctrines:

> P and D enter a contract under which D agrees to deliver certain goods to P on July 1, 2000, and certain other goods on July 1, 2002. D fails to make the first delivery. P sues D for breach of contract and seeks prospective relief only, *i.e.*, an order requiring D to make the initial shipment. D denies the validity of the contract, claiming a lack of consideration. After a trial on this issue, judgment is for P, and D is ordered to make the delivery. D complies. Subsequently, D fails to make the July 1, 2002 delivery. P again sues D. This time P seeks damages for the late 2000 delivery, and an order requiring D to make the 2002 delivery.

First, as to claim preclusion: P's initial suit involved a *claim* for breach of contract based on D's failure to make the 2000 delivery. That claim went to final judgment. The second suit, although it seeks monetary damages, is based in part on the exact same claim, namely, breach of contract based on D's failure to make the 2000 delivery. The doctrine of claim preclusion will prevent P from seeking monetary damages for the 2000 breach. This is so even though the issue of monetary damages was not previously litigated. In essence, the final judgment has fully extinguished all aspects of the claim, both litigated and not. On the other hand, P's claim for the 2002 breach is a factually distinct claim that arose after the first suit was filed. He is not foreclosed from bringing that separate claim even though it involves the same contract and roughly similar circumstances, for despite these similarities, it is not the same claim.

Next, as to issue preclusion: If in the second suit involving the 2002 breach, D again challenges the underlying contract for a lack of consideration, he will be precluded from doing so since in the initial proceeding the *issue* of consideration was actually litigated, decided, and necessary to the judgment. D is bound by that finding. If D wishes to raise another defense, *e.g.*, impossibility due to an intervening act of God, he is free to do so. But under the principle of issue preclusion, a court will not revisit issues previously decided between the same parties, even if those issues arise with respect to different claims.

In short, claim preclusion prevents a party from asserting any part of a previously resolved claim, including those aspects of the claim that may not have been raised or litigated in the initial proceeding. The key is the identity of the parties and a determination of whether the cases involve the same claim. Issue preclusion, on the other hand, is not dependent on the claim litigated in the first suit but on the discrete issues necessarily decided in that suit. When such a previously decided issue is identified, the doctrine prevents the parties from relitigating that issue in a subsequent suit even if it involves a different claim.

Typically, claim and issue preclusion problems arise in the context of successive lawsuits filed in court. Sometimes, however, one of the proceedings is filed before an administrative tribunal. In general, a proceeding before an administrative tribunal will be accorded full res judicata effect—including both claim and issue preclusion—so long as that tribunal provides essentially the same range of procedures and protections available in a traditional judicial forum, including notice, opportunity to be heard, and finality of decision. *See B & B Hardware, Inc. v. Hargis Indus., Inc.*, 135 S. Ct. 1293, 1303 (2015). The preclusive scope of an administrative tribunal's decisions may, however, be limited by statute or other policy considerations. *See generally* RESTATEMENT (SECOND) JUDGMENTS (hereinafter RESTATEMENT) § 83; Lawrence B. Solum, *Recognition and Validity of Judgments, in* 18 MOORE'S FEDERAL PRACTICE § 130.60 (3d ed. 2015).

A.   Claim Preclusion or Res Judicata

As we have noted, once a claim or cause of action between two parties has gone to final judgment, the party asserting the claim, *i.e.*, the claimant, may not reassert it in a subsequent proceeding against the same adversary. If the claimant party prevailed in the initial proceeding, further assertions of the claim are *merged* into the initial judgment (as in our example above); if the claimant lost in the first proceeding, any further assertion of the claim is said to be *barred*. Whether referred to as claim preclusion or res judicata, the result is the same: The party is precluded from again litigating any aspect of the finalized claim.

In an early case, the Supreme Court described the rule as follows:

> [A] judgment, if rendered upon the merits, constitutes an absolute bar to a subsequent action. It is a finality as to the claim or demand in controversy, concluding parties and those in privity with them, not only as to every matter which was offered and received to sustain or defeat the claim or demand, but as to any other admissible matter which might have been offered for that purpose.

Cromwell v. County of Sac, 94 U.S. (4 Otto) 351, 352 (1876). In essence, the full breadth of the claim is forever extinguished other than for purposes of enforcing the actual judgment.

Claim preclusion is not, however, self-executing. It is an affirmative defense that must be raised by the party against whom the challenged claim is being asserted. *See, e.g.,* Fed. R. Civ. P. 8(c)(1); Cal. Civ. Proc. Code § 1908.5; Fla. R. Civ. Proc. 1.110(d); Mass. R. Civ. P. 8(c). A failure to raise the defense in a timely fashion, either by pretrial motion or in the answer, constitutes a waiver. The defense consists of three elements, each of which must be established by the party raising the defense:

- The claim in the second proceeding must be the *same claim* or cause of action as that resolved in the first proceeding;
- The judgment in the first proceeding must have been *final, valid, and on the merits*; and
- The first and second proceedings must involve the *same parties* or those who, for specified reasons, should be treated as the same parties.

We will examine each of these elements in turn.

1.   The Same Claim

Whether claims filed in successive lawsuits are "the same" depends in large part on how one defines the term "claim." The broader the definition, the wider the range of a judgment's preclusive effect, and the more likely it is to create repose and conserve judicial resources—the two primary policies underlying the doctrine. On the other hand, if the definition of "claim" is too broad or too vague, it may unfairly prejudice a party's legitimate right to seek redress for legal wrongs. The ideal definition, therefore, will promote finality and judicial efficiency, while at the same time providing fair notice as to which legal rights are properly considered part of an initially asserted claim. In addition to that notice, however, there must be some opportunity for a party to assert those legal rights in the initial proceeding if they are later to be precluded from litigating them in another suit.

Consider an example:

P and D are involved in an automobile accident in which P sustains a broken arm. P sues D, claiming negligence and seeking damages for her broken arm. After a trial, judgment is entered for P and damages are awarded. In a subsequent lawsuit based on the same accident, P again sues D. This time, in addition to allegations of negligence, P claims that D acted intentionally. In the second suit P seeks redress for damages to her car and for injuries to her back. Is the claim asserted in the second lawsuit the same as the claim asserted in the first? In other words, should P be precluded from bringing all or part of the second action?

Certainly we can see a logical relationship between these lawsuits. There is a substantial factual overlap between the allegations in each, as well as a sense that the controversy between P and D comprises a single, convenient litigation unit. Hence our legal instinct probably tells us that P should have sought relief for all of these various harms in a single proceeding. Yet we can also see that in the second lawsuit P seeks damages for what are literally distinct injuries from those asserted in the first. She also relies in part on a different theory of liability. Should these injuries and theories be considered to be merged into the first proceeding?

From a policy perspective, allowing P to proceed with a second suit promotes an inefficient use of finite judicial resources by requiring a second judicial foray into a previously litigated and seemingly finalized controversy. The resurrection of the controversy also undermines D's legitimate interest in repose. What was once settled has now become unsettled. Both policy factors, therefore, weigh against P and suggest that we adopt an approach to preclusion that encompasses all forms of legal redress P may have had against D related to the accident.

But would such an approach be unfair to P by denying her a day in court for these alleged wrongs? Perhaps. The trick is to devise a definition of "claim" that promotes efficiency and repose, yet at the same time provides P with notice and a fair opportunity to fully litigate her grievances against D. You are probably sensing that there must be (or ought to be) some relationship between the scope of preclusion and the system of joinder under which preclusion is being asserted. For if P is allowed to plead or join the various rights of action in a single suit, any unfairness to her in insisting that she do so will surely be ameliorated.

Not surprisingly, the scope of the doctrine of res judicata has thus always been keyed to the underlying pleading system within which it operates. Under the common law system, the applicability of "res adjudicata" depended on the content of the pleadings in the original proceeding, *i.e.*, on the facts pled and the specific form of action under which the plaintiff proceeded. JOSEPH H. KOFFLER & ALLISON REPPY, COMMON LAW PLEADING 16-17, 406 (1969). In essence, the judge was asked to compare the pleadings from the initial suit with the pleadings in the second suit to determine whether there was an essential identity between the two actions. Yet because joinder under the common law system was relatively limited—only causes of action involving the same writ could be joined—the availability of res judicata was also quite limited. In essence, the requisites of the forms of action, as well as the division between law and equity, sometimes required parties to "split" claims or causes of action into separate suits. On the other hand, parties were not allowed to file successive suits to vindicate the same underlying right, even using different forms of action, if the relief sought was meant to redress the same basic harm. Charles E. Clark, Handbook of the Law of Code Pleading 473-474 (2d ed. 1947). In general, however, res judicata provided a relatively limited remedy at common law.

All of this changed in the mid to late nineteenth century with the adoption of code pleading. The codes eliminated the forms of action and simultaneously promoted liberal joinder of "rights of action." As a consequence of this new liberality, the scope of res judicata began to expand. After all, if a plaintiff could join various rights of action in a single proceeding, why not use the prod of preclusion to compel that joinder in the pursuit of the efficiency and justice that the codes were designed to promote? Over time, two distinct definitions of the preclusive litigation unit emerged, both of which were closely tied to the code-pleading rules of joinder.

The first, generally referred to as the "primary rights" theory, defined a claim or cause of action by reference to the primary right at the heart of the controversy. Primary rights were in turn defined as the basic rights and duties imposed on individuals by the substantive law. John Norton Pomeroy, Remedies and Remedial Rights by the Civil Action 1-4 (2d ed. 1883). Under this approach, each primary right is treated as distinct. Thus every person has a primary right to enter into and enforce contracts, another to be free from personal injury, and yet another to be free from injuries to personal property, etc. The code-pleading statutes allowed for liberal joinder within these classes of primary rights. Given this liberal approach to joinder, it followed that a plaintiff should not be allowed to split factually related claims involving the same primary right into separate lawsuits. On the other hand, the plaintiff could file separate suits to redress the violation of distinct primary rights, even if the violation of those rights was factually related.

Thus, in our hypothetical, applying the primary-rights theory, D's actions violated two of P's primary rights, namely, the right to be free from injury to her person and the right to be free from injury to her property. By failing to join her back-injury claim with her broken-arm claim, P split her cause of action for vindication of the personal-injury primary right. In addition, she also split that cause of action by adopting a new theory of liability in the second proceeding. The allegation that D acted intentionally simply asserts a different theory of recovery for the violation of the same underlying primary right. Therefore, under the primary-rights approach, in the second proceeding P would be precluded from asserting her claim for injury to her back, regardless of the underlying theory for the claim. On the other hand, since the damage to P's car involves a different primary right — injury to personal property — her failure to assert that claim in the first proceeding did not split the cause of action. Under a primary-rights theory, she would be free to proceed with that separate claim in the second lawsuit regardless of the underlying theory of liability.

From a policy perspective, the primary-rights model promotes some efficiencies — the joinder of all claims related to a single primary right — and to that extent it also promotes repose. Yet, given the variety of primary rights, it also has the potential to produce gross inefficiencies, as should be evident from its application in our hypothetical. From a plaintiff's perspective, however, the test is relatively predictable and hence fair, though in application the determination of what constitutes a primary right can sometimes be somewhat tricky, as we will see.

Given the potential lack of efficiency and repose that resulted from use of the primary-rights model, some courts began to move toward a broader definition of "claim." Various verbal formulae surfaced—the same essential facts and issues, the same legal theories, an identity of grounds, a coincidence of issues, or whether the gist of both cases was the same. *See* 18 CHARLES ALAN WRIGHT, ARTHUR R. MILLER & EDWARD H. COOPER, FEDERAL PRACTICE AND PROCEDURE § 4407 (2d ed. 2002 & Supp. 2015). Eventually, these various approaches led to what has been called the "transactional" test, our second major definition of "claim."

The transactional definition of "claim" took its cue from a catchall joinder provision that became part of most code-pleading statutes by the end of the nineteenth century. That provision allowed joinder of rights of action that arose from the "same transaction or transactions," whether or not they involved the same primary right. Given this very liberal rule of joinder, many courts and commentators developed an equally liberal definition of "claim" for purposes of preclusion. Under this approach, a claim came to be defined as the now familiar "group of operative facts giving rise to one or more rights of action." CHARLES E. CLARK, *supra*, at 477.

Applying this fact-driven definition of the claim to our hypothetical, all of the rights asserted by P in the second lawsuit arise from the same operative facts or transactions at issue in the first suit. That the assertions in the second suit may involve different primary rights or different theories of liability is irrelevant. Since all of P's assertions arise out of the same factual or historical narrative, the rights asserted in the second suit are properly considered part of the claim that was resolved in the prior lawsuit. Hence, even though P did not actually raise or assert them, they are nonetheless "merged" into the prior judgment, and further litigation is precluded.

The transactional approach, unlike the primary-rights model, promotes efficiency and repose, but potentially at the cost of fairness. Although this unfairness may not be evident from our hypothetical, you may have seen earlier—in the context of supplemental jurisdiction and compulsory counterclaims—that the concept of "same transaction" is sufficiently flexible to allow a court some latitude in determining what falls within or without the transactional sphere. Given this flexibility and uncertainty, a plaintiff can sometimes be prejudiced by post-judgment applications of the concept. The Restatement has therefore proposed a version of the transactional test that takes much of the unpredictability out of the formula by focusing its application on particular factors. That definition provides:

> (1) When a valid and final judgment rendered in an action extinguishes the plaintiff's claim pursuant to the rules of merger or bar, the claim extinguished includes all rights of the plaintiff to remedies against the defendant with respect to all or any part of the transaction, or series of connected transactions, out of which the action arose.
>
> (2) What factual grouping constitutes a "transaction," and what groupings constitute a "series," are to be determined pragmatically, giving weight to such

considerations as whether the facts are related in time, space, origin, or motivation, whether they form a convenient trial unit, and whether their treatment as a unit conforms to the parties' expectations or business understanding or usage.

RESTATEMENT, *supra*, § 24. The Restatement's definition of transaction, particularly subpart (2), is meant to temper the transactional test's potential reach by imposing what are in essence common-sense limitations on the scope of what may constitute a transaction. The basic message, however, is that a plaintiff should err on the side of joinder to avoid the potential for splitting (and hence losing) a claim under this very liberal test.

There is a third variation on the definition of claim that falls somewhere between the transactional and the primary-rights models: the "same-evidence" test. Under this test, for two claims to be the same, the factual overlap between them must be perfectly coextensive. In other words, the transaction's scope is narrowed to the specific facts used to prove each claim. If the evidence to prove each claim is identical, then the claims are the same; if the evidence is different, then they are not. In essence, the identity of the evidence establishes the identity of the underlying rights or claims. How would our hypothetical be resolved under this approach?

As quasi-sovereign entities, states are free to develop their own principles governing the claim- and issue-preclusive effect of their courts' judgments. *See Richards v. Jefferson Cnty.*, 517 U.S. 793, 797 & n.4 (1996) (stating that subject to limits imposed by the Due Process Clause, "[s]tate courts are generally free to develop their own rules for protecting against the relitigation of common issues or the piecemeal resolution of disputes"). The same holds true for the federal courts. A majority of the states (at least 34), and nearly all federal courts, have now adopted some version of the Restatement's transactional definition of "claim." *See* Lawrence B. Solum, *Claim Preclusion and Res Judicata, in* 18 MOORE'S FEDERAL PRACTICE § 131.20 (3d. ed. 2015) (discussing adoption of Restatement test by federal courts). A small number of states follow some version of the same-evidence test. *See, e.g., Phoenix Newspapers, Inc. v. Department of Corr.*, 934 P.2d 801, 804-806 (Ariz. Ct. App. 1997) (criticizing but applying the same-evidence test). Only one state—California—continues to apply the primary-rights model. *See Mycogen Corp. v. Monsanto Co.*, 51 P.3d 297, 306-310 (Cal. 2002); *City of Oakland v. Oakland Police & Fire Ret. System*, 169 Cal. Rptr. 3d 51, 66-71 (2014). *Cf. Creech v. Addington*, 281 S.W.3d 363, 379-383 (Tenn. 2009) (abandoning primary rights model in favor of transactional definition).

Porn v. National Grange Mutual Insurance Co.

93 F.3d 31 (1st Cir. 1996)

STAHL, Circuit Judge.

Having successfully sued his insurer, National Grange Mutual Insurance Company ("National Grange"), six months earlier for breach of contract in refusing to pay his claim for underinsured motorist benefits incurred during a July

1990 car accident, plaintiff-appellant Daryl E. Porn brought this diversity action in Maine's federal district court against National Grange seeking additional damages for its alleged mishandling of his underinsured motorist claim. The district court granted summary judgment in favor of National Grange based on the doctrines of collateral estoppel (issue preclusion) and res judicata (claim preclusion), concluding that an issue underlying one of Porn's claims had been decided in the earlier proceeding and that all of Porn's claims could have been raised therein. Porn appeals the district court's summary judgment order. Finding no error, we affirm.

I. Background & Prior Proceedings

On July 17, 1990, Porn, a Connecticut resident, was involved in an automobile accident in Portland, Maine, when motorist Lori Willoughby sped through a stop sign and broadsided his vehicle. Because his damages exceeded Willoughby's $20,000 policy limit, Porn made a claim to National Grange under his automobile policy seeking recovery from the underinsured motorist indorsement to the policy. For reasons not apparent in the record, National Grange refused to pay the claim.

Disgruntled by this refusal, Porn wrote to National Grange accusing it of bad faith in handling his claim and threatening legal action. Porn sent copies of his letter to the insurance commissioners of Connecticut and Massachusetts. National Grange, unimpressed, remained steadfast in its refusal to pay, and in November 1993, Porn filed suit against National Grange in Maine's federal district court for breach of the insurance contract ("first action"). [Porn prevailed in that first action and was awarded a judgment of $255,314.40.] . . .

Six months later, Porn commenced this action against National Grange in Maine's federal district court ("second action"). This time Porn alleged that National Grange's conduct in handling his underinsured motorist claim constituted breach of the covenant of good faith, intentional infliction of emotional distress, negligent infliction of emotional distress, and violations of the Connecticut Unfair Insurance Practices Act and the Connecticut Unfair Trade Practices Act. National Grange moved for summary judgment, arguing that the judgment in the first action precluded Porn from bringing the second action. The district court accepted that argument and granted summary judgment in favor of National Grange on the grounds that (1) one aspect of Porn's bad-faith claim was barred by issue preclusion and (2) all of Porn's claims were barred by claim preclusion. . . .

In reaching its broader holding that all five of Porn's claims were barred by claim preclusion, the district court reasoned that once Porn chose to bring the first action against National Grange for breach of contract, he was required to raise all his claims arising from the breach or else forfeit the right to do so. Because it found that Porn's five tort and statutory claims, like the earlier breach of contract claim, involved National Grange's obligations arising under the insurance policy, the district court concluded that they should have been brought in the first action and therefore were barred by claim preclusion from being raised in the second action.

II.   Analysis

Porn appeals the district court's grant of summary judgment in favor of National Grange, arguing that the judgment in the first action for breach of contract does not preclude his bad-faith, emotional distress, and statutory unfair practices claims (collectively "bad-faith claim") against National Grange in this action. Specifically, Porn argues that (1) the facts relevant to his bad-faith claim are separate from those relevant to his contract claim, (2) the bad-faith facts do not form a convenient trial unit with the contract facts, (3) treatment of both sets of facts as a unit does not conform to the parties' expectations, and (4) it was inequitable to apply the res judicata bar where, as here, the insurer's conduct in the contract litigation forms part of the bad-faith action. After reciting the standard of review and setting forth the governing res judicata law, we consider each argument in turn. . . .

Because the judgment in the first action was rendered by a federal court, the preclusive effect of that judgment in the instant diversity action is governed by federal res judicata principles. Under the federal law of res judicata, a final judgment on the merits of an action precludes the parties from relitigating claims that were raised or could have been raised in that action. *Allen v. McCurry*, 449 U.S. 90, 94 (1980). For a claim to be precluded, the following elements must be established: (1) a final judgment on the merits in an earlier action, (2) sufficient identity between the causes of action asserted in the earlier and later suits, and (3) sufficient identity between the parties in the two suits. Because there is no dispute that the first and third elements of the test are established, we focus on the second element: whether the causes of action in the two lawsuits are sufficiently identical.

In defining the cause of action for res judicata purposes, this circuit has adopted the "transactional" approach of the Restatement. Under this approach, a valid and final judgment in the first action will extinguish subsequent claims "with respect to all or any part of the transaction, or series of connected transactions, out of which the action arose." Restatement (Second) Judgments § 24. We determine what factual grouping constitutes a "transaction" pragmatically, giving weight to such factors as "whether the facts are related in time, space, origin, or motivation, whether they form a convenient trial unit, and whether their treatment as a unit conforms to the parties' expectations." Restatement § 24. These factors, however, are merely suggestive; they are not intended to be exhaustive, nor is any one factor determinative. *See* Restatement § 24, cmt. b. Finally, in making this determination, we are mindful that a single transaction may give rise to a multiplicity of claims, and recognize that "the mere fact that different legal theories are presented in each case does not mean that the same transaction is not behind each."

A.   Consideration of the Restatement Factors

With that background, we inquire whether the causes of action asserted in the first and second suits are sufficiently identical, focusing on the three Restatement factors.

1.   *Relation of the Facts in Time, Space, Origin, or Motivation*

The first Restatement factor asks whether the facts underlying the breach of contract and bad-faith claims are related in time, space, origin, or motivation, *i.e.*, whether they arise out of the same transaction, seek redress for essentially the same basic wrong, and rest on the same or a substantially similar factual basis. In this case, our answers to these questions lead us to conclude that the facts underlying the two claims are closely related.

First, we find that both the bad-faith claim and the contract claim derive from the same occurrence: National Grange's refusal to pay Porn the proceeds of his underinsured motorist policy for the July 17, 1990, accident. Second, although the two claims present different legal theories, one sounding in contract and the other in tort, they both seek redress for essentially the same basic wrong. For instance, Porn's contract action sought redress for National Grange's refusal to pay the policy proceeds, while his bad-faith action sought redress for its unreasonable refusal to pay the proceeds. Third, a comparison of the two complaints illustrates that the two claims rest on a similar factual basis. Both complaints, in their factual allegations, outline the circumstances of the accident, the particulars of the insurance policy, and National Grange's conduct in refusing to pay. In sum, the facts underlying the two claims are closely related in time, space, origin, and motivation.

Porn expends considerable effort characterizing the instant action as arising out of a transaction separate from that giving rise to the first action. In particular, Porn maintains that the bad-faith action stems from National Grange's conduct in handling his insurance claim, whereas the contract action stems from the circumstances surrounding the car accident. Porn's definition of the two transactions out of which the claims arise, however, is artificially narrow. For instance, the contract claim arises out of more than the car accident alone. It arises out of the accident in conjunction with National Grange's refusal to pay under the policy. Indeed, without the refusal to pay, no contract breach could exist. Similarly, the factual basis of Porn's bad-faith claim cannot be limited to National Grange's conduct in handling Porn's insurance claim. In this case, the facts of the car accident are also probative of National Grange's reasonableness in refusing to pay Porn's claim. For instance, if, as Porn suggests, the facts of the accident present a clear picture that Willoughby was the legal cause of the accident and Porn was not contributorily negligent, National Grange would have had less reason to contest the claim and therefore its refusal to pay appears less reasonable.[4]

---

4. Porn's argument that the facts underlying the bad-faith and contract claims are not related in time is similarly unpersuasive. Porn argues that the facts underlying the bad-faith action go to National Grange's handling of the claim after the car accident, while the facts underlying the contract action go to the accident itself. However, as we explained above, the factual basis of the contract action is formed by more than just the accident; it also includes National Grange's refusal to pay, and that refusal occurred after the accident. Therefore, the facts underlying the contract action cannot be limited to the accident itself but extend to the time period after the accident as well, thereby minimizing any time differential between the facts underlying the two claims.

Admittedly, each legal theory relies more heavily on some of the underlying facts than others. The accident facts, for example, will likely receive more emphasis in proving the contract claim, while the facts regarding National Grange's conduct in handling Porn's insurance claim will be more focal in proving the bad-faith claim. However, the Restatement makes clear that merely because two claims depend on different shadings of the facts or emphasize different elements of the facts, we should not color our perception of the transaction underlying them, creating multiple transactions where only one transaction exists. Restatement § 24, cmt. c. By focusing exclusively on the facts most critical to each claim, Porn has ignored the other facts underlying each claim. Accordingly, we reject Porn's grouping of the facts underlying the two claims into separate transactions.

2.   *Trial Convenience*

The second Restatement factor directs us to determine whether the facts underlying the contract and bad-faith claims form a convenient trial unit. This factor, aimed at conserving judicial resources, provides that where the witnesses or proof needed in the second action overlap substantially with those used in the first action, the second action should ordinarily be precluded. Restatement § 24, cmt. b. We conclude that Porn's bad-faith claim would use much of the same evidence produced in the first action for breach of the insurance contract, and therefore it would have been convenient and efficient for the district court to have heard the two claims in the same action.

Testimony and exhibits about the circumstances of the accident are relevant to both the contract and bad-faith claims. To establish that National Grange breached the insurance policy in not paying his claim, Porn had to prove that Willoughby's negligence caused the accident and that he was not contributorily negligent. Accordingly, in the first action, Porn presented evidence detailing the circumstances of the accident. This evidence would likely have been repeated in a second action for bad faith, as Porn would have sought to portray the accident facts as so plainly establishing Willoughby's negligence that National Grange had no credible reason for refusing to pay his claim.

The evidence in the contract action and the second action would also overlap as to the terms of Porn's underinsured motorist policy and National Grange's refusal to pay his claim. To prove breach of contract, Porn had to establish that National Grange refused to pay his claim where the terms of the policy so required. Likewise, the reasonableness of National Grange's refusal to pay, *i.e.*, whether it acted in bad faith, depends on what the policy required.

Rather than addressing the degree to which the evidence supporting each claim overlaps, Porn challenges the convenience of bringing the claims together on two other grounds. First, Porn argues that evidence relevant to the bad-faith claim, specifically evidence of the amount of insurance available and the fact of settlement offers and negotiations, would prejudice the insurer's defense of the contract claim, and therefore the two claims do not form a convenient trial unit. However, we agree with the district court that any potential prejudice could be resolved by bifurcating the trial. With bifurcation, the evidence common to both claims, which was considerable, could have been presented at once and not "in separate lawsuits commenced at a distance of months or years."

Second, Porn argues that he had to procure a judgment that National Grange breached the insurance contract before the cause of action for bad faith could accrue and therefore the bad-faith and contract claims could not be joined in the same action. Porn bases this contention on an assumption that, although a Connecticut court has yet to decide this issue, it would follow jurisdictions like Florida and require a judgment of contract breach as a condition precedent to the pursuit of a bad-faith claim. The district court correctly observed, however, that the Connecticut Supreme Court rejected this contention in *Duhaime v. American Reserve Life Ins. Co.*, 200 Conn. 360, 511 A.2d 333, 334-35 (1986). Invoking the doctrine of res judicata, the Connecticut Supreme Court held that Duhaime's earlier action for breach of the insurance policy barred a subsequent action for bad faith. In so holding, the court implicitly acknowledged that a bad-faith action can accrue without a separate judgment of contract breach. Although *Duhaime* involved disability insurance and the instant case involves underinsured motorist insurance, we see nothing unique about underinsured motorist insurance that would preclude *Duhaime*'s holding from governing here.

3. *Parties' Expectations*

The final Restatement factor is whether treating the underlying facts as a trial unit conforms to the parties' expectations. For the following reasons, we conclude that it does.

When he brought his contract suit in November 1993, Porn knew the facts necessary for bringing a bad-faith claim. He knew that National Grange had refused to pay; he knew its alleged reasons for so refusing; and he knew the extent of the delay in payment attributable to the refusal. Therefore, because the two claims arose in the same time frame out of similar facts, one would reasonably expect them to be brought together. See 18 Charles A. Wright & Arthur R. Miller, *Federal Practice and Procedure* § 4407, at 56 (1981) ("Defendants may reasonably demand that disposition of the first suit establish repose as to all matters that ordinary people would intuitively count part of a single basic dispute."). Indeed, in February 1993, nine months before filing the first action, Porn wrote a letter to National Grange in which he made a demand for his policy proceeds and concomitantly threatened to sue for bad faith. In light of this letter, it would not have been unreasonable for National Grange to expect that any subsequent lawsuit that Porn initiated would include claims for both breach of contract and bad faith. Finally, bringing related claims together is arguably more conducive to settlement and therefore, at least in this case, may have had some pragmatic appeal.

In sum, applying the Restatement's transactional test to this case, we conclude that the two lawsuits involved sufficiently identical causes of action. Because the cause of action should not have been split into two lawsuits, Porn's bad-faith claim is barred by claim preclusion.

B.   Equitable Exception

As his final argument, Porn contends that even if we find that res judicata applies, equity demands its suspension in this case. Specifically, Porn argues that because National Grange's decision to proceed to judgment in the contract action with no evidence to support its defense ("litigation conduct") is probative of bad faith, the full nature of National Grange's bad-faith tort was not revealed until judgment was entered in the contract action. Therefore, Porn argues, it would be premature and unfair to require him to bring his bad-faith claim together with his contract claim.

The Supreme Court has counseled us to adhere to traditional principles of res judicata and not to make any "ad hoc determination of the equities in a particular case." *Federated Dep't Stores, Inc. v. Moitie*, 452 U.S. 394, 401 (1981) (refusing to condone an exception to an application of res judicata that would bar relitigation of an unappealed adverse judgment where other plaintiffs in similar actions against common defendants successfully appealed the judgments against them). In a post-*Moitie* decision, however, this court has suggested that an " 'occasional exception' to claim preclusion" may still exist in instances of " 'unusual hardship.'" *Kale v. Combined Ins. Co. of Am.*, 924 F.2d 1161, 1168 (1st Cir. 1991); *but see Johnson v. SCA Disposal Servs., Inc.*, 931 F.2d 970, 977 (1st Cir. 1991) (citing *Moitie* for the proposition that "we cannot relax the principles of claim preclusion even if we find that the equities cry out for us to do so"). Assuming *arguendo* that *Moitie* did not foreclose the possibility of an equitable exception, we find that, in the context of this case, requiring the bad-faith claim to be brought in the first action creates no unusual hardship for Porn and therefore the exception does not apply. . . .

III.   Conclusion

For the reasons stated above, we *affirm* the district court's grant of summary judgment in favor of National Grange.

NOTES AND QUESTIONS

1. *Applying the primary-rights model.*   Was Porn suing for the vindication of more than one primary right? If so, can you identify the separate rights? Would the analysis and/or outcome have changed if the court of appeals had adopted the primary-rights model?

2. *The underlying policies.*   Did the court of appeals adequately consider the policies of efficiency, repose, and fairness? To what extent are those policies served or disserved by the Restatement's approach? Would any or all of those policies have been better served under a primary-rights approach?

Los Angeles Branch NAACP v. Los Angeles Unified School District

750 F.2d 731 (9th Cir. 1984) (en banc), *cert. denied*, 474 U.S. 919 (1985)

CANBY, Circuit Judge:

We took this case en banc to decide the extent to which the doctrine of res judicata bars this class action alleging intentional segregation in the Los Angeles public schools in violation of the United States Constitution. Defendants moved in district court for summary judgment on the ground that plaintiffs were seeking in this action to relitigate the same claim that had been litigated and decided in *Crawford v. Board of Education*, 113 Cal. App. 3d 633 (1980), *aff'd*, 458 U.S. 527 (1982). The district court denied the motion and certified this interlocutory appeal. 28 U.S.C. § 1292(b).

I.   Facts

The *Crawford* litigation began in 1963 as a class action on behalf of black high school students seeking to desegregate a high school in Los Angeles. Before trial, the complaint was amended to assert a desegregation claim on behalf of all black and Hispanic students attending school in the Los Angeles Unified School District. The case was filed in the California courts just months after the California Supreme Court, in *Jackson v. Pasadena City School District*, 59 Cal. 2d 876 (1963), held that school boards in the state were under a state constitutional obligation to take reasonable steps to alleviate racial segregation in the schools, regardless of whether the segregation was de facto or de jure in nature.* The case went to trial in 1968 under a stipulation that permitted the court to consider activities of the defendants occurring from May 1, 1963 to the time of trial. The trial court rendered its decision on May 12, 1970, [Judge Gitelson] finding that the District schools were substantially segregated and concluding that this segregation was both de facto and de jure in origin.

On appeal, the California Supreme Court refused to affirm on the basis of the trial court's conclusion of de jure segregation. *Crawford v. Board of Education*, 17 Cal. 3d 280 (1976) (*Crawford I*). Instead, it chose to affirm on the basis of its previous decision in *Jackson* that the California Constitution imposed a duty upon school boards to take reasonably feasible steps to alleviate segregation in the public schools, regardless of its cause. The court then remanded the cause to the trial court for the development of a reasonably feasible desegregation plan.

On remand, the trial court rejected the largely voluntary desegregation plan submitted by the School District and ordered the implementation of a plan calling

---

* ["De jure segregation" refers to racial segregation that is intentionally imposed by law; "de facto segregation" refers to racial segregation that exists "in fact" but that is not the direct product of intentionally discriminatory laws. Only de jure segregation violates the Fourteenth Amendment of the U.S. Constitution. Some state constitutions, however, prohibit de facto segregation as well. — EDS.]

for large-scale mandatory pupil reassignment and transportation. The court-ordered plan went into effect in the fall of 1978. In October 1979, the trial court began hearings to determine the constitutional sufficiency of its court-ordered plan. On November 6, 1979, before the hearings could be completed, the voters of California approved Proposition I, an initiative measure which amended the California Constitution to limit the power of state courts to order mandatory pupil reassignment and transportation on the basis of race. In effect, the state courts were forbidden to order those measures except in circumstances where federal courts could do so to remedy violations of the United States Constitution. In addition, Proposition I authorized any court having jurisdiction, upon application by any interested person, to modify existing judgments or decrees containing provisions for mandatory pupil reassignment and transportation, unless such modification would be prohibited by the United States Constitution.

Following passage of Proposition I, the School District applied to the California courts for an order halting mandatory pupil reassignment and transportation in the District. On May 19, 1980, the Superior Court denied the application on the ground that the trial court in *Crawford I* had found de jure segregation and thus the elimination of mandatory pupil reassignment and transportation in the District would be prohibited by the United States Constitution. The Superior Court thereafter issued a new order on July 7, 1980, substantially continuing the 1978 desegregation plan.

The California Court of Appeal reversed and vacated the July 7, 1980, desegregation order. *Crawford v. Board of Education*, 113 Cal. App. 3d 633, 643 (1980) (*Crawford II*). The appellate court determined that the 1970 findings by the trial court in *Crawford I* did not support its conclusion of de jure segregation, when viewed in light of subsequent Supreme Court decisions emphasizing the need for showing specific discriminatory intent. Because the Court of Appeal viewed the findings as establishing only de facto segregation in the District schools, it concluded that a federal court would not be authorized under federal law to order pupil assignment and transportation. Consequently, Proposition I barred the state court from doing so. The court thereupon vacated the orders of May 19, 1980, and July 7, 1980, and remanded to the Superior Court "for further proceedings consistent with this opinion." The California Supreme Court refused review on March 11, 1981, and the case was remitted to the Superior Court on the next day.

Following the remittitur, the District submitted a revised desegregation plan with no mandatory pupil reassignment or mandatory busing. The plan was accepted by the Superior Court, with modifications, on September 10, 1981. On November 25, 1981, the Superior Court awarded plaintiffs attorneys' fees and costs and, declaring that the "underlying issues have been resolved," terminated jurisdiction. The *Crawford* plaintiffs appealed the September 10, 1981 order but dropped their appeal on May 24, 1983, thus closing the last chapter of the *Crawford* litigation.

The NAACP filed the present case while *Crawford* was still pending in the California Superior Court following the remittitur from *Crawford II*. The district court refused to give res judicata effect to the *Crawford* litigation because it determined that no final judgment had yet been entered in that case and that retrial of the de jure issue on remand had not been foreclosed by the appellate court's remittitur. A three-judge panel of this court reversed the district court on the ground that the *Crawford* judgment had since become final and that therefore relitigation of the claim that the District was segregated de jure on or before September 10, 1981, was barred by the doctrines of res judicata and collateral estoppel. We granted the NAACP's petition for rehearing en banc and withdrew the opinion of the three-judge panel. Because we agree that relitigation of the de jure claim is barred by the doctrine of res judicata, we reverse the order of the district court. We determine the bar, however, to apply only to events occurring on or before May 2, 1969.

II. Res Judicata

The state court judgment in the *Crawford* litigation is entitled to the same preclusive effect in this court as it would be accorded in a California court, whether the effect is one of claim preclusion or issue preclusion. 28 U.S.C. § 1738. Under California law, the claim preclusion aspect of res judicata, also referred to as bar or merger, precludes the maintenance of a second suit between the same parties on the same cause of action so long as the first suit concluded in a final judgment on the merits. *Agarwal v. Johnson*, 25 Cal. 3d 932, 954 (1979). All issues that were litigated or that might have been litigated as part of the cause of action are barred. The parties no longer dispute that there is now a final judgment on the merits in *Crawford*. We therefore turn our attention to the more complex problem of determining whether this action involves the same cause of action . . . as *Crawford*.

The plaintiffs argue that the claim sued upon in this action is not the same as that in *Crawford*. They contend that the *Crawford* plaintiffs sued for violation of a right arising under the state constitution—the right to be free of de facto segregation. Plaintiffs assert that here they are suing for violation of a right arising under the Federal Constitution—the right to be free of de jure segregation. There are at least two major flaws in plaintiffs' argument.

First, the record in *Crawford* simply does not support the contention that plaintiffs there confined their claim to de facto segregation in violation of state law. The *Crawford* plaintiffs pleaded violations of the Fourteenth Amendment. They successfully moved the state court to be allowed to show bad faith on the part of the School District in maintaining segregation in the schools, injecting the element of defendants' intent into the trial. The findings and conclusions of the state trial judge directly addressed de jure segregation as a violation of the Federal Constitution. It is true that the California Supreme Court in *Crawford I* chose not to rely on the de jure findings, but that fact did not permanently remove the de jure issue from the case. When the School District moved to modify the desegregation plan after the passage of Proposition I, the *Crawford* plaintiffs responded in a memorandum of April 23, 1980, to the state trial court: "In *Crawford*, the Court heard and decided the Fourteenth Amendment issues and defense, and found de jure segregation. The violations and defense were pleaded, argued, and decided.

They cannot now be relitigated by invasion of the final judgment." Thereafter, the California Court of Appeal addressed the de jure issue and held that the trial court's 1970 findings did not support a conclusion of de jure segregation. The de jure issue had to be addressed at that time in order to determine the effect of Proposition I on the existing desegregation plan that included mandatory pupil reassignment and transportation. In view of this record, it is not possible to accept the contention of plaintiffs here that the *Crawford* litigation had nothing to do with de jure segregation in violation of the United States Constitution.

The second major flaw in plaintiffs' argument is that it misconceives the scope of a cause of action under California law. As plaintiffs correctly point out, California follows the "primary rights" theory, under which the right sought to be enforced determines the cause of action. The invasion of more than one primary right gives rise to as many causes of action as rights violated, even though all may arise from a single set of facts. California's rule, however, does not mean that different causes of action are involved just because relief may be obtained under either state or federal law, or under either of two legal theories. . . .

. . . [W]e are unable to accept plaintiffs' contention that they are attempting to enforce a different primary right than were the plaintiffs in *Crawford*. We would adhere to that conclusion even if the *Crawford* litigation had been confined to de facto segregation in violation of state law. The right to be free from de facto segregation is not a thing apart from the right to be free from de jure segregation; the former necessarily encompasses the latter. The California Supreme Court in *Crawford I* held that school boards had an affirmative duty to take reasonable steps to eliminate both de facto and de jure segregation. That duty survived Proposition I. The California Supreme Court clearly regarded the injury from both kinds of segregation to be the same: "[T]here is virtually no dispute that the practical effect of segregated schooling on minority children does not depend upon whether a court finds the segregation de jure or de facto in nature; the isolation and debilitating effects do not vary with the source of the segregation." *Crawford I*, 17 Cal. 3d at 301. We can only conclude that California regards the primary right underlying de jure and de facto claims to be one and the same — "the right to an equal opportunity for education."[8] *Crawford I*, 17 Cal. 3d at 305. Since the primary right enforced in *Crawford* was the same as the primary right asserted in this litigation, the present action is barred as to all matters that might have been litigated by the same parties in *Crawford*.

Our conclusion that the same primary right is involved also puts to rest the contention that the federal claim is not barred because the federal right is narrower than the state right. It is true that federal law does not place school boards under a

---

8. The distinction between de facto and de jure segregation is not unlike that between intentional torts and those involving negligence or strict liability. In each case, the difference consists only in the nature of the defendant's state of mind, and not in the nature of the harm suffered by the plaintiff. It is for this reason that the "primary rights" theory recognizes only one cause of action for a single personal injury regardless of whether defendants' liability might be grounded on several tort theories. By analogy, the same principle is applicable here.

duty to alleviate de facto segregation. The right to desegregate is therefore greater under California law than under the Federal Constitution. . . . But the doctrine of res judicata, in California as elsewhere, not only bars the maintenance of the identical cause of action in a subsequent suit by the same parties. It also bars the maintenance of a subsequent action on any part of the original cause of action, even if that part was not litigated in the prior action. Restatement of Judgments § 62 (1942), cited with approval in *Mattson v. City of Costa Mesa*, 106 Cal. App. 3d at 449. Similarly, a plaintiff with a claim supported by both state and federal law may not bring separate actions on each ground; the first action precludes the second if the first court had jurisdiction to adjudicate both grounds.

Res judicata claim preclusion does not, of course, bar plaintiffs from litigating matters that were not within the scope of the claim litigated in *Crawford*. The *Crawford* claim necessarily included all segregative acts of the District occurring prior to commencement of the *Crawford* litigation in August 1963. The stipulation of the parties, accepted by the trial court, extended the scope of the claim to cover the period from 1963 to the time of trial. The trial court considered the effects of School District inaction up to the end of the trial, and the California Supreme Court in affirming in *Crawford I*, characterized the trial court's findings and conclusions as covering the "relevant time period—which ran through the conclusion of the trial in May 1969." We conclude, therefore, that segregative acts occurring before the close of the *Crawford* trial of the merits on May 2, 1969 fall within the bar of res judicata.

It has been argued, and the three judge panel of this court held, that the bar of the *Crawford* litigation must extend to all segregative acts occurring prior to September 10, 1981, the date that [the] trial court terminated the litigation on the merits and discharged the writ of mandate. We reject that position. The scope of litigation is framed by the complaint at the time it is filed. The rule that a judgment is conclusive as to every matter that might have been litigated "does not apply to new rights acquired pending the action which might have been, but which were not, required to be litigated." *Kettelle v. Kettelle*, 110 Cal. App. 310, 312 (1930). Plaintiffs may bring events occurring after the filing of the complaint into the scope of the litigation by filing a supplemental complaint with leave of court, Cal. Civ. Proc. Code § 464, but there is no requirement that plaintiffs do so. The stipulation of the parties that permitted the court to consider events occurring from 1963 to the time of trial was clearly intended to operate as a supplemental pleading, but it specified that "[t]he rights of petitioners, if any, and the duties of respondent, if any, shall be determined as of the time of trial." It therefore cannot have extended the durational scope of the litigation past the close of trial of the merits on May 2, 1969—the date that the California Supreme Court stated to be the end of the period relevant to the trial court's findings and conclusions.

If the *Crawford* plaintiffs had actually litigated the liability of the District for segregative acts occurring after May 2, 1969, then the res judicata bar would have to expand to encompass those events and others that might have been litigated with them. The record indicates, however, that the *Crawford* plaintiffs did not so open the litigation to later events. Judge Gitelson entered his findings and conclusions on May 12, 1970. The California Supreme Court affirmed on June 28, 1976 (*Crawford I*). The case was then remanded for the adoption and approval of a desegregation plan. All further proceedings were concerned entirely with the appropriateness and legality of various Board plans, before and after passage of Proposition I. . . .

The order of the district court denying claim preclusive effect to the *Crawford* judgment is REVERSED. The case is REMANDED to the district court for further proceedings consistent with this opinion.

[Concurring and dissenting opinions are omitted.]

NOTES AND QUESTIONS

1. *Identifying the "claims."*   Clearly, both *Crawford* and *Los Angeles Branch NAACP* involved challenges to racial segregation in the Los Angeles Unified School District. From the perspective of claim preclusion, the question was whether this coincidence of concern translated into the same claim. To appreciate why the Ninth Circuit held that it did (at least within a specified time frame), it is necessary to understand precisely what transpired in the *Crawford* proceedings. Although there were multiple opinions in *Crawford* as well as various interim decisions, it all boiled down to one final judgment that encapsulated the basic claim being pursued and resolved. Can you describe that claim? Having done that, the next step is to determine what the parties in *Los Angeles Branch NAACP* were asking the federal court to decide. What was their claim? Without applying any "tests," ask yourself how these claims resemble one another and how they differ. Essentially, the court held that the resemblance was more significant than any differences.

2. *The "sameness" of the claims.*   The court in *Los Angeles Branch NAACP* gave two reasons for finding that the two suits involved the same claim. What were those reasons? (*Hint:* The first pertained to what actually transpired in the *Crawford* case and the second pertained to the appropriate measure of sameness.) Can you construct an argument that the right asserted in *Crawford* under the California Constitution involves a different primary right than the right asserted by the plaintiffs in *Los Angeles Branch NAACP* under the Fourteenth Amendment Equal Protection Clause? In other words, how might you argue that each case involves the injury of a distinct interest? Suppose the court had applied the transactional test. Would application of that test have led to a different result?

A NOTE ON CONTINUING CONDUCT

From a temporal perspective, a claim is usually said to include only those events occurring prior to the commencement of litigation. Events occurring after this date give rise to separate claims. *See, e.g., Legnani v. Alitalia Linee Aeree Italiane, S.P.A.*, 400 F.3d 139 (2d Cir. 2005) (finding plaintiff's retaliatory discharge claim not part of a previously filed employment discrimination claim against the same employer since the discharge took place after the employment discrimination suit had been filed). *See generally* 18 MOORE'S FEDERAL PRACTICE, *supra*, § 131.23[3][c]. This general rule can be altered if the initial litigation actually embraced a wider temporal sphere. In *Los Angeles Branch NAACP*, for example, the Ninth Circuit enlarged the presumptive scope of the claim that had been litigated in *Crawford* by extending that scope through the close of trial. This extension was premised on the parties' earlier stipulation that the *Crawford* trial court could consider all "activities of the defendants . . . to the time of trial." *Los Angeles Branch NAACP*, 750 F.2d at 734.

A similar extension may be implied when judgment is entered by agreement of the parties. In such cases, the scope of the claim may be deemed to reach past the date of filing up through the date the settlement judgment is entered. However, events occurring after that date will normally give rise to a new claim that is not precluded by the earlier judgment. For example, in *Lawlor v. National Screen Service Corp.*, 349 U.S. 322 (1955), the plaintiff sued the defendant in federal court in 1949 for engaging in certain monopolistic practices. The district court dismissed the action on the basis of claim preclusion, for in 1942 the plaintiff had filed a similar antitrust suit against the same defendant asserting similar allegations of monopolistic practices. The earlier suit was settled and dismissed with prejudice in 1943. Although the allegations in the 1949 suit were similar to the earlier allegations, because they involved activity that occurred after the 1943 settlement judgment was entered, the Supreme Court held that the new allegations were not part of the original claim or cause of action.

> That both suits involved "essentially the same course of wrongful conduct" is not decisive. Such a course of conduct—for example, an abatable nuisance—may frequently give rise to more than a single cause of action. And so it is here. The conduct presently complained of was all subsequent to the 1943 judgment. . . . While the 1943 judgment precludes recovery on claims arising prior to its entry, it cannot be given the effect of extinguishing claims which did not even then exist and which could not possibly have been sued upon in the previous case.

Id. at 327-328. The district court's judgment dismissing the plaintiff's 1949 action on claim-preclusion grounds was accordingly reversed. *See also Frank v. United Airlines, Inc.*, 216 F.3d 845, 851 (9th Cir. 2000), *cert. denied*, 532 U.S. 914 (2001) (holding that a 1979 settlement judgment for defendant in a class action alleging that airline's weight policy violated female employees' rights under Title VII of the 1964 Civil Rights had no claim-preclusive effect in later action by same class of employees challenging airline's weight policy as implemented after 1980).

Although these general rules are easy to state, there are some conceptual problems. One arises in the context of nuisance actions in which the wrongful conduct continues after the commencement of litigation and sometimes even after the entry of judgment. The question is whether the nuisance should be treated as temporary or permanent. If temporary, the initial claim will cover only that wrongful activity that preceded the lawsuit's commencement; activity of a similar nature that occurs after that date will give rise to a separate claim. If the nuisance is deemed permanent, however, the initial claim will preclude any further relief against the defendant. The problem is that it is not always clear whether a nuisance will be deemed temporary or permanent. The Restatement solves this problem by giving the plaintiff an option: "[I]n a case involving a continuing or recurrent wrong, the plaintiff is given an option to sue once for the total harm, both past and prospective, or to sue from time to time for the damages incurred to the date of suit. . . ." RESTATEMENT, *supra*, § 26(1)(e) & comment h.

A similar issue may arise in the context of contracts that impose continuing obligations. Consistent with the general rule noted above, the claim in a breach-of-contract suit usually includes only those breaches occurring prior to the commencement of litigation. If the breach is deemed "entire" or "material," however, some jurisdictions require the plaintiff to sue for all past and future damages in a single proceeding. In essence, the contract merges with the initial claim, dissolving any future obligations under the contract. *See Jones v. Morris Plan Bank of Portsmouth*, 191 S.E. 608 (Va. 1937). Yet, as with temporary and permanent nuisances, the question of whether a breach is material is not always self-evident. Under the Restatement, therefore, even if a breach is deemed material, the plaintiff has the option of treating the breach as "partial" and suing for only those damages accrued as of the suit's commencement. But if the plaintiff does sue for past *and prospective* damages, *i.e.*, treats the breach as material, it will preclude future litigation on the contract. RESTATEMENT, *supra*, § 26 comment g.

PROBLEMS

13-1. In 1992, the Post-Modern School of Law ("PMSL") filed an application for accreditation with the American Bar Association ("ABA"). Shortly thereafter, an ABA team visited PMSL's campus. The site-visit team recommended that the ABA deny accreditation because PMSL was not in compliance with numerous ABA standards, including those relating to student-faculty ratio, use of part-time instructors, faculty salaries, faculty teaching hours, library facilities, and use of standardized tests as a measure of potential success in law school. In 1993, PMSL brought an antitrust suit against the ABA, claiming that the ABA standards were anticompetitive in violation of the Sherman Act. Eventually, the antitrust suit was dismissed with prejudice. While that case was pending, however, PMSL filed a second suit against the ABA, alleging that the denial of accreditation amounted to a tortious interference with PMSL's business. Should PMSL be permitted to proceed with the second suit? Apply both transactional and primary-rights models. *See Massachusetts Sch. of Law v. American Bar Ass'n*, 142 F.3d 26 (1st Cir. 1998).

13-2. Maharaj and Security Bank founded a corporation named IQ, the purpose of which was to provide investment advice using quantitative methods and proprietary software developed by Maharaj. The bank owned 80 percent of the shares in IQ, with the remaining 20 percent owned by Maharaj. Once the corporation was formed, Maharaj was elected as a director, and was named president and CEO pursuant to a five-year employment agreement with the bank.

After one year, however, the bank terminated Maharaj's employment for failure to abide by the bank's code of conduct. Maharaj commenced a civil suit against the bank seeking damages for breach of the employment agreement. The case proceeded to trial before a jury that returned a verdict in Maharaj's favor, awarding him $390,000. After the complaint in the initial action was filed but before the case had gone to trial, the bank dissolved IQ by filing a certificate of dissolution. The certificate falsely stated that the dissolution had been approved by IQ's "sole" shareholder, namely, the bank. Maharaj, who at that time was an IQ shareholder, was not given notice of the dissolution. Maharaj filed a second suit against the bank alleging three causes of action: failure to give notice of dissolution, conversion, and breach of the stockholders' agreement. Is this second suit precluded by the prior judgment? Apply both transactional and primary-rights models. *See Maharaj v. BankAmerica Corp.*, 128 F.3d 94 (2d Cir. 1997).

A NOTE ON INTERSYSTEM PRECLUSION

"Intersystem preclusion" refers to the application of claim and issue preclusion across jurisdictional lines. What happens, for example, when a court in State A renders a judgment and then in a subsequent case, a court in State B is required to determine that judgment's preclusive reach? The basic rule is that the second court must apply the law of preclusion that the court that first rendered judgment would apply. In other words, in our hypothetical, the court in State B must apply the same claim- and issue-preclusion principles that a State A court would apply had the second suit been filed in State A.

There are three scenarios under which the rules of intersystem preclusion might come into play: state-to-state; state-to-federal; and federal-to-state. We will consider each of these in turn.

State-to-State

Article IV, § 1 of the U.S. Constitution provides that "Full Faith and Credit shall be given in each State to the . . . judicial Proceedings of every other State." U.S. CONST. art. IV, § 1. In the context of state-to-state intersystem preclusion, this means that a state court judgment's preclusive scope must be measured by the law that would apply in the state in which that court sits. In other words, in the hypothetical described above, the State B courts must look to the law that a State A court would apply when attempting to ascertain a State A judgment's preclusive reach. Thus, if State A would follow a primary-rights approach, the State B courts must apply that same model in determining the prior State A judgment's preclusive effect. This remains true even if State B has specifically rejected the primary-rights model for its own judgments. In short, the law applicable in the jurisdiction in which judgment is first rendered determines the scope of claim and issue preclusion.

State-to-Federal

The Full Faith and Credit Clause does not, by its terms, apply to the federal government. However, 28 U.S.C. § 1738 imposes a statutory "full faith and credit" obligation on federal courts. Recall that in *Los Angeles Branch NAACP*, the federal court looked to California law to determine the preclusive scope of the judgment in the initial state court litigation. Therefore, instead of applying the federal transactional rule, the Ninth Circuit applied California's primary-rights theory. In "borrowing" California law, the court was guided by § 1738. In the context of claim and issue preclusion, this means that a federal court must give a prior state court judgment the same preclusive effect as would a court of the rendering state. In other words, the full-faith-and-credit obligation in state-to-federal preclusion is virtually identical to the full-faith-and-credit obligation imposed in state-to-state preclusion. In both circumstances, the applicable law of preclusion is that which would be followed by the jurisdiction in which the rendering state court sits.

Since the federal full-faith-and-credit obligation is statutory rather than constitutional, Congress can make statutory exceptions to the rule. Whether such an exception has been created presents a question of congressional intent, which will not be lightly assumed. For a discussion of this issue, including particular applications, see Susan Bandes, *Intersystem Preclusion, in* 18 MOORE'S FEDERAL PRACTICE §§ 133.31-133.32 (3d. ed. 2015).

Federal-to-State

Neither the Full Faith and Credit Clause nor § 1738 requires state courts to follow a federal court's prior judgment. However, by virtue of the Supremacy Clause, U.S. CONST. art. VI, cl. 2, and the inherent power of an Article III court to determine the scope of its own judgments, it is generally agreed that state courts, when considering the preclusive effect of a prior federal judgment, must adhere to the rules of preclusion that would be followed by that federal court. Again, we see the same pattern as was applied in state-to-state and state-to-federal preclusion: in essence, the rendering court determines the scope of its own judgment.

There is one wrinkle in the federal-to-state context. It is now agreed that if the initial federal judgment arises in a federal question case, the subsequent state court must follow federal rules of preclusion. *Semtek Int'l Inc. v. Lockheed Martin Corp.*, 531 U.S. 497, 507-508 (2001).* There has been some controversy, however, as to the correct approach when the rendering federal court was exercising

---

* Prior to the clarification in *Semtek*, courts often determined the preclusive effect of a prior federal court judgment in a federal question case by applying the preclusion rules of the state in which the federal court sat. In *Los Angeles Branch NAACP*, page 1144, *supra*, decided in 1985, the court in an omitted passage thus cited two cases in which the preclusive effect of prior California federal court judgments in federal question cases was determined by applying California's primary-rights model rather than the federal transactional approach.

diversity jurisdiction. Some commentators have argued that federal preclusion law should apply in this context as well, relying on an Article III court's inherent authority to determine the scope of its own judgments. *See* Ronan E. Degnan, *Federalized Res Judicata*, 85 YALE L.J. 741 (1976). Others have suggested that state law should control, *i.e.*, the second court should apply the rules of preclusion that would be applied by a court of the state in which the federal court sits, at least to the extent that the underlying substantive rights are products of state law. *See* Stephen B. Burbank, *Interjurisdictional Preclusion, Full Faith and Credit and Federal Common Law: A General Approach*, 71 CORNELL L. REV. 733 (1986). In essence, the latter position is based on an application of the *Erie* doctrine, under which rules of preclusion are treated as being substantive or "rules of decision" to the extent that they may affect the litigation's outcome. *See generally* RESTATEMENT, *supra*, § 87 comment b (seeming to endorse the latter approach); Chapter VI, part D.3, page 529, *supra*.

In *Semtek International Inc.*, *supra*, the Supreme Court may have resolved this controversy by adopting a middle-ground position. At issue in *Semtek* was the preclusive effect to be given a California federal court's dismissal of a diversity contract action for failure to file within the forum state's two-year statute of limitations, where the dismissal was designated by the federal court as being "on the merits." When a subsequent suit was then filed on the same claim but in a Maryland state court where the statute of limitations had not yet run, the question was whether the Maryland court had to apply the federal law of preclusion and thus dismiss the case, or whether it could rely instead on the law of the state in which the earlier federal court sat—*i.e.*, California—which might not preclude subsequent litigation in a state whose statute of limitations had not yet run.

The Supreme Court held that while a federal court judgment's preclusive effect is a matter of federal common law in both federal question and diversity cases, in the context of diversity, the content of that law will normally incorporate the forum state's preclusion laws, *i.e.*, the rules that a state court would apply in the state in which the federal court sits. The Court then tempered its holding by noting that "[t]his federal reference to state law will not obtain, of course, in situations in which the state law is incompatible with federal interests," such as a case in which the federal dismissal was imposed as a sanction for failure to comply with a discovery order. *Semtek Int'l Inc.*, 531 U.S. at 509. However, there being no such countervailing interest present in the case before it, the *Semtek* Court held that as a matter of federal law, the preclusive effect of the earlier federal dismissal must be determined by applying the initial forum state's preclusion law.*

---

* Under California law, a dismissal on statute of limitations grounds is not deemed to be on the merits for res judicata purposes. *See Koch v. Rodlin Enterprises, Inc.*, 223 Cal. App. 3d 1591 (Ct. App. 1990). On remand, the Maryland state court therefore ruled that despite the earlier California federal court dismissal, Semtek's action could proceed since Maryland's statute of limitations had not run at the time the suit was refiled there. *Semtek Int'l, Inc. v. Lockheed Martin Corp.*, 2002 WL 32500569, at *1-*2 (Md. Cir. Ct. Mar. 20, 2002).

Although *Semtek* involved a situation where the second action was filed in a state rather than a federal court, the Court's reasoning suggests that the same rule should apply where the second suit is brought in a federal court; otherwise, with respect to the second action, "filing in, or removing to, federal court would be encouraged by the divergent effects that the litigants would anticipate from likely grounds of dismissal." *Id.* at 509. While the lower federal courts are divided on the question, most have thus held that *Semtek* applies in successive federal court diversity actions. *See Hatch v. Trail King Industries, Inc.*, 699 F.3d 38, 44 & n.4 (1st Cir. 2012) (so ruling but noting circuit split).

The federal court of appeals decision in *Porn v. National Grange Mutual Insurance Co.*, page 1137, *supra*, was issued five years before the Supreme Court's decision in *Semtek*. In light of *Semtek*, would the analysis in *Porn* be any different if that case arose today?

PROBLEM

13-3. The front tire of Gabriel's motorcycle exploded while he was trying to navigate a sharp curve on a mountain road in California. The bike careened off the road, throwing him onto an embankment. Gabriel was able to walk away from the accident, but his bike was completely destroyed. He then filed a products liability suit against the tire manufacturer in a California state court seeking to recover for the loss of his bike. After a trial, judgment was entered for Gabriel. He subsequently filed a second suit against the tire manufacturer in a Florida state court, the manufacturer's place of incorporation, seeking damages for back injuries incurred as a result of the accident. Gabriel was unaware of these injuries at the time he filed his first suit. Assume that Florida has adopted the Restatement's definition of claim or cause of action. If the defendant in the Florida action files a motion to dismiss based on claim preclusion, what should the state court do? Explain why. How might your answer differ if the second case had been filed in a Florida federal court based on diversity? Would your answer be different if the first case had been filed in a California federal court and the second in a Florida state court?

2.   Final, Valid, and on the Merits

To have claim-preclusive effect, a judgment must be final, valid, and on the merits. We will briefly examine each of these requirements.

a.   Finality

A claim is final when a trial court has definitively ruled on it, *i.e.*, when all that remains for the court to do is assess costs or execute the judgment. In a majority of jurisdictions, this finality is not altered by the availability of an appeal or by the ability to file a motion to reconsider or vacate the judgment. This is true as to both claim and issue preclusion. In essence, the trial court's decision is the "final" decision until reversed or altered on appeal, or by its own reconsideration. If and when a new judgment is entered on appeal or on reconsideration, that judgment then becomes the final judgment with full preclusive effect. RESTATEMENT § 27 comment o. In some jurisdictions, including federal courts, finality also requires that the judgment be entered on the court's docket.

The Restatement describes finality as follows: "[A] judgment will ordinarily be considered final . . . if it is not tentative, provisional, or contingent and represents the completion of all steps in the adjudication of the claim by the court, short of any steps by way of execution or enforcement that may be consequent upon the particular kind of adjudication." RESTATEMENT, *supra*, § 13 comment b. This is not a technical definition, but a pragmatic one designed to ensure that the initial trial court's adjudication of the claim is in fact complete. Thus a decision imposing liability but not assessing the amount of damages is not final since "all steps in the adjudication of the claim" have not yet been completed. *Id.* On the other hand, a decision entering an injunction is final even though the court retains supervisory authority over the enjoined party, for the adjudication is complete; all that remains for the court to do is to oversee the injunction's enforcement.

Federated Department Stores, Inc. v. Moitie

452 U.S. 394 (1981)

JUSTICE REHNQUIST delivered the opinion of the Court.

The only question presented in this case is whether the Court of Appeals for the Ninth Circuit validly created an exception to the doctrine of res judicata. The court held that res judicata does not bar relitigation of an unappealed adverse judgment where, as here, other plaintiffs in similar actions against common defendants successfully appeal the judgments against them. We disagree with the view taken by the Court of Appeals for the Ninth Circuit and reverse.

I

In 1976 the United States brought an antitrust action against petitioners, owners of various department stores, alleging that they had violated § 1 of the Sherman Act, 15 U.S.C. § 1, by agreeing to fix the retail price of women's clothing sold in northern California. Seven parallel civil actions were subsequently filed by private plaintiffs seeking treble damages on behalf of proposed classes of retail purchasers, including that of respondent Moitie in state court (*Moitie I*) and respondent Brown (*Brown I*) in the United States District Court for the Northern District of California. Each of these complaints tracked almost verbatim the allegations of the Government's complaint, though the *Moitie I* complaint referred solely to state law. All of the actions originally filed in the District Court were assigned to a single federal judge, and the *Moitie I* case was removed there on the basis of diversity of citizenship and federal-question jurisdiction. The District Court dismissed all of the actions "in their entirety" on the ground that plaintiffs had not alleged an "injury" to their "business or property" within the meaning of § 4 of the Clayton Act, 15 U.S.C. § 15.

Plaintiffs in five of the suits appealed that judgment to the Court of Appeals for the Ninth Circuit. The single counsel representing Moitie and Brown, however, chose not to appeal and instead refiled the two actions in state court, *Moitie II* and *Brown II.* Although the complaints purported to raise only state-law claims, they made allegations similar to those made in the prior complaints, including that of the Government. Petitioners removed these new actions to the District Court for the Northern District of California and moved to have them dismissed on the ground of res judicata. In a decision rendered July 8, 1977, the District Court first denied respondents' motion to remand. It held that the complaints, though artfully couched in terms of state law, were "in many respects identical" with the prior complaints, and were thus properly removed to federal court because they raised "essentially federal law" claims. The court then concluded that because *Moitie II* and *Brown II* involved the "same parties, the same alleged offenses, and the same time periods" as *Moitie I* and *Brown I,* the doctrine of res judicata required that they be dismissed. This time, Moitie and Brown appealed.

Pending that appeal, this Court on June 11, 1979, decided *Reiter v. Sonotone Corp.,* 442 U.S. 330, holding that retail purchasers can suffer an "injury" to their "business or property" as those terms are used in § 4 of the Clayton Act. On June 25, 1979, the Court of Appeals for the Ninth Circuit reversed and remanded the five cases which had been decided with *Moitie I* and *Brown I,* the cases that had been appealed, for further proceedings in light of *Reiter.*

When *Moitie II* and *Brown II* finally came before the Court of Appeals for the Ninth Circuit, the court reversed the decision of the District Court dismissing the cases. Though the court recognized that a "strict application of the doctrine of *res judicata* would preclude our review of the instant decision," it refused to apply the doctrine to the facts of this case. It observed that the other five litigants in the *Weinberg* cases had successfully appealed the decision against them. It then asserted that "non-appealing parties may benefit from a reversal when their position is closely interwoven with that of appealing parties," and concluded that "[b]ecause the instant dismissal rested on a case that has been effectively overruled," the doctrine of res judicata must give way to "public policy" and "simple justice." We granted certiorari, to consider the validity of the Court of Appeals' novel exception to the doctrine of res judicata.

II

There is little to be added to the doctrine of res judicata as developed in the case law of this Court. A final judgment on the merits of an action precludes the parties or their privies from relitigating issues that were or could have been raised in that action. Nor are the res judicata consequences of a final, unappealed judgment on the merits altered by the fact that the judgment may have been wrong or rested on a legal principle subsequently overruled in another case. As this Court explained in *Baltimore S.S. Co. v. Phillips*, 274 U.S. 316, 325 (1927), an "erroneous conclusion" reached by the court in the first suit does not deprive the defendants in the second action "of their right to rely upon the plea of *res judicata*. . . . A judgment merely voidable because based upon an erroneous view of the law is not open to collateral attack, but can be corrected only by a direct review and not by bringing another action upon the same cause [of action]." We have observed that "[t]he indulgence of a contrary view would result in creating elements of uncertainty and confusion and in undermining the conclusive character of judgments, consequences which it was the very purpose of the doctrine of *res judicata* to avert." *Reed v. Allen*, 286 U.S. 191, 201 (1932).

In this case, the Court of Appeals conceded that the "strict application of the doctrine of *res judicata*" required that *Brown II* be dismissed. By that, the court presumably meant that the "technical elements" of res judicata had been satisfied, namely, that the decision in *Brown I* was a final judgment on the merits and involved the same claims and the same parties as *Brown II*. The court, however, declined to dismiss *Brown II* because, in its view, it would be unfair to bar respondents from relitigating a claim so "closely interwoven" with that of the successfully appealing parties. We believe that such an unprecedented departure from accepted principles of res judicata is unwarranted. Indeed, the decision below is all but foreclosed by our prior case law.

In *Reed v. Allen, supra*, this Court addressed the issue presented here. The case involved a dispute over the rights to property left in a will. A won an interpleader action for rents derived from the property and, while an appeal was pending, brought an ejectment action against the rival claimant B. On the basis of the decree in the interpleader suit A won the ejectment action. B did not appeal this judgment, but prevailed on his earlier appeal from the interpleader decree and was awarded the rents which had been collected. When B sought to bring an ejectment action against A, the latter pleaded res judicata, based on his previous successful ejectment action. This Court held that res judicata was available as a defense and that the property belonged to A:

> "The judgment in the ejectment action was final and not open to assault collaterally, but subject to impeachment only through some form of direct attack. The appellate court was limited to a review of the interpleader decree; and it is hardly necessary to say that jurisdiction to review one judgment gives an appellate court no power to reverse or modify another and independent judgment. If respondent, in addition to appealing from the [interpleader] decree, had appealed from the [ejectment] judgment, the appellate court, having both cases before it, might have afforded a remedy. . . . But this course respondent neglected to follow." Id., at 198.

This Court's rigorous application of res judicata in *Reed*, to the point of leaving one party in possession and the other party entitled to the rents, makes clear that this Court recognizes no general equitable doctrine, such as that suggested by the Court of Appeals, which countenances an exception to the finality of a party's failure to appeal merely because his rights are "closely interwoven" with those of another party. Indeed, this case presents even more compelling reasons to apply the doctrine of res judicata than did *Reed*. Respondents here seek to be the windfall beneficiaries of an appellate reversal procured by other independent parties, who have no interest in respondents' case, not a reversal in interrelated cases procured, as in *Reed*, by the same affected party. Moreover, in contrast to *Reed*, where it was unclear why no appeal was taken, it is apparent that respondents here made a calculated choice to forgo their appeals.

The Court of Appeals also rested its opinion in part on what it viewed as "simple justice." But we do not see the grave injustice which would be done by the application of accepted principles of res judicata. "Simple justice" is achieved when a complex body of law developed over a period of years is evenhandedly applied. The doctrine of res judicata serves vital public interests beyond any individual judge's ad hoc determination of the equities in a particular case. There is simply "no principle of law or equity which sanctions the rejection by a federal court of the salutary principle of *res judicata*." *Heiser v. Woodruff*, 327 U.S. 726, 733 (1946). The Court of Appeals' reliance on "public policy" is similarly misplaced. This Court has long recognized that "[p]ublic policy dictates that there be an end of litigation; that those who have contested an issue shall be bound by the result of the contest, and that matters once tried shall be considered forever settled as between the parties." *Baldwin v. Traveling Men's Assn.*, 283 U.S. 522, 525 (1931). We have stressed that "[the] doctrine of *res judicata* is not a mere matter of practice or procedure inherited from a more technical time than ours. It is a rule of fundamental and substantial justice, 'of public policy and of private peace,' which should be cordially regarded and enforced by the courts. . . ." *Hart Steel Co. v. Railroad Supply Co.*, 244 U.S. 294, 299 (1917). The language used by this Court half a century ago is even more compelling in view of today's crowded dockets:

> "The predicament in which respondent finds himself is of his own making. . . . [W]e cannot be expected, for his sole relief, to upset the general and well-established doctrine of *res judicata*, conceived in the light of the maxim that the interest of the state requires that there be an end to litigation—a maxim which comports with common sense as well as public policy. And the mischief which would follow the establishment of precedent for so disregarding this salutary doctrine against prolonging strife would be greater than the benefit which would result from relieving some case of individual hardship." *Reed v. Allen*, 286 U.S., at 198-199. . . .

. . . *Brown I* is res judicata as to respondents' federal-law claims. Accordingly, the judgment of the Court of Appeals is reversed, and the cause is remanded for proceedings consistent with this opinion.

It is so ordered.

[The concurring opinion of JUSTICES BLACKMUN and MARSHALL, and the dissenting opinion of JUSTICE BRENNAN, are omitted.]

NOTES AND QUESTIONS

1. Finality and appellate review.   We have already noted that a federal court judgment is final for purposes of preclusion, both as to claims and issues, even while an appeal of that judgment is either available or pending. *See* 18A CHARLES ALAN WRIGHT, ARTHUR R. MILLER & EDWARD H. COOPER, FEDERAL PRACTICE AND PROCEDURE § 4433 (2d ed. 2002 & Supp. 2015). If an appeal is taken and an appellate court renders a decision, that decision supersedes the trial court's decision for purposes of preclusion. When the appellate court affirms, this normally presents no difficulties. But if the appellate court reverses, there is a potential problem if, in the interim, a second court has given preclusive effect to the initial court's (now reversed) judgment. Under such circumstances, the second court's judgment is at best suspect, for it rests on a foundation that no longer exists. Yet that judgment will remain valid unless the parties or the second court take measures designed to ensure otherwise. They may accomplish this by "delaying further proceedings in the second action pending conclusion of the appeal in the first action, by a protective appeal in the second action that is held open pending determination of the appeal in the first action, or by direct action to vacate the second judgment." *Id.* at 89-90. In *Reed v. Allen*, discussed in *Moitie*, the parties failed to take any such protective or curative actions as to the second judgment. As a result, that judgment bound them despite the reversal of the first action on which it had been based.

A minority of states avoid this problem altogether by holding that a decision is not final for purposes of preclusion until the appellate process's completion. As the Virginia Supreme Court explained, "[T]he better rule, which we now adopt, is that a judgment is not final for the purposes of *res judicata* or collateral estoppel when it is being appealed or when the time limits fixed for perfecting the appeal have not yet expired." *Faison v. Hudson*, 417 S.E.2d 302, 305 (Va. 1992); *see also Nathanson v. Hecker*, 121 Cal. Rptr. 2d 773, 776 n.1 (Ct. App. 2002); 7 BERNARD E. WITKIN, CALIFORNIA PROCEDURE, JUDGMENT § 364 (5th ed. 2008). *Cf. Campbell v. Lake Hallowell Homeowners Ass'n*, 852 A.2d 1029, 1039-1041 (Md. App. 2004) (noting split of authority among the states and adopting majority rule that the pendency of an appeal does not affect the finality of a judgment). Which rule better promotes fairness and efficiency?

2. Strict application of the preclusion doctrine.   Do you agree with the *Moitie* Court's strict application of the preclusion doctrine? While the Court in *Moitie* suggested that there are no exceptions to the principle of res judicata as applied to federal court judgments, some lower federal courts have nevertheless suggested that as a matter of equity, an "occasional exception" may still be warranted "in instances of 'unusual hardship.'" *Porn*, 93 F.3d at 37, page 1143, *supra*. However, it is difficult to find cases in which a federal court was willing to conclude that a hardship exception was in fact warranted. State law is sometimes more flexible. *See Parker v. Lyons*, 757 F.3d 701, 706 (7th Cir. 2014) (noting that under Illinois law, claim preclusion "is an equitable doctrine that is not applied when it is 'fundamentally unfair to do so'" (internal citation omitted)). What would be the harm of building in some "equitable" flexibility? Or is it already there within the framework of the doctrine itself?

3. *Strict application of full faith and credit.* The *Moitie* Court's refusal to recognize an equitable exception to the doctrine of claim preclusion was mirrored in a more recent decision involving the scope of the full faith and credit statute, 28 U.S.C. § 1738. In *San Remo Hotel, L.P. v. City and County of San Francisco*, 545 U.S. 323 (2005), the owners of a hotel ("the Owners") raised a federal "takings" claim to a municipal ordinance that required them to pay a $567,000 fee for converting residential rooms into tourist rooms. They began their challenge in state court but then filed an action in a U.S. district court, claiming that the ordinance effected an unconstitutional taking of their property. The federal court dismissed their takings claim as "unripe" since the state had not yet refused to pay compensation for the alleged taking. (If a state pays just compensation for taking private property, there is no violation of the Takings Clause. In other words, the state can take so long as it pays.) The Owners then returned to state court, where they raised challenges to the ordinance under state takings law. The state courts rejected these claims, including the Owners' claim for compensation. The Owners then returned to federal court—their federal claim having now ripened—advancing a series of federal takings claims that depended on issues identical to those previously resolved in the state court proceedings. In order to avoid the application of issue preclusion, the Owners asked the federal court to exempt their federal takings claims from the reach of the full faith and credit statute, 28 U.S.C. § 1738. The Owners argued that since federal law had required them to exhaust their state remedies prior to filing a federal takings claim, the findings in the state proceeding should not be binding in the subsequent federal action. In essence, they argued that they were entitled to assert their federal takings claims in a federal forum, unburdened by the issues previously decided against them in state court. The Supreme Court, relying in part on *Moitie*, rejected the Owners' argument, reasoning that the interest in finality trumped the Owners' desire to litigate in a federal forum. Just as *Moitie* recognized no equitable exceptions to the doctrine of claim preclusion, the *San Remo* Court declined to recognize any exceptions to the operation of the full faith and credit statute.

PROBLEMS

13-4. A group of Mini-Market, Inc. ("Mini-Market") franchisees filed a class action lawsuit in California's Alameda Superior Court against Mini-Market, claiming that it had breached their franchise agreements by failing to share ratably in certain rebates provided to the company by vendors of products sold at retail by the franchisees. While that suit was pending, the plaintiffs discharged some of their original attorneys. Those attorneys then filed a separate breach-of-contract lawsuit in California's San Diego Superior Court against their former clients (the class action plaintiffs) and their former co-counsel, seeking their fair share of attorneys' fees. Eventually, the Alameda Superior Court approved a settlement of the class action, including an award of $4.75 million in attorneys' fees for class coun-sel—part of which were allocated to the discharged attorneys. After the Alameda Superior Court entered a final judgment on the class action settlement, some class members who objected to the settlement agreement, along with the discharged attorneys, appealed that judgment to the California Court of Appeals. While the appeal was pending, the defendants in the San Diego Superior Court proceeding moved to dismiss that suit on the basis of claim preclusion. Assuming that both cases involve the same claim for attorneys' fees due the discharged attorneys, was the Alameda Superior Court judgment final for claim preclusion purposes? *See Franklin & Franklin v. 7-Eleven Owners for Fair Franchising*, 102 Cal. Rptr. 2d 770 (Ct. App. 2000).

13-5. Rebecca filed a federal civil rights suit in a U.S. district court in New York against Ronald, a police officer from the City of Schenectady ("City"), New York. In her lawsuit, Rebecca claimed that Ronald had arrested her solely because she had rejected his personal advances. She further claimed that after arresting her, Ronald had choked her, slammed her against a wall, thrown her to the ground, and struck her while she lay defenseless on the floor. Before the trial, Ronald requested that the City defend and indemnify him against any judgment, but the City declined the request on the ground that Ronald had been acting beyond the scope of his employment. Ronald challenged this refusal in an action filed against the City in a New York state court. The state trial court ruled in favor of the City, and Ronald filed a timely appeal. In addition, Ronald filed a Rule 14 impleader claim for indemnification against the City in the federal proceeding. While the state appeal was pending, the federal civil rights action went to trial. After a trial on the merits, the U.S. district court entered a final judgment awarding Rebecca $1.6 million in compensatory and punitive damages but also upheld Ronald's state-law claim for indemnity from the City. The City has appealed, arguing that the ear-lier state court judgment on indemnification should have been given preclusive effect. Do you agree? What additional information, if any, do you need to answer this question? *See DiSorbo v. Hoy*, 343 F.3d 172 (2d Cir. 2003).

b.   Validity

A judgment is deemed valid if the defendant had proper notice, if the requi-sites of personal jurisdiction were satisfied, and if the rendering court had subject matter jurisdiction over the controversy. RESTATEMENT, *supra*, § 1 ("Requisites of a Valid Judgment"). As we know, however, a party can waive notice and personal jurisdiction if the party makes an appearance and fails to object in a timely fash-ion. Moreover, if an objection to notice or personal jurisdiction is raised, the initial court's resolution of that objection will not generally be subject to collateral attack. Indeed, collateral attack is available only to a party who either did not appear in the initial proceeding or who had no opportunity to raise an objection in that proceed-ing. *See* Chapters II and III, *supra*. Similarly, although subject matter jurisdiction may be challenged throughout the initial proceeding, including at the appellate stage of review, a court's subject matter jurisdiction may be collaterally attacked only under exceptional circumstances, the presumption being that the rendering court has properly decided the issue. *See* Chapter IV, part B.2, page 401, *supra*; *see also* RESTATEMENT, *supra*, § 12. Thus, although validity of a judgment is technically a requirement of claim preclusion, it is seldom a dispositive issue.

A judgment's validity can also be challenged on grounds of fraud, duress, or mistake. However, such challenges are typically addressed to the initial rendering court and not by way of collateral attack. *See, e.g.,* FED. R. CIV. P. 60(b). As a result, a court confronted with a claim-preclusion defense is unlikely to find that a prior judgment by another court was the product of fraud, duress, or mistake.

c. On the Merits

A final, valid judgment will have claim-preclusive effect only if the decision is "on the merits." The latter phrase, however, can be misleading. Every final judgment in favor of a plaintiff is on the merits, including defaults, summary judgments, and directed verdicts. From the perspective of judgments for a plaintiff, "on the merits" thus means simply that the plaintiff won. *See* RESTATEMENT, *supra*, § 18.

The on-the-merits nature of a judgment in favor of a defendant is more complicated. "The prototype case continues to be one in which the merits of the claim are in fact adjudicated against the plaintiff after trial of the substantive issues." RESTATEMENT, *supra*, § 19 comment a. Such a judgment is clearly on the merits and will have full preclusive effect. On the other hand, some judgments for defendants so clearly rest on nonsubstantive grounds—e.g., a dismissal for lack of personal jurisdiction or subject matter jurisdiction—that they will not be deemed on the merits, and claim preclusion will not apply to them. In between these two extremes there lies a range of defense judgments that may or may not be deemed to be on the merits.

Instead of attempting to fashion a definition of "on the merits" that captures the somewhat amorphous realm of defense judgments, the easiest way to understand the on-the-merits requirement's scope is to identify those defense judgments that will *not* have claim-preclusive effect. This is the approach that the Restatement § 20 adopts. Thus a judgment in favor of a defendant, although valid and final, will not trigger claim preclusion:

> (a) When the judgment is one of dismissal for lack of jurisdiction, for improper venue, or for nonjoinder or misjoinder of parties; or
> (b) When the plaintiff agrees to or elects a nonsuit (or voluntary dismissal) without prejudice or the court directs that the plaintiff be nonsuited (or that the action be otherwise dismissed) without prejudice; or
> (c) When by statute or rule of court the judgment does not operate as a bar to another action on the same claim, or does not so operate unless the court specifies, and no such specification is made.

RESTATEMENT, *supra*, § 20(1). Similarly,

[a] valid and final personal judgment for the defendant, which rests on the prematurity of the action or on the plaintiff's failure to satisfy a precondition to suit, does not bar another action by the plaintiff instituted after the claim has matured, or the precondition has been satisfied, unless a second action is precluded by operation of the substantive law.

Id. § 20(2).

Thus the question to ask with respect to any judgment in favor of a defendant is whether it is of a type specified in Restatement § 20, subsection (1), or whether it falls into the prematurity category described in subsection (2). By process of elimination, all other judgments in favor of a defendant are presumptively on the merits. Note, however, that as to subsection (1)(b) "nonsuits," a dismissal is in many jurisdictions, including federal courts, presumed to be with prejudice unless expressly provided to the contrary or unless the dismissal's nonprejudicial character appears clearly from the record. *See* FED. R. CIV. P. 41(b).

There is a peculiarity that arises in the context of dismissals for failure to satisfy an applicable statute of limitations. If, for example, State A would apply a one-year statute of limitations to a particular transaction and State B would apply a two-year statute to that same transaction, then a dismissal in State A for failure to satisfy its shorter statute of limitations will be deemed "with prejudice" or "on the merits" only in State A. The plaintiff, in other words, will be free to file her case in State B. On the other hand, if both State A and State B would apply the same statute of limitations, then a dismissal by a court in either state would bar further proceedings in both states. *See Semtek Int'l, Inc.*, 531 U.S. 497 (2001), discussed at page 1154, *supra; and see* footnote *, at page 1154, *supra.*

PROBLEMS

13-6. Monica filed a breach-of-contract claim against Carlyle, claiming that he failed to deliver clear title to a parcel of real property he had agreed to sell her. Because the complaint did not allege that the agreement was evidenced by a writing signed by Carlyle, as required by the statute of frauds, he moved to dismiss the complaint for failure to state a cause of action. His motion was granted and the case dismissed. Under the approach adopted by the Restatement, was this dismissal on the merits, *i.e.*, would it operate to bar any further action by Monica on this claim?

13-7. Waldo Woo sued Warren Wiggins for breach of contract in a State X court. The contract was to be performed in State Z. Warren decided to ignore the summons since he hadn't been to State X in several years and had no desire to return. After Warren's failure to appear, Waldo filed a motion for default judgment in the State X court. The court held a brief hearing at which Waldo testified under oath regarding the details of the contract and the alleged breach. The court then granted Waldo's motion. Sixty days later, by operation of law, the default became final, although under State X law Warren would still have one year to appear and contest the judgment. Instead of doing so, however, Warren filed an action against Waldo in a State Z court seeking a declaratory judgment that the contract had not been breached. Waldo has filed a motion for summary judgment in that action, arguing that the suit for declaratory relief is merely an effort to revisit the claim that was adjudicated in the State X action. For purposes of claim preclusion, was the State X judgment final, valid, and on the merits?

3.   Same Parties and Persons Who Should Be Treated as Such

If a claim is resolved in a final and valid judgment on the merits, the adverse parties on that claim are bound by the judgment. *See* RESTATEMENT § 34 (Parties to an Action). The claim is either merged in the judgment for the claimant or barred by a judgment for the defense. *See id.* §§ 18 & 19. In either case, further litigation between those parties is forever foreclosed on that claim. But can others be bound by or benefit from the judgment? The short answer is yes. While the general rule is that, as a matter of due process, only the parties to a case are bound by the judgment and only those bound by the judgment can benefit from it, there are exceptional circumstances where nonparties may also be subject to and benefit from a judgment's claim- or issue-preclusive effects. *See id.* §§ 39-61. The next principal case outlines and imposes limits on those circumstances.

Taylor v. Sturgell
553 U.S. 880 (2008)

JUSTICE GINSBURG delivered the opinion of the Court.

"It is a principle of general application in Anglo-American jurisprudence that one is not bound by a judgment *in personam* in a litigation in which he is not designated as a party or to which he has not been made a party by service of process." *Hansberry v. Lee*, 311 U.S. 32, 40 (1940). Several exceptions, recognized in this Court's decisions, temper this basic rule. . . . In this case, we consider for the first time whether there is a "virtual representation" exception to the general rule against precluding nonparties. Adopted by a number of courts, including the courts below in the case now before us, the exception so styled is broader than any we have so far approved.

The virtual representation question we examine in this opinion arises in the following context. Petitioner Brent Taylor filed a lawsuit under the Freedom of Information Act seeking certain documents from the Federal Aviation Administration [and its Acting Administrator, Robert Sturgell]. Greg Herrick, Taylor's friend, had previously brought an unsuccessful suit seeking the same records. The two men have no legal relationship, and there is no evidence that Taylor controlled, financed, participated in, or even had notice of Herrick's earlier suit. Nevertheless, the D.C. Circuit held Taylor's suit precluded by the judgment against Herrick because, in that court's assessment, Herrick qualified as Taylor's "virtual representative."

We disapprove the doctrine of preclusion by "virtual representation," and hold, based on the record as it now stands, that the judgment against Herrick does not bar Taylor from maintaining this suit.

I

The Freedom of Information Act (FOIA) accords "any person" a right to request any records held by a federal agency. . . .

The courts below held the instant FOIA suit barred by the judgment in earlier litigation seeking the same records. Because the lower courts' decisions turned on the connection between the two lawsuits, we begin with a full account of each action.

A

The first suit was filed by Greg Herrick, an antique aircraft enthusiast and the owner of an F-45 airplane, a vintage model manufactured by the Fairchild Engine and Airplane Corporation (FEAC) in the 1930's. In 1997, seeking information that would help him restore his plane to its original condition, Herrick filed a FOIA request asking the Federal Aviation Administration (FAA) for copies of any technical documents about the F-45 contained in the agency's records.

To gain a certificate authorizing the manufacture and sale of the F-45, FEAC had submitted to the FAA's predecessor, the Civil Aeronautics Authority, detailed specifications and other technical data about the plane. Hundreds of pages of documents produced by FEAC in the certification process remain in the FAA's records. The FAA denied Herrick's request, however, upon finding that the documents he sought are subject to FOIA's exemption for "trade secrets and commercial or financial information obtained from a person and privileged or confidential," 5 U.S.C. § 552(b)(4). In an administrative appeal, Herrick urged that FEAC and its successors had waived any trade-secret protection. The FAA thereupon contacted FEAC's corporate successor, respondent Fairchild Corporation ("Fairchild"). Because Fairchild objected to release of the documents, the agency adhered to its original decision.

Herrick then filed suit in the U.S. District Court for the District of Wyoming. Challenging the FAA's invocation of the trade-secret exemption, Herrick placed heavy weight on a 1955 letter from FEAC to the Civil Aeronautics Authority. The letter authorized the agency to lend any documents in its files to the public "for use in making repairs or replacement parts for aircraft produced by Fairchild." This broad authorization, Herrick maintained, showed that the F-45 certification records held by the FAA could not be regarded as "secre[t]" or "confidential" within the meaning of § 552(b)(4).

Rejecting Herrick's argument, the District Court granted summary judgment to the FAA. The 1955 letter, the court reasoned, did not deprive the F-45 certification documents of trade-secret status, for those documents were never in fact released pursuant to the letter's blanket authorization. The court also stated that even if the 1955 letter had waived trade-secret protection, Fairchild had successfully "reversed" the waiver by objecting to the FAA's release of the records to Herrick.

On appeal, the Tenth Circuit agreed with Herrick that the 1955 letter had stripped the requested documents of trade-secret protection. But the Court of Appeals upheld the District Court's alternative determination—*i.e.*, that Fairchild had restored trade-secret status by objecting to Herrick's FOIA request. On that ground, the appeals court affirmed the entry of summary judgment for the FAA.

In so ruling, the Tenth Circuit noted that Herrick had failed to challenge two suppositions underlying the District Court's decision. First, the District Court assumed trade-secret status could be "restored" to documents that had lost protection. Second, the District Court also assumed that Fairchild had regained trade-secret status for the documents even though the company claimed that status only *after* Herrick had initiated his request" for the F-45 records. The Court of Appeals expressed no opinion on the validity of these suppositions.

B

The Tenth Circuit's decision was issued on July 24, 2002. Less than a month later, on August 22, petitioner Brent Taylor—a friend of Herrick's and an antique aircraft enthusiast in his own right—submitted a FOIA request seeking the same documents Herrick had unsuccessfully sued to obtain. When the FAA failed to respond, Taylor filed a complaint [against the FAA and its Administrator] in the U.S. District Court for the District of Columbia. Like Herrick, Taylor argued that FEAC's 1955 letter had stripped the records of their trade-secret status. But Taylor also sought to litigate the two issues concerning recapture of protected status that Herrick had failed to raise in his appeal to the Tenth Circuit.

After Fairchild intervened as a defendant, the District Court in D.C. concluded that Taylor's suit was barred by claim preclusion; accordingly, it granted summary judgment to Fairchild and the FAA. The court acknowledged that Taylor was not a party to Herrick's suit. Relying on the Eighth Circuit's decision in *Tyus v. Schoemehl*, 93 F.3d 449 (1996), however, it held that a nonparty may be bound by a judgment if she was "virtually represented" by a party.

The Eighth Circuit's seven-factor test for virtual representation, adopted by the District Court in Taylor's case, requires an "identity of interests" between the person to be bound and a party to the judgment. Six additional factors counsel in favor of virtual representation under the Eighth Circuit's test, but are not prerequisites: (1) a "close relationship" between the present party and a party to the judgment alleged to be preclusive; (2) "participation in the prior litigation" by the present party; (3) the present party's "apparent acquiescence" to the preclusive effect of the judgment; (4) "deliberat[e] maneuver[ing]" to avoid the effect of the judgment; (5) adequate representation of the present party by a party to the prior adjudication; and (6) a suit raising a "public law" rather than a "private law" issue. These factors, the D.C. District Court observed, "constitute a fluid test with imprecise boundaries" and call for "a broad, case-by-case inquiry."

The record before the District Court in Taylor's suit revealed the following facts about the relationship between Taylor and Herrick: Taylor is the president of the Antique Aircraft Association, an organization to which Herrick belongs; the two men are "close associate[s]"; Herrick asked Taylor to help restore Herrick's F-45, though they had no contract or agreement for Taylor's participation in the restoration; Taylor was represented by the lawyer who represented Herrick in the earlier litigation; and Herrick apparently gave Taylor documents that Herrick had obtained from the FAA during discovery in his suit.

Fairchild and the FAA conceded that Taylor had not participated in Herrick's suit. The D.C. District Court determined, however, that Herrick ranked as Taylor's virtual representative because the facts fit each of the other six indicators on the Eighth Circuit's list. Accordingly, the District Court held Taylor's suit, seeking the same documents Herrick had requested, barred by the judgment against Herrick.

The D.C. Circuit affirmed [applying a slightly different standard]. . . .

We granted certiorari to resolve the disagreement among the Circuits over the permissibility and scope of preclusion based on "virtual representation."

II

The preclusive effect of a federal-court judgment is determined by federal common law. See *Semtek Int'l Inc. v. Lockheed Martin Corp.*, 531 U.S. 497, 507-508 (2001). . . . The federal common law of preclusion is, of course, subject to due process limitations. See *Richards v. Jefferson County*, 517 U.S. 793, 797 (1996).

Taylor's case presents an issue of first impression in this sense: Until now, we have never addressed the doctrine of "virtual representation" adopted (in varying forms) by several Circuits and relied upon by the courts below. Our inquiry, however, is guided by well-established precedent regarding the propriety of nonparty preclusion. . . .

A person who was not a party to a suit generally has not had a "full and fair opportunity to litigate" the claims and issues settled in that suit. The application of claim and issue preclusion to nonparties thus runs up against the "deep-rooted historic tradition that everyone should have his own day in court." *Richards*, 517 U.S., at 798. Indicating the strength of that tradition, we have often repeated the general rule that "one is not bound by a judgment *in personam* in a litigation in which he is not designated as a party or to which he has not been made a party by service of process." *Hansberry*, 311 U.S., at 40.

Though hardly in doubt, the rule against nonparty preclusion is subject to exceptions. For present purposes, the recognized exceptions can be grouped into six categories.

First, "[a] person who agrees to be bound by the determination of issues in an action between others is bound in accordance with the terms of his agreement." 1 Restatement (Second) of Judgments § 40, p. 390 (1980) (hereinafter Restatement). . . .

Second, nonparty preclusion may be justified based on a variety of pre-existing "substantive legal relationship[s]" between the person to be bound and a party to the judgment. Qualifying relationships include, but are not limited to, preceding and succeeding owners of property, bailee and bailor, and assignee and assignor. These exceptions originated "as much from the needs of property law as from the values of preclusion by judgment."[8]

Third, we have confirmed that, "in certain limited circumstances," a nonparty may be bound by a judgment because she was "adequately represented by someone with the same interests who [wa]s a party" to the suit. Representative suits with preclusive effect on nonparties include properly conducted class actions, and suits brought by trustees, guardians, and other fiduciaries.

Fourth, a nonparty is bound by a judgment if she "assume[d] control" over the litigation in which that judgment was rendered. . . .

Fifth, a party bound by a judgment may not avoid its preclusive force by relitigating through a proxy. Preclusion is thus in order when a person who did not participate in a litigation later brings suit as the designated representative of a person who was a party to the prior adjudication. . . .

Sixth, in certain circumstances a special statutory scheme may "expressly foreclos[e] successive litigation by nonlitigants . . . if the scheme is otherwise consistent with due process." Examples of such schemes include bankruptcy and probate proceedings, and *quo warranto* actions or other suits that, "under [the governing] law, [may] be brought only on behalf of the public at large," *Richards*, 517 U.S., at 804.

III

Reaching beyond these six established categories, some lower courts have recognized a "virtual representation" exception to the rule against nonparty preclusion. . . .

The D.C. Circuit, the FAA, and Fairchild have presented three arguments in support of an expansive doctrine of virtual representation. We find none of them persuasive.

A

The D.C. Circuit purported to ground its virtual representation doctrine in this Court's decisions stating that, in some circumstances, a person may be bound by a judgment if she was adequately represented by a party to the proceeding yielding that judgment. But the D.C. Circuit's definition of "adequate representation" strayed from the meaning our decisions have attributed to that term.

In *Richards*, we reviewed a decision by the Alabama Supreme Court holding that a challenge to a tax was barred by a judgment upholding the same tax in a suit

---

8. The substantive legal relationships justifying preclusion are sometimes collectively referred to as "privity." The term "privity," however, has also come to be used more broadly, as a way to express the conclusion that nonparty preclusion is appropriate on any ground. To ward off confusion, we avoid using the term "privity" in this opinion.

filed by different taxpayers. The plaintiffs in the first suit "did not sue on behalf of a class," their complaint "did not purport to assert any claim against or on behalf of any nonparties," and the judgment "did not purport to bind" nonparties. There was no indication, we emphasized, that the court in the first suit "took care to protect the interests" of absent parties, or that the parties to that litigation "understood their suit to be on behalf of absent [parties]." In these circumstances, we held, the application of claim preclusion was inconsistent with "the due process of law guaranteed by the Fourteenth Amendment."

The D.C. Circuit stated, without elaboration, that it did not "read *Richards* to hold a nonparty . . . adequately represented only if special procedures were followed [to protect the nonparty] or the party to the prior suit understood it was representing the nonparty." As the D.C. Circuit saw this case, Herrick adequately represented Taylor for two principal reasons: Herrick had a strong incentive to litigate; and Taylor later hired Herrick's lawyer, suggesting Taylor's "satisfaction with the attorney's performance in the prior case."

The D.C. Circuit misapprehended *Richards*. As just recounted, our holding that the Alabama Supreme Court's application of res judicata to nonparties violated due process turned on the lack of either special procedures to protect the nonparties' interests or an understanding by the concerned parties that the first suit was brought in a representative capacity. *Richards* thus established that representation is "adequate" for purposes of nonparty preclusion only if (at a minimum) one of these two circumstances is present.

We restated *Richards'* core holding in *South Central Bell Telephone Co. v. Alabama*, 526 U.S. 160 (1999). In that case, as in *Richards*, the Alabama courts had held that a judgment rejecting a challenge to a tax by one group of taxpayers barred a subsequent suit by a different taxpayer. In *South Central Bell*, however, the nonparty had notice of the original suit and engaged one of the lawyers earlier employed by the original plaintiffs. Under the D.C. Circuit's decision in Taylor's case, these factors apparently would have sufficed to establish adequate representation. Yet *South Central Bell* held that the application of res judicata in that case violated due process. Our inquiry came to an end when we determined that the original plaintiffs had not understood themselves to be acting in a representative capacity and that there had been no special procedures to safeguard the interests of absentees.

Our decisions recognizing that a nonparty may be bound by a judgment if she was adequately represented by a party to the earlier suit thus provide no support for the D.C. Circuit's broad theory of virtual representation.

B

Fairchild and the FAA do not argue that the D.C. Circuit's virtual representation doctrine fits within any of the recognized grounds for nonparty preclusion. Rather, they ask us to abandon the attempt to delineate discrete grounds and clear rules altogether. Preclusion is in order, they contend, whenever "the relationship between a party and a non-party is 'close enough' to bring the second litigant within the judgment." Courts should make the "close enough" determination, they urge, through a "heavily fact-driven" and "equitable" inquiry. Only this sort of diffuse balancing, Fairchild and the FAA argue, can account for all of the situations in which nonparty preclusion is appropriate.

We reject this argument for three reasons. First, our decisions emphasize the fundamental nature of the general rule that a litigant is not bound by a judgment to which she was not a party. Accordingly, we have endeavored to delineate discrete exceptions that apply in "limited circumstances." Respondents' amorphous balancing test is at odds with the constrained approach to nonparty preclusion our decisions advance. . . .

Our second reason for rejecting a broad doctrine of virtual representation rests on the limitations attending nonparty preclusion based on adequate representation. A party's representation of a nonparty is "adequate" for preclusion purposes only if, at a minimum: (1) the interests of the nonparty and her representative are aligned; and (2) either the party understood herself to be acting in a representative capacity or the original court took care to protect the interests of the nonparty. In addition, adequate representation sometimes requires (3) notice of the original suit to the persons alleged to have been represented. In the class-action context, these limitations are implemented by the procedural safeguards contained in Federal Rule of Civil Procedure 23.

An expansive doctrine of virtual representation, however, would "recogniz[e], in effect, a common-law kind of class action." That is, virtual representation would authorize preclusion based on identity of interests and some kind of relationship between parties and nonparties, shorn of the procedural protections prescribed in *Hansberry*, *Richards*, and Rule 23. These protections, grounded in due process, could be circumvented were we to approve a virtual representation doctrine that allowed courts to "create *de facto* class actions at will."

Third, a diffuse balancing approach to nonparty preclusion would likely create more headaches than it relieves. Most obviously, it could significantly complicate the task of district courts faced in the first instance with preclusion questions. An all-things-considered balancing approach might spark wide-ranging, time-consuming, and expensive discovery tracking factors potentially relevant under [multi]-prong tests. And after the relevant facts are established, district judges would be called upon to evaluate them under a standard that provides no firm guidance. Preclusion doctrine, it should be recalled, is intended to reduce the burden of litigation on courts and parties. "In this area of the law," we agree, " 'crisp rules with sharp corners' are preferable to a round-about doctrine of opaque standards."

C

Finally, . . . the FAA maintains that nonparty preclusion should apply more broadly in "public-law" litigation than in "private-law" controversies. To support this position, the FAA offers two arguments. First, the FAA urges, our decision in *Richards* acknowledges that, in certain cases, the plaintiff has a reduced interest in controlling the litigation "because of the public nature of the right at issue."

When a taxpayer challenges "an alleged misuse of public funds" or "other public action," we observed in *Richards*, the suit "has only an indirect impact on [the plaintiff's] interests." In actions of this character, the Court said, "we may assume that the States have wide latitude to establish procedures . . . to limit the number of judicial proceedings that may be entertained."

Taylor's FOIA action falls within the category described in *Richards*, the FAA contends, because "the duty to disclose under FOIA is owed to the public generally." The opening sentence of FOIA, it is true, states that agencies "shall make [information] available to the public." 5 U.S.C. § 552(a). Equally true, we have several times said that FOIA vindicates a "public" interest. The Act, however, instructs agencies receiving FOIA requests to make the information available not to the public at large, but rather to the "person" making the request. § 552(a)(3)(A). Thus, in contrast to the public-law litigation contemplated in *Richards*, a successful FOIA action results in a grant of relief to the individual plaintiff, not a decree benefiting the public at large.

Furthermore, we said in *Richards* only that, for the type of public-law claims there envisioned, States are free to adopt procedures limiting repetitive litigation. In this regard, we referred to instances in which the first judgment foreclosed successive litigation by other plaintiffs because, "under state law, [the suit] could be brought only on behalf of the public at large."[12] *Richards* spoke of state legislation, but it appears equally evident that *Congress*, in providing for actions vindicating a public interest, may "limit the number of judicial proceedings that may be entertained." It hardly follows, however, that *this Court* should proscribe or confine successive FOIA suits by different requesters. Indeed, Congress' provision for FOIA suits with no statutory constraint on successive actions counsels against judicial imposition of constraints through extraordinary application of the common law of preclusion.

The FAA next argues that "the threat of vexatious litigation is heightened" in public-law cases because "the number of plaintiffs with standing is potentially limitless." FOIA does allow "any person" whose request is denied to resort to federal court for review of the agency's determination. Thus it is theoretically possible that several persons could coordinate to mount a series of repetitive lawsuits.

But we are not convinced that this risk justifies departure from the usual rules governing nonparty preclusion. First, *stare decisis* will allow courts swiftly to dispose of repetitive suits brought in the same circuit. Second, even when *stare decisis* is not dispositive, "the human tendency not to waste money will deter the bringing of suits based on claims or issues that have already been adversely determined against others." This intuition seems to be borne out by experience: The FAA has not called our attention to any instances of abusive FOIA suits in the Circuits that reject the virtual representation theory respondents advocate here.

---

12. Nonparty preclusion in such cases ranks under the sixth exception described above: special statutory schemes that expressly limit subsequent suits.

IV

For the foregoing reasons, we disapprove the theory of virtual representation on which the decision below rested. The preclusive effects of a judgment in a federal-question case decided by a federal court should instead be determined according to the established grounds for nonparty preclusion described in this opinion.

Although references to "virtual representation" have proliferated in the lower courts, our decision is unlikely to occasion any great shift in actual practice. Many opinions use the term "virtual representation" in reaching results at least arguably defensible on established grounds. In these cases, dropping the "virtual representation" label would lead to clearer analysis with little, if any, change in outcomes.

In some cases, however, lower courts have relied on virtual representation to extend nonparty preclusion beyond the latter doctrine's proper bounds. We now turn back to Taylor's action to determine whether his suit is such a case, or whether the result reached by the courts below can be justified on one of the recognized grounds for nonparty preclusion.

A

It is uncontested that four of the six grounds for nonparty preclusion have no application here: There is no indication that Taylor agreed to be bound by Herrick's litigation, that Taylor and Herrick have any legal relationship, that Taylor exercised any control over Herrick's suit, or that this suit implicates any special statutory scheme limiting relitigation. Neither the FAA nor Fairchild contends otherwise.

It is equally clear that preclusion cannot be justified on the theory that Taylor was adequately represented in Herrick's suit. Nothing in the record indicates that Herrick understood himself to be suing on Taylor's behalf, that Taylor even knew of Herrick's suit, or that the Wyoming District Court took special care to protect Taylor's interests. Under our pathmarking precedent, therefore, Herrick's representation was not "adequate." See *Richards*, 517 U.S., at 801-802.

That leaves only the fifth category: preclusion because a nonparty to an earlier litigation has brought suit as a representative or agent of a party who is bound by the prior adjudication. Taylor is not Herrick's legal representative and he has not purported to sue in a representative capacity. He concedes, however, that preclusion would be appropriate if respondents could demonstrate that he is acting as Herrick's "undisclosed agen[t]."

Respondents argue here, as they did below, that Taylor's suit is a collusive attempt to relitigate Herrick's action. The D.C. Circuit considered a similar question in addressing the "tactical maneuvering" prong of its virtual representation test. The Court of Appeals did not, however, treat the issue as one of agency, and it expressly declined to reach any definitive conclusions due to "the ambiguity of the facts." We therefore remand to give the courts below an opportunity to determine whether Taylor, in pursuing the instant FOIA suit, is acting as Herrick's agent. . . .

We have never defined the showing required to establish that a nonparty to a prior adjudication has become a litigating agent for a party to the earlier case.

Because the issue has not been briefed in any detail, we do not discuss the matter elaboratively here. We note, however, that courts should be cautious about finding preclusion on this basis. A mere whiff of "tactical maneuvering" will not suffice; instead, principles of agency law are suggestive. They indicate that preclusion is appropriate only if the putative agent's conduct of the suit is subject to the control of the party who is bound by the prior adjudication.

B

On remand, Fairchild suggests, Taylor should bear the burden of proving he is not acting as Herrick's agent. When a defendant points to evidence establishing a close relationship between successive litigants, Fairchild maintains, "the burden [should] shif[t] to the second litigant to submit evidence refuting the charge" of agency. Fairchild justifies this proposed burden-shift on the ground that "it is unlikely an opposing party will have access to direct evidence of collusion."

We reject Fairchild's suggestion. Claim preclusion, like issue preclusion, is an affirmative defense. Ordinarily, it is incumbent on the defendant to plead and prove such a defense, and we have never recognized claim preclusion as an exception to that general rule. We acknowledge that direct evidence justifying nonparty preclusion is often in the hands of plaintiffs rather than defendants. But "[v]ery often one must plead and prove matters as to which his adversary has superior access to the proof." In these situations, targeted interrogatories or deposition questions can reduce the information disparity. We see no greater cause here than in other matters of affirmative defense to disturb the traditional allocation of the proof burden.

* * *

For the reasons stated, the judgment of the United States Court of Appeals for the District of Columbia Circuit is vacated, and the case is remanded for further proceedings consistent with this opinion.

It is so ordered.

NOTES AND QUESTIONS

1. Six exceptions.   The Court listed six exceptions to the rule that a nonparty cannot be bound by a previous in personam judgment. The first listed exception, an agreement to be bound by the judgment, is not really an exception, but a form of voluntary waiver. In essence, the nonparty's enforceable agreement to be bound waives any potential objection to the application of preclusion against her. *See* RESTATEMENT § 40. Does due process typically permit a voluntary waiver of rights? Under what circumstances might the enforcement of such a waiver violate due process?

The second exception is premised on a preexisting substantive relationship between a party and a nonparty. This exception covers the classic "privity" relationships arising out of the law of property. For example, courts have long recognized that privity exists between successive owners of real or personal property. Suppose A conveys Topeacre to B. Prior to the conveyance, A had been involved in a lawsuit with C, who claimed an easement over Topeacre. Judgment was for A. If C now sues B on the same claim to establish that same easement, B will be allowed to use the prior judgment to preclude C's claim, there being privity between A and B. In other words, B may benefit from the prior judgment for A. Similarly, if the first judgment had been for C, thereby establishing the easement, B would be burdened or bound by that judgment to the same extent as A had been. Under both circumstances, B's privity relationship with A permits a subsequent court to treat B as if B had been a party to the previous action. *See id.* §§ 43-44. Recognition of this privity relationship comports with the basic principle of property law that a conveyance of property carries both the benefits and burdens of the prior owner's title. A similar rule applies when the rights and responsibilities of the party and nonparty are substantively intertwined, as in the relationships of employer and employee, bailor and bailee, indemnitor and indemnitee, etc. *See id.* §§ 45-61.

The third exception involves cases in which a nonparty's interests are represented by a party to the action. This might occur when a trustee represents the interests of a trust beneficiary; so too with respect to executors, administrators, guardians, conservators, or similar fiduciaries and their respective beneficiaries. In addition, a government official or agency may sometimes have authority to represent a nonparty's interests or the interests of the public in general. So too the representative of a class of similarly situated persons who has been designated as such with court approval may represent the interests of nonparties who are members of that class. In all such circumstances, the nonparty "is bound by and entitled to the benefits of a judgment as though he were a party." *Id.* § 41; *but see id.* § 42 (listing exceptions).

The fourth and fifth exceptions—control and agency—are most easily understood as variations on the representational theme. In both cases, the named party litigates as the proxy representative of the nonparty. *Id.* § 39; *see also Montana v. United States*, 440 U.S. 147 (1979) (holding United States bound by prior judgment when it controlled prior litigation by a private contractor).

Finally, the sixth exception encompasses a narrow category of true in rem proceedings in which "all the world" is bound by the prior judgment. One might argue that there are no "nonparties" to such in rem proceedings.

Presumably, virtual representation is something distinct from each of these six exceptions. It seems most like the third exception, which is premised on the representational relationship between a party and a nonparty. How would a virtual relationship differ from the relationship between, for example, a trustee and a beneficiary or a class representative and the members of a designated class? In the virtual-representation setting, is there any comparable judicial oversight to ensure that nonparties' interests are in fact being protected? In other words, why wasn't the Court willing to expand this third exception to embrace virtual representation?

2. *The proceedings on remand.*   Why did the Supreme Court remand the case? Was the issue that still needed to be resolved one that involved virtual representation, or was it a question of whether the case might fall into one of the six recognized grounds for nonparty preclusion? Did the respondents, *i.e.*, the FAA and Fairchild Corp., suggest that if the burden of proof were placed on them, they could not make the requisite showing to allow nonparty preclusion? Might that explain why, on remand, the defendants abandoned their argument that Taylor was acting as Herrick's agent and, with it, their contention that claim preclusion barred Taylor's suit? *See Taylor v. Babbitt*, 673 F. Supp. 2d 20, 23 n.1 (D.D.C. 2009). The district court subsequently granted summary judgment for Taylor. *Taylor v. Babbitt*, 760 F. Supp. 2d 80 (D.D.C. 2011).

3. *The death knell for virtual representation?*   After the decision in *Taylor*, is there any room left under a doctrine of virtual representation that goes beyond the six specific exceptions recognized by the Court in that case? Does *Taylor* purport to establish precedent with respect to the binding effect of judgments of all courts in the United States, state as well as federal? Or does *Taylor* simply refine the federal common law of preclusion as it pertains to the binding effect of federal court judgments—and then only some of them? Whose law of preclusion usually determines the binding effect of federal court judgments in diversity cases? *See* "A Note on Intersystem Preclusion," at pages 1152-1155, *supra*.

The decision in *Taylor* thus leaves the states free to craft their own approaches to virtual representation—approaches that may be more expansive than what the Supreme Court was willing to recognize. As a result, "[s]ome state courts . . . have not altered their preclusion standards after *Taylor*." *Sierra Club v. Two Elk Generation Partners, Ltd. P'ship*, 646 F.3d 1258, 1267 (10th Cir. 2011). Might the Due Process Clause still place limits on how far a state can take the doctrine of virtual representation so as to bind nonparties to a suit? On the ability of states to fashion their own virtual-representation doctrine despite the Supreme Court's decision in *Taylor*, see, *e.g.*, *City of Chicago v. St. John's United Church of Christ*, 935 N.E.2d 1158 (Ill. App. Ct. 2010), *appeal denied*, 943 N.E.2d 1100 (Ill. 2011) (declining to follow *Taylor* and holding that relatives of parties to prior suit were bound on basis of virtual representation); *State ex rel. Schachter v. Ohio Public Employees Retirement Board*, 905 N.E.2d 1210, 1216-1218 (Ohio 2009) (declining to apply *Taylor* to extent it would prevent court from finding privity for claim-preclusion purposes). *See also Dolis v. Robert*, 2014 WL 7530158, at *4 (S.D. Ill. Dec. 8, 2014), *so ordered*, 2015 WL 159697 (S.D. Ill. Jan. 13, 2015) (under Illinois law of virtual representation, interests of defendants in current federal action and those of defendants in prior Illinois state court action "appear to be so closely aligned as to establish privity").

4. *Parties litigating in different capacities.* Not all persons who are named parties are subject to claim preclusion in the same fashion and under all circumstances. For example, a person who is named as a party in one legal capacity, *e.g.*, as an executor of an estate, will not be subject to claim preclusion as to other legal capacities she may hold, *e.g.*, as an individual, unless the substance of the initial case indicates that the party's participation in the litigation included those other

capacities as well. *See* RESTATEMENT, *supra*, § 36. In addition, not all parties are necessarily bound (or benefited) by every claim decided in an action. Rather, the burdens and benefits of claim preclusion apply only to those parties who were adversaries with one another on the claim at issue. Thus parties aligned on the same side of a claim, *e.g.*, co-defendants, may not use claim preclusion against one another unless they were adversaries on that claim by virtue of a cross-claim or the like. *Id.* § 38. Similarly, if a party's personal incapacity, *e.g.*, she is a minor or has been adjudged mentally incompetent, undermines the integrity of the adversarial process, the party will not be bound by the decision despite her technical presence in the suit. *Id.* § 35. The general rule, however, is that named parties are fully subject to the burdens and benefits of claim preclusion. *Id.* § 34.

PROBLEMS

13-8. Fleming fell into an excavation on a sidewalk that was being repaired by a contractor working for the City of Anderson ("the City"). She sued the contractor for negligence and a judgment was entered in favor of the contractor. She then sued the City on a theory of respondeat superior. The City was not a party to the first suit. Should the City be permitted to assert claim preclusion against Fleming? *See City of Anderson v. Fleming*, 67 N.E. 443 (Ind. 1903). Suppose that in the first suit the judgment had been for Fleming against the contractor. To what extent would either Fleming or the City be bound by that judgment in a subsequent suit by Fleming against the City? Now suppose the first suit was filed against the City, with a judgment for the City. Would Fleming be precluded from subsequently suing the contractor?

13-9. The MPA is a labor union that represents police officers in the City of Milwaukee ("the City"). It has filed a lawsuit against the City in Wisconsin state court, seeking an injunction that would require the City to promote qualified police officers in accord with the terms of a Wisconsin labor statute. In a previous suit filed in Wisconsin state court, 23 individual officers, all of whom were MPA members, sued the City for backpay and promotions, alleging that its policies violated the terms of a collective bargaining agreement between the MPA and the City. The MPA was not a party to that suit. After the trial court ruled against the 23 officers on both counts, the officers abandoned their promotion claims but successfully appealed their claims for damages. As a result, each officer received an award for backpay. The injunction sought by the MPA in the current action would include relief for all of the officers adversely affected by the promotion policy, including the 23 who were parties to the earlier suit. The City has moved for summary judgment, arguing that the MPA was in privity with the 23 officers in the first action and that the doctrine of claim preclusion therefore operates as a bar to the current proceeding.

  A. Should the court find that the MPA was in privity with the individual officers who filed and won the first action?

B. If the court finds there was no privity, can the City successfully invoke the doctrine of virtual representation?

C. Assuming there was either privity or virtual representation, can the MPA avoid claim preclusion by successfully arguing that the two suits do not involve the same claim?

D. If the MPA's suit had gone to judgment first, the court ruling in favor of the City, might the individual officers be bound by that judgment on the basis of either privity or virtual representation?

See Pasko v. City of Milwaukee, 643 N.W.2d 72 (Wis. 2002); *Monahan v. N.Y. City Dep't of Corr.*, 214 F.3d 275 (2d Cir.), *cert. denied*, 531 U.S. 1035 (2000).

13-10. Crystal is an 18-year-old exotic dancer who works at The Garter Belt, Inc. ("Garter Belt"), an adult lounge in Van Buren, Michigan. She has filed an action against the Township of Van Buren ("Van Buren") in a Michigan federal district court under 42 U.S.C. § 1983, alleging that Van Buren's Public Indecency Ordinance ("Ordinance"), which prohibits nudity in public establishments that serve alcohol, violates her First Amendment right to engage in expressive activity. Crystal seeks declaratory and injunctive relief and damages. Van Buren has moved for summary judgment on the ground of res judicata, citing *City of Van Buren v. Garter Belt*, a case decided by a Michigan county circuit court seven years ago. In that suit, Van Buren sought an injunction barring Garter Belt from violating the Ordinance. In response, Garter Belt filed an answer and a counterclaim seeking a declaration that the Ordinance was invalid because it prohibited expressive activity protected by the First Amendment. The state court rejected Garter Belt's claim, ruling that the Ordinance "is without constitutional or legal infirmity." After that decision was affirmed by Michigan's appellate courts, the U.S. Supreme Court denied certiorari. In the present § 1983 action, Van Buren contends that under Michigan law, the counterclaim Garter Belt filed in the prior state court suit, involving an identical constitutional challenge to the Ordinance, has claim-preclusive effect here and requires dismissal of Crystal's suit. Crystal objects that she had no knowledge of the earlier suit, that she was only 11 years old at the time, and that she is entitled to her day in court.

A. Though Crystal was not a party to *City of Van Buren v. Garter Belt*, does she fall within any of the six recognized exceptions to the rule against nonparty preclusion?

B. If Crystal does not fall within any of the recognized exceptions to that rule, since she filed this § 1983 action in federal court, can she rely on the Supreme Court's decision in *Taylor v. Sturgell* to defeat Van Buren's motion for summary judgment?

C. Would your answer to the prior question be any different if the *Garter Belt* lawsuit had been removed to and decided by a Michigan federal district court, rather than by a state court?

D. Would it violate Crystal's right to due process of law if the federal district court here allows Van Buren to invoke issue preclusion against Crystal and dismisses her case? What will each side argue on this question? How should the court rule, and why?

See Ludwig v. Township of Van Buren, 682 F.3d 457 (6th Cir. 2012).

13-11. In December 1999, 36 African-American employees of Pemco, a military airplane repair-and-maintenance facility, filed suit in an Alabama federal court against their employer, claiming that Pemco violated their civil rights by subjecting them to racial harassment and other forms of race discrimination ("Case I"). The suit was not brought as a class action. At the same time, the Equal Employment Opportunity Commission (EEOC), a federal agency, was investigating multiple charges of discrimination at Pemco, having uncovered possible evidence of nooses, racially inflammatory graffiti, racial slurs by co-workers and supervisors, and other disconcerting incidents of race-related conduct at Pemco's Alabama facilities. In September 2000, the EEOC brought its own federal court suit ("Case II") against Pemco under Title VII of the 1964 Civil Rights Act, alleging that Pemco subjected its more than 200 black employees to a racially hostile work environment. The EEOC sought injunctive relief and monetary compensation for all of the company's black employees. Case I was tried before a jury in June 2002. During that trial, an EEOC attorney was present in the courtroom about half the time, according to the EEOC, and virtually each day, according to Pemco. EEOC's counsel did not, however, sit at counsel table, offer evidence, examine witnesses, or otherwise participate in the trial of Case I. On the other hand, the EEOC's attorneys had met with counsel for the individual plaintiffs on many occasions prior to the trial. After trial in Case I, a jury concluded that none of the plaintiffs had been subjected to a hostile work environment, and a judgment against them was entered accordingly. Shortly thereafter, Pemco moved for summary judgment in Case II, alleging that the EEOC's suit was barred by claim preclusion in light of the judgment in Case I. How should the district court rule? Was the EEOC a party or in privity with a party to Case I? Might Pemco successfully invoke the doctrine of virtual representation? *See E.E.O.C. v. Pemco Aeroplex, Inc.*, 383 F.3d 1280, 1285-1290 (11th Cir. 2004), *cert. denied*, 546 U.S. 811 (2005).

B.   Issue Preclusion or Collateral Estoppel

As we have seen, claim preclusion extinguishes entire claims or causes of action, including those aspects of a claim that were not previously litigated. Indeed, it most often applies under precisely such circumstances, namely, when a plaintiff "splits" a claim by failing to allege it in its entirety. Issue preclusion, on the other hand, merely forecloses the relitigation of discrete issues that were actually litigated and decided in a previous case, even if that litigation involved different claims. Restatement § 27 defines the scope of issue preclusion as follows:

> When an issue of fact or law is actually litigated and determined by a valid and final judgment, and the determination is essential to the judgment, the determination is

conclusive in a subsequent action between the parties, whether on the same or a different claim.

RESTATEMENT, *supra*, § 27.

At the beginning of this chapter we gave the following example to distinguish claim and issue preclusion:

> P and D enter a contract under which D agrees to deliver certain goods to P on July 1, 2000, and certain other goods on July 1, 2002. D fails to make the first delivery. P sues D for breach of contract and seeks prospective relief only, *i.e.*, an order requiring D to make the initial shipment. D denies the validity of the contract claiming a lack of consideration. After a trial on this issue, judgment is for P, and D is ordered to make the delivery. D complies. Subsequently, D fails to make the July 1, 2002, delivery. P again sues D. This time P seeks damages for the late 2000 delivery, and an order requiring D to make the 2002 delivery.

As we explained, under the doctrine of claim preclusion, the judgment in the first action did not foreclose P's subsequent suit to enforce the July 1, 2002, delivery obligation, since that claim was not the same as the claim asserted in the first action. (You should now be able to explain why this is so.) D would, however, be precluded from relitigating the issue of consideration for the underlying contract, since that issue was actually litigated, decided, and essential to the judgment in that action.

Both claim and issue preclusion are triggered by a decision in a previous case, and in this sense both involve the prior judgment's preclusive effect. But as the above example suggests, the doctrines are in many ways quite different from one another. The easiest way to keep them separate in your mind is to focus on each doctrine's elements. We have already surveyed the elements of claim preclusion. The elements of issue preclusion are both similar and distinct. Specifically, the doctrine of issue preclusion requires that the party asserting it (in the second action) must establish four elements, namely, that

- the *same issue* is involved in both actions;
- the issue was *actually litigated* in the first action;
- the issue was *decided* and *necessary* to a valid judgment in that action; and
- both actions involve the *same parties* or those in *privity* with them.

In addition, it is often said that issue preclusion only applies if the party against whom it is asserted had a full and fair opportunity to litigate that issue in the initial proceeding. Although sometimes stated as a separate element, the full-and-fair-opportunity principle is usually presumed as being satisfied if the other four elements are met. The party resisting issue preclusion may, however, attempt to rebut that presumption by showing that the requisite full and fair opportunity was in fact lacking.

1.   Same Issue

An issue may comprise facts, law, or a combination of both. For two seemingly separate issues to be treated as the "same issue," perfect congruence of facts and law is not necessary, although if there is such a congruence the issues are quite likely to be treated as the same. Rather, there simply must be enough of a factual and legal overlap between the issues that it is reasonable, under the circumstances, to treat them as the same issue for purposes of issue preclusion. The reasonableness inquiry should take into account factual and legal similarities between the issues, the nature of the underlying claims as to each, substantive policies that may argue for or against the application of issue preclusion, and the extent to which application of issue preclusion will promote or undermine principles of fairness and efficiency.

Let's consider a simple example. Case #1 involves a breach-of-contract claim filed by Sellstuff.com ("SC") against Fiona premised on her failure to pay for certain items she ordered from SC. A key issue in the case is whether Fiona had reached the age of majority (18 years of age) as of May 1, 2001, the date on which the contract was entered. This issue is litigated by the parties and submitted to the court. A judgment is entered for SC, the court finding that Fiona had reached majority by the specified date. Case #2 involves a second breach-of-contract suit brought by SC against Fiona. This completely separate contract was entered by the parties on June 1, 2001. Again Fiona defends by claiming that she had not reached majority as of the date the contract was entered. Are the issues involving Fiona's majority status the same in both cases?

The answer is yes. Although the facts are not identical—majority as of May 1 as opposed to majority as of June 1—they are logically the same since a finding that Fiona had reached majority on May 1 necessarily includes a conclusion that she had attained majority by the latter date. There is also no indication that the law defining majority status has changed in the interim. As such, both the facts and the law substantially overlap—indeed, they are the same. Moreover, nothing about the nature of contract law suggests that denying Fiona an opportunity to relitigate this issue in Case #2 would undermine any policy relating to the enforceability of contracts. The opposite would appear to be true. Applying issue preclusion promotes the stability of contracts. Finally, given that Fiona apparently had a full opportunity to litigate this issue in the first proceeding, with an awareness of its consequences, it would seem both fair and efficient to bind her to the first trial court's resolution.

Suppose, however, that in Case #1, the court found that Fiona had not reached majority status as of May 1, 2001. Now, the different dates as to majority status may represent a significant change in the facts, for nonmajority status on May 1 does not exclude the possibility of majority status one month later. Yet allowing relitigation could still lead to an inefficient use of judicial resources. A court might, therefore, require the party against whom issue preclusion is being asserted to show changed circumstances—an intervening birthday—or it might inquire into the evidence adduced in the first proceeding to determine the actual scope of the issue decided. Thus, if that evidence focused on the fact that Fiona was born in 1991, there would seem to be little point in relitigating the majority status issue. On the other hand, if the evidence simply established that Fiona's eighteenth birthday fell some time after May 1, 2001, despite the potential inefficiency, it might be unfair to prevent SC from challenging the factually different defense in the second case.

Consider how this problem would play out if Fiona's incapacity had instead been a mental illness that was found to have existed on May 1, 2001. Should the court simply assume that the incapacity continued through June 1 of that same year? *See* Restatement § 27 comment c, illustrations 7-8.

The point of this example (and its variations) is to make it clear that the determination of whether two issues are the "same issue" involves more than a description of the issues in the abstract. Again, any conclusion as to "sameness" must be premised on an examination of the factual and legal overlap between the issues, the contexts in which they arise, any relevant policy concerns, and the extent to which principles of fairness and efficiency may be advanced or undermined by an application of issue preclusion.

Commissioner of Internal Revenue v. Sunnen
333 U.S. 591 (1948)

Opinion of the Court by Mr. Justice Murphy, announced by Mr. Justice Rutledge.

[A taxpayer granted a corporation the right to market certain of his inventions in exchange for which the corporation agreed to pay him royalties. To this end, the taxpayer entered into two essentially identical contracts with the corporation, one in 1928 and the other in 1929. He then assigned his rights to the royalties under both contracts to his wife, who reported the royalties as income on her separate tax returns for all relevant years. The Internal Revenue Service disputed the royalty assignments' validity, arguing that the royalty income was properly attributable to the husband on his separate return. In a 1935 proceeding involving the 1929-1931 tax years and the 1928 agreement, the tax court held that the royalty income had been properly reported as the wife's separate income. Despite this ruling, the IRS commissioner again challenged the assignments, this time for the tax years 1937-1941. The 1937 tax year involved the same 1928 agreement, while the 1938-1941 tax years involved the essentially identical 1929 agreement. In this second proceeding, the tax court in 1946 agreed with the commissioner that royalties for the 1938-1941 tax years under the 1929 agreement should have been reported as the husband's separate income. However, with respect to the 1937 tax year involving the 1928 agreement, the Tax Court ruled that issue preclusion barred the commissioner from again challenging that assignment's validity. The court of appeals affirmed as to the 1937 tax year but reversed as to the subsequent tax years, holding that the royalties under both agreements were the wife's separate income for all relevant years.] . . .

If the doctrine of *res judicata* is properly applicable so that all the royalty payments made during 1937-1941 are governed by the prior decision of the Board of Tax Appeals, the case may be disposed of without reaching the merits of the controversy. We accordingly cast our attention initially on that possibility, one that has been explored by the Tax Court and that has been fully argued by the parties before us.

It is first necessary to understand something of the recognized meaning and scope of *res judicata*, a doctrine judicial in origin. The general rule of *res judicata* applies to repetitious suits involving the same cause of action. It rests upon considerations of economy of judicial time and public policy favoring the establishment of certainty in legal relations. The rule provides that when a court of competent jurisdiction has entered a final judgment on the merits of a cause of action, the parties to the suit and their privies are thereafter bound "not only as to every matter which was offered and received to sustain or defeat the claim or demand, but as to any other admissible matter which might have been offered for that purpose." *Cromwell v. County of Sac*, 94 U.S. 351, 352 [(1877)]. The judgment puts an end to the cause of action, which cannot again be brought into litigation between the parties upon any ground whatever, absent fraud or some other factor invalidating the judgment.

But where the second action between the same parties is upon a different cause or demand, the principle of *res judicata* is applied much more narrowly. In this situation, the judgment in the prior action operates as an estoppel, not as to matters which might have been litigated and determined, but "only as to those matters in issue or points controverted, upon the determination of which the finding or verdict was rendered." *Cromwell v. County of Sac, supra*, at 353. Since the cause of action involved in the second proceeding is not swallowed by the judgment in the prior suit, the parties are free to litigate points which were not at issue in the first proceeding, even though such points might have been tendered and decided at that time. But matters which were actually litigated and determined in the first proceeding cannot later be relitigated. Once a party has fought out a matter in litigation with the other party, he cannot later renew that duel. In this sense, *res judicata* is usually and more accurately referred to as estoppel by judgment, or collateral estoppel.

These same concepts are applicable in the federal income tax field. Income taxes are levied on an annual basis. Each year is the origin of a new liability and of a separate cause of action. Thus if a claim of liability or non-liability relating to a particular tax year is litigated, a judgment on the merits is *res judicata* as to any subsequent proceeding involving the same claim and the same tax year. But if the later proceeding is concerned with a similar or unlike claim relating to a different tax year, the prior judgment acts as a collateral estoppel only as to those matters in the second proceeding which were actually presented and determined in the first suit. Collateral estoppel operates, in other words, to relieve the government and the taxpayer of "redundant litigation of the identical question of the statute's application to the taxpayer's status." *Tait v. Western Md. R. Co.*, 289 U.S. 620, 624 [(1933)].

But collateral estoppel is a doctrine capable of being applied so as to avoid an undue disparity in the impact of income tax liability. A taxpayer may secure a judicial determination of a particular tax matter, a matter which may recur without substantial variation for some years thereafter. But a subsequent modification of the significant facts or a change or development in the controlling legal principles may make that determination obsolete or erroneous, at least for future purposes. If such a determination is then perpetuated each succeeding year as to the taxpayer involved in the original litigation, he is accorded a tax treatment different from that given to other taxpayers of the same class. As a result, there are inequalities in the administration of the revenue laws, discriminatory distinctions in tax liability, and a fertile basis for litigious confusion. Such consequences, however, are neither necessitated nor justified by the principle of collateral estoppel. That principle is designed to prevent repetitious lawsuits over matters which have once been decided and which have remained substantially static, factually and legally. It is not meant to create vested rights in decisions that have become obsolete or erroneous with time, thereby causing inequities among taxpayers.

And so where two cases involve income taxes in different taxable years, collateral estoppel must be used with its limitations carefully in mind so as to avoid injustice. It must be confined to situations where the matter raised in the second suit is identical in all respects with that decided in the first proceeding and where the controlling facts and applicable legal rules remain unchanged. If the legal matters determined in the earlier case differ from those raised in the second case, collateral estoppel has no bearing on the situation. And where the situation is vitally altered between the time of the first judgment and the second, the prior determination is not conclusive. As demonstrated by *Blair v. Commissioner*, 300 U.S. 5, 9 [(1937)], a judicial declaration intervening between the two proceedings may so change the legal atmosphere as to render the rule of collateral estoppel inapplicable. . . . The supervening decision cannot justly be ignored by blind reliance upon the rule of collateral estoppel. It naturally follows that an interposed alteration in the pertinent statutory provisions or Treasury regulations can make the use of that rule unwarranted.

Of course, where a question of fact essential to the judgment is actually litigated and determined in the first tax proceeding, the parties are bound by that determination in a subsequent proceeding even though the cause of action is different. See *The Evergreens v. Nunan*, 141 F.2d 927 [(2d Cir. 1944)]. And if the very same facts and no others are involved in the second case, a case relating to a different tax year, the prior judgment will be conclusive as to the same legal issues which appear, assuming no intervening doctrinal change. But if the relevant facts in the two cases are separable, even though they be similar or identical, collateral estoppel does not govern the legal issues which recur in the second case. Thus the second proceeding may involve an instrument or transaction identical with, but in a form separable from, the one dealt with in the first proceeding. In that situation, a court is free in the second proceeding to make an independent examination of the legal matters at issue. It may then reach a different result or, if consistency in decision is considered just and desirable, reliance may be placed upon the ordinary rule of *stare decisis*. Before a party can invoke the collateral estoppel doctrine in these circumstances, the legal matter raised in the second proceeding must involve the same set of events or documents and the same bundle of legal principles that contributed to the rendering of the first judgment.

It is readily apparent in this case that the royalty payments growing out of the license contracts which were not involved in the earlier action before the Board of Tax Appeals and which concerned different tax years are free from the effects of the collateral estoppel doctrine. That is true even though those contracts are identical in all important respects with the 1928 contract, the only one that was before the Board, and even though the issue as to those contracts is the same as that raised by the 1928 contract. For income tax purposes, what is decided as to one contract is not conclusive as to any other contract which is not then in issue, however similar or identical it may be. In this respect, the instant case thus differs vitally from *Tait v. Western Md. R. Co., supra*, where the two proceedings involved the same instruments and the same surrounding facts.

A more difficult problem is posed as to the $4,881.35 in royalties paid to the taxpayer's wife in 1937 under the 1928 contract. Here there is complete identity of facts, issues and parties as between the earlier Board proceeding and the instant one. The Commissioner claims, however, that legal principles developed in various intervening decisions of this Court have made plain the error of the Board's conclusion in the earlier proceeding, thus creating a situation like that involved in *Blair v. Commissioner, supra*. This change in the legal picture is said to have been brought about by such cases as *Helvering v. Clifford*, 309 U.S. 331 [1940,] [and] *Helvering v. Horst*, 311 U.S. 112 [1940]. These cases all imposed income tax liability on transferors who had assigned or transferred various forms of income to others within their family groups, although none specifically related to the assignment of patent license contracts between members of the same family. It must therefore be determined whether this *Clifford-Horst* line of cases represents an intervening legal development which is pertinent to the problem raised by the assignment of the 1928 agreement and which makes manifest the error of the result reached in 1935 by the Board. If that is the situation, the doctrine of collateral estoppel becomes inapplicable. A different result is then permissible as to the royalties paid in 1937 under the agreement in question. But to determine whether the *Clifford-Horst* series of cases has such an effect on the instant proceeding necessarily requires inquiry into the merits of the controversy growing out of the various contract assignments from the taxpayer to his wife. To that controversy we now turn. . . .

The principles which have thus been recognized and developed by the *Clifford* and *Horst* cases, and those following them, are directly applicable to the transfer of patent license contracts between members of the same family. They are guideposts for those who seek to determine in a particular instance whether such an assignor retains sufficient control over the assigned contracts or over the receipt of income by the assignee to make it fair to impose income tax liability on him.

Moreover, the clarification and growth of these principles through the *Clifford-Horst* line of cases constitute, in our opinion, a sufficient change in the legal climate to render inapplicable, in the instant proceeding, the doctrine of collateral estoppel relative to the assignment of the 1928 contract. True, these cases did not originate the concept that an assignor is taxable if he retains control over the assigned property or power to defeat the receipt of income by the assignee. But they gave much added emphasis and substance to that concept, making it more suited to meet the "attenuated subtleties" created by taxpayers. So substantial was the amplification of this concept as to justify a reconsideration of earlier Tax Court decisions reached without the benefit of the expanded notions, decisions which are now sought to be perpetuated regardless of their present correctness. Thus in the earlier litigation in 1935, the Board of Tax Appeals was unable to bring to bear on the assignment of the 1928 contract the full breadth of the ideas enunciated in the *Clifford-Horst* series of cases. And, as we shall see, a proper application of the principles as there developed might well have produced a different result, such as was reached by the Tax Court in this case in regard to the assignments of the other contracts. Under those circumstances collateral estoppel should not have been used by the Tax Court in the instant proceeding to perpetuate the 1935 viewpoint of the assignment. . . .

. . . [T]he Tax Court's conclusion that the assignments of the license contracts merely involved a transfer of the right to receive income rather than a complete disposition of all the taxpayer's interest in the contracts and the royalties [was reasonable]. The existence of the taxpayer's power to terminate those contracts and to regulate the amount of the royalties rendered ineffective for tax purposes his attempt to dispose of the contracts and royalties. The transactions were simply a reallocation of income within the family group, a reallocation which did not shift the incidence of income tax liability.

The judgment below must therefore be reversed and the case remanded for such further proceedings as may be necessary in light of this opinion.

Reversed.

MR. JUSTICE FRANKFURTER and MR. JUSTICE JACKSON believe the judgment of the Tax Court is based on substantial evidence and is consistent with the law, and would affirm that judgment. . . .

NOTES AND QUESTIONS

1. Claim preclusion.   Why didn't the doctrine of claim preclusion prevent the IRS from filing its second challenge to the royalty assignments? If you cannot answer this question, go to jail, go directly to jail, and while there re-read the section on claim preclusion.

2. Identifying the issue.   What issue decided in the first tax court proceeding was arguably relevant to the second tax court proceeding? Be precise. Was that issue one of fact, law, or a combination of both?

3. Not the same issue.   There are two ways in which an issue decided in one case can be said to differ from an arguably similar issue in another case: Either the facts have changed (or differ) or the law has changed (or differs). Why did the Supreme Court in *Sunnen* conclude that the issue decided in the first proceeding—the issue you identified in the previous question—was not the same as the arguably similar issue presented with respect to the 1937 tax year? Had the law changed or had the facts changed? Same question regarding the 1938-1941 tax years. As to the latter, what did the Court mean by "separable facts"?

Some authorities have declined to apply *Sunnen's* concept of separable facts outside the tax context. Thus, the Restatement provides, "Preclusion ordinarily is proper if the question is one of the legal effect of a document identical in all relevant respects to another document whose effect was adjudicated in a prior action." RESTATEMENT, *supra*, § 27 comment c. More generally, fact issues in contexts other than tax or customs will be treated as the same so long as there are no material (*i.e.*, substantively relevant) differences between the facts. *See* Lawrence B. Solum, *Issue Preclusion and Collateral Estoppel, in* 18 MOORE'S FEDERAL PRACTICE § 132.02[2] (3d. ed. 2015); 18 WRIGHT, MILLER & COOPER, *supra*, § 4417. In short, absolute identity of facts is not required.

Why should the tax context be treated more strictly? Would it have made more sense in *Sunnen* to have held that although the issues were the same in the first and second proceedings, it would be unfair to allow one taxpayer, who happened to be involved in earlier litigation, to have a continuing benefit not available or no longer available to others? *See* RESTATEMENT, *supra*, § 28(2) (recognizing an exception to issue preclusion designed to "avoid inequitable administration of the laws").

In *United States v. Stauffer Chemical Co.*, 464 U.S. 165 (1984), the Supreme Court applied the more flexible standard of issue identity to successive federal court actions brought by the Environmental Protection Agency (EPA) against Stauffer Chemical. Both suits involved a contention by the EPA that under the Clean Air Act, it was empowered to authorize private contractors to inspect Stauffer chemical plants for potential violations of the act. The first suit involved Stauffer's refusal to allow EPA private contractors to inspect a Stauffer plant in Wyoming. The court upheld Stauffer's right to refuse, concluding that the Clean Air Act did not authorize the use of private contractors under the circumstances presented. The second suit involved a similar refusal with respect to a Stauffer plant in Tennessee. The question before the Supreme Court was whether issue preclusion prevented the EPA from relitigating the "right to refuse" issue in the second action. The government contended that the issues were not the same in both suits since each case involved a different chemical plant, *i.e.*, the facts were separable. However, because there was no showing that this factual difference had any material effect on the underlying legal issue, the Court rejected the government's contention.

> [T]he Government's argument essentially is that two cases presenting the same legal issue must arise from the very same facts or transaction before an estoppel can be applied. Whatever applicability that interpretation may have in the tax context, see *Commissioner v. Sunnen*, 333 U.S. 591, 601-602 (1948) (refusing to apply an estoppel when two tax cases presenting the same issue arose from "separable facts"), we reject its general applicability outside of that context.

Stauffer Chem. Co., *supra*, 464 U.S. at 172 n.5.

4. *Facts, law, and mixed questions of law and fact.*   Issue preclusion clearly applies to pure questions of fact (*e.g.*, Marco was present on Mulberry Street on a

given date), and to mixed questions of law and fact (*e.g.*, Marco negligently caused an accident on Mulberry Street on that date, which mixes the facts of Marco's activities with the law of negligence to arrive at a legal conclusion). The extent to which issue preclusion applies to pure questions of law, *i.e.*, to questions involving the scope or content of the law, is somewhat more difficult. Issue preclusion will apply to pure issues of law when those issues arise in separate cases involving the same historical facts. If, however, the claims presented in two separate cases are substantially unrelated to one another in terms of the underlying facts, a pure issue of law decided in the first case will not have issue-preclusive effect in the subsequent case. So if little Billy sues Bag of Broken Glass, Inc. ("BBG"), for injuries he sustained while playing with a toy manufactured by BBG—"The Exploding Teddy Bear"—and fails to convince the court to adopt a strict liability standard of review, Billy will not be precluded from attempting to convince a subsequent court to adopt that same standard when, three years later, he again sues BBG for injuries caused by another BBG product—"Poke Yer Eye Out." The claims are sufficiently unrelated to permit Billy to seek to change the content of the law. His arguments will, of course, be subject to the more flexible doctrine of stare decisis. *See* RESTATEMENT, *supra*, § 28(2), comment b.

SOME FURTHER THOUGHTS ON THE DIMENSIONS OF AN ISSUE

The breadth with which an issue is defined will determine the scope of that issue's preclusive effect. In *Sunnen*, for example, the Court defined the issue decided by the first tax court relatively narrowly—the tax consequences of an assignment of royalties pursuant to a specific contract. The result was that this narrowly defined issue did not preclude the government from later challenging an assignment of royalties under a virtually identical but separate contract. Although there is no specific method for determining how broadly or narrowly to define an issue, the accepted approach is a pragmatic one that weighs a number of factors, most prominently the principles of fairness and efficiency.

The Restatement gives the following example: "A brings an action against B to recover for personal injuries in an automobile accident. A seeks to establish that B was negligent in driving at an excessive rate of speed. After trial, verdict and judgment are given for B." RESTATEMENT, *supra*, § 27 comment c, illustration 4. If B then sues A for injuries arising out of the same accident—we're assuming there was no compulsory counterclaim rule—may A raise B's negligence as a defense, relying on a theory other than excessive speed such as an allegation that B fell asleep at the wheel? If we define the issue in this example narrowly, *i.e.*, as B's negligence based on excessive speed, then A would not be precluded from raising an alternate theory of B's negligence. Each theory technically presents a different issue. Yet A presumably had a full and fair opportunity to present all of her theories of B's negligence in the first proceeding. And, under claim preclusion, we would certainly say that A split her cause of action if she attempted to sue B for the same injuries on a new theory of negligence. There would seem to be no reason, in terms of fairness or efficiency, to hold otherwise in the context of issue preclusion. A narrow definition of the issue in the first proceeding merely gives A an additional opportunity to establish B's negligence at the unnecessary expense of both B and the judicial system. As a consequence, the issue decided in the first case should be defined as B's negligence, regardless of the underlying theory. A will, therefore, be precluded from raising this issue as a defense.

Other factors a court might consider in determining the dimensions of an issue include the factual and legal similarity of the claims in the two cases, any potential overlap of evidence or arguments, the extent to which pretrial preparation and discovery in the first action should have disclosed the matter asserted in the second proceeding, and, if relevant, the relative length of the time lapse between the cases. *See* RESTATEMENT, *supra*, § 27 comment c; ROBERT C. CASAD & KEVIN M. CLERMONT, RES JUDICATA: A HANDBOOK ON ITS THEORY, DOCTRINE, AND PRACTICE 114-123 (2001).

Lumpkin v. Jordan

57 Cal. Rptr. 2d 303 (Ct. App. 1996)

CHAMPLIN, J.—Reverend Eugene Lumpkin, Jr. (Reverend Lumpkin) appeals after Mayor Frank Jordan (Mayor Jordan) and the City and County of San Francisco (the City) successfully demurred to his complaint. The trial court concluded that the issues raised by Reverend Lumpkin's complaint had been fully litigated in a prior federal action involving the same parties and, therefore, that Reverend Lumpkin was collaterally estopped from relitigating them. Reverend Lumpkin contends that the record fails to establish that the identical issues were necessarily decided in the prior federal action. He further argues that the trial court abused its discretion in applying collateral estoppel to this case. We affirm.

Background

This case concerns the alleged unlawful removal of Reverend Lumpkin from the City's human rights commission (the Commission). The events leading up to Reverend Lumpkin's removal are not in dispute. On August 13, 1992, Mayor Jordan, then mayor of the City, appointed Reverend Lumpkin to serve as a member of the Commission. At the time of his appointment, Reverend Lumpkin was a Baptist minister who served as Pastor of the Ebenezer Baptist Church. Mayor Jordan and Reverend Lumpkin had known one another for over 15 years and, at the time of the appointment, Mayor Jordan was aware that Reverend Lumpkin was a Baptist minister.

On June 26, 1993, the San Francisco Chronicle quoted Reverend Lumpkin as saying: "It's sad that people have AIDS and what have you, but it says right there in the scripture that the homosexual lifestyle is an abomination against God. So I have to preach that homosexuality is a sin." These remarks provoked a public controversy surrounding Reverend Lumpkin's membership on the Commission.

On July 13, 1993, after meeting with Reverend Lumpkin, Mayor Jordan issued a press release announcing that he would not remove Reverend Lumpkin from the Commission. In this statement, Mayor Jordan stated that Reverend Lumpkin "has a solid and unambiguous record as a member of the Human Rights Commission. As a commissioner he has protected and advanced gay and lesbian civil rights."

In reaction to Mayor Jordan's announcement, the San Francisco Board of Supervisors adopted a resolution on July 19, 1993, calling for Reverend Lumpkin's resignation or removal from the Commission. The resolution demanded that Mayor Jordan "restore public confidence in the role and mission of the Commission, especially with regards to the ability of the Commission to consider complaints and lead the community toward equality and respect for all lesbian and gay San Franciscans."

On August 20, 1993, Reverend Lumpkin was interviewed during a live broadcast of a television news show, *Mornings on 2*. After the interviewer identified Reverend Lumpkin as a member of the Commission, he asked him if he believed homosexuality to be an "abomination." Reverend Lumpkin replied, "Sure, I believe, I believe everything the Bible sayeth." The following exchange ensued: "Interviewer: Leviticus also says that a man who sleeps with a man should be put to death. Do you believe that? Reverend Lumpkin: That's what it sayeth. Interviewer: Do you believe that? Reverend Lumpkin: That's—I said that's what the Book sayeth."

Later that day, after learning of the interview, Mayor Jordan asked Reverend Lumpkin to resign from the Commission. In a press release explaining his decision, Mayor Jordan stated: "While religious beliefs are constitutionally protected and cannot be the grounds to remove anyone from elected or appointed public office, the direct or indirect advocacy of violence is not, cannot and will not be condoned by this administration. . . . On the grounds of religious freedom and an unblemished record as a Human Rights Commissioner, I have supported Reverend Lumpkin for holding fundamentalist beliefs which are not my own. We part company when those beliefs imply that attacks against anyone can be justified by the scripture or on any other grounds."

On August 23, 1993, Mayor Jordan met with Reverend Lumpkin, who refused to resign. After this meeting, Mayor Jordan announced his decision to remove Reverend Lumpkin from the Commission.

The Federal Lawsuit

After his removal from the Commission, Reverend Lumpkin brought suit against Mayor Jordan in state court, but the case was removed to federal court at Mayor Jordan's request. An amended complaint was filed in federal court and the City was added as a party. The first cause of action was alleged under the California Fair Employment and Housing Act (FEHA), barring discrimination in employment decisions on the basis of religion. Reverend Lumpkin alleged that he had been terminated "solely because of his religious beliefs" in violation of the FEHA. The second cause of action alleged that defendants, acting under color of state law, deprived Reverend Lumpkin of the right to exercise his constitutionally protected religious beliefs as guaranteed by 42 U.S.C. § 1983.[2] He sought reinstatement to the Commission, compensatory damages, and attorney fees.

The federal court granted summary judgment to Mayor Jordan and the City on all of the causes of action, except for the claims based on [the] FEHA, over which the federal court declined to exercise its supplemental jurisdiction. The state FEHA claims were dismissed without prejudice to refiling in state court.

The operative provisions of the federal opinion granting summary judgment, of which we take judicial notice, are as follows: Reverend Lumpkin's removal from the Commission did not violate his freedom of expression. The court reasoned that he was a policymaker with the Jordan administration and "Reverend Lumpkin's televised remarks regarding homosexuality could reasonably have been interpreted by the Mayor as undermining the very policies of the Commission to promote good will toward all people."

The court's order further held that Reverend Lumpkin's removal did not violate his rights under the free exercise clause. The court found that Mayor Jordan's interest in preventing disruption of the goals of his administration outweighed Reverend Lumpkin's right to religious expression. The court's opinion points out that "[c]ritical to this analysis is the fact that Reverend Lumpkin was not removed solely for exercising his constitutional rights. He is, and at all times was, free to hold and to profess his religious beliefs; however, when the expression of those beliefs clashed with the goals of the Jordan Administration and undermined the public confidence in the ability of the Commission to effect its goals, the Mayor was justified in removing him."

Finally, the court's order held that Reverend Lumpkin's removal did not violate the establishment clause. The court explained that Reverend Lumpkin's removal could not reasonably be construed as sending a message either endorsing or disapproving of religion and that "his removal was based on secular concerns." The court emphasized that Reverend Lumpkin "was not removed because he believed in the inerrancy of the Bible; rather, he was removed because his religious beliefs were at odds with the goals of the Commission and disrupted Mayor Jordan's administration."

Reverend Lumpkin has appealed from this judgment. His appeal is presently pending before the United States Court of Appeal[s], Ninth Circuit, oral argument having been heard on April 8, 1996.*

The State Action

On or about December 14, 1994, Reverend Lumpkin refiled his FEHA claim against Mayor Jordan and the City in state court. They demurred to the complaint,

---

2. Courts have consistently held that employment discrimination claims against state or municipal employers may be brought under the aegis of 42 U.S.C. § 1983 where those claims arise from violations of constitutional or statutory rights.

* [The Ninth Circuit subsequently affirmed the district court's decision. *Lumpkin v. Brown*, 109 F.3d 1498 (9th Cir.), *cert. denied*, 522 U.S. 995 (1997). — EDS.]

arguing that the federal summary judgment finding that Reverend Lumpkin's removal from the Commission was motivated by legitimate, as opposed to discriminatory, reasons negated the necessity of a trial on Reverend Lumpkin's state religious discrimination claims. The trial court agreed, indicating the federal order "is final under federal law and operates as collateral estoppel on this Court on the issue of [Reverend Lumpkin's] removal for religious belief. As a matter of law, [Reverend Lumpkin] was removed for a secular purpose and therefore cannot state a claim under the California Fair Employment and Housing Act." Accordingly, the trial court granted the demurrer to Reverend Lumpkin's complaint without leave to amend. This appeal followed.

Discussion

In general, collateral estoppel (or as it is sometimes known, issue preclusion) precludes a party from relitigating an issue of fact or law if the issue was litigated and decided in a prior proceeding. The rules on application of collateral estoppel are found in the Restatement Second of Judgments. Section 27 of the Restatement provides, "When an issue of fact or law is actually litigated and determined by a valid and final judgment, and the determination is essential to the judgment, the determination is conclusive in a subsequent action between the parties, whether on the same or a different claim." Application of collateral estoppel prevents a litigant from being "subjected to consecutive proceedings raising the same factual allegations."

According to California law, collateral estoppel is only applied if several threshold questions are met with an affirmative answer. First, was the issue decided in the prior adjudication identical with the one presented in the action in question? Second, was the issue actually litigated in the prior proceeding and was there a final judgment on the merits? Third, was the party against whom preclusion is sought the same as, or in privity with, the party to the former proceeding? The party asserting collateral estoppel bears the burden of establishing these requirements.

We believe each of these questions must be answered in the affirmative. The last requirement, privity, is the most easily established. Reverend Lumpkin was, of course, the plaintiff in the prior federal proceeding based upon the same controversy. The requirement that the decision in the former proceeding be final and on the merits is also satisfied. The summary judgment on the complaint is a judgment on the merits.

Furthermore, for collateral estoppel purposes, the federal court's ruling on the summary judgment, even though appealed, must be considered final. "A federal judgment has the same effect in the courts of this state as it would have in a federal court." The federal rule is that "a judgment or order, once rendered, is final for purposes of res judicata until reversed on appeal or modified or set aside in the court of rendition."[5] Because the federal court's ruling on the summary judgment

---

5. Under California law, a judgment is not final for purposes of collateral estoppel while open to direct attack, *e.g.*, by appeal. [*See Los Angeles Branch NAACP v. Los Angeles Unified School District*, 750 F.2d 731 (9th Cir. 1984), at pages 1144, 1146, *supra.* — EDS.]

has not been reversed or modified, the decision is "final." We are therefore left with the question whether the issue decided in the prior adjudication is identical to the one presented in the instant action.

Reverend Lumpkin argues that the summary judgment obtained by Mayor Jordan and the City in federal court did not decide the issues central to his religious discrimination claim under the FEHA. We disagree. The federal court's detailed opinion, taken as a whole, found legitimate, nondiscriminatory reasons had been established for removing Reverend Lumpkin from the Commission. Among those reasons were preventing disruption to the goals of the Commission and the Jordan administration, of avoiding a public controversy, and of securing a new Commissioner who would more effectively implement those goals. In short, the federal court found that Reverend Lumpkin's discharge from the Commission was prompted by a series of events which called into question Reverend Lumpkin's ability to promote the policies of the entity which he served. Accordingly, the court found Reverend Lumpkin had not presented evidence of a discriminatory motive sufficient to proceed to trial.

It is quite true, as Reverend Lumpkin so emphatically asserts, that there exists a significant public interest in this state in fully and vigorously enforcing the FEHA, and that the FEHA is intended to provide an independent remedy to redress employment discrimination. However, the doctrine of collateral estoppel depends on what issues are adjudicated, not the nature of the proceeding or the relief requested. If the rule were otherwise, "litigation finally would end only when a party ran out of counsel whose knowledge and imagination could conceive of different theories of relief based upon the same factual background."

While claims under the FEHA and federal antidiscrimination remedies have their substantive differences, they are generally treated by courts as analogous. What is significant for collateral estoppel purposes is that the issue decided in the federal proceedings—that Reverend Lumpkin was discharged from the Commission for legitimate, nondiscriminatory reasons—is the pivotal factual issue that must be decided in the state FEHA proceedings. Once we give collateral estoppel effect to the prior judicial determination that secular as opposed to religious considerations provided the motivation for Reverend Lumpkin's termination, the outcome of the state FEHA proceedings is preordained.

To the extent that Reverend Lumpkin's arguments go to the correctness of the federal court's ruling, they are misguided. The federal court order is entitled to collateral estoppel effect regardless of our agreement or disagreement with the decision itself. . . . Even if Reverend Lumpkin's analysis of the evidence is correct, it would not change the outcome of this case.

In support of his contention that he retains the right to litigate his FEHA claims in state court, Reverend Lumpkin directs our attention to *Merry v. Coast Community College Dist.* (1979) 97 Cal. App. 3d 214, [158 Cal. Rptr. 603]. In that case the court held that a federal court's summary judgment dismissing a civil rights action did not preclude a subsequent state court action based upon the same operative facts. In so holding, the court noted that "a refusal to exercise pendent jurisdiction over a state claim following pretrial dismissal of a federal claim does not bar litigation of state claims in the state court." However, the *Merry* court's reasoning was based on determining the res judicata effect of the federal dismissal, and whether the mere fact that the federal case had been dismissed barred the plaintiff from further litigation under a state law theory. The *Merry* court expressly declined to resolve whether the cause of action asserted by plaintiff in federal court involved the same issues or operative facts as the cause of action asserted in the state action. By contrast, our case presents a question of issue preclusion—we are dealing with the collateral estoppel effect of a prior judgment on an admittedly different cause of action. Where dispositive factual issues are actually litigated and resolved in the federal action, the losing party is estopped to relitigate those issues in a subsequent state action, and nothing in *Merry* holds to the contrary.

Since the answer to all three pertinent questions is in the affirmative, Mayor Jordan and the City have satisfied their burden of proving the requirements for application of collateral estoppel and Reverend Lumpkin is estopped from pursuing his state action. To prevail in the state action, Reverend Lumpkin would have to prove that Mayor Jordan acted for discriminatory purposes. However, this question of fact has already been resolved against him in the federal proceeding. To subject Mayor Jordan to a second proceeding in state court in which he must defend himself against the very same allegation is unduly burdensome and unjust. We are also concerned with "the possibility of inconsistent judgments which may undermine the integrity of the judicial system. . . ." Applying the doctrine of collateral estoppel, we hold that this finding is conclusive and cannot be relitigated by Reverend Lumpkin in the state action. . . .

The judgment is affirmed.

NOTES AND QUESTIONS

1. Claim preclusion revisited.   Did the FEHA cause of action constitute the same claim as the cause of action under 42 U.S.C. § 1983, which was dismissed by the federal court on summary judgment? Is the answer to this question the same under both the transactional and primary-rights definitions of "claim"? Which of these two definitions would in fact apply here? If the claims were the same, why didn't the *Lumpkin* court dismiss the FEHA claim on grounds of claim preclusion, rather than relying on issue preclusion?

2. Intersystem preclusion revisited.   In footnote 5, the *Lumpkin* court notes that under California law, a decision is not final for purposes of issue preclusion while an appeal is pending. At the time *Lumpkin* was decided, the appeal from the federal summary judgment was still pending. Why did the state court of appeal nonetheless treat the summary judgment order as final? Given your answer to that question, does it make sense for the court in paragraph two of the *"Discussion"* (see page 1192) to have said: "According to California law, collateral estoppel is only applied if several threshold questions are met with an affirmative answer"? *Lumpkin, supra,* 57 Cal. Rptr. 2d at 307.

Suppose that after the state court decision was rendered, the Ninth Circuit reversed the district court and remanded the case for further proceedings. Would the FEHA claim then be allowed to proceed in state court? What avenues would still remain open to Lumpkin? To protect his options, might it have been wise for him to have filed a petition for review with the California Supreme Court? *See* Note 1 following *Federated Department Stores, Inc. v. Moitie*, at page 1160, *supra*.

A NOTE ON FORESEEABILITY—THE *EVERGREENS* PROBLEM

In the famous (or infamous) case of *Evergreens v. Nunan*, 141 F.2d 927 (2d Cir.), *cert. denied*, 323 U.S. 720 (1944), Judge Learned Hand wrote a wonderfully opaque opinion that has baffled judges and lawyers ever since. The essence of that opinion can be distilled as follows: Every case comprises two types of "datum": "mediate facts," *i.e.*, the raw factual materials and findings that lay the foundation for a claim or a defense and from which inferences can be drawn to establish or defeat liability; and "ultimate facts," *i.e.*, the mixed findings of law and fact that in themselves establish legal rights and obligations. For example, in a negligence case, a mediate fact might be that the defendant ran a stop sign or that the defendant was chatting on his cell phone when he entered the intersection. An ultimate fact in that case might be that the defendant was negligent. In *Evergreens*, Judge Hand explained that neither a mediate nor an ultimate fact found in one case could be used to preclude litigation of a mediate fact in another case, *i.e.*, a fact from which other inferences could be drawn. Instead, issue preclusion could be used only to establish the ultimate facts in a subsequent case.

The primary difficulty with this theory was that other than in the simplest case, it is close to impossible to distinguish between mediate facts and ultimate facts. As a result, the *Evergreens* formula has largely been abandoned. Yet there was some wisdom to it. The underlying rationale for the rule framed by Judge Hand was that a party in the second case might be taken by surprise by the unforeseeable use of an issue established in a previous case. An issue that may have seemed trivial in one case, and therefore not worth the expenditure of substantial resources, may loom rather large in a later and very different context. This potential is even greater under the modern law of issue preclusion in which, as we will see, nonparties to the initial action may sometimes use issue preclusion against a party to the first action in a subsequent proceeding. Instead of *Evergreens*'s formalistic rule, the modern approach to the *Evergreens* problem is simply to ask whether it was "sufficiently foreseeable at the time of the initial action that the issue would arise in the context of a subsequent action. . . ." RESTATEMENT, *supra*, § 28(5)(b).

PROBLEMS

13-12. A labor union filed a claim under the Freedom of Information Act (FOIA) against the Internal Revenue Service (IRS) seeking certain documents compiled during the 1980-1981 fiscal year, specifically, all Form 6419s, entitled "Senior Executive Performance Objectives." The district court granted the request but held that under the FOIA the IRS was entitled to redact its employees' names from the forms. No appeal was taken. Subsequently, the union again sued the IRS under the FOIA, this time seeking all Form 6419s for the 1981-1982 fiscal year. The union argues in the second action that redaction of the employees' names from the forms is not proper under the FOIA. Is the question of redaction the "same issue" as that decided in the first case? Would it make any difference if the union legitimately claimed that redaction makes the forms useless and that it was unaware of this fact until it had received the 1980-1981 forms, long after its opportunity to appeal the first decision had expired? *See National Treasury Emps. Union v. I.R.S.,* 765 F.2d 1174 (D.C. Cir. 1985).

13-13. Moser, who attended the Naval Academy as a cadet during the Civil War, retired from the U.S. Navy after 40 years of service. According to federal law, Moser was entitled to an increased retirement salary if he had served "as an officer of the Navy . . . during the civil war. . . ." 30 Stat. 1004, 1007 (1899). Moser claimed that his status as a cadet during that war qualified him for this benefit. The government disagreed. In three separate suits filed by Moser, each involving earlier installments of his pension, the court of claims ruled in his favor on this precise issue. The second and third decisions relied, in essence, on issue preclusion. Despite these rulings the government denied Moser the enhancement benefit on yet another installment of his retirement salary. When he sued a fourth time, the government argued that issue preclusion should not apply since the court of claims' initial judgment was based on a mistaken interpretation of the law. Assuming the government's contention is correct, what should the court do? Under that same assumption, would a ruling in favor of Moser be consistent with the decision in *Sunnen? See United States v. Moser,* 266 U.S. 236 (1924).

13-14. Groucho claimed a 5 percent royalty interest on oil produced by well No. 3 or "any substitute well" located on a small lot in Huntington Beach, California, for which Chico held the leasehold. After well No. 3 burned down, Chico drilled another well on the lot—well No. 4—approximately 50 feet from the location of well No. 3. When Chico refused to pay Groucho any royalties for oil produced from well No. 4, Groucho sued him to collect the royalties. Chico denied that Groucho had any interest in oil produced from wells located on the lot in question. After a trial on the merits, the court entered judgment for Groucho, holding that: he had acquired the claimed royalty interest; that well No. 4 was subject to that interest since it drew oil from the same pool as had well No. 3; and that Groucho was therefore entitled to a 5 percent royalty for all oil produced by well No. 4. When Groucho was again forced to sue Chico for later accruing royalties on the same well, Chico now claimed that well No. 4 was a "whipstock well" drilled diagonally into oil-producing sand under the Pacific Ocean, more than 2,000 feet from the lot, and that it did not draw from the same pool as had well No. 3. Chico offered to prove this by introducing credible evidence that he was paying a royalty to the state of California for oil produced by well No. 4 from state land under the ocean. Should the court allow Chico to introduce this evidence? *See Sutphin v. Speik*, 99 P.2d 652 (Cal.), *reh'g denied*, 101 P.2d 497 (Cal. 1940).

2.   Actually Litigated

Issue preclusion applies only to those issues that were "actually litigated" in the previous proceeding. This requirement is sometimes confused with the same-issue element since if one concludes that the first case does not involve the same issue as the second, it is safe to say that the issue in the second case was not actually litigated in the first. But the requirements are distinct. The same-issue requirement is addressed to identifying the issues, while the actually-litigated requirement focuses on how the identified issue was treated in the first case. Thus, if the same issue is presented in both cases (step one), the party asserting issue preclusion must also establish that the issue was not merely present in that proceeding but also that it was actually litigated there (step two).

For an issue to be actually litigated, it must be (1) properly raised, (2) formally contested between the parties, and (3) submitted to the court for determination. Actual litigation can occur at the trial itself (if there is one) or through a wide variety of pre- and post-trial motions, including motions to dismiss for lack of jurisdiction or venue, failure to state a claim, judgment on the pleadings, summary judgment, directed verdict, and the like. The litigation need not take the form of an adversarial hearing; it may, in fact, occur completely on paper. In short, for an issue to be actually litigated the parties must formally oppose one another on the issue at some point in the litigation process and must submit the issue to the court for a resolution of their dispute.

An issue is not actually litigated if it is admitted by the opposing party or if it is simply not contested by that party. For example, if the plaintiff alleges that the defendant was driving west on Olympic Boulevard at a certain time and the defendant admits the allegation, the fact alleged has not been actually litigated regardless of the case's outcome. In general, in the vast majority of jurisdictions, no issues are actually litigated when a judgment is entered by default, confession, or stipulation, or due to a failure to prosecute. A stipulation can, however, have preclusive effect if the parties so provide.

You should notice some clear distinctions between issue preclusion and claim preclusion in this context. The latter doctrine has no actually-litigated requirement. As we saw earlier, claim preclusion applies even to aspects of a claim or cause of action that were never raised or disputed, *i.e.*, that were never litigated. Indeed, that is the quintessential circumstance under which claim preclusion arises as a defense. In addition, in contrast to issue preclusion, claim preclusion *does* apply to uncontested judgments such as defaults, despite the obvious lack of adversarial litigation in such proceedings. Claim preclusion may, therefore, seem to cut a broader swath than issue preclusion since it applies to matters that were not actually litigated. On the other hand, the on-the-merits requirement of claim preclusion—which does not apply to issue preclusion—prevents claim preclusion from being applied to such pretrial matters as dismissal for a lack of jurisdiction or improper venue, despite the fact that actual and even substantial litigation may have occurred in connection with those dismissals. Issue preclusion does, however, apply to such proceedings.

In addition, to the extent that a judgment of dismissal is not on the merits, the plaintiff may be able to file the same claim against the same defendant again, as long as the statute of limitations has not run. Yet even though the prior dismissal will have no claim-preclusive effect, it may, as a result of issue preclusion, nonetheless prevent the plaintiff from prevailing in the second action. In such cases, because the successive actions involve the same claim, the estoppel, if any, is said to be "direct" rather than "collateral." *See* RESTATEMENT, *supra*, § 27 comment b & illustration 3. Think about this as you do the next problem.

PROBLEM

13-15. Eliot brought a tort action against Pound in a West Virginia state court, claiming that Pound was responsible for injuries Eliot had suffered in an accident Frost had caused. According to Eliot's complaint, Frost was driving Pound's red truck with Pound's permission (an essential element of the tort), Pound well knowing that Frost was wont to drive recklessly on the road less traveled. Pound, who lives in Virginia, moved to dismiss for lack of personal jurisdiction, claiming an absence of minimum contacts. His attached affidavit admitted ownership of the red truck but asserted that Frost drove the truck against Pound's wishes. In contesting the motion to dismiss, Eliot asserted that Pound caused a tortious act within West Virginia by loaning his truck to Frost. In support of his position, Eliot submitted an affidavit in which he averred that immediately after the accident, Frost said he had been driving the truck with Pound's permission. After considering the parties' affidavits, the court—erroneously as it turned out—found that Frost was not driving the red truck with Pound's permission and thus dismissed the suit for lack of minimum contacts. Instead of appealing, Eliot simply refiled his suit in a Virginia state court, making the same claim against Pound under the same provisions of substantive law. May Pound rely on either claim or issue preclusion to defeat Eliot's claim? Would it make any difference if Eliot now claimed that Frost had been driving as Pound's employee at the time of the accident? If estoppel applies here, would it be direct or collateral? *See* Robert Frost, "Stopping by Woods on a Snowy Evening" (1923); *cf.* T.S. Eliot, "The Waste Land" (1922).

3.   Decided and Necessary

A party asserting issue preclusion must establish that the issue on which preclusion is sought was previously resolved ("decided") and that the resolution was essential ("necessary") to the court's ruling or judgment. However, as we have noted, the prior ruling or judgment need not have been on the merits for issue preclusion to apply. Thus an issue can be decided and necessary to a motion to dismiss for lack of personal jurisdiction, and if all other elements of issue preclusion are satisfied, it gives the issue preclusive effect. In addition, issue preclusion may sometimes apply to decisions that are complete but not technically final, so long as it is clear that the court's decision on the issue was "adequately deliberated and firm." RESTATEMENT, *supra*, § 13 comment g. For example, under this principle of "practical finality," in a jurisdiction that severs a trial's liability portion from its damages portion, a finding of liability will be treated as final for purposes of issue preclusion even though the entry of a final judgment must await the determination of damages. Note, however, that such a decision is not "final" for purposes of claim preclusion. *See* 18A WRIGHT, MILLER & COOPER, *supra*, § 4434.

An issue can be expressly or implicitly decided. For example, if a court makes findings of fact or conclusions of law, those findings and conclusions represent express decisions on the particular factual or legal contentions involved. On the other hand, if a jury renders a general verdict, precisely which issues the jury decided may have to be inferred from the logic of the result and an assessment of the issues actually litigated. In such cases, the second court may examine the pleadings or other materials found in the record of the previous case to determine what issues were litigated and decided. When the record is not adequate, extrinsic evidence (*e.g.*, testimony of the lawyers or parties) may be considered as well.

In cases with multiple issues, it may not be possible to determine which issues were decided by a prior judgment. For example, suppose a defendant in a negligence case raises contributory negligence as a complete bar to the plaintiff's recovery and the jury returns a general verdict for the defendant. The verdict may have been based on the plaintiff's failure to prove that the defendant was negligent, or it may have been based on the defendant's affirmative defense. In such a case, even if both issues were actually litigated we cannot say for certain which issue was decided. As a consequence, the decided requirement is not met with respect to either issue.

Once it is clear that an issue has been decided, the next question is whether the decision on that issue was necessary to the court's judgment. Necessary is used synonymously with essential, in the sense that resolution of the issue must be such that the court's judgment could not stand without it. For example, if a court dismisses a case for lack of personal jurisdiction but at the same time finds that the absent defendant did have some contacts with the state (*e.g.*, the defendant owned a vacation home there, was present in the state for two weeks during the previous year, etc.), these findings are not necessary to the judgment of dismissal. Indeed, they have no effect on the judgment entered. These findings may not, therefore, be given preclusive effect in another proceeding. In general, if a court's decision of an issue can be excised from its judgment without altering the case's outcome, that decision was not necessary to the judgment.

The necessity requirement stems from a concern that the gratuitous resolution of an issue may not have been given the full judicial attention it deserves. In addition, the party against whom such an issue was decided may have had little incentive to appeal the decision since a reversal as to that issue would have no effect on

the case's outcome. Moreover, to the extent that party was the winning party—
e.g., a defendant whose motion to dismiss was granted—they may not even have
had the right to appeal, in which case the party would have no ability to correct
a particular finding no matter how erroneous it may have been. Thus, the idea
here is to avoid giving preclusive effect to issues decided by the previous court that
were, in essence, extraneous to the judgment in the sense of being dicta.

Consider several examples:

1. A sues B for breach of contract. B's sole defense is that A procured the contract
through fraud. After a jury trial on that issue, a judgment is entered on a general
verdict for A. The absence of fraud was both decided and necessary to the judgment.
Even though there were no specific findings on the fraud issue, a decision that
no fraud occurred is implicit in the judgment. That decision was also necessary to
the judgment since the court could not have ruled in A's favor without finding an
absence of fraud. Note the close relationship between determining that the decision
of an issue was implicit in the judgment and determining whether that decision was
necessary to the judgment.

2. A sues B for negligence arising out of an automobile accident, claiming that
B was driving at an excessive speed. B asserts that A was contributorily negligent.
Under the applicable law, contributory negligence is a complete bar to a plaintiff's
recovery. After a trial, judgment is entered for A, the jury returning a special verdict
that B was driving at an excessive speed. The excessive speed issue and A's lack of
contributory negligence were both decided and necessary to the judgment. The
first was expressly decided and the second implicitly decided. As to necessity, the
excessive-speed issue is the sole basis for establishing B's liability. Had the finding
been the opposite, the judgment would have been for B. A's lack of contributory
negligence is also necessary to the judgment since that particular judgment could
not have been rendered if A had been found to have been contributorily negligent.

3. In the second example, suppose that A's claim for negligence had asserted
both that B was speeding and that B had failed to properly maintain his vehicle. If
the jury returns a special verdict finding that B was speeding but that B did not fail to
properly maintain his vehicle, the latter finding was not necessary to the judgment,
for the judgment would still have been for A even without it. The finding that B
properly maintained his vehicle would therefore not be entitled to preclusive effect
in a subsequent suit between A and B.

Cunningham v. Outten

2001 WL 428687 (Del. Super. Ct. Mar. 26, 2001)

WITHAM, J.

Presently before the Court is Plaintiff's motion for partial summary judgment
on the issue of liability and Defendant's response thereto. It appears that:

On August 16, 1996, the vehicle operated by Val Cunningham ("Cunningham"
or "Plaintiff") was struck by a vehicle driven by Grace Outten ("Outten" or
"Defendant"). In this civil action, Cunningham alleges that he suffered injuries
in the collision which occurred because of Outten's negligence. As a result of

the collision, Outten was charged with "Inattentive Driving," in violation of 21 Del. C. § 4176(b). On October 21, 1996, this charge was tried before the Court of Common Pleas and Outten was found guilty of "Inattentive Driving." Plaintiff claims that based on the conviction for "Inattentive Driving," the Defendant should be collaterally estopped from denying negligence and liability. Defendant concedes that Outten's conviction for inattentive driving cannot be relitigated, but argue[s] that the Court of Common Pleas' decision is not dispositive as to liability because the causation issue is outstanding and must be determined by the fact finder. . . .

Plaintiff's argument for summary judgment is based upon the doctrine of collateral estoppel. According to the Plaintiff, the Court of Common Pleas' finding that the Defendant was guilty of "Inattentive Driving" establishes negligence and thereby liability. Under collateral estoppel, "if a court has decided an issue of fact necessary to its judgment, that decision precludes relitigation of the issue in a suit on a different cause of action involving a party to the first case." The test for applying collateral estoppel consists of four parts: it requires that "(1) a question of fact essential to the judgment, (2) be litigated and (3) determined (4) by a valid and final judgment." The question before the Court of Common Pleas was whether or not Outten violated 21 Del. C. § 4176(b). The alleged violation of this statute was litigated and the Court below determined in a valid and final judgment following a bench trial that Outten was guilty. This Court has previously noted that under modern law the decision of whether a criminal conviction can be conclusive as to a question of fact in a civil case rests in the sound discretion of the court, particularly in cases involving offensive collateral estoppel.

Collateral estoppel does not apply to liability in this personal injury action because the issue of liability was not before the Court of Common Pleas as "a question of fact essential to the judgment." The issue before the Court of Common Pleas was whether the Defendant violated the statute in question, 21 Del. C. § 4176(b). The finding with respect to the violation of a motor vehicle statute does not include a determination of liability which consists of more than guilt or negligence. The Court of Common Pleas determined that 21 Del. C. § 4176(b) was violated by the Defendant but did not consider or decide whether the violation of that statute caused any of Plaintiff's injuries. The fact that liability was not the issue before the Court of Common Pleas is also evident as the finding did not have to consider any claims of comparative negligence.

The motion for summary judgment on liability also fails because the issue of Plaintiff's alleged negligence has not been determined. Defendant alleges in her Answer and in her response to this summary judgment motion that the Plaintiff was at least partly at fault for this accident. Apportioning liability between the parties involved here has never been done and is the province of the fact finder. Therefore, for collateral estoppel to apply to liability in this action, there must be a valid and final judgment that apportions liability between the parties. [T]he Court [has] stated that "until there is a judicial determination either finding plaintiff not negligent or finding the negligence of plaintiff to be no greater than defendant's negligence, the issue of liability of defendant cannot be resolved." Plaintiff's argument that collateral estoppel should support a judgment as a matter of law for liability is not appropriate because the issue of comparative negligence was not decided by the Court of Common Pleas' ruling. As a practical matter, Defendant could have violated the motor vehicle statute and not have been 100% at fault for this accident. Therefore, it will be up to the jury to determine whose conduct was the ultimate cause of this accident.

The doctrine of collateral estoppel only applies to this case insofar as it shows that Defendant was negligent in violating the statute, driving inattentively. The Court of Common Pleas' finding of guilt does not establish liability. Plaintiff will be entitled to a jury instruction on negligence per se stating that the Defendant violated a motor vehicle statute of the State of Delaware; however, this instruction is not conclusive on the issues of causation and liability. The Defendant will still be permitted to assert a comparative negligence defense and the fact finder will ultimately determine who was at fault or the degree of fault for each party in this accident. The Defendant's violation of the motor vehicle statute will only be one of several factors the jury can use to determine liability for this accident. Therefore, Plaintiff's motion for partial summary judgment is *denied*.

It is so ordered.

NOTES AND QUESTIONS

1. *Identifying the issue that was both decided and necessary.* What was the issue (or issues) that the plaintiff in *Cunningham* sought to preclude the defendant from litigating? On what grounds did the court decline to grant the plaintiff's motion? Was the court nonetheless correct in ruling that the defendant was precluded from denying that she had been driving inattentively? Did the court's ruling preclude the defendant from claiming that the plaintiff was also negligent?

2. *Nonparty assertion of issue preclusion.* Notice that the plaintiff in *Cunningham* was not a party to the prior criminal proceeding. Yet the court allowed the plaintiff to rely on issue preclusion. This is an example of "nonmutual issue preclusion," a subject we will examine in the next section.

3. *Settlement incentives.* The *Cunningham* case went to trial a few weeks after the court ruled on the plaintiff's motion for partial summary judgment. The jury returned a verdict awarding Cunningham $10,000, but since it also found each party to be 50 percent negligent, the court entered judgment for Cunningham in the amount of only $5,000. Under a Delaware court rule designed to encourage settlement, because Outten, well before trial, had offered to settle the case for $6,000 and the plaintiff ended up recovering less than that amount, the court taxed the plaintiff a portion of the defendant's costs—those incurred after the making of the offer—even though the plaintiff was the prevailing party in the case. *See Cunningham v. Outten*, 2001 WL 879999 (Del. Super. Ct. June 28, 2001); DEL. SUPER. CT. CIV. R. 68. While the amount of the defendant's costs taxed came to less than $1,000, the rule also denied the plaintiff the recovery of his own costs. In retrospect, might the plaintiff have done well to settle this case prior to trial?

PROBLEMS

13-16. In 1920, the Fall River Valley Navigation District ("the District") brought a civil action in a California Superior Court against the state of California ("the State") in an effort to establish the District's right to divert water from the Fall River. Under applicable law, the State has the power to issue water-diversion permits to riparian owners on any river in the state to which the property is contiguous. After a trial on the merits in which all claims and issues were fully litigated, the trial court ruled in the District's favor. The court issued a number of findings of fact and conclusions of law, including: that the Fall River is a scenic and non-navigable river in Northern California; that the District is a riparian landowner along the Southwest Fork of the Fall River; and that the State granted the District a special-use permit to divert a certain quantity of water from the Fall River for a period of 20 years. The California Supreme Court affirmed all findings by the trial court. Fifty years later the State brought an action against Mack, seeking to require Mack to remove certain wires and cables extending across the Fall River, on the basis that Mack was obstructing travel on a navigable waterway. Mack moved to dismiss the State's action, arguing that issue preclusion bars the State from asserting that the Fall River is a navigable river. How should the trial court rule? Assume that the same-parties element of issue preclusion has been satisfied. *See People v. Mack*, 97 Cal. Rptr. 448 (Ct. App. 1971).

13-17. Sabek, Inc. ("Sabek"), owned a lot in California. Sabek sued Englehard, a foreign corporation, claiming that the latter was responsible for contaminating the lot. Englehard filed a motion to quash service of process. After a contested hearing, the motion was granted on the ground that Sabek had failed to establish Englehard's minimum contacts with the state. Sabek did not appeal. Instead, it filed a second amended complaint against Englehard alleging additional evidence of minimum contacts. Englehard has again moved to dismiss, this time relying on issue preclusion. What should the court do? Are the first three elements of issue preclusion satisfied? (You may safely assume that the fourth element—same parties—is met.) *See Sabek, Inc. v. Englehard Corp.*, 76 Cal. Rptr. 2d 882 (Ct. App. 1998).

A NOTE ON POTENTIAL EXCEPTIONS BASED ON THE NATURE OF THE PRIOR PROCEEDINGS

Even if an issue is decided and necessary to the judgment, it will not be given preclusive effect if the initial forum in which the litigation took place provided significantly less extensive or less formal procedures for the resolution of the underlying controversy, or if as a matter of law, the party against whom issue preclusion is being asserted could not have appealed the initial judgment. For example, a decision by a small claims court with relatively informal procedures will not have issue-preclusive effect in a subsequent proceeding raising the same issues before a court of record in which the full panoply of procedures are available. (A small claims court decision can, however, have claim-preclusive effect. Why the distinction?) The jurisdictional allocation between two courts may also limit the scope of issue preclusion. If, for example, a probate court decides that a couple was not married for purposes of distributing an estate's assets, that decision will not bind the parties in a subsequent marriage-dissolution proceeding before a family law court. To hold otherwise would undermine the family law court's jurisdictional authority. *See* RESTATEMENT, *supra*, § 28(1) & (3), comments a & d.

That the prior decision was issued by an administrative agency rather than a court will not necessarily prevent it from having full issue-preclusive effect. *B & B Hardware, Inc. v. Hargis Industries, Inc.*, 135 S. Ct. 1293, 1302 (2015) (rejecting view that agency decisions can never have issue-preclusive effect merely because agencies are not Article III courts). As the Court held, "issue preclusion is not limited to those situations in which the same issue is before two *courts*. Rather, where a single issue is before a court and an administrative agency, preclusion also often applies." *Id.* at 1303. In such cases, the "correct inquiry" is not the nature of the first tribunal, as such, but "whether the procedures used in the first proceeding were fundamentally poor, cursory, or unfair." *Id.* at 1309. If those procedures afforded "an adequate opportunity to litigate, the courts have not hesitated to apply res judicata to enforce repose." *Id.* at 1303 (internal quotation marks omitted).

In addition, issue preclusion will not apply if the party against whom it is asserted had a significantly heavier burden of proof in the initial proceeding, or if the party asserting issue preclusion has a significantly heavier burden of proof in the second proceeding, or if the burden of proof has shifted from the party against whom issue preclusion is asserted to her adversary. RESTATEMENT, *supra*, § 28(4) comment f. Thus, in a criminal prosecution, if the government fails to prove "beyond a reasonable doubt" that the defendant used his boat to smuggle explosives into the country, the government will not be precluded from establishing those same facts in a civil proceeding seeking forfeiture of the boat under a preponderance-of-the-evidence standard. The reason is straightforward. The government, the party against whom issue preclusion would be asserted in the second proceeding, had a significantly heavier burden in the first proceeding. *See United States v. One Assortment of 89 Firearms*, 465 U.S. 354, 357-362 (1984). What would occur if the proceedings were reversed and the government failed to meet the preponderance standard in the first proceeding? Could the defendant successfully assert issue preclusion against the government in the second proceeding?

Finally, a court may refuse to apply issue preclusion if the party to be estopped lacked an incentive to litigate the issue seriously in the earlier suit. The Supreme Court has recognized that "[i]ssue preclusion may be inapt if 'the amount in controversy in the first action [was] so small in relation to the amount in controversy in the second that preclusion would be plainly unfair.'" *B & B Hardware, Inc. v. Hargis Industries, Inc., supra*, 135 S. Ct. at 1309 (quoting RESTATEMENT, *supra*, § 28, comment j). However, where the issues in the first suit are "weighty enough," such that "there is good reason to think that both sides will take the matter seriously," preclusion then applies even if the stakes in the second action are greater than they were in the first. *Id.* at 1309-1310.

A NOTE ON ALTERNATIVE DETERMINATIONS

A difficulty arises in determining whether the decision on an issue can be deemed necessary if a court's judgment was premised on alternative findings, either of which would sustain the judgment without reference to the other. For example, suppose A sues B for breach of contract. B denies that there was a contract, citing a lack of consideration, and alternatively asserts that she had not yet reached the age of majority as of the date the alleged contract was entered. Judgment is entered for B, the court finding that the agreement lacked consideration and that at the time of the agreement B had not reached majority. Either of these issues standing alone would support the judgment and, clearly, if only one of them had been decided in B's favor it would be treated as necessary. Should both of these issues be treated as necessary to the judgment since both clearly support the result?

According to the Restatement, "[i]f a judgment of a court of first instance is based on determinations of two issues, either of which standing independently would be sufficient to support the result, the judgment is not conclusive with respect to either issue standing alone." RESTATEMENT, *supra*, § 27 comment i. Thus neither issue will be treated as being necessary to the judgment for purposes of issue preclusion. However, if an appeal is taken and both issues are affirmed on appeal, both will then be treated as necessary. *Id.* at comment o. Thus, in the above hypothetical, neither issue decided in the first proceeding—lack of consideration or B's nonmajority status—will be treated as necessary unless A appeals and the appellate court affirms the decision on both grounds, in which case both will be deemed to have been necessary. And if the appellate court affirms but on only one of the grounds, that ground alone will be treated as necessary. (Of course, the judgment in the first proceeding will still have claim-preclusive effect.)

The rationale for this rule is similar to the rationale for the nonpreclusive effect afforded issues decided unnecessarily. First, there is a danger that the initial trial court did not fully consider the alternative ground for a decision (and it is usually not clear which of the two issues was the "alternative" one), and second, the party against whom the decision was rendered may not have had the incentive to appeal since an affirmance on either issue would be sufficient to sustain the judgment. Thus, if one of the independent issues is unassailable, the defendant is not likely to challenge the resolution of the other issue since a reversal on the potentially "assailable" issue would not alter the judgment.

Aldrich v. State of New York

494 N.Y.S.2d 662 (App. Div. 1985)

WEISS, Justice.

Claimants in these two actions are the owners of separate parcels of real estate along Slaterville Road in the Town of Caroline, Tompkins County. In separate actions commenced October 19, 1982, claimants seek personal injury and property damages stemming from the October 28, 1981 flooding of Six Mile Creek adjacent to their properties. Claimants allege that the flooding was caused, *inter alia*, by the State's negligence in the design, construction and maintenance of a bridge carrying State Route 79 over the creek. The bridge, which originally was a single span across the creek, was replaced in 1963 with a twin box culvert design that claimants challenge as inappropriate. In a previous action, claimants had prosecuted a claim for damages caused by a flood at this same location on July 11, 1976. As in the instant case, claimants alleged in the prior case that the flooding was occasioned by the State's negligence in designing and constructing the subject bridge. After a four-day trial in April 1983, the Court of Claims (Moriarty, J.), held in the prior case (1) that the claimants' damages resulted from an act of God and (2) that "the bridge design was not evolved without adequate study nor was the utilization of a twin culvert design a departure from good engineering practice." Those claims were dismissed and no appeal was pursued.

The State thereafter served a supplemental answer in the instant action and moved for partial summary judgment on the ground that claimants were barred from relitigating so much of their claims as asserted negligence on the State's part in the design and construction of the subject bridge. The Court of Claims denied the motion, finding that the alternative grounds set forth in the earlier decision, each of which was independently sufficient to support the judgment, were not entitled to conclusive effect (*see*, Restatement [Second] of Judgments § 27 comment i [1982]). The court observed that Judge Moriarty's analysis of the negligence issue was essentially secondary and not necessary to the earlier decision, inasmuch as the storm was so severe that the damage would have resulted regardless of any negligence on the State's part.

On this appeal, the critical issue is whether the State's alleged negligence in the design and construction of the bridge was so reviewed in the prior action as to preclude relitigation. In *Malloy v. Trombley*, 50 N.Y.2d 46, 427 N.Y.S.2d 969, 405 N.E.2d 213 [1980], the Court of Appeals rejected a mechanical application of the alternative determination rule adopted in the Restatement, which prevents issue preclusion in an instance of alternative grounds for a prior court's decision. Thus, to the extent that the Court of Claims relied on the Restatement rule as dispositive, it did so improvidently. As clarified by the Court of Appeals in *O'Connor v. G & R Packing Co.*, 53 N.Y.2d 278, 280, 440 N.Y.S.2d 920, 423 N.E.2d 397 [1981], issue preclusion may serve to bar "relitigation of an issue considered alternatively in the prior trial only when it is clear that the prior determination *squarely addressed and specifically decided* the issue" (emphasis supplied). Contrary to the ruling of the Court of Claims, we find that the issue of the State's negligence concerning the bridge design and construction was actually and fully litigated in the prior trial. Several factors support this conclusion.

In the prior action, claimants specifically alleged that the twin culvert design of the new bridge was not in conformance with good engineering practice in view of the debris generated by the geographical characteristics of the upstream watershed. Inasmuch as the claims in the present action had been filed before trial on the initial action, it becomes eminently clear that all parties and the court were cognizant of the possible preclusive effect of the court's ruling on this issue. Nor is there any suggestion that claimants were in any way inhibited from addressing the issue, which involved the essence of their claim. Significantly, a review of Judge Moriarty's decision confirms that the issue was thoroughly and carefully addressed. He specifically outlined the physical characteristics of the new bridge and noted that the stream channel was so altered as to accommodate a larger volume of water. The court reviewed the expert testimony of both sides, accrediting the State's witnesses who opined that the bridge was constructed in accord with proper engineering standards, which would not require consideration of the effects that a storm with a return frequency well in excess of 100 years, such as the one involved in 1976, might have on the bridge. By its terms, Judge Moriarty's decision addressed the negligence issue and, as the statement quoted above indicates, employed the correct standard of governmental liability for bridge design. Judge Moriarty's negligence ruling was not merely a "bald statement" lacking "critical deliberation" as observed by the Court of Claims, but a reasoned assessment of liability premised on extensive expert testimony.

On the basis of the foregoing, we hold that the rule of issue preclusion is applicable even though the issue precluded was the subject of only an alternative ruling by Judge Moriarty. *Accordingly, the decision of the Court of Claims must be reversed and the State's motion for partial summary judgment granted. . . .*

NOTES AND QUESTIONS

1. Alternative views of alternatives.   The original Restatement, contrary to the Restatement (Second), endorsed the view that alternative grounds for a decision should uniformly be treated as necessary to the judgment. RESTATEMENT (FIRST) JUDGMENTS § 68 comment n. New York seems to have adopted a third view. What is it? How does the *Aldrich* court deal with the concern that alternative grounds for a decision may not be reliable when, as in that case, they were never tested on appeal? For several interesting illustrations of the alternative findings problem, see RESTATEMENT, *supra*, § 27 comment i & illustrations 15-16; compare RESTATEMENT (FIRST) JUDGMENTS § 68 comment n & illustrations 7-8.

2. What is an alternative determination?   When a court decides two issues in a case, it does not necessarily follow that those issues are alternative to one another. To be alternatives, each issue standing independently must be sufficient to support the result. Return to our example in which A sued B for breach of contract. B claimed both lack of consideration and that she hadn't reached majority as of the date of the alleged contract. Suppose that this time the court finds for A, concluding that there was consideration and that B had reached the age of majority. Can you explain why these are not alternative holdings? Should one or both of these findings be treated as necessary to the court's judgment?

4.   Same Parties: The Principles of Mutuality and Nonmutuality

In general, the same standards used to determine whether a person was a party or a person who ought to be bound for purposes of claim preclusion are fully applicable to issue preclusion. Thus, for purposes of issue preclusion, a party is "[a] person who is named as a party to an action and subjected to the jurisdiction of the court. . . ." RESTATEMENT, *supra*, § 34(1). And a nonparty who will be bound is someone whose relationship with a party is such that the former will be treated as a party for purposes of preclusion. *Id.* §§ 43-61. In addition, in the specific context of issue preclusion, a person not technically a party (or in privity) who controls a prior litigation or substantially participates in it will also be treated as a party as to those issues over which that control or participation was asserted. *Id.* § 39 & comments a-b; *see Montana v. United States*, 440 U.S. 147 (1979). A few courts have also applied this "control" principle to assertions of claim preclusion.

There is, however, one crucial distinction between claim preclusion and issue preclusion with respect to who may benefit from a prior judgment or decision. The mutuality principle provides that only a person bound by a judgment or decision may benefit from it. Thus, under the mutuality rule, only a party (or someone in privity with a party) may use a judgment in a preclusive manner in a subsequent proceeding. A stranger to the case, who by definition cannot be bound by the judgment or decision, can therefore get no legal benefit from it either, even when the parties are bound as to each other. Mutuality remains the rule in claim preclusion, though its scope has been somewhat eroded by the increasingly broad sweep of privity and by some state courts' willingness to recognize virtual representation. Mutuality was also long the rule for issue preclusion, under what may be described as the traditional approach. Only a person bound by a previously decided issue, *i.e.*, a party or someone in privity with a party, could use issue preclusion to prevent relitigation of that issue in a subsequent case. As the next two cases demonstrate, however, modern courts have moved away from this rigid model.

Bernhard v. Bank of America National Trust & Savings Association
122 P.2d 892 (Cal. 1942)

TRAYNOR, J.—In June, 1933, Mrs. Clara Sather, an elderly woman, made her home with Mr. and Mrs. Charles O. Cook in San Dimas, California. Because of her failing health, she authorized Mr. Cook and Dr. Joseph Zeiler to make drafts jointly against her commercial account in the Security First National Bank of Los Angeles. On August 24, 1933, Mr. Cook opened a commercial account at the First National Bank of San Dimas in the name of "Clara Sather by Charles O. Cook." No authorization for this account was ever given to the bank by Mrs. Sather. Thereafter, a number of checks drawn by Cook and Zeiler on Mrs. Sather's commercial account in Los Angeles were deposited in the San Dimas account and checks were drawn upon that account signed "Clara Sather by Charles O. Cook" to meet various expenses of Mrs. Sather.

On October 26, 1933, a teller from the Los Angeles Bank called on Mrs. Sather at her request to assist in transferring her money from the Los Angeles Bank to the San Dimas Bank. In the presence of this teller, the cashier of the San Dimas Bank, Mr. Cook, and her physician, Mrs. Sather signed by mark an authorization directing the Security First National Bank of Los Angeles to transfer the balance of her savings account in the amount of $4,155.68 to the First National Bank of San Dimas. She also signed an order for this amount on the Security First National Bank of San Dimas "for credit to the account of Mrs. Clara Sather." The order was credited by the San Dimas Bank to the account of "Clara Sather by Charles O. Cook." Cook withdrew the entire balance from that account and opened a new account in the same bank in the name of himself and his wife. He subsequently withdrew the funds from this last mentioned account and deposited them in a Los Angeles Bank in the names of himself and his wife.

Mrs. Sather died in November, 1933. Cook qualified as executor of the estate and proceeded with its administration. After a lapse of several years he filed an account at the instance of the probate court accompanied by his resignation. The account made no mention of the money transferred by Mrs. Sather to the San Dimas Bank; and Helen Bernhard, Beaulah Bernhard, Hester Burton, and Iva LeDoux, beneficiaries under Mrs. Sather's will, filed objections to the account for this reason. After a hearing on the objections the court settled the account, and as part of its order declared that the decedent during her lifetime had made a gift to Charles O. Cook of the amount of the deposit in question.

After Cook's discharge, Helen Bernhard was appointed administratrix with the will annexed. She instituted this action against defendant, the Bank of America, successor to the San Dimas Bank, seeking to recover the deposit on the ground that the bank was indebted to the estate for this amount because Mrs. Sather never authorized its withdrawal. In addition to a general denial, defendant pleaded two affirmative defenses: (1) that the money on deposit was paid out to Charles O. Cook with the consent of Mrs. Sather and (2) that this fact is res judicata by virtue of the finding of the probate court in the proceeding to settle Cook's account that Mrs. Sather made a gift of the money in question to Charles O. Cook and "owned no sums of money whatsoever" at the time of her death. Plaintiff demurred to both these defenses, and objected to the introduction in evidence of the record of the earlier proceeding to support the plea of res judicata. . . . The trial court overruled the demurrers and objection to the evidence, and gave judgment for defendant on the ground that Cook's ownership of the money was conclusively established by the finding of the probate court. Plaintiff has appealed, denying that the doctrine of res judicata is applicable to the instant case or that there was a valid gift of the money to Cook by Mrs. Sather.

Plaintiff contends that the doctrine of res judicata does not apply because the defendant who is asserting the plea was not a party to the previous action nor in privity with a party to that action and because there is no mutuality of estoppel.

The doctrine of res judicata precludes parties or their privies from relitigating a cause of action that has been finally determined by a court of competent jurisdiction. . . . The rule is based upon the sound public policy of limiting litigation by preventing a party who has had one fair trial on an issue from again drawing it into controversy. The doctrine also serves to protect persons from being twice vexed for the same cause. It must, however, conform to the mandate of due process of law that no person be deprived of personal or property rights by a judgment without notice and an opportunity to be heard.

Many courts have stated the facile formula that the plea of res judicata is available only when there is privity and mutuality of estoppel. Under the requirement of privity, only parties to the former judgment or their privies may take advantage of or be bound by it. A party in this connection is one who is "directly interested in the subject matter, and had a right to make defense, or to control the proceeding, and to appeal from the judgment." A privy is one who, after rendition of the judgment, has acquired an interest in the subject matter affected by the judgment through or under one of the parties, as by inheritance, succession, or purchase. The estoppel is mutual if the one taking advantage of the earlier adjudication would have been bound by it, had it gone against him.

The criteria for determining who may assert a plea of res judicata differ fundamentally from the criteria for determining against whom a plea of res judicata may be asserted. The requirements of due process of law forbid the assertion of a plea of res judicata against a party unless he was bound by the earlier litigation in which the matter was decided. He is bound by that litigation only if he has been a party thereto or in privity with a party thereto. There is no compelling reason, however, for requiring that the party asserting the plea of res judicata must have been a party, or in privity with a party, to the earlier litigation.

No satisfactory rationalization has been advanced for the requirement of mutuality. Just why a party who was not bound by a previous action should be precluded from asserting it as res judicata against a party who was bound by it is difficult to comprehend. Many courts have abandoned the requirement of mutuality and confined the requirement of privity to the party against whom the plea of res judicata is asserted. The commentators are almost unanimously in accord. The courts of most jurisdictions have in effect accomplished the same result by recognizing a broad exception to the requirements of mutuality and privity, namely, that they are not necessary where the liability of the defendant asserting the plea of res judicata is dependent upon or derived from the liability of one who was exonerated in an earlier suit brought by the same plaintiff upon the same facts. Typical examples of such derivative liability are master and servant, principal and agent, and indemnitor and indemnitee. Thus, if a plaintiff sues a servant for injuries caused by the servant's alleged negligence within the scope of his employment, a judgment against the plaintiff on the grounds that the servant was not negligent can be pleaded by the master as res judicata if he is subsequently sued by the same plaintiff for the same injuries. Conversely, if the plaintiff first sues the master, a judgment against the plaintiff on the grounds that the servant was not negligent can be pleaded by the servant as res judicata if he is subsequently sued by the plaintiff. In each of these situations the party asserting the plea of res judicata was not a party to the previous action nor in privity with such a party under the accepted definition of a privy set forth above. Likewise, the estoppel is not mutual since the party asserting the plea, not having been a party or in privity with a party to the former action, would not have been bound by it had it been decided the other way. The cases justify this exception on the ground that it would be unjust to permit one who has had his day in court to reopen identical issues by merely switching adversaries.

In determining the validity of a plea of res judicata three questions are pertinent: Was the issue decided in the prior adjudication identical with the one presented in the action in question? Was there a final judgment on the merits? Was the party against whom the plea is asserted a party or in privity with a party to the prior adjudication? . . .

In the present case, therefore, the defendant is not precluded by lack of privity or of mutuality of estoppel from asserting the plea of res judicata against the plaintiff. Since the issue as to the ownership of the money is identical with the issue raised in the probate proceeding, and since the order of the probate court settling the executor's account was a final adjudication of this issue on the merits, it remains only to determine whether the plaintiff in the present action was a party or in privity with a party to the earlier proceeding. The plaintiff has brought the present action in the capacity of administratrix of the estate. In this capacity she represents the very same persons and interests that were represented in the earlier hearing on the executor's account. In that proceeding plaintiff and the other legatees who objected to the executor's account represented the estate of the decedent. They were seeking not a personal recovery but, like the plaintiff in the present action, as administratrix, a recovery for the benefit of the legatees and creditors of the estate, all of whom were bound by the order settling the account. The plea of res judicata is therefore available against plaintiff as a party to the former proceeding, despite her formal change of capacity. "Where a party though appearing in two suits in different capacities is in fact litigating the same right, the judgment in one estops him in the other."

The judgment is affirmed.

NOTES AND QUESTIONS

1. *Identifying the parties.*   The first proceeding in the *Bernhard* case was the probate of Clara Sather's will. One of the issues in that probate proceeding was the legitimacy of the closing of Ms. Sather's bank account with the San Dimas Bank (a most excellent bank). Who were the adversaries on that issue? Was the San Dimas Bank a party to that proceeding or in privity with a party? In the second proceeding, Helen Bernhard sued the Bank of America, which was the San Dimas Bank's successor. Why was Bernhard bound by the judgment in the first proceeding? (There are two reasons.) Which party to the second proceeding was attempting to use issue preclusion? Was that party a party or in privity with a party to the first proceeding?

If not, why does the court allow the "nonparty" to assert issue preclusion? Does the court's reasoning comport with notions of fairness and efficiency? If Bernhard had not been a party or in privity with a party in the first proceeding, would (could) the court have held her bound by an issue decided in that proceeding?

2. *Nonmutuality.*   In the years following the *Bernhard* decision, a majority of jurisdictions, including federal courts, abandoned the mutuality rule. Often that abandonment came with the caveat that a stranger may invoke issue preclusion against a party only if the party had a full and fair opportunity to litigate the issue and had an incentive to do so. *See* CASAD & CLERMONT, *supra*, 169-188. Similarly, the Restatement endorses "nonmutuality" but at the same time recognizes various exceptions. Thus, according to the Restatement, nonmutual issue preclusion should not be allowed (1) if doing so would be incompatible with the scheme of administering the remedies in the actions involved; (2) if the forum in the second action provides procedures that would likely lead to a different determination and that were not available in the first action; (3) if the person seeking to invoke preclusion could easily have joined in the first proceeding; (4) if the decision on the issue was inconsistent with another determination of that same issue; (5) if the relationships among the parties to the first action may have affected the decision, or if the decision was based on a compromise verdict or finding; (6) if doing so might complicate a subsequent action or prejudice the interests of another party thereto; (7) if doing so would inappropriately foreclose obtaining reconsideration of the legal rule upon which it is based; or (8) if there are other compelling circumstances for allowing relitigation of the issues. RESTATEMENT, *supra*, § 29. Yet some states continue to adhere to the mutuality rule. *See, e.g.*, *5F, LLC v. Dresing*, 142 So. 3d 936, 947 (Fla. Ct. App. 2014); *Wilkerson v. Leath*, 2012 WL 2361972, at *5 (Tenn. Ct. App. June 22, 2012); *Bell v. Texaco, Inc.*, 2010 WL 5330729, at *2 (S.D. Miss. Dec. 21, 2010) (applying Mississippi preclusion law); *Rawlings v. Lopez*, 591 S.E.2d 691, 692 (Va. 2004).

PROBLEM

13-18. Return to the facts of Problem 13-16, page 1203, *supra*. Assuming that all other elements of issue preclusion have been satisfied, could Mack assert the doctrine of issue preclusion against the State under the standards established in *Bernhard*?

Parklane Hosiery Co., Inc. v. Shore
439 U.S. 322 (1979)

MR. JUSTICE STEWART delivered the opinion of the Court.

This case presents the question whether a party who has had issues of fact adjudicated adversely to it in an equitable action may be collaterally estopped from relitigating the same issues before a jury in a subsequent legal action brought against it by a new party.

The respondent brought this stockholder's class action against the petitioners in a Federal District Court. The complaint alleged that the petitioners, Parklane Hosiery Co., Inc. (Parklane), and 13 of its officers, directors, and stockholders, had issued a materially false and misleading proxy statement in connection with a merger. The proxy statement, according to the complaint, had violated §§ 14(a), 10(b), and 20(a) of the Securities Exchange Act of 1934, as well as various rules and regulations promulgated by the Securities and Exchange Commission (SEC). The complaint sought damages, rescission of the merger, and recovery of costs.

Before this action came to trial, the SEC filed suit against the same defendants in the Federal District Court, alleging that the proxy statement that had been issued by Parklane was materially false and misleading in essentially the same respects as those that had been alleged in the respondent's complaint. Injunctive relief was requested. After a 4-day trial, the District Court found that the proxy statement was materially false and misleading in the respects alleged, and entered a declaratory judgment to that effect. The Court of Appeals for the Second Circuit affirmed this judgment.

The respondent in the present case then moved for partial summary judgment against the petitioners, asserting that the petitioners were collaterally estopped from relitigating the issues that had been resolved against them in the action brought by the SEC. The District Court denied the motion on the ground that such an application of collateral estoppel would deny the petitioners their Seventh Amendment right to a jury trial. The Court of Appeals for the Second Circuit reversed, holding that a party who has had issues of fact determined against him after a full and fair opportunity to litigate in a nonjury trial is collaterally estopped from obtaining a subsequent jury trial of these same issues of fact. The appellate court concluded that "the Seventh Amendment preserves the right to jury trial only with respect to issues of fact, [and] once those issues have been fully and fairly adjudicated in a prior proceeding, nothing remains for trial, either with or without a jury." Because of an intercircuit conflict, we granted certiorari.

I

The threshold question to be considered is whether, quite apart from the right to a jury trial under the Seventh Amendment, the petitioners can be precluded from relitigating facts resolved adversely to them in a prior equitable proceeding with another party under the general law of collateral estoppel. Specifically, we must determine whether a litigant who was not a party to a prior judgment may nevertheless use that judgment "offensively" to prevent a defendant from relitigating issues resolved in the earlier proceeding.[4]

---

4. In this context, offensive use of collateral estoppel occurs when the plaintiff seeks to foreclose the defendant from litigating an issue the defendant has previously litigated unsuccessfully in an action with another party. Defensive use occurs when a defendant seeks to prevent a plaintiff from asserting a claim the plaintiff has previously litigated and lost against another defendant.

A

Collateral estoppel, like the related doctrine of res judicata,[5] has the dual purpose of protecting litigants from the burden of relitigating an identical issue with the same party or his privy and of promoting judicial economy by preventing needless litigation. Until relatively recently, however, the scope of collateral estoppel was limited by the doctrine of mutuality of parties. Under this mutuality doctrine, neither party could use a prior judgment as an estoppel against the other unless both parties were bound by the judgment. Based on the premise that it is somehow unfair to allow a party to use a prior judgment when he himself would not be so bound,[7] the mutuality requirement provided a party who had litigated and lost in a previous action an opportunity to relitigate identical issues with new parties.

By failing to recognize the obvious difference in position between a party who has never litigated an issue and one who has fully litigated and lost, the mutuality requirement was criticized almost from its inception. Recognizing the validity of this criticism, the Court in *Blonder-Tongue Laboratories, Inc. v. University of Illinois Foundation*, 402 U.S. 313 (1971), abandoned the mutuality requirement, at least in cases where a patentee seeks to relitigate the validity of a patent after a federal court in a previous lawsuit has already declared it invalid. The "broader question" before the Court, however, was "whether it is any longer tenable to afford a litigant more than one full and fair opportunity for judicial resolution of the same issue." The Court strongly suggested a negative answer to that question:

> "In any lawsuit where a defendant, because of the mutuality principle, is forced to present a complete defense on the merits to a claim which the plaintiff has fully litigated and lost in a prior action, there is an arguable misallocation of resources. To the extent the defendant in the second suit may not win by asserting, without contradiction, that the plaintiff had fully and fairly, but unsuccessfully, litigated the same claim in the prior suit, the defendant's time and money are diverted from alternative uses—productive or otherwise—to relitigation of a decided issue. And, still assuming that the issue was resolved correctly in the first suit, there is reason to be concerned about the plaintiff's allocation of resources. Permitting repeated litigation of the same issue as long as the supply of unrelated defendants holds out reflects either the aura of the gaming table or 'a lack of discipline and of disinterestedness on the part of the lower courts, hardly a worthy or wise basis for fashioning rules of procedure.' Although neither judges, the parties, nor the adversary system performs perfectly in all cases, the requirement of determining whether the party against whom an estoppel is asserted had a full and fair opportunity to litigate is a most significant safeguard."

---

5. Under the doctrine of res judicata, a judgment on the merits in a prior suit bars a second suit involving the same parties or their privies based on the same cause of action. Under the doctrine of collateral estoppel, on the other hand, the second action is upon a different cause of action and the judgment in the prior suit precludes relitigation of issues actually litigated and necessary to the outcome of the first action.

7. It is a violation of due process for a judgment to be binding on a litigant who was not a party or a privy and therefore has never had an opportunity to be heard. *Blonder-Tongue Laboratories, Inc. v. University of Illinois Foundation*, 402 U.S. 313, 329; *Hansberry v. Lee*, 311 U.S. 32, 40.

B

The *Blonder-Tongue* case involved defensive use of collateral estoppel—a plaintiff was estopped from asserting a claim that the plaintiff had previously litigated and lost against another defendant. The present case, by contrast, involves offensive use of collateral estoppel—a plaintiff is seeking to estop a defendant from relitigating the issues which the defendant previously litigated and lost against another plaintiff. In both the offensive and defensive use situations, the party against whom estoppel is asserted has litigated and lost in an earlier action. Nevertheless, several reasons have been advanced why the two situations should be treated differently.

First, offensive use of collateral estoppel does not promote judicial economy in the same manner as defensive use does. Defensive use of collateral estoppel precludes a plaintiff from relitigating identical issues by merely "switching adversaries." *Bernhard v. Bank of America Nat. Trust & Savings Assn.*, 19 Cal. 2d, at 813.[12] Thus defensive collateral estoppel gives a plaintiff a strong incentive to join all potential defendants in the first action if possible. Offensive use of collateral estoppel, on the other hand, creates precisely the opposite incentive. Since a plaintiff will be able to rely on a previous judgment against a defendant but will not be bound by that judgment if the defendant wins, the plaintiff has every incentive to adopt a "wait and see" attitude, in the hope that the first action by another plaintiff will result in a favorable judgment. Thus offensive use of collateral estoppel will likely increase rather than decrease the total amount of litigation, since potential plaintiffs will have everything to gain and nothing to lose by not intervening in the first action.

A second argument against offensive use of collateral estoppel is that it may be unfair to a defendant. If a defendant in the first action is sued for small or nominal damages, he may have little incentive to defend vigorously, particularly if future suits are not foreseeable. *The Evergreens v. Nunan*, 141 F.2d 927, 929 (CA 2); cf. *Berner v. British Commonwealth Pac. Airlines*, 346 F.2d 532 (CA2) (application of offensive collateral estoppel denied where defendant did not appeal an adverse judgment awarding damages of $35,000 and defendant was later sued for over $7 million). Allowing offensive collateral estoppel may also be unfair to a defendant if the judgment relied upon as a basis for the estoppel is itself inconsistent with one or more previous judgments in favor of the defendant.[14] Still another situation where it might be unfair to apply offensive estoppel is where the second

---

12. Under the mutuality requirement, a plaintiff could accomplish this result since he would not have been bound by the judgment had the original defendant won.

14. In Professor Currie's familiar example, a railroad collision injures 50 passengers all of whom bring separate actions against the railroad. After the railroad wins the first 25 suits, a plaintiff wins in suit 26. Professor Currie argues that offensive use of collateral estoppel should not be applied so as to allow plaintiffs 27 through 50 automatically to recover.

action affords the defendant procedural opportunities unavailable in the first action that could readily cause a different result.[15]

C

We have concluded that the preferable approach for dealing with these problems in the federal courts is not to preclude the use of offensive collateral estoppel, but to grant trial courts broad discretion to determine when it should be applied. The general rule should be that in cases where a plaintiff could easily have joined in the earlier action or where, either for the reasons discussed above or for other reasons, the application of offensive estoppel would be unfair to a defendant, a trial judge should not allow the use of offensive collateral estoppel.

In the present case, however, none of the circumstances that might justify reluctance to allow the offensive use of collateral estoppel is present. The application of offensive collateral estoppel will not here reward a private plaintiff who could have joined in the previous action, since the respondent probably could not have joined in the injunctive action brought by the SEC even had he so desired. Similarly, there is no unfairness to the petitioners in applying offensive collateral estoppel in this case. First, in light of the serious allegations made in the SEC's complaint against the petitioners, as well as the foreseeability of subsequent private suits that typically follow a successful Government judgment, the petitioners had every incentive to litigate the SEC lawsuit fully and vigorously.[18] Second, the judgment in the SEC action was not inconsistent with any previous decision. Finally, there will in the respondent's action be no procedural opportunities available to the petitioners that were unavailable in the first action of a kind that might be likely to cause a different result.

We conclude, therefore, that none of the considerations that would justify a refusal to allow the use of offensive collateral estoppel is present in this case. Since the petitioners received a "full and fair" opportunity to litigate their claims in the SEC action, the contemporary law of collateral estoppel leads inescapably to the conclusion that the petitioners are collaterally estopped from relitigating the question of whether the proxy statement was materially false and misleading.

---

15. If, for example, the defendant in the first action was forced to defend in an inconvenient forum and therefore was unable to engage in full scale discovery or call witnesses, application of offensive collateral estoppel may be unwarranted. Indeed, differences in available procedures may sometimes justify not allowing a prior judgment to have estoppel effect in a subsequent action even between the same parties, or where defensive estoppel is asserted against a plaintiff who has litigated and lost. The problem of unfairness is particularly acute in cases of offensive estoppel, however, because the defendant against whom estoppel is asserted typically will not have chosen the forum in the first action.

18. After a 4-day trial in which the petitioners had every opportunity to present evidence and call witnesses, the District Court held for the SEC. The petitioners then appealed to the Court of Appeals for the Second Circuit, which affirmed the judgment against them. Moreover, the petitioners were already aware of the action brought by the respondent, since it had commenced before the filing of the SEC action.

II

The question that remains is whether, notwithstanding the law of collateral estoppel, the use of offensive collateral estoppel in this case would violate the petitioners' Seventh Amendment right to a jury trial. . . .

. . . The petitioners contend that since the scope of the Amendment must be determined by reference to the common law as it existed in 1791 [when the Seventh Amendment was ratified], and since the common law permitted collateral estoppel only where there was mutuality of parties, collateral estoppel cannot constitutionally be applied when such mutuality is absent.

The petitioners have advanced no persuasive reason, however, why the meaning of the Seventh Amendment should depend on whether or not mutuality of parties is present. . . . In either case there is no further factfinding function for the jury to perform, since the common factual issues have been resolved in the previous action.

The Seventh Amendment has never been interpreted in the rigid manner advocated by the petitioners. On the contrary, many procedural devices developed since 1791 that have diminished the civil jury's historic domain have been found not to be inconsistent with the Seventh Amendment. See *Galloway v. United States*, 319 U.S. 372, 388-393 [(1943)] (directed verdict does not violate Seventh Amendment); . . . *Fidelity & Deposit Co. v. United States*, 187 U.S. 315, 319-321 [(1902)] (summary judgment does not violate Seventh Amendment).

The law of collateral estoppel, like the law in other procedural areas defining the scope of the jury's function, has evolved since 1791. [T]hese developments are not repugnant to the Seventh Amendment simply for the reason that they did not exist in 1791. Thus if, as we have held, the law of collateral estoppel forecloses the petitioners from relitigating the factual issues determined against them in the SEC action, nothing in the Seventh Amendment dictates a different result, even though because of lack of mutuality there would have been no collateral estoppel in 1791.

The judgment of the Court of Appeals is
Affirmed.

[The opinion of JUSTICE REHNQUIST, dissenting on Seventh Amendment grounds, is omitted.]

NOTES AND QUESTIONS

1. *The distinction between offensive and defensive issue preclusion.* The *Parklane* Court described the plaintiff's attempt to invoke issue preclusion as "offensive." *Parklane Hosiery Co., Inc., supra*, 439 U.S. at 329. By contrast, the use of issue preclusion in *Bernhard* would be described as defensive. What is the distinction between the two? Sometimes this distinction is described as the difference between using issue preclusion as a "sword" or as a "shield." Which is the sword and which is the shield? In any of the earlier cases that we read, did the

plaintiff seek to invoke offensive nonmutual issue preclusion? Did the court allow it? If not, was the court's refusal to do so consistent with the decision in *Parklane*? *See Cunningham v. Outten, supra*, at page 1200, *supra*.

2. *Limiting the scope of offensive issue preclusion.*   Some states that have abandoned mutuality with respect to defensive uses of issue preclusion have not done so with respect to offensive uses. *See, e.g., Sullivan v. Wilson County*, 2012 WL 1868292, at *11 (Tenn. Ct. App. Oct. 11, 2011); *Keywell and Rosenfeld v. Bithell*, 657 N.W.2d 759, 787-788 (Mich. Ct. App. 2002). What concerns might lead a court to draw such a distinction? Might fairness or efficiency play any part in this thinking? Did the *Parklane* Court adequately address the potential downside of permitting nonmutual offensive issue preclusion? To what extent is the *Parklane* ruling consistent or inconsistent with the position adopted by § 29 of the Restatement? *See* Note 2 following *Bernhard*, page 1212, *supra*.

3. *Nonmutual preclusion against the government.*   In *United States v. Mendoza*, 464 U.S. 154 (1984), the Supreme Court refused, as a matter of federal preclusion law, to allow the plaintiff to invoke nonmutual offensive issue preclusion against the U.S. government in the context of an immigration proceeding. The issue in question was one of federal constitutional law that the government had litigated and lost in federal district court seven years earlier, and then chose not to appeal. The Court gave three reasons for refusing to allow preclusion. First, application of issue preclusion under such circumstances would prevent the underlying legal question from percolating and developing in lower federal courts, where conflicting approaches might lend insight into the proper scope of the law. Second, it would undermine the government's discretion to seek or not seek review of adverse judgments by essentially forcing the government's hand in the first case in which a lower court rules against it. And third, to freeze the law at the first decision would hamper the flexibility of successive elected administrations to exercise discretion over the development of policy. Although *Mendoza* involved a potential application of offensive issue preclusion, some lower federal courts have held that the principle of *Mendoza* applies to nonmutual defensive issue preclusion as well. *See, e.g., Kanter v. Commissioner of Internal Revenue*, 590 F.3d 410, 419 (7th Cir. 2009) ("The policy reasons for treating the government differently . . . seem to be just as powerful when applied to defensive preclusion."); *Reich v. D.C. Wiring, Inc.*, 940 F. Supp. 105, 107-108 (D.N.J. 1996) (collecting authorities).

The *Mendoza* Court did not state categorically that the federal government is absolutely immune from all assertions of nonmutual issue preclusion, although the opinion gave no indication of any potential exceptions. A number of lower courts have treated the "rule" as a categorical one. *See* 18A WRIGHT, MILLER & COOPER, *supra*, § 4465.4. Some federal courts, however, have adopted a more flexible approach, reading *Mendoza*'s holding as being qualified rather than absolute. For example in *Gulfstream Aerospace Corp. v. United States*, 981 F. Supp. 654 (Ct. Int'l Trade 1997), the Court of International Trade allowed a private party to use nonmutual offensive issue preclusion against the government, reasoning that the trio of concerns discussed in *Mendoza* were not implicated in the pending case. *Id.* at 660. First, since the issue presented was within the Court of International

Trade's exclusive jurisdiction, there could be no "percolation" of the issue in other courts in any event. Next, the government's discretion to appeal was not undermined since the government did appeal the prior ruling. And finally, the question presented simply involved compliance with the Administrative Procedure Act and did not, therefore, involve the type of policy judgment that should remain within elected officials' discretion. *See also Colorado Springs Prod. Credit Ass'n v. Farm Credit Admin.*, 666 F. Supp. 1475 (D. Colo. 1987) (permitting nonmutual offensive estoppel against the government when the underlying issue does not involve significant policy concerns and when the cases are factually and legally similar). Whether such decisions will survive remains an open question.

The courts are divided as to whether state and local governments should be insulated from nonmutual offensive and defensive issue preclusion, with most courts extending *Mendoza*-type protection to them. *Compare State of Idaho Potato Comm'n v. G & T Terminal Packaging, Inc.*, 425 F.3d 708, 713-714 (9th Cir. 2005) (applying *Mendoza* to bar nonmutual defensive issue preclusion against state agency), *Bogle Farms, Inc. v. Baca*, 925 P.2d 1184, 1190-1191 (N.M. 1996) (applying *Mendoza* to bar nonmutual offensive issue preclusion against state), *Board of Educ. of St. Louis v. City of St. Louis*, 879 S.W.2d 530, 532 (Mo. 1994) (applying *Mendoza* to bar nonmutual offensive issue preclusion against city government), and *Hercules Carriers, Inc. v. Claimant State of Fla. Dep't of Transp.*, 768 F.2d 1558, 1578-1579 (11th Cir. 1985) (applying *Mendoza* to bar nonmutual offensive or defensive issue preclusion against state),*with In re Stevenson*, 40 A.3d 1212, 1222 (Pa. 2012) (declining to extend *Mendoza* and allowing nonmutual offensive issue preclusion against state based on prior federal court judgment holding a state law unconstitutional), and *State v. United Cook Inlet Drift Ass'n*, 895 P.2d 947, 950-952 (Alaska 1995) (declining to extend *Mendoza* and permitting nonmutual offensive issue preclusion against state government based on prior state court judgment). *See generally* Note, *Nonmutual Issue Preclusion Against States*, 109 Harv. L. Rev. 792 (1996).

Smith v. Bayer Corporation

564 U.S. 299 (2011)

Justice Kagan delivered the opinion of the Court.

In this case, a Federal District Court enjoined a state court from considering a plaintiff's request to approve a class action. The District Court did so because it had earlier denied a motion to certify a class in a related case, brought by a different plaintiff against the same defendant alleging similar claims. The federal court thought its injunction appropriate to prevent relitigation of the issue it had decided.

We hold to the contrary. In issuing this order to a state court, the federal court exceeded its authority under the "relitigation exception" to the Anti-Injunction Act. That statutory provision permits a federal court to enjoin a state proceeding only in rare cases, when necessary to "protect or effectuate [the federal court's] judgments." 28 U.S.C. § 2283. Here, that standard was not met for two reasons. First, the issue presented in the state court was not identical to the one decided in the federal tribunal. And second, the plaintiff in the state court did not have the requisite connection to the federal suit to be bound by the District Court's judgment.

I . . .

. . . In August 2001, George McCollins sued respondent Bayer Corporation in the Circuit Court of Cabell County, West Virginia, asserting various state-law claims arising from Bayer's sale of an allegedly hazardous prescription drug called Baycol (which Bayer withdrew from the market that same month). McCollins contended that Bayer had violated West Virginia's consumer-protection statute and the company's express and implied warranties by selling him a defective product. And pursuant to West Virginia Rule of Civil Procedure 23 (2011), McCollins asked the state court to certify a class of West Virginia residents who had also purchased Baycol, so that the case could proceed as a class action.

Approximately one month later, the suit now before us began in a different part of West Virginia. Petitioners Keith Smith and Shirley Sperlazza (Smith for short) filed state-law claims against Bayer, similar to those raised in McCollins' suit, in the Circuit Court of Brooke County, West Virginia. And like McCollins, Smith asked the court to certify under West Virginia's Rule 23 a class of Baycol purchasers residing in the State. Neither Smith nor McCollins knew about the other's suit.

In January 2002, Bayer removed McCollins' case to the United States District Court for the Southern District of West Virginia on the basis of diversity jurisdiction. See 28 U.S.C. §§ 1332, 1441. The case was then transferred to the District of Minnesota pursuant to a preexisting order of the Judicial Panel on Multi-District Litigation, which had consolidated all federal suits involving Baycol (numbering in the tens of thousands) before a single District Court Judge. See § 1407. Bayer, however, could not remove Smith's case to federal court because Smith had sued several West Virginia defendants in addition to Bayer, and so the suit lacked complete diversity.* See § 1441(b).[1] Smith's suit thus remained in the state courthouse in Brooke County.

Over the next six years, the two cases proceeded along their separate pretrial paths at roughly the same pace. By 2008, both courts were preparing to turn to

---

* [While the case later became removable, 28 U.S.C. § 1446(b)'s one-year limitation on removal had by then run. — EDS.]

1. The Class Action Fairness Act of 2005, 119 Stat. 4, which postdates and therefore does not govern this lawsuit, now enables a defendant to remove to federal court certain class actions involving nondiverse parties. See 28 U.S.C. §§ 1332(d), 1453(b).

[Had Smith filed his lawsuit a few years later, after CAFA was enacted, Bayer could in fact have removed the action to federal court despite the lack of complete diversity. *See In re Baycol Prods. Litig.*, 593 F.3d 716, 720 (8th Cir. 2010); Chapter IX, part B.2, "'CAFA' Class Actions and Mass Actions," page 765, *supra*. — EDS.]

their respective plaintiffs' motions for class certification. The Federal District Court was the first to reach a decision.

Applying Federal Rule of Civil Procedure 23, the District Court declined to certify McCollins' proposed class of West Virginia Baycol purchasers. The District Court's reasoning proceeded in two steps. The court first ruled that, under West Virginia law, each plaintiff would have to prove "actual injury" from his use of Baycol to recover. The court then held that because the necessary showing of harm would vary from plaintiff to plaintiff, "individual issues of fact predominate[d]" over issues common to all members of the proposed class, and so the case was not suitable for class treatment. In the same order, the District Court also dismissed McCollins' claims on the merits in light of his failure to demonstrate physical injury from his use of Baycol. McCollins chose not to appeal.

Although McCollins' suit was now concluded, Bayer asked the District Court for another order based upon it, this one affecting Smith's case in West Virginia. In a motion—receipt of which first apprised Smith of McCollins' suit—Bayer explained that the proposed class in Smith's case was identical to the one the federal court had just rejected. Bayer therefore requested that the federal court enjoin the West Virginia state court from hearing Smith's motion to certify a class. According to Bayer, that order was appropriate to protect the District Court's judgment in McCollins' suit denying class certification. The District Court agreed and granted the injunction.

The Court of Appeals for the Eighth Circuit affirmed. The court noted that the Anti-Injunction Act generally prohibits federal courts from enjoining state court proceedings. But the court held that the Act's relitigation exception authorized the injunction here because ordinary rules of issue preclusion barred Smith from seeking certification of his proposed class. According to the court, Smith was invoking a similar class action rule as McCollins had used to seek certification "of the same class" in a suit alleging "the same legal theories"; the issue in the state court therefore was "sufficiently identical" to the one the federal court had decided to warrant preclusion. In addition, the court held, the parties in the two proceedings were sufficiently alike: Because Smith was an unnamed member of the class McCollins had proposed, and because their "interests were aligned," Smith was appropriately bound by the federal court's judgment.

We granted certiorari. . . . We think the District Court erred on both grounds when it granted the injunction, and we now reverse.

II

The Anti-Injunction Act, first enacted in 1793, provides that

> "A court of the United States may not grant an injunction to stay proceedings in a State court except as expressly authorized by Act of Congress, or where necessary in aid of its jurisdiction, or to protect or effectuate its judgments." 28 U.S.C. § 2283.

The statute, we have recognized, "is a necessary concomitant of the Framers' decision to authorize, and Congress' decision to implement, a dual system of federal and state courts." *Chick Kam Choo v. Exxon Corp.*, 486 U.S. 140, 146 (1988). And the Act's core message is one of respect for state courts. . . .

This case involves the last of the Act's three exceptions, known as the relitigation exception. That exception is designed to implement "well-recognized concepts" of claim and issue preclusion. The provision authorizes an injunction to prevent state litigation of a claim or issue "that previously was presented to and decided by the federal court." But in applying this exception, we have taken special care to keep it "strict and narrow." After all, a court does not usually "get to dictate to other courts the preclusion consequences of its own judgment." Deciding whether and how prior litigation has preclusive effect is usually the bailiwick of the *second* court (here, the one in West Virginia). So issuing an injunction under the relitigation exception is resorting to heavy artillery.[5] For that reason, every benefit of the doubt goes toward the state court; an injunction can issue only if preclusion is clear beyond peradventure.

The question here is whether the federal court's rejection of McCollins' proposed class precluded a later adjudication in state court of Smith's certification motion. For the federal court's determination of the class issue to have this preclusive effect, at least two conditions must be met.[6] First, the issue the federal court decided must be the same as the one presented in the state tribunal. And second, Smith must have been a party to the federal suit, or else must fall within one of a few discrete exceptions to the general rule against binding nonparties. In fact, as we will explain, the issues before the two courts were not the same, and Smith was neither a party nor the exceptional kind of nonparty who can be bound. So the courts below erred in finding the certification issue precluded, and erred all the more in thinking an injunction appropriate.[7]

A

In our most recent case on the relitigation exception, *Chick Kam Choo v. Exxon*, we applied the "same issue" requirement of preclusion law to invalidate a federal court's injunction. The federal court had dismissed a suit involving Singapore law on grounds of *forum non conveniens*. After the plaintiff brought the same claim in Texas state court, the federal court issued an injunction

---

5. That is especially so because an injunction is not the only way to correct a state trial court's erroneous refusal to give preclusive effect to a federal judgment. As we have noted before, "the state appellate courts and ultimately this Court" can review and reverse such a ruling. See *Atlantic Coast Line R. Co. v. Locomotive Engineers*, 398 U.S. 281, 287 (1970). [*See also* Chapter IX, "A Note on Enjoining Competing Actions," at page 850, *supra.* —EDS.]

6. We have held that federal common law governs the preclusive effect of a decision of a federal court sitting in diversity. See *Semtek Int'l Inc. v. Lockheed Martin Corp.*, 531 U.S. 497, 508 (2001). Smith assumes that federal common law should here incorporate West Virginia's preclusion law, whereas Bayer favors looking only to federal rules of preclusion because of the federal interests at stake in this case. We do not think the question matters here. Neither party identifies any way in which federal and state principles of preclusion law differ in any relevant respect. Nor have we found any such divergence. We therefore need not decide whether, in general, federal common law ought to incorporate state law in situations such as this.

7. Because we rest our decision on the Anti-Injunction Act and the principles of issue preclusion that inform it, we do not consider Smith's argument, based on *Phillips Petroleum Co. v. Shutts*, 472 U.S. 797 (1985), that the District Court's action violated the Due Process Clause.

barring the plaintiff from pursuing relief in that alternate forum. We held that the District Court had gone too far. "[A]n essential prerequisite for applying the relitigation exception," we explained, "is that the . . . issues which the federal injunction insulates from litigation in state proceedings actually have been decided by the federal court." *Id.*, at 148. That prerequisite, we thought, was not satisfied because the issue to be adjudicated in state court was not the one the federal court had resolved. The federal court had considered the permissibility of the claim under federal *forum non conveniens* principles. But the Texas courts, we thought, "would apply a significantly different *forum non conveniens* analysis"; they had in prior cases rejected the strictness of the federal doctrine. Our conclusion followed: "[W]hether the Texas *state* courts are an appropriate forum for [the plaintiff's] Singapore law claims has not yet been litigated." Because the legal standards in the two courts differed, the issues before the courts differed, and an injunction was unwarranted.

The question here closely resembles the one in *Chick Kam Choo*. The class Smith proposed in state court mirrored the class McCollins sought to certify in federal court: Both included all Baycol purchasers resident in West Virginia. Moreover, the substantive claims in the two suits broadly overlapped: Both complaints alleged that Bayer had sold a defective product in violation of the State's consumer protection law and the company's warranties. So far, so good for preclusion. But not so fast: a critical question—the question of the applicable legal standard—remains. The District Court ruled that the proposed class did not meet the requirements of Federal Rule 23 (because individualized issues would predominate over common ones). But the state court was poised to consider whether the proposed class satisfied *West Virginia* Rule 23. If those two legal standards differ (as federal and state *forum non conveniens* law differed in *Chick Kam Choo*)—then the federal court resolved an issue not before the state court. In that event, much like in *Chick Kam Choo*, "whether the [West Virginia] *state* cour[t]" should certify the proposed class action "has not yet been litigated."

. . . The Eighth Circuit relied almost exclusively on the near-identity of the two Rules' texts. That was the right place to start, but not to end. Federal and state courts, after all, can and do apply identically worded procedural provisions in widely varying ways. If a State's procedural provision tracks the language of a Federal Rule, but a state court interprets that provision in a manner federal courts have not, then the state court is using a different standard and thus deciding a different issue. . . . Smith contends that the source of law is all that matters: a different sovereign must in each and every case "have the opportunity, if it chooses, to construe its procedural rule differently." But if state courts made it crystal clear that they follow the same approach as the federal court applied, we see no need to ignore that determination; in that event, the issue in the two cases would indeed be the same. So a federal court considering whether the relitigation exception applies should examine whether state law parallels its federal counterpart. But as suggested earlier, the federal court must resolve any uncertainty on that score by leaving the question of preclusion to the state courts.

Under this approach, the West Virginia Supreme Court has gone some way toward resolving the matter before us by declaring its independence from federal courts' interpretation of the Federal Rules—and particularly of Rule 23. In *In re W. Va. Rezulin Litigation*, 214 W. Va. 52, 585 S.E.2d 52 (2003) *(In re Rezulin)*, the West Virginia high court considered a plaintiff's motion to certify a class— coincidentally enough, in a suit about an allegedly defective pharmaceutical product. The court made a point of complaining about the parties' and lower court's near-exclusive reliance on federal cases about Federal Rule 23 to decide the certification question. . . . Of course, the state courts might still have adopted an approach to their Rule 23 that tracked the analysis the federal court used in McCollins' case. But absent clear evidence that the state courts had done so, we could not conclude that they would interpret their Rule in the same way. And if that is so, we could not tell whether the certification issues in the state and federal courts were the same. That uncertainty would preclude an injunction.

But here the case against an injunction is even stronger, because the West Virginia Supreme Court has *disapproved* the approach to Rule 23(b)(3)'s predominance requirement that the Federal District Court embraced. Recall that the federal court held that the presence of a single individualized issue—injury from the use of Baycol—prevented class certification. The court did not identify the common issues in the case; nor did it balance these common issues against the need to prove individual injury to determine which predominated. The court instead applied a strict test barring class treatment when proof of each plaintiff's injury is necessary. By contrast, the West Virginia Supreme Court in *In re Rezulin* adopted an all-things-considered, balancing inquiry in interpreting its Rule 23. . . . A state court using the *In re Rezulin* standard would decide a different question than the one the federal court had earlier resolved.[9]

. . . A federal court and a state court apply different law. That means they decide distinct questions. The federal court's resolution of one issue does not preclude the state court's determination of another. It then goes without saying that the federal court may not issue an injunction. The *Anti*-Injunction Act's *re*-litigation exception does not extend nearly so far.

B

The injunction issued here runs into another basic premise of preclusion law: A court's judgment binds only the parties to a suit, subject to a handful of discrete and limited exceptions. The importance of this rule and the narrowness

---

9. . . . Our point is not that *In re Rezulin* dictates the answer to the class certification question here; the two cases are indeed too dissimilar for that to be true. The point instead is that *In re Rezulin* articulated a general approach to the predominance requirement that differs markedly from the one the federal court used. Minor variations in the application of what is in essence the same legal standard do not defeat preclusion; but where, as here, the State's courts "would apply a significantly different . . . analysis," *Chick Kam Choo v. Exxon Corp.*, 486 U.S. 140, 149 (1988), the federal and state courts decide different issues.

of its exceptions go hand in hand. We have repeatedly "emphasize[d] the fundamental nature of the general rule" that only parties can be bound by prior judgments; accordingly, we have taken a "constrained approach to nonparty preclusion." *Taylor v. Sturgell*, 553 U.S. 880, 898 (2008). Against this backdrop, Bayer defends the decision below by arguing that Smith—an unnamed member of a proposed but uncertified class—qualifies as a party to the McCollins litigation. Alternatively, Bayer claims that the District Court's judgment binds Smith under the recognized exception to the rule against nonparty preclusion for members of class actions. We think neither contention has merit.

Bayer's first claim ill-comports with any proper understanding of what a "party" is. In general, "[a] 'party' to litigation is '[o]ne by or against whom a lawsuit is brought,'" *United States ex rel. Eisenstein v. City of New York*, 129 S. Ct. 2230, 2234 (2009), or one who "become[s] a party by intervention, substitution, or third-party practice," *Karcher v. May*, 484 U.S. 72, 77 (1987). And we have further held that an unnamed member of a *certified* class may be "considered a 'party' for the [particular] purpos[e] of appealing" an adverse judgment. *Devlin v. Scardelletti*, 536 U.S. 1, 7 (2002). But as the dissent in *Devlin* noted, no one in that case was "willing to advance the novel and surely erroneous argument that a nonnamed class member is a party to the class-action litigation *before the class is certified.*" Still less does that argument make sense *once certification is denied.* The definition of the term "party" can on no account be stretched so far as to cover a person like Smith, whom the plaintiff in a lawsuit was denied leave to represent.[10] If the judgment in the McCollins litigation can indeed bind Smith, it must do so under principles of *non* party preclusion.

As Bayer notes, one such principle allows unnamed members of a class action to be bound, even though they are not parties to the suit. But here Bayer faces a conundrum. If we know one thing about the McCollins suit, we know that it was *not* a class action. Indeed, the very ruling that Bayer argues ought to be given preclusive effect is the District Court's decision that a class could not properly be certified. So Bayer wants to bind Smith as a member of a class action (because it is only as such that a nonparty in Smith's situation can be bound) to a determination that there could not be a class action. . . .

But wishing does not make it so. McCollins sought class certification, but he failed to obtain that result. Because the District Court found that individual issues predominated, it held that the action did not satisfy Federal Rule 23's

---

10. In support of its claim that Smith counts as a party, Bayer cites two cases in which we held that a putative member of an uncertified class may wait until after the court rules on the certification motion to file an individual claim or move to intervene in the suit [*United Airlines, Inc. v. McDonald*, 432 U.S. 385 (1977); *American Pipe & Constr. Co. v. Utah*, 414 U.S. 538 (1974)]. But these cases, which were specifically grounded in policies of judicial administration, demonstrate only that a person not a party to a class suit may receive certain benefits (such as the tolling of a limitations period) related to that proceeding. That result is consistent with a commonplace of preclusion law—that nonparties sometimes may benefit from, even though they cannot be bound by, former litigation. See *Parklane Hosiery Co. v. Shore*, 439 U.S. 322, 326-333 (1979); *Blonder-Tongue Laboratories, Inc. v. University of Ill. Foundation*, 402 U.S. 313 (1971).

requirements for class proceedings. In these circumstances, we cannot say that a properly conducted class action existed at any time in the litigation. . . . Neither a proposed class action nor a rejected class action may bind nonparties. What does have this effect is a class action approved under Rule 23. But McCollins' lawsuit was never that.

We made essentially these same points in *Taylor v. Sturgell* just a few Terms ago. The question there concerned the propriety of binding nonparties under a theory of "virtual representation" based on "identity of interests and some kind of relationship between parties and nonparties." We rejected the theory unanimously, explaining that it "would 'recogniz[e], in effect, a common-law kind of class action.'" . . . Bayer attempts to distinguish *Taylor* by noting that the party in the prior litigation there did not propose a class action. But we do not see why that difference matters. Yes, McCollins wished to represent a class, and made a motion to that effect. But it did not come to pass. To allow McCollins' suit to bind nonparties would be to adopt the very theory *Taylor* rejected.

Bayer's strongest argument comes not from established principles of preclusion, but instead from policy concerns relating to use of the class action device. Bayer warns that under our approach class counsel can repeatedly try to certify the same class "by the simple expedient of changing the named plaintiff in the caption of the complaint." And in this world of "serial relitigation of class certification," Bayer contends, defendants "would be forced in effect to buy litigation peace by settling."

But this form of argument flies in the face of the rule against nonparty preclusion. That rule perforce leads to relitigation of many issues, as plaintiff after plaintiff after plaintiff (none precluded by the last judgment because none a party to the last suit) tries his hand at establishing some legal principle or obtaining some grant of relief. We confronted a similar policy concern in *Taylor*, which involved litigation brought under the Freedom of Information Act (FOIA). . . . But we rejected this argument, even though the payoff in a single successful FOIA suit—disclosure of documents to the public—could "trum[p]" or "subsum[e]" all prior losses, just as a single successful class certification motion could do. As that response suggests, our legal system generally relies on principles of *stare decisis* and comity among courts to mitigate the sometimes substantial costs of similar litigation brought by different plaintiffs. We have not thought that the right approach (except in the discrete categories of cases we have recognized) lies in binding nonparties to a judgment. . . .

* * *

The Anti-Injunction Act prohibits the order the District Court entered here. The Act's relitigation exception authorizes injunctions only when a former federal adjudication clearly precludes a state-court decision. . . . Under this approach, close cases have easy answers: The federal court should not issue an injunction, and the state court should decide the preclusion question. But this case does not even strike us as close. The issues in the federal and state lawsuits differed because the relevant legal standards differed. And the mere proposal of a class in the federal action could not bind persons who were not parties there. For these reasons, the judgment of the Court of Appeals is

Reversed.

NOTES AND QUESTIONS

1. *The Anti-Injunction Act.*   The issue in *Smith* was whether the Anti-Injunction Act, 28 U.S.C. § 2283, allowed the federal court to enjoin a West Virginia state court from certifying as a class action a suit brought there by Smith against Bayer. How did the question of issue preclusion enter the picture? Did one of the act's exceptions to the ban on federal injunctions against pending state court proceedings turn on the issue-preclusive effect of an earlier federal court judgment in a similar suit brought by McCollins against Bayer? Thus while this case involves the act, the critical question concerns the earlier federal court judgment's proper issue-preclusive effect. According to the Supreme Court, when would such an injunction be appropriate in a case like this?

2. *Issue preclusion.*   In determining the issue-preclusive effect of the earlier federal court judgment, whose law of issue preclusion would apply? Did the Supreme Court have to resolve that question here? What issue did Bayer seek to preclude Smith from litigating in state court? Did this involve offensive or defensive preclusion? Was the issue one of fact, one of law, or a mixed question of fact and law? Were the relevant facts as to that issue essentially identical in both suits? Were the relevant legal principles the same? As to the latter, was it clear that West Virginia Rule 23 was different from Federal Rule 23 or that it would lead to a different class-certification result than the federal court had reached earlier in McCollins's case? If not—*i.e.*, if the two rules, both as written and as applied, might well yield identical results—what was wrong with the federal district court enjoining Smith from seeking class certification in state court?

3. *Virtual representation.*   Since Smith was neither a party to nor in privity with a party to McCollins's earlier federal suit, the argument for binding Smith to the McCollins court's finding that a class action was improper amounted to an argument for virtual representation—a doctrine the Court had rejected a few years earlier in *Taylor v. Sturgell*, page 1165, *supra*. On what bases did Bayer seek to distinguish *Taylor*? Why did the Court reject those arguments? Was *Smith* arguably a more compelling case for allowing virtual representation given the use to which the prior judgment was to be put? In *Taylor*, the preclusion argument went to the merits of the plaintiff's FOIA claim and would have resulted in its dismissal, whereas in *Smith*, preclusion would have applied only to the issue of whether the suit could proceed as a class action. Might the Court have seized on this to allow virtual representation on such procedural issues, while disallowing it on issues going to the merits of a plaintiff's claim? Yet might there be times when those lines blur, *i.e.*, when a procedural issue will be dispositive of the case? *Smith* appears to have been such a case, for the would-be plaintiff class there was suing

only for the small economic loss reflected in the drug's purchase price. As the district court noted, the cost of "litigating an individual . . . refund claim . . . to recover economic damages from purchasing Baycol would dwarf the amount of any individual claim," rendering individual actions infeasible. *In re Baycol Prods. Litig.*, 265 F.R.D. 453, 458 (D. Minn. 2008). The Supreme Court may have been sensitive to this fact, for by barring the federal court from enjoining a class action in state court, it left open the possibility that West Virginia courts might interpret their version of Rule 23 in such a way as to allow Smith's suit to proceed on a class basis there.

4. *Trusting the state courts.*   Since the preclusive effect of the earlier federal judgment in McCollins's case will now be determined by the West Virginia state courts rather than by the federal court that rendered it, what assurance is there that the state courts will give the federal judgment its proper preclusive effect? That Bayer removed Smith's case to federal court suggests that Bayer may have distrusted the state courts' ability to handle the case fairly—a case brought on behalf of ordinary retail purchasers against a large out-of-state corporation. Realistically, what recourse would Bayer have if West Virginia's courts fail to give the earlier federal judgment the preclusive effect to which Bayer thinks it was entitled? Since a federal judgment's preclusive effect in a diversity case is generally determined in accordance with state law, *see* "A Note on Intersystem Preclusion (Federal-to-State)," at page 1153, *supra*), is the Supreme Court likely to grant certiorari if Bayer later claims that the state courts got it wrong? Does this perhaps explain Bayer's efforts to have the federal district court resolve this question, rather than leaving it for the state's courts to decide?

5. *Preclusive effect of putative class actions.*   What rule did the Court announce with respect to when claim or issue preclusion can be invoked against someone who was a member of a putative federal court class action when the class was never certified? Under this rule, is there anything to keep plaintiffs who were members of a putative but uncertified class from suing the same defendant over and over again on the same claim, as long as a different plaintiff brings each suit? Can a defendant like Bayer who wins one or more of these individual actions use issue or claim preclusion against new plaintiffs in subsequent suits? If one of the individual plaintiffs (or a plaintiff class) eventually wins the suit, can other individual or class plaintiffs then use that case as a basis for invoking offensive issue preclusion against the defendant? Does this put defendants like Bayer in an unfair position? To the extent that the defendant wins the early suits, can it at least invoke stare decisis against plaintiffs in later suits? Might such plaintiffs eventually become discouraged from filing after earlier plaintiffs have lost identical actions?

A NOTE ON NONMUTUALITY AND INTERSYSTEM PRECLUSION

Under the general principle of intersystem preclusion, the law of preclusion that would be followed within the jurisdiction of the court first rendering judgment controls the application of preclusion to that judgment by a court from

another jurisdiction. *See* "A Note on Intersystem Preclusion," page 1152, *supra.*
This intersystem principle generally applies equally to both claim and issue preclusion. A few courts have, however, fashioned a slight variation on this theme in
the specific context of issue preclusion and mutuality. These courts have held that
the law of preclusion that would be applied by the initial court merely establishes
the *minimum* amount of preclusion that must be accorded that court's judgment.
Under this view, the second court may thus give the prior judgment *greater* issue-
preclusive effect than would the first or rendering court. Theoretically, because
the additional preclusive effect does not in any way undermine the initial judgment, no violation of full faith and credit occurs. As applied, however, this variation does alter the scope of the initial court's judgment.

The most likely context in which this variation might apply is in that of a mass
tort. Consider the following example:

> Hotrock, Inc., manufactures and distributes car tires nationwide. A number of
> lawsuits have been filed by individuals claiming to have suffered injuries due to
> the defective design of Hotrock's "Ridgerider" tire. These suits have been filed in
> state and federal courts throughout the nation, most of them in the home state
> of the injured party. The first such suit to go to judgment was filed by Smith in
> State X. In that case, after a trial on the merits, the court found that the Ridgerider
> had a dangerous design defect that caused it to explode even under normal driving
> conditions. The court also found that the explosion of a Ridgerider caused Smith's
> car to flip, seriously injuring him. Judgment was entered for Smith.
>
> Jones has filed a similar suit against Hotrock in a State Y court. Relying on the
> State X judgment, Jones argues that Hotrock should be precluded from denying
> that the design of the Ridgerider was dangerously defective. However, State X courts
> have not abandoned the mutuality requirement for offensive use of issue preclusion.
> A State X court, therefore, would not allow someone like Jones to use the judgment
> in *Smith v. Hotrock.* On the other hand, State Y courts have completely abandoned
> the mutuality requirement. In ruling on Jones's motion, may the State Y court apply
> its own law of preclusion or must it adhere to the less preclusive model adopted by
> State X?

Under one view, the State Y court should apply the exact rule that a State X
court would apply under the circumstances. To do otherwise would show a lack
of respect for the judgment of a sister state and perhaps violate the principle of full
faith and credit. *See Columbia Cas. Co. v. Playtex, FP, Inc.,* 584 A.2d 1214, 1218
(Del. 1991) (holding that based on principle of interstate comity, Delaware courts
must respect sister state's mutuality requirement in enforcing that state's judgment,
despite Delaware's having abandoned mutuality); *Rourke v. Amchem Prods., Inc.,*
863 A.2d 926, 934-940 (Md. 2004) (holding that Maryland courts must respect
rendering state court's adherence to mutuality even though Maryland has abandoned that requirement). In accord with this view, the State Y court would not
permit Jones to assert issue preclusion against Hotrock.

Under what is clearly a minority view, however, full faith and credit has been
interpreted as only requiring the State Y court to give the State X judgment at least
as much preclusive effect as would be granted by a State X court. In other words,

State X law merely establishes the minimum preclusive effect of a State X judgment. Adopting this approach, the State Y court could if it wished allow Jones to assert issue preclusion, since doing so would not diminish the State X judgment's preclusive effect. *See Hart v. American Airlines, Inc.*, 304 N.Y.S.2d 810 (Sup. Ct. 1969) (ruling as such). *See also Finley v. Kesling*, 433 N.E.2d 1112, 1116-1118 (Ill. Ct. App. 1982) (giving greater issue-preclusive effect to Indiana state court judgment than Indiana courts would have given it).

The Restatement has not taken a definite position concerning this variation on intersystem preclusion. *See* RESTATEMENT, *supra*, § 86 comment g. *But see* CASAD & CLERMONT, *supra*, 216-217 (describing this variation as "suspect"). In terms of fairness and efficiency, what are the arguments in favor of or opposed to adopting this variation on the general rule of intersystem preclusion?

C.   Claim and Issue Preclusion Review Problems

13-19. Popular Dry Goods brought suit against Davis claiming that Davis had negligently caused a collision with a Popular Dry Goods truck. Davis interposed contributory negligence as a defense and joined Rios as a third-party defendant, claiming that the latter had also been responsible for the collision. Davis sought damages from Rios for damage to Davis's car. Rios asserted that Davis was contributorily negligent. After a trial on these claims and defenses, the jury specifically found that all three parties were guilty of negligence in causing the accident. A judgment was entered denying Popular Dry Goods any recovery against Davis, and denying Davis any recovery against Rios. None of the parties appealed. Rios has now sued Davis to recover damages arising out of the same collision.

A. Is Rios's claim against Davis subject to claim preclusion?
B. If there had been a compulsory counterclaim rule modeled on Federal Rule of Civil Procedure 13(a), would Rios's claim be subject to that rule?
C. Could Davis file a counterclaim against Rios for personal injuries incurred in the same accident?
D. Could either party claim that the first judgment was not final since no appeal was taken?
E. Would your answer to the previous question be the same if the time for filing an appeal had not expired?
F. Assuming Rios is allowed to proceed with his claim, could Davis successfully assert issue preclusion against Rios?
G. Assuming Davis is allowed to proceed with his claim, could Rios successfully assert issue preclusion against Davis?
H. Could Davis or Rios now sue the driver of the Popular Dry Goods truck, claiming that the driver's negligence caused the accident?

I. Would the truck driver be precluded from filing a claim against either Davis or Rios arising out of the same accident?

J. If the truck driver were allowed to file a claim against Davis and Rios, could the driver assert issue preclusion against either of them?

K. Could Davis or Rios assert issue preclusion against the truck driver?

L. If a pedestrian now sues Popular Dry Goods for injuries caused by the collision, may the pedestrian assert issue preclusion against the company? In answering this question, would it matter if the pedestrian's lawsuit were filed in federal court while the initial lawsuit had been filed in a state court that has not abandoned mutuality?

See Rios v. Davis, 373 S.W.2d 386 (Tex. Civ. App. 1963) (addressing the issue-preclusion defense raised by Davis against Rios).

13-20. Between 1957 and 1964, CBS ran a television program called *Have Gun—Will Travel*. The program starred Paladin, a fictional cowboy who dressed in black, carried a derringer pistol, and handed out calling cards with a picture of a chess knight. In 1947, Victor DeCosta began to appear as a cowboy at rodeos, hospitals, and charitable events. DeCosta dressed in black, carried a derringer, handed out cards with a picture of a chess knight, and called himself Paladin. In 1963 DeCosta sued CBS for trademark infringement, claiming that it had unlawfully copied his character. The court found that while CBS did copy DeCosta's idea, DeCosta had failed to show any "likelihood" of buyer "confusion" between his Paladin character and that of CBS's, a necessary element for trademark infringement. As to confusion, the court held that few if any buyers of either "product" (rodeo/personal appearances or television programs) would likely believe that either DeCosta or CBS was the "source" of the other's "service."

In the years that followed, DeCosta registered the Paladin trademark and continued to make public appearances as Paladin. During those same years, CBS transferred the rights to the TV series to Viacom, and in the 1980s Viacom licensed reruns of the series on cable television. In 1990, DeCosta sued Viacom claiming trademark infringement. As part of this case, he argued that his registration of the Paladin trademark carried a presumption of validity, and that this presumption should make it easier for him to prove confusion. In addition, he alleged that since the filing of the first lawsuit, he has gathered significant evidence that the public is in fact confused as to the source of the Paladin character. He relies on witnesses, surveys, and expert testimony from a public relations expert. Moreover, since the time of the first lawsuit, he has engaged in significant additional activity as the Paladin character, distributing 60,000 more calling cards, 15,000 more photographs, 15,000 bumper stickers, and 2,800 pens with a Paladin legend. He has also made personal appearances at rodeos and ice cream stores, and has appeared on two television talk shows and in one television commercial. He argues that "confusion then" is therefore not the same as "confusion now." Finally, he argues that in the first suit he attempted to prove that the confusion emanated from the possibility that people would assume he had endorsed the television series, whereas courts have now shown a willingness to find a type of "reverse confusion" in which the assumption, equally damaging to him, is that the television series has sponsored him.

Does Viacom have a colorable basis on which to argue claim preclusion? To argue issue preclusion? What if the first court had clearly misapplied the law? Could DeCosta preclude Viacom from relitigating the initial court's ruling that CBS had copied DeCosta's character? *See DeCosta v. Viacom Int'l, Inc.*, 981 F.2d 602 (1st Cir. 1992), *cert. denied*, 509 U.S. 923 (1993).

TABLE OF CASES

Principal cases are italicized.

ABB Inc. v. Cooper Industries, LLC, 635 F.3d 1345 (Fed. Cir. 2011), 322, 323

Acridge v. Evangelical Lutheran Good Samaritan Society, 334 F.3d 444 (5th Cir. 2003), 339

Acton S.A. v. Marc Rich & Co., 951 F.2d 504 (2d Cir. 1991), 356

Adams v. New York State Education Department, 630 F. Supp. 2d 333 (S.D.N.Y. 2009), 955

Adkins v. Christie, 488 F.3d 1324 (11th Cir. 2007), 568

Advance Financial Corp. v. Utsey, 2001 WL 102484 (S.D. Ala. Jan. 24, 2001), 589, 620

Advanced Micro Devices v. Intel Corp., 2004 WL 2282320 (N.D. Cal. Oct. 4, 2004), 628

Advanced Tactical Ordinance Systems, LLC v. Real Action Paintball, Inc., 751 F.3d 796 (7th Cir. 2014), 172

Aerogroup International, Inc. v. Marlboro Footworks, Ltd., 956 F. Supp. 427 (S.D.N.Y. 1996), 236

AFTG–TG, LLC v. Nuvoton Technology Corp., 689 F.3d 1358 (Fed. Cir. 2012), 200

Ag Services of America, Inc. v. Nielsen, 231 F.3d 726 (10th Cir. 2000), 976

Aguilar v. Atlantic Richfield Co., 24 P.3d 493 (Cal. 2001), 899

Ahrenholz v. Board of Trustees of the University of Illinois, 219 F.3d 674 (7th Cir. 2000), 1070, 1072

Aldinger v. Howard, 427 U.S. 1 (1976), 386, 389

Aldrich v. State of New York, 494 N.Y.S.2d 662 (App. Div. 1985), 1205, 1207

Alexander v. University/Gainesville Healthcare Center, Inc., 17 F. Supp. 2d 1291 (N.D. Fla. 1998), 515

Allison v. Citgo Petroleum Corp., 151 F.3d 402 (5th Cir. 1998), 830

ALS Scan v. Digital Service Consultants, Inc., 293 F.3d 707 (4th Cir. 2002), 202

Amchem Products, Inc. v. Windsor, 521 U.S. 591 (1997), 781, 790-791, 811-812, 823, 825, 834-835

American Bank Note Holographics, Inc. Securities Litigation, In re, 127 F. Supp. 2d 418 (S.D.N.Y. 2001), 863

American Dredging Co. v. Miller, 510 U.S. 443 (1994), 459, 501

American Express Co. v. Italian Colors Restaurant, 133 S. Ct. 2304 (2013), 879-880

American-European Art Associates, Inc. v. Moquay, 1995 WL 317321 (S.D.N.Y. May 24, 1995), 287

American Family Mutual Insurance Co. v. Roche, 830 F. Supp. 1241 (E.D. Wis. 1993), 711

American Institute of Certified Public Accountants v. Affinity Card, Inc., 8 F. Supp. 2d 372 (S.D.N.Y. 1998), 249, 255, 277

American Pipe & Construction Co. v. Utah, 414 U.S. 538 (1974), 783

American Well Works Co. v. Layne & Bowler Co., 241 U.S. 257 (1916), 312, 314, 317, 321

Americana Art China Co., Inc. v. Foxfire Printing and Packaging, Inc., 743 F.3d 243 (7th Cir. 2014), 863

Americans United for Separation of Church & State v. City of Grand Rapids, 922 F.2d 303 (6th Cir. 1990), 698

Amgen, Inc. v. Connecticut Retirement Plans and Trust Funds, 133 S. Ct. 1184 (2013), 834

Anderson v. Bayer Corp., 610 F.3d 390 (7th Cir. 2010), 771

Anderson v. City of Bessemer City, 470 U.S. 564 (1985), 1089, 1129

Anderson v. Liberty Lobby, Inc., 477 U.S. 242 (1986), 66, 889, 898-900, 908, 987 n., 1007, 1009

Ankenbrandt v. Richards, 504 U.S. 689 (1992), 340

A.O. Smith Corp. v. American Alternative Insurance Corp., 778 So. 2d 615 (La. Ct. App. 2000), 200

Arends v. Mitchell Savings Bank, 1997 WL 754118 (N.D. Ill. Nov. 21, 1997), 366

Arkwright-Boston Manufacturers Mutual Insurance Co. v. City of New York, 762 F.2d 205 (2d Cir. 1985), 724

Arnold v. United Artists Theatre Circuit, Inc., 158 F.R.D. 439 (N.D. Cal. 1994), 830

Asahi Metal Industry Co., Ltd. v. Superior Court of California, 480 U.S. 102 (1987), 181-182, 199-200, 213, 216, 236

Asbestos Products Liability Litigation, In re, 771 F. Supp. 415 (J.P.M.L. 1991), 437

Ash v. Tyson Foods, Inc., 129 Fed. Appx. 529 (11th Cir. 2005), 1043

Ashcroft v. Iqbal, 556 U.S. 662 (2009), 55, 66-67, 68-70, 76, 83, 95, 102, 104, 107

Associated Dry Goods Corp. v. Towers Financial Corp., 920 F.2d 1121 (2d Cir. 1990), 745

Astro-Med, Inc. v. Nihon Kohden America, Inc., 591 F.3d 1 (1st Cir. 2009), 242, 414, 415

AT&T Corp., In re, 455 F.3d 160 (3d Cir. 2006), 863

AT&T Mobility LLC v. Concepcion, 563 U.S. 333 (2011), 863, 867, 878-880

Atlantic Coast Line R.R. v. Brotherhood of Locomotive Engineers, 398 U.S. 281 (1970), 851

Atlantic Marine Construction Co., Inc. v. United States District Court, 134 S. Ct. 568 (2013), 439, 448, 451

Atlantis Development Corp. v. United States, 379 F.2d 818 (5th Cir. 1967), 698

Attorneys Trust v. Videotape Computer Products, Inc., 93 F.3d 593 (9th Cir. 1996), 342

Atwell v. Boston Scientific Corp., 740 F.3d 1160 (8th Cir. 2013), 770

Ault v. Walt Disney World Co., 692 F.3d 1212 (11th Cir. 2012), 781

Aurora Loan Services, Inc. v. Craddieth, 442 F.3d 1018 (7th Cir. 2006), 697, 704

Ava Acupuncture P.C. v. State Farm Mutual Automobile Insurance Co., 592 F. Supp. 2d 522 (S.D.N.Y. 2008), 766

B & B Hardware, Inc. v. Hargis Industries, Inc., 135 S. Ct. 1293 (2015), 1132, 1204

Bacardí International Ltd. v. V. Suárez & Co., Inc., 719 F.3d 1 (1st Cir. 2013), 720

Baer v. First Options of Chicago, Inc., 72 F.3d 1294 (7th Cir 1995), 376

Baidoo v. Blood-Dzraku, 5 N.Y.S.3d 709 (Sup. Ct. 2015), 280

Baird v. Celis, 41 F. Supp. 2d 1358 (N.D. Ga. 1999), 528

Baldwin v. Iowa State Traveling Men's Association, 283 U.S. 522 (1931), 239

Bally Export Corp. v. Balicar, Ltd., 804 F.2d 398 (7th Cir. 1986), 239

Baltimore & Carolina Line v. Redman, 295 U.S. 654 (1935), 1009

Banco Nacional de Cuba v. Sabbatino, 376 U.S. 398 (1964), 501

Bancroft & Masters, Inc. v. Augusta National Inc., 223 F.3d 1082 (9th Cir. 2000), 172

Bank Brussels Lambert v. Chase Manhattan Bank, 175 F.R.D. 34 (S.D.N.Y. 1997), 586

Bank Julius Baer & Co. Ltd. v. WikiLeaks, 2008 WL 413737 (N.D. Cal. Feb. 13, 2008), 279-280

Bank of America National Trust & Savings Association v. Parnell, 352 U.S. 29 (1956), 500-501

Bank of Augusta v. Earle, 38 U.S. (13 Pet.) 519 (1839), 136

Barber v. Miller, 146 F.3d 707 (9th Cir. 1998), 936, 953

Barnes v. American Tobacco Co., 161 F.3d 127 (3d Cir. 1998), 830-831

Barone v. Rich Brothers Interstate Display Fireworks Co., 25 F.3d 610 (8th Cir. 1994), 200, 201

Barry Aviation, Inc. v. Land O' Lakes Municipal Airport Commission, 366 F. Supp. 2d 792 (W.D. Wis. 2005), 389

Bartnicki v. Vopper, 532 U.S. 514 (2001), 925, 1073

Baumgartner v. United States, 322 U.S. 665 (1944), 1107

Baycol Products Litigation, In re, 593 F.2d 716 (8th Cir. 2010), 1220 n., 1228

Beacon Theatres, Inc. v. Westover, 359 U.S. 500 (1959), 971, 975, 976

Beard v. Banks, 548 U.S. 521 (2006), 963

Bedell v. H.R.C. Ltd., 522 F. Supp. 732 (E.D. Ky. 1981), 369

Bell v. Marseilles Elementary School District, 160 F. Supp. 2d 883 (N.D. Ill. 2001), 937

Bell v. Texaco, Inc., 2010 WL 5330729 (S.D. Miss. Dec. 21, 2010), 1212

Bell Atlantic Corp. v. Twombly, 550 U.S. 544 (2007), 42, 53-55, 66, 67, 68-70, 76, 83, 95, 922

Belle-Midwest, Inc. v. Missouri Property & Casualty Insurance Guarantee Association, 56 F.3d 977 (8th Cir. 1995), 954

Bennett v. Schmidt, 153 F.3d 516 (7th Cir. 1998), 41

Bernard v. Gulf Oil Corp., 890 F.2d 735 (5th Cir. 1989), 783

Bernhard v. Bank of America National Trust & Savings Association, 122 P.2d 892 (Cal. 1942), 1208, 1211-1212, 1217

Best Van Lines, Inc. v. Walker, 490 F.3d 239 (2d Cir. 2007), 202

Beverly Hills Fan Co. v. Royal Sovereign Corp., 21 F.3d 1558 (Fed. Cir. 1994), 200

Bhatnagar v. Surrendra Overseas Ltd., 52 F.3d 1220 (3d Cir. 1995), 463

Bieter, In re, 16 F.3d 929 (8th Cir. 1994), 574

Bills v. Aseltine, 52 F.3d 596 (6th Cir. 1995), 1006

Binder v. Shepard's Inc., 133 P.3d 276 (Okla. 2006), 461

Blackmer v. United States, 284 U.S. 421 (1932), 128

Blair v. Equifax Check Services, Inc., 181 F.3d 832 (7th Cir. 1999), 852

Board of Education of the City of St. Louis v. City of St. Louis, 879 S.W.2d 530 (Mo. 1994), 1219

Board of Trustees, Sheet Metal Workers' National Pension Fund v. Elite Erectors, Inc., 212 F.3d 1031 (7th Cir. 2000), 240

Bochetto v. Piper Aircraft Co., 94 A.3d 1044 (Pa. Super. Ct. 2014), 460-461

Bockman v. First American Marketing Corp., 459 Fed. Appx. 157 (3d Cir. 2012), 413-414

Boddie v. Connecticut, 401 U.S. 371 (1971), 287

Boggs v. Divested Atomic Corp., 141 F.R.D. 58 (S.D. Ohio 1991), 806, 812, 822, 829-830

Bogle Farms, Inc. v. Baca, 925 P.2d 1184 (N.M. 1996), 1219

Boit v. Gar-Tec Products, Inc., 967 F.2d 671 (1st Cir. 1992), 200

Book v. Doublestar Dongfeng Tyre Co., Ltd., 860 N.W.2d 576 (Iowa 2015), 200, 201

Borkon v. City of Philadelphia, 2008 WL 4058694 (E.D. Pa. Aug. 29, 2008), 275

Boucher v. Syracuse University, 164 F.3d 113 (2d Cir. 1999), 791

Bowles v. Russell, 551 U.S. 205 (2007), 1029

Boyle v. American Auto Service, Inc., 571 F.3d 734 (8th Cir. 2009), 959

Brady v. Maryland, 373 U.S. 83 (1963), 1124

Braun v. Lorillard, Inc., 84 F.3d 230 (7th Cir. 1996), 586

Brautigan v. Brooks, 38 Cal. Rptr. 784 (Cal. Ct. App. 1964), 19-20

Bridgeport Music Inc. v. Still N the Water Publishing, 327 F.3d 472 (6th Cir. 2003), 200

Briggs Avenue L.L.C. v. Insurance Corp. of Hanover, 516 F.3d 42 (2d Cir. 2008), 476

Briggs Avenue L.L.C. v. Insurance Corp. of Hanover, 550 F.3d 246 (2d Cir. 2008), 477

Brooklyn Legal Services Corp. v. Legal Services Corp., 462 F.3d 219 (2d Cir. 2006), 790

Brown v. Ticor Title Insurance Co., 982 F.2d 386 (9th Cir. 1992), 754

Brown & Caldwell v. Institute for Energy Funding, Ltd., 617 F. Supp. 649 (C.D. Cal. 1985), 385

Brunswick Leasing Corp. v. Wisconsin Central, Ltd., 136 F.3d 521(7th Cir. 1998), 98

Burdick v. Superior Court, 183 Cal. Rptr. 3d 1 (Ct. App. 2015), 174

Burger King Corp. v. Rudzewicz, 471 U.S. 462 (1985), 157, 166-167, 172, 180, 204, 413, 459, 1082

Burlington Northern Railroad Co. v. Strong, 907 F.2d 707 (7th Cir. 1990), 643, 645

Burlington Northern Railroad Co. v. Woods, 480 U.S. 1 (1987), 528

Burnham v. Superior Court, 495 U.S. 604 (1990), 234, 284, 286

Byrd v. Blue Ridge Rural Electric Cooperative, Inc., 356 U.S. 525 (1958), 533, 537

C & K Engineering Contractors v. Amber Steel Co., 587 P.2d 1136 (Cal. 1978), 985

Cabalceta v. Standard Fruit Co., 883 F.2d 1553 (11th Cir. 1989), 357

Calder v. Jones, 465 U.S. 783 (1984), 168, 171-173, 180, 197, 198, 204

Calero-Toledo v. Pearson Yacht Leasing Co.,
416 U.S. 663 (1974), 297

California Department of Water Resources
v. Powerex Corp., 533 F.3d 1087 (9th Cir.
2008), 394

Campbell v. Lake Hallowell Homeowners
Association, 852 A.2d 1029 (Md. App.
2004), 1160

Canal National Bank v. Old Folks' Home
Association of Brunswick, 347 A.2d 428
(Me. 1975), 720

Carden v. Arkoma Associates, 494 U.S. 185
(1990), 343, 353

Cardinale v. Louisiana, 394 U.S. 437 (1969),
1124, 1126

Carimi v. Royal Caribbean Cruise Line,
Inc., 959 F.2d 1344 (5th Cir. 1992), 247

Carlough v. Amchem Products, Inc., 10 F.3d
189 (3d Cir. 1993), 851

Carmouche v. Tamborlee Management, Inc.,
789 F.3d 1201 (11th Cir. 2015), 231

Carney v. Preston, 683 A.2d 47 (Del. Super.
Ct. 1996), 1040

Carnival Cruise Lines, Inc. v. Shute, 499 U.S.
585 (1991), 449

Carson v. American Brands, Inc., 450 U.S. 79
(1981), 1064, 1067, 1068

Carson v. Dunham, 121 U.S. 421 (1887), 309

Case v. State Farm Mutual Auto Insurance
Co., 294 F.2d 676 (5th Cir. 1961), 108

Castaneda v. Burger King Corp., 259 F.R.D.
194 (N.D. Cal. 2009), 586

Catlin v. United States, 324 U.S. 229 (1945),
1048-1049

Catrett v. Johns-Manville Sales Corp., 826
F.2d 33 (D.C. Cir. 1987), 908-909

CBS Inc. v. Snyder, 136 F.R.D. 364 (S.D.N.Y.
1991), 698

Celotex Corp. v. Catrett, 477 U.S. 317 (1986),
889, 901, 908-909, 923, 936-937

Cendant Corp. PRIDES Litigation, In re, 243
F.3d 722 (3d. Cir. 2001), 863

Central West Virginia Energy Co., Inc. v.
Mountain State Carbon, LLC, 636 F.3d
101 (4th Cir. 2011), 344

Cerberus International, Ltd. v. Apollo
Management, L.P., 794 A.2d 1141 (Del.
2002), 899

Chamberlain v. Giampapa, M.D., 210 F.3d
154 (3d Cir. 2000), 528

Chambers v. NASCO, Inc., 501 U.S. 32
(1991), 537

Chandler v. Southwest Jeep-Eagle, Inc., 162
F.R.D. 302 (N.D. Ill. 1995), 775, 780-781,
782-783, 803, 852

Channell v. Citicorp National Services, Inc.,
89 F.3d 379 (7th Cir. 1996), 388, 646

*Chauffeurs, Teamsters and Helpers, Local No.
391 v. Terry*, 494 U.S. 558 (1990), 971, 976,
984-985, 992

Chew v. Dietrich, 143 F.3d 24 (2d Cir. 1998),
210

Chicot County Drainage District v. Baxter
State Bank, 308 U.S. 371 (1940), 401-402,
403

China Nuclear Energy Industry Corp. v.
Andersen, LLP, 11 F. Supp. 2d 1256 (D.
Colo. 1998), 356, 357

Chisholm v. TranSouth Financial Corp., 194
F.R.D. 538 (E.D. Va. 2000), 792

Chmieleski v. City Products Corp., 71 F.R.D.
118 (W.D. Mo. 1976), 791

Christopher v. Cutter Laboratories, 53 F.3d
1184 (11th Cir. 1995), 1005

Christopher Village, L.P. v. United States, 360
F.3d 1319 (Fed. Cir. 2004), 403

Citibank Global Markets, Inc. v. Rodriguez
Santana, 573 F.3d 17 (1st Cir. 2009), 953

Citizens Utilities Co. v. AT&T, 595 F.2d 1171
(9th Cir. 1979), 957

City of Anderson v. Fleming, 67 N.E. 443
(Ind. 1903), 1177

City of Chicago v. St. John's United Church
of Christ, 935 N.E.2d 1158 (Ill. App. Ct.
2010), 1176

City of Colton v. American Promotional
Events, Inc., 2010 WL 4569038 (C.D. Cal.
Nov. 2, 2010), 655

City of Monterey v. Del Monte Dunes at
Monterey, Ltd., 526 U.S. 687 (1999), 992

City of Oakland v. Oakland Police & Fire
Retirement System, 169 Cal. Rptr. 3d 51
(2014), 1137

City of South Bend, Indiana v. Consolidated
Rail Corp., 880 F. Supp. 595 (N.D. Ind.
1995), 369

Clark v. United Parcel Service, Inc., 460 F.3d
1004 (8th Cir. 2006), 935

Clearfield Trust Co. v. United States, 318 U.S.
363 (1943), 500

CMMC v. Salinas, 929 S.W.2d 435 (Tex.
1996), 200

CNA Insurance Companies v. Waters, 926
F.2d 247 (3d Cir. 1991), 711

Coffey v. Freeport McMoran Copper & Gold, 581 F.3d 1240 (10th Cir. 2009), 769

Cohen v. Beneficial Industrial Loan Corp., 337 U.S. 541 (1949), 509, 514, 532, 1047, 1048, 1056-1057

Cohen v. Office Depot, Inc., 184 F.3d 1292 (11th Cir. 1999), 515

Cole v. Gohmann, 727 N.E.2d 1111 (Ind. Ct. App. 2000), 923

Coleman v. American Red Cross, 23 F.3d 1091 (6th Cir. 1994), 958

Colgrove v. Battin, 413 U.S. 149 (1973), 995

Colorado Springs Production Credit Association v. Farm Credit Administration, 666 F. Supp. 1475 (D. Colo. 1987), 1219

Columbia Casualty Co. v. Playtex, FP, Inc., 584 A.2d 1214 (Del. 1991), 1229

Comcast Corp. v. Behrend, 133 S. Ct. 1426 (2013), 835

Commissioner of Internal Revenue v. Sunnen, 333 U.S. 591 (1948), 1182, 1186-1187, 1188

Committee on Children's Television, Inc. v. General Foods Corp., 673 P.2d 660 (Cal. 1983), 21, 31

Condit v. Dunne, 225 F.R.D. 100 (S.D.N.Y. 2004), 559

Conley v. Gibson, 355 U.S. 41 (1957), 32, 34-35, 41, 66

Connecticut v. Doehr, 501 U.S. 1 (1991), 288, 295-297, 299-300

Conover v. Lein, 87 F.3d 905 (7th Cir. 1996), 256

Cook v. Niedert, 142 F.3d 1004 (7th Cir. 1998), 862

Cooper v. Bissell, 16 Johns. 146 (N.Y. Sup. Ct. 1819), 634

Cooper v. Federal Reserve Bank of Richmond, 467 U.S. 867 (1984), 832

Cooper Industries, Inc. v. Leatherman Tool Group, Inc., 532 U.S. 424 (2001), 1098, 1105-1107

Cooper Tire & Rubber Co., In re, 568 F.3d 1180 (10th Cir. 2009), 558

Coopers & Lybrand v. Livesay, 437 U.S. 463 (1978), 1057

Cooter & Gell v. Hartmarx Corp., 496 U.S. 384 (1990), 1088, 1107

Cornelison v. Chaney, 545 P.2d 264 (Cal. 1976), 212

Cossaboon v. Maine Medical Center, 600 F.3d 25 (1st Cir. 2010), 220

Cottman Transmission Systems, Inc. v. Martino, 36 F.3d 291 (3d Cir. 1994), 413, 464

County of Orange, In re, 784 F.3d 520 (9th Cir. 2015), 552

Coury v. Prot, 85 F.3d 244 (5th Cir. 1996), 356

Coventry Sewage Associates v. Dworkin Realty Co., 71 F.3d 1 (1st Cir. 1995), 359, 365-366

Covey v. Town of Somers, 351 U.S. 141 (1956), 265

Cox Broadcasting Corp. v. Cohn, 420 U.S. 469 (1975), 1114, 1119, 1122, 1124

Craigslist, Inc. v. Meyer, 2010 WL 2975938 (N.D. Cal. July 26, 2010), 279

Crawford v. Equifax Payment Services, Inc., 201 F.3d 877 (7th Cir. 2000), 865

Creech v. Addington, 281 S.W.3d 363 (Tenn. 2009), 1137

Crockett v. Long Island Railroad, 65 F.3d 274 (2d Cir. 1995), 1088

Cromwell v. County of Sac, 94 U.S. (4 Otto) 351 (1876), 1133

Crosby v. National Foreign Trade Council, 530 U.S. 363 (2000), 925

Crowder v. Lash, 687 F.2d 996 (7th Cir. 1982), 832

Crown, Cork & Seal Co. v. Parker, 462 U.S. 345 (1983), 783

Cruz v. Chang, M.D., 400 F. Supp. 2d 906 (W.D. Tex. 2005), 529

Cunningham v. Hamilton County, 527 U.S. 198 (1999), 1057

Cunningham v. Outten, 2001 WL 428687 (Del. Super. Ct. Mar. 26, 2001), 1200, 1202, 1218

Cunningham v. Outten, 2001 WL 879999 (Del. Super. Ct. June 28, 2001), 1202

Cunningham v. Whitener, 182 Fed. Appx. 966 (11th Cir. 2006), 955

Curtis v. Express, Inc., 868 F. Supp. 467 (N.D.N.Y. 1994), 615

Curtiss-Wright Corp. v. General Electric Co., 446 U.S. 1 (1980), 1083, 1084

Cutler v. La Crepe Restaurant/Chefs International, Inc., 2004 WL 451855 (S.D. Fla. Feb. 18, 2004), 954

Cybersell, Inc. v. Cybersell, Inc., 130 F.3d 414 (9th Cir. 1997), 202

Daimler A.G. v. Bauman, 134 S. Ct. 746 (2014), 220, 230

Dairy Queen, Inc. v. Wood, 369 U.S. 469 (1962), 975, 976

Daitch v. Benson, 2014 WL 1022110 (Tex. Ct. App. Mar. 11, 2014), 1029

Daniel v. American Board of Emergency Medicine, 428 F.3d 408 (2d Cir. 2005), 416

Daniels v. Philip Morris Companies, Inc., 18 F. Supp. 2d 1110 (S.D. Cal. 1998), 765

Danner v. Anskis, 256 F.2d 123 (3d Cir. 1958), 658

Dart Cherokee Basin Operating Co., LLC v. Owens, 135 S. Ct. 547 (2014), 768

Davis v. Ford Motor Co., 128 F.3d 631 (8th Cir. 1997), 1007

DeCosta v. Viacom International, Inc., 981 F.2d 602 (1st Cir. 1992), 1232

Dehmlow v. Austin Fireworks, 963 F.2d 941 (7th Cir. 1992), 200

Dennis v. Kellogg Co., 697 F.3d 858 (9th Cir. 2012), 838

Des Moines Navigation & R. Co. v. Iowa Homestead Co., 123 U.S. 552 (1887), 403

Deutsche Bank National Trust Co. v. Goldfeder, 86 A.3d 1118 (Del. 2014), 265

Devlin v. Scardelletti, 536 U.S. 1 (2002), 861

D.H. Overmyer Co. v. Frick Co., Inc., 405 U.S. 174 (1972), 280

Diaz v. Paterson, 547 F.3d 88 (2d Cir. 2008), 300

Dice v. Akron, Canton & Youngstown Railroad Co., 342 U.S. 359 (1952), 550

Diet Drugs, In re, 282 F.3d 220 (3d Cir. 2002), 851

Digital Equipment Corp. v. Desktop Direct, Inc., 511 U.S. 863 (1994), 1058

Dimick v. Schiedt, 293 U.S. 474 (1935), 1040

Dioguardi v. Durning, 139 F.2d 774 (2d Cir. 1944), 35, 102

Dionne v. Bouley, 757 F.2d 1344 (1st Cir. 1985), 297

Direct Mail Specialists, Inc. v. Eclat Computerized Technologies, Inc., 840 F.2d 685 (9th Cir. 1988), 255

DiSorbo v. Hoy, 343 F.3d 172 (2d Cir. 2003), 1162

D. Light Design, Inc. v. Boxin Solar Co., Ltd., 2015 WL 526835 (N.D. Cal. Feb. 6, 2015), 279

Doe v. City of Los Angeles, 169 P.3d 559 (Cal. 2007), 21, 28-29, 54, 66, 70

Dolis v. Robert, 2014 WL 7530158 (S.D. Ill. Dec. 8, 2014), *1176*

Dollar Savings & Trust Co. v. Trocheck, 725 N.E.2d 710 (Ohio Ct. App. 1999), 284

Dorwart v. Caraway, 966 P.2d 1121 (Mont. 1998), 297

Dresser Industries, Inc. v. Underwriters at Lloyd's of London, 106 F.3d 494 (3d Cir. 1997), 347

Drexler v. Kozloff, 2000 WL 376608 (10th Cir. Apr. 13, 2000), 240

Duffy v. Ford Motor Co., 218 F.3d 623 (6th Cir. 2000), 956

Dukes v. Wal-Mart Stores, Inc., 222 F.R.D. 137 (N.D. Cal. 2004), 804

Dukes v. Wal-Mart Stores, Inc., 964 F. Supp.2d 1115 (N.D. Cal. 2013), 804

Duncan v. Louisiana, 391 U.S. 145 (1968), 970 n.

Duncan v. Upjohn Co., 155 F.R.D. 23 (D. Conn. 1994), 616

Durfee v. Duke, 375 U.S. 106 (1963), 403

Eagle Energy, Inc. v. District 17, UMW, 177 F.R.D. 357 (S.D. W. Va. 1998), 247

Earl v. Bouchard Transportation Co., Inc., 917 F.2d 1320 (2d Cir. 1990), 1040

Ebrahimi v. City of Huntsville Board of Education, 114 F.3d 162 (11th Cir. 1997), 1084

Edmonson v. Leesville Concrete Co., 500 U.S. 614 (1991), 994

E.E.O.C. v. Pemco Aeroplex, Inc., 383 F.3d 1280 (11th Cir. 2004), 1179

E.I. Dupont de Nemours & Co. v. Shell Oil Co., 1983 WL 8942 (Del. Ch. Dec. 13, 1983), 720

Eisen v. Carlisle & Jacquelin, 417 U.S. 156 (1974), 811, 839

El-Fadl v. Central Bank of Jordan, 75 F.3d 668 (D.C. Cir. 1996), 460

Engl v. Aetna Life Insurance Co., 139 F.2d 469 (2d Cir. 1943), 567

Enochs v. Lampasas County, 641 F.3d 155 (5th Cir. 2011), 388-389

Epstein v. M. Blumenthal & Co., 158 A. 234 (Conn. 1932), 17, 19-20, 36

Erickson v. Pardus, 551 U.S. 89 (2007), 54-55, 76

Ericsson GE Mobile Communications, Inc. v. Motorola Communications & Electronics, Inc., 120 F.3d 216 (11th Cir. 1997), 369

Erie Railroad Co. v. Tompkins, 304 U.S. 64 (1938), 467, 470, 474-477, 488, 496, 497-498, 508-509, 514, 531-532, 533, 546-547, 548, 951

Estate of C.A. v. Grier, 752 F. Supp. 2d 763 (S.D. Tex. 2010), 528

Estate of Davis v. Wells Fargo Bank, 633 F.3d 529 (7th Cir. 2011), 109

Etchieson v. Central Purchasing, LLC, 232 P.3d 301 (Colo. Ct. App. 2010), 200

Ettlin v. Harris, 2013 WL 6178986 (C.D. Cal. Nov. 22, 2013), 394, 398-399

Eubank v. Pella Corp., 753 F.3d 718 (7th Cir. 2014), 853, 862

Eubanks v. Billington, 110 F.3d 87 (D.C. Cir. 1997), 812

Evans v. Stephens, 544 U.S. 942 (2005), 1110

Evergreens, The v. Nunan, 141 F.2d 927 (2d Cir. 1944), 1195

Evolution Online Systems, Inc. v. Koninklijke PTT Nederland N.V., 145 F.3d 505 (2d Cir. 1998), 439

Exxon Corp. v. F.T.C., 588 F.2d 895 (3d Cir. 1978), 414

Exxon Mobil Corp. v. Allapattah Services, Inc., 545 U.S. 546 (2005), 660, 669-671, 731, 765, 769

Exxon Shipping Co. v. Baker, 554 U.S. 471 (2008), 1009-1110

Eze v. Yellow Cab Co. of Alexandria, Va., Inc., 782 F.2d 1064 (D.C. Cir. 1986), 345, 346-347, 356-357

Faison v. Hudson, 417 S.E.2d 302 (Va. 1992), 1160

Falken Industries, Ltd. v. Johnson, 360 F. Supp. 2d 208 (D. Mass. 2005), 356

Farm Labor Organizing Committee v. Ohio State Highway Patrol, 184 F.R.D. 583 (N.D. Ohio 1998), 784

FDIC v. Bathgate, 27 F.3d 850 (3d Cir. 1994), 686

Federated Department Stores, Inc. v. Moitie, 452 U.S. 394 (1981), 1156, 1160, 1161, 1195

Felder v. Casey, 487 U.S. 131 (1988), 548-549

Ferens v. John Deere Co., 494 U.S. 516 (1990), 435, 496

Field v. Volkswagenwerk A.G., 626 F.2d 293 (3d Cir. 1980), 730

Fielding v. Hubert Burda Media, Inc., 415 F.3d 419 (5th Cir. 2005), 172

Finberg v. Sullivan, 634 F.2d 50 (3d Cir. 1980), 297

Finkle v. Gulf & Western Manufacturing Co., 744 F.2d 1015 (3d Cir. 1984), 385

Finley v. Kesling, 433 N.E.2d 1112 (Ill. Ct. App. 1982), 1230

Finley v. United States, 490 U.S. 545 (1989), 386-387, 389

Firestone Tire & Rubber Co. v. Risjord, 449 U.S. 368 (1981), 1062

First of Michigan Corp. v. Bramlet, 141 F.3d 260 (6th Cir. 1998), 409, 413

First Summit Bank v. Samuelson, 580 N.W.2d 132 (N.D. 1998), 283-284

Fischer v. Cingular Wireless, LLC, 446 F.3d 663 (7th Cir. 2006), 957

5F, LLC v. Dresing, 142 So.3d 936 (Fla. Ct. App. 2014), 1212

Florida v. Thomas, 532 U.S. 774 (2001), 1123

Flynt v. Ohio, 451 U.S. 619 (1981), 1120, 1122

Fortner v. Thomas, 983 F.2d 1024 (11th Cir. 1993), 832

Fowler v. UPMC Shadyside, 578 F.3d 203 (3d Cir. 2009), 96

Franchise Tax Board v. Construction Laborers Vacation Trust, 463 U.S. 1 (1983), 325-326

Frank v. United Airlines, Inc., 216 F.3d 845 (9th Cir. 2000), 1150

Frank v. Wilbur-Ellis Co. Salaried Employees LTD Plan, 2008 WL 4370095 (E.D. Cal. Sept. 24, 2008), *100*

Franklin & Franklin v. 7-Eleven Owners for Fair Franchising, 102 Cal. Rptr. 2d 770 (Ct. App. 2000), 1162

Frederico v. Home Depot, 507 F.3d 188 (3d Cir. 2007), 773

Freeman v. Alderson, 119 U.S. 185 (1886), 131

Freeman v. Blue Ridge Paper Products, Inc., 551 F.3d 405 (6th Cir. 2008), 767

Freidrich v. Davis, 767 F.3d 374 (3d Cir. 2014), 339

FTC v. Pecon Software Ltd., 2013 WL 4016272 (S.D.N.Y. Aug. 7, 2013), 280

Fuentes v. Shevin, 407 U.S. 67 (1972), 287

Furnco Construction Corp. v. Waters, 438 U.S. 567 (1978), 84

Gaines v. Chew, 43 U.S. (2 How.) 619 (1844), 635

Galentine v. Holland America Line, 333 F. Supp. 2d 991 (W.D. Wash. 2004), 901

Galloway v. United States, 319 U.S. 372 (1943), 1009

Gammon v. GC Services L.P., 162 F.R.D. 313 (N.D. Ill. 1995), 833

Gandolfo v. U-Haul International, Inc., 978 F. Supp. 558 (D.N.J. 1996), 673

Gardiner v. Tallmadge, 700 S.E.2d 755 (N.C. Ct. App. 2010), 284

Gardner v. United States, 211 F.3d 1305 (D.C. Cir. 2000), 957, 961

Gasperini v. Center for Humanities, Inc., 518 U.S. 415 (1996), 489, 538, 546-547, 1040

Gator.com Corp. v. L.L. Bean, Inc., 341 F.3d 1072 (9th Cir. 2003), 231

Geler v. National Westminster Bank USA, 763 F. Supp. 722 (S.D.N.Y. 1991), 712, 716-718

Geler v. National Westminster Bank USA, 1991 WL 267759 (S.D.N.Y. Dec. 5, 1991), 716 n.

Genentech, Inc., In re, 566 F.3d 1338 (Fed. Cir. 2009), 429

General Engineering Corp. v. Martin Marietta Alumina, Inc., 783 F.2d 352 (3d Cir. 1986), 439 n.

General Motors Corporation Pick-Up Truck Fuel Tank Products Liability Litigation, In re, 55 F.3d 768 (3d Cir. 1995), 824, 861

General Telephone Co. of the Northwest v. E.E.O.C., 446 U.S. 318 (1980), 781

Genesis Healthcare Corp. v. Symczyk, 133 S. Ct. 1523 (2013), 789

Ghazarian v. Wheeler, 177 F.R.D. 482 (C.D. Cal. 1997), 700

Gibson v. Miami Valley Milk Producers, Inc., 299 N.E.2d 631 (Ind. Ct. App. 1973), 700

Gilbert v. Security Finance Co. of Oklahoma, Inc., 152 P.3d 165 (Okla. 2006), 147

Gilmer v. Interstate/Johnson Lane Corp., 500 U.S. 20 (1991), 882

Global NAPs, Inc. v. Verizon New England, Inc., 603 F.3d 71 (1st Cir. 2010), 646

Goldberger v. Integrated Resources, Inc., 209 F.3d 43 (2d Cir. 2000), 863

Goldlawr v. Heiman, 369 U.S. 463 (1962), 436

Goldstein v. Fidelity and Guaranty Insurance Underwriters, Inc., 86 F.3d 749 (7th Cir. 1996), 937, 941

Goldston v. American Motors Corp., 392 S.E.2d 735 (N.C. 1990), 1062-1063

Gordy v. Daily News, L.P., 95 F.3d 829 (9th Cir. 1996), 213

Grafton Partners, L.P. v. Superior Court, 116 P.3d 479 (Cal. 2003), 552

Graham v. Dyncorp International, Inc., 973 F. Supp. 2d 698 (S.D. Tex. 2013), 418, 419, 430, 435

Grand Jury Subpoena Dated July 6, 2005, In re, 510 F.3d 180 (2d Cir. 2007), 585

Granfinanciera, S.A. v. Nordberg, 492 U.S. 33 (1989), 975-976

Grassi v. Ciba-Geigy, Ltd., 894 F.2d 181 (5th Cir. 1990), 342

Gratz v. Bollinger, 539 U.S. 244 (2003), 699

Gray v. American Radiator & Standard Sanitary Corp., 176 N.E.2d 761 (Ill. 1961), 181

Great Atlantic & Pacific Tea Co. v. Town of East Hampton, 178 F.R.D. 39 (E.D.N.Y. 1998), 691, 696-699

Green v. Chicago, Burlington & Quincy Railway, 205 U.S. 530 (1907), 137

Green Tree Financial Corp. v. Bazzle, 539 U.S. 444 (2003), 865-866

Greene v. Lindsey, 456 U.S. 444 (1982), 275

Greene v. Solano County Jail, 513 F.3d 982 (9th Cir. 2008), 943

Griffin v. Bierman, 941 A.2d 475 (Md. 2008), 275

Grupo Dataflux v. Atlas Global Group, L.P., 541 U.S. 567 (2004), 347, 352-353, 356, 400

Grutter v. Bollinger, 188 F.3d 394 (6th Cir. 1999), 699

Grynberg v. Goldman Sachs Group, Inc., 2013 WL 1192585 (D.N.J. Mar. 22, 2013), 418

Guaranteed Systems, Inc. v. American National Can Co., 842 F. Supp. 855 (M.D.N.C. 1994), 489, 687, 690

Guaranty Trust Co. v. York, 326 U.S. 99 (1945), 529, 531-532, 533

Guidi v. Inter-Continental Hotels Corp., 224 F.3d 142 (2d Cir. 2000), 462

Guirguis v. Movers Specialty Services, Inc., 346 Fed. Appx. 774 (3d Cir. 2009), 96

Gulfstream Aerospace Corp. v. United States, 981 F. Supp. 654 (Ct. Int'l Trade 1997), 1218-1219

Gully v. First National Bank of Meridian, 299 U.S. 109 (1936), 317, 321, 332

Gumperz v. Hofmann, 283 N.Y.S. 823 (App. Div. 1935), 286

Gunn v. Minton, 133 S. Ct. 1059 (2013), 326, 332-333

Hadjipateras v. Pacificia, S.A., 290 F.2d 697 (5th Cir. 1961), 1069

Hall v. Helicopteros Nacionales de Colombia, S.A., 638 S.W.2d 870 (Tex. 1982), 147

Hall v. South Orange, 89 F. Supp. 2d 488 (S.D.N.Y. 2000), 437

Halliburton Co. v. Erica P. John Fund, Inc., 134 S. Ct. 2398 (2014), 774

Hamad v. Gates, 2010 WL 4511142 (W.D. Wash. Nov. 2, 2010), 417

Hammett v. Hammett, 424 N.Y.S.2d 913 (App. Div. 1980), 286

Hanlon v. Chrysler Corp., 150 F.3d 1011 (9th Cir. 1998), 840, 847-850, 851, 853, 855, 860-864

Hanna v. Plumer, 380 U.S. 460 (1965), 486, 489, 509, 513-515, 527, 534, 536-537

Hansberry v. Lee, 311 U.S. 32 (1940), 750, 754-755, 781

Hanson v. Denckla, 357 U.S. 235 (1958), 151, 156-157, 172, 199, 743

Harden v. Roadway Package Systems, Inc., 249 F.3d 1137 (9th Cir. 2001), 1046

Harper Macleod Solicitors v. Keaty & Keaty, 260 F.3d 389 (5th Cir. 2001), 240

Harris v. Balk, 198 U.S. 215 (1905), 131, 134-135

Harrison v. M.S. Carriers, Inc., 1999 WL 195539 (E.D. La. Apr. 7, 1999), 656, 658

Hart v. American Airlines, Inc., 304 N.Y.S.2d 810 (Sup. Ct. 1969), 1230

Hart v. Clayton-Parker and Associates, Inc., 869 F. Supp. 774 (D. Ariz. 1994), 647, 649-650

Hartford Life & Accident Insurance Co. v. Eterna Benefits L.L.C., 1997 WL 726441 (N.D. Tex. Nov. 17, 1997), 712

Hartford Steam Boiler Inspection & Insurance Co. v. Quantum Chemical Corp., 1994 WL 494776 (N.D. Ill. Sept. 8, 1994), 677, 682

Hartwell v. Marquez, 498 S.E.2d 1 (W. Va. 1997), 276

Hatch v. Trail King Industries, Inc., 699 F.3d 38 (1st Cir. 2012), 1155

Haywood v. Drown, 556 U.S. 729 (2009), 548

HDNet MMA 2008 LLC v. Zuffa, LLC, 2008 WL 958067 (N.D. Tex. Apr. 9, 2008), 342

Hemme v. Bharti, 183 S.W.3d 593 (Mo. 2006), 655

Henderson v. United States, 517 U.S. 654 (1996), 256

Henry v. Cash Today, Inc., 199 F.R.D. 566 (S.D. Tex. 2000), 835-836

Hercules Carriers, Inc. v. Claimant State of Florida, Department of Transportation, 768 F.2d 1558 (11th Cir. 1985), 1219

Hernandez v. Mario's Auto Sales, Inc., 617 F. Supp. 2d 488 (S.D. Tex. 2009), 969

Herrera v. Lufkin Industries, Inc., 474 F.3d 675 (10th Cir. 2007), 615

Hertz Corp. v. Friend, 559 U.S. 77 (2010), 230, 343

Hess v. Pawloski, 274 U.S. 352 (1927), 135-136, 145

Hickman v. Taylor, 329 U.S. 495 (1947), 574, 581

Hinderlider v. La Plata River & Cherry Creek Ditch Co., 304 U.S. 92 (1938), 498

Hiser v. Franklin, 94 F.3d 1287 (9th Cir. 1996), 832

Hithon v. Tyson Foods, Inc., 566 Fed. Appx. 827 (11th Cir. 2014), 1043

Hoffman v. Blaski, 363 U.S. 335 (1960), 429

Holland v. Cardiff Coal Co., 991 F. Supp. 508 (S.D. W. Va. 1997), 100

Hollinger v. Home State Mutual Insurance Co., 654 F.3d 564 (5th Cir. 2011), 768

Hollow v. Hollow, 747 N.Y.S.2d 704 (Sup. Ct. 2002), 279

HollyAnne Corp. v. TFT, Inc., 199 F.3d 1304 (Fed. Cir. 1999), 436

Honaker v. Smith, 256 F.3d 477 (7th Cir. 2001), 1010, 1021-1022

Horton v. Goose Creek Independent School District, 690 F.2d 470 (5th Cir. 1982), 754

Howlett v. Rose, 496 U.S. 356 (1990), 324, 548

HP Inkjet Printer Litigation, In re, 2014 WL 4949584 (N.D. Cal. Sept. 30, 2014), 864

Hubbard v. Parker, 994 F.2d 529 (8th Cir. 1993), 937

Huckabee v. Time Warner Entertainment Co. LP, 19 S.W.3d 413 (Tex. 2000), 899-900

Huminski v. Rutland City Police Department, 221 F.3d 357 (2d Cir. 2000), 1068

Hunt v. City of Minneapolis, 203 F.3d 524 (8th Cir. 2000), 960

Hutchinson v. Chase & Gilbert, Inc., 45 F.2d 139 (2d Cir. 1930), 137

IMO Industries, Inc. v. Kiekert AG, 155 F.3d 254 (3d Cir. 1998), 172

Indianapolis Colts v. Mayor and City Council of Baltimore, 741 F.2d 954 (7th Cir. 1984), 707, 710-711

Infant Formula Multidistrict Litigation, In re, 2005 WL 2211312 (N.D. Fla. Sept. 8, 2005), 836

Ingraham v. United States, 808 F.2d 1075 (5th Cir. 1987), 98

Intel Corp. v. Advanced Micro Devices, Inc., 542 U.S. 241 (2004), 627-628

Interfund Corp. v. O'Byrne, 462 N.W.2d 86 (Minn. Ct. App. 1990), 129

International Chemical Corp. v. Nautilus Insurance Co., 2010 WL 3070101 (W.D.N.Y. Aug. 3, 2010), 697

International Harvester Co. v. Kentucky, 234 U.S. 579 (1914), 137

International Savings and Loan Association, Ltd. v. Carbonel, 5 P.3d 454 (Haw. Ct. App. 2000), 720

International Shipping Co. v. Hydra Offshore, Inc., 875 F.2d 388 (2d Cir. 1989), 353

International Shoe Co. v. State, 154 P.2d 801 (Wash. 1945), 143

International Shoe Co. v. Washington, 326 U.S. 310 (1945), 137, 138, 143-146, 151, 156, 171, 204, 220, 231, 761-762

International Textbook Co. v. Pigg, 217 U.S. 91 (1910), 136

Iragorri v. International Elevator, Inc., 203 F.3d 8 (1st Cir. 2000), 462

Iragorri v. United Technologies Corp., 274 F.3d 65 (2d Cir. 2001), 462

Iran National Airlines Corp. v. Marschalk Co., Inc. 453 U.S. 919 (1981), 1109

Islamic Republic of Iran v. Pahlavi, 467 N.E.2d 245 (N.Y. 1984), 461

Jackson Lockdown/MCO Cases, In re, 107 F.R.D. 703 (E.D. Mich. 1985), 823

Jaffee v. Redmond, 518 U.S. 1 (1996), 560, 566-567

James v. Stockham Valves & Fittings Co., 559 F.2d 310 (5th Cir. 1977), 1098

Janmark, Inc. v. Reidy, 132 F.3d 1200 (7th Cir. 1997), 172

J.E.B. v. Alabama, 511 U.S. 127 (1994), 994

Jefferson v. Ingersoll International Inc., 195 F.3d 894 (7th Cir. 1999), 849

Jehl v. Southern Pacific Co., 427 P.2d 988 (Cal. 1967), 1040

Jeub v. B/G Foods, Inc., 2 F.R.D. 238 (D. Minn. 1942), 508

Jinks v. Richland County, South Carolina, 538 U.S. 456 (2003), 550

J. McIntyre Machinery, Ltd. v. Nicastro, 131 S. Ct. 2780 (2011), 182, 197-200, 216, 230

Johnson v. City of Shelby, 135 S. Ct. 346 (2014), 103, 104, 108

Johnson v. General Motors Corp., 598 F.2d 432 (5th Cir. 1979), 832

Johnson v. Gmeinder, 191 F.R.D. 638 (D. Kan. 2000), 619

Johnson v. Jones, 515 U.S. 304 (1995), 1062

Johnson v. Tuff N Rumble Management, Inc., 2000 WL 622612 (E.D. La. May 15, 2000), 926, 934, 935

Jones v. Flowers, 107 F.R.D. 703 (E.D. Mich. 1985), 266, 274-276, 278

Jones v. Ford Motor Credit Co., 358 F.3d 205 (2d Cir. 2004), 388, 646

Jones v. Morris Plan Bank of Portsmouth, 191 S.E. 608 (Va. 1937), 1151

Jones v. National Distillers, 56 F. Supp. 2d 355 (S.D.N.Y. 1999), 838

Kalb v. Feuerstein, 308 U.S. 433 (1940), 402-403

Kane v. New Jersey, 242 U.S. 160 (1916), 129

Kanter v. Commissioner of Internal Revenue, 464 U.S. 154 (1984), 1218

Kaplan v. DaimlerChrysler, A.G., 331 F.3d 1251 (11th Cir. 2003), 953

Katchen v. Landy, 382 U.S. 323 (1966), 975-976

Kaufman v. Allstate New Jersey Insurance Co., 561 F.3d 144 (3d Cir. 2009), 768

Keeling v. Esurance Insurance Co., 660 F.3d 273 (7th Cir. 2011), 766

Keeton v. Hustler Magazine, Inc., 465 U.S. 770 (1984), 173, 199, 219

Kellar v. Wills, 186 Fed. Appx. 714 (8th Cir. 2006), 937

Kennedy v. Silas Mason Co., 334 U.S. 249 (1948), 899

Kernan v. Kurz-Hastings, Inc., 175 F.3d 236 (2d Cir. 1999), 219

Keywell and Rosenfeld v. Bithell, 657 N.W.2d 759 (Mich. Ct. App. 2002), 1218

Kilborn v. Woodworth, 5 Johns. 37 (N.Y. 1809), 124-125

King v. South Central Bell Telephone & Telegraph Co., 790 F.2d 524 (6th Cir. 1986), 763, 834

King Vision Pay Per View, Ltd. v. J.C. Dimitri's Restaurant, Inc., 180 F.R.D. 332 (N.D. Ill. 1998), 98, 100

Kirksey v. R.J. Reynolds Tobacco Co., 168 F.3d 1039 (7th Cir. 1999), 104, 107-108

Klaxon Co. v. Stentor Electric Manufacturing Co., 313 U.S. 487 (1941), 475-476, 531

Kmart Corp. v. Aronds, 123 F.3d 297 (5th Cir. 1997), 1082

Knoblauch v. DEF Express Corp., 86 F.3d 684 (7th Cir. 1996), 478

Knoll v. American Telephone & Telegraph Co., 176 F.3d 359 (6th Cir. 1999), 958, 960

Knowlton v. Allied Van Lines, Inc., 900 F.2d 1196 (8th Cir. 1990), 414

Koch v. Rodlin Enterprises, Inc., 223 Cal. App. 3d 1591 (Ct. App. 1990), 1154 n.

Koehler v. Bank of Bermuda, Ltd., 101 F.3d 863 (2d Cir. 1996), 1069

Kontrick v. Ryan, 540 U.S. 443 (2004), 400, 402-403

Kraebel v. New York City Department of Housing Preservation & Development, 1994 WL 132239 (S.D.N.Y. Apr. 14, 1994), 724

Kramer v. Caribbean Mills, Inc., 394 U.S. 823 (1969), 341

Krimstock v. Kelly, 306 F.3d 40 (2d Cir. 2002), 299

Lambert v. Kysar, 983 F.2d 1110 (1st Cir. 1993), 439 n.

Landes v. Capital City Bank, 795 P.2d 1127 (Utah 1990), 720

Lasa per L'Industria del Marmo Societa per Azioni v. Alexander, 414 F.2d 143 (6th Cir. 1969), 686

Law Offices of Jerris Leonard, P.C. v. Mideast Systems, Ltd., 111 F.R.D. 359 (D.D.C. 1986), 638, 641-643, 645

Lawlor v. National Screen Service Corp., 349 U.S. 322 (1955), 1150

Leach v. Pan American World Airways, 842 F.2d 285 (11th Cir. 1988), 976

Leatherman v. Tarrant County Narcotics & Coordination Unit, 507 U.S. 163 (1993), 38, 40-41, 54, 76

Leatherman Tool Group, Inc. v. Cooper Industries, Inc., 285 F.3d 1146 (9th Cir. 2002), 1107

LeBlang Motors, Ltd. v. Subaru of America, Inc., 148 F.3d 680 (7th Cir. 1998), 954

Legal Aid Services of Oregon v. Legal Services Corp., 608 F.3d 1084 (9th Cir. 2010), 790

Legnani v. Alitalia Linee Aeree Italiane, S.P.A., 400 F.3d 139 (2d Cir. 2005), 1149-1150

Lemon v. International Union of Operating Engineers, Local No. 139, 216 F.3d 577 (7th Cir. 2000), 831, 849

Lepone-Dempsey v. Carroll County Commissioners, 476 F.3d 1277 (11th Cir. 2007), 256

Lesnick v. Hollingsworth & Vose Co., 35 F.3d 939 (4th Cir. 1994), 200

Lewis v. Verizon Communications, Inc., 627 F.3d 395 (9th Cir. 2010), 767-768

Liberty Lobby, Inc. v. Anderson, 1991 WL 186998 (D.D.C. May 1, 1991), 899

Liberty Mutual Insurance Co. v. Wetzel, 424 U.S. 737 (1976), 1083

Licciardi v. TIG Insurance Group, 140 F.3d 357 (1st Cir. 1998), 619-620

Lighthouse MGA, L.L.C. v. First Premium Insurance Group, Inc., 448 Fed. Appx. 512 (5th Cir. 2011), 439 n.

Lights of America, Inc. v. U.S. District Court, 130 F.3d 1369 (9th Cir. 1997), 1082

Lillo ex rel. Estate of Lilo v. Bruhn, 413 Fed. Appx. 161 (11th Cir. 2011), 937

Lindley v. Caterpillar, Inc., 93 F. Supp. 2d 615 (E.D. Pa. 2000), 437

Link v. Wabash R.R. Co., 370 U.S. 626 (1962), 957, 958

Little York Gold Washing & Water Co. v. Keyes, 96 U.S. 199 (1877), 309

Littlejohn v. City of New York, 795 F.3d 296 (2d Cir. 2015), 84, 95

Lloyd v. City of Philadelphia, 121 F.R.D. 246 (E.D. Pa. 1988), 812-813

Lodge Hall Music, Inc. v. Waco Wrangler Club, Inc., 831 F.2d 77 (5th Cir. 1987), 925

Lodge on the Green Associates v. Comfed Savings Bank, 121 F.R.D. 3 (D. Mass. 1988), 744

Lorix v. Crompton Corp., 680 N.W.2d 574 (Minn. Ct. App. 2004), 147

Los Angeles Branch NAACP v. Los Angeles Unified School District, 750 F.2d 731 (9th Cir. 1984), 1144, 1149, 1150, 1153

Louisiana v. American National Property & Casualty Co., 746 F.3d 633 (5th Cir. 2014), 767

Louisville & Nashville Railroad Co. v. Mottley, 211 U.S. 149 (1908), 310, 321, 400, 1110

Lowery v. Alabama Power Co., 483 F.3d 1184 (11th Cir. 2007), 770

LSJ Investment Co. v. O.L.D., Inc., 167 F.3d 320 (6th Cir. 1999), 249

Ludwig v. Township of Van Buren, 682 F.3d 457 (6th Cir. 2012), 1179

Lumpkin v. Brown, 109 F.3d 1498 (9th Cir. 1997), 1191 n.

Lumpkin v. Jordan, 57 Cal. Rptr. 2d 303 (Ct. App. 1996), 1189, 1194-1195

Lundquist v. Precision Valley Aviation, Inc., 946 F.2d 8 (1st Cir. 1991), 341

Lungren v. Community Redevelopment Agency for Palm Springs, 56 Cal. Rptr. 2d 786 (Cal. Ct. App. 1997), 720

Lupron Marketing and Sales Practices Litigation, In re, 677 F.3d 21 (1st Cir. 2012), 838

Lyon v. Whisman, 45 F.3d 758 (3d Cir. 1995), 376

Mace v. Van Ru Credit Corp., 109 F.3d 338 (7th Cir. 1997), 839

Mackey v. Compass Marketing, Inc., 892 A.2d 479 (Md. 2006), 147

Maharaj v. BankAmerica Corp., 128 F.3d 94 (2d Cir. 1997), 1152

Makaeff v. Trump University, LLC, 715 F.3d 254 (9th Cir. 2013), 551

Maldonado-Viñas v. National Western Life Insurance Co., 303 F.R.D. 177 (D.P.R. 2014), 725, 730, 741

Mallard v. U.S. District Court, 490 U.S. 296 (1989), 1081

Mallon v. Walt Disney World Co., 42 F. Supp. 2d 143 (D. Conn. 1998), 212

Mann v. Lewis, 108 F.3d 145 (8th Cir. 1997), 961

Marbury v. Madison, 5 U.S. (1 Cranch) 137 (1803), 13

Marek v. Lane, 134 S. Ct. 8 (2013), 838

Margolis v. Caterpillar, Inc., 815 F. Supp. 1150 (C.D. Ill. 1991), 839

Markman v. Westview Instruments, Inc., 517 U.S. 370 (1996), 971, 986, 992

Marlow v. Winston & Strawn, 19 F.3d 300 (7th Cir. 1994), 954-955

Marlow v. Winston & Strawn, 1994 WL 262077 (N.D. Ill. June 10, 1994), 955

Marshall v. Marshall, 547 U.S. 293 (2006), 340, 516

Marshall v. Mulrenin, 508 F.2d 39 (1st Cir. 1974), 516

Marten v. Godwin, 499 F.3d 290 (3d Cir. 2007), 172, 174

Martin v. Blessing, 134 S. Ct. 402 (2013), 781

Maryland v. Baltimore Radio Show, 338 U.S. 912 (1950), 1110

Massachusetts School of Law v. American Bar Association, 142 F.3d 26 (1st Cir. 1998), 1151

Mathews v. Eldridge, 424 U.S. 319 (1976), 295-298, 299

Matrixx Initiatives, Inc. v. Siracusano, 563 U.S. 27 (2011), 37

Matsushita Electric Industrial Co., Ltd. v. Zenith Radio Corp., 475 U.S. 574 (1986), 889, 909, 921-922

Mattel, Inc. v. Bryant, 446 F.3d 1011 (9th Cir. 2006), 701, 703, 743

M.B. Restaurants, Inc. v. CKE Restaurants, Inc., 183 F.3d 750 (8th Cir. 1999), 439 n.

McAdams v. Medtronic, Inc., 2010 WL 3909958 (S.D. Tex. Sept. 29, 2010), 333

McCleary-Evans v. Maryland Department of Transportation, 780 F.3d 582 (4th Cir. 2015), 77, 83-84

McClellan v. Rowell, 99 So. 2d 653 (Miss. 1958), 285

McCorkle v. City of Los Angeles, 449 P.2d 453 (Cal. 1969), 238

McDaniel v. County of Schenectady, 595 F.3d 411 (2d Cir. 2010), 863

McDaniel v. IBP, Inc., 89 F. Supp. 2d 1289 (M.D. Ala. 2000), 415

McDonnell Douglas v. Green, 411 U.S. 792 (1973), 83-84, 95

McDonough v. Celebrity Cruises, Inc., 64 F. Supp. 2d 259 (S.D.N.Y. 1999), 901

McGee v. International Life Insurance Co., 355 U.S. 220 (1957), 149, 150-151, 156, 157, 166, 172, 204

McIntosh v. McIntosh, 1996 WL 689948 (Conn. Super. Ct. Nov. 20, 1996), 287, 451

McKnight v. Gingras, 966 F. Supp. 801 (E.D. Wis. 1997), 943

Medical Mutual of Ohio v. deSoto, 245 F.3d 561 (6th Cir. 2001), 236

Melrose v. Shearson/American Express, Inc., 120 F.R.D. 668 (N.D. Ill. 1988), 935

Mennonite Board of Missions v. Adams, 462 U.S. 791 (1983), 277

Michigan v. Long, 463 U.S. 1032 (1983), 1126

Microsoft Corp. v. Marturano, 2008 WL 2622832 (E.D. Cal. July 1, 2008), 945

Milbert v. Bison Laboratories, Inc., 260 F.2d 431 (3d Cir. 1958), 1069

Milliken v. Meyer, 311 U.S. 457 (1940), 128

Milwaukee v. Illinois and Michigan, 451 U.S. 304 (1981), 498, 501

Mink v. AAAA Development LLC, 190 F.3d 333 (5th Cir. 1999), 202

Miree v. DeKalb County, 433 U.S. 25 (1977), 502

Miserandino v. Resort Properties, Inc., 691 A.2d 208 (Md. 1997), 265

Mississippi & Missouri Railroad Co. v. Ward, 67 U.S. (2 Black) 485 (1862), 369

Mississippi Publishing Corp. v. Murphree, 326 U.S. 438 (1946), 245, 514

Mitchell v. Forsyth, 472 U.S. 511 (1985), 935, 1057

Mitchell v. Gonzales, 819 P.2d 872 (Cal. 1991), 998, 1004

Mitchell v. W.T. Grant Co., 416 U.S. 600 (1974), 288, 296, 297, 299

Mitrano v. Hawes, 377 F.3d 402 (4th Cir. 2004), 415

Mohawk Industries, Inc. v. Carpenter, 558 U.S. 100 (2009), 1050, 1056-1057

Monahan v. New York City Department of Corrections, 214 F.3d 275 (2d Cir. 2000), 1178

Monegro v. Rosa, 211 F.3d 509 (9th Cir. 2000), 463

Montana v. United States, 440 U.S. 147 (1979), 1175, 1208

Montgomery Ward & Co. v. Duncan, 311 U.S. 243 (1940), 1009

Monument Builders of Greater Kansas City, Inc. v. American Cemetery Association, 891 F.2d 1473 (10th Cir. 1989), 408

Monumental Life Insurance Co., In re, 365 F.3d 408 (5th Cir. 2004), 830

Morgenstern v. Wilson, 29 F.3d 1291 (8th Cir. 1994), 1067-1068

Morris v. LandNpulaski, LLC, 309 S.W.3d 212 (Ark. Ct. App. 2009), 275

Morrison v. Allstate Indemnity Co., 228 F.3d 1255 (11th Cir. 2000), 369

Moses H. Cone Memorial Hospital v. Mercury Construction Corp., 460 U.S. 1 (1983), 1061

Moss v. United States Secret Service, 711 F.3d 941 (9th Cir. 2013), 114

M/S Bremen v. Zapata Off-Shore Co., 407 U.S. 1 (1972), 439

Mucha v. King, 792 F.2d 602 (7th Cir. 1986), 1105-1106

Mulbah v. Detroit Board of Education, 261 F.3d 586 (6th Cir. 2001), 958

Mullane v. Central Hanover Bank & Trust Co., 339 U.S. 306 (1950), 257, 263-265, 275, 755

Mycogen Corp. v. Monsanto Co., 51 P.3d 297 (Cal. 2002), 1137

Namas Noor Sdn Bhd v. Williams, 112 F. Supp. 2d 580 (M.D. La. 2000), 942

Nance v. Vieregge, 147 F.3d 589 (7th Cir. 1998), 36

Nathan v. Boeing Co., 116 F.3d 422 (9th Cir. 1997), 497

Nathanson v. Hecker, 121 Cal. Rptr. 2d 773 (Ct. App. 2002), 1160

National Equipment Rental, Ltd. v. Szukhent, 375 U.S. 311 (1964), 129

National Hockey League v. Metropolitan Hockey Club, Inc., 427 U.S. 639 (1976), 960

National Society of Professional Engineers v. United States, 435 U.S. 679 (1978), 500

National Treasury Employees Union v. Internal Revenue Service, 765 F.2d 1174 (D.C. Cir. 1985), 1196

Nazareth Candy Co., Ltd. v. Sherwood Group, Inc., 683 F. Supp. 539 (M.D.N.C. 1988), 357

Neely v. Martin K. Eby Construction Co., 386 U.S. 317 (1967), 1028

Neff v. Pennoyer, 17 F. Cas. 1291 (C.C.D. Ore. 1875) (No. 10,085), 126

Negrete v. Allianz Life Insurance Co. of North America, 523 F.3d 1091 (9th Cir. 2008), 851

Neogen Corp. v. Neo Gen Screening, Inc., 282 F.3d 883 (6th Cir. 2002), 202

Nesbitt v. Bun Basket, Inc., 780 F. Supp. 1151 (W.D. Mich. 1991), 399

New York Access Billing, LLC v. ATX Communications, Inc., 289 F. Supp. 2d 260 (N.D.N.Y. 2013), 418

New York Times Co. v. United States [The Pentagon Papers Case], 403 U.S. 713 (1971), 1110

Newman-Green, Inc. v. Alfonzo-Larrain, 490 U.S. 826 (1989), 347

Newport, State ex rel. v. Wiesman, 627 S.W.2d 874 (Mo. 1982), 147

Nicholson v. HF05, 2009 WL 4842472 (Iowa App. Dec. 17, 2009), 275

Nissan Motor Co., Ltd. v. Nissan Computer Corp., 89 F. Supp. 2d 1154 (C.D. Cal. 2000), 420

Nixon v. Fitzgerald, 457 U.S. 731 (1982), 1057

Norfolk Shipbuilding & Drydock Corp. v. Garris, 531 U.S. 1 (2001), 501

Norgrove v. Board of Education of City School District of City of New York, 881 N.Y.S.2d 802 (Sup. Ct. 2009), 277

North Georgia Finishing, Inc. v. Di-Chem, Inc., 419 U.S. 601 (1975), 288

North River Insurance Co. v. Stefanou, 831 F.2d 484 (4th Cir. 1987), 567

Nowak v. Tak How Investments, Ltd., 94 F.3d 708 (1st Cir. 1996), 204, 210-212, 216, 218-219

Nuskey v. Lambright, 251 F.R.D 3 (D.D.C. 2008), 616

O'Connor v. Sandy Lane Hotel Co., Ltd., 496 F.3d 312 (3d Cir. 2007), 212

Olympia Hotels Corp. v. Johnson Wax Development Corp., 908 F.2d 1363 (7th Cir. 1990), 1084, 1086, 1087

Omni Capital International, Ltd. v. Rudolf Wolff & Co., Ltd., 484 U.S. 97 (1987), 245

On Track Transportation, Inc. v. Lakeside Warehouse & Trucking, Inc., 245 F.R.D. 213 (E.D. Pa. 2007), 240

Oneida Indian Nation of Wisconsin v. New York, 732 F.2d 261 (2d Cir. 1984), 698

Opera Plaza Residential Parcel Homeowners Association v. Hoang, 376 F.3d 831 (9th Cir. 2004), 324

Oppenheimer Fund, Inc. v. Sanders, 437 U.S. 340 (1978), 839

Ormet Corp. v. Ohio Power Co., 98 F.3d 799 (4th Cir. 1996), 322

Ortiz v. Fibreboard Corp., 527 U.S. 815 (1999), 762, 821-822

Osborn v. Bank of the United States, 22 U.S. (9 Wheat.) 738 (1824), 306-308, 321

Owen Equipment & Erection Co. v. Kroger, 437 U.S. 365 (1978), 377, 382-386, 392, 658

Oxford Health Plans LLC v. Sutter, 133 S. Ct. 2064 (2013), 866

Pagel v. Dairy Farmers of America, Inc., 986 F. Supp. 2d 1151 (C.D. Cal. 2013), 766

Pagonis v. United States, 575 F.3d 809 (8th Cir. 2009), 275

Palmer v. Valdez, 560 F.3d 965 (9th Cir. 2009), 552

Pan American Fire & Casualty Co. v. Revere, 188 F. Supp. 474 (E.D. La. 1960), 719

Panavision International, L.P. v. Toeppen, 141 F.3d 1316 (9th Cir. 1998), 203

Paramount Aviation Corp. v. Agusta, 178 F.3d 132 (3d Cir. 1999), 655

Parker v. Lyons, 757 F.3d 701 (7th Cir. 2014), 1160

Parker v. Time Warner Entertainment Co., L.P., 198 F.R.D. 374 (E.D.N.Y. 2001), 836

Parker v. Time Warner Entertainment Co., L.P., 331 F.3d 13 (2d Cir. 2003), 833, 836

Parker v. Time Warner Entertainment Co., L.P., 631 F. Supp. 2d 242 (E.D.N.Y. 2009), 836-837

Parklane Hosiery Co., Inc. v. Shore, 439 U.S. 322 (1979), 1212, 1217-1218

Parrish v. City of Orlando, 53 So. 3d 1199 (Fla. Dist. Ct. App. 2011), 1040

Parson v. Johnson & Johnson, 749 F.3d 879 (10th Cir. 2014), 770-771

Pasko v. City of Milwaukee, 643 N.W.2d 72 (Wis. 2002), 1178

Pavlovich v. Superior Court, 58 P.3d 2 (Cal. 2002), 172

Payne v. Travenol Laboratories, Inc., 673 F.2d 798 (5th Cir. 1982), 783

Peabody v. Hamilton, 106 Mass. 217 (1870), 130

Pebble Beach Co. v. Caddy, 453 F.3d 1151 (9th Cir. 2006), 203

Peckham v. Continental Casualty Insurance Co., 895 F.2d 830 (1st Cir. 1990), 211

Peninsula Cruise, Inc. v. New River Yacht Sales, Inc., 512 S.E.2d 560 (Va. 1999), 147

Pennoyer v. Neff, 95 U.S. 714 (1877), 116, 124-126, 127, 129, 135, 136, 146, 198, 238

Pennzoil Products Co. v. Colelli & Associates, Inc., 149 F.3d 197 (3d Cir. 1998), 200

Pension Committee of University of Montreal Pension Plan v. Banc of America Securities, LLC, 685 F. Supp. 2d 456 (S.D.N.Y. 2010), 608

People v. Mack, 97 Cal. Rptr. 448 (Ct. App. 1971), 1203

Perrain v. O'Grady, 958 F.2d 192 (7th Cir. 1992), 724

Petrucelli v. Bohringer & Ratzinger, 46 F.3d 1298 (3d Cir. 1995), 256

Pettitt v. Boeing Co., 606 F.3d 340 (7th Cir. 2010), 344

Peyton v. Otis Elevator Co., 1998 WL 574378 (N.D. Ill. Aug. 31, 1998), 100

Phar-Mor, Inc. Securities Litigation, In re, 875 F. Supp. 277 (W.D. Pa. 1994), 824

Philadelphia & Reading Railway v. McKibbin, 243 U.S. 264 (1917), 137

Philip Morris USA, Inc. v. Veles Ltd., 2007 WL 725412 (S.D.N.Y. Mar. 12, 2007), 280

Phillips Petroleum Co. v. Shutts, 472 U.S. 797 (1985), 755, 761-763, 772, 829, 851

Phoenix Newspapers, Inc. v. Department of Corrections, 934 P.2d 801 (Ariz. Ct. App. 1997), 1137

Pierce County v. Guillen, 537 U.S. 129 (2003), 1123

Pioneer Investment Services Co. v. Brunswick Associates Limited Partnership, 507 U.S. 380 (1993), 945

Piper Aircraft Co. v. Reyno, 454 U.S. 235 (1981), 451, 459-461, 462, 533

Pit River Tribe v. U.S. Forest Service, 615 F.3d 1069 (9th Cir. 2010), 1081

Poindexter v. Bonsukan, M.D., 145 F. Supp. 2d 800 (E.D. Tex. 2001), 529

Polar Supply Co., Inc. v. Steelmaster Industries, Inc., 127 P.3d 52 (Alaska 2005), 147

Porn v. National Grange Mutual Insurance Co., 93 F.3d 31 (1st Cir. 1996), 1137, 1143, 1155, 1160

Preston v. Tenet Healthsystem Memorial Medical Center, Inc., 485 F.3d 804 (5th Cir. 2007), 769

Proffitt v. Abbott Laboratories, 2008 WL 4401367 (E.D. Tenn. Sept. 23, 2008), 767

Provident Tradesmens Bank & Trust Co. v. Patterson, 390 U.S. 102 (1968), 721, 731, 740-743

Prudential Insurance Co. of America Sales Practices Litigation, In re, 148 F.3d 283 (3d Cir. 1998), 851

Puffer v. Allstate Insurance Co., 614 F. Supp. 2d 905 (N.D. Ill. 2009), 783

Pullman-Standard v. Swint, 456 U.S. 273 (1982), 1089, 1090, 1097-1098, 1105-1106

Pure Oil Co. v. Suarez, 384 U.S. 202 (1966), 408

Pyke v. Cuomo, 209 F.R.D. 33 (N.D.N.Y. 2002), 804

Quackenbush v. Allstate Insurance Co., 517 U.S. 706 (1996), 1058, 1060-1061

"R" Best Produce, Inc. v. DiSapio, 540 F.3d 115 (2d Cir. 2008), 238

Ragan v. Merchants Transfer & Warehouse Co., 337 U.S. 530 (1949), 508, 514, 532

Rainbow Management Group, Ltd. v. Atlantis Submarines Hawaii, L.P., 158 F.R.D. 656 (D. Haw. 1994), 651, 655-656

Randall v. Nelson & Kennard, 2009 WL 2710141 (D. Ariz. Aug. 26, 2009), 650

Rannis v. Recchia, 380 Fed. Appx. 646 (9th Cir. 2010), 780

Rawlings v. Lopez, 591 S.E.2d 691 (Va. 2004), 1212

Ray Haluch Gravel Co. v. Central Pension Fund, 134 S. Ct. 773 (2014), 1049

Realmonte v. Reeves, 169 F.3d 1280 (10th Cir. 1999), 848

Redrup v. New York, 386 U.S. 767 (1967), 1111, 1113-1114

Reeves v. Sanderson Plumbing Products, Inc., 530 U.S. 133 (2000), 1009

Reich v. D.C. Wiring, Inc., 940 F. Supp. 105 (D.N.J. 1996), 1218

Resolution Trust Corp. v. Starkey, 41 F.3d 1018 (5th Cir. 1995), 277

Retirement Systems of Alabama v. J.P. Morgan Chase & Co., 386 F.3d 419 (2d Cir. 2004), 851

Rey v. Classic Cars, 762 F. Supp. 421 (D. Mass. 1991), 399

Reynolds v. Missouri, Kansas & Texas Railway, 113 N.E. 413 (Mass. 1916), 137

Richards v. Aramark Services, Inc., 108 F.3d 925 (8th Cir. 1997), 1088

Richards v. Jefferson County, 517 U.S. 793 (1996), 1137

Richardson-Merrell, Inc. v. Koller, 472 U.S. 424 (1985), 1062, 1063

Rio Properties, Inc. v. Rio International Interlink, 284 F.3d 1007 (9th Cir. 2002), 203, 278-279

Rios v. Davis, 373 S.W.2d 386 (Tex. Civ. App. 1963), 1231

Rivera v. Rochester Genesee Regional Transportation Authority, 743 F.3d 11 (2d Cir. 2012), 389

Robidoux v. Celani, 987 F.2d 931 (2d Cir. 1993), 784, 789, 790, 824

Robinson v. Lattimore, 946 F.2d 1566 (D.C. Cir. 1991), 832

Rodriguez v. Doral Mortgage Corp., 57 F.3d 1168 (1st Cir. 1998), 388

Rodríguez v. Señor Frog's de La Isla, Inc., 642 F.3d 28 (1st Cir. 2011), 335, 339, 366

Rodriguez v. West Publishing Co., 563 F.3d 948 (9th Cir. 2008), 862

Rodriguez-Torres v. American Airlines Corp., 8 F. Supp. 2d 150 (D.P.R. 1998), 420

Rogers v. City of Warren, 302 Fed. Appx. 371 (6th Cir. 2008), 957

Rogers v. Hartford Life & Accident Insurance Co., 167 F.3d 933 (5th Cir. 1999), 945, 950-951

Rogers v. ITT Hartford Life & Accident Co., 178 F.R.D. 476 (S.D. Miss. 1997), 951

Rogers v. Wal-Mart Stores, Inc., 230 F.3d 868 (6th Cir. 2000), 955

Romero v. Philip Morris, Inc., 242 P.3d 280 (N.M. Ct. App. 2010), 899

Ronzio v. Denver & Rio Grande Western Railroad Co., 116 F.2d 604 (10th Cir. 1940), 369

Ross v. Bernhard, 396 U.S. 531 (1970), 986

Rothman v. Emory University, 123 F.3d 446 (7th Cir. 1997), 597

Rourke v. Amchem Products, Inc., 863 A.2d 926 (Md. 2004), 1229

Ruhrgas AG v. Marathon Oil Co., 526 U.S. 574 (1999), 303, 305, 400-401, 460

Ruston Gas Turbines, Inc. v. Donaldson Co., 9 F.3d 415 (5th Cir. 1993), 200

Rybski v. Home Depot USA, Inc., 2012 WL 5416586 (D. Ariz. Oct. 19, 2012), 969

Sabek, Inc. v. Englehard Corp., 76 Cal. Rptr. 2d 882 (Ct. App. 1998), 1203

Salve Regina College v. Russell, 499 U.S. 225 (1991), 1089

San Remo Hotel, L.P. v. City & County of San Francisco, 545 U.S. 323 (2005), 1161

Sanderson-Cruz v. United States, 88 F. Supp. 2d 388 (E.D. Pa. 2000), 97-98

Sandpiper Village Condominium Association v. Louisiana Pacific Corp., 428 F.3d 831 (9th Cir. 2005), 850

Santa Fe Downs, Inc., In re, 611 F.2d 815 (10th Cir. 1980), 20

Schachter, State ex rel. v. Ohio Public Employees Retirement Board, 905 N.E.2d 1210 (Ohio 2009), 1176

Schaefer v. City of Defiance Police Department, 529 F.3d 731 (6th Cir. 2008), 958

Schlagenhauf v. Holder, 379 U.S. 104 (1964), 609, 615

Schoot v. United States, 664 F. Supp. 293 (N.D. Ill. 1987), 675, 677

Schwarzenegger v. Fred Martin Motor Co., 374 F.3d 797 (9th Cir. 2004), 243

Sea-Land Service, Inc. v. Ceramica Europa II, Inc., 160 F.3d 849 (1st Cir. 1998), 238

Seals v. General Motors Corp., 546 F.3d 766 (6th Cir. 2008), 101

Sears, Roebuck & Co. v. Mackey, 351 U.S. 427 (1956), 1083

Seattle Times Co. v. Rhinehart, 467 U.S. 20 (1984), 621, 627

S.E.C. v. Carrillo, 115 F.3d 1540 (11th Cir. 1997), 236

S.E.C. v. McNulty, 137 F.3d 732 (2d Cir. 1998), 945, 951

Sellon v. Smith, 112 F.R.D. 9 (D. Del. 1986), 596

Semmes Motors, Inc. v. Ford Motor Co., 429 F.2d 1197 (2d Cir. 1970), 651

Semtek International, Inc. v. Lockheed Martin Corp., 531 U.S. 497 (2001), 1153, 1154, 1155, 1164

Semtek International, Inc. v. Lockheed Martin Corp., 2002 WL 32500569 (Md. Cir. Ct. Mar. 20, 2002), 1154

Servewell Plumbing, LLC v. Federal Insurance Co., 439 F.3d 786 (8th Cir. 2006), 439 n.

Shady Grove Orthopedic Associates, P.A. v. Allstate Insurance Co., 559 U.S. 393 (2010), 485, 507, 516, 527, 795

Shaffer v. Heitner, **433 U.S. 1986 (1977)**, 232-233

Shawmut Bank of Rhode Island v. Costello, 643 A.2d 194 (R.I. 1994), 298

Sher v. Johnson, 911 F.2d 1357 (9th Cir. 1990), 168

Shoshone Mining Co. v. Rutter, 177 U.S. 505 (1900), 310, 312, 321

Shroder v. Suburban Coastal Corp., 729 F.2d 1371 (11th Cir. 1984), 852

Shull v. Pilot Life Insurance Co., 313 F.2d 445 (5th Cir. 1963), 108

Shute v. Carnival Cruise Lines, 783 P.2d 78 (Wash. 1989), 147

Shute v. Carnival Cruise Lines, 897 F.2d 377 (9th Cir. 1990), 207 *, 210

Sibbach v. Wilson & Company, Inc., 312 U.S. 1 (1941), 503, 506-507, 508, 514, 527, 615

Siems v. City of Minneapolis, 531 F. Supp. 2d 1069 (D. Minn. 2008), 960-961

Sierra Club v. Espy, 18 F.3d 1202 (5th Cir. 1994), 697

Sierra Club v. Two Elk Generation Partners, Ltd. Part., 646 F.3d 1258 (10th Cir. 2011), 1176

Silver Sage Partners, Ltd. v. City of Desert Hot Springs, 251 F.3d 814 (9th Cir. 2001), 1081

Silver Sage Partners, Ltd. v. City of Desert Hot Springs, 339 F.3d 782 (9th Cir. 2003), 1081

Silver Sage Partners, Ltd. v. U.S. District Court, 1998 WL 246526 (9th Cir. May 15, 1998), 1079, 1081

Silverman v. Superior Court, 249 Cal. Rptr. 724 (Ct. App. 1988), 285

Singleton v. Wulff, 428 U.S. 106 (1976), 1046

Sinochem International Co. Ltd. v. Malaysia International Shipping Corp., 549 U.S. 422 (2007), 459-460

Sioux Pharm, Inc. v. Summit Nutritionals International, Inc., 859 N.W.2d 182 (Iowa 2015), 203

Skelly Oil Co. v. Phillips Petroleum Co., 339 U.S. 667 (1950), 322, 326

Skyhawke Technologies, LLC v. DECA International Corp., 2011 WL 1806511 (S.D. Miss. May 11, 2011), 421, 429, 438

Smith v. Bayer Corp., 131 S. Ct. 2368 (2011), 782, 861, 1219, 1227-1228

Smith v. Diamond Offshore Drilling, Inc., 168 F.R.D. 582 (S.D. Tex. 1996), 585

Smith v. Gold Dust Casino, 526 F.3d 402 (8th Cir. 2008), 961

Smith v. Kansas City Title & Trust Co., 255 U.S. 180 (1921), 314, 317, 321, 332

Smith v. Lenches, 263 F.3d 972 (9th Cir. 2001), 954

SmithKline Beecham Corp. v. Abbott Laboratories, 740 F.3d 471 (9th Cir. 2013), 994

Smuck v. Hobson, 408 F.2d 175 (D.C. Cir. 1969), 697

Snider International Corp. v. Town of Forest Heights, 739 F.3d 140 (4th Cir. 2014), 264

Snowney v. Harrah's Entertainment, Inc., 112 P.3d 28 (Cal. 2005), 202

Snyder v. Harris, 394 U.S. 332 (1969), 764

Snyder v. Louisiana, 552 U.S. 472 (2008), 994

Soma Medical International v. Standard Chartered Bank, 196 F.3d 1292 (10th Cir. 1999), 202

Sosa v. Alvarez-Machain, 542 U.S. 692 (2004), 501

Southern Pacific Co. v. Jensen, 244 U.S. 205 (1917), 501

Specialty Cabinets & Fixtures, Inc. v. American Equitable Life Insurance Co., 140 F.R.D. 474 (S.D. Ga. 1991), 812

Sproul v. Rob & Charlies, Inc., 304 P.3d 18 (N.M. Ct. App. 2012), 200

St. Mary's Honor Center v. Hicks, 509 U.S. 502 (1993), 84

St. Paul Mercury Indemnity Co. v. Red Cab Co., 303 U.S. 283 (1938), 358

Standard Fire Insurance Co. v. Knowles, 133 S. Ct. 1345 (2013), 767

Stanko v. LeMond, 1991 WL 152940 (E.D. Pa. Aug. 6, 1991), 286

State v. Lamar Advertising Co. of Louisiana, Inc., 279 So. 2d 671 (La. 1973), 720

State v. United Cook Inlet Drift Association, 895 P.2d 947 (Alaska 1995), 1219

State Farm Fire & Casualty Co. v. Tashire, 386 U.S. 523 (1967), 335, 706, 711, 712, 717

State Farm General Insurance Co. v. JT's Frames, Inc., 104 Cal. Rptr. 3d 573 (Ct. App. 2010), 238

State Farm Mutual Automobile Insurance Co. v. Campbell, 538 U.S. 408 (2003), 836

State Farm Mutual Automobile Insurance Co. v. Powell, 87 F.3d 93 (3d Cir. 1996), 365

State of Idaho Potato Commission v. G & T Terminal Packaging, Inc., 425 F.3d 708 (9th Cir. 2005), 1219

State Street Bank & Trust Co. v. Brockrim, Inc., 87 F.3d 1487 (1st Cir. 1996), 1083

Steers v. Rescue 3, Inc., 934 P.2d 532 (Or. Ct. App. 1997), 720

Stevenson, In re, 40 A.3d 1212 (Pa. 2012), 1219

Stewart v. Cheek & Zeehandelar, LLP, 252 F.R.D. 387 (S.D. Ohio 2008), 833

Stewart v. Ramsay, 242 U.S. 128 (1916), 285

Stewart Organization, Inc. v. Ricoh Corp., 487 U.S. 22 (1988), 483, 490, 495-496, 499, 509

Stolt-Nielsen S.A. v. AnimalFeeds International Corp., 559 U.S. 662 (2010), 866-867

Stone v. First Union Corp., 371 F.3d 1305 (11th Cir. 2004), 698

Stough v. Mayville Community Schools, 138 F.3d 612 (6th Cir. 1998), 957

Strawbridge v. Curtiss, 7 U.S. (3 Cranch) 267 (1806), 335, 346, 706-707

Sullivan v. Wilson County, 2012 WL 1868292 (Tenn. Ct. App. Oct. 11, 2011), 1218

Sumotomo Copper Litigation, In re, 74 F. Supp. 2d 393 (S.D.N.Y. 1999), 863

Supreme Tribe of Ben-Hur v. Cauble, 255 U.S. 356 (1921), 764

Sutphin v. Speik, 99 P.2d 652 (Cal. 1940), 1197

Suttie v. Sloan Sales, Inc., 711 A.2d 1285 (Me. 1998), 147

Swanson v. Citibank, N.A., 614 F.3d 400 (7th Cir. 2010), 70, 76-77, 83

Swierkiewicz v. Sorema N.A., 534 U.S. 506 (2002), 41, 95

Swiger v. Allegheny Energy, Inc., 540 F.3d 179 (3d Cir. 2008), 356

Swift v. Tyson, 41 U.S. (16 Pet.) 1 (1842), 468-470, 475, 478

Swint v. Chambers County Commission, 514 U.S. 35 (1995), 1056, 1062

Szabo v. Bridgeport Machines, Inc., 249 F.3d 672 (7th Cir. 2001), 782

Tafflin v. Levitt, 493 U.S. 455 (1990), 324

Talbott v. GC Services L.P., 191 F.R.D. 99 (W.D. Va. 2000), 833

Tamburo v. Dworkin, 601 F.3d 693 (7th Cir. 2010), 172

Tancredi v. Metropolitan Life Insurance Co., 378 F.3d 220 (2d Cir. 2004), 401

Tango Music, LLC v. DeadQuick Music, Inc., 348 F.3d 244 (7th Cir. 2003), 347

Taylor v. Babbitt, 673 F. Supp. 2d 20 (D.D.C. 2009), 1176

Taylor v. Babbitt, 760 F. Supp. 2d 80 (D.D.C. 2011), 1176

Taylor v. State, 320 N.Y.S.2d 343 (N.Y. App. Div. 1971), 30

Taylor v. Sturgell, 553 U.S. 880 (2008), 1165, 1175-1176, 1178, 1227

TCI Group Life Insurance Plan v. Knoebber, 244 F.3d 691 (9th Cir. 2001), 952

Teamsters Local Union No. 171 v. Keal Driveaway Co., 173 F.3d 915 (4th Cir. 1999), 744

Telectronics Pacing Systems, Inc., In re, 221 F.3d 870 (6th Cir. 2000), 813, 820-821, 822, 823, 847, 852

Telectronics Pacing Systems, Inc., In re, 137 F. Supp. 2d 985 (S.D. Ohio 2001), 816 *

Tellabs, Inc. v. Makor Issues & Rights, Ltd., 551 U.S. 308 (2007), 37

Temple v. Synthes Corp., Ltd., 498 U.S. 5 (1990), 722, 723

Tennessee v. Union & Planters' Bank, 152 U.S. 454 (1894), 310

Tercero v. Catholic Diocese of Norwich, 48 P.3d 50 (N.M. 2002), 147

Terra International, Inc. v. Mississippi Chemical Corp., 119 F.3d 688 (8th Cir. 1997), 450

Tesser v. Board of Education, 190 F. Supp. 2d 430 (E.D.N.Y. 2002), 1029, 1039-1040

Testa v. Katt, 330 U.S. 386 (1947), 548

Textile Workers Union of America v. Lincoln Mills of Alabama, 353 U.S. 448 (1957), 500

Thermtron Products, Inc. v. Hermansdorfer, 423 U.S. 336 (1976), 1061

Thomas v. Bank of America Corp., 570 F.3d 1280 (11th Cir. 2009), 766

Thompson v. American Home Assurance Co., 95 F.3d 429 (6th Cir. 1996), 945

Thompson v. Handa-Lopez, Inc., 998 F. Supp. 738 (W.D. Tex. 1998), 168

Tilley v. TJX Companies, Inc., 345 F.3d 34 (1st Cir. 2003), 813, 1072

Tilt v. Kelsey, 207 U.S. 43 (1907), 130-131

Tobin v. Astra Pharmaceutical Products, Inc., 993 F.2d 528 (6th Cir. 1993), 200

Tomkins v. Basic Research LL, 2008 WL 1808316 (E.D. Cal. Apr. 22, 2008), 766, 852, 883

Tongkook America, Inc. v. Shipton Sportswear, 14 F.3d 781 (2d Cir. 1994), 365, 366

Torres v. Estate of Hill, 2007 WL 1975440 (S.D. Cal. Apr. 18, 2007), 945

Tovar v. United States Postal Service, 3 F.3d 1271 (9th Cir. 1993), 899

Toys "R" Us, Inc. v. Step Two, S.A., 318 F.3d 446 (3d Cir. 2003), 202, 237

Transure, Inc. v. Marsh and McLennan, Inc., 766 F.2d 1297 (9th Cir. 1985), 347

Travelers Insurance Co. v. Intraco, Inc., 163 F.R.D. 554 (S.D. Iowa 1995), 682

Trbovich v. United Mine Workers, 404 U.S. 528 (1972), 698

Tri-County Elevator Co. v. Superior Court, 185 Cal. Rtpr. 208 (Ct. App. 1982), 1029

Troy Bank v. G.A. Whitehead & Co., 222 U.S. 39 (1911), 367

Turkmen v. Hasty, 789 F.3d 218 (2d Cir. 2015), 67

Turner v. Imperial Stores, 161 F.R.D. 89 (S.D. Cal. 1995), 616

Turner v. Safley, 482 U.S. 78 (1987), 962-963

Twentieth Century-Fox Film Corp. v. Taylor, 239 F. Supp. 913 (S.D.N.Y. 1965), 339

Underwood Farmers Elevator v. Leidholm, 460 N.W.2d 711 (N.D. 1990), 281, 284

Union Carbide Corp. Gas Plant Disaster at Bhopal, India, In re, 634 F. Supp. 842 (S.D.N.Y. 1986), 459

Union National Bank v. Pacamor Bearings, Inc., 503 N.Y.S.2d 671 (Sup. Ct. 1986), 266

United Mine Workers of America v. Gibbs, 383 U.S. 715 (1966), 371, 375-377, 383, 388, 391-392

United States v. American Telephone & Telegraph Co., 642 F.2d 1285 (D.C. Cir. 1980), 698

United States v. Any and All Radio Equip. Located at 9613 Madison Avenue, Cleveland, Ohio, 218 F.3d 543 (6th Cir. 2000), 297

United States v. County of Cook, Illinois, 167 F.3d 381 (7th Cir. 1999), 239

United States v. Department of Mental Health, 785 F. Supp. 846 (E.D. Cal. 1992), 698

United States v. $52,000.00, More or Less, in U.S. Currency, 508 F. Supp. 2d 1036 (S.D. Ala. 2007), 924

United States v. James Daniel Good Real Property, 510 U.S. 43 (1993), 296-297

United States v. Kras, 409 U.S. 434 (1973), 1110

United States v. Mendoza, 464 U.S. 154 (1984), 1218-1219

United States v. Mitchell, 17 F. Cas. 1291 (C.C.D. Ore. 1875) (No. 10,085), 126

United States v. Mitchell, 141 F. 666 (C.C.D. Or. 1916), 126

United States v. Moser, 266 U.S. 236 (1924), 1196

United States v. One Assortment of 89 Firearms, 465 U.S. 354 (1984), 1204

United States v. Oregon, 839 F.2d 635 (9th Cir. 1988), 698

United States v. Reynolds, 345 U.S. 1 (1953), 559

United States v. Seale, 558 U.S. 985 (2009), 1109

United States v. Stauffer Chemical Co., 464 U.S. 165 (1984), 1187

United States v. Swiss American Bank, Ltd., 191 F.3d 30 (1st Cir. 1999), 235

United States v. Swiss American Bank, Ltd., 274 F.3d 610 (1st Cir. 2001), 172

United States v. United Shoe Machinery Corp., 89 F. Supp. 357 (D. Mass. 1950), 574

United States v. U.S. Gypsum Co., 333 U.S. 364 (1948), 1089

United States v. West Productions, Ltd., 1997 WL 668210 (S.D.N.Y. Oct. 27, 1997), 659

Unitherm Food Systems, Inc. v. Swift-Eckrich, Inc., 546 U.S. 394 (2006), 1022, 1028

Upjohn Co. v. United States, 449 U.S. 383 (1981), 568, 573-574, 582

Urethane Antitrust Litigation, In re, 663 F. Supp. 2d 1067 (D. Kan. 2009), 848

USHA Holdings, LLC v. Franchise India Holdings Ltd., 11 F. Supp. 3d 244 (E.D.N.Y. 2014), 286

Van Dusen v. Barrack, 376 U.S. 612 (1964), 435, 436

Vanguard Environmental, Inc. v. Kerin, 528 F.3d 756 (10th Cir. 2008), 954

Varney v. R.J. Reynolds Tobacco Co., 118 F. Supp. 2d 63 (D. Mass. 2000), 37

Vega v. T-Mobile USA, Inc., 564 F.3d 1256 (8th Cir. 2009), 780

Verlinden B.V. v. Central Bank of Nigeria, 461 U.S. 480 (1983), 307

Vermeulen v. Renault, U.S.A., Inc., 985 F.2d 1534 (11th Cir. 1993), 200

Vesuvius Technologies, LLC v. SilverCentral, Inc., 2013 WL 1879107 (E.D. Wis. May 3, 2013), 418

Vetrotex Certainteed Corp. v. Consolidated Fiber Glass Products Co., 75 F.3d 147 (1996), 168

Viacom International, Inc. v. Kearney, 212 F.3d 721 (2d Cir. 2000), 691

Vicknair v. Phelps Dodge Industries, Inc., 767 N.W.2d 171 (N.D. 2009), 461

Virmani v. Novant Health Inc., 259 F.3d 284 (4th Cir. 2001), 568

Vizcaino v. United States District Court, 184 F.3d 1070 (9th Cir. 1999), 1081-1082

Volkswagen of America, Inc., In re, 545 F.3d 304 (5th Cir. 2008), 429

Volkswagenwerk Aktiengesellschaft v. Schlunk, 486 U.S. 694 (1988), 254

Wagner v. Truesdell, 574 N.W.2d 627 (S.D. 1998), 266

Walden v. Fiore, 134 S. Ct. 1115 (2014), 174, 180, 198

Walker v. Armco Steel Corp., 446 U.S. 740 (1980), 482

Walker v. City of Lompoc, 42 F.3d 1404 (9th Cir. 1994), 957

Wallkill 5 Assocs. II v. Tectonic Engineering, P.C., 1997 WL 452252 (D.N.J. July 25, 1997), 683, 686-687

Wal-Mart Stores, Inc. v. Dukes, 131 S. Ct. 2541 (2011), 762, 774, 792, 803-805, 812, 822, 825, 829-831, 832-833, 849, 850

Ware v. Jolly Roger Rides, Inc., 857 F. Supp. 462 (D. Md. 1994), 673

Warner v. Pacific Telephone & Telegraph Co., 263 P.2d 465 (Cal. Ct. App. 1953), 730

Warren v. Xerox Corp., 2004 WL 1562884 (E.D.N.Y. Jan. 26, 2004), 791

Washington Metropolitan Area Transit Commission v. Reliable Limousine Service, LLC, 776 F.3d 1 (D.C. Cir. 2015), 596

Watson v. Payne, 2011 WL 1233499 (Tenn. Ct. App. Apr. 1, 2011), 1040

Weaver v. New York, 7 F. Supp. 2d 234 (W.D.N.Y. 1998), 255

Webb v. District of Columbia, 146 F.3d 964 (D.C. Cir. 1998), 597

Weber v. Goodman, 9 F. Supp. 2d 163 (E.D.N.Y. 1998), 839-840, 852

Weber v. Goodman, 1998 WL 1807355 (E.D.N.Y. June 1, 1998), 852

Weichert v. Kimber, 645 N.Y.S.2d 674 (App. Div. 1996), 285

Weigner v. City of New York, 852 F.2d 646 (2d Cir. 1988), 265

Weisgram v. Marley Co., 528 U.S. 440 (2000), 1023, 1027-1028

Weiss v. Glemp, 903 P.2d 455 (Wash. 1995), 256

Westerfeld v. Independent Processing, LLC, 621 F.3d 819 (8th Cir. 2010), 768

Westlands Water District v. United States, 100 F.3d 94 (9th Cir. 1996), 955

Westlands Water District v. United States, 153 F. Supp. 2d 1133 (E.D. Cal. 2001), 955

White v. National Football League, 822 F. Supp. 1389 (D. Minn. 1993), 813

Wilkerson v. Leath, 2012 WL 2361972 (Tenn. Ct. App. June 22, 2012), 1212

Will v. Hallock, 546 U.S. 345 (2006), 1058

Will v. United States, 389 U.S. 90 (1967), 1074, 1081

Williams v. Combined Insurance Co. of America, 84 Fed. Appx. 660 (7th Cir. 2003), 957

Willy v. Coastal Corp., 503 U.S. 131 (1992), 404

Wilson v. Farris, 2010 WL 3463442 (M.D. Fla. Aug. 30, 2010), 276

Wm. T. Thompson Co. v. General Nutrition Corp., Inc., 593 F. Supp. 1443 (C.D. Cal. 1984), 597

Wm. T. Thompson Co. v. General Nutrition Corp., Inc., 104 F.R.D. 119 (C.D Cal. 1985), 597

Wolin v. Jaguar Land Rover North America, LLC, 617 F.3d 1168 (9th Cir. 2010), 781

Wood v. Brosse U.S.A., Inc., 149 F.R.D. 44 (S.D.N.Y. 1993), 366

Wood v. Capital One Services, LLC, 2011 WL 2154279 (N.D.N.Y. Apr. 15, 2011), 599, 607-608

Woods v. Interstate Realty Co., 337 U.S. 535 (1949), 508-509

World-Wide Volkswagen Corp. v. Woodson, 444 U.S. 286 (1980), 181, 213

Wright v. Collins, 766 F.2d 841 (4th Cir. 1985), 832

Wynder v. McMahon, 360 F.3d 73 (2d Cir. 2004), 42

Xuncax v. Gramajo, 886 F. Supp. 162 (D. Mass. 1995), 421

Yahoo! Inc. v. La Ligue Contre Le Racisme et L'Antisemitisme, 433 F.3d 1199 (9th Cir. 2006), 172

Yi Tu v. National Transportation Safety Board, 470 F.3d 941 (9th Cir. 2006), 276

Young v. Schutz, 2015 WL 2265465 (N.D. Ill. May 11, 2015), 724

Zahn v. International Paper Co., 414 U.S. 291 (1973), 764

Zapata v. City of New York, 502 F.3d 192 (2d Cir. 2007), 256

Zippo Manufacturing Co. v. Zippo Dot Com, Inc., 952 F. Supp. 1119 (W.D. Pa. 1997), 202

Zubulake v. UBS Warburg LLC, 217 F.R.D. 309 (S.D.N.Y. 2003), 607-608, 632

Zubulake v. UBS Warburg LLC, 220 F.R.D. 212 (S.D.N.Y. 2003), 608, 632

TABLE OF AUTHORITIES

Adams, Douglas, The Hitchhiker's Guide to the Galaxy (2005), 598 *
Administrative Office of the U.S. Courts, Federal Judicial Caseload Statistics, 1997: 6
_____, Federal Judicial Caseload Statistics, 2001: 334
_____, Federal Judicial Caseload Statistics, 2010: 6
_____, Federal Judicial Caseload Statistics, 2014: 10, 305, 334
_____, Judicial Business of the United States Courts 2000: 10
_____, Judicial Business of the United States Courts 2001: 11
_____, Judicial Business of the United States Courts 2004: 10
_____, Judicial Business of the United States Courts 2014: 4, 11, 965, 996, 1108
_____, Judicial Facts and Figures 2013: 4
Advisory Committee Note, 1963 Amendments, 31 F.R.D. 587: 886
Advisory Committee Note, 1966 Amendments, 39 F.R.D. 69: 277, 674, 724, 744, 754, 834, 835, 848
Advisory Committee Note, 1970 Amendments, 48 F.R.D. 487: 616, 618
Advisory Committee Note, 1993 Amendments, 146 F.R.D. 401: 236, 246, 256, 588, 953
Advisory Committee Note, 2006 Amendments, 234 F.R.D. 296: 599, 607
Advisory Committee Note, 2010 Amendments, 266 F.R.D. 502: 899
Advisory Committee Report of October 1955 on Rule 8(a)(2): 36
Advisory Committee Report of May 8, 2013 on Civil Rules, 596
Advisory Committee Report of May 2, 2014 on Civil Rules, 608
American Bar Association, Model Rules of Professional Conduct (2013), 839
American Bar Association/Brookings Symposium, Charting a Future for the Civil Jury System
    (1992), 995

Bandes, Susan, "Intersystem Preclusion," 18 Moore's Federal Practice (3d ed. 2015), 1153
Bloom, Robert M., "Default; Default Judgment," 10 Moore's Federal Practice (3d ed. 2015), 945
Blume, William W., The Scope of a Civil Action, 42 Mich. L. Rev. 257 (1943), 636
Brazil, Wayne D., "Failure to Make Disclosure or to Cooperate in Discovery: Sanctions," 7
    Moore's Federal Practice (3d ed. 2015), 620-621
Brieant, Charles L. & Martin H. Redish, "Dismissal of Actions," 8 Moore's Federal Practice (3d ed.
    2015), 955, 957, 958, 961
Brunet, Edward J. & Jerry E. Smith, "Intervention," 6 Moore's Federal Practice (3d ed. 2015), 699
Burbank, Stephen B., Interjurisdictional Preclusion, Full Faith and Credit and Federal Common
    Law: A General Approach, 71 Cornell L. Rev. 733 (1986), 1154
_____, The Rules Enabling Act of 1934, 130 U. Penn. L. Rev. 1015 (1982), 467
Burger, Warren E., Thinking the Unthinkable, 31 Loy. L. Rev. 205 (1985), 995

Calabresi, Guido, Federal and State Courts: Restoring a Workable Balance, 78 N.Y.U. L. Rev.
    1293 (2003), 476
Casad, Robert C. & Kevin M. Clermont, Res Judicata: A Handbook on Its Theory, Doctrine, and
    Practice (2001), 1189, 1212, 1230

Charrow, Robert P. & Veda R. Charrow, Making Legal Language Understandable: A Psycholinguistic Study of Jury Instructions, 79 Colum. L. Rev. 1306 (1979), 997

Clark, Charles E., Handbook of the Law of Code Pleading (2d ed. 1947), 13 *, 16, 30, 634-635, 636, 1135, 1136

————, Pleading Under the Federal Rules, 12 Wyo. L. J. 177 (1958), 102

————, The Code Cause of Action, 33 Yale L. J. 817 (1924), 13 *, 16

Clermont, Kevin M. & Theodore Eisenberg, Trial by Jury or Judge: Transcending Empiricism, 77 Cornell L. Rev. 1124 (1992), 995

Cook, Gregory C., ed., The Class Action Fairness Act: Law and Strategy (2013), 772

Days, Drew, III, "Authorization for Three-Judge Courts and Direct Appeals to the Supreme Court," 22 Moore's Federal Practice (3d ed. 2015), 1109

Degnan, Ronan E., Federalized Res Judicata, 85 Yale L. J. 741 (1976), 1154

Development in the Law: The Civil Jury, 110 Harv. L. Rev. 1408 (1997), 996

Dudnik, Robert, Special Verdicts, Rule 49 of the Federal Rules of Civil Procedure, 74 Yale L. J. 483 (1965), 1006

Eliot, T. S., "The Waste Land" (1922), in The Complete Poems and Plays, 1909–1950, at 37 (1952), 1198

Elliot, J., ed., Debates on the Adoption of the Federal Constitution (Elliot's Debates) (1888), 334

Ely, John Hart, The Irrepressible Myth of *Erie*, 87 Harv. L. Rev. 693 (1974), 467

Finberg, James M. & Laura M. Reich, "CAFA Settlement Provisions," in The Class Action Fairness Act: Law and Strategy (Gregory C. Cook ed. 2013), 863-864

Fishman, Clifford S. & Anne T. McKenna, Jones on Evidence (7th ed. 2014), 69

Francis, James C, IV, "Depositions upon Written Questions," 7 Moore's Federal Practice (3d ed. 2015), 593

————, "Physical and Mental Examinations of Persons," 7 Moore's Federal Practice (3d ed. 2015), 615

————, "Production of Documents and Things and Entry upon Land for Inspection and Other Purposes," 7 Moore's Federal Practice (3d ed. 2015), 596

Frank, Jerome, Courts on Trial: Myth and Reality in American Justice (1949), 553, 995, 1006

Freer, Richard, D., "Interpleader," 4 Moore's Federal Practice (3d ed. 2015), 711, 717

————, "Permissive Joinder of Parties," 4 Moore's Federal Practice (3d ed. 2015), 660

————, "Plaintiff and Defendant; Capacity; Public Officers," 4 Moore's Federal Practice (3d ed. 2015), 342, 674

————, "Required Joinder of Parties," 4 Moore's Federal Practice (3d ed. 2015), 724

Friedenthal, Jack H., Mary Kay Kane & Arthur R. Miller, Civil Procedure (4th ed. 2005), 970

Frost, Robert, "Stopping by Woods on a Snowy Evening" (1923), in Complete Poems of Robert Frost 275 (1949), 1198

Geer, Theodore T., Fifty Years in Oregon (1916), 126

Gorelick, Jamie S., Stephen Marzen & Lawrence Solum, Destruction of Evidence (1989 & Supp. 2014), 597

Grossi, Simona, A Modified Theory of the Law of Federal Courts: The Case of Arising Under Jurisdiction, 88 Wash. L. Rev. 961 (2013), 326

————, *Forum Non Conveniens* as a Jurisdictional Doctrine, 75 U. Pitt. L. Rev. 1 (2013), 459

————, Personal Jurisdiction: A Doctrinal Labyrinth with No Exit, 47 Akron L. Rev. 617 (2014), 127

Hamilton, Alexander, The Federalist No. 80 (Clinton Rossiter ed., 1961), 333-334

Hans, Valerie & Neil Vidmar, Judging the Jury (1986), 995

Haydock, Roger S. & David F. Herr, Discovery Practice (4th ed. 2008), 591, 595

Herr, David F., Federal Judicial Center, Manual for Complex Litigation (4th ed. 2014), 783, 851, 862, 863

Higginbotham, Patrick E., "Duty of Disclosure; General Provisions Governing Discovery," 6 Moore's Federal Practice (3d ed. 2015), 559-560, 566, 567, 582, 586, 589, 618, 620

Huber, Peter, Junk Science and the Jury, 1990 U. Chi. Legal Forum 273: 995-996

Ides, Allan, A Critical Appraisal of the Supreme Court's Decision in *J. McIntyre Machinery, Ltd. v. Nicastro*, 45 Loy. L. Rev. 341 (2012), 198

_____, *Bell Atlantic* and the Principle of Substantive Sufficiency Under Federal Rule of Civil Procedure 8(a)(2): Toward a Structured Approach to Federal Pleading Practice, 243 F.R.D. 604 (2007), 55

_____, Judicial Supremacy and the Law of the Constitution, 47 U.C.L.A. L. Rev. 491 (1999), 499

_____, The Supreme Court and the Law to Be Applied in Diversity Cases: A Critical Guide to the Development and Application of the *Erie* Doctrine and Related Problems, 163 F.R.D. 19 (1995), 467

Ides, Allan & Simona Grossi, The Purposeful Availment Trap, 7 Fed. Cts. L. Rev. 118 (2013), 157

James, Fleming, Jr., Civil Procedure (1965), 635, 691

Judicial Council of California, California Civil Jury Instructions (2015), 997, 1001

_____, 2014 Court Statistics Report: Statewide Caseload Trends 2003-2004 through 2012-2013 (2014), 7, 9, 965

Kalven, Harry, Jr. & Hans Zeisel, The American Jury (1966), 995

Keeton, W. Page, Dan B. Dobbs, Robert E. Keeton & David G. Owen, Prosser and Keeton on Torts (5th ed. 1984), 1004

Keigwin, Charles A., Cases in Common Law Pleading (2d ed. 1934), 15

Klonoff, Robert H. & Edward K. M. Bilich, Class Actions and Other Multi-Party Litigation (2d ed. 2006), 749

Koffler, Joseph H. & Allison Reppy, Common Law Pleading (1969), 15, 1134

Lee, Emery G., III & Thomas E. Willging, The Impact of the Class Action Fairness Act of 2005 in the Federal Courts: Fourth Interim Report to the Judicial Council Advisory Committee on Civil Rules (Federal Judicial Center 2008), 771, 772

_____, The Impact of the Class Action Fairness Act of 2005 in the Federal Courts: Third Interim Report to the Judicial Council Advisory Committee on Civil Rules (Federal Judicial Center 2007), 772

Marcus, Richard L., The Revival of Fact Pleading Under the Federal Rules of Civil Procedure, 86 Colum. L. Rev. 433 (1986), 37-38

Marshall, Prentice H. & Thomas D. Rowe, Jr., "Right to Jury Trial; Demand," 8 Moore's Federal Practice (3d ed. 2015), 971

_____, "Special Verdict; General Verdict and Questions," 9 Moore's Federal Practice (3d ed. 2015), 1006, 1007

May, Christopher N., Allan Ides & Simona Grossi, National Power and Federalism (7th ed. 2016), 985

McKelvey, John Jay, Principles of Common Law Pleading (2d ed. 1917), 15

McLaughlin, Joseph M., McLaughlin on Class Actions (2014), 767, 772

Miller, Neal, An Empirical Study of Forum Choices in Removal Cases under Diversity and
      Federal Question Jurisdiction, 41 Am. U. L. Rev. 369 (1992), 334

Morgan, Edmund M., A Brief History of Special Verdicts and Special Interrogatories, 32 Yale L. J.
      575 (1923), 1006

Mullenix, Linda S., Ending Class Actions as We Know Them: Rethinking the American Class
      Action," 64 Emory L. J. 399 (2014), 749

_____, State Class Actions: Practice and Procedure (2007), 749

National Center for State Courts, An Analysis of 2010 State Court Caseloads (2012), 7

_____, An Overview of 2012 State Trial Court Caseloads (2014), 3, 6, 10

_____, Examining the Work of State Courts, 1999–2000: A National Perspective from the
      Court Statistics Project (2001), 9

_____, Examining the Work of State Courts, 2001: A National Perspective from the Court
      Statistics Project (2002), 8

_____, Examining the Work of State Courts, 2003: A National Perspective from the Court
      Statistics Project (2004), 7, 965

_____, State Court Structure Charts (2013), 2, 8

_____, 2012 Appellate Court Caseload Tables (2015), 8

_____, 2012 Trial Courts – Civil Caseload (Statewide Civil Caseloads and Rates) (2014), 6-7

New York Commissioners on Practice & Pleadings, First Report (1848), 15-16

New York State Unified Court System, Annual Report 2013 (2014), 7, 965

Nieland, Robert G., Pattern Jury Instructions: A Critical Look at a Modern Movement to Improve
      the Jury System (1979), 997

Note, Developments in the Law—State Court Jurisdiction, 73 Harv. L. Rev. 911 (1960), 137

Note, Nonmutual Issue Preclusion Against States, 109 Harv. L. Rev. 792 (1996), 1219

Parness, Jeffrey A., "General Rules of Pleading," 2 Moore's Federal Practice (3d ed. 2015), 96

_____, "Pleading Special Matters," 2 Moore's Federal Practice (3d ed. 2015), 36-37

Perdue, Wendy C, Sin, Scandal, and Substantive Due Process: Personal Jurisdiction and *Pennoyer*
      Reconsidered, 62 Wash. L. Rev. 479 (1987), 126

Pomeroy, John Norton, Remedies and Remedial Rights by the Civil Action (2d ed. 1883), 1135

Pratt, George C, "Citing Judicial Dispositions, 20A Moore's Federal Practice (3d ed. 2015), 11

_____, "Interlocutory Orders," 19 Moore's Federal Practice (3d ed. 2015), 1064, 1067, 1068,
      1069

_____, "Standards of Review," 19 Moore's Federal Practice (3d ed. 2015), 1090

Redish, Martin H., "Judgment as a Matter of Law in a Jury Trial; Related Motion for a New Trial;
      Conditional Ruling," 9 Moore's Federal Practice (3d ed. 2015), 1010

_____, "New Trial; Altering or Amending a Judgment," 12 Moore's Federal Practice (3d ed.
      2015), 1029

Restatement (First) of Judgments (1942), 1207

Restatement (Second) of Conflict of Laws (1971), 171, 172, 173, 232, 285

Restatement (Second) of Judgments (1982), 144, 403, 1132, 1136-1137, 1139, 1143, 1151, 1154,
      1155, 1156, 1162, 1163, 1164, 1165, 1174, 1177, 1179-1180, 1182, 1187, 1188-1189, 1195,
      1198, 1199, 1204, 1205, 1207, 1208, 1212, 1218, 1230

Rowe, Thomas D., Jr., "Instructions to the Jury; Objections; Preserving a Claim of Error," 9
      Moore's Federal Practice (3d ed. 2015), 997

Scheindlin, Shira A. & Daniel J. Capra, Electronic Discovery and Digital Evidence in a Nutshell (2009), 598, 608

Schwarzer, William W., Communicating with Juries: Problems and Remedies, 69 Cal. L. Rev. 731 (1981), 997

Scott, Harvey W., 1 History of the Oregon Country (1924), 126

Scott, Robert & John Raimo, 3 Biographical Directory of the Governors of the United States, 1789–1978 (1988), 126

Shadur, Milton I. & Mary P. Squiers, "Defenses and Objections: When and How Presented; Motion for Judgment on the Pleadings; Consolidating Motions; Waiving Defenses; Pretrial Hearing," 2 Moore's Federal Practice (3d ed. 2015), 103

Shapiro, Stephen M., Kenneth S. Geller, Timothy S. Bishop, Edward A. Hartnett & Dan Himmelfarb, Supreme Court Practice (10th ed. 2014), 1109, 1114, 1127

Sherman, Edward F. & Mary P. Squiers, "Counterclaim and Cross-Claim," 3 Moore's Federal Practice (3d ed. 2015), 637, 641, 655, 658

Shipman, Benjamin J., Common-Law Pleading (3d ed. 1923), 15, 634

Siegel, David D., Supplementary Practice Commentaries, 7B McKinney's Consolidated Laws of New York Annotated (Supp. 1995), 1063

Smith, Fern M., "Judgment; Costs," 10 Moore's Federal Practice (3d ed. 2015), 1084

Solimine, Michael E., Revitalizing Interlocutory Appeals in the Federal Courts, 58 Geo. Wash. L. Rev 1165 (1990), 1069

_____ & Christine Oliver Hines, Deciding to Decide: Class Action Certification and the Interlocutory Review by the United States Courts of Appeals Under Rule 23(f), 41 Wm. & Mary L. Rev. 1531 (2000), 1072-1073

Solovy, Jerold S., Ronald L. Marmer, Timothy J. Chorvat & David M. Feinberg, "Class Actions," 5 Moore's Federal Practice (3d ed. 2015), 813, 824, 835, 838, 848, 853, 860, 862

_____ & Laura A. Kaster, "Signing Pleadings, Motions, and Other Papers, Representation to the Court; Sanctions," 2 Moore's Federal Practice (3d ed. 2015), 953

Solum, Lawrence B., "Claim Preclusion and Res Judicata," 18 Moore's Federal Practice (3d ed. 2015), 1137, 1150

_____, "Issue Preclusion and Collateral Estoppel," 18 Moore's Federal Practice (3d ed. 2015), 1187

_____, "Recognition and Validity of Judgments," 18 Moore's Federal Practice (3d ed. 2015), 1132

Sorenson, Charles W., Jr., Disclosure Under Federal Rule of Civil Procedure 26(a)—"Much Ado About Nothing?," 46 Hast. L. J. 679 (1995), 589

Stempel, Jeffrey W., "Depositions Upon Oral Examination," 7 Moore's Federal Practice (3d ed. 2015), 591, 592

_____ & Steven S. Gensler, "Summary Judgment," 11 Moore's Federal Practice (3d ed. 2015), 886, 924, 935

Sunderland, Edson R., The Theory and Practice of Pre-Trial Procedure, 36 Mich. L. Rev. 215 (1937), 967

Sward, Ellen E., The Decline of the Civil Jury (2001), 993, 995

Tiersma, Peter, Communicating with Juries: How to Draft More Understandable Jury Instructions (National Center for State Courts 2006), 998

U.S. Census Bureau, Population by Sex, Age, Nativity, and U.S. Citizenship Status (2014), 345

_____, The Foreign-Born Population in the United States: 2010 (2012), 345

Vairo, Georgene M., "Change of Venue," 17 Moore's Federal Practice (3d ed. 2015), 436, 439 &
    *, 460
_____, Class Action Fairness Act of 2005: A Review and Preliminary Analysis (Matthew Bender
    2005), 772
_____, "Determination of Proper Venue," 17 Moore's Federal Practice (3d ed. 2015), 414, 418,
    637
_____, "Multidistrict Litigation," 17 Moore's Federal Practice (3d ed. 2015), 438
von Moschzisker, Robert, Res Judicata, 38 Yale L. J. 299 (1929), 1131

Weil, Robert I. & Ira A. Brown, Jr., California Practice Guide: Civil Procedure Before Trial (2010),
    20
Werner, Marc A., The Viability and Strategic Significance of Class Action Alternatives Under
    CAFA's Mass Action Provisions, 103 Geo. L. J. 465 (2015), 771
Wilken, Claudia, "Interrogatories to Parties," 7 Moore's Federal Practice (3d ed. 2015), 594
_____, "Requests for Admissions," 7 Moore's Federal Practice (3d ed. 2015), 617
Witkin, Bernard E., California Procedure (5th ed. 2008), 21, 1006, 1062, 1160
Wright, Charles Alan & Mary Kay Kane, The Law of Federal Courts (7th ed. 2011), 888-889
Wright, Charles Alan & Arthur R. Miller, 4 Federal Practice and Procedure (3d ed. 2002), 236
_____, 4A Federal Practice and Procedure (4th ed. 2015), 247, 253, 255, 285
Wright, Charles Alan, Arthur R. Miller & Adam N. Steinman, 4B Federal Practice and Procedure
    (4th ed. 2015), 254
Wright, Charles Alan & Arthur R. Miller, 5 Federal Practice and Procedure (3d ed. 2004), 36
_____, 5A Federal Practice and Procedure (3d ed. 2004), 36-37, 77
_____, 5B Federal Practice and Procedure (3d ed. 2004), 103
Wright, Charles Alan, Arthur R. Miller & Mary Kay Kane, 6 Federal Practice and Procedure (3d
    ed. 2010), 385, 637, 641, 647, 651, 677
_____, 6A Federal Practice and Procedure (3d ed. 2010), 20, 674, 967
Wright, Charles Alan, Arthur R. Miller & Mary Kay Kane, 7 Federal Practice and Procedure (3d
    ed. 2015), 636, 672, 717, 718, 743
_____, 7A Federal Practice and Procedure (3d ed. 2005), 851
_____, 7AA Federal Practice and Procedure (3d ed. 2005), 763, 812, 836, 838
_____, 7B Federal Practice and Procedure (3d ed. 2005), 782, 783, 848, 851
_____, 7C Federal Practice and Procedure (3d ed. 2007), 697, 698, 699
Wright, Charles Alan, Arthur R. Miller & Richard L. Marcus, 8 Federal Practice and Procedure
    (3d ed. 2010), 567, 582, 618
_____, 8A Federal Practice and Procedure (3d ed. 2010), 586, 589, 592, 593, 618, 620, 621
_____, 8B Federal Practice and Procedure (3d ed. 2010), 594, 596, 615, 617
Wright, Charles Alan & Arthur R. Miller, 9 Federal Practice and Procedure (3d ed. 2008), 956,
    958
_____, 9B Federal Practice and Procedure (3d ed. 2008), 1006, 1007, 1022
Wright, Charles Alan, Arthur R. Miller & Mary Kay Kane, 10 Federal Practice and Procedure (4th
    ed. 2014), 1084
_____, 10A Federal Practice and Procedure (3d ed. 2008), 886, 899, 935, 945
_____, 10B Federal Practice and Procedure (3d ed. 1998), 899, 924
_____, 11 Federal Practice and Procedure (3d ed. 2012), 238-239, 240
_____, 11A Federal Practice and Procedure (3d ed. 2013), 401
Wright, Charles Alan, Arthur R. Miller, Edward H. Cooper & Richard D. Freer, 13D Federal
    Practice and Procedure (3d ed. 2008), 376
Wright, Charles Alan, Arthur R. Miller, Edward H. Cooper & Joan E. Steinman, 14B Federal
    Practice and Procedure (4th ed. 2009), 391
_____, 14C Federal Practice and Procedure (4th ed. 2009), 394

Wright, Charles Alan, Arthur R. Miller, Edward H. Cooper & Richard D. Freer, 14D Federal
    Practice and Procedure (4th ed. 2013), 414, 418
_____, 15 Federal Practice and Procedure (4th ed. 2013), 435, 438
Wright, Charles Alan, Arthur R. Miller & Edward H. Cooper, 15A Federal Practice and Procedure
    (2d ed. 1992), 935
_____, 16 Federal Practice and Procedure (3d ed. 2012), 1064, 1069, 1082
_____, 18 Federal Practice and Procedure (2d ed. 2002), 1136, 1187
_____, 18A Federal Practice and Procedure (2d ed. 2002), 832, 1160, 1199, 1218
_____, 19 Federal Practice and Procedure (2d ed. 1996), 476, 477

INDEX

A

Adjudication without trial, *see also* Default
      and default judgment, Dismissal,
      and Summary judgment, 885-963
  Appellate review, 1-11, 1045-1129
  Appellate courts, 1-11
  Final decisions, 1046-49,
    Alternate approach, 1160-61
    Collateral order doctrine, 1046-49
    Cohen factors, 1146-49, 1056-58
      Effectively unreviewable, *1057*
      Importance of the interest, *1057*
    Efficiency rationale, 1049
    Effect of, 1049
    Exceptions, statutory, 1063-86
      All Writs Act, 1073-81
      Certification under Rule 54(b),
       1083-86
      Certification under §1292(b), 1068-73
      Class actions, 1072-73
      Injunctions, 1163-68
      Interlocutory appeals under §1292(a),
       1063-68
      Interlocutory appeals under §1292(b),
       1068-73
      Interlocutory orders, 1046-47
      Mandamus, 1073-81
      Multiple claims or parties, 1083-86
      Non-injunctive court orders, 1068
      Prohibition, 1073-81
    Final judgments compared, 1046-47
    Interlocutory orders, 1046-47
    Remand orders in removed cases, 1061
    State law, appealability, 1062-63
    Surrender of jurisdiction, 1060-61
  Final judgment, 1045-46
  Frivolous appeals, 1045
  Harmless error, 1046
  Issue raised below, 1046

  Standards of review, 1046, 1086-1107
    Abuse of discretion, 1087-88
    Clearly erroneous, 1088-89
    De novo, 1189
    Functional approach, 1105-06
    Mixed questions of fact and law, 1089-90
    Questions involving discretion, 1087-88
    Questions of fact, 1088-89
    Questions of law, 1089
    Single standard, 1106
    Sliding scale, 1090
    Substantial evidence, 1088, 1106
  Summary judgment rulings, 1069, 1072,
    1083
  Supreme Court review, 2-9, 308, 1045-46,
    1107-27
    Adequate and independent state ground,
     1126
    Appellate caseload, 1108
    Article III, 1107-08
    Cert denial, precedential value of, 1110
    Certification, 1109
    Certiorari, petition for, 1109-11
    Derivative jurisdiction, 1110
    Discretion, 1110
    Federal question raised and decided,
     1111, 1124-26
    Final judgment rule, 1111, 1114-24
     Final decisions compared, 1119
    Highest state court in which decision
     could be had, 1111, 1126-27
    Injunctions, orders re, 1108-09
    Review of federal court decisions,
     1108-11
    Review of state court decisions, 1111-27
    Rule of four, 1110
    Substantial federal question, lack of,
     1113-14
    Three-judge district courts, 1108-09

Article III, 304-308, 333-334, 356-58, 660-69, 707, 806, 1107-08
Attachment of property, *see also* Service of process and notice, 287-300
   Basis for jurisdiction, 291-93
   Repossession, 296
   Satisfy a judgment, 297-98
   Security for judgment, 296

C

Claim preclusion, 832-33, 851, 1131-79
   Administrative tribunals, 1132, 1204
   Bar, 1133
   Class actions, 832-33, 851
   Code pleading, under, 1135
   Common law, at, 1134-35
   Due process limitations, 1165, 1164, 1176
   Elements of, 1133
   Equitable exceptions, 1160-61
   Finality, 1155-61
   Intersystem preclusion, 1152-55
      Erie doctrine, 1154
      Federal-to-state, 1153-55
      Full faith and credit, 1248-49
      State-to-federal, 1153
      State-to-state, 1152
   Issue preclusion compared, 1131-32
   Joinder, relationship to, 1134-35
   Merger, 1133
   Merits, on the, 1163-64
   Privity, 754, 1133, 1174-75, 1180, 1208
   Same claim, 1133-52
      Continuing conduct, 1149-51
      Primary rights, 1135-37, 1143
      Same-evidence test, 1137
      Transactional test, 1136-37
   Same parties, 1165-79
      Exceptions, 1174-75
   Validity of judgment, 1162-63
   Virtual representation, 1176
   Waiver, 1133, 1174
Clark, Hon. Charles E., 13, 16, 30-31, 35, 50, 53, 102, 634-36, 1135
Class actions, 344-45, 421, 661-63, 749-883
   Adequacy of representation, 750-55, 781, 789
      Collateral attack based on inadequacy, 754
   Appearance through counsel, 848
   Arbitration, 865-80
   Attorneys fees, 862-63
   Burden of showing compliance with Rule, 804

Certification, 782, 811
   Appealability, 782, 860-61, 1072-73
Class Action Fairness Act (CAFA), 344-45, 421, 854-55
Cohesiveness, 830-31
Commonality, 780, 803
Competing actions, 850-52
Coupon settlements, 863-64
Defining class, 781
Dismissal, 853-65
Dissenting class members, 754
Due process, 829
Fairness concerns, 774, 805, 838
Fluid class, 789
Hybrid cases, 831
Identifiable class, 774
Incidental monetary relief, 830
Incompatible relief, 773, 805, 812
Individualized relief, 829
Injunctive/declaratory relief, 774, 805, 812, 824, 829-33
Jurisdiction over class members, 762
Legal services programs, federally funded, 790
Limited fund, 820-22
Manageability, 838
   Mass Actions, 770-71
Merits, relevance to certification, 803
Monetary relief, 762, 770, 812, 824, 829-31, 849
Mootness, 789
Nationwide class, 803-04
Nonexhaustive factors, predominance and superiority, 837-38
Notice and right to appear or opt out, 763, 838-40, 847-48, 861-62
Numerosity, 780, 789
Opt-out, right to, 755-63, 812-13, 822, 848
Pending litigation, 813, 837
Preclusive effect, 832-33
Predominance, 834-35
Prejudice from individual suits, 773, 805, 812,-13, 837
Privies, binding effect on, 754
Settlement, 823-24, 853-65
Settlement classes, 823-24, 847
Standard of review, certification, 788-89
Statute of limitations, 782-83, 848
Subclasses, 790-91, 811-12
Subject matter jurisdiction, 763-73
   Amount in controversy, 764-66
   Class Action Fairness Act (CAFA), 344-45, 421, 765-773

Diversity, 764-65
Federal question, 764
Removal from state court, 766-68
Supplemental jurisdiction, 764-65
Superiority, 835-37
Typicality, 780-81, 789
Waiver of right to bring, 865-80
Collateral estoppel, *see* Issue preclusion

D

Default and default judgment, 238, 944-52
Setting aside, 951
Seven-day notice, 950
Demurrer, *see also* Dismissal (Failure to state a
claim), 15-16, 25, 28, 102
Directed verdict, *see* Trials (Verdicts, Directed)
Discovery, 13, 34, 39-41, 45-46, 50-53, 55, 59,
62-63, 66-68, 75, 100-01, 553-632
Admissions, requests for, 616-17
Appellate review, 1068-69
Bill of particulars, 554
Common law, at, 554
Compel, motion to, 592, 598, 620-27
Depositions, 591-93
Destruction of evidence, 597
Discovery conference, 587-88
Discovery plan, 555-57, 587-88
Duty to preserve information, 597
Duty to supplement or correct, 619-20
E-discovery, 597-608
Equity, in, 554
Experts, discovery re, 585-86, 617-19
Federal practice, 586-628
Field Code, 554
Foreign and international tribunals, 627-28
History of, 554-55
Interrogatories, 593-94
Judicial discretion to limit, 579, 615
Mandatory disclosure, 588-89
Physical and mental examinations, 608-16
Privilege, 559-586
Asserting, 566-67
Attorney-client, 573-74
Presumption against, 566
State law, 566
Waiver, 566-67
Production and inspection, requests for,
594-97
Proportionality, 558-59
Protective orders, 620-27
Relevance, 557-59
Sanctions, 588, 620-27

Scope of, 557-86
Work product doctrine, 574-86
Attorney-client privilege compared, 581
Information from experts, 585-86
Judicial duty to limit, 582
Witness statements, 581
Dismissal, 952-61
Failure to join a party, *see* Joinder of
claims and parties (Necessary and
indispensable (or required))
Failure to prosecute, 956-60
Failure to state a claim, 622-31, 952
Forum non conveniens, *see* Forum non
conveniens (main entry)
Indispensable party, failure to join, *see*
Joinder of claims and parties
(Necessary and indispensable (or
required) parties)
Jurisdiction over defendant, lack of, *see*
Personal jurisdiction
Motions to dismiss, 622-23
Sanction, dismissal as judicial, 960-61
Subject matter jurisdiction, lack of, *see*
Subject matter jurisdiction
Summary judgment, *see* Summary
judgment
Venue, improper, *see* Venue (Improper,
motion to dismiss for)
Voluntary, 953-56
Due Process Clause, 122, 125-26, 130, 134,
136, 138-43, 145-52, 159-61,
165, 171, 174, 176-77, 182-87,
193-94, 199, 204, 207-08, 212-14,
216, 220-21, 223-24, 229, 232-36,
242, 245, 254, 257-80, 287-301,
754-55, 762-63, 822, 829, 843, 1195,
1225, 1256, 1268

E

Eliot, T.S., 1198
Equity, courts of, 14-15, 30-31
Erie doctrine, 465-552, 951, 1154
Choice of law, 475-77, 479
Comparison of three tracks, chart, 489
Content of state law, 476-77
Federal common law, 497-502
Admiralty and maritime, 501
Constitutional, 499
Foreign relations and customary
international law, 501
Interstate relations, 502
Procedure, 501, 529-47

Statutory, 499
Uniquely federal interests, 500-01
Federal general common law, demise of, 470-78
Federal law in state courts, 465-66, 547-49
Federal Rules of Civil Procedure, 502-29
Overview of doctrine, 478-89
Pre-*Erie* landscape, 467-70
Rules Enabling Act, 483-86, 502-29
Rules of Decision Act, 468, 469, 479, 496, 498, 504
Story, Justice Joseph, 469
Supremacy Clause, 478-79, 490, 496, 498, 529, 547-49
Track-one test, 482-86, 490-97, 547-48
Erie compared, 496
Reverse track-one analysis, 547-49
Track-two test, 483-86, 502-29
Erie compared, 508-09
Track-three test, 486-89, 529-47
Byrd balancing, 533
Outcome-determinative test, 487-89, 532-33, 536-37
Refined outcome-determinative test, 536-37

F

Failure to state a claim, 33-34, 46, 50, 81, 101, 885, 952
Legal sufficiency, 16, 28, 34, 102, 886
Pleading sufficiency, 54, 67-68
Federal Arbitration Act, 865
Federal civil caseload, 9-12, 305, 333
Federal Class Action Fairness Act (CAFA), *see* Class actions
Federal common law, *see Erie* doctrine
Federal judicial system, 3-6, 9-12
Caseloads, trial and appellate courts, 9-12
Court structure, 3-6
Disposition of cases in trial courts, 9-12
Publication of appellate opinions, 8-9, 11
Time to trial, 9-12
Trials, extent and nature of, 9-12
Federal law in state courts, 465-66, 547-49
Field Code, 15, 72, 554, 635
Final judgment, 1111, 1114-24
Forum non conveniens, 450-63
Available alternate forum, 460
State courts, 460-61
Forum selection clauses, 438-50
Fourteenth Amendment, *see* Due Process Clause

Frank, Jerome, 553, 995
Frost, Robert, 1198
Full Faith and Credit Clause, 120, 124-25, 127-28, 132-33, 135, 149, 151-55, 265, 284, 1152, 1229
Full faith and credit statute, 125, 1153, 1161

H

Hand, Hon. Learned, 1195
Holmes, Hon. Oliver Wendell, Jr., 317, 325

I

In personam jurisdiction, *see* Personal jurisdiction
In rem jurisdiction, *see* Personal jurisdiction
Issue preclusion, 1131-32, 1179-1230
Actually litigated, 1180, 1197-98
Administrative tribunals, 1132, 1204
Claim preclusion compared, 1131-32, 1180
Class actions, 832-33, 1175, 1228
Decided and necessary, 1198-1203
Alternative determinations, 1205-07
Defensive use, 1217-18
Elements of, 1180
Exceptions to, 1203-04
Full and fair opportunity to litigate, 1180, 1188
Intersystem preclusion, 1228-30, *see also* Claim Preclusion, Intersystem Preclusion
Necessary, *see* Decided and necessary
Offensive use, 1217-18
Privity, *see* Claim Preclusion, Privity
Same issue, 1180-97
Dimensions of the issue, 1186-89
Evergreens problem, 1195
Fact/law distinction, 1187-88
Foreseeability, 1195
Pragmatic approach, 1180-82
Same parties, 1208-30, *see also* Claim Preclusion, Same Parties
Mutuality, 1208, 1211-1212
Nonmutuality, 1212
Against federal government, 1218-19
Against state and local governments, 1219
Defensive use, 1217-18
Exceptions, 1218
Intersystem preclusion, 1319-20
Offensive use, 1217-18

Virtual representation, 1227, *see also* Claim Preclusion, Virtual Representation

J

Joinder of claims and parties, 633-747
  Claims and counterclaims, 637-51
  Claims by plaintiff, 637
  Class actions, *see* Class actions
  Code joinder, 635-36, 1135
  Common law joinder, 633-34
  Compulsory counterclaims, 637-51
    Amendment to assert, 642-43
    Counterclaim to a counterclaim, 655
    Cross-claim compared, 655
    Default judgment, 641
    Exceptions to rule, 638, 642
    Failure to assert, 641-42
    Full faith and credit, 642
    Logical relationship test, 641, 645
    Parallel proceedings, 651
    Same transaction or occurrence, 638, 642, 646-47
    Supplemental jurisdiction, 646-47
  Compulsory joinder, *see* Necessary and indispensable (or required) parties
  Crossclaims, 651-59
    Counterclaims compared, 655
    Opposing parties, 655
    Plaintiffs, between, 658
    Same transaction or occurrence, 655, 659
    Subject matter jurisdiction, 655-56, 658
    Supplemental jurisdiction, 655-56, 658
    Unrelated cross-claims, 659
  Equity, joinder in, 634-35
  Impleader, 371, 377, 384-85, 683-91
  Interpleader, 704-19, 743
    Adverse claims, 705, 710-11
    Chart, 706
    Defensive, 705, 716-17, 743
    Enjoining other proceedings, 706, 717
    Federal interpleader statute, 705-06
    Federal subject matter jurisdiction, 705-06
      Amount in controversy, 706
      Diversity, 705-06
      Complete, 706
      Minimal, 706
    In rem jurisdiction, 705
    Nationwide service of process, 706
    Personal jurisdiction, 706, 719, 721
    Rule interpleader, 705-06, 711

    Single obligation, 705
    Stages of, 705
    Stake, 704-05
    Stakeholder, 704-05
      As claimant, 705, 717-18
    Statutory interpleader, 705-06, 711
    Tort claims, 711
    Venue, 706
  Intervention, 691-704
    Adequacy of representation, 698
    Conditions on, 699
    Impairment, 698
    Indispensable parties, 703
    Interest of intervenor, 697
    Of right, 691
    Permissive, 691, 698-99
    Procedure, 696
    Statutory, 691
    Subject matter jurisdiction, 700, 703
    Supplemental jurisdiction, 700, 703
    Timeliness, 696-97
  Joinder of parties by defendants, 674-91
    Counterclaims and crossclaims, adding parties to, 674-83
    Impleader, 380, 683-91
      Plaintiffs, impleader by, 690
      Piggybacking, 686
    Mislabeling claims, 686-87
    Necessary and indispensable parties, *see* Necessary and indispensable parties
    Subject matter jurisdiction, 686, 690
    Supplemental jurisdiction, 686
  Joinder of parties by plaintiffs, 659-74
    Impleader by plaintiffs, 690
    Misjoinder, 671-72
    Permissive joinder, 659-73
      Common question, 660
      Complete diversity, 669-70
      Same transaction or occurrence, 659-60
      Supplemental jurisdiction, 669-71
    Real party in interest, 673-74
  Necessary and indispensable (or required) parties, 719-45, 805-06
    Ameliorating prejudice, 742-43
    Collateral attack, 743-44
    Complete relief, 723-24, 730
    Feasibility of joinder, 719, 721, 740-41
    Impair or impede, 730
    Inconsistent obligations, 730
    Indispensablity, 731-45
    Multiple liability, risk of, 705, 711, 717, 720, 740-41

Overview, 719-22
Pragmatic approach, 741
Supplemental jurisdiction, 731, 741
Use of other joinder devices, 721, 742-43
Waiver, 743
Permissive counterclaims, 638, 646-47,
646-47, 649-50
Subject matter jurisdiction, 633, 637-38,
646-47, 649-50, 655-56, 658, 660,
669-72, 674, 682, 686-87, 690, 700,
703, 706-07, 711, 718, 719, 722,
730-31, 741, 743
Venue, 637-38, 659-60, 706, 711, 718, 721,
731
Judgment as a matter of law, 1007-28
Bench trial, use in, 1009
Binding effect, *see also* Claim Preclusion,
Issue preclusion
Constitutionality of, in jury trials, 1009-10
Directed verdict, 1008
Judgment notwithstanding the verdict
(j.n.o.v.), 1008-09, 1021
Motion for new trial compared, 1008,
1039-40
Nonsuit, 1008-09
Reasonable juror standard, 1008-10, 1028
Summary judgment compared, 1007-08
Judgment notwithstanding the verdict (j.n.o.v.),
see Judgment as a matter of law
Jurisdiction over defendant, *see* Personal
jurisdiction
Jury trial, *see* Trials

M

Minimum contacts, *see* Personal jurisdiction
Multidistrict litigation, 437-38

N

Necessary and indispensable parties, *see* Joinder
of Claims and parties (Necessary and
indispensable (or required) parties
New trial, motion for, *see* Trials (New trial,
motion for)
Notice, *see* Service of process and notice

P

Personal jurisdiction, 101, 115-243, 301, 303,
305, 353, 400-01, 407-08, 413,
416-23, 429, 435-36, 459-60,
1162-63, 1199
Challenging personal jurisdiction, 237-241
Burden of proof, 237, 239
Collateral attack, 239-41, 277
Direct attack, 237-39
Confession of judgment, as waiver of, 280-84
Consent to service on an agent, 129
Domicile, 127-28
Due Process Clause, 122, 125-26, 130, 134,
136, 138-143, 145-152, 159-161, 165,
171, 174, 176-77, 182-87, 193-94,
199, 204, 207-08, 212-14, 216,
220-21, 223-24, 229, 232-36, 242
Federal long-arm provisions, 234-36,
705-06
Forum selection clauses, 129, 438-50
Full Faith and Credit Clause, 120, 124-25,
127-28, 132-33, 135, 149, 151-55
General jurisdiction, *see* Minimum contacts
In personam jurisdiction, *see also* Consent to
service on an agent, Domicile, Long-
arm jurisdiction, Minimum contacts,
Physical presence, 124
Internet, 201-03
In rem jurisdiction, 118, 120-25, 130-31,
232-33, 296-97, 1175
Long-arm jurisdiction, *see also* Minimum
contacts, 143, 145-48, 234-36
Federal long-arm provisions, 234-36,
705-06
State long-arm statutes, 143, 145-48
Minimum contacts, 140, 143-45, 147-48,
150, 160-62, 164, 166-67, 170-71,
176-80, 185, 187, 189, 197-98, 203,
214, 216, 223, 231-38, 761-62, 851
Contractual relationships, 149-168
Effects test, 168-80
Federal long-arm provisions, national
contacts, 235-36
General jurisdiction, 220-31
Necessity, 218-19
Reasonableness, 228
Necessity, 218-19
Presumption of jurisdiction, 167, 212,
236
Purposeful availment or purposeful
contacts, *see also* Contractual
relationships, Effects test, Stream
of commerce, 156-57, 166-68, 171,
198
Reasonableness, 212-20, 228
Factors, 213-18
Foreign defendants, 216
General jurisdiction, 228
Variable standard, 216

Relatedness, 145, 167, 204-12, *see also* Specific jurisdiction
Specific jurisdiction, 145, 167, 204
Stream of commerce, 181-201
Traditional bases, minimum contacts, 231-34
   Physical presence, 234
   Quasi in rem, 232-33
Physical presence, 129-30
   Trickery or fraud, immunity, 285-87
   Witness immunity, 285
Quasi in rem in jurisdiction, 130-35, 232-33
Reasonableness, *see* Minimum contacts
Relatedness, *see* Minimum contacts
Specific jurisdiction, *see* Minimum contacts and Relatedness
State long-arm statutes, 143, 145-48,
Statutory basis for, *see also* Long-arm jurisdiction
Subject matter jurisdiction, challenge to it and to personal jurisdiction, 400-01
Territoriality, 116-27
Transient jurisdiction, 129-30, 234, *see also* Physical presence
Voluntary appearance, 128-29
Pleadings, 13-114
Amendments to, 19-20, 97
Answer, 15-16, 31, 96-101
Code pleading, 14-32, 35, 59, 72, 102
   Amendments to pleading, 19-20, 97
   Answer, 15-16
   Civil action, 14-15
   Complaint, 14-15
   Demurrer, 15-16, 28, 102
   Fact pleading, 15-17, 21, 30-31, 54, 72, 102
   Field Code, 15, 72
   Merger of law and equity, 15
   Reply, 16
   Ultimate facts, 16, 20-21, 29
   Variances, 18-20
Common law pleading, 14-15
Clark, Hon. Charles E., *see* Clark, Hon. Charles E. (main entry)
Complaint, 15-102
Demurrer, 15-16, 25, 28, 102
Equity, pleading in, 14-15, 30-31
Fact pleading, 15-17, 21, 30-31, 54, 72, 102
Failure to state a claim, motion to dismiss for, 33-34, 46, 50, 81, 101
Federal court procedure, evolution, 30-31
Notice pleading, 30-109
   Advisory Committee, 31, 35-36

Affirmative defenses, 96-98, 100-01
Amendments to, 19-20, 97
Answer, 96-101
Complaint, 30-96
Demurrer, 102
Exceptions to federal notice pleading, 36-38
Fact pleading compared, 30-32
Heightened pleading standards, 36-38
Plausibility standard, 42-101
Posner, Hon. Richard, 74, 104, 107-108
Pretrial conference, 966-69

Q

Quasi in rem jurisdiction, *see* Personal jurisdiction

R

Res judicata, *see also* Claim preclusion, Issue preclusion, 1131-1232

S

Sanctions, 620-27, 888, 935
Service of process and notice, 245-301
   Attachment of property, *see also* Service of process and notice, 287-300
      Basis for jurisdiction, 291-93
      Repossession, 296
      Satisfy a judgment, 297-98
      Security for judgment, 296
   Burden of proof, when service challenged, 277-78
   Collateral attack, 277-78
   Compliance with rule or statute, 247-57
   Confession of judgment and cognovit clauses, 280-84
      Full faith and credit, 284
   Consent, 280-84
   Corporations, partnerships, associations, 249-54
   Due diligence to effect service, 262
   Due Process Clause, 245, 254, 257-80, 287-301
   E-mail, 278-80
   First-class mail, 264-65
   Foreign country, service in, 254
   Fraud, *see* Trickery or fraud
   Hearing, right to when property attached, 287-300
   Immunity from service, 284-87
   Individuals, 248-49

Insufficiency of process, motion to dismiss
    for, 277-78
Jurisdiction, distinguished, 245
Mechanics of service, 246-57
Posting, 265, 275
Procedural posture of case, relevance of,
    251, 253-54
Publication, 261-265
Reasonably calculated, 260, 264, 278
Restricted delivery mail, 274-76
Statute of limitations, 246-47, 256
Substantial compliance, 254-56
Tailoring to defendant's needs, 265
Time limits for effecting service, 256-57
Trickery or fraud, 285-86
Waiver of objection to service, 277-78
Waiver of right to notice, pre-filing, 280-84
Waiver of service, request for, 246-47
Witness immunity, 285
Settlement, incentives, 1202
State judicial systems, 1-3, 6-9, 304, 401-03
    Caseloads, trial and appellate courts, 6-9
    Court structure, 1-3
    Disposition of cases in trial courts, 6-9
    Publication of appellate court opinions, 9
    Trials, extent and nature of, 7
Story, Justice Joseph, 469
Subject matter jurisdiction, 101, 303-406, 633,
        637-38, 646-47, 649-50, 655-56, 658,
        660, 669-72, 674, 682, 686-87, 690,
        700, 703, 706-07, 711, 718, 719,
        722, 730-31, 741, 743, 763-73
    Ancillary jurisdiction, see Supplemental
        jurisdiction
    Article III, 303-06, 307, 319-20, 321, 327,
        329, 331, 353, 356, 357, 360, 379,
        407-08, 660-69, 707, 806, 1107,
        1108, 1153
    Burden of pleading and proving, 304, 339
    Challenging, 400-04
    Collateral attack, 401-03
    Concurrent jurisdiction, 324
    Courts of general jurisdiction, 303, 324
    Courts of limited jurisdiction, 303-04
    Direct attack, 400-01
    Diversity jurisdiction, 333-70, 408, 435,
        465-67, 560, 656, 669-72, 682, 690,
        700, 703, 706-07, 731, 743, 764-65
        Aliens, 333-35, 345-58
        Amount in controversy, 303, 358-70,
            706, 764-65
            Aggregation, 366-68
            Attorney's fees, 365-66, 862-63

Burden of pleading and proving, 339
Class Action Fairness Act (CAFA),
    344-45, 421, 765-73
Collusive, 341
Domestic relations, 340
Declaratory relief, 368-70
Good faith rule, 358-59, 365
Injunctive relief, 368-70
Interpleader, 705
Legal certainty, 358-59, 365
Standard of review, 366
Subsequent events, 365
Subsequent revelations, 365
Citizens domiciled abroad, 339
Citizens with dual nationality, 356-57
Class actions, 344-45, 379, 764-65
Collusive creation of, 341
Complete diversity, 335, 343, 669-72
Corporations, 342-44
    Dual citizenship, 342-44
    Principal place of business, 343, 357
    Nerve center, 343
Curing lack of, 347
Domestic relations exception, 340
Domicile, 339
Minimal diversity, 335, 344-45, 706, 766
Partnerships, 342-43
Probate exception, 340
Role in federal courts' caseload, 5-6, 305,
    334
State citizenship, diversity of, 335-45
Time of filing rule, 352, 359-65
Unincorporated associations and
    organizations, 342-43
Exclusive jurisdiction, 324
Federal question jurisdiction, 306-33, 764
    Arising under, constitutional, 306-08
    Arising under, statutory, 308-33
    Concurrent and exclusive, re state
        courts, 324
    Creation test, 317, 325-26, 333
    Declaratory judgments, 322-24
    Essential federal ingredient, 326, 332
    Preemption, 323
    Role in federal courts caseload, 5-6,
        305
    Well-pleaded complaint rule, 310, 323,
        325, 332
Motion to dismiss for lack of, 400-01
Pendent jurisdiction, see Personal
        jurisdiction, Supplemental
        jurisdiction
Removal jurisdiction, 390-99

Appealablity of remand orders, 394,
    1061
Citizenship of defendants, 391, 869
Class Action Fairness Act (CAFA),
    766-67
Concurrence of all defendants, 393, 767
Fictitious parties, 391
Mass actions, 766-71
Remand, 392, 394, 1161
State courts, 1-3, 6-9, 303-04, 324, 333-34
Supplemental jurisdiction, 370-90, 646-47,
    655-56, 658, 700, 703, 669-70, 686,
    669-71, 700, 703, 731, 741
    Ancillary jurisdiction, 371, 383-84,
        387-89
    Class actions, 764-65, 769
    Common nucleus, 375-76, 383, 386, 392
    Counterclaims, 646-47
    Cross-claims, 655-56, 658
    Discretion, 376, 383, 388-89, 393-94
    Diversity cases, 391-92, 669-70
    Federal question cases, 390-91
    Intervention, 700, 703
    Pendent jurisdiction, 371, 375-76, 383,
        386-87
    Pendent party jurisdiction, 386-87
    Power, 376, 383
Summary judgment, 885-943
    Basic requirements, 887-88
    Burden of persuasion, 887-88, 897-98,
        908, 941
    Burden of production, 886-88, 897-98, 908,
        921
    Cross-motions, 925-26
    Directed verdict compared, 908, 941
    Evidentiary sufficiency, 886, 888, 898, 921
    Exceptions, 899
    Genuine issue of material fact, 897-98, 921,
        924, 934
    Inferences, 922
    Interlocutory appeal, 934
    Judgment as a matter of law, j.n.o.v., and
        nonsuit, compared, 886
    Motion to dismiss for failure to state a
        claim, compared, 886
    Nonmovant's burden, 898
    Partial summary judgment, 887, 924, 934
    Plaintiff as movant, 923-36
    Reasonable jury standard, 886, 898-99
    Sanctions, 888, 935
    Scintilla of evidence test, 892-93
    State practices, 899-900
    Sua sponte, 936-43

Timing of motion, 887
Variable standard, 898
Supplemental jurisdiction, see Subject matter
    jurisdiction
Supremacy Clause, 306, 308, 323-24, 478-79,
    490, 496, 498, 529, 547-49
Supreme Court review, see Appellate Review

T

Trials, 7, 10-11, 965-1043
    Bench trial, 965, 1009
    Consolidation of actions, 672, 770, 835
    Jury trial, 969-1007, see also Judgment as a
        matter of law
        Additur, 1040
        Challenge for cause, 994
        Composition of juries, 993-95
        Criminal, 970, 996
        Criticism of, 995-96
        Damages, 970-71, 975
        Debate concerning, 995-96
        Equitable claims, 970-71, 975
        Federal courts, use in, 10-11, 965, 995
        Instructions, 996-1004
        Legal claims, 975
        Peremptory challenge, 994
        Remittitur, 1040
        Selection process, 993-95
            Race or gender discrimination, 994
        Seventh Amendment right to, 969-71
            Functional test, 992
            Historical test, 985
            Two-part test, 984-85
        State courts, 7, 985
        Verdicts, 1005-07
            Additur, 1040
            Directed, 1007-1028
            General, 1005
            Interrogatories, 1006-07
            Remittitur, 1040
            Special, 1006-07
        Voir dire, 994
        Waiver of right to, 966
    New trial, motion for, 1028-40
        Additur, 1040
        Judgment as matter of law, compared,
            1039
        Prejudicial errors, 1029
        Remittitur, 1040
    Percentage of cases going to trial, 7, 10-11,
        965
    Pretrial conference process, 966-69

V

Venue, 407-64, 637-38, 659-60, 706, 711, 718, 721, 731
    Aliens as defendants, 409, 420
    Burden of pleading, 414
    Burden of proof, 414
    Change of, *see* Transfer
    Fallback provisions, 416
    Forum non conveniens, 450-63
       Available alternate forum, 460
       State courts, 460-61
    Forum selection clauses, 438-50
    General federal venue statute, 408-21
    Improper, motion to dismiss for, 414, 436
    Interpleader, 706

    Local actions, 408
    Multidistrict litigation, 437-38
    Multiple claims, 409, 414
    Multiple parties, 414
    Removal, 391, 420-21
    Residence, 409, 414
       Defendant entities, 417-21
       Political subdivisions, 420
    Standard of review, 413
    Substantial part of events, 408-15
    Time frame for assessing, 414
    Transfer, 421-37
       Law to be applied, 435-36
       Motion to, 428-29
       Personal jurisdiction, 436
    Waiver of objection, 414

Venu cont:
     all other cases = Transferee courts
choice of law

Pleading: Rule 8.

In the complaint - P must address:

- Jurisdiction
  - Short ~~statement~~ statement of SMJ

- Factual Allegations
  - requires more than "the D unlawfully harmed me." but does not require detailed allegations
  - each allegation simple, concise, and direct - No technical form Req.
  - Pleadings = construed so as to do Justice

- Claim for relief
- Prayer for relief

Answer to Complaint:

- Responses: yes, deny, Not enough info to answer
- Affirmative defenses: yes I did it but .... Alleges new facts which would defeat the claim against them.
- Negative defenses: denies/ challenges P's ability to prove one or more Necessary elements of their claim
- D's own claims

Denial:

- must admit or deny every allegation
- General denial denies everything, even ~~PJ~~ SMJ
- must specifically deny each Allegation
if Not a general denial - or admit each specifically

→

② • A failure to affectively deny, non-response, or failure to properly **confirm**, deny, or NEITA is **an** affirmation.

• some denials-such as those challenging P's capacity or performance of a condition precedent must be made in specifity

EXCEPTIONS to rule 8:
• must state allegations of fraud w/ specifity
• Rule 9 protects a defending party's reputation from harm
• it also discharges meritless fraud accusations

Plausibility Test:
• Possible < Plausible < Probable
• No legal conclusions
• only factual Allegations
• Judicial experience and common sense. OR

① court must Identify the elements of P's claim under sub. law
② Accept factual allegations as true
③ conclusory allegations = No presumption of truth since they merely recite elements of claim
④ court must determine if non-conclusory allegations are suggestive of a plausible claim for relief

③ Motions to DISMISS 12(b): lack of SMJ, lack of PJ, improper venue, insufficien process, insufficient SoP, Failu to state a claim for which reli can be granted (inadequate complaint), Failure to Join a party.

• you only get one chance to file a 12b1-5 motion and once you're notified of denial you have 14 days to answer complai

• should file motion before answering - you can file a 12b motion after answering but if you omit ~~the motion~~ from an already submitted motion what you're trying to dismiss, fail to file motion at all, or fail to include it in your answer to complaint you lose 2-5 and can only file 12b for 1 or 6 or 7

complaint
~~Con~~
2 days ↓   12 (b) 1-7 one try
Answer
↓   12 b 6 or 7 or
Trial   SMJ

SMJ
12 b(6) motions challenge factual plausibility and legal sufficiency of elements (Kirksey)

• winning → case dismissed

④ Joinder of Parties: 20, 24, 14, 13h

Parties added by P:

- must arise out of the same transaction/occurence and be a common question of law or fact (logical Rel. Test)

Parties added by D: Rules (24, 20, 14, 13(h))

- Keep diversity exceptions in mind
- must attach D to counter or crossclaims - Rule 13h acts as Rule 20 for third parties
- New claim must satisfy Rule 20 relating to the claim original D is attaching new D to
- in order to becom co-D's, each D has to sue or be sued by P, meaning a third party D is not a crossclaim bcuz D and D are not co-parties
- D can also join third party to indemnify.

AIC exception:

- where other elements of Jurisdiction are met, A fed. court in diversity can exercise supp. Jurisdiction over Plaintiffs who do not satisfy AIC when standing alone so long as the claims are part of the same case or controversy as the claims of plaintiffs who DO allege a sufficient AIC

1367(b) exception only applies to claims made by a plaintiff against a person made a party by Rules 14, 19, 20, 24

1367(b) does not on its face prohibit a defendant from joining a non-diverse third party defendant to a compulsory CC, only a P from joining a non-diverse party under rule 24, 19, 20, 14 - only claims by P against new parties whose addition would destroy diversity - initially file claims against only diverse parties then adding later non-diverse parties whose presence would have destroyed diversity NOT Allowed.

● Compulsory vs. **Permissive** ✱ Counter Claims ✱

- if it arises out of the same transaction or occurence it is a compulsory counterclaim. you must bring it
- Joinder can be good and SMJ bad
- if not brought in original lawsuit - P loses it unless it has not matured   or is

▸ Pending in a previosly filed suit.

- Permissive Counterclaims donot arise out of same T/O and must establish Jurisdictional basis counter claims in general: Rule 18, 13(a) (b), and (g)

- counter claims are responsive claims in the sense that they are filed in response to a claim previously filed against the counter-claimant in the pending action.
- They are against an opposing party ~~when filing one against~~ ~~a co-plaintiff~~ ~~or co-defendant makes~~ ~~them an opposing party~~
- ~~one party answers a cross claim become opposing parties.~~
- You bring counter claims in an answer, amended answer because amended answers Replace answers
- Thus, a P can assert a counter claim against a D but D would need to file crossclaim first
- P can also file counter claim against co-P so long as co-P cross claimed first

cross claims: 18, 13 (a) (b) (g)

- when co-parties, not opposing parties sue eachother it is a cross-claim
- Must arise out of same T/O as original action
- Rule is limited to substantive cross-claim not ones for indemnity
- first cross must be substantive but response can be for indemnity.

LOGICAL RELATIONSHIP TEST not so much upon immediateness of connection

- totality of circumstances
- Nature of the claims,
- legal basis for recovery
- the law involved
- and respective factual Backgrounds

crossclaims:
    Co-parties become opposing parties within meaning of FRCP after one such party pleads an initial cross-claim against the other where the initial cross-claim includes a substantive claim instead of one for indemnity — it is @ this point that opposing party must bring counter if it is compulsory

indemnity — Rule 14 allows D to add parties who are or may be liable for the claim against them.

• counter claims — compulsory or permissive
~~must still have an jurisdiction whether it be Federal, diversity, or supplemental~~

Joinder of claims: 18, 13a, b, g, (cross, counter, New)

any asserted claims must satisfy an independent jurisdictional basis:

- Federal Question
- Diversity
- supplemental

venue must only be good for original claims

Rule 18: may join 2 claims even if they are contigent on one another - but court may grant Relief only in acordance w/ the parties' Relative substantive rights